Cómo utilizar el diccionario

Todas las **entradas** están ordenadas alfabéticamente y se destacan en negrita.

dato ['da·to] *m* **1.** (*detalle*) fact; ...
dc. d.C. [des·'pwes de 'kris·to] *abr de* **después de Cristo** AD
dcha. [de·'re·tʃa] *abr de* **derecha** R
de [de] *prep* **1.** (*posesión*) ...

Los verbos frasales ingleses van justo después del verbo principal y están marcados con un rombo (♦).
Las cifras arábigas *voladas* diferencian **homógrafos**.
Se emplean los signos de la IPA para la transcripción fonética. En español se indica primero la pronunciación latinoamericana. Los puntos centrados indican la división silábica.
Las indicaciones de las **formas irregulares del plural** y de las **formas irregulares de verbos y adjetivos** están entre paréntesis triangulares. En el apéndice se incluye una lista con modelos de conjugación de los verbos españoles.

era¹ ['e·ra] *f* era
era² ['e·ra] *3. imp de* **ser**
agradecer [a·ɣra·de·'ser, -'θer] *irr como* **crecer** *vt* ...
anillo [a·'ni·jo, -ʎo] *m* ...

club <clubs *o* clubes> ...
merendar <e→ie> ...
fotografiar <1. *pres*: fotografío> ...
adelgazar <z→c> ...

Se indica la forma femenina de los sustantivos y adjetivos. Se indica el género de los sustantivos españoles.

actor, actriz [ak·'tor, ak·'tris, -'triθ] *m, f* actor *m*, actress *f*; ...
antiguo, -a [an·'ti·ɣwo, -a] *adj* ...

Las cifras romanas indican las distintas **categorías gramaticales**. Las cifras arábigas indican las distintas **acepciones**.

abdominal [aβ·do·mi·'nal] **I.** *adj* abdominal **II.** *m* DEP sit-up
abordar [a·βor·'dar] *vt* **1.** (*persona*) to approach **2.** (*tema*) to discuss

La **tilde** sustituye la entrada anterior. El símbolo ► introduce el bloque de las locuciones y los proverbios. Las palabras subrayadas permiten una mejor orientación.

río ['rri·o] *m* river; ~ **abajo/arriba** downstream/upstream ► **cuando el ~ suena, agua lleva** *prov* where there's smoke, there's fire

Se dan numerosas **indicaciones** para dirigir al usuario a la traducción correcta:

- indicaciones de **especialidad**

- **definiciones** o **sinónimos**, **contextos**, **complementos** o **sujetos** típicos de la entrada
- indicaciones de **uso regional** tanto a nivel de la entrada como a nivel de la traducción
- indicaciones de **estilo**

grabación [gra·βa·'sjon, -'θjon] *f* recording; TV shooting; COMPUT copying
bravo, -a ['bra·βo, -a] *adj* **1.** (*valiente*) brave **2.** (*salvaje*) wild; (*mar*) stormy **3.** *AmL* (*picante*) hot
porrista [po·'rris·ta] *mf Méx* DEP fan

recalentado [rre·ka·len·'ta·do] *m Méx*, *inf* leftovers *pl*

Si una entrada o un ejemplo no pueden ser traducidos se dará una **explicación** o una **equivalencia aproximada** (≈).

s. a. (*see also*) y *v.t.* (*véase también*) remiten a una **entrada modelo** para más información.

pochismo [po·'tʃis·mo] *m Méx* **1.** *inf* .. - Anglicism introduced into Spanish
martes ['mar·tes] *m inv* Tuesday; ~ **trece** ≈ Friday the thirteenth; ...
abril [a·'βril] *m* April; *v.t.* **marzo** ...

inwards ['ɪn·wərds] *adv* hacia adentro, para dentro

I/O COMPUT *abbr of* **input/output** E/S

iodine ['aɪ·ə·daɪn] *n* yodo *m*

All **entries** appear in alphabetical order and are printed in bold type.

bring [brɪŋ] <brought, brought> *vt* 1. …
 ◆**bring about** *vt* 1. (*cause*) provocar …

English phrasal verbs come directly after the base verb and are marked with a diamond (◆).

incense[1] ['ɪn·sents] *n* incienso *m*
incense[2] ['ɪn·sents] *vt* indignar

Raised numbers indicate so-called **homographs.**

flexible ['flek·sə·bəl] *adj* (*material, policy*) flexible

The International Phonetic Alphabet is used for all **phonetic transcriptions.** In Spanish, the common Latin-American pronunciation is given first. Centered dots are used for syllable division.

child [tʃaɪld] <children> …
be [bi] <was, been>
uncanny [ʌn·ˈkæn·i] *adj* <-ier, -iest> …

Angle brackets are used to show **irregular plural forms** and **forms of irregular verbs and adjectives.** Model conjugations for Spanish can be found in the appendix.

abrupt [ə·ˈbrʌpt] *adj* 1. (*sudden*) repentino, -a; (*change*) brusco, -a; …
instructor [ɪn·ˈstrʌk·tər] *n* 1. (*teacher*) instructor(a) *m(f)* …
mute [mjut] **I.** *n* MUS sordina *f* **II.** *adj* mudo, -a
honey [hʌn·i] *n* 1. CULIN miel *f* 2. (*term of endearment*) cariño *m*

Feminine forms of nouns and adjectives are shown. Spanish nouns are followed by their gender.

Roman numerals are used for the **parts of speech** of a word, and Arabic numerals for **sense divisions.**

horse [hɔrs] *n* 1. ZOOL caballo *m*; **to ride a ~** montar a caballo … ▶**to get sth straight from the ~'s <u>mouth</u>** saber algo de buena tinta; **don't look a gift ~ in the <u>mouth</u>** *prov* a caballo regalado, no le mires el dentado *prov*; …

The **swung dash** represents the entry word. The ▶ sign introduces **a block of set expressions, idioms and proverbs.** Key words are <u>underlined</u> as a guide.

horn [hɔrn] *n* 1. ZOOL cuerno *m* 2. MUS trompa *f* 3. AUTO bocina *f* …
wild [waɪld] **I.** *adj* 1. (*animal*) salvaje; (*plant*) silvestre; …
celery ['sel·ə·ri] *n* apio *m*, panul *m CSur*

Various kinds of **meaning indicators** are used to guide you to the required translation:
• **Subject labels**

• **Definitions** or **synonyms,** typical **context partners, subjects** or **objects** of the entry
• **Regional vocabulary and variants**

juice [dʒus] *n* 1. (*drink*) zumo *m* 2. (*of meat*) jugo *m* 3. *sl* (*electricity*) luz *f*; (*fuel*) sopa *f* …
ego surfing *n* COMPUT *introducir en un buscador de Internet el propio nombre*
Sunday school *n* REL ≈ catequesis *f inv*

• **Usage Labels**

When a word or expression has no direct translation, an **explanation** or **approximate equivalent** is given (≈).

March [martʃ] *n* marzo *m*; *s.a.* **April**

s. a. (see also) and *v.t. (véase también)* invite the reader to consult a **model entry** for further information.

With the aid of the alphabetical thumb index overleaf (at the edge of the page) you can quickly locate the letter you need to find in the Spanish-English and English-Spanish dictionary. Once you have located the letter you need on the thumb index, simply flip to the correspondingly marked part of the dictionary.

If you are left-handed, you can use the thumb index at the end of this book.

Gracias al índice alfabético del borde derecho (véase al dorso), puede ir directamente a la letra que necesite del diccionario Español-Inglés e Inglés-Español. Una vez localizada en el índice la letra que busca, puede pasar directamente a la parte correspondiente del diccionario.

Si usted es zurdo/a puede utilizar el índice alfabético que hay al final del diccionario.

BARRON'S
FOREIGN LANGUAGE GUIDES

SPANISH–ENGLISH
Pocket Dictionary

~

Diccionario de bolsillo
ESPAÑOL–INGLÉS

BARRON'S Foreign Language Guides
Spanish-English Pocket Dictionary
Diccionario de bolsillo Español-Inglés

First edition for the United States and Canada published in 2008 by Barron's Educational Series, Inc.

© 2008 Ernst Klett Sprachen GmbH, Stuttgart, Germany, and Barron's Educational Series, Inc., Hauppauge, USA.

Editorial management: Dr. Meg Tsiris

Contributors: Almudena García Hernandez, Eugenio Presno Ruiz, William Steinmetz

Typesetting: Mariusz Idzikowski, Poznań; Dörr und Schiller GmbH, Stuttgart

All inquiries should be addressed to:

Barron's Educational Series, Inc.
250 Wireless Boulevard
Hauppauge, NY 11788
www.barronseduc.com

ISBN-13: 978-0-7641-4537-7
ISBN-10: 0-7641-4537-1
Library of Congress Control Number 2008920657

Printed in China
9 8 7 6 5 4 3 2 1

A

A, a *f* (*letra*) A, a; **A de Antonio** A as in Alpha

a [a] *prep* **1.** (*dirección*) to; **ir ~ Caracas** to go to Caracas; **llegar ~ Santiago** to arrive in Santiago; **ir ~ casa de alguien** to go to sb's house; **ir ~ la escuela/~l cine** to go to school/to the movies **2.** (*posición*) at; **estar sentado ~ la mesa** to be sitting at the table; **~ la derecha** on the right; **~l sur (de)** to the south (of); **~l sol** in the sun **3.** (*distancia*) **~ 10 kilómetros de aquí** 10 kilometers (away) from here **4.** (*tiempo*) at; (*hasta*) until; **~ las tres** at three o'clock; **~ mediodía** at noon; **~ los veinte años** at (the age of) twenty; **~l poco rato** shortly after; **¿~ cuántos estamos?** what's the date? **5.** (*modo*) **~ pie** on foot; **~ mano** by hand; **~ oscuras** in the dark **6.** (*precio*) **¿~ cómo está?** how much is it?; **~ 2 pesos el kilo** (at) 2 pesos a [*o* per] kilo **7.** (*complemento (in)directo, con infinitivo*) to; **dio su fortuna ~ los pobres** he/she gave his/her fortune to the poor; **he visto ~ tu hermano** I've seen your brother; **empezó ~ correr** he/she began to run **8.** (*con verbo, expresiones*) **oler ~ gas** to smell of gas; **¡~ que llueve mañana!** I bet it'll rain tomorrow!; **~ Pedro le gusta mucho nadar, ¿~ que sí, Pedro?** Pedro likes swimming a lot. Don't you, Pedro?

abacorar [a·βa·ko·'rar] *vt AmL* to hound

abad(esa) [a·'βad, a·βa·'de·sa] *m(f)* abbot *m*, abbess *f*

abadía [a·βa·'di·a] *f* abbey

abajeño, -a [a·βa·'xe·ɲo, -a] *adj AmL* coastal

abajo [a·'βa·xo] *adv* **1.** (*movimiento*) down; **calle ~** down the street; **cuesta ~** downhill; **de arriba ~** from top to bottom **2.** (*estado*) down (below); (*en casa*) downstairs; **boca ~** face down; **hacia ~** down, downward; **de veinte para ~** twenty or under; **véase más ~** see below

abalear [a·βa·le·'ar] *vt Col* to shoot

abandonar [a·βan·do·'nar] **I.** *vt* **1.** (*dejar*) to leave; (*desamparar*) to abandon **2.** (*renunciar*) to give up **II.** *vr:* **~se** (*ir desaliñado*) to let oneself go

abandono [a·βan·'do·no] *m* **1.** (*abandonamiento*) abandonment **2.** (*renuncia*) renunciation; (*de una idea*) giving-up **3.** (*descuido*) neglect

abanicar(se) <c → qu> [a·βa·ni·'kar·(se)] *vt, (vr)* to fan (oneself)

abanico [a·βa·'ni·ko] *m* fan; **un ~ de posibilidades** a range of possibilities

abaratar [a·βa·ra·'tar] *vt* to make cheaper; (*precios*) to lower; **~ costes** to cut costs

abarcar <c → qu> [a·βar·'kar] *vt* (*comprender*) to include; **~ con la vista** to take in

abarrotar [a·βa·rro·'tar] *vt* **~ algo de algo** to pack sth with sth

abarrote [a·βa·'rro·te] *m Cuba, Méx* grocery store

abarrotería [a·βa·rro·te·'ri·a] *f* **1.** *AmL* (*ferretería*) hardware store **2.** *Guat* (*abacería*) retail grocery

abastecer(se) [a·βas·te·'ser·(se), -'θer·(se)] *irr como crecer vt, (vr)* **~(se) de** [*o* con] **algo** to provide (oneself) with sth

abastero [a·βas·'te·ro] *m Chile* (*de carne*) wholesale livestock dealer; *Méx* (*de artículos*) purveyor

abasto [a·'βas·to] *m* (*provisiones*) provisions *pl*; **no dar ~ con algo** to be unable to cope with sth

abatí [a·βa·'ti] *m Arg, Par* (*maíz*) corn; (*bebida*) corn whisky

abatible [a·βa·'ti·βle] *adj* **asiento ~** folding chair

abatido, -a [a·βa·'ti·do, -a] *adj* dejected

abatir [a·βa·'tir] **I.** *vt* **1.** (*árbol*) to fell; (*avión, pájaro*) to shoot down **2.** (*desmontar*) to dismantle **II.** *vr:* **~se** to become dejected

abdicación [aβ·di·ka·'sjon, -'θjon] *f* abdication

abdicar <c → qu> [aβ·di·'kar] *vt* (*monarca*) to abdicate; (*ideales*) to renounce

abdomen [aβ·'do·men] *m* abdomen

abdominal [aβ·do·mi·'nal] **I.** *adj* abdominal **II.** *m DEP* sit-up

abecé [a·βe·'se, -'θe] *m* ABC, alphabet;

no <u>saber</u> el ~ to have no clue

abecedario [a·βe·se·'da·rjo, a·βe·θe-] *m* alphabet

abedul [a·βe·'dul] *m* BOT birch

abeja [a·'βe·xa] *f* bee

abejorro [a·βe·'xo·rro] *m* bumblebee
▶ <u>ser un</u> ~ to be a pain (in the neck)

aberración [a·βe·rra·'sjon, -'θjon] *f* 1. (*desviación*) aberration 2. (*disparate*) absurdity 3. *AmL* (*error*) mistake

aberrante [a·βe·'rran·te] *adj* aberrant

abertura [a·βer·'tu·ra] *f* 1. (*acción*) opening 2. (*hueco*) hole

abeto [a·'βe·to] *m* BOT fir; ~ **rojo** spruce

abiertamente [a·βjer·ta·'men·te] *adv* 1. (*francamente*) openly 2. (*patentemente*) clearly

abierto, -a [a·'βjer·to, -a] I. *pp de* **abrir** II. *adj* open; (*persona*) open-minded; ~ **a nuevas ideas** open to new ideas

abismal [a·βis·'mal] *adj* enormous

abismo [a·'βis·mo] *m* GEO abyss; **entre tus opiniones y las mías hay un** ~ there's a world of difference between our opinions

abjurar [aβ·xu·'rar] *vi, vt* ~ (**de**) **algo** to renounce sth

ablandar [a·βlan·'dar] I. *vt* (*poner blando*) to soften II. *vr*: ~**se** to soften; (*persona*) to relent

abnegación [aβ·ne·ɣa·'sjon, -'θjon] *f* self-denial; **con** ~ selflessly

abnegado, -a [aβ·ne·'ɣa·do, -a] *adj* selfless

abochornar [a·βo·tʃor·'nar] I. *vt* 1. (*calor*) to oppress 2. (*avergonzar*) to embarrass II. *vr* ~**se** to be embarrassed (**de** by)

abofetear [a·βo·fe·te·'ar] *vt* to slap

abogacía [a·βo·ɣa·'si·a, -'θi·a] *f* legal profession; **ejercer la** ~ to practice law

abogado, -a [a·βo·'ɣa·do, -a] *m, f* 1. JUR lawyer; (*en tribunal*) attorney 2. (*defensor*) advocate

abogar <g → gu> [a·βo·'ɣar] *vi* ~ **por algo** to advocate sth

abolición [a·βo·li·'sjon, -'θjon] *f* abolition

abolir [a·βo·'lir] *irr vt* to abolish

abolladura [a·βo·ja·'du·ra, a·βo·ʎa-] *f* dent

abollar [a·βo·'jar, -'ʎar] *vt* to dent

abombarse [a·βom·'bar·se] *vr* 1. (*abultarse*) to bulge 2. *CSur, Ecua, Nic* (*alimentos*) to go bad

abominable [a·βo·mi·'na·βle] *adj* abominable

abonado, -a [a·βo·'na·do, -a] *m, f* (*a revistas*) subscriber

abonar [a·βo·'nar] I. *vt* 1. (*garantizar*) to guarantee 2. (*pagar*) to pay; ~ **en cuenta** to credit to an account 3. PREN to subscribe to II. *vr*: ~**se** to subscribe (**a** to)

abono [a·'βo·no] *m* 1. *t.* TEAT (*para el tren*) season ticket; ~ **mensual** monthly ticket 2. PREN subscription 3. (*pago*) payment; ~ **en cuenta** credit

abordaje [a·βor·'da·xe] *m* boarding; **tomar al** ~ to board

abordar [a·βor·'dar] *vt* 1. (*persona*) to approach 2. (*tema*) to discuss; (*problema*) to tackle

aborigen [a·βo·'ri·xen] I. *adj* aboriginal II. *mf* aborigine

aborrecer [a·βo·rre·'ser, -'θer] *irr como crecer vt* to loathe

abortar [a·βor·'tar] I. *vi* (*provocado*) to have an abortion; (*espontáneo*) to have a miscarriage II. *vt* to abort

aborto [a·'βor·to] *m* (*provocado*) abortion; (*espontáneo*) miscarriage

abotonar [a·βo·to·'nar] *vt* to button up

abr. *abr de* **abril** Apr.

abra ['a·βra] *f AmL* (*desmonte*) clearing

abrasar [a·βra·'sar] I. *vi* (*sol*) to scorch II. *vt* 1. (*quemar, dolor*) to burn; (*plantas*) to dry up 2. (*odio*) to consume III. *vr*: ~**se** to burn (up)

abrasivo [a·βra·'si·βo] *m* abrasive

abrazar <z → c> [a·βra·'sar, -'θar] I. *vt* 1. (*persona*) to embrace 2. (*contener*) to include II. *vr*: ~**se** to embrace (each other)

abrazo [a·'βra·so, -θo] *m* embrace; **dar un** ~ **a alguien** to give sb a hug; **un** (**fuerte**) ~ (*en cartas*) best regards

abrebotellas [a·βre·βo·'te·jas, -ʎas] *m inv* bottle opener

abrecartas [a·βre·'kar·tas] *m inv* letter opener

abrelatas [a·βre·'la·tas] *m inv* can opener

abreviar [a·βre·'βar] *vt* (*ganado*) to water

abreviado, -a [a·βre·ˈβja·ðo, -a] *adj* abridged

abreviar [a·βre·ˈβjar] **I.** *vt* **1.** (*acortar*) to shorten **2.** (*palabras*) to abbreviate **II.** *vi* to hurry

abreviatura [a·βre·βja·ˈtu·ra] *f* abbreviation

abridor [a·βri·ˈðor] *m* opener

abrigado, -a [a·βri·ˈɣa·ðo, -a] *adj* (*con ropa*) **estar ~** to be wrapped up warm

abrigar <g → gu> [a·βri·ˈɣar] *vt* **1.** (*cubrir*) to cover **2.** (*esperanzas*) to cherish

abrigo [a·ˈβri·ɣo] *m* **1.** (*prenda*) coat; **de ~** warm **2.** (*refugio*) shelter; **al ~ de** protected by

abril [a·ˈβril] *m* April; *v. t.* **marzo**

abrillantar [a·βri·jan·ta·ðo, -a; a·βri·ʎan-] *adj AmL* shining; **fruta abrillantada** *Arg* glazed fruit

abrillantar [a·βri·jan·ˈtar, a·βri·ʎan-] *vt* to polish

abrir [a·ˈβrir] *irr* **I.** *vt* **1.** (*algo cerrado*) to open; (*paraguas*) to put up; (*grifo*) to turn on; (*con la llave*) to unlock; **~ de par en par** to open wide **2.** (*túnel*) to dig **3.** (*inaugurar*) to open; (*curso*) to begin ▶ **en un ~ y cerrar de ojos** in the blink of an eye **II.** *vr:* **~se 1.** (*puerta*) to open (**a** onto) **2.** (*confiar*) to confide **3.** *inf* (*irse*) to beat it

abrochar [a·βro·ˈtʃar] *vt* (*con broches*) to fasten; (*con botones*) to button (up); (*cinturón*) fasten

abrumador(a) [a·βru·ma·ˈðor, -·ˈðo·ra] *adj* (*agobiador*) overwhelming

abrumar [a·βru·ˈmar] *vt* to overwhelm

abrupto, -a [a·ˈβrup·to, -a] *adj* (*camino*) steep; (*carácter*) abrupt

absentismo [aβ·sen·ˈtis·mo] *m* absenteeism

absolución [aβ·so·lu·ˈsjon, -ˈθjon] *f* **1.** JUR acquittal **2.** REL absolution

absolutamente [aβ·so·lu·ta·ˈmen·te] *adv* absolutely, completely; **~ nada** nothing at all

absoluto, -a [aβ·so·ˈlu·to, -a] *adj* absolute ▶ **en ~** not at all

absolver [aβ·sol·ˈβer] *irr como* **volver** *vt* **1.** JUR to acquit **2.** REL to absolve

absorber [aβ·sor·ˈβer] *vt* **1.** (*tierra*) *t.* FÍS to absorb **2.** (*cautivar*) to engross

absorción [aβ·sor·ˈsjon, -ˈθjon] *f* **1.** (*de líquidos*) *t.* FÍS absorption **2.** ECON takeover

absorto, -a [aβ·ˈsor·to, -a] *adj* **1.** (*pasmado*) amazed **2.** (*entregado*) absorbed

abstemio, -a [aβs·ˈte·mjo, -a] *adj* abstemious, teetotal

abstención [aβs·ten·ˈsjon, -ˈθjon] *f* *t.* POL abstention

abstenerse [aβs·te·ˈner·se] *irr como* **tener** *vr* (*privarse de*) *t.* POL to abstain (**de** from); **~ del tabaco** to refrain from smoking

abstinencia [aβs·ti·ˈnen·sja, -θja] *f* abstinence; **síndrome de ~** withdrawal symptoms

abstinente [aβs·ti·ˈnen·te] *adj* abstinent

abstracción [aβs·trak·ˈsjon, -ˈθjon] *f* abstraction

abstracto, -a [aβs·ˈtrak·to, -a] *adj* abstract

abstraer [aβs·tra·ˈer] *irr como* **traer I.** *vt* to abstract **II.** *vr* **~se en algo** to be absorbed in sth

abstraído, -a [aβs·tra·ˈi·ðo, -a] *adj* lost in thought; **estar ~ en algo** to be preoccupied by sth

absurdo [aβ·ˈsur·ðo] *m* absurdity

absurdo, -a [aβ·ˈsur·ðo, -a] *adj* absurd

abuchear [a·βu·tʃe·ˈar] *vt* to boo; (*silbando*) to hiss

abucheo [a·βu·ˈtʃeo] *m* booing; (*silbidos*) hissing

abuelo, -a [a·ˈβwe·lo] *m, f* grandfather *m*, grandmother *f*; **los ~s** the grandparents

abultado, -a [a·βul·ˈta·ðo, -a] *adj* bulky; (*labios*) thick

abultar [a·βul·ˈtar] **I.** *vi* to take up a lot of room **II.** *vt* *fig* (*exagerar*) to exaggerate

abundancia [a·βun·ˈdan·sja, -θja] *f* abundance; (*de bienes*) plenty; **en ~** in abundance; **vivir en la ~** to be affluent

abundante [a·βun·ˈdan·te] *adj* abundant; (*cosecha*) plentiful; **~ en algo** abounding in sth

abundar [a·βun·ˈdar] *vi* to abound; **~ en algo** to be rich in sth

aburrido, -a [a·βu·ˈrri·ðo, -a] *adj* **1.** *estar* (*harto*) bored (**de** with) **2.** *ser* (*pesado*) boring

aburrimiento [a·βu·rri·'mjen·to] *m*
1. (*tedio*) boredom **2.** (*fastidio*) bore

aburrir [a·βu·'rrir] **I.** *vt* **1.** (*hastiar*) to
bore **2.** (*fastidiar*) to tire **II.** *vr:* ~**se**
to be bored

abusar [a·βu·'sar] *vi* **1.** (*usar mal*) ~ **de**
algo to misuse sth; ~ **de su salud** to
abuse one's health **2.** (*aprovecharse*)
~ **de alguien** to take (unfair) advantage
of sb **3.** (*sexualmente*) ~ **de alguien** to
sexually abuse sb

abusivo, -a [a·βu·'si·βo, -a] *adj* improper;
(*precios*) outrageous

abuso [a·'βu·so] *m* abuse

acá [a·'ka] *adv* here; ~ **y allá** here and
there; **para** ~ over here; **¡ven ~!** come
here!

acabado, -a [a·ka·'βa·do, -a] *adj* (*completo, sin futuro*) finished

acabar [a·ka·'βar] **I.** *vi* **1.** (*terminar*)
to end; ~ **bien/mal** to turn out well/
badly; **ella acaba de llegar** she's just
arrived; ~ **con algo** to finish sth off; ~
con alguien to settle with sb **2.** (*finalmente*) ~**ás por comprenderlo** you'll
understand it in the end **II.** *vt* to finish;
(*consumir*) to finish off **III.** *vr:* ~**se; la
mantequilla se ha acabado** there's no
butter left; **todo se acabó** it's all over;
¡se acabó! and that's that!

academia [a·ka·'de·mja] *f* **1.** (*corporación*) academy **2.** (*colegio*) (private)
school

académico, -a [a·ka·'de·mi·ko, -a] *adj*
academic

acaecer [a·kae·'ser, -'θer] *irr como crecer*
vi to happen

acahual [a·ka·'wal] *m Méx* sunflower

acallar [a·ka·'jar, -'ʎar] *vt* **1.** (*hacer callar*)
to silence **2.** (*apaciguar*) to pacify

acalorado, -a [a·ka·lo·'ra·do, -a] *adj*
heated

acalorarse [a·ka·lo·'rar·se] *vr* **1.** (*sofocarse*) to get hot **2.** (*apasionarse*) to get
worked up (**con** over) **3.** (*enfadarse*) to
get angry (**por** about)

acampar [a·kam·'par] *vi* to camp

acantilado [a·kan·ti·'la·do] *m* cliff

acantilado, -a [a·kan·ti·'la·do, -a] *adj*
steep

acaparar [a·ka·pa·'rar] *vt* to hoard

acapillar [a·ka·pi·'jar, -'ʎar] *vt Méx* (*atrapar*) to seize

acariciar [a·ka·ri·'sjar, -'θjar] *vt* **1.** (*persona*) to caress **2.** (*plan*) to toy with

acarrear [a·ka·rre·'ar] *vt* **1.** (*transportar*)
to transport **2.** (*ocasionar*) to cause

acaso [a·'ka·so] **I.** *m* chance; **el ~ hizo
que... +*subj*** as chance would have it...
II. *adv* maybe ▶ **por si** ~ (*en caso de*)
in case; (*en todo caso*) just in case

acatar [a·ka·'tar] *vt* **1.** (*respetar*) to respect **2.** (*obedecer*) to obey **3.** *Col,
Guat, PRico* (*caer en cuenta*) to realize

acatarrarse [a·ka·ta·'rrar·se] *vr* to catch
a cold

acceder [ak·se·'der, ak·θe·] *vi* **1.** (*consentir*) to agree (**a** to) **2.** (*tener acceso*)
to gain access **3.** (*ascender*) to accede;
~ **a un cargo** to take office

accesible [ak·se·'si·βle, ak·θe·] *adj*
1. (*persona*) approachable **2.** (*lugar*)
accessible

accésit [ak·'se·sit, aɣ·'θe·] *m inv* consolation prize

acceso [ak·'se·so, aɣ·'θe·so] *m* **1.** (*a
un lugar*) *t.* COMPUT access; **de fácil** ~
(*easily*) accessible; **libre** ~ open access
2. (*ataque*) attack

accesorio [ak·se·'so·rjo, aɣ·θe·] *m* (*utensilio*) implement

accesorio, -a [ak·se·'so·rjo, -a; aɣ·θe·]
adj accessory

accidentado, -a [ak·si·den·'ta·do, -a;
aɣ·θi·] **I.** *adj* rugged **II.** *m, f* accident victim

accidental [ak·si·den·'tal, aɣ·θi·] *adj*
1. (*no esencial*) incidental **2.** (*casual*)
casual

accidentarse [ak·si·den·'tar·se, aɣ·θi·] *vr*
to have an accident

accidente [ak·si·'den·te, aɣ·θi·] *m* **1.** (*suceso*) accident; **por** ~ by accident; **sufrir
un** ~ to have an accident **2.** ~**s geográficos** geographical features

acción [ak·'sjon, aɣ·'θjon] *f* **1.** (*acto*)
act; **un hombre de** ~ a man of action;
entrar en ~ to go into action; **poner
en** ~ to put into action **2.** (*influencia*)
t. MIL, JUR action **3.** FIN share; ~ **común**
common share

accionar [ak·sjo·'nar, aɣ·θjo·] *vt* TÉC to

operate

accionista [ak·sjo·'nis·ta, aɣ·θjo-] *mf* shareholder

acebo [a·'se·βo, a·'θe-] *m* holly

acechar [a·se·'tʃar, a·θe-] *vt* **1.** (*espiar*) to spy on **2.** (*esperar*) to lie in wait for

acecho [a·'se·tʃo, a·θe-] *m* spying; **estar al ~** to lie in wait

aceite [a·'sei·te, a·'θei-] *m* oil; **~ comestible** cooking oil ▶ **echar ~ al fuego** to add fuel to the flames

aceitoso, -a [a·sei·'to·so, -a; a·θei-] *adj* oily

aceituna [a·sei·'tu·na, a·θei-] *f* olive

aceleración [a·se·le·ra·'sjon, a·θe·le·ra·'θjon] *f* acceleration

acelerador [a·se·le·ra·'dor, a·θe-] *m* gas pedal; **pisar el ~** to step on the gas

acelerar [a·se·le·'rar, a·θe-] *vt, vi* to accelerate; **¡no aceleres tanto!** don't go so fast!

acelga [a·'sel·ɣa, a·'θel-] *f* BOT Swiss chard

acento [a·'sen·to, -'θen·to] *m* **1.** LING (*prosódico*) stress **2.** LING (*signo*) accent **3.** (*pronunciación*) accent

acentuación [a·sen·twa·'sjon, a·θen·twa·'θjon] *f* (*prosódica*) stress; (*ortográfica*) accentuation

acentuado, -a [a·sen·tu·'a·do, -a; a·θen-] *adj* **1.** (*al pronunciar*) stressed; (*al escribir*) with an accent **2.** (*marcado*) marked

acentuar <*1. pres* acentúo> [a·sen·tu·'ar, a·θen-] *vt* **1.** (*al pronunciar*) to stress; (*al escribir*) to write with an accent **2.** (*resaltar*) to highlight

acepción [a·sep·'sjon, a·θep·'θjon] *f* sense, meaning

aceptable [a·sep·'ta·βle, a·θep-] *adj* acceptable

aceptación [a·sep·ta·'sjon, a·θep·ta·'θjon] *f* (*aprobación*) approval

aceptado, -a [a·sep·'ta·do, a·θep-] *interj AmL* (*vale*) OK

aceptar [a·sep·'tar, a·θep-] *vt* **1.** (*recibir*) to accept **2.** (*aprobar*) to approve

acequia [a·'se·kja, a·θe-] *f* irrigation ditch

acera [a·'se·ra, -'θe·ra] *f* sidewalk

acerca [a·'ser·ka, a·'θer-] *prep* **~ de** (*sobre*) about

acercamiento [a·ser·ka·'mjen·to, a·θer-] *m* approach

acercar <*c → qu*> [a·ser·'kar, a·θer-] **I.** *vt* **1.** (*poner cerca*) to bring nearer; (*traer*) to bring over **2.** *inf* (*llevar*) to take, to bring **II.** *vr* **~se a alguien/algo** to approach sb/sth

acero [a·'se·ro, -'θe·ro] *m* steel

acertado, -a [a·ser·'ta·do, -a; a·θer-] *adj* (*atinado*) accurate

acertar <*e → ie*> [a·ser·'tar, a·θer-] **I.** *vi* **1.** (*dar*) to hit; **~ el blanco** to hit the mark **2.** (*hacer con acierto*) to be right **II.** *vt* **1.** (*dar en el blanco*) to hit **2.** (*adivinar*) to get right

acertijo [a·ser·'ti·xo, a·θer-] *m* riddle

acetona [a·se·'to·na, a·θe-] *f* acetone

achacoso, -a [a·tʃa·'ko·so, -a] *adj* sickly; **estar ~** to be ailing

achaque [a·'tʃa·ke] *m* ailment

achicar <*c → qu*> [a·tʃi·'kar] **I.** *vt* **1.** (*empequeñecer*) to make smaller; (*persona*) to intimidate **2.** (*agua*) to bale out **II.** *vr:* **~se 1.** (*empequeñecerse*) to become smaller **2.** (*persona*) to take fright

achicharrar [a·tʃi·tʃa·'rrar] **I.** *vt* **1.** (*calor*) to scorch **2.** (*comida*) to burn **II.** *vr:* **~se 1.** (*comida*) to get burnt **2.** (*persona*) to be sweltering

achichiguar [a·tʃi·tʃi·'ɣwar] *vt Méx* (*malcriar*) to spoil

achicoria [a·tʃi·'ko·rja] *f* chicory

achinado, -a [a·tʃi·'na·do, -a] *adj* (*rasgos*) oriental

achiote [a·'tʃjo·te] *m AmC, Bol, Méx* **1.** BOT annatto tree **2.** (*pigmento*) annatto

achipolarse [a·tʃi·po·'lar·se] *vr Méx* (*personas*) to grow sad

achiquillado, -a [a·tʃi·ki·'ja·do, -a; 'ʎa·do, -a] *adj* **1.** *Méx* (*infantil*) childish **2.** *Chile* (*aniñado*) boyish

achira [a·'tʃi·ra] *f AmS* BOT canna

achís [a·'tʃis] *interj* atchoo

acholado, -a [a·tʃo·'la·do, -a] *adj CSur, Perú, Bol* **1.** (*mestizo*) mestizo **2.** (*acobardado*) intimidated

acholar [a·tʃo·'lar] **I.** *vt Chile, Perú, Bol* (*avergonzar*) to embarrass **II.** *vr:* **~se** *CSur, Perú, Bol* to become intimidated

achucutado, -a [a·tʃu·ku·'ta·do, -a] *adj AmL* (*abatido*) depressed

achumarse [a·tʃu·'mar·se] *vr Ecua* to get drunk

achunchar [a·tʃun·'tʃar] *vt AmL* to humiliate

acicalarse [a·si·ka·'lar·se, a·θi-] *vr* to get dressed up

acidez [a·si·'des, a·θi·'deθ] *f* acidity; ~ **de estómago** MED heartburn

ácido ['a·si·do, 'a·θi-] *m t.* QUÍM acid

ácido, -a ['a·si·do, -a; 'a·θi-] *adj* **1.** (*agrio*) tart; QUÍM acidic **2.** (*tono*) harsh

acierto [a·'sjer·to, a·'θjer-] *m* **1.** (*en el tiro*) accuracy **2.** (*éxito*) success

acitrón [a·si·'tron, a·θi-] *m Méx* CULIN candied citron

aclamación [a·kla·ma·'sjon, -'θjon] *f* applause

aclamar [a·kla·'mar] *vt* to cheer

aclaración [a·kla·ra·'sjon, -'θjon] *f* **1.** (*clarificación*) clarification **2.** (*explicación*) explanation

aclarar [a·kla·'rar] **I.** *vt* **1.** (*hacer más claro*) to lighten; (*la ropa*) to rinse; ~ **la voz** to clear one's throat **2.** (*explicar*) to explain **II.** *vr:* ~**se** to be clarified; *inf* (*entender*) to catch on

aclaratorio, -a [a·kla·ra·'to·rjo, -a] *adj* explanatory

acné [ay·'ne] *m o f* acne

acobardar [a·ko·βar·'dar] **I.** *vt* to frighten **II.** *vr:* ~**se** (*intimidarse*) to be frightened

acogedor(a) [a·ko·xe·'dor, -·'do·ra] *adj* welcoming, inviting

acoger <g → j> [a·ko·'xer] *vt* to welcome; (*recibir*) to receive

acogida [a·ko·'xi·da] *f* welcome; (*recibimiento*) reception

acometer [a·ko·me·'ter] **I.** *vi* to attack **II.** *vt* **1.** (*embestir*) to attack **2.** (*emprender*) to undertake

acomodado, -a [a·ko·mo·'da·do, -a] *adj* well-off

acomodador(a) [a·ko·mo·da·'dor, -·'do·ra] *m(f)* CINE usher

acomodar [a·ko·mo·'dar] **I.** *vt* **1.** (*adaptar*) to adapt **2.** (*colocar*) to place **3.** (*albergar*) to accommodate **II.** *vr:* ~**se** **1.** (*adaptarse*) to adapt oneself **2.** (*ponerse cómodo*) to make oneself comfortable

acomodo [a·ko·'mo·do] *m* **1.** (*arreglo*) arrangement **2.** (*acuerdo*) agreement

acompañado, -a [a·kom·pa·'na·do, -a] *adj* accompanied

acompañante [a·kom·pa·'nan·te] *mf* (*de una dama*) escort; (*en el coche*) passenger

acompañar [a·kom·pa·'nar] *vt* **1.** (*ir con*) MÚS to accompany; ~ **a alguien a casa** to see sb home **2.** (*hacer compañía*) ~ **a alguien** to keep sb company

acompasado, -a [a·kom·pa·'sa·do, -a] *adj* MÚS rhythmic

acomplejado, -a [a·kom·ple·'xa·do, -a] *adj* full of complexes

acomplejar [a·kom·ple·'xar] **I.** *vt* to give (sb) a complex **II.** *vr:* ~**se** to get a complex

aconchar [a·kon·'tʃar] **I.** *vt Méx* to tell (sb) off **II.** *vr:* ~**se** *Chile, Perú* (*sedimentarse*) to settle

acondicionado, -a [a·kon·di·sjo·'na·do, -a; -θjo·'na·do, -a] *adj* **bien/mal** ~ in good/bad condition

acondicionar [a·kon·di·sjo·'nar, -θjo·'nar] *vt* **1.** (*preparar*) to prepare **2.** (*climatizar*) to air-condition

acongojar [a·kon·go·'xar] *vt* to distress

aconsejable [a·kon·se·'xa·βle] *adj* advisable

aconsejar [a·kon·se·'xar] *vt* to advise; ~ **algo a alguien** to recommend sth to sb

acontecer [a·kon·te·'ser, -'θer] *irr como crecer vi* to happen

acontecimiento [a·kon·te·si·'mjen·to, a·kon·te·θi-] *m* event

acopio [a·'ko·pjo] *m* store; **hacer ~ de algo** to stock up on sth

acoplar [a·ko·'plar] *vt* **1.** (*juntar*) to join **2.** (*piezas*) to fit together **3.** ELEC to connect

acorazar <z → c> [a·ko·ra·'sar, -'θar] *vt* to armor-plate

acordar <o → ue> [a·kor·'dar] **I.** *vt* **1.** (*convenir*) to agree **2.** (*decidir*) to

decide II. *vr* ~**se de algo/alguien** to remember sth/sb; **¡acuérdate de decírselo!** remember to tell him/her!

acorde [a·'kor·de] I. *adj* agreed; **estar ~ con alguien** to be in agreement with sb; ~ **con el medio ambiente** in keeping with the environment II. *m* MÚS chord

acordeón [a·kor·de·'on] *m* accordion

acorralar [a·ko·rra·'lar] *vt* 1. (*ganado*) to round up 2. (*rodear*) to corner

acortar [a·kor·'tar] I. *vt* to shorten; (*duración*) to cut down; ~ **camino** to take a short cut II. *vr*: ~**se** to get shorter

acosar [a·ko·'sar] *vt* 1. (*perseguir*) to hound 2. (*asediar*) to harass; ~ **a alguien a preguntas** to pester sb with questions

acoso [a·'ko·so] *m* relentless pursuit; *fig* harassment

acostar <o → ue> [a·kos·'tar] I. *vt* to put to bed II. *vr*: ~**se** 1. (*descansar*) to lie down; **estar acostado** to be lying down 2. (*ir a la cama*) to go to bed; ~**se con alguien** to go to bed with sb

acostumbrado, -a [a·kos·tum·'bra·do, -a] *adj* accustomed; **mal ~** spoiled

acostumbrar [a·kos·tum·'brar] I. *vi* ~ **a hacer algo** to be used to doing sth II. *vr*: ~**se a algo** to get used to sth

acotación [a·ko·ta·'sjon, -'θjon] *f* (*cota*) elevation mark

acre ['a·kre] *m* acre

acreditado, -a [a·kre·di·'ta·do, -a] *adj* reputable

acreditar [a·kre·di·'tar] *vt* 1. (*atestiguar*) to vouch for 2. (*autorizar*) to authorize 3. (*dar reputación*) to do credit

acreedor(a) [a·kre·'dor/a·kre·e·'dor, -·'do·ra] I. *adj* **hacerse ~ a** [*o* **de**] **algo** to be worthy of sth II. *m(f)* FIN creditor

acribillar [a·kri·βi·'jar, -·ʎar] *vt* to riddle (**a** with)

acrílico, -a [a·'kri·li·ko, -a] *adj* acrylic

acriollarse [a·krjo·'jar·se, -·ʎar·se] *vr AmL* to go native

acrobacia [a·kro·'βa·sja, -θja] *f* acrobatics *pl*

acróbata [a·'kro·βa·ta] *mf* acrobat

acrónimo [a·'kro·ni·mo] *m* acronym

acta ['ak·ta] *f* (*de una reunión*) minutes *pl*; **hacer constar en ~** to record in the minutes

actitud [ak·ti·'tud] *f* 1. (*corporal*) posture 2. (*disposición*) attitude 3. (*comportamiento*) behavior

activamente [ak·ti·βa·'men·te] *adv* actively

activar [ak·ti·'βar] *vt* 1. (*avivar*) to stimulate 2. QUÍM, COMPUT to activate

actividad [ak·ti·βi·'dad] *f* activity; (*ocupación*) occupation; ~ **profesional** profession; **entrar en ~** to become active

activo [ak·'ti·βo] *m* FIN assets *pl*; ~ **circulante/fijo** current/fixed assets

activo, -a [ak·'ti·βo, -a] *adj* active; (*medicamento*) effective

acto ['ak·to] *m* 1. (*acción*) action; **hacer ~ de presencia** to put in an appearance 2. (*ceremonia*) ceremony; ~ **conmemorativo** commemoration 3. TEAT act ► ~ **seguido**... immediately after...; **en el ~** immediately, on the spot

actor, actriz [ak·'tor, ak·'tris, -'triθ] *m, f* actor *m*, actress *f*; ~ **de cine** film actor

actor(a) [ak·'tor, -·'to·ra] *m(f)* plaintiff

actuación [ak·twa·'sjon, -'θjon] *f* 1. (*conducta*) conduct; **la ~ de la policía** the police action 2. TEAT performance; ~ **en directo** live performance

actual [ak·tu·'al] *adj* (*de ahora*) present; (*corriente*) current

actualidad [ak·twa·li·dad] *f* present; **en la ~** at present; **de ~** topical

actualizar <z → c> [ak·twa·li·'sar, -'θar] *vt* to update

actualmente [ak·twal·'men·te] *adv* at the moment, currently

actuar <1. *pres* actúo> [ak·tu·'ar] *vi* 1. (*hacer*) to work 2. (*tener efecto*) ~ **sobre algo** to have an effect on sth 3. TEAT to act

acuache [a·'kwa·tʃe] *m Méx* (*compinche*) pal

acuarela [a·kwa·'re·la] *f* watercolor

acuario [a·'kwa·rjo] *m* aquarium

Acuario [a·'kwa·rjo] *m* ASTR Aquarius

acuático, -a [a·'kwa·ti·ko, -a] *adj* aquatic; **parque ~** water park

acuchamarse [a·ku·tʃa·'mar·se] *vr Ven* (*entristecerse*) to get depressed

acuchillar [a·ku·tʃi·'jar, -'ʎar] *vt* (*herir*) to knife; (*matar*) to stab to death

acudir [a·ku·'dir] *vi* to go; **~ a una cita** to keep an appointment; **~ a** (*recurrir*) to turn to

acueducto [a·kwe·'duk·to] *m* aqueduct

acuerdo [a·'kwer·do] *m* **1.** (*convenio*) agreement; **llegar a un ~** POL agreement; **llegar a un ~** to reach an agreement; **estar de ~ con alguien** to agree with sb; **ponerse de ~** to come to an agreement; **de común ~** by mutual consent **2.** (*decisión*) decision; **tomar un ~** to pass a resolution ▶ **¡de ~!** I agree!, OK!; **de ~ con** in accordance with

acuerpado, -a [a·kwer·'pa·do, -a] *adj Bol* (*corpulento*) hefty

acullicar [a·ku·ji·'kar, -ʎi·'kar] *vi Arg, Bol, Chile, Perú* to chew coca leaves

acumuchar [a·ku·mu·'tʃar] *vt Chile* to pile up

acumulación [a·ku·mu·la·'sjon, -'θjon] *f* accumulation; (*de cosas reunidas*) collection

acumular [a·ku·mu·'lar] *vt* **1.** (*reunir*) to collect **2.** (*amontonar*) to accumulate

acunar [a·ku·'nar] *vt* to rock (to sleep)

acuñar [a·ku·'ɲar] *vt* (*monedas*) to mint; (*palabras*) to coin

acupuntura [a·ku·pun·'tu·ra] *f* acupuncture

acurrucarse <c → qu> [a·ku·rru·'kar·se] *vr* to curl up; (*por el frío*) to huddle up

acusación [a·ku·sa·'sjon, -'θjon] *f* **1.** (*inculpación*) accusation **2.** JUR (*en juicio*) charge; (*escrito*) indictment

acusado, -a [a·ku·'sa·do, -a] **I.** *adj* (*claro*) pronounced; (*marcado*) marked **II.** *m, f* accused

acusar [a·ku·'sar] *vt* **1.** (*culpar*) to accuse (**de** of) **2.** (*en juicio*) to charge **3.** ECON to confirm; **~ recibo de un pedido** to acknowledge receipt of an order

acusativo [a·ku·sa·'ti·βo] *m* LING accusative

acuse [a·'ku·se] *m* **~ de recibo** acknowledgement of receipt

acústica [a·'kus·ti·ka] *f* **1.** (*ciencia*) acoustics + *sing vb* **2.** (*de un sitio*)

acoustics + *pl vb*

acústico, -a [a·'kus·ti·ko, -a] *adj* acoustic

acutí [a·ku·'ti] *m Arg, Par, Urug* ZOOL agouti

adaptable [a·dap·'ta·βle] *adj* adaptable

adaptación [a·dap·ta·'sjon, -'θjon] *f* adaptation; **la ~ de una obra de teatro al cine** the film version of a play

adaptador [a·dap·ta·'dor] *m* TÉC adapter

adaptar [a·dap·'tar] **I.** *vt* **1.** (*acomodar*) *t.* LIT to adapt; **bien adaptado al grupo** well adapted to the group; **~ una novela a la pantalla** to adapt a novel for the screen **2.** (*ajustar*) to adjust; **~ algo a algo** to adapt sth to sth **II.** *vr:* **~se** to adapt

adecuado, -a [a·de·'kwa·do, -a] *adj* **1.** (*apto*) appropriate **2.** (*palabras*) fitting

adecuar [a·de·'kwar] *vt, vr:* **~se** to adapt

a. de (J)C. ['an·tes de (xe·su)·'kris·to] *abr de* **antes de (Jesu)cristo** BC

adelantado, -a [a·de·lan·'ta·do, -a] *adj* (*avanzado*) advanced ▶ **por ~** in advance

adelantamiento [a·de·lan·ta·'mjen·to] *m* (*del coche*) passing; **realizar un ~** to pass

adelantar [a·de·lan·'tar] **I.** *vi* **1.** (*progresar*) to progress; **no adelanto nada en francés** I'm not making any progress in French **2.** (*coche*) to pass **II.** *vt* **1.** (*reloj*) to put forward **2.** (*avanzar*) to move forward; **~ unos pasos** to go forward a few steps **3.** (*coche*) to pass **4.** (*viaje*) to bring forward **5.** (*paga*) to advance **6.** (*ganar*) to gain; **¿qué adelantas con esto?** where does that get you? **III.** *vr:* **~se** (*reloj*) to be fast

adelante [a·de·'lan·te] *adv* forward, ahead; **llevar un plan ~** to carry forward a plan; **sacar una familia ~** to provide for a family; **¡~!** come in!; **seguir ~** to go (straight) ahead; **véase más ~** see below

adelanto [a·de·'lan·to] *m* progress; (*anticipo*) advance; **~s técnicos** technical innovations

adelgazar <z → c> [a·del·ɣa·'sar, -'θar] *vi* to lose weight

ademán [a·de·'man] *m* gesture; **hacer ~**

English phonetic symbols –
Símbolos fonéticos del inglés

Vowels/Vocales

[a]	farm, not
[æ]	man, sad
[e]	bed, get, hair, dare
[ə]	ago, better, actor, anonymous, antivirus
[ɜ]	bird, her
[i]	beat, bee, me, belief, hobby
[ɪ]	it, wish, near
[ɔ]	all, law, long, sauce, floor
[u]	do, you, soon
[ʊ]	look, push, sure, tour
[ʌ]	but, son
[ã]	genre

Diphthongs/Diptongos

[aɪ]	life, buy, by
[aʊ]	house, now
[eɪ]	lame, name
[ɔɪ]	boy, oil
[oʊ]	rope, piano, road, toe, show, plateau
[ju]	accuse, beauty

Consonants/Consonantes

[b]	been, blind
[d]	do, had
[ð]	father, this
[dʒ]	cartridge, garbage, jam, object
[f]	father, wolf
[g]	beg, go
[h]	house
[j]	youth
[ʒ]	pleasure
[k]	keep, milk
[l]	ill, lamp, oil
[m]	am, man
[n]	manner, no
[ŋ]	long, sing, prank
[p]	happy, paper
[r]	dry, red, current, player, part
[s]	sand, stand, yes, cent, capacity
[ʃ]	ship, station, fish
[t]	fat, tell
[t̬]	butter, water
[θ]	death, thank
[tʃ]	catch, church
[v]	live, voice
[w]	water, we, which, will, wore
[z]	gaze, these, zeal

Signs/Otros símbolos

[']	primary stress
[,]	secondary stress
[·]	syllable division

Symbol/ Símbolo	Graphic representation/ Representación gráfica	Examples/ Ejemplos	Notes/Notas
[ɣ]	g, gu	paga, agosto, agua, alegre, estigma, alargar,	*Used in the combinations g + a, o, u and gu + e, i in the middle of a word and when not preceded by n.*
[t]	t	letra, tío	
[d]	d	dedo, conde, caldo	
[θ]	c, z	cero, cita, zarza, cruz	*Occurs in the combinations c + e,i as well as in z in all positions in ceceo pronunciation characteristic of Spain.*
[l]	l	libro, bloque, sal	
[ʎ]	ll	llueve, pollo	*Pronounced similarly to lli in million. Used for ll in all positions.*
[s]	s, c	sábado, así, coser, afueras, cebra, cierto, zarza, cruz	*Used for s in all positions; in seseo pronunciation characteristic of Spanish America: for c+e, i and for z in all positions.*
[r]	r	caro, prisa, vivir	*Used in the middle or at the end of a word when not preceded by n, l, s.*
[rr]	r, rr	roca, honrado	*Used for r when it occurs at the beginning of a word; also used for -rr- and -r- at the beginning of a syllable after n, l, s.*
[tʃ]	ch	chino, mucho	
[j]	y, ll	cónyuge, inyección, yunque, llueve, pollo	*Used when y occurs at the beginning of a syllable. Also used for ll in yeísmo.*
[ʃ]	sh	shock	*Like English shock, show.*
[w]	u, w	adecuado, bueno, ruido, arduo, windsurf, whisky	*Used as the first element of the diphthongs wa, we, wi, wo; also in w or wh in some words of foreign origin.*

Triphthongs/Triptongos

Symbol/Símbolo	Graphic representation/Representación gráfica	Examples/Ejemplos	Notes/Notas
[jai]	iái	apreciáis	Pronounced like yi in yikes!
[jei]	iéi	despreciéis	Pronounced like the cheer yay!
[wai]	uay	Paraguay	Pronounced like why
[wie]	uey	buey	Pronounced like way

Consonants/Consonantes

Symbol/Símbolo	Graphic representation/Representación gráfica	Examples/Ejemplos	Notes/Notas
[p]	p	pato	
[b]	b, v	vacío, bola, hombre	Used for b and v at the beginning of a word and for b following m.
[β]	b, v	objeto, pueblo, vivir	Used for all positions except b and v at the beginning of a word and for b following m; pronounced like v in never and with both lips touching.
[m]	m, n	mamá	
[n]	n	nadie, entre	
[ɲ]	ñ	viña, ñácara	Pronounced like ny in canyon.
[f]	f	fabuloso, café	
[k]	c, q, k	casa, cosa, Cuba, actual, que, quinta, kilo	Used in the combinations c + a, o, u, c before a consonant and qu + e, i. Also used in a number of words of foreign origin beginning with k.
[g]	g, gu	garra, gobierno, gubernamental, guerra, guija, mango	Used at the beginning of a word or in the combinations g + a, o, u and gu + e, i. Also used in the middle of a word, preceded by n.
[x]	j, g	justo, rojo, girar, gente, agitar, México	Used for j and for the combinations g + e, i except at the end of a word; sometimes also used for x.

Símbolos fonéticos del español – Spanish phonetic symbols

Vowels/Vocales

Symbol/Símbolo	Graphic representation/Representación gráfica	Examples/Ejemplos
[a]	a	san, acción
[e]	e	pez, saber
[i]	i	sí, mirar
[o]	o	con
[u]	u	tú, dibujo

Diphthongs/Diptongos

Symbol/Símbolo	Graphic representation/Representación gráfica	Examples/Ejemplos	Notes/Notas
[ai]	ai, ay	baile, hay	Pronounced like *i* in *write*
[au]	au	auto, causa	Pronounced like *ow* in *how*
[ei]	ei, ey	aceite, ley	Pronounced like *a* in *rate*
[eu]	eu	deuda	Pronounced similarly to *ay* in *hay*
[oi]	oi, oy	boicoteo, hoy	Pronounced like *oi* in *foil*
[ja]	ia, ya	envidia, adyacente	Pronounced like *ya* in *yard*
[je]	ie, ye	abierto, ayer	Pronounced like *ye* in *yellow*
[jo]	io, yo	aleatorio, apoyo	Pronounced like *Yo* in *York*
[ju]	iu, yu	ciudad, ayuda	Pronounced like *u* in *fuse*
[wa]	ua	adecuado	Pronounced like *wa* in *water*
[we]	ue	bueno, cuerda	Pronounced like *wa* in *wake*
[wi]	ui	ruido	Pronounced like *wee* in *week*
[wo]	uo	arduo	Pronounced like *uo* in *quote*

La pronunciación del español – Spanish pronunciation

Remarkable variations are evident in Spanish pronunciation, both within the regions of the Iberian Peninsula and amongst the individual countries in which Spanish is spoken. Surprisingly, these variations are stronger within Spain itself than between the various Spanish-speaking countries in America. In the bilingual regions of the Iberian Peninsula – Catalonia, Valencia, the Balearic Islands, the Basque Provinces, and Galicia – pronunciation of Spanish is strongly influenced by the native languages of these areas. In other regions, it is the phonetic features of a range of dialects that have been mixed into spoken Spanish. Particularly characteristic of Andalusia, for example, is this dialect's particular variant of so-called *ceceo* pronunciation, in which not only the usual *z* and *c*, but also *s* is pronounced θ (as in *think)*. So, in Andalusia, the words *la casa* ('the house') and *la caza* ('the hunt') are pronounced in exactly the same way.

In the vernacular pronunciation of some areas of Spain and Spanish America, one encounters aspiration of *s* at the end of a word. In the case of *las casas*, for example, the pronunciation would be *lah kása*, instead of *las kásas*. The *s* can even disappear altogether as is the case in the pronunciation *mímo*, instead of *mísmo* for the word *mismo*. Both phenomena are considered nonstandard and should therefore be avoided.

Ceceo (θe·'θeo)

This refers to the pronunciation of *z* in all positions and of *c* before *e* or *i* as θ, e.g., paθ for *paz*, θínko for *cinco* or aθeptáble for *aceptable*. Generally speaking, *ceceo* is associated with Spain.

Pronunciation in Spanish America

Spanish-American pronunciation bears the closest similarity to that of the Andalusian region. Among the phonetic characteristics of Spanish America, the following are the most characteristic:

Seseo (se·'seo)

Seseo refers to the pronunciation of *z* and *c* as *s* (e.g., **pas** instead of paθ for *paz* or **sínko**, instead of θínko for *cinco*). Though this is a characteristic mainly of Spanish America, it also occurs in subregions of Andalusia and on the Canary Islands.

In this dictionary, *seseo* pronunciation is given first and c*eceo* pronunciation is given as a second variant.

Yeísmo

Yeísmo is common not only in Spanish-speaking areas of America but also in various regions of Spain such as Andalusia, the Canary Islands, Extremadura, Madrid, and Castilian subregions. It refers to the pronunciation of *ll* as *y* (e.g., **yovér**, instead of **llovér** for *llover*). However, it would be incorrect to assume that *yeísmo* is a practiced all over Spanish America. As a matter of fact, the standard pronunciation of *ll* is used in the subregions of Chile, Peru, Columbia, and Ecuador.

In this dictionary, *yeísmo* pronunciation is given first and ʎ pronunciation is provided as a second variant.

Also characteristic of Spanish America is the pronunciation of *y* as dʒ (e.g., adʒér, instead of ajér for *ayer*) in Argentina, Uruguay, and subregions of Ecuador and Mexico.

Índice

Contents

de salir to make as if to leave

además [a·ðe·ˈmas] *adv* besides, moreover

adentrarse [a·ðen·ˈtrar·se] *vr* (*tema*) to study thoroughly; ~ **en algo** to go into sth; (*penetrar*) to penetrate into sth

adentro [a·ˈðen·tro] *adv* inside; **mar ~** out to sea; **el grito le salió de muy ~** his/her cry came from deep within

adentros [a·ˈðen·tros] *mpl* innermost being; **para sus ~** inwardly; **guardar algo para sus ~** to keep sth to oneself

adepto, -a [a·ˈðep·to, -a] *m, f* supporter

aderezar <z → c> [a·ðe·re·ˈsar, -ˈθar] *vt* 1. (*preparar*) to prepare 2. (*condimentar*) to season; (*ensalada*) to dress

adeudar [a·ðeu·ˈdar] *vr*: ~**se** to run into debt

adherir [a·ðe·ˈrir] *irr como* sentir I. *vt* to stick II. *vr*: ~**se** (*pegarse*) to adhere

adhesión [a·ðe·ˈsjon] *f* 1. (*adherencia*) adhesion 2. (*a una opinión*) adherence, support; ~ **a alguien** support of sb; ~ **a algo** membership in sth

adhesivo [a·ðe·ˈsi·βo] *m* 1. (*sustancia*) adhesive 2. (*pegatina*) sticker

adhesivo, -a [a·ðe·ˈsi·βo, -a] *adj* adhesive

adicción [a·ðik·ˈsjon, -a·ðiɣ·ˈθjon] *f* addiction; ~ **a las drogas** drug addiction

adición [a·ði·ˈsjon, -ˈθjon] *f t.* MAT addition

adicional [a·ði·sjo·ˈnal, -θjo·ˈnal] *adj* additional

adicto, -a [a·ˈðik·to, -a] I. *adj* addicted; ~ **a las drogas** addicted to drugs II. *m, f* addict

adiestrar [a·ðjes·ˈtrar] *vt* to train

adinerado, -a [a·ði·ne·ˈra·ðo, -a] *adj* wealthy

adiós [a·ˈðjos] I. *interj* (*despedida*) goodbye, bye II. *m* farewell; **decir ~ a alguien** to say goodbye to sb

aditivo [a·ði·ˈti·βo] *m* additive

adivinanza [a·ði·βi·ˈnan·sa, -θa] *f* riddle

adivinar [a·ði·βi·ˈnar] *vt* 1. (*el futuro*) to foretell 2. (*conjeturar*) to guess; **¡adivina cuántos años tengo!** guess how old I am!

adjetivo [ad·xe·ˈti·βo] *m* adjective; ~ **numeral** numeral

adjudicar <c → qu> [ad·xu·ði·ˈkar] I. *vt* (*premio*) to award II. *vr*: ~**se** to appropriate; (*premio*) to win

adjuntar [ad·xun·ˈtar] *vt* to enclose

adjunto, -a [a·ˈðʝun·to, -a] *adj* 1. (*junto*) enclosed 2. (*auxiliar*) assistant; **profesor(a) ~** UNIV associate professor

administración [ad·mi·nis·tra·ˈsjon, -ˈθjon] *f* 1. (*gestión*) administration; **la ~ española** the Spanish authorities; ~ **de una cuenta** managing of an account; ~ **municipal** town/city council 2. (*de medicamentos*) administering 3. *Arg* (*gobierno*) government

administrador(a) [ad·mi·nis·tra·ˈdor] *m(f)* administrator; (*gerente*) manager

administrar [ad·mi·nis·ˈtrar] *vt* 1. (*dirigir*) to administer; ~ **justicia** to dispense justice 2. (*racionar*) to ration 3. (*medicamentos*) to administer

administrativo, -a [ad·mi·nis·tra·ˈti·βo, -a] I. *adj* administrative II. *m, f* clerk

admirable [ad·mi·ˈra·βle] *adj* admirable

admiración [ad·mi·ra·ˈsjon, -ˈθjon] *f* 1. (*respeto*) admiration 2. (*asombro*) amazement 3. (*signo*) exclamation point

admirado, -a [ad·mi·ˈra·ðo, -a] *adj* amazed

admirador(a) [ad·mi·ra·ˈdor, -·ˈdo·ra] *m(f)* admirer

admirar [ad·mi·ˈrar] *vt* 1. (*adorar*) to admire 2. (*asombrar*) to amaze

admisible [ad·mi·ˈsi·βle] *adj* admissible

admisión [ad·mi·ˈsjon] *f* ~ **en algo** admission [*o* acceptance] to sth

admitir [ad·mi·ˈtir] *vt* 1. (*aceptar*) to accept 2. (*reconocer*) to recognize 3. (*permitir*) to permit; ~ **una queja** JUR to accept a complaint

ADN [a·ðe·ˈe·ne] *m abr de* **ácido desoxirribonucleico** DNA

adobar [a·ðo·ˈβar] *vt* (*con salsa*) to marinate; (*carne*) to pickle

adobe [a·ˈðo·βe] *m* adobe

adolecer [a·ðo·le·ˈser, -ˈθer] *irr como* crecer *vi* (*enfermar*) to get sick; (*padecer*) to suffer; **este chico adolece de falta de imaginación** this boy suffers from a lack of imagination

adolescencia [a·ðo·les·ˈsen·sja, -ˈθen·θja] *f* adolescence

adolescente [a·do·les·'sen·te, -'θen·te]
I. *adj* adolescent II. *mf* teenager
adonde [a·'don·de] *adv* where; **el pueblo
~ iremos es muy bonito** the village
we'll go to is very pretty
adónde [a·'don·de] *adv* (*interrogativo*)
where
adopción [a·dop·'sjon, -'θjon] *f* adoption
adoptar [a·dop·'tar] *vt* to adopt
adoptivo, -a [a·dop·'ti·βo, -a] *adj* adopted, foster
adoquín [a·do·'kin] *m* cobblestone
adorable [a·do·'ra·βle] *adj* adorable
adorar [a·do·'rar] *vt* to adore
adormecer [a·dor·me·'ser, -'θer] *irr como
crecer* I. *vt* to make sleepy; (*dolor*) to
numb II. *vr*: **~se** to fall asleep
adormilarse [a·dor·mi·'lar·se] *vr* to doze
adornar [a·dor·'nar] I. *vt* to adorn [o to
decorate] II. *vr*: **~se** to adorn oneself
adorno [a·'dor·no] *m* adornment; **árbol
de ~** ornamental tree; **la lámpara sólo
está de ~** the lamp is just for decoration;
estar de ~ *fig* to be for show
adosado, -a [a·do·'sa·do, -a] *adj* **casa
adosada** duplex
adquirir [ad·ki·'rir] *irr vt* 1. (*conseguir*) to
acquire; **~ un hábito** to acquire a habit
2. (*comprar*) to purchase
adquisición [ad·ki·si·'sjon, -'θjon] *f* acquisition; **este coche es una buena ~**
this car is a good buy
adquisitivo, -a [ad·ki·si·'ti·βo, -a] *adj* ac-
quisitive; **poder ~** purchasing power
adrede [a·'dre·de] *adv* on purpose
adrenalina [a·dre·na·'li·na] *f* adrenalin
Adriático [a·'drja·ti·ko] *m* GEO Adriatic
adscribir [ads·kri·'βir] *irr como escribir
vt* to appoint
aduana [a·'dwa·na] *f* 1. (*tasa*) customs
duty; **declaración de ~s** customs declaration; **despacho de ~** customs clearance; **sin ~** duty-free 2. (*oficina*) customs office
aduanero, -a [a·dwa·'ne·ro, -a] I. *adj*
customs II. *m, f* customs officer
adulador(a) [a·du·la·'dor, -'do·ra] *adj*
flattering
adular [a·du·'lar] *vt* to flatter
adulterar [a·dul·te·'rar] *vt* to falsify; (*alimentos*) to adulterate

adulterio [a·dul·'te·rjo] *m* adultery
adúltero, -a [a·'dul·te·ro, -a] I. *adj* adulterous II. *m, f* adulterer
adulto, -a [a·'dul·to, -a] *adj, m, f* adult
adverbial [ad·βer·'βjal] *adj* adverbial
adverbio [ad·'βer·βjo] *m* adverb; **~ de
modo/de lugar/de tiempo** adverb of
manner/of place/of time
adversario, -a [ad·βer·'sa·rjo, -a] *m, f*
opponent
adversidad [ad·βer·si·'dad] *f* 1. (*contrariedad*) adversity 2. (*desgracia*) setback
adverso, -a [ad·'βer·so, -a] *adj* adverse;
(*clima*) harsh
advertencia [ad·βer·'ten·sja, -θja] *f*
1. (*amonestación*) warning 2. (*indicación*) advice
advertir [ad·βer·'tir] *irr como sentir vt*
1. (*reparar*) to notice; **advirtió mis
intenciones** he/she guessed my intentions 2. (*indicar*) to point out 3. (*avisar*) to warn; **~ algo** to draw attention
to sth
adyacencia [ad·ja·'sen·sja, -'θen·θja] *f*
RíoPl (*proximidad*) proximity; **en las
~s** in the vicinity
adyacente [ad·ja·'sen·te, -'θen·te] *adj*
adjacent
aéreo, -a [a·'e·reo, -a] *adj* aerial; **base aérea** MIL airbase; **compañía aérea** airline
(company); **por vía aérea** (by) airmail
aeróbic [ae·'ro·βik] *m* aerobics + *sing
or pl vb*
aerodinámico, -a [ae·ro·di·'na·mi·ko,
-a] *adj* aerodynamic; (*vehículo*) streamlined
aerolínea [ae·ro·'li·nea] *f* airline
aeroplano [ae·ro·'pla·no] *m* airplane
aeropuerto [ae·ro·'pwer·to] *m* airport
aerosol [ae·ro·'sol] *m* aerosol; (*espray*)
spray
afable [a·'fa·βle] *adj* affable
afamado, -a [a·fa·'ma·do, -a] *adj* famous
afán [a·'fan] *m* 1. (*ahínco*) eagerness; **~
de algo** urge for sth; **~ de lucro** profit
motive; **poner mucho ~ en algo** to put
a lot of effort into sth 2. (*anhelo*) **~ de
algo** longing for sth
afanador(a) [a·fa·na·'dor, -'do·ra] *m(f)*

afanar [a·fa·'nar] I. vt CSur inf to steal, to pinch II. vr: ~se (esforzarse) to toil (away)

afección [a·fek·'sjon, a·fey·'θjon] f 1. MED condition 2. (inclinación) inclination

afectado, -a [a·fek·'ta·do, -a] adj affected

afectar [a·fek·'tar] vt 1. (influir) to concern 2. (dañar) to harm 3. (impresionar) to affect

afectivo, -a [a·fek·'ti·βo, -a] adj 1. (de afecto) affective 2. (cariñoso) affectionate

afecto [a·'fek·to] m emotion; ~ a algo/alguien affection for sth/sb

afecto, -a [a·'fek·to, -a] adj ~ a algo/alguien inclined towards sth/sb

afectuoso, -a [a·fek·tu·'o·so, -a] adj affectionate; (cordial) kind; **afectuosamente** yours affectionately

afeitado [a·fei·'ta·do] m shave

afeitar [a·fei·'tar] I. vt to shave; **máquina de ~** (safety) razor II. vr: ~se to shave

afgano, -a [af·'ɣa·no, -a] adj, m, f afghan

afianzar <z → c> [a·fjan·'sar, -'θar] I. vt (dar firmeza) to strengthen II. vr: ~se (afirmarse) to become established

afiche [a·'fi·tʃe] m AmL poster

afición [a·fi·'sjon, -'θjon] f 1. (inclinación) liking; **tener** [o sentir] **una ~ hacia** [o a] **algo** to be fond of sth 2. (pasatiempo) hobby; **hacer algo por ~** to do sth as a hobby 3. (hinchada) fans pl

aficionado, -a [a·fi·sjo·'na·do, -a; a·fi·θjo-] I. adj amateur; **ser ~ a tocar la flauta** to be fond of playing the flute II. m, f 1. (entusiasta) lover; DEP fan 2. (no profesional) amateur

aficionar [a·fi·sjo·'nar, a·fi·θjo-] I. vt ~ a alguien a algo to get sb interested in sth II. vr: ~se a algo (acostumbrarse) to take a liking to sth

afilado, -a [a·fi·'la·do, -a] adj (cuchillo) sharp; (nariz) pointed; (cara) thin

afilalápices [a·fi·la·'la·pi·ses, -θes] m inv pencil sharpener

afilar [a·fi·'lar] I. vt to sharpen II. vr: ~se to get sharp

afiliación [a·fi·lja·'sjon, -'θjon] f affiliation; ~ **política** political affiliation

afiliado, -a [a·fi·'lja·do, -a] m, f member

afin [a·'fin] adj related

afinar [a·fi·'nar] I. vi (cantando) to sing in tune; (tocando) to play in tune II. vt 1. (hacer más fino) to refine; ~ **la puntería** to sharpen one's aim 2. MÚS to tune

afinidad [a·fi·ni·'dad] f similarity; ~ **de caracteres** relatedness of character

afirmación [a·fir·ma·'sjon, -'θjon] f 1. (confirmación) confirmation 2. (aseveración) assertion

afirmar [a·fir·'mar] I. vt 1. (decir sí) to affirm; (dar por cierto) to confirm; ~ **con la cabeza** to nod in agreement 2. (aseverar) to state II. vr: ~se to be confirmed; ~se en algo to reaffirm sth

afirmativo, -a [a·fir·ma·'ti·βo, -a] adj affirmative; **en caso ~** if so

aflicción [a·flik·'sjon, -ɣ'θjon] f ~ **por algo/alguien** grief for sth/sb

afligir <g → j> [a·fli·'xir] I. vt 1. (apenar) to upset 2. (atormentar) to afflict II. vr ~se por algo to get upset about [o over] sth

aflojar [a·flo·'xar] I. vi to slacken II. vt 1. (nudo) to loosen 2. (velocidad) to reduce; ~ **el paso** to slacken one's pace; **un tira y afloja** a tug-of-war III. vr: ~se to slacken

aflorar [a·flo·'rar] vi 1. (salir) to come to the surface 2. (apuntar) to appear

afluencia [a·'flwen·θja, -sja] f abundance; (gente) crowd

afluente [a·'flwen·te] m tributary

afonía [a·fo·'ni·a] f hoarseness

afónico, -a [a·'fo·ni·ko, -a] adj hoarse

aforo [a·'fo·ro] m (en teatro) capacity; **la sala tiene un ~ de 300 personas** the hall can seat 300 people

afortunado, -a [a·for·tu·'na·do, -a] adj fortunate; **¡qué afortunada eres!** how lucky you are!

afrenta [a·'fren·ta] f affront, insult

afrentar [a·fren·'tar] vt to insult

África ['a·fri·ka] f Africa

africano, -a [a·fri·'ka·no, -a] adj, m, f African

afroamericano, -a [a·fro·a·me·ri·'ka·

no] *adj, m, f* Afro-American, African American

afrodisiaco [a·fro·di·'sja·ko] *m*, **afrodisíaco** [a·fro·di·'si·a·ko] *m* aphrodisiac

afrontar [a·fron·'tar] *vt* to face; **~ un problema** to tackle a problem

afuera [a·'fwe·ra] *adv* outside; **¡~!** *inf* get out of here!

afueras [a·'fwe·ras] *fpl* outskirts *pl;* **~ de la ciudad** outskirts of the city

agachar [a·ɣa·'ʧar] I. *vt* to lower II. *vr:* **~se** (*encogerse*) to crouch

agache [a·'ɣa·ʧe] *m* 1. *Col* (*mentira*) fib 2. *Cuba* **andar de ~** to be on the run 3. *Ecua* (*de tapadillo*) **de ~** on the sly

agalla [a·'ɣa·ja, -ʎa] *f* gill; **tener ~s** *fig* to have guts

agarrada [a·ɣa·'rra·da] *f inf* fight

agarrado, -a [a·ɣa·'rra·do] *adj* stingy

agarrador [a·ɣa·rra·'dor] *m* pot holder

agarrar [a·ɣa·'rrar] I. *vt* 1. (*tomar*) to take 2. (*asir*) to grasp 3. (*enfermedad*) to catch; **~ una borrachera** to get drunk; **~ una pulmonía** to catch pneumonia II. *vr:* **~se** 1. (*asirse*) to hold on 2. *AmL* (*coger*) to catch; (*frutas*) to pluck

agarrotar [a·ɣa·rro·'tar] I. *vt* (*entumecer*) to stiffen up II. *vr:* **~se** (*entumecerse*) to go numb; (*por el miedo*) to stiffen with fear

agasajar [a·ɣa·sa·'xar] *vt* to receive in great style

agatas [a·'ɣa·tas] *adv Par, RíoPl* 1. (*con dificultad*) with great difficulty 2. (*casi no*) hardly; **~ sabe leer** he/she can barely read 3. (*tan sólo*) barely; **~ hace una hora** barely an hour ago

agencia [a·'xen·sja, -θja] *f* 1. (*empresa*) agency; **~ de noticias/de publicidad/ de viajes** news/advertising/travel agency 2. (*sucursal*) branch

agenciarse [a·xen·'sjar·se, -'θjar·se] *vr* to get hold of; **agenciárselas** to manage

agenda [a·'xen·da] *f* 1. (*calendario*) engagement [*o* date] book; **~ de bolsillo** pocket diary; **tener una ~ apretada** to have a tight schedule 2. (*orden del día*) agenda

agente [a·'xen·te] I. *mf* 1. (*representante*) representative; (*de un artista*) agent;

~ de bolsa stockbroker 2. (*funcionario*) **~ de aduanas** customs officer; **~ de policía** police officer II. *m t.* MED agent

ágil ['a·xil] *adj* (*de movimiento*) agile; (*mental*) alert, quick-witted

agilidad [a·xi·li·'dad] *f* (*física*) agility; (*mental*) acumen

agilizar <z → c> [a·xi·li·'sar, -'θar] *vt* to speed up

agitación [a·xi·ta·'sjon, -'θjon] *f* movement; *t.* POL agitation; (*excitación*) excitement

agitado, -a [a·xi·'ta·do, -a] *adj* hectic

agitar [a·xi·'tar] I. *vt* 1. (*mover*) to move; (*bandera*) to wave 2. (*intranquilizar*) to worry 3. (*sublevar*) to rouse II. *vr:* **~se** 1. (*moverse*) to move about; (*bandera*) to wave; (*mar*) to get rough 2. (*excitarse*) to get excited

aglomeración [a·ɣlo·me·ra·'sjon, -'θjon] *f* agglomeration; **~ de gente** crowd of people; **~ urbana** urban sprawl

ago. *abr de* **agosto** Aug.

agobiado, -a [a·ɣo·'βja·do, -a] *adj* exhausted; **estar ~ de trabajo** to be overloaded with work

agobiante [a·ɣo·'βjan·te] *adj* overwhelming; (*persona*) tiresome

agobiar [a·ɣo·'βjar] I. *vt* 1. (*abrumar*) to overwhelm; **¡no me agobies!** *inf* don't keep going on at me! 2. (*calor*) to suffocate II. *vr:* **~se** 1. (*angustiarse*) **~se por algo** to be weighed down with sth 2. (*sentirse abatido*) to feel overwhelmed

agobio [a·'ɣo·βjo] *m* 1. (*carga*) burden 2. (*cansancio*) exhaustion 3. (*opresión*) oppression

agonía [a·ɣo·'ni·a] *f* 1. (*del moribundo*) death throes *pl* 2. (*angustia*) anguish

agónico, -a [a·'ɣo·ni·ko, -a] *adj* **estar ~** to be dying

agonizar <z → c> [a·ɣo·ni·'sar, -'θar] *vi* 1. to be dying; 2. (*terminar*) to be coming to an end

agosto [a·'ɣos·to] *m* August; **hacer su ~** to make a killing; *v. t.* **marzo**

agotado, -a [a·ɣo·'ta·do, -a] *adj* (*producto*) out of stock; (*persona*) exhausted

agotador(a) [a·ɣo·ta·'dor, -·'do·ra] *adj* exhausting

agotamiento [a·ɣo·ta·'mjen·to] *m* exhaustion

agotar [a·ɣo·'tar] I. *vt* 1. (*existencias*) to use up; (*mercancía*) to deplete; (*paciencia*) to exhaust 2. (*cansar*) to tire (out) II. *vr:* ~**se** 1. (*mercancía*) to run out; (*pilas*) to run down [*o* out]; (*fuerzas*) to give out; **esta edición se agotó enseguida** this edition sold out immediately 2. (*cansarse*) to wear oneself out

agraciado, -a [a·ɣra·'sja·do, -a; -'θja·do, -a] *adj* 1. (*gracioso*) graceful 2. (*bien parecido*) attractive 3. (*afortunado*) lucky; **salir ~ en la lotería** to win in the lottery

agradable [a·ɣra·'da·βle] *adj* pleasant; ~ **al paladar** tasty; **es ~ a la vista** it is pleasing to the eye; ~ **con alguien** pleasant to sb

agradar [a·ɣra·'dar] *vi* to please; **me agrada esta gente** I like these people; **quieres ~ a todos** you want to please everyone

agradecer [a·ɣra·de·'ser, -'θer] *irr como crecer vt* to thank; **te agradezco la invitación** thanks for the invitation; **le ~ía mucho que** +*subj* I'd be very grateful if; **el campo ha agradecido la lluvia** the rain has been good for the fields

agradecido, -a [a·ɣra·de·'si·do, -a; -'θi·do, -a] *adj* (*que agradece*) ~ **por algo** grateful for sth; **le estaría muy ~ si me contestara lo antes posible** I would appreciate it very much if you could reply as soon as possible; **le estoy sumamente ~** I am extremely grateful (to you)

agradecimiento [a·ɣra·de·si·'mjen·to, -θi·'mjen·to] *m* gratitude

agrado [a·'ɣra·do] *m* 1. (*afabilidad*) affability; **tratar a alguien con ~** to treat sb kindly 2. (*complacencia*) willingness; **he recibido con ~ su carta** I was very pleased to receive your letter; **esto no es de mi ~** this isn't to my liking

agrandar [a·ɣran·'dar] I. *vt* to make bigger II. *vr:* ~**se** to get bigger

agrario, -a [a·'ɣra·rjo, -a] *adj* agrarian; **población agraria** rural population

agravamiento [a·ɣra·βa·'mjen·to] *m t.* MED worsening

agravar [a·ɣra·'βar] I. *vt* to make worse II. *vr:* ~**se** to worsen

agraviar [a·ɣra·'βjar] I. *vt* to offend II. *vr:* ~**se** to be offended

agravio [a·'ɣra·βjo] *m* offense; ~ **material** material damage

agredir [a·ɣre·'dir] *vt* to attack

agregado [a·ɣre·'ɣa·do] *m* 1. (*conglomerado*) aggregate 2. (*aditamento*) addition

agregado, -a [a·ɣre·'ɣa·do, -a] *m, f* UNIV associate professor

agregar <g → gu> [a·ɣre·'ɣar] *vt* to add

agresión [a·ɣre·'sjon] *f* aggression

agresividad [a·ɣre·si·βi·'dad] *f* aggressiveness

agresivo, -a [a·ɣre·'si·βo, -a] *adj* aggressive

agresor(a) [a·ɣre·'sor] I. *adj* aggressor II. *m(f)* aggressor, assailant

agreste [a·'ɣres·te] *adj* 1. (*campestre*) country 2. (*terreno*) rough, wild

agriar [a·'ɣrjar] I. *vt* (*alimentos*) to sour; (*persona*) to make bitter II. *vr:* ~**se** (*alimentos*) to turn sour; (*persona*) to become embittered [*o* bitter]

agrícola [a·'ɣri·ko·la] *adj* agricultural

agricultor(a) [a·ɣri·kul·'tor, -·'to·ra] *m(f)* farmer

agricultura [a·ɣri·kul·'tu·ra] *f* agriculture

agridulce [a·ɣri·'dul·se, -θe] *adj* bittersweet; CULIN sweet-and-sour

agrietar [a·ɣrje·'tar] I. *vt* to crack II. *vr:* ~**se** to crack; (*pared*) to become cracked; (*piel*) to become chapped

agringarse <g → gu> [a·ɣrin·'gar·se] *vr AmL* to imitate or adopt the customs of a foreigner

agrio, -a ['a·ɣrjo, -a] *adj* 1. (*sabor*) sour 2. (*carácter*) bitter

agrónomo, -a [a·'ɣro·no·mo, -a] *m, f* agronomist

agropecuario, -a [a·ɣro·pe·'kwa·rjo, -a] *adj* agricultural, farming

agroturismo [a·ɣro·tu·'ris·mo] *m* agrotourism

agrupación [a·ɣru·pa·'sjon, -'θjon] *f* 1. (*agrupamiento*) grouping 2. (*conjunto*) group 3. (*asociación*) society

agrupar [a·ɣru·'par] I. *vt* to group (together); ~ **algo por temas** to group sth by subject **II.** *vr*: ~**se** to form a group

agua [ˈa·ɣwa] *f* **1.** (*líquido*) water; ~ **de colonia** eau de cologne; ~ **con gas** sparkling water; ~ **del grifo** tap water; ~ **de mar** seawater; ~ **nieve** sleet; ~ **potable** drinking water; **¡hombre al ~!** man overboard!; **claro como el ~** crystal clear; **esta noche ha caído mucha** ~ it rained a lot last night. *pl* (*mares*) waters *pl*; ~ **interiores** inland waters; ~**s residuales** sewage; ~**s termales** hot baths [*o* springs]; ~**s abajo/arriba** downstream/upstream ▸ **volver las** ~**s a su** <u>cauce</u> to go back to normal; **estoy con el ~ hasta el** <u>cuello</u> I'm up to my neck in it; **como ~ de** <u>mayo</u> very welcome; **no hallar ~ en el** <u>mar</u> to act stupid; **llevar el ~ a su** <u>molino</u> to turn things to one's advantage; **sacar ~ a las** <u>piedras</u> to make something out of nothing; **estar entre** <u>dos</u> ~**s** to be sitting on the fence; **es ~** <u>pasada</u> that's water under the bridge; **hacer ~** (*buque*) to take in water; (*negocio*) to founder

aguacate [a·ɣwa·ˈka·te] *m* avocado

aguacero [a·ɣwa·ˈse·ro, -ˈθe·ro] *m* downpour; **cayó un** ~ there was a cloudburst

aguachento, -a [a·ɣwa·ˈtʃen·to, -a] *adj AmL v.* **aguado**

aguado, -a [a·ˈɣwa·do, -a] *adj* watered-down; (*fruta*) tasteless

aguafiestas [a·ɣwa·ˈfjes·tas] *mf inv inf* spoilsport, party pooper

aguafuerte [a·ɣwa·ˈfwer·te] *m* etching

aguaitar [a·ɣwai·ˈtar] *vt* **1.** *Arg, Cuba* (*acechar*) to lie in wait for **2.** *Col* (*esperar*) to wait

aguamiel [a·ɣwa·ˈmjel] *f Méx* (*jugo del maguey*) maguey juice

aguanieve [a·ɣwa·ˈnje·βe] *f* sleet

aguantadero [a·ɣwan·ta·ˈde·ro] *m Arg, Urug* hide-out

aguantar [a·ɣwan·ˈtar] **I.** *vt* **1.** (*sostener*) to hold; (*sujetar*) to hold tight; ~ **la risa** to hold back one's laughter **2.** (*soportar*) to bear; **no aguanto más** I can't bear it any more; **no poder** ~ **a alguien** not to be able to stand sb; ~ **la mirada de alguien** to hold sb's stare **3.** (*du-*

rar) to last; **este abrigo** ~**á mucho** this coat will last for a long time **II.** *vr*: ~**se 1.** (*contenerse*) to restrain oneself **2.** (*soportar*) to put up with it **3.** (*conformarse*) to resign oneself

aguante [a·ˈɣwan·te] *m* **1.** (*paciencia*) patience; **tener mucho** ~ to be very patient **2.** (*resistencia*) stamina

aguar <g→gü> [a·ˈɣwar] **I.** *vt* **1.** (*mezclar*) to water (down) **2.** (*frustrar*) to spoil **II.** *vr*: ~**se 1.** (*con agua*) to fill with water; **nuestras vacaciones se** ~**on** our vacation was spoiled by rain **2.** (*estropearse*) to be spoiled

aguardar [a·ɣwar·ˈdar] *vt* to wait for; ~ **unos días** to wait a few days; ~ **algo/a alguien** to await sth/sb

aguardiente [a·ɣwar·ˈdjen·te] *m* brandy

aguarrás [a·ɣwa·ˈrras] *m* turpentine

agudeza [a·ɣu·ˈde·sa, -ˈθa] *f* **1.** (*del cuchillo*) sharpness; ~ **visual** keenness of sight **2.** (*ingenio*) wittiness

agudo, -a [a·ˈɣu·do, -a] *adj* **1.** (*afilado*) sharp; **vista aguda** keen sight **2.** (*ingenioso*) witty; (*mordaz*) scathing **3.** (*dolor*) acute **4.** (*sonido*) piercing **5.** (*grave*) severe

agüero [a·ˈɣwe·ro] *m* omen; **de mal** ~ ill-fated

aguijón [a·ɣi·ˈxon] *m* (*punta*) goad; ZOOL sting, stinger

águila [ˈa·ɣi·la] *f* eagle; ~ **real** golden eagle; **ser un** ~ **para los negocios** *fig* to be sharp in business

aguinaldo [a·ɣi·ˈnal·do] *m* tip (*given at Christmas*)

aguja [a·ˈɣu·xa] *f* **1.** (*general*) needle; ~ **de punto** knitting needle; ~ **de la iglesia** church steeple; **buscar una** ~ **en un pajar** to look for a needle in a haystack **2.** (*del reloj*) hand; (*de un instrumento*) pointer **3.** FERRO point **4.** CULIN **carne de** ~ rib roast

agujerear [a·ɣu·xe·re·ˈar] *vt* to make holes in; (*orejas*) to pierce

agujero [a·ɣu·ˈxe·ro] *m* hole; ~ **en la capa de ozono** hole in the ozone layer; **tapar un** ~ to fill a hole

agujetas [a·ɣu·ˈxe·tas] *fpl* stiffness

aguzar <z→c> [a·ɣu·ˈsar, -ˈθar] *vt* **1.** (*afilar*) to sharpen **2.** (*avivar*) ~ **la**

atención to heighten one's attention; ~ **los sentidos** to sharpen one's senses; ~ **la vista** to look more carefully

ahí [a·'i] **I.** *adv* (*lugar*) there; ~ **está** he/she/it is; ~ **viene** there he/she/it comes; ~ **está el problema** that's the problem; **me voy por** ~ I'm going that way ▶ **¡~ es nada!** not bad!; ~ **me den todas** *inf* I couldn't care less; **por** ~, **por** ~ something like that **II.** *conj* **de** ~ **que...** that is why...

ahijado, -a [a·i·'xa·do, -a] *m, f* godchild

ahínco [a·'in·ko] *m* **1.** (*empeño*) effort **2.** (*insistencia*) insistence

ahogado, -a [a·o·'ya·do, -a] *adj* drowned; **estar** ~ **de trabajo** *fig* to be snowed under with work

ahogar <g → gu> [a·o·'yar] **I.** *vt* **1.** (*en el agua*) to drown **2.** (*asfixiar*) to suffocate **II.** *vr:* ~**se** **1.** (*en el agua*) to drown **2.** (*asfixiarse*) to suffocate; ~**se de calor** to be sweltering (in the heat) **3.** (*motor*) to flood ▶ ~**se en un vaso de agua** to make mountains out of molehills

ahondar [a·on·'dar] *vi* ~ **en algo** (*tema*) to go deeply into sth

ahora [a·'o·ra] *adv* now; (*muy pronto*) very soon; ~ **bien** now then; **de** ~ **en adelante** from now on; **hasta** ~ up to now; **por** ~ for the present; **¡**~ **(lo entiendo)!** now I've got it!; ~ **mismo vengo** I'm just coming; **acaba de salir** ~ **mismo** he/she has just gone out; **¡ven** ~ **mismo!** come right now!; **¿y** ~ **qué?** what now?

ahorcar(se) <c → qu> [a·or·'kar(·se)] *vt, (vr)* to hang (oneself)

ahorita [a·o·'ri·ta] *adv AmL* right away

ahorrador, -a [a·o·rra·'dor, -·'do·ra] **I.** *adj* thrifty **II.** *m(f)* saver

ahorrar [a·o·'rrar] **I.** *vt* to save; ~ **fuerzas** to save one's energy; ~ **esfuerzos a alguien** to save sb the trouble; **ahórrame explicaciones** spare me your explanation **II.** *vr:* ~**se** (*evitar*) to save oneself

ahorrativo, -a [a·o·rra·'ti·βo, -a] *adj* thrifty

ahorro [a·'o·rro] *m* (*cantidad*) saving

ahuecar <c → qu> [a·we·'kar] **I.** *vt* (*vaciar*) to hollow out **II.** *vr:* ~**se** **1.** (*ave*)

to ruffle (up) its feathers **2.** (*envanecerse*) to put on airs

ahulado [a·u·'la·do] *m AmC, Méx* (*mantel*) oilcloth tablecloth

ahumado, -a [a·u·'ma·do, -a] *adj* **1.** (*cristal*) tinted **2.** (*salmón*) smoked

ahumar [a·u·'mar] **I.** *vi* to smoke **II.** *vt* CULIN to smoke; (*una colmena*) to smoke out

ahuyentar [a·u·jen·'tar] *vt* **1.** (*espantar*) to frighten off [*o* away] **2.** (*dudas*) to dispel

aimara, aimará [ai·ma·ra] **I.** *adj* Aymara **II.** *mf* Aymara

aindiado, -a [a·in·'dja·do, -a] *adj AmL* Indian-looking

airar [ai·'rar] *irr* **I.** *vt* to anger **II.** *vr:* ~**se** to get angry

aire ['ai·re] *m* **1.** (*atmósfera*) air; ~ **acondicionado** air conditioning; **Ejército del Aire** air force; **al** ~ **libre** in the open air; **echar una moneda al** ~ to toss a coin (into the air); **tomar el** ~ to go for a stroll; **dejar una pregunta en el** ~ to leave a question open; **cambiar de** ~**s** to have a change of scene; **¡**~**!** *inf* beat it! **2.** (*viento*) wind; **corriente de** ~ draft; **corre** ~ it's drafty; **hoy hace** ~ it's windy today **3.** (*aspecto*) appearance; **darse** ~**s de grandeza** to have pretensions of grandeur; **¡tiene unos** ~**s!** he/she is always putting on airs! **4.** (*garbo*) elegance

airear [ai·re·'ar] **I.** *vt* to air **II.** *vr:* ~**se** **1.** (*ventilarse*) to air **2.** (*coger aire*) to get some fresh air

airoso, -a [ai·'ro·so, -a] *adj* graceful; **salir** ~ **de algo** to come out of sth with flying colors

aislado, -a [ais·'la·do, -a] *adj* isolated

aislamiento [ais·la·'mjen·to] *m* **1.** (*retiro*) isolation **2.** *t.* TÉC insulation; ~ **acústico** soundproofing

aislante [ais·'lan·te] **I.** *adj* insulating; **cinta** ~ insulating tape **II.** *m* insulator

aislar [ais·'lar] **I.** *vt* to isolate; TÉC to insulate; **aislado contra el ruido** soundproof **II.** *vr:* ~**se** to isolate oneself

ajedrez [a·xe·'dres, -'dreθ] *m* DEP chess

ajeno, -a [a·'xe·no, -a] *adj* **1.** (*de otro*) somebody else's; **la felicidad ajena**

other people's happiness **2.** estar (*ignorante*) ignorant; **estar ~ a** [*o* **de**] **algo** to be unaware of sth; **vivía ~ a todo lo que pasaba en el mundo** he/she lived unaware of what was happening in the world

ajetreo [a·xe·'treo] *m* (*de personas*) drudgery; (*en un sitio*) bustle

ají [a·'xi] *m AmS, Ant* **1.** (*arbusto*) pepper (plant) **2.** (*pimentón*) chili; (*de las Indias*) cayenne (pepper)

ajillo [a·'xi·jo, -ʎo] *m* CULIN **al ~** prepared with olive oil and garlic

ajo ['a·xo] *m* BOT garlic; (*diente*) clove of garlic ▶ **andar** (**metido**) **en el ~** *inf* **estar en el ~** *inf* to be mixed up in it

ajotar [a·xo·'tar] *vt* **1.** AmC, Ant (*azuzar*) to incite. *Cuba* (*desdeñar*) to scorn

ajuar [a·'xwar] *m* **1.** (*de novia*) trousseau **2.** (*de casa*) furnishings *pl*

ajustable [a·xus·'ta·βle] *adj* adjustable; **sábanas ~s** fitted sheets

ajustado, -a [a·xus·'ta·do, -a] *adj* **1.** (*ropa*) tight **2.** (*adecuado*) fitting

ajustar [a·xus·'tar] **I.** *vi* to fit **II.** *vt* **1.** (*adaptar*) *t.* TÉC to adjust; **~ un vestido** to take in a dress; **~ una correa** to adjust a strap **2.** (*dos piezas*) to fit **III.** *vr:* **~se** (*adaptarse*) to adapt; **no ~se al tema** not to keep to the subject; **~se a la verdad** to stick to the truth

ajuste [a·'xus·te] *m* **1.** (*adaptación*) adjustment **2.** (*graduación*) graduation; **~ de brillo** brightness control **3.** (*encaje*) fitting **4.** (*acuerdo*) compromise; **~ de cuentas** settling of scores

ajusticiar [a·xus·ti·'sjar, -'θjar] *vt* to execute

al [al] = **a** + **el** *v. a.*

ala ['a·la] *f* wing; (*de sombrero*) brim *pl* ▶ **tener demasiadas ~s** to be overconfident; **estar tocado del ~** *inf* to be crazy; **ahuecar el ~** to get going; **cortar las ~s a alguien** to clip sb's wings; **dar ~s a alguien** to encourage sb

Alá [a·'la] *m* REL Allah

alabanza [a·la·'βan·sa, -θa] *f* praise; **deshacerse en ~s para con alguien** to shower praises on sb

alabar [a·la·'βar] **I.** *vt* **~ a alguien por algo** to praise sb for sth; **alabado sea**

el Señor praise be to God **II.** *vr:* **~se** to boast

alabastro [a·la·'βas·tro] *m* alabaster

alacena [a·la·'se·na, -'θe·na] *f* pantry

alacrán [a·la·'kran] *m* ZOOL scorpion

ALALC [a·'lalk] *abr de* **Asociación Latinoamericana de Libre Comercio** LAFTA

alambique [a·lam·'bi·ke] *m* distillery

alambrada [a·lam·'bra·da] *f* wire fence; **~ eléctrica** electric fence

alambre [a·'lam·bre] *m* wire; **~ de espino** barbed wire

alameda [a·la·'me·da] *f* (*lugar*) poplar grove

álamo ['a·la·mo] *m* BOT poplar; **~ temblón** aspen

alarde [a·'lar·de] *m* show; **hacer ~ de algo** to make a show of sth

alardear [a·lar·de·'ar] *vi* **~ de algo** to boast about sth

alargado, -a [a·lar·'ɣa·do, -a] *adj* elongated

alargar <g → gu> [a·lar·'ɣar] **I.** *vt* **1.** (*extensión*) to lengthen; **~ el cuello** to crane one's neck; **~ la mano** to hold out one's hand **2.** (*duración*) to prolong **II.** *vr:* **~se** (*en la extensión*) to lengthen; **no te alargues** to be brief

alarido [a·la·'ri·do] *m* shriek

alarma [a·'lar·ma] *f* **1.** (*general*) alarm; **falsa ~** false alarm; **dar la ~** to raise the alarm; **ha saltado la ~ del banco** the alarm in the bank has gone off **2.** (*susto*) scare

alarmar [a·lar·'mar] **I.** *vt* **1.** (*dar la alarma*) to alarm **2.** (*asustar*) to frighten; **noticia alarmante** terrible news **II.** *vr:* **~se** (*inquietarse*) to get worried; (*asustarse*) to be alarmed

alarmista [a·lar·'mis·ta] *mf* alarmist

alba ['al·βa] *f* dawn; **al rayar** [*o* **romper**] **el ~** at daybreak

albacea [al·βa·'sea, -'θea] *mf* executor

albacora [al·βa·'ko·ra] *f* Chile, Perú, Méx swordfish

albahaca [al·βa·ka/al·βa·'a·ka] *f* BOT basil

albanés, -esa [al·βa·'nes, --'ne·sa] *adj, m, f* Albanian

albañil [al·βa·'nil] *mf* **1.** (*constructor*) builder **2.** (*artesano*) bricklayer

albarán [al·βa·ˈran] *m* delivery note, invoice

albaricoque [al·βa·ri·ˈko·ke] *m* apricot

albedrío [al·βe·ˈðri·o] *m* whim; **libre ~** free will; **a mí ~** just as I like

albergar <g → gu> [al·βer·ˈɣar] **I.** *vt* to house **II.** *vr:* **~se** to lodge

albergue [al·ˈβer·ɣe] *m* refuge; **~ juvenil** youth hostel; **~ de montaña** mountain hut

albino, -a [al·ˈβi·no, -a] *adj, m, f* albino

albóndiga [al·ˈβon·di·ɣa] *f* (*de carne*) meatball

albornoz [al·βor·ˈnoθ,] *m* bathrobe

alborotado, -a [al·βo·ro·ˈta·do, -a] *adj* (*excitado*) excited

alborotar [al·βo·ro·ˈtar] **I.** *vi* to make a racket; (*niños*) to roughhouse **II.** *vt* **1.** (*excitar*) to excite **2.** (*desordenar*) to agitate **3.** (*sublevar*) to stir up **III.** *vr:* **~se 1.** (*excitarse*) to get excited **2.** (*sublevarse*) to riot

alboroto [al·βo·ˈro·to] *m* **1.** (*vocerío*) racket; (*ruido*) noise **2.** (*bulla*) uproar; (*disturbio*) disturbance

alborozo [al·βo·ˈro·so, -θo] *m* joy

albufera [al·βu·ˈfe·ra] *f* lagoon

álbum [ˈal·βun] *m* <álbum(e)s> album

albur [al·ˈβur] *m* ZOOL (*pez*) bleak ▶ **al ~** at random

alburear [al·βu·re·ˈar] **I.** *vt CRi* to disturb **II.** *vi* **1.** Col (*dinero*) to get money **2.** Cuba (*engañar*) to deceive

alcachofa [al·ka·ˈtʃo·fa] *f* **1.** BOT artichoke **2.** (*de ducha*) shower head; (*de regadera*) sprinkler

alcahuete, -a [al·ka·ˈwe·te, -a] *m, f* pimp

alcalde(sa) [al·ˈkal·de, al·kal·ˈde·sa] *m(f)* mayor

alcaldía [al·kal·ˈdi·a] *f* (*oficio, oficina*) mayor's office

alcalino, -a [al·ka·ˈli·no, -a] *adj* alkaline

alcamonero, -a [al·ka·mo·ˈne·ro, -a] *adj* Ven (*entrometido*) nosy; (*de novedades*) newsy

alcance [al·ˈkan·se, -θe] *m* **1.** (*distancia*) range; **misil de corto ~** short-range missile; **al ~ de la mano** within reach; **al ~ de todos los bolsillos** within everybody's means; **tener la victoria a su ~** to have victory within one's grasp **2.** (*importancia*) importance; **de mucho/poco ~** of great/little importance ▶ **la noticia de último ~** the latest news; **dar ~ a alguien** to catch up with sb

alcanfor [al·kan·ˈfor] *m* camphor

alcantarilla [al·kan·ta·ˈri·ja, -ʎa] *f* **1.** (*cloaca*) sewer **2.** (*sumidero*) drain

alcantarillado [al·kan·ta·ri·ˈja·do, -ʎa·do] *m* sewer system, drains *pl*

alcanzar <z → c> [al·kan·ˈsar, -ˈθar] **I.** *vi* to reach; **el dinero no alcanza para pagar la comida** there wasn't enough to pay for the food **II.** *vt* **1.** (*dar alcance*) to catch up (with); **ve tirando, ya te ~é** keep going, I'll catch up with you **2.** (*llegar*) to reach; **~ un acuerdo** to reach an agreement; **el disparo le alcanzó en la pierna** he was shot in the leg; **~ fama** to become famous **3.** (*entender*) to grasp

alcaparra [al·ka·ˈpa·rra] *f* (*fruto*) caper

alcatraz [al·ka·ˈtras, -ˈtraθ] *m* **1.** ZOOL gannet **2.** BOT arum

alcázar [al·ˈka·sar, -θar] *m* MIL fortress

alce [ˈal·se, -θe] *m* ZOOL elk, moose

alcoba [al·ˈko·βa] *f* bedroom

alcohol [al·ˈkol/al·ko·ˈol] *m* alcohol; **bebida sin ~** non-alcoholic drink; **no tomo ~** I don't drink alcohol; **estar bajo los efectos del ~** to be under the influence of alcohol

alcohólico, -a [al·ˈko·li·ko/al·ko·ˈo·li·ko, -a] *adj, m, f* alcoholic

alcoholímetro [al·ko·ˈli·me·tro/al·ko·o·ˈli·me·tro] *m* Breathalyzer®

alcoholismo [al·ko·ˈlis·mo/al·ko·o·ˈlis·mo] *m* alcoholism

alcoholizar <z → c> [al·ko·li·ˈsar/al·ko·o·li·ˈsar, -ˈθar] **I.** *vt* to get (sb) drunk **II.** *vr:* **~se** to become an alcoholic

alcornoque [al·kor·ˈno·ke] *m* BOT cork oak; (*pedazo de*) ~ idiot

alcurnia [al·ˈkur·nja] *f* ancestry; **de ~** of noble birth

aldea [al·ˈde·a] *f* small village

aldeano, -a [al·de·ˈa·no, -a] *m, f* **1.** (*de la aldea*) villager **2.** (*inculto*) country bumpkin

aleación [a·lea·ˈsjon, -ˈθjon] *f* alloy; **~ ligera** light alloy

aleatorio, -a [a·le·a·'to·rjo, -a] *adj* random, fortuitous

alegación [a·le·ɣa·'sjon, -'θjon] *f* JUR (*declaración*) declaration; (*escrito*) statement

alegar <g → gu> [a·le·'ɣar] *vt* to cite; (*pruebas*) to produce

alegoría [a·le·ɣo·'ri·a] *f* allegory

alegrar [a·le·'ɣrar] I. *vt* 1. (*a personas*) to make happy 2. (*cosas*) to brighten up II. *vr* ~**se de algo** to be glad about sth; **me alegro de verle de nuevo** I'm pleased to see you again; **me alegro (por ti)** I'm so happy for you

alegre [a·le·ɣre] *adj* 1. (*contento*) happy; (*divertido*) merry; (*color*) bright; **una cara** ~ a cheerful face; **estoy ~ de que** +*subj* I'm pleased that 2. (*frívolo*) frivolous; **llevar una vida** ~ to lead a free-and-easy life 3. *inf* (*achispado*) merry; **estar** ~ to be tipsy

alegría [a·le·'ɣri·a] *f* (*gozo*) happiness; (*buen humor*) cheerfulness; **llevarse una gran** ~ to be very happy

alejar [a·le·'xar] I. *vt* 1. (*distanciar*) to remove 2. (*ahuyentar*) to drive away; **aleja estos pensamientos de tu cabeza** banish these thoughts from your mind II. *vr* ~**se** to move away; (*retirarse*) to withdraw; **todos se alejan de él** everyone avoids him

aleluya [a·le·'lu·ja] *interj, m o f* REL hallelujah; **estar de** ~ to rejoice

alemán [a·le·'man] *m* German; **decir algo en** ~ to say sth in German

alemán, -ana [a·le·'man, --'ma·na] *adj, m, f* German

Alemania [a·le·'ma·nja] *f* Germany; **República Federal de** ~ Federal Republic of Germany

alentar <e → ie> [a·len·'tar] I. *vt* to encourage II. *vr:* ~**se** (*animarse*) to take heart

alergia [a·'ler·xia] *f* allergy; ~ **al polen** pollen allergy; **esto me da** ~ I'm allergic to this

alérgico, -a [a·'ler·xi·ko, -a] *adj* allergic

alerta [a·'ler·ta] I. *adj* alert II. *f* alert; ~ **por vibración** TEL vibration alert; **dar la** ~ to give the alarm; **poner en** ~ **a alguien** to put sb on the alert III. *interj* watch out

aleta [a·'le·ta] *f* wing; (*de un buzo*) flipper; (*de un pez*) fin

alevosía [a·le·βo·'si·a] *f* treachery; **con** ~ treacherously

alfabético, -a [al·fa·'βe·ti·ko, -a] *adj* alphabetic(al); **estar por orden** ~ to be in alphabetical order

alfabetizar <z → c> [al·fa·βe·ti·'sar, -'θar] *vt* to teach to read and write

alfabeto [al·fa·'βe·to] *m* alphabet

alfalfa [al·'fal·fa] *f* BOT alfalfa

alfarería [al·fa·re·'ri·a] *f* pottery

alfarero, -a [al·fa·'re·ro, -a] *m, f* potter

alférez [al·'fe·res, -reθ] *m* MIL second lieutenant

alfil [al·'fil] *m* (*ajedrez*) bishop

alfiler [al·fi·'ler] *m* 1. (*aguja*) pin 2. (*broche*) brooch; ~ **de corbata** tiepin ► **llevo la lección prendida con ~es** I'm hardly prepared for the exam; **no caber un** ~ to be bursting at the seams

alfombra [al·'fom·bra] *f* carpet

alfombrado [al·fom·'bra·do] *m AmL* carpeting

alfombrilla [al·fom·'bri·ja, -ʎa] *f* 1. (*estera*) mat; ~ **de baño** bath mat 2. COMPUT mousepad

alforja [al·'for·xa] *f* bag; (*de caballería*) saddlebag

alga ['al·ɣa] *f* alga

algarabía [al·ɣa·ra·'βi·a] *f* (*griterío*) uproar

álgebra ['al·xe·βra] *f* MAT algebra

álgido, -a ['al·xi·do, -a] *adj* 1. (*culminante*) **la crisis está en su momento más** ~ the crisis has reached a climax 2. (*muy frío*) freezing

algo ['al·ɣo] I. *pron indef* (*en frases afirmativas*) something; (*en neg., interrog. y condicionales*) anything; ~ **es** ~ it's better than nothing; **¿quieres ~?** do you want anything?; **¿apostamos ~?** do you want to bet?; **me suena de** ~ it seems familiar to me; **se cree** ~ he/she thinks he/she is something; **por** ~ **lo habrá dicho** he/she must have had a reason for saying it II. *adv* a little; **aún falta** ~ **hasta llegar** there's still a bit to go; ~ **así como** something like

algodón [al·ɣo·'don] *m* 1. (*tejido*) cotton; **una camisa de** ~ a cotton shirt; ~ **en rama** raw cotton **2.** (*cosmético*) cotton

alguacil [al·ɣwa·ˈsil, -ˈθil] *mf* bailiff

alguien [ˈal·γjen] *pron indef* (*en frases afirmativas*) somebody, someone; (*en interrog. y condicionales*) anybody, anyone; ¿**hay** ~ **aquí?** is anybody [*o* anyone] there?; ~ **me lo ha contado** somebody [*o* someone] told me; **se cree** ~ he/she thinks he/she is somebody [*o* someone]

algún [al·ˈɣun] *adj v.* **alguno**[1]

alguno, -a[1] [al·ˈɣu·no, -a] *adj* <algún> **1.** (*antepuesto*) some; (*en frases neg. e int.*) any; ¿**alguna pregunta?** any questions?; **de alguna manera** somehow; **en algún sitio** somewhere; **alguna vez** sometimes; **algún día** someday **2.** (*postpuesto: ninguno*) no, not any; **en** ~ **sitio** nowhere; **persona alguna** no one

alguno, -a[2] [al·ˈɣu·no, -a] *pron indef* somebody, someone; ~**s de los presentes** some of those present; ~ **s ya se han ido** some have already gone; ¿**tienes caramelos? — sí, me quedan** ~**s** do you have any candy? — yes, I still have some left; **los niños han vuelto a hacer alguna de las suyas** the children have been up to their tricks again

alhaja [a·ˈla·xa] *f* (*de piedras preciosas*) piece of jewelry; (*de bisutería*) costume jewelry

alhajado, -a [a·la·ˈxa·do, -a] *adj Col* (*rico*) wealthy

alhajera [a·la·ˈxe·ra] *f Arg, Chile* jewel box

aliado, -a [a·li·ˈa·do, -a] **I.** *adj* allied **II.** *m, f* ally

alianza [a·li·ˈan·sa, -θa] *f* **1.** (*pacto*) alliance; **Alianza Atlántica** Atlantic Alliance, NATO **2.** (*anillo*) wedding ring

aliar(se) <*1. pres* alío> [a·li·ˈar·(se)] *vt, (vr)* to ally (oneself)

alias [ˈa·ljas] *adv, m inv* alias

alicaído, -a [a·li·ka·ˈi·do, -a] *adj* weak; (*deprimido*) dejected

alicates [a·li·ˈka·tes] *mpl* pliers *pl*

aliciente [a·li·ˈsjen·te, -ˈθjen·te] *m* incentive

aliento [a·ˈljen·to] *m* **1.** (*respiración*)

breath; **mal** ~ bad breath; **sin** ~ out of breath; **cobrar** ~ to get one's breath back; **esto me quita el** ~ this takes my breath away; **tomar** ~ to take a breath **2.** (*ánimo*) courage; **dar** ~ **a alguien** to encourage sb

aligerar [a·li·xe·ˈrar] **I.** *vi* to hurry (up) **II.** *vt* **1.** (*cargas*) to lighten **2.** (*acelerar*) to quicken; ~ **el paso** to go faster

alimaña [a·li·ˈma·ɲa] *f* **1.** (*animal*) pest; ~**s** vermin **2.** (*persona*) animal, brute

alimentación [a·li·men·ta·ˈsjon, -ˈθjon] *f* **1.** (*nutrición*) food **2.** (*de animales*) feeding **3.** (*de un horno*) stoking; (*de una máquina*) feeding; ~ **de energía** energy supply

alimentar [a·li·men·ˈtar] **I.** *vi* to be nourishing **II.** *vt* **1.** (*nutrir*) to feed; ~ **el odio** to fuel hatred **2.** (*horno*) to stoke; (*máquina*) to feed **III.** *vr* ~**se de algo** to live on sth

alimenticio, -a [a·li·men·ˈti·sjo, -a; ˈθjo, -a] *adj* **1.** (*nutritivo*) nourishing **2.** (*alimentario*) food; **industria alimenticia** food industry; **pensión alimenticia** alimony; **productos** ~**s** foodstuffs *pl*

alimento [a·li·ˈmen·to] *m* **1.** (*sustancia*) food; **los** ~**s** foodstuffs *pl*; ~**s congelados** frozen food **2.** (*alimentación*) nourishment; **de mucho/poco** ~ full of/lacking nutritional value **3.** *pl* JUR (*asistencia financiera*) alimony

alineación [a·li·nea·ˈsjon, -ˈθjon] *f*, **alineamiento** [a·li·nea·ˈmjen·to] *m* **1.** (*general*) alignment **2.** DEP line-up

alinear [a·li·ne·ˈar] **I.** *vt* **1.** (*poner en línea*) to line up **2.** DEP to select; (*para un partido*) to field; **país no alineado** POL non-aligned country **II.** *vr:* ~**se** to line up

aliñar [a·li·ˈɲar] *vt* to season; (*ensalada*) to dress

aliño [a·ˈli·ɲo] *m* seasoning; (*para ensalada*) dressing

alioli [a·li·ˈo·li] *m* mayonnaise made with olive oil and garlic

alisar [a·li·ˈsar] *vt* (*superficie*) to smooth down; (*un terreno*) to level (off); (*el pelo*) to smooth

aliso [a·ˈli·so] *m* t. BOT alder

alistar [a·lis·ˈtar] *vr:* ~**se 1.** (*inscribirse*)

to enroll **2.** MIL to enlist

aliviar [a·li·'βjar] **I.** vt **1.** (*carga*) to lighten **2.** (*de una preocupación*) to relieve **3.** (*dolor*) to alleviate **II.** vr: **~se 1.** (*dolor*) to ease off [*o* up] **2.** (*de una enfermedad*) to recover

alivio [a·'li·βjo] m **1.** (*aligeramiento*) relief **2.** (*de una enfermedad*) recovery; (*mejoría*) improvement ▶ **ser de ~** *inf* to be horrible; **pescar un catarro de ~** *inf* to get an awful cold

allá [a·'ja, a·'ʎa] adv **1.** (*lugar, dirección*) there; **el más ~** REL the hereafter; **¿cuánto se tarda de aquí ~?** how long does it take to go there?; **ponte más ~** move further over **2.** (*tiempo*) back; **~ por el año 1964** around 1964 ▶ **¡~ tú!** *inf* that's your problem!

allanamiento [a·ja·na·'mjen·to, a·ʎa·-] m **1.** (*de un terreno*) leveling **2.** JUR **~ de morada** breaking and entering

allanar [a·ja·'nar, a·ʎa·-] **I.** vt **1.** (*terreno*) to level (out) **2.** (*dificultades*) to remove **3.** JUR **~ una casa** to break into a house **II.** vr: **~se** to agree

allegado, -a [a·je·'ɣa·do, -a; a·ʎe·-] **I.** adj close **II.** m, f relative

allí [a·'ji, a·'ʎi] adv (*lugar, dirección*) there; **~ cerca por ~** over there; **¡~ viene!** he's/she's just coming!; **hasta ~** as far as that

alma ['al·ma] f **1.** (*espíritu*) soul; **agradecer con el ~** to thank with all one's heart; **me arranca el ~** it's heartbreaking; **me llega al ~** I'm deeply touched; **lo siento en el ~** I'm terribly sorry; **no tener ~** to be heartless; **fue el ~ de la fiesta** he/she was the life and soul of the party **2.** (*ánimo*) spirit ▶ **como ~ que lleva el diablo** *inf* like a bat out of hell; **~ en pena** lost soul; **se le cayó el ~ a los pies** *inf* his/her heart sank

almacén [al·ma·'sen, -'θen] m **1.** (*depósito*) warehouse; **tener en ~** to have in stock **2.** (*tienda*) **grandes almacenes** department store

almacenaje [al·ma·se·'na·xe, al·ma·θe·-] m, **almacenamiento** [al·ma·se·na·'mjen·to, al·ma·θe·-] m (*de mercancías*) t. COMPUT storage

almacenar [al·ma·se·'nar, al·ma·θe·-] vt t. COMPUT to store

almeja [al·'me·xa] f ZOOL clam

almendra [al·'men·dra] f (*fruta*) almond

almendro [al·'men·dro] m almond tree

almíbar [al·'mi·βar] m syrup; **melocotón en ~** peach in syrup

almidón [al·mi·'don] m starch; (*cola*) paste

almidonar [al·mi·do·'nar] vt to starch

almirante [al·mi·'ran·te] mf admiral

almirez [al·mi·'res, -'reθ] m mortar

almizcle [al·'mis·kle, al·'miθ-] m musk

almohada [al·mo·'a·da] f pillow ▶ **consultar algo con la ~** *inf* to sleep on sth

almohadilla [al·moa·'di·ja, -'di·ʎa] f (*cojín*) small cushion; (*acerico*) pin cushion

almorranas [al·mo·'rra·nas] fpl piles pl

almorzar [al·mor·'sar, -'θar] irr (*como forzar*) **I.** vi **1.** (*a mediodía*) to have lunch **2.** reg (*desayunar*) to have breakfast **II.** vt **1.** (*a mediodía*) to have for lunch **2.** reg (*desayunar*) to have for breakfast

almuerzo [al·'mwer·so, -θo] m **1.** (*al mediodía*) lunch; **~ de negocios** business lunch; **¿qué hay de ~?** what's for lunch? **2.** reg (*desayunar*) breakfast

aló [a·'lo] interj AmC, AmS TEL hello; **~, ¿quién es?** hello, who's speaking?

alocado, -a [a·lo·'ka·do, -a] adj **1.** (*loco*) crazy **2.** (*imprudente*) reckless

alojamiento [a·lo·xa·'mjen·to] m **1.** (*lugar*) accommodation **2.** (*acción*) housing

alojar [a·lo·'xar] **I.** vt **1.** (*albergar*) to accommodate **2.** (*procurar alojamiento*) to house **3.** (*cosa*) to lodge **II.** vr: **~se** to stay

alondra [a·'lon·dra] f ZOOL (*ave*) lark

alopecia [a·lo·'pe·sja, -θja] f alopecia

alpaca [al·'pa·ka] f **1.** (*tela*) t. ZOOL alpaca **2.** (*aleación*) nickel silver, German silver

alpargata [al·par·'ɣa·ta] f espadrille

Alpes ['al·pes] mpl **los ~** the Alps + pl vb, Alps

alpinismo [al·pi·'nis·mo] m mountain climbing

alpinista [al·pi·'nis·ta] mf mountain climber

alpino, -a [al·'pi·no, -a] *adj* Alpine; **refugio** ~ mountain refuge

alpiste [al·'pis·te] *m* 1. (*para pájaros*) birdseed 2. *inf* (*alcohol*) **le gusta mucho el** ~ he's/she's a boozer

alquilar [al·ki·'lar] I. *vt* 1. (*dejar*) to rent (out), to let 2. (*tomar en alquiler*) to rent II. *vr*: ~**se** to be let; **se alquila** for rent

alquiler [al·ki·'ler] *m* 1. (*acción*) renting, letting; ~ **de coches** car-rental 2. (*precio*) rent, rental

alquimia [al·'ki·mja] *f* alchemy

alquimista [al·ki·'mis·ta] *mf* alchemist

alquitrán [al·ki·'tran] *m* tar

alrededor [al·rre·de·'dor] *adv* 1. (*local*) around; ~ **de la plaza** around the square; **un viaje** ~ **del mundo** a trip around the world 2. (*aproximadamente*) ~ around

alrededores [al·rre·de·'do·res] *mpl* surroundings *pl*; (*de una ciudad*) outskirts *pl*

alta ['al·ta] *f* 1. (*documento*) (certificate of) discharge; **dar el** ~ to discharge; **dar de** ~ **del hospital** to discharge from hospital 2. (*inscripción*) registration; (*ingreso*) membership; **darse de** ~ **en una asociación** to become a member of an association

altamente [al·ta·'men·te] *adv* highly; ~ **cualificado** highly qualified

altanero, -a [al·ta·'ne·ro, -a] *adj* arrogant, haughty

altar [al·'tar] *m* altar

altavoz [al·ta·'βoθ, -'βos] *m* loudspeaker

alteración [al·te·ra·'sjon, -'θjon] *f* 1. (*cambio*) alteration, change 2. (*perturbación*) disturbance 3. (*turbación*) unrest 4. (*irritación*) irritation

alterado, -a [al·te·'ra·do, -a] *adj* upset

alterar [al·te·'rar] I. *vt* 1. (*cambiar*) to alter 2. (*perturbar*) to disturb 3. (*turbar*) to upset II. *vr*: ~**se** 1. ~**se por algo** (*aturdirse*) to get upset over sth; (*irritarse*) to be irritated by sth 2. (*cambiar*) to alter

altercado [al·ter·'ka·do] *m* argument, altercation *form*

alternar [al·ter·'nar] I. *vi* 1. (*turnarse*) to alternate; ~ **en el volante** to take turns at the wheel 2. (*tratar*) ~ **con alguien**

to associate with sb 3. (*en un club*) to go clubbing II. *vt* to alternate; ~ **el trabajo con la diversión** to alternate between periods of work and leisure III. *vr* ~**se en algo** to take turns at sth

alternativa [al·ter·na·'ti·βa] *f* alternative; **no le queda otra** ~ **que...** he/she has no other alternative than...

alternativo, -a [al·ter·na·'ti·βo, -a] *adj* 1. (*opcional*) alternative 2. (*con alternación*) alternating

alterne [al·'ter·ne] *m* **chica de** ~ hostess; **bar de** ~ singles bar

alterno, -a [al·'ter·no, -a] *adj* alternate; **en días** ~**s** every other day

alteza [al·'te·sa, -θa] *f* (*tratamiento*) nobleness; **Su Alteza Real** His/Her/Your Royal Highness

altibajos [al·ti·'βa·xos] *mpl* 1. (*de un terreno*) undulations *pl* 2. (*cambios*) ups *pl* and downs; **es una persona con muchos** ~ **en su estado de ánimo** he's/she's very moody

altiplanicie [al·ti·pla·'ni·sje, -θje] *f*, **altiplano** [al·ti·'pla·no] *m* high plateau

altitud [al·ti·'tud] *f* height, altitude; **a una** ~ **de 1500 metros** at a height of 1,500 meters

altivo, -a [al·'ti·βo, -a] *adj* (*soberbio*) arrogant, haughty

alto, -a ['al·to] I. *interj* halt; ¡~ **el fuego!** cease fire! II. *m* 1. (*descanso*) stop; ~ **el fuego** ceasefire; **dar el** ~ to order to halt 2. (*altura*) height; **medir 8 metros de** ~ to be 8 meters high 3. (*collado*) hill III. *adv* (*en un lugar elevado*) high (up); **ponlo en lo más** ~ put it as high up as possible ▶ **pasar por** ~ to ignore; **pasar una pregunta por** ~ to overlook a question; **por todo lo** ~ splendidly

alto, -a ['al·to, -a] *adj* <más alto o superior, altísimo> 1. (*en general*) high; **un** ~ **cargo** a high-ranking position; **notas altas** MÚS high notes; **artículos de cuero de alta calidad** high-quality leather goods; **tener un** ~ **concepto de alguien** to have a high opinion of sb 2. (*persona*) tall; (*edificio*) high, tall 3. (*en la parte superior*) upper; **clase alta** upper class 4. GEO (*río*) upper; **la alta montaña** the high mountains

5. (*tiempo*) late; **a altas horas de la noche** late at night **6.** (*río*) torrential; (*mar*) rough; **el río está ~** the river is rough **7.** (*sonido*) loud; **hablar en voz alta** to speak loudly

altoparlante [al·to·par·'lan·te] *m AmL* loudspeaker

altramuz [al·tra·'muꞩ, -'muθ] *m* BOT lupin(e)

altruista [al·tru·'is·ta] **I.** *adj* altruistic **II.** *mf* altruist

altura [al·'tu·ra] *f* **1.** (*altitud*) height; **de gran ~** high; **de poca ~** low; **a gran ~** at a great height; **una montaña de 2000 metros de ~** a 2,000-meter-high mountain; **el avión pierde ~** the plane is losing altitude **2.** (*estatura*) height **3.** (*de un sonido*) pitch **4.** *pl* (*cielo*) heaven ▶ **estar a la ~ del betún** *inf* to look really stupid; **estar a la ~ de las circunstancias** to rise to the occasion; **estar a la ~ de Valencia** to be in the vicinity of Valencia; **a estas ~s** at this point

alubia [a·'lu·βja] *f* bean

alucinación [a·lu·si·na·'sjon, -θi·na·'θjon] *f* hallucination

alucinado, -a [a·lu·si·na·do, -a; a·lu·θi-] *adj inf* (*asombrado*) **miraba ~ a la chica** he looked at the girl in amazement; **me quedé ~ al leerlo en el periódico** I was stunned on reading it in the newspaper

alucinante [a·lu·si·'nan·te, a·lu·θi-] *adj inf* **1.** (*estupendo*) fantastic **2.** (*increíble*) incredible

alucinar [a·lu·si·'nar, a·lu·θi-] **I.** *vi inf* **1.** (*hablando*) to hallucinate; **¡tú alucinas!** *fig* you're crazy! **2.** (*quedar fascinado*) to be fascinated **II.** *vt inf* **1.** (*pasmar*) to amaze **2.** (*fascinar*) to fascinate

alud [a·'lud] *m* avalanche; **un ~ de gente** *fig* a throng of people

aludir [a·lu·'dir] *vi* (*referirse*) to allude; (*mencionar*) to mention; **darse por aludido** (*ofenderse*) to take it personally; **no darse por aludido** not to take the hint

alumbrado [a·lum·'bra·do] *m* lighting; **~ público** street lighting

alumbrar [a·lum·'brar] **I.** *vi* (*iluminar*) to give off light; **la lámpara alumbra poco** the lamp doesn't give off much light **II.** *vt* (*iluminar*) to light (up); (*a alguien*) to shine a light on

aluminio [a·lu·'mi·njo] *m* aluminum

alumnado [a·lum·'na·do] *m* (*de escuela*) pupils *pl;* (*de universidad*) students *pl*

alumno, -a [a·'lum·no, -a] *m, f* (*de escuela*) pupil; (*de universidad*) student

alusión [a·lu·'sjon] *f* **1.** (*mención*) **~ a algo** mention of sth **2.** (*insinuación*) allusion; **hacer una ~ a algo** to allude to sth

aluvión [a·lu·'βjon] *m* (*inundación*) *t. fig* flood

alza [ˈal·sa, -θa] *f* (*elevación*) rise; **estar en ~** (*precios*) to be rising; (*persona*) to be up-and-coming

alzamiento [al·sa·'mjento, al·θa-] *m* uprising

alzar <z → c> [al·'sar, -'θar] **I.** *vt* **1.** (*levantar*) to lift (up); (*precio*) to raise **2.** (*poner vertical*) to put up **3.** (*construir*) to erect **II.** *vr:* **~se 1.** (*levantarse*) to rise (up); **allí se alza la universidad** the university buildings rise up over there **2.** *AmL* (*sublevarse*) to revolt

ama [ˈa·ma] *f* (*dueña*) mistress; (*propietaria*) owner; **~ de casa** housewife; **~ de llaves** housekeeper

amabilidad [a·ma·βi·li·'dad] *f* kindness; **tuvo la ~ de avisarme** he/she was kind enough to warn me

amable [a·'ma·βle] *adj* kind; **ser ~ con alguien** to be kind to sb; **¿sería Ud. tan ~ de explicármelo?** would you be so kind as to explain it to me?

amaestrar [a·maes·'trar] *vt* to train; (*caballos*) to break in

amagar <g → gu> [a·ma·'ɣar] *vt* **1.** (*indicar*) **amagó un golpe** he/she made as if to strike **2.** (*amenazar*) to threaten; **~ a alguien con algo** to threaten sb with sth

amago [a·'ma·ɣo] *m* **1.** (*amenaza*) threat **2.** (*indicio*) hint **3.** DEP feint

amainar [a·mai·'nar] *vi* to abate

amalaya [a·ma·'la·ja] *interj AmL* hopefully

amalgama [a·mal·'ɣa·ma] *f* **1.** QUÍM amalgam **2.** (*mezcla*) mixture

amamantar [a·ma·man·'tar] *vt* (*bebé*) to breastfeed; (*cachorro*) to suckle

amanecer [a·ma·ne·'ser, -θer] **I.** *vimpers* to dawn; **está amaneciendo** it's getting light **II.** *m* dawn; **al ~** at dawn

amanecida [a·ma·ne·'si·da, -'θi·da] *f AmL* dawn

amanerado, -a [a·ma·ne·'ra·do, -a] *adj* **1.** (*persona*) affected **2.** (*estilo*) mannered

amansador [a·man·sa·'dor] *m Méx* (*domador*) horse breaker

amansar [a·man·'sar] *vt* **1.** (*animal*) to tame **2.** (*persona*) to subdue; (*sosegar*) to calm down

amante [a·'man·te] **I.** *adj* **soy poco ~ de hablar en público** I don't like speaking in public **II.** *mf* lover; **un ~ de la naturaleza** a nature-lover

amañar [a·ma·'ɲar] **I.** *vt* **1.** (*asunto*) to fix; **~ una solución** to cook up a solution **2.** (*resultado*) to fake **II.** *vr* **amañárselas** (**para todo**) to manage to get by (in everything)

amapola [a·ma·'po·la] *f* poppy

amar [a·'mar] *vt* to love

amargar <g → gu> [a·mar·'ɣar] **I.** *vt* to make bitter; **~ la vida a alguien** to make life difficult for sb **II.** *vr:* **~se** to become bitter

amargo, -a [a·'mar·ɣo] *adj* bitter; **la verdad amarga** the painful truth

amargura [a·mar·'ɣu·ra] *f* bitterness; **llorar con ~** to weep bitterly

amarillento, -a [a·ma·ri·'jen·to, -a; -'ʎen·to, -a] *adj* yellowish; (*papel*) yellowed

amarillo, -a [a·ma·'ri·jo, -'ʎo] *adj* **1.** (*color*) yellow **2.** (*pálido*) pale

amarradero [a·ma·rra·'de·ro] *m* **1.** (*poste*) post, bollard **2.** NÁUT berth

amarrar [a·ma·'rrar] **I.** *vt* **1.** (*atar*) to tie up **2.** NÁUT to moor ▶ **tener a alguien muy amarrado** *inf* to keep sb under tight control **II.** *vr:* **~se** *AmL* to get married

amasar [a·ma·'sar] *vt* **1.** (*masa*) to knead **2.** (*fortuna*) to amass

amasijar [a·ma·si·'xar] *vt AmL inf* (*dar paliza*) to give a beating; (*pegar brutalmente*) to beat to a pulp

amateur [a·ma·'ter] **I.** *adj* amateur **II.** *mf* <amateurs> amateur

amatista [a·ma·'tis·ta] *f* amethyst

amauta [a·'mau·ta] *m Bol, Perú* **1.** (*de los incas*) Incan sage **2.** (*autoridad*) village elder

amazona [a·ma·'so·na, -'θo·na] *f* **1.** (*mujer*) Amazon **2.** DEP rider

ámbar ['am·bar] *adj, m inv* amber

ambición [am·bi·'sjon, -'θjon] *f* ambition; **~ de poder** hunger for power; **mi ~ en la vida es...** my ambition in life is...

ambicioso, -a [am·bi·'sjo·so, -a; am·bi·'θjo-] *adj* ambitious

ambientador [am·bjen·ta·'dor] *m* air freshener

ambientar [am·bjen·'tar] **I.** *vt* **1.** (*novela*) to set; **la novela está ambientada en Lima** the novel is set in Lima **2.** (*fiesta*) to enliven **II.** *vr:* **~se 1.** (*aclimatarse*) to adjust **2.** (*en una fiesta*) to get into the mood

ambiente [am·'bjen·te] *m* **1.** (*aire*) air **2.** (*medio*) surroundings *pl;* **medio ~** environment; **nocivo para el medio ~** harmful to the environment **3.** (*social*) milieu **4.** (*atmósfera*) atmosphere; **dar ~** to create a favorable atmosphere; **no había ~ en la calle** there wasn't much happening in the street

ambigüedad [am·bi·ɣwe·'dad] *f* ambiguity; **sin ~es** unambiguous

ambiguo, -a [am·'bi·ɣwo, -a] *adj* (*de doble significado*) ambiguous

ámbito ['am·bi·to] *m* (*espacio*) area; **en el ~ nacional** on a national level

ambivalente [am·bi·βa·'len·te] *adj* ambivalent

ambos, -as [am·bos, -as] *adj* both

ambulancia [am·bu·'lan·sja, -θja] *f* (*vehículo*) ambulance

ambulante [am·bu·'lan·te] *adj* walking; **circo ~** traveling circus; **vendedor ~** peddler; **venta ~** peddling

ambulatorio [am·bu·la·'to·rjo] *m* outpatient department

ameba [a·'me·βa] *f* ameba

amedrentar [a·me·dren·'tar] *vt* **1.** (*asustar*) to scare **2.** (*intimidar*) to intimidate

amén [a·'men] *m* amen; **decir ~ a todo** to agree to everything

amenaza [a·me·'na·sa, -θa] *f* **1.** (*intimidación*) threat; **bajo la ~ de violencia** under the threat of violence **2.** (*peligro*) menace

amenazador(a) [a·me·na·sa·'dor, -·'do·ra; a·me·na·θa-] *adj* **1.** (*tono*) threatening; **gesto ~** threatening gesture **2.** (*que anuncia peligro*) menacing

amenazar <z → c> [a·me·na·'sar, -'θar] **I.** *vt* (*intimidar*) to threaten; **el jefe lo ha amenazado con despedirle** the boss has threatened him with dismissal **II.** *vi, vt* (*presagiar*) to threaten; **amenaza tormenta** there's a storm ahead

amenizar <z → c> [a·me·ni·'sar, -'θar] *vt* **1.** (*hacer agradable*) to make pleasant **2.** (*entretener*) to entertain

ameno, -a [a·'me·no, -a] *adj* **1.** (*agradable*) pleasant **2.** (*entretenido*) entertaining

América [a·'me·ri·ka] *f* America; **~ Central** Central America; **~ Latina** Latin America; **~ del Norte/del Sur** North/South America

americana [a·me·ri·'ka·na] *f* jacket

americanismo [a·me·ri·ka·'nis·mo] *m* LING Americanism

americano, -a [a·me·ri·'ka·no] *adj, m, f* (*de América del Sur*) South American; (*estadounidense*) American

amerindio, -a [a·me·'rin·djo, -a] *adj, m, f* American Indian, Amerindian

ametralladora [a·me·tra·ja·'do·ra, a·me·tra·ʎa-] *f* machine gun

amigable [a·mi·'ɣa·βle] *adj* friendly

amígdala [a·'miɣ·da·la] *f* tonsil

amigo, -a [a·'mi·ɣo, -a] **I.** *adj* **1.** (*amistoso*) friendly; **es muy amiga mía** she's a good friend of mine; **somos (muy) ~s desde la infancia** we've been (close) friends since our childhood **2.** (*aficionado*) **ser ~ de algo** to be fond of sth; **soy ~ de decir las cosas claras** I'm all for calling a spade a spade ▶ **¡y tan ~s!** and that's that! **II.** *m, f* **1.** (*general*) friend; **~ por correspondencia** pen pal; **hacerse ~ de alguien** to make friends with sb; **poner a alguien cara de pocos ~s** to look grimly at sb **2.** (*amante*) lover **3.** (*adepto*) supporter

amiguete [a·mi·'ɣe·te] *m inf* pal, buddy

aminorar [a·mi·no·'rar] **I.** *vi* to diminish **II.** *vt* to reduce; **~ el paso** to slow down

amistad [a·mis·'tad] *f* **1.** (*entre amigos*) friendship; **tener ~ con alguien** to be friendly with sb **2.** *pl* (*amigos*) friends *pl*

amistoso, -a [a·mis·'to·so, -a] *adj* friendly, amicable; **partido ~** friendly match

amnesia [am·'ne·sja] *f* amnesia

amnistía [am·nis·'ti·a] *f* amnesty; **Amnistía Internacional** Amnesty International

amo ['a·mo] *m* **1.** (*propietario*) owner **2.** (*patrón*) boss; **ser el ~ en algo** to be the boss in sth

amodorrarse [a·mo·do·'rrar·se] *vr* to become drowsy [*o* sleepy]

amoldar [a·mol·'dar] **I.** *vt* **1.** (*ajustar*) to adjust **2.** (*moldear*) to mold **3.** (*acomodar*) to adapt **II.** *vr:* **~se** to adapt oneself

amonestación [a·mo·nes·ta·'sjon, -'θjon] *f* (*advertencia*) warning

amonestar [a·mo·nes·'tar] *vt* (*advertir*) to warn; (*reprender*) to reprimand

amoníaco [a·mo·'ni·a·ko] *m* ammonia

amontonar [a·mon·to·'nar] **I.** *vt* to pile up **II.** *vr:* **~se** to pile up; (*personas*) to crowd together

amor [a·'mor] *m* love; **~ al prójimo** love for one's neighbor; **~ propio** self-esteem; **~ a primera vista** love at first sight; **¡~ mío!** my love!; **hacer el ~ con alguien** *inf* to make love with sb; **hacer algo con ~** to do sth lovingly ▶ **por ~ al arte** for nothing; **¡por ~ de Dios!** for God's sake!; **de mil ~es** with the greatest of pleasure

amoratado, -a [a·mo·ra·'ta·do, -a] *adj* purple; **un ojo ~** a black eye; **tengo los labios ~s de frío** my lips are blue with cold

amordazar <z → c> [a·mor·da·'sar, -'θar] *vt* to gag; *fig* to silence, to gag

amorfo, -a [a·'mor·fo, -a] *adj* shapeless, amorphous

amorío(s) [a·mo·'ri·o(s)] *m(pl) pey* love affair

amoroso, -a [a·mo·'ro·so, -a] *adj* **1.** (*de amor*) loving **2.** (*cariñoso*) **~ con al-**

guien affectionate to/towards sb

amortiguador [a·mor·ti·ɣwa·'dor] *m* AUTO shock absorber

amortiguar <gu → gü> [a·mor·ti·'ɣwar] *vt* (*sonido*) to muffle; (*golpe*) to cushion

amortización [a·mor·ti·sa·'sjon, -θa·'θjon] *f* 1. (*de una deuda*) repayment 2. (*fiscal*) depreciation

amortizar <z → c> [a·mor·ti·'sar, -'θar] *vt* 1. (*deuda*) to pay off 2. (*fiscalmente*) to write off 3. (*inversión*) to recover

amotinar [a·mo·ti·'nar] *vr:* ~se to rebel

amparar [am·pa·'rar] I. *vt* to protect; **la constitución ampara la libertad de religión** the constitution guarantees religious freedom II. *vr:* ~se to seek protection; **se ampara en una ley antigua** he/she has recourse to an old law

amparo [am·'pa·ro] *m* (*protección*) protection; **al ~ de la oscuridad** under cover of darkness

amperio [am·'pe·rjo] *m* amp

ampliación [am·plja·'sjon, -'θjon] *f* 1. (*engrandecimiento*) enlargement; (*de capital*) increase; (*de un territorio*) expansion; (*de una carretera*) extension 2. (*de conocimientos*) broadening 3. (*de un sonido*) amplification; **~ de RAM** COMPUT RAM expansion

ampliar <1. *pres* amplío> [am·pli·'ar] *vt* 1. (*hacer más grande*) to enlarge; (*territorio*) to expand; **edición ampliada** extended edition 2. (*conocimientos*) to broaden 3. (*sonido*) to amplify

amplificador [am·pli·fi·ka·'dor] *m* amplifier

amplificar <c → qu> [am·pli·fi·'kar] *vt* to amplify

amplio, -a ['am·pljo, -a] *adj* 1. (*casa*) spacious; (*parque*) extensive 2. (*vestido*) loose-fitting 3. (*informe*) detailed; (*experiencia*) wide-ranging; (*red*) extensive; (*interés*) broad; **una derrota amplia** a serious defeat; **en un sentido más ~** in a wider sense

amplitud [am·pli·'tud] *f* 1. (*extensión*) extent; (*de conocimientos*) range; **~ de miras** broad-mindedness; **de gran ~** wide-ranging 2. (*de una casa*) roominess; (*de un parque*) extensiveness

3. FÍS amplitude

ampolla [am·'po·ja, -ʎa] *f* 1. (*burbuja*) blister; **tener ~s en los pies** to have blisters on one's feet 2. (*garrafa*) flask 3. (*para inyecciones*) ampoule ▶ **levantar ~** to get people's backs up

ampolleta [am·po·'je·ta, -'ʎe·ta] *f* Arg light bulb

amputar [am·pu·'tar] *vt* to amputate

amuchar [a·mu·'tʃar] *vt* Arg, Bol, Chile to multiply

amueblar [a·mwe·'βlar] *vt* to furnish

amularse [a·mu·'lar·se] *vr* Méx (*mercancía*) to become unsalable; (*persona*) to get stubborn

amuleto [a·mu·'le·to] *m* amulet

amurallar [a·mu·ra·'jar, -'ʎar] *vt* to wall

anabolizante [a·na·βo·li·'san·te, -'θan·te] *m* anabolic steroid

anacardo [a·na·'kar·do] *m* 1. BOT cashew tree 2. (*fruto*) cashew (nut)

anagrama [a·na·'ɣra·ma] *m* anagram

anal [a·'nal] *adj* anal

anales [a·'na·les] *mpl* 1. HIST annals *pl* 2. (*de una sociedad*) records *pl*

analfabetismo [a·nal·fa·βe·'tis·mo] *m* illiteracy

analfabeto, -a [a·nal·fa·'βe·to, -a] *m, f* illiterate (person)

analgésico [a·nal·'xe·si·ko] *m* painkiller

análisis [a·'na·li·sis] *m inv* 1. (*general*) t. MAT analysis 2. MED test

analista [a·na·'lis·ta] *mf* (*que analiza*) analyst; **~ de sistemas** COMPUT systems analyst; **el médico mandó las pruebas al ~** the doctor sent the samples to the laboratory

analítico, -a [a·na·'li·ti·ko, -a] *adj* analytic(al)

analizar <z → c> [a·na·li·'sar, -'θar] *vt* (*examinar*) t. MED to analyze

analogía [a·na·lo·'xi·a] *f* analogy; **por ~ con algo** on the analogy of sth

análogo, -a [a·'na·lo·ɣo, -a] *adj* analogous

ananá(s) [a·na·'na(s)] *m* CSur pineapple

anaranjado, -a [a·na·ran·'xa·do, -a] *adj* orange

anarquía [a·nar·'ki·a] *f* anarchy

anarquismo [a·nar·'kis·mo] *m* anarchism

anarquista [a·nar·ˈkis·ta] *adj, mf* anarchist

anatomía [a·na·to·ˈmi·a] *f* anatomy

anatómico, -a [a·na·ˈto·mi·ko, -a] *adj* 1. MED anatomical 2. (*adaptado al cuerpo*) anatomically designed

anca [ˈan·ka] *f* 1. (*de animal*) haunch; ~**s de rana** frogs' legs 2. (*cadera*) hip 3. *pl inf* (*nalgas*) backside ▶ **montar a las ~s** to sit behind

ancestral [an·ses·ˈtral, an·θes-] *adj* 1. (*de los antepasados*) ancestral 2. (*antiguo*) ancient

ancho [ˈan·tʃo] *m* width; ~ **de vía** FERRO gauge [*o* gage]; **tener** [*o* **medir**] **cinco metros de ~** to be five meters wide

ancho, -a [ˈan·tʃo, -a] *adj* wide; (*vestidos*) loose-fitting; ~ **de espaldas** broadshouldered; **a lo ~** widthwise 2. **en este pueblo estoy a mis anchas** I feel at home in this village; **se queda tan ~ cuando dice tonterías** he remains completely unabashed when he talks nonsense

anchoa [an·ˈtʃoa] *f* anchovy

anchura [an·ˈtʃu·ra] *f* width; (*de un vestido*) looseness

ancianidad [an·sja·ni·ˈdad, an·θja-] *f* old age

anciano, -a [an·ˈsja·no, -a; an·ˈθja-] **I.** *adj* old **II.** *m, f* old man *m*, old woman *f*

ancla [ˈan·kla] *f* anchor; **echar/levar ~s** to drop/weigh anchor

anclar [an·ˈklar] *vi, vt* to anchor; **estar anclado** to be anchored

andadas [an·ˈda·das] *fpl* **volver a las ~** to revert to old habits

ándale [ˈan·da·le] *interj* Méx (*adiós*) bye; (*deprisa*) come on

Andalucía [an·da·lu·ˈsi·a, -ˈθi·a] *f* Andalusia

andaluz(a) [an·da·ˈlus, -·ˈlu·sa; -ˈluθ, -·ˈlu·θa] *adj, m(f)* Andalusian

andamiaje [an·da·ˈmja·xe] *m*, **andamio** [an·ˈda·mjo] *m* scaffolding

andanada [an·da·ˈna·da] *f* **por ~s** Arg in excess

andanza [an·ˈdan·sa, -θa] *f* (*aventura*) adventure

andar [an·ˈdar] *irr* **I.** *vi* 1. (*caminar*) to walk; ~ **a caballo** to ride (a horse); ~ **a gatas** to go on all fours; (*bebés*) to crawl; ~ **de prisa** to go quickly; ~ **detrás de algo** to be after sth; **desde la estación hay 10 minutos andando** it's 10 minutes walk from the station 2. (*coche*) to run; (*máquina*) to work 3. (*estar*) ~ **atareado** to be busy; ~ **metido en un asunto** to be involved in a matter; ~ **haciendo algo** to be doing sth; **te ando llamando desde hace una hora** I've been trying to call you for an hour; ~ **mal de dinero** to be short of money; **~emos por los 30 grados** it must be about 30 degrees; **no andes en mi escritorio** don't go rummaging in my desk ▶ **dime con quien andas y te diré quien eres** *prov* a man is known by the company he keeps; ~ **a la que salta** to seize the opportunity; **¡anda!** good heavens! **II.** *vt* **he andado toda la casa para encontrarte** I've looked all over the house for you **III.** *m* walk, gait

andén [an·ˈden] *m* FERRO platform

Andes [ˈan·des] *mpl* **los ~** the Andes + *pl vb*

andinismo [an·di·ˈnis·mo] *m AmL* mountaineering, mountain climbing

andino, -a [an·ˈdi·no, -a] *adj* Andean

Andorra [an·ˈdo·rra] *f* Andorra

andrajo [an·ˈdra·xo] *m* rag

andrajoso, -a [an·dra·ˈxo·so, -a] *adj* ragged

andurrial [an·du·ˈrrjal] *m* Arg, Ecua, Perú muddy road

anécdota [a·ˈnek·do·ta] *f* anecdote

anemia [a·ˈne·mja] *f* anemia

anémona [a·ˈne·mo·na] *f* anemone

anestesia [a·nes·ˈte·sja] *f* anesthesia

anestesiar [a·nes·te·ˈsjar] *vt* to anesthetize

anestésico [a·nes·ˈte·si·ko] *m* anesthetic

anexión [a·nek·ˈsjon] *f* annexation

anexo [a·ˈnek·so] *m v.* **anejo**

anexo, -a [a·ˈnek·so, -a] *adj v.* **anejo, -a**

anfibio [an·ˈfi·βjo] *m* amphibian

anfibio, -a [an·ˈfi·βjo, -a] *adj* amphibious

anfiteatro [an·fi·te·ˈa·tro] *m* 1. (*local*) amphitheater 2. (*en la universidad*) lecture hall

anfitrión, -ona [an·fi·ˈtrjon] *m, f* host *m*, hostess *f*

ánfora [ˈan·fo·ɾa] f (*cántaro*) amphora

ángel [ˈan·xel] m angel; ~ **de la guarda** guardian angel

angelical [an·xe·li·ˈkal] adj angelic(al)

angina [an·ˈxi·na] f ~ **de pecho** angina (pectoris); ~**s** sore throat

anglicismo [an·gli·ˈsis·mo, -ˈθis·mo] m Anglicism

angosto, -a [an·ˈgos·to, -a] adj narrow

anguila [an·ˈgi·la] f ZOOL eel

angula [an·ˈgu·la] f ZOOL glass eel, elver

angular [an·gu·ˈlar] I. adj angular; **piedra** ~ cornerstone II. m **gran** ~ FOTO wide-angle lens

ángulo [ˈan·gu·lo] m 1. MAT angle; ~ **recto** right angle; **en** ~ angled; ~ **de tiro** DEP angle of fire 2. (*rincón*) corner 3. (*de vista*) angle of vision

angurriento, -a [an·gu·ˈrrjen·to, -a] adj AmL 1. pey (*glotón*) gluttonous; (*hambriento*) greedy 2. (*codicioso*) avaricious

angustia [an·ˈgus·tja] f 1. (*temor*) anguish; ~ **vital** angst 2. (*aflicción*) anxiety

angustiar [an·gus·ˈtjar] I. vt 1. (*acongojar*) to distress 2. (*causar temor*) to frighten 3. (*afligir*) to worry II. vr: ~**se** 1. (*afligirse*) to get worried 2. (*atemorizarse*) to get scared

angustioso, -a [an·gus·ˈtjo·so, -a] adj 1. (*lleno de angustia*) anguished 2. (*inquietante*) worrying

anhelar [a·ne·ˈlar] I. vi to pant II. vt to long for

anhelo [a·ˈne·lo] m ~ **de algo** longing for sth

anidar [a·ni·ˈdar] vi (*hacer nido*) to nest

anilla [a·ˈni·ja, -ʎa] f 1. (*aro*) ring 2. pl DEP rings pl

anillo [a·ˈni·jo, -ʎo] m ring; ~ **de boda** wedding ring ▶ **venir como** ~ **al dedo** to be just right; **ese vestido se te viene como** ~ **al dedo** this dress suits you perfectly; **no se me caen los** ~**s por...** it's not beneath me to...

ánima [ˈa·ni·ma] f soul

animación [a·ni·ma·ˈsjon, -ˈθjon] f 1. (*acción*) animation 2. (*viveza*) liveliness 3. (*actividad*) activity; **había mucha** ~ **en la calle** the street was very busy

animado, -a [a·ni·ˈma·do, -a] adj 1. (*per-sona*) in high spirits; **no estar muy** ~ not to be very cheerful 2. (*lugar*) busy 3. (*actividad*) lively 4. **estar** ~ **a hacer algo** to be keen on doing sth; ~ **por ordenador** COMPUT computer-animated

animador(a) [a·ni·ma·ˈdor, -ˈdo·ɾa] I. adj encouraging II. m(f) 1. (*artista*) entertainer 2. (*presentador*) presenter 3. DEP cheerleader

animal [a·ni·ˈmal] I. adj 1. (*de los animales*) animal; **comportamiento** ~ animal behavior 2. (*grosero*) rude II. m 1. ZOOL animal; ~**es de caza** game; ~ **de compañía** pet; ~ **de presa** predator; **comer como un** ~ inf to eat like a horse 2. pey (*persona ignorante*) fool; (*bruta*) brute

animalada [a·ni·ma·ˈla·da] f inf 1. (*disparate*) (piece of) nonsense 2. (*barbaridad*) disgrace; **¡qué** ~**!** how outrageous! 3. (*cantidad*) massive amount

animar [a·ni·ˈmar] I. vt 1. (*dinamizar*) to liven up 2. (*alentar*) to encourage 3. (*persona*) to cheer up II. vr: ~**se** 1. (*cobrar vida*) to liven up 2. (*atreverse*) to dare; **¡por fin te has animado a escribir!** so you've finally decided to write!; **¿te animas?** are you up to it? 3. (*alegrarse*) to cheer up

ánimo [ˈa·ni·mo] m 1. (*espíritu*) spirit; **no estoy con** ~**s de...** I don't feel like... 2. (*energía*) energy; (*valor*) courage; **dar** ~ to encourage; **¡~!** cheer up! 3. (*intención*) intention; **con** ~ **de...** with the intention of...; **sin** ~ **de lucro** non-profit-making; **sin** ~ **de ofender a nadie** without wishing to offend anyone

aniñado, -a [a·ni·ˈɲa·do, -a] adj childlike; pey childish

aniquilar [a·ni·ki·ˈlar] vt 1. (*destruir*) to annihilate 2. (*desanimar*) to shatter

anís <*anises*> [a·ˈnis] m 1. (*planta*) anise; (*semilla*) aniseed 2. (*licor*) anisette

aniversario [a·ni·βer·ˈsa·ɾjo] m anniversary; ~ **de bodas** wedding anniversary

ano [ˈa·no] m ANAT anus

anoche [a·ˈno·tʃe] adv last night; **antes de** ~ the night before last

anochecer [a·no·tʃe·ˈser, -ˈθer] I. irr como crecer vimpers **anochece** it's getting dark II. m nightfall; **al** ~ at dusk

anodino, -a [a·no·'di·no, -a] *adj* (*cosa*) insipid; (*persona*) bland

anomalía [a·no·ma·'lia] *f* anomaly

anonadar [a·no·na·'dar] I. *vt* to astound; (*maravillar*) to overwhelm; **la noticia me dejó anonadado** I was astonished by the news II. *vr*: **~se 1.** (*descorazonarse*) to be discouraged **2.** (*aniquilarse*) to be destroyed

anonimato [a·no·ni·'ma·to] *m* anonymity; **mantener el ~** to remain anonymous

anónimo [a·'no·ni·mo] *m* (*autor*) anonymous author; (*escrito*) anonymous work

anónimo, -a [a·'no·ni·mo, -a] *adj* anonymous; **sociedad anónima** ECON stock corporation

anorexia [a·no·'rek·sja] *f* anorexia

anormal [a·nor·'mal] *adj* abnormal; **~ (físico/síquico)** physically/mentally handicapped

anotación [a·no·ta·'sjon, -'θjon] *f* **1.** (*acción*) annotation; (*en un registro*) record **2.** (*nota*) note

anotar [a·no·'tar] *vt* to note (down); (*en un registro*) to record

ansia ['an·sja] *f* **1.** (*angustia*) anguish **2.** (*intranquilidad*) anxiety **3.** (*afán*) longing; **~ de poder** craving for power

ansiar <*1. pres* ansío> [an·'sjar] *vt* to long for; **el momento ansiado** the long-awaited moment; **~ el regreso de alguien** to long for sb's return

ansiedad [an·sje·'dad] *f* anxiety

ansioso, -a [an·'sjo·so, -a] *adj* **1.** (*intranquilo*) anxious **2.** (*anheloso*) eager **3.** (*impaciente*) impatient

antagónico, -a [an·ta·'yo·ni·ko, -a] *adj* **1.** (*opuesto*) opposed **2.** (*rival*) antagonistic

antagonista [an·ta·yo·'nis·ta] *mf* antagonist

antaño [an·'ta·no] *adv* long ago

antártico, -a [an·'tar·ti·ko, -a] *adj* Antarctic; **Océano Glacial Antártico** Antarctic Ocean

Antártida [an·'tar·ti·da] *f* Antarctica

ante ['an·te] I. *m* **1.** ZOOL elk **2.** (*piel*) suede II. *prep* **1.** (*posición*) before **2.** (*en vista de*) in view of **3.** (*adversario*) faced with

anteanoche [an·te·a·'no·tʃe] *adv* the night before last

anteayer [an·te·a·'jer] *adv* the day before yesterday

antebrazo [an·te·'βra·so, -θo] *m* ANAT forearm

antecedente [an·te·se·'den·te, an·te·θe·] *m pl* history; (*de una persona*) background; **~s penales** criminal record

anteceder [an·te·se·'der, an·te·θe·] *vt* to precede

antecesor(a) [an·te·se·'sor, --'so·ra; ante·θe-] *m(f)* **1.** (*en un cargo*) predecessor **2.** (*antepasado*) ancestor

antelación [an·te·la·'sjon, -'θjon] *f* **con ~** in advance; **con la debida ~** in good time

antemano [an·te·'ma·no] *adv* **de ~** in advance; **calcular de ~** to calculate in advance

antena [an·'te·na] *f* **1.** ZOOL antenna **2.** (*de televisor*) antenna; **estar en ~** to be on the air; **el programa lleva un año en ~** the program has been running for a year; **estar con las ~s puestas** *irón* to be all ears

antepasado, -a [an·te·pa·'sa·do, -a] *m, f* ancestor

antepenúltimo, -a [an·te·pe·'nul·ti·mo, -a] *adj* antepenultimate, third from last

anteponer [an·te·po·'ner] *irr como* poner I. *vt* **1.** (*poner delante*) **~ algo a algo** to place sth in front of sth **2.** (*dar preferencia*) to give priority to II. *vr*: **~se 1.** (*ponerse delante*) **~se a alguien** to stand in front of sb **2.** (*tener preferencia*) to be preferred

anteproyecto [an·te·pro·'jek·to] *m* draft

anterior [an·te·'rjor] II. *adj* previous; **la noche ~ había llovido** the night before it had rained; **en la página ~** on the preceding [*o* previous] page II. *prep* **~ a** prior to

anterioridad [an·te·rjo·ri·'dad] *f* anteriority; **con ~ a** prior to, before

anteriormente [an·te·rjor·'men·te] *adv* before, previously

antes ['an·tes] I. *adv* **1.** (*de tiempo*) before; (*hace un rato*) just now; (*antiguamente*) formerly; (*primero*) first; **poco ~** shortly before; **piénsate ~ lo que dices**

think before you speak; **ahora como ~** still; **cuanto ~** as soon as possible; **~ de nada** first of all **2.** (*comparativo*) rather **~ de** before **III.** *prep* **~ de** (*temporal*) before; **~ (de) que llegues** before you arrive **IV.** *adj* **el día ~** the previous day

antiaéreo, -a [an·tja·'e·reo, -a] *adj* MIL anti-aircraft

antibalas [an·ti·'βa·las] *adj inv* bullet-proof

antibiótico [an·ti·'βjo·ti·ko] *m* antibiotic

anticiclón [an·ti·si·'klon, -θi·'klon] *m* anticyclone

anticipación [an·ti·si·pa·'sjon, -θi·pa·'θjon] *f* (*de fecha, de suceso*) anticipation

anticipadamente [an·ti·si·pa·da·'men·te, an·ti·θi-] *adv* in advance; **jubilar ~ a alguien** to retire sb early

anticipado, -a [an·ti·si·'pa·do, -a; an·ti·θi-] *adj* early; **pagar por ~** to pay in advance

anticipar [an·ti·si·'par, an·ti·θi-] **I.** *vt* **1.** (*fecha*) to move up **2.** (*suceso*) to anticipate; **no anticipemos los acontecimientos** let's not anticipate events **3.** (*dinero*) to advance; **~ una paga sobre el sueldo** to give an advance on a salary **II.** *vr* **-se a alguien** to beat sb to it; **el verano se ha anticipado este año** summer is early this year

anticipo [an·ti·'si·po, -'θi·po] *m* **1.** (*del sueldo*) advance **2.** (*de un pago*) advance payment

anticonceptivo, -a [an·ti·kon·sep·'ti·βo, -a; -θep·'ti·βo, -a] *adj* contraceptive, birth-control; **píldora anticonceptiva** oral contraceptive, birth control pill

anticongelante [an·ti·kon·xe·'lan·te] *m* antifreeze

anticonstitucional [an·ti·kons·ti·tu·sjo·'nal, -θjo·'nal] *adj* unconstitutional

anticuado, -a [an·ti·'kwa·do, -a] *adj* old-fashioned

anticuario, -a [an·ti·'kwa·rjo, -a] *m, f* antique dealer

anticucho [an·ti·'ku·tʃo] *m* Perú kebob

anticuerpo [an·ti·'kwer·po] *m* antibody

antideportivo, -a [an·ti·de·por·'ti·βo, -a] *adj* unsporting

antidoping [an·ti·'do·piŋ] *adj inv* **control ~** drugs test

antídoto [an·'ti·do·to] *m* antidote

antifaz [an·ti·'fas, -'faθ] *m* mask

antiguamente [an·ti·ɣwa·'men·te] *adv* once, long ago

antigüedad [an·ti·ɣwe·'dad] *f* **1.** (*edad antigua*) antiquity **2.** (*objeto*) antique; **tener una ~ de 100 años** to be 100 years old **3.** (*en una empresa*) seniority; **tengo 5 años de ~ (en el trabajo)** I've been in the company's service for 5 years

antiguo, -a [an·'ti·ɣwo, -a] *adj* <anti-quísimo> **1.** (*viejo*) old; (*relación*) long-standing **2.** (*anticuado*) antiquated; (*muy anticuado*) ancient **3.** (*de la antigüedad*) ancient **4.** (*anterior*) former **5.** (*en un cargo*) **es el más ~ en esta empresa** he's the most senior member of staff in this firm

antiinflamatorio, -a [an·tin·fla·ma·'to·rjo/an·ti·in·fla·ma·'to·rjo] *adj* anti-inflammatory

antílope [an·'ti·lo·pe] *m* antelope

antinatural [an·ti·na·tu·'ral] *adj* unnatural

antipatía [an·ti·pa·'ti·a] *f* antipathy; **~ a alguien** antipathy for sb

antipático, -a [an·ti·'pa·ti·ko, -a] *adj* unpleasant

antirreglamentario, -a [an·ti·rre·ɣla·men·'ta·rjo, -a] *adj* unlawful

antirrobo [an·ti·'rro·βo] *m* anti-theft device

antisemita [an·ti·se·'mi·ta] **I.** *adj* anti-Semitic **II.** *mf* anti-Semite

antiséptico, -a [an·ti·'sep·ti·ko] *adj* antiseptic

antisocial [an·ti·so·'sjal, -'θjal] *adj* antisocial

antiterrorista [an·ti·te·rro·'ris·ta] *adj* antiterrorist; **lucha ~** fight against terrorism

antítesis [an·'ti·te·sis] *f inv* antithesis

antojarse [an·to·'xar·se] *vimpers* (*encapricharse*) **se me antojó un helado** I felt like having an ice cream; **hace siempre lo que se le antoja** he/she always does as he/she pleases

antojitos [an·to·'xi·tos] *mpl* Méx CULIN appetizers *pl*

antojo [an·'to·xo] *m* **1.** (*capricho*) whim; **a mi ~** as I please **2.** (*de una embarazada*) craving **3.** *Méx* (*apetito*) appetite

antología [an·to·lo·'xi·a] *f* anthology

antorcha [an·'tor·tʃa] *f* torch

antro ['an·tro] *m* pey dive; **un ~ de corrupción** a den of iniquity

antropología [an·tro·po·lo·'xi·a] *f* anthropology

antropólogo, -a [an·tro·'po·lo·ɣo, -a] *m, f* anthropologist

anual [a·nu·'al] *adj* annual, yearly; **informe ~** annual report

anualmente [a·nwal·'men·te] *adv* annually, yearly

anuario [a·nu·'a·rjo] *m* yearbook

anudar [a·nu·'dar] **I.** *vt* to knot **II.** *vr:* **~se** to become knotted

anulación [a·nu·la·'sjon, -'θjon] *f* (*de una ley*) repeal; (*de una sentencia*) overturning; (*de un matrimonio*) annulment; (*de un contrato*) cancellation

anular [a·nu·'lar] **I.** *vt* (*ley*) to repeal; (*sentencia*) to overturn; (*matrimonio*) to annul; (*contrato*) to cancel; (*gol*) to disallow **II.** *adj* (*del anillo*) annular

anunciar [a·nun·'sjar, -'θjar] **I.** *vt* **1.** (*comunicar*) to announce; **acaban de ~ la llegada del vuelo** they've just announced the arrival of the flight **2.** (*dar publicidad*) to advertise **II.** *vr:* **~se** (*hacer publicidad*) to be advertised

anuncio [a·'nun·sjo, -θjo] *m* **1.** (*de una noticia*) announcement **2.** (*en la TV*) commercial; (*en un periódico*) advertisement, ad

anverso [am·'ber·so] *m* obverse

anzuelo [an·'swe·lo, -'θwe·lo] *m* **1.** (*para pescar*) (fish-)hook **2.** *inf* (*aliciente*) bait, lure; **echar el ~ a alguien** to lure sb; **morder** [*o* **tragar**] **el ~** to swallow the bait

añadidura [a·ɲa·di·'du·ra] *f* addition; **por ~** in addition

añadir [a·ɲa·'dir] *vt* to add; **a esto hay que ~ que...** there's also the fact that...

añares [a·'ɲa·res] *mpl Arg* ages *pl*

añejo, -a [a·'ɲe·xo, -a] *adj* old; (*vino*) mature

añicos [a·'ɲi·kos] *mpl* fragments *pl;* **hacer algo ~** to smash sth up

año ['a·ɲo] *m* year; **~ bisiesto** leap year; **~ luz** light year; **~ natural** calendar year; **la víspera de ~ nuevo** New Year's Eve; **los ~s 60** the sixties; **en el ~ 1960 en** 1960; **el ~ de la pera** the year one; **cumplir ~s** to have a birthday; **cumplir 60 ~s** to turn sixty; **¿cuántos ~s tienes?** how old are you?; **Juan le saca cinco ~s a Pepe** Juan is five years older than Pepe; **los ~s no pasan en balde** the years take their toll ▶ **un hombre entrado en ~s** an elderly man; **por él no pasan los ~s** he doesn't seem to get any older; **quitarse ~s** to be older than one admits; **a mis ~s** at my age

añoranza [a·ɲo·'ran·sa, -θa] *f* yearning

añorar [a·ɲo·'rar] *vt* to yearn for; **~ los viejos tiempos** to long for the old days

aorta [a·'or·ta] *f* aorta

apacible [a·pa·'si·βle, -'θi·βle] *adj* **1.** (*persona*) placid; (*temperamento*) even **2.** (*tiempo*) mild

apadrinar [a·pa·dri·'nar] *vt* **1.** (*ser padrino*) **~ a alguien** (*en un bautizo*) to be sb's godfather; (*en una boda*) to be sb's best man **2.** (*patrocinar*) to sponsor

apagado, -a [a·pa·'ɣa·do, -a] *adj* (*sonido*) muffled; (*persona*) lifeless; (*color*) dull

apagar <g → gu> [a·pa·'ɣar] **I.** *vt* (*luz*) to put out; **~ el fuego con una manta** to put out the fire with a blanket; (*radio*) to switch off; (*vela*) to snuff ▶ **estar apagado** to not be in form; **¡apaga y vámonos!** that's enough! **II.** *vr:* **~se** (*fuego*) to go out; (*sonido*) to die out

apagón [a·pa·'ɣon] *m* blackout; ELEC power cut

apalabrar [a·pa·la·'βrar] *vt* to arrange

apaleada [a·pa·le·'a·da] *f Arg, Méx,* **apaleamiento** [a·pa·lea·'mjen·to] *m* (*zurra*) drubbing

apantallado, -a [a·pan·ta·'ja·do, -a; -'ʎa·do, -a] *adj Méx* overwhelmed

apañado, -a [a·pa·'ɲa·do, -a] *adj* **1.** (*hábil*) skilful **2.** (*adecuado*) suitable; **estás ~ si crees que te voy a ayudar** *inf* you're quite mistaken if you think I'm going to help you

apañar [a·pa·'nar] **I.** *vt* (*remendar*) to mend **II.** *vr:* **~se** (*arreglárselas*) to manage; **no sé cómo te las apañas** I don't know how you manage

apaño [a·'pa·ɲo] *m* **1.** (*remiendo*) patch; **encontrar un ~** to find a solution **2.** (*chanchullo*) scam

aparato [a·pa·'ra·to] *m* **1.** (*utensilio*) *t.* DEP apparatus; **~ indicador** meter; **~ de precisión** precision instrument; **~ de televisión** television set **2.** TEL receiver; **ponerse al ~** to come to the phone **3.** ANAT system; **~ digestivo** digestive system **4.** (*ostentación*) pomp **5.** POL (*de un partido*) machine

aparatoso, -a [a·pa·ra·'to·so, -a] *adj* **1.** (*ostentación*) ostentatious **2.** (*desmedido*) excessive

aparcamiento [a·par·ka·'mjen·to] *m* **1.** (*acción*) parking **2.** (*lugar*) parking lot

aparcar <c → qu> [a·par·'kar] *vt* **1.** (*coche*) to park **2.** (*decisión*) to put off

aparecer [a·pa·re·'ser, -'θer] *irr como* **crecer I.** *vi* to appear; (*algo inesperado*) to turn up; **~ ante la opinión pública** to appear in public **II.** *vr:* **~se** to appear

aparejador(a) [a·pa·re·xa·'dor, -·'ðo·ra] *m(f)* foreman builder *m*, forewoman builder *f*

aparentar [a·pa·ren·'tar] *vt* to feign; **trata de ~ que es rico** he tries to make out that he's rich; **no aparentas la edad que tienes** you don't look your age

aparente [a·pa·'ren·te] *adj* **1.** (*que parece*) apparent **2.** (*visible*) visible

aparentemente [a·pa·ren·te·'men·te] *adv* apparently, seemingly

aparición [a·pa·ri·'sjon, -'θjon] *f* **1.** (*acción*) appearance **2.** (*visión*) apparition

apariencia [a·pa·'rjen·sja, -θja] *f* appearance; **en ~** apparently; **guardar las ~s** to keep up appearances ▶ **las ~s engañan** appearances can be deceptive

apartado [a·par·'ta·do] *m* **1.** (*párrafo*) paragraph **2.** ADMIN **~ de Correos** post office box

apartado, -a [a·par·'ta·do, -a] *adj* (*lugar*) isolated

apartamento [a·par·ta·'men·to] *m* apartment

apartar [a·par·'tar] **I.** *vt* **1.** (*separar*) to separate; (*la vista*) to avert **2.** (*a un lado*) to put aside; **~ a alguien para de-**

cirle algo to take sb aside to tell him/ her sth; **¡aparta la mano del taladro!** take your hand off the drill! **3.** (*de un cargo*) to remove **II.** *vr:* **~se 1.** (*separarse*) to separate; (*del tema*) to deviate **2.** (*de un camino*) to turn off; **¡apártate!** get out of the way!

aparte [a·'par·te] **I.** *adv* apart; **esta cuestión debe tratarse ~** this question must be dealt with on its own **II.** *prep* **1.** (*separado*) **él estaba ~ del grupo** he was separated from the group **2.** (*además de*) **~ de** apart from; **~ de esto, perdí las llaves** apart from that, I lost the keys **III.** *m* paragraph; **punto y ~** new paragraph **IV.** *adj inv* **1.** (*singular*) special **2.** (*separado*) separate; **en un plato ~** on a separate plate

apasionado, -a [a·pa·sjo·'na·do, -a] **I.** *adj* **1.** (*con pasión*) passionate **2.** (*entusiasta*) enthusiastic **II.** *m, f* enthusiast

apasionante [a·pa·sjo·'nan·te] *adj* exciting

apatía [a·pa·'ti·a] *f* apathy

apático, -a [a·'pa·ti·ko, -a] *adj* apathetic

apátrida [a·'pa·tri·da] *adj* stateless

apeadero [a·pea·'de·ro] *m* FERRO halt

apearse [a·pe·'ar·se] *vr* (*de un vehículo*) to get out; (*de un caballo*) to get off

apechugar <g → gu> [a·pe·tʃu·'ɣar] *vi* **~ con** to put up with stoically; **~ con las consecuencias** to suffer the consequences

apedrear [a·pe·dre·'ar] *vt* to throw stones at; (*lapidar*) to stone (to death)

apegado, -a [a·pe·'ɣa·do, -a] *adj* **estar ~ a alguien** to be attached to sb

apego [a·'pe·ɣo] *m* attachment; **tener un gran ~ a algo** to be very attached to sth

apelación [a·pe·la·'sjon, -'θjon] *f* JUR appeal; **esto no tiene ~** *fig* there's nothing to be done

apelar [a·pe·'lar] *vi* **1.** (*invocar*) to appeal **2.** (*recurrir*) to turn; (*a algo*) to resort; **~ a todos los medios** to try everything **3.** JUR (*recurrir*) to appeal

apellidar [a·pe·ʎi·'dar, -ʎi·'dar] **I.** *vt* to name **II.** *vr:* **~se** to be called; **se apellida Martínez** his/her surname is Martínez

apellido [a·pe·'ji·ðo, -'ʎi·ðo] *m* surname; **~ de soltera** maiden name; **primer ~** father's surname

apenas [a·'pe·nas] *adv* **1.** (*casi no*) hardly; **~ había nadie** there was hardly anybody [*o* anyone] there **2.** (*tan solo*) just; (*escasamente*) barely; **~ hace una hora** barely an hour ago; **tengo ~ 10 dólares en el bolsillo** I have just 10 dollars in my pocket

apéndice [a·'pen·di·se, -θe] *m* **1.** (*de un libro*) appendix; (*tomo separado*) supplement **2.** (*complemento*) appendage **3.** ANAT appendix

apendicitis [a·pen·di·'si·tis, -'θi·tis] *f inv* appendicitis

aperitivo [a·pe·ri·'ti·βo] *m* **1.** (*bebida*) aperitif **2.** (*comida*) appetizer ▶ **¡y ésto es tan solo el ~!** and that's only the beginning!

apertura [a·per·'tu·ra] *f* opening; **~ de un crédito** taking out of a loan

apestar [a·pes·'tar] *vi* **~ a algo** to stink of sth

apestoso, -a [a·pes·'to·so, -a] *adj* **1.** (*que apesta*) stinking, stinky *inf* **2.** (*fastidioso*) annoying

apetecer [a·pe·te·'ser, -'θer] *irr como crecer vi* **1.** (*tener ganas de*) to feel like; **¿qué te apetece?** what would you like?; **me apetece un helado** I feel like an ice cream **2.** (*gustar*) **una copa de vino siempre apetece** a glass of wine is always welcome

apetito [a·pe·'ti·to] *m* **1.** (*de comida*) **~ de algo** appetite for sth; **abrir el ~ to** whet one's appetite **2.** (*deseo*) **~ de algo** desire for sth

apetitoso, -a [a·pe·ti·'to·so, -a] *adj* **1.** (*que da apetito*) appetizing **2.** (*sabroso*) tasty **3.** (*deseable*) desirable

ápice ['a·pi·se, -θe] *m* apex; **no ceder un ~** *fig* not to yield an inch

apicultor(a) [a·pi·kul·'tor, -·'to·ra] *m(f)* beekeeper

apicultura [a·pi·kul·'tu·ra] *f* beekeeping, apiculture

apilar(se) [a·pi·'lar·(se)] *vt, (vr)* to pile up

apio ['a·pjo] *m* celery

apirularse [a·pi·ru·'lar·se] *vr Chile* to dress up

apisonadora [a·pi·so·na·'ðo·ra] *f* steamroller

aplacar <c → qu> [a·pla·'kar] **I.** *vt* **1.** (*persona*) to calm down **2.** (*dolor*) to soothe; (*hambre*) to satisfy; (*sed*) to quench **II.** *vr:* **~se** to calm down

aplanar [a·pla·'nar] *vt* **1.** (*allanar*) to level **2.** (*aplastar*) to flatten

aplastante [a·plas·'tan·te] *adj* overwhelming; (*derrota*) crushing

aplastar [a·plas·'tar] *vt* **1.** (*chafar*) to flatten; (*con la mano*) to squash; (*con el pie*) to crush; **el desprendimiento de piedras aplastó a dos personas** the rockfall crushed two people **2.** (*derrotar*) to overwhelm

aplatanarse [a·pla·ta·'nar·se] *vr Cuba, PRico* (*adoptar las costumbres*) to go native

aplaudir [a·plau·'dir] **I.** *vi* to applaud, to clap **II.** *vt* **1.** (*palmear*) to applaud **2.** (*aprobar*) to approve

aplauso [a·'plau·so] *m* applause; **digno de ~** *fig* worthy of applause

aplazamiento [a·pla·sa·'mjen·to, a·pla·θa-] *m* **1.** (*de fecha*) postponement; (*de reunión*) postponement, adjournment **2.** (*de decisión*) deferment

aplazar <z → c> [a·pla·'sar, -'θar] *vt* **1.** (*fecha*) to postpone; (*reunión*) to postpone, to adjourn *(after having begun)*; **~ el viaje una semana** to postpone the trip by one week **2.** (*decisión*) to defer

aplicación [a·pli·ka·'sjon, -'θjon] *f* **1.** (*de pintura*) application **2.** (*utilización*) use; **las múltiples aplicaciones del plástico** the various applications [*o* uses] of plastic

aplicado, -a [a·pli·'ka·do, -a] *adj* (*trabajador*) hardworking

aplicar <c → qu> [a·pli·'kar] **I.** *vt* **1.** (*poner sobre*) to apply; **~ dando un ligero masaje** apply, massaging lightly **2.** (*utilizar*) to use; **~ una máquina para un trabajo** to use a machine for a job; **~ el freno** to apply the brake **3.** JUR **~ una sanción** to impose; **la ley no se puede ~ en este caso** the law is not applicable in this case **II.** *vr:* **~se 1.** (*esforzarse*) to apply oneself **2.** (*emplearse*) to be used

aplique [a·'pli·ke] *m* wall lamp, sconce

aplomo [a·'plo·mo] *m* self-confidence, composure; **perder el ~** to lose one's composure

apocarse <c → qu> [a·po·'kar·se] *vr* to lose heart

apodar [a·po·'dar] **I.** *vt* to call; (*un apodo*) to nickname **II.** *vr:* ~**se...** (*tener el sobrenombre*) to be called ...; (*el apodo*) to be nicknamed...

apoderado, -a [a·po·de·'ra·do, -a] *m, f* **1.** JUR proxy **2.** COM agent

apoderar [a·po·de·'rar] **I.** *vt* to authorize; JUR to grant power of attorney to **II.** *vr:* ~**se** to take possession; **el espía se apoderó del maletín** the spy seized the briefcase

apodo [a·'po·do] *m* nickname

apogeo [a·po·'xeo] *m* **1.** ASTR apogee **2.** (*cumbre*) summit; **estar en el ~ de su carrera** to be at the peak of one's career

apolismado, -a [a·po·lis·'ma·do, -a] *adj* **1.** *AmL* (*magullado*) damaged **2.** *Col, Méx, PRico* (*raquítico*) sickly **3.** *CRi* (*holgazán*) lazy **4.** *Méx, Ven* (*deprimido*) depressed **5.** *PRico* (*tonto*) stupid

apolítico, -a [a·po·'li·ti·ko, -a] *adj* apolitical

apología [a·po·lo·'xi·a] *f* defense

apoplejía [a·po·ple·'xi·a] *f* stroke

aporrear [a·po·rre·'ar] *vt* (*dar golpes*) to beat; ~ **el piano** to bang on the piano; ~ **la puerta** to bang [*o* hammer] on the door

aportación [a·por·ta·'sjon, -'θjon] *f* **1.** (*contribución*) contribution; ~ **dineraria** cash contribution; **hacer una ~ a un trabajo** to make a contribution to a job **2.** (*donación*) donation

aportar [a·por·'tar] *vt* **1.** (*contribuir*) to contribute; **he aportado algo a la fiesta** I've made a contribution to the party; **no aporta nada ir a esa conferencia** it's not worth going to that conference **2.** (*información*) to provide

aposento [a·po·'sen·to] *m* **1.** (*hospedaje*) lodging; **nos dieron ~** they put us up **2.** (*cuarto*) room

aposición [a·po·si·'sjon, -'θjon] *f* apposition

apósito [a·'po·si·to] *m* (*vendaje*) dressing; (*adhesivo*) adhesive tape

aposta [a·'pos·ta] *adv* on purpose

apostar <o → ue> [a·pos·'tar] **I.** *vi* ~ **por algo/alguien** to back sth/sb **II.** *vt, vr:* ~**se** to bet; **¿qué/cuánto apostamos?** what/how much should we bet?; **¿qué te apuestas a que no lo hace?** I bet you he/she won't do it; ~ **doble contra sencillo que...** I bet you two to one that...

a posteriori [a pos·te·'rjo·ri] *adv* with hindsight

apostilla [a·pos·'ti·ja, -ʎa] *f* marginal note

apóstol [a·'pos·tol] *m* apostle

apóstrofo [a·'pos·tro·fo] *m* LING apostrophe

apoteósico, -a [a·po·te·'o·si·ko, -a] *adj* tremendous; **éxito ~** tremendous success

apoyar [a·po·'jar] **I.** *vt* **1.** (*colocar sobre*) to rest; (*contra*) to lean **2.** (*fundar*) to base **3.** (*patrocinar*) to back; ~ **una moción** to support a motion; ~ **una reforma** to back a reform **II.** *vr:* ~**se 1.** (*descansar*) to rest; ~**se en** [*o* contra] **algo** to lean on sth; ~**se con la mano** to support oneself with one's hand **2.** (*fundarse*) to be based

apoyo [a·'po·jo] *m* **1.** (*sostén*) support **2.** (*respaldo*) backing, support; (*ayuda*) help; **cuenta con mi ~** you can rely on me

apreciable [a·pre·'sja·βle, -'θja·βle] *adj* **1.** (*observable*) noticeable; ~ **al oído** audible **2.** (*considerable*) considerable

apreciación [a·pre·sja·'sjon, -θja·'θjon] *f* **1.** (*juicio*) assessment **2.** (*de una moneda*) appreciation **3.** (*del tamaño*) estimation

apreciado, -a [a·pre·'sja·do, -a; -'θja·do, -a] *adj* (*en cartas*) ~**s Sres** Dear Sirs

apreciar [a·pre·'sjar, -'θjar] *vt* **1.** (*estimar*) to appreciate; **si aprecias tu vida, ¡desaparece de aquí!** if you value your life, get out of here! **2.** (*una moneda*) to appreciate **3.** (*tamaño*) to estimate **4.** (*captar*) to detect; **de lejos no se aprecia ningún sonido** no sound can be heard from afar; **el médico apreció una contusión en el pecho** the doctor detected bruising in the chest **5.** (*valorar*) to assess

aprecio [a·'pre·sjo, -θjo] *m* **1.** (*afecto*) affection; **te tengo un gran ~** I'm very fond of you **2.** (*estima*) esteem; **gran ~** high opinion

aprehensión [a·pren·'sjon/a·pre·en·'sjon] *f* **1.** (*acción de coger*) apprehension; (*del botín*) seizure **2.** (*percepción*) perception

apremiante [a·pre·'mjan·te] *adj* pressing

apremiar [a·pre·'mjar] **I.** *vt* (*acuciar*) to urge (on) **II.** *vi* to be urgent; **el tiempo apremia** time is pressing

aprender [a·pren·'der] *vt* to learn; **fácil de ~** easy to learn; **~ a leer** to learn to read; **~ de la historia** to learn from history; **~ de memoria** to learn by heart

aprendiz(a) [a·pren·'dis, -·'di·sa, -·'diθ, -·'di·θa] *m(f)* apprentice; **entrar de ~** to become an apprentice; **trabajar de ~** to work as an apprentice

aprendizaje [a·pren·di·'sa·xe, -·'θa·xe] *m* **1.** (*acción*) learning **2.** (*formación*) apprenticeship

aprensión [a·pren·'sjon] *f* **1.** (*recelo*) apprehension; **me da ~ decírtelo** I don't dare tell you **2.** (*asco*) disgust; **me da ~ beber de este vaso** I find it disgusting to drink from this glass **3.** (*temor*) fear

aprensivo, -a [a·pren·'si·βo, -a] *adj* overanxious; (*hipocondríaco*) hypochondriac

apresar [a·pre·'sar] *vt* to seize; (*delincuente*) to capture

apresurado, -a [a·pre·su·'ra·do, -a] *adj* hurried; (*con excesiva prisa*) hasty; **andar con paso ~** to walk quickly

apresurar [a·pre·su·'rar] **I.** *vt* (*acelerar*) to speed up; **~ el paso** to quicken one's step **II.** *vr*: **~se** to hurry; **¡no te apresures!** take your time!

apretado, -a [a·pre·'ta·do, -a] *adj* **1.** (*oprimido*) oppressed **2.** (*tornillo*) tight; (*vestido*) close-fitting, tight; (*cuerda*) taut; (*personas*) tight-fisted **3.** (*difícil*) **verse** [*o* **estar**] **muy ~** to be in a very difficult situation **4.** (*apurado*) **estar ~ de dinero** to be short of money;

estar ~ de tiempo to be short of time

apretar <e → ie> [a·pre·'tar] **I.** *vi* **1.** (*calor*) to become oppressive **2.** (*vestido*) to be too tight; **la americana me aprieta por detrás** the jacket is too tight around the back **3.** (*deudas*) **~ a alguien** to weigh heavily on sb **4.** (*esforzarse*) **si aprietas un poco, puedes ganar el partido** if you put more effort into it, you can win the game **5.** (*exigir*) **este profesor aprieta mucho en los exámenes** this professor demands a lot in the examinations **II.** *vt* **1.** (*hacer presión*) to press; **~ un botón** to press a button; **~ algo contra el pecho** to press sth against one's chest; **~ el tubo de la pasta de dientes** to squeeze the toothpaste tube **2.** (*estrechar*) **~ las cuerdas de la guitarra** to tighten the strings of the guitar; **~ los dientes** to grit one's teeth; **~ filas** to close ranks; **~ las manos** to clasp one's hands; **~ el puño** to clench one's fist; **~ un nudo/un tornillo** to tighten a knot/a screw **III.** *vr*: **~se 1.** (*estrecharse*) to become narrower **2.** (*agolparse*) to crowd together **3.** (*ceñirse*) **~se el cinturón** to tighten one's belt

apretón [a·pre·'ton] *m* (*presión*) squeeze

aprieto [a·'prje·to] *m* jam, fix; **~ económico** financial difficulties; **estar en un ~** to be in a jam

a priori [a pri·'o·ri] *adv* a priori

aprisa [a·'pri·sa] *adv* quickly

aprisionar [a·pri·sjo·'nar] *vt* **1.** (*atar*) to bind **2.** (*inmovilizar*) to immobilize; (*pillar*) to catch; **quedarse aprisionado en el barro** to be trapped in the mud

aprobación [a·pro·βa·'sjon, -'θjon] *f* (*de decisión*) approval; (*de una ley*) passing; **murmullo de ~** murmur of approval

aprobado [a·pro·'βa·do] *m* ENS pass; **he sacado un ~ en historia** I've passed history

aprobar <o → ue> [a·pro·'βar] **I.** *vt* **1.** (*decisión*) to approve; (*ley*) to pass; **la solicitud fue aprobada** the application was approved **2.** (*examen*) to pass **II.** *vi* ENS to pass

apronte [a·'pron·te] *m* *AmL* preparation

apropiación [a·pro·pja·'sjon, -'θjon] *f*

appropriation; ~ **indebida** misappropriation

apropiado, -a [a·pro·'pja·do, -a] *adj*
1. (*adecuado*) ~ **a** [*o* **para**] **algo** suitable for sth **2.** (*oportuno*) appropriate

apropiar [a·pro·'pjar] **I.** *vt AmL* (*premio*) to award; (*encargo*) to assign **II.** *vr* ~**se de algo** to appropriate sth

aprovechable [a·pro·βe·'tʃa·βle] *adj* usable

aprovechado, -a [a·pro·βe·'tʃa·do, -a] *adj* (*calculador*) opportunistic

aprovechamiento [a·pro·βe·tʃa·'mjen·to] *m* exploitation

aprovechar [a·pro·βe·'tʃar] **I.** *vi* (*valer*) to be of use ▶ **¡que aproveche!** enjoy your meal!, bon appétit! **II.** *vt* to make good use of; (*abusar*) to exploit; ~ **una idea** to exploit an idea **III.** *vr*: ~**se 1.** (*sacar provecho*) ~**se de algo** to profit by [*o* from] sth **2.** (*abusar*) to take advantage; ~**se de una mujer** to take advantage of a woman **3.** (*explotar*) ~**se de alguien** to exploit sb

aprovisionar [a·pro·βi·sjo·'nar] *vt* ~ **de** [*o* **con**] **algo** to supply with sth

aproximación [a·prok·si·ma·'sjon] *f*
1. (*acercamiento*) approach **2.** (*en una lotería*) consolation prize

aproximado, -a [a·prok·si·'ma·do, -a] *adj* approximate

aproximar [a·prok·si·'mar] **I.** *vt* to bring nearer; ~ **opiniones** to bring opinions closer together **II.** *vr*: ~**se** to approach; **se aproxima a la realidad** it comes close to the truth; **las tropas se aproximan** the troops are getting closer

aptitud [ap·ti·'tud] *f* **1.** (*talento*) aptitude; ~ **para algo** aptitude for sth **2.** (*conveniencia*) suitability

apto, -a ['ap·to, -a] *adj* suitable; ~ **para algo** fit for sth; **la película no es apta para menores** the film is not suitable for minors

apuesta [a·'pwes·ta] *f* **1.** (*juego*) bet; **corredor de ~s** bookmaker **2.** (*cantidad*) bid

apuesto, -a [a·'pwes·to, -a] *adj* handsome

apuntador(a) [a·pun·ta·'dor, ‑·'do·ra] *m(f)* TEAT prompter

apuntar [a·pun·'tar] **I.** *vi* to appear; (*día*) to break; **apunta la primavera** spring is coming **II.** *vt* **1.** (*con un arma*) ~ **algo** to aim at sth; **¡apunten!** take aim! **2.** (*con el dedo*) ~ **a algo** to point at sth **3.** (*anotar*) to note (down) **4.** (*inscribir*) to enroll; (*en una lista*) to enter **5.** TEAT to prompt **6.** (*insinuar*) to hint at **7.** (*indicar*) to point out; **todo apunta en esta dirección** everything points in this direction **III.** *vr*: ~**se 1.** (*inscribirse*) ~**se a algo** to enroll in sth; (*en una lista*) to enter one's name in sth; ~**se a un club** to join a club **2.** (*tanto*) to score; (*victoria*) to achieve

apunte [a·'pun·te] *m* (*escrito*) note; **tomar ~s** to take notes

apuñalar [a·pu·ɲa·'lar] *vt* to stab

apurado, -a [a·pu·'ra·do, -a] *adj* **1.** (*falto*) ~ **de dinero** hard up; ~ **de tiempo** short of time **2.** (*dificultoso*) difficult; **verse** ~ to be in trouble **3.** *AmL* (*apresurado*) hurried; **estar** ~ to be in a hurry

apurar [a·pu·'rar] **I.** *vt* **1.** (*vaso*) to drain; (*plato*) to finish off **2.** (*paciencia*) to exhaust; ~ **todos los medios** to try everything **3.** (*atosigar*) to harass; **¡no me apures, mi paciencia tiene un límite!** don't hassle me, my patience is limited! **4.** (*avergonzar*) to embarrass; **me apura decirle que no tengo dinero** I'm embarrassed to tell him/her that I don't have any money **5.** *AmL* (*dar prisa*) to hurry **II.** *vr*: ~**se 1.** (*preocuparse*) to worry; **¡no te apures por eso!** don't worry about that! **2.** *AmL* (*darse prisa*) to hurry up; **¡no te apures!** there's no hurry

apuro [a·'pu·ro] *m* **1.** (*aprieto*) fix; (*dificultad*) difficulty; **estar en un** ~ to be in a fix; **sacar a alguien de un** ~ to get sb out of a fix **2.** (*estrechez*) financial need; **sufrir grandes ~s** to be in financial difficulties **3.** (*vergüenza*) embarrassment; **me da** ~ **pedirle el dinero** it's embarrassing for me to ask him/her for money **4.** *AmL* (*prisa*) hurry

aquel, -ella [a·'kel, ‑·'ke·ja, ‑·'ke·ʎa] **I.** *adj dem* <aquellos, -as> that, those *pl*; **aquella casa es nuestra** that house is ours; **¿qué fue del hombre ~?** what became of that man?; **¿estabais de acuerdo en ~ punto?** did you agree on that point?; **en aquellos tiempos** in those days **II.** *pron dem v.* **aquél, aquélla, aquello**

aquí [a·'ki] *adv* **1.** (*lugar*) here; (*por*) **~ cerca** around here; **~ dentro** in here; **éste de ~** this guy here; **¡ah, ~ estás!** oh, there you are!; **andar de ~ para allá** to walk up and down; **de ~ hasta allí hay 10 minutos a pie** it's a 10-minute walk from here; **mejor ir por ~** it's better to go this way **2.** (*de tiempo*) **de ~ en adelante** from now on; **de ~ a una semana** a week from now; **hasta ~** up until now

ara¹ ['a·ra] *f* altar ▶ **dar la vida en ~s de una idea** to sacrifice one's life for an idea

ara² ['a·ra] *m AmL* parrot

árabe ['a·ra·βe] **I.** *adj* **1.** (*país*) Arab **2.** (*palabra*) Arabic **3.** (*península*) Arabian **4.** (*de los moros*) Moorish **II.** *mf* (*persona*) Arab **III.** *m* (*lengua*) Arabic

Arabia [a·'ra·βja] *f* Arabia; **~ Saudita** Saudi Arabia

arábigo, -a [a·'ra·βi·ɣo] *adj* Arab; (*número*) Arabic

arado [a·'ra·do] *m* plow

Aragón [a·ra·'ɣon] *m* Aragon

aragonés, -esa [a·ra·ɣo·'nes, -·'ne·sa] *adj, m, f* Aragonese

arancel [a·ran·'sel, -'θel] *m* tariff; (*impuesto*) duty

arándano [a·'ran·da·no] *m* blueberry

araña [a·'ra·ɲa] *f* ZOOL spider; **tela de ~** spider web

arañar(se) [a·ra·'ɲar(·se)] *vt, vi, (vr)* (*rasguñar*) to scratch (oneself)

arañazo [a·ra·'ɲa·so, -θo] *m* scratch; **dar un ~ a alguien** to scratch sb

arar [a·'rar] *vt* to plow

arbitraje [ar·βi·'tra·xe] *m* **1.** (*juicio*) arbitration **2.** (*en fútbol*) refereeing; (*en tenis*) umpiring

arbitral [ar·βi·'tral] *adj* arbitral

arbitrar [ar·βi·'trar] *vt* **1.** (*disputa*) **~ algo** to arbitrate in sth **2.** (*medios*) to provide **3.** DEP (*en fútbol*) to referee; (*en tenis*) to umpire

arbitrariedad [ar·βi·tra·rje·'dad] *f* **1.** (*cualidad*) arbitrariness **2.** (*acción*) arbitrary act

arbitrario, -a [ar·βi·'tra·rjo, -a] *adj* arbitrary

arbitrio [ar·'βi·trjo] *m* (*voluntad*) free will; **dejar algo al ~ de alguien** to leave sth to sb's discretion

árbitro, -a ['ar·βi·tro, -a] *m, f* **1.** (*mediador*) arbitrator **2.** (*fútbol*) referee; (*tenis*) umpire

árbol ['ar·βol] *m* **1.** BOT tree; **~ de Navidad** Christmas tree; **~ genealógico** family tree **2.** TÉC (*eje*) shaft ▶ **los ~es no le dejan ver el bosque** he can't see the wood for the trees; **del ~ caído todos hacen leña** *prov* if a man falls, all will tread on him

arbolado [ar·βo·'la·do] *m*, **arboleda** [ar·βo·'le·da] *f* woods + *sing or pl vb*

arbusto [ar·'βus·to] *m* shrub, bush

arca ['ar·ka] *f* chest; (*para dinero*) safe; **las ~s del estado** the treasury ▶ **~ de Noé** Noah's Ark

arcada [ar·'ka·da] *f* **1.** ARQUIT arcade **2.** *pl* (*náusea*) heaving

arcaico, -a [ar·'kai·ko, -a] *adj* archaic

arce ['ar·se, -θe] *m* maple

arcén [ar·'sen, -'θen] *m* edge; (*de carretera*) shoulder

archipiélago [ar·tʃi·'pje·la·ɣo] *m* archipelago

archivador [ar·tʃi·βa·'dor] *m* **1.** (*mueble*) filing cabinet **2.** (*carpeta*) file

archivador(a) [ar·tʃi·βa·'dor, -·'do·ra] *m(f)* archivist

archivar [ar·tʃi·'βar] *vt* to file; COMPUT to store; (*asunto: por un tiempo*) to put on file; (*para siempre*) to close the file on

archivo [ar·'tʃi·βo] *m* **1.** (*lugar*) archive(s); **constar en los ~s** to be on record **2.** (*documentos*) archives *pl* **3.** COMPUT file

arcilla [ar·'si·ja, -'θi·ʎa] *f* clay

arco ['ar·ko] *m* **1.** ARQUIT, MAT arc; **~ de medio punto** round arch; **~ iris** rainbow; **~ voltaico** arc lamp **2.** (*arma*) *t.* MÚS bow **3.** *AmL* DEP goal

arcón [ar·'kon] *m* large chest

arder [ar·'der] *vi* **1.** (*quemar*) to burn; **~ con fuerza** to blaze; **~ sin llama** to smolder; **~ de fiebre** to have a very high temperature; **~ de pasión** to be inflamed with passion; **~ de rabia** to be mad with rage; **me arde la garganta** my throat is burning **2.** + *en, fig* **ardo en deseos de conocerte** I'm dying to get to know you

ardid [ar·'did] *m* ruse

ardiente [ar·'djen·te] *adj* **1.** (*pasión*) burning **2.** (*persona*) passionate

ardilla [ar·'di·ʎa, -ʎa] *f* squirrel

ardor [ar·'dor] *m* **1.** (*calor*) heat; **~ de estómago** heartburn **2.** (*fervor*) ardor; **el ~ de su mirada** the ardor of his/her look

arduo, -a ['ar·dwo, -a] *adj* arduous

área ['a·rea] *f t.* MAT area; **un ~ de 200 metros cuadrados** an area of 200 square meters; **~ de descanso** AUTO picnic area; **~ de castigo** DEP penalty area; **~ metropolitana** metropolitan area; **~ de no fumadores** non-smoking area

arena [a·'re·na] *f* (*materia*) sand; **~s movedizas** quicksand ▶ **edificar sobre ~** to build on sandy ground

arenal [a·re·'nal] *m* sandy area

arenoso, -a [a·re·'no·so, -a] *adj* sandy

arenque [a·'ren·ke] *m* herring; **~s ahumados** kippers *pl*

arepa [a·'re·pa] *f AmL* cornmeal griddlecake

arequipa [a·re·'ki·pa] *f Col, Méx* rice pudding

arete [a·'re·te] *m* earring

argamasa [ar·ɣa·'ma·sa] *f* mortar

Argentina [ar·xen·'ti·na] *f* Argentina

argentino, -a [ar·xen·'ti·no, -a] *adj, m, f* Argentine

argolla [ar·'ɣo·ja, -ʎa] *f* **1.** (*anilla*) ring **2.** *Chile, Col, Hond, Méx* (*alianza*) wedding ring

argot <argots> [ar·'ɣo(t)] *m* (*marginal*) slang; (*profesional*) jargon

argucia [ar·'ɣu·sja, -θja] *f* **1.** (*argumento*) fallacy **2.** (*truco*) trick

argüende [ar·'ɣwen·de] *m Méx* (*chisme*) gossip

argüir [ar·ɣu·'ir] *irr como huir vt, vi* (*alegar*) to argue

argumentación [ar·ɣu·men·ta·'sjon, -'θjon] *f* line of argument

argumentar [ar·ɣu·men·'tar] *vi, vt* to argue

argumento [ar·ɣu·'men·to] *m* **1.** (*razón*) argument; (*razonamiento*) reasoning **2.** CINE plot

aria ['a·rja] *f* aria

aridez [a·ri·'des, -'deθ] *f* aridity

árido, -a ['a·ri·do, -a] *adj* (*terreno*) arid, dry; (*tema*) dry

Aries ['a·rjes] *m inv* ASTR Aries

arisco, -a [a·'ris·ko, -a] *adj* (*persona*) surly, unfriendly; (*animal*) skittish

aristocracia [a·ris·to·'kra·sja, -θja] *f* aristocracy

aristócrata [a·ris·'to·kra·ta] *mf* aristocrat

aristocrático, -a [a·ris·to·'kra·ti·ko, -a] *adj* aristocratic

aritmética [a·rit·'me·ti·ka] *f* arithmetic

aritmético, -a [a·rit·'me·ti·ko, -a] *adj* arithmetical

arlequín [ar·le·'kin] *m* harlequin

arma ['ar·ma] *f* **1.** (*instrumento*) weapon, arm; **~s de destrucción masiva** weapons of mass destruction; **un ~ homicida** a murder weapon; **~ blanca** knife; **~ de fuego** firearm; **rendir las ~s** to surrender [*o* lay down] one's arms; **tomar las ~s** to take up arms; **¡apunten ~s!** take aim!; **¡descansen ~s!** order arms! **2.** *pl* (*blasón*) arms *pl* ▶ **ser un ~ de doble filo** to be a double-edged sword; **ser de ~s tomar** to be bold

armada [ar·'ma·da] *f* **1.** (*fuerzas navales*) navy **2.** (*escuadra*) fleet; HIST armada

armado, -a [ar·'ma·do] *adj* armed; **~ de algo** armed with sth

armador(a) [ar·ma·'dor, -·'do·ra] *m(f)* shipowner

armadura [ar·ma·'du·ra] *f* **1.** (*de caballero*) armor; **una ~** a suit of armor **2.** (*de edificio*) framework

armamento [ar·ma·'men·to] *m* arms *pl*; (*de un país*) armaments *pl*

armar [ar·'mar] **I.** *vt* **1.** (*ejército*) to arm; **~ a alguien** [*o* con]... to arm sb with... **2.** TÉC to assemble **3.** *inf* (*jaleo*) to stir up; (*ruido*) to raise; **~la** to start an argument **II.** *vr* **~se** to arm oneself with sth ▶ **~se de paciencia** to muster one's patience; **~se de valor** to find courage

armario [ar·'ma·rjo] *m* cupboard; ~ **empotrado** built-in cupboard; ~ (**ropero**) wardrobe

armazón [ar·ma·'son, -'θon] *m o f* (*armadura*) frame; (*de edificio*) skeleton

armiño [ar·'mi·ɲo] *m* **1.** (*animal*) stoat **2.** (*piel*) ermine

armisticio [ar·mis·'ti·sjo, -θjo] *m* armistice

armonía [ar·mo·'ni·a] *f* harmony; **falta de** ~ (*entre personas*) discord; **su comportamiento no estuvo en** ~ **con la solemnidad del acto** his/her behavior wasn't in keeping with the solemnity of the ceremony

armónica [ar·'mo·ni·ka] *f* harmonica, mouth organ

armónico, -a [ar·'mo·ni·ko] *adj* harmonic

armonioso, -a [ar·mo·'njo·so, -a] *adj* harmonious

armonizar <z → c> [ar·mo·ni·'sar, -'θar] **I.** *vi* to harmonize; ~ **con** (*colores*) to blend with **II.** *vt* to harmonize; ~ **ideas** to reconcile ideas

árnica ['ar·ni·ka] *f* BOT arnica

aro ['a·ro] *m* **1.** (*argolla*) ring; (*para jugar*) hoop **2.** *Arg* (*arete*) earring **3.** *AmL* (*anillo de boda*) wedding ring ▶ **entrar** [*o* **pasar**] **por el** ~ to give in

aroma [a·'ro·ma] *m* (*olor*) scent; (*de café*) aroma

aromático, -a [a·ro·'ma·ti·ko, -a] *adj* aromatic

arpa ['ar·pa] *f* harp

arpón [ar·'pon] *m* harpoon

arqueología [ar·keo·lo·'xi·a] *f* archeology

arqueológico, -a [ar·keo·'lo·xi·ko, -a] *adj* archeological

arqueólogo, -a [ar·ke·'o·lo·ɣo, -a] *m, f* archaeologist

arquero, -a [ar·'ke·ro, -a] *m, f* **1.** archer **2.** *Arg* DEP goalkeeper

arquetipo [ar·ke·'ti·po] *m* archetype

arquitecto, -a [ar·ki·'tek·to, -a] *m, f* architect

arquitectónico, -a [ar·ki·tek·'to·ni·ko] *adj* architectural

arquitectura [ar·ki·tek·'tu·ra] *f* architecture

arrabal [a·rra·'βal] *m* (*periferia*) suburb; (*barrio bajo*) slum area; **vivir en los** ~**es** to live on the outskirts

arracachada [a·rra·ka·'tʃa·da] *f* Col silliness

arraigar <g → gu> [a·rrai·'ɣar] *vi, vr:* ~**se** *t. fig* to take root

arrancar <c → qu> [a·rran·'kar] **I.** *vt* **1.** (*planta*) to pull up; **el viento arrancó el árbol** the wind uprooted the tree **2.** (*pegatina*) to tear off; (*página*) to tear out **3.** (*muela*) to extract, to pull (out); **el ladrón le arrancó el bolso de la mano** the thief snatched her handbag from her hand; **la corriente arrancó el puente** the current swept away the bridge **4.** (*vehículo, motor*) to start **5.** (*conseguir*) ~ **una promesa a alguien** to force a promise out of sb; ~ **un secreto a alguien** to get a secret out of sb **II.** *vi* (*vehículo*) to start

arranque [a·'rran·ke] *m* **1.** (*comienzo*) start; **en el** ~ **de la temporada** at the start of the season **2.** AUTO starting; ~ **automático** self-starter **3.** (*arrebato*) outburst; **un** ~ **de cólera** a fit of anger; **en un** ~ impulsively **4.** COMPUT boot (up)

arrasar [a·rra·'sar] **I.** *vt* (*región*) to devastate **II.** *vi* to triumph; POL to sweep the board

arrastrado, -a [a·rras·'tra·do, -a] *adj* poor, miserable

arrastrar [a·rras·'trar] **I.** *vt* **1.** (*tirar de*) to pull; (*algo pesado*) to drag; ~**on la caja montaña arriba** they dragged the box up the mountain; **el agua arrastra las piedras** the water sweeps the stones along; **el viento arrastra las hojas** the wind sweeps away the leaves; ~ **los pies** (*al caminar*) to drag one's feet **2.** (*impulsar*) ~ **a alguien a hacer algo** to lead sb to do sth **II.** *vi* to drag **III.** *vr:* ~**se 1.** (*reptar*) to crawl; ~**se por el suelo** to crawl along; **se arrastró hasta la habitación** he/she dragged himself/herself to the room **2.** (*humillarse*) to grovel

arrastre [a·'rras·tre] *m* dragging; (*en pesca*) trawling ▶ **estar para el** ~ *inf* (*cosa*) to be ruined; (*persona*) to be a wreck

arre [ˈa·rre] *interj* giddy-up

arreada [a·rre·ˈa·da] *f Arg, Chile, Méx* rustling

arrear [a·rre·ˈar] **I.** *vt* (*ganado*) to drive; *inf* (*golpe*) to give **II.** *vi inf* to hurry along

arrebatar [a·rre·βa·ˈtar] *vt* **1.** (*arrancar*) to snatch (away); **~ la vida a alguien** to take sb's life; **~ la victoria a alguien** to snatch victory from sb **2.** (*extasiar*) to captivate

arrebato [a·rre·ˈβa·to] *m* (*arranque*) outburst; **un ~ de cólera** a fit of anger

arrecho, -a [a·ˈrre·tʃo, -a] *adj Col inf* **1.** (*vigoroso*) vigorous **2.** (*cachondo*) horny **3.** (*enfadado*) angry

arreciar [a·rre·ˈsjar, -ˈθjar] *vi* (*viento*) to get stronger; (*lluvia*) to get heavier; (*críticas*) to intensify

arrecife [a·rre·ˈsi·fe, -ˈθi·fe] *m* reef

arreglado, -a [a·rre·ˈɣla·do, -a] *adj* **1.** (*ordenado*) tidy; (*cuidado*) neat **2.** (*elegante*) smart ▶ **¡estamos ~s!** now we're in trouble!; **¡vas ~ si piensas que...!** you're in for a big surprise if you think ...!

arreglar [a·rre·ˈɣlar] **I.** *vt* **1.** (*reparar*) to repair; (*ropa*) to mend **2.** (*ordenar*) to tidy up; **~ la habitación** to tidy up the room; **~ a los niños para salir** to get the children ready to go outside **3.** (*pelo*) to do **4.** (*resolver*) to sort out, to arrange; **~ las cuentas con alguien** to get even with sb **5.** mús to arrange ▶ **¡ya te ~é yo!** *inf* I'll sort you out! **II.** *vr:* **~se 1.** (*vestirse*) to get ready **2.** (*componérselas*) to manage; **no sé cómo te las arreglas** I don't know how you manage **3.** (*ponerse de acuerdo*) to come to an agreement; **al final todo se arregló** everything worked out all right in the end

arreglo [a·ˈrre·ɣlo] *m* **1.** (*reparación*) repair **2.** (*solución*) solution; **no tienes ~** you're a hopeless case; **este trabajo ya no tiene ~** this job is completely botched **3.** (*acuerdo*) agreement; **llegar a un ~** to reach a settlement; **con ~ a lo convenido** as agreed **4.** mús arrangement

arremeter [a·rre·me·ˈter] *vi* (*criticar*) to attack; **~ contra alguien** to attack sb

arrendador(a) [a·rren·da·ˈdor, -·ˈdo·ra] *m(f)* (*de casa*) landlord *m*, landlady *f*; (*de terreno*) t. jur lessor

arrendamiento [a·rren·da·ˈmjen·to] *m* **1.** (*alquiler*) rent; (*de terreno*) lease **2.** (*contrato*) contract

arrendar <e → ie> [a·rren·ˈdar] *vt* (*propietario*) to rent, to let; (*inquilino*) to rent, to lease

arrendatario, -a [a·rren·da·ˈta·rjo, -a] *m, f* (*de una casa*) tenant; (*de un terreno*) t. jur lessee, leaseholder

arrepentido, -a [a·rre·pen·ˈti·do, -a] *adj* sorry; rel repentant; **estar ~ de algo** to be sorry about sth, to regret sth

arrepentimiento [a·rre·pen·ti·ˈmjen·to] *m* (*lamento*) regret; rel repentance

arrepentirse [a·rre·pen·ˈtir·se] *irr como* **sentir** *vr* (*lamentar*) to regret; rel to repent; **~ de algo** to regret sth, rel to repent of sth

arrestar [a·rres·ˈtar] *vt* to arrest

arresto [a·ˈrres·to] *m* **1.** (*detención*) arrest; (*reclusión*) imprisonment; **estar bajo ~** to be under arrest; **~ domiciliario** house arrest **2.** *pl* (*arrojo*) daring; **tener ~s** to be bold

arria [ˈa·rrja] *f AmL* train of pack animals

arriba [a·ˈrri·βa] *adv* **1.** (*posición*) above; (*en una casa*) upstairs; **más ~** higher up; **te espero** I'll wait for you upstairs; **la habitación de ~** (*de encima*) the room above; **el piso de ~** (*el último*) the top floor; **de ~ abajo** from top to bottom; (*persona*) from head to foot; **¡manos ~!** hands up! **2.** (*dirección*) up, upwards; **río ~** upstream; **¡~!** get up! **3.** (*cantidad*) **precios de 100 pesos para ~** prices from 100 pesos upwards **4.** *CSur* **de ~** (*gratis*) free (of charge); (*sin merecerlo*) for no reason

arribar [a·rri·ˈβar] *vi* **1.** náut to reach port **2.** *AmL* (*llegar*) to arrive

arribista [a·rri·ˈβis·ta] *mf* arriviste; (*en sociedad*) social climber

arriesgado, -a [a·rrjes·ˈɣa·do, -a] *adj* **1.** (*peligroso*) risky, dangerous **2.** (*atrevido*) daring

arriesgar <g → gu> [a·rrjes·ˈɣar] **I.** *vt*

1. (*vida*) to risk **2.** (*en el juego*) to stake **3.** (*hipótesis*) to venture **II.** *vr:* **~se** to take a risk; **~se a hacer algo** to risk doing sth

arrimar [a·rri·'mar] **I.** *vt* (*acercar*) to bring closer **II.** *vr:* **~se** (*acercarse*) to come close(r); **~se a algo** to move closer to sth

arrinconar [a·rrin·ko·'nar] *vt* **1.** (*objeto*) to put in a corner **2.** (*enemigo*) to corner

arroba [a·'rro·βa] *f* **1.** comput. at, at sign **2.** *AmL* (*unidad de peso*) arroba *unit of weight from 24 to 36 lbs. depending on the region*

arrodillarse [a·rro·di·'jar·se, -'ʎar·se] *vr* to kneel (down)

arrogancia [a·rro·'ɣan·sja, -θja] *f* arrogance

arrogante [a·rro·'ɣan·te] *adj* arrogant

arrojar [a·rro·'xar] **I.** *vt* **1.** (*lanzar*) to throw **2.** (*emitir*) to emit, to give off [*o out*] **3.** (*expulsar*) to throw out **4.** *AmL inf* (*vomitar*) to throw up **5.** (*un resultado*) to produce; **~ beneficios** to yield profits **II.** *vr:* **~se** to throw oneself; **~se al agua** to jump into the water

arrojo [a·'rro·xo] *m* daring; **con ~** boldly

arrollador(a) [a·rro·ja·'dor, -·'do·ra, a·rro·ʎa-] *adj* **1.** (*mayoría*) overwhelming; (*fuerza*) devastating **2.** (*carácter*) irresistible

arrollar [a·rro·'jar, -'ʎar] *vt* **1.** (*enrollar*) to roll up **2.** (*atropellar*) to run over **3.** dep (*derrotar*) to crush

arrorró [a·rro·'rro] *m AmS* lullaby

arroyo [a·'rro·jo] *m* stream

arroz [a·'rros, -roθ] *m* rice; **~ con leche** rice pudding

arrozal [a·rro·'sal, -'θal] *m* rice field

arruga [a·'rru·ɣa] *f* (*en la piel*) wrinkle; (*en papel*) crease; **este vestido hace ~s** this dress creases

arrugar <g → gu> [a·rru·'ɣar] **I.** *vt* (*piel*) to wrinkle; (*papel*) to crease **II.** *vr:* **~se** **1.** (*piel*) to wrinkle, to get wrinkled; (*papel*) to crease, to get creased **2.** (*achicarse*) to get scared

arruinar [a·rrwi·'nar] **I.** *vt* **1.** (*causar ruina*) to ruin **2.** (*fiesta*) to spoil; (*plan*) to wreck **II.** *vr:* **~se** to be ruined

arrullar [a·rru·'jar, -'ʎar] **I.** *vt* to lull to sleep **II.** *vi* (*paloma*) to coo **III.** *vr:* **~se** to bill and coo

arsenal [ar·se·'nal] *m* arsenal

arsénico [ar·'se·ni·ko] *m* arsenic

arte ['ar·te] *m o f* (*m en sing, f en pl*) **1.** (*disciplina*) art; **~ dramático** drama; **~s plásticas** visual arts; **~ y oficios** arts and crafts; **bellas ~s** fine arts; **el séptimo ~** the cinema **2.** (*habilidad*) skill; **tiene mucho ~ para la pintura** he's quite a skilled painter **3.** (*maña*) trick; **conseguir algo por malas ~s** to obtain sth by trickery; **desplegó todas sus ~s para convencerlo** she used all her wiles to convince him ▶ **como por ~ de magia** as if by magic

artefacto [ar·te·'fak·to] *m* appliance; (*mecanismo*) device; **~ explosivo** explosive device

arteria [ar·'te·rja] *f* **1.** anat artery **2.** (*de tráfico*) thoroughfare

arterio(e)sclerosis [ar·te·rjos·kle·'ro·sis/ar·te·rjo·es·kle·'ro·sis] *f inv* arteriosclerosis

artesanal [ar·te·sa·'nal] *adj* craft; **industria ~** craft industry

artesanía [ar·te·sa·'ni·a] *f* **1.** (*arte*) craftsmanship **2.** (*obras*) handicrafts *pl*

artesano, -a [ar·te·'sa·no, -a] *m, f* artisan, craftsman *m*, craftswoman *f*

ártico ['ar·ti·ko, -a] *m* (*océano*) Arctic Ocean **2.** (*región*) Arctic

ártico, -a ['ar·ti·ko, -a] *adj* Arctic

articulación [ar·ti·ku·la·'sjon, -'θjon] *f* **1.** anat joint **2.** ling articulation

articulado, -a [ar·ti·ku·'la·do] *adj* articulated; **camión ~** tractor-trailer truck

articular [ar·ti·ku·'lar] *vt* **1.** téc to join together **2.** ling to articulate

artículo [ar·'ti·ku·lo] *m* (*objeto*) *t.* pren article; com commodity; **~s de consumo** consumer goods; **~s de lujo** luxury goods; **~s de primera necesidad** basic commodities

artífice [ar·'ti·fi·se, -θe] *mf* artist; *fig* architect

artificial [ar·ti·fi·'sjal, -'θjal] *adj* artificial

artificio [ar·ti·'fi·sjo, -θjo] *m* (*habilidad*) skill; (*truco*) trick; **un ~ técnico** a technical contrivance

artillería [ar·ti·je·'ri·a, ar·ti·ʎe-] *f* artillery

artimaña [ar·ti·'ma·ɲa] *f* (sly) trick

artista [ar·'tis·ta] *mf* (*de bellas artes*) artist; (*de circo*) artist(e) *m(f)*; **es un ~ en su especialidad** he's an expert in his field

artístico, -a [ar·'tis·ti·ko, -a] *adj* artistic

artritis [ar·'tri·tis] *f inv* arthritis

artrosis [ar·'tro·sis] *f inv* arthrosis

arzobispo [ar·so·'βis·po, ar·θo-] *m* archbishop

as [as] *m t. fig* ace; **un ~ del volante** an ace at the wheel

asa ['a·sa] *f* handle

asado [a·'sa·do] *m* 1. CULIN roast 2. *Arg* (*comida*) barbecue

asalariado, -a [a·sa·la·'rja·do, -a] *m, f* wage earner

asaltar [a·sal·'tar] *vt* 1. (*fortaleza*) to storm; (*banco*) to break into, to raid 2. (*persona*) to attack, to assault 3. (*duda*) to assail; **me asaltó el pánico** I was overwhelmed by panic

asalto [a·'sal·to] *m* 1. (*a una fortaleza*) storming; **tomar por** [*o* **al**] **~** to take by storm 2. (*a un banco*) raid; **~ a un banco** raid on a bank 3. (*a una persona*) attack, assault 4. DEP (*en boxeo*) round

asamblea [a·sam·'blea] *f* assembly; **~ general** general assembly; **~ de trabajadores** workers' meeting

asar [a·'sar] I. *vt* CULIN to roast; **~ a la parrilla** to grill II. *vr:* **~se** to roast; **en esta casa se asa uno vivo** *inf* it's absolutely roasting in this house

ascendencia [as·θen·'den·sja, as·θen·'den·θja] *f* (*linaje*) ancestry, descent; **de ~ escocesa** of Scottish descent

ascendente [a·sen·'den·te, as·θen-] *adj* ascending; **en orden ~** in ascending order

ascender <e → ie> [a·sen·'der, as·θen-] I. *vi* 1. (*subir*) to rise; DEP to go up; **el equipo asciende a primera (división)** the team goes up to the first division 2. (*escalar*) to climb 3. (*de empleo*) to be promoted 4. COM **~ a** (*cantidad*) to amount to II. *vt* to promote

ascendiente [a·sen·'djen·te, as·θen-] *mf* (*antepasado*) ancestor

ascensión [a·sen·'sjon, as·θen-] *f* ascent

ascenso [a·'sen·so, as·'θen-] *m* 1. (*de precio*) rise 2. (*a una montaña*) ascent; **el ~ a primera (división)** the promotion to the first division

ascensor [a·sen·'sor, as·θen-] *m* elevator

asco ['as·ko] *m* 1. (*sensación*) disgust, loathing; **este olor me da ~** this smell makes me feel sick; **las espinacas me dan ~** I hate spinach; **este hombre me da ~** I really detest this man; **hacer ~s a algo** to turn up one's nose at sth; **¡qué ~ de gente!** *inf* what dreadful people!; **¡qué ~!** how awful! 2. (*situación*) **estar hecho un ~** (*lugar*) to be a mess; (*persona*) to feel low; **estar muerto de ~** to be bored stiff; **ser un ~** to be disgusting

ascua ['as·kwa] *f* ember ▶ **estar en ~s** to be on tenterhooks; **tener a alguien en ~s** to keep sb on tenterhooks

aseado, -a [a·se·'a·do, -a] *adj* clean, tidy; (*arreglado*) smart

asear [a·se·'ar] I. *vt* to clean up II. *vr:* **~se** to wash (up)

asediar [a·se·'djar] *vt* MIL to besiege

asedio [a·'se·djo] *m* MIL siege

asegurado, -a [a·se·ɣu·'ra·do, -a] *adj, m, f* insured

asegurador(a) [a·se·ɣu·ra·'dor, -·'do·ra] *m(f)* insurance agent

asegurar [a·se·ɣu·'rar] I. *vt* 1. (*fijar*) to secure; **~ una puerta** to secure a door 2. (*afirmar*) to affirm; **asegura no haber dicho nada** she maintains that she did not say anything 3. (*prometer*) to assure; **se lo aseguro** I assure you 4. (*con un seguro*) to insure II. *vr:* **~se** (*comprobar*) to make sure; **~se de que funciona** to make sure that it works

asemejarse [a·se·me·'xar·se] *vr* to be alike; **~ a algo** to resemble sth, to be like sth

asentar <e → ie> [a·sen·'tar] I. *vt* (*poner*) to place; **~ los cimientos** to lay the foundations; **la lluvia ha asentado el polvo** the rain has caused the dust to settle II. *vr:* **~se** to settle

asentir [a·sen·'tir] *irr como sentir* *vi* to agree; **~ a algo** to agree to sth; **~ con la cabeza** to nod in agreement

aseo [a.'seo] *m* **1.** (*acción*) cleaning; (**cuarto de**) ~ bathroom; ~ **personal** personal hygiene **2.** *pl* (*servicios públicos*) restrooms *pl*

aséptico, -a [a.'sep.ti.ko, -a] *adj* MED aseptic; *fig* (*desapasionado*) dispassionate

asequible [a.se.'ki.βle] *adj* **1.** (*precio*) reasonable **2.** (*objetivo*) attainable **3.** (*persona*) approachable

asesinar [a.se.si.'nar] *vt* to murder; (*personaje público*) to assassinate

asesinato [a.se.si.'na.to] *m* murder; (*de personaje público*) assassination

asesino, -a [a.se.'si.no, -a] **I.** *adj t. fig* murderous; **ballena asesina** killer whale **II.** *m, f* murderer; (*de personaje público*) assassin; ~ (**a sueldo**) hit man

asesor(a) [a.se.'sor, -'so.ra] **I.** *adj* advisory **II.** *m(f)* adviser, consultant

asesorar [a.se.so.'rar] **I.** *vt* to advise **II.** *vr* ~**se en algo** to take advice about sth

asesoría [a.se.so.'ri.a] *f* **1.** (*oficio*) consultancy **2.** (*oficina*) consultant's office

asestar [a.ses.'tar] *vt* to deal; ~ **una puñalada a alguien** to stab sb

aseverar [a.se.βe.'rar] *vt* to affirm; (*asegurar*) to assure; (*con energía*) to assert

asfaltar [as.fal.'tar] *vt* to asphalt

asfalto [as.'fal.to] *m* asphalt

asfixia [as.'fik.sja] *f* suffocation, asphyxia

asfixiante [as.fik.'sjan.te] *adj* suffocating; **una atmósfera** ~ a stifling atmosphere; **hace un calor** ~ the heat is suffocating

asfixiar [as.fik.'sjar] **I.** *vt* (*persona*) to suffocate; (*humo*) to asphyxiate **II.** *vr:* ~**se** to suffocate

así [a.'si] **I.** *adv* **1.** (*de este modo*) accordingly; **lo hizo** ~ he/she did it like this; ~ **es como lo hizo** that's how he/she did it; **yo soy** ~ that's the way I am; **no puedes decir esto** ~ **como** ~ you just can't say that; **¡~ es!** that's right!; **¡~ es la vida!** that's life; **¿no es** ~? isn't it?; **por** ~ **decirlo** so to speak **2.** (*de extrañeza*) **¿~ que me dejas?** so you're leaving me? **3.** (*de esta medida*) ~ **de grande** this big ▶ ~ **y todo** even so; ~ ~ so-so **II.** *conj* **1.** (*concesiva*) ~ **se esté muriendo de frío...** even though he's/she's freezing... **2.** (*consecutiva*) **empe-** zó a llover, ~ **que nos quedamos en casa** it began to rain, so we stayed indoors **III.** *adj inv* like this, like that; **un sueldo** ~ a salary of that amount; **una cosa** ~ something like that

Asia ['a.sja] *f* Asia; ~ **menor** Asia Minor

asiático, -a [a.'sja.ti.ko, -a] *adj, m, f* Asian, Asiatic

asidero [a.si.'de.ro] *m* handle; *fig* pretext

asiduo, -a [a.'si.dwo, -a] *adj* frequent; **un** ~ **cliente de este local** a regular in this bar

asiento [a.'sjen.to] *m* (*silla*) seat; ~ **delantero** front seat; ~ **trasero** [*o de atrás*] rear seat; **tomar** ~ to take a seat

asignación [a.siɣ.na.'sjon, -'θjon] *f* **1.** *t.* COMPUT assignment; (*de recursos*) allocation; ~ **de una tecla** assignment of a key **2.** FIN allowance

asignar [a.siɣ.'nar] *vt t.* COMPUT to assign; (*recursos*) to allocate; (*subvención*) to award

asignatura [a.siɣ.na.'tu.ra] *f* subject; ~ **pendiente** failed subject

asilo [a.'si.lo] *m* **1.** POL asylum; **pedir/ conceder** ~ to seek/to grant political asylum **2.** (*de ancianos*) (old people's) home

asimetría [a.si.me.'tri.a] *f* asymmetry

asimétrico, -a [a.si.'me.tri.ko, -a] *adj* asymmetric(al)

asimilar [a.si.mi.'lar] *vt* to assimilate

asimismo [a.si.'mis.mo] *adv* likewise, also

asir [a.'sir] *irr* **I.** *vt* to seize **II.** *vr* ~**se a algo** to seize sth

asistencia [a.sis.'ten.sja, -θja] *f* **1.** (*presencia*) attendance, presence **2.** (*ayuda*) assistance, help; ~ **médica** medical care; ~ **social** social work

asistenta [a.sis.'ten.ta] *f* **1.** (*ayudante*) assistant **2.** (*para limpiar*) cleaning woman

asistente¹ [a.sis.'ten.te] *mf* **1.** (*ayudante*) assistant **2.** (*presentes*) **los** ~**s** those present ▶ ~ **social** social worker

asistente² [a.sis.'ten.te] *m* COMPUT wizard; ~ **de instalacíon** installation wizard; ~ **personal digital** PDA, personal digital assistant

asistido, -a [a·sis·'ti·do, -a] *adj* assisted; **~ por ordenador** computer-assisted; **dirección asistida** power(-assisted) steering; **respiración asistida** artificial respiration

asistir [a·sis·'tir] I. *vi* 1. (*ir*) **~ a algo** to attend sth 2. (*estar presente*) to be present; **asistieron unas 50 personas** some 50 people were present 3. (*presenciar*) **~ a algo** to witness sth II. *vt* (*ayudar*) to help, assist; **~ a un enfermo** to care for a patient

asma ['as·ma] *f* asthma

asno ['as·no] *m* ZOOL donkey, ass

asociación [a·so·sja·'sjon, -θja·'θjon] *f* association; **Asociación de Padres de Alumnos** parent-teacher association

asociar [a·so·'sjar, -'θjar] I. *vt* 1. *t.* POL to associate; **la asocio con alguien** I associate her with sb 2. (*juntar*) to join II. *vr:* **~se** to associate; COM to become partners, to form a partnership; **~se con alguien** (*hacer compañía*) to join sb

asolar <o → ue> [a·so·'lar] *vt* to devastate

asoleada [a·so·le·'a·da] *f Col, Chile, Guat* (*insolación*) sunstroke

asomar [a·so·'mar] I. *vt* 1. (*mostrar*) to show 2. (*destacar*) to stick out; **~ la cabeza por la ventana** to put one's head out of the window II. *vi* (*verse*) to show; (*aparecer*) to appear; **asoma el día** day is breaking III. *vr:* **~se** (*mostrarse*) to show up; **~se al balcón** to come out onto the balcony; **¡asómate!** stick your head out!

asombrar [a·som·'brar] I. *vt* to amaze II. *vr* **~se de algo** to be amazed at sth

asombro [a·som·'bro] *m* amazement; **poner cara de ~** to look amazed; **no salir de su ~** not to get over one's amazement

asombroso, -a [a·som·'bro·so, -a] *adj* amazing

asomo [a·'so·mo] *m* hint; **no pienso en ello ni por ~** I don't give it the slightest thought

asonancia [a·so·'nan·sja, -θja] *f* assonance

asorocharse [a·so·ro·'ʧar·se] *vr AmS* to get altitude sickness

aspa ['as·pa] *f* cross; (*de molino*) sail; **marcar con un ~** to mark with a cross; **en forma de ~** cross-shaped

aspaviento [as·pa·'βjen·to] *m* fuss; **hacer ~s** to make a fuss

aspecto [as·'pek·to] *m* 1. (*apariencia*) appearance; **tener buen/mal ~** to look/not to look well 2. (*punto de vista*) aspect

áspero, -a [as·pe·ro, -a] *adj* 1. (*superficie*) rough 2. (*persona*) harsh; **tener un carácter ~** to be bad-tempered

aspiración [as·pi·ra·'sjon, -'θjon] *f* 1. (*inspiración*) breathing in 2. (*pretensión*) aspiration

aspiradora [as·pi·ra·'do·ra] *f* vacuum cleaner; **pasar la ~** to vacuum

aspirante [as·pi·'ran·te] *mf* aspirant; (*a un empleo*) applicant

aspirar [as·pi·'rar] I. *vt* 1. (*inspirar*) to breathe in, inhale 2. (*aspirador*) to suck in II. *vi* 1. (*inspirar*) to breathe in 2. (*pretender*) to aspire; **~ a mucho en la vida** to have high aims in life

aspirina® [as·pi·'ri·na] *f* aspirin®

asquear [as·ke·'ar] I. *vt* (*dar asco*) to disgust II. *vr:* **~se** to feel disgusted

asquerosidad [as·ke·ro·si·'dad] *f* disgusting mess

asqueroso, -a [as·ke·'ro·so, -a] *adj* disgusting; (*sucio*) filthy

asta ['as·ta] *f* 1. (*de bandera*) flagpole; **a media ~** at half mast 2. (*cuerno*) horn

asterisco [as·te·'ris·ko] *m* asterisk

asteroide [as·te·'roi·de] *m* asteroid

astilla [as·'ti·ja, -ʎa] *f* splinter; **clavarse una ~** to get a splinter

astillero [as·ti·'je·ro, -'ʎe·ro] *m* shipyard

astro ['as·tro] *m t. fig* star

astrología [as·tro·lo·'xi·a] *f* astrology

astrólogo, -a [as·'tro·lo·ɣo, -a] *m, f* astrologer

astronauta [as·tro·'nau·ta] *mf* astronaut

astronomía [as·tro·no·'mi·a] *f* astronomy

astrónomo, -a [as·'tro·no·mo, -a] *m, f* astronomer

astucia [as·'tu·sja, -θja] *f* astuteness, shrewdness

astuto, -a [as·'tu·to, -a] *adj* astute, shrewd; (*con malicia*) crafty

asumir [a·su·'mir] *vt* 1. (*responsabilidad*)

to assume, to take on; (*cargo*) to take over; (*gastos*) to agree to pay **2.** (*suponer*) to assume

asunto [a·'sun·to] *m* **1.** (*cuestión*) matter; **ir al ~** to get to the point; **el ~ es que... la thing is (that)...; ¡~ concluido!** that's the end of it!; **ocúpate de tus ~s** mind your own business **2.** (*negocio*) business; **tener ~s en el extranjero** to have business dealings abroad **3.** (*amorío*) affair **4.** POL **Ministerio/Ministro de Asuntos Exteriores** State Department/Secretary of State

asustadizo, -a [a·sus·ta·'ði·so, -a; -'ði·θo, -a] *adj* jumpy; (*animal*) easily startled

asustar [a·sus·'tar] **I.** *vt* to scare, to frighten; **la responsabilidad no me asusta** I'm not afraid of the responsibility **II.** *vr*: **~se** to be scared, to be frightened; **no te asustes** don't be frightened

atacar <c → qu> [a·ta·'kar] **I.** *vt* (*embestir*) to attack; **~ por la espalda** to attack from behind **II.** *vi* t. DEP to attack; **~ por las bandas** to attack from the wings

atadura [a·ta·'ðu·ra] *f* **1.** (*acción*) tying **2.** (*cuerda*) rope, string **3.** (*entre personas*) tie, bond

atajar [a·ta·'xar] **I.** *vi* to take a short cut **II.** *vt* **1.** (*detener*) to stop **2.** (*cortar el paso*) to head off

atajo [a·'ta·xo] *m* short cut; **ir por un ~** to take a short cut

atalaya [a·ta·'la·ja] *f* **1.** (*torre*) watchtower **2.** (*lugar*) vantage point

atañer <3. pret atañó> [a·ta·'ɲer] *vimpers* **eso no te atañe** that doesn't concern you; **por lo que atañe a tu empleo** as far as your job is concerned

ataque [a·'ta·ke] *m* **1.** (*embestida*) attack; **~ por sorpresa** surprise attack; **pasar al ~** to go on the offensive **2.** *t.* MED attack, fit; **~ al corazón** heart attack; **~ de nervios** nervous breakdown; **~ de tos** fit of coughing

atar [a·'tar] **I.** *vt* **1.** (*sujetar*) to tie; (*cerrar*) to tie up; (*cautivo*) to bind; **~ a alguien las manos a la espalda** to tie sb's hands behind his/her back; **~ al perro** to tie up the dog **2.** (*comprometer*) **esta profesión te ata mucho** this profession ties you down a lot ▶ **~**

corto a alguien to keep a tight rein on sb **II.** *vr*: **~se** to do up; **~se los zapatos** to tie one's shoes

atardecer [a·tar·ðe·'ser, -'θer] **I.** *irr como crecer vimpers* **atardece** it's getting dark **II.** *m* dusk; **al ~** at dusk

atascar <c → qu> [a·tas·'kar] **I.** *vt* to block **II.** *vr*: **~se 1.** (*cañería*) to get blocked (up); **el desagüe se ha atascado** the drain is blocked (up) **2.** (*coche*) to get stuck; (*mecanismo*) to jam

atasco [a·'tas·ko] *m* **1.** (*de un mecanismo*) blocking; **~ de papel** COMPUT paper jam **2.** (*de tráfico*) traffic jam

ataúd [a·ta·'uð] *m* coffin

ate ['a·te] *m Méx* CULIN fruit paste

ateísmo [a·te·'is·mo] *m* atheism

atemorizar <z → c> [a·te·mo·ri·'sar, -'θar] *vt* to scare, to frighten

Atenas [a·'te·nas] *f* Athens

atenazar <z → c> [a·te·na·'sar, -'θar] *vt* (*miedo*) to grip; (*duda*) to torment

atención [a·ten·'sjon, -'θjon] *f* **1.** (*interés*) attention; **falta de ~** inattentiveness; **digno de ~** noteworthy; **¡~, por favor!** your attention please!; **estamos llamando la ~** we're attracting attention; **llamar la ~ de alguien sobre** [*o a*] **algo** to draw sb's attention to sth; **mantener la ~ de alguien** to hold sb's attention; **prestar ~ a algo** to pay attention to sth; **a la ~ de...** for the attention of... **2.** (*cuidado*) attention, care; **~ médica** medical care **3.** (*cortesía*) kindness; **tener muchas atenciones con alguien** to be very nice to sb ▶ **llamar la ~ a alguien** to rebuke sb

atender <e → ie> [a·ten·'der] **I.** *vt* **1.** (*prestar atención a*) to pay attention to **2.** (*consejo*) to heed; (*petición*) to comply with; **~ una solicitud** to grant a request **3.** (*cuidar*) **~ a alguien** to care for sb **4.** (*tratar*) to treat **5.** (*despachar*) to wait on, to help; **¿lo atienden?** are you being served? **6.** (*llamada*) to answer; **~ el teléfono** to answer the telephone **II.** *vi* (*prestar atención*) to pay attention

atenerse [a·te·'ner·se] *irr como tener vr* **~ a** (*reglas*) to abide by; (*lo dicho*) to stand by, to keep to; **~ a lo seguro**

to play (it) safe; **saber a qué ~** (*en un futuro*) to know what to expect; **si no lo haces, atente a las consecuencias** if you don't do it, you'll bear the consequences

atentado [a·ten·'ta·do] *m* attack, assault; (*crimen*) crime; **~ contra alguien** assassination attempt on sb; **~ suicida** suicide attack; **~ terrorista** terrorist attack; **ser víctima de un ~** to be the victim of an assassination attempt

atentamente [a·ten·ta·'men·te] *adv* (*carta*) **(muy)** ~ (*si la carta empieza* "*Dear Sir*") yours truly; (*si la carta empieza* "*Dear Mr. X*") sincerely yours

atentar [a·ten·'tar] *vi* **~ contra alguien** to make an attempt on sb's life; **~ contra la ley** to break the law

atento, -a [a·'ten·to, -a] *adj* **1.** (*observador*) attentive; **estar ~ a la conversación** to follow the conversation closely; **estar ~ al peligro** to be aware of the danger **2.** (*cortés*) kind; **estuvo muy ~ con nosotros** he was very considerate towards us

atenuantes [a·te·nu·'an·te] *f pl* JUR extenuating circumstances *pl*

atenuar <*1. pres* atenúo> [a·te·nu·'ar] *vt* **1.** to attenuate; (*dolor*) to ease **2.** JUR to extenuate

ateo, -a [a·'teo, -a] **I.** *adj* atheistic **II.** *m, f* atheist

aterrador(a) [a·te·rra·'dor, -·'do·ra] *adj* terrifying

aterrar [a·te·'rrar] *vt* to terrify

aterrizaje [a·te·rri·'sa·xe, -·'θa·xe] *m* landing; **~ forzoso** forced landing

aterrizar <z → c> [a·te·rri·'sar, -'θar] *vi* to land

aterrorizar <z → c> [a·te·rro·ri·'sar, -'θar] *vt* **1.** POL, MIL to terrorize **2.** (*causar terror*) to terrify

atestado [a·tes·'ta·do] *m* **~ (policial)** statement

atestiguar <gu → gü> [a·tes·ti·'ɣwar] *vt* to testify to

ático ['a·ti·ko] *m* attic; (*de lujo*) penthouse

atinar [a·ti·'nar] *vi* **1.** (*acertar*) **~ con algo** to hit on sth; **no atiné con la respuesta** I didn't come up with the answer **2.** (*encontrar*) **~ con algo** to find sth **3.** (*ser capaz*) **~ a hacer algo** to manage to do sth

atípico, -a [a·'ti·pi·ko, -a] *adj* atypical

atisbo [a·'tis·βo] *m* **un ~ de esperanza** a glimmer of hope

atizar <z → c> [a·ti·'sar, -'θar] *vt* **1.** (*fuego*) to poke; (*pasión*) to rouse **2.** (*bofetada*) to give

atlántico, -a [at·'lan·ti·ko, -a] *adj* Atlantic

Atlántico [at·'lan·ti·ko] *m* **el ~** the Atlantic

atlas ['at·las] *m inv* atlas

atleta [at·'le·ta] *mf* athlete

atlético, -a [at·'le·ti·ko, -a] *adj* athletic

atletismo [at·le·'tis·mo] *m* athletics

atmósfera [at·'mos·fe·ra] *f* atmosphere

atole [a·'to·le] *m* AmC hot drink prepared with cornmeal

atolladero [a·to·ja·'de·ro, a·to·ʎa-] *m* (*apuro*) jam; **estar en un ~** to be in a fix; **sacar a alguien de un ~** to get sb out of a jam

atolondrado, -a [a·to·lon·'dra·do, -a] *adj* bewildered

atomía [a·to·'mi·a] *f* AmL evil act; **decir ~s** (*decir tonterías*) to talk nonsense

atómico, -a [a·'to·mi·ko, -a] *adj* atomic; **refugio ~** fallout shelter

átomo ['a·to·mo] *m* atom

atónito, -a [a·'to·ni·to, -a] *adj* amazed

átono, -a ['a·to·no, -a] *adj* unstressed

atontado, -a [a·ton·'ta·do, -a] *adj* **1.** (*tonto*) stupid **2.** (*distraído*) inattentive

atontar [a·ton·'tar] **I.** *vt* **1.** (*aturdir*) to stun **2.** (*entontecer*) to bewilder **II.** *vr:* **~se** to become stupid

atormentar(se) [a·tor·men·'tar(·se)] *vt, (vr)* (*mortificar*) to torment (oneself)

atornillador [a·tor·ni·ja·'dor, -ʎa·'dor] *m* screwdriver

atornillar [a·tor·ni·'jar, -'ʎar] *vt* to screw down; (*fijar*) to screw on

atosigar <g → gu> [a·to·si·'ɣar] *vt* to harass; (*importunar*) to pester

atracadero [a·tra·ka·'de·ro] *m* mooring

atracador(a) [a·tra·ka·'dor, -·'do·ra] *m(f)* bank robber

atracar <c → qu> [a·tra·'kar] **I.** *vi* NÁUT to berth **II.** *vt* **1.** NÁUT to moor **2.** (*asaltar*) to hold up **III.** *vr inf* **~se de algo** to stuff oneself with sth

atracción [a·trak·'sjon, -'θjon] *f t.* Fís attraction; **parque de atracciones** amusement park

atraco [a·'tra·ko] *m* hold-up; **~ a un banco** bank robbery; **~ a mano armada** armed robbery

atractivo [a·trak·'ti·βo] *m* attraction

atractivo, -a [a·trak·'ti·βo, -a] *adj* attractive

atraer [a·tra·'er] *irr como* traer *vt* to attract; **el cebo atrae a los peces** the bait lures the fish; **sentirse atraído hacia alguien** to feel drawn towards sb

atrancar <c → qu> [a·traŋ·'kar] I. *vt* (*puerta*) to bolt II. *vr:* **~se** (*tubo*) to become blocked; (*al hablar*) to get stuck

atrapar [a·tra·'par] *vt* to trap; (*ladrón*) to catch; (*animal*) to capture; **el portero atrapó la pelota** the goalkeeper caught the ball

atrás [a·'tras] *adv* 1. (*hacia detrás*) back, backwards; **dar un paso ~** to take a step backwards [*o* back]; **ir marcha ~** to back up; **quedar ~** to fall behind; **volver ~** to go back; **¡~!** get back! 2. (*detrás*) back, behind; **rueda de ~** rear wheel; **dejar ~ a los perseguidores** to leave one's pursuers behind; **quedarse ~** to remain behind; **sentarse ~** to sit at the back 3. (*de tiempo*) **años ~** years ago ► **echarse ~ de un acuerdo** to back out of an agreement

atrasado, -a [a·tra·'sa·do, -a] *adj* 1. (*en el desarrollo*) behind; (*país*) backward; **viven 20 años ~s** they're 20 years behind the times 2. (*pago*) overdue 3. (*tarde*) late; **el reloj va ~** the watch is slow

atrasar [a·tra·'sar] I. *vt* 1. (*aplazar*) to postpone 2. (*reloj*) to put back II. *vr:* **~se** (*retrasarse*) to be late; **el tren se ha atrasado** the train is late

atraso [a·'tra·so] *m* 1. (*de un tren*) delay 2. (*de un país*) backwardness 3. Fin arrears *pl*

atravesar <e → ie> [a·tra·βe·'sar] I. *vt* 1. (*persona*) **~ la calle** to cross the street; **~ un río nadando** to swim across a river; **~ un momento difícil** to go through a difficult time 2. (*cuerpo*) **~ algo con una aguja** to pierce sth

with a needle; **la bala le atravesó el corazón** the bullet went through his/her heart; **una cicatriz le atraviesa el pecho** a scar runs across his/her chest 3. (*poner de través*) to lay across II. *vr:* **~se** 1. (*ponerse*) **no te atravieses en mi camino** don't get in my way; **se me ha atravesado una miga en la garganta** a crumb has gotten stuck in my throat 2. (*no soportar*) **se me atraviesa ese tipo** I can't stand that fellow

atreverse [a·tre·'βer·se] *vr* to dare; **~ a hacer algo** to dare to do sth; **¡no te atreverás!** you wouldn't dare!

atrevido, -a [a·tre·'βi·do, -a] *adj* 1. (*persona*) daring 2. (*insolente*) insolent

atrevimiento [a·tre·βi·'mjen·to] *m* 1. (*audacia*) boldness 2. (*descaro*) nerve *fig*

atribuir [a·tri·βu·'ir] *irr como* huir I. *vt* 1. (*hechos*) to attribute; **~ la culpa de algo a alguien** to blame sth on sb 2. (*funciones*) to confer II. *vr:* **~se** 1. (*hechos*) to claim for oneself 2. (*facultades*) **~se todo el poder** to assume absolute power

atributo [a·tri·'β·u·to] *m t.* Ling attribute

atril [a·'tril] *m* Mús music stand; (*de mesa*) lectern

atrio ['a·trjo] *m* atrium

atrocidad [a·tro·si·'dad, a·tro·θi-] *f* 1. (*cosa*) atrocity 2. (*disparate*) foolish remark; **¡no digas ~es!** don't talk nonsense!

atropellar [a·tro·pe·'jar, -'ʎar] I. *vt* 1. (*vehículo*) to run over 2. (*empujar*) to push past 3. (*agraviar*) to insult II. *vr:* **~se** to rush

atropello [a·tro·'pe·jo, -'pe·ʎo] *m* 1. (*colisión*) collision; (*accidente*) accident 2. (*empujón*) push 3. (*insulto*) insult; **¡esto es un ~!** this is preposterous! 4. (*prisa*) **tomar una decisión sin prisas ni ~s** not to rush a decision

atroz [a·'tros, -'troθ] *adj* 1. (*horroroso*) atrocious 2. (*cruel*) cruel 3. (*enorme*) huge

atufar [a·tu·'far] *vi inf* to stink

atún [a·'tun] *m* tuna (fish)

aturdido, -a [a·tur·'di·do, -a] *adj* 1. (*pasmado*) stunned 2. (*irreflexivo*) thoughtless

aturdir [a·tur·'dir] *vt* 1. (*los sentidos*) to stupefy 2. (*pasmar*) to stun

audacia [au·'da·sja, -θja] *f* boldness, audacity

audaz [au·'das, -'daθ] *adj* bold, audacious

audible [au·'di·βle] *adj* audible

audición [au·di·'sjon, -'θjon] *f* 1. (*acción*) hearing 2. TEAT audition

audiencia [au·'djen·sja, -θja] *f* 1. TEL audience; **nivel de ~** viewing figures *pl* 2. JUR (*sesión*) hearing; (*sala*) courtroom; (*tribunal*) court

audífono [au·'di·fo·no] *m* 1. (*para sordos*) hearing aid 2. *AmL* (*auricular*) receiver

auditivo, -a [au·di·'ti·βo, -a] *adj* ANAT hearing

auditorio [au·di·'to·rjo] *m* 1. (*público*) audience 2. (*sala*) auditorium

auge ['au·xe] *m* (*cumbre*) peak; **en el ~ de su belleza** at the height of her beauty

augurar [au·ɣu·'rar] *vt* to predict

augurio [au·'ɣu·rjo] *m* prediction

aula ['au·la] *f* classroom; (*de universidad*) lecture room; **~ magna** main lecture hall

aullar [au·'jar, -'ʎar] *irr vi* to howl

aumentar [au·men·'tar] I. *vi, vt* 1. (*subir*) to increase; (*precios*) to rise, to increase; **~ de peso** to get heavier; **los disturbios aumentan** the disturbances are spreading 2. (*extender*) to extend II. *vt* to increase; (*precios*) to raise, to increase

aumento [au·'men·to] *m* increase; (*de la temperatura*) rise; (*de valor*) appreciation; (*en la extensión*) expansion; **~ de precio** price rise

aun [aun] I. *adv* even; **~ así** even so II. *conj* **~ cuando** even though

aún [a·'un] *adv* still; **~ más** even more; **~ no** yet; **¿~ no ha llegado?** hasn't he/she arrived yet?

aunar [au·'nar] *irr como aullar* I. *vt* (*unir*) to unite; **~ esfuerzos** to join forces II. *vr:* **~se** to unite

aunque ['aun·ke] *conj* 1. (*concesivo*) even though; **~ es viejo, aún puede trabajar** although he's old, he can still work; **~ parezca extraño** however strange it may seem 2. (*adversativa*) but

aúpa [a·'u·pa] *interj* up!, get up! ▶ **de ~** *inf* tremendous

aupar [au·'par] *irr como aullar* *vt* to lift up

aura ['au·ra] *f* aura; **tiene un ~ misteriosa** he/she has a mysterious aura

aureola [au·re·'o·la] *f* halo

auricular [au·ri·ku·'lar] *m* 1. TEL receiver; **coger/colgar el ~** to pick up/put down the receiver 2. *pl* (*de música*) headphones *pl*

aurora [au·'ro·ra] *f* dawn

auscultar [aus·kul·'tar] *vt* MED **el médico lo auscultó** the doctor listened to his chest (with a stethoscope)

ausencia [au·'sen·sja, -θja] *f* 1. (*estado*) absence 2. (*falta*) lack; **~ de interés** lack of interest 3. PSICO mental blackouts ▶ **brillar por su ~** to be conspicuous by one's absence

ausentarse [au·sen·'tar·se] *vr* to go away; **~ de la ciudad** to leave town

ausente [au·'sen·te] *adj* 1. (*no presente*) absent; **estar ~** to be absent 2. (*distraído*) distracted

auspiciar [aus·pi·'sjar, -'θjar] *vt* 1. (*presagiar*) to predict 2. (*patrocinar*) to back

austeridad [aus·te·ri·'dad] *f* austerity

austero, -a [aus·'te·ro, -a] *adj* austere

austral [aus·'tral] *adj* southern

Australia [aus·'tra·lja] *f* Australia

australiano, -a [aus·tra·'lja·no, -a] *adj, m, f* Australian

Austria ['aus·trja] *f* Austria

austriaco, -a [aus·'trja·ko, -a], **austríaco, -a** [aus·'tri·a·ko, -a] *adj, m, f* Austrian

autenticidad [au·ten·ti·si·'dad, -θi·'dad] *f* authenticity

auténtico, -a [au·'ten·ti·ko, -a] *adj* authentic; **un ~ fracaso** an absolute failure; **es un ~ maestro en su especialidad** he's an absolute expert in his field

autista [au·'tis·ta] *adj* autistic

autobiografía [au·to·βjo·ɣra·'fi·a] *f* autobiography

autobús [au·to·'βus] *m* bus

autocar <autocares> [au·to·'kar] *m* bus

autocarril [au·to·ka·'rril] *m* *Bol, Chile, Nic* divided highway

autóctono, -a [au·'tok·to·no, -a] *adj* indigenous

autodefensa [au·to·de·'fen·sa] *f* self-defense

autoescuela [au·to·es·'kwe·la] *f* driving school

autógrafo [au·'to·ɣra·fo] *m* autograph

autolavado [au·to·la·'βa·do] *m* car wash

automático [au·to·'ma·ti·ko] *m* snap fastener

automático, -a [au·to·'ma·ti·ko, -a] *adj* automatic; **dispositivo ~** automatic mechanism; **fusil ~** automatic rifle; **la puerta se cierra de modo ~** (*en el metro*) the door closes automatically

automatizar <z → c> [au·to·ma·ti·'sar, -'θar] *vt* to automate

automóvil [au·to·'mo·βil] *m* car; **~ de carreras** racing car; **~ eléctrico** electrically powered car; **~ todo terreno** all-terrain vehicle; **Salón del Automóvil** motor show

automovilista [au·to·mo·βi·'lis·ta] *mf* motorist, driver

autonomía [au·to·no·'mi·a] *f* 1. (*personal*) autonomy; **en esta empresa no tengo ~ para tomar decisiones** in this company I cannot make my own decisions 2. (*territorio*) autonomous region

autonómico, -a [au·to·'no·mi·ko, -a] *adj* autonomous; **elecciones autonómicas** regional elections

autónomo, -a [au·'to·no·mo, -a] *adj* 1. POL autonomous 2. (*trabajador*) self-employed; **trabajar de ~** to be self-employed

autopista [au·to·'pis·ta] *f* highway, freeway; **~ de peaje** turnpike

autopsia [au·'toβ·sja] *f* MED autopsy

autor(a) [au·'tor, -·'to·ra] *m(f)* 1. LIT author; **derechos de ~** royalties 2. (*de un crimen*) perpetrator

autoridad [au·to·ri·'dad] *f* 1. (*en general*) authority; **estar bajo la ~ de alguien** to be under sb's control 2. (*pl*) (*policía*) authorities *pl*; **desacato a la ~** contempt (of court) 3. (*experto*) authority

autoritario, -a [au·to·ri·'ta·rjo, -a] *adj* authoritarian

autorización [au·to·ri·sa·'sjon, -θa·'θjon] *f* authorization

autorizado, -a [au·to·ri·'sa·do, -a; -'θa·do, -a] *adj* 1. (*facultado*) authorized; **persona no autorizada** unauthorized person; **de fuentes autorizadas** from approved sources 2. (*oficial*) official

autorizar <z → c> [au·to·ri·'sar, -'θar] *vt* 1. (*consentir*) to approve 2. (*facultar*) to authorize 3. (*dar derecho*) to entitle; **que sea mi jefe no le autoriza para insultarme** even though you're my boss, it doesn't give you the right to insult me

autorretrato [au·to·rre·'tra·to] *m* self-portrait

autoservicio [au·to·ser·'βi·sjo, -θjo] *m* self-service

autostopista [au·tos·to·'pis·ta] *mf* hitch-hiker

autovía [au·to·'βi·a] *f* divided highway

auxiliar[1] [auk·si·'ljar] I. *adj* assistant II. *mf* assistant; **~ administrativo** administrative assistant; **~ de vuelo** flight attendant III. *vt* to help

auxiliar[2] [auk·si·'ljar] *m* LING auxiliary verb

auxilio [auk·'si·ljo] *m* help; **primeros ~s** first aid; **pedir ~** (a alguien) to ask for (sb's) help

avalancha [a·βa·'lan·tʃa] *f* avalanche

avance [a·'βan·se, -θe] *m* t. MIL advance, trailer for sth; **~ informativo** TV news summary

avanzado, -a [a·βan·'sa·do, -a; a·βan·'θa·] *adj* advanced

avanzar <z → c> [a·βan·'sar, -'θar] *vi* 1. (*seguir adelante*) t. MIL to advance; **a medida que el tiempo avanzaba** as time went by 2. (*progresar*) to progress; **no ~ nada** not to make any headway

avaricia [a·βa·'ri·sja, -θja] *f* 1. (*codicia*) greed 2. (*tacañería*) avarice

avaricioso, -a [a·βa·ri·'sjo·so, -a; a·βa·ri·'θjo·] *adj*, **avariento, -a** [a·βa·'rjen·to, -a] *adj* 1. (*codicioso*) greedy 2. (*tacaño*) avaricious

avaro, -a [a·'βa·ro, -a] I. *adj* miserly II. *m, f* miser

avatares [a·βa·'ta·res] *mpl* **los ~es de la vida** life's ups and downs

ave ['a·βe] *f* bird; **~s de corral** poultry; **~ rapaz** [*o* de rapiña] bird of prey

AVE ['a·βe] *m abr de* **Alta Velocidad Es-**

pañola Spanish high-speed train

avecinarse [a·βe·si·'nar·se, -θi·'nar·se] *vr* to approach

avellana [a·βe·'ʎa·na] *f* hazelnut

avemaría [a·βe·ma·'ri·a] *f* Hail Mary

avena [a·'βe·na] *f* oats *pl*

avenida [a·βe·'ni·da] *f* (*calle*) avenue

avenido, -a [a·βe·'ni·do, -a] *adj* **dos personas bien avenidas** two good friends; **una pareja mal avenida** a mismatched couple

avenir [a·βe·'nir] *irr como venir* **I.** *vt* to reconcile **II. ~se 1.** (*entenderse*) to get on **2.** (*ponerse de acuerdo*) **~se en algo** to agree on sth; **no ~se a...** not to agree to...

aventajado, -a [a·βen·ta·'xa·do, -a] *adj* outstanding

aventajar [a·βen·ta·'xar] *vt* (*ser mejor*) to surpass; **~ a todos** to get ahead of everyone

aventar <e → ie> [a·βen·'tar] *vt* to blow away; (*el grano*) to winnow

aventón [a·βen·'ton] *m Méx inf* push; **dar un ~** to give a lift; **ir de ~** to ride free

aventura [a·βen·'tu·ra] *f* adventure; (*amorosa*) affair

aventurar [a·βen·tu·'rar] **I.** *vt* to venture; (*algo atrevido*) to dare **II.** *vr:* **~se** to dare

aventurero, -a [a·βen·tu·'re·ro, -a] **I.** *adj* adventurous; **espíritu** ~ thirst for adventure **II.** *m, f* adventurer

avergonzado, -a [a·βer·ɣon·'sa·do, -a; -'θa·do, -a] *adj* embarrassed; **sentirse ~** to be ashamed

avergonzar [a·βer·ɣon·'sar, -'θar] *irr* **I.** *vt* to shame **II.** *vr* **~se de** [*o por*] **algo/alguien** to be ashamed of sth/sb

avería [a·βe·'ri·a] *f* **1.** AUTO breakdown **2.** (*de mercancía*) damage **3.** TÉC fault

averiar <1. pres averío> [a·βe·ri·'ar] **I.** *vt* to damage **II.** *vr:* **~se** AUTO to break down; TÉC to fail

averiguación [a·βe·ri·ɣwa·'sjon, -'θjon] *f* inquiry

averiguar <gu → gü> [a·βe·ri·'ɣwar] *vt* to inquire into; **averigua a qué hora sale el tren** find out (at) what time the train leaves

aversión [a·βer·'sjon] *f* aversion

avestruz [a·βes·'trus, -'truθ] *m* ostrich

aviación [a·βja·'sjon, -'θjon] *f* **1.** AVIAT aviation; **compañía de ~** airline (company) **2.** MIL air force

aviador(a) [a·βja·'dor, -·'do·ra] *m(f)* aviator

aviar <1. pres avío> [a·βi·'ar] **I.** *vt* (*maleta*) to pack; (*mesa*) to set **II.** *vi* **1.** (*apresurar*) **diles que vayan aviando** tell them to get a move on; **estar aviado** (*en un apuro*) to be in a tight spot **2.** *AmS* (*prestar*) to lend

avicultura [a·βi·kul·'tu·ra] *f* poultry farming

avidez [a·βi·'des, -'deθ] *f* eagerness; **~ de algo** eagerness for sth

ávido, -a ['a·βi·do, -a] *adj* eager; **~ de algo** eager for sth

avinagrarse [a·βi·na·'ɣrar·se] *vr* (*vino*) to turn sour; (*persona*) to become bitter

avión [a·βi·'on] *m* AVIAT airplane; **~ a reacción** jet (plane); **por ~** (*correos*) by airmail; **ir en ~ a La Paz** to fly to La Paz

avioneta [a·βjo·'ne·ta] *f* light aircraft

avisar [a·βi·'sar] *vt* **1.** (*dar noticia*) to notify; **avísame cuando estés de vuelta** let me know when you're back; **llegar sin ~** to arrive unannounced **2.** (*poner sobre aviso*) to warn **3.** (*llamar*) to call

aviso [a·'βi·so] *m* **1.** (*notificación*) notification; (*nota*) notice; (*por altavoz*) announcement; **~ de salida** FERRO departure announcement; **hasta nuevo ~** until further notice; **sin previo ~** without notice **2.** (*advertencia*) warning; **~ de bomba** bomb warning; **estar sobre ~** to be warned; **poner sobre ~** to warn; **servir a alguien de ~** to be a lesson to sb **3.** *AmL* (*en el periódico*) ad(vertisement)

avispa [a·'βis·pa] *f* wasp

avispado, -a [a·βis·'pa·do, -a] *adj* sharp

avistar [a·βis·'tar] *vt* to sight

avivar [a·βi·'βar] *vt* to enliven; (*fuego*) to stoke; (*pasión*) to arouse; (*sentidos*) to sharpen; **~ el paso** to increase one's pace

avizor [a·βi·'sor, -'θor] *adj* **estar ojo ~** to be alert

axila [ak·'si·la] *f* **1.** ANAT armpit **2.** BOT axil

axioma [ak·'sjo·ma] *m* axiom

ay [ai] *interj* **1.** (*de dolor*) ouch **2.** (*de sorpresa*) oh; **¡~, qué divertido!** oh, how funny! **3.** (*de miedo*) oh, my **4.** (*de amenaza*) **¡~ si vienes tarde!** you'll regret it if you come late!; **~ del que...** +*subj* Heaven help anyone who...

ayer [a·'jer] *adv* yesterday; **~ (por la) noche** last night; **~ hace una semana** a week ago yesterday; **de ~ acá** overnight; **¡parece que fue ~!** it seems like only yesterday!; **no he nacido ~** I wasn't born yesterday

ayuda¹ [a·'ju·da] *f* (*auxilio*) help; **eso no me sirve de ninguna ~** that doesn't help me

ayuda² [a·'ju·da] *m* helper

ayudado, -a [a·ju·'da·do, -a] *m, f* Col **1.** (*brujo*) witchdoctor; (*de tribu*) medicine man **2.** (*endemoniado*) possessed person

ayudante [a·ju·'dan·te] *mf* helper; (*cargo*) assistant

ayudar [a·ju·'dar] **I.** *vt* to help; **~ a alguien a levantarse** to help sb up; **~ a alguien a salir del coche** to help sb to get out of the car; **¡Dios me ayude!** God help me!; **¿le puedo ~ en algo?** can I help you with anything? **II.** *vr:* **~se** (*valerse de*) to help oneself

ayunar [a·ju·'nar] *vi* to fast

ayunas [a·'ju·nas] *adv* **estar en ~** to have an empty stomach

ayuno [a·'ju·no] *m* fast

ayuntamiento [a·jun·ta·'mjen·to] *m* **1.** (*corporación*) district council; (*de una ciudad*) town/city council **2.** (*edificio*) town/city hall

azabache [a·sa·'βa·tʃe, a·θa-] *m* jet; **ojos de ~** jet-black eyes

azada [a·'θa·da, a·'θa-] *f* hoe

azafata [a·sa·'fa·ta, a·θa-] *f* AVIAT air hostess; **~ de congresos** conference hostess

azafrán [a·sa·'fran, a·θa-] *m* saffron

azahar [a·'sar, a·sa·'ar; a·'θar, a·θa·'ar] *m* orange blossom

azalea [a·sa·'lea, a·θa-] *f* azalea

azar [a·'sar, -'θar] *m* **1.** (*casualidad*) chance; **juegos de ~** games of chance; **al ~** at random; **por ~** by chance **2.** (*im-*

previsto) misfortune; **los ~es de la vida** life's ups and downs

Azores [a·'so·res, -θo·res] *fpl* **las ~** the Azores + *pl vb*

azoro [a·'so·ro, -θo·ro] *m* **1.** AmC (*fantasma*) ghost **2.** AmC (*aparición*) apparition **3.** Méx, Perú, PRico (*azoramiento*) bewilderment

azotaina [a·so·'tai·na, a·θo-] *f* spanking

azotar [a·so·'tar, a·θo-] *vt* **1.** (*con un látigo*) to whip; (*con la mano*) to thrash, to spank; **el viento me azota (en) la cara** the wind is hitting my face **2.** (*producir daños*) to devastate; **una epidemia azota la región** an epidemic is causing havoc in the region

azote [a·'so·te, -θo·te] *m* **1.** (*látigo*) whip **2.** (*golpe*) lash; (*en las nalgas*) spank

azotea [a·so·'tea, a·θo-] *f* terrace roof ▶ **estar mal de la ~** *inf* to be off one's rocker

azteca [as·'te·ka, aθ-] **I.** *adj* Aztec; **el equipo ~** (*en fútbol*) Mexico **II.** *mf* Aztec

azúcar [a·'su·kar, a·'θu-] *m* sugar; **~ en polvo** icing sugar; **tener el ~ muy alto** MED to have a very high blood-sugar level

azucarero [a·su·ka·'re·ro, a·'θu-] *m* sugar bowl

azucena [a·su·'se·na, a·θu·'θe·na] *f* Madonna lily

azufre [a·'su·fre, a·'θu-] *m* sulfur

azul [a·'sul, a'θul] *adj* blue; **~ celeste** sky blue; **~ marino** navy blue

azulado, -a [a·su·'la·do, -a; a·θu·-] *adj* bluish

azulejo [a·su·'le·xo, a·θu-] *m* **1.** (*para pared*) (glazed) tile **2.** ZOOL (*pez*) blue wrasse

azulgrana [a·sul·'yra·na, a·θul·-] *adj* blue and scarlet; **el equipo ~** DEP Barcelona Soccer Team

azuzar <z → c> [a·su·'sar, a·θu·'θar] *vt* **1.** **~ a los perros a uno** to set the dogs on sb **2.** *fig* (*persona*) to incite, to egg on

B

B, b [be] *f* B, b; **~ de Barcelona** B as in Bravo

baba ['ba·βa] *f* spittle; (*del caracol*) slime; **caerse a alguien la ~ por alguien** *inf* to dote on sb

babero [ba·'βe·ro] *m* bib

babosa [ba·'βo·sa] *f* **1.** ZOOL slug **2.** *AmL* (*tontería*) stupid thing

babosada [ba·βo·'sa·da] *f AmC, Méx* (*bobería*) silliness

babosear [ba·βo·se·'ar] *vi inf* to drool, to dribble

baboso, -a [ba·'βo·so, -a] *adj* **1.** (*con babas*) slimy **2.** *inf* (*zalamero*) fawning **3.** *AmL* (*tonto*) silly

baca ['ba·ka] *f* roof rack, luggage rack

bacalao [ba·ka·'lao] *m* **1.** (*pez*) cod; (*salado*) salt cod **2.** MÚS techno music ▶ **cortar el ~** to run the show

bachatear [ba·tʃa·te·'ar] *vi AmL* to go out on the town

bache ['ba·tʃe] *m* **1.** (*en la calle*) pothole **2.** (*económico, psíquico*) slump

bachillerato [ba·tʃi·je·'ra·to, -ʎe·'ra·to] *m* **1.** (*título*) certificate of secondary education **2.** (*estudios*) high school education for 14-17-year-olds

bacilo [ba·'si·lo, -'θi·lo] *m* bacillus

bacteria [bak·'te·rja] *f* bacteria

badén [ba·'den] *m* dip; (*en carreteras*) drainage channel

bádminton ['bad·min·ton] *m* DEP badminton

bafle ['ba·fle] *m* (loud)speaker

bagaje [ba·'ɣa·xe] *m* **~ cultural** cultural knowledge

bagatela [ba·ɣa·'te·la] *f* trifle

bagre ['ba·ɣre] I. *adj* **1.** *Bol, Col* (*cursi*) coarse **2.** *Guat, Hond, ElSal* (*inteligente*) clever II. *m* **1.** *AmL* ZOOL catfish **2.** *And* (*antipático*) unpleasant person

bah [ba] *interj* **1.** (*incredulidad*) never **2.** (*desprecio*) that's nothing

bahía [ba·'ia] *f* bay

bailador(a) [bai·la·'dor, -'do·ra] I. *adj* dancing II. *m(f)* dancer (of flamenco)

bailar [bai·'lar] I. *vi* **1.** (*danzar*) to dance **2.** (*objetos*) to move; **hacer ~ una**

peonza to spin a top ▶ **~ con la más fea** to get the short end of the stick; **otro que tal ~** he/she is just as bad II. *vt* to dance

bailarín, -ina [bai·la·'rin, --'ri·na] I. *adj* dancing II. *m, f* dancer; (*de ballet*) ballet dancer

baile ['bai·le] *m* **1.** (*acto*) dancing **2.** (*danza*) dance **3.** (*fiesta*) dance party; (*de etiqueta*) ball

baja ['ba·xa] *f* **1.** (*disminución*) decrease **2.** (*de trabajo*) vacancy; **~ por maternidad** maternity leave; **darse de ~** (*por enfermedad*) to be on sick leave **3.** (*en una asociación*) resignation; **dar de ~ a alguien** to expel sb **4.** (*documento*) discharge certificate; (*del médico*) doctor's note **5.** MIL casualty

bajada [ba·'xa·da] *f* **1.** (*descenso*) descent; **~ de tipos de interés** ECON fall in interest rates; **~ de bandera** minimum fare **2.** (*camino*) way down; (*pendiente*) slope

bajar [ba·'xar] I. *vi* **1.** (*ir hacia abajo*) to go down; (*venir hacia abajo*) to come down; **~ en ascensor** to take the elevator down **2.** (*apearse*) **~ de** (*de un caballo*) to dismount, to get down from; (*de un coche*) to get out of **3.** (*disminuir*) to decrease; (*temperatura*) to drop II. *vt* **1.** (*transportar*) to bring down; (*coger*) to take down; **~ las persianas** to lower the blinds **2.** (*precios*) to lower **3.** (*voz*) to lower; (*radio*) to turn down **4.** COMPUT to download III. *vr*: **~se** (*descender*) **~se de** (*de un caballo*) to dismount; (*de un coche*) to get out of

bajativo [ba·xa·'ti·βo] *m AmL* digestive

bajo ['ba·xo] I. *m* **1.** (*instrumento*) bass **2.** (*persona*) bass player **3.** *pl* (*piso*) first floor *Am* **4.** *pl* (*parte inferior*) underneath; (*de una prenda*) hemline II. *adv* **1.** (*posición*) below **2.** (*voz*) quietly III. *prep* **1.** (*debajo*) below **2.** (*por debajo de*) underneath; **~ llave** under lock and key; **~ la lluvia** in the rain; **~ fianza** on bail

bajo, -a <más bajo *o* inferior, bajísimo> ['ba·xo, -a] *adj* **1.** *estar* (*posición*) low **2.** *ser* (*de temperatura*) low; (*de estatura*) short; **baja tensión** ELEC low tension; **con la cabeza baja** with head lowered; **tener la moral baja** to be in poor spirits **3.** (*voz*) low; (*sonido*) soft **4.** (*comportamiento*) mean **5.** (*clase social*) humble **6.** (*calidad*) poor

bajón [ba·ˈxon] *m* (*descenso*) decline; (*de precios*) drop

bala [ˈba·la] *f* (*proyectil*) bullet; **~ de fogueo** blank cartridge; **como una ~** like a flash

balance [ba·ˈlan·se, -θe] *m* **1.** COM (*resultado*) balance; **hacer un ~** to draw up a balance **2.** (*comparación*) comparison; **hacer (el) ~** to take stock of the situation

balancear [ba·lan·se·ˈar, ba·lan·θe·] **I.** *vt* (*mecer*) to sway; (*acunar*) to rock **II.** *vr:* **~se 1.** (*columpiarse*) to swing **2.** NÁUT to roll

balanceo [ba·lan·ˈseo, -ˈθeo] *m* swaying; NÁUT rocking

balanza [ba·ˈlan·sa, -θa] *f* **1.** (*pesa*) scales *pl* **2.** COM balance; **~ de pagos** balance of payments

balar [ba·ˈlar] *vi* to bleat

balazo [ba·ˈla·so, -θo] *m* **1.** (*tiro*) shot **2.** (*herida*) bullet wound

balbucir [bal·βu·ˈsir, -ˈθir] *vi, vt* to stammer; (*niño*) to babble

Balcanes [bal·ˈka·nes] *mpl* **los ~** the Balkans

balcón [bal·ˈkon] *m* balcony

balda [ˈbal·da] *f* shelf

baldado, -a [bal·ˈda·do, -a] *adj* crippled; *inf* (*muy cansado*) exhausted

balde [ˈbal·de] *m* bucket ▶ **obtener algo de ~** to get sth for nothing; **en ~** in vain

baldío, -a [bal·ˈdi·o, -a] *adj* **1.** (*terreno*) uncultivated **2.** (*inútil*) useless; (*en balde*) vain

baldosa [bal·ˈdo·sa] *f* paving stone, floor tile

baldosín [bal·do·ˈsin] *m* tile

balear [ba·le·ˈar] **I.** *vt AmL* **~ a alguien** (*disparar contra*) to shoot at sb; (*herir, matar*) to shoot sb **II.** *vr:* **~se** *AmL* **1.** (*disparar*) to exchange shots **2.** (*disputar*) to argue **III.** *adj* Balearic **IV.** *mf* native/inhabitant of the Balearic Islands

Baleares [ba·le·ˈa·res] *fpl* **las (islas) ~** the Balearic Islands

baleo [ba·ˈleo] *m AmL* (*disparo*) shot

balero [ba·ˈle·ro] *m AmL* (*juego*) cup-and-ball toy

ballena [ba·ˈje·na, -ˈʎe·na] *f* whale

ballet <ballets> [ba·ˈle] *m* ballet

balneario [bal·ne·ˈa·rjo] *m* **1.** (*baños*) spa **2.** (*estación*) health resort

balón [ba·ˈlon] *m* DEP ball ▶ **echar balones fuera** to evade the question

baloncesto [ba·lon·ˈses·to, -ˈθes·to] *m* basketball

balonmano [ba·lon·ˈma·no, ba·lom·ˈma·no] *m* handball

balsa [ˈbal·sa] *f* **1.** (*charca*) pool **2.** NÁUT (*barca*) ferry; (*plataforma*) raft; **~ neumática** rubber dinghy ▶ **ser una ~ de aceite** (*mar*) to be as calm as a millpond

bálsamo [ˈbal·sa·mo] *m* balm

báltico, -a [ˈbal·ti·ko, -a] *adj* Baltic; **el mar ~** the Baltic Sea; **los países ~s** the Baltic countries

baluarte [ba·ˈlwar·te] *m* bastion; **un ~ de la libertad** a bulwark of freedom

balumba [ba·ˈlum·ba] *f AmS* (*barullo*) racket

bambú [bam·ˈbu] *m* bamboo

banal [ba·ˈnal] *adj* banal

banalidad [ba·na·li·ˈdad] *f* banality

banalizar <z → c> [ba·na·li·ˈsar, -ˈθar] *vt* to trivialize

banana [ba·ˈna·na] *f AmL* banana

banca [ˈban·ka] *f* **1.** (*en el mercado*) stall **2.** *AmL* (*asiento*) bench **3.** FIN banking; **~ electrónica** electronic banking **4.** (*en juegos*) bank

bancario, -a [ban·ˈka·rjo, -a] *adj* bank(ing); **cuenta bancaria** bank account

bancarrota [ban·ka·ˈrro·ta] *f* bankruptcy

banco [ˈban·ko] *m* **1.** (*asiento*) bench **2.** FIN bank; **~ emisor** issuing bank; **Banco Mundial** World Bank **3.** TÉC bench, work table; **~ de pruebas** test bed; *fig* testing ground **4.** (*de peces*) shoal ▶ **~ de datos** COMPUT databank; **~ de sangre** blood bank

banda [ˈban·da] *f* **1.** (*cinta*) band; (*insignia*) sash; **~ de frecuencia** RADIO frequency band; ~ **sonora** CINE soundtrack **2.** (*pandilla*) gang; ~ **terrorista** terrorist group **3.** (*de música*) band; (*de música moderna*) group

bandada [ban·da·da] *f* **1.** (*de pájaros*) flock **2.** (*de personas*) gang

bandear [ban·de·ar] *vt AmC* (*perseguir a alguien*) to chase; (*herir de gravedad*) to seriously wound **2.** *Arg, Par, Urug* (*taladrar*) to drill **3.** *Arg, Par, Urug* (*un río*) to cross **4.** *Guat* (*pretender*) to court **5.** *Urug* (*herir con palabras*) to hurt; (*inculpar*) to charge

bandeja [ban·de·xa] *f* tray; ~ **de entrada** in-tray; ~ **de salida** out-tray; **servir en** ~ to hand on a plate

bandera [ban·de·ra] *f* flag ▸ **estar hasta la** ~ *inf* to be packed full

banderola [ban·de·ro·la] *f CSur* (*ventana*) transom

bandido, -a [ban·di·do, -a] *m, f* **1.** (*criminal*) bandit **2.** (*persona pilla*) rogue

bando [ban·do] *m* **1.** (*edicto*) edict **2.** (*partido*) faction

banquero, -a [ban·ke·ro, -a] *m, f* banker

banqueta [ban·ke·ta] *f* **1.** (*taburete*) stool; (*para los pies*) footstool **2.** *AmC* (*acera*) sidewalk

banquete [ban·ke·te] *m* banquet

banquillo [ban·ki·jo, -ʎo] *m* bench; JUR dock

bañadera [ba·ɲa·de·ra] *f AmL* bathtub

bañado [ba·ɲa·do] *m Arg, Bol, Par* marshland

bañador [ba·ɲa·dor] *m* (*de mujer*) swimsuit; (*de hombre*) swimming trunks

bañar [ba·ɲar] **I.** *vt* **1.** (*lavar*) to bathe **2.** (*sumergir*) to immerse **3.** (*mar*) to bathe **4.** (*recubrir*) to coat; **bañado en sudor** bathed in sweat **II.** *vr:* **~se 1.** (*lavarse*) to take a bath, to bathe **2.** (*en el mar*) to take a swim

bañera [ba·ɲe·ra] *f* bathtub

bañista [ba·ɲis·ta] *mf* (*en playa*) swimmer; (*en balneario*) guest at a spa

baño [ba·ɲo] *m* **1.** (*acto*) bathing; ~ **María** CULIN double boiler; ~ **de sangre** bloodbath **2.** (*cuarto*) bathroom; **ir al** ~ to go to the bathroom **3.** (*de pintura*) coat; (*de chocolate*) coating **4.** *pl* (*balneario*) spa; **~s termales** hot springs

bar [bar] *m* **1.** (*café*) café; (*tasca*) bar **2.** FÍS bar

baraja [ba·ra·xa] *f* deck of cards; **una** ~ **de posibilidades** *fig* a range of possibilities

barajar [ba·ra·xar] *vt* **1.** (*naipes*) to shuffle **2.** (*mezclar*) to mix up **3.** (*posibilidades*) to consider

barandilla [ba·ran·di·ja, -ʎa] *f* (*de balcón*) handrail; (*pasamanos*) banister

barato [ba·ra·to] *adv* cheap(ly)

barato, -a [ba·ra·to, -a] *adj* cheap

barba ['bar·βa] *f* **1.** (*mentón*) chin **2.** (*pelos*) beard; **dejarse** ~ to grow a beard; **por** ~ per head ▸ **subirse a las** ~**s de alguien** to be disrespectful to sb

barbacoa [bar·βa·koa] *f* barbecue

barbaridad [bar·βa·ri·dad] *f* **1.** (*crueldad*) barbarity; **¡qué** ~! how terrible! **2.** (*disparate*) nonsense

barbarie [bar·βa·rje] *f* savagery

bárbaro, -a ['bar·βa·ro] **I.** *adj* **1.** (*cruel*) savage **2.** *inf* (*estupendo*) tremendous **II.** *m, f* HIST barbarian

barbería [bar·βe·ri·a] *f* barber's (shop)

barbero [bar·βe·ro] *m* barber

barbilla [bar·βi·ja, -ʎa] *f* chin

barbo ['bar·βo] *m* ZOOL barbel

barbudo, -a [bar·βu·do, -a] *adj* bearded

barca ['bar·ka] *f* (*small*) boat; **dar un paseo en** ~ to take a boat ride

barchilón, -ona [bar·tʃi·lon, --'lo·na] *m, f AmL* (*curandero*) healer

barco ['bar·ko] *m* ship; ~ **cisterna** tanker; ~ **de pasajeros** passenger ship; ~ **de vapor** steamer; ~ **de vela** sailing ship

baremo [ba·re·mo] *m* range of values

barniz [bar·niθ, -niθ] *m* polish; (*para madera*) varnish

barnizar ‹z → c› [bar·ni·sar, -'θar] *vt* to put a gloss on; (*madera*) to varnish

barómetro [ba·ro·me·tro] *m* barometer

barón, -onesa [ba·ron, ba·ro·ne·sa] *m, f* baron *m*, baroness *f*

barquero, -a [bar·ke·ro, -a] *m, f* (*en un bote*) boatman *m*, boatwoman *f*

barquillo [bar·ki·jo, -ʎo] *m* wafer

barra ['ba·rra] *f* **1.** (*pieza*) bar; (*de pan*) loaf; (*de chocolate*) bar; ~ **de labios** lipstick **2.** (*en un bar*) bar **3.** (*raya*) dash; (*signo gráfico*) slash; MÚS bar **4.** COMPUT

~ **de comandos** taskbar; ~ **de desplazamiento** scroll bar; ~ **espaciadora** space bar; ~ **inversa** backslash; ~ **de navegación** navigation bar

barraca [ba·'rra·ka] *f* 1. (*casa*) cabin 2. (*choza*) hut 3. *AmL* MIL barracks

barranco [ba·'rran·ko] *m* 1. (*despeñadero*) cliff 2. (*cauce*) ravine

barrenar [ba·rre·'nar] *vt* to drill

barrendero, -a [ba·rren·'de·ro, -a] *m, f* sweeper

barreño [ba·'rre·ɲo] *m* washbasin

barrer [ba·'rrer] *vt* 1. (*habitación*) to sweep 2. *inf* (*derrotar*) to defeat ▶ ~ **para** [*o* **hacia**] **dentro** to look after number one

barrera [ba·'rre·ra] *f* 1. (*barra*) barrier; ~ **del sonido** sound barrier 2. DEP wall

barriada [ba·'rrja·da] *f* 1. (*barrio*) district 2. *AmL* (*barrio pobre*) shanty town

barricada [ba·rri·'ka·da] *f* barricade

barriga [ba·'rri·ɣa] *f* 1. (*vientre*) belly 2. (*de una vasija*) rounded part ▶ **rascarse la** ~ to laze about, to twiddle one's thumbs

barril [ba·'rril] *m* (*cuba*) barrel; **cerveza de** ~ draught beer

barrio [ba·'rrjo] *m* 1. (*de ciudad*) district, neighborhood; ~ **comercial** business quarter 2. (*arrabal*) suburb ▶ **irse al otro** ~ *inf* to snuff it

barrizal [ba·rri·'sal, -'θal] *m* mire

barro ['ba·rro] *m* 1. (*lodo*) mud 2. (*arcilla*) clay; **de** ~ earthenware

barroco [ba·'rro·ko] *m* baroque

barroco, -a [ba·'rro·ko] *adj* baroque; *fig* overly elaborate, gaudy *pej*

barrote [ba·'rro·te] *m* (heavy) bar; **entre ~s** *fig inf* behind bars

bártulos ['bar·tu·los] *mpl* belongings *pl*

barullo [ba·'ru·jo, -ʎo] *m inf* 1. (*ruido*) din 2. (*desorden*) confusion

basalto [ba·'sal·to] *m* basalt

basar [ba·'sar] I. *vt* to ground II. *vr* ~**se en algo** (*teoría*) to be based on sth; (*persona*) to base oneself on sth

báscula ['bas·ku·la] *f* scales *pl*

base [ba·se] *f* 1. (*fundamento*) basis; ~ **de datos** COMPUT database; **partir de la** ~ **de que...** to start with the assumption that... 2. ARQUIT, MAT base ▶ **a** ~ **de**

bien *inf* really well

básico, -a ['ba·si·ko, -a] *adj* (*t. quím*) basic

basílica [ba·'si·li·ka] *f* basilica

bastante [bas·'tan·te] I. *adj* enough; **tengo** ~ **frío** I'm very cold II. *adv* (*suficientemente*) sufficiently; (*considerablemente*) rather; **con esto tengo** ~ this is enough for me

bastar [bas·'tar] I. *vi* to be enough; ¡**basta**! that's enough! II. *vr* ~**se** (*uno*) **solo** to be self-sufficient

bastardo, -a [bas·'tar·do, -a] I. *adj* 1. (*hijo*) bastard 2. (*vil*) wicked II. *m, f* bastard

bastidor [bas·ti·'ðor] *m* 1. TÉC frame(work); (*de coche*) chassis *inv*; (*de ventana*) frame 2. TEAT wing; **entre ~es** behind the scenes

basto, -a ['bas·to, -a] *adj* 1. (*grosero*) rude; (*vulgar*) coarse 2. (*superficie*) rough

bastón [bas·'ton] *m* 1. (*para andar*) stick; (*para esquiar*) ski pole 2. (*de mando*) baton

bastoncillo [bas·ton·'si·jo, -'θi·ʎo] *m diminutivo de* **bastón** small stick; ~ **de algodón** cotton swab, Q-tip®

bastos ['bas·tos] *mpl* clubs *pl* (*in Spanish deck of cards*) ▶ **pintan** ~ things are getting difficult

basura [ba·'su·ra] *f* 1. (*desperdicios*) garbage; **echar algo a la** ~ to throw sth away 2. (*lo despreciable*) trash

basurero [ba·su·'re·ro] *m* 1. (*vertedero*) garbage dump 2. (*recipiente*) trashcan

basurero, -a [ba·su·'re·ro, -a] *m, f* garbage [*o* trash] collector *mf*, garbage man *m*

bata ['ba·ta] *f* (*albornoz*) dressing gown; (*de laboratorio*) lab coat; (*de hospital*) white coat

batacazo [ba·ta·'ka·so, -θo] *m* 1. (*golpe*) thump 2. (*caída*) heavy fall; **se pegó un** ~ *inf* he/she came a cropper

batalla [ba·'ta·ja, -ʎa] *f* MIL battle; ~ **campal** pitched battle; *fig* bitter dispute

batallón [ba·ta·'jon, -'ʎon] *m* 1. MIL battalion 2. *inf* (*grupo*) group

batata [ba·'ta·ta] *f* 1. (*planta*) sweet potato plant **2.** (*tubérculo*) sweet potato **3.** *CSur* (*susto*) shock **4.** *CSur* (*vergüenza*) embarrassment **5.** *AmL* ~ **de la pierna** calf

bate ['ba·te] *m* DEP bat

batería¹ [ba·te·'ri·a] *f* **1.** *t.* TÉC battery; ~ **de cocina** pots and pans; **aparcar en** ~ to parallel park **I.** MÚS drums *pl*

batería² [ba·te·'ri·a] *mf* drummer

batida [ba·'ti·da] *f* **1.** (*de cazadores*) beat **2.** (*de policía*) raid **3.** *AmL* (*paliza*) beating, thrashing

batido [ba·'ti·do] *m* (*bebida*) milk shake

batidora [ba·ti·'do·ra] *f* (*de mano*) whisk; (*eléctrica*) mixer

batifondo [ba·ti·'fon·do] *m CSur inf* (*alboroto*) uproar; (*disturbio*) commotion; (*zozobra*) uneasiness

batín [ba·'tin] *m* (man's) dressing gown

batir [ba·'tir] **I.** *vt* **1.** (*golpear, metal*) to beat; (*las olas*) to crash against; ~ **palmas** to clap **2.** (*enemigo*) to defeat; MIL to beat; ~ **un récord** to beat a record **3.** (*un terreno*) to comb **4.** *CSur* (*denunciar*) to inform on **II.** *vr*: ~**se 1.** (*combatir*) to fight **2.** (*en duelo*) to fight a duel

batuta [ba·'tu·ta] *f* MÚS baton ▶ **llevar la** ~ to be in charge

baúl [ba·'ul] *m* **1.** (*mueble*) trunk **2.** *AmL* AUT (*portamaletas*) trunk

bausán, -ana [bau·'san, -·'sa·na] *adj AmL* (*perezoso*) lazy

bautismo [bau·'tis·mo] *m* baptism

bautizar <z → c> [bau·ti·'sar, -·'θar] *vt* REL to baptize; (*nombrar*) to christen

bautizo [bau·'ti·so, -·θo] *m* baptism; (*ceremonia*) christening; (*fiesta*) christening party

baya ['ba·ja] *f* berry

bayeta [ba·'je·ta] *f* rag, dishcloth

baza ['ba·sa, -·θa] *f* **1.** (*naipes*) trick; **meter** ~ **en algo** *inf* to butt in on sth **2.** (*provecho*) benefit; **sacar** ~ **de algo** to profit from sth

bazar [ba·'sar, -·'θar] *m* (*mercado*) bazaar

bazo ['ba·so, -·θo] *m* ANAT spleen

beatificar <c → qu> [bea·ti·fi·'kar] *vt* to beatify

beato, -a [be·'a·to, -a] *adj* REL **1.** (*piadoso*) devout **2.** (*beatificado*) beatified

bebe, -a ['be·βe, -a] *m, f AmL* baby

bebé [be·'βe] *m* baby

bebedor(a) [be·βe·'dor, -·'do·ra] *m(f)* drinker

beber [be·'βer] **I.** *vi*, *vt* **1.** (*líquido*) to drink; ~ **de la botella** to drink from the bottle; ~ **a sorbos** to sip; ~ **de un trago** to gulp **2.** (*información*) to absorb **II.** *vr*: ~**se** to drink up

bebida [be·'βi·da] *f* drink, beverage *form*; ~ **alcohólica** alcoholic drink; ~ **energética** energy drink; **darse a la** ~ to take to drink

bebido, -a [be·'βi·do, -a] *adj* (*borracho*) drunk

beca ['be·ka] *f* (*de estudios*) grant; (*por méritos*) scholarship; **conceder una** ~ **a alguien** to award a grant to sb

becario, -a [be·'ka·rjo, -a] *m, f* grant holder; (*por méritos*) scholarship holder

becerro, -a [be·'se·rro, -a; be·'θe-] *m, f* yearling calf

bechamel [be·tʃa·'mel] *f* white sauce

bedel(a) [be·'del, -·'de·la] *m(f)* beadle, proctor

begonia [be·'ɣo·nja] *f* begonia

beicon ['bei·kon] *m* bacon

beige [beis] *adj* beige

béisbol ['beis·βol] *m* DEP baseball

belduque [bel·'du·ke] *m AmL* pointed sword

belén [be·'len] *m* **1.** (*nacimiento*) crib, Nativity scene **2.** *inf* (*confusión*) confusion

Belén [be·'len] *m* Bethlehem

belga ['bel·ɣa] *adj*, *mf* Belgian

Bélgica ['bel·xi·ka] *f* Belgium

Belgrado [bel·'ɣra·do] *m* Belgrade

belicista [be·li·'sis·ta, -·'θis·ta] **I.** *adj* belligerent **II.** *mf* warmonger

bélico, -a ['be·li·ko, -a] *adj* warlike

beligerante [be·li·xe·'ran·te] *adj* belligerent

bellaquear [be·ja·ke·'ar, be·ʎa-] *vi* **1.** (*persona*) to cheat **2.** *AmL* (*caballo*) to shy

belleza [be·'je·sa, -·ʎe·θa] *f* beauty

bello, -a ['be·jo, -a; -ʎo, -a] *adj* beautiful

bellota [be·'jo·ta, -·ʎo·ta] *f* acorn

bembo, -a ['bem·bo, -a] *adj AmL* thick-lipped

bemol [be·'mol] *m* MÚS flat ▶ **tener ~es** to be difficult

benceno [ben·'se·no, ·'θe·no] *m* benzene

bencina [ben·'si·na, ·'θi·na] *f* benzine; *Arg, Chile, Par, Urug* gasoline

bendecir [ben·de·'sir, ·'θir] *irr como* decir *vt* (*sacerdote*) to bless; **~ la mesa** to say grace

bendición [ben·di·'sjon, ·'θjon] *f* **1.** (*acto*) blessing **2.** (*cosa magnífica*) marvel

bendito, -a [ben·'di·to, -a] **I.** *adj* **1.** REL blessed; (*agua*) holy; (*santo*) saintly; **¡~ sea!** *inf* thank God! **2.** (*dichoso*) lucky **II.** *m, f* kind soul

benefactor(a) [be·ne·fak·'tor, ·'to·ra] **I.** *adj* beneficent **II.** *m(f)* benefactor

beneficencia [be·ne·fi·'sen·sja, ·'θen·θja] *f* charity

beneficiar [be·ne·fi·'sjar, ·'θjar] **I.** *vt* **1.** (*favorecer*) to benefit **2.** AmL (*animal*) to slaughter **II.** *vr:* **~se** (*sacar provecho*)**~se de algo** to benefit from sth

beneficiario, -a [be·ne·fi·'sja·rjo, -a; be·ne·fi·'θja·] *m, f* beneficiary; **~ de la pensión** receiver of the pension

beneficio [be·ne·fi·sjo, ·θjo] *m* **1.** (*bien*) good **2.** (*provecho*) *t.* FIN profit **3.** AmL (*matanza*) slaughter

beneficioso, -a [be·ne·fi·'sjo·so, -a; be·ne·fi·'θjo·] *adj* **1.** (*favorable*) beneficial **2.** (*útil*) useful **3.** (*productivo*) profitable

benéfico, -a [be·'ne·fi·ko, -a] *adj* (*caritativo*) charitable

beneplácito [be·ne·'pla·si·to, ·θi·to] *m* (*permiso*) approval

benévolo, -a [be·'ne·βo·lo, -a] *adj* **1.** (*favorable*) benevolent **2.** (*clemente*) indulgent

bengala [ben·'ga·la] *f* flare; (*pequeña*) sparkler

benigno, -a [be·'niɣ·no, -a] *adj* **1.** (*persona*) kind **2.** (*clima*) mild **3.** MED benign

benjamín, -ina [ben·xa·'min] *m, f* **1.** (*hijo menor*) youngest child **2.** (*de un grupo*) youngest member

beodo, -a [be·'o·do, -a] *adj* drunk

berberecho [ber·βe·'re·tʃo] *m* cockle

berenjena [be·ren·'xe·na] *f* eggplant

Berlín [ber·'lin] *m* Berlin

berlina [ber·'li·na] *f* **1.** (*vehículo*) sedan **2.** AmL (*pastel*) jelly donut

berlinés, -esa [ber·li·'nes, ·'ne·sa] **I.** *adj* Berlin **II.** *m, f* Berliner

bermudas [ber·'mu·das] *mpl* Bermuda shorts *pl*

berrear [be·rre·'ar] *vi* **1.** (*animal*) to bellow **2.** (*llorar*) to howl **3.** (*chillar*) to screech

berrinche [be·'rrin·tʃe] *m inf* **1.** (*llorera*) tantrum **2.** (*enfado*) rage

berro ['be·rro] *m* watercress

berza ['ber·sa, ·θa] *f* cabbage

besar [be·'sar] **I.** *vt* to kiss **II.** *vr:* **~se** to kiss one another

beso ['be·so] *m* kiss; **comerse a alguien a ~s** to smother sb with kisses

bestia¹ ['bes·tja] **I.** *adj* stupid **II.** *mf* (*bruto*) brute; (*grosero*) boor

bestia² ['bes·tja] *f* animal; (*salvaje*) (wild) beast

bestial [bes·'tjal] *adj* **1.** (*de una bestia*) bestial **2.** (*muy brutal*) brutal **3.** *inf* (*muy intenso*) tremendous; (*muy grande*) huge; (*muy bueno*) marvelous

bestialidad [bes·tja·li·'ðad] *f* **1.** (*cualidad*) bestiality **2.** (*crueldad*) brutality **3.** *inf* (*gran cantidad*) **una ~ de** lots and lots of

besugo [be·'su·ɣo] *m* **1.** ZOOL bream; **ojos de ~** *inf* bulging eyes **2.** *inf* (*persona*) idiot

besuquear [be·su·ke·'ar] *vt* to cover with kisses

betabel [be·ta·'βel] *f Méx* (*remolacha*) beet; **~ forrajera** fodder beet

betún [be·'tun] *m* **1.** QUÍM bitumen **2.** (*para el calzado*) shoe polish

biaba ['bja·βa] *f Arg, Urug* (*cachetada*) slap; (*paliza*) beating

bianual [bi·a·nu·'al] *adj* biannual; BOT biennial

biberón [bi·βe·'ron] *m* feeding bottle

Biblia ['bi·βlja] *f* Bible

bíblico, -a ['bi·βli·ko, -a] *adj* biblical

bibliografía [bi·βljo·ɣra·'fi·a] *f* bibliography

biblioteca [bi·βljo·'te·ka] *f* **1.** (*local*) library; **~ de consulta** reference library

2. (*estantería*) bookshelves *pl*

bibliotecario, -a [bi·βljo·te·'ka·rjo, -a] *m, f* librarian

bicarbonato [bi·kar·βo·'na·to] *m* bicarbonate; **~ sódico** baking soda, sodium bicarbonate

bíceps ['bi·seps, -θeps] *m inv* ANAT biceps *inv*

bicho ['bi·tʃo] *m* **1.** (*animal*) (small) animal; (*insecto*) bug **2.** *inf* (*persona*) **~ raro** weirdo; **mal ~** rogue

bici ['bi·si, -θi] *f inf abr de* **bicicleta** bike

bicicleta [bi·si·'kle·ta, bi·θi·-] *f* bicycle; **~ estática** exercise bike; **~ de montaña** mountain bike

bicisenda [bi·si·'sen·da, bi·θi·-] *f Arg* bicycle [*o* bike] path

bidón [bi·'don] *m* steel drum

Bielorrusia [bje·lo·'rru·sja] *f* Byelorussia

bien ['bjen] **I.** *m* **1.** (*bienestar*) wellbeing **2.** (*bondad*) good **3.** (*provecho*) benefit **4.** *pl* ECON goods *pl* **5.** *pl* (*posesiones*) property; (*riqueza*) wealth; **~es inmuebles** real estate **II.** *adv* **1.** (*convenientemente*) properly; (*correctamente*) well; **~ mirado** well thought of; **estar ~ de salud** to be in good health; **estar (a) ~ con alguien** to get on well with sb; **hacer algo ~** to do sth well; **hacer ~ en** +*infin* to do well to +*infin* **¡pórtate ~!** behave yourself!; **te está ~** that serves you right **2.** (*con gusto*) willingly **3.** (*seguramente*) surely **4.** (*muy*) very; (*bastante*) quite; **es ~ fácil** it's very simple **5.** (*asentimiento*) all right; **¡está ~!** OK! ▸ **ahora ~** however **III.** *adj* well-off **IV.** *conj* **1.** (*aunque*) **~ que** although; **si ~** even though **2.** (*o...o*) **~...~...** either... or... **V.** *interj* well done

bienestar [bje·nes·'tar] *m* **1.** (*estado*) well-being **2.** (*riqueza*) prosperity; **estado del ~** welfare state

bienhechor(a) [bje·ne·'tʃor, -·'tʃo·ra] **I.** *adj* beneficent **II.** *m(f)* benefactor

bienintencionado, -a [bjen·in·ten·sjo·'na·do, -a; bjen·in·ten·θjo·-] *adj* well-meaning

bienvenida [bjem·be·'ni·da] *f* welcome; **dar la ~ a alguien** to welcome sb

bienvenido, -a [bjem·be·'ni·do, -a] *adj, interj* welcome; **¡~ a España!** welcome to Spain!

bife ['bi·fe] *m CSur* **1.** (*carne*) steak **2.** *inf* (*sopapo*) slap

bifurcación [bi·fur·ka·'sjon, -'θjon] *f* fork

bigamia [bi·'ɣa·mja] *f* bigamy

bigote [bi·'ɣo·te] *m* **1.** (*de hombre*) moustache, mustache **2.** *pl* (*de animal*) whiskers *pl*

bigudí [bi·ɣu·'di] *m* (hair) curler

bikini [bi·'ki·ni] *m* bikini

bilingüe [bi·'lin·gwe] *adj* bilingual

bilingüismo [bi·lin·'gwis·mo] *m* bilingualism

bilis ['bi·lis] *f inv* ANAT bile

billar [bi·'jar, -'ʎar] *m* **1.** (*juego*) billiards; **~ americano** pool **2.** (*mesa*) billiard table

billete [bi·'je·te, -'ʎe·te] *m* **1.** (*pasaje*) ticket; **~ de ida y vuelta** roundtrip ticket; **sacar un ~** to get a ticket **2.** FIN bill **3.** (*de lotería*) ticket; **~ premiado** winning ticket

billetera [bi·je·'te·ra, bi·ʎe·-] *f* billfold

billón [bi·'jon, -'ʎon] *m* **1.** (10^{12}) trillion **2.** (10^9) billion

binario, -a [bi·'na·rjo, -a] *adj* binary

bingo ['bin·go] *m* (*juego*) bingo; (*sala*) bingo hall

binoculares [bi·no·ku·'la·res] *mpl* binoculars *pl*

binóculo [bi·'no·ku·lo] *m* pince-nez

biodegradable [bio·de·ɣra·'da·βle] *adj* biodegradable

biografía [bjo·ɣra·'fi·a] *f* biography

biógrafo [bi'o·ɣra·fo] *m CSur* (*cine*) cinema

biógrafo, -a [bi'o·ɣra·fo, -a] *m, f* (*persona*) biographer

biología [bio·lo·'xi·a] *f* biology

biólogo, -a [bi'o·lo·ɣo, -a] *m, f* biologist

biombo [bi·'om·bo] *m* (folding) screen, bionic

biopsia [bi·'oβ·sja] *f* biopsy

bioquímica [bio·'ki·mi·ka] *f* biochemistry

biosfera [bios·'fe·ra] *f* biosphere

bipartidismo [bi··par·ti·'dis·mo] *m* POL two-party system

biplano [bi·'pla·no] *m* biplane

biquini [bi·'ki·ni] *m* bikini

birlar [bir·'lar] *vt inf* (*hurtar*) to swipe

birome [bi·'ro·me] *m o f CSur* ball-point (pen)

birra ['bi·rra] *f inf* beer

birria ['bi·rrja] *f* 1. (*persona*) drip; **va hecho una ~** he looks really scruffy 2. (*objeto*) rubbish, trash; **la película es una ~** the film is rubbish

birriondo, -a [bi·'rrjon·do, -a] *adj Méx* 1. (*callejero*) street; (*animales*) jumpy 2. (*enamoradizo*) easily infatuated

biruje [bi·'ru·xe] *m AmL*, **biruji** [bi·'ru·xi] *m* cold wind

bis [bis] I. *interj, m* MÚS encore II. *adv* 1. MÚS bis 2. (*piso*) **7 ~** 7A

bisabuelo, -a [bi·sa·'βwe·lo, -a] *m, f* great-grandfather *m*, great-grandmother *f*

bisagra [bi·'sa·γra] *f* hinge

biscote [bis·'ko·te] *m* rusk

bisexual [bi·sek·'swal] *adj* bisexual

bisiesto [bi·'sjes·to] *adj* **año ~** leap year

bisílabo, -a [bi·'si·la·βo, -a] *adj* two-syllable

bisnieto, -a [bis·'nje·to, -a] *m, f* great-grandson *m*, great-granddaughter *f*

bisonte [bi·'son·te] *m* (*americano*) buffalo; (*europeo*) bison

bisturí [bis·tu·'ri] *m* scalpel

bisutería [bi·su·te·'ri·a] *f* costume jewelry

bit [bit] *m* <bits> COMPUT bit; **~ de parada** stop bit

bizco, -a ['bis·ko, -a; 'biθ-] *adj* cross-eyed

bizcocho [biθ·'ko·tʃo, biθ-] I. *adj Méx* (*cobarde*) cowardly II. *m* CULIN sponge cake

blanca ['blaŋ·ka] *f* 1. MÚS half note 2. (*de dominó*) double-blank ► **estar sin ~** *inf* to be broke

blanco ['blaŋ·ko] *m* 1. (*color*) white; **película en ~ y negro** black and white film 2. (*en un escrito*) blank space; **cheque en ~** blank check 3. (*diana*) target; **dar en el ~** *fig* to hit the mark ► **pasar la noche en ~** to have a sleepless night; **~ del ojo** white of the eye; **quedarse en ~** to go blank

blanco, -a ['blaŋ·ko, -a] I. *adj* white;

(*tez*) pale II. *m, f* white man *m*, white woman *f*

blando, -a ['blan·do] *adj* 1. (*objeto*) soft 2. (*carácter*) mild; (*blandengue*) soft; (*cobarde*) cowardly

blanquear [blaŋ·ke·'ar] I. *vi* to whiten II. *vt* 1. (*poner blanco*) to whiten; (*tejido*) to bleach 2. (*dinero*) to launder

blasfemar [blas·fe·'mar] *vi* 1. REL to blaspheme 2. (*maldecir*) **~ de algo** to swear about sth

blasfemia [blas·'fe·mja] *f* 1. REL blasphemy 2. (*injuria*) insult

blasfemo, -a [blas·'fe·mo, -a] *adj* blasphemous

bledo ['ble·do] *m* BOT goosefoot ► (**no**) **me importa un ~** I couldn't care less

blindado, -a [blin·'da·do] *adj* MIL armor-plated; **puerta blindada** reinforced door

blindaje [blin·'da·xe] *m* (*armor*) plating

blindar [blin·'dar] *vt* to plate

bloc [blok] *m* <blocs> (*cuaderno*) notepad

blofear [blo·fe·'ar] *vi AmL* (*engañar*) to bluff

bloque ['blo·ke] *m* 1. block; **~ de viviendas** block of flats 2. POL bloc ► **en ~** en bloc

bloquear [blo·ke·'ar] I. *vt* 1. (*el paso*) *t.* DEP to block; MIL to blockade 2. (*aislar*) to cut off 3. TÉC to jam 4. FIN to freeze 5. (*obstaculizar*) to obstruct II. *vr:* **~se** (*cosa*) to jam; (*persona*) to have a mental block

bloqueo [blo·'keo] *m* 1. (*de paso*) *t.* DEP blocking; MIL blockade; **~ comercial** COM trade embargo 2. (*de un mecanismo*) jamming 3. (*mental*) block

blusa ['blu·sa] *f* blouse

bluyín [blu·'jin] <bluyines> *m* blue jeans *pl*

boa ['boa] *f* boa

bobada [bo·'βa·da] *f* silly thing

bobina [bo·'βi·na] *f* ELEC coil; (*de película*) reel

bobo, -a ['bo·βo] I. *adj* (*tonto*) silly II. *m, f* (*tonto*) fool

boca ['bo·ka] *f* 1. ANAT mouth; **~ abajo** face down(ward); **~ arriba** face up(ward); **estaba tumbada ~ abajo/ arriba** she was lying on her stomach/ on her back; **andar de ~ en ~** to be the subject of gossip **2.** (*abertura*) opening; **~ de metro** subway entrance; **~ de riego** hydrant **3.** (*agujero*) hole; (*de cañón*) muzzle; (*de volcán*) mouth ▶ **quedarse con la ~ abierta** to be dumbfounded; **a pedir de ~** perfectly

bocacalle [bo·ka·'ka·je, -ʎe] *f* (*de una calle*) street entrance; (*calle secundaria*) side street

bocadillo [bo·ka·'di·jo, -ʎo] *m* **1.** (*sándwich*) sandwich **2.** (*tira cómica*) balloon, bubble

bocado [bo·'ka·do] *m* **1.** (*mordisco*) mouthful **2.** (*freno*) bit

bocajarro [bo·ka·'xa·rro] *adv* **a ~** (*tirar*) point-blank

bocanada [bo·ka·'na·da] *f* puff; **echar ~s** *fig* to boast

bocaza(s) [bo·ka·'sa(s), -θa(s)] *mf* (*inv*) loudmouth

boceto [bo·'se·to, bo·'θe-] *m* sketch

boche ['bo·tʃe] *m* *CSur* *inf* (*bronca*) telling-off

bochinche [bo·'tʃin·tʃe] *m* *AmL* piece of gossip

bochorno [bo·'tʃor·no] *m* **1.** METEO sultry weather **2.** (*sofocación*) stifling atmosphere **3.** (*vergüenza*) shame; **me da ~ que esté mirando** it embarrasses me that he/she is looking

bochornoso, -a [bo·tʃor·'no·so, -a] *adj* **1.** METEO sultry **2.** (*vergonzoso*) shameful

bocina [bo·'si·na, bo·'θi-] *f* **1.** (*de coche*) horn; **tocar la ~** to blow the horn **2.** (*megáfono*) megaphone

bocio ['bo·sjo, 'bo·θjo] *m* goiter

boda ['bo·da] *f* **1.** (*ceremonia*) wedding **2.** (*fiesta*) wedding reception; **noche de ~s** wedding night

bodega [bo·'de·ɣa] *f* **1.** (*habitación*) wine cellar **2.** (*tienda*) wine shop; (*taberna*) bar **3.** NÁUT (*en un puerto*) storeroom; (*en un buque*) hold

bodrio ['bo·drjo] *m* **1.** *inf*(*cosa*) rubbish, trash; **esta película es un ~** this film is rubbish **2.** *AmL* (*confusión*) mess

BOE ['bo·e] *m* *abr de* **Boletín Oficial del Estado** ≈ The Congressional Record

bofetada [bo·fe·'ta·da] *f* smack; **dar una ~ a alguien** to slap sb

bofia ['bo·fja] *f* *inf*cops *pl*

boga ['bo·ɣa] *f* (*moda*) vogue; **estar en ~** to be in vogue

bogavante [bo·ɣa·'βan·te] *m* lobster

bogotano, -a [bo·ɣo·'ta·no, -a] **I.** *adj* of/from Bogotá **II.** *m, f* native/inhabitant of Bogotá

Bohemia [bo·'e·mja] *f* Bohemia

bohío [bo·'i·o] *m* *AmL* rustic hut

boicot <boicots> [boi·'ko(t)] *m* boycott

boicotear [boi·ko·te·'ar] *vt* to boycott

boina ['boi·na] *f* beret

bol [bol] *m* (*tazón*) bowl

bola ['bo·la] *f* **1.** (*cuerpo*) ball; **~ del mundo** globe; **~ de nieve** snowball **2.** (*canica*) marble **3.** *inf*(*mentira*) fib; (*rumor*) rumor ▶ **no dar pie con ~** to be unable to do anything right; **ir a su ~** to go one's own way

bolado [bo·'la·do] *m* *AmL* (*asunto*) matter

boleadoras [bo·lea·'do·ras] *fpl* *CSur* bolas *pl*

bolear [bo·le·'ar] *vt* **1.** *CSur* (*cazar*) to hunt; (*atrapar*) to catch with a lasso **2.** *Méx* (*zapatos*) to polish **3.** (*alumno*) to fail

bolera [bo·'le·ra] *f* bowling alley

bolero [bo·'le·ro] *m* MÚS bolero

boleta [bo·'le·ta] *f* *AmL* **1.** (*entrada*) ticket **2.** (*documento*) permit **3.** (*para votar*) ballot (paper)

boletería [bo·le·te·'ri·a] *f* *AmL* (*taquilla*) ticket agency [*o* office]; TEAT box office

boletero, -a [bo·le·'te·ro, -a] *m, f* *AmL* (*taquillero*) ticket clerk

boletín [bo·le·'tin] *m* **1.** (*publicación*) bulletin **2.** (*informe*) report; **~ de noticias** news report

boleto [bo·'le·to] *m* **1.** *AmL* (*entrada*) ticket **2.** (*de quiniela*) coupon **3.** *Arg* (*mentira*) lie

boliche [bo·'li·tʃe] *m* **1.** (*bola*) jack **2.** (*bochas*) bowls; (*bolos*) ninepins *pl* **3.** *AmL* (*establecimiento*) grocery shop **4.** *Arg* *inf*(*bar*) bar

bólido ['bo·li·do] *m* AUTO racing car

bolígrafo [bo·'li·ɣra·fo] *m* (ballpoint) pen

bolillo [bo·'li·jo, -ʎo] *m* 1. (*de encajes*) bobbin 2. Col (*de tambor*) drumstick 3. *Méx* (*panecillo*) bread roll

bolívar [bo·'li·βar] *m* FIN bolivar

Bolivia [bo·'li·βja] *f* Bolivia

boliviano [bo·li·'βja·no] *m* (*moneda*) boliviano

boliviano, -a [bo·li·'βja·no, -a] *adj, m, f* Bolivian

bollería [bo·je·'ri·a, bo·ʎe-] *f* (*tienda*) baker's; (*bollos*) buns, baked goods *pl*

bollo ['bo·jo, -ʎo] *m* 1. (*panecillo*) bun; (*pastelillo*) cake 2. (*abolladura*) dent 3. (*confusión*) mix-up

bolo ['bo·lo] *m* DEP skittle; (*juego de*) ~s ≈ ninepins

bolsa ['bol·sa] *f* 1. (*saco*) bag 2. (*bolso*) handbag, purse; ~ **de plástico** plastic bag; ~ **de la compra** shopping bag; ~**s de los ojos** bags under the eyes 3. FIN stock exchange; ~ **de trabajo** employment bureau; ~ **negra** *AmL* black market; ~ **de valores** stock exchange 4. *AmL* (*bolsillo*) pocket

bolsillo [bol·'si·jo, -ʎo] *m* 1. (*en una prenda*) pocket; **edición de** ~ pocket edition 2. (*monedero*) purse; **rascarse el** ~ *inf* to pay up

bolso ['bol·so] *m* bag; (*pequeño*) handbag, purse; (*en una vela*) bulge

boludo, -a [bo·'lu·do, -a] *inf* I. *adj* Arg, Urug (*imbécil*) dummy II. *m, f* Arg, Urug (*imbécil*) jerk

bomba ['bom·ba] I. *f* 1. *t.* MIL bomb; ~ **de relojería** time bomb 2. TÉC pump; ~ **neumática** air pump 3. *AmL* (*bola*) ball 4. *AmL* (*pompa*) bubble 5. *AmL inf* (*borrachera*) **pegarse una** ~ to get drunk ▸ **a prueba de** ~**s** bomb-proof II. *adj inf* astounding; **pasarlo** ~ to have a great time

bombacha [bom·'ba·tʃa] *f* CSur (*ropa interior*) panties *pl*

bombardear [bom·bar·de·'ar] *vt* 1. MIL to bomb 2. *inf* (*abrumar*) to overwhelm 3. FÍS to bombard

bombardeo [bom·bar·'deo] *m* 1. MIL bombing 2. FÍS bombardment

bombazo [bom·'ba·so, -θo] *m* bomb explosion; *inf* (*sensación*) bombshell

bombear [bom·be·'ar] *vt* 1. (*un líquido*) to pump 2. (*un balón*) to lob

bombero [bom·'be·ro] *m* 1. (*oficio*) fireman 2. *pl* (*cuerpo*) fire brigade; **coche de** ~**s** fire engine

bombilla [bom·'bi·ja, -ʎa] *f* 1. ELEC (light) bulb 2. *AmS* (*caña*) drinking straw

bombín [bom·'bin] *m* bowler hat

bombo ['bom·bo] *m* 1. MÚS (*tambor*) bass drum; (*en un sorteo*) drum 2. (*elogio*) exaggerated praise ▸ **tener la cabeza hecha un** ~ to have a splitting headache

bombón [bom·'bon] *m* 1. (*golosina*) chocolate 2. *inf* (*mujer*) **es un** ~ she's gorgeous

bombona [bom·'bo·na] *f* (*de gas*) cylinder

bonachón, -ona [bo·na·'tʃon, -·'tʃo·na] *adj* 1. (*buenazo*) kindly 2. (*crédulo*) naive

bonaerense [bo·nae·'ren·se] I. *adj* of/from Buenos Aires province II. *mf* native/inhabitant of Buenos Aires province

bondad [bon·'dad] *f* 1. (*de bueno*) goodness 2. (*de amable*) kindness; **tenga la** ~ **de seguirme** be so kind as to follow me

bondadoso, -a [bon·da·'do·so, -a] *adj* good-natured, kind

bongo ['bon·go] *m* *AmL* (*canoa*) small canoe; (*balsa*) small raft

bonificación [bo·ni·fi·ka·'sjon, -'θjon] *f* (*gratificación*) bonus

bonificar <c > qu> [bo·ni·fi·'kar] *vt* (*abonar*) to improve

bonito [bo·'ni·to] I. *m* ZOOL bonito II. *adv* *AmL* nicely

bonito, -a [bo·'ni·to, -a] *adj* pretty

bonitura [bo·ni·'tu·ra] *f* *AmL* (*hermosura*) beauty

bono ['bo·no] *m* voucher; COM bond

bonsái [bon·'sai] *m* <bonsais> bonsai

boquerón [bo·ke·'ron] *m* ZOOL (fresh) anchovy

boquete [bo·'ke·te] *m* opening; (*en pared*) hole

boquiabierto, -a [bo·kja·'βjer·to, -a] *adj* open-mouthed; **dejar a alguien** ~ *fig* to astonish sb

boquilla [bo·'ki·ja, -ʎa] f 1. mús mouthpiece 2. (de cigarrillos) cigarette holder 3. téc nozzle ▶ **decir algo de** ~ to say sth without meaning it

borda ['bor·da] f náut (borde) gunwale; **motor fuera (de)** ~ outboard motor; **echar algo por la** ~ t. fig to throw sth overboard

bordado [bor·'da·ðo] m embroidery

bordar [bor·'dar] vt to embroider; inf to do superbly

borde ['bor·ðe] I. adj inf (persona) difficult, hostile II. m (de camino) verge; (de mesa) edge; (de río) bank

bordear [bor·ðe·'ar] vt 1. (ir por) to skirt; (en coche) to drive along 2. (estar) to border on 3. (aproximarse) to verge on; **su comportamiento bordea la locura** his/her behavior borders on madness

bordillo [bor·'di·jo, -ʎo] m curb

bordo ['bor·ðo] m 1. náut board; **ir a** ~ to go on board 2. Méx (presa) dam

boreal [bo·re·'al] adj northern

borrachera [bo·rra·'tʃe·ra] f 1. (ebriedad) drunkenness; **agarrar una** ~ to get drunk 2. (juerga) drinking binge

borracho, -a [bo·'rra·tʃo, -a] I. adj 1. ser (alcohólico) hard drinking 2. estar (ebrio) drunk; **estar** ~ **como una cuba** inf to be as drunk as a lord; ~ **de algo** fig elated with sth II. m, f drunk

borrador [bo·rra·'ðor] m 1. (escrito) rough draft 2. (cuaderno) scribbling pad 3. (utensilio) duster; (esponja) board rubber

borrar [bo·'rrar] I. vt 1. (con goma) to rub out; (con esponja) to wipe off 2. (tachar) to cross out; comput to delete 3. (huellas) to remove II. vr: ~**se** to blur; ~**se de algo** to resign from sth

borrasca [bo·'rras·ka] f meteo squall; (tempestad) storm

borrascoso, -a [bo·rras·'ko·so, -a] adj meteo stormy

borrego, -a [bo·'rre·ɣo, -a] m, f 1. (cordero) lamb 2. (persona) meek person 3. AmL (noticia falsa) hoax

borrón [bo·'rron] m 1. (mancha) stain 2. (defecto) blemish ▶ **hacer** ~ **y cuenta nueva** to start with a clean

slate

borroso, -a [bo·'rro·so, -a] adj (escritura) unclear; (foto) blurred

Bósforo ['bos·fo·ro] m Bosporus

bosnio, -a ['bos·njo, -a] adj, m, f Bosnian

bosque ['bos·ke] m wood; ~ **frondoso** broad-leaved woodland

bosquejo [bos·'ke·xo] m sketch

bostezar <z → c> [bos·te·'sar, -'θar] vi to yawn

bostezo [bos·'te·so, -θo] m yawn

bota ['bo·ta] I. f 1. (calzado) boot; **ponerse las** ~**s** inf to strike it rich 2. (cuba) large barrel II. adj Méx 1. (torpe) dim 2. (borracho) drunk

botado, -a [bo·'ta·ðo, -a] adj 1. AmC (malgastador) spendthrift 2. Ecua (resignado) resigned; (resuelto) resolute 3. Guat (tímido) shy 4. Méx (barato) dirt cheap

botador(a) [bo·ta·'ðor] adj AmL spendthrift

botánica [bo·'ta·ni·ka] f botany

botánico, -a [bo·'ta·ni·ko, -a] I. adj botanical II. m, f botanist

botar [bo·'tar] I. vi (pelota) to bounce; (persona) to jump ▶ **estar (uno) que bota** to be hopping mad II. vt 1. (pelota) to bounce 2. náut (barco) to launch 3. AmL (tirar) to throw away 4. AmL (expulsar) to fire; **lo** ~**on del colegio** he was expelled from school 5. AmL (derrochar) to squander 6. AmL (extraviar) to lose

bote ['bo·te] m 1. (golpe) blow 2. (salto) jump; **pegar un** ~ to jump 3. (de pelota) bounce; **la pelota dio cuatro** ~**s** the ball bounced four times 4. (vasija) jar 5. (en la lotería) jackpot 6. náut boat; ~ **salvavidas** lifeboat ▶ **a** ~ **pronto** (adj) sudden; (adv) suddenly; **chupar del** ~ inf to feather one's nest; **darse el** ~ inf to beat it; **la tiene en el** ~ inf he has her in his pocket

botella [bo·'te·ja, -ʎa] f bottle; ~ **de cerveza** bottle of beer

botija [bo·'ti·xa] f 1. (vasija) earthenware jug 2. AmL (tesoro) buried treasure

botín [bo·'tin] m 1. (calzado) high shoe 2. mil booty

botiquín [bo·ti·'kin] *m* medicine chest; (*de emergencia*) first-aid kit

botón [bo·'ton] *m* **1.** (*en vestidos*) button **2.** ELEC knob; ~ **de muestra** sample; *fig* illustration; ~ **de opciones** COMPUT option button **3.** MÚS key **4.** CSur *pey* (*policía*) cop

botones [bo·'to·nes] *m inv* errand boy; (*de hotel*) bellhop

boutique [bu·'tik] *f* boutique

bóveda ['bo·βe·da] *f* ARQUIT vault; ~ **celeste** firmament

bovino, -a [bo·'βi·no, -a] *adj* bovine

box [boks] *m* **1.** (*para caballos*) stall **2.** AmL (*boxeo*) boxing **3.** AmC (*postal*) mailbox **4.** *pl* AUTO pits *pl*; **entrar en ~es** to make a pit-stop

boxeador(a) [bok·sea·'dor, --·'do·ra] *m(f)* boxer

boxear [bok·se·'ar] *vi* to box

boxeo [bok·'seo] *m* boxing

boya ['bo·ja] *f* buoy; (*en una red*) float

boyante [bo·'jan·te] *adj* prosperous

boy scout <boy scouts> ['boi es·'kaut] *mf* boy scout

bozal [bo·'sal, -'θal] *m* **1.** (*de perro*) muzzle **2.** AmL (*cabestro*) halter; (*cuerda*) headstall

bracero [bra·'se·ro, -'θe·ro] *m* AmL farmhand; (*peón*) laborer

braga ['bra·ya] *f pl* (*de mujer*) panties *pl*

bragueta [bra·'ye·ta] *f* fly

braille ['brai·le] *m* Braille

bramar [bra·'mar] *vi* (*animal*) to roar; (*persona*) to bluster; (*viento*) to howl

brandy ['bran·di] *m* brandy

branquia ['bran·kja] *f* gill

brasa ['bra·sa] *f* ember; **a la ~** grilled

brasero [bra·'se·ro] *m* **1.** (*estufa*) brazier **2.** AmL (*fuego*) fireplace; (*hogar*) hearth

Brasil [bra·'sil] *m* (**el**) ~ Brazil

brasileño, -a [bra·si·'le·no, -a] *adj, m, f* Brazilian

brava ['bra·βa] *f Cuba* (*golpe*) punch; **dar una ~** to intimidate; **a la ~ por las ~s** by force

bravío [bra·'βi·o] *m* fierceness

bravío, -a [bra·'βi·o, -a] *adj* **1.** (*animal*) wild; (*sin domar*) untamed **2.** (*perso-*

na) impetuous

bravo ['bra·βo] *interj* well done

bravo, -a ['bra·βo, -a] *adj* **1.** (*valiente*) brave **2.** (*salvaje*) wild; (*mar*) stormy **3.** (*picante*) hot

brazalete [bra·sa·'le·te, bra·θa·-] *m* (*pulsera*) bracelet; (*banda*) armband

brazo ['bra·so, -θo] *m* **1.** ANAT arm; ~ **derecho** *fig* right-hand man; **cruzarse de ~s** to fold one's arms; *fig* to stand by and do nothing; **dar el ~ a torcer** to give in; **ir cogidos del ~** to walk arm-in-arm; **recibir a alguien con los ~s abiertos** to welcome sb with open arms **2.** (*de una silla*) arm **3.** GEO (*del río*) branch **4.** (*poder*) power

brea ['brea] *f* tar

brebaje [bre·'βa·xe] *m* (*bebida*) brew; (*medicina*) potion

brecha ['bre·tʃa] *f* **1.** MIL breach **2.** (*abertura*) opening; (*en una pared*) gap **3.** (*herida*) gash ▶ **estar en la ~** to be in the thick of things

brécol(es) ['bre·kol, --·ko·l(es)] *m(pl)* broccoli

bregar <g → gu> [bre·'yar] *vi* **1.** (*reñir*) to quarrel **2.** (*luchar*) to struggle **3.** (*trabajar*) to slave away

Bretaña [bre·'taɲa] *f* Brittany; **Gran ~** Great Britain

breva ['bre·βa] *f* **1.** (*higo*) early fig **2.** (*cigarro*) flat cigar **3.** AmL (*tabaco*) chewing tobacco

breve ['bre·βe] **I.** *adj* (*de duración*) brief; (*de extensión*) short; **en ~** shortly **II.** *m* PREN short news item

brevedad [bre·βe·'dad] *f* (*duración*) brevity; (*extensión*) shortness

bribón, -ona [bri·'βon, --·'bo·na] *adj* **1.** (*pícaro*) rascally **2.** (*vago*) idle

bricolaje [bri·ko·'la·xe] *m* do-it-yourself

brida [bri·'da] *f* **1.** (*de caballo*) bridle **2.** TÉC flange

brigada¹ [bri·'ya·da] *f* **1.** MIL brigade **2.** (*de policía*) squad

brigada² [bri·'ya·da] *m* MIL sergeant major

brillante [bri·'jan·te, -'ʎan·te] **I.** *m* diamond **II.** *adj* **1.** (*luz*) bright; (*joya*) sparkling **2.** (*compañía*) brilliant

brillantez [bri·jan·'tes, bri·ʎan·'teθ] *f t.*

fig brilliance

brillantina [bri·jan·'ti·na, bri·ʎan-] *f* brilliantine, hair cream

brillar [bri·'jar, -'ʎar] *vi* to shine; **~ por su ausencia** *irón* to be conspicuous by one's absence

brillo ['bri·jo, -ʎo] *m* **1.** (*cualidad*) shine; (*reflejo*) glow; **dar ~ a algo** to polish sth **2.** (*gloria*) splendor

brincar <c → qu> [brin·'kar] *vi* to hop; (*hacia arriba*) to jump; **~ de alegría** *fig* to jump for joy

brinco ['brin·ko] *m* hop; **dar ~s** to hop; **de un ~** in one bound; *AmL* right away

brindar [brin·'dar] I. *vi* to drink a toast; **~ por alguien** to drink to sb II. *vt* to offer

brindis ['brin·dis] *m inv* toast; **echar un ~** to drink a toast

brío ['bri·o] *m* **1.** (*energía*) spirit **2.** (*pujanza*) drive

brisa ['bri·sa] *f* breeze

británico, -a [bri·'ta·ni·ko, -a] I. *adj* British; **inglés ~** British English II. *m, f* Briton

brizna ['bris·na, 'briθ-] *f* **1.** (*hebra*) strand; *BOT* blade **2.** (*porción*) scrap **3.** *AmL* (*llovizna*) drizzle

brocha ['bro·ʧa] *f* brush; (*de afeitar*) shaving brush; **pintor de ~ gorda** house painter

broche ['bro·ʧe] *m* **1.** (*en la ropa*) clasp; (*de adorno*) brooch; **~ de oro** *fig* finishing touch **2.** *AmL* (*sujetapapeles*) paper clip **3.** *pl AmL* (*gemelos*) cufflinks *pl*

brocheta [bro·'ʧe·ta] *f* skewer

broma ['bro·ma] *f* **1.** (*gracia*) fun, kidding **2.** (*tontería*) joke; **~ pesada** practical joke; **decir algo en ~** to be kidding; **gastar ~s a alguien** to play jokes on sb; **~s aparte...** joking apart...; **estoy de ~** I'm not serious; **no estoy para ~s** I'm in no mood for jokes; **¡ni en ~!** no way!

bromear [bro·me·'ar] *vi* to joke, to kid; **¿bromeas?** are you kidding?

bromista [bro·'mis·ta] I. *adj* fond of jokes II. *mf* joker

bronca ['bron·ka] *f* **1.** (*riña*) argument **2.** (*reprimenda*) earful **3.** *AmL* (*enfado*) anger

bronce ['bron·se, -θe] *m* bronze

bronceado [bron·se·'a·do, bron·θe-] *m* (*de la piel*) tan

bronceado, -a [bron·se·'a·do, -a; bron·θe-] *adj* (*piel*) tanned

bronceador [bron·sea·'dor, bron·θe-] *m* suntan lotion

broncear [bron·se·'ar, bron·θe-] I. *vt* (*un objeto*) to bronze; (*la piel*) to tan II. *vr:* **~se** to get a (sun)tan

bronco, -a ['bron·ko, -a] *adj* **1.** (*voz*) gruff **2.** (*genio*) surly **3.** *AmL* (*caballo*) untamed

bronquio ['bron·kjo] *m ANAT* bronchial tube

bronquitis [bron·'ki·tis] *f inv MED* bronchitis

broqueta [bro·'ke·ta] *f* skewer

brotar [bro·'tar] *vi* **1.** *BOT* to sprout; (*semilla*) to germinate **2.** (*agua*) to flow **3.** (*enfermedad*) to break out

brote ['bro·te] *m* **1.** *BOT* shoot; **~s de soja** bean sprouts **2.** (*erupción*) outbreak

bruces ['bru·ses, 'bru·θes] *adv* **caer de ~** to fall headlong

bruja ['bru·xa] *f* witch

brujería [bru·xe·'ri·a] *f* witchcraft

brujo ['bru·xo] *m* **1.** (*hechicero*) wizard **2.** *AmL* (*curandero*) medicine man

brújula ['bru·xu·la] *f* compass; **perder la ~** *fig* to lose one's bearings

bruma ['bru·ma] *f* mist

brumoso, -a [bru·'mo·so, -a] *adj* misty

brusco, -a ['brus·ko, -a] *adj* **1.** (*repentino*) sudden **2.** (*persona*) abrupt

Bruselas [bru·'se·las] *f* Brussels

brutal [bru·'tal] *adj* **1.** (*violento*) brutal **2.** *inf* (*enorme*) huge **3.** *inf* (*estupendo*) tremendous

brutalidad [bru·ta·li·'dad] *f* **1.** (*calidad*) brutality **2.** (*acción*) brutal act, crime **3.** (*cantidad*) huge amount

bruto ['bru·to] *m* brute

bruto, -a ['bru·to, -a] *adj* **1.** (*brutal*) brutal **2.** (*rudo*) uncouth **3.** (*estúpido*) stupid **4.** (*inculto*) rough **5.** (*tosco*) uncut; **diamante en ~** rough diamond **6.** (*peso*) gross

buceador(a) [bu·sea·'dor, -·'do·ra; bu·θea-] *m(f)* diver

bucear [bu·se·'ar, bu·θe-] *vi* to dive

buceo [bu·'seo, -'θeo] *m* diving

buche ['bu·tʃe] *m* **1.** (*en las aves*) crop **2.** *inf* (*estómago*) belly

bucle ['bu·kle] *m* (*onda*) curl; COMPUT loop

budismo [bu·'dis·mo] *m* Buddhism

budista [bu·'dis·ta] *adj, mf* Buddhist

buen [bwen] *adj v.* **bueno**

buenaventura [bwe·na·βen·'tu·ra] *f* **1.** (*suerte*) good luck **2.** (*adivinación*) fortune

buenazo, -a [bwe·'na·so, -a; -θo, -a] *m, f* good-natured person

bueno ['bwe·no] *interj* OK

bueno, -a ['bwe·no, -a] *adj* <mejor *o* más bueno, el mejor *o* buenísimo *o* bonísimo> *ante sustantivo masc. sing.:* buen **1.** (*calidad*) good; (*tiempo*) fine; (*constitución*) sound; (*decisión*) right; **~s días** good morning; **buenas tardes/noches** good afternoon/evening; **buen viaje** have a good journey; **hace ~** it's nice weather; **dar algo por ~** to accept sth; **estar de buenas** to be in a good mood; **por las buenas o por las malas** by fair means or foul **2.** (*apropiado*) suitable **3.** (*honesto*) honest; (*bondadoso*) kindly; (*niño*) well-behaved; **es buena gente** he/she is a nice person **4.** (*sano*) healthy **5.** *inf* (*atractivo*) attractive; **está buenísima** she's hot stuff **6.** (*bonito*) fine; **¡buena la has hecho!** *irón* you've done it now!; **¡estaría ~!** *fig* I should think not!

buey [bwei] *m* ZOOL ox

búfalo ['bu·fa·lo] *m* buffalo

bufanda [bu·'fan·da] *f* scarf

bufar [bu·'far] *vi* **1.** (*resoplar*) to snort; **está que bufa** he/she is really furious **2.** *AmL* (*oler mal*) to stink

bufete [bu·'fe·te] *m* **1.** (*escritorio*) desk **2.** (*de abogado*) lawyer's office

bufido [bu·'fi·do] *m* **1.** (*resoplido*) snort **2.** (*exabrupto*) sharp remark

bufón, -ona [bu·'fon, --'fo·na] *m, f* **1.** (*bromista*) joker **2.** TEAT buffoon

buhardilla [bwar·'di·ja, -ʎa] *f* (*vivienda*) garret

búho ['bu·o] *m* ZOOL owl

buitre ['bwi·tre] *m* **1.** ZOOL vulture, buzzard **2.** *inf* (*persona*) sponger

bujía [bu·'xi·a] *f* **1.** (*vela*) candle **2.** AUTO spark plug

bula ['bu·la] *f* (*papal*) bull

bulbo ['bul·βo] *m* bulb

bule ['bu·le] *m* *Méx* BOT gourd

Bulgaria [bul·'ɣa·rja] *f* Bulgaria

búlgaro, -a ['bul·ɣa·ro] *adj, m, f* Bulgarian

bulimia [bu·'li·mja] *f* MED bulimia

bulla ['bu·ja, -ʎa] *f* **1.** (*ruido*) racket **2.** *AmL* (*pelea*) brawl

bullicio [bu·'jis·jo, -'ʎi·θjo] *m* uproar

bullicioso, -a [bu·ji·'sjo·so, -a; bu·ʎi·'θjo-] *adj* noisy

bullir <3. *pret* bulló> [bu·'jir, -'ʎir] *vi* **1.** (*hervir*) to boil; (*borbotar*) to bubble; **le bulle la sangre** (**en las venas**) *fig* he/she is a bundle of energy **2.** (*moverse*) to stir

bulo ['bu·lo] *m* false rumor

bulto ['bul·to] *m* **1.** (*tamaño*) size; **a ~** roughly; **escurrir el ~** *inf* to pass the buck **2.** (*importancia*) importance; **un error de ~** a major error **3.** (*objeto*) mass **4.** (*paquete*) piece of luggage **5.** MED swelling

búnker ['bun·ker] *m* MIL bunker

buñuelo [bu·'nwe·lo] *m* doughnut, donut

buque ['bu·ke] *m* (*barco*) ship; **~ de carga** freighter; **~ de guerra** warship; **~ insignia** flagship

buraco [bu·'ra·ko] *m* *Arg, Par, Urug* hole

burbuja [bur·'βu·xa] *f* bubble

burbujear [bur·βu·xe·'ar] *vi* to bubble

burdel [bur·'del] *m* brothel

burdo, -a ['bur·do, -a] *adj* coarse; (*excusa*) clumsy

burgués, -esa [bur·'ɣes, --'ɣe·sa] *adj t. pey* bourgeois, middle-class

burguesía [bur·ɣe·'si·a] *f* bourgeoisie

burla [bur·la] *f* **1.** (*mofa*) taunt; **hacer ~ de alguien** to make fun of sb **2.** (*engaño*) hoax

burlar [bur·'lar] **I.** *vt* to cheat **II.** *vr:* **~se** to joke

burlón, -ona [bur·'lon, --'lo·na] **I.** *adj* mocking **II.** *m, f* **1.** (*mofador*) mocker **2.** (*guasón*) joker

burocracia [bu·ro·'kra·sja, -θja] *f* bureaucracy

burócrata [bu·ro·'kra·ta] *mf* bureaucrat

burocrático, -a [bu·ro·'kra·ti·ko, -a] *adj* bureaucratic

burrada [bu·'rra·ða] *f inf* silly thing; **de- cir ~s** to talk nonsense

burro ['bu·rro] *m* 1. *AmC* (*escalera*) step ladder 2. *AmC* (*columpio*) swing

burro, -a ['bu·rro, -a] I. *m, f* ZOOL don- key; **~ de carga** *t. fig* beast of burden ▶ **apearse** del **~** to admit to one's mistake; **no ver tres en un ~** to be as blind as a bat II. *adj* 1. (*tonto*) stupid 2. (*obstinado*) obstinate

bursátil [bur·'sa·til] *adj* stock exchange

bus [bus] *m* COMPUT bus

busca[1] ['bus·ka] *f* search; **en ~ de al- guien** in search of sb

busca[2] ['bus·ka] *m* beeper

buscar <c → qu> [bus·'kar] *vi, vt* to look for; **enviar a alguien a ~ algo** to send sb to fetch sth; **ir a ~ algo** to go and look for sth; **me viene a ~ a las 7** he/she is picking me up at 7; **él se lo ha bus- cado** he brought it on himself; **~ tres pies al gato** to complicate matters; **'se busca'** 'wanted'

buscavidas [bus·ka·'βi·ðas] *mf inv* go-getter

buseta [bu·'se·ta] *f* Col, Ven (*pequeño autobús*) minibus

búsqueda ['bus·ke·ða] *f t.* COMPUT search

busto ['bus·to] *m* bust

butaca [bu·'ta·ka] *f* armchair; (*de cine*) seat

butano [bu·'ta·no] I. *adj* orange II. *m* QUÍM butane (gas)

buzo ['bu·so, -θo] *m* diver

buzón [bu·'son, -'θon] *m* (*de correos*) mailbox; **~ (electrónico)** COMPUT mail- box

byte [bait] *m* COMPUT byte

C

C, c [se, θe] *f* C, c; **~ de Carmen** C as in Charlie

C/ ['ka·xe, -ʎe] *abr de* **calle** St

cabalgar <g → gu> [ka·βal·'γar] *vi* to ride horseback

cabalgata [ka·βal·'γa·ta] *f* procession, cavalcade

caballería [ka·βa·je·'ri·a, -ʎe·'ri·a] *f* 1. (*montura*) mount 2. MIL cavalry

caballero [ka·βa·'je·ro, -'ʎe·ro] *m* 1. (*ga- lán*) gentleman 2. HIST knight

caballerosidad [ka·βa·je·ro·si·'dad, ka· βa·ʎe-] *f* gentlemanliness

caballo [ka·'βa·jo, -ʎo] *m* 1. (*animal*) horse; **a ~** on horseback; **ir a ~** to ride; **~ de batalla** *fig* hobby horse 2. (*ajedrez*) knight 3. AUTO horsepower 4. (*naipes*) queen 5. *inf* (*heroína*) smack

cabaña [ka·'βa·ɲa] *f* cabin

cabecear [ka·βe·se·'ar, -θe·'ar] I. *vi* 1. (*mover la cabeza*) to shake one's head 2. (*dormitar*) to nod off II. *vt* DEP to head

cabecera [ka·βe·'se·ra, -'θe·ra] *f* 1. (*de cama*) head 2. (*del periódico*) mast- head; **médico de ~** family doctor

cabecilla [ka·βe·'si·ja, -'θi·ʎa] *mf* ring- leader

cabello [ka·'βe·jo, -ʎo] *m* hair; **se le pu- sieron los ~s de punta** his/her hair stood on end

caber [ka·'βer] *irr vi* (*tener espacio*) **~ en algo** to fit in [*o* into] sth; **no ~ en sí de...** to be beside oneself with...; **esta falda no me cabe** this skirt doesn't fit me

cabeza [ka·'βe·sa, -θa] I. *f* 1. *t.* ANAT, TÉC head; **~ de ajo** bulb of garlic; **~ atómica** atomic warhead; **~ abajo** upside down; **~ arriba** upright; **de ~** headfirst; **por ~** a head; **abrirse la ~** to split one's head open; **asentir con la ~** to nod (one's head); **negar con la ~** to shake one's head; **se me va la ~** I feel dizzy; **de la ~ a los pies** from head to toe; **estar mal de la ~** *inf* to be out of one's mind; **levantar ~** to pull through; **métetelo en la ~** get it into your head; **algo se le pasa a alguien por la ~** sth crosses sb's mind; **quitarse algo de la ~** to put sth out of one's mind; **sentar (la) ~** to settle down; **tener la ~ dura** to be stub- born; **traer a alguien de ~** to drive sb crazy; **este chico tiene ~** this boy is clever **2.** (*extremo*) top; **ir en ~** DEP to be in the lead **3.** AGR (*res*) head **II.** *mf* head; **~ de familia** head of the family; **~ rapada** skinhead

cabezada [ka·βe·'sa·da, -'θa·da] *f* **dar** [*o* **echar**] **una ~** *inf* to take a nap

cabezazo [ka·βe·'sa·so, -θa·θo] *m* blow on the head; DEP header; **darse un ~** to bang one's head

cabezón, -ona [ka·βe·'son, -'θon] *adj* **1.** (*de cabeza grande*) with a big head **2.** *inf* (*obstinado*) pigheaded

cabida [ka·'βi·da] *f* space; **dar ~ a** to make room for

cabina [ka·'βi·na] *f* cabin; (*de gimnasio*) locker; **~ de control** TÉC control room; **~ del piloto** cockpit; **~ de teléfonos** phone booth

cabinera [ka·βi·'ne·ra] *f Col* stewardess *f*, flight attendant

cable ['ka·βle] *m t.* ELEC (*telegrama*) cable; **se le cruzaron los ~s** *inf* he/she lost control; **echar un ~ a alguien** *inf* to help sb out

cabo ['ka·βo] *m* **1.** (*extremo*) end; **al fin y al ~** in the end; **de ~ a rabo** from beginning to end; **llevar a ~** to carry out; **no dejar ningún ~ suelto** to leave no loose ends **2.** GEO cape; **Ciudad del Cabo** Cape Town **3.** MIL corporal **4.** NÁUT rope ▶ **al ~ de** after

cabra ['ka·βra] *f* goat; **estar como una ~** *inf* to be off one's rocker

cabrear [ka·βre·'ar] **I.** *vt inf* to infuriate; **estar cabreado** to be furious **II.** *vr:* **~se** *inf* to get angry

cábula ['ka·βu·la] *f* **1.** *Arg, Par* (*amuleto*) amulet **2.** *Arg* (*cábala*) cabal, intrigue **3.** *Chile, Méx, Perú, PRico* (*ardid*) ruse, trick

caca ['ka·ka] *f inf* **1.** (*excremento*) poop **2.** (*chapuza*) rubbish

cacahuete [ka·ka·'we·te] *m* peanut

cacalote [ka·ka·'lo·te] *m AmC* CULIN popcorn

cacao [ka·'kao] *m* **1.** (*planta*) cacao; (*polvo, bebida*) cocoa **2.** *inf* (*jaleo*) fuss, todo; **pedir ~** *AmL* to give in

cacería [ka·se·'ri·a, ka·θe·] *f* (*partida*) hunting

cacerola [ka·se·'ro·la, ka·θe·] *f* sauce-pan

cacharpas [ka·'tʃar·pas] *fpl AmS* odds *m pl* and ends

cacharro [ka·'tʃa·ro] *m* **1.** (*recipiente*) pot **2.** *pey inf* (*aparato*) gadget **3.** *pey inf* (*trasto*) piece of junk

cachear [ka·tʃe·'ar] *vt* to frisk

cachete [ka·'tʃe·te] *m* **1.** (*golpe*) slap **2.** (*carrillo*) (fat) cheek

cachetear [ka·tʃe·te·'ar] *vt AmL* to slap

cachetón, -ona [ka·tʃe·'ton, -·'to·na] *adj AmL* chubby-cheeked

cachimba [ka·'tʃim·ba] *f AmL* (*pipa*) pipe

cachondeo [ka·tʃon·'deo] *m* **1.** *inf* (*broma*) joke; **tomar algo a ~** to take sth as a joke; **esto es un ~** this is a joke **2.** (*burla*) farce

cachondo, -a [ka·'tʃon·do, -a] **I.** *adj* **1.** *inf* (*sexual*) sexy, horny; **poner a alguien ~** to turn sb on **2.** *inf* (*gracioso*) funny **II.** *m, f inf* (*gracioso*) joker; **es un ~** he's a real laugh

cachorro, -a [ka·'tʃo·rro, -a] *m, f* (*de tigre*) cub; (*de perro*) pup(py)

caco ['ka·ko] *m inf* burglar

cacto ['kak·to] *m* cactus

cada ['ka·da] *adj* each; **~ uno/una** each one; **~ hora** hourly; **~ día** daily; **~ vez más/peor** more and more/worse and worse; **¿~ cuánto?** how often?

cadáver [ka·'da·βer] *m* corpse; (*de animales*) carcass

cadena [ka·'de·na] *f* **1.** *t. fig* chain; **~ alimentaria** BIO food chain; **~ (antideslizante)** AUTO snow chain; **~ hotelera** hotel chain; **~ humana** human chain; **~ perpetua** JUR life imprisonment; **trabajo en ~** assembly-line work; **atar un perro con ~** to chain up a dog; **reacción en ~** chain reaction **2.** GEO mountain chain **3.** RADIO, TV network; **~ de sonido** sound system

cadera [ka·'de·ra] *f* hip

caducar <c → qu> [ka·du·'kar] *vi* **1.** (*documento*) to expire **2.** (*producto*) **la leche está caducada** the milk is past its sell-by date

caducidad [ka·du·si·'dad, ka·ðu·'θi-] *f* **fecha de ~** (*de documento*) date of expiry; (*de productos*) use-by date

caduco, -a [ka·'du·ko, -a] *adj* senile

caer [ka·'er] *irr* I. *vi* 1. (*objeto*) to fall (down); (*precio*) to fall; **~ al suelo** to fall to the ground; **~ en manos de alguien** to fall into sb's hands; **dejarse ~** *inf* to show up; **tu amigo me cae bien/mal** *fig* I like/I don't like your friend; **estar al ~** *inf* to be about to happen; **2.** *inf* (*encontrarse*) to be (located); **¿por dónde cae Jerez?** whereabouts is Jerez? **3.** (*atacar*) **~ sobre algo/alguien** to fall on sth/sb II. *vr:* **~se** to collapse; (*pelo*) to fall out; **se me ha caído el pañuelo** I dropped my handkerchief

café [ka·'fe] *m* 1. (*bebida*) coffee; **~ americano** large black coffee; **~ con leche** coffee with milk; **~ cortado** coffee with a dash of milk; **~ solo** black coffee; **tomar un ~** to have a coffee **2.** (*local*) café

cafeína [ka·fe·'i·na] *f* caffeine

cafetera [ka·fe·'te·ra] *f* (*jarra*) coffee pot; **~ eléctrica** coffeemaker

cafetería [ka·fe·te·'ri·a] *f* café

caída [ka·'i·da] *f* 1. (*acción*) fall; **~ del cabello** hair loss; **~ del sistema** COMPUT system crash; **la ~ del gobierno** the fall of the government **2.** (*de agua*) waterfall

caimán [kai·'man] *m* caiman

Cairo ['kai·ro] *m* El **~** Cairo

caja ['ka·xa] *f* 1. (*recipiente*) box; **~ fuerte** safe; **~ de herramientas** *t.* COMPUT tool box; **~ negra** AVIAT black box **2.** (*carcasa*) case; **~ de cambios** AUTO gearbox; **~ torácica** ANAT thoracic cavity **3.** FIN fund; **~ de ahorros** savings bank

cajero, -a [ka·'xe·ro, -a] *m, f* cashier; **~ automático** cash dispenser

cajeta [ka·'xe·ta] *f* 1. *Arg* (*cepo*) trap **2.** *AmC* CULIN toffee-like candy

cajetilla [ka·xe·'ti·ja, -ʎa] *f* small box; (*de cigarrillos*) pack of cigarettes

cajón [ka·'xon] *m* drawer; **eso es de ~** *inf* that goes without saying

cajuela [ka·'xwe·la] *f Méx* AUTO trunk

cal [kal] *f* lime; **cerrar a ~ y canto** to shut firmly

cala ['ka·la] *f* 1. (*bahía*) cove **2.** NÁUT hold **3.** (*prueba*) probe

calabacín [ka·la·βa·'sin, -'θin] *m* zucchini

calabaza [ka·la·'βa·sa, -θa] *f* BOT pumpkin ► **dar ~ s a alguien** (*un suspenso*) to fail sb; (*una negativa*) to brush sb off

calabozo [ka·la·'βo·so, -θo] *m* 1. (*mazmorra*) dungeon **2.** (*celda*) (prison) cell

calada [ka·'la·da] *f* *inf* (*de humo*) puff; **¿me das una ~?** will you give me a drag?

calaguasca [ka·la·'ɣwas·ka] *f* Col CULIN raw brandy

calamar [ka·la·'mar] *m* squid

calambre [ka·'lam·bre] *m* (*eléctrico*) electric shock; (*muscular*) cramp

calamidad [ka·la·mi·'dad] *f* calamity; *inf* (*persona*) disaster

calar [ka·'lar] I. *vi* to soak in II. *vt* 1. (*líquido*) to soak; **el chaparrón me ha calado la chaqueta** the downpour has drenched my jacket **2.** (*afectar*) **~ a alguien** to make an impression on sb **3.** *inf* (*desenmascarar*) to see through **4.** (*motor*) to stall III. *vr:* **~se** 1. (*mojarse*) to get soaked **2.** (*motor*) to stall **3.** (*gorra*) to pull down

calavera [ka·la·'βe·ra] *f* skull

calcar <c → qu> [kal·'kar] *vt* 1. (*dibujar*) to trace **2.** (*imitar*) to copy

calcetín [kal·se·'tin, kal·θe·-] *m* sock

calcinar(se) [kal·si·'nar·(se), kal·θi·-] *(vt, vr)* to burn

calcio ['kal·sjo, -θjo] *m* calcium

calco ['kal·ko] *m* 1. (*de dibujos*) tracing **2.** (*imitación*) imitation

calculador(a) [kal·ku·la·'dor, --'do·ra] *adj* calculating

calculadora [kal·ku·la·'do·ra] *f* calculator; **~ de bolsillo** pocket calculator

calcular [kal·ku·'lar] *vt* 1. (*computar*) to calculate **2.** (*aproximadamente*) to estimate; **calculo que llegaré sobre las diez** I reckon that I'll arrive around ten

cálculo ['kal·ku·lo] *m* 1. *t.* ECON calculation; ~ **mental** mental arithmetic 2. (*suposición*) conjecture 3. MED stone

caldear [kal·de·'ar] I. *vt* (*calentar*) to heat (up) II. *vr:* ~**se** (*calentarse*) to heat up

caldera [kal·'de·ra] *f* TÉC boiler

calderilla [kal·de·'ri·ja, -ʎa] *f* small change

caldero [kal·'de·ro] *m* caldron

calefacción [ka·le·fak·'sjon, -faɣ·'θjon] *f* heating

calendario [ka·len·'da·rjo] *m* calendar

calentador [ka·len·ta·'dor] *m* heater

calentamiento [ka·len·ta·'mjen·to] *m* warming; DEP warm-up

calentar <e → ie> [ka·len·'tar] I. *vt* to warm II. *vt* 1. (*caldear*) to heat (up); (*con calefacción*) to warm (up) 2. *vulg* (*sexualmente*) to turn on 3. *inf* (*pegar*) to give a good hiding to III. *vr:* ~**se** 1. (*caldearse*) to heat up; DEP to warm up 2. (*enfadarse*) to get angry

calesita [ka·le·'si·ta] *f* *Arg, Par* merry-go-round

caleta [ka·'le·ta] *f* *AmL* (*barco*) coaster

calibrar [ka·li·'βrar] *vt* 1. TÉC (*medir*) to gauge, to gage 2. (*graduar*) to calibrate

calibre [ka·'li·βre] *m* 1. (*diámetro*) caliber; **eso es una mentira de ~** *inf* that's a huge lie 2. (*instrumento*) gauge, gage

calidad [ka·li·'dad] *f* quality; **en ~ de** as

cálido, -a ['ka·li·do, -a] *adj* (*país*) hot; *fig* warm

caliente [ka·'ljen·te] *adj* 1. (*cálido*) warm; (*ardiente*) hot 2. (*acalorado*) heated

calificación [ka·li·fi·ka·'sjon, -'θjon] *f* 1. (*denominación*) description; (*evaluación*) assessment 2. (*nota*) mark, grade

calificado, -a [ka·li·fi·'ka·do, -a] *adj* qualified; (*reconocido*) well-known

calificar <c → qu> [ka·li·fi·'kar] *vt* 1. (*definir*) ~ **de algo** to describe as sth 2. (*evaluar*) to assess; ENS to mark, to grade

calificativo [ka·li·fi·ka·'ti·βo] *m* description, qualifier

California [ka·li·'for·nja] *f* California

caligrafía [ka·li·ɣra·'fi·a] *f* calligraphy

callado, -a [ka·'ja·do, -a; ka·'ʎa-] *adj* (*sin

hablar*) silent; (*silencioso*) quiet

callampa [ka·'jam·pa, ka·'ʎam-] *f* 1. *Col, Chile, Perú* (*seta*) mushroom 2. *Chile* (*sombrero*) felt hat

callana [ka·'ja·na, -'ʎa·na] *f* 1. *AmS* (*vasija*) earthenware pan 2. *Chile* (*reloj*) large pocket watch

callar [ka·'jar, -'ʎar] I. *vi*, *vr* ~**se por algo** (*no hablar*) to keep quiet because of sth; (*enmudecer*) to fall silent due to sth; **¡cállate de una vez!** just shut up! II. *vt* to keep quiet about; **hacer ~ a alguien** to make sb keep quiet

calle ['ka·je, -ʎe] *f* street; (*de autopista*) DEP lane; ~ **de dirección única** one-way street; ~ **peatonal** pedestrian street; ~ **arriba/abajo** up/down the street; **hacer la ~** *inf* to be a streetwalker; **quedarse en la ~** *inf* to be out of a job

callejero [ka·je·'xe·ro, ka·ʎe-] *m* street directory

callejón [ka·je·'xon, ka·ʎe-] *m* alley; ~ **sin salida** blind alley

callo ['ka·jo, -ʎo] *m* 1. (*callosidad*) callus; **dar el ~** *inf* to slave away 2. *pl* CULIN tripe

calma ['kal·ma] *f* 1. (*silencio*) calm; **¡(con) ~!** calm down! 2. *inf* (*indolencia*) indolence

calmante [kal·'man·te] *m* sedative

calmar [kal·'mar] I. *vt* 1. (*tranquilizar*) to calm (down) 2. (*dolor*) to relieve II. *vr:* ~**se** to calm down; (*dolor*) to ease off

caló [ka·'lo] *m* gypsy slang

calor [ka·'lor] *m* 1. (*de un cuerpo*) warmth 2. (*clima*) heat; ~ **sofocante** stifling heat; **hace mucho ~** it's very hot 3. (*entusiasmo*) passion

caloría [ka·lo·'ri·a] *f* calorie; **bajo en ~s** low-calorie

calote [ka·'lo·te] *m* *RíoPl* swindle

caluma [ka·'lu·ma] *f* *Perú* Andean gorge

calumnia [ka·'lum·nja] *f* slander

caluroso, -a [ka·lu·'ro·so, -a] *adj* hot; *fig* warm; **un recibimiento ~** a warm reception

calva ['kal·βa] *f* bald patch

calvario [kal·'βa·rjo] *m* **pasar un ~** to suffer agonies

calvicie [kal·'βi·sje, -θje] *f* baldness

calvo, -a ['kal·βo, -a] *adj* bald

C

calzada [kal·'sa·da, -'θa·da] *f* (*carretera*) (paved) road

calzado [kal·'sa·do, -'θa·do] *m* footwear

calzar <z > c> [kal·'sar, -'θar] I. *vt* 1. (*zapatos*) to put on; (*cuña*) to wedge 2. (*llevar puesto*) to wear II. *vr:* ~**se** to put one's shoes on

calzón [kal·'son] *m AmL* (*pantalón*) trousers *pl*, pants *pl*

calzoncillo(s) [kal·son·'si·jo(s), kal·θon·'θi·ʎo(s)] *m(pl)* men's underpants *pl*

calzoneras [kal·θo·'ne·ras, kal·θo·] *fpl Méx* (*pantalón de montar*) riding pants *pl*

cama ['ka·ma] *f* bed; ~ **elástica** trampoline

camaleón [ka·ma·le·'on] *m t. fig* chameleon

cámara ['ka·ma·ra] I. *f* 1. FOTO camera; ~ **de vídeo** video camera; **a - lenta** in slow motion 2. (*consejo*) house; **Cámara Alta** POL upper house; **Cámara Baja** POL lower house II. *mf* CINE cameraman *m*, camerawoman *f*

camaradería [ka·ma·ra·de·'ri·a] *f* comradeship

camarero, -a [ka·ma·'re·ro, -a] *m, f* 1. (*en restaurantes*) waiter *m*, waitress *f*; ¡~! waiter! 2. (*en la barra*) barman *m*, barmaid *f*

camarón [ka·ma·'ron] *m* shrimp, prawn

camarote [ka·ma·'ro·te] *m* NÁUT cabin, berth

cambiante [kam·'bjan·te] *adj* changeable; *pey* (*veleidoso*) moody

cambiar [kam·'bjar] I. *vi* to change; ~ **de casa** to move (house); ~ **de coche** to buy a new car; ~ **de marcha** AUTO to change gear II. *vt* 1. (*algo comprado*) to change; ~ **dinero** to (ex)change money 2. (*variar*) to change; ~ **algo de lugar** to move sth III. *vr* (*de ropa*) to change; (*de casa*) to move

cambiavía [kam·bja·'βi·a] *m AmL* FERRO switchman

cambio ['kam·bjo] *m* 1. (*transformación*) change; ~ **de aceite** AUTO oil change; ~ **climático** climatic change; ~ **de marchas** shift lever, gearshift; **a las primeras de** ~ at the first opportunity; **¿tiene** ~ **de 100 dólares?** can you change 100 dollars?; **en** ~ however 2. (*intercambio*) exchange; **a** ~ **de algo** in exchange for sth 3. FIN exchange rate; ~ **de divisa** [*o* **de moneda**] foreign exchange 4. TÉC gearshift; ~ **de marchas** gearbox, transmission 5. DEP substitution

camelia [ka·'me·lja] *f* camellia

camello, -a [ka·'me·jo, -ʎo] *m, f* 1. ZOOL camel 2. *inf* (*persona*) drug dealer

camerino [ka·me·'ri·no] *m* TEAT dressing room

Camerún [ka·me·'run] *m* Cameroon

camilla [ka·'mi·ja] *f* stretcher

camilucho, -a [ka·mi·'lu·tʃo, -a] *m, f AmL* Indian day laborer

caminar [ka·mi·'nar] I. *vi* 1. to walk 2. *AmL* (*funcionar*) to work II. *vt* (*distancia*) to cover

caminata [ka·mi·'na·ta] *f* long walk

camino [ka·'mi·no] *m* 1. (*senda*) path; (*estrecho*) track; (*calle*) road; **a medio** ~ halfway (there); **de** ~ **a Londres** on the road to London; **abrirse** ~ to make one's way; **ponerse en** ~ to set out [*o* off]; **ir por buen/mal** ~ *fig* to be on the right/wrong track 2. (*distancia*) way; **está a dos horas de** ~ it's two hours away 3. (*manera*) way; ~ **de ro-sas** bed of roses

camión [ka·'mjon] *m* AUTO truck; ~ **de la basura** garbage truck

camionero, -a [ka·mjo·'ne·ro, -a] *m, f* truck driver

camioneta [ka·mjo·'ne·ta] *f* 1. (*furgoneta*) van; ~ **de reparto** delivery van 2. *AmL* (*autobús*) bus

camisa [ka·'mi·sa] *f* 1. (*prenda*) shirt; ~ **de fuerza** straitjacket; **cambiar de** ~ to change sides 2. (*funda*) case 3. (*de reptil*) slough ▶ **meterse en** ~ **de once varas** to bite off more than one can chew

camiseta [ka·mi·'se·ta] *f* (*exterior*) T-shirt; (*interior*) undershirt; DEP shirt

camisón [ka·mi·'son] *m* nightgown

camote [ka·'mo·te] *m AmL* 1. (*batata*) sweet potato 2. (*molestia*) nuisance 3. (*amante*) lover

camotear [ka·mo·te·'ar] *vi Méx* (*vagabundear*) to roam

campamento [kam·pa·'men·to] *m* camp; ~ **de verano** summer camp

campana [kam·'pa·na] *f* bell; ~ **extractora** (**de humos**) extractor hood; **el coche dio tres vueltas de ~** the car turned over three times

campanario [kam·pa·'na·rjo] *m* bell tower

campante [kam·'pan·te] *adj inf* (*tranquilo*) calm; **quedarse tan ~** not to bat an eyelid

campaña [kam·'pa·na] *f* **1.** (*campo*) countryside; **tienda de ~** tent **2.** POL campaign; ~ **antitabaco** anti-smoking campaign; ~ **electoral** electoral [*o* election] campaign **3.** COM sales drive

campar [kam·'par] *vi* to camp

campear [kam·pe·'ar] *vi* **1.** *AmL* (*ir de acampada*) to camp **2.** *inf* (*arreglárselas*) **ir campeando** to get by

campechana [kam·pe·'tʃa·na] *f Méx, Cuba* (*bebida*) cocktail

campeón, -ona [kam·pe·'on, -·'o·na] *m, f* champion

campeonato [kam·peo·'na·to] *m* championship; **de ~** *inf* terrific

campera [kam·'pe·ra] *f CSur* Windbreaker®

campesino, -a [kam·pe·'si·no, -a] *m, f* man from the country *m*, woman from the country *f*; **los ~s** country people; *t. pey* (*labrador*) peasant

camping ['kam·pin] *m* **1.** (*campamento*) camping site **2.** (*actividad*) **hacer ~** to go camping

campirano, -a [kam·pi·'ra·no, -a] *adj* **1.** *AmL* (*patán, rural*) rustic **2.** *Méx* (*campesino*) peasant **3.** *Méx* (*entendido en el campo*) good at farming **4.** *Méx* (*que maneja bien caballos*) skilled at handling horses

campo ['kam·po] *m* **1.** (*terreno*) countryside; (*de cultivo*) field; *t.* DEP ~ **de tiro** firing range; **gente del ~** country people **2.** *t.* POL, MIL camp; ~ **de concentración** HIST concentration camp; ~ **de trabajo** work camp **3.** *t.* FÍS, COMPUT field; ~ **visual** field of vision

campus ['kam·pus] *m inv* campus

camuflaje [ka·mu·'fla·xe] *m* camouflage

camuflar [ka·mu·'flar] *vt t. fig* to camouflage

cana ['ka·na] *f* **1.** (*pelo*) white hair; **echar**

una ~ al aire *fig* to let one's hair down **2.** *Arg inf* (*policía*) police **3.** *Arg inf* (*prisión*) jail

Canadá [ka·na·'da] *m* (**el**) ~ Canada

canal [ka·'nal] *m* **1.** *t.* ANAT canal **2.** GEO, TV channel; **el Canal de la Mancha** the English Channel; **el Canal de Panamá** the Panama Canal

canalización [ka·na·li·sa'sjon, -θa·'θjon] *f* **1.** (*de un río*) canalization **2.** (*alcantarillado*) sewerage system

canalizar <z → c> [ka·na·li·'sar, -'θar] *vt* to canalize; *fig* to channel

canalla [ka·'na·ja, -ʎa] *mf pey* swine

canalón [ka·na·'lon] *m* gutter

canana [ka·'na·na] *f* (*cinturón*) cartridge belt

Canarias [ka·'na·rjas] *fpl* **las Islas ~** the Canary Islands

canario [ka·'na·rjo] *m* canary

canasta [ka·'nas·ta] *f* basket

canastero, -a [ka·nas·'te·ro, -a] *m, f Chile* (*panadería*) baker's helper

cancelar [kan·se·'lar, kan·θe·] *vt* **1.** (*anular*) to cancel; ~ **una cita** to cancel an appointment **2.** FIN (*una cuenta*) to close; (*una deuda*) to pay (off)

cáncer ['kan·ser, -θer] *m* **1.** *t. fig* MED cancer **2.** ASTR Cancer

cancerígeno, -a [kan·se·'ri·xe·no, -a; kan·θe·] *adj* carcinogenic

canceroso, -a [kan·se·'ro·so, -a; kan·θe·] *adj* cancerous

cancha ['kan·tʃa] *f* **1.** DEP (*de deporte*) sports field; (*de tenis*) court **2.** *AmL* (*hipódromo*) racetrack **3.** *AmL* (*de un río*) broad part of a river **4.** *AmL* (*espacio*) space

canciller [kan·si·'jer, -θi·'ʎer] *mf* **1.** POL chancellor **2.** *AmL* (*de Asuntos Exteriores*) foreign minister

canción [kan·'sjon, -'θjon] *f* song; (**es**) **siempre la misma ~** (it's) always the same old story

cancona [kan·'ko·na] *adj Chile* broadhipped

candado [kan·'da·do] *m* padlock

candelabro [kan·de·'la·βro] *m* candelabra

candelejón, -ona [kan·de·le·'xon, -·'xo·na] *adj Chile, Col, Perú* naïve

candelilla [kan·de·'li·ja, -ʎa] *f* CRI, Chile, Hond (*luciérnaga*) glow-worm

candidato, -a [kan·di·'da·to, -a] *m, f* applicant; POL candidate; ~ **al título** DEP contender for the title

candidatura [kan·di·da·'tu·ra] *f* (*presentación*) application; POL candidature

candil [kan·'dil] *m* **1.** (*lámpara*) oil lamp **2.** AmL (*candelabro*) candelabra

candinga [kan·'diŋ·ga] *f* **1.** Chile (*necedad*) absurdity **2.** Hond (*maraña*) mess

candonga [kan·'doŋ·ga] *f* Col (*pendiente*) earring

caneca [ka·'ne·ka] *f* **1.** Col (*basurero*) trash can **2.** Cuba (*de agua caliente*) hot-water bottle **3.** AmL (*barril*) drum; (*balde*) bucket

canela [ka·'ne·la] *f* cinnamon

canfín [kan·'fin] *m* AmC (*petróleo*) gasoline

cangrejo [kan·'gre·xo] *m* crab; ~ **de río** crayfish

canguro¹ [kan·'gu·ro] *m* ZOOL kangaroo

canguro² [kan·'gu·ro] *mf* inf baby-sitter

caníbal [ka·'ni·βal] *adj, mf* cannibal

canica [ka·'ni·ka] *f* marble

canijo, -a [ka·'ni·xo, -a] *adj* AmL (*malvado*) sly

canilla [ka·'ni·ja, -ʎa] *f* Arg, Par, Urug (*grifo*) tap

canillera [ka·ni·'je·ra, -'ʎe·ra] *f* AmL **1.** (*espinillera*) shin guard **2.** (*temblor*) trembling

canillita [ka·ni·'ji·ta, -'ʎi·ta] *m* AmS newspaper vendor

canjear [kan·xe·'ar] *vt* to exchange

canoa [ka·'noa] *f* **1.** t. DEP (*bote a remo*) canoe **2.** AmL (*artesa*) feeding trough

canoso, -a [ka·'no·so, -a] *adj* grizzled

cansado, -a [kan·'sa·do, -a] *adj* **1.** *estar* (*fatigado*) tired; (*harto*) tired **2.** *ser* (*fatigoso*) tiring; (*aburrido*) boring; (*molesto*) tiresome **3.** AmL **a las cansadas** at long last

cansador(a) [kan·sa·'dor, -'do·ra] *adj* Arg **1.** *ser* (*fatigoso*) tiring **2.** *ser* (*aburrido*) boring **3.** *ser* (*molesto*) tiresome

cansancio [kan·'san·sjo, -θjo] *m* **1.** (*fatiga*) tiredness; **estoy muerto de ~** I'm dead tired **2.** (*hastío*) boredom

cansar [kan·'sar] **I.** *vi* **1.** (*fatigar*) to tire

2. (*hastiar*) to be tiresome **II.** *vt* **1.** (*fatigar*) to tire (out) **2.** (*hastiar*) to bore **III.** *vr:* **~se 1.** (*fatigarse*) to tire oneself out **2.** (*hartarse*) **~se de algo** to get tired of sth

cansera [kan·'se·ra] *f* Col (*tiempo malgastado*) wasted effort

cantábrico, -a [kan·ta·βri·ko, -a] *adj* Cantabrian; **el Mar Cantábrico** the Bay of Biscay

cantante [kan·'tan·te] **I.** *adj* **llevar la voz** ~ *fig* to call the tune **II.** *mf* singer

cantar [kan·'tar] *vi, vt* **1.** (*personas*) to sing; (*gallo*) to crow; (*grillo*) to chirp; **en menos que canta un gallo** *inf* in no time at all **2.** *inf* (*confesar*) to talk **3.** *inf* (*oler mal*) to stink

cántaro ['kan·ta·ro] *m* pitcher; **llover a** ~**s** to rain cats and dogs

cantera [kan·'te·ra] *f* quarry; DEP young local club players

cantidad [kan·ti·'dad] **I.** *f* quantity; (*número*) number; (*dinero*) sum; **una gran** ~ **de** lots of **II.** *adv* inf a lot

cantimplora [kan·tim·'plo·ra] *f* water bottle, canteen

cantina [kan·'ti·na] *f* (*en estaciones*) buffet; (*en cuarteles*) canteen

canto ['kan·to] *m* **1.** (*acción*) singing; (*canción*) song; ~ **de los pájaros** birdsong **2.** (*arista*) edge **3.** (*de cuchillo*) back; (*de libro*) fore-edge; **poner de** ~ to put on end

caña ['ka·ɲa] *f* **1.** AGR reed; (*tallo*) stalk; ~ **de azúcar** sugar cane **2.** (*de la pierna*) shinbone **3.** (*de pescar*) (fishing) rod **4.** (*de cerveza*) glass

cáñamo ['ka·ɲa·mo] *m* **1.** (*planta*) hemp **2.** (*tejido*) canvas

cañería [ka·ɲe·'ri·a] *f* pipe; ~ **del agua** plumbing

caño ['ka·ɲo] *m* tube; (*de la fuente*) spout

cañón [ka·'ɲon] *m* **1.** (*tubo*) tube; ~ **de escopeta** barrel **2.** MIL cannon **3.** GEO canyon; **el Cañón del Colorado** the Grand Canyon

cañonazo [ka·ɲo·'na·so, -θo] *m* cannon shot; *inf* (*en fútbol*) powerful shot

cañonera [ka·ɲo·'ne·ra] *f* AmL (*pistolera*) holster

caoba [ka·'o·βa] *f* 1. (*madera, color*) mahogany 2. (*árbol*) mahogany tree

caos ['ka·os] *m inv* chaos

caótico, -a [ka·'o·ti·ko, -a] *adj* chaotic

capa ['ka·pa] *f* 1. t. TAUR (*prenda*) cape 2. (*cobertura*) covering; (*recubrimiento*) layer; (*baño*) coating; **~ aislante** insulating layer; **~ de nieve** covering of snow; **~ de ozono** ozone layer 3. GEO, MIN stratum ▶ **estar de ~ caída** *inf* to be on the decline

capacidad [ka·pa·si·'dad, ka·pa·θi·] *f* 1. t. FÍS (*cabida*) capacity 2. (*aptitud*) aptitude; **~ adquisitiva** purchasing power

capacitado, -a [ka·pa·si·'ta·do, -a; ka·pa·θi-] *adj* **~ para algo** qualified for [*o* to do] sth

capacitar [ka·pa·si·'tar, ka·pa·θi·] *vt* 1. (*formar*) to train; (*preparar*) to prepare 2. *AmL* JUR (*habilitar*) to capacitate

capar [ka·'par] *vt inf* to castrate

capataz [ka·pa·'tas, -'taθ] *m* foreman

capaz [ka·'pas, -'paθ] *adj* 1. (*en condiciones*) capable 2. *AmL* (*tal vez*) perhaps

capi ['ka·pi] *m* 1. *AmS* (*maíz*) corn 2. *Bol* (*harina*) white corn flour

capilla [ka·'pi·ja, -ʎa] *f* REL chapel; **~ ardiente** funeral chapel

capisayo [ka·pi·'sa·jo] *m Col* (*camiseta*) undershirt

capital¹ [ka·pi·'tal] I. *adj* essential; **pena ~** capital punishment; **de ~ importancia** of prime importance II. *m* capital; **~ fijo** fixed capital

capital² [ka·pi·'tal] *f* capital (city)

capitalismo [ka·pi·ta·'lis·mo] *m* capitalism

capitalista [ka·pi·ta·'lis·ta] *adj* capitalist(ic)

capitán [ka·pi·'tan] *m* MIL, DEP, AVIAT captain

capitular [ka·pi·tu·'lar] *vi* 1. (*acordar*) to agree to [*o* on] 2. MIL to surrender

capítulo [ka·'pi·tu·lo] *m* t. REL chapter

capota [ka·'po·ta] *f* AUTO convertible top

capotera [ka·po·'te·ra] *f Hond* (*percha*) clothespin; (*perchero*) coat rack

capricho [ka·'pri·tʃo] *m* whim; **darse un**

~ to allow oneself sth

caprichoso, -a [ka·pri·'tʃo·so, -a] *adj* capricious; *pey* (*inconstante*) moody

Capricornio [ka·pri·'kor·njo] *m* Capricorn

cápsula ['kaβ·su·la] *f* capsule; **~ espacial** AVIAT space capsule

captar [kap·'tar] *vt* 1. (*recoger*) to collect 2. (*percibir*) to make out; (*comprender*) to grasp

captura [kap·'tu·ra] *f* 1. (*apresamiento*) capture 2. (*detención*) arrest 3. (*piezas cobradas*) catch

capturar [kap·tu·'rar] *vt* 1. (*apresar*) to capture 2. (*detener*) to arrest 3. (*cazar*) to catch

capucha [ka·'pu·tʃa] *f* hood

capullo [ka·'pu·jo, -ʎo] *m* 1. BOT (*de flor*) bud 2. ZOOL cocoon; **salir del ~** to hatch out 3. *vulg* (*canalla*) jerk

cara ['ka·ra] I. *f* 1. (*rostro*) face; **~ a** face to face; (**no**) **dar la ~ por alguien** (not) to come to sb's defense; **echar en ~ to** reproach; **plantar ~ a** to face up to; **partir la ~ a alguien** *inf* to smash sb's face in; **~ de póker** *inf* poker face; **una ~ larga** a long face; **una ~ de pocos amigos** *inf* a sour look; **tener buena/mala ~** to look good/bad 2. (*lado*) side; (*de una moneda*) face; **~ o cruz** heads or tails 3. *inf* (*osadía*) nerve; **¡qué ~!** what nerve!; **tener mucha ~** to have some nerve II. *prep* (**de**) **~ a** facing; **de ~ al futuro** with an eye to the future III. *conj* **de ~ a** +*infin* in order to +*infin*

caracol [ka·ra·'kol] *m* 1. ZOOL snail 2. (*concha*) conch (shell)

caracola [ka·ra·'ko·la] *f* conch

caracolillo [ka·ra·ko·'li·jo, -ʎo] *m AmL* high quality small-bean coffee

carácter <caracteres> [ka·'rak·ter] *m* 1. (*en general*) character; (**no**) **tiene ~** he/she has (no) character 2. (*índole*) nature; **con ~ de** as 3. *AmL* (*personaje*) character

característica [ka·rak·te·'ris·ti·ka] *f* characteristic

característico, -a [ka·rak·te·'ris·ti·ko, -a] *adj* characteristic

caracterizar <z → c> [ka·rak·te·ri·'sar,

-'θar| **I.** vt **1.** (*marcar*) to characterize **2.** TEAT to play **II.** vr: ~**se** to be characterized

caramanchel [ka·ra·man·'tʃel] m **1.** *Perú* (*cobertizo*) shed **2.** *Chile* (*taberna*) canteen

caramba [ka·'ram·ba] *interj inf* ¡(**qué**) ~**!** (*enfado*) damn!; (*extrañeza*) good heavens!

carambola [ka·ram·'bo·la] f cannon; *inf* (*trampa*) trick

caramelo [ka·ra·'me·lo] m (*golosina*) candy; (*azúcar*) caramel

caraota [ka·ra·'o·ta] f *Ven* (*haba*) kidney bean

carapacho [ka·ra·'pa·tʃo] m **1.** ZOOL carapace, shell **2.** *Cuba* CULIN shellfish cooked in the shell

caraqueño, -a [ka·ra·'ke·ɲo, -a] *adj* of/from Caracas

carátula [ka·'ra·tu·la] f (*de un disco*) album [*o* CD] cover

caravana [ka·ra·'βa·na] f **1.** (*remolque*) trailer **2.** (*embotellamiento*) tailback

carbón [kar·'βon] m coal; ~ **de leña** [*o* **vegetal**] charcoal; **papel** ~ carbon paper

carbonato [kar·βo·'na·to] m carbonate

carbonilla [kar·βo·'ni·ja, -ʎa] f *AmL* charcoal

carbono [kar·'βo·no] m carbon; **dióxido de** ~ carbon dioxide

carburador [kar·βu·ra·'dor] m TÉC carburetor

carburante [kar·βu·'ran·te] m fuel

carcajada [kar·ka·'xa·da] f guffaw; **reírse a** ~**s** to roar with laughter; **soltar una** ~ to burst out laughing

carcasa [kar·'ka·sa] f TÉC casing

cárcel ['kar·sel, -θel] f prison; **tres años de** ~ three years imprisonment; **estar en la** ~ to be in prison

carcelero, -a [kar·se·'le·ro, -a; kar·θe·] m, f prison officer, jailer

carcoma [kar·'ko·ma] f ZOOL woodworm

cardenal [kar·de·'nal] m **1.** REL cardinal **2.** (*hematoma*) bruise

cardiaco, -a [kar·'dja·ko, -a] *adj*, **cardíaco, -a** [kar·'di·a·ko, -a] *adj* heart; MED cardiac; **ataque** ~ heart attack; **paro** ~ cardiac arrest

cardinal [kar·di·'nal] *adj* cardinal; **los cuatro puntos** ~**es** the four cardinal points

cardiólogo, -a [kar·'djo·lo·ɣo, -a] m, f MED cardiologist

carecer [ka·re·'ser, -'θer] *irr como crecer* vi ~ **de algo** to lack sth

carencia [ka·'ren·sja, -θja] f lack; (*escasez*) shortage, scarcity; ~ **de algo** MED deficiency in sth

carente [ka·'ren·te] *adj* ~ **de algo** lacking in sth, devoid of sth; ~ **de interés** uninteresting

careo [ka'reo] m confrontation

careta [ka·'re·ta] f mask; **quitar la** ~ **a alguien** *t. fig* to unmask sb

carga ['kar·ɣa] f **1.** (*acto*) loading **2.** (*cargamento*) load; **animal de** ~ pack animal; **buque de** ~ freighter **3.** (*obligación*) obligation; **ser una** ~ **para alguien** to be a burden on sb **4.** MIL charge; ~ **explosiva** explosive charge; ~ **policial** baton charge; **¡a la** ~**!** charge!

cargado, -a [kar·'ɣa·do, -a] *adj* (*lleno*) ~ **con** [*o* **de**] **algo** loaded with sth; **la batería está cargada** the battery is charged; **un café muy** ~ very strong coffee

cargamento [kar·ɣa·'men·to] m (*acto*) loading; (*carga*) load, cargo

cargar <g → gu> [kar·'ɣar] **I.** vi **1.** (*llevar*) ~ **con algo** to carry sth **2.** (*atacar*) ~ **contra alguien** to charge at sb **II.** vt **1.** *t.* MIL to load **2.** (*achacar*) to attribute **3.** FIN (*en una cuenta*) to charge **4.** *inf* a **Paco le han cargado las mates** Paco failed Math **5.** COMPUT to load **6.** *AmL* (*llevar*) to have; **¿cargas dinero?** do you have any money on you? **III.** vr: ~**se 1.** (*llenarse*) ~**se de algo** to fill up with sth **2.** *inf* (*romper*) to smash up; **¡te la vas a** ~**!** *fig* you're in for it! **3.** *inf* (*matar*) to kill

cargo ['kar·ɣo] m **1.** FIN charge; ~ **a cuenta** debit **2.** (*puesto*) post; **desempeñar un** ~ to hold a position **3.** (*cuidado*) **estoy a** ~ **de las correcciones** I'm responsible for the corrections; ~ **de conciencia** feeling of guilt

Caribe [ka·'ri·βe] m **el** (**Mar**) ~ the Caribbean (Sea)

caribeño, -a [ka·ri·'βe·ɲo, -a] *adj* Caribbean

caricatura [ka·ri·ka·'tu·ra] *f* caricature, cartoon

caricia [ka·'ri·sja, -θja] *f* caress

caridad [ka·ri·'ðad] *f* charity; (*limosna*) alms *pl*; **hacer obras de ~** to do works of charity

caries [ka·rjes] *f inv* tooth decay

carimbo [ka·'rim·bo] *m Bol* branding iron

cariño [ka·'ri·ɲo] *m* affection; (*amor*) love; **hacer algo con ~** to do sth lovingly; **sentir ~ por alguien** to be fond of sb; **¡~ (mío)!** (my) dear!; **hacer ~s** *inf* to caress

cariñoso, -a [ka·ri·'ɲo·so, -a] *adj* **~ con alguien** affectionate [*o* tender] towards sb

carioca [ka·'rjo·ka] *adj* of/from Rio de Janeiro; (*brasileño*) Brazilian

carisma [ka·'ris·ma] *m* charisma

caritativo, -a [ka·ri·ta·'ti·βo, -a] *adj* charitable

cariz [ka·'ris, -'riθ] *m* look; **esto toma buen ~** this is looking good

carnal [kar·'nal] *adj* carnal

carnaval [kar·na·'βal] *m* carnival

carnaza [kar·'na·sa, -θa] *f* bait

carne [kar·ne] *f* 1. (*del cuerpo*) flesh; **ser uña y ~** to be inseparable 2. (*alimento*) meat; **~ asada** roast meat; **~ de cerdo/vacuna** pork/beef; **~ picada** ground meat ▶ **poner toda la ~ en el asador** to risk all; **~ de gallina** goose bumps *pl*; **ser de ~ y hueso** (*auténtico*) to be real; (*humano*) to be quite human

carné [kar·'ne] *m* <carnés> identity card; **~ de identidad** identity card; **~ de conducir** driver's license

carnear [kar·ne·'ar] *vt* 1. *CSur* (*matar: un animal*) to slaughter; (*una persona*) to murder brutally 2. *Chile* (*engañar*) to cheat 3. *Méx* (*apuñalar*) to stab (to death)

carnero [kar·'ne·ro] *m* 1. ZOOL ram 2. *CSur* (*débil*) weakling; (*desertor de huelga*) scab

carnet [kar·'ne] *m* <carnets> *v.* **carné**

carnicería [kar·ni·se·'ri·a, kar·ni·θe-] *f* butcher's (shop); *fig* (*masacre*) massacre

carnicero, -a [kar·ni·'se·ro, -a; kar·ni·θe-] I. *adj* carnivorous; *fig* (*sanguinario*) bloodthirsty II. *m, f* butcher

carnitas [kar·'ni·tas] *fpl AmC* CULIN barbecued pork

carnívoro, -a [kar·'ni·βo·ro, -a] *adj* carnivorous; **animal ~** carnivore

caro [ka·ro] *adv* dear(ly); **esto nos costará ~** *fig* this'll cost us dear

caro, -a [ka·ro, -a] *adj* expensive

carozo [ka·'ro·so, -θo] *m CSur* stone (*of fruit*)

carpa [kar·pa] *f* 1. ZOOL carp 2. (*entoldado*) marquee; **~ del circo** big top 3. *AmL* (*tienda de campaña*) tent 4. *AmL* (*puesto de mercado*) market stall

carpeta [kar·'pe·ta] *f* folder

carpincho [kar·'pin·tʃo] *m AmL* ZOOL capybara

carpintería [kar·pin·te·'ri·a] *f* carpentry

carpintero, -a [kar·pin·'te·ro, -a] *m, f* carpenter; **pájaro ~** woodpecker

carpir [kar·'pir] *vt AmL* to hoe

carraspear [ka·rras·pe·'ar] *vi* to clear one's throat

carrasposo, -a [ka·rras·'po·so, -a] *adj* *Col, Ecua, Ven* (*áspero*) rough

carrera [ka·'rre·ra] *f* 1. (*movimiento*) run 2. DEP (*competición*) race; **~ de relevos** relay race; **coche de ~s** racing car 3. (*profesión*) profession; **~ profesional** career 4. (*estudios*) degree course; **hacer una ~** to study 5. (*en medias*) ladder

carreta [ka·'rre·ta] *f* wagon

carrete [ka·'rre·te] *m t.* FOTO spool, reel; **~ de película** roll of film

carretera [ka·rre·'te·ra] *f* (main) road

carretilla [ka·rre·'ti·ja, -ʎa] *f* wheelbarrow

carril [ka·'rril] *m* (*en la carretera*) lane; **~ de adelantamiento/lento** fast/slow lane

carro [ka·rro] *m* 1. (*vehículo*) cart; **~ acorazado** [*o* blindado] armored car; **¡para el ~!** *inf* hold your horses! 2. *AmL* (*coche*) car 3. (*de una máquina*) carriage

carrocería [ka·rro·se·'ri·a, ka·rro·θe-] *f*

bodywork

carroña [ka·'rro·ɲa] f carrion

carroza [ka·'rro·sa, -θa] f carriage

carruaje [ka·'rrwa·xe] m carriage; (de caballos) coach

carrusel [ka·rru·'sel] m (tiovivo) merry-go-round, carousel

carta ['kar·ta] f 1. (escrito) letter; ~ **certificada** registered letter; ~ **de presentación** [o **de recomendación**] letter of introduction; **echar una** ~ to mail a letter; **Carta Magna** Magna Carta; **tomar ~s en un asunto** to intervene in a matter 2. (naipes) card; **jugar a las ~s** to play (at) cards; **echar las ~s a alguien** to tell sb's fortune 3. (menú) menu

cartel [kar·'tel] m poster; (rótulo) sign; TEAT bill; **'prohibido fijar ~es'** ' post no bills'

cártel ['kar·tel] m ECON cartel

cartelera [kar·te·'le·ra] f notice board; TEAT publicity board; **estar en** ~ to be on

cartera [kar·'te·ra] f (de bolsillo) wallet; (de mano) handbag, purse; (escolar) schoolbag; **ministro sin** ~ POL minister without portfolio; ~ **de valores** FIN securities portfolio

carterista [kar·te·'ris·ta] mf pickpocket

cartero, -a [kar·'te·ro, -a] m, f mailman m, letter carrier

cartilla [kar·'ti·ja, -ʎa] f 1. ENS (catón) first reader 2. (cuaderno) notebook; ~ **de ahorros** savings book; ~ **sanitaria** health services card 3. AmL (carnet) identity card

cartón [kar·'ton] m 1. (material) cardboard 2. (envase) carton; ~ **de leche** carton of milk

cartucho [kar·'tu·tʃo] m t. MIL cartridge; ~ **de tinta** ink cartridge; ~ **de fogueo** blank cartridge

cartulina [kar·tu·'li·na] f thin cardboard

casa ['ka·sa] f 1. (edificio) house; ~ **adosada** semi-detached house; ~ **de campo** country house 2. (vivienda) flat 3. (hogar) home; **ir a** ~ to go home; **vengo de** ~ I'm coming from home; **en** ~ at home; **estoy en** ~ **de Paco** I'm at Paco's (place); **no parar en** ~ to be always on the go; **todo queda en** ~ it'll

stay in the family; ~ **real** royal family 4. ECON (empresa) firm; ~ **discográfica** record company

casabe [ka·'sa·βe] m AmL CULIN cassava bread

casar [ka·'sar] I. vi to match II. vt 1. (novios) to marry; **estar casado** to be married; **los recién casados** the newlyweds 2. (combinar) to combine; (piezas) to join together III. vr ~**se con alguien** (por la Iglesia/por lo civil) to get married to sb (in church/in a registry office)

cascabel [kas·ka·'βel] m (little) bell; **serpiente de** ~ rattlesnake ▶ **poner el** ~ **al gato** to bell the cat

cascada [kas·'ka·da] f waterfall; (artificial) cascade

cascanueces [kas·ka·'nwe·ses, -θes] m inv nutcracker

cascar <c → qu> [kas·'kar] I. vt 1. (romper) to crack; ~ **un huevo** to crack an egg 2. inf (pegar) to clout II. vr: ~**se** to crack; (estropearse) to break III. vi inf (charlar) to chatter

cáscara ['kas·ka·ra] f shell; ~ **de huevo** eggshell; ~ **de limón** lemon peel

cascarón [kas·ka·'ron] m shell

cascarudo [kas·ka·'ru·do] m Arg beetle

casco ['kas·ko] m 1. (para cabeza) helmet 2. (pezuña) hoof 3. (de barco) hull 4. (botella) (empty) bottle 5. (de ciudad) center city, downtown; **el** ~ **antiguo** the old city 6. (cascote) piece of rubble 7. pl (auriculares) headphones pl

caserío [ka·se·'ri·o] m farmhouse

casero, -a [ka·'se·ro, -a] I. adj 1. (de casa) homemade; **remedio** ~ household remedy 2. (hogareño) home-loving II. m, f (propietario) landlord m, landlady f

caseta [ka·'se·ta] f hut; (de feria) booth; (de muestras) stand; ~ **del perro** doghouse

casete[1] [ka·'se·te] m o f (cinta) cassette

casete[2] [ka·'se·te] m 1. (aparato) cassette recorder 2. (pletina) cassette deck

casi ['ka·si] adv almost; ~ ~ very nearly

casilla [ka·'si·ja, -ʎa] f (en cuadrícula) box; (en tablero) square; (en casillero) pigeonhole; **sacar a alguien de sus ~s** *fig* to drive sb crazy

casillero [ka·si·'je·ro, -'ʎe·ro] *m* set of pigeonholes

casimba [ka·'sim·ba] *f AmL* (*hoyo*) well; (*manantial*) spring; (*barril*) bucket

casino [ka·'si·no] *m* casino

caso ['ka·so] *m* **1.** (*hecho*) case; **~ aislado** isolated case; **~ de fuerza mayor** case of force majeure; **¡eres un ~!** *inf* you're a right one!; **yo, en tu ~...** if I were you...; **en ~ de** +*infin* in the event of; **dado** [*o* **llegado**] **el ~** if it comes to it; **en ~ contrario** otherwise; **en cualquier ~** in any case; **en ningún ~** on no account; **en último ~** as a last resort; **en tal ~** in such a case; **en todo ~** in any case **2.** (*atención*) notice; **hacer ~ a alguien** (*considerar*) to pay attention to sb; (*obedecer*) to obey sb; (*creer*) to believe sb

caspa ['kas·pa] *f* dandruff

caspiroleta [kas·pi·ro·'le·ta] *f AmL CULIN* eggnog

casta ['kas·ta] *f* **1.** (*raza*) race **2.** (*clase social*) caste

castaña [kas·'ta·ɲa] *f* **1.** (*fruto*) chestnut **2.** *inf* (*golpe*) blow; **darse una ~** to give oneself a knock **3.** *inf* (*borrachera*) drunkenness; **coger una ~** to get tight **4.** *inf* (*rápido*) **a toda ~** flat out

castaño [kas·'ta·ɲo] *m* chestnut tree

castaño, -a [kas·'ta·ɲo, -a] *adj* brown

castañuela [kas·ta·'ɲwe·la] *f* castanet

castellano [kas·te·'ʝa·no, -'ʎa·no] *m* (*español*) Spanish; (*variedad*) Castilian

castellano, -a [kas·te·'ʝa·no, -a; -'ʎa·no, -a] *adj, m, f* Castilian; **la lengua castellana** the Spanish language

castidad [kas·ti·'dad] *f* chastity

castigar <g → gu> [kas·ti·'ɣar] *vt* **1.** (*punir*) **~ por algo** to punish for sth **2.** (*físicamente*) to beat; *fig* to castigate

castigo [kas·'ti·ɣo] *m* **1.** (*punición*) punishment **2.** (*aflicción*) affliction

Castilla [kas·'ti·ja, -ʎa] *f* Castile

castillo [kas·'ti·jo, -ʎo] *m* **1.** castle; **~ de arena** sandcastle; **~ de naipes** house of cards

castor [kas·'tor] *m* beaver

castrar [kas·'trar] *vt t. MED* to castrate

casual [ka·'swal] *adj* chance

casualidad [ka·swa·li·'dad] *f* chance; **de** [*o* **por**] **~** by chance; **¡qué ~!** what a coincidence!; **da la ~ que conozco a tu mujer** it so happens that I know your wife

casualmente [ka·swal·'men·te] *adv* by chance

cata ['ka·ta] *f* sampling; **~ de vinos** wine-tasting

catalán [ka·ta·'lan] *m* (*lengua*) Catalan

catalán, -ana [ka·ta·'lan, --'la·na] *adj, m, f* Catalan, Catalonian

catalizador [ka·ta·li·sa·'dor, ka·ta·li·θa-] *m* catalyst; *AUTO* catalytic converter

catalogar <g → gu> [ka·ta·lo·'ɣar] *vt* to catalog(ue); **~ a alguien de algo** to classify sb as sth

catálogo [ka·'ta·lo·ɣo] *m* catalog(ue)

Cataluña [ka·ta·'lu·ɲa] *f* Catalonia

catapultar [ka·ta·pul·'tar] *vt* to catapult

catar [ka·'tar] *vt* to taste

catarata [ka·ta·'ra·ta] *f* **1.** *GEO* waterfall; **las ~s del Niágara** the Niagara Falls **2.** *MED* cataract

catarro [ka·'ta·rro] *m* cold; *MED* catarrh

catástrofe [ka·'tas·tro·fe] *f* catastrophe

catecismo [ka·te·'sis·mo, -'θis·mo] *m* *REL* catechism

catedral [ka·te·'dral] *f* cathedral; **como una ~** *fig* massive

catedrático, -a [ka·te·'dra·ti·ko, -a] *m, f* *ENS* professor

categoría [ka·te·ɣo·'ri·a] *f* **1.** (*clase*) category **2.** (*calidad*) quality; **de primera ~** first-class; **tener mucha/poca ~** to be important/unimportant

catete [ka·'te·te] *m Chile* **1.** *CULIN* pork-broth porridge **2.** (*diablo*) devil

catolicismo [ka·to·li·'sis·mo, -'θis·mo] *m* *REL* (Roman) Catholicism

católico, -a [ka·'to·li·ko, -a] *adj, m, f* (Roman) Catholic

catorce [ka·'tor·se, -θe] *adj inv m* fourteen; *v. t.* **ocho**

cauce ['kau·se, -θe] *m* **1.** *GEO* (*lecho*) river bed **2.** (*camino*) channel, course; **~ jurídico** *JUR* legal action

cauchal [kau·'ʧal] *m AmL* rubber plantation

caucho ['kau·ʧo] *m* **1.** (*sustancia*) rubber; **árbol del ~** rubber tree **2.** *AmL* (*neumático*) tire

caudal [kau̯'dal] *m* **1.** (*de agua*) volume **2.** (*dinero*) **caja de ~es** safe **3.** (*abundancia*) abundance

caudillaje [kau̯di'ja·xe, -'ʎa·xe] *m Arg, Chile, Perú pey* (*caciquismo*) rule by political bosses

caudillo [kau̯'di·jo, -ʎo] *m* MIL, POL leader

caula ['kau̯·la] *f AmL* (*estratagema*) trick

causa ['kau̯·sa] *f t.* POL (*ideal*) cause; (*motivo*) reason; **a** [*o* **por**] **~ de** on account of; **la ~ de su despido** the reason for his/her dismissal

causar [kau̯'sar] *vt* to cause; **~ daño/ problemas** to cause damage/problems; **~ efecto** to have an effect

cautela [kau̯'te·la] *f* caution

cautivar [kau̯ti'βar] *vt* **1.** (*apresar*) to capture **2.** (*fascinar*) to captivate

cautiverio [kau̯ti'βe·rjo] *m*, **cautividad** [kau̯·ti·βi'ðað] *f* captivity

cautivo, -a [kau̯'ti·βo, -a] *adj, m, f* captive

cauto, -a ['kau̯·to, -a] *adj* cautious

cava ['ka·βa] *m* cava (*Champagne from the northeast of Spain*)

cavar [ka'βar] *vi, vt* to dig

caverna [ka'βer·na] *f* cave; (*gruta*) *t.* MED cavern; **los hombres de las ~s** cavemen

caviar [ka'βjar] *m* caviar

cavilar [ka·βi'lar] *vt* **~ algo** to ponder (on) sth

caza¹ ['ka·sa, -θa] *f* **1.** (*montería*) hunting; **ir de** [*o* **a la**] **~** to go hunting **2.** (*animales*) game

caza² ['ka·sa, -θa] *m* MIL fighter plane

cazador(a) [ka·sa·'dor, ka·θa·-] **I.** *adj* hunting **II.** *m(f)* hunter *m*, huntress *f*; **~ furtivo** poacher

cazadora [ka·sa·'do·ra, ka·θa·-] *f* bomber jacket; **~ de piel** leather jacket

cazar <z → c> [ka'sar, -'θar] *vt* **1.** (*atrapar*) to hunt **2.** (*coger*) to catch; (*conseguir*) to get **3.** *inf* (*engañar*) to take in

cazo ['ka·so, -θo] *m* **1.** (*puchero*) saucepan **2.** (*cucharón*) ladle

cazuela [ka·'swe·la, -'θwe·la] *f* casserole

CE [se·'e, θe·'e] *f* HIST *abr de* **Comunidad Europea** EC

cebada [se·'βa·da, θe·-] *f* barley

cebar [se·'βar, θe·-] **I.** *vt* **1.** (*engordar*) to fatten (up) **2.** (*horno*) to stoke (up) **3.** (*máquina*) to start **II.** *vr:* **~se** (*ira*) to vent one's anger

cebo ['se·βo, θe·-] *m* **1.** (*de anzuelo*) bait; *t. fig* lure **2.** (*en un horno*) fuel

cebolla [se·'βo·ja, θe·'βo·ʎa] *f* **1.** BOT (*comestible*) onion **2.** BOT (*bulbo*) bulb

cebra ['se·bra, 'θe·-] *f* zebra; **paso de ~** AUTO crosswalk

cecear [se·se·'ar, θe·θe·-] *vi* to pronounce Spanish 's' as [θ]

ceder [se·'der, θe·-] **I.** *vi* **1.** (*renunciar*) to renounce; (*de una pretensión*) to give up **2.** (*disminuir*) to diminish; **cedió la lluvia** the rain eased off **3.** (*capitular*) **~ a algo** to give in to sth **4.** (*cuerda*) to give way **II.** *vt* **1.** (*dar*) to hand over; (*balón*) to pass **2.** (*transferir*) to transfer **3.** AUTO **'ceda el paso'** 'yield'

cedrón [se·'dron, θe·-] *m AmS* BOT lemon verbena

cegar [se·'ɣar, θe·-] *irr como* **fregar I.** *vi* to go [*o* become] blind **II.** *vt* (*quitar la vista*) to blind; **le ciega la ira** he/she is blinded by rage

ceguera [se·'ɣe·ra, θe·-] *f t. fig* blindness

ceja ['se·xa, 'θe·-] *f* (*entrecejo*) eyebrow; **fruncir las ~s** to knit one's eyebrows; **tener a alguien entre ~ y ~** *inf* to have it in for sb

celador(a) [se·la·'dor, -·'do·ra; θe·-] *m(f)* watchman *m*, watchwoman *f*; (*de cárcel*) prison guard

celda ['sel·da, 'θel·-] *f* (*celdilla*) cell; (*en prisión*) prison cell; **~ de castigo** solitary confinement

celebración [se·le·βra·'sjon, θe·le·βra·'θjon] *f* (*acto*) celebration

celebrar [se·le·'βrar, θe·-] **I.** *vt* **1.** (*mérito*) to celebrate **2.** (*reuniones*) to hold; **~ una subasta** to hold an auction **3.** (*alegrarse*) to be delighted; (*aplaudir*) to applaud **II.** *vr:* **~se** (*fiesta*) to be celebrated; (*reunión*) to be held

célebre <celebérrimo> ['se·le·βre, 'θe·-] *adj* **~ por algo** famous for sth

celebridad [se·le·βri·'dad, θe·-] *f* **1.** (*personaje*) celebrity **2.** (*renombre*) fame

celeste [se·'les·te, θe-] *adj* **1.** (*célico*) celestial; **cuerpos ~s** heavenly bodies **2.** (*color*) sky blue

celestial [se·les·'tjal, θe-] *adj* (*del cielo*) celestial, heavenly

celibato [se·li·'βa·to, θe-] *m* REL celibacy

celo ['se·lo, 'θe-] *m* **1.** (*afán*) zeal **2.** *pl* (*por amor*) jealousy; **tener ~s** to be jealous **3.** *pl* (*envidia*) envy **4.** ZOOL (*macho*) rut; (*hembra*) heat; **estar en ~** (*macho*) to be in rut; (*hembra*) to be on heat **5.** (*cinta*) adhesive [*o* Scotch®] tape

celoso, -a [se·'lo·so, θe-] *adj* **1.** (*con fervor*) ~ **en algo** zealous in sth **2.** (*exigente*) ~ **de algo** conscientious about sth **3.** (*con celos*) jealous **4.** (*con envidia*) envious

celta ['sel·ta, 'θel-] **I.** *adj* Celtic **II.** *mf* Celt

célula ['se·lu·la, 'θe-] *f* BIO, POL cell

celulitis [se·lu·'li·tis, θe-] *f inv* MED cellulitis

cementerio [se·men·'te·rjo, θe-] *m* (*camposanto*) cemetery

cemento [se·'men·to, θe-] *m* ARQUIT, ANAT cement; ~ **armado** reinforced concrete

cena ['se·na, 'θe-] *f* supper

cenaduría [se·na·du·'ri·a, θe-] *f* Méx eating house (*serving only at night*)

cenar [se·'nar, θe-] **I.** *vi* to have dinner **II.** *vt* to have for dinner

cenicero [se·ni·'θe·ro, θe-] *m* ashtray

cenicienta [se·ni·'sjen·ta, θe·ni·'θjen-] *f*, **Cenicienta** *f t. fig* Cinderella

cenit [se·'nit, θe-] *m* zenith

ceniza [se·'ni·sa, θe·'ni·θa] *f* **1.** (*residuo*) ash; **reducir algo a ~s** to reduce sth to ashes **2.** *pl* (*restos mortales*) ashes *pl*

censar [sen·'sar, θen-] **I.** *vi* to carry out a census **II.** *vt* to take a census of

censo ['sen·so, 'θen-] *m* census; ~ **electoral** POL electoral roll

censura [sen·'su·ra, θen-] *f* **1.** (*crítica*) censorship **2.** (*entidad*) censor's office **3.** POL **moción de ~** motion of censure

censurar [sen·su·'rar, θen-] *vt* to censure; **~on todas las escenas violentas** all the violent scenes were taken out

centavo [sen·'ta·βo, θen-] *m* **1.** (*centésima parte*) hundredth (part) **2.** (*de dólar*) cent, penny **3.** *AmC, CSur* FIN (*moneda*) centavo

centavo, -a [sen·'ta·βo, -a; θen-] *adj* hundredth; *v. t.* **octavo**

centell(e)ar [sen·te·je·'ar, θen·te·ʎe·'ar; sen·te·'jar, θen·te·'ʎar] *vi* **1.** (*relámpago*) to flash **2.** (*fuego*) to spark **3.** (*estrella*) to twinkle **4.** (*ojos*) to glitter

centena [sen·'te·na, θen-] *f* hundred

centenar [sen·te·'nar, θen-] *m* hundred

centenario [sen·te·'na·rjo, θen-] *m* centennial

centenario, -a [sen·te·'na·rjo, -a; θen-] *adj, m, f* centenarian

centeno [sen·'te·no, θen-] *m* rye

centígrado [sen·'ti·ɣra·do, θen-] *m* centigrade; **grado ~** degree centigrade

centímetro [sen·'ti·me·tro, θen-] *m* centimeter

céntimo ['sen·ti·mo, -a; 'θen-] **I.** *adj* hundredth **II.** *m* **1.** (*parte*) hundredth part **2.** FIN (*moneda*) (Euro) cent; *CRi, Par, Ven* centimo; **estar sin un ~** to be broke

centinela [sen·ti·'ne·la; θen-] *mf* MIL sentry

centrado, -a [sen·'tra·do, -a; θen-] *adj* **1.** (*en el centro*) centered **2.** (*forma de ser*) stable

central [sen·'tral, θen-] **I.** *adj* central; **estación ~** main station **II.** *f* **1.** (*oficina*) head office **2.** TÉC plant; ~ **depuradora** waterworks; ~ (**hidro**)**eléctrica/nuclear/térmica** (hydro)electric/nuclear/oil-fired power station

centralismo [sen·tra·'lis·mo, θen-] *m* POL centralism

centralita [sen·tra·'li·ta, θen-] *f* TEL switchboard

centralizar <z → c> [sen·tra·li·'sar, θen·tra·li·'θar] *vt* to centralize

centrar [sen·'trar, θen-] **I.** *vt* **1.** TÉC (*colocar*) to center **2.** (*concentrar*) to concentrate **3.** (*interés*) to focus **II.** *vi, vt* DEP (*fútbol*) to center **III.** *vr:* **~se** **1.** (*basarse*) to center **2.** (*interés*) to focus

céntrico, -a [sen·'tri·ko, -a; 'θen-] *adj t.* TÉC central; **piso ~** an apartment in the center of town

centrifugar <g → gu> [sen·tri·fu·'ɣar, θen-] *vt* to spin-dry

C

centrífugo, -a [sen·'tri·fu·ɣo, -a; θen-] *adj* centrifugal

centro ['sen·tro, 'θen-] *m* **1.** *t.* POL, DEP (*el medio*) center; (*de la ciudad*) center city, downtown; ~ **de gravedad** center of gravity **2.** (*institución*) center; ~ **de enseñanza** teaching institution; ~ **comercial** shopping center, mall **3.** ANAT ~ **nervioso** nerve center

Centroamérica [sen·tro·a·'me·ri·ka, θen-] *f* Central America

centroamericano, -a [sen·tro·a·me·ri·'ka·no, -a; θen-] *adj, m, f* Central American

ceñir [se·'nir, θe-] *irr.* **I.** *vt* (*ponerse*) to put on; (*cinturón*) to buckle on **II.** *vr:* ~**se 1.** (*ajustarse*) to limit oneself; (*al hablar*) to be brief; ~**se al presupuesto** to keep to the budget **2.** (*vestido*) to be close-fitting **3.** (*ponerse*) to put on

ceño ['se·no, 'θe-] *m* frown; **fruncir el** ~ to frown

cepa ['se·pa, 'θe-] *f t.* BOT (*tronco*) stump; **de pura** ~ true

cepillar [se·pi·'jar, θe·pi·'ʎar] **I.** *vt* **1.** (*traje*) to brush; TÉC (*madera*) to plane **2.** *AmL inf* (*adular*) to butter up **3.** *inf* (*ganar*) to win **II.** *vr:* ~**se 1.** *inf* (*devorar*) to polish off **2.** *inf* (*dinero*) to squander **3.** *inf* (*matar*) to bump off

cepillo [se·'pi·jo, θe·pi·'ʎo] *m* **1.** (*para traje*) brush; TÉC (*para madera*) plane; (*de limpiar*) scrubbing brush; ~ **de barrer** broom; ~ **de dientes** toothbrush; **pasar el** ~ to brush **2.** (*en misa*) collection box

cepo ['se·po, 'θe-] *m* **1.** (*caza*) trap **2.** *pl* AUTO wheel clamp

cera ['se·ra, 'θe-] *f* wax; ~ **de los oídos** earwax; ~ **para suelos** wax polish; **museo de** ~ wax museum

cerámica [se·'ra·mi·ka, θe-] *f* ceramics *pl*

cerca ['ser·ka, 'θer-] **I.** *adv* (*en el espacio*) near; **aquí** ~ near here; **mirar de** ~ to look closely at **II.** *prep* **1.** (*lugar*) ~ **de** near **2.** (*cantidad*) ~ **de** about **III.** *f* fence

cercanía [ser·ka·'ni·a, θer-] *f* **1.** (*proximidad*) closeness **2.** *pl* (*alrededores*) outskirts *pl*

cercano, -a [ser·'ka·no, -a; θer-] *adj* near

cercar <c → qu> [ser·'kar, θer-] *vt* **1.** (*vallar*) to fence in **2.** (*rodear*) to surround

cerco ['ser·ko, 'θer-] *m* **1.** (*círculo*) circle; (*borde*) rim **2.** (*valla*) fence **3.** MIL siege

cerdo, -a ['ser·do, -a; 'θer-] **I.** *m, f* **1.** ZOOL pig; **carne de** ~ pork **2.** (*insulto*) swine **II.** *adj* (*sucio*) dirty

cereales [se·re·'a·les, θe-] *mpl* cereals *pl*, grain

cerebro [se·'re·βro, θe-] *m* **1.** ANAT brain **2.** (*inteligencia*) brains *pl*

ceremonia [se·re·'mo·nja, θe-] *f* **1.** (*acto*) ceremony **2.** (*cortesía*) formality; **sin ~s** without any fuss

cereza [se·'re·sa, θe·'re·θa] *f* cherry

cerezo [se·'re·so, θe·'re·θo] *m* (*árbol*) cherry tree; (*madera*) cherry wood

cerilla [se·'ri·ja, θe·'ri·ʎa] *f* (*fósforo*) match

cerillero [se·ri·'je·ro, θe·ri·'ʎe·ro] *m AmL* (*cajita*) matchbox

cero ['se·ro, 'θe-] *m t.* MAT zero; **ocho** (**grados**) **bajo/sobre** ~ eight below/above zero; **partir de** ~ to start from scratch

cerrado, -a [se·'rra·do, -a; θe-] *adj* **1.** *estar* (*no abierto*) closed; (*con llave*) locked; (*cielo*) overcast; **la puerta está cerrada** the door is closed; **a puerta cerrada** behind closed doors; **aquí huele a** ~ it smells stuffy in here **2.** *ser* (*actitud*) reserved **3.** *ser* (*denso*) dense; **noche cerrada** dark night **4.** *ser* (*acento*) broad **5.** *ser* (*curva*) sharp **6.** *ser* (*lerdo*) thick

cerradura [se·rra·'du·ra, θe-] *f* (*dispositivo*) lock

cerrajero, -a [se·rra·'xe·ro, -a; θe-] *m, f* locksmith

cerrar <e → ie> [se·'rrar, θe-] **I.** *vt* **1.** (*puerta*) to close; (*con llave*) to lock; (*carta*) to seal; ~ **el pico** *inf* to keep one's trap shut; ~ **un archivo** COMPUT to close a file; ~ **el paso a alguien** to block sb's way **2.** (*agujero*) to close (up); (*agua*) to turn off **3.** (*terreno*) to close off; (*con un cerco*) to enclose **4.** (*nego-*

ciación) to conclude **II.** *vi* **1.** (*puerta*) to close **2.** (*acabar*) to end **III.** *vr*: ~**se** **1.** (*puerta*) **la puerta se cerró sola** the door closed by itself **2.** (*herida*) to heal (up) **3.** (*obstinarse*) to persist **4.** (*el cielo*) to become overcast **5.** (*agruparse*) to crowd together

cerril [se·'rril, θe-] *adj* **1.** (*obstinado*) obstinate **2.** (*torpe*) dense

cerro ['se·rro, 'θe-] *m* hill; (*peñasco*) crag

cerrojo [se·'rro·xo, θe-] *m* bolt; **echar el** ~ **a la puerta** to bolt the door

certamen [ser·'ta·men, θer-] *m* competition

certeza [ser·'te·sa, θer·'te·θa] *f* certainty

certidumbre [ser·ti·'dum·bre, θer-] *f* certainty

certificado [ser·ti·fi·'ka·do, θer-] *m* certificate; ~ **de asistencia** certificate of attendance; ~ **médico** medical certificate

certificado, -a [ser·ti·fi·'ka·do, -a; θer-] *adj* JUR certified; **carta certificada** (*correos*) registered letter

certificar <c → qu> [ser·ti·fi·'kar, θer-] *vt* **1.** *t.* JUR (*afirmar*) to certify **2.** (*correos*) to register

cervecería [ser·βe·se·'ri·a, θer·βe·θe-] *f* **1.** (*bar*) bar **2.** (*fábrica*) brewery

cervecero, -a [ser·βe·'se·ro, -a; θer·βe·'θe-] *adj* beer; (*industria*) brewing

cerveza [ser·'βe·sa, θer·'βe·θa] *f* beer; ~ **de barril** draft beer; ~ **negra** dark beer, stout; ~ **rubia** lager beer

cervical [ser·βi·'kal, θer-] *adj* **1.** ANAT neck **2.** MED cervical

cesar [se·'sar, θe-] **I.** *vi* **1.** (*parar*) to stop; **sin** ~ ceaselessly **II.** *vt* **1.** (*pagos*) to stop **2.** (*despedir*) to dismiss, to fire

cesárea [se·'sa·rea, θe-] *f* Cesarean, C-section

cese ['se·se, 'θe-] *m* **1.** (*que termina*) cessation; (*interrupción*) suspension; ~ **de pagos** suspension of payments **2.** (*de obrero*) firing; (*de funcionario*) dismissal; ~ **en el cargo** to retire from office

cesión [se·'sjon, θe-] *f* **1.** (*entrega*) transfer **2.** JUR cession

césped ['ses·ped, 'θes-] *m* grass; '**prohibido pisar el** ~' 'keep off the grass'

cesta ['ses·ta, 'θes-] *f* basket

cesto ['ses·to, 'θes-] *m t.* DEP basket

ceta ['se·ta, 'θe-] *f* Z

chabola [ʧa·'βo·la] *f* (*casucha*) shack

chacal [ʧa·'kal] *m* jackal

chacalín [ʧa·ka·'lin] *m* AmC ZOOL shrimp

chácara ['ʧa·ka·ra] *f* Par, Nic, Bol **1.** (*granja*) small farm **2.** MED ulcer

chacarero, -a [ʧa·ka·'re·ro] *m, f* AmL farmer; (*trabajador*) farm laborer

cháchara ['ʧa·ʧa·ra] *f* inf (*charla*) chatter; **andar** [*o* **estar**] **de** ~ to have a chat

chacra ['ʧa·kra] *f* AmL (*granja*) small farm; (*finca*) country estate

chafar [ʧa·'far] **I.** *vt* **1.** (*aplastar*) to flatten *fig*, to squelch; (*arrugar*) to crease; (*deshacer*) to mess up **2.** (*confundir*) to confuse; **quedar(se) chafado** to be speechless **3.** (*estropear*) to spoil **II.** *vr*: ~**se** (*aplastarse*) to be flattened; (*deshacerse*) to be messed up; (*arrugarse*) to be creased

chaflán [ʧa·'flan] *m* **1.** (*bisel*) bevel (edge) **2.** (*en una calle*) street corner; (*en un edificio*) house corner

chagra ['ʧa·ɣra] *mf* Ecua (*labriego*) peasant

cháguar ['ʧa·ɣwar] *m* AmS BOT Paraguayan sisal

chal [ʧal] *m* shawl

chalado, -a [ʧa·'la·do, -a] *adj* inf crazy

chalanear [ʧa·la·ne·'ar] *vt* AmL (*un caballo*) to break in; (*adiestrar*) to train

chalé [ʧa·'le] *m* (*casa unifamiliar*) detached family home; (*de campo*) country house; (*villa*) chalet

chaleco [ʧa·'le·ko] *m* vest; ~ **salvavidas** life jacket

chalina [ʧa·'li·na] *f* Arg, Col, CRi (*chal*) narrow shawl

chamaco, -a [ʧa·'ma·ko, -a] *m, f* Cuba, Méx **1.** (*muchacho*) boy; (*muchacha*) girl **2.** (*novio*) boyfriend; (*novia*) girlfriend

chamagoso, -a [ʧa·ma·'ɣo·so, -a] *adj* Méx (*mugriento*) filthy

chamico [ʧa·'mi·ko] *m* AmL BOT thorn apple

champán [ʧam·'pan] *m* champagne

champiñón [ʧam·pi·'ɲon] *m* mushroom

champú [ʧam·'pu] *m* shampoo; ~ **anti-**

caspa anti-dandruff shampoo

chamuscar <c = qu> [ʧa.mus.'kar] I. *vt* (*quemar*) to scorch II. *vr*: **~se** (*quemarse*) to get scorched

chance ['ʧan.se, -θe] *m o f* AmC (*oportunidad*) chance

chanchería [ʧan.ʧe.'ri.a] *f* AmL pork butcher's shop

chancho ['ʧan.ʧo] *m* AmL pig

chancho, -a ['ʧan.ʧo, -a] *adj* AmL 1. (*marrano*) dirty 2. (*desaseado*) slovenly

chanchullo [ʧan·'ʧu·jo, -ʎo] *m inf* swindle, fiddle

chancla ['ʧan.kla] *f* 1. (*zapato viejo*) old shoe 2. (*zapatilla*) slipper 3. (*de playa*) flip flop

chancleta [ʧan·'kle.ta] *f* 1. (*chinela*) slipper 2. AmL (*bebé*) baby girl 3. *inf* (*persona inepta*) fool

chanclo ['ʧan.klo] *m* 1. (*zueco*) clog 2. (*de goma*) (rubber) overshoe, galosh

chándal ['ʧan.dal] *m* <chándals> tracksuit

changa ['ʧan.ga] *f* 1. Arg (*ocupación*) trade 2. AmS (*transporte*) porterage 3. AmS, Cuba (*broma*) joke

changador [ʧan·ga·'dor] *m* 1. AmS (*cargador*) carrier 2. Arg (*temporero*) casual worker

chantaje [ʧan·'ta.xe] *m* blackmail

chantajear [ʧan·ta·xe·'ar] *vt* to blackmail

chantajista [ʧan·ta·'xis.ta] *mf* blackmailer

chantar [ʧan·'tar] *vt* Chile (*golpe*) to deal

chapa ['ʧa.pa] *f* 1. (*metal*) sheet 2. (*lámina*) plate 3. (*contrachapado*) plywood 4. (*tapón*) (bottle)cap 5. (*placa*) badge 6. AmL (*cerradura*) lock 7. *pl* (*juego*) game played with bottle caps

chaparreras [ʧa·pa·'rre.ras] *fpl* Méx (*pantalones para montar a caballo*) chaps *pl*

chaparrón [ʧa·pa·'rron] *m* 1. (*lluvia*) downpour; (*chubasco*) cloudburst 2. *inf* (*cantidad grande*) barrage

chapetón, -ona [ʧa·pe·'ton] I. *adj* AmL newly arrived II. *m, f* AmL Spaniard in America

chapisca [ʧa·'pis.ka] *f* AmC AGR (*cosecha de maíz*) corn harvest

chapopote [ʧa.po.'po.te] *m* Ant, Méx (*asfalto*) asphalt

chapucero, -a [ʧa.pu.'se.ro, -a; -'θe.ro, -a] *adj* (*trabajando*) shoddy

chapulín [ʧa.pu.'lin] *m* 1. AmL (*langosta*) large cicada 2. AmC (*niño*) child

chapuza [ʧa.'pu.sa, -θa] *f* 1. (*chapucería*) shoddy job 2. (*trabajo*) odd job

chapuzón [ʧa.pu·'son, -'θon] *m* dip; **darse un ~** to go for a dip

chaqueta [ʧa.'ke.ta] *f* jacket; **cambiar de ~** *fig* to change sides

chaquetón [ʧa.ke.'ton] *m* long jacket; (*cazadora*) Windbreaker®

charanga [ʧa·'ran.ga] *f* 1. (*banda*) brass band 2. AmL (*baile*) dance

charca ['ʧar.ka] *f* pond

charco ['ʧar.ko] *m* puddle, pool

charcón, -ona [ʧar.'kon, --'ko.na] *adj* Arg, Bol, Urug (*flaco*) skinny

charcutería [ʧar·ku·te·'ri.a] *f* 1. (*productos*) cooked or cured pork products *pl* 2. (*tienda*) ≈ delicatessen

charla ['ʧar.la] *f* 1. (*conversación*) chat; **estar de ~** to have a chat 2. (*conferencia*) talk

charlar [ʧar·'lar] *vi* 1. (*conversar*) to chat 2. (*parlotear*) to chatter

charlatán, -ana [ʧar.la.'tan, --'ta.na] I. *adj* talkative II. *m, f* 1. (*hablador*) chatterbox 2. (*chismoso*) gossip 3. (*vendedor*) hawker

charol [ʧa·'rol] *m* 1. (*barniz*) varnish 2. (*cuero*) patent leather 3. AmL (*bandeja*) tray

chárter ['ʧar.ter] *adj inv* **vuelo ~** charter flight

chasco ['ʧas.ko] *m* (*decepción*) disappointment

chasco, -a ['ʧas.ko, -a] *adj* CSur crinkly

chasis ['ʧa.sis] *m inv* AUTO chassis

chasqui ['ʧas.ki] *m* AmS (*chasque*) messenger

chasquido [ʧas·'ki.do] *m* 1. (*de lengua*) click 2. (*de la madera*) creak

chatarra [ʧa·'ta.rra] *f* 1. (*metal viejo*) scrap (metal) 2. (*trastos*) junk 3. *inf* (*dinero*) change

chatarrería [ʧa·ta·rre·'ri.a] *f* junkyard

chatarrero, -a [ʧa·ta·'rre.ro, -a] *m, f* junkman *m*, junkwoman *f*

chato, -a ['tʃa·to] **I.** *adj* **1.** (*nariz*) snub **2.** (*persona*) snub-nosed **3.** (*objeto*) blunt; (*aplastado*) flattened **II.** *m, f, inf* (*tratamiento*) kid

chaucha ['tʃau·tʃa] *f AmS* **1.** (*judía verde*) green bean **2.** (*patata*) new potato **3.** *pl* (*calderilla*) small change

chauchera [tʃau·'tʃe·ra] *f Chile, Ecua* (*monedero*) purse

chaval(a) [tʃa·'βal, -'βa·la] *m(f) inf* (*chico*) kid; (*joven*) young man *m*, young woman *f*

che [tʃe] *interj AmS* hey

checo, -a ['tʃe·ko, -a] **I.** *adj* Czech; **República Checa** Czech Republic **II.** *m, f* Czech

chelín [tʃe·'lin] *m* (*moneda*) shilling

chelo ['tʃe·lo] *m* cello

chepa ['tʃe·pa] *f inf* hump ▶ **subirse a la ~ de alguien** to be disrespectful to sb

cheque ['tʃe·ke] *m* check; **~ en blanco** blank check; **~ sin fondo** bounced check; **~ de viaje** traveler's check; **cobrar un ~** to cash a check; **extender un ~** to write a check

chequear [tʃe·ke·'ar] **I.** *vt AmL* (*comprobar*) to check **II.** *vr:* **~se** to get a checkup

chequeo [tʃe·'ke·o] *m* (*de la salud*) checkup; (*de un mecanismo*) service

chequera [tʃe·'ke·ra] *f AmL* checkbook

Chequia ['tʃe·kja] *f* Czech Republic

chévere ['tʃe·βe·re] **I.** *adj Ven inf* terrific **II.** *mf Cuba, PRico, Ven* braggart

chica ['tʃi·ka] **I.** *adj* (*pequeña*) small; (*joven*) young **II.** *f* **1.** (*niña*) girl; (*joven*) young woman **2.** (*criada*) maid

chicano, -a [tʃi·'ka·no, -a] *m, f* Chicano *(person of Mexican origin living in the USA)*

chichón [tʃi·'tʃon] *m* bump

chicle ['tʃi·kle] *m* chewing gum

chico, -a ['tʃi·ko] **I.** *adj* **1.** (*pequeño*) small **2.** (*joven*) young **II.** *m* **1.** (*niño*) boy; (*joven*) young man **2.** (*de los recados*) errand boy

chicote [tʃi·'ko·te] *m AmL* (*látigo*) whip

chiflado, -a [tʃi·'fla·do, -a] *adj inf* crazy

chiflón [tʃi·'flon] *m AmL* (*viento*) gale; (*corriente*) draft; **un ~ de aire** a blast of air

chigüín [tʃi·'ɣwin] *m AmC* (*niño*) kid

chile ['tʃi·le] *m* (*especia*) chili

Chile ['tʃi·le] *m* Chile

chileno, -a [tʃi·'le·no, -a] *adj, m, f* Chilean

chillar [tʃi·'ʎar, -'ʎar] *vi* **1.** (*persona*) to yell; **¡no me chilles!** don't shout at me! **2.** (*animal*) to howl; (*frenos*) to screech; (*puerta*) to creak **3.** (*colores*) to clash

chillido [tʃi·'ʎi·do, -'ʎi·do] *m* **1.** (*de persona*) yell **2.** (*de animal*) howl; (*de frenos*) screech; (*de puerta*) creak

chilote [tʃi·'lo·te] *m Méx* drink made of chili and pulque *(beverage made of agave)*

chimenea [tʃi·me·'nea] *f* **1.** *t. GEO* (*de un edificio*) chimney **2.** (*hogar*) fireplace

chimpancé [tʃim·pan·'se, -'θe] *mf* chimpanzee

china ['tʃi·na] *f* **1.** (*piedra*) pebble **2.** *AmL* (*india*) Indian woman; (*mestiza*) half-caste woman **3.** *AmL* (*amante*) mistress

China ['tʃi·na] *f* (**la**) **~** China

chinchar [tʃin·'tʃar] **I.** *vt inf* to pester **II.** *vr:* **~se** *inf* to get upset; **¡chínchate!** so there!, tough luck!

chinche¹ ['tʃin·tʃe] *m o f ZOOL* bedbug

chinche² ['tʃin·tʃe] *mf inf* (*pelmazo*) pain

chincheta [tʃin·'tʃe·ta] *f* thumbtack

chincol [tʃin·'kol] *f AmS ZOOL* crown sparrow

chingar <g → gu> [tʃin·'ɡar] **I.** *vt* **1.** (*molestar*) to annoy **2.** *inf* (*bebidas*) to drink **II.** *vr:* **~se** *inf* **1.** (*emborracharse*) to get plastered **2.** *AmL* (*frustrarse*) to be a washout **3.** *AmL* (*fallar*) to fail

chingo, -a ['tʃin·ɡo, -a] *adj* **1.** *AmC* (*animal*) with a cropped tail **2.** *AmC, Ven* (*chato*) flat-nosed **3.** *AmC* (*corto*) short **4.** *CRi* (*desnudo*) naked **5.** *Ven* (*ansioso*) anxious **6.** *Col, Cuba* (*pequeño*) tiny **7.** *Nic* (*bajo*) short

chingue ['tʃin·ɡe] *m Chile ZOOL* skunk

chinita [tʃi·'ni·ta] *f Chile* (*insecto*) ladybug

chino ['tʃi·no] *m AmL* (*indio*) Indian; (*mestizo*) mestizo

chino, -a ['tʃi·no, -a] **I.** *adj* Chinese **II.** *m, f* Chinese man *m*, Chinese woman *f* ▶ **engañar** a alguien como a un ~ *inf* to take sb for a ride

chip [tʃip] *m* COMPUT chip

chipichipi [tʃi·pi·'tʃi·pi] *m Méx* (*llovizna*) drizzle

Chipre ['tʃi·pre] *f* Cyprus

chiqueo [tʃi·'keo] *m* **1.** *Cuba, Méx* (*mimo*) pampering **2.** *AmC* (*contoneo*) swagger

chiquillo, -a [tʃi·'ki·jo, -a; -'ki·ʎo, -a] **I.** *adj* young **II.** *m, f* (*niño*) (small) child; (*chico*) (little) boy; (*chica*) (little) girl

chiringuito [tʃi·rin·'gi·to] *m* kiosk *(selling snacks and drinks)*

chiripa [tʃi·'ri·pa] *f inf* stroke of luck; (*casualidad*) fluke

chirola [tʃi·'ro·la] *f* **1.** *Arg* (*moneda*) old coin made of nickel **2.** *Chile* (*moneda*) silver 20 centavo coin **3.** *pl Arg* (*calderilla*) small change

chirona [tʃi·'ro·na] *f inf* jail, clink *inf*

chirriar <*l.* pres *chirrío*> [tʃi·rri·'ar] *vi* **1.** (*metal*) to squeak; (*madera*) to creak **2.** (*pájaros*) to chirp

chisme ['tʃis·me] *m* **1.** (*habladuría*) piece of gossip **2.** (*objeto*) thingamajig; **recoge esos** ~**s** put away those things

chismoso, -a [tʃis·'mo·so, -a] **I.** *adj* gossiping **II.** *m, f* gossip

chispa ['tʃis·pa] *f* **1.** *t.* ELEC spark; **echar** ~**s** to give off sparks; *fig* to be hopping mad **2.** (*ingenio*) wit **3.** *inf* (*borrachera*) drunkenness **4.** (*una pizca*) **una** ~ **de...** a bit of...

chispear [tʃis·pe·'ar] **I.** *vi* **1.** (*centellear*) to spark **2.** (*brillar*) to sparkle **II.** *vimpers* (*lloviznar*) to drizzle

chiste ['tʃis·te] *m* (*cuento*) funny story; (*broma*) joke; ~ **verde** dirty joke

chistoso, -a [tʃis·'to·so, -a] **I.** *adj* funny **II.** *m, f* joker

chiva ['tʃi·βa] *f Col inf* (*noticia*) (piece of) news

chivarse [tʃi·'βar·se] *vr inf* **1.** (*hablar*) to grass **2.** *AmL* (*enojarse*) to get annoyed

chivatear [tʃi·βa·te·'ar] *vi* **1.** *Arg, Chile* (*chillar*) to shout **2.** *AmS* (*alborotar*) to make a ruckus

chivato, -a [tʃi·'βa·to, -a] *m, f inf* (*informador*) stool pigeon; (*en la escuela*) tell-tale

chivo, -a ['tʃi·βo, -a] *m, f* kid; ~ **expiatorio** scapegoat

chocante [tʃo·'kan·te] *adj* (*raro*) strange; (*sorprendente*) startling

chocar <c → qu> [tʃo·'kar] **I.** *vi* (*vehículos*) ~ **contra algo** to collide with sth; (*dar*) to crash into sth; (*coches*) to run into sth **II.** *vt* **1.** (*entrechocar*) ~ **las copas** to clink glasses **2.** (*perturbar*) to startle

chochear [tʃo·tʃe·'ar] *vi* **1.** (*por vejez*) to dodder (around) **2.** (*sentir cariño*) to dote

choclo ['tʃo·klo] *m* **1.** *AmS* (*maíz*) corn; (*mazorca tierna*) ear of corn **2.** *AmS* CULIN sweet tamale

chocolate [tʃo·ko·'la·te] *m* chocolate; *inf* (*hachís*) hash *inf*

chocolatería [tʃo·ko·la·te·'ri·a] *f* (*establecimiento*) café specializing in hot chocolate drinks; (*fábrica*) chocolate factory

chocolatina [tʃo·ko·la·'ti·na] *f* chocolate bar

chofer [tʃo·'fer] *m*, **chófer** ['tʃo·fer] *m* chauffeur

chollo ['tʃo·jo, -ʎo] *m inf* **1.** (*suerte*) luck **2.** (*ganga*) bargain **3.** (*trabajo*) cushy job

cholo, -a ['tʃo·lo, -a] *m, f AmL* **1.** (*indio*) Indian integrated into Creole society **2.** (*mestizo*) mestizo

chomba ['tʃom·ba] *f Arg* (*polo*) polo shirt

chongo ['tʃon·go] *m* **1.** *Méx inf* (*trenza*) braid; (*moño*) knot, bun **2.** *Chile* (*cuchillo*) blunt knife

chopo ['tʃo·po] *m* black poplar

choque ['tʃo·ke] *m* **1.** (*impacto*) impact; (*colisión*) crash **2.** (*encuentro*) clash

chorizo [tʃo·'ri·so, -θo] *m* chorizo *(hard pork sausage)*

chorizo, -a [tʃo·'ri·so, -a; -θo, -a] *m, f inf* petty thief

choro ['tʃo·ro] *m* **1.** *Chile* (*mejillón*) large mussel **2.** *AmS inf* (*ladrón*) thief

chorote [tʃo·'ro·te] *m Méx, Ven* (*chocolate*) chocolate drink

chorrada [tʃo·'rra·da] f 1. inf (tontería) stupid remark 2. inf (cosa superflua) trivial thing

chorrear [tʃo·rre·'ar] vi 1. (fluir) to gush (out) 2. (gotear) to drip

chorro ['tʃo·rro] m 1. (hilo) trickle; (de ingrediente) drop 2. (torrente) stream; t. TÉC jet; **avión a ~** jet plane

choza ['tʃo·sa, -θa] f hut

chubasco [tʃu·'βas·ko] m (heavy) shower

chubasquero [tʃu·βas·'ke·ro] m raincoat

chuchería [tʃu·tʃe·'ri·a] f (dulce) sweet

chucho ['tʃu·tʃo] m 1. inf (perro) mutt 2. AmL (escalofrío) shivers pl; (fiebre) fever

chucrut [tʃu·'kru] m sauerkraut

chufa ['tʃu·fa] f tiger nut

chufla ['tʃu·fla] f joke

chulada [tʃu·'la·da] f inf (cosa estupenda) cool thing

chulear [tʃu·le·'ar] vi, vr: ~**se** (jactarse) to brag

chulería [tʃu·le·'ri·a] f bragging

chuleta [tʃu·'le·ta] f 1. (costilla) chop 2. inf (apunte) crib (sheet)

chuletón [tʃu·le·'ton] m T-bone steak

chulo ['tʃu·lo] m 1. (mal educado) boor 2. inf (proxeneta) pimp

chulo, -a ['tʃu·lo, -a] adj 1. (jactancioso) boastful; (presumido) conceited; **ponerse ~** to get cocky 2. inf (elegante) smart

chungo, -a ['tʃun·go, -a] adj inf (malo) bad

chuño ['tʃu·ɲo] m AmS (fécula) potato flour

chupa-chups® [tʃu·pa·'tʃups] m inv lollipop

chupada [tʃu·'pa·da] f (paja) suck; (cigarrillo) puff

chupado, -a [tʃu·'pa·do, -a] adj 1. (flaco) skinny; (consumido) emaciated 2. inf (fácil) a cinch 3. AmL (borracho) drunk

chupaflor [tʃu·pa·'flor] m AmC ZOOL hummingbird

chupar [tʃu·'par] I. vt 1. (extraer) to suck out; (aspirar) to suck in; (absorber) to absorb 2. (caramelo) to suck; (helado) to lick 3. (cigarrillo) to smoke, to puff on II. vi 1. inf (mamar) to suckle; ~

del bote to line one's pocket 2. AmL inf (beber) to booze III. vr: ~**se** 1. (secarse) to get very thin 2. inf (aguantar) to sit out, to put up with

chupe ['tʃu·pe] m CSur, Ecua, Perú CULIN spicy chowder

chupete [tʃu·'pe·te] m 1. (del bebé) pacifier 2. AmL (piruli) lollipop

churrasco [tʃu·'rras·ko] m steak

churro ['tʃu·rro] m 1. (fritura) ≈ fritter 2. (chapuza) (piece of) shoddy work 3. (suerte) piece of luck 4. Col (persona atractiva) good-looker

chusma ['tʃus·ma] f rabble, riffraff

chutar [tʃu·'tar] I. vt to shoot; **esto va que chuta** inf it's going well II. vr: ~**se** inf to shoot up

chuza ['tʃu·sa, -θa] f 1. Arg, Urug (lanza) pike 2. Arg (gallo) cock's spur 3. Méx (juego: bolos) strike 4. pl Arg (pelo) rats' tails

chuzar <z → c> [tʃu·'sar, -'θar] vt Col to prick

Cía ['si·a, 'θi·a] abr de **compañía** Co.

ciberespacio [si·βer·es·'pa·sjo, θi·βer·es·'pa·θjo] m cyberspace

cibernauta [si·βer·'nau·ta, θi-] mf websurfer, cybernaut

cibernética [si·βer·'ne·ti·ka, θi-] f cybernetics pl

cicatriz [si·ka·'tris, θi·ka·'triθ] f scar

cicatrizar <z → c> [si·ka·tri·'sar, θi·ka·tri·'θar] vt, vi, vr: ~**se** to heal

ciclismo [si·'klis·mo, θi-] m DEP cycling

ciclista [si·'klis·ta, θi-] I. adj cycle II. mf cyclist

ciclo ['si·klo, 'θi-] m cycle; ~ **económico** economic cycle

ciclón [si·'klon, θi-] m cyclone

ciego, -a ['sje·ɣo, 'θje-] I. adj 1. (persona) blind; **quedarse ~** to go blind 2. (taponado) blocked II. m, f blind man m, blind woman f III. adv **a ciegas** blindly

cielo ['sje·lo, 'θje-] I. m 1. (atmósfera) sky; **caído del ~** out of the blue 2. REL Heaven 3. (apelativo) darling II. interj **¡~s!** good heavens!

ciempiés [sjem·'pjes, θjem-] m inv centipede

cien [sjen, θjen] adj inv a (o one) hun-

dred; al ~ por ~ one hundred per cent; v. t. **ochocientos**

ciencia ['sjen·sja, 'θjen·θja] f 1. (saber) knowledge; **a ~ cierta** for sure 2. (disciplina) science; **~s políticas** political science; **~s (naturales)** natural science(s)

ciencia-ficción ['sjen·sja·fik·'sjon, 'θjen·θja·fiɣ·'θjon] f science fiction

científico, -a [sjen·'ti·fi·ko, -a; θjen-] I. adj scientific II. m, f scientist

ciento ['sjen·to, 'θjen-] adj <cien> inv a [o one] hundred; **el cinco por ~** five per cent; v. t. **ochocientos**

cierre ['sje·rre, 'θje-] m 1. (conclusión) closing; (clausura) closure; PREN time of going to press; **~ del ejercicio** close of the financial year; **hora de ~** closing time; **~ centralizado** AUTO central locking 2. Arg (cremallera) zipper

cierto ['sjer·to, 'θjer-] adv certainly; **por ~** by the way

cierto, -a ['sjer·to, -a; 'θjer-] adj <certísimo> 1. (verdadero) true; (seguro) sure; **estar en lo ~** to be right; **lo ~ es que...** the fact is that... 2. (alguno) a certain; **~ día** one day

ciervo, -a ['sjer·βo, -a; 'θjer-] m, f deer

cifra ['si·fra, 'θi-] f (guarismo) figure; **~ de negocios** ECON turnover; **~ de ventas** ECON sales figures

cifrar [si·'frar, θi-] vt 1. (codificar) to code 2. (calcular) to reckon

cigarra [si·'ɣa·rra, θi-] f cicada

cigarrillo [si·ɣa·'rri·jo, θi·ɣa·'rri·ʎo] m cigarette

cigarro [si·'ɣa·rro, θi-] m cigar

cigüeña [si·'ɣwe·ɲa, θi-] f stork

cilindrada [si·lin·'dra·da, θi-] f AUTO cubic capacity

cilindro [si·'lin·dro, θi-] m cylinder

cima ['si·ma, 'θi-] f t. fig summit; **~ del árbol** tree top; **~ del monte** mountain peak

cimarrón, -ona [si·ma·'rron, --'rro·na; θi-] adj AmL wild

cimbronazo [sim·bro·'na·so, θim·bro·'na·θo] m AmL 1. (temblor) jolt; (de tierra) earthquake 2. (tirón) yank

cimiento [si·'mjen·to, θi-] m foundation

cinc [siŋ, θiŋ] m zinc

cincel [sin·'sel, θin·'θel] m chisel

cinco ['siŋ·ko, 'θiŋ-] I. adj inv five II. m five; **¡choca esos ~!** give me five!; v. t. **ocho**

cincuenta [sin·'kwen·ta, θin-] adj inv m fifty; v. t. **ochenta**

cine ['si·ne, 'θi-] m 1. (arte) cinema, movies pl; **~ mudo/sonoro** silent/talking films; **~ negro** film noir; **me gusta el ~** I like the movies 2. (sala) cinema, movie theater; **ir al ~** to go to the movies

cínico, -a ['si·ni·ko, -a; 'θi-] I. adj cynical II. m, f cynic

cinismo [si·'nis·mo, θi-] m cynicism

cinta ['sin·ta, 'θin-] f band; **~ adhesiva** adhesive tape; **~ aislante** insulating tape; **~ métrica** tape measure; **~ del pelo** hair ribbon; **~ de vídeo** videotape; **~ virgen** blank tape; **~ transportadora** conveyor belt

cinto ['sin·to, 'θin-] m belt

cintura [sin·'tu·ra, θin-] f waist

cinturón [sin·tu·'ron, θin-] m belt; **ponerse el ~** to fasten one's seatbelt; **apretarse el ~** fig to tighten one' belt

cipe ['si·pe, 'θi-] adj AmC sickly, runty

ciprés [si·'pres, θi-] m cypress

circo ['sir·ko, 'θir-] m (arena) circus; **~ ambulante** traveling circus

circuito [sir·ku·'i·to, θir-] m 1. t. ELEC circuit; **~ integrado** integrated circuit; **corto ~** short circuit 2. DEP circuit, track

circulación [sir·ku·la·'sjon, θir·ku·la·'θjon] f 1. t. ECON circulation; **~ sanguínea** (blood) circulation; **retirar de la ~** to withdraw from circulation 2. (tránsito) traffic

circular [sir·ku·'lar, θir-] I. adj circular II. vi 1. (recorrer) to circulate 2. (personas) to walk (around); (vehículos) to drive (around); **¡circulen!** move along! III. f circular

circulatorio, -a [θir·ku·la·'to·rjo, -a; θir-] adj MED circulatory

círculo ['θir·ku·lo, 'θir-] m circle; **~ de amistades** circle of friends; **~ vicioso** vicious circle

circunferencia [sir·kun·fe·'ren·sja, θir·kun·fe·'ren·θja] f t. MAT circumference

circunstancia [sir·kuns·'tan·sja, θir·kuns·'tan·θja] f circumstance; **en estas ~s** these circumstances

circunvalación [sir·kum·ba·la·'sjon, θir·kum·ba·la·'θjon] *f* **carretera de** ~ by-pass

ciruela [si·'rwe·la, θi·] *f* plum; ~ **pasa** prune

ciruelo [si·'rwe·lo, θi·] *m* BOT plum tree

cirugía [si·ru·'xi·a, θi·] *f* MED surgery; ~ **estética** cosmetic surgery

cirujano, -a [si·ru·'xa·no, -a; θi·] *m, f* MED surgeon

cisco ['sis·ko, θis·] *m* **1.** (*carbón*) coal dust **2.** (*jaleo*) fight

Cisjordania [sis·xor·'da·nja, θis·] *f* GEO (the) West Bank

cisne ['sis·ne, θis·] *m* swan

cisterna [sis·'ter·na, θis·] *f* tank; **barco** ~ tanker

cita ['si·ta, θi·] *f* **1.** (*convocatoria*) appointment **2.** (*encuentro*) meeting; (*romántico*) date; ~ **anual** annual meeting; ~ **a ciegas** blind date; **tener una ~ con alguien** to be meeting sb; (*romántica*) to have a date with sb **3.** (*mención*) quotation

citación [si·ta·'sjon, θi·ta·'θjon] *f* JUR summons

citar [si·'tar, θi·] **I.** *vt* **1.** (*convocar*) to arrange to meet **2.** (*mencionar*) to quote **3.** JUR to summon **II.** *vr:* ~**se** to arrange to meet

cítrico, -a ['si·tri·ko, -a; 'θi·] *adj* citric

cítricos ['si·tri·kos, 'θi·] *mpl* citrus fruits *pl*

ciudad [sju·'dad, θju·] *f* town; (*más grande*) city; ~ **hermanada** twin town; ~ **industrial** industrial town [*o* city]; ~ **de origen** home town; ~ **universitaria** university campus; ~ **dormitorio** dormitory town

ciudadanía [sju·da·da·'ni·a, θju·] *f* **1.** (*nacionalidad*) citizenship **2.** (*ciudadanos*) citizenry, citizens *pl*

ciudadano, -a [sju·da·'da·no, -a; θju·] **I.** *adj* **1.** (*de la ciudad*) city **2.** (*del ciudadano*) civic **II.** *m, f* **1.** (*residente*) resident **2.** (*súbdito*) citizen

cívico, -a ['si·βi·ko, -a; 'θi·] *adj* (*del ciudadano*) civic

civil [si·'βil, θi·] *adj* civil; **derecho** ~ civil law; **guerra** ~ civil war

civilización [si·βi·li·sa·'sjon, θi·βi·li·θa·'θjon] *f* civilization

civilizar <z → c> [si·βi·li·'sar, θi·βi·li·'θar] *vt* to civilize

civismo [si·'βis·mo, θi·] *m* community spirit, civic-mindedness

cizaña [si·'sa·ɲa, θi·'θa·] *f* **1.** BOT darnel **2.** (*enemistad*) discord

clamar [kla·'mar] **I.** *vi* to cry out **II.** *vt* to demand

clan [klan] *m* clan

clandestino, -a [klan·des·'ti·no, -a] *adj* secret; **reunión clandestina** secret meeting

claqué [kla·'ke] *f* tap dancing

clara ['kla·ra] *f* (*del huevo*) white

claramente [kla·ra·'men·te] *adv* clearly

clarear [kla·re·'ar] **I.** *vi* **1.** (*amanecer*) to grow light; **al ~ el día** at dawn **2.** (*despejarse*) to clear up **II.** *vt* to brighten

clarete [kla·'re·te] *m* rosé (wine)

claridad [kla·ri·'dad] *f* **1.** (*luminosidad*) brightness **2.** (*lucidez*) clarity

clarificar <c → qu> [kla·ri·fi·'kar] *vt* **1.** (*iluminar*) to illuminate **2.** (*aclarar*) to clarify

clarinete [kla·ri·'ne·te] *m* (*instrumento*) clarinet

clarividente [kla·ri·βi·'den·te] *adj* **1.** (*perspicaz*) discerning **2.** (*que percibe*) clairvoyant

claro ['kla·ro] **I.** *interj* of course **II.** *m* **1.** (*hueco*) gap **2.** (*calvero*) clearing **III.** *adv* clearly

claro, -a ['kla·ro, -a] *adj* **1.** (*iluminado*) bright; **azul** ~ light blue **2.** (*evidente*) clear; **poner** [*o* **sacar**] **en** ~ to clarify

clase ['kla·se] *f* **1.** (*tipo*) kind; **trabajos de toda** ~ all kinds of jobs **2.** (*categoría*) class; ~ **turista** tourist class; ~ **media** middle class **3.** ENS class; (*aula*) classroom; **dar** ~**s** to teach

clasicismo [kla·si·'sis·mo, -'θis·mo] *m* classicism

clásico, -a ['kla·si·ko, -a] **I.** *adj* classical; *fig* classic **II.** *m, f* classic

clasificación [kla·si·fi·ka·'sjon, -'θjon] *f* **1.** (*ordenación*) sorting **2.** *t.* BIO classification

clasificar <c → qu> [kla·si·fi·'kar] **I.** *vt* ~ **por algo** (*ordenar*) to sort according to sth; BIO to classify under sth **II.** *vr:* ~**se** to qualify

clasismo [kla.'sis.mo] *m* class-consciousness

claudicar <c → qu> [klau.ði.'kar] *vi* **1.** (*principios*) ~ **de algo** to abandon sth **2.** (*ceder*) to give in

claustro ['klaus.tro] *m* ARTE cloister

claustrofobia [klaus.tro.'fo.βja] *f* claustrophobia

cláusula ['klau.su.la] *f* clause; (*ley*) article

clausura [klau.'su.ra] *f* **1.** (*cierre*) closure; **sesión de ~** closing session **2.** REL cloister

clausurar [klau.su.'rar] *vt* to close

clavar [kla.'βar] *vt* **1.** (*hincar*) to knock in; (*enclavar*) to nail **2.** (*fijar*) to fix; **tener la vista clavada en algo** to have one's eyes set on sth **3.** *inf*(*dar*) to give **4.** *inf*(*cobrar*) to rip off

clave ['kla.βe] I. *adj inv* key II. *f* **1.** (*secreto*) ~ **de algo** key to sth **2.** (*código*) code; ~ **de acceso** password; **en ~** coded **3.** MÚS clef

clavel [kla.'βel] *m* carnation

clavícula [kla.'βi.ku.la] *f* collar bone

clavija [kla.'βi.xa] *f* **1.** TÉC pin; (*enchufe*) plug **2.** MÚS peg ▶ **apretar las ~s a alguien** to put the screws on sb

clavo ['kla.βo] *m* **1.** (*punta*) nail; **dar en el ~** to hit the nail on the head **2.** (*especia*) clove

claxon ['klak.son] *m* horn

clemencia [kle.'men.sja, -θja] *f* mercy

clemente [kle.'men.te] *adj* merciful

cleptómano, -a [klep.'to.ma.no, -a] *adj, m, f* PSICO kleptomaniac

clérigo ['kle.ri.ɣo] *m* clergyman; (*católico*) priest

clero ['kle.ro] *m* clergy

cliché [kli.'tʃe] *m* **1.** (*tópico*) cliché **2.** FOTO negative

cliente, -a [kljen.te] *m, f* customer; (*de un abogado*) client; ~ **fijo** regular customer

clientela [kljen.'te.la] *f* customers *pl*; (*de un abogado*) clients *pl*

clima ['kli.ma] *m* **1.** (*atmósfera*) atmosphere **2.** GEO climate

clínica ['kli.ni.ka] *f* clinic

clip [klip] *m* (*pinza*) clip

cloaca [klo.'a.ka] *f* sewer

clon [klon] *m* BIO clone

clonar [klo.'nar] *vt* to clone

cloro ['klo.ro] *m* chlorine

clorofila [klo.ro.'fi.lja] *f* chlorophyl(l)

club <clubs *o* clubes> [kluβ] *m* club; ~ **deportivo** sports club

cm [sen.'ti.me.tro, θen-] *abr de* **centímetro** cm.

coacción [ko.ak.'sjon, -aɣ.'θjon] *f* coercion

coaccionar [ko.ak.sjo.'nar, ko.aɣ.'θjo-] *vt* to coerce

coagular(se) [ko.a.ɣu.'lar.(se)] *vt, (vr)* to coagulate

coágulo [ko.'a.ɣu.lo] *m* clot

coalición [koa.li.'sjon, -'θjon] *f* coalition

coartada [koar.'ta.da] *f* alibi

coartar [koar.'tar] *vt* (*libertad*) to restrict; (*persona*) to inhibit

coba ['ko.βa] *f* lie; **dar ~ a alguien** to suck up to sb

cobalto [ko.'βal.to] *m* cobalt

cobarde [ko.'βar.de] I. *adj* cowardly II. *m* coward

cobardía [ko.βar.'di.a] *f* cowardice

cobaya [ko.'βa.ja] *m o f* guinea pig

cobija [ko.'βi.xa] *f* **1.** AmL (*manta*) blanket **2.** *pl* AmL (*ropa de cama*) bedclothes *pl*; **pegarse a alguien las ~s** to oversleep

cobijar [ko.βi.'xar] I. *vt* **1.** (*proteger*) to shelter **2.** (*acoger*) to give shelter to II. *vr:* ~**se** to take shelter

cobo ['ko.βo] *m* AmC, Ant **1.** ZOOL giant sea snail **2.** (*persona*) unsociable person

cobra ['ko.βra] *f* cobra

cobrar [ko.'βrar] I. *vt* **1.** (*recibir*) to receive; (*suma*) to collect; (*cheque*) to cash; (*sueldo*) to earn; **¿me cobra, por favor?** how much do I owe you? **2.** (*intereses*) to charge; (*deudas*) to recover **3.** (*conseguir*) ~ **ánimos** to gather courage II. *vi* **1.** (*sueldo*) to get one's wages **2.** *inf*(*una paliza*) to get a beating; **¡que vas a ~!** you're going to get it! III. *vr:* ~**se** to cash up; *fig* to claim

cobre ['ko.βre] *m* **1.** QUÍM copper **2.** AmL (*moneda*) copper coin

cobro ['ko.βro] *m* **1.** (*acto*) recovery

2. FIN (*impuestos*) collection; (*pago*) payment; **llamar a ~ revertido** to reverse the charges **3.** *pl* COM arrears *pl*

cocaína [ko·ka·'i·na] *f* cocaine

cocción [kok·'sjon, koɣ·'θjon] *f* cooking; (*duración*) cooking time

cocer [ko·'ser, -'θer] *irr* I. *vt* (*cocinar*) to cook; (*hervir*) to boil II. *vi* **1.** (*cocinar*) to cook **2.** (*hervir*) to boil III. *vr:* **~se 1.** (*cocinarse*) to be cooked **2.** (*tramarse*) to be going on **3.** *inf* (*pasar calor*) to be sweltering

cocha ['ko·tʃa] *f* AmS (*laguna*) lagoon; (*charco*) puddle

cochayuyo [ko·tʃa·'ju·jo] *m* AmS BOT rockweed

coche ['ko·tʃe] *m* **1.** (*automóvil*) car; **~ de bomberos** fire engine; **~ de carreras** DEP racing car; **ir en ~** to go by car **2.** (*de caballos*) coach, carriage

coche-cama <coches-cama> ['ko·tʃe·'ka·ma] *m* FERRO sleeping car

cochecito [ko·tʃe·'si·to, -'θi·to] *m* baby carriage

coche-patrulla <coches-patrulla> ['ko·tʃe·pa·'tru·ja, -ʎa] *m* patrol car

cochera [ko·'tʃe·ra] *f* garage; **~ de tranvías** tram depot

cochinada [ko·tʃi·'na·da] *f* *inf* filthy thing

cochinillo [ko·tʃi·'ni·jo, -ʎo] *m* piglet; **~ asado** roast suckling pig

cochino, -a [ko·'tʃi·no, -a] I. *adj* *inf* filthy II. *m, f* **1.** ZOOL (*macho*) pig; (*hembra*) sow **2.** *inf* (*guarro*) swine

cocido [ko·'si·do, ko·'θi·do] *m* stew (*made with chickpeas and meat*)

cocina [ko·'si·na, ko·'θi·-] *f* **1.** (*habitación*) kitchen **2.** (*aparato*) stove **3.** (*arte*) cookery, cooking; **libro de ~** cookbook

cocinar [ko·si·'nar, ko·θi·-] *vt, vi* to cook

cocinero, -a [ko·si·'ne·ro, -a; ko·θi·-] *m, f* cook

coco ['ko·ko] *m* **1.** BOT (*fruto*) coconut; (*árbol*) coconut palm **2.** *inf* (*cabeza*) head; **comerse el ~** to worry **3.** *inf* (*ogro*) bogeyman

cocodrilo [ko·ko·'dri·lo] *m* crocodile

cocoliche [ko·ko·'li·tʃe] *m* Arg, Urug LING *pidgin Spanish of Italian immigrants*

cocotero [ko·ko·'te·ro] *m* coconut palm

cóctel <cócteles> ['kok·tel] *m* cocktail

coctelera [kok·te·'le·ra] *f* cocktail shaker

cocuy [ko·'kuj] *m* AmL **1.** BOT agave **2.** (*bebida alcohólica*) corn whiskey

cocuyo [ko·'ku·jo] *m* AmL **1.** ZOOL firefly **2.** AUTO rear light

codazo [ko·'da·so, -θo] *m* nudge (with one's elbow)

codear [ko·de·'ar] I. *vi* to nudge II. *vr:* **~se** to rub shoulders [*o* elbows]

codicia [ko·'di·sja, -θja] *f* greed; (*algo ajeno*) covetousness; **~ de algo** greed for sth

codiciar [ko·di·'sjar, -'θjar] *vt* to covet

codicioso, -a [ko·di·'sjo·so, -a; ko·di·'θjo-] *adj* covetous

codificar <c → qu> [ko·di·fi·'kar] *vt* to code; *t.* COMPUT to encode

código ['ko·di·ɣo] *m* code; **~ de circulación** highway code; **Código Civil** civil code; **~ de barras** bar code; **~ postal** postal code, zip code; **mensaje en ~** coded message

codillo [ko·'di·jo, -ʎo] *m* **1.** ZOOL elbow **2.** CULIN knuckle

codo ['ko·do] *m* **1.** ANAT elbow; **trabajar ~ a ~** to work side by side; **hablar por los ~s** to talk nonstop **2.** TÉC (*doblez*) elbow joint **3.** (*de camino*) bend

codorniz [ko·dor·'nis, -'niθ] *f* quail

coetáneo, -a [koe·'ta·neo, -a] *adj, m, f* contemporary

cofradía [ko·fra·'di·a] *f* **1.** (*hermandad*) brotherhood **2.** (*gremio*) guild

cofre ['ko·fre] *m* chest; (*baúl*) trunk; (*de joyas*) jewel case

coger <g → j> [ko·'xer] I. *vt* **1.** (*agarrar*) to take hold, to seize; (*del suelo*) to pick up; (*flores*) to pick; **le cogió del brazo** he/she took him by the arm; **le cogió en brazos** he/she picked him up in his/her arms **2.** (*quitar*) to take away **3.** (*atrapar*) to catch; (*apresar*) to capture **4.** AUTO (*atropellar*) to knock down, to run over **5.** (*hábito*) to acquire; **~ cariño a alguien** take a liking to sb; **~ el hábito de fumar** to start smoking **6.** (*enfermedad*) to catch; **~ frío** to catch a cold; **ha cogido una gripe** he's/she's caught the flu **7.** (*sorprender*) to find **8.** (*obtener*) to get; **¿vas a ~ el piso?** are you going to take the apartment? **9.** (*tomar*) to take; **~ el tren/autobús** to take the train/bus **II.** *vi* (*tener sitio*) to fit

cognitivo, -a [koɣ·ni·'ti·βo, -a] *adj* cognitive

cogote [ko·'ɣo·te] *m inf* scruff; **estar hasta el ~** *inf* to have had enough

coherencia [ko·e·'ren·sja, -θja] *f* coherence

coherente [ko·e·'ren·te] *adj* coherent

cohesión [ko·e·'sjon] *f* cohesion

cohete [ko·'e·te] *m* rocket

cohibido, -a [koi·'βi·do, -a] *adj* **1.** (*intimidado*) intimidated **2.** (*inhibido*) inhibited

coima ['koi·ma] *f And, CSur* (*soborno*) bribe; (*dinero*) rake-off

coincidencia [koin·si·'den·sja, koin·θi·'den·θja] *f* **1.** (*simultaneidad*) coincidence; **¡qué ~!** what a coincidence! **2.** (*acuerdo*) agreement

coincidir [koin·si·'dir, koin·θi·'dir] *vi* **1.** (*sucesos*) to coincide **2.** (*toparse*) to meet; **~ con alguien** to meet sb **3.** (*concordar*) to agree; **~ con alguien** to agree with sb

coipo ['koi·po] *m Arg, Chile* ZOOL coypu

coito ['koi·to] *m* coitus, (*sexual*) intercourse

cojear [ko·xe·'ar] *vi* (*persona*) to limp; (*mueble*) to wobble; *fig* (*tener defecto*) to have a weak point

cojín [ko·'xin] *m* cushion

cojo, -a ['ko·xo, -a] *adj* (*persona*) lame; (*mueble*) wobbly; **a la pata coja** on one leg

cojudo, -a [ko·'xu·do, -a] *adj AmL* stupid

col [kol] *f* cabbage; **~es de Bruselas** Brussels sprouts

cola ['ko·la] *f* **1.** (*de cometa*) *t.* ANAT tail **2.** (*al esperar*) line; **hacer ~** to line up; **ponerse a la ~** to get in line **3.** (*pegamento*) glue

colaboración [ko·la·βo·ra·'sjon, -'θjon] *f* collaboration; (*periódico*) contribution

colaborador(a) [ko·la·βo·ra·'dor, -'do·ra] **I.** *adj* collaborating **II.** *m(f)* collaborator; LIT contributor

colaborar [ko·la·βo·'rar] *vi* **1.** (*cooperar*) to collaborate **2.** LIT to contribute

colada [ko·'la·da] *f* (*de ropa*) washing

coladera [ko·la·'de·ra] *f Méx* (*alcantarilla*) sewer

colador [ko·la·'dor] *m* sieve, strainer

colapsar [ko·lap·'sar] **I.** *vt* to bring to a standstill; **~ la red** COMPUT to bring down [*o to collapse*] the net **II.** *vi, vr:* **~se 1.** (*tráfico*) to come to a standstill **2.** MED to collapse

colapso [ko·'lap·so] *m* **1.** MED collapse **2.** (*paralización*) standstill

colar <o → ue> [ko·'lar] **I.** *vt* (*filtrar*) to filter; (*metal*) to cast **II.** *vi* **1.** (*líquido*) to seep (through); (*aire*) to get in **2.** *inf* (*información*) to be credible; **a ver si cuela** let's see if it comes off **III.** *vr:* **~se 1.** *inf* (*entrar*) to slip in **2.** (*en una cola*) to jump in line [*o line*] **3.** *inf* (*equivocarse*) to be wrong

colcha ['kol·tʃa] *f* bedspread

colchón [kol·'tʃon] *m* mattress; **~ de agua** water bed

colchoneta [kol·tʃo·'ne·ta] *f* (*neumática*) airbed; (*isoterma*) foam mattress; (*de gimnasia*) mat

colección [ko·lek·'sjon, -leɣ·'θjon] *f* collection

coleccionar [ko·lek·sjo·'nar, ko·leɣ·θjo-] *vt* to collect

coleccionista [ko·lek·sjo·'nis·ta, ko·leɣ·θjo-] *mf* collector

colecta [ko·'lek·ta] *f* collection (for charity); REL collect

colectivo [ko·lek·'ti·βo] *m* **1.** POL collective, group **2.** *Méx* (*microbús*) minibus *(that can be flagged down)*

colectivo, -a [ko·lek·'ti·βo, -a] *adj* collective; **acción colectiva** joint action

colega [ko·'le·ɣa] *mf* **1.** (*compañero*) colleague **2.** (*homólogo*) counterpart **3.** *inf* (*amigo*) pal, buddy

colegial(a) [ko·le·'xjal, -'xja·la] *m(f)* schoolboy *m*, schoolgirl *f*

colegio [ko·'le·xjo] *m* **1.** ENS school; **ir al ~** to go to school **2.** *AmL* (*universidad*) college; **~ mayor** hall of residence **3.** (*profesional*) association; **~ de abogados** bar association

cólera[1] ['ko·le·ra] *m* MED cholera

cólera[2] ['ko·le·ra] *f* (*ira*) anger; **acceso de ~** fit of anger

colesterol [ko·les·te·'rol] *m* cholesterol

colgado, -a [kol·'ɣa·do, -a] *adj* (*cuadro*) hung up; (*bandera*) hung out

colgador [kol·ɣa·'dor] *m* hanger; (*gancho*) (coat)hook; (*percha*) coat-hanger

colgante [kol·'ɣan·te] **I.** *adj* hanging; **puente ~** (*entre dos lados*) suspension bridge; (*de castillo*) drawbridge **II.** *m* pendant

colgar [kol·'ɣar] *irr* **I.** *vt* **1.** (*pender*) **~ algo** to hang sth; (*decorar*) to decorate with sth; **~ el teléfono** to put down the phone **2.** (*dejar*) **~ los libros** to abandon one's studies **3.** (*atribuir*) to attribute **II.** *vi* **1.** (*pender*) to hang; (*lengua*) to droop **2.** TEL (*auricular*) to hang up

colibrí [ko·li·'βri] *m* hummingbird

cólico ['ko·li·ko] *m* MED colic

coliflor [ko·li·'flor] *f* cauliflower

colilla [ko·'li·ja, -ʎa] *f* cigarette butt

colín [ko·'lin] *m* AmC, Ant ZOOL American bobwhite

colina [ko·'li·na] *f* hill

colindar [ko·lin·'dar] *vi* **~ con algo** to adjoin sth

colirio [ko·'li·rjo] *m* eye drops *pl*

colisión [ko·li·'sjon] *f* collision

collage [ko·'laʃ] *m* ARTE collage

collar [ko·'jar, -'ʎar] *m* (*adorno*) necklace; **~ de perlas** string of pearls; **~ de perro** dog collar

colmado [kol·'ma·do] *m* grocery store

colmado, -a [kol·'ma·do, -a] *adj* full; **un año ~ de felicidad** a very happy year

colmena [kol·'me·na] *f* beehive

colmillo [kol·'mi·jo, -ʎo] *m* eyetooth; (*de elefante*) tusk; (*de perro*) fang

colmo ['kol·mo] *m* height ▶ **¡esto es el ~!** this is the last straw!; **para ~** on top of everything

colocado, -a [ko·lo·'ka·do, -a] *adj inf* (*bebido*) plastered; (*drogado*) high, stoned

colocar <c → qu> [ko·lo·'kar] **I.** *vt*

1. (*emplazar*) to place; (*ordenar*) to arrange; (*poner*) to put **2.** COM (*invertir*) to invest; (*mercancías*) to sell **3.** (*empleo*) to find a job for **II.** *vr:* **~se 1.** (*empleo*) to get a steady job **2.** (*sombrero*) to put on **3.** (*posicionarse*) to place oneself **4.** *inf* (*alcohol*) to get plastered; (*drogas*) to get high

Colombia [ko·'lom·bja] *f* Colombia

colombiano, -a [ko·lom·'bja·no, -a] *adj, m, f* Colombian

Colón [ko·'lon] *m* **1.** (*Cristóbal*) Columbus **2.** (*moneda*) colon

colonia [ko·'lo·nja] *f* **1.** (*grupo*) colony **2.** (*barrio*) suburb **3.** (*perfume*) cologne

Colonia [ko·'lo·nja] *f* Cologne; **agua de ~** eau de cologne

coloniaje [ko·lo·'nja·xe] *m AmL* **1.** (*período*) colonial period **2.** (*sistema*) system of colonial government **3.** *pey* (*esclavitud*) slavery

colonialismo [ko·lo·nja·'lis·mo] *m* colonialism

colonización [ko·lo·ni·sa·'sjon, -θa·'θjon] *f* **1.** (*conquista*) colonization **2.** (*población*) settling

colonizador(a) [ko·lo·ni·sa·'dor, -·'do·ra; ko·lo·ni·θa-] **I.** *adj* colonizing **II.** *m(f)* **1.** (*conquistador*) colonizer **2.** (*poblador*) settler

colonizar <z → c> [ko·lo·ni·'sar, -'θar] *vt* **1.** (*conquistar*) to colonize **2.** (*poblar*) to settle

colono [ko·'lo·no, -a] *m* settler; (*labrador*) tenant farmer

coloquial [ko·lo·'kjal] *adj* LING colloquial

coloquio [ko·'lo·kjo] *m* conversation; (*científico*) colloquium

color [ko·'lor] *m* **1.** (*en general*) color; **un hombre de ~** a dark-skinned man; **nuestros ~es** DEP our team; **sacar los ~es a alguien** to embarrass sb **2.** (*sustancia*) dye **3.** POL (*ideología*) hue ▶ **verlo todo de ~ de rosa** to see the world through rose-colored glasses

colorado, -a [ko·lo·'ra·do] *adj* (*rojo*) red; **ponerse ~** to blush

colorante [ko·lo·'ran·te] *adj, m* coloring

colorear [ko·lo·re·'ar] *vt* to color; (*pintar*) to paint

colosal [ko·lo·'sal] *adj* colossal

columna [ko·'lum·na] *f* column; *fig* pillar; ~ **vertebral** ANAT spinal column

columpiar [ko·lum·'pjar] **I.** *vt* **1.** (*balancear*) to swing (to and fro) **2.** (*mecer*) to push on a swing **II.** *vr*: ~**se** to swing

columpio [ko·'lum·pjo] *m* **1.** (*para niños*) swing **2.** *AmL* (*mecedora*) rocking chair

coma[1] ['ko·ma] *m* MED coma

coma[2] ['ko·ma] *f* LING comma

comadre [ko·'ma·dre] *f* **1.** *inf* (*comadrona*) midwife **2.** *inf* (*amiga íntima*) crony **3.** *inf* (*celestina*) go-between

comadrona [ko·ma·'dro·na] *f* midwife

comando [ko·'man·do] *m* MIL, COMPUT command

comarca [ko·'mar·ka] *f* (*zona*) area; (*región*) region

comba [ko·'ba] *f* **1.** (*curvatura*) bend; (*de madera*) warp **2.** (*cuerda*) skipping rope; (*juego*) skipping; **saltar a la** ~ to skip

combar [kom·'bar] *vt, vr*: ~**se** to bend; (*madera*) to warp

combate [kom·'ba·te] *m* **1.** (*lucha*) combat; (*batalla*) battle **2.** DEP match; ~ **de boxeo** boxing match; **fuera de** ~ out of action

combatir [kom·ba·'tir] *vt, vi* to fight

combinación [kom·bi·na·'sjon, -'θjon] *f* **1.** (*composición*) combination; ~ **ganadora** winning combination **2.** (*de transportes*) connection **3.** (*lencería*) slip

combinar [kom·bi·'nar] *vt* **1.** (*componer*) to combine **2.** (*unir*) to unite; ~ **ideas** to link ideas **3.** (*coordinar*) to coordinate; MAT to permute

combustible [kom·bus·'ti·βle] **I.** *adj* combustible **II.** *m* fuel

combustión [kom·bus·'tjon] *f* combustion

comedia [ko·'me·dja] *f* **1.** TEAT (*obra*) play; (*divertida*) comedy **2.** CINE comedy **3.** *inf* (*farsa*) farce; **hacer** ~ to pretend

comediante, -a [ko·me·'djan·te, -a] *m, f* **1.** CINE actor **2.** (*farsante*) fraud

comedor [ko·me·'dor] *m* (*sala*) dining room; (*en una empresa*) cafeteria

comentador(a) [ko·men·ta·'dor, -·'do·ra] *m(f)* commentator

comentar [ko·men·'tar] *vt* **1.** (*hablar*) to talk about; (*hacer comentarios*) to comment on **2.** (*una obra*) to discuss, to review

comentario [ko·men·'ta·rjo] *m* **1.** (*general*) comment **2.** *pl* (*murmuraciones*) gossip

comentarista [ko·men·ta·'ris·ta] *mf* commentator

comenzar [ko·men·'sar, -'θar] *irr como* **empezar** *vt, vi* to begin, to commence; **para** ~ to begin with

comer [ko·'mer] **I.** *vi* **1.** (*alimentarse*) to eat; **dar de** ~ **a un animal** to feed an animal; ~ **caliente** to have a warm meal **2.** (*almorzar*) to have lunch; **antes/después de** ~ before/after lunch **II.** *vt* **1.** (*ingerir*) to eat **2.** *fig* (*consumir*) to consume **3.** (*corroer*) to eat away **4.** (*colores*) to fade **5.** (*en juegos*) to take **III.** *vr*: ~**se 1.** (*ingerir*) to eat up; ~**se a alguien a besos** to smother sb with kisses; **está para comérsela** she looks a treat **2.** (*corroer*) to eat away **3.** (*colores*) to fade **4.** (*palabras*) to skip; (*al pronunciar*) to slur

comercial[1] [ko·mer·'sjal, -'θjal] **I.** *adj* commercial **II.** *mf* sales representative

comercial[2] [ko·mer·'sjal, ·θjal] *m AmL* (*anuncio*) commercial

comercializar <z → c> [ko·mer·sja·li·'sar, -θja·li·'θar] *vt* (*producto*) to market

comerciante, -a [ko·mer·'sjan·te, -a; -'θjan·te, -a] *m, f* shopkeeper; (*negociante*) dealer

comerciar [ko·mer·'sjar, -'θjar] *vi* **1.** (*tener trato con*) ~ **con un país** to trade with a country **2.** (*traficar en*) ~ **en algo** to deal in sth

comercio [ko·'mer·sjo, -θjo] *m* **1.** (*actividad*) trade; ~ **exterior** foreign trade; ~ **justo** fair trade; ~ **al por mayor** wholesale trade **2.** (*tienda*) shop

comestibles [ko·mes·'ti·βles] *mpl* foods; **tienda de** ~ grocer's (shop), grocery

cometa[1] [ko·'me·ta] *m* ASTR comet

cometa[2] [ko·'me·ta] *f* (*de papel*) kite

cometer [ko·me·'ter] *vt* **1.** JUR to commit; (*error*) to make

comezón [ko·me·'son, -'θon] *f* (*picor*) itch

cómic [ˈko·mik] *m* <cómics> comic

comicios [ko·ˈmi·sjos, -θjos] *mpl* elections *pl*

cómico, -a [ˈko·mi·ko, -a] I. *adj* comedy; (*divertido*) comical II. *m, f* comedian

comida [ko·ˈmi·ða] *f* 1. (*alimento*) food; (*plato*) meal; **~ para animales** pet food; **~ basura/rápida** junk/fast food; **~ casera** home-style cooking 2. (*horario*) **~ principal** main meal (of the day) 3. (*almuerzo*) lunch; **~ de negocios** business lunch 4. *Col, Perú, Chile* (*cena*) supper

comienzo [ko·ˈmjen·so, -θo] *m* beginning; **al ~** at first; **a ~s de mes** at the beginning of the month

comino [ko·ˈmi·no] *m* cumin; **no valer un ~** *inf* not to be worth anything

comisaría [ko·mi·sa·ˈri·a] *f* (*edificio*) **~ de policía** police station [*o* precinct]

comisariato [ko·mi·sa·ˈrja·to] *m AmL* company store; (*almacén*) warehouse

comisario, -a [ko·mi·ˈsa·rjo, -a] *m, f* (*de policía*) superintendent, chief of police

comisión [ko·mi·ˈsjon] *f* 1. (*delegación*) commission; (*comité*) committee; **Comisión Europea** European Commission; **~ permanente** standing committee 2. COM commission; **a ~** on a commission basis

comisura [ko·mi·ˈsu·ra] *f* ANAT commissure; **~ de los labios** corner of the mouth

comité [ko·mi·ˈte] *m* committee; **~ de empresa** works committee

comitiva [ko·mi·ˈti·βa] *f* procession; **~ fúnebre** cortege

como [ˈko·mo] I. *adv* 1. (*del modo que*) as, like; **hazlo ~ quieras** do it any way you like; **~ quien dice** so to speak; **blanco ~ la nieve** white as snow 2. (*comparativo*) as; **es tan alto ~ su hermano** he's as tall as his brother 3. (*aproximadamente*) about; **hace ~ un año** about a year ago 4. (*y también*) as well as 5. (*en calidad de*) as; **trabaja ~ camarero** he works as a waiter II. *conj* 1. (*causal*) as, since; **~ no tengo tiempo, no voy** I'm not going because I don't have time 2. (*condicional*) if 3. (*con "si" +subj o con* "*que*") as if

cómo [ˈko·mo] I. *adv* 1. (*modal, exclamativo*) how; **¿~ estás?** how are you?; **¿~ (dice)?** sorry?, pardon? 2. (*por qué*) why; **¡~ no!** certainly! II. *m* **el ~** the how

cómoda [ˈko·mo·ða] *f* chest (of drawers), dresser

comodidad [ko·mo·ði·ˈðað] *f* 1. (*confort*) comfort 2. (*conveniencia*) convenience

comodín [ko·mo·ˈðin] *m* 1. (*en juegos*) joker 2. (*palabra*) all-purpose word 3. COMPUT wild card

cómodo, -a [ˈko·mo·ðo, -a] *adj* 1. *ser* (*cosa*) comfortable; (*conveniente*) convenient 2. *ser* (*perezoso*) lazy 3. *estar* (*a gusto*) comfortable; **¡ponte ~!** make yourself comfortable!

comoquiera [ko·mo·ˈkje·ra] *conj* 1. (*causal*) **~ que** +*subj* since 2. (*concesiva*) **~ que** +*subj* in whatever way; **~ que sea eso** however that may be

compact disc [ˈkom·pak (disk)] *m* compact disc

compacto, -a [kom·ˈpak·to, -a] *adj* compact; (*denso*) dense; (*firme*) firm; **disco ~** compact disc

compadecer [kom·pa·ðe·ˈser, -ˈθer] *irr como crecer* I. *vt* to feel sorry for II. *vr* **~se de alguien/algo** to (take) pity (on) sb/sth

compadre [kom·ˈpa·ðre] *m* (*amigo*) friend, buddy

compadrear [kom·pa·ðre·ˈar] *vi CSur* (*presumir*) to show off

compadrito [kom·pa·ˈðri·to] *m AmS* braggart

compaginar [kom·pa·xi·ˈnar] I. *vt* (*combinar*) to combine II. *vr* **~se** 1. (*combinar*) to combine 2. (*armonizar*) to go together

compañerismo [kom·pa·ɲe·ˈris·mo] *m* companionship; DEP team spirit

compañero, -a [kom·pa·ˈɲe·ro, -a] *m, f* 1. (*persona*) companion; (*amigo*) friend; (*pareja*) partner; **~ de clase** schoolmate; UNIV fellow student; **~ de piso** roommate; **~ de trabajo** fellow worker 2. (*cosa*) other one (of a pair)

compañía [kom·pa·ˈɲi·a] *f* company;

animal de ~ pet; **hacer ~ a alguien** to keep sb company

comparación [kom·pa·ra·'sjon, -'θjon] *f* comparison; **no hay ni punto de ~** there's no comparison

comparar [kom·pa·'rar] I. *vt* to compare II. *vr:* **~se** to be compared

comparativo [kom·pa·ra·'ti·βo] *m* comparative

comparecer [kom·pa·re·'ser, -'θer] *irr como crecer* vi t. JUR to appear (in court)

compartim(i)ento [kom·par·ti·'m(j)en·to] *m* compartment

compartir [kom·par·'tir] *vt* 1. (*tener en común*) to share 2. (*repartirse*) to share (out)

compás [kom·'pas] *m* 1. (*en dibujo*) compass 2. (*ritmo*) beat; MÚS time 3. NÁUT compass

compasión [kom·pa·'sjon] *f* **~ de alguien** pity on sb, compassion [*o* sympathy] with sb; **sin ~** pitiless(ly)

compasivo, -a [kom·pa·'si·βo, -a] *adj* compassionate, sympathetic

compatibilidad [kom·pa·ti·βi·li·'dad] *f* compatibility

compatible [kom·pa·'ti·βle] *adj* compatible

compatriota [kom·pa·'trjo·ta] *mf* compatriot, fellow citizen

compenetración [kom·pe·ne·tra·'sjon, -'θjon] *f* (mutual) understanding

compenetrarse [kom·pe·ne·'trar·se] *vr* (*identificarse*) to reach an understanding

compensación [kom·pen·sa·'sjon, -'θjon] *f* compensation

compensar [kom·pen·'sar] *vt* **~ de algo** to compensate for sth

competencia [kom·pe·'ten·sja, -θja] *f* 1. t. COM competition; (*rivalidad*) rivalry; **~ desleal** unfair competition 2. (*responsabilidad*) responsibility; **esto (no) es de mi ~** I'm not responsible for this

competente [kom·pe·'ten·te] *adj* competent

competición [kom·pe·ti·'sjon, -'θjon] *f* competition

competidor(a) [kom·pe·ti·'dor, -·'do·ra] I. *adj* competing II. *m(f)* t. ECON

competitor

competir [kom·pe·'tir] *irr como pedir* vi 1. (*enfrentarse*) **~ por algo** to compete for sth 2. (*igualarse*) to rival each other

competitividad [kom·pe·ti·ti·βi·'dad] *f* competitiveness

competitivo, -a [kom·pe·ti·'ti·βo, -a] *adj* competitive

compilar [kom·pi·'lar] *vt* t. COMPUT to compile

complacer [kom·pla·'ser, -'θer] *irr como crecer* I. *vt* to please II. *vr* **~se en algo** to be pleased to sth

complaciente [kom·pla·'sjen·te, -'θjen·te] *adj* 1. (*servicial*) obliging 2. (*indulgente*) **~ con alguien** indulgent towards sb

complejidad [kom·ple·xi·'dad] *f* complexity

complejo [kom·'ple·xo] *m* complex

complejo, -a [kom·'ple·xo, -a] *adj* complex

complemento [kom·ple·'men·to] *m* 1. t. LING complement 2. *pl* (*accesorio*) accessory

completamente [kom·ple·ta·'men·te] *adv* completely

completar [kom·ple·'tar] *vt* to complete

completo, -a [kom·'ple·to, -a] *adj* (*íntegro*) complete; (*total*) total; (*lleno*) full; (*espectáculo*) sold out; **pensión completa** full board

complexión [kom·plek·'sjon] *f* 1. (*constitución*) constitution, build 2. *AmL* (*tez*) complexion

complicación [kom·pli·ka·'sjon, -'θjon] *f* t. MED (*problema*) complication

complicar <c → qu> [kom·pli·'kar] I. *vt* (*dificultar*) to complicate II. *vr:* **~se** (*dificultarse*) to get complicated

cómplice ['kom·pli·se, -θe] *mf* t. JUR accomplice

complicidad [kom·pli·θi·'dad, kom·pli·θi-] *f* complicity

componente [kom·po·'nen·te] *m* 1. t. TÉC component 2. (*miembro*) member

componer [kom·po·'ner] *irr como poner* I. *vt* 1. (*formar*) to put together; (*organizar*) to organize 2. (*constituir*) to make up 3. t. MÚS to compose 4. (*asear*) to arrange **5.** *AmL* (*castrar*) to castrate **6.** *AmL* (*hueso*) to set **II.** *vr:* **~se 1.** (*constituirse*) to consist **2.** (*arreglarse*) to tidy oneself up **3.** *AmL* (*mejorarse*) to get better

comportamiento [kom·por·ta·'mjen·to] *m* conduct, behavior; *t.* TÉC performance

comportar [kom·por·'tar] **I.** *vt* to involve; **esto** (**no**) **comporta que** +*subj* this (doesn't) mean(s) that **II.** *vr:* **~se** to behave

composición [kom·po·si·'sjon, -'θjon] *f* *t.* MÚS composition

compositor(a) [kom·po·si·'tor, --'to·ra] *m(f)* composer

compra ['kom·pra] *f* purchase; **~s** shopping; **ir de ~s** to go shopping

comprador(a) [kom·pra·'dor, --'do·ra] *m(f)* buyer; (*cliente*) customer

comprar [kom·'prar] *vt* **1.** (*adquirir*) to buy; **~ al contado** to pay cash; **~ a plazos** to buy on an installment plan **2.** (*corromper*) to buy off

comprender [kom·pren·'der] *vt* **1.** (*entender*) to understand; **hacerse ~** to make oneself understood; **~ mal** to misunderstand **2.** (*contener*) to comprise; (*abarcar*) to take in

comprensible [kom·pren·'si·βle] *adj* understandable, comprehensible

comprensión [kom·pren·'sjon] *f* (*capacidad*) understanding; (*entendimiento*) comprehension

comprensivo, -a [kom·pren·'si·βo, -a] *adj* **1.** (*benévolo*) understanding **2.** (*tolerante*) tolerant

compresa [kom·'pre·sa] *f* **1.** *t.* MED (*apósito*) compress **2.** (*higiénica*) sanitary napkin [*o* pad]

comprimido [kom·pri·'mi·do] *m* pill

comprimir [kom·pri·'mir] *vt* *t.* FÍS, TÉC to compress

comprobación [kom·pro·βa·'sjon, -'θjon] *f* **1.** (*control*) checking **2.** (*verificación*) verification; (*prueba*) proof

comprobante [kom·pro·'βan·te] *m* voucher, proof

comprobar <o → ue> [kom·pro·'βar] *vt* **1.** (*controlar*) to check **2.** (*verificar*) to verify; (*probar*) to prove

comprometedor(a) [kom·pro·me·'te·dor, --'do·ra] *adj* compromising

comprometer [kom·pro·me·'ter] **I.** *vt* **1.** (*implicar*) to involve **2.** (*exponer*) to endanger **3.** (*arriesgar*) to put at risk **4.** (*obligar*) to commit **II.** *vr:* **~se 1.** (*implicarse*) to compromise oneself **2.** (*obligarse*) to commit oneself

compromiso [kom·pro·'mi·so] *m* **1.** (*vinculación*) commitment; (*obligación*) obligation; **visita de ~** formal visit; **sin ~** without obligation **2.** (*promesa*) promise **3.** (*acuerdo*) agreement **4.** (*aprieto*) awkward situation **5.** (*cita*) engagement

compulsar [kom·pul·'sar] *vt* to compare; JUR to certify

compulsivo, -a [kom·pul·'si·βo, -a] *adj* compulsive

computador [kom·pu·ta·'dor] *m* computer

computador(a) [kom·pu·ta·'dor, --'do·ra] *adj* computer

computadora [kom·pu·ta·'do·ra] *f* *AmL* computer

cómputo ['kom·pu·to] *m* calculation; **~ de votos** count of votes

comulgar <g → gu> [ko·mul·'ɣar] *vi* REL to take communion; *fig* (*estar de acuerdo*) to agree

común [ko·'mun] *adj* common; **de ~ acuerdo** by common consent; **sentido ~** common sense; **fuera de lo ~** out of the ordinary; **poco ~** unusual; **por lo ~** usually

comunal [ko·mu·'nal] *adj* communal

comunicación [ko·mu·ni·ka·'sjon, -'θjon] *f* **1.** (*en general*) communication **2.** (*conexión*) connection; **~ telefónica** telephone call **3.** (*de transporte*) link **4.** *pl* *t.* TEL communications *pl*

comunicado [ko·mu·ni·'ka·do] *m* communiqué; **~ de prensa** press release

comunicar <c → qu> [ko·mu·ni·'kar] **I.** *vi* **1.** (*estar unido*) to be joined; (*estar en contacto*) to be connected **2.** (*conectar*) to connect **3.** (*teléfono*) to be busy **II.** *vt* **1.** (*informar*) to inform **2.** (*transmitir*) to communicate **3.** (*unir*) to connect **III.** *vr:* **~se 1.** (*entenderse*) to communicate **2.** (*relacionarse*) to be connected

comunicativo, -a [ko·mu·ni·ka·ˈti·βo, -a] *adj* communicative

comunidad [ko·mu·ni·ˈdad] *f* community; ~ **de vecinos** residents' association

comunión [ko·mu·ˈnjon] *f* communion

comunismo [ko·mu·ˈnis·mo] *m* POL communism

comunista [ko·mu·ˈnis·ta] *adj* POL communist

comunitario, -a [ko·mu·ni·ˈta·rjo, -a] *adj* **1.** (*colectivo*) communal **2.** (*municipal*) community **3.** POL (*Comunidad Europea*) Community

con [kon] **I.** *prep* **1.** (*compañía, modo*) with; ~ **el tiempo...** with time... **2.** MAT **3** ~ **5** 3 point 5 **3.** (*actitud*) (*para*) ~ to, towards **4.** (*circunstancia*) ~ **este tiempo...** in this weather... **5.** (*a pesar de*) in spite of **II.** *conj* + *infin* if; ~ **que** +*subj* as long as

cóncavo, -a [ˈkon·ka·βo, -a] *adj* concave

concebir [kon·se·ˈβir, kon·θe-] *irr como pedir* *vt, vi* to conceive; ~ **esperanzas** to have hopes

conceder [kon·se·ˈder, kon·θe-] *vt* (*otorgar*) to grant; (*asignar*) to give; ~ **la palabra a alguien** to give sb the floor; ~ **un premio** to award a prize

concejal(a) [kon·se·ˈxal, -·ˈxa·la, kon·θe-] *m(f)* councilman *m*, councilwoman *f*

concentración [kon·sen·tra·ˈsjon, -θen·tra·ˈθjon] *f* concentration

concentrar [kon·sen·ˈtrar, kon·θen-] **I.** *vt* to concentrate **II.** *vr*: ~**se 1.** (*reunirse*) to assemble; (*agruparse*) to gather together **2.** (*centrarse*) to concentrate

concepto [kon·ˈsep·to, kon·ˈθep-] *m* **1.** (*noción*) notion; (*plan*) concept **2.** (*opinión*) opinion **3.** (*motivo*) **bajo ningún ~** on no account **4.** (*calidad*) **en ~ de** by way of

concernir [kon·ser·ˈnir, kon·θer-] *irr como cernir* *vi* to concern; **en** [o **por**] **lo que concierne a alguien...** as far as sb is concerned...

concertar <e → ie> [kon·ser·ˈtar, kon·θer-] **I.** *vi* *t.* LING to agree **II.** *vt* (*arreglar*) to arrange

concesión [kon·se·ˈsjon, kon·θe-] *f* *t.*

COM concession

concesionario, -a [kon·θe·sjo·ˈna·rjo, -a; kon·θe-] *m, f* dealer

concha [ˈkon·tʃa] *f* **1.** (*del molusco*) shell; (*de tortuga*) tortoiseshell **2.** AmL (*descaro*) nerve

conchabar [kon·tʃa·ˈβar] *vt* AmL to hire

conchudo, -a [kon·ˈtʃu·do, -a] *adj* **1.** AmL *inf* (*sinvergüenza*) shameless **2.** *Méx, Col inf* (*indolente*) sluggish

conciencia [kon·ˈsjen·sja, -ˈθjen·θja] *f* **1.** (*conocimiento*) awareness **2.** (*moral*) conscience; **a ~** conscientiously; (*sin*) **cargo de ~** (without) remorse

concienciar [kon·sjen·ˈsjar, -θjen·ˈθjar] **I.** *vt* to make aware **II.** *vr*: ~**se 1.** (*convencerse*) to convince oneself **2.** (*sensibilizarse*) to become aware

concienzudo, -a [kon·sjen·ˈsu·do, -a; -θjen·ˈθu·do, -a] *adj* conscientious

concierto [kon·ˈsjer·to, kon·ˈθjer-] *m* **1.** MÚS (*función*) concert; (*obra*) concerto **2.** *t.* ECON (*acuerdo*) agreement

conciliar [kon·si·ˈljar, kon·θi-] *vt* to reconcile; (*armonizar*) to harmonize; ~ **el sueño** *fig* to get to sleep

concilio [kon·ˈsi·ljo, -ˈθi·ljo] *m t.* REL council

conciso, -a [kon·ˈsi·so, -a; kon·ˈθi-] *adj* concise

concluir [kon·klu·ˈir] *irr como huir* **I.** *vt* **1.** (*terminar*) to complete **2.** (*deducir*) ~ **de algo** to conclude from sth **II.** *vi, vr*: ~**se** to end; **¡asunto concluido!** that's settled!

conclusión [kon·klu·ˈsjon] *f* conclusion; **llegar a la ~ de que...** to come to the conclusion that...

concordancia [kon·kor·ˈdan·sja, -θja] *f* concordance

concordar <o → ue> [kon·kor·ˈdar] *vi* to coincide

concordia [kon·ˈkor·dja] *f* harmony

concretar [kon·kre·ˈtar] **I.** *vt* **1.** (*precisar*) to put in concrete form **2.** (*limitar*) to limit **II.** *vr*: ~**se** to limit oneself

concretizar <z → c> [kon·kre·ti·ˈsar, -ˈθar] *vt v.* **concretar**

concreto, -a [kon·ˈkre·to] *adj* concrete; **en ~** specifically

concurrido, -a [kon·ku·ˈrri·do, -a] *adj* crowded

concurrir [kon·ku·'rrir] *vi* 1. (*en un lugar*) to come together; (*en el tiempo*) coincide 2. (*concursar*) ~ **por algo** to compete for sth

concursante [kon·kur·'san·te] *mf* 1. (*aspirante*) candidate 2. (*participante*) competitor, contestant

concursar [kon·kur·'sar] *vi* to compete

concurso [kon·'kur·so] *m* 1. *t.* DEP competition 2. (*oposición*) (public) competition

conde(sa) ['kon·de, kon·'de·sa] *m(f)* count *m*, countess *f*

condecorar [kon·de·ko·'rar] *vt* MIL to decorate

condena [kon·'de·na] *f* sentence, conviction; **cumplir una ~** to serve a sentence

condenado, -a [kon·de·'na·do, -a] I. *adj* *inf*condemned II. *m, f* (*reo*) convicted person, convict

condenar [kon·de·'nar] *vt* (*sentenciar*) to condemn

condensar [kon·den·'sar] *vt, vr:* ~**se** to condense

condesa [kon·'de·sa] *f v.* conde

condición [kon·di·'sjon, -'θjon] *f* 1. (*índole*) nature 2. (*estado*) condition; **a ~ de que** +*subj* on condition that, providing 3. (*situación*) position 4. (*clase*) social class

condicional [kon·di·sjo·'nal, kon·di·θjo-] *adj, m* LING conditional

condicionar [kon·di·sjo·'nar, kon·di·θjo-] *vt* (*supeditar*) ~ **a algo** to make conditional on sth

condimento [kon·di·'men·to] *m* seasoning, flavoring

condolencia [kon·do·'len·sja, -θja] *f* condolence, sympathy

condolerse <o → ue> [kon·do·'ler·se] *vr* ~**se de algo** to sympathize with sth

condón [kon·'don] *m* *inf*condom

condonar [kon·do·'nar] *vt* (*deuda*) to write off

cóndor ['kon·dor] *m* condor

conducción [kon·duk·'sjon, -duɣ'θjon] *f* 1. (*transporte*) transport(ation) 2. (*coche*) driving; ~ **temeraria** reckless driving

conducir [kon·du·'sir, -'θir] *irr como* traducir I. *vt* 1. (*llevar*) to take; (*transportar*) to transport 2. (*guiar*) to guide 3. (*arrastrar*) to lead 4. (*pilotar*) to drive II. *vi* 1. (*dirigir*) to lead 2. (*pilotar*) to drive

conducta [kon·'duk·ta] *f* conduct, behavior

conducto [kon·'duk·to] *m* 1. (*tubo*) pipe 2. MED canal; ~ **auditivo** ear canal 3. (*mediación*) channels *pl*

conductor [kon·duk·'tor] *m* FÍS conductor

conductor(a) [kon·duk·'tor, -·'to·ra] I. *adj* conductive; **hilo ~** conductor wire II. *m(f)* driver

conectar [ko·nek·'tar] I. *vt* 1. (*enlazar*) to connect 2. (*enchufar*) to plug in II. *vi* to communicate

conejo, -a [ko·'ne·xo] *m, f* rabbit

conexión [ko·nek·'sjon] *f* *t.* TEL connection

confabularse [kon·fa·βu·'lar·se] *vr* to plot

confección [kon·fek·'sjon, -feɣ·'θjon] *f* making; (*de vestidos*) dressmaking

confederación [kon·fe·de·ra·'sjon, -'θjon] *f* confederation

conferencia [kon·fe·'ren·sja, -θja] *f* 1. (*charla*) lecture 2. (*encuentro*) conference 3. (*telefónica*) call

conferir [kon·fe·'rir] *irr como* sentir *vt* to confer

confesar <e → ie> [kon·fe·'sar] I. *vt* 1. (*admitir*) to confess 2. REL (*declarar*) to confess II. *vr:* ~**se** to confess; ~**se culpable** to admit one's guilt

confesión [kon·fe·'sjon] *f* confession

confesor [kon·fe·'sor] *m* confessor

confiado, -a [kon·fi·'a·do, -a] *adj* 1. ser (*crédulo*) trusting 2. estar (*de sí mismo*) self-confident

confianza [kon·fi·'an·sa, -θa] *f* 1. (*crédito*) trust; **amiga de ~** close friend 2. (*esperanza*) confidence 3. (*en uno mismo*) self-confidence 4. (*familiaridad*) familiarity

confiar <1. *pres* confío> [kon·fi·'ar] I. *vi* ~ **en algo/alguien** to trust in sth/sb II. *vt* to entrust III. *vr* ~**se a alguien** to confide in sb

confidencia [kon·fi·'den·sja, -θja] *f* secret

confidencial [kon·fi·den·'sjal, -'θjal] *adj* confidential

confidente [kon·fi·'den·te] *mf* (*cómplice*) confidant *m*, confidante *f*

configuración [kon·fi·ɣu·ra·'sjon, -'θjon] *f* **1.** (*formación*) shaping **2.** (*forma*) shape; COMPUT configuration

configurar [kon·fi·ɣu·'rar] **I.** *vt* to shape; COMPUT to configure **II.** *vr*: ~**se** to take shape

confirmación [kon·fir·ma·'sjon, -'θjon] *f* t. REL confirmation

confirmar [kon·fir·'mar] **I.** *vt* t. REL to confirm **II.** *vr*: ~**se** to be confirmed

confiscar <c → qu> [kon·fis·'kar] *vt* to confiscate

confitería [kon·fi·te·'ri·a] *f* cake [*o* pastry] shop, candy shop

conflicto [kon·'flik·to] *m* conflict

conformar [kon·for·'mar] **I.** *vt* **1.** (*dar forma*) to shape **2.** (*ajustar*) to adjust **II.** *vr*: ~**se 1.** (*contentarse*) to be satisfied **2.** (*ajustarse*) to adjust

conforme [kon·'for·me] **I.** *adj* (*adecuado*) **estar ~ con algo** to be satisfied with sth **II.** *prep* ~ **a** according to **III.** *conj* (*como*) as

conformidad [kon·for·mi·'dad] *f* (*aprobación*) approval

confort [kon·'fort] *m* comfort

confortable [kon·for·'ta·βle] *adj* comfortable

confortar [kon·for·'tar] **I.** *vt* **1.** (*vivificar*) to strengthen **2.** (*consolar*) to comfort **II.** *vr*: ~**se** (*consolarse*) to take comfort

confrontación [kon·fron·ta·'sjon, -'θjon] *f* **1.** (*comparación*) comparison **2.** (*enfrentamiento*) confrontation

confrontar [kon·fron·'tar] **I.** *vt* **1.** (*comparar*) to compare **2.** (*enfrentar*) to confront **II.** *vr* ~**se con alguien** to face up to sb

confundir [kon·fun·'dir] **I.** *vt* **1.** (*trastocar*) to mistake **2.** (*mezclar*) to mix up **3.** (*embrollar*) to confuse **II.** *vr*: ~**se 1.** (*mezclarse*) to mix **2.** (*embrollarse*) to get confused

confusión [kon·fu·'sjon] *f* confusion

confuso, -a [kon·'fu·so, -a] *adj* confused

congelación [kon·xe·la·'sjon, -'θjon] *f* **1.** (*solidificación*) freezing **2.** frost-

bite; MED

congelador [kon·xe·la·'dor] *m* **1.** (*electrodoméstico*) freezer **2.** (*de un frigorífico*) freezer compartment

congelar [kon·xe·'lar] **I.** *vt* t. *fig* to freeze **II.** *vr*: ~**se** (*solidificarse*) to freeze

congeniar [kon·xe·'njar] *vi* ~ **con** to get on [*o* along] with

congénito, -a [kon·'xe·ni·to, -a] *adj* congenital

congestión [kon·xes·'tjon] *f* t. MED congestion

congoja [kon·'go·xa] *f* **1.** (*pena*) sorrow **2.** (*desconsuelo*) anguish

congola [kon·'go·la] *f* Col (*pipa de fumar*) pipe

congregar <g → gu> [kon·gre·'ɣar] **I.** *vt* to bring together **II.** *vr*: ~**se** to gather

congresista [kon·gre·'sis·ta] *mf* POL delegate, congressman *m*, congresswoman *f*

congreso [kon·'gre·so] *m* **1.** POL congress **2.** (*reunión*) congress, convention

congrio ['kon·grjo] *m* conger eel

congruencia [kon·'grwen·sja, -θja] *f* coherence

conjetura [kon·xe·'tu·ra] *f* conjecture

conjugación [kon·xu·ɣa·'sjon, -'θjon] *f* conjugation

conjugar <g → gu> [kon·xu·'ɣar] *vt* **1.** (*combinar*) to combine **2.** LING to conjugate

conjunción [kon·xun·'sjon, -'θjon] *f* conjunction

conjuntamente [kon·xun·ta·'men·te] *adv* jointly; ~ **con** together with

conjuntar [kon·xun·'tar] **I.** *vi* to match; ~ **con** to go with **II.** *vt* to harmonize

conjuntivitis [kon·xun·ti·'βi·tis] *f inv* conjunctivitis

conjunto [kon·'xun·to] *m* **1.** (*totalidad*) whole; **en ~** as a whole **2.** TEAT ensemble **3.** (*ropa*) outfit **4.** MAT set

conjurar [kon·xu·'rar] **I.** *vt* **1.** (*invocar*) to beseech **2.** (*alejar*) to ward off **II.** *vr*: ~**se** to conspire

conllevar [kon·je·'βar, kon·ʎe-] *vt* **1.** (*implicar*) to involve **2.** (*soportar*) to bear

conmemoración [kon·me·mo·ra·'sjon, kom·me·-, -'θjon] *f* commemoration

conmemorar [kon·me·mo·'rar, kom·me·mo·'rar] *vt* to commemorate

conmigo [kon·'mi·ɣo, kom·'mi·ɣo] *pron pers* with me

conmoción [kon·mo·'sjon, kom·mo·, -'θjon] *f* 1. MED concussion 2. *fig* shock

conmocionar [kon·mo·sjo·'nar, kom·mo·, -θjo·'nar] *vt* 1. MED to concuss 2. *fig* to shake

conmovedor(a) [kon·mo·βe·'dor, -·'do·ra; kom·mo·] *adj* (*sentimental*) moving

conmover <o → ue> [kon·mo·'βer, kom·mo·] I. *vt* (*emocionar*) to move II. *vr:* ~**se** 1. (*emocionarse*) to be moved 2. (*sacudirse*) to be shaken

cono ['ko·no] *m* cone; **Cono Sur** GEO Southern Cone *(Argentina, Chile, Paraguay and Uruguay)*

conocedor(a) [ko·no·se·'dor, -·'do·ra, ko·no·θe·] I. *adj* ~ **de algo** knowledgeable about sth II. *m(f)* expert

conocer [ko·no·'ser, -'θer] *irr como crecer* I. *vt* 1. (*saber, tratar*) to know; ~ **de vista** to know by sight; **dar a** ~ to make known 2. (*reconocer*) to recognize 3. (*descubrir*) to get to know 4. (*por primera vez*) to meet; **les conocí en una fiesta** I met them at a party II. *vi* ~ **de algo** to know about sth III. *vr:* ~**se** 1. (*tener trato*) to know each other; **se conocieron en una fiesta** they met at a party 2. (*a sí mismo*) to know oneself

conocido, -a [ko·no·'si·do, -a; ko·no·'θi-] I. *adj* (well-)known II. *m, f* acquaintance

conocimiento [ko·no·θi·'mjen·to, ko·no·θi-] *m* 1. (*saber*) knowledge 2. (*entendimiento*) understanding 3. (*consciencia*) consciousness 4. *pl* (*nociones*) knowledge

conque ['kon·ke] *conj inf* so

conquista [kon·'kis·ta] *f* conquest

conquistador(a) [kon·kis·ta·'dor, -·'do·ra] *m(f)* conqueror

conquistar [kon·kis·'tar] *vt* to conquer

consagrar [kon·sa·'ɣrar] I. *vt* (*dedicar*) to dedicate II. *vr:* ~**se** 1. (*dedicarse*) to devote oneself 2. (*acreditarse*) to distinguish oneself

consciencia [kon·'sjen·sja, -'θjen·θja] *f* consciousness

consciente [kon·'sjen·te, kons·'θjen·te] *adj* conscious; **estar** ~ MED to be conscious; **ser** ~ **de algo** to be aware of sth

conscripción [kons·krip·'sjon, -'θjon] *f* Arg (*servicio militar*) conscription

consecución [kon·se·ku·'sjon, -'θjon] *f* attainment

consecuencia [kon·se·'kwen·sja, -θja] *f* 1. (*efecto*) consequence; **a** ~ **de** as a result of 2. (*coherencia*) consistency

consecuente [kon·se·'kwen·te] *adj* consistent

consecutivo, -a [kon·se·ku·'ti·βo, -a] *adj* consecutive

conseguir [kon·se·'ɣir] *irr como seguir* *vt* to get

consejero, -a [kon·se·'xe·ro, -a] *m, f* 1. (*guía*) adviser, counselor, consultant 2. (*miembro de un consejo*) member; ~ **delegado** managing director

consejo [kon·'se·xo] *m* 1. (*recomendación*) piece of advice 2. (*organismo*) council 3. (*reunión*) meeting

consenso [kon·'sen·so] *m* consensus

consentido, -a [kon·sen·'ti·do, -a] *adj* spoiled

consentimiento [kon·sen·ti·'mjen·to] *m* ~ **para algo** consent to sth

consentir [kon·sen·'tir] *irr como sentir* I. *vi* (*admitir*) ~ **en algo** to agree to sth II. *vt* 1. (*autorizar*) to allow; (*tolerar*) to tolerate 2. (*mimar*) to spoil 3. (*aguantar*) to put up with

conserje [kon·'ser·xe] *mf* 1. (*encargado*) janitor 2. (*hotel*) concierge, receptionist 3. (*portero*) (hall) porter

conserjería [kon·ser·xe·'ri·a] *f* 1. (*cargo*) job of caretaker 2. (*oficina*) caretaker's office 3. (*hotel*) reception (desk)

conserva [kon·'serβa] *f* canned food; **en** ~ canned

conservación [kon·ser·βa·'sjon, -'θjon] *f* 1. (*mantenimiento*) maintenance 2. (*guarda*) conservation 3. (*conserva*) preserving

conservador(a) [kon·ser·'·βa·dor] *adj* conservative

conservar [kon·ser·'βar] I. *vt* 1. (*mantener*) to maintain 2. (*guardar*) to conserve 3. (*hacer conservas*) to can II. *vr:* ~**se** (*mantenerse*) to keep

conservatorio [kon·ser·βa·'to·rjo] *m* conservatory

considerable [kon·si·de·'ra·βle] *adj* considerable

consideración [kon·si·de·ra·'sjon, -'θjon] *f* 1. (*reflexión*) consideration; **en ~ a** in consideration of 2. (*respeto*) respect

considerado, -a [kon·si·de·'ra·do, -a] *adj* 1. (*tenido en cuenta*) considered 2. (*apreciado*) respected 3. (*atento*) considerate

considerar [kon·si·de·'rar] *vt, (vr):* ~**se** to consider (oneself)

consigna [kon·'siɣ·na] *f* 1. MIL motto 2. (*de equipajes*) checkroom

consignatario, -a [kon·siɣ·na·'ta·rjo, -a] *m, f* 1. (*destinatario*) addressee 2. COM consignee

consigo [kon·'si·ɣo] *pron pers* **tiene el libro ~** he/she has the book with him/her; **lléveselo ~** take it with you

consiguiente [kon·si·'ɣjen·te] *adj* resulting; **por ~** consequently

consistencia [kon·sis·'ten·sja, -θja] *f* consistency

consistir [kon·sis·'tir] *vi* 1. (*componerse*) ~ **en algo** to consist of sth 2. (*radicar*) ~ **en algo** to lie in sth

consola [kon·'so·la] *f* (*mesa*) console table; ELEC console; (*de videojuegos*) video console

consolar <o → ue> [kon·so·'lar] *vt, vr:* ~**se** to console (oneself)

consolidación [kon·so·li·da·'sjon, -'θjon] *f* consolidation

consolidar [kon·so·li·'dar] I. *vt* to consolidate II. *vr:* ~**se** to be consolidated

consomé [kon·so·'me] *m* consommé

consonancia [kon·so·'nan·sja, -θja] *f* harmony; **en ~ con** in keeping with

consonante [kon·so·'nan·te] *f* LING consonant

consorcio [kon·'sor·sjo, -θjo] *m* consortium

conspiración [kons·pi·ra·'sjon, -'θjon] *f* conspiracy

conspirar [kons·pi·'rar] *vi* to conspire

constancia [kons·'tan·sja, -θja] *f* 1. (*firmeza*) constancy 2. (*perseverancia*) perseverance 3. (*certeza*) certainty 4. (*prueba*) proof; **dejar ~ de algo** to show evidence of sth

constante [kons·'tan·te] *adj* constant

constar [kons·'tar] *vi* 1. (*ser cierto*) to be clear 2. (*figurar*) to be on record; **hacer ~ algo** to put sth on record 3. (*componerse*) to consist

constatar [kons·ta·'tar] *vt* to confirm

constelación [kons·te·la·'sjon, -'θjon] *f* constellation

constipado [kons·ti·'pa·do] *m* cold

constipar [kons·ti·'par] *vr:* ~**se** to catch a cold

constitución [kons·ti·tu·'sjon, -'θjon] *f* 1. *t.* POL constitution 2. (*composición*) make-up

constitucional [kons·ti·tu·sjo'nal, -θjo'nal] *adj* constitutional

constituir [kons·ti·tu·'ir, kons·ti·'twir] *irr como huir* *vt* 1. (*formar*) to constitute 2. (*ser*) to be

construcción [kons·truk·'sjon, -truɣ·'θjon] *f* 1. (*acción*) construction 2. (*edificio*) building

constructivo, -a [kons·truk·'ti·βo, -a] *adj* constructive

constructor(a) [kons·truk·'tor, -·'to·ra] *m(f)* builder

construir [kons·tru·'ir/kons·'trwir] *irr como huir* *vt* (*casa*) to build

consuelo [kon·'swe·lo] *m* consolation

consulado [kon·su·'la·do] *m* (*lugar*) consulate

consulta [kon·'sul·ta] *f* 1. (*acción*) consultation 2. (*de un médico*) surgery; **horas de ~** surgery hours

consultar [kon·sul·'tar] *vt* to consult

consultorio [kon·sul·'to·rjo] *m* 1. (*establecimiento*) consultancy; (*de un médico*) surgery 2. (*en la radio*) phone-in

consumar [kon·su·'mar] *vt* to carry out

consumición [kon·su·mi·'sjon, -'θjon] *f* (*bar*) drink; **~ mínima** minimum charge

consumidor(a) [kon·su·mi·'dor, -·'do·ra] *m(f)* consumer

consumir [kon·su·'mir] I. *vt* 1. (*gastar*) to consume 2. (*acabar*) to use 3. (*comer*) to eat II. *vr:* ~**se** 1. (*persona*) to waste away 2. (*gastarse*) to be consumed

consumo [kon·'su·mo] *m* consumption

contabilidad [kon·ta·βi·li·'dad] *f* 1. (*sistema*) accounting 2. (*profesión*) accountancy

contabilizar <z → c> [kon·ta·βi·li·'sar, -'θar] *vt* to enter

contable [kon·'ta·βle] I. *adj* countable II. *mf* accountant

contactar [kon·tak·'tar] *vi*, *vt* ~ **con alguien** to contact sb

contacto [kon·'tak·to] *m* 1. (*tacto*) contact 2. AUTO ignition

contado [kon·'ta·do] *m* **pagar al** ~ to pay (in) cash

contador [kon·ta·'dor] *m* meter

contagiar [kon·ta·'xjar] *vt* to transmit, to infect

contagio [kon·'ta·xjo] *m* contagion

contagioso, -a [kon·ta·'xjo·so, -a] *adj* contagious

contaminación [kon·ta·mi·na·'sjon, -'θjon] *f* pollution

contaminante [kon·ta·mi·'nan·te] I. *adj* polluting II. *m* pollutant

contaminar [kon·ta·mi·'nar] *vt* 1. (*infestar*) to pollute 2. (*contagiar*) to infect

contar <o → ue> [kon·'tar] I. *vi* 1. (*calcular*) to count 2. (+ *con: confiar*) ~ **con alguien/algo** to rely on sb/sth 3. (+ *con: tener en cuenta*) ~ **con algo** to expect sth II. *vt* 1. (*numerar*) to count 2. (*narrar*) to tell; **¿qué (te) cuentas?** (*saludo*) how's it going?

contemplación [kon·tem·pla·'sjon, -'θjon] *f* 1. (*observación*) contemplation 2. *pl* (*miramientos*) indulgence

contemplar [kon·tem·'plar] *vt* 1. (*mirar*) to look at 2. (*considerar*) to consider

contemporáneo, -a [kon·tem·po·'ra·neo, -a] *adj, m, f* contemporary

contenedor [kon·te·ne·'dor] *m* (*recipiente*) container; (*basura*) dumpster

contener [kon·te·'ner] *irr como* tener I. *vt* 1. (*encerrar*) to contain 2. (*refrenar*) to hold back II. *vr*: ~**se** to contain oneself

contenido [kon·te·'ni·do] *m* 1. (*lo incluido*) contents *pl* 2. (*concentración*) content

contentar [kon·ten·'tar] I. *vt* to satisfy II. *vr*: ~**se** to be contented

contento, -a [kon·'ten·to] *adj* (*alegre*) happy; (*satisfecho*) content

contestación [kon·tes·ta·'sjon, -'θjon] *f* answer

contestador [kon·tes·ta·'dor] *m* answering machine

contestar [kon·tes·'tar] I. *vt* to answer II. *vi* to answer; (*replicar*) to answer back

contexto [kon·'tes·to] *m* context

contienda [kon·'tjen·da] *f* dispute

contigo [kon·'ti·γo] *pron pers* with you

contiguo, -a [kon·'ti·γwo, -a] *adj* adjoining

continental [kon·ti·nen·'tal] *adj* continental

continente [kon·ti·'nen·te] *m* GEO continent

continuación [kon·ti·nwa·'sjon, -'θjon] *f* continuation; **a** ~ (*después*) next; (*en un escrito*) as follows

continuar <1. pres continúo> [kon·ti·nu·'ar] *vt, vi* to continue

continuidad [kon·ti·nwi·'dad] *f* continuity

continuo, -a [kon·'ti·nwo] *adj* continuous

contorno [kon·'tor·no] *m* (*de una figura*) outline

contra¹ ['kon·tra] I. *prep* against; **tener algo en** ~ to object II. *m* **los pros y los** ~**s** the pros and the cons

contra² ['kon·tra] *f* (*dificultad*) snag

contraataque [kon·tra·'ta·ke/kon·tra·a·'ta·ke] *m* MIL counterattack

contrabajo [kon·tra·'βa·xo] *m* (*instrumento*) double bass; (*rock*) bass guitar

contrabando [kon·tra·'βan·do] *m* (*comercio*) smuggling; **pasar algo de** ~ to smuggle sth in

contracción [kon·trak·'sjon, -tray·'θjon] *f t.* LING contraction

contracorriente [kon·tra·ko·'rrjen·te] *f* crosscurrent

contradecir [kon·tra·de·'sir, -'θir] *irr como* decir *vt, (vr):* ~**se** to contradict (oneself)

contradicción [kon·tra·dik·'sjon, -diγ·'θjon] *f* contradiction

contradictorio, -a [kon·tra·dik·'to·rjo, -a] *adj* contradictory

contraer [kon·tra·'er] *irr como* traer I. *vt* 1. (*encoger*) to contract 2. (*enferme-*

dad) to catch, to contract *form* **II.** *vr:* ~se to contract

contraindicación [kon·tra·in·di·ka·'sjon, -'θjon] *f* MED contraindication

contramedida [kon·tra·me·'di·da] *f* countermeasure

contraoferta [kon·tra·o·'fer·ta] *f* counteroffer

contraorden [kon·tra·'or·den] *f* countermand *form*

contrapartida [kon·tra·par·'ti·da] *f* compensation

contrapeso [kon·tra·'pe·so] *m* counterweight

contraproducente [kon·tra·pro·du·'sen·te, -'θen·te] *adj* counterproductive

contrariar <*1. pres* contrarío> [kon·tra·ri·'ar] *vt* (*disgustar*) to upset

contrariedad [kon·tra·rje·'dad] *f* **1.** (*inconveniente*) obstacle **2.** (*disgusto*) annoyance

contrario, -a [kon·'tra·rjo, -a] **I.** *adj* (*opuesto*) contrary; (*perjudicial*) harmful; **al ~** on the contrary; **en caso ~** otherwise; **de lo ~** or else; **llevar la contraria a alguien** to oppose [*o* contradict] sb **II.** *m, f* opponent

contrarrestar [kon·tra·rres·'tar] *vt* to counteract

contraseña [kon·tra·'se·ɲa] *f* password

contrastar [kon·tras·'tar] **I.** *vi* to contrast **II.** *vt* (*peso*) to verify

contraste [kon·'tras·te] *m t.* FOTO contrast

contratación [kon·tra·ta·'sjon, -'θjon] *f* contracting

contratar [kon·tra·'tar] *vt* **1.** (*trabajador*) to hire; (*artista*) to sign up **2.** (*encargar*) to contract

contratiempo [kon·tra·'tjem·po] *m* setback

contrato [kon·'tra·to] *m* contract; **~ de alquiler** lease

contravenir [kon·tra·βe·'nir] *irr como venir vt* to contravene

contribución [kon·tri·βu·'sjon, -'θjon] *f* **1.** (*aportación*) contribution **2.** (*impuesto*) tax

contribuir [kon·tri·βu·'ir] *irr como huir vt, vi* (*ayudar*) to contribute

contribuyente [kon·tri·βu·'jen·te] *mf* taxpayer

contrincante [kon·trin·'kan·te] *mf* opponent

control [kon·'trol] *m* control; (*inspección*) inspection

controlar [kon·tro·'lar] **I.** *vt* (*revisar*) to check; (*gobernar*) to control **II.** *vr:* ~se to control oneself

controversia [kon·tro·'βer·sja] *f* controversy

controvertido, -a [kon·tro·βer·'ti·do, -a] *adj* controversial

contundencia [kon·tun·'den·sja, -θja] *f* force

contundente [kon·tun·'den·te] *adj* contusive; *fig* convincing

contusión [kon·tu·'sjon] *f* MED bruise

convalecencia [kom·ba·le·'sen·sja, -'θen·θja] *f* convalescence

convalidación [kom·ba·li·da·'sjon, -'θjon] *f* **1.** (*de un título*) (re)validation **2.** (*confirmación*) confirmation, recognition

convalidar [kom·ba·li·'dar] *vt* **1.** (*título*) to (re)validate **2.** (*confirmar*) to confirm, to recognize

convencer <c → z> [kom·ben·'ser, -'θer] **I.** *vt* **1.** (*persuadir*) to persuade **2.** (*satisfacer*) **no me convence ese piso** I'm not at all sure about that flat **II.** *vr:* ~se to be convinced

convencido, -a [kom·ben·'si·do, -a; -'θi·do, -a] *adj* sure

convencimiento [kom·ben·si·'mjen·to, kom·ben·θi·] *m* conviction; **tengo el ~ de que...** I'm convinced that...

convención [kom·ben·'sjon, -'θjon] *f* convention

convencional [kom·ben·sjo·'nal, kom·ben·θjo·] *adj* conventional

conveniencia [kom·be·'njen·sja, -θja] *f* usefulness

conveniente [kom·be·'njen·te] *adj* **1.** (*adecuado*) suitable **2.** (*provechoso*) advisable; (*útil*) useful

convenio [kom·'be·njo] *m* agreement

convenir [kom·be·'nir] *irr como venir vi* **1.** (*acordar*) to agree **2.** (*ser oportuno*) to be advisable

convento [kom·'ben·to] *m* (*de monjes*) monastery; (*de monjas*) convent

convergencia [kom·ber·'xen·sja, -θja] *f* convergence

converger <g → j> [kom·ber·'xer] *vi*, **convergir** <g → j> [kom·ber·'xir] *vi* 1. (*líneas*) to converge 2. (*coincidir*) to coincide

conversación [kom·ber·sa·'sjon, -'θjon] *f* conversation

conversar [kom·ber·'sar] *vi* to talk

conversión [kom·ber·'sjon] *f* conversion

convertir [kom·ber·'tir] *irr como sentir* I. *vt* 1. (*transformar*) ~ **en algo** to turn into sth 2. COM, TÉC to convert II. *vr:* ~**se** 1. (*transformarse*) ~**se en algo** to turn into sth 2. REL to convert

convexo, -a [kom·'bek·so, -a] *adj* convex

convicción [kom·bik·'sjon, -biɣ·'θjon] *f* conviction

convicto, -a [kom·'bik·to, -a] *adj* convicted

convidar [kom·bi·'dar] *vt* to invite

convincente [kom·bin·'sen·te, -'θen·te] *adj* convincing

convivencia [kom·bi·'βen·sja, -θja] *f* living together; *fig* co-existence

convivir [kom·bi·'βir] *vi* to live together; *fig* to coexist

convocar <c → qu> [kom·bo·'kar] *vt* 1. (*citar*) to summon 2. (*concurso*) to announce

convocatoria [kom·bo·ka·'to·rja] *f* 1. (*citación*) summons 2. (*de un concurso*) official announcement 3. (*de una conferencia*) notification

convulsión [kom·bul·'sjon] *f* 1. MED convulsion 2. POL upheaval 3. GEO tremor

conyugal [kon·ju·'ɣal] *adj* marital

cónyuge ['kon·ju·xe] *mf* spouse

coña ['ko·ɲa] *f vulg* (*broma*) joking; **tomar algo a** ~ to take sth as a joke; **¡ni de** ~! no way!

coñac [ko·'nak] *m* <coñacs> cognac

cooperación [ko·pe·ra·'sjon/ko·o·pe·ra·'sjon, -'θjon] *f* cooperation

cooperar [ko·pe·'rar/ko·o·pe·'rar] *vi* to cooperate

cooperativa [ko·pe·ra·'ti·βa/ko·o·pe·ra·'ti·βa] *f* cooperative, co-op

cooperativo, -a [ko·pe·ra·'ti·βo, -a/ko·o·pe·ra·'ti·βo, -a] *adj* cooperative

coordenada [kor·de·'na·da/ko·or·de·'na·da] *f* MAT coordinate

coordinación [kor·di·na·'sjon/ko·or·di·na·'sjon, -'θjon] *f* coordination

coordinador(a) [kor·di·na·'dor/ko·or·di·na·'dor, --·'do·ra] *m(f)* coordinator

coordinar [kor·di·'nar/ko·or·di·'nar] *vt* to coordinate

copa ['ko·pa] *f* 1. (*vaso*) glass; **una ~ de vino** a glass of wine; **ir de ~s** to go out for a drink; **tener una ~ de más** to have had one too many 2. (*de árbol*) top 3. *t.* DEP (*de sujetador*) cup

Copenhague [ko·pe·'na·ɣe] *m* Copenhagen

copetín [ko·pe·'tin] *m* 1. *Méx* (*copa de licor*) glass of liquor; (*aperitivo*) aperitif 2. *Arg* (*cóctel*) cocktail

copia ['ko·pja] *f* copy; FOTO print; ~ **de seguridad** COMPUT back-up copy

copiar [ko·'pjar] *vt* 1. (*general*) to copy 2. (*fotocopiar*) to photocopy, to xerox

copiloto, -a [ko·pi·'lo·to, -a] *m, f* AVIAT copilot; AUTO co-driver

copo ['ko·po] *m* flake; ~ **de nieve** snowflake; ~**s de maíz** cornflakes

copucha [ko·'pu·tʃa] *f* *Chile* 1. (*mentira*) lie 2. (*vejiga de animal*) bladder

copular [ko·pu·'lar] *vi* to copulate

coquetear [ko·ke·te·'ar] *vi* to flirt

coqueto, -a [ko·'ke·to, -a] *adj* 1. (*que coquetea*) flirtatious 2. (*vanidoso*) vain 3. (*objeto*) pretty

coracha [ko·'ra·tʃa] *f* AmL leather bag

coraje [ko·'ra·xe] *m* 1. (*valor*) courage 2. (*ira*) anger; **dar** ~ to make angry

coral [ko·'ral] I. *adj* (*color*) coral II. *m t.* ZOOL coral III. *f* (*coro*) choir

Corán [ko·'ran] *m* REL Koran

corazón [ko·ra·'son, -'θon] *m* 1. *t. fig* ANAT heart; **de todo** ~ with all one's heart; **con el ~ en la mano** with one's heart on one's sleeve; **hacer algo de** ~ to do sth willingly; **tener un ~ de oro** to have a heart of gold; **no tener** ~ to be heartless; ~ (**mío**) darling 2. BOT core

corazonada [ko·ra·so·'na·da, ko·ra·θo·]

f (*presentimiento*) hunch

corbata [kor·'βa·ta] f tie

corchea [kor·'tʃea] f quaver

corchete [kor·'tʃe·te] m 1. (*broche*) hook and eye 2. TIPO square bracket

corcho ['kor·tʃo] m cork

cordel [kor·'del] m cord

cordero [kor·'de·ro] m (*carne*) mutton, lamb

cordero, -a [kor·'de·ro, -a] m, f lamb

cordial [kor·'djal] adj, m cordial

cordialidad [kor·dja·li·'dad] f cordiality

cordillera [kor·di·'ʎe·ra, -'ʎe·ra] f mountain range

cordillerano, -a [kor·di·ʎe·'ra·no, -a; kor·di·ʎe-] adj AmL GEO Andean

córdoba ['kor·do·βa] m Nic (*moneda*) cordoba

cordobés, -esa [kor·do·'βes, --'βe·sa] adj, m, f Cordovan

cordón [kor·'don] m 1. (*cordel*) cord; (*de zapatos*) shoelace; ~ **umbilical** ANAT umbilical cord 2. MIL cordon

cordura [kor·'du·ra] f (*razón*) good sense

coreografía [ko·reo·ɣra·'fi·a] f choreography

coreógrafo, -a [ko·re·'o·ɣra·fo, -a] m, f choreographer

corista [ko·'ris·ta] mf MÚS chorister

córnea [kor·nea] f cornea

córner ['kor·ner] m DEP corner

corneta [kor·'ne·ta] f cornet; (*en el ejército*) bugle

corneta [kor·'ne·ta] m cornet player; MIL bugler

cornudo, -a [kor·'nu·do, -a] adj (*animal*) horned

coro ['ko·ro] m choir; **a ~** in unison

corona [ko·'ro·na] f 1. (*real*) crown; (*de flores*) garland, wreath 2. (*de los dientes*) crown

coronar [ko·ro·'nar] vt to crown

coronel(a) [ko·ro·'nel, --'ne·la] m(f) colonel

corotos [ko·'ro·tos] mpl AmL (*bártulos*) things pl

corporación [kor·po·ra·'sjon, -'θjon] f t. COM corporation

corporal [kor·po·'ral] adj physical

corporativo, -a [kor·po·ra·'ti·βo, -a] adj corporate

corpulento, -a [kor·pu·'len·to, -a] adj (*persona*) hefty

corral [ko·'rral] m 1. (*cercado*) yard; (*redil*) stockyard; (*para gallinas*) chicken run 2. (*para niños*) playpen

corralón [ko·rra·'lon] m CSur (*maderería*) lumberyard

correa [ko·'rrea] f 1. (*tira*) strap 2. (*cinturón*) belt; ~ **de transmisión** TÉC driving belt, drive

corrección [ko·rrek·'sjon, -reɣ·'θjon] f 1. correction; TIPO proofreading 2. (*cualidad*) correctness

correcto, -a [ko·'rrek·to, -a] adj correct

corrector(a) [ko·rrek·'tor] I. adj correcting II. m(f) TIPO proofreader

corredor [ko·rre·'dor] m corridor

corredor(a) [ko·rre·'dor, --'do·ra] m(f) 1. DEP runner 2. COM agent, broker

correduría [ko·rre·du·'ri·a] f 1. (*oficio*) brokerage 2. (*comisión*) commission

corregir [ko·rre·'xir] irr como elegir I. vt t. TIPO to correct II. vr: ~**se** (*en la conducta*) to change one's ways

correlación [ko·rre·la·'sjon, -'θjon] f correlation

correlativo, -a [ko·rre·la·'ti·βo, -a] adj elev correlative

correntada [ko·rren·'ta·da] f AmL (*rápido*) rapids pl

correo [ko·'rreo] m 1. (*correspondencia*) mail; ~ **aéreo** airmail; ~ **basura** COMPUT spam; ~ **certificado** certified mail; ~ **electrónico** e-mail; ~ **urgente** special delivery; **echar al** ~ to mail 2. (*persona*) courier

Correos [ko·'rreos] mpl post office

correr [ko·'rrer] I. vi 1. (*caminar*) to run; **salir corriendo** to run out; **a todo** ~ at top speed 2. (*conducir*) to go fast 3. (*líquido*) to flow 4. (*camino*) to run 5. (*rumor*) to circulate 6. (*estar a cargo de*) **eso corre de** [o **por**] **mi cuenta** (*gastos*) I'm paying for that II. vt 1. (*un mueble*) to move; (*una cortina*) to draw; (*un cerrojo*) to slide 2. (*tener*) ~ **la misma suerte** to suffer the same fate; **corre prisa** it's urgent ► **dejar** ~ **algo** not to worry about sth **III.** *vr:* **~se 1.** (*moverse*) to move **2.** (*colores*) to run

correspondencia [ko·rres·pon·'den·sja, -θja] *f* **1.** (*correo, cartas*) mail; **curso por ~** correspondence course **2.** (*equivalente*) correspondence

corresponder [ko·rres·pon·'der] **I.** *vi* **1.** (*equivaler*) to correspond **2.** (*armonizar*) to match **3.** (*convenir*) to tally **4.** (*incumbir*) to concern; **no me corresponde criticarlo** it's not for me to criticize him **II.** *vr:* **~se** (*equivaler, escribir*) to correspond; (*armonizar*) to match

correspondiente [ko·rres·pon·'djen·te] *adj* **1.** (*oportuno*) corresponding **2.** (*respectivo*) respective

corresponsal [ko·rres·pon·'sal] *mf* correspondent

corrida [ko·'rri·da] *f* **1.** TAUR bullfight **2.** (*carrera*) run **3.** *vulg* (*orgasmo*) orgasm

corriente [ko·'rrjen·te] **I.** *adj* **1.** (*fluente*) running **2.** (*actual*) current; (*moneda*) valid; **estar al ~ de algo** to be aware of sth; **ponerse al ~ de algo** to get to know about sth **3.** (*ordinario*) ordinary **4.** (*normal*) normal **II.** *f* **1.** (*de fluido*) current; **~ de aire** draft; **~ alterna** alternating current; **hace ~** there's a draft; **ir contra la ~** to swim against the tide; **seguir** [*o* **llevar**] **la ~ a alguien** to play along with sb **2.** (*tendencia*) tendency

corrimiento [ko·rri·'mjen·to] *m* GEO slipping; **~ de tierras** landslide

corro ['ko·rro] *m* **1.** (*círculo*) circle, to form a circle; (*hacer sitio*) to make room **2.** (*juego*) ring-around-the-rosy

corroborar [ko·rro·βo·'rar] *vt* to corroborate

corroer [ko·rro·'er] *irr como* roer *vt* **1.** (*un material*) to corrode **2.** (*una persona*) consume; **el remordimiento lo corroe** he's consumed by remorse

corromper [ko·rrom·'per] *vt* **1.** (*descomponer*) to rot **2.** (*sobornar*) to bribe **3.** (*enviciar*) to debauch; (*pervertir*) to corrupt

corronchoso, -a [ko·rron·'tʃo·so, -a] *adj AmL* (*basto*) coarse

corrosca [ko·'rros·ka] *f Col* broad-brimmed straw hat

corrosión [ko·rro·'sjon] *f* corrosion

corrosivo, -a [ko·rro·'si·βo, -a] *adj* (*sustancia*) corrosive

corrupción [ko·rrup·'sjon, -rruβ·'θjon] *f* **1.** (*descomposición*) decay **2.** (*moral*) corruption

corrupto, -a [ko·'rrup·to, -a] *adj* corrupt

corsé [kor·'se] *m* corset

cortacésped [kor·ta·'ses·ped, -'θes·ped] *m* lawnmower

cortada [kor·'ta·da] *f AmL* (*herida*) cut

cortado [kor·'ta·do] *m* CULIN coffee with only a little milk

cortado, -a [kor·'ta·do, -a] *adj* **1.** (*leche*) sour **2.** (*tímido*) shy

cortafuegos [kor·ta·'fwe·ɣos] *m inv* **1.** AGR firebreak, fire lane **2.** COMPUT firewall

cortar [kor·'tar] **I.** *vt* **1.** (*tajar*) *t.* COMPUT to cut; (*por el medio*) to cut through; (*en pedazos*) to cut up; (*un traje*) to cut out; (*un árbol*) to cut down; (*leña*) to chop; (*el césped*) to mow; (*pelo*) to trim; **¡corta el rollo!** that's enough! **2.** DEP (*la pelota*) to slice **3.** (*el agua*) to cut off; (*la corriente*) to switch off; (*carretera*) to cut; (*comunicación*) to cut off **II.** *vi* cut; **ha cortado con su novio** *inf* she has split up with her boyfriend **III.** *vr:* **~se 1.** (*persona*) to cut oneself **2.** (*turbarse*) to become embarrassed; **no se cortó ni un pelo** he/she wasn't embarrassed in the least **3.** (*leche*) to turn **4.** TEL to get cut off

cortaúñas [kor·ta·'u·ɲas] *m inv* nail clippers *pl*

corte[1] ['kor·te] *m* **1.** (*herida*) cut **2.** (*de pelo*) haircut **3.** TÉC section; **~ transversal** cross section **4.** ELEC **~ de corriente** power cut ► **hacer a alguien un ~ de mangas** ≈ to give sb the V-sign; **dar ~** to embarrass

corte[2] ['kor·te] *f* court

cortejar [kor·te·'xar] *vt* to court

Cortes ['kor·tes] *fpl* POL Spanish parliament

cortés [kor·'tes] *adj* polite

cortesía [kor·te·'si·a] *f* courtesy; (*gentileza*) politeness

corteza [kor·'te·sa, -θa] *f* (*de un tronco*) bark; (*del pan*) crust; **la ~ terrestre** GEO the earth's crust

cortijo [kor·'ti·xo] *m* (*finca*) country estate; (*casa*) country house

cortina [kor·'ti·na] *f* curtain; **correr/ descorrer la ~** to draw/to draw back the curtain

corto, -a ['kor·to] *adj* 1. (*pequeño*) short; **~ de vista** short-sighted 2. (*breve*) brief 3. (*poco listo*) slow

cortocircuito [kor·to·sir·'kwi·to/kor·to· sir·ku·'i·to, kor·to·θir-] *m* ELEC short circuit

cosa ['ko·sa] *f* 1. (*en general*) thing; **eso es ~ tuya/mía** that's your/my affair; **¿sabes una ~?** do you know what?; **no me queda otra ~ que...** I have no alternative but...; **no valer gran ~** not to be worth much; **tal como están las ~s...** as things stand...; **como si tal ~** as if nothing had happened; **esas son ~s de Inés** that's typical of Inés 2. *pl* (*pertenencias*) things *pl*

coscacho [kos·'ka·tʃo] *m AmS inf* (*capón*) rap on the head

coscorrón [kos·ko·'rron] *m* (*golpe*) bump

cosecha [ko·'se·tʃa] *f* 1. AGR harvest 2. (*conjunto de frutos*) crop; **de ~ propia** home-grown

cosechar [ko·se·'tʃar] *vi, vt* to harvest

coser [ko·'ser] I. *vt* 1. (*un vestido*) to sew; (*un botón*) to sew on; (*un roto*) to sew up; **~ a alguien a balazos** to riddle sb with bullets 2. MED to stitch (up) II. *vi* to sew

cosmética [kos·'me·ti·ka] *f* cosmetics *pl*

cosmopolita [kos·mo·po·'li·ta] *adj, mf* cosmopolitan

cosmos ['kos·mos] *m inv* cosmos

cosquillas [kos·'ki·jas, -ʎas] *fpl* **hacer ~** to tickle; **tener ~** to be ticklish; **buscar las ~ a alguien** *fig* to try to stir sb up

costa ['kos·ta] *f* 1. GEO coast 2. FIN cost; **a toda ~** at any price

costado [kos·'ta·do] *m* (*lado*) side; **por los cuatro ~s** through and through

costalearse [kos·ta·le·'ar·se] *vr Chile* 1. (*recibir un costalazo*) to fall heavily 2. *fig* (*sufrir una decepción*) to be disappointed

costanera [kos·ta·'ne·ra] *f Arg* (*paseo marítimo*) jetty

costar <o → ue> [kos·'tar] *vi, vt* 1. (*valer*) to cost; **~ caro** to be expensive; **esto te va a ~ caro** this is going to cost you dear; **cueste lo que cueste** cost what it may 2. (*ser difícil*) **me cuesta convencerlo** I find it difficult to persuade him

Costa Rica [kos·ta·rri·'ka] *f* Costa Rica

costarriqueño, -a [kos·ta·rri·'ke·ɲo, -a] *adj, m, f* Costa Rican

coste ['kos·te] *m* 1. (*costo*) cost 2. (*precio*) price

costear [kos·te·'ar] I. *vt* to pay for II. *vi* NÁUT to sail along the coast III. *vr*: **~se** to cover the expenses

costero, -a [kos·'te·ro] *adj* coastal

costilla [kos·'ti·ja, -ʎa] *f* 1. ANAT rib 2. CULIN chop

costo ['kos·to] *m* 1. (*coste*) cost 2. *AmL* (*esfuerzo*) effort

costoso, -a [kos·'to·so, -a] *adj* 1. (*en dinero*) expensive 2. (*en esfuerzo*) difficult

costra ['kos·tra] *f* 1. MED scab 2. (*corteza*) crust

costumbre [kos·'tum·bre] *f* 1. (*hábito*) habit; **como de ~** as usual 2. (*tradición*) custom

costura [kos·'tu·ra] *f* 1. (*efecto*) seam 2. (*acción*) sewing, needlework 3. (*confección*) dressmaking; **alta ~** haute couture

cotejar [ko·te·'xar] *vt* to compare

cotidiano, -a [ko·ti·'dja·no, -a] *adj* daily

cotilla [ko·'ti·ja, -ʎa] *mf inf* gossip

cotillear [ko·ti·je·'ar, ko·ti·ʎe-] *vi inf* gossip

cotilleo [ko·ti·'jeo, -'ʎeo] *m inf* gossip

cotización [ko·ti·sa·'sjon, -θa·'θjon] *f* 1. (*de acciones*) price 2. (*pago*) contribution

cotizar <z → c> [ko·ti·'sar, -'θar] I. *vt* FIN **~ a algo** to stand at sth II. *vi* to pay contributions III. *vr*: **~se** 1. FIN **~ a algo** to sell at sth 2. (*ser popular*) to be valued

coto ['ko·to] *m* (*vedado*) **~ de caza** game [*o* hunting] preserve

cototo [ko·'to·to] *m AmL inf* (*chichón*) bump

coxis ['kok·sis] *m inv* ANAT coccyx

coyote [ko·'jo·te] *m* coyote

coyuntura [ko·jun·'tu·ra] *f* (*situación*) situation, circumstances *pl*

coyuntural [ko·jun·tu·'ral] *adj* ECON current

coz [kos, koθ] *f* (*patada*) kick; **dar coces** to kick

crack [krak] *m* 1. ECON crash 2. (*droga*) crack

cráneo ['kra·neo] *m* ANAT skull

cráter ['kra·ter] *m* crater

creación [krea·'sjon, -'θjon] *f* creation

creador(a) [krea·'dor,-·'do·ra] I. *adj* creative II. *m(f)* creator

crear [kre·'ar] I. *vt* 1. (*hacer*) to create; ~ **archivo** COMPUT to make a new file 2. (*fundar*) to establish II. *vr*: ~**se** to be created

creatividad [krea·ti·βi·'dad] *f* creativity

creativo, -a [krea·'ti·βo, -a] *adj* creative

crecer [kre·'ser, -'θer] *irr* III. *vi* 1. (*aumentar*) to grow, to increase 2. (*luna*) to wax 3. (*agua*) to rise II. *vr*: ~**se** (*persona*) to grow more confident

creces ['kre·ses, -θes] *fpl* **con** ~ fully

crecimiento [kre·si·'mjen·to, kre·θi·] *m* t. ECON growth

credencial [kre·den·'sjal, -'θjal] I. *adj* accrediting II. *fpl* credentials

credibilidad [kre·di·βi·li·'dad] *f* credibility

crédito ['kre·di·to] *m* 1. FIN (*préstamo*) credit; **pedir un** ~ to ask for a loan 2. (*fama*) reputation 3. (*confianza*) **dar** ~ **a algo/alguien** to believe in sth/sb

credo ['kre·do] *m* 1. (*creencias*) beliefs *pl* 2. (*oración*) creed

crédulo, -a ['kre·du·lo, -a] *adj* credulous

creencia [kre·'en·sja, -θja] *f* belief

creer [kre·'er] *irr como* leer I. *vi* ~ **en Dios/alguien** to believe in God/sb II. *vt* 1. (*dar por cierto*) to believe; **¡quién iba a ~lo!** who would have believed it!; **no te creo** I don't believe you; **hacer** ~ **algo a alguien** to make sb believe sth 2. (*pensar*) **¡ya lo creo!** I should think so! III. *vr*: ~**se** (*considerarse*) to believe oneself to be

creíble [kre·'i·βle] *adj* credible, believable

creído, -a [kre·'i·do, -a] *adj inf* (*vanidoso*) conceited

crema ['kre·ma] *f* 1. cream; ~ **antiarrugas** anti-wrinkle cream 2. (*natillas*) custard; **la** ~ **y la nata** *fig* the crème de la crème

cremallera [kre·ma·'je·ra, -'ʎe·ra] *f* (*cierre*) zipper

crematorio [kre·ma·'to·rjo] *m* crematorium

crematorio, -a [kre·ma·'to·rjo, -a] *adj* **horno** ~ crematorium

cremoso, -a [kre·'mo·so, -a] *adj* creamy

crepúsculo [kre·'pus·ku·lo] *m* twilight, dusk; ~ **matutino** dawn

cresta ['kres·ta] *f* 1. (*del gallo*) (cocks) comb 2. (*de ola, montaña*) crest 3. (*plumas*) crest 4. (*cabello*) tuft

Creta ['kre·ta] *f* Crete

cretino, -a [kre·'ti·no, -a] *m, f* t. *fig* cretin

creyente [kre·'jen·te] *mf* believer

cría ['kri·a] *f* 1. (*acción*) rearing, raising 2. (*cachorro*) baby animal 3. (*camada*) litter

criado, -a [kri·'a·do, -a] *m, f* servant

criandera [krjan·'de·ra] *f AmL* wet nurse

criar <1. pres crío> [kri·'ar] I. *vt* 1. (*alimentar*) to feed; (*mamíferos*) to suckle 2. (*reproducir*) to breed 3. (*educar*) to bring up II. *vr*: ~**se** to grow up

criatura [krja·'tu·ra] *f* t. *fig* creature; (*niño*) child

criba ['kri·βa] *f* sieve; *fig* selection process

cribar [kri·'βar] *vt* to sieve

crimen ['kri·men] *m* crime

criminal [kri·mi·'nal] *adj*, *mf* criminal

criminalidad [kri·mi·na·li·'dad] *f* criminality

crío, -a ['kri·o, -a] *m, f inf* kid

criollo, -a [kri·'o·jo, -a; -·'o·ʎo, -a] *adj*, *m, f* Creole

cripta ['krip·ta] *f* crypt

críptico, -a ['krip·ti·ko, -a] *adj* cryptic

crisis ['kri·sis] *f inv* crisis; ~ **nerviosa** nervous breakdown

crispación [kris·pa·'sjon, -'θjon] *f* (*irritación*) tension

crispar [kris·'par] I. *vt* 1. (*exasperar*)

to exasperate **2.** (*contraer*) to contract **II.** *vr:* **~se 1.** (*exasperarse*) to become exasperated **2.** (*contraerse*) to contract

cristal [kris·'tal] *m* **1.** (*cuerpo*) crystal **2.** (*vidrio*) glass

cristianismo [kris·tja·'nis·mo] *m* Christianity

cristiano [kris·'tja·no, -a] *m inf* **1.** (*persona*) person **2.** (*castellano*) Spanish; **hablar en ~** *fig* to speak plainly

cristiano, -a [kris·'tja·no, -a] *adj, m, f* Christian

cristo ['kris·to] *m* crucifix; **todo ~** *inf* everyone

Cristo ['kris·to] *m* Christ

criterio [kri·'te·rjo] *m* **1.** (*norma*) criterion **2.** (*discernimiento*) judgment **3.** (*opinión*) opinion

crítica ['kri·ti·ka] *f* **1.** (*juicio*) criticism **2.** (*prensa*) review, write-up

criticar <c → qu> [kri·ti·'kar] **I.** *vt* to criticize **II.** *vi* to gossip

crítico, -a ['kri·ti·ko, -a] **I.** *adj* critical **II.** *m, f* critic

Croacia [kro·'a·sja, -·θja] *f* Croatia

croar [kro·'ar] *vi* to croak

croata [kro·'a·ta] *adj, mf* Croat(ian)

cromo ['kro·mo] *m* **1.** QUÍM chromium **2.** (*estampa*) (picture) card; **~s de béisbol** baseball cards; **estar** [*o* **ir**] **hecho un ~** to look wonderful *iron*

cromosoma [kro·mo·'so·ma] *m* chromosome

crónica ['kro·ni·ka] *f* **1.** HIST chronicle **2.** (*prensa*) (feature) article; (*reportaje*) report

crónico, -a ['kro·ni·ko, -a] *adj t.* MED chronic

cronista [kro·'nis·ta] *mf* **1.** HIST chronicler **2.** (*periodista*) journalist

cronología [kro·no·lo·'xi·a] *f* chronology, sequence of events

cronológico, -a [kro·no·'lo·xi·ko, -a] *adj* chronological

cronometrar [kro·no·me·'trar] *vt* to time

cronómetro [kro·'no·me·tro] *m* chronometer; DEP stopwatch

croqueta [kro·'ke·ta] *f* ≈ croquette

croquis ['kro·kis] *m inv* sketch, outline

cruasán [krwa·'san/kru·'san] *m* croissant

cruce ['kru·se, -·θe] *m* **1.** (*acción*) cross-

ing **2.** (*intersección*) crossing, intersection **3.** (*mezcla*) crossing, cross; **~ de peatones** pedestrian crossing **4.** BIO cross

crucero [kru·'se·ro, -·'θe·ro] *m* **1.** (*buque*) cruiser **2.** (*viaje*) cruise

crucial [kru·'θjal, -·'sjal] *adj* crucial

crucificar <c → qu> [kru·si·fi·'kar, kru·θi-] *vt* to crucify

crucifijo [kru·si·'fi·xo, kru·θi-] *m* crucifix

crucigrama [kru·si·'γra·ma, kru·θi-] *m* crossword (puzzle)

crudeza [kru·'de·sa, -·θa] *f* (*rigor*) harshness

crudo ['kru·do] *m* crude oil

crudo, -a ['kru·do, -a] *adj* **1.** (*sin cocer*) raw **2.** (*tiempo*) harsh

cruel [kru·'el] *adj* <crudelísimo> **~ con alguien** cruel to sb

crueldad [krwel·'dad] *f* **~ con alguien** cruelty to sb

crujido [kru·'xi·do] *m* (*de papel*) rustling; (*de madera*) creaking

crujiente [kru·'xjen·te] *adj* (*pan*) crunchy

crujir [kru·'xir] *vi* (*papel*) to rustle; (*madera*) creak

cruz [krus, kruθ] *f* **1.** (*figura*) cross; **~ gamada** swastika; **Cruz Roja** Red Cross **2.** (*de moneda*) reverse; **¿cara o ~?** heads or tails? **3.** (*de animal*) withers *pl* **4.** (*suplicio*) burden; **llevar una ~** to have a cross to bear

cruzada [kru·'sa·da, -·'θa·da] *f* crusade

cruzado, -a [kru·'sa·do, -a; -·'θa·do, -a] *adj* **animal ~** BIO crossbred animal; **chaqueta cruzada** double-breasted jacket

cruzar <z → c> [kru·'sar, -·'θar] **I.** *vt, vi* to cross; **~ los brazos** to cross one's arms **II.** *vr:* **~se 1.** (*caminos*) to cross **2.** (*encontrarse*) to meet; **~se con alguien** to pass sb **3.** *t.* MAT to intersect

cu [ku] *f* (name of the letter) q

cuaderno [kwa·'der·no] *m* notebook; **~ de bitácora** NÁUT logbook

cuadra ['kwa·dra] *f* **1.** (*establo*) stable **2.** (*caballos*) stables *pl* **3.** (*lugar*) pigsty **4.** AmL (*manzana de casas*) block (of houses)

cuadrado [kwa·'dra·do] *m t.* ASTR square; **elevar al ~** to square

cuadrado, -a [kwa·'dra·do, -a] *adj*

1. (*forma*) square; **tener la cabeza cuadrada** to be pigheaded 2. (*corpulento*) hefty

cuadrángulo [kwa·'dran·gu·lo] *m* quadrangle

cuadrar [kwa·'drar] I. *vi* 1. (*convenir*) to fit in 2. (*coincidir*) to tally II. *vt t.* MAT to square III. *vr:* ~se *inf* (*plantarse*) to dig one's heels in

cuadrícula [kwa·'dri·ku·la] *f* grid squares *pl*

cuadrilla [kwa·'dri·ja, -ʎa] *f* (*de amigos*) group; (*de maleantes*) gang

cuadro ['kwa·dro] *m* 1. (*cuadrado*) square; **a ~s** plaid, check(er)ed 2. (*pintura*) painting 3. (*marco*) frame 4. (*escena*) scene 5. (*descripción*) description; ~ **sinóptico** synoptic chart 6. TÉC panel

cuajada [kwa·'xa·da] *f* curd

cuajar [kwa·'xar] I. *vi* 1. (*espesarse*) to thicken 2. *inf* (*realizarse*) to come off II. *vt* (*leche*) to curdle III. *vr:* ~se to coagulate; (*leche*) to curdle

cual [kwal] *pron rel* 1. (*explicativo*) **el/la** ~ (*persona*) who, whom; (*cosa*) which; **lo** ~ which; **los/las ~es** (*personas*) who, whom; (*cosas*) which; **cada** ~ everyone 2. (*correlativo*) **hazlo tal ~ te lo digo** do it just as I tell you (to); **sea** ~ **sea su intención** whatever his/her intention may be

cuál [kwal] I. *pron interrog* which (one); ¿~ **es el tuyo?** which is yours? II. *pron indef* (*distributivo*) ~ **más** ~ **menos** some more, some less

cualesquier(a) [kwa·les·'kje·ra] *pron indef pl de* **cualquiera**

cualidad [kwa·li·'dad] *f* quality

cualificación [kwa·li·fi·ka·'sjon, -'θjon] *f* qualification

cualificar <c → qu> [kwa·li·fi·'kar] *vt* to qualify

cualitativo, -a [kwa·li·ta·'ti·βo, -a] *adj* qualitative

cualquiera [kwal·'kje·ra] I. *pron indef* (*ante sustantivo:* **cualquier**) any; **en un lugar** ~ anywhere; **a cualquier hora** at any time; **cualquier cosa** anything; **de cualquier modo** whichever way; (*de todas maneras*) anyway; ¡~ **lo puede**

hacer! anybody can do it! II. *mf* **ser una** ~ *pey* to be a whore

cuando ['kwan·do] *conj* 1. (*presente, pasado*) when; **de** ~ **en** ~ from time to time 2. (*futuro; +subj*) when; ~ **quieras** when(ever) you want 3. (*relativo*) **el lunes es** ~ **no trabajo** I don't work on Mondays 4. (*condicional*) if; ~ **más** [*o* **mucho**] at (the) most; ~ **menos** at least 5. (*aunque*) **aun** ~ even if

cuándo ['kwan·do] *adv* when

cuantía [kwan·'ti·a] *f* amount

cuantificar <c → qu> [kwan·ti·fi·'kar] *vt* to quantify

cuantioso, -a [kwan·'tjo·so, -a] *adj* substantial

cuantitativo, -a [kwan·ti·ta·'ti·βo, -a] *adj* quantitative

cuanto ['kwan·to] I. *adv* ~ **antes** as soon as possible; ~ **antes mejor** the sooner the better; ~ **más lo pienso, menos me gusta** the more I think about it, the less I like it II. *prep* **en** ~ **a** as regards III. *conj* (*temporal*) **en** ~ (**que**) as soon as

cuanto, -a ['kwan·to, -a] I. *pron rel* 1. (*neutro*) all that (which); **tanto...** ~ as much as...; **dije** (**todo**) ~ **sé** I said all that I know 2. *pl* all those that; **la más hermosa de cuantas conozco** the most beautiful of those I know II. *pron indef* **unos ~s/unas cuantas** some, several

cuánto ['kwan·to] *adv* 1. (*interrogativo*) how much 2. (*exclamativo*) how; ¡~ **llueve!** how hard it's raining!

cuánto, -a ['kwan·to, -a] I. *adj* ¿~ **vino?** how much wine?; ¿~**s libros?** how many books?; ¿~ **tiempo?** how long?; ¿**cuántas veces?** how often? II. *pron interrog* how much [*o* many]; ¿~ **hay de aquí a Veracruz?** how far is it from here to Veracruz?

cuarenta [kwa·'ren·ta] I. *adj inv* forty II. *m* forty; *v. t.* **ochenta**

cuarentena [kwa·ren·'te·na] *f* 1. (*aislamiento*) quarantine 2. (*conjunto*) **una** ~ **de veces** about forty times

cuaresma [kwa·'res·ma] *f* REL Lent

cuartel [kwar·'tel] *m* 1. MIL (*acuartelamiento*) encampment; ~ **general** headquarters pl 2. MIL (edificio) barracks pl

cuartelillo [kwar·te·'li·jo, -ʎo] m police station

cuarteto [kwar·'te·to] m MÚS quartet

cuartilla [kwar·'ti·ja, -ʎa] f (hoja) sheet of paper

cuarto ['kwar·to] m 1. (habitación) room; ~ de baño bathroom; ~ de estar living room; ~ trastero lumber room 2. (pl) inf (dinero) money, dough inf 3. (de un caballo) ~s delanteros forequarters pl; ~s traseros hindquarters pl

cuarto, -a ['kwar·to, -a] I. adj fourth II. m, f quarter; ~ creciente/menguante first/last quarter; ~s de final DEP quarterfinal; un ~ de hora a quarter of an hour; es la una y/menos ~ it's a quarter past/to one; v. t. octavo

cuarzo ['kwar·so, -θo] m quartz

cuate, -a ['kwa·te, -a] m, f 1. Méx (gemelo) twin 2. Guat, Méx (amigo) buddy

cuatrero, -a [kwa·'tre·ro, -a] m, f rustler

cuatrimestre [kwa·tri·'mes·tre] m four-month period

cuatro ['kwa·tro] adj inv m four; v. t. ocho

cuatrocientos, -as [kwa·tro·'sjen·tos, -as; kwa·tro·'θjen-] adj four hundred; v. t. ochocientos

cuba ['ku·βa] f (tonel) barrel; estar como una ~ inf (borracho) to be plastered

Cuba ['ku·βa] f Cuba

cubano, -a [ku·'βa·no, -a] adj, m, f Cuban

cubertería [ku·βer·te·'ri·a] f cutlery, silverware

cúbico, -a ['ku·βi·ko, -a] adj t. MAT cubic

cubierta [ku·'βjer·ta] f 1. (cobertura) cover; (de libro) jacket; (de rueda) tire; ~ de cama bedspread 2. NÁUT deck

cubierto [ku·'βjer·to] m 1. t. CULIN place setting; poner un ~ to set a place; los ~s the cutlery, the silverware 2. (techumbre) ponerse a ~ to take cover

cubierto, -a [ku·'βjer·to, -a] I. pp de cubrir II. adj (cielo) overcast

cubilete [ku·βi·'le·te] m (en juegos) cup

cubismo [ku·'βis·mo] m ARTE cubism

cubitera [ku·βi·'te·ra] f ice tray

cubito [ku·'βi·to] m ~ de hielo ice cube

cubo ['ku·βo] m 1. (recipiente) bucket; ~ de basura trashcan 2. t. MAT cube

cubrir [ku·'βrir] irr como abrir I. vt 1. (tapar) to cover 2. (vacante) to fill II. vr: ~se 1. (taparse) to cover oneself 2. (cielo) to become overcast 3. (protegerse) to cover oneself; MIL to take cover

cucaracha [ku·ka·'ra·tʃa] f cockroach

cuchara [ku·'tʃa·ra] f spoon; ~ de palo wooden spoon; ~ sopera soup spoon

cucharada [ku·tʃa·'ra·da] f (porción) spoonful; una ~ grande/pequeña a tablespoonful/teaspoonful; a ~s in spoonfuls

cucharilla [ku·tʃa·'ri·ja, -ʎa] f teaspoon

cuchichear [ku·tʃi·tʃe·'ar] vi to whisper

cuchilla [ku·'tʃi·ja, -ʎa] f 1. (hoja) blade; (de afeitar) 2. (de carnicero) cleaver, razor blade

cuchillo [ku·'tʃi·jo, -ʎo] m knife; ~ de cocina kitchen knife

cuchitril [ku·tʃi·'tril] m pigsty; fig (habitación) hole

cuchuco [ku·'tʃu·ko] m Col CULIN pork and barley soup

cuclillas [ku·'kli·jas, -ʎas] fpl estar en ~ to be squatting

cuco ['ku·ko] m cuckoo

cuco, -a ['ku·ko, -a] adj 1. (astuto) crafty 2. (bonito) pretty

cuello ['kwe·jo, -ʎo] m 1. ANAT neck; ~ de botella fig bottleneck; alargar el ~ to crane one's neck; estar con el agua al ~ to be in a tight spot 2. (de una prenda) collar; ~ alto turtleneck; ~ de pico V-neck; ~ redondo crew neck

cuenca ['kwen·ka] f 1. GEO basin; ~ del río river basin 2. (región) valley 3. (de los ojos) socket

cuenco ['kwen·ko] m 1. (vasija) bowl 2. (concavidad) hollow

cuenta ['kwen·ta] f 1. (cálculo) counting; ~ atrás countdown; ~s atrasadas outstanding debts pl; pagar la ~ to pay the bill; trabajar por ~ propia to be self-employed; establecerse por su ~ to set up one's own business; echar ~s to reflect; dar ~ de algo to report on sth; ajustar las ~s a alguien to get even with sb; ajuste de ~s act of revenge;

caer en la ~ to catch on; **hablar más de la ~** to talk too much; **a fin de ~s** after all; **en resumidas ~s** in short; **perder la ~** to lose count **2.** (*en el banco*) account; **~ corriente** current account; **~ de crédito** loan account; **abonar en ~** to credit; **abrir una ~** to open an account **3.** (*consideración*) **tener en ~** to bear in mind; **tomar en ~** to take into consideration; **darse ~ de algo** to realize sth **4.** (*de un collar*) bead

cuentagotas [kwen·ta·'ɣo·tas] *m inv* dropper; **con** [*o* **a**] **~** *fig* bit by bit

cuento ['kwen·to] *m* LIT (*historieta*) story; **~ chino** *inf* tall story; **~ de hadas** fairy tale [*o* story]; **~ de nunca acabar** never-ending story; **tener mucho ~** *inf* (*presumir*) to boast a lot; (*exagerar*) to exaggerate everything; **dejarse de ~s** to stop beating about the bush ▶ **eso es como el ~ de la** lecheʀa don't count your chickens before they're hatched; **no** venir **a ~** to be beside the point

cuerda ['kwer·da] *f* **1.** (*gruesa*) rope; (*delgada*) string; **~ floja** tightrope; **andar en la ~ floja** *fig* to be in an unstable position; **bajo ~** secretly **2.** (*del reloj*) spring; **dar ~ al reloj** to wind up one's watch; **dar ~ a alguien** to encourage sb **3.** ANAT **~s vocales** vocal chords **4.** (*de instrumentos*) string; **juego de ~s** set of strings

cuerdo, -a ['kwer·do, -a] *adj* sensible; **estar ~** to be sane

cueriza [kwe·'ri·sa, -θa] *f AmL* (*zurra*) beating

cuerno ['kwer·no] *m* **1.** ZOOL horn; **poner a alguien los ~s** *inf* to be unfaithful to sb **2.** *inf* (*exclamativo*) **¡un ~!** my foot!; **irse al ~** to be ruined; (*plan*) to fall through

cuero ['kwe·ro] *m* leather; **~ cabelludo** scalp; **estar en ~s** *inf* to be stark naked

cuerpo ['kwer·po] *m* **1.** (*organismo*) body; (*tronco*) trunk; (*cadáver*) corpse, cadaver; **una foto de ~ entero** a full-length photo(graph); **luchar ~ a ~** to fight hand-to-hand; **tomar ~** to take shape; **estar de ~ presente** to lie in state; **hacer de(l) ~** to relieve oneself;

haz lo que te pida el ~ do what you feel like doing **2.** (*objeto, corporación*) body; **~ de bomberos** fire department; **~ diplomático** diplomatic corps **3.** (*grosor*) thickness; **tener poco ~** to be thin ▶ **vivir a ~ de rey** to live like a king

cuervo ['kwer·βo] *m* raven, crow

cuesta ['kwes·ta] *f* slope; **~ abajo/arriba** downhill/uphill; **un camino en ~** an uphill road; **llevar algo a ~s** to carry sth on one's back

cuestión [kwes·'tjon] *f* question, matter; **~ de gustos** question of taste; **eso es otra ~** that's another matter; **la ~ es pasarlo bien** the main thing is to enjoy oneself

cuestionable [kwes·tjo·'na·βle] *adj* questionable

cuestionar [kwes·tjo·'nar] *vt* to question

cuestionario [kwes·tjo·'na·rjo] *m* questionnaire

cuete ['kwe·te] *m Méx* **1.** (*loncha de carne*) slice of meat **2.** (*borrachera*) drunken spree; **traer un ~** to be plastered

cueva ['kwe·βa] *f* cave

cuidado [kwi·'ða·ðo] *m* care; **¡~!** careful!; **¡~ con el escalón!** mind the step!; **de ~** serious; **eso me tiene sin ~** I couldn't care less about that

cuidador(a) [kwi·ða·'ðor] *m(f)* caregiver; *Arg* nurse

cuidadoso, -a [kwi·ða·'ðo·so, -a] *adj* careful

cuidar [kwi·'ðar] **I.** *vt* to look after **II.** *vr:* **~se** to look after oneself; **¡cuídate!** take care!

culminación [kul·mi·na·'sjon, -'θjon] *f* culmination

culminante [kul·mi·'nan·te] *adj* **punto ~** high point

culo ['ku·lo] *m* bottom; (*de vaso*) bottom; **caer de ~** to fall on one's backside; *fig* to be amazed

culpa ['kul·pa] *f* fault; JUR guilt; **echar la ~ a alguien** to blame sb; **y ¿qué ~ tengo yo?** and how am I to blame (for that)?

culpabilidad [kul·pa·βi·li·'dad] *f* guilt

culpable [kul·'pa·βle] **I.** *adj* guilty; **decla-**

rar ~ to find guilty **II.** *mf* culprit

culpar [kul·'par] **I.** *vt* ~ **de** [*o por*] **algo** to blame for sth **II.** *vr* ~**se de** [*o por*] **algo** to be to blame for sth

cultivar [kul·ti·'βar] *vt t. fig* AGR to cultivate; ~ **la tierra** to farm the land

cultivo [kul·'ti·βo] *m* AGR (*acto*) cultivation; (*resultado*) crop; (*de bacterias*) culture; ~ **de regadío** irrigated crop

culto ['kul·to] *m* worship

culto, -a ['kul·to, -a] *adj* educated, cultured

cultura [kul·'tu·ra] *f* culture; ~ **general** general knowledge

cultural [kul·tu·'ral] *adj* cultural

cuma ['ku·ma] *f* **1.** AmC (*machete*) long knife **2.** Perú (*comadre*) godmother

cumbre ['kum·bre] *f* **1.** (*cima*) summit **2.** (*reunión*) summit meeting **3.** (*culminación*) height

cumiche [ku·'mi·tʃe] *m* AmC baby of the family

cumpleaños [kum·ple·'a·ɲos] *m inv* birthday

cumplido [kum·'pli·do] *m* compliment; **hacer algo por** ~ to do sth out of courtesy

cumplido, -a [kum·'pli·do, -a] *adj* **1.** (*acabado*) completed; **¡misión cumplida!** mission accomplished! **2.** (*cortés*) courteous

cumplimentar [kum·pli·men·'tar] *vt* **1.** (*felicitar*) to congratulate **2.** (*visitar*) to pay one's respects **3.** (*una orden*) to carry out **4.** (*un impreso*) to complete

cumplir [kum·'plir] **I.** *vi* **1.** (*satisfacer*) ~ **con su deber/su promesa** to do one's duty/to keep one's promise; **hacer algo sólo por** ~ to do sth as a matter of form **2.** (*plazo*) to end **II.** *vt* **1.** (*orden*) to carry out **2.** (*promesa*) to keep **3.** (*plazo*) to keep to **4.** (*una pena*) to serve **5.** (*las leyes*) to observe **6.** (*años*) **en mayo cumplo treinta años** I'm thirty years old in May **III.** *vr:* ~**se** to be fulfilled

cuna ['ku·na] *f* cradle; **canción de** ~ lullaby

cundir [kun·'dir] *vi* **1.** (*dar de sí*) to be productive **2.** (*trabajo*) to go well

cuneta [ku·'ne·ta] *f* ditch

cuña ['ku·ɲa] *f* (*traba*) wedge

cuñado, -a [ku·'ɲa·do, -a] *m, f* brother-in-law *m*, sister-in-law *f*

cuota ['kwo·ta] *f* **1.** (*porción*) quota; ~ **de crecimiento** rate of increase; ~ **de mercado** market share **2.** (*contribución*) fee; ~ **de socio** membership fee

cupo [ku·po] *m* **1.** 3. *pret de* **caber** **II.** *m* **1.** ECON quota **2.** MIL draft

cupón [ku·'pon] *m* coupon; (*de lotería*) lottery ticket

cúpula ['ku·pu·la] *f* ARQUIT dome; ~ **dirigente** POL top management

cura[1] [ku·ra] *m* priest

cura[2] [ku·ra] *f* **1.** (*curación*) cure **2.** (*tratamiento*) treatment

curación [ku·ra·'sjon, -'θjon] *f* treatment

curado, -a [ku·'ra·do, -a] *adj* **1.** (*alimento*) cured **2.** AmL (*borracho*) drunk

curandero, -a [ku·ran·'der·o, -a] *m, f* healer

curar [ku·'rar] **I.** *vt* **1.** (*tratar*) to treat; (*sanar*) to cure **2.** (*alimentos*) to cure; (*pieles*) to tan **II.** *vr:* ~**se** to recover; ~**se en salud** to take precautions

curativo, -a [ku·ra·'ti·βo, -a] *adj* curative

curiosidad [ku·rjo·si·'dad] *f* curiosity; **despertar la** ~ **de alguien** to arouse sb's curiosity

curioso, -a [ku·'rjo·so, -a] **I.** *adj* curious; **¡qué** ~**!** how curious! **II.** *m, f* **1.** (*indiscreto*) busybody, snoop **2.** (*mirón*) onlooker, bystander **3.** AmL (*curandero*) quack doctor

currante [ku·'rran·te] *mf inf* worker

currar [ku·'rrar] *vi inf* to work

currículo [ku·'rri·ku·lo] *m* curriculum

curro ['ku·rro] *m inf* job

curry ['ku·rri] *m* curry

cursar [kur·'sar] *vt* **1.** (*cursos*) to take **2.** (*orden*) to issue; (*telegrama*) to send; (*solicitud*) to pass on

cursi ['kur·si] **I.** *adj inf* affected **II.** *mf inf* affected person

cursillo [kur·'si·jo, -ʎo] *m* short course

cursiva [kur·'si·βa] *f* italics *pl*

curso ['kur·so] *m* **1.** (*transcurso*) course; ~ **de agua** watercourse; **estar en** ~ to be going on; FIN to be in circulation;

tomar un ~ **favorable** to go favorably; **dar ~ a una solicitud** to deal with an application **2.** ENS course; **~ acelerado** crash course; **asistir a un ~** to take part in a course

cursor [kur·'sor] *m* COMPUT cursor

curtir [kur·'tir] I. *vt* to tan; *fig* to harden II. *vr:* ~**se 1.** (*piel*) to become tanned **2.** (*a la vida dura*) to become inured

curva ['kur·βa] *f* curve

cusma ['kus·ma] *f* AmS coarse woolen Indian shirt

cúspide ['kus·pi·de] *f* **1.** MAT apex **2.** *fig* pinnacle

custodia [kus·'to·dja] *f* (*guarda*) custody; **bajo ~** in custody; **estar bajo la ~ de alguien** to be in sb's care

custodiar [kus·to·'djar] *vt* to guard

cususa [ku·'su·sa] *f* AmC uncured rum

cutis ['ku·tis] *m inv* skin, complexion

cuyo, -a ['ku·jo, -a] *pron rel* whose; **por cuya causa** for which reason

D

D, d [de] *f* D, d; **D de Dolores** D as in Delta

D. [don] *abr de* **Don** Mr.

Dª ['do·ɲa] *abr de* **Doña** Mrs.

dactilar [dak·ti·'lar] *adj* **huellas ~es** fingerprints *pl*

dado[1] ['da·ðo] *m* die; (**jugar a los**) ~**s** (to play) dice

dado, -a *conj* **1.** (+ *inf*) ~ **que llueve...** given that it's raining... **2.** (+ *subj*) ~ **que sea posible...** assuming it were possible...

dado, -a ['da·ðo, -a] *adj* (*supuesto*) given; **en el caso ~** in this particular case

▶ **no ser ~** *Méx* to be brave

daga ['da·ɣa] *f* dagger; *PRico* machete

daiquiri [dai·'ki·ri] *m* CULIN daiquiri

dalia ['da·lja] *f* dahlia

dálmata ['dal·ma·ta] *m* ZOOL dalmatian

daltónico, -a [dal·'to·ni·ko, -a] *adj* color-blind

dama ['da·ma] *f* **1.** (*señora*) lady; ~ **de honor** bridesmaid **2.** *pl* (*juego*) checkers *pl*

damnificar [dam·ni·fi·'kar] *vt* (*persona*) to injure; (*cosa*) to damage

danés, -esa [da·'nes, -·'ne·sa] I. *adj* Danish II. *m, f* Dane

danza ['dan·sa, -θa] *f* dance

danzar [dan·'sar, -'θar] *vi, vt* to dance

dañar [da·'ɲar] I. *vi* to harm II. *vt* (*cosa*) to damage; (*persona*) to injure III. *vr:* ~**se** to get damaged

dañero, -a [da·'ɲe·ro, -a] *adj* Ven misleading

dañino, -a [da·'ɲi·no, -a] *adj* harmful

daño ['da·ɲo] *m* **1.** (*perjuicio*) damage; ~**s y perjuicios** JUR damages **2.** (*dolor*) hurt; **hacer ~ a alguien** to hurt sb; **hacerse ~** to hurt oneself

dar [dar] *irr* I. *vt* **1.** (*entregar*) to give; ~ **forma a algo** to shape sth; ~ **importancia a algo** to consider sth important **2.** (*producir*) **la vaca da leche** the cow yields milk; **este árbol da naranjas** this tree bears oranges **3.** (*celebrar*) to give; ~ **clases** to teach **4.** (*causar*) ~ **miedo** to be frightening; **me das pena** I feel sorry for you **5.** (*película*) to show **6.** (*una noticia*) to give; ~ **las buenas noches** to say goodnight; ~ **recuerdos** to send one's regards **7.** (+ *'un'*) **un paseo** to take a walk; (*encender*) to turn on **8.** (*reloj*) to strike **9.** (+ *'a'*) ~ **a conocer algo** to let sth be known; ~ **a entender algo a alguien** to let sb know sth II. *vi* **1.** (+ *'a'*) **el balcón da a la calle** the balcony faces the street; **la ventana da al patio** the window opens onto the courtyard **2.** (+ *'con'*) ~ **con la solución** to find the solution **3.** ~ **contra algo** to hit sth **4.** (*caer*) ~ **de espaldas** to land on one's back **5.** (*acertar*) ~ **en el blanco** *fig* to hit the target; ~ **en el clavo** *fig* to hit the nail on the head **6.** (+ *'para'*) **da para vivir** it's enough to live on **7.** (+ *'por'* + *adj*) ~ **a alguien por inocente** to assume sb is innocent **8.** (+ *'por'* + *vb*) **le ha dado por dejarse el pelo largo** he/she has decided to grow his/her hair long **9.** (+ *'que'* + *vb*) ~ **que decir/pensar** to give cause for comment/thought; ~ **que hablar** to be the topic of conversation; ~

que hacer to be a lot of work ▶ **¡qué más da!** inf what does it matter? **III.** vr: **~se 1.** (suceder) to happen **2.** (+ 'a') to devote oneself; (entregarse) to surrender **3.** (+ 'con(tra)') **~se con(tra) algo** to hit sth **4.** (+ 'por' + adj) **~se por vencido** to give up **5.** (+ 'a' + vb) **~se a conocer** (persona) to make oneself known; (noticia) to become known; **~se a entender** to hint **6.** (+ 'de') **~se de alta/de baja** to sign up/off; **dárselas de valiente** inf to pretend to be brave **7.** (+ subst) **~se un baño** to take a bath; **~se cuenta de algo** to realize sth; **~se prisa** to hurry up

dardo ['dar·do] m dart

datar [da·'tar] vi, vt to date

dátil ['da·til] m date

dato ['da·to] m **1.** (detalle) fact; **~s personales** personal details **2.** (cantidad) figure **3.** pl COMPUT data pl; **elaborar ~s** to compile data

dC, d.C. [des·'pwes de 'kris·to] abr de **después de Cristo** AD

dcha. [de·'re·tʃa] abr de **derecha** R

de [de] prep **1.** (posesión) **el reloj ~ mi padre** my father's watch **2.** (origen) from; **ser ~ Italia** to come from Italy; **~ Caracas a Bogotá** from Caracas to Bogotá; **un libro ~ Allende** a book by Allende **3.** (material, cualidad) of; **~ oro** of gold, golden **4.** (temporal) from; **~ niño** as a child **5.** (finalidad) **máquina ~ lavar** washing machine; **hora ~ comer** mealtime **6.** (causa) of, from **7.** (condición) **~ haber sabido no habríamos ido** if we had known we wouldn't have gone **8.** (partitivo) **dos platos ~ sopa** two bowls of soup **9.** (+ nombre propio) **la ciudad ~ Cuzco** the city of Cuzco; **pobre ~ mí** poor me

deambular [de·am·bu·'lar] vi to wander around

debajo [de·'βa·xo] **I.** adv underneath **II.** prep **~ de** below, under; (con movimiento) under; **pasar por ~ de** to go under

debate [de·'βa·te] m **1.** POL debate **2.** (charla) discussion

debatir [de·βa·'tir] vt **1.** POL to debate **2.** (considerar) to discuss

deber [de·'βer] **I.** vi (suposición) **debe de estar al llegar** he/she should arrive soon; **deben de ser las nueve** it must be nine o'clock **II.** vt **1.** (obligación) to have to; **no ~ías haberlo dicho** you shouldn't have said it **2.** (tener que dar) to owe **III.** vr: **~se 1.** (tener por causa) **~se a algo** to be due to sth; (gracias a) to be thanks to sth **2.** (obligación) to have a duty **IV.** m **1.** (obligación) duty **2.** pl (tareas) homework

debido [de·'βi·do] prep **~ a** due to

debido, -a [de·'βi·do, -a] adj **como es ~** as is proper

débil ['de·βil] adj weak; (sonido) faint; (luz) dim

debilidad [de·βi·li·'dad] f weakness (**por** for)

debilitar [de·βi·li·'tar] vt to weaken

debitar [de·βi·'tar] vt AmL to debit

débito ['de·βi·to] m debit; (deuda) debt

debocar <c → qu> [de·βo·'kar] vi Arg, Bol to vomit

debut <debuts> [de·'βu(t)] m debut; (teatro) opening

debutar [de·βu·'tar] vi to make one's debut

década ['de·ka·da] f decade

decadencia [de·ka·'den·sja, -θja] f **1.** (declive) decay; **~ moral** decadence **2.** (de un imperio) decline

decadente [de·ka·'den·te] adj (en declive) declining; (moralmente) decadent

decaer [de·ka·'er] irr como caer vi to decline; **~ el ánimo** to lose heart

decaído, -a [de·ka·'i·do, -a] adj **1.** (abatido) downhearted **2.** (débil) weak

decano, -a [de·'ka·no, -a] m, f UNIV dean

decapitar [de·ka·pi·'tar] vt to decapitate

decatlón [de·kad·'lon] m decathlon

decena [de·'se·na, -'θe·na] f ten; **una ~ de huevos** ten eggs

decencia [de·'sen·sja, -'θen·θja] f decency

decente [de·'sen·te, -'θen·te] adj **1.** (decoroso) decent **2.** (honesto) upright

decepción [de·sep·'sjon, -θeβ·'θjon] f disappointment

decepcionante [de·sep·sjon'an·te, -θeβ·θjon-] adj disappointing

D

decepcionar [de·sep·sjo·'nar, -θeβ·θjo·'nar] *vt* to disappoint

decibel(io) [de·si·'βel, -·'βe·ljo, de·θi-] *m* decibel

decididamente [de·si·di·da·'men·te, de·θi-] *adv* 1. (*resueltamente*) resolutely 2. (*definitivamente*) decidedly

decidido, -a [de·θi·'di·do, -a; de·θi-] *adj* determined

decidir [de·si·'dir, de·θi-] I. *vi* to decide II. *vt* 1. (*determinar, acordar*) to decide 2. (*mover a*) to persuade III. *vr* **~se por/en contra de algo** to decide in favor of/against sth

décima ['de·si·ma, de·θi-] *f* tenth

decimal [de·si·'mal, de·θi-] *adj, m* decimal

décimo, -a ['de·si·mo, -a; de·θi-] I. *adj* tenth II. *m, f* tenth; (*de lotería*) tenth share of a lottery ticket; *v. t.* **octavo**

decimonono, -a [de·si·mo·'no·no, -a; de·θi-], **decimonoveno, -a** [de·si·mo·no·'βe·no, -a; de·θi-] *adj* nineteenth; *v. t.* **octavo**

decimoquinto, -a [de·si·mo·'kin·to, -a; de·θi-] *adj* fifteenth; *v. t.* **octavo**

decimotercero, -a [de·si·mo·ter·'se·ro, -a; de·θi·mo·ter·'θe-], **decimotercio, -a** [de·si·mo·'ter·sjo, -a; de·θi·mo·'ter·θjo, -a] *adj* thirteenth; *v. t.* **octavo**

decir [de·'sir, -θir] *irr* I. *vi* 1. (*expresar*) **~ algo de alguien** to say sth about sb; **~ que sí** to say yes; **diga** [*o* **dígame**] TEL hello; **es** [*o* **quiere**] **~** in other words; **¡no me digas!** *inf* really!; **¡quién lo diría!** who would have thought it!; **y que lo digas** you can say that again; **y no digamos** not to mention 2. (*llevar escrito*) to say; **un letrero que dice 'Bienvenidos'** a sign that says "Welcome" II. *vt* (*expresar*) to say; (*comunicar*) to tell; **dicho y hecho** no sooner said than done III. *vr* **¿cómo se dice en inglés?** how do you say it in English? IV. *m* saying ▶ **ser un ~** to be a manner of speaking

decisión [de·si·'sjon, de·θi-] *f* 1. (*resolución*) resolution; (*acuerdo*) decision; **tomar una ~** to make a decision 2. (*firmeza*) determination

decisivo, -a [de·si·'si·βo, -a; de·θi-] *adj* decisive

declaración [de·kla·ra·'sjon, -'θjon] *f* 1. (*a la prensa*) declaration; **hacer declaraciones** to make a statement 2. JUR statement 3. **~ de la renta** income tax return

declarar [de·kla·'rar] I. *vi* 1. (*testigo*) to testify, to give evidence 2. (*a la prensa*) to make a statement II. *vt* 1. (*manifestar*) to declare; **~ a alguien culpable/inocente** to convict/acquit sb 2. (*ingresos, aduanas*) to declare III. *vr:* **~se** (*manifestarse*) to declare oneself; **~se en huelga** to go on strike; **~se inocente** to plead innocent

declinación [de·kli·na·'sjon, -'θjon] *f* 1. (*disminución*) decline 2. LING declension

declinar [de·kli·'nar] *vi, vt* (*disminuir*) to decline

declive [de·'kli·βe] *m* 1. (*del terreno*) slope; **en (fuerte) ~** (steeply) sloping 2. (*decadencia*) decline

decodificador [de·ko·di·fi·ka·'dor] *m* decoder

decolaje [de·ko·'la·xe] *m AmL* take-off

decolar [de·ko·'lar] *vi AmL* to take off

decolorar [de·ko·lo·'rar] I. *vt* 1. QUÍM to discolor 2. (*el sol*) to bleach II. *vr:* **~se** to fade

decoración [de·ko·ra·'sjon, -'θjon] *f* decoration

decorado [de·ko·'ra·do] *m* TEAT set

decorador(a) [de·ko·ra·'dor, -·'do·ra] *m(f)* decorator; TEAT set designer; **~ de interiores** interior designer

decorar [de·ko·'rar] *vt* (*adornar*) to decorate

decorativo, -a [de·ko·ra·'ti·βo, -a] *adj* decorative

decoro [de·'ko·ro] *m* 1. (*dignidad*) dignity 2. (*respeto*) respect; **guardar el ~** to show respect 3. (*pudor*) decency; **con ~** decently

decoroso, -a [de·ko·'ro·so, -a] *adj* 1. (*decente*) decent 2. (*digno*) dignified

decrecer [de·kre·'ser, -'θer] *irr vi* (*crecer*) to decrease; (*nivel, fiebre*) to fall

decrépito, -a [de·'kre·pi·to, -a] *adj* 1. (*persona*) decrepit 2. (*sociedad*) declining

decretar [de·kre·'tar] *vt* to decree

decreto [de·'kre·to] *m* decree

dedal [de·'dal] *m* thimble

dedear [de·de·'ar] *vt Méx* to finger

dedicación [de·di·ka·'sjon, -'θjon] *f* 1. (*consagración*) consecration 2. (*entrega*) dedication, commitment

dedicar <c → qu> [de·di·'kar] I. *vt* 1. (*destinar*) to dedicate 2. (*consagrar*) to consecrate II. *vr:* ~**se** to devote oneself; ~**se a algo** (*profesionalmente*) to work at sth; ~**se a la enseñanza** to be a teacher; **¿a qué se dedica Ud.?** what do you do?

dedicatoria [de·di·ka·'to·rja] *f* dedication

dedillo [de·'di·jo, -ʎo] *m inf* **saberse algo al** ~ to know sth inside out

dedo ['de·do] *m* (*de mano*) finger; (*de pie*) toe; (*pulgar*) thumb ▶ **hacer** [*o* **ir a**] ~ to hitch-hike; **no** <u>mover</u> **un** ~ to not lift a finger; <u>nombrar</u> **a** ~ to hand-pick

deducción [de·duk·'sjon, -duɣ·'θjon] *f* t. ECON deduction; ~ **estándar/por hijo** basic/child tax allowance

deducir [de·du·'sir, -'θir] *irr como* **traducir** *vt* 1. (*derivar*) to deduce 2. (*descontar*) to deduct

defecar <c → qu> [de·fe·'kar] *vi* to defecate

defecto [de·'fek·to] *m* 1. (*carencia*) lack; **en** ~ **de** in the absence of; **en su** ~ (*cosa*) if it is unavailable; (*persona*) in his/her absence 2. (*falta*) defect

defectuoso, -a [de·fek·tu·'o·so, -a] *adj* faulty, defective

defender <e → ie> [de·fen·'der] I. *vt* 1. (*ideas, intereses*) t. JUR to defend 2. (*proteger*) to protect II. *vr:* ~**se** 1. (*contra ataques*) to defend oneself 2. (*arreglárselas*) to get by

defensa[1] [de·'fen·sa] *f* 1. (*contra ataques*) t. JUR, DEP defense; **en legítima** ~ JUR in self-defense 2. *pl* t. BIO defenses *pl;* **tener** ~**s** to have resistance 3. *Méx* (*paragolpes*) bumper, fender

defensa[2] [de·'fen·sa] *mf* DEP defender

defensiva [de·fen·'si·βa] *f* (**a la** ~) (on the) defensive

defensivo, -a [de·fen·'si·βo, -a] *adj* defensive

defensor(a) [de·fen·'sor, --'so·ra] I. *adj* defending II. *m(f)* defender

deferencia [de·fe·'ren·sja, -θja] *f* (*consideración*) deference; (*cortesía*) courtesy

deficiencia [de·fi·'sjen·sja, -θja] *f* 1. (*insuficiencia*) lack 2. (*defecto*) deficiency

deficiente [de·fi·'sjen·te, -'θjen·te] I. *adj* 1. (*insuficiente*) lacking 2. (*defectuoso*) deficient II. *mf* ~ **mental** mentally disabled person

déficit ['de·fi·sit, -θit] *m inv* FIN ~ (**presupuestario**) (budget) deficit 2. (*escasez*) shortage

deficitario, -a [de·fi·si·'ta·rjo, -a; de·fi·θi-] *adj* (*empresa*) loss-making; (*cuenta*) in deficit

definición [de·fi·ni·'sjon, -'θjon] *f* (*aclaración*) t. TV definition

definir [de·fi·'nir] *vt* to define

definitivo, -a [de·fi·ni·'ti·βo, -a] *adj* 1. (*irrevocable*) final 2. (*decisivo*) decisive ▶ **en definitiva** in short

deforestación [de·fo·res·ta·'sjon, -'θjon] *f* deforestation

deformación [de·for·ma·'sjon, -'θjon] *f* 1. (*alteración*) distortion 2. (*desfiguración*) deformation; ~ **física** physical deformity

deformar [de·for·'mar] I. *vt* 1. (*alterar*) to distort 2. (*desfigurar*) to deform II. *vr:* ~**se** to become deformed

deforme [de·'for·me] *adj* 1. (*imagen*) distorted 2. (*cuerpo*) deformed

deformidad [de·for·mi·'dad] *f* deformity

defraudar [de·frau·'dar] *vt* 1. (*estafar*) to cheat; ~ **a Hacienda** to evade one's taxes 2. (*decepcionar*) to disappoint

defunción [de·fun·'sjon, -'θjon] *f* death

degeneración [de·xe·ne·ra·'sjon, -'θjon] *f* degeneration

degenerar [de·xe·ne·'rar] *vi* to degenerate

degollar <o → ue> [de·ɣo·'jar, -'ʎar] *vt* (*decapitar*) to behead; (*cortar la garganta*) to slit sb's throat

degradación [de·ɣra·da·'sjon, -'θjon] *f* (*humillación*) humiliation

degradante [de·ɣra·'dan·te] *adj* demeaning

degradar [de·ɣra·'dar] **I.** *vt* **1.** (*en el cargo*) to demote **2.** (*calidad*) to worsen; ~ **el medio ambiente** to damage the environment **3.** (*humillar*) to humiliate **II.** *vr* to degrade [*o* demean] oneself

degustación [de·ɣus·ta·'sjon, -'θjon] *f* ~ (**de vinos**) (wine) tasting

degustar [de·ɣus·'tar] *vt* to taste

dehesa [de·'e·sa] *f* pasture

deidad [dei·'dad] *f* (*dios*) deity

dejadez [de·xa·'des, -'deθ] *f* **1.** (*falta de aseo*) slovenliness **2.** (*pereza*) laziness **3.** (*negligencia*) neglect

dejado, -a [de·'xa·do, -a] *adj* **1.** *ser* (*descuidado*) slovenly **2.** *estar* (*abatido*) dejected

dejar [de·'xar] **I.** *vi* ~ **de hacer algo** to stop doing sth; **no dejes de escribirles** don't fail to write them **II.** *vt* **1.** (*en general*) to leave; ~ **caer** to drop; ~ **claro** to make clear; ~ **a deber** to owe; ~ **en libertad** to set free; **¡déjanos en paz!** leave us alone! **2.** (*abandonar*) to leave; ~ **la carrera** to drop out of university **3.** (*ganancia*) to give **4.** (*permitir*) to allow, to let; **no me dejan salir** they won't let me go out **5.** (*entregar*) to give; (*prestar*) to lend; (*en herencia*) to leave **III.** *vr:* ~**se 1.** (*descuidarse*) to neglect oneself **2.** (*olvidar*) to forget ▶ ~**se** <u>llevar</u> to let oneself get carried away

deje ['de·xe] *m* lilt; **se te nota un ~ argentino** you have a slight Argentine accent

dejo ['de·xo] *m* **1.** (*entonación*) lilt; (*acento*) accent **2.** (*regusto*) *t. fig* aftertaste

del [del] *v.* = **de + el** *v.* **de**

delantal [de·lan·'tal] *m* apron

delante [de·'lan·te] **I.** *adv* **1.** (*en la parte delantera*) in front; **de** ~ from the front; **abierto por** ~ open at the front **2.** (*enfrente*) opposite **II.** *prep* ~ **de** in front of; ~ **mío** [*o* **de mí**] in front of me

delantera [de·lan·'te·ra] *f* **1.** (*parte anterior*) front (part) **2.** (*primera fila*) front row **3.** (*distancia*) lead **4.** DEP forward line

delantero [de·lan·'te·ro] *m* (*parte anterior*) front (part)

delantero, -a [de·lan·'te·ro] *m, f* DEP forward; ~ **centro** center forward

delatar [de·la·'tar] **I.** *vt* **1.** (*denunciar*) to inform on **2.** (*manifestar*) to reveal **II.** *vr:* ~**se** to give oneself away

delegación [de·le·ɣa·'sjon, -'θjon] *f* **1.** (*comisión*) delegation **2.** *Méx* (*comisaría*) police station; (*ayuntamiento*) council

delegado, -a [de·le·'ɣa·do, -a] *m, f* delegate; ~ **gubernamental** government representative

delegar <g → gu> [de·le·'ɣar] *vt* ~ **algo en alguien** to delegate sth to sb

deleitar(se) [de·lei·'tar(·se)] *vt, vr* to delight (**con/en** in)

deleite [de·'lei·te] *m* delight

deletrear [de·le·tre·'ar] *vt* to spell

delfín [del·'fin] *m* dolphin

delgado, -a [del·'ɣa·do, -a] *adj* thin; (*esbelto*) slender

deliberado, -a [de·li·βe·'ra·do, -a] *adj* **1.** (*tratado*) considered **2.** (*intencionado*) deliberate

deliberar [de·li·βe·'rar] *vi, vt* **1.** (*reflexionar*) to deliberate **2.** (*discutir*) ~ **sobre** [*o* **acerca de**] **algo** to discuss sth

delicadeza [de·li·ka·'de·sa, -θa] *f* **1.** (*finura*) delicacy; **con** ~ delicately **2.** (*miramiento*) attentiveness; **tener la** ~ **de...** to be thoughtful enough to...

delicado, -a [de·li·'ka·do, -a] *adj* **1.** (*fino, frágil*) delicate **2.** (*enfermizo*) frail

delicia [de·'li·sja, -θja] *f* delight

delicioso, -a [de·li·'sjo·so, -a; -'θjo·so, -a] *adj* (*comida*) delicious; (*agradable*) delightful

delictivo, -a [de·lik·'ti·βo, -a] *adj* **acto** ~ criminal act

delimitar [de·li·mi·'tar] *vt* **1.** (*terreno*) to mark out **2.** (*definir*) to define

delincuencia [de·lin·'kwen·sja, -θja] *f* crime; ~ **juvenil** juvenile delinquency

delincuente [de·lin·'kwen·te] *adj, mf* criminal

delinear [de·li·ne·'ar] *vt* to draw

delirar [de·li·'rar] *vi* (*desvariar*) to be delirious

delirio [de·'li·rjo] *m* delirium; ~**s de gran-**

deza delusions of grandeur

delito [de·'li·to] *m* crime; **~ común** common offence

delta ['del·ta] *m* GEO delta

demagogia [de·ma·'ɣo·xja] *f* demagoguery

demanda [de·'man·da] *f* 1. (*petición*) request; **~ de empleo** job application 2. COM demand; **tener mucha ~** to be in great demand 3. JUR lawsuit; **presentar una ~ contra alguien** to bring an action against sb

demandado, -a [de·man·'da·do, -a] I. *adj* (*solicitado*) requested II. *m, f* JUR defendant

demandante [de·man·'dan·te] I. *adj* JUR **parte ~** plaintiff II. *mf* claimant; JUR plaintiff

demandar [de·man·'dar] *vt* 1. (*pedir*) to ask for; (*solicitar*) to request 2. JUR **~ por algo** to sue for sth

demarcación [de·mar·ka·'sjon, -'θjon] *f* demarcation

demás [de·'mas] *adj* other; **y ~...** and other...; **y ~** and so on; **por lo ~** otherwise

demasiado [de·ma·'sja·do] *adv* (+ *adj*) too; (+ *verbo*) too much

demasiado, -a [de·ma·'sja·do] *adj* too much; **~s** too many; **hace ~ calor** it's too hot

demencia [de·'men·sja, -θja] *f* dementia; **~ senil** senile dementia

demencial [de·men·'sjal, -'θjal], **demente** [de·'men·te] *adj* insane

democracia [de·mo·'kra·sja, -θja] *f* democracy

demócrata [de·'mo·kra·ta] I. *adj* democratic II. *mf* democrat

democrático, -a [de·mo·'kra·ti·ko, -a] *adj* democratic

democratizar <z → c> [de·mo·kra·ti·'sar, -'θar] I. *vt* to democratize II. *vr:* **~se** to become democratic

demográfico, -a [de·mo·'ɣra·fi·ko, -a] *adj* demographic

demoler <o → ue> [de·mo·'ler] *vt* to demolish

demonio [de·'mo·njo] *m* 1. (*espíritu*) demon 2. (*diablo*) devil ▶ **de mil ~s** dreadful; **cómo/dónde/qué ~s...** how/where/what the hell...

demora [de·'mo·ra] *f* delay

demorar [de·mo·'rar] I. *vt* to delay II. *vr* **~se en hacer algo** to delay in doing sth

demostración [de·mos·tra·'sjon, -'θjon] *f* 1. (*prueba*) test 2. (*argumentación*) proof 3. (*exteriorización*) display

demostrar <o → ue> [de·mos·'trar] *vt* 1. (*probar*) to demonstrate 2. (*mostrar*) to show

denegar [de·ne·'ɣar] *irr como fregar vt* 1. (*negar*) to deny 2. (*rechazar*) to refuse; (*solicitud*) to reject

denominar [de·no·mi·'nar] I. *vt* to name II. *vr:* **~se** to be called

denotar [de·no·'tar] *vt* to denote

densidad [den·si·'dad] *f* density

denso, -a ['den·so, -a] *adj* 1. (*compacto*) dense 2. (*espeso*) thick

dentadura [den·ta·'du·ra] *f* teeth *pl*; **~ postiza** false teeth

dental [den·'tal] *adj* dental

dentera [den·'te·ra] *f* (*grima*) **dar ~ a alguien** to give sb the shivers

dentista [den·'tis·ta] *mf* dentist

dentro ['den·tro] I. *adv* inside; **desde ~** from within; **por ~** inside II. *prep* 1. (*local*) **~ de** inside 2. (*con movimiento*) **~ de** into 3. (*temporal*) **~ de** within

denuncia [de·'nun·sja, -θja] *f* 1. (*acusación*) accusation 2. (*injusticia*) denunciation

denunciar [de·nun·'sjar, -'θjar] *vt* 1. (*acusar*) **~ a alguien por algo** to accuse sb of sth 2. (*hacer público*) to expose; (*robo*) to report

deparar [de·pa·'rar] *vt* to bring

departamento [de·par·ta·'men·to] *m* 1. (*sección*) *t.* UNIV department 2. *AmL* (*apartamento*) apartment

dependencia [de·pen·'den·sja, -θja] *f* 1. (*sujeción*) dependency 2. (*sección*) section 3. *pl* rooms *pl*

depender [de·pen·'der] *vi* to depend (**de** on); **depende de ti** it's up to you

dependiente [de·pen·'djen·te] *adj* dependent (**de** on)

dependiente, -a [de·pen·'djen·te, -a] *m, f* dependent; (*de una tienda*) shop assistant

depilación [de·pi·la·'sjon, -'θjon] *f* hair removal

depilar [de·pi·'lar] **I.** *vt* (*con pinzas*) to pluck; (*con cera*) to wax; (*afeitarse*) to shave **II.** *vr* **~se las cejas** top pluck one's eyebrows; **~se las piernas** (*con cera*) to wax one's legs; (*con maquinilla*) to shave one's legs

deponer [de·po·'ner] *irr como poner vt* (*destituir*) to remove

deportación [de·por·ta·'sjon, -'θjon] *f* deportation

deportar [de·por·'tar] *vt* to deport

deporte [de·'por·te] *m* sport; **hacer ~** to practice sports

deportista [de·por·'tis·ta] **I.** *adj* sporty **II.** *mf* sportsman, sportswoman *m*

deportivo, -a [de·por·'ti·βo, -a] *adj* sporting; **noticias deportivas** sports news

depositar [de·po·si·'tar] **I.** *vt* to put; FIN to deposit; (*cadáver*) to lay out; (*confianza*) to place **II.** *vr:* **~se** to settle

depósito [de·'po·si·to] *m* **1.** (*almacén*) warehouse **2.** AUTO gas tank **3.** FIN deposit

depravar [de·pra·'βar] **I.** *vt* to corrupt **II.** *vr:* **~se** to become depraved

depre ['de·pre] *f inf* **estar con la ~** to be feeling down

depredador(a) [de·pre·da·'dor, -·'do·ra] *adj* predatory

depresión [de·pre·'sjon] *f* **1.** (*tristeza*) depression **2.** ECON, METEO depression; **~ económica** recession

depresivo, -a [de·pre·'si·βo, -a] *adj* **1.** (*que deprime*) depressing **2.** (*persona*) depressive

deprimente [de·pri·'men·te] *adj* (*que deprime*) depressing

deprimir [de·pri·'mir] **I.** *vt* (*abatir*) to depress **II.** *vr:* **~se** to become depressed

deprisa [de·'pri·sa] *adv* quickly

depuradora [de·pu·ra·'do·ra] *f* water-treatment plant

depurar [de·pu·'rar] *vt* (*purificar*) to purify

derecha [de·'re·tʃa] *f* **1.** (*lado*) right-hand side; **a la ~** (*estar*) on the right; (*ir*) to the right; **doblar a la ~** to turn right **2.** POL right (wing); **de ~(s)** right-wing

derechista [de·re·'tʃis·ta] **I.** *adj* right-wing **II.** *mf* right-winger

derecho [de·'re·tʃo] **I.** *adv* straight **II.** *m* **1.** (*legitimidad*) right **2.** (*jurisprudencia, ciencia*) **estudiar ~** to study law **3.** (*de un papel, una tela*) right side **4.** *pl* (*impuestos*) duties *pl* **5.** *pl* (*honorarios*) fee(s); **~s de autor** copyright

derecho, -a [de·'re·tʃo, -a] *adj* **1.** (*diestro*) right; **lado ~** right-hand side **2.** (*recto*) straight **3.** (*erguido*) upright

derivado [de·ri·'βa·do] *m* derivative

derivar [de·ri·'βar] **I.** *vi, vt* (*proceder*) to derive; **~ hacia algo** to turn towards sth **II.** *vr:* **~se de algo** to come from sth

dermatólogo, -a [der·ma·'to·lo·ɣo, -a] *m, f* dermatologist

dérmico, -a ['der·mi·ko, -a] *adj* dermal

derogar <g → gu> [de·ro·'ɣar] *vt* to repeal

derramamiento [de·rra·ma·'mjen·to] *m* spilling; (*sangre, lágrimas*) shedding (**de** of)

derramar [de·rra·'mar] **I.** *vt* (*verter*) to pour; (*sin querer*) to spill; (*lágrimas, sangre*) to shed **II.** *vr:* **~se** (*esparcirse*) to spill; **~ en algo** to leak onto sth

derrame [de·'rra·me] *m* **1.** *v.* **derramamiento** **2.** MED hemorrhage

derrapar [de·rra·'par] *vi* to skid

derretir(se) [de·rre·'tir(·se)] *irr como pedir vt, vr* to melt

derribar [de·rri·'βar] *vt* (*edificio*) to demolish; (*puerta*) to batter down; (*árbol*) to fell

derrocar <c → qu> [de·rro·'kar] *vt* (*destituir*) to remove

derrochador(a) [de·rro·tʃa·'dor, -·'do·ra] *adj, m(f)* spendthrift

derrochar [de·rro·'tʃar] *vt* **1.** (*despilfarrar*) to squander **2.** *inf* (*irradiar*) to be brimming with

derroche [de·'rro·tʃe] *m* **1.** (*despilfarro*) waste **2.** (*abundancia*) profusion

derrota [de·'rro·ta] *f* defeat

derrotar [de·rro·'tar] *vt* to defeat

derruir [de·rru·'ir] *irr como huir vt* to tear down

derrumbar [de·rrum·'bar] **I.** *vt* to knock down **II.** *vr:* **~se** to fall down; (*esperanzas*) to collapse

desab(o)rido, -a [de·sa·'β(o)·ri·do, -a]

adj **1.** (*comida*) insipid **2.** (*persona*) disagreeable

desabrochar(se) [de·sa·βro·'tʃar(·se)] *vt, vr* to undo; (*cordones*) to untie

desacato [de·sa·'ka·to] *m* disrespect (**a** for)

desacierto [de·sa·'sjer·to, -'θjer·to] *m* mistake

desacreditar [de·sa·kre·di·'tar] *vt* to discredit

desactivar [des·ak·ti·'βar] *vt* (*explosivos*) to defuse

desacuerdo [de·sa·'kwer·do] *m* disagreement; **estar en ~** to disagree

desafiar <*1. pres desafío*> [de·sa·fi·'ar] **I.** *vt* **1.** (*retar*) to challenge **2.** (*hacer frente a*) to defy **II.** *vr:* **~se** to challenge each other

desafinado, -a [de·sa·fi·'na·do, -a] *adj* out of tune

desafinar [de·sa·fi·'nar] *vi* to sing/play out of tune

desafío [de·sa·'fi·o] *m* challenge; (*duelo*) duel

desafortunado, -a [de·sa·for·tu·'na·do, -a] *adj* unlucky

desagradable [de·sa·ɣra·'da·βle] *adj* unpleasant

desagradar [de·sa·ɣra·'dar] *vi* to displease

desagradecido, -a [de·sa·ɣra·de·'si·do, -a; -'θi·do, -a] *adj* ungrateful

desagüe [de·'sa·ɣwe] *m* drain

desahogado, -a [de·sa·o·'ɣa·do, -a] *adj* **1.** (*lugar*) spacious **2.** (*adinerado*) well-off

desahogar <g → gu> [de·sa·o·'ɣar] **I.** *vt* **1.** (*aliviar*) to relieve **2.** (*consolar*) to console **II.** *vr* **~se con alguien** to tell one's troubles to sb

desahogo [de·sa·'o·ɣo] *m* **1.** (*alivio*) relief **2.** (*reposo*) rest

desahuciar [de·sau·'sjar, -'θjar] *vt* (*inquilino*) to evict

desajuste [de·sa·'xus·te] *m* **1.** (*desorden*) imbalance **2.** (*desconcierto*) confusion

desalentador(a) [de·sa·len·ta·'dor, -·'do·ra] *adj* discouraging

desalentar <e → ie> [de·sa·len·'tar] **I.** *vt* to discourage **II.** *vr:* **~se** to lose heart

desaliñado, -a [de·sa·li·'ɲa·do, -a] *adj* shabby

desalmado, -a [de·sal·'ma·do, -a] **I.** *adj* heartless **II.** *m, f* swine

desalojar [de·sa·lo·'xar] *vt* (*casa*) to vacate; (*persona*) to eject

desamparado, -a [des·am·pa·'ra·do, -a] *adj* defenseless

desamparar [des·am·pa·'rar] *vt* **1.** (*dejar*) to abandon **2.** (*desasistir*) to fail to help

desamparo [des·am·'pa·ro] *m* **1.** (*desprotección*) defenselessness **2.** (*abandono*) abandonment

desangrar [de·san·'grar] **I.** *vt* **1.** (*animales*) to bleed **2.** (*arruinar*) to impoverish, to bleed white **II.** *vr:* **~se** to bleed heavily

desanimado, -a [de·sa·ni·'ma·do, -a] *adj* **1.** (*persona*) downhearted **2.** (*lugar*) lifeless

desanimar [de·sa·ni·'mar] **I.** *vt* to discourage **II.** *vr:* **~se** to lose heart

desánimo [de·'sa·ni·mo] *m* dejection

desaparecer [de·sa·pa·re·'ser, -'θer] *irr como crecer vi* to disappear; (*en guerra*) to go missing

desaparecido, -a [de·sa·pa·re·'si·do, -a; -'θi·do, -a] *adj* missing

desaparición [de·sa·pa·ri·'sjon, -'θjon] *f* disappearance

desapercibido, -a [de·sa·per·si·'βi·do, -a; de·sa·per·θi-] *adj* **1.** (*inadvertido*) unnoticed; **pasar ~** to go unnoticed **2.** (*desprevenido*) unprepared; **coger ~** to catch unawares

desaprensivo, -a [de·sa·pren·'si·βo, -a] *adj* unscrupulous

desaprovechar [de·sa·pro·βe·'tʃar] *vt* to waste

desarmador [des·ar·ma·'dor] *m Méx* screwdriver

desarmar [des·ar·'mar] *vt* **1.** (*dejar sin armas*) to disarm **2.** (*desmontar*) to take apart

desarme [des·'ar·me] *m* disarmament

desarraigar <g → gu> [de·sa·rrai·'ɣar] *vt* **1.** (*árbol, persona*) to uproot **2.** (*costumbre, creencia*) to eradicate

desarraigo [de·sa·'rrai·ɣo] *m* **1.** (*de árbol, persona*) uprooting **2.** (*de costumbre, creencia*) eradication

desarrollar [de·sa·rro·'ʝar, -'ʎar] I. vt
1. (aumentar) to develop 2. (exponer)
to expound II. vr: ~se 1. (progresar) to
develop 2. (ocurrir) to take place

desarrollo [de·sa·'rro·jo, -ʎo] m 1. development; **país en vías de ~** developing country 2. (crecimiento) growth

desarticular [des·ar·ti·ku·'lar] I. vt
1. (mecanismo) to dismantle 2. (grupo)
to break up II. vr: ~se 1. (mecanismo)
to come apart 2. (articulación) to become dislocated 3. (grupo) to break up

desasosiego [de·sa·so·'sje·ɣo] m unease

desastre [de·'sas·tre] m disaster; **ser un
~** inf (alguien) to be hopeless; (algo)
to be a flop

desastroso, -a [de·sas·'tro·so, -a] adj
disastrous

desatado, -a [de·sa·'ta·do, -a] adj
1. (desligado) untied 2. (desenfrenado) wild

desatar [de·sa·'tar] I. vt 1. (soltar) to
untie; (nudo) to undo 2. (causar) to
unleash II. vr: ~se 1. (soltarse) to untie
oneself; (nudo) to come undone 2. (tormenta) to break; (crisis) to erupt

desatascar <c → qu> [de·sa·tas·'kar] vt
to unblock

desatender <e → ie> [de·sa·ten·'der] vt
1. (desoír) to ignore 2. (abandonar)
to neglect

desatento, -a [de·sa·'ten·to, -a] adj
1. (distraído) inattentive; (negligente) careless 2. (descortés) impolite
(con s)

desatino [de·sa·'ti·no] m (error) mistake;
(torpeza) blunder

desatornillador [de·sa·tor·ni·ja·'dor, -ʎa·
'dor] m AmL screwdriver

desatornillar [de·sa·tor·ni·'jar, -'ʎar] vt
to unscrew

desatrancar <c → qu> [de·sa·tran·'kar]
vt to unblock

desavenencia [de·sa·βe·'nen·sja, -θja] f
1. (desacuerdo) disagreement 2. (discordia) friction

desayunar [de·sa·ju·'nar] I. vi to have
breakfast II. vt ~ **algo** to have sth for
breakfast

desayuno [de·sa·'ju·no] m breakfast

desbancar <c → qu> [des·βan·'kar] vt
to oust

desbarajuste [des·βa·ra·'xus·te] m chaos

desbaratar [des·βa·ra·'tar] I. vt 1. (desunir, dispersar) to break up 2. (arruinar)
to ruin II. vr: ~se 1. (separarse) to
break up 2. (fracasar) to fail

desbloquear [des·βlo·ke·'ar] vt to unblock; FIN to unfreeze

desbocar <c → qu> [des·βo·'kar] I. vt
(enloquecer) to drive mad II. vr: ~se to
go crazy; (caballo) to bolt

desbordamiento [des·βor·da·'mjen·to]
m overflowing

desbordar [des·βor·'dar] I. vi, vr: ~se to
overflow II. vt to exceed

descabellado, -a [des·ka·βe·'ja·do, -a;
-'ʎa·do, -a] adj preposterous

descafeinado, -a [des·ka·fei·'na·do, -a]
adj decaffeinated

descalcificar <c → qu> [des·kal·si·fi·'kar,
-θi·fi·'kar] vt decalcify

descalificación [des·ka·li·fi·ka·'sjon,
-'θjon] f disqualification

descalificar <c → qu> [des·ka·li·fi·'kar]
vt to disqualify

descalzar <z → c> [des·kal·'sar, -'θar] vr:
~se to take one's shoes off

descalzo, -a [des·'kal·so, -a; -θo, -a]
adj barefoot

descambiar [des·kam·'bjar] vt to change
back

descaminar [des·ka·mi·'nar] vr: ~se
1. (perderse) to get lost; **ir descamina-
do** to be on the wrong track 2. (descarriarse) to go astray

descampado [des·kam·'pa·do] m piece
of open ground

descansar [des·kan·'sar] vi 1. (reposar) to rest 2. (recuperarse) to recover
3. (dormir) to sleep; **¡que descanses!**
sleep well! 4. (apoyar) to rest

descanso [des·'kan·so] m 1. (reposo) rest 2. (recuperación) recovery
3. (tranquilidad) peace 4. (pausa) t. DEP
break 5. (alivio) relief

descapotable [des·ka·po·'ta·βle] m convertible

descarado, -a [des·ka·'ra·do, -a] adj
1. (desvergonzado) shameless 2. (evidente) blatant

descarga [des·'kar·ɣa] *f* **1.** (*de mercancías*) unloading **2.** ELEC, FÍS, FIN discharge **3.** COMPUT download

descargar <g → gu> [des·kar·'ɣar] I. *vt* **1.** (*carga*) to unload **2.** ELEC, FÍS to discharge **3.** COMPUT to download II. *vr:* **~se 1.** (*vaciarse*) to empty; ELEC, FÍS to discharge; (*pila*) to run out **2.** (*librarse*) to unburden oneself; (*desahogarse*) to let off steam

descaro [des·'ka·ro] *m* cheek

descarriarse <*1. pres* descarrío> [des·ka·rri·'ar·se] *vr* **1.** (*perderse*) to get lost **2.** (*descaminarse*) to go astray

descarrilar [des·ka·rri·'lar] *vi* to be derailed

descartar [des·kar·'tar] *vt* (*propuesta*) to reject; (*posibilidad*) to rule out

descendencia [de·sen·'den·sja, -θen·'den·θja] *f* descendents *pl;* **tener ~** to have offspring

descendente [de·sen·'den·te, des·θen·] *adj* **1.** (*en caída*) descending **2.** (*en disminución*) diminishing

descender <e → ie> [de·sen·'der, des·θen·] I. *vi* **1.** (*bajar*) to descend **2.** (*disminuir*) to diminish **3.** (*proceder*) to be descended II. *vt* to take down; (*escalera*) to go down

descendiente [de·sen·'djen·te, des·θen·] *mf* descendant

descenso [des·'sen·so, des·'θen·so] *m* **1.** (*bajada*) descent **2.** (*cuesta*) slope **3.** (*disminución*) decline; ECON downturn

descentralizar <z → c> [de·sen·tra·li·'sar, des·θen·tra·li·'θar] *vt* to decentralize

descifrar [de·si·'frar, des·θi·] *vt* to decipher

descocado, -a [des·ko·'ka·do, -a] *adj* impudent

descodificador [des·ko·di·fi·ka·'dor] *m* decoder

descodificar <c → qu> [des·ko·di·fi·'kar] *vt* to decode

descojonante [des·ko·xo·'nan·te] *adj inf* hilarious

descojonarse [des·ko·xo·'nar·se] *vr inf* to die laughing

descolgar [des·kol·'ɣar] *irr como* colgar *vt* (*teléfono*) to pick up

descolorar [des·ko·lo·'rar], **descolorir** [des·ko·lo·'rir] *vt, vr:* **~se** *v.* decolorar

descomponer [des·kom·po·'ner] *irr como* poner I. *vt* **1.** (*desordenar*) to mess up **2.** (*separar*) to take apart **3.** (*corromper*) *t.* QUÍM to decompose II. *vr:* **~se 1.** (*desmembrarse*) to come apart **2.** (*corromperse*) to decay

descomposición [des·kom·po·si·'sjon, -'θjon] *f* **1.** (*separación*) separation; QUÍM decomposition **2.** (*corrupción*) decay

descompuesto, -a [des·kom·'pwes·to, -a] I. *pp de* **descomponer** II. *adj* **1.** (*desordenado*) untidy **2.** (*podrido*) rotten

descomunal [des·ko·mu·'nal] *adj* enormous

desconcertar <e → ie> [des·kon·ser·'tar, des·kon·θer·] *vt* **1.** (*desbaratar*) to ruin **2.** (*pasmar*) to confuse; **estar desconcertado** to be disconcerted

desconcierto [des·kon·'sjer·to, -'θjer·to] *m* **1.** (*desarreglo*) disorder **2.** (*desorientación*) confusion

desconectar [des·ko·nek·'tar] I. *vt* to disconnect; (*radio, tele*) to switch off II. *vi inf* to switch off

desconfiado, -a [des·kon·fi·'a·do, -a] *adj* distrustful

desconfiar <*1. pres* desconfío> [des·kon·fi·'ar] *vi* **~ de alguien/algo** to mistrust sb/sth

descongelar [des·kon·xe·'lar] I. *vt* **1.** (*comida*) to thaw out; (*nevera*) to defrost **2.** FIN to unfreeze II. *vr:* **~se** (*comida*) to thaw out; (*nevera*) to defrost

descongestionar [des·kon·xes·tjo·'nar] *vt* to unblock; MED to clear

desconocer [des·ko·no·'ser, -'θer] *irr como* crecer *vt* **1.** (*ignorar*) to be unaware of **2.** (*no reconocer*) to not recognize

desconocido, -a [des·ko·no·'si·do, -a; -'θi·do, -a] I. *adj* unknown; **estar ~** to be unrecognizable II. *m, f* stranger

desconsiderado, -a [des·kon·si·de·'ra·do, -a] *adj* inconsiderate

desconsolado, -a [des·kon·so·'la·do, -a] *adj* disconsolate

descontado, -a [des·kon·'ta·do, -a] *adj* (*descartado*) discounted ▶ **dar**

algo por ~ to take sth for granted; **por ~** of course

descontar <o → ue> [des·kon·'tar] *vt* **1.** (*restar*) to take away **2.** (*descartar*) to disregard

descontento [des·kon·'ten·to] *m* dissatisfaction

descontento, -a [des·kon·'ten·to, -a] *adj* dissatisfied

descontrol [des·kon·'trol] *m* chaos

descontrolarse [des·kon·tro·'lar·se] *vr* (*máquina*) to go out of control; (*persona*) to go wild

descorazonar [des·ko·ra·so·'nar, des·ko·ra·θo·-] **I.** *vt* to discourage **II.** *vr*: **~se** to lose heart

descorchador [des·kor·ʧa·'dor] *m* corkscrew

descorchar [des·kor·'ʧar] *vt* to uncork

descorrer [des·ko·'rrer] *vt* to draw; (*cortinas*) to draw back

descortés [des·kor·'tes] *adj* impolite

descortesía [des·kor·te·'si·a] *f* discourtesy

descoser [des·ko·'ser] **I.** *vt* to unstitch **II.** *vr*: **~se** to come apart at the seam

descosido, -a [des·ko·'si·do] *adj* **como un ~** like mad

descrédito [des·'kre·di·to] *m* discredit

descreído, -a [des·kre·'i·do, -a] *adj* skeptical

describir [des·kri·'βir] *irr como* **escribir** *vt* **1.** (*explicar*) to describe **2.** (*trazar*) to trace

descripción [des·krip·'sjon, -kriβ·'θjon] *f* description

descuartizar <z → c> [des·kwar·ti·'sar, -'θar] *vt* to cut up

descubierto [des·ku·'βjer·to] *m* **1.** (*lugar*) **al ~** in the open **2.** (*en evidencia*) **poner algo al ~** to bring sth into the open; **quedar al ~** to be revealed

descubierto, -a [des·ku·'βjer·to, -a] *pp de* **descubrir** **II.** *adj* open; (*sin techo*) open-air; (*cielo*) clear

descubrimiento [des·ku·βri·'mjen·to] *m* **1.** (*invento*) discovery **2.** (*revelación*) disclosure

descubrir [des·ku·'βrir] *irr como* **abrir** **I.** *vt* **1.** (*destapar*) to uncover **2.** (*encontrar*) to discover **3.** (*averiguar*) to

find out **4.** (*inventar*) to invent **5.** (*desenmascarar*) to unmask **II.** *vr*: **~se** **1.** (*salir a la luz*) to come out **2.** (*delatarse*) to give oneself away

descuento [des·'kwen·to] *m* discount

descuidado, -a [des·kwi·'da·do, -a] *adj* **1.** *ser* (*despistado*) inattentive; (*sin cuidado*) careless; (*imprudente*) negligent; (*desaseado*) slovenly; (*desaliñado*) untidy **2.** *estar* (*abandonado*) neglected; (*desprevenido*) unprepared

descuidar [des·kwi·'dar] **I.** *vi* ¡**descuida!** don't worry! **II.** *vt* to neglect **III.** *vr*: **~se** (*distraerse*) to be distracted

descuido [des·'kwi·do] *m* (*falta de atención*) inattentiveness; (*de cuidado*) carelessness; (*imprudencia*) negligence; **por ~** inadvertently

desde ['des·de] **I.** *prep* **1.** (*temporal*) since; (*a partir de*) from; **~... hasta...** from... until...; **~ ahora/ya** from now on; **¿~ cuándo?** since when?; **~ entonces** since then; **~ hace...** for...; **~ hace poco/mucho** for a short/long time; **~ hoy/mañana** from today/tomorrow; **~ el principio** from the beginning **2.** (*local*) from **II.** *adv* **~ luego** of course **III.** *conj* **~ que** since

desdén [des·'den] *m* disdain

desdeñar [des·de·'ɲar] *vt* **1.** (*despreciar*) to scorn **2.** (*rechazar*) to spurn

desdicha [des·'di·ʧa] *f* **1.** (*desgracia*) misfortune **2.** (*miseria*) misery

desdichado, -a [des·di·'ʧa·do, -a] *adj* unfortunate

deseable [de·se·'a·βle] *adj* desirable

desear [de·se·'ar] *vt* to want, to desire; **~ suerte a alguien** to wish sb luck; **hacerse ~** to play hard to get; **¿desea algo más?** would you like anything else?; **dejar mucho que ~** to leave a lot to be desired

desecar <c → qu> [de·se·'kar] **I.** *vt* to dry; (*pantano*) to dry out **II.** *vr*: **~se** to dry up

desechable [de·se·'ʧa·βle] *adj* disposable

desechar [de·se·'ʧar] *vt* **1.** (*tirar*) to throw away **2.** (*descartar*) to rule out; (*desestimar*) to reject

desechos [de·'se·ʧos] *mpl* (*restos*) remains *pl*; (*residuos*) residue; (*basura*) waste

desembalar [des·em·ba·'lar] *vt* to unpack

desembarcar <c → qu> [des·em·βar·'kar] **I.** *vi* to disembark **II.** *vt* to unload

desembarco [des·em·'bar·ko] *m*, **desembarque** [des·em·'bar·ke] *m* landing

desembocadura [des·em·bo·ka·'du·ra] *f* mouth

desembocar <c → qu> [des·em·bo·'kar] *vi* **1.** (*río*) ~ **en** to flow into **2.** (*situación*) ~ **en** to result in

desembolso [des·em·'bol·so] *m* **1.** (*pago*) payment **2.** (*gasto*) expense

desembrollar [des·em·bro·'jar, -'ʎar] *vt inf* **1.** (*madeja*) to untangle **2.** (*asunto*) to sort out

desembuchar [des·em·bu·'tʃar] *vi, vt inf* (*confesar*) to come clean (about); **¡desembucha de una vez!** out with it!

desempacar <c → qu> [des·em·pa·'kar] *vt AmL* to unpack

desempaquetar [des·em·pa·ke·'tar] *vt* to unwrap

desempate [des·em·'pa·te] *m* breakthrough

desempeñar [des·em·pe·'ɲar] *vt* to carry out; (*cargo*) to hold; (*papel*) to play; (*préstamo*) to pay off

desempleado, -a [des·em·ple·'a·do, -a] **I.** *adj* unemployed **II.** *m, f* unemployed person

desempleo [des·em·'ple·o] *m* unemployment

desencadenar [des·en·ka·de·'nar] **I.** *vt* **1.** (*soltar*) to unleash **2.** (*provocar*) to trigger **II.** *vr:* ~**se** to break loose

desencajar [des·en·ka·'xar] **I.** *vt* to dismantle; MED to dislocate; (*cara*) to distort **II.** *vr:* ~**se** to come apart; MED to dislocate

desencantar [des·en·kan·'tar] **I.** *vt* (*desilusionar*) to disillusion; (*decepcionar*) to disappoint **II.** *vr:* ~**se** to become disillusioned

desencanto [des·en·'kan·to] *m* **1.** (*decepción*) disappointment **2.** (*desilusión*) disillusion

desenchufar [des·en·tʃu·'far] *vt* to unplug

desencriptar [des·eŋ·krip·'tar] *vt* COMPUT to decrypt

desenfadado, -a [des·en·fa·'da·do, -a] *adj* **1.** (*desenvuelto*) self-assured **2.** (*carácter*) easy-going **3.** (*ropa*) casual

desenfado [des·en·'fa·do] *m* openness; (*naturalidad*) naturalness

desenfocado, -a [des·en·fo·'ka·do, -a] *adj* out of focus

desenfrenado, -a [des·en·fre·'na·do, -a] *adj* frantic

desenfreno [des·en·'fre·no] *m* lack of restraint

desenganchar [des·en·gan·'tʃar] **I.** *vt* **1.** (*gancho*) to unhook **2.** (*soltar*) to take off **II.** *vr:* ~**se** *inf* to get off drugs

desengañar [des·en·ga·'ɲar] **I.** *vt* (*desilusionar*) to disillusion **II.** *vr:* ~**se** to be disappointed; **pronto te** ~**ás** you'll soon see the truth

desengaño [des·en·'ga·ɲo] *m* disillusion

desengrasar [des·en·gra·'sar] *vt* to remove the grease from

desenlace [des·en·'la·se, -θe] *m* outcome

desenmascarar [des·en·mas·ka·'rar/ des·em·mas·ka·'rar] *vt* to unmask; *fig* to expose

desenredar [des·en·rre·'dar] *vt* to unravel; (*pelo*) to untangle

desenroscar <c → qu> [des·en·rros·'kar] *vt* to unscrew; (*desenrollar*) to unwind

desentenderse <e → ie> [des·en·ten·'der·se] *vr* **1.** (*despreocuparse*) ~ **de algo** to want nothing to do with sth; ~ **de un problema** to wash one's hands of a problem **2.** (*fingir ignorancia*) ~ **de algo** to pretend to not know about sth

desenterrar <e → ie> [des·en·te·'rrar] *vt* to dig up; (*cadáver*) to exhume

desentonar [des·en·to·'nar] *vi* **1.** (*cantar*) to sing out of tune; (*tocar*) to play out of tune **2.** (*no combinar*) to not match

desentrañar [des·en·tra·'ɲar] *vt* to unravel

desenvolver [des·em·bol·'βer] *irr como volver* **I.** *vt* **1.** (*desempaquetar*) to unwrap **2.** (*desenrollar*) to unwind; (*desdoblar*) to unfold **II.** *vr:* ~**se** (*manejarse*) to handle oneself

deseo [de·'seo] *m* **1.** (*anhelo*) wish **2.** (*necesidad*) need **3.** (*ansia*) longing **4.** (*sexual*) desire

deseoso, -a [de·se·'o·so, -a] *adj* **estar ~ de hacer algo** to be eager to do sth

desequilibrado, -a [de·se·ki·li·'βra·do, -a] *adj* unbalanced; (*trastornado*) (mentally) disturbed

desequilibrar [de·se·ki·li·'βrar] **I.** *vt* **1.** (*descompensar*) to unbalance **2.** (*trastornar*) to disturb **II.** *vr:* **~se 1.** (*descompensarse*) to unbalance **2.** (*psíquicamente*) to become disturbed

desequilibrio [de·se·ki·li·'βrjo] *m* **1.** (*falta de equilibrio*) lack of balance; (*descompensación, desproporción*) imbalance **2.** (*trastorno*) disturbance; **~ mental** mental instability

desertar [de·ser·'tar] *vi* to desert

desértico, -a [de·'ser·ti·ko, -a] *adj* desert

desertor(a) [de·ser·'tor, -·'to·ra] *m(f)* deserter

desesperación [des·es·pe·ra·'sjon, -'θjon] *f* **1.** (*desmoralización*) desperation, despair; **con ~** desperately **2.** (*enojo*) exasperation

desesperado, -a [des·es·pe·'ra·do, -a] *adj* **1.** (*desmoralizado*) desperate; (*situación*) hopeless **2.** (*enojado*) exasperated

desesperante [des·es·pe·'ran·te] *adj* **1.** (*sin esperanza*) hopeless **2.** (*exasperante*) exasperating

desesperar [des·es·pe·'rar] **I.** *vt* **1.** (*desesperanzar*) to cause to lose hope **2.** (*exasperar*) to exasperate **II.** *vi* to despair **III.** *vr:* **~se 1.** (*desesperanzarse*) to give up hope **2.** (*despecharse*) to despair

desestimar [des·es·ti·'mar] *vt* **1.** (*despreciar*) to have a low opinion of **2.** (*rechazar*) to reject

desfachatez [des·fa·tʃa·'tes, -'teθ] *f* cheek

desfallecer [des·fa·je·'ser, -ʎe·'θer] *irr como crecer vi* **1.** (*debilitarse*) to weaken **2.** (*colapsar*) to collapse; (*desmayarse*) to faint **3.** (*desanimarse*) to lose heart

desfasado, -a [des·fa·'sa·do, -a] *adj* (*per-*

sona) old-fashioned; (*cosa*) antiquated; **estar ~** to be behind the times

desfase [des·'fa·se] *m* (*diferencia*) gap; **~ con la realidad** lack of realism; **¡que ~!** *inf* wild!

desfavorable [des·fa·βo·'ra·βle] *adj* unfavorable

desfavorecer [des·fa·βo·re·'ser, -'θer] *irr como crecer vt* to discriminate against

desfigurar [des·fi·yu·'rar] *vt* **1.** (*afear*) to disfigure **2.** (*deformar*) to deface; (*imagen, realidad*) to distort

desfiguro [des·fi·'yu·ro] *m Méx* (*ridiculez*) silly stunt; **hacer un ~** to make a fool of oneself

desfiladero [des·fi·la·'de·ro] *m* gorge

desfilar [des·fi·'lar] *vi* **1.** (*marchar*) to walk in file **2.** (*salir*) to file out

desfile [des·'fi·le] *m* **1.** (*acción*) marching; (*de tropas*) march-past; **~ de modelos** fashion show **2.** (*personas*) procession

desgana [des·'ya·na] *f* **1.** (*inapetencia*) lack of appetite **2.** (*desinterés*) lack of enthusiasm

desgarbado, -a [des·yar·'βa·do, -a] *adj* gangling

desgarrador(a) [des·ya·rra·'dor, -·'do·ra] *adj* heartrending

desgarrar [des·ya·'rrar] **I.** *vt* to tear **II.** *vr:* **~se** to tear

desgarro [des·'ya·rro] *m* **1.** (*rotura*) tear **2.** *AmL* (*esputo*) spittle

desgastar [des·yas·'tar] **I.** *vt* **1.** (*estropear, cansar*) to wear out **2.** (*consumir*) to use up **II.** *vr:* **~se** to wear out; (*color*) to fade

desgaste [des·'yas·te] *m* **1.** (*fricción*) wear **2.** (*consumo*) consumption

desgracia [des·'yra·sja, -θja] *f* **1.** (*mala suerte*) bad luck; **por ~** unfortunately **2.** (*acontecimiento*) misfortune **3. caer en ~** to fall from grace [*o* into disgrace] **▶ las ~s nunca vienen solas** *prov* when it rains, it pours *prov*

desgraciadamente [des·yra·sja·da·'men·te, des·yra·θja-] *adv* unfortunately

desgraciado, -a [des·yra·'sja·do, -a; des·yra·θja-] **I.** *adj* **1.** (*sin suerte*) unlucky **2.** (*infeliz*) miserable **3.** (*con desgracias*) unfortunate **4.** (*pobre*) poor

II. *m, f* 1. (*sin suerte*) unlucky person 2. (*infeliz*) poor devil 3. (*pobre*) poor person

desgraciar [des·ɣra·'θjar, -'θjar] I. *vt* 1. (*estropear*) to ruin 2. (*disgustar*) to displease II. *vr:* ~**se** to be ruined

desgravable [des·ɣra·'βa·βle] *adj* tax-deductible

desgravación [des·ɣra·'βa·sjon, -θjon] *f* 1. (*de impuestos*) tax allowance 2. (*de gastos*) tax relief

desgravar [des·ɣra·'βar] *vt* 1. (*suprimir*) to exempt from 2. (*reducir*) ~ **el tabaco** (*bajar el impuesto*) to reduce the tax on tobacco; (*el arancel*) to reduce the duties on tobacco

desgreñado, -a [des·ɣre·'ɲa·do, -a] *adj* disheveled

desguace [des·'ɣwa·se, -θe] *m* 1. (*lugar*) junkyard 2. (*acción*) wrecking

desguazar <z → c> [des·ɣwa·'sar, -'θar] *vt* to scrap; (*para reutilizar*) to use sth for scrap

deshabitado, -a [des·a·βi·'ta·do, -a] *adj* empty

deshabitar [des·a·βi·'tar] *vt* to empty; (*edificio*) to abandon; (*casa*) to vacate

deshacer [des·a·'ser, -'θer] *irr como* **hacer** I. *vt* 1. (*nudo*) to undo; (*cama*) to mess up; (*aparato*) to dismantle; (*maleta*) to unpack; (*error*) to rectify 2. (*romper*) to break; (*en pedazos*) to tear apart; (*cortar*) to cut up 3. (*arruinar*) to ruin; (*plan*) to spoil 4. (*disolver*) to dissolve; (*hielo*) to melt II. *vr:* ~**se** 1. (*descomponerse*) to come apart; (*hielo*) to melt; (*desaparecer*) to disappear 2. (*romperse*) to break; (*nudo*) to come undone 3. (*desprenderse*) to come away; ~**se de** (*vender*) to offload; (*librarse de, asesinar*) to get rid of

deshecho, -a [des·'e·tʃo, -a] I. *pp de* **deshacer** II. *adj* 1. (*deprimido*) devastated; **dejar a alguien ~** to leave sb shattered 2. (*cansado*) exhausted

deshelar <e → ie> [des·e·'lar] I. *vt* to melt II. *vr:* ~**se** (*hielo*) to melt; (*nieve*) to thaw

desheredar [des·e·re·'dar] *vt* to disinherit

deshidratar [des·i·dra·'tar] I. *vt* to dry;

(*cuerpo*) to dehydrate II. *vr:* ~**se** to dry out; (*cuerpo*) to dehydrate

deshielo [des·'je·lo] *m* thawing; METEO, POL thaw

deshilachar [des·i·la·'tʃar] *vt, vr:* ~**se** to fray

deshinchar [des·in·'tʃar] I. *vt* 1. (*vaciar*) to deflate 2. (*por una inflamación*) to reduce II. *vr:* ~**se** 1. (*perder aire*) to deflate 2. (*una inflamación*) to go down

deshojar [des·o·'xar] I. *vt* BOT to strip the leaves from; (*flor*) to pull the petals off 2. (*libro*) to tear the pages out of II. *vr:* ~**se** to lose its leaves/petals/pages

deshonesto, -a [des·o·'nes·to, -a] *adj* 1. (*inmoral*) indecent 2. (*tramposo*) dishonest

deshonor [des·o·'nor] *m*, **deshonra** [des·'on·rra] *f* dishonor; (*afrenta*) disgrace

deshonrar [des·on·'rrar] *vt* to disgrace; (*ofender*) to offend; (*humillar*) to humiliate; (*desacreditar*) to bring disgrace on

deshonroso, -a [des·on·'rro·so, -a] *adj* disgraceful; (*deshonesto*) dishonest

deshora [des·'o·ra] *f* inconvenient time; **venir a ~(s)** (*tarde*) to arrive too late; **dormir a ~s** to sleep at odd hours

desidia [de·'si·dja] *f* 1. (*descuido*) carelessness 2. (*pereza*) laziness

desierto [de·'sjer·to] *m* 1. GEO desert 2. (*despoblado*) wasteland

desierto, -a [de·'sjer·to, -a] *adj* 1. (*sin gente*) deserted 2. (*árido*) desert

designación [de·siɣ·na·'sjon, -'θjon] *f* 1. (*nombramiento*) appointment 2. (*nombre*) name

designar [de·siɣ·'nar] *vt* 1. (*dar un nombre*) to designate 2. (*destinar*) to assign; (*elegir*) to choose; (*fecha*) to set; (*nombrar*) to appoint (**para** to); (*candidato*) to select; (*representante*) to nominate

designio [de·'siɣ·njo] *m* 1. (*plan*) plan 2. (*propósito*) intention 3. (*deseo*) wish

desigual [de·si·'ɣwal] *adj* 1. (*distinto*) unequal 2. (*injusto*) unfair 3. (*irregular*) uneven 4. (*inconstante*) inconsistent

desigualdad [de·si·ɣwal·'dad] *f* 1. (*dife-*

rencia) inequality **2.** (*injusticia*) unfairness **3.** (*irregularidad*) unevenness

desilusión [de·si·lu·'sjon] *f* **1.** (*desengaño*) disappointment **2.** (*desencanto*) disillusion

desilusionante [de·si·lu·sjo·'nan·te] *adj* disillusioning

desilusionar [de·si·lu·sjo·'nar] **I.** *vt* **1.** (*desencantar*) to disillusion **2.** (*decepcionar*) to disappoint **II.** *vr:* **~se** **1.** (*perder la ilusión*) to become disilusioned; (*ver claro*) to see things for what they are **2.** (*decepcionarse*) to be disappointed

desinfectante [des·in·fek·'tan·te] *m* disinfectant

desinfectar [des·in·fek·'tar] *vt* to disinfect

desinflado, -a [des·in·'fla·do, -a] *adj* flat

desinflar [des·in·'flar] **I.** *vt* to deflate **II.** *vr:* **~se** to go down

desintegración [des·in·te·ɣra·'sjon, -'θjon] *f* **1.** disintegration; (*erosión*) erosion; QUÍM decomposition **2.** (*territorio, grupo*) breakup

desintegrar [des·in·te·'ɣrar] **I.** *vt* to disintegrate; (*grupo, país*) to break up **II.** *vr:* **~se** to disintegrate; (*edificio, muro*) to fall down; QUÍM to decompose; (*grupo*) to break up

desinterés [des·in·te·'res] *m* **1.** (*indiferencia*) indifference **2.** (*altruismo*) altruism; (*generosidad*) generosity

desinteresado, -a [des·in·te·re·'sa·do, -a] *adj* **1.** (*indiferente*) indifferent **2.** (*altruista*) altruistic; (*generoso*) generous

desintoxicación [des·in·tok·si·ka·'sjon, -'θjon] *f* detoxification

desintoxicar <c → qu> [des·in·tok·si·'kar] **I.** *vt* to detoxify **II.** *vr:* **~se** **1.** to undergo detoxification; (*de alcohol*) to dry out **2.** *fig* to get away from it all

desistir [de·sis·'tir] *vi* **~ de** (*proyecto*) to give up; (*derecho*) to waive; (*cargo*) to resign

desleal [des·le·'al] *adj* (*infiel*) disloyal; (*traidor*) treacherous; (*competencia*) unfair; (*publicidad*) misleading

deslealtad [des·leal·'tad] *f* **1.** (*infidelidad*) disloyalty **2.** (*injusticia*) unfairness

desleír [des·le·'ir] *irr como reír* *vt*, *vr:* **~se** to dissolve

deslenguado, -a [des·len·'gwa·do, -a] *adj* **1.** (*desvergonzado*) foul-mouthed **2.** (*chismoso*) gossipy

desligar <g → gu> [des·li·'ɣar] **I.** *vt* to separate **II.** *vr:* **~se** (*de un compromiso*) to be released; **no poder ~se de algo** to be unable to get out of sth

desliz [des·'lis, -'liθ] *m* slip

deslizante [des·li·'san·te, -'θan·te] *adj* **1.** (*resbaladizo*) slippery **2.** (*corredizo*) sliding

deslizar <z → c> [des·li·'sar, -'θar] **I.** *vt* **~ la mano sobre algo** to run one's hand over sth; **~ un sobre por debajo de una puerta** to slip an envelope under the door **II.** *vi* to slip **III.** *vr:* **~se** **1.** (*resbalar*) **~ sobre algo** to slide over sth **2.** (*escaparse*) to slip away **3.** (*cometer un error*) to slip up

deslomar [des·lo·'mar] **I.** *vt* **~ a alguien** to break sb's back **II.** *vr:* **~se** to break one's back

deslucido, -a [des·lu·'si·do, -a; -'θi·do, -a] *adj* (*ropa*) shabby; (*actuación*) lackluster

deslucir [des·lu·'sir, -'θir] *irr como lucir* **I.** *vt* **1.** (*estropear*) to ruin; (*metal*) to tarnish; (*tejidos, colores*) to fade **2.** (*desacreditar*) to discredit **II.** *vr:* **~se** **1.** (*fracasar*) to fail **2.** (*deslustrarse*) to lose its shine; (*colores*) to fade; (*metal*) to become dull **3.** (*desacreditarse*) to be discredited

deslumbrador(a) [des·lum·bra·'dor, -·'do·ra], **deslumbrante** [des·lum·'bran·te] *adj* (*impresionante*) dazzling; (*despampanante*) stunning

deslumbrar [des·lum·'brar] *vt* to dazzle

deslustrar [des·lus·'trar] *v.* **deslucir**

desmadrado, -a [des·ma·'dra·do, -a] *adj* wild

desmadrarse [des·ma·'drar·se] *vr* to go wild

desmadre [des·'ma·dre] *m* outrageous behavior; (*caos*) chaos

desmalezar <z → c> [des·ma·le·'sar] *vt* *AmL* to weed

desmantelar [des·man·te·'lar] *vt* **1.** (*derribar*) to knock down; (*edificio*) to demolish **2.** (*desmontar*) to take apart; (*bomba*) to dismantle

desmaquillador [des·ma·ki·ja·'dor, des·ma·ki·ˈʎa-] *m* make-up remover

desmayado, -a [des·ma·'ja·do, -a] *adj* **1.** (*inconsciente*) unconscious **2.** (*sin fuerza*) exhausted; (*de hambre*) faint with hunger

desmayar [des·ma·'jar] **I.** *vi* to lose heart **II.** *vr:* **~se** to faint

desmayo [des·'ma·jo] *m* faint; (*desánimo*) dismay

desmedido, -a [des·me·'di·do, -a] *adj* excessive

desmejorar [des·me·xo·'rar] **I.** *vt* (*estropear*) to ruin; (*gastar*) to wear out **II.** *vi* to deteriorate **III.** *vr:* **~se 1.** (*estropearse*) to be ruined; (*gastarse*) to wear out **2.** (*de salud*) to deteriorate

desmembrar <e → ie> [des·mem·'brar] **I.** *vt* **1.** (*desunir*) to break up; (*un cuerpo*) to dismember **2.** (*escindir*) to separate **II.** *vr:* **~se 1.** (*desunirse*) to break up **2.** (*escindirse*) to separate (**de** from)

desmentir [des·men·'tir] *irr como* sentir *vt* (*negar*) to deny; (*contradecir*) to contradict; (*probar que es falso*) to refute

desmenuzar <z → c> [des·me·nu·'sar, -'θar] **I.** *vt* **1.** (*deshacer*) to break into small pieces; (*pez*) to flake; (*con un cuchillo*) to chop up; (*con los dedos*) to crumble; (*raspar*) to grate; (*moler*) to grind **2.** (*analizar*) to scrutinize **II.** *vr:* **~se** to crumble

desmerecer [des·me·re·'ser, -'θer] *irr como* crecer **I.** *vt* to not deserve **II.** *vi* (*decaer*) to decline

desmesurado, -a [des·me·su·'ra·do, -a] *adj* **1.** (*enorme*) enormous **2.** (*excesivo*) excessive; (*ambición*) boundless **3.** (*desvergonzado*) shameless; (*descortés*) rude

desmigajar [des·mi·ɣa·'xar] *vt, vr:* **~se** to crumble

desmilitarizar <z → c> [des·mi·li·ta·ri·'sar, -'θar] *vt* to demilitarize

desmontar [des·mon·'tar] **I.** *vt* **1.** (*mecanismo*) to disassemble **2.** (*una pieza: quitar*) to detach; (*sacar*) to remove **3.** (*estructura*) to take down **II.** *vi, vr:*

~se to dismount

desmoralizador(a) [des·mo·ra·li·sa·'dor, -·'do·ra; des·mo·ra·li·θa-] *adj* **1.** (*que desanima*) demoralizing **2.** (*que corrompe*) corrupting

desmoralizar <z → c> [des·mo·ra·li·'sar, -'θar] **I.** *vt* **1.** (*desanimar*) to demoralize **2.** (*corromper*) to corrupt **II.** *vr:* **~se 1.** (*desanimarse*) to lose heart; (*perder la confianza*) to lose one's confidence **2.** (*corromperse*) to be corrupted

desmoronamiento [des·mo·ro·na·'mjen·to] *m* ruin; (*edificio*) collapse; (*imperio, ideología*) decline; (*persona*) breakdown; (*sentimiento*) weakening

desmoronar [des·mo·ro·'nar] **I.** *vt* to wear away; (*edificio*) to ruin **II.** *vr:* **~se** to fall to pieces; (*edificio, muro*) to fall down; (*imperio, ideología*) to decline; (*persona*) to fall apart

desnatado [des·na·'ta·do] *vt* skimmed, low-fat

desnatar [des·na·'tar] *vt* to skim

desnivel [des·ni·'βel] *m* **1.** (*diferencia de altura*) drop; (*pendiente*) slope **2.** (*desequilibrio*) imbalance **3.** (*altibajo*) unevenness

desnivelar [des·ni·βe·'lar] **I.** *vt* **1.** (*terreno*) to make uneven **2.** (*desequilibrar*) to unbalance **II.** *vr:* **~se** (*torcerse*) to twist

desnucar <c → qu> [des·nu·'kar] **I.** *vt* **~ a alguien** to break sb's neck **II.** *vr:* **~se** to break one's neck

desnudar [des·nu·'dar] **I.** *vt* **1.** (*desvestir*) to undress **2.** (*descubrir*) to strip **II.** *vr:* **~se** to undress

desnudez [des·nu·'des, -'deθ] *f* nudity; *fig* bareness

desnudo, -a [des·'nu·do, -a] *adj* **1.** naked, nude **2.** (*despojado*) bare; **~ de algo** devoid of sth

desnutrición [des·nu·tri·'sjon, -'θjon] *f* malnutrition

desnutrido, -a [des·nu·'tri·do, -a] *adj* undernourished

desobedecer [des·o·βe·de·'ser, -'θer] *irr como* crecer *vi, vt* to disobey

desobediencia [de·so·βe·'djen·sja, -θja] *f* disobedience

desobediente [des·o·βe·'djen·te] *adj*

disobedient

desocupación [de·so·ku·pa·'sjon, -'θjon] f 1. (paro) unemployment 2. (ociosidad) leisure

desocupado, -a [de·so·ku·'pa·do, -a] I. adj 1. (parado) unemployed 2. (vacío) empty; (vivienda) vacant 3. (ocioso) idle II. m, f unemployed person

desocupar [de·so·ku·'par] I. vt 1. (abrir paso) to clear 2. (vaciar) to empty; (vivienda) to vacate II. vr: ~se 1. (de una tarea) to get away 2. (quedarse libre) to be vacant III. vi AmL (parir) to give birth

desodorante [de·so·do·'ran·te] adj, m deodorant

desoír [de·so·'ir] irr como oír vt to not listen to

desolación [de·so·la·'sjon, -'θjon] f 1. (devastación) desolation 2. (desconsuelo) distress

desolado, -a [de·so·'la·do, -a] adj 1. (desierto) desolate 2. (desconsolado) devastated

desolar <o → ue> [de·so·'lar] I. vt to devastate II. vr: ~se to be devastated

desollar <o → ue> [de·so·'jar, -'ʎar] vt to skin

desorbitado, -a [des·or·βi·'ta·do, -a] adj exaggerated; (precio) exorbitant; (ojos) bulging

desorbitar [des·or·βi·'tar] vt, vr: ~se to exaggerate; (asunto) to get out of hand

desorden [des·'or·den] m mess; (confusión) chaos

desordenado, -a [des·or·de·'na·do, -a] adj jumbled; (persona, suceso) messy

desordenar [des·or·de·'nar] vt (turbar) to mess up; (mezclar) to mix up

desorganización [des·or·ya·ni·sa·'sjon, -θa·'θjon] f lack of organization

desorganizar <z → c> [des·or·ya·ni·'sar, -'θar] I. vt to disrupt; (planes) to disturb II. vr: ~se to be disorganized

desorientación [de·so·rjen·ta·'sjon, -'θjon] f 1. (extravío) disorientation 2. (confusión) confusion 3. (falta de orientación) loss of direction

desorientar [de·so·rjen·'tar] I. vt 1. (extraviar) to disorient 2. (confundir) to confuse II. vr: ~se 1. (extraviarse) to become disoriented 2. (confundirse) to become confused

desovar [de·so·'βar] vi to lay eggs; (pez, anfibio) to spawn

despabilado, -a [des·pa·βi·'la·do, -a] adj v. **espabilado**

despabilar [des·pa·βi·'lar] v. **espabilar**

despachante [des·pa·'tʃan·te] mf RíoPl customs officer

despachar [des·pa·'tʃar] I. vt 1. (enviar) to send; (mercancías) to dispatch 2. (concluir) to finish off 3. (atender) to serve; (vender) to sell 4. (matar) to kill 5. (despedir) to fire II. vi 1. (acabar) to finish 2. (atender) to do business

despacho [des·pa·'tʃo] m 1. (oficina) office; (en casa) study 2. (envío) sending; (pedido) dispatch 3. (de un asunto) resolution 4. (de clientes) service 5. (venta) sale 6. (taquilla) ticket office; (tienda) shop

despacio [des·'pa·sjo, -θjo] I. adv 1. (lentamente) slowly 2. (calladamente) quietly II. interj take it easy

despampanante [des·pam·pa·'nan·te] adj stunning

desparejado, -a [des·pa·re·'xa·do, -a] adj odd

desparpajo [des·par·'pa·xo] m 1. (desenvoltura) self-confidence; (en el hablar) ease; **con ~** confidently 2. (habilidad) skill; **con ~** skillfully 3. (frescura) cheek; **con ~** flippantly

desparramar [des·pa·rra·'mar] I. vt 1. (dispersar) to scatter; (líquido) to spill 2. (malgastar) to waste 3. Arg, Méx, PRico (diluir) to dilute II. vr: ~se 1. (dispersarse) to scatter; (líquido) to spill 2. (divertirse) to enjoy oneself

despatarrado, -a [des·pa·ta·'rra·do, -a] adj estar ~ to straddle; (en un sofá) to sprawl (out)

despavorido, -a [des·pa·βo·'ri·do, -a] adj terrified

despecho [des·'pe·tʃo] m despair

despectivo, -a [des·pek·'ti·βo] adj (despreciativo) contemptuous; (desdeñoso) disdainful; (tono) derogatory

despedazar <z → c> [des·pe·da·'sar, -'θar] I. vt to smash; (en mil pedazos) to tear to pieces; (con cuchillo/tijeras) to cut up; (*con las manos*) to tear up **II.** *vr*: ~se to smash; (*en mil pedazos*) to fall to pieces

despedida [des·pe·'ði·ða] *f* **1.** (*separación*) farewell **2.** (*acto oficial*) send-off; (*fiesta*) going-away party; ~ **de soltero/ soltera** stag/hen party

despedir [des·pe·'ðir] *irr como pedir* **I.** *vt* **1.** (*decir adiós*) to say goodbye; **vino a ~me al aeropuerto** he/she came to the airport to see me off **2.** (*echar*) to throw out; (*de un empleo*) to dismiss **3.** (*difundir*) to give off; (*emitir*) to emit **4.** (*lanzar*) to launch **II.** *vr*: ~se **1.** (*decir adiós*) to say goodbye **2.** (*dejar un empleo*) to leave **3.** ~se de (**hacer**) **algo** forget about (doing) sth

despegado, -a [des·pe·'ɣa·ðo, -a] *adj* **1.** (*frío*) distant **2.** (*áspero*) unfriendly **3.** (*suelto*) unstuck

despegar <g → gu> [des·pe·'ɣar] **I.** *vt* to unstick **II.** *vi* to take off **III.** *vr*: ~se **1.** (*desprenderse*) to come off; (*deshacerse*) to come apart **2.** ~se de alguien to lose one's feelings for sb

despegue [des·'pe·ɣe] *m* take-off; (*cohete*) blast-off

despeinado, -a [des·pei·'na·ðo, -a] *adj* unkempt

despeinar [des·pei·'nar] **I.** *vt* to ruffle **II.** *vr* to get one's hair messed up

despejado, -a [des·pe·'xa·ðo, -a] *adj* **1.** (*sin nubes/obstáculos*) clear **2.** (*ancho*) wide **3.** (*listo*) smart **4.** (*despierto*) alert; (*cabeza*) clear

despejar [des·pe·'xar] **I.** *vt* **1.** (*lugar, mesa*) to clear; (*sala*) to tidy up **2.** (*situación*) to clarify; (*misterio*) to clear up **II.** *vr*: ~se **1.** (*cielo, misterio*) to clear up **2.** (*espabilarse*) to wake up; (*mentalmente*) to sharpen one's wits **3.** (*un enfermo*) to improve

despeje [des·'pe·xe] *m* DEP clearance

despellejar [des·pe·je·'xar, des·pe·ʎe-] **I.** *vt* **1.** (*desollar*) to flay **2.** *inf* (*desvalijar*) to fleece **II.** *vr*: ~se to peel

despelotarse [des·pe·lo·'tar·se] *vr inf* to strip off; (*de risa*) to split one's sides

despeluz(n)ar [des·pe·lus·'(n)ar, des·pe·luθ-] **I.** *vt* **1.** (*asustar*) to terrify **2.** *Cuba* (*desplumar*) to pluck **II.** *vr* to

be terrified

despensa [des·'pen·sa] *f* **1.** pantry **2.** *Arg* (*almacén*) shop

despeñadero [des·pe·ɲa·'ðe·ro] *m* **1.** GEO precipice **2.** (*riesgo*) danger

despeñar [des·pe·'ɲar] **I.** *vt* to throw down **II.** *vr*: ~se to throw oneself down

desperdiciar [des·per·di·'sjar, -'θjar] *vt* to waste; (*ocasión*) to miss

desperdicio [des·per·'di·sjo, -θjo] *m* **1.** waste; **no tener ~** to be good from start to finish **2.** *pl* garbage

desperdigar <g → gu> [des·per·di·'ɣar] *vt, vr*: ~se to scatter

desperezarse <z → c> [des·pe·re·'sar·se, -'θar·se] *vr* to stretch

desperfecto [des·per·'fek·to] *m* **1.** (*deterioro*) damage **2.** (*defecto*) fault

despertador [des·per·ta·'ðor] *m* alarm clock

despertar <e → ie> [des·per·'tar] **I.** *vt, vr*: ~se to wake up **II.** *m* awakening

despiadado, -a [des·pja·'ða·ðo, -a] *adj* (*inhumano*) ruthless; (*cruel*) cruel

despido [des·'pi·ðo] *m* dismissal; ~ **colectivo** mass layoff

despierto, -a [des·'pjer·to, -a] *adj* **1.** (*insomne*) awake **2.** (*listo*) smart; (*mente*) sharp

despilfarrador(a) [des·pil·fa·rra·'ðor, -·'ðo·ra] **I.** *adj* wasteful; (*con el dinero*) spendthrift **II.** *m(f)* wasteful person; (*con el dinero*) spendthrift

despilfarrar [des·pil·fa·'rrar] *vt* to waste; (*dinero*) to squander

despilfarro [des·pil·'fa·rro] *m* waste; (*de dinero*) squandering

despintar [des·pin·'tar] **I.** *vt* **1.** (*color*) to run **2.** (*la realidad*) to misrepresent **3.** *Chile, PRico* (*apartar la mirada*) to look away from; (*perder de vista*) to lose sight of **II.** *vr*: ~se (*borrarse*) to fade

despistado, -a [des·pis·'ta·ðo, -a] *adj, m, f* absent-minded

despistar [des·pis·'tar] **I.** *vt* (*confundir*) to confuse; (*desorientar*) to mislead **II.** *vr*: ~se (*perderse*) to get lost; (*desconcertarse*) to become confused

despiste [des·'pis·te] *m* **1.** (*distracción*) absentmindedness **2.** (*error*) slip

desplazado, -a [des·pla·'sa·do, -a; -'θa·do, -a] *adj* (*no integrado*) out of place; (*trasladado*) displaced

desplazamiento [des·pla·sa·'mjen·to, des·pla·θa-] *m* movement; (*persona*) displacement

desplazar <z → c> [des·pla·'sar, -'θar] *vt* 1. (*mover*) to move 2. (*suplantar*) to displace

desplegable [des·ple·'ɣa·βle] *adj* folding

desplegar [des·ple·'ɣar] *irr como fregar vt* 1. (*abrir*) to open out; (*desdoblar*) to unfold 2. MIL to deploy 3. (*desarrollar*) to develop

despliegue [des·'plje·ɣe] *m* unfolding; MIL deployment

desplomarse [des·plo·'mar·se] *vr* to collapse

desplumar [des·plu·'mar] *vt* 1. (*plumas*) to pluck 2. (*robar*) to fleece; **~ a alguien jugando a las cartas** to clean sb out at cards

despoblado [des·po·'βla·do] *m* deserted place

despoblado, -a [des·po·'βla·do, -a] *adj* depopulated

despoblar <o → ue> [des·po·'βlar] *vt* to depopulate; (*bosque*) to clear

despojar [des·po·'xar] I. *vt* to strip; **~ de un derecho a alguien** to deprive sb of a right II. *vr:* **~se** 1. (*desistir*) to give up 2. (*quitar*) to remove; (*ropa*) to take off

despojo [des·'po·xo] *m* 1. spoils *pl* 2. *pl* (*restos*) leftovers *pl*; (*mortales*) mortal remains *pl*

desposeer [des·po·se·'er] *irr como leer* I. *vt* 1. (*expropiar, destituir*) to dispossess; **~ a alguien de su cargo** to remove sb from his/her position 2. (*no reconocer*) to not recognize; **la desposeyeron de sus derechos** they deprived her of her rights 3. (*quitar*) to fleece II. *vr:* **~se** 1. (*renunciar*) to give up 2. (*desapropiarse*) to relinquish

despostar [des·pos·'tar] *vt AmS* to joint

déspota ['des·po·ta] *mf* despot

despotismo [des·po·'tis·mo] *m* despotism

despotricar <c → qu> [des·po·tri·'kar] *vi*

inf ~ de algo/alguien to rant and rave about sth/sb

despreciable [des·pre·'sja·βle, -'θja·βle] *adj* contemptible; **nada ~** to not be sneered at

despreciar [des·pre·'sjar, -'θjar] I. *vt* 1. (*menospreciar*) to despise 2. (*rechazar*) to spurn; (*oferta*) to turn down II. *vr:* **~se** to run oneself down

despreciativo, -a [des·pre·sja·'ti·βo, -a; des·pre·θja-] *adj* disdainful

desprecio [des·'pre·sjo, -θjo] *m* contempt

desprender [des·pren·'der] I. *vt* 1. (*soltar*) to release 2. (*olor, gas*) to give off 3. (*deducir*) to deduce II. *vr:* **~se** 1. (*soltarse*) to untie oneself 2. (*deshacerse*) to come undone; (*librarse*) to rid oneself of; (*renunciar*) to part with 3. **de tu comportamiento se desprende de que...** your behavior shows that...

desprendido, -a [des·pren·'di·do, -a] *adj* (*generoso*) generous; (*altruista*) disinterested

desprendimiento [des·pren·di·'mjen·to] *m* 1. (*separación*) separation; **~ de tierras** landslide; **~ de retina** detached retina 2. (*generosidad*) generosity

despreocupación [des·preo·ku·pa·'sjon, -'θjon] *f* 1. (*indiferencia*) indifference 2. (*insensatez*) carelessness

despreocupado, -a [des·preo·ku·'pa·do, -a] *adj* 1. (*negligente*) careless 2. (*tranquilo*) unconcerned

despreocuparse [des·preo·ku·'par·se] *vr* to stop worrying; **~ de** to neglect

despresar [des·pre·'sar] *vt AmS* to carve

desprestigiar [des·pres·ti·'xjar] I. *vt* to discredit II. *vr:* **~se** to fall into discredit; (*la reputación*) to see one's reputation suffer

desprevenido, -a [des·pre·βe·'ni·do, -a] *adj* unprepared; **coger a alguien ~** to catch sb unawares

desproporción [des·pro·por·'sjon, -'θjon] *f* disproportion

desproporcionado, -a [des·pro·por·sjo·'na·do, -a; des·pro·por·θjo-] *adj* disproportionate

despropósito [des·pro·'po·si·to] *m* stupid remark

desproveer [des·pro·βe·'er] *irr como proveer vt* to deprive

desprovisto, -a [des·pro·'βis·to, -a] *adj* ~ **de** lacking

después [des·'pwes] **I.** *adv* after; **una hora** ~ an hour later; ~ **de la torre** behind the tower; ~ **de todo** after all **II.** *conj* ~ **(de) que** +*subj* after

despuntar [des·pun·'tar] **I.** *vi* 1. (*amanecer*) to dawn 2. (*distinguirse*) to stand out; **despunta en inglés** he/she excels at English **II.** *vr:* ~**se** to become blunt

desquiciado, -a [des·ki·'sja·ðo, -a; -'θja·ðo, -a] *adj* disturbed

desquiciar [des·ki·'sjar, -'θjar] **I.** *vt* 1. (*desencajar*) to unhinge 2. (*alterar*) to disturb **II.** *vr:* ~**se** to become unstable

desquitar [des·ki·'tar] *vt, vr:* ~**se** 1. (*resarcir*) to win back; ~ **de algo** to make up for sth 2. (*vengar*) to get even with

desquite [des·'ki·te] *m* 1. (*satisfacción*) satisfaction 2. (*venganza*) revenge

desrielar [des·rrje·'lar] *vi AmL* to derail

destacable [des·ta·'ka·βle] *adj* outstanding

destacado, -a [des·ta·'ka·ðo, -a] *adj* outstanding

destacamento [des·ta·ka·'men·to] *m* MIL detail

destacar <c → qu> [des·ta·'kar] **I.** *vi* to stand out; ~ **en el deporte** to excel at sports **II.** *vt* (*realzar*) to emphasize **III.** *vr:* ~**se** to stand out

destajo [des·'ta·xo] *m* piecework; **trabajar a** ~ *fig* to work hard; **hablar a** ~ to talk nineteen to the dozen; **a** ~ *Arg, Chile* by guesswork

destapar [des·ta·'par] **I.** *vt* 1. (*abrir*) to open 2. (*desabrigar*) to uncover 3. (*secretos*) to reveal **II.** *vr:* ~**se** 1. (*perder la tapa*) to lose its lid 2. *inf* (*desnudarse*) to strip off 3. (*descubrirse*) to be revealed

destartalado, -a [des·tar·ta·'la·ðo, -a] *adj* ramshackle

destellar [des·te·'jar, -'ʎar] *vi* to sparkle

destello [des·'te·jo, -ʎo] *m* 1. (*rayo*) ray 2. (*reflejo*) glint 3. (*resplandor*) sparkle

destemplado, -a [des·tem·'pla·ðo, -a] *adj* 1. (*sonido*) out of tune 2. (*voz*) harsh 3. (*tiempo*) unpleasant 4. (*persona*) bad-tempered

desteñido, -a [des·te·'ɲi·ðo, -a] *adj* (*descolorido*) faded; (*manchado*) discolored

desteñir [des·te·'ɲir] *irr como ceñir* **I.** *vi* (*descolorarse*) to fade; (*despintar*) to run **II.** *vt* 1. (*descolorar*) to fade 2. (*manchar*) to stain **III.** *vr:* ~**se** (*descolorarse*) to fade; (*despintar*) to run

desternillarse [des·ter·ni·'jar·se, -'ʎar·se] *vr* ~ **de risa** to laugh one's head off

desterrar <e → ie> [des·te·'rrar] *vt* 1. (*exiliar*) to exile 2. (*alejar*) to banish

destetar [des·te·'tar] *vt* to wean

destiempo [des·'tjem·po] *m* **a** ~ at the wrong moment

destierro [des·'tje·rro] *m* 1. (*pena*) exile 2. (*lugar*) (place of) exile

destilación [des·ti·la·'sjon, -'θjon] *f* (*alcohol*) distillation; (*petróleo*) refining

destilar [des·ti·'lar] *vi, vt* to distill

destilería [des·ti·le·'ri·a] *f* distillery; ~ **de petróleo** oil refinery

destinar [des·ti·'nar] *vt* 1. (*dedicar*) to dedicate; (*asignar*) to assign 2. (*enviar*) to send 3. (*designar*) to appoint 4. MIL to post

destinatario, -a [des·ti·na·'ta·rjo, -a] *m, f* addressee; (*de mercancías*) consignee

destino [des·'ti·no] *m* 1. (*hado*) fate 2. (*empleo*) position 3. (*meta*) destination; **con** ~ **a** to 4. (*finalidad*) purpose

destitución [des·ti·tu·'sjon, -'θjon] *f* dismissal; ~ **del cargo** removal from office

destituir [des·ti·tu·'ir] *irr como huir vt* to dismiss

destornillador [des·tor·ni·ja·'ðor, -ʎa·'ðor] *m* screwdriver; ~ **de estrella** Philips screwdriver

destornillar [des·tor·ni·'jar, -'ʎar] *vt* to unscrew

destreza [des·'tre·sa, -θa] *f* skill; ~ **manual** dexterity; **con** ~ skillfully

destripar [des·tri·'par] *vt* 1. (*animal*) to disembowel; (*pez*) to gut 2. (*final*) to spoil

destrozar <z → c> [des·tro·'sar, -'θar] *vt*

1. (*despedazar*) to smash; (*ropa*) to tear up; (*vehículo*) to smash up 2. (*emocionalmente*) to shatter; **estar destrozado** to be an emotional wreck 3. (*físicamente*) to shatter; **estoy destrozado** I'm beat 4. (*planes*) to ruin

destrozo [des·'tro·so, -θo] *m* 1. (*daño*) damage 2. (*acción*) destruction

destrucción [des·truk·'sjon, -truɣ·'θjon] *f* destruction

destructivo, -a [des·truk·'ti·βo, -a] *adj* destructive

destruir [des·tru·'ir] *irr como* huir *I*. *vt* 1. (*destrozar*) to destroy 2. (*física o moralmente*) to shatter 3. (*aniquilar*) to annihilate

desubicado, -a [de·su·βi·'ka·do, -a] *adj* disoriented

desunir [de·su·'nir] *I*. *vt* 1. (*separar*) to separate 2. **~ a dos personas** to cause discord between two people *II*. *vr*: **~se** 1. (*separarse*) to separate 2. (*enemistarse*) to fall out

desuso [de·'su·so] *m* **caer en ~** to fall into disuse; (*máquina*) to become obsolete

desvalido, -a [des·βa·'li·do, -a] *adj* needy

desvalijar [des·βa·li·'xar] *vt* to clean out

desvalorización [des·βa·lo·ri·sa·'sjon, -θa·'θjon] *f* depreciation

desvalorizar <z → c> [des·βa·lo·ri·'sar, -'θar] *vt* to devalue

desván [des·'βan] *m* loft

desvanecer [des·βa·ne·'ser, -'θer] *irr como* crecer *I*. *vt* 1. (*color*) to tone down 2. (*dudas*) to dispel; (*sospechas*) to allay *II*. *vr*: **~se** to disappear; (*color, esperanza*) to fade; **el entusiasmo se desvaneció pronto** the enthusiasm soon abated

desvanecimiento [des·βa·ne·si·'mjen·to, -θi·'mjen·to] *m* 1. (*desaparición*) disappearance 2. (*mareo*) faint

desvariar <1. pres desvarío> [des·βa·ri·'ar] *vi* to talk nonsense; MED to be delirious

desvarío [des·βa·'ri·o] *m* craziness; MED delirium

desvelar [des·βe·'lar] *I*. *vt* 1. (*revelar*) to reveal 2. (*sueño*) to keep awake *II*. *vr*:

~se to stay awake

desvelo [des·'βe·lo] *m* 1. (*insomnio*) insomnia 2. (*despabilamiento*) alertness

desventaja [des·βen·'ta·xa] *f* disadvantage

desventura [des·βen·'tu·ra] *f* misfortune

desventurado, -a [des·βen·tu·'ra·do, -a] *adj* unfortunate

desvergonzado, -a [des·βer·ɣon·'sa·do, -θa·do, -a] *adj* shameless; (*descarado*) brazen

desvergüenza [des·βer·'ɣwen·sa, -θa] *f* shamelessness

desvestir [des·βes·'tir] *irr como* pedir *vt, vr*: **~se** to undress

desviación [des·βja·'sjon, -'θjon] *f* 1. (*torcedura*) deviation; (*columna vertebral*) curvature 2. (*del tráfico*) diversion; (*bocacalle*) turning

desviado, -a [des·βi·'a·do, -a] *adj* deviant

desviar <1. pres desvío> [des·βi·'ar] *I*. *vt* (*camino, dinero*) to divert; (*propósito*) to distract; (*cuestión, problema*) to avoid *II*. *vr*: **~se** 1. (*extraviarse*) to get lost 2. **~se de** (*camino*) to stray off; (*idea, intención*) to stray from; (*tema*) to depart from 3. **se desviaron hacia la izquierda** they turned towards the left

desvincular [des·βin·ku·'lar] *I*. *vt* to dissociate *II*. *vr*: **~se** to dissociate oneself

desvío [des·'βi·o] *m* detour

desvirtuar <1. pres desvirtúo> [des·βir·tu·'ar] *vt* 1. (*tergiversar*) to distort; (*argumento, prueba*) to undermine 2. (*desmentir: rumor*) to scotch

detallado, -a [de·ta·'ja·do, -a; de·ta·'ʎa-] *adj* detailed; (*lista*) itemized

detalle [de·'ta·je, -ʎe] *m* 1. (*pormenor*) detail; **en** [*o* **al**] **~** in detail; **entrar en ~s** to go into details 2. (*finura*) nice gesture; **qué ~ regalarme las flores** it was so kind of you to give me the flowers

detallista [de·ta·'jis·ta, -'ʎis·ta] *I*. *adj* precise; *pey* pedantic *II*. *mf* 1. (*minucioso*) perfectionist 2. (*considerado*) thoughtful person

detectar [de·tek·'tar] *vt* to detect

detective [de·tek·'ti·βe] *mf* detective

detector [de·tek·'tor] *m* detector

detención [de·ten·'sjon, -'θjon] *f* 1. (*parada*) stopping 2. (*arresto*) arrest; ~ **ilegal** false imprisonment; ~ **preventiva** preventive detention 3. (*dilación*) delay

detener [de·te·'ner] *irr como* tener I. *vt* 1. (*parar*) to stop 2. (*arrestar*) to arrest 3. (*retener*) to keep II. *vr:* ~**se** 1. (*pararse*) to stop 2. (*entretenerse*) ~**se en algo** to spend one's time doing sth

detenido, -a [de·te·'ni·do, -a] I. *adj* 1. (*minucioso*) thorough 2. (*arrestado*) arrested II. *m, f* person under arrest

detenimiento [de·te·ni·'mjen·to] *m* (*minuciosidad*) care; **con ~** thoroughly

detergente [de·ter·'xen·te] *adj, m* detergent; ~ **lavavajillas** dishwashing liquid

deteriorar [de·te·rjo·'rar] I. *vt* 1. (*empeorar*) to worsen 2. (*romper*) to break 3. (*gastar*) to wear out II. *vr:* ~**se** 1. (*empeorarse*) to worsen 2. (*estropearse*) to spoil

deterioro [de·te·'rjo·ro] *m* 1. (*desmejora*) deterioration; ~ **de calidad** decline in quality 2. (*daño*) damage 3. (*desgaste*) wear and tear

determinación [de·ter·mi·na·'sjon, -'θjon] *f* 1. (*fijación*) establishment 2. (*decisión*) decision; **tomar una ~** to make a decision; **con ~** determinedly 3. (*audacia*) determination

determinado, -a [de·ter·mi·'na·do, -a] *adj* 1. (*cierto*) t. LING definite 2. (*preciso*) specific 3. *estar* determined (**a** to)

determinante [de·ter·mi·'nan·te] I. *adj* decisive II. *m* decisive factor

determinar [de·ter·mi·'nar] I. *vt* 1. (*fijar*) to establish; (*plazo*) to fix 2. (*decidir*) to decide 3. (*motivar*) to determine II. *vr* decide (**a** to, **por** in favor of)

detestable [de·tes·'ta·βle] *adj* loathsome

detestar [de·tes·'tar] *vt* to detest

detonación [de·to·na·'sjon, -'θjon] *f* 1. (*acción*) detonation 2. (*ruido*) explosion

detonador [de·to·na·'dor] *m* detonator

detonante [de·to·'nan·te] I. *adj* 1. (*explosivo*) explosive 2. *AmL* (*que molesta*) discordant II. *m* cause

detonar [de·to·'nar] *vi, vt* to detonate

detractor(a) [de·trak·'tor, -·'to·ra] I. *adj*

denigrating II. *m(f)* detractor

detrás [de·'tras] I. *adv* 1. (*local*) behind; **me asaltaron por ~** they attacked me from behind 2. (*por orden*) **el que está ~** the next one 3. *prep* ~ **de** 1. (*local*) behind; **ir ~ de alguien** to be looking for sb; **hablar mal (por) ~ de alguien** to criticize sb behind his/her back 2. (*por orden*) after; **uno ~ de otro** one after another

detrimento [de·tri·'men·to] *m* 1. (*daño*) harm 2. (*perjuicio*) detriment; **en ~ de alguien** to sb's detriment; **en ~ de su salud** to the detriment of his/her health

deuda ['deu·da] *f* 1. (*débito*) debt; ~ **activa/pendiente** productive/outstanding debt; ~ **externa/interna/pública** foreign/internal/national debt; ~ **a pagar** debt due; **cargado de** ~ burdened with debt; **contraer** ~**s** to get into debt 2. (*moral*) debt; **estar en ~ con alguien** to be indebted to sb; **lo prometido es ~** a promise is a promise

deudor(a) [deu·'dor, -·'do·ra] I. *adj* indebted II. *m(f)* debtor

devaluación [de·βa·lwa·'sjon, -'θjon] *f* devaluation

devaluar <1. *pres* devalúo> [de·βa·lu·'ar] *vt* to devalue

devaneo [de·βa·'neo] *m* flirtation

devastación [de·βas·ta·'sjon, -'θjon] *f* devastation

devastar [de·βas·'tar] *vt* to devastate

devenir [de·βe·'nir] *irr como* venir *vi* to occur; ~ **en algo** to become sth

devoción [de·βo·'sjon, -'θjon] *f* 1. (*religión*) religious belief; **tener ~ a un santo** to venerate a saint; **con ~** devoutly 2. (*fervor*) fervor 3. (*afición*) attachment

devolución [de·βo·lu·'sjon, -'θjon] *f* return; FIN refund; ~ **de impuestos** tax refund; **'no se admiten devoluciones'** "no refunds"

devolver [de·βol·'βer] *irr como* volver I. *vt* to return; *fig* to restore; ~ **un favor** to return a favor II. *vi* to throw up III. *vr:* ~**se** *AmL* (*volver*) to return; ~**se a casa** to go back home

devorar [de·βo·'rar] *vt* to devour; ~ **la**

comida to wolf down one's food

devoto, -a [de·'βo·to, -a] **I.** adj **1.** (religioso) devout **2.** (adicto) devoted; **~ admirador** loyal fan **II.** m, f **1.** (creyente) devotee **2.** (admirador) enthusiast

día ['di·a] m day; **~ libre/de baja** day off; **al otro ~** by the next day; **un ~ sí y otro no ~ por medio** AmL every other day; **el ~ de mañana** in the future; **un buen ~** [o **el ~ menos pensado**] one fine day; **un ~ de estos** one of these days; **el otro ~** the other day; **en su ~** in his/her day; **hoy (en) ~** nowadays; **hace buen ~** it's nice weather; **de ~** by day; **del ~** today's; **~ a ~** [o **~ tras** [o **por**] ~] day after day; **¡buenos ~s!** good morning!; **¡hasta otro ~!** until another day!; **al ~** up to date

diabetes [dja·'βe·tes] f inv diabetes

diabético, -a [dja·'βe·ti·ko, -a] adj, m, f diabetic

diablo [di·'a·βlo] m devil; **de mil ~s** hellish; **¡vete al ~!** go to hell!; **¿cómo ~s...?** how on earth...?; **¡qué ~s!** hell!; **¡~s!** damn!

diablura [dja·'βlu·ra] f prank

diabólico, -a [dja·'βo·li·ko, -a] adj diabolic(al)

diadema [dja·'de·ma] f diadem; (del pelo) hair band

diafragma [dja·'fraγ·ma] m diaphragm

diagnosis [djaγ·'no·sis] f inv diagnosis

diagnosticar <c → qu> [djaγ·nos·ti·'kar] vt to diagnose

diagnóstico [djaγ·'nos·ti·ko] m diagnosis

diagonal [dja·γo·'nal] adj, f diagonal; **en ~** diagonally

diagrama [dja·'γra·ma] m diagram

dial [di·'al] m dial

dialectal [dja·lek·'tal] adj dialect

dialéctica [dja·'lek·ti·ka] f dialectics pl

dialecto [dja·'lek·to] m dialect

diálisis [di·'a·li·sis] f inv dialysis

dialogar <g → gu> [dja·lo·'γar] vi to talk

diálogo [di·'a·lo·γo] m conversation; LIT dialog(ue)

diamante [dja·'man·te] m diamond

diametralmente [dja·me·tral·'men·te] adv diametrically; **~ opuesto** diametrically opposed

diámetro [di·'a·me·tro] m diameter

diana [di·'a·na] f **1.** (blanco) target; (centro) bull's-eye; **hacer ~** to hit the bull's-eye **2.** MIL reveille

diapasón [dja·pa·'son] m range; (objeto) tuning fork

diapositiva [dja·po·si·'ti·βa] f slide

diariero, -a [dja·'rje·ro, -a] m, f AmS newspaper vendor

diario [di·'a·rjo] m **1.** (periódico) (daily) newspaper **2.** (agenda) diary

diario, -a [di·'a·rjo, -a] adj daily; **a ~** daily; **de ~** everyday

diarismo [dja·'ris·mo] m AmL journalism

diarrea [dja·'rrea] f diarrhea

dibujante [di·βu·'xan·te] mf draftsman, draftswoman m, f; (de caricaturas, animaciones) cartoonist

dibujar [di·βu·'xar] vt, vi to draw

dibujo [di·'βu·xo] m **1.** (acción, resultado) drawing; **~s animados** cartoons **2.** (ilustración) illustration; **con ~s** illustrated **3.** (estampado) pattern

dic. abr de **diciembre** Dec.

diccionario [dik·sjo·'na·rjo, diγ·θjo-] m dictionary; **~ enciclopédico** encyclopedic dictionary; **~ de inglés-español** English-Spanish dictionary

dicha ['di·tʃa] f luck; **nunca es tarde si la ~ es buena** prov better late than never prov

dicharachero, -a [di·tʃa·ra·'tʃe·ro, -a] **I.** adj funny **II.** m, f joker

dicho ['di·tʃo] m observation; (refrán) saying

dicho, -a ['di·tʃo, -a] **I.** pp de **decir** **II.** adj **dicha gente** the said people; **~ y hecho** no sooner said than done

dichoso, -a [di·'tʃo·so, -a] adj happy; irón blessed

diciembre [di·'sjem·bre, -'θjem·bre] m December; v. t. **marzo**

dictado [dik·'ta·do] m dictation; fig dictate

dictador(a) [dik·ta·'dor, -·'do·ra] m(f) dictator

dictadura [dik·ta·'du·ra] f dictatorship

dictamen [dik·'ta·men] m opinion; (informe) report; **~ judicial** legal judgment

dictaminar [dik·ta·mi·'nar] vi to render

judgment

dictar [dik·'tar] *vt* **1.** (*dictado*) to dictate **2.** (*sentencia*) to pass **3.** (*ley*) to enact **4.** (*discurso*) to give **5.** *AmS* (*clases*) to teach

didáctico, -a [di·'dak·ti·ko, -a] *adj* didactic; **material ~** teaching material

diecinueve [dje·si·'nwe·βe, dje·θi-] *adj inv* nineteen; *v. t.* **ocho**

dieciocho [dje·si·'o·tʃo, dje·θi-] *adj inv* eighteen; *v. t.* **ocho**

dieciséis [dje·si·'seis, dje·θi-] *adj inv m* sixteen; *v. t.* **ocho**

dieciseisavo, -a [dje·si·sei·'sa·βo, dje·θi-] *adj, m, f* (*fraction*) sixteenth; *v. t.* **octavo**

diecisiete [dje·si·'sje·te, dje·θi-] *adj inv* seventeen; *v. t.* **ocho**

diecisieteavo, -a [dje·si·sje·te·'a·βo, -a; dje·θi-] *adj, m, f* (*fraction*) seventeenth; *v. t.* **octavo**

diente ['djen·te] *m* tooth; **~ de leche** milk tooth; **~ picado** decayed tooth; **~s postizos** false teeth; (*ajo*) clove; **~ de león** dandelion; **decir algo entre ~s** to mumble sth; **poner los ~s largos a alguien** to make sb green with envy; **pelar el ~** *AmL inf* to smile flirtatiously; **volar ~** *AmL* to stuff one's face

diesel ['die·sel] *m* diesel

diestro, -a ['djes·tro, -a] *adj* <d(i)estrísimo> **1.** (*no zurdo*) right-handed; **a ~ y siniestro** left, right and center **2.** (*hábil*) skillful **3.** (*astuto*) cunning

dieta [di·'e·ta] *f* diet; (*equilibrada*) balanced; **a ~** on a diet

dietético, -a [dje·'te·ti·ko, -a] *adj* dietary; **régimen ~** diet

diez [djes, djeθ] *adj inv m* ten; *v. t.* **ocho**

diezmar [djes·'mar, djeθ-] *vt* to decimate

difamación [di·fa·ma·'sjon, -'θjon] *f* defamation

difamar [di·fa·'mar] *vt* to defame

difamatorio, -a [di·fa·ma·'to·rjo, -a] *adj* defamatory

diferencia [di·fe·'ren·sja, -θja] *f* **1.** *t.* MAT difference; **a ~ de algo** unlike sth **2.** (*desacuerdo*) disagreement; **arreglar (las) ~s** to settle one's differences

diferencial [di·fe·ren·'sjal, 'θjal-] **I.** *adj* variable; MAT differential **II.** *f* differential

diferenciar [di·fe·ren·'sjar, -'θjar] **I.** *vi* to differentiate **II.** *vt* to distinguish; MAT to differentiate **III.** *vr:* **~se** to differ

diferendo [di·fe·'ren·do] *m AmS* dispute

diferente [di·fe·'ren·te] **I.** *adj* different; **~s veces** several times **II.** *adv* differently

diferir [di·fe·'rir] *irr como* **sentir** **I.** *vi* to differ; **~ de algo** to be different from sth **II.** *vt* to postpone; **en diferido** pre-recorded

difícil [di·'fi·sil, -θil] *adj* difficult; **~ de explicar** difficult to explain; **de ~ acceso** hard to get to

difícilmente [di·fi·sil·'men·te, di·fi·θil-] *adv* with difficulty; (*apenas*) hardly

dificultad [di·fi·kul·'tad] *f* difficulty; **en ~es** in difficulty; **con ~** with difficulty; **poner ~es a alguien** to put sb in a difficult position

dificultar [di·fi·kul·'tar] *vt* to hinder; (*tráfico*) to obstruct

dificultoso, -a [di·fi·kul·'to·so, -a] *adj* difficult; (*laborioso*) arduous

difteria [dif·'te·rja] *f* diphtheria

difuminar [di·fu·mi·'nar] *vt* (*dibujo*) to stump; (*luz*) to diffuse

difundir [di·fun·'dir] *vt, vr:* **~se** to spread; (*gas*) to give off; TV, RADIO to broadcast

difunto, -a [di·'fun·to, -a] **I.** *adj* deceased; **mi ~ padre** my late father **II.** *m, f* deceased person; **día de ~s** All Souls' Day **misa de ~s** Requiem (mass)

difusión [di·fu·'sjon] *f* dissemination; TV, RADIO broadcast

difuso, -a [di·'fu·so, -a] *adj* widespread; (*vago*) diffuse

digerir [di·xe·'rir] *irr como* **sentir** *vt* (*comida*) to digest

digestión [di·xes·'tjon] *f* digestion; **corte de ~** stomach cramp

digestivo, -a [di·xes·'ti·βo, -a] *adj* digestive; **aparato ~** digestive system

digital [di·xi·'tal] *adj* finger; **huellas ~es** fingerprints; COMPUT, TÉC digital

digitalizar <z → c> [di·xi·ta·li·'sar, -'θar] *vt* to digitalize

dígito ['di·xi·to] *m* digit

dignarse [diɣ·'nar·se] *vr* ~ (a) **hacer algo** to condescend to do sth

dignidad [diɣ·ni·'dad] *f* dignity

digno, -a ['diɣ·no, -a] *adj* 1. (*merecedor*) deserving; ~ **de confianza** trustworthy; ~ **de ver** worth seeing 2. (*adecuado*) fitting 3. (*noble*) noble

dilación [di·la·'sjon, -'θjon] *f* (*aplazamiento*) postponement; (*retraso*) delay; **sin** ~ without delay

dilapidar [di·la·pi·'dar] *vt* to squander

dilatación [di·la·ta·'sjon, -'θjon] *f* expansion; MED dilation

dilatar [di·la·'tar] **I.** *vt* 1. (*extender*) to expand; MED to dilate 2. (*prolongar*) to prolong **II.** *vr*: ~**se** 1. (*extenderse*) to expand 2. (*alargarse*) to be prolonged 3. *AmL* (*tardar*) to take long

dilema [di·'le·ma] *m* dilemma

diligencia [di·li·'xen·sja, -θja] *f* 1. (*esmero*) diligence 2. (*agilidad*) skill 3. ADMIN paperwork; ~**s policiales** police proceedings 4. JUR procedure; ~ **judicial/policial** legal/police procedures

diligente [di·li·'xen·te] *adj* diligent

dilucidar [di·lu·si·'dar, di·lu·θi-] *vt* to elucidate

diluir [di·lu·'ir] *irr como huir vt* to dissolve; (*líquidos, colores*) to dilute; **sin** ~ undiluted

diluviar [di·lu·'βjar] *vimpers* to pour down

diluvio [di·'lu·βjo] *m* downpour; *fig* shower

dimanar [di·ma·'nar] *vi* to emanate

dimensión [di·men·'sjon] *f* dimension; *fig* magnitude; **de grandes dimensiones** large; **la** ~ **cultural** the cultural aspect

diminutivo [di·mi·nu·'ti·βo] *m* diminutive

diminuto, -a [di·mi·'nu·to, -a] *adj* tiny

dimisión [di·mi·'sjon] *f* resignation; **presentar la** ~ to resign

dimitir [di·mi·'tir] *vi, vt* to resign (**de** from)

Dinamarca [di·na·'mar·ka] *f* Denmark

dinamarqués, -esa [di·na·mar·'kes, -·'ke·sa] **I.** *adj* Danish **II.** *m, f* Dane

dinámica [di·'na·mi·ka] *f* dynamics *pl*

dinámico, -a [di·'na·mi·ko, -a] *adj* dynamic

dinamismo [di·na·'mis·mo] *m* dynamism

dinamita [di·na·'mi·ta] *f* dynamite

dinamitar [di·na·mi·'tar] *vt* to dynamite

dinamizar [di·na·mi·'sar, -'θar] *vt* to vitalize

dinamo [di·'na·mo] *f*, **dínamo** ['di·na·mo] *f* dynamo

dinastía [di·nas·'ti·a] *f* dynasty

dineral [di·ne·'ral] *m* fortune

dinero [di·'ne·ro] *m* money; ~ **electrónico** e-cash; ~ **en metálico** [*o* **contante y sonante**] hard cash; ~ **negro** undeclared money; ~ **suelto** loose change; **estar mal de** ~ to be short of money; **de** ~ rich

dinosaurio [di·no·'sau·rjo] *m* dinosaur

dintel [din·'tel] *m* lintel

dio [djo] 3. *pret de* **dar**

diócesis [di·'o·se·sis, -θe·sis] *f inv* diocese

dioptría [djop·'tri·a] *f* diopter

dios(a) [djos, 'djo·sa] *m(f)* god, goddess *m, f*

Dios [djos] *m* God; **¡~ mío!** my God!; **¡ay ~!** oh dear!; **como ~ lo trajo al mundo** stark naked; **¡(vaya) por ~!** for God's sake!; **todo** ~ everyone; ~ **dirá** time will tell; **hacer algo como ~ manda** to do sth properly; **vivir como ~** to live like a lord

dióxido [di·'ok·si·do] *m* dioxide

diploma [di·'plo·ma] *m* diploma; ~ **de bachiller(ato)** ≈ *high school diploma;* ~ **universitario** university diploma

diplomacia [di·plo·'ma·sja, -θja] *f* diplomacy; (*cuerpo*) diplomatic corps

diplomado, -a [di·plo·'ma·do, -a] *adj* qualified

diplomático, -a [di·plo·'ma·ti·ko, -a] **I.** *adj* diplomatic **II.** *m, f* diplomat

diptongo [dip·'ton·go] *m* diphthong

diputación [di·pu·ta·'sjon, -'θjon] *f* deputation; *Méx* (*edificio*) town hall

diputado, -a [di·pu·'ta·do, -a] *m, f* member of parliament

dique ['di·ke] *m* dike

dirección [di·rek·'sjon, -reɣ·'θjon] *f* 1. (*rumbo*) direction; ~ **única** one-way; ~ **prohibida** no entry; **en** ~ **contra-**

ria/opuesta in the opposite direction; **salir con ~ a España** to leave for Spain **2.** ADMIN direction; **~ central** central control; **~ general** head office; **~ comercial** business management **3.** (*guía*) direction; TEAT artistic direction; **bajo la ~ de** directed by **4.** (*señas*) address; **~ comercial** business address; **~ de correo electrónico** e-mail address **5.** AUTO steering; **~ asistida** power steering

directiva [di·rek·'ti·βa] *f* **1.** (*dirección*) board (of directors) **2.** (*instrucción*) directive

directivo, -a [di·rek·'ti·βo, -a] **I.** *adj* managing; **junta directiva** managing committee **II.** *m, f* (*ejecutivo*) director; (*gerente*) manager

directo, -a [di·'rek·to, -a] *adj* **1.** (*recto*) straight **2.** (*inmediato, franco*) direct; **en ~** live; **un tren;** a through train; **el camino más ~** the shortest way

director(a) [di·rek·'tor, -·'to·ra] *m(f)* rector; (*jefe*) manager; ENS principal; CINE, TEAT director; **~ administrativo/general/técnico** administrative/managing/technical director; **~ de departamento** department manager; **~ de orquesta** conductor; **~ de tesis** doctoral advisor

directorio [di·rek·'to·rjo] *m* **1.** COMPUT directory **2.** (*agenda*) address book; *AmL* telephone book

directriz [di·rek·'triθ] *f* guideline, instruction

dirigente [di·ri·'xen·te] *mf* leader; **los ~s** the leadership

dirigir <g → j> [di·ri·'xir] **I.** *vt* **1.** (*coche, buque*) to steer **2.** (*tráfico*) to direct **3.** (*envío, palabras*) to address **4.** (*vista*) to turn **5.** (*empresa*) to manage; (*finca*) to run; (*orquesta, debate*) to conduct **6.** (*por un camino*) to lead **7.** CINE, TEAT, TV to direct **II.** *vr* **~se a** to head for; **~se a alguien** to address sb

discapacitado, -a [dis·ka·pa·si·'ta·do, -a; dis·ka·pa·θi·] *adj* handicapped

discernir [di·ser·'nir, dis·θer·] *irr como* **cernir** *vt, vi* to distinguish

disciplina [di·si·'pli·na, dis·θi·] *f* discipline

disciplinado, -a [di·si·pli·'na·do, -a; dis·

θi-] *adj* disciplined

disciplinar [di·si·pli·'nar, dis·θi·] *vt* to discipline

disciplinario, -a [di·si·pli·'na·rjo, -a; dis·θi·] *adj* disciplinary; **sanción disciplinaria** disciplinary measure

discípulo, -a [di·'si·pu·lo, -a; dis·'θi·] *m, f* disciple

disc-jockey <dis yoqueis> [dis 'jo·kei] *mf* disc jockey

disco ['dis·ko] *m* **1.** (*aro*) disk **2.** MÚS record **3.** COMPUT disk; **~ de arranque** boot disk; **~ duro** hard disk

discográfico, -a [dis·ko·'γra·fi·ko, -a] *adj* record

disconforme [dis·kon·'for·me] *adj* in disagreement; (*cosas*) incompatible

disconformidad [dis·kon·for·mi·'dad] *f* disagreement; (*de cosas*) incompatibility

discontinuidad [dis·kon·ti·nwi·'dad] *f* **1.** (*inconstancia*) discontinuity **2.** (*interrupción*) interruption

discontinuo, -a [dis·kon·'ti·nwo, -a] *adj* **1.** (*inconstante*) discontinuous **2.** (*interrumpido*) interrupted

discordancia [dis·kor·'dan·sja, -θja] *f* disagreement; MÚS discordance

discordante [dis·kor·'dan·te] *adj* conflicting; MÚS discordant

discordia [dis·'kor·dja] *f* discord

discoteca [dis·ko·'te·ka] *f* **1.** (*local*) disco **2.** (*discos*) record collection

discreción [dis·kre·'sjon, -'θjon] *f* discretion

discrepancia [dis·kre·'pan·sja, -θja] *f* **1.** (*entre cosas*) discrepancy **2.** (*entre personas*) disagreement

discrepante [dis·kre·'pan·te] *adj* divergent

discrepar [dis·kre·'par] *vi* **1.** (*diferenciarse*) to differ **2.** (*disentir*) to dissent

discreto, -a [dis·'kre·to, -a] *adj* discreet

discriminación [dis·kri·mi·na·'sjon, -'θjon] *f* discrimination

discriminar [dis·kri·mi·'nar] *vt* **1.** (*diferenciar*) to differentiate (between) **2.** (*perjudicar*) to discriminate against

discriminatorio, -a [dis·kri·mi·na·'to·rjo, -a] *adj* discriminatory

disculpa [dis·'kul·pa] *f* apology; **admi-**

tir una ~ to accept an apology; **pedir ~s** to apologize; **eso no tiene ~** there is no excuse

disculpar [dis·kul·'par] I. vt 1. (*perdonar*) to forgive 2. (*justificar*) to justify II. vr: **~se** to apologize

discurrir [dis·ku·'rrir] vi 1. (*pensar*) ~ **sobre algo** to ponder sth 2. (*andar*) to roam; (*río*) to flow 3. (*transcurrir*) to pass

discurso [dis·'kur·so] m t. LING speech; ~ **de clausura/recepción** closing/opening speech; **pronunciar un ~** to make a speech

discusión [dis·ku·'sjon] f 1. (*debate*) discussion 2. (*riña*) argument

discutible [dis·ku·'ti·βle] adj 1. (*disputable*) debatable 2. (*dudoso*) doubtful

discutido, -a [dis·ku·'ti·do, -a] adj controversial

discutir [dis·ku·'tir] vi, vt to argue; (*hablar*) to discuss; **siempre me discutes lo que digo** you always contradict what I say

disecar <c → qu> [di·se·'kar] vt to stuff; ANAT to dissect

disección [di·sek·'sjon, -sey·'θjon] f dissection

diseminar [di·se·mi·'nar] vt, vr: ~se to spread; (*semillas*) to disperse

disentería [di·sen·te·ri·a] f dysentery

disentir [di·sen·'tir] irr como sentir vi to dissent

diseñador(a) [di·se·ɲa·'dor, -·'do·ra] m(f) 1. (*dibujante*) artist 2. (*decorador*) designer

diseñar [di·se·'ɲar] vt 1. (*crear*) to design 2. (*dibujar*) to draw; (*delinear*) to draft 3. (*proyectar*) to plan

diseño [di·'se·ɲo] m 1. (*dibujo*) drawing; (*boceto*) sketch; (*esbozo*) outline; ~ **de página** page design 2. (*forma*) design 3. (*en tejidos*) pattern

disertación [di·ser·ta·'sjon, -'θjon] f (*escrita*) dissertation; (*oral*) presentation

disfraz [dis·'fras, -'fraθ] m disguise; (*en fiestas*) fancy dress; fig pretense

disfrazar <z → c> [dis·fra·'sar, -'θar] I. vt, vr to disguise II. vr: ~**se de** to disguise oneself as

disfrutar [dis·fru·'tar] vi, vt ~ (**de**) **algo**

1. (*gozar, sacar provecho*) to enjoy 2. (*poseer*) to have 3. (*utilizar*) to use

disfrute [dis·'fru·te] m 1. (*goce*) enjoyment 2. (*aprovechamiento*) benefit

disgregar <g → gu> [dis·yre·'yar] vt, vr: ~**se** to disintegrate; (*gente*) to disperse

disgustar [dis·yus·'tar] I. vt 1. (*desagradar*) to displease; **me disgusta** I don't like it 2. (*enfadar*) to anger; (*ofender*) to offend II. vr: ~**se** 1. (*enfadarse*) to get angry (**por** about); (*ofenderse*) to be offended (**por** about) 2. (*reñir*) to quarrel (**con** with)

disgusto [dis·'yus·to] m (*desagrado*) displeasure; **estar a ~** to be ill at ease; (*aflicción*) suffering; (*molestia*) annoyance; (*enfado*) anger; **dar un ~ a alguien** (*afligir*) to cause sb suffering; (*fastidiar*) to annoy sb

disidencia [di·si·'den·sja, -θja] f dissent

disidente [di·si·'den·te] adj, mf dissident

disimulación [di·si·mu·la·'sjon, -'θjon] f 1. (*fingimiento*) pretense 2. (*ocultación*) concealment

disimular [di·si·mu·'lar] I. vi to pretend II. vt to conceal; ~ **el miedo** to hide one's fear; **no ~ algo** to not hide sth

disimulo [di·si·'mu·lo] m (*fingimiento*) pretense; (*engaño*) deceit; **con ~** furtively

disipar [di·si·'par] I. vt (*nubes, niebla*) to disperse; (*dudas*) to dispel II. vr: ~**se** to disperse; (*dudas*) to vanish; (*fracasar*) to go up in smoke

dislexia [dis·'lek·sja] f dyslexia

disléxico, -a [dis·'lek·si·ko, -a] adj, m, f dyslexic

dislocación [dis·lo·ka·'sjon, -'θjon] f dislocation

dislocar <c → qu> [dis·lo·'kar] vt, vr: ~**se** to dislocate

disminución [dis·mi·nu·'sjon, -'θjon] f decrease; ~ **de los gastos/precios/producción/ventas** fall in spending/prices/production/sales; ~ **de la natalidad** decline in the birth rate; ~ **de la pena** remission of sentence; **ir en ~** to diminish

disminuir [dis·mi·nu·'ir] irr como huir I. vi (*intensidad*) to diminish; (*número*) to decrease **II.** *vt* to diminish; (*precio, sueldo*) to lower; (*velocidad*) to reduce

disociación [di·so·sja·'sjon, -θja·'θjon] *f* separation

disociar [di·so·'sjar, -'θjar] *vt, vr:* **~se** to separate

disoluble [di·so·'lu·βle] *adj* soluble; (*contrato*) rescindable

disolución [di·so·lu·'sjon, -'θjon] *f* dissolution; (*familia*) break-up; (*costumbres*) dissoluteness; (*contrato*) rescission; QUÍM solution

disolvente [di·sol·'βen·te] *m* solvent; (*para pintura*) thinner

disolver [di·sol·'βer] *irr como volver vt, vr:* **~se** to dissolve; (*reunión*) to break up

disonancia [di·so·'nan·sja, -θja] *f* discord; MÚS dissonance

dispar [dis·'par] *adj* dissimilar

disparado, -a [dis·pa·'ra·do, -a] *adj* **salir ~** to rush off

disparador [dis·pa·ra·'dor] *m* trigger; FOTO shutter release

disparar [dis·pa·'rar] **I.** *vt, vi* to fire (**contra** at) **II.** *vr:* **~se** (*desbocarse*) to blow one's top; (*arma*) to go off; (*precios*) to shoot up

disparatado, -a [dis·pa·ra·'ta·do, -a] *adj* **1.** (*absurdo*) nonsensical **2.** (*desmesurado*) outrageous

disparate [dis·pa·'ra·te] *m* **1.** (*acción/comentario/idea*) foolish act/remark/idea **2.** *inf* **me gusta un ~** I really love him/her/it; **costar un ~** to cost a fortune

disparidad [dis·pa·ri·'dad] *f* disparity

disparo [dis·'pa·ro] *m* **1.** (*acción*) firing **2.** (*tiro*) shot

dispensador [dis·pen·sa·'dor] *m*, **dispensadora** [dis·pen·sa·'do·ra] *f* dispenser

dispensar [dis·pen·'sar] *vt* **1.** (*otorgar*) to give out **2.** (*librar*) to release; (*cargo, molestias*) to relieve **3.** (*excusar*) to forgive

dispensario [dis·pen·'sa·rjo] *m* dispensary; (*sanitario*) clinic

dispersar [dis·per·'sar] **I.** *vt* to spread; (*personas, animales*) to disperse; (*manifestación*) to break up; FÍS to scatter

II. *vr:* **~se** (*semillas*) to be dispersed; (*personas, animales*) to disperse

dispersión [dis·per·'sjon] *f* dispersion; FÍS diffusion

disperso, -a [dis·'per·so, -a] *adj* scattered

disponer [dis·po·'ner] *irr como poner* **I.** *vi* to have (the use) **II.** *vt* **1.** (*colocar*) to place **2.** (*preparar*) to prepare **3.** (*determinar*) to stipulate **III.** *vr:* **~se 1.** (*colocarse*) to position oneself **2.** (*prepararse*) to get ready

disponibilidad [dis·po·ni·βi·li·'dad] *f* availability; *pl* cash

disponible [dis·po·'ni·βle] *adj* available

disposición [dis·po·si·'sjon, -'θjon] *f* **1.** (*colocación*) arrangement **2.** (*ánimo, salud*) disposition **3.** (*preparativo*) preparation; **estar en ~ de hacer algo** to be ready to do sth **4.** (*disponibilidad*) availability; **de libre ~** freely available; **estoy a su ~** I am at your disposal; **poner a ~** to make available **5.** (*talento*) aptitude (**para** for) **6.** (*resolución*) agreement; **~ legal** legal provision

dispositivo [dis·po·si·'ti·βo] *m* device; **~ intrauterino** intrauterine device

dispuesto, -a [dis·'pwes·to, -a] **I.** *pp de disponer* **II.** *adj* **1.** (*preparado*) ready; **estar ~ a trabajar/negociar** to be prepared to work/negotiate **2.** (*habilidoso*) capable

disputa [dis·'pu·ta] *f* argument; (*pelea*) fight; JUR dispute

disputar [dis·pu·'tar] **I.** *vi* to argue **II.** *vt, vr:* **~se** to compete for; **~ una carrera** to contest a race

disquete [dis·'ke·te] *m* floppy disk

disquetera [dis·ke·'te·ra] *f* disk drive

distancia [dis·'tan·sja, -θja] *f t. fig* distance; **¿a qué ~?** how far?; **acortar ~s** to close the gap; **guardar las ~s** to keep one's distance

distanciado, -a [dis·tan·'sja·do, -a; -'θja·do, -a] *adj t. fig* distant

distanciamiento [dis·tan·sja·'mjen·to, dis·tan·θja-] *m fig* distance

distanciar [dis·tan·'sjar, -'θjar] **I.** *vt* to distance **II.** *vr:* **~se** to move away; *fig* to drift apart

distante [dis·'tan·te] *adj t. fig* distant

distar [dis·'tar] *vi* to be distant

distender <e → ie> [dis·ten·'der] *vt fig* to relax

distensión [dis·ten·'sjon] *f* easing of tension; POL détente

distinción [dis·tin·'sjon, -'θjon] *f* 1. (*diferenciación*) distinction; **a ~ de algo** in contrast to sth; **no hacer ~** to make no distinction; **sin ~ de** irrespective of 2. (*claridad*) clarity 3. (*honor*) distinction

distinguido, -a [dis·tin·'gi·do, -a] *adj* 1. (*ilustre*) distinguished 2. (*elegante*) refined 3. (*en cartas*) Dear

distinguir <gu → g> [dis·tin·'gir] I. *vt* 1. (*diferenciar*) to distinguish; **no ~ lo blanco de lo negro** to not be able to tell left from right 2. (*divisar*) to make out II. *vr*: **~se** (*ser visible/diferente*) to be noticeable/different

distintivo [dis·tin·'ti·βo] *m* emblem

distintivo, -a [dis·tin·'ti·βo, -a] *adj* distinguishing

distinto, -a [dis·'tin·to, -a] *adj* different (**a** from)

distorsión [dis·tor·'sjon] *f* distortion

distorsionar [dis·tor·sjo·'nar] *vt* to distort

distracción [dis·trak·'sjon, -traɣ·'θjon] *f* distraction; (*hobby*) pastime

distraer [dis·tra·'er] I. *vt* 1. (*entretener*) to entertain 2. (*despistar*) to distract II. *vr*: **~se** 1. (*entretenerse*) to amuse oneself 2. (*no atender*) to be distracted

distraído, -a [dis·tra·'i·do, -a] I. *adj* 1. (*desatento*) distracted 2. (*entretenido*) entertaining 3. *Chile, Méx* (*mal vestido*) badly dressed II. *m, f* **hacerse el ~** to pretend to not notice

distribución [dis·tri·βu·'sjon, -'θjon] *f* t. COM, CINE, TEC distribution; FIN sharing out; **~ de beneficios** profit breakdown

distribuidor [dis·tri·βwi·'dor] *m* distributor; (*automático*) COM dealer; **~ oficial** official dealer; **~ exclusivo** exclusive distributor; **~ industrial** industrial retailer

distribuidora [dis·tri·βwi·'do·ra] *f* distribution company

distribuir [dis·tri·βu·'ir] *irr como huir*

I. *vt t.* COM to distribute; (*disponer*) to arrange; (*tarea*) to allocate; (*correo*) to deliver II. *vr*: **~se** to divide up

distributivo, -a [dis·tri·βu·'ti·βo, -a] *adj* distributive

distrito [dis·'tri·to] *m* district; **~ electoral** constituency; **~ industrial** industrial area; **~ judicial** jurisdiction

disturbio [dis·'tur·βjo] *m* disturbance

disuadir [di·swa·'dir] *vt* to dissuade (**de** from)

disuasión [di·swa·'sjon] *f* dissuasion; POL, MIL deterrence

disuasivo, -a [di·swa·'si·βo, -a] *adj* dissuasive; POL, MIL deterrent; **poder ~** deterrent

dita ['di·ta] *f* AmC, Chile debt

DIU ['diu] *m abr de* **dispositivo intrauterino** IUD

diurético, -a [dju·'re·ti·ko, -a] *adj* diuretic

diurno, -a [di·'ur·no, -a] *adj* daily; **trabajo ~** day work

divagación [di·βa·ɣa·'sjon, -'θjon] *f* digression; *pl* ramblings

divagar <g → gu> [di·βa·'ɣar] *vi* to digress; (*al hablar*) to ramble

diván [di·'βan] *m* divan

divergencia [di·βer·'xen·sja, -θja] *f* divergence

divergente [di·βer·'xen·te] *adj* divergent; (*opiniones*) differing

divergir <g → j> [di·βer·'xir] *vi t.* MAT to diverge; (*opiniones*) to differ; (*personas*) to disagree

diversidad [di·βer·si·'dad] *f* diversity

diversificación [di·βer·si·fi·ka·'sjon, -'θjon] *f* diversity; ECON diversification

diversificar <c → qu> [di·βer·si·fi·'kar] *vt, vr*: **~se** to diversify

diversión [di·βer·'sjon] *f* entertainment; (*pasatiempo*) pastime

diverso, -a [di·'βer·so, -a] *adj* distinct; **~s** many

divertido, -a [di·βer·'ti·do, -a] *adj* 1. (*alegre*) amusing 2. (*que hace reír*) funny 3. *AmL* (*achispado*) tipsy

divertir [di·βer·'tir] *irr como sentir* I. *vt* to amuse II. *vr*: **~se** to amuse oneself; **¡que te diviertas!** enjoy yourself!

dividendo [di·βi·'den·do] *m* dividend

dividir [di·βi·'dir] I. vt 1. (*partir*) to divide 2. (*distribuir*) to distribute 3. (*separar*) to separate; (*sembrar discordia*) to disunite 4. (*agrupar*) to divide up 5. MAT ~ **algo entre** [*o por*] **dos** to divide sth by two II. vr: ~**se** 1. (*partirse*) to divide 2. (*agruparse*) to divide up into 3. (*enemistarse*) to fall out

divinidad [di·βi·ni·'dad] f divinity; (*deidad*) deity

divino, -a [di·'βi·no, -a] adj divine

divisa [di·'βi·sa] f currency

divisar [di·βi·'sar] vt to make out

divisible [di·βi·'si·βle] adj divisible

división [di·βi·'sjon] f 1. (*partición*) t. MAT, MIL division 2. (*separación*) separation 3. (*parte*) portion

divisorio, -a [di·βi·'so·rjo, -a] adj dividing

divo, -a ['di·βo, -a] m, f leading opera singer m,f, diva f

divorciado, -a [di·βor·'sja·do, -a; -'θja·do, -a] I. adj divorced II. m, f divorcee

divorciarse [di·βor·'sjar·se, -'θjar·se] vr to get divorced

divorcio [di·'βor·sjo, -θjo] m divorce

divulgación [di·βul·ɣa·'sjon, -'θjon] f disclosure; (*publicación*) publication; **libro de** ~ popularizing book

divulgar <g → gu> [di·βul·'ɣar] I. vt to spread; (*dar a conocer*) to make known II. vr: ~**se** to spread; (*conocerse*) to become known

DNI [de·ne·'i/de·e·ne·'i] m abr de **Documento Nacional de Identidad** ID

Dña. ['do·ɲa] abr de **doña** ≈ Ms.

dobladillo [do·βla·'di·jo, -ʎo] m hem

doblaje [do·'βla·xe] m CINE dubbing

doblar [do·'βlar] I. vt 1. (*arquear*) to bend 2. (*plegar*) to fold 3. (*duplicar*) to double 4. CINE to dub 5. (*rodear*) to go around II. vi 1. (*redoblar*) to double 2. (*torcer*) to turn (a towards)

doble ['do·βle] adj, mf t. CINE double; ~ **nacionalidad** dual citizenship; ~ **personalidad** split personality

doblegar <g → gu> [do·βle·'ɣar] I. vt to subdue II. vr: ~**se** to give in

doblez [do·'βles, -'βleθ] m fold

doce ['do·se, -θe] adj inv m twelve; v. t. **ocho**

doceavo, -a [do·se·'a·βo, -a; do·θe·-] adj (*fracción*) twelfth; v. t. **octavo**

docena [do·'se·na, -'θe·na] f dozen

docencia [do·'sen·sja, -'θen·θja] f teaching; **dedicarse a la** ~ to be a teacher

docente [do·'sen·te, -'θen·te] I. adj teaching II. mf teacher; UNIV professor

dócil ['do·sil, -θil] adj docile; (*sumiso*) obedient

docilidad [do·si·li·'dad, do·θi·-] f docility; (*sumisión*) obedience

docto, -a ['dok·to, -a] adj learned; ~ **en leyes** well-versed in the law

doctor(a) [dok·'tor, --'to·ra] m(f) doctor

doctorado [dok·to·'ra·do] m doctorate; **curso de** ~ doctoral course

doctoral [dok·to·'ral] adj **tesis** ~ doctoral thesis

doctorarse [dok·to·'rar·se] vr to do a doctorate (**en** in)

doctrina [dok·'tri·na] f doctrine

documentación [do·ku·men·ta·'sjon, -'θjon] f 1. (*estudio*) information 2. (*documentos*) documentation; (*del coche*) vehicle documents pl

documentado, -a [do·ku·men·'ta·do, -a] adj 1. (*identificado*) documented; (*personas*) with papers 2. (*informado*) informed

documental [do·ku·men·'tal] adj, m documentary

documentar [do·ku·men·'tar] I. vt 1. (*probar*) to document 2. (*instruir*) to inform II. vr: ~**se** to inform oneself

documento [do·ku·'men·to] m document; **Documento Nacional de Identidad** identity card

dogma ['doɣ·ma] m dogma

dogmático, -a [doɣ·'ma·ti·ko, -a] adj dogmatic

dogo ['do·ɣo] m bulldog

dólar ['do·lar] m dollar

dolencia [do·'len·sja, -θja] f ailment

doler <o → ue> [do·'ler] I. vi to hurt; **me duele la cabeza** I have a headache II. vr: ~**se de** 1. (*quejarse*) to complain about 2. (*arrepentirse*) to regret

dolido, -a [do·'li·do, -a] adj hurt

dolor [do·'lor] m pain; ~ **de cabeza** headache

dolorido, -a [do·lo·'ri·do, -a] *adj* painful; (*apenado*) sad

doloroso, -a [do·lo·'ro·so, -a] *adj* painful

dom. *abr de* **domingo** Sun.

domar [do·'mar] *vt* to tame

domesticar <c → qu> [do·mes·ti·'kar] *vt* to domesticate; (*personas*) to bring under control

doméstico, -a [do·'mes·ti·ko, -a] *adj* domestic; **vuelo ~** national flight; **animal ~** pet; **gastos ~s** household expenses

domiciliar [do·mi·si·'ljar, -θi·'ljar] I. *vt* 1. (*recibo*) to pay by direct debit; (*alquiler*) to pay by standing order; (*nómina*) to pay direct into sb's account 2. (*dar domicilio*) to house II. *vr:* **~se** to reside

domiciliario, -a [do·mi·si·'lja·rjo, -a; do·mi·θi·-] *adj* home; **arresto ~** house arrest

domicilio [do·mi·'si·ljo, -'θi·ljo] *m* residence; (*de empresa*) address; **reparto a ~** home delivery

dominación [do·mi·na·'sjon, -'θjon] *f* domination

dominante [do·mi·'nan·te] *adj* dominant

dominar [do·mi·'nar] I. *vi* 1. (*imperar*) to rule 2. (*sobresalir*) to stand out 3. (*predominar*) to predominate II. *vt* 1. (*conocer*) to have a good knowledge of; (*idioma*) to have a good command of 2. (*reprimir*) to control 3. (*sobresalir*) to dominate

domingo [do·'min·go] *m* Sunday; *v. t.* **lunes**

dominguero, -a [do·min·'ge·ro, -a] *m, f pey* Sunday tripper

dominical [do·mi·ni·'kal] I. *adj* Sunday II. *m* Sunday supplement

dominicano, -a [do·mi·ni·'ka·no, -a] *adj, m, f* Dominican

dominio [do·'mi·njo] *m* 1. (*dominación*) control 2. (*poder*) authority 3. (*territorio*) domain 4. (*campo*) subject 5. (*posesión*) ownership; **ser de ~ público** to be common knowledge

dominó <dominós> [do·mi·'no] *m* (*juego*) dominoes *pl*

don [don] *m* gift; **tener ~ de gentes** to

have a way with people

don, doña [don, 'do·ɲa] *m, f* ≈ Mr., ≈ Mrs. *m, f + first name*

donación [do·na·'sjon, -'θjon] *f* donation

donaire [do·'nai·re] *m* grace

donante [do·'nan·te] *mf* donor

donar [do·'nar] *vt* to donate

donativo [do·na·'ti·βo] *m* donation

doncella [don·'se·ja, -'θe·ʎa] *f* maid

donde ['don·de] *adv* where; **a** [*o* **hacia**] **~...** where... to; **de ~...** where... from; **en ~** where; **estuve ~ Luisa** I was at Luisa's

dónde ['don·de] *pron interrog, rel* where; **¿a** [*o* **hacia**] **~?** where to?; **¿de ~?** where from?; **¿en ~?** where?

dondequiera [don·de·'kje·ra] *adv* 1. (*en cualquier parte*) anywhere 2. (*donde*) wherever

donut ['do·nu(t)] *m* <donuts> doughnut

doña ['do·ɲa] *f v.* **don**

doparse [do·'par·se] *vr* to take drugs

doping ['do·pin] *m* drug-taking

dorada [do·'ra·da] *f* gilthead

dorado, -a [do·'ra·do] *adj* golden

dorar [do·'rar] I. *vt* to brown II. *vr:* **~se** to go brown

dormilón, -ona [dor·mi·'lon, --'lo·na] *m, f* sleepyhead

dormir [dor·'mir] *irr* I. *vi* to sleep; **quedarse dormido** to fall asleep; **~ la siesta** to take a nap; (*pernoctar*) to spend the night II. *vr:* **~se** to fall asleep; **se me ha dormido el brazo** my arm fell asleep; (*descuidarse*) to not pay attention

dormitorio [dor·mi·'to·rjo] *m* bedroom

dorsal [dor·'sal] I. *adj* dorsal; **espina ~** backbone II. *m* DEP number

dorso ['dor·so] *m* t. ANAT back; **véase al ~** please turn over

dos [dos] *adj inv* two; **de ~ en ~** two by two; **cada ~ por tres** all the time; **los/las ~** both

doscientos, -as [do·'sjen·tos, -as; dos·'θjen·-] *adj* two hundred; *v. t.* **ochocientos**

dosificar <c → qu> [do·si·fi·'kar] *vt* to measure out

dosis ['do·sis] *f inv* dose; **una buena ~ de paciencia** a lot of patience; (*dro-*

ga) fix *sl*

dotado, -a [do·'ta·do, -a] *adj* gifted

dotar [do·'tar] *vt* ~ **de** [*o* **con**] **algo** to equip with sth

dote[1] ['do·te] *m o f* dowry

dote[2] ['do·te] *f* gift; ~ **de mando** leadership ability

doy [doi] *1. pres de* **dar**

Dpto. [de·par·ta·'men·to] *AmL abr de* **departamento** administrative district

Dr(a). [dok·'tor, -·'to·ra] *abr de* **doctor(a)** Dr.

dragón [dra·'ɣon] *m* dragon

drama ['dra·ma] *m* drama; TEAT play

dramático, -a [dra·'ma·ti·ko, -a] *adj* dramatic; **autor** ~ playwright

dramatizar <z → c> [dra·ma·ti·'sar, -'θar] *vt* dramatize

dramaturgo, -a [dra·ma·'tur·ɣo, -a] *m, f* playwright

drástico, -a ['dras·ti·ko] *adj* drastic

drenaje [dre·'na·xe] *m* drainage

drenar [dre·'nar] *vt* to drain

droga ['dro·ɣa] *f* drug

drogadicto, -a [dro·ɣa·'dik·to, -a] I. *adj* addicted to drugs II. *m, f* drug addict

drogar <g → gu> [dro·'ɣar] I. *vt* to drug II. *vr:* ~**se** to take drugs

drogodependencia [dro·ɣo·de·pen·'den·sja, -θja] *f* drug addiction

droguería [dro·ɣe·'ri·a] *f* drugstore

dromedario [dro·me·'da·rjo] *m* dromedary

ducha ['du·tʃa] *f* shower

ducharse [du·'tʃar·se] *vr* to take a shower

ducho, -a ['du·tʃo, -a] *adj* skilled

duda ['du·da] *f* doubt; **salir de** ~**s** to dispel one's doubts; **no cabe la menor** ~ there is not the slightest doubt; **poner algo en** ~ to question sth

dudar [du·'dar] I. *vi* 1. (*desconfiar*) ~ **de algo** to doubt sth 2. (*vacilar*) to hesitate II. *vt* to doubt

dudoso, -a [du·'do·so, -a] *adj* 1. (*inseguro*) doubtful 2. (*indeciso*) undecided 3. (*sospechoso*) suspicious

duelo ['dwe·lo] *m* 1. (*desafío*) duel 2. (*funeral*) mourning

duende ['dwen·de] *m* elf

dueño, -a ['dwe·ɲo, -a] *m, f* owner; (*amo*) boss; **hacerse** ~ **de algo** (*apro-*

piarse/dominar) to take possession/command of sth

dulce ['dul·se, -θe] I. *adj* 1. (*sabor*) sweet 2. (*suave*) soft 3. (*agradable*) pleasant 4. (*agua*) fresh II. *m* 1. (*postre*) dessert 2. (*golosina*) candy

dulzor [dul·'sor, -'θor] *m*, **dulzura** [dul·'su·ra, -'θu·ra] *f* sweetness; (*ternura*) softness

duna ['du·na] *f* dune

dundera [dun·'de·ra] *f AmL* stupidity

dundo, -a ['dun·do, -a] *adj AmL* silly

dúo ['duo] *m* duet

duodécimo, -a [duo·'de·si·mo, -a; -'de·θi·mo, -a] *adj* twelfth; *v. t.* **octavo**

dúplex ['du·pleks] *m* duplex

duplicado [du·pli·'ka·do] *m* duplicate; **por** ~ in duplicate

duplicar <c → qu> [du·pli·'kar] *vt, vr:* ~**se** to duplicate

duque(sa) ['du·ke, du·'ke·sa] *m(f)* duke, duchess *m, f*

durabilidad [du·ra·βi·li·'dad] *f* durability

duración [du·ra·'sjon, -'θjon] *f* length; **de larga** ~ long-term

duradero, -a [du·ra·'de·ro, -a] *adj* long-lasting

durante [du·'ran·te] *prep* during; ~ **una hora** for an hour

durar [du·'rar] *vi* to last; (*permanecer*) to stay

durazno [du·'ras·no] *m AmL* (*fruta*) peach; (*árbol*) peach tree

dureza [du·'re·sa, -'re·θa] *f* hardness; MED hard skin

duro ['du·ro] *adv* hard

duro, -a ['du·ro, -a] *adj* hard; ~ **de oído** hard of hearing; **a duras penas** barely

DVD [de·u·βe·'de] *m abr de* **videodisco digital** DVD

E

E [e], **e** *f* E, e; **E de España** E as in Echo

e [e] *conj* (*before 'i' or 'hi'*) **Eva** ~ **Inés** Eva and Inés

E ['es·te] *abr de* **Este** E

ebanista [e·βa·'nis·ta] *mf* cabinetmaker

ébano ['e·βa·no] *m* ebony

ebrio, -a ['e·βrjo, -a] *adj* inebriated; **~ de** beside oneself with; (*ciego*) blind with

ebullición [e·βu·ʝi·'sjon, -ʎi·'θjon] *f* boiling

echado, -a [e·'tʃa·do] *adj* lying down; **~ para adelante** pushy

echar [e·'tʃar] **I.** *vt* **1.** (*tirar*) to throw; (*carta*) to mail; (*a la basura, al suelo*) to throw out; **la suerte está echada** the die is cast **2.** (*verter*) to pour (**en** into) **3.** (*expulsar*) to throw out **4.** (*pelo*) to grow; (*hojas, flores*) to sprout **5.** (*emitir*) to give off; (*humo*) to let out **6.** CINE, TV to show; TEAT to stage **II.** *vi* (*lanzar*) to throw; (*verter*) to pour; **~ a correr** to break into a run **III.** *vr:* **~se 1.** (*tumbarse*) to lie down **2.** (*lanzarse*) to jump; **~se sobre algo/alguien** to fall upon sth/sb; **~se a los pies de alguien** to throw oneself down before sb; **~se atrás** *fig* to have second thoughts **3.** (*empezar*) to begin; **~se a llorar** to burst into tears; **~se a la bebida** to take to drink; **~se (un) novio** to get a boyfriend

echarpe [e·'tʃar·pe] *m AmL* shawl

eclesiástico, -a [e·kle·'sjas·ti·ko, -a] *adj* ecclesiastical

eclipsar [e·kliβ·'sar] **I.** *vt* **1.** ASTR to eclipse **2.** (*oscurecer*) to darken **3.** *fig* to outshine **II.** *vr:* **~se 1.** ASTR to be eclipsed **2.** (*decaer*) to decline

eclipse [e·'kliβ·se] *m* eclipse

eco ['e·ko] *m* **1.** *t. fig* echo; **tener ~** *fig* to arouse interest; **~s de sociedad** PREN gossip column **2.** (*repercusión*) consequence; **hacer ~** to have an impact

ecografía [e·ko·ɣra·'fi·a] *f* ultrasound scan

ecología [e·ko·lo·'xi·a] *f* ecology

ecológico, -a [e·ko·'lo·xi·ko, -a] *adj* ecological; **daños ~s** environmental damage; **producción ecológica** organic farming

ecologismo [e·ko·lo·'xis·mo] *m* green movement

ecologista [e·ko·lo·'xis·ta] **I.** *adj* ecological **II.** *mf* ecologist

economía [e·ko·no·'mi·a] *f* **1.** (*situación, sistema*) economy; **~ de desechos** recycling industry; **~ forestal** forestry sector; **~ sumergida** black economy; **~ de escala** economy of scale; **~ de oferta** supply-side economy **2.** (*ciencia*) economics; **~ política/de la empresa** political/business economics **3.** (*ahorro*) saving; **hacer ~s** to economize

económico, -a [e·ko·'no·mi·ko, -a] *adj* **1.** ECON economic; **año ~** financial year; **estudiar Ciencias Económicas** to study economics **2.** (*barato*) cheap; (*ahorrador*) economical; (*persona*) thrifty

economista [e·ko·no·'mis·ta] *mf* economist

economizar <z → c> [e·ko·no·mi·'sar, -'θar] *vi, vt* to economize; **no ~ esfuerzos** to spare no effort; **~ esfuerzos** to save one's efforts

ecosistema [e·ko·sis·'te·ma] *m* ecosystem

ecuación [e·kwa·'sjon, -'θjon] *f* equation

ecuador [e·kwa·'dor] *m* equator

Ecuador [e·kwa·'dor] *m* Ecuador

ecuánime [e·'kwa·ni·me] *adj* fair

ecuanimidad [e·kwa·ni·mi·'dad] *f* impartiality

ecuatorial [e·kwa·to·'rjal] *adj* equatorial

ecuatoriano, -a [e·kwa·to·'rja·no, -a] *adj, m, f* Ecuadorean

ecuménico, -a [e·ku·'me·ni·ko, -a] *adj* universal

edad [e·'dad] *f* **1.** age; **~ para jubilarse** retirement age; **~ del pavo** adolescence; **mayor de ~** adult; **menor de ~** minor; **ser mayor/menor de ~** to be of/under age; **a la ~ de...** at the age of...; **¿qué ~ tiene?** how old is he/she?; **de mi ~** of my age; **de cierta ~** getting up there (in age); **llegar a la mayoría de ~** to come of age; **de mediana ~** middle-aged; **la tercera ~** old [*o* retirement] age **2.** (*época*) age, era; **la Edad Media** the Middle Ages

edén [e·'den] *m* Eden; *fig* paradise

edición [e·di·'sjon, -'θjon] *f* edition; **~ de bolsillo** paperback edition; **la presente ~ del Festival de Cine** this year's Film Festival

edificación [e·di·fi·ka·'sjon, -'θjon] *f* con-

construction

edificante [e·di·fi·'kan·te] *adj* edifying

edificar <c → qu> [e·di·fi·'kar] *vt* to build

edificio [e·di·'fi·sjo, -θjo] *m* building

edil(a) [e·'dil, e·'di·la] *m(f)* councilman, councilwoman *m, f*

editar [e·di·'tar] *vt* 1. (*publicar*) to publish 2. (*revisar*) to edit

editor(a) [e·di·'tor, -·'to·ra] *m(f)* 1. (*que publica*) publisher 2. (*que revisa*) editor

editorial¹ [e·di·to·'rjal] I. *adj* publishing II. *f* publisher

editorial² [e·di·to·'rjal] *m* editorial

Edo. [es·'ta·do] *Méx, Ven abr de* **Estado** State

edredón [e·dre·'don] *m* eiderdown; ~ **nórdico** quilt

educación [e·du·ka·'sjon, -'θjon] *f* 1. (*instrucción*) education; ~ **de adultos** adult education; ~ **ambiental** environmental education; ~ **física** ENS physical education; ~ **a distancia** distance learning; ~ **permanente** permanent education; **Educación General Básica** HIST education for children aged 6 to 14; **educación preescolar** preschool education; ~ **vial** road education 2. (*modales*) manners *pl*; **este niño no tiene** ~ this child has no manners

educado, -a [e·du·'ka·do, -a] *adj* 1. (*cortés*) (**bien**) ~ polite; **mal** ~ rude 2. (*culto*) cultivated

educar <c → qu> [e·du·'kar] *vt* to educate; (*criar*) to bring up; **debes ~ tu oído** you should train your ear

educativo, -a [e·du·ka·'ti·βo, -a] *adj* educational

edulcorante [e·dul·ko·'ran·te] *m* sweetener

EE.UU. [es·'ta·dos u·'ni·dos] *mpl abr de* **Estados Unidos** USA

efectivamente [e·fek·ti·βa·'men·te] *adv* in fact

efectividad [e·fek·ti·βi·'dad] *f* effectiveness

efectivo [e·fek·'ti·βo] *m* (*dinero*) cash; **en** ~ (in) cash; ~ **electrónico** electronic cash

efectivo, -a [e·fek·'ti·βo, -a] *adj* 1. (*que hace efecto*) effective 2. (*real*) real; **un éxito** ~ a real success; **hacer** ~ to put into action; (*cheque*) to cash

efecto [e·'fek·to] *m* effect; ~ **invernadero** greenhouse effect; ~ **retardado** delayed reaction; ~**s secundarios** side effects; **hacer** ~ to have an effect; **hacer buen** ~ (*impresión*) to make a good impression; **tener** ~ to take effect; **llevar a** ~ to carry out; **en** ~ indeed; **para los** ~**s** effectively; **con** ~**s retroactivos** retroactively

efectuar <1. *pres* efectúo> [e·fek·tu·'ar] I. *vt* to carry out; ~ **una compra** to make a purchase II. *vr:* ~**se** (*tener lugar*) to take place; (*realizarse*) to be carried out

efervescente [e·fer·βe·'sen·te, -'θen·te] *adj* fizzy; (*pastilla*) dissoluble

eficacia [e·fi·'ka·sja, -θja] *f t.* ECON, TÉC efficiency; (*medida*) effectiveness; **con** ~ effectively; **sin** ~ inefficiently

eficaz [e·fi·'kas, -'kaθ] *adj* efficient; (*medida*) effective

eficiencia [e·fi·'sjen·sja, -'θjen·θja] *f* efficiency; (*medida*) effectiveness

eficiente [e·fi·'sjen·te, -'θjen·te] *adj* efficient; (*medida*) effective

efusión [e·fu·'sjon] *f* effusion; **con gran** ~ very effusively

efusivo, -a [e·fu·'si·βo, -a] *adj* effusive

Egeo [e·'xe·o] *m* Aegean

egipcio, -a [e·'xip·sjo, -a; -'xiβ·θjo, -a] *adj, m, f* Egyptian

Egipto [e·'xip·to] *m* Egypt

ego ['e·γo] *m* ego

egocéntrico, -a [e·γo·'sen·tri·ko, -a; -'θen·tri·ko, -a] *adj* egocentric

egoísmo [e·γo·'is·mo] *m* selfishness

egoísta [e·γo·'is·ta] I. *adj* selfish II. *mf* egoist

egresado, -a [e·γre·'sa·do, -a] *m, f* Arg, Chile graduate

egresar [e·γre·'sar] *vi* Arg, Chile to graduate

eh [e] *interj* ¡~! hey!; ¿~? eh?; **no vuelvas a hacerlo, ¿~?** don't do it again, OK?

ej. [e·'xem·plo] *abr de* **ejemplo** example

eje ['e·xe] *m* (*de rueda*) axle; *fig* ~ **del debate** crux of the discussion; **ser el** ~ **de**

atención to be the center of attention

ejecución [e·xe·ku·'sjon, -'θjon] *f* t. JUR execution; (*proyecto*) implementation; (*pedido*) carrying out; **poner en ~** to carry out

ejecutar [e·xe·ku·'tar] *vt* to execute; (*ley*) to enforce

ejecutivo, -a [e·xe·ku·'ti·βo, -a] **I.** *adj* t. JUR executive; **comité ~** executive committee; **poder ~** executive power **II.** *m, f* (*directivo*) executive; (*empleado*) manager; **~ de marketing** marketing executive

ejemplar [e·xem·'plar] **I.** *adj* exemplary; **un alumno ~** a model student **II.** *m* specimen; (*libro*) copy; (*revista*) issue; **~ de muestra** sample

ejemplarizar <z → c> [e·xem·pla·ri·'sar] *vi AmL* to serve as an example

ejemplificar <c → qu> [e·xem·pli·fi·'kar] *vt* to exemplify

ejemplo [e·'xem·plo] *m* example; **dar buen ~** to set a good example; **poner por ~** to give as an example; **por ~** for example; **sin ~** unprecedented; **predicar con el ~** to practice what one preaches; **tomar por ~** to take as an example

ejercer <c → z> [e·xer·'ser, -'θer] **I.** *vt* (*profesión*) to practice; (*derechos*) to exercise **II.** *vi* to practice; (*profesor*) to work

ejercicio [e·xer·'si·sjo, -'θi·θjo] *m* **1.** (*de una profesión*) practice; **en ~** practicing **2.** DEP, ENS exercise; **tener falta de ~** to be out of practice **3.** ECON **~ contable** tax year; **~ (económico)** financial year

ejercitar [e·xer·si·'tar, -θi·'tar] **I.** *vt* **1.** (*profesión*) to practice; (*actividad*) to carry out **2.** (*adiestrar*) to train **II.** *vr*: **~se** to train

ejército [e·'xer·si·to, -θi·to] *m* army; (*fuerzas armadas*) armed forces

ejote [e·'xo·te] *m AmC, Méx* string bean

el [el], **la** [la], **lo** [lo] <los, las> *art def* **1.** the; **la mesa** the table; **los amigos** as the friends; **~ azul** the blue one **2.** *lo + adj* **lo bueno/malo** the good/bad (thing); **lo antes posible** as soon as possible **3.** + *nombres geográficos* **la India** India **4.** + *días de semana* **llegaré el**

domingo I'll arrive on Sunday; **los sábados no trabajo** I don't work on Saturdays **5.** + *nombre propio inf* **he visto a la Carmen** I saw Carmen **6.** + *que* **lo que digo es...** what I'm saying is...

él [el] *pron pers,* 3. *sing m* he; + *prep* him; **el libro es de ~** the book is his

elaboración [e·la·βo·ra·'sjon, -'θjon] *f* manufacture; (*de comidas*) preparation; **de ~ casera** homemade

elaborar [e·la·βo·'rar] *vt* to manufacture; (*preparar*) to prepare

elación [e·la·'sjon] *f AmL* exaltation

elasticidad [e·las·ti·si·'dad, -θi·'dad] *f* elasticity

elástico [e·'las·ti·ko] *m* elastic

elástico, -a [e·'las·ti·ko, -a] *adj* elastic; (*tela*) stretch

elección [e·lek·'sjon, -ley·'θjon] *f* (*selección*) choice; **lo dejo a su ~** the choice is yours; POL election; **elecciones generales/legislativas** general election; **~ parcial** by-election

electo, -a [e·'lek·to, -a] *adj* elect

elector(a) [e·lek·'tor, -·'to·ra] **I.** *adj* electing **II.** *m(f)* voter

electorado [e·lek·to·'ra·do] *m* electorate

electoral [e·lek·to·'ral] *adj* electoral

electricidad [e·lek·tri·si·'dad, -θi·'dad] *f* electricity

electricista [e·lek·tri·'sis·ta, -'θis·ta] *mf* electrician

eléctrico, -a [e·'lek·tri·ko, -a] *adj* electric; (*aparato, instalación*) electrical

electrificar <c → qu> [e·lek·tri·fi·'kar] *vt*, **electrizar** <z → c> [e·lek·tri·'sar, -'θar] *vt* to electrify

electrocardiograma [e·lek·tro·kar·djo·'yra·ma] *m* electrocardiogram

electrocución [e·lek·tro·ku·'sjon, -'θjon] *f* electrocution

electrocutar [e·lek·tro·ku·'tar] *vt* to electrocute

electrodo [e·lek·'tro·do] *m* electrode

electrodoméstico [e·lek·tro·do·'mes·ti·ko] *m* household appliance

electrón [e·lek·'tron] *m* electron

electrónica [e·lek·'tro·ni·ka] *f* electronics

electrónico, -a [e·lek·'tro·ni·ko, -a] *adj* electronic; (*microscopio*) electron;

correo ~ e-mail

elefante, -a [e·le·'fan·te, -a] *m, f* elephant; ~ **marino** elephant seal

elegancia [e·le·'ɣan·sja, -ɵja] *f* elegance; (*buen gusto*) tastefulness

elegante [e·le·'ɣan·te] *adj* elegant; (*con buen gusto*) tasteful

elegantoso, -a [e·le·ɣan·'to·so, -a] *adj infra*ritzy

elegir [e·le·'xir] *irr vi, vt* to choose; **a ~ entre** to be chosen from; POL to elect

elementado, -a [e·le·men·'ta·do, -a] *adj Chile, Col* bewildered

elemental [e·le·men·'tal] *adj* basic

elemento [e·le·'men·to] *m* element; ~ **base** basic element; **tener ~s de juicio** to be able to judge; ~ **decisivo** crucial factor; **los ~** the elements; ~**s de matemáticas** basic mathematics

elenco [e·'len·ko] *m* 1. TEAT cast 2. *AmL* (*personal*) staff 3. *Chile, Perú* (*equipo*) team

elepé [e·le·'pe] *m* LP

elevación [e·le·βa·'sjon, -'θjon] *f* rise; GEO elevation

elevado, -a [e·le·'βa·do, -a] *adj* elevated; (*nivel, estilo*) refined; MAT ~ **a** raised to the power of

elevador [e·le·βa·'dor] *m AmC* elevator

elevalunas [e·le·βa·'lu·nas] *m inv* automatic window

elevar [e·le·'βar] **I.** *vt* to raise; (*protesta*) to lodge; MAT ~ **a** to raise to the power of **II.** *vr:* ~**se** to rise; ~**se a** (*precio*) to amount to; (*cotización*) to stand at

eliminación [e·li·mi·na·'sjon, -'θjon] *f* elimination; (*basura, residuos*) disposal

eliminar [e·li·mi·'nar] *vt* 1. to eliminate; ~ **la competencia** to eliminate the competition 2. DEP to knock out; **fueron eliminados en la cuarta prueba** they went out in the fourth round

eliminatoria [e·li·mi·na·'to·rja] *f* playoff

elipse [e·'liβ·se] *f* ellipse

elite [e·'li·te] *f*, **élite** [e·'li·te] *f* elite; **de ~** top-class

elitista [e·li·'tis·ta] *adj* elitist

elixir [e·lik·'sir] *m* elixir

ella ['e·ja, -ʎa] *pron pers, 3. sing f* she; + *prep* her; **el abrigo es de ~** the coat is hers

ellas ['e·jas, -ʎas] *pron pers, 3. pl f* they; + *prep* them; **el coche es de ~** the car is theirs

ello ['e·jo, -ʎo] *pron pers, 3. sing neutro* it; **para ~** for it; **por ~** that is why; **estar en ~** to be doing it; **¡a ~!** let's do it!

ellos ['e·jos, -ʎos] *pron pers, 3. pl m* they; + *prep* them; **estos niños son de ~** these children are theirs

elocuencia [e·lo·'kwen·sja, -θja] *f* eloquence; **con ~** eloquently

elocuente [e·lo·'kwen·te] *adj* eloquent; **las pruebas son ~s** the evidence speaks for itself

elogiar [e·lo·'xjar] *vt* to praise

elogio [e·'lo·xjo] *m* praise; **hacer ~s** to eulogize; **recibir ~s** to be praised; **digno de ~** praiseworthy

elote [e·'lo·te] *m AmC* corncob

eludir [e·lu·'dir] *vt* to elude; (*preguntas*) to evade; (*responsabilidad*) to shirk

e-mail [i·'meil] *m abr de* **electronic mail** e-mail

emanar [e·ma·'nar] *vi* 1. (*escaparse*) ~ **de** to emanate from *form*; (*líquido*) to ooze from 2. (*originarse*) ~ **de** to stem from

emancipación [e·man·si·pa·'sjon, -θi·pa·'θjon] *f* emancipation

emanciparse [e·man·si·'par·se, e·man·θi-] *vr* to become emancipated

embadurnar [em·ba·dur·'nar] **I.** *vt* ~ **algo de** [*o* **con**] **algo** to smear sth with sth **II.** *vr:* ~**se de** [*o* **con**] **algo** to be smeared with sth

embajada [em·ba·'xa·da] *f* embassy

embajador(a) [em·ba·xa·'dor, -·'do·ra] *m(f)* ambassador

embalaje [em·ba·'la·xe] *m* packaging; (*acción*) packing

embalar [em·ba·'lar] **I.** *vt* to pack **II.** *vr:* ~**se** (*correr*) to dash off

embalsamar [em·bal·sa·'mar] *vt* to embalm

embalsar [em·bal·'sar] *vt* to dam

embalse [em·'bal·se] *m* reservoir; *Arg* dam

embarazada [em·ba·ra·'sa·da, -'θa·da] **I.** *adj* pregnant; **estar ~ de seis meses** to be six months pregnant; **quedarse ~** to get pregnant **II.** *f* pregnant woman

embarazo [em·ba·'ra·so, -θo] *m* pregnancy; **interrupción del ~** abortion; *fig* **causar ~ a alguien** to make sb feel awkward

embarazoso, -a [em·ba·ra·'so·so, -a; -'θo·so, -a] *adj* awkward

embarcación [em·bar·ka·'sjon, -'θjon] *f* vessel; **~ de recreo** pleasure craft

embarcadero [em·bar·ka·'de·ro] *m* pier

embarcar <c → qu> [em·bar·'kar] **I.** *vi* to go on board; (*avión*) to board **II.** *vt* (*barco*) to stow; (*avión*) to put on board; (*asunto*) to involve **III.** *vr:* **~se** (*barco*) to embark; (*avión*) to board; (*asunto*) to become involved

embargar <g → gu> [em·bar·'ɣar] *vt* to confiscate

embargo [em·'bar·ɣo] **I.** *m* confiscation; COM embargo **II.** *conj* **sin ~** however

embarque [em·'bar·ke] *m* **1.** (*material*) loading **2.** (*personas*) boarding; **tarjeta de ~** boarding card

embarrada [em·ba·'rra·da] *f* *Cuba, PRico, And* (*desliz*) blunder; (*tontería*) foolishness

embaucador(a) [em·bau·ka·'dor, --'do·ra] **I.** *adj* deceitful **II.** *m(f)* cheat

embaucar <c → qu> [em·bau·'kar] *vt* to cheat

embelesar [em·be·le·'sar] *vi, vt* to captivate

embellecer [em·be·je·'ser, -ʎe·'θer] *irr como crecer vt* to beautify

embestida [em·bes·'ti·da] *f* onslaught

embestir [em·bes·'tir] *irr como pedir* **I.** *vi* to charge **II.** *vt* (*atacar*) to attack; (*coche*) to crash into

emblema [em·'ble·ma] *m* emblem; (*logotipo*) logo

embobar [em·bo·'βar] **I.** *vt* (*asombrar*) to amaze; (*fascinar*) to fascinate **II.** *vr* **~se en** [*o con*] **algo** to be amazed by sth; (*fascinación*) to be fascinated by sth

embolarse [em·bo·'lar·se] *vr AmC* to get drunk

embolia [em·'bo·lja] *f* embolism; **~ cerebral** brain clot

embolsar [em·bol·'sar] *vt* to pocket

emborrachar [em·bo·rra·'tʃar] **I.** *vt* to make drunk; CULIN to soak (**con** in) **II.** *vr:* **~se** to get drunk

emborronar [em·bo·rro·'nar] *vt* to blot, to smudge

emboscada [em·bos·'ka·da] *f* ambush

embotellado, -a [em·bo·te·'ja·do, -'ʎa·do] *adj* bottled

embotellamiento [em·bo·te·ja·'mjen·to, em·bo·te·ʎa·-] *m* **1.** (*de bebidas*) bottling **2.** (*de tráfico*) jam

embotellar [em·bo·te·'jar, -'ʎar] **I.** *vt* **1.** (*bebidas*) to bottle **2.** (*tráfico*) to block **II.** *vr:* **~se** (*tráfico*) to get congested

embrague [em·'bra·ɣe] *m* clutch

embriagar <g → gu> [em·brja·'ɣar] **I.** *vi, vt* **1.** (*emborrachar*) to inebriate **2.** (*enajenar*) to hypnotize **II.** *vr:* **~se** (*emborracharse*) to get drunk

embriaguez [em·brja·'ɣes, -'ɣeθ] *f* **1.** (*borrachera*) inebriation; **en estado de ~** inebriated **2.** (*enajenación*) delight

embrión [em·bri·'on] *m* embryo

embrollar [em·bro·'jar, -'ʎar] **I.** *vt* **1.** (*liar*) to mess up; **embrollas todo lo que tocas** you mess everything up; **lo embrollas más de lo necesario** you're overcomplicating things **2.** *CSur* (*engañar*) to deceive **II.** *vr:* **~se** to get tangled up; **~se en algo** to get involved in sth

embrollo [em·'bro·jo, -'ʎo] *m* **1.** (*lío*) mess; **meterse en un ~** to get into a mess **2.** (*embuste*) swindle; **no me vengas con ~s** don't try and fool me

embromado, -a [em·bro·'ma·do, -a] *adj* *AmL inf* **1.** (*difícil*) hard **2.** (*molesto*) annoyed

embromar [em·bro·'mar] *vt AmL* to annoy

embroncarse [em·bron·'kar·se] <c → qu> *vr Arg inf* to get mad

embrujado, -a [em·bru·'xa·do, -a] *adj* bewitched; (*casa*) haunted

embrujar [em·bru·'xar] *vt* to bewitch

embudo [em·'bu·do] *m* funnel; **en forma de ~** funnel-shaped; **aplicar la ley del ~** to apply one-sided rule

embuste [em·'bus·te] *m* lie; (*estafa*) swindle

embustero, -a [em·bus·'te·ro, -a] **I.** *adj* lying; **¡qué tío más ~!** what a swindler! **II.** *m, f* liar; (*estafador*) swindler

embute [em·'bu·te] *m Méx inf* bribe

embutido [em·bu·'ti·do] *m* sausage

embutir [em·bu·'tir] *vt* to stuff

emergencia [e·mer·'xen·sja, -θja] *f* emergency; **estado de ~** state of emergency; **plan de ~** emergency plan

emergente [e·mer·'xen·te] *adj* emergent

emerger <g → j> [e·mer·'xer] *vi* to emerge; (*submarino*) to surface; **mi jefe emergió de la nada** my boss is a self-made man

emigración [e·mi·ɣra·'sjon, -'θjon] *f* emigration; (*animales*) migration

emigrante [e·mi·'ɣran·te] *mf* emigrant; POL émigré

emigrar [e·mi·'ɣrar] *vi* to emigrate; (*animales*) to migrate

emilio [e·'mi·ljo] *m inf* e-mail; **escribir/mandar un ~** to write/send an e-mail

eminencia [e·mi·'nen·sja, -θja] *f* Eminence; *fig* expert; **ser una ~ en su campo** to be an expert in one's field

eminente [e·mi·'nen·te] *adj* outstanding

emisión [e·mi·'sjon] *f* 1. TV, RADIO broadcast; (*de programas*) program 2. FÍS emission; **emisiones contaminantes** pollution

emisor(a) [e·mi·'sor] *adj* broadcasting; (*banco*) issuing

emisora [e·mi·'so·ra] *f* broadcasting station; **~ clandestina** pirate station; **~ de radio** radio station; **~ de televisión** television station

emitir [e·mi·'tir] *vt* 1. TV, RADIO to broadcast 2. FÍS to emit, to give off 3. (*humo*) to let off; (*grito*) to let out; (*dictamen*) to give

emoción [e·mo·'sjon, -'θjon] *f* emotion; (*ilusión*) excitement; **lleno de emociones** full of thrills; **palabras llenas de ~** words full of emotion; **llorar de ~** to cry with emotion; **sin ~** without emotion; **sentir una honda ~** to feel a deep emotion; **dar rienda suelta a sus emociones** to give free rein to one's emotions

emocional [e·mo·sjo·'nal, e·mo·θjo-] *adj* emotional

emocionante [e·mo·sjo·'nan·te, e·mo·θjo-] *adj* exciting; (*conmovedor*) moving

emocionar [e·mo·sjo·'nar, e·mo·θjo-] **I.** *vt* 1. (*apasionar*) to excite; **este libro no me emociona** this book doesn't do anything for me 2. (*conmover*) to move; **los espectadores estaban emocionados** the spectators were moved; **tus palabras me ~on** I found your words very moving **II.** *vr:* **~se** to get excited; (*conmoverse*) to be moved

emotivo, -a [e·mo·'ti·βo, -a] *adj* emotional; (*palabras*) moving

empacar <c → qu> [em·pa·'kar] *vi, vt AmL* to pack

empachado, -a [em·pa·'tʃa·do, -a] *adj* **estoy ~** (*indigestado*) I have indigestion; (*harto*) I'm so full I feel sick

empachar [em·pa·'tʃar] **I.** *vt* to give indigestion **II.** *vr:* **~se** to get indigestion; (*comer demasiado*) to eat too much

empacho [em·pa·'tʃo] *m* indigestion; **tengo un ~ de dulces** I've eaten too many sweets; (*saturación*) saturation; **tengo un ~ de televisión** I'm sick of watching television

empadronamiento [em·pa·dro·na·'mjen·to] *m* registration in local census bureau

empadronar [em·pa·dro·'nar] *vt, vr:* **~se** to register (for a census)

empalagar <g → gu> [em·pa·la·'ɣar] **I.** *vi* (*alimento*) to be oversweet **II.** *vr* **~se de** [*o* con] **algo** to get sick of sth

empalagoso, -a [em·pa·la·'ɣo·so, -a] *adj* (*alimento*) oversweet; (*persona*) cloying; (*película*) treacly

empalmar [em·pal·'mar] **I.** *vi* **~ con** to meet; (*carretera*) to join up with **II.** *vr:* **~se** to get a hard-on

empalme [em·'pal·me] *m* 1. join; (*teléfono*) connection 2. (*erección*) hard-on

empanada [em·pa·'na·da] *f* ≈ pie

empanadilla [em·pa·na·'di·ʝa, -ʎa] *f* halfmoon-shaped savory turnover

empanar [em·pa·'nar] *vt* to coat in breadcrumbs

empañetar [em·pa·ɲe·'tar] *vt AmL* to plaster

empapar [em·pa·'par] **I.** *vt* to soak; **la lluvia ha empapado el suelo** the rain has soaked the floor; (*absorber*) to soak up **II.** *vr:* **~se** to get soaked; **~se de**

algo *fig* to become versed in sth

empapelar [em·pa·pe·'lar] I. *vi, vt* to (wall)paper II. *vt* 1. to wrap up 2. *inf* (*expedientar*) to book

empaque [em·'pa·ke] *m AmL* (*cara dura*) cheek

empaquetar [em·pa·ke·'tar] *vt* to pack

emparedado [em·pa·re·'da·do] *m AmL* sandwich

emparejar [em·pa·re·'xar] I. *vt* 1. (*juntar*) to pair up; **ya estoy emparejado** I already have a partner 2. (*nivelar*) to level II. *vr:* ~**se** to make a pair

emparentado, -a [em·pa·ren·'ta·do, -a] *adj* related (**con** to)

empastar [em·pas·'tar] *vt* (*muela*) to fill; (*libro*) to bind

empaste [em·'pas·te] *m* filling

empatar [em·pa·'tar] I. *vi* 1. DEP to draw; ~ **a uno** to draw one-all 2. POL to tie II. *vt* 1. *AmL* (*cuerdas*) to tie together; ~ **mentiras** to tell one lie after another 2. *CRi, PRico* (*amarrar*) to moor 3. *Ven, Col* (*importunar*) to annoy

empate [em·'pa·te] *m* 1. DEP draw 2. POL tie

empatía [em·pa·'ti·a] *f* empathy

empavonar [em·pa·βo·'nar] I. *vt AmL* to grease II. *vr:* ~**se** *AmC* to get dressed up

empedernido, -a [em·pe·der·'ni·do, -a] *adj* incorrigible; (*bebedor*) hardened; (*fumador*) chain; (*solterón*) confirmed

empeine [em·'pei·ne] *m* instep

empelotado, -a [em·pe·lo·'ta·do, -a] *adj AmL inf* stark naked; *Méx* (*enamorado*) infatuated

empeñar [em·pe·'ɲar] I. *vt* to pawn; ~ **la palabra** to give one's word II. *vr:* ~**se** to insist (**en** on); **se empeña en hablar contigo** he/she insists on speaking to you; **no te empeñes** don't go on about it

empeño [em·'pe·ɲo] *m* 1. (*afán*) determination; **con** ~ determinedly; **poner** ~ **en** to try one's best; **tengo** ~ **por** [*o* **en**] **sacar la mejor nota** I'm determined to get the highest mark 2. (*de objetos*) pawning; **casa de** ~**s** pawnbroker's

empeorar [em·peo·'rar] I. *vt* to make

worse II. *vi, vr:* ~**se** to worsen

empequeñecer [em·pe·ke·ɲe·'ser, -'θer] *irr como crecer vt* to make smaller; (*quitar importancia*) to trivialize

emperador [em·pe·ra·'dor] *m* emperor

emperatriz [em·pe·ra·'tris, -'triθ] *f* empress

emperrarse [em·pe·'rrar·se] *vr* to be bent dead set on

empezar [em·pe·'sar, -'θar] *irr vi, vt* to begin, to start; **empezó de la nada** he/she started with nothing; **¡no empieces!** don't start!; ~ **con buen pie** to get off to a good start; **para** ~ **me leeré el periódico** to begin with, I'll read the newspaper; **para** ~ **no tengo dinero y, además, no tengo ganas** first of all, I have no money, and what's more, I don't feel like it

empiezo [em·'pje·so] *m Col, Ecua, Guat* beginning

empinado, -a [em·pi·'na·do, -a] *adj* steep

empinar [em·pi·'nar] *vt* to raise; ~ **la cabeza** to raise one's head; ~ **el codo/una botella** *inf* to take a drink

empipada [em·pi·'pa·da] *f AmL* binge

empiparse [em·pi·'par·se] *vr AmL* to go on a binge

empírico, -a [em·'pi·ri·ko, -a] *adj* empirical

emplazamiento [em·pla·sa·'mjen·to, em·pla·θa·] *m* location

emplazar <z → c> [em·pla·'sar, -'θar] *vt* to locate; **este monumento no está bien emplazado aquí** this isn't the best place for this monument

empleado, -a [em·ple·'a·do, -a] *m, f* employee; ~ **de oficina** office worker; ~ **de ventanilla** clerk; **los** ~**s de una empresa** company staff

empleador(a) [em·plea·'dor, -·'do·ra] *m(f) AmL* employer

emplear [em·ple·'ar] I. *vt* 1. (*medio, técnica, método*) to use; (*tiempo*) to spend; (*dinero*) to invest; **¡podrías** ~ **mejor el tiempo!** you could make better use of your time!; **¡te está bien empleado!** it serves you right!; **dar algo por bien empleado** to be satisfied with the results of sth; **he empleado todo el dine-**

ro en la casa I've put all my money into the house **2.** (*dar trabajo*) to employ; **en estos momentos no estoy empleado** I'm unemployed at the moment **II.** *vr:* **~se** to be used; **~se de** [*o como*] **algo** to be employed as sth; **~se a fondo** to put everything into sth

empleo [em·'pleo] *m* employment; (*un trabajo*) job; **pleno ~** full employment; **no tener ~** to be out of work; **crear ~** to create jobs; **solicitud de ~** job application; **modo de ~** instructions for use

emplomadura [em·plo·ma·'ðu·ɾa] *f AmL* filling

emplomar [em·plo·'maɾ] *vt* **1.** *AmL* to fill **2.** *Col, Guat* (*enredar*) to entangle

empobrecer [em·po·βɾe·'seɾ, -'θeɾ] *irr como crecer* **I.** *vt* to impoverish; **la edad empobrece los reflejos** age slows one's reflexes **II.** *vi, vr:* **~se** to become poorer; **este terreno se ha empobrecido** this soil has become less fertile

empobrecimiento [em·po·βɾe·si·'mjen·to, -θi·'mjen·to] *m* impoverishment

empollar [em·po·'ʎaɾ, -'ʝaɾ] **I.** *vi* **1.** *inf* (*estudiar*) to work hard **2.** *AmL* (*ampollar*) to blister **II.** *vt* **1.** (*ave*) to brood **2.** *inf* (*estudiarse*) to work hard at

empollón, -ona [em·po·'ʎon, -·'ʝo·na; -·'ʎo·na, -·'ʝo·na] *m, f inf* brain

emponchado, -a [em·pon·'tʃa·do, -a] *adj* **1.** *Arg, Ecua, Perú, Urug* (*con poncho*) wearing a poncho **2.** *Arg, Bol, Perú* (*sospechoso*) suspicious

emporio [em·'po·ɾjo] *m AmC* store

empotrado, -a [em·po·'tɾa·do, -a] *adj* built-in

empotrar [em·po·'tɾaɾ] **I.** *vt* to build in **II.** *vr:* **~se con(tra)** to crash into

emprendedor(a) [em·pɾen·de·'doɾ, -·'do·ɾa] *adj* enterprising

emprender [em·pɾen·'deɾ] *vt* (*trabajo*) to begin; (*negocio*) to set up; **~ la marcha** to set out; **~ la vuelta** to go back; **~ el vuelo** to take off; **al anochecer la emprendimos hacia la casa** at nightfall we set off back to the house; **~la con alguien** to take it out on sb; **~la a insultos con alguien** to begin insulting sb

empresa [em·'pɾe·sa] *f* enterprise; (*com-*

pañía) company; **pequeña/mediana ~** small/medium-sized company; **~ matriz/pública** parent/state-owned company; **~ privada** private enterprise; **~ de mensajería** courier company

empresarial [em·pɾe·sa·'ɾjal] *adj* business

empresario, -a [em·pɾe·'sa·ɾjo, -a] *m, f* businessman, businesswoman *m, f*

empujar [em·pu·'xaɾ] *vi, vt* to push; (*con violencia*) to shove; (*multitud*) to elbow

empuje [em·'pu·xe] *m* **1.** (*acción*) pushing **2.** fís force **3.** (*energía*) energy; (*resolución*) drive

empujón [em·pu·'xon] *m* push; (*violento*) shove; **dar un ~ a alguien** to give sb a shove; **entrar en un local a empujones** to push one's way into a place

empuntar [em·pun·'taɾ] **I.** *vt Col, Ecua* to direct towards; **~las** to beat it **II.** *vr:* **~se** *Ven* to dig one's heels in

empuñar [em·pu·'ɲaɾ] *vt* to grip; **~ las armas** to take up arms

empurrarse [em·pu·'rrar·se] *vr AmC* to get angry

emulación [e·mu·la·'sjon, -'θjon] *f* emulation

emular [e·mu·'laɾ] *vt* to emulate

emulsión [e·mul·'sjon] *f* emulsion

en. *abr de* **enero** Jan.

en [en] *prep* **1.** (*lugar: dentro*) in; (*encima de*) on; (*con movimiento*) in, into; **el libro está ~ el cajón** the book is in the drawer; **pon el libro ~ el cajón** put the book in the drawer; **he dejado las llaves ~ la mesa** I left the keys on the table; **coloca el florero ~ la mesa** put the vase on the table; **~ la pared hay un cuadro** there is a painting on the wall; **pon el póster ~ la pared** put the poster on the wall; **estar ~ el campo/~ la ciudad/~ una isla** to be in the countryside/in the city/on an island; **~ España** in Spain; **vacaciones ~ el mar** holidays at the seaside; **jugar ~ la calle** to play in the street; **estoy ~ casa** I'm at home; **trabajo ~ una empresa japonesa** I work at a Japanese company **2.** (*tiempo*) in; **~ el año 2005** in 2005; **~ mayo** in May; **~ otra ocasión** on another occasion; ~ **aquellos tiempos** in those times [o days]; ~ **un mes** in a month; **lo terminaré ~ un momento** I'll finish it in a minute; ~ **todo el día** all [o the whole] day **3.** (modo, estado) ~ **absoluto** not at all; ~ **construcción** under construction; ~ **flor** in flower; ~ **venta** for sale; ~ **vida** while living; ~ **voz alta** aloud; **de dos ~ dos** two at a time; **decir algo ~ español** to say something in Spanish; **pagar ~ pesos** to pay in pesos **4.** (medio) ~ **tren** by train; **lo reconocí ~ la voz** I recognized him by his voice **5.** (ocupación) **doctor ~ filosofía** PhD in Philosophy; **trabajo ~ ingeniería** I work in engineering; **estar ~ la policía** to be in the police force; **estar ~ la mili** to be doing military service; **trabajar ~ Correos** to work in the postal service **6.** (con verbo) **pienso ~ ti** I am thinking of you; **no confío ~ él** I don't trust him; **ingresar ~ un partido** to join a party; **ganar ~ importancia** to gain in importance **7.** (cantidades) **aumentar la producción ~ un 5%** to increase production by 5%; **me he equivocado sólo ~ 3 dólares** I was off by just 3 dollars

enajenación [e·na·xe·na·'sjon, -'θjon] *f* derangement; ~ **mental** insanity

enajenar [e·na·xe·'nar] **I.** *vt* to drive crazy **II.** *vr:* ~**se** to go crazy

enamoradizo, -a [e·na·mo·ra·'di·so, -a; -'di·θo, -a] *adj* always falling in love

enamorado, -a [e·na·mo·'ra·do, -a] **I.** *adj* in love (**de** with) **II.** *m, f* lover; **día de los ~s** Valentine's Day

enamorar [e·na·mo·'rar] **I.** *vt* to win the heart of **II.** *vr:* ~**se** (**de**) to fall in love (with)

enano, -a [e·'na·no, -a] **I.** *adj* tiny **II.** *m, f* **1.** dwarf **2.** *inf* (niño) kid

enardecer [e·nar·de·'ser, -'θer] *irr como* **crecer I.** *vt* to fire with enthusiasm **II.** *vr:* ~**se** to be kindled; ~**se por** to become enthusiastic about

encabezado [en·ka·βe·'sa·do] *m Guat, Méx* headline

encabezamiento [en·ka·βe·sa·'mjen·to, -θa·'mjen·to] *m* headline; (de una carta) letterhead; (primeras líneas) opening

encabezar <z → c> [en·ka·βe·'sar, -'θar] *vt* (lista, grupo) to head; (institución) to be the head of

encabritarse [en·ka·βri·'tar·se] *vr* to lose one's temper

encadenar [en·ka·de·'nar] *vt* to chain (up); *fig* to link up

encajar [en·ka·'xar] **I.** *vi* to fit; **la puerta encaja mal** the door doesn't fit properly; (datos, hechos) to fit in; **las dos declaraciones encajan** the two statements fit together; **este chiste no encaja aquí** this joke is uncalled for here **II.** *vt* **1.** to fit; ~ **en algo** to clamp into sth; ~ **dos piezas** to fit two pieces together; ~ **la ventana en el marco** to fit the window into the frame; ~ **el sombrero en la cabeza** to stick a hat on one's head; ~ **la funda en la máquina** to put the covering over the machine **2.** (dar) ~ **un golpe a alguien** to hit sb; ~ **una reprimenda a alguien** to give sb a talking-to; ~ **una tarea a alguien** to palm a task off on sb **3.** (aceptar) **no ~ la muerte de alguien** not to take sb's death well; **no sabes ~ una broma** you don't know how to take a joke **III.** *vr:* ~**se 1.** *AmL inf* (aprovecharse) to go too far **2.** (atascarse) to jam

encaje [en·'ka·xe] *m* lace

encalambrarse [en·ka·lam·'brar·se] *vr AmL* to cramp up; (de frío) to become numb

encaminar [en·ka·mi·'nar] **I.** *vt* to direct; ~ **sus pasos hacia el pueblo** to head towards the village; ~ **la mirada/la conversación hacia un punto** to direct one's gaze/the conversation towards a point; ~ **los esfuerzos hacia una meta** to focus one's efforts on a goal; ~ **los negocios hacia algo** to steer one's business towards sth **II.** *vr:* ~**se a/hacia** to head for/towards; ~**se a la meta** to focus on the goal

encamotarse [en·ka·mo·'tar·se] *vr AmL inf* to fall in love (**de** with)

encandilar [en·kan·di·'lar] **I.** *vt* to dazzle; **escuchar encandilado** to listen in rapture **II.** *vr:* ~**se 1.** (luz, emociones) to light up **2.** *AmL* (asustarse) to be scared **3.** *PRico* (enfadarse) to get angry

encanecer [en·ka·ne·'ser, -'θer] *irr como crecer* I, *vr*: ~**se** to go gray; **pelo encanecido** gray hair

encantado, -a [en·kan·'ta·do, -a] *adj* 1. delighted; **¡~ (de conocerle)!** pleased to meet you!; **estoy ~ con mi nuevo trabajo** I love my new job; **estoy ~ de la vida** I am thrilled 2. (*embrujado*) haunted

encantador(a) [en·kan·ta·'dor, -·'do·ra] *adj* lovely; (*persona*) charming

encantamiento [en·kan·ta·'mjen·to] *m* spell

encantar [en·kan·'tar] *vt* (*gustar*) **me encanta viajar** I love to travel; (*cautivar*) to captivate; (*fascinar*) to fascinate

encanto [en·'kan·to] *m* charm; **¡es un ~ de niño!** what an adorable child!

encapricharse [en·ka·pri·'tʃar·se] *vr* ~**se con algo** to be taken by sth; ~**se con alguien** to become infatuated with sb

encapuchado, -a [en·ka·pu·'tʃa·do, -a] *adj* hooded

encarar [en·ka·'rar] I. *vt* to bring face to face; (*riesgo, dificultad*) to face up to II. *vr*: ~**se** to be face to face

encarcelamiento [en·kar·se·la·'mjen·to, en·kar·θe-] *m* imprisonment

encarcelar [en·kar·se·'lar, en·kar·θe-] *vt* to imprison

encarecer [en·ka·re·'ser, -'θer] *irr como crecer* *vt* to raise the price of

encarecidamente [en·ka·re·si·da·'men·te, en·ka·re·θi-] *adv* strongly; **le ruego ~...** I have to insist...

encarecimiento [en·ka·re·si·'mjen·to, -θi·'mjen·to] *m* 1. COM price increase 2. (*acentuación*) emphasis; **con ~** insistently

encargado, -a [en·kar·'ɣa·do, -a] I. *adj* in charge II. *m, f* person in charge; ~ **de negocios** chargé d'affaires; ~ **de campo** groundskeeper; ~ **de curso** course director; ~ **de obras** site manager; ~ **de prensa** press officer

encargar <g → gu> [en·kar·'ɣar] I. *vt* 1. (*encomendar*) to put in charge; **lo ~on del departamento de ventas** they put him in charge of the sales department; **encargó a su hija a una vecina** he asked a neighbor to look af-

ter his daughter 2. (*comprar*) to order 3. (*mandar*) to ask II. *vr* ~**se de algo** to take responsibility for sth; **tengo que ~me aún de un par de cosas** I still have to get a couple of things done

encargo [en·'kar·ɣo] *m* 1. (*pedido*) order; ~ **por anticipado** advance order; **hacer un nuevo ~** to make another order 2. (*trabajo*) job; **traje de ~** tailor-made suit; **de ~** to order; **por ~ de** at the request of; **hacer ~s** to run errands; **tener ~ de hacer algo** to be commissioned to do sth

encariñado, -a [en·ka·ri·'ɲa·do, -a] *adj* **estar ~ con algo** to be very attached to sth; **estar ~ con alguien** to be fond of sb

encariñarse [en·ka·ri·'ɲar·se] *vr* ~ **con algo/alguien** to grow fond of sth/sb

encarnación [en·kar·na·'sjon, -'θjon] *f* incarnation

encarnado, -a [en·kar·'na·do] *adj* (*color carne*) skin-tone; (*rosado*) pink; (*rojo*) red

encarnar [en·kar·'nar] *vt* to represent; CINE, TEAT to play the role of

encarnizado, -a [en·kar·ni·'sa·do, -a; -'θa·do, -a] *adj* bloody

encarpetar [en·kar·pe·'tar] *vt* AmL to shelve

encarrilar [en·ka·rri·'lar] *vt* to guide

encasillar [en·ka·si·'jar, -'ʎar] I. *vt* to classify; (*persona, idea*) to pigeon-hole II. *vr* ~**se en** to limit oneself to

encausar [en·kau·'sar] *vt* to prosecute

encauzar <z → c> [en·kau·'sar, -'θar] *vt* (*corriente*) to channel; (*debate*) to lead; (*vida*) to sort out

encéfalo [en·'se·fa·lo, en·'θe-] *m* brain

encendedor [en·sen·de·'dor, en·θen-] *m* lighter

encender <e → ie> [en·sen·'der, en·θen-] I. *vi* to catch fire; (*motor*) to fire II. *vt* to switch on; (*cigarrillo*) to light III. *vr*: ~**se** 1. (*desencadenarse*) to break out 2. (*arder*) to ignite

encendido [en·sen·'di·do, en·θen-] *m* ignition

encendido, -a [en·sen·'di·do, -a; en·θen-] *adj* 1. (*conectado*) **estar ~** to be on 2. (*ardiente*) burning; (*cigarrillo*) lighted; (*apasionado*) passionate

encerado [en·se·'ra·do, en·θe·] *m* blackboard

encerar [en·se·'rar, en·θe·] *vt* to wax

encerrar <e → ie> [en·se·'rrar, en·θe·] **I.** *vt* to lock in [*o* up]; **~ entre paréntesis** to put in parentheses; (*contener*) to contain; **la oferta encerraba una trampa** the was a cacht to the offer **II.** *vr:* **~se** to lock oneself in

encerrona [en·se·'rro·na, en·θe·] *f* trap

encestar [en·se·'tar, en·θes·] *vi* to score a basket

enchastrar [en·tʃas·'trar] *vt* CSur to dirty

enchilada [en·tʃi·'la·da] *f* AmC enchilada

enchilado, -a [en·tʃi·'la·do, ·a] *adj* Méx **1.** (*bermejo*) ruddy **2.** (*colérico*) angry

enchilar [en·tʃi·'lar] **I.** *vt* AmC **1.** CULIN to season with chili **2.** (*molestar*) to annoy **3.** (*decepcionar*) to disappoint **II.** *vr:* **~se** AmC to blow one's top

enchinar [en·tʃi·'nar] Méx **I.** *vt* to curl **II.** *vr:* **~se 1.** (*escalofríos*) to get goose bumps **2.** (*acobardarse*) to be frightened

enchinchar [en·tʃin·'tʃar] **I.** *vt* **1.** Guat, RDom (*incomodar*) to annoy **2.** Méx **~ a alguien** to waste sb's time **II.** *vr:* **~se 1.** Arg (*malhumorarse*) to be in a bad mood **2.** Guat, Méx, Perú, PRico (*llenarse de chinches*) to be infested with bugs

enchironar [en·tʃi·ro·'nar] *vt* to throw in jail

enchivarse [en·tʃi·'βar·se] *vr* Col, Ecua to get furious

enchufar [en·tʃu·'far] *vt* **1.** ELEC to plug in **2.** TÉC to connect **3.** (*acoplar*) to couple **4. ~ a alguien** to get sth for sb by pulling strings

enchufe [en·'tʃu·fe] *m* **1.** (*clavija*) plug **2.** (*toma*) socket **3. tener ~** to have connections

enchutar [en·tʃu·'far] *vt* AmC to introduce; **~ de algo** to fill with sth

encía [en·'si·a, ·'θi·a] *f* gum

enciclopedia [en·si·klo·'pe·dja, en·θi·] *f* encyclopedia

enciclopédico, -a [en·si·klo·'pe·di·ko, ·a; en·θi·] *adj* encyclopedic

encierro [en·'sje·rro, ·'θje·rro] *m* (*reclu-*

sión) confinement; (*prisión*) imprisonment; (*aislamiento*) isolation

encima [en·'si·ma, ·'θi·ma] **I.** *adv* **1.** (*arriba: tocando*) on top; (*sin tocar*) above **2.** (*además*) besides; **te di el dinero y ~ una botella de vino** I gave you the money and a bottle of wine into the bargain **3.** *fig* **echarse ~ de alguien** to attack sb; **se nos echa el tiempo ~** time is running out; **quitarse algo de ~** (*librarse*) to get sth off one's back; **quitar a alguien un peso de ~** to take a weight off sb's mind; **tener algo ~** to be saddled with sth; **ya tenemos bastante ~** we have enough on our plate; **llevaba mucho dinero ~** he/she had a lot of money on him/her; **por ~ superficial(ly) II.** *prep* **1.** (*local: con contacto*) **~ de** on top of; **con queso ~** with cheese on top; **el libro está ~ de la mesa** the book is on the table; **el rascacielos está por ~ de la catedral** the skyscraper is higher than the cathedral; **estar ~ de alguien** *fig* to be on sb's case [*o* back] **2.** (*sin contacto*) **(por) ~ de** above; **por ~ de todo** above all; **por ~ de la media** above average **3.** (*con movimiento*) **(por) ~ de** over; **pon esto ~ de la cama** put this over the bed; **cuelga la lámpara ~ de la mesa** hang the light above the table; **¡por ~ de mí!** *fig* over my dead body!; **ése pasa por ~ de todo** *fig* he only cares about himself

encina [en·'si·na, en·'θi·] *f* holm oak

encinta [en·'sin·ta, ·'θin·ta] *adj* pregnant

enclave [en·'kla·βe] *m* enclave

enclenque [en·'klen·ke] *adj* (*enfermizo*) sickly; (*débil*) weak

encoger <g → j> [en·ko·'xer] **I.** *vi, vt* to shrink **II.** *vr:* **~se 1.** (*contraerse*) to contract; (*persona*) to cringe; **~se de hombros** to shrug one's shoulders **2.** (*reducirse*) to shrink

encolerizar <z → c> [en·ko·le·ri·'sar, ·'θar] **I.** *vt* to incense **II.** *vr:* **~se** to be incensed

encomendar <e → ie> [en·ko·men·'dar] *vt* to recommend; **~ algo a alguien** to entrust sth to sb

encomienda [en·ko·'mjen·da] *f* AmL parcel

encontrar <o → ue> [en·kon·'trar] I. vt 1. (hallar) to find 2. (considerar) to find II. vr: ~se 1. (estar) to be 2. (sentirse) to feel 3. ~se con alguien to meet sb; (casualmente) to run into sb 4. (hallar) to find; ~se con algo to come across sth

encontronazo [en·kon·tro·'na·so, -θo] m inf crash; (enfrentamiento) clash

encorvado, -a [en·kor·'βa·do, -a] adj hunched; (persona) stooped

encorvar [en·kor·'βar] I. vt to bend; (persona) to stoop II. vr: ~se to become bent; (madera) to warp; (persona) to become hunched

encuadernación [en·kwa·der·na·'sjon, -'θjon] f binding; (cubierta) cover

encuadernador(a) [en·kwa·der·na·'dor, -·'do·ra] m(f) bookbinder

encuadernar [en·kwa·der·'nar] vt to bind; sin ~ unbound

encuadrar [en·kwa·'drar] vt 1. to frame 2. (incluir) to include

encubierto, -a [en·ku·'bjer·to, -a] I. pp de **encubrir** II. adj una acusación **encubierta** a veiled accusation

encubrir [en·ku·'brir] irr como abrir vt (ocultar) to hide; (silenciar) to hush up; (escándalo, crimen) to cover up; (delincuente) to harbor

encuentro [en·'kwen·tro] m 1. (acción) encounter; **ir al ~ de alguien** to go to meet sb 2. (cita, reunión) meeting 3. DEP match

encuerado, -a [en·kwe·'ra·do, -a] adj Cuba, Méx 1. (desharrapado) shabby 2. (desnudo) naked

encuerar [en·kwe·'rar] vt, vr: ~se AmL to undress

encuerista [en·kwe·'ris·ta] mf AmL stripper

encuesta [en·'kwes·ta] f opinion poll

encularse [en·ku·'lar·se] vr Arg inf ~ **por algo** to get ticked off about sth

enculebrado, -a [en·ku·'le·bra·do, -a] adj Col inf indebted

encumbrar [en·kum·'brar] I. vt to raise; (socialmente) to elevate II. vr: ~se (elevarse) to rise; (engrandecerse) to be ennobled

endeble [en·'de·βle] adj (débil) weak;

(enfermizo) sickly

endémico, -a [en·'de·mi·ko, -a] adj endemic

endemoniado, -a [en·de·mo·'nja·do, -a] adj 1. (poseso) possessed 2. (malo) evil 3. inf (difícil) awful; (travieso) naughty

endenantes [en·de·'nan·tes] adv AmL inf a bit before

enderezar <z → c> [en·de·re·'sar, -'θar] vt to straighten; (corregir) to straighten out

endeudarse [en·deu·'dar·se] vr to get into debt

endiablado, -a [en·dja·'βla·do, -a] adj v. **endemoniado**

endibia [en·'di·βja] f endive

endilgar <g → gu> [en·dil·'γar] vt, **endiñar** [en·di·'ɲar] vt inf ~ **algo a alguien** to unload sth onto sb; **me ~on el trabajo sucio** I got stuck with the dirty work

endrogarse <g → gu> [en·dro·'γar·se] vr 1. AmL (drogarse) to take drugs 2. Méx, Perú (endeudarse) to get into debt

endulzar <z → c> [en·dul·'sar, -'θar] vt to sweeten

endurecer [en·du·re·'ser, -'θer] irr como crecer I. vt 1. (poner duro) to harden; TÉC to chill 2. (hacer resistente) to strengthen; (mente) to toughen; (persona) to inure II. vr: ~se 1. (ponerse duro) to get tough; (sentimientos) to become hardened 2. (hacerse resistente) to be strengthened 3. (agudizarse) to become more intense

endurecimiento [en·du·re·si·'mjen·to, -θi·'mjen·to] m 1. (dureza) hardness 2. (proceso) hardening 3. (resistencia) harshness

ene ['e·ne] adj inv ~ **veces** x times

eneldo [e·'nel·do] m dill

enema [e·'ne·ma] m enema

enemigo, -a [e·ne·'mi·γo, -a] I. adj enemy; **país ~** hostile country II. m, f enemy; DEP, POL opponent; ~ **acérrimo** sworn enemy; ~**s mortales** mortal enemies pl; **ser ~ de algo** to be opposed to sth

enemistad [e·ne·mis·'tad] f enmity; (hostilidad) animosity

enemistar [e·ne·mis·'tar] I. vt to make

enemies of **II.** *vr:* ~**se** to become enemies

energético, -a [e·ner·'xe·ti·ko, -a] *adj* energy; **valor** ~ calories

energía [e·ner·'xi·a] *f* energy; (*fuerza*) force; ~ **nuclear** nuclear energy; ~ **eólica** wind power; **con** ~ *fig* forcefully; **con toda su** ~ with all one's force; **sin** ~ *fig* feebly; **la energía da** ~ glucose gives you energy; **emplear todas las** ~**s en algo** to put all one's energies into sth

enérgico, -a [e·'ner·xi·ko, -a] *adj* energetic; (*decidido*) firm

energúmeno, -a [e·ner·'yu·me·no, -a] *m, f inf* berserk; **gritando como un** ~ shouting like a maniac

enero [e·'ne·ro] *m* January; *v. t.* **marzo**

enervante [e·ner·'βan·te] *adj* annoying

enésimo, -a [e·'ne·si·mo, -a] *adj* nth; **por enésima vez** for the umpteenth time

enfadar [en·fa·'dar] **I.** *vt* **1.** to anger; **estar enfadado con alguien** to be angry with sb **2.** *AmL* to bore **II.** *vr:* ~**se** to get angry; ~**se con alguien** to get angry with sb

enfado [en·'fa·do] *m* anger; (*molestia*) annoyance

énfasis ['en·fa·sis] *m inv* emphasis; (*insistencia*) insistence

enfático, -a [en·'fa·ti·ko, -a] *adj* emphatic; (*insistente*) insistent

enfatizar <z → c> [en·fa·ti·'sar, -'θar] *vt, vi* to emphasize

enfermar [en·fer·'mar] **I.** *vi, vr* to get sick **II.** *vt* to make sick

enfermedad [en·fer·me·'dad] *f* illness; (*específica*) disease

enfermería [en·fer·me·'ri·a] *f* infirmary

enfermero, -a [en·fer·'me·ro, -a] *m, f* nurse

enfermizo, -a [en·fer·'mi·so, -a; -'mi·θo, -a] *adj* sickly; (*morboso*) sick

enfermo, -a [en·'fer·mo, -a] **I.** *adj* ill; ~ **del corazón** suffering heart disease; ~ **de gravedad** seriously ill; **caer** ~ **de algo** to come down with sth; **ponerse** ~ to get ill; **esta situación me pone** ~ this situation is really getting me down **II.** *m, f* ill person; (*paciente*) patient

enfilar [en·fi·'lar] *vt* (*en fila*) to put in a row; (*en línea*) to line up

enfocar <c → qu> [en·fo·'kar] *vt* **1.** (*ajustar*) to focus; **mal enfocado** out of focus **2.** (*iluminar*) to shine light upon **3.** (*considerar*) to consider; (*cuestión*) to approach; **no enfocas bien el problema** you're not addressing the issue properly

enfoque [en·'fo·ke] *m* (*posición*) stance; (*planteamiento*) approach; (*concepción*) conception

enfrentamiento [en·fren·ta·'mjen·to] *m* confrontation; (*pelea*) fight; ~**s callejeros** street-fighting

enfrentar [en·fren·'tar] **I.** *vt* to face **II.** *vr:* ~**se 1.** (*encararse*) to come face to face **2.** (*hacer frente*) to face up to **3.** (*pelearse*) to fight; **estar enfrentado a alguien** to be up against sb

enfrente [en·'fren·te] **I.** *adv* opposite; **allí** ~ over there; **la casa de** ~ the house opposite; **tendrás a tu familia** ~ *fig* your family will be against you **II.** *prep* ~ **de** opposite; ~ **del teatro** opposite the theater; **vivo** ~ **del parque** I live opposite the park; **ponerse** ~ **de alguien** *fig* to be opposed to sb

enfriamiento [en·frja·'mjen·to] *m* cooling; (*catarro*) cold

enfriar <*l. pres* enfrío> [en·fri·'ar] **I.** *vi,* to cool (down) **II.** *vr:* ~**se 1.** (*perder calor*) to cool (down) **2.** (*calmarse*) to cool off **3.** (*acatarrarse*) to catch a cold

enfundar [en·fun·'dar] *vt* to sheathe; (*pistola*) to put back in the holster

enfurecer [en·fu·re·'ser, -'θer] *irr como* **crecer I.** *vt* to enrage **II.** *vr:* ~**se** to be furious

engajado, -a [en·ga·'xa·do, -a] *adj Col, CRi* curly

engalanar [en·ga·la·'nar] **I.** *vt* (*decorar*) to decorate; (*adornar*) to embellish **II.** *vr:* ~**se** to get dressed up

enganchar [en·gan·'tʃar] **I.** *vt* **1.** (*sujetar*) to hook; (*remolque*) to hitch up **2.** (*prender*) to catch on **3.** *inf* (*atrapar*) to catch; (*convencer*) to persuade **II.** *vr:* ~**se 1.** (*sujetarse*) ~**se de algo** to get hooked on sth **2.** (*prenderse*) ~**se de** [*o* **con**] **algo** to get caught on sth **3.** (*involucrarse*) to get caught up **4.** *inf* (*droga*) ~**se a** to get hooked on; **estar engan-**

chado to be hooked

enganche [en·ˈgan·tʃe] *m* **1.** (*gancho*) hook **2.** (*acto*) hooking

engañabobos [en·ga·ɲa·ˈβo·βos] *mf inv inf* con artist

engañar [en·ga·ˈɲar] **I.** *vi* to deceive; **las apariencias engañan** appearances can be deceptive **II.** *vt* **1.** (*desorientar*) to confuse **2.** (*mentir*) to deceive; (*estafar*) to cheat; **~ a alguien** (*ser infiel*) to cheat on sb; (*burlarse*) to laugh at sb; **~ el hambre** to stave off one's hunger; **dejarse ~** to fall for it **III.** *vr:* **~se** to deceive oneself; **¡no te engañes con esta oferta!** don't get all excited about this offer!

engañifa [en·ga·ˈɲi·fa] *f inf*, **engañifla** [en·ga·ˈɲi·fla] *f Chile* trap

engaño [en·ˈga·ɲo] *m* **1.** (*mentira*) deceit **2.** (*truco*) trick **3.** (*ilusión*) illusion

engañoso, -a [en·ga·ˈɲo·so, -a] *adj* misleading; **publicidad engañosa** false advertising; (*persona*) deceitful

engaratusar [en·ga·ra·tu·ˈsar] *vt AmC, Col* to coax

engarzar <z → c> [en·gar·ˈsar, -ˈθar] **I.** *vt* **1.** (*trabar*) to join together **2.** (*montar*) to set **II.** *vr:* **~se** to get caught up

engatusar [en·ga·tu·ˈsar] *vt* to sweet-talk; **~ a alguien para que haga algo** to coax sb into doing sth

engavetar [en·ga·βe·ˈtar] *vt Guat* to pigeon-hole

engendrar [en·xen·ˈdrar] *vt* to beget; *fig* to give rise to

engendro [en·ˈxen·dro] *m* freak

englobar [en·glo·ˈβar] *vt* (*incluir*) to comprise; (*reunir*) to bring together

engolillarse [en·go·li·ˈjar·se, -ˈʎar·se] *vr* **1.** *Cuba* (*endeudarse*) to get into debt **2.** *Perú* (*encolerizarse*) to lose one's temper

engomar [en·go·ˈmar] *vt* to put glue on; (*pelo*) to put gel on

engordar [en·gor·ˈdar] *vi* (*ponerse gordo*) to get fat; (*ganar peso*) to gain weight

engorroso, -a [en·go·ˈrro·so, -a] *adj* awkward; (*molesto*) bothersome

engranaje [en·gra·ˈna·xe] *m* cogs *pl;* TÉC gear

engrandecer [en·gran·de·ˈser, -ˈθer] *irr*

como crecer vt (*aumentar*) to increase; (*acrecentar*) to enlarge; (*exagerar*) to exaggerate

engrasar [en·gra·ˈsar] *vt* to grease; AUTO, TÉC to lubricate

engrase [en·ˈgra·se] *m* greasing; AUTO, TÉC lubrication

engreído, -a [en·gre·ˈi·do, -a] *adj* conceited; *AmL* (*mimado*) spoiled

engreír [en·gre·ˈir] *irr como reír vt AmL* to pamper

engrifarse [en·gri·ˈfar·se] *vr* **1.** *Col* (*volverse altivo*) to become arrogant **2.** *Méx* (*irritarse*) to get annoyed

engualichar [en·gwa·li·ˈtʃar] *vt Arg* **~ a alguien** to put a spell on sb; (*al amante*) to have power over sb

enguandocar [en·gwan·do·ˈkar] *vt Col* to adorn; (*recargar*) to overload

enguaraparse [en·gwa·ra·ˈpar·se] *vr AmC* to ferment

engullir <3. pret engulló> [en·gu·ˈjir, -ˈʎir] *vt* to swallow; (*devorar*) to devour; (*zamparse*) to gobble down

enharinar [en·a·ri·ˈnar] *vt* to coat with flour

enhebrar [en·e·ˈβrar] *vt* to thread

enhorabuena [en·o·ra·ˈβwe·na] *f* congratulations *pl;* **dar la ~ a alguien** to congratulate sb; **estar de ~** to be on top of the world

enigma [e·ˈniɣ·ma] *m* enigma; **descifrar/plantear un ~** to unravel/to pose an enigma

enigmático, -a [e·niɣ·ˈma·ti·ko, -a] *adj* enigmatic; (*misterioso*) mysterious

enjabonar [en·xa·βo·ˈnar] *vt* to soap

enjambre [en·ˈxam·bre] *m* swarm; *fig* throng

enjaular [en·xau·ˈlar] *vt* to cage

enjetarse [en·xe·ˈtar·se] *vr Arg, Méx* (*enojarse*) to get angry; (*ofenderse*) to take offense

enjuagar <g → gu> [en·xwa·ˈɣar] *vt* to rinse

enjuague [en·ˈxwa·ɣe] *m* rinse; **~ bucal** mouthwash

enjugamanos [en·xu·ɣa·ˈma·nos] *m inv AmL* hand-towel

enjugar <g → gu> [en·xu·ˈɣar] *vt, vr:* **~se** to dry

enjuiciar [en·xwi·ˈsjar, -ˈθjar] *vt* to analyze; JUR to prosecute

enjutarse [en·xu·ˈtar·se] *vr Guat, Ven* (*adelgazar*) to become thin; (*achicarse*) to get smaller; (*encoger*) to shrink

enjuto, -a [en·ˈxu·to, -a] *adj* scrawny

enlace [en·ˈla·se, -θe] *m* **1.** connection **2.** ELEC, FERRO, COMPUT link **3.** (*boda*) wedding

enlatados [en·la·ˈta·dos] *mpl Col* canned food

enlatar [en·la·ˈtar] *vt* to can; TV **enlatado** prerecorded

enlazar <z → c> [en·la·ˈsar, -ˈθar] **I.** *vi* to link up **II.** *vt* to tie; ELEC, TÉC to connect

enloquecer [en·lo·ke·ˈser, -ˈθer] *irr como* *crecer* **I.** *vi, vr:* ~**se** to go crazy; ~ **de** **dolor** to be in terrible pain; ~ **de rabia** to be a lunatic; ~ **por alguien** to be crazy about sb **II.** *vt* to drive crazy

enlozado [en·lo·ˈsa·do] *m AmL* glaze

enlozar <z → c> [en·lo·ˈsar] *vt AmL* to enamel

enmarcar <c → qu> [en·mar·ˈkar, em·mar·ˈkar] *vt* to frame

enmascarar [en·mas·ka·ˈrar, em·mas·ka·ˈrar] **I.** *vt* (*disfrazar*) to disguise; (*ocultar*) to hide; (*encubrir*) to cover up **II.** *vr:* ~**se** to disguise oneself; (*encubrirse*) to cover one's tracks

enmendar <e → ie> [en·men·ˈdar, em·men·ˈdar] **I.** *vt* (*corregir*) to correct; (*modificar*) to modify; JUR to amend **II.** *vr:* ~**se** to mend one's ways

enmicar [en·mi·ˈkar, em·mi·ˈkar] <c → qu> *vt Méx* to cover in plastic

enmienda [en·ˈmjen·da, em·ˈmjen·da] *f* JUR amendment

enmohecer [en·mo·e·ˈser, em·mo·e·ˈser; -ˈθer] *irr como crecer* *vi, vr:* ~**se** to go moldy

enmudecer [en·mu·de·ˈser, em·mu·de·ˈser; -ˈθer] *irr como crecer* **I.** *vi* to become speechless **II.** *vt* to silence

ennegrecer [en·ne·ɣre·ˈser, -ˈθer] *irr como crecer vt, vr:* ~**se** to blacken; (*oscurecer*) to darken

enojar [e·no·ˈxar] **I.** *vt* to anger **II.** *vr:* ~**se** to get angry

enojo [e·ˈno·xo] *m* anger

enojón, -ona [e·no·ˈxon, -·ˈxo·na] **I.** *adj* Chile, Ecua, Méx touchy **II.** *m, f* Chile, Ecua, Méx quick-tempered person

enojoso, -a [e·no·ˈxo·so, -a] *adj* annoying

enorgullecer [e·nor·ɣu·je·ˈser, -ʎe·ˈθer] *irr como crecer* **I.** *vt* to fill with pride **II.** *vr:* ~**se** to be proud

enorme [e·ˈnor·me] *adj* huge; *fig* remarkable

enrabiar [en·rra·ˈβjar] **I.** *vt* to enrage **II.** *vr:* ~**se** to lose one's temper

enraizado, -a [en·rrai·ˈsa·do, -a; -ˈθa·do, -a] *adj* rooted; (*tradición*) deep-seated

enrastrojarse [en·rras·tro·ˈxar·se] *vr AmL* to get dirty

enredadera [en·rre·da·ˈde·ra] *f* climbing plant

enredar [en·rre·ˈdar] **I.** *vt* (*liar*) to mix up; (*confundir*) to confuse **II.** *vr:* ~**se** (*cuerda, asunto*) to get mixed up; (*planta*) to climb

enredo [en·ˈrre·do] *m* tangle; (*engaño*) deceit

enrejado [en·rre·ˈxa·do] *m* grating

enrevesado, -a [en·rre·βe·ˈsa·do, -a] *adj* complicated; (*camino*) winding

enriquecer [en·rri·ke·ˈser, -ˈθer] *irr como crecer* **I.** *vt* to enrich **II.** *vr:* ~**se** to get rich

enriquecimiento [en·rri·ke·si·ˈmjen·to, -θi·ˈmjen·to] *m* enrichment

enrojecer [en·rro·xe·ˈser, -ˈθer] *irr como crecer vt, vi, vr:* ~**se** to redden; (*persona*) to blush

enrolar [en·rro·ˈlar] *vt* NÁUT to enroll; MIL to enlist

enrollar [en·rro·ˈjar, -ˈʎar] **I.** *vt* (*cartel*) to roll up; (*cuerda*) to coil **II.** *vr:* ~**se** *inf* **1.** (*tener rollo*) to go on and on **2.** (*ligar*) ~**se con alguien** to take up with sb **3.** (*ser guay*) to get on well

enroscar <c → qu> [en·rros·ˈkar] **I.** *vt* (*tornillo*) to screw in; (*tapa*) to twist on **II.** *vr:* ~**se** to curl up

enrostrar [en·rros·ˈtrar] *vt AmL* to throw in one's face

enrular [en·rru·ˈlar] *vt CSur* to curl

ensalada [en·sa·ˈla·da] *f* salad

ensaladera [en·sa·la·ˈde·ra] *f* salad bowl

ensalzar <z → c> [en·sal·ˈsar, -ˈθar] **I.** *vt*

to dignify **II.** vr: ~**se** to boast

ensamblar [en·sam·'blar] vt to assemble

ensanchar [en·san·'t∫ar] vt, vr: ~**se** to widen

ensanche [en·'san·t∫e] m widening

ensangrentar <e → ie> [en·san·gren·'tar] vt to cover in blood

ensartar [en·sar·'tar] vt **1.** (perlas) to string **2.** (pinchar) to skewer

ensayar [en·sa·'jar] vt to rehearse

ensayo [en·'sa·jo] m **1.** rehearsal; ~ **general** dress rehearsal **2.** LIT essay **3.** (prueba) test; (experimento) experiment

enseguida [en·se·'ɣi·da] adv right away

ensenada [en·se·'na·da] f **1.** inlet **2.** Arg (corral) meadow

enseñanza [en·se·'ɲan·sa, -θa] f **1.** (sistema) education; ~ **primaria/secundaria/superior/universitaria** primary/secondary/higher/university education; ~ **privada/pública** private/public education **2.** (docencia) teaching; ~ **a distancia** distance learning; ~ **universitaria** university education; **método de** ~ teaching method; **dedicarse a la** ~ to be a teacher **3.** (lección) lesson

enseñar [en·se·'ɲar] vt **1.** (dar clase) to teach; (explicar) to explain; **ella me enseñó a tocar la flauta** she taught me how to play the flute; **hay que** ~ **con el ejemplo** you have to lead by example; **¡la vida te** ~**á!** life is the best teacher!; **¡ya te** ~**é yo a obedecer!** I'll teach you to be obedient! **2.** (mostrar) to show; ~ **el camino a alguien** to show sb the way

enseres [en·'se·res] mpl belongings pl; (útiles) tools pl

ensimismarse [en·si·mis·'mar·se] vr **1.** to become absorbed; ~ **en recuerdos/una lectura** to become engrossed in one's memories/reading **2.** Col, Chile (engreírse) to become vain

ensombrecer [en·som·bre·'ser, -'θer] irr como crecer **I.** vt to darken; fig to cast a shadow over **II.** vr: ~**se** to darken; fig to become sad

ensopar [en·so·'par] **I.** vt AmS to soak **II.** vr: ~**se** AmS to get soaked

ensordecedor(a) [en·sor·de·se·'dor, -·'dor·; en·sor·de·θe·-] adj deafening

ensordecer [en·sor·de·'ser, -'θer] irr como crecer vi to go deaf

ensortijado, -a [en·sor·ti·'xa·do, -a] adj curly

ensuciar [en·su·'sjar, -'θjar] **I.** vt to dirty **II.** vr: ~**se** to get dirty; ~**se de algo** to be stained with sth

ensueño [en·'swe·ɲo] m dream; **de** ~ fantastic

entablar [en·ta·'βlar] vt (conversación) to strike up; (negociación) to begin; (amistad, comercio) to establish

entablillar [en·ta·βli·'jar, -'ʎar] vt to splint

entallado, -a [en·ta·'ja·do, -a; en·ta·'ʎa·do] adj fitted at the waist

entarimado [en·ta·ri·'ma·do] m floorboards pl

ente ['en·te] m (ser) being

entendederas [en·ten·de·'de·ras] fpl inf **es muy corto de** ~ he's pretty dumb

entender <e → ie> [en·ten·'der] **I.** vi **1.** (comprender) to understand; **si entiendo bien Ud. quiere decir que...** am I right in saying that what you mean is that... **2.** (saber) ~ **mucho de algo** to know a lot about sth; **no** ~ **nada de algo** to know nothing about sth **II.** vt **1.** (comprender) to understand (por by); **dar a** ~ **que...** to imply that...; **dar a** ~ **a alguien que...** to lead sb to believe that...; **lo entendieron mal** they misunderstood it; **¿qué entiende Ud. por 'acuerdo'?** what do you understand by 'agreement'?; **ellos ya se harán** ~ they'll soon make themselves understood; **no** ~ **ni jota/papa** inf not to understand a thing; **no entiende una broma** he/she can't take a joke **2.** (creer) to think; **yo entiendo que sería mejor si** +subj I think it would be better if; **yo no lo entiendo así** that's not the way I see it; **tengo entendido que...** (según creo) I believe that...; (según he oído) I've heard that... **III.** vr: ~**se 1.** (llevarse bien) to get on **2.** (ponerse de acuerdo) to agree; **para el precio entiéndete con mi socio** as regards the price, reach an agreement with my partner **3.** **¡yo me entiendo!** I know what I'm doing!; **¡que se las entienda!** let him/her get on with it!; **pero ¿cómo se entiende?** *inf* but what does it mean?; **eso se entiende por sí mismo** this is self-explanatory **IV.** *m* opinion; **a mi ~** the way I see it

entendido, -a [en·ten·'di·do, -a] **I.** *adj* clever; **~ en algo** expert on sth **II.** *m, f* expert; **hacerse el ~** to act smart

entendimiento [en·ten·di·'mjen·to] *m* **1.** (*razón*) reason; **obrar con ~** to go about things reasonably; **un hombre de mucho ~** a very reasonable man **2.** (*acuerdo*) agreement

enterado, -a [en·te·'ra·do, -a] *adj* **~ de algo** aware of sth; **yo ya estaba ~ del incidente** I already knew about the incident; **no se dio por ~** he pretended he didn't understand

enteramente [en·te·ra·'men·te] *adv* wholly

enterar [en·te·'rar] **I.** *vt* **1.** **~ de algo** to tell about sth **2.** *Méx, CRi, Hond* to pay **II.** *vr:* **~se de** (*descubrir*) to find out about; (*saber*) to hear about; **no me enteré de nada hasta que me lo dijeron** I wasn't aware of anything until they told me; **pasa las hojas sin ~se de lo que lee** he/she turns the pages without taking anything in; **¡para que se entere!** *inf* that'll teach him/her/you!; **para que te enteres...** for your information...

entereza [en·te·'re·sa, -'re·θa] *f* (*determinación*) strength (of mind); (*integridad*) integrity

enternecer [e·ter·ne·'ser, -'θer] *irr como* **crecer** **I.** *vt* to move **II.** *vr:* **~se** to be touched

entero, -a [en·'te·ro] *adj* whole; **el mundo ~** the whole world; **por ~** completely; **se pasa días ~s sin decir ni una palabra** he/she goes for days at a time without speaking; **el espejo salió ~ de aquí** when the mirror left here it was in one piece; **la comisión entera se declaró a favor** the whole committee declared themselves in favor; **el juego de café no está ~** some of the coffee service is missing

enterrador(a) [en·te·rra·'dor] *m(f)* gravedigger

enterrar <e → ie> [en·te·'rrar] *vt* to bury; (*poco profundo*) to cover up

enterratorio [en·te·rra·'to·rjo] *m AmS* Indian burial ground

entidad [en·ti·'dad] *f* organization; **~ aseguradora** insurance firm; **~ crediticia** credit company; **~ jurídica** legal entity; **~ bancaria** bank

entierro [en·'tje·rro] *m* burial; (*funeral*) funeral

entonación [en·to·na·'sjon, -'θjon] *f* intonation

entonar [en·to·'nar] **I.** *vi* **1.** (*canción*) to sing in tune **2.** (*armonizar*) to go well **II.** *vt* (*canción*) to sing

entonces [en·'ton·ses, -θes] *adv* then; **desde ~** from then on; **hasta ~** until then; **en** [*o* **por**] **aquel ~** at that time; **¿y ~ qué pasó?** and what happened next?; **¿pues ~ por qué no vienes?** then why don't you come?; **¡~!** well, then!

entornar [en·tor·'nar] *vt* to leave slightly open

entorno [en·'tor·no] *m* surroundings *pl*; (*medio ambiente*) environment; (*mundillo*) sphere

entorpecer [en·tor·pe·'ser, -'θer] *irr como* **crecer** *vt* (*dificultar*) to hamper; (*sentidos*) to dull

entrabar [en·tra·'βar] *vt AmS* to interfere

entrada [en·'tra·da] *f* **1.** (*puerta, acción*) entrance; **hacer una ~** to make an entrance; **~ trasera** back door; (*autopista*) (entry) ramp; **prohibida la ~** no entry **2.** (*comienzo*) entry; **~ en funciones** starting date; **~ en vigor** coming into force; **de ~** right from the start; **así de ~ tu idea no me pareció mal** at first your idea didn't strike me as bad **3.** (*ticket*) ticket; **~ gratuita** free entry; **en el estreno hubo una gran ~** the premiere was packed **4.** CULIN first course **5.** (*pelo*) **tiene ~s** his/her hair is receding **6.** **la ~ del coche** the down-payment on the car; **~s de dinero** income; **~s y salidas** income and costs **7.** COMPUT input

entrado, -a [en·'tra·do, -a] *adj* **~ en años** elderly; **entrada la noche** already dark

entrador(a) [en·tra·'dor, -·'do·ra] *adj*

1. AmS (*animoso*) spirited; (*atrevido*) daring **2.** Arg (*simpático*) friendly **3.** AmL (*enamoradizo*) romantic **4.** Chile (*entremetido*) interfering **5.** Guat, Nic (*compañero*) companionable

entramparse [en·tram·'par·se] *vr* to get into debt

entrante [en·'tran·te] **I.** *adj* next **II.** *m* starter

entrañable [en·tra·'na·βle] *adj* endearing; (*recuerdo*) fond

entrañar [en·tra·'nar] *vt* to involve; (*peligro*) to entail

entrañas [en·'tra·nas] *fpl* entrails *pl*; **en las ~ s de la tierra** in the bowels of the earth

entrar [en·'trar] **I.** *vi* **1.** (*pasar*) to enter; **~ por la ventana** to come in through the window; **~ por la fuerza** to break in; **el tren entra en la estación** the train enters the station; **me entró por un oído y me salió por otro** it went in one ear and out the other; **~ con buen pie** to start off on the right foot; **¡entre!** come in! **2.** (*caber*) to fit; **no me entra el anillo** I can't get the ring on; **el corcho no entra en la botella** the cork won't fit into the bottle; **por fin he hecho ~ el tapón** I finally got the lid on **3.** (*penetrar*) to go in; **el clavo entró en la pared** the nail went into the wall; **¡no me entra en la cabeza!** I can't understand it! **4.** (*empezar*) to begin; **~ en relaciones** to start a relationship; **el verano entra el 21 de junio** summer begins on the 21st of June; **después entré a trabajar en una casa más rica** afterwards I started working in a wealthier household; **cuando entró de alcalde** when he was elected mayor; **no ~ en detalles** not to go into details; **~ en calor** to warm up; **~ en vigor** to come into force; **me entró la tentación** I was tempted; **me entró un mareo** I became dizzy; **me entró el hambre** I became hungry **5.** (*como miembro*) **~ en algo** to become a member of sth; **~ en la Academia de Ciencias** to be admitted to the Royal Academy of Science **6.** (*formar parte*) **en un kilo en-** **tran tres panochas** you can get three corncobs to the kilo; **eso no entraba en mis cálculos** I hadn't planned on this **7.** COMPUT to access **8.** (*dar*) **esperemos que no te entre la gripe** we hope you don't get the flu; **le ha entrado la costumbre de...** he/she's gotten into the habit of... **9.** *inf* (*entender*) **las matemáticas no me entran** I can't get the hang of mathematics **10.** *inf* (*soportar*) **su hermano no me entra** I can't stand his/her brother **11.** *inf* (*relacionarse, tratar*) **no sabe ~ a las chicas** he doesn't know how to pick up girls; **a él no sabes como ~le** you don't know how to deal with him **12.** (*opinar*) **yo en eso no entro** [*o* **ni entro ni salgo**] *inf* I have nothing to do with this **II.** *vt* to put; **~ el coche en el garaje** to put the car into the garage

entre ['en·tre] *prep* **1.** (*dos cosas*) between; (*más de dos cosas*) among; **salir de ~ las ramas** to emerge from the branches; **pasar por ~ las mesas** to go between the tables; **~ semana** during the week; **ven ~ las cinco y las seis** come between five and six; **~ tanto** meanwhile; **lo cuento ~ mis amigos** I consider him as one of my friends; **un ejemplo ~ muchos** one of many examples; **el peor ~ todos** the worst of the lot; **llegaron veinte ~ hombres y mujeres** twenty men and women arrived; **se la llevaron ~ cuatro hombres** she was carried off by four men; **lo hablaremos ~ nosotros** we'll talk it over with each other; **~ el taxi y la entrada me quedé sin dinero** what with the taxi and the ticket I had no money left; **¡guárdalo ~ los libros!** keep it with your books; **me senté ~ los dos** I sat down between the two of them **2.** MAT **ocho ~ dos son cuatro** eight divided by two is four

entreabierto, -a [en·tre·a·'βjer·to, -a] *adj* ajar

entreabrir [en·tre·a·'βrir] *irr como* **abrir** *vt* to open slightly

entreacto [en·tre·'ak·to] *m* interval

entrecejo [en·tre·'sexo, -'θe·xo] *m* brow

entrecomillar [en·tre·ko·mi·'jar, -'ʎar] *vt*

to put in quotes

entrecortado, -a [en·tre·kor·'ta·do, -a] *adj* (*respiración*) uneven; (*voz*) halting

entrecruzar <z → c> [en·tre·kru·'sar, -'θar] *vt, vr*: ~**se** to interweave; (*miradas*) to cross

entredicho [en·tre·'di·tʃo] *m* **poner algo en ~** to cast doubt on sth

entrega [en·'tre·ɣa] *f* **1.** (*dedicación*) dedication **2.** (*fascículo*) installment; **novela por ~s** serialized novel **3.** (*reparto*) delivery; **~ de premios** giving of prizes; **~ de títulos** UNIV graduation ceremony; **hacer ~ de algo** to hand sth over; **~ a domicilio** home delivery; **talón de ~** delivery sheet; **pagadero a la ~** payable on delivery; **~ contra reembolso** collect on delivery

entregar <g → gu> [en·tre·'ɣar] **I.** *vt* (*dar*) to give; (*correos*) to deliver **II.** *vr*: ~**se** to surrender; ~**se a la bebida** to take to drink; ~**se a la policía** to give oneself up

entrelazar <z → c> [en·tre·la·'sar, -'θar] *vt, vr*: ~**se** to (inter)weave

entremedias [en·tre·'me·djas] *adv* **1.** (*local*) between **2.** (*temporal*) meanwhile

entremeses [en·tre·'me·ses] *mpl* appetizers *pl*

entremeterse [en·tre·me·'ter·se, -'θer·se] *vr* to interfere

entremetido, -a [en·tre·me·'ti·do, -a] **I.** *adj* interfering **II.** *m, f* busybody

entremezclar [en·tre·mes·'klar, en·tre·meθ-] *vt* to intermingle

entrenador(a) [en·tre·na·'dor] *m(f)* coach

entrenamiento [en·tre·na·'mjen·to] *m* training

entrenar [en·tre·'nar] *vt, vr*: ~**se** to train

entrepierna [en·tre·'pjer·na] *f* **1.** crotch **2.** *Chile* swimsuit

entresacar <c → qu> [en·tre·sa·'kar] *vt* to pick out

entresuelo [en·tre·'swe·lo] *m* mezzanine

entretanto [en·tre·'tan·to] *adv* meanwhile

entretecho [en·tre·'te·tʃo] *m CSur* attic

entretejer [en·tre·te·'xer] *vt* to interweave

entretener [en·tre·te·'ner] *irr como tener*

I. *vt* **1.** (*divertir*) to entertain **2.** (*distraer*) to distract **II.** *vr*: ~**se 1.** (*divertirse*) to amuse oneself **2.** (*tardar*) to delay; **¡no se entretenga!** don't dilly dally! **3.** (*distraerse*) to be distracted

entretenido, -a [en·tre·te·'ni·do, -a] *adj* entertaining

entretenimiento [en·tre·te·ni·'mjen·to] *m* entertainment; (*pasatiempo*) activity

entretiempo [en·tre·'tjem·po] *m* between season

entrever [en·tre·'βer] *irr como ver* *vt* to glimpse; (*sospechar*) to surmise

entrevero [en·tre·'βe·ro] *m CSur* **1.** (*confusión*) jumble **2.** (*riña*) brawl **3.** (*escaramuza*) skirmish

entrevista [en·tre·'βis·ta] *f* **1.** (*prensa, trabajo*) interview **2.** (*reunión*) meeting

entrevistar [en·tre·βis·'tar] **I.** *vt* to interview **II.** *vr*: ~**se** to have a meeting

entristecer [en·tris·te·'ser, -'θer] *irr como crecer* **I.** *vt* to sadden **II.** *vr*: ~**se** to be saddened

entrometerse [en·tro·me·'ter·se] *vr* to interfere

entrometido, -a [en·tro·me·'ti·do, -a] *adj, m, f* v. **entremetido**

entroncar <c → qu> [en·tron·'kar] *vi AmL* to connect

entronque [en·'tron·ke] *m AmL* connection

entrucharse [en·tru·'tʃar·se] *vr Méx* ~ **en algo** to interfere with sth; ~ **de alguien** to fall in love with sb

entuerto [en·'twer·to] *m* offense

entumecerse [en·tu·me·'ser·se, -'θer·se] *irr como crecer* *vr* to stiffen; (*de frío*) to go numb

entumecido, -a [en·tu·me·'si·do, -a; -'θi·do, -a] *adj* stiff; (*de frío*) numb

enturbiar [en·tur·'βjar] *vt* to darken

entusiasmar [en·tu·sjas·'mar] **I.** *vt* to enthuse **II.** *vr*: ~**se** to get enthusiastic

entusiasmo [en·tu·'sjas·mo] *m* enthusiasm

entusiasta [en·tu·'sjas·ta] **I.** *adj* enthusiastic **II.** *mf* enthusiast

enumeración [e·nu·me·ra·'sjon, -'θjon] *f* enumeration

enumerar [e·nu·me·'rar] *vt* to enumerate

enunciado [e·nun·'sja·do, -'θja·do] *m* setting out

enunciar [e·nun·'sjar, -'θjar] *vt* to set out; (*expresar*) to state

envasar [em·ba·'sar] *vt* to package; (*en latas*) to can; (*en botellas*) to bottle

envase [em·'ba·se] *m* **1.** (*paquete*) package; (*recipiente*) container; (*botella*) bottle **2.** (*acción*) packing; ~ **al vacío** vacuum packing

envejecer [em·be·xe·'ser, -'θer] *irr como* **crecer** *vt, vr:* ~**se** to age

envenenar [em·be·ne·'nar] *vt* to poison

envergadura [em·ber·ya·'du·ra] *f* magnitude; **de gran** ~ far-reaching

envés [em·'bes] *m* back

enviado, -a [em·bi·'a·do, -a] *m, f* envoy; ~ **especial** special correspondent

enviar <*1. pres* envío> [em·bi·'ar] *vt* to send; ~ **por correo** to mail

envidia [em·'bi·dja] *f* envy; **tener** ~ **a alguien** to envy sb; **tener** ~ **de algo** to be jealous of sth; **daba** ~ **verlo de lo guapo que iba** it made me envious to see how handsome he looked; **lo corroe la** ~ he is eaten up by jealousy

envidiable [em·bi·'dja·βle] *adj* enviable

envidiar [em·bi·'djar] *vt* to envy

envidioso, -a [em·bi·'djo·so, -a] *adj* envious

envío [em·'bi·o] *m* sending; ~ **a domicilio** home delivery; ~ **contra reembolso** cash on delivery; ~ **urgente** urgent delivery; ~ **con valor declarado** declared value delivery; **gastos de** ~ shipping and handling

enviudar [em·bju·'dar] *vi* to be widowed

envoltorio [em·bol·'to·rjo] *m* wrapping

envoltura [em·bol·'tu·ra] *f* (*capa exterior*) covering

envolver [em·bol·'βer] *irr como* **volver** *vt* (*en papel*) to wrap; ~ **con** [*o* **en**] **algo** to wrap up in sth; ~ **para regalo** to gift-wrap

envuelto, -a [em·'bwel·to] *pp de* **envolver**

enyesar [en·je·'sar] *vt* to plaster

enzarzar [en·sar·'sar, -θar·'θar] *vr:* ~**se en** to get entangled in

enzima [en·'si·ma, -'θi·ma] *m o f* enzyme

eólico, -a [e·'o·li·ko, -a] *adj* wind; **central eólica** wind power plant

epa ['e·pa] *interj AmL* (*saludo*) hi!; (*llamada*) hey!; (*accidente*) (wh)oops!

épica ['e·pi·ka] *f* epic

epicentro [e·pi·'sen·tro, -'θen·tro] *m* epicenter

épico, -a ['e·pi·ko, -a] *adj* epic

epidemia [e·pi·'de·mja] *f* epidemic

epidermis [e·pi·'der·mis] *f inv* epidermis

epilepsia [e·pi·'leβ·sja] *f* epilepsy

epiléptico, -a [e·pi·'lep·ti·ko, -a] *adj, m, f* epileptic

epílogo [e·'pi·lo·yo] *m* epilog(ue)

episodio [e·pi·'so·djo] *m* episode; (*etapa*) stage

época ['e·po·ka] *f* **1.** time; ~ **de lluvias** rainy season; **es la** ~ **más calurosa del año** it is the hottest time of the year; **en aquella** ~ at that time **2.** HIST age; **coches de** ~ classic cars *pl;* **muebles de** ~ antique furniture; **trajes de** ~ period costumes *pl;* **un invento que hizo** ~ a revolutionary invention

epopeya [e·po·'pe·ja] *f* epic

equidad [e·ki·'dad] *f* fairness; (*precios*) equity

equilibrado, -a [e·ki·li·'βra·do, -a] *adj* balanced; (*sensato*) sensible

equilibrar [e·ki·li·'βrar] *vt, vr:* ~**se** to balance

equilibrio [e·ki·li·'βrjo] *m* balance; **mantener/perder el** ~ to keep/lose one's balance

equilibrista [e·ki·li·'βris·ta] *mf* tightrope artist

equino, -a [e·'ki·no] *adj* equine

equipaje [e·ki·'pa·xe] *m* baggage, luggage; **entrega de** ~**s** baggage check-in; **exceso de** ~ excess baggage; **registro de** ~ baggage inspection; **hacer el** ~ to pack; ~ **de mano** hand baggage

equipal [e·ki·'pal] *m Méx* (*de mimbre*) rustic wicker chair; (*de cuero*) leather chair

equipamiento [e·ki·pa·'mjen·to] *m* ~ **de serie** standard equipment

E

equipar [e·ki·'par] *vt* to equip

equiparable [e·ki·pa·'ra·βle] *adj* comparable

equiparar [e·ki·pa·'rar] *vt* **1.** (*igualar*) to put on the same level **2.** (*comparar*) to compare

equipo [e·'ki·po] *m* **1.** (*de personas*) team; **~ gestor** management team; **~ de investigadores** research team; **trabajo en ~** teamwork; **carrera por ~s** team race; **el ~ de casa/de fuera** the home/visiting team **2.** (*utensilios*) equipment; **~ de alta fidelidad** hi-fi system; **~ productivo** productive equipment; **bienes de ~** capital goods

equis ['e·kis] *inv* **I.** *adj* X; **~ dólares** X number of dollars **II.** *f* Col snake

equitación [e·ki·ta·'sjon, -'θjon] *f* horseback riding

equitativamente [e·ki·ta·ti·βa·'men·te] *adv* equitably

equitativo, -a [e·ki·ta·'ti·βo, -a] *adj* equitable; **hicieron un reparto ~ de las ganancias** they split the profits equally

equivalencia [e·ki·βa·'len·sja, -'θja] *f* equivalence

equivalente [e·ki·βa·'len·te] **I.** *adj* equivalent (**a** to) **II.** *m* equivalent (**a/de** of)

equivaler [e·ki·βa·'ler] *irr como valer vi* to be equivalent (**a** to); **lo que equivale a decir que...** which is the same as saying that...

equivocación [e·ki·βo·ka·'sjon, -'θjon] *f* mistake; (*error*) error; **por ~** by mistake

equivocado, -a [e·ki·βo·'ka·ðo, -a] *adj* mistaken; **número ~** wrong number

equivocar <c → qu> [e·ki·βo·'kar] **I.** *vt* **1.** (*confundir*) to get wrong; **equivoqué los sobres de las cartas** I got the envelopes for the letters mixed up **2.** (*desconcertar*) to throw **II.** *vr:* **~se** to be wrong; **~se en** [o *de*] **algo** to be wrong about sth; **~se de camino** to take the wrong way; **~se al escribir/al hablar** to make a mistake (when) writing/when speaking; **~se al leer** to misread; **~se de número** (**de teléfono**) to dial the wrong number; **~se de tranvía** to take the wrong tram; **~se de puerta** to take the wrong door

equívoco [e·'ki·βo·ko] *m* (*doble sentido*) ambiguity; (*malentendido*) misunderstanding

era¹ ['e·ra] *f* era

era² ['e·ra] *3. imp de* **ser**

erección [e·rek·'sjon, -rey·'θjon] *f* **1.** (*del pene*) erection **2.** (*de monumentos*) building

erecto, -a [e·'rek·to, -a] *adj* erect; (*cuerpo*) upright

eres ['e·res] *2. pres de* **ser**

erguido, -a [er·'ɣi·ðo, -a] *adj* upright

erigir <g → j> [e·ri·'xir] *vt* **1.** (*construir*) to build **2.** (*fundar*) to establish

erizado, -a [e·ri·'sa·ðo, -a; e·ri·'θa-] *adj* on end

erizarse <z → c> [e·ri·'sar·se, -'θar·se] *vr* (*pelo*) to stand on end

erizo [e·'ri·so, -θo] *m* hedgehog; **~ de mar** sea urchin

ermita [er·'mi·ta] *f* hermitage

ermitaño [er·mi·'ta·ɲo] *m* hermit crab

erogación [e·ro·ɣa·'sjon, -'θjon] *f* **1.** *Arg, Méx, Par* (*pago*) costs *pl* **2.** *Ven, Col* (*donativo*) contribution

erogar <g → gu> [e·ro·'ɣar] *vt Arg, Col* (*pagar*) to pay

erógeno, -a [e·'ro·xe·no, -a] *adj* erogenous

erosión [e·ro·'sjon] *f* GEO erosion

erosionar [e·ro·sjo·'nar] *vt* **1.** (*desgastar*) to wear away **2.** GEO to erode

erótico, -a [e·'ro·ti·ko, -a] *adj* erotic

erotismo [e·ro·'tis·mo] *m* eroticism

erradicar <c → qu> [e·rra·di·'kar] *vt* to eradicate; (*enfermedad*) to stamp out

errar [e·'rrar] *irr vi* **1.** **~ en algo** to make a mistake in sth; **~ en la respuesta** to give the wrong answer; **~ en el camino** to take the wrong road; *fig* to make the wrong choice; (*vagar*) to wander; **~ por algo** to roam around sth; **ir errando por las calles** to wander the streets

errata [e·'rra·ta] *f* errata

erróneo, -a [e·'rro·ne·o, -a] *adj* erroneous *form*, wrong

error [e·'rror] *m* **1.** (*falta*) fault; **~ de cálculo** miscalculation; **~ de operación** COMPUT operative error; **~ ortográfico** spelling mistake; **~ freudiano** Freudian slip; **cometer un ~** to make a mistake; **has cometido un ~ muy grave** you have made a very serious mistake **2.** (*equivocación*) mistake; (*descuido*) oversight; **estar en el ~** to be wrong; **por ~** by mistake; **~ judicial** miscarriage of justice; **~ de imprenta** misprint **3.** FÍS, MAT error

eructar [e·ruk·'tar] *vi* to burp

eructo [e·'ruk·to] *m* burp

erudito, -a [e·ru·'di·to, -a] **I.** *adj* erudite; (*obra*) scholarly **II.** *m, f* scholar

erupción [e·rup·'sjon, -ruβ·'θjon] *f* **1.** GEO eruption **2.** MED rash

es [es] *3. pres de* **ser**

esa(s) ['e·sa(s)] *adj, pron dem v.* **ese, -a**

ésa(s) ['e·sa(s)] *pron dem v.* **ése**

esbelto, -a [es·'βel·to, -a] *adj* slender; **un hombre ~** a well-proportioned man

esbozar <z → c> [es·βo·'sar, -'θar] *vt* to sketch

esbozo [es·'βo·so, -θo] *m* sketch; (*de un proyecto*) outline

escabechar [es·ka·βe·'tʃar] *vt* to marinate

escabeche [es·ka·'βe·tʃe] *m* marinade; **en ~** marinated; (*pescado*) pickled

escabroso, -a [es·ka·'βro·so, -a] *adj* (*terreno*) uneven; (*asunto*) thorny

escabullirse <3. pret se escabulló> [es·ka·βu·'ʝir·se, -'ʎir·se] *vr* to slip away

escacharrar [es·ka·tʃa·'rrar] *vt, vr:* **~se** *inf* to break (down)

escafandra [es·ka·'fan·dra] *f* diving suit; (*espacial*) space suit

escala [es·'ka·la] *f* **1.** *t.* MÚS scale; **~ de colores** range of colors, color scale; **~ de cuotas** payment scale; **~ de descuentos** range of discounts; **~ de grados** degree scale; **~ impositiva** tax bracketing; **~ de reproducción** scale of reproduction; **~ de Richter** Richter scale; **~ de salarios** salary scale; **~ de valores** set of values; **a ~** to scale; **hacer ~s** to do scales; **un mapa a 1:100.000** a map with a scale of 1:100,000; **~ milimétrica** millimeter scale **2.** (*medida*) level; **a ~ mundial** on a world scale; **a ~ nacional** on a national scale; **en gran ~** on a large scale; **comprar en gran ~** to buy in bulk; **fabricación en gran ~** large-scale production; **ser de mayor ~** to be on a large

scale **3.** (*parada*) stop; AVIAT stopover; **~ forzada** forced landing; **el avión tuvo que hacer ~ en París** the plane had to land in Paris; **hacer ~ en un puerto** to make a stop at a port **4.** (*escalera*) ladder; **~ de cuerda** rope ladder

escalada [es·ka·'la·da] *f* climb; **~ libre** free climbing; **~ en roca** rock climbing; **se produjo una ~ de la violencia** there was an escalation of violence

escalar [es·ka·'lar] *vt, vi* to climb

escaldado, -a [es·kal·'da·do, -a] *adj* scalded; **salir ~** to learn one's lesson

escaldadura [es·kal·da·'du·ra] *f* Arg chafing

escalera [es·ka·'le·ra] *f* **1.** (*escalones*) staircase, stairs; AVIAT stairway; **~ abajo** downstairs; **~ arriba** upstairs; **~ de caracol** spiral staircase; **~ mecánica** [*o* **automática**] escalator; **~ de servicio** service stairs **2.** (*escala*) ladder; **~ de bomberos** firemen's ladder; **~ de cuerda** rope ladder; **~ doble** stepladder; **~ de incendios** fire escape; **~ de mano** ladder; **~ de tijera** stepladder; **subir la ~** to go up the ladder **3.** (*naipes*) run; **~ de color real** royal flush

escalinata [es·ka·li·'na·ta] *f* staircase

escalofriante [es·ka·lo·'frjan·te] *adj* chilling; (*película*) scary

escalofrío [es·ka·lo·'fri·o] *m* chill; MED shiver; **al abrir la ventana sentí ~s** I felt a chill when I opened the window; **el libro me produjo ~s** the book sent shivers down my spine; **cierra la puerta, tengo ~s** close the door, I feel chilly

escalón [es·ka·'lon] *m* step; (*peldaño*) rung; **subir un ~** *fig* to move up the ladder; **este libro es un ~ hacia el éxito** this book is a stepping stone on the way to success; **descender un ~ en la opinión pública** to go down in the eyes of the public

escalonado, -a [es·ka·lo·'na·do, -a] *adj* terraced; (*tarifa*) graded

escalope [es·ka·'lo·pe] *m* escalope

escalpelo [es·kal·'pe·lo] *m* scalpel

escama [es·'ka·ma] *f* scale

escamado, -a [es·ka·'ma·do] *adj inf* cautious

escamar [es·ka·'mar] **I.** *vt* **1.** (*pescado*)

to scale **2.** *inf* to make suspicious **II.** *vr:* ~**se** *inf* to smell a rat

escamocha [es·ka·'mo·tʃa] *f Méx* leftovers *pl*

escampar [es·kam·'par] *vimpers* **espera hasta que escampe** wait until it clears

escandalizar <z → c> [es·kan·da·li·'sar, -'θar] **I.** *vt* to shock **II.** *vr:* ~**se** to be shocked (**de/por** by)

escándalo [es·'kan·da·lo] *m* **1.** scandal; ~ **público** public scandal; **causar** ~ to cause a scandal; **la piedra del** ~ the root of the scandal; **estos precios son un** ~ these prices are outrageous; **tu comportamiento es un** ~ your behavior is a disgrace; **de** ~ scandalous; **¡qué** ~**!** can you believe it? **2.** (*ruido*) uproar; **armar un** [*o* **dar el**] ~ to make a scene; **se armó un** ~ there was a terrible uproar

escandaloso, -a [es·kan·da·'lo·so, -a] *adj* **1.** (*ruidoso*) noisy **2.** (*inmoral*) scandalous **3.** (*precios*) outrageous

Escandinavia [es·kan·di·'na·βja] *f* Scandinavia

escandinavo, -a [es·kan·di·'na·βo, -a] *adj, m, f* Scandinavian

escanear [es·ka·ne·'ar] *vt* to scan

escáner [es·'ka·ner] *m* scanner

escaño [es·'ka·ɲo] *m* seat

escapada [es·ka·'pa·da] *f* escape

escapar [es·ka·'par] **I.** *vi* to escape; (*ocultamente*) to get away; **logré** ~ I managed to escape; **es imposible** ~ **a esta ley** it is impossible to dodge this law; ~ **de casa** to run away from home **II.** *vr:* ~**se 1.** to escape; (*ocultamente*) to get away; (*agua, gas*) to leak; ~**se de casa** to run away from home; **algunas cosas se escapan al poder de la voluntad** some things are beyond one's power; **no se te escapa ni una** you don't miss a thing **2.** (*sin querer*) **se me ha escapado que te vas a casar** I let it slip that you were getting married; **se escapó un tiro** a shot was let loose; **se me ha escapado su nombre** I've forgotten your name; **se me ha escapado el autobús** I missed the bus; **se me ha escapado la mano** my hand slipped; **se me ha escapado la risa** I couldn't help

laughing; **se me escapó un suspiro** I let out a sigh

escaparate [es·ka·pa·'ra·te] *m* **1.** shop window **2.** *AmL* (*armario*) dresser

escapatoria [es·ka·pa·'to·rja] *f* way out

escape [es·'ka·pe] *m* leak

escarabajo [es·ka·ra·'βa·xo] *m* beetle

escaramuza [es·ka·ra·'mu·sa, -θa] *f* skirmish

escarapelar [es·ka·ra·pe·'lar] **I.** *vt* **1.** *Col, CRi, Méx* (*descascarar*) to peel **2.** *Col* (*manosear*) to handle; ~ **de viviendas** to wear out **II.** *vr:* ~**se** *Méx, Perú* **1.** (*atemorizarse*) to be scared **2.** (*temblar*) to shudder

escarbar [es·kar·'βar] *vi, vt* ~ (**en**) **algo** to dig sth; *fig* to investigate sth

escarcha [es·'kar·tʃa] *f* frost

escarlata [es·kar·'la·ta] *adj* scarlet

escarmentar <e → ie> [es·kar·men·'tar] **I.** *vi* to learn one's lesson **II.** *vt* to punish

escarmiento [es·kar·'mjen·to] *m* lesson

escarola [es·ka·'ro·la] *f* curly endive, escarole

escarpado, -a [es·kar·'pa·do, -a] *adj* rugged

escasamente [es·ka·sa·'men·te] *adv* scarcely

escasear [es·ka·se·'ar] *vi* to be scarce

escasez [es·ka·'ses, -'seθ] *f* shortage; ~ **de lluvias** lack of rain; ~ **de viviendas** housing shortage; **una región con** ~ **de agua** a region with scarce rainfall; **vivir con** ~ to live in need

escaso, -a [es·'ka·so, -a] *adj* insufficient; ~ **de palabras** of few words; **viento** ~ light wind; **andar** ~ **de dinero** to be short of money; **estar** ~ **de tiempo** to be short of time; **tener escasas posibilidades de ganar** to have little chance of winning; **en dos horas escasas** in only two hours

escatimar [es·ka·ti·'mar] *vt* to skimp

escayola [es·ka·'jo·la] *f* plaster; *MED* cast

escayolar [es·ka·jo·'lar] *vt* to put a cast on; **un brazo escayolado** an arm in a cast

escena [e·'se·na, es·'θe-] *f* **1.** (*parte del teatro*) stage; **aparecer en** ~ to appear on stage; **poner en** ~ to stage; **puesta**

en ~ staging; **salir a la ~** to go on stage; **salir de la ~** to go off stage **2.** (*lugar, parte de una obra*) scene; **~ final** final scene; **~ del crimen** scene of the crime; **desaparecer de ~** (*marcharse*) to leave the scene; (*morirse*) to pass away; **poner en ~** to put on stage; **salir a ~** (*aparecer*) to make an appearance **3.** (*arte*) theater; **dedicarse a la ~** to devote oneself to the stage **4.** LIT scene **5.** (*suceso, reproche*) scene; **~ de celos** display of jealousy; **hacer una ~ ridícula** to make a ridiculous scene

escenario [es·e·'na·rjo, es·'θe·-] *m* **1.** scene; **~ del crimen** scene of the crime; **un cambio de ~** a change of scene **2.** TEAT stage

escénico, -a [e·'se·ni·ko, -a; es·'θe·] *adj* stage

escepticismo [es·ep·ti·'sis·mo, es·θep·ti·'θis-] *m* skepticism

escéptico, -a [e·'sep·ti·ko, -a; es·'θep-] **I.** *adj* skeptical **II.** *m, f* skeptic

escindirse [e·sin·'dir·se, es·θin-] *vr* to split (**en** into)

escisión [e·si·'sjon, es·θi-] *f* MED excision

esclarecer [es·kla·re·'ser, -'θer] *irr como crecer* *vt* to clear up; (*crimen, misterio*) to shed light upon

esclarecimiento [es·kla·re·si·'mjen·to, -θi·'mjen·to] *m* explanation

esclavitud [es·kla·βi·'tud] *f* slavery

esclavizar <z → c> [es·kla·βi·'sar, -'θar] **I.** *vt* to enslave **II.** *vr:* **~se** to become a slave

esclavo, -a [es·'kla·βo, -a] **I.** *adj* slave; (*dominado*) dependent; (*obediente*) obedient; **eres esclava de tu familia** you do everything your family wants; **ser ~ del alcohol** to be a slave to alcohol **II.** *m, f* slave; **ser un ~ de algo** *fig* to be dependent on sth

escoba [es·'ko·βa] *f* broom

escobazo [es·ko·'βa·so, -θo] *m* Arg, Chile **dar un ~ al suelo** to give the floor a quick sweep

escobilla [es·ko·'βi·ja, -ʎa] *f* brush

escobillar [es·ko·βi·'jar, -'ʎar] *vi* AmL to tap or shuffle the feet

escocer [es·ko·'ser, -'θer] *irr como cocer* *vi* to sting

escocés [es·ko·'ses, -'θes] *m* (Scottish) Gaelic; (*whisky*) Scotch

escocés, -esa [es·ko·'ses, -·'se·sa; -'θes, -·'θe·sa] **I.** *adj* Scottish **II.** *m, f* Scot, Scotsman, Scotswoman *m, f*

Escocia [es·'ko·sja, -θja] *f* Scotland

escoger <g → j> [es·ko·'xer] *vi, vt* to choose; **no has sabido ~** you've made the wrong choice

escogido, -a [es·ko·'xi·do, -a] *adj* finest; **estos plátanos están ya muy ~s** all the good bananas are gone

escolar [es·ko·'lar] **I.** *adj* academic; **curso ~** academic year; **edad ~** school age **II.** *mf* schoolboy, schoolgirl *m, f*

escolaridad [es·ko·la·ri·'dad] *f* schooling; **la ~ es obligatoria** education is compulsory

escolarización [es·ko·la·ri·sa·'sjon, -θa·'θjon] *f* education

escolarizar <z → c> [es·ko·la·ri·'sar, -'θar] *vt* to educate

escollar [es·ko·'jar, -'ʎar] *vi* Arg, Chile to fail

escollo [es·'ko·jo, -ʎo] *m* pitfall

escolta [es·'kol·ta] *f* t. MIL escort; (*guardaespaldas*) bodyguard; (*guardia*) guard

escoltar [es·kol·'tar] *vt* to escort

escombro(s) [es·'kom·bro(s)] *m(pl)* rubble; **hacer ~** Arg to exaggerate

esconder [es·kon·'der] *vt, vr:* **~se** to hide; **el fondo del mar esconde muchas riquezas** the ocean bed has many secret treasures

escondidas [es·kon·'di·das] *adv* **a ~** secretly; **a ~ del profesor** behind the teacher's back

escondido(s) [es·kon·'di·do(s)] *m(pl)* AmL hide and seek

escondite [es·kon·'di·te] *m* **1.** (*juego*) hide and seek **2.** (*lugar*) hiding place

escondrijo [es·kon·'dri·xo] *m* hideout

escopeta [es·ko·'pe·ta] *f* shotgun; **~ de aire comprimido** air gun

escopetear [es·ko·pe·te·'ar] *vt* **1.** Méx (*con indirectas*) to be snide about **2.** Ven (*contestar mal*) to give an unpleasant reply to

escorchar [es·kor·'tʃar] *vt* Arg to annoy

escoria [es·'ko·rja] *f* scum

Escorpio [es·'kor·pjo] *m* Scorpio

escorpión [es·kor·'pjon] *m* scorpion

escotado [es·ko·'ta·do] *m* neckline

escotado, -a [es·ko·'ta·do, -a] *adj* with a low neckline

escote [es·'ko·te] *m* neckline

escotilla [es·ko·'ti·ja, -ʎa] *f* hatchway

escozor [es·ko·'sor, -'θor] *m* burning

escrachar [es·kra·'tʃar] *vt* 1. *AmL* (*tachar*) to strike out 2. *PRico* (*estropear*) to ruin 3. *Arg inf* (*arruinar*) to wreck

escracho [es·'kra·tʃo] *m RíoPl* 1. (*cara fea*) mug *inf* 2. (*esperpento*) fright

escribanía [es·kri·βa·'ni·a] *f AmL* notary

escribir [es·kri·'βir] *irr* I. *vi, vt* write; **~ algo a mano** to write sth by hand; **~ algo a máquina** to typewrite sth; **escrito a mano** handwriting; **escrito a máquina** typewriting; **¿cómo se escribe tu nombre?** how do you spell your name? II. *vr:* **~se** to write (to each other); **se escriben mucho** they write to each other a lot; **estaba escrito que acabarían casándose** it was in their stars to get married

escrito [es·'kri·to] *m* text

escrito, -a [es·'kri·to, -a] I. *pp de* **escribir** II. *adj* written; **por ~** in writing

escritor(a) [es·kri·'tor, -·'to·ra] *m(f)* writer

escritorio [es·kri·'to·rjo] *m* desk; COMPUT desktop

escritura [es·kri·'tu·ra] *f* 1. (*acto*) writing 2. (*signos*) script 3. (*documento*) deed; **~ de propiedad/hipoteca** title/mortgage deeds; **~ de seguro** insurance certificate; **~ social** company registration; **mediante ~** in writing

escriturar [es·kri·tu·'rar] *vt* to execute by deed

escroto [es·'kro·to] *m* scrotum

escrúpulo [es·'kru·pu·lo] *m* 1. (*duda*) scruple; **~s de conciencia** pangs of conscience; **ser una persona sin ~s** to be completely unscrupulous; **no tener ~s en hacer algo** to have no qualms about doing sth 2. (*asco*) disgust; **me da ~ beber de latas** I think it's disgusting to drink out of cans

escrupuloso, -a [es·kru·pu·'lo·so, -a] *adj* 1. (*meticuloso*) scrupulous 2. (*quisquilloso*) fussy

escrutar [es·kru·'tar] *vt* (*votos*) to count

escrutinio [es·kru·'ti·njo] *m* scrutiny; (*votos*) count

escuadra [es·'kwa·dra] *f* bracket; (*para dibujar*) set square

escuadrón [es·kwa·'dron] *m* squadron

escuálido, -a [es·'kwa·li·do] *adj* scrawny

escucha [es·'ku·tʃa] *f* listening; **~ telefónica** telephone tapping; **estar a la ~** to be listening

escuchar [es·ku·'tʃar] I. *vi* to listen; (*en secreto*) to eavesdrop II. *vt* to listen to; (*en secreto*) to eavesdrop; **~ un concierto** to listen to a concert; **~ una conversación telefónica** to tap into a telephone conversation; **~ (la) radio** to listen to the radio; **¡escúchame bien!** pay attention to what I'm saying!

escudar [es·ku·'dar] I. *vt* to shield II. *vr* **~se en algo** to use sth as an excuse

escudo [es·'ku·do] *m* 1. (*arma*) shield 2. (*moneda*) escudo *(monetary unit of Chile)*

escudriñar [es·ku·dri·'nar] *vt, vi* to scrutinize; **~ en la intimidad de alguien** to invade sb's privacy

escuela [es·'kwe·la] *f* school; (*de primaria*) primary/elementary school; **~ de idiomas/conducir/párvulos** language/driving/nursery school; **Escuela de Bellas Artes** School of Fine Arts; **~ normal** teacher training college; **~ técnica superior** polytechnic; **~ taller** workshop; **la vida es la mejor ~** life is the best teacher; **la ~ holandesa/de Durero** the Dutch school/the Dürer school; **su ejemplo ha hecho ~** his/her work has set an example

escueto, -a [es·'kwe·to, -a] *adj* bare; (*lenguaje*) concise; **escuetamente** briefly

escuincle [es·'kwin·kle, -a] *m Méx inf* kid

escular <c → qu> [es·kul·'kar] *vt AmC, Col, Méx* to go through

esculpir [es·kul·'pir] *vt* to sculpt; **~ a cincel** to sculpt using a chisel; **~ en madera** to carve in wood; **~ una figura en**

mármol to sculpt a figure in marble

escultor(a) [es·kul·'tor, -·'to·ra] *m(f)* sculptor, sculptress *m, f*; **~ de madera** wood carver

escultura [es·kul·'tu·ra] *f* sculpture; **~ de madera** wood carving

escultural [es·kul·tu·'ral] *adj* sculptural; *(bello)* statuesque

escupidera [es·ku·pi·'de·ra] *f* chamber pot

escupir [es·ku·'pir] **I.** *vi* **1.** to spit **2.** *inf (contar)* to spit it out **II.** *vt* to spit out; **~ sangre** to spit blood; **~ fuego** to belch smoke; **escupe lo que sabes** spill the beans

escurreplatos [es·ku·rre·'pla·tos] *m inv* plate rack

escurridizo, -a [es·ku·rri·'di·so, -a; -'di·θo, -a] *adj* slippery

escurrido, -a [es·ku·'rri·do] *adj* **1.** *(flaco)* thin **2.** *Méx, PRico (avergonzado)* embarrassed

escurridor [es·ku·rri·'dor] *m* drainer

escurrir [es·ku·'rrir] **I.** *vi* to drip; *(verdura)* to drain **II.** *vt* **1.** to drain; *(ropa)* to wring out **2.** *(deslizar)* to slip; **~ la mano por encima de algo** to run one's hand over sth **III.** *vr:* **~se 1.** *(resbalar)* to slip **2.** *(escaparse)* to slip out; **el pez se me escurrió de las manos** the fish slipped out of my hands

ése, ésa, eso <ésos, -as> *pron dem* that (one); **¿por qué no vamos a otro bar? — ~ no me gusta** why don't we go to another bar? — I don't like that one; **llegaré a eso de las doce** I'll be there at about twelve o'clock; **¡no me vengas con ésas!** come off it!; **¡ni por ésas!** not on your life!; **lejos de eso** just the opposite; **no es eso** it's not that; **por eso (mismo)** that's why; **¡eso sí que no!** definitely not!; *v. t.* **ese, -a**

ese ['e·se] *f* **ir haciendo ~s** to stagger from side to side

ese, -a ['e·se, -a] **I.** *adj* <eses, -as> that; **¿~ coche es tuyo?** is that car yours?; **el chico ~ no me cae bien** I don't like that boy **II.** *pron dem v.* **ése, ésa, eso**

esencia [e·'sen·sja, -θja] *f* essence

esencial [e·sen·'sjal, -'θjal] *adj* funda-

mental; **lo ~** the main thing; **alimento/aceite/elemento ~** essential food/oil/element

esencialmente [e·sen·sjal·'men·te, e·sen·θjal-] *adv* essentially

esfera [es·'fe·ra] *f* **1.** MAT sphere **2.** *(ámbito)* field; **~ de actividad** area of activity; **~ de influencia** sphere of influence; **las altas ~s** the upper classes

esferográfico [es·fe·ro·'ɣra·fi·ko, -a] *m* AmS ball-point pen

esfinge [es·'fin·xe] *f* sphinx

esforzar [es·for·'sar, -'θar] *irr como* forzar **I.** *vt* to force; *(vista, voz)* to strain **II.** *vr:* **~se** *(moralmente)* to strive; *(físicamente)* to make an effort

esfuerzo [es·'fwer·so, -θo] *m* effort; **sin ~** effortlessly; **hacer un ~** to make an effort; *(económico)* to tighten one's belt

esfumarse [es·fu·'mar·se] *vr:* **~se** to fade away; *inf* to beat it

esgrima [es·'ɣri·ma] *f* fencing; **practicar la ~** to do fencing

esgrimir [es·ɣri·'mir] *vt* to wield; *(argumento)* to use

esgrimista [es·ɣri·'mis·ta] *mf* AmL fencer

esguince [es·'ɣin·se, -θe] *m* sprain; **hacerse un ~ en el tobillo** to sprain one's ankle

eslabón [es·la·'βon] *m* link; **el ~ perdido** the missing link; *fig* step

eslavo, -a [es·'la·βo, -a] *adj, m, f* Slav

eslogan [es·'lo·ɣan] *m* slogan

eslovaco, -a [es·lo·'βa·ko, -a] **I.** *adj* Slovakian **II.** *m, f* Slovak

Eslovaquia [es·lo·'βa·kja] *f* Slovakia

Eslovenia [es·lo·'βe·nja] *f* Slovenia

esloveno, -a [es·lo·'βe·no, -a] *adj, m, f* Slovene

esmaltar [es·mal·'tar] *vt* to enamel

esmalte [es·'mal·te] *m* **1.** *(barniz)* varnish; *(en metal, porcelana, dientes)* enamel; **sin ~** mat(te) **2.** *(de uñas)* nail polish **3.** *(color)* smalt

esmerado, -a [es·me·'ra·do, -a] *adj* painstaking; *(obra)* professional

esmeralda [es·me·'ral·da] *adj, f* emerald

esmerarse [es·me·'rar·se] *vr* to make an effort (**en** with)

esmero [es-'me·ro] *m* care; **con ~** with great care

esmirriado, -a [es-mi·'rrja·do, -a] *adj (flaco) (raquítico)* puny

esmoquin [es-'mo·kin] *m* tuxedo

esnifar [es-ni·'far] *vt inf* to sniff; *(cocaína)* to snort

esnob [es-'noβ] **I.** *adj* snobbish **II.** *mf* snob

esnobismo [es-no·'βis·mo] *m* snobbery

eso ['e·so] *pron dem v.* **ése**

esófago [e·'so·fa·ɣo] *m* esophagus

esos ['e·sos] *adj v.* **ese**

ésos ['e·sos] *pron dem v.* **ése**

esotérico, -a [e·so·'te·ri·ko, -a] *adj* esoteric

esoterismo [e·so·te·'ris·mo] *m* esoteric nature

espabilada [es·pa·βi·'la·da] *f Col* blink; **en una ~** in a second

espabilado, -a [es·pa·βi·'la·do, -a] *adj* **1.** *(listo)* smart **2.** *(despierto)* awake

espabilar [es·pa·βi·'lar] **I.** *vt* **1.** *(despertar)* to wake up **2.** *(avivar)* to sharpen up **II.** *vi* **1.** *(darse prisa)* to hurry up **2.** *(avivar)* to shape up **III.** *vr:* **~se 1.** *(despertarse)* to wake oneself up **2.** *(avivar)* to liven up **3.** *AmL (irse)* to head off

espaciador [es·pa·sja·'dor, es·pa·θja-] *m* COMPUT space bar

espacial [es·pa·'sjal, -'θjal] *adj* space

espaciar [es·pa·'sjar, -'θjar] *vt (sillas)* to separate; *(letras)* to space out; *(visitas)* to stagger

espacio [es·'pa·sjo, -θjo] *m* **1.** *t.* ASTR space; *(superficie)* area; **~ exterior/vital** outer/living space; **a doble ~** double-spaced; **~ virtual** cyberspace; **~ web** web site; **a doble ~** double-spaced; **la bici ocupa demasiado ~** the bike takes up too much room [*o* space] **2.** *(de tiempo)* period; **en el ~ de dos meses** in a period of two months; **por ~ de tres horas** for a three-hour period **3.** *(programa)* program; **~ informativo** news bulletin; **~ publicitario** advertising spot

espacioso, -a [es·pa·'sjo·so, -a, es·pa·'θjo-] *adj* spacious, roomy

espada [es·'pa·da] *f* sword; *(naipes)* spade

espadachín, -ina [es·pa·da·'tʃin, -·'tʃi·na] *m, f* swordsman, swordswoman *m, f*

espagueti(s) [es·pa·'ɣe·ti(s)] *m(pl)* spaghetti

espalda [es·'pal·da] *f* **1.** back; **ancho de ~s** broad-shouldered; **ser cargado de ~s** to be hunched; **andar de ~s** to walk backwards; **con las manos en la ~** with one's hands clasped behind one's back; **estar a ~s de alguien** to be behind sb; **estar de ~s a la pared** to have one's back to the wall; **atacar por la ~** to attack from the rear; **coger a alguien por la ~** *fig* to take sb by surprise; **doblar la ~** *fig* to put one's back into a task; **volver la ~ a alguien** *fig* to turn one's back on sb; **hablar a ~s de alguien** to talk behind sb's back; **me caí de ~s al oír eso** *inf* I was astonished to hear that; **tener las ~s muy anchas** *fig* to put up with a lot; **tener las ~s bien guardadas** *inf* to have friends in high places; **la responsabilidad recae sobre mis ~s** the responsibility is on my shoulders; **vivir de ~s a la realidad** to live in the clouds **2.** DEP backstroke; **100 metros ~** 100-meters backstroke; **¿sabes nadar ~?** can you do the backstroke?

espaldero [es·pal·'de·ro] *m Ven* bodyguard

espanglis [es·'pan·lis] *m* Spanglish

espantapájaros [es·pan·ta·'pa·xa·ros] *m inv* scarecrow

espantar [es·pan·'tar] **I.** *vt* **1.** *(dar susto)* to shock; *(dar miedo)* to frighten **2.** *(ahuyentar)* to shoo away **II.** *vr* **~se de** [*o* por] **algo** *(personas)* to be scared of sth; *(animales)* to be shooed away

espanto [es·'pan·to] *m* **1.** fright; **¡qué ~!** how awful!; **hace un calor de ~** it's terribly hot; **los precios son de ~** prices are outrageous; **estar curado de ~s** *inf* to have been around a few years **2.** *AmL (fantasma)* ghost

espantosidad [es·pan·to·si·'dad] *f AmC, Col, PRico* horror

espantoso, -a [es·pan·'to·so, -a] *adj* horrible; *(feo)* hideous

España [es·'pa·ɲa] *f* Spain

español [es·pa·'ɲol] *m* Spanish; **clases**

de ~ Spanish classes; **aprender** ~ to learn Spanish; **traducir al** ~ to translate into Spanish

español(a) [es·pa·'ɲol, -·'ɲo·la] **I.** *adj* Spanish; **a la ~a** Spanish-style **II.** *m(f)* Spaniard

esparadrapo [es·pa·ra·'dra·po] *m* adhesive tape

esparcimiento [es·par·si·'mjen·to, -θi·'mjen·to] *m* **1.** spreading ~ **2.** (*diversión*) fun

esparcir <c → z> [es·par·'sir, -'θir] **I.** *vt* to spread out; (*líquido*) to spill; (*noticia*) to spread; **el viento ha esparcido los papeles de la mesa** the wind has blown the papers off the table **II.** *vr:* **~se** to spread out; (*noticias*) to spread

espárrago [es·'pa·rra·yo] *m* asparagus; ~ **triguero** wild asparagus; **¡vete a freír ~s!** *inf* get lost!; **estar hecho un ~** *fig* to be as thin as a rake

espartillo [es·par·'ti·jo, -ʎo] *AmL,* **esparto** [es·'par·to] *m* esparto

espasmo [es·'pas·mo] *m* spasm

espasmódico, -a [es·pas·'mo·di·ko, -a] *adj* spasmodic

espátula [es·'pa·tu·la] *f* spatula

especia [es·'pe·sja, -θja] *f* spice

especial [es·pe·'sjal, -'θjal] *adj* special; (*adecuado*) perfect; (*raro*) peculiar; **edición/comisión/escuela** ~ special edition/committee/school; **en** ~ in particular

especialidad [es·pe·sja·li·'dad, es·pe·θja·] *f* specialty; (*rama*) field

especialista [es·pe·sja·'lis·ta, es·pe·θja·] *mf* **1.** specialist **2.** CINE, TV stuntman, stuntwoman *m, f*

especialización [es·pe·sja·li·sa·'sjon, -θja·li·θa·'θjon] *f* specialization

especializar <z → c> [es·pe·sja·li·'sar, es·pe·θja·li·'θar] *vi, vr:* **~se** to specialize; **personal especializado** skilled staff

especialmente [es·pe·sjal·'men·te, es·pe·θjal-] *adv* especially

especie [es·'pe·sje, -'pe·θje] *f* **1.** *t.* BOT, ZOOL species *inv;* ~ **amenazada de extinción** endangered species **2.** (*tipo*) kind; **pagar en** ~s to pay in kind

especificación [es·pe·si·fi·ka·'sjon, -θi·fi·ka·'θjon] *f* **1.** (*precisión*) specification

2. (*explicación*) explanation

especificar <c → qu> [es·pe·si·fi·'kar, es·pe·θi·] *vt* (*explicar*) to explain; (*citar*) to specify; (*enumerar*) to enumerate

específico, -a [es·pe·'si·fi·ko, -'θi·fi·ko] *adj* specific

espécimen [es·'pe·si·men, -θi·men] *m* <especímenes> specimen; (*muestra*) sample

espectacular [es·pek·ta·ku·'lar] *adj* spectacular

espectáculo [es·pek·'ta·ku·lo] *m* **1.** TEAT show; ~ **de variedades** variety show; ~ **deportivo** sporting event **2.** (*visión*) sight **3.** *inf* (*escándalo*) **dar el** ~ to make a scene

espectador(a) [es·pek·ta·'dor, -·'do·ra] *m(f)* spectator

espectro [es·'pek·tro] *m* specter

especulación [es·pe·ku·la·'sjon, -'θjon] *f* speculation

especulador(a) [es·pe·ku·la·'dor, -·'do·ra] *m(f)* speculator

especular [es·pe·ku·'lar] *vi* **1.** *t.* FIN to speculate; ~ **en la Bolsa** to speculate on the stock market **2.** (*meditar*) to speculate

especulativo, -a [es·pe·ku·la·'ti·βo, -a] *adj* speculative; (*teórico*) theoretical

espejismo [es·pe·'xis·mo] *m* **1.** (*óptico*) mirage **2.** (*imaginario*) illusion

espejo [es·'pe·xo] *m* mirror; ~ **retrovisor** car mirror; **mirarse al** ~ to look at oneself in the mirror

espeluznante [es·pe·lus·'nan·te, es·pe·luθ-] *adj* horrific

espera [es·'pe·ra] *f* wait; **tuvimos dos horas de** ~ we had a two-hour wait; **a la** ~ waiting; **lista de** ~ waiting list; **esta** ~ **me saca de quicio** this waiting around is really getting to me

esperanza [es·pe·'ran·sa, -θa] *f* hope; ~ **de vida** life expectancy; **no tener** ~s to have no hope; **poner las** ~**s en algo** to put one's hopes into sth; **tener** ~**s de conseguir un puesto de trabajo** to have hopes of getting a job; **veo el futuro con** ~ I'm hopeful about the future

esperanzador(a) [es·pe·ran·sa·'dor, -·'do·ra; -θa·dor, -·'do·ra] *adj* hopeful

esperanzar <z → c> [es·pe·ran·'sar, -'θar]

I. *vt* to give hope to **II.** *vr* ~**se en algo** to become hopeful about sth

esperar [es·pe·'rar] **I.** *vi* **1.** (*aguardar*) to wait; **hacerse** ~ to keep people waiting; **es de** ~ **que** +*subj* it is to be expected that; **¡que se espere!** let him/her wait!; **¿a qué esperas?** what are you waiting for?; **espera, que no lo encuentro** hold on, I can't find it; **ganaron la copa tan esperada** they won the long-awaited cup **2.** (*confiar*) to hope **II.** *vt* **1.** (*aguardar*) to wait for; **hace una hora que lo espero** I've been waiting for him for an hour; **hacer** ~ **a alguien** to keep sb waiting; **la respuesta no se hizo** ~ the answer was not long in coming; **me van a** ~ **al aeropuerto** they're meeting me at the airport; **nos esperan malos tiempos** there are bad times in store for us; **te espera una prueba dura** a hard test awaits you **2.** (*un bebé, anticipar*) to expect; **ya me lo esperaba** I expected it **3.** (*confiar*) to hope; **espero que nos veamos pronto** I hope to see you soon; **esperando recibir noticias tuyas...** looking forward to hearing from you...; **espero que sí** I hope so

esperma [es·'per·ma] *m* sperm

esperpento [es·per·'pen·to] *m* fright

espesar [es·pe·'sar] **I.** *vt* (*líquido*) to thicken **II.** *vr:* ~**se** (*bosque*) to become denser

espeso, -a [es·'pe·so, -a] *adj* **1.** thick **2.** *Arg, Perú, Ven* (*molesto*) bothersome

espesor [es·pe·'sor] *m* **1.** (*grosor*) thickness; (*nieve*) depth **2.** (*densidad*) density

espesura [es·pe·'su·ra] *f* **1.** thickness; (*líquido*) density **2.** (*bosque*) thicket

espía [es·'pi·a] *mf* spy; (*de la policía*) informer; (*infiltrado*) infiltrator; ~ **doble** double agent

espiantar [es·pjan·'tar] **I.** *vi, vr:* ~**se** *CSur inf* (*alejarse*) to head off; (*huir*) to escape **II.** *vt* *CSur* (*hurtar*) to steal

espiar <*1. pres* **espío**> [es·pi·'ar] **I.** *vi* to spy **II.** *vt* to spy on; (*para la policía*) to inform on

espichar [es·pi·'tʃar] *vt* *Col inf* to squash

espiga [es·'pi·ɣa] *f* ear

espina [es·'pi·na] *f* **1.** (*de pescado*) bone **2.** BOT thorn **3.** ANAT ~ (**dorsal**) spine **4.** (*inconveniente*) problem; **esto me da mala** ~ I don't like the look of this **5.** (*pesar*) frustration; **tener una** ~ **clavada** to have sth hanging over one

espinaca [es·pi·'na·ka] *f* spinach

espinal [es·pi·'nal] *adj* spinal; **médula** ~ spinal chord

espinazo [es·pi·'na·so, -θo] *m* spinal column

espinilla [es·pi·'ni·ja, -ʎa] *f* **1.** ANAT shin; **dar a alguien una patada en la** ~ to kick sb in the shin **2.** (*grano*) blackhead

espino [es·'pi·no] *m* **alambre de** ~ barbed wire

espinoso, -a [es·pi·'no·so, -a], **espinudo, -a** [es·pi·'nu·do, -a] *adj* *AmC, CSur* (*planta*) thorny; (*pescado*) bony; (*problema*) tricky

espionaje [es·pjo·'na·xe] *m* espionage; ~ **industrial** industrial espionage

espiración [es·pi·ra·'sjon, -'θjon] *f* exhalation

espiral [es·pi·'ral] **I.** *adj* spiral; **escalera** ~ spiral staircase **II.** *f* spiral

espirar [es·pi·'rar] **I.** *vi* to exhale **II.** *vt* (*olor*) to give off

espiritismo [es·pi·ri·'tis·mo] *m* spiritualism; **sesión de** ~ séance

espiritista [es·pi·ri·'tis·ta] *adj* spiritualist

espíritu [es·'pi·ri·tu] *m* spirit; (*alma*) soul; ~ **de compañerismo** brotherly spirit; ~ **emprendedor** hardworking nature; ~ **deportivo** sportsmanship; **el Espíritu Santo** the Holy Spirit

espiritual [es·pi·ri·tu·'al] *adj* spiritual

espléndido, -a [es·'plen·di·do, -a] *adj* **1.** splendid; (*día*) beautiful; (*ocasión, idea, resultado*) excellent **2.** (*generoso*) generous

esplendor [es·plen·'dor] *m* splendor

esplendoroso, -a [es·plen·do·'ro·so, -a] *adj* splendid

espliego [es·'plje·ɣo] *m* lavender

espolvorear [es·pol·βo·re·'ar] *vt* to sprinkle

esponja [es·'pon·xa] *f* sponge; **beber como una** ~ to drink like a fish

esponjoso, -a [es·pon·'xo·so, -a] *adj*

(*masa*) fluffy; (*pan*) light

espontaneidad [es·pon·ta·nei·'dad] *f* spontaneity

espontáneo, -a [es·pon·'ta·neo, -a] *adj* spontaneous; (*saludo*) natural

espora [es·'po·ra] *f* spore

esporádico, -a [es·po·'ra·di·ko, -a] *adj* sporadic

esportivo, -a [es·por·'ti·βo, -a] *adj AmL* **1.** (*deportivo*) sporting **2.** (*descuidado*) casual

esposar [es·po·'sar] *vt* to handcuff

esposas [es·'po·sas] *fpl* handcuffs *pl*

esposo, -a [es·'po·so, -a] *m, f* husband, wife *m, f*, spouse; **los ~s** husband and wife

espray [es·'prai] *m* spray; (*envase*) aerosol

esprint [es·'prin(t)] *m* sprint

espuma [es·'pu·ma] *f* foam; **~ de afeitar** shaving foam; (*de las olas*) spray; (*de jabón*) lather; (*de cerveza*) head; **crecer como la ~** to grow very quickly

espumarajo [es·pu·ma·'ra·xo] *m pey* froth; (*de la boca*) foam

espumilla [es·pu·'mi·ja, -ʎa] *f AmL* meringue

espumoso, -a [es·pu·'mo·so, -a] *adj* foamy; (*líquido*) sparkling

esqueje [es·'ke·xe] *m* cutting

esquela [es·'ke·la] *f* notice of death; ~ (**mortuoria**) obituary notice

esquelético, -a [es·ke·'le·ti·ko, -a] *adj* scrawny; ANAT skeletal

esqueleto [es·ke·'le·to] *m* **1.** ANAT skeleton **2.** (*avión, barco*) shell; (*edificio*) framework

esquema [es·'ke·ma] *m* (*gráfico*) sketch; (*lista*) summary; **romper los ~s** to shake up sb's ideas

esquemático, -a [es·ke·'ma·ti·ko, -a] *adj* schematic

esquematizar [es·ke·ma·ti·'sar, -'θar] *vt* to outline

esquí [es·'ki] *m* **1.** (*patín*) ski; ~ **de fondo** cross-country ski **2.** (*deporte*) skiing; ~ **acuático** water-skiing

esquiador(a) [es·kja·'dor, --'do·ra] *m(f)* skier

esquiar <*1. pres* esquío> [es·ki·'ar] *vi* to ski

esquilar [es·ki·'lar] *vt* to shear

esquimal [es·ki·'mal] **I.** *adj* Eskimo; *Can* Inuit; **perro ~** husky **II.** *mf* Eskimo; *Can* Inuit

esquina [es·'ki·na] *f* corner; **que hace ~** on the corner; **a la vuelta de la ~** around the corner; **doblar la ~** to turn the corner

esquinazo [es·ki·'na·so, -θo] *m inf* **dar ~ a alguien** to avoid sb

esquivar [es·ki·'βar] *vt* (*golpe*) to dodge; (*problema*) to shirk; (*persona*) to avoid

esquivo, -a [es·'ki·βo, -a] *adj* **1.** (*huidizo*) evasive **2.** (*arisco*) aloof

esquizofrenia [es·ki·so·'fre·nja, es·ki·θo-] *f* schizophrenia

esquizofrénico, -a [es·ki·so·'fre·ni·ko, -a; es·ki·θo-] *adj, m, f* schizophrenic

esta ['es·ta] *adj v.* **este, -a**

ésta ['es·ta] *pron dem v.* **éste**

estabilidad [es·ta·βi·li·'dad] *f* stability

estabilización [es·ta·βi·li·sa·'sjon, -θa·'θjon] *f* stabilization

estabilizar <z → c> [es·ta·βi·li·'sar, -'θar] *vt, vr:* ~**se** to stabilize

estable [es·'ta·βle] *adj* stable; (*trabajo*) steady

establecer [es·ta·βle·'ser, -'θer] *irr como crecer* **I.** *vt* **1.** (*fundar*) to establish; (*negocio*) to open; (*principio, récord*) to set; (*escuela*) to found **2.** (*colocar*) to place; (*campamento*) to set up; (*colonos*) to settle; (*conexión*) to establish **II.** *vr* ~**se** to settle

establecimiento [es·ta·βle·si·'mjen·to, -θi·'mjen·to] *m* establishment

establo [es·'ta·βlo] *m* **1.** stable **2.** *Cuba* (*cochera*) depot; (*parking*) garage

estaca [es·'ta·ka] *f* post

estacada [es·ta·'ka·da] *f* **en la ~** in the lurch

estación [es·ta·'sjon, -'θjon] *f* **1.** (*período*) season; ~ **de las lluvias** rainy season **2.** RADIO, TV, FERRO station; (*parada*) stop; ~ **de autobuses/metro** bus/subway station; ~ **central** central station; ~ **de destino** destination **3.** (*centro*) ~ **meteorológica/espacial** weather/space station; ~ **de servicio** gas station

estacionamiento [es·ta·sjo·na·'mjen·to, es·ta·θjo·] *m* AUTO (*acción*) parking; (*es-*

pacio) parking space; (*lugar*) parking lot; (*edificio*) parking garage

estacionar [es·ta·sjo·'nar, es·ta·θjo·] **I.** *vt* AUTO to park **II.** *vr:* ~**se 1.** to stabilize **2.** AUTO to park

estada [es·'ta·da] *AmL*, **estadía** [es·ta·'di·a] *f* (*estancia*) stay

estadio [es·'ta·djo] *m* DEP stadium

estadística [es·ta·'dis·ti·ka] *f* statistics *pl*

estadístico, -a [es·ta·'dis·ti·ko, -a] **I.** *adj* statistical **II.** *m, f* statistician

estado [es·'ta·do] *m* **1.** (*condición*) condition; **en buen ~** in good condition; (*situación*) state; ~ **civil** marital status; ~ **gaseoso** gaseous state; ~ **de guerra** state of war; **en ~ de embriaguez** in a state of inebriation **2.** POL state; ~ **comunitario/miembro/totalitario** community/member/police state

Estados Unidos [es·'ta·dos u·'ni·dos] *mpl* United States of America *pl + sing vb*

estadounidense [es·ta·do·u·ni·'den·se] **I.** *adj* of/from the US, American **II.** *mf* native/inhabitant of the US, American

estafa [es·'ta·fa] *f* swindle

estafador(a) [es·ta·fa·'dor, -·'do·ra] *m(f)* swindler

estafar [es·ta·'far] *vt* to swindle

estagnación [es·tay·na·'sjon, -·'θjon] *f* AmC stagnation

estaje [es·'ta·xe] *m AmL* piecework

estajear [es·ta·xe·'ar] *vi AmL* to do as piecework

estajero, -a [es·ta·'xe·ro, -a] *m, f* AmL pieceworker

estalactita [es·ta·lak·'ti·ta] *f* stalactite

estalagmita [es·ta·lay·'mi·ta] *f* stalagmite

estallar [es·ta·'jar, -'ʎar] *vi* (*globo*) to burst; (*bomba*) to explode; (*tormenta*) to break; (*revolución, incendio, guerra*) to break out

estallido [es·ta·'ji·do, -'ʎi·do] *m* explosion; (*globo*) bursting; (*revolución/cólera*) outbreak

estampa [es·'tam·pa] *f* **1.** (*dibujo*) illustration **2.** (*impresión*) impression

estampado [es·tam·'pa·do] *m* print; (*diseño*) design; (*en metal*) engraving

estampado, -a [es·tam·'pa·do, -a] *adj* printed

estampar [es·tam·'par] **I.** *vt* (*en papel,* *tela*) to print; (*con relieve*) to stamp **II.** *vr* ~**se con(tra)** *algo inf* to crash into sth

estampilla [es·tam·'pi·ja, -ʎa] *f* AmL stamp

estancamiento [es·tan·ka·'mjen·to] *m* **1.** stagnation **2.** ECON recession

estancar <c → qu> [es·tan·'kar] *vt* to stagnate; **aguas estancadas** stagnant water; (*proceso*) to hold up **II.** *vr:* ~**se** (*río*) to be held back; (*negocio*) to falter; **quedarse estancado** to get stuck

estancia [es·'tan·sja, -θja] *f* **1.** (*permanencia*) stay **2.** (*cuarto*) room **3.** AmL (*hacienda*) estate **4.** Cuba, Ven (*quinta*) country house

estanciero, -a [es·tan·'sje·ro, -a; -'θje·ro, -a] *m, f* CSur, Col, Ven **1.** (*ganadero*) cattle farmer **2.** (*latifundista*) landowner

estanco [es·'tan·ko] *m* tobacconist's

estándar [es·'tan·dar] *adj, m* standard; **tipo** ~ standard version

estandarizar <z → c> [es·tan·da·ri·'sar, -'θar] *vt* to standardize

estanque [es·'tan·ke] *m* pool; (*para regar*) tank

estanquillo [es·tan·'ki·jo, -ʎo] *m Méx* shop

estante [es·'tan·te] *m* shelf

estantería [es·tan·te·'ri·a] *f* shelves *pl;* (*para libros*) bookcase

estañar [es·ta·'nar] *vt Ven* to wound

estaño [es·'ta·no] *m* tin; ~ **para soldar** solder

estar [es·'tar] *irr* **I.** *vi* **1.** to be; (*de pie*) to stand; (*tumbado*) to lie; (*colgando*) to hang; **Valencia está en la costa** Valencia is on the coast; **¿está Pepe?** is Pepe there?; **¿está la comida?** is lunch ready? **2.** (*sentirse*) **¿cómo estás?** how are you?; **ya estoy mejor** I'm better **3.** (+ *adjetivo, participio*) ~ **cansado/** **sentado** to be tired/sitting; **el asado** **está delicioso** the roast is delicious **4.** (+ *bien, mal*) ~ **mal de azúcar** to be running out of sugar; ~ **mal de dinero** to be short of money; ~ **mal de la cabeza** to be out of one's mind; **eso te** **está bien empleado** it serves you right; **esa blusa te está bien** that blouse suits you **5.** (+ *a*) ~ **al caer** (*persona*) to be about to arrive; (*suceso*) to be about to happen; ~ **al día** to be up to date; **estamos a uno de enero** it's the first of January; **¿a qué estamos?** what day is it?; **las peras están a 10 pesos el kilo** pears cost 10 pesos a kilo; **las acciones están a 12 dólares** the shares are at 12 dollars; **Caracas está a 40 grados** it is 40 degrees in Caracas **6.** (+ *con*) **estoy con mi novio** I'm with my boyfriend; **estoy contigo en este punto** I agree with you on that point **7.** (+ *de*) ~ **de broma/charla/viaje** to be joking/chatting/traveling; ~ **de mal humor** to be in a bad mood; ~ **de parto** to be in labor; ~ **de pie/suerte** to be standing/lucky; ~ **de secretario** to be working as a secretary; **en esta reunión estoy de más** I'm not needed in this meeting **8.** (+ *en*) **siempre estás en todo** you never miss a thing **9.** (+ *para*) **hoy no estoy para bromas** today I'm in no mood for jokes; **el tren está para salir** the train is about to leave **10.** (+ *por*) **estoy por llamarle** I think we should call him; **eso está por ver** we don't know that yet; **este partido está por la democracia** this party believes in democracy **11.** (+ *gerundio*) **¿qué estás haciendo?** what are you doing?; **siempre estás viendo la tele** you're always watching TV; **¡lo estaba viendo venir!** I saw it coming! **II.** *vr:* ~**se** (*permanecer*) to stay; **¡estate quieto!** keep still!; **¡estate callado!** shut up!

estatal [es·taˈtal] *adj* state

estático, -a [esˈta·ti·ko, -a] *adj* static

estatua [esˈta·twa] *f* statue

estatuilla [es·ta·ˈtwi·ja, -ʎa] *f* statuette

estatura [es·taˈtu·ra] *f* stature; (*altura*) height; **¿qué ~ tienes?** how tall are you?; **de ~ pequeña** short

estatus [esˈta·tus] *m inv* status

estatuto [es·taˈtu·to] *m* JUR, POL statute

éste, ésta, esto <**éstos, -as**> *pron dem* him, her, this; (a) **éstos no los he visto nunca** I've never seen them; ~ **se cree muy importante** this guy thinks he's very important; **antes yo también tenía una camisa como ésta** I used to

have a shirt like this, too; *v. t.* **este, -a**

este [ˈes·te] *m* east; (*viento*) easterly

este, -a [ˈes·te, -a] **I.** *adj* <**estos, -as**> this; ~ **perro es mío** this dog is mine **II.** *pron dem v.* **éste, ésta, esto**

estela [esˈte·la] *f* trail; (*de avión*) slipstream; NÁUT wake

estelar [es·teˈlar] *adj* stellar; **invitado/programa ~** star guest/program

estelaridad [es·te·la·ri·ˈdad] *f Chile* stardom

estepa [esˈte·pa] *f* steppe

estera [esˈte·ra] *f* matting

estéreo [esˈte·reo] *adj, m* stereo

estereotipado, -a [es·te·reo·ti·ˈpa·do, -a] *adj* stereotyped; **frase estereotipada** hackneyed expression

estereotipo [es·te·reo·ˈti·po] *m* stereotype

estéril [esˈte·ril] *adj* (*persona*) sterile; (*tierra*) barren; (*trabajo*) mundane; (*esfuerzo*) useless; (*discusión*) pointless

esterilidad [es·te·ri·li·ˈdad] *f* (*persona*) sterility; (*tierra*) barrenness

esterilizar [es·te·ri·li·ˈsar, -ˈθar] <z → c> *vt* to sterilize

esterilla [es·teˈri·ja, -ʎa] *f* **1.** mat; ~ **de camping** camping mat **2.** *Ecua* **silla de ~** wicker chair

esterlina [es·terˈli·na] *adj* **libra ~** pound sterling

esternón [es·terˈnon] *m* sternum, breastbone

estero [esˈte·ro] *m* **1.** *AmL* (*pantano*) bog **2.** *Cuba* (*ría*) estuary **3.** *Chile, Ecua* (*arroyo*) stream **4.** *Ven* (*aguazal*) pool

esteroide [es·teˈroi·de] *m* steroid

estética [esˈte·ti·ka] *f* esthetics

estético, -a [esˈte·ti·ko, -a] *adj* esthetic; **cirugía estética** plastic surgery

estetoscopio [es·te·tos·ˈko·pjo] *m* stethoscope

estiércol [esˈtjer·kol] *m* manure

estigma [esˈtiɣ·ma] *m* stigma

estigmatizar [es·tiɣ·ma·ti·ˈsar, -θar] <z → c> *vt* to stigmatize

estilista [es·tiˈlis·ta] *mf* stylist

estilístico, -a [es·tiˈlis·ti·ko, -a] *adj* stylistic

estilizar [es·ti·li·ˈsar, -ˈθar] <z → c> *vt* to stylize

estilo [es·'ti·lo] *m* **1.** *t.* ARTE, LIT, DEP style; **al ~ de** in the style of; **~ de vida** lifestyle; **por el ~** like that; **algo por el ~** something similar **2.** LING **~ directo/indirecto** direct/indirect speech

estilográfica [es·ti·lo·'ɣra·fi·ka] *f* fountain pen

estima [es·'ti·ma] *f* esteem; **tener a alguien en mucha ~** to hold sb in high esteem

estimación [es·ti·ma·'sjon, -'θjon] *f* **1.** (*aprecio*) esteem **2.** (*evaluación*) estimate; **~ de ventas** sales forecast

estimado, -a [es·ti·'ma·do, -a] *adj* **~ Señor** Dear Sir

estimar [es·ti·'mar] **I.** *vt* **1.** (*apreciar*) to appreciate **2.** (*tasar*) to estimate **3.** (*valorar*) **~ en algo** to value at sth **4.** (*juzgar*) to consider **II.** *vr:* **~se en algo** to be valued at sth

estimulante [es·ti·mu·'lan·te] *m* stimulant

estimular [es·ti·mu·'lar] *vt t.* ECON to stimulate; (*animar*) to encourage

estímulo [es·'ti·mu·lo] *m* incentive; MED stimulus

estío [es·'ti·o] *m elev* summer

esti(p)tiquez [es·ti(p)·ti·'kes, -'keθ] *f AmL* constipation

estipulación [es·ti·pu·la·'sjon, -'θjon] *f* agreement; JUR stipulation

estipular [es·ti·pu·'lar] *vt* **1.** (*acordar*) to stipulate **2.** (*fijar*) to fix

estirado, -a [es·ti·'ra·do, -a] *adj* snooty

estirar [es·ti·'rar] **I.** *vi, vr:* **~se** to stretch **II.** *vt* **1.** (*alargar*) to stretch out; (*suma*) to spin out; **~ el bolsillo** to spin out one's resources; **voy a ~ un poco las piernas** I'm going to stretch my legs a little; **~ la pata** to kick the bucket **2.** (*alisar*) to smoothen; (*masa*) to roll out **3.** (*extender*) to stretch **4.** (*tensar*) to tighten

estirón [es·ti·'ron] *m* **1.** (*tirón*) pull **2.** (*crecimiento*) **dar un ~** to shoot up

estirpe [es·'tir·pe] *f* stock

estival [es·ti·'βal] *adj* summer

esto ['es·to] *pron dem v.* **éste**

estofado [es·to·'fa·do] *m* (meat) stew

estofar [es·to·'far] *vt* to stew

estoico, -a [es·'toi·ko, -a] *adj* stoical

estomacal [es·to·ma·'kal] *adj* stomach; **trastorno ~** stomach upset

estómago [es·'to·ma·ɣo] *m* stomach; **dolor de ~** stomach-ache

Estonia [es·'to·nja] *f* Estonia

estonio, -a [es·'to·njo, -a] *adj, m, f* Estonian

estorbar [es·tor·'βar] **I.** *vi* **1.** (*obstaculizar*) to get in the way **2.** (*molestar*) to be annoying **II.** *vt* **1.** (*obstaculizar*) to hinder **2.** (*molestar*) to bother

estorbo [es·'tor·βo] *m* **1.** (*molestia*) nuisance **2.** (*obstáculo*) obstacle

estornudar [es·tor·nu·'dar] *vi* to sneeze

estornudo [es·tor·'nu·do] *m* sneeze

estos ['es·tos] *adj v.* **este**, **éste**

estrabismo [es·tra·'βis·mo] *m* squint

estrado [es·'tra·do] *m* dais; **~ del testigo** witness box

estrafalario, -a [es·tra·fa·'la·rjo, -a] *adj inf* **1.** (*ropa*) shabby **2.** (*extravagante*) outlandish; (*ridículo*) preposterous

estragón [es·tra·'ɣon] *m* tarragon

estragos [es·'tra·ɣos] *m pl* damage

estrambótico, -a [es·tram·'bo·ti·ko, -a] *adj* eccentric

estramonio [es·tra·'mo·njo] *m* thorn apple

estrangulación [es·tran·gu·la·'sjon, -'θjon] *f*, **estrangulamiento** [es·tran·gu·la·'mjen·to] *m* strangulation

estrangular [es·tran·gu·'lar] *vt* to strangle

estraperlista [es·tra·per·'lis·ta] *mf* black-marketeer

estraperlo [es·tra·'per·lo] *m* black market

estratagema [es·tra·ta·'xe·ma] *m* ploy

estrategia [es·tra·'te·xja] *f* strategy

estratégico, -a [es·tra·'te·xi·ko, -a] *adj* strategic

estrato [es·'tra·to] *m* stratum

estrechamente [es·tre·tʃa·'men·te] *adv* **1.** (*íntimamente*) closely **2.** (*rigurosamente*) strictly

estrechar [es·tre·'tʃar] **I.** *vt* **1.** (*angostar*) to narrow **2.** (*abrazar*) to hug; (*mano*) to shake **II.** *vr:* **~se 1.** (*camino*) to become narrower **2.** (*en un asiento*) to squeeze in

estrechez [es·tre·'tʃes, -'tʃeθ] *f* **1.** (*espacial*) narrowness **2.** (*escasez*) shortage;

(*económica*) neediness

estrecho [es.'tre.tʃo] *m* strait

estrecho, -a [es.'tre.tʃo, -a] *adj* 1. (*angosto*) narrow; (*amistad*) close; (*ropa, lugar*) tight 2. (*sexualmente*) prudish

estregar [es.tre.'ɣar] *irr como* fregar *vt v.* **restregar**

estrella [es.'tre.ja, -ʎa] *f* 1. ASTR, CINE star; ~ **fugaz** shooting star; **ver las ~s** *fig* to see stars; **tener buena/mala ~** to be lucky/unlucky 2. TIPO asterisk 3. ~ **de mar** starfish

estrellado, -a [es.tre.'ʝa.ðo, -a; es.tre.'ʎa-] *adj* 1. (*esteliforme*) star-shaped 2. (*cielo*) starry 3. (*vehículo*) crashed

estrellar [es.tre.'jar, -'ʎar] I. *adj* star II. *vt* to smash; (*coche*) to crash III. *vr* ~**se** (**contra** [*o* **en**] **algo**) to crash (into sth)

estremecedor(a) [es.tre.me.se.'dor, -'ðo.ra, es.tre.me.θe-] *adj* harrowing

estremecer [es.tre.me.'ser, -'θer] *irr como* crecer I. *vt* to make shudder II. *vr:* ~**se** to be shocked; (*temblar*) to shiver

estremecimiento [es.tre.me.si.'mjen.to, -θi.'mjen.to] *m* shock; (*de frío, miedo*) shivering

estrenar [es.tre.'nar] I. *vt* 1. to use for the first time; (*ropa*) to wear for the first time; (*trabajo*) to start; ~ **un piso** to move into a new apartment; **sin ~** brand new 2. CINE, TEAT to premiere II. *vr:* ~**se** (*artista*) to make one's debut; (*obra*) to be premiered

estreno [es.'tre.no] *m* 1. (*uso*) first use 2. (*artista*) debut; (*obra*) premiere

estreñido, -a [es.tre.'ni.ðo, -a] *adj* constipated

estreñimiento [es.tre.ni.'mjen.to] *m* constipation

estreñir [es.tre.'nir] *irr como* ceñir *vt* to constipate; **las judías me estriñen** green beans give me constipation

estrépito [es.'tre.pi.to] *m* din

estrepitoso, -a [es.tre.pi.'to.so, -a] *adj* loud; (*fracaso*) spectacular

estrés [es.'tres] *m* stress

estresante [es.tre.'san.te] *adj* stressful

estresar [es.tre.'sar] *vt* to stress

estrías [es.'tri.as] *f pl* grooves *pl*

estribillo [es.tri.'βi.jo, -ʎo] *m* chorus

estribor [es.tri.'βor] *m* starboard

estribos [es.'tri.βos] *m pl* **perder los ~** to fly off the handle

estricto, -a [es.'trik.to, -a] *adj* strict; (*exacto*) exact

estridente [es.tri.'den.te] *adj* shrill

estripazón [es.tri.pa.'son] *m AmC* 1. (*apertura*) opening 2. (*destrozo*) mutilation

estrofa [es.'tro.fa] *f* (*poema*) stanza; (*canción*) verse

estropajo [es.tro.'pa.xo] *m* scourer

estropear [es.tro.pe.'ar] I. *vt* to spoil; (*aparato*) to break; (*cosecha*) to ruin II. *vr:* ~**se** 1. (*deteriorarse*) to spoil 2. (*averiarse*) to break down; (*comida*) to go off; (*planes*) to be spoiled

estructura [es.truk.'tu.ra] *f* structure; (*edificio*) framework

estructural [es.truk.tu.'ral] *adj* structural

estructurar [es.truk.tu.'rar] I. *vt* to structure; (*clasificar*) to classify II. *vr:* ~**se** to be structured

estruendo [es.'trwen.do] *m* 1. (*ruido*) din 2. (*alboroto*) uproar

estrujar [es.tru.'xar] I. *vt* to squeeze; (*papel*) to crumple up; (*machacar*) to crush II. *vr:* ~**se** (*apretujarse*) to squeeze together; ~**se los sesos** to rack one's brains

estuche [es.'tu.tʃe] *m* case; (*cajita*) little box

estudiante [es.tu.'djan.te] *mf* pupil; (*universitario*) student

estudiantil [es.tu.djan.'til] *adj* student

estudiar [es.tu.'djar] *vi, vt* to study; ~ **para médico** to study to be a doctor; **lo ~é** I'll think about it

estudio [es.'tu.djo] *m* 1. (*aprendizaje*) studying 2. (*obra*) study; (*investigación*) research; **estar en ~** to be under study 3. ARTE, TV, TALLER studio 4. *pl* studies *pl*; **cursar ~s** to study; **tener ~s** to have an education

estudioso, -a [es.tu.'djo.so, -a] I. *adj* studious II. *m, f* scholar

estufa [es.'tu.fa] *f* heater

estupefacción [es.tu.pe.fak.'sjon, -faɣ.'θjon] *f* (*asombro*) amazement; (*sorpresa*) surprise; (*espanto*) fright

estupefaciente [es·tu·pe·fa·'sjen·te, -'θjen·te] *m* narcotic; (*ilegal*) drug

estupefacto, -a [es·tu·pe·'fak·to, -a] *adj* (*atónito*) amazed; (*espantado*) shocked

estupendo, -a [es·tu·'pen·do, -a] *adj* fantastic; ¡~! great!

estupidez [es·tu·pi·'des, -'deθ] *f* stupidity

estúpido, -a [es·'tu·pi·do, -a] I. *adj* stupid II. *m, f* idiot

estupor [es·tu·'por] *m* amazement; MED stupor

esturión [es·tu·'rjon] *m* sturgeon

esvástica [es·'βas·ti·ka] *f* swastika

etapa [e·'ta·pa] *f* (*fase*) stage; (*época*) phase; **por ~s** in stages

etarra [e·'ta·rra] *mf* ETA member

etc. [et·'se·te·ra, et·'θe·] *abr de* **etcétera** etc.

etcétera [et·'se·te·ra, et·'θe·] etcetera

éter ['e·ter] *m* ether

etéreo, -a [e·'te·reo, -a] *adj* ethereal

eternidad [e·ter·ni·'dad] *f* eternity; **tardar una ~** to take a lifetime

eternizar <z → c> [e·ter·ni·'sar, -'θar] I. *vt* to make last forever II. *vr* ~**se** (**en algo**) to take ages (doing sth)

eterno, -a [e·'ter·no, -a] *adj* eternal

ética ['e·ti·ka] *f* ethics

ético, -a ['e·ti·ko, -a] *adj* ethical

etílico, -a [e·'ti·li·ko, -a] *adj* alcoholic; QUÍM ethyl

etimología [e·ti·mo·lo·'xi·a] *f* etymology

etimológico, -a [e·ti·mo·'lo·xi·ko, -a] *adj* etymological

etiqueta [e·ti·'ke·ta] *f* 1. label 2. (*convenciones*) etiquette; **de ~** (*solemne*, *traje*) formal; (*ceremonioso*) ceremonial

etiquetar [e·ti·ke·'tar] *vt* to label; (*encasillar*) to stereotype

etnia ['ed·nja] *f* ethnic group

étnico, -a ['et·ni·ko, -a] *adj* ethnic

etnología [et·no·lo·'xi·a] *f* ethnology

eucalipto [eu·ka·'lip·to] *m* eucalyptus

eufemismo [eu·fe·'mis·mo] *m* euphemism

euforia [eu·'fo·rja] *f* euphoria

eufórico, -a [eu·'fo·ri·ko, -a] *adj* euphoric

Eurasia [eu·'ra·sja] *f* Eurasia

euro ['eu·ro] *m* euro

Europa [eu·'ro·pa] *f* Europe

europeo, -a [eu·ro·'peo, -a] *adj, m, f* European

Euskadi [eus·'ka·di] *m* Basque Provinces

euskera [eus·'ke·ra], **eusquera** [eus·'ke·ra] *m* Basque language

eutanasia [eu·ta·'na·sja] *f* euthanasia

evacuación [e·βa·kwa·'sjon, -'θjon] *f* evacuation

evacuar [e·βa·'kwar] *vt* (*ciudad, población*) to evacuate

evadir [e·βa·'dir] I. *vt* to avoid; (*peligro*) to avert II. *vr*: ~**se** to get away

evaluación [e·βa·lwa·'sjon, -'θjon] *f* valuation; ENS assessment

evaluar <*l. pres* evalúo> [e·βa·lu·'ar] *vt* to value; ENS to assess

evangélico, -a [e·βan·'xe·li·ko, -a] I. *adj* evangelical II. *m, f* evangelist

evangelio [e·βan·'xe·ljo] *m* Gospel

evaporación [e·βa·po·ra·'sjon, -'θjon] *f* evaporation

evaporar [e·βa·po·'rar] I. *vt* to evaporate II. *vr*: ~**se** 1. to evaporate 2. (*desaparecer*) to vanish; (*persona*) to disappear into thin air

evasión [e·βa·'sjon] *f* evasion; ~ **de la realidad** escape from reality

evasiva [e·βa·'si·βa] *f* evasions; (*pretexto*) excuse

evasivo, -a [e·βa·'si·βo, -a] *adj* evasive; (*ambiguo*) non-committal

evento [e·'βen·to] *m* event; DEP meeting

eventual [e·βen·'twal] *adj* (*posible*) possible; (*accidental*) fortuitous; (*adicional*) extra

eventualmente [e·βen·twal·'men·te] *adv* fortuitously; (*tal vez*) possibly

evidencia [e·βi·'den·sja, -θja] *f* evidence; **poner a alguien en ~** to make sb look bad

evidenciar [e·βi·den·'sjar, -'θjar] *vt* to show

evidente [e·βi·'den·te] *adj* evident; (*prueba*) manifest

evidentemente [e·βi·den·te·'men·te] *adv* evidently

evitar [e·βi·'tar] I. *vt* to avoid; (*prevenir*) to prevent II. *vr*: ~**se** to avoid; (*personas*) to avoid each other

evocación [e·βo·ka·'sjon, -'θjon] *f* evocation

evocar <c → qu> [e·βo·'kar] *vt* to evoke

evolución [e·βo·lu·'sjon, -'θjon] *f* **1.** *t.* MED progress **2.** (*cambio*) transformation **3.** BIO evolution

evolucionar [e·βo·lu·sjo·'nar, -θjo·'nar] *vi* **1.** (*desarrollarse*) to progress **2.** (*cambiar*) to transform **3.** MED to evolve

ex [eks] **I.** *adj* ex-; **~ novia** ex-girlfriend **II.** *mf* ex

exactitud [ek·sak·ti·'tud] *f* (*precisión*) accuracy; (*veracidad*) exactitude

exacto, -a [ek·'sak·to, -a] *adj* **1.** (*preciso*) accurate **2.** (*correcto*) correct

exageración [ek·sa·xe·ra·'sjon, -'θjon] *f* exaggeration

exagerado, -a [ek·sa·xe·'ra·do, -a] **I.** *adj* exaggerated; (*precio*) steep **II.** *m, f* **¡eres un ~!** I don't exaggerate!

exagerar [ek·sa·xe·'rar] *vi, vt* to exaggerate; **¡anda, anda, no exageres tanto!** come on, stop exaggerating!

exaltación [ek·sal·ta·'sjon, -'θjon] *f* enthusiasm

exaltado, -a [ek·sal·'ta·do, -a] *adj* overexcited; (*violento*) extreme

exaltarse [ek·sal·'tar·se] *vr* **~ con algo** to become excited about sth

examen [ek·'sa·men] *m* **1.** *t.* MED examination; **~ de conducir** driving test; **~ de ingreso** entrance exam; **~ de selectividad** *university entrance exam*; **presentarse a un ~** to sit for an exam; **someterse a un ~ médico** to have a check-up **2.** TÉC test; AUTO check

examinador(a) [ek·sa·mi·na·'dor, -·'do·ra] *m(f)* examiner

examinar [ek·sa·mi·'nar] **I.** *vt* **1.** MED, ADMIN, JUR to examine; **para/al ~lo** for/upon examination **2.** TÉC, AUTO to inspect **II.** *vr:* **~se** to take an exam; **volver a ~se** to retake an exam

exasperación [ek·sas·pe·ra·'sjon, -'θjon] *f* exasperation

exasperante [ek·sas·pe·'ran·te] *adj* exasperating

exasperar [ek·sas·pe·'rar] **I.** *vt* to exasperate **II.** *vr:* **~se** to get exasperated

excarcelar [es·kar·se·'lar, es·kar·θe·-] *vt* to release from prison

excavación [es·ka·βa·'sjon, -'θjon] *f* excavation; (*arqueológica*) dig

excavadora [es·ka·βa·'do·ra] *f* excavator

excavar [es·ka·'βar] *vt* to excavate; (*en arqueología*) to dig

excedencia [es·e·'den·sja, es·θe·'den·θja] *f* leave

excedente [es·e·'den·te, es·θe·-] *adj, m* surplus

exceder [es·e·'der, es·θe·-] **I.** *vi* to be greater; **~ de algo** to exceed sth **II.** *vt* (*persona*) to outdo; (*cosa*) to be better than **III.** *vr:* **~se** (*pasarse*) to go too far

excelente [es·e·'len·te, es·θe·-] *adj* excellent

excentricidad [es·en·tri·si·'dad, es·θen·tri·θi-] *f* eccentricity

excéntrico, -a [e·'sen·tri·ko, -a; es·'θen·-] *adj, m, f* eccentric

excepción [es·ep·'sjon, es·θeβ·'θjon] *f* exception; **de ~** unique; **a** [*o* **con**] **~** with the exception of

excepcional [es·ep·sjo·'nal, es·θeβ·θjo·-] *adj* exceptional; (*raro*) unusual

excepto [e·'sep·to, es·'θep-] *adv* except; **todos ~ yo** everybody except me

excesivo, -a [e·se·'si·βo, -a; es·θe·-] *adj* excessive

exceso [e·'se·so, -'θe·so] *m* **1.** excess; **~ de alcohol** excessive drinking; **~ de capacidad** overcapacity; **~ de equipaje/peso** excess baggage/weight; **~ de velocidad** speeding; **en ~** in excess **2.** FIN surplus

excitación [e·si·ta·'sjon, es·θi·ta·'θjon] *f* excitement

excitar [e·si·'tar, es·θi·-] *vt* to incite; (*apetito*) to stimulate

exclamación [es·kla·ma·'sjon, -'θjon] *f* **1.** cry **2.** LING exclamation; **signo de ~** exclamation mark

exclamar [es·kla·'mar] *vi, vt* to exclaim

excluir [es·klu·'ir] *irr como huir vt* to exclude; (*descartar*) to rule out

exclusión [es·klu·'sjon] *f* **1.** (*eliminación*) exclusion; **con ~ de** excluding **2.** (*rechazo*) rejection

exclusiva [es·klu·si·βa] *f* **1.** (*privilegio*) sole rights *pl* **2.** (*monopolio*) monopoly **3.** PREN exclusive

exclusivamente [es·klu·si·βa·'men·te] *adv* exclusively

exclusive [es·klu·'si·βe] *adv* exclusively; **cerrado hasta el 27 de mayo ~** closed up to and including the 26th of May

exclusivo, -a [es·klu·'si·βo, -a] *adj* exclusive

excremento [es·kre·'men·to] *m* excretion

exculpar [es·kul·'par] *vt* to acquit

excursión [es·kur·'sjon] *f* excursion; **~ a pie** hike; **ir de ~** to go on an excursion

excursionista [es·kur·sjo·'nis·ta] *mf* (*turista*) tourist; (*para un día*) day-tripper; (*a pie*) hiker

excusa [es·'ku·sa] *f* 1. (*pretexto*) excuse 2. (*disculpa*) apology 3. (*justificación*) justification

excusar [es·ku·'sar] *vt* 1. (*justificar*) to justify 2. (*disculpar*) to excuse 3. (*eximir*) to let off

exento, -a [ek·'sen·to, -a] *adj* exempt; **~ de impuestos** tax free

exfoliar [es·fo·'ljar] I. *vt* to exfoliate II. *vr:* **~se** (*pintura*) to peel; (*corteza*) to flake

exhalar [ek·sa·'lar] *vt* to exhale; (*suspiro*) to let out

exhaustivo, -a [ek·saus·'ti·βo, -a] *adj* exhaustive; **de forma exhaustiva** thoroughly

exhausto, -a [ek·'saus·to, -a] *adj* exhausted

exhibición [ek·si·βi·'sjon, -'θjon] *f* exhibition; (*presentación*) show; **~ cinematográfica/deportiva** film/sports festival

exhibir [ek·si·'βir] *vt* to exhibit; (*ostentar*) to show off

exhumar [ek·su·'mar] *vt* to exhume

exigencia [ek·si·'xen·sja, -θja] *f* 1. (*demanda*) demand 2. (*requisito*) requirement

exigente [ek·si·'xen·te] *adj* demanding

exigir <g → j> [ek·si·'xir] *vt* to demand

exil(i)ado [ek·si·'la·do/ek·si·'lja·do, -a] I. *adj* exiled II. *m, f* exile

exil(i)ar [ek·si·'lar/ek·si·'ljar] I. *vt* to exile II. *vr:* **~se** to go into exile

exilio [ek·'si·ljo] *m* exile

eximir [ek·si·'mir] *vt* to exempt (**de** from)

existencia [ek·sis·'ten·sja, -θja] *f* 1. existence 2. *pl* stock

existencial [ek·sis·ten·'sjal, -'θjal] *adj* existential

existir [ek·sis·'tir] *vi* to exist, to be

éxito ['ek·si·to] *m* success; **con ~** successfully; **sin ~** without success; **tener ~** to be successful

exitoso, -a [ek·si·'to·so, -a] *adj* successful

éxodo ['ek·so·do] *m* exodus; **~ rural** rural depopulation

exorbitante [ek·sor·βi·'tan·te] *adj* excessive; (*precio*) exorbitant

exótico, -a [ek·'so·ti·ko, -a] *adj* exotic

exotismo [ek·so·'tis·mo] *m* exoticism

expandir [es·pan·'dir] I. *vt* to spread; (*dilatar*) to expand II. *vr:* **~se** to spread; (*dilatarse*) to expand

expansión [es·pan·'sjon] *f* expansion; POL enlargement

expatriar <1. *pres* expatrío> [es·pa·tri·'ar] *vt* to exile; (*quitar la ciudadanía*) to deprive of citizenship

expectación [es·pek·ta·'sjon, -'θjon] *f* 1. (*expectativa*) expectation; **con ~** expectantly 2. (*emoción*) excitement

expectante [es·pek·'tan·te] *adj* expectant

expectativa [es·pek·ta·'ti·βa] *f* 1. (*expectación*) expectation; **estar a la ~ de algo** to be on the lookout for sth 2. (*perspectiva*) prospect; **~ de vida** life expectancy

expedición [es·pe·di·'sjon, -'θjon] *f* 1. (*viaje, grupo*) expedition 2. (*remesa*) shipment; (*acción*) shipping 3. (*documento*) issue

expediente [es·pe·'djen·te] *m t.* ADMIN file; UNIV record; (*judicial*) proceedings *pl*

expedir [es·pe·'dir] *irr como pedir vt* to send; (*pedido*) to ship; (*documento*) to issue

expeditar [es·pe·di·'tar] *vt* 1. *AmL* (*acelerar*) to speed up 2. *AmC, Méx* (*despachar*) to send

expendedor(a) [es·pen·de·'dor, -·'do·ra] I. *adj* **máquina ~a de billetes/tabaco** ticket/cigarette vending machine

II. *m(f)* vendor; **~ automático** vending machine

expendio [es·'pen·djo] *m And, Méx, Ven* store

expensas [es·'pen·sas] *fpl* costs *pl*; **a ~ de** at the expense of; **vivir a ~ de alguien** to live off sb

experiencia [es·pe·'rjen·sja, -θja] *f* experience; **(falta de) ~ laboral** (lack of) work experience; **saber algo por ~ propia** to know sth from experience; *(experimento)* experiment

experimentado, -a [es·pe·ri·men·'ta·do, -a] *adj* 1. experienced 2. *(probado)* tested; **no ~ en animales** not tested on animals

experimental [es·pe·ri·men·'tal] *adj* experimental

experimentar [es·pe·ri·men·'tar] I. *vi* to experiment II. *vt* 1. *(sentir)* to experience 2. *(hacer experimentos)* to experiment with; *(probar)* to test 3. *(en estadísticas)* to register; **~ un aumento/una pérdida** to register an increase/a loss

experimento [es·pe·ri·'men·to] *m* experiment

experto, -a [es·'per·to, -a] *adj, m, f* expert; *(perito)* specialist

expirar [es·pi·'rar] *vi* to expire

explanada [es·pla·'na·da] *f* flat area

explayarse [es·pla·'jar·se] *vr* to speak at length; **~se con alguien** to talk openly to sb

explicación [es·pli·ka·'sjon, -'θjon] *f* 1. *(aclaración)* explanation 2. *(motivo)* reason; **dar explicaciones** to justify; **sin dar explicaciones** without giving any reason

explicar <c → qu> [es·pli·'kar] I. *vt* 1. *(manifestar)* to tell 2. *(aclarar)* to explain 3. *(justificar)* to justify II. *vr:* **~se** 1. *(disculparse)* to apologize 2. *(expresarse)* to express oneself; **¿me explico?** do I make myself clear?; **no me lo explico** I don't understand it

explicativo, -a [es·pli·ka·'ti·βo, -a] *adj* explanatory

explícito, -a [es·'pli·si·to, -a; -θi·to, -a] *adj* explicit

exploración [es·plo·ra·'sjon, -'θjon] *f* exploration; MED examination

explorador(a) [es·plo·ra·'dor] *m(f)* explorer; MIL scout

explorar [es·plo·'rar] *vt* to explore; MED to analyze

explosión [es·plo·'sjon] *f* 1. *(estallido)* explosion; **~ demográfica** population boom; **hacer ~** to explode 2. *(detonación)* detonation; **~ fallida** dud 3. *(arrebato)* outburst

explosionar [es·plo·sjo·'nar] *vi, vt* to explode

explosivo, -a [es·plo·'si·βo, -a] *adj, m, f* explosive

explotación [es·plo·ta·'sjon, -'θjon] *f* exploitation

explotar [es·plo·'tar] I. *vi* 1. to explode 2. *(persona)* to blow up *inf* II. *vt* to exploit; AGR to cultivate; *(empresa)* to manage

exponente [es·po·'nen·te] *m* example; MAT exponent

exponer [es·po·'ner] *irr como* poner I. *vt* 1. *(mostrar)* to show 2. *(hablar)* to set out 3. *(exhibir)* to exhibit 4. *(arriesgar)* to endanger II. *vr:* **~se** 1. *(descubrirse)* to expose oneself 2. *(arriesgarse)* to endanger oneself

exportación [es·por·ta·'sjon, -'θjon] *f* export

exportador(a) [es·por·ta·'dor, -·'do·ra] I. *adj* exporting II. *m(f)* exporter

exportar [es·por·'tar] *vt* to export

exposición [es·po·si·'sjon, -'θjon] *f* 1. *(explicación)* explanation 2. *(informe)* report 3. *(exhibición)* exhibition; **~ universal** world('s) fair 4. FOTO exposure

exprés [es·'pres] *adj, m inv* express; **olla ~** pressure cooker

expresamente [es·pre·sa·'men·te] *adv* 1. *(literalmente)* clearly 2. *(deliberadamente)* expressly

expresar [es·pre·'sar] I. *vt* to express II. *vr:* **~se** to express oneself

expresión [es·pre·'sjon] *f* expression

expresionismo [es·pre·sjo·'nis·mo] *m* expressionism

expresionista [es·pre·sjo·'nis·ta] *adj, mf* expressionist

expresivo, -a [es·pre·'si·βo, -a] *adj* expressive; (*afectuoso*) affectionate

expreso, -a [es·'pre·so, -a] *adj* express; (*claro*) clear; (**tren**) ~ express train; **enviar por** (**correo**) ~ to send by special delivery

exprimidor [es·pri·mi·'dor] *m* squeezer

exprimir [es·pri·'mir] *vt* (*fruta*) to squeeze; (*persona*) to bleed (dry)

expropiación [es·pro·pja·'sjon, -'θjon] *f* expropriation

expropiar [es·pro·'pjar] *vt* to expropriate

expuesto, -a [es·'pwes·to, -a] I. *pp de* **exponer** II. *adj* 1. (*peligroso*) risky 2. (*sin protección*) exposed 3. (*sensible*) vulnerable

expulsar [es·pul·'sar] *vt* to expel; (*del país*) to deport; (*excluir*) to bar

expulsión [es·pul·'sjon] *f* expulsion; (*del país*) deportation

exquisitez [es·ki·si·'tes, -'teθ] *f* exquisiteness; (*manjar*) delicacy

exquisito, -a [es·ki·'si·to, -a] *adj* exquisite; (*comida*) delicious

éxtasis ['eks·ta·sis] *m inv* ecstasy

extender <e → ie> [es·ten·'der] I. *vt* 1. (*untar, alisar, propagar*) to spread 2. (*desplegar*) to unfold; ~ **la mano** to reach out one's hand 3. (*ensanchar*) to widen; (*agrandar*) to enlarge II. *vr:* ~**se** 1. to extend; ~**se por algo** to extend over sth 2. (*prolongarse*) to last

extendido, -a [es·ten·'di·do, -a] *adj* 1. (*amplio*) widespread; **estar muy** ~ to be very well-known 2. (*prolongado*) long; (*detallado*) extensive 3. (*mano, brazos*) outstretched

extensible [es·ten·'si·βle] *adj* extensible; **mesa** ~ folding table

extensión [es·ten·'sjon] *f* 1. (*dimensión*) extent; (*longitud, duración*) length; **por** ~ by extension 2. (*difusión*) spreading 3. (*ampliación*) *t.* POL expansion 4. TEL, ELEC extension

extenso, -a [es·'ten·so, -a] *adj* extensive

extenuar <*l. pres* extenúo> [es·te·nu·'ar] *vt* (*agotar*) to exhaust; (*debilitar*) to weaken

exterior [es·te·'rjor] I. *adj* 1. (*externo*) external; (*aspecto*) external; (*espacio*) outer 2. (*extranjero*) foreign; **Ministerio de Asuntos Exteriores** State Department

II. *m* exterior; **en el** ~ abroad

exteriorizar <z → c> [es·te·rjo·ri·'sar, -'θar] *vt* (*manifestar*) to show; (*revelar*) to reveal

exteriormente [es·te·rjor·'men·te] *adv* externally

exterminar [es·ter·mi·'nar] *vt* to exterminate

exterminio [es·ter·'mi·njo] *m* extermination

externo, -a [es·'ter·no, -a] *adj* external; **de uso** ~ external use only

extinción [es·tin·'sjon, -'θjon] *f* 1. ECOL extinction; **en vías de** ~ threatened by extinction 2. ~ **de incendios** fire extinguishing 3. (*contrato*) termination

extinguir <gu → g> [es·tin·'gir] I. *vt* to terminate; (*apagar*) to extinguish II. *vr:* ~**se** 1. ECOL to become extinct; (*finalizar*) to be terminated 2. (*apagarse*) to be extinguished

extinto, -a [es·'tin·to, -a] *adj* 1. extinct; (*fuego*) extinguished 2. AmS, Méx (*muerto*) deceased

extintor [es·tin·'tor] *m* ~ **de incendios** fire extinguisher

extirpación [es·tir·pa·'sjon, -'θjon] *f* extraction; (*de un miembro*) amputation

extirpar [es·tir·'par] *vt* to extract; (*miembro*) to amputate

extorsión [es·tor·'sjon] *f* extortion

extorsionar [es·tor·sjo·'nar] *vt* to extort; (*molestar*) to bother

extra ['es·tra] I. *adj* extra; **horas** ~**s** overtime; **paga** ~ bonus II. *m* 1. *t.* CINE, TV extra; (*en periódico, revista*) special supplement 2. (*paga*) bonus 3. (*ayudante*) helper

extracción [es·trak·'sjon, -'θjon] *f* removal; (*diente, mineral*) extraction; ~ **de sangre** drawing of blood

extraconyugal [es·tra·kon·ju·'ɣal] *adj* extramarital

extracto [es·'trak·to, -a] *m t.* QUÍM extract; (*resumen*) summary

extractor [es·trak·'tor] *m* ~ **de humo** exhaust fan

extradición [es·tra·di·'sjon, -'θjon] *f* extradition

extraditar [es·tra·di·'tar] *vt* to extradite

extraer [es·tra·'er] *irr como* traer *vt* to extract

extraescolar [es·tra·es·ko·'lar] *adj* extracurricular

extralimitarse [es·tra·li·mi·'tar·se] *vr* to go too far

extranjería [es·tran·xe·'ri·a] *f* **ley de ~** immigration law

extranjero, -a [es·tran·'xe·ro, -a] **I.** *adj* foreign **II.** *m, f* foreigner; **(en) el ~** abroad

extrañar [es·tra·'ɲar] **I.** *vt* **1.** (*sorprender*) to surprise **2.** (*echar de menos*) to miss **II.** *vr* **~se de algo** to find sth strange

extrañeza [es·tra·'ɲe·sa, -θa] *f* strangeness; **causar ~** to cause surprise

extraño, -a [es·tra·'ɲo, -a] **I.** *adj* (*raro*) strange; (*peculiar*) peculiar; (*extraordinario*) remarkable **II.** *m, f* stranger

extraoficial [es·tra·o·fi·'sjal, -'θjal] *adj* unofficial

extraordinario, -a [es·tra·or·di·'na·rjo, -a] *adj* extraordinary; (*muy bueno*) fantastic

extrarradio [es·tra·'rra·djo] *m* outskirts *pl*

extrasensorial [es·tra·sen·so·'rjal] *adj* extrasensory

extraterrestre [es·tra·te·'rres·tre] *adj, mf* extraterrestrial

extravagancia [es·tra·βa·'ɣan·sja, -θja] *f* eccentricity

extravagante [es·tra·βa·'ɣan·te] **I.** *adj* **1.** (*raro*) odd **2.** (*excéntrico*) eccentric **II.** *mf* eccentric

extraviado, -a [es·tra·βi·'a·do, -a] *adj* lost; (*animal*) stray

extraviar <*1. pres* extravío> [es·tra·βi·'ar] **I.** *vt* **1.** (*despistar*) to confuse **2.** (*perder*) to lose **II.** *vr:* **~se** to get lost; (*descarriarse*) to stray, *fig* to go astray

extremado, -a [es·tre·'ma·do, -a] *adj* (*excesivo*) excessive; (*exagerado*) extreme

extremar [es·tre·'mar] *vt* to carry to extremes; (*medidas de seguridad*) to tighten; **~ la prudencia** to be extremely cautious

extremidad [es·tre·mi·'dad] *f* limb

extremismo [es·tre·'mis·mo] *m* extremism; (*religioso*) fundamentalism

extremista [es·tre·'mis·ta] *adj, mf* extremist

extremo [es·'tre·mo] *m* (*cabo*) end; (*punto límite*) extreme; **con** [*o* **en**] **~** a lot

extremo, -a [es·'tre·mo, -a] *adj* extreme; (*distante*) furthest

extrínseco, -a [es·'trin·se·ko, -a] *adj* extrinsic(al)

extrovertido, -a [es·tro·βer·'ti·do, -a] *adj* outgoing

exuberancia [ek·su·βe·'ran·sja, -θja] *f* exuberance

exuberante [ek·su·βe·'ran·te] *adj* exuberant; (*vegetación*) lush

eyaculación [e·ja·ku·la·'sjon, -'θjon] *f* ejaculation

eyacular [e·ja·ku·'lar] *vi* to ejaculate

F

F, f ['e·fe] *f* F, f, F, f; **F de Francia** F as in Foxtrot

fabada [fa·'βa·da] *f* Asturian bean stew with pork sausage, blood sausage and pork chops

fábrica ['fa·βri·ka] *f* factory; **~ de cerveza** brewery; (*de ladrillo, piedra*) masonry; **en** [*o* **ex**] **~** direct from the factory

fabricación [fa·βri·ka·'sjon, -'θjon] *f* manufacturing; **~ en masa** mass production

fabricante [fa·βri·'kan·te] *mf* manufacturer

fabricar <c → qu> [fa·βri·'kar] *vt* to manufacture; **~ cerveza** to brew beer

fábula ['fa·βu·la] *f* fable; (*invención*) tale; **¡de ~!** terrific!

fabuloso, -a [fa·βu·'lo·so, -a] *adj* fabulous

facción [fak·'sjon, -'θjon] *f* **1.** POL faction **2.** *pl* (*facial*) features *pl*

faceta [fa·'se·ta, fa·'θe·] *f* facet; (*aspecto*) side

faceto, -a [fa·'se·to, -a] *adj Méx* **1.** (*chistoso*) facetious **2.** (*presuntuoso*) cocksure

facha[1] ['fa·tʃa] *adj, mf pey inf* fascist

facha[2] ['fa·tʃa] *f inf* look; **estar hecho una ~** to look terrible

fachada [fa·'tʃa·da] *f* façade; **su buen humor es pura ~** his/her good mood is pure pretense

facial [fa·'sjal, -'θjal] *adj* facial

fácil ['fa·sil, -θil] *adj* **1.** (*simple*) easy; **es más ~ de decir que de hacer** *prov* easier said than done *prov* **2.** (*cómodo*) undemanding **3.** (*probable*) probable; **es ~ que** +*subj* it is likely that **4.** (*de seducir*) loose

facilidad [fa·si·li·'dad, fa·θi·-] *f* **1.** (*sin dificultad*) ease **2.** (*dotes*) facility; **tener ~ para algo** to have an ability for sth; (*idiomas*) to have a flair for languages **3.** **~es de pago** payment arrangements *pl*; **ofrecer** [*o* **dar**] **~es a alguien para algo** to facilitate sth for sb

facilitar [fa·si·li·'tar, fa·θi·-] *vt* (*favorecer*) to facilitate; (*posibilitar*) to make possible; (*suministrar*) to supply

fácilmente [fa·sil·'men·te, fa·θil·-] *adv* easily; (*seguramente*) probably

factible [fak·'ti·βle] *adj* feasible

factor [fak·'tor] *m* factor; **~ de riesgo** risk factor

factoría [fak·to·'ri·a] *f* factory

factura [fak·'tu·ra] *f* (*cuenta*) bill; (*recibo*) receipt; **pasar ~** to render an account; **su holgazanería le pasa ahora ~** *inf* he/she is now having to pay the price for his/her idleness; **esta chaqueta es de buena ~** this jacket is well made

facturación [fak·tu·ra·'θjon, -'sjon] *f* AVIAT check-in

facturar [fak·tu·'rar] *vt* **1.** (*cobrar*) to bill; **~ los gastos de transporte** to bill for transport costs; **nuestra compañía factura tres millones de pesos al mes** our company is bringing in three million pesos a month **2.** (*ganar*) to earn **3.** **~** (*el equipaje*) to check in

facultad [fa·kul·'tad] *f* **1.** *t.* UNIV faculty; *pl* faculties; **recobró sus ~es** he/she recovered his/her faculties **2.** (*atribuciones*) authority; **tener ~ para hacer algo** to have the authority to do sth; **conceder ~es a alguien (para hacer algo)** to authorize sb (to do sth); **este título me faculta para ejercer la abogacía** this qualification entitles me to practice law

facultar [fa·kul·'tar] *vt* to authorize

faena [fa·'e·na] *f* **1.** task; **~s domésticas** chores *pl* **2.** *inf* dirty trick; **hacer una ~ a alguien** to play a dirty trick on sb

faenar [fae·'nar] *vi* to work; (*pescar*) to fish

faenero, -a [fae·'ne·ro, -a] *m, f* Chile field worker

failear [fai·le·'ar] *vt* AmC, RíoPl (*documentos*) to file; (*en una carpeta*) to put in a folder

faisán [fai·'san] *m* pheasant

faja ['fa·xa] *f* corset

fajada [fa·'xa·da] *f* **1.** Ant (*ataque*) attack **2.** Arg *inf* (*paliza*) beating **3.** Ven (*chasco*) disappointment

fajar [fa·'xar] **I.** *vt* AmL (*golpear*) to strike **II.** *vr:* **~se** (*pelearse*) to fight

fajilla [fa·'xi·ja, -ʎa] *f* AmL wrapper

fajo ['fa·xo] *m* bundle; **~ de billetes** wad of bills

falange [fa·'lan·xe] *f* phalanx

falda ['fal·da] *f* **1.** skirt; **~ pantalón** culottes; **~ plisada** pleated skirt; **~ tubo/recta** straight skirt **2.** (*regazo*) lap **3.** (*de la mesa*) table cover **4.** (*de una montaña*) lower slope

faldeo [fal·'deo] *m* Arg, Chile mountainside

faldero [fal·'de·ro] *m* womanizer; **perro ~** lapdog

fálico, -a ['fa·li·ko, -a] *adj* phallic

falla ['fa·ja, -ʎa] *f t.* GEO fault

fallar [fa·'jar, -'ʎar] *vi* **1.** to go wrong; (*proyecto*) to fail; (*plan, intento*) to miscarry; **le ~on los nervios** his/her nerves failed him/her; **algo le falla** there is sth wrong with him/her; **no falla nunca** (*cosa*) it never fails; (*persona*) you can always count on her/him; **~ a alguien** to let sb down; (*en una cita*) to stand sb up **2.** JUR to render judgment

fallecer [fa·je·'ser, -ʎe·'θer] *irr como crecer vi* to pass away

fallecido, -a [fa·je·'si·do, -a; -ʎe·'θi·do, -a] *adj, m, f* deceased

fallecimiento [fa·je·si·'mjen·to, -ʎe·θi·'mjen·to] *m* death

fallido, -a [fa·'ji·do, -a; fa·'ʎi·-] *adj* (*proyecto*) unsuccessful; (*intento*) abortive; (*deuda*) bad

fallo ['fa·jo, -ʎo] *m* **1.** error; (*fracaso*) failure; **~ humano** human error; **este asunto solo tiene un pequeño ~**

this matter only has one small shortcoming; TÉC breakdown **2.** JUR sentence **3.** ~ **cardíaco/renal** heart/kidney failure

falluto, -a [fa·'ʎu·to, -a; fa·'ʎu-] *adj RíoPl inf* unreliable; (*falso*) two-faced

falsear [fal·se·'ar] *vt* to misrepresent; (*verdad*) to distort; (*falsificar*) to counterfeit

falsedad [fal·se·'ðað] *f* falseness; (*hipocresía*) hypocrisy

falsificación [fal·si·fi·ka·'sjon, -'θjon] *f* forgery; ~ **de billetes** counterfeiting of banknotes

falsificador(a [fal·si·fi·ka·'ðor, -'ðo·ra] *m(f)* forger; (*de billetes*) counterfeiter

falsificar <c → qu> [fal·si·fi·'kar] *vt* to falsify; (*verdad*) to distort

falso ['fal·so] *adv* en ~ (*falsamente*) falsely; **jurar en** ~ to commit perjury; **coger a alguien en** ~ to catch sb out [o in a lie]; **dar un golpe en** ~ (*movimiento*) to miss the mark; **dar un paso en** ~ (*tropezar*) to stumble; (*equivocarse*) to make a mistake; **sonar** ~ to ring false

falso, -a ['fal·so, -a] **I.** *adj* false; **¡~!** not true!; (*no natural*) artificial **II.** *m, f* liar; (*hipócrita*) hypocrite

falta ['fal·ta] *f* **1.** (*carencia*) lack; (*ausencia*) absence; ~ **de dinero** shortage of money; ~ **de educación** lack of education; **echar en** ~ to miss; **hacer** ~ to need; **me hace** ~ **dinero** I need money; **¡ni** ~ **que hace!** there is absolutely no need! **2.** (*fallo*) error; ~ **ortográfica** spelling error; **sin** ~**s** with no mistakes; **sin** ~ without fail **3.** DEP foul **4.** JUR default

faltar [fal·'tar] *vi* **1.** (*no estar*) to be missing; (*persona*) to be absent; ~ **a clase** to miss class; ~ **a una cita** not to turn up to an appointment; **me faltan mis llaves** my keys are missing **2.** (*necesitarse*) ~ (**por**) **hacer** to be still to be done; **nos falta dinero para...** we do not have enough money to...; **me faltan diez céntimos** I'm ten cents short; **me falta tiempo para hacerlo** I need time to do it; **no falta quien...** there is always sb who...; **falta** (**por**) **saber si...** we need

to know if...; **¡no** ~**ía** [*o* faltaba] **más!** that is the limit!; (*respuesta a agradecimiento*) you are welcome!; (*asentir amablemente*) of course!; **por si algo faltaba...** as if it were not enough already...; **¡lo que faltaba!** that is the last straw! **3.** (*temporal: quedar*) to be left; **faltan cuatro días para tu cumpleaños** your birthday is in four days; **falta poco para las doce** it is nearly twelve o'clock; **falta diez para las nueve** *AmL* it is ten to nine; **poco le faltó para llorar** he/she was on the verge of tears **4.** (*no cumplir*) ~ **a una promesa** to break a promise; **nunca falta a su palabra** she/he never goes back on his/her word **5.** (*ofender*) ~ **a alguien** to be disrespectful to sb

falto, -a ['fal·to, -a] *adj* (*escaso*) ~ **de algo** short of sth; (*desprovisto*) lacking in sth; ~ **de recursos** lacking in resources; ~ **de cariño** lacking affection

faltón, -ona [fal·'ton, -·to·na] *adj inf* **1.** fly-by-night *AmL* **2.** do-nothing

fama ['fa·ma] *f* **1.** fame; (*gloria*) glory; **tener** ~ to be famous; **dar** ~ **a algo/alguien** to make sth/sb famous; **unos tienen la** ~ **y otros cardan la lana** *prov* some do all the work while others reap all the glory *prov* **2.** (*reputación*) reputation; **tener** ~ **de...** to have a reputation of being...; **ser de mala** ~ to have a bad reputation

familia [fa·'mi·lja] *f* family; (*parentela*) relatives *pl*; ~ **numerosa** large family; **cabeza de** ~ head of the household; ~ **política** in-laws *pl*; **de buena** ~ from a good family; **eso viene de** ~ that runs in the family; **en** ~ with the family; **ser de la** ~ to be one of the family; **acordarse de la** ~ **de alguien** *inf* to insult sb

familiar [fa·mi·'ljar] **I.** *adj* **1.** (*íntimo*) intimate; **asunto** ~ personal matter; **economía** ~ domestic economy **2.** (*conocido*) familiar **II.** *mf* relative

familiaridad [fa·mi·lja·ri·'ðað] *f* familiarity; (*confianza*) intimacy

familiarizarse <z → c> [fa·mi·lja·ri·'sar·se, -'θar·se] *vr* to familiarize oneself (**con** with)

famoso, -a [fa.'mo.so, -a] adj famous; (sonado) talked-of; ~ **por algo** famous for sth

fan [fan] mf <fans> fan

fanático, -a [fa.'na.ti.ko, -a] **I.** adj fanatical **II.** m, f fan; pey fanatic; **es una fanática del rock** she is crazy about rock

fanatismo [fa.na.'tis.mo] m fanaticism

fané [fa.'ne] adj AmL inf (arrugado) crumpled; (marchito) withered

fanfarrón, -ona [fan.fa.'rron, -.'rro.na] **I.** adj swanky **II.** m, f swank

fanfarronear [fan.fa.rro.ne.'ar] vi inf to brag

fango ['fan.go] m mud

fantasear [fan.ta.se.'ar] vi to fantasize; (presumir) to boast

fantasía [fan.ta.'si.a] f imagination; (cosa imaginada) fantasy; **¡déjate de ~s!** come down to earth!

fantasioso, -a [fan.ta.'sjo.so, -a] **I.** adj **1.** (inventado) fanciful **2.** (fachendoso) swanky inf **II.** m, f show-off

fantasma [fan.'tas.ma] m **1.** ghost; (visión) phantom; **andar como un ~** to be lifeless; **aparecer como un ~** to appear out of nowhere **2.** inf boaster

fantasmada [fan.tas.'ma.da] f inf pose

fantasmagórico, -a [fan.tas.ma.'ɣo.ri.ko, -a] adj phantasmagorical; TEAT with optical illusion

fantasmal [fan.tas.'mal] adj phantom

fantasmón, -ona [fan.tas.'mon, -.'mo.na] inf **I.** adj presumptuous **II.** m, f show-off

fantástico, -a [fan.'tas.ti.ko, -a] adj fantastic

fantochada [fan.to.'tʃa.da] f **1.** (fantasmada) pose **2.** (tontería) silly act

fantoche [fan.'to.tʃe] m **1.** (títere) puppet **2.** (mamarracho) sight

FAO ['fao] f abr de **Organización para la Agricultura y la Alimentación** FAO

faramallear [fa.ra.ma.je.'ar] vi Chile, Méx to brag

faraón [fa.ra.'on] m Pharaoh

fardar [far.'dar] vi inf to boast; (impresionar) to make an impression

fardo ['far.do] m package; (de tela) bundle

fardón, -ona [far.'don, -.'do.na] adj inf **1.** (chulo) swanky **2.** (vistoso) showy; (coche) flashy

farfullar [far.fu.'jar, -'ʎar] inf **I.** vi to stutter **II.** vt to botch

faringe [fa.'rin.xe] f pharynx

faringitis [fa.rin.'xi.tis] f inv pharyngitis

fariña [fa.'ri.ɲa] f AmS coarse cassava flour

farmacéutico, -a [far.ma.'seu.ti.ko, -a; far.ma.'θeu-] **I.** adj pharmaceutical; **industria farmacéutica** pharmaceutical industry; **productos ~s** pharmaceutical products **II.** m, f druggist

farmacia [far.'ma.sja, -θja] f **1.** (tienda) drugstore; ~ **de guardia** ≈ 24-hour drugstore **2.** (ciencia) pharmacy

fármaco ['far.ma.ko] m drug

farmacodependencia [far.ma.ko.de.pen.'den.sja, -θja] f drug dependence

faro ['fa.ro] m **1.** AUTO headlight; ~ **antiniebla** fog light **2.** NÁUT lighthouse

farol [fa.'rol] m **1.** (lámpara) lamp; (de calle) streetlight **2.** inf (fanfarronada) swank; (patraña) tall story; **tirarse un ~** to show off **3.** pl AmL eyes; **¡adelante con los ~es!** inf go for it!

farola [fa.'ro.la] f street light; (poste) lamppost

farolazo [fa.ro.'la.so] m AmC, Méx swig of liquor

farolear [fa.ro.le.'ar] vi to swank

farolero, -a [fa.ro.'le.ro, -a] inf **I.** adj bragging **II.** m, f show-off

farrear [fa.rre.'ar] inf **I.** vi CSur to paint the town red **II.** vr: ~**se** RíoPl (dinero) to blow inf

farrista [fa.'rris.ta] adj, mf CSur fun-loving

farruto, -a [fa.'rru.to, -a] adj Bol, Chile puny

farsa ['far.sa] f sham

farsante [far.'san.te] **I.** adj sham **II.** m, f charlatan

FAS [fas] fpl MIL abr de **Fuerzas Armadas** the (armed) forces

fascículo [fa.'si.ku.lo, fas.'θi-] m installment

fascinación [fa.si.na.'sjon, fas.θi.na.'θjon] f fascination; **sentir ~ por algo** to be fascinated by sth

fascinador(a) [fa·si·na·'dor, -·'do·ra, fas-θi-], **fascinante** [fas·θi·'nan·te] adj fascinating; (persona) captivating; (libro) enthralling

fascinar [fa·si'nar, fas·θi-], vt to fascinate; (libro) enthrall

fascismo [fa·'sis·mo, fas·'θis-] m fascism

fascista [fa·'sis·ta, fas·'θis-] I. adj fascist(ic) II. mf fascist

fase [fa·se] f phase

fast food [fas fud] m o f fast food

fastidiado, -a [fas·ti·'dja·do, -a] adj inf 1. (enfermo) unwell 2. (molesto) annoyed 3. (estropeado) broken; **andar ~ de...** to have a bad...; **ando ~ de dinero/tiempo estos días** I don't have enough money/time these days; **anda ~ de la rodilla** he has a bad knee

fastidiar [fas·ti·'djar] inf I. vt 1. (molestar) to annoy; **¡no te fastidia!** you must be kidding! 2. (estropear) ruin II. vr: **-se** 1. (enojarse) to get cross 2. (aguantarse) to put up with it; **¡fastídiate!** get lost!; **¡hay que ~se!** it's unbelievable! 3. AmL (perjudicarse) to harm

fastidio [fas·'ti·djo] m 1. (disgusto) bother; **¡vaya ~!** what a nuisance!; (mala suerte) misfortune 2. (aburrimiento) bore

fastidioso, -a [fas·ti·'djo·so, -a] adj 1. (molesto) annoying 2. (aburrido) boring 3. (pesado) dull

fatal [fa·'tal] I. adj 1. (inevitable) unavoidable; **el momento ~** the fateful moment 2. (muy mal) awful 3. (funesto) fatal; (mortal) mortal; **mujer ~** femme fatale II. adv inf awfully; **el examen me fue ~** my exam was a disaster

fatalidad [fa·ta·li·'dad] f misfortune

fatídico, -a [fa·'ti·di·ko, -a] adj (terrible) horrible

fatiga [fa·'ti·ɣa] f 1. weariness, fatigue; **~ visual** eye strain 2. pl hardship

fatigado, -a [fa·ti·'ɣa·do, -a] adj worn-out; (sofocado) short of breath

fatigar <g → gu> [fa·ti·'ɣar] I. vt to tire, to fatigue; (molestar) to annoy II. vr: **-se** 1. (agotarse) to wear oneself out; (ojos) to strain 2. (esforzarse) to ex-

ert oneself 3. (sofocarse) to get short of breath

fatigoso, -a [fa·ti·'ɣo·so, -a] adj tiring; (persona) tiresome

fauces ['fau·ses, -θes] fpl 1. fauces pl 2. AmL (dientes) teeth

fauna ['fau·na] f fauna

favela [fa·'βe·la] f 1. AmL shanty 2. pl shanty town

favor [fa·'βor] m 1. (servicio) favor; (ayuda) good turn; **por ~** please; **hacer un ~ a alguien** to do sb a favor; **¡hágame el ~ de dejarme en paz!** would you please leave me alone!; **te lo pido por ~** I am begging you; **hagan el ~ de ser puntuales** please be punctual 2. (gracia) favor; **a [o en] ~ de alguien** in sb's favor; **tener a alguien a tu ~** to have sb on your side; **a ~ del viento/de la corriente** with the wind/the current 3. (beneficio) **voto a ~** vote for; **votar a ~ de alguien** to vote for sb; **estar a ~ de algo** to be in favor of sth

favorable [fa·βo·'ra·βle] adj favorable; (optimista) promising

favorecer [fa·βo·re·'ser, -'θer] irr como crecer I. vt 1. (beneficiar) to benefit 2. (ayudar) to help 3. (dar preferencia) to favor 4. (ropa) to become II. vr: **~se** to benefit

favorecido, -a [fa·βo·re·'si·do, -a; -'θi·do, -a] adj favored; **has salido ~ en la foto** you came out well in the picture

favoritismo [fa·βo·ri·'tis·mo] m nepotism; (parcialidad) favoritism

favorito, -a [fa·βo·'ri·to, -a] I. adj favorite; **plato ~** favorite dish II. m, f **~ del público** the public's darling; DEP (the) favorite

fax [faks] m inv fax; **mandar un ~ a una empresa/a Suecia** to send a fax to a company/to Sweden

fayuca [fa·'ju·ka] f Méx inf black market; **tabaco de ~** contraband tobacco

fayuquero, -a [fa·ju·'ke·ro, -a] m, f Méx inf smuggler

faz [fas, faθ] f countenance

fe [fe] f t. REL faith; **~ en Dios** faith in God; **digno de ~** worthy of trust; **dar ~ a algo/alguien** to vouch for sth/sb; **dar ~ de algo** to certify sth; **tener ~**

en alguien to believe in sb; **de buena/mala ~** in good/bad faith; **~ de erratas** errata

fealdad |feal·'dad| f ugliness

feb. *abr de* **febrero** Feb.

febrero |fe·'βre·ro| m February; *v. t.* **marzo**

febril |fe·'βril| *adj* feverish; (*actividad*) hectic; **acceso ~** sudden temperature

fecal |fe·'kal| *adj* fecal; **sustancias ~es** fecal matter

fecha |'fe·tʃa| f (*data*) t. ECON date; (*señalada*) day; **~ de caducidad** expiration date; (*de comida*) sell-by date; **~ de cierre** closing date; **~ clave** decisive day; **~ de las elecciones** Election day; **~ de entrega** date of delivery; **~ límite** [*o* **tope**] deadline; **sin ~** undated; **en la ~ fijada** on the agreed day; **hasta la ~** until now, so far; **adelantar/atrasar la ~ de algo** to bring forward/put back the date of sth; **¿cuál es la ~ de hoy?** what is the date today?; **a 30 días ~** at 30 days' sight; **en estas ~s** around this time

fechable |fe·'tʃa·βle| *adj* datable

fechado, -a |fe·'tʃa·do, -a| *adj* **~ el...** dated...

fechar |fe·'tʃar| *vt* to date

fechoría |fe·tʃo·'ri·a| f prank; JUR misdemeanor

fécula |'fe·ku·la| f starch

fecundación |fe·kun·da·'sjon, -'θjon| f fertilization

fecundar |fe·kun·'dar| *vt* to fertilize

fecundidad |fe·kun·di·'dad| f fertility; (*abundancia*) abundance

fecundo, -a |fe·'kun·do, -a| *adj* prolific; (*tierra*) fertile; (*campo*) productive

federación |fe·de·ra·'sjon, -'θjon| f federation

federado, -a |fe·de·'ra·do, -a| *adj* federate

federal |fe·de·'ral| I. *adj* federal; **estado ~** federal state; **república ~** federal republic II. *mf* federalist

federalismo |fe·de·ra·'lis·mo| m federalism

federalizar <z → c> |fe·de·ra·li·'sar, -'θar| I. *vt* to federalize II. *vr:* **~se** to form a federation

federar |fe·de·'rar| I. *vt* to unite; (*federa-lizar*) to federate II. *vr:* **~se** to become a member; (*federalizarse*) to form a federation

federativo, -a |fe·de·ra·'ti·βo, -a| *adj* federative

felación |fe·la·'sjon, -'θjon| f fellatio

felicidad |fe·li·si·'dad, fe·li·θi·-| f happiness; (*dicha*) good fortune; **¡~es!** congratulations!; (*cumpleaños*) happy birthday; **te deseamos muchas ~es** we wish you all the best

felicitación |fe·li·si·ta·'sjon, -θi·ta·'θjon| f congratulation; (*tarjeta*) greetings card

felicitar |fe·li·si·'tar, fe·li·θi·-| I. *vt* **~ alguien por algo** to congratulate sb on sth II. *vr* **~se por algo** to be glad about sth

felino, -a |fe·'li·no, -a| *adj* feline

feliz |fe·'lis, -'liθ| *adj* happy; (*exitoso*) fortunate; **¡~ Navidad!** merry Christmas!; **¡~ viaje!** have a good trip!

felpa |'fel·pa| f plush

felpeada |fel·pe·'a·da| f Arg, Urug, CSur inf dressing-down

felpudo |fel·'pu·do| m doormat

femenino |fe·me·'ni·no| m feminine

femenino, -a |fe·me·'ni·no, -a| *adj* **1. equipo ~** women's team **2.** (*afemi-nado*) effeminate **3.** LING feminine

feminidad |fe·mi·ni·'dad| f femininity

feminismo |fe·mi·'nis·mo| m feminism; (*movimiento*) feminist movement

feminista |fe·mi·'nis·ta| *adj, mf* feminist

fémur |'fe·mur| m femur

fenomenal |fe·no·me·'nal| *adj* (*extraordi-nario*) incredible; (*estupendo*) terrific

fenómeno |fe·'no·me·no| I. *adj inv inf* marvelous; **¡~!** terrific! II. m **1.** t. FILOS, MED phenomenon; (*maravilla*) marvel **2.** (*genio*) genius III. *adv* marvelously

feo |'feo| I. m *inf* insult; **hacer un ~ a alguien** to snub sb II. *adv AmL* bad, badly

feo, -a |'feo, -a| I. *adj* **1.** ugly; **dejar ~ a alguien** to show sb up; **la cosa se está poniendo fea** things aren't looking too good **2.** (*malo*) bad; **está muy ~ lo que hiciste** what you did was really nasty II. m, f ugly man, ugly woman m, f; ugly child mf

féretro |'fe·re·tro| m coffin

feria ['fe·rja] *f* **1.** (*exposición, verbena*) fair; **~ de muestras** trade fair **2.** (*fiesta*) festival; **puesto de ~** stand

feriado, -a [fe·'rja·do, -a] *adj AmL* holiday; **día ~** bank holiday

ferial [fe·'rjal] **I.** *adj* fair; **recinto ~** trade fair pavilion **II.** *m* fair; (*lugar*) fairground

feriante [fe·'rjan·te] *mf* (*que exhibe*) exhibitor; (*en la verbena*) stall holder; (*que compra*) fairgoer

fermentación [fer·men·ta·'sjon, -'θjon] *f* fermentation

fermentar [fer·men·'tar] *vi, vt* to ferment

fermento [fer·'men·to] *m* fermenting agent

ferocidad [fe·ro·si·'dad, fe·ro·θi·-] *f* ferocity; (*crueldad*) savagery

feroz [fe·'ros, -'roθ] *adj* fierce; (*cruel*) savage

férreo, -a ['fe·reo, -a] *adj* iron

ferretería [fe·re·te·'ri·a] *f* hardware store

ferrocarril [fe·ro·ka·'rril] *m* railroad; **por ~** by rail

ferrocarrilero, -a [fe·ro·ka·rri·'le·ro, -a] *adj AmL inf* railroad; **el transporte ~** rail transport

ferroviario, -a [fe·ro·'βja·rjo, -a] **I.** *adj* railroad **II.** *m, f* railroad worker

ferry ['fe·rri] *m* ferry

fértil ['fer·til] *adj* fertile; **estar en edad ~** to be of reproductive age

fertilidad [fer·ti·li·'dad] *f* fertility; (*tierra*) productiveness

fertilización [fer·ti·li·sa·'sjon, -θa·'θjon] *f* fertilization; **~ in vitro** in vitro fertilization

fertilizante [fer·ti·li·'san·te, -'θan·te] *m* fertilizer

fertilizar <z → c> [fer·ti·li·'sar, -'θar] *vt* to fertilize

ferviente [fer·'βjen·te] *adj* fervent

fervor [fer·'βor] *m* fervor; (*entusiasmo*) enthusiasm; **con ~** ardently

festejar [fes·te·'xar] *vt* **1.** to celebrate **2.** *AmL* (*azotar*) to beat

festejo [fes·'te·xo] *m* **1.** celebration **2.** *pl* public festivities *pl*

festín [fes·'tin] *m* celebration; (*banquete*) feast

festinar [fes·ti·'nar] *vt AmC* **1.** (*agasajar*) to wine and dine **2.** (*arruinar*) to ruin

3. (*apremiar*) to hasten

festival [fes·ti·'βal] *m* festival; **~ de cine** film festival

festividad [fes·ti·βi·'dad] *f* festivity; (*día*) feast

festivo, -a [fes·'ti·βo, -a] *adj* **1.** festive; **día ~** bank holiday **2.** (*humorístico*) humorous; (*persona*) witty

feta ['fe·ta] *f Arg* slice

fetal [fe·'tal] *adj* fetal

fetiche [fe·'ti·tʃe] *m* fetish

fetichismo [fe·ti·'tʃis·mo] *m* fetishism

fétido, -a ['fe·ti·do, -a] *adj* foul smelling

feto ['fe·to] *m* fetus

feúcho, -a [fe·'u·tʃo, -a] *adj inf* plain

feudal [feu·'dal] *adj* feudal

feudalismo [feu·da·'lis·mo] *m* **1.** (*sistema*) feudalism **2.** (*época*) feudal era

fiabilidad [fja·βi·li·'dad] *f* **1.** (*persona*) trustworthiness **2.** (*empresa, datos*) reliability

fiable [fi·'a·βle] *adj* **1.** (*persona*) trustworthy **2.** (*empresa*) reliable

fiaca [fi·'a·ka] *f Arg inf* laziness

fiambre [fi·'am·bre] *m* **1.** CULIN cold meat **2.** *inf* stiff

fiambrera [fjam·'bre·ra] *f* (*cesta*) picnic basket; (*para el almuerzo*) lunch pail; (*táper*) Tupperware® container

fianza [fi·'an·sa, -θa] *f* **1.** (*depósito*) deposit **2.** (*garantía*) security **3. en libertad bajo ~** free on bail

fiar <*1. pres* fío> [fi·'ar] **I.** *vi* **1.** (*al vender*) to give credit **2.** (*confiar*) to trust; **es de ~** he/she is trustworthy **II.** *vt* **1.** (*garantizar*) to stand surety for **2.** (*dar crédito*) to sell on credit **3.** (*confiar*) to entrust **III.** *vr* **~se de algo/alguien** to trust sth/sb; **no te fíes de lo que dice** don't trust what he/she says

fiasco ['fjas·ko] *m* fiasco

fibra ['fi·βra] *f* **1.** *t.* BIO, MED fiber; **~ muscular** muscle fiber; **~ de vidrio** fiberglass **2.** (*vigor*) energy; **no tiene ~ suficiente para llevar la empresa** he/she doesn't have the drive to run the business

ficción [fik·'sjon, -'θjon] *f* **1.** (*simulación*) simulation **2.** (*invención*) invention; LIT, CINE fiction

ficha ['fi·tʃa] *f* **1.** (*de ruleta*) chip; (*de do-*

minó) domino; (*de ajedrez*) piece; (*para una máquina*) token **2.** (*tarjeta*) card; ~ **policial** police record; ~ **técnica** technical specifications

fichaje [fi·'tʃa·xe] *m* signing (up)

fichar [fi·'tʃar] **I.** *vi* **1.** DEP to sign **2.** (*en el trabajo*) to clock in **II.** *vt* **1.** (*registrar*) to enter; **estar fichado** to have a police record; ~ **a alguien** to open a file on sb **2.** DEP to sign up

fichero [fi·'tʃe·ro] *m* filing-cabinet; (*caja*) box file; COMPUT file

ficticio, -a [fik·'ti·sjo, -a; -θjo, -a] *adj* fictitious

fidedigno, -a [fi·de·'diɣ·no, -a] *adj* reliable

fidelidad [fi·de·li·'dad] *f* **1.** (*lealtad*) fidelity, faithfulness **2.** (*precisión*) precision; **alta** ~ high fidelity

fideo [fi·'deo] *m* fine noodle

fiebre ['fje·βre] *f* fever; ~ **del heno** hay fever; ~ **del juego** compulsive gambling; ~ **del oro** gold rush; ~ **palúdica** malaria; **tener** ~ to have a fever; **tener poca** ~ to have a slight temperature

fiel [fjel] **I.** *adj* (*persona, retrato*) faithful; (*memoria*) accurate; **ser** ~ **a una promesa** to keep a promise; **siempre me han sido** ~**es** they have always been loyal to me **II.** *m* **los** ~**es** the faithful

fieltro ['fjel·tro] *m* felt

fiera ['fje·ra] *f* wild animal; (*persona*) animal; (*astuto*) wizard

fiero, -a ['fje·ro, -a] *adj* fierce; (*cruel*) cruel

fierro ['fje·rro] *m* AmL iron

fiesta ['fjes·ta] *f* **1.** (*día*) holiday; **¡Felices Fiestas!** Merry Christmas and a Happy New Year!; **hoy hago** ~ I have taken the day off today **2.** (*celebración*) celebration; ~ (**mayor**) festival; **aguar la** ~ to be a wet blanket; **tengamos la** ~ **en paz** let's agree to differ

fifi [fi·'fi] *m* AmL playboy

fifiriche [fi·fi·'ri·tʃe] *adj* AmL weak

fig. [fi·ɣu·ra·'ti·βo] *abr de* **figurado** fig

figura [fi·'ɣu·ra] *f* **1.** *t.* ARTE, MAT figure; **las grandes** ~**s del deporte** great sports figures; **un vestido que realza la** ~ a dress that enhances the figure **2.** (*cara, mueca*) face; (*aspecto*) counte-

nance **3.** (*imagen*) image; **se distinguía la** ~ **de un barco** you could make out the shape of a boat

figurado, -a [fi·ɣu·'ra·do, -a] *adj* figurative; **en sentido** ~ in a figurative sense; (*lenguaje*) metaphorical

figurar [fi·ɣu·'rar] **I.** *vi* **1.** (*encontrarse*) to figure; **no figura en la lista** it is not on the list; **figura en el puesto número tres** he appears in third place **2.** (*destacar*) to stand out **3.** (*aparentar*) to pose; **le gusta un montón** ~ he loves putting on airs **II.** *vt* **1.** (*representar*) to represent **2.** TEAT to appear **3.** (*simular*) to pretend **III.** *vr*: ~**se** to imagine; **¡figúrate!** just think!; **no vayas a** ~**te que...** don't go thinking that...

figuroso, -a [fi·ɣu·'ro·so, -a] *adj Chile, Méx* loud-dressing

fijación [fi·xa·'sjon, -'θjon] *f t. fig* fixation; **tener una** ~ **por alguien** to have a fixation on sb; (*precio, regla*) fixing; (*mirada*) fixedness

fijador [fi·xa·'dor] *m* **1.** (*para el pelo*) hair gel **2.** (*de pintura*) fixative **3.** FOTO fixer

fijar [fi·'xar] **I.** *vt t.* QUÍM to fix; (*residencia, precio*) to establish; ~ **con chinchetas** to stick up with drawing pins; ~ **una placa en la pared** to fix a plaque on the wall; **prohibido** ~ **carteles** bill posters prohibited; ~ **la atención en algo** to concentrate on sth **II.** *vr*: ~**se 1.** (*en un lugar*) to establish oneself **2.** (*atender*) to pay attention; **no se ha fijado en mi nuevo peinado** he/she has not noticed my new hairdo; **ese se fija en todo** nothing escapes him; **fíjate bien en lo que te digo** listen carefully to what I have to say **3.** (*mirar*) to notice; **no se fijó en mí** he/she did not notice me

fijo, -a ['fi·xo, -a] **I.** *adj* stable; (*cliente*) regular; (*idea, precio*) fixed; (*mirada*) steady; (*trabajador*) permanent **II.** *adv* with certainty; **saber algo de** ~ to know sth for sure

fila ['fi·la] *f* **1.** *t.* MAT row; ~ **de coches** line of cars; **en** ~ **india** in single file; **aparcar en doble** ~ to double-park; **en** ~ in line; **salir de la** ~ to step out of line **2.** MIL rank; **llamar a** ~**s** to draft **3.** *pl* (de un partido) ranks pl

filántropo [fi·lan·tro·po, -a] *m* philanthropist

filarmónico, -a [fi·lar·'mo·ni·ko, -a] *adj* Philharmonic

filatelia [fi·la·'te·lja] *f* philately

filete [fi·'le·te] *m* filet; (solomillo) steak

filetear [fi·le·te·'ar] *vt* to filet

filial [fi·'ljal] I. *adj* filial II. *f* subsidiary

film(e) ['fil·m(e)] *m* film, movie; ~ **transparente** plastic wrap

filmar [fil·'mar] *vt* to film

filo ['fi·lo] *m* 1. (de cuchillo) blade; **un arma de dos** ~**s** a double-edged sword 2. (entre dos partes) dividing line 3. *AmC* (hambre) hunger

filología [fi·lo·lo·'xi·a] *f* philology; ~ **hispánica** Hispanic language and literature

filólogo, -a [fi·'lo·lo·ɣo, -a] *m, f* philologist

filoso, -a [fi·'lo·so, -a] *adj AmL* sharp

filosofía [fi·lo·so·'fi·a] *f* philosophy; **tomar las cosas con** ~ to be philosophical about things

filosófico, -a [fi·lo·'so·fi·ko, -a] *adj* philosophical

filósofo, -a [fi·'lo·so·fo, -a] *m, f* philosopher

filtrar [fil·'trar] I. *vi* to leak; (luz) to filter II. *vt* to filter; (llamadas) to screen; (datos) to leak; (noticia) to percolate III. *vr*: ~**se** (líquido) to seep; (luz) to filter; (noticia) to percolate; (dinero) to dwindle

filtro ['fil·tro] *m* 1. filter; **cigarrillo con** ~ filter tip cigarette; ~ **solar** sunscreen 2. (poción) philter

filudo, -a [fi·'lu·do, -a] *adj AmL* sharp

fin [fin] *m* 1. (término) end; ~ **de semana** weekend; **a** ~**(es) de mes** at the end of the month; **algo toca a su** ~ sth is coming to an end; **poner** ~ **a algo** to put an end to sth; **sin** ~ never-ending; **al** ~ **y al cabo a** ~ **de cuentas** after all 2. (propósito) aim; ~**es deshonestos** immoral purposes; **a** ~ **de que** +subj so that

finado, -a [fi·'na·do, -a] *m, f* deceased

final [fi·'nal] I. *adj* (producto, resultado) end; (fase, examen) final; (solución)

ultimate II. *m* 1. end; (libro, película) ending; **película con** ~ **feliz** film with a happy ending; **al** ~ **no nos lo dijo** in the end he/she did not tell us 2. (partido) final; (ronda) finals pl

finalidad [fi·na·li·'dad] *f* purpose

finalista [fi·na·'lis·ta] *mf* finalist

finalización [fi·na·li·sa·'sjon, -θa·'θjon] *f* finalization; ~ **de contrato** completion of a contract

finalizar <z > c> [fi·na·li·'sar, -'θar] I. *vi* to finish; (plazo) to end II. *vt* to end; (discurso) to conclude

finalmente [fi·nal·'men·te] *adv* finally

financiación [fi·nan·sja·'sjon, -θja·'θjon] *f* financing, funding; ~ **de los partidos** political party financial backing

financiador(a) [fi·nan·sja·'dor, -·'do·ra, fi·nan·θja-] *m(f)* financial backer

financiar [fi·nan·'sjar, -'θjar] *vt* to finance

financiero, -a [fi·nan·'sje·ro, -a; -'θje·ro, -a] I. *adj* financial II. *m, f* financier

financista [fi·nan·'sis·ta] *mf AmL* financial expert; (financiador) financier

finanzas [fi·'nan·sas, -θas] *fpl* finance

finca ['fin·ka] *f* (urbana) (town) property; (rústica) (country) estate

finés, -esa [fi·'nes] I. *adj* Finnish II. *m, f* Finn

fingido, -a [fin·'xi·do, -a] *adj* fake, make-believe; (persona) false

fingir <g > j> [fin·'xir] *vi, vt* to pretend; (sentimiento) to feign

finiquitar [fi·ni·ki·'tar] *vt* 1. (cuenta) to settle 2. inf (asunto) to wind up

finiquito [fi·ni·'ki·to] *m* settlement; (documento) final discharge

finito, -a [fi·'ni·to, -a] *adj* finite

finlandés, -esa [fin·lan·'des] I. *adj* Finnish II. *m, f* Finn

Finlandia [fin·'lan·dja] *f* Finland

fino, -a [fi·'no, -a] *adj* 1. (delgado) fine 2. (liso) smooth 3. (de calidad) excellent; (oro) refined; (metal) precious; (sentido) acute; (paladar) discriminating 4. (cortés) polite; **modales** ~**s** refined manners 5. (astuto) shrewd

finolis [fi·'no·lis] *inv inf* I. *adj* la-di-da II. *mf* affected person

finura [fi·'nu·ra] *f* 1. (delgadez) fineness 2. (suavidad) smoothness 3. (calidad)

F

excellence **4.** (*cortesía*) refinement **5.** (*astucia*) shrewdness

firma ['fir·ma] *f* **1.** (*en documentos*) signature **2.** (*de un acuerdo*) signing **3.** (*empresa*) firm

firmamento [fir·ma·'men·to] *m* firmament

firmante [fir·'man·te] *mf* signatory; **el/la abajo ~** the undersigned

firmar [fir·'mar] *vi, vt* to sign; **~ autógrafos** to sign autographs; **~ un cheque** (*para pagar*) to sign a check; (*para cobrar*) to endorse a check; **~ un tratado/un acuerdo** to sign a treaty/an agreement

firme ['fir·me] **I.** *adj* (*fijo*) firm; (*estable*) steady; (*seguro*) secure; (*recto*) straight; (*carácter*) resolute; (*amistad*) strong; **con mano ~** with a firm hand; **esta mesa no está ~** this table is unsteady; **es ~ en sus propósitos** he/she is resolute in his/her intentions **II.** *m* road surface **III.** *adv* **de ~** (*fuertemente*) strongly; (*sin parar*) steadily; **el calor aprieta de ~** the heat is intense

firmeza [fir·'me·sa, -θa] *f* **1.** solidity; (*mueble*) sturdiness; (*creencia*) firmness; **~ de carácter** resolution **2.** (*perseverancia*) perseverance

fiscal [fis·'kal] **I.** *adj* fiscal; (*de impuestos*) tax **II.** *mf* public prosecutor; **Fiscal General del Estado** Attorney General

fiscalidad [fis·ka·li·'dad] *f* taxation

fisgar <g → gu> [fis·'ɣar] *vi* **~ en algo** to snoop around sth

fisgón, -ona [fis·'ɣon, -·'ɣo·na] *m, f* nosy parker

fisgonear [fis·ɣo·ne·'ar] *vi* **~ en algo** to pry into sth

física ['fi·si·ka] *f* physics *pl*

físicamente [fi·si·ka·'men·te] *adv* physically

físico ['fi·si·ko] *m* physique

físico, -a ['fi·si·ko, -a] **I.** *adj* physical; **educación física** physical education **II.** *m, f* physicist

fisiología [fi·sjo·lo·'xi·a] *f* physiology

fisonomía [fi·so·no·'mi·a] *f* v. **fisonomía**

fisioterapeuta [fi·sjo·te·ra·'peu·ta] *mf* physiotherapist

fisioterapia [fi·sjo·te·'ra·pja] *f* physiotherapy

fisonomía [fi·so·no·'mi·a] *f* physiognomy *form*, features *pl*

fisura [fi·'su·ra] *f* **1.** crack **2.** MED hairline fracture; (*en el ano*) fissure

flác(c)ido, -a ['flak·si·do, -a; 'flay·θi·do, -a] *adj* (*carnes*) flabby; (*piel*) flaccid

flaco, -a ['fla·ko, -a] *adj* thin; **punto ~** weak spot

flacucho, -a [fla·'ku·tʃo, -a] *adj* skinny

flamante [fla·'man·te] *adj inf* flamboyant; **nuevo ~** brand-new

flamenco [fla·'men·ko] *m* **1.** ZOOL flamingo **2.** (*cante, baile*) flamenco **3.** (*lengua*) Flemish

flan [flan] *m* crème caramel

flaquear [fla·ke·'ar] *vi* **1.** (*fuerzas*) to flag; (*salud*) to decline; (*ánimo*) to lose heart; (*demanda*) to slacken **2.** (*en un examen*) to be poor

flash [flaʃ] *m inv* flash

flato ['fla·to] *m* **1. tener ~** to have a stitch **2.** *AmC* melancholy

flatoso, -a [fla·'to·so, -a] *adj AmL* apprehensive

flatulencia [fla·tu·'len·sja, -θja] *f* flatulence

flauta ['flau·ta] *f* (*dulce*) recorder; (*travesera*) flute

flecha ['fle·tʃa] *f* arrow

flechazo [fle·'tʃa·so, -θo] *m* **1.** (*de flecha*) arrow shot **2.** (*de amor*) love at first sight

fleco ['fle·ko] *m* **1.** fringe **2.** *pl* frayed edges *pl*

flema ['fle·ma] *f* **1.** (*calma*) imperturbability **2.** (*mucosidad*) phlegm

flemón [fle·'mon] *m* conjunctivitis; (*dental*) gumboil

flequillo [fle·'ki·jo, -ʎo] *m* fringe

fleta ['fle·ta] *f AmC* **1.** (*friega*) rubbing **2.** (*zurra*) thrashing; (*castigo*) spanking

fletar [fle·'tar] **I.** *vt* **1.** (*avión*) to charter **2.** COM to freight **3.** *AmL* (*vehículo*) to rent **4.** *CSur* (*despedir*) to fire **II.** *vr:* **~se** *AmC* to get annoyed

flete ['fle·te] *m AmL* (*tarifa*) hire charge

flexibilidad [flek·si·βi·li·'ðað] *f* flexibility; (*músculo*) suppleness

flexible [flek·'si·βle] *adj* flexible; (*músculo*) supple; **horario ~** flextime

flexión [flek·'sjon] *f* flexion

flexionar [flek·sjo·'nar] *vt* to flex

flexo ['flek·so] *m* flexible table lamp

flojear [flo·xe·'ar] *vi* to diminish; (*calor*) to ease up; **~ en algo** to be poor at sth

flojera [flo·'xe·ra] *f inf* (*debilidad*) weakness; (*pereza*) slackness

flojo, -a ['flo·xo, -a] *adj* 1. (*vino, café, argumento*) weak; (*cuerda*) slack; (*nudo*) loose; (*viento*) light; **estoy ~ en inglés** I am weak in English 2. *AmL* (*cobarde*) cowardly

flor [flor] *f* 1. BOT flower; (*planta*) flowering plant; **estar en ~** to be in flower [*o* bloom]; **camisa de ~es** flowery shirt; **la ~ de la vida** the prime of life; **la ~ y nata de la sociedad** the cream of society; **la ~ de la canela** *fig* the best 2. (*piropo*) compliment 3. (*nivel*) **pasó volando a ~ de tierra** the plane skimmed over the ground; **tengo los nervios a ~ de piel** my nerves are frayed

flora ['flo·ra] *f* flora

florear [flo·re·'ar] *vi AmL* to flower

florecer [flo·re·'ser, -'θer] *irr como crecer* I. *vi* to flower, to bloom; (*industria*) to flourish II. *vr*: **~se** to grow mold

floreciente [flo·re·'sjen·te, -'θjen·te] *adj* flowering; (*industria*) flourishing

florecimiento [flo·re·si·'mjen·to, -θi·'mjen·to] *m* flowering; (*industria*) flourishing

florería [flo·re·'ri·a] *f CSur, Bol, Perú* florist's

florero [flo·'re·ro] *m* vase; (*maceta*) flowerpot

florido, -a [flo·'ri·ðo, -a] *adj* flowery

florista [flo·'ris·ta] *mf* florist

floristería [flo·ris·te·'ri·a] *f* florist's

flota ['flo·ta] *f* fleet

flotador [flo·ta·'ðor] *m* 1. float; (*para niños*) rubber ring 2. *RíoPl inf* roll of fat

flotar [flo·'tar] *vi* (*activamente*) to stay afloat; (*pasivamente*) to be suspended; (*en el aire*) to float

fluctuación [fluk·twa·'sjon, -'θjon] *f* 1. fluctuation 2. (*irresolución*) uncertainty

fluidez [flwi·'des, -'deθ] *f* fluidity; **hablar con ~** to speak fluently

fluido ['flwi·ðo] *m* 1. (*líquido*) fluid; (*expresión*) fluent 2. ELEC current

fluido, -a ['flwi·ðo, -a] *adj* 1. (*alimento*) liquid; **es ~ de palabra** he speaks with ease 2. (*tráfico*) free-flowing

fluir [flu·'ir] *irr como huir vi* to flow; (*correr*) to run

flujo ['flu·xo] *m* 1. flow; **~ de datos** data flow; **~ de palabras** stream of words 2. MED discharge

flúor ['fluor] *m* fluorine

fluorescente [flwo·re·'sen·te, -s'θen·te] I. *adj* fluorescent; **tubo ~** fluorescent tube II. *m* fluorescent light

flus [flus] *m Ant, Col, Ven* suit of clothes

fluvial [flu·'βjal] *adj* fluvial; **puerto ~** river port

FM [e·fe·'me, e·fe·'eme] *f abr de* **Frecuencia Modulada** FM

FMI [e·fe·m·e'i] *m abr de* **Fondo Monetario Internacional** IMF

fobia ['fo·βja] *f* aversion; MED phobia

foca ['fo·ka] *f* 1. seal 2. *pey* whale

focalizar <z → c> [fo·ka·li·'sar, -'θar] *vt* to focus on

foco ['fo·ko] *m* 1. FÍS, MAT focus 2. (*centro*) focal point; **~ de infección** source of infection 3. (*lámpara*) light; (*en estadio*) floodlight; (*en teatro*) spotlight 4. *AmL* (*bombilla*) light bulb

fofo, -a ['fo·fo, -a] *adj* flabby

fogaje [fo·'ya·xe] *m Arg, Col, PRico, Ven* stifling heat

fogata [fo·'ya·ta] *f* bonfire

fogón [fo·'yon] *m* 1. (*cocina*) stove 2. *AmL* (*fogata*) fire

fogueado, -a [fo·ye·'a·ðo, -a] *adj AmL* expert

fogueo [fo·'yeo] *m* **bala de ~** blank (cartridge)

foguerear [fo·ye·re·'ar] *vt Chile, Cuba* to burn off

foja ['fo·xa] *f AmL* sheet; **~ de servicios** record

folclor(e) [fol·'klor, --'klo·re] *m* folklore

folclórico, -a [fol·'klo·ri·ko, -a] *adj* folk

fólder ['fol·der] *f AmL* folder

folio ['fo·ljo] *m* sheet (of paper); (*de un libro*) leaf

folk [folk] *m* folk music

follaje [fo·'ja·xe, fo·'ʎa·] *m* foliage

follar [fo·'jar, -'ʎar] *vi, vt, vr:* **~se** to fuck; (*suspender*) to screw up

folletín [fo·je·'tin, fo·ʎe-] *m* newspaper serial; **novela de ~** pulp novel

folleto [fo·'je·to, fo·'ʎe-] *m* pamphlet; **~ publicitario** advertising leaflet

follón [fo·'jon, -'ʎon] *m inf* ruckus; (*lío*) trouble; **armar un ~** to cause a commotion

fome ['fo·me] *adj Arg, Chile* boring

fomentar [fo·men·'tar] *vt* (*empleo*) to promote; (*economía*) to boost; (*discordias*) to foment

fomento [fo·'men·to] *m* (*empleo*) promotion; (*economía*) boosting; (*discordias*) fueling

fondeado, -a [fon·de·'a·do, -a] *adj AmL* well-heeled

fondo ['fon·do] *m* 1. (*río*) bed; (*valle*) bottom; (*edificio*) depth; **los bajos ~s** the underworld; **tocar ~** to hit bottom; **al ~ del pasillo** at the end of the corridor; **al ~ de la casa** at the back of the house; **en el ~ de su corazón** in his/her heart of hearts; **en este asunto hay mar de ~** there are underlying issues in this matter 2. (*lo esencial*) essence; **artículo de ~** editorial; **en el ~** at bottom; **ir al ~ del asunto** to go to the heart of the matter; **tratar un tema a ~** to seriously discuss a subject; **hay un ~ de verdad en lo que dices** there is sth of truth in what you say 3. (*de un cuadro*) background; **ruido/música de ~** background noise/music 4. DEP long-distance; **corredor de ~** long-distance runner; **esquiador de ~** cross-country skier 5. FIN, POL fund; **común** kitty; **Fondo Monetario Internacional** International Monetary Fund; **a ~ perdido** non-recoverable 6. *pl* funds *pl*; **~s públicos** public funds; **cheque sin ~s** bad check

fonema [fo·'ne·ma] *m* phoneme

fonética [fo·'ne·ti·ka] *f* phonetics *pl*

fonología [fo·no·lo·'xi·a] *f* phonology

fontanería [fon·ta·ne·'ri·a] *f* plumbing; (*establecimiento*) plumber's

fontanero, -a [fon·ta·'ne·ro, -a] *m, f* plumber

footing ['fu·tin] *m* jogging; **hacer ~** to jog

forajido, -a [fo·ra·'xi·do, -a] I. *adj* outlawed II. *m, f* outlaw

foráneo, -a [fo·'ra·neo, -a] *adj* (*de fuera*) outside; (*extraño*) alien

forastero, -a [fo·ras·'te·ro, -a] I. *adj* (*de fuera*) outside; (*extranjero*) foreign; (*extraño*) alien II. *m, f* stranger; (*extranjero*) foreigner

forcejear [for·se·xe·'ar, for·θe-] *vi* 1. (*esforzarse*) to struggle 2. (*resistir*) to resist

forcejeo [for·se·'xeo, for·θe-] *m* 1. (*esfuerzo*) struggle 2. (*resistencia*) resistance

forense [fo·'ren·se] I. *adj* forensic; **médico ~** forensic surgeon II. *mf* pathologist

forestal [fo·res·'tal] *adj* forest; **camino ~** forest track; **repoblación ~** reforestation; **guarda ~** forest ranger

forja ['for·xa] *f* 1. (*fragua*) forge 2. (*ferrería*) ironworks *pl* 3. (*creación*) forging

forjar [for·'xar] I. *vt* (*fraguar, crear*) to forge; (*inventar*) to invent II. *vr:* **~se** to shape; **~ ilusiones** to build castles in the air

forma ['for·ma] *f* 1. (*figura*) form, shape; **en ~ de gota** in the shape of a drop; **dar ~ a** to shape 2. (*manera*) way; **~ de comportamiento** demeanor; **~ de pago** method of payment; **defecto de ~** JUR defect of form; **de ~ libre** freely; **en ~ escrita** written; **en (buena y) debida ~** duly; **de ~ que** so that; **de todas ~s,...** anyway,...; **lo haré de una ~ u otra** I will do it one way or another; **no hay ~ de abrir la puerta** this door is impossible to open 3. (*comportamiento*) manners *pl* 4. **en ~** fit; **en baja ~** off form

formación [for·ma·'sjon, -'θjon] *f*

1. (*creación*) creation; GEO formation; **~ de humo** forming of smoke **2.** *t.* MIL (*de personas*) formation; **~ política** political group **3.** (*educación*) education; **~ escolar/de adultos** school/adult education; **~ profesional** vocational training

formal [for·'mal] *adj* **1.** (*de la forma*) formal; **requisito ~** formal requirement **2.** (*serio*) serious; (*educado*) educated; (*cumplidor*) reliable **3.** (*oficial*) official; **una invitación ~** a formal invitation; **tiene novio ~** she has a steady boyfriend

formalidad [for·ma·li·'dad] *f* **1.** (*seriedad*) seriousness; (*exactitud*) correctness **2.** *pl* formalities *pl*

formalizar <z → c> [for·ma·li·'sar, -'θar] **I.** *vt* **1.** *to* formalize; **~ un contrato/una solicitud** to formalize a contract/motion **2.** (*solemnizar*) to solemnize; **~ un noviazgo** (*comprometerse*) to become engaged **II.** *vr:* **~se 1.** (*formarse*) to be formalized **2.** (*volverse formal*) to grow up

formar [for·'mar] **I.** *vt* **1.** *to* form; **~ parte de** to form part of **2.** (*educar*) to train; (*enseñar*) to teach **II.** *vr:* **~se 1.** (*crearse, hacerse*) to form; **~se una idea de algo** to form an impression of sth **2.** (*educarse*) to be educated; **se ha formado a sí mismo** he is self-taught **3.** (*desarrollarse*) to develop

formatear [for·ma·te·'ar] *vt* to format

formato [for·'ma·to] *m* format; (*tamaño*) size; **~ de datos/texto** data/text format; **~ vertical** vertical format

formidable [for·mi·'da·βle] *adj* **1.** (*estupendo*) fantastic **2.** (*enorme*) enormous **3.** (*temible*) awesome

fórmula ['for·mu·la] *f* **1.** formula; **coche de ~ 1** Formula One car **2.** *AmL* MED prescription

formular [for·mu·'lar] *vt* **1.** to formulate; (*demanda*) to file; (*denuncia*) to lodge **2.** MAT, FÍS to express with a formula **3.** *AmL* (*recetar*) to prescribe

formulario [for·mu·'la·rjo] *m* form; (*de fórmulas*) formulary; (*de recetas*) recipe form

fornicar <c → qu> [for·ni·'kar] *vi* to forni-

cate; (*adulterio*) to commit adultery

fornido, -a [for·'ni·do, -a] *adj* well-built

foro ['fo·ro] *m* **1.** (*plaza, internet, romano*) forum **2.** TEAT upstage area

forofo, -a [fo·'ro·fo, -a] *m, f* fan

forrar [fo·'rrar] **I.** *vt* (*exterior, pared*) to face; (*interior, prenda*) to line; (*butaca*) to upholster; (*libro*) to cover **II.** *vr:* **~se** *inf* to make a packet

forro ['fo·rro] *m* (*exterior, pared*) facing; (*interior, prenda*) lining; (*butaca*) upholstery; (*libro*) cover; **ni por el ~** at all

fortachón, -ona [for·ta·'tʃon, -·'tʃo·na] *adj inf* beefy

fortalecer [for·ta·le·'ser, -'θer] *irr como crecer* **I.** *vt* **1.** (*vigorizar*) to invigorate **2.** (*animar*) to encourage **3.** (*reforzar*) to fortify **II.** *vr:* **~se** to become stronger; (*vigorizarse*) to fortify oneself

fortaleza [for·ta·'le·sa, -θa] *f* **1.** (*fuerza*) strength **2.** (*virtud*) fortitude **3.** (*robustez*) robustness **4.** MIL fortress

fortificación [for·ti·fi·ka·'sjon, -'θjon] *f* strengthening; MIL fortification

fortísimo, -a [for·'ti·si·mo, -a] *adj superl de* **fuerte**

fortuito, -a [for·'twi·to, -a/for·tu·'i·to, -a] *adj* fortuitous

fortuna [for·'tu·na] *f* (*suerte, capital*) fortune; (*destino*) fate; **por ~** fortunately; (*por casualidad*) luckily; **probar ~** to try one's luck

forzado, -a [for·'sa·do, -a; -'θa·do, -a] *adj* (*artificial*) forced; **trabajos ~s** hard labor

forzar [for·'sar, -'θar] *irr* **I.** *vt* (*obligar, esforzar*) to force; (*voz*) to strain; (*puerta, ventana*) to force open; (*acontecimiento*) to bring about **II.** *vr:* **~se 1.** (*obligarse*) to force oneself **2.** (*esforzarse*) to push oneself

forzosamente [for·so·sa·'men·te, for·θo-] *adv* (*inevitablemente*) unavoidably; (*obligatoriamente*) necessarily

forzoso, -a [for·'so·so, -a; for·'θo-] *adj* forced; **aterrizaje ~** forced landing; **venta forzosa** forced sale

forzudo, -a [for·'su·do, -a; for·'θu-] *adj* strong

fosa ['fo·sa] *f* **1.** pit; MIL, GEO trench;

~ **séptica** septic tank **2.** (*sepultura*) grave; ~ **común** common grave **3.** ANAT fossa; ~ **nasal** nostril

fosforescente |fos·fo·re·'sen·te, -res·'θen·te| *adj* phosphorescent; **pintura** ~ luminous paint

fósforo |'fos·fo·ro| *m* match; QUÍM phosphorus

fósil |'fo·sil| *adj, m* fossil

foso |'fo·so| *m* **1.** hole; (*alargado*) ditch; MIL trench **2.** MÚS, TEAT orchestra pit

foto |'fo·to| *f* photo

fotocopia |fo·to·'ko·pja| *f* photocopy

fotocopiadora |fo·to·ko·pja·'do·ra| *f* photocopier

fotocopiar |fo·to·ko·'pjar| *vt* to photocopy

fotogénico, -a |fo·to·'xe·ni·ko, -a| *adj* photogenic

fotografía |fo·to·γra·'fi·a| *f* **1.** photograph; ~ **aérea** aerial photograph; ~ **en color** color photograph; ~ (**tamaño**) **carnet** passport photograph; **álbum de** ~**s** photo(graph) album **2.** (*arte*) photography

fotografiar <*1. pres* fotografío> |fo·to·γra·fi·'ar| **I.** *vi, vt* to photograph **II.** *vr:* ~**se** to have one's picture taken

fotográfico, -a |fo·to·'γra·fi·ko, -a| *adj* photographic; **máquina fotográfica** camera; **papel** ~ photographic paper

fotógrafo, -a |fo·'to·γra·fo, -a| *m, f* photographer

fotograma |fo·to·'γra·ma| *m* **1.** CINE still **2.** FOTO photogram

fotomatón |fo·to·ma·'ton| *m* photo booth; (*mecanismo*) photo automaton

fotomontaje |fo·to·mon·'ta·xe| *m* photomontage

fotosíntesis |fo·to·'sin·te·sis| *f inv* photosynthesis

FP |e·fe·'pe| *f abr de* **Formación Profesional** vocational training, technical education

frac |frak| *m* <fracs *o* fraques> tails *pl*

fracasar |fra·ka·'sar| *vi* to fail; ~ **en un examen** to fail an exam; **la película fracasó** the film was a flop

fracaso |fra·'ka·so| *m* **1.** (*acción*) failure **2.** (*fiasco*) fiasco **3.** (*desastre*) disaster

fracción |frak·'sjon, -'θjon| *f* **1.** (*división*) division; (*ruptura*) rupture; (*de una cantidad*) splitting up **2.** (*parte*) t. MAT, QUÍM fraction; (*de un objeto*) fragment; (*de una organización*) splinter group; ~ **parlamentaria** parliamentary faction

fractura |frak·'tu·ra| *f* break; GEO fault; MED fracture; ~ **simple/complicada** closed/compound fracture

fragancia |fra·'γan·sja, -θja| *f* fragrance; (*perfume*) perfume; (*vino*) bouquet

fragata |fra·'γa·ta| *f* frigate

frágil |'fra·xil| *adj* fragile; (*constitución, salud*) delicate; (*anciano*) frail; (*carácter*) weak

fragilidad |fra·xi·li·'dad| *f* fragility; (*constitución, salud*) delicacy; (*anciano*) frailty; (*carácter*) weakness

fragmentación |fray·men·ta·'sjon, -'θjon| *f* fragmentation; (*en muchos pedazos*) breaking up; (*cristal*) shattering

fragmentar |fray·men·'tar| **I.** *vt* to fragment; (*en muchos pedazos*) to break up; (*romper*) to break; (*roca*) to split **II.** *vr:* ~**se** (*cristal*) to shatter; (*roca*) to split

fragmento |fray·'men·to| *m* t. LIT, MÚS fragment; (*cristal*) splinter; (*roca*) chip; (*tejido*) remnant; (*papel*) scrap

fragua |'fra·γwa| *f* forge

fraile |'frai·le| *m* friar

frambuesa |fram·'bwe·sa| *f* raspberry

francés, -esa |fran·'ses, -·'se·sa; -'θes, -·'θe·sa| **I.** *adj* French; **tortilla francesa** plain omelet **II.** *m, f* Frenchman, Frenchwoman *m, f*

Francia |'fran·sja, -θja| *f* France

franco, -a |'fran·ko, -a| *adj* **1.** (*sincero*) frank **2.** (*generoso*) generous **3.** (*libre*) free; **puerto** ~ free port; ~ **a bordo** free on board; ~ **de derechos** duty-free; ~ **en fábrica** ex-factory **4.** (*claro*) patent

francotirador, -a |fran·ko·ti·ra·'dor, -·'do·ra| *m(f)* sniper

franela |fra·'ne·la| *f* **1.** flannel **2.** AmL T-shirt

franelear |fra·ne·le·'ar| *vi* Arg, Urug *inf* to pet

franja |'fran·xa| *f* **1.** (*guarnición*) border **2.** (*tira*) strip; ~ **horaria** time zone

franquear |fran·ke·'ar| *vt* **1.** (*carta*) to pay postage on; **a** ~ **en destino** postage paid at destination **2.** (*abrir*) to clear; ~

el paso to open the way; (*río*) to cross; (*obstáculo*) to get around **3.** (*conceder*) to grant

franqueo [fran·'keo] *m* **1.** (*sellos*) postage; **sin ~** without stamps **2.** (*acción: de una carta*) franking; (*de una salida*) opening

franqueza [fran·'ke·sa, -θa] *f* **1.** (*sinceridad*) frankness; **admitir algo con ~** to openly admit sth **2.** (*generosidad*) generosity **3.** (*familiaridad*) intimacy

franquicia [fran·'ki·sja, -θja] *f* exemption; **~ postal** free postage; ECON franchise

frasco ['fras·ko] *m* **1.** flask; **~ de perfume** perfume bottle; **~ pulverizador** sprayer **2.** *AmL* 2.37 liters

frase ['fra·se] *f* sentence; (*locución*) expression; (*refrán*) saying; **~ hecha** idiom; (*locución*) proverb

fraternal [fra·ter·'nal] *adj* fraternal

fraternidad [fra·ter·ni·'dad] *f* fraternity

fraternizar <z → c> [fra·ter·ni·'sar, -'θar] *vi* **1.** (*unirse*) to mingle with; POL to sympathize with **2.** (*alternar*) to fraternize

fraude ['frau·de] *m* fraud; **~ fiscal** tax fraud; **cometer ~** to commit a fraudulent act

fraudulento, -a [frau·du·'len·to, -a] *adj* fraudulent; **publicidad fraudulenta** misleading advertising

frazada [fra·'sa·da] *f* *AmL* blanket

frecuencia [fre·'kwen·sja, -θja] *f* t. FÍS frequency; **con ~** frequently

frecuentar [fre·kwen·'tar] *vt* to frequent; (*a alguien*) to be in touch with

frecuente [fre·'kwen·te] *adj* **1.** (*repetido*) frequent **2.** (*usual*) common

fregadero [fre·ɣa·'de·ro] *m* (kitchen) sink

fregado [fre·'ɣa·do] *m* **1.** cleaning **2.** *inf* (*lío*) mess; (*pelea*) brawl

fregado, -a [fre·'ɣa·do, -a] *adj* **1.** *AmL* (*descarado*) cheeky; (*fastidioso*) tiresome; (*astuto*) sly **2.** *AmC* (*severo*) strict

fregar [fre·'ɣar] *irr* *vt* **1.** (*frotar*) to rub **2.** (*suelo*) to scrub; (*con fregona*) to mop; (*platos*) to wash **3.** *AmL inf* to annoy

fregona [fre·'ɣo·na] *f* mop

freidora [frei·'do·ra] *f* fryer

freír [fre·'ir] *irr* **I.** *vt* to fry; (*en mucho aceite*) to deep-fry **II.** *vr:* **~se 1.** to fry **2.** *inf* to find it hot; **aquí te fríes** it's boiling here

frenada [fre·'na·da] *f* *Arg, Chile* sudden braking

frenar [fre·'nar] **I.** *vt* to stop; (*impulso, persona*) to restrain; (*desarrollo*) to curb **II.** *vi* to brake; **~ en seco** to slam on the brakes **III.** *vr* **~se en algo** to restrain oneself from sth

frenazo [fre·'na·so, -θo] *m* sudden braking

frenesí [fre·ne·'si] *m* (*exaltación*) frenzy; (*locura*) wildness

frenético, -a [fre·'ne·ti·ko, -a] *adj* **1.** (*exaltado*) frenzied; **aplauso ~** frenzied applause **2.** (*loco*) wild **3.** (*furioso*) furious

freno ['fre·no] *m* brake; **~ de mano** hand brake; (*contención*) curb; **tirar del ~ a alguien** to hold sb back; **no tener ~** not to hold back

frente¹ ['fren·te] *f* forehead; **a ~** face to face; **fruncir la ~** to frown; **bajó la ~** he/she bowed his/her head

frente² ['fren·te] **I.** *m* t. POL, METEO, MIL front; **al ~** (*dirección*) ahead; (*lugar*) in front; **de ~** head-on; **ponerse al ~** to take charge; **estar al ~ de algo** to be in charge of sth; **hacer ~ a alguien** to stand up to sb; **hacer ~ a algo** to face up to sth; **no tener dos dedos de ~** to be as thick as two short planks; **un ~ frío** a cold front **II.** *prep* **1. ~ a** (*enfrente*) opposite; (*delante*) in front of; (*contra*) as opposed to; (*ante*) in the face of **2. en ~** opposite

fresa ['fre·sa] *f* strawberry

fresco ['fres·ko] *m* **1.** freshness; (*frío moderado*) coolness; **salir a tomar el ~** to go out to get some fresh air **2.** ARTE fresco **3.** *AmL* soft drink

fresco, -a ['fres·ko, -a] **I.** *adj* **1.** (*frío*) cool; **estar ~** *inf* to be wrong **2.** (*reciente, descansado, desvergonzado*) fresh; **noticia fresca** up-to-date news; **queso ~** cottage cheese **II.** *m, f inf* cheeky person

frescor [fres·'kor] *m* freshness; (*frío moderado*) coolness

frescura [fres·'ku·ra] f 1. freshness; (*frío moderado*) coolness 2. (*desvergüenza*) cheek 3. (*desembarazo*) naturalness; **con ~** freely

fresquería [fres·ke·'ri·a] f AmL store where drinks are made and sold

frialdad [frjal·'dad] f 1. (*frío*) coldness 2. (*despego, impasibilidad*) coolness; **me trató con ~** he/she was cool towards me

fricción [frik·'sjon, -'θjon] f 1. (*resistencia, desavenencia*) friction 2. (*del cuerpo*) rub; (*con linimento*) massage

friega ['frje·ɣa] f 1. (*fricción*) rub 2. AmL (*molestia*) bother 3. inf (*zurra*) beating

friegaplatos [frje·ɣa·'pla·tos] m inv dishwasher

frigidez [fri·xi·'des, -'deθ] f frigidity

frígido, -a ['fri·xi·do, -a] adj frigid

frigorífico [fri·ɣo·'ri·fi·ko] m fridge; (*cámara*) cold store

frigorífico, -a [fri·ɣo·'ri·fi·ko, -a] adj refrigerated; **camión ~** refrigerated truck

frijol [fri·'xol], **frijol** ['fri·xol] m AmL bean

friki ['fri·ki] inf I. adj freaky II. m freak

frío ['fri·o] m cold; **tener ~** to be cold; **hace ~** it is cold; **hace un ~ que pela** it is bitterly cold; **coger ~** to catch cold

frío, -a ['fri·o, -a] adj 1. cold; (*relación*) cool; (*ambiente*) impersonal 2. (*sin sentimientos*) indifferent; (*impasible*) impassive

friolento, -a [frjo·'len·to, -a] AmL, **friolero, -a** [frjo·'le·ro, -a] adj sensitive to the cold

frisa ['fri·sa] f 1. Arg, Chile (*pelo*) nap 2. PRico, RDom (*manta*) blanket

fritanga [fri·'tan·ga] f pey (greasy) fried food

frito ['fri·to] m fry

frito, -a ['fri·to, -a] I. pp de **freír** II. adj 1. (*comida*) fried 2. inf (*dormido*) **quedarse ~** to fall fast asleep 3. inf (*muerto*) **quedarse ~** to kick the bucket 4. inf (*harto*) **estar ~ con algo** to be fed up with sth

frivolidad [fri·βo·li·'dad] f frivolity; (*trivialidad*) triviality

frívolo, -a ['fri·βo·lo, -a] adj frivolous

frondoso, -a [fron·'do·so, -a] adj (*planta, árbol*) leafy; (*bosque*) lush

frontal [fron·'tal] adj head-on; ANAT frontal

frontera [fron·'te·ra] f border; **atravesar la ~** to cross the frontier

fronterizo, -a [fron·te·'ri·so, -a, -'ri·θo, -a] adj frontier; **paso ~** border post; (*país*) border(ing)

frontón [fron·'ton] m 1. DEP jai alai, pelota 2. ARQUIT pediment

frotar [fro·'tar] I. vt to rub; (*con cepillo*) to brush; (*con estropajo*) to scrub II. vr: **~se** to rub oneself

fructífero, -a [fruk·'ti·fe·ro, -a] adj fruitful

fructificar <c → qu> [fruk·ti·fi·'kar] vi (*planta*) to bear fruit; (*esfuerzo*) to come to fruition

fruncir <c → z> [frun·'sir, -'θir] vt (*tela*) to shirr; (*labios*) to purse; (*frente*) to wrinkle; **~ el ceño/entrecejo** to frown

frustración [frus·tra·'sjon, -'θjon] f 1. failure; (*planes*) thwarting; (*esperanza*) frustration 2. (*desilusión*) disappointment

frustrado, -a [frus·'tra·do, -a] adj frustrated; (*intento*) failed

frustrar [frus·'trar] I. vt 1. to thwart; (*esperanzas*) to frustrate 2. (*decepcionar*) to discourage II. vr: **~se** (*plan*) to fail; (*esperanzas*) to be disappointed

fruta ['fru·ta] f fruit; **~ del tiempo** seasonal fruit; **~s tropicales** tropical fruits

frutal [fru·'tal] I. adj fruit II. m fruit tree

frutería [fru·te·'ri·a] f greengrocer's

frutero [fru·'te·ro] m fruit bowl

frutero, -a [fru·'te·ro, -a] I. adj fruit; **es muy ~** he eats a lot of fruit II. m, f fruit seller

frutilla [fru·'ti·ja, -ʎa] f AmL strawberry

fruto ['fru·to] m 1. fruit 2. (*hijo*) offspring 3. (*rendimiento*) fruit; (*resultado*) result 4. (*ganancia*) profit; (*provecho*) benefit

fucsia ['fuk·sja] I. adj fuchsia-colored II. m fuchsia III. f fuchsia

fue [fwe] 1. 3. pret de **ir** 2. 3. pret de **ser**

fuego ['fwe·ɣo] m 1. fire; **¿me das ~?** can you give me a light?; **~s artificiales** fireworks; **a ~ lento** over a low heat; fig little by little; **prender** [o **pegar**] **~ a algo** to set sth on fire; **echar ~ por los**

ojos to look daggers at sb; **en el ~ de la discusión** in the heat of the discussion 2. MIL firing; **arma de ~** firearm; **estar entre dos ~s** to be caught in the crossfire

fuel ['fwel] m refined oil

fuente ['fwen·te] f 1. (manantial) spring 2. (construcción) fountain 3. (plato llano) platter; (plato hondo) (serving) dish 4. (origen) source; **~s bien informadas** reliable sources

fuera ['fwe·ra] I. adv 1. (lugar) outside; **por ~** on the outside; **de ~** from the outside; **el nuevo maestro es de ~** the new teacher is not from here; **estar ~ de lugar** to be out of place 2. (dirección) out; **¡~!** out!; **¡~ con esto!** no way!; **¡~ de mi vista!** out of my sight!; **echar a alguien ~** to throw sb out; **hacia ~** outwards; **salir ~** to go out 3. (tiempo) out; **~ de plazo** past the deadline 4. (de viaje) away; **me voy ~ una semana** I am going away for a week II. prep 1. (lugar) out of; **~ de casa** away from home; **~ de juego** offside; **~ de serie** exceptional 2. (excepto) **~ de** outside of III. conj **~ de que** +subj apart from the fact that IV. m boo

fuereño, -a [fwe·'re·ɲo, -a] I. adj AmL inf outside II. m, f AmL inf outsider

fuerte ['fwer·te] I. adj <fortísimo> 1. (resistente, musculoso) strong; (robusto) tough; **caja ~** safe; **hacerse ~** to entrench oneself; **~ de carácter** strongwilled; **tener un carácter** [o **genio**] **muy ~** to be quick-tempered 2. (intenso) intense; (sonido) loud; (comida, golpe) heavy; (abrazo, beso) big; **un vino ~** a full-bodied wine 3. (valiente) brave 4. (sólido) solid; (duro) hard; (tela) thick 5. (poderoso) powerful 6. (expresión) nasty; (palabra) rude II. m 1. (de una persona) strong point 2. MIL fort III. adv 1. (con fuerza) strongly; (con intensidad) intensely; **desayunar ~** to have a large breakfast 2. (en voz alta) aloud

fuerza ['fwer·sa, -θa] f 1. t. FÍS (capacidad física) strength; t. FÍS (potencia) force; ELEC power; **~ de ánimo** strength of mind; **~ de voluntad** willpower; **sin ~s**

drained; **se le va la ~ por la boca** he/she is all talk 2. (resistencia) toughness; (eficacia) effectiveness; (poder) power; (intensidad) intensity; **~ de disuasión** powers of dissuasion; **~ mayor** force majeure 3. (violencia) force; **a** [o **por**] **la ~** any which way; **por ~** (por necesidad) out of necessity; (con violencia) by force; **recurrir a la ~** to resort to violence; **a ~ de** by means of; **a ~ de trabajo** through hard work 4. pl POL political groups pl; MIL forces pl; **~s del orden público** forces of law and order; **Fuerzas Armadas** the (armed) forces

fuete ['fwe·te] m AmL whip

fuga ['fu·ya] f 1. flight; (de la cárcel) escape; **darse a la ~** to run away; **~ capital** flight of capital; **~ de cerebros** brain drain 2. (escape) leak; (de líquido) leakage; (de gas) escape; **la cañería tiene una ~** the pipe has a leak

fugacidad [fu·ya·si·'dad, -θi·'dad] f brevity

fugarse <g → gu> [fu·'yar·se] vr to flee; (de casa) to run away; (para casarse) to elope; **~ de la cárcel** to escape from prison

fugaz [fu·'yas, -'yaθ] adj fleeting; **estrella ~** shooting star

fugitivo, -a [fu·xi·'ti·βo, -a] I. adj fugitive; (belleza) transitory II. m, f fugitive; (de la cárcel) escapee

fulana [fu·'la·na] f whore

fulano, -a [fu·'la·no, -a] m, f 1. (evitando el nombre) so-and-so 2. (persona indeterminada) John Doe; **no me importa lo que digan ~ y mengano** I don't care what Tom, Dick or Harry say

fulero, -a [fu·'le·ro, -a] adj inf 1. (embustero) lying 2. (chapucero) **eres muy ~** you are a bungler

fulgor [ful·'yor] m (resplandor) radiance; (centelleo) sparkle; (de una superficie) gleam

fulgurante [ful·yu·'ran·te] adj rapid; (dolor) intense; **su carrera fue ~** he/she rose rapidly in his/her career

fullería [fu·je·'ri·a, fu·ʎe-] f 1. (trampa) trick; (en el juego) cheating; **hacer ~s** to cheat 2. (treta) ruse

fullero, -a [fu·'je·ro, -a; fu·'ʎe-] I. adj

1. (*tramposo*) tricky 2. (*astuto*) crafty
II. *m, f* 1. (*tramposo*) trickster; (*en el juego*) cheat 2. (*astuto*) crafty individual

fulminante [ful·mi·'nan·te] *adj* 1. *t.* MED (*inesperado*) sudden 2. (*explosivo*) explosive; (*mirada*) withering

fulminar [ful·mi·'nar] I. *vi* to explode II. *vt* (*dañar*) to strike down; (*aniquilar*) to destroy; (*matar*) to electrocute

fumador(a) [fu·ma·'dor, -·'do·ra] *m(f)* smoker; **no ~es** non-smoker; **zona de no ~es** no-smoking area

fumar [fu·'mar] *vi, vt, vr:* **~se** to smoke; **~se la clase** to play hooky from school

fumigar <g → gu> [fu·mi·'ɣar] *vt* to fumigate

función [fun·'sjon, -'θjon] *f* 1. *t.* BIO, MAT (*rol*) function; **el precio está en ~ de la calidad** the price depends on the quality 2. (*cargo*) office; (*tarea*) duty; **el ministro en funciones** the acting minister; **entrará en ~ mañana** he/she will start work tomorrow; (*cargo*) he/she will take office tomorrow 3. (*actuación*) function; CINE showing; TEAT performance; **~ doble** double feature; **~ de noche** late show

funcional [fun·sjo·'nal, fun·θjo-] *adj* functional

funcionalidad [fun·sjo·na·li·'dad, fun·θjo-] *f* functionality

funcionamiento [fun·sjo·na·'mjen·to, fun·θjo-] *m* 1. (*marcha*) running; **~ administrativo** running of the administration; **~ del mercado** market organization; **poner en ~** to bring into operation 2. (*rendimiento*) performance; (*manera de funcionar*) operation; (*máquina*) working; **en estado de ~** in working order

funcionar [fun·sjo·'nar, fun·θjo-] *vi* to work; **la radio no funciona** the radio does not work; **'no funciona'** "out of order"

funcionario, -a [fun·sjo·'na·rjo, -a; fun·θjo-] *m, f* employee; (*público*) civil servant

funda ['fun·da] *f* cover; (*libro*) (dust) jacket; (*almohada*) pillowcase; (*butaca*) loose cover; (*gafas*) glasses case; ~

nórdica duvet

fundación [fun·da·'sjon, -'θjon] *f* foundation

fundado, -a [fun·'da·do, -a] *adj* well-founded

fundador(a) [fun·da·'dor, -·'do·ra] *adj, m(f)* founder

fundamental [fun·da·men·'tal] *adj* fundamental; (*esencial*) essential; (*básico*) basic; (*argumento*) key; (*conocimientos*) rudimentary

fundamentalismo [fun·da·men·ta·'lis·mo] *m* fundamentalism

fundamentalista [fun·da·men·ta·'lis·ta] *adj, mf* fundamentalist

fundamentar [fun·da·men·'tar] *vt* (*basar*) to base; (*establecer*) to establish

fundamento [fun·da·'men·to] *m* 1. (*base*) basis 2. (*motivo*) grounds; **sin ~** groundless; **hablar sin ~** not to talk seriously 3. *pl* fundamentals *pl*

fundar [fun·'dar] I. *vt t.* TÉC to found; (*basar*) to base II. *vr:* **~se** (*basarse*) to be founded; (*asentarse*) to be established

fundición [fun·di·'sjon, -'θjon] *f* 1. (*de un metal*) smelting; (*en una forma*) casting 2. (*taller*) foundry

fundillo [fun·'di·jo, -ʎo] *m Méx* bottom

fundir [fun·'dir] I. *vt* 1. (*derretir*) to melt; (*dar forma*) to cast 2. (*unir*) to unite; (*empresas*) to merge II. *vr:* **~se** 1. (*derretirse*) to melt 2. (*bombilla*) to fuse; (*plomos*) to blow 3. (*unirse*) to unite; (*empresas*) to merge 4. *inf* (*gastar*) to squander

fundo ['fun·do] *m Chile, Perú* country property

fúnebre ['fu·ne·βre] *adj* 1. (*triste*) mournful; (*sombrío*) gloomy 2. (*de los difuntos*) funerary; **coche ~** hearse; **pompas ~s** (*ceremonia*) funeral; (*empresa*) undertaker's

funeral [fu·ne·'ral] I. *adj* funerary II. *m* 1. burial 2. *pl* funeral

funeraria [fu·ne·'ra·rja] *f* funeral parlor

funesto, -a [fu·'nes·to, -a] *adj* (*aciago*) ill-fated; (*desgraciado*) terrible

fungir <g → j> [fun·'xir] *vi* 1. *AmL* (*en cargo*) to hold the post 2. *AmC* (*presumir*) to put on airs

furgón [fur·'ɣon] *m* 1. (*carro*) wagon; (*camioneta*) van **2.** (*para el equipaje*) baggage car; (*para mercancías*) freight car

furgoneta [fur·ɣo·'ne·ta] *f* van

furia ['fu·rja] *f* fury; **estaba hecha una ~** she was furious

furioso, -a [fu·'rjo·so, -a] *adj* **1.** (*furibundo*) furious **2.** (*loco*) beside oneself **3.** (*violento*) violent; (*tempestad*) raging

furor [fu·'ror] *m* **1.** (*ira*) fury; (*locura*) frenzy **2.** (*auge*) craze; **hacer ~** to be the (latest) thing **3.** MED **~ uterino** nymphomania

furtivo, -a [fur·'ti·βo, -a] *adj* furtive; **cazador ~** poacher

fusible [fu·'si·βle] *m* fuse

fusil [fu·'sil] *m* rifle

fusilar [fu·si·'lar] *vt* **lo fusilaron** he was executed by firing squad

fusión [fu·'sjon] *f* fusion; (*unión*) union; ECON merger

fusionar [fu·sjo·'nar] **I.** *vi* to fuse **II.** *vt, vr:* **~se** to fuse; (*empresas*) to merge

fustán [fus·'tan] *m AmL* lady's slip

fútbol ['fud·βol] *m* soccer; **~ americano** football

futbolín [fud·βo·'lin] *m* table football

futbolista [fud·βo·'lis·ta] *mf* soccer player

futbolístico, -a [fud·βo·'lis·ti·ko, -a] *adj* soccer

fútbol-sala ['fud·βol·'sa·la] *m* indoor soccer

fútil ['fu·til] *adj* trivial

futileza [fu·ti·'le·sa] *f Chile* trifle

futilidad [fu·ti·li·'dad] *f* triviality

futre ['fu·tre] *m AmL pey* stuck-up person

futuro [fu·'tu·ro] *m* future

futuro, -a [fu·'tu·ro, -a] **I.** *adj* future **II.** *m, f* intended

G

G, g [xe] *f* (*letra*) G, g; **G de Granada** G as in Golf

g. ['gra·mo] *abr de* **gramo** g.

gabardina [ga·βar·'di·na] *f* raincoat

gabinete [ga·βi·'ne·te] *m* **1.** (*estudio*) study; **~ de prensa** press office **2.** POL cabinet

gacela [ga·'se·la, ga·'θe·-] *f* gazelle

gaceta [ga·'se·ta, ga·'θe·-] *f* gazette

gachas ['ga·tʃas] *fpl* ≈ porridge

gachí <gachís> [ga·'tʃi] *f inf* chick

gachó [ga·'tʃo] *m inf* bloke

gafar [ga·'far] *vt inf* to jinx

gafas ['ga·fas] *fpl* glasses *pl*; **~ de bucear** diving mask; **llevar ~** to wear glasses

gafe ['ga·fe] *m* (*cenizo*) jinx; (*aguafiestas*) party-pooper

gaita ['gai·ta] *f* bagpipes *pl*

gajo ['ga·xo] *m* (*de naranja*) segment

gala ['ga·la] *f* **1.** (*fiesta*) gala **2.** (*garbo*) elegance; **hacer ~ de algo** to take pride in sth **3.** *pl* finery

galáctico, -a [ga·'lak·ti·ko, -a] *adj* galactic

galán [ga·'lan] *m* handsome man; (*novio*) beau

galante [ga·'lan·te] *adj* **1.** (*hombre*) gallant **2.** (*mujer*) flirtatious

galantería [ga·lan·te·'ri·a] *f* **1.** (*cortesía*) gallantry **2.** (*amabilidad*) politeness **3.** (*cumplido*) compliment

galápago [ga·'la·pa·yo] *m* sea turtle

galardón [ga·lar·'don] *m* prize

galardonar [ga·lar·do·'nar] *vt* to award a prize to; **~ a alguien con un título** to confer a title on sb

galaxia [ga·'lak·sja] *f* galaxy

galera [ga·'le·ra] *f* **1.** galley **2.** *AmL* (*cobertizo*) shed **3.** *AmL* (*de copa*) top hat; (*de hongo*) bowler hat

galería [ga·le·'ri·a] *f* **1.** (*corredor; de arte*) *t.* MIN, TEAT gallery **2.** *pl* (*grandes almacenes*) department store; (*centro comercial*) mall **3.** *pl* (*bulevar*) arcade

galerón [ga·le·'ron] *m* **1.** *AmS* (*romance*) ballad **2.** *Col, Ven* MÚS folkdance and song **3.** *CRi, ElSal* (*cobertizo*) shed

galés, -esa [ga·'les, --'le·sa] **I.** *adj* Welsh **II.** *m, f* Welshman, Welshwoman *m, f*; **Gales** ['ga·les] *m* Wales

galgo, -a ['gal·ɣo, -a] *m, f* greyhound; **échale un ~!** ¡no way!

galguerías [gal·ɣe·'ri·as] *fpl* candies *pl*

Galicia [ga·'li·sja, -θja] *f* Galicia

galimatías [ga·li·ma·'ti·as] *m inv* gibberish

gallardía [ga·jar·'di·a, ga·ʎar-] f (*garbo*) style; (*valentía*) bravery

gallardo, -a [ga·'jar·do, -a; ga·'ʎar-] adj 1. (*de aspecto*) elegant 2. (*garboso*) dashing 3. (*valiente*) brave 4. (*generoso*) noble

gallego, -a [ga·'je·ɣo, -a; ga·'ʎe-] m, f 1. (*de Galicia*) Galician 2. AmS pey Spaniard

galleta [ga·'je·ta, -'ʎe·ta] f 1. (*dulce*) cookie; (*salada*) cracker 2. inf (*bofetada*) smack

gallina [ga·'ji·na, -'ʎi·na] f 1. hen 2. inf (*cobarde*) chicken

gallinero [ga·ji·'ne·ro, ga·ʎi-] m (*corral*) chicken coop

gallito [ga·'ji·to, -'ʎi·to] m inf **ser un ~** to be a tough guy; **ponerse ~** to act tough

gallo ['ga·jo, -ʎo] m 1. (*ave*) cock; **~ de pelea** fighting cock; **en menos que <u>canta</u> un ~** in a flash 2. (*engreído*) show-off 3. MÚS false note; **soltar un ~** to let out a squeak 4. AmL (*fuerte*) tough guy

galón [ga·'lon] m gallon

galopar [ga·lo·'par] vi to gallop

galope [ga·'lo·pe] m gallop

galpón [gal·'pon] m AmL shed

galuchar [ga·lu·'tʃar] vi Col, Cuba, PRico, Ven to gallop

gama [ga·'ma] f 1. range; **una amplia ~ de productos** a wide range of products 2. MÚS gamut; (*escala*) scale

gamba ['gam·ba] f shrimp

gamberrada [gam·be·'rra·da] f act of hooliganism; **hacer ~s** to horse around inf

gamberro, -a [gam·'be·rro, -a] m, f hooligan

gambeta [gam·'be·ta] f AmL 1. (*distensión*) swerve 2. (*evasiva*) dodge 3. (*fútbol*) dummy; **hacer ~s** to dribble

gamín, -ina [ga·'min, -'mi·na] m, f Col urchin

gamo ['ga·mo] m fallow deer

gamonal [ga·mo·'nal] m AmL local political boss

gamonalismo [ga·mo·na·'lis·mo] m AmL caciquism

gana ['ga·na] f desire; **tener ~s de hacer algo** to feel like doing sth; **me quedé con las ~s de verlo** I wish I'd been able to see him; **no me da la (real) ~** inf I can't be bothered

ganadería [ga·na·de·'ri·a] f 1. (*ganado*) livestock 2. (*crianza*) livestock farming

ganadero, -a [ga·na·'de·ro, -a] I. adj livestock II. m, f (*criador*) cattle farmer; (*tratante*) cattle merchant

ganado [ga·'na·do, -a] m 1. (*reses*) livestock pl; **~ bovino** [o **vacuno**] cattle pl; **~ caprio** goats pl; **~ ovino** sheep inv; **~ porcino** pigs pl 2. AmL inf (*personas*) crowd

ganador(a) [ga·na·'dor, -·'do·ra] I. adj winning II. m(f) winner

ganancia [ga·'nan·sja, -θja] f (*beneficio*) profit; (*sueldo*) earnings pl

ganancial [ga·nan·'sjal, -'θjal] adj profit; **bienes ~es** property acquired by marriage

ganar [ga·'nar] I. vi to win; (*mejorar*) **~ en algo** to improve at sth II. vt 1. (*trabajando*) to earn; **con ese negocio consiguió ~ mucho dinero** he/she made a lot of money out of that business 2. (*jugando*) win; (*a alguien*) to beat 3. (*adquirir*) to gain; (*libertad*) to win; **~ peso** to put on weight 4. (*aventajar*) **~ a alguien en algo** to be better than sb at sth III. vr: **~se** 1. (*dinero*) to earn; **¡te la vas a ~!** inf you're for it 2. (*a alguien*) to win over

ganchillo [gan·'tʃi·jo, -ʎo] m 1. (*gancho*) hook 2. (*labor*) crochet; **hacer ~** to crochet

gancho ['gan·tʃo] m 1. (*instrumento*) hook; **tener ~** to be attractive 2. DEP (*boxeo*) hook; (*baloncesto*) hook shot 3. (*que atrae*) bait 4. AmL (*horquilla*) hairpin

gandido, -a [gan·'di·do, -a] adj Col pey gluttonous

gandinga [gan·'din·ga] f Cuba, PRico liver stew

gandul(a) [gan·'dul, -·'du·la] I. adj lazy II. m(f) loafer

gandulear [gan·du·le·'ar] vi to loaf around

ganga ['gan·ga] f bargain; **a precio de ~** at a bargain price

ganglio ['gaŋ·gljo] *m* ganglion; **~ linfáti-co** lymph gland

gangoso, -a [gaŋ·'go·so, -a] *adj* nasal

gángster ['gaŋs·ter] *mf* gangster

gansada [gan·'sa·da] *f* silly thing; **ha-cer ~s** to clown around; **decir ~s** to talk nonsense

gansear [gan·se·'ar] *vi inf* **1.** (*hacer gan-sadas*) to clown around **2.** (*decir gansa-das*) to talk nonsense

ganso, -a ['gan·so, -a] *m, f* **1.** goose; (*macho*) gander **2.** *inf* dummy; **hacer el ~** to clown around

ganzúa [gan·'su·a, -'θu·a] *f* picklock

gañán [ga·'ɲan] *m* farmhand; *pey* brute

garabato [ga·ra·'βa·to] *m* (*al escribir*) scribble; (*al dibujar*) doodle

garaje [ga·'ra·xe] *m* garage

garante [ga·'ran·te] **I.** *adj* responsible **II.** *mf* guarantor

garantía [ga·ran·'ti·a] *f* (*seguridad*) *t.* COM, FIN guarantee; (*caución*) surety; **~s constitucionales** POL constitutional rights

garantizar <z → c> [ga·ran·ti·'sar, -'θar] *vt* to guarantee; JUR to act as guaran-tor for

garapiña [ga·ra·'pi·ɲa] *f* **1.** sugar coating **2.** *AmL* iced pineapple drink

garapiñar [ga·ra·pi·'ɲar] *vt* to coat with sugar

garbanzo [gar·'βan·so, -θo] *m* chickpea

garbo ['gar·βo] *m* elegance; (*de movi-miento*) grace(fulness); (*de un escri-to*) style

garete [ga·'re·te] *inf* **ir**(**se**) **al ~** to go down the tubes

garfio ['gar·fjo] *m* hook

gargajo [gar·'ɣa·xo] *m inf* phlegm

garganta [gar·'ɣan·ta] *f* throat; (*cuello*) neck; **se me hizo un nudo en la ~** I had a lump in my throat

gargantilla [gar·ɣan·'ti·ja, -ʎa] *f* (short) necklace

gárgaras ['gar·ɣa·ras] *fpl* gargles *pl*; **ha-cer ~** to gargle

gargarear [gar·ɣa·re·'ar] *vi* Chile, Guat, Perú to gargle

gárgola ['gar·ɣo·la] *f* gargoyle

garito [ga·'ri·to] *m* nightclub; (*de juego*) gambling den

garra ['ga·rra] *f* **1.** claw; *pey* (*mano*) paw; **caer en las ~s de alguien** to fall into sb's clutches **2.** *pl AmL* (*harapos*) rags *pl* **3.** *inf* **tener ~** to be compelling

garrafa [ga·'rra·fa] *f* (*pequeña*) carafe; (*grande*) demijohn; **vino de ~** cheap wine

garrafal [ga·rra·'fal] *adj* (*enorme*) enor-mous; (*fatal*) terrible

garrapata [ga·rra·'pa·ta] *f* tick

garrapiña [ga·rra·'pi·ɲa] *f v.* garapiña

garúa [ga·'ru·a] *f AmL* drizzle

garuar [ga·'rwar] *vimpers AmL* to drizzle

G

garza ['gar·sa, -θa] *f* heron

garzón, -ona [gar·'son, -·'so·na] *m, f AmL* waiter, waitress *m, f*

gas [gas] *m* **1.** gas; **~ natural** natural gas; **bombona/cocina de ~** gas cylinder/stove; **agua con/sin ~** carbonated/still water **2.** *inf* **dar ~** to accelerate; **ir a todo ~** to go at full speed **3.** *pl* wind

gasa ['ga·sa] *f* gauze; MED lint; (*pañal*) diaper liner

gaseosa [ga·se·'o·sa] *f* soda

gaseoso, -a [ga·se·'o·so, -a] *adj* gaseous; (*bebida*) fizzy

gasfitería [gas·fi·te·'ri·a] *f AmL* plumbing

gasoducto [ga·so·'duk·to] *m* gas pipeline

gasoil [gas·'oil], **gasóleo** [ga·'so·leo] *m* diesel

gasolina [ga·so·'li·na] *f* gas(oline); **~ súper/sin plomo** premium/unleaded gasoline; **echar ~** to get gas

gasolinera [ga·so·li·'ne·ra] *f* gas station

gastado, -a [gas·'ta·do, -a] *adj* worn out; (*neumático*) bare; (*pila*) used up

gastar [gas·'tar] **I.** *vt* **1.** to wear out; (*di-nero, tiempo*) to spend; (*electricidad*) to use **2.** (*consumir, usar*) use; **¿qué talla [o número] gastas?** what size are you? **II.** *vr*: **~se** to run out; (*dinero*) to spend; (*ropa*) to wear out

gasto ['gas·to] *m* **1.** *pl* (*de dinero*) spend-ing; (*en un negocio*) costs *pl*; (*de fuerza*) *t.* ECON, COM expenditure; **~s adiciona-les** extra charges; **~s pagados** all ex-penses paid; **~s de inscripción** registra-tion fees *pl*; **el ~ público** public expen-diture **2.** (*consumo*) consumption

gastroenteritis [gas·tro·en·te·'ri·tis] *f inv* gastroenteritis

gastronomía [gas·tro·no·'mi·a] *f* gastronomy

gastronómico, -a [gas·tro·'no·mi·ko, -a] *adj* gastronomic

gatas ['ga·tas] **andar a ~** to crawl

gatear [ga·te·'ar] *vi* to crawl; *AmL* to seduce

gatera [ga·'te·ra] *f AmL* vegetable seller

gatillo [ga·'ti·jo, -ʎo] *m* trigger; **apretar el ~** to pull the trigger

gato ['ga·to] *m* **1.** cat; *(macho)* tomcat; **dar ~ por liebre a alguien** to rip sb off; **aquí hay ~ encerrado** there's something fishy going on here **2.** *(de coche)* jack; *(de carpintero)* vice

gatuno, -a [ga·'tu·no, -a] *adj* catlike

gaucho ['gau·tʃo] *m AmL* **1.** *(campesino)* gaucho **2.** *(jinete)* skilled horseman

gaucho, -a ['gau·tʃo, -a] *adj* **1.** gaucho **2.** *AmL (grosero)* coarse **3.** *AmL (astuto)* cunning

gavilán [ga·'βi·lan] *m* sparrow hawk

gaviota [ga·'βjo·ta] *f* (sea)gull

gay [gai] *m* gay

gazpacho [gas·'pa·tʃo, gaθ-] *m* gazpacho

GB [dʒi·γa·'bait] *m* **1.** *abr de* **gigabyte** GB **2.** *abr de* **Gran Bretaña** GB

géiser ['xei·ser] *m* geyser

gel [xel] *m* gel

gelatina [xe·la·'ti·na] *f* gelatin; CULIN *(dulce)* jelly; *(salado)* aspic

gelatinoso, -a [xe·la·ti·'no·so, -a] *adj* gelatinous

gélido, -a ['xe·li·do, -a] *adj* icy

gema ['xe·ma] *f* gem

gemelo, -a [xe·'me·lo, -a] *adj, m, f* identical twin; **hermanos ~s** twin brothers

gemelos [xe·'me·los] *mpl* **1.** *(anteojos)* binoculars *pl;* **~ de teatro** opera glasses **2.** ANAT calves *pl*

gemido [xe·'mi·do] *m (de dolor)* groan; *(de pena, de placer)* moan; *(al llorar)* wail

Géminis ['xe·mi·nis] *m* Gemini

gemir [xe·'mir] *irr como* **pedir** *vi (de dolor)* to groan; *(de pena, de placer)* to moan

gen [xen] *m* gene

genealógico, -a [xe·nea·'lo·xi·ko, -a] *adj* genealogical; **árbol ~** family tree

generación [xe·ne·ra·'sjon, -'θjon] *f* generation

generador [xe·ne·ra·'dor] *m* generator

generador(a) [xe·ne·ra·'dor, -'do·ra] *adj* productive; **medidas ~as de empleo** employment creation measures; ELEC generating

general [xe·ne·'ral] *adj, m* general; **cuartel ~** headquarters; **cultura ~** general knowledge; **por lo** *[o* **en]** **~** in general, generally; **por regla ~** as a (general) rule; **en ~ me siento satisfecho** overall, I'm satisfied; **tengo una idea ~ del tema** I have a general idea about the subject

generalización [xe·ne·ra·li·sa·'sjon, -θa·'θjon] *f* generalization; *(difusión)* spread

generalizar <z → c> [xe·ne·ra·li·'sar, -'θar] *vt* to generalize; *(difundir)* to spread

generalmente [xe·ne·ral·'men·te] *adv* generally; *(ampliamente)* widely

generar [xe·ne·'rar] *vt (producir)* to generate; *(provocar)* to provoke

genérico, -a [xe·'ne·ri·ko, -a] *adj* generic

género ['xe·ne·ro] *m* **1.** BIO genus; **~ humano** mankind **2.** *(clase)* sort **3.** LING gender **4.** LIT, ARTE genre **5.** COM *(artículo)* article; *(mercancía)* goods *pl*

generosidad [xe·ne·ro·si·'dad] *f* generosity

generoso, -a [xe·ne·'ro·so, -a] *adj* generous

genética [xe·'ne·ti·ka] *f* genetics

genético, -a [xe·'ne·ti·ko, -a] *adj* genetic

genial [xe·'njal] *adj* great; *(idea)* brilliant

genialidad [xe·nja·li·'dad] *f* genius

genio ['xe·njo] *m* **1.** *(carácter)* character; **tener mal ~** to be bad-tempered **2.** *(persona)* genius **3.** *(duende)* genie

genital [xe·ni·'tal] *adj* genital

genitales [xe·ni·'ta·les] *mpl* genitals *pl*

genocidio [xe·no·'si·djo, -'θi·djo] *m* genocide

gente ['xen·te] *f* **1.** people *pl;* **¿qué tal tu ~?** how are your folks? **2.** *AmL* honest people

gentileza [xen·ti·'le·sa, -θa] *f* kindness; **¿tendría Ud. la ~ de ayudarme?** would you be so kind as to help me?

gentío [xen·'ti·o] *m* crowd

gentuza [xen·'tu·sa, -θa] *f* rabble

genuino, -a [xe·'nwi·no, -a] *adj* genuine

geografía [xeo·γra·'fi·a] *f* geography

geográfico, -a [xeo·'γra·fi·ko, -a] *adj* geographical

geología [xeo·lo·'xi·a] *f* geology

geológico, -a [xeo·'lo·xi·ko, -a] *adj* geological

geólogo, -a [xe·'o·lo·γo, -a] *m, f* geologist

geometría [xeo·me·'tri·a] *f* geometry

geométrico, -a [xeo·'me·tri·ko, -a] *adj* geometric(al)

geranio [xe·'ra·njo] *m* geranium

gerencia [xe·'ren·sja, -θja] *f* management

gerente [xe·'ren·te] *mf* director, general manager; (*pequeña empresa*) manager; (*departamento*) head

geriatra [xe·'rja·tra] *mf* geriatrician

geriatría [xe·rja·'tri·a] *f* geriatrics *pl*

geriátrico, -a [xe·'rja·tri·ko, -a] *adj* geriatric

germánico, -a [xer·'ma·ni·ko, -a] *adj*, **germano, -a** [xer·'ma·no, -a] *adj* German; HIST Germanic

germen ['xer·men] *m* origin; BIO germ

germinar [xer·mi·'nar] *vi* to germinate

gerundio [xe·'run·djo] *m* gerund

gestación [xes·ta·'sjon, -'θjon] *f* gestation

gesticular [xes·ti·ku·'lar] *vi* to gesticulate; (*con la cara*) to pull faces

gestión [xes·'tjon] *f* management; (*diligencia*) measure; **hacer gestiones** to take measures

gestionar [xes·tjo·'nar] *vt* to manage; (*asunto*) to conduct

gesto ['xes·to] *m* gesture; (*con la cara*) expression

gestor(a) [xes·'tor, -·'to·ra] I. *adj* managing II. *m(f)* agent

gigabyte [dʒi·ya·'bait] *m* gigabyte

gigante [xi·'yan·te] I. *adj* gigantic II. *m* giant

gigantesco, -a [xi·yan·'tes·ko, -a] *adj* gigantic

gigoló [dʒi·γo·'lo] *m* gigolo

gilipollas [xi·li·'po·jas, -ʎas] *mf inv argot* dimwit

gilipollez [xi·li·po·'jes, -'ʎeθ] *f inf* nonsense

gimnasia [xim·'na·sja] *f* ENS gym; **hacer ~** to do exercises; DEP gymnastics *pl*; **~ rítmica** rhythm gymnastics

gimnasio [xim·'na·sjo] *m* gym

gimnasta [xim·'nas·ta] *mf* gymnast

gimotear [xi·mo·te·'ar] *vi* to whimper; (*gemir*) to groan

ginebra [xi·'ne·βra] *f* gin

ginecólogo, -a [xi·ne·'ko·lo·γo, -a] *m, f* gynecologist

gira ['xi·ra] *f* tour; **estar de ~** to be on tour

girar [xi·'rar] I. *vi* 1. (*dar vueltas*) to revolve; **~ en torno a algo** to revolve around sth; (*con rapidez*) to spin 2. (*torcer*) to turn II. *vt* to turn

girasol [xi·ra·'sol] *m* sunflower

giratorio, -a [xi·ra·'to·rjo, -a] *adj* revolving

giro ['xi·ro] *m* turn; COM draft; **~ postal** money order

gitano, -a [xi·'ta·no, -a] *adj, m, f* gypsy

glaciación [gla·sja·'sjon, -θja·'θjon] *f* glaciation

glaciar [gla·'sjar, -'θjar] *m* glacier

glándula ['glan·du·la] *f* gland

global [glo·'βal] *adj* overall; (*mundial*) global; (*cantidad, valoración*) total; (*informe*) comprehensive

globalidad [glo·βa·li·'dad] *f* totality

globalización [glo·βa·li·sa·'sjon, -θa·'θjon] *f* globalization

globo ['glo·βo] *m* 1. sphere; **~ ocular** eyeball 2. (*mapa*) globe 3. (*para niños*) balloon; (*tebeos*) speech balloon; **~ (aerostático)** hot-air balloon 4. *inf* rubber

gloria ['glo·rja] *f* glory; **estar en la ~** to be in seventh heaven

glorieta [glo·'rje·ta] *f* (*small*) square; (*rotonda*) traffic circle, rotary *reg*

glosario [glo·'sa·rjo] *m* glossary

glotón, -ona [glo·'ton, -·'to·na] I. *adj* gluttonous II. *m, f* glutton

glotonear [glo·to·ne·'ar] *vi* to be gluttonous

glotonería [glo·to·ne·'ri·a] *f* gluttony

glucosa [glu·'ko·sa] *f* glucose

glúteo ['glu·teo] *m* gluteus

G

gobernador(a) [go·βer·na·'dor, -·'do·ra]
I. *adj* governing II. *m(f)* governor

gobernanta [go·βer·'nan·ta] *f AmL* (*niñera*) nanny; (*institutriz*) governess; (*ama de llaves*) housekeeper

gobernante [go·βer·'nan·te] *mf* ruler

gobernar <e ➝ ie> [go·βer·'nar] *vt* to govern

gobierno [go·'βjer·no] *m* 1. POL government; ~ **autonómico/central** regional/central government 2. (*ministros*) cabinet 3. (*del gobernador*) governorship

goce [go·se, -θe] *m* enjoyment

godo, -a ['go·do, -a] *m, f* 1. Goth 2. *AmC pey* Spaniard

gofre ['go·fre] *m* waffle

gol [gol] *m* goal; ~ **del empate** equalizer; **meter un ~** to score (a goal)

golazo [go·'la·so, -θo] *m* great goal

goleador(a) [go·lea·'dor, -·'do·ra] *m(f)* goal scorer

golf [golf] *m* golf

golfo ['gol·fo] *m* gulf

golfo, -a ['gol·fo, -a] I. *adj* naughty II. *m, f* 1. (*pilluelo*) urchin 2. (*vagabundo*) tramp

golondrina [go·lon·'dri·na] *f* swallow

golosina [go·lo·'si·na] *f* candy

goloso, -a [go·'lo·so, -a] I. *adj* sweet-toothed; **es una oferta muy golosa** it's a very tempting offer II. *m, f* **ser un ~** to have a sweet tooth

golpe ['gol·pe] *m* 1. (*impacto*) blow; (*choque*) bump; ~ **de Estado** coup (d'état); **abrirse de ~** to fly open; **dar un ~** to strike; **me he dado un ~ en la cabeza** I banged my head; **me lo tragué de un ~** I downed it in one gulp 2. (*ruido*) bang 3. (*atraco*) hold-up

golpear [gol·pe·'ar] I. *vi* to hit II. *vt* to hit; (*puerta*) to knock on III. *vr* ~**se la cabeza** to bang one's head

goma ['go·ma] *f* 1. rubber; ~ **de borrar** eraser; ~ **elástica** elastic band 2. *AmL* (*resaca*) hangover

gomaespuma [go·ma·es·'pu·ma] *f* foam rubber

gomina® [go·'mi·na] *f* hair gel

gominola [go·mi·'no·la] *f* gumdrop

góndola ['gon·do·la] *f AmL* bus

gordo ['gor·do] *m* 1. fat 2. (*lotería*) **el** ~ the jackpot

gordo, -a ['gor·do, -a] I. *adj* fat; (*tejido*) thick; (*salario, mentira*) big; **ha pasado algo muy ~** sth serious has happened II. *m, f* fat man, fat woman *m, f*

gorila [go·'ri·la] *m* 1. gorilla 2. *inf* (*portero*) bouncer; (*guardaespaldas*) bodyguard; (*matón*) thug

gorra ['go·rra] *f* cap; (*para niños*) bonnet; **de** ~ *inf* free

gorrear [go·rre·'ar] *vi, vt inf* to scrounge; **¿te puedo ~ un cigarrillo?** can I get a cigarette from you?

gorrinada [go·rri·'na·da] *f* dirty trick

gorrino, -a [go·'rri·no, -a] *m, f* pig

gorrión [go·'rri·'on] *m* 1. sparrow 2. *AmC* (*colibrí*) hummingbird

gorro ['go·rro] *m* hat; (*de uniforme*) cap; (*para bebés*) bonnet; ~ **de natación** bathing cap

gorrón, -ona [go·'rron, -·'rro·na] *m, f* scrounger; *AmC* selfish person

gorronear [go·rro·ne·'ar] *vi v.* **gorrear**

gota ['go·ta] *f* drop; **parecerse como dos ~s de agua** to be like two peas in a pod; **no queda ni ~ de agua** there's not a drop of water left; ~ **fría** cold front; **la ~ que colma el vaso** the last straw

gotear [go·te·'ar] I. *vi* to drip; (*salirse*) to leak II. *vimpers* **está goteando** it's drizzling

goteo [go·'teo] *m* drip

gotera [go·'te·ra] *f* 1. leak; (*mancha*) stain 2. *pl AmL* outskirts *pl*

gótico, -a ['go·ti·ko, -a] *adj* Gothic

gozada [go·'sa·da, -'θa·da] *f inf* delight

gozar <z ➝ c> [go·'sar, -'θar] *vi* to enjoy oneself; ~ **de algo** to enjoy sth; ~ **de una increíble fortuna** to be incredibly wealthy

gr. ['gra·mo] *abr de* **gramo** g.

grabación [gra·βa·'sjon, -'θjon] *f* recording; TV shooting; COMPUT copying

grabado [gra·'βa·do] *m* 1. (*acción*) engraving 2. (*copia*) print 3. (*ilustración*) illustration

grabador(a) [gra·βa·'dor] *m(f)* engraver

grabadora [gra·βa·'do·ra] *f* tape recorder

grabar [gra·'βar] *vt* 1. to record 2. ARTE to engrave; (*en madera*) to cut 3. COMPUT to copy

gracia [ˈgra·sja, -θja] f 1. pl ¡~s! thanks!; ¡muchas ~s! thanks a lot!; ~s a thanks to 2. (chiste) joke; no tiene (ni) pizca de ~ it's not the least bit funny; no me hace nada de ~ I don't find it funny in the least; la ~ es que... the funny thing is that...

gracioso, -a [gra·ˈsjo·so, -a; gra·ˈθjo-] adj funny; no te hagas el ~ conmigo don't try to play the clown with me

grada [ˈgra·da] f 1. (de un estadio) tier; las ~s the terraces 2. pl AmL courtyard

gradación [gra·da·ˈsjon, -ˈθjon] f gradation

grado [ˈgra·do] m 1. (nivel, parentesco, alcohol) t. MAT, LING degree; ~ centígrado degree centigrade; ~ de confianza degree of trust; quemaduras de primer ~ first-degree burns; en ~ sumo greatly 2. ENS year; UNIV degree 3. MIL rank

graduable [gra·du·ˈa·βle] adj adjustable

graduación [gra·dwa·ˈsjon, -ˈθjon] f 1. (regulación) adjustment 2. (en grados) graduation; (en niveles, de personas) grading; (de precios) regulation; ~ alcohólica alcohol content 3. UNIV graduation

graduado, -a [gra·du·ˈa·do, -a] I. adj graduate(d) II. m, f graduate; ~ escolar school diploma

gradual [gra·du·ˈal] adj gradual

gradualmente [gra·dwal·ˈmen·te] adv 1. (en grados) by degrees 2. (progresivamente) gradually

graduar <1. pres gradúo> [gra·du·ˈar] I. vt 1. (regular) to regulate 2. TÉC to graduate; ~ la vista a alguien to test sb's eyesight 3. (en niveles) to classify; (precios) to regulate II. vr: ~se to graduate

grafía [gra·ˈfi·a] f writing; (ortografía) spelling

gráfica [ˈgra·fi·ka] f graph

gráfico [ˈgra·fi·ko] m graph; COMPUT graphic

gráfico, -a [ˈgra·fi·ko, -a] adj 1. (de la escritura) written 2. (del dibujo) illustrated; diccionario ~ visual dictionary; tarjeta gráfica graphics card 3. (claro)

graphic 4. fig expressive

grafito [gra·ˈfi·to] m graphite

gragea [gra·ˈxea] f (sugar-coated) pill

grajo [ˈgra·xo] m 1. rook 2. AmL (soba-quina) body odor

gral. [xe·ne·ˈral] adj abr de **general** gen.

gramática [gra·ˈma·ti·ka] f grammar

gramatical [gra·ma·ti·ˈkal] adj grammatical; regla ~ grammatical rule

gramilla [gra·ˈmi·ja, -ʎa] f AmL lawn

gramo [ˈgra·mo] m gram

gran [gran] adj v. **grande**

granada [gra·ˈna·da] f 1. pomegranate 2. (de mano) grenade; (de artillería) shell

granadilla [gra·na·ˈdi·ja, -ʎa] f AmC passionflower

granate [gra·ˈna·te] I. adj burgundy II. m garnet

Gran Bretaña [gram bre·ˈta·ɲa] f Great Britain

grande [ˈgran·de] adj <más grande o mayor, grandísimo> (ante sust sing: gran) 1. (de tamaño) big; (número, cantidad, habitación) large; gran ciudad big city; a gran velocidad at high speed; vino gran cantidad de gente a lot of people came; tengo un gran interés por... I'm very interested in...; no me preocupa gran cosa I'm not very worried about it 2. (de edad) grown-up 3. (moralmente) great; un gran hombre a great man; una gran idea a great idea ▶ pasarlo en ~ to have a great time

grandeza [gran·ˈde·sa, -θa] f greatness; (tamaño) size

grandiosidad [gran·djo·si·ˈdad] f grandeur

grandioso, -a [gran·ˈdjo·so, -a] adj impressive; (rimbombante) grandiose

grandullón, -ona [gran·du·ˈjon, -·ˈjo·na; -ˈʎon, -·ˈʎo·na] adj oversized

granel [gra·ˈnel] a ~ (sin envase) loose; (líquido) by volume; (en abundancia) in abundance

granero [gra·ˈne·ro] m granary; (de granja) barn

granito [gra·ˈni·to] m granite

granizado [gra·ni·ˈsa·do, -ˈθa·do] m iced drink; ~ de café ≈ iced coffee

granizar <z → c> [gra·ni·'sar, -'θar] *vimpers* to hail

granizo [gra·'ni·so, -θo] *m* hail

granja ['gran·xa] *f* farm

granjero, -a [gran·'xe·ro, -a] *m, f* farmer

grano ['gra·no] *m* t. TÉC grain; (*café*) bean; (*de piel*) pimple; **ir al ~** to get to the point

granuja [gra·'nu·xa] *m* (*pilluelo*) rascal; (*bribón*) scoundrel

grapa ['gra·pa] *f* **1.** (*para papeles*) staple **2.** (*licor*) grappa

grapadora [gra·pa·'do·ra] *f* stapler

grapar [gra·'par] *vt* to staple

grasa ['gra·sa] *f* **1.** fat; **~ de cerdo** pork fat **2.** TÉC oil, grease **3.** (*mugre*) grime

grasiento, -a [gra·'sjen·to, -a] *adj* fatty; (*de aceite*) greasy

graso, -a ['gra·so, -a] *adj* fatty; (*piel*) oily; (*pelo*) greasy

gratificación [gra·ti·fi·ka·'sjon, -'θjon] *f* **1.** (*recompensa*) reward **2.** (*del sueldo*) bonus **3.** (*propina*) tip **4.** (*satisfacción*) gratification

gratificante [gra·ti·fi·'kan·te] *adj* gratifying

gratificar <c → qu> [gra·ti·fi·'kar] *vt* **1.** (*recompensar*) **~ a alguien por algo** to reward sb for sth **2.** (*en el trabajo*) **~ a alguien** to give sb a bonus

gratinar [gra·ti·'nar] *vt* to cook au gratin

gratis ['gra·tis] *adv* free

gratitud [gra·ti·'tud] *f* gratitude

grato, -a ['gra·to, -a] *adj* pleasant

gratuito, -a [gra·'twi·to, -a] *adj* free

grava ['gra·βa] *f* gravel

gravable [gra·'βa·βle] *adj* taxable

gravar [gra·'βar] *vt* to tax

grave ['gra·βe] *adj* serious; (*sonido*) deep; **está ~** he/she is very sick

gravedad [gra·βe·'dad] *f* **1.** t. MED seriousness; **de ~** seriously **2.** FÍS gravity **3.** MÚS depth

gravilla [gra·'βi·ja, -ʎa] *f* gravel

gravitación [gra·βi·ta·'sjon, -'θjon] *f* gravitation

graznar [gras·'nar, graθ-] *vi* (*cuervo*) to caw; (*ganso*) to honk; (*pato*) to quack

graznido [gras·'ni·do, graθ-] *m* (*de cuervo*) caw; (*de ganso*) honk; (*de pato*) quack

greca ['gre·ka] *f* AmL coffee machine

Grecia ['gre·sja, -θja] *f* Greece

grecorromano, -a [gre·ko·rro·'ma·no, -a] *adj* Greco-Roman

gremio ['gre·mjo] *m* association; (*sindicato*) trade union

greña ['gre·ɲa] *f* matted hair

griego, -a ['grje·ɣo] *adj, m, f* Greek

grieta ['grje·ta] *f* (*en la pared, una taza*) crack; (*piel*) chap

grifo ['gri·fo] *m* **1.** tap; **agua del ~** tap water; **he dejado el ~ abierto** I left the faucet running **2.** Perú, Ecua, Bol gas station

grillarse [gri·'jar·se, -'ʎar·se] *vr inf* to go nuts

grillo ['gri·jo, -ʎo] *m* ZOOL cricket

grima ['gri·ma] *f* **me da ~** (*asco*) it's disgusting; (*dentera*) it gets on my nerves

gringada [grin·'ga·da] *f* AmL inf group of gringos; (*faena*) dirty trick

gringo [grin·go] *m* AmL inf gibberish; **hablar en ~** to speak gibberish

gringo, -a ['grin·go, -a] *m, f* AmL inf gringo; (*de EE.UU.*) Yank(ee)

gripa ['gri·pa] *f* AmL flu

gripal [gri·'pal] *adj* flu

gripe ['gri·pe] *f* flu; **~ aviar** bird flu

gris [gris] *adj, m* gray

grisáceo, -a [gri·'sa·seo, -θeo] *adj* grayish

grisma ['gris·ma] *f* Chile, Guat, Hond pinch

gritadera [gri·ta·'de·ra] *f* Col, Ven loud shouting

gritar [gri·'tar] **I.** *vt* to shout at; (*reprender*) to tell off **II.** *vi* to shout, to yell

criterio [gri·te·'ri·o] *m* uproar

grito ['gri·to] *m* shout; **pegar un ~** to shout; **a ~s** in a very loud voice; **a ~ limpio** [*o* **pelado**] at the top of one's voice; **~ de protesta** cry of protest; **la región está pidiendo a ~s ayuda internacional** the region is crying out for international support; **ser el último ~** to be the (latest) rage

groenlandés, -esa [groen·lan·'des, -·'de·sa] **I.** *adj* Greenland **II.** *m, f* Greenlander

Groenlandia [groen·'lan·dja] *f* Greenland

grogui ['gro·ɣi] *adj* groggy

grosella [gro·'se·ja, -ʎa] *f* currant

grosería [gro·se·'ri·a] *f* **1.** (*descortesía*) rudeness **2.** (*ordinariez*) vulgarity **3.** (*observación*) rude comment; (*palabrota*) swearword

grosero, -a [gro·'se·ro, -a] *adj* rude; (*ordinario*) vulgar

grosor [gro·'sor] *m* thickness

grotesco, -a [gro·'tes·ko, -a] *adj* grotesque

grúa ['gru·a] *f* **1.** (*máquina*) crane **2.** (*vehículo*) wrecker

grueso, -a [‘grwe·so, -a] *adj* thick; (*persona*) stout; **mar gruesa** heavy seas

grulla ['gru·ja, -ʎa] *f* crane

grumo ['gru·mo] *m* lump

gruñido [gru·'ɲi·do] *m* grunt; (*queja*) grumble; (*perro*) growl; (*puerta*) creak

gruñir <3. pret gruñó> [gru·'ɲir] *vi* to grunt; (*quejarse*) to grumble; (*perro*) to growl; (*puerta*) to creak

gruñón, -ona [gru·'ɲon, --'ɲo·na] *inf* **I.** *adj* grumbling **II.** *m, f* grumbler

grupo ['gru·po] *m* group; ~ (**industrial**) corporation; ~ **parlamentario** parliamentary group; **trabajo en** ~ group work

gruta ['gru·ta] *f* cave; (*artificial*) grotto

guaca ['gwa·ka] *f AmL* **1.** (*tumba*) tomb **2.** (*tesoro*) buried treasure **3.** (*hucha*) money box; **hacer** ~ to make money

guacal [gwa·'kal] *m AmC, Col, Ven* gourd

guacamayo [gwa·ka·'ma·jo] *m* macaw

guacamol(e) [gwa·ka·'mol, --'mo·le] *m* guacamole

guacamote [gwa·ka·'mo·te] *m Méx* manioc

guachada [gwa·'tʃa·da] *f AmL inf* dirty trick

guachimán [gwa·tʃi·'man] *m AmL* watchman

guacho, -a ['gwa·tʃo, -a] *m, f AmS* orphan; (*expósito*) abandoned child

guadaña [gwa·'da·na] *f* scythe; **la Guadaña** the Grim Reaper

guagua ['gwa·ɣwa] *f* **1.** *AmC* bus **2.** *CSur* baby

guajiro, -a [gwa·'xi·ro, -a] *adj, m, f Cuba* (white) peasant

guamazo [gwa·'ma·so] *m Méx* punch

guamúchil [gwa·'mu·tʃil] *m* BOT *Méx* camachile

guanábano [gwa·'na·βa·no] *m AmL* soursop tree; (*fruta*) custard apple

guanaco [gwa·'na·ko] *m* guanaco

guanaco, -a [gwa·'na·ko, -a] **I.** *adj AmL* simple; (*lento*) slow **II.** *m, f* **1.** *AmL* simpleton **2.** *AmC pey* Salvadoran

guanajo, -a [gwa·'na·xo, -a] *m, f Cuba, PRico* turkey

guandoca [guan·'do·ka] *f Col* prison

guango, -a ['guan·go, -a] *adj Méx* baggy

guano ['gwa·no] *m* guano; *CSur* dung

guantada [gwan·'ta·da] *f* slap; **dar una** ~ **a alguien** to slap sb

guantazo [gwan·'ta·so, -θo] *m v.* **guantada**

guante ['gwan·te] *m* glove

guantear [gwan·te·'ar] *vt AmL* to slap (around)

guantera [gwan·'te·ra] *f* glove compartment

guaperas [gwa·'pe·ras] *inv inf* **I.** *adj* good-looking **II.** *m* heart-throb

guaperío [gwa·pe·'ri·o] *m* **el** ~ the jet set

guapo, -a ['gwa·po, -a] *adj* **1.** handsome, pretty **estar** [*o* **ir**] ~ to look smart **2.** *AmL* bully

guaraca [gwa·'ra·ka] *f AmL* (*honda*) catapult; (*látigo*) whip

guaraná [gwa·ra·'na] *f* guarana

guarangada [gwa·ran·'ga·da] *f AmL* rude comment

guaraní [gwa·ra·'ni] *adj, m* Guarani; (*moneda*) guarani

guarapo [gwa·'ra·po] *m AmL* sugar-cane juice; (*licor*) sugar-cane liquor

guarda ['gwar·da] *mf* guard; (*cuidador*) keeper; ~ **jurado** security guard

guardabarros [gwar·da·'βa·rros] *m inv* fender

guardabosque(s) [gwar·da·'βos·ke(s)] *mf (inv)* forest ranger; (*de caza*) gamekeeper

guardacostas [gwar·da·'kos·tas] *m inv* coastguard

guardaespaldas [gwar·da·es·'pal·das] *mf inv* bodyguard

G

guardameta [gwar·da·'me·ta] *mf* goalkeeper

guardar [gwar·'dar] I. *vt* 1. (*vigilar*) to guard; (*proteger*) to protect 2. (*conservar, quedarse con*) to keep; ~ **un sitio** to keep a place; ~ **un trozo de pastel a alguien** to save a piece of cake for sb; **¿dónde has guardado las servilletas?** where did you put the napkins?; ~ **algo en el bolsillo** to put sth in one's pocket; ~ **las fuerzas** to save one's strength 3. COMPUT to save II. *vr* ~**se de algo/alguien** to be on one's guard against sth/sb; ~**se de hacer algo** to be careful not to do sth

guardarropa [gwar·da·'rro·pa] *m* checkroom; (*armario*) wardrobe

guardería [gwar·de·'ri·a] *f* nursery

guardia[1] ['gwar·dja] *f* 1. duty; DEP guard; **¿cuál es la farmacia de ~?** which pharmacy is open tonight?; **estar de ~** to be on duty; **estar en ~** to be on one's guard; **bajar la ~** to lower one's guard 2. **la Guardia Civil** the Civil Guard; ~ **municipal** [*o* **urbana**] local police

guardia[2] ['gwar·dja] *mf* ~ **civil** civil guard; ~ **municipal** [*o* **urbano**] local policeman; ~ **de tráfico** traffic policeman, -woman *m, f*

guardián, -ana [gwar·'djan, -·'dja·na] *m, f* guardian; **perro** ~ watchdog; (*en el zoo*) (zoo)keeper

guarecerse [gwa·re·'ser·se, -'θer·se] *irr como crecer vr* to take refuge; ~**se de la lluvia** to take shelter from the rain

guarida [gwa·'ri·da] *f* hideout; (*de animales*) den

guarnición [gwar·ni·'sjon, -'θjon] *f* 1. CULIN *accompaniment to a main dish* 2. MIL garrison

guarro, -a ['gwa·rro, -a] I. *adj* 1. disgusting; **chiste** ~ dirty joke 2. (*persona*) dirty; (*moralmente*) smutty II. *m, f* pig

guasa ['gwa·sa] *f* joke; **estar de** ~ to be joking; **tiene** ~ **que... +***subj* it's ironic that...

guasanga [gwa·'san·ga] *f* AmL hubbub

guasca ['gwas·ka] *f* AmL whip

guasería [gwa·se·'ri·a] *f* Arg, Chile obscenity

guaso, -a ['gwa·so, -a] *adj* CSur peasant;

(*tosco*) coarse

guata ['gwa·ta] *f* AmL belly

Guatemala [gwa·te·'ma·la] *f* Guatemala

guatemalteco, -a [gwa·te·mal·'te·ko, -a] *adj, m, f* Guatemalan

guay [gwai] *adj inf* cool

guayaba [gwa·'ja·βa] *f* 1. guava; (*jalea*) guava jelly 2. AmL (*mentira*) lie

guayabo [gwa·'ja·βo] *m* guava tree

guayacán [gwa·ja·'kan] *m* guaiacum

Guayana [gwa·'ja·na] *f* Guyana

guayarse [gwa·'jar·se] *vr* PRico to get drunk

gubernamental [gu·βer·na·men·'tal] *adj* governmental

guepardo [ge·'par·do] *m* cheetah

güero, -a ['gwe·ro, -a] AmL I. *adj* blond(e); (*de piel*) fair II. *m, f* blond, blonde *m, f*

guerra ['ge·rra] *f* war; **en** ~ at war; **la Primera/Segunda Guerra Mundial** the First/Second World War; ~ **química/psicológica/biológica** chemical/psychological/biological warfare; **dar mucha** ~ *inf* to be a real handful

guerrero, -a [ge·'rre·ro, -a] *m, f* warrior

guerrilla [ge·'rri·ja, -·ʎa] *f* guerrilla band

guerrillero, -a [ge·rri·'je·ro, -a, ·ʎe·ro, -a] *m, f* guerrilla (fighter)

gueto ['ge·to] *m* ghetto

guía[1] ['gi·a] *mf* guide; ~ **turístico** tourist guide

guía[2] ['gi·a] *f* 1. (*pauta*) guideline 2. (*manual*) handbook; ~ **comercial/telefónica** trade/telephone directory; ~ **de ferrocarriles** train schedule; ~ **turística** travel guide(book) 3. TÉC guide 4. PRico (*volante*) steering wheel

guiar <*1. pres* **guío**> [gi·'ar] I. *vt* to guide; (*conversación*) to direct II. *vr* ~**se por algo** to be guided by sth; **me guío por mi instinto** I follow my instincts

guijarro [gi·'xa·rro] *m* pebble

guillotina [gi·jo·'ti·na, gi·ʎo-] *f* guillotine

guinda ['gin·da] *f* morello cherry; **poner la ~ a algo** to top sth off

guindilla [gin·'di·ja, -·ʎa] *f* chili pepper

guineo [gi·'neo] *m* AmL banana

guiñapo [gi·'na·po] *m* rag; **estar hecho un ~** to be a wreck

guiñar [gi·'nar] I. *vt* ~ **el ojo a alguien**

to wink at sb **II.** *vi* to wink

guiño ['gi·ɲo] *m* wink

guiñol [gi·'ɲol] *m* puppet; (*obra*) puppet show

guión [gi·'on] *m* **1.** outline; CINE, TV script **2.** LING hyphen; (*en diálogo*) dash

guionista [gjo·'nis·ta] *mf* CINE screenwriter; TV scriptwriter

guiri ['gi·ɾi] *mf* *inf* foreign tourist

guirigay [gi·ɾi·'ɣai] *m* <guirigayes *o* gurigáis> *inf* **1.** (*lenguaje*) gibberish **2.** (*griterío*) uproar; (*barullo*) hubbub

guirnalda [giɾ·'nal·da] *f* garland

guisado [gi·'sa·ðo] *m* stew

guisante [gi·'san·te] *m* pea

guisar [gi·'saɾ] *vt* to cook; (*con salsa*) to stew

guiso ['gi·so] *m* dish; (*en salsa*) stew

guita ['gi·ta] *f* twine; *inf* (*dinero*) dough

guitarra [gi·'ta·rra] *f* guitar

guitarrista [gi·ta·'rris·ta] *mf* guitarist

gula ['gu·la] *f* gluttony

guripa [gu·'ɾi·pa] *m* *inf* cop

gurú [gu·'ɾu] *m* guru

gusanillo [gu·sa·'ni·jo, -ʎo] *m* **matar el ~** (*comiendo*) to have a snack; (*bebiendo*) to quench one's thirst

gusano [gu·'sa·no] *m* worm; (*oruga*) caterpillar

gustar [gus·'taɾ] *vi* **me gusta nadar/el helado** I like swimming/ice cream; **me gustan estos zapatos** I like these shoes; **así me gusta!** ¡well done!; **me gusta tu hermano** I think your brother is handsome; **me gustas** I like you; **me ~ía saber...** I would like to know...

gustazo [gus·'ta·so, -θo] *m* great pleasure; **darse el ~ de algo** to treat oneself to sth

gustillo [gus·'ti·jo, -ʎo] *m* **1.** (*sabor*) aftertaste **2.** (*sensación*) kick

gusto ['gus·to] *m* **1.** (*sentido, sabor*) taste; **una broma de mal ~** a joke in bad taste; **no hago nada a su ~** nothing I do pleases him/her; **~ a algo** taste of sth **2.** (*placer*) pleasure; **con ~** with pleasure; **coger ~ a algo** to take a liking to sth; **estar a ~** to feel comfortable; **tanto ~ en conocerla — el ~ es mío** pleased to meet you — the pleasure is all mine; **cantan que da ~** they sing

wonderfully

gustoso, -a [gus·'to·so, -a] *adj* **1.** (*sabroso*) savory **2.** (*agradable*) pleasant; **te acompañaré ~** I'd be glad to accompany you

H

H, h ['a·tʃe] *f* H, h; **~ de Huelva** H as in Hotel

haba ['a·βa] *f* broad bean

Habana [a·'βa·na] *f* **La ~** Havana

habanero, -a [a·βa·'ne·ro, -a] *adj, m, f* Havanan

habano [a·'βa·no] *m* Havana cigar

haber [a·'βeɾ] *irr* **I.** *aux* **1.** to have; **ha ido al cine** he/she has gone to the cinema; **he comprado el periódico** I bought the newspaper **2.** *elev* **~ de hacer algo** to have to do sth; **han de llegar pronto** they should be here soon **3.** (*imperativo*) **no tengo sitio — ¡~ venido antes!** there's no room — you should have come earlier! **II.** *vimpers* **1.** (*ocurrir*) to take place; **ha habido un terremoto** there has been an earthquake; **¿qué hay?** what's the news?; **¿qué hay, Pepe?** how's it going, Pepe? **2.** (*existir, estar*) **hay** there is/are; **había** there was/were; **no hay de qué** not at all; **no hay quien me gane al ping-pong** nobody can beat me at table tennis; **había una vez...** once upon a time there was... **3.** (*obligatoriedad*) **¡hay que ver cómo están los precios!** my God! look at those prices!; **hay que trabajar más** we have to work harder; **no hay que olvidar que...** we must not forget that... **III.** *m* **tener algo en su ~** to have sth (to one's credit)

habichuela [a·βi·'tʃwe·la] *f* (kidney) bean; (*blanca*) haricot bean

hábil ['a·βil] *adj* **1.** (*diestro*) skilled (*para, en* at) **2.** (*astuto*) shrewd **3.** **días ~es** working days

habilidad [a·βi·li·'dad] *f* **1.** (*destreza*) skill **2.** (*facultad*) ability **3.** (*astucia*) shrewdness

habilidoso, -a [a·βi·li·'do·so, -a] *adj*, ha-

biloso, -a [a·βi·'lo·so, -a] *adj AmL* skillful; (*astuto*) shrewd

habitación [a·βi·ta·'sjon, -'θjon] *f* room; (*dormitorio*) bedroom; ~ **individual** single room

habitante [a·βi·'tan·te] *mf* inhabitant; ¿**cuántos habitantes tiene Chile?** what is the population of Chile?

habitar [a·βi·'tar] **I.** *vi* to live **II.** *vt* to live in

hábitat ['a·βi·tat] *m* <hábitats> habitat

hábito ['a·βi·to] *m* habit; **he dejado el ~ de fumar** I've given up smoking

habitual [a·βi·tu·'al] *adj* regular; **bebedor/cliente ~** regular drinker/client

habituar <1. *pres* habitúo> [a·βi·tu·'ar] **I.** *vt* **a alguien a algo** to get somebody used to something **II.** *vr* **~se a algo** to get used to sth

habla [a·βla] *f* speech; **quedarse sin ~** to be left speechless; **un país de ~ inglesa** an English-speaking country; **¡Juan al ~!** Juan speaking!; (*manera, dialecto*) way of speaking

hablado, -a [a·'βla·do, -a] *adj* spoken; **bien ~** well-spoken; **el francés ~** spoken French; **ser mal ~** to be foulmouthed

hablador(a) [a·βla·'dor, -'do·ra] **I.** *adj* talkative **II.** *m(f)* **1.** (*cotorra*) chatterbox **2.** (*chismoso*) gossip

habladuría [a·βla·du·'ri·a] *f* rumor; **~s** gossip

hablante [a·'βlan·te] *mf* speaker

hablantina [a·βlan·'ti·na] *f Col, Ven* chatterbox

hablar [a·'βlar] **I.** *vi* **1.** (*decir*) to speak, to talk; **~ a gritos** to shout; **~ alto/bajo** to speak loudly/softly; **~ entre dientes** to mutter; **déjeme terminar de ~** let me finish what I have to say; **~ claro** to speak frankly; **el autor no habla de este tema** the author does not address this topic; **la policía lo ha hecho ~** the police made him talk; **los números hablan por sí solos** the figures speak for themselves; **¡no ~ás en serio!** you must be joking!; **por no ~ de...** not to mention...; **¡y no se hable más!** and that's an end to it; **¡ni ~!** no way! **2.** (*conversar*) **~ con alguien** to talk to sb; **~**

con franqueza to talk sincerely; **~ por teléfono** to talk on the telephone; **no he podido ~ con él** I haven't managed to speak to him; **~ por los codos** *inf* to talk nineteen to the dozen **II.** *vt* to say; (*idioma*) to speak; **~ a alguien (de algo/alguien)** to talk to sb (about sth/sb); **no me habló en toda la noche** he/she didn't say a word to me all night; **lo hablaré con tu padre** I'll talk about it with your father **III.** *vr:* **~se** to talk to each other; **no se hablan** they are not on speaking terms; **nos hablamos de tú** we are on familiar terms

hacendoso, -a [a·sen·'do·so, -a; a·θen-] *adj* hard-working

hacer [a·'ser, -'θer] *irr* **I.** *vt* **1.** (*producir*) to make, to manufacture; **la casa está hecha de madera** the house is made of wood **2.** (*realizar*) to do; (*libro*) to write; **¿qué hacemos hoy?** what shall we do today?; **~ una llamada** to make a phone call; **demuestra lo que sabes ~** show us what you can do; **hazlo por mí** do it for me; **a medio ~** half-finished; **hicimos la trayectoria en tres horas** we did the trip in three hours; **lo hecho, hecho está** there's no use crying over spilled milk; **puedes ~ lo que quieras** you can do whatever you want; **¿qué haces por aquí?** what are you doing around here?; **¡me la has hecho!** you've let me in for it; **la ha hecho buena** he's/she's really messed things up **3.** (*pregunta*) to ask; (*observación*) to make; (*discurso*) to make, to give; (*dinero, amigos*) to make; (*ruido*) to make; (*daño*) to cause; **~ destrozos** to wreak havoc; **~ sombra** to cast a shadow; **no puedes ~me esto** you can't do this to me; **¿puedes ~me sitio?** can you fit me in? **4.** (*construir*) to build **5.** (*transformar*) **~ pedazos algo** to smash sth up; **estás hecho un hombre** you're a man now **6.** (*llegar*) **~ puerto** to clear harbor; **~ noche en...** to spend the night in... **7.** (+ *sust*) **~ el amor** to make love; **~ caso a alguien** to pay heed to sb; **~ cumplidos** to pay compliments; **~ deporte** to do sports; **~ frente a algo/alguien** to face up to sth/sb; **~ la maleta** to pack; **~ uso de algo** to make use of sth **8.** (+ *verbo*) **~ creer algo a alguien** to make [*o* have] sb believe sth; **~ venir a alguien** to make sb come; **hazlo pasar** let him in; **no me hagas contarlo** don't make me say it **9.** (*limpiar*) **hacer las escaleras** *inf* to do the steps **10.** TEAT **~ una obra** to do [*o* put on] a play; **~ el papel de Antígona** to play the role of Antigone **11.** ENS (*carrera*) to study, to do; **¿haces francés o inglés?** are you doing French or English? **12.** CULIN (*comida, pastel*) to make; (*patatas*) to do; **quiero la carne bien hecha** I want the meat well done **II.** *vi* **1.** (*convenir*) **eso no hace al caso** that's not relevant **2.** (*oficio*) **~ de algo** to work as sth **3.** (*con preposición*) **por lo que hace a Juan...** regarding Juan...; **hizo como que no me vio** he/she pretended he/she didn't seen me **III.** *vr:* **~se 1.** (*volverse*) to become; **~se del Madrid** to become a Madrid fan **2.** (*crecer*) to grow **3.** (*simular*) to pretend; **se hace a todo** he's/she's always pretending; **~se la víctima** to act like a victim **4.** (*habituarse*) **~se a algo** to get used to sth **5.** (*dejarse hacer*) **~se una foto** to have one's picture taken **6.** (*conseguir*) **~se respetar** to instill respect; **~se con el poder** to seize power **7.** (*resultar*) **se me hace muy difícil creer eso** it's very difficult for me to believe that **IV.** *vimpers* **1.** (*tiempo*) **hace frío/calor** it's cold/hot; **hoy hace un buen día** it's a nice day today **2.** (*temporal*) **hace tres días** three days ago; **no hace mucho** not long ago; **desde hace un día** since yesterday

hacha ['a·tʃa] *f* axe

hachís [xa·'tʃis] *m* hashish

hacia ['a·sja, -θja] *prep* **1.** (*dirección*) towards, to; **el pueblo está más ~ el sur** the village lies further to the south; **el pueblo está yendo ~ Cuzco** the village is on the way to Cuzco; **fuimos ~ allí** we went that way; **vino ~ mí** he/she came towards me **2.** (*cerca de*) near **3.** (*respecto a*) regarding

hacienda [a·'sjen·da, a·'θjen-] *f* **1.** (*finca*) country estate **2.** (*bienes*) **~ pública**

public finance

Hacienda [a·'sjen·da, a·'θjen-] *f* (*ministerio*) Treasury; (*administración*) Internal Revenue Service; **el Ministro de Economía y ~** the Minister of Finance; **¿pagas mucho a ~?** do you pay a lot of tax?

hacinamiento [a·si·na·'mjen·to, a·θi-] *m* **1.** (*de haces*) piling **2.** (*de objetos*) stacking; (*de personas*) (over)crowding

hacinar [a·si·'nar, a·θi-] **I.** *vt* to pile **II.** *vr:* **~se** (*personas*) to (over)crowd; (*objetos*) to stack

hacker ['xa·ker] *mf* hacker

hada ['a·da] *f* fairy; **cuento de ~s** fairy tale; **~ madrina** fairy godmother

Haití [ai·'ti] *m* Haiti

hala ['a·la] *interj* **1.** (*sorpresa*) wow! **2.** (*prisa*) come on!

halagar <g → gu> [a·la·'ɣar] *vt* to flatter

halago [a·'la·ɣo] *m* **1.** (*acción*) flattery **2.** (*palabras*) flattering words *pl*, compliment

halcón [al·'kon] *m* falcon

hall [xol] *m* hall

hallar [a·'jar, -'ʎar] **I.** *vt* **1.** (*encontrar*) to find; (*sin buscar*) to come across; (*tierra*) to discover **2.** (*inventar*) to invent **3.** (*averiguar*) to check **4.** (*darse cuenta*) to realize **II.** *vr:* **~se 1.** (*sitio*) to be **2.** (*estado*) to feel; **se halló con la resistencia de su partido** he/she met opposition from his/her party

hallazgo [a·'jas·ɣo, a·'ʎaθ-] *m* **1.** discovery **2.** *pl* findings *pl*

halterofilia [al·te·ro·'fi·lja] *f* weightlifting

hamaca [a·'ma·ka] *f* **1.** (*cama*) hammock **2.** (*tumbona*) deckchair **3.** *AmL* (*mecedora*) rocking chair

hamacar <c → qu> [a·ma·'kar] *vt, vr:* **~se** *AmS, Guat* to rock

hambre ['am·bre] *f* **1.** (*apetito*) hunger; **huelga de ~** hunger strike; **matar el ~** to satisfy one's hunger; **me ha entrado (el) ~** I'm getting hungry; **morirse de ~** to die of hunger; **tener ~** to be hungry **2.** (*de la población*) starvation **3.** (*deseo*) **~ de algo** longing for sth; **~ de poder** hunger for power

hambrear [am·bre·'ar] *vi AmL* to starve;

(*mendigar*) to be hungry

hambriento, -a [am·'brjen·to, -a] *adj*
hungry; (*muerto de hambre*) starving;
estar ~ de poder to be hungry for
power

hambruna [am·'bru·na] *f* famine

hamburguesa [am·bur·'ɣe·sa] *f* hamburger; **~ con queso** cheeseburger

hamburguesería [am·bur·ɣe·se·'ri·a] *f*
hamburger restaurant

haragán, -ana [a·ra·'ɣan, -·'ɣa·na] *m, f*
(*persona*) loafer

harapo [a·'ra·po] *m* rag

hardware ['xard·wer] *m* hardware

harem [a·'ren], **harén** [a·'ren] *m* harem

harina [a·'ri·na] *f* 1. CULIN flour; **~ integral** whole-wheat flour; **~ de trigo**
wheat flour 2. (*polvo*) powder

harinear [a·ri·ne·'ar] *vimpers Ven* to
drizzle

harmonía [ar·mo·'ni·a] *f* harmony

hartar [ar·'tar] *irr* I. *vt* 1. (*saciar*) **~ a alguien** to give sb their fill 2. (*fastidiar*)
me harta con sus chistes I'm getting
sick of his/her jokes II. *vr:* **~se** 1. (*sa-
ciarse*) to eat one's fill; (*en exceso*) to eat
too much 2. (*cansarse*) to get fed up;
~se de reír to laugh oneself silly; **me
he hartado del tiempo que hace en
Nueva York** I'm sick of [*o* fed up with]
this New York weather

harto, -a ['ar·to, -a] I. *adj* 1. (*repleto*)
full; (*en exceso*) too full 2. (*sobrado*)
tengo hartas razones I have plenty
of reasons 3. (*cansado*) **estar ~ de al-
guien/algo** to be sick of [*o* fed up with]
sb/sth II. *adv* (*sobrado*) (more than)
enough; (*muy*) a lot of

hasta ['as·ta] I. *prep* 1. (*de lugar*) to;
te llevo ~ la estación I'll give you a
lift to the station; **volamos ~ Madrid**
we're flying to Madrid; **~ cierto punto**
to a certain degree, up to a point 2. (*de
tiempo*) until, up to until; **~ ahora** up to
now; **~ el próximo año** up until next
year 3. (*en despedidas*) **¡~ luego!** see
you later!; **¡~ la vista!** see you again!;
¡~ la próxima! until next time! II. *adv*
even III. *conj* **~ cuando come lee el
periódico** he/she even reads the newspaper while he's/she's eating; **no con-**

siguió un trabajo fijo **~ que cumplió
40 años** he/she didn't get a steady job
until he/she was forty

hastiar <*1. pres* hastío> [as·ti·'ar] I. *vt*
1. (*aburrir*) to bore 2. (*hartar, repugnar*)
to sicken II. *vr* **~se de alguien/algo** to
get fed up with sb/sth

hastío [as·'ti·o] *m* 1. (*tedio*) boredom;
¡qué ~! what a bore! 2. (*repugnancia*) disgust

Hawai [xa·'wai] *m* Hawaii

hawaiano, -a [xa·wa·'ja·no, -a] *adj, m, f*
Hawaiian

haya ['a·ja] *f* beech; (*madera*) beech
wood

haz [as, aθ] *m* bunch; (*de papeles*) sheaf

hazaña [a·'sa·ɲa, a·'θa-] *f* feat, exploit

hazmerreír [as·me·rre·'ir, aθ·me·] *m inv*
laughing stock; **es el ~ de la gente**
he's/she's the butt of everyone's jokes

he [e] *1. pres de* **haber**

hebilla [e·'βi·ja, -ʎa] *f* buckle

hebra [e·'βra] *f* 1. (*hilo*) thread 2. (*fibra*)
fiber; **tabaco de ~** loose tobacco

hebreo, -a [e·'βreo, -a] *adj, m, f* Hebrew

heces ['e·ses, 'e·θes] *fpl* (*excrementos*)
feces *pl*

hechicero, -a [e·tʃi·'se·ro, -a; -'θe·ro, -a]
m, f 1. (*brujo*) sorcerer 2. (*de tribu*)
witch doctor

hechizar <z → c> [e·tʃi·'sar, -'θar] *vt*
1. (*encantar*) to cast a spell on 2. (*fascinar*) captivate, to enchant

hechizo [e·'tʃi·so, -θo] *m* spell; **romper
el ~** to break the spell

hecho ['e·tʃo] *m* 1. (*circunstancia*) fact
2. (*acto*) action, deed; **~ delictivo** criminal act 3. (*suceso*) event; JUR deed;
exposición de los ~s statement of
events; **lugar de los ~s** scene of the
crime; **los ~s que causaron el incendio** the events that gave rise to the fire
▶ **de ~** in fact

hecho, -a ['e·tʃo, -a] *adj* 1. (*maduro*) mature; **vino ~** mature wine 2. (*cocido*)
cooked; **me gusta la carne hecha** I like
meat well done; **el pollo está demasiado ~** the chicken is overcooked 3. (*acabado*) finished; **frase hecha** idiom; **traje
~** ready-made suit 4. (*adulto*) **un hom-**

bre ~ y derecho a real man

hectárea [ek·'ta·re·a] *f* hectare

hedonista [e·do·'nis·ta] **I.** *adj* hedonistic **II.** *mf* hedonist

hedor [e·'dor] *m* stench; **~ a huevos podridos** stench of rotten eggs

hegemonía [e·xe·mo·'ni·a] *f* hegemony

helada [e·'la·da] *f* frost; **las primeras ~s del año** the first frosts of the year; **anoche cayó una ~** there was a frost last night

heladera [e·la·'de·ra] *f* fridge

heladería [e·la·de·'ri·a] *f* ice cream parlor

helado [e·'la·do] *m* ice cream; (*sorbete*) sherbe(r)t

helado, -a [e·'la·do, -a] *adj* **1.** (*frío*) freezing; (*congelado*) frozen; **estoy ~** I'm freezing; **el lago está ~** the lake is frozen; **las cañerías están heladas** the pipes are frozen **2.** (*pasmado*) **me quedé ~** I was left speechless; (*de miedo*) I was petrified **3.** (*altivo*) aloof

helaje [e·'la·xe] *m Col* frost

helar <e → ie> [e·'lar] **I.** *vt* **1.** (*congelar*) to freeze **2.** (*pasmar*) to astonish **II.** *vimpers* to freeze **III.** *vr*: **~se 1.** (*congelarse*) to freeze; **el lago se ha helado** the lake has frozen over **2.** (*morir*) to freeze to death **3.** (*pasar frío*) to be frozen [*o* ice cold]; **~se de frío** to get chilled to the bone

helecho [e·'le·tʃo] *m* bracken

hélice [e·'li·se, -θe] *f* propeller

helicóptero [e·li·'kop·te·ro] *m* helicopter

helio [e·'ljo] *m* helium

helipuerto [e·li·'pwer·to] *m* heliport

helvético, -a [el·'βe·ti·ko, -a] *adj, m, f* Swiss

hematoma [e·ma·'to·ma] *m* bruise; MED hematoma

hembra ['em·bra] *f* t. ZOOL, ELEC, TÉC (*tornillo*) nut

hemiplejia [e·mi·'ple·xja] *f*, **hemiplejía** [e·mi·ple·'xi·a] *f* MED hemiplegia, semiparalysis

hemisferio [e·mis·'fe·rjo] *m* hemisphere

hemorragia [e·mo·'rra·xia] *f* hemorrhage

hemorroides [e·mo·'rroi·des] *fpl* hemorrhoids *pl*

heno ['e·no] *m* hay; **fiebre del ~** hay fever

hepatitis [e·pa·'ti·tis] *f inv* hepatitis

herbicida [er·βi·'si·da, -'θi·da] *m* herbicide

herbívoro [er·'βi·βo·ro] *m* herbivore

herbolario [er·βo·'la·rjo] *m* health food store, herbalist's

heredar [e·re·'dar] *vt* to inherit; **propiedad heredada** inherited property; **problemas heredados del franquismo** problems handed down from Franco's time

heredero, -a [e·re·'de·ro, -a] *m, f* heir; **el ~ del trono** the heir to the throne; **el príncipe ~** the crown prince

hereditario, -a [e·re·di·'ta·rjo, -a] *adj* hereditary; **enfermedad hereditaria** hereditary disease

herencia [e·'ren·sja, -θja] *f* **1.** JUR inheritance **2.** (*legado*) legacy; **una ~ de la antigüedad** a legacy of the past

herida [e·'ri·da] *f* **1.** (*lesión*) wound; **tocar a alguien en la ~** *fig* to find somebody's weak [*o* sore] spot **2.** (*ofensa*) affront

herido, -a [e·'ri·do, -a] **I.** *adj* **1.** (*lesionado*) injured; MIL wounded; **~ de gravedad** seriously injured; MIL mortally wounded **2.** (*ofendido*) hurt, offended **II.** *m, f* injured person; MIL wounded soldier; **los ~s** the wounded; **en el atentado no hubo ~s** nobody was wounded in the attack

herir [e·'rir] *irr como sentir* **I.** *vt* **1.** (*lesionar*) to injure; MIL to wound **2.** (*golpear*) to hit **3.** (*flecha*) to sink into **4.** (*sol*) to beat down **5.** (*ofender*) to hurt, to offend **II.** *vr*: **~se** to be injured

hermafrodita [er·ma·fro·'di·ta] *adj, m* hermaphrodite

hermanastro, -a [er·ma·'nas·tro, -a] *m, f* stepbrother, stepsister *m, f*

hermandad [er·man·'dad] *f* (*de hombres*) brotherhood; (*de mujeres*) sisterhood

hermano, -a [er·'ma·no, -a] *m, f* brother, sister *m, f*; **~ de padre** paternal half-brother; **~ político** brother-in-law; **~ de leche** foster brother; **~s siameses** Siamese twins; **mi ~ mayor/pequeño**

my elder/younger brother; **tengo tres ~s** (*sólo chicos*) I have three brothers; (*chicos y chicas*) I have three brothers and sisters; **medio ~** half-brother; **lenguas hermanas** sister tongues

hermético, -a [er·'me·ti·ko, -a] *adj* hermetic(al); (*al aire*) airtight; (*al agua*) watertight

hermoso, -a [er·'mo·so, -a] *adj* (*paisaje, mujer*) beautiful; (*hombre*) handsome; (*día*) lovely; (*niño*) pretty; (*sanote*) robust

hermosura [er·mo·'su·ra] *f* beauty

hernia ['er·nja] *f* hernia

herniarse [er·'njar·se] *vr* to rupture oneself; *irón* to work very hard; **¡no te herniarás, no!** *irón* don't burst a blood vessel!

héroe ['e·roe] *m* hero; (*protagonista*) main character

heroico, -a [e·'roi·ko, -a] *adj* heroic

heroína [e·ro·'i·na] *f* **1.** (*de héroe*) heroine; (*protagonista*) main character **2.** (*droga*) heroin

heroinómano, -a [e·roi·'no·ma·no, -a] *m, f* heroin addict

herpes ['er·pes] *m of inv* herpes

herradura [e·rra·'du·ra] *f* horseshoe; **camino de ~** bridle path

herramienta [e·rra·'mjen·ta] *f* tool; **~ agrícola** agricultural machinery; **caja de (las) ~s** tool box

herrero [e·'rre·ro] *m* blacksmith

hervido [er·'βi·do] *m AmS* stew

hervir [er·'βir] *irr como sentir* **I.** *vi* **1.** (*alimentos*) to boil; (*a fuego lento*) to simmer **2.** (*burbujear*) to bubble **3.** (*persona*) to get angry; **~ en cólera** to lose one's temper; **le hierve la sangre** his/her blood is boiling **4.** (*abundar*) **esta calle hierve en rumores** the street is buzzing with rumors **II.** *vt* **1.** (*bullir*) to boil **2.** (*desinfectar*) to sterilize

hervor [er·'βor] *m* **1.** (*acción*) boil; **dar un ~ a algo** to bring sth to the boil; **levantar el ~** to come to the boil; **le falta un ~** *fig* he's has a loose screw **2.** (*burbujeo*) bubbling **3.** (*de la juventud*) fervor

heterogéneo, -a [e·te·ro·'xe·neo, -a] *adj* heterogeneous

heterosexual [e·te·ro·sek·su·'al] *adj, mf* heterosexual

heterosexualidad [e·te·ro·sek·swa·li·'dad] *f* heterosexuality

hibernación [i·βer·na·'sjon, -'θjon] *f* hibernation

hibernar [i·βer·'nar] *vi* to hibernate

hibisco [i'βis·ko] *m* hibiscus

híbrido, -a [i'βri·do, -a] *adj, m, f* hybrid

hidratante [i·dra·'tan·te] *adj* moisturizing; **crema ~** moisturizer

hidratar [i·dra·'tar] *vt* to moisturize

hidrato [i·'dra·to] *m* hydrate

hidráulico, -a [i·'drau·li·ko, -a] *adj* hydraulic

hidroavión [i·dro·a·βi·'on] *m* seaplane

hidroeléctrico, -a [i·dro·e·'lek·tri·ko, -a] *adj* hydroelectric; **central hidroeléctrica** hydroelectric power station

hidrógeno [i·'dro·xe·no] *m* hydrogen

hidrográfico, -a [i·dro·'yra·fi·ko, -a] *adj* hydrographic

hiedra ['je·dra] *f* ivy

hiel [jel] *f* **1.** (*bilis*) bile **2.** (*amargura*) bitterness; **echar la ~** to sweat blood

hielera [je·'le·ra] *f* **1.** *Chile, Méx* ice bucket **2.** *Arg* (*cubitera*) ice cube tray

hielo ['je·lo] *m* **1.** ice; **~ en la carretera** black ice; **~ picado** crushed ice; **el barco ha quedado aprisionado en el ~** the ship is trapped in the ice; **capa** [*o* **manta**] **de ~** icecap; **romper el ~** to break the ice **2.** *pl* (*helada*) frost, cold spell

hiena ['je·na] *f* hyena

hierba ['jer·βa] *f* (*planta, marihuana*) grass; *t.* MED herb; **~ medicinal** medicinal herb; **infusión de ~s** herbal tea; **mala ~** weed; **tenis sobre ~** lawn tennis ▶ **como la mala** ~ like wildfire

hierbabuena [jer·βa·'βwe·na] *f* mint

hierbajo [jer·'βa·xo] *m* weed

hierra ['je·rra] *f AmL* branding

hierro ['je·rro] *m* **1.** iron; **edad del ~** Iron Age; **salud de ~** iron constitution; **voluntad de ~** iron will **2.** (*del ganado*) branding iron **3.** (*para marcar*) brand

hígado ['i·ya·do] *m* liver

higiene [i·'xje·ne] *f* hygiene; **~ personal** personal hygiene

higiénico, -a [i·'xje·ni·ko, -a] *adj* hygienic;

compresa higiénica sanitary napkin; **papel ~** toilet paper

higienizar <z → c> [i·xje·ni·'sar, -'θar] *vt* to clean

higo ['i·ɣo] *m* **1.** (*fruto*) fig; **~ chumbo** prickly pear **2.** *inf* (*cosa sin valor*) **esto me importa un ~** I don't give a hoot; **esto no vale un ~** this is pure nonsense **3.** (*algo arrugado*) **estar hecho un ~** (*persona*) to be withered (up); (*ropa*) to be crumpled

higuera [i·'ɣe·ra] *f* fig tree

hijastro, -a [i·'xas·tro, -a] *m, f* stepson, stepdaughter *m, f*

hijo, -a ['i·xo, -a] *m, f* **1.** (*parentesco*) son, daughter *m, f;* **~ adoptivo** adopted son; **un ~ de papá** Daddy's boy; **~ político** son-in-law; **~ predilecto** (*de una ciudad*) favorite son; **~ de puta** *vulg* bastard; **~ único** only child; **pareja sin ~s** childless couple; **como cualquier ~ de vecino** just like everybody else; **es ~ de Madrid** he's from Madrid **2.** *pl* (*descendencia*) children *pl*, offspring

híjole ['i·xo·le] *interj Méx inf* Jesus!

hilacha [i·'la·tʃa] *f,* **hilacho** [i·'la·tʃo] *m* loose thread

hilar [i·'lar] *vt* **1.** (*hilo, araña*) to spin **2.** (*inferir*) to work out **3.** (*cavilar*) to ponder; **~ fino** *fig* to split hairs

hilera [i·'le·ra] *f* (*fila, de cosas iguales*) row, line; MIL file; **colocarse en la ~** to get into line

hilo ['i·lo] *m* **1.** (*para coser*) thread; (*más resistente*) yarn; **~ bramante** twine; **~ dental** dental floss; **~ de perlas** string of pearls; **cortar el ~ de la vida a alguien** *fig* to cut short sb's life; **mover los ~s** *fig* to pull the strings; **pender de un ~** *fig* to hang by a thread **2.** (*tela*) linen **3.** TÉC wire; **~ conductor** thread **4.** (*de un discurso*) gist; **no sigo el ~ de la película** I'm not following the plot of this movie; **perder el ~** (*de la conversación*) to lose the thread (of the conversation) **5. ~ musical** piped music, Muzak®

himen ['i·men] *m* hymen

himno ['im·no] *m* hymn; **~ nacional** national anthem

hincapié [in·ka·'pje] *m* hold; **hacer ~ en**

algo to emphasize sth

hincar <c → qu> [in·'kar] **I.** *vt* **1.** (*clavar*) to stick; **~ el diente en algo** *fig inf* to get one's teeth into sth **2.** (*pie*) to get a strong foothold, to stand firmly **II.** *vr* **~se de rodillas** to kneel down

hincha ['in·tʃa] *mf* (*seguidor*) fan

hinchable [in·'tʃa·βle] *adj* inflatable; **colchón ~** air mattress

hinchado, -a [in·'tʃa·do, -a] *adj* (*pie, madera*) swollen; (*estilo*) verbose; (*persona*) pompous

hinchar [in·'tʃar] **I.** *vt* **1.** (*globo*) to blow up; (*neumático*) to inflate; (*estómago*) to swell; **~ la bici** to inflate the bike tires **2.** (*exagerar*) to exaggerate; **¡no lo hinches!** come off it! **3.** *AmL* (*molestar*) to bother **II.** *vr:* **~se 1.** (*pierna*) to swell; **se me ha hinchado mucho el pie** my foot's really swollen **2.** (*engreírse*) to become conceited **3.** *inf* (*de comer*) **~se** (**de algo**) to stuff oneself (with sth) **4.** (*hacer mucho*) **~se de mirar/escuchar algo** to look at/to listen to sth non-stop; **~se de insultar a alguien** to go overboard insulting sb

hinchazón [in·tʃa·'son, -'θon] *f* (*pie, madera*) swelling

hindi ['in·di] *m* Hindi

hindú [in·'du] *mf* **1.** (*indio*) Indian **2.** (*hinduista*) Hindu

hinduismo [in·du·'is·mo] *m* Hinduism

hinojo [i·'no·xo] *m* fennel

hipar [i·'par] *vi* to have the hiccups

hiperactivo, -a [i·per·ak·'ti·βo, -a] *adj* hyperactive

hiperenlace [i·per·en·'la·se, -θe] *m* hyperlink

hipermercado [i·per·mer·'ka·do] *m* superstore

hipermétrope [i·per·'me·tro·pe] *adj* farsighted

hipermetropía [i·per·me·tro·'pi·a] *f* farsightedness

hipersensible [i·per·sen·'si·βle] *adj* hypersensitive

hipertensión [i·per·ten·'sjon] *f* high blood pressure

hipertexto [i·per·'tes·to] *m* hypertext

hípica ['i·pi·ka] *f* (*general*) horsemanship; (*montar*) riding; (*carreras*) horse racing

H

hípico, -a ['i·pi·ko, -a] *adj* equestrian

hípido [i·'pi·do] *m* whimper

hipnosis [iβ·'no·sis] *f inv* hypnosis

hipnótico, -a [iβ·'no·ti·ko, -a] *adj* hypnotic

hipnotizador(a) [iβ·no·ti·sa·'dor, –·'do·ra; iβ·no·ti·θa·–] *m(f)* hypnotizer

hipnotizar [z > c] [iβ·no·ti·'sar, –·'θar] *vt* to hypnotize

hipo ['ipo] *m* **1.** *(fisiológico)* hiccup; **tener ~** to have the hiccups **2.** *(deseo)* **~ de algo** longing for sth; **...que quita el ~** *fig* ... that takes your breath away

hipocondríaco, -a [i·po·kon·'dri·a·ko, -a] *adj, m, f* hypochondriac

hipocrático, -a [i·po·'kra·ti·ko, -a] *adj* **el juramento ~** the Hippocratic oath

hipocresía [i·po·kre·'si·a] *f* hypocrisy

hipócrita [i·'po·kri·ta] **I.** *adj* hypocritical **II.** *mf* hypocrite

hipopótamo [i·po·'po·ta·mo] *m* hippopotamus

hipoteca [i·po·'te·ka] *f* mortgage

hipotecar [c > qu] [i·po·te·'kar] *vt* to mortgage; **si haces eso ~ás tu libertad** if you do that you're signing away your freedom

hipotensión [i·po·ten·'sjon] *f* low blood pressure

hipotenusa [i·po·te·'nu·sa] *f* hypotenuse

hipotermia [i·po·'ter·mja] *f* hypothermia; **muerte por ~** death from hypothermia

hipótesis [i·'po·te·sis] *f inv* hypothesis

hipotético, -a [i·po·'te·ti·ko, -a] *adj* hypothetical; **es totalmente ~ que...** we cannot be at all sure that...

hippie ['xi·pi], **hippy** ['xi·pi] **I.** *adj* hippy; **moda ~** hippy style **II.** *mf* hippy

hirviente [ir·'βjen·te] *adj* boiling

hispánico, -a [is·'pa·ni·ko, -a] *adj* Hispanic; *(de España)* Spanish; **Filología Hispánica** Spanish Language and Literature

hispano, -a [is·'pa·no, -a] **I.** *adj* Hispanic; *(español)* Spanish **II.** *m, f* Hispanic; *(español)* Spaniard

Hispanoamérica [is·pa·no·a·'me·ri·ka] *f* Spanish America

hispanoamericano, -a [is·pa·no·a·me·ri·'ka·no, -a] *adj, m, f* Spanish American

hispanohablante [is·pa·no·a·'βlan·te]
I. *adj* Spanish-speaking; **los países ~s** Spanish-speaking countries **II.** *mf* Spanish speaker

histeria [is·'te·rja] *f* hysteria

histérico, -a [is·'te·ri·ko, -a] **I.** *adj* hysterical **II.** *m, f* hysterical person

historia [is·'to·rja] *f* **1.** *(antigüedad)* history; **~ natural** natural history; **~ universal** universal *[o world]* history; **pasar a la ~** *(ser importante)* to go down in history; *(no ser actual)* to be out of date **2.** *t. inf* story; **cuenta la ~ completa** tell the whole story; **ésa es la misma ~ de siempre** it's the same old story; **eso sólo son ~s** that doesn't prove anything; **ya sabes la ~** you know what I'm talking about; **¡déjate de ~s!** stop fooling around; **¡no me vengas con ~s!** come off it

historiador(a) [is·to·rja·'dor, –·'do·ra] *m(f)* historian

historial [is·to·'rjal] **I.** *adj* historical **II.** *m* **1.** *(antecedentes)* file, record; **~ delictivo** police record **2.** *(currículo)* curriculum vitae; **~ profesional** professional background; **este hecho no empañará el ~ de esta institución** this will not tarnish the reputation of this institution; **él tiene un ~ intachable** he has an impeccable record

historiar [is·to·'rjar] *vt AmL* to complicate

histórico, -a [is·'to·ri·ko, -a] *adj* historical; *(acontecimiento)* historic; **un miembro ~ del partido** a longstanding party member

historieta [is·to·'rje·ta] *f* **1.** *(anécdota)* anecdote **2.** *(con viñetas)* comic strip

hito ['i·to] *m* milestone

hobby ['xo·βi] *m* <hobbies> hobby

hocico [o·'si·ko, o·'θi–] *m* muzzle; *(de cerdo)* snout; *inf* mug; **caer de ~s** to fall on one's face; **estar de ~s** to be in a bad mood; **meter el ~ en todo** *fig* to stick one's nose in everything

hocicudo, -a [o·si·'ku·do, -a] *adj AmL* **1.** *(persona)* thick-lipped **2.** *(animal)* long-snouted

hockey ['xo·kei] *m* hockey; **~ sobre hielo/hierba** ice/field hockey

hogar [o·'ɣar] *m* **1.** *(casa)* home; **~ del pensionista** old people's home; **~ de**

adopción foster home; **artículos para el ~** household items; **persona sin ~** homeless person **2.** (*familia*) family; **la vida de ~** family life; **crear un ~** to start a family

hoguera [o·'ɣe·ɾa] *f* bonfire; **morir en la ~** to be burnt at the stake

hoja ['o·xa] *f* **1.** (*de planta*) leaf; (*pétalo*) petal; **~s del bosque** forest leaves; **árbol sin ~s** leafless tree; **los árboles vuelven a echar ~s** the leaves on the trees are sprouting again **2.** (*de papel*) sheet; **~ de lata** tinplate; **~ volante** leaflet, flyer; **~ de una mesa** (**extensible**) table flap; **pasar la ~** to turn the page; **no hay** [*o* **tiene**] **vuelta de ~** *fig* there's no doubt about it **3.** (*formulario*) form; **~ de estudios** educational record; **~ de pedido** order form; **~ de servicios** service record **4.** (*de arma*) blade; **~ de afeitar** razor blade

hojalata [o·xa·'la·ta] *f* tinplate

hojaldre [o·'xal·dɾe] *m* (*pasta*) puff pastry; **pastel de ~** puff pastry

hojarasca [o·xa·'ɾas·ka] *f* fallen leaves

hojear [o·xe·'aɾ] *vt* to browse through

hojuela [o·'xwe·la] *f* *AmC* puff pastry

hola ['o·la] *interj* hello

holán [o·'lan] *m* *AmC* canvas

Holanda [o·'lan·da] *f* the Netherlands

holandés, -esa [o·lan·des, -·'de·sa] **I.** *adj* Dutch; **la escuela holandesa** ARTE the Dutch school **II.** *m, f* Dutchman, Dutchwoman *m, f*

holgado, -a [ol·'ɣa·do, -a] *adj* spacious; (*ropa*) loose; **en este coche se va ~** there's lots of space in this car; **ir ~ de tiempo** to have plenty of time

holgazán, -ana [ol·ɣa·'san, -·'sa·na; -'θan, -·'θa·na] *m, f* loafer

holgazanear [ol·ɣa·sa·ne·'aɾ, ol·ɣa·θa·] *vi* to loaf around

holgura [ol·'ɣu·ɾa] *f* looseness; **vivir con ~** to live comfortably

holocausto [o·lo·'kaus·to] *m* holocaust

hombre ['om·bɾe] **I.** *m* man; (*especie humana*) **el ~** mankind; **el ~ de la calle** *fig* the man in the street; **~ de las cavernas** caveman; **~ de confianza** right-hand man; **~ de estado** statesman; **~ del montón** nobody special; **~ de**

negocios businessman; **~ de paja** front man; **el ~ medio** the average man; **el ~ del saco** the boogeyman; **ser ~ de dos caras** to be two-faced; **el ~ del tiempo** the weatherman; **el defensa fue al ~** DEP the defender went for the man; **¡está hecho un ~!** he's become a man!; **hacer un ~ de alguien** to make a man out of sb; **¡~ al agua!** man overboard! **II.** *interj* (*sorpresa*) well, well; (*duda*) well...; **¡~!, ¿qué tal?** hey! how's it going?; **¡cállate, ~!** c'mon, give it a rest; **¡pero, ~!** but, come on!; **¡sí, ~!** yes, of course!

hombrera [om·'bɾe·ɾa] *f* shoulder pad; (*de uniforme*) epaulet(te)

hombro ['om·bɾo] *m* shoulder; **ancho de ~s** broad-shouldered; **cargado de ~s** round-shouldered; **encogerse de ~s** to shrug one's shoulders; **llevar algo a ~s** to carry sth on one's shoulders; **arrimar el ~** to lend a hand; **mirar a alguien por encima del ~** to snub sb

homenaje [o·me·'na·xe] *m* tribute; **hacer una fiesta en ~ de alguien** to celebrate in honor of sb; **rendir ~ a alguien** to pay homage to sb

homenajear [o·me·na·xe·'aɾ] *vt* to pay tribute to

homeopático, -a [o·meo·'pa·ti·ko, -a] *adj* homeopathic

homicida [o·mi·'si·da, -'θi·da] **I.** *adj* homicidal; **el arma ~** the murder weapon **II.** *mf* murderer

homicidio [o·mi·'si·djo, -'θi·djo] *m* homicide; **~ planeado** murder; **~ no planeado** manslaughter; **~ frustrado** attempted murder; **brigada de ~s** murder squad

homo ['o·mo] *adj* *inf* gay

homogeneidad [o·mo·xe·nei·'dad] *f* homogeneity

homogeneizar <z → c> [o·mo·xe·nei·'saɾ, -'θaɾ] *vt* **1.** *t.* QUÍM to homogenize **2.** (*uniformar*) to standardize

homogéneo, -a [o·mo·'xe·neo, -a] *adj* homogeneous

homologable [o·mo·lo·'ɣa·βle] *adj* equivalent

homologar <g → gu> [o·mo·lo·'ɣaɾ] **I.** *vt* **1.** ENS to validate **2.** TÉC to authorize **II.** *vr:* **~se** to be officially recognized

H

homólogo, -a [o·'mo·lo·ɣo, -a] **I.** *adj* equivalent **II.** *m, f* counterpart

homosexual [o·mo·sek·'swal] *adj, mf* homosexual

homosexualidad [o·mo·sek·swa·li·'dad] *f* homosexuality

honda ['on·da] *f* sling

hondo, -a ['on·do, -a] *adj* deep

hondonada [on·do·'na·da] *f* GEO depression

Honduras [on·'du·ras] *f* Honduras

hondureño, -a [on·du·'re·ɲo, -a] *adj, m, f* Honduran

honestidad [o·nes·ti·'dad] *f* honesty

honesto, -a [o·'nes·to, -a] *adj* honest

hongo ['on·ɡo] *m* fungus; (*comestible*) mushroom

honor [o·'nor] *m* honor; **cuestión de ~** matter of honor; **¡palabra de ~!** word of honor!; **¡por mí ~!** on my honor!; **hacer ~ a su fama** to honor his/her name; **es para mí un gran ~** it is a great honor for me; **hacer los ~es** to do the honors

honorable [o·no·'ra·βle] *adj* honorable

honorario, -a [o·no·'ra·rjo] *adj*, **honorífico, -a** [o·no·'ri·fi·ko, -a] *adj* honorary; **cónsul ~** honorary consul

honra ['on·rra] *f* honor; **¡a mucha ~!** I'm proud of it!; **~s fúnebres** funeral proceedings

honradez [on·rra·'des, -'deθ] *f* (*honestidad*) honesty; (*integridad*) integrity; **falta de ~** lack of integrity

honrado, -a [on·'rra·do, -a] *adj* honorable; (*decente*) upright; **llevar una vida honrada** to lead an honorable life

honrar [on·'rrar] **I.** *vt* to honor; **nos honra con su presencia** h/she honors us with his/her presence **II.** *vr* **~se con** [*o de*] **algo** to be an honor for sb

hora ['o·ra] *f* **1.** (*del día*) hour; **~s de consulta** surgery hours; **~s extraordinarias** overtime; **~ feliz** happy hour; **~(s) punta** rush hour; **un cuarto de ~** a quarter of an hour; **media ~** half an hour; **una ~ y media** an hour and a half; **a última ~** at the last minute; **a primera/última ~ de la tarde** in the early/late afternoon; **noticias de última ~** last-minute news; **el pueblo está a dos ~s de camino** the village is a two-hour

walk from here; **estuve esperando ~s y ~s** I was waiting for hours and hours; **a la ~** on time **2.** (*de reloj*) time; **¿qué ~ es?** what time is it?, what's the time?; **¿a qué ~ vendrás?** what time are you coming?; **adelantar la ~** to put [*o set*] the clock forward; **poner el reloj en ~** to set one's watch; **retrasar la ~** to put [*o set*] the clock back; **me ha dado** [*o tengo*] **~ para el martes** I have an appointment for Tuesday **3.** (*tiempo*) time; **a la ~ de la verdad...** when it comes down to it...; **comer entre ~s** to eat between meals; **estar en ~s bajas** to be feeling down; **no lo dejes para última ~** don't leave it till the last minute; **tener** (**muchas**) **~s de vuelo** *fig* to have a lot of experience; **ven a cualquier ~** come at any time; **ya va siendo ~ que tomes tus propias decisiones** it is about time that you made your own decisions

horario ['o·ra·rjo] *m* timetable, schedule; (*de consulta*) surgery hours; **~ de atención al público** opening hours; **~ flexible** flextime; **~ de oficina** office hours; **¿qué ~ hacen?** what hours do they work?; **tenemos ~ de tarde** we work evenings; **franja horaria** time zone

horario, -a ['o·ra·rjo, -a] *adj* hourly

horca ['or·ka] *f* gallows *pl*

horizontal [o·ri·son·'tal, o·ri·θon-] **I.** *adj* horizontal **II.** *f* horizontal position

horizonte [o·ri·'son·te, -'θon·te] *m* horizon

hormiga [or·'mi·ɣa] *f* ant; **~ blanca** white ant; **ser una ~** *fig* to be always working

hormigón [or·mi·'ɣon] *m* concrete; **~ armado** reinforced concrete

hormigueo [or·mi·'ɣeo] *m* **1.** (*picor*) pins and needles; **tengo un ~ en la espalda** my back is itching **2.** (*multitud*) swarming

hormiguero [or·mi·'ɣe·ro] *m* **1.** (*de hormigas*) anthill **2.** (*de gente*) swarm; **la plaza era un ~ de gente** the square was crawling with people

hormiguero, -a [or·mi·'ɣe·ro, -a] *adj* related to ants; **oso ~** anteater

hormona [or·'mo·na] *f* hormone

hormonal [or·mo·'nal] *adj* hormone, hormonal

hornalla [or·'na·ʝa, -ʎa] f AmL 1. (parrilla) barbecue 2. (del fogón) hot plate 3. (horno) oven

hornear [or·ne·'ar] vt to bake

hornillo [or·'ni·to·pjo, -ʎo] m (cocina) stove; (de una cocina) ring; ~ de gas gas ring; ~ portátil hot plate

horno ['or·no] m 1. oven; ~ microondas microwave oven; recién salido del ~ fresh from the oven; asar al ~ to oven roast 2. TÉC furnace; ~ crematorio cremation furnace; alto ~ blast furnace; (para cerámica) kiln

horóscopo [o·'ros·ko·po] m horoscope

horquilla [or·'ki·ja, -ʎa] f (del pelo) bobby pin; (de moño) hairpin

horrendo, -a [o·'rren·do, -a] adj v. horroroso

horrible [o·'rri·βle] adj 1. (horroroso) horrible; un crimen ~ a ghastly crime; una historia ~ a horrible story 2. (muy feo) grotesque

horripilante [o·rri·pi·'lan·te] adj horrifying

horror [o·'rror] m 1. (miedo, aversión) horror; tener ~ a algo to have a horror of sth; siento ~ a la oscuridad I'm terrified of the dark; me da ~ verte con esta corbata you look terrible with that tie on; el diseño moderno me parece un ~ I don't like modern design at all; ¡qué ~! inf how horrible!; los ~es de la guerra the atrocities of war 2. inf (mucho) ganar un ~ de dinero to earn a lot of money; hoy hace un ~ de frío it's freezing cold today; me cuesta ~es it's very hard for me; me gusta ~es el regalo I absolutely love the gift

horrorizar <z → c> [o·rro·ri·'sar, -'θar] I. vt to horrify; me horrorizó ver el accidente I was horrified by the accident II. vr ~se de algo to be horrified by sth

horroroso, -a [o·rro·'ro·so, -a] adj horrifying; una escena horrorosa a terrible scene; su última novela es horrorosa his/her last novel is awful

hortaliza [or·ta·'li·sa, -θa] f vegetable

hortelano, -a [or·te·'la·no, -a] m, f truck gardener; ~ aficionado amateur gardener

hortensia [or·'ten·sja] f BOT hydrangea

hortera [or·'te·ra] inf I. adj tasteless II. m vulgar person

horterada [or·te·'ra·da] f inf tasteless thing; esta película es una ~ this movie is so tacky

hortícola [or·'ti·ko·la] adj horticultural; productos ~s horticultural produce

hospedaje [os·pe·'da·xe] m 1. (acción, situación) residence; dar ~ a alguien to put sb up 2. (coste) rent

hospedar [os·pe·'dar] I. vt to accommodate II. vr: ~se to stay

hospicio [os·'pi·sjo, -θjo] m 1. (para niños) children's home 2. (para pobres, en un monasterio) hospice

hospital [os·pi·'tal] m hospital; ~ militar military hospital

hospitalario, -a [os·pi·ta·'la·rjo, -a] adj 1. (acogedor) welcoming, hospitable 2. (de hospital) hospital

hospitalidad [os·pi·ta·li·'dad] f hospitality

hospitalización [os·pi·ta·li·sa·'sjon, -θa·'θjon] f 1. (envío) hospitalization 2. (estancia) stay in hospital

hospitalizar <z → c> [os·pi·ta·li·'sar, -'θar] vt to hospitalize; ayer ~on a mi madre yesterday my mother went into hospital; estoy hospitalizado desde el domingo I've been in hospital since Sunday

hostal [os·'tal] m cheap hotel

hostelería [os·te·le·'ri·a] f 1. ECON hotel business 2. ENS hotel management; escuela superior de ~ school of hotel management

hostelero, -a [os·te·'le·ro, -a] I. adj hotel II. m, f hotelier

hostia ['os·tja] f 1. REL host 2. inf smack; (golpe) bash; darse una ~ (chocar) to smash

hostiar [os·'tjar] vt inf to belt

hostigante [os·ti·'ɣan·te] adj Col (sabor) sickly; (persona) annoying

hostigoso, -a [os·ti·'ɣo·so, -a] adj Chile, Guat, Perú cloying

hostil [os·'til] adj hostile; un recibimiento ~ a hostile reception

hostilidad [os·ti·li·'dad] f hostility

hostión [os·'tjon] m inf heavy clout

H

hotel [o·'tel] *m* hotel; ~ **residencia** guesthouse

hotelero, -a [o·te·'le·ro, -a] **I.** *adj* hotel; **industria hotelera** hotel business **II.** *m, f* hotelier, hotelkeeper

hoy [oi] *adv* today; ~ (**en**) **día** nowadays; **llegará de** ~ **a mañana** it will arrive any time now; **de** ~ **en adelante** from now on; **los niños de** ~ (**en día**) children nowadays; **llegará de** ~ **a mañana** it will arrive today or tomorrow

hoyo ['o·jo] *m* **1.** (*concavidad*) hollow **2.** (*agujero*) hole **3.** (*sepultura*) grave

hoyuelo [o·'jwe·lo] *m* dimple

hoz [os, oθ] *f* sickle

huacal [wa·'kal] *m* And, Méx wooden box

huarache [wa·'ra·t∫e] *m* Méx sandal; CULIN corn dough filled with fried beans

huarmi ['war·mi] *f* AmS hardworking woman; (*ama de casa*) housewife

huasca ['was·ka] *f* AmL whip

huaso, -a ['wa·so, -a] *adj, m, f* AmS peasant

hubo ['u·βo] *3. pret de* **haber**

hucha ['u·t∫a] *f* **1.** (*alcancía*) piggy bank **2.** (*ahorros*) savings

hueco ['we·ko] *m* **1.** (*agujero*) hole; ~ **del ascensor** elevator shaft; ~ **de la mano** hollow of the hand **2.** (*sitio*) space; **hazme un** ~ move over **3.** (*tiempo*) time; **hazme un** ~ **para mañana** make time for me tomorrow

hueco, -a ['we·ko, -a] *adj* (*ahuecado*) hollow; (*vacío*) empty; (*sonido*) resonant; (*tierra*) soft; (*palabras*) empty; (*persona*) vain; **ponerse** ~ to become conceited; **tener la cabeza hueca** to be dense

huelga ['wel·ɣa] *f* strike; ~ **de advertencia** warning strike; ~ **de brazos caídos** sit-down strike; ~ **general** general strike; ~ **de hambre** hunger strike; ~ **salvaje** wildcat strike; **convocar una** ~ to call a strike; **declararse en** [o **hacer**] ~ to go on strike

huelguista [wel·'ɣis·ta] *mf* striker

huella ['we·ʎa, -ʎa] *f* **1.** (*señal*) mark; ~ **de un animal** animal track; ~ **dactilar** fingerprint **2.** (*vestigio*) trace; (*pa-*

sos) footsteps; **seguir las** ~**s de alguien** to follow sb's footsteps

huérfano, -a ['wer·fa·no, -a] **I.** *adj* orphan; **ser** ~ **de padre** to have no father; **quedarse** ~ to become an orphan; **la ciudad se queda huérfana en invierno** the city empties in winter **II.** *m, f* orphan

huerta ['wer·ta] *f*, **huerto** ['wer·to] *m* (*hortalizas*) vegetable patch; (*frutales*) orchard; ~ **familiar** allotment

hueso ['we·so] *m* **1.** ANAT bone; **carne sin** ~ boneless meat; **estar en los** ~**s** to be a rack of bones; **un** ~ **duro de roer** a hard nut to crack; **este profesor es un** ~ this teacher's really strict **2.** (*de fruto*) pit **3.** AmL (*trabajo*) hard work

huésped ['wes·ped] *mf* guest; BIO host

huesudo, -a [we·'su·do, -a] *adj* big-boned; (*carne*) bony

hueva ['we·βa] *f* roe

huevada [we·'βa·da] *f* AmL inf stupid thing

huevear [we·βe·'ar] *vi* AmS inf to fool around

huevo ['we·βo] *m* egg; ~ **duro** hard-boiled egg; ~**s fritos** fried eggs; ~ **pasado por agua** soft-boiled egg; ~**s revueltos** scrambled eggs; **clara de** ~ egg white; **ir pisando** ~**s** to go very slowly and/or carefully; **poner un** ~ to lay an egg; **poner algo a alguien a** ~ to make sth very easy for sb; **me costó un** ~ (*de dinero*) it cost loads; (*de dificultades*) it was damn difficult

huida [u·'i·da] *f* flight; ~ **del lugar del accidente** flight from the scene of the accident; **no hay** ~ **posible** there's no way out

huir [u·'ir] *irr* **I.** *vi* (*escapar*) to flee; ~ **de casa** to run away from home; **el tiempo huye** time flies; **pudieron** ~ **de sus perseguidores** they managed to give their pursuers the slip **II.** *vi, vt* (*evitar*) ~ (**de**) **algo** to keep away from sth; ~ (**de**) **alguien** to avoid sb

huiro ['wi·ro] *m* AmS seaweed

hule ['u·le] *m* **1.** oilcloth; (*para la mesa*) tablecloth **2.** AmL (*caucho*) rubber

hulero, -a [u·'le·ro, -a] *m, f* AmL rubber gatherer

hulla [ˈu.ʝa, -ʎa] *f* fossil coal; **~ blanca** white coal

humanamente [u.ma.naˈmen.te] *adv* humanly; **hacer todo lo ~ posible** to do everything humanly possible

humanidad [u.ma.niˈdad] *f* **1.** (*género humano*) **la ~** mankind; **un crimen contra la ~** a crime against humanity **2.** (*naturaleza, caridad humana*) humanity **3.** *pl* (*letras*) arts

humanismo [u.maˈnis.mo] *m* humanism

humanista [u.maˈnis.ta] *mf* humanist

humanitario, -a [u.ma.niˈta.rjo, -a] *adj* humanitarian; **organización humanitaria** humanitarian organization

humanizar <z → c> [u.ma.niˈsar, -ˈθar] **I.** *vt* to humanize **II.** *vr:* **~se** to become human

humano, -a [uˈma.no, -a] *adj* human; (*manera de ser*) humane

humanoide [u.maˈnoi.de] *m* humanoid

humareda [u.maˈre.da] *f* cloud of smoke

humazo [uˈma.so, -θo] *m* thick smoke

humear [u.meˈar] *vi* to smoke; (*vapor*) to steam

humedad [u.meˈdad] *f* humidity; (*agradable*) moisture; (*desagradable*) dampness

humedal [u.meˈdal] *m* wetland

humedecer [u.me.deˈser, -ˈθer] *irr como* **crecer** *vt* to moisten

húmedo, -a [ˈu.me.do, -a] *adj* wet; (*agradable*) moist; (*desagradable*) damp; (*con vapor*) humid; (*aire*) muggy

humildad [u.milˈdad] *f* humility, humbleness; (*social*) lowliness

humilde [uˈmil.de] *adj* **1.** (*modesto*) humble; **un ~ trabajador** a humble worker **2.** (*condición social*) poor; **ser de orígenes ~s** to be of humble origin

humillación [u.mi.ʎaˈsjon, -ʎaˈθjon] *f* humiliation; (*vergüenza*) shame

humillante [u.mi.ˈʎan.te, -ˈʎan.te] *adj* humiliating

humillar [u.miˈʝar, -ˈʎar] **I.** *vt* to humiliate; (*avergonzar*) to shame **II.** *vr:* **~se** to lower oneself

humo [ˈu.mo] *m* **1.** smoke; (*vapor*) steam; **señal de ~** smoke signal; **en ese bar siempre hay ~** it's always smoky in that bar; **la chimenea echa ~** the chimney pours out smoke; **tragar el ~ al fumar** to inhale cigarette smoke **2.** *pl* conceit; **bajar los ~s a alguien** to take sb down a peg; **subirse los ~s a la cabeza** to put on airs

humor [uˈmor] *m* **1.** humor; **~ negro** black humor; **¡pero no tienes sentido del ~ o qué!** don't you have a sense of humor? **2.** (*ánimo*) mood; **estar de buen/mal ~** to be in a good/bad mood; **no estoy de ~ para bailar** I'm not in the mood for dancing

humorado, -a [u.moˈra.do, -a] *adj* **bien/mal ~** (*por un momento*) in a good/bad mood; (*carácter*) even-tempered/bad-tempered

humorista [u.moˈris.ta] *mf* comic, humorist; (*dibujante*) cartoonist

humorístico, -a [u.moˈris.ti.ko, -a] *adj* comic

humus [ˈu.mus] *m* humus

hundido, -a [unˈdi.do, -a] *adj* (*ojos*) deep-set; (*techo*) collapsed; (*persona*) downcast, demoralized

hundimiento [un.diˈmjen.to] *m* **1.** (*barco*) sinking; (*edificio*) *t.* ECON collapse **2.** GEO hollow

hundir [unˈdir] **I.** *vt* **1.** (*barco*) to sink; (*suelo*) to cave in; **~ la mano en el agua** to put one's hand in the water; **~ los pies en el barro** to sink one's feet into the mud **2.** (*arruinar*) to ruin; (*proyecto*) to cause to fail; (*empresa*) to bankrupt; (*esperanzas*) to destroy; **la crisis económica ha hundido a muchos empresarios** the economic crisis has ruined many businessmen **II.** *vr:* **~se 1.** (*barco*) to sink; (*edificio*) to collapse; (*suelo*) to cave in; **el rublo se hunde** the ruble is plummeting **2.** (*fracasar*) to fail, to lose it; **me he hundido en el tercer set** I lost it in the third set

húngaro, -a [ˈun.ga.ro, -a] *adj, m, f* Hungarian

Hungría [unˈgri.a] *f* Hungary

huracán [u.raˈkan] *m* hurricane; (*persona*) whirlwind of energy

H

huracanado, -a [u·ra·ka·'na·do, -a] *adj* tempestuous; **vientos ~s** hurricane winds

huraño, -a [u·'ra·ɲo, -a] *adj* **1.** (*insociable*) unsociable **2.** (*hosco*) surly

hurgar <g → gu> [ur·'ɣar] **I.** *vi, vt* **1.** (*remover*) ~ **en algo** to poke around in sth; **~ el fuego** to poke the fire **2.** (*fisgonear*) ~ **en algo** to rummage through sth **II.** *vr* **~se la nariz** to pick one's nose

hurguetear [ur·ɣe·te·'ar] *vt AmL* **~ algo** to rummage around in sth

hurón, -ona [u·'ron, -·'ro·na] *m, f* **1.** ferret **2.** *inf* (*husmeador*) nosy parker; (*huraño*) unsociable

hurra ['u·rra] *interj* hooray!

hurtadillas [ur·ta·'di·ʝas, -ʎas] **a ~** secretly

hurtar [ur·'tar] *vt* to steal; (*en tiendas*) to shoplift

hurto ['ur·to] *m* stealing; (*en tiendas*) shoplifting; (*cosa*) stolen property

husmear [us·me·'ar] **I.** *vt* (*perro*) to sniff **II.** *vi* (*perro*) to sniff around; (*fisgonear*) to nose around

huy [ui] *interj* (*accidente*) oops!; (*de asombro*) wow!

I

I, i [i] *f* I, i; **~ de Italia** I as in India; **~ griega** y

I+D [i mas de] *abr de* **Investigación y Desarrollo** R & D

ibérico, -a [i·'βe·ri·ko, -a] *adj* Iberian; **Península Ibérica** Iberian Peninsula

Iberoamérica [i·βe·ro·a·'me·ri·ka] *f* Latin America

iberoamericano, -a [i·βe·ro·a·me·ri·'ka·no, -a] *adj, m, f* Latin American

iceberg [i·se·'βeɾ, i·θe-] *m* <icebergs> iceberg

icono [i·'ko·no] *m* REL, COMPUT icon

ida ['i·da] *f* departure; **billete de ~** one-way ticket; **billete de ~ y vuelta** return (ticket)

idea [i·'dea] *f* **1.** idea; **ni ~** no idea **2.** (*propósito*) intention; **mudar de ~** to change one's mind; **tener ~ de hacer algo** to intend to do sth

ideal [i·de·'al] *adj, m* ideal

idealismo [i·dea·'lis·mo] *m* idealism

idealista [i·dea·'lis·ta] *adj* idealistic

idealizar <z → c> [i·dea·li·'sar, -'θar] *vt* to idealize

idear [i·de·'ar] *vt* **1.** (*concebir*) to conceive **2.** (*inventar*) to think up **3.** (*un plan*) to devise

idéntico, -a [i·'den·ti·ko, -a] *adj* identical; **es ~ a su madre** he looks just like his mother

identidad [i·den·ti·'dad] *f* identity; **carné de ~** identity card

identificación [i·den·ti·fi·ka·'sjon, -'θjon] *f* identification

identificar <c → qu> [i·den·ti·fi·'kar] **I.** *vt* to identify **II.** *vr:* **~se** to identify; **~se con alguien/algo** to identify oneself with sb/sth

ideología [i·deo·lo·'xi·a] *f* ideology

idílico, -a [i·'di·li·ko, -a] *adj* idyllic

idilio [i·'di·ljo] *m* idyll; (*relación amorosa*) love affair

idioma [i·'djo·ma] *m* language

idiota [i·'djo·ta] **I.** *adj* idiotic, stupid **II.** *mf* idiot

idiotez [i·djo·'tes, -'teθ] *f* idiocy

ido, -a ['i·do, -a] *adj inf* crazy

idolatrar [i·do·la·'trar] *vt* to worship; (*adorar*) to adore

ídolo ['i·do·lo] *m* idol

idóneo, -a [i·'do·neo, -a] *adj* apt

iglesia [i·'ɣle·sja] *f* church; **casarse por la ~** to have a church wedding

iglú [i·'ɣlu] *m* igloo

ignición [iɣ·ni·'sjon, -'θjon] *f* ignition

ignorancia [iɣ·no·'ran·sja, -θja] *f* ignorance; (*incultura*) lack of culture [*o* education]

ignorante [iɣ·no·'ran·te] *adj* **1.** (*desconocer*) ~ **de algo** ignorant about [*o* of] sth **2.** (*inculto*) uncultured, uneducated

ignorar [iɣ·no·'rar] *vt* **1.** (*desconocer*) ~ **algo** to be ignorant of sth **2.** (*no hacer caso*) to ignore

igual [i·'ɣwal] **I.** *adj* **1.** (*idéntico*) identical; (*semejante*) same; MAT equal; **nunca he visto cosa ~** I've never seen anything like it **2.** (*lo mismo*) **¡es ~!** it doesn't matter ▶ **al ~ que...** as well as... **II.** *mf* equal; **no tiene ~** he/she has no equal **III.** *adv inf (quizá)* **~ no viene** he/she might not come

igualado, -a [i·ɣwa·ˈla·ðo, -a] *adj (empatado)* level

igualar [i·ɣwa·ˈlar] **I.** *vt* **1.** *(hacer igual)* to equalize; *(equiparar)* to match **2.** *(allanar)* to flatten (out); *(nivelar)* to level **3.** *(ajustar)* to even out **II.** *vr:* **~se 1.** *(parecerse)* **~se a** [*o* con] **alguien** to be similar to sb **2.** *(ponerse al igual)* to make equal, to equate

igualdad [i·ɣwal·ˈdað] *f* equality; *(semejanza)* **~ de derechos** equal rights; **estar en ~ de condiciones** to be on an equal footing

igualitario, -a [i·ɣwa·li·ˈta·rjo, -a] *adj* egalitarian

igualmente [i·ɣwal·ˈmen·te] **I.** *interj* and the same to you **II.** *adv* equally

iguana [i·ˈɣwa·na] *f* iguana

ilegal [i·le·ˈɣal] *adj* illegal, unlawful

ilegible [i·le·ˈxi·βle] *adj* unreadable

ilegítimo, -a [i·le·ˈxi·ti·mo, -a] *adj (asunto)* illegal; *(hijo)* illegitimate

ileso, -a [i·ˈle·so, -a] *adj* unharmed, unhurt; **salir** [*o* **resultar**] **~** to be unscathed

ilícito, -a [i·ˈli·si·to, -a; -θi·to, -a] *adj* illegal, illicit

ilimitado, -a [i·li·mi·ˈta·ðo, -a] *adj* unlimited

ilógico, -a [i·ˈlo·xi·ko, -a] *adj* illogical

iluminación [i·lu·mi·na·ˈsjon, -ˈθjon] *f* illumination; *(alumbrado)* lighting; *(como adorno)* illuminations *pl*

iluminado, -a [i·lu·mi·ˈna·ðo] *adj* illuminated; *(un monumento)* lit up

iluminar [i·lu·mi·ˈnar] *vt* to illuminate; *fig* to enlighten; *(un monumento)* to light up

ilusión [i·lu·ˈsjon] *f* **1.** *(alegría)* excitement; **ese viaje me hace mucha ~** I'm excited about the journey **2.** *(esperanza)* hope; **hacerse ilusiones** to get one's hopes up **3.** *(sueño)* illusion; *(espejismo)* (optical) illusion

ilusionar [i·lu·sjo·ˈnar] **I.** *vt* **1.** *(entusiasmar)* to excite; **estar ilusionado con algo** to be excited about sth **2.** *(hacer ilusiones)* to raise false hopes **II.** *vr:* **~se**

(alegrarse) to be excited

ilusionismo [i·lu·sjo·ˈnis·mo] *m* illusionism, conjuring

ilusionista [i·lu·sjo·ˈnis·ta] *mf* illusionist

iluso, -a [i·ˈlu·so, -a] *adj* gullible

ilustración [i·lus·tra·ˈsjon, -ˈθjon] *f* **1.** *(imagen, instrucción)* illustration; *(explicación)* explanation **2.** HIST **la Ilustración** the Enlightenment

ilustrado, -a [i·lus·ˈtra·ðo, -a] *adj (con imágenes)* illustrated

ilustrar [i·lus·ˈtrar] *vt* **1.** *(con imágenes)* to illustrate **2.** *(instruir)* to enlighten

ilustrativo, -a [i·lus·tra·ˈti·βo, -a] *adj* illustrative

ilustre [i·ˈlus·tre] *adj (famoso)* illustrious

imagen [i·ˈma·xen] *f* **1.** *(representación mental)* image; **ser la viva ~ de alguien** to be the spitting image of sb **2.** TV picture

imaginable [i·ma·xi·ˈna·βle] *adj* imaginable

imaginación [i·ma·xi·na·ˈsjon, -ˈθjon] *f* imagination

imaginar [i·ma·xi·ˈnar] **I.** *vt* to imagine **II.** *vr:* **~se** *(figurarse)* to imagine, to suppose; **me lo imagino** I can imagine [*o* picture] it

imaginario, -a [i·ma·xi·ˈna·rjo, -a] *adj* imaginary

imaginativo, -a [i·ma·xi·na·ˈti·βo, -a] *adj* imaginative

imán [i·ˈman] *m* **1.** *t. fig (hierro)* magnet **2.** REL imam

imantar [i·man·ˈtar] *vt* to magnetize

imbatible [im·ba·ˈti·βle] *adj* unbeatable

imbécil [im·ˈbe·sil, -θil] *adj, mf* imbecile

imborrable [im·bo·ˈrra·βle] *adj* indelible; *(acontecimiento)* unforgettable

imbuir [im·bu·ir] *irr como huir* **I.** *vt* to imbue **II.** *vr* **~se de algo** to imbibe sth

imitable [i·mi·ˈta·βle] *adj* imitable

imitación [i·mi·ta·ˈsjon, -ˈθjon] *f* imitation

imitador(a) [i·mi·ta·ˈðor, -·ˈðo·ra] *m(f)* imitator; *(parodista)* impersonator

imitar [i·mi·ˈtar] *vt* to imitate, to copy; *(parodiar)* to impersonate; **~ una firma** to forge a signature

impaciencia [im·pa·ˈsjen·sja, -ˈθjen·θja] *f* impatience

impacientar [im·pa·sjen·'tar, -θjen·'tar] **I.** vt to make impatient **II.** vr: ~**se** to become impatient

impaciente [im·pa·'sjen·te, -'θjen·te] adj impatient; **estamos ~s por empezar** we are eager to start

impactar [im·pak·'tar] vt **1.** (un acontecimiento) to make an impact **2.** (un proyectil) to strike

impacto [im·'pak·to] m (choque) impact; (golpe emocional) shock; (huella) damage; fig repercussions pl; ~ **medioambiental** environmental impact

impago [im·'pa·yo] m nonpayment

impar [im·'par] adj (número) odd

imparable [im·pa·'ra·βle] adj unstoppable

imparcial [im·par·'sjal, -'θjal] adj impartial; (sin prejuicios) unbiased

imparcialidad [im·par·sja·li·'dad, -θja·li·'dad] f impartiality, fairness

impartir [im·par·'tir] vt to give; (conferir) to impart form

impasible [im·pa·'si·βle] adj impassive

impecable [im·pe·'ka·βle] adj **1.** ser (correcto) impeccable **2.** estar (nuevo) **el motor está** ~ the engine is in perfect condition

impedido, -a [im·pe·'di·do, -a] adj disabled; **estar** ~ **para algo** to be incapacitated for sth

impedimento [im·pe·di·'men·to] m **1.** (que imposibilita algo) restraint **2.** (obstáculo) impediment, hindrance

impedir [im·pe·'dir] irr como pedir vt **1.** (imposibilitar) to prevent, to keep from **2.** (obstaculizar) to impede, to hinder

impenetrable [im·pe·ne·'tra·βle] adj impenetrable

impensable [im·pen·'sa·βle] adj unthinkable

imperar [im·pe·'rar] vi to reign; fig to prevail

imperativo [im·pe·ra·'ti·βo] m **1.** LING imperative **2.** pl (necesidad) imperative

imperativo, -a [im·pe·ra·'ti·βo, -a] adj imperative

imperceptible [im·per·sep·'ti·βle, im·per·θep-] adj **1.** (inapreciable) imperceptible **2.** (minúsculo) minute

imperdible [im·per·'di·βle] m safety pin

imperdonable [im·per·do·'na·βle] adj unpardonable, inexcusable

imperfección [im·per·fek·'sjon, -'θjon] f imperfection, flaw

imperfecto [im·per·'fek·to] m LING imperfect

imperfecto, -a [im·per·'fek·to, -a] adj imperfect, flawed

imperial [im·pe·'rjal] adj imperial

imperialismo [im·pe·rja·'lis·mo] m POL imperialism

imperio [im·'pe·rjo] m (territorio) empire

impermeable [im·per·me·a·βle] **I.** adj impermeable **II.** m raincoat

impersonal [im·per·so·'nal] adj t. LING impersonal

impertinencia [im·per·ti·'nen·sja, -'nen·θja] f (insolencia) impertinence, impudence

impertinente [im·per·ti·'nen·te] adj (insolente) impertinent, impudent

imperturbable [im·per·tur·'βa·βle] adj imperturbable

ímpetu ['im·pe·tu] m **1.** (vehemencia) vehemence **2.** (brío) impetus, energy

impetuoso, -a [im·pe·tu·o·so, -a] adj rash

implacable [im·pla·'ka·βle] adj implacable; (riguroso) relentless

implantar [im·plan·'tar] **I.** vt **1.** t. MED to implant **2.** (asentar) to establish **3.** (instituir) to found, to institute **4.** (introducir) to introduce **II.** vr: ~**se** to become established

implementar [im·ple·men·'tar] vt AmL (método) to introduce; (plan) to implement

implicación [im·pli·ka·'sjon, -'θjon] f (inclusión) inclusion; (en un delito) implication

implicar <c → qu> [im·pli·'kar] **I.** vt **1.** (incluir) to involve **2.** (significar) to imply; **eso implica que...** this means that... **II.** vr: ~**se** to be [o become] involved

implícito, -a [im·'pli·si·to, -a; -θi·to, -a] adj implicit

implorar [im·plo·'rar] vt (a alguien) to implore; (algo) to beg

mponente [im·po·'nen·te] adj (*impresionante*) imposing; (*que infunde respeto*) awesome; (*grandioso*) grand

imponer [im·po·'ner] irr como poner I. vt to impose; (*respeto*) to command; ~ **a** [o sobre] **alguien** (*carga, impuestos*) to impose on [o upon] sb II. vi to impress III. vr: ~**se** 1. (*hacerse ineludible*) to become unavoidable 2. (*hacerse obedecer*) **se impuso a los demás** he/she made his/her authority felt 3. (*prevalecer*) ~**se a algo** to prevail over sth

impopular [im·po·pu·'lar] adj unpopular

importación [im·por·ta·'sjon, -'θjon] f 1. (*acción*) importation 2. (*producto*) import

importador(a) [im·por·ta·'dor, --'do·ra] m(f) importer

importancia [im·por·'tan·sja, -θja] f 1. (*interés*) importance; **sin ~** unimportant; **restar** [o quitar] ~ **a algo** to play sth down 2. (*extensión*) scope, magnitude 3. (*trascendencia*) significance

importante [im·por·'tan·te] adj 1. (*de gran interés*) important 2. (*dimensión*) considerable 3. (*cantidad*) significant

importar [im·por·'tar] I. vt (*mercancía*) to import II. vi to matter, to mind; **no importa la hora que sea** it doesn't matter what time it is; **¿a ti qué te importa?** what does it have to do with you?; **¿te importa esperar?** do you mind waiting?

importe [im·'por·te] m (*cuantía*) value; (*total*) amount

importunar [im·por·tu·'nar] vt to pester, to importune *form*

imposibilitar [im·po·si·βi·li·'tar] vt (*impedir*) to impede, to make impossible

imposible [im·po·'si·βle] adj 1. (*irrealizable*) impossible 2. inf (*insoportable*) impossible, unbearable

imposición [im·po·si·'sjon, -'θjon] f imposition

impositivo, -a [im·po·si·'ti·βo, -a] adj FIN tax

impostor(a) [im·pos·'tor, --to·ra] m(f) impostor, imposter

impotencia [im·po·'ten·sja, -θja] f 1. (*falta de poder*) t. MED impotence 2. (*incapacidad*) incapacity; (*indefensión*) helplessness

impotente [im·po·'ten·te] adj 1. (*sin poder*) impotent, powerless 2. (*incapaz*) incapable 3. (*desvalido*) helpless 4. MED impotent

impracticable [im·prak·ti·'ka·βle] adj 1. (*irrealizable*) unfeasible 2. (*intransitable*) impassable

imprecisión [im·pre·si·'sjon, -θi·'sjon] f 1. (*falta de precisión*) inexactness 2. (*falta de determinación*) vagueness

impreciso, -a [im·pre·'si·so, -a; -'θi·so, -a] adj 1. (*no preciso*) imprecise 2. (*indefinido*) vague

impredecible [im·pre·de·'si·βle, -'θi·βle] adj unpredictable; (*suceso*) unforeseeable

impregnar [im·preɣ·'nar] I. vt 1. (*empapar*) to impregnate, to saturate 2. (*penetrar*) to penetrate II. vr: ~**se** to become impregnated

imprenta [im·'pren·ta] f printing; (*taller*) printer's; (*impresión*) print

imprescindible [im·pre·sin·'di·βle, im·pres·θin-] adj (*ineludible*) essential; (*insustituible*) indispensable

impresentable [im·pre·sen·'ta·βle] adj unpresentable

impresión [im·pre·'sjon] f 1. (*huella*) imprint 2. TIPO printing, impression; COMPUT print-out 3. (*sensación*) impression; **cambiar impresiones** to compare notes

impresionante [im·pre·sjo·'nan·te] adj (*emocionante*) impressive, striking; (*magnífico*) magnificent

impresionar [im·pre·sjo·'nar] vt to impress

impresionismo [im·pre·sjo·'nis·mo] m ARTE impressionism

impreso [im·'pre·so] m 1. (*formulario*) form 2. (*envío*) printed matter

impreso, -a [im·'pre·so, -a] pp de **imprimir**

impresora [im·pre·'so·ra] f COMPUT printer; ~ **de inyección de tinta** ink-jet printer; ~ **láser** laser printer

imprevisible [im·pre·βi·'si·βle] adj unforeseeable; (*persona*) unpredictable

imprevisto [im·pre·'βis·to] m 1. (*algo inesperado*) contingency, sth unexpected

2. *pl* (*gastos*) unexpected expenses

imprevisto, -a [im·pre·'βis·to, -a] *adj* (*no previsto*) unforeseen; (*inesperado*) unexpected

imprimir [im·pri·'mir] *irr vt* **1.** TIPO, COMPUT to print **2.** (*editar*) to publish **3.** *t. fig* (*un sello*) to stamp

improbable [im·pro·'βa·βle] *adj* improbable, unlikely

improcedente [im·pro·se·'den·te, im·proθe-] *adj* **1.** (*inadecuado*) inappropriate **2.** (*antirreglamentario*) irregular; JUR inadmissible

improductivo, -a [im·pro·duk·'ti·βo, -a] *adj* **1.** (*no productivo*) unproductive **2.** (*antieconómico*) unprofitable

impropio, -a [im·'pro·pjo, -a] *adj* improper, unfitting; (*inadecuado*) inappropriate; **ese comportamiento es ~ en él** that behavior is unusual for him

improvisación [im·pro·βi·sa·'sjon, -'θjon] *f* improvisation

improvisar [im·pro·βi·'sar] *vt* to improvise; TEAT to ad-lib

improviso, -a [im·pro·'βi·so, -a] *adj* unexpected; **de ~** unexpectedly

imprudencia [im·pru·'den·sja, -θja] *f* **1.** (*irreflexión*) imprudence, carelessness **2.** JUR **~ temeraria** criminal negligence; (*conduciendo*) reckless driving

imprudente [im·pru·'den·te] *adj* **1.** (*irreflexivo*) imprudent; (*insensato*) unwise **2.** (*incauto*) incautious

impuesto [im·'pwes·to] *m* FIN tax; **~ sobre la renta** income tax; **~ sobre la propiedad** property tax; **Impuesto sobre el Valor Añadido** Value Added Tax; **libre de ~s** tax-free, duty-free; **sujeto a ~s** taxable, dutiable

impugnar [im·puɣ·'nar] *vt* **1.** *t.* JUR to contest **2.** (*combatir*) to dispute; (*una teoría*) to challenge

impulsar [im·pul·'sar] *vt* **1.** (*empujar*) to impel **2.** (*estimular*) to motivate; (*promover*) to instigate

impulsivo, -a [im·pul·'si·βo, -a] *adj* impulsive

impulso [im·'pul·so] *m* (*estímulo*) impulse, stimulus

impulsor(a) [im·pul·'sor] *adj* **fuerza ~a** driving force

impune [im·'pu·ne] *adj* unpunished

impunidad [im·pu·ni·'dad] *f* impunity

impureza [im·pu·'re·sa, -'re·θa] *f* impurity

impuro, -a [im·'pu·ro, -a] *adj t.* REL impure

imputar [im·pu·'tar] *vt* to impute

inaccesible [in·ak·se·'si·βle, in·ak·θe-] *adj* inaccessible, unapproachable; (*inalcanzable*) beyond one's reach

inaceptable [in·a·sep·'ta·βle, in·a·θep-] *adj* unacceptable

inactivo, -a [in·ak·'ti·βo, -a] *adj* inactive; (*volcán*) dormant

inadecuado, -a [in·a·de·'kwa·do, -a] *adj* inadequate

inadmisible [in·ad·mi·'si·βle] *adj* inadmissible

inadvertido, -a [in·ad·βer·'ti·do, -a] *adj* **1.** (*descuidado*) inadvertent; **me cogió ~** it caught me unprepared **2.** (*desapercibido*) unnoticed

inagotable [in·a·yo·'ta·βle] *adj* inexhaustible; (*persona*) tireless

inaguantable [in·a·ɣwan·'ta·βle] *adj* unbearable, intolerable

inalámbrico, -a [in·a·'lam·bri·ko, -a] *adj* TEL cordless, wireless

inalcanzable [in·al·kan·'sa·βle, -'θa·βle] *adj* unattainable, beyond one's reach

inalterable [in·al·te·'ra·βle] *adj* unalterable; (*imperturbable*) impassive

inalterado, -a [in·al·te·'ra·do, -a] *adj* unchanged

inamovible [in·a·mo·'βi·βle] *adj* fixed, immovable

inanición [i·na·ni·'sjon, -'θjon] *f* starvation

inanimado, -a [in·a·ni·'ma·do, -a] *adj* inanimate

inapelable [in·a·pe·'la·βle] *adj* **1.** JUR unappealable, not open to appeal **2.** (*inevitable*) inevitable

inapetencia [in·a·pe·'ten·sja, -θja] *f* loss [*o* lack] of appetite

inapreciable [in·a·pre·'sja·βle, -'θja·βle] *adj* **1.** (*imperceptible*) inappreciable **2.** (*de gran valor*) priceless

inasequible [in·a·se·'ki·βle] *adj* out of reach

inaudible [in·au·'di·βle] *adj* inaudible

naudito, -a [in·au·'di·to, -a] *adj* **1.** (*sin precedente*) unprecedented **2.** (*vituperable*) outrageous

inauguración [in·au·yu·ra·'sjon, -'θjon] *f* **1.** (*puente, exposición*) opening; (*estatua*) unveiling **2.** (*comienzo*) inauguration

inaugurar [in·au·yu·'rar] *vt* **1.** (*puente*) to open; (*estatua*) to unveil **2.** (*comenzar*) to inaugurate

inca ['in·ka] *adj, m* Inca

incalculable [in·kal·ku·'la·βle] *adj* incalculable

incandescente [in·kan·de·'sen·te, -des·'θen·te] *adj* FÍS (*metal*) incandescent

incansable [in·kan·'sa·βle] *adj* tireless

incapacidad [in·ka·pa·si·'dad, in·ka·paθi-] *f* **1.** (*ineptitud*) incompetence **2.** (*psíquica*) incapacity; (*física*) disability **3.** (*falta de habilidad*) inability, incapability

incapacitado, -a [in·ka·pa·si·'ta·do, -a; -θi·'ta·do, -a] *adj* (*incapaz*) incapacitated; (*incompetente*) incompetent

incapacitar [in·ka·pa·si·'tar, -θi·'tar] *vt* to incapacitate

incapaz [in·ka·'pas, -'paθ] *adj* **1.** (*inepto*) incapable **2.** JUR (*sin capacidad legal*) incapacitated, incompetent **3.** (*sin talento*) inept

incautarse [in·kau·'tar·se] *vr* **~ de algo** (*confiscar*) to confiscate sth; (*adueñarse*) to appropriate sth

incauto, -a [in·'kau·to, -a] *adj* (*sin cautela*) incautious; (*confiado*) credulous

incendiar [in·sen·'djar, in·θen-] **I.** *vt* to set fire to **II.** *vr:* **~se** to catch fire

incendio [in·'sen·djo, in·'θen-] *m* fire; **~ intencionado** arson

incentivar [in·sen·ti·'βar, in·θen-] *vt* to motivate, to offer incentives to

incentivo [in·sen·'ti·βo, in·θen-] *m* incentive

incertidumbre [in·ser·ti·'dum·bre, in·θer-] *f* incertitude

incesante [in·se·'san·te, in·θe-] *adj* incessant

incesto [in·'ses·to, in·'θes-] *m* incest

incidencia [in·si·'den·sja, in·θi-] *f* **1.** *t.* MAT incidence **2.** (*consecuencia*) repercussion

incidente [in·si·'den·te, in·θi-] *m* incident

incidir [in·si·'dir, in·θi-] *vi* **~ en algo** (*consecuencias*) to impinge on [*o* affect] sth; (*tema*) to touch on sth

incienso [in·'sjen·so, -'θjen·so] *m* incense

incierto, -a [in·'sjer·to, -a; in·'θjer-] *adj* (*dudoso*) doubtful, uncertain; (*falso*) untrue

incineradora [in·si·ne·ra·'do·ra, in·θi-] *f* (*para basuras*) incinerator

incinerar [in·si·ne·'rar, in·θi-] *vt* to incinerate; (*cadáveres*) to cremate

incisión [in·si·'sjon, in·θi-] *f* *t.* MED incision

inciso [in·'si·so, in·'θi-] *m* (*al relatar*) aside

incitar [in·si·'tar, in·θi-] *vt* (*instigar*) to incite

inclemencia [in·kle·'men·sja, -θja] *f* inclemency

inclinación [in·kli·na·'sjon, -'θjon] *f* **1.** (*declive*) slope **2.** (*afecto*) ~ por alguien/algo inclination for [*o* to] sb/sth **3.** (*tendencias*) propensity, tendency

inclinado, -a [in·kli·'na·do, -a] *adj* inclined; **~ a algo** inclined to [*o* towards] sth

inclinar [in·kli·'nar] **I.** *vt* to incline **II.** *vr:* **~se 1.** (*reverencia*) to bow; (*árboles*) to bend **2.** (*propender*) to incline **3.** (*preferir*) **~se por algo** to have a penchant for sth

incluir [in·klu·ir] *irr como huir* *vt* to include, to enclose, to contain; **todo incluido** all-inclusive

inclusive [in·klu·'si·βe] *adv* inclusively

incluso [in·'klu·so] *prep* including; **han aprobado todos, ~ tú** everybody has passed, even you

incluso, -a [in·'klu·so, -a] *adj* included

incógnita [in·'koɣ·ni·ta] *f* enigma; (*secreto*) secret; **despejar la ~** (*secreto*) to disclose the secret

incógnito, -a [in·'koɣ·ni·to] *adj* incognito

incoherencia [in·ko·e·'ren·sja, -θja] *f* incoherence

incoherente [in·ko·e·'ren·te] *adj* incoherent

incoloro, -a [in·ko·'lo·ro, -a] *adj* colorless

incomodar [in·ko·mo·'dar] *vt* to inconvenience

incomodidad [in·ko·mo·di·'dad] *f* discomfort

incómodo, -a [in·'ko·mo·do, -a] *adj* **1.** (*inconfortable*) uncomfortable **2.** (*molesto*) tiresome

incomparable [in·kom·pa·'ra·βle] *adj* incomparable

incompatible [in·kom·pa·'ti·βle] *adj* incompatible

incompetencia [in·kom·pe·'ten·sja, -θja] *f* incompetence

incompetente [in·kom·pe·'ten·te] *adj* incompetent

incompleto, -a [in·kom·'ple·to, -a] *adj* incomplete

incomprensible [in·kom·pren·'si·βle] *adj* incomprehensible

incomprensión [in·kom·pren·'sjon] *f* (*no querer comprender*) unwillingness to understand; (*no poder comprender*) incomprehension

incomunicado, -a [in·ko·mu·ni·'ka·do, -a] *adj* incommunicado; **el preso estuvo 6 días** ~ the prisoner spent 6 days in solitary confinement

incomunicar <c → qu> [in·ko·mu·ni·'kar] *vt* **1.** (*aislar*) to isolate **2.** (*bloquear*) to cut off

inconcebible [in·kon·se·'βi·βle, -θe-'βi·βle] *adj* **1.** (*inimaginable*) inconceivable **2.** (*inadmisible*) unacceptable

inconcluso, -a [in·kon·'klu·so, -a] *adj* unfinished

incondicional [in·kon·di·sjo·'nal, -θjo·'nal] *adj* unconditional

inconexo, -a [in·ko·'nek·so, -a] *adj* unconnected

inconformista [in·kon·for·'mis·ta] *mf* nonconformist

inconfundible [in·kon·fun·'di·βle] *adj* unmistakable

incongruente [in·kon·'grwen·te] *adj* incongruous

inconsciencia [in·kon·'sjen·sja, -kons·'θjen·θja] *f* **1.** (*desmayo*) unconsciousness **2.** (*insensatez*) senselessness; (*irresponsabilidad*) thoughtlessness

inconsciente [in·kon·'sjen·te, -kons·'θjen·te] *adj* **1.** *estar* (*desmayado*) unconscious **2.** *ser* (*insensato*) senseless; (*irresponsable*) thoughtless **3.** *ser* (*gesto*) involuntary

inconsistente [in·kon·sis·'ten·te] *ad* **1.** (*irregular*) uneven **2.** (*poco sólido*) flimsy; (*argumento*) weak

inconsolable [in·kon·so·'la·βle] *adj* inconsolable, broken-hearted

incontable [in·kon·'ta·βle] *adj* **1.** (*innumerable*) countless **2.** LING uncountable

incontinencia [in·kon·ti·'nen·sja, -θja] *t.* MED incontinence

incontrolado, -a [in·kon·tro·'la·do, -a] *adj* uncontrolled; (*violento*) violent

inconveniencia [in·kom·be·'njen·sja, -θja] *f* (*no adecuado*) inappropriateness

inconveniente [in·kom·be·'njen·te] **I.** *adj* (*no adecuado*) inappropriate **II.** *m* disadvantage; (*obstáculo*) inconvenience

incordiar [in·kor·'djar] *vt* to bother

incordio [in·'kor·djo] *m inf* bother, pest

incorporación [in·kor·po·ra·'sjon, -'θjon] *f* **1.** (*al enderezarse*) straightening up, (*al sentarse*) sitting up **2.** (*integración*) incorporation

incorporar [in·kor·po·'rar] **I.** *vt* (*a un grupo*) ~ **a algo** to incorporate in [*o* into] sth **II.** *vr:* ~**se 1.** (*enderezarse*) to sit up **2.** (*en el trabajo*) ~**se al trabajo** to start a new job **3.** (*agregarse*) ~**se a algo** to join sth

incorrecto, -a [in·ko·'rrek·to, -a] *ad* **1.** (*erróneo*) erroneous **2.** (*descortés*) impolite

incorregible [in·ko·rre·'xi·βle] *adj* incorrigible

incrédulo, -a [in·'kre·du·lo, -a] *adj* incredulous

increíble [in·kre·'i·βle] *adj* incredible

incrementar [in·kre·men·'tar] *vt, vr:* ~**se** to increase

incremento [in·kre·'men·to] *m* (*aumento*) increment; (*crecimiento*) increase

increpar [in·kre·'par] *vt* to rebuke

incriminar [in·kri·mi·'nar] *vt* JUR to incriminate

incrustación [in·krus·ta·'sjon, -'θjon] *f* (*proceso*) embedding; ARTE inlaying; MED incrustation

incrustar [in·krus·'tar] I. *vt* (*con madera*) to inlay II. *vr*: ~**se** to embed itself; MED to encrust

incubadora [in·ku·βa·'do·ra] *f* incubator

incubar [in·ku·'βar] *vt, vr*: ~**se** to incubate

incuestionable [in·kwes·tjo·'na·βle] *adj* unquestionable

inculcar <c → qu> [in·kul·'kar] *vt* (*enseñar*) to instill; (*infundir*) to inculcate

inculpar [in·kul·'par] *vt* to accuse

inculto, -a [in·'kul·to, -a] *adj* uneducated

incumbencia [in·kum·'ben·sja, -θja] *f* responsibility, incumbency *form;* **no es de tu ~** it's none of your business

incumbir [in·kum·'bir] *vi* to concern

incumplimiento [in·kum·pli·'mjen·to] *m* non-compliance; ~ **de contrato** breach of contract

incumplir [in·kum·'plir] *vt* to breach

incurable [in·ku·'ra·βle] *adj* incurable

incurrir [in·ku·'rrir] *vi* ~ **en una falta** to commit an error

incursión [in·kur·'sjon] *f* incursion, strike

indagar <g → gu> [in·da·'ɣar] *vt* ~ **algo** to look into sth

indebido, -a [in·de·'βi·do, -a] *adj* wrongful; (*ilícito*) illicit

indecencia [in·de·'sen·sja, -'θen·θja] *f* indecency

indecente [in·de·'sen·te, -'θen·te] *adj* indecent

indecisión [in·de·si·'sjon, in·de·θi·] *f* (*vacilación*) indecision

indeciso, -a [in·de·'si·so, -a; 'θi·so, -a] *adj* **1.** (*irresoluto*) irresolute **2.** (*que vacila*) indecisive

indecoroso, -a [in·de·ko·'ro·so, -a] *adj* indecorous

indefenso, -a [in·de·'fen·so, -a] *adj* defenseless

indefinidamente [in·de·fi·ni·da·'men·te] *adv* indefinitely

indefinido, -a [in·de·fi·'ni·do, -a] *adj t.* LING indefinite

indemne [in·'dem·ne] *adj* (*persona*) unharmed; (*cosa*) undamaged

indemnización [in·dem·ni·sa·'sjon, -θa·'θjon] *f* indemnity, indemnification

indemnizar <z → c> [in·dem·ni·'sar, -'θar] *vt* (*daños y perjuicios*) to indemnify; ~ **por algo** to indemnify for sth

independencia [in·de·pen·'den·sja, -θja] *f* independence; **con ~ de algo** independently of sth

independiente [in·de·pen·'djen·te] *adj* independent

independizar <z → c> [in·de·pen·di·'sar, -'θar] I. *vt* to make independent II. *vr*: ~**se** to become independent

indescifrable [in·de·si·'fra·βle, in·des·θi·'fra·βle] *adj* indecipherable

indescriptible [in·des·krip·'ti·βle] *adj* indescribable

indeseable [in·de·se·'a·βle] *adj* undesirable

indestructible [in·des·truk·'ti·βle] *adj* indestructible

indeterminación [in·de·ter·mi·na·'sjon, -'θjon] *f* indeterminacy; (*indecisión*) indecision

indeterminado, -a [in·de·ter·mi·'na·do, -a] *adj* indeterminate; (*indeciso*) indecisive

India ['in·dja] *f* **la ~** India; **las ~s** the Indies

indicación [in·di·ka·'sjon, -'θjon] *f* **1.** (*señal*) indication; (*por escrito*) observation; (*consejo*) advice **2.** *pl* (*instrucciones*) instructions *pl*

indicado, -a [in·di·'ka·do, -a] *adj* (*aconsejable*) advisable; (*adecuado*) indicated; **eso es lo más ~** that is the most suitable

indicador [in·di·ka·'dor] *m* indicator; TÉC gauge, gage; ECON index

indicar <c → qu> [in·di·'kar] *vt* **1.** TÉC (*aparato*) to register **2.** (*señalar, sugerir*) to indicate; (*mostrar*) to show

índice ['in·di·se, -θe] *m* **1.** (*biblioteca, catálogo*) index, catalog; (*libro*) table of contents **2.** (*dedo*) index finger, forefinger **3.** (*estadísticas*) rate; ~ **de audiencia** audience ratings

indicio [in·'di·sjo, -θjo] *m* sign; JUR indication; (*vestigio*) trace

indiferencia [in·di·fe·'ren·sja, -θja] *f* indifference

indiferente [in·di·fe·'ren·te] *adj* indifferent; **me es ~** it doesn't make any difference to me

indígena [in·'di·xe·na] *adj* indigenous, native; (*en Latinoamérica*) Indian

indigente [in·di·'xen·te] *mf* destitute person

indigestar [in·di·xes·'tar] **I.** *vt* to cause indigestion to **II.** *vr:* ~**se 1.** (*empacharse*) ~**se de** [*o* **por**] **algo** to get indigestion from sth **2.** *inf* (*hacerse antipático*) to be detestable

indigestión [in·di·xes·'tjon] *f* MED indigestion

indignación [in·diɣ·na·'sjon, -'θjon] *f* indignation

indignado, -a [in·diɣ·'na·do, -a] *adj* ~ **por algo** indignant about [*o* at] sth

indignante [in·diɣ·'nan·te] *adj* infuriating, outrageous

indignar [in·diɣ·'nar] **I.** *vt* to infuriate, to outrage **II.** *vr* ~**se por algo** to become indignant [*o* infuriated] about sth

indigno, -a [in·'diɣ·no, -a] *adj* **1.** (*desmerecedor*) unworthy **2.** (*vil*) contemptible

indio, -a ['in·djo, -a] **I.** *adj* **1.** (*de la India*) Indian **2.** (*de Norteamérica*) American Indian; (*de América Central, Suramérica*) Indian, Amerindian **II.** *m, f* **1.** (*de la India*) Indian **2.** (*de Norteamérica*) American Indian; (*de América Central, Suramérica*) Indian, Amerindian ► **hacer el ~** (*tonterías*) to fool around [*o* about]

indirecta [in·di·'rek·ta] *f inf* hint, insinuation; **lanzar** [*o* **soltar**] **una ~** to drop a hint

indirecto, -a [in·di·'rek·to, -a] *adj* indirect

indisciplinado, -a [in·di·si·pli·'na·do, -a; in·dis·θi-] *adj* undisciplined

indiscreción [in·dis·kre·'sjon, -'θjon] *f* indiscretion

indiscreto, -a [in·dis·'kre·to, -a] *adj* imprudent; (*que no guarda secretos*) indiscreet

indiscutible [in·dis·ku·'ti·βle] *adj* indisputable

indispensable [in·dis·pen·'sa·βle] *adj* indispensable; **lo** (**más**) ~ the most es-

sential; **el requisito ~ es...** the key requisite is...

indisponer [in·dis·po·'ner] *irr como* **poner I.** *vt* **1.** (*enemistar*) ~ **a uno contra otro** to set one person against another **2.** (*de salud*) to indispose **II.** *vr:* ~**se 1.** (*enemistarse*) to quarrel **2.** (*ponerse mal*) to become indisposed

indispuesto, -a [in·dis·'pwes·to, -a] *adj* indisposed; (*reacio*) unwilling

indistintamente [in·dis·tin·ta·'men·te] *adv* indiscriminately; **se aplica a todos los niños** ~ it applies to all the children without distinction

indistinto, -a [in·dis·'tin·to, -a] *adj* indistinguishable

individual [in·di·βi·'dwal] *adj* **1.** (*personal*) personal; (*peculiar*) individual **2.** (*simple*) single

individualista [in·di·βi·dwa·'lis·ta] *mf* individualist

individualizar <z → c> [in·di·βi·dwa·li·'sar, -'θar] *vt* to individualize

individuo [in·di·'βi·dwo] *m* individual; *pey* (*sujeto*) individual, character

indivisible [in·di·βi·'si·βle] *adj* indivisible

indocumentado, -a [in·do·ku·men·'ta·do, -a] *adj* **estar** ~ to be without papers [*o* means of identification]

índole ['in·do·le] *f* nature, kind

indomable [in·do·'ma·βle] *adj* (*que no se somete*) indomitable; (*indomesticable*) untameable

inducir [in·du·'sir, -'θir] *irr como* **traducir** *vt* **1.** ELEC (*corriente*) to induce **2.** (*instigar*) to induce; ~ **a error** to lead astray, to mislead

indudable [in·du·'da·βle] *adj* undeniable; **es ~ que...** it is certain that...

indulgencia [in·dul·'xen·sja, -θja] *f* indulgence

indultar [in·dul·'tar] *vt* JUR (*perdonar*) to pardon

indulto [in·'dul·to] *m* (*perdón total*) pardon; (*perdón parcial*) remission

indumentaria [in·du·men·'ta·rja] *f* clothing, clothes *pl*; (*vestir*) dress

industria [in·'dus·trja] *f* industry

industrial [in·dus·'trjal] *adj* industrial; **polígono** ~ industrial estate, industrial park

industrializar <z → c> [in·dus·trja·li·'sar,

-'θar] *vt, vr:* ~**se** to industrialize

inédito, -a [i·'ne·di·to, -a] *adj (no publicado)* unpublished

ineficacia [in·e·fi·'ka·sja, -θja] *f* **1.** *(sin resultado)* ineffectiveness **2.** com *(sin rentabilidad)* lack of profitability **3.** *(de una persona)* inefficiency

ineficaz [in·e·fi·'kas·'kaθ] *adj* **1.** *(cosa)* ineffective **2.** *(persona)* ineffectual

ineficiente [in·e·fi·'sjen·te, -'θjente] *adj* inefficient

INEM [i·'nem] *m abr de* **Instituto Nacional de Empleo** national employment agency

ineptitud [i·nep·ti·'tud] *f* ~ **para algo** *(incapacidad)* ineptitude in sth; *(incompetencia)* incompetence in sth

inepto, -a [i·'nep·to, -a] *adj* ~ **para algo** *(incapaz)* inept at sth; *(incompetente)* incompetent at sth

inequívoco, -a [in·e·'ki·βo·ko, -a] *adj* unequivocal; *(inconfundible)* unmistakable

inercia [i·'ner·sja, -θja] *f.* fís inertia; **por** ~ mechanically

inerte [i·'ner·te] *adj (sin vida)* inanimate; *(inmóvil)* inert

inesperado, -a [in·es·pe·'ra·do, -a] *adj* unexpected

inestable [in·es·'ta·βle] *adj* **1.** *(frágil)* t. téc fragile **2.** *(variable)* unstable

inestimable [in·es·ti·'ma·βle] *adj* inestimable

inevitable [in·e·βi·'ta·βle] *adj* inevitable, unavoidable

inexacto, -a [in·ek·'sak·to, -a] *adj* inexact; *(erróneo)* inaccurate

inexistente [in·ek·sis·'ten·te] *adj* non-existent

inexperiencia [in·es·pe·'rjen·sja, -θja] *f* inexperience

inexperto, -a [in·es·'per·to, -a] *adj* inexpert; *(sin experiencia)* inexperienced

inexplicable [in·es·pli·'ka·βle] *adj* inexplicable

inexpresivo, -a [in·es·pre·'si·βo, -a] *adj* inexpressive

infalible [in·fa·'li·βle] *adj* infallible

infame [in·'fa·me] *adj* **1.** *(vil)* wicked **2.** *(muy malo)* vile

infamia [in·'fa·mja] *f* infamy; *(deshon-*

ra) dishonor

infancia [in·'fan·sja, -θja] *f (niñez, niños)* childhood

infantería [in·fan·te·'ri·a] *f* mil infantry

infanticida [in·fan·ti·'si·da, -'θi·da] **I.** *adj* infanticidal **II.** *mf person who commits infanticide*

infantil [in·fan·'til] *adj* **1.** *(referente a la infancia)* infant; **trabajo** ~ child labor **2.** *pey (ingenuo)* infantile

infarto [in·'far·to] *m* heart attack

infatigable [in·fa·ti·'γa·βle] *adj* tireless

infección [in·fek·'sjon, -'θjon] *f* contagion; *(afección)* infection

infeccioso, -a [in·fek·'sjo·so, -a; -'θjo·so, -a] *adj* infectious; **enfermedad infecciosa** contagious disease

infectar [in·fek·'tar] **I.** *vt (contagiar)* to transmit; *inf(contaminar)* to infect; *(corromper)* to corrupt **II.** *vr:* ~**se 1.** *(contagiarse)* ~**se de SIDA** to catch AIDS **2.** *(inflamarse)* to become infected

infelicidad [in·fe·li·si·'dad, -θi·'dad] *f* unhappiness

infeliz [in·fe·'lis, -liθ] *adj* **1.** *(no feliz)* unhappy **2.** *inf (ingenuo)* ingenuous

inferior [in·fe·'rjor] *adj* **1.** *(debajo)* lower; **labio** ~ lower lip **2.** *(de menos calidad)* inferior **3.** *(menos)* ~ **a algo** lesser than sth **4.** *(subordinado)* subordinate **II.** *mf* inferior

inferioridad [in·fe·rjo·ri·'dad] *f* inferiority; **estar en** ~ **de condiciones** to be at a disadvantage

infernal [in·fer·'nal] *adj* infernal

infestar [in·fes·'tar] *vt* ~ **de algo** *(inundar)* to overrun with sth; *(infectar)* to infect with sth; *(corromper)* to corrupt with sth

infidelidad [in·fi·de·li·'dad] *f* infidelity, unfaithfulness

infiel [in·'fjel] **I.** *adj* <infidelísimo> **1.** *(desleal)* unfaithful **2.** *(pagano)* heathen **II.** *mf* infidel

infierno [in·'fjer·no] *m t.* rel hell; **me mandó al** ~ he/she told me to go to hell

infiltrar [in·fil·'trar] **I.** *vt* to infiltrate, to penetrate **II.** *vr:* ~**se en algo** *(penetrar)* to penetrate sth; *(introducirse)* to infiltrate sth

infinidad [in·fi·ni·'dad] *f* 1. (*cualidad de infinito*) infinity 2. (*gran número*) enormous quantity

infinitivo [in·fi·ni·'ti·βo] *m* infinitive

infinito [in·fi·'ni·to] *m* t. MAT infinity

infinito, -a [in·fi·'ni·to, -a] *adj* 1. (*ilimitado*) limitless; (*cosas no materiales*) boundless 2. (*incontable*) infinite

inflación [in·fla·'sjon, -'θjon] *f* t. ECON inflation

inflamable [in·fla·'ma·βle] *adj* (in)flammable

inflamación [in·fla·ma·'sjon, -'θjon] *f* 1. t. MED inflammation 2. TÉC ignition

inflamar [in·fla·'mar] I. *vt* 1. (*encender*) to ignite 2. (*excitar*) t. MED to inflame II. *vr:* ~**se** t. MED to become inflamed

inflar [in·'flar] I. *vt* 1. (*llenar de aire*) to inflate 2. (*exagerar*) to exaggerate II. *vr* 1. (*hincharse*) ~**se de algo** to swell with sth 2. *inf* (*de comida*) to stuff oneself

inflexible [in·flek·'si·βle] *adj* 1. (*rígido*) inflexible 2. (*firme*) firm

inflexión [in·flek·'sjon] *f* 1. (*de la voz*) t. MAT, LING inflection, inflexion 2. (*torcimiento*) bend

infligir <g → j> [in·fli·'xir] *vt* (*dolor*) to inflict; ~ **un castigo** to inflict a punishment; ~ **daño** to cause injury

influencia [in·'flwen·sja, -θja] *f* influence; **tener** ~ to be influential

influenciar [in·flwen·'sjar, -θjar] *vt* to influence; **dejarse** ~ to be influenced

influir [in·flu·'ir] *irr como huir* I. *vi* ~ **en** [*o* **sobre**] **algo** (*contribuir*) to have a hand in sth; (*actuar*) to have an influence on sth II. *vt* to influence

influyente [in·flu·'jen·te] *adj* influential

información [in·for·ma·'sjon, -'θjon] *f* information; TEL directory assistance

informal [in·for·'mal] *adj* 1. (*desenfadado*) informal, casual 2. (*no cumplidor*) unreliable

informar [in·for·'mar] I. *vt* to inform II. *vr* ~**se de algo** to find out about sth

informática [in·for·'ma·ti·ka] *f* computer [*o* computing] science

informático, -a [in·for·'ma·ti·ko, -a] I. *adj* **fallo** ~ computer error II. *m, f* computer expert

informativo [in·for·ma·'ti·βo] *m* news broadcast; **el** ~ **de las nueve** the nine o'clock news

informativo, -a [in·for·ma·'ti·βo, -a] *adj* informative; **boletín** ~ (*por escrito, radial*) (news) bulletin

informatizar <z → c> [in·for·ma·ti·'sar, -'θar] *vt* to computerize

informe [in·'for·me] *m* report

infortunado, -a [in·for·tu·'na·do, -a] *adj* unfortunate

infortunio [in·for·'tu·njo] *m* misfortune, adversity

infracción [in·frak·'sjon, -'θjon] *f* infraction; (*administrativa*) breach; ~ **de tráfico** traffic violation

infractor(a) [in·frak·'tor, --'to·ra] *m(f)* offender

infraestructura [in·fra·es·truk·'tu·ra] *f* infrastructure

infrahumano, -a [in·fra·u·'ma·no, -a] *adj* subhuman

infranqueable [in·fran·ke·'a·βle] *adj* impassable, insurmountable *fig*

infrarrojo, -a [in·fra·'rro·xo, -a] *adj* infrared

infravalorar [in·fra·βa·lo·'rar] *vt* to undervalue, to underestimate

infringir <g → j> [in·frin·'xir] *vt* to infringe; ~ **la ley** to break the law

infructuoso, -a [in·fruk·tu·'o·so, -a] *adj* fruitless

infundado, -a [in·fun·'da·do, -a] *adj* unfounded

infundir [in·fun·'dir] *vt* (*deseo*) to infuse; (*respeto*) to command; (*sospechas*) to instill

infusión [in·fu·'sjon] *f* infusion; (*de hierbas*) herb(al) tea

ingeniar [in·xe·'njar] I. *vt* to devise II. *vr:* ~**se** to contrive, to manage

ingeniería [in·xe·nje·'ria] *f* engineering

ingeniero, -a [in·xe·'nje·ro, -a] *m, f* engineer

ingenio [in·'xe·njo] *m* (*inventiva*) ingenuity; (*maña*) aptitude

ingenioso, -a [in·xe·'njo·so, -a] *adj* 1. (*hábil*) skillful 2. (*listo*) ingenious

ingenuidad [in·xe·nwi·'dad] *f* 1. (*inocencia*) candor 2. (*torpeza*) naivety

ingenuo, -a [in·'xe·nwo, -a] *adj* ingenuous, candid

ingerir [in·xe·'rir] *irr como sentir* *vt* to ingest; (*medicamentos*) to take

ingestión [in·xes·'tjon] *f* ingestion, consumption; (*medicamentos*) taking, intake

Inglaterra [in·gla·'te·rra] *f* England

ingle ['in·gle] *f* ANAT groin

inglés, -esa [in·'gles, -·'gle·sa] **I.** *adj* English **II.** *m, f* Englishman *m*, Englishwoman *f*

ingratitud [in·gra·ti·'tud] *f* ingratitude

ingrato, -a [in·'gra·to, -a] *adj* (*persona*) ungrateful; (*tarea*) thankless

ingravidez [in·gra·βi·'des, -'deθ] *f* weightlessness, lack of gravity

ingrediente [in·gre·'djen·te] *m* ingredient

ingresar [in·gre·'sar] **I.** *vi* **1.** (*inscribirse*) ~ **en algo** to become a member of sth **2.** (*hospitalizarse*) to be admitted to hospital **II.** *vt* **1.** FIN (*cheque*) to pay in, to deposit **2.** (*hospitalizar*) to hospitalize **3.** (*percibir*) to earn

ingreso [in·'gre·so] *m* **1.** (*inscripción*) entry; (*alta*) incorporation; **examen de ~** entrance exam **2.** (*en una cuenta*) deposit **3.** *pl* (*retribuciones*) income

inhabilitar [in·a·βi·li·'tar] *vt* JUR **1.** (*incapacitar*) ~ **para algo** to incapacitate for sth **2.** (*prohibir*) ~ **a** (**hacer**) **algo** to disqualify from (doing) sth

inhabitado, -a [in·a·βi·'ta·do, -a] *adj* uninhabited

inhalador [in·a·la·'dor] *m* MED inhaler

inhalar [in·a·'lar] *vt* t. MED to inhale, to breathe in

inhibición [in·i·βi·'sjon, -'θjon] *f* (*represión*) repression; (*abstención*) abstention; MED, JUR inhibition

inhibir [in·i·'βir] **I.** *vt* to repress; BIO, JUR to inhibit **II.** *vr* ~**se de algo** to abstain from sth; ~**se de hacer algo** to refrain from doing sth

inhospitalario, -a [in·os·pi·ta·'la·rjo, -a] *adj* inhospitable, unfriendly

inhóspito, -a [in·'os·pi·to, -a] *adj* inhospitable

inhumación [in·u·ma·'sjon, -'θjon] *f* inhumation, burial

inhumano, -a [in·u·'ma·no, -a] *adj* (*no humano*) inhuman; (*sin compasión*) inhumane

iniciación [i·ni·sja·'sjon, -θja·'θjon] *f* **1.** (*comienzo*) beginning, commencement **2.** (*introducción*) ~ **a** [*o* en] **algo** initiation to sth

iniciado, -a [i·ni·'sja·do, -a; -'θja·do, -a] **I.** *adj* initiated **II.** *m, f* initiate

inicial [i·ni·'sjal, -'θjal] *adj* initial

iniciar [i·ni·'sjar, -'θjar] **I.** *vt* **1.** (*comenzar*) to begin **2.** (*introducir*) to initiate; COMPUT to log in [*o* on] **II.** *vr:* ~**se 1.** (*comenzar*) to begin **2.** (*introducirse en*) ~ **en algo** to learn sth on one's own

iniciativa [i·ni·sja·'ti·βa, i·ni·θja·-] *f* initiative

inicio [i·'ni·sjo, -θjo] *m* beginning

inigualable [in·i·γwa·'la·βle] *adj* incomparable, unrivaled

inimaginable [in·i·ma·xi·'na·βle] *adj* unimaginable

ininteligible [in·in·te·li·'xen·te] *adj* unintelligible; (*escritura*) illegible

ininterrumpido, -a [in·in·te·rrum·'pi·do, -a] *adj* uninterrupted

injerto [in·'xer·to] *m* (*brote*) t. MED graft

injuria [in·'xu·rja] *f* (*con palabras*) insult, affront; (*con acciones*) harm; JUR slander

injusticia [in·xus·'ti·sja, -θja] *f* injustice, unfairness

injustificado, -a [in·xus·ti·fi·'ka·do, -a] *adj* unjustified

injusto, -a [in·'xus·to, -a] *adj* (*no justo*) unjust, unfair

inmaculado, -a [in·ma·ku·'la·do, -a, im·ma-] *adj* immaculate

inmadurez [in·ma·du·'res, -reθ; im·ma-] *f* immaturity

inmaduro, -a [in·ma·'du·ro, -a, im·ma-] *adj* immature

inmediaciones [in·me·dja·'sjo·nes, -'θjo·nes; im·me-] *fpl* surroundings *pl*, vicinity

inmediatamente [in·me·dja·ta·'men·te, im·me-] *adv* **1.** (*sin demora*) immediately **2.** (*directamente*) directly

inmediato, -a [in·me·'dja·to, -a, im·me-] *adj* **1.** (*sin demora*) immediate; **de ~** immediately, right away **2.** (*directo*) direct **3.** (*próximo*) adjacent

inmejorable [in·me·xo·'ra·βle, im·me-] *adj* unbeatable, excellent

inmensidad [in·men·si·'dad, im·men-] *f* 1. (*extensión*) immensity 2. (*cantidad*) vastness

inmenso, -a [in·'men·so, -a/im·'men·so, -a] *adj* immense

inmerecido, -a [in·me·re·'si·do, -a, -'θi·do, -a; im·me- ime-] *adj* undeserved

inmersión [in·mer·'sjon, im·mer-] *f* (*sumersión*) immersion

inmerso, -a [in·'mer·so, -a/im'mer·so, -a] *adj* immersed; *fig* involved

inmigración [in·mi·γra·'sjon, -'θjon; im·mi-] *f* immigration

inmigrante [in·mi·'γran·te, im·mi-] *mf* immigrant

inmigrar [in·mi·'γrar, im·mi-] *vi* to immigrate

inminente [in·mi·'nen·te; im·mi·'nen·te] *adj* imminent

inmiscuir [in·mis·ku·'ir, im·mi-] *irr como huir* I. *vt* to put in II. *vr*: ~se to interfere, to meddle

inmobiliaria [in·mo·βi·'lja·rja, im·mo-] *f* real estate agency

inmobiliario, -a [in·mo·βi·'lja·rjo, -a; im·mo-] *adj* property

inmoral [in·mo·'ral, im·mo-] *adj* immoral

inmortal [in·mor·'tal, im·mor-] *adj* immortal

inmortalidad [in·mor·ta·li·'dad, im·mor-] *f* immortality

inmortalizar <z → c> [in·mor·ta·li·'sar, -'θar; im·mor-] *vt* to immortalize

inmóvil [in·'mo·βil, im·'mo-] *adj* immobile

inmovilizar <z → c> [in·mo·βi·li·'sar, -'θar; im·mo-] *vt* (*paralizar*) to paralyze; ~ **a alguien** to put sb out of action

inmueble [in·'mwe·βle, im·'mwe-] *adj, m* property

inmundo, -a [in·'mun·do, -a; im·'mun·do, -a] *adj* filthy; (*asqueroso*) disgusting

inmune [in·'mu·ne/im·'mu·ne] *adj* immune

inmunidad [in·mu·ni·'dad, im·mu·ni-] *f* immunity

inmunizar <z → c> [in·mu·ni·'θar, im·mu·ni-] *vt* to immunize

inmunodeficiencia [in·mu·no·de·fi·'sjen·sja, -'θjen·θja; im·mu·no-] *f* MED immunodeficiency; **síndrome de ~ adquirida** Acquired Immune Deficiency Syndrome

inmutable [in·mu·'ta·βle, im·mu-] *adj* immutable

inmutar [in·mu·'tar, im·mu·'tar] I. *vt* 1. (*afectar*) to affect 2. (*variar*) to alter II. *vr*: ~se to be affected; **sin ~se** without batting an eyelash

innato, -a [in·'na·to, -a] *adj* innate, inborn; **tiene un talento ~** he/she has a natural talent

innecesario, -a [in·ne·se·'sa·rjo, -a; in·ne·θe-] *adj* unnecessary

innegable [in·ne·'ya·βle] *adj* undeniable

innovación [in·no·βa·'sjon, -'θjon] *f* innovation

innovador(a) [in·no·βa·'dor, -·'do·ra] *adj* innovative, novel

innovar [in·no·'βar] *vt* to innovate

innumerable [in·nu·me·'ra·βle] *adj* innumerable

inocencia [i·no·'sen·sja, -'θen·θja] *f* (*falta de culpabilidad/malicia*) innocence

inocentada [i·no·sen·'ta·da, i·no·θen-] *f* (*engaño*) blunder; (*broma*) **gastar una ~ a alguien** to play a practical joke on sb

inocente [i·no·'sen·te, -'θen·te] *adj* innocent

inocuo, -a [i·'no·kwo, -a] *adj* innocuous, harmless

inodoro [i·no·'do·ro] *m* (*recipiente*) toilet

inodoro, -a [i·no·'do·ro, -a] *adj* odorless

inofensivo, -a [in·o·fen·'si·βo, -a] *adj* inoffensive

inolvidable [in·ol·βi·'da·βle] *adj* unforgettable

inoportuno, -a [in·o·por·'tu·no, -a] *adj* (*fuera de lugar*) inappropriate; (*fuera de tiempo*) inopportune, untimely

inorgánico, -a [in·or·'ya·ni·ko, -a] *adj* (*no viviente*) inorganic

inoxidable [in·ok·si·'da·βle] *adj* rustproof; (*acero*) stainless

input ['im·put] *m* <inputs> COMPUT input

inquietante [in·kje·'tan·te] *adj* (*preocupante*) worrying; (*perturbador*) disturbing

inquietar [in·kje·'tar] I. *vt* to worry II. *vr*

~se por algo to worry about sth

inquieto, -a [in·'kje·to, -a] *adj* 1. *estar* (*intranquilo*) anxious 2. *ser* (*desasosegado*) restless

inquietud [in·kje·'tud] *f* 1. (*intranquilidad*) anxiety 2. (*desasosiego*) restlessness 3. *pl* (*anhelos*) aspirations *pl*

inquilino, -a [in·ki·'li·no] *m, f* tenant, lessee

Inquisición [in·ki·si·'sjon, -'θjon] *f* Inquisition

insaciable [in·sa·'sja·βle, -'θja·βle] *adj* insatiable; (*sed*) unquenchable

insalubre [in·sa·'lu·βre] *adj* unhealthy, insalubrious *form*

insalvable [in·sal·'βa·βle] *adj* unsalvageable; (*obstáculo*) insuperable

insano, -a [in·'sa·no, -a] *adj* 1. (*insalubre*) unhealthy 2. (*loco*) insane

insatisfacción [in·sa·tis·fak·'sjon, -'θjon] *f* dissatisfaction

insatisfecho, -a [in·sa·tis·'fe·tʃo, -a] *adj* dissatisfied

inscribir [ins·kri·'βir] *irr como* **escribir** I. *vt* 1. (*registrar*) to register 2. (*grabar*) to inscribe; **~ en algo** to inscribe on sth 3. (*alistar*) to enroll; **~ en algo** to enroll in sth II. *vr*: **~se** 1. (*registrarse*) to register; **se inscribió en la oficina de empleo** he registered with the employment agency 2. *t. univ* (*alistarse*) to enroll; **~se en algo** to enroll in sth

inscripción [ins·krip·'sjon, -krip·'θjon] *f* 1. (*registro*) registration 2. (*alistamiento*) *t. univ* enrollment; **~ en un curso** registration in a course 3. (*escrito grabado*) inscription

inscrito, -a [ins·'kri·to, -a] *pp de* **inscribir**

insecticida [in·sek·ti·'si·da, -'θi·da] *m* insecticide

insecto [in·'sek·to] *m* insect

inseguridad [in·se·ɣu·ri·'dad] *f* insecurity

inseguro, -a [in·se·'ɣu·ro, -a] *adj* insecure

inseminación [in·se·mi·na·'sjon, -'θjon] *f* insemination

insensatez [in·sen·sa·'tes, -'teθ] *f* 1. (*falta de sensatez*) foolishness 2. (*disparate*) stupidity

insensato, -a [in·sen·'sa·to, -a] *adj* foolish

insensibilizar <z → c> [in·sen·si·βi·li·'sar, -'θar] I. *vt* to render insensitive; med to desensitize II. *vr*: **~se** (*no sentir*) to become insensitive

insensible [in·sen·'si·βle] *adj* (*física o afectivamente*) insensitive

inseparable [in·se·pa·'ra·βle] *adj* inseparable

inserción [in·ser·'sjon, -'θjon] *f* (*inclusión*) inclusion; **~ social** social insertion

insertar [in·ser·'tar] *vt* 1. (*llave, moneda, texto*) to insert 2. (*anuncio*) to place

inservible [in·ser·'βi·βle] *adj* useless

insignia [in·'siɣ·nja] *f* 1. (*de asociación*) badge; (*honorífica*) decoration; (*militar*) insignia 2. (*bandera*) flag, ensign

insignificante [in·siɣ·ni·fi·'kan·te] *adj* insignificant

insinuación [in·si·nwa·'sjon, -'θjon] *f* 1. (*alusión*) allusion 2. (*engatusamiento*) insinuation

insinuar <1. *pres* insinúo> [in·si·nu·'ar] I. *vt* to insinuate; **¿qué estás insinuando?** what are you insinuating? II. *vr*: **~se** 1. (*engatusar*) **~se a alguien** to get in with sb; *inf* (*amorosamente*) to flirt with sb 2. (*cosa*) to be discernible

insípido, -a [in·'si·pi·do, -a] *adj* 1. (*comida*) insipid 2. (*persona: aburrida*) dull; (*sin espíritu*) listless

insistencia [in·sis·'ten·sja, -θja] *f* 1. (*perseverancia*) persistence 2. (*énfasis*) insistence

insistente [in·sis·'ten·te] *adj* 1. (*perseverante*) persistent; (*machacón*) insistent 2. (*con énfasis*) pressing

insistir [in·sis·'tir] *vi* to persist; **~ en algo** (*perseverar*) to persist in sth; (*exigir*) to insist on sth

insobornable [in·so·βor·'na·βle] *adj* incorruptible

insolación [in·so·la·'sjon, -'θjon] *f* med sunstroke

insolencia [in·so·'len·sja, -θja] *f* impertinence, disrespect; (*arrogancia*) arrogance

insolente [in·so·'len·te] *adj* impertinent; (*arrogante*) insolent

insolidario, -a [in·so·li·'da·rjo, -a] *adj* (*egoísta*) selfish

insólito, -a [in·'so·li·to, -a] *adj* (*inhabitual*) unusual, uncommon

insoluble [in·so·'lu·βle] *adj* insoluble

insolvencia [in·sol·'βen·sja, -θja] *f* ECON insolvency

insolvente [in·sol·'βen·te] *adj* ECON insolvent

insomnio [in·'som·njo] *m* MED insomnia, sleeplessness

insonorizar <z → c> [in·so·no·ri·'sar, -'θar] *vt* to soundproof

insoportable [in·so·por·'ta·βle] *adj* unbearable

insospechable [in·sos·pe·'tʃa·βle] *adj* (*imprevisible*) unforeseeable

insospechado, -a [in·sos·pe·'tʃa·ðo, -a] *adj* 1. (*no esperado*) unexpected 2. (*no sospechado*) unsuspected, unforeseen

insostenible [in·sos·te·'ni·βle] *adj* untenable

inspección [ins·pek·'sjon, -'θjon] *f* t. TÉC inspection; (*de equipaje*) check; **Inspección Técnica de Vehículos** motor vehicle inspection

inspeccionar [ins·pek·sjo·'nar, -θjo·'nar] *vt* t. TÉC to inspect; (*equipaje*) to check

inspector(a) [ins·pek·'tor, --'to·ra] *m(f)* inspector; ENS school inspector

inspiración [ins·pi·ra·'sjon, -'θjon] *f* 1. (*de aire*) inhalation 2. (*ideas*) inspiration

inspirar [ins·pi·'rar] I. *vt* 1. (*aire*) to inhale 2. (*ideas, confianza*) to inspire II. *vr* ~**se en algo/alguien** to be inspired by sth/sb

instalación [ins·ta·la·'sjon, -'θjon] *f* 1. (*acción*) installation; (*de baño*) plumbing 2. (*lo instalado*) TÉC fitting; (*objeto fijo*) fixture 3. *pl* (*edificio*) facility

instalador(a) [ins·ta·la·'dor, --'do·ra] *m(f)* installer, fitter

instalar [ins·ta·'lar] I. *vt* 1. (*calefacción, teléfono*) to install; (*baño*) to plumb, to fit 2. (*alojar*) to accommodate II. *vr* ~**se** to settle; (*negocio*) to set up; **me instalé en un sillón** I settled into an armchair

instancia [ins·'tan·sja, -θja] *f* 1. (*acción de instar*) urging 2. (*solicitud*) application; (*petición formal*) petition 3. JUR instance; **en última ~** *fig* as a last resort

instantánea [ins·tan·'ta·nea] *f* FOTO snapshot

instantáneo, -a [ins·tan·'ta·neo, -a] *adj* instantaneous; (*efecto, café*) instant

instante [ins·'tan·te] *m* instant; **en un ~** in an instant; **a cada ~** constantly; **¡un ~!** one moment!

instar [ins·'tar] *vi, vt* to urge; ~ **a algo** to press for sth

instaurar [ins·tau·'rar] *vt* (*imperio*) to found; (*democracia*) to establish; (*plan*) to implement

instigar <g → gu> [ins·ti·'ɣar] *vt* to instigate; (*a algo malo*) to incite

instintivo, -a [ins·tin·'ti·βo, -a] *adj* instinctive

instinto [ins·'tin·to] *m* instinct

institución [ins·ti·tu·'sjon, -'θjon] *f* 1. (*social*) institution; ~ **penitenciaria** prison 2. (*fundación*) foundation

institucional [ins·ti·tu·sjo·'nal, -θjo·'nal] *adj* institutional

instituir [ins·ti·tu·'ir] *irr como huir* *vt* 1. (*fundar*) to found 2. (*establecer: comisión*) to set up; (*derecho*) to institute; (*norma*) to introduce

instituto [ins·ti·'tu·to] *m* 1. ENS (*de bachillerato*) secondary school, high school 2. (*científico*) institute

instrucción [ins·truk·'sjon, -'θjon] *f* 1. (*enseñanza*) teaching; (*en una máquina*) instruction 2. *pl* (*órdenes*) instructions *pl*, directions *pl*

instructivo, -a [ins·truk·'ti·βo, -a] *adj* instructive, educational

instructor(a) [ins·truk·'tor, --'to·ra] I. *m(f)* instructor II. *adj* instructional

instruido, -a [ins·tru·'i·ðo, -a] *adj* educated

instruir [ins·tru·'ir] *irr como huir* *vt* 1. (*enseñar*) to teach; (*en una máquina*) to instruct; (*en tarea específica*) to train 2. (*informar*) to inform

instrumental [ins·tru·men·'tal] *adj* t. MÚS instrumental

instrumento [ins·tru·'men·to] *m* instrument

insuficiencia [in·su·fi·'sjen·sja, -'θjen·θja] *f* insufficiency; MED failure

insuficiente [in·su·fi·'sjen·te, -'θjen·te]
I. *adj* insufficient II. *m* ENS fail; **sacar un ~** to get an F

insufrible [in·su·'fri·βle] *adj* insufferable

insular [in·su·'lar] *adj* insular

insulina [in·su·'li·na] *f* insulin

insulso, -a [in·'sul·so, -a] *adj* (*comida*) insipid, tasteless; (*persona, película*) dull

insultante [in·sul·'tan·te] *adj* insulting

insultar [in·sul·'tar] *vt* to insult; (*con injurias*) to abuse

insulto [in·'sul·to] *m* insult; (*injuria*) abuse

insuperable [in·su·pe·'ra·βle] *adj* insuperable, insurmountable; (*resultado*) unbeatable

insurrección [in·su·rrek·'sjon, -'θjon] *f* insurrection

insustituible [in·sus·ti·tu·'i·βle] *adj* irreplaceable

intachable [in·ta·'tʃa·βle] *adj* irreproachable; (*comportamiento*) faultless

intacto, -a [in·'tak·to, -a] *adj* (*no tocado*) untouched; (*no dañado*) intact

intangible [in·tan·'xi·βle] *adj* (*intocable, inmaterial*) intangible

integración [in·te·ɣra·'sjon, -'θjon] *f* integration

integral [in·te·'ɣral] *adj* 1. (*completo*) integral, full 2. (*pan*) wholegrain 3. (*elemento*) integral, intrinsic 4. MAT integral

integrar [in·te·'ɣrar] I. *vt* 1. (*constituir*) to constitute, to comprise 2. (*en conjunto*) *t.* MAT to integrate II. *vr:* **~se** to integrate

integridad [in·te·ɣri·'dad] *f* 1. (*totalidad*) entirety 2. (*honradez*) integrity 3. (*física*) physical well-being

integrismo [in·te·'ɣris·mo] *m* (*ideológico*) fundamentalism

íntegro, -a ['in·te·ɣro, -a] *adj* (*completo*) whole; (*persona*) honest, upright

intelectual [in·te·lek·tu·'al] *adj, mf* intellectual

inteligencia [in·te·li·'xen·sja, -θja] *f* *t.* POL intelligence; **servicio de ~** intelligence agency [*o* bureau]

inteligente [in·te·li·'xen·te] *adj* intelligent

inteligible [in·te·li·'xi·βle] *adj* comprehen-

sible; (*sonido*) *t.* FILOS intelligible

intemperie [in·tem·'pe·rje] *f* (*el aire libre*) **a la ~** out in the open

intención [in·ten·'sjon, -'θjon] *f* intention; (*propósito firme*) resolution; **sin ~** unintentionally; **con ~** deliberately; **tener buenas intenciones** to mean well

intencionado, -a [in·ten·sjo·'na·do, -a; -θjo·'na·do, -a] *adj* intentional; **bien ~** (*acción*) well-meant; (*persona*) well-meaning; **mal ~** unkind; (*persona*) malicious

intensidad [in·ten·si·'dad] *f* *t.* FÍS intensity; (*de tormenta*) severity; (*de viento*) force

intensificar <c → qu> [in·ten·si·fi·'kar] I. *vt* to intensify II. *vr:* **~se** (*tráfico, calor*) to increase; (*conflicto*) to intensify

intensivo, -a [in·ten·'si·βo, -a] *adj* intensive

intenso, -a [in·'ten·so, -a] *adj* (*fuerza, olor*) strong; (*frío, calor*) intense

intentar [in·ten·'tar] *vt* 1. (*probar*) to attempt, to try 2. (*proponerse*) to intend, to mean

intento [in·'ten·to] *m* attempt, try

intentona [in·ten·'to·na] *f* *inf* reckless attempt

interacción [in·ter·ak·'sjon, -'θjon] *f* interaction

interactivo, -a [in·ter·ak·'ti·βo, -a] *adj* interactive

intercalar [in·ter·ka·'lar] *vt* (*en un periódico*) to insert

intercambiar [in·ter·kam·'bjar] *vt* to interchange; (*opiniones*) to exchange; (*cosas*) to swap

intercambio [in·ter·'kam·bjo] *m* exchange

interceder [in·ter·se·'der, -θe·'der] *vi* to intercede; **~ en favor de alguien** to intercede on behalf of sb

interceptar [in·ter·sep·'tar, -θep·'tar] *vt* (*comunicaciones*) to cut off; (*el paso de algo*) to intercept

intercultural [in·ter·kul·tu·'ral] *adj* intercultural

interdisciplinar [in·ter·di·si·pli·'nar, -dis·θi·pli·'nar] *adj*, **interdisciplinario, -a** [in·ter·di·si·pli·'na·rjo, -a; in·ter·dis·θi·] *adj* interdisciplinary

interés [in·te·'res] *m* **1.** (*importancia*) concern **2.** (*deseo, atención*) interest; **tengo ~ por saber...** I'm interested in knowing... **3.** (*provecho*) interest; **el ~ público** the public's interest; **esto redunda en ~ tuyo** this redounds to your credit **4.** FIN interest; (*rendimiento*) yield; **un 10% de ~** 10% interest

interesado, -a [in·te·re·'sa·do, -a] **I.** *adj* **1.** (*con interés*) interested **2.** (*egoísta*) selfish, self-seeking **II.** *m, f* **1.** the interested party, the person concerned **2.** (*egoísta*) selfish person

interesante [in·te·re·'san·te] *adj* interesting

interesar [in·te·re·'sar] **I.** *vi* to be of interest **II.** *vr:* **~se 1.** (*mostrar interés*) **~se por algo** to become interested in sth **2.** (*preguntar por*) **~se por algo** to ask about sth

interferencia [in·ter·fe·'ren·sja, -θja] *f* t. FÍS, LING interference

interferir [in·ter·fe·'rir] *irr como* **sentir** *vi* t. FÍS to interfere; **eso no interfiere en mi decisión** that does not influence my decision

interfono [in·ter·'fo·no] *m* intercom

interino, -a [in·te·'ri·no, -a] **I.** *adj* **1.** (*funcionario*) temporary **2.** POL interim **II.** *m, f* **1.** (*suplente*) stand-in **2.** (*funcionario*) temporary [*o* acting] incumbent; (*maestro*) substitute teacher

interior [in·te·'rjor] **I.** *adj* interior; (*sin costa*) inland; **mercado ~** COM (*de la UE*) internal market; **ropa ~** underwear **II.** *m* interior; **Ministerio del Interior** POL Department of the Interior; **en el ~ de...** inside...

interiores [in·te·'rjo·res] *mpl Col* (*calzoncillos*) men's underpants *pl*

interiorizar <z → c> [in·te·rjo·ri·'sar, -'θar] *vt* to internalize

interjección [in·ter·xek·'sjon, -'θjon] *f* LING interjection, exclamation

interlocutor(a) [in·ter·lo·ku·'tor, -·'to·ra] *m(f)* speaker, interlocutor *form*

intermediario, -a [in·ter·me·'dja·rjo, -a] *m, f* **1.** (*mediador*) mediator, intermediary **2.** (*enlace*) go-between **2.** (*comerciante*) middleman

intermedio [in·ter·'me·djo] *m* interval

intermedio, -a [in·ter·'me·djo, -a] *adj* **1.** (*capa*) intermediate **2.** (*período de tiempo*) intervening

interminable [in·ter·mi·'na·βle] *adj* interminable, endless

intermitencia [in·ter·mi·'ten·sja, -θja] *f* **1.** (*calidad*) intermittency **2.** MED intermittence

intermitente [in·ter·mi·'ten·te] *m* intermittence; AUTO turn signal

internacional [in·ter·na·sjo·'nal, -θjo·'nal] *adj* international

internado [in·ter·'na·do] *m* boarding school

internado, -a [in·ter·'na·do, -a] *m, f* **1.** (*alumno*) boarder **2.** (*demente*) inmate

internar [in·ter·'nar] *vt* **~ en** (*hospital*) to admit to; (*asilo*) to commit to

internauta [in·ter·'nau·ta] *mf* COMPUT Internet user

internet [in·ter·'net] *f* COMPUT Internet

interno, -a [in·ter·no, -a] *adj* internal; **régimen ~** (*de una empresa*) internal management; (*de un partido*) internal affairs

interponer [in·ter·po·'ner] *irr como* **poner** **I.** *vt* **1.** (*entre varias cosas*) to interpose; (*entre dos cosas: silla*) to place **2.** (*en un asunto*) to intervene **3.** JUR to bring, to lodge **II.** *vr:* **~se** to intervene

interposición [in·ter·po·si·'sjon, -'θjon] *f* **1.** (*entre varias cosas*) interposition; (*de una silla*) placing between; (*de un papel*) insertion; (*de alguien*) coming between **2.** (*en un asunto*) intervention **3.** JUR bringing, lodging

interpretación [in·ter·pre·ta·'sjon, -'θjon] *f* **1.** (*de texto*) interpretation; (*traducción oral*) interpreting **2.** TEAT performance; MÚS rendering; **escuela de ~** TEAT stage [*o* acting] school

interpretar [in·ter·pre·'tar] *vt* **1.** (*texto, traducir oralmente*) to interpret **2.** TEAT to perform; MÚS to render

intérprete [in·'ter·pre·te] *mf* (*actor*) performer; (*traductor*) interpreter

interprofesional [in·ter·pro·fe·sjo·'nal] *adj* **Salario Mínimo Interprofesional** minimum wage

interpuesto, -a [in·ter·'pwes·to, -a] *pp*

de **interponer**

interrelacionado, -a [in·te·rre·la·sjo·'na·do, -a; -θjo·'na·do, -a] *adj* interrelated

interrogación [in·te·rro·γa·'sjon, -'θjon] *f* (*signo*) question mark

interrogante [in·te·rro·'γan·te] *m* question

interrogar <g → gu> [in·te·rro·'γar] *vt* to question; (*policía*) to interrogate

interrogatorio [in·te·rro·γa·'to·rjo] *m* interrogation, (cross-)examination

interrumpir [in·te·rrum·'pir] *vt* (*cortar*) to interrupt; (*bruscamente al hablar*) to break

interrupción [in·te·rrup·'sjon, -rruβ·'θjon] *f* (*corte*) break; **sin ~** uninterruptedly

interruptor [in·te·rrup·'tor] *m* ELEC switch

intersección [in·ter·sek·'sjon, -'θjon] *f* intersection

interurbano, -a [in·ter·ur·'βa·no, -a] *adj* intercity

intervalo [in·ter·'βa·lo] *m t.* MÚS interval; **a ~s** at intervals

intervención [in·ter·βen·'sjon, -'θjon] *f* **1.** (*participación*) participation **2.** (*en conflicto*) intervention **3.** (*mediación*) mediation **4.** POL intervention **5.** MED operation **6.** (*del teléfono*) tapping

intervenir [in·ter·βe·'nir] *irr como* venir **I.** *vi* **1.** (*tomar parte*) to participate **2.** (*en conflicto*) to intervene **3.** (*mediar*) to mediate **II.** *vt* **1.** MED to operate on **2.** (*incautar*) to seize **3.** (*teléfono*) to tap **4.** COM to audit

intestinal [in·tes·ti·'nal] *adj* intestinal

intestino [in·tes·'ti·no] *m* **1.** ANAT intestine; **el ~ delgado/grueso** the small/large intestine **2.** *pl* (*tripas*) intestines *pl*, bowels *pl*

intimar [in·ti·'mar] *vi* to become intimate [*o* friendly]

intimidación [in·ti·mi·da·'sjon, -'θjon] *f* intimidation

intimidad [in·ti·mi·'dad] *f* **1.** (*asuntos*) personal matters *pl*; (*privacidad*) privacy **2.** (*vida privada*) private life

intimidar [in·ti·mi·'dar] **I.** *vt* to intimidate **II.** *vr:* **~se** to be intimidated

intimidatorio, -a [in·ti·mi·da·'to·rjo, -a] *adj* intimidating

íntimo, -a ['in·ti·mo, -a] *adj* **1.** (*interior,*

interno) inner, innermost **2.** (*amigo*) intimate, close **3.** (*velada*) intimate

intocable [in·to·'ka·βle] *adj* untouchable

intolerable [in·to·le·'ra·βle] *adj* intolerable

intolerancia [in·to·le·'ran·sja, -θja] *f* intolerance

intolerante [in·to·le·'ran·te] *adj* intolerant

intoxicación [in·tok·si·ka·'sjon, -'θjon] *f* (*alimentos*) food poisoning; (*alcohol*) intoxication

intoxicar <c → qu> [in·tok·si·'kar] *vt, vr:* **~(se)** to poison

intranquilizar <z → c> [in·tran·ki·li·'sar, -'θar] *vt, vr:* **~(se)** to worry

intranquilo, -a [in·tran·'ki·lo, -a] *adj* **1.** (*preocupado*) worried, uneasy **2.** (*excitado*) agitated, restless

intransferible [in·trans·fe·'ri·βle] *adj* untransferable

intransigente [in·tran·si·'xen·te] *adj* intransigent; (*intolerante*) intolerant

intrascendente [in·tra·sen·'den·te, -tras·θen·'den·te] *adj* trivial

intratable [in·tra·'ta·βle] *adj* (*persona*) impossible

intrépido, -a [in·'tre·pi·do, -a] *adj* intrepid

intriga [in·'tri·γa] *f* **1.** (*maquinación*) intrigue **2.** (*de una película*) suspense

intrigante [in·tri·'γan·te] *adj* (*película*) gripping

intrigar <g → gu> [in·tri·'γar] **I.** *vi* to scheme **II.** *vt* to intrigue

introducción [in·tro·duk·'sjon, -'θjon] *f* introduction; COMPUT (*de datos*) input; (*de mercancías*) launching; (*de libro*) preface

introducir [in·tro·du·'sir, -'θir] *irr como* traducir **I.** *vt* (*llave*) to insert, to put in; (*medidas*) to introduce; COMPUT (*datos*) to enter, to input **II.** *vr:* **~se** (*meterse*) to get in(to); **~se en algo** to enter into sth

intromisión [in·tro·mi·'sjon] *f* interference

introvertido, -a [in·tro·βer·'ti·do, -a] *adj* introverted

intruso, -a [in·'tru·so, -a] *m, f* intruder; (*en reunión*)

intuición [in·twi·'sjon, -'θjon] *f* intuition

intuir [in·tu·'ir] *irr como huir vt* (*presentir*) to sense; **intuyo que...** I have a hunch that...

intuitivo, -a [in·twi·'ti·βo, -a] *adj* intuitive

inundación [i·nun·da·'sjon, -'θjon] *f* flood(ing)

inundar [i·nun·'dar] *vt* to flood

inusitado, -a [i·nu·si·'ta·do, -a] *adj* **1.** (*no habitual*) unusual, uncommon **2.** (*extraordinario*) unwonted

inusual [i·nu·su·'al] *adj* **1.** (*no habitual*) unusual **2.** (*extraordinario*) unwonted

inútil [in·'u·til] **I.** *adj* **1.** (*que no sirve*) useless **2.** (*esfuerzo*) vain **3.** (*sin sentido*) futile **II.** *mf* (*torpe*) incompetent person

inutilizar [z → c] [in·u·ti·li·'sar, -'θar] *vt* **1.** (*objeto*) to render useless **2.** (*al enemigo*) to defeat

invadir [im·ba·'dir] *vt* (*país*) to invade; (*entrar en gran número*) to overrun; (*privacidad*) to intrude on; **los hinchas invadieron el campo** the fans invaded the pitch [*o* field]

invalidar [im·ba·li·'dar] *vt* to invalidate

invalidez [im·ba·li·'des, -'deθ] *f* invalidity; MED disability

inválido, -a [im·'ba·li·do, -a] *adj* invalid; MED disabled

invariable [im·ba·'rja·βle] *adj t.* MAT invariable

invasión [im·ba·'sjon] *f t.* MIL, MED invasion; (*en privacidad*) intrusion

invasor(a) [im·ba·'sor, -·so·ra] *m(f)* invader

invencible [im·ben·'si·βle, -'θi·βle] *adj* invincible; (*insuperable*) unbeatable; (*obstáculo*) insurmountable

invención [im·ben·'sjon, -'θjon] *f* invention

inventar [im·ben·'tar] *vt* to invent

inventario [im·ben·'ta·rjo] *m* inventory

inventiva [im·ben·'ti·βa] *f* inventiveness

invento [im·'ben·to] *m* invention

inventor(a) [im·ben·'tor, -·to·ra] *m(f)* inventor

invernadero [im·ber·na·'de·ro] *m* greenhouse; **el efecto ~** the greenhouse effect

invernal [im·ber·'nal] *adj* winter; (*tiempo*) wintry

invernar [e → ie] [im·ber·'nar] *vi* to winter

inverosímil [im·be·ro·'si·mil] *adj* implausible; (*que no parece verdad*) improbable, hard to believe

inversión [im·ber·'sjon] *f* **1.** COM, FIN investment **2.** (*efecto de invertir*) inversion

inverso, -a [im·'ber·so] *adj* inverse, opposite; **a la inversa** inversely; **y a la inversa** vice versa; **en orden ~** in reverse order

inversor(a) [im·ber·'sor, -·so·ra] *m(f)* investor

invertido, -a [im·ber·'ti·do, -a] *adj* (*al revés*) inverted; (*volcado*) upside-down

invertir [im·ber·'tir] *irr como sentir vt* **1.** (*orden*) to invert **2.** (*volcar*) to turn upside down **3.** (*dinero*) to invest

investigación [im·bes·ti·ɣa·'sjon, -'θjon] *f* **1.** (*indagación*) investigation; (*averiguación*) inquiry **2.** (*ciencia*) research

investigador(a) [im·bes·ti·ɣa·'dor, -·do·ra] **I.** *adj* investigative; **comisión ~a** investigatory commission **II.** *m(f)* investigator, researcher

investigar [g → gu] [im·bes·ti·'ɣar] *vt* **1.** (*indagar*) to investigate; (*averiguar*) to inquire **2.** (*en la ciencia*) to research

inviable [im·bi·'a·βle] *adj* non-viable, unfeasible

invicto, -a [im·'bik·to, -a] *adj* unbeaten

invidente [im·bi·'den·te] *adj* blind

invierno [im·'bjer·no] *m* winter; *AmL* (*lluvias*) rainy season

invisibilidad [im·bi·si·βi·li·'dad] *f* invisibility

invisible [im·bi·'si·βle] *adj* invisible

invitación [im·bi·ta·'sjon, -'θjon] *f* invitation

invitado, -a [im·bi·'ta·do, -a] *m, f* guest

invitar [im·bi·'tar] **I.** *vt* **1.** (*convidar*) to invite **2.** (*instar*) to press; (*rogar*) to beg **II.** *vi* to invite; **esta vez invito yo** this time it's on me

invocar [c → qu] [im·bo·'kar] *vt* to invoke; (*suplicar*) to implore, to appeal; (*alegar*) to allege

involucrar [im·bo·lu·'krar] **I.** *vt* to involve **II.** *vr:* **~se** to interfere; (*intervenir*) to become [o get] involved

involuntario, -a [im·bo·lun·'ta·rjo, -a] *adj* involuntary; (*sin querer*) unintentional

invulnerable [im·bul·ne·'ra·βle] *adj* invulnerable

inyección [in·jek·'sjon, -'θjon] *f* **1.** MED injection **2.** TÉC fuel injection

inyectar [in·jek·'tar] *vt* to inject

ión [i·'on] *m* ion

ir [ir] *irr* **I.** *vi* **1.** (*general*) to go; **¡voy!** I'm coming!; **¡vamos!** let's go!, come on!; ~ **a pie** to go on foot; ~ **en bicicleta** to go by bicycle; ~ **a caballo** to go on horseback; **tengo que ~ a París** I have to go to Paris **2.** (*ir a buscar*) **iré por el pan** I'll go and get the bread **3.** (*progresar*) to go; **¿cómo va la tesina?** how is the dissertation going?; **¿cómo te va?** how are things?; **en lo que va de año** so far this year **4.** (*referirse*) **eso no va por ti** I'm not referring to you; **¿tú sabes de lo que va?** do you know what it is about? **5.** (*interj: sorpresa*) **¡qué va!** of course not! **6.** (*con verbo*) **iban charlando** they were chatting; **voy a hacerlo** I'm going to do it **II.** *vr:* ~**se 1.** (*marcharse*) to leave **2.** (*dirección*) to go; ~**se por las ramas** to beat about the bush

ira ['i·ra] *f* anger

irascible [i·ra·'si·βle, ···ras·'θi·βle] *adj* irascible

irgo ['ir·γo] *1. pres de* **erguir**

irguió [ir·'γjo] *3. pret de* **erguir**

iris ['i·ris] *m inv* ANAT iris; **arco** ~ rainbow

Irlanda [ir·'lan·da] *f* Ireland

irlandés, -esa [ir·lan·'des, -·'de·sa] **I.** *adj* Irish **II.** *m, f* Irishman *m*, Irishwoman *f*

ironía [i·ro·'ni·a] *f* irony

irónico, -a [i·'ro·ni·ko, -a] *adj* ironic

ironizar [<z → c>] [i·ro·ni·'sar, -'θar] *vt* to be ironic

irracional [i·rra·sjo·'nal, -θjo·'nal] *adj* irrational; **número** ~ MAT irrational number

irreal [i·rre·'al] *adj* unreal

irrealizable [i·rrea·li·'θa·βle, -'θa·βle] *adj* unrealizable, unfeasible

irrebatible [i·rre·βa·'ti·βle] *adj* irrefutable

irreconocible [i·rre·ko·no·'si·βle, -'θi·βle]

adj unrecognizable

irreflexivo, -a [i·rre·flek·'si·βo, -a] *adj* reckless; (*persona*) rash

irrefutable [i·rre·fu·'ta·βle] *adj* irrefutable

irregular [i·rre·γu·'lar] *adj* irregular

irrelevante [i·rre·le·'βan·te] *adj* irrelevant

irremediable [i·rre·me·'dja·βle] *adj* irremediable

irreparable [i·rre·pa·'ra·βle] *adj* irreparable

irrepetible [i·rre·pe·'ti·βle] *adj* unique

irreprimible [i·rre·pri·'mi·βle] *adj* irrepressible

irreprochable [i·rre·pro·'tʃa·βle] *adj* irreproachable

irresistible [i·rre·sis·'ti·βle] *adj* (*atractivo*) irresistible

irrespetuoso, -a [i·rres·pe·tu·'o·so, -a] *adj* disrespectful

irrespirable [i·rres·pi·'ra·βle] *adj* (*por tóxico*) unbreathable; (*aire*) stale, suffocating

irresponsable [i·rres·pon·'sa·βle] *adj* irresponsible

irreverente [i·rre·βe·'ren·te] *adj* irreverent

irreversible [i·rre·βer·'si·βle] *adj* irreversible

irrevocable [i·rre·βo·'ka·βle] *adj* irrevocable

irrisorio, -a [i·rri·'so·rjo, -a] *adj* derisory; **a precios** ~**s** at ridiculous prices

irritable [i·rri·'ta·βle] *adj* irritable

irritación [i·rri·ta·'sjon, -'θjon] *f* **1.** MED (*órgano*) inflammation; (*de piel*) irritation **2.** (*enfado*) irritation

irritante [i·rri·'tan·te] *adj* irritating

irritar [i·rri·'tar] **I.** *vt* **1.** (*enojar, molestar*) to irritate **2.** MED (*órgano*) to inflame **II.** *vr:* ~**se 1.** (*enojarse*) to become irritated **2.** MED (*órgano*) to become inflamed

irrompible [i·rrom·'pi·βle] *adj* unbreakable

irrumpir [i·rrum·'pir] *vi* ~ **en algo** to burst into sth

isla ['is·la] *f* island

Islam [is·'lan] *m* REL Islam

islámico, -a [is·'la·mi·ko, -a] *adj* Islamic

islandés, -esa [is·lan·'des, -·'de·sa] I. *adj* Icelandic II. *m, f* Icelander

Islandia [is·'lan·dja] *f* Iceland

isleño, -a [is·'le·ɲo, -a] *m, f* islander

islote [is·'lo·te] *m* islet

Israel [i·rra·'el/is·rra·'el] *m* Israel

israelí [i·rrae·'li/is·rrae·'li] *adj, mf* Israeli

Italia [i·'ta·lja] *f* Italy

italiano, -a [i·ta·'lja·no, -a] *adj, m, f* Italian

itinerancia [i·ti·ne·'ran·sja, -θja] *f* TEL roaming *no pl*

itinerante [i·ti·ne·'ran·te] *adj* itinerant, traveling

itinerario [i·ti·ne·'ra·rjo] *m* itinerary, schedule; (*vuelo*) route

ITV [i·te·'u·βe] *f abr de* **Inspección Técnica de Vehículos** MOT test

IVA ['i·βa] *m abr de* **Impuesto sobre el Valor Añadido** VAT

izar <z → c> [i·'sar, -'θar] *vt* to hoist

izqda. *adj,* **izqdo.** [is·'kjer·da, iθ-] *adj abr de* **izquierda, izquierdo** left

izquierda [is·'kjer·da, iθ-] *f* **1.** (*mano*) left hand **2.** POL left **3.** (*lado*) left side; **a la ~** to the left

izquierdo, -a [is·'kjer·do, -a; iθ-] *adj* left; (*zurdo*) left-handed; **levantarse con el pie ~** to get up on the wrong side of the bed

J

J, j ['xo·ta] *f* J, j; ~ **de Juan** J as in Juliet

ja [xa] *interj* ha

jabalí [xa·βa·'li] *m* <jabalíes> wild boar

jabalina [xa·βa·'li·na] *f* DEP javelin

jabón [xa·'βon] *m* **1.** (*para lavar*) soap; **pastilla de ~** bar of soap **2.** PRico, Arg (*susto*) fright ▸ **dar ~ a alguien** to soft-soap sb

jabonar [xa·βo·'nar] *vt* to soap

jacal [xa·'kal] *m Méx, Ven* hut

jacinto [xa·'sin·to, -'θin·to] *m* BOT hyacinth

jaco ['xa·ko] *m pey* (*caballo*) nag

jactancioso, -a [xak·tan·'sjo·so, -a; -'θjo·so, -a] *adj* boastful

jactarse [xak·'tar·se] *vr* ~ **de algo** to boast of [*o* about] sth

jade ['xa·de] *m* jade

jadear [xa·de·'ar] *vi* to pant

jaguar [xa·'ɣwar] *m* ZOOL jaguar

jagüey [xa·'ɣwei] *m AmL* (*balsa*) pool; (*cisterna*) cistern

jaiba [xa·i·βa] I. *adj* **1.** *Ant, Méx* (*astuto*) cunning **2.** *Cuba* (*perezoso*) lazy II. *f AmL* (*cangrejo*) crab

jalado, -a [xa·'la·do, -a] *adj* **1.** *Méx, Ven* (*exagerado*) exaggerated **2.** *AmL* (*demacrado*) emaciated **3.** *AmL* (*obsequioso*) obliging **4.** *AmL* (*borracho*) drunk

jalar [xa·'lar] I. *vt* **1.** *AmL* (*una cuerda*) to pull **2.** *AmL* (*una persona*) to attract **3.** *inf* (*comer*) to guzzle, to wolf down II. *vi Bol, PRico, Urug, Ven* (*largarse*) to clear off III. *vr:* **~se** *AmL* to get drunk

jalea [xa·'lea] *f* jelly

jalear [xa·le·'ar] *vt* (*animar*) to encourage

jaleo [xa·'leo] *m* **1.** (*barullo*) commotion; **armar ~** to make a scene **2.** (*desorden*) confusion

jamás [xa·'mas] *adv* never; ~ **de los jamases** never in your life; **nunca digas nunca ~** never (ever) say never; **nunca ~** never again

jamelgo [xa·'mel·ɣo] *m inf* (*caballo*) nag

jamón [xa·'mon] *m* ham; ~ **de York** boiled ham; ~ **serrano** cured ham ▸ **¡y un ~!** *inf* get away!

Japón [xa·'pon] *m* Japan

japonés, -esa [xa·po·'nes, -·'ne·sa] *adj, m, f* Japanese

jaque ['xa·ke] *m* check; ~ **mate** checkmate; **dar ~** to check ▸ **tener a alguien en ~** *fig* to keep sb in check

jaqueca [xa·'ke·ka] *f* (severe) headache, migraine

jara ['xa·ra] *f Guat, Méx* (*flecha*) arrow

jarabe [xa·'ra·βe] *m* syrup; (*para la tos*) cough mixture [*o* syrup]; ~ **de arce** maple syrup ▸ **dar ~ de palo a alguien** *inf* to give sb a thrashing

jarana [xa·'ra·na] *f* **1.** *inf* (*juerga*) spree **2.** *Méx* MÚS small guitar **3.** *AmL* (*burla*) joke **4.** *AmC* (*deuda*) debt **5.** *Col* (*embuste*) trick

jardín [xar'din] *m* garden; ~ **de infancia** (*hasta los tres años*) nursery school; (*a partir de tres años*) kindergarten; **los jardines de una ciudad** the municipal parks

jardinear [xar·di·ne·'ar] *vt AmL* to garden

jardinera [xar·di·'ne·ra] *f* (*maceta*) window box

jardinería [xar·di·ne·'ri·a] *f* gardening

jardinero, -a [xar·di·'ne·ro, -a] *m, f* gardener

jareta [xa·'re·ta] *f CRi, Par* (*bragueta*) fly, zipper

jarocho, -a [xa·'ro·tʃo, -a] *adj AmL* (*arrogante*) rude

jarra ['xa·rra] *f* jar; (*de agua*) jug, pitcher ▶ **ponerse en ~s** to stand with arms akimbo

jarro ['xa·rro] *m* jug, pitcher; **echar un ~ de agua fría** *fig* to pour cold water on

jarrón [xa·'rron] *m* vase

jauja ['xau·xa] *f* earthly paradise; **para ti la vida es Jauja** you're living in clover

jaula ['xau·la] *f* (*para animales*) cage

jauría [xau·'ri·a] *f* pack of hounds

jazmín [xas·'min, xaθ-] *m* jasmine

jazz [dʒas] *m* jazz

J.C. [xe·su·'kris·to] *abr de* **Jesucristo** J.C.

jebe ['xe·βe] *m AmL* (*caucho*) rubber

jefatura [xe·fa·'tu·ra] *f* **1.** (*cargo*) leadership **2.** (*sede*) ~ **del gobierno** seat of government; ~ **de policía** police headquarters

jefazo, -a [xe·'fa·so, -a; -θo, -θa] *m, f inf* big boss

jefe, -a ['xe·fe, -a] *m, f* head, boss; (*de una banda*) leader; ~ **de filas** DEP team captain; ~ **de gobierno** head of the government; ~ **de(l) Estado** head of state; **redactor ~** editor-in-chief

jeque ['xe·ke] *m* sheik(h)

jerarca [xe·'rar·ka] *mf* high official

jerarquía [xe·rar·'ki·a] *f* hierarchy

jerárquico, -a [xe·'rar·ki·ko, -a] *adj* hierarchical

jerez [xe·'res, -'reθ] *m* sherry

jerga ['xer·ɣa] *f* jargon

jeringa [xe·'rin·ga] *f* (*instrumento*) syringe

jeringuilla [xe·rin·'gi·ja, -ʎa] *f* syringe

jeroglífico [xe·ro·'ɣli·fi·ko] *m* hieroglyph(ic); (*pasatiempo*) rebus, puzzle

jersey [xer·'sei] *m* pullover; ~ **de cuello alto** turtleneck sweater

Jesucristo [xe·su·'kris·to] *m* Jesus Christ

Jesús [xe·'sus] *m* Jesus ▶ ¡~! (*al estornudar*) bless you!; (*interjección*) good heavens!

jeta ['xe·ta] *f inf* (*cara*) mug, dial; **ése tiene una ~ increíble** *fig* what incredible cheek that guy has

jíbaro, -a ['xi·βa·ro, -a] *adj* **1.** *AmL* (*campesino*) country, peasant; (*costumbres, vida*) rural **2.** *AmL* (*planta, animal*) wild **3.** *Ant, Méx* (*huraño*) shy

jícama ['xi·ka·ma] *f Méx* BOT jicama, Mexican turnip

jícaro ['xi·ka·ro] *m AmC* (*árbol*) calabash tree

jilguero [xil·'ɣe·ro] *m* goldfinch

jinete [xi·'ne·te] *m* (*persona*) horseman; (*profesional*) rider

jinetear [xi·ne·te·'ar] *vt AmL* to break in (horses)

jirafa [xi·'ra·fa] *f* giraffe

jirón [xi·'ron] *m* shred; **hacer algo jirones** to tear sth to shreds

jitomate [xi·to·'ma·te] *m Méx* (*tomate*) tomato

JJ.OO. ['xwe·ɣos o·'lim·pi·kos] *abr de* **Juegos Olímpicos** Olympic Games

jo [xo] *interj* **1.** (*so*) whoa **2.** (*sorpresa*) ¡~! well, well!

jockey ['xo·kei] *m* jockey

jocoso, -a [xo·'ko·so, -a] *adj* humorous, jocular

jolgorio [xol·'ɣo·rjo] *m* merriment

jolín [xo·'lin] *interj*, **jolines** [xo·'li·nes] *interj* sugar

jopé [xo·'pe] *interj* sugar

jornada [xor·'na·da] *f* **1.** (*de trabajo*) working day; (*tiempo trabajado*) hours of work; ~ **continua** continuous schedule without lunch break, finishing early; ~ **partida** split shift; **trabajo media ~** I work half a day [*o* part-time] **2.** (*viaje*) day's journey **3.** pl (congreso, simposio) conference

jornal [xor·'nal] m (paga) day's wage [o pay]

jornalero, -a [xor·na·'le·ro, -a] m, f day laborer

joroba [xo·'ro·βa] f (de persona) hunched back; (de camello) hump

jorobado, -a [xo·ro·'βa·do, -a] adj hunchbacked

jorobar [xo·ro·'βar] **I.** vt inf to annoy **II.** vr: ~se inf **1.** (enojarse) to get annoyed **2.** (aguantar) to put up with it; **si no le gusta, ¡que se jorobe!** if he doesn't like it, he can lump it!

jorongo [xo·'ron·go] m Méx poncho

jota ['xo·ta] f (letra) j ▶ **no entender** [o **saber**] **ni ~** inf not to have a clue

joto ['xo·to] m **1.** Col (paquete) bundle **2.** Méx pey (homosexual) queer

joven ['xo·βen] **I.** adj young; **de muy ~** in early youth **II.** mf young man m, young woman f

jovial [xo·'βjal] adj cheerful, jovial

joya ['xo·ja] f (alhaja) jewel; **las ~s** jewelry; **esta mujer de la limpieza es una ~** this cleaning lady [o cleaner] is a gem

joyería [xo·je·'ri·a] f (tienda) jeweler's (shop)

joyero [xo·'je·ro] m jewel case

joyero, -a [xo·'je·ro, -a] m, f jeweler

juanete [xwa·'ne·te] m (del pie) bunion

jubilación [xu·βi·la·'sjon, -'θjon] f **1.** (acción) retirement **2.** (pensión) pension

jubilado, -a [xu·βi·'la·do, -a] m, f pensioner, retiree

jubilar [xu·βi·'lar] **I.** vt to pension off **II.** vr: ~se **1.** (retirarse) to retire **2.** AmC (hacer novillos) to play truant

júbilo ['xu·βi·lo] m joy, jubilation

jubiloso, -a [xu·βi·'lo·so, -a] adj jubilant

judía [xu·'di·a] f BOT bean; ~ **verde** green bean

judicial [xu·di·'sjal, -'θjal] adj judicial

judío, -a [xu·'di·o, -a] **I.** adj Jewish **II.** m, f Jew

judo ['dʒu·do] m DEP judo

juego ['xwe·ɣo] m **1.** (diversión) game; ~ **de mesa** board game; **hacer ~s malabares** to juggle **2.** DEP play; ~ **en blanco** zero-zero tie; ~ **limpio** fair play; ~ **sucio** foul play; **fuera de ~** (persona) offside **3.** (conjunto) set; ~ **de café** coffee set; **hacer ~** to match

juerga ['xwer·ɣa] f spree; **ayer estuve de ~** inf I was (out) partying yesterday

jueves ['xwe·βes] m inv Thursday; **Jueves Santo** Maundy Thursday; v. t. **lunes**

juez [xwes, xweθ] mf t. JUR judge; ~ **de instrucción** JUR examining magistrate; ~ **de línea** DEP linesman

jugada [xu·'ɣa·da] f **1.** DEP play **2.** (jugarreta) bad turn; **hacer** [o **gastar**] **una ~ a alguien** to play a dirty trick on sb

jugador(a) [xu·ɣa·'do, -·'do·ra] m(f) t. DEP player

jugar [xu·'ɣar] irr **I.** vi **1.** (a un juego, deporte) to play; ~ **limpio/sucio** to play fair/unfairly; **¿quién juega?** (juego de mesa) whose move is it?; (partido en la TV, radio) who's playing?; **¿puedo ~?** can I join in? **2.** (bromear) to play about **3.** ~ **a la bolsa** to speculate on the stock exchange **II.** vt **1.** (un juego, una partida) to play **2.** (apostar) to gamble; ~ **fuerte** to play for high stakes **III.** vr: ~se **1.** (la lotería) to be drawn **2.** (apostar) ~se **algo** to gamble [o to bet] on sth **3.** (arriesgar) to risk; ~se **el todo por el todo** to stake one's all ▶ **jugársela a alguien** to take sb for a ride

jugarreta [xu·ɣa·'rre·ta] f inf dirty trick

jugo ['xu·ɣo] m **1.** (de fruta, carne) juice **2.** (esencia) essence; **declaraciones con mucho ~** fig important declarations

jugoso, -a [xu·'ɣo·so, -a] adj juicy

juguete [xu·'ɣe·te] m toy

juguetear [xu·ɣe·te·'ar] vi **1.** (con las llaves, una pelota) to play **2.** (los niños) to romp

juguetería [xu·ɣe·te·'ri·a] f toyshop

juguetón, -ona [xu·ɣe·'ton, -·'to·na] adj playful

juicio ['xwi·sjo, -θjo] m **1.** (facultad

para juzgar) reason **2.** (*razón*) sense; **falta de ~** lack of common sense; **recobrar el ~** to come to one's senses; **tú no estás en tu sano ~** you're not in your right mind **3.** (*opinión*) opinion; **a mi ~** to my mind; **emitir un ~ sobre algo** to pass judgment on sth **4.** JUR trial; **llevar a alguien a ~** to take sb to court; **el (día del) Juicio final** REL the Last Judgment

juicioso, -a [xwiˈsjoˑso, -a; -ˈθjoˑso, -a] *adj* (*sensato*) sensible; (*acertado*) fitting

julepe [xuˈleˑpe] *m AmL* **1.** (*miedo*) scare **2.** (*ajetreo*) drudgery; **dar un ~ a alguien** *inf* to make sb sweat

julio [ˈxuˑljo] *m* **1.** (*mes*) July; *v. t.* **marzo 2.** FÍS joule

juma [ˈxuˑma] *f AmL inf* drunkenness

jumarse [xuˈmarˑse] *vr Col, Cuba* to get drunk

junco [ˈxunˑko] *m* BOT reed

jungla [ˈxunˑgla] *f* jungle

junio [ˈxuˑnjo] *m* June; *v. t.* **marzo**

júnior [ˈdʒuˑnjor] *m* <juniors> junior

junta [ˈxunˑta] *f* **1.** (*comité*) committee; (*consejo*) council; **~ directiva** COM board of directors **2.** (*reunión*) meeting; **~ general** general meeting; **~ de accionistas** shareholders' meeting

juntar [xunˈtar] **I.** *vt* **1.** (*aproximar*) **la mesa a la pared** to move the table over to the wall; **~ las sillas** to put the chairs together **2.** (*unir*) to join **3.** (*reunir: personas*) to assemble; (*objetos*) to put together; (*dinero*) to collect **II.** *vr:* **~se 1.** (*reunirse*) to meet **2.** (*unirse*) to come together **3.** (*aproximarse*) to come closer **4.** (*vivir juntos*) to move in (together)

junto [ˈxunˑto] **I.** *adv* **hacerlo todo ~** to do it all at the same time **II.** *prep* **1.** (*local*) **~ a** near to; **estábamos ~ a la entrada** we were at the entrance; **pasaron ~ a nosotros** they walked past us **2.** (*con movimiento*) **~ a** beside; **pon la silla ~ a la mesa** put the chair next to the table **3.** (*con, en compañía de*) **~ con** together with

junto, -a [ˈxunˑto, -a] *adj* joined; **nos sentamos todos ~s** we all sat together

jura [ˈxuˑra] *f* oath; (*acto*) swearing in

jurado [xuˈraˑdo] *m* **1.** JUR (*miembro*) juror; (*tribunal*) jury **2.** (*de un examen*) qualified examiner **3.** (*de un concurso*) panel member

jurado, -a [xuˈraˑdo, -a] *adj* qualified; **intérprete ~** sworn interpreter

juramento [xuraˈmenˑto] *m* **1.** *t.* JUR (*jura*) oath; **falso ~** perjury; **estar bajo ~** to be on oath; **tomar ~ a alguien** to swear sb in **2.** (*blasfemia*) swearword

jurar [xuˈrar] *vi, vt* to swear; **~ por alguien** to swear by sb; **jurársela a alguien** *inf* to swear vengeance on sb

jurídico, -a [xuˈriˑdiˑko, -a] *adj* legal, lawful

jurisdicción [xurisdikˈsjon, -ˈθjon] *f* **1.** JUR (*potestad*) jurisdiction **2.** (*territorio*) administrative district

jurisdiccional [xurisdiksjoˈnal, -θjoˈnal] *adj* jurisdictional, judicial; **aguas ~es** territorial waters

jurisprudencia [xurispruˈdenˑsja, -θja] *f* **1.** (*legislación*) jurisprudence **2.** (*ciencia*) science of law

jurista [xuˈrisˑta] *mf* jurist

justamente [xustaˈmenˑte] *adv* justly; (*precisamente*) precisely

justicia [xusˈtiˑsja, -θja] *f* justice; (*derecho*) law; **hacer ~ a alguien** to do sb justice

justificable [xustifiˈkaˑβle] *adj* justifiable

justificación [xustifikaˈsjon, -ˈθjon] *f* justification; **no hay ~ para lo que has hecho** there's no excuse for what you've done

justificante [xustifiˈkanˑte] *m* (*de ausencia*) note of absence

justificar <c → qu> [xustifiˈkar] **I.** *vt* (*disculpar*) to justify; **mi desconfianza es justificada** my distrust is vindicated **II.** *vr:* **~se** to justify oneself

justo [ˈxusˑto] *adv* **1.** (*exactamente*) right; **llegué ~ a tiempo** I arrived just in time **2.** (*escasamente*) scarcely; **tengo ~ para vivir** I have just enough to live on

justo, -a [ˈxusˑto, -a] *adj* **1.** (*persona, decisión*) just **2.** (*exacto*) exact; (*acertado*) correct; **el peso ~** the correct weight; **tener el dinero ~** to have exact change **3.** (*escaso*) **ha venido muy justo el dinero** money's been very tight **4.** (*ajustado*) close-fitting; **este abrigo me viene ~** this coat is rather tight for me

juvenil [xu·βe·'nil] **I.** *adj* youthful, young **II.** *mf* DEP **juego con los ~es** I'm in the junior team

juventud [xu·βen·'tud] *f* **1.** (*edad*) youth **2.** (*estado*) early life **3.** (*jóvenes*) young people

juzgado [xus·'ɣa·do, xuθ-] *m* court; **~ de guardia** police court

juzgar <g → gu> [xus·'ɣar, xuθ-] *vt* **1.** (*juez: decidir*) to judge; (*condenar*) to sentence **2.** (*opinar sobre*) to judge; (*considerar*) to consider, to deem; **~ mal a alguien** to misjudge sb; **no te juzgo capaz de hacerlo** I don't think you're capable of doing it

K

K, k [ka] *f* K, k; **~ de Kenia** K as in Kilo

kaki [ka·ki] *adj* khaki

karaoke [ka·ra·'o·ke] *m* karaoke

karate [ka·'ra·te] *m*, **kárate** ['ka·ra·te] *m* DEP karate

kayak [ka·'jak] *m* <kayaks> DEP kayak

keroseno [ke·ro·'se·no] *m* kerosene

ketchup ['ked·tʃup] *m* <ketchups> ketchup

kg [ki·lo·'ɣra·mo] *abr de* **kilogramo** kg

kikiriki [ki·ki·ri·'ki] *m* cock-a-doodle-doo

kilo ['ki·lo] *m* kilo

kilocaloría [ki·lo·ka·lo·'ri·a] *f* kilocalorie

kilogramo [ki·lo·'ɣra·mo] *m* kilogram

kilohercio [ki·lo·'er·sjo, -θjo] *m* kilohertz

kilolitro [ki·lo·'li·tro] *m* kiloliter

kilometraje [ki·lo·me·'tra·xe] *m* AUTO mileage

kilométrico, -a [ki·lo·'me·tri·ko] *adj* kilometric

kilómetro [ki·'lo·me·tro] *m* kilometer

kilovatio [ki·lo·'βa·tjo] *m* kilowatt

kinder ['kin·der] *m inv AmL*, **kindergarten** [kin·der·'ɣar·ten] *m inv* kindergarten, nursery school

kit [kit] *m* <kits> kit

kleenex® ['kli·neks] *m inv*, **klínex** ['kli·neks] *m inv* Kleenex®, tissue

km [ki·'lo·me·tro] *abr de* **kilómetro** km.

km/h [ki·'lo·me·tro por 'o·ra] *abr de* **kilómetro por hora** km/h

L

L, l ['e·le] *f* L,l; **~ de Lisboa** L as in Lima

l ['li·tro] *abr de* **litro(s)** l

la [la] **I.** *art def v.* **el, la II.** *pron pers, f sing* **1.** *objeto directo: f sing* her; (*cosa*) it; **¡tráeme~!** bring her/it to me!; **mi bicicleta y ~ tuya** my bicycle and yours **2.** (*con relativo*) **~ que...** the one that...; **~ cual** which **III.** *m* MÚS A; **en ~ bemol menor** in A flat minor

laberinto [la·βe·'rin·to] *m* **1.** (*lugar*) labyrinth, maze **2.** (*maraña*) tangle

labia ['la·βja] *f inf* glibness; **tener mucha ~** to be a smooth talker

labial [la·'βjal] *adj* labial

lábil ['la·βil] *adj* **1.** *t.* QUÍM (*carácter*) labile **2.** (*frágil*) frail

labio ['la·βjo] *m* **1.** (*boca*) lip; **estar sin despegar los ~s** to not say a word **2.** (*borde*) rim **3.** *pl* (*vulva*) labia *pl*

labor [la·'βor] *f* work; (*de coser*) needlework; (*labranza*) plowing; **no estoy por la ~** I don't feel like it

laborable [la·βo·'ra·βle] *adj* **día ~** working day

laboral [la·βo·'ral] *adj* labor

laboratorio [la·βo·ra·'to·rjo] *m* laboratory, lab

laborioso, -a [la·βo·'rjo·so, -a] *adj* hard-working, industrious; (*difícil*) arduous

labrador(a) [la·βra·'dor, --do·ra] *m(f)* farmhand

labranza [la·'βran·sa, -θa] *f* (*cultivo*) tillage

labrar [la·'βrar] *vt* **1.** (*un material*) to work; (*cristal*) to etch; **sin ~** plain **2.** (*cultivar, en jardín*) to work; (*arar*) to plow

labriego, -a [la·ˈβrje·ɣo, -a] *m, f* farm worker

laburar [la·βu·ˈrar] *vi Arg, Urug inf* to work

laburo [la·ˈβu·ro] *m Arg, Urug inf* work

laca [ˈla·ka] *f* **1.** (*pintura*) lacquer, shellac **2.** (*para el pelo*) hairspray

lacayo [la·ˈka·jo] *m* footman; *pey* (*adulador*) lackey

lacho [ˈla·tʃo] *m Chile, Perú* (*enamorado*) lover; (*pisaverde*) dandy

lacio, -a [ˈla·sjo, -a; ˈla·θjo-] *adj* (*cabello*) straight, lank

lacónico, -a [la·ˈko·ni·ko, -a] *adj* brief; (*persona*) laconic

lacra [ˈla·kra] *f* **1.** (*de una enfermedad*) mark **2.** (*vicio*) blight

lacrar [la·ˈkrar] *vt* (*cerrar*) to seal

lacre [ˈla·kre] *m* sealing wax

lacrimógeno, -a [la·kri·ˈmo·xe·no, -a] *adj* tear; **gas ~** tear gas

lactancia [lak·ˈtan·sja, -θja] *f* breastfeeding; (*período*) lactation

lactante [lak·ˈtan·te] **I.** *adj* nursing; **mujer ~** nursing mother **II.** *mf* nursling

lácteo, -a [ˈlak·teo, -a] *adj* milk, dairy; *fig* milky; **vía láctea** ASTR Milky Way

lactosa [lak·ˈto·sa] *f* lactose

ladeado, -a [la·de·ˈa·do, -a] *adj* tilted

ladear [la·de·ˈar] **I.** *vt* **1.** (*inclinar*) to slant **2.** (*desviar*) to skirt **II.** *vr:* **~se** **1.** (*inclinarse*) to lean **2.** *Chile* (*enamorarse*) **~se de alguien** to fall in love with sb

ladera [la·ˈde·ra] *f* slope, hillside

ladilla [la·ˈdi·ja, -ʎa] *f* crab louse

ladino, -a [la·ˈdi·no] *adj* cunning

lado [ˈla·do] *m* **1.** *t.* MAT side; **a ambos ~s** on both sides; **por el ~ materno** on the mother's side; **ir de un ~ a otro** to go back and forth; **por todos ~s** everywhere; **al ~** nearby; **la casa de al ~** the house next-door; **al ~ de** (*junto a*) beside, next to; **al ~ mío, a mi ~** next to me, by my side; **por un ~..., y por el otro ~...** on the one hand..., and on the other hand... **2.** *ir a algún otro ~* to go somewhere else; **~ a ~** side by side **3.** (*punto de vista*) side; **el ~ bueno de la vida** the good side of life; **su ~ débil** his/her weak spot **4.** (*camino*) direc-

tion; **ir por otro ~** to go another way **5.** (*partido*) **me puse de tu ~** I sided with you ▶ **dejar de ~ a alguien** to ignore sb; **mirar de ~ a alguien** to look out of the corner of one's eye at sb

ladrar [la·ˈdrar] *vi* to bark

ladrido [la·ˈdri·do] *m* bark

ladrillo [la·ˈdri·jo, -ʎo] *m* brick

ladrón [la·ˈdron] *m* (*enchufe*) multiple socket

ladrón, -ona [la·ˈdron, -·ˈdro·na] *m, f* thief, robber

lagar [la·ˈɣar] *m* **1.** (*aceite*) oil press; (*vino*) winepress **2.** (*edificio*) press house

lagartija [la·ɣar·ˈti·xa] *f* small lizard

lagarto [la·ˈɣar·to] *m* **1.** (*reptil*) lizard **2.** *AmL* (*caimán*) alligator

lago [ˈla·ɣo] *m* lake

lágrima [ˈla·ɣri·ma] *f* tear ▶ **deshacerse en ~s** to burst into tears

lagrimal [la·ɣri·ˈmal] *m* corner of the eye

laguna [la·ˈɣu·na] *f* **1.** (*agua salada*) lagoon; (*dulce*) small lake **2.** (*omisión*) gap; **~ en la memoria** memory lapse

laico, -a [ˈlai·ko, -a] *adj* lay

lamentable [la·men·ˈta·βle] *adj* regrettable

lamentación [la·men·ta·ˈsjon, -ˈθjon] *f* lamentation

lamentar [la·men·ˈtar] **I.** *vt* to regret; **lo lamento** I'm sorry **II.** *vr* **~se de algo** to complain about sth

lamento [la·ˈmen·to] *m* lament

lamer [la·ˈmer] *vt* to lick

lamido, -a [la·ˈmi·do] *m* licking

lámina [ˈla·mi·na] *f* **1.** (*hojalata*) tin plate; (*hoja de metal*) sheet; (*segmento*) lamina **2.** (*ilustración*) print

laminar [la·mi·ˈnar] **I.** *adj* **1.** (*en forma de lámina*) laminar **2.** (*formado de láminas*) laminated **II.** *vt* **1.** (*cortar*) to split **2.** (*guarnecer*) to laminate

lámpara [ˈlam·pa·ra] *f* lamp, light; **~ fluorescente** fluorescent lamp; **~ de pie** floor lamp

lamparilla [lam·pa·ˈri·ja, -ʎa] *f* (*luz*) small lamp

lamparón [lam·pa·ˈron] *m* (*mancha*) grease stain

lana [ˈla·na] *f* **1.** (*material, tela*) wool

2. inf (dinero) dough; **tienen mucha ~** they're loaded

lanar [la·'nar] adj wool-bearing; **ganado ~** sheep

lance ['lan·se, 'lan·θe] m throw; **~ de amor** love affair; **~ de fortuna** stroke of luck

lancha ['lan·tʃa] f motorboat; **~ a remolque** barge; **~ de salvamento** lifeboat

langosta [laŋ·'gos·ta] f **1.** (insecto) locust **2.** (crustáceo) lobster

langostino [laŋ·gos·'ti·no] m prawn

langucia [laŋ·'gu·sja, -θja] f AmL hunger

lánguido, -a ['laŋ·gido, -a] adj **1.** (débil) weak **2.** (espíritu) languid

lanilla [la·'ni·ja, -ʎa] f nap

lanoso, -a [la·'no·so, -a] adj, **lanudo, -a** [la·'nu·do, -a] adj woolly; (oveja) wool-bearing

lanza ['lan·sa, -θa] f lance ▶ **romper una ~ en favor de alguien** to stick up for sb

lanzacohetes [lan·sa·ko·'e·tes, lan·θa-] m inv rocket launcher

lanzadera [lan·sa·'de·ra, lan·θa-] f shuttle; (plataforma) platform, launch(ing) pad

lanzado, -a [lan·'sa·do, -a; lan·'θa-] adj **1.** (decidido) determined; (emprendedor) enterprising **2.** (impetuoso) impetuous; (fogoso) forward

lanzador(a) [lan·sa·'dor, lan·'θa-] m(f) thrower; (béisbol) bowler, pitcher

lanzallamas [lan·sa·'ja·mas, lan·θa·ʎa-] m inv flamethrower

lanzamiento [lan·sa·'mjen·to, lan·θa-] m throw; **~ comercial** commercial promotion, product launch; **~ espacial** space launch; **~ de peso** DEP shot put

lanzamisiles [lan·sa·mi·'si·les, lan·θa-] m inv missile-launcher

lanzar <z → c> [lan·'sar, -'θar] **I.** vt **1.** (arrojar) **~ algo/alguien** to throw at [o to] sth/sb **2.** (al mercado) to launch **II.** vr **~se a/sobre algo/alguien** to throw oneself at/against sth/sb; **~se al agua** to dive into the water; **~se en paracaídas** to parachute; **~se en picado** to nosedive; **~se a algo** to undertake sth

lapa ['la·pa] f ZOOL limpet; **pegarse como**

una ~ inf (persona) to stick like a leech

lapicero [la·pi·'θe·ro, -·'θe·ro] m pencil

lápida ['la·pi·da] f stone tablet, gravestone

lapidar [la·pi·'dar] vt to stone

lápiz ['la·pis, 'la·piθ] m pencil; **~ de labios** lipstick; **~ de ojos** eye pencil; **~ de color** crayon

lapso ['lap·so] m **1.** (período) ~ (de tiempo) lapse **2.** v. lapsus

lapsus ['lap·sus] m inv blunder

largar <g → gu> [lar·'ɣar] **I.** vt **1.** (soltar) to release **2.** inf (golpe) to land; (bofetada) to let fly **3.** inf (discurso) to give **II.** vr: **~se** **1.** (irse) to leave; (de casa) to leave home **2.** AmL (comenzar) to begin; **~se a hacer algo** to start to do sth **III.** vi inf to yak

largo ['lar·ɣo] **I.** adv plenty; **tenemos comida para ~** we have plenty of food; **~ y tendido** at length ▶ **a lo ~ de la playa** along the beach; **a lo ~ del día** throughout the day; **¡~!** (de aquí) clear off! **II.** m length; **nadar tres ~s** to swim three lengths of the pool; **diez metros de ~** ten meters long

largo, -a ['lar·ɣo, -a] adj long; **a ~ plazo a la larga** in the long term [o run]; **dar largas a algo** to put off doing sth; **el pantalón te está ~** your pants are too long for you; **ir de ~** to be in a long dress; (de gala) to be in formal dress; **pasar de ~** to pass by; fig to ignore; **tener las manos largas** (pegar) to be free with one's hands; (robar) to be light-fingered

largometraje [lar·ɣo·me·'tra·xe] m full-length [o feature] film

larguero [lar·'ɣe·ro] m DEP crossbar

largura [lar·'ɣu·ra] f length

laringe [la·'rin·xe] f larynx

larva ['lar·βa] f larva

las [las] **I.** art def v. **el, la II.** pron pers f pl **1.** (objeto directo) them; **¡míra~!** look at them! **2.** (con relativo) **~ que...** the ones that...; **~ cuales** those which

lascivo, -a [la·'si·βo, las·'θi·βo, -a] adj lascivious

láser ['la·ser] m laser

lástima ['las·ti·ma] f pity; **dar ~** to inspire

pity; **su último libro da ~** his/her latest book is pathetic; **¡qué ~!** what a pity!

lastimar [las·ti·'mar] I. vt 1. (herir) to hurt 2. (agraviar) to offend II. vr: **~se** 1. (herirse) to hurt oneself 2. (quejarse) **~se de algo** to complain about sth

lastimero, -a [las·ti·'me·ro, -a] adj, **lastimoso, -a** [las·ti·'mo·so, -a] adj pitiful

lastre [las·tre] m (estorbo) dead weight; **ser un ~** to be a burden

lata ['la·ta] f 1. (metal) tin 2. (envase) can 3. inf (pesadez) bore; **dar la ~** to be a nuisance; **¡vaya ~!** (fastidio) what a pain!

latazo [la·'ta·so, -θo] m inf **ser un ~** (pesado) to be a drag; (fastidioso) bother; (aburrido) bore; **dar el ~** to be a nuisance

latear [la·te·'ar] vi AmL to bore; **se pasa el día lateando** he/she spends all day blabbing away

latente [la·'ten·te] adj latent

lateral [la·te·'ral] adj lateral

latido [la·'ti·do] m (corazón) heartbeat

latifundio [la·ti·'fun·djo] m large estate

latifundista [la·ti·fun·'dis·ta] mf owner of a large estate

latigazo [la·ti·'ɣa·so, -'ɣa·θo] m (golpe) whiplash; (chasquido) crack of a whip

látigo ['la·ti·ɣo] m whip

latín [la·'tin] m Latin

latino, -a [la·'ti·no, -a] I. adj Latin; **América Latina** Latin America II. m, f Latin; AmL (latinoamericano) Latin American

Latinoamérica [la·ti·no·a·'me·ri·ka] f Latin America

latinoamericano, -a [la·ti·no·a·me·ri·'ka·no, -a] adj, m, f Latin American

latir [la·'tir] vi (corazón) to beat

latitud [la·ti·'tud] f latitude; (extensión) breadth

latón [la·'ton] m brass

latoso, -a [la·'to·so, -a] adj bothersome

laúd [la·'ud] m MÚS lute

laureado, -a [lau·re·'a·do, -a] adj (premiado) laureate, prize-winning

laurel [lau·'rel] m (árbol) laurel; (condimento) bay leaf; **dormirse en los ~es** to rest on one's laurels

lava ['la·βa] f (volcán) lava

lavabo [la·'βa·βo] m 1. (pila) sink 2. (cuarto) lavatory

lavacoches [la·βa·'ko·tʃes] m inv (instalación) car wash

lavadero [la·βa·'de·ro] m (de ropa) laundry; (en el río) washing place

lavado [la·'βa·do] m wash; **~ en seco** dry-cleaning; MED washing; **~ de cerebro** fig brainwashing; **~ de cara** fig facelift

lavadora [la·βa·'do·ra] f washing machine

lavanda [la·'βan·da] f lavender

lavandería [la·βan·de·'ri·a] f laundromat

lavaplatos [la·βa·'pla·tos] m inv 1. (electrodoméstico) dishwasher 2. Col inf (fregadero) (kitchen) sink

lavar [la·'βar] I. vt to wash; **~ los platos** to do the dishes II. vr: **~se** to wash; **~se la cabeza** to wash one's hair; **~se los dientes** to brush one's teeth

lavarropas [la·βa·'rro·pas] f inv Arg washing machine

lavativa [la·βa·'ti·βa] f (enema) enema

lavatorio [la·βa·'to·rjo] m AmL washroom

lavavajillas [la·βa·βa·'xi·jas, -ʎas] m inv 1. (electrodoméstico) dishwasher 2. (detergente) dish detergent

laxante [lak·'san·te] m laxative

laxo, -a [lak·so, -a] adj slack; (moral) lax

lazada [la·'sa·da, -'θa·da] f (de zapato) bow

lazo ['la·so, 'la·θo] m 1. (nudo) bow 2. (para caballos) lasso 3. (cinta) ribbon 4. (vínculo) tie; **~s afectivos** emotional bonds

le [le] pron pers 1. objeto indirecto: m sing him; f sing her; forma cortés you; **¡da~ un beso!** give him/her a kiss!; **~ puedo llamar el lunes** I can call you on Monday 2. reg, objeto directo: m sing him 3. forma cortés you

leal [le·'al] adj loyal

lealtad [le·al·'tad] f loyalty

lección [lek·'sjon, -'θjon] f lesson; **tomar lecciones de matemáticas** to take mathematics classes; **dar una ~ a alguien** to teach sb a lesson; **¡que te sirva de ~!** let that be a lesson to you!

lechada [le·'tʃa·da] f (argamasa) grout

lechal [le·'tʃal] I. adj (cachorro) suckling II. m (cordero) baby lamb

leche ['le·tʃe] f 1. (líquido) milk; ~ **en polvo** powdered milk; ~ **entera** whole milk; ~ **desnatada** skimmed milk; ~ **semidesnatada** partially skimmed milk 2. inf (golpe) blow; **¡te doy una ~!** I'm going to belt you one! 3. inf (hostia) **ser la ~** to be too much; **estar de mala ~** to be in a foul mood; **tener mala ~** to be vindictive; **a toda ~** at full speed

lechería [le·tʃe·'ri·a] f dairy

lechero, -a [le·'tʃe·ro, -a] m, f milkman m, milkwoman f

lecho ['le·tʃo] m bed; (río) riverbed

lechón, -ona [le·'tʃon, -·'tʃo·na] m, f suckling pig

lechuga [le·'tʃu·ɣa] f lettuce ▶ **fresco como una ~** as fresh as a daisy

lechuza [le·'tʃu·sa, -θa] f barn owl

lectivo, -a [lek·'ti·βo, -a] adj **día ~** school day

lector [lek·'tor] m COMPUT reader; ~ **de CD** CD player

lector(a) [lek·'tor, -·to·ra] m(f) 1. (que lee) reader; (en voz alta) lector 2. (profesor) conversation assistant

lectorado [lek·to·'ra·do] m assistantship

lectura [lek·'tu·ra] f 1. t. COMPUT (acción) reading 2. (obra) reading material

leer [le·'er] irr vt to read; ~ **en voz alta** to read aloud

legado [le·'ɣa·do] m legacy

legajo [le·'ɣa·xo] m dossier

legal [le·'ɣal] adj 1. (determinado por la ley) legal; (conforme a la ley) lawful 2. (fiel) trustworthy

legalidad [le·ɣa·li·'dad] f legality; **fuera de la ~** unlawful

legalización [le·ɣa·li·θa·'θjon] f (autorización) legalization

legalizar <z → c> [le·ɣa·li·'sar, -'θar] vt 1. (autorizar) to legalize 2. (atestar) to authenticate

legaña [le·'ɣa·ɲa] f sleep, rheum; **tienes ~s** you have sleep in your eyes

legar <g → gu> [le·'ɣar] vt (legado) to bequeath

legendario, -a [le·xen·'da·rjo] adj legendary; (famoso) renowned

legible [le·'xi·βle] adj legible

legión [le·'xjon] f legion; **hay comida para una ~** there's enough food to feed an army

legionario, -a [le·xjo·'na·rjo, -a] m, f legionnaire

legionella [le·xjo·'ne·la] f MED Legionnaire's disease

legislación [le·xis·la·'sjon, -'θjon] f legislation

legislador(a) [le·xis·la·'dor, -·'do·ra] I. adj legislative II. m(f) 1. (que legisla) legislator 2. AmL (parlamentario) member of parliament

legislar [le·xis·'lar] vi to legislate

legislativo, -a [le·xis·la·'ti·βo, -a] adj legislative; **poder ~** legislative power

legislatura [le·xis·la·'tu·ra] f 1. (período) term of office 2. AmL (parlamento) legislative body

legitimación [le·xi·ti·ma·'sjon, -'θjon] f 1. (legalización) authentication 2. (habilitación) recognition 3. (hijo) legitimization

legitimar [le·xi·ti·'mar] vt 1. (dar legitimidad) to authenticate 2. (habilitar) to recognize 3. (hijo) to make legitimate

legítimo, -a [le·'xi·ti·mo, -a] adj 1. (legal) legitimate; **defensa legítima** self-defense 2. (verdadero) genuine 3. (hijo) legitimate

legua ['le·ɣwa] f league; **a la ~** miles away

legumbre [le·'ɣum·bre] f 1. (planta) legume 2. (seca) pulse

leído, -a [le·'i·do, -a] adj 1. (persona) well-read 2. (revista) widely-read

lejanía [le·xa·'ni·a] f distance

lejano, -a [le·'xa·no, -a] adj faraway; (parentesco) distant; **en un futuro no muy ~** in the not-so-distant future

lejía [le·'xi·a] f (para lavar) bleach

lejos [le·'xos] I. adv far; ~ **de algo** far from sth; **a lo ~** in the distance; **de ~** from afar; **ir demasiado ~** t. fig to go too far; **es de ~ la mejor soprano** she is by far the best soprano; **llegar ~** fig to go far; **sin ir más ~** fig to take an obvious example II. prep ~ **de** far from

lelo, -a ['le·lo, -a] adj inf 1. ser (tonto) silly, goofy 2. estar (pasmado) stunned;

(*mareado*) dizzy

lema ['le·ma] *m* (*tema*) theme; (*mote*) motto

lencería [len·se·'ri·a, len·θe·] *f* 1. (*ropa interior*) lingerie 2. (*ropa blanca*) linen

lengua ['len·gwa] *f* 1. ANAT tongue; **lo tengo en la punta de la ~** I have it on the tip of my tongue; **morderse la ~** *t. fig* to bite one's tongue; **sacar la ~ a alguien** to stick one's tongue out at sb; **se me trabó la ~** I got tongue-tied; **tener la ~ demasiado larga** *fig* to talk too much 2. LING tongue; **~ materna** mother tongue; **~ oficial** official language 3. (*forma*) tongue; **~ de agua** tongue of water ► **tener la ~ de trapo** *inf* to stutter and stammer; **estar con la ~ fuera** to be out of breath; **dar a la ~** to gab; **aquí alguien se ha ido de la ~** sb here has spilled the beans; **tirar a alguien de la ~** to pump sb for information

lenguado [len·'gwa·do] *m* sole

lenguaje [len·'gwa·xe] *m* language

lengüeta [len·'gwe·ta] *f* (*zapato*) tongue; MÚS reed

lengüetear [len·gwe·te·'ar] *vi AmL inf* to stick one's tongue out

lente ['len·te] *f* 1. (*gafas*) eyeglasses *pl*; **llevar ~s** to wear glasses 2. *t.* FOTO (*cristal*) lens; **~ de aumento** magnifying glass

lenteja [len·'te·xa] *f* lentil

lentejuela [len·te·'xwe·la] *f* sequin, spangle

lentilla [len·'ti·ja, ·ʎa] *f* contact lens

lentitud [len·ti·'tud] *f* slowness; *fig* slow-wittedness; **con ~** slowly

lento, -a ['len·to] *adj* slow; *fig* slow-witted; **a paso ~** slowly; **cocinar a fuego ~** to cook over low heat [*o* a low flame]; **quemar a fuego ~** *fig* to burn slowly

leña ['le·ɲa] *f* 1. (*madera*) firewood; **echar ~ al fuego** to add more firewood; *fig* to add fuel to the flames 2. (*castigo*) beating; **dar ~** to give a beating; **repartir ~** to dish out blows; **recibir ~** to get beaten up ► **hacer ~ del árbol caído** to kick somebody when he is down

leñador(a) [le·ɲa·'dor, ·'do·ra] *m(f)* woodcutter, lumberjack

leñazo [le·'ɲa·so, ·θo] *m inf* bash; **darse un ~ en la cabeza** to bash one's head

Leo ['le·o] *m* Leo

león [le·'on] *m* lion; **~ (marino)** sea lion

leonera [leo·'ne·ra] *f* (*habitación*) messy room

leopardo [leo·'par·do] *m* leopard

leotardo(s) [leo·'tar·do(s)] *m* 1. (*pl*) leotards *pl* 2. DEP (*malla*) tights *pl*

lépero, -a ['le·pe·ro, ·a] I. *adj* 1. *AmC* (*grosero*) coarse; (*vil*) rotten 2. *Cuba* (*perspicaz*) shrewd 3. *Ecua inf* (*arruinado*) broke II. *m, f AmC* pauper

lepra ['le·pra] *f* MED leprosy

leproso, -a [le·'pro·so, ·a] I. *adj* leprous II. *m, f* leper

lerdear [ler·de·'ar] *vi AmC, Arg* to be sluggish; (*demorarse*) to take a long time

lerdo, -a ['ler·do, ·a] *adj* slow, sluggish

les [les] *pron pers* 1. *m pl reg* (*objeto directo*) them; (*forma cortés*) you 2. *mf pl* (*objeto indirecto*) them; (*forma cortés*) you

lesbiana [les·'βja·na] *f* lesbian

lésbico, -a ['les·βi·ko, ·a] *adj* lesbian

lesear [le·se·'ar] *vi Chile* to fool around

lesera [le·'se·ra] *f AmL* stupidity

lesión [le·'sjon] *f* (*herir*) injury

lesionar [le·sjo·'nar] I. *vt* (*herir*) to injure; (*dañar*) to damage II. *vr:* **~se** to get hurt

letal [le·'tal] *adj elev* lethal

letárgico, -a [le·'tar·xi·ko, ·a] *adj* lethargic

letargo [le·'tar·ɣo] *m* lethargy

Letonia [le·'to·nja] *f* Latvia

letra ['le·tra] *f* 1. (*signo*) letter; **con ~ mayúscula/minúscula** in capitals/small letters; **al pie de la ~** to the letter; **~ por ~** word for word 2. (*escritura*) handwriting; **de su puño y ~** in his own handwriting 3. *pl* (*saber*) learning, letters; UNIV arts *pl*; **hombre de ~s** man of letters 4. MÚS lyrics *pl* 5. COM **~ (de cambio)** bill of exchange; **~ al portador** draft payable to the bearer

letrado, -a [le·'tra·do, ·a] *m, f* lawyer

letrero [le·'tre·ro] *m* notice, sign

leucemia [leu·'se·mja, ·'θe·mja] *f* MED leukemia

levadizo, -a [le·βa·'di·so, ·a; ·'di·θo, ·a] *adj* **puente ~** drawbridge

L

levadura [le.βa.'du.ra] *f* leavening yeast;
~ **en polvo** baking powder

levantamiento [le.βan.ta.'mjen.to] *m*
1. (*amotinamiento*) uprising **2.** (*alzar*) lifting

levantar [le.βan.'tar] **I.** *vt* **1.** (*alzar*)
lift, to raise; (*del suelo*) to pick up; (*polvo, telón*) to raise; (*un campamento*) to
strike; **el vuelo** to take off; **después
del fracaso ya no levantó cabeza**
he/she never recovered from the fiasco
2. (*despertar, provocar*) to awaken; **no
queremos ~ sospechas** we don't want
to arouse suspicion **3.** (*construir*) to
build; (*monumento*) to erect; (*muro*) to
put up **4.** (*suprimir*) to remove; (*embargo, castigo*) to lift **5.** (*voz, mirada*) to
raise; **~ la voz a alguien** to raise one's
voice to sb **II.** *vr:* **~se 1.** (*de la cama*) to
get up; **~se con el pie izquierdo** *fig* to
get out of bed on the wrong side **2.** (*sublevarse*) to rebel **3.** (*viento, telón*) to
rise **4.** (*sesión*) to adjourn; **se levanta
la sesión** the meeting is closed, court
is adjourned

levante [le.'βan.te] *m* east; (*viento*) east
wind

levar [le.'βar] *vt* **~ anclas** to weigh anchor

leve ['le.βe] *adj* (*enfermedad*) mild; (*peso, sanción*) light; (*error*) slight

levitar [le.βi.'tar] *vi* to levitate

léxico ['lek.si.ko] *m* vocabulary

ley [lei] *f* **1.** JUR, REL, FÍS law; **Ley Fundamental** Fundamental Law; **~ orgánica**
constitutional law; **la ~ de la oferta y
demanda** the law of supply and demand; **la ~ seca** the Prohibition; **la ~
de la selva la ~ del más fuerte** the law
of the jungle; **fuerza de ~** force of law;
proyecto de ~ bill; **hacer algo con todas las de la ~** to do sth properly; **hecha la ~, hecha la trampa** every law
has its loophole; **según la ~ vigente** in
accordance with the law currently in
force; **ser de ~** *inf* to be reliable **2.** (*oro*)
legal standard of fineness; (*monedas*)
genuine; **oro de ~** standard gold

leyenda [le.'jen.da] *f* LIT, REL legend

liana [li.'a.na] *f* liana

liar <*1. pres* lío> [li.'ar] **I.** *vt* **1.** (*fardo*) to
tie up; (*paquete*) to wrap up **2.** (*cigarrillo*) to roll **3.** *inf* (*engañar*) to take in;
(*enredar*) to mix up; **¡ahora sí que la
hemos liado!** we've really done it now!
II. *vr:* **~se 1.** *inf* (*juntarse*) to become
lovers **2.** (*embarullarse*) to get complicated **3.** (*ponerse a*) **~se a golpes con
alguien** to start fighting with sb

libélula [li.'βe.lu.la] *f* dragonfly

liberación [li.βe.ra.'sjon, -'θjon] *f* liberation, release

liberal [li.βe.'ral] *adj t.* POL liberal

liberalizar <z → c> [li.βe.ra.li.'sar, -'θar]
vt to liberalize

liberar [li.βe.'rar] *vt* to liberate, to set free;
(*eximir*) to exempt

libertad [li.βer.'tad] *f* (*libre arbitrio*) liberty, freedom; **~ de expresión** freedom
of speech; **~ de prensa** freedom of the
press; **en ~ bajo fianza** on bail; **en ~
condicional** on parole; **poner en ~** to
set free; **tomarse demasiadas ~es** to
take too many liberties

libertar [li.βer.'tar] *vt* to liberate

libertario, -a [li.βer.'ta.rjo, -a] *adj, m, f*
libertarian

libertinaje [li.βer.ti.'na.xe] *m* libertinage

libertino, -a [li.βer.'ti.no, -a] *adj* dissolute

libido [li.'βi.do] *f* libido

libra ['li.βra] *f* pound; **~ esterlina** pound
sterling

Libra ['li.βra] *f* Libra

librado, -a [li.'βra.do, -a] *adj* **salir bien ~
de algo** to come out of sth unscathed, to
be successful in sth; **salir mal ~** to come
out the worse for wear, to fail

librar [li.'βrar] **I.** *vt* (*dejar libre*) **~ de
algo/alguien** to free from sth/sb; (*salvar*) to save from sth/sb **II.** *vi inf* (*tener
libre*) **hoy libro** I have today off **III.** *vr*
~se de algo/alguien (*deshacerse*) to
get rid of sth/sb; (*salvarse*) to escape
from sth/sb

libre <libérrimo> ['li.βre] *adj* free; **~ de
franqueo** no postage necessary; **dar vía
~** to give the green light; **eres bien ~ de
hacerlo** you are quite free to do so

librecambio [li.βre.'kam.bjo] *m* free trade

librería [li.βre.'ri.a] *f* bookshop

librero, -a [li.'βre.ro] *m, f* bookseller

libreta [li·'βre·ta] f 1. (cuaderno) notebook; (para notas) notepad 2. (de ahorros) bank book

libro ['li·βro] m book; ~ de bolsillo paperback; ~ de cocina cookbook; ~ de consulta reference book; ~ de escolaridad school record; ~ de texto textbook ▶ hablar como un ~ cerrado not to express oneself clearly

licencia [li·'sen·sja, -'θen·θja] f (permiso) license; (para un libro) authorization; ~ de conducir Méx, Cuba driver's license

licenciado, -a [li·sen·'sja·ðo, -a; li·θen·'θja-] m, f 1. (estudiante) graduate; ~ en economía Economics graduate 2. (soldado) discharged soldier

licenciar [li·sen·'sjar, -'θjar] I. vt (despedir) to dismiss; (soldado) to discharge II. vr: ~se to graduate; se licenció en psicología he got a degree in psychology

licenciatura [li·sen·sja·'tu·ra, li·θen·θja·] f (título) degree; (carrera) university studies pl

lícito, -a ['li·si·to, -a; -θi·to, -a] adj allowed; (justo) fair

licor [li·'kor] m liquor; (de frutas) liqueur

licuadora [li·kwa·'ðo·ra] f (batidora) blender; (para fruta) liquidizer

licuar <1. pres licúo> [li·'kwar] vt 1. Fís to liquate 2. (fruta) to liquefy

líder ['li·ðer] mf leader; la empresa ~ the leading company

liderar [li·ðe·'rar] vt to lead; (dirigir) to head; el equipo que lidera la clasificación the team at the top of the table

liderato [li·ðe·'ra·to] m, liderazgo [li·ðe·'ras·ɣo, -'raθ·ɣo] m leadership; capacidad de ~ leadership capability

lidia ['li·ðja] f fight; TAUR bullfight

liebre [lje·'βre] f hare ▶ levantar la ~ to let the cat out of the bag; donde menos se piensa salta la ~ things always happen when you least expect them to

lienzo ['ljen·so, -θo] m (tela) cloth; (para cuadros) canvas; (óleo) painting

liga ['li·ɣa] f 1. (alianza) t. DEP league 2. (prenda) suspender, garter

ligamento [li·ɣa·'men·to] m ANAT ligament

ligar <g → gu> [li·'ɣar] I. vi inf (tontear) to flirt II. vt 1. (atar) to tie 2. (unir) to join III. vr: ~se 1. (unirse) to join 2. inf (tontear) to flirt

ligereza [li·xe·'re·sa, -θa] f 1. (rapidez) swiftness 2. (levedad) lightness

ligero, -a [li·'xe·ro, -a] adj 1. (leve, ingrávido) light; ir muy ~ de ropa to be scantily clad, not to be wearing much 2. (ágil) nimble ▶ hacer algo a la ligera to do sth without thinking; tomarse algo a la ligera to not take sth seriously

ligón [li·'ɣon, -ona] m womanizer; ser un ~ to be a Don Juan

ligue [li·'ɣe] m inf 1. (acción) pick-up; tener un ~ con alguien to have an affair with sb 2. (persona) chat-up, pick-up

liguero [li·'ɣe·ro] m garter belt

liguero, -a [li·'ɣe·ro, -a] adj DEP league

lija ['li·xa] f sandpaper

lijadora [li·xa·'ðo·ra] f sander

lijar [li·'xar] vt to sand

lila ['li·la] I. adj lilac II. f BOT lilac

lima ['li·ma] f 1. (instrumento) file; rebajar con la ~ to file down 2. BOT (fruta) lime; (árbol) lime tree ▶ comer como una ~ to eat like a horse

limar [li·'mar] vt to file; fig to perfect

limbo ['lim·bo] m REL limbo; estar en el ~ (distraído) to be distracted; (no enterarse) to be oblivious

limeño, -a [li·'me·ɲo, -a] I. adj of/from Lima II. m, f native/inhabitant of Lima

limitación [li·mi·ta·'sjon, -'θjon] f limitation; (de una norma) restriction; sin limitaciones unlimited

limitado, -a [li·mi·'ta·ðo, -a] adj (poco) scant; (medios) limited; un número ~ a limited number

limitar [li·mi·'tar] I. vi ~ con algo to border on sth II. vt to limit; (libertad) to restrict III. vr: ~se to confine oneself

límite ['li·mi·te] m limit; situación ~ extreme situation; sin ~s limitless; fecha ~ de entrega delivery deadline

limítrofe [li·'mi·tro·fe] adj bordering; países ~s neighboring countries

limón [li·'mon] adj, m lemon

limonada [li·mo·'na·da] f lemonade

L

limonero [li·mo·'ne·ro] *m* lemon tree

limosna [li·'mos·na] *f* alms *pl*; **pedir ~ to** beg

limosnero, -a [li·mos·'ne·ro, -a] *m, f AmL (pedigüeño)* beggar

limpiabotas [lim·pja·'βo·tas] *mf inv* bootblack

limpiacristales [lim·pja·kris·'ta·les] *m inv (producto)* window cleaning fluid

limpiador [lim·pja·'dor] *m* cleaner

limpiaparabrisas [lim·pja·pa·ra·'βri·sas] *m inv* windshield wiper

limpiar [lim·'pjar] I. *vt* to clean; *(dientes)* to brush; **~ el polvo** to dust; **~ en seco** to dry-clean II. *vi* to clean III. *vr:* **~se** to clean; *(nariz)* to wipe; *(dientes)* to brush

limpieza [lim·'pje·sa, -θa] *f* 1. *(lavar)* washing; *(casa, zapatos)* cleaning; **~ a fondo** thorough cleaning; **señora de la ~** cleaning lady, cleaner 2. *(estado)* cleanness, cleanliness 3. *(eliminación)* cleansing; POL purge

limpio [lim·pjo] *adv (sin trampas)* fairly; **jugar ~** to play fair ▶ **¿qué has sacado en ~ de todo este asunto?** what do you make of all this?

limpio, -a [lim·pjo, -a] *adj* clean; *(aire)* pure ▶ **lo dejaron ~** *inf (sin dinero)* they cleaned him out

limusina [li·mu·'si·na] *f* AUTO limousine

linaje [li·'na·xe] *m* lineage

lince [lin·se, -θe] *m* lynx; **tener ojos de ~** to be sharp-eyed

linchamiento [lin·tʃa·'mjen·to] *m* lynching

linchar [lin·'tʃar] *vt* to lynch

lindar [lin·'dar] *vi* **~ con algo** to border on sth

lindo, -a [lin·do, -a] *adj* pretty; *(niño)* lovely, cute

línea [li·ne·a] *f. t.* MAT, MIL, ECON *(raya)* line; **~ de meta** DEP *(atletismo)* finishing line; **~ recta** straight line 2. *(renglón)* line; **~ en blanco** blank line; **leer entre ~s** to read between the lines 3. *(de transporte)* line; *(trayecto)* route; **~ aérea** airline; **~ férrea** railroad line 4. TEL telephone line; **no hay ~** the line is dead [*o* down] 5. *(pariente)* line; **por ~ materna** on his mother's side

6. *(tipo)* figure; **guardar la ~** to watch one's figure 7. *(fábrica)* **~ de montaje** assembly line

lineal [li·ne·'al] *adj t.* MAT, ARTE linear

lingote [lin·'go·te] *m* ingot

lingüística [lin·'gwis·ti·ka] *f* linguistics

lingüístico, -a [lin·'gwis·ti·ko, -a] *adj* linguistic

linimento [li·ni·'men·to] *m* liniment

lino [li·no] *m* 1. BOT flax 2. *(tela)* linen

linterna [lin·'ter·na] *f* lantern; *(a pila)* flashlight

lío [li·o] *m* 1. *(embrollo)* mess; **¡déjame de ~s!** don't come to me with your problems!; **hacerse un ~ con algo** to get into a jam with sth 2. *inf (relación)* affair

lipidia [li·'pi·dja] *f* 1. *AmC (pobreza)* poverty; *(miseria)* misery 2. *Cuba, Méx (impertinencia)* impertinence

lipotimia [li·po·'ti·mja] *f* blackout

liquidación [li·ki·da·'sjon, -'θjon] *f* 1. *(de una mercancía)* sale; **~ total** clearance sale 2. *(de una factura)* payment; *(cuenta)* settlement

liquidar [li·ki·'dar] *vt* 1. *inf (acabar)* to liquidate; *(matar)* to kill; **lo ~on** *inf* they bumped him off 2. *(mercancía)* to sell; **~ las existencias** to sell off all merchandise 3. *(cerrar)* to close 4. *(factura)* to settle

liquidez [li·ki·'des, 'deθ] *f* 1. *(agua)* fluidity 2. COM liquidity

líquido [li·ki·do] *m* 1. *(agua)* liquid; **~ de frenos** brake fluid 2. *(saldo)* cash; **~ imponible** taxable income

líquido, -a [li·ki·do, -a] *adj* 1. *(material)* liquid 2. *(dinero)* cash; **renta líquida** disposable income

lira [li·ra] *f* 1. *(moneda)* lira 2. *(instrumento)* lyre

lírica [li·ri·ka] *f* poetry

lírico, -a [li·ri·ko, -a] *adj* 1. LIT lyric(al) 2. MÚS lyrical

lirio [li·rjo] *m* lily

lirón [li·'ron] *m* dormouse; **dormir como un ~** to sleep like a log

Lisboa [lis·'βoa] *f* Lisbon

lisboeta [lis·βo·'e·ta] I. *adj* of/from Lisbon II. *mf* native/inhabitant of Lisbon

lisiado, -a [li·'sja·do, -a] *adj* crippled

lisiar [li·'sjar] *vr*: ~**se** to become disabled
liso, -a ['li·so, -a] *adj* **1.** (*superficie*) smooth; (*pelo*) straight; **los 100 metros** ~**s** the 100 meter flat race **2.** (*tela*) plain
lisonjero, -a [li·son·'xe·ro, -a] **I.** *adj* flattering **II.** *m, f* flatterer
lista ['lis·ta] *f* (*enumeración*) list; ~ **de la compra** shopping list; **estar en la** ~ **de espera** to be on the waiting list; **pasar** ~ (*leer*) to take roll call
listado [lis·'ta·do] *m* list
listar [lis·'tar] *vt* to list
listillo, -a [lis·'ti·jo, -a; -ʎo, -a] *m, f* smart aleck
listín [lis·'tin] *m* (*de teléfonos*) directory
listo, -a ['lis·to, -a] *adj* **1.** *ser* (*inteligente*) clever; (*sagaz*) shrewd; **pasarse de** ~ to be too clever by half **2.** *estar* (*preparado*) ready; ~ **para despegar** ready for takeoff; **estás** ~ **si crees que...** *inf* you have another think coming if you think that...
listón [lis·'ton] *m* lath; **poner el** ~ **muy alto** *fig* to set very high standards
litera [li·'te·ra] *f* (*cama*) bunk; FERRO couchette; NÁUT berth
literal [li·te·'ral] *adj* literal
literario, -a [li·te·'ra·rjo, -a] *adj* literary
literatura [li·te·ra·'tu·ra] *f* literature
litigar <g → gu> [li·ti·'ɣar] *vt t.* JUR to dispute
litigio [li·'ti·xjo] *m* **1.** (*disputa*) dispute; **en** ~ in dispute **2.** (*juicio*) lawsuit
litoral [li·to·'ral] *m* (*costa*) coast; (*playa*) shore
litro ['li·tro] *m* liter; **un** ~ **de leche** a liter of milk
liturgia [li·'tur·xja] *f* liturgy
liviano, -a [li·'βja·no, -a] *adj* light
lívido, -a ['li·βi·do, -a] *adj* **1.** (*amoratado*) livid; ~ **de frío** livid with cold **2.** (*pálido*) ashen
llaga ['ja·ɣa, ʎa-] *f* (*herida*) wound
llama ['ja·ma, ʎa-] *f* **1.** (*fuego*) flame **2.** ZOOL llama
llamada [ja·'ma·da, ʎa-] *f* **1.** (*voz*) call; ~ **al orden** call to order **2.** (*de teléfono*) phone call; ~ **a cobro revertido** collect call; ~ **interurbana** long-distance call; ~ **local** local call **3.** (*a la puerta golpeando*) knock; (*con el timbre*) ring

llamado, -a [ja·'ma·do, ʎa-] *adj* (*conocido como*) called; (*supuesto*) so-called
llamado [ja·'ma·do, -a; ʎa-] *m AmS v.* **llamamiento**
llamador [ja·ma·'dor, ʎa-] *m* doorknocker
llamamiento [ja·ma·'mjen·to, ʎa-] *m* **1.** (*exhortación*) appeal; **hacer un** ~ **a todos** to issue an appeal to all **2.** MIL ~ **a filas** call to arms **3.** JUR (*citación*) summons, subpoena
llamar [ja·'mar, ʎa-] **I.** *vt* **1.** (*voz, teléfono*) to call; ~ **a filas** MIL to draft; **te llaman al teléfono** you're wanted on the phone **2.** (*denominar*) to call; **lo llamé idiota** I called him an idiot **3.** (*despertar*) to wake up; ~ **la atención** (*reprender*) to reprimand; (*ser llamativo*) to attract attention; ~ **la atención sobre algo** to draw attention to sth **II.** *vi* (*a la puerta golpeando*) to knock; (*con el timbre*) to ring; **¿quién llama?** who is it? **III.** *vr*: ~**se** to be called; **¿cómo te llamas?** what's your name?
llamarada [ja·ma·'ra·da, ʎa-] *f* blaze
llamativo, -a [ja·ma·'ti·βo, -a; ʎa-] *adj* (*traje*) flashy; (*color*) loud
llana ['ja·na, ʎa-] *f* trowel
llanca ['jan·ka, ʎa-] *f* Chile bluish-green copper ore
llanito, -a [ja·'ni·to, -a; ʎa-] *m, f* *inf* Gibraltarian
llano ['ja·no, ʎa-] *m* plain
llano, -a ['ja·no, -a; ʎa-] *adj* **1.** (*liso*) flat; (*terreno*) level **2.** LING paroxytone **3.** (*sencillo*) **el pueblo** ~ the common people
llanta ['janta, 'ʎan-] *f* **1.** AmL (*rueda*) tire **2.** (*cerco*) (metal) rim; ~ **de aleación** alloy wheel
llanto ['jan·to, 'ʎan-] *m* crying
llanura [ja·'nu·ra, ʎa-] *f* plain
llave ['ja·βe, 'ʎa-] *f* **1.** *t. fig* (*instrumento*) key; ~ **de contacto** AUTO ignition key; **ama de** ~**s** housekeeper; **en mano** (*coche*) on the road; **echar la** ~ to lock; **estar bajo** ~ to be under lock and key; **la** ~ **no entra** the key doesn't fit; **meter/sacar la** ~ to put in/pull out the key **2.** (*grifo*) faucet **3.** (*tuerca*) wrench; ~ **inglesa** monkey wrench **4.** (*interruptor*) switch

L

llavero [ʎa·ˈβe·ro, ˌʎa-] *m* key ring

llegada [ʎe·ˈɣa·ða, ˌʎe-] *f* arrival; (*meta*) finishing line

llegar <g → gu> [ʎe·ˈɣar, ˌʎe-] **I.** *vi* **1.** (*al destino, el correo*) to arrive; ~ **a la meta** DEP to reach the finishing line; **estar al** ~ to be about to arrive; ~ **a Madrid/al hotel** to arrive in Madrid/at the hotel; ~ **tarde** to be late; **¡todo llegará!** all in good time!; **¡hasta ahí podíamos** ~! that's the limit! **2.** (*recibir*) **no me ha llegado el dinero** I haven't received the money **3.** (*durar*) to live; ~ **a viejo** to live to old age; **el enfermo no** ~**á a la primavera** the patient won't make it to spring **4.** (*ascender*) to amount to; **no llega a 20 dólares** it's less than 20 dollars **5.** (*lograr*) **ese** ~**á lejos** that fellow will go far; ~ **a ser muy rico** to become very rich; **llegamos a recoger 8.000 firmas** we managed to get 8,000 signatures **6.** (*ser suficiente*) to be enough **7.** (*tocar*) ~ **a** [*o* **hasta**] **algo** to reach sth; **no me llegas ni a la suela de los zapatos** you can't hold a candle to me **II.** *vr:* ~**se** (*ir*) to go; ~**se por casa de alguien** to stop by sb's house

llenador, -a [ʎe·na·ˈðor, -·ˈðo·ra, ˌʎe-] *adj* Csur filling; **esta tarta es muy llenadora** this pie is very filling

llenar [ʎe·ˈnar, ˌʎe-] **I.** *vt* **1.** (*atestar*) to fill; ~ **de algo** to fill with sth **2.** (*cumplimentar*) to fill in [*o* out] **3.** (*colmar*) ~ **de algo** to overwhelm with sth; **nos llenó de regalos** we were showered with gifts **4.** (*satisfacer*) to satisfy **II.** *vi* (*comida*) to be filling; **la pasta llena mucho** pasta is very filling **III.** *vr:* ~**se de algo** *inf* (*comida*) to stuff oneself with sth

lleno [ˈʎe·no, ˌʎe-] *m* (*teatro, auditorio*) full house

lleno, -a [ˈʎe·no, -a; ˌʎe-] *adj* full; **luna llena** full moon; ~ **de** full of, filled with; **el autobús iba** ~ the bus was full; **estoy** ~ *inf* I'm full

llevadero, -a [ʎe·βa·ˈðe·ro, -a; ˌʎe-] *adj* bearable

llevar [ʎe·ˈβar, ˌʎe-] **I.** *vt* **1.** (*a un destino, acompañar*) to take; (*transportar*) to transport; (*en brazos*) to carry; (*comida*) to take out; ~ **a alguien en el coche** to give sb a lift; ~ **algo a alguien** to take sth to sb; **dos pizzas para** ~, **por favor** two pizzas to go, please **2.** (*costar*) to cost; **este trabajo lleva mucho tiempo** this work takes a lot of time **3.** (*tener*) ~ **consigo** to be carrying, to have **4.** (*conducir*) to lead; ~ **de la mano** to lead by the hand; **esto no lleva a ninguna parte** this isn't getting us anywhere **5.** (*ropa*) to wear **6.** (*coche*) to drive **7.** (*estar*) to have been; **llevo cuatro días aquí** I've been here for four days **8.** (*gestionar*) to manage; ~ **las cuentas** to manage the accounts; **el abogado que lleva el caso** the lawyer handling the case **9.** (*inducir*) ~ **a algo** to lead to sth, to induce sth; **me llevó a pensar que...** it led me to think that... **10.** (*exceder*) to exceed; **te llevo dos años** I'm two years older than you **11.** (*tener como ingrediente*) **¿lleva picante?** does it have hot pepper? ▶ **dejarse** ~ **por algo** to be carried away with sth; **dejarse** ~ **por alguien** to let sb influence you; ~ **las de perder** to be fighting a losing battle; **¿qué tal lo llevas?** how are you holding up? **II.** *vr:* ~**se 1.** (*coger*) to take; ~**se algo por delante** to crush sth **2.** (*ganar*) to win; ~**se la mejor/ peor parte** to get the best/worst of it **3.** (*estar de moda*) to be in fashion; **ya no se llevan estos zapatos** those shoes are no longer in fashion **4.** (*soportarse*) ~**se bien** to get along well; ~**se a matar** to hate each other ▶ **...y me llevo cuatro** MAT ... and carry four

lliclla [ˈʎik·ja, ˌʎik·ʎa] *f* Bol, Ecua, Perú blanket *(carried on the back by Indian women)*

llicta [ˈʎik·ta, ˌʎik-] *f* Bol potato meal cake *(type of hard cake eaten while chewing coca to give flavor to the coca ball)*

llorar [ʎo·ˈrar, ˌʎo-] **I.** *vi* to cry; **me lloran los ojos** my eyes are watering; ~ **de alegría** to cry for joy; ~ **por algo/alguien** to cry over sth/sb; *fig* to mourn sb/ sb; **lloramos de risa** we laughed until we cried ▶ **quien no llora no mama** *inf* the squeaky wheel gets the oil *prov* **II.** *vt* **1.** (*lágrimas*) ~ **la muerte de al-**

guien to mourn sb's death **2.** (*quejarse*) to whine; (*lamentar*) to bemoan

llorica [jo·'ri·ka, ʎo-] *mf inf* crybaby

lloriquear [jo·ri·ke·'ar, ʎo-] *vi* to whimper

lloriqueo [jo·ri·'keo, ʎo-] *m* whimpering

lloro(s) ['jo·ro(s), ʎo-] *m(pl)* crying; **con estos ~s no conseguirás nada** this crying won't get you anywhere

llorón, -ona [jo·'ron, -o·na; ʎo-] **I.** *adj* **sauce ~** weeping willow **II.** *m, f* crybaby

lloroso, -a [jo·'ro·so, -a; ʎo-] *adj* tearful

llover <o → ue> [jo·'βer, ʎo-] *vi, vt, vimpers* to rain; **está lloviendo** it's raining; **llueve a mares** [*o a cántaros*] it's pouring; **siempre llueve sobre mojado** it never rains but it pours; **como llovido del cielo** heaven sent; **me escucha como quien oye ~** *inf* in one ear and out the other; **ya ha llovido mucho desde entonces** *fig* a lot has happened since then

llovida [jo·'βi·da, ʎo-] *f AmL* rain; **¡qué ~!** what a downpour!

llovizna [jo·'βis·na, ʎo-'βiθ·na] *f* drizzle

lloviznar [jo·βis·'nar, ʎo·βiθ·'nar] *vimpers* está **lloviznando** it's drizzling

lluvia ['ju·βja, 'ʎu-] *f* **1.** (*chubasco*) rain; **~ de estrellas** meteor shower; **época de las ~s** rainy season; **~ ácida** acid rain; **~ radiactiva** fallout; **hubo una ~ de protestas** there was a shower of protests **2.** *AmL* (*ducha*) shower

lluvioso, -a [ju·'βjo·so, -a; ʎu-] *adj* rainy

lo [lo] **I.** *art def v.* **el, la, lo II.** *pron pers m y neutro sing* **1.** (*objeto: masculino*) him; (*neutro*) it; **¡lláma~!** call him!; **¡haz~!** do it! **2.** (*con relativo*) **~ que...** what; **~ cual** which; **~ que quiero decir es que...** what I mean is that...

loable [lo·'a·βle] *adj* commendable

lobo, -a ['lo·βo] *m, f* wolf; **~ de mar** old salt; **meterse en la boca del ~** to go into the lion's den; **ser un ~ con piel de oveja** to be a wolf in sheep's clothing; **tener un hambre de ~** to be as hungry as a wolf

lóbulo ['lo·βu·lo] *m ANAT* lobe; **~ de la oreja** earlobe

local [lo·'kal] **I.** *adj* local **II.** *m* locale; COM

premises *pl*; **~ público** public building

localidad [lo·ka·li·'dad] *f* **1.** (*municipio*) town **2.** (*entrada*) ticket; (*asiento*) seat

localización [lo·ka·li·sa·'sjon, -θa·'θjon] *f* (*búsqueda*) finding; AVIAT tracking; **~ de software** COMPUT software localization

localizar <z → c> [lo·ka·li·'sar, -'θar] *vt* **1.** (*encontrar*) to find; **~ por teléfono** to get in touch by phone **2.** (*limitar*) to localize; (*fuego, epidemia*) to confine

locería [lo·se·'ri·a, loθe-] *f AmL* crockery

loción [lo·'sjon, -'θjon] *f* lotion; **~ capilar** hair lotion; **~ bronceadora** suntan lotion; **~ hidratante** moisturizing cream

loco, -a ['lo·ko, -a] *I.* *adj* mad, crazy; **a lo tontas y a locas** any old way; **estar ~ de atar** to be raving mad; **estar ~ por la música** to be crazy about music; **estar ~ de contento** to be elated; **estar medio ~** to be not all there; **tener una suerte loca** to be incredibly lucky **II.** *m, f* madman *m*, madwoman *f*; **casa de ~s** *fig* madhouse; **cada ~ con su tema** to each his own; **hacerse el ~** to act dumb; **hacer el ~** to act the fool

locomoción [lo·ko·mo·'sjon, -'θjon] *f* locomotion

locomotora [lo·ko·mo·'to·ra] *f* locomotive

locro ['lo·kro] *m AmS* meat and vegetable stew

locuaz [lo·'kwas, -'kwaθ] *adj* loquacious; (*charlatán*) talkative

locución [lo·ku·'sjon, -'θjon] *f* (*expresión*) phrase

locura [lo·'ku·ra] *f* **1.** (*enajenación mental*) madness; **querer con ~** to be madly in love with **2.** (*disparate*) crazy thing; **andar haciendo ~s** to be doing foolish things

locutor(a) [lo·ku·'tor, -·'to·ra] *m(f)* speaker

locutorio [lo·ku·'to·rjo] *m* TEL telephone booth

lodazal [lo·da·'sal, -'θal] *m* quagmire

lodo ['lo·do] *m* mud

lógica ['lo·xi·ka] *f* logic

lógico, -a ['lo·xi·ko, -a] *adj* logical; (*normal*) natural

logística [lo·'xis·ti·ka] *f* logistics *pl*

logístico, -a [lo·'xis·ti·ko, -a] *adj* logistic

logopeda [lo·ɣo·'pe·ða] *mf* speech therapist

logopedia [lo·ɣo·'pe·ðja] *f* speech therapy

logotipo [lo·ɣo·'ti·po] *m* logotype; (*de una empresa, un producto*) logo

logrado, -a [lo·'ɣra·ðo, -a] *adj* successful, well done

lograr [lo·'ɣrar] *vt* to achieve; **logré convencerla** I managed to convince her

logro [ˈlo·ɣro] *m* achievement

loma [ˈlo·ma] *f* hill

lombriz [lom·ˈbris, -ˈbriθ] *f* worm; **~ intestinal** tapeworm; **~ de tierra** earthworm

lomo [ˈlo·mo] *m* back; (*de libro*) spine; (*solomillo*) loin

lona [ˈlo·na] *f* canvas

loncha [ˈlon·tʃa] *f* slice; (*beicon*) rasher

londinense [lon·di·ˈnen·se] **I.** *adj* London **II.** *mf* Londoner

Londres [ˈlon·dres] *m* London

longaniza [lon·ɡa·ˈni·sa, -ˈni·θa] *f* spicy pork sausage

longevidad [lon·xe·βi·ˈðað] *f* longevity

longevo, -a [lon·ˈxe·βo, -a] *adj* (*que dura*) long-lived; (*viejo*) very old

longitud [lon·xi·ˈtuð] *f* length; **salto de ~** DEP long jump; **cuatro metros de ~** four meters long; **cincuenta grados ~ este/oeste** fifty degrees longitude east/west

longitudinal [lon·xi·tu·di·ˈnal] *adj* **corte ~** longitudinal section

lonja [ˈlon·xa] *f* COM public exchange

loquera [lo·ˈke·ra] *f* AmL madness

loro [ˈlo·ro] *m* ZOOL parrot; **repetir como un ~** to repeat parrot fashion; **hablar como un ~** to talk non-stop

los [los] **I.** *art def v* **el, la, lo II.** *pron pers m y neutro pl* **1.** (*objeto directo*) them; **¡lláma~!** call them! **2.** (*con relativo*) **~ que...** the ones that...; **~ cuales** which

losa [ˈlo·sa] *f* **1.** (*piedra*) slab; (*lápida*) gravestone **2.** (*baldosa*) tile

lote [ˈlo·te] *m* **1.** (*parte*) share; COM lot **2.** (*toqueteo*) **darse** [*o* **pegarse**] **el ~** to get off with

lotería [lo·te·ˈri·a] *f* lottery; **~ primitiva** weekly lottery; **administración de ~**

office selling lottery tickets; **me tocó la ~** I won the lottery; **un décimo de ~** a tenth share of a lottery number; **¡con ese hijo te tocó la ~!** you really struck gold with that son of yours!; **jugar a la ~** to play the lottery

loza [ˈlo·sa, ˈlo·θa] *f* earthenware; (*vajilla*) crockery; **~ fina** china

lubina [lu·ˈβi·na] *f* sea bass

lubricante [lu·βri·ˈkan·te] *m* lubricant

lubricar <c → qu> [lu·βri·ˈkar] *vt* to lubricate

lucero [lu·ˈse·ro, -ˈθe·ro] *m* (*estrella*) bright star

lucha [ˈlu·tʃa] *f* fight; DEP wrestling; **~ cuerpo a cuerpo** hand-to-hand fighting [*o* combat]; **~ contra la droga** the fight against drugs

luchador(a) [lu·tʃa·ˈðor, -·ˈðo·ra] *m(f)* fighter; DEP wrestler

luchar [lu·ˈtʃar] *vi* **~ por algo** to fight for sth, to struggle for sth

luche [ˈlu·tʃe] *m* Chile **1.** (*juego*) hopscotch **2.** BOT, CULIN sea lettuce

lucidez [lu·si·ˈðes, lu·θi·ˈðeθ] *f* **1.** (*estado*) lucidity **2.** (*clarividencia*) clarity; (*sagacidad*) clear-headedness

lúcido, -a [ˈlu·si·ðo, -a; ˈlu·θi-] *adj* **1.** (*clarividente*) clear-sighted; (*sagaz*) astute **2.** (*sobrio*) clear-headed

luciérnaga [lu·ˈsjer·na·ɣa, lu·ˈθjer-] *f* firefly

lucio [ˈlu·sjo, -θjo] *m* pike

lucir [lu·ˈsir, -ˈθir] *irr* **I.** *vi* **1.** (*brillar*) to shine **2.** (*verse*) to look good; **el vestido no le luce** the dress doesn't look good on her; **es un trabajo pesado y que no luce** it's hard work, though it doesn't look it **II.** *vt* (*exhibir*) to display; **lucía un bronceado impecable** he/she was showing off his/her perfect tan **III.** *vr*: **~se 1.** (*exhibirse*) to display **2.** (*destacarse*) to stand out; **¡ahora sí que nos hemos lucido!** *irón* now we've really made a mess of it!

lucrativo, -a [lu·kra·ˈti·βo, -a] *adj* lucrative; **sin fines ~s** non-profit making

lucro [ˈlu·kro] *m* profit; **organización sin ánimo de ~** non-profit organization

lúdico, -a [ˈlu·di·ko, -a] *adj* relating to games

luego [ˈlwe·ɣo] **I.** *adv* **1.** (*después*)

later; **¡hasta ~!** see you later! **2.** (*entonces*) then **3.** (*por supuesto*) **desde ~** of course **II.** *conj* **1.** (*así que*) and so **2.** (*después de*) **~ que** as soon as

lugar [lu·'yar] *m* place; **en primer/segundo ~** first/second; **tener ~** to take place; **en algún ~ de la casa** somewhere in the house; **la observación está fuera de ~** that comment is out of place; **en ~ de** instead of; **yo en ~ de usted...** if I were you...; **no des ~ a que te reprendan** don't give them any cause for reproach

lúgubre ['lu·yu·βre] *adj* gloomy

lujo ['lu·xo] *m* luxury; **permitirse el ~ de...** to treat oneself to the luxury of...; **con gran ~ de detalles** with a wealth of detail

lujoso, -a [lu·'xo·so, -a] *adj* luxurious

lujuria [lu·'xu·rja] *f* lechery, lust

lujurioso, -a [lu·xu·'rjo·so, -a] *adj* lecherous

lumbago [lum·'ba·yo] *m* MED lumbago

lumbar [lum·'bar] *adj* lumbar

lumbre ['lum·bre] *f* (*llamas*) fire; (*brasa*) glow

luminoso, -a [lu·mi·'no·so, -a] *adj* (*brillante*) bright, luminous; (*día*) light; **anuncio ~** illuminated [*o* neon] sign

luna ['lu·na] *f* **1.** ASTR moon; (*luz*) moonlight; **~ creciente/menguante** waxing/waning moon; **~ llena/nueva** full/new moon; **~ de miel** honeymoon; **media ~** half moon; **a la luz de la ~** in the moonlight; **estar en la ~** to be daydreaming **2.** (*cristal*) plate glass; **~s del coche** car windows

lunar [lu·'nar] **I.** *adj* lunar **II.** *m* (*en la piel*) mole; (*en una tela*) polka-dot

lunático, -a [lu·'na·ti·ko, -a] *adj* lunatic

lunes ['lu·nes] *m inv* Monday; **el ~** on Monday; **el ~ pasado** last Monday; **el ~ que viene** next Monday; **el ~ por la noche/al mediodía/por la mañana/por la tarde** Monday night/at noon/morning/afternoon; (**todos**) **los ~** every Monday, on Mondays; **en la noche del ~ al martes** in the small hours of Tuesday; **el ~ entero** all day Monday; **cada dos ~** every other Monday; **hoy es ~, once de marzo** today is Monday,

March 11th

lupa ['lu·pa] *f* magnifying glass; **mirar con ~** *fig* to examine meticulously

lustrabotas [lus·tra·'βo·tas] *mf inv AmL* shoeshine

lustrar [lus·'trar] *vt* to polish; (*zapatos*) to shine

lustro ['lus·tro] *m* lustrum; **en el último ~** *elev* in the last five years

lustroso, -a [lus·'tro·so, -a] *adj* shiny; **estar ~** *fig* to be radiant

luto ['lu·to] *m* mourning; **ir de ~** to wear mourning; **estar de ~ por alguien** to be in mourning for sb

luxación [luk·sa·'sjon, -'θjon] *f* MED dislocation

Luxemburgo [luk·sem·'bur·yo] *m* Luxembourg

luxemburgués, -esa [luk·sem·bur·'yes, --'ye·sa] *adj* Luxembourgish, Luxembourgian

luz [lus, luθ] *f* **1.** (*resplandor*) light; **~ corta** dipped headlights; **~ larga** full beam; **~ natural** natural light; **~ trasera** tail light; **traje de luces** bullfighter's suit; **a la ~ del día** in daylight; **a media ~** in subdued light; **dar a ~** to give birth; **¡~ de mis ojos!** the apple of my eye!; **sacar a la ~** *fig* to bring to light; **salir a la ~** *fig* to come to light; **a la ~ de los nuevos datos...** in the light of the new data... **2.** (*energía*) electricity; **¡da la ~!** turn on the light!; **se fue la ~** the power went off; **apagar/encender la ~** to turn off/on the light **3.** *pl* (*inteligencia*) intelligence; **el Siglo de las Luces** the Age of Enlightenment; **ser de pocas luces** to be dim-witted; **tener pocas luces** to be stupid; **a todas luces** evidently

M

M, m ['eme] *f* M, m; **~ de María** M as in Mike

Mª [ma·'ri·a] *abr de* **María** abbreviation for the name Mary

macabro, -a [ma·'ka·βro, -a] *adj* macabre

macagua [ma·'ka·ɣwa] *f* 1. *AmS* (*ave*) laughing falcon 2. *Ven* (*serpiente*) large poisonous snake 3. *Cuba* BOT macaw-tree

macanudo, -a [ma·ka·'nu·do, -a] *adj AmL inf* fantastic, super

macarra [ma·'ka·rra] *m inf* 1. (*chorizo*) roughneck 2. (*chulo*) pimp

macarrón [ma·ka·'rron] *m* (*pasta*) macaroni

macedonia [ma·se·'do·nja, ma·θe-] *f* ~ (**de frutas**) fruit salad

maceta [ma·'se·ta, -'θe·ta] *f* 1. (*tiesto*) flowerpot 2. *Chile* (*ramo*) bunch of flowers

macetero [ma·se·'te·ro, ma·θe-] *m* flowerpot stand; *AmL* flowerpot

machacar <c → qu> [ma·tʃa·'kar] I. *vt* 1. (*triturar*) to pound 2. (*insistir*) to insist on, to harp on 3. (*destruir*) to crush II. *vr*: ~**se** *inf* to wear oneself out

machete [ma·'tʃe·te] *m* 1. machete 2. *Arg, Urug, Col inf* (*chuleta*) crib (sheet)

machetear [ma·tʃe·te·'ar] I. *vi, vt Arg, Col inf* (*copiar*) to copy II. *vr*: ~**se** *Méx* (*trabajar*) to work; *inf* (*empollar*) to cram

machetero, -a [ma·tʃe·'te·ro, -a] *m, f* 1. *Arg inf* (*copión*) copycat 2. *Méx* (*empollón*) plodder

machismo [ma·'tʃis·mo] *m* male chauvinism

machista [ma·'tʃis·ta] *adj* (male) chauvinistic

macho ['ma·tʃo] *m* 1. ZOOL (*masculino*) male 2. *inf* (*machote*) tough guy

machote [ma·'tʃo·te] *m inf* (*hombre*) (tough) guy

macizo [ma·'si·so, -'θi·θo] *m* GEO massif

macizo, -a [ma·'si·so, -a; -'θi·θo, -a] *adj* 1. (*puerta*) solid; **de plata maciza** of solid silver 2. (*persona*) robust

macuto [ma·'ku·to] *m* 1. (*mochila*) backpack; MIL knapsack 2. *Ven* (*de los mendigos*) begging basket

madeja [ma·'de·xa] *f* skein

madera [ma·'de·ra] *f* (*de los árboles*) wood; ~ **prensada** particle board, chip-board; (*cortada*) timber, lumber; **de** ~ wooden; **¡toca** ~**!** knock on wood!; **tener** ~ **de** to have the makings of

madrastra [ma·'dras·tra] *f* stepmother

madre ['ma·dre] *f* mother; ~ **de alquiler** surrogate mother; ~ **de leche** wet nurse; ~ **política** mother-in-law; **futura** ~ mother-to-be; **¡**~**! (mía)!** goodness me!; **¡viva la** ~ **que te parió!** *inf* well done!; **sacar a alguien de** ~ *inf* to drive sb mad [*o* nuts]; **los alquileres se están saliendo de** ~ *inf* rents are becoming ridiculously high

Madrid [ma·'drid] *m* Madrid

madriguera [ma·dri·'ɣe·ra] *f* 1. (*guarida*) den; (*de conejo*) burrow; (*de ratón*) hole; (*de zorro*) earth 2. (*escondrijo*) lair

madrileño, -a [ma·dri·'le·ɲo, -a] *adj* of/ from Madrid

madrina [ma·'dri·na] *f* (*de bautismo*) godmother; ~ (**de boda**) maid of honor

madrugada [ma·dru·'ɣa·da] *f* dawn; **en la** [*o* **de**] ~ in the early morning; **salimos de viaje de** ~ we set off in the early hours; **a las cinco de la** ~ at five in the morning

madrugador(a) [ma·dru·ɣa·'dor, -·'do·ra] *adj* **ser muy** ~ to be an early riser [*o* early bird]

madrugar <g → gu> [ma·dru·'ɣar] *vi* to get up early ▶ **a quien madruga, Dios le ayuda** *prov* the early bird catches the worm *prov*; **no por mucho** ~ **amanece más temprano** *prov* ≈ everything will happen at its appointed time

madrugón [ma·dru·'ɣon] *m* **darse un** ~ to get up very early

madurar [ma·du·'rar] I. *vt* 1. (*hacer maduro: fruta*) to ripen; (*persona*) to mature 2. (*reflexionar sobre*) to think over II. *vi* 1. (*volverse maduro: fruta*) to ripen; (*persona*) to mature

madurez [ma·du·'res, -'reθ] *f* (*de fruta*) ripeness; (*de persona*) maturity; (*de un plan*) readiness; **estar en la** ~ to be middle-aged

maduro, -a [ma·'du·ro, -a] *adj* (*fruta*) ripe; (*persona: prudente*) mature; (*plan*) ready; **una manzana demasiado ma-**

dura an overripe apple; **estar a las duras y a las maduras** to take the bad with the good

maestría [maes·'tri·a] f (*habilidad*) mastery; **con ~** skillfully

maestro, -a [ma·'es·tro, -a] I. *adj* **obra maestra** masterpiece II. *m, f* 1. (*profesor*) teacher; **la vida es la mejor maestra** life is the best school 2. (*persona de gran conocimiento*) master 3. (*capataz*) overseer; **~ de cocina** master chef; **~ de obras** foreman

mafioso, -a [ma·'fjo·so, -a] *m, f* Mafioso

magdalena [mag·da·'le·na] f (*pastel*) sweet muffin

magia ['ma·xja] f magic; **como por arte de ~** as if by magic

mágico, -a ['ma·xi·ko, -a] *adj* 1. (*misterioso*) magic; **varita mágica** magic wand 2. (*maravilloso*) marvelous

magisterio [ma·xis·'te·rjo] *m* **dedicarse al ~** to be a teacher; **estudiar ~** to study to become a teacher

magistrado, -a [ma·xis·'tra·do, -a] *m, f* JUR (*juez*) magistrate; (*miembro del Tribunal Supremo*) Supreme Court judge

magistral [ma·xis·'tral] *adj* (*con maestría*) masterly

magma ['mag·ma] *m* magma

magnate [mag·'na·te] *m* tycoon; **~ de la prensa** press baron

magnesio [mag·'ne·sjo] *m* magnesium

magnético, -a [mag·'ne·ti·ko, -a] *adj* magnetic

magnetismo [mag·ne·'tis·mo] *m* magnetism

magnetizar <z → c> [mag·ne·ti·'sar, -'θar] *vt* to magnetize; (*retener la atención*) to captivate

magnífico, -a [mag·'ni·fi·ko, -a] *adj* (*excelente*) magnificent

magnitud [mag·ni·'tud] f magnitude

magnolia [mag·'no·lja] f magnolia

mago, -a ['ma·go, -a] *m, f* magician; **los Reyes Magos** the Magi, the Three Wise Men

magrear [ma·yre·'ar] *vt* vulg to feel up

magro ['ma·yro] *m* (*como el lomo*) tenderloin; inf (*carne magra*) lean meat

magro, -a ['ma·yro, -a] *adj* lean

maguey [ma·'gei] *m* AmL BOT maguey

magulladura [ma·yu·ja·'du·ra, ma·yu·ʎa-] f bruising

magullar [ma·yu·'jar, -'ʎar] *vt* to bruise

mahometano, -a [ma·o·me·'ta·no, -a] *adj, m, f* Muslim

mahonesa [ma·o·'ne·sa] f mayonnaise

maíz [ma·'is, -'iθ] *m* corn

majadería [ma·xa·de·'ri·a] f (*tontería*) idiocy

majadero, -a [ma·xa·'de·ro] *adj* (*porfiado*) pestering; (*imprudente*) foolish; (*loco*) crazy

majagua [ma·'xa·ywa] f Cuba 1. (*árbol*) type of linden tree 2. (*chaqueta*) suit jacket

majara [ma·'xa·ra], **majareta** [ma·xa·'re·ta] *adj* inf crazy, nuts

majarete [ma·xa·'re·te] *m* 1. Cuba (*galanteador*) Don Juan 2. PRico (*confusión*) commotion 3. Ant, Ven (*postre*) blancmange (*made with corn, milk and sugar*)

majestad [ma·xes·'tad] f Majesty; **Su Majestad** Your Majesty

majestuoso, -a [ma·xes·tu·'o·so, -a] *adj* majestic

majo, -a ['ma·xo, -a] *adj* 1. (*bonito*) lovely; (*guapo*) attractive 2. (*agradable*) pleasant

mal [mal] I. *adj v.* **malo** II. *m* 1. (*daño*) harm; (*injusticia*) wrong; (*sufrimiento*) suffering; **hacer ~ a alguien** to do sb harm 2. (*lo malo*) bad thing; **el ~ menor** the lesser evil; **menos ~** thank goodness 3. (*enfermedad*) illness; **~ de montaña** mountain sickness; **~ de vientre** stomach complaint 4. (*desgracia*) misfortune ▶ **el ~ de ojo** the evil eye; **no hay ~ que por bien no venga** *prov* every cloud has a silver lining III. *adv* 1. (*de mala manera, insuficientemente*) badly; **dejar ~ a alguien** to show sb in a bad light; **estar ~ de dinero** to be badly off; **esto acabará ~** this will end badly; **ir de ~ en peor** to go from bad to worse; **sentar ~** to upset; **ella me cae ~** I don't like her 2. (*equivocadamente*) wrongly 3. (*+ a mal*) **tomarse algo a ~** to take sth badly; **estoy a ~ con mi vecino** I'm on bad terms with my neighbor 4. (*mal que bien*) **~ que bien, el nego-**

M

cio sigue funcionando better or worse, the business is still working; **aprobar los exámenes más ~ que bien** to scrape through the exams

malabarismo [ma·la·βa·'ris·mo] *m* juggling

malabarista [ma·la·βa·'ris·ta] *mf* juggler

malaconsejar [mal·a·kon·se·'xar] *vt* to badly advise

malacostumbrado, -a [mal·a·kos·tum·'bra·ðo, -a] *adj* **estar ~** (*mimado*) to be spoiled; (*vicioso*) to have bad habits

malacostumbrar [mal·a·kos·tum·'brar] **I.** *vt* **1.** (*mimar*) to spoil **2.** (*educar mal*) to bring up badly **II.** *vr:* **~se** to get into a bad habit

malapata [ma·la·'pa·ta] *mf* clumsy oaf; **tener ~** (*poca destreza*) to be maladroit; (*malas intenciones*) to have wicked intentions; (*mala suerte*) to be unlucky; **la cosa tiene ~** *fig* it is ill-starred [*o* fated]

malaria [ma·'la·rja] *f* malaria

malcriado, -a [mal·kri·'a·ðo, -a] *adj* (*mal educado*) spoiled

malcriar <*1. pres* malcrío> [mal·kri·'ar] *vt* to bring up badly; (*mimar*) to spoil

maldad [mal·'dað] *f* evil, wickedness

maldecir [mal·de·'sir, -'θir] *irr* **I.** *vt* to curse, to damn **II.** *vi* **1.** (*jurar*) to swear **2.** (*quejarse*) **~ de algo/alguien** to complain about sth/sb

maldición [mal·di·'sjon, -'θjon] *f* **1.** (*imprecación*) curse; **me ha caído una ~** a curse has been put on me **2.** (*juramento*) swear word; **soltar una ~ contra alguien** to swear at sb

maldito, -a [mal·'di·to] **I.** *pp de* **maldecir II.** *adj* **1.** (*endemoniado*) damned; **¡maldita sea!** *inf* damn (it)!; **¡~ seas!** *vulg* damn you!; **¡maldita la gracia (que me hace)!** I don't find it funny at all! **2.** (*maligno*) wicked; **¡vete, ~!** get out of here!

maldoso, -a [mal·'do·so, -a] *adj Méx* wicked

maleable [ma·le·'a·βle] *adj* **1.** (*forjable*) malleable; (*flexible*) pliable **2.** (*dócil*) pliant

maleante [ma·le·'an·te] *adj* (*delincuen-*

te) delinquent; (*persona maligna*) miscreant

malecón [ma·le·'kon] *m* dyke; (*rompeolas*) breakwater

maleducado, -a [mal·e·du·'ka·ðo, -a] *adj* ill-mannered; (*niño*) ill-bred; (*mimado*) spoiled; (*descortés*) rude

maleducar [mal·e·du·'kar] *vt* to spoil

maleficio [ma·le·'fi·sjo, -θjo] *m* (*hechizo*) curse; (*daño*) harm

maléfico, -a [ma·'le·fi·ko, -a] *adj* evil

malentendido [mal·en·ten·'di·ðo] *m* misunderstanding

malestar [ma·les·'tar] *m* malaise; (*espiritual*) uneasiness

maleta [ma·'le·ta] *f* suitcase; **hacer la ~** to pack one's suitcase

maletera [ma·le·'te·ra] *f Col, Méx*, **maletero** [ma·le·'te·ro] *m* AUTO trunk

maletero, -a [ma·le·'te·ro, -a] *m, f Chile* (*ladrón*) thief

maletín [ma·le·'tin] *m* **1.** briefcase; **~ (de viaje)** overnight bag **2.** (*de aseo*) toilet bag

malévolo, -a [ma·'le·βo·lo, -a] *adj* malevolent

maleza [ma·'le·sa, -θa] *f* weeds *pl*; (*matorral*) thicket

malgastar [mal·ɣas·'tar] *vt* to waste; **~ todo el dinero en tabaco** to squander all the money on cigarettes; **~ una oportunidad** to waste an opportunity

malhechor(a) [mal·e·'tʃor(a)] *m(f)* delinquent, wrongdoer

malherir [mal·e·'rir] *irr como sentir vt* to seriously injure

malhumorado, -a [mal·u·mo·'ra·ðo, -a] *adj* bad-tempered

malicia [ma·'li·sja, -θja] *f* **1.** (*intención malévola*) malice **2.** (*maldad*) wickedness **3.** (*picardía*) mischievousness; **tener mucha ~** to be full of mischief

malicioso, -a [ma·li·'sjo·so, -a; -θjo·so, -a] *adj* malicious; (*maligno*) malign

maligno, -a [ma·'liɣ·no] *adj* (*pernicioso*) malign; MED malignant

malinchista [ma·lin·'tʃis·ta] *mf Méx* person who favors foreign things

malintencionado, -a [mal·in·ten·sjo·'na·do, -a, -θjo·'na·do, -a] *adj* unkind

malinterpretar [mal·in·ter·pre·'tar] *vt* to misinterpret

malla ['ma·ja, -'ʎa] *f* **1.** (*de un tejido*) mesh, weave; **de ~ ancha/estrecha/fina** open/close/fine weave **2.** *pl* (*pantalones*) leggings *pl* **3.** *AmL* (*de baño*) swimsuit

Mallorca [ma·jor·'ka, ma·ʎor-] *f* Majorca

mallorquín, -ina [ma·jor·'kin, ma·ʎor-] *adj* of/from Majorca

malo, -a ['ma·lo, -a] I. *adj* <peor, pésimo> (*precediendo un sustantivo masc. sing: mal*) **1.** (*en general*) bad; **fumar es ~ para la salud** smoking is bad for your health; **de mala gana** unwillingly; **me gusta la casa, lo ~ es que es demasiado cara** I like the house, the problem is that it is too expensive; **tener mala mano para algo** to have no talent for sth; **tener mala suerte** to be unlucky; **hace un tiempo malísimo** the weather is really bad; **hacer un trabajo de mala manera** to do a job badly **2.** *ser* (*falso*) false **3.** *ser* (*malévolo*) nasty; **tener mal genio** to have a bad temper; **una mala persona** a nasty person; **venir de malas** to have a hostile attitude **4.** *estar* (*enfermo*) ill **5.** *ser* (*travieso*) naughty **6.** *estar* (*estropeado*) spoiled; (*leche*) sour ▶ **más vale ~ conocido que** <u>bueno</u> **por conocer** *prov* better the devil you know II. *adv* **podemos llegar a un acuerdo por las buenas o por las malas** we can reach an agreement by fair means or foul; **andar a malas** to be on bad terms III. *m, f* (*persona*) bad man *m*, bad woman *f*; CINE baddie; **los ~s de la peli** the bad guys

malograr [ma·lo·'ɣrar] I. *vt* **1.** (*desaprovechar*) to waste; (*frustrar*) to frustrate; **has malogrado la ocasión** you have wasted the occasion **2.** (*estropear*) to ruin II. *vr:* **~se 1.** (*fallar*) to fail; **se han malogrado mis esperanzas** my hopes have come to nothing **2.** (*estropearse*) to be ruined

maloliente [mal·o·'ljen·te] *adj* foul-smelling

malparar [mal·pa·'rar] *vt* (*persona*) to come off badly; **salió malparado de la pelea** he came off worse in the fight

malpensado, -a [mal·pen·'sa·do, -a] *adj* evil-minded; **no seas tan ~** don't be so cynical

malsano, -a [mal·'sa·no, -a] *adj* unhealthy; (*moralmente*) unwholesome

malsonante [mal·so·'nan·te] *adj* (*sonido*) jarring; (*palabra*) nasty

malta ['mal·ta] *f* **1.** *t.* AGR malt **2.** *Arg* (*cerveza*) beer

maltratar [mal·tra·'tar] *vt* to maltreat; **~** (*de palabra*) to abuse (verbally)

maltrato [mal·'tra·to] *m* maltreatment, abuse; (*insulto*) (verbal) abuse

maltrecho, -a [mal·'tre·tʃo, -a] *adj* (*golpeado*) battered

malva ['mal·βa] I. *adj* mauve II. *f* mallow; **estar criando ~s** *inf* to be pushing up daisies; **ser (como) una ~** *inf* to be meek and mild

malvado, -a [mal·'βa·do, -a] *adj* wicked

malvender [mal·βen·'der] *vt* to sell at a loss

malversar [mal·βer·'sar] *vt* to misappropriate, to embezzle

Malvinas [mal·'βi·nas] *fpl* Falkland Islands *pl*

malvón [mal·'βon] *m Arg, Méx, Par, Urug* BOT geranium

mama ['ma·ma] *f* (*pecho*) breast; (*ubre*) udder

mamá [ma·'ma] *f inf* mom(my)

mamada [ma·'ma·da] *f* **1.** (*acción*) breastfeeding **2.** (*cantidad mamada*) breastfeed **3.** *AmL* (*ganga*) bargain; **¡vaya ~!** what a bargain!

mamadera [ma·ma·'de·ra] *f AmL* baby bottle

mamar [ma·'mar] I. *vi, vt* (*en el pecho*) to breastfeed II. *vr:* **~se** *vulg* (*emborracharse*) to get sloshed

mamarracho [ma·ma·'rra·tʃo] *m inf* ridiculous person

mamífero [ma·'mi·fe·ro] *m* mammal

mamografía [ma·mo·ɣra·'fi·a] *f* MED mammogram, mammography

mamón, -ona [ma·'mon] *m, f* **1.** *vulg* (*insulto*) jerk **2.** *AmL inf* (*borracho*) drunk

M

mampara [mam·'pa·ra] f screen (door), (room) divider

mamporro [mam·'po·rro] m inf clout; **darse un ~ contra algo** to bash oneself against sth

mamut <mamuts> [ma·'mut] m mammoth

manada [ma·'na·da] f (rebaño de vacas, ciervos) herd; (de peces) shoal; (de lobos) pack; **~ de gente** crowd of people; **pasamos la frontera en ~** we crossed over the border en masse

manantial [ma·nan·'tjal] m spring; **~ caliente** hot spring

manar [ma·'nar] I. vt to flow with; **la herida no paraba de ~ sangre** the wound wouldn't stop flowing with blood II. vi 1. (surgir) to well; **el agua manaba sucia de la fuente** dirty water welled from the fountain 2. (fluir fácilmente) to flow; **las palabras manaban de su boca** the words flowed from his/her mouth

manazas [ma·'nasas, -θas] mf inv inf clumsy person, klutz; **ser un ~** to be clumsy

mancha ['man·tʃa] f 1. (en la ropa, piel) dirty mark; (de tinta) stain; (salpicadura) spot 2. (toque de color) fleck; **este perro es blanco con ~s negras** this dog is white with black patches

Mancha ['man·tʃa] f **el canal de la ~** the (English) Channel

manchado, -a [man·'tʃa·do, -a] adj (ropa, mantel) stained; (cara, fruta) dirty

manchar [man·'tʃar] I. vt to dirty II. vr: **~se** (ensuciarse) to get dirty

mancillar [man·si·'jar, -θi·'ʎar] vt to sully

manco, -a ['man·ko] adj (de un brazo) one-armed; (de una mano) one-handed; **no ser** (**cojo ni**) **~** (ser hábil) to be dexterous; (ser largo de manos) to be light-fingered

mancomunidad [man·ko·mu·ni·'dad] f (comunidad) community

mandamás [man·da·'mas] mf pey inf big shot

mandamiento [man·da·'mjen·to] m 1. (orden) order; **~ judicial** court order 2. (precepto) precept 3. REL commandment

mandar [man·'dar] vt 1. (ordenar) to order; **~ a alguien que** +subj to order sb to; **lo que Ud. mande** whatever you say 2. (dirigir) to lead; (gobernar) to govern 3. (encargar) to ask to get/do/come 4. (enviar) to send; **~ al cuerno** inf to send to hell

mandarina [man·da·'ri·na] f mandarin, tangerine

mandatario, -a [man·da·'ta·rjo, -a] m, f agent; **primer ~** POL head of state

mandato [man·'da·to] m 1. (orden) order; **~ judicial** injunction 2. POL mandate; **~ parlamentario** parliamentary mandate

mandíbula [man·'di·βu·la] f ANAT jaw

mandil [man·'dil] m AmL (de caballería) cloth (used to rub down a horse)

mandinga [man·'din·ga] m 1. AmL inf (diablo) devil 2. Arg inf (muchacho) scamp

mando ['man·do] m 1. (poder) control; MIL command; (del presidente) term of office; **don de ~** leadership qualities; **estar al ~ de** to be in command of; **estar bajo el ~ de alguien** to be under sb's command 2. (quien lo tiene) **alto ~** MIL high command 3. TÉC control; **~ a distancia** remote control

mandón, -ona [man·'don, --'do·na] adj bossy

manecilla [ma·ne·'si·ja, -'θi·'ʎa] f (del reloj) hand; TÉC pointer

manejable [ma·ne·'xa·βle] adj user-friendly; (persona) tractable

manejar [ma·ne·'xar] I. vt 1. (usar) to use; (máquina) to operate; fig to handle; **~ un cuchillo** to use a knife; **manejas bien las cifras** you are good with numbers; **'¡manéjese con cuidado!'** 'handle with care!' 2. (dirigir) to handle 3. (a alguien) to manage; **maneja al marido a su antojo** she can twist her husband around her little finger 4. AmL (un coche) to drive II. vr: **~se** to manage; **saber ~se en la vida** to know how to get on in life

manejo [ma·'ne·xo] m 1. (uso) use; (de una máquina) operation; fig handling 2. COMPUT management; **~ de la memoria** memory management 3. AmL (de un coche) driving

manera [ma·'ne·ra] *f* 1. (*forma, modo*) manner, way; ~ **de decir** way of saying; ~ **de pensar** way of thinking; ~ **de proceder** way of acting; **es su** ~ **de ser** that's the way he/she is; **a la** ~ **de sus abuelos** in the way their grandparents did; **a mi** ~ my way; **de la** ~ **sea** somehow or other; **de cualquier** ~ **de todas** ~**s** anyway; **de esta** ~ that way; **de** ~ **que** (*finalidad*) so that; **¿de** ~ **que sacaste mala nota?** so you got a bad mark, did you?; **de ninguna** ~ no way; **se echó a gritar de tal** ~ **que...** *inf* he/she started to shout in such a way that...; **de una** ~ **o de otra** one way or another; **en cierta** ~ in a way; **en gran** ~ largely; **no hay** ~ **de...** there is no way that...; **¡qué** ~ **de llover!** just look at the rain!; **sobre** ~ a lot; **primero se lo dije de buena** ~ first I said it to him nicely; **contestar de mala** ~ to answer rudely; **hacer las cosas de mala** ~ to do things badly 2. *pl* (*modales*) manners *pl*; **¡estas no son** ~**s!** this is no way to behave!

manga ['man·ga] *f* 1. (*del vestido*) sleeve; **de** ~ **corta/larga** short-/long-sleeved; **estar en** ~**s de camisa** to be in shirt-sleeves; **andar** ~ **por hombro** *inf* to be a mess; **poner algo** ~ **por hombro** *inf* to turn sth inside out; **sacarse algo de la** ~ *fig* to come up with sth; **hacer un corte de** ~**s a alguien** ≈ to give sb the finger; **tener (la) [o ser de] la** ~ **ancha** *fig* to be lenient; **tienen algo en la manga** they are keeping sth up their sleeve 2. METEO *fig* ~ **de viento** tornado; ~ **de agua** waterspout 3. *Arg pey* (*grupo de personas*) mob

manganeta [man·ga·'ne·ta] *f Hond* trick

mangante [man·'gan·te] *mf inf* (*ladrón*) thief

manganzón, -ona [man·gan·'son, -·'so·na; -'θon, -·'θo·na] *m, f AmL* loafer

mangar <g → gu> [man·'gar] *vt inf* to swipe; (*en tiendas*) to shoplift

mangle ['man·gle] *m AmL* BOT mangrove tree

mango ['man·go] *m* 1. (*puño*) knob; (*alargado*) handle; **tener la sartén por**

el ~ *fig* to hold the reins 2. (*árbol*) mango tree; (*fruta*) mango

mangonear [man·go·ne·'ar] *inf* I. *vi* 1. (*entrometerse*) to meddle 2. (*vaguear*) to loaf II. *vt* to wangle; **está mangoneando todo** he/she has a finger in every pie

mangoneo [man·go·'ne·o] *m inf* 1. (*entremetimiento*) meddling 2. (*vagancia*) idleness

manguera [man·'ge·ra] *f* (*tubo*) hose

maní [ma·'ni] *m* peanut

manía [ma·'ni·a] *f* 1. (*locura*) mania 2. (*extravagancia*) eccentricity, quirk 3. (*obsesión*) obsession 4. *inf* (*aversión*) aversion; **tener** ~ **a alguien** not to be able to stand sb; **coger** ~ **a alguien** to take a dislike to sb

maniaco, -a [ma·'nja·ko, -a], **maníaco, -a** [ma·'ni·a·ko, -a] *m, f* maniac

maniatar [ma·nja·'tar] *vt* ~ **a alguien** to tie sb's hands up

maniático, -a [ma·'nja·ti·ko, -a] *m, f* 1. (*extravagante*) fusspot 2. (*loco*) maniac; **un** ~ **de la limpieza** a cleaning maniac

manicomio [ma·ni·'ko·mjo] *m* psychiatric hospital; *fig* (*casa de locos*) madhouse

manicura [ma·ni·'ku·ra] *f* manicure

manifestación [ma·ni·fes·ta·'sjon, -'θjon] *f* 1. (*expresión*) expression; **como** ~ **de cariño** as an expression of love 2. (*reunión*) demonstration

manifestante [ma·ni·fes·'tan·te] *mf* demonstrator

manifestar <e → ie> [ma·ni·fes·'tar] I. *vt* 1. (*declarar*) to declare 2. (*mostrar*) to show II. *vr:* ~**se** 1. (*declararse*) to declare oneself; ~**se a favor/en contra de algo** to declare oneself for/against sth 2. (*revelarse*) to show oneself 3. (*política*) to demonstrate

manifiesto [ma·ni·'fjes·to] *m* manifesto

manifiesto, -a [ma·ni·'fjes·to, -a] *adj* (*evidente*) manifest; **poner de** ~ (*revelar*) to show [*o* make clear]; (*expresar*) to declare

manigua [ma·'ni·ɣwa] *f Cuba* jungle

manija [ma·'ni·xa] *f* handle

manilla [ma·'ni·ja, -ʎa] *f* (*del reloj*) hand

M

manillar [ma·ni·'jar, -ʎar] *m* handlebars *pl*

maniobra [ma·ni·o·βra] *f* 1. (*operación manual*) handling 2. (*ardid*) ploy 3. MIL maneuver; **estar de ~s** to be on maneuvers 4. (*vehículo*) maneuver

maniobrar [ma·njo·'βrar] I. *vi* MIL to carry out maneuvers II. *vt* 1. (*manejar*) to handle 2. (*manipular*) to manipulate

manipulación [ma·ni·pu·la·'sjon, -'θjon] *f* 1. (*empleo*) use, handling 2. (*alteración*) manipulation

manipular [ma·ni·pu·'lar] *vt* 1. (*máquina*) to operate 2. (*alterar*) to manipulate 3. (*interferir*) ~ **algo** to interfere with sth 4. (*manosear*) ~ **algo** to fiddle with sth

maniquí <maniquíes> [ma·ni·'ki] *m* (*para ropa*) mannequin

manirroto, -a [ma·ni·'rro·to, -a] *adj* spendthrift

manitas [ma·'ni·tas] **hacer** ~ *inf* to neck; **ser un** ~ *inf* to be dexterous, to be good with one's hands

manito [ma·'ni·to] *m Méx* pal

manivela [ma·ni·'βe·la] *f* handle

manjar [man·'xar] *m* food; (*exquisitez*) delicacy

mano ['ma·no] *f* 1. ANAT hand; **a ~ alzada** (*votación*) by a show of hands; **a ~ armada** armed; **a ~s llenas** in abundance; **alzar la ~ contra alguien** to raise one's hand to sb; **apretón de ~s** handshake; **coger a alguien con las ~s en la masa** to catch sb red-handed; **cogidos de las ~s** hand in hand; **comer de la ~ de alguien** *fig* to eat out of sb's hand; **me lo prometió con la ~ en el corazón** he/she promised me with his/her hand on his/her heart; **echar una ~ a alguien** to give sb a hand; **dejar algo en ~s de alguien** to leave sth in sb's hands; **echar ~ de alguien** to make use of sb; **estar al alcance de la ~** to be within (arm's) reach; **estar ~ sobre ~** *fig* to be idle; **hecho a ~** hand-made; **su vida se le había ido de las ~s** his/her life has gotten out of hand; **se le ha ido la ~** (*desmesura*) he/she has overdone it; (*violencia*) he/she has lost control; **lavarse las ~s (en algo)** to wash one's hands of sth; **llevar a alguien de la ~** to lead sb by the hand; *fig* to guide sb; ~

a ~ *fig* hand in hand; **¡~s a la obra!** to work!; **meter ~ a alguien** *inf* to touch sb up; **pedir la ~ de alguien** to ask for sb's hand in marriage; **poner la ~ en el fuego por alguien** to stick one's neck out for someone; **echar ~ de algo** to draw on sth; **traer algo entre ~s** to be up to sth!; **¡venga esa ~!** let's shake on it! 2. ZOOL (*de un mono*) hand; (*de un perro*) paw; ~ **de cerdo** pig's trotter 3. (*lado*) ~ **derecha/izquierda** right-/left-hand side; **a la** *o* **de la ~ derecha** on the right(-hand side) 4. (*capa*) coat; **una ~ de pintura** a coat of paint 5. (*trabajador*) hand; ~ **de obra** labor 6. (*habilidad*) skill; **tener buena ~ para coser** to be good at sewing; **tener ~ izquierda** to be tactful; **tener ~ con** to have a way with; ~ **de santo** sure remedy 7. (*de naipes*) hand; **ser** ~ to lead

manojo [ma·'no·xo] *m* bunch; ~ **de llaves** bunch of keys; **ser un** ~ **de nervios** to be a bundle of nerves

manopla [ma·'no·pla] *f* mitten; (*para lavarse*) washcloth

manoseado, -a [ma·no·se·'a·do, -a] *adj* (*sobado*) worn; (*trillado*) hackneyed

manosear [ma·no·se·'ar] *vt* to handle

manotazo [ma·no·'ta·so, -θo] *m* smack

mansarda [man·'sar·da] *f AmC, AmS* attic

mansión [man·'sjon] *f* (*casa suntuosa*) mansion

manso, -a ['man·so] *adj* docile; (*animales*) tame; (*aguas*) quiet

manta¹ ['man·ta] *f* blanket; **a** ~ in abundance; **liarse la** ~ **a la cabeza** (*actuar con decisión*) to take it on oneself to do sth; (*de modo irreflexivo*) to recklessly decide to do sth; **tirar de la** ~ to let the cat out of the bag

manta² ['man·ta] *mf* (*persona torpe*) oaf

manteca [man·'te·ka] *f* 1. (*grasa*) fat; ~ **de cerdo** lard 2. *RíoPl* (*mantequilla*) butter

mantel [man·'tel] *m* tablecloth

mantener [man·te·'ner] *irr como* tener I. *vt* 1. (*conservar, relaciones*) to maintain; (*orden*) to keep; **mantiene la línea** he/she keeps his/her figure; ~ **la calma**

to keep calm **2.** (*perseverar*) ~ **algo** to keep sth up **3.** (*sustentar*) to maintain **4.** (*sostener*) to support **5.** (*proseguir*) to continue; ~ **una conversación con alguien** to hold a conversation with sb **II.** *vr:* **~se 1.** (*sostenerse*) to support oneself **2.** (*continuar*) to continue **3.** (*perseverar*) to keep; **se mantiene en sus trece** *inf* he/she is sticking to his/her guns

mantenimiento [man·te·ni·'mjen·to] *m* **1.** (*alimentos*) sustenance **2.** TÉC maintenance; ~ **de datos** COMPUT database update; **sin** ~ maintenance-free **3.** (*de una propiedad*) upkeep

mantequilla [man·te·'ki·ja, -ʎa] *f* butter

mantilla [man·'ti·ja, -ʎa] *f* **1.** (*de mujer*) mantilla **2.** (*de niño*) swaddling clothes *pl*

manto ['man·to] *m* **1.** (*prenda*) cloak **2.** (*capa*) layer; ~ **terrestre** earth's crust

mantón [man·'ton] *m* shawl

manual [ma·nu·'al] **I.** *adj* manual, hand; **trabajos** ~**es** handicrafts *pl* **II.** *m* manual, handbook; ~ **de instrucciones** instruction manual

manufacturar [ma·nu·fak·tu·'rar] *vt* to manufacture

manuscrito [ma·nus·'kri·to] *m* manuscript

manuscrito, -a [ma·nus·'kri·to, -a] *adj* handwritten

manutención [ma·nu·ten·'sjon, -'θjon] *f* **1.** (*alimentos*) keep **2.** TÉC maintenance

manzana [man·'sa·na, -'θa·na] *f* **1.** (*fruta*) apple; **sano como una** ~ as fit as a fiddle **2.** (*conjunto de casas*) block; **dar la vuelta a la** ~ to go around the block **3.** *AmL* ANAT (*nuez*) Adam's apple

manzanilla [man·sa·'ni·ja, man·θa·'ni·ʎa] *f* **1.** (*planta*) chamomile; (*flor*) chamomile flower; (*infusión*) chamomile tea **2.** (*vino*) manzanilla

manzano [man·'sa·no, -'θa·no] *m* apple tree

maña ['ma·ɲa] *f* **1.** (*habilidad*) skill, dexterity; **tener** ~ **para algo** to have a knack for sth **2.** (*astucia*) craftiness **3.** *pl* (*caprichos*) whims *pl*; **tiene** ~**s** he/she has his/her little whims ▶ **más**

vale ~ **que fuerza** *prov* better brains than brawn

mañana¹ [ma·'ɲa·na] **I.** *f* (*temprano*) early morning; (*hasta el mediodía*) morning; **a las 5 de la** ~ at 5 a.m.; **de la noche a la** ~ overnight; **por la** ~ in the morning; **todas las** ~**s** every morning; ~ **por la** ~ tomorrow morning **II.** *adv* **1.** (*día*) tomorrow; **¡hasta** ~**!** see you tomorrow!; ~ **será otro día** tomorrow is another day; **pasado** ~ the day after tomorrow **2.** (*futuro*) tomorrow ▶ **no dejes para** ~ **lo que puedas hacer hoy** *prov* do not leave for tomorrow what you can do today

mañana² [ma·'ɲa·na] *m* tomorrow; **el día de** ~ in the future

mañanero, -a [ma·ɲa·'ne·ro, -a] *adj* **1.** (*madrugador*) early-rising **2.** (*de la mañana*) morning

mañero, -a [ma·'ɲe·ro, -a] *adj Arg inf* fussy

mañoso, -a [ma·'ɲo·so, -a] *adj* (*hábil*) dexterous, handy

mapa ['ma·pa] *m* map; ~ **del tiempo** weather map; **borrar del** ~ (*matar*) to wipe off the face of the earth; **desaparecer del** ~ to vanish into thin air; **no estar en el** ~ *fig* to be out of this world

mapache [ma·'pa·tʃe] *m* raccoon

maqueta [ma·'ke·ta] *f* **1.** ARQUIT (*scale*) model **2.** (*formato*) format

maquetación [ma·ke·ta·'sjon, -'θjon] *f* layout

maquillaje [ma·ki·'ja·xe, -ʎa·xe] *m* **1.** (*acción*) application of make-up **2.** (*producto*) make-up

maquillar [ma·ki·'jar, -ʎar] **I.** *vt* **1.** to apply make-up to **2.** (*disimular*) to disguise **II.** *vr:* **~se** to put on make-up

máquina ['ma·ki·na] *f* **1.** (*artefacto*) machine; ~ **de afeitar** electric shaver [*o* razor]; ~ **de coser/lavar** sewing/washing machine; ~ **de escribir** (**automática**) (electric) typewriter; **a toda** ~ (at) full speed; **escrito a** ~ typed; **hecho a** ~ machine-made **2.** ~ **de tabaco** cigarette dispenser; ~ **tragaperras** *inf* slotmachine

maquinar [ma·ki·'nar] *vt* (*urdir*) to scheme

M

maquinaria [ma·ki·'na·rja] *f* (*máquinas*) machinery

maquinilla [ma·ki·'ni·ja, -ʎa] *f* (safety) razor

maquinista [ma·ki·'nis·ta] *mf* (*conductor*) machinist

mar [mar] *m o f* **1.** GEO sea; **Mar Antártico** Antarctic Ocean; **Mar Báltico** Baltic Sea; **Mar de Irlanda** Irish Sea; **Mar Mediterráneo** Mediterranean Sea; **Mar del Norte** North Sea; **en alta ~** offshore; **~ adentro** high seas; **~ gruesa/picada/rizada** heavy/rough/choppy sea; *fig* unrest; **por ~** by sea; **hacerse a la ~** to put out to sea; **al otro lado del ~** overseas **2.** *inf* **la ~ de...** loads of...; **llueve a ~es** it is raining cats and dogs; **lloró a ~es** he/she cried his/her eyes out; **sudar a ~es** to pour with sweat; **ser la ~ de aburrido** to be excruciatingly boring

maraña [ma·'ra·ɲa] *f* (*lío*) mess; **~ de cabello** tangle of hair; **~ de hilo** tangle of threads

maratón [ma·ra·'ton] *m o f* marathon

maravilla [ma·ra·'βi·ja, -ʎa] *f* (*portento*) marvel; **a las mil ~s de ~** marvelously; **hablar ~s de alguien** to speak extremely well of sb; **hacer ~s** *fig* to work wonders

maravillar [ma·ra·βi·'jar, -ʎar] I. *vt* to amaze II. *vr* **~se de algo** to marvel at sth

maravilloso, -a [ma·ra·βi·'jo·so, -a; -ʎo·so, -a] *adj* marvelous

marca ['mar·ka] *f* **1.** (*distintivo*) mark; **~ de agua** watermark; **~ de ganado** brand **2.** (*de productos*) brand; **~ registrada** registered trademark; **ropa de ~** designer label **3.** (*huella*) impression **4.** DEP record

marcación *f* **~ por voz** TEL voice dialing

marcado, -a [mar·'ka·do] *adj* (*señalado*) marked; (*evidente*) clear

marcador [mar·ka·'dor] *m* **1.** (*tablero*) scoreboard; **abrir el ~** to open the scoring **2.** *Arg* (*rotulador*) marker pen

marcaje [mar·'ka·xe] *m* DEP marking, cover(age)

marcapaso(s) [mar·ka·'pa·so(s)] *m (inv)* pacemaker

marcar <c → qu> [mar·'kar] I. *vt* **1.** (*señalar*) to mark; (*ganado*) to brand; (*mercancías*) to label; **~ una época** to denote an era; **~ el compás** to beat time **2.** (*resaltar*) to emphasize **3.** (*teléfono*) to dial **4.** DEP **~ un gol** to score a goal; **~ un punto** to score a point **5.** DEP (*a un jugador*) to mark, to cover II. *vr*: **~se** to show

marcha ['mar·tʃa] *f* **1.** (*movimiento*) progress; **poner en ~** to start **2.** (*caminata*) hike **3.** (*curso*) course; **la ~ de los acontecimientos** the course of events; **sobre la ~** along the way **4.** (*velocidad*) gear; **~ atrás** reverse; **a toda ~** at full speed **5.** *t.* MIL, MÚS march; **~ silenciosa** silent march **6.** (*salida*) departure; **¡en ~!** let's go! **7.** *inf* (*acción*) action; **¡aquí hay mucha ~!** this is where the action is!; **ir de ~** to go out on the town; **tener ~** to be full of go

marchar [mar·'tʃar] I. *vi* **1.** (*ir*) to go; **¡marchando!** let's go! **2.** (*funcionar*) to work; **~ sobre ruedas** *fig* to go like clockwork II. *vr*: **~se** (*irse*) to leave

marchitar [mar·tʃi·'tar] I. *vi* (*plantas*) to wither; (*personas*) to be on the wane II. *vr*: **~se** to wither

marchito, -a [mar·'tʃi·to, -a] *adj* withered

marchoso, -a [mar·'tʃo·so, -a] *adj inf* fun-loving

marcial [mar·'sjal, -'θjal] *adj* martial; **artes ~es** martial arts; **ley ~** martial law

marciano, -a [mar·'sja·no, -a; 'θja·no, -a] *adj, m, f* Martian

marco ['mar·ko] *m* **1.** (*recuadro*) frame; (*armazón*) framework; **el ~ legal** the legal framework **2.** (*ambiente*) background

marea [ma·'rea] *f* (*mar*) tide; **~ alta** high tide; **~ baja** low tide; **~ creciente** rising tide; **~ menguante** ebb tide; **~ negra** oil slick [*o* spill]; **una ~ humana** a flood of people

mareado, -a [ma·re·'a·do, -a] *adj* **1.** (*in-*

marear [ma·re·'ar] **I.** vt **1.** inf (molestar) to pester **2.** MED (aturdir) to make dizzy; fig to confuse **II.** vr: ~ **se 1.** (enfermarse) to feel sick; (en el mar) to get seasick; (al viajar) to get travel-sick **2.** (quedar aturdido) to become dizzy; fig to become confused **3.** (emborracharse) to get tipsy

marejada [ma·re·'xa·da] f swell

maremoto [ma·re·'mo·to] m tidal wave; (seísmo) seaquake

mareo [ma·'reo] m **1.** (malestar) nausea; (en el mar) seasickness; (al viajar) travel-sickness, motion sickness **2.** (vértigo) dizziness

marfil [mar·'fil] m ivory

margarina [mar·ya·'ri·na] f margarine

margarita [mar·ya·'ri·ta] f **1.** BOT daisy; **deshojar la ~** to play 'he/she loves me, he/she loves me not' **2.** (bebida) margarita

margen ['mar·xen] m o f **1.** (borde) edge; **el ~ del río** the riverside [o riverbank]; **al ~** apart; **dejar al ~** to leave out; **mantenerse al ~ de algo** fig to keep out of sth **2.** (página) margin **3.** (libertad) leeway; **dar ~** to give leeway **4.** (ganancia) profit margin; **~ de seguridad** safety margin

marginado, -a [mar·xi·'na·do, -a] adj **1.** (excluido) excluded, marginalized **2.** (aislado) isolated

marginal [mar·xi·'nal] adj **1.** (al margen) apart **2.** (secundario) secondary

marginar [mar·xi·'nar] vt (ignorar algo) to disregard; (a alguien) to marginalize

maría [ma·'ri·a] f inf (marihuana) grass, pot

mariachi [ma·'rja·tʃi] m Méx mariachi musician

marido [ma·'ri·do] m husband

mariguana [ma·ri·'ɣwa·na], **marihuana** [ma·ri·'wa·na] f marijuana, marihuana

marimba [ma·'rim·ba] f **1.** MÚS (de maderas) marimba; (tambor) African drum **2.** Arg (paliza) beating

marina [ma·'ri·na] f navy; **la ~ mercante** the merchant marine

marinero [ma·ri·'ne·ro] m sailor; **~ de agua dulce** irón landlubber

marinero, -a [ma·ri·'ne·ro, -a] adj **1.** (relativo al mar) marine; **pueblo ~** coastal town **2.** (relativo a la marina) marine; **nudo ~** sailor's knot

marino [ma·'ri·no] m sailor, seaman

marino, -a [ma·'ri·no, -a] adj marine

marioneta [ma·rjo·'ne·ta] f (títere) puppet, marionette

mariposa [ma·ri·'po·sa] f ZOOL butterfly ► **¡a otra cosa ~!** let's change the subject!

mariquita [ma·ri·'ki·ta] f (insecto) ladybug

marisco [ma·'ris·ko] m seafood

marisma [ma·'ris·ma] f marsh

marisquería [ma·ris·ke·'ri·a] f (tienda) seafood shop; (restaurante) seafood restaurant

marital [ma·ri·'tal] adj marital; **vida ~** married life

marítimo, -a [ma·'ri·ti·mo, -a] adj maritime, marine; **ciudad marítima** seaside town

marmita [mar·'mi·ta] f pot

mármol ['mar·mol] m marble; **de ~** of marble

marmota [mar·'mo·ta] f marmot

marqués, -esa [mar·'kes, -·'ke·sa] m, f marquis m, marquise f

marquesina [mar·ke·'si·na] f (glass) canopy, marquee

marranada [ma·rra·'na·da] f inf filthiness

marrano [ma·'rra·no] m (cerdo) pig; pey inf (hombre sucio) dirty man; (grosero) rude man

marrano, -a [ma·'rra·no, -a] adj filthy

marrón [ma·'rron] adj brown

marroquí [ma·rro·'ki] adj, mf Moroccan

Marruecos [ma·'rrwe·kos] m Morocco

marrullero, -a [ma·rru·'je·ro, a-; -ˈʎe·ro, -a] adj flattering; (con labia) glib

marsopa [mar·'so·pa] f porpoise

marsupial [mar·su·'pjal] m marsupial

marta ['mar·ta] f ZOOL marten

Marte ['mar·te] m Mars

M

martes ['mar·tes] *m inv* Tuesday; **~ y tre-ce** ≈ Friday the thirteenth; *v. t.* **lunes**

martill(e)ar [mar·ti·'jar, -ʎar; mar·ti·je·'ar, -ʎe·'ar] *vt* to hammer

martillo [mar·'ti·jo, -ʎo] *m* hammer; **pez ~** hammerhead; **repetir algo a macha ~** to repeat sth ad nauseam

mártir ['mar·tir] *mf* martyr

martirio [mar·'ti·rjo] *m* REL martyrdom; *fig* torture

martirizar <z → c> [mar·ti·ri·'sar, -'θar] *vt* to torture

maruja [ma·'ru·xa] *f pey inf* housewife *(whose sole interests are her home, family, personal appearance and gossip)*

marzo ['mar·so, -θo] *m* March; **en ~** in March; **a principios/a mediados/a fin(al)es de ~** at the beginning/in the middle/at the end of March; **el 21 de ~** the 21st of March; **el mes de ~ tiene 31 días** the month of March has 31 days; **el pasado ~ fue muy frío** last March was very cold

mas [mas] *conj* LIT but, yet

más [mas] I. *adv* 1. *(cantidad)* more; **~ dinero/zapatos** more money/shoes 2. *(comparativo)* more; **~ inteligen-te/complicado** more intelligent/complicated; **~ grande/pequeño** bigger/smaller; **~ temprano/tarde** earlier/later; **correr ~** to run more; **esto me gusta ~** I like this better; **~ acá** closer; **~ adelante** *(local)* further forward [*o* on]; *(temporal)* later; **es ~ guapo que tú** he is more handsome than you; **cada día** [*o* vez] **~** more and more; **cuanto ~ mejor** the more the merrier; **~ allá de esto** beyond this; **~ de la cuenta** too much 3. *(superlativo)* **el/la ~** the most; **el ~ listo de la clase** the smartest in the class; **lo que ~ me gusta** what I most like [*o* like most]; **lo que ~ quieras** what you most want; **lo ~ probable es que llueva** it is likely to rain; **lo ~ pronto posible** as early as possible; **~ que nunca** more than ever; **a ~ no poder** to the utmost; **a ~ tardar** at the latest; **todo lo ~** at most 4. *(con numerales, cantidad)* **~ de treinta** more than thirty; **son ~ de las diez** it is after

ten 5. *(tan)* **¡está ~ guapa!** she looks so beautiful; **¡qué tarde ~ apacible!** what a peaceful afternoon! 6. *(con pronombre interrogativo, indefinido)* **¿algo ~?** anything else?; **no, nada ~** no, nothing else 7. *(en frases negativas)* **no puedo ~** I have had it; **nunca ~** never again 8. MAT plus; **tengo tres libros, ~ los que he prestado** I have three books, plus those I have lent 9. *(de más)* **de ~** spare, more than enough; **hay comida de ~** there is food to spare; **estar de ~** not to be needed; **de lo ~** very 10. *(más bien)* **~ bien** rather; **no es muy delgado; es ~ bien gordo** he is not very thin; rather he is fat 11. *(más o menos)* **~ o menos** *(aproximadamente)* more or less; **le va ~ o menos** he/she is doing so-so; **ni ~ ni menos** exactly 12. *(por más que)* **por ~ que lo intento, no consigo dormirme** however hard I try, I cannot sleep ▶ **el ~ allá** the beyond; **el que ~ y el que menos** every single one; **quien ~ y quien menos** everyone; **es ~ aún** what is more; **el no va ~** *(de la moda)* the latest fashion; **como el que ~** as well as the next man; **sin ~ ni ~** without more ado; **¿qué ~ da?** what difference does it make? II. *m* MAT plus sign

masa ['ma·sa] *f* 1. *(pasta)* mixture; *(para hornear)* dough; **coger a alguien con las manos en la ~** to catch sb red-handed 2. *(volumen, muchedumbre)* mass; **medios de comunicación de ~s** mass media; **en ~** en masse

masacrar [ma·sa·'krar] *vt* to massacre

masacre [ma·'sa·kre] *f* massacre

masaje [ma·'sa·xe] *m* massage; **dar ~s** to massage

masajista [ma·sa·'xis·ta] *mf* masseur *m*, masseuse *f*

mascada [mas·'ka·ða] *f* 1. *AmL (tabaco)* quid of chewing tobacco 2. *Col, Cuba, Chile (bocado)* bite 3. *Méx (pañuelo)* silk kerchief

mascar <c → qu> [mas·'kar] *vt (masti-car)* to chew

máscara ['mas·ka·ra] *f* mask; **quitar la ~ a alguien** *fig* to unmask sb; **quitarse la ~** *fig* to reveal oneself

mascarilla [mas·ka·'ri·ja, -ʎa] f 1. (máscara) mask 2. (protección) face mask 3. (cosmética) ~ **exfoliante** face scrub; ~ **facial** face pack

mascota [mas·'ko·ta] f mascot; (animal de compañía) pet

masculinidad [mas·ku·li·ni·'dad] f masculinity

masculino [mas·ku·'li·no] m LING masculine

masculino, -a [mas·ku·'li·no, -a] adj (de hombre) masculine; **moda masculina** men's fashion

mascullar [mas·ku·'jar, -ʎar] vt to mumble

masificación [ma·si·fi·ka·'sjon, -'θjon] f overcrowding

masita [ma·'si·ta] f AmS CULIN small cake

masivo, -a [ma·'si·βo, -a] adj (grande) massive; (fuerte) strong; (de masas) mass

masón, -ona [ma·'son, -·'so·na] m, f Mason, Freemason

masoquista [ma·so·'kis·ta] adj masochistic

máster <másters> ['mas·ter] m master's degree

masticar <c → qu> [mas·ti·'kar] vt to chew; (meditar) to ponder

mástil ['mas·til] m mast, spar; (poste) post, pole

mastín [mas·'tin] m mastiff

masturbación [mas·tur·βa·'sjon, -'θjon] f masturbation

masturbarse [mas·tur·'βar·se] vr to masturbate

mata ['ma·ta] f clump; (arbusto) bush

matadero [ma·ta·'de·ro] m slaughterhouse; **ir al** ~ fig to put one's life in danger; **llevar al** ~ fig to send sb to his/her death

matador(a) [ma·ta·'dor, -·'do·ra] m(f) TAUR matador

matamoscas [ma·ta·'mos·kas] m inv (insecticida) fly-spray; (objeto) fly-swatter

matanza [ma·'tan·sa, -θa] f 1. (el matar) killing; (en batallas) slaughter; **hacer una** ~ to massacre 2. (carneada) slaughter; **hacer la** ~ to slaughter an animal

matar [ma·'tar] I. vt 1. (quitar la vida) to kill; ~ **a golpes** to beat to death; ~ **a palos** to club to death; ~ **a puñaladas** to knife [o stab] to death; ~ **a tiros** to shoot dead; ~ **a disgustos** to be the death of 2. (carnear) to slaughter 3. (saciar) to assuage; (hambre) to satisfy; (sed) to quench 4. (el tiempo) to kill II. vr: ~**se** 1. (suicidarse) to kill oneself 2. (trabajar sin descanso) ~**se a trabajar** to work oneself to death; ~**se por algo** to go out of one's way to do sth 3. (por accidente) to get killed

matarife [ma·ta·'ri·fe] mf butcher

matarratas [ma·ta·'rra·tas] m inv 1. (raticida) rat poison 2. pey inf (alcohol de mala calidad) rotgut, hooch

matasanos [ma·ta·'sa·nos] mf inv, irón inf quack

matasellos [ma·ta·'se·jos, -ʎos] m inv postmark

match [matʃ] m match

mate ['ma·te] I. adj dull II. m 1. (ajedrez) mate; **jaque** ~ checkmate 2. (acabado) matte 3. pl inf (matemáticas) math 4. AmS (bebida) maté

matemáticas [ma·te·'ma·ti·kas] fpl mathematics

matemático, -a [ma·te·'ma·ti·ko, -a] I. adj mathematical II. m, f mathematician

materia [ma·'te·rja] f 1. t. FÍS matter; ~ **gris** ANAT grey matter; ~ **prima** raw material 2. (tema) subject, matter; **en** ~ **de** in the matter of 3. t. ENS (disciplina) subject

material [ma·te·'rjal] I. adj (real) tangible; **daño** ~ physical damage; **el autor** ~ **del hecho** the actual perpetrator of the deed II. m material; ~**es de construcción** building materials; ~ **de oficina** office equipment

materialista [ma·te·rja·'lis·ta] adj materialistic

materializar <z → c> [ma·te·rja·li·'sar, -'θar] I. vt to bring into being; (realizar) to carry out; (hacer aparecer) to produce II. vr: ~**se** to materialize

materialmente [ma·te·rjal·'men·te] adv materially; **ser** ~ **posible** to be physically possible

M

maternal [ma·ter·'nal] *adj* maternal, motherly

maternidad [ma·ter·ni·'dad] *f* maternity; (*hospital*) maternity hospital; (*sala*) maternity ward

materno, -a [ma·'ter·no, -a] *adj* maternal; **abuelo ~** maternal grandfather; **lengua materna** mother tongue

matinal [ma·ti·'nal] *adj* morning; **sesión ~** (*congreso*) morning session; CINE, TEAT matinee

matiz [ma·'tis, -'tiθ] *m* **1.** (*gradación*) shade; (*toque*) touch **2.** (*sentido*) nuance

matizar <z → c> [ma·ti·'sar, -'θar] *vt* **1.** (*combinar colores o tonos*) to blend; **~ de rojo** to tinge with red **2.** (*graduar*) to tint **3.** (*de un sentido*) to tinge

matón [ma·'ton] *m* thug

matorral [ma·to·'rral] *m* thicket

matrícula [ma·'tri·ku·la] *f* **1.** (*documento*) registration document **2.** (*inscripción*) enrollment; UNIV matriculation **3.** AUTO (*placa*) license plate; **número de la ~** license number

matricular [ma·tri·ku·'lar] I. *vt* to register; UNIV to enroll II. *vr* **~se en la universidad** to enroll in the university

matrimonial [ma·tri·mo·'njal] *adj* matrimonial, marriage; **agencia ~** dating agency

matrimonio [ma·tri·'mo·njo] *m* **1.** (*institución*) marriage; **contraer ~** to marry **2.** (*marido y mujer*) married couple; **cama de ~** double bed

matriz [ma·'tris, -'triθ] *f* **1.** (*útero*) womb **2.** (*molde*) cast **3.** TIPO, MAT matrix

matrona [ma·'tro·na] *f* (*comadrona*) midwife

maturrango, -a [ma·tu·'rran·go, -a] *adj* **1.** AmS (*mal jinete*) **ser ~** to be a poor rider **2.** *Chile* (*tosco*) clumsy

matutino, -a [ma·tu·'ti·no, -a] *adj* morning; **sesión matutina** morning session

maullar [mau·'jar, -ʎar] *irr como aullar vi* to meow

maullido [mau·'ji·do, -ʎido] *m* meow

mausoleo [mau·so·'leo] *m* mausoleum

maxilar [mak·si·'lar] I. *adj* maxillary II. *m* jaw

máxima ['mak·si·ma] *f* maxim

máxime ['mak·si·me] *adv* particularly

máximo, -a ['mak·si·mo, -a] I. *adj* maximum; **rendimiento ~** maximum output; **pon la radio al ~** turn the radio as high as it goes II. *m, f* maximum; **como ~** at most; (*temporal*) at the latest

mayo ['ma·jo] *m* May; *v. t.* **marzo**

mayonesa [ma·jo·'ne·sa] *f* mayonnaise

mayor [ma·'jor] *adj* **1.** (*tamaño*) bigger; **la ~ parte** the majority, most; **el ~ barco** the largest boat; **mal ~** greater evil; **~ que** bigger than; **comercio al por ~** wholesale trade **2.** (*edad*) older; **~ que** older than; **mi hermano ~** my older [*o* big] brother; **el ~ de mis hermanos** the eldest of my brothers and sisters; **ser ~** to be grown-up; **ser ~ de edad** to be an adult, to be of legal age; **persona ~** elderly person; **los ~es** the adults, the grown-ups; **ya es ~ para esos juguetes** he/she is too old for [*o* has outgrown] those toys **3.** MÚS major; **escala en do ~** scale of C major

mayorcito, -a [ma·jor·'si·to, -a; -θi·to, -a] *adj inf* **¡si ya eres ~!** what a big boy/girl you are now!

mayordomo, -a [ma·jor·'do·mo] *m, f* (*de una mansión*) butler

mayoría [ma·jo·'ri·a] *f* majority; **~ de edad** (age of) majority; **llegar a la ~ de edad** to come of age; **~ relativa** relative majority

mayorista [ma·jo·'ris·ta] I. *adj* wholesale; **comercio ~** wholesale business II. *mf* wholesaler

mayoritario, -a [ma·jo·ri·'ta·rjo, -a] *adj* majority

mayormente [ma·jor·'men·te] *adv* especially, particularly

mayúscula [ma·'jus·ku·la] *f* capital (letter); **escribirse con ~** to be written with a capital (letter)

mayúsculo, -a [ma·'jus·ku·lo, -a] *adj* big; **letra mayúscula** capital letter

maza ['ma·sa, -θa] *f* (*porra*) club; (*para machacar*) pestle; (*percusor*) hammer

mazacotudo, -a [ma·sa·ko·'tu·do, -a; ma·θa-] *adj* AmL clumsy

mazapán [ma·sa·'pan, ma·θa-] *m* marzipan

mazmorra [mas·'mo·rra, maθ-] *f* dungeon

mazo ['ma·so, 'ma·θo] *m* **1.** (*martillo*) mallet **2.** (*del mortero*) pestle; (*grande*) sledgehammer

mazorca [ma·'sor·ka, -'θor·ka] *f* (*del maíz*) cob; **~ de maíz** corncob, ear of corn

me [me] **I.** *pron pers* **1.** (*objeto directo*) me; **¡míra~!** look at me! **2.** (*objeto indirecto*) me; **da~ el libro** give me the book **II.** *pron reflexivo* **~ lavo** I wash myself; **~ voy** I am going; **~ lavo el pelo** I wash my hair

meada [me·'a·da] *f* **1.** *inf* (*pis*) pee; **echar una ~** to take a piss **2.** (*mancha de orina*) piss; **aquí hay una ~ de gato** a cat took a piss here

meadero [mea·'de·ro] *m vulg* urinal

meandro [me·'an·dro] *m* (*curva*) meander

mear [me·'ar] *vi, vr*: **~se** *inf* to piss; **~se de risa** to die laughing

mecánico, -a [me·'ka·ni·ko, -a] **I.** *adj* mechanical **II.** *m, f* mechanic

mecanismo [me·ka·'nis·mo] *m* mechanism; (*dispositivo*) device

mecanizar <z → c> [me·ka·ni·'sar, -'θar] *vt* to mechanize

mecanografía [me·ka·no·ɣra·'fi·a] *f* typewriting

mecate [me·'ka·te] *m AmC, Col, Méx, Ven* rope

mecedora [me·se·'do·ra, me·θe·] *f* rocking chair

mecenas [me·'se·nas, -'θe·nas] *mf inv* patron

mecer <c → z> [me·'ser, -'θer] **I.** *vt* (*balancear*) to rock; (*columpiar*) to swing **II.** *vr*: **~se** (*balancearse*) to rock; (*columpiarse*) to swing

mecha ['me·tʃa] *f* **1.** (*pabilo*) wick; (*de explosivos*) fuse **2.** (*gasa*) swab **3.** (*mechón*) tuft **4.** *pl* (*mechones teñidos*) highlights *pl*, streaks *pl*; **hacerse ~s** to have highlights [*o* streaks] put in **5.** *inf* (*prisa*) **a toda ~** very fast

mechero [me·'tʃe·ro] *m* (*encendedor*) lighter

mechón [me·'tʃon] *m* tuft

medalla [me·'da·ja, -ʎa] *f* medal; **~ (militar)** military decoration

medallista [me·da·'jis·ta, -ʎis·ta] *mf* medal winner, medalist

medallón [me·da·jon, -ʎon] *m* medallion

media ['me·dja] *f* **1.** (*promedio*) average **2.** (*calceta*) stocking; *AmL* (*calcetín*) sock

mediación [me·dja·'sjon, -'θjon] *f* mediation

mediado, -a [me·'dja·do, -a] *adj* **1.** (*medio lleno*) half-full (**de** of) **2.** (*trabajo*) half-completed; **para ~s de semana** by the middle of the week [*o* by midweek]

mediador(a) [me·dja·'dor, -·'do·ra] *m(f)* mediator

mediano, -a [me·'dja·no, -a] *adj* **1.** (*calidad*) average **2.** (*tamaño*) medium

medianoche [me·dja·'no·tʃe] *f* (*hora*) midnight; **a ~** at midnight

mediante [me·'djan·te] *prep* by means of; (*a través de*) through

mediar [me·'djar] *vi* **1.** (*intermediar*) to mediate **2.** (*interceder*) **~ por alguien** to intercede on behalf of sb

medicación [me·di·ka·'sjon, -'θjon] *f* medication

medicamento [me·di·ka·'men·to] *m* medicine

medicar <c → qu> [me·di·'kar] **I.** *vt* to medicate **II.** *vr*: **~se** to take medicine

medicina [me·di·'si·na, -'θi·na] *f* medicine

medicinal [me·di·si·'nal, -θi·'nal] *adj* medicinal; **balón ~** medicine ball; **hierba ~** medicinal plant

medición [me·di·'sjon, -'θjon] *f* measurement

médico, -a ['me·di·ko, -a] **I.** *adj* medical; **cuerpo ~** medical corps **II.** *m, f* doctor; **~ de cabecera** general practitioner; **~ forense** forensic surgeon

medida [me·'di·da] *f* **1.** (*medición*) measurement **2.** (*dimensión*) measurement; **a la ~** (*ropa*) made-to-measure; **tomar la(s) ~(s)** to take the measurement(s); **hasta cierta ~** up to a point; **en la ~ de lo posible** as far as possible; **a ~ que** as **3.** (*moderación*) moderation; **con ~** with care; **sin ~** without moderation **4.** (*acción*) measure; **tomar ~s** to take measures

M

medidor [me·di·'dor] *m* **1.** (*instrumento*) gauge **2.** *AmL* (*contador*) meter

medieval [me·dje·'βal] *adj* medieval

medio ['me·djo] *m* **1.** (*mitad*) middle; **en ~ de** in the middle of; **meterse por ~** to intervene; **quitar de en ~** to get rid of **2.** (*instrumento*) means; **~ de transporte** means of transport; **por ~ de** by means of **3.** PREN, RADIO, TV medium; **los ~s de comunicación** the media **4.** (*entorno*) surroundings *pl;* **~ ambiente** environment **5.** *Cuba* (*moneda*) five cent coin **6.** *pl* (*fuentes*) sources *pl;* (*capital*) means *pl*

medio, -a ['me·djo, -a] **I.** *adj* **1.** (*mitad*) half; **a las cuatro y media** at half past four; **litro y ~** one and a half liters; **mi media naranja** *fig* my better half **2.** (*promedio*) ciudadano ~ average person **II.** *adv* half; **~ vestido** half dressed; **~ dormido** half asleep; **ir a medias** to go halves

medioambiental [me·djo·am·bjen·'tal] *adj* environmental

mediocre [me·'djo·kre] *adj* mediocre

mediodía [me·djo·'di·a] *m* midday; **al ~ at** noon

medir [me·'dir] *irr como pedir* **I.** *vt* **1.** (*calcular*) to measure; **¿cuánto mides?** how tall are you? **2.** (*sopesar*) to weigh; **~ los riesgos** to weigh up the risks **3.** (*moderar*) to moderate **II.** *vi* to measure **III.** *vr* **~se con alguien** to measure oneself against sb

meditación [me·di·ta·'sjon, -'θjon] *f* meditation

meditar [me·di·'tar] *vi, vt* to meditate

mediterráneo, -a [me·di·te·'rra·neo, -a] *adj* Mediterranean

Mediterráneo [me·di·te·'rra·neo] *m* Mediterranean

medrar [me·'drar] *vi* (*crecer*) to grow; (*avanzar*) to thrive

médula ['me·du·la] *f* **1.** ANAT marrow; **~ espinal** spinal cord **2.** (*meollo*) core; **hasta la ~** to the core

medusa [me·'du·sa] *f* jellyfish

megáfono [me·'ɣa·fo·no] *m* megaphone

mejicano, -a [me·xi·'ka·no, -a] *adj, m, f* Mexican

Méjico ['me·xi·ko] *m* Mexico

mejilla [me·'xi·ja, -ʎa] *f* cheek; **poner la otra ~** to turn the other cheek

mejillón [me·xi·'jon, -ʎon] *m* mussel

mejor [me·'xor] **I.** *adj* **1.** (*compar*) better; **~ que** better than; **es ~ que no vayas** +*subj* it is better that you don't go; **cambiar a ~** to change for the better; **pasar a ~ vida** to pass away **2.** (*superl*) **el/la/lo ~** the best; **el ~ alumno** the best student **II.** *adv* better; **a lo ~** maybe; **~ que ~** better still [*o* yet]; **en el ~ de los casos** at best

mejora [me·'xo·ra] *f* improvement

mejorable [me·xo·'ra·βle] *adj* improvable

mejorar [me·xo·'rar] **I.** *vt* **1.** (*perfeccionar*) to improve **2.** (*superar*) to surpass; (*subasta*) to outbid **II.** *vi, vr:* **~se** (*enfermo*) to get better; **¡que se mejore!** I hope you get better soon!

mejoría [me·xo·'ri·a] *f* improvement

melancolía [me·lan·ko·'li·a] *f* melancholy

melancólico, -a [me·lan·'ko·li·ko, -a] *adj* melancholic

melanoma [me·la·'no·ma] *m* MED melanoma

melena [me·'le·na] *f* **1.** (*crin*) mane **2.** (*pelo*) long hair *(shoulder-length or longer, worn loose);* **soltarse la ~** *t. fig* to let one's hair down

mella ['me·ja, -ʎa] *f* **hacer ~** to make an impression

mellizo, -a [me·'ji·so, -a; -ʎi·θo, -a] *m, f* twin

melocotón [me·lo·ko·'ton] *m* peach

melocotonero [me·lo·ko·to·'ne·ro] *m* peach tree

melodía [me·lo·'di·a] *f* melody

melódico, -a [me·'lo·di·ko, -a] *adj* melodic

melón [me·'lon] *m* melon; *inf* (*cabeza*) noggin

melón, -ona [me·'lon, -ona] *m, f* *inf* loony

membrana [mem·'bra·na] *f* membrane

membrete [mem·'bre·te] *m* letterhead

membrillo [mem·'bri·jo, -ʎo] *m* (*árbol*) quince tree; (*fruto*) quince; **carne** [*o* **dulce**] **de ~** quince jelly

memela [me·'me·la] *f* *Méx* CULIN thin

corn tortilla

memo, -a ['me.mo, -a] *adj* idiotic

memorable [me·mo·'ra·βle] *adj* memorable

memoria [me·'mo·rja] *f* 1. (*facultad, recuerdo*) memory; **a la** [*o* **en**] **~ de** in memory of; **de ~** by heart; **hacer ~** to try and remember; **traer a la ~** to bring to mind; **venir a la ~** to come to mind 2. (*informe*) report 3. COMPUT memory 4. *pl* (*autobiografía*) memories

memorizar <z → c> [me·mo·ri·'sar, -'θar] *vt* to memorize

menaje [me·'na·xe] *m* household furnishings *pl*; **~ de cocina** kitchen utensils

mención [men·'sjon, -'θjon] *f* mention; **digno de ~** worth mentioning; **hacer ~ de** to mention

mencionar [men·sjo·'nar, -θjo·'nar] *vt* to mention

menda ['men·da] **I.** *pron pers inf* yours truly; **aquí el** [*o* **este**] **~ no dijo nada** yours truly didn't say anything **II.** *pron indef inf* **un ~** a guy

mendigar <g → gu> [men·di·'ɣar] *vi, vt* **~ algo** to beg for sth

mendigo, -a [men·'di·ɣo, -a] *m, f* beggar

mendrugo [men·'dru·ɣo] *m* (*trozo de pan*) crust

menear [me·ne·'ar] **I.** *vt* to move; (*cabeza*) to shake; **~ la cola** to wag one's tail **II.** *vr:* **~se** to move; *inf*(*apresurarse*) to get a move on

meneo [me·'neo] *m* (*brusco*) jolt

menestra [me·'nes·tra] *f* vegetable stew

mengano, -a [men·'ga·no, -a] *m, f* **fulano y ~** so-and-so

menguante [men·'gwan·te] *f* 1. (*marea*) ebb; (*estiaje*) low water level 2. (*mengua*) decrease

menguar <gu → gü> [men·'gwar] **I.** *vi* to diminish **II.** *vt* to decrease; (*punto*) to reduce

meningitis [me·nin·'xi·tis] *f inv* MED meningitis

menisco [me·'nis·ko] *m* ANAT meniscus

menopausia [me·no·'pau·sja] *f* MED menopause, change of life

menor [me·'nor] **I.** *adj* 1. (*tamaño*) smaller; **~ que** smaller than; (*número*) smaller; **al por ~** COM retail; **no dar**

la ~ importancia a algo not to give sth the least importance; **Asia Menor** Asia Minor 2. (*edad*) younger; **~ que** younger than; **~ de edad** underage; **el ~ de mis hermanos** the youngest of my brothers 3. MÚS minor **II.** *mf* (*persona*) minor; **no apto para ~es** not suitable for children

menos ['me·nos] **I.** *adv* 1. (*contrario de más*) less; **a ~ que** unless; **el/la ~** the least; **el coche ~ caro** the least expensive car; **eso es lo de ~** that is the least important thing; **lo ~** the least; **al** [*o* **por lo**] **~** at least; **aún ~** even less; **cuanto ~... (tanto) más** the less... the more; **de ~** short; **echar de ~** to miss; **en ~ de nada** in no time; **ir a ~** to decrease; **~ de 20 personas** fewer than 20 people; **~ de una hora** less than an hour; **~ mal** thank goodness; **¡ni mucho ~!** not at all!; **son las ocho ~ diez** it's ten minutes to eight; **cada vez ~ tiempo/casos** less and less time/fewer and fewer cases 2. MAT minus 3. (*excepto*) except; **todo ~ eso** anything but that **II.** *m* MAT minus

menospreciar [me·nos·pre·'sjar, -'θjar] *vt* to underrate; (*subestimar*) to underestimate

menosprecio [me·nos·'pre·sjo, -θjo] *m* underrating; (*subestimación*) underestimate

mensaje [men·'sa·xe] *m* message; **~ de error** COMPUT error message; **~ (de) radio** radio communication; **~ de socorro** SOS message

mensajero, -a [men·sa·'xe·ro, -a] **I.** *adj* messenger; **paloma mensajera** messenger [*o* carrier] pigeon **II.** *m, f* messenger

menso, -a ['men·so, -a] *adj Méx* (*necio*) stupid

menstruación [mens·trwa·'sjon, -'θjon] *f* menstruation

menstruar <1. pres menstrúo> [mens·tru·'ar] *vi* to menstruate

mensual [men·su·'al] *adj* monthly

mensualidad [men·swa·li·'dad] *f* (*pago*) monthly payment; (*compra aplazada*) monthly installment; **~ del alquiler** month's rent

menta ['men·ta] *f* mint; (*infusión*) mint tea; (*extracto*) menthol; **caramelo de ~** mint

mental [men·'tal] *adj* mental; **cálculo ~** mental arithmetic

mentalidad [men·ta·li·'dad] *f* mentality

mentalizar <z → c> [men·ta·li·'sar, -'θar] **I.** *vt* (*preparar*) to prepare (mentally); (*concienciar*) to make aware; **~ a alguien de algo** to make sb aware of sth **II.** *vr*: **~se** (*prepararse*) to prepare oneself (mentally); (*concienciarse*) to make oneself aware

mentar <e → ie> [men·'tar] *vt* to mention

mente ['men·te] *f* **1.** (*pensamiento*) mind; **tener en (la) ~** to have in mind; **quitarse algo de la ~** to get sth out of one's head; **tengo la ~ en blanco** my mind is a complete blank; **traer a la ~** to bring to mind **2.** (*intelecto*) intellect

mentecato, -a [men·te·'ka·to, -a] *adj* silly

mentir [men·'tir] *irr como* **sentir** *vi* to lie; **miente más que habla** he/she is a compulsive liar; **¡miento!** I tell a lie!, I am wrong!

mentira [men·'ti·ra] *f* lie; **~ piadosa** white lie; **¡parece ~!** I can hardly believe it!

mentiroso, -a [men·ti·'ro·so, -a] **I.** *adj* (*persona*) lying **II.** *m, f* liar

mentol [men·'tol] *m* menthol

mentón [men·'ton] *m* chin

mentor [men·'tor] *m* mentor

menú [me·'nu] *m* <menús> *t.* COMPUT menu

menudencia [me·nu·'den·sja, -θja] *f* (*pequeñez*) trifle; (*meticulosidad*) meticulousness

menudo, -a [me·'nu·do, -a] *adj* minuscule; (*pequeño y delgado*) slight; **¡menuda película!** what a movie!; **¡~ lío has armado!** what a fuss you have created! ▶ **a ~** often

meñique [me·'ɲi·ke] *m* little finger, pinky

meollo [me·'o·jo, -ʎo] *m* **1.** (*sesos*) brains *pl* **2.** (*médula*) marrow **3.** (*fundamen-* *to*) essence, crux

mequetrefe [me·ke·'tre·fe] *m inf* good-for-nothing

meramente [me·ra·'men·te] *adv* merely

mercader [mer·ka·'der] *m* merchant

mercadillo [mer·ka·'di·jo, -ʎo] *m* street market, flea market

mercado [mer·'ka·do] *m* market; **~ de divisas** foreign exchange market; **~ exterior/interior** overseas/domestic market; **~ alcista/bajista** bull/bear market; **~ de trabajo** labor market; **~ único europeo** European Single Market; **~ de valores** securities market; **hay ~ los sábados** there is a market on Saturdays

mercancía [mer·kan·'si·a, -'θi·a] *f* goods *pl*; **tren de ~s** goods [*o* freight] train

mercante [mer·'kan·te] *adj* mercantile

mercantil [mer·kan·'til] *adj* mercantile

merced [mer·'sed, -'θed] *f* mercy; **~ a** thanks to; **estar a ~ de alguien** to be at sb's mercy

mercenario, -a [mer·se·'na·rjo, -a; mer·θe·] *adj, m, f* mercenary

mercería [mer·se·'ri·a, mer·θe·] *f* notions *pl*; (*tienda*) notions store

mercurio [mer·'ku·rjo] *m* mercury

Mercurio [mer·'ku·rjo] *m* Mercury

merecedor(a) [me·re·se·'dor, -·'do·ra; me·re·θe·] *adj* deserving; **hacerse ~ de algo** to earn sth

merecer [me·re·'ser, -'θer] *irr como* **crecer** **I.** *vt* to deserve; (*valer*) to be worthy of; **merece respeto de nuestra parte** he/she deserves our respect; **no merece la pena** it is not worth it **II.** *vr*: **~se** to deserve

merecido [me·re·'si·do, -'θi·do] *m* deserts *pl*; **se llevó su ~** he/she got his/her just deserts

merendar <e → ie> [me·ren·'dar] **I.** *vt* to have for tea, to have for an afternoon snack **II.** *vi* to have tea, to have an afternoon snack; (*en el campo*) to picnic **III.** *vr*: **~se** *inf* to wangle; **~se a alguien** to get the better of sb

merengue [me·'ren·ge] *m* **1.** (*dulce*) meringue **2.** *CSur inf* (*lío*) mess

meridiano [me·ri·'dja·no] *m* meridian

meridional [me·ri·djo·'nal] *adj* south

merienda [me·'rjen·da] *f* **1.** (*comida por la tarde*) tea, afternoon snack **2.** (*picnic*) picnic; **ir de ~** to go for a picnic

mérito ['me·ri·to] *m* merit; (*valor*) worth; **hacer ~s** to prove oneself worthy

merlo ['mer·lo] *m AmL* ZOOL wrasse

merluza [mer·'lu·sa, ·θa] *f* **1.** ZOOL hake **2.** *inf* (*borrachera*) **coger una buena ~** to get sloshed

merluzo, -a [mer·'lu·so, ·a; ·θo, ·a] *adj inf* silly

mermar [mer·'mar] *vt* to lessen

mermelada [mer·me·'la·da] *f* jam; **~ de naranja** orange marmalade

mero ['me·ro] **I.** *adv* **1.** *AmC, Méx* (*pronto*) soon **2.** *Méx* (*muy*) very **3.** *Méx* (*precisamente*) precisely **II.** *m* **1.** ZOOL grouper **2.** *Méx* (*jefe*) boss

mero, -a ['me·ro, ·a] *adj* **1.** (*sencillo*) simple **2.** (*sin nada más*) mere; **la mera verdad** the plain truth **3.** *Méx* (*preciso*) precise **4.** *Méx* (*propio*) own

merodear [me·ro·de·'ar] *vi* to prowl; **~ por un sitio** to hang about a place

mes [mes] *m* month; **a principios/a mediados/a fin(al)es de ~** at the beginning/in the middle/at the end of the month; **5.000 pesos al ~** 5,000 pesos a month; **todos los ~es** every month; **el ~ que viene** next month; **el ~ pasado** last month; **hace un ~** a month ago; **con un ~ de anticipo** a month's salary in advance; **tengo el ~** *inf* I have my period

mesa ['me·sa] *f* **1.** (*mueble*) table; **vino de ~** table wine; **bendecir la ~** to say grace; **poner la ~** to lay [*o* set] the table; **quitar la ~** to clear the table; **en la ~** (*comiendo*) at the table; **¡a la ~!** food's ready!; **servir una ~** to serve a table **2.** POL **~ electoral** *officials in charge of a polling station*

mesero, -a [me·'se·ro, ·a] *m, f Méx* (*camarero*) waiter *m*, waitress *f*

meseta [me·'se·ta] *f* GEO plateau

mesilla [me·'si·ja, ·ʎa] *f* small table; **~ de noche** nightstand

mesón [me·'son] *m* inn, tavern

mesonero, -a [me·so·'ne·ro, ·a] *m, f* innkeeper

mestizo, -a [mes·'ti·so, ·a; ·θo, ·a] **I.** *adj* **1.** (*entre blancos e indios*) mestizo **2.** (*entre dos razas*) mixed-race **II.** *m, f* **1.** (*entre blancos e indios*) mestizo **2.** (*entre dos razas*) person of mixed race

mesura [me·'su·ra] *f* **1.** (*moderación*) moderation **2.** (*cortesía*) courtesy, civility **3.** (*calma*) calm

meta ['me·ta] *f t. fig* winning post; (*portería*) goal; **la ~ de su vida** his/her aim in life; **fijarse una ~** to set oneself a goal

metabolismo [me·ta·βo·'lis·mo] *m* metabolism

metafísica [me·ta·'fi·si·ka] *f* FILOS metaphysics

metafísico, -a [me·ta·'fi·si·ko, ·a] *adj* metaphysical

metáfora [me·'ta·fo·ra] *f* metaphor

metafórico, -a [me·ta·'fo·ri·ko, ·a] *adj* metaphorical

metal [me·'tal] *m* metal; **~ noble** precious metal; **~ pesado** heavy metal; **el vil ~** (*dinero*) filthy lucre

metálico [me·'ta·li·ko] *m* **en ~** in cash; **premio en ~** cash prize

metálico, -a [me·'ta·li·ko, ·a] *adj* metallic

metalúrgico, -a [me·ta·'lur·xi·ko, ·a] *adj* metallurgical

metamorfosis [me·ta·mor·'fo·sis] *f inv* metamorphosis; (*en una persona*) transformation

metano [me·'ta·no] *m* methane

metástasis [me·'tas·ta·sis] *f inv* MED metastasis

metedura [me·te·'du·ra] *f* **¡vaya ~ de pata!** *inf* what a blooper!

meteórico, -a [me·te·'o·ri·ko, ·a] *adj* (*rápido*) meteoric

meteorito [me·teo·'ri·to] *m* meteorite

meteorología [me·teo·ro·lo·'xi·a] *f* meteorology

meteorológico, -a [me·teo·ro·'lo·xi·ko, ·a] *adj* meteorological; **informe ~** weather forecast; **estación meteorológica** weather station

meteorólogo, -a [me·teo·'ro·lo·ɣo, ·a] *m, f* meteorologist

M

meter [me·'ter] I. vt 1. (*introducir*) to insert; (*poner*) to put; ~ **en una caja** to put in a box; **¡mete el enchufe!** put the plug in!; ~ **un clavo en la pared** to hammer a nail into the wall; ~ **a alguien en la cárcel** to put sb in jail; ~ **un gol** DEP to score a goal; ~ **dinero en el banco** to put money in the bank 2. inf (*encasquetar*) to palm off; (*vender*) to sell; (*enjaretar*) to foist; **le metieron tres meses de cárcel** they gave him/ her three months in jail 3. inf (*pegar*) ~ **un puñetazo a alguien** to punch sb 4. (*provocar*) ~ **miedo/un susto a alguien** to frighten/startle sb; ~ **prisa a alguien** to hurry sb (up) 5. (*hacer participar*) to involve; ~ **a toda la familia en el asunto** to involve the whole family in the matter 6. (*emplear*) to employ; ~ **a uno a trabajar** to put sb to work (**de as**) ▶ ~ <u>a todo</u> ~ inf as fast as possible II. vr: ~**se** 1. (*introducirse*) to put; ~**se el dedo en la nariz** to stick one's finger in one's nose; **se le ha metido en la cabeza que...** he/she has gotten it into his/ her head that... 2. (*entrar en un lugar*) to enter; **lo vi** ~**se en un cine** I saw him go into a movie theater; ~**se entre la gente** to mingle with the people; **¿dónde se habrá metido?** where has he/she gotten to? 3. (*entrar indebidamente*) to enter unlawfuly 4. (*inmiscuirse*) to meddle; **¡no te metas donde no te llaman!** mind your own business! 5. (*provocar*) ~**se con alguien** to provoke sb 6. (*comenzar un oficio*) ~**se a actor** to become an actor

metiche [me·'ti·tʃe] adj Méx (*entrometido*) meddlesome

meticuloso, -a [me·ti·ku·'lo·so, -a] adj meticulous

metido, -a [me·'ti·do, -a] adj estar ~ **en un negocio** to be involved in a business; ~ **en carnes** chubby; ~ **en años** elderly; **la llave está metida** the key is in

metódico, -a [me·'to·di·ko, -a] adj methodical

método ['me·to·do] m method; **un** ~ **de guitarra** (*libro*) a guitar manual

metodología [me·to·do·lo·'xi·a] f methodology

metralla [me·'tra·ja, -ʎa] f 1. (*munición*) shell; **fuego de** ~ shellfire 2. (*trozos*) shrapnel

metralleta [me·tra·'je·ta, -ʎeta] f submachine gun

métrico, -a ['me·tri·ko, -a] adj metric

metro ['me·tro] m 1. (*unidad*) meter; ~ **cuadrado** square meter; ~ **cúbico** cubic meter 2. (*para medir*) ruler; ~ **de cinta** tape measure; ~ **plegable** folding ruler 3. FERRO subway

metrópoli [me·'tro·po·li] f (*urbe*) metropolis; (*capital*) capital

metropolitano [me·tro·po·li·'ta·no] m subway

metropolitano, -a [me·tro·po·li·'ta·no, -a] adj (*de la capital*) metropolitan; (*de la urbe*) city

mexicano, -a [me·xi·'ka·no, -a] adj, m, f v. **mejicano**

México ['me·xi·ko] m Mexico

mezcal [mes·'kal, meθ-] m Méx BOT mescal

mezcla ['mes·kla, 'meθ-] f mixture; ~ **explosiva** t. fig explosive mixture

mezclar [mes·'klar, meθ-] I. vt 1. (*unir*) to blend; CULIN (*añadir*) to mix 2. (*revolver*) to muddle; (*confundir*) to mix up 3. (*involucrar*) to involve II. vr: ~**se** 1. (*inmiscuirse*) to meddle; ~**se entre los espectadores** to mingle with the spectators; ~**se con gente de mucho dinero** to mix with wealthy people 2. (*revolverse*) to mix

mezcolanza [mes·ko·'lan·sa, meθ·ko·'lan·θa] f pey hodgepodge

mezquino, -a [mes·'ki·no, -a; meθ-] adj 1. (*tacaño*) stingy 2. (*innoble*) ignoble; (*miserable*) small-minded

mezquita [mes·'ki·ta; meθ-] f mosque

mi [mi] I. adj (*antepuesto*) my; ~ **amigo/casa** my friend/house; ~**s amigos** my friends II. m inv MÚS E; ~ **mayor** E major; ~ **menor** E minor

mí [mi] pron pers me; **a** ~ (*objeto directo*) me; (*objeto indirecto*) to me; **para** ~ for me; **¿y a** ~ **qué?** so what?; **para (que)...** I think (that)...; **por** ~ as far as I'm concerned; **por** ~ **mismo** by myself; **¡a** ~ **con esas!** don't give me that!; **¡a** ~ **!**

(¡socorro!) help!

miau [mjau] meow

miche ['mi.tʃe] m 1. CRi (pendencia) brawl 2. Chile (juego) game of marbles

mico ['mi.ko] m ZOOL long-tailed monkey

micro ['mi.kro] m (micrófono) mike

microbio [mi.'kro.βjo] m microbe

microbús [mi.kro.'βus] m minibus

microchip [mi.kro.'tʃip] m microchip

microficha [mi.kro.fi.tʃa] f microfiche

microfilm [mi.kro.'film] m <microfilm(e)s> microfilm

micrófono [mi.'kro.fo.no] m microphone

microonda [mi.kro.'on.da/mi.'kron.da] f t. FÍS (cocina) microwave; (horno) ~s microwave (oven)

microorganismo [mi.kro.or.ɣa.'nis.mo] m micro-organism

microscópico, -a [mi.kros.'ko.pi.ko, -a] adj microscopic

microscopio [mi.kros.'ko.pjo] m microscope; ~ de 60 aumentos microscope with x60 magnification; ~ electrónico electron microscope

microtenis [mi.kro.'te.nis] m inv AmL table tennis

miedo ['mje.ðo] m fear; por ~ a [o de] for fear of; por ~ de que +subj for fear that; meter ~ a alguien to frighten sb; dar ~ to be frightening; morirse de ~ to be petrified; el concierto estuvo de ~ the concert was terrific; hace un frío de ~ inf (terrible) it is awfully cold

miedoso, -a [mje.'do.so, -a] adj ser fearful

miel [mjel] f honey; luna de ~ honeymoon; quedarse con la ~ en los labios to be left wanting more ▶ ~ sobre <u>hojuelas</u> even better

miembro ['mjem.bro] m 1. pl (extremidades) limbs pl 2. (pene) ~ (viril) male member 3. t. LING, MAT (socio) member; no ~ non-member; ~ de pleno derecho full member; hacerse ~ de to join

mientras ['mjen.tras] I. adv meanwhile; ~ (tanto) in the meantime II. conj ~ (que) while; ~ (que) +subj as long as

miércoles ['mjer.ko.les] m inv Wednesday; ~ de ceniza Ash Wednesday; ~ santo Easter Wednesday; v. t. lunes

mies [mjes] f 1. (cereal maduro) (ripe) corn 2. (temporada) harvest (time) 3. pl (campos) cornfields pl

miga ['mi.ɣa] f bread (not the crust); (trocito) crumb; hacer buenas/malas ~s con alguien to get along well/badly with sb; estar hecho ~ (cansado) to be shattered; hacer ~s to destroy; esto tiene su ~ (esencia) there is something to this

migaja [mi.'ɣa.xa] f 1. (trocito) crumb; una ~ de algo a scrap of sth 2. pl (sobras) leftovers pl

migración [mi.ɣra.'sjon, -'θjon] f ZOOL migration

migraña [mi.'ɣra.ɲa] f migraine

mijo ['mi.xo] m millet

mil [mil] I. adj inv thousand; dos ~ millones two billion; ya se lo he dicho ~ veces I have already told him/her hundreds of times II. m thousand; ~es thousands; a ~es by the thousands; ~es y ~es thousands and thousands; varios ~es de dólares several thousand dollars; a las ~ very late

milagro [mi.'la.ɣro] m miracle; hacer ~s to work wonders; contar la vida y ~s de alguien to tell all the gory details about sb's life; esta vez se escapó de ~ this time he/she had a lucky escape

milagroso, -a [mi.la.'ɣro.so, -a] adj miraculous; (maravilloso) marvelous

milenario, -a [mi.le.'na.rjo, -a] adj millennial

milenio [mi.'le.njo] m millennium

mili ['mi.li] f inf military service; ir a [o hacer] la ~ to do military service

milicia [mi.'li.sja, -θja] f military; ~ nacional (ciudadanos) militia

miligramo [mi.li.'ɣra.mo] m milligram

mililitro [mi.li.'li.tro] m milliliter

milímetro [mi.'li.me.tro] m millimeter

militar [mi.li.'tar] I. vi 1. (cumplir el servicio) to serve 2. (en un partido) to be an active member of; ~ en favor de/ contra algo to campaign for/against sth II. adj military; los altos mandos

M

~es the military high command **III.** *m* soldier

milla ['mi·ja, -ʎa] *f* mile; **~ marina** nautical mile

millar [mi·'jar, -ʎar] *m* thousand

millón [mi·'jon, -'ʎon] *m* million; **mil millones** a billion; **cuatro millones de habitantes** four million inhabitants

millonada [mijo·'na·da, mi·ʎo-] *f inf* fortune

millonario, -a [mijo·'na·rjo, -a; mi·ʎo-] *m, f* millionaire

milpa ['mil·pa] *f AmL* **1.** (*campo*) cornfield **2.** (*planta*) corn

milpiés [mil·'pjes] *m inv* millipede

mimar [mi·'mar] *vt* to indulge; (*excesivamente*) to spoil

mimbre ['mim·bre] *m* wicker; **muebles de ~** wicker furniture

mimeógrafo [mi·me·'o·ɣra·fo] *m AmL* mimeograph

mímica ['mi·mi·ka] *f* **1.** (*facial*) mime **2.** (*señas*) sign language **3.** (*ademanes*) gesticulation

mimo ['mi·mo] *m* **1.** (*actor*) mimic **2.** (*caricia*) caress; (*condescendencia*) spoiling; **necesitar mucho ~** to need a lot of affection; **le dan demasiado ~** they spoil him/her; **realizo mi trabajo con ~** I carry out my work with love

mimoso, -a [mi·'mo·so, -a] *adj* **1.** (*mimado*) spoiled **2.** *ser* (*cariñoso*) affectionate **3.** *estar* (*apegado*) clinging

mina ['mi·na] *f* **1.** MIN mine; **~ de carbón** coal mine; **este negocio es una ~** this business is a gold mine **2.** (*explosivo*) mine **3.** (*de lápiz*) lead

minar [mi·'nar] **I.** *vt* **1.** (*excavar, colocar minas*) to mine **2.** (*debilitar*) to undermine **II.** *vr:* **~se** *inf* (*hartarse*) to become fed up

mineral [mi·ne·'ral] **I.** *adj* mineral; **agua ~** mineral water **II.** *m* GEO mineral

minería [mi·ne·'ri·a] *f* mining

minero, -a [mi·'ne·ro, -a] *m, f* miner

miniatura [mi·nja·'tu·ra] *f* miniature

minibús [mi·ni·'βus] *m* minibus

minifalda [mi·ni·'fal·da] *f* miniskirt

minifundio [mi·ni·'fun·djo] *m* smallholding

minigolf [mi·ni·'ɣolf] *m* miniature golf

minimizar <z → c> [mi·ni·mi·'sar, -'θar] *vt* to minimize

mínimo ['mi·ni·mo] *m* minimum; **un ~ de respeto** a minimum of respect; **como ~** (*cantidad*) as a minimum; **como ~ podrías llamar por teléfono** you could at least phone; **reducir al ~** to reduce to the bare minimum

mínimo, -a ['mi·ni·mo, -a] *adj superl de* **pequeño** minimum; **la mínima obligación posible** the slightest obligation possible; **sin el más ~ ruido** without the least noise; **no ayudar en lo más ~** to be no help at all

ministerio [mi·nis·'te·rjo] *m* **1.** (*cartera, edificio*) ministry **2.** (*cargo*) ministerial office

ministro, -a [mi·'nis·tro, -a] *m, f* minister; **primera ministra** prime minister; **~ sin cartera** minister without portfolio; **Ministro de Economía y Hacienda** Treasury Secretary; **Ministro de Educación y Ciencia** Education Secretary; **Ministro del Interior** Secretary of the Interior

minoría [mi·no·'ri·a] *f* minority; **~ de edad** minority

minorista [mi·no·'ris·ta] **I.** *adj* retail **II.** *mf* retailer

minoritario, -a [mi·no·ri·'ta·rjo, -a] *adj* minority

minucioso, -a [mi·nu·'sjo·so, -a; -θjo·so, -a] *adj* meticulous

minúscula [mi·'nus·ku·la] *f* LING lower case; **en ~s** in lower case [*o* small] letters; **escribirse con ~** to be written in lower case

minúsculo, -a [mi·'nus·ku·lo, -a] *adj* minuscule, minute; **letra minúscula** lower-case [*o* small] letter

minusvalía [mi·nus·βa·'li·a] *f* **1.** (*física*) handicap, disability **2.** COM capital loss

minusválido, -a [mi·nus·'βa·li·do, -a] *adj* handicapped

minusvalorar [mi·nus·βa·lo·'rar] *vt* to undervalue

minuta [mi·'nu·ta] *f* (*cuenta*) lawyer's bill

minutero [mi·nu·'te·ro] *m* minute hand

minuto [mi·'nu·to] *m* minute; **sin perder un ~** at once; **vuelvo en un ~** I will be right back

mío, -a ['mi·o, -a] *pron pos* **1.** (*de mi propiedad*) mine; **la botella es mía** the bottle is mine; **¡ya es ~!** I have it! **2.** (*tras artículo*) **el ~/la mía** mine; **los ~s** (*cosas*) mine; (*parientes*) my family; **ésta es la mía** *inf* this is just what I want; **eso es lo ~** that is my strong point **3.** (*tras sustantivo*) of mine; **una amiga mía** a friend of mine; **¡amor ~!** my darling!; **(no) es culpa mía** it is (not) my fault

miocardio [mjo·'kar·djo] *m* ANAT myocardium

miope [mi·o·pe] *adj* myopic, short-sighted

miopía [mjo·'pi·a] *f* myopia, short-sightedness

mira ['mi·ra] *f* **1.** MIL watchtower; **estar en la ~ de alguien** to be in sb's sights **2.** (*mirada*) gaze; **con amplias ~s** broad-minded; **de ~s estrechas** narrow-minded; **con ~s a** with a view to **3.** (*pl*) (*intención*) intention; **con ~s desinteresadas** disinterestedly

mirada [mi·'ra·da] *f* look; **~ perdida** faraway look; **devorar con la ~** to gaze hungrily at; **echar una ~ a algo** to glance at sth; **levantar la ~** to look up; **apartar la ~** to look away; **volver la ~ atrás** to look back

mirado, -a [mi·'ra·do, -a] *adj* **estar bien/mal ~** (*persona*) to be well/badly thought of; **bien ~,...** all things considering [*o* considered],...

mirador [mi·ra·'dor] *m* (*atalaya*) viewpoint

miramiento [mi·ra·'mjen·to] *m* **1.** (*consideración*) consideration; **tener ~ con alguien** to have[*o* show] consideration for sb; **sin ~** inconsiderately; **andar con ~s** to tread carefully **2.** (*cuidado*) discretion; **sin ~** indiscreetly

mirar [mi·'rar] **I.** *vt* **1.** (*observar*) to observe; (*ver*) to look at; **~ fijamente a alguien** to stare at sb; **~ algo por encima** to give sth a quick look (over) **2.** (*buscar*) to look for **3.** (*prestar atención*) to watch; **¡pero mira lo que estás haciendo!** but look what you are doing! **4.** (*meditar*) to think about; **mirándolo bien, bien mirado** taking everything into consideration **5.** (*tener en cuen-*

ta) to take into account; **~ el dinero** to be careful of the money **6.** (*estimar*) **~ bien/mal** to have a good/poor opinion of; **~ con buena/mala cara** to approve/disapprove of **II.** *vi* **1.** (*dirigir la vista*) to look; **~ por la ventana** to look out of the window; **~ por un agujero** to look through a hole; **~ atrás** to look back; **~ alrededor** to look around **2.** (*buscar*) to look for; **siempre miramos por nuestros hijos** we always look out for our children **3.** (*dar*) **la casa mira al este** the house faces east **4.** (*de aviso, exclamativo*) **¡mira! ya llega** look! here he/she/it comes; **mira, mira, déjate de tonterías** that is enough, stop being silly; **¡pues, mira por donde...!** surprise, surprise...!; **mire, ya se lo he explicado tres veces** look, I have explained it to you three times already **5.** (*tener en cuenta*) **mira que si se cae este jarrón** just imagine if the vase fell **6.** (*mira que*) **mira que es tonta, ¿eh?** she really is silly, isn't she? ▶ **ser de mírame y no me toques** to be very delicate **III.** *vr:* **~se** (*verse*) to look at oneself; **~se a los ojos** to look into another's eyes; **~se en el espejo** to look at oneself in the mirror

mirilla [mi·'ri·ja, -ʎa] *f* (*en la puerta*) peephole; FOTO viewer

mirlo ['mir·lo] *m* blackbird

mirón, -ona [mi·'ron, -ona] *m, f* (*espectador curioso*) onlooker; *pey* (*de intimidades*) snoop; (*voyeur*) peeping Tom

misa ['mi·sa] *f* mass; **~ de difuntos** requiem mass; **ir a ~** to go to mass; **cantar ~** to sing mass; **decir ~** to say mass ▶ **no saber de la ~ la** media [*o* **la mitad**] not to know the half [*o* the first thing] of it; **eso** va **a ~** *inf* and that's a fact

miserable [mi·se·'ra·βle] *adj* **1.** (*pobre*) poor **2.** (*lamentable*) pitiful **3.** (*tacaño*) stingy **4.** (*poco, mísero*) miserable; **un sueldo ~** a miserable wage

miseria [mi·'se·rja] *f* **1.** (*pobreza*) poverty; **caer en la ~** to become impoverished; **vivir en la ~** to live in poverty **2.** (*poco dinero*) pittance

misericordia [mi·se·ri·'kor·dja] *f* **1.** (*com-*

pasión) compassion **2.** (*perdón*) forgiveness

misericordioso, -a [mi·se·ri·kor·'djo·so, -a] *adj* **1.** (*que siente*) compassionate **2.** (*que perdona*) forgiving

mísero, -a ['mi·se·ro, -a] *adj v.* **miserable**

misil [mi·'sil] *m* missile; **~ antiaéreo** anti-aircraft missile

misión [mi·'sjon] *f* mission

misionero, -a [mi·sjo·'ne·ro, -a] *m, f* missionary

mismo ['mis·mo] *adv* **1.** (*incluso*) even **2.** (*manera*) **así ~** in that way **3.** (*justamente*) **ahí ~** just there; **aquí ~** right here; **ayer ~** only yesterday; **nos podemos ver el miércoles ~** we could meet on Wednesday, say

mismo, -a ['mis·mo, -a] *adj* **1.** (*idéntico*) **el/lo ~/la misma** the same; **al ~ tiempo** at the same time; **da lo ~** it does not matter; **por lo ~** for that reason; **lo ~ José que María** both José and María; **lo ~ no vienen** they might not come; **quedamos** [*o* **seguimos**] **en las mismas** we are where we were **2.** (*semejante*) **el ~/la misma/lo ~** the same; **llevar la misma falda** to wear an identical skirt **3.** (*reflexivo*) myself; **te perjudicas a ti ~** you harm yourself; **yo misma lo vi** I myself saw him/it; **lo hizo por sí misma** she did it (all) by herself; **lo podemos hacer nosotros ~s** we can do it ourselves **4.** (*precisamente*) **este ~ perro fue el que me mordió** that very dog was the one that bit me; **¡eso ~!** exactly! **5.** (*hasta*) actual; **el ~ embajador asistió a la fiesta** the ambassador himself attended the party

misterio [mis·'te·rjo] *m* mystery

misterioso, -a [mis·te·'rjo·so, -a] *adj* mysterious

mística ['mis·ti·ka] *f* mysticism

místico, -a ['mis·ti·ko] *adj* mystical

mitad [mi·'tad] *f* **1.** (*parte igual*) half; **~ hombre ~ bestia** half man, half beast; **a ~ de precio** at half price; **mezcla harina y agua, ~ y ~** mix flour and water, half and half [*o* in equal amounts]; **reducir a la ~** to halve **2.** (*medio*) middle; **en ~ del bosque** in the middle of the

forest; **cortar por la ~** to cut in half

mítico, -a ['mi·ti·ko, -a] *adj* mythical, mythological

mitigar <g > gu> [mi·ti·'yar] **I.** *vt* **1.** (*dolores*) to alleviate; (*sed*) to quench; (*hambre*) to take the edge off; (*temperamento*) to pacify; **~ la inquietud de alguien** to put sb's mind at rest **2.** (*colores, luz*) to subdue; (*calor*) to mitigate **II.** *vr:* **~se 1.** (*dolores*) to lessen **2.** (*color, luz*) to become subdued

mitin ['mi·tin] *m* political meeting, rally

mito ['mi·to] *m* myth

mitología [mi·to·lo·'xi·a] *f* mythology

mitológico, -a [mi·to·'lo·xi·ko, -a] *adj* mythological

mitote [mi·'to·te] *m Méx* **1.** (*jaleo*) uproar; (*caos*) riot **2.** (*danza*) ritual Aztec dance

mixto, -a ['mis·to, -a] *adj* mixed

mobiliario [mo·βi·'lja·rjo] *m* furniture

mocasín [mo·ka·'sin] *m* moccasin

mochila [mo·'tʃi·la] *f* backpack

mochuelo [mo·'tʃwe·lo] *m* small owl; **cargar a alguien con el ~** *inf* to let sb else do all the dirty work

moción [mo·'sjon, -'θjon] *f t.* POL motion; **presentar una ~ de censura** to put forward a censure motion

moco ['mo·ko] *m* **1.** (*materia*) mucus; (*de la nariz*) snot; **limpiarse los ~s** to wipe one's nose **2.** (*del pavo*) wattle; **no es ~ de pavo** *fig* you can't laugh this one off ▶ **llorar a ~ tendido** *inf* to cry one's eyes out

mocoso, -a [mo·'ko·so, -a] *m, f* pey brat

moda ['mo·da] *f* fashion; **estar de ~** to be fashionable; **ponerse/pasar de ~** to come into/go out of fashion; **ir a la (última) ~** to follow the (latest) fashion

modal [mo·'dal] **I.** *adj* modal **II.** *mpl* manners *pl*; **¡qué ~es son estos!** what manners are these!

modalidad [mo·da·li·'dad] *f* form; **~es de un contrato** types of contract

modelar [mo·de·'lar] *vt* to model; *fig* to fashion

modelo [mo·'de·lo] *mf* **1.** (*de modas*) model **2.** ARTE, FOTO model

modelo [mo·'de·lo] *m* **1.** (*ejemplo*) model; **un político ~** a model politician **2.** (*esquema*) design

módem ['mo·den] *m* COMPUT modem

moderación [mo·de·ra·ˈsjon, -ˈθjon] *f* moderation; **comer con ~** to eat in moderation

moderado, -a [mo·de·ˈra·do, -a] *adj* (*propuesta, persona, velocidad*) moderate; (*precio, petición*) reasonable

moderador(a) [mo·de·ra·ˈdor] *m(f)* TV, RADIO moderator

moderar [mo·de·ˈrar] **I.** *vt* **1.** (*disminuir*) to moderate **2.** TV, RADIO to present; (*debate*) to chair **II.** *vr:* **~se** to calm down

modernismo [mo·der·ˈnis·mo] *m* modernism

modernización [mo·der·ni·sa·ˈsjon, -θa·ˈθjon] *f* modernization

modernizar <z → c> [mo·der·ni·ˈsar, -ˈθar] **I.** *vt* to modernize **II.** *vr:* **~se** to modernize oneself, to come up to date

moderno, -a [mo·ˈder·no, -a] *adj* modern; **edad moderna** present day

modestia [mo·ˈdes·tja] *f* modesty; **~ aparte** modesty apart [*o* aside]

modesto, -a [mo·ˈdes·to, -a] *adj* modest

módico, -a [ˈmo·di·ko, -a] *adj* moderate

modificación [mo·di·fi·ka·ˈsjon, -ˈθjon] *f* (*de plan*) modification; (*de tema*) alteration

modificar <c → qu> [mo·di·fi·ˈkar] *vt* (*plan*) to modify; (*tema*) to alter

modismo [mo·ˈdis·mo] *m* idiom

modista [mo·ˈdis·ta] *mf* dressmaker

modisto [mo·ˈdis·to] *m* fashion designer

modo [ˈmo·do] *m* **1.** (*manera*) way; **~ de andar/hablar/pensar** way of walking/talking/thinking; **hazlo a tu ~** do it your way; **de este ~** in this way; **de ningún ~** no way; **hacer algo de cualquier ~** to do sth any old how; **encontrar un ~ de resolver el problema** to find a way to solve the problem; **de cualquier ~ no hubieran ido** anyway they would not have gone; **de ~ que lo has conseguido** so you have managed it; **utilizar el paraguas a ~ de espada** to use the umbrella as a sword; **en cierto ~** in a way; **de un ~ u otro** one way or another; **de todos ~s es mejor que te vayas** in spite of everything it would be better

for you to go **2.** LING mood **3.** COMPUT mode **4.** *pl* (*comportamiento*) manners *pl;* **decir algo con buenos/malos ~s** to say sth politely/rudely

modorra [mo·ˈdo·rra] *f* drowsiness

modular [mo·du·ˈlar] *vi*, *vt* to modulate

módulo [ˈmo·du·lo] *m* **1.** *t.* ARQUIT, ELEC (*de un mueble*) unit **2.** ENS, COMPUT module

mofar [mo·ˈfar] *vi*, *vr* **~se de algo/alguien** to scoff at sth/sb

mofeta [mo·ˈfe·ta] *f* ZOOL skunk

moflete [mo·ˈfle·te] *m* chubby cheek

mogolla [mo·ˈɣo·ja, -ʎa] *m* Col CULIN dark wholegrain bread

mogollón [mo·ɣo·ˈjon, -ˈʎon] *m inf* **1.** (*cantidad*) load(s); **había ~ de público en el pabellón** there were masses of spectators in the pavilion **2.** (*lío*) mess

moho [ˈmo(o)] *m* mold; **no** (**dejar**) **criar ~** (*alimentos*) to be eaten immediately; (*un objeto*) to be in constant use

mohoso, -a [mo·ˈo·so, -a] *adj* moldy

mojar [mo·ˈxar] **I.** *vt* to wet; (*ligeramente*) to moisten; (*el pan*) to dunk **II.** *vr:* **~se 1.** (*con un líquido*) to get wet **2.** *inf* (*comprometerse*) to get involved

mojarra [mo·ˈxa·rra] *f* Arg short broad knife

mojigato, -a [mo·xi·ˈɣa·to, -a] *adj* (*gazmoño*) prudish; (*hipócrita*) hypocritical

molar [mo·ˈlar] **I.** *adj* **1.** (*de muela*) **diente ~** molar **2.** (*de moler*) grinding **II.** *m* molar **III.** *vi inf* (*gustar*) **este libro mola** this book is really cool; **me molan las rubias** I am into [*o* I go for] blonds

molde [ˈmol·de] *m* TÉC, CULIN mold; TIPO form; **pan de ~** sliced bread; **romper ~s** to break the mold

moldear [mol·de·ˈar] *vt* to mold

moldura [mol·ˈdu·ra] *f* **1.** (*listón*) trim **2.** ARQUIT molding

mole¹ [ˈmo·le] *f* (*masa*) mass

mole² [ˈmo·le] *m* Méx CULIN **1.** (*salsa*) sauce; **~ verde** green sauce **2.** (*guiso*) stew

molécula [mo·ˈle·ku·la] *f* molecule

molecular [mo·le·ku·ˈlar] *adj* molecular

moler <o → ue> [mo·ˈler] *vt* **1.** (*café, trigo*) to grind; (*aceitunas*) to press **2.** (*fatigar*) to exhaust; **estoy molido de la**

excursión the trip has exhausted me

molestar [mo·les·'tar] I. *vt* (*estorbar*) to inconvenience; (*fastidiar*) to bother; (*dolores*) to hurt; (*enfadar*) to annoy; **esta camisa me molesta** this shirt annoys me II. *vr:* **~se 1.** (*tomarse la molestia*) to bother; **ni siquiera te has molestado en comprobarlo** you didn't even bother check it; **no tendrías que haberte molestado** you shouldn't have bothered **2.** (*ofenderse*) to take offense; **se ha molestado por tu comentario** he/she has taken offense at what you said

molestia [mo·'les·tja] *f* **1.** (*fastidio*) bother; (*por dolores*) discomfort; **ser una ~** to be a nuisance **2.** (*inconveniente*) trouble; **no es ninguna ~ (para mí)** it is no trouble (for me); **tomarse la ~** to take the trouble; **perdonen las ~s** we apologize for the inconvenience caused

molesto, -a [mo·'les·to, -a] *adj* **1.** *ser* (*desagradable*) unpleasant; (*fastidioso*) troublesome **2.** *estar* (*enfadado*) **~ por algo** annoyed about sth; (*ofendido*) hurt by sth

molinero, -a [mo·li·'ne·ro, -a] *m, f* miller

molinillo [mo·li·'ni·jo, -ʎo] *m* **~ de café** coffee grinder

molino [mo·'li·no] *m* mill; **~ de papel** paper mill

mollera [mo·'je·ra, -'ʎe·ra] *f* (*seso*) brain; **eso no me entra en la ~** I just don't get it; **ser duro de ~** to be stubborn

molo ['mo·lo] *m Chile* (*rompeolas*) breakwater; (*dique*) seawall

molusco [mo·'lus·ko] *m* mollusk

momentáneo, -a [mo·men·'ta·neo, -a] *adj* **1.** (*instantáneo*) momentary **2.** (*provisional*) provisional; **hacer un arreglo ~** to find a provisional solution **3.** (*temporal*) temporary

momento [mo·'men·to] *m* **1.** (*instante*) instant, moment; **¡espera un ~!** wait a moment!; **de un ~ a otro** at any time now; **al ~** immediately; **en cualquier** [*o* **en todo**] **~** at any time; **en el ~ adecuado** at the appropriate time; **en este ~ estaba pensando en ti** I was just thinking about you; **de ~, no te puedo decir nada** for the moment, I can't tell

you anything; **en un ~ de flaqueza** in a moment of weakness; **la tensión aumentaba por ~s** the tension was growing ever stronger [*o* stronger and stronger]; **aparecer en el último ~** to arrive at the last moment; **en todo ~ mantuvo la calma** at all times he/she remained calm; **no tengo un ~ libre** I do not have one free moment; **hace un ~ que ha salido** he/she left a moment ago; **a cada ~** all the time **2.** (*período*) period; **atravieso un mal ~** I am going through a bad patch **3.** (*actualidad*) present; **la música del ~** present-day music

momia ['mo·mja] *f* mummy

mona ['mo·na] *f* **1.** ZOOL female monkey **2.** *inf* (*borrachera*) drunken state; **coger una ~** to get drunk; **estar como una ~** to be drunk; **dormir la ~** to sleep off a hangover ▶ **aunque la ~ se vista de seda, ~ se queda** *prov* you can't make a silk purse from a sow's ear

monada [mo·'na·da] *f* **es una ~ de chica** that girl is a beauty; **¡qué ~ de vestido!** what a gorgeous dress!

monaguillo, -a [mo·na·'ɣi·jo, -a; -ʎo, -a] *m, f* altar boy *m*, altar girl *f*

monarca [mo·'nar·ka] *mf* monarch

monarquía [mo·nar·'ki·a] *f* monarchy

monárquico, -a [mo·'nar·ki·ko, -a] *adj* **1.** (*de la monarquía*) monarchic **2.** (*partidario*) monarchist

monasterio [mo·nas·'te·rjo] *m* monastery

monda ['mon·da] *f* **1.** (*acción*) peeling **2.** (*peladura*) peel ▶ **ser la ~** *inf* to be terrific

mondadientes [mon·da·'djen·tes] *m inv* toothpick

mondar [mon·'dar] I. *vt* **1.** (*plátano, patata, palo*) to peel **2.** (*árbol*) to prune II. *vr:* **~se** to peel; **~se los dientes** to clean one's teeth with a toothpick; **~se (de risa)** *inf* to die laughing

moneda [mo·'ne·da] *f* **1.** (*pieza*) coin; **~ de cinco peniques** five pence coin; **~ de 5/10/25 centavos** nickel/dime/quarter; **~ suelta** change; **teléfono de ~s** pay phone; **pagar a alguien con la misma ~** *fig* to pay sb back tit for tat; **la otra cara de la ~** the other side of the coin **2.** (*de un país*) currency; ~ **de curso legal** legal tender; ~ **extranjera** foreign currency; ~ **fuerte/débil** strong/weak currency; ~ **nacional** local currency; ~ **única europea** single currency

monedero [mo·ne·'de·ro] *m* purse

monetario, -a [mo·ne·'ta·rjo] *adj* monetary; **institución monetaria** monetary institution

mongólico, -a [mon·'go·li·ko, -a] *adj* MED of Down's syndrome

mongolismo [mon·go·'lis·mo] *m* MED Down's syndrome

monigote [mo·ni·'ɣo·te] *m* **hacer ~s** (*figuras humanas*) to draw stick figures; (*borrones*) to doodle

monitor [mo·ni·'tor] *m* TÉC monitor; COMPUT (*pantalla*) screen

monitor(a) [mo·ni·'tor(a)] *m(f)* (*de un deporte*) coach, trainer; (*de un campamento*) camp leader; ~ **de natación** swimming instructor

monja ['mon·xa] *f* nun, sister

monje ['mon·xe] *m* monk, brother

mono ['mo·no] *m* **1.** ZOOL monkey; **¿tengo ~s en la cara?** *inf* what are you staring at?; **en esta casa soy el último ~** in this house I am a nobody **2.** (*traje*) overalls *pl*; (*de mecánico*) coveralls *pl*; (*de calle*) jumpsuit **3.** *inf* (*de drogas*) withdrawal symptoms *pl*; **tener el ~** to be suffering from withdrawal symptoms

mono, -a ['mo·no, -a] *adj* good-looking; (*niño*) cute; (*chica*) pretty; (*vestido*) lovely

monogamia [mo·no·'ɣa·mja] *f* monogamy

monógamo, -a [mo·'no·ɣa·mo, -a] *adj* monogamous

monografía [mo·no·ɣra·'fi·a] *f* monograph

monólogo [mo·'no·lo·ɣo] *m* monologue; TEAT soliloquy

monopatín [mo·no·pa·'tin] *m* skateboard

monopolio [mo·no·'po·ljo] *m* monopoly

monopolizar <z → c> [mo·no·po·li·'sar, -'θar] *vt* COM to monopolize, to corner (a market); ~ **la atención de alguien** to monopolize sb's attention

monosílabo [mo·no·'si·la·βo] *m*

syllable; **responder con ~s** to answer in monosyllables

monosílabo, -a [mo·no·'si·la·βo, -a] *adj* monosyllabic

monotonía [mo·no·to·'ni·a] *f* monotony

monótono, -a [mo·'no·to·no, -a] *adj* monotonous

monóxido [mo·'nok·si·do, -a] *m* monoxide

monstruo ['mons·trwo] *m* monster; (*persona fea*) hideous person; (*persona perversa*) fiend; (*artista*) superstar

monstruosidad [mons·trwo·si·'dad] *f* monstrosity

monstruoso, -a [mons·tru·'o·so, -a] *adj* (*desfigurado*) disfigured; (*terrible*) monstrous; (*enorme*) huge

monta ['mon·ta] *f* **de poca ~** unimportant

montacargas [mon·ta·'kar·ɣas] *m inv* (freight) elevator

montaje [mon·'ta·xe] *m* **1.** TÉC assembly; CINE editing; FOTO montage **2.** (*engaño*) set-up

montante [mon·'tan·te] *m* **1.** (*importe*) total **2.** (*de puerta*) jamb; (*de ventana*) mullion

montaña [mon·'ta·ɲa] *f* (*monte*) mountain; (*zona*) mountains *pl*; ~ **rusa** big dipper; **la fe mueve ~s** faith will move mountains ▶ **hacer una ~ de un grano de arena** to make a mountain out of a molehill

montañero, -a [mon·ta·'ɲe·ro, -a] *m, f* mountaineer

montañés, -esa [mon·ta·'ɲes, -·'ɲe·sa] *adj* highlander

montañismo [mon·ta·'ɲis·mo] *m* mountaineering

montañoso, -a [mon·ta·'ɲo·so, -a] *adj* mountainous

montar [mon·'tar] **I.** *vi* **1.** (*subir a una bici, un caballo*) to get on; (*en un coche*) to get in; ~ **en** (*una bici, un caballo*) to get onto; (*en un coche*) to get into **2.** (*ir a caballo*) to ride; ~ **en bici** to ride a bicycle **II.** *vt* **1.** (*subir en un caballo*) to mount **2.** (*ir a caballo*) to ride **3.** (*acaballar, cubrir*) to cover **4.** (*máquina*) to assemble **5.** (*clara de huevo*) to beat;

M

(*nata*) to whip **6.** (*negocio*) to set up **7.** *inf* (*lío*) ~**la** to kick up a fuss; ~ **un número** to make a scene **III.** *vr:* ~**se 1.** (*subir*) to climb **2.** *inf* (*arreglárselas*) **¿cómo te lo montas con el trabajo?** how do you manage with the work?

monte ['mon·te] *m* **1.** (*montaña*) mountain; **el ~ de los Olivos** the Mount of Olives **2.** (*bosque*) ~ **alto** woodland; ~ **bajo** scrub; **batir el ~** (*cazar*) to go hunting; **echarse al ~** to take to the hills **3.** *pl* (*cordillera*) mountain range ▶ **no todo el ~ es orégano** *prov* all that glitters is not gold

montés, -esa [mon·'tes, -·'te·sa] *adj* wild; **cabra montesa** mountain goat; **gato ~** wildcat

montículo [mon·'ti·ku·lo] *m* mound

monto ['mon·to] *m* total

montón [mon·'ton] *m* heap; **un ~ de ropa** a heap of clothes; **había un ~ de gente** there were a lot of people; **tengo problemas a montones** *inf* I have loads of problems; **ser del ~** to be ordinary

montura [mon·'tu·ra] *f* (*arnés*) harness; (*silla*) saddle; (*de gafas*) frame

monumental [mo·nu·men·'tal] *adj* (*grande, de importancia*) monumental; (*error*) tremendous

monumento [mo·nu·'men·to] *m* memorial; (*grande*) monument; **los ~s de una ciudad** the sights of a city; **esta casa es un ~ nacional** this house is a listed building; **esta chica es un ~** this girl is beautiful

monzón [mon·'son, -'θon] *m* monsoon

moño ['mo·ɲo] *m* **1.** (*pelo*) bun **2.** (*lazo*) bow **3.** *Col* (*capricho*) whim **4.** *Chile* (*pelo*) hair; (*copete*) forelock **5.** *inf* **estar hasta el ~ de algo** to be fed up to the back teeth with sth

moqueta [mo·'ke·ta] *f* carpet

mora ['mo·ra] *f* (*del moral*) mulberry; (*de la zarzamora*) blackberry

morada [mo·'ra·da] *f* **1.** (*casa*) abode **2.** (*residencia*) residence **3.** (*estancia*) stay

morado, -a [mo·'ra·do, -a] *adj* purple; **poner un ojo ~ a alguien** to give sb a black eye; **ponerse ~** (*comiendo*) *inf* to stuff oneself

moral [mo·'ral] **I.** *adj* **1.** (*ético*) moral; **código ~** code of ethics **2.** (*espiritual*) spiritual **II.** *f* morals *pl*; **levantar la ~ a alguien** to boost sb's morale; **hay que tener ~ para hacer eso** you have to be sure of yourself to do that

moraleja [mo·ra·'le·xa] *f* moral

moratón [mo·ra·'ton] *m* bruise

morbo ['mor·βo] *m* **1.** (*enfermedad*) illness **2.** (*interés malsano*) morbid fascination; **esto tiene mucho ~** this has created a lot of unhealthy interest

morboso, -a [mor·'βo·so, -a] *adj* (*placer, imaginación*) morbid

morcilla [mor·'si·ja, -'θi·ʎa] *f* **1.** CULIN blood sausage **2.** *Cuba* (*mentira*) lie **3.** *inf* (*fastidiar*) **¡que te den ~!** go fly a kite!

mordaz [mor·'das, -'daθ] *adj* (*comentario*) caustic; (*crítica*) scathing

mordaza [mor·'da·sa, -'da·θa] *f* gag; **quieren ponerme una ~** *fig* they want to shut me up

mordedura [mor·de·'du·ra] *f* bite

morder <o → ue> [mor·'der] **I.** *vt* **1.** (*con los dientes*) to bite; **está que muerde** *inf* he/she is furious **2.** *AmL* (*estafar*) to cheat **II.** *vr:* ~**se** to bite; **¡no te muerdas las uñas!** don't bite your nails; **tuve que ~me la lengua** I had to bite my tongue

mordida [mor·'di·da] *f* **1.** *Méx inf* (*acción*) bite; (*dinero*) bribe **2.** *Arg v.* **mordisco**

mordisco [mor·'dis·ko] *m* bite, nibble

mordisquear [mor·dis·ke·'ar] *vt* ~ **algo** to nibble at sth

moreno, -a [mo·'re·no, -a] *adj* brown; (*de piel*) dark-skinned; (*de cabello*) dark-haired; (*de ojos*) brown-eyed

morete [mo·'re·te] *m* *AmC*, **moretón** [mo·re·'ton] *m* *inf* bruise

morfema [mor·'fe·ma] *m* LING morpheme

morfina [mor·'fi·na] *f* morphine

morgue ['mor·ɣe] *f* *AmL* morgue

moribundo, -a [mo·ri·'βun·do, -a] *adj* dying

morir [mo·'rir] *irr* **I.** *vi* (*perecer*) to die; (*en catástrofe, guerra, accidente*) to be killed; ~ **de hambre/sed** to die of starvation/thirst; ~ **ahogado** (*en agua*) to drown; (*en humo*) to asphyxiate, to suffocate; **~ de viejo** to die of old age **II.** *vr:* **~se 1.** (*perecer*) to die; (*planta*) to wither **2.** (*con 'de'*) **~se de hambre/de sed** to die of starvation/thirst; **~se de frío** to freeze to death; **~se de risa** to die laughing; **~se de pena** to pine away **3.** (*con 'por'*) **me muero (de ganas) por saber lo que me dijo** I am dying to know what she/he said to you; **me muero por ella** I am crazy about her

mormón, -ona [mor·'mon, -·'mo·na] *adj, m, f* Mormon

moro, -a ['mo·ro, -a] **I.** *adj* Moorish **II.** *m, f* Moor; **~ y cristianos** *Cuba* rice with black beans ▶ **¡no hay ~s en la costa!** the coast is clear!; **ser un ~** *inf* to be chauvinistic

moroso, -a [mo·'ro·so, -a] *m, f* debtor in arrears, defaulter

morral [mo·'rral] *m* (*de las caballerías*) nosebag

morrear [mo·rre·'ar] *vt, vr:* **~se** *vulg* to French-kiss

morriña [mo·'rri·ɲa] *f inf* homesickness

morro ['mo·rro] *m* **1.** *zool* (*hocico*) snout *pl* (*de persona*) **~s** (*labios*) lips; (*boca*) mouth; **beber a ~** to drink straight from the bottle; **me caí de ~s** I fell flat on my face; **estar de ~(s)** *fig* to be angry; **torcer el ~** *fig* to pout; **tiene un ~ que se lo pisa** *inf* he/she has a real nerve; **lo hizo así, por el ~** *inf* he/she did it like that, quite brazenly

morrón [mo·'rron] *adj* **pimiento ~** sweet red pepper

morsa ['mor·sa] *f* walrus

morse ['mor·se] *m* Morse code

mortadela [mor·ta·'de·la] *f* mortadella, ≈ bologna, ≈ baloney

mortaja [mor·'ta·xa] *f* **1.** (*sábana*) shroud; (*vestidura*) burial garments *pl* **2.** *AmL* (*de cigarrillo*) cigarette paper

mortal [mor·'tal] **I.** *adj* **1.** (*sujeto a la muerte*) mortal; **los restos ~es** the mortal remains **2.** (*que la causa*) mortal, lethal; **peligro ~** mortal danger **II.** *mf* mortal; **los ~es** mankind

mortalidad [mor·ta·li·'dad] *f* (*cualidad*) mortality; (*número*) mortality rate

mortero [mor·'te·ro] *m t.* MIL (*cuenco*) mortar

mortífero, -a [mor·'ti·fe·ro, -a] *adj* deadly

mortificar <c → qu> [mor·ti·fi·'kar] **I.** *vt* **1.** (*atormentar*) to torment **2.** (*humillar*) to mortify **II.** *vr:* **~se 1.** (*atormentarse*) to be tormented **2.** REL to mortify oneself **3.** *Méx* (*avergonzarse*) to be ashamed

mortuorio, -a [mor·tu·'o·rjo, -a] *adj* death

moruno, -a [mo·'ru·no, -a] *adj* Moorish; **pincho ~** spicy meat kebab

mosaico [mo·'sai·ko] *m* mosaic

mosca ['mos·ka] *f* ZOOL fly; **por si las ~s** *inf* just in case; **tener la ~ detrás de la oreja** *inf* to be nagged by sth; **estar ~** *inf* (*receloso*) to be suspicious; (*enfadado*) to be cross; **¿qué ~ te ha picado?** what's bugging you?; **~ cojonera** *vulg* pest; **~ muerta** hypocrite

moscada [mos·'ka·da] *adj* **nuez ~** nutmeg

moscovita [mos·ko·'βi·ta] *adj, mf* Muscovite

Moscú [mos·'ku] *m* Moscow

mosqueado, -a [mos·ke·'a·do, -a] *adj inf* cross; **estar ~ con alguien** to be cross with sb

mosquearse [mos·ke·'ar·se] *vr inf* (*ofenderse*) to take offense; (*enfadarse*) to get angry

mosqueo [mos·'keo] *m* anger

mosquita [mos·'ki·ta] *f* **~ muerta** hypocrite

mosquitero [mos·ki·'te·ro] *m* mosquito net(ting)

mosquito [mos·'ki·to] *m* mosquito; (*pequeño*) gnat

mostaza [mos·'ta·sa, -'ta·θa] *f* mustard; (**de**) **color ~** mustard(-yellow)

mosto ['mos·to] *m* must

mostrador [mos·tra·'dor] *m* (*tienda*) counter; (*bar*) bar; (*ventanilla*) window

mostrar <o → ue> [mos·'trar] **I.** *vt* (*enseñar*) to show; (*presentar*) to display **II.** *vr:* **~se** to appear; **~se amigo** to be friendly

mota ['mo·ta] *f* (*partícula*) speck; **~ (de polvo)** speck of dust

mote ['mo·te] *m* **1.** (*apodo*) nickname; **~ cariñoso** pet name **2.** *AmL* (*maíz*) boiled corn

moteado, -a [mo·te·'a·do, -a] *adj* (*ojos*) flecked; (*tela*) dotted; (*huevos*) speckled

motel [mo·'tel] *m* motel

motín [mo·'tin] *m* uprising; (*militar*) mutiny; **un ~ en la cárcel** a prison riot

motivación [mo·ti·βa·'sjon, -'θjon] *f* motivation

motivar [mo·ti·'βar] *vt* **1.** (*incitar*) to motivate **2.** (*provocar*) to cause

motivo [mo·'ti·βo] *m* **1.** (*causa*) reason behind; (*crimen*) motive; **con ~ de...** on the occasion of...; **por este ~** for this reason **2.** (*tela*) motif

moto [mo·to] *f* *inf* motorbike; **~ acuática** Jet Ski®; **ir en ~** to ride a motorbike; **iba como una ~** *inf* he/she was going like a bat out of hell; **ponerse como una ~** (*enfadado*) to get furious

motocicleta [mo·to·si·'kle·ta, -θi·'kle·ta] *f* motorcycle; **ir en ~** to go by motorcycle

motociclismo [mo·to·si·'klis·mo, -θi·'klis·mo] *m* motorcycling

motociclista [mo·to·si·'klis·ta, -θi·'klis·ta] *mf* motorcyclist

motoneta [mo·to·ne·'ta] *f* *AmL* motor scooter

motor [mo·'tor] *m* *t. fig* motor; **~ de búsqueda** COMPUT search engine; **~ de reacción** jet engine

motor(a) [mo·'tor, --'to·ra] *adj* motor

motora [mo·'to·ra] *f* motorboat

motorista [mo·to·'ris·ta] *mf* **1.** *t.* DEP motorcyclist **2.** (*policía*) motorized policeman

motorizar <z → c> [mo·to·ri·'sar, -'θar] *vt* to motorize; **estar motorizado** *inf* to have wheels [*o* a car]

motosierra [mo·to·'sje·rra] *f* chain saw

motriz [mo·'tris, -'triθ] *adj* driving; **fuerza ~** driving force

movedizo, -a [mo·βe·'di·so, -a, -'di·θo, -a] *adj* (*móvil*) moving; **arenas movedizas** quicksand; *fig* dangerous ground

mover <o → ue> [mo·'βer] **I.** *vt* **1.** (*desplazar*) to move; **~ archivo** COMPUT move file; **~ la cola** to wag one's tail; **~ la cabeza** (*asentir*) to nod (one's head); (*negar*) to shake one's head **2.** (*incitar*) to rouse **II.** *vr:* **~se** to move; **¡venga,**

¡muévete! come on! get a move on!

movida [mo·'βi·da] *f* **1.** *inf* fuss; **¡qué ~!** (*lío*) what a business! **2.** (*ambiente*) scene

movido, -a [mo·'βi·do, -a] *adj* **1.** (*foto*) blurred **2.** (*activo*) active; (*vivo*) lively; **he tenido un día muy ~** I have had a very busy day

móvil ['mo·βil] **I.** *adj* (*que se mueve*) mobile **II.** *m* **1.** (*crimen*) motive **2.** TEL cell (phone)

movilidad [mo·βi·li·'dad] *f* mobility

movilización [mo·βi·li·sa·'sjon, -θa·'θjon] *f* **1.** (*recursos, tropas*) mobilization **2.** (*huelga*) industrial action

movilizar <z → c> [mo·βi·li·'sar, -'θar] *vt* to mobilize; (*dinero*) to release

movimiento [mo·βi·'mjen·to] *m* **1.** *t.* FÍS movement; **~ vibratorio** vibratory movement; **poner en ~** to put [*o* set] in motion; **había mucho ~ en las tiendas** the shops were busy **2.** COM movement; **~s bursátiles** stock-market movements

mozo, -a ['mo·so, -θo] *m* servant; **~ (de estación)** porter; **~ de hotel** bellboy

mozo, -a ['mo·θo, -a; -θo, -a] *m, f* (*chico*) lad; (*chica*) girl; (*joven*) youth, young person; **¡pero si estás hecho un ~!** (*a un chico*) what a strapping lad you are!

mu [mu] **I.** *interj* (*vaca*) moo **II.** *m* **no decir ni ~** *inf* not to say a word

mucamo, -a [mu·'ka·mo, -a] *m, f* *AmL* (*criado*) servant; (*criada*) maid

muchacho, -a [mu·'tʃa·tʃo, -a] *m, f* (*chico*) boy; (*chica*) girl

muchedumbre [mu·tʃe·'dum·bre] *f* (*de personas*) crowd; (*de cosas*) collection

mucho, -a ['mu·tʃo, -a] **I.** *adj* a lot of; **~ vino** a lot of wine, much wine; **~s libros** a lot of books, many books; **esto es ~ para ella** this is too much for her; **hace ya ~ tiempo que...** it has been a long time since...; **muchas veces** lots of times **II.** *adv* (*intensidad*) very; **trabajar/esforzarse ~** to work/to try hard; (*cantidad*) a lot; (*mucho tiempo*) for a long time; (*muchas veces*) many times; (*a menudo*) often; **lo sentimos ~** we are very sorry; **no hace ~ estuvo aquí**

he/she was here not long ago; **es con ~ el más simpático** he is by far the most pleasant; **por ~ que se esfuercen, no lo conseguirán** however hard they try, they will not manage it; **ni ~ menos** far from it; **como ~** at (the) most

mucosa [mu·'ko·sa] *f* mucus

muda [mu·ða] *f* 1. (*ropa interior*) change of underwear; (*cama*) change of sheets 2. (*serpiente*) slough, shedding of skin 3. (*pájaro, pelo*) molt

mudanza [mu·'dan·sa, -θa] *f* move; **camión de ~s** moving van; **estar de ~** to be in the middle of a move

mudar [mu·'dar] I. *vi, vt* to change; **~ (de) pluma** to molt; **~ (de) piel** to slough, to shed II. *vr*: **~se** 1. (*casa*) to move; **nos mudamos (de aquí)** we are moving (away); **~se a Ecuador** to move to Ecuador 2. (*ropa*) **~se (de ropa)** to change clothes

mudo, -a ['mu·ðo, -a] *adj* mute; **cine ~** silent movies; **quedarse ~ de asombro** to be speechless with amazement

mueble ['mwe·βle] I. *m* 1. (*pieza*) piece of furniture; **~ bar** drinks cabinet; **~ de cocina** kitchen unit 2. *pl* furniture; **con/sin ~s** furnished/unfurnished II. *adj* JUR **bienes ~s** movable goods, personal property

mueca ['mwe·ka] *f* face; **hacer ~s** to pull faces; (*de dolor, disgusto*) grimace

muela ['mwe·la] *f* (*diente*) molar; **~s del juicio** wisdom teeth; **~ picada** molar with tooth decay; **dolor de ~s** toothache

muelle ['mwe·je, -ʎe] *m* 1. (*resorte*) spring 2. (*puerto*) wharf; **~ flotante** floating quay

muérdago ['mwer·da·ɣo] *m* mistletoe

muerte ['mwer·te] *f* death; **pena de ~** death penalty; **condenar a ~** to condemn [o sentence] to death; **morir de ~ natural** to die of natural causes; **hasta que la ~ os separe** (*matrimonio*) till death do you part ▶ **de mala ~** lousy, crummy; **a ~** to death; **a ese tipo lo odio a ~** I detest that man; **llevarse un susto de ~** to be scared to death

muerto, -a ['mwer·to, -a] I. *pp de* **morir** II. *adj* dead; **horas muertas** period

of inactivity; **naturaleza muerta** still life; **estar ~ (de cansancio)** to be exhausted; **estar ~ de hambre/sed** to be ravenous/dying of thirst; **caerse ~** to drop dead; **no tener dónde caerse ~** *inf* to be penniless; **punto ~** AUTO neutral III. *m, f* dead person; (*difunto*) deceased; (*cadáver*) corpse; **ahora me cargan el ~ a mí** *inf* now they are laying the blame on me; **hacerse el ~** (*quieto, t. fig*) to play dead; **ser un ~ de hambre** to be a nobody

muesca ['mwes·ka] *f* nick; (*ranura*) groove

muestra ['mwes·tra] *f* 1. (*mercancía*) sample; (*gratuita*) free sample; **feria de ~s** trade fair 2. (*prueba*) proof; **~ de amistad** token of friendship 3. (*demostración*) demonstration; **dar ~(s) de valor** to give a demonstration of courage 4. (*de labores*) example 5. MED **~ de sangre/orina** blood/urine sample

muestrario [mwes·'tra·rjo] *m* collection of samples

muestreo [mwes·'treo] *m* sampling

mugir <g → j> [mu·'xir] *vi* (*vaca*) to moo

mugre ['mu·ɣre] *f* grime

mugriento, -a [mu·'ɣrjen·to, -a] *adj* grubby

mujer [mu·'xer] *f* woman; (*esposa*) wife; **~ fatal** femme fatale; **~ de la limpieza** cleaning lady, cleaner; **está hecha toda una ~** she really is grown-up; **esto es cosa de ~es** this is women's stuff

mujeriego [mu·xe·'rje·ɣo] *m* womanizer

mulato, -a [mu·'la·to, -a] *m, f* mulatto

mulero, -a [mu·'le·ro, -a] *m, f* RíoPl *inf* 1. (*mentiroso*) liar 2. (*tramposo*) cheat

muleta [mu·'le·ta] *f* 1. (*apoyo*) crutch; **andar con ~s** to walk with crutches 2. TAUR red cloth attached to a stick used by a matador

muletilla [mu·le·'ti·ja, -ʎa] *f* (*coletilla*) tag; (*palabra*) pet word; (*frase*) catch phrase

mullido, -a [mu·'ji·ðo, -ʎi·ðo] *adj* soft

mulo, -a ['mu·lo, -a] *m, f* (*caballo y asna*) hinny; (*asno y yegua*) mule

multa ['mul·ta] *f* fine; **poner una ~ a alguien** to fine sb

M

multar [mul·'tar] *vt* to fine; **me han mul-tado con 3.000 pesos** I've been fined 3,000 pesos

multicolor [mul·ti·ko·'lor] *adj* multicolored; TIPO polychromatic

multilingüe [mul·ti·'lin·gwe] *adj* multilingual

multimedia [mul·ti·'me·dja] *adj inv* multimedia

multimillonario, -a [mul·ti·mi·jo·'na·rjo, -a, mul·ti·mi·ʎo-] *m, f* multimillionaire

multinacional [mul·ti·na·sjo·'nal, -θjo·'nal] *adj, f* multinational

múltiple ['mul·ti·ple] *adj* multiple; **~s ve-ces** numerous times

multiplicación [mul·ti·pli·ka·'sjon, -'θjon] *f t.* MAT multiplication

multiplicar <c → qu> [mul·ti·pli·'kar] **I.** *vi, vt* **1.** MAT **~ por algo** to multiply by sth; **tabla de ~** multiplication table **2.** (*reproducir, aumentar*) to multiply **II.** *vr:* **~se 1.** (*reproducirse*) to multiply **2.** (*desvivirse*) to be everywhere at the same time

múltiplo, -a ['mul·ti·plo, -a] *adj, m, f* multiple

multitud [mul·ti·'tud] *f* **1.** (*cantidad*) multitude; **una ~ de flores** a great number of flowers **2.** (*gente*) multitude, crowd; (*vulgo*) masses *pl*

multitudinario, -a [mul·ti·tu·di·'na·rjo, -a] *adj* multitudinous

multiuso [mul·ti·'u·so] *adj inv* multipurpose

mundanal [mun·da·'nal] *adj*, **mundano, -a** [mun·'da·no, -a] *adj* **1.** (*del mundo*) of the world; (*terrenal*) worldly **2.** (*ex-travagante*) society

mundial [mun·'djal] *adj* world; **campeonato ~ de fútbol** World Cup; **guerra ~** world war; **a nivel ~** worldwide

mundillo [mun·'di·jo, -ʎo] *m inf* (*ambiente*) world; **en el ~ de la música** in musical circles

mundo ['mun·do] *m* **1.** (*tierra*) earth; (*planeta*) planet; (*globo*) world; **~ profesional** professional world; **el otro ~** the next world; **dar la vuelta al ~** to go around the world; **venir al ~** to be born; **irse de este ~** to die; **ver ~** to travel a lot; **recorrer medio ~** to visit many countries; **con la mayor tranquilidad del ~** with the utmost calm; **vive en otro ~** *fig* he/she lives in a world of his/her own; **este ~ es un pañuelo** it is a small world; **desde que el ~ es ~** since the world began; **hacer un ~ de algo** to make a mountain out of a molehill; **así va** [*o* **anda**] **el ~** that is the way things are; **no es nada del otro ~** it is nothing out of this world; **por nada del ~** not for the world **2.** (*humanidad*) **todo el ~** everyone, everybody; **a la vista de todo el ~** for the whole world to see **3.** (*experiencia*) worldliness; **Lola tiene mucho ~** Lola is worldly-wise

munición [mu·ni·'sjon, -'θjon] *f* ammunition

municipal [mu·ni·si·'pal, -θi·'pal] *adj* municipal; **parque ~** municipal park; **término ~** municipality

municipio [mu·ni·'si·pjo, -θi·pjo] *m* **1.** (*población*) municipality, borough **2.** (*ayuntamiento*) town hall **3.** (*concejo*) town council

muñeca [mu·'ɲe·ka] *f* **1.** (*brazo*) wrist **2.** (*juguete*) doll; **~ hinchable** inflatable doll **3.** *fig* (*niña*) doll, cutie

muñeco [mu·'ɲe·ko] *m* **1.** (*juguete*) doll; **~ articulado** jointed doll; **~ de nieve** snowman **2.** *pey* (*monigote*) puppet

muñequera [mu·ɲe·'ke·ra] *f* wristband

muñón [mu·'ɲon] *m* stump

mural [mu·'ral] *m* mural

muralla [mu·'ra·ja, -ʎa] *f* wall

murciélago [mur·'sje·la·ɣo, -mur·'θje·] *m* bat

murmullo [mur·'mu·jo, -ʎo] *m* **1.** (*voz*) whisper; (*cuchicheo*) murmur **2.** (*hojas*) rustling; (*agua*) murmur

murmuración [mur·mu·ra·'sjon, -'θjon] *f* (*calumnia*) slander; (*cotilleo*) gossip

murmurar [mur·mu·'rar] **I.** *vi, vt* (*entre dientes*) to mutter; (*susurrar*) to murmur; **~ al oído de alguien** to whisper in sb's ear **II.** *vi* **1.** (*gruñir*) to grumble **2.** (*criticar*) to criticize; (*chismorrear*) to gossip **3.** (*agua*) to murmur; (*hojas*) to rustle

muro ['mu·ro] *m* wall; **~ de contención** retaining wall; **Muro de las Lamenta-**

ciones the Wailing Wall

mus [mus] *m card game*

musa ['mu·sa] *f* muse

musaraña [mu·sa·'ra·ɲa] *f* 1. ZOOL shrew 2. *fig* (*bicho*) small animal; **pensar en las ~s** *fig* to have one's head in the clouds

muscular [mus·ku·'lar] *adj* muscular

musculatura [mus·ku·la·'tu·ra] *f* musculature

músculo ['mus·ku·lo] *m* muscle; **ser ~ puro** to be all muscle

musculoso, -a mus·ku·'lo·so, -a] *adj* muscular

museo [mu·'seo] *m* museum

musgo ['mus·ɣo] *m* moss

música ['mu·si·ka] *f* music; **~ folclórica** traditional music; **~ de cámara** chamber music; **~ ligera** easy listening; **banda de ~** band; **caja de ~** music box; **tener talento para la ~** to be musical

musical [mu·si·'kal] **I.** *adj* musical; **composición ~** musical composition **II.** *m* musical

músico, -a ['mu·si·ko, -a] *m, f* musician; (*compositor*) composer

musitar [mu·si·'tar] *vi* (*balbucear*) to mumble; (*susurrar*) to whisper; **~ al oído de alguien** to whisper in sb's ear

muslo ['mus·lo] *m* (*persona*) thigh; (*animal*) leg

mustio, -a ['mus·tjo, -a] *adj* 1. (*flores*) wilting 2. (*triste*) low

musulmán, -ana [mu·sul·'man, -·'ma·na] *adj, m, f* Muslim

mutación [mu·ta·'sjon, -'θjon] *f* mutation

mutilado, -a [mu·ti·'la·do, -a] *m, f* cripple; **~ de guerra** disabled war veteran

mutilar [mu·ti·'lar] *vt* 1. (*cuerpo*) to mutilate 2. (*recortar*) to cut

mutis ['mu·tis] *m inv* TEAT exit; **~ por el foro** quick exit; **hacer ~** to exit

mutualidad [mu·twa·li·'dad] *f* 1. (*cooperativa*) mutual benefit society 2. (*reciprocidad*) mutuality

mutuo, -a ['mu·two, -a] *adj* mutual

muy [mwi] *adv* very; **es ~ improbable que... +*subj* it is very unlikely that...; ~ a pesar mío** much to my dismay; **~ de**

tarde en tarde once in a blue moon; **~ de mañana** in the very early morning; **le saluda ~ atentamente,** (*en cartas*) sincerely yours,; **es Ud. ~ libre de hacer lo que quiera** you are completely free to do as you please

N

N, n ['e·ne] *f* N, n; **~ de Navarra** N as in November

nabo ['na·βo] *m* BOT turnip

nácar ['na·kar] *m* mother-of-pearl, nacre; **de ~** nacreous, pearly

nacatamal [na·ka·ta·'mal] *m AmC, Méx* CULIN pork tamale

nacer [na·'ser, -θer] *irr como crecer vi* 1. (*venir al mundo*) to be born; **nací el 29 de febrero** I was born on the 29th of February; **haber nacido para la música** to be a natural for music; **volver a ~** to have a very narrow escape 2. ASTR to be created; (*día*) to rise; **nace una estrella** a star is born; **al ~ el día** at the break of day 3. (*originarse*) to stem; (*arroyo*) to begin; (*surgir*) to arise ▶ **nadie nace enseñado** *prov* we all have to learn

nacido, -a [na·'si·do, -a; -θi·do, -a] **I.** *adj* **bien ~** (*origen*) born into a good family; (*comportamiento*) noble **II.** *m, f* **recién ~** newborn; **los ~s el 2 de abril** those born on the 2nd of April; **un mal ~** a born villain

nacimiento [na·si·'mjen·to, na·θi-] *m* 1. (*venida al mundo*) birth; **de ~** by birth; **ciego de ~** born blind; **lugar de ~** birthplace; **partida de ~** birth certificate; (*belén*) Nativity scene 2. (*linaje*) family; **ser de humilde ~** to be of humble birth 3. (*comienzo*) beginning

nación [na·'sjon, -'θjon] *f* nation; (**la Organización de) las Naciones Unidas** the United Nations (Organization)

nacional [na·sjo·'nal, -θjo·'nal] *adj* national; **carretera ~** (*en los Estados Unidos*) highway; **renta ~** national income; **vuelos ~es** domestic flights

nacionalidad [na·sjo·na·li·'dad, na·θjo-]

f (*ciudadanía*) nationality, citizenship; **ser de ~ española** to have Spanish nationality

nacionalismo [na·sjo·na·ˈlis·mo, na·θjo-] *m* nationalism

nacionalista [na·sjo·na·ˈlis·ta, na·θjo-] *adj, mf* nationalist

nacionalizar <z > c> [na·sjo·na·li·ˈsar, na·θjo·na·li·ˈθar] I. *vt* (*persona*) to naturalize, to nationalize II. *vr* **~se español** to obtain Spanish nationality

nada [ˈna·da] I. *pron indef* nothing; **¡gracias! — ¡de ~!** thank you! — you're welcome!; **¡pues ~!** all well right then; **por ~ se queja** he/she complains about the slightest thing; **como si ~** as if nothing had happened; **~ menos que el director** the director himself; **no servir para ~** to be useless II. *adv* not at all; **~ más** (*solamente*) only; (*no más*) no more; **¡~ más!** enough!; **~ de ~** absolutely nothing; **no ser ~ difícil** not to be difficult at all; **¡~ de eso!** none of that!; **¡y ~ de llegar tarde!** no arriving late!; **¡casi ~!** hardly anything!; **antes de ~** (*sobre todo*) above all; (*primero*) first of all; **para ~** not in the slightest III. *f* nothing, nothingness; **salir de la ~** to appear out of nowhere

nadador(a) [na·da·ˈdor, -·ˈdo·ra] *m(f)* swimmer

nadar [na·ˈdar] *vi* to swim

nadie [ˈna·dje] *pron indef* nobody, anybody, no one; **no vi a ~** I didn't see anybody, I saw nobody; **no vino ~** nobody came; **tú no eres ~ para decir...** who are you to say ...?; **un don ~** a nobody; **tierra de ~** no man's land

nado [ˈna·do] *adv* **a ~** afloat, swimming

nagual [na·ˈɣwal] *f* *Méx, Hond* witch doctor

nailon [ˈnai·lon] *m* nylon

naipe [ˈnai·pe] *m* (*carta*) (playing) card

nalga [ˈnal·ɣa] *f* buttock; **~s** bottom

nana [ˈna·na] *f* **1.** (*canción*) lullaby **2.** (*niñera*) nanny

nanay [na·ˈnai] *interj inf* no way!

nanotecnología [na·no·tek·no·lo·ˈxi·a] *f* nanotechnology

napia(s) [ˈna·pja(s)] *f(pl) inf* conk

naranja [na·ˈran·xa] I. *f* orange ▶ **¡~s**

(de la China)! no way!; **tu media ~** your better half II. *adj* (**de color**) ~ orange

naranjada [na·ran·ˈxa·da] *f* orangeade

naranjo [na·ˈran·xo] *m* orange tree

narcisismo [nar·si·ˈsis·mo, nar·θi-] *m* narcissism, egoism

narcisista [nar·si·ˈsis·ta, nar·θi-] *adj* narcissistic

narco [ˈnar·ko] *m inf* drug dealer

narcótico [nar·ˈko·ti·ko] *m* narcotic

narcótico, -a [nar·ˈko·ti·ko, -a] *adj* narcotic

narcotraficante [nar·ko·tra·fi·ˈkan·te] *mf* drug dealer

narcotráfico [nar·ko·ˈtra·fi·ko] *m* drug dealing

nariz [na·ˈriθ] *f* **1.** ANAT nose; **~ chata** flat nose; **~ respingona** turned-up nose; **~ aguileña** aquiline nose; **dar a alguien con la puerta en las narices** to slam the door in sb's face; **sonarse/limpiarse la ~** to blow/wipe one's nose; **no ver más allá de sus narices** *inf* to not be able to see further than the end of one's nose; **quedarse con un palmo de narices** *inf* to be let down; **me da en la ~ que...** I have a funny feeling that... **2.** *inf* (*eufemismo por 'cojones'*) **estar hasta las narices** to have had it up to here; **¡(qué) narices!** no way; **tener narices** to be too much; **¡tócate las narices!** would you believe it?

narración [na·rra·ˈsjon, -ˈθjon] *f* narration

narrador(a) [na·rra·ˈdor, -·ˈdo·ra] *m(f)* narrator; (*que cuenta la historia*) storyteller

narrar [na·ˈrrar] *vt* to narrate; (*informar*) to tell

narrativa [na·rra·ˈti·βa] *f* literature

nasal [na·ˈsal] *adj* nasal

nata [ˈna·ta] *f* **1.** (*producto*) cream; **~ montada** whipped cream; **la crema y ~ de la sociedad** the crème de la crème of society **2.** (*sobre un líquido*) film

natación [na·ta·ˈsjon, -ˈθjon] *f* DEP swimming

natal [na·ˈtal] *adj* native, home; **ciudad ~** home town; **país ~** native country [*o* land]

natalidad [na·ta·li·'dad] f birth; **índice de ~** birth rate

natillas [na·'ti·jas, -ʎas] fpl custard

nativo, -a [na·'ti·βo, -a] **I.** adj native, home; **lengua nativa** native [o mother] tongue **II.** m, f AmL native

nato, -a ['na·to, -a] adj born; **un triunfador ~** a born winner

natural [na·tu·'ral] adj **1.** (no artificial, sencillo) natural; (fruto) fresh; (flor) real; **de tamaño ~** life-sized; **esto es lo más ~ del mundo** (normal) it is the most natural thing in the world **2.** (nacido) **ser ~ de Madrid** to be a native of Madrid

naturaleza [na·tu·ra·'le·sa, -θa] f **1.** (campo) nature; **~ muerta** still life; **en plena ~** in the heart of the countryside **2.** (manera) nature **3.** (índole) type

naturalidad [na·tu·ra·li·'dad] f naturalness; **lo dijo con mucha ~** he/she said it very naturally

naufragar <g → gu> [nau·fra·'ɣar] vi **1.** (hundirse) to sink **2.** (no hundir del todo) to be wrecked; (personas) to be shipwrecked **3.** (fracasar) to fall through

naufragio [nau·'fra·xjo] m (accidente) shipwreck

náufrago, -a ['nau·fra·ɣo, -a] m, f shipwrecked sailor, castaway

nauseabundo, -a [nau·sea·'βun·do, -a] adj nauseating

náuseas ['nau·seas] fpl sick feeling; **tengo ~** I feel sick; **dar ~ a alguien** to make sb feel sick

náutico, -a ['nau·ti·ko, -a] adj nautical; **club ~** yacht club

navaja [na·'βa·xa] f (pocket) knife; **~ automática** switchblade

navajazo [na·βa·'xa·θo] m **1.** (golpe) stabbing **2.** (herida) stab [o knife] wound, gash

naval [na·'βal] adj naval

nave ['na·βe] f **1.** NÁUT, AVIAT ship, vessel; **~ (espacial)** spaceship, spacecraft **2.** (en una iglesia) nave **3.** (almacén) warehouse ▶ **quemar las ~s** to burn one's bridges

navegable [na·βe·'ɣa·βle] adj navigable

navegación [na·βe·ɣa·'sjon, -'θjon] f navigation

navegador [na·βe·ɣa·'dor] m COMPUT browser

navegante [na·βe·'ɣan·te] mf navigator

navegar <g → gu> [na·βe·'ɣar] vi, vt to navigate; **~ veinte nudos por hora** to sail at 20 knots an hour; **~ contra la corriente** to go against the flow; **~ por la web** to surf the net

Navidad [na·βi·'dad] f Christmas; **¡feliz ~!** merry Christmas!

navideño, -a [na·βi·'de·ɲo, -a] adj Christmas

navío [na·'βi·o] m ship

neblina [ne·'βli·na] f mist; fig haze

necedad [ne·θe·'dad] f stupidity

necesariamente [ne·θe·sa·rja·'men·te] adv necessarily

necesario, -a [ne·θe·'sa·rjo, -a] adj necessary

neceser [ne·θe·'ser] m (de aseo) toilet bag; (de afeitar) shaving kit; (de maquillaje) cosmetic bag

necesidad [ne·θe·si·'dad] f **1.** (ser preciso) need, necessity; **de primera ~** essential **2.** (requerimiento) need; **tener ~ de algo** to be in need of sth **3.** pl (evacuación corporal) **hacer sus ~es** to relieve oneself

necesitado, -a [ne·θe·si·'ta·do, -a] **I.** adj (pobre) needy; **estar ~ de amor** to be in need of love **II.** m, f poor person; **los ~s** the poor

necesitar [ne·θe·si·'tar] vt **1.** (precisar) to need **2.** (tener que) to need to; **necesitas comer algo** you have to eat something

necio, -a ['ne·sjo, -a; neθ-] adj idiotic

necrológico, -a [ne·kro·'lo·xi·ko, -a] adj necrological

néctar ['nek·tar] m nectar

nectarina [nek·ta·'ri·na] f nectarine

neerlandés, -esa [ne(e)r·lan·'des, -·'de·sa] **I.** adj Dutch **II.** m, f Dutchman m, Dutchwoman f

nefasto, -a [ne·'fas·to, -a] adj awful; (día) horrible

negación [ne·ɣa·'sjon, -'θjon] f **1.** (desmentir) denial **2.** (denegar) refusal **3.** LING negative

negado, -a [ne·'ɣa·do, -a] adj **~ para**

algo useless at sth

negar [ne·'ɣar] *irr como* **fregar** I. *vt* 1. (*desmentir*) to deny 2. (*rehusar*) to refuse; (*rechazar*) to reject; ~ **con la cabeza** to shake one's head II. *vr:* **~se** to refuse

negativa [ne·ɣa·'ti·βa] *f* (*negación*) denial; (*rehusamiento*) refusal; (*rechazo*) rejection

negativo [ne·ɣa·'ti·βo] *m* FOTO negative

negativo, -a [ne·ɣa·'ti·βo, -a] *adj* negative; **tu respuesta fue negativa** your answer was negative

negligencia [ne·ɣli·'xen·sja, -θja] *f* (*descuido*) carelessness; JUR negligence

negligente [ne·ɣli·'xen·te] *adj* 1. (*descuidado*) careless 2. JUR negligent

negociable [ne·ɣo·'θja·βle] *adj* negotiable; **el precio es ~** the price is open to negotiation

negociación [ne·ɣo·sja·'sjon, -θja·'θjon] *f* negotiation; ~ **colectiva** collective bargaining

negociador(a) [ne·ɣo·θja·'dor, -·'do·ra] *m(f)* 1. (*comerciante*) merchant 2. (*mediador*) negotiator

negociante [ne·ɣo·'θjan·te] *mf* (*comerciante*) dealer

negociar [ne·ɣo·'θjar, -'θjar] I. *vi* (*comerciar*) to deal II. *vi, vt* (*dialogar, concertar*) to negotiate

negocio [ne·'ɣo·sjo, -θjo] *m* 1. (*comercio*) business; **hombre/mujer de ~s** businessman/businesswoman 2. (*asunto*) matter ▶ **hacer un ~ redondo** *inf* to do a good bit of business

negrero, -a [ne·'ɣre·ro, -a] *m, f* 1. (*que trata con esclavos*) slave dealer; (*tirano*) slave driver 2. CSur (*aprovechado*) parasite

negrilla [ne·'ɣri·ja, -ʎa] *f*, **negrita** [ne·'ɣri·ta] *f* TIPO bold face

negro, -a [ne·'ɣro] I. *adj* black; ~ **como la boca del lobo** pitch-black; ~ **como el carbón** as black as coal ▶ **estar/ponerse ~** *inf* to be/get furious; **pasarlas negras** *inf* to have a terrible time; **verse ~ para hacer algo** *inf* to have a hard time doing sth; **verlo todo ~** to be very pessimistic II. *m, f* 1. (*persona*) black; **trabajar como un ~** *inf* to work like a

slave 2. (*escritor*) ghost writer 3. *Arg inf* (*cariño*) darling

negrura [ne·'ɣru·ra] *f* blackness

nene, -a [ˈne·ne, -a] *m, f inf* (*niño*) baby; (*expresión de cariño*) darling

neocapitalismo [neo·ka·pi·ta·'lis·mo] *m* ECON neocapitalism

neoclásico, -a [neo·'kla·si·ko, -a] *adj* neoclassical

neón [ne·'on] *m* neon

neoyorquino, -a [neo·jor·'ki·no, -a] *m, f* New Yorker

nervio ['ner·βjo] *m* 1. (*conductor*) nerve; **ataque de ~s** nervous breakdown; **ponerse de los ~s** to get nervous [*o* flustered]; **estar atacado de los ~s** to be a nervous wreck; **tener ~s de acero** to have nerves of steel 2. (*tendón*) sinew 3. (*ímpetu*) impetus; **esta empresa tiene ~** this company is dynamic

nerviosismo [ner·βjo·'sis·mo] *m* nervousness

nervioso, -a [ner·'βjo·so, -a] *adj* 1. *t.* ANAT nervous; **el sistema ~** the nervous system 2. (*intranquilo*) excitable

neto, -a ['ne·to] *adj* (*no bruto*) net

neumático [neu·'ma·ti·ko] I. *adj* pneumatic; **martillo ~** pneumatic drill II. *m* tire

neumonía [neu·mo·'ni·a] *f* MED pneumonia

neurología [neu·ro·lo·'xi·a] *f* MED neurology

neurólogo, -a [neu·'ro·lo·ɣo, -a] *m, f* MED neurologist

neurona [neu·'ro·na] *f* ANAT neuron

neurótico, -a [neu·'ro·ti·ko, -a] *adj, m, f* neurotic

neutral [neu·'tral] *adj, mf* neutral

neutralidad [neu·tra·li·'dad] *f* neutrality

neutralizar <z → c> [neu·tra·li·'sar, -'θar] I. *vt* to neutralize II. *vr:* **~se** to be neutralized

neutro, -a ['neu·tro, -a] *adj* 1. *t.* QUÍM neutral 2. LING **género ~** neuter gender

neutrón [neu·'tron] *m* FÍS neutron

nevada [ne·'βa·da] *f* snowfall; (*tormenta*) snowstorm

nevado, -a [ne·'βa·do] *adj* (*cubierto*) snow-covered; (*montaña*) snow-capped

nevar <e → ie> [ne·'βar] *vimpers* to snow

nevera [ne·'βe·ra] *f* (*frigorífico*) fridge; **este cuarto es una ~** this room is freezing

neviscar <c → qu> [ne·βis·'kar] *vimpers* to snow lightly

nexo ['nek·so] *m* nexus; LING connective

ni [ni] *conj* **~... ~...** neither... nor...; **no fumo ~ bebo** I don't smoke or drink, I neither smoke nor drink; **~** (*siquiera*) not even; **¡~ lo pienses!** don't even let it cross your mind!; **sin más ~ más** without any further ado; **~ bien...** *Arg* as soon as...

Nicaragua [ni·ka·'ra·ɣwa] *f* Nicaragua

nicaragüense [ni·ka·ra·'ɣwen·se] *adj, mf* Nicaraguan

nicho ['ni·tʃo] *m* niche

nicotina [ni·ko·'ti·na] *f* nicotine

nido ['ni·do] *m* **1.** (*nidal*) nest **2.** (*lecho*) den; **~ de ladrones** den of thieves

niebla ['nje·βla] *f* fog; **hay ~** it is foggy

nieto, -a ['nje·to, -a] *m, f* grandchild, grandson *m*, grand-daughter *f*; **los nietos** the grandchildren

nieve ['nje·βe] *f* **1.** (*precipitación*) snow; **copo de ~** snowflake **2.** *inf* (*cocaína*) coke, snow **3.** *AmC* (*helado*) ice cream

NIF [nif] *m abr de* **Número de Identificación Fiscal** Fiscal Identity Number

nimio, -a ['ni·mjo, -a] *adj* insignificant

ninfa ['nin·fa] *f* (*mitología*) *t.* ZOOL nymph

ningún [nin·'ɡun] *adj indef v.* **ninguno**

ninguno, -a [nin·'ɡu·no, -a] **I.** *adj indef* (*precediendo a un sustantivo masculino singular: ningún*) any; **por ningún lado** anywhere; **de ninguna manera** no way; **ninguna vez** never; **en ningún sitio** nowhere; **no hay ningún peligro** there is no danger **II.** *pron indef* anything, nothing; (*personas*) anybody, nobody; **no quiso venir ~** nobody wanted to come

niña ['ni·na] *f* **1.** (*chica, persona no adulta*) girl **2.** ANAT pupil; **eres como las ~s de mis ojos** *fig* you are the apple of my eye

niñera [ni·'ne·ra] *f* nanny; (*canguro*) babysitter

niñería [ni·ne·'ri·a] *f* **1.** (*de niños*) childish act **2.** *inf* (*pequeñez*) triviality

niñez [ni·'neθ] *f* childhood; *fig* infancy

niño ['ni·no] *m* boy; **~ bien** *inf* rich kid; **~ mimado** (*favorito*) spoiled child; **~ probeta** test tube baby; **¡no seas ~!** don't act like a child!

nipón, -ona [ni·'pon, -·'po·na] *adj* Japanese

níquel ['ni·kel] *m* nickel

niqui ['ni·ki] *m* (*camiseta*) T-shirt

nitidez [ni·ti·'deθ] *f* brightness; FOTO clarity

nítido, -a ['ni·ti·do, -a] *adj* bright; FOTO clear

nitrato [ni·'tra·to] *m* nitrate

nítrico, -a ['ni·tri·ko, -a] *adj* nitric; **ácido ~** nitric acid

nitrógeno [ni·'tro·xe·no] *m* nitrogen

nivel [ni·'βel] *m* **1.** (*estándar*) standard; **~ de vida** standard of living; **estar al ~ de lo exigido** to rise to the occasion **2.** (*horizontalidad, grado, cota*) level; **~ estilístico** stylistic level; **paso a ~** grade crossing; **sobre el ~ del mar** above sea level

nivelar [ni·βe·'lar] **I.** *vt* to level **II.** *vr:* **~se** to level out

nixtamal [nis·ta·'mal] *m Méx* corn (*specially processed for tortilla-making*)

NO [no·ro·'es·te] *abr de* **Noroeste** NW

no [no] *adv* **1.** (*respuesta*) no; **¡que ~!** I tell you it isn't! **2.** + *adjetivo* non-; **~ protegido** non-protected **3.** + *verbo* not; **~... nada** not... anything; **~... nadie** not... anyone; **~... nunca** not... ever, never; **~ ya** not only; **ya ~** not any more, no longer; **hoy ~ tengo clase** I don't have class today; **~ tiene más que un abrigo** she only has one coat **4.** (*retórica*) **¿~?** isn't he/she?, don't we/they? ► **el ~ va más** the best, the state-of-the-art; **tener un ~ sé qué** to have something special; **a ~ ser que** +*subj* unless; **¡a que ~!** do you want to bet?; **¿cómo ~?** of course; **o, si ~** otherwise

nº ['nu·me·ro] *abr de* **número** No.

noble ['no·βle] **I.** *adj* <nobilísimo> **1.** *t.* QUÍM (*aristócrata*) noble **2.** (*bueno*) upright **3.** (*honesto*) honest **II.** *mf* nobleman *m*, noblewoman *f*

nobleza [no·'βle·sa, -θa] *f* **1.** (*linaje, hi-*

N

dalguía) nobility **2.** (*bondad*) uprightness **3.** (*honestidad*) honesty

noche ['no·t∫e] *f* **1.** (*contrario de día*) night; **buenas ~s** (*saludo*) good evening; (*despedida*) good night; **turno de ~** night shift; **media ~** midnight; **a media ~** at midnight; **por la ~** at night; **toda la ~** all night long; **ayer** (**por la**) **~** last night; **hacerse de ~** to get dark; **hacer ~ en** to spend the night in **2.** (*tarde*) evening **3.** (*oscuridad*) darkness; **es de ~** it's dark ▸ **ser como la ~ y el día** to be like night and day; **de la ~ a la mañana** overnight; **pasar la ~ en blanco** to stay up all night

Nochebuena [no·t∫e·'βwe·na] *f* Christmas Eve; **en ~** on Christmas Eve

Nochevieja [no·t∫e·'βje·xa] *f* New's Year's Eve

noción [no·'sjon, -'θjon] *f* **1.** (*idea*) idea; **perder la ~ del tiempo** to lose track of the time **2.** *pl* (*fundamentos*) base; **tengo nociones de francés** I know a little French

nocivo, -a [no·'θi·βo, -a] *adj* harmful; **~ para la salud** damaging to health

noctámbulo, -a [nok·'tam·bu·lo, -a] *adj* **ser ~** to be a night-bird

nocturno [nok·'tur·no] *m* MÚS nocturne

nocturno, -a [nok·'tur·no, -a] *adj* **1.** (*de noche*) night; **la vida nocturna** nightlife **2.** BOT, ZOOL nocturnal

nodo ['no·do] *m* node

nodriza [no·'dri·sa, -θa] *f* **1.** (*ama*) wet-nurse **2.** (*transporte*) **avión ~** mother airplane; **buque ~** supply ship

nogal [no·'γal] *m*, **noguera** [no·'γe·ra] *f* walnut tree

nómada ['no·ma·da] **I.** *adj* nomadic; **pueblo ~** nomadic people **II.** *mf* nomad

nomás [no·'mas] *adv AmL* **1.** (*solamente*) only; **~ que** +*subj* unless; **¡pase ~!** come straight in! **2.** (*nada más*) and that was all **3.** (*apenas*) hardly

nombrado, -a [nom·'bra·do, -a] *adj* famous

nombramiento [nom·bra·'mjen·to] *m* (*designación*) appointment

nombrar [nom·'brar] *vt* **1.** (*citar*) to quote; (*mencionar*) to mention **2.** (*llamar*) to call **3.** (*designar*) to appoint

nombre ['nom·bre] *m* **1.** (*designación*) name; **~ y apellido** name and surname, full name; **~ de pila** primer **~** first name; **~ de soltera** maiden name; **de ~** by name; **~ artístico** stage name; **sin ~** nameless; **en ~ de** on behalf of; **dar su ~** to give one's name; **poner un ~ a alguien** to give sb a name; **llamar a las cosas por su ~** *fig* to call a spade a spade; **tu conducta no tiene ~** your behavior is a disgrace; **reservar a ~ de X** to book in X's name **2.** (*reputación*) reputation; **de ~** famous **3.** LING noun; **~ común** common noun; **~ propio** proper noun

nomenclatura [no·men·kla·'tu·ra] *f* nomenclature

nomeolvides [no·meol·'βi·des] *f inv* forget-me-not

nómina ['no·mi·na] *f* **1.** (*lista*) list; (*de sueldos*) payroll **2.** (*haberes*) salary

nominación [no·mi·na·'sjon, -'θjon] *f* appointment, nomination

nominal [no·mi·'nal] *adj* **1.** (*relativo al nombre*) nominal; **valor ~** nominal value **2.** LING noun

nominar [no·mi·'nar] *vt* to nominate

nominativo [no·mi·na·'ti·βo] *m* LING nominative

nominativo, -a [no·mi·na·'ti·βo, -a] *adj* nominative

non [non] **I.** *adj* odd **II.** *m* odd number; **decir** (**que**) **~es** *fig* to say no

noquear [no·ke·'ar] *vt* to knock out

nordeste [nor·'des·te] *m* (*dirección*) North East; (*viento*) northeasterly

nórdico, -a ['nor·di·ko, -a] *adj* northern, northerly

noreste [nor·'es·te] *m v.* **nordeste**

noria ['no·rja] *f* **1.** (*para agua*) water wheel **2.** *inf* (*trabajo*) treadmill *fig* **3.** (*columpio*) Ferris wheel

norma ['nor·ma] *f* rule; (*general*) norm, standard; **~s de circulación** road safety manual; **~ técnica** technical norm; **observar la ~** to follow the rules; **como ~** (**general**) as a rule

normal [nor·'mal] *adj* normal; **gasolina ~** regular gas

normalizar <z → c> [nor·ma·li·'sar, -'θar] *vt* **1.** (*volver normal*) to normalize

2. (*reglar*) to regulate

normalmente [nor·mal·'men·te] *adv* normally; (*habitualmente*) usually

normativa [nor·ma·'ti·βa] *f* rules *pl*; ~ **comunitaria** POL Community regulations *pl*; **según la ~ vigente** according to current rules

normativo, -a [nor·ma·'ti·βo, -a] *adj* normative

noroeste [no·ro·'es·te] *m* (*dirección*) North West

norte ['nor·te] *m* **1.** (*punto cardinal*) north; **el ~ de España** Northern Spain; **al ~ de** north of **2.** (*guía*) aim; **ha perdido el ~** *fig* he/she has lost his/her way; **sin ~** aimless

norteamericano, -a [nor·te·a·me·ri·'ka·no, -a] *adj, m, f* North American; (*de los EE.UU.*) American

Noruega [no·'rwe·ɣa] *f* Norway

noruego, -a [no·'rwe·ɣo] *adj, m, f* Norwegian

nos [nos] **I.** *pron pers* us; **tu primo ~ pegó** your cousin hit us; ~ **escribieron una carta** they wrote a letter to us **II.** *pron reflexivo* ourselves, each other

nosocomio [no·so·'ko·mjo] *m AmL* hospital

nosotros, -as [no·'so·tros, -as] *pron pers, 1. pl* **1.** (*sujeto*) we **2.** (*tras preposición*) us

nostalgia [nos·'tal·xja] *f* (*de lugar*) homesickness; (*del pasado*) nostalgia

nostálgico, -a [nos·'tal·xi·ko, -a] *adj* (*de un lugar*) homesick; (*del pasado*) nostalgic; **sentimiento ~** sentimental longing

nota ['no·ta] *f* **1.** (*anotación*) note; ~ **al pie de la página** footnote **2.** (*apunte*) note; **tomar** (**buena**) ~ **de algo** to take (good) note of sth **3.** (*aviso*) letter **4.** (*calificación*) mark, grade; **sacar malas ~s** to get bad marks [*o* grades] **5.** (*factura*) receipt **6.** (*cuenta*) bill **7.** (*detalle*) touch; **una ~ individual** a personal touch **8.** MÚS note ▶ **dar la ~** to stand out (in a negative way)

notable [no·'ta·βle] **I.** *adj* remarkable; (*suma*) considerable **II.** *m* ENS very good (*7 or 8 out of 10 in the Spanish grading system*)

notación [no·ta·'sjon, -'θjon] *f* **1.** (*sistema*) notation; ~ **musical** musical notation **2.** MAT, QUÍM annotation

notar [no·'tar] *vt* to notice; (*calor*) to feel; **hacer ~** to point out; **hacerse ~** to stand out

notaría [no·ta·'ria] *f* notary's office

notarial [no·ta·'rjal] *adj* JUR legal; (*hecho por el notario*) notarial

notario, -a [no·'ta·rjo, -a] *m, f* notary

noticia [no·'ti·sja, -θja] *f* (piece of) news; **las ~s** the news; **ser ~** to be in the news; **~s de última hora** latest news; **tener ~ de algo** to have heard about sth

noticiario [no·ti·'sja·rjo, -'θja·rjo] *m* RADIO, TV news program

notificación [no·ti·fi·ka·'sjon, -'θjon] *f* notification; ~ **por escrito** written notification

notificar <c → qu> [no·ti·fi·'kar] *vt* to notify

notorio, -a [no·'to·rjo, -a] *adj* **1.** (*conocido*) well-known **2.** (*evidente*) obvious

novatada [no·βa·'ta·da] *f* (*broma*) hazing; **gastar la ~ a alguien** to play a trick on sb; **pagar la ~** to learn the hard way

novato, -a [no·'βa·to, -a] *m, f* (*en un lugar*) new guy *m*, new girl *f*; (*en una actividad*) beginner

novecientos, -as [no·βe·'θjen·tos, -as] *adj* nine hundred; *v. t.* **ochocientos**

novedad [no·βe·'dad] *f* **1.** (*acontecimiento*) new development; **¿hay alguna ~?** anything new?; **las últimas ~es** the latest **2.** (*cosa*) novelty; (*libro*) new publication

novedoso, -a [no·βe·'do·so, -a] *adj AmL* novel

novela [no·'βe·la] *f* novel; ~ **corta** novella; ~ **policíaca** detective story; ~ **rosa** romance

novelista [no·βe·'lis·ta] *mf* novelist

noveno, -a [no·'βe·no, -a] *adj, m, f* ninth; *v. t.* **octavo**

noventa [no·'βen·ta] *adj inv m* ninety; *v. t.* **ochenta**

noviazgo [no·'βjaθ·ɣo] *m* **1.** (*para casarse*) engagement **2.** *inf* (*relación*) relationship

novicio, -a [no·'βi·sjo, a; -θjo, -a] *m, f* **1.** REL novice **2.** (*principiante*) beginner

noviembre [no·'βjem·bre] *m* November; *v. t.* marzo

novillada [no·βi·'ja·da, -'ʎa·da] *f* TAUR bullfight with young bulls and less experienced bullfighters

novillo, -a [no·'βi·jo, -a; -ʎo, -a] *m, f* young bull ▸ **hacer** ~s to play truant

novio, -a ['no·βjo, -a] *m, f* **1.** (*para casarse*) bridegroom *m*, bride *f*; **los** ~ (*en la boda*) the bride and groom; (*después de la boda*) the newly-weds; **viaje de** ~s honeymoon **2.** (*en relación amorosa*) boyfriend *m*, girlfriend *f*; **echarse novia** to get a girlfriend ▸ **compuesta y sin** ~ all dressed up and nowhere to go

nube ['nu·βe] *f* cloud ▸ **bajar de las** ~s to come back down to earth; **estar por las** ~s (*precios*) to be sky-high; **poner a alguien por las** ~s to praise sb to the skies

nublado [nu·'βla·do] *adj* cloudy

nublar [nu·'βlar] **I.** *vt* **1.** (*nubes*) to cloud **2.** (*mente*) to get confused; (*ojos*) to mist over **II.** *vr:* ~**se 1.** (*nubes*) to cloud over **2.** (*mente*) to get confused; (*ojos*) to mist over; **se me nubló la vista** my eyes clouded over

nubosidad [nu·βo·si·'dad] *f* cloudiness

nuboso, -a [nu·'βo·so, -a] *adj* cloudy

nuca ['nu·ka] *f* ANAT nape, back of the neck

nuclear [nu·kle·'ar] *adj* nuclear; **energía** ~ nuclear energy [o power]

núcleo ['nu·kleo] *m* **1.** QUÍM nucleus **2.** (*centro*) hub; ~ **urbano** town

nudillo [nu·'di·jo, -ʎo] *m* ANAT knuckle

nudo ['nu·do] *m* **1.** *t.* NÁUT (*atadura*) knot; ~ **corredizo** slipknot; **deshacer el** ~ to untie the knot **2.** (*madera*) knot; **sin** ~s smooth **3.** (*punto de reunión*) center; ~ **de comunicaciones** communications center; ~ **ferroviario** junction **4.** (*dificultad*) **el** ~ **del problema es...** the crux of the problem is...

nuera ['nwe·ra] *f* daughter-in-law

nuestro, -a ['nwes·tro, -a] **I.** *adj pos antepuesto* our; ~ **hijo/nuestra hija** our son/daughter; ~**s nietos** our grandchildren; **por nuestra parte** on our side **II.** *pron pos* **1.** (*propiedad*) **la casa es nuestra** the house is ours; **¡ya es** ~!

fig we got it/him! **2.** *tras artículo* **el** ~**/la nuestra/lo** ~ ours; **los** ~**s** our people; (*parientes*) our family **3.** *tras substantivo* of ours, our; **una amiga nuestra** a friend of ours; **es culpa nuestra** it is our fault

nuevamente [nwe·βa·'men·te] *adv* **1.** (*otra vez*) again **2.** (*últimamente*) recently

Nueva York [nwe·βa·'jork] *f* New York

Nueva Zelanda [nwe·βa·se·'lan·da] *f* New Zealand

nueve ['nwe·βe] *adj inv m* nine; *v. t.* ocho

nuevo, -a ['nwe·βo, -a] *adj* new; **de** ~ again; **sentirse como** ~ to feel like a new man; **¿qué hay de** ~**?** what's new?; **hasta** ~ **aviso** until further notice

nuez [nweθ] *f* **1.** BOT walnut; ~ **de coco** coconut; ~ **moscada** nutmeg; **cascar nueces** to crack nuts **2.** ANAT Adam's apple

nulidad [nu·li·'dad] *f* **1.** (*no válido*) nullity; **declarar la** ~ **de algo** to declare sth invalid **2.** *inf* (*persona*) nonentity; **ser una** ~ to be useless

nulo, -a ['nu·lo, -a] *adj* **1.** (*inválido*) null; **voto** ~ invalid vote **2.** (*incapaz*) useless; **soy** ~ **para el deporte** I'm no good at sports

numeración [nu·me·ra·'sjon, -'θjon] *f* (*sistema*) numbering system

numeral [nu·me·'ral] **I.** *adj* numeral **II.** *m* LING number

numerar [nu·me·'rar] *vt* to number; **sin** ~ unnumbered

numérico, -a [nu·'me·ri·ko, -a] *adj* numerical

número ['nu·me·ro] *m* **1.** MAT number; ~ **cardinal** cardinal number; ~ **primo** prime number; **en** ~**s redondos** in round numbers; **hacer** ~s to do one's sums **2.** (*cantidad*) number; ~ **de habitantes** number of inhabitants; **sin** ~ innumerable **3.** *t.* LING (*cifra, edición*) number; ~ **de matrícula** enrollment number; ~ **de identificación personal** PIN (personal identification number); ~ **de zapatos** shoe size; ~ **suelto** odd number **4.** (*ejemplar*) copy; ~ **atrasado** back issue **5.** (*actuación*) ~ **de baile** dance number; **montar un** ~ to make a scene

numeroso, -a [nu·me·'ro·so, -a] *adj* numerous; **familia numerosa** large family

nunca ['nun·ka] *adv* never; ~ **jamás** never ever; **más que** ~ more than ever

nupcial [nup·'sjal, -'β·βjal] *adj* nuptial

nurse ['nur·se] *f AmL* **1.** (*niñera*) nanny; (*extranjera*) au-pair **2.** (*enfermera*) nurse

nutria ['nu·trja] *f* otter

nutrición [nu·tri·'sjon, -'θjon] *f* nutrition

nutrido, -a [nu·'tri·do, -a] *adj* **1.** (*alimentado*) fed; **bien** ~ well-fed; **mal** ~ undernourished **2.** (*numeroso*) ample; (*biblioteca*) well-stocked

nutrir [nu·'trir] **I.** *vt* **1.** (*alimentar*) to feed; (*piel*) to nourish **2.** (*fortalecer*) to strengthen **II.** *vr* **~se de** [*o* **con**] **algo** to feed off sth

nutritivo, -a [nu·tri·'ti·βo, -a] *adj* nutritious; **valor** ~ nutritional value

Ñ

Ñ, ñ ['e·ɲe] *f* Ñ, ñ

ña [ɲa] *f AmC, AmS inf* (*señora*) lady, Missis

ñangotarse [ɲan·go·'tar·se] *vr* **1.** *PRico, RDom* (*ponerse en cuclillas*) to squat **2.** *PRico* (*someterse*) to yield **3.** *PRico* (*perder el ánimo*) to lose heart

ñapango, -a [ɲa·'pan·go, -a] *adj Col* mestizo, half-breed

ñata ['ɲa·ta] *f AmL inf* beak

ñeque ['ɲe·ke] **I.** *adj AmC* strong **II.** *m* **1.** *Chile, Ecua, Perú* (*fuerza*) strength; (*energía*) vim **2.** *Perú* (*valor, coraje*) courage

ño [ɲo] *m AmC, AmS inf* (*señor*) abbreviated form of 'señor' used only before the first name

ñoño, -a ['ɲo·ɲo, -a] **I.** *adj inf* **1.** (*soso*) insipid; (*aburrido*) boring **2.** (*tonto*) inane **3.** (*remilgado*) prudish **II.** *m, f inf* **1.** (*tonto*) idiot **2.** (*aburrido*) bore

ñu [ɲu] *m* gnu

O

O, o [o] *f* O, o; ~ **de Oviedo** O as in Oscar ▶ **no saber hacer la 'o' con un canuto** not to know a thing

o, ó [o] *conj* or; **~..., ~...** either..., or...; ~ **sea** in other words; ~ **bien** or else

O [o·'es·te] *abr de* **oeste** W

oasis [o·'a·sis] *m inv* oasis

obcecar [c → qu] [oβ·θe·'kar] **I.** *vt* to blind **II.** *vr:* ~**se** to be blinded, to stubbornly insist

obedecer [o·βe·de·'ser, -θer] *irr como crecer* **I.** *vt* (*orden, a alguien*) to obey; (*instrucciones*) to follow; **hacerse** ~ to make people obey **II.** *vi* (*provenir*) to be due; (*responder*) to respond

obediencia [o·βe·'djen·sja, -θja] *f* obedience

obediente [o·βe·'djen·te] *adj* obedient

obesidad [o·βe·si·'dad] *f* obesity

obeso, -a [o·'βe·so, -a] *adj* obese

obispo [o·'βis·po] *m* REL bishop

objeción [oβ·xe·'sjon, -'θjon] *f* objection; ~ **de conciencia** conscientious objection; **poner** ~ **a algo** to object to sth

objetar [oβ·xe·'tar] *vt* to object; **tengo algo que** ~ I have an objection

objetividad [oβ·xe·ti·βi·'dad] *f* objectivity

objetivo [oβ·xe·'ti·βo] *m* **1.** (*finalidad*) goal; **tener como** ~ to have as one's goal **2.** FOTO lens **3.** (*blanco*) target

objetivo, -a [oβ·xe·'ti·βo, -a] *adj* objective

objeto [oβ·'xe·to] *m* **1.** (*cosa*) object; ~ **de lujo** luxury item; ~ **de valor** valuables *pl*; **la mujer** ~ woman as an object; **~s perdidos** lost property **2.** (*motivo*) purpose; **con** (**el**) [*o* **al**] ~ **de...** in order to...; **tener por** ~ to have as one's aim **3.** LING object

objetor(a) [oβ·xe·'tor, -·'to·ra] *m(f)* dissenter; ~ **de conciencia** conscientious objector

oblicuo, -a [o·'βli·kwo, -a] *adj* oblique, slanted

obligación [o·βli·ɣa·'sjon, -'θjon] *f* **1.** (*deber*) obligation; **contraer una** ~ to undertake an obligation; **cumplir con**

una ~ to fulfill an obligation; **dedicarse a sus obligaciones** to devote oneself to one's duties; **faltar a sus obligaciones** to neglect one's duties; **tener la ~ de hacer algo** to be obliged to do sth **2.** (*deuda*) liability; (*documento*) bond

obligado, -a [o·βli·'γa·do, -a] *adj* **1.** *estar* obliged **2.** *ser* (*imprescindible*) obligatory

obligar <g → gu> [o·βli·'γar] **I.** *vt* **1.** (*forzar*) to force; (*comprometer*) to oblige **2.** *Chile, Arg* (*invitar*) to invite to drink **II.** *vr:* **~se** to commit oneself

obligatorio, -a [o·βli·γa·'to·rjo, -a] *adj* obligatory; **asignatura obligatoria** compulsory subject; **es ~ llevar puesto el casco** helmets must be worn

oboe [o·'βoe] *m* MÚS oboe; (*músico*) oboist

obra ['o·βra] *f* **1.** (*creación, labor*) work; **~ de arte** work of art; **~ benéfica** charitable act; **~s completas** collected [*o* complete] works; **~ de consulta** reference work; **~ maestra** masterpiece; **~ de teatro** play; **por ~ (y gracia) de** thanks to; **¡manos a la ~!** let's get to work! **2.** (*construcción*) building work; (*lugar en construcción*) construction site; (*edificio*) building; **~s públicas** public works; **mano de ~** labor; **estar en ~s** to be under construction

obradera [o·βra·'de·ra] *f Col, Guat, Pan* (*diarrea*) diarrhea

obrar [o·'βrar] **I.** *vi* (*actuar*) to act; **~ a tontas y a locas** *inf* to act rashly **II.** *vi, vt* **1.** (*hacer efecto*) to have an effect on; **~ buen efecto** to be effective; **~ sobre alguien/algo** to act on sb/sth **2.** (*construir*) to build **3.** (*hacer*) to do; (*trabajar*) to work; **sin ~** unworked

obrero, -a [o·'βre·ro, -a] **I.** *adj* (*relativo al trabajo*) working; (*relativo al obrero*) working-class **II.** *m, f* worker; **~ asalariado** day laborer; **~ especializado** [*o* cualificado] skilled worker; **~ fijo** permanent employee

obscenidad [oβs·θe·ni·'dad] *f* obscenity

obsceno, -a [oβs·'θe·no, -a] *adj* obscene

obsequiar [oβ·se·'kjar] *vt* **1.** (*con atenciones*) to honor; (*con regalos*) to be-

stow **2.** (*agasajar*) to lavish attention on; (*festejar*) to celebrate; **~ con su presencia** to honor with one's presence **3.** *AmL* (*regalar*) to give

obsequio [oβ·se·'kjo] *m* **1.** (*regalo*) gift **2.** (*agasajo*) attention; **en ~ de alguien** in honor of sb

observación [oβ·ser·βa·'sjon, -'θjon] *f* **1.** (*contemplación, vigilancia*) observation **2.** (*comentario*) remark

observador(a) [oβ·ser·βa·'dor, --'do·ra] **I.** *adj* observant **II.** *m(f)* observer

observar [oβ·ser·'βar] *vt* **1.** (*contemplar, cumplir*) to observe **2.** (*orden*) to follow; (*normas, plazos*) to adhere to **3.** (*notar*) to notice; **hacer ~ algo a alguien** to bring sth to sb's attention

observatorio [oβ·ser·βa·'to·rjo] *m* observatory; **~ astronómico** observatory; **~ meteorológico** weather station

obsesión [oβ·se·'sjon] *f* obsession

obsesionar [oβ·se·sjo·'nar] **I.** *vt* to obsess; **el fútbol lo obsesiona** he is obsessed with [*o* by] soccer **II.** *vr:* **~se** to be obsessed; **~se con algo/alguien** to be obsessed by [*o* with] sth/sb

obsesivo, -a [oβ·se·'si·βo, -a] *adj* obsessive

obsoleto, -a [oβ·so·'le·to, -a] *adj* obsolete

obstaculizar <z → c> [oβs·ta·ku·li·'sar, -'θar] *vt* to hinder; **~ la carretera** to obstruct [*o* block] the road; **el progreso** to hinder progress

obstáculo [oβs·'ta·ku·lo] *m* obstacle; DEP hurdle; **salvar un ~** to overcome an obstacle; **poner ~s a alguien** to hinder sb

obstante [oβs·'tan·te] *adv* **no ~** nevertheless

obstinado, -a [oβs·ti·'na·do, -a] *adj* obstinate

obstinarse [oβs·ti·'nar·se] *vr* to persist; **~ en su silencio** to remain silent

obstrucción [oβs·truk·'sjon, -'θjon] *f* obstruction; MED blockage

obstruir [oβs·tru·'ir] *irr como huir* **I.** *vt* **1.** (*el paso, acción*) to obstruct **2.** (*una tubería*) to block **II.** *vr:* **~se** to get blocked

obtención [oβ·ten·'sjon, -'θjon] *f* obtaining; QUÍM extraction; **~ de datos** data collection

obtener [oβ·te·'ner] *irr como* tener *vt* to obtain; QUÍM to extract; (*resultado, ventaja*) to gain; **difícil de ~** not easily obtainable

obturar [oβ·tu·'rar] *vt* to close; (*bloquear*) to block; (*los dientes*) to fill

obviar [oβ·'βjar] **I.** *vi* to stand in the way **II.** *vt* (*evitar*) to avoid; (*eliminar*) to remove; **~ un problema** to get around a problem

obvio, -a ['oβ·βjo, -a] *adj* obvious; **es ~** it's obvious

oca ['o·ka] *f* **1.** ZOOL goose **2.** (*juego*) ≈ snakes *pl* and ladders

ocasión [o·ka·'sjon] *f* occasion; **coche de ~** second hand car; **libros de ~** bargain [*o* cut-price] books; **aprovechar la ~** to make the most of the opportunity; **desperdiciar la ~** to waste the opportunity; **en esta ~** on this occasion; **en ocasiones** sometimes; **con ~ de** on the occasion of

ocasional [o·ka·sjo·'nal] *adj* (*no habitual*) occasional; **trabajo ~** temporary work

ocasionar [o·ka·sjo·'nar] *vt* **~ algo** to cause sth, to bring sth about

occidental [ok·θi·den·'tal] *adj* western

occidente [ok·θi·'den·te] *m* GEO west; **el ~** the West

Oceanía [o·θea·'ni·a] *f* Oceania

océano [o·'θea·no] *m* **1.** (*mar*) ocean **2.** *fig* (*cantidad*) sea; **un ~ de gente** a sea of people

ochenta [o·'tʃen·ta] **I.** *adj inv* **1.** eighty; **los años ~** the eighties; **un hombre de alrededor de ~ años** a man of about eighty years of age; **una mujer en sus ~ años** a woman in her eighties **2.** (*octogésimo*) eightieth **II.** *m* eighty

ocho ['o·tʃo] **I.** *adj inv* eight; **jornada de ~ horas** eight-hour day; **~ veces mayor/menor que...** eight times bigger/smaller than...; **a las ~** at eight (o'clock); **son las ~ y media de la mañana/tarde** it is half past eight in the morning/evening; **las ~ y cuarto/menos cuarto** a quarter past/to eight; **a las ~ en punto** at eight o'clock precisely [*o* on the dot]; **el ~ de agosto** the eighth of

August ▶ **ser más chulo que un ~** *inf* to be a real showoff; **dar igual ~ que ochenta** not to care less **II.** *m* eight

ochocientos, -as [o·tʃo·'θjen·tos, -as] *adj* eight hundred; **esta basílica fue construida hace ~ años** this basilica was built eight hundred years ago; **vinieron más de ochocientas personas** more than eight hundred people came

ocio ['o·sjo, -θjo] *m* leisure; **horas de ~** spare time

ocioso, -a [o·'sjo·so, -a; -'θjo·so, -a] *adj* **1.** *estar* (*inactivo*) idle **2.** *ser* (*inútil*) useless

ocote [o·'ko·te] *m Méx* BOT ocote pine

octágono [ok·'ta·γo·no] *m* octagon

octava [ok·'ta·βa] *f* LIT, MÚS octave

octavilla [ok·ta·'βi·ʝa, -ʎa] *f* (*volante*) leaflet

octavo, -a [ok·'ta·βo] **I.** *adj* eighth; **en ~ lugar** in eighth place; (*enumeración*) eighth; **la octava parte** an eighth **II.** *m, f* eighth

octogésimo, -a [ok·to·'xe·si·mo, -a] *adj* eightieth; *v. t.* **octavo**

octubre [ok·'tu·βre] *m* October; *v. t.* **marzo**

ocular [o·ku·'lar] *adj* ocular; **examen ~** eye test; **testigo ~** eyewitness

oculista [o·ku·'lis·ta] *mf* MED ophthalmologist

ocultar [o·kul·'tar] **I.** *vt* (*cosa*) to hide; (*información, delito*) to conceal; **~ la cara entre** [*o* con] **las manos** to cover one's face with one's hands **II.** *vr*: **~se** to hide

oculto, -a [o·'kul·to, -a] *adj* (*escondido*) hidden; (*secreto*) secret; **traerse algo ~** to keep sth hidden

ocupación [o·ku·pa·'sjon, -'θjon] *f* **1.** (*trabajo*) occupation; **sin ~** unemployed **2.** (*apoderamiento*) *t.* MIL occupation; **zona de ~** occupation zone

ocupado, -a [o·ku·'pa·do, -a] *adj* **1.** (*sitio*) occupied **2.** (*persona*) busy **3.** (*línea de teléfono*) busy

ocupante [o·ku·'pan·te] **I.** *adj* MIL occupying **II.** *mf* **1.** (*de vehículo*) occupant; (*de tren, avión*) passenger **2.** (*de un edificio*) resident

ocupar [o·ku·'par] **I.** *vt* **1.** (*lugar, telé-*

fono) *t.* MIL to occupy **2.** (*un cargo*) to hold; (*vacante*) to fill **3.** (*tiempo, espacio, asiento*) to take up **4.** (*a una persona*) to keep busy **II.** *vr* ~se de [*o* con] algo to busy oneself with sth; ~se de alguien (*cuidar*) to look after sb; ella se ocupó de todo she took care of everything

ocurrencia [o·ku·'rren·sja, -θja] *f* (*idea*) idea; se bañó en el mar en pleno invierno, ¡qué ~! he/she swam in the sea in the middle of winter, what a thing to do!; tener la ~ de... to have the bright idea of...

ocurrir [o·ku·'rrir] **I.** *vi* to happen; ¿qué ocurre? what's wrong?; ¿qué te ocurre? what's the matter?; lo que ocurre es que... the thing is that... **II.** *vr:* ~se to occur; no se me ocurre nada I can't think of anything; ¿cómo se te ocurrió esa tontería? what on earth made you think of a stupid thing like that?; nunca se me hubiese ocurrido pensar que... I never would have imagined that...

odiar [o·'djar] *vt* to hate; ~ a alguien a muerte to have an undying hatred for sb, to hate sb's guts *inf*

odio ['o·djo] *m* hate, hatred

odioso, -a [o·'djo·so, -a] *adj* **1.** (*hostil*) nasty **2.** (*repugnante*) horrible **3.** *AmL* (*fastidioso*) annoying

odisea [o·di·'sea] *f* odyssey

odontólogo, -a [o·don·'to·lo·γo, -a] *m, f* MED dentist

oeste [o·'es·te] *m* **1.** (*punto*) west; el lejano ~ the wild [*o* far] west; película del ~ western; hacia el ~ westward(s); al ~ de... west of... **2.** (*viento*) westerly

ofender [o·fen·'der] **I.** *vt* (*humillar*) to offend; hacerse el ofendido to take offense **II.** *vr:* ~se to take offense; ¡no te ofendas conmigo! don't get angry with me!

ofensa [o·'fen·sa] *f* offense

ofensiva [o·fen·'si·βa] *f* offensive; tomar la ~ to go on the offensive

ofensivo, -a [o·fen·'si·βo, -a] *adj* **1.** (*hiriente*) offensive **2.** (*dañino*) damaging; ~ para el medio ambiente environ-

mentally damaging **3.** (*que ataca*) attacking

oferta [o·'fer·ta] *f* **1.** (*propuesta*) offer; ~ de empleo job offer; estar de ~ to be on special offer **2.** COM tender, bid **3.** ECON supply; ~ y demanda supply and demand

ofertar [o·fer·'tar] *vt* to offer

oficial [o·fi·'θjal] *adj* official; boletín ~ official gazette

oficial(a) [o·fi·'θjal, -·'θja·la] *m(f)* **1.** (*oficio manual*) (skilled) worker; (*administrativo*) clerk; ~ de obra building worker **2.** MIL officer **3.** (*funcionario*) civil servant

oficina [o·fi·'θi·na] *f* office; ~ de asistencia social social security office; ~ de correos post office; ~ de empleo employment agency

oficinista [o·fi·si·'nis·ta, o·fiθ-] *mf* office worker

oficio [o·'fi·sjo, -θjo] *m* **1.** (*trabajo manual*) trade; ~ especializado skilled trade; ejercer un ~ to have a trade; sin ~ ni beneficio out of work **2.** (*profesión*) profession; gajes del ~ occupational hazards **3.** (*función*) function; defensor de ~ JUR public defender; de ~ ex officio **4.** (*escrito*) official document **5.** REL service; Santo Oficio Holy Office

oficioso, -a [o·fi·'sjo, -a; -θjo·so, -a] *adj* **1.** (*extraoficial*) unofficial **2.** (*servicial*) obliging

ofrecer [o·fre·'ser, -θer] *irr como crecer* **I.** *vt* to offer; ~ un banquete to give a meal; ~ grandes dificultades to present a lot of difficulties; ~ un sacrificio to offer up a sacrifice **II.** *vr:* ~se (*brindarse*) to offer oneself; ¿qué se le ofrece? may I help you?

ofrecimiento [o·fre·θi·'mjen·to] *m* offer; REL offering

ofrenda [o·'fren·da] *f* offering; (*sacrificio*) sacrifice

oftalmólogo, -a [of·tal·'mo·lo·γo, -a] *m, f* MED ophthalmologist

ofuscar <c > qu> [o·fus·'kar] **I.** *vt* **1.** (*cegar*) to blind **2.** (*la mente*) to confuse; ~ (la mente) a alguien to confuse sb **II.** *vr* ~se en algo to insist on sth

ogro [o·ɣro] *m t. fig* ogre

oída [o·ˈi·ða] *f* **conocer a alguien de ~s** to have heard about sb; **saber algo de ~s** to have heard about sth

oído [o·ˈi·ðo] *m* **1.** (*sentido*) hearing; **aprender de ~** to learn by ear; **aplicar el ~** to listen carefully; **aguzar el ~** to prick up one's ears; **tener buen ~** to have a good ear; **duro de ~** hard of hearing **2.** ANAT ear; **~ interno/medio/externo** inner/middle/outer ear; **cerrar los ~s a algo** to turn a deaf ear to sth; **dar ~s a alguien** (*escuchar*) to listen to sb; (*creer*) to believe sb; **llegar a ~s de alguien** to come to sb's notice [*o* attention]; **ser todo ~s** to be all ears ▸ **¡~ al parche!** look out!

oír [o·ˈir] *irr vt* (*sentir*) to hear; (*escuchar*) to listen; **¡oye!** hey!; **¿oyes?** do you understand?; **¡oiga!** excuse me!; **¡Dios te oiga!** may your prayers be answered!; **como lo oyes** believe it or not; **~ decir que...** to hear that...; **ya me oirá** he/she hasn't heard the last of me; **no se oye el vuelo de una mosca** you could hear a pin drop ▸ **como quien oye llover** not to be listening

ojal [o·ˈxal] *m* **1.** (*para botones*) buttonhole **2.** (*ojete*) eyelet

ojalá [o·xa·ˈla] *interj* I hope so, I wish; **¡~ tuvieras razón!** if only you were right!

ojeada [o·xe·ˈa·ða] *f* glance; **echar una ~ a algo** to glance at sth

ojear [o·xe·ˈar] *vt* **1.** (*mirar con atención*) to stare at **2.** (*pasar la vista*) to glance at

ojeras [o·ˈxe·ras] *fpl* bags *pl* (under the eyes); **tener ~** to have dark circles under one's eyes

ojo [o·xo] **I.** *m* **1.** ANAT eye; **~ morado** black eye; **~s rasgados** almond [*o* slanting] eyes; **~s saltones** bulging eyes; **a ~** by eye; **mirar con buenos/malos ~s** to approve/disapprove of; **pasar los ~s por algo** to run one's eyes over sth; **¡qué ~ tienes!** you don't miss a thing!; **tener ~ clínico** to be a good diagnostician; *fig* to be very observant **2.** (*agujero*) hole; **~ de aguja** eye of a needle; **~ de cerradura** keyhole; **~ del huracán** eye of the storm ▸ **donde pone el ~,**

pone la bala he/she is a good shot; **no parecerse ni en el blanco de los ~s** to be like night and day; **poner los ~s en blanco** to roll one's eyes; **costar un ~ de la cara** to cost an arm and a leg; **~s que no ven, corazón que no siente** *prov* out of sight, out of mind *prov*; **a ~ de buen cubero** roughly; **mirar con unos ~s redondos como platos** to look wide-eyed; **a ~s cerrados** without thinking; **con los ~s cerrados** with complete confidence; **andar con cien ~s** to be on one's guard; **cuatro ~s** *pey* four-eyes; **cuatro ~s ven más que dos** *prov* two heads are better than one *prov*; **ser el ~ derecho de alguien** to be the apple of sb's eye; **¡dichosos los ~s que te ven!** *irón* it's great to see you after so long!; **a ~s vistas** visibly; **en un abrir y cerrar de ~s** in a flash; **andar con ~** to be careful; **cerrar los ~s a algo** to shut one's eyes to sth; **clavar los ~s en algo** to lay eyes on sth; **comerse con los ~s** to devour with one's eyes; **echar el ~ a algo/alguien** to have one's eye on sth/sb; **echar un ~ a algo/alguien** to take a look at sth/sb; (*vigilar*) to keep an eye on sth/sb; **meter algo a alguien por los ~s** to shove sth down sb's throat; **no pegar ~** to not sleep a wink; **sacarle los ~s a alguien** to kill sb; **tener ~** (*cuidado*) to be careful; **~ por ~ (y diente por diente)** *prov* an eye for an eye (a tooth for a tooth) **II.** *interj* (be) careful, look out; **¡~ con ese tipo!** watch out for that guy!

ojota [o·ˈxo·ta] *f AmL* (*sandalia*) sandal

okupa [o·ˈku·pa] *mf inf* squatter

ola [ˈo·la] *f* wave; **~ de calor** heat wave; **~ de frío** cold spell

olé [o·ˈle] *interj* ≈ bravo

oleada [o·le·ˈa·ða] *f t. fig* wave; **~ de gente** throng of people

oleaje [o·le·ˈa·xe] *m* swell, surf

óleo [ˈo·leo] *m* ARTE oil paint; **cuadro al ~** oil painting; **pintar al ~** to paint in oil

oler [o·ˈler] *irr* **I.** *vi* to smell; **~ a algo** to smell of sth; **~ bien** to smell good **II.** *vt* to smell; **~ una flor** to smell a flower; **~ el peligro** to smell danger

olfatear [ol·fa·te·ˈar] **I.** *vt* to sniff; (*hus-*

mear) to smell out **II.** *vi* to sniff; (*curiosear*) to pry

olfato [ol·'fa·to] *m* sense of smell; **tener (buen) ~** *fig* to have a good nose [o instinct]

olimpiada [o·lim·'pja·da] *f* Olympics + *pl vb*

olímpico, -a [o·'lim·pi·ko, -a] *adj* Olympic

oliva [o·'li·βa] **I.** *adj* (*verde*) **~ olive** (green) **II.** *f* BOT (*fruta*) olive

olivo [o·'li·βo] *m* olive tree; **el Monte de los Olivos** REL the Mount of Olives

olla ['o·ja, -ʎa] *f* **1.** (*para cocinar*) pot; **~ exprés** pressure cooker **2.** CULIN stew

olmo ['ol·mo] *m* elm

olor [o·'lor] *m* smell; **buen ~** good smell; (*fragancia*) scent; **~ corporal** body odor; **tener ~ a** to smell of

oloroso, -a [o·lo·'ro·so] *adj* fragrant

olote [o·'lo·te] *m Méx* corncob

olvidadizo, -a [ol·βi·da·'di·so, -a; -'di·θo, -a] *adj* forgetful

olvidar [ol·βi·'dar] *vt, vr*: **~se** to forget; **no ~ que...** (*considerar*) to remember that...; **se me ha olvidado tu nombre** I've forgotten your name

olvido [ol·'βi·do] *m* **1.** (*falta de memoria*) forgetfulness **2.** (*omisión*) oversight, forgetting; **caer en (el) ~** to sink into oblivion; **enterrar en el ~** to forget forever

ombligo [om·'bli·ɣo] *m* navel, belly button *inf*; **el ~ del mundo** the center of the world; **contemplarse el ~** to self-gratify

omisión [o·mi·'sjon] *f* **1.** (*supresión*) omission **2.** (*negligencia*) negligence

omiso, -a [o·'mi·so, -a] *adj* (*negligente*) negligent; **hacer caso ~ de algo** to take no notice of sth

omitir [o·mi·'tir] *vt* **1.** (*no hacer*) to fail to do **2.** (*pasar por alto*) to omit

ómnibus ['om·ni·βus] *m* AUTO bus

omnipotente [om·ni·po·'ten·te] *adj* almighty, omnipotent

omnipresente [om·ni·pre·'sen·te] *adj* ubiquitous

omoplato [o·mo·'pla·to] *m*, **omóplato** [o·'mo·pla·to] *m* ANAT scapula, shoulder blade

once ['on·θe] **I.** *adj inv* eleven ▶ **estar a las ~** (*ropa*) to be askew **II.** *m* eleven; *v. t.* **ocho**

ONCE ['on·θe] *f abr de* **Organización Nacional de Ciegos Españoles** *Spanish national organization for the blind*

onceno, -a [on·'θe·no, -a] *adj* eleventh; *v. t.* **octavo**

onda ['on·da] *f.t.* FÍS, RADIO wave; **~ explosiva** [o **expansiva**] shockwave; **~s del pelo** waves *pl* of hair ▶ **¡qué buena ~!** *inf* that's really cool!; **estar en la misma ~** to be on the same wavelength; **estar en la ~ de algo** *inf* (*seguir*) to keep up with sth

ondear [on·de·'ar] *vi* (*formar*) to undulate; (*moverse*) to ripple; (*bandera*) to flutter

ondulado, -a [on·du·'la·do, -a] *adj* wavy; **cartón ~** corrugated cardboard

ONG [o·e·ne·'xe] *f abr de* **Organización No Gubernamental** NGO

ONU ['o·nu] *f abr de* **Organización de las Naciones Unidas** UNO

onza [on·sa, -θa] *f* ounce

opa ['o·pa] *mf CSur* **1.** (*retrasado mental*) mental retard **2.** (*simple*) fool

opacar <c → qu> [o·pa·'kar] *vt* **1.** *AmL* (*hacer opaco*) to darken **2.** *Méx* (*superar*) to outshine

opaco, -a [o·'pa·ko, -a] *adj* **1.** (*no transparente*) opaque **2.** (*sin brillo*) dull; (*oscuro*) gloomy **3.** (*persona, voz*) gloomy

opción [op·'sjon, -β·'θjon] *f* **1.** (*elección*) choice; (*posibilidad*) option; **~ del menú** COMPUT menu option **2.** (*derecho*) right **3.** ECON, JUR option; **~ de compra** option to purchase

opcional [op·sjo·'nal, oβ·θjo-] *adj* optional

OPEP [o·'pep] *f abr de* **Organización de Países Exportadores de Petróleo** OPEC

ópera ['o·pe·ra] *f* opera; **teatro de la ~** opera house; **~ prima** CINE, LIT author's first work

operación [o·pe·ra·'sjon, -'θjon] *f* **1.** MAT, MED operation; **~ quirúrgica** surgical operation **2.** (*actividad*) activity; (*negocio*) transaction; **~ de saneamiento** cleanup operation

operador(a) [o·pe·ra·'dor] *m(f)* COMPUT, TEL operator

operar [o·pe·'rar] **I.** *vi* **1.** (*actuar*) *t.* MIL to operate **2.** COM to do business **3.** (*tener efecto*) to take effect **II.** *vt* MED to operate on **III.** *vr*: **~se** to have an operation

operario, -a [o·pe·'ra·rjo, -a] *m, f* worker

operativo, -a [o·pe·ra·'ti·βo] *adj* **1.** (*efectivo*) operative **2.** COMPUT **sistema ~** operating system

opinar [o·pi·'nar] *vi, vt* to think; **~ bien/mal de algo/alguien** to have a good/bad opinion of sth/sb; **¿tú qué opinas de** [*o* **sobre**] **esto?** what do you think about this?; **¿puedo ~?** can I say what I think?

opinión [o·pi·'njon] *f* opinion; (*postura*) stance; (*punto de vista*) viewpoint; **en mi ~** in my opinion; **cambiar de ~** to change one's opinion [*o* mind]; **dar su ~ (sobre algo)** to express an opinion (about sth); **ser de otra/la misma ~** to be of a different/the same opinion; **tener buena/mala ~ de algo/alguien** to have a good/bad opinion of sth/sb

opio [o·'pjo] *m* opium

oponente [o·po·'nen·te] *mf* opponent

oponer [o·po·'ner] *irr como* **poner I.** *vt* **1.** (*enfrentar*) to oppose; (*confrontar*) to confront **2.** (*objetar*) to object; **~ resistencia** to offer resistance **II.** *vr*: **~se 1.** (*rechazar*) to object; **~se a algo** to oppose sth **2.** (*enfrentarse*) to oppose each other **3.** (*obstaculizar*) to hinder **4.** (*ser contrario*) to be opposed **5.** (*estar enfrente*) to be opposite

oporto [o·'por·to] *m* CULIN port (wine)

oportunidad [o·por·tu·ni·'dad] *f* **1.** (*posibilidad*) chance; (*ocasión*) opportunity; **una segunda ~** a second chance; **aprovechar la ~** to make the most of the opportunity; **(no) tener ~ de...** (not) to have the opportunity of... **2.** (*cualidad*) opportuneness; (*temporal*) timeliness; (*adecuación*) appropriateness

oportuno, -a [o·por·'tu·no, -a] *adj* **1.** (*adecuado, apropiado*) appropriate; **en el momento ~** at the right moment **2.** (*propicio*) opportune **3.** (*al caso*) relevant

oposición [o·po·si·'sjon, -'θjon] *f* **1.** (*resistencia*) *t.* POL opposition; **encontrar ~** to meet opposition; **presentar ~** to oppose **2.** (*objeción*) objection **3.** (*contraposición*) comparison **4.** (*pl*) UNIV (*competitive*) examination (*for a public-sector job*); **por ~** by examination

opositar [o·po·si·'tar] *vi* **~ a algo** to sit an examination for sth

opositor(a) [o·po·si·'tor, -·'to·ra] **I.** *adj* opposing; **partido ~** opposing party **II.** *m(f)* **1.** (*oponente*) *t.* POL opponent **2.** (*candidato*) candidate (*in examination for a public-sector job*)

opresión [o·pre·'sjon] *f* **1.** (*angustia*) anxiety **2.** (*represión*) oppression **3.** (*presión*) pressure

opresor(a) [o·pre·'sor, -·'so·ra] **I.** *adj* oppressive **II.** *m(f)* oppressor

oprimir [o·pri·'mir] *vt* **1.** (*presionar*) to press **2.** (*agobiar*) to weigh down **3.** (*reprimir*) to oppress

optar [op·'tar] *vi* **1.** (*escoger*) **~ por algo/alguien** to opt for sth/sb **2.** (*aspirar*) to aspire **3.** (*solicitar*) **~ a un cargo** to apply for a position

optativo, -a [op·ta·'ti·βo, -a] *adj* optional; (*asignatura*) **optativa** optional subject

óptica ['op·ti·ka] *f* **1.** FÍS optics *pl* **2.** (*establecimiento*) optician's **3.** (*punto de vista*) viewpoint; **bajo esta ~** according to this point of view

óptico, -a ['op·ti·ko, -a] **I.** *adj* **1.** ANAT optic; **nervio ~** optic nerve **2.** FÍS optical **II.** *m, f* optician

optimismo [op·ti·'mis·mo] *m* optimism

optimista [op·ti·'mis·ta] *adj* optimistic

optimizar [op·ti·mi·'sar, -'θar] *vt* to optimize

óptimo ['op·ti·mo] *m* optimum

óptimo, -a ['op·ti·mo, -a] **I.** *superl de* **bueno II.** *adj* (*very*) best; (*excelente*) excellent

opuesto, -a [o·'pwes·to] **I.** *pp de* **oponer II.** *adj* **1.** (*enfrente*) opposite; **al lado ~** on the other side; **en dirección opuesta** in the opposite direction **2.** (*diverso*) different; (*contrario, enfrentado*) opposing; **polo ~** *t. fig* opposite pole; **el sexo ~** the opposite sex **3.** (*enemigo*) enemy

O

oración [o.ra.'sjon, -'θjon] f 1. REL prayer; **decir una ~** to say a prayer 2. (*frase*) sentence; LING clause; **~ coordinada/subordinada** coordinate/subordinate clause; **~ simple/compuesta** simple/compound sentence

oráculo [o.'ra.ku.lo] m oracle

orador(a) [o.ra.'dor, -'do.ra] m(f) orator

oral [o.'ral] adj oral; **por vía ~** MED orally

órale ['o.ra.le] interj Méx (*animar*) come on; (*oiga*) hey; (*acuerdo*) OK, right

orar [o.'rar] vi elev **~ por algo** to pray for sth

órbita ['or.βi.ta] f 1. ASTR, FÍS orbit; **~ terrestre** terrestrial orbit; **poner en ~** to put into orbit; **estar en ~** fig to be up to date; **estar fuera de ~** fig to be out of touch 2. (*ámbito*) sphere 3. ANAT eye socket; **se me salían los ojos de las ~s** fig I couldn't believe my eyes

orca ['or.ka] f killer whale

orden¹ <órdenes> ['or.den] m 1. (*organización*) t. REL order; **en ~** in order; **llamar al ~** to call to order; **poner en ~** to put in order; **ser persona de ~** to be orderly; fig to be upright 2. (*sucesión*) order; **en** [o **por**] **su** (**debido**) **~** in the right order; **por ~** by order; **por ~ de antigüedad** in order of seniority 3. (*categoría*) rank; **de primer/segundo ~** first-rate/second-rate; **del ~ de** in the order of

orden² <órdenes> ['or.den] f 1. (*mandato*) order; **~ de registro** search warrant; **órdenes son órdenes** orders are orders; **¡a la ~!** yes, sir!; **dar/cumplir una ~** to give/obey an order; **estar a las órdenes de alguien** to be at sb's command; **hasta nueva ~** until further notice; **estar a la ~ del día** fig to be the order of the day 2. COM, REL order; **~ de entrega** delivery order; **~ de pago** payment order; **por ~** by order; **por ~ de** to the order of; **entrar en una ~** (*religiosa*) to join a religious order

ordenado, -a [or.de.'na.do, -a] adj 1. estar (*en orden*) tidy, neat 2. ser (*persona*) organized

ordenador [or.de.na.'dor] m computer; **~ de a bordo** car computer; **~ personal** personal computer; **~ portátil**

laptop computer; **asistido por ~** computer-aided

ordenar [or.de.'nar] vt 1. (*arreglar*) to organize; (*habitación, armario*) to tidy; (*colocar*) to arrange; (*clasificar*) to order 2. (*mandar*) to order 3. REL to ordain

ordeñar [or.de.'nar] vt to milk

ordinal [or.di.'nal] adj, m ordinal

ordinario, -a [or.di.'na.rjo, -a] adj 1. (*habitual*) usual; **de ~** usually 2. (*grosero*) rude 3. t. JUR (*regular*) ordinary

orégano [o.'re.ɣa.no] m oregano

oreja [o.'re.xa] f 1. ANAT ear; **aguzar las ~s** to prick up one's ears; **calentar las ~s a alguien** to box sb's ears; fig to give sb an earful 2. (*lateral*) ear ▶ **ver las ~s al lobo** to have a close shave; **con las ~s gachas** with one's tail between one's legs; **agachar las ~s** to lose heart

orfanato [or.fa.'na.to] m orphanage

orfebre [or.'fe.βre] mf (*orífice*) goldsmith; (*platero*) silversmith

orgánico, -a [or.'ɣa.ni.ko, -a] adj organic; **Ley Orgánica del Estado** basic law

organillo [or.ɣa.'ni.jo, -ʎo] m barrel organ

organismo [or.ɣa.'nis.mo] m 1. ANAT, BIO organism 2. (*institución*) body; **~ oficial** official body

organización [or.ɣa.ni.sa.'sjon, -θa.'θjon] f organization; **Organización del Tratado del Atlántico Norte** North Atlantic Treaty Organization; **Organización No Gubernamental** Non-Governmental Organization

organizado, -a [or.ɣa.ni.'sa.do, -a; -'θa.do, -a] adj organized

organizador(a) [or.ɣa.ni.sa.'dor, -θa.'dor] I. adj organizing; **comité ~** organizing committee II. m(f) (*de un evento*) organizer

organizar <z → c> [or.ɣa.ni.'sar, -'θar] I. vt to organize; (*una fiesta*) to hold II. vr: **~se** 1. (*asociarse*) to organize oneself 2. (*surgir*) to break out; **¡menuda se organizó!** all hell broke loose! 3. (*ordenar*) to arrange; **~se el tiempo** to organize one's time

organizativo, -a [or.ɣa.ni.sa.'ti.βo, -a; or.ɣa.ni.θa-] adj organizing

órgano ['or.ɣa.no] m 1. (*organismo*) t.

ANAT organ; **~ judicial** judicial body; **~s sexuales** sexual organs **2.** MÚS organ; **~ electrónico** electric organ

orgasmo [or-'yas-mo] *m* orgasm

orgía [or-'xi-a] *f* orgy; (*desenfreno*) wildness, disinhibition

orgullo [or-'yu-ʝo, -ʎo] *m* **1.** (*satisfacción*) pride; **sentir ~ por alguien/algo** to be proud of sb/sth; **tener el ~ de...** to be proud to...; **~ propio** self-respect **2.** (*soberbia*) arrogance

orgulloso, -a [or-yu-'ʝo-so, -a; -ʎo-so, -a] *adj* **1.** *estar* (*satisfecho*) proud; **sentirse ~ de algo/alguien** to feel proud of sth/sb **2.** *ser* proud; (*soberbio*) arrogant

orientación [o-rjen-ta-'sjon, -'θjon] *f* **1.** (*situación*) situation **2.** (*posición*) position **3.** (*ajuste*) adjustment **4.** (*asesoramiento*) advice; (*dirección*) management; **~ profesional** career [*o* vocational] guidance **5.** (*tendencia*) inclination; **~ política** political orientation; **~ sexual** sexual orientation

oriental [o-rjen-'tal] *adj* **1.** (*del Este*) eastern **2.** (*del Extremo Oriente*) oriental

orientar [o-rjen-'tar] **I.** *vt* **1.** (*dirigir*) to direct; **orientado a la práctica** with a practical focus **2.** (*ajustar*) to adjust **3.** (*asesorar*) to advise **4.** (*dirigir*) to manage **II.** *vr:* **~se 1.** (*dirigirse*) to orient oneself; *fig* to find one's bearings; **~se bien** to have a good sense of direction; **se orientó muy bien en el trabajo** he/she settled in well in the job **2.** (*tender*) to tend

oriente [o-'rjen-te] *m* **1.** GEO east; **Oriente Próximo** the Near East; **el Lejano Oriente** the Far East **2.** (*viento*) easterly

orificio [o-ri-'fi-sjo, -θjo] *m* orifice; (*abertura*) opening; **~ de salida** outlet

origen [o-'ri-xen] *m* **1.** (*principio*) origin; **texto/idioma de ~** source text/language **2.** (*causa*) cause; **dar a algo a** to give rise to sth; **tener su ~ en algo** to have its origins in sth **3.** (*ascendencia*) descent **4.** (*procedencia*) origin; **de ~ español** of Spanish origin

original [o-ri-xi-'nal] **I.** *adj* **1.** (*auténtico, creativo*) original; **versión ~** original version **2.** (*originario*) originating **3.** (*singular*) peculiar **II.** *m* original; **fiel al ~** faithful to the original

originalidad [o-ri-xi-na-li-'dad] *f* **1.** (*autenticidad, creatividad*) originality **2.** (*singularidad*) peculiarity

originar [o-ri-xi-'nar] **I.** *vt* **1.** (*causar*) to cause **2.** (*provocar*) to provoke **II.** *vr:* **~se 1.** (*tener el origen*) to originate **2.** (*surgir*) to arise **3.** (*proceder*) **~se en algo** to spring from sth

originario, -a [o-ri-xi-'na-rjo, -a] *adj* **1.** (*oriundo*) native; **es ~ de Chile** he comes from Chile **2.** (*de origen*) **país ~** country of origin

orilla [o-'ri-ʝa, -ʎa] *f* **1.** (*borde*) edge **2.** (*ribera*) bank; **a ~s del Orinoco** on the banks of the Orinoco **3.** *pl AmL* (*arrabales*) outskirts *pl*

orillero, -a [o-ri-'ʝe-ro, -a; -ʎe-ro, -a] **I.** *adj AmL pey* **1.** (*arrabalero*) low class **2.** (*grosero*) coarse **II.** *m, f AmL pey* **1.** (*arrabalero*) common person **2.** (*grosero*) ill-bred person

orina [o-'ri-na] *f* <orines> urine

orinal [o-ri-'nal] *m* chamber pot; (*de niño*) potty

orinar [o-ri-'nar] **I.** *vi, vt* to urinate **II.** *vr:* **~se** to wet oneself; **~se en la cama** to wet the bed

orla ['or-la] *f* (*foto*) graduating-class photo [*o* picture]

oro ['o-ro] *m* gold; **~ de ley** fine gold; **bañado en ~** gold-plated; **de ~** gold; **color ~** golden; **hacerse de ~** to make one's fortune ▸ **prometer a alguien el ~ y el moro** to promise sb the earth; **mi palabra es ~** my word is my honor; **guardar como ~ en paño** to treasure; **no es ~ todo lo que reluce** *prov* all that glitters is not gold *prov*

orquesta [or-'kes-ta] *f* MÚS orchestra

orquídea [or-'ki-dea] *f* orchid

ortiga [or-'ti-ya] *f* nettle

ortodoncia [or-to-'don-sja, -θja] *f* MED orthodontics *pl*

ortodoxo, -a [or-to-'dok-so, -a] **I.** *adj* orthodox **II.** *m, f* orthodox

ortografía [or-to-yra-'fi-a] *f* spelling; **falta de ~** spelling mistake

ortográfico, -a [or-to-'yra-fi-ko, -a] *adj* spelling

O

ortopeda [or·to·'pe·ða] *mf* MED orthopedist

ortopedia [or·to·'pe·ðja] *f* MED orthopedics

ortopédico, -a [or·to·'pe·ði·ko, -a] *adj* MED orthopedic; **pierna ortopédica** artificial leg

oruga [o·'ru·ɣa] *f* 1. ZOOL caterpillar 2. TÉC caterpillar track

orujo [o·'ru·xo] *m* 1. (*residuo*) marc 2. (*aguardiente*) ≈ grappa

os [os] *pron* I. *pron pers* (*objeto directo e indirecto*) you II. *pron reflexivo* yourselves; **¿~ marcháis?** are you leaving?

osadía [o·sa·'ði·a] *f* daring

osado, -a [o·'sa·ðo, -a] *adj* daring

osar [o·'sar] *vi* to dare; **¿cómo osas decir esto?** how dare you say that!

oscilación [os·θi·la·'θjon] *f* 1. (*vaivén*) oscillation 2. (*variación*) fluctuation 3. (*indecisión*) indecision

oscilar [os·θi·'lar] *vi* 1. (*en vaivén*) to oscillate 2. (*péndulo*) to swing 3. (*variar*) to fluctuate

oscilatorio, -a [os·θi·la·'to·rjo, -a] *adj* oscillatory

oscurecer [os·ku·re·'θer, -θer] *irr como* **crecer** I. *vimpers* to get dark II. *vt t. fig* (*privar de luz*) to darken III. *vr:* **~se** *t. fig* (*volverse oscuro*) to darken IV. *m* dusk; **al ~** at dusk

oscurecimiento [os·ku·re·θi·'mjen·to] *m t. fig* darkening

oscuridad [os·ku·ri·'ðað] *f* 1. (*falta de luz*) darkness; **en la ~** in the dark 2. (*falta de claridad*) obscurity

oscuro, -a [os·'ku·ro, -a] *adj* dark; *fig* obscure; **azul ~** dark blue; **a oscuras** in the dark; **de ~ origen** of obscure origin

óseo, -a [o·'se·o, -a] *adj* bony

oso [o·so] *m* bear; **~ de peluche** teddy bear; **fuerte como un ~** as strong as an ox

ostensible [os·ten·'si·βle] *adj* obvious; **hacer ~** to make evident

ostentar [os·ten·'tar] *vt* 1. (*mostrar*) to show; (*jactarse*) to flaunt 2. (*poseer*) to have; (*puesto, poder*) to hold

ostentoso, -a [os·ten·'to·so, -a] *adj* 1. (*jactancioso*) ostentatious 2. (*llamativo*) showy

ostra ['os·tra] *f* oyster ▶ **aburrirse como una ~** *inf* to be bored to death; **¡~s!** *inf* Jesus!

OTAN [o·'tan] *f abr de* **Organización del Tratado del Atlántico Norte** NATO

otitis [o·'ti·tis] *f inv* MED (*dolor*) earache; (*infección*) ear infection

otomano, -a [o·to·'ma·no, -a] *adj, m, f* Ottoman

otomía [o·to·'mi·a] *f Arg, Col* atrocity

otoñal [o·to·'pal] *adj* autumnal

otoño [o·'to·po] *m* autumn, fall; **a fin(al) es de ~** at the end of autumn [*o* fall]; **el ~** (**de la vida**) the autumn (of one's life)

otorgar <g → gu> [o·tor·'ɣar] *vt* 1. (*conferir*) to confer; **~ poderes** to confer powers 2. (*conceder*) to concede; (*ayudas*) to offer 3. (*expedir*) to issue; **~ licencia** to grant a license 4. (*acceder*) **~ algo** to agree to sth

otorrinolaringólogo, -a [o·to·rri·no·la·rin·'ɣo·lo·ɣo, -a] *m, f* MED ear, nose and throat specialist

otro, -a ['o·tro, -a] I. *adj* another, other; **al ~ día** the next day; **el ~ día** the other day; **en otra ocasión** another time; **la otra semana** the other week; **en ~ sitio** in another place, somewhere else; **otra cosa** another thing; **~ tanto** as much again; **otra vez** again; **¡otra vez será!** maybe another time!; **eso ya es otra cosa** that is much better; **¡hasta otra (vez)!** until the next time! II. *pron indef* 1. (*distinto: cosa*) another (one); (*persona*) someone else; **~s** others; **el ~/la otra/lo ~** the other (one); **ninguna otra persona** nobody else; **de un sitio a ~** from one place to another; **no ~ que...** none other than...; **ésa es otra** (*cosa distinta*) that is different 2. (*uno más*) another; **otras tres personas** three more people; **¡otra, otra!** more!

ovación [o·βa·'sjon, -'θjon] *f* ovation; **dar/recibir una ~** to give/receive an ovation

oval [o·'βal] *adj*, **ovalado, -a** [o·βa·'la·ðo, -a] *adj* oval

ovario [o·'βa·rjo] *m* ANAT ovary

oveja [o·'βe·xa] *f* sheep *inv*; (*hembra*)

ewe; **la ~ negra de la familia** the black sheep of the family ▶ **cada ~ con su pareja** *prov* birds of a feather flock together *prov*

ovillo [o·'βi·jo, -ʎo] *m* ball; *fig* tangle; **hacerse un ~** (*enredarse*) to get tangled up; (*encogerse*) to curl up into a ball

ovino, -a [o·'βi·no, -a] *adj* sheep; **ganado ~** sheep *pl*

ovni ['oβ·ni] *m* UFO

ovulación [o·βu·la·'sjon, -'θjon] *f* ovulation

óvulo ['o·βu·lo] *m* ANAT ovule

oxidación [ok·si·da·'sjon, -'θjon] *f* 1. QUÍM oxidation 2. (*metal*) rusting

oxidar [ok·si·'dar] I. *vt* 1. QUÍM to oxidize 2. (*metal*) to rust; **un hierro oxidado** a piece of rusty iron II. *vr:* **~se** 1. (*metal*) to rust; (*mente*) to go rusty 2. QUÍM to oxidize

óxido ['ok·si·do] *m* 1. QUÍM oxide 2. (*orín*) rust

oxigenar [ok·si·xe·'nar] I. *vt* 1. (*cabello*) to bleach 2. QUÍM to oxygenate; **agua oxigenada** (hydrogen) peroxide II. *vr:* **~se** *inf* to get some fresh air

oxígeno [ok·'si·xe·no] *m* QUÍM oxygen

oyente [o·'jen·te] *mf* listener

ozono [o·'θo·no] *m* QUÍM ozone; **el agujero en la capa de ~** the hole in the ozone layer

P

P, p [pe] *f* P, p; **~ de París** P as in Papa

pabellón [pa·βe·'jon, -'ʎon] *m* 1. (*tienda*) bell tent 2. (*bandera*) flag 3. ARQUIT pavilion

pacer [pa·'ser, -θer] *irr como crecer vi, vt* to graze

pacha [pa·'tʃa] *f* 1. *Nic*, *Méx* (*botella aplanada*) flask 2. *Nic* (*biberón*) baby's bottle

pachacho, -a [pa·'tʃa·tʃo, -a] *adj Chile* short-legged

pachanga [pa·'tʃan·ga] *f* 1. *Cuba* (*danza*) Cuban dance 2. *Col inf* (*fiesta*) party

pachón, -ona [pa·'tʃon, --'tʃo·na] *adj AmL* (*peludo*) hairy

pachucho, -a [pa·'tʃu·tʃo, -a] *adj* 1. *inf* (*persona*) off-color 2. (*fruta*) overripe

paciencia [pa·'sjen·sja, --'θjen·θja] *f* patience; **se me ha acabado la ~** I've run out of patience

paciente [pa·'sjen·te, 'θjen·te] I. *adj* patient; **ser ~ con alguien** to be patient with sb II. *mf* patient

pacífico, -a [pa·'si·fi·ko, -a, -θi·fi·ko -a] *adj* peaceful

Pacífico [pa·'si·fi·ko, -θi·fi·ko] *m* Pacific (Ocean)

pacifismo [pa·si·'fis·mo, -θi·'fis·mo] *m* pacifism

pacifista [pa·si·'fis·ta, -θi'fista] *adj*, *mf* pacifist

pacotilla [pa·ko·'ti·ja, -ʎa] *f* 1. (*calidad inferior*) trashiness; **de ~** (*mercancía*) shoddy; (*restaurante*) second-rate 2. *AmL* (*chusma*) rabble

pactar [pak·'tar] I. *vi* to come to an agreement II. *vt* to agree on

pacto ['pak·to] *m* agreement; (*contrato*) contract; **~ antiterrorista** antiterrorism pact

padecer [pa·de·'ser, -θer] *irr como crecer* I. *vi* to suffer II. *vt* 1. (*sufrir*) to suffer; **~ algo** to suffer from sth 2. (*soportar*) to endure

padecimiento [pa·de·θi·'mjen·to] *m* 1. (*sufrimiento*) suffering 2. (*enfermedad*) ailment

padrastro [pa·'dras·tro] *m* (*marido de madre*) stepfather

padre ['pa·dre] *m* 1. *t.* REL father; **¡tu ~!** *inf* up yours! 2. *pl* (*padre y madre*) parents *pl*

padrenuestro [pa·dre·'nwes·tro] *m* Lord's Prayer

padrillo [pa·'dri·jo, -ʎo] *m CSur* stallion

padrino [pa·'dri·no] *m* (*de bautizo*) godfather; (*de boda*) best man; **tener buenos ~s** *fig* to know the right people

padrote [pa·'dro·te] *m AmC*, *Méx* 1. (*equino*) stallion; (*bovino*) breeding bull 2. *inf* (*alcahuete*) pimp

paella [pa·'e·ja, -ʎa] *f* paella *(Spanish dish of rice, meat and fish, flavored and colored with saffron)*

paellera [pae·je·ra, -ʎera] *f* paella dish

pág. ['pa·xi·na] *abr de* **página** p.

P

paga ['pa·ɣa] f 1. (sueldo) pay 2. (acto) payment

pagano, -a [pa·'ɣa·no, -a] adj pagan

pagar ⟨g → gu⟩ [pa·'ɣar] vt 1. (gastos) to pay; (una deuda) to repay; **~ un anticipo** to make an advance payment 2. (expiar) to atone for; **¡me las ~ás!** you'll pay for this! 3. (recompensar) to repay; (una visita) to return; **¡Dios se lo pague!** God will reward you!

pagaré [pa·ɣa·'re] m promissory note, IOU

página ['pa·xi·na] f page; **pasar (la) ~** to turn the page; **~s blancas** telephone directory; **~s amarillas** TEL yellow pages; **~ web** COMPUT web site

pago ['pa·ɣo] m 1. payment; **~ adicional** supplement; **~ inicial** down payment; **~ a plazos** payment in installments; **día de ~** pay day; **anticipar el ~** to pay in advance; **sujeto a ~** subject to payment; **~ anticipado** advance payment 2. fig (recompensa) reward; **¿éste es el ~ que me das?** is this how you repay me? 3. Arg, Perú (de nacimiento) home region

paila ['pai·la] f AmL (sartén) frying pan

país [pa·'is] m country; **~ comunitario** member state (of the European Union); **~ industrializado** industrialized country; **~ limítrofe** neighboring country; **~ en vías de desarrollo** developing country; **~ en vías de industrialización** industrializing country

paisa ['pai·sa] m AmL v. paisano

paisaje [pai·'sa·xe] m landscape

paisano, -a [pai·'sa·no, -a] m, f 1. (no militar) civilian; **ir de ~** to be in plain clothes 2. (compatriota) compatriot 3. (campesino) peasant

Países Bajos [pa·'i·ses 'βa·xos] mpl Netherlands

paja ['pa·xa] f straw; **no dormirse en las ~s** inf to be alert

pajar [pa·'xar] m haystack; (lugar) hayloft; **buscar una aguja en un ~** fig to search for a needle in a haystack

pajarita [pa·xa·'ri·ta] f bow tie

pájaro ['pa·xa·ro] m bird; **~ bobo** penguin; **~ carpintero** woodpecker; **tener la cabeza llena de ~s** to be scatter-brained ▸ **más vale ~ en mano que ciento volando** prov a bird in the hand is worth two in the bush

pajita [pa·'xi·ta] f (drinking) straw

pajonal [pa·xo·'nal] m CSur scrubland

pajuela [pa·'xwe·la] f 1. Bol (cerilla) match 2. Bol, Col (mondadientes) toothpick

pajuerano, -a [pa·xwe·'ra·no, -a] m, f Arg, Bol, Urug pey (paleto) country bumpkin, hick

pala ['pa·la] f 1. (para cavar) spade; (cuadrada) shovel; **~ mecánica** mechanical shovel; AmL bulldozer 2. (del timón) rudder 3. (raqueta) racket

palabra [pa·'la·βra] f word; **~ clave** t. COMPUT keyword, password; **~s cruzadas** crossword; **~s mayores** strong words; **juego de ~s** pun, play on words; **de pocas ~s** quiet; **ahorrar ~s** not to waste one's words; **coger a alguien la ~** to take sb at his/her word; **cumplir la ~** to be as good as one's word; **dirigir la ~ a alguien** to speak to sb; **faltar a la ~** to go back on one's word; **llevar la ~** to speak; **medir las ~s** to choose one's words carefully; **no entender ~** not to understand a single word; **quitar a alguien la ~ de la boca** to take the words right out of sb's mouth ▸ **dejar a alguien con la ~ en la boca** to interrupt sb; **a ~s necias oídos sordos** prov sticks and stones will break my bones, but names will never hurt me prov; **decir la última ~** to have the last word; **de ~** (oral) by word of mouth; (que cumple sus promesas) honorable

palabrota [pa·la·'βro·ta] f swearword

palacio [pa·'la·sjo, -θjo] m palace; **Palacio de Justicia** law courts; **~ municipal** town hall

paladar [pa·la·'dar] m palate; **tener buen ~** (vino) to be smooth on the palate; (persona) to have a discerning palate

paladear [pa·la·de·'ar] vt to savor

palanca [pa·'lan·ka] f 1. (pértiga) lever; (palanqueta) crowbar; **~ de mando** AVIAT, COMPUT joystick; **~ de cambio** gearshift 2. AmL (influencia) influence; **tener mucha ~** to have a lot of influence

palangana [pa·lan·'ga·na] *f* washbasin

palanquear [pa·lan·ke·'ar] *vt AmL* **1.** (*apalancar*) to lever **2.** (*influenciar*) to influence

palco ['pal·ko] *m* TEAT box

Palestina [pa·les·'ti·na] *m* Palestine

palestino, -a [pa·les·'ti·no, -a] *adj, m, f* Palestinian

paleta [pa·'le·ta] *f* **1.** (*pala*) (small) shovel; (*del albañil*) trowel **2.** (*del pintor*) palette **3.** (*de turbinas*) blade **4.** (*omóplato*) shoulder blade **5.** *Col inf* (*helado*) popsicle

paletilla [pa·le·'ti·ja, -ʎa] *f* (*omóplato*) shoulder blade

paleto [pa·'le·to] *m* fallow deer

paliacate [pa·lja·'ka·te] *m Méx* large brightly colored scarf

paliar <1. pres *palio*, *palio*> [pa·'ljar] *vt* (*enfermedad*) to alleviate

palidecer [pa·li·de·'ser, -ɵer] *irr como crecer vi* **1.** (*persona*) to turn pale **2.** (*cosa*) to fade

pálido, -a ['pa·li·do, -a] *adj* pale; (*estilo*) flat

palillo [pa·'li·jo, -ʎo] *m* (small) stick; (*para los dientes*) toothpick; (*para el tambor*) drumstick

palique [pa·'li·ke] *m inf* chat; **estar de ~ con alguien** to chat to sb

paliza [pa·'li·sa, -ɵa] *f* beating; *inf* (*esfuerzo*) slog; **dar una buena ~** (*pegar*) to beat up; (*derrotar*) to thrash; **¡no me des la ~!** *fig* give me a break!; **pegarse una ~ con algo** *inf* to exhaust oneself with sth

palma ['pal·ma] *f* **1.** (*palmera*) palm (tree); (*hoja de palmera*) palm leaf; **llevarse la ~** to be the best **2.** ANAT palm; **conocer algo como la ~ de su mano** *inf* to know sth like the back of one's hand **3.** *pl* (*ruido*) clapping; (*aplauso*) applause; **tocar las ~s** to clap

palmada [pal·'ma·da] *f* (*golpe*) pat

palmar [pal·'mar] *vi inf* **-la** to kick the bucket

palmera [pal·'me·ra] *f* palm (tree)

palmo ['pal·mo] *m* (hand)span ▸ **dejar a alguien con un ~ de narices** to disappoint sb badly; **~ a ~** inch by inch

palo ['pa·lo] *m* **1.** (*bastón*) stick; (*vara*) pole; (*garrote*) club; (*estaca*) post; **~ de la escoba** broomstick; **~ de hockey** hockey stick; **~ de la portería** goalpost **2.** (*paliza*) beating; **dar ~s de ciego** *fig* to grope in the dark; **dar un ~ a alguien** *fig* to tear a strip off sb; (*cobrar mucho*) to rip sb off; **echar a alguien a ~s** to throw sb out; **liarse a ~s con alguien** to come to blows with sb; **moler a alguien a ~s** to beat sb black and blue ▸ **~ de agua** *AmL* downpour; **no dar un ~ al agua** not to do a stick of work; **de tal ~, tal astilla** *prov* like father, like son; **ser un ~** to be a setback

paloma [pa·'lo·ma] *f* (*ave*) pigeon; (*blanca, como símbolo*) dove; **~ mensajera** carrier pigeon

palomitas [pa·lo·'mi·tas] *fpl* CULIN popcorn

palpable [pal·'pa·βle] *adj* palpable; (*evidente*) clear

palpar [pal·'par] *vt* **1.** (*tocar*) to touch **2.** (*percibir*) to feel; **se palpaba el entusiasmo** you could feel the enthusiasm

palpitar [pal·pi·'tar] *vi* (*contraerse*) to shudder; (*corazón, pulso*) to throb

palta ['pal·ta] *f AmS* BOT avocado (pear)

palto ['pal·to] *m CSur* BOT avocado pear tree

paludismo [pa·lu·'dis·mo] *m* MED malaria

palurdo, -a [pa·'lur·do, -a] *m, f* yokel, hick

pampa ['pam·pa] *f* GEO pampas + *sing/ pl vb*

pampear [pam·pe·'ar] *vi CSur* to travel over the pampas

pampero, -a [pam·'pe·ro] *adj* of/from the Pampas

pamplina [pam·'pli·na] *f inf* (*pamema*) silly thing

pan [pan] *m* bread; **~ de azúcar** sugar loaf; **~ integral** wholegrain bread; **~ con mantequilla** bread and butter; **~ de molde** sliced bread; **~ rallado** breadcrumbs *pl*; **estar a ~ y agua** to be on (a strict diet of) bread and water; **ganarse el ~** to earn one's living ▸ **no sólo de ~ vive el hombre** man cannot live by

P

bread alone; **a falta de ~, buenas son <u>tortas</u>** *prov* half a loaf is better than none; (*llamar*) **al ~, ~ y al <u>vino</u>, vino** *inf* to call a spade a spade; **ser más <u>bueno que el</u> ~** to be very good-natured; **ser ~ <u>comido</u>** *inf* to be dead easy; **con su ~ se lo <u>coma</u>** *inf* that's his/her lookout [*o* problem]

pana ['pa·na] *f* corduroy

panacea [pa·na·'sea, -'θea] *f* panacea, cure-all

panadería [pa·na·de·'ri·a] *f* bakery

panadero, -a [pa·na·'de·ro, -a] *m, f* baker

panal [pa·'nal] *m* honeycomb

Panamá [pa·na·'ma] *m* Panama

panameño, -a [pa·na·'me·ɲo, -a] *adj, m, f* Panamanian

pancarta [pan·'kar·ta] *f* placard

pancho ['pan·tʃo] *m Arg* (*perrito caliente*) hotdog

pancho, -a ['pan·tʃo, -a] *adj* calm

páncreas ['pan·kreas] *m inv* pancreas

panda¹ ['pan·da] *m* ZOOL panda

panda² ['pan·da] *f v.* **pandilla**

pandereta [pan·de·'re·ta] *f*, **pandero** [pan·'de·ro] *m* MÚS tambourine

pandilla [pan·'di·ʝa, -ʎa] *f* band; (*de amigos*) group; **~ de ladrones** gang of thieves

panecillo [pa·ne·'si·ʝo, -'θi·ʎo] *m* roll

panel [pa·'nel] *m* panel; **~ de control** control panel

panela [pa·'ne·la] *f* 1. (*bizcocho*) corn cake 2. *Col, CRi, Hond* (*azúcar*) brown sugar loaf

pánfilo, -a ['pan·fi·lo, -a] *adj* 1. (*fácil de engañar*) gullible 2. (*lento*) slow

panfleto [pan·'fle·to] *m* pamphlet; *fig* propaganda

pánico ['pa·ni·ko] *m* panic; **tener ~ a algo** to be terrified of sth

pánico, -a ['pa·ni·ko, -a] *adj* panic

panocha [pa·'no·tʃa] *f*, **panoja** [pa·'no·xa] *f* 1. (*de maíz*) corncob 2. (*espiga*) ear of corn; (*racimo*) cornstalk

panoli [pa·'no·li] *adj inf* idiotic

panorama [pa·no·'ra·ma] *m* panorama; *fig* outlook

pantaleta(s) [pan·ta·'le·ta(s)] *f(pl) Méx, Ven* (*bragas*) panties *pl*

pantalla [pan·'ta·ja, -ʎa] *f* 1. (*de la lámpara*) shade 2. (*protección*) screen 3. COMPUT, TV, CINE screen; **~ panorámica** wide screen; **pequeña ~** *inf* TV

pantalón [pan·ta·'lon] *m* trousers *pl*, pants *pl*, pair of pants; **~ tejano** [*o* **vaquero**] jeans *pl*; **llevar los pantalones** *fig* to wear the trousers [*o* pants]

pantano [pan·'ta·no] *m* (*ciénaga*) marsh; (*laguna*) swamp

pantanoso, -a [pan·ta·'no·so, -a] *adj* marshy

panteón [pan·te·'on] *m* 1. HIST pantheon 2. (*sepultura*) tomb; **~ de familia** family vault 3. *AmL* (*cementerio*) cemetery

pantera [pan·'te·ra] *f* panther

pantimedia(s) [pan·ti·'me·dja(s)] *f(pl) Méx* pantyhose

pantis ['pan·tis] *mpl inf* pantyhose

pantomima [pan·to·'mi·ma] *f* pantomime

pantorrilla [pan·to·'rri·ja, -ʎa] *f* calf

pantufla [pan·'tu·fla] *f* slipper

panucho [pa·'nu·tʃo] *m Méx* meat and bean stuffed tortilla

panza ['pan·sa, -θa] *f* 1. (*barriga*) belly 2. ZOOL stomach; (*rumiantes*) rumen

pañal [pa·'ɲal] *m* diaper; **estar aún en ~es** *fig* to be still in its infancy

pañetar [pa·ɲe·'tar] *vt Col* (*una pared*) to plaster

paño ['pa·ɲo] *m* (*tejido, trapo*) cloth; **~ de cocina** (*para fregar*) dishcloth; (*para secar*) dish towel ▶ **~s <u>menores</u>** underwear

pañoleta [pa·ɲo·'le·ta] *f* fichu

pañuelo [pa·'ɲwe·lo] *m* 1. (*moquero*) handkerchief; **el mundo es un ~** it's a small world 2. (*pañoleta*) fichu; (*de cabeza*) headscarf, scarf

papa¹ ['pa·pa] *m* pope

papa² ['pa·pa] *f* 1. *reg, AmL* (*patata*) potato; **no entender ni ~** not to understand a thing 2. *pl* (*comida*) purée

papá [pa·'pa] *m inf* dad; **Papá Noel** Santa Claus; **los ~s** mom and dad

papada [pa·'pa·da] *f* (*de la persona*) double chin, jowl; (*del animal*) dewlap

papagayo [pa·pa·'ɣa·jo] *m* 1. (*loro*) parrot 2. (*hablador*) chatterbox

papaya [pa·'pa·ja] *f* pawpaw, papaya

papel [pa·'pel] *m* **1.** (*para escribir, material*) paper; (*hoja*) piece of paper; (*escritura*) piece of writing; ~ **de calcar** tracing paper; ~ **de envolver** wrapping paper; ~ **de regalo** gift-wrap; ~ **de estraza** brown paper; ~ **de aluminio** aluminum [*o* tin] foil; ~ **de seda** tissue paper; ~ **higiénico** toilet paper; ~ **de lija** sandpaper; ~ **moneda** banknotes *pl*, bills *pl*; ~ **pintado** wallpaper; ~ **de plata** silver paper; ~ **reciclado** recycled paper; ~ **secante** blotting paper; ~ **mojado** *fig* worthless scrap of paper **2.** (*rol*) role; ~ **protagonista** leading role; ~ **secundario** supporting role; **hacer su** ~ to play one's part; **hacer buen/mal** ~ to make a good/bad impression **3.** *pl* (*documentos*) documentation; (*de identidad*) identity papers *pl*

papeleo [pa·pe·'leo] *m* paperwork

papelera [pa·pe·'le·ra] *f* **1.** (*cesto*) wastepaper basket; (*en la calle*) litter bin **2.** (*fábrica*) paper mill

papelería [pa·pe·le·'ri·a] *f* stationer's

papelerío [pa·pe·le·'ri·a] *m AmL* mass of papers

papeleta [pa·pe·'le·ta] *f* (*cédula*) slip of paper; ~ **de propaganda** flier

papera [pa·'pe·ra] *f* MED **1.** *pl* (*enfermedad*) mumps *pl* **2.** (*bocio*) goiter

papilla [pa·'pi·ja, -ʎa] *f* baby food; **echar la** (**primera**) ~ *inf* to be as sick as a dog; **hacer** ~ **a alguien** *fig* to beat hell out of sb; **estar hecho** ~ *fig* to be smashed to a pulp

papiro [pa·'pi·ro] *m* papyrus

papo ['pa·po] *m* **1.** *inf* (*bocio*) goiter **2.** (*papada*) double chin, jowl

paquete [pa·'ke·te] *m* **1.** *t. fig* (*atado*) packet; ~ **postal** parcel **2.** *inf* (*castigo*) **meter un** ~ **a alguien** (*reprender*) to tell sb off; (*castigar*) to punish sb heavily **3.** *vulg* (*genitales*) basket; **marcar** ~ to show one's basket

paquete, -a [pa·'ke·te, -a] *adj Arg* smart

paquetear [pa·ke·te·'ar] *vi Arg, Urug inf* to show off one's outfit

paquete-bomba [pa·'ke·te·'βom·ba] *m* <paquetes-bomba> mail [*o* letter] bomb

par [par] **I.** *adj* **1.** (*número*) even; **~es o**

nones odds or evens **2.** (*igual*) equal; **a la** ~ at the same time; **sin** ~ without equal ▶ **de** ~ **en** ~ wide open **II.** *m* **1.** (*dos cosas*) pair; **un** ~ **de zapatos/pantalones** a pair of shoes/pants **2.** (*algunos*) **un** ~ **de minutos** a couple of minutes

para ['pa·ra] **I.** *prep* **1.** (*destino*) for; **un regalo** ~ **el niño** a present for the child **2.** (*finalidad*) for; **servir** ~ **algo** to be useful for sth; **¿~ qué es esto?** what is this for? **3.** (*dirección*) to; **voy** ~ **Madrid** I'm going to Madrid; **mira** ~ **acá** look over here **4.** (*duración*) for; ~ **siempre** forever; **vendrá** ~ **Navidad/finales de marzo** he/she will come for Christmas/towards the end of March; **estará listo** ~ **el viernes** it will be ready for [*o* by] Friday; **diez minutos** ~ **las once** *AmL* ten to eleven **5.** (*contraposición*) for; **es muy activo** ~ **la edad que tiene** he is very active for his age **6.** (*trato*) ~ (**con**) with; **es muy amable** ~ **con nosotros** he/she is very kind to us **7.** (+ *estar*) **estar** ~... (*disposición*) to be ready to...; (*a punto de*) about to...; **no estoy** ~ **bromas** I'm in no mood for jokes **8.** (*a juicio de*) ~ **mí, esto no es lo mismo** in my opinion, this is not the same **II.** *conj* **1.** + *infin* to; **he venido** ~ **darte las gracias** I came to thank you **2.** ~ **que** +*subj* so that; **te mando al colegio** ~ **que aprendas algo** I send you to school so that you learn sth

parábola [pa·'ra·βo·la] *f* **1.** (*alegoría*) parable **2.** MAT curve, parabola

parabólica [pa·ra·'βo·li·ka] *f* satellite dish

parabrisas [pa·ra·'βri·sas] *m inv* AUTO windshield

paracaídas [pa·ra·ka·'i·das] *m inv* parachute

paracaidismo [pa·ra·kai·'dis·mo] *m* parachuting

paracaidista [pa·ra·kai·'dis·ta] *mf* DEP parachutist; MIL paratrooper

parachoques [pa·ra·'tʃo·kes] *m inv* AUTO bumper

parada [pa·'ra·da] *f* **1.** (*de un autobús*) stop; ~ **de taxis** taxi rank **2.** (*acción de parar*) stopping; ~ **de una fábrica** factory stoppage; **hacer una ~ para descansar** to make a rest stop

paradero [pa·ra·'de·ro] *m* whereabouts; **está en ~ desconocido** his/her whereabouts are unknown

paradisíaco, -a [pa·ra·di·'si·a·ko, -a] *adj* heavenly

parado, -a [pa·'ra·do, -a] **I.** *adj* **1.** (*que no se mueve*) stationary; **estar ~** to be motionless; **quedarse ~** to remain motionless **3.** (*remiso*) slow **4.** (*tímido*) shy **5.** *AmL* standing (up) ▶ **salir bien/mal ~ de algo** to come out of sth well/badly; **ser el peor ~** to be the worst off **II.** *m, f* unemployed person

paradoja [pa·ra·'do·xa] *f* paradox

parador [pa·ra·'dor] *m* inn; (*en España*) state-run luxury hotel

paragolpes [pa·ra·'ɣol·pes] *m inv AmL* bumper

parágrafo [pa·'ra·ɣra·fo] *m* paragraph

paraguas [pa·ra·ɣwas] *m inv* umbrella

Paraguay [pa·ra·'ɣwai] *m* Paraguay

paraguayo, -a [pa·ra·'ɣwa·jo, -a] *adj, m, f* Paraguayan

paragüero [pa·ra·'ɣwe·ro] *m* umbrella stand

paraíso [pa·ra·'i·so] *m* **1.** (*en el cielo*) heaven; **~ terrenal** earthly paradise **2.** *Méx* (*gallinero*) henhouse

paraje [pa·'ra·xe] *m* (*lugar*) place; (*punto*) spot

paralelo, -a [pa·ra·'le·lo, -a] *adj* parallel; **líneas paralelas** parallel lines; **conexión en ~** ELEC parallel connection; **seguir caminos ~s** to develop along similar lines

parálisis [pa·'ra·li·sis] *f inv* paralysis

paralítico, -a [pa·ra·'li·ti·ko, -a] *adj* (*persona*) paralyzed

paralización [pa·ra·li·sa·'sjon, -θa·θjon] *f* (*de un proceso*) halting

paralizar <z → c> [pa·ra·li·'sar, -'θar] **I.** *vt* **1.** (*persona*) to paralyze; **el miedo/el frío la paralizó** she was paralyzed by fear/by the cold **2.** (*cosa*) to stop; **~ un transporte** to paralyze a means of transport **II.** *vr* **1.** (*persona*) to be paralyzed **2.** (*cosa*) to stop

parámetro [pa·'ra·me·tro] *m* parameter

páramo ['pa·ra·mo] *m* **1.** (*terreno desierto*) wilderness; (*infértil*) wasteland **2.** (*lugar desamparado*) exposed place

paranoia [pa·ra·'noja] *f* paranoia

paranoico, -a [pa·ra·'noi·ko, -a] *adj* paranoid

parapetarse [pa·ra·pe·'tar·se] *vr* to protect oneself

parapeto [pa·ra·'pe·to] *m* MIL parapet; (*barricada*) barricade

parapléjico, -a [pa·ra·'ple·xi·ko, -a] *adj, m, f* paraplegic

parar ['pa·rar] **I.** *vi* **1.** (*detenerse, cesar*) to stop; **la máquina funciona sin ~** the machine works non-stop; **mis hijos no me dejan ~** my kids never give me a break; **ha parado de llover** it has stopped raining; **no para (de trabajar)** he/she never stops (working) **2.** (*acabar*) to finish; **ir a ~ a...** to end up in...; **¿dónde iremos a ~?** what's the world coming to?; **¿en qué irá a ~ esto?** where will it all end?; **salir bien/mal parado de algo** to come out of sth well/badly; **¿dónde quieres ir a ~?** what are you getting at? **3.** (*alojarse, estar*) to live; **nunca para en casa** he/she is never at home; **siempre para en el mismo hotel** he/she always stays at the same hotel **II.** *vt* (*detener*) to stop; (*un golpe*) to block; (*un gol*) to save; (*el motor*) to turn off **III.** *vr* **1.** (*detenerse*) to stop; **~se a pensar** to stop and think; **~se a descansar** to stop to rest **2.** *AmL* (*levantarse*) to get up

pararrayos [pa·ra·'rra·jos] *m inv* lightning conductor

parásito [pa·'ra·si·to] *m t. fig* parasite

parasol [pa·ra·'sol] *m* sunshade; (*en el coche*) sun visor

parcela [par·'se·la, -'θe·la] *f* plot; **~ edificable** building plot

parcelar [par·se·'lar, par·θe·] *vt* to parcel out

parche ['par·tʃe] *m* **1.** (*pegote*) patch; **~ para el ojo** eye patch; **poner un ~** to patch up **2.** (*retoque*) makeshift remedy; (*de pintura*) dab; **poner ~s** to paper over the cracks

parchís [par·'tʃis] *m* Parcheesi®

parcial [par·'sjal, -'θjal] *adj* **1.** (*incomple-*

to) partial **2.** (*arbitrario*) biased

parco, -a [ˈpar.ko, -a] *adj* **1.** (*moderado*) moderate; (*sobrio*) frugal **2.** (*escaso*) meager; **~ en palabras** of few words

pardiez [par.ˈdjes, -ˈdjeθ] *interj* HIST good gracious

pardillo [par.ˈdi.jo, -ʎo] *m* linnet

pardillo, -a [par.ˈdi.jo, -a; -ʎo, -a] *adj inf* **1.** (*palurdo*) uncouth **2.** (*ingenuo*) simple **II.** *m, f* **1.** (*palurdo*) yokel **2.** (*ingenuo*) simpleton

pardo, -a [ˈpar.do] **I.** *adj* grayish-brown; **oso ~** brown bear; **de ojos ~s** brown-eyed **II.** *m, f* AmL mulatto

parear [pa.re.ˈar] *vt* **1.** (*formar parejas*) to pair; (*atar*) to tie together; (*ropa*) to match up **2.** BIO to mate **3.** (*igualar*) to match

parecer [pa.re.ˈser, -ˈθer] **I.** *irr como crecer vi* to seem; (*aparentar*) to appear; **parece mayor de lo que es** he/she seems older than he/she is; **parece mentira que** +*subj* it seems incredible that; **aunque parezca mentira** though it may seem incredible; **parece que va a llover** it looks like rain; **¿qué te parece?** what do you think?; **si te parece bien,...** if you agree,... **II.** *irr como crecer vr* to look alike; **te pareces mucho a tu madre** you look very much like your mother **III.** *m* **1.** (*opinión*) opinion; (*juicio*) judgment; **a mi ~** in my opinion; **esto es cuestión de ~es** this is a matter of opinion **2.** (*aspecto, apariencia*) appearance; **ser de buen ~** to be good-looking; **al ~** apparently

parecido [pa.re.ˈsi.do, -ˈθi.do] *m* similarity, likeness

parecido, -a [pa.re.ˈsi.do, -a; -ˈθi.do, -a] *adj* **1.** (*semejante*) similar **2.** (*de aspecto*) **ser bien/mal ~** (*persona*) to be good/bad-looking

pared [pa.ˈred] *f* wall; (*de una montaña*) face; (*separación*) partition; **~ abdominal** stomach wall; **~ maestra** (load-)bearing wall ▶ **entre** **cuatro ~es** cooped up; **quedarse** **pegado a la ~** to be put on the spot; **hablar a la ~** to talk to a brick wall; **¡cuidado, que estas ~es** **oyen!** careful, walls have ears!; **subirse por las ~es** to go up the wall;

(*enfadarse*) to blow one's top; (*estar nervioso*) to be [*o* go] stir crazy

pareja [pa.ˈre.xa] *f* **1.** (*par*) couple; **~ de hecho** common law couple; **~s mixtas** DEP mixed doubles; **hacen buena ~** they make a good couple; **¿dónde está la ~ de este guante?** where is the other glove? **2.** (*compañero*) partner **3.** (*en los dados*) pair

parentesco [pa.ren.ˈtes.ko] *m* relationship, kinship

paréntesis [pa.ˈren.te.sis] *m inv* **1.** (*signo*) bracket; **poner algo entre ~** to put sth in brackets; **abrir/cerrar el ~** to open/close brackets; *fig* to introduce/finish a digression **2.** (*interrupción*) interruption; **hicimos un ~ para almorzar** we had a break for lunch

paridad [pa.ri.ˈdad] *f* **1.** FIN, ECON parity **2.** (*igualdad*) equality; (*semejanza*) similarity; **~ de fuerzas** parity of strength

pariente, -a [pa.ˈrjen.te, -a] **I.** *adj* related **II.** *m, f* **1.** (*familiar*) relative; **los** **~s** the relations, the relatives; **~lejano/cercano** distant/close relative **2.** *inf* (*marido, mujer*) other half; **mi parienta** my missus

paripé [pa.ri.ˈpe] *m* show; **hacer el ~** to put on a show; (*fingir*) to pretend

parir [pa.ˈrir] **I.** *vt* to give birth to **II.** *vi* to give birth ▶ **poner a alguien a ~** *inf* to run sb down

París [pa.ˈris] *m* Paris

parisiense [pa.ri.ˈsjen.se] *adj, mf* Parisian

parking [ˈpar.kin] *m* <parkings> parking lot

parlamentario, -a [par.la.men.ˈta.rjo, -a] *adj* parliamentary; **debate ~** parliamentary debate

parlamento [par.la.ˈmen.to] *m* parliament; **Parlamento Europeo** European Parliament

parlanchín, -ina [par.lan.ˈtʃin, -.ˈtʃi.na] *adj inf* talkative

paro [ˈpa.ro] *m* **1.** (*parar: una fábrica*) shutdown; (*de trabajar*) stopping **2.** (*desempleo*) unemployment; **estar** **en ~** to be unemployed; **cobrar el ~** to be on the dole

parodia [pa.ˈro.dja] *f* parody

parpadear [par·pa·de·'ar] *vi* **1.** (*ojos*) to blink; **sin ~** *fig* without a second thought **2.** (*luz, llama*) to flicker

parpadeo [par·pa·'deo] *m* **1.** (*de los ojos*) blinking **2.** (*de luz, llama*) flicker

párpado ['par·pa·do] *m* eyelid

parque ['par·ke] *m* **1.** (*jardín*) park; **~ de atracciones** amusement park; **~ natural** National Park; **~ zoológico** zoo **2.** (*depósito*) depot; **~ de bomberos** fire department; **~ militar** military depot **3.** (*conjunto*) collection; **~ industrial** industrial park; **~ de maquinaria** pool of machinery; **~ de vehículos** fleet of vehicles, car pool **4.** (*para niños*) playpen

parqué [par·'ke] *m* parquet

parqueadero [par·kea·'de·ro] *m* AmL parking lot

parquímetro [par·'ki·me·tro] *m* parking meter

parra ['pa·rra] *f* (grape)vine; **subirse a la ~** (*enfadarse*) to hit the roof; (*darse importancia*) to put on airs

párrafo ['pa·rra·fo] *m v.* **parágrafo**

parranda [pa·'rran·da] *f* spree; **ir de ~** to go out on the town

parrilla [pa·'rri·ja, -ʎa] *f* **1.** (*para la brasa*) grill; (*de un horno*) oven rack **2.** (*establecimiento*) grill(room) **3.** DEP **~** (*de salida*) (starting) grid **4.** AmL AUTO roof-rack

parrillada [pa·rri·'ja·da, -'ʎa·da] *f* grill; **~ de pescado** grilled fish; **~ de carne** mixed grill

párroco ['pa·rro·ko] *m* parish priest

parroquia [pa·'rro·kja] *f* **1.** (*territorio, fieles*) parish **2.** (*iglesia*) parish church

parsimonia [par·si·'monja] *f* **1.** (*calma*) calm; (*lentitud*) deliberation; **con ~** calmly **2.** (*prudencia*) care; (*moderación*) moderation

parte¹ ['par·te] *f* **1.** (*porción, elemento*) part; (*de repuesto*) spare (part); **una cuarta ~** a quarter; **de varias ~s** of several parts; **en ~** in part; **en gran ~** largely; **en mayor ~** for the most part; **por ~** bit by bit; **tomar ~ en algo** to be involved in sth **2.** (*repartición*) division; **~ hereditaria** share of the inheritance; **tener ~ en algo** to have a share in sth;

llevarse la peor/mejor **~** to come off (the) worst/best **3.** (*lugar*) part; **¿a qué ~ vas?** where are you going?; **a ninguna ~** nowhere; **en ninguna ~** nowhere; **en cualquier ~** anywhere; **por todas (las) ~s** everywhere; **en otra ~** somewhere else; **¿de qué ~ de Colombia eres?** which part of Colombia is your family from?; **no llevar a ninguna ~** *fig* to lead nowhere **4.** *t.* JUR (*bando*) party; (*en una discusión*) participant; **~ contratante** contracting party **5.** (*lado*) side; **dale recuerdos de mi ~** give him/her my regards; **estar de ~ de alguien** to be on sb's side; **ponerse de ~ de alguien** to take sb's side; **me tienes de tu ~** I'm on your side; **de ~ a ~** (*de un lado a otro*) from side to side; **por otra ~** on the other hand; (*además*) what's more **6.** (*sección*) section; (*tomo*) volume; (*capítulo*) chapter **7.** TEAT, MÚS (*papel*) part **8.** *pl* (*genitales*) (private) parts *pl*

parte² ['par·te] *m* **1.** (*comunicado*) message; **dar ~** to report **2.** RADIO, TV report; **~ meteorológico** weather report

partición [par·ti·'sjon, -'θjon] *f* partition; MAT division

participación [par·ti·si·pa·'sjon, -θi·pa·'θjon] *f* **1.** (*intervención*) participation; **~ en los beneficios** profit-sharing **2.** (*parte*) share

participante [par·ti·si·'pan·te, par·ti·θi-] *mf* participant

participar [par·ti·si·'par, par·ti·θi-] *vi* **1.** (*tomar parte*) to participate; **~ en un juego** to take part in a game **2.** (*tener parte*) to have a part; **~ en una herencia** to share in an inheritance

partícipe [par·'ti·si·pe, -θi·pe] **I.** *adj* involved **II.** *mf* participant; **hacer a alguien ~ de algo** (*compartir*) to share sth with sb; (*informar*) to inform sb of sth

participio [par·ti·'si·pjo, -'θi·pjo] *m* LING participle; **~ activo** [*o* de presente] present participle; **~ pasivo** [*o* de pretérito] past participle

partícula [par·'ti·ku·la] *f* **1.** *t.* FÍS, QUÍM particle; **~s de polvo** dust particles **2.** LING particle

particular¹ [par·ti·ku·'lar] **I.** *adj* **1.** (*pro*-

pio) peculiar; (*individual*) individual; (*típico*) typical; (*personal*) personal; **el sabor ~ del azafrán** the special flavor of saffron **2.** (*raro*) peculiar **3.** (*extraordinario*) unusual **4.** (*privado*) private; **envíamelo a mi domicilio ~** send it to my home address **5.** (*determinado*) particular; **un problema ~** a particular problem; **en ~** in particular **II.** *mf* private individual

particular² [par·ti·ku·'lar] *m* matter

particularidad [par·ti·ku·la·ri·'dad] *f* **1.** (*especialidad*) specialty; (*singularidad*) distinctive feature; (*peculiaridad*) peculiarity **2.** (*rareza*) peculiarity **3.** (*detalle*) detail; (*circunstancia*) circumstance; **las ~es del crimen** the circumstances of the crime

particularmente [par·ti·ku·lar·'men·te] *adv* particularly

partida [par·'ti·da] *f* **1.** (*salida*) departure **2.** (*envío*) consignment **3.** FIN item; **~ doble** double entry **4.** (*certificado*) certificate; **~ de defunción** death certificate **5.** (*juego*) game; **jugar una ~ de ajedrez** to play a game of chess

partidario, -a [par·ti·da·rjo, -a] **I.** *adj* (*seguidor*) **ser ~ de algo** to be in favor of sth **II.** *m, f* (*seguidor*) follower; (*afiliado*) member; (*de una idea*) supporter

partido [par·'ti·do] *m* **1.** POL party; **~ de derecha(s)/de izquierda(s)** right-wing/left-wing party; **~ obrero** worker's party **2.** (*grupo*) group; **esta idea tiene mucho ~** this idea has a lot of supporters **3.** DEP (*juego*) match; **~ amistoso** friendly **4.** (*para casarse*) match; **encontrar un buen ~** to make quite a catch **5.** (*determinación*) determination; **tomar ~ a favor de algo/alguien** (*inclinarse*) to lean towards sth/sb **6.** (*provecho*) advantage; **sacar ~ de algo** to put sth to use; **saqué ~ del asunto** I profited from the affair **7.** *AmL* (*del pelo*) parting

partir [par·'tir] **I.** *vt* **1.** *t.* MAT (*dividir*) to divide; **~ por la mitad** to divide into two halves **2.** (*romper*) to break; (*madera*) to chop; (*una nuez*) to crack; **~ la cabeza a alguien** to crack sb's head open

3. (*una baraja*) to cut **II.** *vi* **1.** (*tomar como base*) to start; **a ~ de ahora** from now on; **a ~ de mañana** from tomorrow; **a ~ de las seis** from six o'clock onwards; **a ~ de entonces** since then **2.** (*salir de viaje*) to leave; (*ponerse en marcha*) to start; **partimos de Cádiz a las cinco** we left Cadiz at five o'clock **III.** *vr* to split; (*cristal*) to crack; **~se** (*de risa*) *inf* to split one's sides laughing

partitura [par·ti·'tu·ra] *f* MÚS score; (*hojas*) sheet music

parto ['par·to] *m* birth; **estar de ~** to be in labor

parvulario [par·βu·'la·rjo] *m* kindergarten; (*educación preescolar*) nursery school, preschool

párvulo, -a ['par·βu·lo, -a] *m, f* infant; **escuela de ~s** nursery school, preschool

pasa ['pa·sa] *f* raisin; **estar hecho una ~** *inf* to be as shriveled as a prune

pasable [pa·'sa·βle] *adj* passable

pasada [pa·'sa·da] *f* **1.** (*paso*) passing; **hacer varias ~s** to make several passes; **de ~** when passing; *fig* in passing **2.** (*mano*) going-over; (*pintura*) coat; **dar una ~ a algo** to give sth another going-over **3.** *inf* (*comportamiento*) excess; **¡vaya (mala) ~!** what a thing to do!; **hacer una mala ~ a alguien** to play a dirty trick on sb **4.** *inf* (*exageración*) **¡es una ~!** it's way over the top!

pasadizo [pa·sa·'di·so, -θo] *m* (*pasillo*) corridor; (*entre dos calles*) alley; **~ secreto** secret passageway

pasado [pa·'sa·do] *m* past; LING past (tense); **en el ~** in the past; **son cosas del ~** it's all in the past

pasado, -a [pa·'sa·do, -a] *adj* **1.** (*de atrás*) past; **el año ~** last year; **~ mañana** the day after tomorrow; **~s dos meses** after two months; **~ de moda** out of fashion **2.** (*estropeado: alimentos*) bad; (*fruta*) overripe; (*leche*) off, sour; (*mantequilla*) rancid; **el yogur está ~ de fecha** the yogurt is past its sell-by date **3.** (*muy cocido*) overcooked; **un huevo ~ por agua** a soft-boiled egg

pasador [pa·sa·'dor] *m* **1.** (*alfiler*) pin; (*imperdible*) safety pin; (*broche*) clip;

P

(*de corbata*) tiepin **2.** (*para el cabello*) hairclip, barrette **3.** (*cerrojo*) bolt **4.** (*colador*) colander

pasaje |pa·'sa·xe| *m* **1.** (*derecho*) toll **2.** (*billete de avión*) (plane) ticket; (*de barco*) (boat) ticket; (*precio*) fare **3.** (*pasajeros*) passengers *pl* **4.** (*pasillo*) passage; ~ **subterráneo** underground passage **5.** (*estrecho*) strait

pasajero, -a |pa·sa·'xe·ro, -a| **I.** *adj* (*transitorio, breve*) passing; (*fugaz*) fleeting **II.** *m, f* (*viajero*) passenger; **tren de ~s** passenger train

pasamano(s) |pa·sa·'ma·no(s)| *m(pl)* handrail

pasamontañas |pa·sa·mon·'ta·ɲas| *m inv* ski mask

pasapalos |pa·sa·'pa·los| *m inv* *Méx, Ven* appetizer

pasaporte |pa·sa·'por·te| *m* passport; **dar (el) ~ a alguien** *inf* (*despedirlo*) to give sb their marching orders; (*matarlo*) to bump sb off

pasar |pa·'sar| **I.** *vi* **1.** (*por delante*) to pass; ~ **desapercibido** to go unnoticed; ~ **de largo** to go past; **dejar ~** (*por delante*) to allow to go past; ~ **por encima de** (*un obstáculo*) to overcome; (*una persona*) to overlook; ~ **por alto** *fig* to leave out; **no dejes ~ la oportunidad** don't miss the opportunity **2.** (*por un hueco*) to go through; **el sofá no pasa por la puerta** the sofa won't go through the door; **el Ebro pasa por Zaragoza** the Ebro flows through Zaragoza; ~ **por una crisis** to go through a crisis **3.** (*trasladarse*) to move; **pasemos al comedor** let's go to the dining room **4.** (*acaecer*) to happen; **¿qué pasa?** what's up?; **¿qué te pasa?** what's wrong?; **pase lo que pase** whatever happens; **dejar ~ algo** to allow sth to happen; **lo que pasa es que...** the thing is that... **5.** (*acabar*) to pass; **cuando pasen las vacaciones...** when the holidays are over... **6.** (*el tiempo*) to pass; **lo pasado, pasado** what's done is done **7.** (*aparentar*) to pass for; **pasa por nuevo** it looks new; **hacerse ~ por médico** to pass oneself off as a doctor **8.** (*cambiar*) to go; **paso a explicar por qué** and now I will (go

on to) explain why; ~ **a mayores** to go from bad to worse **9.** (*ser admisible*) to pass; **arreglándolo aún puede ~** if we fix it, it should still be okay **10.** (*no jugar*) to pass **11.** *inf* (*no necesitar*) **yo paso de salir** I don't want to go out; **pasa de todo** he/she couldn't care less about anything **II.** *vt* **1.** (*atravesar*) to cross; ~ **el puente** to cross the bridge; ~ **el semáforo en rojo** to go through a red light **2.** (*por un hueco*) to go through; ~ **la tarjeta por la ranura** to swipe the card through the slot; ~ **algo por debajo de la puerta** to slide sth under the door **3.** (*trasladar*) to transfer; ~ **a limpio** to make a fair copy **4.** (*dar*) to pass; ~ **la pelota** to pass the ball **5.** (*una temporada*) to spend; ~ **el invierno en el Caribe** to spend the winter in the Caribbean; ~**lo bien/mal** to have a good/bad time; ~**lo en grande** to have a whale of a time; **¡que lo paséis bien!** enjoy yourselves! **6.** (*sufrir*) to experience; ~ **hambre** to go hungry; ~ **frío** to feel the cold; **pasé un mal rato** I went through a difficult time **7.** (*transmitir*) to send; (*dinero*) to give; ~ **un recado** to pass on a message; **me has pasado el resfriado** you've given me your cold; **le paso a la Sra. Ortega** I'll put you through to Mrs. Ortega **8.** (*sobrepasar*) to exceed; **he pasado los treinta** I am over thirty; **te paso en altura** I am taller than you **9.** (*hacer deslizar*) ~ **la mano por la mesa** to run one's hand over the table; ~ **la aspiradora** to vacuum **10.** (*tolerar*) to allow to pass **11.** (*aprobar*) to pass **12.** (*omitir*) to overlook **13.** (*colar*) to strain **14.** (*las hojas de un libro*) to turn **III.** *vr* **1.** (*acabarse*) to pass; **ya se le ~á el enfado** his anger will soon subside; ~**se de fecha** to miss a deadline **2.** (*exagerar*) to go too far; ~**se de la raya** to go over the line; ~**se de listo** to be too clever by half **3.** (*por un sitio*) to visit; **me pasé un rato por casa de mi tía** I popped by my aunt's house for a while; **se me pasó por la cabeza que...** it occurred to me that...; ~**se la mano por el pelo** to run one's hand through one's hair **4.** *t.* MIL (*cam-*

biar) to go over **5.** (*olvidarse*) to be forgotten; **se me pasó tu cumpleaños** I forgot your birthday **6.** (*estropearse: alimentos, leche*) to go off; (*fruta*) to overripen; (*mantequilla*) to go rancid; (*flores*) to wilt; **se ha pasado el arroz** the rice is overcooked **7.** (*escaparse*) to be missed; **se me pasó la oportunidad** I missed my chance

pasarela [pa·sa·'re·la] *f* **1.** (*para desfiles*) catwalk **2.** (*de un barco*) gangway **3.** (*puente provisional*) temporary bridge; (*para peatones*) walkway

pasatiempo [pa·sa·'tjem·po] *m* **1.** (*diversión*) pastime; **los pasatiempos del periódico** the games and puzzles section of the newspaper **2.** (*hobby*) hobby

pascana [pas·'ka·na] *f* **1.** *AmS* (*etapa de un viaje*) stage **2.** *Arg, Bol, Perú* (*posada*) wayside inn

Pascua ['pas·kwa] *f* **1.** (*de resurrección*) Easter; **de ~s a Ramos** once in a blue moon; **hacer la ~ a alguien** *inf* to do the dirty on sb **2.** *pl* (*navidad*) Christmas time; **dar las ~s a alguien** to wish sb a merry Christmas **3.** *pl* (*pentecostés*) Whitsun ▶ **¡y santas ~s!** and that's that!; **estar como una(s) ~(s)** to be over the moon

pase ['pa·se] *m* **1.** (*desfile*) parade; (*de moda*) fashion show **2.** DEP pass **3.** *t.* MIL pass; (*licencia*) license; (*para entrar gratis*) free pass; **~ (de transporte)** travel pass **4.** *AmL* (*pasaporte*) passport

paseante [pa·se·'an·te] *adj* fond of walking

pasear [pa·se·'ar] **I.** *vt* (*en coche*) to take for a ride; (*a pie*) to take for a walk; **~ al perro** to walk the dog **II.** *vi, vr* (*a pie*) to go for a walk; (*en coche*) to go for a drive; (*a caballo*) to ride

paseo [pa·'se·o] *m* **1.** (*a pie*) walk; (*en coche, a caballo*) ride; (*en bici*) trip; **dar un ~** to go for a walk; **¡vete a ~!** get lost! **2.** (*para pasear*) avenue; **~ marítimo** promenade, esplanade

pasillo [pa·'si·ʝo, -ʎo] *m* (*corredor*) passage; (*entre habitaciones*) corridor, hallway

pasión [pa·'sjon] *f* passion; **con ~** passionately; **sin ~** without enthusiasm;

sentir ~ por el fútbol to be passionate about soccer

pasional [pa·sjo·'nal] *adj* passionate

pasividad [pa·si·βi·'ðað] *f* passivity, passiveness

pasivo [pa·'si·βo] *m* liabilities *pl*; (*en balance*) debit side

pasivo, -a [pa·'si·βo, -a] *adj t.* LING passive; **verbo ~** passive verb; **voz pasiva** passive

pasmar [pas·'mar] *vt* (*asombrar*) to astonish; **me has dejado pasmado** you have left me completely stunned

paso ['pa·so] *m* **1.** (*acción de pasar*) passing; **ceder el ~** (*a una persona*) to make way; (*en el tráfico*) to yield; **estar de ~** to be passing through; **nadie salió al ~ de sus mentiras** nobody put a stop to his/her lies **2.** (*movimiento*) step; (*progreso*) progress; **ir al ~** to keep in step; **marcar el ~** to mark the rhythm [*o* time]; **a cada ~** at every step; **~ a ~** step by step; **dar un ~ adelante/atrás** to take a step forwards/backwards; **dar un ~ en falso** to trip; *fig* to make a false move; **vive a dos ~s de mi casa** he/she lives very near to my house; **dar todos los ~s necesarios** *fig* to take all the necessary steps **3.** (*velocidad*) pace; **a ~s agigantados** with giant steps; *fig* by leaps and bounds; **a buen ~** quickly; **a ~ de tortuga** at snail's pace; **a este ~ no llegarás** at this speed you'll never get there **4.** (*pasillo*) passage; (*en el mar*) strait; (*entre montañas*) pass; **~ subterráneo** underground passage; **abrirse ~** to open up a path for oneself; *fig* to make one's way; **¡prohibido el ~!** (*pasar*) no thoroughfare!; (*entrar*) no entry!; **salir del ~ (con algo)** to get out of a jam (with sth) **5.** (*para atravesar algo*) crossing; **~ de cebra** zebra crossing; **a nivel** level crossing; **¡~!** make way! **6.** (*de un contador*) unit; **marcar los ~s** to count the units

pasota [pa·'so·ta] *mf inf* drop-out; **es un ~ total** he doesn't give a damn about anything

pasta ['pas·ta] *f* **1.** (*masa*) paste; (*para un pastel*) pastry; (*para paredes*) filler; (*para madera*) putty; **~ de dientes** toothpaste

P

2. (*comida italiana*) pasta **3.** (*pastelería*) pastries *pl* **4.** (*encuadernación*) cover; **de ~ dura/blanda** hardback/paperback **5.** *inf* (*dinero*) dough **6.** (*madera*) pulp; **tener ~ para algo** to be cut out for sth; **tener buena ~** to be good-natured

pastar [pas·'tar] *vi, vt* to graze

pastel [pas·'tel] *m* **1.** (*tarta*) cake; (*bollo*) pastry; (*de carne*) pie; **descubrir el ~** to catch on **2.** (*lápiz*) pastel crayon **3.** (*pintura*) pastel

pastelería [pas·te·le·'ri·a] *f* pastry shop

pastelero, -a [pas·te·'le·ro, -a] *m, f* (*repostero*) pastry chef

pastilla [pas·'ti·ja, -ʎa] *f* **1.** (*medicinal*) tablet; **~ contra el dolor** painkiller; **~ para la garganta** throat lozenge; **~ para la tos** cough drop **2.** (*dulce*) candy **3.** (*trozo*) piece; **~ de caldo** stock cube; **~ de jabón** bar of soap; **ir a toda ~** *inf* to go at full speed

pasto ['pas·to] *m* **1.** (*pastizal*) pasture **2.** (*hierba*) grass; **~ seco** fodder; **ser ~ de las llamas** to go up in flames

pastor [pas·'tor] *m* **1.** REL minister **2.** ZOOL **perro ~** sheepdog

pastor(a) [pas·'tor, -·'to·ra] *m(f)* (*de ganado*) herdsman *m;* (*de ovejas*) shepherd

pastorear [pas·to·re·'ar] *vt* **1.** (*el ganado*) to graze **2.** *AmC* (*mimar*) to spoil **3.** *AmL* (*atisbar*) to spy on

pastoso, -a [pas·'to·so, -a] *adj* **1.** (*voz*) mellow; **lengua pastosa** furred tongue **2.** *AmL* (*región*) grassy

pata ['pa·ta] *f* (*de un perro*) paw; (*de una silla*) leg; **~s de gallo** (*en el rostro*) crow's feet; **~ de palo** wooden leg; **mala ~** *inf* bad luck; **estirar la ~** *inf* to kick the bucket; **ir a ~** *inf* to go on foot; **~s arriba** upside down; **a la ~ coja** hopping; **a cuatro ~s** on all fours; **meter la ~** *inf* to put one's foot in it

patada [pa·'ta·da] *f* (*contra algo*) kick; (*en el suelo*) stamp; **dar una ~ contra la pared** to kick the wall; **dar ~s en el suelo** to stamp one's feet; **romper una puerta a ~s** to kick a door down; **echar a alguien a ~s** to kick sb out; **tratar a alguien a ~s** to treat sb like dirt; **a ~s** *fig* by the bucket load

patalear [pa·ta·le·'ar] *vi* to kick; (*en el suelo*) to stamp one's feet

patata [pa·'ta·ta] *f* potato; **~s fritas** French fries *pl;* **una bolsa de ~s fritas** a bag of potato chips; **tortilla de ~** Spanish omelet; **puré de ~** mashed potatoes **2.** ¡~! (*al hacer una foto*) cheese!

patatús [pa·ta·'tus] *m inv inf* (*desmayo*) faint; **le dio un ~** he/she fainted

patear [pa·te·'ar] **I.** *vt* **1.** (*dar golpes*) to kick **2.** (*pisotear*) to trample **3.** (*tratar rudamente*) to trample on **II.** *vi* **1.** (*en el suelo*) to stamp **2.** (*andar mucho*) to tramp around

patentar [pa·ten·'tar] *vt* to patent

patente [pa·'ten·te] **I.** *adj* **1.** (*visible*) clear **2.** (*evidente*) patent; **hacer ~** to establish; (*comprobar*) to prove; (*revelar*) to reveal **II.** *f* **1.** (*documento*) license; (*permiso*) permit; **~ de comercio** business license; **~ de sanidad** bill of health **2.** JUR patent; **~ industrial** industrial patent; **solicitar la ~** to apply for a patent

patera [pa·'te·ra] *f* small boat

paternal [pa·ter·'nal] *adj* paternal

paternidad [pa·ter·ni·'dad] *f* **1.** (*relación*) fatherhood; JUR paternity **2.** (*calidad*) fatherliness

paterno, -a [pa·'ter·no, -a] *adj* paternal; **mi abuelo ~** my paternal grandfather

patero, -a [pa·'te·ro, -a] *m, f* Chile bootlicker

patético, -a [pa·'te·ti·ko, -a] *adj pey* pathetic

patíbulo [pa·'ti·βu·lo] *m* scaffold; (*horca*) gallows *pl*

patilla [pa·'ti·ja, -ʎa] *f* **1.** (*de gafas*) sidepiece; (*de madero*) peg **2.** *pl* (*pelo*) sideburns *pl*

patín [pa·'tin] *m* **1.** (*de hielo*) ice skate; (*de ruedas*) roller skate; **patines en línea** rollerblades **2.** TÉC shoe

patinaje [pa·ti·'na·xe] *m* (*sobre hielo*) (ice) skating; (*sobre ruedas*) (roller) skating; **~ artístico** (*sobre hielo*) figure skating; **~ de velocidad** speed skating

patinar [pa·ti·'nar] *vi* **1.** (*sobre patines de hielo*) to (ice) skate; (*sobre patines de ruedas*) to (roller) skate **2.** (*deslizarse*) to slip; (*un vehículo*) to skid **3.** (*equivocarse*) to slip up

patinazo [pa·ti·'na·so, -θo] m 1. (*deslizamiento*) slip; (*de un vehículo*) skid 2. *inf* (*equivocación*) blunder

patinete [pa·ti·'ne·te] m scooter

patio ['pa·tjo] m (*interior*) courtyard; (*entre dos casas*) back yard; **~ de recreo** playground

pato, -a ['pa·to] m, f 1. ZOOL duck; (*macho*) drake 2. *inf* (*torpe*) clumsy person ▶ **pagar el ~** *inf* to carry the can

patógeno, -a [pa·'to·xe·no, -a] *adj* MED pathogen; **germen ~** harmful germ

patojo [pa·'to·xo] m, f Col, Guat kid *inf*

patológico, -a [pa·to·'lo·xi·ko, -a] *adj t. fig* pathological

patoso, -a [pa·'to·so, -a] *adj* 1. (*soso*) boring 2. (*torpe*) clumsy

patraña [pa·'tra·ɲa] f lie, pack of lies

patria ['pa·trja] f native land; **madre ~** mother country; *AmL* Spain

patrimonio [pa·tri·'mo·njo] m 1. (*herencia*) inheritance; **~ cultural** cultural heritage 2. (*riqueza*) wealth

patriota [pa·'trjo·ta] mf patriot

patriótico, -a [pa·'trjo·ti·ko, -a] *adj* patriotic

patriotismo [pa·trjo·'tis·mo] m patriotism

patrocinador(a) [pa·tro·si·na·'dor, -·'do·ra; patroθi-] m(f) t. DEP sponsor

patrocinar [pa·tro·si·'nar, pa·tro·θi·] vt t. DEP to sponsor

patrocinio [pa·tro·'si·njo, -'θi·njo] m 1. (*protección*) patronage 2. DEP sponsorship

patrón [pa·'tron] m (*modelo*) model; (*de costura*) pattern

patrón, -ona [pa·'tron, -·'tro·na] m, f 1. (*que protege*) patron m, patroness f 2. (*jefe*) boss 3. (*de una casa*) head; (*de una pensión*) landlord m, landlady f

patronal [pa·tro·'nal] I. *adj* (*empresario*) employers'; **cierre ~** lockout II. f (*asociación*) employers' organization

patrono, -a [pa·'tro·no, -a] m, f 1. (*jefe*) boss 2. (*de un feudo*) landowner 3. (*miembro del patronato*) board member 4. REL patron saint

patrulla [pa·'tru·ja, -ʎa] f t. MIL patrol;

estar de ~ to be on patrol

patrullar [pa·tru·'jar, -'ʎar] vi, vt to patrol

paturro, -a [pa·'tu·rro, -a] *adj* Col short and stocky

paulatino, -a [pau·la·'ti·no, -a] *adj* gradual

pausa ['pau·sa] f pause

pauta ['pau·ta] f 1. (*modelo*) guide 2. (*normas*) standard; **marcar la ~** to set the example [o standard] 3. (*regla*) rule

pava ['pa·βa] f 1. ZOOL v. **pavo. pava** 2. *AmL* (*olla*) pot; (*tetera*) tea kettle 3. *AmL* (*sombrero*) straw hat 4. *And, AmC* (*flecos*) fringe

pavimentar [pa·βi·men·'tar] vt (*con losas*) to pave; (*con asfalto*) to surface

pavimento [pa·βi·'men·to] m 1. (*recubrimiento: en una casa*) flooring; (*en la carretera*) surfacing 2. (*material: en una casa*) floor; (*en una carretera*) surface

pavo ['pa·βo] m *inf* (*dólar*) buck

pavo, -a ['pa·βo, -a] m, f turkey; (*persona*) idiot; **~ real** peacock; **estar en la edad del ~** *inf* to be at an awkward stage *(of one's adolescence)*; **no es moco de ~** *inf* it's not to be scoffed at [o sneezed]; **ir de ~** *AmL* to mooch a ride

pavor [pa·'βor] m terror

payada [pa·'ja·da] f CSur MÚS improvised song between two competing musicians, accompanied by guitars

payasada [pa·ja·'sa·da] f clowning; *pey* idiotic behavior

payaso, -a [pa·'ja·so, -a] m, f clown; **¡deja de hacer el ~!** stop fooling around!

payo, -a ['pa·jo, -a] m, f non-gypsy *(gypsy term to refer to people who are not gypsies)*

paz [pas, paθ] f peace; **hacer las paces** to make up; **estar en ~ con alguien** to be even with sb; **¡déjame en ~!** leave me alone!; **¡...y en ~!** ... and that's that!; **que en ~ descanse** may he/she rest in peace

P.D. [pos·'da·ta] *abr de* **posdata** P.S.

pe [pe] f p; **de ~ a pa** *inf* from A to Z

peaje [pe·'a·xe] m toll

peatón, -ona [pea·'ton, -·'to·na] *m, f* pedestrian

peca ['pe·ka] *f* freckle

pecado [pe·'ka·do] *m* sin; ~ **capital** deadly sin; ~ **original** original sin; **pagar sus** ~**s** to pay for one's sins; **sería un** ~ **rechazarlos** it would be a crying shame to reject them

pecador(a) [pe·ka·'dor, -·'do·ra] **I.** *adj* sinning **II.** *m(f)* sinner

pecar <c → qu> [pe·'kar] *vi* to sin; ~ **por exceso** to go too far; **peca por exceso de confianza** he/she is too confident by half

pecarí [pe·ka·'ri] *m AmL* ZOOL peccary

pecera [pe·'se·ra, -θe·ra] *f* fish tank; (*en forma de globo*) fishbowl

pecho ['pe·tʃo] *m* breast, chest; **dar el** ~ **al bebé** to breastfeed the baby; **a** ~ **descubierto** (*sin armas*) unarmed; *fig* openly; **tomarse algo muy a** ~ to take sth to heart

pechuga [pe·'tʃu·ɣa] *f* (*de ave*) breast; ~ **de pollo** chicken breast

pechugón, -ona [pe·tʃu·'ɣon] *adj* **1.** *AmL* (*descarado*) shameless **2.** *AmL* (*franco*) outspoken

pecoso, -a [pe·'ko·so, -a] *adj* freckly

pectoral [pek·to·'ral] **I.** *adj* **1.** ANAT pectoral **2.** (*contra la tos*) cough **II.** *m* MED pectoral

peculiar [pe·ku·'ljar] *adj* **1.** (*especial*) distinctive **2.** (*raro*) peculiar

peculiaridad [pe·ku·lja·ri·'dad] *f* **1.** (*singularidad*) peculiarity **2.** (*distintivo*) distinguishing feature

pedagogía [pe·da·ɣo·'xi·a] *f* pedagogy

pedagógico, -a [pe·da·'ɣo·xi·ko, -a] *adj* pedagogical

pedal [pe·'dal] *m* pedal; **pisar el** ~ AUTO to accelerate

pedalear [pe·da·le·'ar] *vi* to pedal

pedante [pe·'dan·te] *adj* pretentious, pedantic

pedazo [pe·'da·θo] *m* (big) piece; ~ **de papel** piece of paper; **caerse a** ~**s** to fall apart, to fall to pieces; **hacerse** ~**s** to fall to pieces; **hacer** ~**s** to break; (*madera*) to smash up; (*papel*) to tear up; **ser un** ~ **de pan** to be very good-natured; **¡**~

de bruto! *inf* you brute!

pedestal [pe·des·'tal] *m* pedestal; (*apoyo*) base; **poner a alguien en un** ~ to put sb on a pedestal

pediatra [pe·'dja·tra] *mf* pediatrician

pediatría [pe·dja·'tri·a] *f* pediatrics

pedicura [pe·di·'ku·ra] *f* pedicure; **hacerse la** ~ to get a pedicure

pedida [pe·'di·da] *f* ~ **de mano** asking for sb's hand in marriage

pedido [pe·'di·do] *m* COM order; (*de un servicio*) reservation; **enviar sobre** ~ to supply on request; **a** ~ to order

pedido, -a [pe·'di·do, -a] *adj* (*solicitado*) requested; (*encargado*) ordered

pedigrí [pe·di·'ɣri] *m* pedigree

pedir [pe·'dir] *irr vt* **1.** (*rogar*) to ask for; ~ **algo a alguien** to ask sb for sth; ~ **prestado** to borrow; **a** ~ **de boca** just right; ~ **la mano de alguien** to ask for sb's hand in marriage; ~ **limosna** to beg **2.** (*exigir*) to demand; (*necesitar*) to need; (*solicitar*) to request; ~ **a gritos algo** *fig* to be crying out for sth **3.** (*encargar*) to order

pedo ['pe·do] *m inf* **1.** (*ventosidad*) fart; **tirarse un** ~ to fart **2.** (*borrachera*) drunkenness

pedrada [pe·'dra·da] *f* throw of a stone; **matar a alguien a** ~**s** to stone sb to death

pedregullo [pe·dre·'ɣu·jo, -ʎo] *m CSur* gravel

pega ['pe·ɣa] *f* **1.** *inf* (*dificultades*) difficulty; **poner** ~**s a** to find fault with; **de** ~ fake **2.** *CSur, Méx inf* (*trabajo*) job

pegadizo, -a [pe·ɣa·'di·so, -a; -di·θo, -a] *adj* (*pegajoso*) sticky; (*enfermedad*) contagious; **melodía pegadiza** catchy tune

pegajoso, -a [pe·ɣa·'xo·so, -a] *adj* **1.** (*adhesivo*) sticky, adhesive **2.** (*persona*) tiresome; (*niño*) clinging

pegamento [pe·ɣa·'men·to] *m* glue; ~ **en barra** stick glue; ~ **de contacto** bonding cement

pegar <g → gu> [pe·'ɣar] **I.** *vt* **1.** (*aglutinar*) to stick; ~ **un sello** to attach a stamp; **no** ~ **ojo** not to sleep a wink **2.** (*muebles*) ~ **la mesilla a la cama**

to put the side table right next to the bed **3.** (*contagiar*) to give **4.** (*golpear*) to hit; **~ una paliza a alguien** to beat sb up **5.** (*un grito*) to let out; (*un tiro*) to fire; **~ una bofetada** to slap; **~ un salto** to jump; **~ un susto a alguien** to frighten sb **6.** COMPUT to paste **7.** *AmL inf* (*tener suerte*) to be lucky; **~la** to get what one wants **8.** *Méx* (*atar*) to tie **II.** *vi* **1.** (*hacer juego*) to go together; **esto no pega ni con cola** this really doesn't go **2.** (*rozar*) **~ en algo** to brush against sth; (*tocar*) to touch sth **3.** (*golpear*) to beat; **¡cómo pega el sol!** *inf* the sun is burning hot! **4.** *inf* (*currar*) to work hard; **no ~ golpe** not to do a thing **III.** *vr* **1.** (*impactar*) **~se con algo** to bump into sth; **~se con alguien** to fight with sb **2.** (*quemarse*) to stick to the pot **3.** (*acompañar siempre*) **~se a alguien** to stick to sb (like glue); (*perseguir*) to follow sb **4.** (*contagiarse*) **se me pegó el sarampión** I caught [*o* got] the measles **5.** *inf* (*engañar*) **pegársela a alguien** *inf* to trick sb **6.** *inf* (*darse*) **~se la gran vida** to live it up; **~se un tiro** to shoot oneself

pegatina [pe·ɣa·'ti·na] *f* sticker

pegote [pe·'ɣo·te] *m* **esa corbata es un ~** that tie just doesn't go; **tirarse ~s** to show off

peinado [pei·'na·do] *m* hairstyle, hairdo

peinado, -a [pei·'na·do, -a] *adj* combed

peinar [pei·'nar] **I.** *vt* to comb; (*acicalar*) to style **II.** *vr* to comb one's hair; (*arreglar el pelo*) to style [*o* to do] one's hair

peine ['pei·ne] *m* comb; **¡te vas a enterar de lo que vale un ~!** *fig* you'll soon find out what's what!

peineta [pei·'ne·ta] *f* Spanish ornamental comb

p.ej. [por e·'xem·plo] *abr de* **por ejemplo** e.g.

pela ['pe·la] *f inf* (*dinero*) **no me quedan más ~s** I have no money left

pelado [pe·'la·do] *m inf* poor wretch

pelado, -a [pe·'la·do, -a] *adj* **1.** (*rapado*) shorn **2.** (*escueto*) bare **3.** *inf* (*sin dinero*) broke

pelambrera [pe·lam·'bre·ra] *f* mop

pelapatatas [pe·la·pa·'ta·tas] *m inv* potato peeler

pelar [pe·'lar] **I.** *vt* **1.** (*pelo*) to cut; (*rapar*) to shear; (*frutas*) to peel; **ser duro de ~** to be a hard nut to crack **2.** *AmL inf* (*dar una paliza*) to beat up **3.** *Andinf* (*morir*) to kick the bucket **II.** *vr* **1.** (*el pelo*) to have one's hair cut **2.** (*la piel*) to peel **3.** *inf* (*intensificador*) **corre que se las pela** he/she is a really fast runner; **pelárselas por algo** to be crazy about sth

peldaño [pel·'da·no] *m* step

pelea [pe·'le·a] *f* fight; (*verbal*) quarrel, argument; **buscar ~** to be looking for trouble

pelear [pe·le·'ar] **I.** *vi* to fight; (*discutir*) to argue; **~ por algo** (*trabajar*) to struggle for sth **II.** *vr* **1.** (*con violencia*) **~se por algo** to fight over sth; (*verbal*) to argue about sth **2.** (*enemistarse*) to fall out

pelele [pe·'le·le] *m* **1.** (*muñeco*) rag doll **2.** *inf* (*persona*) puppet

peletería [pe·le·te·'ri·a] *f* **1.** (*costura*) furrier's; (*venta*) fur shop **2.** *AmC* (*zapatería*) shoe store

pelícano [pe·'li·ka·no] *m* pelican

película [pe·'li·ku·la] *f* film, movie; **~ en blanco y negro** black and white movie; **~ muda** silent film [*o* movie]; **~ de suspense** thriller; **~ de terror** horror film [*o* movie]; **~ del oeste** western; **de ~** *inf* sensational; **como de ~** like sth out of the movies; **poner en ~** to film; **echar una ~** to show a film

peligrar [pe·li·'ɣrar] *vi* to be in danger; **hacer ~** to endanger

peligro [pe·'li·ɣro] *m* danger; **~ de incendio** fire risk; **correr ~** to run a risk; **estar en ~ de muerte** to be in mortal danger; **fuera de ~** out of danger; **poner en ~** to endanger; **poniendo en ~ su propia vida** risking his/her own life

peligroso, -a [pe·li·'ɣro·so, -a] *adj* dangerous

pelillo [pe·'li·jo, -ʎo] *m inf* trifle; **¡~s a la mar!** let bygones be bygones!

P

pelirrojo, -a [pe·li·'rro·xo, -a] *adj* red-haired

pellejo [pe·'je·xo, -'ʎe·xo] *m* **1.** (*de animal*) hide **2.** (*de persona*) skin; **no tener más que el ~** to be all skin and bones; **no caber en su ~** *fig* to be bursting with pride; **si yo estuviera en tu ~...** *inf* if I were in your shoes...; **salvar el ~** *inf* to save one's skin; **arriesgar el ~** to risk one's neck **3.** (*odre*) wineskin **4.** (*fruta*) peel; (*salchicha*) skin

pellizcar <c → qu> [pe·jis·'kar, -ʎiθ·'kar] **I.** *vt* **1.** (*repizcar*) to pinch **2.** *inf* (*pizcar algo*) to take a pinch of **II.** *vr* to pinch oneself

pellizco [pe·'jis·ko, -ʎiθ·ko] *m* **1.** (*pizco*) pinch; **dar un ~ a alguien** to pinch sb **2.** (*poquito: de sal*) pinch; (*de bocadillo*) nibble

pelma ['pel·ma] *mf inf*, **pelmazo, -a** [pel·'ma·so, -a; -θo, -θa] *m, f inf* bore, drag

pelo ['pe·lo] *m* **1.** (*cabello*) hair; (*de animal*) fur; (*de barba*) whisker; **tener el ~ rubio** to have fair hair; **cortarse el ~** to get one's hair cut; **soltarse el ~** to let one's hair down; *fig* to show one's true colors **2.** (*vello*) fluff; (*pelusa*) fluff; (*de alfombra*) pile **3.** (+ *al*) **al ~** perfectly; **todo irá al ~** everything will be fine; **venir al ~** to be just right, to happen [*o* come] at just the right time **4.** *inf* (*poco*) **por un ~ te caes** you very nearly fell; **escaparse por un ~** to escape by the skin of one's teeth ▸ **no tener ~s en la lengua** *inf* not to mince words; **un hombre de ~ en pecho** a real man; **ponerle a uno los ~s de punta** to make one's hair stand on end; **no tocar un ~ (de la ropa) a alguien** *inf* not to lay a finger on sb; **contar algo con ~s y señales** *inf* to describe sth in great detail; **no tener (un) ~ de tonto** *inf* to be nobody's fool; **estar hasta los ~s** *inf* to be fed up; **tomar el ~ a alguien** *inf* to pull sb's leg; **a ~** (*la cabeza descubierta*) bare-headed; (*sin prepararse*) unprepared

pelota¹ [pe·'lo·ta] *f* **1.** (*balón*) ball; **devolver la ~ a alguien** (*argumentar*) to turn the tables on sb; (*vengarse*) to give sb a taste of their own medicine; **la ~ sigue en el tejado** *fig* things are still up in the air **2.** (*juego*) pelota

pelota² [pe·'lo·ta] *m inf* crawler

pelotazo [pe·lo·'ta·so, -θo] *m* **1.** (*con el pie*) shot; (*tirando*) throw; (*con la raqueta*) stroke **2.** *inf* (*bebida*) slug; **meterse un ~** to have a drink

pelotear [pe·lo·te·'ar] *vi* (*tenis*) to toss back and forth; (*fútbol*) to kick around

pelotera [pe·lo·'te·ra] *f inf* fight

pelotón [pe·lo·'ton] *m* (*de gente*) crowd; (*en carreras*) pack; **~ de ejecución** firing squad

peluca [pe·'lu·ka] *f* wig

peluche [pe·'lu·tʃe] *m* (*juguete*) soft toy; **oso de ~** teddy bear

peludo, -a [pe·'lu·do] *adj* **1.** hairy **2.** *AmC inf* (*difícil*) tricky

peluquería [pe·lu·ke·'ri·a] *f* hairdresser's; **ir a la ~** to go to the hairdresser's

peluquero, -a [pe·lu·'ke·ro, -a] *m, f* hairdresser

pelusa [pe·'lu·sa] *f* (*vello*) down; (*tejido*) fluff; (*de polvo*) fluff; **sentir ~** to be jealous

pelvis ['pel·βis] *f inv* pelvis

pena ['pe·na] *f* **1.** (*tristeza*) sorrow; **ahogar las ~s** to drown one's sorrows **2.** (*lástima*) **ser una ~** to be a pity; **¡qué ~!** what a shame!; **ella me da ~** I feel really sorry for her **3.** (*sanción*) punishment; **~ capital** capital punishment **4.** (*dificultad*) trouble; **a duras ~s** with great difficulty; (*apenas*) scarcely; **sin ~ ni gloria** undistinguished; **valer la ~** to be worth the effort [*o* the trouble] **5.** *AmL* (*vergüenza*) shame; **tener ~** to be ashamed

penal [pe·'nal] **I.** *adj* JUR penal; **antecedentes ~es** criminal record **II.** *m* **1.** (*prisión*) prison **2.** *AmL* (*falta*) foul (*inside the penalty area*)

penalización [pe·na·li·sa·'sjon, -θa·'θjon] *f* penalization

penalizar <z → c> [pe·na·li·'sar, -'θar] *vt* to penalize

penalti [pe·'nal·ti] *m* **1.** (*falta*) foul (*inside the penalty area*) **2.** (*sanción*)

penalty; casarse de ~ inf to have a shotgun wedding

penar [pe·'nar] **I.** *vt* to punish **II.** *vi* **1.** (*padecer*) to suffer **2.** (*ansiar*) ~ **por algo** to long for sth

pendejada [pen·de·'xa·da] *f* AmL inf **1.** (*disparate*) stupidity **2.** (*acto cobarde*) cowardly act

pendejear [pen·de·xe·'ar] *vi* Col, Méx inf to mess [*o* to fool] around

pendejo, -a [pen·'de·xo] *m, f* Arg inf fool

pender [pen·'der] *vi* to hang

pendiente¹ [pen·'djen·te] **I.** *adj* **1.** (*colgado*) hanging **2.** (*problema, asunto*) unresolved; (*trabajo, pedido*) outstanding; **una cuenta ~ de pago** an outstanding account; **quedar ~ una asignatura** to have one subject left to pass *(as a resit or carried over to next year)* **3.** *inf* (*ocuparse*) **estate ~ del arroz** keep an eye on the rice **4.** (*depender*) **estamos ~s de lo que digan nuestros padres** it all depends on what our parents say **II.** *m* (*de oreja*) earring; (*de nariz*) nose ring

pendiente² [pen·'djen·te] *f* (*cuesta, del tejado*) slope; **de mucha ~** steep

pendón [pen·'don] *m* banner

péndulo ['pen·du·lo] *m* pendulum

penetrante [pe·ne·'tran·te] *adj* **1.** (*profundo*) deep; (*dolor*) fierce **2.** (*frío*) biting; (*hedor*) strong; (*olor*) penetrating **3.** (*sonido*) penetrating; (*grito*) piercing

penetrar [pe·ne·'trar] *vi, vt* (*atravesar*) to penetrate

penicilina [pe·ni·si·'li·na, pe·ni·θi-] *f* MED penicillin

península [pe·'nin·su·la] *f* GEO peninsula; **la Península Ibérica** the Iberian Peninsula

peninsular [pe·nin·su·'lar] *adj* peninsular

penique [pe·'ni·ke] *m* penny

penitencia [pe·ni·'ten·sja, -θja] *f* **1.** (*pena*) punishment **2.** REL penance; **hacer ~** to do penance **3.** (*arrepentimiento*) penitence

penitenciario, -a [pe·ni·ten·'sja·rjo, -'θja·rjo] *adj* (*relativo a la penitenciaría*) penitentiary

penoso, -a [pe·'no·so, -a] *adj* **1.** (*ar-*

duo) laborious **2.** (*dificultoso*) difficult **3.** AmL (*vergonzoso*) shameful

pensado, -a [pen·'sa·do, -a] *adj* **1.** (*reflexionado*) considered; **lo tengo bien ~** I have thought it through thoroughly; **tener ~ hacer algo** to have it in mind to do sth; **el día menos ~ volverá** just when it's least expected he/she will return **2.** (*persona*) **ser un mal ~** to always be ready to think the worst

pensamiento [pen·sa·'mjen·to] *m* **1.** (*acción, idea, objeto*) thought **2.** (*intención*) intention **3.** (*mente*) mind; **¿cuándo te vino esa idea al ~?** when did that idea occur to you? **4.** BOT pansy

pensar <e → ie> [pen·'sar] **I.** *vi, vt* **1.** (*formar un juicio, reflexionar*) ~ **(en) algo** to think (about) sth; **¡ni ~lo!** don't even think about it!; **¡no quiero ni ~lo!** I don't even want to think about it!; **dar mucho que ~** to give people a lot to think about; **esto hay que ~lo bien** this needs to be thought out carefully; **lo hicimos sin ~lo** we did it without thinking; **pensándolo bien** on reflection; **pienso que deberíamos irnos** I think we should go **2.** (*considerar*) to consider **II.** *vi* (*opinar, suponer*) to think; ~ **muy mal de alguien** to think very badly of sb **III.** *vt* **1.** (*intención*) to think of; **pensábamos venir este fin de semana** we were thinking of coming this weekend **2.** (*inventar, tramar*) to think up

pensativo, -a [pen·sa·'ti·βo, -a] *adj* thoughtful, pensive

pensión [pen·'sjon] *f* **1.** (*paga*) pension; ~ **de viudez** widow's pension; **aún no cobra la ~** (*no recibe la paga*) he/she doesn't get a pension yet **2.** (*para huéspedes*) guesthouse **3.** (*precio por alojamiento*) (charge for) board and lodging; ~ **completa** full board

pensionista [pen·sjo·'nis·ta] *mf* (*jubilado*) pensioner

pentágono [pen·'ta·γo·no] *m* pentagon

pentagrama [pen·ta·'γra·ma] *m* MÚS stave, staff

Pentecostés [pen·te·kos·'tes] *m* REL **1.** (*cristiano*) Whitsun **2.** (*judío*) Pentecost

penúltimo, -a [pe.'nul·ti·mo, -a] *adj* penultimate, next-to-last

penumbra [pe.'num·bra] *f* semi-darkness; ASTR penumbra

penuria [pe.'nu·rja] *f* 1. (*escasez*) scarcity; **pasar muchas ~s** to suffer great hardship 2. (*pobreza*) poverty

peña ['pe·ɲa] *f* 1. (*roca*) crag 2. (*grupo*) group; (*de aficionados*) club; *inf* (*de jóvenes*) gang

peñasco [pe.'ɲas·ko] *m* boulder

peñón [pe.'ɲon] *m* 1. (*peñasco*) crag; **el Peñón** the Rock (of Gibraltar) 2. (*monte*) mountain

peón [pe.'on] *m* 1. (*obrero*) unskilled laborer; *Méx* (*aprendiz*) apprentice 2. (*en ajedrez*) pawn

peonza [pe.'on·sa, -θa] *f* (*juguete*) top

peor [pe.'or] *adv, adj comp de* **mal(o)** worse; **en matemáticas soy ~ que tú** I am worse at math than you are; **el ~ de la clase** the worst in the class; **y verás, será ~ aún** you'll see, it will get even worse; **en el ~ de los casos** at worst; **pero lo ~ de todo fue...** but the worst thing of all was...; **vas de mal en ~** you're going from bad to worse

pepinillo [pe·pi·'ni·jo, -ʎo] *m* gherkin

pepino [pe.'pi·no] *m* cucumber; **eso me importa un ~** *inf* I don't give a hoot about that

pepita [pe.'pi·ta] *f* seed

pequeñajo, -a [pe.ke.'ɲa·xo, -a] *m, f inf* kid

pequeñez [pe.ke.'ɲes, -'ɲeθ] *f* 1. (*tamaño*) littleness 2. (*bagatela*) trifle

pequeño, -a [pe.'ke·ɲo, -a] **I.** *adj* small, little; **ya desde ~ solía venir a este sitio** I've been coming here since I was little; **esta camisa me queda pequeña** this shirt is too small for me **II.** *m, f* little one

pequinés [pe.ki.'nes] *m* ZOOL Pekinese

pequinés, -esa [pe.ki.'nes, -·'ne·sa] *adj, m, f* Pekinese

pera ['pe·ra] *f* BOT pear ▶ **pedir ~s al olmo** *inf* to ask for the impossible; **eso es la ~** *inf* that's the limit

peral [pe.'ral] *m* pear tree

percance [per.'kan·se, -θe] *m* (*contratiempo*) setback

per cápita [per 'ka.pi·ta] *adv* per capita; **consumo ~** per capita consumption

percatarse [per.ka.'tar·se] *vr* **~ de algo** (*darse cuenta*) to notice sth; (*comprender*) to realize sth

percepción [per.sep.'sjon, -θeθ.'θjon] *f* 1. (*acción*) perception 2. (*impresión*) impression 3. FIN receipt

percha ['per·tʃa] *f* 1. (*en el armario*) hanger 2. (*perchero*) coat stand; (*en la tienda*) clothes rail 3. *AmC* (*chaqueta*) jacket 4. *inf* (*tipo*) build; **tener buena ~** to have a good figure

perchero [per.'tʃe·ro] *m* **~ (de pared)** coat rack; **~ (de pie)** coat stand

percibir [per.si.'βir, per.θi-] *vt* 1. (*notar*) to perceive 2. (*darse cuenta*) to notice 3. (*cobrar*) to receive

percusión [per.ku.'sjon] *f* MÚS percussion; **instrumento de ~** percussion instrument

perdedor(a) [per.'de·dor, -·'do·ra] *m(f)* loser

perder <e → ie> [per.'der] **I.** *vt* 1. (*en general, peso, costumbre*) to lose; **~ la cuenta** to lose count; **he perdido mis gafas** I lost my glasses; **~ terreno** *fig* to lose ground 2. (*malgastar*) to waste 3. (*oportunidad, tren*) to miss 4. (*ocasionar daños*) to destroy; **esa equivocación nos perdió** that mistake was our undoing; **el juego lo ~á** gambling will be his undoing **II.** *vi* 1. (*en general*) to lose; **Portugal perdió por 1 a 2 frente a Italia** Portugal lost 2-1 against Italy; **vas a salir perdiendo** you're going to come off worst; **llevar todas las de ~** to be fighting a losing battle; **lo echó todo a ~** he/she spoiled everything; **la comida se echó a ~** the food was completely ruined 2. (*decaer*) to decline; **~ en salud** to decline in health **III.** *vr* 1. (*extraviarse*) to get lost; **¡qué se le habrá perdido por allí?** *fig* what is he/she doing there? 2. (*bailando, leyendo*) to lose oneself 3. (*desaparecer*) to disappear 4. (*desperdiciarse*) to be wasted; **se pierde mucha agua por falta de conciencia ecológica** a lot of water is wasted through lack of environmental awareness 5. (*ocasión*) to miss

out; **si no te vienes, tú te lo pierdes** if you don't come, you'll be the one who misses out **6.** (*anhelar*) **~se por algo/ alguien** to be crazy about sth/sb

perdición [per·di·ˈsjon, -ˈθjon] *f* **1.** (*acción*) loss; (*daño*) ruin **2.** (*moral*) perdition

pérdida [ˈper·di·da] *f* loss; **~ de cabello** hair loss; **esto es una ~ de tiempo** this is a waste of time; **es fácil de encontrar, no tiene ~** it's easy to find, you can't miss it; **~s humanas** victims

perdido, -a [per·ˈdi·do, -a] *adj* **1.** (*que no se encuentra*) lost; **dar algo/a alguien por ~** to give sth/sb up for lost; *fig* to give up on sth/sb; **estar ~** to be lost **2.** (*vicioso, sin salida*) lost; **estar loco ~** *inf* to be completely insane **3.** (*sucio*) **poner algo ~** *inf* to make sth completely dirty; **ponerse ~ de pintura** *inf* to get covered in paint

perdiz [per·ˈdis, -ˈdiθ] *f* partridge; **...y fueron felices y comieron perdices** ...and they lived happily ever after

perdón [per·ˈdon] *m* **1.** (*absolución, indulto*) pardon **2.** (*disculpa*) **¡~!** sorry!; **¿~?** pardon?; **¡con ~!** if you'll excuse me!; **pedir ~ a alguien** to ask for sb's forgiveness; (*disculparse*) to apologize to sb

perdonar [per·do·ˈnar] *vt* **1.** (*ofensa, deuda*) to forgive; (*pecado, pena*) to pardon; **no te perdono** I don't forgive you; **perdona que te interrumpa** forgive me for interrupting; **perdona, ¿puedo pasar?** excuse me, can I come through? **2.** (*obligación*) to let off; **te perdono los 20 dólares** I'll forget about the 20 dollars you owe me **3.** (*dejar pasar*) **no ~ ningún medio** to use all possible means

perdurar [per·du·ˈrar] *vi* **1.** (*todavía*) to persist **2.** (*indefinidamente*) to last for ever; **su recuerdo ~á para siempre entre nosotros** his/her memory will always be with us

perecedero, -a [pe·re·se·ˈde·ro, -a; pe·re·θe-] *adj* **1.** (*pasajero*) transitory **2.** (*alimento*) perishable

perecer [pe·re·ˈser, -ˈθer] *irr como crecer* *vi* (*morir*) to perish

peregrinación [pe·re·ɣri·na·ˈsjon, -ˈθjon] *f* REL pilgrimage

peregrinar [pe·re·ɣri·ˈnar] *vi* REL to make a pilgrimage

peregrino, -a [pe·re·ˈɣri·no, -a] *m, f* pilgrim

perejil [pe·re·ˈxil] *m* BOT parsley

perenne [pe·ˈren·ne] *adj* everlasting; BOT perennial

pereza [pe·ˈre·sa, -θa] *f* (*gandulería*) laziness; **me dio ~ ir** I didn't feel like going

perezosa [pe·re·ˈso·sa, -ˈθo·sa] *f* Arg, Perú, Urug deck chair

perezoso, -a [pe·re·ˈso·so, -ˈθo·so] *adj* (*gandul*) lazy; **y ni corto ni ~** *inf* without giving it a thought

perfección [per·fek·ˈsjon, -ˈθjon] *f* perfection; **hacer algo a la ~** to do sth to perfection

perfeccionamiento [per·fek·sjo·na·ˈmjen·to, -θjo·na·ˈmjen·to] *m* perfection; (*técnica, sistema*) improvement; (*profesional*) further training

perfeccionar [per·fek·sjo·ˈnar, -θjo·ˈnar] *vt* to perfect; (*de técnica, sistema*) to improve

perfeccionista [per·fek·sjo·ˈnis·ta, -θjo·ˈnis·ta] *adj, mf* perfectionist

perfectamente [per·fek·ta·ˈmen·te] *adv* perfectly; **sabes ~ que...** you know perfectly well that...

perfecto [per·ˈfek·to] *m* LING perfect tense

perfecto, -a [per·ˈfek·to, -a] *adj* **1.** perfect; **nadie es ~** nobody is perfect; **habla un inglés ~** he/she speaks perfect English; **un ~ caballero** a perfect gentleman; **eres un ~ idiota** you are a complete idiot **2.** LING **pretérito ~** past perfect

perfil [per·ˈfil] *m* **1.** *t.* TÉC (*de cara*) profile; **de ~** in profile **2.** (*contorno*) outline **3.** (*de personalidad*) characteristics *pl*; **el ~ del candidato** the description of the candidate

perfilar [per·fi·ˈlar] **I.** *vt* **1.** (*retocar*) to touch up **2.** (*sacar perfil*) to outline; TÉC to streamline **II.** *vr* **1.** (*distinguirse*) to stand out **2.** (*tomar forma*) to take shape

perforar [per·fo·'rar] *vt* (*con máquina*) to drill; (*oreja*) to pierce; (*papel*) to punch; (*para decorar, arrancar*) to perforate

perfumar [per·fu·'mar] *vt* to perfume; **las flores perfuman la habitación** the smell of flowers fills the room

perfume [per·'fu·me] *m* **1.** (*sustancia*) perfume **2.** (*olor*) fragrance

perfumería [per·fu·me·'ri·a] *f* perfume shop

pericial [pe·ri·'sjal, -'θjal] *adj* expert; **informe ~** expert report

periferia [pe·ri·'fe·rja] *f* periphery; (*de ciudad*) outskirts *pl*

perilla [pe·'ri·ja, -ʎa] *f* goatee ▶ **venir de ~s** to be just what was needed

perímetro [pe·'ri·me·tro] *m* MAT perimeter

periódico [pe·'rjo·di·ko] *m* newspaper

periódico, -a [pe·'rjo·di·ko, -a] *adj* periodic; **sistema ~** QUÍM periodic table

periodismo [pe·rjo·'dis·mo] *m* journalism

periodista [pe·rjo·'dis·ta] *mf* journalist

periodístico, -a [pe·rjo·'dis·ti·ko, -a] *adj* **1.** (*de los periodistas*) journalistic **2.** (*de los periódicos*) newspaper; **reportaje ~** newspaper report

periodo [pe·'rjo·do] *m*, **período** [pe·'ri·o·do] *m t.* MAT, FÍS, GEO period; **~ álgido** critical period; **~ glacial** ice age; **~ de prueba** trial period

peripecia [pe·ri·'pe·sja, -θja] *f* vicissitude; **pasar por muchas ~s** to go through many ups and downs

periquete [pe·ri·'ke·te] *m* **estoy lista en un ~** I'll be ready in a jiffy

periquito [pe·ri·'ki·to] *m* parakeet

periscopio [pe·ris·'ko·pjo] *m* periscope

perito, -a [pe·'ri·to, -a] *m, f* (*experto*) expert

perjudicar <c → qu> [per·xu·di·'kar] *vt* **1.** (*causar daño*) to damage; (*intereses*) to harm; **fumar perjudica la salud** smoking is bad for your health **2.** (*causar desventaja*) to disadvantage

perjudicial [per·xu·di·'sjal, -'θjal] *adj* **1.** (*que causa daño*) harmful **2.** (*desventajoso*) disadvantageous

perjuicio [per·'xwi·sjo, -θjo] *m* **1.** (*daño: de imagen, naturaleza*) harm; (*de obje-*

to) damage; **causar ~s** to cause harm **2.** (*detrimento*) detriment; **ir en ~ de alguien** to be to sb's detriment

perjurio [per·'xu·rjo] *m* **1.** (*en falso*) perjury **2.** (*faltar al juramento*) breaking one's word

perla ['per·la] *f* pearl; **~ cultivada** cultured pearl; **eso viene de ~s** that is just what was needed

permanecer [per·ma·ne·'ser, -'θer] *irr como crecer vi* to remain; **~ quieto** to keep still; **~ invariable** to remain unchanged; **~ dormido** to carry on sleeping; **~ sentado** to remain seated

permanencia [per·ma·'nen·sja, -θja] *f* **1.** (*estancia*) stay; (*duración*) duration; **lograr la ~ en primera** DEP to stay in the first division

permanente [per·ma·'nen·te] **I.** *adj* permanent; **estado ~** permanent state **II.** *f* perm

permeable [per·me·'a·βle] *adj* permeable

permisividad [per·mi·si·βi·'dad] *f* permissiveness

permisivo, -a [per·mi·'si·βo, -a] *adj* permissive

permiso [per·'mi·so] *m* **1.** (*aprobación, autorización*) permission; **me dio ~ para hacerlo** he/she gave me permission to do it; **pedir ~ a alguien** to ask sb for permission **2.** (*licencia*) permit; **~ de conducir** driver's license; **~ de residencia/de trabajo** residence/work permit **3.** (*vacaciones*) leave; **estar de ~** MIL to be on leave

permitir [per·mi·'tir] **I.** *vt* **1.** (*consentir*) to permit; **¿me permite pasar/entrar/salir?** may I get past/enter/leave?; **no está permitido fumar** smoking is not allowed; **si me permite la expresión** if you will excuse the phrase **2.** (*autorizar*) to authorize **3.** (*hacer posible, tolerar*) to allow; **esta máquina permite trabajar el doble** this machine allows you to do twice as much work; **no permito que me levantes la voz** I won't allow you to raise your voice to me **II.** *vr* to allow oneself

pernera [per·'ne·ra] *f* (*pant*) leg

pernicioso, -a [per·ni·'sjo·so, -a; -'θjo·so,

-a] *adj* damaging

pernoctar [per·nok·'tar] *vi* to spend the night

pero ['pe·ro] **I.** *conj* but; (*sin embargo*) however; ¡~ **si todavía es una niña!** but she is still only a child!; ¿~ **qué es lo que quieres?** what do you want? **II.** *m* (*objeción*) objection; **el proyecto tiene sus** ~**s** there are lots of problems with the project; **sin un** ~ no buts; **poner** ~**s a algo** to object to sth; ¡**no hay** ~ **que valga!** there are no buts about it!; **poner** ~**s a todo** to object to everything

peroné [pe·ro·'ne] *m* fibula

perpendicular [per·pen·di·ku·'lar] *adj, f* perpendicular

perpetrar [per·pe·'trar] *vt* to perpetrate

perpetuar <*1. pres* perpetúo> [per·pe·tu·'ar] **I.** *vt* **1.** (*recuerdo, memoria, nombre*) to preserve **2.** (*situación, error, mentira*) to perpetuate **II.** *vr* to be perpetuated

perpetuidad [per·pe·twi·'dad] *f* **1.** (*continuidad*) continuity **2.** (*eternidad*) perpetuity; **a** ~ in perpetuity; **condenar a** ~ to condemn to life imprisonment

perpetuo, -a [per·'pe·two, -a] *adj* **1.** (*incesante*) perpetual; **nieves perpetuas** permanent snow **2.** (*vitalicio*) life; **cadena perpetua** life sentence

perplejo, -a [per·'ple·xo, -a] *adj* perplexed

perra ['pe·rra] *f* **1.** ZOOL bitch; *v. t.* **perro** I. **2.** *inf* (*rabieta*) tantrum; **coger una** ~ to throw a tantrum **3.** (*mujer malvada*) bitch **4.** *inf* (*dinero*) penny; **no tener una** ~ to be broke

perrera [pe·'rre·ra] *f* (*de perros callejeros*) dog pound

perrito [pe·'rri·to] *m* = **caliente** hot dog

perro, -a ['pe·rro] **I.** *m, f* (*macho*) dog; (*hembra*) bitch; ~ **callejero** stray dog; ~ **faldero** lapdog; ~ **lazarillo** guide-dog; **morir como un** ~ *inf* to die a lonely death ▶ **se llevan como el** ~ **y el gato** *inf* they fight like cat and dog; **ser como el** ~ **del hortelano** to be a dog in the manger; **humor de** ~**s** *inf* filthy mood; **a** ~ **flaco todo son pulgas** *prov* misfortunes never come singly; **tiempo de** ~**s** *inf* filthy weather; ~ **ladrador,**

poco mordedor *prov* his bark is worse than his bite; **muerto el** ~ **se acabó la rabia** *prov* dead dogs don't bite; **ser** ~ **viejo** *inf* to be an old hand **II.** *adj* lousy; **llevar una vida perra** to lead a wretched life

persa ['per·sa] *adj* Persian; **alfombra** ~ Persian rug

persecución [per·se·ku·'sjon, -'θjon] *f* pursuit; (*acoso*) persecution; ~ **en coche** car chase

perseguir [per·se·'ɣir] *irr como seguir vt* to chase; (*contrato, chica*) to pursue; **la policía persigue al fugitivo** the police are pursuing the fugitive; **me persigue la mala suerte** I am dogged by bad luck; **el jefe me persigue todo el día** the boss is always on my back; ¡**qué persigues con esto?** what do you hope to achieve by this?

perseverancia [per·se·βe·'ransja, -θja] *f* **1.** (*insistencia*) ~ **en algo** insistence on sth **2.** (*en trabajo, actividad*) ~ **en algo** perseverance in sth **3.** (*firmeza*) resolve

perseverante [per·se·βe·'ran·te] *adj* **1.** (*insistente*) insistent **2.** (*constante*) persevering **3.** (*firme*) determined

perseverar [per·se·βe·'rar] *vi* **1.** (*insistir*) to insist **2.** (*mantener*) ~ **en algo** to persevere in sth

Persia ['per·sja] *f* Persia

persiana [per·'sja·na] *f* blind

persignarse [per·siɣ·'nar·se] *vr* to cross oneself

persistencia [per·sis·'ten·sja, -θja] *f* persistence

persistente [per·sis·'ten·te] *adj* persistent

persistir [per·sis·'tir] *vi* to persist

persona [per·'so·na] *f* person; ~ **de contacto** contact; ~ (**non) grata** persona (non) grata; **en** ~ in person; ~ **jurídica** legal entity; ~ **mayor** adult, grown-up; ~ **física** individual; **ser buena/mala** ~ to be good/bad; **había muchas** ~**s** there were a lot of people; **no había ninguna** ~ **allí** there was nobody there; **ese es una** ~ **de cuidado** you need to be careful with him

personaje [per·so·'na·xe] *m* personality; TEAT, LIT character; **es todo un** ~ he/she is a real character

P

personal [per·so·'nal] **I.** *adj* personal; **datos ~es** personal details; **pronombre ~** personal pronoun **II.** *m* **1.** (*plantilla*) personnel; (*en empresa*) staff; **~ docente** teaching staff **2.** *inf* (*gente*) people *pl*

personalidad [per·so·na·li·'dad] *f* personality

personalizar <z → c> [per·so·na·li·'sar, ·'θar] *vt* **1.** (*hacer personal*) to personalize **2.** (*aludir*) to get personal

personarse [per·so·'nar·se] *vr* to appear; **~ en juicio** to appear before the court; **persónese ante el director** report to the director

personificar <c → qu> [per·so·ni·fi·'kar] *vt* to personify; **personifica la maldad** he/she is evil personified

perspectiva [pers·pek·'ti·βa] *f* **1.** (*general*) perspective **2.** (*vista*) view **3.** *pl* (*posibilidad*) prospects *pl*

perspicacia [pers·pi·'ka·sja, ·θja] *f* insight

perspicaz [pers·pi·'kas, ·'kaθ] *adj* **1.** (*vista*) keen **2.** (*persona*) perceptive

persuadir [per·swa·'dir] **I.** *vt* **1.** (*inducir*) to encourage; **lo ~é para que no lo haga** I will persuade him not to do it **2.** (*convencer*) to persuade **II.** *vr* to be persuaded

persuasión [per·swa·'sjon] *f* (*acto*) persuasion; **emplear todo su poder de ~** to use all one's powers of persuasion

persuasivo, -a [per·swa·'si·βo, ·a] *adj* persuasive

pertenecer [per·te·ne·'ser, ·'θer] *irr como crecer* vi (*ser de*) to belong; **esta casa me pertenece** this house belongs to me

perteneciente [per·te·ne·'sjen·te, ·'θjen·te] *adj* ~ a belonging to; **los países ~s a la ONU** the countries that are members of the UN; **todo lo ~ al caso** everything that is relevant to the case

pertenencia [per·te·'nen·sja, ·θja] *f* **1.** (*acción*) belonging **2.** *pl* (*bienes*) belongings *pl* **3.** *pl* (*accesorios*) accessories *pl*

pértiga ['per·ti·ɣa] *f t.* DEP pole; **salto de ~** pole vault; **saltar con ~** to pole vault

pertinente [per·ti·'nen·te] *adj* **1.** (*opor-* *tuno*) appropriate **2.** (*datos, pregunta, comentario*) relevant, pertinent **3.** (*relativo*) **en lo ~ a...** with regard to...

perturbado, -a [per·tur·'βa·do, ·a] *m, f* **~** (*mental*) mentally disturbed person

perturbar [per·tur·'βar] *vt* to disturb; (*confundir*) to confuse

Perú [pe·'ru] *m* Peru

peruano, -a [pe·'rwa·no, ·a] *adj, m, f* Peruvian

perversidad [per·βer·si·'dad] *f* (*sexual*) perversity

perversión [per·βer·'sjon] *f* **1.** (*acción*) perversion **2.** (*cualidad*) perversity

perverso, -a [per·'βer·so, ·a] *adj* (*sexual*) perverse

pervertido, -a [per·βer·'ti·do, ·a] *adj* perverted

pervertir [per·βer·'tir] *irr como sentir* **I.** *vt* to corrupt **II.** *vr* to become corrupt; (*depravarse*) to become perverted

pesa ['pe·sa] *f t.* DEP weight; **hacer ~s** to do weight training; **levantamiento de ~s** weightlifting

pesadez [pe·sa·'des, ·'deθ] *f* **1.** (*de objeto*) heaviness **2.** (*de movimiento*) slowness, sluggishness **3.** (*de sueño*) drowsiness **4.** (*de tarea*) boring nature **5.** (*de persona*) tiresome nature **6.** (*de viaje*) tediousness **7.** (*de lectura*) density; (*aburrido*) dullness **8.** (*de estómago*) (acid) indigestion

pesadilla [pe·sa·'di·ja, ·ʎa] *f* nightmare

pesado, -a [pe·'sa·do, ·a] *adj* **1.** (*que pesa*) heavy; **tengo la cabeza pesada** my head feels rather stuffy; **tengo el estómago ~** my stomach is uncomfortably full **2.** (*lento*) slow **3.** (*molesto*) tiresome **4.** (*duro*) hard; **un trabajo ~** hard work **5.** (*aburrido*) boring **6.** (*sueño*) deep; (*tiempo*) oppressive; (*viaje*) tedious; (*lectura*) heavy going

pésame ['pe·sa·me] *m* condolences *pl*; **dar el ~** to offer one's condolences; **reciba mi más sincero ~** please accept my heartfelt condolences

pesar [pe·'sar] **I.** *vi* to weigh; **esta caja pesa mucho** this box is very heavy; **pon encima lo que no pese** put the lightest things on top; **~ sobre alguien** to weigh heavily on sb; (*problemas*) to weigh sb down **II.** *vt* to weigh; (*cantidad concreta*) to weigh out; ¿me puede ~ la fruta? could you weigh this fruit for me?; **me pesa haberte mentido** I regret having lied to you; **pese a quien pese** come what may; **pese a que...** although... **III.** *m* **1.** (*pena*) sorrow; **muy a ~ mío** to my great sadness **2.** (*remordimiento*) regret ▶ **a ~ de** in spite of

pesca ['pes·ka] *f* fishing; (*captura*) capture; **ir de ~** to go fishing; **~ de altura** deep-sea fishing; **~ de arrastre** trawling; **~ de bajura** inshore fishing; **y toda la ~** *fig inf* and all the rest of the crew

pescadería [pes·ka·de·'ri·a] *f* (*tienda*) fish market

pescado [pes·'ka·do] *m* fish

pescador(a) [pes·ka·'dor, -·'do·ra] *m(f)* (*de caña*) angler; (*de mar*) fisherman

pescar <c → qu> [pes·'kar] *vt* **1.** (*con caña, en barco*) to fish for; **ir a ~ sardinas** to fish for sardines **2.** (*sorprender*) to catch out; (*resfriado*) to catch **3.** *inf* (*novio*) to land **4.** *inf* (*entender*) to understand

pescuezo [pes·'kwe·so, -θo] *m* (scruff of the) neck; **retorcer el ~ a alguien** *inf* to wring sb's neck; **salvar el ~** *fig* to save one's skin

pese ['pe·se] *adv* **~ a** in spite of, despite

pesebre [pe·'se·βre] *m* manger; (*de Navidad*) Nativity scene

peseta [pe·'se·ta] *f* peseta

pesetero, -a [pe·se·'te·ro, -a] *m, f* money-grubbing; **eres un ~** all you think about is money

pesimismo [pe·si·'mis·mo] *m* pessimism

pesimista [pe·si·'mis·ta] *adj* pessimistic

pésimo, -a ['pe·si·mo, -a] *adj* dreadful

peso ['pe·so] *m* **1.** (*de objeto*) weight; **coger/perder ~** to gain/lose weight; **¿qué ~ tiene?** how much does it weigh?; **vender a ~** to sell by weight; **eso cae por su propio ~** that goes without saying **2.** (*pesadez*) heaviness **3.** (*importancia*) weight; **tener una razón de ~** to have a good reason **4.** (*carga*) burden; **llevar el ~ de algo** to bear the burden of sth; **me saco un ~ de encima** that's taken a load off my mind

5. DEP (*bola*) shot **6.** DEP (*boxeo*) weight **7.** (*moneda*) peso ▶ **comprar a ~ de oro** to pay way over the odds

pesquero [pes·'ke·ro] *m* fishing boat

pesquisa[^1] [pes·'ki·sa] *f* inquiry; **hacer ~s** to make inquiries

pesquisa[^2] [pes·'ki·sa] *m* *Arg, Ecua, Par* detective

pestaña [pes·'ta·ɲa] *f* eyelash; **quemarse las ~s** *fig* to burn the midnight oil

pestañear [pes·ta·'ɲar/pes·ta·ɲe·'ar] *vi* to blink; **sin ~** without batting an eyelid

peste ['pes·te] *f* **1.** *t.* MED (*plaga*) plague; **~ bubónica** bubonic plague **2.** (*olor*) stench; **aquí hay una ~ increíble** it really stinks here **3.** (*crítica*) **echar ~s de alguien** to heap abuse on sb

pestillo [pes·'ti·jo, -ʎo] *m* bolt; **echar el ~** to shoot the bolt

petaca [pe·'ta·ka] *f* **1.** (*para cigarros*) cigarette case; (*para tabaco*) tobacco pouch **2.** *AmL* (*caja*) box; (*baúl*) chest; (*cesto*) basket **3.** *AmC* (*joroba*) hump

pétalo ['pe·ta·lo] *m* petal

petardo [pe·'tar·do] *m* **1.** (*de fiesta*) firecracker; **tirar ~s** to set off firecrackers **2.** *inf* (*persona o cosa mala*) **ser un ~** to be a pain

petate [pe·'ta·te] *m* (*de soldado, marinero*) kit bag

petición [pe·ti·'sjon, -'θjon] *f* (*ruego, solicitud*) request; (*escrito*) petition; **a ~ de...** at the request of...

petiso, -a [pe·'ti·so] *adj* *Arg, Urug* (*pequeño*) small; (*muy pequeño*) tiny; (*enano*) short

peto ['pe·to] *m* (*de bebé, delantal*) bib

petrificar <c → qu> [pe·tri·fi·'kar] *vt* *t. fig* to petrify

petróleo [pe·'tro·leo] *m* **1.** (*carburante*) petroleum, (crude) oil **2.** (*de lámpara*) paraffin

petrolero [pe·tro·'le·ro] *m* (*barco*) oil tanker

petrolífero, -a [pe·tro·'li·fe·ro, -a] *adj* oil-bearing; (*zona*) ~ oilfield; **industria petrolífera** oil industry

petulante [pe·tu·'lan·te] *adj* **1.** (*arrogante*) arrogant **2.** (*insolente*) insolent

peyorativo, -a [pe·jo·ra·'ti·βo, -a] *adj*

P

[^1]: pesquisa¹
[^2]: pesquisa²

pejorative; **un comentario ~** a derogatory remark

peyote [pe·'jo·te] *m AmL* BOT peyote cactus

pez [pes, peθ] *m* ZOOL fish; **estar como ~ en el agua** to be in one's element; **estar ~ en español** *inf* to have no idea of Spanish; **un ~ gordo** a big shot

pezón [pe·'son, ·'θon] *m* 1. (*de mujer*) nipple 2. (*de animal*) teat

pezuña [pe·'su·ɲa, pe·'θu·] *f* 1. (*de vaca, oveja*) hoof 2. *pl inf* (*de persona*) feet *pl*

piadoso, -a [pja·'do·so, -a] *adj* 1. (*misericordioso*) merciful; (*bondadoso*) compassionate 2. (*devoto*) pious

pial [pja·'lar] *vt AmL* to lasso

pianista [pja·'nis·ta] *mf* pianist

piano [pi·'a·no] *m* piano; **~ de cola** grand piano

piar <1. *pres* pío> [pi·'ar] *vi* (*pájaro*) to chirp

piara [pi·'a·ra] *f* herd (of pigs)

PIB [pe·i·'βe] *m abr de* **Producto Interior Bruto** GDP

pibe, -a [pi·'βe, -a] *m, f Arg* (*chico*) boy; (*chica*) girl

picadero [pi·ka·'de·ro] *m* (*para adiestrar*) ring; (*escuela*) riding school

picadillo [pi·ka·'di·jo, -ʎo] *m* (*carne picada*) ground meat; **hacer ~ a alguien** *inf* to make mincemeat of sb

picadura [pi·ka·'du·ra] *f* 1. (*de insecto*) sting; (*de serpiente*) bite 2. (*en ropa, metal*) hole 3. (*caries*) cavity

picante [pi·'kan·te] I. *adj* spicy, hot; *fig* risqué II. *m* CULIN spicy food

picaporte [pi·ka·'por·te] *m* 1. (*aldaba*) doorknocker 2. (*tirador*) door handle 3. (*pestillo*) latch

picar <c → qu> [pi·'kar] I. *vi* 1. (*sol*) to sting 2. (*pimienta*) to be hot 3. (*pez*) to take the bait 4. (*de la comida*) to snack 5. (*tener picazón*) to itch; **me pica la espalda** my back is itchy 6. (*golpear*) **~ a la puerta** to knock on the door 7. (*aspirar*) **~ muy alto** to aim too high II. *vt* 1. (*insecto*) to sting; (*serpiente*) to bite 2. (*ave*) to peck 3. (*desmenuzar*) to chop up; (*carne*) to mince 4. (*ofender*) to irritate; **estar picado con alguien** to

be annoyed with sb; **¿qué mosca te ha picado?** what's eating you? 5. (*incitar*) to goad III. *vr* 1. (*metal*) to rust; (*muela*) to decay; (*vino*) to turn sour 2. (*mar*) to become choppy 3. (*ofenderse*) to become irritated; (*mosquearse*) to become angry; **~se por nada** to get irritated about the slightest thing

picardía [pi·kar·'di·a] *f* 1. (*malicia*) roguishness 2. (*travesura*) **una ~** a dirty trick

picaresco, -a [pi·ka·'res·ko, -a] *adj* 1. (*astuto*) cunning 2. (*comentario*) mischievous

pícaro, -a [pi·ka·ro, -a] I. *adj* 1. (*granuja*) roguish 2. (*astuto*) cunning 3. (*comentario*) naughty II. *m, f* rogue

picazón [pi·ka·'son, -'θon] *f* itch

pichanga [pi·'tʃan·ga] *f* 1. *Arg* (*vino*) wine (*not fully fermented*) 2. *Bol* (*fácil*) **ser ~** to be a cinch *inf*

pichichi [pi·'tʃi·tʃi] *m* DEP top goal-scorer

pichín [pi·'tʃin] *m CSur inf* pee

pichincha [pi·'tʃin·tʃa] *f* 1. *Arg* (*ganga*) bargain 2. *Chile* (*cantidad pequeña*) tiny bit

picnic [piɣ·nik] *m* picnic

pico [pi·ko] *m* 1. (*del pájaro*) beak 2. *inf* (*boca*) mouth; **~ de oro** the gift of gab; **alguien se fue del ~** sb let the cat out of the bag 3. (*herramienta*) pickax 4. (*montaña*) peak; **cortado a ~** sheer 5. (*de jarra*) lip 6. (*cantidad*) **llegar a las cuatro y ~** to arrive just after four o'clock; **tiene cuarenta y ~ años** he/she is forty-something; **salir por un ~** to cost a lot

picor [pi·'kor] *m* (*en la piel*) itching; (*en la boca*) stinging, burning

picotazo [pi·ko·'ta·so, -θo] *m* **pegar un ~** (*ave*) to peck; **arrancar a ~s** to peck off

picotear [pi·ko·te·'ar] I. *vi* (*comer*) to nibble II. *vt* to peck

picudo, -a [pi·'ku·do, -a] *adj* pointed; (*anguloso*) angular

pie [pje] *m* 1. (*extremidad, medida*) foot; **tener los pies** flat feet; **¿qué ~ calza Ud.?** what shoe size do you take?; **a ~ de obra** on the spot; **a ~ on** foot; **quedarse de ~** to remain standing; **estar**

de ~ to be standing; **ponerse de** ~ to stand up; **ya sabemos de qué** ~ **cojea** *fig* now we know his/her weak spot; **tener los** ~**s en el suelo** *fig* to be realistic; **se marchó por su propio** ~ he/she left on his own; **no hacer** ~ (*en una piscina*) to be out of one's depth; **estoy cansada:** **no me tengo en** ~ I am so tired I can barely stand; **con buen** ~ *fig* on the right footing; **estar en** ~ **de guerra** to be on a war footing; **ya tiene un** ~ **en el hoyo** *inf* he/she already has one foot in the grave **2.** TIPO ~ **de imprenta** imprint; ~ **de página** foot of the page **3.** (*métrica*) foot **4.** (*trípode*) leg ▸ **hoy no doy** ~ **con** **bola** I can't seem to do anything right today; **no tener ni** ~**s ni** **cabeza** to make no sense; **estar al** ~ **del** **cañón** to be ready for action; **buscar tres** ~**s al** **gato** (*daño*) to ask for trouble; (*complicaciones*) to complicate matters; **seguir algo al** ~ **de la** **letra** to follow sth to the letter; **andarse con** ~**s de** **plomo** to tread very carefully; **parar los** ~**s a alguien** *inf* to put sb in his/her place; ~**s, ¿para qué os** **quiero?** time to leave!; **salir por** ~**s** *inf* to beat it; **de a** ~ ordinary

piedad [pje·'dad] *f* REL piety; (*compasión*) pity; **¡ten** ~ **de nosotros!** have pity on us!

piedra ['pje·dra] *f* stone; ~ **pómez** pumice stone; ~ **preciosa** precious stone; **cartón** ~ papier-mâché; **Edad de Piedra** Stone Age; **poner la primera** ~ to lay the foundation stone; ~ **angular** *fig* cornerstone; ~ **filosofal** *fig* philosopher's stone; ~ **de toque** *fig* touchstone; **no dejar** ~ **sobre** ~ to raze to the ground; **quedarse de** ~ to be stunned; **tirar la** ~ **y esconder la mano** to play the innocent; **tirarse** ~**s a su propio tejado** to foul one's own nest; **pasar a alguien por la** ~ *inf* to lay sb

piel [pjel] *f* (*de persona, fruta*) skin; (*de animal*) skin, hide; (*con pelo*) fur; (*cuero*) leather; **dejarse la** ~ **en algo** *inf* to work oneself into the ground for sth; **un abrigo de** ~**es** a fur coat ▸ ~ **de** **gallina** goose-pimples *pl*

pienso ['pjen·so] *m* fodder; ~ **completo**

compound feed

pierna ['pjer·na] *f* leg; ~ **ortopédica** artificial leg; **estirar las** ~**s** to stretch one's legs; **con las** ~**s cruzadas** with one's legs crossed; **dormir a** ~ **suelta** to be fast asleep

pieza ['pje·sa, -θa] *f* **1.** (*pedazo*) *t.* MÚS, TEAT piece; ~ **de recambio** spare part; **un traje de dos** ~**s** a two-piece suit; ~ **por** ~ piece by piece; **¡menuda** ~ **está hecho ese!** *inf* what a little rascal he is! **2.** *AmL* (*habitación*) room ▸ **quedarse de una** ~ to be absolutely dumbfounded

pifia ['pi·fja] *f* (*error*) blunder

pigmento [piɣ·'men·to] *m* pigment

pijada [pi·'xa·da] *f* *inf* piece of nonsense

pijama [pi·'xa·ma] *m* pajamas *pl*

pijo, -a ['pi·xo, -a] *adj* pey, *inf* stuck-up; **niño** ~ spoiled brat

pila ['pi·la] *f* **1.** (*recipiente*) basin; (*lavadero*) sink; (*bautismal*) font; **nombre de** ~ first name, Christian name **2.** FÍS battery; **ponerse las** ~**s** *inf* to get one's act together **3.** (*montón*) pile; **una** ~ **de libros** a pile of books

pilar [pi·'lar] *m* **1.** (*columna*) pillar **2.** (*apoyo*) prop **3.** (*en camino*) milestone

pilcha ['pil·tʃa] *f* CSur *inf* fine clothes *pl*

píldora ['pil·do·ra] *f* pill; **la** ~ (*anticonceptiva*) the pill; **dorar la** ~ **a alguien** *inf* to sweeten the pill

pillar [pi·'jar, -'ʎar] *vt* **1.** (*atropellar*) to knock down, to run over **2.** (*encontrar*) to find; (*en flagrante*) to catch; **me pillas de buen humor** you've caught me in a good mood; **eso no me pilla de sorpresa** that doesn't surprise me; **tu casa nos pilla de camino** your house is on our way **3.** (*entender*) to grasp **4.** *Arg* (*orinar*) to piss

pillastre [pi·'jas·tre, -'ʎas·tre] *m* *inf* rascal

pillín, -ina [pi·'jin, -·'ji·na; -·'ʎin, -·'ʎi·na] *adj* *inf* crafty

pillo, -a ['pi·jo, -a; -ʎo, -a] **I.** *adj* *inf* crafty **II.** *m, f* *inf* rascal

pilmama [pil·'ma·na] *f* *Méx* nanny

pilotar [pi·lo·'tar] *vt* (*barco*) to steer; (*co-*

che) to drive; (avión) to fly

piloto¹ [pi·'lo·to] I. mf 1. NÁUT navigator; (oficial) first mate; (práctico) (coast) pilot 2. AVIAT pilot; **poner el ~ automático** to set the automatic pilot 3. AUTO driver; **~ de carreras** racing driver II. adj (de prueba) test; (de modelo) show, model; **piso ~** model apartment

piloto² [pi·'lo·to] m Arg (impermeable) raincoat

pimentón [pi·men·'ton] m paprika

pimienta [pi·'mjen·ta] f pepper; **~ en grano** peppercorns pl

pimiento [pi·'mjen·to] m pepper; **me importa un ~** I couldn't care less

pinacoteca [pi·na·ko·'te·ka] f art gallery

pinar [pi·'nar] m pine grove

pincel [pin·'sel, -'θel] m (paint)brush; **estar hecho un ~** to be stylishly dressed

pincelada [pin·se·'la·da, pin·θe-] f brushstroke; **dar las últimas ~s** fig to apply the finishing touches

pinchar [pin·'tʃar] I. vi (rueda) to get a flat (tire) ▶ **ni ~ ni cortar** inf to not count for anything II. vt 1. (alfiler) to prick 2. (estimular) to prod; (mortificar) to wound 3. (inyección) to give an injection; **tengo que ir al médico para que me pinche** I have to go to the doctor's for an injection 4. (teléfono) to tap III. vr 1. (alfiler) to prick oneself 2. (rueda) **se nos ha pinchado una rueda** one of our tires has a flat 3. (insulina) to give oneself an injection 4. inf (drogarse) to shoot up

pinchazo [pin·'tʃa·so, -'tʃa·θo] m 1. (espina) prick; **me dieron unos ~s en el estómago** I had some shooting pains in the stomach 2. (neumático) flat (tire)

pinche ['pin·tʃe] mf cook's helper

pinchito [pin·'tʃi·to] m (tapa) snack

pincho ['pin·tʃo] m 1. (erizo) sting; (rosa) thorn 2. v. **pinchito**

pingo ['pin·go] m 1. inf (harapo) rag 2. CSur (caballo) horse ▶ **poner a alguien hecho un ~** to run sb down

ping-pong [pin·'pon] m ping-pong

pingüino [pin·'gwi·no] m penguin

pino ['pi·no] m 1. (árbol, madera) pine; **~ piñonero** stone pine 2. DEP handstand ▶ **en el quinto ~** in the back

of beyond

pinta ['pin·ta] f 1. t. ZOOL (mancha) spot; (gota) drop 2. inf (aspecto) appearance; **tener ~ de caro** to look expensive; **tener buena ~** (plato) to look tasty; (persona) to be attractive

pintada [pin·'ta·da] f (pared) (piece of) graffiti

pintado, -a [pin·'ta·do] adj (animal) spotted; **papel ~** wallpaper; **el traje te sienta que ni ~** inf the suit really suits you

pintalabios [pin·ta·'la·βjos] m inv lipstick

pintar [pin·'tar] I. vi 1. ARTE to paint 2. (bolígrafo) to write II. vt 1. (pared) to paint; (con dibujos) to decorate; **~ de azul** to paint blue; **¡recién pintado!** wet paint! 2. (cuadro) to paint; **¿qué pinta eso aquí?** fig what's that doing here?; **no ~ nada** fig (persona) to have no influence; (asunto) to be completely irrelevant 3. (describir) to describe III. vr to do one's make-up

pinto, -a ['pin·to, -a] adj spotted

pintor(a) [pin·'tor, -·'to·ra] m(f) painter

pintoresco, -a [pin·to·'res·ko, -a] adj picturesque, colorful

pintura [pin·'tu·ra] f 1. (arte, cuadro) painting; **~ al óleo** oil painting; **~ rupestre** cave painting; **voy a clases de ~** I go to painting classes; **no lo puedo ver ni en ~** inf I can't stand him 2. (color) paint; **caja de ~s** paint box; **dar una capa de ~ a algo** to give sth a coat of paint

pinza(s) ['pin·sa(s), -θa(s)] f(pl) 1. (tenacilla) tongs pl; TÉC pincers pl 2. (para la ropa) clothespin 3. (para depilar) tweezers pl 4. (de cangrejo) claw

piña ['pi·ɲa] f 1. (pino) pine cone 2. (fruta) pineapple

piñón [pi·'ɲon] m 1. (pino) pine nut; **estar a partir un ~ con alguien** inf to be thick as thieves 2. TÉC pinion

pío [pi·o] m cheep; **no decir ni ~** not to say a word; **¡~, ~, ~!** tweet, tweet!

pío, -a [pi·o, -a] adj pious

piojo ['pjo·xo] m louse

piojoso, -a [pjo·'xo·so, -a] adj louse-infested; (sucio) seedy

piola ['pjo·la] I. adj Arg inf (astuto) clever

II. f AmS (cuerda) cord

pionero, -a [pjo·'ne·ro, -a] m, f pioneer

pipa ['pi·pa] f 1. (fumador) pipe; **fumar en ~** to smoke a pipe 2. (de fruta) pip, seed 3. CRi inf (cabeza) head 4. inf (muy bien) **lo pasamos ~** we had a great time

pipí [pi·'pi] m inf pee sl

pique ['pi·ke] m 1. (rivalidad) rivalry; **menudo ~ se traen entre ellos** they really hate each other 2. Arg, Par, Nic (camino) trail 3. (hundirse) **irse a ~** (barco) to sink; (plan) to fail

piqueta [pi·'ke·ta] f pickax

piquete [pi·'ke·te] m (strike) picket

pira ['pi·ra] f pyre; **~ funeraria** funeral pyre

pirado, -a [pi·'ra·do, -a] adj inf crazy

piragua [pi·'ra·ɣwa] f canoe

pirámide [pi·'ra·mi·de] f pyramid

piraña [pi·'ra·ɲa] f piranha

pirarse [pi·'rar·se] vr inf to clear off

pirata [pi·'ra·ta] I. mf pirate II. adj pirate; **emisora ~** pirate radio station

pirenaico, -a [pi·re·'nai·ko, -a] adj Pyrenean

Pirineos [pi·ri·'neos] mpl Pyrenees

piripi [pi·'ri·pi] adj inf tipsy

pirómano, -a [pi·'ro·ma·no, -a] m, f pyromaniac

piropo [pi·'ro·po] m inf flirtatious comment; **echar ~s** to make flirtatious comments

pirotecnia [pi·ro·'teɣ·nja] f pyrotechnics

pirrarse [pi·'rrar·se] vr inf **~ por alguien** to be crazy about sb

pirueta [pi·'rwe·ta] f pirouette

piruleta [pi·ru·'le·ta] f, **pirulí** [pi·ru·'li] m <pirulís> lollipop

pis [pis] m inf piss

pisada [pi·'sa·da] f 1. (acción) footstep 2. (huella) footprint; **seguir las ~s de alguien** fig to follow in sb's footsteps

pisapapeles [pi·sa·pa·'pe·les] m inv paperweight

pisar [pi·'sar] vt 1. (poner el pie) to step, to tread; **¡no pises las flores!** don't step on the flowers!; **me han pisado en el bus** sb stepped on my foot in the bus; **ir pisando huevos** fig to watch one's step; **~ los talones a alguien** fig to follow

on sb's heels; **~ fuerte** fig to make a big impact 2. (entrar) to enter 3. (humillar) to walk all over 4. inf (planes) to pre-empt; **me han pisado el tema** they have stolen my topic

piscina [pi·'si·na, pis·'θi·na] f swimming pool; **~ cubierta** indoor swimming pool

Piscis ['pi·sis, 'pis·θis] m inv Pisces

pisco ['pis·ko] m 1. (aguardiente) strong Peruvian liquor 2. Col, Ven (pavo) turkey 3. Col pey (hombre) guy

piso ['pi·so] m 1. (pavimento) floor; (calle) surface 2. (planta) floor, story; **de dos ~s** with two floors 3. (vivienda) apartment

pisotear [pi·so·te·'ar] vt to trample; fig to walk all over

pisotón [pi·so·'ton] m stamp; **dar un ~ a alguien** to tread on sb's foot

pista ['pis·ta] f 1. (huella) trail; (indicio) clue; **seguir la ~ a alguien** to follow sb's trail 2. (de circo) ring; (para atletismo, coches) track; (de tenis) court; (de baile) floor; **~ de aterrizaje** runway; **~ de esquí** ski slope; **~ de hielo** ice rink 3. (camino) trail 4. COMPUT track

pistacho [pis·'ta·tʃo] m pistachio

pistola [pis·'to·la] f 1. (arma) pistol 2. (del pintor) spray gun

pistolero [pis·to·'le·ro, -a] m gunman

pistoletazo [pis·to·le·'ta·so, -'ta·θo] m pistol shot; **~ de salida** fig starting signal

pistón [pis·'ton] m 1. (émbolo) piston 2. (de arma) percussion cap 3. MÚS key

pita ['pi·ta] f BOT agave, century plant

pitar [pi·'tar] I. vi, vt 1. (claxon) to blow; **me pitan los oídos** my ears are buzzing 2. AmS (fumar) to smoke 3. Chile (engañar) to cheat II. vi inf (deprisa) **salir pitando** to rush off

pitido [pi·'ti·do] m whistle

pitillera [pi·ti·'je·ra, -·'ʎe·ra] f cigarette case

pitillo [pi·'ti·jo, -ʎo] m cigarette

pito ['pi·to] m 1. (silbato) whistle; (claxon) horn; **entre ~s y flautas** inf what with one thing and another; **tomar a alguien por el ~ del sereno** inf to take no notice of sb

pitón [pi·'ton] *m* **1.** ZOOL python **2.** (*cuerno*) budding horn

pitorrearse [pi·to·rre·'ar·se] *vr inf* to make fun

pitorreo [pi·to·'rreo] *m inf* joking; **¡esto es un ~!** this is a joke!

pitufo [pi·'tu·fo] *m inf* shrimp

piyama [pi·'ja·ma] *m AmL* pajamas *pl*

pizarra [pi·'sa·rra, -'θa·rra] *f* **1.** (*roca*) slate **2.** (*encerado*) blackboard

pizarrón [pi·sa·'rron, pi·θa-] *m AmL* blackboard

pizca ['pis·ka, 'piθ-] *f* **1.** *inf* (*poco*) pinch, little bit; **una ~ de sal** a pinch of salt; **ni ~** not a bit; **no tienes ni ~ de vergüenza** you have no shame whatsoever **2.** *Méx* (*cosecha*) harvest

pizza ['pi·tsa] *f* pizza

placa ['pla·ka] *f* **1.** (*lámina, plancha*) sheet; FOTO plate; COMPUT board; **~ base** COMPUT motherboard **2.** (*cartel*) plaque; **~ conmemorativa** commemorative plaque **3.** MED **~ dental** (dental) plaque

placenta [pla·'sen·ta, -'θen·ta] *f* placenta

placentero, -a [pla·sen·'te·ro, -a; pla·θen-] *adj* pleasant

placer [pla·'ser, -'θer] **I.** *m* pleasure **II.** *irr como crecer vi* to please; **¡haré lo que me plazca!** I will do as I please!

placero, -a [pla·'se·ro, -a; -'θe·ro, -a] *m, f AmL* street trader

plácido, -a ['pla·si·do, -a; -θi·do, -a] *adj* calm

plaga ['pla·ɣa] *f* **1.** AGR plague **2.** (*calamidades*) disaster; (*lacra*) blight **3.** (*abundancia*) glut

plagado, -a [pla·'ɣa·do -a] *adj* infested; **el texto estaba ~ de faltas** the text was full of mistakes

plagar <g → gu> [pla·'ɣar] **I.** *vt* to infest; **~ de algo** to fill with sth **II.** *vr:* **~se** to become infested; **el pueblo se plagó de ratas** the village became infested with rats

plagiar [pla·'xjar] *vt* (*copiar*) to plagiarize

plagio ['pla·xjo] *m* (*copia*) plagiarism

plan [plan] *m* **1.** (*proyecto*) plan; **¿tienes ~ para esta noche?** do you have

any plans for tonight **2.** *inf* (*actitud*) **esto no es ~** it's just not on; **en ~ de...** as...; **está en un ~ que no lo soporto** I can't stand him/her when he/she behaves like this

plancha ['plan·tʃa] *f* **1.** (*lámina*) sheet; TIPO plate **2.** (*para ropa*) iron **3.** *inf* (*desacierto*) blunder **4.** CULIN grill; **a la ~** grilled

planchar [plan·'tʃar] *vt* to iron

planeador [pla·nea·'dor] *m* AVIAT glider

planear [pla·ne·'ar] **I.** *vi* (*ave*) to hover; AVIAT to glide **II.** *vt* to plan

planeta [pla·'ne·ta] *m* planet

planetario [pla·ne·'ta·rjo] *m* planetarium

planetario, -a [pla·ne·'ta·rjo, -a] *adj* planetary

planicie [pla·'ni·sje, -θje] *f* plain

planificación [pla·ni·fi·ka·'sjon, -'θjon] *f* planning

planificar <c → qu> [pla·ni·fi·'kar] *vt* to plan

plano ['pla·no] *m* **1.** MAT plane **2.** (*mapa*) map CINE **primer ~** close-up; **en primer ~** (*delante*) in the foreground **4.** (*totalmente*) **de ~** directly; (*negar*) flatly

plano, -a ['pla·no, -a] *adj* flat; **superficie plana** flat surface

planta ['plan·ta] *f* **1.** BOT plant; **~ de interior** houseplant; **~ medicinal** medicinal plant; **~ trepadora** climbing plant **2.** (*pie*) sole **3.** (*fábrica*) plant; **~ de energía atómica/hidráulica** atomic/hydraulic power station; **~ incineradora** incineration plant; **~ de reciclaje de basuras** recycling plant **4.** (*piso*) floor, story; **~ baja** ground floor, first floor *Am* **5.** (*aspecto*) **tener buena ~** to be good-looking

plantación [plan·ta·'sjon, -'θjon] *f* plantation

plantar [plan·'tar] **I.** *vt* **1.** (*bulbo*) to plant **2.** (*clavar*) to stick in; **~ una tienda de campaña** to pitch a tent **3.** *inf* (*golpe*) to land; **~ un tortazo a alguien** to slap sb **4.** *inf* (*cita*) to stand up; **desapareció y me dejó plantado** he/she disappeared and left me standing; **lo ~on en la calle** they chucked him out **II.** *vr:* **~se** **1.** (*resistirse*) **~se ante algo**

to stand firm in the face of sth **2.** (*aparecer*) to get to; **se ~on en mi casa en un periquete** they arrived at my house in no time **3.** (*en los naipes*) to stick; **aquí me planto** I'm sticking

planteamiento [plan·tea·'mjen·to] *m* **1.** (*enfoque*) approach **2.** MAT solution

plantear [plan·te·'ar] **I.** *vt* **1.** (*asunto, problema*) to put forward; **este problema está mal planteado** this problem has been incorrectly formulated **2.** (*causar*) to cause **3.** (*proponer*) to put forward, to pose **II.** *vr* **1.** (*reflexionar*) to think about **2.** (*cuestión*) to ask oneself; **ahora me planteo si...** now I ask myself whether...

plantilla [plan·'ti·ja, -ʎa] *f* **1.** (*empleados*) staff **2.** (*de zapato*) insole **3.** (*patrón*) pattern **4.** (*equipo*) squad

plantón [plan·'ton] *m inf* long wait; **dar un ~ a alguien** to stand sb up

plasma ['plas·ma] *m* plasma

plasmar [plas·'mar] *vt* (*moldear*) to mold

plasta ['plas·ta] *mf pey* bore, drag

plástico ['plas·ti·ko] *m* plastic; (*para envolver*) plastic wrap

plástico, -a ['plas·ti·ko, -a] *adj* **1.** (*materia*) plastic **2.** (*expresivo*) expressive; **las artes plásticas** the plastic arts

plastificar <c → qu> [plas·ti·fi·'kar] *vt* to laminate

plastilina® [plas·ti·'li·na] *f* modeling clay

plata ['pla·ta] *f* **1.** (*metal*) silver; **~ de ley** sterling silver; **bodas de ~** silver wedding anniversary **2.** AmL (*dinero*) money; **¡adiós mi ~!** CSur inf what a disaster! ▸ **hablar en ~** to talk bluntly

plataforma [pla·ta·'for·ma] *f t.* POL platform; **~ petrolífera** oil rig; **~ de lanzamiento** launch pad

platal [pla·'tal] *m AmL* fortune

plátano ['pla·ta·no] *m* (*árbol*) banana tree; (*fruta*) banana

plateado, -a [pla·te·'a·do] *adj* silver-plated; (*color*) silver

plática ['pla·ti·ka] *f* chat; **estar de ~** to be chatting

platillo [pla·'ti·jo, -ʎo] *m* **1.** (*de taza*) saucer **2.** (*de balanza*) pan **3.** MÚS cymbal

platino [pla·'ti·no] *m* QUÍM platinum

plato ['pla·to] *m* **1.** (*vajilla*) plate; (*para taza*) saucer; **tiro al ~** DEP clay pigeon shooting; **pagar los ~s rotos** *fig* to pay the consequences **2.** (*comida*) dish; **~ combinado** dish usually consisting of meat or fish and vegetables; **~ fuerte** main dish; *fig* main part

plató [pla·'to] *m* CINE (film) set

platónico, -a [pla·'to·ni·ko, -a] *adj* platonic

platudo, -a [pla·'tu·do, -a] *adj AmL* well-heeled

plausible [plau·'si·βle] *adj* (*admisible*) acceptable

playa ['pla·ja] *f* **1.** (*mar*) beach **2.** AmL (*espacio*) open space; **~ de estacionamiento** parking lot

playeras [pla·'je·ras] *fpl* gym shoes *pl*

plaza ['pla·sa, -θa] *f* **1.** (*espacio*) square; (*de mercado*) marketplace; (*de toros*) bullring; **~ de abastos** (central) food market **2.** (*asiento*) seat; (*de garaje*) space **3.** (*empleo*) position **4.** (*en instituciones, viajes*) place

plazo ['pla·so, -θo] *m* **1.** (*vencimiento*) period; **~ de entrega** delivery date; **a corto/largo ~** in the short/long term; **en el ~ de un mes** within a month; **depósito a ~ fijo** fixed-term deposit; **el ~ vence el día...** the deadline is on... **2.** (*cantidad*) installment; **a ~s** in installments

plebe ['ple·βe] *f pey* (*chusma*) rabble

plebeyo, -a [ple·'βe·jo, -a] *adj* **1.** *t.* HIST plebeian **2.** (*sin linaje*) common **3.** (*inculto*) uneducated; (*grosero*) uncouth

plebiscito [ple·βi·'si·to, -'θi·to] *m* plebiscite

plegable [ple·'ɣa·βle] *adj* (*papel*) foldable; (*mueble*) folding; **silla ~** folding chair

plegar [ple·'ɣar] *irr como fregar vt* (*doblar*) to fold; (*muebles*) to fold away

plegaria [ple·'ɣa·rja] *f* prayer

pleito ['plei·to] *m* **1.** JUR lawsuit **2.** (*disputa*) dispute

plenario, -a [ple·'na·rjo] *adj* plenary; **sesión plenaria** plenary session

plenitud [ple·ni·'tud] *f* **1.** (*totalidad*) fullness **2.** (*apogeo*) height; **~ vital** full vigor

pleno ['ple·no] *m* plenary session; **apro-**

P

bar algo en ~ to approve sth in a full session

pleno, -a ['ple·no, -a] *adj* full; **~ empleo** full employment; **a plena luz del día** in broad daylight; **en ~ verano** at the height of summer

pletórico, -a [ple·'to·ri·ko, -a] *adj* full; **~ de salud** bursting with health

pliego ['plje·ɣo] *m* 1. (*hoja*) sheet 2. (*documento*) document

pliegue ['plje·ɣe] *m t.* GEO fold

plomero [plo·'me·ro] *m Arg* plumber

plomo ['plo·mo] *m* 1. (*metal*) lead; **gasolina sin ~** unleaded gas; **caer a ~** to fall heavily 2. *inf* (*pesado*) **ser un ~** to be a real drag 3. *pl* ELEC fuse

pluma ['plu·ma] *f* 1. (*ave*) feather; **cambiar la ~** to molt 2. (*escribir*) pen; **~ estilográfica** fountain pen

plumaje [plu·'ma·xe] *m* (*ave*) plumage

plumear [plu·me·'ar] *vt AmC* to write

plumero [plu·'me·ro] *m* (*para limpiar*) feather duster ▶ **vérsele el ~ a alguien** to be obvious what sb is up to

plural [plu·'ral] I. *adj* plural II. *m* plural; **~ mayestático** royal 'we'

plus [plus] *m* 1. (*gratificación*) bonus 2. (*ventaja*) advantage

pluscuamperfecto [plus·kwam·per·'fek·to] *m* LING pluperfect

plusmarquista [plus·mar·'kis·ta] *mf* DEP record holder

plusvalía [plus·βa·'li·a] *f* ECON appreciation

plutonio [plu·'to·njo] *m* plutonium

PN ['pe·so 'ne·to] *m abr de* **peso neto** net weight

PNB [pe·ne·'be, pe·en·e·'be] *m abr de* **producto nacional bruto** GNP

población [po·βla·'sjon, -'θjon] *f* 1. BIO (*habitantes*) population; **~ activa** ECON working population 2. (*localidad: ciudad*) city; (*ciudad pequeña*) town; (*pueblo*) village

poblado [po·'βla·do] *m* (*pueblo*) village; (*colonia*) settlement

poblado, -a [po·'βla·do, -a] *adj* 1. (*habitado*) inhabited 2. (*cejas*) bushy

poblar <o → ue> [po·'βlar] I. *vi, vt* 1. (*colonizar*) to colonize 2. (*de plantas*) to plant 3. (*habitar*) to inhabit;

distintas especies pueblan el fondo del mar various species inhabit the sea bed II. *vr:* **~se** to fill; **la costa se pobló rápidamente** the coast quickly filled with people

pobre ['po·βre] I. *adj* 1. (*no rico*) poor 2. (*desgraciado*) unfortunate 3. (*humilde*) humble 4. (*exclamaciones*) **¡~ de ti si dices mentiras!** you'll be sorry if you lie! II. *mf* poor person; **los pobres** the poor *pl*

pobreza [po·'βre·sa, -θa] *f* (*necesidad*) poverty

pochismo [po·'tʃis·mo] *m Méx* 1. *inf* (*angloamericanismo*) Anglicism introduced into Spanish 2. *inf* (*característica de los pochos*) characteristic of Americanized Mexicans

pocho, -a ['po·tʃo, -a] I. *m, f Méx pey* Americanized Mexican II. *adj* 1. (*fruta*) overripe 2. (*persona*) off-color

pocilga [po·'sil·ɣa, po·'θil-] *f t. fig* pigsty

pócima ['po·si·ma, -θi·ma] *f,* **poción** [po·'sjon, -'θjon] *f* potion; *pey* (*brebaje*) brew; **la ~ mágica** the magic potion

poco ['po·ko] I. *m* 1. (*cantidad*) **un ~ de azúcar** a little sugar; **espera un ~** wait a little 2. *pl* few; **~s de los presentes lo sabían** few of those present knew it; **los ~s que vinieron...** the few who came... II. *adv* little; **escribir ~** to write little; **es ~ simpático** he is not very friendly; **~ a ~** bit by bit, little by little; **~ a ~ dejamos de creerle** we gradually stopped believing him; **a ~ de llegar...** shortly after arriving...; **~ después** shortly afterwards; **dentro de ~** soon; **desde hace ~** since recently; **hace ~** recently, not long ago; **a ~ que se esfuerce lo conseguirá** with a little bit of effort he/she will get it; **por ~ me estrello** I very nearly crashed; **y por si fuera ~...** and as if that wasn't enough...

poco, -a <poquísimo> ['po·ko, -a] *adj* little; **~s** few; **queda poca comida** there's not much food left; **hay pocas colecciones mejores que ésta** there are few collections better than this one; **tiene pocas probabilidades de aprobar** he/she has little chance of passing

podar [po·'dar] *vt* to prune
poder [po·'der] **I.** *irr vi* to be able to; **puedo** I can; **puedes** you can; **yo a ti te puedo** *inf* I'm stronger than you; **no ~ con el alma** to be completely exhausted; **no puedes cogerlo sin permiso** you can't take it without permission; **no podemos abandonarlo** we can't abandon him; **¡bien pod(r)ías habérmelo dicho!** you could have told me!; **bien puede haber aquí un millón de abejas** there could easily be a million bees here; **no puedo con mi madre** I can't cope with my mother; **la sala se llenó a más no ~** the room filled to bursting point; **de ~ ser, no dudes que lo hará** if it is at all possible, have no doubt that he/she will do it; **no pude menos que preguntar** I couldn't help but asking; **lo menos que puedes hacer es llamar** the least you can do is call; **no puede ser** it is impossible; **a ~ ser** if possible **II.** *irr vimpers* **puede ser** maybe; **¡puede!** maybe!; **¿se puede?** may I (come in)? **III.** *m* **1.** *t.* POL (*autoridad*) power; **~ absoluto** absolute power; **~ ejecutivo** executive power; **~ judicial** judicial power; **~ legislativo** legislative power; **la división de ~es** the separation of powers; **el partido en el ~** the party in power; **subir al ~** to achieve power; **los documentos están en ~ del juez** the documents are in the hands of the judge; **haré todo lo que está en mi ~** I will do everything in my power **2.** (*autorización*) authority; **~ notarial** power of attorney; **por ~es** by proxy; **~ de decisión** decision-making power **3.** (*fuerza*) strength; **~ adquisitivo** ECON buying [*o* purchasing] power
poderío [po·de·'ri·o] *m* (*fuerza*) strength
poderoso, -a [po·de·'ro·so, -a] *adj* **1.** (*influyente*) powerful **2.** (*rico*) wealthy **3.** (*eficaz*) effective
podio ['po·djo] *m* podium
podrido, -a [po·'dri·do, -a] *adj* **1.** (*descompuesto*) *t. fig* rotten; **estar ~ de dinero** *inf* estar **~ en plata** *Arg inf* to be filthy rich **2.** *Arg inf* (*aburrido*) fed up
poema [po·'e·ma] *m* poem; **estar hecho un ~** to be a real sight

poesía [poe·'si·a] *f* **1.** (*género*) poetry **2.** (*poema*) poem
poeta, -isa [po·'e·ta, poe·'ti·sa] *m, f* poet *m(f)*, poetess *f*
poético, -a [po·'e·ti·ko, -a] *adj t. fig* poetic
póker ['po·ker] *m* poker; **poner cara de ~** to look poker-faced
polaco, -a [po·'la·ko, -a] *adj* Polish
polar [po·'lar] *adj* polar; **Círculo Polar Ártico/Antártico** Arctic/Antarctic Circle; **la estrella ~** Polaris, Pole Star
polaridad [po·la·ri·'dad] *f* polarity
polarizar <z > c> [po·la·ri·'sar, -'θar] *vt t.* FÍS to polarize; (*atención*) to focus
polea [po·'le·a] *f* pulley
polémica [po·'le·mi·ka] *f* controversy, polemic
polémico, -a [po·'le·mi·ko, -a] *adj* polemical
polemizar <z > c> [po·le·mi·'sar, -'θar] *vi* to argue
polen ['po·len] *m* pollen; **alergia al ~** hay fever
polera [po·'le·ra] *f* **1.** *Chile* (*camiseta*) T-shirt **2.** *Arg* (*de cuello alto*) turtleneck
poli ['po·li] *f inf abr de* **policía** cops *pl*
policía¹ [po·li·'si·a, -'θi·a] *f* police; **agente de ~** police officer; **coche de ~** police car; **comisaría de ~** police station
policía² [po·li·'si·a, -'θi·a] *mf* policeman *m*, policewoman *f*; **perro ~** police dog
policiaco, -a [po·li·'sja·ko, -a; -'θja·ko, -a] *adj,* **policíaco, -a** [po·li·'si·a·ko, -a] *adj* police; **película/novela policíaca** detective film/novel
policial [po·li·'sjal, -'θjal] *adj v.* **policíaco**
policlínica [po·li·'kli·ni·ka] *f* hospital
polideportivo [po·li·de·por·'ti·βo] *m* sports center
polifacético, -a [po·li·fa·'se·ti·ko, -a; po·li·fa·'θe·] *adj* multi-faceted; (*persona*) many-sided
poligamia [po·li·'ɣa·mja] *f* polygamy
políglota [po·'li·ɣlo·ta] *adj* polyglot
polígono [po·'li·ɣo·no] *m* **1.** MAT polygon **2.** (*terreno*) site; **~ industrial** industrial estate [*o* park]
polilla [po·'li·ja, -ʎa] *f* moth

polinesio, -a [po·li·'ne·sjo, -a] *adj, m, f* Polynesian

polio ['po·ljo] *f inv* MED polio, poliomyelitis

pólipo ['po·li·po] *m* MED polyp

polisemia [po·li·'se·mja] *f* LING polysemy

política [po·'li·ti·ka] *f* politics; ~ **interior/exterior** domestic/foreign policy

político, -a [po·'li·ti·ko, -a] I. *adj* 1. POL political; **ciencias políticas** political science 2. (*parentesco*) in-law; **hermano ~** brother-in-law; **hermana política** sister-in-law II. *m, f* politician

póliza ['po·li·sa, -θa] *f* policy; ~ **de seguros** insurance policy

polizón [po·li·'son, -'θon] *mf* stowaway

polla ['po·ja, -ʎa] *f* 1. *inf* (*chica*) chick 2. *AmL* (*carrera*) horse race

pollera [po·'je·ra, -'ʎe·ra] *f Arg* (*falda*) skirt

pollo ['po·jo, -ʎo] *m* 1. CULIN chicken; ~ **asado** roast chicken 2. *inf* (*mozo*) boy; **¿quién es ese ~?** who's that guy?

polo ['po·lo] *m* 1. GEO, FÍS, ASTR pole; ~ **norte** North Pole; ~ **sur** South Pole 2. DEP polo 3. (*camiseta*) polo neck 4. (*helado*) popsicle

Polonia [po·'lo·nja] *f* Poland

polución [po·lu·'sjon, -'θjon] *f* pollution

polvareda [pol·βa·'re·da] *f* dust cloud; **levantar una ~** *fig* to cause an uproar

polvo ['pol·βo] *m* 1. (*suciedad*) dust; **quitar el ~** to dust; **hacer ~** (*algo*) to smash; (*a alguien*) to annihilate; **estoy hecho ~** *inf* I'm exhausted; **hacer morder el ~ a alguien** to humiliate sb 2. (*sustancia*) powder; **levadura en ~** powdered yeast 3. *pl* (*cosmética*) powder

pólvora ['pol·βo·ra] *f* gunpowder; **no haber inventado la ~** *inf* to be a bit dim

polvorín [pol·βo·'rin] *m* powder magazine; **estamos sentados sobre un ~** *fig* we're sitting on a powder keg

polvorón [pol·βo·'ron] *m crumbly almond shortbread, eaten at Christmas*

polvoso, -a [pol·'βo·so, -a] *adj AmL* dusty

pomada [po·'ma·da] *f* ointment

pomelo [po·'me·lo] *m* grapefruit

pómez ['po·mes, -meθ] *f* pumice

pompa ['pom·pa] *f* 1. (*esplendor*) pomp; (*ostentación*) display; **~s fúnebres** (*funeraria*) funeral parlor 2. (*burbuja*) bubble

pompis ['pom·pis] *m inv inf* bottom, tush(y) *sl*

pompo, -a ['pom·po, -a] *adj Col, Ecua* (*sin filo*) blunt

pomposo, -a [pom·'po·so, -a] *adj* magnificent; (*estilo*) pompous

pómulo ['po·mu·lo] *m* cheekbone

ponche ['pon·tfe] *m* punch

poncho ['pon·tfo] *m* poncho

poncho, -a ['pon·tfo, -a] *adj AmL* lazy

ponderar [pon·de·'rar] *vt* 1. (*sopesar*) to weigh up 2. (*encomiar*) to praise

ponencia [po·'nen·sja, -θja] *f* (*conferencia*) paper; (*informe*) report

ponente [po·'nen·te] *mf* (*en conferencia*) speaker

poner [po·'ner] *irr* I. *vt* 1. (*colocar*) to put; (*horizontalmente*) to lie; (*inyección*) to give; (*sellos, etiqueta*) to stick on; (*tirita*) to put on; (*huevos*) to lay; **pon la ropa en el tendedero** hang the clothes on the line; **¿dónde habré puesto...?** where can I have put ...?; **lo pongo en tus manos** *fig* I leave it in your hands 2. (*disponer*) to place; (*la mesa*) to lay, to set; ~ **algo a disposición de alguien** to make sth available to sb 3. (*encender*) to switch on; **pon el despertador para las cuatro** set the alarm for four o'clock; ~ **en marcha** to start 4. (*convertir*) to make; ~ **de mal humor a alguien** to put sb in a bad mood; **el sol te pondrá moreno** the sun will give you a tan 5. (*suponer*) to assume; **pongamos** (**por caso**) **que no llegue a tiempo** let's consider what happens if he/she doesn't arrive on time 6. (*exponer*) ~ **la leche al fuego** to put the milk on the stove; ~ **en peligro** to endanger 7. (*contribuir*) to put in; (*juego*) to bet; **pusimos todo de nuestra parte** we did all that we could 8. (*una expresión*) to take on; ~ **mala cara** to look angry 9. (*tratar*) to treat; ~ **de**

idiota *pey* to treat sb like a fool **10.** (*denominar*) to give; **¿qué nombre le van a ~?** what are they going to call him/her? **11.** (*espectáculo*) to put on; **¿qué ponen hoy en el cine?** what's on at the cinema today? **12.** (*imponer*) to impose; **nos han puesto muchos deberes** they have given us a lot of homework; **~ una multa** to impose a fine; **~ condiciones** to impose conditions **13.** (*instalar*) to install **14.** (*a trabajar*) **tendré que ~te a trabajar** I will have to put you to work **15.** (*añadir*) to add **16.** (*escribir*) to write; **~ entre comillas** to put in inverted commas; **~ la firma** to sign; **~ un anuncio** to place an advertisement; **~ por escrito** to put in writing **17.** (*estar escrito*) to say **18.** (*vestido, zapato*) to put on; **le pusieron el collar** they put its collar on **19.** (*teléfono*) to put through **II.** *vr:* **~se 1.** (*vestido, zapato*) to put on **2.** ASTR to set; **el sol se pone por el oeste** the sun sets in the west **3.** (*comenzar*) to begin; **se puso a llover** it started to rain **4.** (*con adjetivo o adverbio*) to become; **ponte cómodo** make yourself comfortable; **ponte guapo** make yourself look nice

pongo ['pon·go] *I. pres de* **poner**

poni ['po·ni] *m* pony

poniente [po·'njen·te] *m* (*oeste*) west

popa [po·'pa] *f* (*barco*) stern; **viento en ~** following wind; **a ~** astern

popular [po·pu·'lar] *adj* **1.** (*del pueblo*) folk **2.** (*conocido*) well-known; (*admirado*) popular

popularidad [po·pu·la·ri·'dad] *f* popularity

popularizar <z → c> [po·pu·la·ri·'sar, -'θar] **I.** *vt* to popularize **II.** *vr:* **~se** to become popular

poquito [po·'ki·to] *adv* a little; **bébelo ~ a poco** drink it a little bit at a time

por [por] *prep* **1.** (*lugar: a través de*) through; (*vía*) via; (*en*) in; **~ aquí** near here; **limpia la botella ~ dentro/fuera** clean the inside/outside of the bottle; **pasé ~ Madrid** I passed through Madrid; **adelantar ~ la izquierda** to overtake on the left; **volar ~ encima de los Alpes** to fly over the Alps; **la co-**gió **~ la cintura** he grasped her waist **2.** (*tiempo*) in; **~ la(s) mañana(s)** in the morning; **mañana ~ la mañana** tomorrow morning; **~ la tarde** in the evening; **ayer ~ la noche** last night; **~ fin** finally **3.** (*a cambio de*) for; (*en lugar de*) instead of; (*sustituyendo a alguien*) in place of; **cambié el libro ~ el álbum** I exchanged the book for the album **4.** (*agente*) by; **hecho ~ mí** done by me **5.** MAT (*multiplicación*) by **6.** (*reparto*) per; **toca a cuatro ~ cabeza** it comes out at four each; **el ocho ~ ciento** eight per cent **7.** (*finalidad*) for **8.** (*causa*) because of; (*en cuanto a*) regarding; **~ lo hago ~ ti** I'm doing it for you; **~ consiguiente** consequently; **~ eso ~ lo tanto** therefore, because of that; **~ mí que se vayan** as far as I'm concerned, they can go **9.** (*preferencia*) in favor; **estoy ~ comprarlo** I think I should buy it; **estar loco ~ alguien** to be crazy about sb **10.** (*dirección*) **voy (a) ~ tabaco** I'm going to get some cigarettes **11.** (*pendiente*) **este pantalón está ~ lavar** these pants need to be washed **12.** (*aunque*) however; **~ muy cansado que esté lo haré** however tired I am, I'll get it done **13.** (*medio*) by means of; (*alguien*) through; **poner ~ escrito** to put in writing; **al ~ mayor** wholesale **14.** (*interrogativo*) **¿~ (qué)?** why? **15.** **~ si acaso** just in case **16.** (*casi*) **~ poco** almost

porcelana [por·se·'la·na, por·θe·-] *f* porcelain

porcentaje [por·sen·'ta·xe, por·θen·-] *m* percentage

porcentual [por·sen·tu·'al, por·θen·-] *adj* percentage

porche ['por·tʃe] *m* **1.** (*pórtico*) porch **2.** (*cobertizo*) arcade

porcino, -a [por·'si·no, -'θi·no] *adj* pig; **ganado ~** swine *pl*

porción [por·'sjon, -'θjon] *f* portion; CULIN serving

pordiosero, -a [por·djo·'se·ro, -a] *m, f* beggar

pormenorizado, -a [por·me·no·ri·'sa·do, -a; -θa·do, -a] *adj* detailed

porno ['por·no] *adj inv m inf* porn

P

pornografía [por·no·ɣra·'fi·a] f pornography

pornográfico, -a [por·no·'ɣra·fi·ko, -a] adj pornographic

poro ['po·ro] m pore

poroso, -a [po·'ro·so, -a] adj porous

poroto [po·'ro·to] m Chile bean

porque ['por·ke] conj **1.** (causal) because; **lo hizo ~ sí** he/she did it because he/she wanted to **2.** +subj (final) so that; **recemos ~ llueva** let us pray that it rains

porqué [por·'ke] m reason

porquería [por·ke·'ri·a] f inf **1.** (suciedad) filth **2.** (comida) pigswill **3.** (cacharro) piece of junk

porra ['po·rra] f (bastón) truncheon; **¡vete a la ~!** go to hell!

porrazo [po·'rra·so, -θo] m blow; **de golpe y ~** all of a sudden; **de un ~** in one go

porrista [po·'rris·ta] mf Méx fan

porro ['po·rro] m inf (canuto) joint

porrón [po·'rron] m glass wine jar with a long spout

portaaviones [por·ta·βi·'o·nes; por·ta·a·βi-] m inv aircraft carrier

portada [por·'ta·da] f TIPO title page; PREN cover

portaequipaje(s) [por·ta·e·ki·'pa·xe(s)] m (inv) (baca, en tren) luggage rack; (en bicicleta) carrier

portafolios [por·ta·'fo·ljos] m inv briefcase

portal [por·'tal] m (zaguán) hall; COMPUT portal; **~ de Belén** REL Nativity scene

portalámpara [por·ta·'lam·pa·ra] m inv (de bombilla) socket

portaligas [por·ta·'li·ɣas] m inv AmL garter belt

portamaletas [por·ta·ma·'le·tas] m inv AUTO trunk

portaminas [por·ta·'mi·nas] m inv mechanical pencil

portar [por·'tar] vr: **~se** to behave; **~se bien con alguien** to treat sb well; **el niño se porta bien/mal** the child is well-/badly behaved; **~se como un hombre** to act like a man; **nuestro equipo se ha portado** our team performed well

portátil [por·'ta·til] adj portable; (ordenador) ~ laptop

portavoz [por·ta·'βos, -'βoθ] mf spokesperson, spokesman m, spokeswoman f

portazo [por·'ta·so, -θo] m slam (of the door); **dar un ~** to slam the door

porte ['por·te] m **1.** (transporte) transport; **~ aéreo** air freight; **gastos de ~** shipping costs; **a ~ debido** carriage forward **2.** (gastos de transporte) shipping costs pl **3.** (correo) postage; **~ suplementario** additional postage **4.** (aspecto) appearance; **es un hombre de ~ distinguido** he has a distinguished air

portento [por·'ten·to] m marvel; **ser un ~ de energía** to be full of energy

porteño, -a [por·'te·ɲo, -a] **I.** adj of/from Buenos Aires **II.** m, f native/inhabitant of Buenos Aires

portería [por·te·'ri·a] f **1.** (en edificio) porter's lodge **2.** DEP goal

portero, -a [por·'te·ro, -a] m, f **1.** (conserje) caretaker; (en un edificio de viviendas) porter; **~ automático** intercom **2.** Arg (administrador) building manager **3.** DEP goalkeeper

portorriqueño, -a [por·to·rri·'ke·ɲo, -a] adj, m, f Puerto Rican

Portugal [por·tu·'ɣal] m Portugal

portugués, -esa [por·tu·'ɣes, -·'ɣe·sa] adj, m, f Portuguese

porvenir [por·βe·'nir] m future; **tener el ~ asegurado** to have a secure future; **un joven de ~** a young man with great prospects

pos [pos] **I.** adv ir en ~ de algo/alguien to pursue sth/sb; **van en ~ del éxito** they are striving for success **II.** conj Méx inf v. **pues**

posada [po·'sa·da] f **1.** (parador, fonda) inn; (pensión) guest house **2.** (hospedaje) lodging; **dar ~ a alguien** to give sb lodging

posar [po·'sar] **I.** vi (modelo) to pose **II.** vt (poner suavemente) to place; (mirada) to rest **III.** vr: **~se** to settle; **el gorrión se posó en la rama** the sparrow alighted on the branch

posdata [pos·'da·ta] f postscript

pose ['po·se] f (postura) pose

poseer [po·'ser/po·se·'er] irr como leer vt

to possess, to have

poseído, -a [po·se·'i·ðo, -a] *adj* possessed; **~ de odio** full of hatred

posesión [po·se·'sjon] *f* possession; **estar en ~ de algo** to be in possession of sth

posesivo, -a [po·se·'si·βo, -a] *adj t.* LING possessive

poseso, -a [po·'se·so, -a] **I.** *adj* possessed **II.** *m, f* madman *m*, madwoman *f*

posguerra [pos·'ɣe·rra] *f* postwar period

posibilidad [po·si·βi·li·'ðað] *f* **1.** (*lo posible*) possibility **2.** (*aptitud, facultad*) capability; **esto está por encima de mis ~es** this is beyond my capabilities **3.** *pl* (*medios económicos*) means *pl*; **estás viviendo por encima de tus ~es** you are living beyond your means

posibilitar [po·si·βi·li·'tar] *vt* to make possible

posible [po·'si·βle] *adj* possible; **hacer ~** to make possible; **hacer todo lo ~** to do everything one can; **es muy ~ que lleguen tarde** they may very well arrive late; **es ~ que** +*subj* it is possible that; **es muy ~ que** +*subj* it is very likely that; **¡no es ~!** I can't believe it!; **¿será ~?** surely not?; **si es ~** if possible; **en lo ~** as far as possible; **lo antes ~** as soon as possible

posiblemente [po·si·βle·'men·te] *adv* possibly

posición [po·si·'sjon, -'θjon] *f t.* MIL position; **la ~ económica** the economic situation; **la ~ geográfica** the geographic location; **mi ~ ante este asunto...** my opinion on this affair...; **tomar ~** to adopt a stance

positivo [po·si·'ti·βo] *m* FOTO print

positivo, -a [po·si·'ti·βo, -a] *adj t.* MAT, FÍS positive

poso ['po·so] *m* sediment; (*de café*) grounds *pl*; (*de vino*) lees *pl*

posponer [pos·po·'ner] *irr como poner vt* **1.** (*postergar*) to relegate **2.** (*aplazar*) to postpone

postal [pos·'tal] **I.** *adj* mail **II.** *f* postcard

poste ['pos·te] *m t.* TEL post; ELEC pylon; **~ indicador** signpost

póster ['pos·ter] *m* poster

postergar <g → gu> [pos·ter·'ɣar] *vt* (*aplazar*) to postpone; **~ la fecha** to put back the date

posteridad [pos·te·ri·'ðað] *f* **1.** (*descendencia*) descendants *pl*; (*generaciones venideras*) future generations *pl* **2.** (*futuro*) posterity; **pasar a la ~** to be remembered by posterity

posterior [pos·te·'rjor] *adj* **1.** (*de tiempo*) later; **~ a** after **2.** (*de lugar*) back; **la parte ~ de la cabeza** the back of the head

posteriormente [pos·te·rjor·'men·te] *adv* subsequently, later

postizo, -a [pos·'ti·so, -a; -θo, -a] *adj* artificial; **dentadura postiza** false teeth; **pelo ~** wig

postor(a) [pos·'tor, --'to·ra] *m(f)* bidder; **mejor ~** highest bidder

postrado, -a [pos·'tra·ðo, -a] *adj* prostrate; **~ de dolor** (*dolor físico*) in great pain; (*pena*) beside oneself with grief; **~ en cama** laid up in bed

postre ['pos·tre] *m* dessert; **a la ~** *fig* in the end, when all is said and done; **llegar a los ~s** *fig* to arrive too late

postular [pos·tu·'lar] *vt* **1.** (*pedir*) to request; (*donativos*) to collect **2.** (*solicitar*) **~ algo** to petition for sth

póstumo, -a ['pos·tu·mo, -a] *adj* posthumous; **fama póstuma** posthumous fame

postura [pos·'tu·ra] *f* **1.** (*colocación*) position; (*del cuerpo*) posture **2.** (*actitud*) attitude

post-venta [pos·'βen·ta] *adj* after-sales; **servicio ~** after-sales service

potable [po·'ta·βle] *adj* drinkable; **agua ~** drinking water

potaje [po·'ta·xe] *m* **1.** CULIN (*sopa*) soup; (*guiso*) stew *(containing pulses and vegetables)* **2.** *inf* (*mezcla*) mixture

potasio [po·'ta·sjo] *m* potassium

pote ['po·te] *m* pot; (*para plantas*) flowerpot

potencia [po·'ten·sja, -θja] *f* **1.** (*fuerza*) strength; (*capacidad*) capacity; **~ de carga** capacity; **~ del motor** engine capacity; **~ motriz** motive power **2.** (*poder*) power; **gran ~** great power **3.** COMPUT **~ de entrada/de salida** input/output

P

capacity **4.** FILOS possibility; **en ~** potential **5.** MAT power; **elevar a la cuarta ~** to raise to the power of four

potencial [po·ten·'sjal, -'θjal] **I.** *adj* **1.** (*que tiene potencia*) powerful **2.** (*posible*) potential **II.** *m* **1.** (*poder, capacidad*) power; **~ financiero** financial muscle **2.** FÍS potential energy; ELEC potential difference

potente [po·'ten·te] *adj* **1.** (*poderoso*) powerful **2.** (*eficiente*) efficient **3.** (*sexualidad*) potent

potrear [po·tre·'ar] *vt* **1.** AmL (*domar*) to break **2.** Guat, Perú (*pegar*) to beat

potro ['po·tro] *m* **1.** ZOOL colt **2.** DEP vaulting horse **3.** (*de tortura*) rack

poza ['po·sa, -θa] *f* (*charca*) puddle

pozo ['po·so, -θo] *m* **1.** (*manantial*) well **2.** (*hoyo profundo*) shaft; **~ de extracción** extraction shaft; **~ negro** cesspool; **~ petrolífero** oil well; **~ séptico** septic tank; **ser un ~ sin fondo** *fig* to be a bottomless pit **3.** CSur (*bache*) pothole

práctica ['prak·ti·ka] *f* **1.** (*experiencia*) experience; **adquirir ~** to gain experience; **perder la ~** to get out of practice; **tener ~ en algo** to have experience of sth **2.** (*ejercitación*) practice; **~ profesional** professional practice **3.** (*cursillo*) practical course **4.** (*realización*) practice; **en la ~** in practice; **llevar a la ~** to carry out; **poner en ~** to put into practice **5.** (*costumbre*) practice; **~ judicial** normal legal practice; **la ~ de los negocios** business norms **6.** (*modo*) manner; (*método*) method; **la ~ comercial** business methods

practicar <c → qu> [prak·ti·'kar] *vi, vt* to practice; **~ deporte** to play sport, to do sports; **estudió medicina, pero no practica** he/she studied medicine, but he/she doesn't work as a doctor; **~ el español** to practice Spanish

práctico ['prak·ti·ko] *m* NÁUT pilot; **~ de puerto** coast pilot

práctico, -a ['prak·ti·ko, -a] *adj* practical

pradera [pra·'de·ra] *f* grassland, prairie

prado ['pra·do] *m* (*para ganado*) meadow; (*para pasear*) park

pragmático, -a [pray·'ma·ti·ko, -a] *adj* pragmatic

preámbulo [pre·'am·bu·lo] *m* introduction, preamble; **sin ~s** *fig* without further ado; **no andarse con ~s** not to beat around the bush

precalentar <e → ie> [pre·ka·len·'tar] *vt* to preheat

precario, -a [pre·'ka·rjo, -a] *adj* precarious

precaución [pre·kau·'sjon, -'θjon] *f* precaution; **tomar precauciones** to take precautions

precaver [pre·ka·'βer] **I.** *vt* (*prevenir*) to prevent; (*evitar*) to avoid **II.** *vr* **hay que ~se de todas las eventualidades** you have to be prepared for all eventualities

precavido, -a [pre·ka·'βi·do, -a] *adj* cautious

precedente [pre·se·'den·te, pre·θe·-] **I.** *adj* preceding **II.** *m* precedent; **sentar un ~** to establish a precedent; **sin ~s** unprecedented

preceder [pre·se·'der, pre·θe·-] *vt* **1.** (*anteceder*) to precede **2.** (*tener primacía*) **~ a algo/alguien** to have priority over sth/sb; **~ en categoría** to have a higher position

precepto [pre·'sep·to, -'θep·to] *m* (*mandamiento*) order; (*norma*) precept

precintar [pre·sin·'tar, -'θin·tar] *vt* to seal

precinto [pre·'sin·to, 'θin·to] *m* seal

precio ['pre·sjo, -θjo] *m* price; **~ al consumidor** retail price; **~ al contado** cash price; **~ de fábrica** price ex-works, factory price; **~ al por mayor** wholesale price; **~ recomendado** recommended price; **~ de venta al público** retail price; **a buen ~** for a good price; **a mitad de ~** at half price; **a ~ de oro** for a very high price; **poner el ~** to set the price; **¿qué ~ tiene el libro?** how much does this book cost?; **no tener ~** *fig* to be priceless; **querer conseguir algo a cualquier ~** to want sth at any price; **poner ~ a la cabeza de alguien** to put a price on sb's head

preciosidad [pre·sjo·si·'dad, pre·θjo·-] *f* value; **esta chica es una ~** this girl is lovely

precioso, -a [pre·'sjo·so, -a; pre·'θjo·-] *adj* **1.** (*valioso*) valuable **2.** (*hermo-*

_so_) lovely

precipicio [pre·si·'pi·sjo, -θi·'pi·θjo] _m_ precipice; **estar al borde del ~** _fig_ to be on the brink of disaster

precipitación [pre·si·pi·ta·'sjon, -θi·pi·ta·'θjon] _f_ 1. (_prisa_) haste; **con ~** hastily 2. METEO rainfall

precipitadamente [pre·si·pi·ta·da·'men·te, pre·θi·] _adv_ hastily

precipitado, -a [pre·si·pi·'ta·do, pre·θi·] _adj_ hasty

precipitar [pre·si·pi·'tar, pre·θi·] I. _vt_ 1. (_arrojar_) to throw down; **lo ~on por la ventana** they threw him out of the window 2. (_apresurar_) to hasten; (_acelerar_) to hurry II. _vr:_ **~se** 1. (_arrojarse_) to throw oneself down; **~se sobre algo/alguien** to hurl oneself at sth/sb 2. (_acontecimientos_) to happen very quickly; (_personas_) to act hastily; **¡no se precipite!** don't be hasty!

precisamente [pre·si·sa·'men·te, pre·θi·] _adv_ exactly; **¿tiene que ser ~ hoy?** does it have to be today, of all days? **~ por eso** for that very reason

precisar [pre·si·'sar, pre·θi·] _vt_ 1. (_determinar_) to specify; **no lo puedo ~** I can't put my finger on it 2. (_necesitar_) to need; **preciso tu ayuda** I need your help

precisión [pre·si·'sjon, pre·θi·] _f_ 1. (_exactitud_) precision; **~ de** (_tiempo_) accuracy; **instrumento de ~** precision instrument; **hablar con ~** to speak clearly 2. (_determinación_) clarification; **hacer precisiones** to clarify matters

preciso, -a [pre·'θi·so, -a, pre·'θi·] _adj_ 1. (_necesario_) necessary; **es ~ que nos veamos** we need to see each other; **si es ~...** if necessary... 2. (_exacto_) precise

precocinado, -a [pre·ko·si·'na·do, -a, pre·ko·θi·] _adj_ pre-cooked

preconcebido, -a [pre·kon·se·'βi·do, -a, pre·kon·θe·] _adj_ preconceived; **tener ideas preconcebidas** to have preconceived ideas

precordillera [pre·kor·di·'je·ra, -'ʎe·ra] _f Arg_ Andean foothills _pl_

precoz [pre·'kos, -'koθ] _adj_ precocious; (_diagnóstico, cosecha_) early; **eyacula-ción ~** premature ejaculation

precursor(a) [pre·kur·'sor, -·'so·ra] I. _adj_ preceding II. _m(f)_ precursor

predecesor(a) [pre·de·se·'sor -·'so·ra, -θe·'sor, -·'so·ra] _m(f)_ 1. (_en el cargo_) predecessor 2. (_antepasados_) ancestor

predecir [pre·de·'sir, -'θir] _irr como decir_ _vt_ to predict; (_tiempo_) to forecast

predestinado, -a [pre·des·ti·'na·do, -a] _adj_ predestined

predeterminar [pre·de·ter·mi·'nar] _vt_ to predetermine

predicado [pre·di·'ka·do] _m_ LING predicate

predicar <c → qu> [pre·di·'kar] _vt_ to preach; **~ en desierto** to preach in the wilderness; **~ con el ejemplo** to practice what one preaches

predicción [pre·dik·'sjon, -'θjon] _f_ prediction

predilecto, -a [pre·di·'lek·to, -a] _adj_ favorite; **hijo ~** favorite son

predisponer [pre·dis·po·'ner] _irr como poner_ I. _vt_ 1. (_fijar por anticipado_) to agree beforehand; **venía predispuesto a pelearse** he arrived in a mood for a quarrel 2. (_influir_) to predispose; **~ a alguien a favor/en contra de alguien** to bias sb in favor of/against sb 3. (_inclinar_) to make receptive; MED to predispose II. _vr_ 1. (_prepararse_) **~se a algo** to prepare oneself for sth 2. (_tomar partido_) to have a bias; **~se a favor/en contra de alguien** to be biased in favor of/against sb

predisposición [pre·dis·po·si·'sjon, -'θjon] _f t._ MED predisposition; (_tendencia_) tendency; **tener ~ a engordar** to have a tendency to put on weight

predispuesto, -a [pre·dis·'pwes·to, -a] I. _pp de_ **predisponer** II. _adj_ 1. **ser ~** (_sensible_) predisposed 2. **estar ~** (_prevenido_) prejudiced; **estar (mal) ~ contra alguien** to be prejudiced against sb

predominar [pre·do·mi·'nar] _vi, vt_ 1. (_prevalecer_) to predominate; **aquí predomina la corrupción** corruption is very common here; **~ en número** to be most numerous 2. (_sobresalir_) to stand out; **~ en algo/sobre alguien** to stand

P

out at sth/over sb

predominio [pre·do·'mi·njo] *m* **1.** (*poder*) predominance **2.** (*preponderancia*) preponderance **3.** (*superioridad*) ~ **sobre alguien** superiority over sb

preescolar [pres·ko'lar/pre·es·ko'lar] *adj* pre-school

preestreno [pres·'tre·no/pre·es·tre·no] *m* preview

prefabricado, -a [pre·fa·βri·'ka·do, -a] *adj* prefabricated; **casa prefabricada** prefabricated house

preferencia [pre·fe·'ren·sja, -θja] *f* **1.** (*elección, trato*) preference; **mostrar ~ por alguien** to show a preference for sb **2.** (*predilección*) predilection; **sentir ~ por alguien** to be biased in favor of sb **3.** (*prioridad*) priority; ~ **de paso** right of way; **dar ~** to give preference

preferentemente [pre·fe·ren·te·'men·te] *adv* preferably

preferible [pre·fe·'ri·βle] *adj* preferable; **sería ~ que lo hicieras** it would be best if you did it

preferiblemente [pre·fe·ri·βle·'men·te] *adv* preferably

preferido, -a [pre·fe·'ri·do, -a] *adj* favorite

preferir [pre·fe·'rir] *irr como sentir vt* to prefer; **prefiero ir a pie** I prefer to walk; **prefiero que no venga** I would rather he/she didn't come

prefijar [pre·fi·'xar] *vt* to decide (in advance), to prearrange

prefijo [pre·'fi·xo] *m* **1.** LING prefix **2.** TEL area code

pregón [pre·'ɣon] *m* proclamation

pregonar [pre·ɣo·'nar] *vt* **1.** (*en público*) to proclaim **2.** (*lo que estaba oculto*) to make public; ~ **a los cuatro vientos** *inf* to proclaim for all to hear **3.** (*alabar*) to praise publicly

pregunta [pre·'ɣun·ta] *f* **1.** (*demanda*) question; ~ **capciosa** trick question **2.** (*de datos*) inquiry

preguntar [pre·ɣun·'tar] **I.** *vt* to ask; ~ **a alguien la lección** to test sb; ~ **por alguien** to ask after sb **II.** *vr* ~**se si/cuándo/qué...** to wonder if/when/what...

prehistórico, -a [pre·is·'to·ri·ko, -a] *adj*

prehistoric

prejuicio [pre·'xwi·sjo, -θjo] *m* prejudice

prejuzgar <g → gu> [pre·xus·'ɣar, pre·xuθ-] *vt* to prejudge

premamá [pre·ma·'ma] *adj inv* **vestido ~** maternity dress

prematuro, -a [pre·ma·'tu·ro, -a] *adj* premature; (*persona*) precocious; **nacimiento ~** premature birth

premeditación [pre·me·di·ta·'sjon, -'θjon] *f* premeditation; **con ~** premeditated

premeditado, -a [pre·me·di·'ta·do, -a] *adj* premeditated

premeditar [pre·me·di·'tar] *vt* (*planear*) to plan; JUR to premeditate

premiado, -a [pre·'mja·do, -a] *adj* prize-winning

premiar [pre·'mjar] *vt* to reward; (*dar un premio*) to give [*o* award] a prize to

premio [pre·'mjo] *m* **1.** (*galardón*) prize; ~ **Nobel** (**de literatura**) Nobel Prize (for/in literature); **conceder un ~** to award a prize **2.** (*recompensa*) reward **3.** (*lotería*) prize; **el ~ gordo** the jackpot

premisa [pre·'mi·sa] *f* (*condición*) premise

premonición [pre·mo·ni·'sjon, -'θjon] *f* premonition

premunir [pre·mu·'nir] **I.** *vt AmL* ~ **de algo** to provide with sth **II.** *vr AmL* ~**se de algo** to provide oneself with sth

prenda ['pren·da] *f* **1.** (*fianza*) guarantee; **en ~** as security; **soltar ~** to commit oneself; **no soltar ~** *inf* not to say a word **2.** (*pieza de ropa*) garment; ~**s interiores** underwear

prendar [pren·'dar] **I.** *vt* **1.** (*tomar como prenda*) to take as security **2.** (*ganar el afecto*) to captivate **II.** *vr* ~**se de alguien** *elev* to fall in love with sb

prendedor [pren·de·'dor] *m* (*broche*) brooch, pin; (*de corbata*) tiepin

prender [pren·'der] *vt* **1.** (*sujetar*) to hold down; (*con alfileres*) to pin; (*en un gancho*) to hang; ~ **un alfiler de corbata** to put a tiepin on **2.** (*detener*) to catch **3.** (*fuego*) **el coche prendió fuego** the car caught fire **4.** *AmL* (*encender*) to light; (*luz*) to turn on; ~ **un cigarrillo**

to light a cigarette

prensa ['pren·sa] *f* **1.** (*máquina*) press **2.** (*imprenta*) printer's, press; **estar en ~** to be at the printer's **3.** PREN press; **~ amarilla** tabloids *pl*; **rueda de ~** press conference; **libertad de ~** freedom of the press; **secretario de ~** press secretary; **tener buena/mala ~** *fig* to get a good/bad press

prensar [pren·'sar] *vt* to press

preñada [pre·'ɲa·ða] *adj* (*mujer*) pregnant

preñar [pre·'ɲar] *vt* **1.** (*mujer*) to make pregnant **2.** (*animal*) to impregnate

preocupación [preo·ku·pa·'sjon, -'θjon] *f* **1.** worry; **~ por algo/alguien** worry about sth/sb; **sin preocupaciones** unworried **2.** (*obsesión*) concern; **tu única ~ es el dinero** the only thing you care about is money

preocupado, -a [preo·ku·'pa·ðo, -a] *adj* worried; **~ por algo/alguien** worried about sth/sb; **mi padre anda bastante ~** my father is quite worried

preocupante [preo·ku·'pan·te] *adj* worrying

preocupar [preo·ku·'par] **I.** *vt* to worry; **~ a alguien** to make sb worry **II.** *vr* **1.** (*inquietarse*) **~se por algo/alguien** to worry about sth/sb; **¡no te preocupes tanto!** don't worry so much! **2.** (*encargarse*) to take care; **no se preocupa de arreglar el asunto** he/she doesn't do anything to solve the problem

preparación [pre·pa·ra·'sjon, -'θjon] *f* **1.** (*de asunto, comida*) preparation **2.** (*formación*) training; **~ académica** education; **sin ~** untrained

preparado [pre·pa·'ra·ðo] *m* preparation

preparado, -a [pre·pa·'ra·ðo, -a] *adj* (*listo*) ready; **tener ~** to have ready

preparar [pre·pa·'rar] **I.** *vt* **1.** (*disponer*) to prepare; **~ el camino** to prepare the way; **~ un discurso** to write a speech; **~ las maletas** to pack one's bags **2.** QUÍM, ANAT to prepare **II.** *vr* to get ready; **prepárate para salir** get ready to leave; **se prepara una tormenta** there's a storm brewing

preparativo [pre·pa·ra·'ti·βo] *m* preparation

preparativo, -a [pre·pa·ra·'ti·βo, -a] *adj* preparatory

preposición [pre·po·si·'sjon, -'θjon] *f* preposition

prepotente [pre·po·'ten·te] *adj* arrogant

presa ['pre·sa] *f* **1.** (*acción*) capture; **ser ~ del terror** to be seized by terror **2.** (*objeto, de caza*) prey; **animal de ~** prey; **ave de ~** bird of prey **3.** (*dique*) dam **4.** (*acequia*) channel **5.** DEP hold; **~ de brazo** (*judo*) arm hold

presagiar [pre·sa·'xjar] *vt* to betoken *form*; **estas nubes presagian tormenta** these clouds mean there will be a storm

presagio [pre·'sa·xjo] *m* **1.** (*señal*) warning sign **2.** (*presentimiento*) premonition

prescindible [pre·sin·'di·βle, pres·θin-] *adj* dispensable

prescindir [pre·sin·'dir, pres·θin-] *vi* **1.** (*renunciar a*) **~ de algo/alguien** to do without sth/sb; **no podemos ~ de él** we can't do without him **2.** (*no contar*) **~ de algo/alguien** to disregard sth/sb

prescribir [pres·kri·'βir] *irr como* **escribir** **I.** *vi* (*plazo*) to expire **II.** *vt* (*indicar*) *t.* MED to prescribe; **prescrito por la ley** prescribed by law

prescripción [pres·krip·'sjon, -kriβ·'θjon] *f* **1.** (*indicación*) indication **2.** MED prescription **3.** (*plazo*) expiry

presencia [pre·'sen·sja, -θja] *f* **1.** (*asistencia*) presence; **sin la ~ del ministro** without the minister being present; **hacer acto de ~** to put in an appearance **2.** (*aspecto*) appearance; **buena ~** good looks

presencial [pre·sen·'sjal, -'θjal] *adj* **testigo ~** eyewitness

presenciar [pre·sen·'sjar, -'θjar] *vt* **1.** (*ver*) to witness **2.** (*asistir*) to attend; **10.000 personas ~on el concierto** 10,000 people attended the concert

presentable [pre·sen·'ta·βle] *adj* presentable; **ponerse ~** to make oneself presentable

presentación [pre·sen·ta·'sjon, -'θjon] *f* **1.** (*de una novela, una película*) launch(ing) **2.** (*de un número artístico*) presentation; TEAT show **3.** (*de instancia, dimisión*) submission; **el plazo de ~ de solicitudes finaliza hoy** the period for presenting requests ends today **4.** (*de argumentos, documento, propuesta*) presentation **5.** (*de personas*) introduction **6.** (*aspecto*) appearance **7.** *AmL* (*súplica*) petition

presentador(a) [pre·sen·ta·ˈdor, -·ˈdo·ra] *m(f)* (*de programa*) presenter; (*de telediario*) newsreader

presentar [pre·senˈtar] I. *vt* **1.** (*mostrar*) to show **2.** (*ofrecer*) to offer; **el viaje presenta dificultades** the journey poses difficulties **3.** TV, RADIO to present; TEAT to put on; (*presentador*) to introduce **4.** (*instancia, dimisión*) to submit **5.** (*argumentos*) to put forward; (*pruebas, propuesta*) to submit **6.** (*pasaporte, documento*) to show **7.** (*persona*) to introduce; **te presento a mi marido** may I introduce you to my husband? **8.** (*candidato*) to propose II. *vr:* **~se 1.** (*comparecer*) to present oneself; (*aparecer*) to turn up **2.** (*para elecciones*) **~se a** to run for

presente [pre·ˈsen·te] I. *adj* **1.** (*que está*) present; **¡~!** present!; **estar ~** to be present **2.** (*actual*) current **3.** (*este*) **la ~ edición** this edition **4.** (*a considerar*) **ten ~ lo que te he dicho** bear in mind what I have told you **5.** (*en una carta*) **por la ~ deseo comunicarle que...** I write in order to tell you that... II. *m* **1.** (*actualidad*) present; **hasta el ~** until now **2.** LING present (tense) **3.** (*regalo*) present, gift

presentimiento [pre·sen·ti·ˈmjen·to] *m* premonition; **tengo el ~ de que...** I have a feeling that...

presentir [pre·senˈtir] *irr como sentir vt* to have a premonition of; **presiento que mañana lloverá** I have a feeling it's going to rain tomorrow

preservar [pre·ser·ˈβar] *vt* to protect

preservativo [pre·ser·βa·ˈti·βo] *m* condom

presidencia [pre·si·ˈðen·sja, -ˈθja] *f* **1.** (*mandato*) presidency; **asumir la ~** to take over the presidency **2.** (*de organización, asamblea: conjunto*) board;

(*individuo*) chairperson, president; **asumir la ~** to take the chair

presidencial [pre·si·ðen·ˈsjal, -·ˈθjal] *adj* POL presidential

presidente [pre·si·ˈðen·te, -a] *mf* **1.** POL president; **~ del gobierno** prime minister **2.** (*de asociación*) chairperson

presidiario, -a [pre·si·ˈðja·rjo, -a] *m, f* convict

presidio [pre·ˈsi·ðjo] *m* prison

presidir [pre·si·ˈðir] *vt* **1.** (*ocupar presidencia*) to be president of **2.** (*mandar*) to rule

presión [pre·ˈsjon] *f* pressure; **~ arterial** blood pressure; **~ social** social pressure; **grupo de ~** pressure group; **zona de altas presiones** METEO high pressure area; **cerrado a ~** pressurized; **¿a qué ~ llevas las ruedas?** what is your tire pressure?; **estar bajo ~** to be under pressure; **hacer ~ sobre alguien** to put pressure on sb

presionar [pre·sjo·ˈnar] *vt* **1.** (*apretar*) to press **2.** (*coaccionar*) to put pressure on

preso, -a [ˈpre·so, -a] *m, f* prisoner, (prison) inmate

prestación [pres·ta·ˈsjon, -ˈθjon] *f* **1.** (*de ayuda, servicio*) provision; **~ por desempleo** unemployment benefit **2.** *pl* (*de coche*) features *pl*; **un coche con todas las últimas prestaciones** a car with all the latest features

prestado, -a [pres·ˈta·ðo, -a] *adj* borrowed; **dar algo ~** to lend sth; **pedir algo ~** to borrow sth

prestamista [pres·ta·ˈmis·ta] *mf* moneylender

préstamo [ˈpres·ta·mo] *m* **1.** (*acción*) lending **2.** *t.* FIN (*lo prestado: por exposición*) loan; **~ hipotecario** mortgage; **~ a interés fijo** fixed-interest loan

prestar [pres·ˈtar] I. *vt* **1.** (*dejar*) to lend; **¿me prestas la bici, por favor?** can I borrow your bike?; **el banco me ha prestado el dinero** I have borrowed money from the bank **2.** (*dedicar*) **~ ayuda** to help; **~ servicios** to provide services; **~ apoyo** to support **3.** (*declaración*) to make; (*juramento*) to swear **4.** (*atención*) to pay; **~ silencio** to remain silent **II.** *vr:* **~se 1.** (*ofrecerse*) to offer oneself; **se prestó a ayudarme** he/she offered to help me **2.** (*avenirse*) to accept **3.** (*dar motivo*) to give rise to; **tus palabras se prestan a confusión** your words lend themselves to misinterpretation

prestigio [pres·'ti·xjo] *m* prestige

prestigioso, -a [pres·ti·'xjo·so, -a] *adj* prestigious

presumido, -a [pre·su·'mi·do, -a] *adj* (*vanidoso*)

presumir [pre·su·'mir] **I.** *vi:* **~ de algo** to boast about sth **II.** *vt* to presume

presunto, -a [pre·'sun·to, -a] *adj* (*supuesto*) presumed; **el ~ asesino** the alleged murderer

presuntuoso, -a [pre·sun·tu·'o·so] *adj* conceited

presuponer [pre·su·po·'ner] *irr como* **poner** *vt* **1.** (*suponer*) to presuppose **2.** (*calcular*) to suppose

presupuesto [pre·su·'pwes·to] *m* **1.** POL, ECON budget; **~ anual** annual budget **2.** (*cálculo*) estimate

pretender [pre·ten·'der] *vt* **1.** (*aspirar a*) to aspire to **2.** (*pedir*) to expect; **¿qué pretendes que haga?** what do you want me to do? **3.** (*tener intención*) to mean; **no pretendía molestar** I didn't mean to disturb you **4.** (*intentar*) to try to

pretendiente [pre·ten·'djen·te] *m* (*de trabajo*) applicant; (*de mujer*) suitor; (*a la corona*) pretender

pretensión [pre·ten·'sjon] *f* **1.** (*derecho*) claim; **~ económica** financial demand **2.** (*ambición*) ambition; (*aspiración*) aim; **es una persona con muchas pretensiones** he/she is very ambitious

pretérito [pre·'te·ri·to] *m* LING past

pretérito, -a [pre·'te·ri·to, -a] *adj* past

pretexto [pre·'tes·to] *m* pretext

prevalecer [pre·βa·le·'ser, -'θer] *irr como* **crecer** *vi* **1.** (*imponerse*) to prevail; **la verdad prevaleció sobre la mentira** truth prevailed over lies **2.** (*predominar*) to predominate; **esta regla prevalece sobre las demás** this rule takes precedence over the others

prevaricación [pre·βa·ri·ka·'sjon, -·'θjon]

f **1.** JUR perversion of the course of justice **2.** (*del deber*) dereliction of duty

prevención [pre·βen·'sjon, -·'θjon] *f* **1.** (*precaución*) precaution **2.** *t.* MED (*acción*) prevention; **~ del cáncer** cancer prevention; **~ de accidentes** accident prevention

prevenido, -a [pre·βe·'ni·do, -a] *adj* **1.** *estar* (*alerta*) **estar ~** to be prepared **2.** *ser* (*previsor*) prudent ▶ **hombre ~ vale por dos** *prov* forewarned is forearmed *prov*

prevenir [pre·βe·'nir] *irr como* **venir** *vt* **1.** (*protegerse de*) to prevent **2.** (*advertir*) to warn **3.** (*predisponer*) to prejudice; **~ a alguien a favor de alguien/ en contra de alguien** to bias sb in sb's favor/against sb ▶ **más vale ~ que curar** *prov* prevention is better than cure, a stitch in time saves nine *prov*

preventivo, -a [pre·βen·'ti·βo, -a] *adj* preventive, preventative; **medida preventiva** preventive measure; **prisión preventiva** preventive remand

prever [pre·'βer] *irr como* **ver** *vt* to foresee

previo ['pre·βjo] *m* TV, CINE playback

previo, -a ['pre·βjo, -a] *adj* previous; (**sin**) **~ aviso** (without) prior warning; **~ pago de la matrícula** on payment of the matriculation fee

previsible [pre·βi·'si·βle] *adj* **1.** (*probable*) predictable **2.** (*que se puede prever*) foreseeable; **era ~** it was to be expected

previsión [pre·βi·'sjon] *f* **1.** (*de prever*) prediction; **esto supera todas las previsiones** this surpasses all the predictions **2.** (*precaución*) precaution **3.** (*cálculo*) forecast; **las previsiones económicas** the economic forecasts

previsor(a) [pre·βi·'sor, -·'so·ra] *adj* **1.** (*con visión*) far-sighted **2.** (*precavido*) prudent

previsto, -a [pre·'βis·to, -a] *adj* predicted; **todo lo necesario está ~** everything necessary has been prepared

prieto, -a ['prje·to, -a] *adj* (*apretado*) tight

prima ['pri·ma] *f* **1.** (*pariente*) (girl) cousin; **~ hermana/segunda** first/second cousin **2.** FIN bonus; (*seguro*) insurance premium

primacía [pri·ma·'sia, -'θia] *f t.* MIL, POL supremacy

primar [pri·'mar] **I.** *vi* to be of great importance; **en esta escuela prima el orden** in this school the most important thing is good behavior **II.** *vt* to reward

primario, -a [pri·'ma·rjo, -a] *adj* primary; **enseñanza primaria** primary education; **necesidades primarias** basic necessities

primate [pri·'ma·te] *m* primate

primavera [pri·ma·'βe·ra] *f* spring; **estar en la ~ de la vida** *fig* to be in the prime of life

primaveral [pri·ma·βe·'ral] *adj* to spring(-like)

primer [pri·'mer] *adj v.* **primero, -a**

primera [pri·'me·ra] *f* **1.** AUTO first (gear); **ir en ~** to be in first (gear) **2.** FERRO, AVIAT first class; **viajar en ~** to travel first class

primero [pri·'me·ro] *adv* **1.** (*en primer lugar*) first; **~..., segundo...** first..., second...; **~ dice una cosa, luego otra** first he/she says one thing, then another **2.** (*antes*) rather

primero, -a [pri·'me·ro, -a] **I.** *adj* (*ante sustantivo masc. sing.: primer*) first; **primera calidad** top quality; **primera edición** first edition; **el Primer Ministro** the Prime Minister; **a primera hora (de la mañana)** first thing (in the morning); **a ~s de mes** at the beginning of the month; **de primera** first-rate; **de primera calidad** top quality; **desde un primer momento** from the outset; **en primer lugar** in the first place; **lo ~ es lo ~** first things first; **lo ~ es ahora la familia** the most important thing now is the family **II.** *m, f* first; **el ~ de la clase** the top of the class; **estar entre los ~s** to be among the leaders

primicia [pri·'mi·sja, -θja] *f* PREN, TV, RADIO scoop

primitivo, -a [pri·mi·'ti·βo, -a] *adj* primitive; **lotería primitiva** Spanish state lottery

primo ['pri·mo] *m* **1.** (*pariente*) (boy) cousin; **~ hermano/segundo** first/second cousin **2.** *inf* (*ingenuo*) mug; **hacer el ~** to get taken for a ride

primo, -a ['pri·mo, -a] *adj* **materia prima** raw material; **número ~** MAT prime number

primogénito, -a [pri·mo·'xe·ni·to, -a] *adj, m, f* first-born

primor [pri·'mor] *m* **1.** (*habilidad*) skill **2.** (*esmero*) care

primordial [pri·mor·'djal] *adj* **1.** (*más importante*) supreme; **este asunto es de interés ~** this affair is of fundamental concern **2.** (*fundamental*) essential, fundamental

princesa [prin·'se·sa, -'θe·sa] *f v.* **príncipe, princesa**

principado [prin·si·'pa·do, prin·θi-] *m* principality

principal [prin·si·'pal, prin·θi-] *adj* **1.** (*más importante*) principal; **el problema ~** the main problem; **lo ~ es que...** the main priority is... **2.** (*esencial*) essential

principalmente [prin·si·pal·'men·te, prin·θi-] *adv* mainly, principally

príncipe, princesa ['prin·si·pe, -θi·pe; prin·'se·sa, -'θe·sa] *m, f* prince *m*, princess *f*; **~ heredero** crown prince; **el Príncipe de Asturias** the Prince of Asturias (*title held by the heir to the Spanish ish throne*); **~ azul** Prince Charming

principiante [prin·si·'pjan·te, prin·θi-] *mf* beginner, novice

principio [prin·'si·pjo, -'θi·pjo] *m* **1.** (*comienzo*) beginning; **al ~** at the beginning; **ya desde el ~** right from the beginning; **desde un ~** from the first; **a ~s de diciembre** at the beginning of December **2.** (*causa*) cause; (*origen*) origin; **el ~ de la discusión** the cause of the argument **3.** (*de ética*) principle; **sin ~s** unprincipled; **hombre de ~s a** man of principle(s); **por ~** on principle **4.** *t.* FÍS (*fundamento*) principle

pringar <g → gu> [prin·'gar] **I.** *vt* (*manchar*) **~ de/con algo** to smear with sth **II.** *vi* AmL (*lloviznar*) to drizzle **III.** *vr:* **~se** (*mancharse*) **~se de/con algo** to cover oneself with sth

pringoso, -a [prin·'go·so, -a] *adj* greasy

prioridad [prjo·ri·'dad] *f* **1.** (*anteriori-*

dad) priority; **de máxima ~** top priority; **dar ~ a un asunto** to give a matter priority; **tener ~ sobre** to have priority over **2.** AUTO (*de paso*) right of way

prioritario, -a [pri·o·ri'ta·rjo, -a] *adj* priority; **este plan es ~** this plan has priority

prisa ['pri·sa] *f* hurry; **a toda ~** at full speed; **de ~** quickly; **de ~ y corriendo** (*con demasiada prisa*) in a rush; (*rápidamente*) quickly; **no corre ~** there's no hurry; **¡date ~!** hurry up!; **meter ~ a alguien** to hurry sb; **tengo ~** I'm in a hurry

prisión [pri'sjon] *f* **1.** (*reclusión*) imprisonment; **~ preventiva** remand **2.** (*edificio*) prison; **~ de alta seguridad** high-security prison; **estar en ~** to be in prison

prisionero, -a [pri·sjo'ne·ro, -a] *m, f* prisoner; **hacer ~ a alguien** to take sb prisoner

prisma ['pris·ma] *m* (*figura*) prism

prismáticos [pris·'ma·ti·kos] *mpl* binoculars *pl*

privación [pri·βa·'sjon, -'θjon] *f* **1.** (*desposesión*) deprivation; **~ de libertad** JUR loss of liberty **2.** (*carencia*) privation

privado, -a [pri·'βa·do, -a] *adj* **1.** (*reunión, fiesta*) private; (*sesión*) closed **2.** (*personal, confidencial*) private; **vida privada** private life; **en ~** in private **3.** (*falto*) **~ de...** without...; **~ de medios** without means

privar [pri·'βar] **I.** *vt* **1.** (*desposeer*) to deprive; **~ a alguien de un derecho** to deprive sb of a right **2.** (*prohibir*) to forbid **3.** (*gustar*) to delight; **está privado por esa chica** he's crazy about that girl **II.** *vr* to deny oneself; **no se privan de nada** they don't want for anything

privatizar <z → c> [pri·βa·ti·'sar, -'θar] *vt* to privatize

privilegiado, -a [pri·βi·le·'xja·do, -a] *adj* privileged; (*memoria*) exceptional

privilegio [pri·βi·'le·xjo] *m* privilege; **~ fiscal** tax concession

pro [pro] *m, f* **1.** (*provecho*) advantage; **valorar los ~s y los contras** to weigh the pros and cons **2.** (*de bien*) **un hombre de ~** an honest man

II. *prep* for

proa ['pro·a] *f* NÁUT bow; AVIAT nose

probabilidad [pro·βa·βi·li'dad] *f* **1.** (*verosimilitud*) probability; **con toda ~** in all likelihood **2.** (*posibilidad*) prospect; **hay ~es de ganar** there is a good chance of winning

probable [pro·'βa·βle] *adj* (*verosímil*) probable; **un resultado ~** a likely result; **lo más ~ es que...** chances are that...

probablemente [pro·βa·βle·'men·te] *adv* probably

probado, -a [pro·'βa·do, -a] *adj* proven

probador [pro·βa·'dor] *m* fitting room

probar <o → ue> [pro·'βar] **I.** *vt* **1.** (*demostrar*) to prove **2.** (*experimentar*) to try; (*aparato*) to test **3.** (*a alguien*) to test **4.** (*vestido*) to try on **5.** CULIN to taste; **no he probado nunca una paella** I have never tried paella **II.** *vi* (*intentar*) to try

problema [pro·'βle·ma] *m* problem; **~ liquidez** cash flow problem

problemático, -a [pro·βle·'ma·ti·ko, -a] *adj* problematic

procedencia [pro·se·'den·sja, pro·θe·'den·θja] *f* (*origen*) origin

procedente [pro·se·'den·te, pro·θe-] *adj* **1.** (*oportuno*) appropriate **2.** (*que viene de*) **~ de** from; **el tren ~ de Nueva York con destino a Chicago** the train from New York to Chicago **3.** JUR fitting

proceder [pro·se·'der, pro·θe-] **I.** *m* **1.** (*comportamiento*) behavior **2.** (*actuación*) (course of) action **II.** *vi* **1.** (*familia*) to descend; (*de un lugar*) to come **2.** (*actuar*) to act **3.** (*ser oportuno*) to be appropriate; **no ~** to be inappropriate; **táchese lo que no proceda** delete as applicable **4.** (*pasar a*) to proceed

procedimiento [pro·se·di·'mjen·to, pro·θe-] *m* **1.** (*actuación*) procedure; **seguir un ~** to follow a procedure **2.** (*método*) method **3.** JUR proceedings *pl*

procesado, -a [pro·se·'sa·do, -a; pro·θe·-] *m, f* JUR defendant; **el ~** the accused

procesador [pro·se·sa·'dor, pro·θe-] *m* computer; **~ de textos** word processor

procesamiento [pro·se·sa·'mjen·to, pro·θe-] *m* **1.** JUR prosecution **2.** COMPUT processing

procesar [pro·se·'sar, pro·θe-] vt **1.** JUR to prosecute; **le procesan por violación** he is being prosecuted for rape **2.** TÉC to process

procesión [pro·se·'sjon, pro·θe-] f **1.** t. REL (*marcha*) procession **2.** (*hilera*) line; (*de personas*) procession **3.** inf (*preocupación*) **permaneció tranquilo aunque la ~ iba por dentro** he remained outwardly calm, but he was actually rather worried

proceso [pro·'se·so, pro·'θe-] m **1.** (*método*) process **2.** (*procedimiento*) procedure **3.** JUR (*causa*) trial

proclamación [pro·kla·ma·'sjon, -'θjon] f proclamation

proclamar [pro·kla·'mar] **I.** vt **1.** (*hacer público*) to announce; **~ la República** to proclaim a Republic **2.** (*aclamar*) to acclaim **3.** (*sentimiento*) to declare **4.** (*ganador*) to declare; **fue proclamado Premio Nobel** he was awarded the Nobel Prize **II.** vr **~se ganador** to declare oneself the winner

procrear [pro·kre·'ar] vt to procreate

procurador(a) [pro·ku·ra·'dor, -·'do·ra] m(f) attorney; (*en negocios*) agent

procurar [pro·ku·'rar] **I.** vt **1.** (*intentar*) to try; **procura que no te oigan** make sure they don't hear you **2.** (*proporcionar*) to obtain **II.** vr to secure (for oneself)

prodigar <g → gu> [pro·di·'ɣar] **I.** vt **1.** (*malgastar*) to waste **2.** (*dar*) to lavish **II.** vr **se prodigó en toda clase de atenciones con nosotros** he attended to our every need; **se prodigó en elogios hacia él** he/she showered him with praise

prodigio [pro·'di·xjo] m prodigy; **niño ~** child prodigy

prodigioso, -a [pro·di·'xjo·so, -a] adj **1.** (*sobrenatural*) miraculous **2.** (*extraordinario*) marvelous

pródigo, -a ['pro·di·ɣo, -a] adj **1.** (*malgastador*) wasteful; **el hijo ~** the prodigal son **2.** (*generoso*) generous; **la pródiga naturaleza** bountiful nature

producción [pro·duk·'sjon, -'θjon] f **1.** t. TÉC, CINE production; **~ en cadena** assembly line production; **~ en masa** mass

production **2.** (*productos*) output

producir [pro·du·'sir, -'θir] irr como traducir **I.** vt **1.** t. TÉC, CINE to produce; (*energía*) to generate **2.** (*beneficios*) to generate; (*intereses*) to yield **3.** (*alegría, impresión*) to create; (*aburrimiento, miedo*) to produce; (*daño, tristeza*) to cause **II.** vr: **~se 1.** (*fabricarse*) to be produced **2.** (*tener lugar*) to take place; **se produjo una crisis** a crisis occurred

productividad [pro·duk·ti·βi·'dad] f productivity

productivo, -a [pro·duk·'ti·βo, -a] adj productive

producto [pro·'duk·to] m **1.** t. QUÍM, MAT product; **~s básicos** commodities; **~s alimenticios** foodstuffs pl; **~ de belleza** beauty product; **~ de marca** brand-name product; **~s químicos** chemicals pl; **~ (semi)manufacturado** manufactured good; **~ derivado** [o **secundario**] by-product **2.** (*de un negocio*) profit; (*de una venta*) proceeds pl; **Producto Interior Bruto** Gross Domestic Product; **Producto Nacional Bruto** Gross National Product

productor(a) [pro·duk·'tor, -·'to·ra] **I.** adj producing **II.** m(f) producer

profano, -a [pro·'fa·no, -a] adj **1.** (*secular*) secular **2.** (*irreverente*) irreverent **3.** (*ignorante*) ignorant; **soy ~ en esta materia** I am not an expert in this subject

profecía [pro·fe·'si·a, -'θi·a] f prophecy

profesar [pro·fe·'sar] vt (*religión, doctrina*) to profess

profesión [pro·fe·'sjon] f **1.** (*empleo*) profession; **de ~ by** profession **2.** (*de religión, doctrina*) profession

profesional [pro·fe·sjo·'nal] **I.** adj professional; **ética ~** professional ethics; **secreto ~** trade secret **II.** mf professional

profesor(a) [pro·fe·'sor, -·'so·ra] m(f) (*no universitario*) teacher; (*universitario*) professor; (*catedrático*) senior teacher

profeta, -isa [pro·'fe·ta, pro·fe·'ti·sa] m, f prophet m(f), prophetess f; **nadie es ~ en su tierra** no one is a prophet in his own land

profundamente [pro·fun·da·'men·te] *adv* profoundly; **~ ofendido** deeply offended

profundidad [pro·fun·di·'dad] *f* depth; **analizar en ~** to analyze in depth; **tener una ~ de cinco metros** to be five meters deep

profundizar <z → c> [pro·fun·di·'sar, -'θar] I. *vt* (*hoyo, zanja*) to make deeper; *fig* to study in depth II. *vi* **~ en algo** (*o to go into*) sth in depth

profundo, -a [pro·'fun·do] *adj* (*hoyo, lago, voz*) deep; (*observación*) incisive; (*pena*) heartfelt; (*pensamiento, misterio*) profound; (*conocimiento*) thorough; **en lo más ~ de mi corazón** from the very bottom of my heart

profusión [pro·fu·'sjon] *f* profusion; **con ~ de detalles** with a wealth of details; **hay gran ~ de noticias** there is a lot of news

progenitor(a) [pro·xe·ni·'tor, -·'to·ra] *m(f)* **1.** (*antepasado*) for(e)bear **2.** (*mayor*) father *m*, mother *f*; **los ~es** the parents

programa [pro·'ɣra·ma] *m* program; **~ de las clases (de la Universidad)** (university) class schedule; **~ de estudios** study plan; **~ de trabajo** work schedule; **~ antivirus** COMPUT antivirus program

programación [pro·ɣra·ma·'sjon, -'θjon] *f* **1.** (*acción*) programming **2.** TV, RADIO program

programador(a) [pro·ɣra·ma·'dor, -·'do·ra] *m(f)* programmer

programar [pro·ɣra·'mar] *vt* to plan; **la conferencia está programada para el domingo** the talk is scheduled for Sunday; **¿qué tienes programado para esta tarde?** what do you have planned for this evening?

progresar [pro·ɣre·'sar] *vi* to make progress; (*enfermedad, ciencia*) to develop; **~ profesionalmente** to progress [*o get ahead*] in one's career

progresión [pro·ɣre·'sjon] *f* **1.** (*avance*) progress **2.** MAT, MÚS progression

progresista [pro·ɣre·'sis·ta] *adj* progressive

progresivo, -a [pro·ɣre·'si·βo, -a] *adj t.* FIN (*que progresa*) progressive; (*que aumenta*) increasing

progreso [pro·'ɣre·so] *m* progress

prohibición [pro·i·βi·'sjon, -'θjon] *f* prohibition

prohibido, -a [pro·i·'βi·do, -a] *adj* **~ fumar** no smoking; **fruto ~** forbidden fruit; **prohibida la entrada** no entry

prohibir [pro·i·'βir] *irr vt* to prohibit, to ban

prohibitivo, -a [pro·i·βi·'ti·βo, -a] *adj* prohibitive; **a precio ~** prohibitively expensive

prójimo ['pro·xi·mo] *m* (*semejante*) fellow man; **amor al ~** love of one's neighbor

proletario, -a [pro·le·'ta·rjo, -a] *adj* proletarian; **barrio ~** working-class area

proliferación [pro·li·fe·ra·'sjon, -'θjon] *f* **1.** (*en cantidad*) proliferation; **tratado de no ~ de armas nucleares** nuclear non-proliferation treaty **2.** *t.* MED (*incontrolada*) spread

proliferar [pro·li·fe·'rar] *vi* **1.** (*en cantidad*) to proliferate **2.** (*epidemia, rumor*) to spread

prólogo ['pro·lo·ɣo] *m* (*de libro*) foreword; TEAT, DEP prelude

prolongación [pro·lon·ga·'sjon, -'θjon] *f* extension; (*de decisión*) postponement

prolongado, -a [pro·lon·'ga·do, -a] *adj* prolonged; **un sobre ~** a long envelope

prolongar <g → gu> [pro·lon·'gar] I. *vt* to extend; (*decisión*) to postpone; (*un estado*) to prolong II. *vr:* **~se** to continue; (*un estado*) to be prolonged; (*reunión*) to overrun; **las negociaciones se están prolongando demasiado** the negotiations are dragging on for too long

promediar [pro·me·'djar] I. *vt* **1.** (*repartir*) to divide in two **2.** (*sacar promedio*) to average out II. *vi* **1.** (*mediar*) to mediate **2.** (*temporal*) **antes de ~ el año** before the year was halfway through

promedio [pro·'me·djo] *m* average; **veo la tele un ~ de dos horas al día** I watch an average of two hours' TV a day

promesa [pro·'me·sa] *f* promise; REL vow; **el jefe me ha dado su ~ de que...** the boss has promised me that...

prometedor(a) [pro·me·te·'dor, -·'do·ra] *adj* promising

prometer [pro·me·'ter] I. *vt* to promise;

REL to vow; **te prometo que lo haré** I promise you I'll do it; **~ el oro y el moro** to promise the earth ▶ **lo prometido es deuda** *prov* a promise is a promise II. *vi* **este negocio promete** this business is promising III. *vr* (*novios*) to get engaged

prometido, -a [pro·me·'ti·do] *m, f* fiancé *m*, fiancée *f*

promiscuidad [pro·mis·kwi·'dad] *f* (*sexual*) promiscuity

promoción [pro·mo·'sjon, -'θjon] *f* 1. (*de empresa, categoría, producto*) promotion 2. (*de licenciados*) year, graduating class; **ser de la misma ~** to have graduated in the same year

promocionar [pro·mo·sjo·'nar, -θjo·'nar] *vt* (*empresa, producto*) to promote; **está promocionando su nueva película** she is promoting her new film

promotor(a) [pro·mo·'tor] *m(f)* (*patrocinador*) sponsor; (*deportivo, artístico, de espectáculo*) promoter

promover <o → ue> [pro·mo·'βer] *vt* 1. (*querella, escándalo*) to cause; (*proceso*) to advance 2. (*en el cargo*) to promote

promulgar <g → gu> [pro·mul·'γar] *vt* to enact; (*divulgar*) to announce

pronombre [pro·'nom·bre] *m* LING pronoun

pronosticar <c → qu> [pro·nos·ti·'kar] *vt* to forecast

pronóstico [pro·'nos·ti·ko] *m* t. ECON forecast; MED prognosis; DEP prediction

pronto ['pron·to] I. *adv* 1. (*rápido*) quickly 2. (*enseguida*) at once 3. (*temprano*) early ▶ **de ~** suddenly; **¡hasta ~!** see you!; **por de** [*o* **por lo**] **~** for the time being II. *conj* **tan ~ como** as soon as

pronto, -a ['pron·to, -a] *adj* 1. (*rápido*) quick; (*despierto*) sharp 2. (*dispuesto*) ready; **estar ~** *CSur* to be ready

pronunciación [pro·nun·sja·'sjon, -θja·'θjon] *f* LING pronunciation

pronunciado, -a [pro·nun·'sja·do, -a, -'θja·do, -a] *adj* pronounced; (*pendiente, cuesta*) steep; **acento ~** strong [*o* marked] accent; **una curva pronunciada** a sharp bend; **rasgos ~s** strong features

pronunciar [pro·nun·'sjar, -'θjar] I. *vt* 1. (*articular*) to pronounce; **~ un discurso** to make a speech; **~ unas palabras** to say a few words; **~ sentencia** to pass sentence 2. (*resaltar*) to emphasize II. *vr:* **~se** 1. (*opinar*) **~se sobre algo** to state one's opinion on sth 2. (*acentuarse*) to become more pronounced

propagación [pro·pa·ya·'sjon, -'θjon] *f* (*multiplicación, reproducción*) propagation

propaganda [pro·pa·'yan·da] *f* 1. (*publicidad*) publicity; **hacer ~** to advertise, to publicize 2. MIL, POL propaganda

propagar <g → gu> [pro·pa·'yar] I. *vt* (*multiplicar*) to propagate; **~ un rumor** to spread a rumor II. *vr:* **~se** (*multiplicarse*) to propagate

propano [pro·'pa·no] *m* propane

propasar [pro·pa·'sar] *vr:* **~se** (*extralimitarse*) to go too far; **~se con alguien** to take liberties with sb

propenso, -a [pro·'pen·so, -a] *adj* (*a enfermedades*) susceptible; (*dispuesto*) inclined; **ser ~ a algo** to be prone to sth

propiamente [pro·pja·'men·te] *adv* ~ **dicho** strictly speaking

propiciar [pro·pi·'sjar, -'θjar] *vt* (*favorecer*) to favor; (*posibilitar*) to make possible; **el viento propició la extensión de las llamas** the wind helped the flames to spread

propicio, -a [pro·'pi·sjo, -a; -θjo, -a] *adj* 1. (*favorable*) favorable; **en el momento ~** at the right moment 2. (*dispuesto*) inclined; **mostrarse (poco) ~ para...** (not) to be prepared to...

propiedad [pro·pje·'dad] *f* 1. (*pertenencia, cualidad*) FÍS property; **~ exclusiva** exclusive ownership; **~ intelectual** intellectual property; **~ inmobiliaria** real estate; **un piso de mi ~** an apartment that I own; **tener algo en ~** to own sth; **ser ~ de alguien** to be sb's property 2. (*corrección*) correctness; (*exactitud*) precision; **expresarse con ~** to speak correctly

propietario, -a [pro·pje·'ta·rjo, -a] *m, f* owner; (*terrateniente*) landowner; (*casero*) landlord

propina [pro·'pi·na] *f* tip; **dejar ~** to leave a tip; **de ~** *fig* for good measure

propinar [pro·pi·'nar] *vt* (*golpes*) to give

propio, -a ['pro·pjo, -a] *adj* 1. (*de uno mismo*) own; **en defensa propia** in self-defense; **lo he visto con mis ~s ojos** I have seen it with my own eyes; **tengo piso ~** I own my apartment 2. (*mismo*) same; **lo ~** the same; **el ~ jefe** the boss himself; **nombre ~** LING proper noun 3. (*característico*) characteristic; **eso (no) es ~ de ti** that is (not) like you 4. (*apropiado*) proper

proponer [pro·po·'ner] *irr como* **poner** I. *vt* 1. (*sugerir, presentar*) to propose; **~ un brindis por alguien** to propose a toast in sb's honor 2. (*plantear*) to put forward; **~ una cuestión** to set out a matter II. *vr* to propose; (*tener intención*) to intend; **¿qué te propones?** what are you trying to do?

proporción [pro·por·'sjon, -'θjon] *f* 1. (*relación, porcentaje*) proportion; **no guardar ~ con algo** to be out of proportion with sth; **en una ~ de 8 a 1** in a ratio of 8 to 1 2. *pl* (*dimensión*) proportions *pl;* **un accidente de enormes proporciones** a major accident

proporcional [pro·por·sjo·'nal, -θjo·'nal] *adj* proportional; **reparto ~** proportional distribution; **sistema ~** POL proportional representation

proporcionar [pro·por·sjo·'nar, -θjo·'nar] *vt* 1. (*facilitar*) to provide; **~ víveres a alguien** to provide sb with supplies 2. (*ocasionar*) to cause; **~ disgustos a alguien** to upset sb

proposición [pro·po·si·'sjon, -'θjon] *f* 1. (*propuesta*) proposal; **~ de ley** bill 2. LING (*oración*) sentence; (*parte*) clause

propósito [pro·'po·si·to] I. *m* 1. (*intención*) intention; **buenos ~s** good intentions; **tener el ~ de...** to intend to... 2. (*objetivo*) objective ▸ **a ~** (*adrede*) on purpose; (*por cierto*) by the way II. *prep* **a ~ de** with regard to

propuesta [pro·'pwes·ta] *f* proposal; (*oferta*) offer; **a ~ de alguien** on sb's suggestion; **formular una ~** to draw up a proposal

propulsar [pro·pul·'sar] *vt* 1. TÉC to propel 2. (*fomentar*) to promote

propulsión [pro·pul·'sjon] *f* TÉC propulsion; **~ a hélice** propeller power; **~ por reacción** jet propulsion

prórroga ['pro·rro·ɣa] *f* 1. ECON extension 2. (*aplazamiento*) deferral 3. DEP extra time, overtime

prosa ['pro·sa] *f* prose

proseguir [pro·se·'ɣir] *irr como* **seguir** I. *vi* to continue II. *vt* 1. (*continuar*) *t.* JUR to continue 2. (*un fin*) to pursue

prospecto [pros·'pek·to] *m* prospectus; (*de un medicamento*) directions *pl* for use

prosperar [pros·pe·'rar] *vi* (*florecer*) to thrive; (*tener éxito*) to prosper

prosperidad [pros·pe·ri·'dad] *f* (*bienestar*) prosperity; **~ económica** economic prosperity

próspero, -a ['pros·pe·ro, -a] *adj* (*floreciente*) thriving; (*con éxito*) prosperous; **¡Próspero Año Nuevo!** Happy New Year!

próstata ['pros·ta·ta] *f* prostate

prostíbulo [pros·'ti·βu·lo] *m* brothel

prostitución [pros·ti·tu·'sjon, -'θjon] *f* prostitution; **ejercer la ~** to be a prostitute

prostituir [pros·ti·tu·'ir] *irr como* **huir** I. *vt* to prostitute II. *vr:* **~se** *t.* *fig* to prostitute oneself

prostituto, -a [pros·ti·'tu·to, -a] *m, f* male prostitute *m*, prostitute *f*

protagonista [pro·ta·ɣo·'nis·ta] I. *adj* **el papel ~** the leading role II. *mf* key participant; CINE, TEAT leading actor *m*, leading actress *f;* LIT main character

protagonizar [<z > c> [pro·ta·ɣo·ni·'sar, -'θar] *vt* to play; **~ una película** to star in a film

protección [pro·tek·'sjon, -'θjon] *f* protection; **~ sanitaria** health cover; **crema de alta ~** high-protection sun cream; **poner a alguien bajo ~** to place sb under protection; **tomar a alguien bajo su ~** to take sb into one's protection

protector [pro·tek·'tor] *m* protector; **~ solar** sunscreen

protector(a) [pro·tek·'tor, -·'to·ra] I. *adj* protective; **casco ~** protective helmet;

sociedad ~a de animales society for the prevention of cruelty to animals II. *m(f)* protector; (*mecenas*) patron

proteger <g → j> [pro·te·'xer] I. *vt* to protect; *vr:* ~**se** to protect oneself; ~**se los ojos** to protect one's eyes

protegido, -a [pro·te·'xi·do, -a] I. *adj* protected; ~ **contra escritura** COMPUT write-protected II. *m, f* protégé *m*, protégée *f*

proteína [pro·te·'i·na] *f* protein

prótesis ['pro·te·sis] *f inv* prosthesis

protesta [pro·'tes·ta] *f* protest; JUR objection

protestante [pro·tes·'tan·te] *adj, mf* REL Protestant

protestar [pro·tes·'tar] I. *vi* to protest II. *vt* JUR to raise an objection

protestón, -ona [pro·tes·'ton, --'to·na] *adj inf* grumbling

protocolo [pro·to·'ko·lo] *m* protocol

protón [pro·'ton] *m* proton

prototipo [pro·to·'ti·po] *m* prototype

provecho [pro·'βe·tʃo] *m* use; (*ventaja*) advantage; (*beneficio*) benefit; **de ~** useful; **nada de ~** nothing of use; **en ~ de alguien** to sb's advantage; **sacar ~ de algo/alguien** to do benefit from sth/sb, to profit from sth/sb; **¡buen ~!** enjoy your meal!, bon appétit!

provechoso, -a [pro·βe·'tʃo·so, -a] *adj* beneficial; (*útil*) useful

proveedor(a) [pro·βe·'dor/pro·βe·'e·dor] *m(f)* 1. (*suministrador*) supplier 2. COMPUT provider

proveer [pro·'βer/pro·βe·'er] *irr* I. *vi* to provide II. *vt:* ~**se** 1. (*abastecer*) to supply; ~ **de algo** to furnish with sth; (*dotar*) to provide with sth 2. (*un puesto*) to fill III. *vr* to supply oneself; ~**se de algo** to provide oneself with sth

proveniente [pro·βe·'njen·te] *adj* **el tren ~ de Madrid** the train from Madrid

provenir [pro·βe·'nir] *irr como* venir *vi* ~ **de** to come from, to stem from

proverbio [pro·'βer·βjo] *m* proverb

provincia [pro·'βin·sja, -θja] *f* province; *AmS* (*estado*) state

provisión [pro·βi·'sjon] *f* (*reserva*) sup-

ply; **provisiones** provisions *pl*

provisional [pro·βi·sjo·'nal] *adj* provisional; **gobierno ~** provisional government; **medida ~** temporary measure

provisto, -a [pro·'βis·to, -a] I. *pp de* **proveer** II. *adj* provided; ~ **al efecto** provided for the purpose

provocación [pro·βo·ka·'sjon, -'θjon] *f* provocation

provocador [pro·βo·ka·'dor] *m* stirrer

provocar <c → qu> [pro·βo·'kar] I. *vt* 1. (*incitar*) to provoke; **¡no me provoques!** don't provoke me! 2. (*causar*) *t.* MED to cause, to induce; ~ **risa a alguien** to make sb laugh; ~ **un cambio** to bring about a change; ~ **una guerra** to start a war; ~ **un incendio** to start a fire II. *vi* AmL (*apetecer*) (**no**) **me provoca** I (don't) feel like it

provocativo, -a [pro·βo·ka·'ti·βo, -a] *adj* provocative

próximamente [prok·si·ma·'men·te] *adv* soon

proximidad [prok·si·mi·'dad] *f* proximity; **en las ~es** in the vicinity

próximo, -a ['prok·si·mo, -a] *adj* 1. (*cercano*) near, neighboring; (*temporal*) close; **estar ~ a...** to be close to... 2. (*siguiente*) next; **el ~ año** next year; **el ~ viernes** next Friday; **la próxima vez** the next time; **¡hasta la próxima!** see you soon!

proyección [pro·jek·'sjon, -'θjon] *f* 1. FÍS, ARQUIT, CINE, PSICO projection; (*sesión*) screening 2. (*influencia*) influence; **una empresa de ~ internacional** a business with a global presence

proyectar [pro·jek·'tar] I. *vt* 1. FÍS, FOTO, CINE to project 2. (*lanzar*) to throw 3. (*luz*) to shine; (*sombra*) to cast 4. (*planear*) to plan 5. *t.* TÉC (*diseñar*) to design II. *vr:* ~**se** 1. (*luz*) to be shone; (*sombra*) to be cast 2. PSICO ~**se en algo** to project onto sth

proyectil [pro·jek·'til] *m* projectile

proyecto [pro·'jek·to] *m* plan; ~ **de fin de carrera** UNIV final year project; ~ **de ley** bill; **en ~** planned

proyector [pro·jek·'tor] *m* FOTO, CINE projector; ~ **de cine** film projector; **de diapositivas** slide projector; ~ **de luz**

floodlight

prudencia [pru·'den·sja, -θja] *f* prudence

prudencial [pru·den·'sjal, -'θjal] *adj* (*razonable*) reasonable

prudente [pru·'den·te] *adj* prudent

prueba ['prwe·βa] *f* **1.** *t.* TÉC (*test*) test; (*experimento*) experiment; **~ de alcoholemia** Breathalyzer® test; **~ de aptitud** aptitude test; **~ de paternidad** paternity test; **período de ~** trial period; **poner a ~** to try out; **someter a ~** to test; **sufrir una dura ~** to be put through a stern test; **a ~ de agua** waterproof; **a ~ de balas** bullet-proof; **a ~ de robo** theft-proof; **~ de fuego** *fig* acid test **2.** (*comprobación*) proof **3.** (*examen*) exam; **~ de acceso** entry exam **4.** DEP (*competición*) event; **~ clasificatoria/eliminatoria** qualifier/eliminator **5.** TIPO proof; **~ de imprenta** proof **6.** (*testimonio*) piece of evidence; **~ circunstancial** circumstantial evidence; **en ~ de nuestro reconocimiento** as a token of our gratitude; **tener ~s de que...** to have evidence that...

(p)**seudónimo** [seu·'do·ni·mo] *m* pseudonym

(p)**sicoanálisis** [si·ko·a·'na·li·sis] *m* psychoanalysis

(p)**sicoanalista** [si·ko·a·na·'lis·ta] *mf* psychoanalyst

(p)**sicología** [si·ko·lo·'xi·a] *f* psychology; **~ infantil** child psychology

(p)**sicológico, -a** [si·ko·lo·'xi·ko, -a] *adj* psychological

(p)**sicólogo, -a** [si·ko·lo·ɣo, -a] *m, f* psychologist

(p)**sicópata** [si·'ko·pa·ta] *mf* psychopath

(p)**sicosis** [si·'ko·sis] *f inv* psychosis; **~ colectiva** collective psychosis

(p)**sicosomático, -a** [si·ko·so·'ma·ti·ko, -a] *adj* psychosomatic

(p)**sicoterapia** [si·ko·te·'ra·pja] *f* psychotherapy

(p)**sique** [si·'ke] *f* psyche

(p)**siquiatra** [si·'kja·tra] *mf* psychiatrist

(p)**siquiatría** [si·kja·'tri·a] *f* psychiatry

(p)**siquiátrico** [si·'kja·tri·ko] *m* (*hospital*) mental [*o* psychiatric] hospital

(p)**síquico, -a** ['si·ki·ko, -a] *adj* psychic, mental

púa ['pu·a] *f* (*de planta*) thorn; (*de animal*) spine, quill; (*del peine*) tooth; (*de tenedor*) prong; MÚS plectrum

pub <pubs> [paβ] *m* bar, cocktail lounge

pubertad [pu·βer·'tad] *f* puberty

pubis ['pu·βis] *m inv* pubis

publicación [pu·βli·ka·'sjon, -'θjon] *f* publication

publicar <c → qu> [pu·βli·'kar] **I.** *vt* to publish **II.** *vr:* **~se** to be published

publicidad [pu·βli·si·'dad, -θi·'dad] *f* **1.** (*carácter público*) publicity; **este programa le ha dado mucha ~** this program has given him/her a lot of publicity **2.** (*propaganda*) advertising; **hacer ~ de algo** to advertise sth

publicitario, -a [pu·βli·si·'ta·rjo, -a; pu·βli·θi-] *adj* advertising

público ['pu·βli·ko] *m* public; **en ~** in public; **el gran ~** the general public; **para todos los ~s** for all audiences; CINE G-rated; **abierto/cerrado al ~** open/closed to the public; **hoy hay poco ~** there aren't many people today

público, -a ['pu·βli·ko, -a] *adj* public; **deuda pública** national debt; **relaciones públicas** public relations; **el sector ~** the public sector; **transporte ~** public transport; **escándalo ~** public scandal; **hacer ~** to make public; **hacerse ~** to become known; **ser del dominio ~** to be public domain

pucha ['pu·tʃa] *interj* CSur **¡la ~!** damn!

pucherazo [pu·tʃe·'ra·so, -θo] *m* – electoral electoral fraud

puchero [pu·'tʃe·ro] *m* (*olla*) pot; CULIN stew; **hacer ~s** *inf* (*gestos*) to pout

pudor [pu·'dor] *m* (*recato*) shyness; (*vergüenza*) shame

pudrir [pu·'drir] *irr* **I.** *vt t. fig* to rot **II.** *vr:* **~se** *t. fig* to rot; *Arg inf* (*aburrirse*) to get bored; **~se en la cárcel** *inf* to rot in prison

pueblo ['pwe·βlo] *m* **1.** (*nación*) people; **un hombre del ~** a man of the people **2.** (*aldea*) village; (*población*) (small) town; **~ costero** seaside town; **~ de mala muerte** *inf* dead-end town; **de ~**

from a small town; **pey** small-town

puente ['pwen·te] *m* **1.** *t.* NÁUT, ELEC (*construcción, de las gafas*) bridge; **~ levadizo** drawbridge; **~ colgante** suspension bridge; **~ aéreo** (*servicio*) shuttle; MIL airlift; **~ dental** bridge; **~ de mando** (*compass*) bridge; **hacer un ~ a un coche** to hot-wire a car **2.** (*fiesta*) long weekend *(a public holiday plus an additional day off);* **hacer/tener ~** to take/ have a long weekend

puenting ['pwen·tin] *m* bungee jumping

puerco, -a ['pwer·ko, -a] *m, f* **1.** (*cerdo*) pig; (*macho*) hog; (*hembra*) sow; **~ espín** porcupine **2.** *inf* (*persona sucia u obscena*) pig **3.** *inf* (*canalla*) swine

puericultor(a) [pwe·ri·kul·'tor, -·'to·ra] *m(f)* MED pediatrician

pueril [pwe·'ril] *adj* infant

puerro [pwe·rro] *m* leek

puerta ['pwer·ta] *f* door; **~ de la calle** front door; **~ corredera** sliding door; **~ de servicio** service door; **~ giratoria** revolving door; **día de ~s abiertas** open day; **quinta ~** AUTO rear door; **escuchar detrás de la ~** to eavesdrop; **a la ~ de casa** at the front door; **a ~ cerrada** JUR in private; **a las ~s de la muerte** at death's door; **estar a las ~s** *fig* to be on the brink; **dar a alguien con la ~ en las narices** to slam the door in sb's face; **de ~s adentro** *fig* in private; **ir de ~ en ~** to go from door to door; **cerrar las ~s a alguien** *fig* to block sb's path; **por la ~ grande** *t. fig* in triumph; **tiene todas las ~s abiertas** *fig* he has a wealth of opportunities; **disparo a ~** DEP shot at goal

puerto ['pwer·to] *m* **1.** NÁUT harbor; (*ciudad*) port; **~ deportivo** marina; **~ franco** free port; **~ marítimo** seaport; **tomar ~** to come into port **2.** (*de montaña*) pass **3.** COMPUT port

puertorriqueño, -a [pwer·to·rri·'ke·ɲo, -a] *adj, m, f* Puerto Rican

pues [pwes] **I.** *adv* **1.** (*entonces*) then; (*así que*) so; **he vuelto a suspender — ~ estudia más** I've failed again — well, you should study more; **~ entonces, nada** well that's it, then **2.** (*ilativo*) so;

~ bien okay; **la consecuencia es, ~,...** so the result is... **3.** (*causal*) **estudio inglés — ¡ah, ~ yo también!** I study English — ah, me too!; **¿quién es? — no sé** who is it? — I don't know **4.** (*expletivo*) well; **¿estuvisteis por fin en Toledo? — ~ no/sí** did you end up going to Toledo? — no, I didn't/yes, I did; **¡~ esto no es nada!** this is nothing compared with what's to come! **5.** (*exclamativo*) **¡~ no faltaría más!** (*naturalmente*) but of course!; (*el colmo*) that's all we (etc.) need! **6.** (*interrogativo*) **¿y ~?** and? **7.** (*atenuación*) well; **¿nos vemos mañana? — ~ no sé todavía** shall we meet tomorrow? — well, I'm not sure yet **8.** (*insistencia*) **~ así es** well that's how it is; **~ claro** but of course; **¡~ entonces!** for that very reason! **II.** *conj* **no voy de viaje, ~ no tengo dinero** I'm not going on holiday because I don't have any money

puesta ['pwes·ta] *f* putting; (*de aves*) laying; **~ a cero** resetting; **~ al día** updating; **~ en escena** TEAT staging; **~ en hora** setting *(of time);* **~ en libertad** release; **~ en marcha** start button; AUTO starter; **~ en práctica** putting into effect; **~ a punto** final check; AUTO service; **~ de sol** sunset

puesto ['pwes·to] *m* **1.** (*lugar*) place; (*posición*) position; **~ de observación** ASTR observation station; MED observation post **2.** (*empleo*) job; (*cargo, posición*) position **3.** (*tenderete*) stall; (*feria de muestras*) stand; (*chiringuito*) open-air bar; **~ de periódicos** newspaper stand **4.** MIL post **5.** (*guardia*) post; **~ de socorro** first-aid station

puesto, -a ['pwes·to, -a] **I.** *pp de* **poner** **II.** *adj* **1.** *inf* (*arreglado*) **ir muy bien ~** to be very smartly dressed; **tenerlos muy bien ~s** *vulg* to be a real man **2.** *inf* (*entendido*) **estar ~ en un tema** to be well-informed about a subject; **~ al día** up to date **III.** *conj* **~ que** given that

puja ['pu·xa] *f* (*en una subasta*) bid

pujar [pu·'xar] *vi* (*en una subasta*) to bid

pulcro, -a <pulquérrimo> ['pul·kro, -a]

adj (*aseado*) tidy

pulga ['pul·ɣa] *f* flea; COMPUT bug; **tener ~s** to be restless; **tener malas ~s** *inf* to be bad-tempered; **buscar las ~s a alguien** *inf* to tease sb

pulgada [pul·'ɣa·da] *f* (*medida*) inch

pulgar [pul·'ɣar] *adj*, *m* thumb

pulir [pu·'lir] *vt* to polish; (*perfeccionar*) to polish up

pulla ['pu·ja, -ʎa] *f* gibe

pulmón [pul·'mon] *m* lung; **gritar a pleno ~** to shout at the top of one's lungs

pulmonar [pul·mo·'nar] *adj* MED pulmonary

pulmonía [pul·mo·'ni·a] *f* MED pneumonia

pulóver [pu·'lo·βer] *m AmL* pullover

pulpa ['pul·pa] *f* (*de la fruta*) flesh

pulpero, -a [pul·'pe·ro, -a] *m, f AmL* grocer

púlpito ['pul·pi·to] *m* pulpit

pulpo ['pul·po] *m* octopus

pulque ['pul·ke] *m Méx* CULIN *drink made from fermented agave cactus juice*

pulsación [pul·sa·'sjon, -'θjon] *f* 1. ANAT (*latido*) beat, throbbing 2. (*de una tecla*) striking; (*mecanografía*) keystroke

pulsar [pul·'sar] *vt* to press; (*teclado*) to strike; **~ el timbre** to ring the bell

pulsera [pul·'se·ra] *f* bracelet; **reloj de ~** wristwatch

pulso ['pul·so] *m* wrist; *fig* steadiness of hand; **a ~** (*sin apoyarse*) freehand; (*por su propio esfuerzo*) on one's own; **con ~** carefully; **tener buen ~** to have a steady hand; **tomar el ~ a alguien** to take sb's pulse; **echar un ~ a alguien** to arm wrestle sb

pulverizador [pul·βe·ri·sa·'dor, -θa·'dor] *m* sprayer; (*atomizador*) atomizing spray

pulverizar <z → c> [pul·βe·ri·'sar, -'θar] *vt* 1. (*reducir a polvo*) to pulverize 2. (*atomizar*) to atomize

puma ['pu·ma] *m* puma

puna [pu·na] *f AmS* 1. (*altiplano*) Andean plateau 2. (*malestar*) altitude sickness

punta ['pun·ta] *f* 1. (*extremo*) end; (*de lengua, iceberg*) tip; (*de tierra*) headland; **hora(s) ~** rush hour; **de ~ a ~** from end to end; **lo tenía en la ~ de la lengua** it was on the tip of my tongue 2. (*pico*) point; **a ~ de navaja** at knifepoint; **a ~ de pistola** at gunpoint; **acabar en ~** to come to a point; **sacar ~** (*afilar*) to sharpen

puntada [pun·'ta·da] *f* (*costura*) stitch; (*pinchazo*) prick; *fig* hint

puntapié [pun·ta·'pje] *m* kick; **pegar un ~ a alguien** to kick sb

puntería [pun·te·'ri·a] *f* (*destreza*) marksmanship; **tener buena/mala ~** to be a good/bad shot

puntero, -a [pun·'te·ro, -a] *adj* leading; **tecnología puntera** cutting-edge technology; **el equipo ~** DEP the top team

puntiagudo, -a [pun·tja·'ɣu·do, -a] *adj* (sharp-)pointed

puntilla [pun·'ti·ja, -ʎa] *f* 1. (*encaje*) lace (edging) 2. (*del pie*) **andar/ponerse de ~s** to walk/stand on tiptoe

punto ['pun·to] *m* 1. (*general*) point; **~ álgido** crucial moment; **~ cardinal** point of the compass; **~ clave** key point; **no hay ~ de comparación** there's no comparison; **~ de destino** destination; **~ de ebullición** boiling point; **~ de encuentro** meeting place; **~ fuerte** strong point; **~ de intersección** intersection; **~ muerto** AUTO neutral; **~ de referencia** reference point; **~ de venta** point of sale; **~ de vista** point of view; **ganar por ~s** to win on points; **hasta tal ~ que...** to such a degree that...; **la una en ~** exactly one o'clock; **hasta cierto ~** up to a point; **¿hasta qué ~?** how far?; **a ~ de** on the point of; **está a ~ de llover** it's about to rain; **¡~ en boca!** *inf* mum's the word!; **¡y ~!** *inf* and that's that!; **en su ~** *fig* just right 2. TIPO full stop; **~ y aparte** full stop, new paragraph; **~ y coma** semicolon; **~ final** full stop (*end of paragraph*); **poner ~ final a algo** *fig* to bring sth to an end; **~ y seguido** full stop (*no new paragraph*); **~s suspensivos** suspension points, dot, dot, dot *inf*; **dos ~s** colon; **poner los ~s sobre las íes** *fig* to dot one's i's and cross one's t's **3.** (*calceta, labor*) knitting; **chaqueta de ~** knitted jacket; **hacer ~** to knit **4.** (*puntada*) stitch; **~ de sutura** MED stitch **5.** CULIN **a/en su ~** done **6.** (*preparado*) **a ~** ready; **poner a ~** TÉC to fine-tune; (*ajustar*) to adjust **7.** COMPUT dot

puntocom [pun·to·'kom] *f* COMPUT (**compañía**) [*o* **empresa**] **~** dotcom company

puntuación [pun·twa·'sjon, -'θjon] *f* **1.** LING punctuation; **signo de ~** punctuation mark **2.** (*calificación*) mark, grade; DEP score; **sistema de ~** scoring system

puntual [pun·tu·'al] *adj* **1.** (*concreto*) specific **2.** (*exacto*) precise **3.** (*sin retraso*) punctual

puntualidad [pun·twa·li·'ðað] *f* punctuality

puntualizar <z → c> [pun·twa·li·'sar, -'θar] *vt* to specify; (*aclarar*) to clarify

puntuar <1. *pres* puntúo> [pun·tu·'ar] *vt* **1.** (*un escrito*) to punctuate **2.** (*conseguir puntos*) to score **3.** (*calificar*) to mark, to grade; DEP to score

punzada [pun·'sa·ða, -θa·ða] *f* (*dolor*) sharp pain; (*en los costados*) stitch

punzante [pun·'san·te, -θan·te] *adj* **1.** (*puntiagudo*) sharp **2.** (*mordaz*) scathing

puñado [pu·'ɲa·ðo] *m* handful; **a ~s** (*mucho*) by the handful; **un ~** *inf* (*mucho*) a lot

puñal [pu·'ɲal] *m* dagger

puñalada [pu·ɲa·'la·ða] *f* stab; (*herida*) stab wound; *fig* blow; **coser a ~s** to stab repeatedly; **dar una ~ trapera a alguien** *fig* to stab sb in the back

puñetazo [pu·ɲe·'ta·so, -θo] *m* punch

puño [pu·'ɲo] *m* **1.** (*mano*) fist; **~ cerrado** clenched fist; **con el ~ en alto** with one's fist raised; **apretar los ~s** *fig* to struggle hard; **como un ~** (*huevo, mentira*) enormous; (*casa, habitación*) tiny; **verdades como ~s** fundamental truths; **de su ~ y letra** in his/her own hand; **meter a alguien en un ~** *fig* to intimidate sb **2.** (*mango*) handle; (*pomo*) hilt **3.** (*de la ropa*) cuff; **~ vuelto** turned-up cuff

pupa ['pu·pa] *f* **1.** (*ampolla*) blister; (*heridilla*) small wound **2.** *inf* (*dolor*) pain; **¡~!** ouch! **3.** ZOOL pupa

pupila [pu·'pi·la] *f* pupil

pupilo, -a [pu·'pi·lo, -a] *m, f* ward

pupitre [pu·'pi·tre] *m* (*escritorio*) desk

purasangre [pu·ra·'san·gre] *adj, m* thoroughbred

puré [pu·'re] *m* purée; **~ de patatas** mashed potatoes; **hacer ~** to purée; *fig* to beat to a pulp; **estar hecho ~** *fig* to be knackered

pureza [pu·'re·sa, -θa] *f* purity

purgante [pur·'ɣan·te] *adj, m* purgative

purgar <g → gu> [pur·'ɣar] *vt t. fig* to clean; MED to purge; (*evacuar*) to empty; (*aguas*) to drain

purgatorio [pur·ɣa·'to·rjo] *m* purgatory

purificador [pu·ri·fi·ka·'ðor] *m* purifier; **~ de humos** smoke filter

purificar <c → qu> [pu·ri·fi·'kar] **I.** *vt t. fig* to purify **II.** *vr:* **~se** to be purified; *fig* to purify oneself

puro ['pu·ro] *m* cigar

puro, -a ['pu·ro, -a] *adj* pure; (*auténtico*) authentic; **pura lana** pure wool; **la pura verdad** the honest truth; **pura casualidad** sheer chance; **de ~ miedo** from sheer terror; **se cae de ~ bueno/tonto** he is unbelievably kind/stupid

púrpura ['pur·pu·ra] *adj, f* purple

pus [pus] *m* MED pus

puta ['pu·ta] *f vulg* whore; **casa de ~s** brothel

puzzle ['pus·le, 'puθ-] *m* jigsaw (puzzle)

PVP ['pre·sjo de 'βen·ta al 'pu·βli·ko, 'pre·θjo] *m abr de* **Precio de Venta al Público** RRP

Q

Q, q [ku] *f* Q, q; **~ de Queso** Q as in Quebec

qm [kin·'tal 'me·tri·ko] *abr de* **quintal métrico** 100 kg

que [ke] I. *pron rel* 1. (*con antecedente: personas, cosas*) that, which *(often omitted when referring to object)*; **la pelota ~ está pinchada** the ball that is punctured; **la pelota ~ compraste** the ball you bought; **la historia de ~ te hablé** the story I told you about; **reacciones a las ~ estamos acostumbrados** reactions which we are accustomed to; **el proyecto en el ~ trabajo** the project that I am working on; **la empresa para la ~ trabajo** the company that I work for 2. (*con antecedente: personas*) that, who *(often omitted when referring to the object)*; **la mujer que conocí** the woman that [o who] I met 3. (*sin antecedente*) **el/la/lo ~...** the one (that/who/which)...; **los ~ hayan terminado** those who have finished; **el ~ quiera, ~ se marche** whoever wants to, can leave; **es de los ~...** he/she/it is the type that...; **el ~ más y el ~ menos** every single one; **es todo lo ~ sé** that's all I know; **lo ~ haces** what you do; **no sabes lo difícil ~ es** you don't know how difficult it is 4. (*con preposición*) **de lo ~ hablamos** what you are talking about II. *conj* 1. (*completivo*) that; **me pidió ~ la ayudara** she asked me to help her 2. (*estilo indirecto*) that; **ha dicho ~...** he/she said that... 3. (*comparativo*) **más alto ~** taller than; **lo mismo ~** the same as 4. (*porque*) because; **lo ayudaré, ~ se lo he prometido** I'll help him, because I promised 5. (*de manera que*) **corre ~ vuela** he/she runs like the wind 6. (*o, ya*) **~ paguen, ~ no paguen, eso ya se verá** we'll see whether they pay or not 7. (*frecuentativo*) **y él dale ~ dale con la guitarra** and he kept on playing and playing the guitar 8. (*explicativo*) **hoy no vendré, es ~ estoy cansado** I'm not coming in today because I'm tired; **no es ~ no pueda, es ~ no quiero** it's not that I can't, it's that I don't want to; **¿es ~ no puedes venir?** can't you come then? 9. (*enfático*) **¡~ sí/no!** I said "yes"/"no"!; **sí ~ lo hice** I did it 10. (*de duda*) **¿~ no está en casa?** are you saying he/she isn't at home? 11. (*exclamativo*) **¡~ me canso!** I'm getting tired!; **¡~ sea yo el que tenga que hacerlo!** I would be the one who has to do it! 12. (*con verbo*) **hay ~ trabajar más** you/we/they have to work harder; **tener ~ hacer algo** to have to do something; **dar ~ hablar** to give people something to talk about ▶ **a la ~ llegue** as soon as he/she arrives; **a menos ~** +*subj* unless; **antes (de) ~** +*subj* before; **con tal (de) ~** +*subj* as long as; **por mucho ~** as much as; **por tú digas...** no matter what you say...; **yo ~ tú...** if I were you...

qué [ke] *adj, pron interrog* 1. (*general*) what; (*cuál*) which; (*qué clase de*) what kind of; **¿por ~?** why?; **¿en ~ piensas?** what are you thinking about?; **¿para ~?** what for?; **¿de ~ hablas?** what are you talking about?; **¿a ~ esperas?** what are you waiting for?; **¿~ día llega?** what day is he/she arriving?; **¿~ cerveza tomas?** what kind of beer do you drink?; **¿a ~ vienes?** what are you here for?; **¿~ edad tienes?** how old are you? 2. (*exclamativo*) **¡~ alegría/gracia!** how nice/funny!; **¡~ suerte!** what luck!; **¡cuán ~ magnífica vista!** what a magnificent view!; **¡mira ~ contento está!** look how happy he is! 4. (*cuánto*) **¡~ de gente!** what a lot of people! ▶ **¿~ tal?** how are you?, how are things?; **¿~ tal si salimos a cenar?** how about going out to dinner?; **¿y ~?** so what?; **¿y a mí ~?** and what about me?, **~, ¿vienes o no?** well, are you coming, or not?

quebrada [ke·'βra·da] *f AmL* stream

quebradizo, -a [ke·βra·'ði·so, -a; -'ði·θo, -a] *adj* 1. (*objeto*) brittle 2. (*persona mayor*) frail 3. (*voz*) faltering

quebrado [ke·'βra·ðo] *m MAT* fraction

quebrado, -a [ke·'βra·ðo, -a] *adj* 1. (*em-*

presa) bankrupt; (*terreno*) rough **2.** (*herniado*) ruptured

quebrantar [ke·βran·'tar] *vt* **1.** (*romper*) to break; (*cascar*) to crack; (*machacar*) to crush **2.** (*ley, secreto*) to break; (*obligación*) to violate; (*autoridad*) to breach; (*salud*) to debilitate

quebrar <e → ie> [ke·'βrar] **I.** *vt* (*romper*) to break **II.** *vi* **1.** (*con alguien*) to break up **2.** COM to go bankrupt **3.** *Méx* (*darse por vencido*) to give in **III.** *vr*: **~se** MED to rupture oneself; **~se de dolor** to double over with pain

quebrazón [ke·βra·'son] *m AmL* **1.** (*resultado*) breakage **2.** (*acción*) shattering

quechua ['ke·tʃwa] **I.** *adj* Quechua **II.** *mf* Quechuan

quedada [ke·'da·da] *f inf* **1.** joke **2.** *Méx pey* old maid

quedado, -a [ke·'da·do, -a] *adj Arg, Chile* slow

quedar [ke·'dar] **I.** *vi* **1.** (*permanecer*) to remain; **los problemas quedan atrás** the problems are a thing of the past; **¿cuánta gente queda?** how many people are left?; **~ a deber algo** to owe sth **2.** (*sobrar*) to be left; **no nos queda otro remedio que...** there's nothing left for us to do but...; **no queda ningún ejemplar** there are no copies left **3.** (*resultar*) **todo quedó en una simple discusión** it ended up in a mere argument; **~ acordado** to be arranged; **~ cojo** to go lame; **~ eliminado** to be eliminated; **~ en ridículo** to make a fool of oneself **4.** (*acordar*) **~ en algo** to agree to sth; **¿en qué habéis quedado?** what have you decided?; **quedamos a las 10** we agreed to meet at 10; **a ver, ¿en qué quedamos?** make up your mind! **5.** (*estar situado*) to lie; **queda por/hacia el norte** it lies to the north; **quedar lejos de aquí** to be a long way from here **6.** (*faltar*) **quedan aún 100 km para llegar a casa** there are still 100 km left before we get home; **aún queda mucho por hacer** there's still a lot to do; **por mí que no quede** I'll do all that I can **7.** (*terminar*) to end; **~ bien/mal**

to turn out well/badly **8.** (*+ por*) **~ por cobarde** to come across as a coward; **algo queda por ver** sth remains to be seen **9.** (*+ como*) **~ como un señor** to behave like a real gentleman; **~ como un idiota** to look like a fool **II.** *vr*: **~se 1.** (*permanecer*) to stay; **~se atrás** to stay behind; **~se colgado** COMPUT to block; **durante la tormenta nos quedamos a oscuras** during the storm the lights went out; **cuando me lo dijo me quedé mudo** when he told me I was speechless **2.** (*resultar*) **~se ciego** to go blind; **~se viuda/viudo** to become a widow/widower; **al freír la carne se ha quedado en nada** when the meat was fried it shrunk to almost nothing **3.** (*conservar, adquirir*) **me quedo con el coche pequeño** I'll take the small car; **quédate con el libro** keep the book; **~se sin nada** to be left with nothing; **entre el mar y la montaña me quedo con el mar** if I have to choose between the sea and the mountains, I'll take the sea **4.** (*burlarse*) **~se con alguien** to make fun of sb

quehacer [ke·a·'ser, -'θer] *m* chores *pl*; **los ~es de la casa** the housework; **dar ~ a alguien** to assign work to sb

queja ['ke·xa] *f* complaint

quejarse [ke·'xar·se] *vr* **~ de algo** to complain about sth; (*gemir*) to moan about sth; **se queja del frío** he complains about the cold

quejica [ke·'xi·ka] **I.** *adj* complaining; (*por dolor*) moaning; **¡no seas ~, hombre!** stop whining! **II.** *mf* complainer; (*criticón*) picky

quejido [ke·'xi·do] *m* moan; (*constante*) lament; **~ de dolor** cry of pain; **dar ~s** to groan

quejoso, -a [ke·'xo·so, -a] *adj* complaining; **estar ~ de alguien** to be annoyed at sb

quelite [ke·'li·te] *m Méx* greens *pl*

quema ['ke·ma] *f* burning

quemada [ke·'ma·da] *f* **1.** *Arg, Méx* (*ridículo*) embarrassment **2.** *Méx* (*quemadura*) burn

quemado, -a [ke·'ma·do] *adj* burnt; *fig* exhausted; **este político está ~** *inf* this politician is finished

quemadura [ke·ma·'du·ra] *f* burn; ~ **de primer grado** first-degree burn

quemar [ke·'mar] **I.** *vi* to burn; **cuidado, esta sopa quema** be careful, the soup is boiling hot **II.** *vt* **1.** to burn; (*casa*) to burn down; (*planta*) to scorch; ~ **un bosque** to set fire to a forest; **este chili quema la garganta/la lengua** this chili burns my throat/tongue **2.** (*fastidiar*) to mess up **3.** *AmC* (*denunciar*) ~ **a alguien** to inform against sb **III.** *vr:* ~**se 1.** (*arder*) to burn; **el bosque se quema** the forest is on fire; **me he quemado los cabellos** I've singed my hair **2.** (*herir*) to be hurt **3.** (*comida*) to burn; (*ligeramente*) to singe **4.** (*tener calor*) **me estoy quemando** I'm burning up **5.** (*por una pasión*) ~**se de amor** to burn with love **6.** (*acertar*) **¡que te quemas!** you're getting warmer!

quemarropa [ke·ma·'rro·pa] **disparar a** ~ to shoot at close range; **hacerle preguntas a alguien a** ~ to fire questions at sb

quemazón [ke·ma·'son, -'θon] *f* **1.** (*quema*) burning **2.** (*calor*) intense heat **3. siento una** ~ **en el estómago** I have a burning sensation in my stomach

quemo ['ke·mo] *m Arg* **¡que** ~**!** how embarrassing!

quemón [ke·'mon] *m Méx* dope smoker

quena ['ke·na] *f* reed flute used in Andean music

quepo ['ke·po] *1. pres de* **caber**

queque ['ke·ke] *m Chile, Perú, AmC* cake

querella [ke·'re·ja, -ʎa] *f* dispute; *JUR* lawsuit; ~ **criminal** criminal action; **poner una** ~ **contra alguien** to sue sb

querencia [ke·'ren·sja] *f AmL* (*aprecio*) attachment; (*cariño*) affection; (*afición*) liking; **tomar** ~ **a algo/alguien** to take a liking to sth/sb

querendón, -ona [ke·ren·'don, -·'do·na] *adj AmL* loving, affectionate

querer [ke·'rer] *irr* **III. I.** *vt* **1.** (*desear*) to desire; (*más suave*) to want; **como tú quieras** as you like; **has ganado, ¿qué**

más quieres? you win, what more do you want?; **hacer algo queriendo/sin** ~ to do something on purpose/unintentionally; **quisiera tener 20 años menos** I wish I were 20 years younger; **eso es lo que quería decir** that's what I meant to say; **quiero que sepáis que...** I want you to know that ...; **donde quiera que esté** wherever he/she/it may be; **¡por lo que más quieras, deja ese tema!** for God's sake, change the subject! **2.** (*amar*) to like; (*más fuerte*) to love; **te quiero con locura** I'm madly in love with you **3.** (*pedir, precisar*) to require; **estas plantas quieren mucha agua** these plants need a lot of water ▶ ~ **es poder** *prov* where there's a will, there's a way; **como quiera que sea** anyhow **II.** *vimpers* **parece que quiere llover** it looks like rain **III.** *m* love

querido, -a [ke·'ri·do, -a] **I.** *adj* dear **II.** *m, f* (*amante*) lover; (*como vocativo*) darling

queroseno [ke·ro·'se·no] *m* kerosene

quesadilla [ke·sa·'di·ja, -ʎa] *f* **1.** (*pastel*) cheesecake; (*pastelillo*) pastry **2.** *AmL* (*tortilla*) quesadilla

queso ['ke·so] *m* **1.** cheese; ~ **de bola** Edam cheese **2.** *inf* (*pie*) foot

quicio ['ki·sjo, -θjo] *m* **sacar las cosas de** ~ to make a mountain out of a molehill; **sacar a alguien de** ~ to drive sb up the wall *sl*

quico ['ki·ko] *m* toasted corn snack

quid [kid] *m* crux; **el** ~ **de la cuestión** the crux of the matter; **dar en el** ~ to hit the nail on the head

quiebra ['kje·βra] *f* COM bankruptcy; **dar en** ~ to go bankrupt

quien [kjen] *pron rel* **1.** (*con antecedente*) who, that *(often omitted when referring to object)*; **el chico de** ~ **te hablé** the boy I told you about; **las chicas con** ~**es...** the girls with whom ... **2.** (*sin antecedente*) that; **hay** ~ **dice que...** some people say that...; **no hay** ~ **lo aguante** nobody can stand him; ~ **opine eso...** whoever thinks so...

quién [kjen] *pron interrog* who; **¿**~ **es?** (*llama*) who is it?; **¿**~**es son tus pa-**

dres? who are your parents?; **¿a ~ has visto?** who did you see?; **¿a ~ se lo has dado?** who did you give it to?; **¿~ eres tú para decirme esto?** who are you to tell me this?; **¿por ~ me tomas?** what do you take me for?; **¡~ tuviera 20 años!** If only I were 20!

quienquiera <quienesquiera> [kjen·'kje·ra] *pron indef* whoever; **~ que sea que pase** whoever it is, come in

quieto, -a [kje·to, -a] *adj* **1.** (*tranquilo*) calm **2.** (*parado*) still; **no puede estar nunca ~** he can never keep still; **quedarse ~** to stand still

quietud [kje·'tuð] *f* **1.** (*inmovilidad*) stillness **2.** (*calma*) calm

quijada [ki·'xa·da] *f* jaw(bone)

quilate [ki·'la·te] *m* karat

quilco ['kil·ko] *m Chile* (large) basket

quilla [ki·ja, -ʎa] *f* keel

quillango [ki·'jan·go, -'ʎan·go] *m CSur* fur blanket

quillay [ki·'jai, -'ʎai] *m Arg, Chile* BOT soapbark tree

quilo ['ki·lo] *m* **1.** (*peso*) kilo(gram) **2.** *inf* (*dinero*) million

quilombo [ki·'lom·bo] *m* **1.** *Chile* (*burdel*) whorehouse **2.** *Ven* (*choza*) hut **3.** *Arg* (*lío*) mess

quiltro ['kil·tro] *m Chile pey* mutt

quimba ['kim·ba] *f* **1.** *AmL* (*garbo*) grace **2.** *AmL* (*sandalia*) sandal **3.** *pl Col* (*conflicto*) difficulties *pl*

quimbo ['kim·bo] *m Cuba* machete

química ['ki·mi·ka] *f* chemistry

químico, -a ['ki·mi·ko, -a] **I.** *adj* chemical; **productos ~s** chemicals *pl* **II.** *m, f* chemist

quimioterapia [ki·mjo·te·'ra·pja] *f* chemotherapy

quimono [ki·'mo·no] *m* kimono

quince ['kin·se, -θe] **I.** *adj inv* fifteen; **dentro de ~ días** in two weeks **II.** *m* fifteen; *v. t.* **ocho**

quincena [kin·'se·na, kin·'θe-] *f* two weeks

quincenal [kin·se·'nal, kin·θe-] *adj* every two weeks; **revista ~** semimonthly journal

quingos ['kin·gos] *m inv AmL* zigzag

quiniela [ki·'nje·la] *f* **1.** (*juego*) sports

pools *pl*; (*boleto*) pools coupon; **jugar a las ~s** to do the pools **2.** *CSur* lottery

quinientos, -as [ki·'njen·tos, -as] *adj* five hundred; *v. t.* **ochocientos**

quino ['ki·no] *m AmL* cinchona tree

quinqué [kin·'ke] *m* oil lamp

quinqui ['kin·ki] *mf inf* crook

quinta [kin·ta] *f* **1.** (*casa*) country house **2.** MIL draft

quintal [kin·'tal] *m* quintal; **~ métrico** 100 kg

quinteto [kin·'te·to] *m* quintet

quinto, -a ['kin·to, -a] *adj, m, f* fifth; *v. t.* **octavo**

quinto ['kin·to] *m* draftee

quiosco ['kjos·ko] *m* **1.** (*de jardín*) gazebo **2.** (*de periódicos*) news-stand

quirófano [ki·'ro·fa·no] *m* operating room; **pasar por el ~** to be operated on

quirquincho [kir·'kin·tʃo] *m CSur* **1.** ZOOL small armadillo **2.** (*guitarra*) charango

quirúrgico, -a [ki·'rur·xi·ko, -a] *adj* surgical

quiso ['ki·so] *3. pret de* **querer**

quisque ['kis·ke] *pron indef inf*, **quisqui** ['kis·ki] *pron indef inf* **todo ~** anyone and everyone; **se lo dijo a todo ~** he told every Tom, Dick and Harry

quisquilloso, -a [kis·ki·'jo·so, -a; -'ʎo·so, -a] *adj* (*susceptible*) touchy; (*meticuloso*) fussy

quiste ['kis·te] *m* cyst

quitaesmalte [ki·ta·es·'mal·te] *m* nail varnish remover

quitagusto [ki·ta·'ɣus·to] *m Ecua, Perú* killjoy

quitamanchas [ki·ta·'man·tʃas] *m inv* stain remover

quitanieves [ki·ta·'nje·βes] *f inv* snowplow

quitar [ki·'tar] **I.** *vt* **1.** (*piel, funda, obstáculo*) to remove; (*sombrero, tapa, ropa*) to take off; (*botón*) to pull off **2.** (*mancha*) to get out; (*dolor*) to relieve; (*vida*) to take; (*mesa*) to clear; **una capucha de quita y pon** a detachable hood **3.** (*desposeer*) to take; (*robar*) to steal; **me lo has quitado de la boca** you took the words right out of my mouth; **el café me quita el sueño** coffee keeps me up at night; **ese asunto me quita el sueño**

that matter is keeping me awake at night **4.** (*de plan, horario, texto*) to leave out **5.** (*apartar*) to get out of the way; (*mueble*) to remove; **¡quita!** (*no me molestes*) don't bother me!; (*deja eso*) leave that alone!; (*déjate de tonterías*) stop it! **6.** MAT to subtract; **quitando dos** taking away two ▶ **ni ~ ni** poner **en algo** not to have any say in sth **II.** *vr:* **~se** (*sombrero, gafas, ropa*) to take off; (*barba*) to shave off; **~se la vida** to commit suicide; **~se de la bebida** to give up drinking; **~se de encima algo/a alguien** to get rid of sth/sb; **quítate de mi vista** get out of my sight

quizá(s) [ki·ˈsa(s), -ˈθa(s)] *adv* perhaps, maybe

R

R, r [ˈe·rre] *f* R, r; **~ de Ramón** R as in Romeo

rabadilla [rra·βa·ˈdi·ja, -ʎa] *f* coccyx

rabanito [rra·βa·ˈni·to] *m* radish

rábano [ˈrra·βa·no] *m* radish; **~ picante** [*o* **blanco**] horseradish **2.** *inf* me **importa un ~** I couldn't care less; **¡y un ~!** no way!

rabí <rabíes> [rra·ˈβi] *m* rabbi

rabia [ˈrra·βja] *f* **1.** (*furia*) rage; **¡qué ~!** how infuriating! **2.** (*enfado, manía*) **tener ~ a alguien** (*enfado*) to be furious with sb; (*manía*) not to be able to stand sb; **me da ~ sólo pensarlo** just thinking about it makes me mad; **con ~** angrily

rabiar [rra·ˈβjar] *vi* to be furious; **hacer ~ a alguien** to infuriate sb; **~ de...** to be dying of...; **~ de dolor** to be in great pain ▶ **está que rabia** *inf* it's incredibly hot; **a ~** incredibly

rabieta [rra·ˈβje·ta] *f* tantrum; **coger una ~** to throw a tantrum

rabimocho, -a [rra·βi·ˈmo·tʃo, -a] *adj* *AmL* short

rabino [rra·ˈβi·no] *m* rabbi

rabioso, -a [rra·ˈβjo·so, -a] *adj* **1.** furious; **un tema de rabiosa actualidad** a highly topical issue **2.** *inf* (*picante*)

really hot

rabo [ˈrra·βo] *m* **1.** (*cola*) tail; **salir con el ~ entre las piernas** to go away with one's tail between one's legs **2.** (*extremo*) end **3.** (*tallo*) stem

rabona [rra·ˈβo·na] *f* *CSur inf* **hacer(se) la ~** to play hook(e)y

rácano, -a [ˈrra·ka·no, -a] *adj inf* (*tacaño*) mean; (*gandul*) lazy

racha [ˈrra·tʃa] *f* (*fase*) series; **tener buena/mala ~** to have a good/bad run; **a [*o* por] ~s** in fits and starts; **~ de aire** gust of wind

racial [rra·ˈsjal, -ˈθjal] *adj* racial; **disturbios ~es** race riots

racimo [rra·ˈsi·mo, rra·ˈθi-] *m* bunch

raciocinio [rra·sjo·ˈsi·njo, -θjo·ˈθi·njo] *m* **1.** (*facultad, razón*) reason **2.** (*proceso mental*) reasoning

ración [rra·ˈsjon, -ˈθjon] *f* portion; (*en casa*) helping; (*en restaurante*) plate; **una ~ de patatas fritas** a side of French fries

racional [rra·sjo·ˈnal, rra·θjo·] *adj* rational; (*razonable*) reasonable

racionalización [rra·sjo·na·li·sa·ˈsjon, -θjo·na·li·θa·ˈθjon] *f* rationalization

racionalizar <z → c> [rra·sjo·na·li·ˈsar, -θjo·na·li·ˈθar] *vt* to rationalize

racionamiento [rra·sjo·na·ˈmjen·to, rra·θjo-] *m* rationing

racionar [rra·sjo·ˈnar, rra·θjo-] *vt* **1.** (*repartir*) to ration out **2.** (*limitar*) to ration

racismo [rra·ˈsis·mo, -ˈθis·mo] *m* racism

racista [rra·ˈsis·ta, -ˈθis·ta] *adj, mf* racist

radar [rra·ˈdar] *m* radar

radiación [rra·dja·ˈsjon, -ˈθjon] *f* radiation

radiactividad [rra·djak·ti·βi·ˈdad] *f* radioactivity

radiactivo, -a [rra·djak·ˈti·βo, -a] *adj* radioactive

radiador [rra·dja·ˈdor] *m* radiator

radial [rra·ˈdjal] *adj* **1.** radial **2.** *AmL* radio

radiante [rra·ˈdjan·te] *adj* radiant; **~ de alegría/felicidad** radiant with joy/happiness; **estás ~ con ese vestido** you look wonderful in that dress

radiar [rra·ˈdjar] **I.** *vi* to radiate **II.** *vt*

R

1. (*irradiar*) to radiate **2.** RADIO to broadcast; **un debate radiado** a radio debate **3.** *AmL* (*eliminar*) to delete

radical [rra·di·'kal] **I.** *adj* **1.** *t.* BOT, MAT radical **2.** (*fundamental*) drastic **II.** *m* **1.** LING root **2.** MAT, QUÍM, PSICO radical **III.** *mf* POL radical; ~ **de derecha** extreme right-winger

radicalizar <z → c> [rra·di·ka·li·'sar, -'θar] **I.** *vt* to radicalize **II.** *vr:* ~**se** to become radical

radicar <c → qu> [rra·di·'kar] *vi* ~ **en algo** (*basarse*) to be based on sth; (*consistir*) to consist of sth; **el problema radica en su comportamiento** the problem lies in his/her behavior

radicheta [rra·di·'tʃe·ta] *f* *Arg*, *Urug* chicory

radio¹ ['rra·djo] *f* RADIO, TEL **1.** radio; ~ **del coche** car radio; **dirigido por** ~ radio-controlled; **retransmitir por** ~ to send by radio **2.** (*emisora*) radio station; ~ **pirata** pirate radio

radio² ['rra·djo] *m* MAT, ANAT radius; **en un** ~ **de varios kilómetros** within a radius of several kilometers **2.** (*en la rueda*) spoke **3.** (*ámbito*) range; ~ **de acción** operational range; *fig* sphere of influence; ~ **de alcance** reach

radioactivo, -a [rra·djo·ak·'ti·βo, -a] *adj* radioactive

radioaficionado, -a [rra·djo·a·fi·sjo·'na·do, -a; -θjo·'na·do, -a] *m, f* radio ham

radiocomunicación [rra·djo·ko·mu·ni·ka·'sjon, -'θjon] *f* radio communication

radiodespertador [rra·djo·des·per·ta·'dor] *m* radio alarm (clock)

radiodifusión [rra·djo·di·fu·'sjon] *f* broadcasting

radiodifusora [rra·djo·di·fu·'so·ra] *f* *AmL* radio transmitter

radioescucha [rra·djo·es·'ku·tʃa] *mf* listener

radiografía [rra·djo·γra·'fi·a] *f* **1.** (*técnica*) radiography **2.** (*placa*) radiograph

radiografiar <*1. pres* radiografío> [rra·djo·γra·fi·'ar] *vt* to radiograph; MED to X-ray

radiólogo, -a [rra·djo·lo·γo, -a] *m, f* MED radiologist

radiopatrulla [rra·djo·pa·'tru·ja, -ʎa] *f* patrol car

radiotaxi [rra·djo·'tak·si] *m* radio taxi

radioterapia [rra·djo·te·'ra·pja] *f* MED radiotherapy

radioyente [rra·djo·'jen·te] *mf* listener

R.A.E. ['rra·e] *f* *abr de* **Real Academia Española** Spanish Royal Academy

raer [rra·'er] *irr vt* (*raspar*) to scrape; (*desgastar*) to wear out

ráfaga ['rra·fa·γa] *f* **1.** (*de aire*) gust **2.** (*de luz, inspiración*) flash

ragú <ragús> [rra·'γu] *m* ragout

raído, -a [rra·'i·do, -a] *adj* (*deslucido*) spoilt; (*gastado*) worn-out

raíl [rra·'il] *m* rail

raíz [rra·'is, -'iθ] *f* **1.** ANAT, BOT *t. fig* root; **tener sus raíces en un lugar** *fig* to have one's roots in a place **2.** (*causa*) cause; (*origen*) origin; **a** ~ **de** because of; **tener su** ~ **en algo** to be due to sth **3.** MAT, LING root; ~ **cuadrada/cúbica** square/cube root ▶ **de** ~ completely; **arrancar de** ~ to destroy

raja ['rra·xa] *f* **1.** (*grieta*) crack; (*hendedura*) split **2.** (*abertura*) opening; (*separación*) gap

rajada [rra·'xa·da] *f* *inf* **1.** *Arg* (*fuga*) flight **2.** *Méx* (*cobardía*) chickening out **3.** *Col* (*examen*) fail

rajadiablo(s) [rra·xa·'dja·βlos] *m (inv)* *Chile* young rogue

rajante [rra·'xan·te] *adj* *Arg* definitive

rajar [rra·'xar] **I.** *vi inf* (*charlar*) to chatter; ~ **de alguien** to slag sb off **II.** *vt* (*cortar*) to cut; (*abrir*) to cut open; (*hender*) to split; (*partir*) to cut up; (*en rajas*) to slice **III.** *vr:* ~**se 1.** (*abrirse*) to split open; (*agrietarse*) to crack **2.** *inf* (*echarse atrás*) to back out

rajatabla [rra·xa·'ta·βla] **a** ~ (*estrictamente*) strictly; (*exactamente*) to the letter

raje ['rra·xe] *m* *Arg* **1.** *inf* (*huida*) flight; **al** ~ in a rush **2.** *inf* (*despido*) sacking; **dar el** ~ **a alguien** to get rid of sb

rajo ['rra·xo] *m* *AmC* (*desgarrón*) tear; (*rotura*) rip

rajón, -ona [rra·'xon, -·'xo·na] *adj* **1.** *AmC*, *Méx* (*fanfarrón*) bragging **2.** *AmC* (*ostentoso*) lavish **3.** *Cuba*, *Méx* (*cobarde*) chicken *inf* **4.** *Méx* (*poco fiable*) unreliable

ralea [rra·'lea] *f pey* sort

ralentí [rra·len·'ti] *m* **al ~** AUTO ticking over; CINE in slow motion

rallador [rra·ja·'dor, rra·ʎa-] *m* grater

ralladura [rra·ja·'du·ra, rra·ʎa-] *f* gratings *pl;* **~ de queso** grated cheese

rallar [rra·'jar, -'ʎar] *vt* to shred; (*fino*) to grate

rally(e) <rallys> ['rra·li] *m* rally

ralo, -a ['rra·lo, -a] *adj* **1.** scarce; (*cabello*) thin **2.** CSur (*insustancial*) flimsy

rama ['rra·ma] *f t.* BOT, MAT branch; (*sector*) *t.* ECON sector; **~s secas** brushwood; **por la ~ materna/paterna** on the mother's/father's side ▶ **andarse por las ~s** to beat about the bush; **irse por las ~s** to go off on a tangent

ramada [rra·'ma·da] *f* Chile festival stand

ramaje [rra·'ma·xe] *m* branches *pl;* (*follaje*) foliage

rambla ['rram·bla] *f* boulevard

ramera [rra·'me·ra] *f pey* whore

ramificación [rra·mi·fi·ka·'sjon, -'θjon] *f* ramification

ramificarse [rra·mi·fi·'kar·se] <c → qu> *vr* to branch out

ramillete [rra·mi·'je·te, -'ʎe·te] *m* bouquet

ramo ['rra·mo] *m* (*de flores*) bunch

rampa ['rram·pa] *f* ramp; **en ~** sloping

rampla ['rram·pla] *f* Chile hand truck

rana ['rra·na] *f* frog ▶ **cuando las ~s críen pelo** when pigs fly

ranchera [rran·'tʃe·ra] *f* AmL **1.** (*canción*) typical popular Mexican song **2.** (*furgoneta*) station wagon

ranchería [rran·tʃe·'ri·a] *f* Col (*chabolas*) shantytown; (*barraca*) bunkhouse

ranchero, -a [rran·'tʃe·ro, -a] *m, f* rancher

rancho ['rran·tʃo] *m* (*granja*) ranch

ranciarse [rran·'sjar·se, -'θjar·se] *vr* to go rancid

rancio, -a ['rran·sjo, -a; -θjo, -a] *adj* rancid; (*anticuado*) old-fashioned

rancotán [rran·ko·'tan] *adv* AmL in cash

rango ['rran·go] *m* (*categoría, puesto*) rank; (*ordenación*) order; **de primer/segundo ~** first/second-level; **de (alto) ~** high-ranking

rangoso, -a [rran·'go·so, -a] *adj* AmC **1.** (*generoso*) generous **2.** (*ostentoso*) ostentatious

ranura [rra·'nu·ra] *f* groove; (*junta*) joint; (*fisura*) slot

rapacidad [rra·pa·si·'dad, rra·pa·θi-] *f* rapacity

rapar [rra·'par] *vt* to shave; **~se el pelo** (*afeitar*) to shave one's head; (*cortar*) to have one's hair cut very short

rapaz [rra·'pas, -'paθ] **I.** *adj* **1.** (*ávido*) greedy **2.** (*expoliador*) rapacious **II.** *f* bird of prey

rapaz(a) [rra·'pas, -'pa·sa; -'paθ, -'pa·θa] *m(f)* kid

rape ['rra·pe] *m* **1.** ZOOL monkfish **2.** **al ~** (*pelo*) closely cropped

rapear [rra·pe·'ar] *vi* MÚS to rap

rapidez [rra·pi·'des, -'deθ] *f* speed; **~ de reflejos** quick reflexes; **con (gran) ~** (very) quickly

rápido ['rra·pi·do] *m* **1.** (*tren*) express **2.** *pl* (*de un río*) rapids *pl*

rápido, -a ['rra·pi·do, -a] *adj* **1.** (*veloz*) fast **2.** (*breve*) quick

rapiña [rra·'pi·ɲa] *f* robbery

raposo, -a [rra·'po·so, -a] *m, f* **1.** ZOOL fox **2.** (*astuto*) sly fox

raptar [rrap·'tar] *vt* to kidnap

rapto ['rrap·to] *m* kidnapping; **~ de un niño** child abduction

raptor(a) [rrap·'tor, -'to·ra] *m(f)* kidnapper

raque ['rra·ke] *adj* Ven scrawny

raqueta [rra·'ke·ta] *f* **1.** DEP (*pala*) bat **2.** (*para nieve*) snowshoe

raquítico, -a [rra·'ki·ti·ko, -a] *adj inf* (*enclenque*) sickly; (*débil*) weak

raramente [rra·ra·'men·te] *adv* (*casi nunca*) rarely, seldom

rareza [rra·'re·sa, -θa] *f* **1.** (*cualidad*) rarity **2.** (*peculiaridad*) peculiarity

rarífico, -a [rra·'ri·fi·ko, -a] *adj* Chile implausible

raro, -a ['rra·ro, -a] *adj* **1.** (*extraño, inesperado*) strange; **¡(qué) cosa más rara!** how strange! **2.** (*inusual*) unusual; (*poco común*) rare; **no es ~ que...** **+subj** it's not surprising that...

ras [rras] *m* level; **a(l) ~ de** on a level with; **a ~ de agua/tierra** at water/ground level; **volar a ~ de suelo** to hedgehop; **al ~** level

rasante [rra·'san·te] f slope; **cambio de ~** brow of a hill

rasar [rra·'sar] vt to level

rasca ['rras·ka] f 1. inf (frío) cold; **¡vaya ~ que hace!** it's freezing! 2. AmL (mona) drunkenness; **pegarse una ~** to get plastered

rascacielos [rras·ka·'sje·los, -'θje·los] m inv skyscraper

rascar <c → qu> [rras·'kar] I. vt to scrape; (con las uñas) to scratch II. vr: **~se** 1. to scratch 2. AmS (achisparse) to get tipsy

rascón, -ona [rras·'kon, -·'ko·na] adj Méx troublemaker

rascuache [rras·'kwa·tʃe] adj Méx inf 1. (pobre) wretched 2. (de baja calidad) cheap

rasgar <g → gu> [rras·'ɣar] I. vt to tear; (en dos) to tear in two; (en pedazos) to tear to pieces; (cortar) to cut; **ojos rasgados** almond eyes II. vr: **~se** 1. to tear 2. AmL vulg (diñarla) to kick the bucket

rasgo ['rras·ɣo] m 1. (del rostro) feature; (del carácter) trait 2. (trazo) stroke; **a grandes ~s** in outline

rasguñar [rras·ɣu·'ɲar] I. vt 1. (arañar) to scratch; (herir) to wound; (cortar) to cut 2. ARTE to sketch II. vr: **~se** (arañarse) to scratch oneself; (herirse) to wound oneself; **~se con algo** to graze oneself against sth

rasguño [rras·'ɣu·ɲo] m (arañazo) scratch; (rasponazo) scrape; (excoriación) chafing; **sin un ~** unscathed

raso ['rra·so] m satin

raso, -a ['rra·so, -a] adj 1. (liso) smooth; (llano) flat 2. (cielo) clear; **al ~** in the open air 3. (al borde) level; **una cucharada rasa** a level spoonful

raspa ['rras·pa] f 1. backbone 2. AmL prostitute; (ratero) pickpocket

raspada [rras·'pa·da] f Méx, PRico scolding

raspar [rras·'par] I. vi (ser rasposo) to be rough; (en sorteos) to scratch II. vt 1. (rascar) to scratch 2. AmL inf (mangar) to swipe 3. AmS inf (abroncar) to yell at III. vr: **~se** to scratch oneself

raspón [rras·'pon] m 1. (arañazo) scratch

2. Col (sombrero) (large) straw hat

rasposo, -a [rras·'po·so, -a] adj rough

rasquetear [rras·ke·te·'ar] vt 1. AmL (almohazar) to groom 2. Arg (raer) to scrape 3. AmS (caballo) to curry

rasquiña [rras·'ki·ɲa] f AmL itch

rastras ['rras·tras] fpl **a ~s** unwillingly; **llevar a alguien a ~s** to drag sb along

rastrear [rras·tre·'ar] vt 1. (seguir) to track 2. (investigar) to make inquiries about

rastrero, -a [rras·'tre·ro, -a] adj pey (canallesco) base; (despreciable) despicable; (servil) cringing

rastrillo [rras·'tri·jo, -ʎo] m rake

rastro ['rras·tro] m 1. (indicio, pista) trace; **ni ~** not a trace; **sin dejar (ni) ~** without trace; **seguir el ~ a [o de] alguien** to follow sb's trail 2. (mercadillo) flea market

rastrojo [rras·'tro·xo] m stubble

rasurar [rra·su·'rar] AmL I. vt to shave II. vr: **~se** to shave

rata¹ ['rra·ta] f ZOOL rat ► **~ de biblioteca** bookworm; **más pobre que las ~s** as poor as a church mouse; **hacerse la ~** AmL to play truant

rata² ['rra·ta] mf inf (rácano) miser

ratear [rra·te·'ar] vt 1. inf (mangar) to nick 2. inf (racanear) **~ algo** to be stingy with sth

ratero, -a [rra·'te·ro, -a] m, f petty thief

raticida [rra·ti·'si·da, -'θi·da] m rat poison

ratificación [rra·ti·fi·ka·'sjon, -'θjon] f 1. JUR, POL ratification 2. (confirmación) confirmation

ratificar <c → qu> [rra·ti·fi·'kar] I. vt 1. (confirmar) to confirm 2. JUR, POL to ratify II. vr: **~se** JUR, POL to be ratified

rato ['rra·to] m while; (momento) moment; **a ~s de ~ en ~** from time to time; **a cada ~** all the time; **al (poco) ~** shortly after; **todo el ~** the whole time; **un buen ~** for quite a time; **pasar un buen/mal ~** to have a good/bad time; **hacer pasar un mal ~ a alguien** to give sb a rough time; **pasar el ~** to pass the time ► **aún hay para ~** there's still plenty left to do; **tener para ~** to have lots to do

ratón [rra'ton] *m t.* COMPUT mouse; **~ de campo** field mouse ▶ **~ de** <u>biblioteca</u> bookworm

ratonera [rra·to·'ne·ra] *f* **1.** (*trampa*) mousetrap; *fig* trap; **caer en la ~** to fall into the trap **2.** (*agujero*) mousehole

raudal [rrau·'dal] *m* torrent; **~ de palabras** flood of words ▶ **a ~es** in floods

raya ['rra·ja] *f* **1.** (*línea*) line; (*guión*) dash; **a ~s** (*papel*) lined; (*jersey*) striped; **tres en ~** (*juego*) tic(k)-tac(k)-toe **2.** (*del pelo*) line **3.** ZOOL ray **4.** (*cocaína*) line ▶ **pasar(se) de la ~** to go too far

rayar [rra·'jar] **I.** *vi* **1.** (*lindar*) **~ con algo** to border on sth **2.** (*asemejarse*) **~ en algo** to come close to sth **3.** (*amanecer*) **al ~ el día** at the break of day **II.** *vt* **1.** (*con rayas*) to line **2.** (*tachar*) to cross out **3.** (*arañar*) to scratch **III.** *vr:* **~se** to get scratched

rayo ['rra·jo] *m* **1.** (*de luz*) ray; **~ de luna** shaft of moonlight **2.** (*radiación*) **~s infrarrojos** infrared rays; **~s X** X-rays; **~ láser** laser beam **3.** (*relámpago*) (bolt of) lightning; **ha caído un ~ en la torre** the tower was hit by lightning

raza ['rra·sa, -θa] *f* (*casta*) race; (*estirpe*) strain; **de ~** (*perro*) pedigree; (*caballo*) thoroughbred

razón [rra·'son, -'θon] **I.** *f* **1.** (*discernimiento*) reason; (*entendimiento*) understanding **2.** (*razonamiento*) reasoning; **(no) atender a razones** (not) to listen to reason **3.** (*motivo*) **la ~ por la que...** the reason why...; **sin ~** without justification; **por razones de seguridad** for security reasons; **por una u otra ~** for one reason or another; **tener razones para...** to have cause to... **4.** (*acierto*) **tener** [*o* **llevar la**] **~** to be right; **tener mucha ~** to be absolutely right; **dar la ~ a alguien** to agree with sb **5.** (*información*) (*recado*) message; **~ aquí** inquire here; **pedir ~ de alguien** to ask sb for information **6.** MAT ratio; **a ~ de 2 pesos el kilo** at 2 pesos per kilo ▶ **entrar en ~** to come to one's senses; **hacer perder la ~ a alguien** to make sb lose control **II.** *prep* **en ~ de** (*en cuanto a*) as far as; (*a causa de*) because of

razonable [rra·so·'na·βle, rra·θo·] *adj* (*sensato*) reasonable; (*justo*) fair; (*adecuado*) sufficient

razonamiento [rra·θo·na·'mjen·to, rra·θo·] *m* reasoning; **tus ~s no son convincentes** your argument is not convincing

razonar [rra·θo·'nar, rra·θo·] **I.** *vi* to reason; (*reflexionar*) to reflect **II.** *vt* (*exponer*) to show; (*fundamentar*) to establish

RDSI [e·rre·de·se·'i/e·rre·de·e·se·'i] *f abr de* **Red Digital de Servicios Integrados** ISDN

reabrir [rre·a·'βrir] *irr como abrir vt* to reopen

reacción [rre·ak·'sjon, -aɣ·'θjon] *f* reaction; **~ en cadena** chain reaction; **~ excesiva** overreaction

reaccionar [rre·ak·sjo·'nar, -aɣ·θjo·'nar] *vi* **~ a** [*o* **ante**] **algo** to react to sth; (*responder*) to respond to sth

reaccionario, -a [rre·ak·sjo·'na·rjo, -a; -aɣ·θjo·'na·rjo, -a] *adj, m, f* reactionary

reacio, -a [rre·a·sjo, -a; -θjo, -a] *adj* reluctant

reactivar [rre·ak·ti·'βar] *vt* to reactivate; ECON to boost

reactivo [rre·ak·'ti·βo] *m* reagent

reactor [rre·ak·'tor] *m* **1.** (*motor*) jet engine; (*avión*) jet **2.** FÍS reactor

readaptación [rre·a·dap·ta·'sjon, -'θjon] *f* readjustment

readaptar [rre·a·dap·'tar] *vt, vr:* **~se** to readapt; **~ a algo** to reintegrate into sth

readmisión [rre·ad·mi·'sjon] *f* readmission; (*de despedidos*) re-employment

readmitir [rre·ad·mi·'tir] *vt* to readmit; (*despedidos*) to re-employ

reafirmar [rre·a·fir·'mar] **I.** *vt* **1.** to make firm; (*piel*) to tone up **2.** (*apoyar*) to reaffirm **II.** *vr:* **~se** to reaffirm; **~se en algo** to insist on sth

reagrupar [rre·a·ɣru·'par] *vt, vr:* **~se** to regroup

reajustar [rre·a·xus·'tar] *vt* to readjust

reajuste [rre·a·'xus·te] *m* readjustment; TÉC, ECON adjustment; **~ salarial** wage settlement

real [rre·'al] *adj* **1.** real; **basado en hechos ~es** based on a true story **2.** (*del rey*) royal

R

realce [rre·'al·se, -θe] *m* relief; (*esplendor*) splendor; **dar ~** to highlight

realengo, -a [rrea·'len·go, -a] *adj AmL* (*sin amo*) ownerless; (*vagabundo*) stray

realeza [rrea·'le·sa, -θa] *f* (*dignidad*) royalty

realidad [rrea·li·'dad] *f* reality; **~ virtual** virtual reality; **ajeno a la ~** far removed from reality; **hacer ~** to make come true; **hacerse ~** to happen; **en ~** in fact

realismo [rrea·'lis·mo] *m* realism

realista [rrea·'lis·ta] **I.** *adj* realistic **II.** *mf* realist

realizable [rrea·li·'sa·βle, -'θa·βle] *adj* **1.** (*practicable*) practical; (*factible*) feasible **2.** ECON saleable; **bienes ~s** saleable goods

realización [rrea·li·sa·'sjon, -θa·'θjon] *f* **1.** (*ejecución*) execution **2.** (*materialización*) realization; *t.* ECON realization; (*cumplimiento*) fulfillment; **~ de un pedido** fulfillment of an order

realizador(a) [rrea·li·sa·'dor, -·'do·ra; rrea·li·θa-] *m(f)* producer

realizar <z → c> [rrea·li·'sar, -'θar] **I.** *vt* **1.** (*efectuar*) to carry out; (*hacer*) to make **2.** (*hacer realidad*) to make real; (*sueños*) to fulfill **3.** ECON to realize **4.** CINE, TV to produce *AmL* (*notar*) to notice **II.** *vr:* **~se 1.** (*desarrollarse*) to be carried out **2.** (*materializarse*) to happen; (*hacerse realidad*) to come true

realmente [rre·al·'men·te] *adv* really; (*de hecho*) in fact

realquilar [rre·al·ki·'lar] *vt* to sublet

realzar <z → c> [rre·al·'sar, -'θar] *vt* **1.** (*labrar*) to emboss **2.** (*acentuar*) to bring out **3.** (*subrayar*) to highlight

reamargo, -a [rrea·'mar·γo, -a] *adj AmL* very bitter

reamigo, -a [rre·a·'mi·γo, -a] *m, f AmL* very close friend; **son ~s del director** they are very close friends of the director

reanimación [rre·a·ni·ma·'sjon, -'θjon] *f* **1.** revival **2.** MED resuscitation; (*posoperatorio*) reanimation; **unidad de ~** intensive care unit

reanimar [rre·a·ni·'mar] **I.** *vt* to revive; (*animar*) to liven up; MED to resuscitate

II. *vr:* **~se** to regain consciousness; (*animarse*) to liven up

reanudar [rre·a·nu·'dar] *vt* to resume

reaparición [rre·a·pa·ri·'sjon, -'θjon] *f* reappearance; TEAT, CINE comeback

reapertura [rre·a·per·'tu·ra] *f* reopening

reavivar [rre·a·βi·'βar] *vt, vr:* **~se** to revive

rebaja [rre·'βa·xa] *f* (*oferta*) sale; (*descuento*) discount; **~s de verano** summer sales; **estar de ~s** to have a sale on

rebajar [rre·βa·'xar] **I.** *vt* **1.** (*abaratar*) to reduce **2.** (*humillar*) to put down **3.** *t.* FOTO (*mitigar*) to soften; (*debilitar*) to weaken; (*bebidas*) to dilute **II.** *vr:* **~se 1.** (*humillarse*) to be humiliated **2.** (*condescender*) to lower oneself

rebanada [rre·βa·'na·da] *f* slice

rebanar [rre·βa·'nar] *vt* (*hacer rebanadas*) to slice; (*partir*) to cut up

rebañar [rre·βa·'ɲar] *vt* to finish off; **~ el plato** to wipe the plate clean

rebaño [rre·'βa·ɲo] *m* herd

rebasar [rre·βa·'sar] *vt* to exceed; **~ el límite** to overstep the mark; **esto rebasa los límites de mi paciencia** this is trying my patience

rebatir [rre·βa·'tir] *vt* (*discutir*) to contest; (*refutar*) to refute; (*rechazar*) to reject

rebelarse [rre·βe·'lar·se] *vr* to rebel; (*oponerse*) to be opposed

rebelde [rre·'βel·de] **I.** *adj* **1.** (*indócil*) unruly **2.** (*insurrecto*) rebellious **II.** *mf* rebel

rebeldía [rre·βel·'di·a] *f* **1.** (*cualidad*) rebelliousness **2.** (*oposición*) opposition **3.** *t.* MIL (*insubordinación*) insubordination

rebelión [rre·βe·'ljon] *f* rebellion

reblandecer [rre·βlan·de·'ser, -'θer] *irr como crecer vt, vr:* **~se** to soften

rebobinar [rre·βo·βi·'nar] *vt* to rewind

rebosar [rre·βo·'sar] *vi* to overflow; **~ de** to be brimming with; **le rebosa el dinero** he/she is rolling in money; (*lleno*) **a ~ (de)** full to the brim (with)

rebotar [rre·βo·'tar] **I.** *vi* **1.** (*botar*) to bounce; (*bala*) to ricochet **2.** (*chocar*) **~ en** [*o* **contra**] **algo** to bump into sth **3.** COMPUT to be returned as undeliverable **II.** *vt* **1.** (*botar*) to bounce **2.** *inf* (*enfadar*) to anger **III.** *vr:* ~**se** *inf* to get angry

rebote [rre-'βo-te] *m* bounce; DEP rebound; **de** ~ on the rebound

rebozar <z → c> [rre-βo-'sar, -'θar] *vt* to coat with breadcrumbs

rebumbio [rre-'βum-bjo] *m Méx* commotion

rebuscado, -a [rre-βus-'ka-do, -a] *adj* pedantic; (*palabras*) obscure; (*estilo*) contrived

rebuscar <c → qu> [rre-βus-'kar] **I.** *vi* to search thoroughly **II.** *vt* to search for **III.** *vr* **rebuscárselas** *CSur* to get by

rebuznar [rre-βus-'nar, rre-βuθ-'] *vi* to bray

recabar [rre-ka-'βar] *vt* **1.** (*obtener*) to manage to obtain **2.** (*pedir*) to ask for

recadero, -a [rre-ka-'de-ro, -a] *m, f* messenger

recado [rre-'ka-do] *m* **1.** (*mensaje*) message; **dar un** ~ **a alguien** to give a message to sb **2.** (*encargo*) errand; **hacer** ~**s** to do errands

recaer [rre-ka-'er] *irr como* caer *vi* **1.** (*enfermedad*) to relapse **2.** (*delito*) to commit a repeat offense; ~ **en el mismo error una y otra vez** to repeat the same mistake again and again

recaída [rre-ka-'i-da] *f* relapse

recalar [rre-ka-'lar] **I.** *vi AmL* to appear **II.** *vt* to soak **III.** *vr:* ~**se** to get soaked

recalcar <c → qu> [rre-kal-'kar] *vt* to stress

recalcitrante [rre-kal-si-'tran-te, rre-kal-θi-] *adj* recalcitrant

recalentado [rre-ka-len-'ta-do] *m Méx inf* leftovers *pl*

recalentar <e → ie> [rre-ka-len-'tar] **I.** *vt* (*comida*) to reheat; (*aparato*) to overheat **II.** *vr:* ~**se** to overheat

recámara [rre-'ka-ma-ra] *f* **1.** (*para ropa*) dressing room **2.** (*arma*) chamber

recamarera [rre-ka-ma-'re-ra] *f Méx* chambermaid

recambiar [rre-kam-bi-'ar] *vt* to substitute

recambio [rre-'kam-bjo] *m* spare (part); (*envase*) refill

recapacitar [rre-ka-pa-si-'tar, -θi-'tar] **I.** *vt* to consider **II.** *vi* to think things over

recapitulación [rre-ka-pi-tu-la-'sjon, -'θjon] *f* summary

recapitular [rre-ka-pi-tu-'lar] *vt* to summarize

recargado, -a [rre-kar-'ɣa-do, -a] *adj* overelaborate; (*lenguaje*) overblown

recargar <g → gu> [rre-kar-'ɣar] *vt* **1.** (*pila*) to recharge; (*impuesto*) to increase **2.** (*decorar*) to overdecorate **3.** (*carga*) to overload; ~ **de trabajo** to overload with work

recargo [rre-'kar-ɣo] *m* (*tasas*) increase; (*sobreprecio*) surcharge; **llamada sin** ~ toll-free call

recatado, -a [rre-ka-'ta-do, -a] *adj* **1.** (*modesto*) modest **2.** (*cauto*) cautious

recato [rre-'ka-to] *m* (*cautela*) caution; (*pudor*) modesty

recaudación [rre-kau-da-'sjon, -'θjon] *f* **1.** (*acción*) collection **2.** (*cantidad*) takings *pl*; (*de impuestos*) receipts *pl*

recaudar [rre-kau-'dar] *vt* to collect

recaudería [rre-kau-de-'ri-a] *f Méx* grocery store

recelo [rre-'se-lo, rre-'θe-] *m* mistrust; **mirar algo con** ~ to be suspicious of sth

receloso, -a [rre-se-'lo-so, -a; rre-'θe-] *adj* distrustful; **estar** ~ **de alguien** to be suspicious of sb; **ponerse** ~ to become suspicious

recepción [rre-sep-'sjon, -θeβ-'θjon] *f* reception

recepcionista [rre-sep-sjo-'nis-ta, -θeβ-θjo-'nis-ta] *mf* receptionist

receptividad [rre-sep-ti-βi-'dad, rre-θep-] *f* receptiveness

receptivo, -a [rre-sep-'ti-βo, -a; rre-θep-] *adj* receptive

receptor [rre-sep-'tor, rre-θep-] *m* receiver

receptor(a) [rre-sep-'tor, --'to-ra, rre-θep-] *m(f)* recipient

recesión [rre-se-'sjon, rre-θe-] *f* recession

receso [rre-'se-so] *m AmL* recess

receta [rre-'se-ta, rre-'θe-] *f* recipe; MED prescription; **con** ~ **médica** on prescription

recetar [rre-θe-'tar, rre-θe-] *vt* to prescribe

recetario [rre-θe-'ta-rjo, rre-θe-] *m* CULIN

cookbook; MED prescription pad

rechazar <z → c> [rre·tʃa·'sar, -'θar] vt to reject; (*denegar, no tolerar*) to refuse; (*ataque*) to repel

rechazo [rre·'tʃa·so, -θo] m rejection; (*denegación*) refusal

rechinar [rre·tʃi·'nar] I. vi to squeak; (*puerta*) to creak II. vt ~ **los dientes** to grind one's teeth

rechistar [rre·tʃis·'tar] vi to grumble; **sin** ~ without complaining

rechupete [rre·tʃu·'pe·te] **de** ~ delicious

recibidor [rre·si·βi·'dor, rre·θi-] m lobby; (*en casa*) entry (hall)

recibimiento [rre·si·βi·'mjen·to, rre·θi-] m welcome

recibir [rre·si·'βir, rre·θi-] I. vt to receive; (*personas*) to welcome; (*aceptar*) to accept II. vr ~**se de algo** AmL to graduate as sth; (*médico, abogado*) to qualify as sth

recibo [rre·'si·βo, rre·'θi-] m receipt; (*de la luz, del agua*) bill; ~ **de entrega** delivery note; **acusar** ~ to acknowledge receipt

reciclaje [rre·si·'kla·xe, rre·θi-] m recycling

reciclar [rre·si·'klar, rre·θi-] vt to recycle

recién [rre·'sjen, -'θjen] adv **1.** recently; ~ **pintado** freshly painted; **los** ~ **casados** the newly weds; **el** ~ **nacido** the newborn baby **2.** AmL (*en cuanto*) as soon as

reciente [rre·'sjen·te, rre·'θjen-] adj recent; (*nuevo*) new; **un libro de** ~ **publicación** a book which has recently been published

recientemente [rre·sjen·te·'men·te, rre·θjen-] adv recently

recinto [rre·'sin·to, rre·'θin-] m enclosure; ~ **universitario** university campus; ~ **ferial** fairgrounds

recio, -a [rre·'re·sjo, -a; -θjo, -a] adj (*fuerte*) strong; (*rígido*) stiff; **en lo más** ~ **del invierno** in the depths of winter

recipiente [rre·si·'pjen·te, rre·θi-] m container; (*de vidrio, barro*) vessel

reciprocidad [rre·si·pro·si·'dad, rre·θi·pro·θi-] f reciprocity

recíproco, -a [rre·'si·pro·ko, -a; rre·'θi-] adj reciprocal

recital [rre·θi·'tal, rre·θi-] m concert

recitar [rre·si·'tar, rre·θi-] vt to recite

reclamación [rre·kla·ma·'sjon, -'θjon] f complaint; (*recurso*) protest

reclamar [rre·kla·'mar] I. vi to protest; ~ **por algo** to complain about sth II. vt (*pedir*) to claim; (*deuda*) to demand; ~ **daños** to sue for damages

reclame [rre·'kla·me] m Arg, Urug ad(vertisement)

reclamo [rre·'kla·mo] m **1.** (*grito*) decoy call; **acudir al** ~ to answer the call **2.** COM ad(vertisement)

reclinar [rre·kli·'nar] vt, vr: ~**se** to lean; (*hacia atrás*) to lean back; (*apoyar(se)*) to rest

recluir [rre·klu·'ir] irr como huir I. vt to imprison II. vr: ~**se** to shut oneself away

reclusión [rre·klu·'sjon] f imprisonment; (*aislamiento*) seclusion

recluso, -a [rre·'klu·so, -a] I. adj imprisoned II. m, f prisoner

recluta [rre·'klu·ta] mf (*voluntario*) recruit; (*obligado*) conscript

reclutamiento [rre·klu·ta·'mjen·to] m recruiting

reclutar [rre·klu·'tar] vt to recruit

recobrar [rre·ko·'βrar] I. vt to recover; ~ **el sentido/las fuerzas** to regain consciousness/one's strength; ~ **las pérdidas** to make good one's losses; ~ **las ganas de vivir** to recover one's enthusiasm for life II. vr: ~**se** to recover

recodo [rre·'ko·do] m bend

recoger <g → j> [rre·ko·'xer] I. vt **1.** (*buscar*) to collect; **te voy a** ~ **a la estación** I'll meet you at the station **2.** (*coger*) to collect; (*guardar*) to keep; ~ **del suelo** to pick up from the floor; (*cosecha*) to gather **3.** (*juntar*) to gather together; (*cabello*) to gather up **4.** (*acoger*) to take in II. vr ~**se** (*a casa*) to go home; (*a la cama*) to go to bed

recogida [rre·ko·'xi·da] f collection; ~ **de basuras** garbage collection; ~ **de equipajes** baggage claim

recogido, -a [rre·ko·'xi·do] adj (*lugar*) secluded

recolección [rre·ko·lek·'sjon, -leɣ·'θjon] f harvest

recolectar [rre·ko·lek·'tar] *vt* to gather; (*cosechar*) to harvest

recomendable [rre·ko·men·'da·βle] *adj* recommendable

recomendación [rre·ko·men·da·'sjon, -'θjon] *f* recommendation; **por ~ de mi médico** on my doctor's advice

recomendado, -a [rre·ko·men·'da·do, -a] *adj* recommended

recomendar <e → ie> [rre·ko·men·'dar] *vt* to advise; **nos recomendó no salir de casa** he/she advised us not to leave the house

recompensa [rre·kom·'pen·sa] *f* reward

recompensar [rre·kom·pen·'sar] *vt* to reward; (*por un daño*) to compensate

reconciliación [rre·kon·si·lja·'sjon, -θi·lja·'θjon] *f* reconciliation; **en señal de ~** as a sign of reconciliation

reconciliar [rre·kon·si·'ljar, rre·kon·θi·] I. *vt* to reconcile II. *vr*: **~se** to be reconciled

recóndito, -a [rre·kon·di·to, -a] *adj* hidden; **la casa está en lo más ~ del bosque** the house is hidden away in the depths of the forest

reconfortar [rre·kon·for·'tar] *vt* to comfort

reconocer [rre·ko·no·'ser, -'θer] *irr como crecer* I. *vt* 1. (*identificar*) to recognize; **~ a alguien por algo** to recognize sb by sth 2. (*admitir*) to accept; (*error*) to acknowledge; **~ como hijo** to recognize as one's son 3. (*examinar*) to check; MED to examine II. *vr*: **~se** 1. (*declararse*) to admit; **~se culpable** to admit one's guilt 2. (*identificarse*) to recognize oneself

reconocimiento [rre·ko·no·si·'mjen·to, -θi·'mjen·to] *m* 1. POL, JUR, COMPUT recognition 2. (*exploración*) inspection; **~ médico** medical examination; **vuelo de ~** reconnaissance flight 3. (*gratitud*) gratefulness; **en ~ de mi labor** in recognition of my work

reconquista [rre·kon·'kis·ta] *f* reconquest

reconquistar [rre·kon·kis·'tar] *vt* to reconquer; *fig* to win back

reconstituir [rre·kons·ti·tu·'ir/rre·kons·ti·'twir] *irr como huir vt* to re-establish

reconstituyente [rre·kons·ti·tu·'jen·te] *m*

MED restorative

reconstrucción [rre·kons·truk·'sjon, -truγ·'θjon] *f* rebuilding

reconstruir [rre·kons·tru·'ir/rre·kons·'trwir] *irr como huir vt* to reconstruct; (*reedificar*) to rebuild

recontra [rre·'kon·tra] *AmL inf* **¡idiota!** — **¡que te ~!** idiot! — the same to you!

recontrabueno, -a [rre·kon·tra·'βwe·no, -a] *adj AmL inf* really good

recontracaro, -a [rre·kon·tra·'ka·ro, -a] *adj AmL inf* really expensive

Recopa [rre·'ko·pa] *f* Cup-Winners' Cup

recopilación [rre·ko·pi·la·'sjon, -'θjon] *f* compilation

recopilar [rre·ko·pi·'lar] *vt* to compile

récord <récords> ['rre·kord] *m* record

recordar <o → ue> [rre·kor·'dar] I. *vi, vt* 1. (*acordarse*) to remember 2. (*traer a la memoria, semejar*) to remind; **recuérdale a mamá que me traiga el libro** remind mom to bring me the book; **este paisaje me recuerda a Cuba** this landscape reminds me of Cuba II. *vi, vr*: **~se** *Arg, Méx* (*despertarse*) to wake up

recorrer [rre·ko·'rrer] *vt* to cross; (*viajar por*) to travel around; (*trayecto*) to travel; **recorrimos tres kilómetros a pie** we walked three kilometers

recortar [rre·kor·'tar] *vt* 1. (*figuras*) to cut out; (*barba, uñas*) to trim; (*quitar*) to cut off 2. (*disminuir*) to cut (down)

recorte [rre·'kor·te] *m* 1. (*periódico*) cutting 2. (*rebajamiento*) cut(back); **~ de personal** downsizing

recostar <o → ue> [rre·kos·'tar] *vt, vr*: **~se** to rest; **~(se) contra/en algo** to lean against/on sth

recova [rre·'ko·βa] *f* 1. *CSur* (*arcadas*) arcade 2. *And, Urug* (*mercado*) market

recoveco [rre·ko·'βe·ko] *m* 1. (*escondrijo*) nook 2. **sin ~s** frankly; **persona con ~** complicated person 3. (*vuelta*) bend

recreación [rre·krea·'sjon, -'θjon] *f* reproduction; (*diversión*) recreation

recrear [rre·kre·'ar] I. *vt* 1. (*reproducir*) to reproduce 2. (*divertir*) to entertain II. *vr*: **~se** to entertain oneself; **se re-**

crea contemplando cuadros he/she enjoys looking at pictures

recreativo, -a [rre·krea·'ti·βo, -a] *adj* recreational; **(salón de juegos)** ~**s** amusement arcade

recreo [rre·'kreo] *m* ENS break

recriminación [rre·kri·mi·na·'sjon, -'θjon] *f* reproach

recriminar [rre·kri·mi·'nar] *vt* to reproach

recrudecer [rre·kru·de·'ser, -'θer] *irr como crecer vi, vr:* ~**se** to worsen; *(conflicto)* to intensify

recta ['rek·ta] *f* straight; **entrar en la ~ final** to enter the final straight

rectamente [rek·ta·'men·te] *adv* justly

rectangular [rek·tan·gu·'lar] *adj* rectangular

rectángulo [rek·'tan·gu·lo] *m* rectangle

rectángulo, -a [rek·'tan·gu·lo, -a] *adj* rectangular

rectificación [rek·ti·fi·ka·'sjon, -'θjon] *f* correction

rectificar <c → qu> [rek·ti·fi·'kar] *vt* to correct

rectilíneo, -a [rek·ti·'li·neo, -a] *adj* rectilinear; *(persona)* rigid

rectitud [rek·ti·'tud] *f* *(honradez)* uprightness

recto¹ ['rek·to] *adv* straight; **siga todo ~** go straight ahead

recto² ['rek·to, -a] *m* rectum

recto, -a ['rek·to, -a] *adj* straight; *(persona)* upright; **línea recta** straight line; **ángulo ~** right angle

rector(a) [rek·'tor, -·'to·ra] *m(f)* rector; UNIV president

recuadro [rre·'kwa·dro] *m* box

recubrimiento [rre·ku·βri·'mjen·to] *m* covering

recubrir [rre·ku·'βrir] *irr como abrir vt* to cover

recuento [rre·'kwen·to] *m* count; **hacer el ~ de votos** to count the votes

recuerdo [rre·'kwer·do] *m* **1.** *(evocación)* memory; **tener un buen ~ de algo** to have good memories of sth **2.** *(de un viaje)* souvenir **3.** *pl (saludos)* regards *pl;* **dales muchos ~s de mi parte** send them my regards

recuperación [rre·ku·pe·ra·'sjon, -'θjon] *f* recovery; ~ **de datos** data retrieval;

~ **de las cotizaciones** share price recovery; ~ **de los precios** rally of prices; **examen de** ~ makeup (exam)

recuperar [rre·ku·pe·'rar] **I.** *vt* to recover; *(tiempo)* to make up **II.** *vr:* ~**se** to recover **(de** from)

recurrir [rre·ku·'rrir] *vi* **1.** ~ **a** *(una persona)* to turn to; *(una institución)* to resort to; ~ **a la justicia** to turn to the law **2.** JUR to appeal

recursivo, -a [rre·kur·'si·βo, -a] *adj* Co resourceful

recurso [rre·'kur·so] *m* **1.** JUR appeal **2.** *(remedio)* solution; **no me queda otro** ~... **que...** I have no alternative but...; **como último** ~ as a last resor **3.** *pl (bienes)* means *pl;* **familias sin ~s** families without means **4.** *pl (reservas)* resources *pl;* ~**s naturales/minerales** natural/mineral resources

recusar [rre·ku·'sar] *vt* to reject; JUR to challenge

red [rred] *f* **1.** net; **caer en las ~es de alguien** to fall into sb's clutches **2.** *(sistema)* network; **la Red** the Net; ~ **comercial/vial** business/road network; **una** ~ **de carteristas** a gang of pickpockets **3.** ELEC power lines *pl;* **avería en la** ~ power failure

redacción [rre·dak·'sjon, -day·'θjon] *f* **1.** ENS writing; **hacer una** ~ **sobre el mar** to write a composition on the sea **2.** PREN editing

redactar [rre·dak·'tar] *vt* to write; *(documento)* to edit; *(testamento)* to draw up

redactor(a) [rre·dak·'tor, -·'to·ra] *m(f)* writer; PREN editor

redada [rre·'da·da] *f* raid

rededor [rre·de·'dor] *m* **al** *[o* **en]** ~ **(de)** around

redistribución [rre·dis·tri·βu·'sjon, -'θjon] *f* redistribution

redoble [rre·'do·βle] *m* drum roll

redomón [rre·do·'mon] *adj AmS* half-trained

redonda [rre·'don·da] *f* **en tres kilómetros a la** ~ for three kilometers in all directions

redondear [rre·don·de·'ar] *vt* to round off; ~ **por defecto/por exceso** to round up/down

redondel [rre·don·'del] *m* circle

redondela [rre·don·'de·la] *f* **1.** *Arg, Chile* round object **2.** *Chile inf* circle

redondo, -a [rre·'don·do] *adj* round; (*redondeado*) rounded ▶ **un negocio ~** a great deal; **caer(se) ~** to fall flat; **negarse en ~** to flatly deny

reducción [rre·duk·'sjon, -duɣ·'θjon] *f* **1.** reduction; (*rebaja*) discount; (*de personal*) cut **2.** JUR remission

reducido, -a [rre·du·'si·do, -a; -'θi·do, -a] *adj* (*pequeño*) small; (*estrecho*) narrow; **tarifas reducidas** reduced rates

reducidor(a) [rre·du·θi·'dor, --'do·ra] *m(f) AmS* fence

reducir [rre·du·'sir, -'θir] *irr como* traducir **I.** *vt* **1.** to reduce; (*personal, gastos*) to cut; (*precios*) to lower; **~/quedar reducido a cenizas/escombros** to reduce/ be reduced to ashes/rubble **2.** (*someter*) to subdue; **la policía redujo al agresor** the police overpowered the assailant **3.** (*resumir*) to summarize; (*acortar*) to abbreviate **II.** *vi* AUTO to downshift **III.** *vr:* **~se** to come down

redundancia [rre·dun·'dan·sja, -θja] *f* redundancy

redundante [rre·dun·'dan·te] *adj* redundant

reeditar [rre·di·'tar/rre·e·di·'tar] *vt* to republish; (*imprimir*) to reprint

reelección [rre·lek·'sjon/rre·e·lek·'sjon, -leɣ·'θjon] *f* re-election

reelegir [rre·le·'xir/rre·e·le·'xir] *irr como* elegir *vt* to re-elect

reembolsar [rrem·bol·'sar/rre·em·bol·'sar] *vt* to reimburse

reembolso [rrem·'bol·so/rre·em·'bol·so] *m* repayment; **enviar algo contra ~** to send sth cash on delivery

reemplazante [rrem·pla·'san·te; rre·em-] *mf Méx* replacement

reemplazar <z → c> [rrem·pla·'sar/rre·em·pla·'sar, -'θar] *vt* to replace; (*representar*) to substitute

reemplazo [rrem·'pla·so/rre·em·'pla·so, -θo] *m* replacement; DEP substitution

reencontrar <o → ue> [rren·kon·'trar, rre·en-] **I.** *vt* to find again **II.** *vr:* **~se** to meet again

reencuentro [rren·'kwen·tro/rre·en-·'kwen·tro] *m* reunion

reenviar <*1. pres* reenvío> [rrem·bi·'ar/ rre·em·bi·'ar] *vt* to forward; (*devolver*) to return

reestructurar [rres·truk·tu·'rar/rre·es·truk·tu·'rar] *vt* to restructure

refacción [rre·fak·'sjon] *f* **1.** *AmL* refurbishment **2.** *Méx* spare (part)

refaccionar [rre·fak·sjo·'nar] *vt AmL* to refurbish

refectorio [rre·fek·'to·rjo] *m* refectory

referencia [rre·fe·'ren·sja, -θja] *f* **1.** reference; **punto de ~** point of reference; **con ~ a** with reference to; **hacer ~ a algo** to refer to sth **2.** *pl* (*informes*) report

referéndum <referéndums> [rre·fe·'ren·dun] *m* referendum

referente [rre·fe·'ren·te] *adj* regarding; **(en lo) ~ a su queja** with regard to your complaint

referí [rre·fe·'ri] *m AmL* referee

referir [rre·fe·'rir] *irr como* sentir **I.** *vt* **1.** (*relatar*) to recount **2.** (*remitir*) to refer **II.** *vr:* **~se** to refer; **en** [*o por*] **lo que se refiere a...** with regard to...

refinado, -a [rre·fi·'na·do] *adj* refined

refinar [rre·fi·'nar] **I.** *vt* to refine **II.** *vr:* **~se** to become refined

refinería [rre·fi·ne·'ri·a] *f* refinery

reflector [rre·flek·'tor] *m* spotlight

reflector(a) [rre·flek·'tor, --'to·ra] *adj* reflective

reflejar [rre·fle·'xar] **I.** *vi, vt* to reflect; **tus palabras reflejan miedo** your words show fear **II.** *vr:* **~se** to be reflected

reflejo [rre·'fle·xo] *m* reflection; MED, PSICO reflex

reflejo, -a [rre·'fle·xo, -a] *adj* reflective; **movimiento ~** reflex

reflexión [rre·flek·'sjon,] *f* reflection; **sin ~** without thinking

reflexionar [rre·flek·sjo·'nar] *vi, vt* to reflect; **reflexiona bien antes de dar ese paso** think carefully before doing that

reflexivo, -a [rre·flek·'si·βo, -a] *adj* thoughtful; LING reflexive

reflujo [rre·'flu·xo] *m* ebb; MED reflux

reforma [rre·'for·ma] *f* **1.** reform; **~ educativa/monetaria** educational/ monetary reform **2.** ARQUIT rebuilding;

R

(*renovación*) renovation; **hacer una ~ en el cuarto de baño** to have one's bathroom refurbished

reformar [rre·for·'mar] I. *vt* 1. to reform; **~ su conducta** to change one's ways 2. ARQUIT to rebuild; (*renovar*) to renovate II. *vr*: **~se** to mend one's ways

reformatorio [rre·for·ma·'to·rjo] *m* reformatory; **~ para delincuentes juveniles** reform school (for juvenile delinquents)

reformista [rre·for·'mis·ta] *adj, mf* reformist

reforzar [rre·for·'sar, -'θar] *irr como* forzar I. *vt* to reinforce II. *vr*: **~se** to be reinforced

refractar [rre·frak·'tar] *vt* to refract

refrán [rre·'fran] *m* proverb

refregar [rre·fre·'ɣar] *irr como* fregar I. *vt* 1. (*frotar*) to rub; (*con cepillo/estropajo*) to scrub 2. *inf* (*reprochar*) **~ algo a alguien (por las narices)** to rub sb's nose in sth II. *vr*: **~se** to rub; **~se los ojos** to rub one's eyes

refrescante [rre·fres·'kan·te] *adj* refreshing

refrescar [rre·fres·'kar] I. *vt* to refresh; **~ la memoria** to refresh one's memory; (*cosas olvidadas*) to brush up; **el baño me ha refrescado** the bath has revived me II. *vi* to refresh; (*aire, viento*) to cool down III. *vr*: **~se** to cool down; (*tomar el fresco*) to get some fresh air IV. *vimpers* **por la tarde refresca** in the evening it gets cooler

refresco [rre·'fres·ko] *m* soft drink

refriega [rre·'frje·ɣa] *f inf* scuffle

refrigeración [rre·fri·xe·ra·'sjon, -'θjon] *f* refrigeration; **~ por aire/agua** air/water-cooling

refrigerador [rre·fri·xe·ra·'dor] *m* refrigerator; (*cámara*) cool room; AUTO cooling system

refrigerador(a) [rre·fri·xe·ra·'dor, -·'do·ra] *adj* **aparato ~** refrigerator; (*para habitaciones*) air-cooling unit

refrigerar [rre·fri·xe·'rar] I. *vt* to refrigerate; (*habitación*) to air-condition II. *vr*: **~se** to cool down

refrigerio [rre·fri·'xe·rjo] *m* snack

refuerzo [rre·'fwer·so, -θo] *m* 1. (*viga*) strengthening; (*parche*) patch 2. (*ayu-*

da) support 3. *pl* MIL reinforcements *pl*

refugiado, -a [rre·fu·'xja·do, -a] *m, f* refugee

refugiarse [rre·fu·'xjar·se] *vr* to take refuge; **~ de algo** to flee from sth

refugio [rre·'fu·xjo] *m* refuge; *t.* MIL shelter; **~ (montañero)** mountain shelter; **~ nuclear** [*o* atómico] fallout shelter

refundirse [rre·fun·'dir·se] *vr* 1. (*reunirse*) to be joined 2. *AmC* (*perderse*) to be lost

refunfuñar [rre·fun·fu·'ɲar] *vi* to grumble

refutación [rre·fu·ta·'sjon, -'θjon] *f* refutation

refutar [rre·fu·'tar] *vt* to refute

regadera [rre·ɣa·'de·ra] *f* 1. watering can 2. *AmC, Col, Méx, Ven* shower

regaderazo [rre·ɣa·de·'ra·so] *m Méx* shower

regadío [rre·ɣa·'di·o, -a] *m* irrigation; **estos campos son de ~** these fields are irrigated

regalado, -a [rre·ɣa·'la·do, -a] *adj* 1. (*cómodo*) easy; **llevar una vida regalada** to lead a life of luxury 2. (*barato*) very cheap; **vender algo a precio ~** to sell sth for a knock-down price

regalar [rre·ɣa·'lar] *vt* to give

regaliz [rre·ɣa·'lis, -'liθ] *m* licorice

regalo [rre·'ɣa·lo] *m* 1. present, gift 2. (*gusto*) pleasure; **un ~ para la vista** a sight for sore eyes

regañadientes [rre·ɣa·ɲa·'djen·tes] **a ~** reluctantly, grudgingly

regañar [rre·ɣa·'ɲar] *vt* to scold

regañina [rre·ɣa·'ɲi·na] *f* reprimand; **echar una ~ a alguien** to tell sb off; **tener una ~ por algo** to quarrel about sth

regar [rre·'ɣar] *irr como* fregar *vt* to water; (*las calles*) to hose down; AGR to irrigate

regata [rre·'ɣa·ta] *f* regatta

regatear [rre·ɣa·te·'ar] I. *vi* 1. (*mercadear*) to haggle 2. DEP to dribble II. *vt* to haggle over

regateo [rre·ɣa·'teo] *m* haggling, dribbling

regazo [rre·'ɣa·so, -θo] *m* lap

regencia [rre·'xen·sja, -θja] *f* management; POL regency

regeneración [rre·xe·ne·ra·'sjon, -'θjon]
f regeneration

regenerar [rre·xe·ne·'rar] **I.** *vt* to regenerate; (*a alguien*) to reform **II.** *vr:* ~**se** to regenerate; (*cabello*) to grow back

regentar [rre·xen·'tar] *vt* to manage; POL to govern

regente [rre·'xen·te] *mf* director; (*negocio*) manager; POL regent

régimen ['rre·xi·men] *m* <regímenes>
1. (*sistema*) system; (*reglamentos*) regulations *pl;* POL regulation; ~ **penitenciario** prison system; ~ **abierto** open regime 2. diet; **a** ~ on a diet

regimiento [rre·xi·'mjen·to] *m* regiment

región [rre·'xjon] *f* region; (*espacio*) area; ~ **abdominal** abdominal region

regional [rre·xjo·'nal] *adj* regional

regir [rre·'xir] *irr como* elegir **I.** *vt* 1. (*gobernar*) to govern; (*dirigir*) to direct; (*guiar*) to lead 2. LING to take **II.** *vr:* ~**se** to be guided

registrador(a) [rre·xis·tra·'dor, -·'do·ra] *adj* registering; **caja** ~**a** cash register

registrar [rre·xis·'trar] **I.** *vt* 1. (*examinar*) to search 2. (*inscribir, grabar*) to record; (*empresa, patente*) to register **II.** *vr:* ~**se** 1. (*inscribirse*) to register 2. (*observarse*) to be reported

registro [rre·'xis·tro] *m* 1. (*inspección*) search 2. (*medición*) measurement 3. (*inscripción, grabación*) recording; (*inclusión*) inclusion; (*empresa, patente*) registration 4. (*protocolo*) record; ~ **de entrada/de salida** note of arrival/ departure 5. (*libro*) register; ~ **electoral/de la propiedad** electoral/land register 6. (*oficina, archivo*) registry; ~ **civil** registry office

regla ['rre·ɣla] *f* 1. (*instrumento*) ruler 2. (*norma*) rule; **por** ~ **general** as a general rule; ~ **de tres** rule of three 3. (*período*) period; **está con la** ~ she has her period ▶ **la excepción confirma la** ~ the exception confirms the rule; **estar/ poner en** ~ to be/to put in order

reglamentación [rre·ɣla·men·ta·'sjon, -'θjon] *f* 1. (*acción*) regulation 2. (*reglas*) rules *pl*

reglamentar [rre·ɣla·men·'tar] *vt* to regulate

reglamento [rre·ɣla·'men·to] *m* rules *pl;* (*de una organización*) regulations *pl;* ~ **de tráfico** traffic regulations

regocijo [rre·ɣo·'si·xo, -'θi·xo] *m* delight; (*júbilo*) rejoicing

regodeón, -ona [rre·ɣo·de·'on] *adj* Chile, Col *inf* fussy

regresar [rre·ɣre·'sar] **I.** *vi* to return, to go back **II.** *vt* Méx to give back **III.** *vr:* ~**se** AmL to return

regresión [rre·ɣre·'sjon] *f* regression

regresivo, -a [rre·ɣre·'si·βo, -a] *adj* regressive

regreso [rre·'ɣre·so] *m* return; (**viaje de**) ~ return journey; **estar de** ~ to have returned

reguero [rre·'ɣe·ro] *m* trail; **expandirse como un** ~ **de pólvora** to spread like wildfire

regulación [rre·ɣu·la·'sjon, -'θjon] *f* 1. (*reglamentación*) regulation; ~ **administrativa** administrative regulations 2. (*organización, ajuste*) t. TÉC adjustment

regulador [rre·ɣu·la·'dor] *m* regulator; (*mecanismo*) control knob

regular [rre·ɣu·'lar] **I.** *vt* 1. (*organizar, ajustar*) t. TÉC to adjust 2. (*reglamentar*) to regulate **II.** *adj* 1. regular; **verbos** ~**es** regular verbs 2. (*mediano*) average; (*mediocre*) mediocre; **de tamaño** ~ normal size **III.** *adv* so-so

regularidad [rre·ɣu·la·ri·'dad] *f* compliance; **con** ~ regularly; (*mediocridad*) mediocrity

regularizar <z → c> [rre·ɣu·la·ri·'sar, -'θar] **I.** *vt* (*poner en orden*) to regularize; (*normalizar*) to standardize **II.** *vr:* ~**se** (*regularse*) to be regulated; (*normalizarse*) to become standardized

regularmente [rre·ɣu·lar·'men·te] *adv* (*normalmente*) usually

rehabilitación [rre·a·βi·li·ta·'sjon, -'θjon] *f* rehabilitation; (*edificio*) refurbishment

rehabilitar [rre·a·βi·li·'tar] **I.** *vt* 1. *t.* JUR, MED to rehabilitate 2. (*una cosa*) to repair; (*edificio*) to refurbish **II.** *vr:* ~**se** to be rehabilitated

rehacer [rre·a·'ser, -'θer] *irr como* hacer **I.** *vt* to redo; (*reconstruir*) to rebuild;

R

(*edificio*) to refurbish; (*reparar*) to repair; **~ su vida con alguien** to rebuild one's life with sb **II.** *vr* **~se de una desgracia** to recover from a misfortune

rehecho, -a [rre·'e·tʃo, -a] **I.** *pp de* **rehacer II.** *adj* thickset

rehén [rre·'en] *m* hostage

rehogar ⟨g → gu⟩ [rre·o·'ɣar] *vt* to sauté

rehuir [rre·u·'ir] *irr como huir vt* to avoid; (*obligación*) to shirk; (*rechazar*) to reject

rehusar [rre·u·'sar] *vt* to refuse; (*invitación*) to decline; **¡rehusado!** rejected!

reimpresión [rre·im·pre·'sjon] *f* reprint

reimprimir [rre·im·pri·'mir] *irr como imprimir vt* to reprint

reina ['rrei·na] *f* queen

reinado [rrei·'na·do] *m* reign

reinar [rrei·'nar] *vi* to reign; (*ambiente*) t. METEO to prevail

reincidencia [rre·in·si·'den·sja, -θi·'den·θja] *f* relapse; JUR repeat offense

reincidente [rre·in·si·'den·te, rre·in·θi-] **I.** *adj* repeat **II.** *mf* repeat offender

reincidir [rre·in·si·'dir, rre·in·θi-] *vi* **~ en algo** to relapse into sth; **~ en un delito** to repeat an offence

reincorporar [rre·in·kor·po·'rar] **I.** *vt* **~ a algo** to reincorporate into sth; **~ a alguien a un puesto** to restore sb to a position **II.** *vr:* **~se** to return; (*a una organización*) to rejoin

reino ['rrei·no] *m* realm; POL kingdom; **Reino Unido** United Kingdom

reintegrar [rre·in·te·'ɣrar] **I.** *vt* **1.** (*reincorporar*) to reintegrate; (*en un cargo*) to reinstate **2.** (*devolver*) to return; (*dinero*) to repay; (*desembolsos*) to reimburse **II.** *vr:* **~se** to return; (*a una organización*) to rejoin

reintegro [rre·in·'te·ɣro] *m* **1.** (*reintegración*) reintegration; (*en un cargo*) reinstatement **2. me tocó un ~** I won back my stake **3.** (*pago*) reimbursement; (*de la cuenta*) withdrawal; (*devolución*) repayment

reír [rre·'ir] *irr* **I.** *vi* to laugh; **echarse a ~** to burst out laughing; **no me hagas ~** *fig* don't make me laugh ▶ **el que ríe último ríe mejor** he who laughs last laughs longest [*o* best] **II.** *vr* **~se de**

algo to laugh at sth; **~se a carcajadas** to laugh loudly **III.** *vt* to laugh at

reiteradamente [rrei·te·ra·da·'men·te] *adv* repeatedly

reiterar [rrei·te·'rar] **I.** *vt* to repeat; **reiteró su intención de ayudarme** he/she repeated his/her intention of helping me **II.** *vr:* **~se** to repeat; **se reiteró en su decisión de dejar de fumar** he/she reaffirmed his/her decision to stop smoking

reivindicación [rrei·βin·di·ka·'sjon, -'θjon] *f* claim (**de** to)

reivindicar ⟨c → qu⟩ [rrei·βin·di·'kar] to claim; (*exigir*) to demand

reja ['rre·xa] *f* grill; **entre ~s** *inf* behind bars

rejego [rre·'xe·ɣo] *adj AmC, Méx* **1.** (*indomable*) wild; (*alzado*) untamed **2.** (*intratable*) unmanageable; (*enojadizo*) cranky

rejilla [rre·'xi·ja, -ʎa] *f* grating; (*parrilla*) grill

rejo ['rre·xo] *m AmL* whip

rejuvenecer [rre·xu·βe·ne·'ser, -'θer] *irr como crecer* **I.** *vt* to rejuvenate; **este peinado te rejuvenece** this haircut makes you look much younger **II.** *vr:* **~se** to be rejuvenated

relación [rre·la·'sjon, -'θjon] *f* relationship; **con ~ a su petición** with regard to your/his/her request; **calidad-precio** value for money; (**no**) **guardar ~ con** to bear (no) relation to; **relaciones públicas** public relations; **mantienen relaciones** they are going out with each other; **mantener relaciones sexuales con alguien** to have a sexual relationship with sb

relacionar [rre·la·sjo·'nar, rre·la·θjo-] **I.** *vt* to relate **II.** *vr:* **~se 1.** (*estar relacionado*) to be related **2.** (*iniciar relaciones*) to strike up a relationship; (*mantener relaciones*) to mix; **~se mucho** (*amigos*) to have lots of friends; (*influyentes*) to have lots of contacts

relajación [rre·la·xa·'sjon, -'θjon] *f* **1.** relaxation **2.** (*malas costumbres*) slackness

relajadura [rre·la·xa·'du·ra] *f Méx* rupture

relajar [rre·la·'xar] I. *vt* to relax; (*suavizar*) to ease II. *vr:* ~**se** to relax; (*suavizarse*) to ease

relamer [rre·la·'mer] I. *vt* to lick II. *vr:* ~**se** to lick one's lips; (*animal*) to lick its chops

relámpago [rre·'lam·pa·ɣo] *m* flash of lightning

relance [rre·'lan·se] *m* 1. *Chile* flirtatious compliment 2. *Col* **de** ~ in cash

relatar [rre·la·'tar] *vt* to report; (*historia*) to tell

relatividad [rre·la·ti·βi·'ðað] *f* relativity

relativo [rre·la·'ti·βo] *m* relative pronoun; **oración de** ~ relative clause

relativo, -a [rre·la·'ti·βo, -a] *adj* relative; **ser** ~ **a algo** to be relative to sth; **un artículo** ~ **a...** an article about...; **pronombre** ~ relative pronoun

relato [rre·'la·to] *m* report; LIT story; ~ **corto** short story

relegar <g → gu> [rre·le·'ɣar] *vt* ~ **algo a un plano secundario** to push sth into the background

relevancia [rre·le·'βan·sja, -θja] *f* relevance

relevante [rre·le·'βan·te] *adj* important; (*sobresaliente*) outstanding

relevar [rre·le·'βar] I. *vt* 1. (*liberar*) to exempt 2. (*destituir*) to remove; ~ **a alguien de un cargo** to relieve sb of his/her post 3. (*reemplazar*) to place; MIL to relieve; DEP to substitute II. *vr:* ~**se** to take turns

relevo [rre·'le·βo] *m* 1. change; **tomar el** ~ **de alguien** to take over from sb 2. (*pl*) DEP relay; **carrera de** ~**s** relay race

relicario [rre·li·'ka·rjo] *m AmL* locket

relieve [rre·'lje·βe] *m* relief ▶ **poner de** ~ to emphasize

religión [rre·li·'xjon] *f* religion

religioso, -a [rre·li·'xjo·so, -a] I. *adj* religious II. *m, f* monk(nun) *m(f)*

reliquia [rre·'li·kja] *f* relic; (*antigüedad*) collector's item; **una** ~ **de familia** a family heirloom

rellano [rre·'ʝa·no, -'ʎano] *m* landing

rellena [rre·'ʝe·na, -'ʎe·na] *f Col, Méx* blood sausage

rellenar [rre·ʝe·'nar, rre·ʎe-] *vt* 1. ~ **de** [o **con**] **algo** to fill with sth; CULIN to stuff with sth 2. (*por completo*) to fill up 3. (*completar*) to fill out

relleno [rre·'ʝe·no, rre·'ʎe-] *m* filling stuffing

relleno, -a [rre·'ʝe·no, -a; rre·'ʎe-] *adj* 1. full; CULIN stuffed 2. *inf* chubby

reloj [rre·'lox] *m* clock; (*de pulsera*) watch; ~ **despertador** alarm clock; **contra** ~ against the clock

relojear [rre·lo·xe·'ar] *vt Arg* 1. (*cronometrar*) to time 2. *inf* (*controlar, espiar*) to keep tabs on; ~ **a alguien de arriba abajo** to look sb up and down

relojería [rre·lo·xe·'ri·a] *f* clockmaker's; (*de pulsera*) watchmaker's

reluciente [rre·lu·'sjen·te, -'θjen·te] *adj* shining; ~ **de limpio** shiny clean

relucir [rre·lu·'sir, -'θir] *irr como lucir vi* to shine; (*sobresalir*) to stand out ▶ **sacar algo a** ~ to bring sth up; **salir a** ~ to come up

relumbrar [rre·lum·'brar] *vi* to shine; (*sobresalir*) to stand out

remachado, -a [rre·ma·'tʃa·ðo] *adj Col* quiet

remachar [rre·ma·'tʃar] I. *vt* 1. (*golpear*) to hammer 2. (*sujetar*) to rivet II. *vr:* ~**se** *Col* to remain silent

remangar <g → gu> [rre·man·'gar] I. *vt* to roll up II. *vr:* ~**se** *t. fig* to roll up one's sleeves

remanso [rre·'man·so] *m* (*represa*) pool; (*agua muerta*) stagnant water

remar [rre·'mar] *vi* to row

rematar [rre·ma·'tar] I. *vt* to finish off; (*terminar de hacer*) to put the finishing touches to; DEP to shoot II. *vi* to end; DEP to shoot

remate [rre·'ma·te] *m* 1. conclusion; (*de un producto*) finishing touch 2. DEP shot ▶ **estar loco de** ~ to be as mad as a hatter; **para** ~ to top it all off; **por** ~ finally

remecer [rre·me·'ser] *irr como crecer vt, vr:* ~**se** *AmL* to shake

remediar [rre·me·'djar] *vt* 1. (*evitar*) to prevent; **no puedo** ~**lo** I can't help it 2. (*acabar con*) to finish off; (*reparar*) to repair; (*compensar*) to make up for 3. (*corregir*) to correct

remedio [rre·'me·djo] *m t.* MED remedy; (*solución*) solution; **no tener ~** to be a hopeless case; **la crisis no tiene ~** there is no solution to the crisis; **no tenemos** [*o* **no hay**] **más ~ que...** there is no choice but to...; **sin ~** (*inútil*) hopeless; (*sin falta*) inevitable ▶ **es peor el ~ que la enfermedad** *prov* the remedy is worse than the disease; **¿qué ~?** what choice is there?

rememorar [rre·me·mo·'rar] *vt* to remember

remendar <e → ie> [rre·men·'dar] *vt* to mend; (*con parches*) to patch; (*zurcir*) to darn

remera [rre·'me·ra] *f Arg* T-shirt

remesa [rre·'me·sa] *f* consignment; FIN remittance

remezón [rre·me·'son] *m AmL* shake

remilgos [rre·'mil·yos] *mpl* **sin ~** without making a fuss; **hacer ~** to make a fuss

remite [rre·'mi·te] *m* sender's name and address

remitente [rre·mi·'ten·te] *mf* sender

remitir [rre·mi·'tir] I. *vt* 1. (*enviar*) to send; FIN to remit 2. (*referirse*) to refer 3. (*de una obligación*) to forgive 4. (*aplazar*) to postpone II. *vi* (*calmarse*) to let up III. *vr:* ~se to refer

remo ['rre·mo] *m* oar; (*sin soporte*) paddle; DEP rowing

remodelación [rre·mo·de·la·'sjon, -'θjon] *f* redesign

remodelar [rre·mo·de·'lar] *vt* to redesign

remojar [rre·mo·'xar] I. *vt* to soak; (*empapar*) to drench; (*ablandar*) to soften; (*galleta*) to dip II. *vr:* ~se to get wet; (*bañarse*) to have a dip

remojo [rre·'mo·xo] *m* soaking; (*baño*) dip; **poner en ~** to leave to soak

remolacha [rre·mo·'la·tʃa] *f* beet; (*roja*) beetroot; (*de azúcar*) (sugar) beet

remolcar <c → qu> [rre·mol·'kar] *vt* to tow; (*barco*) to tug

remolienda [rre·mo·'ljen·da] *f Arg, Urug* binge

remolino [rre·mo·'li·no] *m* whirl; (*de agua*) whirlpool; (*de viento, persona*) whirlwind

remolonear [rre·mo·lo·ne·'ar] *vi, vr:* ~se 1. (*vaguear*) to be lazy 2. (*evitar*) to shirk

remolque [rre·'mol·ke] *m* 1. (*arrastre*) tow; **llevar a ~** to tow 2. (*vehículo*) trailer

remontar [rre·mon·'tar] I. *vt* 1. (*superar*) to overcome 2. (*subir*) to go up; **~ el vuelo** to soar II. *vr:* ~se to go back to; **la construcción de la iglesia se remonta al siglo pasado** the construction of the church dates from the past century

remorder <o → ue> [rre·mor·'der] *vt* **me remuerde** (**la conciencia**) I feel guilty

remordimiento [rre·mor·di·'mjen·to] *m* remorse; **tener ~s** (**de conciencia**) **por algo** to feel remorseful about sth

remoto, -a [rre·'mo·to, -a] *adj* remote; **en tiempos ~s** long ago; **ni la más remota posibilidad/idea** not the slightest possibility/idea

remover <o → ue> [rre·mo·'βer] I. *vt* 1. (*agitar*) to shake; (*dar vueltas*) to stir; (*ensalada*) to toss 2. (*mover*) to remove II. *vi* to investigate

remunerable [rre·mu·ne·'ra·βle] *adj* remunerable

remuneración [rre·mu·ne·ra·'sjon, -'θjon] *f* remuneration; (*recompensa*) compensation

remunerar [rre·mu·ne·'rar] *vt* to remunerate; **~ a alguien por un servicio** to pay sb for a service; (*recompensar*) to compensate

renacer [rre·na·'ser, -'θer] *irr como crecer vi* to revive; **sentirse ~** to feel completely revived

renacimiento [rre·na·si·'mjen·to, -θi·'mjen·to] *m* revival; ARTE, LIT renaissance

renacuajo, -a [rre·na·'kwa·xo, -a] *m, f* pey inf (*niño pequeño*) shrimp

renal [rre·'nal] *adj* renal

rencor [rren·'kor] *m* ill feeling; **guardar ~ a alguien** to bear a grudge against sb

rencoroso, -a [rren·ko·'ro·so, -a] *adj* (*vengativo*) spiteful; (*resentido*) resentful

rendición [rren·di·'sjon, -'θjon] *f* surrender; (*fatiga*) exhaustion

rendido, -a [rren·'di·do, -a] *adj* exhausted; (*sumiso*) submissive

rendija [rren·'di·xa] *f* crack

rendimiento [rren·di·'mjen·to] *m*

1. (*productividad*) yield; ECON capacity; **a pleno ~** at full capacity **2.** (*beneficio*) profit; **de gran ~** very profitable **3.** *pl* (*ingresos*) income

rendir [rren·'dir] *irr como pedir* **I.** *vt* **1.** (*rentar*) to yield; **~ utilidad** to be useful; **~ fruto** to bear fruit **2.** (*trabajar*) to produce; **estas máquinas rinden mucho** these machines are very productive **3.** (*tributar*) to attribute; **~ importancia a algo** to attribute importance to sth **4.** **~ cuentas** to settle the accounts; (*fig*) to account for one's actions **5.** (*cansar*) to exhaust **II.** *vr:* **~se** to surrender; **~se a la evidencia de algo** to bow to the evidence of sth; **~se a las razones de alguien** to yield to sb's arguments

renegado, -a [rre·ne·'ɣa·do] *inf* **I.** *adj* bad-tempered **II.** *m, f* grouch

renegar [rre·ne·'ɣar] *irr como fregar* **I.** *vi* **~ de algo** (*protestar*) to protest against sth; (*renunciar*) to renounce sth **II.** *vt* (*negar*) to deny; (*detestar*) to detest

renglón [rren·'glon] *m* line

rengo, -a [rren·go, -a] *adj* CSur lame

renguear [rren·ge·'ar] *vi* CSur (*cojear*) to limp

renguera [rren·'ge·ra] *f* CSur limp

reno ['rre·no] *m* reindeer

renombrado, -a [rre·nom·'bra·do, -a] *adj* renowned

renombre [rre·'nom·bre] *m* renown; **una empresa de gran ~** a very well-known company; **una persona de ~** a famous person

renovación [rre·no·βa·'sjon, -'θjon] *f* renewal

renovar <o → ue> [rre·no·'βar] *vt* to renew; (*casa*) to renovate; (*país*) to modernize; **~ un pedido/aviso** to repeat a request/warning

renta ['rren·ta] *f* **1.** (*beneficio*) profit; (*ingresos*) income; (*pensión*) pension; **~ per cápita** per capita income **2.** (*alquiler*) rent; **en ~** for rent; **tomar a ~ un negocio** to lease out a business

rentabilidad [rren·ta·βi·li·'dad] *f* profitability

rentable [rren·'ta·βle] *adj* profitable

rentar [rren·'tar] *vt* AmL to rent

rentero, -a [rren·'te·ro, -a] *m, f* **1.** (*arren-*

---

datario) tenant farmer **2.** Arg (*contribuyente*) taxpayer

renuncia [rre·'nun·sja, -θja] *f* **~ a** [*o de*] **algo** resignation from sth; **~ al contrato** withdrawal from the contract; **presentar su ~** to resign

renunciar [rre·nun·'sjar, -'θjar] *vi* **~ a algo** (*desistir*) to renounce sth; (*rechazar*) to reject sth; **~ a un cargo** to resign from a post

reñido, -a [rre·'ɲi·do, -a] *adj* **1.** (*lucha, partida*) tough **2.** (*en oposición*) **estar ~ con...** to be incompatible with...

reñir [rre·'ɲir] *irr como ceñir* **I.** *vi* to quarrel **II.** *vt* to scold

reo, -a ['rreo, -a] **I.** *adj* accused **II.** *m, f* (*culpado*) defendant; (*autor*) culprit; **~ habitual** persistent offender; **~ preventivo** remand prisoner

reojo [rre·'o·xo] *m* **mirar de ~** (*con hostilidad*) to look askance (at); (*con disimulo*) to look out of the corner of one's eye (at)

reorganización [rre·or·ɣa·ni·sa·'sjon, -θa·'θjon] *f* reorganization; **~ del gobierno** government reshuffle

reorganizar <z → c> [rre·or·ɣa·ni·'sar, -'θar] *vt* to reorganize; (*gobierno*) to reshuffle

reparación [rre·pa·ra·'sjon, -'θjon] *f* repair; (*indemnización*) compensation

reparar [rre·pa·'rar] **I.** *vt* **1.** (*arreglar*) to repair; **~ el daño** to repair the damage **2.** (*indemnizar*) to compensate **3.** **~ fuerzas** to recover one's strength **II.** *vi* **~ en** (*advertir*) to notice; (*considerar*) to consider; **sin ~ en gastos** regardless of the cost; **no ~ en sacrificios/gastos** to spare no effort/expense

reparo [rre·'pa·ro] *m* **1.** (*inconveniente*) problem; **sin ~ alguno** without any difficulty; **tener ~s para** to be reluctant [*o hesitant*] **to 2.** (*objeción*) objection; **sin ~** without reservation; **no andar con ~s** to have no reservations; **poner ~s a algo** to raise objections to sth

repartición [rre·par·ti·'sjon, -'θjon] *f* **1.** *v.* **repartimiento 2.** AmL office

repartimiento [rre·par·ti·'mjen·to] *m* (*distribución*) distribution; (*división*) division

repartir [rre·par·'tir] I. *vt* to distribute; (*correos*) to deliver II. *vr:* ~**se** to divide up

reparto [rre·'par·to] *m* distribution; (*división*) division; ~ **postal/a domicilio** mail/home delivery

repasador [rre·pa·sa·'dor] *m Arg, Urug* dish cloth

repasar [rre·pa·'sar] *vt* to revise; (*cuenta*) to check; (*carta*) to reread; (*ropa*) to mend

repaso [rre·'pa·so] *m* 1. (*revisión*) review 2. (*inspección*) check

repatriar [rre·pa·'trjar] *vt* to repatriate

repeinar [rre·pei·'nar] I. *vt* to comb carefully II. *vr:* ~**se** to comb one's hair carefully

repelente [rre·pe·'len·te] I. *adj* 1. (*rechazador*) repellent 2. (*repugnante*) repulsive 3. (*redicho*) affected II. *mf* know-it-all

repeler [rre·pe·'ler] *vt* 1. (*rechazar*) to repel; **los imanes se repelen mutuamente** magnets repel one another 2. (*repugnar*) to disgust

repensar <e → ie> [rre·pen·'sar] *vt* to reconsider

repente [rre·'pen·te] *m* **de** ~ suddenly

repentino, -a [rre·pen·'ti·no, -a] *adj* sudden

repercusión [rre·per·ku·'sjon] *f* repercussion; **tener gran** ~ to meet with great success

repercutir [rre·per·ku·'tir] *vi* ~ **en algo** to have an effect on sth; ~ **en la salud** to affect one's health

repertorio [rre·per·'to·rjo] *m* repertoire; (*lista*) list

repetición [rre·pe·ti·'sjon, -'θjon] *f* repetition

repetido, -a [rre·pe·'ti·do, -a] *adj* repeated; **repetidas veces** again and again; **tengo muchos sellos** ~**s** I have doubles of lots of my stamps

repetir [rre·pe·'tir] *irr como* **pedir** I. *vi* 1. (*sabor*) to repeat; **los ajos repiten mucho** garlic comes back on you 2. (*plato*) to have second helpings II. *vt* (*reiterar, recitar*) to repeat; ~ **curso** to stay down; ~ **un pedido** to reorder goods III. *vr:* ~**se** to repeat oneself

repicar <c → qu> [rre·pi·'kar] *vi, vt* to ring

repisa [rre·'pi·sa] *f* shelf; ~ **de chimenea** mantelpiece; ~ **de ventana** window ledge

replantear [rre·plan·te·'ar] *vt* to rethink; (*asunto*) to raise again; (*plan*) to revise

replegar [rre·ple·'yar] *irr como* **fregar** I. *vt* 1. (*doblar*) to fold 2. (*para atrás*) to fold back II. *vr:* ~**se** to fall back

repleto, -a [rre·'ple·to, -a] *adj* ~ **de algo** full of sth; (*demasiado*) crammed with sth; **el tren está** ~ the train is packed; **estoy** ~ I'm full up

réplica ['rre·pli·ka] *f* rebuttal; ARTE replica

replicar <c → qu> [rre·pli·'kar] I. *vt* to answer II. *vi* to reply; (*contradecir*) to contradict; **obedecer sin** ~ to obey without argument

repoblación [rre·po·βla·'sjon, -'θjon] *f* repopulation; (*de plantas*) replanting; ~ **forestal** reforestation

repoblar <o → ue> [rre·po·'βlar] *vt* to repopulate; (*plantas*) to replant; (*árboles*) to reforest

repollo [rre·'po·jo, -ʎo] *m* cabbage

reponer [rre·po·'ner] *irr como* **poner** I. *vt* to replace; (*fuerzas*) to get back II. *vr:* ~**se** to recover

reportaje [rre·por·'ta·xe] *m* report; PREN article; ~ **gráfico** illustrated report; (*documental*) documentary

reportar [rre·por·'tar] *vt AmL* to report

reportear [rre·por·te·'ar] *vt AmL* to interview

reportero, -a [rre·por·'te·ro, -a] *m, f* reporter; ~ **gráfico** press photographer

reposar [rre·po·'sar] I. *vi* to rest; **aquí reposan los restos mortales de...** here lie the mortal remains of... II. *vt* to settle; ~ **la comida** to let one's food settle III. *vr:* ~**se** to settle; (*vino*) to lie

reposera [rre·po·'se·ra] *f AmL* deckchair

reposición [rre·po·si·'sjon, -'θjon] *f* 1. replacement; ~ **de existencias** replenishment of stocks; (*mercado, persona*) recovery; (*situación*) stabilization 2. TEAT revival; TV rerun; CINE rerelease

reposo [rre·'po·so] *m* peace; (*descanso*)

rest; **~ en cama** rest in bed

repostada [rre·pos·'ta·da] *f AmC* rude reply

repostar [rre·pos·'tar] *vt* to stock up with; (*vehículo*) to refuel

repostería [rre·pos·te·'ri·a] *f* pastries *pl*; (*pastelería*) pastry shop

reprender [rre·pren·'der] *vt* to reprimand

represalia [rre·pre·'sa·lja] *f* reprisal; **en ~ por...** in retaliation for...

representación [rre·pre·sen·ta·'sjon, -'θjon] *f* 1. representation; **por** [*o* **en**] **~ de** representing 2. TEAT performance 3. (*reproducción*) reproduction; (*ilustración*) illustration; **~ digital** digital display

representante [rre·pre·sen·'tan·te] *mf* representative; TEAT, CINE agent, manager; COM dealer

representar [rre·pre·sen·'tar] *vt* 1. (*sustituir*) to represent 2. (*actuar*) to act; (*obra*) to perform 3. (*significar*) to mean 4. (*encarnar*) to embody; (*reproducir*) to reproduce; (*ilustrar*) to illustrate

representativo, -a [rre·pre·sen·ta·'ti·βo, -a] *adj* representative

represión [rre·pre·'sjon] *f* (*contención*) suppression; (*limitación*) repression

reprimenda [rre·pri·'men·da] *f* reprimand

reprimir [rre·pri·'mir] **I.** *vt* to suppress **II.** *vr:* **~se** to control oneself

reprochable [rre·pro·'tʃa·βle] *adj* reprehensible

reprochar [rre·pro·'tʃar] *vt* to reproach

reproche [rre·'pro·tʃe] *m* reproach

reproducción [rre·pro·duk·'sjon, -duɣ·'θjon] *f* reproduction; **~ radiofónica** radio reproduction; (*repetición*) repetition; **~ sexual** sexual reproduction; (*de un libro*) copy (of a book); (*documentos*) duplication

reproducir [rre·pro·du·'sir, -'θir] *irr como traducir* **I.** *vt* 1. (*procrear*) to reproduce 2. (*repetir*) to repeat; (*copiar*) to reproduce; (*libro*) to print; (*documento*) to duplicate 3. (*representar*) to represent **II.** *vr:* **~se** to reproduce

reproductor [rre·pro·duk·'tor] *m* **~ de discos compactos** compact disc player

reptar [rrep·'tar] *vi* to crawl

reptil [rrep·'til] *m* reptile

república [rre·'pu·βli·ka] *f* republic

republicano, -a [rre·pu·βli·'ka·no, -a] *adj, m, f* republican

repudiar [rre·pu·'djar] *vt* to reject; (*parientes*) to disown

repudio [rre·'pu·djo] *m* rejection; (*de parientes*) repudiation

repuesto [rre·'pwes·to] *m* spare part; **rueda de ~** spare tire

repuesto, -a [rre·'pwes·to, -a] *pp de* reponer

repugnancia [rre·puɣ·'nan·sja, -θja] *f* **~ a algo** repugnance for sth; (*asco*) disgust for sth

repugnante [rre·puɣ·'nan·te] *adj* disgusting

repugnar [rre·puɣ·'nar] *vi* to disgust; **me repugna la carne grasosa** fatty meat makes me sick

repulsión [rre·pul·'sjon] *f* aversion; (*asco*) disgust

repulsivo, -a [rre·pul·'si·βo, -a] *adj* repulsive

repunte [rre·'pun·te] *m RíoPl* rise

reputación [rre·pu·ta·'sjon, -'θjon] *f* reputation; **tener muy buena/mala ~** to have a very good/bad reputation

requemar [rre·ke·'mar] **I.** *vt* (*asar bien*) to roast; (*demasiado*) to burn; **~ la garganta/la lengua** to burn one's throat/tongue **II.** *vr:* **~se** to scorch

requenete [rre·ke·'ne·te] *adj Ven* (*rechoncho*) tubby

requerimiento [rre·ke·ri·'mjen·to] *m* **~ de algo** demand for sth; (*escrito*) writ for sth; **~ de información** request for information; **a ~ de...** on the request of...

requerir [rre·ke·'rir] *irr como sentir vt* to require; **esto requiere toda la atención** this calls for our fullest attention

requesón [rre·ke·'son] *m* cottage cheese

requetebueno, -a [rre·ke·te·'βwe·no, -a] *adj AmL inf* really good

requetecaro, -a [rre·ke·te·'ka·ro, -a] *adj AmL inf* really expensive

réquiem ['re·kjen] *m* requiem

requisar [rre·ki·'sar] *vt* to confiscate

requisito [rre·ki·'si·to] *m* requirement; (*condición*) condition; **ser ~ indispen-**

R

sable to be absolutely essential; **~ previo** prerequisite; **cumplir con los ~s** to fulfill the requirements

res [rres] *f* **1.** beast; **carne de ~** beef **2.** *AmL* head of cattle

resaca [rre·'sa·ka] *f* undertow; *inf* hangover

resaltar [rre·sal·'tar] *vi, vt* to stand out; **hacer ~** to highlight

resalte [rre·'sal·te] *m*, **resalto** [rre·'sal·to] *m* projection, ledge

resarcir <c → z> [rre·sar·'sir, -'θir] I. *vt* to repay; **~ de algo** to compensate for sth II. *vr* **~se de algo** to make up for sth

resbalada [rres·βa·'la·da] *f AmL inf* slip

resbaladilla [rres·βa·la·'di·ja, -ʎa] *f Méx* slide

resbaladizo, -a [rres·βa·la·'di·so, -a; -θo, -a] *adj* slippery

resbalar [rres·βa·'lar] *vi* to slide; (*sin querer*) to slip; (*coche*) to skid

resbalín [rres·βa·'lin] *m Chile* slide

rescatar [rres·ka·'tar] *vt* **1.** (*prisionero*) to rescue; (*con dinero*) to pay the ransom for; (*un cadáver, algo perdido*) to recover; (*náufrago*) to pick up **2.** (*deuda*) to pay off; *AmL* (*mercancías*) to peddle

rescate [rres·'ka·te] *m* recovery; (*prisionero*) rescue; (*con dinero*) ransoming

rescindir [rre·sin·'dir, rres·θin-] *vt* (*ley*) to repeal; (*contrato*) to annul

rescisión [rresi·'sjon, rresθi-] *f* (*ley*) repeal; (*contrato*) annulment; (*deuda*) cancellation

resecar <c → qu> [rre·se·'kar] *vt* to dry out

resentido, -a [rre·sen·'ti·do, -a] *adj* **1.** *estar* (*ofendido*) resentful; (*débil*) worn out **2.** *ser* bitter

resentimiento [rre·sen·ti·'mjen·to] *m* resentment

resentirse [rre·sen·'tir·se] *irr como sentir vr* **1.** (*ofenderse*) **~ por** [*o* **de**] **algo** to feel resentful about sth **2.** (*sentir dolor*) **~ de** [*o* **con**] **algo** to suffer from sth **3.** (*debilitarse*) to be weakened

reseña [rre·'se·ɲa] *f* **1.** (*de un libro*) review **2.** (*de una persona*) description **3.** (*narración*) report

reseñar [rre·se·'ɲar] *vt* to summarize; (*libro*) to review; (*persona*) to describe

resero, -a [rre·'se·ro, -a] *m, f CSur* cowhand

reserva [rre·'ser·βa] *f* **1.** (*previsión*) reservation; **~ de equipajes** *AmL* left luggage; **tener algo en ~** to hold sth in reserve **2.** FIN reserve; (*fondos*) reserves *pl* **3.** (*de plazas*) reservation; **hacer una ~** to book **4.** (*biológica*) reserve; (*para animales*) wildlife reserve **5.** (*vino*) vintage

reservado, -a [rre·ser·'βa·do, -a] *adj* **1.** reserved; (*confidencial*) confidential; **quedan ~s todos los derechos** all rights reserved **2.** (*callado*) reserved; (*cauteloso*) cautious

reservar [rre·ser·'βar] I. *vt* **1.** (*plaza*) to reserve **2.** (*guardar*) to put by II. *vr:* **~se** to save oneself

resfriado [rres·fri·'a·do] *m* cold

resfriarse <3. *pres* resfría> [rres·fri·'ar·se] *vr* to catch a cold

resfrío [rres·'fri·o] *m AmL* cold

resguardar [rres·ɣwar·'dar] I. *vt* to protect (**de** from) II. *vr* **~se de algo** to protect oneself from sth; **~se tras un muro** to shelter behind a wall

resguardo [rres·'ɣwar·do] *m* receipt; **~ de entrega/de transferencia** proof of delivery/transfer

residencia [rre·si·'den·sja, -θja] *f* residence; (*colegio*) boarding school; UNIV dormitory; **~ habitual** usual place of residence; **cambiar de ~** to change one's address; **~ de ancianos** old people's home

residente [rre·si·'den·te] *adj, mf* resident; **no ~** non-resident

residir [rre·si·'dir] *vi* to reside; **~ en** *fig* to lie in

residual [rre·si·du·'al] *adj* residual; **aguas ~es** sewage

residuo [rre·'si·dwo] *m* **1.** residue; QUÍM residuum **2.** *pl* waste; **~s industriales/radiactivos** industrial/radioactive waste

resignación [rre·siɣ·na·'sjon, -'θjon] *f* resignation

resignarse [rre·siɣ·'nar·se] *vr* to resign oneself (**con, a** to)

resina [rre·'si·na] *f* resin

resistencia [rre·sis·'ten·sja, -θja] *f* resistance; **~ a la autoridad** opposition to the authorities; **oponer ~** to offer resistance; **~ física** stamina; **carrera de ~** endurance race

resistente [rre·sis·'ten·te] *adj* resistant; **~ al calor/a la luz** heat-/light-resistant

resistir [rre·sis·'tir] I. *vi, vt* to resist II. *vr:* **~se** to resist

resolana [rre·so·'la·na] *f AmL* **1.** (*sol reflejado*) reflection **2.** (*lugar a pleno sol*) sunny, windless spot **3.** (*resplandor*) sun glare

resolución [rre·so·lu·'sjon, -'θjon] *f* **1.** (*firmeza*) resolve **2.** (*decisión*) decision; POL resolution; **~ judicial** adjudication; **tomar una ~** to reach a decision **3.** (*solución*) solution

resolver [rre·sol·'βer] *irr como* volver I. *vt* **1.** (*acordar*) to agree **2.** (*solucionar*) to solve; (*dudas*) to resolve II. *vr:* **~se 1.** (*solucionarse*) to be solved **2.** (*decidirse*) to decide

resonancia [rre·so·'nan·sja, -θja] *f* resonance; **tener ~** (*suceso*) to have an impact

resonante [rre·so·'nan·te] *adj* important; **con éxito ~** with tremendous success

resonar <o → ue> [rre·so·'nar] *vi* to resound

resorte [rre·'sor·te] *m Méx* elastic

resortera [rre·sor·'te·ra] *f Méx* slingshot

respaldar [rres·pal·'dar] I. *vt* to support; (*proteger*) to protect II. *vr:* **~se** to lean; (*hacia atrás*) to lean back

respaldo [rres·'pal·do] *m* support; (*protección*) protection; **en el ~** on the back

respectar [rres·pek·'tar] *vi* (*verbo defectivo*) to regard; **por** [*o* **en**] **lo que respecta a...** with regard to...

respectivamente [rres·pek·ti·βa·'men·te] *adv* respectively

respectivo, -a [rres·pek·'ti·βo, -a] *adj* respective

respecto [rres·'pek·to] *m* (**con**) **~ a** with regard to; **con ~ a eso** in that regard; **a este ~** in this regard

respetable [rres·pe·'ta·βle] *adj* respectable; (*notable*) considerable

respetar [rres·pe·'tar] *vt* **1.** (*honrar*) to respect; **hacerse ~** to command respect **2.** (*cumplir*) to observe

respeto [rres·'pe·to] *m* respect; **falta de ~** lack of respect; **tener mucho ~ a las tormentas** to be well aware of the dangers of storms ▶ faltar **al ~ a alguien** to be disrespectful to(wards) sb; **de ~** respectable

respetuoso, -a [rres·pe·tu·'o·so, -a] *adj* respectful

respiración [rres·pi·ra·'sjon, -'θjon] *f* breathing; (*aliento*) breath; **~ artificial** artificial respiration; **~ boca a boca** mouth to mouth resuscitation

respirar [rres·pi·'rar] *vi* to breathe; **~ aliviado** to breathe easily ▶ **¡déjame que respire!** give me a break!; **sin ~** without stopping

respiratorio, -a [rres·pi·ra·'to·rjo, -a] *adj* respiratory; **vías respiratorias** air passages

resplandecer [rres·plan·de·'ser, -'θer] *irr como* crecer *vi* to shine

resplandor [rres·plan·'dor] *m* brightness

responder [rres·pon·'der] *vi* **1.** (*contestar*) to reply **2.** (*contradecir*) to contradict **3.** (*corresponder*) to correspond **4.** **~ por algo** to answer for sth

responsabilidad [rres·pon·sa·βi·li·'dad] *f* responsibility; (*por un daño*) liability

responsabilizar <z → c> [rres·pon·sa·βi·li·'sar, -'θar] I. *vt* **~ de algo** to make responsible for sth II. *vr* **~se de algo** to accept the responsibility for sth

responsable [rres·pon·'sa·βle] I. *adj* **~ de algo** responsible for sth II. *mf* person in charge; (*culpable*) culprit

respuesta [rres·'pwes·ta] *f* answer; **~ negativa** negative reply; **en ~ a su carta del...** in reply to your letter of...

resquicio [rres·'ki·sjo, -θjo] *m* **1.** (*abertura*) crack **2.** (*ocasión*) opening; **~ de esperanza** glimmer of hope

resta [rres·ta] *f* subtraction

restablecer [rres·ta·βle·'ser, -'θer] *irr como* crecer I. *vt* to re-establish; (*democracia, paz*) to restore II. *vr:* **~se** to recover

restablecimiento [rres·ta·βle·si·'mjen·to, -θi·'mjen·to] *m* re-establishment; (*régimen, paz*) restoration

restante [rres·'tan·te] I. *adj* remain-

R

ing; **cantidad ~** remainder II. *m* remainder

restar [rres·'tar] I. *vi* to remain; **restan dos días para...** there are two days left until... II. *vt* to take away; MAT to subtract; **~ importancia a algo** to play sth down

restauración [rres·tau·ra·'sjon, -'θjon] *f* restoration

restaurante [rres·tau·'ran·te] *m* restaurant

restaurar [rres·tau·'rar] *vt* to restore

restitución [rres·ti·tu·'sjon, -'θjon] *f* return; (*reposición*) replacement

resto ['rres·to] *m* rest; MAT remainder; **~s mortales** mortal remains; **los ~s de la torre** the tower ruins; **lo recordaré el ~ de mis días** I will remember him for the rest of my life

restregar [rres·tre·'ɣar] *irr como fregar vt, vr:* **~se** to rub; **~se los ojos** to rub one's eyes

restricción [rres·trik·'sjon, -triɣ·'θjon] *f* restriction; (*recorte*) cutback; **sin restricciones** freely

restringir <g → j> [rres·trin·'xir] *vt* to restrict

resucitar [rre·su·θi·'tar, rre·su·θi·] *vi, vt* to resuscitate

resuelto, -a [rre·'swel·to, -a] I. *pp de* **resolver** II. *adj* determined

resultado [rre·sul·'ta·do] *m* result; **dar buen/mal ~** to work/fail

resultar [rre·sul·'tar] *vi* to work; **~ de algo** to result from sth; **~ muerto en un accidente** to be killed in an accident

resumen [rre·'su·men] *m* summary; **en ~** in short

resumidero [rre·su·mi·'de·ro] *m AmL* (*alcantarilla*) drain; (*pozo ciego*) cesspool

resumir [rre·su·'mir] *vt* to summarize

resurgir <g → j> [rre·sur·'xir] *vi* to reappear

resurrección [rre·su·rrek·'sjon, -reɣ·'θjon] *f* resurrection

retacón, -ona [rre·ta·'kon, -·'ko·na] *adj CSur* stubby

retaguardia [rre·ta·'ɣwar·dja] *f* rearguard ▶ **estar a la ~ de algo** to lag behind sth; **ir a la ~** to bring up the rear; **quedarse en la ~** to stay in the background;

a [*o* **en**] **~** (*tarde*) late

retar [rre·'tar] *vt* to challenge

retardar [rre·tar·'dar] I. *vt* to delay II. *vr:* **~se** to be late

retardo [rre·'tar·do] *m* delay; **sufrir un ~** to be delayed; **tener ~ con algo** to be late doing sth

rete ['rre·te] *adj Méx* very; **su hija es ~ alta** their daughter is very tall

retención [rre·ten·'sjon, -'θjon] *f* retention; FIN deduction; **~ fiscal** tax retention

retener [rre·te·'ner] *irr como tener vt* to retain; (*pasaporte*) to withhold; (*detener*) to detain

reticente [rre·ti·'sen·te, -'θen·te] *adj* reluctant

retina [rre·'ti·na] *f* retina; **desprendimiento de ~** detached retina

retintín [rre·tin·'tin] *m* sarcastic tone

retirada [rre·ti·'ra·da] *f* abandonment; (*eliminación*) withdrawal; MIL retreat

retirado, -a [rre·ti·'ra·do, -a] *adj* 1. (*lejos*) remote 2. (*jubilado*) retired

retirar [rre·ti·'rar] I. *vt* 1. (*apartar*) to remove; (*dinero*) to withdraw 2. (*recoger, quitar*) to take away 3. (*negar*) to deny II. *vr:* **~se** 1. (*abandonar*) to withdraw 2. (*retroceder*) to retreat 3. (*jubilarse*) to retire

retiro [rre·'ti·ro] *m* withdrawal; (*refugio*) retreat

reto ['rre·to] *m* challenge

retobado, -a [rre·to·'βa·do, -a] *adj* 1. *AmC, Méx, Ecua* (*respondón*) insolent 2. *AmC, Cuba, Ecua* (*indómito*) wild 3. *Arg, Méx, Urug* (*enconado*) ticked off *inf*

retobar [rre·to·'βar] I. *vt CSur* to cover with leather II. *vi Méx* to talk back

retocar <c → qu> [rre·to·'kar] *vt* to perfect; FOTO to retouch

retoñar [rre·to·'ɲar] *vi* to sprout

retoque [rre·'to·ke] *m* alteration; FOTO retouch

retorcer [rre·tor·'ser, -'θer] *irr como cocer* I. *vt* to twist; (*enroscar*) to twine II. *vr:* **~se** to twist; **~ de dolor** to writhe

retorcido, -a [rre·tor·'si·do, -a; rre·tor·'θi-] *adj* 1. (*complicado*) complicated 2. (*maligno*) twisted; (*mente*) warped

retórica [rre·'to·ri·ka] f rhetoric

retornable [rre·tor·'na·βle] adj **botella (no) ~** (non-)returnable bottle

retornar [rre·tor·'nar] vi, vt to return

retorno [rre·'tor·no] m return

retractar [rre·trak·'tar] I. vt to take back; JUR to retract II. vr **~se de algo** to withdraw from sth

retraer [rre·tra·'er] irr como traer I. vt 1. (encoger) to withdraw 2. (impedir) to hinder 3. JUR to retract II. vr: **~se** to retreat; **~se de algo** to withdraw from sth; **~se a** [o **en**] **algo** to withdraw into sth

retraído, -a [rre·tra·'i·do, -a] adj reserved; (poco sociable) withdrawn

retraimiento [rre·trai·'mjen·to] m reserve

retransmisión [rre·trans·mi·'sjon] f broadcast; **~ deportiva** sports program; **~ en directo/diferido** live/pre-recorded broadcast

retransmitir [rre·trans·mi·'tir] vt to broadcast

retrasado, -a [rre·tra·'sa·do, -a] adj 1. (atrasado) backward; (subdesarrollado) underdeveloped; **~ mental** mentally retarded 2. (tarde) behind schedule

retrasar [rre·tra·'sar] I. vt to delay; (reloj) to set back II. vr: **~se** to be late

retraso [rre·'tra·so] m 1. (demora) delay; **tener ~ en los pagos** to be in arrears 2. (subdesarrollo) underdevelopment

retratar [rre·tra·'tar] vt 1. (describir) to depict 2. (fotografiar) to photograph 3. (pintar) to paint a portrait of

retrato [rre·'tra·to] m portrait ▶ **ser el vivo ~ de alguien** to be the spitting image of sb

retrete [rre·'tre·te] m (recipiente) lavatory; (habitación)

retribución [rre·tri·βu·'sjon, -'θjon] f reward; (sueldo) remuneration

retribuir [rre·tri·βu·'ir] irr como huir vt 1. to remunerate 2. AmL to compensate

retroactivo, -a [rre·tro·ak·'ti·βo, -a] adj retroactive

retroalimentación [rre·tro·a·li·men·ta·'sjon, -'θjon] f feedback

retroceder [rre·tro·se·'der, -θe·'der] vi to go back

retroceso [rre·tro·'se·so, -'θe·so] m reversal; MED relapse; (negociaciones) setback

retrógrado, -a [rre·'tro·γra·do, -a] adj, m, f reactionary

retrospectivo, -a [rre·tros·pek·'ti·βo, -a] adj retrospective

retrovisor [rre·tro·βi·'sor] m rearview mirror; **~ exterior** side mirror

retumbar [rre·tum·'bar] vi to boom; (resonar) to resound

reuma ['rreu·ma] m o f, **reúma** [rre·'u·ma] m o f rheumatism

reumático, -a [rreu·'ma·ti·ko, -a] adj rheumatic

reumatismo [rreu·ma·'tis·mo] m rheumatism

reunificación [rre·u·ni·fi·ka·'sjon, -'θjon] f reunification

reunificar <c → qu> [rre·u·ni·fi·'kar] vt to reunify

reunión [rreu·'njon] f meeting; **celebrar una ~** to hold a meeting

reunir [rreu·'nir] irr I. vt to assemble; (unir) to gather; **~ las cualidades necesarias** to have the necessary qualities II. vr: **~se** to meet; (informal) to get together; (unirse) to gather

revaloración [rre·βa·lo·ra·'sjon, -'θjon] f re-evaluation; FIN revaluation

revalorización [rre·βa·lo·ri·sa·'sjon, -θa·'θjon] f appreciation

revancha [rre·'βan·tʃa] f revenge; DEP return match

revelación [rre·βe·la·'sjon, -'θjon] f revelation

revelado [rre·βe·'la·do] m developing

revelar [rre·βe·'lar] vt to reveal; FOTO to develop

revellín [rre·βe·'jin, -'ʎin] m Cuba (dificultad) difficulty ▶ **echar ~** to provoke anger

revenir [rre·βe·'nir] irr como venir vi, vr: **~se** 1. (encoger) to shrink 2. (agriarse) to sour 3. (secarse) to dry out

reventa [rre·'βen·ta] f resale; (entradas) scalping

reventadero [rre·βen·ta·'de·ro] m 1. Col, Méx (hervidero) bubbling spring 2. Chile (rompiente) shoal

R

reventado, -a [rre·βen·'ta·do, -a] *adj* 1. *inf* (*hecho polvo*) wiped out 2. *Arg* (*sinuoso*) devious

reventar <e → ie> [rre·βen·'tar] I. *vi* to break; (*globo, neumático*) to burst; **lleno hasta ~** full to bursting II. *vt* 1. to break; (*globo, neumático*) to burst 2. *inf* to annoy III. *vr:* ~**se** to break; (*globo, neumático*) to burst

reverbero [rre·βer·'βe·ro] *m AmL* (*hornillo*) spirit stove

reverencia [rre·βe·'ren·sja, -θja] *f* bow

reverendo [rre·βe·'ren·do] *m* Reverend

reversa [rre·'βer·sa] *f Chile, Col, Méx* reverse

reversible [rre·βer·'si·βle] *adj* reversible

reversión [rre·βer·'sjon] *f* reversion

reverso [rre·'βer·so] *m* other side

revertir [rre·βer·'tir] *irr como sentir vi* to revert

revés [rre·'βes] *m* 1. (*reverso*) other side; **al** [*o* **del**] ~ back to front; (*con lo de arriba abajo*) upside down; (*dentro para fuera*) inside out; **te has puesto el jersey del** ~ you have put your jumper on back to front 2. (*golpe*) blow with the back of the hand 3. DEP backhand 4. (*infortunio*) setback; ~ **de fortuna** stroke of bad luck

revirado, -a [rre·βi·'ra·do, -a] *adj Arg, Urug* nutty

revire [rre·'βi·re] *m Arg, Urug inf* crazy idea; **le dio uno de sus ~s** he/she had one of his/her crazy ideas

revisada [rre·βi·'sa·da] *f AmL* check

revisar [rre·βi·'sar] *vt* to check; TÉC to inspect; (*textos, edición*) to revise

revisión [rre·βi·'sjon] *f* check; TÉC inspection; JUR, TIPO revision

revisor(a) [rre·βi·'sor, -·'so·ra] *m(f)* inspector; FERRO ticket inspector

revista [rre·'βis·ta] *f* magazine; **las ~s del corazón** the gossip magazines; ~ **electrónica** e-zine; ~ **especializada** special interest magazine

revivir [rre·βi·'βir] I. *vi* to revive II. *vt* to revive; (*evocar*) to relive

revocar <c → qu> [rre·βo·'kar] *vt* to revoke

revolcar [rre·βol·'kar] *irr como volcar* I. *vt* (*derribar*) to knock over II. *vr* ~**se**

por algo to roll around in sth

revolear [rre·βo·le·'ar] *vt Méx, CSur* to whirl around

revoloteo [rre·βo·lo·'teo] *m* fluttering

revoltijo [rre·βol·'ti·xo] *m* jumble

revoltoso, -a [rre·βol·'to·so, -a] I. *adj* mischievous; (*rebelde*) rebellious II. *m, f* troublemaker

revoltura [rre·βol·'tu·ra] *f Méx* mixture

revolución [rre·βo·lu·'sjon, -'θjon] *f* revolution

revolucionar [rre·βo·lu·sjo·'nar, rre·βo·lu·θjo-] *vt* to revolutionize; (*amotinar*) to stir up

revolucionario, -a [rre·βo·lu·sjo·'na·rjo, -a; rre·βo·lu·θjo-] *adj, m, f* revolutionary

revoluta [rre·βo·'lu·ta] *f AmC v.* **revolución**

revolvedora [rre·βol·βe·'do·ra] *f Arg, Méx* cement mixer

revolver [rre·βol·'βer] *irr como volver* I. *vt* 1. (*mezclar*) to mix; (*desordenar*) to mess up 2. (*investigar*) to investigate II. *vr:* ~**se** to toss and turn; **se me revuelve el estómago** it makes my stomach turn

revólver [rre·'βol·βer] *m* revolver

revuelo [rre·'βwe·lo] *m* disturbance; **causar** ~ to disturb

revuelta [rre·'βwel·ta] *f* (*tumulto*) disturbance; (*rebelión*) revolt

revuelto, -a [rre·'βwel·to, -a] I. *pp de* **revolver** II. *adj* (*agitado*) shaken; (*desordenado*) chaotic; (*tiempo*) unsettled; (*huevos*) scrambled

revulsar [rre·βul·'sar] *vi, vt Méx* to throw up

rey [rrei] *m* king; **los ~es** The King and Queen; **los Reyes Magos** the Three Wise Men; **el día de Reyes** Epiphany

rezagado, -a [re·sa·'ɣa·do, -a; re·θa-] *m, f* straggler

rezar <z → c> [rre·'sar, -'θar] *vi, vt* to pray

rezo ['rre·so, -θo] *m* prayer

rezongar <g → gu> [rre·son·'gar, rre·θon-] *vi* to grumble

ría ['rri·a] *f* ≈ estuary

riachuelo [rrja·'tʃwe·lo] *m* stream

riada [rri·'a·da] *f* flood

ribera [rri·'βe·ra] *f* (*orilla*) bank; (*tierra*) riverside; (*vega*) fertile plain

ricamente [rri·ka·'men·te] *adv* richly; (*con placer*) splendidly

rico, -a ['rri·ko, -a] **I.** *adj* **1.** (*acaudalado, abundante*) rich **2.** (*sabroso*) delicious **3.** (*simpático*) lovely **II.** *m, f* (*rico*) rich person; **los ricos** the rich

ricota [rri·'ko·ta] *f Arg* ricotta cheese

ridiculizar <z → c> [rri·di·ku·li·'sar, -'θar] *vt* to ridicule

ridículo, -a [rri·'di·ku·lo, -a] *adj* ridiculous; **poner(se) en ~** to make a fool of (oneself)

riego ['rrje·ɣo] *m* irrigation; **~ sanguíneo** blood flow

riel [rrjel] *m* rail

rienda ['rrjen·da] *f* rein; **tener las ~s del poder** to hold the reins of power ▶ **a ~ suelta** wildly; **dar ~ suelta a** to give free rein to...; **llevar las ~s** to be in control

riesgo ['rrjes·ɣo] *m* risk; **a ~ de que... +subj** at the risk of...; **por cuenta y ~ propios** at one's own risk and expense; **asumir un ~** to assume a risk; **estar asegurado a todo ~** to have full coverage insurance; **correr un ~** to run a risk

riesgoso, -a [rrjes·'ɣo·so, -a] *adj AmL* (*arriesgado*) risky; (*peligroso*) dangerous

rifa ['rri·fa] *f* raffle

rifar [rri·'far] *vt* to raffle

rifle ['rri·fle] *m* rifle

rigidez [rri·xi·'des, -'deθ] *f* rigidity; (*severidad*) strictness

rígido, -a ['rri·xi·do, -a] *adj* rigid; (*severo*) strict

rigor [rri·'ɣor] *m* (*severidad*) strictness; (*exactitud*) rigorousness ▶ **de ~** de rigueur

riguroso, -a [rri·ɣu·'ro·so, -a] *adj* (*severo*) strict; (*exacto*) rigorous

rima ['rri·ma] *f* rhyme

rimar [rri·'mar] *vi, vt* to rhyme

rímel® ['rri·mel] *m* mascara

rin [rrin] *m* **1.** *Ven* (*llanta*) rim **2.** *Perú* (*ficha*) telephone token

rincón [rrin·'kon] *m* corner; *fig* nook; **por todos los rincones** in every nook and cranny

rinoceronte [rri·no·se·'ron·te, rri·no·θe] *m* rhinoceros

riña ['rri·ɲa] *f* quarrel

riñón [rri·'ɲon] *m* **1.** kidney **2.** *pl* (*espalda*) lower back ▶ **costar un ~** to cost an arm and a leg

riñonera [rri·ɲo·'ne·ra] *f* fanny pack *inf*

río ['rri·o] *m* river; **~ abajo/arriba** downstream/upstream ▶ **cuando el ~ suena, agua lleva** where there's smoke, there's fire

rioplatense [rrio·pla·'ten·se] **I.** *adj* of/ from the River Plate region **II.** *mf* native/inhabitant of the River Plate region

riqueza [rri·'ke·sa, -θa] *f* riches *pl*

risa [rri·'sa] *f* laughter; **estar muerto de ~** to be laughing one's head off; **tener un ataque de ~** to have a fit of the giggles; **tomar algo a ~** to treat sth as a joke; **¡qué ~!** what a joke!; **no estoy para ~s** I'm in no mood for jokes

risco ['rris·ko] *m* crag

ríspido, -a ['rris·pi·do, -a] *adj AmL* coarse

ristra ['rris·tra] *f* string; **una ~ de ajos/ mentiras** a string of garlic/lies

risueño, -a [rri·'swe·ɲo, -a] *adj* smiling

rítmico, -a ['rrid·mi·ko, -a] *adj* rhythmic

ritmo ['rrid·mo] *m* rhythm

rito ['rri·to] *m* ritual; REL rite

ritual [rri·tu·'al] *adj, m* ritual

rival [rri·'βal] *adj, mf* rival

rivalidad [rri·βa·li·'dad] *f* rivalry

rizado, -a [rri·'sa·do, rri·'θa-] *adj* curly

rizo ['rri·so, -θo] *m* curl; **rizar el ~** to overcomplicate things

rizo, -a [rri·θo, -a] *adj* curly

robar [rro·'βar] *vt* **1.** to steal; (*a alguien*) to rob; (*con violencia*) to mug; **me ~on en París** I was robbed in Paris; **me robó la novia** he stole my girlfriend **2.** (*estafar*) to cheat **3.** (*en juegos*) to draw

roble ['rro·βle] *m* oak; **estar como un ~** to be as fit as a fiddle

robo ['rro·βo] *m* robbery; **~ a mano armada** armed robbery; (*estafa*) swindle; **ser un ~** (*muy caro*) to be a rip-off

robot <robots> [rro·'βot] *m* robot; **~ de cocina** food processor

R

robusto, -a [rro·'βus·to, -a] *adj* robust

roca ['rro·ka] *f* rock

roce ['rro·θe, -θe] *m* **1.** (*fricción*) brush **2.** (*huella*) scrape **3.** (*contacto*) contact **4.** (*pelea*) scrape

rochar [rro·'tʃar] *vt Chile* to catch red-handed

rochela [rro·'tʃe·la] *f Col, PRico, Ven* hullabaloo

rociar <3. pres rocía> [rro·si·'ar, rro·θi-] *vt* to sprinkle

rocío [rro·'si·o, -'θi·o] *m* dew

rock [rrok] *adj, m* rock

rocoso, -a [rro·'ko·so, -a] *adj* rocky; **Montañas Rocosas** Rocky Mountains

rocote [rro·'ko·te] *m*, **rocoto** [rro·'ko·to] *m Bol, Ecua, Perú* (large) green pepper

rodaja [rro·'da·xa] *f* slice

rodaje [rro·'da·xe] *m* shooting

rodar <o → ue> [rro·'dar] **I.** *vi* to roll; (*sobre un eje*) to turn; (*deslizarse*) to slide; ~ **por el suelo** to roll across the floor **II.** *vt* to roll; (*coche*) to run in; (*película*) to shoot

rodear [rro·de·'ar] **I.** *vi* to go around **II.** *vt* ~ **de algo** to surround with sth; (*tema*) to avoid **III.** *vr* ~**se de algo/alguien** to surround oneself with sth/sb

rodeo [rro·'deo] *m* **1.** (*desvío*) detour; **dar un** ~ to take a detour **2.** (*evasiva*) evasion **3.** DEP rodeo ▶ **andar(se) con** ~**s** to beat about the bush; **dejarse de** ~**s** to stop beating about the bush; **sin** ~**s** without beating about the bush

rodilla [rro·'di·ja, -ʎa] *f* knee; **de** ~**s on** one's knees; **ponerse de** ~**s** to kneel

rodillo [rro·'di·jo, -ʎo] *m* roller; (*de cocina*) rolling pin

roedor [rroe·'dor] *m* rodent

roer [rro·'er] *irr vt* to gnaw at

rogar <o → ue> [rro·'ɣar] *vt* to request; (*con humildad*) to beg; JUR to plead; **le gusta hacerse de** ~ he/she likes playing hard to get

rojizo, -a [rro·'xi·so, -a; -θo, -a] *adj* reddish

rojo, -a ['rro·xo] *adj* red; (*persona*) red-headed ▶ **al** ~ (**vivo**) red-hot; **poner** ~ **a alguien** to make sb blush; **ponerse** ~ to go red

rol [rrol] *m* role; **desempeñar un** ~ to play a role; **juego de** ~ role-playing game

rollo ['rro·jo, -ʎo] *m* **1.** roll **2.** *inf* (*pesadez*) bore; **¡qué** ~ **de película!** what a boring film!; **soltar siempre el mismo** ~ to always come out with the same old stuff **3.** *inf* (*tipo de vida*) lifestyle; (*asunto*) affair; **ir a su** ~ to do as one likes; **tener un** ~ **con alguien** *argot* to have a fling with sb; **traerse un mal** ~ to be in a mess

Roma ['rro·ma] *f* Rome

romance [rro·'man·se, -θe] **I.** *adj* LING Romance **II.** *m* romance; **tiene un** ~ **con la vecina** he's having an affair with his neighbor

románico, -a [rro·'ma·ni·ko, -a] *adj* Romanesque

romano, -a [rro·'ma·no] *adj, m, f* Roman

romanticismo [rro·man·ti·'sis·mo, -'θis·mo] *m* romanticism

romántico, -a [rro·'man·ti·ko, -a] *adj, m, f* romantic

rombo ['rrom·bo] *m* rhombus; **en forma de** ~ diamond-shaped

romería [rro·me·'ri·a] *f* pilgrimage; (*fiesta*) festival

romerito [rro·me·'ri·to] *m Méx* vegetables *pl*

romero [rro·'me·ro] *m* rosemary

romero, -a [rro·'me·ro, -a] *adj, m, f* pilgrim

romo, -a ['rro·mo, -a] *adj* blunt

rompecabezas [rrom·pe·ka·'βe·sas, -θas] *m inv* (*juego*) brainteaser; (*acertijo*) riddle

romper [rrom·'per] **I.** *vi* to break; (*separarse*) to break up; **al** ~ **el día** at the break of day; ~ **a llorar** to burst into tears **II.** *vt* to break; (*cristal*) to shatter; (*plato*) to smash; (*papel, tela*) to tear; (*negociaciones, relaciones*) to break off; ~ **algo a golpes** to bash sth to pieces; ~ **el silencio/el encanto** to break the silence/the spell **III.** *vr*: ~**se** to break; ~**se la pierna** to break one's leg; ~**se la cabeza** *fig* to rack one's brains

rompope [rrom·'po·pe] *m AmC, Ecua, Méx* eggnog

ron [rron] *m* rum

roncar <c → qu> [rron·'kar] *vi* to snore

roncear [rron·se·'ar, rron·θe·'ar] *vt Arg, Chile, Méx* to move by levering

roncha ['rron·tʃa] *f* bruise

ronco, -a ['rron·ko, -a] *adj* hoarse; (*afónico*) voiceless

roncón, -ona [rron·'kon, --'ko·na] *m, f Col, Ven* bragging

ronda ['rron·da] *f* round; **pagar una ~** to buy a round

rondar [rron·'dar] **I.** *vi* to prowl about; (*patrullando*) to be on patrol **II.** *vt* to surround; **roda los setenta años** he/she is about seventy years old

rondín [rron·'din] *m* **1.** *Bol, Ecua, Perú* (*armónica*) harmonica **2.** *Bol, Chile* (*vigilante*) watchman

ronquido [rron·'ki·do] *m* snore

ronronear [rron·rro·ne·'ar] *vi* to purr

roña ['rro·na] **I.** *f* filth **II.** *mf* stingy

roñoso, -a [rro·'no·so, -a] *adj* **1.** (*tacaño*) tight **2.** (*sucio*) filthy **3.** (*sarnoso*) scabby **4.** (*oxidado*) rusty

ropa ['rro·pa] *f* clothes *pl*; **~ interior** underwear; **~ de cama** sheets; **cambiar(se) la ~** to change one's clothes; **poner(se) la ~** to get dressed; **~ de abrigo** warm clothing

ropero [rro·'pe·ro] *m* wardrobe

rosa ['rro·sa] **I.** *adj* pink **II.** *f* rose
▶ **no hay ~ sin espinas** every rose has its thorn

rosado, -a [rro·'sa·do, -a] *adj* pink; **vino ~** rosé (wine)

rosal [rro·'sal] *m* rosebush

rosario [rro·'sa·rjo] *m* rosary

rosca ['rros·ka] *f* **1.** TÉC thread; **el tornillo se pasó de ~** the screw stripped the thread **2.** (*espiral*) coil **3.** (*aro*) ring; (*bollo*) bread roll; (*torta*) sponge ring; **~ de Reyes** *Méx* cake eaten on Epiphany ▶ **no comerse una ~** not to get off with anyone; **pasarse de ~** to go too far

roscón [rros·'kon] *m* sponge ring; **~ de Reyes** cake eaten on Epiphany

rosedal [rro·se·'dal] *m Arg, Urug* rose garden

rosquilla [rros·'ki·ja, -ʎa] *f* doughnut
▶ **venderse como ~s** to sell like hot cakes

rosticería [rros·ti·se·'ri·a] *f Chile, Méx v.* **rotisería**

rostro ['rros·tro] *m* face

rotación [rro·ta·'sjon, -'θjon] *f* rotation; **~ de cultivos** crop rotation

rotería [rro·te·'ri·a] *f Chile* **1.** (*acción*) inconsiderate act **2.** (*plebe*) the masses

rotisería [rro·ti·se·'ri·a] *f Arg* shop that sells roast chicken, beef and other dishes

roto ['rro·to] *m* tear; (*agujero*) hole

roto, -a ['rro·to, -a] **I.** *pp de* **romper** **II.** *adj* **1.** broken; (*vestido*) torn **2.** (*andrajoso*) wretched **3.** (*destrozado*) destroyed

rotonda [rro·'ton·da] *f* traffic circle

rotoso, -a [rro·'to·so, -a] **I.** *adj AmL* tattered **II.** *m, f* wretch

rotulador [rro·tu·la·'dor] *m* felt-tip pen

rótulo ['rro·tu·lo] *m* sign

rotundo, -a [rro·'tun·do, -a] *adj* emphatic; (*éxito, palabras*) resounding; **una negativa rotunda** a flat refusal

rotura [rro·'tu·ra] *f* (*acción*) breaking; (*parte quebrada*) break; **~ de hueso** fracture; **~ de ligamento** torn ligament

rouge [rruʃ] *m Arg, Chile* blusher

roza ['rro·sa] *f,* **rozado** [rro·'sa·do, -'θa·do] *m Arg* cleared ground

rozar <z → c> [rro·'sar, -'θar] **I.** *vi* to rub; **rozar (por) los cincuenta** to be pushing fifty **II.** *vt* **1.** *t. fig* (*tocar ligeramente*) to brush; **~ la ridiculez** *fig* to border on the ridiculous **2.** (*frotar*) to rub **III.** *vr:* **~se** to rub

ruana ['rrwa·na] *f AmS* poncho

rubéola [rru·'βeo·la] *f* German measles

rubí [rru·'βi] *m* ruby

rubio, -a [rru·'βjo, -a] **I.** *adj* fair; **tabaco ~** Virginia tobacco **II.** *m, f* blond, blonde *m, f*

rublo ['rru·βlo] *m* ruble

rubor [rru·'βor] *m* **1.** (*color*) bright red; (*de vergüenza*) blush **2.** (*vergüenza*) shame; (*bochorno*) embarrassment

ruborizado, -a [rru·βo·ri·'sa·do, -a; -'θa·do, -a] *adj* blushing

R

ruborizar <z → c> [rru·βo·ri·'sar, -'θar] I. *vt* to cause to blush II. *vr:* ~**se** to blush

rúbrica ['rru·βri·ka] *f* signature; (*después del nombre*) flourish

rubro ['rru·βro] *m AmL* heading; COM area

ruca ['rru·ka] *f Arg, Chile* shack

ruco, -a ['rru·ko, -a] *adj AmC* old

rudimentario, -a [rru·di·men·'ta·rjo, -a] *adj* rudimentary

rudo, -a ['rru·do, -a] *adj* 1. (*material*) rough; (*sin trabajar*) raw 2. (*persona tosca*) coarse; (*brusca*) rude; (*torpe*) clumsy

rueda ['rrwe·da] *f* 1. wheel; ~ **de repuesto** spare tire 2. (*de personas, orden*) ring; ~ **de prensa** press conference ▶ **todo** <u>marcha</u> **sobre ~s** everything is going smoothly

ruego ['rrwe·ɣo] *m* request

rugby ['rruɣ·βi] *m* rugby

rugido [rru·'xi·do] *m* (*del león*) roar; (*del viento*) howl

rugir <g → j> [rru·'xir] *vi* to roar; (*viento*) to howl

rugoso, -a [rru·'ɣo·so, -a] *adj* 1. (*arrugado*) wrinkled 2. (*áspero*) rough 3. (*ondulado*) wavy

ruido ['rrwi·do] *m* noise; ~ **de fondo** background noise ▶ **mucho ~ y pocas** <u>nueces</u> much ado about nothing

ruidoso, -a [rrwi·'do·so, -a] *adj* noisy; *fig* sensational

ruin [rrwin] *adj* 1. (*malvado*) wicked; (*vil*) despicable 2. (*tacaño*) mean

ruina ['rrwi·na] *f* 1. (*destrucción*) destruction; **este hombre está hecho una** ~ this man is a wreck 2. ARQUIT ruin; **convertir una ciudad en ~s** to raze a city to the ground; **declarar una casa en** ~ to condemn a house 3. (*perdición*) downfall; **causar la** ~ **de alguien** to cause sb's downfall; **estar en la** ~ to be bankrupt; **salvar a alguien de la** ~ to save sb from disaster

ruinoso, -a [rrwi·'no·so, -a] *adj* 1. (*edificios*) dilapidated 2. (*perjudicial*) disastrous; ECON ruinous

ruiseñor [rrwi·se·'ɲor] *m* nightingale

rulenco, -a [rru·'len·ko, -a] *adj Chile* weak; (*raquítico*) stunted

rulero [rru·'le·ro] *m AmS* hair curler

ruleta [rru·'le·ta] *f* roulette

ruletear [rru·le·te·'ar] *vi AmC, Méx* to drive a taxi

ruletero, -a [rru·le·'te·ro, -a] *m, f AmC, Méx* taxi driver

rulo ['rru·lo] *m* roller

ruma ['rru·ma] *f AmS* **una** ~ **de...** a pile of...; ~**s de...** lots of...

Rumania [rru·'ma·nja] *f*, **Rumanía** [rru·ma·'ni·a] *f* Romania

rumano, -a [rru·'ma·no] *adj, m, f* Romanian

rumba ['rrum·ba] *f* rumba

rumbo ['rrum·bo] *m* direction; *t. fig* AVIAT, NÁUT course; **con ~ a** bound [*o* headed] for

rumiante [rru·'mjan·te] *m* ruminant

rumor [rru·'mor] *m* 1. (*chisme*) rumor; **corren ~es de que...** it is rumored that... 2. (*ruido*) murmur; (*del viento*) whistle; (*del bosque*) rustle; ~ **de voces** buzz of conversation

rumorearse [rru·mo·re·'ar·se] *vr* **se rumorea que...** it is rumored that...

rundún [rrun·'dun] *m Arg, Chile, Méx, Perú* (*juguete*) bullroarer

ruptura [rrup·'tu·ra] *f* breaking; (*de relaciones*) breaking-off

rural [rru·'ral] I. *adj* rural; **vida** ~ country life II. *m* 1. *AmL t. pey* yokel 2. *pl Méx* rural police

Rusia ['rru·sja] *f* Russia

ruso, -a ['rru·so, -a] *adj, m, f* Russian; **ensaladilla rusa** Russian salad

rústico, -a ['rrus·ti·ko, -a] I. *adj* 1. (*campestre*) rural; **finca rústica** farmhouse 2. (*tosco*) rough II. *m, f* peasant; *pey* yokel

ruta ['rru·ta] *f* route; ~ **federal** *AmL* federal highway; ~ **de vuelo** flight path

rutina [rru·'ti·na] *f* routine

rutinario, -a [rru·ti·'na·rjo, -a] *adj* routine; **un hombre** ~ a man of habit; (*aburrido*) an unimaginative man

S

S, s ['e·se] *f* S, s; **~ de Soria** S as in Sierra

S. [san] *abr de* **San** St

S.A. [e·se·'a] *f abr de* **Sociedad Anónima** ≈ Inc.

sáb. *abr de* **sábado** Sat.

sábado ['sa·βa·ðo] *m* Saturday; *v. t.* lunes

sabana [sa·'βa·na] *f* savanna(h)

sábana ['sa·βa·na] *f* sheet; **~ ajustable** fitted sheet; **se me han pegado las ~s** *inf* I've overslept

sabandija [sa·βan·'di·xa] *f* wretch

sabático, -a [sa·'βa·ti·ko, -a] *adj* sabbatical

sabelotodo [sa·βe·lo·'to·ðo] *mf inv inf* know-it-all

saber [sa·'βer] *irr* **I.** *vt* **1.** (*conocer*) to know; **¿sabes mi nombre?** do you know my name?; **~ (mucho) de algo** to know (a lot) about sth; **¿se puede ~ dónde/cómo/quién...?** can sb tell me where/how/who ...?; **vete tú/ vaya usted a ~** it's anyone's guess; (*al menos*) **que yo sepa** as far as I know; **para que lo sepas** for your information; **¡y qué sé yo!** how should I know! **2.** (*poder*) **sabe (hablar) ruso** he/she can speak Russian **3.** (*noticia*) to find out; **lo supe por mi hermano** I heard about it from my brother; **no sé nada de Ana** I have no news of Ana **II.** *vi* **1.** **~ a algo** to taste of sth; **sabe bien/ mal** it tastes good/bad **2.** (*agradar*) **me supo a poco** it should have been longer; **me supo mal aquella respuesta** that reply upset me **3.** (*poder*) **~ de algo** to know how to do sth **III.** *vr* to know; **sabérselas todas** *inf* to know all the tricks **IV.** *m* knowledge ▶ **el ~ no ocupa lugar** *prov* you can't know too much

sabichoso, -a [sa·βi·'tʃo·so, -a] *adj Cuba, PRico* pedantic; (*sabiondo*) know-it-all

sabiduría [sa·βi·ðu·'ri·a] *f* knowledge; (*sensatez*) wisdom

sabiendas [sa·'βjen·das] **a ~** knowingly

sabi(h)ondo, -a [sa·'βjon·do, -a] *m, f* know-it-all; (*niño*) smarty pants

sabio, -a ['sa·βjo, -a] **I.** *adj* wise **II.** *m, f*

scholar

sable ['sa·βle] *m* saber

sabor [sa·'βor] *m* taste (**a** of); **dejar un mal ~ de boca** to leave a nasty taste in one's mouth

saborear [sa·βo·re·'ar] *vt* to savor; (*triunfo*) to relish

sabotaje [sa·βo·'ta·xe] *m* sabotage

sabotear [sa·βo·te·'ar] *vt* to sabotage

sabroso, -a [sa·'βro·so, -a] *adj* tasty

sabueso [sa·'βwe·so, -a] *m* bloodhound; *fig* sleuth

sacabuche [sa·ka·'βu·tʃe] *m Méx* pointed knife

sacacorchos [sa·ka·'kor·tʃos] *m inv* corkscrew

sacapuntas [sa·ka·'pun·tas] *m inv* pencil sharpener

sacar <c → qu> [sa·'kar] **I.** *vt* **1.** (*de un sitio*) to take out, to remove; (*agua*) to draw; (*diente*) to pull (out); (*entrada, billete, votos*) to get; (*mancha*) to remove; (*foto*) to take; (*parte del cuerpo*) to stick out; **~ a bailar** to invite to dance; **~ a alguien de la cama/cárcel** to get sb out of bed/jail; **~ a pasear** to take out for a walk; **¿de dónde lo has sacado?** where did you get it from? **2.** (*de una situación*) to get; **~ adelante** (*persona*) to look after; (*negocio*) to run; (*niño*) to bring up **3.** (*obtener*) to obtain; MIN to extract; **~ en claro (de)** to gather (from); **no ~ ni para vivir** not to make enough to live on; **~ a alguien 10 dólares** to squeeze 10 dollars out of sb **4.** (*producto*) to bring out; **~ a la venta** to put on sale [*o* the market]; (*libro*) to publish **5.** (*mostrar*) to show; (*desenterrar*) to unearth; **~ algo a relucir** to bring sth up **II.** *vi* (*tenis*) to serve; (*fútbol: portero*) to take a goal kick; (*fútbol: saque de banda*) to take a throw-in

sacarina [sa·ka·'ri·na] *f* saccharin

sacerdote [sa·ser·'do·te, sa·θer-] *m* priest

saciar [sa·'sjar, -'θjar] **I.** *vt* (*hambre, curiosidad*) to satisfy; (*instintos sexuales*) to satiate; (*sed*) to quench **II.** *vr:* **~se** to satiate oneself

saciedad [sa·sje·'ðad, sa·θje-] *f* satiation; **repetir hasta la ~** to repeat over and over

saco ['sa·ko] *m* 1. sack; ~ **de dormir** sleeping bag; **entrar a** ~ to loot 2. *AmL* (*prenda*) jacket ▶ **en el mismo** ~ in the same boat

sacón, -ona [sa·'kon, -·'ko·na] *m, f Méx inf* chicken

sacramento [sa·kra·'men·to] *m* sacrament

sacrificar <c → qu> [sa·kri·fi·'kar] I. *vt* to sacrifice; *fig* to give up; (*animal*) to slaughter II. *vr* ~**se por algo/alguien** to sacrifice oneself for sth/sb

sacrificio [sa·kri·'fi·sjo, -·'fi·θjo] *m* sacrifice

sacrilegio [sa·kri·'le·xjo] *m* sacrilege

sacudida [sa·ku·'di·da] *f* shake; ~ **eléctrica** electric shock; ~ **sísmica** earthquake; **el coche pegaba** ~**s** the car was jolting; **dale una** ~ **a la alfombra** shake the carpet

sacudir [sa·ku·'dir] *vt* to shake

sádico, -a ['sa·di·ko, -a] I. *adj* sadistic II. *m, f* sadist

sadomasoquismo [sa·do·ma·so·'kis·mo] *m* sadomasochism

safari [sa·'fa·ri] *m* safari

sagaz [sa·'ɣas, -'ɣaθ] *adj* astute

sagitario [sa·xi·'ta·rjo] *m* Sagittarius

sagrado, -a <sacratísimo> [sa·'ɣra·do] *adj* sacred

sagú [sa·'ɣu] *m AmC* arrowroot; (*harina*) sago

sal [sal] *f* 1. salt; ~ **marina** sea salt; ~ **gorda** [*o* **gruesa**] *Méx* coarse [*o* rock] salt; ~**es de baño** bath salts 2. (*gracia*) wit; (*encanto*) charm 3. *AmL* (*fario*) bad luck

sala ['sa·la] *f* 1. room; (*grande*) hall; ~ **de espera/de estar** waiting/living room 2. *JUR* courtroom; **Sala de lo Civil/Penal** Civil/Criminal Court

salado, -a [sa·'la·do, -a] *adj* 1. salty 2. (*gracioso*) witty; (*encantador*) charming 3. *AmL* (*infortunado*) unfortunate

salamanca [sa·la·'man·ka] *f* 1. *Arg* ZOOL flat-headed salamander 2. *CSur* (*cueva*) natural cave

salamandra [sa·la·'man·dra] *f* salamander; ~ **acuática** newt

salame [sa·'la·me] *adj Arg inf* fool

salar [sa·'lar] *vt* 1. to add salt to; (*para conservar*) to salt 2. *AmL* (*echar a perder*) to spoil

salarial [sa·la·'rjal] *adj* wage

salario [sa·'la·rjo] *m* wages *pl*

salchicha [sal·'tʃi·tʃa] *f* sausage; **perro** ~ *inf* dachshund

salchichón [sal·tʃi·'tʃon] *m* ≈ salami

saldar [sal·'dar] *vt* (*cuenta*) to pay; (*deuda*) to pay off

saldo ['sal·do] *m* balance; (*pago*) payment; ~ **de la cuenta** account balance

salero [sa·'le·ro] *m* salt shaker; (*gracia*) wit

saleroso, -a [sa·le·'ro·so, -a] *adj inf* (*ingenioso*) witty; (*encantador*) charming

salida [sa·'li·da] *f* 1. (*puerta*) way out; **a la** ~ **del teatro** coming out of the theater; **callejón sin** ~ dead end; ~ **de emergencia** emergency exit 2. AVIAT, FERRO departure; (*barco*) sailing 3. ASTR rising; ~ **del sol** sunrise 4. DEP start 5. COM sale; (*partida*) consignment; ~ **de capital** capital outflow

salidor(a) [sa·li·'dor, -·'do·ra] *adj AmL* party-loving; **es muy** ~ he likes to go out a lot

salina [sa·'li·na] *f* salt works; (*mina*) salt mine

salir [sa·'lir] *irr* I. *vi* 1. (*al exterior*) to go out; (*irse*) to go away; ~ **a dar una vuelta** to go out for a stroll; ~ **con alguien** to go out with sb; ~ **adelante** to make progress; ~ **de un programa** to exit a program 2. (*de viaje*) to leave; (*avión*) to depart; **para** ~ **de dudas...** to clear up any doubts...; ~ **ganando/perdiendo/ileso** to come out the better/the worse/unscathed 3. (*flores, fuente*) to come out; (*sol*) to rise; ~ **a la luz** to come to light; ~ **en la tele** to be on TV 4. **este niño ha salido a su padre** the boy takes after his father 5. DEP to start 6. (*costar*) to cost II. *vr* ~**se** to spill; (*líquido*) to overflow; (*leche*) to boil over ▶ ~**se con la suya** to get one's own way

saliva [sa·'li·βa] *f* saliva

salmo ['sal·mo] *m* psalm

salmón [sal·'mon] I. *adj* salmon-pink II. *m* salmon

salmuera [sal·'mwe·ra] *f* brine

salón [sa·'lon] *m* hall; (*en casa*) living-room; ~ **de actos** assembly hall

salpicadera [sal·pi·ka·'de·ra] *f* *Méx* mudguard

salpicar <c → qu> [sal·pi·'kar] *vt* (*rociar*) to sprinkle; (*pintura*) to splash; (*manchar*) to spatter

salpicón [sal·pi·'kon] *m* 1. ≈ salmagundi 2. *Col, Ecua* cold drink of fruit juice

salpimentar <e → ie> [sal·pi·men·'tar] *vt* to add salt and pepper

salsa ['sal·sa] *f* 1. sauce; (*caldo*) gravy; ~ **verde** parsley sauce (*to accompany fish*); *Méx* sauce made of green tomatoes, chili, garlic and cilantro; ~ **de tomate** tomato sauce 2. (*gracia*) humor 3. MÚS salsa ▶ **estar en su propia** ~ to be in one's element

salsamentaría [sal·sa·men·ta·'ri·a] *f* *Col* delicatessen

saltamontes [sal·ta·'mon·tes] *m inv* grasshopper

saltar [sal·'tar] I. *vi* 1. to jump; ~ **de alegría** to jump for joy; ~ **a la cuerda** to skip; ~ **al agua** to jump into the water; ~ **con paracaídas** to make a parachute jump 2. (*explotar*) to explode; ~ **en pedazos** to break into pieces; ~ **por los aires** to blow up; (*plomos*) to blow; (*chispas*) to fly up 3. (*desprenderse*) to come off ▶ **estar a la que salta** to look out for an opportunity II. *vt* to jump (over); (*animal*) to cover III. *vr:* ~**se** to come off; **se me** ~**on las lágrimas** my eyes filled with tears; (*ley, norma*) to break; (*línea, párrafo*) to skip

salto ['sal·to] *m* 1. jump; **de** [*o* **en**] **un** ~ with one jump; **dar un** ~ to jump; *fig* to jump with fright; **dar** ~**s de alegría** to jump for joy; ~ **de altura/longitud** high/long jump; ~ **mortal** somersault; ~ **del potro** vault; ~ **de cama** negligee; ~ **de página** page break 2. (*omisión*) gap ▶ ~ **de agua** waterfall

salubridad [sa·lu·βri·'dad] *f* *AmL* hygiene

salud [sa·'lud] *f* health; ¡~! (*al estornudar*) bless you!; (*al brindar*) good health!

saludable [sa·lu·'da·βle] *adj* healthy

saludar [sa·lu·'dar] *vt* 1. to greet; (*con la mano*) to wave; **estos ya ni se saludan** they don't even speak to each other now 2. (*recibir*) to welcome 3. (*mandar saludos*) to send regards to

saludo [sa·'lu·do] *m* greeting; **con un cordial** ~ yours sincerely; ¡**dele** ~**s de mi parte!** give him/her my regards; **tu madre te manda** ~**s** your mother sends her love

salvación [sal·βa·'sjon, -'θjon] *f* rescue

Salvador [sal·βa·'dor] *m* **El** ~ El Salvador

salvadoreño, -a [sal·βa·do·'re·ɲo, -a] *adj, m, f* Salvadoran

salvaguardar [sal·βa·ɣwar·'dar] *vt* to safeguard; (*derechos, intereses*) to protect

salvaje [sal·'βa·xe] I. *adj* (*planta, animal*) wild; (*persona*) uncivilized; (*acto*) savage II. *mf* savage; (*persona ruda*) barbarian

salvamento [sal·βa·'men·to] *m* rescue

salvar [sal·'βar] I. *vt* to save; ~ **del peligro** to save from danger; (*foso*) to jump across; (*distancia*) to cover; (*obstáculo, problema*) to overcome; ~ **las apariencias** to keep up appearances II. *vr:* ~**se** to save oneself; ¡**sálvese quien pueda!** every man for himself!

salvavidas [sal·βa·'βi·das] I. *m inv* lifebelt; **bote** ~ lifeboat; **chaleco** ~ lifejacket II. *mf inv* lifeguard

salvedad [sal·βe·'dad] *f* exception; **con la** ~ **de que...** with the proviso that...

salvo ['sal·βo] *prep* except; ~ **que** +*subj* unless

salvo, -a ['sal·βo, -a] *adj* **poner a** ~ to put in a safe place; **sano y** ~ safe and sound

samba ['sam·ba] *f* samba

sambumbia [sam·'bum·bja] *f* 1. *Col* **volver algo** ~ to smash sth to pieces 2. *Cuba* drink of cane syrup, water and peppers 3. *Méx* pineapple cordial

san [san] *adj* Saint

sanar [sa·'nar] I. *vi* ~ **de algo** to recover from sth II. *vt* to cure

sanatorio [sa·na·'to·rjo] *m* sanatorium

sanción [san·'sjon, -'θjon] *f* 1. (*multa*) penalty; ECON sanction 2. (*ley*) passing

sancionar [san·sjo·'nar, san·θjo·] *vt* (*cas-*

tigar) to punish; ECON to impose sanctions on; JUR to ratify

sancochar [san·ko·'tʃar] *vt AmL* to parboil

sancocho [san·'ko·tʃo] *m* **1.** *AmC, PRico, Ven* fuss **2.** *And, Ven* parboiled meat

sandalia [san·'da·lja] *f* sandal

sándalo ['san·da·lo] *m* **1.** (*árbol*) sandalwood tree **2.** (*madera*) sandalwood

sandez [san·'des, -'deθ] *f inf* **no decir más que sandeces** to say nothing but foolish things

sandía [san·'di·a] *f* watermelon

sandinista [san·di·'nis·ta] *adj, mf* Sandinista

sandunga [san·'dun·ga] *f Col, Chile, PRico inf* celebration

sándwich ['san·gwitʃ] *m* toasted sandwich

saneamiento [sa·nea·'mjen·to] *m* (*edificio*) repair; (*terreno*) drainage; (*de economía*) reform

sanear [sa·ne·'ar] *vt* (*edificio*) to clean up; (*tierra*) to drain; (*economía*) to reform

sangrar [san·'grar] **I.** *vi* to bleed; **estar sangrando por la nariz** to have a nosebleed **II.** *vt* to bleed; (*dinero*) to bleed dry; (*agua*) to drain off

sangre ['san·gre] *f* blood; **a ~ fría** in cold blood; **animales de ~ caliente/fría** warm/cold-blooded animals; (**caballo de**) **pura ~** thoroughbred (horse); **dar** [*o* **donar**] **~** to give [*o* donate] blood; **hacer ~** to draw blood; **llevar algo en la ~** to have sth in the blood; (*de familia*) to run in the family; **le hierve la ~** his/her blood boils ▸ **sudar ~** to go through hardships; **tener mala ~** to be bad-tempered

sangría [san·'gri·a] *f* **1.** TIPO indentation **2.** (*bebida*) sangria

sangriento, -a [san·'grjen·to, -a] *adj* bloody

sangriligero, -a [san·gri·li·'xe·ro, -a] *adj AmC* nice

sangripesado, -a [san·gri·pe·'sa·do, -a] *adj AmC* disagreeable

sangrón, -ona [san·'gron, -·'gro·na] *adj Méx inf* boring; **su novio es un ~, no lo soporto** her boyfriend is a bore, I can't stand him

sanguaraña [san·gwa·'ra·ɲa] *f Ecua, Perú* evasion; **déjate de ~s** stop beating around the bush

sanguijuela [san·gi·'xwe·la] *f* leech; *pey* bloodsucker

sanguíneo, -a [san·'gi·neo, -a] *adj* blood; **grupo ~** blood type

sanidad [sa·ni·'dad] *f* health; **~ (pública)** public health

sanitario, -a [sa·ni·'ta·rjo, -a] **I.** *adj* health; (*aparatos, medidas*) sanitary **II.** *m, f* health worker

sanitarios [sa·ni·'ta·rjos] *mpl* bathroom fixtures

sano, -a ['sa·no, -a] *adj* healthy; (*no roto*) intact; **cortar por lo ~** to take extreme measures; **salir ~ y salvo** to emerge safe and sound

santiaguino, -a [san·tja·'yi·no, -a] **I.** *adj* of/from Santiago (in Chile) **II.** *m, f* native/inhabitant of Santiago (in Chile)

santiamén [san·tja·'men] *m* **en un ~** in a jiffy

santidad [san·ti·'dad] *f* holiness

santo, -a ['san·to, -a] **I.** *adj* holy; (*piadoso*) saintly; **campo ~** cemetery; **Jueves Santo** Maundy Thursday; **Semana Santa** Easter; **Viernes Santo** Good Friday **II.** *m, f* saint; **día de Todos los Santos** All Saint's Day; **el día de mi ~** my saint's day ▸ **no ser ~ de la devoción de alguien** to not be particularly fond of sb; **ser mano de ~** to be good at everything

santuario [san·tu·'a·rjo] *m* **1.** (*templo*) shrine; (*capilla*) chapel **2.** (*refugio*) sanctuary **3.** *Col* (*tesoro*) buried treasure

saña ['sa·ɲa] *f* (*ira*) anger; (*rencor*) viciousness; **lo hizo con toda la mala ~** he/she did it with great cruelty

sapo ['sa·po] *m* toad

saque ['sa·ke] *m* (*fútbol*) goal kick; (*fútbol americano*) kick-off; (*tenis*) serve; **~ de esquina** corner kick

saquear [sa·ke·'ar] *vt* to loot

saqueo [sa·'keo] *m* looting

sarampión [sa·ram·'pjon] *m* measles

sarape [sa·'ra·pe] *m Méx* blanket

sarazo, -a [sa·'ra·so, -a] *adj Col, Cuba, Méx, Ven* ripening

sarcasmo [sar·'kas·mo] *m* sarcasm

sarcástico, -a [sar·'kas·ti·ko, -a] *adj* sarcastic

sardina [sar·'di·na] *f* sardine; (**estar**) **como ~s en lata** to be packed like sardines

sargento [sar·'xen·to] *m* sergeant

sarpullido [sar·pu·'ʝi·ðo, -'ʎi·ðo] *m* rash

sarro ['sa·rro] *m* tartar

sarta ['sar·ta] *f* **una ~ de mentiras** a string of lies

sartén [sar·'ten] *f* frying pan ▶ **tener la ~ por el mango** to have the whip hand

sastre, -a ['sas·tre, -a] *m, f* tailor

sastrería [sas·tre·'ri·a] *f* tailor's shop

satánico, -a [sa·'ta·ni·ko, -a] *adj* satanic

satélite [sa·'te·li·te] *m* satellite

sátira ['sa·ti·ra] *f* satire

satírico, -a [sa·'ti·ri·ko, -a] I. *adj* satirical II. *m, f* satirist

satisfacción [sa·tis·fak·'sjon, -faɣ·'θjon] *f* satisfaction; (*alegría*) happiness; **a mi entera ~** to my complete satisfaction

satisfacer [sa·tis·fa·'ser, -'θer] *irr como* **hacer** I. *vt* to satisfy; (*sed*) to quench; (*demanda*) to settle; (*requisitos*) to meet II. *vr:* **~se** to satisfy oneself

satisfactorio, -a [sa·tis·fak·'to·rjo, -a] *adj* satisfactory; **no ser ~** to be unsatisfactory; **resulta ~...** it is pleasing...

satisfecho, -a [sa·tis·'fe·t∫o, -a] I. *pp de* **satisfacer** II. *adj* contented; (*exigencias, deseo sexual*) satisfied; **~ de sí mismo** self-satisfied; **estar ~** (*harto*) to have had enough

saturación [sa·tu·ra·'sjon, -'θjon] *f* saturation

saturar [sa·tu·'rar] *vt* to saturate

sauce ['sau·se, 'sau·θe] *m* willow; **~ llorón** weeping willow

saúco [sa·'u·ko] *m*, **sauco** [sau·ko] *m* elder

saudí <saudíes> [sau·'di], **saudita** [sau·'di·ta] I. *adj* Saudi; **Arabia Saudí** Saudi Arabia II. *mf* Saudi

sauna [sau·na] *f* sauna

savia ['sa·βja] *f* sap; (*energía*) vitality

saxofón [sak·so·'fon] *m*, **saxófono** [sak·'so·fo·no] *m* saxophone

sazón [sa·'son, -'θon] *f* **1.** (*condimento*) flavor **2.** (*madurez*) ripeness; **estar en ~** to be ripe ▶ **fuera de ~** out of season; **a la ~** at that time

sazonar [sa·so·'nar, sa·θo·-] *vt* to season; (*madurar*) to ripen

se [se] *pron pers* **1.** *reflexivo:* *m sing* himself; *f sing* herself; *de cosa* itself; *pl* themselves; *de Uds.* yourself; *de Uds.* yourselves **2.** *objeto indirecto:* *m sing* to him; *f sing* to her; *a una cosa* to it; *pl* to them; *a Ud., Uds.* to you; **mi hermana ~ lo prestó a su amiga** my sister lent it to her friend **3.** (*impers*) you; **~ aprende mucho aquí** you learn a lot here **4.** (*pasiva*) **~ confirmó la sentencia** the sentence was confirmed; **~ dice que...** it is said that...

sé [se] *1. pres de* **saber**

SE *abr de* **sudeste** SE

sebo ['se·βo] *m* grease; **hacer ~** *Arg inf* to idle

seca ['se·ka] *f AmL* drought; (*temporada*) dry season

secador [se·ka·'dor] *m* (*de ropa*) clothes horse; (*de pelo*) hairdryer

secadora [se·ka·'do·ra] *f* tumble dryer

secante¹ [se·'kan·te] *adj* drying; **línea ~** secant; **papel ~** blotting paper

secante² [se·'kan·te] *f MAT* drying

secar <c → qu> [se'kar] I. *vt* to dry; (*herida*) to heal; (*enjugar*) to wipe II. *vr:* **~se** to dry up; (*fuente*) to run dry; (*herida*) to heal up; (*enjugar*) to wipe up

sección [sek·'sjon, seɣ·'θjon] *f* **1.** (*parte*) section **2.** (*departamento*) branch **3.** (*corte*) cross-section

seco, -a ['se·ko, -a] *adj* **1.** dry; **golpe ~** dull blow; **limpiar en ~** to dry clean **2.** (*desecado, río*) dried up; **frutos ~s** dried fruit and nuts **3.** (*marchito*) withered **4.** (*flaco*) skinny **5.** (*tajante*) curt ▶ **a secas** on its own; **en ~** suddenly; **frenar en ~** to pull up sharply

secreción [se·kre·'sjon, -'θjon] *f* segregation; (*sustancia*) secretion

secretaría [se·kre·ta·'ri·a] *f* **1.** (*oficina*) secretary's office **2.** (*cargo*) secretary position **3.** (*gobierno, organismo*) secretariat

secretariado [se·kre·ta·'rja·do] *m* secretary's office; (*cargo*) secretary position

S

secretario, -a [se·kre·'ta·rjo] *m, f* secretary

secretear [se·kre·te·'ar] *vi inf* to exchange secrets

secreto [se·'kre·to] *m* secret; (*reserva*) secrecy; **~ profesional** trade secret; **~ a voces** open secret; **en ~** in secret; **mantener en ~** to keep secret; **guardar un ~** to keep a secret

secreto, -a [se·'kre·to, -a] *adj* secret

secta ['sek·ta] *f* sect

sectario, -a ['sek·'ta·rjo, -a] I. *adj* sectarian; (*fanático*) fanatical II. *m, f* member of a sect; (*fanático*) fanatic

sector [sek·'tor] *m* sector; (*grupo*) group; **~ económico/servicios** economic/service sector; **~ hotelero** hotel industry; **~ multimedia/de la informática** multimedia/computing sector

secuela [se·'kwe·la] *f* consequence; (*enfermedad*) after-effect; **dejar ~s** to have after-effects

secuencia [se·'kwen·sja, -θja] *f* sequence; (*palabras*) word order; **~ de caracteres** series of characters

secuestrador(a) [se·kwes·tra·'dor, -·'do·ra] *m(f)* kidnapper

secuestrar [se·kwes·'trar] *vt* to kidnap

secuestro [se·'kwes·tro] *m* kidnapping

secular [se·ku·'lar] *adj* secular; *fig* age-old

secundar [se·kun·'dar] *vt* to second

secundario, -a [se·kun·'da·rjo] *adj* secondary; (*cargo*) minor; **papel ~** supporting role; **esto es ~** that's of minor importance

sed [sed] *f* thirst; **tener ~** to be thirsty; **~ de algo** longing for sth; **~ de venganza/riquezas** thirst for vengeance/riches

seda ['se·da] *f* silk; **de ~ natural** of pure silk; **como una ~** (*tacto*) as smooth as silk; (*persona*) sweet-tempered; (*sin tropiezos*) smoothly

sedante [se·'dan·te] I. *adj* (**de efecto**) **~** soothing II. *m* sedative

sedar [se·'dar] *vt* to sedate

sede ['se·de] *f* seat; (*empresa*) headquarters *pl*

sedentario, -a [se·den·'ta·rjo, -a] *adj* sedentary

sediento, -a [se·'djen·to, -a] *adj* thirsty;

~ de algo thirsty for sth

sedimentación [se·di·men·ta·'sjon, -'θjon] *f* sedimentation

sedimento [se·di·'men·to] *m* sediment

sedoso, -a [se·'do·so, -a] *adj* silky

seducción [se·duk·'sjon, -duɣ·'θjon] *f* seduction

seducir [se·du·'sir, -'θir] *irr como* **traducir** *vt* to seduce; (*fascinar*) to captivate

seductor(a) [se·duk·'tor, -·'to·ra] I. *adj* seductive; (*tentador*) tempting; (*idea*) captivating II. *m(f)* seducer; (*encantador*) charmer

segar [se·'ɣar] *irr como* **fregar** *vt* to reap; (*hierba*) to mow

segmentar [seɣ·men·'tar] *vt* to divide into segments

segmento [seɣ·'men·to] *m* segment

segregar <g → gu> [se·ɣre·'ɣar] *vt* to segregate

seguido, -a [se·'ɣi·do, -a] *adj* **1.** consecutive; **un año ~** a whole year **2.** (*recto*) straight; **todo ~** straight on

seguidor(a) [se·ɣi·'dor] *m(f)* supporter; DEP fan

seguimiento [se·ɣi·'mjen·to] *m* chase; **~** (**médico**) (medical) follow-up

seguir [se·'ɣir] *irr* I. *vt* **1.** to follow; **~ un curso de informática** to take a computing course **2.** (*perseguir*) to chase **3.** **~ adelante** to carry on; **¡que sigas bien!** I hope you keep well! II. *vi* **sigue por esta calle** follow this street

según [se·'ɣun] I. *prep* according to; **~ la ley** in accordance with the law II. *adv* **1.** (*como*) as; **~ lo convenido** as we agreed **2.** (*mientras*) while; **podemos hablar ~ vamos andando** we can talk as we walk **3.** (*eventualidad*) **~** it depends; **~ el trabajo iré o no** I'll go if work permits

segunda [se·'ɣun·da] *f* AUTO second gear; FERRO second class ▶ **con ~s** with veiled meaning

segundo [se·'ɣun·do] *m* second

segundo, -a [se·'ɣun·do, -a] I. *adj* second; **primo ~** second cousin; **vivir en el ~** to live on the second floor II. *m, f* second (one); *v. t.* **octavo**

seguramente [se·ɣu·ra·'men·te] *adv* certainly; (*probablemente*) probably

seguridad [se·ɣu·ri·'dað] *f* **1.** (*protección*) security; **Seguridad Social** Social Security **2.** (*certeza*) certainty; **para mayor ~** to be sure of it **3.** (*firmeza*) confidence; **habla con mucha ~** he/she speaks with great self-confidence

seguro [se·'ɣu·ro] **I.** *m* **1.** (*contrato*) insurance; **~ médico** medical [*o* health] insurance; **~ a riesgo parcial/a todo riesgo** third-party/comprehensive insurance **2.** (*mecanismo*) safety device **II.** *adv* for sure; **a buen** [*o* de] **~** surely; **sobre ~** on safe ground

seguro, -a [se·'ɣu·ro, -a] *adj* **1.** (*sin peligro*) safe **2.** (*firme*) secure **3.** (*sólido*) solid **4.** (*convencido*) certain; **~ de sí mismo** confident; **¿estás ~?** are you sure?

seis [seis] *adj inv m* six; *v. t.* **ocho**

seiscientos, -as [sei·'sjen·tos, -as; -'θjen·tos, -as] *adj* six hundred; *v. t.* **ochocientos**

seísmo [se·'is·mo] *m* (*temblor*) tremor; (*terremoto*) earthquake

selección [se·lek·'sjon, -ley·'θjon] *f* selection; **~ nacional** national team

seleccionar [se·lek·sjo·'nar, -ley·θjo·'nar] *vt* to select

selectividad [se·lek·ti·βi·'dad] *f* university entrance exam

selectivo, -a [se·lek·'ti·βo] *adj* selective; **método ~** selective criterion

selecto, -a [se·'lek·to, -a] *adj* select; (*ambiente*) exclusive

sellar [se·'jar, -'ʎar] *vt* **1.** (*timbrar*) to stamp **2.** (*concluir*) to end **3.** (*precintar*) to seal; (*cerrar*) to close

sello ['se·jo, -ʎo] *m* **1.** stamp; **~ de garantía** seal of guarantee; **esta película lleva el ~ de su director** this film carries the stamp of its director **2.** (*precinto*) seal

selva ['sel·βa] *f* forest; (*tropical*) jungle; **~ virgen** virgin forest

semáforo [se·'ma·fo·ro] *m* traffic lights *pl*

semana [se·'ma·na] *f* week; **fin de ~** weekend

semanal [se·ma·'nal] *adj* weekly

semanario [se·ma·'na·rjo] *m* weekly (magazine)

semanario, -a [se·ma·'na·rjo, -a] *adj* weekly

semántica [se·'man·ti·ka] *f* semantics

semblante [sem·'blan·te] *m* face; (*expresión*) appearance; **tener un ~ alegre** to look cheerful

sembrar <e → ie> [sem·'brar] *vt* to sow; (*esparcir*) to scatter; **~ para el futuro** to sow for the future; **~ el terror** to spread terror

semejante [se·me·'xan·te] **I.** *adj* similar; (*tal*) such; **~ persona** such a person **II.** *m* fellow man

semejanza [se·me·'xan·sa, -θa] *f* similarity; (*física*) resemblance

semejar [se·me·'xar] **I.** *vi* to resemble **II.** *vr*: **~se** to look alike; **~se a alguien** to look like sb

semen ['se·men] *m* semen

semental [se·men·'tal] **I.** *adj* breeding; **caballo ~** stud **II.** *m* stud

semestral [se·mes·'tral] *adj* half-yearly

semestre [se·'mes·tre] *m* six-month period; UNIV semester

semicírculo [se·mi·'sir·ku·lo, -'θir·ku·lo] *m* semicircle

semifinal [se·mi·fi·'nal] *f* semi-final; **pasar a la ~** to get through to the semi-final

semilla [se·'mi·ja, -ʎa] *f* seed

seminario [se·mi·'na·rjo] *m* seminary

sémola ['se·mo·la] *f* semolina

senado [se·'na·do] *m* senate

senador(a) [se·na·'dor, -·'do·ra] *m(f)* senator

sencillamente [sen·si·ja·'men·te, sen·θi·ʎa·] *adv* simply

sencillez [sen·si·'jes, sen·θi·'ʎeθ] *f* simplicity; (*naturalidad*) naturalness

sencillo, -a [sen·'si·jo, -a; -'θi·ʎo, -a] *adj* simple; (*fácil*) easy; **gente sencilla** unaffected people

senda ['sen·da] *f*, **sendero** [sen·'de·ro] *m* path; (*método*) way

sendos, -as ['sen·dos, -as] *adj* each of two; **llegamos en ~ coches** we both arrived by car

senil [se·'nil] *adj* senile

senilidad [se·ni·li·'dad] *f* senility

seno ['se·no] *m* **1.** (*concavidad*) hollow **2.** ANAT, MAT sinus **3.** (*matriz*) womb **4.** (*pecho*) breast

S

sensación [sen·sa·'sjon, -'θjon] *f* **1.** (*sentimiento*) feeling **2.** (*novedad*) sensation; **causar ~** to cause a sensation

sensacional [sen·sa·sjo·'nal, sen·sa·θjo-] *adj* sensational

sensacionalismo [sen·sa·sjo·na·'lis·mo, sen·sa·θjo-] *m* sensationalism

sensacionalista [sen·sa·sjo·na·'lis·ta, sen·sa·θjo-] *adj* sensationalist; **prensa ~** tabloid press

sensatez [sen·sa·'tes, -'teθ] *f* good sense

sensato, -a [sen·'sa·to, -a] *adj* sensible

sensibilidad [sen·si·βi·li·'dad] *f* sensitivity

sensibilizar <z → c> [sen·si·βi·li·'sar, -'θar] *vt* to sensitize

sensible [sen·'si·βle] *adj* sensitive; (*impresionable*) impressionable

sensiblemente [sen·si·βle·'men·te] *adv* **1.** (*perceptible*) perceptibly **2.** (*evidente*) markedly

sensitivo, -a [sen·si·'ti·βo, -a] *adj* sensory

sensor [sen·'sor] *m* sensor

sensorial [sen·so·'rjal] *adj* sensory; **órgano ~** sense organ

sensual [sen·su·'al] *adj* sensual

sensualidad [sen·swa·li·'dad] *f* sensuality

sentado, -a [sen·'ta·do, -a] *adj* **dar algo por ~** to take sth for granted

sentador(a) [sen·ta·'dor, -·'do·ra] *adj Arg, Chile* becoming

sentar <e → ie> [sen·'tar] **I.** *vi* (*ropa*) to suit; **esa chaqueta me sienta bien/mal** that jacket suits/doesn't suit me; **~ bien/mal a alguien** (*comida*) to agree/disagree with sb; **~ como un tiro** to be as welcome as a hole in the head **II.** *vt* to sit; **estar sentado** to be sitting down; **estar bien sentado** *fig* to be well established **III.** *vr:* **~se 1.** to sit down; **¡siéntese!** have a seat! **2.** (*establecerse*) to settle down

sentencia [sen·'ten·sja, -θja] *f* sentence; **dictar ~** to pronounce sentence

sentenciar [sen·ten·'sjar, -θjar] *vt* (*condenar*) to sentence; (*decidir*) to give one's opinion on [*o* about]

sentido [sen·'ti·do] *m* **1.** (*facultad, significado*) sense; **~ común** common sense; **~ del deber/humor** sense of duty/humor; **doble ~** (*significado*) double meaning; (*dirección*) two-way; **con los cinco ~s** (**en**) totally absorbed (in); **estar sin ~** to be unconscious; **perder el ~** to lose consciousness; **sexto ~** sixth sense **2.** (*dirección*) direction; **en el ~ de la flecha** in the direction of the arrow; **en el ~ de las agujas del reloj** clockwise; **~ único** one-way

sentido, -a [sen·'ti·do, -a] *adj* (*conmovido*) deeply felt; (*sensible*) sensitive

sentimental [sen·ti·men·'tal] *adj* sentimental

sentimentalismo [sen·ti·men·ta·'lis·mo] *m* sentimentality

sentimiento [sen·ti·'mjen·to] *m* feeling; **sin ~s** unfeeling; (*pena*) sorrow; **le acompaño en el ~** please accept my condolences

sentir [sen·'tir] *irr* **I.** *vt* to feel; **sin ~** without noticing; (*lamentar*) to be sorry for; **lo siento mucho** I am very sorry; **siento que** +*subj* I'm sorry that **II.** *vr:* **~se** to feel; **~se bien/mal** to feel good/bad **III.** *m* opinion; (*sentimiento*) feeling

seña ['se·ɲa] *f* sign; **hacer ~s** to signal; **hablar por ~s** to talk in sign language

señal [se·'ɲal] *f* **1.** (*particularidad*) distinguishing mark **2.** (*signo*) sign; **~ de tráfico** road sign; **en ~ de** as a sign of; **dar ~es de vida** *fig* to show oneself **3.** TEL tone; **~ de comunicar** busy signal **4.** (*huella*) mark; **ni ~** no trace **5.** (*adelanto*) deposit; **paga y ~** first payment; **dejar una ~** to leave a deposit

señalado, -a [se·ɲa·'la·do, -a] *adj* **una fecha señalada** a special day

señalar [se·ɲa·'lar] *vt* **1.** (*anunciar*) to announce **2.** (*marcar, estigmatizar*) to mark **3.** (*mostrar*) to show **4.** (*indicar*) to point out **5.** (*fijar*) to fix

señalización [se·ɲa·li·sa·'sjon, -θa·'θjon] *f* signposting

señalizar <z → c> [se·ɲa·li·'sar, -'θar] *vt* to signpost

señor(a) [se·'ɲor, -·'ɲo·ra] **I.** *adj inf* **1.** (*noble*) lordly **2.** (*enorme*) huge **II.** *m(f)* **1.** (*dueño*) owner **2.** (*hombre*) (gentle)man; (*mujer*) wife; (*dama*) lady; **¡~as y ~es!** ladies and gentlemen! **3.** (*título*) Mister, Mistress *m, f* **4. el Señor** Our Lord

señoría [se·ɲo·'ri·a] *f* rule; **Su Señoría** Your Lordship

señori(a)l [se·ɲo·'ril/se·ɲo·'rjal] *adj* lordly; **casa ~** stately home

señorito, -a [se·ɲo·'ri·to, -a] *m, f* young master, young lady *m, f;* (*título*) Master, Miss *m, f*

señuelo [se·'ɲwe·lo] *m* decoy; *fig* lure

separación [se·pa·ra·'sjon, -'θjon] *f* separation; (*espacio*) distance

separado [se·pa·'ra·do] *adv* **por ~** separately

separar [se·pa·'rar] **I.** *vt* **1.** (*desunir*) to separate; **~ algo de algo** to separate sth from sth **2.** (*apartar*) to remove **II.** *vr:* **~se** to separate

separo [se·'pa·ro] *m Méx* cell

sepia ['se·pja] *f* cuttlefish; **de color ~** sepia

sept. *abr de* **septiembre** September

septentrional [sep·ten·trjo·'nal] *adj elev* northern

septiembre [sep·'tjem·bre] *m* September; *v. t.* **marzo**

séptimo, -a ['sep·ti·mo, -a] *adj, m, f* seventh; *v. t.* **octavo**

sepulcral [se·pul·'kral] *adj* (*silencio*) deathly

sepulcro [se·'pul·kro] *m* tomb

sepultar [se·pul·'tar] *vt* to bury; (*cubrir*) to conceal

sepultura [se·pul·'tu·ra] *f* burial; (*tumba*) grave; **dar ~ a alguien** to bury sb

sequía [se·'ki·a] *f* drought

séquito ['se·ki·to] *m* retinue

ser [ser] *irr* **I.** *aux* **las casas fueron vendidas** the houses were sold; **era de esperar** it was to be expected; **es de esperar que** +*subj* it is to be hoped that **II.** *vi* **1.** *aux* **éramos cuatro** there were four of us; **¿quién es?** who is it?; TEL who's calling?; **soy Pepe** it's me, Pepe; TEL this is Pepe; **es de noche** it's night time; **son las cuatro** it's four o'clock; **el que fue director** the former director; **el concierto es en el pabellón** the concert is in the pavilion; **eso fue en 2000** that was in 2000; **¿cuán-**

to es todo? how much is everything? **2.** MAT **cuatro y cuatro son ocho** four and four make four **3.** (*convertirse*) **¿qué quieres ~ de mayor?** what do you want to be when you grow up?; **llegó a ~ ministro** he became a minister; **¿qué es de él?** what's he doing now?; **¿qué ha sido de ella?** whatever happened to her? **4.** (+ *de*) **~ de México** to be from Mexico; **¿de quién es esto?** whose this is?; **el paquete es de él** the parcel belongs to him; **el anillo es de plata** the ring is made of silver; **el coche es de color azul** the car is blue; **yo soy de los que piensan que...** I'm one of those who think that...; **de no haber sido por ti** if it hadn't been for you; **manera de ~** manner; **razón de ~** raison d'être **5.** (+ *para*) **la película no es para niños** it's not a film for children; **¿para quién es el vino?** who is the wine for?; **no es para ponerse así** there's no need to get so angry; **es como para no hablarte más** it's enough to never speak to you again **6.** (+ *que*) **esto es que no lo has visto bien** you can't have seen it properly; **es que ahora no puedo** the thing is I can't at the moment; **si es que merece la pena** if it's worthwhile; **¡y es que tenía unas ganas de acabarlo!** I was longing to finish it!; **es que** longing to finish it!; **es que ahora no puedo** the thing is I can't at the moment; **si es que merece la pena** if it's worthwhile; **¡y es que tenía unas ganas de acabarlo!** I was longing to finish it! **7.** (*futuro*) **¿~á capaz?** will he/she be up to it? **8.** (*infin*) **todo puede ~** everything is possible; **¡no puede ~!** that can't be!; **por lo que pueda ~** just in case **9.** (*indicativo, condicional*) **es más** what is more; **siendo así** that being so; **es igual** it doesn't matter; **sería un buen líder** he'd be a fine leader **10.** (*subj*) **si yo fuera tú** if I were you; **si no fuera por eso...** if it weren't for that...; **si por mí fuera** if it were up to me; **me tratas como si fuera un niño** you treat me like a child; **sea quien/lo que sea** whoever/whatever it is; **por listo que sea...** however clever he is...; **o sea...** I mean...; **cómprame un chupa-chups o lo que sea** buy me a lollipop or something **III.** *m* being; FILOS life; **~ vivo** living creature; **~ humano** human being

serenarse [se·re·'nar·se] *vr* to calm down

serenata [se·re·'na·ta] *f* serenade

serenidad [se·re·ni·'dad] *f* calmness

sereno, -a [se·'re·no, -a] *adj* calm; *(sin nubes)* clear

serial [se·'rjal] *m* serial

serie ['se·rje] *f* 1. *t.* TV series *inv*; **asesino en ~** serial killer; **fuera de ~** outstanding 2. *(gran cantidad)* set; **fabricar en ~** to mass produce

seriedad [se·rje·'dad] *f* seriousness; **falta de ~** irresponsibility

serio, -a ['se·rjo, -a] *adj* 1. *(grave, sin bromas)* serious; **¿en ~?** are you serious?; **esto va en ~** this is in earnest 2. *(severo)* solemn 3. *(formal)* reliable 4. *(responsable)* trustworthy

sermón [ser·'mon] *m* sermon; **echar un ~ a alguien** to preach to sb

sermonear [ser·mo·ne·'ar] *vt inf* to lecture

seropositivo, -a [se·ro·po·si·'ti·βo, -a] *adj* HIV-positive

serpentear [ser·pen·te·'ar] *vi* to creep; *fig* to wind

serpentina [ser·pen·'ti·na] *f* streamer

serpiente [ser·'pjen·te] *f* snake; **~ de cascabel** rattlesnake

serranía [se·rra·'ni·a] *f* mountainous area

serrano, -a [se·'rra·no, -a] *adj* highland; **jamón ~** cured ham

serrar <e → ie> [se·'rrar] *vt* to saw

serrín [se·'rrin] *m* sawdust

serruchar [se·rru·'tʃar] *vt Arg, Chile, PRico* to saw

serrucho [se·'rru·tʃo] *m* handsaw

servible [ser·'βi·βle] *adj* serviceable

servicial [ser·βi·'sjal, -'θjal] *adj* obliging

servicio [ser·'βi·sjo, -θjo] *m* 1. service; **~ civil sustitutorio** community service; **~ a domicilio** home delivery; **estar de ~** to be on duty; **hacer un ~ a alguien** to do sb a service 2. *(retrete)* lavatory 3. DEP serve

servidor [ser·βi·'dor] *m* server

servidor(a) [ser·βi·'dor, -'do·ra] *m(f)* servant; **¿quién es el último? — ~** who is last in line? — I am

servidumbre [ser·βi·'dum·bre] *f* 1. *(per-*

sonal) servants *pl* 2. *(esclavitud)* servitude

servil [ser·'βil] *adj* servile

servilismo [ser·βi·'lis·mo] *m* servility

servilleta [ser·βi·'je·ta, -'ʎe·ta] *f* napkin

servir [ser·'βir] *irr como pedir* I. *vi* 1. *(ser útil)* to be of use; **no sirve de nada** it's no use; **no sirve para nada** it's useless [*o* no use at all] 2. *(prestar un servicio)* to serve; **¿en qué puedo ~le?** can I help you? II. *vi, vt (comida)* to serve; *(bebida)* to pour out III. *vr:* **~se** 1. *(en la mesa)* to help oneself (to) 2. **sírvase cerrar la ventana** please close the window

sésamo ['se·sa·mo] *m* sesame

sesear [se·se·'ar] *vi* to pronounce the Spanish 'c' before 'e' and 'i' and 'z' in all positions as 's'

sesenta [se·'sen·ta] *adj inv m* sixty; *v. t.* **ochenta**

sesera [se·'se·ra] *f inf* 1. *(cerebro)* brainpan 2. *(cabeza)* brains *pl*

sesgar <g → gu> [ses·'ɣar] *vt* to cut down; *(torcer)* to slant

sesión [se·'sjon] *f* 1. *(reunión)* session; **~ a puerta cerrada** private session 2. *(representación)* show(ing); **~ de tarde** matinee

seso ['se·so] *m* 1. ANAT brain 2. *(inteligencia)* brains *pl* ▶ **tener sorbido el ~ a alguien** *inf* to have complete control over sb

set [set] *m* <sets> service; DEP set

seta ['se·ta] *f* mushroom; *(venenosa)* toadstool

setecientos, -as [se·te·'sjen·tos, -as; se·te·'θjen-] *adj* seven hundred; *v. t.* **ochocientos**

setenta [se·'ten·ta] *adj inv m* seventy; *v. t.* **ochenta**

setiembre [se·'tjem·bre] *m v.* **septiembre**

seto ['se·to] *m* fence; **~ vivo** hedge

seudónimo [seu·'do·ni·mo] *m* pseudonym; *(escritor)* pen name

severidad [se·βe·ri·'dad] *f* severity; *(brusquedad)* roughness; *(rigurosidad)* strictness

severo, -a [se·'βe·ro, -a] *adj* harsh; *(brusco)* rough; *(riguroso)* strict

sexismo [sek·'sis·mo] *m* sexism

sexista [sek·'sis·ta] *adj, mf* sexist

sexo ['sek·so] *m* sex; **~ seguro** safe sex; ANAT genitals *pl*

sexto, -a ['ses·to, -a] *adj, m, f* sixth; *v. t.* octavo

sexual [sek·su·'al] *adj* sexual; **órganos ~es** sex organs

sexualidad [sek·swa·li·'dad] *f* sexuality

shock [ʃok/tʃok] *m* shock

short *m AmL* shorts *pl*

si [si] *conj* **1.** if; **~ no** if not; **por ~ (acaso)** (just) in case...; **~ bien** although; **como ~...** +*subj* as if...; **¿y si ...?** what if ...?; **¡~ hiciera un poco más de calor!** if only it were a little warmer! **2.** (*protesta, sorpresa*) but; **¡pero ~ ella se está riendo!** but she's laughing! **3.** (*énfasis*) **fíjate ~ es tonto que...** he's so stupid that...

sí [si] **I.** *adv* yes; **¡~ que está buena la tarta!** the cake tastes really good!; **¡(claro) que ~!** of course!; **creo que ~** I think so; **¡eso ~ que no!** certainly not!; **porque ~** because that's the way it is; (*lo digo yo*) because I say so; **volver en ~** to regain consciousness **II.** *pron pers m sing* himself; *f sing* herself; *cosa* itself; **a ~ mismo** to himself; **dar de ~** to be extensive; (*tela*) to give; **fuera de ~** beside oneself; **hablar entre ~** to talk among themselves; **por ~** in itself **III.** *m* consent

siamés, -esa [sja·'mes, -·'me·sa] *adj* Siamese; **gato ~** Siamese cat; **hermanos siameses** Siamese twins

Sicilia [si·'si·lja, si·'θi-] *f* Sicily

siciliano, -a [si·si·'lja·no, -a; si·θi-] *adj, m, f* Sicilian

sicología [si·ko·lo·'xi·a] *f v.* (p)sicología

sida ['si·da], **SIDA** ['si·da] *m abr de* síndrome de inmunodeficiencia adquirida AIDS

siderurgia [si·de·'rur·xja] *f* iron and steel industry

sidoso, -a [si·'do·so, -a] **I.** *adj* AIDS **II.** *m, f* AIDS sufferer

sidra ['si·dra] *f* cider

siega ['sje·ɣa] *f* reaping; (*tiempo*) harvest time

siembra ['sjem·bra] *f* sowing; (*tiempo*) sowing time

siempre ['sjem·pre] *adv* always; **de ~** always; **a la hora de ~** at the usual time; **una amistad de ~** a lifelong friendship; **¡hasta ~!** see you!; **por ~ (jamás)** for ever (and ever); **~ que** +*subj* as long as

sien [sjen] *f* temple

sierra ['sje·rra] *f* saw; GEO mountain range

siervo, -a ['sjer·βo, -a] *m, f* servant; (*esclavo*) slave

siesta ['sjes·ta] *f* siesta; **echar** [*o* **dormir**] **la ~** to have a nap; **(la hora de) la siesta** the hottest part of the day

siete ['sje·te] **I.** *adj inv* seven; *v. t.* ocho **II.** *m* seven

sietemesino, -a [sje·te·me·'si·no, -a] *m, f* baby born 2 months premature

sífilis ['si·fi·lis] *f* syphilis

sigilo [si·'xi·lo] *m* discretion; (*secreto*) stealth

sigla ['si·ɣla] *f* initial; (*acrónimo*) acronym

siglo ['si·ɣlo] *m* century; **el ~ XXI** the 21st century; **hace un ~ que no te veo** I haven't seen you for ages

signatura [siɣ·na·'tu·ra] *f* catalog number; TIPO signature

significación [siɣ·ni·fi·ka·'sjon, -'θjon] *f* meaning; (*importancia*) significance

significado [siɣ·ni·fi·'ka·do] *m* meaning

significar <c → qu> [siɣ·ni·fi·'kar] *vi, vt* to mean; **¿qué significa eso?** what's the meaning of this?

signo ['siɣ·no] *m* sign; **~ de enfermedad** sign of illness; **~ de más/menos/multiplicar** plus/minus/multiplication sign; **~ de puntuación** punctuation mark

siguiente [si·'ɣjen·te] **I.** *adj* following; **de la ~ manera** in the following way **II.** *mf* next; **¡el ~!** next please!

sílaba ['si·la·βa] *f* syllable

silbar [sil·'βar] *vi, vt* to whistle; (*abuchear*) to boo; (*serpiente*) to hiss; (*flecha, bala*) to whiz(z)

silbato [sil·'βa·to] *m* whistle

silbido [sil·'βi·do] *m* whistle; (*serpiente*) hiss; (*viento*) whistling; **me silban los oídos** I've got a ringing in my ears

S

silenciador [si·len·sja·'dor, si·len·θja·] *m* silencer

silenciar [si·len·'sjar, -'θjar] *vt* (*suceso*) to hush up; (*persona*) to silence

silencio [si·'len·sjo, -θjo] *m* silence; **en ~** in silence; **guardar ~** to remain silent; **guardar ~ sobre algo** to keep silent about sth; **romper el ~** to break the silence; **¡~!** quiet!

silencioso, -a [si·len·'sjo·so, -a; -'θjo·so, -a] *adj* 1. (*poco hablador*) quiet 2. (*callado*) silent 3. (*sin ruido*) soundless; (*motor*) noiseless

silicona [si·li·'ko·na] *f* silicone

silla ['si·ja, -ʎa] *f* chair; (*montura*) saddle; **~ de ruedas** wheelchair

sillón [si·'jon, -'ʎon] *m* armchair

silueta [si·'lwe·ta] *f* silhouette

silvestre [sil·'βes·tre] *adj* wild

sima ['si·ma] *f* abyss

simbólico, -a [sim·'bo·li·ko, -a] *adj* symbolic

simbolismo [sim·bo·'lis·mo] *m* symbolism

simbolizar <z → c> [sim·bo·li·'sar, -'θar] *vt* to symbolize

símbolo ['sim·bo·lo] *m* symbol

simetría [si·me·'tri·a] *f* symmetry

simétrico, -a [si·'me·tri·ko, -a] *adj* symmetrical

símil ['si·mil] *m* simile

similar [si·mi·'lar] *adj* similar

similitud [si·mi·li·'tud] *f* similarity; (*física*) resemblance

simio ['si·mjo] *m* ape

simpatía [sim·pa·'ti·a] *f* 1. (*agrado*) liking; **tener ~ por alguien** to have a liking for sb 2. (*carácter*) friendliness

simpático, -a [sim·'pa·ti·ko] *adj* friendly; **hacerse el ~** to ingratiate oneself

simpatizar <z → c> [sim·pa·ti·'sar, -'θar] *vi* 1. (*congeniar*) to get along 2. (*identificarse*) to sympathize

simple <simplísimo> ['sim·ple] I. *adj* 1. (*sencillo*) simple 2. (*fácil*) easy 3. (*mero*) pure; **a ~ vista** with the naked eye II. *m* simpleton

simpleza [sim·'ple·sa, -θa] *f* trifle; (*tontería*) silliness

simplicidad [sim·pli·si·'dad, sim·pli·θi·] *f* simplicity; (*ingenuidad*) plainness

simplificar <c → qu> [sim·pli·fi·'kar] *vt* to simplify; MAT to break down

simposio [sim·'po·sjo] *m* symposium

simulación [si·mu·la·'sjon, -'θjon] *f* simulation; (*fingimiento*) feigning

simulacro [si·mu·'la·kro] *m* (*de incendio*) fire drill

simulador [si·mu·la·'dor] *m* simulator

simular [si·mu·'lar] *vt* to simulate

simultaneidad [si·mul·ta·nei·'dad] *f* simultaneity

simultáneo, -a [si·mul·'ta·neo, -a] *adj* simultaneous

sin [sin] *prep* without; **~ dormir** without sleep; **~ querer** unintentionally; **~ más** nothing more; **estar ~ algo** to be out of sth

sinagoga [si·na·'yo·ya] *f* synagogue

sincerarse [sin·se·'rar·se, sin·θe·] *vr* **~ ante alguien** to be completely honest with sb

sinceridad [sin·se·ri·'dad, sin·θe·] *f* sincerity; **con toda ~** in all sincerity

sincero, -a [sin·'se·ro, -a; sin·'θe·] *adj* sincere; **seré ~ contigo** I'll be honest with you

sincrónico, -a [sin·'kro·ni·ko, -a] *adj* synchronous

sincronizar <z → c> [sin·kro·ni·'sar, -'θar] *vt* to synchronize

sindical [sin·di·'kal] *adj* union

sindicalismo [sin·di·ka·'lis·mo] *m* trade unionism; (*doctrina*) syndicalism

sindicalista [sin·di·ka·'lis·ta] I. *adj* (*sindical*) union II. *mf* trade unionist

sindicato [sin·di·'ka·to] *m* labor union

síndrome ['sin·dro·me] *m* syndrome; **~ de abstinencia** withdrawal symptoms; **síndrome de Down** Down's syndrome; **~ de inmunodeficiencia adquirida** Acquired Immune Deficiency Syndrome

sinfonía [sin·fo·'ni·a] *f* symphony

sinfónico, -a [sin·'fo·ni·ko, -a] *adj* symphonic; **orquesta sinfónica** symphony orchestra

singular [sin·gu·'lar] I. *adj* 1. (*único*) singular 2. (*excepcional*) outstanding; **en ~** in the singular 3. (*extraño*) peculiar II. *m* singular

singularidad [sin·gu·la·ri·'dad] *f* 1. (*uni-*

siniestro [si·'njes·tro] *m* accident; (*catástrofe*) natural disaster; (*incendio*) fire

siniestro, -a [si·'njes·tro, -a] *adj* evil; (*funesto*) disastrous; **un personaje ~** a sinister character

sinnúmero [sin·'nu·me·ro] *m* huge number

sino ['si·no] I. *m* fate II. *conj* 1. (*al contrario*) but 2. (*solamente*) **no espero ~ que me creas** I only hope that you believe me 3. (*excepto*) except

sinónimo [si·'no·ni·mo] *m* synonym

sinónimo, -a [si·'no·ni·mo, -a] *adj* synonymous

sinopsis [si·'noβ·sis] *f inv* synopsis; (*esquema*) diagram

sinrazón [sin·rra·'son, -'θon] *f* injustice; (*absurdo*) unreasonableness

sinsentido [sin·sen·'ti·do] *m* absurdity

sintáctico, -a [sin·'tak·ti·ko, -a] *adj* syntactic

sintaxis [sin·'tak·sis] *f inv* syntax

síntesis ['sin·te·sis] *f inv* synthesis; **en ~** in a word

sintético, -a [sin·'te·ti·ko, -a] *adj* synthetic

sintetizador [sin·te·ti·sa·'dor, sin·te·ti·θa-] *m* synthesizer

sintetizar <z → c> [sin·te·ti·'sar, -'θar] *vt* to summarize; QUÍM to synthesize

síntoma ['sin·to·ma] *m* symptom

sintomático, -a [sin·to·'ma·ti·ko, -a] *adj* symptomatic

sintonía [sin·to·'ni·a] *f* 1. (*adecuación*) tuning 2. (*señal sonora, melodía*) signature tune 3. (*entendimiento*) **estar en ~ (con alguien)** to be on the same wavelength (as sb)

sintonizar <z → c> [sin·to·ni·'sar, -'θar] I. *vt* to tune in to; **~ una emisora** to pick up a radio station II. *vi* to tune in, curve

sinuoso, -a [si·nu·'o·so, -a] *adj* (*curvado*) winding; (*retorcido*) devious

sinvergüenza [sim·ber·'ɣwen·sa, -θa] *pey* I. *adj* shameless II. *mf* lowlife

síquico, -a ['si·ki·ko, -a] *adj* v. **(p)síquico**

siquiera [si·'kje·ra] *adv* at least; **ni ~** not even

sirena [si·'re·na] *f* siren; (*mujer pez*) mermaid

sirope [si·'ro·pe] *m AmC, Col* syrup

sirviente [sir·'βjen·te] *mf* servant

sisar [si·'sar] *vt* to pilfer

sisirisco [si·si·'ris·ko] *m Méx* anus; (*miedo*) fright

sísmico, -a ['sis·mi·ko, -a] *adj* seismic; **movimiento ~** earth tremor

sismo ['sis·mo] *m* tremor; (*terremoto*) earthquake

sistema [sis·'te·ma] *m* system; **~ antibloqueo de frenos** antilock brake system; **~ inmunitario/operativo/solar** immune/operating/solar system; **~ montañoso** mountain range

sistemático, -a [sis·te·'ma·ti·ko, -a] *adj* systematic

sistematizar <z → c> [sis·te·ma·ti·'sar, -'θar] *vt* to systematize

sitio ['si·tjo] *m* (*lugar*) place; (*espacio*) room; **en cualquier/en ningún ~** anywhere/nowhere; **en todos los ~s** everywhere; **guardar el ~ a alguien** to keep sb's place; **hacer ~** to make room; **ocupar mucho ~** to take up a lot of room; **poner a alguien en su ~** to put sb in his/her place; **~ (de taxis)** *Méx* taxi stand

sito, -a ['si·to, -a] *adj* **~ en** situated in

situación [si·twa·'sjon, -'θjon] *f* situation; (*ubicación*) location

situado, -a [si·tu·'a·do, -a] *adj* situated

situar <1. pres sitúo> [si·tu·'ar] I. *vt* (*colocar*) to place; (*emplazar*) to locate II. *vr:* **~se** to situate oneself; (*abrirse paso*) to make one's way

smog [es·'moɣ] *m* smog

s/n *abr de* **sin número** no street number

snorkeling [es·'nor·ke·lin] *m* snorkeling; **practicar ~** to snorkel

so [so] I. *interj* whoa! II. *m inf* **¡~ imbécil!** you idiot!

SO [su·do·'es·te] *abr de* **sudoeste** SW

soba ['so·βa] *f inf* 1. (*a una persona*) pawing; (*de un objeto*) fingering 2. (*zurra*) beating

sobaco [so·'βa·ko] *m* armpit

sobado, -a [so·'βa·do, -a] *adj* worn; (*papel*) dog-eared; (*tema*) well worn

sobajar [so·βa·'xar] *vt Méx* to humiliate

sobar [so·'βar] **I.** *vt* (*persona*) to paw; (*objeto*) to finger **II.** *vi* (*persona*) to sleep

soberanamente [so·βe·ra·na·'men·te] *adv* supremely

soberanía [so·βe·ra·'ni·a] *f* sovereignty

soberano, -a [so·βe·'ra·no, -a] *adj, m, f* sovereign

soberbia [so·'βer·βja] *f* (*orgullo*) pride; (*suntuosidad*) magnificence

soberbio, -a [so·'βer·βjo, -a] *adj* (*orgulloso*) proud; (*suntuoso*) magnificent

sobornar [so·βor·'nar] *vt* to bribe

soborno [so·'βor·no] *m* bribe; (*acción*) bribery

sobra ['so·βra] *f* **1.** surplus; **de ~** more than enough; **saber algo de ~** to know sth only too well **2.** *pl* (*desperdicios*) leftovers *pl*; (*restos*) remnants *pl*

sobrador(a) [so·βra·'dor, -·'do·ra] *m(f) Arg, Urug* conceited person

sobrante [so·'βran·te] **I.** *adj* spare; (*de más*) excess; COM, FIN surplus **II.** *m* remainder; (*superávit*) surplus

sobrar [so·'βrar] *vi* **1.** (*quedar*) to remain; **nos sobra bastante tiempo** we have plenty of time **2.** (*abundar*) to be more than enough; **me sobran cinco kilos** I've got five kilos left over **3.** (*estar de más*) to be superfluous; **creo que sobras aquí** I think you're not needed here

sobre ['so·βre] **I.** *m* **1.** (*carta*) envelope; **un ~ de levadura** a packet of yeast **2.** *inf* bed; **irse al ~** to go off to bed **II.** *prep* **1.** (*encima*) on; **~ la mesa** on the table **2.** (*cantidad, hora*) about; **pesar ~ los cien kilos** to weigh about a hundred kilos; **llegar ~ las tres** to arrive at about three o'clock **3.** (*acerca*) about; **~ ello** about it **4.** (*superioridad*) **el boxeador triunfó ~ su adversario** the boxer triumphed over his opponent **5.** MAT out of; **tres ~ cien** three out of a hundred

sobreabundancia [so·βre·a·βun·'dan·sja, -·θja] *f* superabundance

sobrealimentación [so·βre·a·li·men·ta·'sjon, -·'θjon] *f* overfeeding

sobrecarga [so·βre·'kar·ɣa] *f* excess; ELEC overload; COM surcharge

sobrecargar [so·βre·kar·'ɣar] **I.** *vt* to overload; (*por esfuerzo*) to overburden **II.** *vr:* **~se** to overload oneself; **~se de trabajo** to take on too much work

sobrecoger [so·βre·ko·'xer] **I.** *vt* (*sorprender*) to take by surprise; (*espantar*) to frighten **II.** *vr:* **~se** (*asustarse*) to be startled; (*sorprenderse*) to be surprised (**de** by)

sobredosis [so·βre·'do·sis] *f inv* overdose

sobreentender [so·βre·en·ten·'der] <e → ie> **I.** *vt* (*presuponer*) to presuppose; (*adivinar*) to infer; **de todo ello sobreentendemos que...** we understand from all this that... **II.** *vr:* **~se** to be obvious; **aquí queda sobreentendido que...** it is implied here that...

sobreestimar [so·βre·es·ti·'mar] *vt* to overestimate

sobrehumano, -a [so·βre·u·'ma·no, -a] *adj* superhuman

sobrellevar [so·βre·je·'βar, -ʎe·'βar] *vt* to bear; **~ mal/bien** to take badly/well

sobremanera [so·βre·ma·'ne·ra] *adv* exceedingly

sobremesa [so·βre·'me·sa] *f* **1.** (*mantel*) table cover **2.** (*postre*) dessert **3.** (*tarde*) after-lunch; **programa de ~** afternoon program **4.** COMPUT desktop

sobrenatural [so·βre·na·tu·'ral] *adj* **1.** supernatural; **ciencias ~es** occult sciences **2.** (*extraordinario*) incredible

sobrenombre [so·βre·'nom·bre] *m* nickname

sobrentender <e → ie> [so·βren·ten·'der/so·βre·en·ten·'der] *vt, vr v.* **sobreentender**

sobrepasar [so·βre·pa·'sar] *vt* **1.** (*en cantidad*) to surpass; (*límite*) to exceed **2.** (*aventajar*) to pass; (*récord, al mejor*) to beat

sobreponer [so·βre·po·'ner] *irr como* **poner I.** *vt* **~ a algo/alguien** to place above sth/sb; (*anteponer*) to prefer to sth/sb; **~ a todos los demás** to put sb before everyone else **II.** *vr:* **~se 1.** (*calmarse*) to pull oneself together **2.** (*al enemigo, a una enfermedad*) to overcome; (*al miedo, a un susto*) to recover from

sobreprecio [so·βre·'pre·sjo, -θjo] *m* surcharge

sobresaliente [so·βre·sa·'ljen·te] **I.** *adj* outstanding **II.** *m* ENS distinction

sobresalir [so·βre·sa·'lir] *irr como salir vi* to stand out (**de** from); **~ en algo** to be outstanding at sth

sobresaltar [so·βre·sal·'tar] **I.** *vi* to start **II.** *vt* to startle **III.** *vr* **~se con** [*o de*] **algo** to be startled at sth

sobresalto [so·βre·'sal·to] *m* (*susto*) scare; (*turbación*) sudden shock; **con ~** shocked; **de ~** suddenly

sobrestimar [so·βres·ti·'mar] *vt* to overestimate

sobresueldo [so·βre·'swel·do] *m* extra pay

sobretasa [so·βre·'ta·sa] *f* surcharge

sobrevenir [so·βre·βe·'nir] *irr como venir vi* (*epidemia*) to ensue; (*desgracia, guerra*) to happen unexpectedly; (*tormenta*) to break; **me sobrevino una gran tristeza** a feeling of deep sadness came over me

sobrevida [soβ·re·'βida] *f* survival time

sobreviviente [so·βre·βi·'βjen·te] *mf* survivor

sobrevivir [so·βre·βi·'βir] *vi* to survive; (*a alguien*) to outlive

sobrevolar <o → ue> [so·βre·βo·'lar] *vt* to fly over

sobriedad [so·βrje·'dad] *f* soberness; (*prudencia*) restraint; (*estilo*) plainness

sobrino, -a [so·'βri·no, -a] *m, f* nephew, niece *m, f*

sobrio, -a ['so·βrjo, -a] *adj* sober; (*prudente*) restrained; (*estilo*) plain

socar <c → qu> [so·'kar] *AmC* **I.** *vt* to compress **II.** *vr:* **~se** to get drunk

socavar [so·ka·'βar] *vt* to dig under; *fig* to undermine

sociable [so·'sja·βle, so·'θja·] *adj* sociable; (*afable*) friendly

social [so·'sjal, -'θjal] *adj* **1.** (*relativo a la sociedad*) society; (*a la convivencia*) social **2.** (*estatal*) **asistencia/asistente ~** social work/worker; **Estado Social** Welfare State

socialdemócrata [so·sjal·de·'mo·kra·ta, so·θjal·] **I.** *adj* social-democratic **II.** *mf* social democrat

socialismo [so·sja·'lis·mo, so·θja·] *m* socialism

socialista [so·sja·'lis·ta, so·θja·] *adj, mf* socialist

socializar <z → c> [so·sja·li·'sar, -θja·li·'θar] *vt* to socialize

sociedad [so·sje·'dad, so·θje·] *f* **1.** (*población, humanidad*) society **2.** (*trato*) company; **la ~ con la que tratas** the company you keep **3.** (*empresa*) company; **~ anónima** corporation **4.** (*asociación*) association

socio, -a ['so·sjo, -a; -θjo, -a] *m, f* (*de asociación*) member; (*de empresa*) partner

socioeconómico, -a [so·sjo·e·ko·'no·mi·ko, -a; so·θjo·] *adj* socioeconomic

sociología [so·sjo·lo·'xi·a, so·θjo·] *f* sociology

sociólogo, -a [so·'sjo·lo·γo, -a; so·'θjo·] *m, f* sociologist

sociopolítico, -a [so·sjo·po·'li·ti·ko, -a; so·θjo·] *adj* sociopolitical

socollón [so·ko·'jon, -'ʎon] *m AmC, Cuba* jolt

socorrer [so·ko·'rrer] *vt* to come to the aid of

socorrido, -a [so·ko·'rri·do, -a] *adj* helpful; (*útil*) useful

socorrista [so·ko·'rris·ta] *mf* lifeguard; (*en piscinas*) pool attendant

socorro [so·'ko·rro] *m* help; (*salvamento*) rescue; **puesto de ~** first-aid post; **¡~!** help!

socoyote [so·ko·'jo·te] *m Méx* youngest child

soda ['so·da] *f* soda water

sodio ['so·djo] *m* sodium

sofá <sofás> [so·'fa] *m* sofa

sofá-cama <sofás-cama> [so·fa·'ka·ma] *m* sofa-bed

sofisticado, -a [so·fis·ti·'ka·do, -a] *adj* sophisticated

sofocado, -a [so·fo·'ka·do, -a] *adj* stifled

sofocante [so·fo·'kan·te] *adj* stifling; (*ambiente, aire*) suffocating; (*avergonzante*) shameless

sofocar <c → qu> [so·fo·'kar] **I.** *vt* **1.** (*asfixiar*) to suffocate **2.** (*frenar*) to stifle; (*fuego*) to put out; (*revolución*) to crush

3. (*avergonzar*) to embarrass **II.** *vr:* ~**se 1.** (*sonrojarse*) to blush **2.** (*agobiarse*) to get worked up **3.** (*enojarse*) to get angry **4.** (*ahogarse*) to suffocate

sofoco [so·'fo·ko] *m* **1.** (*ahogo*) suffocation; (*jadeo*) panting **2.** (*calor*) heat flush

soga ['so·ɣa] *f* rope; **estar con la ~ al cuello** to have one's back to the wall

sois [sois] *2. pres pl de* **ser**

soja ['so·xa] *f* soy; **salsa/semilla/brote de ~** soy sauce/soybean/bean sprout

sol [sol] *m* **1.** sun; (*luz*) sunlight; **de ~ a ~** from dawn to dusk; **hace ~** it's sunny; **día de ~** sunny day; **al ~** in the sun; **tomar el ~** to sunbathe **2.** ~ **y sombra** brandy and anisette **3.** (*moneda*) sol **4.** *inf* **es un ~** he/she is an angel ▶ **no dejar a alguien ni a ~ ni a <u>sombra</u>** not to leave sb alone

solamente [so·la·'men·te] *adv* only; (*expresamente*) expressly

solapa [so·'la·pa] *f* lapel; (*libro*) flap

solapar [so·la·'par] **I.** *vi* to overlap **II.** *vt* (*cubrir*) to cover up; (*disimular*) to conceal

solar [so·'lar] **I.** *adj* solar **II.** *m* **1.** (*terreno*) plot **2.** (*casa*) family seat **3.** *AmC* (*patio*) yard

soldado, -a [sol·'da·do, -a] *m, f* soldier; ~ **raso** private

soldador [sol·da·'dor] *m* soldering iron

soldador(a) [sol·da·'dor, -·'do·ra] *m(f)* welder

soldar <o → ue> [sol·'dar] **I.** *vt* (*con metal*) to weld; (*unir*) to join **II.** *vr:* ~**se** (*herida*) to heal; (*huesos*) to knit together

soleado, -a [so·le·'a·do, -a] *adj* sunny

soledad [so·le·'dad] *f* solitude; (*sentimiento*) loneliness

solemne [so·'lem·ne] *adj* solemn; (*discurso*) formal; (*mentira*) monstrous; (*error*) monumental

solemnidad [so·lem·ni·'dad] *f* **1.** solemnity **2.** *pl* formalities *pl*

to catch the train

solfeo [sol·'feo] *m* solfeggio; (*fragmento*) sol-fa

solicitante [so·li·si·'tan·te, so·li·θi-] *mf* petitioner; (*para un trabajo*) applicant

solicitar [so·li·si·'tar, so·li·θi-] *vt* to ask for; (*gestionar*) to solicit; (*un trabajo*) to apply for; ~ **un médico** to call for a doctor; (*compañía, atención*) to seek; **te solicitan en todas partes** you're in great demand

solícito, -a [so·'li·si·to, -a; so·li·θi-] *adj* diligent; (*cuidadoso*) solicitous

solicitud [so·li·si·'tud, so·li·θi-] *f* request; (*formal*) petition; ~ **de empleo** job application

solidaridad [so·li·da·ri·'dad] *f* solidarity

solidario, -a [so·li·'da·rjo, -a] *adj* solidary

solidarizarse <z → c> [so·li·da·ri·'sar·se, 'θar·se] *vr* to feel solidarity

solidez [so·li·'des, -'deθ] *f* solidity; (*estabilidad*) firmness

solidificar <c → qu> [so·li·di·fi·'kar] *vt, vr:* ~**se** to solidify; *fig* to harden

sólido ['so·li·do] *m* solid

sólido, -a ['so·li·do, -a] *adj* solid; (*color*) fast; (*precios*) stable; (*voz*) strong

solista [so·'lis·ta] *mf* soloist

solitaria [so·li·'ta·rja] *f* tapeworm

solitario [so·li·'ta·rjo] *m* solitaire

solitario, -a [so·li·'ta·rjo, -a] **I.** *adj* alone; (*abandonado*) lonely; (*lugar*) isolated; **en ~** single-handed **II.** *m, f* loner

sollozar <z → c> [so·jo·'sar, so·ʎo·'θar] *vi* to sob

sollozo [so·'jo·so, -'ʎo·θo] *m* sob

solo ['so·lo] *m* solo

solo, -a ['so·lo, -a] *adj* **1.** (*persona*) alone; (*sin familia*) orphaned; (*solitario*) lonely; **por sí ~** on one's own; **lo hace como ella sola** she does it as only she can **2.** (*único*) only; **ni una sola vez** not once **3.** (*sin añadir nada*) on its own; (*café*) black; (*alcohol*) straight ▶ **estar más ~ que la <u>una</u>** to be completely on one's own; **más vale ~ que mal <u>acompañado</u>** better to be alone than in bad company

sólo ['so·lo] *adv* only; (*expresamente*) expressly; ~ **que...** except that...; **tan**

~ just; **aunque ~ sea(n)...** even if it's only...

solsticio [sols·'ti·sjo, -θjo] *m* solstice

soltar [sol·'tar] *irr* I. *vt* to let go of; (*liberar*) to free; (*dejar caer*) to drop; (*nudo*) to untie; (*grito, pedo, embrague*) to let out; (*frenos*) to release; (*cinturón*) to undo; (*tacos*) to come out with; *inf* (*dinero*) to cough up; **¡suéltame!** let me go!; **~ una carcajada** to burst out laughing; **~ un golpe** to strike; **~ una bofetada a alguien** to slap sb; **no ~ prenda** to give nothing away II. *vr:* **~se 1.** (*liberarse*) to escape; (*librarse*) to free oneself **2.** (*nudo*) to come undone; (*tiro*) to go off **3.** (*al hablar*) to let oneself go; **se me soltó la lengua** I found my tongue

soltero, -a [sol·'te·ro, -a] I. *adj* single II. *m, f* bachelor, single woman *m, f*

solterón, -ona [sol·te·'ron, -'ro·na] *m, f* confirmed bachelor, spinster *m, f*

soltura [sol·'tu·ra] *f* ease; (*hablando*) fluency; (*pelo*) looseness

soluble [so·'lu·βle] *adj* soluble; **~ en agua** water-soluble; **café ~** instant coffee

solución [so·lu·'sjon, -'θjon] *f* solution; **este problema no tiene ~** there's no solution to this problem; **no hay más ~** there's nothing more to be done

solucionar [so·lu·sjo·'nar, so·lu·θjo·-] *vt* to solve

solvencia [sol·'βen·sja, -θja] *f* trustworthiness; FIN solvency

solventar [sol·βen·'tar] *vt* (*problema*) to resolve; (*asunto*) to settle; (*desavenencia*) to end; (*deuda, cuenta*) to pay

solvente [sol·'βen·te] *adj, m* solvent

somatada [so·ma·'ta·da] *f AmC* blow

sombra ['som·bra] *f* **1.** (*proyección*) shadow; **~ de ojos** eye shadow; **~ de duda** shadow of doubt; **se ha convertido en mi ~** he/she follows me everywhere **2.** (*penumbra*) shade; **hacer** [*o* **dar**] **~** to give shade; **hacer ~ a alguien** *fig* to put sb in the shade; **a la ~ de** in the shade of; **no fiarse ni de su** (*propia*) **~** to be extremely suspicious; **trabajar en la ~** to work illegally **3.** *pl* darkness **4.** ARTE shading **5.** (*cárcel*) **a la ~** in the slammer; **poner a la ~** to lock

up ▸ **tener mala ~** to be a nasty bit of work; (*tener mala suerte*) to be unlucky; **¡vete por la ~!** watch how you go!

sombrero [som·'bre·ro] *m* hat; **~ de copa** top hat; **~ hongo** derby; **quitarse el ~ ante algo** to take one's hat off to sth

sombrilla [som·'bri·ja, -ʎa] *f* parasol

sombrío, -a [som·'bri·o, -a] *adj* shady; (*oscuro*) dark; (*pesimista*) gloomy

someter [so·me·'ter] I. *vt* **1.** (*dominar*) to force to submit; (*subyugar*) to conquer **2.** (*proyecto, ideas, tratamiento*) to submit **3.** (*subordinar*) to subordinate; **todo está sometido a tu decisión** everything is subject to your decision II. *vr:* **~se** to give in; **~se a algo** to undergo sth; (*decisión, opinión*) to bow; **~se a las órdenes/la voluntad de alguien** to bow to sb's orders/will

somnífero [som·'ni·fe·ro] *m* sleeping pill

somnífero, -a [som·'ni·fe·ro, -a] *adj* sleep-inducing

somnolencia [som·no·'len·sja, -θja] *f* drowsiness

somos ['so·mos] *1. pres pl de* **ser**

son [son] I. *m* sound; (*rumor, voz*) rumor; **venir en ~ de paz** to come in peace ▸ **bailar al ~ que tocan** to toe the line; **hacer algo a su ~** to do sth one's own way; **sin ~** for no reason at all II. *3. pres pl de* **ser**

sonajero [so·na·'xe·ro] *m* (baby's) rattle

sonambulismo [so·nam·bu·'lis·mo] *m* sleepwalking

sonámbulo, -a [so·nam·bu·lo, -a] I. *adj* sleepwalking II. *m, f* sleepwalker

sonante [so·'nan·te] *adj* **dinero contante y ~** (hard) cash

sonar <o → ue> [so·'nar] I. *vi* **1.** to ring; (*instrumento*) to be heard; **me suenan las tripas** my stomach is rumbling **2.** *t.* LING, MÚS (*parecerse*) to sound; **~ a algo** to sound like sth; **~ a hueco** to sound hollow; **esto me suena** this sounds familiar; (*tal y*) **como suena** as I'm telling you II. *vt* to play; (*nariz*) to blow III. *vr:* **~se** to blow one's nose

sonata [so·'na·ta] *f* sonata

sonda ['son·da] *f* sounding; MED probe

sondeo [son·'deo] *m* **1.** investigation; **~**

S

de mercado/la opinión pública market/public opinion survey **2.** MED probing **3.** MIN boring **4.** NÁUT sounding

songa-songa ['son·ga·'son·ga] *AmC, Chile, Ecua* a la ~ underhand

songo, -a ['son·go] *adj Col, Méx* stupid; (*taimado*) sly

sonido [so·'ni·do] *m* **1.** sound **2.** *t.* MÚS (*manera de sonar*) tone **3.** FÍS resonance

sonoro, -a [so·'no·ro, -a] *adj* **1.** (*que suena*) *t.* FÍS resonant; (*acústico*) acoustic; (*bóveda*) echoing **2.** (*fuerte*) loud; (*agradable*) sonorous; **una voz sonora/poco sonora** a rich/thin voice **3.** LING voiced **4.** CINE **banda sonora** soundtrack

sonreír [son·rre·'ir] *irr como* reír **I.** *vi, vr:* ~se to smile; ~ **a alguien** to smile at sb; ~ **maliciosamente** to smile maliciously; ~ **de felicidad** to beam with happiness **II.** *vi* to smile; **le sonríe la fortuna** fortune smiles on him/her

sonrisa [son·'rri·sa] *f* smile; (*maliciosa*) smirk; ~ **de oreja a oreja** (broad) grin

sonrojar [son·rro·'xar] **I.** *vt* to make blush **II.** *vr:* ~se to blush

sonrojo [son·'rro·xo] *m* blush

sonsear [son·se·'ar] *vi CSur* to behave stupidly

sonsera [son·'se·ra] *f Arg* foolishness

sonso, -a ['son·so, -a] *m, f CSur* stupid

soñado, -a [so·'ɲa·do, -a] *adj* dreamt-of

soñador(a) [so·ɲa·'dor, -·'do·ra] **I.** *adj* dreamy **II.** *m(f)* dreamer

soñar <o → ue> [so·'ɲar] *vi, vt* to dream (**con** of); ~ **despierto** to daydream; **¡ni ~lo!** no way!; **siempre he soñado con ser médico** I've always dreamt of being a doctor

soñoliento, -a [so·ɲo·'ljen·to, -a] *adj* drowsy

sopa ['so·pa] *f* soup; ~**s de leche** bread and milk ▶ **comer la** [*o* **andar a la**] ~ **boba** to live off other people; **estar** ~ to be tight; **ver hasta en la** ~ to see everywhere; **como** [*o* **hecho**] **una** ~ soaked to the skin

sopera [so·'pe·ra] *f* soup tureen

sopero, -a [so·'pe·ro, -a] **I.** *adj* soup **II.** *m, f* soup plate

soplar [so·'plar] **I.** *vi* to blow **II.** *vt* **1.** to

blow on; (*apartar*) to blow away; (*velas*) to blow out; (*hinchar*) to blow up; (*fuego*) to blow on **2.** (*en un examen*) to whisper; TEAT to prompt **3.** *inf* (*delatar*) to squeal on; (*alumnos*) to tell on **4.** *inf* (*hurtar*) to swipe; (*cobrar*) to sting for **III.** *vr:* ~**se** *inf* (*comer*) to wolf down; (*beber*) to knock back

soplete [so·'ple·te] *m* blow torch; ~ **soldador** welding torch

soplo ['so·plo] *m* **1.** puff; **de un** ~ with one puff; ~ **de viento** breath of wind; **como un** ~ like a flash **2.** (*denuncia*) tip-off

soplón, -ona [so·'plon, -·'plo·na] *m, f* tattletale; (*policía*) informer; TEAT prompter

sopor [so·'por] *m* lethargy

soportable [so·por·'ta·βle] *adj* bearable

soportar [so·por·'tar] *vt* to support; (*aguantar*) to stand

soporte [so·'por·te] *m* support; (*pilar*) support pillar; (*de madera*) beam; ~ **físico** hardware; ~ **lógico** software

soprano [so·'pra·no] **I.** *m* soprano **II.** *f* soprano

soquete [so·'ke·te] *m AmL* anklet

sor [sor] *f* sister

sorber [sor·'βer] *vt* to sip; (*con pajita*) to suck; (*empapar*) to soak up; (*nariz*) to sniff; MED to inhale

sorbo ['sor·βo] *m* sip; **beber a** ~**s** to sip; **tomar de un** ~ to drink in one go

sordera [sor·'de·ra] *f* loss of hearing; (*total*) deafness

sordo, -a ['sor·do, -a] **I.** *adj* **1.** deaf; (*que oye mal*) hard of hearing; ~ **de un oído** deaf in one ear; **hacer oídos** ~**s** to turn a deaf ear; ~ **como una tapia** as deaf as a post; **quedarse** ~ to go deaf **2.** (*silencioso*) noiseless; **un golpe** ~ a dull thud **3.** LING voiceless **II.** *m, f* deaf person; **hacerse el** ~ to pretend not to hear; **no hay peor** ~ **que el que no quiere oír** there are none so deaf as those who will not hear

sordomudo, -a [sor·do·'mu·do, -a] **I.** *adj* deaf and dumb **II.** *m, f* deaf mute

sorprendente [sor·pren·'den·te] *adj* **1.** unexpected; (*asombroso*) amazing; (*desarrollo, evolución*) surprising; (**no**)

es ~ que +*subj* it's (hardly) surprising that **2.** (*que salta a la vista*) striking; **poseer una estatura ~** to be surprisingly tall

sorprender [sor·pren·'der] I. *vt* **1.** (*coger desprevenido*) to take by surprise; (*asombrar*) to startle; (*extrañar*) to surprise; **no me ~ía que viniera** I wouldn't be surprised if he/she came **2.** (*descubrir*) to come across **3.** (*pillar*) to catch II. *vr:* **~se** to be surprised; **~se de algo** to be amazed at sth

sorpresa [sor·'pre·sa] *f* surprise; (*efecto*) suddenness; (*asombro*) amazement; **coger a alguien de** [*o por*] **~** to take sb by surprise

sorpresivo, -a [sor·pre·'si·βo, -a] *adj AmL* unexpected

sortear [sor·te·'ar] *vt* **1.** (*decidir*) to draw lots for; (*rifar*) to raffle **2.** (*esquivar*) to avoid

sorteo [sor·'te·o] *m* drawing of lots; (*rifa*) raffle

sortija [sor·'ti·xa] *f* ring

sosegado, -a [so·se·'ɣa·do, -a] *adj* (*apacible*) peaceful; (*tranquilo*) calm

sosegar [so·se·'ɣar] *irr como* **fregar** I. *vt* to calm II. *vi, vr:* **~se** (*descansar*) to rest III. *vr:* **~se** (*calmarse*) to calm down

sosegate [so·se·'ɣa·te] *m Arg, Urug* **dar** [*o pegar*] **un ~ a alguien** to tell sb off

sosiego [so·'sje·ɣo] *m* calm; **con ~** calmly

soso, -a ['so·so, -a] *adj* **1.** (*sin sal*) unsalted; (*sin sabor*) insipid **2.** (*persona*) dull

sospecha [sos·'pe·tʃa] *f* supposition; (*desconfianza*) mistrust; (*de crimen*) suspicion; **bajo ~ de asesinato** suspected of murder

sospechar [sos·pe·'tʃar] I. *vt* (*suponer*) to suppose; (*recelar*) to suspect; **¡ya lo sospechaba!** I thought as much! II. *vi* to be suspicious

sospechoso, -a [sos·pe·'tʃo·so, -a] *adj* suspicious; **me resulta ~ que** +*subj* I find it suspicious that **II.** *m, f* suspect

sostén [sos·'ten] *m AmL* bra

sostener [sos·te·'ner] *irr como* **tener** I. *vt* **1.** (*sujetar*) to support **2.** (*aguantar*) to bear; (*por debajo*) to hold up **3.** (*afir-*

mar) to maintain; (*idea, teoría*) to stick to **4.** (*lucha, velocidad, posición*) to keep up; **~ una conversación** to have a conversation II. *vr:* **~se 1.** (*sujetarse*) to hold oneself up **2.** (*aguantar*) to keep going **3.** (*en pie*) to stand up **4. apenas me puedo ~** (*de puro cansado*) (I'm so tired) I can hardly stand

sota ['so·ta] *f* jack

sótano ['so·ta·no] *m* (*piso*) basement; (*habitación*) cellar

sotreta [so·'tre·ta] *adj Arg, Bol, Urug* (*holgazán*) idle; (*no fiable*) untrustworthy

soturno, -a [so·'tur·no, -a] *adj Ven* taciturn

soy [soi] *1. pres de* **ser**

spray [es·'prai] *m* <sprays> spray

squash [es·'kwaʃ] *m* squash

Sr. [se·'ɲor] *abr de* **señor** Mr.

Sra. [se·'ɲo·ra] *abr de* **señora** Mrs.

Srta. [se·ɲo·'ri·ta] *f abr de* **señorita** Miss

Sta. ['san·ta] *f abr de* **santa** St.

status [es·'ta·tus] *m inv* status

su [su] *adj* (*de él*) his; (*de ella*) her; (*de cosa, animal*) its; (*de ellos*) their; (*de Ud, Uds.*) your; (*de uno*) one's; **~ familia** his/her/their family

suampo ['swam·po] *m AmC* swamp

suave [su·'a·βe] *adj* (*superficie, piel, aterrizaje*) smooth; (*jersey, pelo, droga*) soft; (*viento, noche, curva, subida*) gentle; (*sopa, salsa, temperatura, tabaco*) mild

suavidad [swa·βi·'dad] *f* (*superficie, piel, aterrizaje*) smoothness; (*jersey, cabello*) softness; (*viento, caricia, subida, temperatura*) gentleness

suavizante [swa·βi·'san·te, -'θan·te] I. *adj* **crema ~** conditioner II. *m* conditioner; (*para ropa*) fabric softener

suavizar [swa·βi·'sar, -'θar] <z → c> *vt* to smooth; (*pelo, piel*) to soften; (*situación*) to ease; (*persona*) to mollify; (*recorrido, trabajo*) to make easy; (*velocidad*) to moderate

subalimentación [suβ·a·li·men·ta·'sjon, -'θjon] *f* undernourishment

subarrendar <e → ie> [suβ·a·rren·'dar] *vt* (*piso*) to sublet; (*finca*) to sublease

subasta [su·'βas·ta] *f* auction; (*de con-*

trato público) tender; **sacar a ~ pública** to put up for auction

subastar [suβas·'tar] *vt* to auction; (*contrato público*) to put out to tender

subcampeón, -ona [suβ·kam·pe·'on, -·'o·na] *m, f* runner-up; **~ mundial** world number two

subconsciencia [suβ·kon·'sjen·sja, -'θjen·θja] *f* subconscious

subconsciente [suβ·kon·'sjen·te, -'θjen·te] *adj* subconscious

subcultura [suβ·kul·'tu·ra] *f* subculture

subdesarrollado, -a [suβ·de·sa·rro·'ja·do, -a; -'ʎa·do, -a] *adj* underdeveloped

subdirector(a) [suβ·di·rek·'tor, -·'to·ra] *m(f)* assistant director

súbdito, -a ['suβ·di·to, -a] *m, f* vassal

subdividir [suβ·di·βi·'dir] *vt* to subdivide

subestimar [suβ·es·ti·'mar] **I.** *vt* to underestimate **II.** *vr:* **~se** to underestimate oneself

subida [su·'βi·da] *f* **1.** (*calle, río*) rise; (*precios, temperaturas, costes*) increase **2.** (*cuesta*) slope; **la calle hace ~** the street slopes **3.** (*ascenso*) ascent; (*en coche, teleférico*) climb; **~ al poder** rise to power

subir [su·'βir] **I.** *vi* (*calle, cuesta*) to go up; (*sol, pastel, globo, río*) to rise; **~ a la cima** to climb to the peak; **la marea ha subido** the tide has come in; **sube a por tus cosas** go up and get your things; **~ en algo** to increase by sth; **la gasolina ha subido** gas has gone up; (*al coche*) to get in; (*al caballo, tren, bici*) to get on; **~ a un árbol** to climb a tree **II.** *vt* to go up; (*llevar*) to take up; (*voz, precio, persiana*) to raise; (*música*) to turn up; (*montaña*) to climb; (*brazos*) to lift up; (*cabeza, pesas*) to lift; **~ a un niño en brazos** to lift up a child; **~ al tercer piso** to go up to the third floor **III.** *vr:* **~se** (*coche*) to get in; (*tren, bici*) to get on; **~se a un árbol/a una silla** to climb a tree/onto a chair; **se me ha subido el vino a la cabeza** the wine has gone to my head

súbito ['su·βi·to] *adv* **de ~** suddenly; (*inesperadamente*) unexpectedly

súbito, -a ['su·βi·to, -a] *adj* sudden; (*inesperado*) unexpected

subjefe, -a [suβ·'xe·fe, -a] *m, f* assistant manager

subjetividad [suβ·xe·ti·βi·'dad] *f* subjectivity

subjetivo, -a [suβ·xe·'ti·βo, -a] *adj* subjective

subjuntivo [suβ·xun·'ti·βo] *m* subjunctive

sublevación [su·βle·βa·'sjon, -'θjon] *f* uprising

sublevar [su·βle·'βar] *vr:* **~se** to revolt

sublimación [su·βli·ma·'sjon, -'θjon] *f* praise; PSICO, QUÍM sublimation

sublimar [su·βli·'mar] *vt* to praise; PSICO, QUÍM to sublimate

sublime [su·'βli·me] *adj* sublime

subliminal [su·βli·mi·'nal] *adj* subliminal

submarinismo [suβ·ma·ri·'nis·mo/sum·ma·ri·'nis·mo] *m* scuba-diving; **hacer ~** to go scuba-diving

submarino, -a [suβ·ma·'ri·no/sum·ma·'ri·no, -a] *adj* submarine; (*vida*) underwater

submarino [suβ·ma·'ri·no/sum·ma·'ri·no] *m* submarine

subnormal [suβ·nor·'mal] **I.** *adj* subnormal **II.** *mf* subnormal person; **¡eres un ~!** you moron!

subordinación [su·βor·di·na·'sjon, -'θjon] *f* subordination; (*obediencia*) obedience

subordinado, -a [su·βor·di·'na·do, -a] *adj, m, f* subordinate; **oración subordinada** subordinate clause

subordinar [su·βor·di·'nar] *vt* to subordinate

subrayado [suβ·rra·'ja·do] *m* underlining

subrayar [suβ·rra·'jar] *vt* to underline; (*recalcar*) to emphasize

subsanar [suβ·sa·'nar] *vt* (*falta*) to make up for; (*error*) to rectify; (*defecto*) to repair; (*mal*) to remedy; (*dificultad*) to overcome

subscripción [suβs·krip·'sjon, -kriβ·'θjon] *f v.* **suscripción**

subsecretario, -a [suβ·se·kre·'ta·rjo, -a] *m, f* assistant; POL undersecretary

subsidiar [suβ·si·'djar] *vt* to subsidize

subsidio [suβ·'si·djo] *m* subsidy; **~ de paro** [*o* **desempleo**] unemployment compensation

subsiguiente [suβ·si·'yjen·te] *adj* subsequent

subsistencia [suβ·sis·'ten·sja, -θja] *f* subsistence

subsistente [suβ·sis·'ten·te] *adj* surviving

subsistir [suβ·sis·'tir] *vi* to subsist

substancia [suβs·'tan·sja, -θja] *f v.* **sustancia**

substantivo [suβs·tan·'ti·βo] *adj, m. v.* **sustantivo**

substitución [suβs·ti·tu·'sjon, -'θjon] *f v.* **sustitución**

substraer [suβs·tra·'er] *irr como* traer *vt v.* **sustraer**

subsuelo [suβ·'swe·lo] *m* subsoil

subterráneo, -a [suβ·te·'rra·neo, -a] *adj* underground

subtítulo [suβ·'ti·tu·lo] *m* subtitle

subtropical [suβ·tro·pi·'kal] *adj* subtropical

suburbano, -a [suβ·ur·'βa·no] *adj* suburban

suburbio [su·'βur·βjo] *m* (poor) suburb; (*barrio*) slum area; **vivir en los ~s de Lima** to live on the edge of Lima

subvención [suβ·βen·'sjon, -'θjon] *f* grant; POL subsidy

subvencionar [suβ·βen·sjo·'nar, -θjo·'nar] *vt* to aid; POL to subsidize; ADMIN to finance with a grant

subversión [suβ·βer·'sjon] *f* subversion

subversivo, -a [suβ·βer·'si·βo, -a] *adj* subversive

subyacente [suβ·ja·'sen·te, -'θen·te] *adj elev* underlying; (*problema*) hidden

subyugar <g → gu> [suβ·ju·'yar] *vt* to subjugate

succionar [suk·sjo·'nar, suɣ·θjo·] *vt* to suck; (*tierra, esponja*) to soak up

sucedáneo [su·se·'da·neo, su·θe·] *m* substitute

sucedáneo, -a [su·se·'da·neo, -a; su·θe·] *adj* substitute

suceder [su·se·'der, su·θe·] I. *vi* 1. (*seguir*) to succeed; (*en cargo*) to follow on 2. (*ocurrir*) to happen; **¿qué sucede?** what's happening?; **por lo que pueda ~** just in case; **suceda lo que suceda** whatever happens; **lo más que puede**

~ es que +*subj* the worst thing that can happen is II. *vt* to succeed

sucesión [su·se·'sjon, su·θe·] *f* succession; (*serie*) series *inv*

sucesivo, -a [su·se·'si·βo, -a; su·θe·] *adj* following; **en lo ~** henceforth; **en dos días ~s** on two consecutive days

suceso [su·'se·so, -'θe·so] *m* (*hecho*) event; (*repentino*) incident; (*crimen*) crime; **sección de ~s** accident and crime reports

sucesor(a) [su·se·'sor, --'so·ra; su·θe·] *m(f)* successor; (*heredero*) heir

suche ['su·tʃe] I. *adj Ven* bitter II. *m Chile* 1. (*subalterno*) assistant 2. (*rufián*) pimp

suciedad [su·sje·'dad, su·θje·] *f* dirtiness; (*porquería*) dirt

sucio ['su·sjo, -θjo] *adv* **jugar ~** to play dirty

sucio, -a ['su·sjo, -a; -θjo, -a] *adj* dirty; (*jugada*) foul; **apuntes en ~** notes in rough; **hacer el trabajo ~** to do the dirty work

sucucho [su·'ku·tʃo] *m AmL* shanty

suculento, -a [su·ku·'len·to, -a] *adj* tasty; (*jugoso*) succulent

sucumbir [su·kum·'bir] *vi* to succumb; (*morir*) to die

sucursal [su·kur·'sal] *f* department; (*de empresa*) subsidiary; (*de banco, negocio*) branch

sucusumucu [su·ku·su·'mu·ku] *adv Col, Cuba, PRico* **a lo ~** playing dumb

Sudamérica [su·da·'me·ri·ka] *f* South America

sudamericano, -a [su·da·me·ri·'ka·no, -a] *adj, m, f* South American

sudar [su·'dar] I. *vi, vt* to sweat; *inf* (*trabajar*) to sweat it out; **me sudan los pies** my feet are sweating; **estoy sudando a chorros** I'm dripping with sweat II. *vt* to make sweaty; **gano mucho pero lo sudo** I earn good money but I have to work for it

sudeste [su·'des·te] *m* south-east

sudoeste [su·do·'es·te] *m* south-west

sudor [su·'dor] *m* sweat; **con el ~ de mi frente** with the sweat of my brow

sudoroso, -a [su·do·'ro·so, -a] *adj* sweaty

Suecia ['swe·sja, -θja] *f* Sweden

S

sueco, -a ['sweko] **I.** adj Swedish **II.** m, f Swede ▶ **hacerse el** ~ to pretend not to hear [o see]

suegro, -a ['sweɣro, -a] m, f father-in-law, mother-in-law m, f; **los ~s** the in-laws

suela ['swela] f sole; **tú no me llegas a la ~ del zapato** you can't hold a candle to me; **como la ~ de un zapato** tough as shoe leather

suelazo [swe'laso] m Chile, Col, Ecua, Ven hard fall

sueldo ['sweldo] m pay; (mensual) salary; (semanal) wage; ~ **base** basic salary; ~ **fijo** regular wage; **aumento de** ~ pay raise

suelo ['swelo] m **1.** (de la tierra) ground; (de casa) floor; **está muy hondo, no toco (el)** ~ it's very deep, I can't reach the bottom **2.** (terreno) land; ~ **edificable** building land ▶ **estar por los** ~**s** (deprimido) to feel very down; (de precio) to be dirt cheap

suelto ['swelto] m loose change

suelto, -a ['swelto, -a] adj **1.** loose; (broche) unfastened; (arroz) fluffy; (ropa) loose-fitting; (lenguaje) fluent; (dinero) ready; **no dejar ni un cabo** ~ to leave no loose ends; **un prisionero anda** ~ a prisoner is on the loose; **tener la lengua suelta** to be talkative **2.** (separado) separate; **pieza suelta** individual piece

sueño ['sweɲo] m **1.** sleep; **me cogió el** ~ sleep overcame me; **entre ~s** half asleep; **tener el** ~ **ligero/pesado** to be a light/heavy sleeper **2.** (cansancio) sleepiness; **tener** ~ to be sleepy; **me entró** ~ I got sleepy; **caerse de** ~ to be falling asleep; **me quita el** ~ it keeps me awake **3.** (fantasía) dream; **ni en ~s** not even in your wildest dreams; **los ~s, ~s son** dreams are dreams

suero ['swero] m whey; MED serum

suerte ['swerte] f **1.** (fortuna) luck; **¡(buena)** ~! good luck!; **estar de** ~ to be in luck; **no estar de** ~ to be out of luck; **tener buena/mala** ~ to be lucky/unlucky; **traer/dar buena/mala** ~ to bring/give good/bad luck; **por** ~ fortunately; **probar** ~ to try one's luck; **ser cuestión de** ~ to be a matter of luck; **la**

~ **está echada** the die is cast **2.** (destino) fate; **echar algo a ~(s)** to draw lots for sth **3.** (casualidad) chance

suertero, -a [swer'tero, -a] adj Ecua, Hond, Perú lucky

suéter ['sweter] m sweater

suficiente [sufi'sjente, -'θjente] **I.** adj enough; (presumido) self-important **II.** m pass

sufijo [su'fixo] m suffix

sufragar <g → gu> [sufra'ɣar] **I.** vt to aid; (gastos) to meet; (tasa) to pay **II.** vi AmL ~ **por alguien** to vote for sb

sufragio [su'fraxjo] m **1.** (voto) vote **2.** (derecho) suffrage; ~ **universal** universal suffrage **3.** (sistema) election

sufrido, -a [su'friðo, -a] adj uncomplaining; **eres demasiado** ~ you're too long-suffering; (marido) complaisant

sufrimiento [sufri'mjento] m suffering

sufrir [su'frir] vt **1.** (aguantar) to bear; (peso) to support; (a alguien) to put up with **2.** (padecer) to suffer; (cambio) to undergo; (desengaño, accidente) to have; (pena) to be stricken with; ~ **de celos** to suffer from jealousy; ~ **quejas** to receive complaints; ~ **las consecuencias** to suffer the consequences; ~ **una operación** to have an operation

sugerencia [suxe'rensja, -θja] f suggestion

sugerir [suxe'rir] irr como sentir vt to suggest; (insinuar) to hint; (evocar) to prompt

sugestión [suxes'tjon] f suggestion

sugestionar [suxestjo'nar] **I.** vt to influence **II.** vr: ~**se** to indulge in autosuggestion

suiche ['switʃe] m Méx switch; AUTO ignition key

suicida [swi'siða, swi'θi-] **I.** adj suicidal **II.** mf suicidal person; (muerto) person who has committed suicide

suicidarse [swisi'ðarse, swiθi'-] vr to commit suicide

suicidio [swi'θiðjo, swi'θi-] m suicide; **intento de** ~ suicide attempt

suite [swit] f suite

Suiza ['swisa, -θa] f Switzerland

suizo, -a ['swiθo, -a; -θo, -a] adj, m, f Swiss

sujetador [su·xe·ta·'dor] *m* bra

sujetar [su·xe·'tar] I. *vt* to hold; (*asegurar*) to support; (*pelo*) to hold in place; ~ **por algo** to seize by sth II. *vr*: ~**se** to subject oneself; ~**se a algo** to abide by sth

sujeto [su·'xe·to] *m* individual

sujeto, -a [su·'xe·to, -a] *adj* subject; ~ **a comprobación/fluctuaciones** subject to checking/fluctuation; ~ **a la inflación** affected by inflation

sulfato [sul·'fa·to] *m* sulfate

sulfuro [sul·'fu·ro] *m* sulfide

sultán, -ana [sul·'tan, --'ta·na] *m, f* sultan, sultana *m, f*

suma ['su·ma] *f* adding (up); (*resultado*) total; (*cantidad*) sum

sumamente [su·ma·'men·te] *adv* extremely

sumar [su·'mar] I. *vt* to add (up) II. *vr* ~**se a** to join; (*discusión*) to participate in

sumario [su·'ma·rjo] *m* criminal proceedings *pl*

sumergible [su·mer·'xi·βle] I. *adj* submersible; (*reloj*) waterproof II. *m* submarine

sumergir <g → j> [su·mer·'xir] *vt, vr*: ~**se** to submerge

sumidero [su·mi·'de·ro] *m* drain; (*de la calle*) sewer

suministrar [su·mi·nis·'trar] *vt* to supply; (*abastecer*) to stock

suministro [su·mi·'nis·tro] *m* supply; (*abastecimiento*) stock

sumir [su·'mir] I. *vt* to sink (**en** into); ~ **en la miseria/desesperación a alguien** to plunge sb into poverty/despair II. *vr*: ~**se** to sink (**en** into); ~**se en el trabajo** to become absorbed in one's work

sumisión [su·mi·'sjon] *f* **1.** (*acción*) submission **2.** (*carácter*) submissiveness **3.** (*obediencia*) obedience

sumo, -a ['su·mo] *adj* (*más alto*) high(est); (*mayor*) great; **a lo ~** at most; **en grado ~** highly

sungo, -a ['sun·go, -a] *adj Col* Black

suntuosidad [sun·two·si·'dad] *f* sumptuousness

suntuoso, -a [sun·tu·'o·so, -a] *adj* sumptuous; (*opulento*) lavish

supeditar [su·pe·di·'tar] I. *vt* **1.** to subordinate; (*someter*) to subdue **2.** (*condicionar*) to condition II. *vr*: ~**se** to submit

súper ['su·per] I. *adj inf* super II. *m* supermarket III. *f* Premium (gas)

superabundancia [su·per·a·βun·'dan·sja, -θja] *f* superabundance

superación [su·pe·ra·'sjon, -'θjon] *f* (*de récord*) improvement; (*de situación*) surmounting

superar [su·pe·'rar] I. *vt* to surpass; (*límite*) to exceed; (*récord*) to beat; (*prueba*) to pass; (*situación*) to overcome II. *vr*: ~**se** to excel oneself

superávit [su·pe·'ra·βit] *m* surplus

superdotado, -a [su·per·do·'ta·do, -a] *adj* extremely gifted

superficial [su·per·fi·'sjal, -'θjal] *adj* superficial; (*detalle*) minor; **herida ~** flesh wound

superficie [su·per·'fi·sje, -θje] *f* surface; ~ **cultivable** arable area; **salir a la ~** to surface; (*apariencia*) external appearance

superfluo, -a [su·'per·flwo, -a] *adj* superfluous; (*gastos*) unnecessary

superior [su·pe·'rjor] *adj* higher; (*en calidad*) better; (*en inteligencia, rango*) superior; (*excelente*) excellent; **el curso ~ de un río** the upper course of a river; **el piso ~ al mío** the apartment above mine

superior(a) [su·pe·'rjor, --'rjo·ra] *m(f)* superior

superioridad [su·pe·rjo·ri·'dad] *f* superiority (**sobre** over); **hablar con un tono de ~** to speak in a superior tone of voice

superlativo [su·per·la·'ti·βo] *m* superlative

superlativo, -a [su·per·la·'ti·βo, -a] *adj* superlative

supermercado [su·per·mer·'ka·do] *m* supermarket

superpoblación [su·per·po·βla·'sjon, -'θjon] *f* overpopulation

superponer [su·per·po·'ner] *irr como poner vt* to give more importance to; ~ **algo a algo** to superimpose sth on sth

S

superpotencia [su·per·po·'ten·sja, -θja] f superpower

superproducción [su·per·pro·duk·'sjon, -duɣ·'θjon] f **1.** COM overproduction **2.** CINE big-budget movie

supersónico, -a [su·per·'so·ni·ko, -a] adj supersonic

superstición [su·pers·ti·'sjon, -'θjon] f superstition

supersticioso, -a [su·pers·ti·'sjo·so, -a; -'θjo·so, -a] adj superstitious

supervisar [su·per·βi·'sar] vt to supervise

supervisión [su·per·βi·'sjon] f supervision

supervisor(a) [su·per·βi·'sor, --'so·ra] m(f) supervisor; (funcionario) inspector

supervivencia [su·per·βi·'βen·sja, -θja] f survival

superviviente [su·per·βi·'βjen·te] **I.** adj surviving **II.** mf survivor

suplantar [su·plan·'tar] vt to supplant

suplementario, -a [su·ple·men·'ta·rjo, -a] adj supplementary; **tomo ~** additional volume

suplemento [su·ple·'men·to] m **1.** supplement; (tomo) supplementary volume; **~ en color** color supplement **2.** (precio) extra charge; (del tren) excess fare

suplencia [su·'plen·sja, -θja] f substitution

suplente [su·'plen·te] adj, mf substitute

súplica ['su·pli·ka] f plea; (escrito) request

suplicar <c → qu> [su·pli·'kar] vt to implore; **~ algo de rodillas** to beg on one's knees for sth

suplicio [su·'pli·sjo, -θjo] m torment; **el viaje fue un ~** we had a terrible journey

suplir [su·'plir] vt **1.** (completar) to make up for **2.** (sustituir) to substitute

supo ['su·po] 3. pret de **saber**

suponer [su·po·'ner] irr como poner vt **1.** (dar por sentado) to suppose; **vamos a ~ que...** let's suppose that...; **se supone que...** it is assumed that...; **suponiendo que...** supposing that...; **supongamos que...** let us assume that... **2.** (figurar) to imagine; **supongo que sí** I suppose so; **no supongo que...** +subj

I don't imagine...; **no lo suponía tan fuerte** I didn't realize he was so strong **3.** (significar) to mean; **~ un duro golpe para alguien** to be a real blow for sb; **esto me supone 60 pesos al mes** this amounts to 60 pesos a month for me; **no ~ molestia alguna** to be no trouble

suposición [su·po·si·'sjon, -'θjon] f supposition; (presunción) assumption

supositorio [su·po·si·'to·rjo] m suppository

supremacía [su·pre·ma·'si·a, -'θi·a] f supremacy; (prioridad) priority

supremo, -a [su·'pre·mo] adj highest; fig supreme; **Tribunal Supremo** Supreme Court

suprimir [su·pri·'mir] vt **1.** (poner fin) to suppress; (fronteras) to eliminate; (controles, obstáculos, amenaza) to remove; (regla) to abolish **2.** (omitir) to omit **3.** (silenciar) to silence

supuesto [su·'pwes·to] m assumption; (hipótesis) hypothesis

supuesto, -a [su·'pwes·to, -a] adj (pretendido) so-called; (ladrón, asesino) alleged; (testigo, nombre) assumed; (causa) supposed; **por ~ de** course; **dar algo por ~** to take sth for granted; **~ que** since

supurar [su·pu·'rar] vi to suppurate

sur [sur] m south; (viento) south wind; **América del Sur** South America

surcar <c → qu> [sur·'kar] vt (tierra) to plow; (mares) to sail

surco ['sur·ko] m furrow; (arruga) wrinkle

sureste [sur·'es·te] m south-east

surf [surf] m surfing; **hacer ~** to windsurf

surgir <g → j> [sur·'xir] vi (agua) to gush; (dificultad, posibilidad) to arise; (pregunta) to come up

suroeste [sur·o·'es·te] m south-west

surrealismo [su·rrea·'lis·mo] m surrealism

surrealista [su·rrea·'lis·ta] adj, mf surrealist

surtido [sur·'ti·do] m assortment

surtido, -a [sur·'ti·do, -a] adj **1.** mixed; (variado) varied; **galletas surtidas** assorted biscuits **2.** (bien provisto) well-stocked

surtidor [sur·ti·'dor] *m* gas station; (*aparato*) gas pump

surtir [sur·'tir] **I.** *vt* ~ **de algo** to supply with sth; ~ **efecto** to work; (*palabras*) to have the desired effect **II.** *vr* ~**se de algo** to provide oneself with sth

surumbo, -a [su·'rum·bo, -a] *adj Guat, Hond* stunned

surupa [su·'ru·pa] *f Ven* cockroach

susceptibilidad [su·sep·ti·βi·li·'dad, sus·θep-] *f* susceptibility

susceptible [su·sep·'ti·βle, sus·θep-] *adj* sensitive; (*irritable*) touchy; ~ **de mejora** capable of improvement; **materiales ~s de ser reutilizados** material which can be reused

suscitar [su·si·'tar, sus·θi-] *vt* to cause; (*discusión*) to start; (*escándalo, comentarios*) to provoke; (*odio, conflicto*) to stir up; (*problema*) to raise; (*antipatías, curiosidad*) to arouse

suscribirse [sus·kri·'βir·se] *irr como escribir vr* to subscribe (**a** to)

suscripción [sus·krip·'sjon, -kriβ·'θjon] *f* subscription; (*de acciones*) taking up

suscri(p)tor(a) [sus·krip·'tor, -'to·ra] *m(f)* subscriber

suspender [sus·pen·'der] *vt* 1. to fail; **he suspendido matemáticas** I've flunked math 2. (*trabajador, deportista*) to suspend; (*sesión*) to adjourn; (*tratamiento*) to break off; **se ha suspendido la función de esta noche** tonight's show has been called off 3. ~ **de algo** to hang from sth

suspensión [sus·pen·'sjon] *f* 1. (*acción de colgar*) suspension 2. (*interrupción: tratamiento*) interruption; (*producción*) break; ~ **de armas** truce; ~ **de la pena** annulment of the penalty; ~ **de pagos** temporary receivership

suspenso [sus·'pen·so] *m* 1. fail; **sacar un ~** to fail 2. *AmL* suspense

suspicacia [sus·pi·'ka·sja, -θja] *f* suspicion

suspicaz [sus·pi·'kas, -'kaθ] *adj* suspicious

suspirar [sus·pi·'rar] *vi* to sigh; ~ **por algo** to long for sth

suspiro [sus·'pi·ro] *m* sigh

sustancia [sus·'tan·sja, -θja] *f* substance; **en ~** in essence

sustancial [sus·tan·'sjal, -'θjal] *adj* vital; (*fundamental*) essential; (*comida*) substantial; (*libro*) meaty

sustancioso, -a [sus·tan·'sjo·so, -a; -'θjo·so, -a] *adj* substantial

sustantivo [sus·tan·'ti·βo] *m* noun

sustentar [sus·ten·'tar] **I.** *vt* to hold up; (*columna*) to support; (*esperanza*) to sustain; (*familia*) to feed **II.** *vr*: ~**se** to sustain oneself; ~**se en algo** to rely on sth

sustento [sus·'ten·to] *m* maintenance; (*apoyo*) support

sustitución [sus·ti·tu·'sjon, -'θjon] *f* replacement; (*temporal*) substitution

sustituir [sus·ti·tu·'ir] *irr como huir vt* to substitute; (*temporalmente*) to stand in for; (*definitivamente*) to replace

sustituto, -a [sus·ti·'tu·to, -a] *m, f* substitute

susto ['sus·to] *m* scare; **poner cara de ~** to look scared; **pegarle un ~ a alguien** [*o* **darle**] to give sb a fright; **pegarse** [*o* **llevarse**] **un ~** to get scared; **no ganar para ~s** to have one problem after another

sustraer [sus·tra·'er] *irr como traer* **I.** *vt* 1. (*restar*) to subtract 2. (*robar*) to steal 3. (*privar*) to remove 4. (*separar*) to abduct **II.** *vr* ~**se de algo** to get away from sth

susurrar [su·su·'rrar] **I.** *vi* to whisper; (*no claro*) to mutter; (*viento*) to murmur **II.** *vr*: ~**se** to be rumored **III.** *vimpers* **se susurra que...** it is rumored that...

susurro [su·'su·rro] *m* whisper; (*no claro*) mutter; (*del viento*) murmur

sutil [su·'til] *adj* (*sabor*) subtle; (*aroma*) delicate; (*diferencia, ironía*) fine

sutileza [su·ti·'le·sa, -θa] *f*, **sutilidad** [su·ti·li·'dad] *f* 1. (*de sabor*) subtlety; (*de aroma*) delicacy 2. (*de diferencia, ironía*) fineness; (*de jugada, sistema*) refinement 3. (*de persona*) sharpness

suyo, -a ['su·jo, -a] *adj, pron* (*de él*) his; (*de ella*) hers; (*de cosa, animal*) its; (*de ellos*) theirs; (*de Ud., Uds.*) yours; (*de uno*) one's; **este encendedor es ~** this lighter is his/hers/theirs; **siempre habla de los ~s** he/she is always talking about his/her family; **darle a alguien lo ~ to give** sb what belongs to him/her; *fig* to give sb what he/she deserves; **ya ha hecho otra de las suyas** he/she has been up to his/her tricks again; **Albert es muy ~** Albert keeps to himself; **eso es muy ~** that's typical of him/her; **ir a lo ~** to go one's own way

T

T, t [te] *f* T, t; **~ de Tarragona** T as in Tango

tabacal [ta·βa·ˈkal] *m AmL* tobacco plantation

tabaco [ta·ˈβa·ko] *m* tobacco; (*cigarrillos*) cigarettes *pl;* **~ rubio/de mascar** Virginia/chewing tobacco; **¿tienes ~?** do you have any cigarettes?

tabanco [ta·ˈβaŋ·ko] *m AmC* attic

taberna [ta·ˈβer·na] *f* tavern

tabique [ta·ˈβi·ke] *m* partition; **~ nasal** nasal septum

tabla [ˈta·βla] *f* 1. board; **~ de cocina/planchar** cutting/ironing board; **~ de surf/windsurf** surfboard/sailboard 2. (*lista*) list; (*cuadro*) table; (*de libro*) table of contents 3. *pl* draw ▶ **a raja ~** to the letter; **hacer ~ rasa de algo** to wipe the slate clean

tablada [ta·ˈβla·da] *f CSur* stockyard

tablao [ta·ˈβlao] *m* stage

tablero [ta·ˈβle·ro] *m* board; **~ de anuncios/ajedrez** bulletin/chess board

tableta [ta·ˈβle·ta] *f* 1. bar 2. *AmL* tablet

tabloide [ta·ˈβloi·de] *m AmL* tabloid

tablón [ta·ˈβlon] *m* 1. plank; (*de anuncios*) bulletin board 2. *AmL* patch; (*grande*) plot

tabú [ta·ˈβu] *m* <tabúes> taboo

tabulador [ta·βu·la·ˈdor] *m* tab

tacañería [ta·ka·ɲe·ˈri·a] *f* stinginess

tacaño, -a [ta·ˈka·ɲo, -a] I. *adj* stingy II. *m, f* miser

tachar [ta·ˈtʃar] *vt* to cross out; **~ de algo** to brand as sth; **lo ~on de incompe-**

tente they accused him of being incompetent

tachero [ta·ˈtʃe·ro] *m Arg inf* taxi driver

tacho [ˈta·tʃo] *m* 1. *AmL* (*vasija*) metal basin 2. *AmL* (*hojalata*) tin 3. *AmL* (*cubo*) trash can 4. *Arg inf* taxi; **irse al ~** to collapse

tachón [ta·ˈtʃon] *m* crossing out

tácito, -a [ˈta·si·to, -a; ˈta·θi-] *adj* tacit

taciturno, -a [ta·si·ˈtur·no, -a; ˈta·θi-] *adj* taciturn; (*melancólico*) glum

taco [ˈta·ko] *m* 1. (*pedazo*) piece 2. (*de billar*) cue 3. (*de bota*) stud 4. (*de papel*) pad; (*calendario*) tear-off desk; (*fajo*) wad 5. (*de jamón*) cube; (*bocado*) bite to eat 6. *inf* (*palabrota*) swearword; **decir** [*o* **soltar**] **~s** to swear 7. *inf* (*lío*) mess; **estar hecho un ~** to be all mixed up 8. *AmL* (*tacón*) heel 9. *pl inf* years; **¡ya tengo mis 40 ~s!** I'm already past 40!

tacón [ta·ˈkon] *m* heel; **~ de aguja** spike heel; **zapatos de ~ alto** high-heel(ed) shoes

táctica [ˈtak·ti·ka] *f* tactic(s); **ir con ~** to move strategically

táctico, -a [ˈtak·ti·ko, -a] I. *adj* tactical II. *m, f* tactician

táctil [ˈtak·til] *adj* tactile

tacto [ˈtak·to] *m* 1. touch; **sentido del ~** sense of touch; **al ~** to the touch; **ser áspero al ~** to feel rough 2. (*habilidad*) tact; **no tener ~** to be tactless

tacuache [ta·ˈkwa·tʃe] *m Cuba, Méx zool* almique

tacuaco, -a [ta·ˈkwa·ko, -a] *adj Chile* chubby

taita [ˈtai·ta] *m* 1. *CSur* expert 2. *Arg* bully 3. *Ven* head of the family

tajada [ta·ˈxa·da] *f* 1. (*porción*) slice; (*corte*) cut; **llevarse la mejor ~** to take the lion's share; **sacar ~ de algo** to take advantage of sth 2. *inf* (*ronquera*) **tener una ~** to be hoarse; (*borrachera*) **pilló una buena ~** he/she got smashed

tajante [ta·ˈxan·te] *adj* sharp; (*respuesta*) categorical; (*actitud*) dogmatic; (*medidas*) unequivocal

tajar [ta·ˈxar] *vt* to cut; *AmL* (*afilar*) to sharpen

tajo [ˈta·xo] *m* 1. cut; **darse un ~ en el**

dedo to cut one's finger **2.** GEO gorge **3.** *inf* work; **ir al ~** to go to work

tal [tal] **I.** *adj* **1.** (*igual*) such; **en ~ caso** in that case; **no digas ~ cosa** don't say any such thing; **no he dicho nunca ~ cosa** I never said anything of the kind **2.** (*tanto*) so; **la distancia es ~ que...** it's so far away that... **3.** (*cierto*) certain; **un ~ Pérez llamó** somebody called Perez called **II.** *pron* **1.** (*alguien*) **~ o cual** someone or other **2.** (*cosa*) **hablar de ~ y cual** to talk about one thing and another; **y ~ (y cual)** and so on (and so forth) **III.** *adv* **1.** (*así*) so **2.** (*de la misma manera*) just; **es ~ cual lo buscaba** it's just what I was looking for; **son ~ para cual** they're two of a kind; **estar ~ cual** to be just as it was; **lo dejé ~ cual** I left it just as it was; **~ y como** just as; **~ y como suena** just as I'm telling you **3.** (*cómo*) **¿qué ~ (te va)?** how are things?; **¿qué ~ si tomamos una copa?** why don't we have sth to drink?; **¿qué ~ es tu nuevo jefe?** what's your new boss like?; **~ y como están las cosas** the way things are now **IV.** *conj* **con ~ de** +*infin* **con ~ de que** +*subj* as long as; **~ vez** maybe

tala ['ta·la] *f* felling

taladrar [ta·la·'drar] *vt* to drill; **un ruido que taladra los oídos** an ear-splitting noise

taladro [ta·'la·dro] *m* drill

talante [ta·'lan·te] *m* disposition; (*humor*) mood; **de buen/mal ~** in a good/bad mood; **de buen ~** willingly

talar [ta·'lar] *vt* to fell

talco ['tal·ko] *m* talc; (*polvos*) talcum powder

talento [ta·'len·to] *m* talent; **de gran ~** very talented; **tener ~ para los idiomas** to have a gift for languages

talentoso, -a [ta·len·'to·so, -a] *adj* talented

talero [ta·'le·ro] *m* Arg, Chile, Urug whip

talismán [ta·lis·'man] *m* talisman

talla ['ta·ja, -ʎa] *f* **1.** (*madera*) carving; (*piedra*) sculpting; (*diamante*) cutting **2.** (*estatura*) height; (*moral, intelectual*) stature; **ser de poca ~** to be short; **no dar la ~** not to be good enough **3.** (*de ropa*) size; **un abrigo de la ~ 42** a size 42 coat

tallar [ta·'jar, -'ʎar] *vt* (*diamante*) to cut; (*madera*) to carve; (*piedra*) to sculpt

tallarín [ta·ja·'rin, ta·ʎa-] *m* noodle

talle ['ta·je, -ʎe] *m* waist; (*figura*) figure

taller [ta·'jer, -'ʎer] *m* **1.** workshop; **~ artesanal** craft workshop; **~es gráficos** printing works **2.** ENS seminar **3.** (*auto*) garage

tallo ['ta·jo, -ʎo] *m* stem; (*renuevo*) shoot

talón [ta·'lon] *m* **1.** heel; **pisar a alguien los talones** to be hot on sb's heels **2.** check; **hazme un ~ de 10.000 pesos** make me out a check for 10,000 pesos; **~ sin fondos** bad check **3.** (*resguardo*) voucher; (*recibo*) receipt

tamal [ta·'mal] *m* AmC, Méx tamale

tamalada [ta·ma·'la·da] *f* Méx tamale party

tamango [ta·'man·go] *m* CSur coarse leather shoe

tamaño? [ta·'ma·ɲo] *m* size; **¿de qué ~ es?** what size is it?; **de gran ~** large

tamaño, -a [ta·'ma·ɲo, -a] *adj* **1.** (*grande*) such a big **2.** (*pequeño*) such a small **3.** (*semejante*) such a; **tamaña tontería** such a stupid thing; **~ disparate** such an absurd idea

tambache [tam·'ba·tʃe] *m* Méx *inf* bundle; **un ~ de ropa/hojas** a pile of clothes/papers; **hacer ~ a alguien** to play a dirty trick on sb

tambalear [tam·ba·le·'ar] *vi, vr*: **~se** to stagger; *fig* to totter

tambarria [tam·'ba·rrja] *f* Perú party

también [tam·'bjen] *adv* also, as well, too; **yo lo ví ~** I also saw him, I saw him too [o as well]

tambocha [tam·'bo·tʃa] *f* Col, Ven poisonous red-headed ant

tambor [tam·'bor] *m* drum

tamiz [ta·'mis, -'miθ] *m* sieve

tamizar <z → c> [ta·mi·'sar, -'θar] *vt* to sift

tampoco [tam·'po·ko] *adv* not either, nor, neither; **ni puedo ni ~ quiero** I neither can nor do I want to; **~ me gusta éste** I don't like this one either; **si tú no lo haces yo ~** if you don't do it, neither will I

T

tampón [tam-'pon] *m* tampon

tamuga [ta-'mu-ɣa] *f* **1.** *AmC* (*fardo*) bundle; (*mochila*) knapsack **2.** *AmL* (*marihuana*) joint

tan [tan] *adv* so; **~... como...** as... as...; **de ~ simpático me resulta insoportable** he/she is so nice I find him/her unbearable; **~ siquiera una vez** just once

tanate [ta-'na-te] *m* **1.** *AmC, Méx* (*cesto*) pannier **2.** *AmC* (*fardo*) bundle **3.** *pl AmC* (*cachivaches*) gear, stuff

tanda ['tan-da] *f* **1.** (*turno*) shift; **estar en la ~ de día** to be on the day shift **2.** (*serie*) series *inv*; **por ~s** in batches; **en ~s de ocho** in groups of eight **3.** (*de trabajo, capa*) layer

tanga ['tan-ga] *m* thong

tangente [tan-'xen-te] *f* tangent; **salirse** [*o* **irse**] **por la ~** to go off on a tangent

tangible [tan-'xi-βle] *adj* tangible; *fig* concrete

tango ['tan-go] *m* tango

tano, -a ['ta-no, -a] *adj, m, f Arg, Urug inf* Italian

tanque ['tan-ke] *m* **1.** MIL tank **2.** (*cisterna*) tanker; (*vehículo*) road-tanker **3.** *inf* (*de cerveza*) large glass **4.** *AmL* (*estanque*) pool

tanquear [tan-ke'-ar] *vi Col* to get gas

tantear [tan-te-'ar] *vt* **1.** to calculate; (*a ojo*) to size up; (*tamaño, volumen*) to gauge; (*precio*) to estimate **2.** (*probar*) to try out; (*sondear*) to sound out; **~ el terreno** to get the lay of the land **3.** (*ir a tientas*) to grope; **tuvimos que bajar la escalera tanteando** we had to feel our way down the stairs

tanteo [tan-'te·o] *m* **1.** (*cálculo: cantidad*) calculation; (*de tamaño, volumen*) weighing up; (*a ojo*) sizing up; (*de precio*) estimate; **al** [*o* **por**] **~** by trial and error **2.** (*sondeo*) sounding out **3.** DEP (*de puntos*) score; (*de goles*) scoring; **~ final** final score

tanto ['tan-to] **I.** *m* **1.** (*cantidad*) certain amount; COM rate; **~ por ciento** percentage; **costar otro ~** to cost as much again; **un ~** a bit; **estar un ~ harto de algo** to be rather fed up with sth; **estoy un ~ sorprendido** I'm somewhat sur-

prised **2.** (*punto*) point; (*gol*) goal; **un ~ a favor de alguien** a point in sb's favor ▶ **estar al ~ de algo** to be up to date on sth **II.** *adv* **1.** so much; **no es para ~** there's no need to make such a fuss **2.** (*de duración*) so long; **tu respuesta tardó ~ que...** your answer took so long that... **3.** (*comparativo*) **~ mejor/peor** so much the better/worse; **~ como** as much as; **~ si llueve como si no...** whether it rains or not... ▶ **¡ni ~ ni tan calvo!** neither one extreme nor the other!; **~... como...** both... and...; **en ~ (que +subj)** as long as; **entre ~** meanwhile; **por (lo) ~** therefore; **por lo ~ mejor callar** so best keep quiet

tanto, -a ['tan-to, -a] **I.** *adj* **1.** so much; **tantas posibilidades** so many possibilities; **¡hace ~ tiempo que no te veo!** I haven't seen you for so long!; **~ gusto en conocerle** a pleasure to meet you **2.** (*comparativo*) as much, as many; **no tengo ~ dinero como tú** I don't have as much money as you; **tenemos ~s amigos como ellos** we have as many friends as they do **3.** *pl* **en mil novecientos ochenta y ~s** in nineteen eighty-something; **uno de ~s** one of many; **tener 40 y ~s años** to be 40-odd years old; **a las tantas de la madrugada** in the wee hours of the morning; **quedarse despierto hasta las tantas** to stay up until all hours ▶ **~ tienes, ~ vales** a man's worth is the worth of his land **II.** *pron dem* **~s** as many; **coge ~s como quieras** take as many as you like; **no llego a ~** I won't go that far

tapa ['ta-pa] *f* **1.** lid; **~ de rosca** screw-top; **de ~s duras** hardback **2.** (*de zapato*) heelpiece **3.** CULIN appetizer; **una ~ de aceitunas** a side of olives; **~ de ternera** round of beef

tapado [ta-'pa·do] *m Arg* coat

tapar [ta-'par] **I.** *vt* **1.** to cover; (*olla*) to put a lid on; (*manta*) to cover up; (*desagüe*) to obstruct; (*agujero*) to fill in; (*botella*) to put the cap on **2.** (*ocultar*) to hide; **¿te tapo?** am I blocking your view?; **la pared nos tapa el viento** the wall protects us from the wind **II.** *vr:* **~se** (*con ropa*) to wrap up; (*con* *mantas*) to cover up; (*completamente*) to hide; (*oídos, nariz*) to get blocked; **~se la cara/los ojos** to cover one's face/eyes

taparrabo(s) [ta·pa·'rra·βo(s)] *m (inv)* loincloth

tape ['ta·pe] *m* 1. *Arg, Urug* Indian-looking person 2. *Cuba, PRico* (*tapa*) lid 3. *RíoPl* (*cinta*) tape

tapeo [ta·'peo] *m* **ir de ~** to go bar-hopping

tapia ['ta·pja] *f* wall; (*de jardín*) garden wall; **estar más sordo que una ~** to be as deaf as a doorknob

tapicería [ta·pi·se·'ri·a, ta·pi·θe-] *f* 1. (*tapices*) tapestries *pl* 2. (*tienda: de tapices*) tapestry shop; (*de muebles*) upholstery; (*taller*) upholsterer's

tapisca [ta·'pis·ka] *f AmC* corn harvest

tapiz [ta·'pis, -'piθ] *m* tapestry; (*en el suelo*) rug

tapizar <z → c> [ta·pi·'sar, -'θar] *vt* to upholster; (*acolchar*) to quilt

tapón [ta·'pon] *m* 1. stopper; (*de fregadero*) drain plug; (*corcho*) cork; AUTO oil drain plug 2. *inf* short stubby person 3. MED tampon; (*para el oído*) earplug 4. (*de tráfico*) traffic jam

taponar [ta·po·'nar] *vt* to plug; (*corcho*) to cork; (*plástico*) to seal; (*desagüe*) to clog

tapujo [ta·'pu·xo] *m* **andar con ~s** to behave deceitfully; **no andarse con ~s** to speak plainly

taquear [ta·ke·'ar] *AmL* I. *vi* 1. *inf* (*jugar*) to shoot pool 2. (*arma*) to ram 3. (*llenar*) to stuff II. *vr:* **~se** to tap one's heels

taquería [ta·ke·'ri·a] *f* 1. *Cuba* uninhabitedness 2. *Méx* taco stand

taquicardia [ta·ki·'kar·dja] *f* tachycardia

taquilla [ta·'ki·ja, -ʎa] *f* 1. TEAT, CINE box office; DEP gate money; FERRO ticket window; **éxito de ~** box-office hit 2. (*recaudación*) receipts *pl*

tara ['ta·ra] *f* defect; (*peso*) tare

tarado, -a [ta·'ra·do, -a] I. *adj* crazy II. *m, f* nitwit

tarantín <tarantines> [ta·ran·'tin] *m* 1. *Ven* (*tenducha*) stall 2. *pl AmC, Cuba, PRico* (*cachivaches*) odds and

ends *pl*

tarántula [ta·'ran·tu·la] *f* tarantula

tararear [ta·ra·re·'ar] *vt* to la-la-la; (*con labios cerrados*) to hum

tarascón [ta·ras·'kon] *m AmS* bite; (*herida*) bite wound

tardanza [tar·'dan·sa, -θa] *f* delay; **perdona la ~ en escribirte** forgive me for taking so long to write

tardar [tar·'dar] *vi* to take time; **~ en llegar** to take a long time to arrive; **~on tres semanas en contestar** it took them three weeks to answer; **~on mucho en arreglarlo** it took them a long time to fix it; **no tardo nada** I won't be long; **no ~é en volver** I'll be right back; **¡no tardes!** don't be gone long!; **a más ~** at the latest

tarde ['tar·de] I. *f* (*sobremesa*) afternoon; (*tarde-noche*) evening; **por la ~** in the afternoon; **¡buenas ~s!** good afternoon!, good evening!; **los viernes por la ~** Friday evenings II. *adv* late; **~ o temprano** sooner or later; **de ~ en ~** now and then; **se me hace ~** it's getting late ▶ **más vale ~ que nunca** better late than never

tardío, -a [tar·'di·o, -a] *adj* late; (*lento*) slow; **un consejo ~** a belated piece of advice

tarea [ta·'rea] *f* task; (*trabajo*) job; ENS homework; **¿has hecho tus ~s?** have you done your homework?; **~s de la casa** housework

tareco [ta·'re·ko] *m Cuba, Ecua, Ven* 1. (*herramienta*) tool of trade 2. (*trasto*) old thing

tarifa [ta·'ri·fa] *f* rate; (*transporte*) fare

tarima [ta·'ri·ma] *f* platform

tarja ['tar·xa] *f AmL* business card

tarjeta [tar·'xe·ta] *f* 1. card; **~ de crédito/visita/gráficos** credit/calling/graphics card; **~ de embarque** boarding pass; **~ postal** postcard 2. COMPUT **~ de memoria** memory chip

tarro ['ta·rro] *m* 1. pot; (*cristal*) jar; (*metal*) tin 2. *inf* head; **comer el ~ a alguien** to brainwash sb; **¿estás mal del ~?** are you crazy?

tarta ['tar·ta] *f* cake; (*pastel*) pie

tartamudear [tar·ta·mu·de·'ar] *vi* to stutter

tartamudo, -a [tar·ta·'mu·do, -a] I. *adj* stuttering II. *m, f* stutterer

tasa ['ta·sa] *f* 1. (*valoración*) valuation 2. (*precio, derechos*) fee; (*impuesto*) tax 3. (*porcentaje*) rate; ~ **de desempleo/ interés/natalidad** unemployment/interest/birth rate

tasajear [ta·sa·xe·'ar] *vt AmL* to cut; (*carne*) to jerk

tasar [ta·'sar] *vt* 1. (*precio*) to fix the price of; (*impuesto*) to tax 2. (*valorar*) to value; ~ **en exceso** to overrate

tasca ['tas·ka] *f* bar

tata ['ta·ta] *m AmL* daddy

tatarabuelo, -a [ta·ta·ra·'βwe·lo, -a] *m, f* great-great-grandfather

tataranieto, -a [ta·ta·ra·'nje·to, -a] *m, f* great-great-grandson

tatuaje [ta·tu·'a·xe] *m* tattoo

tatuar <*1. pres* tatúo> [ta·tu·'ar] *vt* to tattoo

tauca ['tau·ka] *f* 1. *Bol, Chile, Ecua* heap; **una ~ de papeles** a pile of papers 2. *Chile* sack

taurino, -a [tau·'ri·no, -a] *adj* bull-like; (*del toreo*) bullfighting

Tauro ['tau·ro] *m* Taurus

taxi ['tak·si] *m* taxi

taxista [tak·'sis·ta] *mf* taxi driver

taza ['ta·sa, -θa] *f* cup; (*grande*) mug; **una ~ de café** a coffee cup; (*con café*) a cup of coffee; (*del wáter*) bowl; (*de fuente*) basin

te [te] I. *pron pers* you; ¡**míra~!** look at yourself! II. *pron reflexivo* — **vistes** you get dressed; ~ **levantas** you get up; **no ~ hagas daño** don't hurt yourself

té [te] *m* tea

teatral [tea·'tral] *adj* theatre; (*efecto, experiencia, autor*) stage; *fig* theatrical

teatro [te·'a·tro] *m* theater; (*escenario*) stage; **obra de ~** play; **hacer ~** to work in the theater; *fig* to playact; (*exagerar*) to exaggerate

techar [te·'tʃar] *vt* to roof

techo ['te·tʃo] *m* ceiling; (*tejado*) roof; **vivir bajo el mismo ~** to live under the same roof

tecla ['te·kla] *f* key; ~ **de mayúsculas/ retroceso/intro** shift/backspace/enter key; **pulsar una ~** to press a key

teclado [te·'kla·do] *m* keyboard

teclear [te·kle·'ar] *vi* (*piano*) to play; (*ordenador*) to type; (*dedos*) to drum

técnica [tek·ni·ka] *f* technique; (*tecnología*) technology

tecnicismo [tek·ni·'sis·mo, -θis·mo] *m* technicality; (*término*) technical term

técnico, -a [tek·ni·ko, -a] I. *adj* technical II. *m, f* specialist; TÉC technician; DEP trainer; ~ **de inserción laboral** employment services assistant

tecnología [tek·no·lo·'xi·a] *f* technology; (*técnica*) technique; ~ **punta** leading-edge technology

tecnológico, -a [tek·no·'lo·xi·ko, -a] *adj* technological; (*técnico*) technical; **parque ~** technology park

tecolote [te·ko·'lo·te] *m AmC, Méx* owl

tedioso, -a [te·'djo·so, -a] *adj* tedious

teja ['te·xa] *f* roof tile

tejado [te·'xa·do] *m* roof; **empezar la casa por el ~** to put the cart before the horse

tejano, -a [te·'xa·no] *adj, m, f* Texan; ~**s** jeans

te(j)aván [te·xa·'βan] *m AmL* 1. (*cobertizo*) shed 2. (*corredor*) corridor 3. (*alero*) eaves *pl* 4. (*casa*) rustic house with tiled roof

tejemaneje [te·xe·ma·'ne·xe] *m inf* 1. (*actividad*) to-do; **traerse un ~ increíble con los papeles** to make such a fuss with the papers 2. (*intriga*) scheming; **se deben de traer algún ~** they must be up to sth

tejer [te·'xer] *vt* to knit; (*en un telar*) to weave; (*araña*) to spin; (*cesto, trenza*) to plait; (*plan*) to plot

tejido [te·'xi·do] *m* tissue; (*tela*) fabric; **los ~s** textiles *pl*

tela ['te·la] *f* 1. fabric; ~ **de araña** spider web; ~ **metálica** wire screen; ~ **de punto** knit; **lo cubrieron con una ~ blanca** they covered it with a white cloth 2. *inf* matter; **hay ~ para rato** (*para discutir*) there's plenty to talk about; (*para trabajar*) there's a lot to be done; **este problema tiene ~** this isn't an easy problem 3. *inf* (*dinero*) dough ▸ **poner algo en ~ de juicio** (*dudar*) to question sth; (*tener reparos*) to raise objections about sth

telar [te·'lar] *m* loom

telaraña [te·la·'ra·ɲa] *f* spiderweb; **tener ~s en los ojos** *fig* to be blind to what is going on

tele ['te·le] *f inf abr de* **televisión** TV; **ver la ~** to watch TV

teleadicto, -a [te·le·a·'dik·to, -a] *adj inf* couch potato

telecabina [te·le·ka·'βi·na] *f* cable car

telecomedia [te·le·ko·'me·dja] *f* sitcom

telecompra [te·le·'kom·pra] *f* teleshopping

telecomunicación [te·le·ko·mu·ni·ka·'sjon, -'θjon] *f* telecommunication; **ingeniero de Telecomunicaciones** telecommunications engineer

telediario [te·le·di·'a·rjo] *m* TV news; **el ~ de las tres** the 3 o'clock news

teleférico [te·le·'fe·ri·ko] *m* cable car

telefonazo [te·le·fo·'na·so, -θo] *m inf* ring; **dar un ~ a alguien** to give sb a ring

telefonía [te·le·fo·'ni·a] *f* telephony

telefónico, -a [te·le·'fo·ni·ko, -a] *adj (de teléfono)* telephone; *(de telefonía)* telephonic; **cabina/guía/llamada telefónica** phone booth/book/call

teléfono [te·'le·fo·no] *m* 1. telephone; **~ móvil/público/de tarjeta** cell/public/card phone; **~ rojo** hotline; **(número de) ~** phone number; **por ~** over the phone; **hablar por ~** to talk on the phone; **llamar por ~** to telephone 2. *pl* telephone company

telegrafiar <3. pret telegrafió> [te·le·ɣra·fi·'ar] *vi, vt* to telegraph

telegrama [te·le·'ɣra·ma] *m* telegram

telenovela [te·le·no·'βe·la] *f* soap opera

telenque [te·'len·ke] **I.** *adj* 1. *Chile (temblón)* shaking; *(enfermizo)* sickly 2. *ElSal (torcido)* crooked **II.** *m Guat (cachivache)* junk

teleobjetivo [te·le·oβ·xe·'ti·βo] *m* telephoto lens

telepatía [te·le·pa·'ti·a] *f* telepathy

telepático, -a [te·le·'pa·ti·ko, -a] *adj* telepathic

telescópico, -a [te·les·'ko·pi·ko, -a] *adj* telescopic

telescopio [te·les·'ko·pjo] *m* telescope

telespectador(a) [te·les·pek·ta·'dor, -·'do·ra] *m(f)* TV viewer

televidente [te·le·βi·'den·te] *mf v.* **telespectador**

televisar [te·le·βi·'sar] *vt* to broadcast; *(en directo)* to televise live

televisión [te·le·βi·'sjon] *f* television; **~ digital** digital television; **~ de pago** pay-television; **~ en color** color TV

televisor [te·le·βi·'sor] *m* television set

telón [te·'lon] *m* curtain

tema ['te·ma] *m* theme; **cada loco con su ~** to each his own; **alejarse del ~** to stray from the issue; **~s de actualidad** current issues

temario [te·'ma·rjo] *m* program; *(para examen)* list of topics

temática [te·'ma·ti·ka] *f* subjects *pl*

temblar <e → ie> [tem·'blar] *vi* to tremble; **~ de miedo** to tremble with fear; **~ de frío** to shiver (with cold); **~ de pensarlo** to shudder just to think of it; **~ como un flan** to shake like a leaf

tembleque [tem·'ble·ke] *m inf* shaking; **me dio un ~** I got the shakes

temblor [tem·'blor] *m* tremor; *(escalofrío)* shiver; **~ de frío** shivers; **~ (de tierra)** earthquake

tembloroso, -a [tem·blo·'ro·so] *adj* shaky

temer [te·'mer] **I.** *vt* to fear; *(sospechar)* to be afraid **II.** *vi* to be afraid; **~ por alguien** to fear for sb **III.** *vr:* **~se** to be afraid; **me temo que sí/no** I'm afraid so/not

temeroso, -a [te·me·'ro·so, -a] *adj* fearful; **~ de que...** *+subj* fearful that...

temible [te·'mi·βle] *adj* fearsome

temor [te·'mor] *m* fear; *(sospecha)* suspicion; **por ~ a** for fear of

témpano ['tem·pa·no] *m* ice floe; **quedarse como un ~** to be chilled to the bone; **él es como un ~** he is as cold as stone

temperamental [tem·pe·ra·men·'tal] *adj* temperamental; *(persona)* spirited

temperamento [tem·pe·ra·'men·to] *m* temperament; **tener mucho ~** to have a strong character

temperante [tem·pe·'ran·te] **I.** *adj AmS* abstemious **II.** *mf AmS* teetotaler

temperatura [tem·pe·ra·'tu·ra] *f* tem-

T

perature; (*fiebre*) fever

tempestad [tem·pes·'tad] *f* storm; (*marejada*) gale; (*agitación*) turmoil

templado, -a [tem·'pla·do, -a] *adj* lukewarm; (*moderado*) moderate

templar [tem·'plar] **I.** *vt* **1.** (*moderar*) to moderate **2.** (*calentar*) to warm up **II.** *vr*: **~se 1.** (*moderarse*) to control oneself **2.** (*calentarse*) to get warm **3.** *AmL* (*enamorarse*) to fall in love **4.** *Col, Perú* (*emborracharse*) to get drunk

temple ['tem·ple] *m* **1.** courage; **estar de buen/mal ~** to be in a good/bad mood **2.** (*acero*) temper; (*proceso*) tempering **3.** ARTE tempera

templo ['tem·plo] *m* temple; **una verdad como un ~** the naked truth

temporada [tem·po·'ra·da] *f* season; (*época*) period; **~ alta/baja** high/low season; **fruta de ~** seasonal fruit; **están pasando por una ~ difícil** they're going through a difficult period

temporal [tem·po·'ral] **I.** *adj* temporal; (*no permanente*) temporary; **contrato ~** temporary contract **II.** *m* storm; (*marejada*) stormy seas *pl*

temporario, -a [tem·po·'ra·rjo, -a] *adj AmL* temporary

temprano [tem·'pra·no] *adv* early; **llegar (demasiado) ~** to arrive (too) early

temprano, -a [tem·'pra·no, -a] *adj* early; **a edad temprana** at an early age

tenacidad [te·na·si·'dad, te·na·θi-] *f* tenacity

tenaz [te·'nas, -'naθ] *adj* tenacious; (*resistente*) resistant

tenaza(s) [te·'na·sa(s), -θa(s)] *f(pl)* pliers *pl*

tencha ['ten·tʃa] *f Guat* jail

tendajón [ten·da·'xon] *m Méx* small shop

tendear [ten·de·'ar] *vi Méx* to window-shop

tendencia [ten·'den·sja, -θja] *f* tendency; **tener ~ a fazer algo** to have a tendency to to sth; **~ a algo** trend toward sth; **~ al alza/a la baja** upward/downward trend; **las últimas ~s de la moda** the latest fashion trends

tender <e → ie> [ten·'der] **I.** *vt* **1.** (*ropa*)

to hang out; (*cuerda*) to stretch **2.** (*tumbar*) to lay; (*de golpe*) to throw down **3. ~ sobre algo** to spread over sth; **~ la cama/mesa** *AmL* to make the bed/to lay the table **4.** (*aproximar*) to hold out; **~ la mano a alguien** *fig* to give sb a hand **II.** *vi* to tend; MAT to tend toward; **tiendo a ser optimista** I more of an optimistic type **III.** *vr*: **~se** to stretch out

tendido [ten·'di·do] *m* **1.** (*de un cable*) laying; (*cables*) wiring **2.** *AmL* (*sábanas*) bed linen

tendón [ten·'don] *m* tendon

tenebroso, -a [te·ne·'βro·so, -a] *adj* dark; (*tétrico*) gloomy

tenedor [te·ne·'dor] *m* fork

tenedor(a) [te·ne·'dor, --'do·ra] *m(f)* holder; **~ de tierras** landowner

tenencia [te·'nen·sja, -θja] *f* possession; **~ ilícita de armas** illegal possession of arms

tener [te·'ner] *irr* **I.** *vt* **1.** to have; **~ los ojos azules** to have blue eyes; **~ 29 años** to be 29 years old; **~ hambre/sed/calor/sueño** to be hungry/thirsty/hot/sleepy; **~ poco de tonto** to be no fool; **¿(con que) ésas tenemos?** so that's the way it is?; **~la tomada con alguien** *inf* to have it in for sb; **no ~las todas consigo** not to be sure of something; **no ~ nada que perder** to have nothing to lose; **no ~ precio** to be priceless; **~ cariño a alguien** to be fond of sb; **~ la culpa de algo** to be to blame for sth; **¿tienes frío?** are you cold?; **le tengo lástima** I feel sorry for him/her; **el frasco ya no tiene miel** there's no honey left in the jar; **~ un niño** to have a baby **2.** (*considerar*) to consider; **~ por algo** to consider sth; **~ a alguien en menos/mucho** to think all the less/more of sb; **ten por seguro que...** rest assured that...; **tengo para mí que...** I think that... **3.** (*coger*) to take; **ten esto** take this; (*sujetar*) to hold; **~ a alguien por el brazo** to hold sb by the arm **4.** (*hacer sentir*) **me tienes preocupado** I'm worried about you; **me tienes loca** you're driving me mad! **II.** *vr*: **~se 1. ~se por algo** to consider oneself sth; **~se en mucho** to think highly of oneself

2. (*sostenerse*) to stand; **~se de pie** to stand; **~se firme** to stand upright; *fig* to stand firm; **estoy que no me tengo** I'm exhausted **3.** (*dominarse*) to control oneself **4.** (*atenerse*) to adhere **III. aux 1.** (+ *participio*) **~ pensado hacer algo** to plan to do sth; **ya tengo comprado todo** I've bought everything already; **~se algo callado** to keep quiet about sth; **ya me lo tenía pensado** I had already thought of that **2. ~ que** to have to; **~ mucho que hacer** to have a lot to do; **¿qué tiene que ver esto conmigo?** what does this have to do with me?

tenida [te·'ni·da] *f* Chile meeting; (*traje*) suit; (*uniforme*) uniform

teniente [te·'njen·te] *m* lieutenant; **~ coronel** lieutenant-colonel

tenis ['te·nis] *m* tennis; **~ de mesa** table tennis

tenor [te·'nor] *m* tenor; **a ~ de** according to

tensar [ten·'sar] *vt* (*músculo*) to tense; (*cuerda*) to tighten

tensión [ten·'sjon] *f* **1.** stress; (*impaciencia*) anxiety; (*cuerda, piel*) tautness; (*nervios, músculos*) tension; **película de ~** thriller; **estar en ~** (*nervioso*) to be nervous; (*impaciente*) to be anxious **2.** Fís tension **3. ~ arterial** blood pressure **4.** ELEC voltage **5.** *pl* strained relations *pl*

tenso, -a ['ten·so, -a] *adj* tense; (*cuerda, piel*) taut; (*impaciente*) anxious

tentación [ten·ta·'sjon, -'θjon] *f* temptation; **me dan tentaciones de...** I'm tempted to...; **caer en la ~** to give in to the temptation

tentáculo [ten·'ta·ku·lo] *m* tentacle

tentar [ten·'tar] *vt* **1.** (*palpar*) to feel **2.** (*atraer*) to tempt; (*seducir*) to entice

tentativa [ten·ta·'ti·βa] *f* attempt; **~ de robo** attempted robbery

tenue ['te·nwe] *adj* delicate; (*sutil*) subtle; (*débil*) weak; (*luz*) faint

teñir [te·'ɲir] *irr como ceñir vt, vr:* **~se** to dye; **~(se) de rojo** to dye red; **~ de tristeza** to tinge with sadness

teología [teo·lo·'xi·a] *f* theology

teólogo, -a [te·'o·lo·γo, -a] **I.** *adj* theo-

logical **II.** *m, f* theologian

teorema [teo·'re·ma] *m* theorem

teoría [teo·'ri·a] *f* theory; **en ~** in theory

teórico, -a [te·'o·ri·ko, -a] *adj* theoretical

tepache [te·'pa·tʃe] *m Méx* tepache (*drink made of fermented agave cactus juice, water, pineapple and cloves*)

tequesquite [te·kes·'ki·te] *m Méx* rock salt

tequiche [te·'ki·tʃe] *m Ven* dish made with toasted corn, coconut milk and butter

tequila [te·'ki·la] *m* tequila

tequio ['te·kjo] *m AmC, Méx* (*molestia*) bother; (*daño*) harm

tequioso, -a [te·'kjo·so, -a] *adj AmC* **1.** (*travieso*) mischievous; (*niño*) trying **2.** (*molesto*) bothersome

terapeuta [te·ra·'peu·ta] *mf* therapist

terapia [te·'ra·pja] *f* therapy; **~ en** [*o de*] **grupo** group therapy

tercer [ter·'ser, -'θer] *adj v.* **tercero**

tercermundista [ter·ser·mun·'dis·ta, ter·θer-] *adj* third-world

Tercer Mundo [ter·'ser 'mun·do, -'θer] *m* Third World

tercero [ter·'se·ro, ter·'θe·-] **I.** *m* third party **II.** *adv* third

tercero, -a [ter·'se·ro, -a; ter·'θe·-] **I.** *adj* (+ *subst m: tercer*) third; **terceras personas** third parties; **en tercer lugar** thirdly; **viven en el ~** they live on the third floor; **tercera edad** retirement years ▸ **a la tercera va la vencida** third time lucky **II.** *m, f* third; *v. t.* **octavo**

terciar [ter·'sjar, -'θjar] **I.** *vt AmL* to water down **II.** *vi* to intervene; (*participar*) to take part **III.** *vr, vimpers:* **~se** to arise; **si se tercia** should the occasion arise

tercio ['ter·sjo, -θjo] *m* **1.** third; *v. t.* **octavo 2.** (*cerveza*) 1/3 liter bottle

terciopelo [ter·sjo·'pe·lo, ter·θjo-] *m* velvet

terco, -a ['ter·ko, -a] *adj* stubborn; (*niño*) unruly; (*animal*) balky; (*cosa*) tough

tereque [te·'re·ke] *m Col, RDom, PRico, Ven* utensil

tergiversar [ter·xi·βer·'sar] *vt* to misrepresent; (*verdad*) to distort

termas ['ter·mas] *fpl* hot baths *pl*

térmico, -a ['ter·mi·ko, -a] *adj* thermal; **central térmica** thermal power plant

terminación [ter·mi·na·'sjon, -'θjon] *f* termination; (*proyecto*) completion; (*final*) end

terminal [ter·mi·'nal] **I.** *adj* terminal; **enfermo ~** terminally ill patient **II.** *m* COMPUT terminal **III.** *f* terminal; **~ aérea** air terminal; FERRO station

terminar [ter·mi·'nar] **I.** *vt* to finish; (*proyecto*) to complete; **¿cuándo terminas?** when will you be done?; (*consumir*) to finish up; (*beber*) to drink up; (*comer*) to eat up **II.** *vi* **1.** (*tener fin*) to finish; (*plazo, contrato*) to end; **~ bien/mal** to have a happy/an unhappy ending; **~ en punta** to end in a point; (*haber hecho*) **~ de hacer algo** to finish doing sth; (*haber hecho*) to have just done sth; **~ por hacer algo** to end up doing sth; **la escuela termina a las dos** school is out at 2 pm; **el tabaco va a ~ contigo** tobacco is going to be the end of you! **2.** (*estar acabando*) to be ending; **ya termina la película** the film is almost over **3.** (*poner fin*) to put an end to **III.** *vr:* **~se 1.** (*estar acabando*) to be almost over **2.** (*no haber más*) to be no more; **se terminaron las galletas** there aren't any more biscuits (left); **se me está terminando la paciencia** I'm running out of patience

término ['ter·mi·no] *m* **1.** (*fin*) end; **dar ~ a algo** to finish sth off; **llevar a ~** to carry out; **poner ~ a algo** to put an end to sth; **en el ~ de quince días** within 15 days **2.** (*linde*) boundary **3.** ADMIN district; **~ municipal** township **4.** LING, MAT term; **en buenos/malos ~s** on good terms/rudely; **en otros ~s** in other words **5.** *pl* (*de un contrato*) terms *pl* ▶ **estar en buenos/malos ~s** to be on good/bad terms; **en ~s generales** generally speaking; **~ medio** compromise; **en primer ~** first of all; **en último ~** as a last resort; **por ~ medio** on the average

terminología [ter·mi·no·lo·'xi·a] *f* terminology

termita [ter·'mi·ta] *f* termite

termo ['ter·mo] *m* thermos

termómetro [ter·'mo·me·tro] *m* thermometer

termostato [ter·mos·'ta·to] *m*, **termóstato** [ter·'mos·ta·to] *m* thermostat

ternejo, -a [ter·'ne·xo, -a] *adj Ecua, Perú* lively

ternera [ter·'ne·ra] *f* beef

ternero, -a [ter·'ne·ro, -a] *m, f* calf

ternura [ter·'nu·ra] *f* **1.** tenderness; (*dulzura*) sweetness; (*delicadeza*) gentleness **2.** *Chile, Ecua, Guat* (*inmadurez*) greenness

terquedad [ter·ke·'dad] *f* obstinacy

terraplén [te·rra·'plen] *m* slope

terráqueo, -a [te·'rra·keo, -a] *adj* earth; **globo ~** globe

terrateniente [te·rra·te·'njen·te] *mf* landowner

terraza [te·'rra·sa, -θa] *f* terrace; (*azotea*) flat roof

terregal [te·rre·'ɣal] *m Méx* loose topsoil

terremoto [te·rre·'mo·to] *m* earthquake

terrenal [te·rre·'nal] *adj* worldly

terreno [te·'rre·no] *m* land; GEO terrain; (*espacio*) lot; (*parcela*) plot of land; DEP playing field; **~ edificable** buildable land; **vehículo todo ~** all-terrain vehicle; *fig* sphere; **~ desconocido** unfamiliar territory; **en su propio ~** on one's own ground ▶ **ceder/ganar/ perder ~** to give up/gain/lose ground; **explorar el ~** to see how the land lies; **preparar el ~ para algo** to pave the way for sth

terrestre [te·'rres·tre] **I.** *adj* **1.** (*de la Tierra*) terrestrial **2.** (*en la tierra*) earthly; **animal ~** land animal; **transporte ~** ground transport **3.** (*terrenal*) earthly **II.** *mf* terrestrial

terrible [te·'rri·βle] *adj* terrible; **hace un frío ~** it's terribly cold

territorial [te·rri·to·'rjal] *adj* territorial

territorio [te·rri·'to·rjo] *m t.* ZOOL territory; POL region; JUR district; **en todo el ~ nacional** nationwide

terror [te·'rror] *m* terror; **película de ~** horror film; **las arañas me dan ~** I'm terrified of spiders

terrorismo [te·rro·'ris·mo] *m* terrorism

terrorista [te·rro·'ris·ta] *adj, mf* terrorist

terso, -a ['ter·so, -a] *adj* smooth

tertulia [ter·'tu·lja] *f* gathering; **estar**

de ~ to talk

tesis [ˈte·sis] *f inv* theory; EDUC, FILOS thesis

tesón [te·ˈson] *m* tenacity; **con ~** diligently

tesonero, -a [te·so·ˈne·ro, -a] *adj AmL* persevering; (*tenaz*) tenacious

tesorería [te·so·re·ˈri·a] *f* treasury; (*despacho*) treasurer's office

tesoro [te·ˈso·ro] *m* treasure; **~ (público)** (public) treasury; **sí, ~** yes, darling

testamento [tes·ta·ˈmen·to] *m* will; **hacer ~** to make one's will

testar [tes·ˈtar] *vi* to make a will

testículo [tes·ˈti·ku·lo] *m* testicle

testificar [c → qu] [tes·ti·fi·ˈkar] **I.** *vt* **1.** (*declarar*) to testify; (*documento*) to bear witness **2.** (*demostrar*) to give evidence **II.** *vi* to testify

testigo [tes·ˈti·ɣo] **I.** *mf* witness; **~ ocular** eyewitness; **ser ~ de algo** to witness sth; **poner a alguien por ~** to cite sb as witness **II.** *m* baton

testimonial [tes·ti·mo·ˈnjal] *adj* attesting; (*que prueba*) evidentiary

testimoniar [tes·ti·mo·ˈnjar] **I.** *vt* **1.** (*declarar*) to testify **2.** (*afirmar*) to attest **3.** (*probar*) to evidence **II.** *vi* to bear witness

testimonio [tes·ti·ˈmo·njo] *m* **1.** (*declaración*) testimony; (*afirmación*) statement; **dar ~** to bear witness **2.** (*prueba*) evidence

testosterona [tes·tos·te·ˈro·na] *m* testosterone

teta [ˈte·ta] *f inf* breast; (*ubre*) udder; **dar la ~** to breast-feed

tétano(s) [ˈte·ta·no(s)] *m (inv)* tetanus

tetera [te·ˈte·ra] *f* **1.** teapot; (*para hervir*) kettle **2.** *AmL* (*pezón*) nipple **3.** *AmL v.* **tetero**

tetero [te·ˈte·ro] *m AmL* baby's bottle

tétrico, -a [ˈte·tri·ko, -a] *adj* dismal

textil [tes·ˈtil] *adj, m* textile

texto [ˈtes·to] *m* text; (*pasaje*) extract; **libro de ~** textbook

textual [tes·tu·ˈal] *adj* textual; (*literal*) word-for-word; **con las palabras ~es** with those exact words

textura [tes·ˈtu·ra] *f* structure; (*tejido*) weave; GEO, QUÍM texture

tez [tes, teθ] *f* complexion; **de ~ morena** dark

ti [ti] *pron pers* **a ~** you; **de ~** from you; **para/por ~** for you

tianguis [ˈtjan·gis] *m inv Méx* street market

tibia [ˈti·βja] *f* tibia

tibiarse [ti·ˈβjar·se] *vr AmC, Ven* to get cross

tibiera [ti·ˈβje·ra] *f Ven* (*molestia*) irritation; (*fastidio*) nuisance

tibio, -a [ˈti·βjo, -a] *adj* **1.** lukewarm **2.** *AmL inf* angry ▶ **poner ~ a alguien** to lay in to sb

tibor [ti·ˈβor] *m AmL* chamber pot

tiburón [ti·βu·ˈron] *m* shark

tico, -a [ˈti·ko, -a] *adj, m, f AmL inf* Costa Rican

tiempo [ˈtjem·po] *m* **1.** time; **~ libre/de ocio** spare/leisure time; **al poco ~** shortly after; **los buenos ~s** the good old days; **a ~** in time; **con ~** in good time; **a ~ parcial** part-time; **todo a su ~** all in good time; **al (mismo) ~** [*o* **a un ~**] at the same time; **al ~ que** while; **antes de ~** early; **desde hace mucho ~** for a long time; **en estos ~s** nowadays; **en mis ~s** in my time; **en otros ~s** in the past; **dar ~ a ~** to give it time; **hace ~ que...** it's a long time since...; **¡cuánto ~ sin verte!** long time no see!; **matar el/hacer ~** to kill time; **perder el ~** to waste time; **sin perder ~** losing no time; **si me da ~** if I have enough time **2.** METEO weather; **hoy hace mal ~** the weather is bad today **3.** LING tense **4.** DEP (*medio*) ~ half-time; **~ muerto** time out **5.** TÉC stroke; **motor de dos ~s** two-stroke engine ▶ **a(l) mal ~ buena cara** you have to look on the bright side of things; **el ~ es oro** time is money; **el ~ no perdona** time and tide wait for no man

tienda [ˈtjen·da] *f* **1.** shop, store; **ir de ~s** to go shopping **2.** ~ **(de campaña)** tent; **montar/desmontar una ~** to put up/take down a tent

tiento [ˈtjen·to] *m* **a ~** gropingly; **con ~** carefully

tierno, -a [ˈtjer·no, -a] **I.** *adj* **1.** tender; (*blando*) soft; (*pan, dulces*) fresh; (*cari-*

ñoso) affectionate **2.** *Chile, Ecua, Guat* (*inmaduro*) green **II.** *m, f Guat, Nic* newborn

tierra ['tje·rra] *f* **1.** earth; **~ de nadie** no-man's-land; **~s altas/bajas** highlands/lowlands; **echar por ~** *fig* to ruin **2.** (*firme*) mainland; **~ adentro** inland; **quedarse en ~** to be left behind **3.** (*región*) land; **Tierra Santa** Holy Land; **~** (*natal*) native land **4.** (*hacienda*) property

tierral [tje·'rral] *m AmL* cloud of dust

tieso, -a ['tje·so, -a] *adj* (*rígido*) stiff; (*erguido*) erect; **dejar ~ a alguien** *inf* (*matar*) to bump sb off; (*sorprender*) to dumbfound; **quedarse ~** (*frío*) to be frozen stiff; (*miedo*) to be scared stiff; (*morirse*) to croak

tiesto ['tjes·to] *m* **1.** flowerpot **2.** *Chile* pot

tifón [ti·'fon] *m* typhoon

tifus ['ti·fus] *m inv* typhus

tigre ['ti·γre] *m* tiger; *AmL* jaguar; *And* (*café*) black coffee with a dash of milk; **oler a ~** to stink

tigresa [ti·'γre·sa] *m* tigress; *AmL* jaguar

tijeras [ti·'xe·ras] *f* scissors *pl*; (*grandes*) shears *pl*

tilde ['til·de] *f* accent; (*de la ñ*) tilde

tiliches [ti·'li·tʃes] *mpl AmC, Méx* junk

tilingo, -a [ti·'lin·go, -a] *adj* **1.** *CSur, Méx* (*atolondrado*) silly **2.** *Arg* (*demente*) soft in the head

timar [ti·'mar] *vt* to con

timba ['tim·ba] *f AmL* belly

timbre ['tim·bre] *m* **1.** bell; (*de la puerta*) doorbell; **han tocado el ~** somebody rang the bell **2.** (*sonido*) timbre **3.** (*sello*) stamp

timidez [ti·mi·'des, -'deθ] *f* shyness

tímido, -a ['ti·mi·do, -a] *adj* shy

timón [ti·'mon] *m* rudder

tímpano ['tim·pa·no] *m* eardrum

tina ['ti·na] *f* vat; *AmL* bathtub

tincanque [tin·'kan·ke] *m Chile inf* flip, flick

tincar <c → qu> [tin·'kar] *vt* **1.** *Chile* (*presentir*) to have a hunch **2.** *Arg, Chile* (*pelota*) to drive

tincazo [tin·'ka·so] *m Arg, Ecua inf* flick

tinga ['tin·ga] *f Méx* uproar

tingo ['tin·go] *Méx* **del ~ al tango** from pillar to post

tiniebla [ti·'nje·βla] *f* darkness

tino ['ti·no] *m* aim; (*destreza*) skill; **a buen ~** by guesswork; **sin ~** recklessly

tinoso, -a [ti·'no·so, -a] *adj Col, Ven* (*hábil*) skillful; (*sensato*) sensible

tinta ['tin·ta] *f* ink; **~ china** Indian ink; **sobre este asunto han corrido ríos de ~** much has been written about this matter; **medias ~s** half-tones; *fig* half measures

tinte ['tin·te] *m* **1.** (*teñidura*) dye **2.** (*colorante*) coloring **3.** (*matiz*) tinge

tinterillo [tin·te·'ri·jo, -ʎo] *m AmL pey inf* shyster

tintero [tin·'te·ro] *m* inkwell; **dejar(se) algo en el ~** to leave sth unsaid

tinto, -a ['tin·to, -a] *adj* dark red; (*uvas, vino*) red

tintorería [tin·to·re·'ri·a] *f* dry cleaner's

tío, -a ['ti·o, -a] *m, f* **1.** uncle, aunt *m, f*; **~ abuelo** great-uncle; **tía abuela** great-aunt; **mis ~s** my aunt and uncle **2.** *inf* guy, girl *m, f*; **¡oye, ~!** hey, man!; **~ bueno** good-looking guy

tipear [ti·pe·'ar] *vi AmC, AmS* to type

típico, -a ['ti·pi·ko, -a] *adj* typical; **plato ~** local or traditional dish

tipo ['ti·po] *m* **1.** (*modelo*) model **2.** (*muestra*) sample; (*espécimen*) type; **un impreso/una carta ~** a standard form/letter **3.** (*cuerpo*) build; **aguantar el ~** to hold out; **mover el ~** *inf* to get moving; **tener buen ~** to have a good figure; **él tiene buen ~** he's well-built **4.** (*clase*) type, kind **5.** FIN rate; **~ de cambio** exchange rate **6.** TIPO type

tipo, -a ['ti·po, -a] *m, f* **1.** *inf* guy, girl *m, f* **2.** *pey* character; **~ raro** weirdo

tiquear [ti·ke·'ar] *vt* **1.** *AmC, PRico, Col* (*chequear*) to check **2.** *Chile* (*perforar*) to punch

tira ['ti·ra] *f* strip; **~ cómica** comic strip

tirabuzón [ti·ra·βu·'son, -'θon] *m* ringlet

tirada [ti·'ra·da] *f* **1.** (*edición*) print run; **de una ~** *fig* without stopping **2.** (*distancia*) stretch

tiradero [ti·ra·'de·ro] *m Méx* garbage dump

tirado, -a [ti·'ra·do, -a] **I.** *adj* **1.** estar

inf (*barato*) dirt cheap; (*fácil*) very easy; **ese ejercicio está ~** that exercise is very easy; **dejar ~ a alguien** to leave sb in the lurch 2. **ser** *pey* slovenly II. *m, f inf* bum

tiranía [ti·ra·'ni·a] *f* tyranny

tiranizar <z → c> [ti·ra·ni·'sar, -'θar] *vt* to tyranize

tirano, -a [ti·'ra·no, -a] I. *adj* tyrannical II. *m, f* tyrant

tirante [ti·'ran·te] I. *adj* 1. (*tieso*) taut; **el pantalón me está ~** the pants are tight on me 2. (*conflictivo*) tense II. *m* strap; **~s** (*elásticos*) suspenders *pl*

tirantez [ti·ran·'tes, -'teθ] *f* strain

tirar [ti·'rar] I. *vi* 1. **~ de algo** to pull on sth; (*sacar*) to pull out sth; **tira y afloja** give and take; **~ de la lengua a alguien** to draw sb out; **aquí cada uno tira por su lado** here everyone takes his/her own turning 2. to attract; **no me tiran los libros** I'm not very interested in books; **~ a rojo** to tend toward red 3. (*disparar*) to shoot; **~ al blanco** to target shoot ▶ **¿qué tal? — vamos tirando** *inf* how are you? — we're managing II. *vt* 1. (*lanzar*) to throw; **~ piedras a alguien** to throw stones at sb 2. (*malgastar*) to waste 3. (*desechar*) to throw away 4. (*disparar*) to shoot 5. (*derribar*) to knock down; (*edificio*) to pull down 6. FOTO to take 7. (*derramar*) to spill III. *vr:* **~se** 1. (*lanzarse*) to throw oneself 2. (*echarse*) to lie down 3. (*pasar*) to spend; **~se una hora esperando** to spend an hour waiting 4. *inf* **~se a alguien** to lay sb

tiritar [ti·ri·'tar] *vi* to shiver

tiro ['ti·ro] *m* shot; **~ con arco** archery; **a ~ in** range; *fig* accessible; **dar** [*o* **pegar**] **un ~** to fire a shot; **me salió el ~ por la culata** it backfired on me ▶ **sentar a alguien como un ~** (*comida*) to disagree with sb; (*noticia*) to upset sb; **ni a ~s** not on a long shot

tiroides [ti·'roi·des] *adj, m inv* (**glándula**) **~** thyroid (gland)

tiroteo [ti·ro·'teo] *m* shooting

titanio [ti·'ta·njo] *m* titanium

titeo [ti·'teo] *m Arg, Bol, Urug* (*burla*) mocking; (*tomadura de pelo*) teasing;

tomar a alguien para el ~ to make fun of sb

títere ['ti·te·re] *m* 1. puppet; **no dejar ~ con cabeza** to spare no one 2. *pl* puppet show

titipuchal [ti·ti·pu·'tʃal] *m Méx inf* throng

titubear [ti·tu·βe·'ar] *vi* to hesitate

titubeo [ti·tu·'βeo] *m* hesitation

titulación [ti·tu·la·'sjon, -'θjon] *f* title; (*académica*) qualifications *pl*

titulado, -a [ti·tu·'la·do, -a] I. *adj* titled II. *m, f* degree holder; **~ (universitario)** university graduate

titular¹ [ti·tu·'lar] *mf* holder; **~ de acciones** shareholder

titular² [ti·tu·'lar] I. *m* headline; **ocupar los ~es** to be in all the newspapers II. *vt* to title III. *vr:* **~se** to be entitled

título ['ti·tu·lo] *m* title; (*diploma*) diploma; **~ universitario** university degree; **~ de propiedad** (*property*) deeds; **a ~ de** by way of; **¿a ~ de qué hace Ud. eso?** why are you doing that?

tiza ['ti·sa, -θa] *f* chalk

tizate [ti·'sa·te] *m Guat, Hond, Nic* chalk

tiznado, -a [tis·'na·do, -a] *adj AmC* drunk

tizne ['tis·ne, -θne] *amb* soot

tlachique [tla·'tʃi·ke] *m Méx* agave cactus juice

tlacote [tla·'ko·te] *m Méx* 1. (*absceso*) boil 2. (*tumor*) tumor

tlapalería [tla·pa·le·'ri·a] *f Méx* hardware store

TLCAN *abr de* **Tratado de Libre Comercio de América del Norte** NAFTA

toalla [to·'a·ja, -ʎa] *f* towel; **~ de lavabo/baño** hand/bath towel; **arrojar la ~** to throw in the towel

tobillera [to·βi·'je·ra, -'ʎe·ra] *f* ankle support

tobillo [to·'βi·jo, -ʎo] *m* ankle

tobo ['to·βo] *m Ven* bucket

tobogán [to·βo·'ɣan] *m* slide

tocadiscos [to·ka·'dis·kos] *m inv* record player

tocado [to·'ka·do] *m* hairdo

tocado, -a [to·'ka·do, -a] *adj* touched; **estar ~ (de la cabeza)** to be not all there

tocador [to·ka·'dor] *m* dressing table

tocar <c → qu> [to·'kar] I. *vt* 1. (*palpar*) to touch; **¡no lo toques!** don't touch it!;

~ **fondo** to hit bottom **2.** MÚS to play; (*campana, timbre*) to ring; (*tambor*) to beat; **el reloj tocó las tres** the clock struck three **3.** (*modificar*) to change **II.** *vi* **te toca jugar** it's your turn; **hoy me toca barrer** today I have to sweep; **toca irse ya** it's time to go; **le tocó a él hacerlo** it fell to him to do it; **le tocó el premio** he/she won the prize; ~ **en** to verge on **III.** *vr*: ~**se** to touch ▶ **los extremos se tocan** extremes meet

tocayo, -a [to·'ka·jo, -a] *m, f* namesake

tocineta [to·si·'ne·ta] *f Col, Cuba* [to·si·no, to·'θi·] *m* pork fat; (*carne*) bacon

todavía [to·da·'βi·a] *adv* still; ~ **no** not yet; **pero** ~ however; **es** ~ **más caro que...** it is even more expensive than...

todo ['to·do] **I.** *pron indef* all; ~ **cuanto** [*o* **lo que**]... all...; (*o*) ~ **o nada** all or nothing; **ante** [*o* **sobre**] ~ above all; ~ **lo contrario** quite the contrary; **después de** ~ after all; **con** ~ nevertheless; **estar en** ~ to be on the ball; **para** ~ all-purpose **II.** *adv inf* completely **III.** *m* the whole; **del** ~ completely; **no del** ~ not entirely

todo, -a ['to·do, -a] *art indef* **1.** (*entero*) all; **toda la familia** the whole family; **toda Argentina** all of Argentina; **en toda Europa** all over Europe; **a toda prisa** [*o* **a** ~ **correr**] as fast as possible **2.** (*cada*) every; **a toda costa** at all cost; ~ **Dios** [*o* **quisqui**] *inf* absolutely everyone; **toda precaución es poca** you can't be careful enough **3.** *pl all*; **a** ~**s los niños les gusta el chocolate** all children like chocolate; ~**s los niños de la clase tomaron chocolate** all of the children in the class had chocolate; ~**y cada uno** each and every one; **a todas horas** at all hours; **en todas partes** everywhere; **de** ~**s modos** anyway

todoterreno [to·do·te·'rre·no] **I.** *adj inv* versatile **II.** *m* all-terrain vehicle

toldillo [tol·'di·jo, -ʎo] *m Col* mosquito net

toldo ['tol·do] *m* marquee; (*en balcón*) canopy; (*en tienda*) awning

tolerancia [to·le·'ran·sja, -θja] *f* tolerance

tolerar [to·le·'rar] *vt* tolerate

tolete [to·'le·te] *m* **1.** *AmL* (*garrote*) bludgeon **2.** *Col, Cuba* (*trozo*) piece

tolvanera [tol·βa·'ne·ra] *f AmC, Méx* cloud of dust

toma [to·ma] *f* **1.** (*adquisición*) taking; ~ **de conciencia** awareness; ~ **de datos** data acquisition; ~ **de decisiones** decision making; ~ **de poder** takeover **2.** (*dosis*) dose **3.** TÉC inlet; ~ **de tierra** ground **4.** (*grabación*) take; FOTO shot

tomacorriente [to·ma·ko·'rrjen·te] *m* **1.** *AmL* (*colector*) collector **2.** *Arg, Perú* (*enchufe*) plug

tomar [to·'mar] **I.** *vi* **1. toma** here you are **2.** *AmL* to drink ▶ **¡toma! well! II.** *vt* **1.** (*coger, quitar, llevar, interpretar*) to take (**por** for); (*préstamo*) to borrow; (*decisión*) to make; (*actitud*) to adopt; ~ **a la ligera** to take lightly; ~ **algo a mal** to take offense at sth; ~ **muy a pecho** to take to heart; ~ **en serio/a risa** to take seriously/as a joke; ~ **conciencia de algo** to become aware of sth; ~ **cariño/manía a alguien** to take a like/dislike to sb **2.** (*contratar*) to hire **3.** (*hacerse cargo*) to take over **4.** *AmL* ~**la** to get drunk ▶ ~**la con algo/alguien** to take it out on sth/sb **III.** *vr*: ~**se 1.** (*coger*) to take **2.** (*beber, comer*) to have; ~**se la cena** to have dinner **3.** *AmL* **tomársela** to get drunk

tomate [to·'ma·te] *m* tomato ▶ **ponerse** <u>rojo</u> **como un** ~ to turn as red as a beetroot

tómbola ['tom·bo·la] *f* charity raffle

tomillo [to·'mi·jo, -ʎo] *m* thyme

tomo [to·mo] *m* volume; **de cuatro** ~**s** in four volumes

tonada [to·'na·da] *f* **1.** tune **2.** *AmL* (*tonillo*) accent

tonalidad [to·na·li·'dad] *f* **1.** LING intonation **2.** MÚS tonality **3.** ARTE shade

tonel [to·'nel] *m* barrel; *inf* fatso

tonelada [to·ne·'la·da] *f* ton

tónica ['to·ni·ka] *f* tonic water

tónico [to·ni·ko] *m* tonic

tonificar <c → qu> [to·ni·fi·'kar] *vt* to tone up

tonina [to·'ni·na] *f Arg, Urug* dolphin

tono ['to·no] *m* tone; ~ **agudo/grave**

high/low pitch; **~ mayor/menor** major/minor key; **bajar el ~** to lower one's voice; **en ~ de reproche** reproachfully; **fuera de ~** out of place; **a ~ con** in tune with; **subirse de ~** to become heated; **de mal ~** vulgar

tontear [ton·te·'ar] *vi* to fool around; *inf* to flirt

tontería [ton·te·'ri·a] *f* trifle; (*memez*) stupidity

tonto, -a ['ton·to] **I.** *adj* silly; **a tontas y a locas** without thinking; **ponerse ~** *inf* to get silly **II.** *m, f* fool; **hacer el ~** to clown around; **hacerse el ~** to play dumb

topacio [to·'pa·sjo, -θjo] *m* topaz

topadora [to·pa·'do·ra] *f Arg, Méx, Urug* bulldozer

topar(se) [to·'par·(se)] *vi, vr* **~ con algo** to run into sth; **~ con alguien** to bump into sb; **~ contra algo** to bump against sth

tope ['to·pe] **I.** *adj* maximum; **fecha ~** latest date **II.** *m* **1.** end; **lleno hasta el ~** [*o* **los ~s**] full to bursting; **estoy a ~ de trabajo** I'm swamped with work **2.** obstacle; (*puerta*) doorstop

tópico ['to·pi·ko] *m* cliché

tópico, -a ['to·pi·ko, -a] *adj* trite; **de uso ~** for external use only

topinambur [to·pi·nam·'bur] *m Arg, Bol* Jerusalem artichoke

topo ['to·po] *m* mole; **ver menos que un ~** to be as blind as a bat

topocho, -a [to·'po·tʃo, -a] *adj Ven* plump

topografía [to·po·ɣra·'fi·a] *f* topography

topón [to·'pon] *m* **1.** *Chile, Col, Hond* (*topetazo*) butt **2.** *Col* (*puñetazo*) punch

topónimo [to·'po·ni·mo] *m* place name

toposo, -a [to·'po·so, -a] *adj Ven* (*entrometido*) meddlesome; (*pedante*) pretentious

toque ['to·ke] *m* (*roce, matiz*) touch; (*golpe*) tap; **dar un ~ en la puerta** to tap on the door; **~ de queda** curfew; **~ de tambor** drumbeat; **~** (*de atención*) warning; **dame un ~ más tarde** give me a call later; **dar los últimos ~s a algo** to put the finishing touches on sth

toquetear [to·ke·te·'ar] *vt inf* to finger

tórax ['to·raks] *m inv* thorax

torbellino [tor·βe·'ʝi·no, -'ʎi·no] *m* whirlwind; **ser un ~** to be a bundle of energy

torcedura [tor·se·'ðu·ra, tor·θe-] *f* sprain

torcer [tor·'ser, -'θer] *irr como* cocer **I.** *vi* to turn; **~ a la izquierda** to turn left **II.** *vt* to turn; (*doblar*) to bend **III.** *vr*: **~se 1.** to bend; **me torcí el tobillo** I've twisted my ankle **2.** (*corromperse*) to go astray; (*fracasar*) to go wrong

torcido, -a [tor·'si·do, tor·'θi-] *adj* lopsided; (*encorvado*) crooked

torear [to·re·'ar] **I.** *vi* to bullfight **II.** *vt* to bullfight; (*tomar el pelo*) to tease

toreo [to·'reo] *m* bullfighting

torero, -a [to·'re·ro, -a] **I.** *adj* bullfighting **II.** *m, f* bullfighter; **saltarse algo a la torera** *inf* to blatantly ignore sth

tormenta [tor·'men·ta] *f* storm; (*agitación*) turmoil; **una ~ en un vaso de agua** a storm in a teacup

tormento [tor·'men·to] *m* anguish; (*castigo*) torment

torna ['tor·na] *f* **1.** (*devolución*) restitution **2.** (*regreso*) return ▶ **se han cambiado las ~s** the shoes are on the other foot; **volver las ~s a alguien** to turn the tables on sb; **volverse las ~s** to turn the tables

tornado [tor·'na·do] *m* tornado

tornarse [tor·'nar·se] *vr* to turn

torneo [tor·'neo] *m* tournament

tornillo [tor·'ni·jo, -ʎo] *m* screw; **apretar los ~s a alguien** to put pressure on sb; **te falta un ~** you have a screw loose

torno ['tor·no] *m* lathe; (*de alfarero*) potter's wheel ▶ **en ~ a** about; **en ~ a ese tema** with regard to this subject

toro ['to·ro] *m* **1.** bull; **coger el ~ por los cuernos** to take the bull by the horns; **fuerte como un ~** strong as an ox **2.** *pl* bullfighting; **ir a los ~s** to go to bullfights

torpe ['tor·pe] *adj* clumsy; (*tonto*) slow

torpedo [tor·'pe·do] *m* torpedo

torpeza [tor·'pe·sa, -θa] *f* clumsiness; (*tontería*) stupidity

torre ['to·rre] *f* tower; **~ de alta tensión** electricity pylon; **~ de mando** control

T

tower; (*ajedrez*) rook

torreja [to·'rre·xa] *f AmL* ≈ French toast

torrencial [to·rren·'sjal, -'θjal] *adj* torrential

torrente [to·'rren·te] *m* torrent; *fig* flood

torrentoso, -a [to·rren·'to·so, -a] *adj AmL* (*lluvia*) torrential; (*caudal*) fast-flowing

torso ['tor·so] *m* torso; ARTE bust

torta ['tor·ta] *f* 1. *AmL* pie 2. *inf* slap; **darse una ~** to bang oneself; **llevar una ~** to be plastered ▶ **no saber ni ~** *inf* not to know a thing

tortilla [tor·'ti·ja, -ʎa] *f* ≈ omelet; *AmL* tortilla ▶ **dar la vuelta a la ~** to change things completely; **se ha vuelto la ~** the tables have turned

tórtola ['tor·to·la] *f* turtledove; **tortolitos** lovebirds

tortuga [tor·'tu·ɣa] *f* turtle; **a paso de ~** at a snail's pace

tortura [tor·'tu·ra] *f* torture

torturar [tor·tu·'rar] *vt* to torture

tos [tos] *f* cough

tosco, -a ['tos·ko, -a] *adj* coarse

tosedera [to·se·'de·ra] *f AmL* nagging cough

toser [to·'ser] *vi* to cough

tostada [tos·'ta·da] *f* toast; *Méx* fried tortilla

tostador [tos·ta·'dor] *m* toaster

tostar <o → ue> [tos·'tar] I. *vt* to roast; (*pan*) to toast II. *vr:* **~se** to tan

total [to·'tal] I. *adj* total; **en ~** in all; **¡ha sido ~!** *inf* it was great! II. *m* sum III. *adv* so, in the end

totalidad [to·ta·li·'dad] *f* totality; **en su ~** in its entirety

totalitario, -a [to·ta·li·'ta·rjo, -a] *adj* totalitarian

totora [to·'to·ra] *f AmS* reed

toxicidad [tok·si·si·'dad, tok·si·θi·] *f* toxicity

tóxico ['tok·si·ko] *m* toxic substance

tóxico, -a ['tok·si·ko, -a] *adj* toxic

toxicomanía [tok·si·ko·ma·'ni·a] *f* drug addiction

toxicómano, -a [tok·si·'ko·ma·no, -a] I. *adj* addicted to drugs II. *m, f* drug addict

toxina [tok·'si·na] *f* toxin

traba ['tra·βa] *f* 1. hindrance; **poner**

~ s a... to put obstacles in the way of... 2. *AmL* grass; (*efecto*) high

trabajador(a) [tra·βa·xa·'dor, --'do·ra] I. *adj* hard-working II. *m(f)* worker

trabajar [tra·βa·'xar] I. *vi* to work; **~ de guía** to work as a guide; **en edad de ~** of working age; **~ como un condenado** to work like a slave; **~ por horas** to be paid by the hour; **~ por cuenta propia** to be self-employed; **~ a tiempo completo/parcial** to work full-time/part-time II. *vt* to work; (*máquina*) to operate; **tienes que ~ el acento** you have to work on your accent III. *vr:* **~se** to work for; (*persona*) to work on

trabajo [tra·'βa·xo] *m* work; (*puesto*) job; **~s manuales** handicrafts; **con/sin ~** employed/unemployed; **~ en equipo** teamwork; **~ fijo** steady job; **hacer un buen ~** to do a good job; **tener ~ atrasado** to have a backlog; **¡buen ~!** well done!; **quedarse sin ~** to be let go; **costar ~** to be difficult; **tomarse el ~ de** to take the trouble to; **ahorrarse el ~ de** to spare oneself the trouble of

trabalenguas [tra·βa·'len·gwas] *m inv* tongue twister

trabar [tra·'βar] I. *vt* 1. (*juntar*) to join 2. (*impedir*) to impede II. *vi* to take hold III. *vr:* **~se** to get stuck; **~se la lengua** to get tongue-tied

trácala ['tra·ka·la] *f* 1. *Ecua* (*multitud*) mob 2. *Méx, PRico* (*fullería*) fraud 3. *Méx* (*fullero*) trickster

tracalada [tra·ka·'la·da] *f* 1. *AmC, AmS* (*multitud*) crowd 2. *Méx* (*fullería*) trickery

tracalero, -a [tra·ka·'le·ro, -a] *m, f Méx, PRico* cheat

tracción [trak·'sjon, -'θjon] *f* drive; **~ delantera/trasera/a cuatro ruedas** front/rear-wheel/four-wheel drive

tractor [trak·'tor] *m* tractor

tradición [tra·di·'sjon, -'θjon] *f* tradition

tradicional [tra·di·sjo·'nal, tra·di·θjo·] *adj* traditional

traducción [tra·duk·'sjon, -duɣ·'θjon] *f* translation; **~ al/del inglés** translation into/from English

traducir [tra·du·'sir, -'θir] *irr vt* to translate; **~ al/del español** to translate into/

from Spanish

traductología [tra·duk·to·lo·'xi·a] *f* translation science

traductor(a) [tra·duk·'tor, -·'to·ra] *m(f)* translator; ~ **de bolsillo** pocket-size electronic translating device; ~ **jurado** sworn translator

traer [tra·'er] *irr* irr I. *vt* **1.** to bring; (*vestido*) to wear; **trae** give it to me; **lo traigo en la cartera** I've got it in my briefcase; **¿qué te trae por aquí?** what brings you here?; **me trae sin cuidado** I couldn't care less; **me la trae floja** *vulg* I don't give a damn **2.** (*ir a por*) to fetch **3.** (*ocasionar*) to cause **4.** (+ *adj*) to have; ~ **de cabeza a alguien** *inf* to be driving sb mad **5.** (+ *subst*) **retraso/prisa/hambre** to be late/in a hurry/hungry; ~ **cara de...** to look...; ~ **a la memoria** to bring to mind II. *vr*: ~**se** to bring; (*ir a por*) to fetch; ~**se algo entre manos** to be up to something; **este examen se las trae** the exam is really tough

traficante [tra·fi·'kan·te] *mf* dealer; (*de drogas*) drug dealer; (*de personas, coches*) smuggler

traficar <c → qu> [tra·fi·'kar] *vi* to deal; (*con drogas*) to traffic; (*con personas*) to smuggle

tráfico ['tra·fi·ko] *m* **1.** (*vial*) traffic; ~ **por carretera** road traffic **2.** com trade; (*drogas*) traffic; (*personas, coches*) smuggling; ~ **de influencias** graft

tragaluz [tra·ɣa·'lus, -·'luθ] *m* transom; (*grande*) skylight

traganíqueles [tra·ɣa·'ni·ke·les] *f inv Nic* inf slot machine

tragar <g → gu> [tra·'ɣar] I. *vt, vr*: ~**se** to swallow; (*historia, mentira*) to fall for; **¡trágame tierra!** I wish the ground would open up and swallow me!; **tuvimos que** ~ **toda la conferencia** we had to sit through the whole conference II. *vt* to down; ~ **saliva** to eat crow; **no** ~ **a alguien** to not be able to stand sb

tragedia [tra·'xe·dja] *f* tragedy

trágico, -a ['tra·xi·ko, -a] *adj* tragic; **no te pongas** ~ don't get all melodramatic

trago ['tra·ɣo] *m* (*sorbo*) swig; (*bebida*) drink; **de un** ~ in one gulp; **tomar un** ~

de más to have one drink too many; **pasar un mal** ~ to have a bad time of it

traición [trai·'sjon, -·'θjon] *f* treachery; (*delito*) treason

traicionar [trai·sjo·'nar, trai·θjo·-] *vt* to betray; **le traicionó su acento** his/her accent gave him/her away

traicionero, -a [trai·sjo·'ne·ro, -a; trai·θjo·-] I. *adj* perfidious; (*acción*) traitorous; (*memoria*) unreliable; (*animal*) dangerous II. *m, f* traitor

traidor(a) [trai·'dor, -·'do·ra] *m(f)* traitor

traje ['tra·xe] *m* dress; (*de hombre*) suit; (*de mujer*) outfit; ~ **de noche/de etiqueta** evening dress/suit; ~ **típico/de época** regional/period costume

trajeado, -a [tra·xe·'a·do, -a] *adj* **ir bien/mal** ~ to be well/badly dressed

trajín [tra·'xin] *m* haulage; (*ajetreo*) rush

trajinera [tra·xi·'ne·ra] *f Méx* (*canoa*) ≈ canoe

trama ['tra·ma] *f* plot

tramar [tra·'mar] *vt* to plot; (*intriga, plan*) to scheme; **¿qué estarán tramando?** what are they up to?; **aquí se está tramando algo** something's cooking here

tramitar [tra·mi·'tar] *vt* to attend to; (*negocio*) to transact; (*expediente*) to process; **está tramitando el divorcio** he/she has started divorce proceedings

trámite ['tra·mi·te] *m* formality; **en** ~**s de hacer algo** in the process of doing sth; **pasar por todos los** ~**s** to go through the whole procedure

tramo ['tra·mo] *m* stretch; FERRO section; (*escalera*) flight

trampa ['tram·pa] *f* **1.** trap; **caer en la** ~ to fall into the trap; **poner una** ~ to set a trap **2.** (*trampilla*) trapdoor **3.** (*fullería*) cheating; **hacer** ~ to cheat **4.** *inf* (*deuda*) bad debt ▶ **sin** ~ **ni cartón** with no catches; **hecha la ley hecha la** ~ laws are made to be broken

trampolín [tram·po·'lin] *m* (*piscina*) diving board

tramposo, -a [tram·'po·so, -a] I. *adj* cheating II. *m, f* swindler; (*fullero*) cheat

tranca ['tran·ka] *f* binge; **coger una** ~ to get plastered

trance ['tran·se, -θe] *m* trance

tranque ['tran·ke] *m Chile* reservoir

tranquilidad [tran·ki·li·'dad] *f* peace; **con ~** calmly; **para mayor ~** to be on the safe side

tranquilizante [tran·ki·li·'san·te, -'θan·te] *m* tranquilizer

tranquilizar <z → c> [tran·ki·li·'sar, -'θar] **I.** *vt* to calm down; (*con palabras*) to reassure **II.** *vr:* **~se** to calm down

tranquillo [tran·'ki·ʝo, -ʎo] *m* **coger el ~ a algo** to get the knack of sth

tranquilo, -a [tran·'ki·lo, -a] *adj* calm; (*sereno*) serene; (*despreocupada*) unconcerned; **tú ~** don't worry; **¡déjame ~!** leave me alone!

transa ['tran·sa] *f* **1.** *AmL* (*compromiso*) commitment **2.** *Méx* (*engaño*) deceit **3.** *RíoPl* (*transacción*) transaction; (*de droga*) drug dealing

transacción [tran·sak·'sjon, -'θjon] *f* **1.** JUR settlement **2.** POL agreement **3.** COM deal **4.** FIN transaction

transar [tran·'sar] *vi AmL* to compromise

transatlántico [trans·at·'lan·ti·ko] *m* ocean liner

transbordar [trans·βor·'dar] *vt, vi* to transfer

transbordo [trans·'βor·do] *m* change; (*mercancías*) transfer; **hay que hacer ~ en el aeropuerto** you have to change planes at the airport

transcender <e → ie> [tran·sen·'der, trans·θen-] *vi v.* **trascender**

transcribir [trans·kri·'βir] *irr como escribir vt* to transcribe

transcripción [trans·krip·'sjon, -kriβ·'θjon] *f* (*acción*) transcription; (*resultado*) transcript

transcurrir [trans·ku·'rrir] *vi* to elapse; (*acontecer*) to take place

transeúnte [tran·se·'un·te] *mf* passer-by

transferencia [trans·fe·'ren·sja, -θja] *f* transfer

transferir [trans·fe·'rir] *irr como sentir vt* **1.** (*trasladar*) to transfer **2.** (*posponer*) to postpone **3.** FIN to make over; (*propiedad, derecho*) to transfer

transformación [trans·for·ma·'sjon, -'θjon] *f* transformation

transformar [trans·for·'mar] *vt* to transform

transfusión [trans·fu·'sjon] *f* transfusion

transgresión [trans·ɣre·'sjon] *f* transgression

transición [tran·si·'sjon, -'θjon] *f* transition

transigente [tran·si·'xen·te] *adj* broadminded; (*tolerante*) tolerant

transigir <g → j> [tran·si·'xir] *vi* **~ con algo** to tolerate sth; JUR, POL to compromise

transistor [tran·sis·'tor] *m* ELEC transistor

transitable [tran·si·'ta·βle] *adj* open to traffic; (*a pie*) passable

transitar [tran·si·'tar] *vi* **~ por** to go/walk along; **muy transitado** very busy

transitivo, -a [tran·si·'ti·βo, -a] *adj* transitive

tránsito ['tran·si·to] *m* t. COM transit; (*circulación*) traffic; **de mucho ~** very busy

transitorio, -a [tran·si·'to·rjo, -a] *adj* temporary

translúcido, -a [trans·'lu·si·do, -a; -θi·do, -a] *adj* translucent

transmisión [trans·mi·'sjon] *f* transmission; (*noticia*) broadcast

transmisor [trans·mi·'sor] *m* transmitter

transmitir [trans·mi·'tir] *vt* to transmit; (*noticia*) to broadcast

transparencia [trans·pa·'ren·sja, -θja] *f* transparency; (*de intención*) openness

transparentar [trans·pa·ren·'tar] **I.** *vt* to reveal **II.** *vi, vr:* **~se** to be transparent **III.** *vr:* **~se** (*dejarse ver, adivinar*) to show through

transparente [trans·pa·'ren·te] *adj* transparent

transpirar [trans·pi·'rar] *vi* to perspire

transponer [trans·po·'ner] *irr como poner* **I.** *vt* to move **II.** *vr:* **~se 1.** to move **2.** (*dormirse*) to doze off

transportar [trans·por·'tar] **I.** *vt* to transport; (*en brazos*) to carry **II.** *vr:* **~se** to be transported

transporte [trans·'por·te] *m* transport; **~ por carretera** road transport; **~s públicos** public transportation

transportista [trans·por·'tis·ta] *mf* carrier

transpuesto, -a [trans·'pwes·to, -a] **I.** *pp de* **transponer** **II.** *adj* **quedarse**

~ to doze off

transversal [trans·βer·'sal] *adj* crosswise; **calle** ~ cross street

tranvía [tram·'bi·a] *m* streetcar

trapear [tra·pe·'ar] *vt AmL* to mop

trapecio [tra·'pe·sjo, -θjo] *m* trapeze

trapiche [tra·'pi·tʃe] *m AmL* sugar mill

trapichear [tra·pi·tʃe·'ar] *vi* **1.** *inf* (*enredos*) to be mixed up in shady business; ~ **en los negocios** to have crooked dealings **2.** (*comerciar*) to buy and sell small scale

trapo ['tra·po] *m* rag; (*para limpiar*) cleaning cloth; ~ **de cocina** dish towel; **a todo** ~ at top speed; (*música*) on full blast ▸ **tener manos de** ~ to be a butterfingers; **estar hecho un** ~ to be worn out; **sacar los** ~**s sucios a relucir** to wash one's dirty linen in public

tráquea ['tra·kea] *f* windpipe

traquetear [tra·ke·te·'ar] **I.** *vi* (*chapa, vajilla*) to clatter; (*motor, ametralladora*) to rattle; (*sillas, carro*) to jolt **II.** *vt* to shake

tras [tras] *prep* after; (*espacial*) behind; **ir** ~ **alguien** to go after sb; **poner uno** ~ **otro** to put one after the other

trasbocar <c → qu> [tras·βo·'kar] *vt AmC, AmS* to throw up

trascendencia [tra·sen·'den·sja, -θen·'den·θja] *f* consequence; **no tener** ~ to be of little importance

trascendental [tra·sen·den·'tal, tras·θen-] *adj* important

trascender <e → ie> [tra·sen·'der, tras·θen-] *vi* to become known; ~ **a algo** to have a wide effect on sth; ~ **de algo** to go beyond sth

trasera [tra·'se·ra] *f* back

trasero [tra·'se·ro] *m* hindquarters *pl*; (*persona*) backside

trasero, -a [tra·'se·ro, -a] *adj* back; **parte trasera** rear; **rueda trasera** rear wheel

trasfondo [tras·'fon·do] *m* background

trasladar [tras·la·'dar] **I.** *vt* to move; (*tienda*) to relocate; (*preso, funcionario*) to transfer **II.** *vr*: ~**se** to go; (*mudarse*) to move

traslado [tras·'la·do] *m* **1.** movement; (*preso, funcionario*) transfer **2.** (*mudanza*) removal

trasluz [tras·'lus, -'luθ] *m* **mirar algo al** ~ to hold sth up to the light

trasnochar [tras·no·'tʃar] *vi* to spend a sleepless night; (*ir de juerga*) to have a night out; (*acostarse tarde*) to stay up late

traspapelar [tras·pa·pe·'lar] **I.** *vt* to mislay **II.** *vr*: ~**se** to get mislaid

traspasar [tras·pa·'sar] *vt* **1.** (*atravesar*) to go through; (*penetrar, perforar*) to pierce; (*líquido*) to soak through; (*límite*) to go beyond **2.** (*pasar a*) to transfer; FIN to make over

traspaso [tras·'pa·so] *m* transfer; (*límite*) exceeding

traspatio [tras·'pa·tjo] *m AmL* backyard

traspié(s) [tras·'pje(s)] *m* (*inv*) stumble; *fig* slip-up; **dar un** ~ to stumble *fig*, to slip up

trasplantar [tras·plan·'tar] *vt* to transplant

trasplante [tras·'plan·te] *m* transplanting; MED transplant

trastada [tras·'ta·da] *f* dirty trick; (*travesura*) prank; **hacer una** ~ **a alguien** to play a prank on sb

traste ['tras·te] *m AmL* piece of junk ▸ **dar al** ~ **con algo** to spoil sth; **irse al** ~ to fall through

trastero [tras·'te·ro] *m* lumber room

trasto ['tras·to] *m* piece of junk; **tus** ~**s** your stuff; **tirarse los** ~**s a la cabeza** to have a knock down drag out fight

trastornado, -a [tras·tor·'na·do, -a] *adj* confused; PSICO disturbed

trastornar [tras·tor·'nar] **I.** *vt* **1.** to disarrange; (*de arriba abajo*) to turn upside down; (*orden, plan, ideas*) disrupt; (*orden público*) to disturb **2.** PSICO to traumatize; (*por amor*) to lose one's head over sb; **la muerte de su marido la trastornó** she was traumatized by her husband's death; **me trastornan los coches** I'm crazy about cars **II.** *vr*: ~**se** **1.** (*enloquecer*) to go mad **2.** (*estropearse*) to fall through

trasvasijar [tras·βa·si·'xar] *vt Chile* to decant

tratable [tra·'ta·βle] *adj* sociable

tratado [tra·'ta·do] *m* treaty; (*científico*) treatise; ~ **de no agresión** nonaggression treaty; **~ comercial** trade agreement

tratamiento [tra·ta·'mjen·to] *m* **1.** *t.* MED, QUÍM treatment **2.** *t.* COMPUT (*elaboración*) processing **3.** (*de cortesía*) form of address

tratante [tra·'tan·te] *mf* dealer

tratar [tra·'tar] **I.** *vt* **1.** (*manejar, portarse*) to deal with **2.** MED, QUÍM to treat **3.** *t.* COMPUT (*elaborar, agua, minerales*) to process **4.** (*dirigirse*) to address **5.** (*tema, asunto*) to discuss **II.** *vi* **1. ~ de** [*o sobre*] **algo** to be about sth **2.** (*intentar*) to try; **trata de concentrarte** try to concentrate **3.** (*con alguien*) to have contact with **4.** COM to deal **III.** *vr:* **~se** to have to do; **¿de qué se trata?** what's it about?; **tratándose de ti...** in your case...

tratativas [tra·ta·'ti·βas] *fpl* Arg, Par negotiations *pl;* **siguen en ~** they are still discussing terms

trato ['tra·to] *m* **1.** (*comportamiento*) treatment; **malos ~s** abuse; **recibir un buen ~** to be well-treated **2.** (*contacto*) contact; **romper el ~ con alguien** to break off relations with sb; **no querer ~s con alguien** to want nothing to do with sb **3.** (*pacto*) agreement; (*negocio*) deal; **cerrar un ~ con alguien** to close a deal with sb; **¡~ hecho!** it's a deal!

trauma ['trau·ma] *m* trauma

traumático, -a [trau·'ma·ti·ko, -a] *adj* traumatic

traumatismo [trau·ma·'tis·mo] *m* injury; **~ cervical** traumatism

través [tra·'βes] *prep* **a ~ de** across; (*de alguien*) from

travesti [tra·'βes·ti] *mf,* **travestí** [tra·βes·'ti] *mf,* **travestido, -a** [tra·βes·'ti·do, -a] *m, f* transvestite

travesura [tra·βe·'su·ra] *f* prank

travieso, -a [tra·'βje·so, -a] *adj* naughty; **correr a campo traviesa** to run cross-country

trayecto [tra·'jek·to] *m* (*trecho*) distance; (*ruta*) route; (*recorrido*) itinerary; **final de ~** end of the line

trayectoria [tra·jek·'to·rja] *f* path; ASTRON, FÍS trajectory; (*profesional*) career

traza ['tra·sa, -θa] *f* **1.** *t.* ARQUIT plan

2. (*habilidad*) ability **3.** (*aspecto*) appearance

trazado [tra·'sa·do, tra·'θa-] *m* **1.** *t.* ARQUIT design **2.** (*recorrido*) route; FERRO line

trazar <z → c> [tra·'sar, -'θar] *vt* **1.** (*líneas*) to trace; (*esquemáticamente*) to outline; (*dibujos*) to sketch **2.** *t.* ARQUIT (*plan*) to draw up **3.** (*describir*) to describe

trazo ['tra·so, -θo] *m* stroke; **de ~s suaves** with soft features

trébol ['tre·βol] *m* clover; (*cartas*) clubs *pl*

trece ['tre·se, -θe] **I.** *adj inv* thirteen; **seguir en sus ~** to stand firm; **en el siglo ~** in the thirteenth century; **martes y ~** ≈ Friday the thirteenth **II.** *m* thirteen; *v. t.* **ocho**

trecho ['tre·tʃo] *m* distance; (*tramo*) stretch

tregua ['tre·ɣwa] *f* truce; (*descanso*) respite; **sin ~** relentlessly

treinta ['trein·ta] *adj inv* thirty; *v. t.* **ochenta**

treintavo, -a [trein·'ta·βo, -a] *adj* thirtieth; *v. t.* **ochentavo**

tremendo, -a [tre·'men·do, -a] *adj* (*temible*) frightful; (*enorme*) tremendous; (*respetable*) imposing; (*niño*) full of mischief ▶ **tomar las cosas a la tremenda** to make such a fuss over things

tren [tren] *m* train; **~ interurbano/rápido/directo** intercity/express/through train; **~ de cercanías/de alta velocidad** suburban/high-speed train; **coger el ~** to catch [*o* take] the train; **ir en ~** to go by train; **perder el último ~** *fig* to miss the boat; **~ de lavado** carwash; **~ de vida** lifestyle; **estar como un ~** *inf* to be very good-looking; **hay sangría como para parar un ~** there's plenty of sangria

trenza ['tren·sa, -θa] *f* braid

trenzar <z → c> [tren·'sar, -'θar] *vt* to plait; (*pelo*) to braid

trepa¹ ['tre·pa] *f* (*astucia*) cunning

trepa² ['tre·pa] *m pey inf* climber

trepador(a) [tre·pa·'dor] **I.** *adj* planta **~a** climbing plant **II.** *m(f)* go-getter

trepar [tre·'par] *vi, vt* to climb; (*planta*) to creep

trepe ['tre·pe] *m* CRI (*regaño*) scolding; **echar un ~ a alguien por algo** to tell sb off for sth

trepidar [tre·pi·'dar] *vi AmL* to hesitate

tres [tres] **I.** *adj inv* three; **no me sale ni a la de ~** I just can't do this no matter how I try; **de ~ al cuarto** two-bit; **~ en raya** (*juego*) tic(k)-tac(k)-toe **II.** *m inv* three; *v. t.* **ocho**

trescientos, -as [tre·'sjen·tos, -as; -'θjen·tos, -as] *adj* three hundred; *v. t.* **ochocientos**

triangular [trian·gu·'lar] *adj* triangular

triángulo [tri·'an·γu·lo] *m* triangle

triates ['trja·tes] *mpl Méx* triplets *pl*

tribu ['tri·βu] *f* tribe

tribuna [tri·'βu·na] *f* stand; (*en parlamento*) rostrum; **~ de jurados/de la prensa** jury/press box

tribunal [tri·βu·'nal] *m* court; **llevar a los ~es** to take to court; **~ examinador** board of examiners

tributar [tri·βu·'tar] *vt* to pay; **~ un homenaje a alguien** to pay tribute to sb

tributario, -a [tri·βu·'ta·rjo, -a] *adj* tributary; (*imponible*) tax; **agencia tributaria** Inland Revenue

tributo [tri·'βu·to] *m* tax; (*homenaje*) tribute

triciclo [tri·'si·klo, tri·'θi-] *m* tricycle

tricolor [tri·ko·'lor] *adj* tricolor

tricota [tri·'ko·ta] *f AmL* sweater

tridimensional [tri·di·men·sjo·'nal] *adj* three-dimensional

trifulca [tri·'ful·ka] *f* rumpus

trigal [tri·'γal] *m* wheat field

trigo ['tri·γo] *m* wheat; **no ser ~ limpio** not to be totally above board

trigueño, -a [tri·'γe·ɲo, -a] *AmL* **I.** *adj* light brown; (*pelo*) dark blond; (*piel*) olive-skinned **II.** *m, f* colored person

trilla ['tri·ja, -ʎa] *f AmL inf* thrashing

trillar [tri·'jar, -'ʎar] *vt AmL inf* to beat

trillizo [tri·'ji·so, -a; -'ʎi·θo, -a] *m* triplet

trillo ['tri·jo, -ʎo] *m AmC* narrow path

trimestral [tri·mes·'tral] *adj* three-month; (*cada tres meses*) quarterly

trimestre [tri·'mes·tre] *m* quarter; ENS term

trinar [tri·'nar] *vi* to warble; **está que trina** *inf* he/she is completely crazy

trinca ['trin·ka] *f* **1.** And, CSur (*pandilla*) gang **2.** AmL inf (*embriaguez*)

drunkenness **3.** CSur (*canicas*) game of marbles

trincar <c → qu> [trin·'kar] **I.** *vt* **1.** *inf* (*robar*) to steal **2.** *inf* (*pillar*) to nab **3.** AmL (*apretar*) to be too tight **II.** *vr:* **~se** *inf* (*copular*) to screw

trinchera [trin·'tʃe·ra] *f* trench

trineo [tri·'neo] *m* sled

trinidad [tri·ni·'dad] *f* trinity

trinitaria [tri·ni·ta·'rja] *f* **1.** pansy **2.** Col, PRico, Ven bougainvillea

trino ['tri·no] *m* warble

trío ['tri·o] *m* trio

tripa ['tri·pa] *f* **1.** (*intestino*) gut **2.** *pl* (*vísceras*) entrails *pl*; *fig* insides *pl*; **me suenan las ~s** my stomach's rumbling; **se me revuelven las ~s** it turns my stomach **3.** *inf* (*vientre*) tummy; **echar ~** to get a paunch; **llenar(se) la ~** to eat one's fill

triple ['tri·ple] **I.** *adj* triple; (*de tres capas*) three-ply **II.** *m* triple; **ser el ~ de grande** to be three times as large

triplicar <c → qu> [tri·pli·'kar] *vt, vr:* **~se** to triple

trípode ['tri·po·de] *m* tripod

tripón, -ona [tri·'pon, --'po·na] *m, f* **1.** *Méx* *inf* little boy or girl; **los tripones** the kids **2.** *inf* (*gordo*) fatty

tripulación [tri·pu·la·'sjon, -'θjon] *f* crew

tripulina [tri·pu·'li·na] *f Chile* hubbub

trisca ['tris·ka] *f AmC* surreptitious sneer

triscar <c → qu> [tris·'kar] *vt AmC* to make fun of

triste ['tris·te] *adj* sad; **un ~ sueldo** a miserable salary; **ni un ~...:** not a single...; **es ~ que no podamos ir** it's too bad we can't go

tristeza [tris·'te·sa, -θa] *f*, **tristura** [tris·'tu·ra] *f AmL* sadness

trituradora [tri·tu·ra·'do·ra] *f* grinder; TÉC crusher; **~ de carne** meat grinder; **~ de papel** paper shredder; **~ de basura** waste-disposal unit; **~ de hielo** ice crusher

triturar [tri·tu·'rar] *vt* to chop; (*moler*) to grind; (*al masticar*) to chew

triunfador(a) [trjun·fa·'dor, --'do·ra] *m(f)* winner

triunfar [trjun·'far] *vi* to triumph; **~ en algo** to win at sth; (*tener éxito*) to succeed; **~ en la vida** to succeed in life

triunfo ['trjun·fo] *m* triumph, victory; (*éxito*) success

trivialidad [tri·βja·li·'dad] *f* triviality; (*dicho*) trite remark

triza ['tri·sa, -θa] *f* shred; **estar hecho ~s** to feel washed out; **hacer ~s** to tear into shreds; **hacerse ~s** to smash to bits

trocar [tro·'kar] *irr como* volcar *vt* **1.** ~ **por algo** to exchange for sth **2.** *CSur* (*vender*) to sell

trofeo [tro·'feo] *m* trophy

troglodita [tro·ɣlo·'di·ta] *m* **1.** troglodyte **2.** *inf* lout

tromba ['trom·ba] *f* ~ **(de agua)** water spout; (*aguacero*) downpour

trombón [trom·'bon] *m* trombone

trombosis [trom·'bo·sis] *f inv* thrombosis

trompa¹ ['trom·pa] *f* **1.** ZOOL trunk; ~ **de Falopio** Fallopian tube **2.** *inf* (*nariz*) conk **3.** *AmL inf* (*labios*) lips *pl* **4.** *inf* drunkenness; **coger una ~** to get smashed; **estar ~** to be drunk

trompa² ['trom·pa] *mf* *CSur inf* boss

trompada [trom·'pa·da] *f,* **trompazo** [trom·'pa·so, -θo] *m* (*porrazo*) bash; (*choque*) crash

trompear [trom·pe·'ar] *AmL, inf* **I.** *vt* to punch **II.** *vr:* ~**se** to get plastered; (*pelearse*) to fight

trompeta [trom·'pe·ta] *f* trumpet

trompicón [trom·pi·'kon] *m* **1. a trompicones** in fits and starts **2.** *AmC* punch

trompis ['trom·pis] *m inv* *Arg, Urug* punch; **agarrarse a ~** to start punching each other

trompiza [trom·'pi·sa] *f* *AmS* fight

trompo ['trom·po] *m* spinning top

trompudo, -a [trom·'pu·do, -a] *adj AmL* thick-lipped

tronado, -a [tro·'na·do, -a] *adj inf* **estar ~** (*loco*) to be cracked; (*arruinado*) to be broke; *AmL* (*drogado*) to be high on drugs

tronar <o → ue> [tro·'nar] *vi, vimpers* to thunder

troncha ['tron·tʃa] *f* *Arg, Chile, Perú* slice

tronchar [tron·'tʃar] **I.** *vt* (*tronco*) to cut down; (*rama*) to snap; (*vida*) to cut

short; (*esperanzas*) to shatter **II.** *vr:* ~**se** to split; ~**se de risa** to split one's sides laughing

troncho ['tron·tʃo] *m* **1.** stalk **2.** *CSur* (*trozo*) chunk

tronco [tron·ko] *m* **1.** BOT, ANAT trunk; (*leño*) log; **dormir como un ~** *inf* to sleep like a log **2.** *inf* buddy; **tranqui ~** cool it, pal

tronera [tro·'ne·ra] *f* *Méx* chimney

trono ['tro·no] *m* throne; *inf* john

tropa ['tro·pa] *f* crowd; *pey* horde; MIL troop

tropel [tro·'pel] *m* throng; **en ~** in a mad rush; **salieron en ~ del estadio** they came pouring out of the stadium

tropero [tro·'pe·ro] *m* *Arg* cowboy

tropezar [tro·pe·'sar, -'θar] *irr como* empezar **I.** *vi* to trip **II.** *vr* ~**se con** to run into

tropezón [tro·pe·'son, -'θon] *m* **1.** (*acción*) stumble; **dar un ~** to trip; **a tropezones** by fits and starts; *fig* falling and rising; **hablaba a tropezones** he/she spoke falteringly **2.** (*error*) mistake; (*desliz*) lapse **3.** CULIN small chunk, esp of meat

tropical [tro·pi·'kal] *adj* tropical

trópico ['tro·pi·ko] *m* tropic; **pasar los ~s** *AmC* to have a hard time

tropiezo [tro·'pje·so, -θo] *m* **dar un ~** to trip; (*error*) blunder

tropilla [tro·'pi·ja, -ʎa] *f* *CSur* drove

trotar [tro·'tar] *vi* to trot

trozo ['tro·so, -θo] *m* piece, bit; **a ~s** in pieces

trucar [tru·'kar] *vt* **1.** (*amañar*) to fix; FOTO to alter **2.** AUTO to soup up

trucha ['tru·tʃa] *f* **1.** trout; ~ **asalmonada** salmon trout **2.** *AmC* stand

trucho, -a ['tru·tʃo, -a] *adj Arg, Col* crafty

truco ['tru·ko] *m* trick; **esto tiene ~** there's a trick to this ▶ **coger el ~ a** to get the hang of sth; (*a alguien*) to catch on to sb

trueno ['trwe·no] *m* clap of thunder

trueque ['trwe·ke] *m* exchange

trufa ['tru·fa] *f* truffle

truncar <c → qu> [trun·'kar] *vt* to truncate; (*desarrollo*) to stunt; (*esperanzas*, *ilusiones*) to shatter

trusa ['tru·sa] *f Méx, Perú* girdle

tu [tu] *art pos* your; ~ **padre/blusa/libro** your father/blouse/book; ~**s hermanos/as** your brothers/sisters

tú [tu] *pron pers* you; **yo que ~** if I were you; **de ~ a ~** on equal footing

tuba ['tu·βa] *f* tuba

tubérculo [tu·'βer·ku·lo] *m* tuber; MED tubercle

tuberculosis [tu·βer·ku·'lo·sis] *f inv* tuberculosis

tubería [tu·βe·'ri·a] *f* pipe

tubo ['tu·βo] *m* 1. tube; ~ **digestivo** alimentary canal; ~ **de ensayo/escape** test/exhaust tube; **alucinar por un** ~ *inf* to really flip; **tenemos trabajo por un** ~ *inf* we have loads of work to do 2. *AmL* TEL receiver

tucán [tu·'kan] *m* toucan

tuerca ['twer·ka] *f* nut

tuerto, -a ['twer·to] *adj* one-eyed

tuétano ['twe·ta·no] *m* 1. (*médula*) marrow 2. (*corazón, esencia*) core; **hasta los ~s** through and through; **enamorado hasta los ~s** head over heels in love; **llegar al ~ de un asunto** to get to the crux of a matter; **calado hasta los ~s** soaked to the skin

tufo ['tu·fo] *m* stink

tulipa [tu·'li·pa] *f* tulip-shaped lampshade

tulipán [tu·li·'pan] *m* tulip

tumba ['tum·ba] *f* 1. grave; **soy una** ~ my lips are sealed 2. *AmL* (*tala*) felling of trees; (*claro*) tree clearing

tumbar [tum·'bar] I. *vt* 1. to knock down; **estar tumbado** to be lying down 2. *AmL* to fell; (*tierra*) to clear II. *vr:* ~**se** to lie down

tumbo ['tum·bo] *m* (*caída*) tumble; (*vaivén*) roll; **dar un** ~ to jolt; **ir por la vida dando** ~**s** to go through life moving from one hardship to another

tumor [tu·'mor] *m* tumor

tumulto [tu·'mul·to] *m* tumult

tunda ['tun·da] *f* beating; **darse una** ~ to wear oneself out

túnel [tu·'nel] *m* tunnel; ~ **de lavado** car wash

túnica ['tu·ni·ka] *f* tunic

tuntún [tun·'tun] *m inf* **al** (**buen**) ~ any old way; **juzgar al buen** ~ to jump to conclusions

tupé [tu·'pe] *m* pompadour

tupí [tu·'pi] *mf AmL* Tupi

tupido, -a [tu·'pi·do, -a] *adj* 1. thick 2. *AmL* blocked 3. *Méx* frequent

tupirse [tu·'pir·se] *vr AmL* to get blocked up

turbación [tur·βa·'sjon, -'θjon] *f* confusion; (*agitación*) concern

turbante [tur·'βan·te] *m* turban

turbar [tur·'βar] I. *vt* to disturb; (*avergonzar*) to embarrass II. *vr:* ~**se** to be disturbed; (*avergonzarse*) to get embarrassed

turbina [tur·'βi·na] *f* turbine

turbio, -a ['tur·βjo, -a] *adj* (*líquido*) cloudy; (*asunto*) turbid; (*negocio*) shady

turbulencia [tur·βu·'len·sja, -θja] *f* turbulence; (*alboroto*) commotion

turbulento, -a [tur·βu·'len·to, -a] *adj* 1. (*agua, aire*) turbulent 2. (*alborotado*) stormy 3. (*rebelde*) disorderly

turismo [tu·'ris·mo] *m* 1. tourism; ~ **verde** ecotourism; **industria del** ~ tourist trade; **oficina de** ~ visitors' bureau; **hacer** ~ to travel as a tourist 2. AUTO private car

turista [tu·'ris·ta] *mf* tourist

turístico, -a [tu·'ris·ti·ko, -a] *adj* tourist; **viaje** ~ sightseeing trip

turnar [tur·'nar] *vi, vr:* ~**se** to take turns

turno ['tur·no] *m* 1. (*laboral*) shift; **cambio de** ~ shift change; **estar de** ~ to be on duty; ~ **de día/noche** day/night shift 2. (*orden*) turn; **por** ~**s** by turns; **hacer algo por** ~**s** to take turns doing sth; **apareció con la novia de** ~ he showed up with his latest girlfriend

turquesa¹ [tur·'ke·sa] I. *adj* turquoise II. *m* (*color*) turquoise blue

turquesa² [tur·'ke·sa] *f* MIN (*piedra*) turquoise

turrón [tu·'rron] *m* ≈ nougat

turulato, -a [tu·ru·'la·to, -a] *adj inf* dazed; **dejar a alguien** ~ to leave sb flabbergasted

tusar [tu·'sar] I. *vi Guat* to murmur II. *vt AmL* to scalp *fig*

tuso, -a ['tu·so, -a] *adj* 1. *Col, PRico* (*pelón*) cropped 2. *Col, Ven* (*viruelas*)

T

pockmarked **3.** *PRico* (*rabón*) bob-tailed

tutear [tu·te·'ar] **I.** *vt* to address in the familiar manner using '*tú*' **II.** *vr:* ~**se** to be on familiar terms

tutela [tu·'te·la] *f* protection; **bajo la ~ de** under the protection of

tutelaje [tu·te·'la·xe] *m* *CSur, Guat, Méx* guardianship

tuteo [tu·'teo] *m* familiar use of '*tú*'

tutilimundi [tu·ti·li·'mun·di] *m* *AmL inf* everybody

tutor(a) [tu·'tor, -·'to·ra] *m(f)* JUR guardian; ENS tutor

tutoría [tu·to·'ri·a] *f* JUR guardianship; ENS tutorship

tuyo, -a ['tu·jo, -a] *pron pos* **1.** yours; **el perro es ~** the dog is yours **2.** (*tras artículo*) **el ~/la tuya/lo ~** yours; **mi coche está roto, vamos en el ~** my car isn't working, let's take yours; **los ~s** (*parientes*) your family; **tú a lo ~** mind your own business; **esto no es lo ~** this isn't your strong point **3.** (*tras subst*) of yours; **una amiga tuya** a friend of yours; **es culpa tuya** it's your fault

U

U, u [u] *f* <úes> U, u; **~ de Uruguay** U as in Uniform

U *abr de* **Universidad** U.

u [u] *conj ante 'o', 'ho'* or; **diez u once** ten or eleven

ubicación [u·βi·ka·'sjon, -'θjon] *f* **1.** location; (*de empresa*) site **2.** *AmL* (*colocación*) placing

ubicar <c → qu> [u·βi·'kar] **I.** *vi* **estar ~** to be situated **II.** *vt* *AmL* to situate; (*guardar*) to place **III.** *vr:* ~**se** to be situated

ubre [u·'βre] *f* udder

UCI ['u·si, -θi] *abr de* **Unidad de Cuidados Intesivos** ICU

Ud(s). [us·'ted, -·'te·des] *abr de* **usted(es)** you

UE [u·'e] *f abr de* **Unión Europea** EU

úlcera ['ul·se·ra, 'ul·θe-] *f* ulcer

ulterior [ul·te·'rjor] *adj* subsequent

últimamente ['ul·ti·ma·'men·te] *adv* recently, lately; (*por último*) lastly

ultimar [ul·ti·'mar] *vt* **1.** to complete; (*acuerdo*) to conclude **2.** *AmL* to murder

ultimátum [ul·ti·'ma·tun] *m* <inv *o* ultimatos> ultimatum

último, -a ['ul·ti·mo, -a] *adj* last; **el ~** the last; **por última vez** for the last time; **la última moda** the latest fashion; **por ~** lastly; **la última fila** the last row; **en el ~ piso** on the top floor; **ocupar la última posición de la tabla** to be at the bottom of the chart ▶ **estar en las últimas** to be at death's door

ultra ['ul·tra] **I.** *adj* extreme **II.** *mf* neofascist **III.** *adv* extremely

ultracongelado, -a [ul·tra·kon·xe·'la·do, -a] *adj* deep-frozen

ultraconservador(a) [ul·tra·kon·ser·βa·'dor, -·'do·ra] *adj* ultraconservative

ultrajar [ul·tra·'xar] *vt* to insult; **~ de palabra** to revile

ultraje [ul·'tra·xe] *m* abuse

ultramar [ul·tra·'mar] *m* overseas

ultramarinos [ul·tra·ma·'ri·nos] *mpl* grocery store

ultramoderno, -a [ul·tra·mo·'der·no, -a] *adj* extremely modern

ultranza [ul·'tran·sa, -θa] *f* **luchar a ~** to fight to the death; **ser un ecologista a ~** to be a radical ecologist

ultrarrápido, -a [ul·tra·'rra·pi·do, -a] *adj* extra fast

ultrasónico, -a [ul·tra·'so·ni·ko, -a] *adj* ultrasonic

ultrasonido [ul·tra·so·'ni·do] *m* ultrasound

ultravioleta [ul·tra·βjo·'le·ta] *adj inv* ultraviolet

umbilical [um·bi·li·'kal] *adj* umbilical

umbral [um·'bral] *m* threshold; (*principio*) beginning

umbrío, -a [um·'bri·o, -a] *adj* shady

UME ['u·me] *f abr de* **Unión Monetaria Europea** EMU

un [un], **una** ['u·na] <unos, -as> **I.** *art indef* **1.** a; (*ante vocal o h muda*) an; **un perro** a dog; **una chica** a girl **2.** *pl* (*algunos*) some, a few **3.** *pl* (*aproximadamente*) approximately, about; **unos**

30 pesos about 30 pesos **II.** *adj v.* **uno, -a**

unánime [u·'na·ni·me] *adj* unanimous

unanimidad [u·na·ni·mi·'ðað] *f* unanimity; **por ~** unanimously

UNED [u·'neð] *f abr de* **Universidad Nacional de Educación a Distancia** ≈ OU

ungir <g → j> [un·'xir] *vt* to anoint

ungüento [un·'gwen·to] *m* salve; MED ointment

únicamente [u·ni·ka·'men·te] *adv* solely

unicameral [u·ni·ka·me·'ral] *adj* single-chamber

único, -a ['u·ni·ko, -a] *adj* only; (*extraordinario*) unique; **hijo ~** only child; **heredero ~** sole heir; **dirección única** one-way

unicornio [u·ni·'kor·njo] *m* unicorn

unidad [u·ni·'ðað] *f* 1. MIL, MAT, TÉC, COMPUT unit; **Unidad de Cuidados Intensivos** [*o de* **Vigilancia Intensiva**] intensive care unit 2. (*armonía*) unity

unidimensional [u·ni·di·men·sjo·'nal] *adj* one-dimensional

unido, -a [u·'ni·do, -a] *adj* united; **estamos muy ~s** we are very close; **mantenerse ~s** to stay together

unifamiliar [u·ni·fa·mi·'ljar] *adj* single-family; (*casa*) detached

unificación [u·ni·fi·ka·'sjon, -'θjon] *f* unification; (*uniformización*) standardization

unificar <c → qu> [u·ni·fi·'kar] *vt* to unite; (*uniformar*) to standardize; (*posiciones*) to unify

uniformar [u·ni·for·'mar] *vt* to standardize

uniforme [u·ni·'for·me] *adj, m* uniform

uniformidad [u·ni·for·mi·'ðað] *f* (*constancia*) regularity; (*similaridad*) uniformity

uniformizar <z → c> [u·ni·for·mi·'sar, -'θar] *vt* to standardize; (*mezclar*) to blend

unilateral [u·ni·la·te·'ral] *adj* one-sided; POL unilateral

unión [u·'njon] *f* 1. *t.* TÉC (*de dos elementos*) joint 2. *t.* ECON, POL (*territorial*) union; **Unión Europea** European Union; **Unión de Repúblicas Socialistas Soviéticas** Union of Soviet Socialist Republics; **~ monetaria** monetary union; **en ~ con** (together) with 3. (*matrimonio*) marriage 4. COM merger 5. (*armonía*) unity ► **la ~ hace la fuerza** united we stand

unir [u·'nir] **I.** *vt* 1. (*dos elementos*) to join 2. (*territorios, familia*) to unite; (*esfuerzos*) to combine **II.** *vr:* **~se** to unite; ECON to merge; **~se en matrimonio** to marry

unisex [u·ni·'seks] *adj* unisex

unísono [u·'ni·so·no] *m* unison; **al ~** in unison

unitario, -a [u·ni·'ta·rjo, -a] *adj* unitary

universal [u·ni·βer·'sal] *adj* 1. (*del universo*) universal 2. (*del mundo*) worldwide; **historia ~** world history 3. (*amplio*) widespread

universalidad [u·ni·βer·sa·li·'ðað] *f* universality

universalizar <z → c> [u·ni·βer·sa·li·'sar, -'θar] *vt* to make universal

universidad [u·ni·βer·si·'ðað] *f* university; **ir a la ~** to go to college [*o* university]; **Universidad Nacional de Educación a Distancia** ≈ Open University

universitario, -a [u·ni·βer·si·'ta·rjo, -a] **I.** *adj* university; **tener estudios ~s** to have studied at university **II.** *m, f* university student

universo [u·ni·'βer·so] *m* universe

unívoco, -a [u·'ni·βo·ko, -a] *adj* unanimous

uno ['u·no] *m* one

uno, -a ['u·no, -a] **I.** *adj* one; **a la una** at one o'clock; **¡(a la) una, (a las) dos y (a las) tres!** ready, set, go! **II.** *pron indef* 1. one; **cada ~** each (one), every one; **~s cuantos** some; **~..., el otro...** one..., the other...; **~ de tantos** one of many; **aquí hay ~ que pregunta por ti** there's sb here asking for you; **una de dos, o... o...** the choice is simple, either... or....; **una que otra vez** once in a while; **de ~ en ~** one by one; **no acierto una** I can't do anything right; **lo ~ por lo otro** what goes around comes around 2. *pl* some

untar [un·'tar] **I.** *vt* to spread; (*mojar*) to dip; (*grasa*) to grease **II.** *vr* **~se de algo**

U

to become smeared with sth; **~se con/ de algo** (*crema*) to rub sth in

uña [u·ņa] *f* nail; ZOOL claw; **comerse las ~s** to bite one's nails; *fig* to become furious ▶ **ser ~ y carne** to be inseparable; **defenderse con ~s y dientes** to fight tooth and nail to defend oneself

upa [u·pa] **I.** *interj* oops-a-daisy; **llevar a ~ un niño** to carry a child **II.** *adj Ecua, Perú* idiot

uranio [u·ra·njo] *m* uranium

urbanícola [ur·βa·ni·ko·la] *mf* city dweller

urbanidad [ur·βa·ni·dad] *f* urbanity

urbanismo [ur·βa·nis·mo] *m* town planning

urbanístico, -a [ur·βa·nis·ti·ko, -a] *adj* town-planning; **desarrollo ~** urban development; **plan ~** development plan

urbanización [ur·βa·ni·sa·sjon, -θa·'θjon] *f* urbanization; (*residencial*) housing estate

urbanizar <z → c> [ur·βa·ni·sar, -'θar] *vt* to urbanize

urbano [ur·βa·no] *m* traffic policeman

urbano, -a [ur·βa·no, -a] *adj* urban

urbe ['ur·βe] *f* metropolis

urgencia [ur·xen·sja, -θja] *f* **1.** (*cualidad*) urgency **2.** (*caso*) emergency **3.** *pl* emergency room

urgente [ur·xen·te] *adj* urgent; (*envío*) express; **un pedido ~** a rush order

urgir <g → j> [ur·xir] *vi* to be urgent

urinario [u·ri·na·rjo] *m* urinal

urinario, -a [u·ri·na·rjo, -a] *adj* urinary; **aparato ~** urinary tract

urna ['ur·na] *f* glass case; (*para cenizas*) urn; POL ballot box

urogallo [u·ro·'ɣa·jo, -ʎo] *m* ZOOL capercaillie

urología [u·ro·lo·'xi·a] *f* urology

urraca [u·'rra·ka] *f* magpie; *inf* chatterbox

URSS [urs] *f abr de* **Unión de Repúblicas Socialistas Soviéticas** USSR

urticaria [ur·ti·'ka·rja] *f* hives *pl*

Uruguay [u·ru·'ɣwai] *m* Uruguay

uruguayo, -a [u·ru·'ɣwa·jo, -a] *adj, m, f* Uruguayan

usado, -a [u·'sa·do, -a] *adj* secondhand; (*gastado*) worn; (*sello*) used

usanza [u·'san·sa, -θa] *f* usage

usar [u·'sar] **I.** *vt* to use; (*ropa, gafas*) to wear; **de ~ y tirar** disposable; **sin ~** brand new **II.** *vr*: **~se** to use; **esta palabra ya no se usa** this word is no longer in use; **los escotes ya no se usan** low necklines are out of fashion

usina [u·'si·na] *f AmL* (*de gas*) gasworks; (*de electricidad*) power plant

uso ['u·so] *m* use; (*costumbre*) *t.* LING usage; **de ~ externo** for external application; **hacer ~ de algo** to make use of sth; **una expresión de ~ corriente** an everyday expression

usted [us·'ted] *pron* **1.** *sing* you; **~es** you; **tratar de ~** to address courteously **2.** *pl AmL* (*vosotros*) you

usual [u·su·'al] *adj* usual; (*común*) common

usuario, -a [u·su·'a·rjo, -a] *m, f* user

usura [u·'su·ra] *f* usury

usurero, -a [u·su·'re·ro, -a] *m, f* usurer

usurpar [u·sur·'par] *vt* to usurp

utensilio [u·ten·'si·ljo] *m* utensil; (*herramienta*) tool

uterino, -a [u·te·'ri·no, -a] *adj* ANAT, MED uterine; **furor ~** nymphomania

útero ['u·te·ro] *m* uterus; **el cuello del ~** the cervix

útil ['u·til] **I.** *adj* useful; (*ayuda*) helpful; **¿en qué puedo serle ~?** can I be of any help to you? **II.** *mpl* tools *pl*

utilidad [u·ti·li·'dad] *f* utility; **ser de ~** to be useful

utilizable [u·ti·li·'sa·βle, -'θa·βle] *adj* usable

utilización [u·ti·li·sa·'sjon, -θa·'θjon] *f* utilization

utilizar <z → c> [u·ti·li·'sar, -'θar] **I.** *vt* to use; (*tiempo, a alguien*) to make use of sth **II.** *vr*: **~se** to be used

utopía [u·to·'pi·a] *f* utopia

utópico, -a [u·'to·pi·ko, -a] *adj* utopian

uva ['u·βa] *f* grape; **~ pasa** raisin **2.** *inf* **estar de mala ~** to be in a bad mood; **tener mala ~** to be bad-tempered

UVI ['u·βi] *f abr de* **Unidad de Vigilancia Intensiva** ICU

V

V, v [u·βe] f V, v; **~ de Valencia** V as in Victor

vaca ['baka] f cow; (*carne*) beef; **síndrome de las ~s locas** mad cow disease; **~ gordas/flacas** prosperous/lean period; **ponerse como una ~** to get as fat as a cow

vacaciones [baka·'sjones, -'θjones] fpl vacation; **de ~** on vacation

vacante [ba·'kante] I. adj vacant II. f vacancy; (*puesto*) unfilled post

vaciado [ba·si·'a·do, ba·θi-] m 1. (*molde*) cast 2. (*ahuecamiento*) hollowing out 3. COMPUT dumping

vaciar <1. pres vacío> [ba·si·'ar, ba·θi-] vt to empty; (*verter*) to pour; (*escultura*) to cast

vacilación [ba·si·la·'sjon, -θi·la·'θjon] f hesitation; **sin vacilaciones** unhesitatingly

vacilada [ba·si·'la·da, ba·θi-] f inf ¡**menuda ~!** cool!; Méx (*borrachera*) binge; (*chiste*) joke; (*chiste verde*) dirty joke; (*timo*) rip-off; **me dieron una ~** they really ripped me off

vacilante [ba·si·'lan·te, ba·θi-] adj hesitant; (*voz*) faltering

vacilar [ba·si·'lar, ba·θi-] vi 1. (*dudar*) to hesitate 2. inf **~ a alguien** to pull sb's leg; **¡no me vaciles!** don't give me that!

vacío [ba·'si·o, -'θi·o] m emptiness; FÍS vacuum; (*abismo*) void; **~ legal** legal void; **~ de poder** political vacuum; **envasado al ~** vacuum-packed

vacío, -a [ba·'si·o, -a; -'θi·o, -a] adj empty; (*hueco*) hollow; (*insustancial*) insubstantial; **con las manos vacías** emptyhanded; **de ~** empty-handed

vacuna [ba·'ku·na] f (*sustancia*) vaccine; (*vacunación*) vaccination; **poner una ~** to vaccinate

vacunación [ba·ku·na·'sjon, -'θjon] f vaccination; **cartilla de ~** vaccination certificate

vacunar [ba·ku·'nar] I. vt to vaccinate II. vr: **~se** to get vaccinated; **se ha vacunado contra la gripe** he/she got vaccinated against flu

vacuno [ba·'ku·no] m cattle

vacuno, -a [ba·'ku·no, -a] adj cow; **ganado ~** cattle

vado ['ba·do] m **~ permanente** keep clear

vagabundear [ba·ɣa·βun·de·'ar] vi to wander; pey to be a tramp

vagabundo, -a [ba·ɣa·'βun·do, -a] I. adj wandering; (*perro*) stray; fig, pey vagrant II. m, f wanderer; fig tramp

vagancia [ba·'ɣan·sja, -θja] f laziness

vagar [ba·'ɣar] <g → gu> vi to wander

vagina [ba·'xi·na] f vagina

vago, -a ['ba·ɣo] I. adj lazy; (*impreciso*) vague II. m, f lazybones; **hacer el ~** to laze about

vagón [ba·'ɣon] m car; (*de mercancías*) freight car; **~ restaurante** dining car

vaguear [ba·ɣe·'ar] vi to laze about

vaguedad [ba·ɣe·'dad] f vagueness

vahído [ba·'i·do] m dizzy spell

vaho ['ba·o] m vapor

vaina ['bai·na] f BOT pod

vainica [bai·'ni·ka] f CRi string bean

vainilla [bai·'ni·ja, -ʎa] f vanilla

vaivén [bai·'βen] m swaying; (*sacudida*) lurch

vajilla [ba·'xi·ja, -ʎa] f dishes, dishware

vale ['ba·le] m voucher

valedero, -a [ba·le·'de·ro, -a] adj valid; (*vigente*) in force

valedura [ba·le·'du·ra] f Méx (*favor*) favor; (*protección*) protection; (*ayuda*) help

valenciana [ba·len·'sja·na] f 1. CSur (*encaje*) fine cotton lace 2. Méx (*dobladillo*) pant cuff

valentía [ba·len·'ti·a] f bravery

valer [ba·'ler] irr I. vt to cost; (*equivaler*) to equal ▶ **más vale que te olvides de él** you'd best forget him; **¡vale ya!** that's enough!; **¡vale!** OK! II. vi 1. to be of use; (*tener validez*) to be valid; **no vale** it's no good 2. (*tener mérito*) to be worthy; **no ~ nada** to be worthless; **~ poco** to be worth little 3. (*permitirse*) to be allowed III. vr: **~se** 1. (*servirse*) to make use 2. (*desenvolverse*) to manage; **ya no puede ~se solo** he can't fend for himself any longer

valeriana [ba·le·'rja·na] *f* valerian

valeroso, -a [ba·le·'ro·so, -a] *adj* brave

valía [ba·'li·a] *f* worth

validar [ba·li·'dar] *vt* to validate

validez [ba·li·'des, -'deθ] *f* validity; **dar ~ a** to validate; **tener ~** to be valid; (*ley*) to be in force

válido, -a [ba·'li·do, -a] *adj* valid

valiente [ba·'ljen·te] *adj* brave

valija [ba·'li·xa] *f* case; (*del cartero*) mailbag; **~ diplomática** diplomatic bag

valioso, -a [ba·'ljo·so, -a] *adj* valuable

valla ['ba·ja, -ʎa] *f* (*tapia*) wall; (*alambrada*) fence; DEP hurdle

vallado [ba·'ja·do, -'ʎa·do] *m* fence

vallar [ba·'jar, -'ʎar] *vt* to fence in

valle ['ba·je, -ʎe] *m* valley

vallunco, -a [ba·'jun·ko, -a; ba·'ʎun-] *adj* AmC rustic

valona [ba·'lo·na] *f* Méx **hacer a alguien la ~** *inf* to put in a good word for sb

valor [ba·'lor] *m* **1.** bravery; **armarse de ~** to pluck up courage **2.** (*morro*) cheek **3.** (*valía*) value; (*cuantía*) amount **4.** (*significado*) meaning **5.** *pl* FIN securities *pl*; **~es inmuebles** real estate **6.** **~es morales** moral principles; **escala de ~es** scale of values

valoración [ba·lo·ra·'sjon, -'θjon] *f* valuation; (*análisis*) assessment

valorar [ba·lo·'rar] *vt* to value (**en** at); **valoro muchísimo tu ayuda** I greatly appreciate your help

valorizar <z → c> [ba·lo·ri·'sar, -'θar] *vt v.* **valorar**

vals [bals] *m* waltz

válvula ['bal·βu·la] *f* valve

vampiro [bam·'pi·ro] *m* vampire

vanagloriarse [ba·na·ɣlo·'rjar·se] *vr* to boast

vanamente [ba·na·'men·te] *adv* vainly

vandalismo [ban·da·'lis·mo] *m* vandalism

vándalo, -a ['ban·da·lo, -a] *adj, m, f* vandal

vanguardia [ban·'gwar·dja] *f* forefront; LIT avant-garde; **de ~** ultra-modern

vanguardista [ban·gwar·'dis·ta] I. *adj* ultra-modern II. *mf* pioneer

vanidad [ba·ni·'dad] *f* vanity

vanidoso, -a [ba·ni·'do·so, -a] *adj* vain

vano ['ba·no] *m* space

vano, -a ['ba·no, -a] *adj* vain; (*infundado*) groundless

vánova ['ba·no·βa] *f* Arg bedspread

vapor [ba·'por] *m* steam; **cocer al ~** to steam

vaporizador [ba·po·ri·sa·'dor, ba·po·ri·θa-] *m* vaporizer

vaporizar <z → c> [ba·po·ri·'sar, -'θar] I. *vt* to vaporize; (*spray*) to spray II. *vr:* **~se** to vaporize

vaporizo [ba·po·'ri·so] *m* Méx, PRico **1.** (*vaho*) vapor; (*para inhalar*) inhalation **2.** (*calor*) sultry heat

vaporoso, -a [ba·po·'ro·so, -a] *adj* steamy; (*tela*) light

vapulear [ba·pu·le·'ar] *vt* to beat

vapuleo [ba·pu·'leo] *m* beating

vaquería [ba·ke·'ri·a] *f* AmS cattle-rearing; (*lechería*) dairy

vaquero, -a [ba·'ke·ro, -a] I. *adj* cattle II. *m, f* cowboy, cowgirl *m, f*

vaquero(s) [ba·'ke·ro(s)] *m(pl)* jeans *pl*

vaquetón, -ona [ba·ke·'ton, --'to·na] *adj* Méx *inf* (*lento*) sluggish; (*vago*) shiftless; (*descarado*) shameless

vaquilla [ba·'ki·ja, -ʎa] *f*, **vaquillona** [ba·ki·'jo·na, -'ʎo·na] *f* Arg, Chile, Nic, Perú heifer

vara ['ba·ra] *f* stick

varar [ba·'rar] *vi* **1.** to run aground **2.** AmL to break down

varear [ba·re·'ar] *vt* (*fruta*) to knock down; (*lana*) to sell by the yard

varejón [ba·re·'xon] *m* AmS, Nic switch

variable [ba·ri·'a·βle] I. *adj* variable; (*carácter*) changeable II. *f* variable

variación [ba·rja·'sjon, -'θjon] *f* oscillation; MAT, MÚS variation

variado, -a [ba·ri·'a·do, -a] *adj* varied; (*mezclado*) assorted

variante [ba·ri·'an·te] *f* version; (*variedad*) variety; LING variant

variar <1. pres varío> [ba·ri·'ar] *vi, vt* to vary; **y para ~...** and for a change...

varicela [ba·ri·'se·la, -'θe·la] *f* chickenpox

variedad [ba·rje·'dad] *f* variety; **una gran ~ de** a wide range of ▶ **en la ~ está el gusto** variety is the spice of life

variopinto, -a [ba·rjo·'pin·to, -a] *adj* di-

verse; (*color*) colorful

varios, -as |'ba·rjos, -as| *adj pl* some; (*diferentes*) several

variz |ba·'ris, -'riθ| *f* varicose vein

varón |ba·'ron| *m* male

varonil |ba·ro·'nil| *adj* virile; (*mujer*) mannish

vasallo, -a |ba·'sa·jo, -a; -ʎo, -a| *m, f* vassal

vasija |ba·'si·xa| *f* container

vaso |'ba·so| *m* glass; **un ~ de agua** a glass of water; **~ de papel** paper cup; ANAT vessel

vástago |'bas·ta·ɣo| *m* scion; **~s** offspring

vasto, -a |'bas·to, -a| *adj* vast; (*saber*) wide

váter |'ba·ter| *m* (*recipiente*) toilet; (*habitación*) washroom

vaticinar |ba·ti·si·'nar, ba·ti·θi-| *vt* to prophesy

vatio |'ba·tjo| *m* watt; **una bombilla de 100 ~s** a 100-watt bulb

Vd. |us·'ted| *pron pers abr de* **usted** you

vda. |'bju·da| *abr de* **viuda** widow

Vds. |us·'te·des| *pron pers abr de* **ustedes** you

vecindad |be·sin·'dad, be·θin-| *f* neighborhood

vecindario |be·sin·'da·rjo, be·θin-| *m* neighborhood

vecino, -a |be·'si·no, -a; be·'θi-| **I.** *adj* **~ de algo** near sth; **~ a algo** similar to sth **II.** *m, f* neighbor; (*habitante*) resident

vector |bek·'tor| *m* vector

veda |'beda| *f* prohibition; **levantar la ~ de animales de caza** to open the hunting season

vedado |be·'da·do| *m* reserve

vedar |be·'dar| *vt* to ban

vedette |be·'det/be·'de·te| *f* (music hall) star

vega |'be·ɣa| *f* **1.** fertile plain **2.** *Cuba* tobacco plantation **3.** *Chile* marshland

vegetación |be·xe·ta·'sjon, -'θjon| *f* vegetation

vegetal |be·xe·'tal| **I.** *adj* plant; **aceite ~** vegetable oil; **carbón ~** charcoal **II.** *m* vegetable

vegetar |be·xe·'tar| *vi* BOT to grow

vegetariano, -a |be·xe·ta·'rja·no, -a| *adj, m, f* vegetarian

vehemencia |be·'men·sja/be·e·'men·sja, -θja| *f* **1.** (*ímpetu*) impetuosity **2.** (*entusiasmo*) eagerness **3.** (*fervor*) vehemence

vehemente |be·'men·te/be·e·'men·te| *adj* impetuous; (*ardiente*) passionate

vehículo |be·'i·ku·lo| *m* vehicle

veinte |'bein·te| *adj inv* twenty; **v. t. ochenta**

veintena |bein·'te·na| *f* **una ~ de personas** about twenty people

vejación |be·xa·'sjon, -'θjon| *f*, **vejamen** |be·'xa·men| *m* **1.** (*molestia*) annoyance **2.** (*humillación*) humiliation

vejar |be·'xar| *vt* to humiliate

vejatorio, -a |be·xa·'to·rjo, -a| *adj* humiliating

vejestorio, -a |be·xes·'to·rjo, -a| *m, f pey* old crock

vejez |be·'xes, -'xeθ| *f* old age; (*envejecimiento*) aging

vejiga |be·'xi·ɣa| *f* blister; ANAT bladder

vela |'be·la| *f* **1.** NÁUT sail **2.** (*luz*) candle ▶ **pasar la** <u>noche</u> **en ~** to have a sleepless night; **estar a** <u>dos</u> **~s** to be broke

velada |be·'la·da| *f* evening (gathering)

veladora |be·la·'do·ra| *f AmL* candlestick

velar |be·'lar| **I.** *vi* to stay awake; **~ por algo** to watch over sth **II.** *vt* to keep watch over; **~ a un muerto** to hold a wake **III.** *vr:* **~se** to blur

velatorio |be·la·'to·rjo| *m* wake

velero |be·'le·ro| *m* sailing ship

veleta |be·'le·ta| *f* weather vane

veliz |be·'lis| *m Méx* (*de cuero*) valise; (*de metal*) case

vello |'be·jo, -ʎo| *m* (body) hair

velludo, -a |be·'ju·do, -a; -'ʎu·do, -a| *adj* hairy

velo |'be·lo| *m* veil; **correr un (tupido) ~ sobre** to draw a veil over

velocidad |be·lo·θi·'dad| *f* **1.** speed; **~ de transmisión de datos** data transfer rate; **exceso de ~** speeding; **a gran/ toda ~** at high/full speed **2.** AUTO gear

velocímetro |be·lo·'si·me·tro, be·lo·'θi-| *m* speedometer

velódromo |be·'lo·dro·mo| *m* cycle track

V

veloz [be·'loθ, -'loθ] *adj* swift; **raudo y ~** in a flash

vena ['be·na] *f* 1. vein 2. (*inspiración*) talent 3. *inf* mood; **dar la ~ a uno** to take it into one's head

venado [be·'na·do] *m* deer; (*carne*) venison

vencedor(a) [ben·se·'dor, -·'do·ra, ben·θe·] I. *adj* winning II. *m(f)* winner

vencejo [ben·'se·xo, -'θe·xo] *m* swift

vencer <c → z> [ben·'ser, -'θer] I. *vi* to win; (*plazo*) to expire II. *vt* to win; (*enemigos*) to defeat; (*obstáculo, sueño*) to overcome ▶ **a la tercera va la vencida** third time lucky

vencimiento [ben·si·'mjen·to, -θi·'mjen·to] *m* expiry

venda ['ben·da] *f* bandage

vendaje [ben·'da·xe] *m* bandaging

vendar [ben·'dar] *vt* to bandage

vendaval [ben·da·'βal] *m* strong wind; (*huracán*) hurricane

vendedor(a) [ben·de·'dor, -·'do·ra] *m(f)* seller; **~ ambulante** hawker; **~ a domicilio** door-to-door salesman

vender [ben·'der] I. *vt, vi* to sell II. *vr:* **~se** 1. to sell; **se vende** for sale 2. (*persona*) to give oneself away

vendimia [ben·'di·mja] *f* grape harvest

vendimiar [ben·di·'mjar] *vi* to harvest grapes

veneno [be·'ne·no] *m* poison

venenoso, -a [be·ne·'no·so, -a] *adj* poisonous

venerable [be·ne·'ra·βle] *adj* venerable

veneración [be·ne·ra·'sjon, -'θjon] *f* worship; (*respeto*) veneration

venerar [be·ne·'rar] *vt* to worship; (*respetar*) to venerate

venéreo, -a [be·'ne·reo, -a] *adj* venereal

venezolano, -a [be·ne·so·'la·no, -a; be·ne·θo-] *adj, m, f* Venezuelan

Venezuela [be·ne·'swe·la, -'θwe·la] *f* Venezuela

vengador(a) [ben·ga·'dor, -·'do·ra] I. *adj* vindictive II. *m(f)* avenger

venganza [ben·'gan·sa, -θa] *f* vengeance

vengar <g → gu> [ben·'gar] I. *vt* to avenge; **~ la muerte de alguien** to avenge sb's death II. *vr:* **~se** to take revenge

vengativo, -a [ben·ga·'ti·βo, -a] *adj* vindictive

venida [be·'ni·da] *f* arrival; (*vuelta*) return

venidero, -a [be·ni·'de·ro, -a] *adj* future; **en años venideros** in years to come

venir [be·'nir] *irr* I. *vi* 1. to come; (*llegar*) to arrive; **vengo (a) por la leche** I've come to fetch the milk; **me vinieron ganas de reír** I felt like laughing; **el mes que viene** next month; **ya viene la primavera** spring is on its way; **vienen a ser unos 300 pesos** it works out at about 300 pesos 2. (*figurar*) to appear; **no viene en la guía** it's not in the guide 3. (*prenda*) to suit 4. (*persistir*) to keep on; **ya te lo vengo advirtiendo hace mucho tiempo** I've been warning you for a long time 5. **me viene muy bien** it comes in very handy; **¿te viene bien mañana?** would tomorrow suit you?; **me viene mal** it doesn't suit me ▶ **a mí eso ni me va ni me viene** to me that's neither here nor there; **¿a qué viene...?** why...? II. *vr:* **~se** to come back; **~se abajo** to collapse; *fig* to fail

venta ['ben·ta] *f* sale; **~ al contado** cash sale; **~ a plazos** purchase on an installment plan; **~ al por menor/mayor** retail/wholesale; **en** [*o* **a la**] **~** for sale

ventaja [ben·'ta·xa] *f* advantage; **sacar ~ de** to take advantage of; **tener ~ sobre** to have an advantage over

ventajoso, -a [ben·ta·'xo·so, -a] *adj* advantageous; (*negocio*) profitable

ventana [ben·'ta·na] *f* window ▶ **tirar la casa por la ~** to go to great expense

ventanal [ben·ta·'nal] *m* large window

ventanilla [ben·ta·'ni·ja, -λa] *f* 1. small window; (*de coche*) side window 2. (*taquilla*) ticket office; (*mostrador*) counter

ventilación [ben·ti·la·'sjon, -'θjon] *f* ventilation

ventilador [ben·ti·la·'dor] *m* fan

ventilar [ben·ti·'lar] I. *vt* 1. (*airear*) to ventilate 2. (*resolver*) to clear up II. *vr:* **~se** to air; (*persona*) to get some air

ventisca [ben·'tis·ka] *f* blizzard

ventolera [ben·to·'le·ra] *f* gust of wind; **le ha dado la ~ de...** he/she has taken it into his/her head to...

ventosa [ben·'to·sa] *f* sucker

ventosear [ben·to·se·'ar] *vi* to break wind

ventosidad [ben·to·si·'ðað] *f* fart

ventura [ben·'tu·ra] *f* fortune; **por ~** fortunately

veo-veo ['beo·'βeo] *m* **jugar al ~** to play I-spy

ver [ber] *irr* **I.** *vi*, *vt* to see; (*observar*) to watch; (*encontrarse*) to meet; **lo nunca visto** something unheard of; **no veas lo contenta que se puso** you should have seen how happy she was; **a ~** let's see; **bueno, ya ~emos** well, we'll see; **te veo venir** *fig* I know what you're up to; **tener que ~ con** to have to do with; **eso está por ~** [*o* habrá que ~lo] that remains to be seen ▶ **tengo un hambre/un sueño que no veo** I'm really tired/hungry; **si te he visto, no me acuerdo** out of sight, out of mind; **¡hay que ~!** it just goes to show!; **hay que ~ lo tranquilo que es** he is such a quiet fellow; **¡vamos a ~!** let's see!; **¡a ~, escuchadme todos!** come on, listen to me everybody!; **¡para que veas!** so there!; **luego ya ~emos** we'll see about that later **II.** *vr*: **~se 1.** (*encontrarse*) to meet **2.** (*estado*) to be; **~se apurado** to be in a jam **3.** (*imaginarse*) to imagine **4.** (*parecer*) **se ve que...** it seems... **5.** *AmL* (*aspecto*) to look **6. véase...** **; no se ve ni torta** you can't see a thing **III.** *m* opinion; (*aspecto*) appearance

vera ['be·ra] *f* **1.** (*orilla*) bank; **~ de un río** river bank **2.** (*lado*) edge; **a la ~ de** beside

veracidad [be·ra·si·'ðað, be·ra·θi·-] *f* truthfulness; (*declaración*) veracity

veraneante [be·ra·ne·'an·te] *mf* vacationer

veranear [be·ra·ne·'ar] *vi* to spend the summer

veraneo [be·ra·'neo] *m* summer vacation; **lugar de ~** vacation spot

veraniego, -a [be·ra·'nje·γo, -a] *adj* summer

veranillo [be·ra·'ni·jo, -ʎo] *m* **~ de San Miguel** [*o* de San Juan *AmL*] Indian summer

verano [be·'ra·no] *m* summer

veras ['be·ras] *fpl* **de ~** really

veraz [be·'ras, -'raθ] *adj* true; (*persona*) truthful

verbalizar <z → c> [ber·βa·li·'sar, -'θar] *vt* to verbalize

verbena [ber·'βe·na] *f* street party; BOT verbena

verbo ['ber·βo] *m* verb

verdad [ber·'dad] *f* truth; **ser ~** to be true; **una ~ a medias** a half truth; **a decir ~** to tell you the truth; **de ~** really; **un héroe de ~** a real hero; **¿~?** isn't it? ▶ **~es como puños** self-evident truths; **decir cuatro ~es a alguien** to give sb a piece of one's mind

verdaderamente [ber·da·de·ra·'men·te] *adv* truly

verdadero, -a [ber·da·'de·ro, -a] *adj* true; (*real*) real

verde ['ber·de] **I.** *adj* green; (*chiste*) dirty; **viejo ~** dirty old man ▶ **~ de envidia** green with envy; **poner ~ a alguien** to badmouth sb **II.** *m* **1.** green; (*del árbol*) foliage **2.** *CSur* (*pasto*) pasture; (*mate*) maté; (*ensalada*) salad **3.** *AmC, Méx* (*campo*) countryside

verdear [ber·de·'ar] *vi* *CSur* to drink maté

verdor [ber·'dor] *m* greenness

verdoso, -a [ber·'do·so, -a] *adj* greenish

verdugo [ber·'du·γo] *m* executioner

verdulero, -a [ber·du·'le·ro, -a] *m, f* greengrocer

verdura [ber·'du·ra] *f* vegetable

vereda [be·'re·da] *f* **1.** path **2.** *AmL* sidewalk ▶ **entrar en ~** to start to lead an orderly life

veredicto [be·re·'dik·to] *m* verdict

vergonzoso, -a [ber·γon·'so·so, -a; 'θo·so, -a] *adj* shy; (*acción*) disgraceful

vergüenza [ber·'γwen·sa, -θa] *f* **1.** (*rubor*) shame; **se me cae la cara de ~** I feel so ashamed; **me da ~...** I'm ashamed to...; **pasar ~** to feel embarrassed; **tener poca ~** to have no shame; **pasar ~ ajena** to be embarrassed for sb

V

else **2.** (*pudor*) shyness **3.** (*escándalo*) disgrace **4.** pl private parts pl

verídico, -a [be·'ri·di·ko, -a] *adj* true

verificación [be·ri·fi·ka·'sjon, -'θjon] *f* inspection; (*prueba*) testing

verificar <c → qu> [be·ri·fi·'kar] *vt* to check; (*controlar*) to verify

verja ['ber·xa] *f* grating; (*cerca*) grille; (*puerta*) iron gate

vermú [ber·'mu] *m*, **vermut** [ber·'mu] *m* <vermús> **1.** vermouth **2.** *And, CSur* early performance

vernáculo, -a [ber·'na·ku·lo, -a] *adj* vernacular

verosímil [be·ro·'si·mil] *adj* (*probable*) likely; (*creíble*) credible

verosimilitud [be·ro·si·mi·li·'tud] *f* likelihood

verraco [be·'rra·ko] *m AmC, CSur* wild boar

verraquera [be·rra·'ke·ra] *f AmC, Col inf* drunken bout

verruga [be·'rru·ɣa] *f* wart

versado, -a [ber·'sa·do, -a] *adj* ~ **en algo** expert in sth

versar [ber·'sar] *vi* **1.** to deal (**sobre** with) **2.** *AmC* (*escribir*) to versify; (*charlar*) to chat **3.** *Méx* (*bromear*) to crack jokes

versátil [ber·'sa·til] *adj* flexible; (*persona*) versatile

versículo [ber·'si·ku·lo] *m* verse

versión [ber·'sjon] *f* version; (*descripción*) account; ~ **resumida** abridged version; ~ **original** in the original language

verso ['ber·so] *m* line; **en** ~ in verse; (*género*) verse

vértebra ['ber·te·βra] *f* vertebra

vertebrado [ber·te·'βra·do] *m* vertebrate

vertebral [ber·te·'βral] *adj* vertebral; **columna** ~ spinal column

vertedero [ber·te·'de·ro] *m* garbage dump

verter <e → ie> [ber·'ter] **I.** *vt* to empty; (*líquido*) to pour; (*sin querer*) to spill; (*basura*) to dump; (*ideas, conceptos*) to transfer **II.** *vi* to flow

vertical [ber·ti·'kal] *adj, f* vertical

vértice ['ber·ti·se, -θe] *m* vertex

vertiente [ber·'tjen·te] *f* **1.** slope **2.** (*punto de vista*) perspective **3.** *And, CSur,*

Méx fountain

vertiginoso, -a [ber·ti·xi·'no·so, -a] *adj* giddy; (*velocidad*) excessive

vértigo ['ber·ti·ɣo] *m* vertigo; **causar** ~(**s**) to cause dizziness

vesícula [be·'si·ku·la] *f* vesicle; ~ **biliar** gall bladder

vespa® ['bes·pa] *f* motor scooter

vespasiana [bes·pa·'sja·na] *f Arg, Chile* public urinal

vespertino, -a [bes·per·'ti·no] *adj* crepuscular

vestíbulo [bes·'ti·βu·lo] *m* hall; (*hotel*) lobby

vestido [bes·'ti·do] *m* dress; (*ropa*) clothing

vestidor [bes·ti·'dor] *m* dressing room

vestiduras [bes·ti·'du·ras] *f* **rasgarse las** ~ to make a great show of being shocked

vestigio [bes·'ti·xjo] *m* vestige; (*señal*) trace

vestimenta [bes·ti·'men·ta] *f* clothing

vestir [bes·'tir] *irr como pedir* **I.** *vt* to wear; (*cuerpo, persona*) to dress; ~ **do de pirata** dressed as a pirate ▸ **vísteme despacio que tengo prisa** *prov* make haste slowly **II.** *vi* to dress; ~ **de blanco** to dress in white; ~ **de uniforme** to wear a uniform; ~ **siempre muy bien** to always be very well-dressed **III.** *vr*: ~**se** to get dressed; ~**se a la moda** to dress according to fashion; ~**se de azul** to dress in blue

vestuario [bes·'twa·rjo] *m* wardrobe; TEAT dressing room; DEP changing room

veta ['be·ta] *f* vein; (*madera*) grain

vetar [be·'tar] *vt* to veto

vetarro, -a [be·'ta·rro, -a] *adj Méx inf* old; **ya están muy** ~**s** they're getting up there

veterano [be·te·'ra·no] *m* veteran

veterano, -a [be·te·'ra·no, -a] **I.** *adj* experienced; MIL veteran **II.** *m, f* old hand; MIL veteran

veterinaria [be·te·ri·'na·rja] *f* veterinary science

veterinario, -a [be·te·ri·'na·rjo, -a] *m, f* veterinarian, vet *inf*

veto ['be·to] *m* veto

vez [bes, beθ] *f* **1.** time; **una** ~ once;

dos veces twice; **a la ~** at the same time; **a veces** sometimes; **alguna (que otra) ~** occasionally; **de una ~** in one go; *(por fin)* once and for all; **de ~ en cuando** from time to time; **otra ~** again; **por primera ~** for the first time; **aquella ~** on that occasion; **muchas veces** many times; **¿cuántas veces ...?** how many times ...?; **rara ~** seldom; **tal ~** perhaps; **una y otra ~** time and time again; **de una ~ por todas** once and for all 2. *(turno)* turn; **en ~ de** instead of ▸ **una ~ al año no hace daño** *prov* once won't do any harm

vía ['bi·a] *f* road; *(calle)* street; FERRO track; **Vía Láctea** Milky Way; **~ pública** public thoroughfare; **en ~s de** in the process of; **a Dublín ~ Londres** to Dublin via London; **por ~ férrea/aérea/oral** by rail/air/mouth; **por ~ judicial** by legal means

viable [bi·'a·βle] *adj* viable

viada [bi·'a·da] *f And* speed

viaducto [bja·'duk·to] *m* viaduct

viajante [bja·'xan·te] *mf* traveling salesman

viajar [bja·'xar] *vi* to travel (**en** by, **por** around)

viaje [bi·'a·xe] *m* 1. travel; **estar de ~** to be away; **irse de ~** to go on a trip; **~ de negocios** business trip; **~ organizado** package tour; **~ de ida/ida y vuelta** outgoing/round trip; **¡buen ~!** have a good trip! 2. *(carga)* load; *(recorrido)* trip; **de un ~** *AmC* in one go 3. *inf (drogas)* trip

viajero, -a [bja·'xe·ro, -a] **I.** *adj* traveling **II.** *m, f* traveler; *(pasajero)* passenger

vial [bi·'al] *adj* road; FERRO line

viaraza [bja·'ra·sa] *f AmL* fit of rage; **me dio la ~** I just felt like it

víbora ['bi·βo·ra] *f* viper

viborear [bi·βo·re·'ar] *vi* 1. *AmL inf (murmurar)* to backbite 2. *CSur (serpentear)* to snake

vibración [bi·βra·'sjon, -'θjon] *f* vibration

vibrador [bi·βra·'dor] *m* vibrator

vibrante [bi·'βran·te] *adj* vibrant

vibrar [bi·'βrar] *vi* to vibrate

vicario [bi·'ka·rjo] *m* vicar

vicedirector(a) [bi·se·di·rek·'tor, -·'to·ra; bi·θe-] *m(f)* COM deputy manager

vicepresidente, -a [bi·se·pre·si'den·te, -a; bi·θe-] *m, f* vice president

vicerrector(a) [bi·se·rrek·'tor, -·'to·ra, bi·θe-] *m(f)* UNIV vice president

viceversa [bi·se·'βer·sa, bi·θe-] *adv* vice versa

vichar [bi·'tʃar] *vt Arg, Urug (espiar)* to spy on; *(ver)* to peep at; *(buscar con la mirada)* to look around for

viciado, -a [bi·'sja·do, -a; bi·'θja-] *adj* stuffy

viciarse [bi·'sjar·se, -'θjar·se] *vr:* **~se** 1. *(costumbres)* to deteriorate; *(persona)* to get a bad habit 2. **~se con algo** to become addicted to sth; **~se con la televisión** to get hooked on television

vicio ['bi·sjo, -θjo] *m* bad habit; *(adicción)* vice

vicioso, -a [bi·'sjo·so, -a; bi·'θjo-] *adj* dissolute

vicisitudes [bi·si·si·'tu·des, bi·θi-] *fpl* ups and downs *pl*

víctima ['bik·ti·ma] *f* victim

victimar [bik·ti·'mar] *vt AmL* to injure; *(matar)* to kill

victimario, -a [bik·ti·'ma·rjo, -a] *m, f AmL* murderer

victoria [bik·'to·rja] *f* victory

victorioso, -a [bik·to·'rjo·so, -a] *adj* victorious

vid [bid] *f* (grape)vine

vida ['bi·da] *f* life; **~ íntima** private life; *(grape)* **¿cómo te va la ~?** how's life treating you?; **con ~** alive; **salir con ~** to survive; **buscarse la ~** to get by on one's own ▸ **estar entre la ~ y la muerte** to be fighting for one's life; **de por ~** for life

vidente [bi·'den·te] *mf* sighted person; *(adivino)* clairvoyant

vídeo ['bi·deo] *m* video recorder

videocámara [bi·deo·'ka·ma·ra] *f* video camera

videocasete [bi·deo·ka·'se·te] *m* videocassette

videoclip [bi·deo·'klip] *m* music video

videoconferencia [bi·deo·kon·fe·'ren·sja, -θja] *f* video conference

videojuego [bi·deo·'xwe·ɣo] *m* video game

V

vidorria [bi·'do·rrja] f **1.** Chile, RíoPl (vida fácil) easy life **2.** Col, PRico, Ven (vida dura) dog's life

vidriera [bi·'drje·ra] f **1.** stained-glass window **2.** AmL shop window

vidrio ['bi·drjo] m glass ▶ **pagar los ~s rotos** to take the rap

vidurria [bi·'du·rrja] f Arg inf life of leisure

viejera [bje·'xe·ra] f PRico **1.** (vejez) old age **2.** (cosa inservible) old piece of junk

viejo, -a ['bje·xo, -a] **I.** adj old; (usado) used; (gastado) worn-out; **hacerse ~** to get old; **Noche Vieja** New year's Eve **II.** m, f old man, old woman m, f; **mi ~/vieja** my old man/lady; **mis ~s** my folks

viento ['bjen·to] m **1.** wind; **hace ~** it's windy; **~s alisios** trade winds; **¡vete a tomar ~!** inf get lost! **2.** AmC MED flatulence ▶ **contra ~ y marea** come hell or high water; **ir ~ en popa** to go swimmingly

vientre ['bjen·tre] m abdomen; (matriz) womb; (barriga) belly; **danza del ~** belly-dancing

viern. abr de **viernes** Fri.

viernes ['bjer·nes] m inv Friday; v. t. **lunes**

viga ['bi·ɣa] f (madera) beam; (metal) girder

vigencia [bi·'xen·sja, -θja] f validity; **estar en ~** to be valid; **entrar en ~** to come into effect

vigente [bi·'xen·te] adj valid

vigía¹ [bi·'xi·a] f watchtower

vigía² [bi·'xi·a] mf lookout

vigilancia [bi·xi·'lan·sja, -θja] f vigilance; **bajo ~** under surveillance

vigilante [bi·xi·'lan·te] **I.** adj alert **II.** mf **1.** guard; (cárcel) warden; **~ de seguridad** security guard **2.** CSur policeman, policewoman m, f

vigilar [bi·xi·'lar] vt to guard; (niños) to watch

vigilia [bi·'xi·lja] f wakefulness

vigor [bi·'ɣor] m vigor; **con ~** with vigor; **entrar en ~** to come into effect

vigorizar <z → c> [bi·ɣo·ri·'sar, -'θar] vt **1.** (fortalecer) to strengthen **2.** (re-

vitalizar) to invigorate **3.** (animar) to encourage

vigoroso, -a [bi·ɣo·'ro·so, -a] adj vigorous

VIH [u·βe·i·'a·tʃe] m abr de **virus de inmunodeficiencia humana** HIV

vil [bil] adj vile; (bajo) base; (infame) despicable

vileza [bi·'le·sa, -θa] f vileness; (acción) vile act

villa ['bi·ja, -ʎa] f town; (casa) villa

villancico [bi·jan·'si·ko, bi·ʎan·'θi·ko] m (Christmas) carol

villano, -a [bi·'ja·no, -a; -'ʎa·no, -a] adj villainous

vilo ['bi·lo] adv (**tener**) **en ~** (to keep) in suspense; **estar en ~** to be up in the air

vinagre [bi·'na·ɣre] m vinegar; (persona) disagreeable person

vinagrera [bi·na·'ɣre·ra] f **1.** vinegar bottle **2.** AmL indigestion

vinagreta [bi·na·'ɣre·ta] f vinaigrette

vincha ['bin·tʃa] f AmS hair band

vinchuca [bin·'tʃu·ka] f Arg, Chile, Par ZOOL barbeiro, assassin bug

vinculación [bin·ku·la·'sjon, -'θjon] f link

vincular [bin·ku·'lar] vt to link; (unir) to join; **~ a** [o con] **algo** to link to sth

vínculo ['bin·ku·lo] m **1.** (unión) tie; **~s familiares** family ties; **los ~s con el extranjero** links with foreign countries **2.** COMPUT link **3.** (obligación) bond

vinería [bi·ne·'ri·a] f And, CSur wine store

vinícola [bi·'ni·ko·la] **I.** adj wine; (cultivo) wine-growing **II.** mf wine-grower

vinicultor(a) [bi·ni·kul·'tor, -·'to·ra] m(f) wine producer

vinicultura [bi·ni·kul·'tu·ra] f wine production

vino ['bi·no] m wine; **~ rosado/tinto/de mesa** rosé/red/table wine; **~ espumoso/peleón/de la casa** sparkling/cheap/house wine; **~ caliente** hot punch; **~ de Jerez** sherry

viña ['bi·na] f, **viñedo** [bi·'ne·do] m vineyard; (planta) vine

viñatero, -a [bi·na·'te·ro, -a] m, f Arg, Perú winegrower

viola ['bjo·la] f MÚS viola; BOT violet

violación [bjo·la·'sjon, -'θjon] *f* violation; (*ley*) breaking; (*contrato*) breach; (*sexual*) rape

violar [bjo·'lar] *vt* **1.** (*forzar*) to rape **2.** (*ley, principio, sepultura*) to violate; (*contrato*) to break

violencia [bjo·'len·sja, -'θja] *f* violence; **~ de género** gender violence; **no ~** nonviolence; **con ~** by force

violentar [bjo·len·'tar] *vt* to force; (*sexualmente*) to assault

violento, -a [bjo·'len·to, -a] *adj* **1.** violent; (*impetuoso*) impetuous; (*temperamento*) fiery; (*acto*) embarrassing; (*cohibido*) embarrassed; **me resulta ~ decirle que no** I find it very hard to say no to him/her **2.** *AmL* (*de repente*) suddenly

violeta [bjo·'le·ta] *adj, f* violet

violín [bjo·'lin] *m* violin

violonc(h)elo [bjo·lon·'se·lo, -'θe·lo/bjo·lon·'tʃe·lo] *m* cello

VIP [bip] *m abr de* **Very Important Person** VIP; **sala ~** VIP lounge

viraje [bi·'ra·xe] *m* turn; (*curva*) bend; NÁUT tack

virar [bi·'rar] *vi, vt* to turn; NÁUT to tack

virgen [bir·xen] **I.** *adj* virgin; (*cinta*) blank **II.** *f* **la Virgen** the Virgin

virginal [bir·xi·'nal] *adj* virginal

virginidad [bir·xi·ni·'dad] *f* virginity

Virgo [bir·ɣo] *m* Virgo

viril [bi·'ril] *adj* virile; (*enérgico*) vigorous

viringo, -a [bi·'rin·go, -a] *adj Col* (*sin ropa*) naked; (*sin piel*) skinned; (*sin pelo*) hairless

virrey, -reina [bi·'rrei] *m, f* viceroy, vicereine *m, f*

virtual [bir·tu·'al] *adj* virtual

virtud [bir·'tud] *f* virtue; **en ~ de** by virtue of

virtuoso, -a [bir·tu·'o·so, -a] *adj* virtuous; MUS virtuoso

viruela [bi·'rwe·la] *f* smallpox

virus ['bi·rus] *m inv* virus; **virus de inmunodeficiencia humana** human immunodeficiency virus

viruta [bi·'ru·ta] *f* shaving

visa ['bi·sa] *m o f AmL*, **visado** [bi·'sa·do] *m* visa; **~ de entrada/salida** entry/exit visa

vísceras ['bi·se·ras, 'bis·θe·-] *fpl* entrails *pl*

viscosa [bis·'ko·sa] *f* viscose

viscoso, -a [bis·'ko·so, -a] *adj* viscous; (*espeso*) thick

visera [bi·'se·ra] *f* peak

visibilidad [bi·si·βi·li·'dad] *f* visibility

visible [bi·'si·βle] *adj* visible

visillo [bi·'si·jo, -ʎo] *m* net curtain

visión [bi·'sjon] *f* (*vista*) sight, vision; (*punto de vista*) view

visita [bi·'si·ta] *f* visit; (*visitante*) visitor; **~ guiada** guided tour; **hacer una ~** to pay a visit

visitante [bi·si·'tan·te] *mf* visitor

visitar [bi·si·'tar] *vt* to visit

vislumbrar [bis·lum·'brar] *vt* to distinguish

visón [bi·'son] *m* mink

visor [bi·'sor] *m* viewfinder; **~ de luz infrarroja** infrared sights

víspera ['bis·pe·ra] *f* (*noche*) eve; (*día*) day before

vista ['bis·ta] *f* **1.** (*visión*) sight, vision; **tener la ~ cansada** to have eye strain; **al/fuera del alcance de la ~** within view/out of sight; **a la ~** visible; **de ~** by sight; **apartar la ~** to take one's eyes off; **perder de ~** to lose sight of; **a primera ~** at first sight; **a simple ~** just by looking; **con ~s a** with a view to; **en ~ de que** in view of; **alzar/bajar la ~** to look up/down; **volver la ~ (atrás)** to look back **2.** (*panorama*) view ▶ **~ de pájaro** bird's-eye view; **hacer la ~ gorda** to turn a blind eye; **tener ~** to be shrewd

vistazo [bis·'ta·so, -θo] *m* look; **de un ~** at a glance; **echar** [*o* **dar**] **un ~ a algo** to have a (quick) look at sth

visto, -a ['bis·to, -a] **I.** *pp de* **ver** **II.** *adj* common; **está muy ~** that's old hat; **está ~ que...** it's clear that... ▶ **nunca ~** unknown; (*inaudito*) unheard of; **~ y no** ~ in a flash; **por lo** ~ apparently that... **conj ~ que...** since...

visto bueno ['bis·to 'βwe·no] *m* approval; **dar el ~ a algo** to give sth the go-ahead

vistoso, -a [bis·'to·so, -a] *adj* colorful; (*llamativo*) striking

visual [bi·su·'al] *adj* visual; **campo ~** field of vision

V

visualización [bi·swa·li·sa·'sjon, -θa·'θjon] *f* visualization; COMPUT visual display

visualizar <z → c> [bi·swa·li·'sar, -'θar] *vt* 1. to visualize; COMPUT to display 2. *AmL* (*divisar*) to make out

vital [bi·'tal] *adj* vital; **constantes ~es** vital signs

vitalicio, -a [bi·ta·'li·sjo, -a; -θjo, -a] *adj* life

vitalidad [bi·ta·li·'ðað] *f* vitality

vitalizar <z → c> [bi·ta·li·'sar, -'θar] *vt* to revitalize; (*fortalecer*) to strengthen

vitamina [bi·ta·'mi·na] *f* vitamin; **pobre/rico en ~s** low/rich in vitamins

viticultor(a) [bi·ti·kul·'tor, --'to·ra] *m(f)* vine grower

vítor ['bi·tor] *m* cheer

vitorear [bi·to·re·'ar] *vt* to cheer

vitrina [bi·'tri·na] *f* glass cabinet; *AmL* shop window

vituperar [bi·tu·pe·'rar] *vt* ~ **a alguien** to vituperate against sb

viudedad [bju·ðe·'ðað] *f*, **viudez** [bju·'ðes, -'ðeθ] *f* widowhood

viudo, -a [bju·ðo, -a] I. *adj* widowed; **quedarse ~** to be widowed II. *m, f* widower, widow *m, f*

viva [bi·'βa] *interj* hurray!

vivacidad [bi·βa·si·'dad, bi·βa·θi-] *f* liveliness

vivaracho, -a [bi·βa·'ra·ʧo, -a] *adj*, **vivaz** [bi·'βas, -'βaθ] *adj* vivacious; (*enérgico*) lively

vivencia [bi·'βen·sja, -θja] *f* experience

víveres ['bi·βe·res] *mpl* provisions *pl*

vivero [bi·'βe·ro] *m* nursery; (*de peces*) hatchery

viveza [bi·'βe·sa, -θa] *f* vivid

vívido, -a [bi·'βi·do, -a] *adj* vivid

vivienda [bi·'βjen·da] *f* 1. residence; **sin ~** homeless; **el problema de la ~** the housing problem 2. *AmL* way of life

viviente [bi·'βjen·te] *adj* living

vivir [bi·'βir] I. *vi* to live; (*estar vivo*) to be alive; (*perdurar*) to live on; ~ **a lo grande** to live it up; ~ **de rentas** to live off the rent II. *vt* to live III. *m* life

vivo, -a ['bi·βo, -a] *adj* 1. alive; **ser ~** living being; **al rojo ~** red-hot; **en ~** live; **ser la viva imagen de alguien** to be

the spitting image of sb 2. (*vivaz*) lively 3. (*color*) bright 4. (*avispado*) sharp

V.O. [ber·'sjon o·ri·xi·'nal] *abr de* **versión original** original version

vocablo [bo·'ka·βlo] *m* word

vocabulario [bo·ka·βu·'la·rjo] *m* vocabulary

vocación [bo·ka·'sjon, -'θjon] *f* vocation

vocal [bo·'kal] I. *adj* vocal II. *f* vowel

voceador(a) [bo·se·a·'dor, --'do·ra, bo·θe-] *m(f)* *AmL* news hawker

vocear [bo·se·'ar, bo·θe-] I. *vi* to shout II. *vt* to express; ~ **algo** to boast of sth

vocerío [bo·se·'ri·o, bo·θe-] *m* clamor

vocero, -a [bo·'se·ro, -a] *m, f* *AmL* spokesperson

vociferar [bo·si·fe·'rar, bo·θi-] *vi, vt* to yell

vodka ['bod·ka] *m o f* vodka

vol. *abr de* **volumen** vol.

volado, -a [bo·'la·do] *adj* 1. *inf* (*loco*) crazy 2. *AmL* (*ausente*) absent-minded; (*enamorado*) lovesick 3. *CSur* ~ **de genio** *inf* quick-tempered

volador(a) [bo·la·'dor, --'do·ra] *adj* flying

volandas [bo·'lan·das] *fpl* **en ~** up in the air; (*deprisa*) in a rush; **llevar en ~** to carry shoulder-high

volante [bo·'lan·te] I. *adj* flying II. *m* 1. AUTO steering wheel; **ir al ~** to be at the wheel 2. (*adorno*) flounce 3. (*escrito*) leaflet 4. *AmL* winger

volantón [bo·lan·'ton, --'to·na] *m* *AmL* 1. (*cometa*) kite 2. (*voltereta*) somersault; (*acrobacia*) acrobatics *pl*

volar <o → ue> [bo·'lar] I. *vi* 1. to fly; **echar a ~** to fly off; **el dinero ha volado** the money has vanished 2. (*apresurarse*) to dash 3. *inf* to be high II. *vt* to blow up; **hacer ~ una cometa** to fly a kite III. *vr:* ~**se** to vanish; *AmL* to get mad

volátil [bo·'la·til] *adj* 1. (*volador*) flying 2. QUÍM volatile 3. (*inconstante*) unpredictable

volatilizar <z → c> [bo·la·ti·li·'sar, -'θar] *vt, vr:* ~**se** to volatilize

volcán [bol·'kan] *m* 1. volcano; ~ **activo/inactivo** active/dormant volcano 2. *AmL* loads *pl*

volcánico, -a [bol·'ka·ni·ko, -a] *adj* volcanic

volcar [bol·'kar] *irr* I. *vi* to overturn II. *vt* to turn over; (*tirar*) to knock over; (*líquido*) to spill III. *vr*: ~**se** to overturn; ~**se en** [*o con*] **alguien** to be extremely kind to sb; ~**se en algo** to throw oneself into sth

voleibol [bo·lei·'βol] *m* volleyball

voleiplaya [bo·lei·'pla·ja] *m* beach volleyball

voleo [bo·'leo] *m* **a** ~ at random

voltaje [bol·'ta·xe] *m* voltage

voltario, -a [bol·'ta·rjo, -a] *adj* Chile 1. (*gastador*) spendthrift; (*dadivoso*) generous 2. (*obstinado*) self-willed

volteado [bol·te·'a·do] *m Méx inf* fag

voltear [bol·te·'ar] *AmL* I. *vi* 1. (*torcer*) to turn 2. (*girarse*) to turn around 3. (*pasear*) to go for a walk 4. ~ **a hacer algo** to do sth again II. *vt* 1. (*volcar*) to knock over 2. (*volver*) to turn; ~ **la espalda a alguien** to turn one's back on sb; ~ **las campanas** to ring the bells 3. (*lanzar al aire*) to throw into the air III. *vr*: ~**se** 1. (*volcar*) to overturn 2. (*darse la vuelta*) to turn around

voltereta [bol·te·'re·ta] *f* handspring; (*en el aire*) somersault

voltio ['bol·tjo] *m* volt

volumen [bo·'lu·men] *m* (*tamaño*) size; (*cantidad*) amount; (*pelo*) body; FÍS, MAT volume; **a todo** ~ (at) full volume; **en dos volúmenes** in two volumes; ~ **de ventas** turnover

voluminoso, -a [bo·lu·mi·'no·so, -a] *adj* sizeable

voluntad [bo·lun·'tad] *f* will; (*fuerza de voluntad*) will-power; **contra su** ~ against one's will; **por propia** ~ of one's own free will

voluntario, -a [bo·lun·'ta·rjo, -a] I. *adj* voluntary II. *m, f* volunteer; **ofrecerse** ~ to volunteer

voluntarioso, -a [bo·lun·ta·'rjo·so, -a] *adj* willing

voluptuoso, -a [bo·lup·tu·'o·so, -a] *adj* voluptuous

volver [bol·'βer] *irr* I. *vi* 1. (*dar la vuelta*) to go back; ~ **atrás** to turn back 2. (*regresar*) to return; ~ **a casa** to go home;

~ **en sí** to come to 3. ~ **a hacer algo** to do sth again II. *vt* 1. (*dar la vuelta*) to turn over; (*poner del revés*) to turn inside out; ~ **la vista a algo** to look back at sth 2. (*transformar*) to make; ~ **loco a alguien** to drive sb crazy III. *vr*: ~**se** 1. to return; ~**se a** [*o hacia*] **algo** to turn (around) towards sth; ~**se contra alguien** to turn against sb 2. (*convertirse*) to become; ~**se viejo** to grow old

vomitar [bo·mi·'tar] I. *vi* to vomit II. *vt* to bring up

vomitivo, -a [bo·mi·'ti·βo] *adj* emetic; *inf* revolting

vómito ['bo·mi·to] *m* vomit; (*acción*) vomiting

voracidad [bo·ra·si·'dad, bo·ra·θi·] *f* voraciousness; (*avaricia*) greed

vorágine [bo·'ra·xi·ne] *f* (*remolino*) whirlpool; (*confusión*) whirl

voraz [bo·'ras, -'raθ] *adj* voracious

vos [bos] *pron pers AmL* you

vosear [bo·se·'ar] to address in the familiar manner using 'vos'

vosotros, -as [bo·'so·tros, -as] *pron pers, pl* you; **para** ~ for you

votación [bo·ta·'sjon, -'θjon] *f* vote; **someter a** ~ to put to the vote

votar [bo·'tar] *vi, vt* to vote (**a, por**)

voto ['bo·to] *m* 1. vote; (*acción*) voting; ~ **a favor/en contra** vote in favor/against; ~ **en blanco** unmarked ballot; ~ **por correo** mail vote 2. REL vow

voy [boi] *1. pres de* **ir**

voz [bos, boθ] *f* 1. *t.* LING voice; **aclarar la** ~ to clear one's throat; **levantar/bajar la** ~ to raise/lower one's voice; **en** ~ **alta/baja** aloud/softly; **tener** ~ **en algo** to have a say in sth 2. (*grito*) shout; **a** ~ **en grito** at the top of one's voice; **dar voces** to shout

vozarrón [bo·sa·'rron, bo·θa·] *m* booming voice

vudú [bu·'du] *m* voodoo

vuelco ['bwel·ko] *m* turning over; (*cambio*) drastic change

vuelo ['bwe·lo] *m* flight; ~ **regular** scheduled flight; **levantar** [*o alzar*] **el** ~ to fly off

vuelta ['bwel·ta] *f* 1. (*giro*) turn; **el camión dio una** ~ **de campana** the

V

truck flipped over; **a la ~ de la esquina** around the corner; **dar la ~** (*rodear*) to go around; (*volver*) to turn back; (*volcar*) to put face down; **dar media ~** to turn around; **dar una ~** to have a walk around; **la cabeza me da ~s** my head is spinning **2.** (*regreso*) return; (*viaje*) trip; **a la ~** on the way back; **de ~ a casa** back home; **estar de ~** to be back **3.** (*dinero, cambio*) change; **la vida da muchas ~s** life has many ups and downs ▶ **dar muchas ~s a algo** to think over sth again and again

vuelto ['bwel·to, -a] *m AmL* change; **dar el ~** to give change

vuestro, -a ['bwes·tro, -a] **I.** *adj* your; **~ coche** your car; **vuestras monedas** your coins **II.** *pron pos* **1.** yours; **¿es ~?** is this yours?; **el ~** yours **2.** (*tras subst*) (of) yours; **un amigo ~** a friend of yours

vulcanizadora [bul·ka·ni·sa·'do·ra] *f Méx* vulcanizer

vulgar [bul·'ɣar] *adj* common; (*ordinario*) vulgar

vulgaridad [bul·ɣa·ri·'dad] *f* ordinariness; *pey* vulgarity

vulgarizar <z → c> [bul·ɣa·ri·'sar, -'θar] *vt* to popularize

vulnerable [bul·ne·'ra·βle] *adj* vulnerable

vulneración [bul·ne·ra·'sjon, -'θjon] *f* violation

vulnerar [bul·ne·'rar] *vt* to hurt; (*derecho*) to violate

vulva ['bul·βa] *f* vulva

W

W, w ['u·βe 'do·βle] *f* W, w; **~ de Washington** W as in Whiskey

walkie-talkie ['wal·ki 'tal·ki] *m* walkie-talkie

wampa ['wam·pa] *f Méx* swamp

wáter ['ba·ter] *m* (*recipiente*) toilet; (*habitación*) washroom

waterpolo [ba·ter·'po·lo] *m* water polo

watt [bat] *m* watt

web [ueb] *m o f* web

wélter ['bel·ter] *AmL* **I.** *adj* **peso ~** welterweight **II.** *m* welterweight

whisky ['wis·ki] *m* whisky

windsurf ['win(d)·surf] *m* windsurfing; **tabla de ~** windsurfer

wing [win] *m AmL* **1.** (*extremo delantero*) winger **2.** (*extrema delantera*) wing

WWW *abr de* **World Wide Web** WWW

X

X, x ['e·kis] *f* **1.** X, x; **~ de xilófono** X as in X-ray; **rayos ~** X-rays *pl* **2.** MAT X **3.** *fig* x; **le presté x pesos** I lent him/her x pesos

xenofobia [se·no·'fo·βja] *f* xenophobia

xenófobo, -a [se·'no·fo·βo, -a] *adj* xenophobic

xilófono [si·'lo·fo·no] *m* xylophone

xilografía [si·lo·ɣra·'fi·a] *f* xylography

xirgo, -a ['sir·ɣo, -a] *adj Méx* (*desaseado*) untidy; (*hirsuto*) hairy

xocoyote [so·ko·'jo·te] *m Méx* youngest child

Y

Y, y [i 'ɣrje·ɣa] *f* Y, y; **~ de Yema** Y as in Yankee

y [i] *conj* and; **¿~ qué?** so what?; **¿~ tu trabajo?** how's work?; **¿~ tu marido?** and how is your husband?; **¿~ mi monedero?** where's my wallet?; **~ eso que...** despite that...; **¡~ tanto!** you bet!

ya [ja] **I.** *adv* (*pasado*) already; (*pronto*) soon; (*ahora*) now; **~ es hora de que cambies** it's time you changed; **~ no fumo** I don't smoke any more; **~, ~** OK; *irón* oh, sure!; **¡ah, ~!** I get it now!; **¡anda ~!** come off it! **II.** *conj* **~ que** since; (*aprovechando que*) now; **~ por..., ~ por...** either by... or... **III.** *interj* that's it!

yacaré [ja·ka·'re] *m Arg, Bol, Par, Urug* caiman

yacer [ja·'ser, -'θer] *irr vi elev* to lie

yacimiento [ja·si·'mjen·to, -θi·'mjen·to] *m* deposit

yagua ['ja·ɣwa] *f AmL* royal palm; *(fibras)* palm leaf

yagual [ja·'ɣwal] *m AmC* padded ring *(for carrying heavy loads on the head)*

yagüé [ja·ɣu·'re] *m AmL* skunk

yanqui ['jan·ki] I. *adj* Yankee II. *mf* Yank

yapa ['ja·pa] *f AmL* bonus; *(objeto)* extra; **de ~** as an addition

yapar [ja·'par] *vt AmL* **~ algo** *(el precio)* to give sth as a bonus; *(un objeto)* to add sth as an extra

yarda ['jar·da] *f* yard

yate ['ja·te] *m* yacht

yedra ['je·dra] *f* ivy

yegua ['je·ɣwa] *f* ZOOL mare; *AmC* cigar stub

yema ['je·ma] *f* yolk; *(de un dedo)* fingertip; BOT young shoot

yendo [jen·do] *gerundio de* **ir**

yerba ['jer·βa] *f* grass; **~ mate** *AmS* maté herb

yerbal [jer·'βal] *m RíoPl*, **yerbatal** [jer·βa·'tal] *m Arg* maté plantation

yerbatero, -a [jer·βa·'te·ro, -a] I. *adj AmL* maté II. *m, f AmS* 1. *(curandero)* folk healer 2. *(vendedor)* herbalist; *(de mate)* grower of maté

yerbear [jer·βe·'ar] *vi AmL* to drink maté

yerbera [jer·'βe·ra] *f RíoPl* maté (tea) gourd

yerbero, -a [jer·'βe·ro, -a] *m, f Méx* herb doctor

yergo ['jer·ɣo] *1. pres de* **erguir**

yermo ['jer·mo] *m* waste land

yermo, -a ['jer·mo, -a] *adj* uninhabited; AGR uncultivated

yerno ['jer·no] *m* son-in-law

yérsey ['jer·sei] *m*, **yersi** [jer·'si] *m AmC, AmS* jersey

yeso ['je·so] *m* plaster; GEO gypsum

yeta ['je·ta] *f Arg, Urug* bad luck

yé-yé [je·'je] *adj inf* cool; **hoy vas muy ~** you look very hip today

yin ['jin] *yines m* jeans *pl*

yira ['ji·ra] *f Arg, Urug pey inf* slut

yo [jo] I. *pron pers* I; **~ que tú...** if I were you...; **¿quién fue? — ~ no** who was it? — not me; **soy ~,** Susan it's me, Susan;

~ mismo myself II. *m* ego

yocalla [jo·'ka·ja, -ʎa] *m Bol (niño callejero)* street urchin; *(mestizo)* half-breed

yodo ['jo·do] *m* iodine

yoga ['jo·ɣa] *m* yoga

yogur ['jo·ɣur] *m* yogurt; **~ natural** plain yogurt

yolo ['jo·lo] *m Méx inf* darling; **¡~ mío!** my darling!

yonqui ['jon·ki] *mf* junkie

yoyó [jo·'jo] *m* yoyo

yuca ['ju·ka] *f* yucca

yudo ['ju·do] *m* judo

yugo ['ju·ɣo] *m* yoke

yugular [ju·ɣu·'lar] *f* jugular vein

yunga ['jun·ga] *mf Bol, Chile, Ecua, Perú* warm valleys native

yungas ['jun·gas] *fpl Bol, Chile, Ecua, Perú* warm valleys *pl*

yunque ['jun·ke] *m* anvil

yuntas ['jun·tas] *fpl PRico, Urug, Ven* cufflinks *pl*

yuppy ['ju·pi] *mf* yuppie

yute ['ju·te] *m* jute

yuxtaponer [jus·ta·po·'ner] *irr como* **poner** I. *vt (a otra cosa)* to join; *(dos cosas)* to juxtapose II. *vr:* **~se** to join together

yuxtaposición [jus·ta·po·si·'sjon, -'θjon] *f* juxtaposition

yuxtapuesto, -a [jus·ta·'pwes·to, -a] *adj* juxtaposed

yuyero, -a [ju·'je·ro, -a] *m, f Arg, CSur* herbalist

yuyo ['ju·jo] *m* 1. *CSur (yerbajo)* weed 2. *pl Col, Ecua (condimento)* seasoning 3. *pl Perú (verdura)* herbs *pl* 4. *AmC (ampolla)* blister

Z

Z, z ['se·ta, 'θe·/'se·da, 'θe-] *f* Z, z; **~ de Zaragoza** Z as in Zulu

zabuir [sa·'bwir] *vi PRico* to plunge

zacatal [sa·ka·'tal] *m AmC, Méx* pasture

zacate [sa·ka·te] *m AmL* hay

zafacoca [sa·fa·'ko·ka] *f* 1. *AmC, AmS, Méx (pelea)* fight 2. *Chile (alboroto)* commotion

W
X
Y
Z

zafacón [sa·fa·'kon] *m PRico, RDom* trash can

zafado, -a [sa·'fa·do, -a] *adj Arg* sassy

zafadura [sa·fa·'du·ra] *f AmL* dislocation

zafar [sa·'far, θa·] *vr* **1. ~se de** to get away; (*compromiso*) to get out of **2.** *AmL* (*dislocarse*) to dislocate

zafarrancho [sa·fa·'rran·tʃo, θa·] *m inf* (*limpieza*) clearing up; (*riña*) quarrel; (*destrozo*) mess

zafiro [sa·'fi·ro, θa·] *m* sapphire

zafo ['θa·fo] *adv AmL* except

zaga ['sa·ɣa, 'θa·] *f* **a la ~** behind

zagal(a) [sa·'ɣal, --'ɣa·la; θa·] *m(f)* boy, girl *m, f*

zaino, -a ['sai·no, -a; 'θai·] *adj* treacherous; **mirar a lo ~** to look shifty

zalamero, -a [sa·la·'me·ro, -a; θa·] **I.** *adj* flattering **II.** *m, f* flatterer

zambo, -a ['sam·bo, -a; 'θam·] *adj* bow-legged

zambullir <*3. pret* zambulló> [sam·bu·'jir, θam·bu·'ʎir] **I.** *vt* to submerge **II.** *vr:* **~se** to dive; (*en un asunto*) to plunge (**en** into)

zampar [sam·'par, θam·] **I.** *vt* to scarf down **II.** *vr:* **~se** to scoff

zampón, -ona [sam·'pon, -'po·na; θam·] *inf* **I.** *adj* greedy **II.** *m, f* glutton

zanahoria [sa·na·'o·rja, θa·] **I.** *f* carrot **II.** *m RíoPl* idiot

zanca ['san·ka, 'θan·] *f* shank; *inf* long leg

zancada [san·'ka·da, θan·] *f* stride; **dar ~s** to stride

zancadilla [san·ka·'di·ja, θan·ka·'di·ʎa] *f* **poner la ~ a alguien** to trip sb up

zanco ['san·ko, 'θan·] *m* stilt

zancudo [san·'ku·do] *m AmL* mosquito; (*ave*) wader

zancudo, -a [san·'ku·do, -a; θan·] *adj* long-legged

zanganear [san·ga·ne·'ar, θan·] *vi inf* to idle

zángano ['san·ga·no, 'θan·] *m* drone; (*vago*) idler

zanja ['san·xa, θan·] *f* ditch; *AmL* watercourse

zanjar [san·'xar, θan·] *vt* (*asunto*) to settle; (*disputa*) to end

zapallo [sa·'pa·jo] *m* **1.** *AmL* (*calabaza*) pumpkin **2.** *Arg, Chile* (*chiripa*) fluke

zapata [sa·'pa·ta, θa·] *f* shoe

zapatear [sa·pa·te·'ar, θa·] *vi* to tap dance

zapatería [sa·pa·te·'ri·a, θa·] *f* shoe store; (*taller*) shoemaker's

zapatero [sa·pa·'te·ro, θa·] *m* shoe rack

zapatero, -a [sa·pa·'te·ro, -a; θa·] *m, f* shoemaker

zapatilla [sa·pa·'ti·ja, sa·pa·'ti·ʎa] *f* slipper; (*de deporte*) sneaker

zapato [sa·'pa·to, θa·] *m* shoe; **un par de ~s** a pair of shoes ▶ **tú no me llegas a la suela del ~** you can't hold a candle to me

zapear [sa·pe·'ar, θa·] *vt* to channel surf

zapping ['sa·pin, 'θa·] *m* channel surfing

zar, zarina [sar, θar; sa·'ri·na, θa·] *m, f* tsar, tsarina *m, f*

zarandear [sarande'ar, θa·] *vt* to shake hard; *AmL* to mock

zarina [sa·'ri·na, θa·] *f v.* **zar**

zarpa ['sar·pa, 'θar·] *f* paw; *inf* mitt; **echar la ~** to grab

zarpar [sar·'par, θar·] *vi* to set sail

zarrapastroso, -a [sa·rra·pas·'tro·so, -a; θar·] *adj inf* dirty

zarza ['sar·sa, 'θar·θa] *f* bramble

zas [sas, θas] *interj* whoosh!; (*golpe*) bang!

zigzag [siɣ·'saɣ, θiɣ·'θaɣ] *m* <zigzags> zigzag

zigzaguear [siɣ·sa·ɣe·'ar, θiɣ·θa·] *vi* to zigzag

zinc [sin, θin] *m* zinc

zíper ['si·per] *m Méx* zipper

zócalo ['θo·ka·lo, 'θo·] *m* **1.** skirting board; *ARQUIT* pedestal **2.** *Méx* (town) square

zodíaco [so·'dia·ko, θo·] *m* zodiac

zombi ['som·bi, 'θom·] *m* zombie; **estar ~** to be like a zombie

zona ['so·na, 'θo·] *f* zone; (*terreno*) belt; (*área*) region; **~ de influencia** area of influence; **~ verde** green belt

zoncera [son·'se·ra] *f AmL*, **zoncería** [son·se·'ri·a] *f* foolishness

zonzo, -a ['son·so, -a; 'θon·θo, -a] *adj* dull; *AmL* stupid

zoo ['so·o, 'θo·o] *m* zoo

zoología [so·lo·'xi·a/so·o·lo·'xi·a; θo·] *f* zoology

zoológico, -a [so·'lo·xi·ko/so·o·'lo·xi·ko, -a; θo-] *adj* zoological; **parque ~** zoo

zoólogo, -a [so·o·lo·γo, -a; θo-] *m, f* zoologist

zopenco, -a [so·'pen·ko, -a; θo-] **I.** *adj* oafish **II.** *m, f* dolt

zopilote [so·pi·'lo·te] *m Méx* turkey vulture

zoquete [so·'ke·te, θo-] *m* blockhead; *Arg* sock

zorrillo [so·'rri·jo] *m AmL* skunk

zorro ['so·rro, 'θo-] *m* fox; *inf* (*astuto*) crafty fellow

zote ['so·te, 'θo-] **I.** *adj* foolish **II.** *mf* fool

zozobra [so·'so·βra, θo·'θo-] *f* anxiety

zozobrar [so·so·'βrar, θo·θo-] **I.** *vi* to capsize; (*persona*) to hesitate **II.** *vt* to sink

zueco ['swe·ko, 'θwe-] *m* clog

zumba ['sum·ba, 'θum-] *f AmL* beating

zumbado, -a [sum·'ba·do, -a; θum-] *adj* **estar ~** to be nuts

zumbar [sum·'bar, θu-] **I.** *vi* to buzz; **salir zumbando** to zoom off; (*oídos*) to hum **II.** *vt AmL* to throw; (*expulsar*) to chuck out

zumbido [sum·'bi·do, θum-] *m* hum; **~ de los oídos** ringing in the ears

zumo ['su·mo, 'θu-] *m* juice

zupay [su·'pai] *m AmL* devil

zurcir <c → z> [sur·'sir, θur·'θir] *vt* to mend; *inf* **¡que te zurzan!** get lost!

zurdo, -a ['sur·do, -a; 'θur-] **I.** *adj* left-handed **II.** *m, f* left-handed person

zurra ['su·rra, 'θur-] *f* hiding

zurrar [su·'rrar, θu-] *vt* to beat

zurullo [su·'ru·jo, θu·'ru·ʎo] *m inf* (*grumo*) lump

Z

A

A, a [eɪ] *n* 1. (*letter*) A, a *f*; **~ as in Alpha** A de Antonio 2. SCHOOL ≈ sobresaliente *m*

a [ə, *stressed:* eɪ] *indef art before consonant,* **an** [ən, *stressed:* æn] *before vowel* 1. (*in general*) un, una; **~ car** un coche; **~ house** una casa 2. (*not translated*) **do you have ~ car?** ¿tienes coche?; **she is ~ teacher** es maestra 3. (*to express prices, rates*) **$2 ~ dozen** 2 dólares la docena; **$6 ~ week** 6 dólares por semana 4. (*before person's name*) **~ Mr. Robinson** un tal Sr. Robinson

aback [əˈbæk] *adv* **to take sb ~** coger a alguien de improviso; **to be taken ~** quedarse desconcertado (**by** por)

abandon [əˈbæn·dən] *vt* (*vehicle, place, person*) abandonar; (*give up: plan*) renunciar a; (*game*) suspender; **to ~ oneself to sth** entregarse a algo

abandoned [əˈbæn·dənd] *adj* abandonado, -a; (*person*) desamparado, -a

abbreviate [əˈbri·vi·eɪt] *vt* abreviar

abbreviation [ə·ˌbri·vɪ·ˈeɪ·ʃən] *n* abreviatura *f*

abdomen [ˈæb·də·mən] *n* ANAT abdomen *m*

abdominal [æbˈdam·ə·nəl] *adj* abdominal

abduct [æbˈdʌkt] *vt* secuestrar, plagiar *AmL*

abduction [æbˈdʌk·ʃən] *n* secuestro *m*, plagio *m AmL*

abide [əˈbaɪd] <-d *or* abode, -d *or* abode> *vt* soportar; **I can't ~ her** no la soporto ◆ **abide by** *vt* (*rule, decision*) atenerse a; (*promise*) cumplir

ability [əˈbɪl·ə·ti] <-ies> *n* 1. (*capability*) capacidad *f*; **to the best of one's ~** lo mejor que uno pueda 2. (*talent*) aptitud *f* 3. *pl* dotes *fpl*

ablaze [əˈbleɪz] *adj* en llamas; *fig* resplandeciente

able [ˈeɪ·bəl] *adj* capaz; **to be ~ to do sth** (*have ability, manage*) poder hacer algo; (*have knowledge*) saber hacer algo

able-bodied *adj* fuerte y sano, -a

abnormal [æbˈnɔr·məl] *adj* (*feature*) anómalo, -a; (*person*) anormal

abnormality [ˌæb·nɔrˈmæl·ə·t̬i] <-ies> *n* anomalía *f*; (*unusualness*) anormalidad *f*

aboard [əˈbɔrd] I. *adv* a bordo II. *prep* a bordo de; **to go ~ a boat/plane** subir a una barca/un avión

abode [əˈboʊd] *vi pt, pp of* **abide**

abolish [əˈbal·ɪʃ] *vt* abolir

abolition [æb·ə·ˈlɪʃ·ən] *n* abolición *f*

abominable [əˈbam·ə·nə·bəl] *adj* abominable

abomination [ə·ˌbam·ə·ˈneɪ·ʃən] *n* 1. (*abominable thing*) abominación *f* 2. (*disgust*) aversión *f*

Aborigine [ˌæb·ə·ˈrɪdʒ·ə·ni] *n* aborigen *mf* (de Australia)

abort [əˈbɔrt] *vt, vi* MED abortar; COMPUT abandonar

abortion [əˈbɔr·ʃən] *n* MED aborto *m*

about [əˈbaʊt] I. *prep* 1. (*on subject of*) sobre, acerca de; **a book ~ football** un libro sobre fútbol; **what is the film ~?** ¿de qué trata la película? 2. (*characteristic of*) **that's what I like ~ him** eso es lo que me gusta de él 3. (*surrounding*) alrededor de; **the garden ~ the house** el jardín alrededor de la casa 4. (*in and through*) por; **to go ~ a place** andar por un lugar ▶ **how ~ that!** ¡vaya!; **how ~ a drink?** ¿qué tal si tomamos algo?; **what ~ it?** (*suggestion*) ¿quieres/queréis?; (*so what?*) ¿y qué? II. *adv* 1. (*approximately*) aproximadamente; **~ my size** más o menos de mi tamaño; **~ 5 years ago** hace unos cinco años; **~ twenty** unos veinte; **to have had just ~ enough of sth** estar harto de algo; **that's ~ it for today** eso es todo por hoy 2. (*almost*) casi; **to be (just) ~ ready** estar casi listo 3. (*on the point of*) **to be ~ to do sth** estar a punto de hacer algo 4. (*around*) **all ~** por todas partes; **to be somewhere ~** estar por aquí

above [əˈbʌv] I. *prep* 1. (*on top of*) encima de 2. (*over*) sobre; **~ suspicion** por encima de toda sospecha 3. (*greater than, superior to*) por encima de; **~ 3** más de 3; **he is not ~ lying** es muy capaz de mentir; **~ all** sobre todo II. *adv* encima; **the floor** ~ la planta de arriba; **up** ~ **sth** por encima de algo; **see** ~ véase más arriba

abovementioned *adj* anteriormente mencionado, -a

abrasive [ə-'breɪ-sɪv] *adj* abrasivo, -a; (*in manner*) agresivo, -a

abreast [ə-'brest] *adv* **two/three** ~ en fila de a dos/tres; **to be/keep** ~ **of sth** estar/mantenerse al corriente de algo

abroad [ə-'brɔd] *adv* **from** ~ del extranjero; **to be** ~ estar en el extranjero; **to go** ~ ir al extranjero; **at home and** ~ dentro y fuera del país

abrupt [ə-'brʌpt] *adj* **1.** (*sudden*) repentino, -a; (*change*) brusco, -a; (*end*) inesperado, -a **2.** (*brusque*) brusco, -a **3.** (*steep*) abrupto, -a

ABS [ˌeɪ-biː-'es] *n abbr of* **antilock braking system** ABS *m*

absence ['æb-səns] *n* **1.** (*not being present*) ausencia *f*; **in the** ~ **of** en ausencia de **2.** (*lack of*) carencia *f*; **in the** ~ **of** a falta de

absent[1] ['æb-sənt] *adj* ausente

absent[2] [əb-'sent] *vt* **to** ~ **oneself** ausentarse (**from** de)

absentee ballot, absentee voting *n* voto *m* por correo

absent-minded *adj* despistado, -a, volado, -a *AmL*

absolute ['æb-sə-luːt] *adj* **1.** POL absoluto, -a; (*denial*) rotundo, -a; (*trust, power, confidence*) pleno, -a **2.** CHEM puro, -a

absolutely *adv* absolutamente; (*very*) totalmente; ~! *inf* ¡claro que sí!; ~ **not!** ¡de ninguna manera!

absorb [əb-'sɔrb] *vt* **1.** (*liquid*) absorber; (*shock*) amortiguar **2.** (*understand*) asimilar **3.** (*engross*) ocupar; **to be ~ed in one's thoughts** estar absorto en sus pensamientos

absorbent [əb-'sɔr-bənt] *adj* absorbente

absorbing *adj* (*book, story*) apasionante

absorption [əb-'sɔrp-ʃən] *n* **1.** (*of liquid*) absorción *f* **2.** (*in book, story*) concentración *f*; (*in work*) dedicación *f* absoluta

abstention [əb-'sten-ʃən] *n a.* POL abstención *f*

abstinence ['æb-stə-nəns] *n* abstinencia *f*

abstract[1] ['æb-strækt] **I.** *adj* abstracto, -a **II.** *n* (*summary*) extracto *m*

abstract[2] [æb-'strækt] *vt* **1.** *a.* CHEM extraer **2.** (*summarize*) resumir

abstracted [æb-'stræk-tɪd] *adj* distraído, -a

abstraction [əb-'stræk-ʃən] *n* **1.** (*concept*) abstracción *f* **2.** (*absent-mindedness*) distracción *f*

absurd [əb-'sɜrd] *adj* absurdo, -a

absurdity [əb-'sɜr-də-ti] <-ies> *n* **1.** absurdo *m*; (*idea, situation*) ridiculez *f* **2.** (*absurd thing*) disparate *m*

abundance [ə-'bʌn-dəns] *n* abundancia *f*

abundant [ə-'bʌn-dənt] *adj* abundante

abuse[1] [ə-'bjus] *n* **1.** (*insults*) insultos *mpl*, insultadas *fpl AmL* **2.** (*mistreatment*) maltrato *m* **3.** (*misuse*) abuso *m*; **sexual** ~ abuso sexual

abuse[2] [ə-'bjuz] *vt* **1.** (*insult*) insultar **2.** (*mistreat*) maltratar **3.** (*sexually, misuse*) abusar de

abusive [ə-'bju-sɪv] *adj* (*language*) ofensivo, -a; (*person*) agresivo, -a

abysmal [ə-'bɪz-məl] *adj* pésimo, -a

abyss [ə-'bɪs] *n a. fig* abismo *m*

academic [ˌæk-ə-'dem-ɪk] *adj* **1.** UNIV académico, -a; SCHOOL escolar **2.** (*intellectual*) erudito, -a

academy [ə-'kæd-ə-mi] <-ies> *n* **1.** academia *f*; (*prep school*) instituto *m* **2. the Academy Awards** los Óscars

accelerate [ək-'sel-ə-reɪt] **I.** *vi* acelerar; (*growth*) acelerarse **II.** *vt* acelerar

accelerator [ək-'sel-ə-reɪ-tər] *n* AUTO acelerador *m*, chancleta *f Ven, Col*

accent ['æk-sent] **I.** *n* LING acento *m*; LIT énfasis *m inv* **II.** *vt* enfatizar; LING acentuar

accentuate [æk-'sen-tʃu-eɪt] *vt* acentuar

accept [ək-'sept] **I.** *vt* **1.** (*take when offered*) aceptar **2.** (*approve*) aprobar **3.** (*believe*) creer en **4.** (*acknowledge*) reconocer **II.** *vi* aceptar

acceptable *adj* aceptable; (*explanation*) admisible

acceptance [ək-'sep-təns] *n* aceptación *f*; (*approval*) aprobación *f*

access ['æk-ses] **I.** *n* entrada *f*, aproches *mpl AmL*; *a.* COMPUT acceso *m*;

Internet ~ acceso a Internet; **to gain** ~ **to sth** acceder a algo; **to have** ~ **to sth** tener acceso a algo; **with easy** ~ de fácil acceso **II.** *vt* acceder a

accessible [ək·'ses·ə·bəl] *adj* accesible

accessory [ək·'ses·ə·ri] <-ies> *n* **1.** accesorio *m* **2.** LAW cómplice *mf*

accident ['æk·sɪ·dənt] *n* accidente *m;* ~ **insurance** seguro *m* contra accidentes; **by** ~ sin querer; (*by chance*) por casualidad

accidental [,æk·sɪ·'den·təl] *adj* accidental; (*discovery*) fortuito, -a

accident-prone *adj* propenso, -a a tener accidentes

acclaim [ə·'kleɪm] *vt* aclamar; **critically** ~**ed** elogiado por la crítica

acclamation [,æk·lə·'meɪ·ʃən] *n* aclamación *f*

acclimate [ə·'klaɪ·mɪt] **I.** *vi* aclimatarse **II.** *vt* aclimatar

accommodate [ə·'kam·ə·deɪt] *vt* alojar; **to** ~ **oneself to sth** adaptarse a algo

accommodation [ə·,kam·ə·'deɪ·ʃən] *n* **1.** *pl* alojamiento *m* **2.** (*on vehicle, plane*) asientos *mpl*

accompany [ə·'kʌm·pə·ni] <-ie-> *vt* acompañar

accomplice [ə·'kam·plɪs] *n* cómplice *mf*

accomplish [ə·'kam·plɪʃ] *vt* lograr; (*finish*) concluir; (*task*) realizar

accomplished [ə·'kam·plɪʃt] *adj* consumado, -a

accomplishment *n* **1.** (*achievement*) logro *m* **2.** (*completion*) conclusión *f;* (*task*) realización *f* **3.** (*skill*) talento *m*

accord [ə·'kɔrd] **I.** *n* acuerdo *m;* (*treaty*) convenio *m* **II.** *vi* to ~ **with sth** concordar con algo

accordance [ə·'kɔr·dəns] *n* **in** ~ **with** conforme a

accordingly *adv* **1.** (*appropriately*) en consecuencia **2.** (*therefore*) por consiguiente

according to [ə·'kɔr·dɪŋ·tə] *prep* según; ~ **her/what I read** según ella/lo que leí; **to go** ~ **plan** salir según lo previsto; ~ **the law** con arreglo a la ley

accordion [ə·'kɔr·di·ən] *n* MUS acordeón *m,* filarmónica *f Méx*

account [ə·'kaʊnt] *n* **1.** (*with bank*) cuenta *f* **2.** (*bill*) factura *f* **3.** *pl* (*financial records*) cuentas *fpl;* **to keep an** ~ **of sth** llevar la cuenta de algo **4. to give an** ~ **of sth** informar sobre algo **5. to take sth into** ~ tomar [*or* tener] algo en cuenta; **to take no** ~ **of sth** no tomar [*or* tener] en cuenta algo; **on** ~ **of sth** por causa de algo **6.** responsabilidad *f;* **on one's own** ~ por cuenta propia; **on sb's** ~ a cuenta de alguien ▶ **to be called to** ~ tener que rendir cuentas (**for** de); **to settle** ~**s with sb** ajustar cuentas con alguien

◆ **account for** *vt* **1.** (*explain*) explicar **2.** (*constitute*) representar

accountable [ə·'kaʊn·tə·bəl] *adj* responsable

accountant [ə·'kaʊn·tənt] *n* contable *mf,* contador(a) *m(f) And*

account book *n* libro *m* de cuentas

accumulate [ə·'kjum·jə·leɪt] **I.** *vt* acumular **II.** *vi* acumularse

accumulation [ə·,kjum·jə·'leɪ·ʃən] *n* acumulación *f;* (*quantity*) cúmulo *m*

accuracy ['æk·jər·ə·si] *n* precisión *f*

accurate ['æk·jər·ɪt] *adj* **1.** (*on target*) certero, -a **2.** (*correct*) exacto, -a **3.** (*careful*) cuidadoso, -a

accusation [,æk·ju·'zeɪ·ʃən] *n* acusación *f*

accuse [ə·'kjuz] *vt* acusar; **she is** ~**d of...** se la acusa de...

accused [ə·'kjuzd] *n* **the** ~ el acusado, la acusada

accustomed [ə·'kʌs·təmd] *adj* **1.** acostumbrado, -a; **to be/to grow** ~ **to doing sth** estar acostumbrado/acostumbrarse a hacer algo **2.** (*usual*) usual

ace [eɪs] **I.** *n* as *m* ▶ **to have an** ~ **up one's sleeve** tener un as en la manga; **to come within an** ~ **of** estar a punto (**of** de) **II.** *adj inf* experto, -a **III.** *vt sl* (*exam, interview*) bordar

ache [eɪk] **I.** *n* dolor *m* **II.** *vi* doler

achieve [ə·'tʃiv] *vt* lograr; (*task*) llevar a cabo; (*success*) alcanzar

achievement *n* logro *m;* (*achieving*) realización *f*

acid ['æs·ɪd] **I.** *n a. sl* ácido *m* **II.** *adj* **1.** ácido, -a **2.** (*sarcastic*) mordaz

acidity [ə·'sɪd·ə·t̬i] *n* acidez *f; fig* mordacidad *f*

acid rain n lluvia f ácida

acid rock n MUS acid rock m

acid-washed adj deslavado, -a, destinado, -a Méx

acknowledge [ək·'nal·ıdʒ] vt (admit) admitir; (guilt) confesar

acknowledg(e)ment n 1. reconocimiento m; (of guilt) confesión f 2. pl agradecimientos mpl

acne ['æk·ni] n acné m

acorn ['eɪ·kɔrn] n bellota f

acoustic(al) [ə·'ku·stɪk(əl)] I. adj acústico, -a II. npl acústica f

acoustics [ə·'ku·stɪks] n + sing vb (science) acústica f; + pl vb (of an enclosed space) acústica f

acquaint [ə·'kweɪnt] vt to be/become ~ed with conocer

acquaintance [ə·'kweɪn·təns] n (relationship) relación f; (person) conocido, -a m, f

acquire [ə·'kwaɪr] vt adquirir; to ~ a taste for sth tomarle el gusto a algo

acquisition [ˌæk·wɪ·'zɪʃ·ən] n adquisición f

acquit [ə·'kwɪt] <-tt-> vt to ~ sb of a charge absolver a alguien de una acusación; to ~ oneself well/badly salir bien/mal parado

acquittal [ə·'kwɪt̬·əl] n absolución f

acre ['eɪ·kər] n acre m (4047 metros cuadrados)

acrobat ['æk·rə·bæt] n acróbata mf

acrobatic [ˌæk·rə·'bæt̬·ɪk] adj acrobático, -a

acronym ['æk·rə·nɪm] n sigla f

across [ə·'krɔs] I. prep 1. (on other side of) al otro lado de; just ~ the street justo al otro lado de la calle; ~ from enfrente de 2. (from one side to other) a través de; to walk ~ the bridge cruzar el puente andando II. adv de un lado a otro; to run/swim ~ cruzar corriendo/a nado; to come ~ sth encontrar(se) algo

across-the-board adj global

acrylic [ə·'krɪl·ɪk] n acrílico m

acrylic paint n pintura f acrílica

act [ækt] I. n 1. (action) a. THEAT acto m; ~ of charity obra f de caridad; to catch sb in the ~ pillar a alguien in fraganti 2. (performance) número m

3. (pretence) fingimiento m 4. LAW ley f ▶ to get one's ~ together arreglárselas; to get in on the ~ meterse en el asunto II. vi 1. (take action) a. THEAT actuar; to ~ for sb representar a alguien 2. (behave) portarse 3. (take effect) dar resultado 4. (pretend) fingir III. vt THEAT representar; to ~ the fool hacer el tonto

◆**act on** vt obrar de acuerdo con

◆**act out** vt representar

◆**act up** vi inf hacer de las suyas; (machine) fallar; (knee, back) doler

acting ['æk·tɪŋ] I. adj en funciones II. n arte m dramático

action ['æk·ʃən] n 1. (activeness) acción f; out of ~ inactivo; (machine) fuera de servicio; to spring into ~ ponerse en marcha; to take ~ tomar medidas 2. MIL combate m 3. (motion) movimiento m 4. LAW demanda f; to bring an ~ interponer una demanda (against contra) 5. inf (exciting events) bullicio m ▶ ~s speak louder than words obras sus amores y no buenas razones

action-packed adj lleno, -a de acción

activate ['æk·tə·veɪt] vt a. CHEM activar

active ['æk·tɪv] adj activo, -a; to be ~ in sth participar en algo

actively adv 1. (in a lively manner) activamente 2. (energetically) enérgicamente 3. (consciously) de forma activa

activist ['æk·tə·vɪst] n activista mf

activity [æk·'tɪv·ɪ·t̬i] <-ies> n actividad f

actor ['æk·tər] n actor m

actress ['æk·trɪs] n actriz f

actual ['æk·tʃu·əl] adj (real) verdadero, -a; (precise) exacto, -a

actually ['æk·tʃu·ə·li] adv en realidad; ~ I saw her yesterday pues la vi ayer

acupuncture ['æk·ju·pʌŋk·tʃər] n acupuntura f

acute [ə·'kjut] I. adj (pain, disease, hearing, sight, angle) agudo, -a; (anxiety) extremo, -a; (embarrassment) hondo, -a; (difficulties) grande; (shortage) fuerte II. n acento m agudo

acutely adv extremadamente; to be ~ aware of sth ser plenamente consciente de algo

ad [æd] n inf abbr of **advertisement**

anuncio *m*

A.D. [ˌeɪ-ˈdiː] *abbr of* **anno Domini** d.C.

adapt [ə-ˈdæpt] **I.** *vt* adaptar **II.** *vi* adaptarse

adaptable *adj* adaptable

adaptation [ˌæd-æp-ˈteɪ-ʃən] *n* adaptación *f*

adapter, adaptor [ə-ˈdæp-tər] *n* adaptador *m;* (*for several plugs*) ladrón *m*

add [æd] *vt* **1.** añadir, agregar *AmL* **2.** MATH sumar

◆ add up *vi, vt* sumar; **to ~ to...** ascender a...

adder [ˈæd-ər] *n* víbora *f*

addict [ˈæd-ɪkt] *n* adicto, -a *m, f;* **drug ~** drogadicto *m;* **to be a movie ~** ser un apasionado del cine

addicted [ə-ˈdɪk-tɪd] *adj* adicto, -a; **to be ~ to sth** ser adicto a algo; *fig* ser muy aficionado a algo

addiction [ə-ˈdɪk-ʃən] *n* adicción *f;* **drug ~** drogadicción *f*

addictive [ə-ˈdɪk-tɪv] *adj* adictivo, -a

addition [ə-ˈdɪʃ-ən] *n* **1.** adición *f;* (*added thing*) añadido *m;* **in ~ (to)** además (de); **an ~ to the family** uno más en la familia **2.** MATH suma *f*

additional [ə-ˈdɪʃ-ən-əl] *adj* adicional

additionally [ə-ˈdɪʃ-ən-əl-i] *adv* por añadidura; **and ~** y además

additive [ˈæd-ɪ-tɪv] *n* aditivo *m*

address¹ [ˈæd-res] *n* dirección *f*

address² [ə-ˈdres] **I.** *vt* **1.** (*letter*) dirigir **2.** (*speak to*) dirigirse a **II.** *n* **form of ~** tratamiento *m*

addressee [ˌæd-re-ˈsi] *n* destinatario, -a *m, f*

adept [ə-ˈdept] *adj* experto, -a; **to be ~ at sth** ser hábil para algo

adequate [ˈæd-ɪ-kwət] *adj* **1.** (*sufficient*) suficiente **2.** (*good enough*) adecuado, -a

adhere [æd-ˈhɪr] *vi* adherirse; *fig* aferrarse

adhesive [æd-ˈhi-sɪv] *adj* adhesivo, -a

ad infinitum [æd-ɪn-ˌfə-ˈnaɪ-təm] *adv* ad infinítum

adjacent [ə-ˈdʒeɪ-sənt] *adj* contiguo, -a; MATH adyacente

adjective [ˈædʒ-ɪk-tɪv] *n* adjetivo *m*

adjoining *adj* (*room*) contiguo, -a; (*field*)

colindante

adjourn [ə-ˈdʒɜrn] **I.** *vt* aplazar **II.** *vi* **1.** aplazarse **2.** (*go*) desplazarse

adjust [ə-ˈdʒʌst] **I.** *vt* **1.** *a.* TECH ajustar **2.** (*rearrange*) arreglar **3.** (*change*) modificar **II.** *vi* adaptarse (**to** a)

adjustable *adj* ajustable

adjustable wrench *n* llave *f* inglesa

adjustment *n* ajuste *m;* (*mental*) adaptación *f*

ad lib [ˌæd-ˈlɪb] *adv* improvisando

admin [æd-ˈmɪn] *abbr of* **administration** admón.

administer [æd-ˈmɪn-ɪ-stər] *vt* (*funds, estate, medicine*) administrar; (*punishment*) aplicar; (*first aid*) prestar

administration [æd-ˌmɪn-ɪ-ˈstreɪ-ʃən] *n a.* POL administración *f;* (*time in power*) mandato *m*

administrative [æd-ˈmɪn-ɪ-streɪ-tɪv] *adj* administrativo, -a

administrator [æd-ˈmɪn-ɪ-streɪ-tər] *n* administrador(a) *m(f)*

admirable [ˈæd-mər-ə-bəl] *adj* admirable

admiral [ˈæd-mər-əl] *n* almirante *m*

admiration [ˌæd-mə-ˈreɪ-ʃən] *n* admiración *f;* **in ~** lleno de admiración

admire [əd-ˈmaɪr] *vt* admirar (**for** por)

admirer [əd-ˈmaɪr-ər] *n* admirador(a) *m(f)*

admissible [æd-ˈmɪs-ə-bəl] *adj* admisible

admission [æd-ˈmɪʃ-ən] *n* **1.** (*entry, entrance fee*) entrada; (*to college, organization*) ingreso *m* **2.** (*acknowledgement*) confesión *f*

admit [æd-ˈmɪt] <-tt-> **I.** *vt* **1.** (*acknowledge*) reconocer; (*crime*) confesar **2.** (*allow entrance to*) dejar entrar **3.** (*permit*) admitir **II.** *vt* **to ~ to sth** confesarse culpable de algo

admittance [æd-ˈmɪt-əns] *n* entrada *f;* **no ~** se prohíbe la entrada

admittedly [æd-ˈmɪt-ɪd-li] *adv* es cierto que

ado [ə-ˈdu] *n* **1.** (*commotion*) embrollo *m* **2.** (*delay*) demora *f* ▶ **much ~ about nothing** mucho ruido y pocas nueces

adobe [ə-ˈdoʊ-bi] *n* adobe *m;* (*building*) construcción *f* de adobe

adolescence [ˌæd-əl-ˈes-əns] *n* adolescencia *f*

adolescent [ˌæd·əl·ˈes·ənt] *adj, n* adolescente *mf*

adopt [ə·ˈdapt] *vt* adoptar; (*candidate*) nombrar

adoption [ə·ˈdap·ʃən] *n* adopción *f;* (*of candidate*) nombramiento *m*

adorable [ə·ˈdɔr·ə·bəl] *adj* encantador(a)

adoration [ˌæd·ə·ˈrei·ʃən] *n* adoración *f*

adore [ə·ˈdɔr] *vt* adorar; **I just ~ the theater** me encanta el teatro

adoring [ə·ˈdɔr·ɪŋ] *adj* cariñoso, -a

adrenaline [ə·ˈdren·ə·lɪn] *n* adrenalina *f*

adrift [ə·ˈdrɪft] *adv* a la deriva; **to go ~** *fig* fallar

adult [ə·ˈdʌlt] **I.** *n* adulto, -a *m, f* **II.** *adj* adulto, -a; (*explicit*) para adultos

adultery [ə·ˈdʌl·tə·ri] <-ies> *n* adulterio *m*

advance [əd·ˈvæns] **I.** *vi* avanzar (**on** hacia) **II.** *vt* **1.** avanzar; (*interest, cause*) promover **2.** (*pay*) anticipar **III.** *n* **1.** (*forward movement*) avance *m;* **in ~** por adelantado **2.** FIN anticipo *m* **3.** *pl* (*flirtation*) insinuaciones *fpl* **IV.** *adj* adelantado, -a; **without ~ warning** sin previo aviso

advanced [əd·ˈvænst] *adj* avanzado, -a

advancement [əd·ˈvæns·mənt] *n* **1.** (*improvement*) avance *m* **2.** (*promotion*) fomento *m*

advance notice *n* aviso *m* (previo)

advance payment *n* anticipo *m*

advantage [əd·ˈvæn·tɪdʒ] *n* ventaja *f* (**over** sobre); **to take ~** aprovecharse (**of** de)

adventure [æd·ˈven·tʃər] *n* aventura *f*

adventurous [əd·ˈven·tʃər·əs] *adj* aventurero, -a; (*decision*) arriesgado, -a

adverb [ˈæd·vɜrb] *n* adverbio *m*

adversary [ˈæd·vər·ser·i] <-ies> *n* adversario, -a *m, f*

adverse [æd·ˈvɜrs] *adj* adverso, -a; (*reaction*) hostil

adversity [æd·ˈvɜr·sə·ti] <-ies> *n* adversidad *f*

advertent [æd·ˈvɜr·tənt] *adj* atento, -a

advertise [ˈæd·vər·taɪz] **I.** *vt* anunciar **II.** *vi* hacer publicidad

advertisement [ˌæd·vər·ˈtaɪz·mənt] *n* anuncio *m*, aviso *m* AmL; **job ~** oferta *f* de empleo

advertiser [ˈæd·vər·taɪ·zər] *n* anunciante *mf*

advertising [ˈæd·vər·ˌtaɪ·zɪŋ] *n* publicidad *f*

advice [æd·ˈvaɪs] *n* **1.** consejo *m;* **a piece of ~** un consejo; **to ask for ~** pedir consejo (**on** sobre); **on her ~** siguiendo su consejo **2.** COM aviso *m*

advisable [æd·ˈvaɪ·zə·bəl] *adj* aconsejable; **it is (not) ~** (no) es aconsejable

advise [æd·ˈvaɪz] **I.** *vt* aconsejar; (*specialist*) asesorar (**on** sobre); **to ~ against** desaconsejar **II.** *vi* dar un consejo

adviser, advisor [əd·ˈvaɪ·zər] *n* asesor(a) *m(f)*

advocacy [ˈæd·və·kəsi] *n* (*of cause, idea*) defensa *f*

advocate¹ [ˈæd·və·keɪt] *vt* **to ~ (doing sth)** recomendar (hacer algo)

advocate² [ˈæd·və·kət] *n* defensor(a) *m(f);* (*lawyer*) abogado, -a *m, f* defensor(a)

aerial [ˈer·i·əl] **I.** *adj* aéreo, -a **II.** *n* antena *f*

aerobics [ə·ˈrou·bɪks] *n + sing/pl vb* aeróbic *m*, aerobic *m;* **to do ~** hacer aeróbic

aerodynamic [ˌer·ou·daɪ·ˈnæm·ɪk] *adj* aerodinámico, -a

aerodynamics *n + sing vb* aerodinámica *f*

aeronautic [ˈer·ə·nɔ·t̬ik] *adj* aeronáutico, -a

aeronautics *n + sing vb* aeronáutica *f*

aerosol [ˈer·ə·sɔl] *n* aerosol *m*

aesthetics *n + sing vb* estética *f*

afar [ə·ˈfar] *adv* lejos

affable [ˈæf·ə·bəl] *adj* afable

affair [ə·ˈfer] *n* **1.** (*matter*) asunto *m* **2.** (*scandal*) escándalo *m* **3.** (**to have) an ~** (tener) una aventura (**with** con) **4.** (*event*) acontecimiento *m*

affect [ə·ˈfekt] *vt* **1.** afectar; **to be ~ed by sth** (*be moved*) conmoverse por algo **2.** (*simulate*) fingir

affected [ə·ˈfek·tɪd] *adj* (*behavior, accent*) amanerado, -a; (*emotion*) fingido, -a; (*style, smile*) forzado, -a

affection [ə·ˈfek·ʃən] *n* cariño *m*

affectionate [ə·ˈfek·ʃə·nɪt] *adj* cariñoso, -a

affiliate¹ [ə·ˈfɪl·i·eɪt] *vt* afiliar (**with** a)

affiliate² [ə·'fɪl·i·ɪt] n filial f

affirm [ə·'fɜrm] vt afirmar

affirmation [ˌæf·ər·'meɪ·fən] n afirmación f

affirmative [ə·'fɜr·mə·tɪv] I. adj afirmativo, -a II. n in the ~ afirmativamente

affix [ə·'fɪks] vt poner; (stick) pegar; (clip) clavar

afflict [ə·'flɪkt] vt afligir; **to be ~ed** padecer (**with** de)

affluent ['æf·lʊ·ənt] adj rico, -a; (lifestyle) acomodado, -a; (society) opulento, -a

afford [ə·'fɔrd] vt 1. (money, time) permitirse 2. (provide) proporcionar

affordable [ə·'fɔr·də·bəl] adj asequible

afforest [ə·'fɔr·əst] vt forestar

afield [ə·'fild] adv far/further ~ muy/más lejos

afloat [ə·'floʊt] adj a flote

afoot [ə·'fʊt] adj there's sth ~ se está tramando algo

aforementioned [əˌfɔr·'men·fənd], **aforesaid** [ə·'fɔr·sed] form I. adj dicho, -a II. n inv the ~ el mencionado/la mencionada; (person) el susodicho/la susodicha

afraid [ə·'freɪd] adj 1. (scared) to be ~ tener miedo (of a); to be ~ of doing [or to do] sth tener miedo de hacer algo 2. (sorry) I'm ~ so/not me temo que sí/no

Africa ['æf·rɪ·kə] n África f

African ['æf·rɪ·kən] adj, n africano, -a m, f

African American, Afro-American adj, n afroamericano, -a m, f

aft [æft] adv (go) a popa; (be) en popa

after ['æf·tər] I. prep 1. (later, following) después de; ~ **two days** al cabo de dos días; (shortly) ~ **breakfast** (poco) después de desayunar; **to have argument** ~ **argument** tener pelea tras pelea; ~ **all** después de todo; **to ask** ~ **sb** preguntar por alguien 2. (behind) detrás de II. adv después; **soon** ~ poco después III. conj después de que +subj

afterbirth n placenta f

aftercare ['æf·tər·ker] n MED asistencia f postoperatoria

aftereffects ['æf·tər·ɪˌfekts] npl (drugs) efectos m pl secundarios; (accident) secuelas fpl

afterglow n 1. (after sunset) arrebol m

2. PHYS luminiscencia f

after-hours adj fuera de horas

afterlife ['æf·tər·laɪf] n the ~ el más allá

after-market n venta f de repuestos y accesorios [or Méx de refacción]

aftermath ['æf·tər·mæθ] n secuelas fpl

afternoon [ˌæf·tər·'nun] I. n tarde f; this ~ esta tarde; in the ~ por la tarde; all ~ toda la tarde; tomorrow/yesterday ~ mañana/ayer por la tarde; 4 o'clock in the ~ las 4 de la tarde; good ~! ¡buenas tardes! II. adj de la tarde; ~ nap siesta f

after-shave ['æf·tər·feɪv] n aftershave m

aftershock n réplica f

aftertaste ['æf·tər·teɪst] n a. fig regusto m

afterward, afterwards [ˈæf·tər·wərd(z)] adv después; **shortly** ~ poco después

again [ə·'gen] adv otra vez; (one more time) de nuevo; **never** ~ nunca más; **once** ~ otra vez; ~ **and** ~ una y otra vez

against [ə·'genst] I. prep 1. contra; **to be** ~ estar en contra (de); ~ **the light** a contraluz; ~ **the clock** contrarreloj; **to run** ~ **a wall** estrellarse contra una pared; **to lean** ~ **a tree** apoyarse en un árbol 2. (protection) **to protect oneself** ~ **rain** protegerse de la lluvia 3. (in comparison with) **the dollar rose/fell** ~ **the euro** el dólar subió/bajó respecto al euro II. adv en contra; **9 votes** ~ 9 votos en contra

age [eɪdʒ] I. n 1. (of person, object) edad f; old ~ vejez f; when I was her ~ cuando tenía su edad; to be under ~ ser menor de edad 2. (era) época f; I haven't seen you in ~s! ¡hace siglos que no te veo! II. vi, vt envejecer; CULIN madurar

age bracket n see age group

aged¹ [eɪdʒd] adj de ... años de edad; CULIN curado, -a; (wine) añejo, -a

aged² ['eɪ·dʒɪd] I. adj viejo, -a II. n the ~ los ancianos

age group n grupo m de edad

agency ['eɪ·dʒən·si] <-ies> n agencia f; **travel** ~ agencia de viajes; **government** ~ organismo gubernamental

agenda [ə·'dʒen·də] n orden m del día; **to be at the top of the** ~ fig ser un asunto prioritario

agent ['eɪ·dʒənt] n agente mf

age-old adj antiguo, -a

aggravate ['æg·rə·veɪt] vt agravar; inf fastidiar

aggravating adj molesto, -a

aggravation [ˌæg·rə·'veɪ·ʃən] n inf fastidio m

aggregate¹ ['æg·rɪ·gɪt] I. n 1. FIN, ECON conglomerado m; (sum, value) total m 2. MATH suma f II. adj total

aggregate² ['æg·rɪ·geɪt] vt sumar

aggression [ə·'greʃ·ən] n (feelings) agresividad f; (violence) agresión f

aggressive [ə·'gres·ɪv] adj agresivo, -a

aggressor [ə·'gres·ər] n agresor(a) m(f)

agile ['ædʒ·əl] adj ágil

agility [ə·'dʒɪl·ə·ti] n agilidad f

aging I. adj envejecido, -a II. n envejecimiento m

agitation [ˌædʒ·ɪ·'teɪ·ʃən] n agitación f

agnostic [æg·'nɑs·tɪk] adj, n agnóstico, -a m, f

ago [ə·'goʊ] adv a minute/year ~ hace un minuto/año; **a long time ~, long ~** hace mucho tiempo; **how long ~ was that?** ¿cuánto tiempo hace de eso?

agog [ə·'gɑg] adj **to watch/listen ~** mirar/escuchar con avidez

agonizing ['æg·ə·naɪ·zɪŋ] adj (pain) atroz; (delay, decision) angustiante

agony ['æg·ə·ni] <-ies> n agonía f; **to be in ~** sufrir fuertes dolores

agony column n sección f de desaparecidos

agrarian [ə·'grer·i·ən] adj agrario, -a

agree [ə·'gri] I. vi 1. estar de acuerdo; **to ~ on sth** (be in agreement) estar de acuerdo en algo; (reach agreement) acordar algo; **to ~ to do sth** (reach agreement) acordar hacer algo; (consent) acceder a hacer algo 2. (be good for) **to ~ with sb** sentar bien a alguien 3. (match up) a. LING concordar II. vt acordar; **at the ~d time** a la hora fijada

agreement n 1. acuerdo m; **to be in ~** estar de acuerdo (**with** con); **to reach an ~** llegar a un acuerdo 2. LING concordancia f

agriculture ['æg·rɪ·kʌl·tʃər] n agricultura f

agritourism [ˌæg·rɪ·'tʊr·ɪzəm] n agroturismo m

aground [ə·'graʊnd] adv **to run ~** encallar; fig fracasar

ah [ɑ] interj ah

aha [ɑ·'hɑ] interj ajá

ahead [ə·'hed] adv 1. (in front) delante 2. (with movement) adelante; **to go ~** adelantarse 3. (in the future) **to look ~** anticiparse

ahead of prep 1. (in front of) delante de; (way) **~ sb/sth** (muy) por delante de alguien/algo 2. (before) antes de; **~ time** antes de tiempo; **to be a minute ~ sb** llevar un minuto a alguien; **to be ~ one's time** anticiparse a su época 3. **to keep ~ sth** estar al tanto de algo

ahoy [ə·'hɔɪ] interj **land/ship ~!** ¡tierra/barco a la vista!

AI [ˌeɪ·'aɪ] n abbr of **artificial intelligence** IA

aid [eɪd] I. n ayuda f; **to/with the ~ of** en/con ayuda de; **financial ~** asistencia f financiera; **hearing ~** audífono m II. vt ayudar

aid convoy n convoy m humanitario

AIDS [eɪdz] n abbr of **Acquired Immune Deficiency Syndrome** sida m

ailing ['eɪ·lɪŋ] adj enfermo, -a; (company, economy) debilitado, -a

aim [eɪm] I. vi (weapon) apuntar (**at** a); **to ~ at** [or **for**] **sth** tener algo como objetivo II. vt apuntar; **to ~ sth at sb/sth** (point a weapon) apuntar algo hacia alguien/algo; (direct at) dirigir algo hacia alguien; **to be ~ed at doing sth** ir encaminado a hacer algo III. n 1. (ability) puntería f 2. (goal) objetivo m

aimless ['eɪm·lɪs] adj sin objetivo(s)

ain't [eɪnt] inf 1. (to be) see **am not, are not, is not** 2. (to have) see **have not, has not**

air [er] I. n aire m; **by ~** por aire; **to travel by ~** viajar en avión; **to be on the ~** estar en el aire; **to have an ~ of confidence/danger** envolverse en un aire de confianza/peligro ▶ **out of thin ~** de la nada; **to disappear into thin ~** desaparecer como por arte de magia II. adj aéreo, -a III. vt 1. TV, RADIO emitir 2. (expose to air) airear IV. vi 1. TV, RADIO emitirse 2. (be exposed to air) ventilarse

air ball n (*in basketball*) pelota que no toca ni el aro

air base n base f aérea

airborne ['er-bɔrn] *adj* aerotransporta-do, -a; **to be ~** volar

airbrush n aerógrafo m

air bus n aerobús m

air-conditioned *adj* climatizado, -a

air conditioning n aire m acondicionado

aircraft ['er-kræft] n avión m

airdrome ['er-droum] n aeródromo m

air-dry vt secar al aire

airfare n precio m del billete de avión [*or Méx, Col* del tiquete]

airfield n aeródromo m

airframe n armazón m

airfreight n carga f aérea

airhead n inf cabeza mf hueca

air lane n vía f aérea

airlift I. n puente m aéreo II. vt aero-transportar

airline n línea f aérea, aerolínea f AmL

airmail I. n correo m aéreo II. vt enviar por correo aéreo

air mass n masa f de aire

air mattress n colchón m inflable

air piracy n piratería f aérea

airplane n avión m

air pocket n bolsa f de aire

air pollution n contaminación f at-mosférica

airport n aeropuerto m

airport terminal n terminal f aérea

air pump n bomba f de aire

air rifle n rifle m de aire comprimido

airship n zepelín m

air show n exhibición f aérea

airsick *adj* mareado, -a; **to get ~** marear-se (en avión)

airspace n espacio m aéreo

airstrip n pista f de aterrizaje

air taxi n aerotaxi m

airtight *adj* hermético, -a

airtime n TV tiempo m en antena

airway ['er-weɪ] n ruta f aérea; ANAT vía f respiratoria

airy ['er-i] *adj* 1. ARCHIT espacioso, -a 2. (*light*) ligero, -a 3. (*lacking sub-stance*) etéreo, -a

aisle [aɪl] n pasillo m ▶ **to take sb down the ~** llevar al altar a alguien

ajar [ə-'dʒɑr] *adj* entreabierto, -a

AK n abbr of **Alaska** Alaska f

AKA, aka abbr of **also known as** alias

akin [ə-'kɪn] *adj* **~ to** parecido a

AL n abbr of **Alabama**

Alabama [ˌæl-ə-'bæm-ə] n Alabama f

à la mode [ˌɑ-lə-'moud] *adj* con helado

alarm [ə-'lɑrm] I. n 1. alarma f; **to cause sb ~** alarmar a alguien; **fire ~** alarma de incendios; **burglar ~** dispositivo m antirrobo 2. (*clock*) reloj m desper-tador II. vt alarmar; **to be ~ed** estar alarmado

alarming *adj* alarmante

Alaska [ə-'læs-kə] n Alaska f

albacore ['æl-bə-ˌkɔr] n ZOOL albacora f

albino [æl-'baɪ-nou] *adj, n* albino, -a m, f

album ['æl-bəm] n álbum m

alcohol ['æl-kə-hɔl] n alcohol m

alcohol-free *adj* sin alcohol

alcoholic [ˌæl-kə-'hɔ-lɪk] *adj, n* alcohó-lico, -a m, f

alcoholism n alcoholismo m

ale [eɪl] n cerveza f

alert [ə-'lɜrt] I. *adj* despierto, -a; **to keep ~** mantenerse alerta II. n (**on the**) **~** alerta f; (*alarm*) alarma f III. vt alertar

alfalfa [æl-'fæl-fə] n BOT alfalfa f

alfresco [æl-'fres-kou] *adv* al aire libre

alga ['æl-gə] n <algae> pl alga f

algebra ['æl-dʒə-brə] n álgebra f

alias ['eɪ-li-əs] *adv,* n alias m inv

alibi ['æl-ə-baɪ] n coartada f

alien ['er-li-ən] I. *adj* (*foreign*) extran-jero, -a; (*strange*) extraño, -a; **~ to sb** ajeno a alguien II. n (*foreigner*) ex-tranjero, -a m, f; (*extraterrestrial*) ex-traterrestre mf

alienate ['er-li-ə-neɪt] vt distanciar; (*prop-erty*) enajenar

alienation [ˌer-li-ə-'ner-ʃən] n distancia-miento m; (*of property*) enajenación f

alight [ə-'laɪt] I. *adj* **to be ~** estar ardien-do; **to set sth ~** prender fuego a algo; (*with enthusiasm, joy*) resplandeciente II. vi (*on branch*) posarse; (*from ve-hicle*) apearse

alignment n alineación f; **to be out of ~** no estar alineado

alike [ə-'laɪk] I. *adj* **to look ~** parecerse; **Clara and Carl ~** tanto Clara como Carl

II. *adv* por igual

alimony ['æl·ɪ·mou·ni] *n* pensión *f* alimenticia

alive [ə·'laɪv] *adj* **1.** to be ~ estar vivo **2.** (*active*) activo, -a; **to make sth come** ~ dar vida a algo **3.** (*aware*) **to be ~ to sth** ser consciente de algo

alkaline ['æl·kə·laɪn] *adj* alcalino, -a

all I. *adj* todo, -a; ~ **the wine** todo el vino; ~ **my sisters** todas mis hermanas **II.** *pron* **1.** (*everybody*) todos, -as; ~ **but him** todos menos él; **once and for** ~ de una vez por todas **2.** (*everything*) todo; **most of** ~ sobre todo; **for** ~ **I know** que yo sepa **3.** (*the whole quantity*) todo, -a; ~ **of Cuba** toda Cuba; ~ **I want is...** lo único que quiero es... **4.** SPORTS **two** ~ **two** dos a dos **III.** *adv* totalmente; **it's** ~ **the same** me da igual

Allah ['æl·ə] *n* REL Alá *m*

all-day *adj* que dura todo el día

allegation [,æl·ɪ·'geɪ·ʃən] *n* acusación *f*

allege [ə·'ledʒ] *vt* afirmar; **it is** ~**d that...** se dice que...

alleged [ə·'ledʒd] *adj* supuesto, -a

allegedly [ə·'ledʒ·ɪd·li] *adv* (según) se dice

allegiance [ə·'li·dʒəns] *n* lealtad *f*

allegorical [,æl·ɪ·'gɔr·ɪk·əl] *adj* alegórico, -a

allegory ['æl·ɪ·gɔr·i] <-ies> *n* alegoría *f*

allergic [ə·'lɜr·dʒɪk] *adj* alérgico, -a

allergist ['æl·ər·dʒɪst] *n* alergólogo, -a *m, f*

allergy ['æl·ər·dʒi] <-ies> *n* alergia *f*

alleviate [ə·'li·vi·eɪt] *vt* aliviar

alley ['æl·i] *n* callejón *m;* (*in garden*) paseo *m;* **blind** ~ callejón sin salida ▶ **to be (right) up one's** ~ ser lo suyo

alleyway *n* callejón *m*

alliance [ə·'laɪ·əns] *n* alianza *f*

allied ['æl·aɪd] *adj* aliado, -a; ~ **with** [*or* **to**] **sth** unido a algo

alligator ['æl·ɪ·geɪ·tər] *n* caimán *m*

alligator pear *n* aguacate *m*, palta *f Arg, Bol, Chile, Ecua, Perú, Urug*

all-inclusive [,ɔl·ɪn·'klu·sɪv] *adj* todo incluido; ~ **rate** precio con todo incluido

alliteration *n* aliteración *f*

all-night *adj* que dura toda la noche; (*open*) abierto, -a toda la noche

all-nighter *n inf* **to pull an** ~ tirarse toda la noche (haciendo algo)

allocate ['æl·ə·keɪt] *vt* **1.** (*assign*) asignar **2.** (*distribute*) repartir

allocation [,æl·ə·'keɪ·ʃən] *n* **1.** (*assignment*) asignación *f* **2.** (*distribution*) distribución *f*

allot [ə·'lat] <-tt-> *vt* asignar

allotment *n* adjudicación *f*

all-out [ɔl·'aʊt] *adj* total

allow [ə·'laʊ] *vt* **1.** (*permit*) permitir; **to** ~ **sb to do sth** dejar a alguien hacer algo; **smoking is not** ~**ed** se prohíbe fumar **2.** (*allocate*) asignar; **please** ~ **up to 7 days for delivery** entrega en un plazo máximo de 7 días **3.** (*admit*) **to** ~ **that...** reconocer que...

◆ allow for *vt* tener en cuenta

allowable *adj* (*error*) permisible; (*expenses*) deducible

allowance [ə·'laʊ·əns] *n* **1.** (*permitted amount*) cantidad *f* permitida **2.** (*pocket money*) paga *f* **3.** (*preparation*) **to make** ~**(s) for sth** tener algo en cuenta **4.** (*excuse*) **to make** ~**s for sb** ser indulgente con alguien; **to make** ~**s for sth** tolerar algo

all-purpose [ɔl·'pɜr·pəs] *adj* multiuso

all right I. *adj* bien; **that's** ~ (*after thanks*) de nada; (*after excuse*) no pasa nada; **to be** ~ (*healthy*) estar bien; (*safe*) estar sano y salvo **II.** *interj* de acuerdo **III.** *adv* **1.** (*well*) bien **2.** (*certainly*) con (toda) seguridad **3.** (*in answer*) vale

allspice ['ɔl·spaɪs] *n* pimienta *f* de Jamaica

all-star *adj* estelar

all-terrain vehicle *n* vehículo *m* todoterreno

allude [ə·'lud] *vi* aludir (**to** a)

alluring [ə·'lʊr·ɪŋ] *adj* (*attractive*) atractivo, -a; (*enticing*) tentador(a)

all-weather *adj* para todo tiempo

ally ['æl·aɪ] **I.** <-ies> *n* **1.** (*country*) aliado, -a *m, f* **2.** (*supporter*) partidario, -a *m, f* **II.** <-ie-> *vt* **to** ~ **oneself with sb** aliarse con alguien

alma mater ['æl·mə·ma·tər] *n* alma máter *f*

almighty [ɔl·'maɪ·t̬i] *adj* todopoderoso, -a

almond ['a·mənd] *n* almendra *f;* (*tree*) almendro *m*

almost ['ɔl·moust] *adv* casi; ~ **half** casi

la mitad; **we're ~ there** casi hemos llegado

aloe vera [ˌæl·ou·'ver·ə] *n* áloe *m* vera

aloha [ə·'lou·ə] *interj Hawaiian* aloha

alone [ə·'loun] **I.** *adj* **1.** (*without others*) solo, -a; **to leave ~** dejar en paz **2.** (*unique*) *Jane ~ can do that* Jane es la única que sabe hacerlo ▶ **let ~** mucho menos **II.** *adv* sólo

along [ə·'laŋ] **I.** *prep* por; **all ~** a lo largo de; **I lost it ~ the way** lo perdí por el camino; **it's ~ here** está por aquí **II.** *adv* **all ~** todo el tiempo; **to go ~** seguir adelante; **he will be ~ in an hour** llegará en una hora; **come ~!** ¡vente!

alongside [ə·'lɔŋ·saɪd] **I.** *prep* junto a **II.** *adv* al lado

aloof [ə·'luf] *adj* distante

aloud [ə·'laud] *adv* en voz alta

alphabet ['æl·fə·bet] *n* alfabeto *m*

alphabetical [ˌæl·fə·'bet·ɪ·kəl] *adj* alfabético, -a; **in ~ order** por orden alfabético

alphabetize *vt* alfabetizar

alpine ['æl·paɪn] *adj* alpino, -a

already [ɔl·'red·i] *adv* ya

alright [ɔl·'raɪt] *adv see* **all right**

also ['ɔl·sou] *adv* también; **~ known as** alias

altar ['ɔl·tər] *n* altar *m*

altar boy *n* monaguillo *f*

altar girl *n* monaguilla *f*

alter ['ɔl·tər] **I.** *vt* cambiar; (*paint*) retocar; (*dress, suit*) hacer ajustes a; (*dog, cat*) castrar **II.** *vi* cambiarse

alteration [ˌɔl·tər·'eɪ·ʃən] *n* modificación *f*; (*in house*) reforma *f*

altercation [ˌɔl·tər·'keɪ·ʃən] *n* altercado *m*

alter ego [al·tər·ˌi·gou] *n* **1.** PSYCH álter ego *m* **2.** (*close friend*) amigo *m* íntimo

alternate ['ɔl·tər·neɪt] **I.** *vi, vt* alternar **II.** *adj* **1.** (*by turns*) alterno, -a; **on ~ days** en días alternos **2.** (*alternative*) alternativo, -a

alternating ['ɔl·tər·neɪ·tɪŋ] *adj* alterno, -a

alternating current *n* ELEC corriente *f* alterna

alternative [ɔl·'tɜr·nə·tɪv] **I.** *n* alternativa *f*; **to have no ~ but to do sth** no tener otra alternativa que hacer algo

II. *adj* alternativo, -a

alternative-fuel *adj* compatible con combustibles menos contaminantes

alternatively *adv* si no

alternator ['ɔl·tər·neɪ·tər] *n* alternador *m*

although [ɔl·'ðou] *conj* aunque

altitude ['æl·tə·tud] *n* altitud *f*

alto ['æl·tou] *n* contralto *mf*

altogether [ˌɔl·tə·'geð·ər] *adv* (*completely*) totalmente; (*in total*) en total; **not ~** no del todo **II.** *n* **in the ~** en cueros

altruism ['æl·tru·ɪz·əm] *n* altruismo *m*

altruist ['æl·tru·ɪst] *n* altruista *mf*

altruistic [ˌæl·tru·'ɪs·tɪk] *adj* altruista

aluminum [ə·'lu·mə·nəm] *n* aluminio *m*

aluminum foil *n* papel *m* de plata

aluminum oxide *n* alúmina *f*

always ['ɔl·weɪz] *adv* siempre

Alzheimer's disease ['alts·haɪ·mərz] *n* Alzheimer *m*

am [əm, *stressed:* æm] *vi* 1. pers sing of **be**

amateur ['æm·ə·tʃər] *adj, n* **1.** aficionado, -a *m, f* **2.** *pej* chapucero, -a *m, f*

amateurish [ˌæm·ə·'tʃɜr·ɪʃ] *adj* chapucero, -a

amaze [ə·'meɪz] *vt* (*astound*) asombrar; (*surprise*) sorprender

amazement *n* asombro *m*; **to stare at sth in ~** quedarse boquiabierto mirando algo; **to my ~** para mi asombro

amazing *adj* asombroso, -a, sorpresivo, -a *AmL*; **truly ~** realmente increíble

Amazon ['æm·ə·zan] *n* GEO **the ~** el Amazonas

ambassador [æm·'bæs·ə·dər] *n* embajador(a) *m(f)*

amber ['æm·bər] *n* ámbar *m*

ambidextrous [ˌæm·bɪ·'dek·strəs] *adj* ambidextro, -a

ambient ['æm·bi·ənt] *adj* ambiental

ambiguity [ˌæm·bə·'gju·ə·ti] <-ies> *n* ambigüedad *f*

ambiguous [æm·'bɪg·ju·əs] *adj* ambiguo, -a

ambition [æm·'bɪʃ·ən] *n* ambición *f*; **she has no ~** no es nada ambiciosa

ambitious [æm·'bɪʃ·əs] *adj* ambicioso, -a

ambulance ['æm·bju·ləns] *n* ambulancia *f*

ambush ['æm·bʊʃ] **I.** vt tender una emboscada **II.** n <-es> emboscada f

amen [eɪ·'men] interj amén; ~ **to that!** ¡así es!

amend [ə·'mend] vt (text, constitution) enmendar; (plan) modificar

amendment n (to text, constitution) enmienda f; (to plan) modificación f

America [ə·'mer·ɪ·kə] n Estados m Unidos pl; **the ~s** las Américas

American [ə·'mer·ɪ·kən] **I.** n americano, -a m, f; (from USA) estadounidense mf; LING inglés m de EEUU **II.** adj americano, -a

Americanism n americanismo m

amiable ['eɪ·mi·ə·bəl] adj amable

amicable ['æm·ɪ·kə·bəl] adj amistoso, -a

amid(st) [ə·'mɪd(st)] prep en medio de, entre

amiss [ə·'mɪs] **I.** adj **there's something ~** algo va mal **II.** adv **to take sth ~** tomar algo a mal; **a little courtesy would not go ~** no vendría mal un poco de cortesía

ammonia [ə·'moʊn·jə] n amoníaco m

ammunition [ˌæm·jə·'nɪʃ·ən] n munición f; fig argumentos mpl

amnesia [æm·'ni·ʒə] n amnesia f

amnesty ['æm·nɪ·sti] <-ies> n amnistía f

amok [ə·'mʌk] adv see **amuck**

among(st) [ə·'mʌŋ(st)] prep entre; ~ **friends** entre amigos; (just) **one ~ many** (sólo) uno entre tantos; ~ **Canadians** entre los canadienses; ~ **other things** entre otras cosas

amorous ['æm·ər·əs] adj amoroso, -a

amount [ə·'maʊnt] **I.** n (quantity) cantidad f; (of money) importe m; **a check in the ~ of...** un cheque por valor de...; **any ~ of** grandes cantidades de **II.** vi **1.** (add up to) **to ~ to sth** ascender a algo **2.** (be successful) **to ~ to sth** llegar a algo

amp 1. abbr of **ampere** amperio m **2.** inf abbr of **amplifier** bafle m

ampere ['æm·pɪr] n amperio m

ampersand [ˌæm·pər·'sænd], **ampersat** [ˌæm·pər·'sæt] n COMPUT arroba f

amphetamine [æm·'fet·ə·min] n anfetamina f

amphibian [æm·'fɪb·i·ən] n anfibio m

amphibious [æm·'fɪb·i·əs] adj anfibio, -a

amphitheater ['æm·fə·θi·ə·tər] n anfiteatro m

ample ['æm·pəl] adj **1.** (plentiful) abundante **2.** (large) amplio, -a **3.** (enough) suficiente

amplifier ['æm·plə·faɪ·ər] n amplificador m

amplify ['æm·plə·faɪ] <-ie-> vt MUS amplificar; (idea) desarrollar; (remark) aclarar

amplitude ['æm·plɪ·tud] n amplitud f

amputate ['æm·pju·teɪt] vt amputar

amuck [ə·'mʌk] adv de forma descontrolada; **to run ~** descontrolarse

amuse [ə·'mjuz] vt **1.** (entertain) entretener **2.** (cause laughter) divertir; **I'm not ~d** no me hace gracia

amusement [ə·'mjuz·mənt] n **1.** (entertainment) entretenimiento m, entretención f AmL; **for one's own ~** para entretenerse **2.** (mirth) diversión f; **to conceal one's ~** aguantarse la risa

amusement park n parque m de atracciones

amusing adj divertido, -a

an [ən, stressed: æn] indef art before vowel see **a**

anagram ['æn·ə·græm] n anagrama m

anal ['eɪ·nəl] adj anal

analgesic [ˌæn·əl·'dʒi·zɪk] **I.** adj analgésico, -a **II.** n analgésico m

analogy [ə·'næl·ə·dʒi] <-ies> n analogía f

analysis [ə·'næl·ə·sɪs] <-ses> n análisis m inv; (psychoanalysis) psicoanálisis m inv ▶ **in the final** [or **last**] ~ a fin de cuentas

analyst ['æn·ə·lɪst] n analista mf; **financial ~** analista de inversiones; PSYCH psicoanalista mf

analytic [ˌæn·ə·'lɪt·ɪk], **analytical** [ˌæn·ə·'lɪt·ɪ·kəl] adj analítico, -a

analyze ['æn·ə·laɪz] vt analizar; PSYCH psicoanalizar

anarchic [æn·'ar·kɪk], **anarchical** [æn·'ar·kɪ·kəl] adj anárquico, -a

anarchist ['æn·ər·kɪst] adj, n anarquista mf

anarchy ['æn·ər·ki] n anarquía f

anatomical [ˌæn·ə·'tam·ɪ·kəl] adj anatómico, -a

anatomy [ə·'næt·ə·mi] <-ies> n anatomía f

ancestor ['æn·ses·tər] n precursor(a) m(f); (of person) antepasado, -a m, f

ancestral [æn·'ses·trəl] adj ancestral

anchor ['æn·kər] I. n ancla f; to be at ~ estar anclado; fig sostén m; (news ~) presentador(a) m(f) de noticias II. vt 1. NAUT anclar 2. (rope, tent) sujetar 3. RADIO, TV presentar III. vi anclar

anchorman ['æn·kər·mæn] <-men> n RADIO, TV presentador m

anchorwoman ['æn·kər·ˌwʊm·ən] <-men> n RADIO, TV presentadora f

anchovy ['æn·tʃoʊ·vi] <-ies> n anchoa f; (fresh) boquerón m

ancient ['eɪn·ʃənt] adj antiguo, -a; inf prehistórico, -a; since ~ times desde tiempos remotos

and [ən, ənd, stressed: ænd] conj y; (before 'i' or 'hi') e; food ~ drink comida y bebida; parents ~ children padres e hijos; 2 ~ 3 is 5 2 más 3 son 5; four hundred ~ twelve cuatrocientos doce; more ~ more cada vez más; better ~ better cada vez mejor; I tried ~ tried lo intenté una y otra vez ► ~ **so** on [or forth] etcétera

Andean ['æn·di·ən] adj andino, -a

Andes ['æn·diz] npl Andes mpl

android ['æn·drɔɪd] n androide m

anecdotal [ˌæn·ɪk·'doʊt·əl] adj anecdótico, -a

anecdote ['æn·ɪk·doʊt] n anécdota f

anemia [ə·'ni·mi·ə] n anemia f

anemic [ə·'ni·mɪk] adj anémico, -a

anesthesia [ˌæn·ɪs·'θi·ʒə] n anestesia f

anesthetic [ˌæn·ɪs·'θet·ɪk] n anestésico m; to be under ~ estar bajo los efectos de la anestesia

anesthetist [ə·'nes·θɪ·tɪst] n anestesista mf

anesthetize [ə·'nes·θɪ·taɪz] vt anestesiar

anew [ə·'nu] adv de nuevo

angel ['eɪn·dʒl] n ángel m

angelic [æn·'dʒel·ɪk] adj angelical

anger ['æŋ·gər] I. n enfado m, enojo m AmL; (stronger) ira f; to speak in ~ hablar indignado II. vt enfadar, enojar AmL

angina [æn·'dʒaɪ·nə] n angina f; ~ pectoris angina de pecho

angle ['æŋ·gəl] I. n 1. ángulo m; at an ~ (picture) torcido, -a; (hat) ladeado, -a; to see sth from a different ~ ver algo desde otro ángulo; she knows all the ~s se las sabe todas 2. (opinion) punto m de vista II. vt, vi 1. (to fish) pescar 2. (information) dirigir; this article is ~d towards teenagers este artículo se dirige a los adolescentes

Anglican ['æŋ·glɪ·kən] adj, n anglicano, -a m, f; **Anglican Church** Iglesia f Anglicana

Anglophone n Can anglohablante mf en Canadá

Anglo-Saxon [ˌæŋ·gloʊ·'sæk·sən] adj, n anglosajón, -ona m, f

angry ['æŋ·gri] adj enfadado, -a, enojado, -a AmL; (crowd) enfurecido, -a; (sky) tormentoso, -a; (sea) embravecido, -a; to make sb ~ enfadar [or AmL enojar] a alguien; to get ~ enfadarse, enojarse AmL (with con, about por)

angst [æŋkst] n angustia f

anguish ['æŋ·gwɪʃ] n angustia f; to be in ~ estar angustiado (over por)

angular ['æŋ·gjʊ·lər] adj angular; (face) anguloso, -a

animal ['æn·ɪ·məl] I. n a. fig animal m II. adj animal; (desires) carnal

animate[1] ['æn·ɪ·meɪt] vt animar

animate[2] ['æn·ɪ·mɪt] adj animado, -a

animated adj animado, -a; to become ~ animarse

animation [ˌæn·ɪ·'meɪ·ʃən] n animación f; **computer** ~ animación por ordenador [or computadora] AmL

anime [ə·'nim] n anime m

animosity [ˌæn·ɪ·'mas·ə·ti] n animosidad f

aniseed, anise seed ['æn·ɪ·sid] n anís m

ankle ['æŋ·kəl] n tobillo m

anklet ['æŋ·klɪt] n 1. (chain) tobillera f 2. (sock) calcetín m corto

annex ['æn·eks] I. n <-es> 1. (building) edificio m anexo 2. (of document) anexo m II. vt (territory) anexionar; (document) adjuntar

annexation [ˌæn·ɪk·'seɪ·ʃən] n anexión f

annihilate [ə·'naɪ·ə·leɪt] vt aniquilar

annihilation [ə-ˌnaɪ-ə-ˈleɪ-ʃən] n aniquilación f

anniversary [ˌæn-ə-ˈvɜr-sə-ri] <-ies> n aniversario m

annotation [ˌæn-ə-ˈteɪ-ʃən] n anotación f

announce [ə-ˈnaʊns] vt anunciar; (result) comunicar

announcement n anuncio m; **official ~** comunicado m oficial

announcer [ə-ˈnaʊn-sər] n locutor(a) m(f)

annoy [ə-ˈnɔɪ] vt molestar, embromar AmL; **to get ~ed** enfadarse [or enojarse] AmL

annoyance [ə-ˈnɔɪ-əns] n fastidio m, enojo m AmL

annoying adj (noise, fact) molesto, -a, chocante AmL; (person) pesado, -a; **it's ~ to think that...** me da rabia pensar que...; **how ~!** ¡qué fastidio!

annual [ˈæn-ju-əl] I. adj anual II. n anuario m; BOT planta f anual

annually [ˈæn-ju-ə-li] adv anualmente

annuity [ə-ˈnu-ə-ti] <-ies> n renta f anual

annul [ə-ˈnʌl] <-ll-> vt anular

anoint [ə-ˈnɔɪnt] vt untar

anointing n unción f

anomaly [ə-ˈnam-ə-li] <-ies> n anomalía f

anonymity [ˌæn-ə-ˈnɪm-ɪ-ti] n anonimato m

anonymous [ə-ˈnan-ə-məs] adj anónimo, -a; **to remain ~** permanecer en el anonimato

anorexia [ˌæn-ə-ˈrek-si-ə] n anorexia f

anorexic [ˌæn-ə-ˈrek-sɪk] adj anoréxico, -a

another [ə-ˈnʌð-ər] I. pron 1. otro, -a; **it's always one thing or ~** siempre pasa algo 2. (mutual) **one ~** uno a otro; **they love one ~** se quieren II. adj otro, -a; **~ pastry?** ¿otro pastel?; **~ $30** otros 30 dólares

answer [ˈæn-sər] I. n 1. (reply) respuesta f; **in ~ to your question** como respuesta a tu pregunta 2. (solution) solución f II. vt responder a; (door) abrir; (need) satisfacer III. vi responder

♦**answer back** vi contestar; **don't ~!** ¡no repliques!

♦**answer for** vt (action, situation) responder de; (person) responder por

♦**answer to** vt 1. (obey) obedecer a 2. (fit) corresponder a

answerable [ˈæn-sər-ə-bəl] adj **to be ~ for sth** ser responsable de algo; **to be ~ to sb** tener que rendir cuentas a alguien

answering machine n contestador m automático

ant [ænt] n hormiga f ▶ **to have ~s in one's pants** ser un manojo de nervios

antagonistic [ænˌtæg-ə-ˈnɪs-tɪk] adj antagónico, -a

antagonize [ænˈtæg-ə-naɪz] vt enfadar, enojar AmL

Antarctic [æntˈark-tɪk] I. adj antártico, -a II. n **the ~** el Antártico

Antarctica [æntˈark-tɪ-kə] n la Antártida

anteater [ˈænt-iˌtər] n oso m hormiguero

antelope [ˈæn-tɪ-loʊp] <-(s)> n antílope m

antenna [ænˈten-ə] <-nae or -s> n antena f

anteroom [ˈæn-tɪ-rum] n antesala f

anthem [ˈæn-θəm] n himno m

anthill [ˈænt-hɪl] n hormiguero m

anthropology [ˌæn-θrə-ˈpal-ə-dʒi] n antropología f

anti [ˈæn-ti] I. adj **(to be) ~** (estar) en contra II. prep en contra de

antiabortion [ˌæn-ti-ə-ˈbɔr-ʃən] adj antiabortista

antiaging cream n crema f antiarrugas

antiaircraft [ˌæn-tɪ-ˈer-kræft] adj antiaéreo, -a

anti-American adj antiamericano, -a

antibiotic [ˌæn-tɪ-baɪ-ˈaṭ-ɪk] I. n antibiótico m II. adj antibiótico, -a

antibody [ˈæn-tɪ-bad-i] <-ies> n anticuerpo m

anticipate [ænˈtɪs-ə-peɪt] vt 1. (plan) tener previsto 2. (look forward to) esperar (con ilusión) 3. (act in advance of) anticiparse a

anticipation [ænˌtɪs-ə-ˈpeɪ-ʃən] n 1. (foresight) previsión f 2. (funds) anticipo m 3. (excitement) ilusión f; **to wait in ~** esperar con gran ilusión

anticlimax [ˌæn-tɪ-ˈklaɪ-mæks] <-es> n

decepción f

antidote ['æn·tɪ·doʊt] n antídoto m (**to** contra)

antiestablishment adj antisistema

antifreeze ['æn·tɪ·friz] n anticongelante m

antihero [æn·tɪ·'hɪr·oʊ] <-es> n antihéroe m

antihistamine [,æn·tɪ·'hɪs·tə·,mɪn] n antihistamínico m

anti-inflammatory [,æn·tɪ·ɪn·'flæm·ə·tɔr·i] adj antiinflamatorio, -a

Antilles [æn·'tɪl·iz] npl the ~ las Antillas

antilock braking system n AUTO sistema m antibloqueo de frenos

antimatter ['æn·tɪ·mæt·ər] n antimateria f

antipasto [æn·tɪ·'pæs·ti] n entrada f

antiperspirant [,æn·tɪ·'pɜr·spər·ənt] n antitranspirante m

antipollution adj anticontaminante

antiquated ['æn·tɪ·kweɪ·ţɪd] adj anticuado, -a

antique [æn·'tik] I. n antigüedad f; (old-fashioned) antigualla f II. adj antiguo, -a; (old-fashioned) anticuado, -a

antiquity [æn·'tɪk·wə·ţi] <-ies> n antigüedad f

antirust [,æn·tɪ·'rʌst] adj antioxidante

anti-Semitism [æn·tɪ·'sem·ə·tɪz·əm] n antisemitismo m

antiseptic [,æn·tə·'sep·tɪk] I. n antiséptico m II. adj antiséptico, -a

antisocial [,æn·tɪ·'soʊ·ʃəl] adj antisocial

antithetic [,æn·tɪ·'θeţ·ɪk], **antithetical** [,æn·tɪ·'θeţ·ɪ·kəl] adj antitético, -a

antivirus [,æn·tɪ·'vaɪ·rəs] adj COMPUT antivirus inv

antiwar [,æn·tɪ·'wɔr] adj antibélico, -a

antiwrinkle cream [,æn·tɪ·'rɪŋ·kəl·,krim] n crema f antiarrugas

antler ['ænt·lər] n cuerno m; ~s cornamenta f

anus ['eɪ·nəs] n ano m

anvil ['æn·vɪl] n yunque m

anxiety [æŋ·'zaɪ·ə·ţi] n 1. (concern) inquietud f; PSYCH ansiedad f 2. (desire) ansia f (to, for de)

anxious ['æŋk·ʃəs] adj 1. (concerned) preocupado, -a (about por) 2. (eager) ansioso, -a; **to be ~ for sth/to do sth** estar ansioso por algo/por hacer algo

any ['en·i] I. adj 1. (some) algún, alguna; **do they have ~ money?** ¿tienen dinero?; **do you want ~ more soup?** ¿quieres más sopa? 2. (not important which) cualquier; **come at ~ time** ven cuando quieras 3. (in negatives) ningún, ninguna; **I don't have ~ money** no tengo dinero II. adv 1. (not) **she doesn't come here ~ more** ya no viene 2. (at all) **does she feel ~ better?** ¿se siente algo mejor? III. pron 1. (some) alguno, alguna; **~ of you** alguno de vosotros; **~ but him would have gone** cualquier otro habría ido 2. (in negatives) ninguno, ninguna

anybody ['en·i·bad·i] pron indef 1. (someone) alguien, alguno 2. (not important which) cualquiera; **~ but him** cualquiera menos él; **~ else** cualquier otro 3. (no one) nadie, ninguno

anyhow ['en·i·haʊ] adv 1. (in any case) de todas maneras 2. (well) bueno; **~, as I was saying...** bueno, como iba diciendo... 3. (disorderly) de cualquier manera

anyone ['en·i·wʌn] pron indef see **anybody**

anyplace ['en·i·pleɪs] adv 1. (interrogative) en alguna parte; **have you seen my glasses ~?** ¿has visto mis gafas en alguna parte? 2. (affirmative) en cualquier parte; **I can sleep ~** puedo dormir en cualquier sitio 3. (negative) en ninguna parte; **you won't see this ~** no verás esto en ningún sitio

anything ['en·i·θɪŋ] pron indef 1. (something) algo; **~ else?** ¿algo más?; **is there ~ new?** ¿alguna novedad? 2. (each thing) cualquier cosa; **it is ~ but funny** es todo menos gracioso; **~ and everything** cualquier cosa; **to be as fast as ~** inf ser rapidísimo 3. (nothing) nada; **hardly ~** casi nada; **for ~** (in the world) por nada (del mundo)

anytime ['en·i·taɪm] adv a cualquier hora

anyway(s) ['en·i·weɪ(z)] adv 1. (in any case) de todas maneras 2. (well) bueno; **~, as I was saying...** bueno, como iba diciendo...

anywhere ['en·i·wer] adv 1. (interrogative) en alguna parte; **are we ~ near**

finished yet? *inf* ¿nos queda mucho para terminar? **2.** (*positive*) en cualquier parte; **its value is ~ between $25 and $30** vale entre los 25 y los 30 dólares; **to live miles from ~** vivir en el quinto pino; **~ else** en cualquier otro sitio **3.** (*negative*) en ninguna parte

apart [əˈpɑrt] *adv* **1.** (*separated*) aparte; **all joking ~** bromas aparte; **to be 20 miles ~** estar a 20 millas; **far ~** lejos; **to move ~** apartarse; **you and me ~** excepto tú y yo **2. to be ~ from sth** estar apartado de algo; **to set sth ~** apartar algo; **to stand ~** mantenerse apartado **3. to come ~** desprenderse; **to take sth ~** desmontar algo

apart from *prep* **1.** (*except*) excepto; **~ that** excepto eso **2.** (*in addition*) aparte de **3.** (*separate*) separado, -a de; **to live ~ sb** vivir separado de alguien

apartheid [əˈpɑrt·heɪt] *n* apartheid *m*

apartment *n* apartamento *m*, departamento *m AmL*

apathetic [ˌæp·əˈθeţ·ɪk] *adj* apático, -a

apathy [ˈæp·ə·θi] *n* apatía *f* (**about** respecto)

ape [eɪp] **I.** *n* simio *m* ▶ **to go ~** *inf* irse de la olla **II.** *vt* imitar

aperitif [əˌper·əˈtif] *n* aperitivo *m*

aperture [ˈæp·ər·tʃʊr] *n* rendija *f*; PHOT abertura *f*

aphrodisiac [ˌæf·rəˈdɪ·zi·æk] **I.** *n* afrodisiaco *m* **II.** *adj* afrodisiaco, -a

apiculture [ˈæp·ɪˌkʌl·tʃər] *n* apicultura *f*

apiece [əˈpis] *adv* cada uno; (*per person*) por cabeza

apologetic [əˌpɑl·əˈdʒeţ·ɪk] *adj* de disculpa; **to be ~ about sth** disculparse por algo

apologetically *adv* disculpándose

apologize [əˈpɑl·ə·dʒaɪz] *vi* disculparse; **to ~ to sb for sth** pedir perdón a alguien por algo; **I (do) ~ if...** pido disculpas si...

apology [əˈpɑl·ə·dʒi] <-ies> *n* disculpa *f*; **to make an ~** disculparse; **please accept my apologies** le ruego (que) me disculpe

apostrophe [əˈpɑs·trə·fi] *n* apóstrofo *m*

Appalachia [ˌæp·əˈleɪ·ʃə] *n* los Apalaches *mpl*

appall [əˈpɔl] *vt* horrorizar; **to be ~ed** estar horrorizado [*or* por] (**at** de/por)

appalling *adj* (*behavior*) escandaloso, -a; (*conditions*) horroroso, -a

apparatus [ˌæp·əˈræţ·əs] *n* equipo *m*; **a piece of ~** un aparato

apparent [əˈpær·ənt] *adj* **1.** (*clear*) evidente; **to become ~ that** hacerse evidente que **2.** (*seeming*) aparente; **for no ~ reason** sin motivo aparente

appeal [əˈpil] **I.** *vi* **1.** (*attract*) atraer; **the idea doesn't ~ to me** no me atrae la idea **2.** LAW apelar **II.** *n* **1.** (*attraction*) atractivo *m*; **to have ~** tener gancho *inf* **2.** LAW apelación *f*; **court of ~s** tribunal *m* de apelación **3.** (*request*) petición *f*

appealing [əˈpi·lɪŋ] *adj* (*smile*) atractivo, -a; (*idea*) tentador(a); (*eyes*) suplicante

appealingly *adv* (*dress*) con estilo; (*look*) de manera suplicante; (*speak*) con tono suplicante

appear [əˈpɪr] *vi* **1.** (*be seen*) aparecer **2.** (*newspaper*) salir; (*book*) publicarse; (*film*) estrenarse **3.** LAW comparecer (**before** ante) **4.** (*seem*) parecer; **it ~s to me that...** me parece que...; **it ~s so** eso parece

appearance [əˈpɪr·əns] *n* **1.** (*instance of appearing*) aparición *f* **2.** LAW comparecencia *f* **3.** (*looks*) aspecto *m* **4.** (**to keep up**) **~s** (guardar las) apariencias **5.** (*performance*) actuación *f*; **stage ~** aparición *f* en escena ▶ **~s can be deceptive** las apariencias engañan

append [əˈpend] *vt* (*document, note*) adjuntar; (*signature*) añadir

appendage [əˈpen·dɪdʒ] *n* apéndice *m*

appendicitis [əˌpen·dɪˈsaɪ·tɪs] *n* apendicitis *f inv*

appendix [əˈpen·dɪks] *n* **1.** <-es> ANAT apéndice *m* **2.** <-dices *or* -es> TYPO apéndice

appetite [ˈæp·ə·taɪt] *n* apetito *m*, antojo *m Méx*, afán *m*

appetizer [ˈæp·ə·taɪ·zər] *n* (*first course*) entrante *m*; (*snack*) aperitivo *m*, botana *f Méx*, pasabocas *m inv Col*

appetizing [ˈæp·ə·taɪ·zɪŋ] *adj* apetitoso, -a

applaud [əˈplɔd] *vi, vt* aplaudir

applause [əˈplɔz] *n* aplauso *m*; **loud ~**

fuerte aplauso

apple ['æp-əl] *n* manzana *f* ▶ **to be the ~ of sb's eye** ser la niña de los ojos de alguien; **the Big Apple** la Gran Manzana

apple pie *n* pastel *m* de manzana

apple polisher *n inf* pelota *mf*, regalado, -a *m, f* Col, barbero, -a *m, f* Méx

applesauce *n* compota *f* de manzana

apple tree *n* manzano *m*

appliance [ə-'plaɪ-əns] *n* aparato *m;* **electrical ~** electrodoméstico *m*

applicable [ə-'plɪ-kə-bəl] *adj* aplicable; **delete where not ~** táchese lo que no proceda; **those rules are not ~ anymore** esas normas ya no están vigentes

applicant ['æp-lɪ-kənt] *n* solicitante *mf;* (*for job*) candidato, -a *m, f*

application [æp-lɪ-'keɪ-ʃən] *n* **1.** (*request*) solicitud *f;* **on ~** mediante solicitud **2.** (*coating*) *a.* COMPUT aplicación *f* **3.** (*use*) uso *m* **4.** (*perseverance*) diligencia *f*

application form *n* (hoja *f* de) solicitud *f*

applied [ə-'plaɪd] *adj* aplicado, -a

apply [ə-'plaɪ] **I.** *vi* **1.** (*request*) presentarse; (*college, company*) solicitar plaza; **to ~ for a job** solicitar un puesto **2.** (*be relevant*) **to ~ to sb** concernir a alguien **II.** *vt* aplicar; (*pressure*) ejercer; **to ~ oneself** dedicarse (to a)

appoint [ə-'pɔɪnt] *vt* **1.** (*select*) nombrar; **to ~ sb as heir** nombrar a alguien heredero **2.** (*designate*) fijar; **at the ~ed time** a la hora señalada

appointment [ə-'pɔɪnt-mənt] *n* **1.** (*to position*) nombramiento *m* **2.** (*meeting*) cita *f;* **dentist's ~** cita *f* con el dentista; **to keep an ~** acudir a una cita; **by ~ only** previa cita

appointment book *n* libro *m* de visitas

appraisal [ə-'preɪ-zəl] *n* (*evaluation*) evaluación *f;* (*estimation*) estimación *f;* (*performance, evidence*) valoración *f;* (*property*) tasación *f*

appreciable [ə-'pri-ʃə-bəl] *adj* apreciable; (*change*) notorio, -a; (*progress*) considerable

appreciate [ə-'pri-ʃi-eɪt] **I.** *vt* **1.** (*value*) apreciar **2.** (*understand*) comprender

3. (*be grateful for*) agradecer **II.** *vi* revalorizarse

appreciation [ə-ˌpri-ʃi-'eɪ-ʃən] *n* **1.** (*gratitude*) agradecimiento *m* **2.** (*understanding*) aprecio *m*

appreciative [ə-'pri-ʃə-t̬ɪv] *adj* agradecido, -a

apprehend [æp-rɪ-'hend] *vt form* **1.** (*arrest*) detener **2.** (*comprehend*) concebir

apprehension [ˌæp-rɪ-'hen-ʃən] *n* **1.** (*arrest*) detención *f* **2.** (*fear*) temor *m* (**about** por) **3.** *form* (*comprehension*) comprensión *f*

apprehensive [æp-rɪ-'hen-sɪv] *adj* aprensivo, -a, flatoso, -a *AmL;* **to be ~ about sth** estar inquieto por algo

apprentice [ə-'pren-t̬ɪs] *n* aprendiz(a) *m(f)*, peón, -ona *m, f* Méx

approach [ə-'proʊtʃ] **I.** *vt* **1.** (*get close to*) acercarse a **2.** (*ask*) dirigirse a **3.** (*deal with*) abordar **II.** *vi* acercarse **III.** *n* **1.** (*coming*) aproximación *f;* **at the ~ of winter** al acercarse el invierno **2.** (*access*) acceso *m* **3.** (*proposition*) propuesta *f* **4.** (*methodology*) enfoque *m*

approachable [ə-'proʊ-tʃə-bəl] *adj* accesible

appropriate [ə-'proʊ-pri-ət] *adj ~* (**to the occasion**) apropiado (para la ocasión)

approval [ə-'pru-vəl] *n* aprobación *f;* **to meet with sb's ~** obtener la aprobación de alguien

approve [ə-'pruv] **I.** *vi* estar de acuerdo (**of** con) **II.** *vt* aprobar

approvingly [ə-'pru-vɪŋ-li] *adv* con aprobación

approx. [ə-'prak-sɪ-met-li] *n abbr of* **approximately** aprox.

approximate¹ [ə-'prak-sɪ-mət] *adj* aproximado, -a

approximate² [ə-'prak-sɪ-meɪt] *vt* aproximarse a

approximately *adv* aproximadamente

approximation [ə-ˌprak-sɪ-'meɪ-ʃən] *n* aproximación *f*

Apr. ['eɪ-prəl] *n abbr of* **April** abr.

apricot ['eɪ-prɪ-kat] *n* albaricoque *m*, chabacano *m* Méx, damasco *m* AmS

April ['eɪ-prəl] *n* abril *m;* **in ~** en abril; **at**

the beginning/end of ~ a principios/
finales de abril; **on** (**the**) **fourth** el
cuatro de abril

apron ['eɪ·prən] *n* (*clothing*) delantal *m*

apt [æpt] *adj* **1.** (*appropriate*) apropiado,
-a; (*comment*) oportuno, -a **2.** (*clever*)
inteligente **3. to be ~ to do sth** tener
tendencia a hacer algo

apt. [ə·'part·mənt] *n abbr of* **apartment**
apto.

aptitude ['æp·tɪ·tud] *n* aptitud *f*

aquacize ['æk·wə·saɪz] *n* aeróbic *m* en
el agua

Aqua-Lung® ['æk·wə·lʌŋ] escafandra *f*
autónoma

aquaplaning [ˌæk·wə·'pleɪ·nɪŋ] *n* ≈ esquí
m acuático

aquarium [ə·'kwer·i·əm] <-s *or* -ria> *n*
acuario *m*

Aquarius [ə·'kwer·i·əs] *n* ASTR Acuario *m*

aquatic [ə·'kwæt·ɪk] *adj* acuático, -a

aquatics *npl* deportes *m* acuáticos *pl*

aqueduct ['æk·wɪ·dʌkt] *n* acueducto *m*

AR *abbr of* **Arkansas** Arkansas *f*

Arab ['ær·əb] *adj, n* árabe *mf*

Arabian *adj* árabe

Arabic ['ær·ə·bɪk] *n* árabe *m*

arbitrary ['ar·bɪ·trer·i] *adj* arbitrario, -a

arbitrate ['ar·bɪ·treɪt] *vi, vt* mediar

arbitration [ˌar·bɪ·'treɪ·ʃən] *n* mediación *f*

arbitrator ['ar·bɪ·treɪ·tər] *n* árbitro, -a *m, f*

arc [ark] **I.** *n* arco *m* **II.** *vi* arquearse

arcade [ar·'keɪd] *n* **1.** (*of shops*) galería *f* comercial **2.** (*around square*)
soportales *mpl* **3.** (*with games*) recrea-
tivos *mpl*

arch [artʃ] **I.** *n* arco *m* **II.** *vi* arquearse **III.** *vt* arquear **IV.** <-er, -est> *adj*
burlón, -ona

archaeology [ˌar·ki·'al·ə·dʒi] *n* arqueología *f*

archbishop [ˌartʃ·'bɪʃ·əp] *n* arzobispo *m*

archenemy <-ies> *n* archienemigo,
-a *m, f*

archeologist [ˌar·ki·'al·ə·dʒɪst] *n* arqueólogo, -a *m, f*

archeology [ˌar·ki·'al·ə·dʒi] *n see* **archaeology**

archer ['ar·tʃər] *n* arquero, -a *m, f*

archery ['ar·tʃə·ri] *n* tiro *m* con arco

architect ['ar·kə·tekt] *n* arquitecto, -a *m, f*;

fig artífice *mf*

architecture ['ar·kə·tek·tʃər] *n* arquitectura *f*

archive ['ar·kaɪv] *n* archivo *m*

archway ['artʃ·weɪ] *n* (*entrance*) arco *m*

Arctic ['ark·tɪk] **I.** *n* **the ~** el Ártico
II. *adj* ártico, -a

Arctic Circle *n* círculo *m* polar ártico

Arctic Ocean *n* Océano *m* Glacial Ártico

ardent ['ar·dənt] *adj* ferviente; (*desire,
plea*) vehemente

arduous ['ar·dʒu·əs] *adj* arduo, -a

are [ər, *stressed:* ar] *vi see* **be**

area ['er·i·ə] *n* **1.** *a.* MATH, SPORTS área *f*
2. (*field*) campo *m*

area rug *n* alfombra *f*

arena [ə·'ri·nə] *n* arena *f*

aren't [arnt] = **are not** *see* **be**

Argentina [ˌar·dʒən·'ti·nə] *n* Argentina *f*

Argentine ['ar·dʒən·tin], **Argentin-
ean** [ˌar·dʒən·'tɪn·i·ən] *adj, n* argentino, -a *m, f*

arguable ['ar·gju·ə·bəl] *adj* discutible

arguably *adv* posiblemente

argue ['ar·gju] **I.** *vi* **1.** (*disagree*) discutir, alegar *AmL* **2.** (*reason*) razonar;
to ~ against/for sth abogar contra/a
favor de algo **II.** *vt* **to ~ that...** sostener
que...; **to ~ sb into doing sth** persuadir
a alguien de hacer algo

argument ['ar·gjə·mənt] *n* **1.** (*disagreement*) discusión *f* **2.** (*reasoning*) argumento *m* **3.** LAW alegato *m*

argumentative [ˌar·gjə·'men·tə·tɪv] *adj*
discutidor(a)

arid ['ær·ɪd] *adj* árido, -a

Aries ['er·iz] *n* ASTR Aries *m*

arise [ə·'raɪz] <arose, arisen> *vi* surgir
(**from** de)

arisen [ə·'rɪz·ən] *pp of* **arise**

aristocracy [ˌær·ɪ·'stak·rə·si] <-ies> *n* +
sing/pl vb aristocracia *f*

aristocrat [ə·'rɪs·tə·kræt] *n* aristócrata *mf*

aristocratic [e·ˌrɪs·tə·'kræt·ɪk] *adj* aristocrático, -a

arithmetic [ə·'rɪθ·mɪ·tɪk] **I.** *n* aritmética *f*
II. *adj* aritmético, -a

arithmetical [ˌær·ɪθ·'met·ɪ·kəl] *adj* aritmético, -a

Arizona [ˌær·ɪ·'zou·nə] *n* Arizona *f*

ark [ark] *n* arca *f*; **Noah's ~** el Arca de Noé

Arkansas ['ar·kən·sɔ] *n* Arkansas *f*

arm[1] [arm] *n* **1.** ANAT, GEO brazo *m*; **~ in ~** del brazo **2.** (*sleeve*) manga *f* ▸ **to welcome with open ~s** recibir con los brazos abiertos; **to cost an ~ and a leg** costar un ojo de la cara; **to keep sb at ~'s length** guardar las distancias con alguien

arm[2] [arm] MIL **I.** *vt* armar **II.** *n* arma *f*; **under ~s** en armas; **to lay down one's ~s** rendir las armas; **to take up ~s** tomar las armas (**against** contra); **to be up in ~s about** poner el grito en el cielo contra

armadillo [ar·mə·'dɪl·ou] *n* armadillo *m*

armaments ['ar·mə·mənts] *npl* armamento *m*

armchair ['arm·tʃer] *n* sillón *m*

armed [armd] *adj* armado, -a

armful ['arm·ful] *n* brazada *f*

armload *n* brazada *f*

armor ['ar·mər] *n* **1.** (*protective covering*) blindaje *m* **2.** MIL, ZOOL armadura *f* **3.** (*tanks*) carros *m pl* blindados

armored *adj* (*car*) blindado, -a; (*train*) acorazado, -a

armpit ['arm·pɪt] *n* axila *f*, sobaco *m*

armrest ['arm·rest] *n* apoyabrazos *m inv*

arm-wrestle *vi* echar [*or Col* hacer] un pulso, jugar a las vencidas *Méx*

arm wrestling *n* pulso *m*

army ['ar·mi] <-ies> *n* ejército *m*; *fig* multitud *f*; **to join the ~** alistarse

aroma [ə·'rou·mə] *n* aroma *m*

aromatherapy [ə·ˌrou·mə·'θer·ə·pi] *n* aromaterapia *f*

aromatic [ˌær·ə·'mæt·ɪk] *adj* aromático, -a

arose [ə·'rouz] *pt of* **arise**

around [ə·'raund] **I.** *prep* **1.** (*surrounding, approximately*) alrededor de; **~ May 10th** sobre el 10 de mayo; **to go ~ the corner** doblar la esquina **2.** (*move within*) por; **to drive ~ Mexico** viajar (en coche) por México **II.** *adv* **1.** (*all over*) alrededor; **all ~** en todas partes; **for miles ~** en millas a la redonda; **to be the other way ~** ser justo lo contrario **2.** (*aimlessly*) **to walk ~** dar una

vuelta; **to stand/hang ~** estar/andar por ahí; **to have been ~** haber visto mundo; (*be experienced*) tener mucha experiencia **3.** (*near by*) por ahí; **to be still ~** seguir ahí

arouse [ə·'rauz] *vt* suscitar; (*anger*) provocar; (*sexually*) excitar

arraign [ə·'rein] *vt* hacer comparecer

arrange [ə·'reindʒ] **I.** *vt* **1.** (*organize*) organizar; (*date*) acordar **2.** (*put in order*) arreglar **II.** *vi* **to ~ (for)** disponer; **to ~ to do sth** quedar en hacer algo

arrangement *n* **1.** *pl* preparativos *mpl*; **to make ~s** hacer los preparativos (**for** de) **2.** (*agreement*) acuerdo *m* **3.** (*method of organizing sth*) arreglo *m*

arrears [ə·'rirz] *npl* FIN atraso *m*

arrest [ə·'rest] **I.** *vt* detener; **to ~ sb's attention** captar la atención de alguien **II.** *n* detención *f*; **to be under ~** estar detenido

arrival [ə·'raɪ·vəl] *n* llegada *f*; **on his ~** a su llegada; **new ~** recién llegado *m*

arrive [ə·'raɪv] *vi* llegar; (*be born*) nacer

arrogance ['ær·ə·gəns] *n* arrogancia *f*

arrogant ['ær·ə·gənt] *adj* arrogante

arrow ['ær·ou] *n* flecha *f*, jara *f Guat, Méx*

arrowroot *n* maranta *f*

arson ['ar·sən] *n* incendio *m* provocado

art [art] *n* arte *f*

artery ['ar·tə·ri] <-ies> *n* arteria *f*

art gallery *n* (*for exhibits*) museo *m* de arte; (*for selling*) galería *f* de arte

arthritic [ar·'θrɪt·ɪk] *adj* artrítico, -a

arthritis [ar·'θraɪ·tɪs] *n* artritis *f inv*

artichoke ['ar·tɪ·tʃouk] *n* alcachofa *f*

article ['ar·tɪ·kəl] *n* artículo *m*; **~ of clothing** prenda *f* de vestir

articulate[1] [ar·'tɪk·jə·lət] *adj* (*person*) que se expresa muy bien; (*speech*) claro, -a; TECH, ANAT articulado, -a

articulate[2] [ar·'tɪk·jə·leɪt] *vt* expresar; (*sound, idea*) articular

artifact ['ar·tə·fækt] *n* artefacto *m*

artificial [ˌar·tə·'fɪʃ·əl] *adj* artificial; **~ insemination/intelligence** inseminación *f*/inteligencia *f* artificial

artificial respiration *n* respiración *f* asistida

artillery [ar·'tıl·ə·ri] n artillería f

artisan ['ar·tɪ·zən] n artesano, -a m, f

artist ['ar·tɪst] n artista mf

artiste [ar·'tist] n THEAT artista mf

artistic [ar·'tɪs·tɪk] adj artístico, -a

artistry ['ar·tɪ·stri] n arte f

arts and crafts n trabajos m pl manuales

artsy ['art·si] adj see **arty**

artwork ['art·wɜrk] n ilustraciones fpl

arty ['ar·ti] <-ier, -iest> adj 1. inf relacionado con la creación de objetos decorativos o de obras de arte 2. pej pseudoartístico, -a; (film) pretencioso, -a

as [əz, stressed: æz] I. prep como; **dressed ~ a clown** vestido de payaso; **~ a baby, I was...** de bebé, yo era... II. conj 1. (in comparison) como; **the same name ~** el mismo nombre que; **~ fast ~ much** tan rápido como; **to eat ~ much ~ sb** comer tanto como alguien; **~ soon ~ possible** lo antes posible 2. (like) (tal) como; **~ it is** tal como es; **~ if it were true** como si fuese verdad 3. (because) como 4. (while) mientras 5. (although) aunque ▶ **~ far ~** (to the extent that) en la medida en que; (concerning) respecto a; **~ for me** en lo que a mí respecta III. adv **~ well** también; **~ long as** mientras que +subj; **~ much as** tanto como; **~ soon as** en cuanto

ASAP [ˌeɪ·es·eɪ·'pi] abbr of **as soon as possible** lo antes posible

asbestos [æs·'bes·təs] n amianto m

ascend [ə·'send] vt, vi ascender; **in ~ing order** en orden ascendente

ascent [ə·'sent] n 1. (climb) ascenso f 2. (slope) pendiente f

ascertain [ˌæs·ər·'teɪn] vt 1. (find out) averiguar 2. (make sure) comprobar

ascot ['æs·kat] n FASHION ≈ fular m

ash[1] [æʃ] n (from fire) ceniza f

ash[2] [æʃ] n BOT fresno m

ashamed [ə·'ʃeɪmd] adj avergonzado, -a; **to be ~ of oneself** avergonzarse de uno mismo

ashore [ə·'ʃɔr] I. adj en tierra II. adv a tierra

ashtray ['æʃ·treɪ] n cenicero m

Asia ['eɪ·ʒə] n Asia f

Asian ['eɪ·ʒən] adj, n asiático -a m, f

Asian American n residente en EEUU de origen asiático

Asiatic [ˌeɪ·ʒi·'æt·ɪk] adj asiático, -a

aside [ə·'saɪd] adv a un lado; **to stand** [or **step**] **~** hacerse a un lado; **to leave sth ~** dejar algo a un lado

aside from prep aparte de

ask [æsk] I. vt 1. (inquire) preguntar; **to ~ (sb) a question about sth** hacer (a alguien) una pregunta acerca de algo 2. (request) pedir; **to ~ a favor/sb's advice** pedir un favor/consejo a alguien; **~ 100 dollars for sth** pedir 100 dólares por algo; **to ~ too much of sb** pedir demasiado de alguien 3. (invite) invitar; **to ~ sb to do sth** invitar a alguien a hacer algo II. vi 1. (inquire) preguntar 2. (request) pedir

◆**ask for** vt (request) pedir

asking ['æs·kɪŋ] n petición f; **it's yours for the ~ing** lo tienes a pedir de boca

asking price n precio m de venta

asleep [ə·'slip] adj dormido, -a; **to be/to fall ~** estar/quedarse dormido

asocial [eɪ·'sou·ʃəl] adj asocial; (antisocial) antisocial

asparagus [ə·'spær·ə·gəs] n espárrago m; (plant) esparraguera f

aspect ['æs·pekt] n 1. (point of view) punto m de vista 2. (feature) faceta f 3. (direction) orientación f 4. (appearance) aspecto m

asphyxiation [əs·ˌfɪk·si·'eɪ·ʃən] n asfixia f

aspic ['æs·pɪk] n áspic m

aspire [ə·'spaɪr] vi aspirar (to a)

aspirin ['æs·pə·rɪn] n aspirina f

ass [æs] <-es> n 1. ZOOL (donkey) asno m 2. inf (idiot) burro, -a m, f

assassinate [ə·'sæs·ə·neɪt] vt asesinar

assassination [ə·ˌsæs·ɪ·'neɪ·ʃən] n magnicidio m

assault [ə·'sɔlt] I. n ataque m; **to make an ~ on** asaltar II. vt atacar

assemble [ə·'sem·bəl] I. vi congregarse II. vt 1. (collect) reunir 2. (put together) armar

A

assembly [ə·'sem·bli] <-ies> n 1. (meeting) reunión f 2. TECH montaje m

assent [ə·'sent] I. n consentimiento m II. vi asentir (to a)

assert [ə·'sɜrt] vt afirmar; **to ~ oneself** imponerse

assertion [ə·'sɜr·ʃən] n afirmación f

assertive [ə·'sɜr·tɪv] adj confiado, -a

assess [ə·'ses] vt calcular; (evaluate) evaluar

assessment n 1. (calculation) valoración f 2. (evaluation) evaluación f

asset ['æs·et] n 1. ventaja f; **he is an ~ to the team** es una valiosa aportación al equipo 2. pl activo m

assign [ə·'saɪn] vt 1. asignar, apropiar AmL; **to ~ sb to a position** destinar a alguien a un puesto; **to ~ the blame for sth to sb** atribuir la culpa de algo a alguien 2. LAW ceder

assignment n 1. (task) tarea f; **foreign ~** cargo m en el extranjero; **an ~ to do sth** un encargo de hacer algo 2. (attribution) asignación f

assimilate [ə·'sɪm·ə·leɪt] I. vt asimilar II. vi asimilarse

assist [ə·'sɪst] I. vt ayudar (with con) II. vi ayudar (with en)

assistance [ə·'sɪs·təns] n asistencia f; **to be of ~** ser de ayuda

assistant n 1. (helper) ayudante mf, suche sm Chile 2. COMPUT asistente m

assn. [ə·,soʊ·si·'eɪ·ʃən] n abbr of **association** asoc.

associate¹ [ə·'soʊ·ʃi·ɪt] adj, n asociado, -a m, f; **business ~** socio, -a m, f

associate² [ə·'soʊ·ʃi·eɪt] I. vt asociar; **to ~ oneself with sth** relacionarse con algo II. vi relacionarse

associate's degree n (college) ≈ primer ciclo m

association n asociación f; (involvement) colaboración f

assorted [ə·'sɔr·tɪd] adj surtido, -a

assortment [ə·'sɔrt·mənt] n surtido m

asst. [ə·'sɪs·tənt] n abbr of **assistant** ayudante

assume [ə·'sum] vt 1. (suppose) suponer, asumir AmL; **let's ~ that...** supongamos que... 2. (alias, identity) adoptar 3. (undertake) asumir; (power) tomar

assumed [ə·'sumd] adj supuesto, -a

assumption [ə·'sʌmp·ʃən] n 1. (supposition) supuesto m; **on the ~ that...** en el supuesto de que... 2. (hypothesis) suposición f 3. (of office, power) toma f

assurance [ə·'ʃʊr·əns] n (self-confidence) seguridad f; **to have ~** tener confianza 2. (promise) garantía f

assure [ə·'ʃʊr] vt garantizar

assuredly adv ciertamente

asterisk ['æs·tə·rɪsk] n asterisco m

astern [ə·'stɜrn] adv (to go) **~** (ir) hacia atrás; **~ of** detrás de

asteroid ['æs·tə·rɔɪd] n asteroide m

asthma ['æz·mə] n asma m

asthmatic [æz·'mæt·ɪk] adj, n asmático, -a m, f

astigmatism [ə·'stɪg·mə·tɪz·əm] n astigmatismo m

astonish [ə·'stɑn·ɪʃ] vt asombrar

astonishing adj asombroso, -a

astonishment n asombro m

astound [ə·'staʊnd] vt asombrar; **to be ~ed** quedarse atónito

astray [ə·'streɪ] adv **to go ~** (letter) extraviarse; (person) descarriarse; **to lead sb ~** llevar a alguien por mal camino

astride [ə·'straɪd] adv a horcajadas

astrologer [ə·'strɑl·ə·dʒər] n astrólogo, -a m, f

astrology [ə·'strɑl·ə·dʒi] n astrología f

astronaut ['æs·trə·nɔt] n astronauta mf

astronomer [ə·'strɑn·ə·mər] n astrónomo, -a m, f

astronomical [,æs·trə·'nɑm·ɪ·kəl] adj astronómico, -a

astronomy [ə·'strɑn·ə·mi] n astronomía f

AstroTurf® ['æs·troʊ·,tɜrf] n césped m artificial

astute [ə·'stut] adj astuto, -a

asylum [ə·'saɪ·ləm] n asilo m; **insane ~** manicomio m

at¹ [ət, æt] prep 1. (place) en; **~ the dentist's** en el dentista; **~ home/school** en casa/la escuela 2. (time) **~ Christmas** en Navidad; **~ night** por la noche; **~ once** enseguida; **all ~ once** de repente; **~ present** en este momento; **~ the time** en el momento; **~ the same time** al mismo tiempo; **~ three o'clock** a las tres 3. (towards) **to laugh ~ sb** reírse de alguien; **to look ~ sth/sb** mirar algo/a alguien; **to point ~ sb** señalar a alguien **4.** (*in reaction to*) **~ sb's request** a petición de alguien; **to be astonished/annoyed ~ sth** estar asombrado/molesto por algo; **to be mad ~ sb** estar enfadado con alguien **5.** (*in amount of*) **~ all** para nada; **~ $10 a kilo** a $10 el kilo; **~ 120 mph** a 120 m/h **6.** (*in state of*) **~ best/worst** en el mejor/peor de los casos; **~ first** al principio; **~ least** al menos; **~ ease** tranquilo; **to be ~ a loss** estar sin saber qué hacer **7. to be good/bad ~ French** ser bueno/malo en francés ▶ **~ all** en realidad; **nobody ~ all** nadie en absoluto; **not ~ all!** ¡para nada!; (*as answer to thanks*) de nada

at² [æt] (*email*) arroba *f*
at bat *n* (*baseball*) turno *m* de bateo
ate [eɪt] *pt of* **eat**
atheism ['eɪ·θi·ɪz·əm] *n* ateísmo *m*
atheist ['eɪ·θi·ɪst] *adj, n* ateo, -a *m, f*
athlete ['æθ·lit] *n* atleta *mf*
athletic [æθ·'let·ɪk] *adj* atlético, -a
athletics *npl* atletismo *m*
Atlanta [æt·'læn·tə] *n* Atlanta *f*
Atlantic [ət·'læn·tɪk] **I.** *n* the **~** (**Ocean**) el (Océano) Atlántico **II.** *adj* atlántico, -a
atlas ['æt·ləs] <-es> *n* atlas *m inv*
atmosphere ['æt·mə·sfɪr] *n* atmósfera *f*; *fig* ambiente *m*
atmospheric [ˌæt·mə·'sfer·ɪk] *adj* atmosférico, -a; *fig* evocador(a)
atom ['æt·əm] *n* átomo *m*
atomic [ə·'tam·ɪk] *adj* atómico, -a
atrocious [ə·'troʊ·ʃəs] *adj* atroz
atrocity [ə·'tras·ə·ti] <-ies> *n* atrocidad *f*
at sign *n* arroba *f*
attach [ə·'tætʃ] *vt* **1.** (*fix onto*) fijar **2.** (*connect*) ligar **3.** COMPUT adjuntar **4.** (*join*) unir; **to be ~ed to** tener mucho apego a **5.** (*assign*) destinar
attaché [ˌæt·ə·'ʃeɪ] *n* agregado, -a *m, f*
attachment [ə·'tætʃ·mənt] *n* **1.** (*fondness*) apego *m*; **to form an ~ to sb** coger cariño a alguien **2.** (*support*) adhesión *f* **3.** (*union*) fijación *f* **4.** (*attached device*) accesorio *m* **5.** LAW incautación *f* **6.** COMPUT anexo *m*
attack [ə·'tæk] **I.** *n* ataque *m* **II.** *vt* ata-

car, cachorrear *Col*; (*problem*) afrontar **III.** *vi* atacar
attain [ə·'teɪn] *vt* alcanzar
attainable *adj* alcanzable
attainment *n* logro *m*
attempt [ə·'tempt] **I.** *n* **1.** (*try*) intento *m*; **to make an ~ at doing sth** intentar hacer algo **2.** (*attack*) atentado *m* **II.** *vt* intentar
attend [ə·'tend] **I.** *vt* asistir a **II.** *vi* asistir
attendance [ə·'ten·dəns] *n* (*presence*) asistencia *f*
attendant [ə·'ten·dənt] *n* asistente, -a *m, f*
attention [ə·'ten·ʃən] *n* **1.** (*maintenance*) cuidado *m* **2.** (*care, notice*) atención *f*; **to pay ~** prestar atención; **to turn one's ~s to sth** dirigir la atención hacia algo
attentive [ə·'ten·tɪv] *adj* atento, -a; **to be ~ to sb** ser atento con alguien
attest [ə·'test] *vt, vi* (*demonstrate*) testimoniar; (*authenticate*) atestiguar
attic ['æt·ɪk] *n* desván *m*, tabanco *m AmC*, entretecho *m CSur*
attitude ['æt·ɪ·tud] *n* **1.** (*opinion*) actitud *f* (**towards** hacia) **2.** (*position*) postura *f*
attorney [ə·'tɜr·ni] *n* abogado, -a *m, f*
attorney-at-law *n* <attorneys-at-law> abogado, -a *m, f*
attract [ə·'trækt] *vt* atraer, jalar *AmL*; **to be ~ed** sentirse atraído (**by** por)
attraction [ə·'træk·ʃən] *n* atracción *f*; (*appeal*) atractivo *m*; **to feel an ~ to sb** sentirse atraído por alguien
attractive [ə·'træk·tɪv] *adj* atractivo, -a
attribute [ə·'trɪb·jut] *vt* atribuir; **to ~ sth to sb** atribuir algo a alguien; **to ~ importance to sth** dar importancia a algo
ATV [ˌeɪ·ti·'vi] *n abbr of* **all terrain vehicle** vehículo *m* todoterreno
at-will *adj* (*contract, basis*) rescindible sin previo aviso; (*employee, employment*) cuyo contrato es rescindible sin previo aviso
auction ['ɔk·ʃən] **I.** *n* subasta *f* **II.** *vt* subastar
audacious [ɔ·'deɪ·ʃəs] *adj* **1.** (*bold*) audaz **2.** (*impudent*) descarado, -a
audible ['ɔ·də·bəl] *adj* perceptible
audience ['ɔ·di·əns] *n* audiencia *f*; (*spec-*

tators) público m; (of book) lectores mpl

audio ['ɔ·dɪ·oʊ] I. adj inv de audio II. n audio m

audio-visual adj audiovisual

audition [ɔ·'dɪʃ·ən] THEAT I. n audición f II. vi hacer una prueba

auditor ['ɔ·də·tər] n UNIV oyente mf

auditorium [ɔ·də·'tɔ·ri·əm] <-s or auditoria> n auditorio m

Aug. n abbr of **August** ago. m

au gratin [oʊ·'gra·tən] adj gratinado, -a

August ['ɔ·gəst] n agosto m; s. a. **April**

aunt [ænt] n tía f

au pair [oʊ·'per] n au pair mf

aura ['ɔr·ə] n aura f

aural ['ɔr·əl] adj auditivo, -a

aurora borealis [ɔ·'rɔr·ə·ˌbɔr·i·'æl·ɪs] <aurora borealises or aurorae borealis> n aurora f boreal

austere [ɔ·'stɪr] adj austero, -a

austerity [ɔ·'ster·ə·ṭi] <-ies> n austeridad f

Australia [ɔ·'streɪl·jə] n Australia f

Australian adj, n australiano, -a m, f

Austria ['ɔ·stri·ə] n Austria f

Austrian adj, n austriaco, -a m, f

authentic [ɔ·'θen·tɪk] adj auténtico, -a

authenticity [ɔ·θən·'tɪs·ə·ṭi] n autenticidad f

author ['ɔ·θər] I. n autor(a) m(f); fig creador(a) m(f) II. vt escribir

authoritarian [ə·ˌθɔr·ə·'ter·i·ən] adj, n autoritario, -a m, f

authoritative [ə·'θɔr·ə·ter·ṭɪv] adj 1. (assertive) autoritario, -a 2. (reliable) autorizado, -a

authority [ə·'θɔr·ə·ṭi] <-ies> n 1. (power) autoridad f; **the authorities** las autoridades f 2. (permission) autorización f ▶ **to have sth on good ~** saber algo de buena tinta; **to have sth on sb's ~** saber algo a través de alguien

authorization [ɔ·θər·ɪ·'zeɪ·ʃən] n autorización f

authorize ['ɔ·θə·raɪz] vt autorizar

autobiographical [ɔ·tə·baɪ·ə·'græf·ɪ·kəl] adj autobiográfico, -a

autobiography [ɔ·tə·baɪ·'ag·rə·fi] n autobiografía f

autocross n autocross m

autograph ['ɔ·tə·græf] I. n autógrafo m II. vt autografiar

automated adj automatizado, -a

automated teller machine n cajero m automático

automatic [ɔ·tə·'mæṭ·ɪk] I. n máquina f; (car) coche m automático II. adj automático, -a

automobile ['ɔ·tə·moʊ·bil] n automóvil m; **~ accident** accidente de coche

automotive [ɔ·tə·'moʊ·ṭɪv] adj inv automovilístico, -a

autonomous [ɔ·'tan·ə·məs] adj autónomo, -a

autonomy [ɔ·'tan·ə·mi] n autonomía f

autopsy ['ɔ·tap·si] <-ies> n autopsia f

autumn ['ɔ·təm] n otoño m; **in (the) ~** en (el) otoño

autumnal [ɔ·'tʌm·nəl] adj otoñal

auxiliary [ɔg·'zɪl·jə·ri] <-ies> adj, n auxiliar mf

av. 1. abbr of **average** media f 2. abbr of **avenue** Avda.

avail [ə·'veɪl] n provecho m; **to no ~** en vano

available [ə·'veɪ·lə·bəl] adj 1. (obtainable) disponible; **to make sth ~ to sb** poner algo a disposición de alguien 2. (free) libre; **to be ~ to do sth** tener tiempo para hacer algo 3. (single) **to be ~** estar libre y sin compromiso

avalanche ['æv·ə·læntʃ] n avalancha f

ave. abbr of **avenue** Avda.

avenge [ə·'vendʒ] vt vengar; **to ~ oneself** vengarse

avenue ['æv·ə·nu] n 1. avenida f, carrera f AmL 2. (possibility) vía f

average ['æv·ər·ɪdʒ] I. n promedio m; **above/below ~** por encima/por debajo de la media; **on ~** por término medio II. adj 1. medio, -a; **~ Joe** un tipo corriente 2. (mediocre) mediocre

aversion [ə·'vɜr·ʒən] n aversión f (**to** hacia)

avert [ə·'vɜrt] vt prevenir; (eyes, thoughts) apartar

aviary ['eɪ·vi·er·i] n pajarera f

aviation [ˌeɪ·vi·'eɪ·ʃən] n aviación f

avid ['æv·ɪd] adj ávido, -a

avocado [ˌæv·ə·'ka·doʊ] <-s or -es> n aguacate m

avoid [əˈvɔɪd] *vt* evitar; (*when moving*) esquivar; **to ~ doing sth** evitar hacer algo

avoidable *adj* evitable

avoidance *n* evasión *f*

await [əˈweɪt] *vt* aguardar; **eagerly ~ed** esperado con ansiedad

awake [əˈweɪk] I. <awoke *or* awaked, awoken *or* awaked> *vi* despertarse; **to ~ to sth** *fig* darse cuenta de algo II. *vt* despertar III. *adj* 1. despierto, -a; **to stay/lie ~** mantenerse despierto 2. *fig* alerta; **to be ~ to sth** estar alerta ante algo

awakening [əˈweɪ·kə·nɪŋ] *n* despertar *m*

award [əˈwɔrd] I. *n* premio *m;* (*reward*) recompensa *f;* MIL condecoración *f* II. *vt* otorgar; (*grant*) conceder

aware [əˈwer] *adj* **to be ~ that** saber que; **not that I'm ~ of** no, que yo sepa; **to be ~ of sth** ser consciente de algo

awareness [əˈwer·nɪs] *n* conciencia *f*

away [əˈweɪ] *adv* 1. (*distant*) **5 miles ~** a 5 millas; **far ~** lejos; **to be miles ~** *fig* no prestar atención 2. (*absent*) fuera; **to be ~ on vacation** estar de vacaciones 3. (*future*) **it's only a week ~** sólo queda una semana; **right ~!** ¡enseguida! 4. (*continuously*) **to read/eat ~** leer/comer sin cesar

away from *prep* lejos de; **~ the town** lejos del pueblo; **~ each other** alejados el uno del otro; **to stay ~ sth/sb** mantenerse alejado de algo/alguien; **to go ~ sth** alejarse de algo

awe [ɔ] *n* sobrecogimiento *m;* **to hold sb in ~** tener un gran respeto por alguien

awe-inspiring *adj* imponente

awesome [ˈɔ·səm] *adj* imponente; *inf* fabuloso

awful [ˈɔ·fəl] *adj* terrible; **an ~ lot** muchísimo

awfully [ˈɔ·fə·li] *adv* terriblemente; (*very*) muy; **I'm ~ sorry** lo siento muchísimo

awhile [əˈhwaɪl] *adv* **to wait ~** esperar un rato

awkward [ˈɔk·wərd] *adj* 1. (*difficult*) difícil 2. (*embarrassed*) incómodo, -a; (*question*) delicado, -a 3. (*inconvenient*) inoportuno, -a 4. (*clumsy*) torpe

awl [ɔl] *n* punzón *m*

awning [ˈɔ·nɪŋ] *n* toldo *m*

awoke [əˈwouk] *pt of* **awake**

awoken [əˈwou·kən] *pp of* **awake**

ax(e) [æks] I. *n* hacha *f;* **the ~** el hacha ▶ **to get the ~** *inf* (*worker*) ser despedido; (*project*) ser anulado II. *vt* recortar <axing>

axis [ˈæk·sɪs] *n* eje *m*

axle [ˈæk·səl] *n* eje *m,* cardán *m AmC, Ven, Col;* **back/front ~** eje trasero/delantero

aye [aɪ] *n* **the ~s** los votos a favor

AZ *n abbr of* **Arizona** Arizona *f*

B

B, b [bi] *n* 1. (*letter*) B, b *f;* **~ as in Bravo** B de Barcelona 2. SCHOOL ≈ notable *m*

babble [ˈbæb·əl] *vi* (*baby*) balbucear; (*adult*) parlotear

babe [beɪb] *n* 1. bebé *m* 2. (*woman*) tía *f* 3. (*dear*) cariño *m,* mamita *Col*

baboon [bæˈbun] *n* babuino *m*

baby [ˈbeɪ·bi] *n* 1. bebé *m;* **to expect/have a ~** esperar/tener un bebé 2. (*dear*) nene, -a *m, f*

baby carriage *n* cochecito *m* de bebé, carriola *f Méx*

babysitter [ˈbeɪ·bɪ·ˌsɪt·ər] *n* canguro *mf,* nana *f Méx*

bachelor [ˈbætʃ·ə·lər] *n* soltero *m;* UNIV licenciado, -a *m, f* (**of** en)

back [bæk] I. *n* 1. (*opposite of front*) parte *f* trasera; (*hand, paper, envelope*) dorso *m;* (*chair*) respaldo *m;* (*reverse side*) revés *m;* **~ to front** al revés; **to know sth ~ to front** saberse algo al derecho y al revés 2. ANAT espalda *f;* (*animal*) lomo *m;* **to be on one's ~** estar boca arriba; **to break one's ~** deslomarse; **to do sth behind sb's ~** hacer algo a espaldas de alguien; **to turn one's ~ on sb** dar la espalda a alguien 3. SPORTS defensa *mf* ▶ **to know sth like the ~ of one's hand** conocer algo al dedillo; **to have one's ~ against the wall** estar entre la espada y la pared; **you scratch my ~ and I'll scratch yours** hoy por ti, mañana por mí II. *adj* trasero, -a;

MED dorsal **III.** *adv* **1. to be ~** estar de vuelta; **to come ~** volver; **to want sb ~** querer que alguien vuelva; **I want the money ~** quiero que me devuelvan el dinero; **to bring ~ memories** traer viejos recuerdos a la memoria **2.** (*behind*) detrás, atrás; **~ and forth** atrás y adelante; **to look ~** mirar (hacia) atrás; **to sit ~** recostarse **3.** (*in return*) de vuelta **4.** (*into the past*) atrás **IV.** *vt* respaldar

◆**back away** *vi* echarse atrás
◆**back down** *vi* retirarse
◆**back off** *vi* retroceder; (*personally*) mantener las distancias
◆**back out of** *vt* salir de; *fig* retirarse de
◆**back up** *vt* **1.** (*reverse*) dar marcha atrás **2.** COMPUT hacer copias de seguridad de **3.** (*support*) respaldar

backbone *n* columna *f* vertebral; *fig* pilar *m*
back door *n* puerta *f* trasera
backer ['bæk·ər] *n* partidario, -a *m, f*
backfire ['bæk·faɪr] *vi* fallar; (*plan*) fracasar; AUTO petardear, detonar *AmL*
backgammon ['bæk·gæm·ən] *n* backgammon *m*
background ['bæk·graʊnd] *n* **1.** (*rear view*) fondo *m*; **in the ~** en segundo plano **2.** (*education*) educación *f*; (*training*) formación *f* **3.** (*circumstances*) antecedentes *mpl*
background music *n* música *f* de fondo
backhand ['bæk·hænd] *n* revés *m*
backing ['bæk·ɪŋ] *n* apoyo *m*
backlash *n* **1.** (*reaction*) reacción *f* violenta **2.** TYPO barra *f* inversa
backlog *n* atraso *m*
backpack ['bæk·pæk] **I.** *n* mochila *f* **II.** *vi* viajar con mochila
backpacker *n* mochilero, -a *m, f*
back pay *n* atrasos *m pl* de sueldo
back seat *n* asiento *m* trasero
backside *n inf* trasero *m*
backspace (**key**) *n* tecla *f* de retroceso
backstabbing ['bæk·ˌstæb·ɪŋ] *n* habladurías *f pl* a espaldas de alguien, víboreo *m Méx*
backstage [bæk·ˈsteɪdʒ] *adv* entre bastidores

backstory *n* historia *f* de fondo
back talk *n* réplicas *fpl*
backup ['bæk·ʌp] *n* **1.** COMPUT copia *f* de seguridad **2.** (*support*) apoyo *m*
backward ['bæk·wərd] *adj* **1.** (*to the rear*) hacia atrás **2.** (*slow in learning*) retrasado, -a **3.** (*underdeveloped*) atrasado, -a
backward(s) ['bæk·wərdz] *adv* **1.** (*towards the back*) hacia atrás; (*step*) atrás **2.** (*in reverse order*) al revés **3.** (*from better to worse*) a peor **4.** (*into the past*) atrás en el tiempo
backyard *n* jardín *m* trasero
bacon ['beɪ·kən] *n* beicon *m*, tocino *m AmL*
bacteria [bæk·ˈtɪr·i·ə] *npl* bacteria *f*
bad [bæd] <worse, worst> **I.** *adj* **1.** (*not good*) malo, -a; (*marriage, times*) difícil; (*pain*) fuerte; (*accident, mistake*) grave; **to go ~** echarse a perder; **to feel ~** sentirse mal; **to look ~** tener mal aspecto; **too ~!** ¡qué lástima!; **to use ~ language** decir palabrotas; **~ luck** mala suerte, macacoa *f PRico*; **in ~ taste** de mal gusto; **to have a ~ temper** tener mal carácter; **to have a ~ heart/back** estar mal del corazón/de la espalda **2.** (*harmful*) perjudicial (**for** para) ▸ **to go from ~ to worse** ir de mal en peor **II.** *adv inf* mal
bad dream *n* pesadilla *f*
badge [bædʒ] *n* insignia *f*, placa *f Méx*
badger ['bædʒ·ər] **I.** *n* tejón *m* **II.** *vt* importunar
badly ['bæd·li] <worse, worst> *adv* **1.** mal; **to think ~ of sb** pensar mal de alguien; **to come out of sth ~** salir mal parado de algo **2.** (*very much*) desesperadamente
badminton ['bæd·mɪn·tən] *n* bádminton *m*
baffle ['bæf·əl] **I.** *vt* **1.** (*confuse*) desconcertar **2.** (*hinder*) impedir **II.** *n* deflector *m*; (*audio*) bafle *m*
baffling *adj* desconcertante
bag [bæg] *n* **1.** bolsa *f*, busaca *f Col, Ven*; (*handbag*) bolso *m*; (*sack*) saco *m*; **to pack one's ~s** hacer las maletas; *fig* marcharse **2.** (*under eyes*) ojera *f* **II.** *vt* <-gg-> **1.** (*groceries*) meter en una bol-

sa **2.** *inf* (*obtain*) agenciarse

baggage ['bæg·ɪdʒ] *n* equipaje *m;* **excess ~** exceso *m* de equipaje

baggage car *n* vagón *m* de equipaje, breque *m Ecua, Perú, RíoPl*

baggage check *n* documentación *f* del equipaje

baggage claim *n* recogida *f* del equipaje

baggy ['bæg·i] *adj* (*pants*) ancho, -a

bagpipes *npl* gaita *f*

baguette [bæ·'get] *n* pan *m* francés

Bahamas [bə·'ha·məz] *npl* **the ~** las Bahamas

Bahamian [bə·'hæ·mi·ən] *adj, n* bahameño, -a *m, f*

bail [beɪl] *n* fianza *f;* **on ~** bajo fianza

bait [beɪt] **I.** *n* cebo *m; fig* señuelo *m;* **to swallow the ~** morder el anzuelo **II.** *vt* cebar; (*person*) acosar

bake [beɪk] **I.** *vi* cocerse; *inf* (*place*) ser un horno **II.** *vt* hornear; (*harden*) tostar

baker ['beɪ·kər] *n* panadero, -a *m, f*

bakery ['beɪ·kə·ri] *n* panadería *f*

baking *adj* **it's ~ hot** hace un calor asfixiante

baking powder *n* levadura *f*

baking soda *n* bicarbonato *m* de sodio

balance ['bæl·ənts] **I.** *n* **1.** (*device*) balanza *f* **2.** *fig* equilibrio *m;* **to lose one's ~** perder el equilibrio **3.** (*in bank account*) saldo *m* **4.** (*to be paid*) balance *m* **II.** *vi* mantener el equilibrio **III.** *vt* **1.** (*compare*) contrapesar; **to ~ sth against sth** comparar algo con algo **2.** (*keep in a position*) estabilizar **3.** (*achieve equilibrium*) equilibrar; **to ~ the books** hacer cuadrar las cuentas; **to ~ working and having a family** compaginar el trabajo con la familia

balanced *adj* equilibrado, -a; **a ~ diet** una dieta equilibrada

balance sheet *n* balance *m*

balcony ['bæl·kə·ni] *n* balcón *m*

bald [bɔld] *adj* **1.** calvo, -a, pelón, -ona *Méx;* **to go ~** quedarse calvo **2.** (*plain*) escueto, -a

baldness ['bɔld·nɪs] *n* calvicie *f,* pelada *f CSur*

bale [beɪl] **I.** *n* fardo *m* **II.** *vt* embalar

ball [bɔl] *n* **1.** SPORT pelota *f;* (*big*) balón *m;* **to play ~** jugar a la pelota; *fig* cooperar **2.** (*round form*) bola *f* **3.** (*dance*) baile *m* ▶ **to have a ~** divertirse; **to get the ~ rolling** poner las cosas en marcha

ballad ['bæl·əd] *n* balada *f*

balladeer [,bæl·ə·'dɪr] *n* cantautor(a) *m(f)*

ballast ['bæl·əst] *n* NAUT lastre *m*

ballerina [,bæl·ə·'ri·nə] *n* bailarina *f*

ballet dancer *n* bailarín, -ina *m, f*

ball game *n* partido *m* de béisbol

ballistic [bə·'lɪs·tɪk] *adj* balístico, -a ▶ **to go ~** *sl* ponerse como un basilisco

balloon [bə·'lun] **I.** *n* globo *m* ▶ **to go over like a lead ~** fracasar estrepitosamente **II.** *vi* inflarse

balloonist *n* ascensionista *mf*

ballot ['bæl·ət] *n* **1.** (*paper*) papeleta *f* **2.** (*election*) sufragio *m* **3.** (*process*) votación *f*

ballot box *n* urna *f*

ballot paper *n* papeleta *f*

ballpark *n* estadio *m* de béisbol; **a ~ figure** una cifra aproximada

ballplayer *n* jugador(a) *m(f)* de béisbol

ballpoint (pen) *n* bolígrafo *m*, birome *m RíoPl*

ballroom *n* salón *m* de baile

balm [bam] *n* MED bálsamo *m; fig* consuelo *m*

bamboo [bæm·'bu] *n* bambú *m*

ban [bæn] **I.** *n* prohibición *f* **II.** *vt* <-nn-> prohibir; **she was ~ned from driving** le prohibieron conducir

banal [bə·'nal] *adj* banal

banana [bə·'næn·ə] *n* plátano *m*, banana *f AmL* ▶ **to go ~s** *sl* irse de la olla

band[1] [bænd] *n* **1.** (*strip, range*) *a.* TEL banda *f* **2.** (*stripe*) franja *f* **3.** (*ribbon*) cinta *f;* **head ~** cinta *f* del pelo; **waist ~** faja *f* **4.** (*ring*) anillo *m;* **wedding ~** alianza *f*

band[2] [bænd] *n* MUS grupo *m;* (*of friends*) pandilla *f;* (*of robbers*) banda *f*

◆ **band together** *vi* agruparse

bandage ['bæn·dɪdʒ] **I.** *n* vendaje *m* **II.** *vt* vendar

Band-Aid® *n* tirita *f*

bandit ['bæn·dɪt] *n* bandido, -a *m, f*, carrilano, -a *m, f Chile*

bandstand n quiosco m (de música)

bandwagon n to jump on the ~ subirse al carro

bandwidth n ancho m de banda

bandy ['bæn·di] I. <-ier, -iest> adj patizambo, -a II. vt <-ies, -ied> intercambiar

bang [bæŋ] I. n 1. golpe m; (explosion) detonación f 2. ~s flequillo m, pollina f PRico, Ven ▶ to go over with a ~ salir a las mil maravillas II. adv 1. smack ~ in the middle of the road en el mismísimo centro de la calzada 2. to go ~ estallar III. interj bang IV. vi (make noise) dar golpes; (explode) estallar; (slam) cerrarse de golpe V. vt golpear; to ~ one's head against/on sth darse un golpe en la cabeza contra/con algo

banish ['bæn·ɪʃ] vt a. fig desterrar; to ~ sth from one's mind apartar algo de la mente

banister ['bæn·ə·stər] n pasamano m

bank¹ [bæŋk] I. n 1. FIN banco m; GAMES banca f 2. (storage) depósito m; blood/data ~ banco de sangre/datos ▶ to be laughing all the way to the ~ ganar mucha pasta II. vi to ~ with tener una cuenta en; to ~ on sb/sth for sth contar con alguien/algo para algo III. vt depositar

bank² [bæŋk] I. n (edge) orilla f II. vi AVIAT ladearse

bank³ [bæŋk] n (earth, snow) montículo m; (fog) banco m; (clouds) masa f

◆ **bank up** I. vi amontonarse II. vt amontonar

bank account n cuenta f bancaria

bankbook n libreta f bancaria

bank charges n gastos m pl bancarios

banker ['bæŋ·kar] n banquero, -a m, f

bank holiday n día m festivo

banking n banca f

bank manager n gerente mf de banco

bank note n billete m

bankrupt ['bæŋk·rʌpt] I. n quebrado, -a m, f II. vt llevar a la bancarrota III. adj to be ~ estar en quiebra; to go ~ quebrar

bankruptcy ['bæŋk·rəp·si] n <-ies> bancarrota f

bank transfer n transferencia f bancaria

banner ['bæn·ər] n 1. (flag) bandera f 2. (placard) pancarta f 3. (Internet) anuncio m

banquet ['bæŋ·kwət] n banquete m

baptism ['bæp·tɪz·əm] n bautismo m

Baptist ['bæp·tɪst] n bautista mf; the Baptist Church la Iglesia Bautista

baptize ['bæp·taɪz] vt bautizar

bar¹ [bar] I. n 1. (metal, wood) barra f; (cage, prison) reja f; (chocolate) tableta f; (gold) lingote m; (soap) pastilla f; (color) franja f; (sand) banco m; to be behind ~s estar entre rejas 2. (restriction) obstáculo m 3. (nightclub) bar m; (counter) barra f; (in store) mostrador m 4. task/scroll/space ~ barra de tareas/de desplazamiento/espaciadora II. vt <-rr-> 1. (obstruct) obstruir; (door, window) atrancar; (way, path) obstaculizar 2. to ~ sb from doing sth prohibir a alguien hacer algo 3. (exclude) excluir

bar² [bar] prep excepto; ~ none sin excepción

Bar [bar] n abogacía f

barb [barb] n (insult) comentario m hiriente

barbaric [bar·'ber·ɪk] adj bárbaro, -a

barbecue ['bar·bɪ·kju] n barbacoa f, parrillada f Col, Ven, asado m Chile

barbed [barbd] adj de púas; fig mordaz

barber ['bar·bər] n barbero, -a m, f

bar code n código m de barras

bare [ber] I. adj 1. (naked) desnudo, -a; (uncovered) descubierto, -a; with one's ~ hands con sus propias manos; the ~ facts [or truth] la pura verdad; the ~ minimum lo mínimo; the ~ necessities las necesidades básicas 2. (empty) vacío, -a; to be ~ of sth estar desprovisto de algo II. vt desnudar

barefoot ['ber·fut] adv descalzo, -a

barely ['ber·li] adv 1. (hardly) apenas, agatas Arg, Urug, Par 2. (scantily) escasamente

bargain ['bar·gɪn] I. n 1. (agreement) trato m; to drive a hard ~ saber regatear; to strike a ~ cerrar un trato 2. (item) ganga f, pichincha f Arg, Bol, Par, Urug, mamada f AmC, Bol, Chile,

Perú ▶ **into** the ~ por si fuera poco II. *vi* negociar; (*haggle*) regatear; **to ~ away** malvender

◆**bargain for, bargain on** *vi* contar con

bargain basement *n* sección *f* de ofertas

bargain sale *n* rebajas *fpl*

barge [bardʒ] I. *n* barcaza *f* II. *vt* empujar; **to ~ one's way through sth** abrirse paso por algo

◆**barge in** *vi* (*intrude*) colarse; **sorry to ~** *fig* disculpe si me entrometo

◆**barge into** *vi* chocar con

◆**barge through** *vi* abrirse paso a empujones

bar graph *n* gráfico *m* de barras

bark[1] [bark] I. *n* ladrido *m* ▶ **his ~ is worse than his** bite perro ladrador poco mordedor *prov* II. *vi* ladrar; (*person*) gritar III. *vt* gritar

◆**bark out** *vt* gritar

bark[2] [bark] *n* (*tree*) corteza *f*

barkeeper ['bar·ki·pər] *n* (*owner*) tabernero, -a *m, f;* (*bartender*) camarero, -a *m, f*

barley ['bar·li] *n* cebada *f*

barman ['bar·mən] *n* <-men> camarero *m*

barn [barn] *n* granero *m*

barnyard *n* corral *m*

baroque [bə·'rouk] *adj* a. *fig* barroco, -a

barrage [bə·'raʒ] *n fig* aluvión *m*

barrel ['bær·əl] I. *n* barril *m;* (*gun*) cañón *m* ▶ **to be a ~ of** fun [*or* laughs] ser una panzada de reír; **to** have **sb over a ~** tener a alguien en un puño II. *vi* <-l-> *inf* ir disparado; **to ~ along** ir a toda pastilla [*or a* mil] *Col, Méx* III. *vt* <-l-> embarrilar

barren ['bær·ən] *adj* (*infertile*) estéril; (*landscape*) árido, -a; ~ **years** años perdidos

barricade ['bær·ə·keɪd] I. *n* barricada *f* II. *vt* atrincherar

barrier ['bær·i·ər] *n* barrera *f;* **language ~** barrera lingüística

barring ['bar·ɪŋ] *prep* ~ **accidents** a menos que surja un imprevisto; ~ **complications** a menos que se presenten complicaciones; ~ **delays** a menos que se produzcan retrasos

bartender ['bar·ten·dər] *n* camarero, -a *m, f*

barter ['bar·tər] I. *n* trueque *m* II. *vi* comerciar III. *vt* cambiar (**for** por)

base [beɪs] I. *n* 1. (*lower part*) a. MIL base *f;* (*of a company*) sede *f* 2. (*bottom*) fondo *m* 3. (*support*) apoyo *m* 4. (*basis*) fundamento *m* ▶ **to be off ~** ir desencaminado; **to** touch **~** tocar fondo II. *vt* basar; **to be ~d** (*company*) tener su sede; (*person*) trabajar (**in** en) III. *adj* vil; (*metal*) impuro, -a

baseball ['beɪs·bɔl] *n* béisbol *m*

baseless ['beɪs·lɪs] *adj* sin fundamento; (*accusation*) infundado, -a

base pay *n* salario *m* base

bash [bæʃ] I. *n* porrazo *m; sl* juerga *f* II. *vt* (*thing*) golpear; (*person*) pegar

◆**bash into** *vi insep* estrellarse contra

◆**bash up** *vt inf* (*car*) estrellar

bashful ['bæʃ·fəl] *adj* tímido, -a

basic ['beɪ·sɪk] *adj* básico, -a; **a ~ command of** conocimientos básicos de

basically *adv* básicamente

basil ['beɪ·zəl] *n* albahaca *f*

basilica [bə·'sɪl·ɪ·kə] *n* basílica *f*

basin ['beɪ·sɪn] *n* 1. (*for washing*) lavadero *m* 2. (*sink*) lavabo *m* 3. GEO cuenca *f*

basis ['beɪ·sɪs] *n* <bases> base *f;* **on a weekly ~** semanalmente

bask [bæsk] *vi* **to ~ in the sun** tomar el sol

basket ['bæs·kət] *n* cesta *f;* SPORTS canasta *f*

basketball ['bæs·kət·bɔl] *n* baloncesto *m*

bass[1] [beɪs] *n* MUS bajo *m*

bass[2] [bæs] *n* ZOOL lubina *f*

bassoon [bə·'sun] *n* fagot *m*

bastard ['bæs·tərd] *n* (*child*) bastardo, -a *m, f*

bat[1] [bæt] I. *n* murciélago *m* ▶ **to have ~s in the** belfry estar mal de la azotea; **to be as** blind **as a ~** no ver tres en un burro II. *vt* **to ~ one's eyelashes** pestañear; (*at sb*) guiñar un ojo

bat[2] [bæt] SPORTS I. *n* bate *m;* (*blow*) golpe *m* ▶ **right off the ~** al instante II. *vt, vi* <-tt-> batear

batch [bætʃ] *n* <-es> tanda *f;* COM, COMPUT lote *m*

bated ['beɪ·tɪd] *adj* **with ~ breath** conteniendo la respiración

bath [bæθ] *n* (*action*) baño *m*, bañada *f Méx*; **to take a ~** bañarse

bathe [beɪð] I. *vi* bañarse II. *vt* bañar; (*wound, eyes*) lavar

bathing *n* **~ prohibited** prohibido bañarse

bathing cap *n* gorro *m* de baño

bathing suit *n* bañador *m*, malla *f RíoPl*, vestido *m* de baño *Col*

bathing trunks *npl* bañador *m*

bath mat *n* alfombrilla *f* de baño

bathrobe *n* albornoz *m*, bata *f Col, Méx*

bathroom *n* (*cuarto m de*) baño *m*; (*lavatory*) aseo *m*; (*public*) servicio *m*

bath towel *n* toalla *f* de baño

bathtub *n* bañera *f*, tina *f AmL*

baton [bə·'tan] *n* **1.** MUS batuta *f* **2.** (*of a policeman*) porra *f* **3.** SPORTS testigo *m*

batsman ['bæts·mən] <-men> *n* bateador *m*

batter[1] ['bæt·ər] I. *n* masa *f*; (*for fried food*) rebozado *m* II. *vt* rebozar

batter[2] ['bæt·ər] I. *n* SPORTS bateador(a) *m(f)* II. *vt* apalear; (*person, pet*) maltratar; **to ~ the door in** [*or* **down**] echar la puerta abajo III. *vi* **to ~ at the door** aporrear la puerta

battered ['bæt·ərd] *adj* **1.** maltratado, -a; (*hat, clothes*) estropeado, -a; (*reputation, image*) maltrecho, -a **2.** CULIN rebozado, -a

battery ['bæt·ə·ri] <-ies> *n* pila *f*; AUTO batería *f*; **a ~ of questions** una sarta de preguntas

battery charger *n* cargador *m*

battle ['bæt·əl] I. *n* lucha *f*; MIL batalla *f* ▶ **that's half the ~** con eso ya hay medio camino andado; **to fight a** <u>losing</u> **~** luchar por una causa perdida II. *vi* pelear; (*nonviolently*) luchar III. *vt* combatir

battlefield, battleground *n* campo *m* de batalla

battleship *n* acorazado *m*

batty ['bæt·i] *adj sl* grillado, -a; **to go ~** volverse majara

bawl [bɔl] I. *vi* vociferar; (*weep*) berrear II. *vt* gritar; **to ~ out** echar la bronca

bay[1] [beɪ] *n* GEO bahía *f*

bay[2] [beɪ] *n* ZOOL caballo *m* zaino

bay[3] [beɪ] *vi* (*dog, wolf*) aullar

bay leaf *n* hoja *f* de laurel

bay window *n* mirador *m*

bazaar [bə·'zar] *n* **1.** (*market*) bazar *m* **2.** (*event*) venta *f* benéfica, bazar *m Col*

BBQ ['bar·bɪ·kju] *n abbr of* **barbecue** (*event*) barbacoa *f*, parrillada *f Col, Ven*, asado *m Chile*

B.C. [‚bi·'si] *adv abbr of* **before Christ** a.C.

be [bi] <was, been> I. *vi* **1.** + *n/adj* (*permanent state, quality, identity*) ser; **she's Spanish a cook** es española/ cocinera; **to ~ good** ser bueno; **to ~ able to do sth** ser capaz de hacer algo; **what do you want to ~ when you grow up?** ¿qué quieres ser de mayor?; **to ~ married/single** [*or CSur* **ser**] casado/soltero; **to ~ a widow** ser viuda **2.** + *adj* (*mental and physical states*) estar; **to ~ fat/happy** estar gordo/contento; **to ~ hungry/thirsty** tener hambre/sed; **don't ~ too long** no tardes mucho **3.** (*age*) tener; **I'm 21** tengo 21 años **4.** **to ~ for/against sth** estar a favor/en contra de algo **5.** (*calculation, cost*) **two and two is four** dos y dos son cuatro; **these glasses are $2 each** estos vasos cuestan $2 cada uno; **how much is that?** ¿cuánto es? **6.** (*measurement*) medir; (*weight*) pesar **7.** (*exist, live*) **there is/are** hay; **to let ~** dejar en paz; **to ~ or not to ~** ser o no ser **8.** (*location, situation*) estar; **to ~ in Ohio** estar en Ohio; **to ~ in a bad situation** estar en una mala situación; **I've never ~en to Mexico** nunca he estado en Méjico **9.** (*take place*) ser, tener lugar **10.** + *on* **to ~ on the pill** tomar la píldora; **to ~ on vacation/on a diet** estar de vacaciones/a régimen II. *impers vb* **it's cloudy** está nublado; **it's sunny** hace sol; **it's two o'clock** son las dos; **it's ~en so long!** ¡cuánto tiempo!; **it's ten minutes by bus to the market** el mercado está a diez minutos en autobús III. *aux vb* **1.** (*continuation*) estar; **to ~ doing sth** estar haciendo algo; **you're always complaining** siempre te estás quejando **2.** (*passive*) ser; **to ~ discovered by sb** ser descubierto por alguien; **he was asked...** le preguntaron... **3.** (*future*) **we are to visit Peru in the May** vamos a ir a Perú en mayo; **she's leaving tomorrow** se va mañana; **she was never to see her brother again** nunca más volvería a ver a su hermano; **you are to come here right now** vas a venir aquí ahora mismo **4.** (*tag question*) **she is tall, isn't she?** es alta, ¿verdad?

beach [biːʧ] *n* playa *f*

bead [biːd] *n* **1.** (*drop*) gota *f* **2.** *pl* collar *m* de cuentas

beak [biːk] *n* pico *m*; *inf* napia *f*, naso *m* RíoPl

be all *n* **the ~ (and end all)** la única cosa que importa

beam [biːm] **I.** *n* **1.** (*ray*) rayo *m*; **high/low** ➞ AUTO luces *f pl* largas/cortas, luces altas/bajas *Chile, Col* **2.** ARCHIT viga *f* **II.** *vt* transmitir **III.** *vi* brillar; (*smile*) sonreír

beaming *adj* **to be ~** estar radiante

bean [biːn] **I.** *n* **1.** (*green*) judía *f* verde, habichuela *f* *Col*, ejote *m* *Méx*, chaucha *f* *RíoPl*, poroto *m* verde *Chile*, vainita *f* *Ven* **2.** (*dried*) alubia *f* **3. coffee ~** grano *m* de café; **vanilla ~** vaina *f* de vainilla ➞ *inf* **to be full of ~s** estar lleno de vida; **to not have a ~** estar pelado; **to spill the ~s** descubrir el pastel **II.** *vt sl* dar un mamporro

beanbag *n* (*toy*) bolsa rellena de alubias usada como pelota; (*chair*) puf *m*

bean sprout *n* brote *m* de soja

bear[1] [beə] *n* oso, -a *m, f*

bear[2] [beə] <bore, borne> **I.** *vt* **1.** (*carry*) llevar; (*weight, responsibility, blame*) cargar con; (*cost*) correr con **2.** (*have*) tener; **to ~ a resemblance to** parecerse a; **to ~ in mind** tener presente; **to ~ sb a grudge** guardar rencor a alguien **3. to ~ oneself** comportarse **4.** (*tolerate*) soportar **5.** (*give birth to*) tener **6.** *a. fig* (*fruit*) dar **II.** *vi* **to ~ east** dirigirse al este; **to ~ right** torcer a la derecha

◆**bear on** *vt* (*be relevant*) tener que ver con; (*affect*) afectar a

◆**bear up** *vi* aguantar

◆**bear with** *vi* tener paciencia con

bearable [ˈbeə·rə·bəl] *adj* soportable

beard [bɪrd] *n* barba *f*

bearded *adj* barbudo, -a

bearing [ˈbeə·rɪŋ] *n* **1.** NAUT rumbo *m*; **to get/lose one's ~s** orientarse/desorientarse **2.** (*behavior*) comportamiento *m* ➞ **to have some ~ on sth** tener que ver con algo

beast [biːst] *n* bestia *f*

beat [biːt] <beat, beaten> **I.** *n* **1.** (*heart*) latido *m*; (*pulse*) pulsación *f* **2.** MUS tiempo *m*; (*rhythm*) ritmo *m* **3.** (*police*) ronda *f* **II.** *adj* reventado, -a **III.** *vt* **1.** (*strike*) golpear; (*drum*) tocar **2.** (*wings, record*) *a.* CULIN batir **3.** **to ~ a path** abrirse paso **4.** (*defeat*) ganar; **to ~ sb in** [*or* at] **sth** superar a alguien en algo **5.** (*arrive before*) **she ~ me to the door** llegó antes que yo a la puerta ➞ **if you can't ~ them, join them** si no puedes vencerlos, únete a ellos; **that ~s everything** ¡eso es el colmo!; **~ it!** *sl* ¡lárgate!; **it ~s me how/why...** no me entra cómo/por qué... **IV.** *vi* (*rain*) caer; (*person*) golpear; (*heart, pulse*) latir

◆**beat back** *vt* rechazar

◆**beat down** **I.** *vi* (*hail, rain*) caer con fuerza; (*sun*) picar **II.** *vt* (*door*) derribar; **I managed to beat him down to 50 cents** conseguí que me lo dejara a 50 centavos

◆**beat off** *vt* rechazar

◆**beat up** (**on**) *vt* dar una paliza a

beaten [ˈbiː·tən] *pp* of **beat**

beating [ˈbiː·tɪŋ] *n* **1.** (*assault, defeat*) paliza *f*, zumba *f* *AmL* **2.** (*heart*) latido *m*

beautician [bjuːˈtɪʃ·ən] *n* esteticista *mf*

beautiful [ˈbjuː·tə·fəl] *adj* precioso, -a

beauty [ˈbjuː·ti] <-ies> *n* **1.** (*property*) belleza *f* **2.** *inf* (*specimen*) maravilla *f* **3.** (*advantage*) **the ~ of** lo bueno de ➞ **~ is in the eye of the beholder** *prov* todo es según el color del cristal con que se mira; **~ is only skin-deep** la belleza está en el interior

beauty parlor, beauty salon, beauty shop *n* salón *m* de belleza

beauty spot *n* lugar *m* pintoresco; (*on the skin*) lunar *m*

beaver ['bi·vər] I. n zool castor m; inf (**eager**) ~ persona trabajadora II. vi to ~ **away** trabajar como una hormiguita

became [bɪ·'keɪm] pt of **become**

because [bɪ·'kɔz] I. conj porque; **just** ~ **he's smiling doesn't mean he is in love** que sonría no significa que esté enamorado; ~ **I said that, I had to leave** como dije eso, tuve que irme; **not** ~ **I am sad but...** no porque esté triste, sino... II. prep ~ **of** por; ~ **of me** por mi culpa

beckon ['bek·ən] I. vt llamar por señas; **to** ~ **sb over** hacer señas a alguien para que se acerque II. vi hacer señas (**to** a)

become [bɪ·'kʌm] <became, become> vi 1. (+ adj) volverse; (+ n) llegar a ser; **to** ~ **angry** enfadarse; **to** ~ **famous/old** hacerse famoso/viejo; **to** ~ **sad/happy** ponerse triste/feliz; **to** ~ **interested** interesarse (**in** por) 2. ~ **of** ser de; **what ever became of her?** ¿qué fue de ella?

becoming [bɪ·'kʌm·ɪŋ] adj 1. (clothes, haircut) favorecedor(a), sentador(a) Arg, Chile 2. (behavior) apropiado, -a

becquerel [bə·'krel] n becquerel m

bed [bed] n cama f; (ocean) fondo m; (river) lecho m; **to get out of** ~ levantarse de la cama; **to go to** ~ (**with sb**) acostarse (con alguien); **to make the** ~ hacer la cama ▶ **a** ~ **of nails** un calvario; **a** ~ **of roses** un lecho de rosas; **to get up on the wrong side of the** ~ levantarse con el pie izquierdo

◆**bed down** vi acostarse

bed and breakfast n pensión f

bedclothes npl, **bedding** ['bed·ɪŋ], **bed linen** n ropa f de cama, cobijas fpl AmL

bedraggled [bɪ·'dræg·əld] adj 1. (wet) empapado, -a 2. (disheveled) desaliñado, -a

bedridden ['bed·ˌrɪd·ən] adj postrado, -a en cama

bedroom ['bed·rum] n dormitorio m, recámara f Méx

bedside ['bed·saɪd] n cabecera f

bedside lamp n lámpara f de noche

bedside table n mesita f de noche, no-

chero m Col, Chile, Urug, buró m Méx

bedspread ['bed·spred] n colcha f

bedtime ['bed·taɪm] n hora f de acostarse; **it's (way) past your** ~ hace rato que deberías estar durmiendo

bee [bi] n 1. abeja f 2. (group) círculo m ▶ **to be a busy** ~ iron estar muy atareado

beech [bitʃ] n haya f

beef [bif] I. n ternera f, res f AmC, Méx; **ground** ~ carne f picada de ternera; **roast** ~ rosbif m II. vi sl refunfuñar (**about** por)

◆**beef up** vt mejorar

beehive ['bi·haɪv] n colmena f

been [bɪn] pp of **be**

beep [bip] I. n pitido m II. vi pitar

beer [bɪr] n cerveza f

beer belly n barriga f cervecera

beer garden n terraza f de verano

beeswax ['biz·wæks] n cera f de abeja

beet [bit] n remolacha f, betabel f Méx; **to turn as red as a** ~ ponerse rojo como un tomate

beetle ['bit·əl] n escarabajo m

before [bɪ·'fɔr] I. prep 1. (earlier, preceding) antes de; **to leave** ~ **sb** salir antes que alguien; ~ **doing sth** antes de hacer algo; **to put sth** ~ **sth else** anteponer algo a algo; ~ **Christ** antes de Cristo 2. (in front of) delante de; ~ **our eyes** ante nuestros ojos II. adv antes; **I've seen it** ~ lo he visto anteriormente; **the day** ~ el día anterior; **two days** ~ dos días antes III. conj antes de +subj; **he spoke** ~ **she went out** habló antes de que ella se fuera; **he had a glass** ~ **he went** se tomó una copa antes de irse; **it was a week** ~ **he came** pasó una semana antes de que llegara; **he'd die** ~ **he'd tell the truth** preferiría morir a decir la verdad

beforehand [bɪ·'fɔr·hænd] adv de antemano

befriend [bɪ·'frend] vt hacerse amigo de

beg [beg] <-gg-> I. vt rogar; **to** ~ **sb to do sth** rogar a alguien que haga algo II. vi 1. (beggar) pedir (limosna) 2. (request) implorar

◆**beg off** vi excusarse (**from** de)

began [bɪ·'gæn] pt of **begin**

beggar ['beg·ər] n mendigo, -a m, f, limosnero, -a m, f AmL ▶ ~s can't be **choosers** a buen hambre no hay pan duro

begin [bɪ·'gɪn] <began, begun> I. vt empezar; (conversation) entablar; **to ~ doing sth** empezar a hacer algo II. vi empezar; **to ~ with** en primer lugar

beginner [bɪ·'gɪn·ər] n principiante mf; **~'s luck** la suerte del principiante

beginning I. n 1. (start) principio m, empiezo m Arg, Col, Ecua, Guat; **at** [or **in**] **the ~** al principio; **from ~ to end** de principio a fin 2. (origin) origen m II. adj inicial

begrudge [bɪ·'grʌdʒ] vt (envy) tener envidia de

begun [bɪ·'gʌn] pp of **begin**

behalf [bɪ·'hæf] n **on ~ of** (for) en beneficio de; (from) de parte de

behave [bɪ·'heɪv] vi 1. (act) comportarse; **to ~ badly/well** portarse mal/bien; **~ yourself!** ¡pórtate bien! 2. (function) funcionar

behavior [bɪ·'heɪv·jər] n comportamiento m

behind [bɪ·'haɪnd] I. prep 1. a. fig detrás de; **right ~ sb/sth** justo detrás de alguien/algo; **~ the wheel** al volante; **there is somebody ~ this** hay alguien detrás de todo esto 2. **to be ~ sb/sth** (all the way) estar con alguien/algo (hasta el final) 3. **~ time** retrasado; **to be ~ schedule** ir con retraso 4. **to be ~ sb/the times** estar atrasado con respecto a alguien/la época II. adv detrás; **to fall ~** (be slower) quedarse atrás; (in work, studies) atrasarse; **to leave sb ~** dejar a alguien atrás; **to be ~** estar atrasado (in en) III. n inf trasero m

behindhand [bɪ·'haɪnd·hænd] adv **to be ~** estar atrasado

beige [beɪʒ] adj beige

being [bi·ɪŋ] I. n ser m II. pres p of **be** III. adj **after n for the time ~** por el momento

belated [bɪ·'leɪ·tɪd] adj tardío, -a

belch [beltʃ] I. n inf eructo m II. vi inf soltar un eructo

belfry ['bel·fri] n campanario m

Belgian ['bel·dʒən] adj, n belga mf

Belgium ['bel·dʒəm] n Bélgica f

belief [bɪ·'lif] n opinión f; REL creencia f; **in the ~ that** con la convicción de que

believable [bɪ·'li·və·bəl] adj creíble

believe [bɪ·'liv] I. vt creer; **would you ~ it?** ¡no lo puedo creer!; **she couldn't ~ her eyes/ears** no podía dar crédito a sus ojos/oídos; **~ it or not** aunque parezca mentira II. vi creer (in en)

believer [bɪ·'li·vər] n REL creyente mf 2. (supporter) partidario, -a m, f (in de)

belittle [bɪ·'lɪt̮·əl] vt menospreciar

bell [bel] n campana f; (round) cascabel m; (bicycle, door) timbre m ▶ **as clear as a ~** más claro que el agua; **his name/face rings a ~** me suena su nombre/cara

bellboy n botones m inv

bellhop n botones mf inv

bellow ['bel·oʊ] I. vt gritar II. vi bramar III. n grito m; (of animal) bramido m

bell pepper n pimiento m [or pimentón m Col] dulce

belly ['bel·i] <-ies> n inf panza f

bellyache inf I. n dolor m de barriga II. vi quejarse

bellybutton n ombligo m

belly flop n panzazo m

belong [bɪ·'lɑŋ] vi 1. **to ~ to** pertenecer a; (club) ser socio de; (political party) estar afiliado a 2. **where do these spoons ~?** ¿dónde pongo estas cucharas?; **this doesn't ~ here** esto no va aquí; **they ~ together** están hechos el uno para el otro

belongings npl pertenencias fpl

beloved[1] [bɪ·'lʌv·ɪd] n amado, -a m, f

beloved[2] [bɪ·'lʌvd] adj amado, -a

below [bɪ·'loʊ] I. prep 1. (lower than, underneath) debajo de; **~ us** debajo de nosotros; **the river ~ the town** el río más abajo del pueblo 2. (less than) **~ average** por debajo de la media; **it's 4 degrees ~ zero** estamos a 4 grados bajo cero; **children ~ the age of twelve** menores de doce años II. adv abajo; **from ~** desde abajo; **the family ~** los vecinos de abajo

belt [belt] I. n 1. FASHION cinturón m 2. TECH correa f 3. (area) zona f 4. sl (punch) tortazo m II. vt sl zurrar III. vi *sl* correr a todo tren

bench [bentʃ] *n* banco *m;* SPORTS banquillo *m;* (*worktable*) mesa *f* de trabajo

bend [bend] <bent, bent> I. *n* curva *f;* **to go/be around the** ~ *sl* volverse/estar chiflado II. *vi* doblarse; (*road*) hacer una curva III. *vt* (*arms, legs*) doblar; (*head*) inclinar ► **to** ~ **sb's ear** comerle la oreja a alguien

◆**bend back** *vt* doblar hacia atrás

◆**bend down** *vi* inclinarse

◆**bend over** *vi* inclinarse ► **to** ~ **backwards** (**to help sb**) mover cielo y tierra (por alguien)

beneath [bɪ·ˈniθ] I. *prep* 1. (*lower than, underneath*) debajo de 2. (*inferior to*) por debajo de II. *adv* abajo

benefit [ˈben·ɪ·fɪt] I. *n* beneficio *m;* **to derive** (**much**) ~ **from** sacar (mucho) provecho (**from** a); **to be of** ~ ser de utilidad (**to** a); **for the** ~ **of sb** a beneficio de alguien II. <-t- *or* -tt-> *vi* beneficiarse (**from** de) III. <-t- *or* -tt-> *vt* beneficiar

bent [bent] I. *pt, pp of* **bend** II. *n* inclinación *f* III. *adj* torcido, -a; **to be** ~ **on** (**doing**) **sth** estar empeñado en (hacer) algo

bereavement [bɪ·ˈriv·mənt] *n* muerte *f* de un familiar

Bermuda [bər·ˈmju·də] *n* las Bermudas

Bermuda shorts *n* bermudas *fpl*

berry [ˈber·i] <-ies> *n* baya *f*

berserk [bər·ˈsɜrk] *adj* **to go** ~ ponerse como loco (**over** por); **Mary goes** ~ **over chocolate** a Mary le chifla el chocolate

berth [bɜrθ] *n* camarote *m;* RAIL litera *f*

beside [bɪ·ˈsaɪd] *prep* 1. (*next, in comparison to*) al lado de 2. (*together with*) junto a 3. **to be** ~ **oneself** estar fuera de sí; **to be** ~ **the point** no venir al caso

besides [bɪ·ˈsaɪdz] I. *prep* (*in addition to*) además de; (*except for*) excepto II. *adv* además; **nothing** ~ nada más

best [best] I. *adj superl of* **good;** **the** ~ el/la mejor; **the** ~ **days of my life** los mejores días de mi vida; ~ **wishes!** ¡felicidades! II. *adv superl of* **well** mejor; **the** ~ lo mejor; **as** ~ (**as**) **you can** lo mejor que puedas; **at** ~ como mucho, a lo

mucho *Méx* III. *n* SPORTS récord *m*

bestial [ˈbes·tʃəl] *adj* bestial

bestiality [ˌbes·tʃi·ˈæl·ə·t̬i] *n* bestialidad *f*

best man *n* padrino *m* (de boda)

bestseller *n* éxito *m* de ventas

bet [bet] <bet *or* -ted, bet *or* -ted> I. *n* apuesta *f;* **to make a** ~ hacer una apuesta (**with** con). II. *vt* apostar; **I** ~ **you don't!** ¡a que no lo haces! III. *vi* apostar (**on** por) ► **I'll** ~! ¡seguro!; **you** ~! ¡ya lo creo!

beta version *n* versión *f* beta

betray [bɪ·ˈtreɪ] *vt* 1. traicionar; (*promise*) romper; (*trust*) defraudar; (*husband*) engañar 2. (*reveal*) delatar; **to** ~ **sth to sb** revelar algo a alguien

betrayal [bɪ·ˈtreɪ·əl] *n* (*disloyalty*) traición *f*

better [ˈbet̬·ər] I. *adj comp of* **good** mejor; **to be** ~ MED estar mejor; **it's** ~ **that way** es mejor así II. *adv comp of* **well** mejor; **I like this** ~ me gusta más esto; **we'd** ~ **stay here** lo mejor es quedarse aquí; **or** ~ **yet...** o mejor aún... III. *n* el/la mejor; **to change for the** ~ cambiar para bien; **the sooner, the** ~ cuanto antes, mejor; **so much the** ~ tanto mejor ► **for** ~ **or** (**for**) **worse** para bien o para mal IV. *vt* **to** ~ **oneself** superarse; (*financially*) prosperar

between [bɪ·ˈtwin] I. *prep* entre; **to eat** ~ **meals** comer entre horas; ~ **the two of us** entre nosotros dos II. *adv* (**in**) ~ en medio de; (*time*) a mitad de

beware [bɪ·ˈwer] *vi* tener cuidado; ~ **of pickpockets!** ¡cuidado con los carteristas!

bewilder [bɪ·ˈwɪl·dər] *vt* desconcertar

bewildered *adj* desconcertado, -a

bewildering *adj* desconcertante

bewilderment *n* desconcierto *m*, azoro *m Méx,* Perú, PRico

bewitch [bɪ·ˈwɪtʃ] *vt* hechizar; *fig* fascinar

bewitching *adj* fascinante

beyond [bɪ·ˈjand] I. *prep* 1. (*on the other side*) más allá de; ~ **the mountain** al otro lado de la montaña 2. (*after*) después de; (*more than*) más de; ~ **lunchtime** después del almuerzo; **to stay** ~ **a week** quedarse más de una semana **3.** (*further*) más allá de; **~ the reach** fuera del alcance (**of** de); **~ belief** increíble; **he is ~ help** a. *iron* es un caso perdido; **the shadow of a doubt** sin lugar a dudas **4.** (*difficult*) **to be ~ sb** ser demasiado para alguien **5.** (*more than*) por encima de **II.** *adv* **1.** (*past*) **the house ~** la casa de más allá **2.** (*future*) **the next ten years and ~** los próximos diez años y más

biannual [,baɪ·'æn·jʊ·əl] *adj* semestral

bias ['baɪ·əs] **I.** *n* **1.** (*prejudice*) prejuicio *m* **2.** (*one-sidedness*) parcialidad *f*; **without ~** imparcialmente **II.** <-s-> *vt* influir; **to ~ sb towards/against sb** predisponer a alguien a favor de/en contra de alguien

biased *adj* parcial

bib [bɪb] *n* babero *m*

Bible ['baɪ·bəl] *n* **the ~** la Biblia

bibliographic [,bɪb·lɪ·ə·'græf·ɪk], **bibliographical** *adj* bibliográfico, -a

bibliography [,bɪb·li·'ag·rə·fi] <-ies> *n* bibliografía *f*

bicarbonate [,baɪ·'kar·bə·nɪt] *n* bicarbonato *m*

bicarbonate of soda *n* bicarbonato *m* de soda

bicentenary [baɪ·'sen·ten·ə·ri] <-ies> *n*, **bicentennial** [baɪ·sen·'ten·i·əl] **I.** *n* bicentenario *m* **II.** *adj* bicentenario, -a

biceps ['baɪ·seps] *n inv* bíceps *m inv*

bicker ['bɪk·ər] *vi* reñir

bickering *n* riñas *fpl*

bicycle ['baɪ·sɪk·əl] *n* bicicleta *f*; **to ride a ~** montar en bicicleta; **by ~** en bicicleta

bicycle lane *n* carril *m* bici

bid [bɪd] **I.** *n* **1.** (*offer*) oferta *f* **2.** (*attempt*) intento *m* **II.** <bid, bid> *vi* hacer una oferta; (*auction*) pujar **III.** <bid, bid> *vt* **1.** pujar **2.** *form* **to ~ sb farewell** despedirse de alguien; **to ~ sb welcome** dar la bienvenida a alguien

bidden ['bɪd·ən] *pp of* bid

bidder ['bɪd·ər] *n* postor(a) *m(f)*; **to the highest ~** al mejor postor

bidding ['bɪd·ɪŋ] *n* FIN puja *f*

bidet [bɪ·'deɪ] *n* bidé *m*

biennial [baɪ·'en·i·əl] *adj, n* bienal *f*

bifocal ['baɪ·foʊ·kəl] *adj* bifocal

big [bɪg] <-ger, -gest> *adj* **1.** (*in size,*

amount) grande; (*before sing noun*) gran; **a ~ book** un libro grande; **~ letters** mayúsculas; **the ~ger the better** cuanto más grande mejor **2.** (*older*) mayor; **~ boy/sister** chico/hermana mayor **3.** (*significant*) gran(de); **a ~ day** un gran día; **a ~ decision** una decisión importante ▸ **to have a ~ heart** tener un buen corazón; **to have a ~ mouth** ser un bocazas; **to think ~** tener grandes aspiraciones

bigamy ['bɪg·ə·mi] *n* bigamia *f*

Big Dipper *n* **the ~** el Carro

bigoted *adj* intolerante; REL fanático, -a

big shot *n* pez *m* gordo

big toe *n* dedo *m* gordo del pie

bike [baɪk] *n* bici *f*; (*motorcycle*) moto *f*

biker ['baɪ·kər] *n inf* motero, -a *m, f*

bikini [bɪ·'ki·ni] *n* bikini *m*

bilateral [,baɪ·'læt·ər·əl] *adj* bilateral

bile [baɪl] *n* ANAT bilis *f inv*

bilingual [baɪ·'lɪŋ·gwəl] *adj* bilingüe

bill [bɪl] **I.** *n* **1.** (*invoice*) factura *f*; **phone ~** factura del teléfono; **the ~, please** la cuenta, por favor **2.** (*bank note*) billete *m* **3.** (*bird*) pico *m* **4.** POL, LAW proyecto *m* de ley **II.** *vt* pasar la cuenta a

bill collector *n* cobrador(a) *m(f)* (de deudas)

billfold *n* cartera *f*

billiards ['bɪl·jərdz] *n* billar *m*

billion ['bɪl·jən] *n* mil millones *mpl*

billy club *n* porra *f*

bimonthly [,baɪ·'mʌnθ·li] **I.** *adj* (*twice a month*) quincenal; (*every two months*) bimestral **II.** *adv* (*twice a month*) quincenalmente; (*once every two months*) bimestralmente

bin [bɪn] *n* trash **~** cubo *m* de basura, basurero *m* Méx

binary ['baɪ·nə·ri] *adj* binario, -a

binary code *n* código *m* binario

bind [baɪnd] **I.** *n inf* lío *m*; **to be in a ~** estar en un lío **II.** <bound, bound> *vi* unirse **III.** <bound, bound> *vt* **1.** (*tie together*) atar; (*book*) encuadernar **2.** (*unite*) unir **3.** (*commit*) vincular

binder ['baɪn·dər] *n* (*notebook*) carpeta *f*

binding ['baɪn·dɪŋ] *adj* vinculante

binge [bɪndʒ] *inf* **I.** *n* (*drink*) borrache-

ra f, vacilada f Méx; (food) comilona f;
to go on a ~ ir de parranda **II.** vi atiborrarse

bingo ['bɪŋ.goʊ] interj, n bingo m

binoculars [bɪ·'nak·jə·lərz] npl prismáticos mpl, binoculares mpl AmL

biochemistry [ˌbaɪ·oʊ·'kem·ɪ·stri] n bioquímica f

biodegradable [ˌbaɪ·oʊ·dɪ·'greɪ·də·bəl] adj biodegradable

biodiversity [ˌbaɪ·oʊ·dɪ·'vɜr·sə·t̬i] n biodiversidad f

bioengineering [ˌbaɪ·oʊ·en·dʒɪ·'nɪr·ɪŋ] n ingeniería f biológica

biography [baɪ·'ag·rə·fi] <-ies> n biografía f

biological [ˌbaɪ·ə·'ladʒ·ɪ·kəl] adj biológico, -a

biologist [baɪ·'al·ə·dʒɪst] n biólogo, -a m, f

biology [baɪ·'al·ə·dʒi] n biología f

biorhythm ['baɪ·oʊ·rið·əm] n biorritmo m

bird [bɜrd] n pájaro m; (larger) ave f; **a strange ~** inf un bicho raro ► **~s of a <u>feather</u> flock together** Dios los cría y ellos se juntan; **to kill two ~s with one <u>stone</u>** matar dos pájaros de un mismo tiro

bird bath n alberquilla f

birdcage n jaula f

bird flue n gripe f aviar

bird's-eye view n vista f panorámica

bird watching n observación f de aves

birth [bɜrθ] n nacimiento m, paritorio m Cuba, Ven; MED parto m; **by/ from/of ~** de nacimiento; **to give ~ to a child** dar a luz a un bebé

birth certificate n certificado m de nacimiento

birth control n control m de natalidad

birthday ['bɜrθ·deɪ] **I.** n cumpleaños m inv; **happy ~!** ¡feliz cumpleaños! **II.** adj de cumpleaños

birthrate n tasa f de natalidad

biscuit ['bɪs·kɪt] n bizcocho m

bisexual [ˌbaɪ·'sek·ʃʊ·əl] adj, n bisexual mf

bishop ['bɪʃ·əp] n obispo m; (chess) al-

fil m

bit[1] [bɪt] n **1.** (piece) trozo m; **little ~s** pedacitos mpl; **to smash sth to ~s** romper algo en pedazos **2.** (some) **a ~ of** un poco de; **a ~ of trouble** un problemilla; **a ~ stupid** un poco tonto; **quite a ~** bastante; **not a ~** en absoluto **3.** (part) parte f; **~ by ~** poco a poco; **to do one's ~** poner su granito de arena **4.** (short time) momentito m

bit[2] [bɪt] n COMPUT bit m

bit[3] [bɪt] pt of bite

bitch [bɪtʃ] **I.** n ZOOL perra f **II.** vi sl quejarse (**about** de)

bitchy ['bɪtʃ·i] adj sl con mala leche

bite [baɪt] **I.** <bit, bitten> vt, vi morder; (insect) picar; **to ~ one's nails/ lips** morderse las uñas/los labios **II.** n **1.** (dog) mordisco m; (insect) picadura f **2.** (mouthful) bocado m

biting ['baɪ·t̬ɪŋ] adj (wind) cortante; (criticism) mordaz

bitten ['bɪt·ən] pp of bite

bitter ['bɪt̬·ər] adj <-er, -est> **1.** (in taste) agrio, -a **2.** (painful) amargo, -a; **to be ~ about sth** estar amargado por algo **3.** (dispute) encarnizado, -a; (wind) cortante

bitterly adv **1.** (resentfully) con rencor **2.** (intensely) intensamente

bitterness n **1.** (animosity) amargura f; (resentment) resentimiento m (**towards** contra) **2.** (taste) amargor m

biweekly [ˌbaɪ·'wik·li] **I.** adj **1.** (every two weeks) quincenal **2.** (twice a week) bisemanal **II.** adv **1.** (every two weeks) quincenalmente **2.** (twice a week) bisemanalmente

bizarre [bɪ·'zar] adj extraño, -a; (clothes) estrafalario, -a

blab [blæb] <-bb-> vi inf **1.** (reveal secret) chivarse **2.** (talk too much) irse de la lengua

blabber ['blæb·ər] vi irse de la lengua

blabbermouth n chivato, -a m, f; (talkative) parlanchín, -ina m, f

black [blæk] **I.** adj **1.** (color) negro, -a; **~ man/woman** negro, -a m, f **2.** (dark) oscuro, -a **3.** (hands) mugriento, -a, mugroso, -a Méx ► **to beat sb ~ and blue** moler a alguien a palos **II.** vt en-

negrecer **III.** n **1.** negro m; **in ~** de negro; **in ~ and white** en blanco y negro **2.** (person) negro, -a m, f
♦**black out** vi desmayarse

blackberry ['blæk·ˌber·i] <-ies> n zarzamora f; (plant) zarza f

blackbird n mirlo m

blackboard n pizarra f

blacken ['blæk·ən] **I.** vt ennegrecer; (slander) desacreditar **II.** vi ennegrecerse

black hat n COMPUT sombrero m negro

blackhead ['blæk·hed] n espinilla f

black hole n agujero m negro

blackish ['blæk·ɪʃ] adj negruzco, -a

black light n luz f negra

blacklist ['blæk·lɪst] **I.** n lista f negra **II.** vt poner en la lista negra

blackmail ['blæk·meɪl] **I.** n chantaje m **II.** vt chantajear; **to ~ sb into doing sth** chantajear a alguien para que haga algo

blackmailer ['blæk·meɪ·lər] n chantajista mf

black mark n punto m en contra

black market n mercado m negro

black markete(e)r n estraperlista mf

blackness ['blæk·nɪs] n negrura f; (darkness) oscuridad f

blackout ['blæk·aʊt] n **1.** (faint) desmayo m; **to have a ~** sufrir un desmayo **2.** ELEC apagón m **3.** (censorship) bloqueo m; **news ~** bloqueo informativo

black sheep n oveja f negra

bladder ['blæd·ər] n vejiga f

blade [bleɪd] n (tool, weapon) hoja f; (grass) brizna f

blah [blɑ] inf **I.** adj pesado, -a **II.** interj bla

blame [bleɪm] **I.** vt culpar; **to ~ sb for sth, to ~ sth on sb** echar a alguien la culpa de algo; **to be to ~** tener la culpa (for de); **I don't ~ you** te comprendo **II.** n culpa f; **to lay the ~ for sth on sb** echar a alguien la culpa de algo

blameless ['bleɪm·lɪs] adj libre de culpa; (life) intachable

bland [blænd] adj (mild) suave; (dull) soso, -a

blank [blæŋk] **I.** adj **1.** (empty) en blanco; (look) inexpresivo, -a; **to go ~** quedarse en blanco **2.** (complete) absoluto, -a; (despair) completo, -a **II.** n

espacio m

blanket ['blæŋ·kɪt] **I.** n manta f, frisa f RDom, PRico, cobija f Méx; (snow) capa f **II.** vt cubrir (in con)

blasphemy ['blæs·fə·mi] n blasfemia f

blast [blæst] **I.** vt volar; (criticize) hacer polvo **II.** n **1.** (detonation) explosión f **2.** (wind) ráfaga f **3.** sl (party) juerga f, tambarria f AmC, AmS; **to have a ~** pasarlo bomba [or Méx padre] ▶ **(at) full ~** (volume) a todo volumen; (speed) a toda marcha

blasted adj inf maldito, -a

blastoff ['blæst·ɔf] n despegue m

blaze [bleɪz] **I.** vi brillar; (fire) arder; **to ~ with anger** echar chispas **II.** n (fire) fuego m; (flames, light) llamarada f

blazing ['bleɪ·zɪŋ] adj resplandeciente; (heat) abrasador(a); (fire) vivo, -a; **to have a ~ temper** tener muy mal carácter

bleach [blitʃ] **I.** vt blanquear **II.** n lejía f; (for hair) decolorante m

bleak [blik] adj (future) sombrío, -a; (weather) gris; (landscape) desolador(a)

bleary ['blɪr·i] adj <-ier, -iest> (person) cansado, -a; (eyes) lagañoso, -a

bleary-eyed adj to be ~ estar medio dormido

bleat [blit] **I.** vi balar; (complain) quejarse **II.** n balido m; (complaint) quejido m

bled [bled] pt, pp of **bleed**

bleed [blid] <bled, bled> **I.** vi sangrar; (color) destintar **II.** vt to ~ **sb dry** dejar seco a alguien

bleep [blip] **I.** n pitido m **II.** vi pitar **III.** vt censurar con pitidos

blemish ['blem·ɪʃ] **I.** n mancha f; **a reputation without ~** una reputación intachable **II.** vt manchar

blend [blend] **I.** n mezcla f **II.** vt mezclar **III.** vi armonizar; **to ~ in** no desentonar

blender ['blen·dər] n licuadora f

bless [bles] vt bendecir ▶ **(God) ~ you!** (sneeze) ¡Jesús!

blessed ['bles·ɪd] adj **1.** (holy) bendito, -a **2.** inf dichoso, -a; **the whole ~ day** todo el santo día

blessing ['bles·ɪŋ] n bendición f ▶ **it's**

a ~ in **disguise** no hay mal que por bien no venga

blew [blu] *pt of* **blow**

blimp [blɪmp] *n* zepelín *m*; (*obese*) obeso, -a *m, f*

blind [blaɪnd] I. *n* 1. the ~ los ciegos 2. (*window*) persiana *f* II. *vt* cegar III. *adj* ciego, -a; (*without knowledge*) a tientas; **to be ~ in one eye** ser tuerto; **to be ~ to sth** no (querer) ver algo IV. *adv* a ciegas; **to be ~ drunk** estar más borracho que una cuba

blind date *n* cita *f* a ciegas

blindfold ['blaɪnd·foʊld] I. *n* venda *f* II. *vt* vendar los ojos a III. *adj* con los ojos vendados

blinding *adj* (*light*) cegador(a); (*color*) deslumbrante

blindman's buff *n* gallina *f* ciega

blindness *n* ceguera *f*

blind spot *n* punto *m* ciego

bling [blɪŋ] *sl* I. *n* joyas *f pl* llamativas y ostentosas II. *adj pred* (*look, outfit*) recargado, -a; (*person*) emperifollado, -a

blink [blɪŋk] I. *vt, vi* **to ~ (one's eyes)** parpadear; **she didn't even ~** ni se inmutó II. *n* parpadeo *m* ▸ **in the ~ of an eye** en un abrir y cerrar de ojos

blinker ['blɪŋ·kər] *n* AUTO intermitente *m*, direccional *f Col, Méx*; **to turn on the ~** poner el intermitente

blissful ['blɪs·fəl] *adj* feliz

blister ['blɪs·tər] *n* burbuja *f*; ANAT ampolla *f*

blizzard ['blɪz·ərd] *n* ventisca *f*

blob [blab] *n* goterón *m*

block [blak] I. *n* (*solid lump, building*) a. COMPUT bloque *m*; (*group of buildings*) manzana *f*, cuadra *f AmL*; (*barrier*) a. SPORTS bloqueo *m* II. *vt* 1. (*road, pipe*) bloquear; (*progress*) obstaculizar 2. COMPUT **to ~ and copy** seleccionar y copiar

◆**block off** *vt* cortar

◆**block out** *vt* (*name*) suprimir; (*memory*) borrar

◆**block up** I. *vt* tapar II. *vi* atascarse, atorozarse *AmC*; MED taponarse

blockade [bla·'keɪd] I. *n* bloqueo *m* II. *vt* bloquear; (*block off*) cortar

blockage ['blak·ɪdʒ] *n* obstrucción *f*

block letters *n* letras *f pl* mayúsculas de imprenta

blond(e) [bland] *adj, n* rubio, -a *m, f*, güero, -a *m, f Méx, Guat, Ven*

blood [blʌd] *n* sangre *f* ▸ **to have ~ on one's hands** tener las manos manchadas de sangre; **bad ~** mala sangre; **in cold ~** a sangre fría; **her ~ ran cold** se le heló la sangre; **it makes my ~ boil** hace que me hierva la sangre; **to sweat ~** sudar tinta

blood clot *n* coágulo *m* de sangre

blood donor *n* donante *mf* de sangre

blood group *n* grupo *m* sanguíneo

blood pressure *n* tensión *f* arterial

bloodshed *n* derramamiento *m* de sangre

bloodshot ['blʌd·ʃat] *adj* (*eyes*) rojo, -a

bloodstained ['blʌd·steɪnd] *adj* manchado, -a de sangre

blood test *n* análisis *m inv* de sangre

bloodthirsty ['blʌd·θɜr·sti] *adj* sanguinario, -a

blood transfusion *n* transfusión *f* de sangre

bloody ['blʌd·i] <-ier, -iest> *adj* ensangrentado, -a; (*battle*) sangriento, -a

bloom [blum] I. *n* flor *f* II. *vi* florecer

blooming ['blu·mɪŋ] *adj* floreciente

blossom ['blas·əm] I. *n* flor *f*; **in ~** en flor; **orange ~** azahar *m* II. *vi* florecer; (*mature*) madurar

blot [blat] I. *n* borrón *m*; (*reputation*) mancha *f* II. *vt* emborronar; (*dry*) secar

blouse [blaʊs] *n* blusa *f*

blow¹ [bloʊ] *n* golpe *m*, zuque *m Col*

blow² [bloʊ] I. <blew, blown> *vi* soplar; (*tire*) reventar II. *vt* 1. MUS tocar 2. **to ~ one's nose** sonarse la nariz 3. (*tire*) reventar 4. *sl* (*spend*) pulirse 5. (*mess up*) echar a perder ▸ *inf* **it blew my mind!** ¡me dejó de piedra!; **to ~ one's top** [*or* **lid**] salirse de sus casillas

◆**blow away** *vt* (*wind*) arrancar

◆**blow down** *vt* derribar

◆**blow out** I. *vt* apagar II. *vi* apagarse

◆**blow up** I. *vt* (*storm*) levantarse; (*bomb*) explotar II. *vt* (*balloon*) inflar

blow-by-blow *adj* **a ~ account** una descripción con todo lujo de detalles

blow-dry *vt* secar con secador

blow dryer n secador m [or Méx secadora f] (de pelo)

blowgun n cerbatana f

blown [bloʊn] vt, pp of **blow**

blowout n 1. (tire) pinchazo m 2. sl fiestón m, pachangón m Méx inf, rumba f Col inf

blowup n PHOT ampliación f

blubber ['blʌb·ər] vi lloriquear

blue [blu] I. adj 1. azul; light/dark/pale/deep ~ azul claro/oscuro/pálido/intenso 2. (sad) triste II. n azul m; sky ~ azul cielo; the door is painted ~ la puerta está pintada de azul ► out of the ~ cuando menos se espera

blueberry ['blu·ber·i] <-ies> n arándano m

bluff [blʌf] I. vi tirarse un farol II. vt engañar III. n 1. farol m, bluff m AmL 2. (cliff) acantilado m IV. <-er, -est> adj campechano, -a

bluish ['blu·ɪʃ] adj azulado, -a

blunder ['blʌn·dər] I. n error m garrafal, embarrada f AmL II. vi cometer un error garrafal; to ~ into sth tropezar con algo

blunt [blʌnt] adj 1. (not sharp) desafilado, -a, pompo, -a Ecua, Col 2. (direct) directo, -a

bluntly adv sin rodeos

blur [blɜr] I. vi <-rr-> desdibujarse II. vt <-rr-> desdibujar; (picture) desenfocar III. n (memory) vago recuerdo m

blurb [blɜrb] n propaganda f

blurred [blɜrd] adj borroso, -a

blush [blʌʃ] I. vi ruborizarse II. n rubor m; (makeup) colorete m

boar [bɔr] n cerdo m; (wild) ~ jabalí m

board [bɔrd] I. n 1. (wood) tabla f 2. (blackboard) pizarra f; (notice board) a. GAMES tablero m 3. ADMIN junta f; ~ of trade Cámara f de Comercio 4. room and ~ pensión f completa 5. on ~ a bordo ► to **take** sth on ~ adoptar algo II. vt (ship, plane) subir a bordo de; (bus, train) subir a III. vi (stay) alojarse; (in school) estar interno

♦ **board up** vt entablar

boarder ['bɔr·dər] n huésped mf; (at a school) interno, -a m, f

board game n juego m de mesa

boarding house n pensión f

boarding pass n tarjeta f de embarque

boarding school n internado m

boardroom n sala f de juntas

boast [boʊst] I. vi alardear II. vt enorgullecerse de; this house ~s 10 rooms esta casa cuenta con 10 habitaciones III. n alarde m

boastful ['boʊst·fəl] adj fanfarrón, -ona, bocatero, -a AmL

boat [boʊt] n barco m; (small) barca f; (large) buque m; to go by ~ ir en barco ► to be in the **same** ~ estar en la misma situación; to **miss** the ~ perder la oportunidad

boathouse n cobertizo m

bob [bab] <-bb-> I. vi to ~ (up and down) agitarse II. n (movement) meneo m

bobby pin n horquilla f, pinza f Col

body ['bad·i] <-ies> n 1. ANAT, ASTR, CHEM cuerpo m; (dead) cadáver m; fig (person) 2. ADMIN, POL unidad f; (governing) organismo m 3. (amount) cantidad f 4. AUTO carrocería f ► to **keep** ~ and **soul** together sobrevivir; to throw oneself ~ and **soul** into sth entregarse a algo en cuerpo y alma; **over my dead** ~ ¡por encima de mi cadáver!; to **sell** one's ~ prostituirse

bodybuilding n culturismo m

bodyguard n guardaespaldas mf inv, espaldero, -a m, f Ven

body language n lenguaje m corporal

body lotion n loción f corporal

body suit n body m

bog [bag] n ciénaga f

♦ **bog down** <-gg-> vt to get bogged down in sth atrancarse en algo

boggle ['bag·əl] I. vi quedarse atónito II. vt to ~ the mind ser increíble

boggy ['bag·i] <-ier, -iest> adj pantanoso, -a

bohemian [boʊ·'hi·mi·ən] adj, n bohemio, -a m, f

boil [bɔɪl] I. vi, vt hervir; a hard/soft ~ed egg un huevo duro/pasado por agua II. n to bring sth to a ~ calentar algo hasta que hierva; to be at a ~ estar hirviendo

◆**boil away** *vi* evaporarse

◆**boil down** I. *vi* **it all boils down to...** todo se reduce a... II. *vt* reducir

◆**boil over** *vi* 1. CULIN irse 2. (*person*) perder el control; (*situation*) estallar

◆**boil up** *vt* hervir

boiler ['bɔɪ·lər] *n* caldera *f*

boiling *adj* hirviendo; (*day, weather*) abrasador(a); **I am ~** me estoy asando; **to be ~ (mad)** estar que echa chispas

boisterous ['bɔɪ·stər·əs] *adj* bullicioso, -a; (*sea*) enfurecido, -a

bold [boʊld] <-er, -est> *adj* 1. (*brave*) audaz; (*color*) llamativo, -a 2. (*not shy*) atrevido, -a; (*cheeky*) descarado, -a 3. **in ~** en negrita

boldness *n* audacia *f*

bole [boʊl] *n* (*tree*) tronco *m*

Bolivia [bə·'lɪv·i·ə] *n* Bolivia *f*

Bolivian [bə·'lɪv·i·ən] *adj, n* boliviano, -a *m, f*

bolt [boʊlt] I. *vi* huir II. *vt* 1. (*lock*) cerrar con pestillo 2. (*fasten down*) atornillar III. *n* 1. (*on a door*) pestillo *m* 2. (*screw*) tornillo *m* 3. (*of lightning*) rayo *m* ▶ **to make a ~ for it** correr hacia algo IV. *adv* **~ upright** rígido

◆**bolt down** *vt* (*food*) engullir

bomb [bam] I. *n* 1. (*aerosol*) bomba *f*; (*aerosol*) aerosol *m* 2. *sl* (*failure*) fiasco *m* II. *vt* bombardear

bomb crater *n* cráter *m* de bomba

bombing *n* atentado *m* con bomba; MIL bombardeo *m*

bombproof *adj* a prueba de bombas

bomb scare *n* alerta *f* de bomba

bombshell ['bam·ʃel] *n* obús *m*; (*surprise*) bombazo *m* *inf*

bond [band] I. *n* 1. (*connection*) vínculo *m*; (*friendship, love*) lazo *m* 2. (*obligation*) obligación *f*; **to break one's ~** romper sus cadenas 3. FIN bono *m* II. *vt* 1. (*stick*) pegar 2. **to ~ (together)** vincular III. *vi* adherirse

bone [boʊn] I. *n* hueso *m*; (*of a fish*) espina *f* ▶ **~ of contention** manzana de la discordia; **to feel sth in one's ~s** tener un presentimiento de algo II. *adj* óseo III. *adv* muy IV. *vt* deshuesar; (*fish*) quitar las espinas a

◆**bone up for** *vt* (*exam*) empollar

bonfire ['ban·faɪr] *n* hoguera *f*

bonk [baŋk] *inf* I. *vt* (*hit on head*) dar un golpe en la cabeza II. *n* golpe *m* en la cabeza

bonnet ['ban·ɪt] *n* gorrito *m*

bonus ['boʊ·nəs] I. *n* 1. (*money*) prima *f*, abono *m AmL*; (*for Christmas*) paga *f* extraordinaria; **productivity ~** plus *m* 2. (*advantage*) ventaja *f* II. *adj* de regalo

bony ['boʊ·ni] *adj* <-ier, -iest> huesudo, -a; (*fish*) con muchas espinas

boo [bu] I. *interj inf* bu II. *vi, vt* abuchear, pifiar *Chile, Méx*

boob tube *n sl* caja *f* tonta

booger ['bʊg·ər] *n* *sl* 1. (*dried mucus*) moco *m* seco 2. (*person*) desgraciado, -a *m, f*

book [bʊk] I. *n* libro *m*; **the ~s** COM, FIN las cuentas ▶ **to be a closed ~** ser un misterio (**to para**) II. *vt* 1. (*reserve*) reservar 2. (*register*) fichar III. *vi* reservar

◆**book up** *vt* **~ed up** completo

bookie ['bʊk·i] *n inf* corredor(a) *m(f)* de apuestas

booking ['bʊk·ɪŋ] *n* reserva *f*; **to make/cancel a ~** hacer/cancelar una reserva

bookkeeper *n* contable *mf*

bookkeeping *n* contabilidad *f*

booklet ['bʊk·lɪt] *n* folleto *m*

bookmaker *n* corredor(a) *m(f)* de apuestas

bookmark *n* marcador *m*

bookseller *n* librero, -a *m, f*; (*shop*) librería *f*

bookshelf <-shelves> *n* estante *m*

bookshop, bookstore *n* librería *f*

boom¹ [bum] ECON I. *vi* estar en auge II. *n* boom *m* III. *adj* en alza; (*time, town*) próspero, -a

boom² [bum] I. *n* (*sound*) estruendo *m* II. *vi, vt* **to ~ (out)** tronar

boom box *n* minicadena *f*, grabadora *f Méx, Col*

boomerang ['bu·mə·ræŋ] I. *n* bumerán *m* II. *vi* **it ~ed on her/him** le salió el tiro por la culata

boondocks *n pl* **the ~** la conchinchina,

la chingada *Méx*

boost [bust] I. *n* 1. (*lift*) to give sb a ~ subir a alguien 2. (*increase*) impulso *m* II. *vt* 1. subir; (*process*) estimular 2. *inf* (*promote*) promover

boot [but] I. *n* 1. (*dismissal*) bota *f;* **ankle** ~ botín *m* 2. *inf* (*kick*) puntapié *m* 3. (*dismissal*) to get the ~ estar despedido; to give sb the ~ echar a alguien 4. COMPUT arranque *m* ▶ to be too **big** for one's ~s tener muchos humos; to **lick** sb's ~s hacer la pelota a alguien II. *vt* 1. (*kick*) dar un puntapié a 2. *sl* (*fire*) echar 3. COMPUT arrancar ▶ **to** ~ por si fuera poco

◆**boot out** *vt* poner de patitas en la calle

boot-cut *adj* de campana

booth [buð] *n* cabina *f;* (*fair, market*) caseta *f*

bootlace ['but·leɪs] *n* cordón *m*

bootleg ['but·leg] <-gg-> *adj* de contrabando; (*recording, software*) pirata

booze [buz] *sl* I. *n* bebida *f* alcohólica; **to be on the** ~ darle al trago II. *vi* empinar el codo, chupar *AmL*

boozer ['bu·zər] *n sl* borrachín, -ina *m, f*

border ['bɔr·dər] I. *n* 1. POL frontera *f* 2. (*edge*) borde *m* 3. (*in a garden*) arriate *m* II. *adj* fronterizo, -a III. *vt* limitar con

◆**border on** *vt* limitar con; *fig* rayar en

bordering *adj* limítrofe

borderland ['bɔr·dər·lænd] *n* zona *f* fronteriza

borderline ['bɔr·dər·laɪn] I. *n* frontera *f* II. *adj* dudoso, -a

bore¹ [bɔr] I. *n* 1. (*thing*) aburrimiento *m;* (*task*) lata *f;* **what a** ~! ¡qué lata! 2. (*person*) pesado, -a *m, f* II. <bored> *vt* aburrir

bore² [bɔr] *pp of* **bear**

bored *adj* aburrido, -a

boredom ['bɔr·dəm] *n* aburrimiento *m*

boring ['bɔr·ɪŋ] *adj* aburrido, -a, cansador(a) *Arg, Chile, Urug*

born [bɔrn] *adj* 1. nacido, -a; **to be** ~ nacer; **where were you** ~? ¿dónde naciste? 2. (*ability*) nato, -a; (*quality, sympathy*) innato, -a ▶ **I wasn't** ~

yesterday no nací ayer

borne [bɔrn] *pt of* **bear**

borough ['bɜr·oʊ] *n* municipio *m*

borrow ['bar·oʊ] *vt* 1. tomar prestado; (*ask for*) pedir prestado; **may I** ~ **your bag?** ¿me prestas tu bolso? 2. MATH llevarse 3. LING tomar

boss [bas] I. *n* jefe, -a *m, f;* (*bossy person*) mandón, -ona *m, f* II. *vt inf* **to** ~ **around** mandonear

bossy ['ba·si] <-ier, -iest> *adj* mandón, -ona

botanical [bə·'tæn·ɪ·kəl] *adj* botánico, -a

botany ['bat·ən·i] *n* botánica *f*

botch [batʃ] I. *n* chapuza *f* II. *vt* hacer una chapuza con

both [boʊθ] I. *adj, pron* ~ (*of them*) los dos, las dos, ambos, ambas; ~ **of us** nosotros dos II. *adv* ~ **Cathy and Julie** tanto Cathy como Julie; **to be** ~ **sad and pleased** estar a la vez triste y satisfecho

bother ['bað·ər] I. *n* molestia *f,* friega *f AmL;* **it is not worth the** ~ no vale la pena II. *vi* molestarse; **to** (**not**) ~ **to do sth** (no) molestarse en hacer algo; **why** ~? ¿para qué molestarse? III. *vt* 1. (*annoy*) molestar; (*body part*) doler 2. (*worry*) preocupar; **he doesn't seem to be** ~**ed by...** no parece que le preocupe...

bothersome ['bað·ər·səm] *adj* molesto, -a, tequioso, -a *AmC*, espeso, -a *Perú, Ven*

bottle ['bat̬·əl] I. *n* 1. botella *f;* (*ink, perfume*) frasco *m;* (*baby's*) biberón *m* 2. *inf* **the** ~ la bebida; **to hit the** ~ empinar el codo II. *vt* embotellar; (*emotions*) reprimir

bottled ['bat̬·əld] *adj* embotellado, -a

bottle green *adj* verde botella

bottleneck ['bat̬·əl·nek] I. *n* cuello *m* de botella II. *vi* embotellarse, trancarse *Col*

bottle opener *n* abrebotellas *m inv*

bottom ['bat̬·əm] *n* 1. (*sea, street, glass*) fondo *m;* (*chair*) asiento *m;* (*stairs, page*) pie *m;* **to touch** ~ hacer pie; *fig* tocar fondo 2. (*lower part*) parte *f* inferior; **from top to** ~ de arriba (a) abajo

3. (*buttocks*) trasero *m* ▶ **from the ~ of one's heart** de todo corazón; **~s up!** ¡al centro y pa'dentro! *inf*; **to get to the ~ of sth** llegar al fondo de algo

bottomless ['bɑt̬·əm·lɪs] *adj* 1. (*without limit*) infinito, -a 2. (*very deep*) sin fondo; **a ~ pit** *fig* un pozo sin fondo

bought [bɔt] *vt pt of* **buy**

boulder ['boʊl·dər] *n* roca *f*

boulevard ['bʊl·ə·vɑrd] *n* bulevar *m*

bounce [baʊnts] **I.** *vi, vt* rebotar; (*jump*) dar saltos **II.** *n* 1. bote *m*; **to give sb the ~** poner a alguien de patitas en la calle 2. (*vitality*) vitalidad *f*

◆**bounce back** *vi* recuperarse

bouncer ['baʊn·tsər] *n sl* gorila *m*

bouncing *adj* robusto, -a

bound¹ [baʊnd] **I.** *vi* 1. (*leap*) saltar 2. (*bounce: ball*) rebotar *AmL* **II.** *n* salto *m*; **with one ~** de un salto

bound² [baʊnd] *vt* **to be ~ed by sth** estar rodeado por algo

bound³ [baʊnd] *adj* **to be ~ for** ir rumbo a; **north/south-bound traffic** tráfico que va hacia el norte/sur

bound⁴ [baʊnd] **I.** *pt, pp of* **bind II.** *adj* **she's ~ to come** seguro que viene; **to be ~ to do sth** estar obligado a hacer algo; **it was ~ to happen sooner or later** tarde o temprano tenía que suceder

boundary ['baʊn·dri] <-ies> *n* (*line*) a. *fig* límite *m*; (*border*) frontera *f*

boundless ['baʊnd·lɪs] *adj* (*love, patience*) sin límites; (*energy*) inagotable; (*universe*) infinito, -a

bounty ['baʊn·t̬i] <-ies> *n* 1. (*reward*) recompensa *f* 2. (*gift*) regalo *m*

bouquet [boʊ·'keɪ] *n* (*flowers*) ramo *m*

bout [baʊt] *n* 1. SPORTS combate *m*; (*fencing*) asalto *m* 2. (*illness, coughing*) ataque *m*

boutique [bu·'tik] *n* boutique *f*

bovine ['boʊ·vaɪn] *adj* (*of cows*) bovino, -a

bow¹ [boʊ] *n* arco *m*; (*knot*) lazo *m*, moño *m* *AmL*

bow² [baʊ] *n* NAUT proa *f*

bow³ [baʊ] **I.** *vi* hacer una reverencia (**to** ante); *fig* ceder; **to ~ to sth** someterse a algo ▶ **to ~ and scrape** hacer la pelo-

ta [*or Méx* barba] **II.** *vt* (*head*) agachar **III.** *n* reverencia *f*, venia *f* *CSur, Col*, caravana *f* *Méx*

◆**bow out** *vi* retirarse

bowel ['baʊ·əl] *n* MED intestino *m* grueso

bowl¹ [boʊl] *n* 1. (*dish*) cuenco *m*; **fruit/ salad ~** frutero/ensaladera *f* 2. (*of toilet*) taza *f*; (*for washing*) palangana *f* 3. (*stadium*) estadio *m*

bowl² [boʊl] SPORTS **I.** *vi* jugar a los bolos; (*throw*) lanzar la bola **II.** *vt* lanzar **III.** *n* bola *f*

bow-legged [ˌboʊ·'legd] *adj* (*person*) patizambo, -a, cascorvo, -a *Col*

bowling *n* bolos *mpl*

bowling alley *n* bolera *f*

bowling ball *n* bola *f* de bolos

bow tie *n* pajarita *f*, corbatín *m* *Col*, moñita *f* *Urug*

box¹ [baks] **I.** *vi* boxear **II.** *vt* SPORTS boxear con [*or* contra] **III.** *n* sopapo *m*

box² [baks] **I.** *n* 1. (*container*) caja *f*; **tool ~** caja de herramientas 2. (*rectangular space*) casilla *f*; **dialog ~** cuadro de diálogo 3. *pej* (*small space*) agujero *m* 4. THEAT palco *m*; (*booth*) cabina *f* 5. (*TV*) **the ~** la caja tonta 6. (*mailbox*) buzón *m* ▶ **to think outside of the ~** tener ideas innovadoras **II.** *vt* poner en una caja

◆**box in** *vt* cerrar el paso a

◆**box up** *vt* poner en una caja

boxer ['bak·sər] *n* boxeador(a) *m(f)*; (*dog*) bóxer *mf*

boxer shorts *npl* bóxer *m*

boxing ['bak·sɪŋ] *n* boxeo *m*, box *m* *AmL*

boxing match *n* combate *m* de boxeo

boxing ring *n* cuadrilátero *m*

box lunch *n* comida *f* en una fiambrera [*or* en una lonchera *f* *Col, Méx*]

box office *n* taquilla *f*, boletería *f* *AmL*

boy [bɔɪ] **I.** *n* (*child*) niño *m*; (*young man*) chico *m*, muchacho *m*, chamaco, -a *m, f* *Méx*, pibe *m* *Arg*, (*boyfriend*) novio *m* ▶ **the old ~ network** el amiguismo, la rosca *Col*; **~s will be ~s** así son los niños **II.** *interj* (**oh**) **~!** ¡vaya!

boycott ['bɔɪ·kat] **I.** *vt* boicotear **II.** *n* boicot *m*

boyfriend ['bɔɪ·frend] *n* novio *m*

bra [bra] *n* sujetador *m*, brasier *m* *Col*,

Méx, corpiño *m RíoPl*

brace [breɪs] **I.** *vt* to ~ oneself for sth prepararse para algo **II.** *n* **1.** ~s *(for teeth, back)* aparato *m* **2.** *(clamp)* abrazadera *f* **3.** TYPO llave *f*

bracelet ['breɪs·lɪt] *n* pulsera *f*

bracket ['bræk·ɪt] **I.** *n* **1.** TYPO paréntesis *m inv;* **angle** ~ corchete *m;* **curly** ~ llave *f;* **in** ~s entre paréntesis **2.** *(category)* categoría *f* **II.** *vt* agrupar; TYPO poner entre paréntesis

brag [bræg] <-gg-> **I.** *vi* fardar *(about* de) **II.** *vt* to ~ that... jactarse de que... **III.** *n* chulería *f;* *(person)* fanfarrón, -ona *m, f*

Braille [breɪl] *n* braille *m*

brain [breɪn] *n* **1.** cerebro *m;* ~s sesos *mpl* **2.** *(intelligence)* cabeza *f* **3.** *inf (genius)* lumbrera *f* ► **to have sth on the** ~ tener algo metido en la cabeza; **to rack one's** ~ devanarse los sesos

brain trust *n* grupo *m* de peritos

brainwashing ['breɪn·wɑʃ·ɪŋ] *n* lavado *m* de cerebro

brainwave ['breɪn·weɪv] *n* onda *f* cerebral; *fig* idea *f* genial, lamparazo *m Col*

brainy ['breɪ·ni] <-ier, -iest> *adj* inteligente

brake [breɪk] **I.** *n* freno *m;* **to put on the** ~s frenar; **to put a** ~ **on sth** poner freno a algo **II.** *vi* frenar

braking *n* frenado *m*

bran [bræn] *n* salvado *m*

branch [bræntʃ] **I.** *n* **a.** *fig* rama *f;* *(river, road)* ramal *m;* *(company, library)* sucursal *f;* *(union, government department)* delegación *f* **II.** *vi* echar ramas; *(river, road)* bifurcarse

♦ **branch off** *vi* bifurcarse; **to ~ from a subject** salirse de un tema

♦ **branch out** *vi* diversificarse; **to ~ on one's own** establecerse por su cuenta

branch office *n* sucursal *f*

brand [brænd] **I.** *n* **1.** COM marca *f* **2.** *fig* clase *f* **3.** *(mark)* hierro *m* **II.** *vt* **1.** *(label)* tachar *((as)* de) **2.** *(cattle)* marcar

brand-new *adj* nuevo, -a flamante; ~ **baby** recién nacido

brandy ['bræn·di] <-ies> *n* brandy *m;* **French** ~ coñac *m*

brash [bræʃ] *adj (attitude)* chulo, -a; *(col-*

ors) chillón, -ona

brass [bræs] *n* latón *m*

brass band *n* banda *f* de música, orfeón *m Chile*

brat [bræt] *n inf* mocoso, -a *m, f;* **he is a spoiled** ~ es un niño mimado, es un sute *Col, Ven*

brave [breɪv] **I.** *adj* valiente **II.** *vt* afrontar

bravery ['breɪ·və·ri] *n* valentía *f*

brawl [brɔl] **I.** *n* pelea *f,* bulla *f AmL* **II.** *vi* pelearse

brawling *n* alboroto *m*

bray [breɪ] **I.** *vi* rebuznar; ~**ing laugh** risa estridente **II.** *n* rebuzno *m*

brazen ['breɪ·zən] *adj* descarado, -a

Brazil [brə·'zɪl] *n* Brasil *m*

Brazilian [brə·'zɪl·jən] *adj, n* brasileño, -a *m, f*

breach [britʃ] **I.** *n* **1.** *(infraction)* infracción *f;* *(contract, promise, agreement)* incumplimiento *m;* *(confidence)* abuso *m* **2.** *(opening)* brecha *f* **II.** *vt (law)* infringir; *(contract, promise, agreement)* incumplir; *(security)* poner en peligro

bread [bred] **I.** *n* **1.** pan *m;* **a loaf of** ~ una barra de pan **2.** *sl (money)* pasta *f* **II.** *vt* empanar

bread and butter *n* sustento *m*

breadbasket, breadbox *n* panera *f*

breadcrumb *n* miga *f* (de pan); ~s pan *m* rallado

breadth [bredθ] *n* **1.** anchura *f;* **to be 5 feet in** ~ tener 5 pies de ancho **2.** *fig* amplitud *f*

break [breɪk] **I.** *n* **1.** *(crack, gap)* grieta *f* **2.** *(escape)* fuga *f;* **to make a** ~ correr *(for/towards* hacia) **3.** *(interruption)* interrupción *f;* *(commercial)* pausa *f* **4.** *(rest period)* descanso *m;* **coffee/lunch** ~ pausa *f* del café/para comer **5.** *(vacation)* vacaciones *fpl* **6.** *(divergence)* ruptura *f;* **a** ~ **from sth** un descanso de algo ► **to make a clean** ~ cortar por lo sano; **give me a** ~! ¡déjame en paz! **II.** <broke, broken> *vt* **1.** romper; **to** ~ **(in)to pieces** hacer añicos; *(circuit)* cortar; *(strike)* poner fin a; *(habit)* dejar; *(agreement)* incumplir; *(date)* no acudir a; *(code)* descifrar; *(bill)* cambiar **2.** *(tell)* decir;

to ~ **the news to sb** dar la noticia a alguien III. <broke, broken> vi 1. romperse; **to ~ into pieces** hacerse añicos; (wave) romper; (fever) bajar; (weather) cambiar 2. (interrupt) **shall we ~ for lunch?** ¿paramos para comer? ▶ **to ~ even** salir sin ganar ni perder; **to ~ free** liberarse; **to ~ loose** soltarse

◆ **break away** vi desprenderse; (faction, region) escindirse

◆ **break down** I. vi 1. (stop working) averiarse 2. (marriage) romperse; (negotiations) fracasar 3. (physically, psychologically) derrumbarse 4. CHEM descomponerse II. vt (door) echar abajo; (opposition, resistance) acabar con; (process) dividir

◆ **break in** vi 1. (burglar) entrar a robar 2. (interrupt) **to ~ (on)** interrumpir

◆ **break into** vi (car) entrar a robar; (business) introducirse en; **to ~ laughter/tears** echarse a reír/llorar

◆ **break off** I. vt partir; (relationship) romper II. vi 1. (become detached) desprenderse 2. (stop speaking) callarse

◆ **break out** vi escaparse; (prison) fugarse; (war, storm, laughing) estallar; **he broke out in spots** se salieron granos

◆ **break through** I. vi penetrar; (sun) salir II. vt atravesar; **to ~ the crowd** abrirse paso entre la multitud

◆ **break up** I. vt (meeting, strike) terminar; (coalition, union) disolver; (family) separar; (gang, cartel) desarticular; **break it up!** inf ¡basta ya!; **to break sb up** hacer reír a alguien II. vi separarse; (marriage) fracasar; (meeting) terminar

breakable ['breɪ·kə·bəl] adj frágil

breakage ['breɪ·kɪdʒ] n roturas fpl

breakaway ['breɪk·ə·weɪ] adj POL disidente

breakdown ['breɪk·daʊn] n 1. (collapse) ruptura f 2. TECH avería f 3. **give me a ~ of the situation** detállame la situación 4. (decomposition) descomposición f 5. (nervous) ~ crisis f inv nerviosa

breakfast ['brek·fəst] n desayuno m; **to have ~** desayunar

breaking point n límite m; **to reach the ~** llegar al límite

breakneck ['breɪk·nek] adj vertiginoso, -a

to ~ **the news to sb** dar la noticia a alguien III. <broke, broken> vi 1. romperse; **to ~ into pieces** hacerse añicos;

breakthrough ['breɪk·θru] n adelanto m

breakup ['breɪk·ʌp] n desintegración f; (family) separación f; (group, empire) disolución f; (talks) fracaso m

breast [brest] n pecho m; CULIN pechuga f

breastfeed ['brest·fid] vt amamantar

breath [breθ] n aliento m; **to be out of ~** estar sin aliento; **to be short of ~** ahogarse; **to hold one's ~** contener la respiración; **to take a deep ~** respirar hondo; **to go out for a ~ of fresh air** salir para que le dé a uno el aire ▶ **to take sb's ~ away** dejar a alguien sin habla

breathalyze ['breθ·ə·laɪz] vt hacer la prueba de la alcoholemia a

Breathalyzer® n alcoholímetro m

breathe [brið] vi, vt respirar; **to ~ again** [or **easily**] respirar tranquilo

breather ['bri·ðər] n respiro m

breathing n respiración f

breathless ['breθ·lɪs] adj sin aliento

breathtaking adj imponente

bred [bred] pt, pp of **breed**

breed [brid] I. vt <bred, bred> criar; (disease, violence) engendrar II. vi <bred, bred> reproducirse; (violence) generarse III. n tipo m; ZOOL raza f; BOT variedad f

breeding n educación f; ZOOL cría f

breeze [briz] n (wind) brisa f; **to be a ~** ser pan comido, ser un bollo RíoPl ▶ **to shoot the ~** estar de palique

brew [bru] I. n inf (beer) birra f II. vi 1. (beer) fermentar 2. (tea) reposar; **to let the tea ~** dejar reposar el té 3. (storm, trouble) avecinarse; **there's something ~ing** se está cociendo algo III. vt (beer) elaborar; (tea) hacer

brewery ['bru·ə·ri] n (company) cervecería f, cervecera f Méx; (place) fábrica f de cerveza

brewski ['bru·ski] <-ies or -s> n sl birra f, bironga f Méx

bribe [braɪb] I. vt sobornar; **to ~ sb into doing sth** sobornar a alguien para que haga algo II. n soborno m

bribery ['braɪ·bə·ri] n soborno m, coima f Perú, CSur, mordida f Méx

brick [brɪk] n ladrillo m

◆ **brick in** vt tapiar

bricklayer *n* albañil *mf*

bridal shower *n* despedida *f* de soltera

bride [braɪd] *n* novia *f*

bridegroom ['braɪd-ˌgrum] *n* novio *m*

bridesmaid ['braɪdz-ˌmeɪd] *n* dama *f* de honor

bridge [brɪdʒ] *n* ARCHIT, MED, MUS puente *m*; GAMES bridge *m*

bridge loan *n* crédito *m* puente

brief [brif] **I.** *adj* (*short*) breve; (*concise*) conciso, -a; **be ~!** ¡sé breve!; **in ~** en resumen **II.** *n* (*instructions*) instrucciones *fpl* **III.** *vt* informar; (*instructions*) dar instrucciones a

briefcase ['brif-keɪs] *n* maletín *m*

briefing *n* **1.** (*instructions*) instrucciones *fpl* **2.** (*session*) reunión *f* informativa; (*for reporters*) rueda *f* de prensa

briefly *adv* (*for short time*) por poco tiempo; (*concisely*) brevemente; **~,...** en resumen,...

briefness *n* brevedad *f*

brigade [brɪ-ˈgeɪd] *n* brigada *f*

bright [braɪt] **I.** *adj* (*light, idea, person*) brillante; (*room*) con mucha luz; (*day*) soleado; (*future*) prometedor(a); (*color*) vivo, -a, fuerte; **to go ~ red** ponerse rojo como un tomate ▶ **to look on the ~ side** of sth mirar [*or* ver] el lado bueno de algo **II.** *n* **~s** AUTO largas *fpl*, altas *fpl* And

brighten (up) ['braɪt-ən (ʌp)] **I.** *vt* iluminar; (*become cheerful*) animar **II.** *vi* hacerse más brillante; (*become cheerful*) animarse; (*eyes, face*) iluminarse; (*future, weather*) mejorar

brightness *n* (*lightness*) brillo *m*

brilliance ['brɪl-jəns] *n* **1.** (*cleverness*) brillantez *f* **2.** (*brightness*) resplandor *m*

brilliant ['brɪl-jənt] *adj* **1.** (*color, idea, person*) brillante; (*sunlight, smile*) radiante; (*water*) resplandeciente **2.** *inf* (*excellent*) fantástico, -a

brim [brɪm] **I.** *n* borde *m*; **to fill sth to the ~** llenar algo hasta el borde **II.** *vi* <-mm-> **to ~ with happiness/energy** rebosar de felicidad/energía

♦ **brim over** *vi a. fig* rebosar

brimful [ˌbrɪm-ˈfʊl] *adj* repleto, -a; (*life, confidence*) rebosante

brine [braɪn] *n* CULIN salmuera *f*

bring [brɪŋ] <brought, brought> *vt* **1.** (*come with, cause*) traer; **to ~ sb in** hacer pasar a alguien; **to ~ sth in** meter algo; **to ~ poverty/fame to a town** traer pobreza/fama a un pueblo; **to ~ sb luck** traer suerte a alguien; **to ~ oneself to do sth** obligarse a hacer algo **2.** (*take*) llevar **2.** LAW interponer; (*complaint*) formular

♦ **bring about** *vt* (*cause*) provocar; (*achieve*) lograr

♦ **bring along** *vt* traer

♦ **bring around** *vt* **1.** MED hacer volver en sí **2.** (*persuade*) convencer

♦ **bring back** *vt* **1.** (*reintroduce*) reintroducir **2.** (*remind*) recordar **3.** (*return*) devolver

♦ **bring down** *vt* **1.** (*reduce*) reducir; (*temperature*) bajar **2.** (*knock down*) tirar; (*tree*) talar; (*government*) derrocar **3.** (*make sad*) deprimir

♦ **bring forward** *vt* **1.** (*to earlier date*) adelantar **2.** (*for discussion*) presentar **3.** FIN transferir

♦ **bring in** *vt* **1.** (*introduce*) introducir **2.** (*call in*) llamar **3.** **to ~ a profit** reportar un beneficio

♦ **bring off** *vt inf* lograr

♦ **bring on** *vt* (*cause*) causar; (*improve*) mejorar

♦ **bring out** *vt* **1.** COM introducir (en el mercado); (*book*) publicar **2.** **to ~ the best/worst in sb** hace salir lo mejor/peor de alguien

♦ **bring over** *vt* **1.** (*person*) convencer **2.** (*take with*) traer

♦ **bring up** *vt* **1.** (*child*) criar **2.** (*mention*) sacar **3.** *inf* (*vomit*) devolver

brink [brɪŋk] *n* borde *m*; **to drive sb to the ~ of sth** llevar a alguien al borde de algo; **to be on the ~ of bankruptcy/war** estar al borde de la bancarrota/la guerra

brisk [brɪsk] *adj* (*pace*) rápido, -a; (*walk*) a paso ligero; (*breeze*) fresco, -a; (*manner, voice*) enérgico, -a

bristle ['brɪs-əl] *vi* (*fur, hair*) erizarse; **to ~ with anger** enfurecerse

Britain ['brɪt-ən] *n* Gran Bretaña *f*

British ['brɪt-ɪʃ] **I.** *adj* británico, -a; **~**

English inglés británico **II.** *n pl* **the ~** los británicos

broad |brɔd| *adj* **1.** (*wide*) ancho, -a **2.** (*spacious, wide-ranging*) amplio, -a **3.** **a ~ hint** una clara indirecta; **a ~ mind** una mente abierta

broadcast |'brɔd·kæst| **I.** *n* programa *m* **II.** *vi, vt* <broadcast *or* broadcasted, broadcast *or* broadcasted> transmitir; (*rumor*) difundir(se)

broadcasting *n* TV transmisión *f*; RADIO radiodifusión *f*

broadcasting station *n* emisora *f*

broaden |'brɔd·ən| **I.** *vi* ampliarse **II.** *vt* (*street*) ensanchar; (*horizons*) ampliar; (*mind*) abrir

broadly |'brɔd·li| *adv* **1.** (*generally*) en líneas generales **2.** (*smile*) de oreja a oreja

broad-minded *adj* con mentalidad abierta

broccoli |'brak·ə·li| *n* brócoli *m*, brécol *m*

brochure |broʊ·'ʃʊr| *n* folleto *m*

broiler |'brɔɪ·lər| *n* (*grill*) parrilla *f*

broke |broʊk| **I.** *pt of* **break II.** *adj* *inf* pelado, -a, planchado, -a *Chile* ▶ **to go ~** *inf* arruinarse

broken |'broʊ·kən| **I.** *pp of* **break II.** *adj* roto, -a; (*interrupted*) interrumpido, -a; **in ~ English** en inglés mal hablado

broken-down *adj* averiado, -a, en pana *Chile*, varado, -a *Col*; (*building*) ruinoso, -a

broken-hearted *adj* destrozado, -a

bronchial tubes *npl* bronquios *mpl*

bronze |branz| **I.** *n* bronce *m* **II.** *adj* de bronce; (*hair*) dorado, -a; (*skin*) bronceado, -a

brooch |broʊtʃ| *n* broche *m*

brood |brud| **I.** *n* ZOOL camada *f*; (*birds*) nidada *f*; *iron* prole *f* **II.** *vi* **to ~ over sth** dar vueltas a algo

brook |brʊk| *n* arroyo *m*

broom |brum| *n* escoba *f*

broth |brɔθ| *n* caldo *m*

brother |'brʌð·ər| *n* **1.** hermano *m* **2.** (*friend*) colega *m*

brother-in-law <brothers-in-law *or* brother-in-laws> *n* cuñado *m*, cuño *m AmL*

brotherly |'brʌð·ər·li| *adj* fraternal

brought |brɔt| *pp, pt of* **bring**

brown |braʊn| **I.** *n* marrón *m* **II.** *adj* marrón; (*hair*) castaño, -a; (*bread, rice*) integral **III.** *vi* broncearse; CULIN dorarse **IV.** *vt* broncear; CULIN dorar

brownnose |'braʊn·noʊz| **I.** *vi inf* ser un pelota [*or* lambón] *Col* **II.** *vt* hacer la pelota [*or Méx* barba] a, echar cepillo a *Col*

brownout |'braʊn·aʊt| *n* apagón *m* (parcial)

browse |braʊz| **I.** *vi* mirar; **to ~ through** echar un vistazo; (*book, magazine*) hojear **II.** *n* ojeada *f*; **to have a ~ through** echar una ojeada a; (*book, magazine*) hojear

browser |'braʊ·zər| *n* navegador *m*

bruise |bruz| **I.** *n* cardenal *m* **II.** *vt* MED hacerse una contusión en

brunt |brʌnt| *n* impacto *m*

brush |brʌʃ| **I.** *n* **1.** (*for hair*) cepillo *m* **2.** (*broom*) escoba *f* **3.** (*for painting*) pincel *m*; (*bigger*) brocha *f* **II.** *vt* **1.** (*hair*) cepillar; **to ~ one's teeth** lavarse los dientes **2.** (*touch lightly*) rozar

◆ **brush against** *vt* rozar

◆ **brush aside** *vt* **1.** (*push to one side*) apartar **2.** (*disregard*) hacer caso omiso de

◆ **brush away** *vt* quitar

◆ **brush off** *vt* (*dust*) quitar; (*person*) no hacer caso a

brush-off *n* **to give sb the ~** dar calabazas a alguien

brusque |brʌsk| *adj* brusco, -a

brusqueness *n* brusquedad *f*

Brussels |'brʌs·əlz| *n* Bruselas *f*

brutal |'bruṭ·əl| *adj* brutal; (*words*) cruel; (*truth*) crudo, -a

brutality |bru·'tæl·ə·ṭi| *n* (*cruelty*) brutalidad *f*; (*words*) crueldad *f*; (*harshness*) crudeza *f*

brute |brut| **I.** *n* bestia *f* **II.** *adj* **~ force** fuerza *f* bruta

bubble |'bʌb·əl| **I.** *n* burbuja *f*; (*comic*) bocadillo *m*; **to live in a ~** vivir en una burbuja **II.** *vi* borbotear

bubble bath *n* sales *f pl* de baño; (*bath*) baño *m* de espuma

bubblegum *n* chicle *m*

bubble-jet printer *n* impresora *f* de inyección

bubbly ['bʌb·li] I. *n inf* champán *m* II. *adj* burbujeante; *fig* animado, -a

buck [bʌk] *n inf* dólar *m;* **to make a fast ~** hacer dinero fácil; **to pass the ~** escurrir el bulto

◆**buck up** *vt inf* **to buck sb up** levantar el ánimo a alguien; **to ~ one's ideas** espabilarse

bucket ['bʌk·ɪt] *n* cubo *m* ▶ **a drop in the ~** un grano de arena en el desierto; **to kick the ~** estirar la pata

bucketful ['bʌk·ɪt·fʊl] <-s *or* bucketsful> *n* cubo *m* (lleno)

buckle ['bʌk·əl] I. *n* hebilla *f* II. *vt* **1.** (*fasten*) abrochar **2.** (*bend*) torcer III. *vi* **1.** (*fasten*) abrocharse **2.** (*bend*) torcerse; (*knees*) doblarse

◆**buckle down** *vi* ponerse ya en serio

◆**buckle up** *vi* abrocharse el cinturón

bud [bʌd] I. *n* BIO brote *m;* (*flower*) capullo *m* II. *vi* <-dd-> echar brotes

Buddhism ['bu·dɪz·əm] *n* budismo *m*

Buddhist *adj, n* budista *mf*

buddy ['bʌd·i] *n inf* colega *m,* cuate *m Méx*

budge [bʌdʒ] I. *vi* moverse; (*opinion*) cambiar de opinión (**from** en) II. *vt* mover; (*opinion*) hacer cambiar de opinión a

budgerigar ['bʌdʒ·ə·rɪ·gɑr] *n* periquito *m*

budget ['bʌdʒ·ɪt] I. *n* presupuesto *m* II. *vt* presupuestar; (*wages, time*) administrar III. *vi* **to ~ for** presupuestar IV. *adj* económico, -a

budget deficit *n* déficit *m inv* presupuestario

buffalo ['bʌf·ə·lou] <-(es)> *n* búfalo *m*

buffer ['bʌf·ər] I. *n* **1.** (*barrier*) barrera *f* **2.** (*intermediary*) mediador(a) *m(f)* **3.** COMPUT búfer *m* II. *vt* proteger

buffet[1] [bə·'feɪ] *n* **1.** (*meal*) buffet *m* **2.** (*bar*) cafetería *f*

buffet[2] ['bʌf·ɪt] *vt* zarandear

bug [bʌg] I. *n* **1.** ZOOL chinche *f;* (*any insect*) bicho *m* **2.** MED microbio *m* **3.** COMPUT error *m* II. *vt* <-gg-> **1.** escuchar clandestinamente; (*telephone*)

pinchar **2.** (*annoy*) chinchar

bugaboo ['bʌg·ə·bu] *n* pesadilla *f*

buggy ['bʌg·i] *n* <-ies> cochecito *m*

build [bɪld] I. *vt* <built, built> **1.** (*make*) construir; (*fire*) hacer; (*car*) fabricar **2.** (*establish*) conseguir; (*relationship*) establecer II. *vi* <built, built> **1.** (*construct*) edificar **2.** (*increase*) aumentar III. *n* complexión *f*

◆**build in** *vt* incorporar

◆**build on** *vt* **to build sth on sth** agregar algo a algo

◆**build up** I. *vt* desarrollar; (*accumulate*) acumular; **to build sb up** poner a alguien por las nubes II. *vi* (*increase*) ir en aumento; (*accumulate*) acumularse

builder ['bɪl·dər] *n* (*company*) constructor(a) *m(f);* (*worker*) albañil *mf*

building *n* edificio *m*

building permit *n* permiso *m* de obras

building site *n* obra *f*

build-up *n* **1.** (*accumulation*) acumulación *f;* (*pressure*) aumento *m* **2.** (*publicity*) propaganda *f*

built [bɪlt] I. *pp, pt of* **build** II. *adj* **slightly ~** menudo; **well ~** de complexión robusta; **he's/she's** (**really**) **built!** ¡vaya un cuerpazo que tiene!

built-in *adj* (*cabinets*) empotrado, -a; (*feature*) incorporado, -a; (*advantage*) intrínseco, -a

built-up *adj* (*area*) edificado, -a; (*heels, shoes*) con alza

bulb [bʌlb] *n* **1.** BOT bulbo *m* **2.** ELEC bombilla *f,* bombillo *m AmL*

Bulgaria [bʌl·'ger·i·ə] *n* Bulgaria *f*

Bulgarian [bʌl·'ger·i·ən] I. *adj* búlgaro, -a II. *n* **1.** (*person*) búlgaro, -a *m, f* **2.** LING búlgaro *m*

bulge [bʌldʒ] I. *vi* sobresalir; **to ~ with** estar repleto de II. *n* **1.** (*swelling*) bulto *m* **2.** (*increase*) alza *f*

bulging *adj* abultado, -a; (*bag, box*) repleto, -a; **~ eyes** ojos saltones

bulimia [buˈliˑmiˑə] *n* bulimia *f*

bulk [bʌlk] I. *n* (*magnitude*) volumen *m;* (*mass*) mole *f;* **the ~ of** la mayor parte de; **in ~** a granel; ECON al por mayor II. *vi* **to ~ large** ser importante

III. *adj* (*mailing, order*) grande; (*goods*) en grandes cantidades

bulky ['bʌl·ki] <-ier, iest> *adj* voluminoso, -a; (*heavy*) pesado, -a; (*person*) corpulento, -a

bull [bʊl] *n* 1. (*bovine*) toro *m* 2. (*male*) macho *m*; **~ whale** ballena macho ► **to take the ~ by the horns** coger [*or AmL* agarrar] el toro por los cuernos

bulldog ['bʊl·dɔg] *n* bulldog *m*

bulldoze ['bʊl·doʊz] *vt* 1. ARCHIT demoler 2. *fig* **to ~ sth through** conseguir algo a la fuerza; **to ~ sb into doing sth** forzar a alguien a hacer algo

bullet ['bʊl·ɪt] *n* bala *f*

bulletin ['bʊl·ə·tɪn] *n* boletín *m*

bulletin board *n* tablón *m* de anuncios

bulletproof ['bʊl·ɪt·pruf] *adj* blindado, -a; (*glass, vest*) antibalas

bullfight ['bʊl·faɪt] *n* corrida *f* de toros

bullfighter ['bʊl·faɪ·tər] *n* torero, -a *m, f*

bully ['bʊl·i] I. <-ies> *n* matón, -ona *m, f* II. <-ie-> *vt* **to ~ sb** (**into doing sth**) intimidar a alguien (para que haga algo) III. *interj inf* **~ for you!** ¡bravo!

bum [bʌm] I. *n* 1. (*lazy*) vago, -a *m, f* 2. (*homeless*) vagabundo, -a *m, f* II. <-mm-> *vt sl* gorronear [*or* lagartear] *Col* (**off a**) III. *vi inf* **to ~ sb** gorronear a alguien; **to ~ around** vagabundear; (*laze around*) pasar el rato

bumblebee ['bʌm·bəl·bi] *n* abejorro *m*

bummed out *adj sl* depre

bump [bʌmp] I. *n* 1. (*lump*) bulto *m*; (*head*) chichón *m*; (*road*) bache *m* 2. *inf* (*blow*) porrazo *m* II. *vt* chocar contra; **to ~ one's head** darse un golpe en la cabeza (**on/against** con/contra)

◆**bump into** *vt insep* 1. (*collide with*) chocar contra 2. (*meet accidentally*) topar con

◆**bump off** *vt sl* cargarse

bumper ['bʌm·pər] I. *n* AUTO parachoques *m inv*, paragolpes *m inv AmL*, defensa *f Méx* II. *adj* abundante; (*edition*) especial

bumpkin ['bʌmp·kɪn] *n* paleto, -a *m, f*

bumpy ['bʌm·pi] <-ier, iest> *adj* (*surface*) desigual; (*road*) lleno, -a de baches; (*journey*) movidito *inf*

bun [bʌn] *n* 1. (*pastry*) bollo *m*; (*roll*) panecillo *m*, pancito *m CSur* 2. (*hair*) moño *m*, chongo *m Méx*

bunch [bʌntʃ] <-es> I. *n* 1. (*grapes*) racimo *m*; (*carrots, keys*) manojo *m*; (*flowers*) ramo *m* 2. (*group*) grupo *m*; (*of friends*) pandilla *f* 3. **a** (*whole*) **~ of problems** un montón de problemas II. *vt* agrupar III. *vi* **to ~** (**together**) amontonar

bundle ['bʌn·dəl] *n* (*clothes*) fardo *m*; (*money*) fajo *m* ► **to be a ~ of nerves** ser un manojo de nervios

bung [bʌŋ] I. *n* tapón *m* II. *vt* taponar

bungalow ['bʌŋ·gə·loʊ] *n* bungalow *m*, bóngalo *m AmL*

bungee jumping ['bʌn·dʒɪ,dʒʌm·pɪŋ] *n* puenting *m*

bungle ['bʌŋ·gəl] *vt* chapucear

bungler *n* chapucero, -a *m, f*

bungling *adj* torpe

bunk [bʌŋk] *n* litera *f*, cucheta *f RíoPl*

◆**bunk down** *vi inf* irse a sobar

bunker ['bʌŋ·kər] *n* búnker *m*

bunny (**rabbit**) ['bʌn·i·('ræb·ɪt)] *n* conejito *m*

buoyant ['bɔɪ·jənt] *adj* (*cheerful*) optimista

burble ['bɜr·bəl] *vi* borbotar; (*talk*) parlotear

burden ['bɜr·dən] I. *n* carga *f*; **to be a ~ on** [*or* to] **sb** ser una carga para alguien II. *vt* cargar; *fig* estorbar

bureau ['bjʊr·oʊ] <-s> *n* 1. (*office*) agencia *f*; POL departamento *m* 2. (*chest of drawers*) cómoda *f*

bureaucracy [bjʊ·'rak·rə·si] *n* burocracia *f*

bureaucratic [,bjʊr·ə·'kræt̬·ɪk] *adj* burocrático, -a

burger ['bɜr·gər] *n inf abbr of* **hamburger** hamburguesa *f*

burglar ['bɜr·glər] *n* ladrón, -ona *m, f*

burglar alarm *n* alarma *f* antirrobo

burglarize ['bɜr·glə·raɪz] *vt* robar; **five houses have been ~d** han entrado a robar en cinco casas

B

burglary ['bɜr·glə·ri] <-ies> n robo m

burgle ['bɜr·gəl] vt see **burglarize**

burial ['ber·i·əl] n entierro m

burial ground n cementerio m

burial service n funerales mpl

burlesque [bɜr·'lesk] adj burlesco, -a

burly ['bɜr·li] <-ier, -iest> adj fornido, -a

burn [bɜrn] I. <burnt or -ed, burnt or -ed> vi 1. (be in flames) quemarse 2. (be hot) arder 3. estar encendido, -a; **he left all the lights ~ing** dejó todas las luces encendidas 4. **to be ~ing to do sth** estar deseando hacer algo; **to ~ with desire** desear ardientemente; **his face ~ed with anger/shame** se puso rojo de furia/vergüenza II. <burnt or -ed, burnt or -ed> vt quemar; (building) incendia; **to be ~ed** (by the sun) quemarse; (injured) sufrir quemaduras III. n quemadura f, quemada f Méx; **severe/minor ~s** quemaduras graves/leves

◆**burn away** I. vi quemarse; (candle) consumirse II. vt quemar

◆**burn down** I. vt incendiar II. vi incendiarse; (fire, candle) apagarse

◆**burn out** vi quemarse; (fire, candle) apagarse; (bulb) fundirse

◆**burn up** vt 1. quemar; (fuel) consumir 2. inf reventar

burner ['bɜr·nər] n fogón m; TECH quemador m

burning ['bɜr·nɪŋ] adj ardiente; (sun) abrasador; (issue, question) candente; **to be ~ hot** estar ardiendo

burnt [bɜrnt] I. pt, pp of **burn** II. adj quemado, -a; **a ~ smell/taste** un olor/sabor a quemado

burp [bɜrp] I. n eructo m; **to let out a ~** soltar un eructo II. vi eructar

burrow ['bɜr·oʊ] I. n madriguera f II. vt, vi excavar

burst [bɜrst] I. n explosión f; **a ~ of laughter** una carcajada; **a ~ of anger** un arranque de cólera II. <burst, burst> vi (balloon, tire) reventar; (storm) desatarse; **to ~ into tears** romper a llorar; **to be ~ing to do sth** morirse de ganas de hacer algo III. <burst, burst> vt reventar

◆**burst in** vi entrar de sopetón

◆**burst out** vi saltar; **to ~ laughing/cry-**

ing echarse a reír/llorar

bury ['ber·i] <-ie-> vt enterrar; (hide) ocultar

bus [bʌs] <-es> n autobús m, camión m Méx, colectivo m Arg, Ven, guagua f Cuba, ómnibus m Perú, Urug; **school ~** autobús escolar; **to catch/miss the ~** coger/perder el autobús; **to go by ~** [or **to take the ~**] ir en autobús ▸ **to miss the ~** perder el autobús

bus driver n conductor(a) m(f) de autobús

bush [bʊʃ] <-es> n arbusto m; (hair) mata f; (land) **the ~** el monte ▸ **to beat around the ~** andarse con rodeos

bushy ['bʊʃ·i] <-ier, -iest> adj tupido, -a; (beard, mustache) espeso, -a; (eyebrows) poblado, -a

busily adv afanosamente

business ['bɪz·nɪs] n 1. (trade, commerce) negocios mpl; **to be away on ~** estar de viaje de negocios; **to go out of ~** cerrar; **to set up a ~** montar un negocio 2. <-es> (sector) industria f; **the frozen food ~** la industria de los congelados 3. <-es> (company) empresa f; **to start up/run a ~** poner/llevar un negocio 4. (matter) asunto m; **an unfinished ~** un asunto pendiente; **it's none of your ~!** ¡no es asunto tuyo!; **mind your own ~!** ¡no te metas donde no te llaman! ▸ **~ before pleasure** prov antes es la obligación que el placer

business address n dirección f comercial

business card n tarjeta f comercial

business hours n horas f pl de oficina

businesslike ['bɪz·nɪs·laɪk] adj 1. (serious) formal 2. (efficient) eficiente

businessman <-men> n hombre m de negocios

business trip n viaje m de negocios

businesswoman <-women> n mujer f de negocios

busk [bʌsk] vi tocar un instrumento en la calle

busker ['bʌs·kər] n músico, -a m, f callejero, -a

bus service n servicio m de autobuses

bus station n estación f de autobuses

bus stop n parada f de autobús

bust[1] [bʌst] n ART busto m

bust[2] [bʌst] I. adj sl destrozado, -a; (bankrupt) en bancarrota; **to go ~** quebrar II. vt inf 1. (break) destrozar 2. (raid) realizar una redada en ▶ **to ~ one's** <u>butt</u> (doing sth/to do sth) partirse la espalda (haciendo algo)

bustle ['bʌs·əl] I. vi **to ~ around** ir y venir; **to ~ with activity** rebosar de actividad II. n ajetreo m; **hustle and ~** bullicio m

busy ['bɪz·i] <-ier, -iest> adj 1. (occupied) atareado, -a; **to be ~ doing sth** estar muy ocupado haciendo algo; **to be ~ with sth** estar ocupado con algo 2. (full of activity) activo, -a; (exhausting) agotador(a); (street) concurrido, -a; (day) ajetreado, -a 3. TEL ocupado

busybody ['bɪz·i,bad·i] <-ies> n inf entrometido, -a m, f; **to be a ~** ser un metomentodo

but [bʌt] I. prep excepto; **all ~ one** todos excepto uno; **anything ~ ...** lo que sea menos...; **nothing ~ ...** nada más que... II. conj 1. pero; **he has paper ~ no pen** tiene papel, pero no pluma 2. **not... but...** no... sino...; **it is not red ~ pink** no es rojo sino rosa III. adv sólo IV. n pero m; **there are no ~s about it!** ¡no hay peros que valgan!

butane ['bju·teɪn] n butano m

butcher ['bʊtʃ·ər] n carnicero, -a m, f

butler ['bʌt·lər] n mayordomo m

butt [bʌt] I. n 1. (rifle) culata f; (cigarette) colilla f 2. (blow with the head) cabezazo m 3. **to be the ~ of sth** ser el blanco de algo 4. (container) tonel m II. vt darse un cabezazo contra

butter ['bʌt·ər] I. n mantequilla f II. vt untar con mantequilla

◆**butter up** vt dar coba a, cepillar AmL

butterfingers n inv manazas mf inv

butterfly ['bʌt·ər·flaɪ] <-ies> n mariposa f; fig frívolo, -a m, f ▶ **to have butterflies in one's** <u>stomach</u> estar con los nervios a flor de piel

buttock ['bʌt·ək] n nalga f

button ['bʌt·ən] I. n botón m; **start ~** botón de inicio; **right/left mouse ~** botón derecho/izquierdo del ratón; **to push**

a **~** apretar un botón II. vi abrocharse III. vt abrochar

◆**button up** vt abrochar

buttonhole ['bʌt·ən·hoʊl] n ojal m

buy [baɪ] I. n compra f; **a good ~** una ganga II. <bought, bought> vt 1. comprar (from, off a) 2. inf **did the teacher ~ your excuse?** ¿se tragó el profesor tu excusa?

◆**buy into** vt comprar acciones de; fig aceptar como válido

◆**buy off** vt always sep sobornar

◆**buy up** vt insep acaparar

buyer ['baɪ·ər] n comprador(a) m(f)

buzz [bʌz] I. vi 1. (hum) zumbar; (bell) sonar; **my ears were ~ing** me zumbaban los oídos 2. sl **to be ~ed** ir borracho II. vt inf TEL llamar; (signal to) dar un toque a III. n 1. (noise) zumbido m; (low noise) rumor m 2. inf **to give sb a ~** echar a alguien el teléfono 3. inf (thrill) subidón m

◆**buzz off** vi inf largarse

buzzer ['bʌz·ər] n timbre m

by [baɪ] I. prep 1. (near) cerca de; **close** [or **near**] **~...** cerca de... 2. (at) junto a; **~ the sea** junto al mar 3. **~ day/night** durante el día/la noche 4. (at the latest) para; **~ tomorrow/midnight** para mañana/la medianoche; **~ then/now** para entonces/ahora 5. (cause) por; **a novel ~** Joyce una novela de Joyce; **to be seen ~ sth/sb** ser visto por algo/alguien; **surrounded ~ dogs** rodeado de perros 6. **~ train/plane/bus** en tren/avión/autobús; **~ hand** a mano; **~ doing sth** haciendo algo 7. (through) **~ chance/mistake** por suerte/error; **what does he mean ~ that?** ¿a qué se refiere con eso? 8. (to be) **~ oneself** (estar) solo 9. MAT **to divide ~ 6** dividir entre 6; **to increase ~ 10%** aumentar en un 10%; **to multiply ~ 4** multiplicar por 4; **paid ~ the hour/day** pagado por hora/día; **one ~ one** uno a uno II. adv 1. (aside) cerca; **to put/lay sth ~** poner/dejar algo a mano 2. **~ and ~** dentro de poco 3. **to go/pass ~** pasar

bye [baɪ], **bye-bye** [,baɪ·'baɪ] interj inf adiós

bylaw n reglamento m local; (*organization's rule*) estatuto m

bypass ['baɪ·pæs] **I.** n AUTO circunvalación f **II.** vt evitar

byproduct ['baɪ·prɑd·əkt] n subproducto m; *fig* derivado m

byroad ['baɪ·roʊd] n carretera f secundaria

bystander ['baɪ·stæn·dər] n espectador(a) m(f)

byte [baɪt] n byte m

byway ['baɪ·weɪ] n carretera f secundaria

byword ['baɪ·wɜrd] n ejemplo m; **to be a ~ for sth** ser sinónimo de algo

C

C, c [si] n **1.** (*letter*) C, c f; **~ as in Charlie** C de Carmen **2.** SCHOOL ≈ bien m

C *after n abbr of* **Celsius, centigrade** C

c. 1. *abbr of* **circa** (*by numbers*) aprox.; (*by dates*) hacia **2.** *abbr of* **cent** cent **3.** *abbr of* **cup** taza f (aprox. 250 ml)

C. *abbr of* **century** s.

CA n *abbr of* **California** California f

cab [kæb] n taxi m; **by ~** en taxi

cabaret [ˌkæb·ə·'reɪ] n cabaret m

cabbage ['kæb·ɪdʒ] n repollo m

cabbie, cabby ['kæb·i], **cabdriver** n taxista mf

cabin ['kæb·ɪn] n cabaña f; NAUT, AVIAT cabina f

cabin cruiser n yate m de motor

cabinet ['kæb·ɪ·nɪt] n **1.** (*cupboard*) armario m; (*glass*) vitrina f **2.** + *sing/pl vb* POL gabinete m

cabinetmaker n ebanista mf

cable ['keɪ·bəl] n cable m

cable car n teleférico m

cable network n cableado m

cable railway n funicular m

cable television, cable TV n televisión f por cable

caboodle [kə·'bud·əl] n *inf* **the whole** (**kit and**) **~** toda la pesca

cabriolet [ˌkæb·ri·ə·'leɪ] n descapotable m

cache [kæʃ] n **1.** (*place*) escondite m; (*stockpile*) alijo m **2.** COMPUT caché m

cackle ['kæk·əl] **I.** vi (*hen*) cacarear; (*laugh*) reírse escandalosamente **II.** n (*hen*) cacareo m; (*laugh*) risotada f

cactus ['kæk·təs] <-es *or* cacti> n cactus m *inv*, ulala f *Bol*

cafe, café [kæ·'feɪ] n cafetería f

cafeteria [ˌkæf·ɪ·'tɪr·i·ə] n self-service m

caffeine [kæ·'fin] n cafeína f

cage [keɪdʒ] **I.** n jaula f **II.** vt enjaular

cagey ['keɪ·dʒi] <-ier, -iest> adj *inf* reservado, -a

cahoots [kə·'huts] n **to be in ~** estar compinchado(s) (**with** con)

cake [keɪk] n pastel m; **frosted ~** tarta f helada; **sponge ~** bizcocho m, queque m *AmL* ▶ **to sell like hot ~s** venderse como rosquillas

cal. n *abbr of* **calorie** cal.

Cal. *abbr of* **California** California f

calamity [kə·'læm·ə·ti] <-ies> n calamidad f

calcium ['kæl·si·əm] n calcio m

calculate ['kæl·kjə·leɪt] vt, vi calcular (**at** en)

calculated adj **1.** (*likely*) probable **2.** MATH calculado, -a; **a ~ risk** un riesgo calculado

calculating adj calculador(a)

calculation [ˌkæl·kjə·'leɪ·ʃən] n cálculo m

calculator ['kæl·kjə·leɪ·tər] n calculadora f

calendar ['kæl·ən·dər] n calendario m, exfoliador m *Chile, Méx*

calendar year n año m civil

calf [kæf] <calves> n ZOOL ternero, -a m, f; ANAT pantorrilla f

caliber ['kæl·ə·bər] n calibre m

Calif. [ˌkæl·ə·'fɔr·njə] *abbr of* **California** California f

California [ˌkæl·ə·'fɔr·njə] n California f

call [kɔl] **I.** n **1.** a. TEL llamada f; **a ~ for help** una llamada de socorro; **to give sb a ~** llamar a alguien (por teléfono) **2.** (*visit*) visita f; **to be on a ~/on ~** estar de visita/de guardia **3.** (*shout*) grito m ▶ **to have a close ~** salvarse por los pelos **II.** vt **1.** (*name, address as*) llamar; **what's that actor ~ed?** ¿cómo se llama ese actor?; **to ~ sb's attention** llamar la atención de alguien;

you ~ this a party? ¿a esto lo llamas fiesta? **2.** TEL llamar, telefonear *AmL;* to ~ sb collect llamar a alguien a cobro revertido **3.** (*meeting*) convocar; (*strike*) declarar; to ~ a halt to sth suspender algo **III.** *vi* **1.** TEL llamar **2.** (*drop by*) pasar **3.** (*shout*) gritar

◆ call back *vt* **1.** TEL devolver la llamada a **2.** (*ask to return*) hacer volver

◆ call for *vt insep* **1.** (*come to get*) pasar a recoger **2.** (*ask*) pedir; (*demand, require*) exigir; this calls for a celebration esto hay que celebrarlo

◆ call in *vt* (*ask to come*) llamar

◆ call off *vt* (*cancel*) suspender

◆ call out **I.** *vt* gritar **II.** *vi* gritar; to call out for sth *fig* exigir algo

◆ call up *vt* TEL llamar

call center *n* TEL centro *m* de atención de llamadas

calligraphy [kə·ˈlɪg·rə·fi] *n* caligrafía *f*

calling card *n* tarjeta *f* telefónica

calm [kam] **I.** *adj* **1.** (*not nervous*) tranquilo, -a **2.** to keep ~ mantener la calma **2.** (*peaceful*) pacífico, -a **3.** (*not windy*) sin viento **II.** *n* tranquilidad *f* **III.** *vt* tranquilizar; to ~ oneself calmarse

calorie [ˈkæl·ə·ri] *n* caloría *f*

calorie-laden *adj* rico, -a en calorías

camcorder [ˈkæm·kɔr·dər] *n* videocámara *f*

came [keɪm] *vi pt of* come

camel [ˈkæm·əl] *n* **1.** ZOOL camello *m* **2.** (*color*) beige *m*

camera [ˈkæm·ər·ə] *n* PHOT, CINE cámara *f*

camouflage [ˈkæm·ə·flaʒ] **I.** *n* camuflaje *m* **II.** *vt* camuflar

camp [kæmp] **I.** *n* **1.** (*encampment*) campamento *m;* summer ~ campamento de verano **2.** (*group*) bando *m;* to go over to the other ~ pasarse al otro bando **II.** *vi* to ~ (out) acampar; to go ~ing ir de acampada, campear *AmL*

campaign [kæm·ˈpeɪn] **I.** *n* campaña *f;* ~ trail campaña electoral **II.** *vi* hacer campaña (for a favor de)

camper [ˈkæm·pər] *n* campista *mf;* AUTO caravana *f*

campground *n* camping *m,* campamento *m Col, Méx*

camping [ˈkæm·pɪŋ] *n* camping *m;* to go ~ ir de acampada

campsite [ˈkæmp·saɪt] *n* campamento *m,* camping *m*

campus [ˈkæm·pəs] <-es> *n* campus *m inv*

can¹ [kæn] **I.** *n* **1.** (*container*) lata *f* **2.** *sl* (*toilet*) trono *m* **3.** *inf* (*prison*) trullo *m* **II.** <-nn-> *vt* **1.** enlatar **2.** *sl* ~ it! ¡basta ya!

can² [kən] <could, could> *aux* **1.** (*be able to*) poder; if I could si pudiera; I think she ~ help you creo que ella te puede ayudar; I could have kissed her habría podido besarla **2.** (*be permitted to*) poder; you can't go no puedes ir; can I look at it? ¿podría verlo? **3.** (*know how to*) saber; ~ you swim? ¿sabes nadar?

Canada [ˈkæn·ə·də] *n* Canadá *m*

Canadian [kə·ˈneɪ·di·ən] *adj, n* canadiense *mf*

canal [kə·ˈnæl] *n* canal *m*

canalization [ˌkæn·ə·lɪ·ˈzeɪ·ʃən] *n* canalización *f*

canary [kə·ˈner·i] <-ies> *n* canario *m*

cancel [ˈkæn·səl] <-ll-, -l-> *vt a.* COMPUT cancelar; (*party, concert*) suspender; (*result, license*) anular

cancellation [ˌkæn·sə·ˈleɪ·ʃən] *n* cancelación *f;* (*party, concert*) suspensión *f;* (*license*) anulación *f;* (*contract*) rescisión *f*

cancer [ˈkæn·sər] *n* cáncer *m,* cangro *m Col, Guat*

Cancer [ˈkæn·sər] *n* Cáncer *m*

candid [ˈkæn·dɪd] *adj* franco, -a; (*talk*) sincero, -a; (*picture*) natural

candidacy [ˈkæn·dɪ·də·si] *n* candidatura *f*

candidate [ˈkæn·dɪ·dət] *n a.* POL candidato, -a *m, f*

candid camera *n* cámara *f* indiscreta

candle [ˈkæn·dəl] *n* vela *f* ▶ she can't hold a ~ to him no le llega ni a la suela del zapato

candlelight [ˈkæn·dəl·laɪt] *n* luz *f* de una vela; by ~ a la luz de las velas

candlepower [ˈkæn·dəl·paʊ·ər] *n* candela *f*

candlestick [ˈkæn·dəl·stɪk] *n* candelabro *m*

candy ['kæn·di] I. <-ies> n golosinas fpl II. vt escarchar

candy store n tienda f de golosinas

cane [keɪn] n 1. (plant) caña f 2. (furniture) mimbre m 3. (stick) bastón m

cane sugar n azúcar m de caña

canister ['kæn·ɪ·stər] n (metal) lata f; (plastic) bote m

cannabis ['kæn·ə·bɪs] n cannabis m

canned [kænd] adj enlatado, -a; (fruit, vegetables) en conserva; (food, meat, beer) de lata

cannibal ['kæn·ɪ·bəl] n caníbal mf

cannibalism ['kæn·ɪ·bəl·ɪz·əm] n canibalismo m

cannibalize ['kæn·ɪ·bə·laɪz] vt AUTO desguazar

cannon ['kæn·ən] n cañón m

cannot ['kæn·ɑt] aux = **can not** see **can²**

canny ['kæn·i] <-ier, -iest> adj (clever) astuto, -a

canoe [kə·'nu] n canoa f

canoeing n piragüismo m

canon ['kæn·ən] n REL, MUS canon m

can opener ['kæn·ˌou·pə·nər] n abrelatas m inv

can't [kænt] = **cannot**

canteen [kæn·'tin] n (container) cantimplora f

canvas ['kæn·vəs] <-es> n 1. (cloth) lona f 2. ART lienzo m, holán m AmC

canvass ['kæn·vəs] I. vt 1. (information) sondear; **to ~ sth** hacer una encuesta de algo 2. (votes) escrutar II. vi POL hacer campaña

canyon ['kæn·jən] n cañón m

cap¹ [kæp] I. n 1. gorro m; (with peak) gorra f 2. (cover) tapón m 3. (limit) tope m II. <-pp-> vt (limit) limitar; (cover) tapar; **to ~ it all** para colmo

cap² [kæp] n abbr of **capital letter** mayúscula f

capability [ˌkeɪ·pə·'bɪl·ə·ti] <-ies> n (ability) capacidad f

capable ['keɪ·pə·bəl] adj 1. (competent) competente 2. (able) capaz; **to be ~ of doing sth** ser capaz de hacer algo

capacity [kə·'pæs·ə·ti] <-ies> n 1. capacidad f; (mental) aptitud f; **seating ~** aforo m; **filled** [or **full**] **to ~** comple-

tamente lleno 2. (output) rendimiento m; **to work at full ~** trabajar a pleno rendimiento

cape¹ [keɪp] n GEO cabo m

cape² [keɪp] n (cloak) capa f

caper ['keɪ·pər] n BOT alcaparra f

capital ['kæp·ə·təl] I. n 1. (city) capital f 2. TYPO mayúscula f 3. ARCHIT capitel m 4. FIN capital m II. adj 1. (principal) primordial 2. TYPO mayúscula f

capital investment n inversión f de capital

capitalism ['kæp·ə·təl·ɪz·əm] n capitalismo m

capitalist ['kæp·ə·təl·ɪst] adj, n capitalista mf

capital letter ['kæp·ə·təl·'le·tər] n mayúscula f; **in ~s** en mayúsculas

capital punishment n pena f de muerte

cappuccino [ˌkæp·ə·'tʃi·nou] n capuchino m

Capricorn ['kæp·rɪ·kɔrn] n Capricornio m

caps. n abbr of **capital letter** mayúsc.

capsize ['kæp·saɪz] vi, vt fig volcar

capsule ['kæp·səl] n cápsula f

captain ['kæp·tɪn] n capitán, -ana m, f

caption ['kæp·ʃən] n TYPO, PUBL título m; CINE subtítulo m

captivate ['kæp·tə·veɪt] vt cautivar

captive ['kæp·tɪv] adj, n cautivo, -a m, f; **to hold sb ~** tener prisionero a alguien

captivity [kæp·'tɪv·ə·ti] n cautiverio m; **to be in ~** estar en cautividad

capture ['kæp·tʃər] I. vt 1. (take prisoner) apresar 2. (take possession of) capturar; (city) conquistar 3. (gain) a. ART captar 4. COMPUT recoger II. n captura f; (city) conquista f

car [kar] n coche m, carro m AmL; RAIL vagón m

caramel ['kar·məl] I. n (sweet) caramelo m II. adj de caramelo

carat <-(s)> n see **karat**

caravan ['kær·ə·væn] n (travelers) caravana f

carbon ['kar·bən] n CHEM carbono m

carbon dioxide n dióxido m de carbono

carbon monoxide n monóxido m de carbono

carburetor ['kar·bə·reɪ·tər] n carburador *m*

carcinogenic [ˌkar·sɪn·ə·ˈdʒen·ɪk] *adj* cancerígeno, -a

card [kard] *n* 1. (*greetings*) a. FIN, COMPUT tarjeta *f*; (*index* ~) ficha *f* 2. GAMES carta *f*; **pack of** ~s baraja; **to play** ~s jugar a las cartas 3. (*identity*) carnet *m*; **membership** ~ carnet de socio 4. tarjeta *f* ▶ **to have a** ~ **up one's sleeve** tener un as en la manga; **to put one's** ~s **on the table** poner las cartas sobre la mesa; **to play one's** ~s **right** jugar bien sus cartas

cardboard [ˈkard·bɔrd] *n* cartón *m*

cardiac [ˈkar·dɪ·æk] *adj* cardíaco, -a; (*disease*) cardiovascular

cardigan [ˈkar·dɪ·gən] *n* rebeca *f*

cardinal [ˈkar·dɪn·əl] *n* REL, ZOOL cardenal *m*; MAT cardinal *m*

cardinal number *n* número *m* cardinal

cardinal points *npl* puntos *m pl* cardinales

card index [ˈkard·ˌɪn·deks] <-es> *n* fichero *m*

cardiogram [ˈkar·dɪ·ə·græm] *n* cardiograma *m*

care [ker] I. *n* 1. (*attention*) cuidado *m*; **to take** ~ **of** cuidar de; (*object*) guardar; (*situation*) encargarse de; **take** ~ (**of yourself**)! ¡cuídate!; **handle with** ~ frágil 2. (*worry*) preocupación *f* II. *vi* 1. (*concern*) preocuparse (**about** por); **as if I** ~**d**! ¿y a mí qué?; **who** ~**s**? ¿qué más da? 2. (*affection*) importar 3. **to** ~ **to do sth** estar dispuesto a hacer algo

career [kə·ˈrɪr] *n* 1. (*profession*) profesión *f* 2. (*working life*) carrera *f*

carefree [ˈker·fri] *adj* despreocupado, -a

careful [ˈker·fəl] *adj* 1. (*cautious*) cuidadoso, -a; (*driver*) prudente; **to be** ~ **of sth** tener cuidado con algo; **to be** ~ **to do sth** procurar hacer algo 2. (*meticulous*) meticuloso, -a; (*worker*) esmerado, -a

careless [ˈker·lɪs] *adj* distraído, -a; (*carefree*) despreocupado, -a

carelessness *n* (*lack of attention*) falta *f* de atención; (*of concern*) despreocupación *f*

caress [kə·ˈres] I. <-es> *n* caricia *f* II. *vi*, *vt* acariciar, barbear *AmC*

caretaker [ˈker·ˌter·kər] *n* vigilante *mf*, guachimán *m Col, CRi, Chile, Pan, GuinEc, Nic*

car ferry <-ies> *n* transbordador *m*

cargo [ˈkar·goʊ] <-(e)s> *n* (*goods*) carga *f*; (*load*) cargamento *m*

Caribbean [ˌker·ɪ·ˈbi·ən] I. *n* the ~ el Caribe II. *adj* caribeño, -a, caribe *AmL*

caricature [ˈker·ə·kə·tjʊr] *n* caricatura *f*

caries [ˈker·iz] *n* caries *f inv*

caring *adj* compasivo, -a

car insurance *n* seguro *m* de vehículos

carnival [ˈkar·nə·vəl] *n* carnaval *m*, chaya *f Arg, Bol, Chile*

carnivorous [kar·ˈnɪv·ər·əs] *adj* carnívoro, -a

carol [ˈker·əl] *n* (*song*) villancico *m*

carp [karp] <-(s)> *n* ZOOL carpa *f*

carpenter [ˈkar·pən·tər] *n* carpintero, -a *m, f*

carpentry [ˈkar·pən·tri] *n* carpintería *f*

carpet [ˈkar·pət] I. *n* alfombra *f*; (*fitted*) moqueta *f* ▶ **to sweep sth under the** ~ correr un velo sobre algo II. *vt* enmoquetar, alfombrar *AmL*

car rental *n* alquiler *m* de coches

carriage [ˈker·ɪdʒ] *n* (*vehicle*) carruaje *m*

carrier [ˈkær·i·ər] *n* 1. (*company*) empresa *f* de transportes 2. MED portador(a) *m(f)*

carrot [ˈker·ət] *n* CULIN zanahoria *f*

carry [ˈker·i] <-ies, -ied> *vt* 1. (*bear*) llevar; (*bring*) traer; **to** ~ **a child** esperar un hijo; **to** ~ **consequences** tener consecuencias 2. (*transport*) transportar 3. MED transmitir

◆**carry along** *vt* llevar

◆**carry away** *vt* 1. (*remove*) arrastrar 2. **to be carried away** (**by**) (*be overcome*) dejarse llevar (por); (*be enchanted*) entusiasmarse (con)

◆**carry forward** *vt* FIN transferir

◆**carry off** *vt* (*sb*) llevarse; (*sth*) salir airoso de

◆**carry on** I. *vt insep* seguir II. *vi* 1. (*continue*) seguir; **to** ~ **doing sth** continuar haciendo algo 2. *inf* (*make a fuss*) montar un número

◆**carry out** *vt* (*repairs*) hacer; (*plan, attack*) llevar a cabo; (*job*) realizar; (*or-*

der) cumplir

◆**carry over** vt **1.** FIN transferir **2.** (*postpone*) posponer

◆**carry through** vt **1.** (*support*) sostener **2.** (*complete*) llevar a término

carryall ['kær·i·ɔl] n bolso m grande

carryover n **1.** FIN pérdida trasladada al ejercicio siguiente **2.** (*remnant*) remanente m

cart [kart] **I.** n carro m **II.** vt acarrear

carte blanche [kart·'blɑnʃ] n carta f blanca

cartel [kar·'tel] n cártel m

cartilage ['kar·təl·ɪdʒ] n cartílago m

carton ['kar·tən] n caja f de cartón; (*juice, milk*) brik m

cartoon [kar·'tun] n viñeta f; CINE dibujos m pl animados

cartridge ['kar·trɪdʒ] n cartucho m, cachimba f AmL

carve [karv] **I.** vt cortar; (*stone, wood*) tallar; (*meat*) trinchar **II.** vi cortar

carving n escultura f; **wood ~** talla f

car wash <-es> n tren m de lavado

cascade [kæs·'keɪd] n cascada f

case[1] [keɪs] n a. MED, LING, LAW caso m; **in any ~** en cualquier caso; **just in ~** por si acaso; **in ~ it rains** en caso de que llueva

case[2] [keɪs] n (*container*) caja f; (*jewels, glasses*) estuche m; (*camera, guitar*) funda f

casebook n diario m; MED registro m

cash [kæʃ] **I.** n dinero m en efectivo **II.** vt cobrar

◆**cash in** **I.** vt insep canjear **II.** vi **to ~ on sth** sacar provecho de algo

cash cow n sl gallina f de los huevos de oro

cashew ['kæʃ·u] n anacardo m, acajú m Cuba, Méx, PRico, RDom

cashier [kæ·'ʃɪr] n cajero, -a m, f

cash register n caja f registradora

casing ['keɪ·sɪŋ] n cubierta f; (*machine*) carcasa f

casino [kə·'si·noʊ] n casino m

casserole ['kæs·ə·roʊl] n cazuela f

cassette [kə·'set] n cinta f

cast [kæst] **I.** n **1.** THEAT, CINE reparto m **2.** (*mold*) molde m **3.** MED escayola f **II.** <cast, cast> vt **1.** (*throw*) lanzar;

2. (*direct: vote*) emitir; **to ~ doubt on sth** poner algo en duda; **to ~ a shadow on sth** ensombrecer algo; **to ~ light on sth** proyectar luz sobre algo; *fig* echar luz sobre algo

◆**cast aside, cast away** vt (*rid oneself of*) dejar de lado; (*free oneself of*) desechar

casting ['kæs·tɪŋ] n **1.** ART vaciado m **2.** THEAT reparto m de papeles

cast-iron adj de hierro fundido; (*evidence*) irrefutable; (*alibi*) a toda prueba; (*promise*) firme

castle ['kæs·əl] **I.** n castillo m; (*chess*) torre f ► **to build ~s in the air** construir castillos en el aire **II.** vi enrocar

castoff ['kæst·af] **I.** n **~s** ropa desechada f **II.** adj desechado, -a

castor ['kæs·tər] n ruedecita f

castrate [kæs·'treɪt] vt castrar, componer AmL

casual ['kæʒ·u·əl] adj **1.** (*relaxed*) relajado, -a **2.** (*chance*) casual; (*meeting*) fortuito, -a **3.** (*not habitual*) de vez en cuando **4.** (*informal*) informal; (*clothes*) informal

casually adv de forma relajada

casualty ['kæʒ·u·əl·ti] <-ies> n (*victim*) víctima f; MIL baja f; (*injured*) herido, -a m, f

cat [kæt] n gato, -a m, f ► **to let the ~ out of the bag** descubrir el pastel; (*carelessly*) irse de la lengua; **to fight like ~s and dogs** llevarse como (el) perro y (el) gato; **to rain ~s and dogs** llover a cántaros; **has the ~ got your tongue?** ¿te ha comido la lengua el gato?, ¿te comieron la lengua los ratones? Col, Méx

catalog ['kæt·əl·ag] **I.** n catálogo m; (*repeated events*) serie f; **a ~ of mistakes** un error detrás de otro **II.** vt catalogar

catastrophe [kə·'tæs·trə·fi] n catástrofe f

catastrophic [kæt·ə·'straf·ɪk] adj catastrófico, -a

catcall ['kæt·kɔl] n (*booing*) abucheo m; (*whistling*) silbido m

catch [kætʃ] **I.** n **1.** (*fish*) pesca f; **he's a good ~** *fig* es un buen partido **2.** (*door*) pestillo m; (*window*) cierre m **II.** <caught, caught> vt **1.** (*object*) agarrar; (*animal, person*) atrapar; **to ~ sb**

at a bad moment pillar a alguien en un mal momento **2.** (*entangle*) involucrar; **to get caught in sth** quedar atrapado en algo; **to get caught up in sth** verse involucrado en algo; **to get caught on sth** engancharse a algo **3.** (*notice*) darse cuenta de; (*hear*) pillar **4.** (*attract*) atraer **5.** (*get*) coger, tomar *AmL*; **to ~ the bus** coger el autobús **6. to ~ sb** (**doing sth**) pillar a alguien (haciendo algo); **to ~ sb red-handed** pillar a alguien con las manos en la masa **7.** MED pillar

◆**catch on** *vi* **1.** (*become popular*) ponerse de moda **2.** *inf* (*understand*) pillar

◆**catch up with** *vi* ponerse al día en; (*person*) alcanzar el nivel de

catch phrase [ˈkætʃ.freɪz] *n* eslogan *m*

catchy [ˈkætʃ·i] <-ier, -iest> *adj* pegadizo, -a

categorical [ˌkæt·ə·ˈɡɔr·ɪ·kəl] *adj* categórico, -a

category [ˈkæt·ə·ɡɔr·i] <-ies> *n* categoría *f*

cater [ˈkeɪ·tər] *vi* llevar el catering

catering [ˈkeɪ·tər·ɪŋ] *n* catering *m*

caterpillar [ˈkæt·ər·pɪl·ər] *n* ZOOL oruga *f*

catfish *n* siluro *m*, bagre *m Col, Méx*

cathedral [kə·ˈθi·drəl] *n* catedral *f*

Catholic [ˈkæθ·ə·lɪk] *adj, n* católico, -a *m, f*

Catholicism [kə·ˈθɑl·ə·sɪz·əm] *n* catolicismo *m*

catsup [ˈketʃ·əp] *n see* ketchup

cattle [ˈkæt·əl] *npl* ganado *m;* **beef ~** ganado vacuno

cattle breeder *n* ganadero, -a *m, f*

cattle breeding *n* ganadería *f*

cattle car *n* vagón *m* de ganado

catty [ˈkæt·i] <-ier, -iest> *adj* (*hurtful*) malicioso, -a

catwalk [ˈkæt·wɔk] *n* FASHION pasarela *f*

caught [kɔt] *pt, pp of* catch

cauliflower [ˈkɔ·lɪ·flaʊ·ər] *n* coliflor *f*

cause [kɔz] **I.** *n* causa *f;* **he is the ~ of all her woes** él es el causante de todas sus penas; **this is no ~ for...** esto no justifica... **II.** *vt* provocar; (*harm*) ocasionar; **to ~ sb/sth to do sth** hacer que alguien/algo haga algo

caution [ˈkɔ·ʃən] *n* **1.** (*carefulness*) cau-

tela *f;* **with ~** con cuidado **2.** (*warning*) advertencia *f;* **a note of ~** un aviso; **~!** ¡cuidado!

cautious [ˈkɔ·ʃəs] *adj* prudente (**about** con)

cave [keɪv] *n* cueva *f*

cave dweller *n* cavernícola *mf*

cave-in *n* derrumbamiento *m*

caveman [ˈkeɪv·mæn] <-men> *n* cavernícola *m*

cavern [ˈkæv·ərn] *n* caverna *f*

cavity [ˈkæv·ɪ·ti] <-ies> *n* **1.** *a.* ANAT cavidad *f;* **nasal ~** fosa *f* nasal **2.** MED caries *f inv*

cayenne [kaɪ·ˈen] *n* cayena *f*

CD [ˌsi·ˈdi] *n abbr of* compact disc CD *m;* **on ~** en CD

CD-ROM [ˌsi·di·ˈram] *n abbr of* compact disc read-only memory CD-ROM *m*

cease [sis] *form* **I.** *vi* cesar; **to ~ to do sth** cesar de (hacer) algo **II.** *vt* suspender; **it never ~s to amaze me** nunca deja de sorprenderme **III.** *n* **without ~** sin cesar

ceaseless [ˈsis·lɪs] *adj* incesante

ceiling [ˈsi·lɪŋ] *n* **1.** techo *m* **2.** (*upper limit*) tope *m;* (*on prices*) límite *m* ▸ **to hit the ~** subirse por las paredes

celebrate [ˈsel·ɪ·breɪt] *vi, vt* celebrar

celebrated *adj* célebre

celebration [ˌsel·ɪ·ˈbreɪ·ʃən] *n* celebración *f;* (*of an event*) conmemoración *f;* **this calls for** (**a**) **~!** ¡esto hay que celebrarlo!

celebrity [sə·ˈleb·rə·ti] *n* <-ies> (*person*) famoso, -a *m, f* **2.** (*fame*) celebridad *f*

celery [ˈsel·ə·ri] *n* apio *m*, panul *m CSur*

celery root *n* apio *m* nabo

cell [sel] *n* **1.** (*prison*) celda *f*, separo *m Méx* **2.** BIO, POL célula *f;* **grey ~s** materia gris

cellar [ˈsel·ər] *n* sótano *m;* (*for wine*) bodega *f*

cello [ˈtʃel·oʊ] <-s *or* -li> *n* violonchelo *m*

cellophane [ˈsel·ə·feɪn] *n* celofán *m*

cell phone [ˈsel·foʊn] *n* móvil *m*, celular *m Col*

cellular phone *n* móvil *m*, celular *m Col*

cellulite ['sel.jə.laɪt] *n* celulitis *f inv*

celluloid ['sel.jʊ.lɔɪd] *n* celuloide *m*

cellulose ['sel.jʊ.loʊs] *n* celulosa *f*

Celsius ['sel.si.əs] *adj* Celsius

cement [sɪ'ment] **I.** *n* **1.** ARCHIT cemento *m* **2.** (*glue*) cola *f* **3.** MED empaste *m* **II.** *vt* **1.** (*stabilize*) fortalecer; (*friendship*) consolidar **2.** MED empastar

cemetery ['sem.ə.ter.i] <-ies> *n* cementerio *m*, panteón *m AmL*

censor ['sen.sər] **I.** *n* censor(a) *m(f)* **II.** *vt* censurar

censorship ['sen.sər.ʃɪp] *n* censura *f*

censure ['sen.ʃər] *vt* censurar

census ['sen.səs] <-es> *n* censo *m*

cent [sent] *n* centavo *m*; (*euro*) céntimo *m*

centenarian [,sen.tə'ner.i.ən] *n* centenario, -a *m, f*

centenary [sen'ten.ə.ri] <-ies>, **centennial** [sen'ten.i.əl] *n* centenario *m*

center ['sen.tər] **I.** *n* centro *m*; (*of population*) núcleo *m* **II.** *vt* centrar; (*efforts*) concentrar

♦**center around** *vi* girar en torno a

♦**center on** *vi* concentrarse en

centigrade ['sen.tə.greɪd] *adj* centígrado, -a

centigram ['sen.tə.græm] *n* centigramo *m*

centimeter ['sen.tə.mi.tər] *n* centímetro *m*

central ['sen.trəl] *adj* **1.** (*at the middle*) central; **in ~ Boston** en el centro de Boston **2.** (*important*) vital (**to** para); **the ~ character** el protagonista **3.** (*bank, air conditioning, unit*) central

century ['sen.tʃə.ri] <-ies> *n* siglo *m*; **the twentieth ~** el siglo XX

ceramic [sə'ræm.ɪk] *adj* de cerámica

cereal ['sɪr.i.əl] *n* cereal *m*; (*breakfast*) cereales

ceremonial [,ser.ə'moʊ.ni.əl] *adj, n* ceremonial *m*

ceremony ['ser.ə.moʊ.ni] <-ies> *n* ceremonia *f*

certain ['sɜr.tən] **I.** *adj* **1.** (*sure*) seguro, -a; **for ~** con certeza; **it is quite ~ (that)...** es muy probable que... +*subj*; **to be ~ about sb** confiar en alguien; **to be ~ about sth** estar convencido de algo;

to feel ~ (that...) estar convencido (de que...); **to make ~ (that...)** asegurarse (de que...) **2.** (*undeniable*) cierto, -a; **it is ~ that...** es cierto que...; **the disaster seemed ~** el desastre parecía inevitable **3.** (*specified*) cierto, -a; **to a ~ extent** hasta cierto punto; **a ~ Steve** un tal Steve **II.** *pron* cierto, -a

certainly *adv* desde luego; **~ not!** ¡desde luego que no!; **why, ~!** ¡claro que sí!

certainty ['sɜr.tən.ti] <-ies> *n* certeza *f*; **with ~** a ciencia cierta

certificate [sər'tɪf.ɪ.kət] *n* certificado *m*, (*birth, death*) partida *f*; (*ownership, school*) título *m*

certification [,sɜr.tə.fɪ'keɪ.ʃən] *n* (*process*) certificación *f*; (*document*) certificado *m*

certify ['sɜr.tə.faɪ] <-ie-> *vt* certificar

cervical ['sɜr.vɪ.kəl] *adj* cervical; **~ collar** collarín *m*

cesarean [sə'zer.i.ən] *n* **a ~ section** una cesárea

chador [tʃə'dɔr] *n* chador *m*

chain [tʃeɪn] **I.** *n* **1. a.** *fig* cadena *f* **2.** GEO cordillera *f* **II.** *vt* encadenar; **to be ~ed to a desk** *fig* estar encerrado en un despacho

chain mail *n* cota *f* de malla

chain reaction *n* reacción *f* en cadena; **to set off a ~** provocar una reacción en cadena

chain saw *n* motosierra *f*

chain smoker *n* fumador(a) *m(f)* empedernido, -a

chair [tʃer] **I.** *n* **1.** (*seat*) silla *f* **2.** (*head*) presidente, -a *m, f* **3.** UNIV cátedra *f* **II.** *vt* presidir

chairlift *n* telesilla *m*

chairman ['tʃer.mən] <-men> *n* presidente *m*

chairperson ['tʃer.pɜr.sən] *n* presidente, -a *m, f*

chairwoman <-women> *n* presidenta *f*

chalet [ʃæ'leɪ] *n* chalet *m*

chalk [tʃɔk] *n* tiza *f*, gis *m Méx*; GEO caliza

challenge ['tʃæl.ɪndʒ] **I.** *n* desafío *m*; **to pose a ~ to sth** poner algo en tela de juicio **II.** *vt* **1.** (*ask to compete*) desafiar **2.** (*question*) cuestionar

challenging *adj* desafiante; (*course, task*) exigente; (*book*) que hace pensar

chamber ['tʃeɪm·bər] *n a.* ANAT, POL, ECON cámara *f*

chameleon [kə·'mi·li·ən] *n* camaleón *m*

chamomile ['kæm·ə·mil] *n* ~ (**tea**) manzanilla *f*

champ [tʃæmp] **I.** *n inf* campeón, -ona *m, f* **II.** *vi, vt* mascar

champagne [ʃæm·'peɪn] **I.** *n* champán *m* **II.** *adj* color champán

champion ['tʃæm·pi·ən] **I.** *adj, n* campeón, -ona *m, f* **II.** *vt* defender

championship ['tʃæm·pi·ən·ʃɪp] *n* campeonato *m*; (*of cause*) defensa *f*

chance [tʃæns] **I.** *n* **1.** (*random*) casualidad *f*; **a ~ encounter** un encuentro casual; **a game of ~** un juego de azar; **to leave nothing to ~** no dejar nada al azar; **by ~** por casualidad **2.** (*likelihood*) probabilidad *f*; **the ~s are that she's already gone** lo más probable es que ya se haya marchado; **on the off ~ that** con la esperanza de que; **to stand a ~ of doing sth** tener posibilidades de hacer algo; **not a ~!** ¡ni de coña! **3.** (*opportunity*) oportunidad *f* (**to do sth** de hacer algo); **to give sb a ~** dar a alguien una oportunidad; **to have the ~** tener la oportunidad; **to miss one's ~** perder la oportunidad; **to jump at the ~** no dejar escapar la oportunidad; **to take a ~** arriesgarse **II.** *vt* arriesgar; **to ~ it** arriesgarse **III.** *vi* ocurrir (por casualidad)

chancellor ['tʃæn·sə·lər] *n* canciller *mf*; UNIV rector(a) *m(f)*

chancy ['tʃæn·si] <-ier, -iest> *adj* arriesgado, -a

change ['tʃeɪndʒ] **I.** *n* **1.** (*alteration*) cambio *m*; **for a ~** para variar **2.** (*coins*) suelto *m*, sencillo *m* AmL, feria *f* Méx; **small ~** calderilla *f inf*; **a dollar in ~** un dólar en monedas; **have you got ~ for a twenty-dollar bill?** ¿tienes cambio de 20 dólares? **3.** (*money returned*) vuelta *f*, vuelto *m* AmL; **no ~ given** no (se) devuelve cambio; **to have exact ~** tener el importe exacto **II.** *vt* cambiar; **to ~ places with sb** *fig* ponerse en el lugar de alguien; **to ~ sth/sb into sth** convertir algo/a alguien en algo; **to ~ trains/**

gear(s) cambiar de tren/marcha **III.** *vi* **1.** cambiar; **to ~ into sth** convertirse en algo; **the traffic light ~d back to red** el semáforo se puso en rojo **2.** (*train/plane*) hacer transbordo **3.** (*clothes*) cambiarse (de ropa)

changeable ['tʃeɪn·dʒə·bəl] *adj* cambiante

changeover ['tʃeɪndʒ·ˌoʊ·vər] *n* transición *f*

changing ['tʃeɪn·dʒɪŋ] *adj* cambiante; ~ **room** vestuario *m*; (*shop*) probador *m*

channel ['tʃæn·əl] **I.** *n a.* TV canal *m*; **irrigation ~** acequia *f*; **through diplomatic ~s** por la vía diplomática **II.** <-ll-, -l-> *vt* canalizar; *fig* encauzar

chaos ['keɪ·as] *n* caos *m inv*

chaotic [keɪ·'at·ɪk] *adj* caótico, -a

chap [tʃæp] <-pp-> **I.** *vi* agrietarse, pasparse *RíoPl* **II.** *vt* agrietar

chapel ['tʃæp·əl] *n* capilla *f*; **funeral ~** capilla ardiente

chapter ['tʃæp·tər] *n* capítulo *m*

chapter house *n* UNIV sala *f* de reuniones

character ['ker·ək·tər] *n* **1.** (*qualities*) *a.* TYPO carácter *m*; **to be in/out of ~ with sb/sth** ser/no ser típico de alguien/algo **2.** (*moral integrity*) reputación *f* **3.** (*representation*) personaje *m*, carácter *m* Col, Méx; **in the ~ of** en el papel de

characteristic [ˌker·ək·tə·'rɪs·tɪk] **I.** *n* característica *f* **II.** *adj* característico, -a; **with her ~ dignity** con la dignidad que la caracteriza

charcoal ['tʃar·koʊl] *n* **1.** carbón *m* vegetal **2.** ART carboncillo *m*, carbonilla *f RíoPl*; **to draw in ~** dibujar al carboncillo

charge [tʃardʒ] **I.** *n* **1.** (*cost*) precio *m*; **at no extra ~** sin cargo adicional; **free of ~** gratis **2.** LAW cargo *m*; **to bring ~s** presentar cargos (**against** contra) **3.** MIL, ELEC carga *f*; SPORTS ofensiva *f* **4.** (*authority*) responsabilidad *f*; **to be in ~ of sb/sth** tener algo/a alguien a su cargo; **who is in ~ here?** ¿quién es el responsable aquí? **II.** *vi* **1.** FIN cobrar **2.** (*attack*) arremeter; MIL cargar (**at** contra) **3.** ELEC cargarse **III.** *vt* **1.** FIN cobrar; **to ~ sth to**

sb's account cargar algo en la cuenta de alguien **2.** LAW acusar; **she's been ~d with murder** se la acusa de asesinato **3.** ELEC cargar

chargeable [ˈtʃɑr·dʒə·bəl] *adj* ~ **to the customer** a cargo del cliente; **to be ~ to tax** estar sujeto a impuestos

charge card n tarjeta f de pago

charged *adj* cargado, -a

charisma [kəˈrɪz·mə] n carisma m

charity [ˈtʃer·ə·ti] <-ies> n caridad f; (*organization*) institución f benéfica

charm [tʃɑrm] **I.** n encanto m **II.** vt cautivar; **to ~ sb into doing sth** embelesar a alguien para que haga algo

charming [ˈtʃɑr·mɪn] *adj* encantador(a)

chart [tʃɑrt] **I.** n **1.** tabla f **2.** MUS **the ~s** la lista de éxitos **II.** vt trazar

charter flight n vuelo m chárter

chase [tʃeɪs] **I.** n persecución f; (*hunt*) a. *fig* caza f; **to give ~** dar caza **II.** vi **they ~ed after her** fueron tras ella **III.** vt perseguir; **to ~ away sb/sth** ahuyentar a alguien/algo

chaste [tʃeɪst] *adj* casto, -a

chat [tʃæt] **I.** n charla f; COMPUT chat m **II.** vi <-tt-> charlar, versar *AmC*; **to ~ away** estar de cháchara, echar la chorcha *Méx*; COMPUT chatear

chatroom n foro m de chat

chatter [ˈtʃæt̬·ər] **I.** n cháchara f **II.** vi charlar

chatty [ˈtʃæt̬·i] <-ier, -iest> *adj inf* hablador(a)

cheap [tʃip] *adj* barato, -a; **dirt ~** tirado, -a de precio; ~ **labor** mano de obra barata

cheaply *adv* de forma barata

cheat [tʃit] **I.** n **1.** (*person*) estafador(a) *m(f)* **2.** (*trick*) trampa f **II.** vi hacer trampa(s) (**at** en); **to ~ on a test** copiar en un examen **III.** vt engañar

check [tʃek] **I.** n **1.** (*inspection, restraint*) control m; **security ~** control de seguridad; **to keep sth in ~** mantener algo bajo control; (*of facts*) verificación f; **to run a ~** realizar una inspección **2.** (*deposit receipt*) resguardo m **3.** (*paper money*) cheque m; **to pay by ~** pagar con cheque **4.** (*bill*) cuenta f **5.** (*chess*) jaque m **II.** *adj* a

cuadros **III.** vt **1.** (*inspect*) comprobar, chequear *AmL* **2.** (*prevent*) frenar **3.** (*deposit*) dejar en consigna; AVIAT facturar **IV.** vi **1.** (*examine*) revisar **2.** (*ask*) consultar

◆**check in** vi (*airport*) facturar; (*hotel*) registrarse

◆**check out I.** vi **to ~ of a room** dejar libre una habitación **II.** vt (*investigate*) investigar

◆**check up on** vt controlar

checkbook [ˈtʃek·bʊk] n talonario m de cheques

checked *adj* a cuadros

checkerboard [ˈtʃek·ər·bɔrd] n tablero m de ajedrez

checkers [ˈtʃek·ərz] n + *sing vb* damas fpl

check-in [ˈtʃek·ɪn] n facturación f

checking account n cuenta f corriente

check-in time n hora f de facturación

checklist [ˈtʃek·lɪst] n lista f

checkmate I. n (jaque m) mate m; (*defeat*) fracaso m **II.** vt dar (jaque) mate a; *fig* ganar

checkout counter n caja f

checkpoint [ˈtʃek·pɔɪnt] n punto m de control

checkroom n (*for coats*) guardarropa m; (*for luggage*) consigna f

checkup [ˈtʃek·ʌp] n comprobación f; MED chequeo m

cheek [tʃik] n mejilla f; (*impertinence*) descaro m, empaque m *AmL*; **to have the ~ to do sth** tener la cara dura de hacer algo

cheekbone [ˈtʃik·boʊn] n pómulo m

cheeky [ˈtʃi·ki] <-ier, -iest> *adj* descarado, -a, fregado, -a *AmL* (**to** con)

cheep [tʃip] vi piar

cheer [tʃɪr] **I.** n **1.** (*shout*) ovación f; **three ~s for the champion!** ¡tres hurras por el campeón!; **to give a ~** vitorear **2.** (*joy*) alegría f; **to be of good ~** estar animado **II.** *interj* ~**s** salud **III.** vi **to ~ for sb** animar a alguien

cheerful [ˈtʃɪr·fʊl] *adj* alegre; (*encouraging*) alentador(a); (*color*) vivo, -a

cheerfulness n alegría f

cheering I. n aplausos mpl **II.** *adj* alentador(a)

cheerleader [ˈtʃɪr·li·dər] n animadora f

cheery ['tʃɪr·i] <-ier, -iest> *adj* alegre

cheese [tʃiz] *n* queso *m*; **hard/melted ~** queso curado/fundido

cheesecake ['tʃiz·keɪk] *n* tarta *f* de queso

cheese-paring ['tʃiz·ˌper·ɪŋ] *n* tacaño, -a *m, f*

cheesy ['tʃi·zi] <-ier, -iest> *adj* **1.** como queso **2.** (*cheap and shoddy*) chungo, -a

cheetah ['tʃi·tə] *n* guepardo *m*

chef [ʃef] *n* jefe, -a *m, f* de cocina

chemical ['kem·ɪ·kəl] **I.** *n* sustancia *f* química; (*additive*) aditivo *m* **II.** *adj* químico, -a

chemist ['kem·ɪst] *n* químico, -a *m, f*

chemistry ['kem·ɪ·stri] *n* química *f*

cherry ['tʃer·i] <-ies> *n* cereza *f*; (*tree*) cerezo *m*

cherry tomato *n* tomate *m* cherry

chess [tʃes] *n* ajedrez *m*

chessman <-men>, **chess piece** *n* pieza *f* de ajedrez

chest [tʃest] *n* **1.** ANAT pecho *m* **2.** (*trunk*) baúl *m*, petaca *f* AmL; **medicine ~** botiquín *m* ▶ **to get sth off one's ~** desahogarse confesando algo

chestnut ['tʃes·nʌt] **I.** *n* castaña *f*; (*tree, color*) castaño *m* **II.** *adj* castaño, -a

chesty ['tʃes·ti] <-ier, -iest> *adj* inf pechugona, bustona *Col, Méx*

chew [tʃu] *vt* masticar

◆**chew out** *vt sl* echar la bronca a

chewing gum ['tʃu·ɪŋ·gʌm] *n* chicle *m*

chic [ʃik] *adj* a la moda

Chicano [tʃɪ·ˈkɑ·noʊ] *n adj* chicano, -a *m, f*

chick [tʃɪk] *n* **1.** (*chicken*) pollito, -a *m, f*; (*bird*) polluelo, -a *m, f* **2.** *sl* tía *f*

chicken ['tʃɪk·ən] *n* **1.** (*farm bird*) pollo *m*; **fried/roasted/grilled ~** pollo frito/asado/a la brasa **2.** *inf* rajado, -a *m, f*, rajón, -ona *m, f Cuba, Méx*

chicken feed *n* **1.** pienso *m* **2.** (*money*) calderilla *f*

chickenpox *n* varicela *f*

chicken run *n* gallinero *m*

chickpea ['tʃɪk·pi] *n* garbanzo *m*

chicory ['tʃɪk·ə·ri] *n* BOT endivia *f*

chief [tʃif] **I.** *n* jefe, -a *m, f* **II.** *adj* (*top*) primero, -a; (*major*) principal

chiefly *adv* principalmente

child [tʃaɪld] <children> *pl n* niño, -a *m, f*

child abuse ['tʃaɪld·ə·bjus] *n* maltrato *m* infantil; (*sexual*) abuso *m* infantil

childbearing *n* maternidad *f*

childbirth *n* parto *m*, parición *f AmL*

child-care *n* cuidado *m* de los niños

childhood *n* infancia *f*

childish ['tʃaɪl·dɪʃ] *adj pej* infantil, achiquillado, -a *Méx*

childless ['tʃaɪld·lɪs] *adj* sin hijos

childlike ['tʃaɪld·laɪk] *adj* infantil

children ['tʃɪl·drən] *n pl of* **child**

child's play *n fig* juego *m* de niños

chile, chili ['tʃɪl·i] <-es> *n* guindilla *f*, chile *m AmL*, ají *m AmS, Ant*

Chile ['tʃɪl·i] *n* Chile *m*

Chilean [tʃɪ·ˈleɪ·ən] *adj, n* chileno, -a *m, f*

chill [tʃɪl] **I.** *n* **1.** (*coldness*) frío *m*; **to catch a ~** resfriarse; **to take the ~ off of something** caldear algo **2.** (*shiver*) escalofrío *m*; **to send a ~ down someone's spine** dar escalofríos a alguien **II.** *adj* frío, -a; (*frightening*) estremecedor(a) **III.** *vt* enfriar

chilly ['tʃɪl·i] <-ier, -iest> *adj a. fig* frío, -a; **to feel ~** tener frío

chime [tʃaɪm] **I.** *vi* repicar **II.** *vt* **to ~ eleven** dar las once

chimney ['tʃɪm·ni] *n* chimenea *f*, tronera *f Méx*

chimpanzee [tʃɪm·ˈpæn·zi] *n* chimpancé *m*

chin [tʃɪn] *n* barbilla *f* ▶ **to keep one's ~ up** no desanimarse

china ['tʃaɪ·nə] *n* (*porcelain*) porcelana *f*; (*dishes*) vajilla *f*

China ['tʃaɪ·nə] *n* China *f*

Chinatown ['tʃaɪ·nə·ˌtoʊn] *n* barrio *m* chino

Chinese [tʃaɪ·ˈniz] **I.** *adj* chino, -a **II.** *n* **1.** (*person*) chino, -a *m, f* **2.** LING chino *m*

Chinese cabbage *n* col *f* china

chink [tʃɪŋk] **I.** *n* **1.** (*thin opening*) hendidura *f* **2.** (*noise*) tintineo *m* **II.** *vi* tintinear

chip [tʃɪp] **I.** *n* **1.** (*flake*) pedazo *m*; (*wood*) astilla *f* **2.** COMPUT chip *m* **3.** (*token*) ficha *f* ▶ *inf* **he's a ~ off the old block** de tal palo, tal astilla; **when the**

~s **are** <u>down</u> a la hora de la verdad **II.** *vt* <-pp-> desportillar **III.** *vi* <-pp-> desportillarse

chirpy ['tʃɜrpi] <-ier, -iest> *adj* animado, -a

chitchat ['tʃɪt·tʃæt] *inf* **I.** *n* cháchara *f* **II.** *vi* **to ~ about sth** estar de palique sobre algo

chlorine ['klɔr·in] *n* cloro *m*

chloroform ['klɔr·ə·fɔrm] *n* cloroformo *m*

chock [tʃak] *n* cuña *f*

chock-a-block [,tʃak·ə·'blak] *adj* **~ with people** abarrotado de gente

chocolate ['tʃak·lət] *n* chocolate *m*; **dark ~** chocolate negro; (*candy*) bombón *m*

choice [tʃɔɪs] **I.** *n* **1.** (*option*) elección *f*; **to make a ~** elegir; **to have no ~** no tener alternativa; **she didn't have much ~** no tenía muchas opciones **2.** (*selection*) selección *f*; **a wide ~** un amplio surtido **3.** (*selected person or thing*) preferencia *f* **II.** *adj* (*top quality*) selecto, -a

choir ['kwaɪr] *n* coro *m*

choke [tʃoʊk] **I.** *vi* sofocarse **II.** *vt* **1.** (*stifle*) estrangular **2.** (*block*) obstruir
◆ **choke back** *vt* ahogar
◆ **choke off** *vt* cortar
◆ **choke up** *vt* obstruir

choker ['tʃoʊ·kər] *n* gargantilla *f*

cholesterol [kə·'les·tə·rəl] *n* colesterol *m*

choose [tʃuz] <chose, chosen> *vt, vi* elegir

choos(e)y ['tʃu·zi] <-ier, -iest> *adj inf* quisquilloso, -a

chop [tʃap] **I.** *vt* <-pp-> cortar; (*wood*) partir; (*meat*) picar **II.** *vi* <-pp-> cortar **III.** *n* **1.** CULIN chuleta *f* **2.** (*blow*) golpe *m*
◆ **chop away** *vt* cortar
◆ **chop down** *vt* talar
◆ **chop off** *vt* tronchar

chop-chop [,tʃap·'tʃap] *interj inf* ¡vamos, que nos vamos!

chopper ['tʃap·ər] *n* **1.** (*tool*) hacha *f* **2.** *inf* helicóptero *m*

chopsticks ['tʃap·stɪks] *npl* palillos *mpl*

chord [kɔrd] *n* MUS acorde *m*

chore [tʃɔr] *n* **1.** tarea *f*; **household**

~s quehaceres domésticos **2.** (*tedious task*) lata *f*

choreography [,kɔr·i·'ag·rə·fi] *n* coreografía *f*

chorus ['kɔr·əs] <-es> *n* **1.** (*refrain*) estribillo *m* **2.** + *sing/pl vb* (*singers*) coro *m*; **in ~** a coro

chose [tʃoʊz] *pt of* **choose**

chosen ['tʃoʊ·zən] *pp of* **choose**

Christ [kraɪst] **I.** *n* Cristo *m* **II.** *interj*: **for ~'s sake** ¡por Dios!

christen ['krɪs·ən] *vt* **1.** (*baptize*) bautizar **2.** (*give name to*) llamar **3.** (*use for first time*) estrenar

christening ['krɪs·ə·nɪŋ] *n* bautizo *m*

Christian ['krɪs·tʃən] *adj, n* cristiano, -a *m, f*

Christianity [,krɪs·tʃi·'æn·ə·ti] *n* cristianismo *m*

Christmas ['krɪs·məs] <-es *or* -ses> *n* Navidad *f*; **at ~** en Navidad; **Merry ~!** ¡Feliz Navidad!; **Father ~** Papá Noel

Christmas carol *n* villancico *m*

Christmas Day *n* día *m* de Navidad [*or Perú, Chile* Pascua]

Christmas Eve *n* Nochebuena *f*

chromosome ['kroʊ·mə·soʊm] *n* cromosoma *m*

chronic ['kran·ɪk] *adj* crónico, -a; (*liar*) empedernido, -a

chronicle ['kran·ɪ·kəl] *n* crónica *f*

chronological [,kran·ə·'ladʒ·ɪ·kəl] *adj* cronológico, -a; **in ~ order** en orden cronológico

chubby ['tʃʌb·i] <-ier, -iest> *adj* regordete, -a

chuck [tʃʌk] *inf* **I.** *vt* tirar **II.** *n* tiro *m*

chuckhole *n* bache *m*, pozo *m Csur*

chuckle ['tʃʌk·əl] **I.** *n* risita *f* **II.** *vi* reírse

chug [tʃʌg] **I.** <-gg-> *vi* resoplar **II.** *n* resoplido *m*

chum[1] [tʃʌm] *n inf* colega *mf*, cuate *m Méx*

chum[2] [tʃʌm] *n* (*bait*) cebo *m*

chummy ['tʃʌm·i] <-ier, -iest> *adj inf* simpático, -a; **to get ~ with sb** hacerse amigo de alguien

chump [tʃʌmp] *n inf* tontorrón, -ona *m, f*

chump change *n sl* calderilla *f*

chunk [tʃʌŋk] *n* **1.** (*cheese, bread, meat*) trozo *m*, troncho *m CSur* **2.** *inf* (*large* part) cacho m

chunky [ˈtʃʌŋ.ki] <-ier, -iest> adj (person) macizo, -a; CULIN con trocitos

church [tʃɜrtʃ] I. n iglesia f; **to go to ~** ir a misa II. adj (parade, celebration) religioso, -a

churchgoer [ˈtʃɜrtʃˌgoʊ.ər] n practicante mf

churchyard [ˈtʃɜrtʃ.jard] n cementerio m

chute [ʃut] n 1. (sloping tube) rampa f; **garbage ~** vertedero m de basuras 2. (swimming pool) tobogán m 3. inf AVIAT paracaídas m inv

cicada <-s or -dae> [sɪˈkeɪdə] n cigarra f

cider [ˈsaɪ.dər] n **sweet ~** zumo m de manzana

cigar [sɪˈgar] n puro m

cigar box <-es> n, **cigar case** n pitillera f

cigar cutter n cortapuros m inv

cigarette [ˌsɪg.əˈret] n cigarrillo m

cigarette butt n colilla f

cigarette case n pitillera f

cigarette holder n boquilla f

cigarette paper n papel m de fumar, mortaja f AmL

cigarillo [ˌsɪg.əˈrɪl.oʊ] n purito m

cinema [ˈsɪn.ə.mə] n cine m, biógrafo m Arg, Chile, Urug

cinnamon [ˈsɪn.ə.mən] n canela f; **ground/stick ~** canela en polvo/en rama

cipher [ˈsaɪ.fər] n clave f; **in ~** en clave

circa [ˈsɜr.kə] prep hacia; **~ 1850** hacia (el año) 1850

circle [ˈsɜr.kəl] I. n círculo m; **to go around in ~s** dar vueltas; **to run around in ~s** fig dar vueltas y más vueltas a algo ► **to come full ~** volver al punto de partida II. vt rodear III. vi dar vueltas

circuit [ˈsɜr.kɪt] n 1. ELEC, SPORTS circuito m 2. POL distrito m

circuit board n placa f base

circular [ˈsɜr.kjə.lər] adj, n circular f

circulate [ˈsɜr.kjə.leɪt] I. vt divulgar II. vi circular

circulation [ˌsɜr.kjʊˈleɪ.ʃən] n circulación f; **to be out of ~** estar fuera de circulación

circulatory [ˈsɜr.kjə.lə.tɔr.i] adj circulatorio, -a

circumstance [ˈsɜr.kəmˌstæns] n circunstancia f; **under no ~s** bajo ningún concepto

circus [ˈsɜr.kəs] <-es> n circo m

cirrhosis [səˈroʊ.sɪs] n cirrosis f inv

cistern [ˈsɪs.tərn] n cisterna f, jagüel m AmL

citizen [ˈsɪt.ɪ.zən] n 1. (subject) ciudadano, -a m, f 2. (resident of town) habitante mf

citizens' band n banda f ciudadana

citizenship [ˈsɪt.ɪ.zən.ʃɪp] n ciudadanía f

citrus [ˈsɪt.rəs] <citrus or citruses> I. n cítrico m II. adj cítrico, -a

city [ˈsɪt.i] <-ies> I. n ciudad f II. adj urbano, -a

city hall n ayuntamiento m

civic [ˈsɪv.ɪk] <inv> adj cívico, -a; (authorities) civil

civil [ˈsɪv.əl] adj civil; (courteous) cortés

civil court n Sala f de lo Civil

civilian [sɪˈvɪl.jən] <inv> I. n civil mf II. adj civil; (clothes) de paisano, -a

civilization [ˌsɪv.ə.lɪˈzeɪ.ʃən] n civilización f

civil servant n funcionario, -a m, f

civil service n Administración f Pública

clad [klæd] I. adj vestido, -a II. vt pt, pp of **clothe**

claim [kleɪm] I. n 1. (assertion) afirmación f 2. (demand) demanda f; (insurance) reclamación f; **to put in a ~** presentar una demanda (**for** por) 3. (right) derecho m; **to lay to ~** reivindicar II. vt 1. (assert) asegurar 2. (declare ownership, demand) reclamar; (right, reward, title) reivindicar; **to ~ damages** reclamar daños y perjuicios 3. (require) requerir III. vi **to ~ for** reclamar

claimant [ˈkleɪ.mənt] n solicitante mf

clam [klæm] n 1. almeja f 2. sl dólar m ► **to be happy as a ~** estar feliz como una lombriz

clamber [ˈklæm.bər] vi trepar

clammy [ˈklæm.i] <-ier, -iest> adj (feet) sudoroso, -a; (weather) bochornoso, -a

clamp [klæmp] vt (impose) imponer

◆**clamp down** vi tomar medidas drásticas (**on** contra)

clan [klæn] *n* clan *m*

clandestine [klæn·'des·tɪn] *adj* clandestino, -a

clang [klæŋ] I. *vi* repicar II. *n* estruendo *m* metálico

clank [klæŋk] I. *vi* hacer ruido II. *vt* hacer sonar III. *n* ruido *m* metálico

clap [klæp] I. <-pp-> *vt* aplaudir; **to ~ one's hands (together)** hacer palmas II. <-pp-> *vi* hacer palmas; (*applaud*) aplaudir III. *n* (*slap*) palmada *f*; (*applause*) aplauso *m*

claptrap ['klæp·træp] *n inf* chorradas *fpl argot*

clarify ['kler·ɪ·faɪ] <-ie-> *vt* 1. (*make clearer*) aclarar 2. (*explain*) explicar

clarity ['kler·ə·ti] *n* claridad *f*

clash [klæʃ] *vi* 1. (*fight*) pelearse; (*argue*) discutir (**over** por) 2. (*compete*) enfrentarse; (*views*) contradecirse; (*colors*) desentonar II. <-es> *n* 1. (*encounter*) enfrentamiento *m* 2. (*contest*) contienda *f* 3. (*conflict*) conflicto *m* 4. (*incompatibility*) choque *m* 5. (*noise*) estruendo *m*

clasp [klæsp] I. *n* cierre *m*; (*of hands*) apretón *m* II. *vt* 1. (*grip*) agarrar; **to ~ one's hands** darse un apretón de manos; **to ~ sb in one's arms** estrechar a alguien entre sus brazos 2. (*fasten*) abrochar

class [klæs] <-es> *n* clase *f* II. *vt* catalogar (**as** de)

classic ['klæs·ɪk] I. *adj* clásico, -a; (*typical*) típico, -a; *inf* (*joke, story*) genial II. *n* clásico *m*

classical ['klæs·ɪ·kəl] *adj* clásico, -a

classification [ˌklæs·ə·fɪ·'keɪ·ʃən] *n* clasificación *f*

classified ['klæs·ɪ·faɪd] <inv> *adj* clasificado, -a; (*confidential*) confidencial

classified advertisement *n* anuncio *m* clasificado

classify ['klæs·ɪ·faɪ] <-ie-> *vt* clasificar

classmate *n* compañero, -a *m, f* de clase

classroom *n* aula *f*

clatter ['klæt̬·ər] I. *vi* hacer ruido II. *n* estruendo *m*

clause [klɔz] *n* cláusula *f*; LING oración *f*

claustrophobia [ˌklɔ·strə·'foʊ·bi·ə] *n*

claustrofobia *f*

claustrophobic *adj* claustrofóbico, -a

clavicle ['klæv·ɪ·kəl] *n* clavícula *f*

claw [klɔ] I. *n* garra *f*; (*crab, lobster*) pinza *f*; **to show one's ~s** *fig* sacar las uñas *fpl* II. *vt* arañar

clay [kleɪ] I. *n* 1. arcilla *f* 2. SPORTS tierra *f* batida *f*. *adj* de arcilla

clean [klin] I. *adj* 1. (*not dirty, fair, smooth*) limpio, -a; **to make a ~ break with sth** romper por completo con algo 2. (*morally acceptable*) decente; (*reputation*) sin tacha II. *n* limpieza *f* III. *adv* completamente IV. *vt, vi* limpiar

◆**clean out** *vt* 1. limpiar; (*with water*) lavar 2. *sl* (*make penniless*) dejar sin blanca a

◆**clean up** I. *vt* 1. limpiar; (*tidy up*) ordenar; **to clean oneself up** asearse 2. (*eradicate*) acabar con II. *vi* 1. limpiar 2. *sl* (*make profit*) barrer con todo

cleaner ['kli·nər] *n* limpiador(a) *m(f)*; (*substance*) producto *m* de limpieza

cleaning ['kli·nɪŋ] *n* limpieza *f*

cleaning lady <-ies>, **cleaning woman** <women> *n* mujer *f* de la limpieza

cleanly ['klen·li] *adv* limpiamente

cleanse [klenz] *vt* limpiar; (*morally*) purificar

clean-shaven ['klin·'ʃeɪ·vən] *adj* bien afeitado, -a

cleansing cream *n* leche *f* limpiadora

cleansing tissue *n* toallita *f* desmaquilladora

cleanup ['klin·ʌp] *n* limpieza *f*

clear [klɪr] I. *n* **to be in the ~** estar fuera de peligro II. *adv* claramente; **to get ~** deshacerse (**of** de); **to stand ~** mantenerse a distancia (**of** de) III. *adj* 1. (*transparent, obvious*) claro, -a; (*picture*) nítido, -a; **to make oneself ~** explicarse con claridad; **as ~ as day** más claro que el agua 2. (*conscience*) tranquilo, -a; **to be ~ of debt** estar libre de deudas IV. *vt* 1. (*make free*) despejar; (*drain, pipe*) desatascar 2. (*remove doubts*) aclarar; **to ~ one's head** despejar la cabeza 3. (*acquit*) absolver V. *vi* (*water*) aclararse; (*weather*) despejarse

◆**clear away** I. *vt* quitar II. *vi* irse

◆**clear off** I. *vi inf* largarse, jalar *Bol*,

PRico, Urug II. vt liquidar

◆clear out I. vt limpiar; (throw away) vaciar II. vi irse

◆clear up I. vt aclarar; (tidy) ordenar II. vi despejarse

clearance ['klɪr·əns] n 1. (space) espacio m libre 2. (permission) autorización f

clearance sale n liquidación f

clearheaded adj perspicaz

clearing ['klɪr·ɪŋ] n claro m

clearly ['klɪr·li] adv claramente

clef [klef] n MUS clave f

clench [klentʃ] vt presionar; (one's fist) apretar

clerical ['kler·ɪ·kəl] adj 1. REL clerical 2. (of offices) de oficina; ~ worker oficinista mf

clerk [klɜrk] n (in office) oficinista mf; (in hotel) recepcionista mf; (in shop) dependiente mf

clever ['klev·ər] adj 1. (intelligent) listo, -a 2. (skillful) hábil; (invention) ingenioso, -a 3. pej astuto, -a; to be too ~ by half pasarse de listo

cleverness n inteligencia f; (skill) habilidad f

cliché [kli·'ʃeɪ] n cliché m; (platitude) tópico m

click [klɪk] I. n clic m II. vi 1. (sound) chasquear 2. COMPUT pinchar 3. (become friendly) congeniar; (become popular) tener éxito 4. (become clear) caer en la cuenta III. vt (tongue) chasquear; (heels) taconear; COMPUT pinchar

client ['klaɪ·ənt] n cliente mf

cliff [klɪf] n precipicio m; (on coast) acantilado m

climactic [ˌklaɪ·'mæk·tɪk] adj culminante

climate ['klaɪ·mɪt] n clima m; the ~ of opinion la opinión general

climatic [klaɪ·'mæt̬·ɪk] adj climático, -a

climax ['klaɪ·mæks] I. <-es> n clímax m inv II. vi culminar

climb [klaɪm] I. n subida f; (to power) ascenso m II. vt (stairs) subir; (tree) trepar a; (mountain) escalar III. vi subir

◆climb down vi bajar(se) de; fig echarse atrás

climb-down ['klaɪm·daʊn] n vuelta f atrás

climber ['klaɪ·mər] n 1. alpinista mf, andinista mf AmL; (for higher status) arribista mf 2. (plant) enredadera f

climbing ['klaɪ·mɪŋ] I. n (mountains) alpinismo m, andinismo m AmL; (rock faces) escalada f II. adj (plant) trepador(a); (boots) de montaña

climbing iron n see crampon

clinch [klɪntʃ] I. <-es> n abrazo m II. vt (settle) resolver; (deal) cerrar

clincher ['klɪn·tʃər] n inf factor m decisivo

cling [klɪŋ] <clung, clung> vi to ~ to (embrace) abrazarse a; (hold) agarrarse a; fig aferrarse a; (stick) adherirse a; (stay close) pegarse a; (follow closely) no separarse de

clinging adj (clothes) ajustado, -a; (person) pegajoso, -a

clinic ['klɪn·ɪk] n clínica f

clinical ['klɪn·ɪ·kəl] adj clínico, -a; (emotionless) frío, -a

clink [klɪŋk] I. vt, vi tintinear II. n 1. tintineo m 2. sl (prison) chirona f

clip¹ [klɪp] I. n (fastener) clip m; (hair) horquilla f; (jewelry) broche m II. <-pp-> vt sujetar

clip² [klɪp] <-pp-> I. vt 1. (cut) recortar; (hair, nails) cortar; (ticket) picar 2. (reduce) abreviar II. n (trim) recorte m; (extract) fragmento m

clipboard ['klɪp·bɔrd] n portapapeles m inv

clique [klik] n pandilla f

clitoris ['klɪt̬·ər·əs] <-es> n clítoris m inv

cloak [kloʊk] I. n capa f; (covering) manto m II. vt (hide) encubrir

cloakroom ['kloʊk·rum] n guardarropa m

clobber ['klab·ər] vt sl endiñar

clock [klak] I. n 1. reloj m; alarm ~ despertador m; around the ~ las 24 horas; against the ~ contrarreloj 2. (speedometer) velocímetro m; (odometer) cuentakilómetros m inv II. vt cronometrar; (reach) alcanzar

◆clock in vi fichar

◆clock out vi fichar (al salir del trabajo); inf salir del trabajo

◆clock up vt insep (attain) alcanzar; (travel) recorrer

clock radio n radio despertador f

clockwise adj, adv en el sentido de las agujas del reloj

clockwork n mecanismo m de relojería; **as regular as ~** como un reloj

clog [klag] **I.** <-gg-> vi atascarse **II.** <-gg-> vt atascar

clone [kloʊn] **I.** n clon m **II.** vt clonar

close[1] [kloʊs] **I.** adj **1.** (near) cercano, -a; (friend) íntimo, -a **2.** (almost even) raspado, -a **3.** (similar) parecido, -a **II.** adv cerca; (in time) casi; **to move ~** acercarse

close[2] [kloʊz] **I.** n (end) fin m **II.** vt (shut) cerrar; (end) terminar; **to ~ a deal** cerrar un trato **III.** vi (shut) cerrarse; (end) terminarse

◆**close down I.** vi cerrarse (definitivamente) **II.** vt cerrar (definitivamente)

◆**close in** vi **1.** (surround) rodear **2.** (get shorter) acortar

◆**close off** vt cerrar

◆**close up I.** vi (people) arrimarse; (wound) cicatrizar **II.** vt cerrar del todo

closed adj cerrado, -a; **behind ~ doors** a puerta cerrada

closed-door adj a puerta cerrada

closedown n cierre m

close-knit adj unido, -a

closely ['kloʊs·li] adv **1.** (near) de cerca **2.** (intimately) estrechamente **3.** (carefully) atentamente

closet ['klaz·ɪt] n (cupboard) armario m; (for food) alacena f ► **to come out of the ~** salir del armario

close to I. prep cerca de; **~ doing sth** cerca de hacer algo; **~ tears** a punto de llorar; **to be ~ sb** estar unido a alguien **II.** adv (almost) casi

close-up ['kloʊs·ʌp] n primer plano m

closing I. adj último, -a; (speech) de clausura **II.** n **1.** (ending) conclusión f; (act) clausura f **2.** COM cierre m

closing date n fecha f límite

closing time n hora f de cierre

closure ['kloʊ·ʒər] n (closing) cierre m; (end) fin m

clot [klat] **I.** n coágulo m **II.** <-tt-> vi cuajar; (blood) coagularse

cloth [klɔθ] **I.** n tela f; (for cleaning) trapo m **II.** adj de tela

clothe [kloʊð] vt vestir; fig revestir de

clothes [kloʊz] npl ropa f

clothes hanger n percha f

clotheshorse n tendedero m plegable

clothesline n cuerda f para tender

clothespin n pinza f

clothing ['kloʊ·ðɪŋ] n ropa f; **article of ~** prenda f

cloud [klaʊd] **I.** n nube f ► **every ~ has a silver lining** no hay mal que por bien no venga; **to be on ~ nine** estar en el séptimo cielo; **to be under a ~** estar bajo sospecha **II.** vt a. fig nublar

◆**cloud over** vi nublarse; fig ensombrecerse

cloudburst n chaparrón m

clouded ['klaʊ·dɪd] adj nublado, -a; (liquid) turbio, -a; (mind) confuso, -a

cloudless ['klaʊd·lɪs] adj despejado, -a

cloudy ['klaʊ·di] <-ier, -iest> adj nublado, -a; (liquid) turbio, -a

clout [klaʊt] **I.** n **1.** inf (hit) tortazo m **2.** (power) influencia f **II.** vt inf dar un tortazo a

clove [kloʊv] n clavo m; (garlic) diente m

clover ['kloʊ·vər] n trébol m

clown [klaʊn] **I.** n payaso m, f **II.** vi **to ~ around** hacer el payaso

club [klʌb] n **1.** (group) asociación f, club m **2.** (team, disco) club **3.** (playing card) trébol m

clubbing vi **to go ~** salir de clubs

clue [klu] n **1.** (evidence) indicio m; (hint) pista f **2.** (secret) clave f **3.** (idea) idea f; **I don't have a ~** no tengo ni idea

◆**clue in** vt informar (on de)

clueless ['klu·lɪs] adj inf despistado, -a

clump [klʌmp] **I.** vt **to ~ together** agrupar **II.** vi **to ~ together** agruparse

clumsy ['klʌm·zi] <-ier, -iest> adj desgarbado, -a; (bungling) torpe

clung [klʌŋ] pp, pt of **cling**

cluster ['klʌs·tər] **I.** n grupo m; (fruits) racimo m **II.** vi agruparse

clutch [klʌtʃ] **I.** vi agarrarse (at a) **II.** vt agarrar **III.** n **1.** AUTO embrague m **2. to be in the ~es of** estar en las garras de; **to come through in the ~** salir airoso

clutter ['klʌt̮·ər] I. n desorden m II. vt desordenar

cm inv abbr of **centimeter** cm

c'mon inf = **come on**

CO n abbr of **Colorado** Colorado m

co. [kou] 1. abbr of **company** cía. 2. GEO abbr of **county** condado m

coach [koutʃ] I. <-es> n 1. (bus) autocar m 2. (carriage) carruaje m 3. RAIL vagón m 4. (teacher) profesor(a) m(f) particular; SPORTS entrenador(a) m(f) II. vt to ~ sb (in sth) enseñar (algo) a alguien III. vi dar clases particulares

coaching n preparación f

coal [koul] n carbón m

coalition [ˌkou·ə·'lɪʃ·ən] n coalición f

coarse [kɔrs] <-r, -st> adj basto, -a; (sand) grueso, -a; (skin) áspero, -a

coast [koust] n costa f ▶ **the ~ is clear** no hay moros en la costa

coastal ['kou·stəl] adj costero, -a, abajeño, -a AmL

coaster ['kou·stər] n 1. (for glasses) posavasos m inv 2. (roller coaster) montaña f rusa

coast guard ['koust·gard] n, **Coast Guard** ['koust·gard] n guardacostas mf inv

coastline n línea f de costa

coat [kout] I. n 1. (overcoat) abrigo m, tapado m AmS; (jacket) chaqueta f 2. (animal's skin) pelaje m 3. (layer) capa f; (paint) mano f; (chocolate) baño m II. vt cubrir (in de)

coated ['kou·t̮ɪd] adj cubierto, -a

coat hanger n percha f

coating ['kou·t̮ɪŋ] n see **coat** I,3

coauthor [kou·'ɔ·θər] I. n coautor(a) m(f) II. vt escribir conjuntamente

coax [kouks] vt convencer; **to ~ sth out of sb** sonsacarle algo a alguien

cob [kɔb] n (corn) mazorca f, elote m AmC, Méx

cobble ['kab·əl] I. n adoquín m II. vt adoquinar; (shoe) remendar

cobbler ['kab·lər] n zapatero m remendón

cobweb ['kab·web] n telaraña f

cocaine [kou·'keɪn] n cocaína f

cock [kak] I. n (chicken) gallo m II. vt 1. (turn) ladear 2. (gun) amartillar

cockfight n pelea f de gallos

cockpit ['kak·pɪt] n 1. AVIAT cabina f 2. MIL campo m de batalla

cockroach ['kak·routʃ] <-es> n cucaracha f, surupa f Ven

cocktail ['kak·teɪl] n cóctel m

cocky ['kak·i] <-ier, -iest> adj gallito, -a

cocoa ['kou·kou] n cacao m; (drink) chocolate m

coconut ['kou·kə·nʌt] n coco m

coconut milk n leche f de coco

cocoon [kə·'kun] n capullo m

cod [kad] n inv bacalao m

code [koud] I. n a. LAW código m II. vt cifrar

coded adj codificado, -a

codeine ['kou·din] n codeína f

code name n nombre m en clave

code number n prefijo m

code word n palabra f en clave

codify ['kad·ɪ·faɪ] <-ie-> vt codificar

coed ['kou·ed] adj inf mixto, -a

coeducation [ˌkou·edʒ·ʊ·'keɪ·ʃən] n educación f mixta

coeducational [ˌkou·edʒ·ə·'keɪ·ʃən·əl] adj mixto, -a

coerce [kou·'ɜrs] vt coaccionar

coexist [ˌkou·ɪg·'zɪst] vi coexistir

coexistence [ˌkou·ɪg·'zɪs·təns] n coexistencia f

coffee ['kɔ·fi] n café m

coffee bean n grano m de café

coffee break n pausa f del café

coffee-colored adj de color café

coffee cup n taza f de café

coffee grinder n molinillo m de café

coffeehouse n cafetería f

coffeemaker n cafetera f, greca f AmL

coffeepot n cafetera f

coffee shop n cafetería f

coffin ['kɔ·fɪn] n ataúd m

cog [kag] n TECH diente m; (wheel) piñón m

cognac ['koun·jæk] n coñac m

cohabit [kou·'hæb·ɪt] vi cohabitar

coherence [kou·'hɪr·əns] n coherencia f

coherent [kou·'hɪr·ənt] adj coherente

coherently adv coherentemente

cohesion [kou·'hi·ʒən] n cohesión f

cohesive [kou·'hi·sɪv] adj cohesivo, -a

coil [kɔɪl] **I.** n rollo m; ELEC bobina f **II.** vi enrollarse **III.** vt enrollar

coin [kɔɪn] **I.** n moneda f; **to toss a ~** echar a cara o cruz **II.** vt acuñar

coincide [ˌkoʊ·ɪn·ˈsaɪd] vi coincidir; (agree) estar de acuerdo

coincidence [koʊ·ˈɪn·sɪ·dəns] n coincidencia f

coincidental [koʊ·ˌɪn·sɪ·ˈden·təl] adj coincidente

coitus [ˈkoʊ·ə·təs] n coito m

coke [koʊk] n **1.** (drink) refresco m de cola **2.** sl coca f

col. [kal] n abbr of **column** columna f

cold [koʊld] **I.** adj frío, -a; **to be ~** tener frío; **to go ~** enfriarse; **I'm getting cold** me está dando frío; **it's bitterly ~** hace un frío que pela ► **to leave sb ~** dejar frío a alguien **II.** n **1.** **the ~** el frío **2.** MED resfriado m; **to catch a ~** resfriarse ► **to leave sb out in the ~** dejar a alguien al margen

cold-blooded adj de sangre fría

cold feet n pl miedîtis f, cululío m Col, Nic, Ecua, Pan, ElSal

cold-hearted adj insensible

coldish [ˈkoʊl·dɪʃ] adj fresquito, -a

cold turkey n sl mono m

collaborate [kə·ˈlæb·ə·reɪt] vi colaborar

collaboration [kə·ˌlæb·ə·ˈreɪ·ʃən] n colaboración f

collaborator [kə·ˈlæb·ə·reɪ·tər] n **1.** colaborador(a) m(f) **2.** pej colaboracionista mf

collage [kə·ˈlaʒ] n collage m

collapse [kə·ˈlæps] **I.** vi **1.** MED sufrir un colapso; PSYCH hundirse **2.** (building) derrumbarse **3.** (fail) fracasar **II.** n **1.** MED colapso m **2.** (people, building) hundimiento m **3.** (failure) fracaso m

collapsible [kə·ˈlæp·sɪ·bəl] adj plegable

collar [ˈkal·ər] **I.** n **1.** FASHION cuello m **2.** (dog, cat) collar m **II.** vt sl agarrar

collarbone n clavícula f

collateral [kə·ˈlæt·ər·əl] adj colateral

colleague [ˈkal·ig] n colega mf

collect [kə·ˈlekt] **I.** vt **1.** (gather) reunir; (money) recaudar; (stamps) coleccionar **2.** (pick up) recoger **II.** vi **1.** (gather) reunirse **2.** (money) cobrar; (contributions) hacer una colecta [or Col vaca]

III. adj, adv (call) a cobro revertido

collected [kə·ˈlek·tɪd] adj sosegado, -a

collection [kə·ˈlek·ʃən] n **1.** (money) recaudación f; REL colecta f **2.** (objects) colección f **3.** (large number) montón m **4.** (act of getting) recogida f

collective [kə·ˈlek·tɪv] **I.** adj colectivo, -a **II.** n colectivo m

collector [kə·ˈlek·tər] n coleccionista mf; (payments) cobrador(a) m(f)

college [ˈkal·ɪdʒ] n colegio m; (university) universidad f

collide [kə·ˈlaɪd] vi chocar

collision [kə·ˈlɪʒ·ən] n colisión f

colloquial [kə·ˈloʊ·kwi·əl] adj familiar; (language) coloquial

Colo. [ˌkal·ə·ˈrad·oʊ] abbr of **Colorado** Colorado f

cologne [kə·ˈloʊn] n colonia f

Colombia [kə·ˈlʌm·bi·ə] n Colombia f

Colombian [kə·ˈlʌm·bi·ən] adj, n colombiano, -a m, f

colon [ˈkoʊ·lən] n ANAT colon m; LING dos puntos m

colonel [ˈkɜr·nəl] n coronel mf

colonization [ˌkal·ə·nɪ·ˈzeɪ·ʃən] n colonización f

colonize [ˈkal·ə·naɪz] vt colonizar

colony [ˈkal·ə·ni] <-ies> n colonia f

color [ˈkʌl·ər] **I.** n **1.** color m; **what ~ is it?** ¿de qué color es? **2.** (vigor) colorido m **3.** (dye) tinte m **II.** vt **1.** (change color) colorear; **to ~ a room blue** pintar una habitación de azul **2.** (dye) teñir **III.** vi sonrojarse

Colorado [ˌkal·ə·ˈrad·oʊ] n Colorado m

colorblind adj daltónico, -a

colored adj coloreado, -a; (pencil, people) de color

color filter n filtro m de color

colorful [ˈkʌl·ər·fəl] adj **1.** (full of color) colorido, -a **2.** (lively) vivo, -a; (countryside) pintoresco, -a

coloring [ˈkʌl·ər·ɪŋ] n color m; (chemical) colorante m

colorless [ˈkʌl·ər·lɪs] adj incoloro, -a; (bland) soso, -a

color scheme n combinación f de colores

colt [koʊlt] n potro m, potranco m AmL

column [ˈkal·əm] n columna f; **spinal ~**

columna vertebral

coma [ˈkoʊ·mə] *n* coma *m*; **to go into a ~** entrar en coma; **to wake up out of one's ~** salir del coma

comb [koʊm] I. *n* peine *m*; ZOOL cresta *f* II. *vt* **to ~ one's hair** peinarse; **to ~ an area** peinar una zona

combat [ˈkɑm·bæt] I. *n* combate *m* II. *vt* luchar contra; (*crime*) combatir; (*desire*) resistir

combination [ˌkɑm·bə·ˈneɪ·ʃən] *n* combinación *f*

combine [kəm·ˈbaɪn] I. *vt* combinar; **to ~ forces** unir fuerzas (**against** contra) II. *vi* asociarse

combined [kəm·ˈbaɪnd] *adj* combinado, -a; (*efforts*) conjunto, -a

come [kʌm] <came, come, coming> *vi* 1. venir (**towards** hacia); **are you coming to the game with us?** ¿te vienes al partido? 2. (*arrive*) llegar; **the year to ~** el próximo año; **to ~ to an agreement/a decision** llegar a un acuerdo/una decisión; **to ~ home** volver a casa 3. (*happen*) pasar; **to ~ to pass** suceder; **~ what may** pase lo que pase; **how ~?** *inf* ¿cómo es?; **nothing came of it** todo quedó en nada 4. (*become*) hacerse; **to ~ true** hacerse realidad; **to ~ open** abrirse 5. *inf* (*climax*) correrse, acabar *AmL* ▶ **~ again?** *inf* ¿cómo?; **to ~ clean** (**about** acerca de); **to have it coming** tenerlo merecido

◆ **come about** *vi* suceder

◆ **come across** I. *vt insep* encontrarse con; (*problem*) topar con II. *vi* **to ~ with** proporcionar

◆ **come along** *vi* 1. (*hurry*) darse prisa; **~!** ¡venga! 2. (*go too*) venirse 3. (*progress*) progresar

◆ **come apart** *vi* separarse

◆ **come around** *vi* 1. (*change mind*) cambiar de opinión 2. MED volver en sí

◆ **come at** *vt insep* atacar

◆ **come away** *vi* irse; **to ~ from** desprenderse de

◆ **come back** *vi* volver; (*be remembered*) volver (a la memoria)

◆ **come by** I. *vt insep* conseguir II. *vi* visitar

◆ **come down** *vi* 1. bajar; (*roof*) hundirse; (*rain, snow*) caer 2. (*land*) aterrizar

◆ **come forward** *vi* avanzar; **to ~ to do sth** ofrecerse para hacer algo

◆ **come from** *vt* ser de; (*family*) descender de; **where do you ~?** ¿de dónde eres?

◆ **come in** *vi* 1. (*enter*) entrar 2. (*arrive*) llegar 3. (*fashion*) ponerse de moda 4. (*be useful*) servir 5. (*participate*) participar

◆ **come into** *vt insep* 1. (*enter*) entrar en; (*power*) tomar; **to ~ fashion** ponerse de moda 2. (*inherit*) heredar

◆ **come off** I. *vi* 1. *inf* (*succeed*) triunfar 2. (*end up*) terminar 3. (*become detached*) desprenderse II. *vt insep* (*complete*) terminar; (*injury*) recuperarse de ▶ **~ it!** ¡anda ya!

◆ **come on** *vi* 1. (*improve*) progresar 2. THEAT, CINE aparecer 3. (*film, program*) empezar; **I've got a headache coming on** me está empezando a dar dolor de cabeza II. *vt insep* encontrarse III. *interj* (*hurry*) ¡date prisa!, ¡ándale! *Méx*, (*encouragement*) ¡ánimo!, ¡órale! *Méx* (*annoyance*) ¡venga ya!

◆ **come out** *vi* 1. (*be) in favor of/against sth* pronunciarse a favor/en contra de algo 2. **how did your painting ~?** ¿cómo quedó tu cuadro? 3. + *n* **to ~ a mess** resultar un desastre 4. + *adj* **to ~ wrong/right** salir mal/bien 5. (*become known*) darse a conocer; **to ~ that...** revelarse que... 6. (*stamp, book, moon, stars*) salir

◆ **come over** I. *vi* 1. (*come nearer*) acercarse 2. (*visit*) visitar 3. (*feel*) sentir II. *vt* apoderarse de

◆ **come through** I. *vi* 1. (*show*) mostrar 2. (*arrive*) llegar 3. (*survive*) sobrevivir II. *vt insep* superar

◆ **come to** I. *vt insep* 1. (*reach*) llegar a; **to come down/up to sth** bajar/subir a algo; **to ~ rest** irse a dormir; **to ~ nothing** quedarse en nada 2. (*amount to*) ascender a II. *vi* MED volver en sí

◆ **come up** *vi* 1. (*be mentioned*) mencionarse 2. (*happen*) suceder; (*holiday*) llegar

◆ **come upon** *vt* encontrarse con

comeback [ˈkʌm·bæk] *n* 1. vuelta *f*

2. (*retort*) réplica *f*

comedian [kə·ˈmi·di·ən] *n* **1.** humorista *mf* **2.** (*funny person*) payaso, -a *m, f*

comedown [ˈkʌm·daʊn] *n inf* **1.** (*anticlimax*) revés *m* **2.** (*decline in status*) humillación *f*

comedy [ˈkam·ə·di] <-ies> *n* comedia *f*; (*funny situation*) comicidad *f*

come-on [ˈkʌm·ɔn] *n sl* (*sexual*) insinuación *f*

comet [ˈkam·ɪt] *n* cometa *m*

comeuppance [kʌm·ˈʌp·ənts] *n* **to get one's** ~ llevarse su merecido

comfort [ˈkʌm·fərt] **I.** *n* comodidad *f*; (*mental*) consuelo *m* **II.** *vt* consolar

comfortable [ˈkʌm·fər·tə·bəl] *adj* cómodo, -a; **to make oneself** ~ ponerse cómodo; (*financially*) acomodado, -a

comfortably [ˈkʌm·fər·tə·bli] *adv* cómodamente; **to live** ~ vivir de forma acomodada

comforting [ˈkʌm·fər·tɪŋ] *adj* reconfortante

comfy [ˈkʌm·fi] <-ier, -iest> *adj inf* cómodo, -a

comic [ˈkam·ɪk] **I.** *n* cómic *m*; (*person*) cómico, -a *m, f* **II.** *adj* cómico, -a; ~ **play** comedia *f*

comical [ˈkam·ɪ·kəl] *adj* cómico, -a; (*idea*) divertido, -a

comic book *n* tebeo *m*

comic strip *n* tira *f* cómica

coming [ˈkʌm·ɪŋ] **I.** *adj* **1.** (*next*) próximo, -a; **the** ~ **year** el año que viene **2.** (*approaching*) venidero, -a **II.** *n* llegada *f*; ~**s and goings** idas y venidas

comma [ˈkam·ə] *n* coma *f*

command [kə·ˈmænd] **I.** *vt* **1. to** ~ **sb to do sth** ordenar a alguien que haga algo; **to** ~ **that** mandar que +*subj* **2.** (*have authority*) estar al mando de **3.** (*have*) disponer de **4.** (*view*) tener; (*respect*) imponer; (*sympathy*) inspirar **II.** *n* **1.** (*order*) orden *f*; **at/under sb's** ~ a/bajo las órdenes de alguien **2.** (*control*) mando *m*; **to be in** ~ estar al mando (**of** de) **3.** COMPUT comando *m* **4.** (*knowledge*) dominio *m*

commandant [ˈkam·ən·dænt], **commander** [kə·ˈmæn·dər] *n* comandante *mf*

commanding [kə·ˈmæn·dɪŋ] *adj* **1.** (*authoritative*) dominante; (*voice*) imponente **2.** (*considerable*) abrumador(a)

command key *n* tecla *f* de comando

commando [kə·ˈmæn·doʊ] <-s *or* -es> *n* comando *m*

commemorate [kə·ˈmem·ə·reɪt] *vt* conmemorar

commemorative [kə·ˈmem·ər·ə·tɪv] *adj* conmemorativo, -a

commence [kə·ˈmens] *vi* dar comienzo

commend [kə·ˈmend] *vt* **1.** (*praise*) elogiar **2.** (*entrust*) encomendar **3.** (*recommend*) recomendar

comment [ˈkam·ent] **I.** *n* comentario *m*; **no** ~ sin comentarios **II.** *vi* comentar

commentary [ˈkam·ən·ter·i] <-ies> *n* comentario *m*; RADIO, TV comentarios

commentate [ˈkam·ən·teɪt] *vi* **to** ~ **on sth** hacer un reportaje sobre algo

commentator [ˈkam·ən·teɪ·tər] *n* comentarista *mf*

commerce [ˈkam·ərs] *n* comercio *m*

commercial [kə·ˈmɜr·ʃəl] **I.** *adj* comercial; RADIO, TV publicitario, -a **II.** *n* anuncio *m*, comercial *m AmL*

commercialization [kə·ˌmɜr·ʃə·lɪ·ˈzeɪ·ʃən] *n* comercialización *f*

commercialize [kə·ˈmɜr·ʃə·laɪz] *vt* comercializar

commission [kə·ˈmɪʃ·ən] **I.** *vt* (*order*) encargar **II.** *n* **1.** (*order*) encargo *m* **2.** ADMIN, COM comisión *f*

commissioner [kə·ˈmɪʃ·ə·nər] *n* comisario, -a *m, f*

commit [kə·ˈmɪt] <-tt-> *vt* cometer; **to** ~ **suicide** suicidarse; **to** ~ **oneself** comprometerse (**to** a); **to** ~ **sb to a hospital/to prison** internar a alguien en un hospital/en prisión

commitment [kə·ˈmɪt·mənt] *n* **1.** (*dedication*) dedicación *f* **2.** (*obligation*) compromiso *m*

committee [kə·ˈmɪt·i] *n* comité *m*

commode [kə·ˈmoʊd] *n* **1.** (*drawers*) cómoda *f* **2.** (*toilet*) taza *f*

common [ˈkam·ən] *adj* **1.** común; **to be** ~ **knowledge** ser de dominio público; **by** ~ **assent** por unanimidad; **for the** ~ **good** en beneficio común **2.** (*vulgar*) vulgar

commonly *adv* normalmente

commonplace ['kam·ən·pleɪs] *adj* corriente

common sense *n* sentido *m* común; (*solution*) lógico, -a

communal [kə·'mju·nəl] *adj* comunal

communicate [kə·'mju·nɪ·keɪt] I. *vt* comunicar; MED transmitir II. *vi* comunicarse

communication [kə·ˌmju·nɪ·'keɪ·ʃən] *n* comunicación *f*

communicative [kə·'mju·nə·keɪ·tɪv] *adj* comunicativo, -a

communism ['kam·jə·nɪz·əm] *n* comunismo *m*

communist ['kam·jə·nɪst] *adj, n* comunista *mf*

community [kə·'mju·nə·ti] <-ies> *n* **1.** (*of people*) comunidad *f*; **the local ~** el vecindario *m* **2.** (*of animals, plants*) colonia *f* **3.** (*togetherness*) colectividad *f*

community center *n* centro *m* social

commute [kə·'mjut] I. *vi* desplazarse al trabajo II. *n* desplazamiento *m* al trabajo III. *vt* (*change*) convertir

compact¹ ['kam·pækt] I. *adj* compacto, -a II. *vt* condensar III. *n* AUTO utilitario *m*

compact² ['kam·pækt] *n* (*agreement*) acuerdo *m*

compact disk *n* compact *m*

compact disk player *n* reproductor *m* de CD

companion [kəm·'pæn·jən] *n* **1.** compañero, -a *m, f*; **traveling ~** compañero de viaje **2.** (*guidebook*) guía *f*

company ['kʌm·pə·ni] <-ies> *n* **1.** (*firm, enterprise*) empresa *f*; **Duggan and Company** Duggan y Compañía **2.** (*companionship*) compañía *f*; **to keep sb ~** hacer compañía a alguien; **he's been keeping bad ~** va con malas compañías ► **two's ~ (three's a crowd)** *prov* dos son compañía, tres son multitud

comparable ['kam·pər·ə·bəl] *adj* comparable; **~ to** equiparable a

comparative [kəm·'per·ə·tɪv] *adj* comparativo, -a

comparatively *adv* en comparación; (*relatively*) relativamente

compare [kəm·'per] I. *vt* comparar (**to, with** con) II. *vi* compararse

comparison [kəm·'per·ɪ·sən] *n* comparación *f*; **by ~ with** en comparación con; **there's no ~ between the two restaurants** no hay ni punto de comparación entre los dos restaurantes

compartment [kəm·'part·mənt] *n* compartimento *m*

compass ['kʌm·pəs] <-es> *n* brújula *f*

compassion [kəm·'pæʃ·ən] *n* compasión *f*

compassionate [kəm·'pæʃ·ə·nɪt] *adj* compasivo, -a

compatibility [kəm·ˌpæt·ə·'bɪl·ə·ti] *n* compatibilidad *f*

compatible [kəm·'pæt·ə·bəl] *adj* compatible

compel [kəm·'pel] <-ll-> *vt* (*force*) obligar

compelling *adj* (*reason*) imponente

compensate ['kam·pən·seɪt] *vt, vi* compensar; (*for loss, damage*) indemnizar

compensation [ˌkam·pen·'seɪ·ʃən] *n* **1.** (*award*) compensación *f*; (*for loss, damage*) indemnización *f*; **in ~ for** en compensación por **2.** (*recompense*) recompensa *f*; **in ~** como recompensa

compete [kəm·'pit] *vi* **1.** (*strive*) competir (**for** por) **2.** (*take part*) participar

competence ['kam·pɪ·təns] *n*, **competency** *n* competencia *f*

competent ['kam·pɪ·tənt] *adj* competente (**at** en)

competition [ˌkam·pə·'tɪʃ·ən] *n* **1.** (*competing*) competencia *f* **2.** (*rivalry*) rivalidad *f* **3.** (*contest*) concurso *m*; **beauty ~** concurso de belleza; **to enter a ~** presentarse a un concurso

competitive [kəm·'pet·ɪ·tɪv] *adj* competitivo, -a; **~ sports** deportes de competición

competitiveness [kəm·'pet·ə·tɪv·nɪs] *n* competitividad *f*

competitor [kəm·'pet·ə·tər] *n* **1.** *a.* ECON competidor(a) *m(f)*; SPORTS rival *mf*; (*participant*) participante *mf*

compilation [ˌkam·pə·'leɪ·ʃən] *n* (*collection*) recopilación *f*

compile [kəm·'paɪl] *vt* recopilar; COMPUT compilar

compiler [ˌkəm·'pi·lər] *n* COMPUT compilador *m*

complain [kəm·'pleɪn] *vi* quejarse (**about, of** de)

complaint [kəm·'pleɪnt] *n* **1.** queja *f* (**about** sobre) **2.** LAW querella *f* **3.** (*illness*) enfermedad *f*

complement ['kam·plɪ·mənt] *vt* complementar

complementary [,kam·plə·'men·tə·ri] *adj* complementario, -a

complete [kəm·'plit] **I.** *vt* **1.** (*add*) completar **2.** (*finish*) terminar; **to ~ doing sth** terminar de hacer algo **3.** (*fill out*) rellenar **II.** *adj* completo, -a

completely *adv* totalmente

completion [kəm·'pli·ʃən] *n* finalización *f*; **to be nearing ~** estar a punto de terminarse

complex ['kam·pleks] **I.** *adj* complejo, -a **II.** <-es> *n* PSYCH, ARCHIT complejo *m*; **guilt/inferiority ~** complejo de culpabilidad/inferioridad; **to have a ~** estar acomplejado (**about** por); **I've got a real ~ about spiders** tengo verdadera fobia a las arañas

complexion [kəm·'plek·ʃən] *n* **1.** (*skin*) cutis *m inv* **2.** (*character*) cariz *m*; (*of people*) aspecto *m*

complexity [kəm·'plek·sə·ti] *n* complejidad *f*

compliant [kəm·'plaɪ·ənt] *adj* sumiso, -a

complicate ['kam·plə·keɪt] *vt* complicar; (*make worse*) empeorar

complicated *adj* complicado, -a

complication [,kam·plə·'keɪ·ʃən] *n* complicación *f*; **if any ~s arise...** si surge alguna dificultad...

complicity [kəm·'plɪs·ə·ti] *n* complicidad *f*

compliment ['kam·plə·mənt] **I.** *n* **1.** (*praise*) cumplido *m*; (*flirt*) piropo *m*; **to pay/repay a ~** hacer/devolver un cumplido **2.** ~**s** saludos *mpl* **II.** *vt* felicitar (**on** por)

complimentary [,kam·plə·'men·tə·ri] *adj* **1.** (*praising*) positivo, -a **2.** (*free*) gratuito, -a

comply [kəm·'plaɪ] <-ie-> *vi* cumplir; **to refuse to ~** negarse a obedecer; **to ~ with the law/the rules** acatar la ley/las normas

component [kəm·'poʊ·nənt] *n* compo-

nente *m*; **key ~** pieza clave

compose [kəm·'poʊz] **I.** *vi* componer **II.** *vt* **1.** (*music, poetry*) componer **2.** (*write*) redactar **3. to be ~d of sth** constar de algo **4. to ~ oneself** calmarse

composed [kəm·'poʊzd] *adj* tranquilo, -a

composer [kəm·'poʊ·zər] *n* compositor(a) *m(f)*

composition [,kam·pə·'zɪʃ·ən] *n* composición *f*; (*of a group*) formación *f*; SCHOOL redacción *f*

composure [kəm·'poʊ·ʒər] *n* compostura *f*; **to lose/regain one's ~** perder/recobrar la compostura

compound¹ [,kam·'paʊnd] *vt* **1.** (*make worse*) agravar **2.** (*mix*) combinar **3. to be ~ed of sth** constar de algo

compound² ['kam·paʊnd] *n* **1.** (*mix*) mezcla *f*; CHEM compuesto *m* **2.** (*enclosure*) recinto *m*

comprehend [,kam·prɪ·'hend] *vi, vt* comprender

comprehensible [,kam·prɪ·'hen·sə·bəl] *adj* comprensible

comprehension [,kamprɪ·'henʃən] *n* comprensión *f*; **beyond ~** incomprensible; **he has no ~ of the size of the problem** no es consciente de la envergadura del problema

comprehensive [,kam·prɪ·'hen·sɪv] *adj* exhaustivo, -a

compress¹ [kəm·'pres] *vt* **1.** a. COMPUT comprimir **2.** (*make shorter*) resumir

compress² ['kam·pres] <-es> *n* compresa *f*

comprise [kəm·'praɪz] *vt* (*consist of*) constar de; (*include*) comprender

compromise ['kam·prə·maɪz] **I.** *n* **1.** (*concession*) transigencia *f*; **to make a ~** hacer una concesión **2.** (*agreement*) compromiso *m*; **to reach a ~** llegar a un acuerdo **II.** *vi* transigir **III.** *vt* **1.** (*betray*) comprometer; **to ~ one's beliefs/principles** dejar de lado sus creencias/principios **2.** (*endanger*) poner en peligro; **to ~ one's reputation** poner en entredicho su reputación

compromising *adj* comprometido, -a

compulsion [kəm·'pʌl·ʃən] *n* obligación *f*;

to be under no ~ to do sth no estar obligado a hacer algo

compulsive [kəm·'pʌl·sɪv] *adj* compulsivo, -a

compulsory [kəm·'pʌl·sə·ri] *adj* obligatorio, -a; **~ education** enseñanza obligatoria; **~ by law** preceptivo por ley

compute [kəm·'pjut] *vt* computar

computer [kəm·'pju·tər] *n* ordenador *m*, computador(a) *m(f) AmL*; **by ~** por ordenador

computer-aided *adj* asistido, -a por ordenador

computer game *n* juego *m* de ordenador

computer graphics *n + sing/pl vb* gráficos *m pl* por ordenador [*or AmL* por computadora]

computerize [kəm·'pju·tə·raɪz] I. *vt* informatizar II. *vi* informatizarse

computer network *n* red *f* de ordenadores [*or* computadoras] *AmL*

computer program *n* programa *m* (de ordenador)

computer programmer *n* programador(a) *m(f)*

computer science *n* informática *f*

computer scientist *n* informático, -a *m, f*

computer virus <-es> *n* virus *m inv* informático

computing *n* informática *f*

comrade ['kam·ræd] *n* compañero, -a *m, f*

comradeship ['kam·ræd·ʃɪp] *n* compañerismo *m*

con¹ [kan] <-nn-> *vt inf* **to ~ sb (into doing sth)** engañar a alguien (para que haga algo); **to ~ sb into believing that...** hacer creer a alguien que...; **to ~ sb out of sth** estafar algo a alguien

con² [kan] *n* (*against*) contra *m;* **the pros and ~s of sth** los pros y los contras de algo

con³ [kan] *n sl* (*convict*) convicto, -a *m, f*

concave [kan·keɪv] *adj* cóncavo, -a

conceal [kən·'sil] *vt* esconder; (*surprise*) contener; (*truth*) encubrir

concede [kən·'sid] I. *vt* **1.** (*acknowledge*) admitir **2.** (*surrender*) ceder; **to ~ sth to sb** otorgar algo a alguien **3.** (*permit*) conceder II. *vi* darse por vencido

conceited [kən·'si·tɪd] *adj* vanidoso, -a

conceivable [kən·'siv·ə·bəl] *adj* verosímil

conceive [kən·'siv] I. *vt* concebir; (*devise*) idear; (*arrange*) preparar II. *vi* **1.** (*think*) formarse un concepto (**of** de) **2.** (*devise*) imaginar(se)

concentrate ['kan·sən·treɪt] I. *vi* **1.** (*focus attention*) concentrarse (**on** en) **2.** (*gather*) reunirse II. *vt* concentrar III. *n* concentrado *m*

concentrated *adj a. fig* concentrado, -a

concentration [ˌkan·sən·'treɪ·ʃən] *n* concentración *f* (**on** en, of de); **to lose (one's) ~** perder la concentración

concept ['kan·sept] *n* concepto *m;* **to grasp a ~** coger una idea

conception [kən·'sep·ʃən] *n a.* BIO concepción *f*

conceptual [kən·'sep·tʃu·əl] *adj* conceptual

concern [kən·'sɜrn] I. *vt* **1.** (*apply to*) referirse a; **to ~ oneself** interesarse (**about** por) **2.** (*affect*) incumbir; (*be about*) tener que ver con; **to be ~ed** ocuparse (**with** de); **as far as I'm ~ed** por lo que a mí respecta **3.** (*worry*) preocuparse; **to be ~ed** estar preocupado (**about** por) II. *n* **1.** (*matter*) asunto *m;* **it's no ~ of mine** eso no es de mi incumbencia; **that's none of your ~** no es asunto tuyo; **to be of ~ to** interesar **2.** (*worry*) preocupación *f* (**for** por); **a major ~** una grave preocupación; **a matter of ~** un asunto de interés

concerning *prep* acerca de

concert ['kan·sərt] *n* concierto *m;* **~ tour** gira *f;* **in ~** en concierto; (*all together*) conjuntamente (**with** con)

concerted [kən·'sɜr·tɪd] *adj* **1.** (*joint*) concertado, -a; (*action*) conjunto, -a; (*exercise*) acordado, -a **2.** (*resolute*) resuelto, -a; (*effort*) enérgico, -a

concession [kən·'seʃ·ən] *n* **1.** (*tax*) desgravación *f* **2.** (*compromise*) concesión *f*

concise [kən·'saɪs] *adj* conciso, -a

conciseness *n,* **concision** [kən·'sɪʒ·ən] *n* concisión *f*

conclude [kən·'klud] I. *vi* concluir; **to**

~ **by doing sth** terminar haciendo algo
II. vt **1.** (finish) finalizar **2.** (decide) resolver **3.** (infer) **to** ~ **(from sth) that** deducir (de algo) que **4.** (ratify) pactar; (contract) firmar

concluding [kənˈkluˌʒən] adj final; (chapter) último, -a

conclusion [kənˈkluˌʒən] n **1.** (end, inference) conclusión f; (story) final m; **to come to a** ~ llegar a una conclusión **2.** (decision) decisión f **3.** (ratification) ratificación f; (contract) firma f **4. in** ~ en conclusión; **in** ~, **I would like to...** para terminar, me gustaría...

conclusive [kənˈkluˌsɪv] adj concluyente

concrete [ˈkanˌkrit] **I.** n hormigón m **II.** adj de hormigón

concur [kənˈkɜr] <-rr-> vi **to** ~ **with sb** (**in sth**) coincidir con alguien (en algo)

concurrent [kənˈkʌrˌənt] adj concurrente

concussion [kənˈkʌʃˌən] n conmoción f cerebral

condemn [kənˈdem] vt condenar; **to be** ~**ed to death** ser condenado a muerte; (building) declarar en ruina

condemnation [ˌkanˌdemˈneɪˌʃən] n (reproof) condena f; (reason) motivo m de crítica

condensation [ˌkanˌdenˈseɪˌʃən] n a. CHEM, PHYS condensación f

condense [kənˈdens] **I.** vt (shorten) sintetizar; (liquid) condensar **II.** vi condensarse

condescend [ˌkanˌdɪˈsend] vi **to** ~ **to do sth** rebajarse a hacer algo

condescending [ˌkanˌdɪˈsenˌdɪŋ] adj condescendiente

condition [kənˈdɪʃˌən] **I.** n condición f; (mental or physical) estado m; **in perfect** ~ en perfecto estado; **in peak** ~ en condiciones óptimas; **in terrible** ~ en un estado deplorable; **to be out of** ~ estar en mal estado; (person) estar en baja forma; **to be in no** ~ **to do sth** no estar en condiciones de hacer algo; **to make a** ~ poner una condición; **on the** ~ **that** con la condición de que +subj **II.** vt (train) preparar; (influence) condicionar

conditional [kənˈdɪʃˌəˌnəl] adj, n con-dicional m

conditionally [kənˈdɪʃˌəˌnəˌli] adv con reservas

conditioner [kənˈdɪʃˌəˌnər] n (hair) acondicionador m, bálsamo m Col, Méx

condolences [kənˈdouˌlənˌsiz] npl pésame m; **to offer one's** ~ dar el pésame

condom [ˈkanˌdəm] n condón m

conduct¹ [ˌkanˈdʌkt] vt **1.** (carry out) llevar a cabo **2.** (direct) dirigir **3. to** ~ **oneself** comportarse **4.** ELEC, PHYS conducir

conduct² [ˈkanˈdʌkt] n **1.** (management) dirección f **2.** (behavior) conducta f (**to-wards** hacia)

conductive [kənˈdʌkˌtɪv] adj conductor(a)

conductor [kənˈdʌkˌtər] n **1.** (director) director(a) m(f) **2.** PHYS, ELEC conductor m **3.** (bus, train) revisor(a) m(f)

cone [koʊn] n cono m; BOT piña f

confection [kənˈfekˌʃən] n form **1.** COM confección f **2.** CULIN dulce m

confectionery [kənˈfekˌʃəˌnerˌi] n confitería f

confederacy [kənˈfedˌərˌəˌsi] <-ies> n confederación f

confederate [kənˈfedˌərˌət] adj confederado, -a

confederation [kənˌfedˌəˈreɪˌʃən] n + sing/pl vb POL confederación f

confer [kənˈfɜr] <-rr-> **I.** vi consultar **II.** vt otorgar

conference [ˈkanˈfərˌəns] n conferencia f

confess [kənˈfes] **I.** vi confesarse **II.** vt confesar

confession [kənˈfeʃˌən] n confesión f

confetti [kənˈfetˌi] n confeti m

confide [kənˈfaɪd] vt confiar

confidence [ˈkanˈfəˌdəns] n **1.** (trust) confianza f; **to win sb's** ~ ganarse la confianza de alguien; **he certainly doesn't lack** ~ desde luego no le falta confianza en sí mismo **2.** (secrecy) ~**s** confidencia f

confident [ˈkanˈfəˌdənt] adj **1.** (sure) seguro, -a; **to be** ~ estar seguro (**about** de) **2.** (self-assured) confiado, -a; **to be** ~ **about oneself** tener confianza en uno mismo

confidential [ˌkan·fə·'den·ʃəl] *adj* confidencial

confidentially [ˌkan·fə·'den·ʃə·li] *adv* confidencialmente

configuration [kən·ˌfɪg·jə·'reɪ·ʃən] *n* configuración *f*

confine [kən·'faɪn] **I.** *vt* confinar; **to ~ sth to sth** restringir algo a algo; **to be ~d to doing sth** limitarse a hacer algo **II.** *n* **the ~s** los confines

confinement [kən·'faɪn·mənt] *n* (*act*) reclusión *f*; (*state*) confinamiento *m*

confirm [kən·'fɜrm] **I.** *vt* confirmar **II.** *vi* confirmarse

confirmation [ˌkan·fər·'meɪ·ʃən] *n* confirmación *f*

confirmed [kən·'fɜrmd] *adj* **1.** (*established*) firme **2.** (*chronic*) empedernido, -a **3.** (*proved*) confirmado, -a

confiscate ['kan·fə·skeɪt] *vt* confiscar

conflict¹ ['kan·flɪkt] *n* conflicto *m*; (*opinions*) discrepancia *f*

conflict² [kən·'flɪkt] *vi* chocar (**with** con)

conflicting [kən·'flɪk·tɪŋ] *adj* opuesto, -a; (*evidence*) contradictorio, -a

conform [kən·'fɔrm] *vi* conformarse; **to ~ to the law** ser conforme a la ley

conformist [kən·'fɔr·mɪst] *adj, n* conformista *mf*

confront [kən·'frʌnt] *vt* enfrentarse a

confuse [kən·'fjuz] *vt* **1.** (*perplex*) desconcertar **2.** (*mix up*) confundir

confused [kən·'fjuzd] *adj* (*perplexed*) confundido, -a; (*disordered*) confuso, -a

confusing [kən·'fju·zɪŋ] *adj* confuso, -a

confusion [kən·'fju·ʒən] *n* confusión *f*

congested [kən·'dʒes·tɪd] *adj a.* MED congestionado, -a; (*people*) abarrotado, -a

congestion [kən·'dʒes·tʃən] *n a.* MED congestión *f*; (*road*) caravana *f*

congratulate [kən·'græt·ʃə·leɪt] *vt* felicitar (**on** por)

congratulation [kən·ˌgræt·ʃə·'leɪ·ʃən] *n* felicitación *f*; **~s!** ¡enhorabuena!

congregate ['kaŋ·grɪ·geɪt] *vi* congregarse

congregation [ˌkaŋ·grɪ·'geɪ·ʃən] *n* congregación *f*

congress ['kaŋ·gres] *n* congreso *m*

congressman ['kaŋ·gres·mən] *n* <-men> congresista *m*

congresswoman *n* <-women> congresista *f*

conical ['kan·ɪ·kəl] *adj* cónico, -a

conjugate ['kan·dʒə·geɪt] *vt* conjugar

conjunction [kən·'dʒʌŋk·ʃən] *n* conjunción *f*; **in ~ with** conjuntamente con

conjunctivitis [kən·ˌdʒʌŋk·tə·'vaɪ·tɪs] *n* conjuntivitis *f inv*

conjure ['kan·dʒər] *vt* conjurar; *fig* evocar

◆ **conjure up** *vt* invocar; (*memories*) evocar

conk [kaŋk] *n sl* (*blow*) coscorrón *m*

◆ **conk out** *vi sl* **1.** (*break down*) escacharrarse **2.** (*person*) quedarse frito

con man ['kan·ˌmæn] *n abbr of* **confidence man** estafador *m*

Conn. *n abbr of* **Connecticut** *abbr of* Connecticut

connect [kə·'nekt] **I.** *vi* conectar(se); **to ~ to the Internet** conectarse a Internet **II.** *vt* **1.** (*join*) conectar **2.** (*associate*) asociar (**with** con) **3.** (*in tourism*) enlazar

connected *adj* conectado, -a; **to be ~d to sb** tener relación con alguien

Connecticut [kə·'net·ɪ·kət] *n* Connecticut *m*

connecting *adj* comunicado, -a

connection [kə·'nek·ʃən] *n* **1.** *a.* ELEC, COMPUT conexión *f* **2.** (*relation*) relación *f*

connector *n* conector *m*

connoisseur [ˌkan·ə·'sɜr] *n* entendido, -a *m, f*

conquer ['kaŋ·kər] *vt* conquistar; (*problem*) acabar con

conquest ['kan·kwest] *n* conquista *f*

conscience ['kan·ʃəns] *n* conciencia *f*; **a guilty ~** remordimientos; **to prey on sb's ~** pesar en la conciencia de alguien

conscientious [ˌkan·tʃi·'en·tʃəs] *adj* concienzudo, -a; **~ objector** objetor de conciencia

conscious ['kan·ʃəs] *adj* **1.** (*deliberate*) expreso, -a **2.** (*aware*) consciente; **to be/become ~ of sth** ser consciente/darse cuenta de algo

consciousness ['kan·ʃəs·nɪs] *n* **1.** MED

conocimiento *m;* **to lose/regain** ~ perder/recobrar el conocimiento **2.** (*awareness*) conciencia *f;* **political/social** ~ conciencia política/social; **to raise one's** ~ concienciarse

consecutive [kən-'sek-jə-ṭɪv] *adj* consecutivo, -a

consecutively *adv* consecutivamente

consensus [kən-'sen-səs] *n* consenso *m*

consent [kən-'sent] **I.** *n* consentimiento *m;* **by common** ~ de común acuerdo **II.** *vi* **to** ~ **to do sth** consentir en hacer algo

consequence ['kan-sɪ-kwənts] *n* consecuencia *f;* **as a** ~ como consecuencia; **in** ~ por consiguiente

consequent ['kan-sɪ-kwənt], **consequential** [,kan-sɪ-'kwen-tʃəl] *adj* consiguiente

consequently *adv* por consiguiente

conservation [,kan-sər-'veɪ-ʃən] *n* conservación *f;* **environmental** ~ preservación *f* del medio ambiente

conservative [kən-'sɜr-və-ṭɪv] *adj* **1.** *a.* POL (*traditional*) conservador(a) **2.** (*cautious*) cauteloso, -a

conservatory [kən-'sɜr-və-tɔr-i] *n* conservatorio *m*

conserve [kən-'sɜrv] *vt* conservar

consider [kən-'sɪd-ər] *vt* **1.** (*contemplate*) considerar **2.** (*examine*) examinar **3.** (*show regard for*) tener en cuenta **4.** (*regard as*) **to be** ~ed **to be the best** ser considerado el mejor; **to** ~ **that...** creer que...

considerable [kən-'sɪd-ər-ə-bəl] *adj* considerable

considerate [kən-'sɪd-ər-ət] *adj* considerado, -a

consideration [kən-,sɪd-ə-'reɪ-ʃən] *n* consideración *f;* **to take into** ~ tener en cuenta

considered [kən-'sɪd-ərd] *adj* considerado, -a

considering [kən-'sɪd-ər-ɪŋ] **I.** *prep* teniendo en cuenta; ~ **the weather** en vista del tiempo **II.** *adv* a pesar de todo **III.** *conj* ~ (**that**)... teniendo en cuenta que...

consist [kən-'sɪst] *vi* consistir (**of** en)

consistency [kən-'sɪs-tən-si] *n* **1.** (*firm-*

ness) consistencia *f* **2.** (*coherence*) coherencia *f*

consistent [kən-'sɪs-tənt] *adj* consecuente (**with** con)

consolation [,kan-sə-'leɪ-ʃən] *n* consuelo *m;* ~ **prize** premio de consolación; **if it's of any** ~... si te sirve de consuelo...

console[1] [kən-'soʊl] *vt* (*comfort*) consolar

console[2] ['kan-soʊl] *n* (*switch panel*) consola *f*

consolidate [kən-'sal-ə-deɪt] **I.** *vi* **1.** (*reinforce*) consolidarse **2.** (*unite*) fusionarse **II.** *vt* consolidar

consonant ['kan-sə-nənt] *n* consonante *f*

consortium [kən-'sɔr-ṭi-əm] *n* <consortiums *or* consortia> consorcio *m*

conspiracy [kən-'spɪr-ə-si] <-ies> *n* conspiración *f*

conspire [kən-'spaɪr] *vi* conspirar (**against** contra)

constant ['kan-stənt] **I.** *n* constante *f* **II.** *adj* **1.** (*continuous, frequent*) constante; ~ **use** uso frecuente **2.** (*unchanging*) inalterable

constantly *adv* constantemente

constellation [,kan-stə-'leɪ-ʃən] *n* constelación *f*

consternation [,kan-stər-'neɪ-ʃən] *n* consternación *f*

constipated *adj* estreñido, -a

constitution [,kan-stə-'tu-ʃən] *n* constitución *f*

constitutional [,kan-stə-'tu-ʃə-nəl] *adj* constitucional

constrain [kən-'streɪn] *vt* **to be/feel** ~ed **to do sth** verse/sentirse obligado a hacer algo

construct [kən-'strʌkt] **I.** *n* construcción *f* **II.** *vt* construir

construction [kən-'strʌk-ʃən] *n* **1.** *a.* LING construcción *f* **2.** (*building*) edificio *m*

constructive [kən-'strʌk-ṭɪv] *adj* constructivo, -a

consul ['kan-səl] *n* cónsul *mf*

consulate ['kan-sə-lət] *n* consulado *m*

consult [kən-'sʌlt] *vi, vt* consultar

consultancy [kən-'sʌl-tən-si] <-ies> *n* asesoría *f*

consultant [kən-'sʌl-tənt] *n* asesor(a) *m(f);* **tax** ~ asesor fiscal

consume [kən·'sum] vt consumir; **to be ~d by sth** estar consumido por algo; **to be ~d by envy** estar muerto de envidia

consumer [kən·'su·mər] n consumidor(a) m(f)

consumption [kən·'sʌmp·ʃən] n consumo m

contact ['kan·tækt] I. n contacto m; (connection) relación f; **to have ~s** tener contactos; **to come into ~ with sth** entrar en contacto con algo II. vt contactar con

contact lens n lentilla f

contagious [kən·'teɪ·dʒəs] adj contagioso, -a

contain [kən·'teɪn] vt contener

container [kən·'teɪ·nər] n recipiente m; (for transport) contenedor m

contaminate [kən·'tæm·ə·neɪt] vt contaminar

contamination [kən·ˌtæm·ɪ·'neɪ·ʃən] n contaminación f

contemplate ['kan·tem·pleɪt] vt contemplar; **to ~ doing sth** tener la intención de hacer algo

contemplation [ˌkan·tem·'pleɪ·ʃən] n contemplación f

contemporary [kən·'tem·pə·rer·i] adj, n contemporáneo, -a m, f

contempt [kən·'tempt] n desprecio m; **to be beneath ~** ser despreciable; **to hold in ~** despreciar

contend [kən·'tend] vi 1. (compete) competir (for por) 2. (struggle) luchar (against contra)

content[1] ['kan·tent] n contenido m

content[2] [kən·'tent] I. vt satisfacer; **to ~ oneself** contentarse (with con) II. adj satisfecho (with con) III. n **to one's heart's ~** a más no poder

contented adj satisfecho, -a

contentious [kən·'ten·ʃəs] adj conflictivo, -a

contentment [kən·'tent·mənt] n satisfacción f

contest ['kan·test] n (competition) concurso m; **sports ~** competición f deportiva

contestant [kən·'tes·tənt] n sports contrincante mf; pol candidato, -a m, f; tv concursante mf

context ['kan·tekst] n contexto m

continent ['kan·tə·nənt] n geo continente m

continental [ˌkan·tə·'nen·təl] adj continental; **the ~ United States** Estados Unidos continental

contingency [kən·'tɪn·dʒən·si] <-ies> n contingencia f

continual [kən·'tɪn·ju·əl] adj continuo, -a

continually adv continuamente

continuation [kən·ˌtɪn·ju·'eɪ·ʃən] n continuación f

continue [kən·'tɪn·ju] I. vi seguir; **to ~ to do** [or **doing**] **sth** seguir haciendo algo; **to ~ (on) one's way** seguir su camino; **to be ~d** continuará; **he ~d by saying that...** prosiguió diciendo que... II. vt 1. (go on) seguir con 2. (lengthen) prolongar

continuous [kən·'tɪn·ju·əs] adj continuo, -a

contraceptive [ˌkan·trə·'sep·tɪv] n anticonceptivo m

contract[1] [kən·'trækt] I. vi contraerse II. vt a. med contraer

contract[2] ['kan·trækt] I. n contrato m; **~ of employment** contrato laboral; **temporary ~** contrato temporal II. vt contratar

◆**contract out** vt subcontratar

contraction [kən·'træk·ʃən] n contracción f

contradict [ˌkan·trə·'dɪkt] I. vi contradecirse II. vt contradecir; **to ~ oneself** contradecirse

contradiction [ˌkan·trə·'dɪk·ʃən] n contradicción f

contradictory [ˌkan·trə·'dɪk·tə·ri] adj contradictorio, -a

contrary ['kan·trer·i] I. n **on the ~** al contrario; **quite the ~!** ¡todo lo contrario!; **to the ~** en contra II. adj contrario, -a (to a)

contrary to prep al contrario de; **~ all our expectations** contra todo pronóstico

contrast[1] [kən·'træst] vt contrastar

contrast[2] ['kan·træst] n contraste m; **by** [or **in**] **~** en contraste; **in ~ to** [or **with**] a diferencia de

contribute [kən·'trɪb·jut] I. vi 1. (*money, time*) contribuir (**towards** en) 2. (*participate*) intervenir II. vt (*money*) contribuir; (*article*) escribir; (*information*) aportar; **to ~ (sth) to sth** contribuir (con algo) a algo; **to ~ sth towards sth** aportar algo a algo

contribution [ˌkan·trɪ·'bju·ʃən] n 1. contribución f 2. (*for publication*) colaboración f

contributor [kən·'trɪb·jə·tər] n 1. contribuyente mf 2. (*writer*) colaborador(a) m(f)

contributory [kən·'trɪb·jə·tɔr·i] adj contributivo, -a

control [kən·'troʊl] I. n 1. control m; **to bring under ~** controlar; **to go out of ~** descontrolarse; **to have/lose ~** tener/perder el control (**over** sobre) 2. (*leadership*) mando m; **to be in ~** mandar 3. **~s** TECH mandos; **to be at the ~s** llevar los mandos II. vt <-ll-> a. MED, ECON, FIN controlar; (*vehicle*) conducir; (*anger*) dominar

control panel n panel m de control

controversial [ˌkan·trə·'vɜr·ʃəl] adj polémico, -a

controversy ['kan·trə·vɜr·si] n <-ies> polémica f

convenience [kən·'vin·jəns] n conveniencia f; (*practicality*) comodidad f; (*advantage*) ventaja f

convenient [kən·'vin·jənt] adj 1. (*suitable*) conveniente 2. (*practical*) práctico, -a 3. (*close*) bien situado, -a

convent ['kan·vənt] n convento m

convention [kən·'ven·ʃən] n 1. convención f; (*custom*) convenciones

conventional [kən·'ven·ʃə·nəl] adj convencional

converge [kən·'vɜrdʒ] vi converger; (*persons*) reunirse

conversation [ˌkan·vər·'seɪ·ʃən] n conversación f, plática f AmL; **to strike up a ~** entablar conversación (**with** con)

conversion [kən·'vɜr·ʒən] n conversión f

convert [kən·'vɜrt] I. vi convertirse II. vt convertir

converter [kən·'vɜr·tər] n ELEC transformador m

convertible [kən·'vɜr·tə·bəl] I. n AUTO descapotable m II. adj a. FIN, ECON convertible; **~ sofa** sofá cama, convertible m AmL

convex ['kan·veks] adj convexo, -a

convey [kən·'veɪ] vt 1. (*transport*) transportar; (*electricity*) conducir 2. (*communicate*) transmitir

convict[1] ['kan·vɪkt] n presidiario, -a m, f

convict[2] [kən·'vɪkt] vt condenar

conviction [kən·'vɪk·ʃən] n 1. LAW condena f 2. (*belief*) convicción f; **to have a ~** estar convencido (**about** de)

convince [kən·'vɪns] vt convencer

convincing [kən·'vɪn·sɪŋ] adj convincente

convoy ['kan·vɔɪ] n convoy m; **in ~** en caravana

cook [kʊk] I. n cocinero, -a m, f II. vi hacerse; **how long does pasta take to ~?** ¿cuánto tarda en hacerse la pasta? ▶ **what's ~ing?** sl ¿qué pasa? III. vt cocinar, asar; (*meat*) **to ~ lunch** hacer la comida

cookbook ['kʊk·bʊk] n libro m de cocina

cookery ['kʊk·ə·ri] n cocina f

cookie ['kʊk·i] n 1. (*biscuit*) galleta f 2. sl (*person*) tipo, -a m, f 3. COMPUT cookie m

cooking ['kʊk·ɪŋ] n **to do the ~** hacer la comida

cool [kul] I. adj 1. (*drink, evening*) fresco, -a; (*color, greeting*) frío, -a 2. (*calm*) tranquilo, -a; **keep ~** tómatelo con calma 3. inf (*fashionable*) **to be ~** estar en la onda II. interj inf ¡qué guay! III. n 1. (*coolness*) fresco m 2. (*calm*) calma f IV. vt enfriar; **just ~ it** inf ¡calma! V. vi enfriarse; **to ~ down** [*or* **off**] enfriarse; (*become calmer*) calmarse

cool-headed [ˌkul·'hed·ɪd] adj sereno, -a

cooling ['ku·lɪŋ] adj refrescante; (*breeze*) fresco, -a

coolness ['kul·nɪs] n 1. METEO fresco m 2. (*unfriendliness*) frialdad f

coop [kup] I. n gallinero m II. vt encerrar

cooperate [koʊ·'ap·ə·reɪt] vi cooperar

cooperation [koʊ·ˌap·ə·'reɪ·ʃən] n cooperación *f*

cooperative [kou·'ap·ər·ə·ţɪv] **I.** *n* cooperativa *f* **II.** *adj* cooperativo, -a

coordinate [ˌkou·'ɔr·dɪn·eɪt] **I.** *n* coordenada *f* **II.** *vi, vt* coordinar(se); (*match*) combinar **III.** *adj* coordinado, -a; (*equal*) igual

coordination [ˌkou·ˌɔr·də·'neɪ·ʃən] *n* coordinación *f*

coordinator *n* coordinador(a) *m(f)*

cop [kap] *n inf* poli *mf*; **to play ~s and robbers** jugar a polis y cacos

copartner ['kou·ˌpart·nər] *n* copartícipe *mf*

cope [koup] *vi* aguantar; **to ~ with** poder con; (*situation*) enfrentarse a; (*problem*) hacer frente a; (*pain*) soportar

copilot ['kou·ˌpaɪ·lət] *n* copiloto *mf*

copper ['kap·ər] **I.** *n* (*metal*) cobre *m* **II.** *adj* (*color*) cobrizo, -a

copulate ['kap·jə·leɪt] *vi* copular

copulation [ˌkap·jə·'leɪ·ʃən] *n* cópula *f*

copy ['kap·i] **I.** <-ies> *n* **1.** *a.* COMPUT copia *f*; (*book*) ejemplar *m*; ART imitación *f*; **hard ~** copia impresa *f* **2.** (*text to be published*) original *m* **II.** <-ie-> *vt* **1.** *a.* COMPUT copiar **2.** (*imitate*) imitar **III.** *vi* copiar

copy protection *n* protección *f* contra escritura

copyright *n* derechos *m pl* de autor

coral ['kɔr·əl] **I.** *n* coral *m* **II.** *adj* (*color*) coralino, -a

cord [kɔrd] *n* (*rope*) cuerda *f*, piola *f AmS*; ELEC cable *m*; **umbilical ~** cordón *m* umbilical

cordless ['kɔrd·lɪs] *adj* inalámbrico, -a

cordon ['kɔr·dən] **I.** *n* cordón *m*; **police ~** cordón policial **II.** *vt* acordonar

corduroy ['kɔr·də·rɔɪ] *n* pana *f*

core [kɔr] *n* **1.** (*center*) centro *m*; (*apple, pear*) corazón *m*; **to the ~** *fig* hasta la médula; **to be at the ~ of the problem** llegar al quid de la cuestión **2.** PHYS núcleo *m*

coriander ['kɔr·i·æn·dər] *n* cilantro *m*

cork [kɔrk] **I.** *n* **1.** corcho *m* **2.** (*stopper*) tapón *m* **II.** *vt* **1.** (*put stopper*) taponar **2.** (*restrain*) contener

corkscrew ['kɔrk·skru] *n* sacacorchos *m inv*

corn[1] [kɔrn] *n* **1.** (*crop*) maíz *m*, choclo *m AmS*, abatí *m Arg* **2.** *sl* (*trite*) sensiblería *f*

corn[2] [kɔrn] *n* MED callo *m*

corn bread *n* pan *m* de maíz

corncob *n* mazorca *f* de maíz

cornea ['kɔr·ni·ə] *n* córnea *f*

corner ['kɔr·nər] **I.** *n* **1.** (*of roads*) esquina *f*; **to be around the ~** estar a la vuelta de la esquina; **to turn the ~** doblar la esquina **2.** (*of a room*) rincón *m*; **a distant ~ of the globe** un rincón remoto de la tierra; **the four ~s of the world** todos los rincones del mundo **3.** SPORTS córner *m* **4.** (*difficulty*) **to be in a tight ~** estar en un aprieto; **to drive sb into a (tight) ~** poner a alguien entre la espada y la pared **5.** (*periphery*) **out of the ~ of one's eye** con el rabillo del ojo; **out of the ~ of sb's mouth** en la comisura de los labios ▶ **to cut ~s** ahorrar esfuerzos **II.** *vt* **1.** (*hinder escape*) acorralar **2.** ECON **to ~ the market** acaparar el mercado

cornered ['kɔr·nərd] *adj* acorralado, -a

cornflakes ['kɔrn·fleɪks] *npl* copos *m pl* de maíz

corn poppy <-ies> *n* amapola *f*

cornstarch *n* maicena *f*

corny ['kɔr·ni] <-ier, -iest> *adj* **1.** *inf* viejo, -a **2.** (*emotive*) sensiblero, -a

corp. *abbr of* **corporation** sociedad *f* anónima

corporate ['kɔr·pər·ət] *adj* colectivo, -a; (*of corporation*) empresarial

corporation [ˌkɔr·pə·'reɪ·ʃən] *n + sing/ pl vb* **1.** FIN sociedad *f* anónima; **multinational ~** empresa *f* multinacional [*or AmL* transnacional] **2.** POL ayuntamiento *m*

corpse [kɔrps] *n* cadáver *m*

correct [kə·'rekt] **I.** *vt* corregir **II.** *adj* correcto, -a

correction [kə·'rek·ʃən] *n* corrección *f*; (*improvememt*) rectificación *f*

correction fluid *n* líquido *m* corrector

correctly [kə·'rekt·li] *adv* correctamente

correspond [ˌkɔr·ə·'spand] *vi* **1.** (*equal*) corresponder a **2.** (*write*) mantener correspondencia

correspondence [ˌkɔr·ə·'span·dəns] *n*

correspondencia *f;* **business ~** correspondencia comercial

correspondent [ˌkɔr·ə·ˈspan·dənt] *n* corresponsal *mf;* **special ~** enviado, -a *m, f* especial

corresponding [ˌkɔr·ə·ˈspan·dɪŋ] *adj* correspondiente

corridor [ˈkɔr·ɪ·dər] *n* (*passage*) pasillo *m*

corrosion [kə·ˈrou·ʒən] *n* corrosión *f; fig* deterioro *m*

corrosive [kə·ˈrou·sɪv] *adj* corrosivo, -a; *fig* destructivo, -a

corrupt [kə·ˈrʌpt] I. *vt* 1. (*debase*) corromper 2. (*bribe*) sobornar 3. (*document*) dañar II. *vi* corromper III. *adj* corrupto, -a; (*document*) dañado, -a

corruption [kə·ˈrʌp·ʃən] *n* corrupción *f*

cosmetic [kaz·ˈmet·ɪk] I. *n* cosmético *m* II. *adj* cosmético, -a; (*superficial*) superficial

cosmonaut [ˈkaz·mə·nɔt] *n* cosmonauta *mf*

cosmopolitan [ˌkaz·mə·ˈpal·ɪ·tən] *adj, n* cosmopolita *mf*

cosmos [ˈkaz·mous] *n* cosmos *m inv*

cost [kɔst] I. *vt* 1. <cost, cost> costar; **to ~ a fortune** costar un ojo de la cara; **to ~ sb dearly** salir muy caro a alguien *fig* 2. <costed, costed> calcular el coste de II. *n* 1. coste *m;* **at ~** a precio de coste; **at no extra ~** sin costes adicionales; **to cut ~s** (*or* **the ~**) recortar costes 2. (*sacrifice*) (**only**) **at the ~ of doing sth** (sólo) a costa de hacer algo; **at all ~s** a toda costa

costly [ˈkɔst·li] <-ier, -iest> *adj* costoso, -a; **to prove ~** *a. fig* salir muy caro

costume [ˈkas·tum] *n* 1. traje *m;* **to dress in ~** ir trajeado 2. (*fancy dress*) disfraz *m*

cot [kat] *n* (*camp bed*) cama *f* plegable

cottage [ˈkat·ɪdʒ] *n* **country ~** casa *f* de campo

cottage cheese *n* requesón *m*

cotton [ˈkat·ən] *n* algodón *m*

cotton candy *n* algodón *m* de azúcar

cotton-picking *adj inf* **~ fool** tonto, -a *m, f* de remate

couch [kautʃ] <-es> *n* sofá *m*

cough [kɔf] I. *n* tos *f* II. *vi* toser

could [kʊd] *pt, pp* can²

council [ˈkaun·səl] *n* consejo *m;* **city ~** ayuntamiento *m*

counsel [ˈkaun·səl] I. <-ll-, -l-> *vt* aconsejar II. *n* 1. (*advice*) consejo *m* 2. (*lawyer*) abogado, -a *m, f*

count¹ [kaunt] *n* conde *m*

count² [kaunt] I. *n* 1. recuento *m;* **to keep/lose ~** llevar/perder la cuenta (**of** de) 2. (*sum*) total *m* II. *vt* 1. (*number*) contar 2. (*consider*) considerar; **to ~ sth a success/failure** considerar algo un éxito/fracaso; **to ~ sb as a friend** tener a alguien como amigo III. *vi* contar; **that's what ~s** eso es lo que cuenta; **to not ~** no tener ni voz ni voto

♦**count on** *vt* (*depend on*) contar con

♦**count out** *vt always sep* contar; **to count sb out** no contar con alguien

countdown [ˈkaunt·daun] *n* cuenta *f* atrás

counter [ˈkaun·tər] I. *n* 1. (*service point*) mostrador *m;* **over the ~** sin receta médica; **under the ~** *fig* clandestinamente 2. (*machine*) caja *f;* TECH contador *m* II. *vt* contrarrestar III. *adv* en contra

counterattack [ˈkaun·tər·ə·ˌtæk] I. *n* contraataque *m* II. *vt, vi* contraatacar

counterclockwise [ˌkaun·tər·ˈklak·waɪz] *adj* en sentido contrario a las agujas del reloj

counterfeit [ˈkaun·tər·fɪt] I. *adj* falsificado, -a; (*money*) falso, -a II. *vt* falsificar III. *n* falsificación *f*

countermeasure [ˈkaun·tər·ˌmeʒ·ər] *n* medida *f* en contra

counterpart [ˈkaun·tər·ˌpart] *n* contrapartida *f;* POL homólogo, -a *m, f*

counterproductive [ˌkaun·tər·prə·ˈdʌk·tɪv] *adj* contraproducente

counterterrorism [ˌkaun·tər·ˈter·ər·ɪz·əm] *n* lucha *f* antiterrorista

countless [ˈkaunt·lɪs] *adj* incontable

country [ˈkʌn·tri] I. *n* 1. (*rural area*) campo *m* 2. <-ies> POL país *m* 3. (*area*) territorio *m* 4. MUS country *m* II. *adj* rural; MUS country

country folk *n + pl vb* gente *f* de campo

countryside [ˈkʌn·tri·saɪd] *n* campo *m,*

verde m AmC, Méx

county ['kaʊn·ti] <-ies> n condado m

county fair n feria f del condado

coup [ku] <coups> n golpe m; **~ de grâce** golpe de gracia/Estado

couple ['kʌp·əl] I. n 1. (a few) par m; **the first ~ of weeks** las primeras dos semanas 2. + sing/pl vb (two people) pareja f; (married) matrimonio m II. vt 1. RAIL, AUTO enganchar 2. (connect) conectar 3. (link) unir

coupon ['ku·pan] n cupón m

courage ['kʌr·ɪdʒ] n coraje m

courageous [kə·'reɪ·dʒəs] adj valiente; (act) valeroso, -a

courier ['kʊr·i·ər] I. n mensajero, -a m, f II. adj **~ service** servicio m de mensajería

course [kɔrs] n 1. (direction) recorrido m; (river) curso m; **to be off ~** a. fig desviarse; **to set ~** poner rumbo (for hacia); **your best ~ of action would be...** lo mejor que podrías hacer sería... 2. (development) transcurso m; **over the ~ of time** con el tiempo 3. (treatment) tratamiento m 4. SPORTS pista f; (golf) campo m 5. (part of meal) plato m ▶ **to let sth run its ~** dejar que algo siga su curso; **of ~** por supuesto; **of ~ not** desde luego que no

court [kɔrt] n 1. (room) juzgado m 2. (judicial body) tribunal m 3. SPORTS cancha f; (tennis) pista f 4. HIST corte f

courteous ['kɜr·ṭi·əs] adj cortés

courtesy ['kɜr·ṭə·si] <-ies> n cortesía f; (decency) decencia f

courthouse ['kɔrt·haʊs] n juzgado m

court of appeals n tribunal m de apelación

court of law n tribunal m de justicia

courtyard n patio m

cousin ['kʌz·ɪn] n primo, -a m, f

cover ['kʌv·ər] I. n 1. (top) tapa f; (book) cubierta f; (magazine) portada f 2. (bedding) colcha m 3. (concealment) abrigo m; **to break ~** salir al descubierto; **to take ~** guarecerse II. vt 1. (hide) tapar; (head) cubrir; (book) forrar 2. (keep warm) abrigar 3. (travel) recorrer 4. (include) incluir ▶ sl **to ~**

one's ass cubrirse las espaldas

◆**cover over** vt cubrir

◆**cover up** I. vt tapar II. vi encubrir (for a)

coverage ['kʌv·ər·ɪdʒ] n cobertura f

coveralls ['kʌv·ər·ɔlz] npl mono m

covered adj cubierto, -a

covering n capa f

cover letter n carta f adjunta

cover-up ['kʌv·ər·ʌp] n encubrimiento m

cow[1] [kaʊ] n 1. vaca f 2. (female) hembra f

cow[2] [kaʊ] vt intimidar

coward ['kaʊ·ərd] n cobarde mf

cowardice ['kaʊ·ər·dɪs] n cobardía f

cowboy ['kaʊ·bɔɪ] n vaquero m, tropero m Arg

co-worker ['koʊ·ˌwɜr·kər] n compañero, -a m, f de trabajo

cowshed ['kaʊ·ʃed] n establo m

coy [kɔɪ] <-er, -est> adj 1. (secretive) reservado, -a 2. (flirtatious) coqueto, -a

coyote [kaɪ·'oʊ·ṭi] n coyote m

coziness ['koʊ·zi·nɪs] n comodidad f

cozy ['koʊ·zi] I. <-ier, -iest> adj 1. (comfortable) cómodo, -a; (place) acogedor(a) 2. pej de conveniencia II. <-ies> n tapadera f

CPU [ˌsi·pi·'ju] n abbr of **central processing unit** CPU f

crab[1] [kræb] n cangrejo m, jaiba f AmL

crab[2] [kræb] <-bb-> vi rezongar

crab louse n ladilla f

crack [kræk] I. n 1. (fissure) grieta f 2. (sound) crujido m 3. (drug) crack m 4. inf (attempt) intento m II. adj de primera III. vt 1. (break) romper; (egg) cascar; (nuts) partir; (safe) forzar; (code) descifrar; (joke) contar 2. (resolve) resolver 3. (hit) pegar IV. vi 1. (break) rajarse; (paintwork) agrietarse 2. (break down) venirse abajo 3. (make noise) chasquear ▶ **to get ~ing** poner manos a la obra

◆**crack up** vi (laugh) reírse a carcajadas

crackdown ['kræk·daʊn] n ofensiva f

cracked [krækt] adj rajado, -a; (lips) agrietado, -a

cracker ['kræk·ər] n 1. (biscuit) galleta f 2. COMPUT cracker mf

crackle ['kræk·əl] I. *vi, vt* crujir II. *n* crujido *m;* TEL ruido *m*

crackling ['kræk·lɪŋ] *n* crujido *m;* RADIO ruido *m*

cradle ['kreɪ·dəl] I. *n* 1. (*bed*) cuna *f;* **from the ~ to the grave** durante toda la vida 2. (*framework*) andamio *m* II. *vt* acunar

craft [kræft] I. *n* 1. (*means of transport*) nave *f* 2. (*skill*) arte *m* 3. (*trade*) oficio *m* 4. (*ability*) destreza *f* II. *vt* construir

craftsman ['kræfts·mən] <-men> *n* artesano *m*

craft store *n* tienda *f* de artesanía

crafty ['kræf·ti] <-ier, -iest> *adj* astuto, -a

cram [kræm] <-mm-> I. *vt* meter; **to ~ sth with sth** llenar algo de algo II. *vi* memorizar

cramp [kræmp] I. *vt* poner obstáculos a; **to ~ sb's style** cortar las alas a alguien II. *n* calambre *m*

crampon ['kræm·pan] *n* crampón *m*

cranberry ['kræn·ˌber·i] <-ies> *n* arándano *m*

crane [kreɪn] *n* grúa *f;* ZOOL grulla *f*

crank [kræŋk] *n* (*person*) maniático, -a *m, f*

cranky ['kræŋ·ki] <-ier, -iest> *adj* maniático, -a

crash [kræʃ] I. *n* <-es> 1. (*accident*) accidente *m* 2. (*noise*) estrépito *m* 3. COM crac *m* 4. COMPUT caída *f* (del sistema) II. *vi* 1. (*vehicle*) chocar; (*plane*) estrellarse 2. (*make noise*) retumbar 3. (*break*) derrumbarse 4. COM colapsarse 5. COMPUT colgarse III. *vt* 1. (*damage*) chocar 2. (*make noise*) hacer ruido

crash course *n* curso *m* intensivo

crash landing *n* aterrizaje *m* forzoso

crate [kreɪt] I. *n* cajón *m* II. *vt* embalar

crater ['kreɪ·tər] *n* cráter *m*

crave [kreɪv] *vt* ansiar; (*attention*) reclamar

craving ['kreɪ·vɪŋ] *n* ansia *f*

crawl [krɔl] *vi* 1. (*go on all fours*) gatear 2. (*move slowly*) arrastrarse 3. **to ~ (up) to sb** hacer la pelota a alguien; **to**

be ~ing with sth estar plagado de algo, nadar a crol

crayfish ['kreɪ·fɪʃ] *n inv* cangrejo *m* de río

crayon ['kreɪ·an] *n* lápiz *m* II. *vt* colorear III. *vi* dibujar

craze [kreɪz] *n* manía *f*

crazed [kreɪzd] *adj* de loco, -a

crazy ['kreɪ·zi] <-ier, -iest> *adj* loco, -a, tarado, -a *AmL;* **to go ~** volverse loco

creak [krik] I. *vi* crujir; (*door*) chirriar II. *n* crujido *m;* (*door*) chirrido *m*

creaky ['kri·ki] <-ier, -iest> *adj* 1. (*squeaky*) chirriante 2. (*decrepit*) decrépito, -a

cream [krim] I. *n* 1. FOOD nata *f* 2. (*cosmetic*) crema *f* II. *adj* 1. (*containing cream*) cremoso, -a 2. (*color*) de color crema III. *vt* (*butter*) batir; (*milk*) desnatar; (*coffee*) añadir crema

cream cheese *n* queso *m* de untar

cream-colored *adj* de color crema

creamy ['kri·mi] <-ier, -iest> *adj* (*smooth*) cremoso, -a; (*skin*) hidratado, -a

crease [kris] I. *n* (*fold*) arruga *f* II. *vt* arrugar III. *vi* arrugarse

create [kri·'eɪt] *vt* 1. (*produce*) crear 2. (*cause*) causar

creation [kri·'eɪ·ʃən] *n* 1. (*making*) creación *f* 2. (*product*) producción *f* 3. FASHION modelo *m*

creative [kri·'eɪ·tɪv] *adj* creativo, -a

creator [kri·'eɪ·tər] *n* creador(a) *m(f)*

creature ['kri·tʃər] *n* criatura *f*

credentials [krɪ·'den·ʃəlz] *npl* credenciales *fpl*

credibility [ˌkred·ə·'bɪl·ə·ti] *n* credibilidad *f*

credible ['kred·ə·bəl] *adj* creíble

credit ['kred·ɪt] I. *n* 1. (*belief*) a. FIN crédito *m;* **to give ~** dar crédito (**to** a); **on ~** a plazos 2. (*recognition*) mérito *m;* **to be a ~ to sb** ser un honor para alguien; **to sb's ~** en favor de alguien; **to take (the) ~** atribuirse el mérito (**for** de) 3. **~s** CINE créditos II. *vt* 1. (*believe*) creer; **he is ~ed with...** se le atribuye... 2. **to ~ sb with 2000 dollars** abonar 2000 dólares en cuenta a alguien

creditable ['kred·ɪ·tə·bəl] *adj* 1. (*believable*) digno, -a de crédito 2. (*commend-*

able) digno, -a de elogio

credit card n tarjeta f de crédito

credit slip n nota f de crédito

creditworthy ['kred·ɪt·ˌwɜr·ði] adj solvente

creep [krip] **I.** <crept, crept> vi **1.** (crawl) arrastrarse; (snake) reptar; (baby) ir a gatas; (plant) trepar **2.** (move imperceptibly) deslizarse **II.** n **1.** sl (sycophant) pelotillero, -a m, f, lambiscón, -ona m, f Méx, lambón, -ona m, f Col **2.** sl (pervert) pervertido, -a m, f ▶ inf **to give sb the ~s** poner a alguien la carne de gallina

◆**creep into** vt insep entrar sigilosamente en

◆**creep up** vi acercarse sigilosamente (**on** a)

creeper ['kri·pər] n BOT enredadera f

creepy ['kri·pi] <-ier, -iest> adj inf espeluznante

cremate ['kri·meɪt] vt incinerar

cremation [krɪ·ˈmeɪ·ʃən] n incineración f

crematorium [ˌkri·mə·ˈtɔr·i·əm] <-s or -ria> n crematorio m

crematory ['kri·mə·tɔr·i] **I.** n crematorio m **II.** adj crematorio, -a

crepe [kreɪp] n CULIN crêpe m o f

crept [krept] pp, pt of **creep**

crest [krest] **I.** n (peak) cima f; (wave, bird) cresta f **II.** vt coronar

crew [kru] n + sing/pl vb **1.** NAUT, AVIAT tripulación f; RAIL personal m; **ground/flight ~** personal de tierra/de vuelo **2.** inf (gang) peña f

crib [krɪb] n **1.** (bed) cuna f **2.** sl (home) keli m **3.** inf SCHOOL chuleta f, chancho m Col, acordeón m Méx, machete m RíoPl

cricket ['krɪk·ɪt] n **1.** SPORTS cricket m **2.** ZOOL grillo m, siripita f Bol

crime [kraɪm] n **1.** LAW delito m; (murder) crimen m; **~ of passion** crimen pasional; **to commit a ~** cometer un delito; **the scene of the ~** la escena del crimen **2.** (criminal activity) delincuencia f; **~ rate** índice de criminalidad; **organized ~** crimen organizado

criminal ['krɪm·ə·nəl] **I.** n delincuente mf; (serious offender) criminal mf **II.** adj **1.** (illegal) delictivo, -a; (more

serious) criminal **2.** LAW penal; **~ court** juzgado m de lo penal; **~ record** antecedentes penales **3.** fig (shameful) vergonzoso, -a; **to be ~ to do sth** ser un crimen hacer algo

criminality [ˌkrɪm·ə·ˈnæl·ə·ti] n criminalidad f

crimson ['krɪm·zən] **I.** n carmesí m **II.** adj **1.** (color) carmesí **2.** (red-faced) colorado, -a

crinkle ['krɪŋ·kəl] **I.** vt arrugar **II.** vi **to ~ (up)** arrugarse **III.** n arruga f

cripple ['krɪp·əl] **I.** n lisiado, -a m, f **II.** vt **1.** (disable) lisiar; (machine, object) inutilizar **2.** (paralyze) paralizar

crisis ['kraɪ·sɪs] <crises> n crisis f inv (**over** provocada por); **to go through a ~** atravesar una crisis

crisp [krɪsp] **I.** <-er, -est> adj **1.** (crunchy) crujiente **2.** (fresh) fresco, -a; (shirt, pants) recién planchado, -a; (banknote) nuevo, -a **3.** (sharp) nítido, -a **4.** (lively) animado, -a **5.** (concise) escueto, -a; (manner) seco, -a; (style) conciso, -a **II.** vt FOOD tostar ligeramente

crispy ['krɪs·pi] <-ier, -iest> adj crujiente

crisscross ['krɪs·kras] **I.** vt entrecruzar **II.** vi entrecruzarse **III.** adj entrecruzado, -a **IV.** <-es> n fig enredo m

criterion [kraɪ·ˈtɪr·i·ən] <-ria> n criterio m

critic ['krɪt·ɪk] n crítico, -a m, f

critical ['krɪt·ɪ·kəl] adj crítico, -a; **to be (highly) ~ of sth/sb** criticar (duramente) algo/a alguien; **to be ~ to sth** ser crítico para algo; **to be in ~ condition** estar en estado crítico

criticism ['krɪt·ɪ·sɪz·əm] n crítica f

criticize ['krɪt·ɪ·saɪz] vt, vi criticar

croak [kroʊk] **I.** vi **1.** (crow) graznar; (frog) croar; (person) gruñir **2.** sl (die) palmar **II.** vt decir con voz ronca **III.** n (crow) graznido m; (frog) croar m; (person) gruñido m

Croatia [kroʊ·ˈeɪ·ʃə] n Croacia f

Croatian [kroʊ·ˈeɪ·ʃən] adj, n croata m/f

crochet [kroʊ·ˈʃeɪ] n ganchillo m

crockery ['krak·ə·ri] n vajilla f de barro

crocodile ['krak·ə·daɪl] <-(s)> n cocodrilo m

croissant [krwa·'saŋ] n croissant m

crook [krʊk] I. n 1. (criminal) delincuente mf 2. inf (rogue) sinvergüenza mf 3. (curve) recodo m II. vt doblar

crooked ['krʊk·ɪd] adj 1. (not straight) torcido, -a; (back) encorvado, -a; (path) tortuoso, -a 2. inf (dishonest) deshonesto, -a

crop [krap] I. n 1. AGR cultivo m; (harvest) cosecha f 2. (group) montón m; a ~ of lies una sarta de mentiras II. <-pp-> vt 1. AGR cultivar 2. (cut) cortar; (hair) cortar al uno; (plant) podar III. vi AGR darse; (land) rendir

♦**crop up** vi surgir

cross [krɔs] I. vt 1. cruzar; to ~ one's legs/fingers cruzar las piernas/los dedos; to ~ one's arms cruzarse de brazos 2. (oppose) contrariar 3. (mark with a cross) marcar con una cruz II. vi 1. (intersect) cruzarse 2. (go across) cruzar III. n 1. a. REL cruz f; to bear one's ~ cargar con su cruz 2. (streets, roads) cruce m 3. BIO cruce, cruza f AmL 4. (mixture) mezcla f IV. adj enfadado, -a (about por); to get ~ enfadarse (with con)

♦**cross out** vt tachar

♦**cross over** vi, vt cruzar

crossbar ['krɔs·bar] n travesaño m; (bicycle) barra f

cross-country adj, adv a campo traviesa

cross-cultural adj intercultural

crosscurrent n contracorriente f

cross-dress vi travestirse

cross-dresser n travesti mf

cross-eyed adj bizco, -a

crossfire n fuego m cruzado; to be caught in the ~ fig estar entre dos fuegos

crossing ['krɔ·sɪŋ] n 1. (place to cross, journey) paso m; border/level/pedestrian ~ paso fronterizo/a nivel/de peatones 2. (crossroads) cruce m 3. ARCHIT crucero m

cross-legged [‚krɔs·'leg·ɪd] adj con las piernas cruzadas

crossover n paso m; fig fusión f

cross-purposes npl to be talking at ~ estar hablando de cosas distintas

cross-reference n remisión f

crossroads n inv cruce m; fig encrucijada f

cross section n sección f transversal; fig muestra f representativa

crosswalk n paso m de cebra

crossword (puzzle) n crucigrama m

crouch [kraʊtʃ] I. vi to ~ (down) agacharse; to be ~ing estar en cuclillas II. n to lower oneself into a ~ agacharse

crow¹ [kroʊ] n ZOOL cuervo m ▶ as the ~ flies en línea recta

crow² [kroʊ] <crowed, crowed> I. n grito m (de alegría); (baby) gorjeo m; (cock) cacareo m II. vi 1. (cry) gritar de entusiasmo; (baby) gorjear; (cock) cacarear 2. (boast) alardear

crowd [kraʊd] I. n + sing/pl vb 1. (throng) multitud f; there was quite a ~ había mucha gente 2. fig to stand out from the ~ destacar(se); to follow the ~ dejarse llevar por los demás 3. inf (group) grupo m; the usual ~ los de siempre 4. inf (large number) montón m; a ~ of things un montón de cosas 5. (audience) público m II. vi aglomerarse; to ~ into a place entrar en tropel en un sitio; to ~ around sb/sth apiñarse alrededor de alguien/algo III. vt 1. (fill) llenar; to ~ the streets/a stadium abarrotar las calles/un estadio 2. (cram) amontonar 3. inf (pressure) atosigar

♦**crowd out** vt 1. (exclude) excluir 2. to be crowded out estar abarrotado

crowded adj lleno, -a; ~ together amontonado; the bar was ~ el bar estaba abarrotado

crowd-pleaser n inf (song) hit m

crown [kraʊn] I. n 1. corona f 2. (peak) cima f; (hat, tree) copa f; (head) coronilla f; (bird) cresta f 3. (culmination) culminación f II. vt 1. (coronate) coronar 2. (complete) rematar; the prize ~ed his career el premio fue la culminación de su carrera 3. inf (hit) dar un coscorrón

crown prince n príncipe m heredero

crow's feet ['kroʊz·fit] npl patas f pl de gallo

crucial ['kru·ʃəl] adj crucial (to para);

it is ~ that... es de vital importancia que... +*subj*

crucify ['kru·sɪ·faɪ] <-ie-> *vt* crucificar; **if she ever finds out, she'll ~ me** si alguna vez lo descubre, me matará

crude [krud] I. *adj* 1. (*rudimentary*) rudimentario, -a 2. (*unrefined*) bruto, -a; (*oil*) crudo, -a 3. (*vulgar*) basto, -a; (*manners*) grosero, -a II. *n* crudo *m*

cruel ['kru·əl] <-(l)ler, -(l)lest> *adj* cruel (**to** con)

cruelty ['kru·əl·ti] <-ies> *n* crueldad *f* (**to** con); **society for the prevention of ~ to animals** sociedad protectora de animales

cruise [kruz] I. *n* crucero *m;* **to go on a ~** hacer un crucero II. *vi* 1. NAUT hacer un crucero; (*at constant speed*) ir a una velocidad de crucero 2. (*police*) patrullar 3. *inf* (*drive around*) dar una vuelta en coche

cruising *adj* de crucero

crumb [krʌm] *n* 1. (*bread*) miga *f* 2. (*small amount*) pizca *f;* **a small ~ of...** un poco de...

crumble ['krʌm·bəl] I. *vt* desmenuzar II. *vi* (*cliff*) derrumbarse; (*empire*) desmoronarse; (*resistance, opposition*) venirse abajo

crummy ['krʌm·i] <-ier, -iest> *adj sl* cutre

crumple ['krʌm·pəl] I. *vt* arrugar; (*metal*) abollar II. *vi* 1. (*fabric, face*) arrugarse 2. (*collapse*) desplomarse

crunch [krʌntʃ] I. *vt* 1. (*eat*) masticar (haciendo ruido) 2. (*grind*) triturar II. *vi* crujir III. *n* 1. (*sound*) crujido *m* 2. (*crisis*) **the ~** la hora de la verdad

crunchy ['krʌn·tʃi] <-ier, -iest> *adj* crujiente

crush [krʌʃ] I. *vt* 1. (*compress*) aplastar; (*paper*) estrujar; (*dress*) arrugar; (*person*) apretujar 2. (*grind: garlic*) machacar; (*grapes, olives*) prensar; (*stone*) triturar; (*ice*) picar 3. (*shock severely*) abatir 4. (*defeat, suppress*) reprimir; (*rebellion, revolution*) reprimir; (*opponent*) derrotar; (*hopes*) frustrar; (*rumor*) acallar II. <-es> *n* 1. (*throng*) muchedumbre *f*; **there was a great ~** había una gran aglomeración 2. *inf* (*infatuation*) enamoramiento *m;* **to have a ~ on**

sb encapricharse de alguien
♦ **crush up** *vt* triturar

crushing *adj* aplastante; (*reply, argument*) contundente

crust [krʌst] *n* 1. CULIN, BOT, GEO corteza *f* 2. (*layer*) capa *f*; **a ~ of ice/dirt** una capa de hielo/suciedad 3. ZOOL caparazón *m* 4. MED costra *f*

crustacean [krʌ·'steɪ·ʃən] *n* crustáceo *m*

crusty ['krʌs·ti] <-ier, -iest> *adj* 1. CULIN crujiente 2. (*person*) malhumorado, -a

crutch [krʌtʃ] <-es> *n* 1. muleta *f;* **to be on ~es** andar con muletas 2. *fig* apoyo *m*

cry [kraɪ] I. <-ie-> *vi* 1. (*weep*) llorar; **to ~ for joy** llorar de alegría 2. (*shout*) gritar; (*animal*) aullar II. <-ie-> *vt* (*shout*) gritar ▶ **to ~ one's eyes out** llorar a lágrima viva III. *n* 1. (*weeping*) llanto *m;* **to have a ~** llorar 2. (*shout*) grito *m;* **to give a ~** dar un grito; **a ~ for help** una llamada de socorro
♦ **cry down** *vt* (*decry*) menospreciar
♦ **cry for** *vt insep* pedir
♦ **cry off** *vi inf* echarse atrás; **to ~ a deal** romper un trato
♦ **cry out** I. *vi* gritar; **to ~ against sth** clamar contra algo; **to ~ for sth** pedir algo a gritos II. *vt* gritar

crying ['kraɪ·ɪŋ] *n* lloro *m*

crystal ['krɪs·təl] *n* cristal *m*

crystalline ['krɪs·tə·laɪn] *adj* cristalino, -a

crystallize ['krɪs·tə·laɪz] *vt, vi* cristalizar; (*plan, thought*) materializar

CT *n abbr of* **Connecticut** Connecticut *m*

ct. 1. *abbr of* **cent** centavo *m* 2. *abbr of* **karat** quilate *m*

cub [kʌb] *n* cachorro *m*

Cuba ['kju·bə] *n* Cuba *f*

Cuban ['kju·bən] *adj, n* cubano, -a *m, f*

cubbyhole ['kʌb·ɪ·hoʊl] *n* cuchitril *m*

cube [kjub] I. *n* cubo *m;* (*cheese*) taco *m;* (*sugar*) terrón *m;* (*ice*) cubito *m;* **~ root** raíz cúbica II. *vt* 1. CULIN cortar en tacos 2. MATH elevar al cubo

cubic ['kju·bɪk] *adj* (*cube-shaped*) cúbico, -a

cubicle ['kju·bɪ·kəl] *n* (*changing room*) probador *m*

cuckoo ['ku·ku] I. *n* cuco *m* II. *adj inf* chiflado, -a

cuckoo clock n reloj m de cuco

cucumber ['kju·kʌm·bər] n pepino m
► (as) **cool** as a ~ más fresco que
una lechuga

cuddle ['kʌd·əl] I. vt abrazar II. vi abrazarse III. n abrazo m

cue [kju] n 1. THEAT pie m 2. MUS entrada f 3. (billiards) taco m; ~ **ball** bola blanca ► to **take** one's ~ **from** sb seguir el ejemplo de alguien; (right) **on** ~ en el momento justo

cuff [kʌf] I. n 1. (sleeve) puño m 2. ~s inf (handcuffs) esposas fpl ► **off the** ~ improvisado, -a II. vt inf esposar

cul-de-sac ['kʌl·də·sæk] <-s or culs-de-sac> n callejón m sin salida

culminate ['kʌl·mɪ·neɪt] vi culminar (in en)

culmination [ˌkʌl·mɪ·'neɪ·ʃən] n culminación f

culprit ['kʌl·prɪt] n culpable mf

cult [kʌlt] n culto m; (sect) secta f

cultivate ['kʌl·tə·veɪt] vt cultivar

cultivated adj 1. AGR cultivado, -a
2. (person) culto, -a

cultural ['kʌl·tʃər·əl] adj cultural

culture ['kʌl·tʃər] I. n 1. cultura f 2. AGR cultivo m II. vt cultivar

cultured ['kʌl·tʃərd] adj 1. AGR cultivado, -a 2. (intellectual) culto, -a; (taste) refinado, -a

culture shock n choque m cultural

cumin ['kju·mɪn] n comino m

cumulative ['kju·mjə·lə·tɪv] adj 1. (increasing) acumulativo, -a 2. (accumulated) acumulado, -a

cunning ['kʌn·ɪŋ] I. adj 1. (ingenious) ingenioso, -a 2. (sly) taimado, -a II. n astucia f

cup [kʌp] n 1. (container) taza f; tea ~ taza de té; **egg** ~ huevera f 2. SPORTS copa f; the **World Cup** la copa del mundo

cupboard ['kʌb·ərd] n armario m; built-in ~ armario empotrado; kitchen ~ armario de cocina

cupful ['kʌp·fʊl] n taza f; a ~ **of** sugar una taza de azúcar

curable ['kjʊr·ə·bəl] adj curable

curb [kɜrb] I. vt (anger, passion) dominar; (inflation, appetite) controlar;
(expenditure) frenar II. n 1. (control) freno m; to keep a ~ on refrenar; to put a ~ poner freno (on a) 2. (obstacle) estorbo m 3. (at roadside) bordillo m, cordón m CSur

curd [kɜrd] n cuajada f; ~ **cheese** requesón m

cure [kjʊr] I. vt curar; (problem) remediar; (leather) curtir II. vi sanar; FOOD curarse III. n cura f; (return to health) curación f

curfew ['kɜr·fju] n toque de queda m

curiosity [ˌkjʊr·i·'as·ə·ti] <-ies> n curiosidad f ► ~ **killed** the **cat** la curiosidad mató al gato

curious ['kjʊr·i·əs] adj curioso, -a; to be ~ sentir curiosidad (about/por); it is ~ that es curioso que +subj

curl [kɜrl] I. n 1. (hair) rizo m 2. (sinuosity) serpenteo m 3. (spiral) espiral f 4. (of lips) mueca f de desprecio II. vi (hair) rizarse; (path) serpentear III. vt (hair) rizar; to ~ **oneself up** acurrucarse ► to ~ **one's lip** hacer una mueca de desprecio

curler ['kɜr·lər] n rulo m

curly ['kɜr·li] <-ier, -iest> adj rizado, -a

currant ['kɜr·ənt] n 1. (dried grape) pasa f de Corinto 2. (berry) grosella f

currency ['kɜr·ən·si] <-ies> n 1. FIN moneda f; **foreign** ~ divisas; ~ **market** mercado de divisas; ~ **unit** unidad monetaria 2. (acceptance) difusión f; to **gain** ~ extenderse

current ['kɜr·ənt] I. adj 1. (present) actual; **in** ~ **use** en uso 2. (latest) último, -a 3. (prevalent) generalizado, -a 4. (valid) vigente II. n 1. a. ELEC corriente f 2. (tendency) tendencia f ► to **drift with the** ~ dejarse llevar por la corriente; to **swim against the** ~ nadar contra corriente

currently adv 1. (at present) actualmente 2. (commonly) comúnmente

curry ['kɜr·i] <-ies> n curry m; **chicken** ~ pollo al curry

curse [kɜrs] I. n 1. (word) palabrota f, grosería f Col 2. (evil spell) maldición f; to put a ~ echar una maldición (on a) II. vt 1. (swear) insultar 2. (wish evil) maldecir III. vi (swear) soltar palabrotas

cursor ['kɜr·sər] n cursor m

cursory ['kɜr·sə·ri] adj rápido, -a

curt [kɜrt] adj (rudely brief) seco, -a; (refusal) tajante

curtain ['kɜr·tən] n 1. a. fig cortina f 2. THEAT telón m; **to raise/lower the ~** subir/bajar el telón ▶ **it's ~s for you** estás acabado

curve [kɜrv] I. n curva f II. vi estar curvado; (river, road) hacer una curva III. vt curvar

cushion ['kʊʃ·ən] I. n 1. cojín m 2. (billiards) banda f II. vt 1. (blow) amortiguar 2. (protect) proteger

cushy ['kʊʃ·i] <-ier, -iest> adj inf fácil; **a ~ job** un chollo

custard ['kʌs·tərd] n ≈ natillas fpl

custody ['kʌs·tə·di] n 1. (care) cuidado m; **in the ~ of sb** al cuidado de alguien 2. (guardianship) custodia f 3. LAW detención f; **to take into ~** detener

custom ['kʌs·təm] n 1. (tradition) costumbre f; **it is his ~ to get up late** tiene por costumbre levantarse tarde 2. LAW derecho m consuetudinario 3. ~**s** (place) aduana f; (tax) aranceles mpl; **to get through ~s** pasar por la aduana

customary ['kʌs·tə·mer·i] adj 1. (traditional) tradicional; **it is ~ to invite...** es costumbre invitar... 2. (usual) habitual

customer ['kʌs·tə·mər] n 1. cliente, -a m, f; **regular ~** cliente habitual 2. inf (person) tío, -a m, f

customer service n servicio m de atención al cliente

custom(s)house n aduana f

cut [kʌt] I. n 1. (incision) a. FASHION, MED, CINE corte m; **to get a ~** cortarse 2. (portion) parte f; (slice) tajada f; **to take one's ~ of sth** sacar tajada de algo; **cold ~s** fiambres m 3. (decrease) reducción f; **a ~ in production** una disminución de la producción; **a ~ in staff** una reducción de plantilla; **wage/budget ~** recorte salarial/presupuestario II. adj cortado, -a; (glass, diamond) tallado, -a III. <cut, cut, -tt-> vt 1. (make an incision) cortar; (tree) talar;

(corn) segar; **to ~ in half** partir por la mitad; **to ~ to pieces** trocear; **to have one's hair ~** cortarse el pelo 2. (cause moral pain) herir 3. (decrease) reducir; (costs, budget, wages) recortar; (prices) bajar 4. shorten, acortar 5. (diamond) tallar; (benefits) repartir; (motor, lights) apagar; (class) saltarse IV. <cut, cut, -tt-> vi 1. (slice) **this knife ~s well** este cuchillo corta bien; **this cheese ~s easily** este queso se corta con facilidad 2. GAMES, CINE cortar ▶ **to ~ to the left/right** torcer a la izquierda/derecha 4. (morally wound) herir ▶ **to ~ both ways** ser un arma de doble filo; **to ~ and run** salir pitando

◆**cut across** vt insep 1. (take short cut) atajar por 2. (transcend) trascender

◆**cut away** vt cortar

◆**cut back** vt 1. (trim down) recortar; (bushes, branches) podar 2. (reduce) reducir; **to ~ (on) costs** recortar costes

◆**cut down** I. vt 1. (tree) talar 2. (reduce) reducir; **to ~ expenses** recortar gastos 3. (destroy) destruir II. vi reducir el consumo (**on** de)

◆**cut in** vi **to ~ (on)** interrumpir

◆**cut into** vt insep 1. (cake) dar el corte 2. (interrupt) interrumpir

◆**cut off** vt 1. (sever) a. ELEC, TEL cortar 2. (amputate) amputar 3. (interrupt) interrumpir 4. (separate) aislar; **to cut oneself off** aislarse (**from** de); **to be ~ by the snow** estar incomunicado por la nieve 5. AUTO cortar el paso a

◆**cut out** I. vt 1. (slice) cortar 2. (suppress) eliminar 3. inf (stop) dejar; **cut it out!** ¡basta ya! II. vi (engine) pararse; (machine) apagarse

◆**cut short** vt acortar

◆**cut up** I. vt 1. (slice) cortar en pedazos; (meat) trinchar 2. (hurt) herir II. vi (clown) payasear

cut-and-dried [,kʌt·ən·'draɪd] adj preparado, -a de antemano; (idea) preconcebido, -a

cutback ['kʌt·bæk] n 1. (reduction) reducción f 2. CINE flashback m

cute [kjut] adj mono, -a inf; (remark, idea) ingenioso, -a

cutey <-ies>, **cutie** ['kju·ʈi] n inf (wom-

an) bombón *m*; (*child*) monada *f*

cutlery ['kʌt·lə·ri] *n* cubiertos *fpl*

cutlet ['kʌt·lɪt] *n* chuleta *f*

cutoff ['kʌt·ɔf] *n a.* TECH corte *m*; ~ **date** fecha límite; ~ **point** tope *m*

cutout *n* **1.** (*design*) recortable *m* **2.** ELEC cortacircuitos *m inv*

cut-rate *adj* rebajado, -a

cutting ['kʌt·ɪŋ] I. *n* **1.** (*act*) corte *m* **2.** (*piece*) recorte *m*; (*cloth*) retal *m* **3.** BOT esqueje *m* II. *adj* cortante; *fig* hiriente

cuttlefish ['kʌt·əl·fɪʃ] *n inv* sepia *f*

cyanide ['saɪ·ə·naɪd] *n* cianuro *m*

cybercafé ['saɪ·bər·kæ.feɪ] *n* cibercafé *m*

cybercash ['saɪ·bər·kæʃ] *n* dinero *m* electrónico

cybernaut [ˌsaɪ·bər·'nɔt] *n* cibernauta *mf*

cybernetics [ˌsaɪ·bər·'net·ɪks] *n + sing vb* cibernética *f*

cycle ['saɪ·kəl] I. *n* **1.** (*bike*) bicicleta *f* **2.** (*of life, seasons*) ciclo *m* **3.** ASTR órbita *f* II. *vi* ir en bicicleta

cyclic ['saɪ·klɪk] *adj*, **cyclical** *adj* cíclico, -a

cycling *n* ciclismo *m*

cyclist ['saɪ·klɪst] *n* ciclista *mf*

cyclone ['saɪ·kloʊn] *n* ciclón *m*

cylinder ['sɪl·ɪn·dər] *n* **1.** MATH, AUTO, TECH cilindro *m* **2.** (*container: of gas*) bombona *f*, garrafa *f Arg, Urug*, (*of water*) tanque *m*

cylindrical [sɪ·'lɪn·drɪ·kəl] *adj* cilíndrico, -a

cynic ['sɪn·ɪk] *adj, n* cínico, -a *m, f*, valemadrista *mf Méx*

cynical ['sɪn·ɪ·kəl] *adj* cínico, -a

cynicism ['sɪn·ɪ·sɪz·əm] *n* cinismo *m*

cypress ['saɪ·prəs] <-es> *n* ciprés *m*

Czech [tʃek] I. *n* **1.** (*person*) checo, -a *m, f* **2.** (*language*) checo *m* II. *adj* checo, -a

Czech Republic *n* República *f* Checa

D

D, d [di] *n* **1.** (*letter*) D, d *f*; ~ **as in Delta** D de Dolores **2.** SCHOOL ≈ suficiente *m*

d *abbr of* **diameter** d

dab [dæb] I. <-bb-> *vt* tocar ligeramente II. <-bb-> *vi* dar toquecitos (**at** a) III. *n* **1.** (*pat*) toque *m* **2.** (*tiny bit*) pizca *f*; (*liquid*) gota *f*

dad [dæd] *n* papá *m*

daddy ['dæd·i] *n* papi *m*, tata *m AmL*

daffodil ['dæf·ə·dɪl] *n* narciso *m*

dagger ['dæɡər] *n* puñal *m* ▶ **to look** ~s **at sb** fulminar a alguien con la mirada

daily ['deɪ·li] I. *adj* diario, -a; **on a ~ basis** por días II. *adv* a diario; **twice** ~ dos veces al día III. <-ies> *n* diario *m*

dairy ['der·i] I. *n* **1.** (*farm*) vaquería *f*, tambo *m Arg* **2.** (*shop*) lechería *f* II. *adj* **1.** (*made from milk*) lácteo, -a **2.** (*producing milk*) lechero, -a; (*farm, herd*) de vacas

dairy farm *n* vaquería *f*, tambo *m Arg*

dairy products *npl* productos *m pl* lácteos

daisy ['deɪ·zi] <-ies> *n* margarita *f* ▶ **to feel as fresh as a** ~ sentirse fresco como una rosa; **to be pushing up daisies** criar malvas

dam [dæm] I. *n* (*barrier*) presa *f*; (*reservoir*) embalse *m* II. <-mm-> *vt* represar; *fig* contener

damage ['dæm·ɪdʒ] I. *vt* **1.** (*harm, hurt*) dañar; (*health, reputation*) perjudicar **2.** (*ruin*) estropear II. *n* **1.** (*harm*) daño *m*; (*to pride, reputation*) perjuicio *m*; **to do ~ to sb/sth** hacer daño a alguien/dañar algo **2.** *pl* LAW daños *m pl* y perjuicios ▶ **the ~ is done** el daño ya está hecho; **what's the ~?** *inf* ¿qué se debe?

damn [dæm] *sl* I. *interj* ¡mierda! II. *adj* maldito, -a III. *vt* **1.** (*God vulg*) ~ **it!** ¡me cago en la puta!; ~ **him!** he took **my bike!** ¡ese idiota se ha llevado mi bici! **2.** REL condenar IV. *adv* muy; **to be ~ lucky** tener una suerte increíble; **you know ~ well that...** sabes perfectamente que... V. *n* **I don't give a ~ what he says!** ¡me importa un comino lo que diga!

damnation [dæm·'neɪ·ʃən] *interj* ¡maldición!

damned *adj sl* maldito, -a; (*for emphasis*) puto, -a *vulg*

damp [dæmp] I. *adj* húmedo, -a II. *vt*

1. (*moisten*) humedecer **2.** *a. fig* PHYS, TECH amortiguar **3. to ~ (down)** (*fire*) sofocar; (*enthusiasm*) apagar

dampen ['dæm·pən] *vt* **1.** (*moisten*) humedecer **2.** (*lessen*) desanimar; (*enthusiasm*) apagar; (*expectations*) frustrar **3.** *a. fig* PHYS, TECH amortiguar

dance [dæns] **I.** <-cing> *vi* **1.** bailar (**to** al compás de); **to go dancing** ir a bailar; **to ~ with joy** dar saltos de alegría **2.** (*bob*) agitarse; **the daffodils were dancing in the breeze** los narcisos se mecían con la brisa **II.** <-cing> *vt* bailar **III.** *n* baile *m*

dancer ['dæn·sər] *n* bailarín, -ina *m, f*

dancing *n* baile *m*

dandelion ['dæn·də·laɪ·ən] *n* diente *m* de león

dandruff ['dæn·drəf] *n* caspa *f*

Dane [deɪn] *n* danés, -esa *m, f*

danger ['deɪn·dʒər] *n* peligro *m* (**to** para); **the ~s of sth** los peligros de algo; **to be in ~** correr peligro; **to be out of ~** estar fuera de peligro; **there's no ~ of him knowing that** no hay peligro de que lo sepa

dangerous ['deɪn·dʒər·əs] *adj* peligroso, -a, riesgoso, -a *AmL*

dangle ['dæŋ·gəl] **I.** <-ling> *vi* (*hang*) colgar (**from** de) **II.** <-ling> *vt* **1.** (*hang*) hacer oscilar **2.** (*tempt*) **to ~ sth in front of sb** tentar a alguien con algo

Danish ['deɪ·nɪʃ] **I.** *adj* danés, -esa **II.** *n* **1.** (*person*) danés, -esa *m, f* **2.** LING danés *m*

dare [der] **I.** <-ring> *vt* **1.** (*risk doing*) atreverse a **2.** (*challenge*) desafiar; **to ~ sb (to do sth)** retar a alguien (a hacer algo) **II.** <-ring> *vi* atreverse; **to ~ to do sth** atreverse a hacer algo; **I don't ~ go there** no me atrevo a ir; **just you ~!** ¡atrévete y verás!; **how ~ you...** ¿cómo te atreves a...? ▶ **don't you ~!** ¡ni se te ocurra! **III.** *n* desafío *m*; **to take a ~** aceptar un reto

daredevil ['der·dev·əl] *inf* **I.** *n* balarrasa *mf* **II.** *adj* temerario, -a

daresay ['der·seɪ] *vt* suponer

daring ['der·ɪŋ] **I.** *adj* **1.** (*courageous*) temerario, -a **2.** (*provocative*) atrevido, -a **II.** *n* osadía *f*

dark [dark] **I.** *adj* **1.** (*without light, black*) oscuro, -a; **~ blue** azul oscuro; (*coffee*) solo; (*chocolate*) negro, -a; (*complexion, hair*) moreno, -a **2.** (*depressing*) sombrío, -a; (*evil*) tenebroso, -a; **to have a ~ side** tener un lado oscuro; **to look on the ~ side of things** ver el lado malo de las cosas **3.** (*evil*) tenebroso, -a **4.** (*unknown*) oculto, -a **II.** *n* **1.** (*darkness*) oscuridad *f*; **to be in the ~** estar a oscuras **2.** (*time of day*) **at ~** al caer la noche; **before/after ~** antes/después de que anochezca ▶ **to keep sb in the ~ about sth** ocultar algo a alguien

darken ['dar·kən] **I.** *vi* oscurecerse; *fig* ensombrecerse **II.** *vt* oscurecer; *fig* ensombrecer

darkly *adv* **1.** (*mysteriously*) misteriosamente **2.** (*gloomily*) tristemente; (*look*) con aire sombrío

darkness *n* oscuridad *f*; *fig* tinieblas *fpl*

darling ['dar·lɪŋ] **I.** *n* **1.** (*person*) amor *m* **2.** (*term of endearment*) cariño *mf* **II.** *adj* **1.** (*beloved*) querido, -a **2.** (*cute*) mono, -a; **a ~ little room** una monada de habitación

darn [darn] *vt inf* **~ it!** ¡carajo!; **I'll be ~ed if I'll do it!** ¡no lo hago ni que me maten!

dart [dart] **I.** *n* **1.** dardo *m*; **to play ~s** jugar a los dardos; **a game of ~s** una partida de dardos **2.** (*quick run*) movimiento *m* fugaz **II.** *vi* precipitarse (**for** hacia); **to ~ away** salir disparado **III.** *vt* lanzar

dash [dæʃ] **I.** <-es> *n* **1.** (*rush*) carrera *f*; **to make a ~ for** precipitarse hacia; **to make a ~ for it** huir precipitadamente **2.** (*pinch*) pizca *f*; **a ~ of color** un toque de color **3.** (*flair*) brío *m* **4.** TYPO guión *m* **II.** *vi* **1.** (*hurry*) precipitarse **2.** (*slam*) romperse (**against** contra) **III.** *vt* (*shatter*) romper; (*hopes*) defraudar; (**to ~ off a note**) escribir una nota corriendo

dashboard ['dæʃ·bɔrd] *n* salpicadero *m*

dashing ['dæʃ·ɪŋ] *adj* gallardo, -a

data ['deɪ·tə] *npl + sing/pl vb a.* COMPUT datos *mpl*

data bank *n*, **databank** *n* banco *m* de datos

database n base f de datos
data file n fichero m de datos
data processing n procesamiento m de datos
date¹ [deɪt] I. n 1. (calendar day) fecha f; **expiration ~** fecha de vencimiento; **what ~ is it today?** ¿cuál es la fecha de hoy?; **to be out of ~** FASHION estar pasado de moda 2. FIN plazo m 3. (appointment) cita f; **to have a ~** tener una cita; **to make a ~** quedar (with con) 4. inf(person) novio, -a m, f II. vt 1. fechar 2. inf to ~ sb salir con alguien III. vi 1. to ~ back to remontarse a 2. FASHION pasarse de moda 3. (go out) salir con alguien
date² [deɪt] n (fruit) dátil m
dated ['deɪ·tɪd] adj anticuado, -a
daughter ['dɔ·tər] n hija f
daughter-in-law <daughters-in-law> n nuera f
dawn [dɔn] I. n alba m, amanezca f Méx; fig nacimiento m; **from ~ to dusk** de sol a sol; **at ~** al alba II. vi amanecer; fig nacer; **it ~ed on him that...** cayó en la cuenta de que...
day [deɪ] n 1. día m; **~ after/by ~** día tras/a día; **all ~ (long)** todo el día; **any·now** cualquier día de estos; **by ~** de día; **by the ~** diariamente; **for a few ~s** por unos días; **from this ~ forth** de ahora en adelante; **from one ~ to the next** de un día para otro; **one ~** algún día; **two ~s ago** hace dos días; **the ~ before yesterday** anteayer; **the ~ after tomorrow** pasado mañana; **in the (good) old ~s** en los viejos tiempos 2. (working period) jornada f; **to take a ~ off** tomarse un día de descanso ▶ **in this ~ and age** en los tiempos que corren; **to have seen better ~s** haber conocido tiempos mejores; **to call it a ~** dejarlo para otro día; **~ in ~ out** un día sí y otro también
daybreak ['deɪ·breɪk] n alba m
day camp n campamento m de día
daydream ['deɪ·drim] vi soñar despierto
daylight ['deɪ·laɪt] n luz f del día; **in broad ~** a plena luz del día ▶ **to scare the** <u>living</u> **~s out of sb** dar un susto de muerte a alguien
day shift n turno m de día

daytime ['deɪ·taɪm] n día m; **in the ~** de día
day-to-day adj cotidiano, -a
day trip n excursión f
daze [deɪz] I. n to be in a ~ estar aturdido II. vt aturdir
dazzle ['dæz·əl] I. vt deslumbrar II. n deslumbramiento m
dazzled adj deslumbrado, -a
dB n abbr of **decibel** dB
DE n abbr of **Delaware** Delaware m
dead [ded] I. adj 1. (not alive) muerto, -a 2. inf(inactive) parado, -a; (fire) apagado, -a; (battery) descargado, -a; (line) cortado, -a 3. inf (boring) muerto, -a 4. (numb) dormido, -a 5. (complete: silence) profundo, -a; **to be a ~ loss** ser un desastre total; **to come to a ~ stop** pararse en seco II. n the ~ los muertos ▶ **in the ~ of night/winter** en plena noche/pleno invierno III. adv 1. inf (totally) completamente; **to be ~ set against/on sth** estar completamente en contra de/decidido a algo 2. (directly) justo; **~ ahead** justo al frente
dead-end adj sin salida
dead end n callejón m sin salida
dead heat n empate m
deadline ['ded·laɪn] n fecha f límite; **to meet/miss the ~** cumplir/incumplir el plazo
deadlock ['ded·lak] n punto m muerto
deadly ['ded·li] I. <-ier, -iest> adj 1. mortal; (weapon) mortífero, -a; (silence) sepulcral 2. inf (boring) aburridísimo, -a II. <-ier, -iest> adv extremadamente
deaf [def] I. adj sordo, -a; **to go ~** quedarse sordo; **to be ~ to sth** fig hacer oídos sordos a algo II. npl the ~ los sordos
deafen ['def·ən] vt ensordecer
deafening adj ensordecedor(a)
deaf-mute [ˌdef·'mjut] n sordomudo, -a m, f
deafness n sordera f
deal¹ [dil] n (amount) cantidad f; **a great ~ of** una gran cantidad; **a great ~ of effort** mucho esfuerzo
deal² [dil] <dealt, dealt> I. n 1. COM negocio m; **a big ~** un negocio impor-

tante **2.** (*agreement*) pacto *m*; **to do a ~** hacer un trato (**with** con) **3.** GAMES **it's your ~** te toca dar a ti ▶ **big ~!** *iron* ¡menuda cosa!; **it's not big ~!** *sl* ¡no es para tanto! **II.** *vi* **1.** (*do business*) negociar; **to ~ with sb** hacer negocios con alguien; **to ~ in sth** comerciar con algo **2.** GAMES repartir **3.** *sl* (*cope*) arreglárselas (**with** con) **III.** *vt* **1.** GAMES repartir **2.** (*give*) dar

◆ **deal out** *vt* repartir

◆ **deal with** *vt* (*problem*) ocuparse de; (*person*) tratar con; (*book*) tratar de

dealer ['di·lər] *n* COM negociante *mf*; **drug ~** traficante de drogas; **antique ~** marchante de antigüedades

dealing ['di·lɪŋ] *n* **1.** COM comercio *m* **2. ~s** FIN transacciones *fpl* **3. ~s** (*relations*) relaciones *fpl*; **to have ~s with sb** tratar con alguien

dealt [delt] *pt, pp of* **deal**

dean [din] *n* UNIV decano, -a *m, f*

dear [dɪr] **I.** *adj* **1.** (*loved*) querido, -a; **it is ~ to me** le tengo mucho cariño **2.** (*in letters*) estimado, -a; **Dear Sarah** Querida Sarah **3.** (*expensive*) caro, -a **II.** *adv* caro **III.** *interj inf* oh ~! ¡Dios mío! **IV.** *n* encanto *m*; **she is a ~** es encantadora; **be a ~ and...** hazme el favor de...

dearly *adv* mucho; *fig* caro; **he paid ~ for his success** su éxito le costó caro

death [deθ] *n* muerte *f*; **scared/bored to ~** muerto de miedo/aburrimiento ▶ **to be at ~'s door** estar a las puertas de la muerte; **to be the ~ of** acabar con

deathblow *n* golpe *m* mortal

death certificate *n* certificado *m* de defunción

deathly ['deθ·li] *adv, adj* de muerte

death penalty *n* pena *f* de muerte

death rate *n* tasa *f* de mortalidad

debatable [dɪ·'beɪ·tə·bəl] *adj* discutible

debate [dɪ·'beɪt] **I.** *n* debate *m* (**over** sobre) **II.** *vt, vi* debatir (**about** acerca de)

debit ['deb·ɪt] **I.** *n* débito *m* **II.** *vt* **the bank ~ed my account for the rent** el banco cargó a mi cuenta el alquiler

debt [det] *n* deuda *f*; **to be in ~** (*person*) tener deudas; (*business*) estar en números rojos

debt collector *n* cobrador(a) *m(f)* (de deudas)

debtor ['det·ər] *n* deudor(a) *m(f)*

debug [ˌdi·'bʌg] <-gg-> *vt* COMPUT depurar

debut [deɪ·'bju] **I.** *n* debut *m* **II.** *vi* debutar (**in/as** en/como)

Dec. *n abbr of* **December** dic.

decade ['dek·eɪd] *n* década *f*

decadence ['dek·ə·dəns] *n* decadencia *f*

decadent ['dek·ə·dənt] *adj* decadente

decaf ['di·kæf] *adj, n inf abbr of* **decaffeinated** descafeinado, -a

decaffeinated [di·'kæf·ɪ·neɪ·tɪd] *adj* descafeinado, -a

decathlon [dɪ·'kæθ·lɑn] *n* decatlón *m*

decay [dɪ·'keɪ] **I.** *n* (*food*) descomposición *f*; (*building, intellect*) deterioro *m*; (*dental*) caries *f inv*; (*civilization*) decadencia *f* **II.** *vi* (*food*) pudrirse; (*building, intellect*) deteriorarse **III.** *vt* descomponer

decease [dɪ·'sis] *n* fallecimiento *m*

deceased [dɪ·'sist] *adj, n* difunto, -a *m, f*

deceit [dɪ·'sit] *n* engaño *m*, transa *f Méx*

deceitful [dɪ·'sit·fəl] *adj* engañoso, -a

deceive [dɪ·'siv] *vt* engañar; **to ~ oneself** engañarse a sí mismo ▶ **appearances can ~** las apariencias engañan

December [dɪ·'sem·bər] *n* diciembre *m*; *s. a.* **April**

decency ['di·sən·si] *n* decencia *f*

decent ['di·sənt] *adj* **1.** (*socially acceptable*) decente; **are you ~?** *fig* ¿estás presentable? **2.** *inf* (*kind*) amable **3.** *inf* (*salary, living, wage*) decente

deception [dɪ·'sep·ʃən] *n* engaño *m*

deceptive [dɪ·'sep·tɪv] *adj* engañoso, -a

decibel ['des·ə·bəl] *n* decibelio *m*

decide [dɪ·'saɪd] **I.** *vi* decidirse (**on** por) **II.** *vt* decidir

decimal ['des·ə·məl] *adj, n* decimal *m*

decipher [dɪ·'saɪ·fər] *vt* descifrar

decision [dɪ·'sɪʒ·ən] *n* **1.** (*choice, resolution*) decisión *f*; **to make a ~** tomar una decisión **2.** LAW fallo *m*

decisive [dɪ·'saɪ·sɪv] *adj* (*factor*) decisivo, -a; (*manner*) categórico, -a; (*victory, defeat*) contundente; (*change*) rotundo, -a

deck [dek] **I.** *n* **1.** NAUT cubierta *f*

2. (*porch*) terraza *f* **3.** (*cards*) baraja *f* **4.** MUS, ELEC platina *f* **II.** *vt* adornar; **to ~ oneself out** engalanarse

deck chair *n* tumbona *f*, reposera *f* Arg

declaration [ˌde·klə·ˈreɪ·ʃən] *n* declaración *f*

declare [dɪ·ˈkler] **I.** *vt* declarar; **to ~ war** declarar la guerra (**on** a); **to ~ oneself** (**to be**) **bankrupt** declararse en bancarrota **II.** *vi* declararse

decline [dɪ·ˈklaɪn] **I.** *vi* **1.** (*price*) bajar; (*power, influence*) disminuir; (*civilization*) decaer; **to ~ in value** disminuir de valor **2.** MED debilitarse **3.** (*refuse*) rehusar **II.** *vt* **1.** (*refuse*) rehusar **2.** LING declinar **III.** *n* **1.** (*price, power, influence*) disminución *f*; (*civilization*) decadencia *f*; **to be in ~** estar en declive **2.** MED debilitación *f*

decode [ˌdi·ˈkoʊd] *vi, vt* descodificar

decoder *n* decodificador *m*

decompose [ˌdi·kəm·ˈpoʊz] **I.** *vi* descomponerse **II.** *vt* descomponer

decomposition [ˌdi·kam·pə·ˈzɪʃ·ən] *n* descomposición *f*

decompress [ˌdi·kəm·ˈpres] *vt a.* COMPUT descomprimir

decontaminate [ˌdi·kən·ˈtæm·ɪ·neɪt] *vt* descontaminar

decontamination [ˌdi·kən·ˌtæm·ɪ·ˈneɪ·ʃən] *n* descontaminación *f*

decorate [ˈdek·ə·reɪt] **I.** *vt* **1.** (*adorn*) decorar; (*paint*) pintar; (*wallpaper*) empapelar **2.** (*honor*) condecorar **II.** *vi* (*paint*) pintar; (*wallpaper*) empapelar

decoration [ˌdek·ə·ˈreɪ·ʃən] *n* **1.** decoración *f*; (*ornament*) adorno *m* **2.** (*medal*) condecoración *f*

decorative [ˈdek·ər·ə·t̬ɪv] *adj* decorativo, -a

decorator [ˈdek·ə·reɪ·t̬ər] *n* decorador(a) *m(f)*

decoy [ˈdi·kɔɪ] *n* señuelo *m;* **to act as a ~** hacer de señuelo

decrease¹ [dɪ·ˈkris] *vi, vt* disminuir; (*prices*) bajar

decrease² [ˈdi·kris] *n* disminución *f*

decree [dɪ·ˈkri] **I.** *n* decreto *m* **II.** *vt* decretar

decrepit [dɪ·ˈkrep·ɪt] *adj* destartalado, -a; (*person*) decrépito, -a

dedicate [ˈded·ɪ·keɪt] *vt* **1.** dedicar; **to ~ oneself/one's life to sth** dedicarse/consagrar su vida a algo **2.** (*formally open*) inaugurar

dedication [ˌded·ɪ·ˈkeɪ·ʃən] *n* **1.** (*devotion*) dedicación *f* **2.** (*inscription*) dedicatoria *f*

deduct [dɪ·ˈdʌkt] *vt* deducir

deductible *adj* deducible

deduction [dɪ·ˈdʌk·ʃən] *n* deducción *f*; **$1000 after ~s** $1000 netos

deed [did] *n* **1.** (*act*) acto *m*; (*remarkable*) hazaña *f* **2.** LAW escritura *f*

deejay [ˈdi·dʒeɪ] *n inf* pincha *mf*

deep [dip] **I.** *adj* **1.** (*not shallow: a. intellectually*) profundo, -a; **to be in ~ breath** respirar hondo; **to be in ~ thought** estar absorto en sus pensamientos **2.** (*extending back*) **the dresser is 2 feet ~** la cómoda tiene 61 cm de fondo **3.** (*extreme: love, disappointment*) gran(de); **to be in ~ trouble** estar metido en un buen lío **4.** (*dark*) oscuro, -a; **~ red** rojo intenso **II.** *adv* **1.** (*far down*) mucho más abajo; **~ in the forest** en lo más profundo del bosque **2.** (*extremely*) mucho; **to be ~ in debt** estar cargado de deudas ▶ **to go ~ into sth** ahondar en algo

deep freeze *n* congelador *m*

deep-frozen *adj* ultracongelado, -a

deep-fry *vt* freír en abundante aceite

deeply *adv* profundamente; (*breathe*) hondo

deer [dɪr] *n inv* ciervo *m*

default [dɪ·ˈfɔlt] *n* (*omission*) omisión *f*; **by** por defecto; **~ value** valor por defecto

defeat [dɪ·ˈfit] **I.** *vt* derrotar; (*hopes*) frustrar; (*proposal*) rechazar **II.** *n* derrota *f*; (*plans*) fracaso *m;* **to admit ~** darse por vencido

defecate [ˈdef·ə·keɪt] *vi* defecar

defect¹ [ˈdi·fekt] *n a.* TECH, MED defecto *m*

defective [dɪ·ˈfek·t̬ɪv] *adj* defectuoso, -a

defend [dɪ·ˈfend] *vt, vi a.* LAW, SPORTS defender; **to ~ oneself** defenderse (**from** de)

defendant [dɪ·ˈfen·dənt] *n* (*civil case*) demandado, -a *m, f*; (*criminal case*) acusado, -a *m, f*

defense [dɪˈfens] *n* a. LAW, MED, SPORTS defensa *f*; **the body's ~s** las defensas del organismo; **counsel for the ~** abogado(a) *m(f)* defensor(a)

defenseless [dɪˈfens·lɪs] *adj* indefenso, -a

defense mechanism *n* PSYCH mecanismo *m* de defensa

defensive [dɪˈfen·sɪv] I. *adj* defensivo, -a II. *n* **to be/go on the ~** estar/ponerse a la defensiva

defer [dɪˈfɜr] <-rr-> *vt* aplazar

deferred *adj* aplazado, -a

defiant [dɪˈfaɪ·ənt] *adj* (*person*) rebelde; (*attitude*) desafiante

deficiency [dɪˈfɪʃ·ən·si] *n* deficiencia *f*

deficient [dɪˈfɪʃ·ənt] *adj* deficiente; **to be ~ in sth** carecer de algo

deficit [ˈdef·ɪ·sɪt] *n* déficit *m*

define [dɪˈfaɪn] *vt* 1. (*give definition of*) definir 2. (*explain*) determinar; (*rights*) formular 3. (*characterize*) caracterizar

definite [ˈdef·ɪ·nɪt] *adj* 1. (*certain*) seguro, -a; (*opinion*) claro, -a; **it's ~ that...** no hay duda de que... 2. (*final*) definitivo, -a

definitely *adv* definitivamente

definition [ˌdef·ɪˈnɪʃ·ən] *n* definición *f*; **to give ~ to sth** realzar algo; **her ideas lack ~** sus ideas no son muy claras

definitive [dɪˈfɪn·ɪ·tɪv] *adj* definitivo, -a, rajante *Arg*

definitively *adv* definitivamente

deflect [dɪˈflekt] I. *vt* desviar II. *vi* desviarse (**off** de)

deflection [dɪˈflek·ʃən] *n* desviación *f*

defog [ˌdiˈfɔg] *vt* desempañar

defogger [ˌdiˈfɔ·gər] *n* dispositivo *m* antivaho

deforest [ˌdiˈfɔr·ɪst] *vt* deforestar

deforestation [ˌdiˌfɔr·ɪˈsteɪ·ʃən] *n* deforestación *f*

deform [dɪˈfɔrm] I. *vt* deformar II. *vi* deformarse

deformation [ˌdi·fɔr·ˈmeɪ·ʃən] *n* deformación *f*

defraud [dɪˈfrɔd] *vt* estafar; **to ~ sb (of sth)** estafar (algo) a alguien

defrost [ˌdiˈfrɔst] I. *vt* deshelar; (*fridge, food*) descongelar; (*windshield*) desempañar II. *vi* deshelarse; (*fridge, food*) descongelarse

defy [dɪˈfaɪ] *vt* 1. (*authority, gravity*) desafiar 2. (*resist*) resistirse a; **it defies description** es indescriptible 3. (*disobey*) desobedecer

degenerate[1] [dɪˈdʒen·ə·reɪt] *vi* degenerar (**into** en); (*health*) deteriorarse

degenerate[2] [dɪˈdʒen·ər·ət] *adj, n* degenerado, -a *m, f*

degeneration [dɪˌdʒen·əˈreɪ·ʃən] *n* degeneración *f*

degrade [dɪˈgreɪd] I. *vt* a. CHEM degradar II. *vi* degradarse

degree [dɪˈgri] *n* 1. MATH, METEO, MED grado *m*; **5 ~s below zero** 5 grados bajo cero 2. (*amount*) nivel *m* 3. (*extent*) **I agree with you to some ~** estoy de acuerdo contigo hasta cierto punto; **by ~s** gradualmente; **to the last ~** en grado sumo 4. UNIV título *m*; **to have a ~/master's ~** ser licenciado/tener un máster (**in** en); **to do a ~ in chemistry** estudiar química

dehydrated *adj* deshidratado, -a; (*milk*) en polvo; **to become ~** deshidratarse

deice [ˌdiˈaɪs] *vt* deshelar

dejected *adj* desanimado, -a

dejection [dɪˈdʒek·ʃən] *n* desánimo *m*

Del. [del·əˈwer] *n abbr of* **Delaware** Delaware *m*

delay [dɪˈleɪ] I. *vt* aplazar; **to be ~ed** retrasarse; **to ~ doing sth** posponer hacer algo II. *vi* tardar; **to ~ in doing sth** dejar algo para más tarde; **don't ~!** ¡no te entretengas! III. *n* tardanza *f*; **without ~** sin dilación; **a two-hour ~** un retraso de dos horas

delegate[1] [ˈdel·ɪ·gət] *n a.* POL delegado, -a *m, f*

delegate[2] [ˈdel·ɪ·geɪt] *vt* delegar

delegation [ˌdel·ɪˈgeɪ·ʃən] *n* delegación *f*

delete [dɪˈlit] *vt* borrar; COMPUT suprimir; (*file*) eliminar

deletion [dɪˈli·ʃən] *n* 1. (*action*) eliminación *f* 2. (*removal*) supresión *f*

deli [ˈdel·i] *n inf see* **delicatessen**

deliberate[1] [dɪˈlɪb·ər·ət] *adj* 1. (*intentional*) deliberado, -a; (*decision*) meditado, -a 2. (*unhurried*) lento, -a; (*movement*) pausado, -a

deliberate[2] [dɪˈlɪb·ə·reɪt] I. *vi* reflexionar (**on** sobre) II. *vt* deliberar sobre

deliberately adv (intentionally) adrede

deliberation [dɪˌlɪb·ə·ˈreɪ·ʃən] n 1. (formal discussion) deliberación f 2. (consideration) reflexión f; **after due ~** después de pensarlo bien 3. (unhurried manner) parsimonia f

delicacy [ˈdel·ɪ·kə·si] n 1. (tact) delicadeza f; **the ~ of the situation** lo delicado de la situación 2. (food) manjar m

delicate [ˈdel·ɪ·kət] adj 1. (fragile) frágil; **to be in ~ health** estar delicado (de salud) 2. (fine) primoroso, -a; (soft) suave; (aroma) exquisito, -a 3. (balance, situation) a. PSYCH delicado, -a

delicatessen [ˌdel·ɪ·kə·ˈtes·ən] n delicatessen m o f inv

delicious [dɪ·ˈlɪʃ·əs] adj exquisito, -a

delight [dɪ·ˈlaɪt] I. n placer m; **to do sth with ~** hacer algo con gusto; **to take ~** disfrutar (**in** con) II. vt encantar; **to be ~ed** estar encantado (**with** con)

delighted adj encantado, -a

delightful [dɪ·ˈlaɪt·fəl] adj delicioso, -a; (person) encantador(a)

delimit [dɪ·ˈlɪm·ɪt] vt delimitar

delirious [dɪ·ˈlɪr·i·əs] adj **to be ~** delirar; **to be ~ with joy** estar delirante de alegría

deliriously adv MED delirantemente; fig locamente; **she was ~ happy** estaba loca de alegría

delirium [dɪ·ˈlɪr·i·əm] n delirio m

deliver [dɪ·ˈlɪv·ər] I. vt 1. (hand over) entregar; (letter, package) repartir (a domicilio) 2. (lecture) dar; (speech, verdict) pronunciar 3. (direct) **to ~ a blow** asestar un golpe; SPORTS lanzar 4. **to ~ a baby** (mother) tener un bebé 5. (save) librar 6. (produce) **to ~ a promise/the goods** cumplir una promesa/lo acordado II. vi 1. COM **we ~** entrega a domicilio 2. (give birth) dar a luz

delivery [dɪ·ˈlɪv·ə·ri] n 1. (distribution) reparto m; **~ charges** gastos de envío; **~ man/woman** repartidor(a) m(f); **to pay on ~** pagar contra reembolso; **to take ~ of** recibir 2. SPORTS lanzamiento m 3. (birth) parto m

delivery room n sala f de partos

delivery service n servicio m de reparto a domicilio

delivery truck n furgoneta f de reparto

delta [ˈdel·tə] n delta m

delude [dɪ·ˈlud] vt engañar; **to ~ sb into believing sth** hacer creer algo a alguien

deluge [ˈdel·judʒ] I. n (downpour) diluvio m; (flood) inundación f; fig avalancha f II. vt a. fig inundar; **to be ~d with tears** estar bañado en lágrimas; **she is ~d with offers** le llueven las ofertas

delusion [dɪ·ˈlu·ʒən] n 1. (wrong idea) error m 2. PSYCH alucinación f

deluxe [dɪ·ˈlʌks] adj de lujo

demand [dɪ·ˈmænd] I. vt 1. exigir; (a right) reclamar; **to ~ that...** exigir que... +subj; **she demanded to see...** insistió en ver a... 2. (ask) preguntar II. n 1. (request) exigencia f; **on ~** a petición; **to make a ~ for** exigir; **to make a ~ that...** hacer una petición de que... +subj; **to make heavy ~s on sb's time** ocupar gran parte del tiempo de alguien; **to meet a ~** satisfacer las exigencias (**for** de); **by popular ~** a petición del público 2. COM demanda f; **to be in ~** tener mucha demanda; (person) estar muy solicitado

demanding adj exigente

demean [dɪ·ˈmin] vt degradar; **to ~ one-self** rebajarse

dementia [dɪ·ˈmen·ʃə] n demencia f

demo [ˈdem·oʊ] n inf see **demonstration** COMPUT demo f; (music) maqueta f, demo m Méx, Col

democracy [dɪ·ˈmak·rə·si] n democracia f

democrat [ˈdem·ə·kræt] n demócrata mf

democratic [ˌdem·ə·ˈkræt̬·ɪk] adj democrático, -a

demolish [dɪ·ˈmal·ɪʃ] vt demoler; fig echar por tierra

demolition [ˌdem·ə·ˈlɪʃ·ən] n demolición f; fig destrucción f

demon [ˈdi·mən] n demonio m; **child-hood ~s** fantasmas de la infancia ▶ **to be a ~ at sth** ser un hacha haciendo algo; **to work like a ~** trabajar como una fiera

demonstrate [ˈdem·ən·streɪt] I. vt (show) mostrar; (prove) demostrar II. vi manifestarse

demonstration [ˌdem·ən·ˈstreɪ·ʃən] n

demostración *f*; POL manifestación *f*; **to hold a ~** manifestarse

demonstrative [dɪ·'man·strə·tɪv] *adj* **1.** (*illustrative*) concluyente **2.** (*effusive*) efusivo, -a

demonstrator ['dem·ən·streɪ·ɾər] *n* (*protester*) manifestante *mf*

demoralize [dɪ·'mɔr·ə·laɪz] *vt* desmoralizar

den [den] *n* **1.** (*animal*) guarida *f* **2.** *a. iron* (*place for vice*) antro *m* **3.** (*small room*) salita *f*

denial [dɪ·'naɪ·əl] *n* negación *f*; (*refusal*) negativa *f*; **to issue a ~ of** desmentir

denim ['den·ɪm] *n* **1.** (*cloth*) tela *f* vaquera *f* **2. ~s** mono *m*

Denmark ['den·mark] *n* Dinamarca *f*

denominator [dɪ·'nam·ə·neɪ·ɾər] *n* denominador *m*

denounce [dɪ·'naʊns] *vt* **1.** (*condemn*) censurar **2.** (*inform*) denunciar

dense [dens] *adj* **1.** (*thick*) espeso, -a **2.** (*closely packed*) denso, -a; (*compact*) compacto, -a **3.** (*complex*) difícil

densely *adv* densamente

density ['den·sə·ti] *n* densidad *f*; **to be high/low in ~** ser de alta/baja densidad

dent [dent] **I.** *n* abolladura *f*; *fig* mella *f* **II.** *vt* abollar; *fig* hacer mella en

dental ['den·təl] *adj* dental

dental floss *n* hilo *m* dental

dentist ['den·tɪst] *n* dentista *mf*

dentistry ['den·tɪ·stri] *n* odontología *f*

dentures ['den·tʃərz] *npl* dentadura *f* postiza

deny [dɪ·'naɪ] *vt* **1.** negar; (*report*) desmentir; **to ~ having done sth** negar haber hecho algo; **she denies that she saw it** niega haberlo visto **2.** (*refuse*) denegar; **to ~ oneself sth** privarse de algo; **to ~ sb a right** privar a alguien de un derecho **3.** (*disown*) renegar de

deodorant [di·'oʊ·dər·ənt] *n* desodorante *m*

depart [dɪ·'part] *vi* partir; (*plane*) despegar; (*train*) salir; (*ship*) zarpar

♦ **depart from** *vi* desviarse de

departed I. *adj* **1.** (*dead*) difunto, -a **2.** (*past*) pasado, -a **II.** *n* **the ~** los difuntos

department [dɪ·'part·mənt] *n* **1.** (*division*) departamento *m*; (*of a shop*) sección *f* **2.** ADMIN, POL ministerio *m* **3.** *inf* (*domain*) terreno *m* **4. Department of Motor Vehicles** ≈ Dirección General de Tráfico *f*

department store *n* grandes almacenes *mpl*, tienda *f* por departamentos *AmS*

departure [dɪ·'par·tʃər] *n* **1.** (*person*) partida *f*; (*vehicle*) salida *f*; (*plane*) despegue *m*; **to make one's ~** marcharse **2.** (*deviation*) desviación *f*; **to be a new ~** ser una novedad (**for** para)

departure gate *n* puerta *f* de embarque

departure lounge *n* sala *f* de embarque

departure time *n* hora *f* de salida

depend [dɪ·'pend] *vi* **1.** depender (**on** de); **~ing on the weather** según el tiempo que haga; **he depends on his father for money** depende del dinero de su padre **2.** (*trust*) confiar (**on** en)

dependable [dɪ·'pen·də·bəl] *adj* fiable; (*person*) serio, -a

dependent [dɪ·'pen·dənt] *adj* dependiente; **to be ~ on** depender de; **to be ~ on drugs** ser drogadicto; **she has two children** tiene dos niños a su cargo

depict [dɪ·'pɪkt] *vt* representar

depiction [dɪ·'pɪk·ʃən] *n* representación *f*

depleted *adj* agotado, -a

deplorable [dɪ·'plɔr·ə·bəl] *adj* deplorable

deplore [dɪ·'plɔr] *vt* deplorar

deploy [dɪ·'plɔɪ] *vt* utilizar; (*troops*) desplegar; (*skills*) demostrar

deployment [dɪ·'plɔɪ·mənt] *n* utilización *f*; (*troops*) despliegue *m*

depopulate [di·'pap·jə·leɪt] *vt* despoblar

deport [dɪ·'pɔrt] *vt* deportar

deportation [ˌdi·pɔr·'teɪ·ʃən] *n* deportación *f*

deportee [ˌdi·pɔr·'ti] *n* deportado, -a *m, f*

depose [dɪ·'poʊz] *vt* destituir

deposit [dɪ·'paz·ɪt] **I.** *vt* **1.** depositar; (*luggage*) guardar en consigna **2.** FIN ingresar; **to ~ $1000** dejar 1000 dólares en depósito **II.** *n* **1.** (*sediment*) sedimento *m* **2.** GEO yacimiento *m* **3.** (*payment*) depósito *m*; **to make/leave a ~** efectuar/dejar un depósito; **to leave**

sth as a ~ dejar algo en garantía; **on ~** en depósito

depositor [dɪ·'paz·ə·tər] n cuentahabiente mf

deprave [dɪ·'preɪv] vt pervertir

depraved adj depravado, -a

depreciate [dɪ·'pri·ʃi·eɪt] I. vi depreciarse II. vt depreciar

depreciation [dɪ·ˌpri·ʃi·'eɪ·ʃən] n depreciación f

depress [dɪ·'pres] vt 1. (sadden) deprimir; **it ~es me that...** me deprime que... +subj 2. (reduce activity) disminuir; (economy) paralizar; (prices) bajar 3. (press) presionar; (pedal, button) apretar

depressed adj deprimido, -a, apolismado, -a Méx, Ven; **to feel ~** sentirse abatido; (period) de depresión; (economy) en crisis

depressing adj deprimente

depression [dɪ·'preʃ·ən] n 1. PSYCH, FIN depresión f; METEO zona f de bajas presiones 2. (hollow) hoyo m

deprive [dɪ·'praɪv] vt privar (of de); (dignity) despojar; (sleep) quitar

deprived adj desvalido, -a

depth [depθ] n 1. a. fig profundidad f; **in the ~ of winter** en pleno invierno; **the ~s of the ocean** las profundidades del océano 2. (intensity) intensidad f ▶ **in ~** en detalle

deputize ['dep·jə·taɪz] vi suplir (for a)

deputy ['dep·jə·ti] n delegado, -a m, f

derail [dɪ·'reɪl] vi descarrilar; fig fracasar

derailment [dɪ·'reɪl·mənt] n descarrilamiento m; fig fracaso m

derange [dɪ·'reɪndʒ] vt perturbar

deranged adj trastornado, -a

derelict ['der·ə·lɪkt] adj (building) abandonado, -a

derision [dɪ·'rɪʒ·ən] n burla f; **to meet sth with ~** burlarse de algo

derisory [dɪ·'raɪ·sə·ri] adj irrisorio, -a

derivation [dɪ·'raɪv] I. vt obtener (**from** de) II. vi derivar (**from** de)

derogatory [dɪ·'rag·ə·tɔr·i] adj desdeñoso, -a

descale [ˌdi·'skeɪl] vt desincrustar

descend [dɪ·'send] I. vi 1. (go down) descender; (fall) caer 2. (lower oneself) **to ~ to stealing** rebajarse a robar 3. (come from) provenir (**from** de) II. vt descender; (ladder) bajar

descendant [dɪ·'sen·dənt] n descendiente mf

descent [dɪ·'sent] n 1. AVIAT descenso m 2. (decline) declive m 3. (ancestry) origen m

describe [dɪ·'skraɪb] vt 1. describir; (experience) relatar; **to ~ sb as stupid** calificar a alguien de tonto 2. (draw) trazar

description [dɪ·'skrɪp·ʃən] n descripción f; **to answer a ~** encajar con una descripción; **of every ~** de todo tipo

descriptive [dɪ·'skrɪp·tɪv] adj descriptivo, -a

desert¹ [dɪ·'zɜrt] I. vi MIL desertar II. vt 1. MIL desertar de 2. (abandon) abandonar; **to ~ sb** dejar a alguien (**for** por)

desert² ['dez·ərt] n desierto m

deserted adj desierto, -a; (person) abandonado, -a

deserts [dɪ·'zɜrts] npl merecido m; **to get one's just ~** tener su merecido

deserve [dɪ·'zɜrv] vt merecer; **what have I done to ~ this?** ¿qué he hecho yo para merecer esto?

deservedly adv merecidamente

deserving adj digno (**of** de)

design [dɪ·'zaɪn] I. vt 1. (plan) diseñar 2. (intend) concebir II. n 1. (plan) diseño m; (sketch) bosquejo m 3. (pattern) motivo m 4. (intention) propósito m; **to do sth by ~** hacer algo adrede 5. **~s** inf malas intenciones fpl III. adj de diseño

designate ['dez·ɪg·neɪt] vt (appoint) nombrar; (indicate) señalar

designation [ˌdez·ɪg·'neɪ·ʃən] n (appointment) nombramiento m

designer [dɪ·'zaɪ·nər] I. n diseñador(a) m(f) II. adj de marca

desirable [dɪ·'zaɪ·rə·bəl] adj 1. (necessary) conveniente; **it is ~ that...** sería deseable que... +subj 2. (attractive) deseable 3. (popular) codiciado, -a

desire [dɪ·'zaɪr] I. vt desear; **to ~ sb** desear a alguien; **to ~ that...** desear que... +subj; **I ~ you to leave** le ruego que se vaya II. n 1. (craving) deseo m 2. (request) petición f

desired adj deseado, -a

desk |desk| n 1. (table) escritorio m; SCH pupitre m 2. (counter) mostrador m

desk lamp n flexo m

desktop n ~ (**computer**) (ordenador m) portátil m

desolate[1] ['des·ə·lət] adj desolado, -a; (prospect) desolador, a; **to feel** ~ sentirse desconsolado

desolate[2] ['des·ə·leɪt] vt desolar

despair [dɪ·'sper] I. n desesperación f; **to be in** ~ estar desesperado (**about** por); **to drive sb to** ~ desesperar a alguien ► **to be the** ~ **of sb** traer de cabeza a alguien II. vi perder las esperanzas (**of** con)

despairing adj desesperado, -a; (glance) de desesperación

desperate ['des·pər·ɪt] adj desesperado, -a; (great) extremo, -a; **to be** ~ **for sth** necesitar algo con suma urgencia

desperation [,des·pə·'reɪ·ʃən] n desesperación f; **in** ~ en su desesperación; **to drive sb to** ~ desesperar a alguien

despise [dɪ·'spaɪz] vt despreciar (**for** por)

despite [dɪ·'spaɪt] prep a pesar de

despondent [dɪ·'span·dənt] adj desalentado, -a; **to feel** ~ sentirse desanimado (**about** por)

dessert [dɪ·'zɜrt] n postre m

destination [,des·tə·'neɪ·ʃən] n destino m

destine ['des·tɪn] vt **to be** ~**d for** estar destinado a algo; **we're** ~**d for Denver** nos dirigimos a Denver; **to be** ~**d to fail/succeed** estar destinado al fracaso/éxito

destiny ['des·tə·ni] n destino m; **to fight one's** ~ luchar contra el destino; **to shape one's** ~ hacerse su propio destino

destitute ['des·tɪ·tut] I. adj necesitado, -a II. n **the** ~ los indigentes

destroy [dɪ·'strɔɪ] vt 1. (demolish) destruir 2. (kill) matar 3. (ruin) arruinar

destructible [dɪ·'strʌk·tə·bəl] adj destructible

destruction [dɪ·'strʌk·ʃən] n destrucción f; **mass** ~ destrucción en masa

destructive [dɪ·'strʌk·tɪv] adj destructivo, -a

detach [dɪ·'tætʃ] vt separar

detachable adj separable

detached adj 1. (separated) separado, -a 2. (aloof) indiferente 3. (impartial) imparcial

detail [dɪ·'teɪl] I. n 1. (information, feature) detalle m; **in** ~ en detalle; **to go into** ~ entrar en detalles 2. (unimportant) minucia f; **gory** ~**s** iron intimidades fpl II. vt detallar

detailed adj detallado, -a

detain [dɪ·'teɪn] vt 1. (prisoner) retener 2. (delay) entretener

detainee [,di·ter·'ni] n detenido, -a m, f

detect [dɪ·'tekt] vt 1. (note) advertir; (presence) percibir 2. (discover) descubrir

detectable [dɪ·'tek·tə·bəl] adj perceptible

detection [dɪ·'tek·ʃən] n detección f

detective [dɪ·'tek·tɪv] n detective mf; (police) agente mf

detective novel, detective story n novela f policíaca

detector [dɪ·'tek·tər] n detector m

detention [dɪ·'ten·ʃən] n detención f; SCHOOL castigo f

detention home n correccional m

deter [dɪ·'tɜr] <-rr-> vt disuadir

detergent [dɪ·'tɜr·dʒənt] n detergente m

deteriorate [dɪ·'tɪr·i·ə·reɪt] vi 1. (wear out) deteriorarse 2. (worsen) empeorar

determinant [dɪ·'tɜr·mə·nənt] n adj determinante m

determinate [dɪ·'tɜr·mə·nɪt] adj determinado, -a

determination [dɪ·,tɜr·mɪ·'neɪ·ʃən] n terminación f

determine [dɪ·'tɜr·mɪn] I. vi 1. decidirse (**on** por) 2. LAW expirar II. vt 1. (decide) decidir 2. (find out) fijar 3. (influence) determinar

determined [dɪ·'tɜr·mɪnd] adj decidido, -a; **to be** ~ **to do sth** estar resuelto a hacer algo

deterrent [dɪ·'tɜr·ənt] I. n freno m; **to act as a** ~ **to sb** disuadir a alguien II. adj disuasivo, -a

detest [dɪ·'test] vt detestar

detestable [dɪ·'tes·tə·bəl] adj detestable

detonate ['det·ə·neɪt] vi, vt detonar

detonation [ˌdet·ə·'neɪ·ʃən] n detonación f

detour ['di·tʊr] n desvío m; **to make a ~** dar un rodeo

detoxify [di·'tak·sɪ·faɪ] vt desintoxicar

detractor [dɪ·'træk·tər] n detractor(a) m(f)

detrimental [ˌdet·rɪ·'men·təl] adj nocivo, -a

deuce [dus] n GAMES dos m; SPORTS empate m

devalue [ˌdi·'væl·ju] vt devaluar

devastate ['dev·ə·steɪt] vt devastar

devastating adj (destructive) desolador(a); (powerful) devastador(a); (stunning) abrumador(a)

devastation [ˌdev·ə·'steɪ·ʃən] n devastación f

develop [dɪ·'vel·əp] I. vi (grow) desarrollarse; (advance) progresar; **to ~ into** transformarse en II. vt 1. (expand) desarrollar; (improve) ampliar 2. (create) crear 3. (show) revelar; (illness) contraer 4. PHOT revelar

developed adj desarrollado, -a; **~ countries** países desarrollados

developing adj **~ countries** países en vías de desarrollo

development [dɪ·'vel·əp·mənt] n 1. (process) desarrollo m; (growth) crecimiento m; (growth stage) avance m; (skills) evolución f 2. (progress) progreso m 3. (event) acontecimiento m 4. (building of) construcción f; (of land) urbanización f

deviate ['di·vi·eɪt] vi apartarse; **to ~ from** desviarse de

device [dɪ·'vaɪs] n 1. (mechanism) dispositivo m; **input/output ~** dispositivo de entrada/salida 2. (method) recurso m ▶ **to leave sb to their own ~s** abandonar a alguien a su suerte

devil ['dev·əl] n 1. REL diablo m 2. (evil spirit or person) demonio m; **lucky ~!** ¡qué suerte!; **the poor ~!** ¡pobre diablo! 3. **to have a ~ of a time doing sth** costar un huevo hacer algo inf; **to be full of the ~** estar lleno de coraje ▶ **between the ~ and the deep blue sea** entre la espada y la pared; **to sell one's soul to the ~** vender el alma al diablo; **to go**

to the ~ irse al infierno; **to play the ~ with sth** estropear algo; **speak of the ~** hablando del rey de Roma; **how/who/ what/where the ~...?** ¿cómo/quién/ qué/dónde diablos...?; **like the ~** como el demonio

devilish ['dev·ə·lɪʃ] adj 1. (evil) diabólico, -a 2. (mischievous) malvado, -a 3. (extreme) extremo, -a

devil's food cake n pastel m de chocolate

devious ['di·vi·əs] adj 1. (dishonest) taimado, -a 2. (winding) tortuoso, -a

devise [dɪ·'vaɪz] I. n legado m II. vt idear; LAW legar

devoid [dɪ·'vɔɪd] adj **to be ~ of** estar desprovisto de

devolution [ˌdev·ə·'lu·ʃən] n transferencia f

devote [dɪ·'voʊt] vt dedicar; **to ~ oneself to sth** dedicarse a algo

devoted [dɪ·'voʊ·t̬ɪd] adj dedicado, -a; (husband, mother) devoto, -a

devotion [dɪ·'voʊ·ʃən] n (loyalty) lealtad f; (admiration) fervor m; (great attachment) dedicación f; REL devoción f

devour [dɪ·'vaʊ·ər] vt devorar; **to be ~ed by jealousy** estar consumido por los celos

devout [dɪ·'vaʊt] adj ferviente; REL devoto, -a

dew [du] n rocío m

dextrose ['dek·stroʊs] n dextrosa f

diabetes [ˌdaɪ·ə·'bi·t̬iz] n diabetes f inv

diabetic [ˌdaɪ·ə·'bet̬·ɪk] adj, n diabético, -a m, f

diabolic(al) [ˌdaɪ·ə·'bal·ɪk(əl)] adj diabólico, -a

diagnose [ˌdaɪ·əg·'noʊs] I. vi hacer un diagnóstico II. vt diagnosticar

diagnosis [ˌdaɪ·əg·'noʊ·sɪs] <-ses-> n (process) diagnosis f inv; (result) diagnóstico m

diagonal [daɪ·'æg·ə·nəl] adj, n diagonal f

diagram ['daɪ·ə·græm] n 1. (drawing) diagrama m; (plan) esquema m 2. (chart) gráfico m

dial ['daɪ·əl] I. n RADIO dial m II. <-l- or -ll-, -l- or -ll-> vi marcar, discar Arg, Perú, Urug III. vt TEL marcar; RADIO sintonizar

D

◆ **dial in** *vi* conectar (**to** con)

dialect ['daɪ·ə·lekt] *n* dialecto *m*

dialog(ue) ['daɪ·ə·lag] *n a.* POL diálogo *m*; **to engage in** ~ dialogar

dial tone *n* tono *m* de marcado

dialysis [daɪ·'æl·ə·sɪs] *n* diálisis *f inv*

diameter [daɪ·'æm·ə·tər] *n* diámetro *m*

diametrically [ˌdaɪ·ə·'met·rɪ·kə·li] *adv* diametralmente; (*completely*) en su totalidad

diamond ['daɪ·ə·mənd] *n* 1. *a.* GAMES diamante *m* 2. (*rhombus*) rombo *m* ▶ **a** ~ **in the rough** un diamante en bruto

diaper ['daɪ·pər] *n* pañal *m*

diaphragm ['daɪ·ə·fræm] *n* diafragma *m*

diarrhea [ˌdaɪ·ə·'ri·ə] *n* diarrea *f*

diary ['daɪ·ə·ri] *n* diario *m*

dice [daɪs] *npl* GAMES dados *mpl*; **to roll the** ~ tirar los dados

dicey ['daɪ·si] <-ier, -iest> *adj inf* arriesgado, -a

dictate ['dɪk·teɪt] **I.** *n* dictado *m* **II.** *vi* 1. (*command*) mandar 2. (*read*) dictar **III.** *vt* 1. (*command, read*) dictar 2. (*make necessary*) imponer

dictation [dɪk·'teɪ·ʃən] *n* SCHOOL dictado *m*

dictator ['dɪk·teɪ·tər] *n* dictador(a) *m(f)*

dictatorship [dɪk·'teɪ·tər·ʃɪp] *n* dictadura *f*

dictionary ['dɪk·ʃə·ner·i] *n* diccionario *m*

did [dɪd] *pt of* **do**

didactic [daɪ·'dæk·tɪk] *adj* didáctico, -a

diddle around *vi* pasar el tiempo; (*unproductively*) perder el tiempo

didn't ['dɪd·ənt] = **did not** *see* **do**

die[1] [daɪ] <dice> *n* 1. dado *m* 2. TECH molde *m* ▶ **the** ~ **is** cast la suerte está echada

die[2] [daɪ] <dying, died> *vi* 1. morir; **to** ~ **a violent/natural death** morir de muerte violenta/natural; **I'm dying for a cup of tea** me muero por una taza de té 2. (*end*) desaparecer; **the secret will** ~ **with her** se llevará el secreto a la tumba 3. (*appliance*) estropearse; (*battery*) gastarse ▶ **to** ~ **hard** persistir; **never say** ~! ¡nunca te rindas!; **to** do **or** ~ vencer o morir

◆ **die away** *vi* desaparecer; (*enthusiasm*)

decaer; (*wind*) amainar; (*sound*) apagarse

◆ **die back** *vi* secarse

◆ **die down** *vi* apagarse

◆ **die off** *vi* (*species*) extinguirse; (*customs*) desaparecer

◆ **die out** *vi* extinguirse

dieback ['daɪ·bæk] *n* muerte *f* de los bosques

die-hard *n* intransigente *mf*

diesel ['di·zəl] *n* diesel *m*

diesel engine *n* motor *m* diesel

diet ['daɪ·ət] *n* dieta *f*; **to be/go on a** ~ estar/ponerse a dieta

dietetic [ˌdaɪ·ə·'tet·ɪk] *adj* dietético, -a

differ ['dɪf·ər] *vi* 1. diferenciarse (**from** de) 2. (*disagree*) discrepar (**about** en)

difference ['dɪf·ər·əns] *n* 1. (*dissimilarity, amount, disagreement*) diferencia *f*; **to pay the** ~ pagar la diferencia; **to put aside** ~**s** dejar de lado las diferencias 2. (*distinction*) distinción *f*; **that makes all the** ~ eso lo cambia todo; **to make a** ~ importar; **to not make any** ~ dar igual 3. (*new feature*) singularidad *f*

different ['dɪf·ər·ənt] *adj* 1. (*not the same*) diferente; **to do something** ~ romper la rutina 2. (*distinct*) distinto, -a ▶ **to be as** ~ **as** night **and day** ser la noche y el día

differentiate [ˌdɪf·ə·'ren·tʃi·eɪt] *vi, vt* distinguir

difficult ['dɪf·ɪ·kəlt] *adj* difícil

difficulty ['dɪf·ɪ·kəl·ti] <-ies> *n* dificultad *f*; (*problem*) obstáculo *m*; **to have** ~ **doing sth** tener problemas para hacer algo

diffract [dɪ·'frækt] *vt* difractar

diffuse[1] [dɪ·'fjuz] **I.** *vi* difundirse **II.** *vt* difundir

diffuse[2] [dɪ·'fjus] *adj* difuso, -a

diffusion [dɪ·'fju·ʒən] *n* difusión *f*; CHEM, PHYS dispersión *f*

dig [dɪg] **I.** *n* 1. (*poke*) empujón *m* 2. (*excavation*) excavación *f* **II.** <-gg-, dug, dug> *vi* 1. (*excavate*) cavar; **to** ~ **deeper** *fig* ahondar 2. (*poke*) empujar **III.** *vt* 1. (*excavate*) cavar; (*machine*) excavar 2. (*stab, poke*) clavar;

to ~ one's elbow into... dar un codazo en... **3.** *sl* (*like*) molar ▶ **to ~ one's own grave** cavarse su propia tumba

◆**dig into** I. *vi* clavar ▶ **to dig** (**deeper**) **into one's pockets** poner (más) dinero de su propio bolsillo II. *vt always sep inf* atacar ▶ **to dig oneself into a hole** meterse en un problema

◆**dig out** *vt* extraer; (*hole*) excavar

◆**dig up** *vt* **1.** (*from ground*) desenterrar **2.** (*excavate*) excavar **3.** *fig* (*find out*) descubrir

digest[1] ['daɪ·dʒest] *n* (*of essays*) resumen *m*

digest[2] [daɪ·'dʒest] I. *vi* digerirse; (*person*) hacer la digestión II. *vt* **1.** (*food*) digerir **2.** *inf* (*understand*) asimilar

digestible [daɪ·'dʒes·tə·bəl] *adj* digerible

digestion [daɪ·'dʒes·tʃən] *n* digestión *f*

digger ['dɪg·ər] *n* (*machine*) excavadora *f*

digit ['dɪdʒ·ɪt] *n* **1.** dígito *m* **2.** ANAT dedo *m*

digital ['dɪdʒ·ɪ·təl] *adj* digital

digitalize ['dɪdʒ·ɪ·təl·aɪz] *vt* digitalizar

dignified ['dɪg·nɪ·faɪd] *adj* (*honorable*) digno, -a; (*solemn*) solemne

dignity ['dɪg·nə·ti] *n* (*state*) dignidad *f*; (*respect*) respeto *m*

digress [daɪ·'gres] *vi* desviarse (**from** de)

dike [daɪk] *n* dique *m*

dilapidated [dɪ·'læp·ɪ·deɪ·tɪd] *adj* destartalado, -a

dilate ['daɪ·leɪt] I. *vi* dilatarse II. *vt* dilatar

dilemma [dɪ·'lem·ə] *n* dilema *m*; **to be in a ~** estar en un dilema

diligent ['dɪl·ɪ·dʒənt] *adj* (*careful*) concienzudo, -a; (*hard-working*) diligente

dill [dɪl] *n* eneldo *m*

dilly-dally ['dɪl·i·dæl·i] *vi inf* **1.** (*waste time*) perder el tiempo **2.** (*be indecisive*) vacilar

dilute [daɪ·'lut] I. *vt* diluir II. *vi* diluirse III. *adj* diluido, -a

dilution [daɪ·'lu·ʃən] *n a. fig* disolución *f*

dim [dɪm] I. <-mm-> *adj* (*lights*) apagarse

II. *vt* apagar III. <-mm-> *adj* **1.** (*not bright*) tenue **2.** (*unclear*) borroso, -a **3.** (*stupid*) tonto, -a **4.** (*unfavorable*) sombrío, -a

dime [daɪm] *n* moneda *f* de diez centavos ▶ **they're a ~ a dozen** los hay a patadas

dimension [dɪ·'men·ʃən] *n* dimensión *f*

diminish [dɪ·'mɪn·ɪʃ] *vi, vt* disminuir; **to** (**greatly**) **~ in value** perder (mucho) valor

diminution [dɪm·ə·'nu·ʃən] *n* disminución *f*

diminutive [dɪ·'mɪn·jə·tɪv] I. *n* diminutivo *m* II. *adj* diminuto, -a

dimple ['dɪm·pəl] *n* hoyuelo *m*

din [dɪn] *n* estrépito *m*

dine [daɪn] *vi* cenar

diner ['daɪ·nər] *n* **1.** (*person*) comensal *mf* **2.** (*restaurant*) bar *m* de carretera

dinghy ['dɪŋ·i] *n* <-ies> bote *m*

dingy ['dɪn·dʒi] <-ier, -iest> *adj* deslustrado, -a

dining room *n* comedor *m*

dinner ['dɪn·ər] *n* cena *f*, comida *f AmS*; **to make ~** hacer la cena [*or* el almuerzo *AmS*]

dinner jacket *n* esmoquin *m*

dinner party *n* cena *f*

dinner service *n* vajilla *f*

dinnertime *n* hora *f* de cenar

dinnerware *n* vajilla *f*

dinosaur ['daɪ·nə·sɔr] *n* dinosaurio *m*; *fig* antigualla *f*

dip [dɪp] I. *n* **1.** (*dunking*) baño *m* **2.** (*drop*) caída *f* **3.** (*sauce*) salsa *f* **4.** (*swim*) chapuzón *m* II. *vi* **1.** (*drop down*) descender; (*prices*) caer **2.** (*slope down*) inclinarse **3.** (*swim*) zambullirse III. *vt* **1.** (*immerse*) sumergir; CULIN mojar **2.** (*put into*) meter

◆**dip into** *vt* **1.** *always sep* (*put*) meter **2. to ~ one's savings** echar mano de los ahorros **3. I'll just ~ this store** voy a echar un vistazo en esta tienda

diphthong ['dɪf·θɑŋ] *n* LING diptongo *m*

diploma [dɪ·'plou·mə] *n* diploma *m*

diplomacy [dɪ·'plou·mə·si] *n* **1.** POL diplomacia *f* **2.** (*tact*) tacto *m*

diplomat ['dɪp·lə·mæt] *n* diplomático,

-a m, f

diplomatic [ˌdɪp·lə·ˈmæt̬·ɪk] *adj* diplomático, -a

dippy [ˈdɪp·i] *adj sl* flipado, -a, ahuevado, -a *Col, Perú, Nic, Pan*

direct [dɪˈrekt] I. *vt* 1. (*point, intend*) dirigir (at a); **to ~ sb to a place** indicar a alguien en el camino hacia un sitio 2. (*command*) ordenar II. *adj* 1. (*straight, frank*) directo, -a 2. (*exact*) exacto, -a; **the ~ opposite** justo lo contrario III. *adv* directamente

direct deposit *n* depósito *m* directo

direct hit *n* blanco *m*

direction [dɪˈrek·ʃən] *n* 1. dirección *f*; **in the ~ of** en dirección a, en sentido de la orientación 2. *pl* instrucciones *fpl*; **can you give me ~s?** ¿me puedes indicar el camino?

directive [dɪˈrek·tɪv] *n* directriz *f*, directiva *f AmL*

directly [dɪˈrekt·li] *adv* 1. (*without deviation*) directamente 2. (*immediately*) inmediatamente 3. (*exactly*) exactamente

director [dɪˈrek·tər] *n* director(a) *m(f)*; **board of ~s** junta directiva

directory [dɪˈrek·tə·ri] *n* 1. guía *f*, directorio *m Méx* 2. COMPUT directorio

directory assistance *n* información *f* (telefónica)

dirt [dɜrt] *n* 1. (*earth*) tierra *f* 2. (*unclean substance*) suciedad *f* 3. (*excrement, worthless thing*) porquería *f*; **to treat sb like ~** tratar a alguien como a un perro 4. (*scandal, gossip*) trapos *m pl* sucios *fig*

dirt cheap *adj inf* tirado, -a, botado, -a *Méx*

dirty [ˈdɜr·t̬i] I. *vt* ensuciar; **to ~ one's hands** ensuciarse las manos II. <-ier, -iest> *adj* 1. (*not clean, unpleasant*) sucio, -a, chancho, -a *AmL*; **to do the work** hacer el trabajo sucio 2. (*mean, nasty*) bajo, -a 3. (*lewd*) obsceno, -a; **~ joke/old man** chiste/viejo verde III. *adv* suciamente; **to play ~** jugar sucio

disability [ˌdɪs·ə·ˈbɪl·ə·t̬i] *n* invalidez *f*

disable [dɪsˈeɪ·bəl] *vt* incapacitar; COMPUT deshabilitar

disabled I. *npl* **the ~** los discapacitados II. *adj* incapacitado, -a

disadvantage [ˌdɪs·əd·ˈvæn·tɪdʒ] I. *n* desventaja *f*; **to be at a ~** estar en desventaja II. *vt* perjudicar

disadvantaged *adj* desfavorecido, -a

disadvantageous [ˌdɪs·ˌæd·væn·ˈteɪ·dʒəs] *adj* desfavorable

disagree [ˌdɪs·ə·ˈɡri] *vi* 1. (*not agree*) no estar de acuerdo (on/with en/con), discrepar *elev* 2. (*differ*) diferir; **the answers ~** las respuestas no concuerdan 3. (*food*) sentar mal; **spicy food ~s with me** la comida picante me sienta mal

disagreeable [ˌdɪs·ə·ˈɡri·ə·bəl] *adj* desagradable

disagreement [ˌdɪs·ə·ˈɡri·mənt] *n* 1. (*lack of agreement*) desacuerdo *m* 2. (*argument*) discusión *f* 3. (*discrepancy*) discrepancia *f*

disallow [ˌdɪs·ə·ˈlaʊ] *vt* rechazar; LAW, SPORTS anular

disappear [ˌdɪs·ə·ˈpɪr] *vi* desaparecer; **to ~ from sight/without a trace** desaparecer de la vista/sin dejar rastro

disappearance [ˌdɪs·ə·ˈpɪr·əns] *n* desaparición *f*

disappoint [ˌdɪs·ə·ˈpɔɪnt] *vt* decepcionar, enchilar *AmC*

disappointed *adj* decepcionado, -a (**in** con)

disappointing *adj* decepcionante

disappointment [ˌdɪs·ə·ˈpɔɪnt·mənt] *n* decepción *f*

disapproval [ˌdɪs·ə·ˈpru·vəl] *n* desaprobación *f*

disapprove [ˌdɪs·ə·ˈpruv] *vi* **to ~ of** desaprobar

disarmament [dɪsˈar·mə·mənt] *n* desarme *m*

disarray [ˌdɪs·ə·ˈreɪ] *n* (*disorder*) desorden *m*; (*confusion*) confusión *f*

disaster [dɪˈzæs·tər] *n* desastre *m*; **~ area** zona *f* catastrófica

disastrous [dɪˈzæs·trəs] *adj* desastroso, -a

disbelief [ˌdɪs·bɪ·ˈlif] *n* incredulidad *f*

disc [dɪsk] *n* disco *m*

discard [dɪˈskard] *vt* desechar; GAMES descartar

discerning [dɪ·ˈsɜr·nɪŋ] *adj* (*discriminating*) exigente; (*acute*) perspicaz

discharge¹ [ˈdɪs·ˌtʃɑrdʒ] *n* **1.** (*hospital*) alta *f;* (*job*) despido *m;* (*prison*) puesta *f* en libertad **2.** MED secreción *f* **3.** ECON liquidación *f* **4.** ELEC descarga *f*

discharge² [dɪs·ˈtʃɑrdʒ] **I.** *vi* **1.** (*ship*) descargar **2.** MED segregar **II.** *vt* **1.** *a.* LAW (*release*) liberar **2.** MIL, ECON despedir; (*duty*) cumplir; (*debt*) liquidar **3.** (*let out*) emitir **4.** (*cancel*) cancelar

disciple [dɪ·ˈsaɪ·pəl] *n* seguidor(a) *m(f);* REL, PHILOS discípulo, -a *m, f*

disciplinary [ˈdɪs·ə·plə·ner·i] *adj* disciplinario, -a

discipline [ˈdɪs·ə·plɪn] **I.** *n* disciplina *f* **II.** *vt* disciplinar; **to ~ oneself to do sth** obligarse a hacer algo

disc jockey *n* pinchadiscos *mf inv*

disclaim [dɪs·ˈkleɪm] *vt* **1.** (*deny*) negar **2.** LAW renunciar a

disclose [dɪs·ˈkloʊz] *vt* revelar

disclosure [dɪs·ˈkloʊ·ʒər] *n* revelación *f*

disco [ˈdɪs·koʊ] *n* discoteca *f;* (*music*) música *f* disco

discolor [dɪs·ˈkʌl·ər] **I.** *vi* desteñirse **II.** *vt* decolorar

discomfort [dɪs·ˈkʌm·fərt] *n* **1.** (*uneasiness*) malestar *m* (**at** respecto a) **2.** (*inconvenience*) molestia *f*

disconcert [ˌdɪs·kən·ˈsɜrt] *vt* desconcertar

disconnect [ˌdɪs·kə·ˈnekt] *vt* (*unplug*) desenchufar; (*phone*) desconectar

disconnected *adj* desconectado, -a; (*incoherent*) inconexo, -a

disconsolate [dɪs·ˈsan·sə·lət] *adj* desconsolado, -a

discontent [ˌdɪs·kən·ˈtent] *n* descontento *m*

discontented *adj* descontento, -a

discontinue [ˌdɪs·kən·ˈtɪn·ju] **I.** *vi* desistir **II.** *vt* suspender

discord [ˈdɪs·kɔrd] *n* (*disagreement*) discordia *f*

discotheque [ˈdɪs·kə·tek] *n* discoteca *f*

discount¹ [ˈdɪs·kaʊnt] *n* descuento *m;* **at a ~** con descuento

discount² [dɪs·ˈkaʊnt] *vt* **1.** (*price*) rebajar **2.** (*disregard*) descartar

discourage [dɪs·ˈkɜr·ɪdʒ] *vt* desanimar; **to ~ sb from doing sth** disuadir a alguien

de hacer algo

discouraging *adj* desalentador(a)

discourteous [dɪs·ˈkɜr·ti·əs] *adj* descortés

discover [dɪ·ˈskʌv·ər] *vt* descubrir

discovery [dɪ·ˈskʌv·ə·ri] <-ies> *n* descubrimiento *m*

discredit [dɪs·ˈkred·ɪt] **I.** *n* (*disrepute*) desprestigio *m;* (*disgrace*) vergüenza *f* **II.** *vt* desacreditar

discreditable [dɪs·ˈkred·ɪ·tə·bəl] *adj* deshonroso, -a

discreet [dɪ·ˈskrit] *adj* discreto, -a

discrepancy [dɪ·ˈskrep·ən·si] <-ies> *n* discrepancia *f*

discretion [dɪ·ˈskreʃ·ən] *n* **1.** (*behavior*) discreción *f* **2.** (*judgment*) criterio *m*

discriminate [dɪ·ˈskrɪm·ə·neɪt] *vi* discernir; **to ~ against sb** discriminar a alguien

discrimination [dɪˌskrɪm·ɪ·ˈneɪ·ʃən] *n* **1.** (*unfair treatment*) discriminación *f* **2.** (*good judgment*) criterio *m*

discriminatory [dɪ·ˈskrɪm·ɪ·nə·tɔr·i] *adj* discriminatorio, -a

discuss [dɪ·ˈskʌs] *vt* discutir; (*consider*) abordar

discussion [dɪ·ˈskʌʃ·ən] *n* discusión *f,* argumento *m AmL*

disdainful [dɪs·ˈdeɪn·fəl] *adj* desdeñoso, -a

disease [dɪ·ˈziz] *n* enfermedad *f*

diseased *adj* enfermo, -a

disembark [ˌdɪs·ɪm·ˈbɑrk] *vi* desembarcar

disentangle [ˌdɪs·ɪn·ˈtæŋ·gəl] *vt* **1.** (*release*) librar; **to ~ oneself from** librarse de **2.** (*untangle*) desenredar

disfavor [dɪs·ˈfeɪ·vər] *vt* desfavorecer

disgrace [dɪs·ˈgreɪs] *n* vergüenza *f*

disgraceful [dɪs·ˈgreɪs·fəl] *adj* vergonzoso, -a

disguise [dɪs·ˈgaɪz] **I.** *n* disfraz *m;* **to be in ~** ir disfrazado **II.** *vt* **1.** disfrazar; **to ~ oneself** disfrazarse (**as** de) **2.** (*hide*) encubrir

disgust [dɪs·ˈgʌst] **I.** *n* **1.** (*repugnance*) asco *m;* **in ~** con asco **2.** (*indignation*) indignación *f* (**at** por) **II.** *vt* **1.** (*sicken*) dar asco **2.** (*be offensive*) indignar

disgusting *adj* **1.** (*repulsive*) repugnante, chocante *AmL* **2.** (*unacceptable*) indignante

dish [dɪʃ] <-es> *n* **1.** (*for food*) plato *m*; **to do the ~es** fregar los platos **2.** TEL parabólica *f* **3.** *sl* (*person*) bombón *m*

◆**dish out** *vt* (*serve*) servir

◆**dish up** *vt inf* (*serve*) servir; (*offer*) ofrecer

dish antenna *n* parabólica *f*

dishcloth [ˈdɪʃˌklɑθ] *n* paño *m* de cocina, repasador *m Arg, Urug*

dishearten [dɪsˈhɑrtən] *vt* descorazonar

dishonest [dɪsˈanɪst] *adj* deshonesto, -a

dishonor [dɪsˈanər] **I.** *n* deshonor *m* **II.** *vt* **1.** (*disgrace*) deshonrar **2.** (*not keep*) incumplir; (*not pay*) impagar

dishwasher *n* (*appliance, person*) lavaplatos *m inv*

disillusion [ˌdɪsɪˈluːʒən] **I.** *vt* desilusionar **II.** *n* desilusión *f*

disillusioned *adj* desilusionado, -a

disinclined [ˌdɪsɪnˈklaɪnd] *adj* **to be ~ to do sth** tener pocas ganas de hacer algo

disinfect [ˌdɪsɪnˈfekt] *vt* desinfectar

disinfectant [ˌdɪsɪnˈfektənt] *adj, n* desinfectante *m*

disinfection [ˌdɪsɪnˈfekʃən] *n* desinfección *f*

disintegrate [dɪsˈɪntəɡreɪt] **I.** *vi* desintegrarse **II.** *vt* desintegrar

disintegration [dɪsˌɪntəˈɡreɪʃən] *n* desintegración *f*

disinterested [dɪsˈɪntrɪstɪd] *adj* desinteresado, -a

disjointed [dɪsˈdʒɔɪntɪd] *adj* inconexo, -a

disk [dɪsk] *n* disco *m*; **hard/start-up ~** disco duro/de arranque

dislike [dɪsˈlaɪk] **I.** *vt* tener aversión a **II.** *n* aversión *f*

dislocate [ˈdɪsloʊkeɪt] *vt* **1.** (*displace*) desplazar; *fig* trastornar **2.** MED dislocarse

dislodge [dɪsˈlɑdʒ] *vt* desalojar

dismal [ˈdɪzməl] *adj* **1.** (*depressing*) deprimente **2.** *inf* (*awful*) terrible; (*truth*) triste

dismantle [dɪsˈmæntəl] *vt* desmontar; (*system*) desmantelar

dismay [dɪsˈmeɪ] **I.** *n* consternación *f*

II. *vt* consternar

dismiss [dɪsˈmɪs] *vt* **1.** (*job*) despedir **2.** (*reject*) descartar **3.** LAW desestimar

dismissal [dɪsˈmɪsəl] *n* (*school*) expulsión *f*; (*job*) despido *m*

dismount [dɪsˈmaʊnt] *vi* desmontar(se)

disobedience [ˌdɪsəˈbiːdiəns] *n* desobediencia *f*

disobedient [ˌdɪsəˈbiːdiənt] *adj* desobediente

disobey [ˌdɪsəˈbeɪ] *vi, vt* desobedecer

disorder [dɪsˈɔrdər] *n* **1.** desorden *m*, desparramo *m CSur* **2.** MED trastorno *m*

disordered *adj* desordenado, -a

disorderly [dɪsˈɔrdərli] *adj* **1.** (*untidy*) desordenado, -a **2.** (*unruly*) escandaloso, -a

disorganized [dɪsˈɔrɡənaɪzd] *adj* desorganizado, -a

disoriented *adj* desorientado, -a

disown [dɪsˈoʊn] *vt* repudiar

dispatch [dɪˈspætʃ] **I.** <-es> *n* (*delivery*) envío *m* **II.** *vt a. fig* despachar

dispel [dɪˈspel] <-ll-> *vt* disipar; (*rumor*) desmentir

dispensable [dɪˈspensəbəl] *adj* prescindible

dispense [dɪˈspens] *vt* (*give out*) repartir; (*medicine*) administrar

◆**dispense with** *vt* prescindir de

dispenser [dɪˈspensər] *n* máquina *f* expendedora

disperse [dɪˈspɜrs] **I.** *vt* dispersar **II.** *vi* dispersarse

dispirited [dɪˈspɪrɪtɪd] *adj* desanimado, -a

displace [dɪsˈpleɪs] *vt* desplazar; (*replace*) reemplazar

display [dɪˈspleɪ] **I.** *vt* **1.** (*show*) exhibir **2.** (*express*) demostrar **II.** *n* **1.** (*arrangement*) exposición *f*; **firework ~** exhibición *f* pirotécnica **2.** (*demonstration*) demostración *f* **3.** COMPUT pantalla *f*

display window *n* escaparate *m*

displease [dɪsˈpliːz] *vt* disgustar; **to be ~d** estar disgustado (**by** con)

displeasure [dɪsˈpleʒər] *n* disgusto *m*

disposable [dɪˈspoʊzəbəl] *adj* desechable

disposal [dɪ'spoʊ·zəl] n eliminación f; (garbage) trituradora f ▶ **to be at sb's ~** estar a disposición de alguien

dispose [dɪ'spoʊz] I. vt **1.** (place) disponer **2.** (incline) predisponer II. vi to **~ of** (throw away) desechar; (get rid) deshacerse de

dispossess [,dɪs·pə·'zes] vt desposeer

disproportionate [,dɪs·prə·'pɔr·ʃə·nɪt] adj desproporcionado, -a

disprove [dɪs·'pruv] vt refutar

disputable [dɪ·'spju·t̬ə·bəl] adj discutible

dispute [dɪ·'spjut] I. vt (argue) discutir; (doubt) poner en duda II. vi discutir (with/over con/sobre) III. n discusión f

disqualification [dɪs·,kwal·ə·fɪ·'keɪ·ʃən] n **1.** SPORTS descalificación f **2.** (incapacity) impedimento m

disqualify [dɪs·'kwal·ə·faɪ] <-ie-> vt descalificar (**from** de)

disquieting adj inquietante

disregard [dɪs·rɪ·'gard] I. vt desatender II. n despreocupación f

disrepair [,dɪs·rɪ·'per] n deterioro m; to **be in a state of ~** estar en mal estado

disreputable [dɪs·'rep·jə·t̬ə·bəl] adj de mala fama

disrepute [,dɪs·rɪ·'pjut] n desprestigio m

disrespect [,dɪs·rɪ·'spekt] n falta f de respeto

disrespectful [,dɪs·rɪ·'spekt·fəl] adj descortés

disrupt [dɪs·'rʌpt] vt (disturb) trastornar; (interrupt) interrumpir

disruption [dɪs·'rʌp·ʃən] n (disturbance) perturbación f; fig (disorder) desorganización f; (interruption) interrupción f

disruptive [dɪs·'rʌp·tɪv] adj perturbador

dissatisfaction [dɪs·,sæt̬·ɪs·'fæk·ʃən] n insatisfacción f

dissatisfied [dɪs·'sæt̬·ɪs·faɪd] adj insatisfecho, -a

dissect [dɪ·'sekt] vt diseccionar; fig examinar

dissection [dɪ·'sek·ʃən] n disección f

dissent [dɪ·'sent] I. n disconformidad f II. vi discrepar (**from** de)

dissident ['dɪs·ɪ·dənt] adj, n disidente mf

dissimilar [,dɪ·'sɪm·ɪ·lər] adj distinto (**to** a, de)

dissimulation [,dɪ·sɪm·jə·'leɪ·ʃən] n disimulo m

dissolve [dɪ·'zalv] I. vi disolverse; fig (disappear) desvanecerse II. vt disolver

dissuade [dɪ·'sweɪd] vt disuadir

distance ['dɪs·təns] I. n distancia f; his **house is within walking ~** se puede ir andando a su casa; **to keep one's ~** guardar las distancias; **in the ~** de lejos II. vt **to ~ oneself** distanciarse (**from** de)

distant ['dɪs·tənt] adj distante; (relative) lejano, -a

distantly adv de lejos; fig distantemente

distasteful [dɪs·'teɪst·fəl] adj desagradable

distillery [dɪ·'stɪl·ə·ri] n destilería f

distinct [dɪ·'stɪŋkt] adj **1.** (separate) distinto, -a **2.** (marked) definido, -a

distinction [dɪ·'stɪŋk·ʃən] n **1.** distinción f; **of great ~** de gran renombre **2.** (honors) sobresaliente m

distinctive [dɪ·'stɪŋk·tɪv] adj característico, -a

distinguish [dɪ·'stɪŋ·gwɪʃ] vi, vt distinguir; **to ~ oneself** destacar (**in** en)

distinguishable adj distinguible

distinguished adj distinguido, -a

distort [dɪ·'stɔrt] vt torcer; (facts, truth) tergiversar

distortion [dɪ·'stɔr·ʃən] n distorsión f

distract [dɪ·'strækt] vt distraer

distracted adj distraído, -a

distraction [dɪ·'stræk·ʃən] n **1.** (disturbance) distracción f **2.** (pastime) entretenimiento m

distress [dɪ·'stres] I. n **1.** aflicción f **2.** (danger) apuro m II. vt afligir

distressed adj **1.** (unhappy) afligido, -a **2.** (in difficulties) apurado, -a

distressful, distressing adj **1.** (causing worry) angustioso, -a **2.** (painful) doloroso, -a

distribute [dɪ·'strɪb·jut] vt distribuir; (share) repartir

distribution [dɪs·trɪ·'bju·ʃən] n **1.** (giving out) reparto m **2.** (spread) distribución f

distributor [dɪ·'strɪb·jə·t̬ər] n distribuidor(a) m(f)

district ['dɪs·trɪkt] *n* **1.** (*defined area*) distrito *m* **2.** (*region*) región *f*

district attorney *n* fiscal *m* del distrito

distrust [dɪs·'trʌst] **I.** *vt* desconfiar de **II.** *n* desconfianza *f*

distrustful [dɪs·'trʌst·fəl] *adj* desconfiado, -a

disturb [dɪ·'stɜrb] *vt* **1.** (*interrupt*) molestar **2.** (*worry*) preocupar **3.** (*move around*) perturbar

disturbance [dɪ·'stɜr·bəns] *n* **1.** (*interruption*) molestia *f* **2.** (*incident*) disturbio *m*

disturbed *adj* **1.** PSYCH trastornado, -a **2.** (*restless*) inquieto, -a

disturbing *adj* **1.** (*annoying*) molesto, -a **2.** (*worrying*) preocupante

disunity [dɪs·'ju·nə·t̬i] *n* desunión *f*

disuse [dɪs·'jus] *n* desuso *m*

disused [dɪs·'juzd] *adj* en desuso

ditch [dɪtʃ] **I.** <-es> *n* (*trench*) zanja *f*; (*by a road*) cuneta *f*; **irrigation ~** acequia *f* **II.** *vt sl* **1.** (*discard*) deshacerse de; (*idea*) descartar; (*boyfriend*) cortar con **2.** (*escape*) zafarse de

dither ['dɪð·ər] *vi inf* **1.** (*indecisive*) vacilar **2.** (*nervous*) ponerse nervioso

ditsy ['dɪt·si] *adj sl* empanado, -a, elevado, -a *Col*

dive [daɪv] **I.** *n* **1.** (*in swimming*) salto *m* [*or AmL* clavado *m*] de cabeza **2.** (*submerge*) inmersión *f* **3.** **to take a ~** (*for*) caer en picado; **to make a ~ for...** precipitarse hacia... **II.** *vi* <dived *or* dove, dived *or* dove> **1.** (*in swimming*) tirarse de cabeza **2.** (*submerge*) sumergirse; **to ~ under sth** bucear por debajo de algo **3.** (*drop*) bajar en picado

diver ['daɪ·vər] *n* buzo *mf*

diverge [dɪ·'vɜrdʒ] *vi* divergir; **to ~ from** apartarse de

divergence [dɪ·'vɜr·dʒəns] *n* divergencia *f*

diverse [dɪ·'vɜrs] *adj* **1.** (*varied*) diverso, -a **2.** (*not alike*) diferente

diversion [dɪ·'vɜr·ʃən] *n* (*change of direction*) desviación *f*

diversity [dɪ·'vɜr·sə·t̬i] *n* diversidad *f*

divert [dɪ·'vɜrt] *vt* **1.** (*change direction*) desviar **2.** (*distract*) distraer

diverting [dɪ·'vɜr·t̬ɪŋ] *adj* ameno, -a

divide [dɪ·'vaɪd] **I.** *vt* **1.** *a.* MATH dividir (**into** en) **2.** (*allot*) repartir **II.** *vi* dividirse; **their paths ~d** sus caminos se separaron ▶ **~ and conquer** divide y vencerás

♦**divide off** *vt always sep* dividir

♦**divide out, divide up** *vt always sep* (re)partir

divided *adj* (*opinion*) dividido, -a

dividend ['dɪv·ɪ·dend] *n* MATH, FIN dividendo *m*

dividing line *n* línea *f* divisoria

diving *n* (*jumping*) zambullida *f*; (*swimming*) buceo *m*

diving board *n* trampolín *m*

diving suit *n* escafandra *f*

divisible [dɪ·'vɪz·ə·bəl] *adj* divisible

division [dɪ·'vɪʒ·ən] *n* **1.** *a.* MIL, MATH, SPORTS división *f* **2.** (*splitting up*) reparto *m* **3.** (*disagreement*) discordia *f*

divorce [dɪ·'vɔrs] **I.** *n* divorcio *m* **II.** *vt* **to get ~d** divorciarse (**from** de); **he ~d her for infidelity** se divorció de ella por infidelidad **III.** *vi* divorciarse

divorced *adj* divorciado, -a

dizzy ['dɪz·i] <-ier, -iest> *adj* **1.** (*having vertigo*) mareado, -a **2.** (*causing vertigo*) vertiginoso, -a **3.** *sl* (*silly*) lelo, -a

DJ ['di·dʒeɪ] *n abbr of* **disc jockey** DJ *mf*

DNA [ˌdi·en·'eɪ] *n abbr of* **deoxyribonucleic acid** ADN *m*

do [du] **I.** *n* **the ~s and don'ts** el conjunto de normas **II.** <does, did, done> *aux* **1.** (*in questions*) **~ you own a dog?** ¿tienes perro? **2.** (*in negatives*) **Frida ~esn't like olives** a Frida no le gustan las aceitunas **3.** (*in imperatives*) **~ your homework!** ¡haz los deberes!; **~ come in!** pero pasa, por favor **4.** (*for emphasis*) **he did ~ it** sí que lo hizo **5.** (*replacing a repeated verb*) **so/neither ~ I** yo también/tampoco; **she speaks more fluently than he ~es** ella habla con mayor fluidez que él **6.** (*requesting affirmation*) ¿verdad?; **you ~n't want to answer, ~ you?** no quieres contestar, ¿verdad? **III.** <does, did, done> *vt* **1.** (*act, carry out*) hacer; **to ~ one's best** emplearse a fondo; **to ~ something for sb/sth** hacer algo por alguien/algo **2.** (*deal with*) encargarse de; **if you ~ the washing up, I'll ~ the drying** si tú lavas los platos, yo los seco **3.** (*finish*) terminar **4.** (*put in order*) ordenar; (*clean*) limpiar; (*make neat*) arreglar; **to do one's hair** peinarse **5.** (*Europe, Florida*) visitar **6.** (*be satisfactory*) **I only have beer, will that ~ you?** sólo tengo cerveza, ¿te va bien? **7.** (*sell, offer*) ofrecer **8.** (*cook*) cocinar **9.** (*cause*) **to ~ sb a good turn** echar una mano a alguien; **to ~ sb good** sentar bien a alguien **10.** *sl* (*sex*) **to ~ it** hacerlo ▶ **what's ~ne is ~ne** a lo hecho, pecho; **that ~es it** eso es el colmo **IV.** <*does, did, done*> *vi* **1.** (*behave, act*) hacer **2.** (*manage*) salir adelante; **to ~ well in school** ir bien en la escuela; **mother and baby are ~ing well** la madre y el bebé se encuentran bien; **how are you ~ing?** ¿qué tal estás? **3.** (*finish with*) **to be ~ne with sb/sth** haber terminado con alguien/algo **4.** (*be satisfactory*) **this behavior just won't ~!** ¡no se puede tolerar este comportamiento! **5.** (*function as*) **it'll ~ for a spoon** servirá de cuchara **6.** *inf* (*going on*) **to be ~ing** pasar **7.** (*treat*) **to ~ badly/well by sb** tratar mal/bien a alguien ▶ **that will never ~** eso no sirve; **that will ~!** ¡ya basta!

◆ **do away with** *vi* **1.** (*dispose of*) suprimir **2.** *inf* (*kill*) liquidar

◆ **do in** *vt always sep, sl* **1. to do sb in** acabar con alguien **2.** (*ruin*) arruinar **3.** (*exhaust*) agotar

◆ **do out** *vt always sep* **1.** (*adorn*) decorar **2. to do sb out of sth** sacar algo a alguien

◆ **do over** *vt always sep, inf* (*redo*) volver a hacer

◆ **do up** *vt* (*button*) abrochar; (*tie*) anudar; (*shoes*) atarse; (*zipper*) cerrar; (*hair*) arreglar; **to do oneself up** acicalarse

◆ **do with** *vi* **1. to have to ~ sth** tener que ver con algo; (*book*) tratar de algo **2.** *inf* **I could ~ a drink** me hace falta tomar algo

◆ **do without** *vi* apañarse sin

doable ['du·ə·bəl] *n inf* realizable

dock [dak] **I.** *n* **1.** NAUT muelle *m* **2. to**

be in the ~ *fig* estar en apuros **II.** *vt, vi* NAUT atracar

dockyard ['dak·jard] *n* astillero *m*

doctor ['dak·tər] **I.** *n* **1.** MED médico, -a *m, f;* **to go to the ~'s** ir al médico **2.** UNIV doctor(a) *m(f)* **II.** *vt* (*fix*) **to ~ sth** (**up**) hacer un apaño a algo

doctorate ['dak·tər·ət] *n* doctorado *m*

docudrama *n* docudrama *m*

document ['dak·jə·mənt] **I.** *n* documento *m* **II.** *vt* documentar

documentary [ˌdak·jə·'men·tə·ri] <-ies> *adj, n* documental *m*

dodge [dadʒ] **I.** *vt* esquivar; *fig* eludir; **to ~ doing sth** escaquearse de hacer algo *inf* **II.** *vi* SPORTS regatear **III.** *n* treta *f*

does [dʌz] *vt, vi, aux 3. pers sing of* **do**

doesn't ['dʌz·ənt] = **does not** *see* **do**

dog [dɔg] **I.** *n* **1.** perro, -a *m, f* **2.** *sl* (*ugly*) callo *m;* (*mean*) **the** (**dirty**) **~!** ¡el muy canalla!; (*failure*) fiasco *m* ▶ **he doesn't have a ~'s chance** *inf* no tiene la más remota posibilidad; **every ~ has its day** *prov* a cada uno le llega su momento de gloria; **to lead a ~'s life** llevar una vida de perros; **to be a ~ in the manger** ser como el perro del hortelano; **it's a ~ eat ~ world** este mundo es un lugar despiadado **II.** <-gg-> *vt* perseguir; *fig* acosar

do-gooder *n inf* tonto, -a de tan bueno, -a *m*

dog-tired *adj* hecho, -a polvo

doing ['du·ɪŋ] *n* **1. to be** (**of**) **sb's ~** ser cosa de alguien **2. ~s** actividades *fpl*

do-it-yourself *n* bricolaje *m*

doll [dal] *n* **1.** muñeco, -a *m, f* **2.** *sl* encanto *m*

◆ **doll up** *vt* emperifollar; **to doll oneself up** ponerse de punta en blanco

dollar ['dal·ər] *n* dólar *m* ▶ **to feel like a million ~s** sentirse a las mil maravillas; **to look like a million ~s** estar despampanante; **to earn a quick ~** ganar dinero fácil

dollhouse *n* casa *f* de muñecas

dollop ['dal·əp] *n* (*amount*) porción *f*

dolly ['dal·i] <-ies> *n* childspeak muñequita *f*

dolphin ['dal·fɪn] *n* delfín *m*, bufeo *m* Perú

domain [dou·'mein] n 1. POL, COMPUT, MAT dominio m 2. (scope) campo m; **to be in the public ~** ser de dominio público

dome [doum] n 1. ARCHIT cúpula f 2. sl cabeza f

domestic [də·'mes·tɪk] adj 1. (of the house) doméstico, -a 2. (home-loving) casero, -a 3. (produce, flight, news) nacional; (trade, policy) interior

domestic market n mercado m nacional

dominant ['dam·ə·nənt] adj dominante

dominate ['dam·ə·neɪt] vi, vt dominar

domination [ˌdam·ə·'neɪ·ʃən] n dominación f

Dominican [də·'mɪn·ɪ·kən] adj, n dominicano, -a m, f

Dominican Republic n República f Dominicana

dominion [də·'mɪn·jən] n dominio m; **to have ~ over sb/sth** tener a alguien/ algo bajo su dominio

domino ['dam·ə·nou] <-es> n ~es dominó m; ~ **effect** efecto dominó

donate ['dou·neɪt] vt donar

donation [dou·'neɪ·ʃən] n 1. (contribution) donativo m 2. (act) donación f

done [dʌn] pp of **do**

donkey ['daŋ·ki] n a. fig burro, -a m, f

donkeywork n sl trabajo m pesado

donor ['dou·nər] n donante mf

don't [dount] = **do not** see **do**

donut ['dou·nʌt] n donut m

doodad ['du·dæd] n inf la cosa esa

doodle ['du·dəl] I. vi garabatear II. n garabato m

doom [dum] I. n (destiny) sino m; (death) muerte f II. vt condenar

door [dɔr] n puerta f; **front/back ~** puerta principal/trasera; **revolving/sliding ~** puerta giratoria/corredera; **to knock at** [or **on**] **the ~** llamar a la puerta; **there's someone at the ~** llaman a la puerta; **to answer the ~** abrir la puerta; **to show sb the ~** echar a alguien; **out of ~s** al aire libre; **behind closed ~s** a puerta cerrada ▶ **to slam the ~ in sb's face** dar a alguien con la puerta en las narices; **to lay sth at sb's ~** echar a alguien la culpa de algo

doorbell n timbre m

doorjamb n marco m de la puerta

doorkeeper n see **doorman**

doorknob n pomo m

doorman <-men> n portero m

doormat n felpudo m

doorstep n **to be right on sb's ~** estar a la vuelta de la esquina

door-to-door adj, adv de puerta en puerta

doorway n entrada f

dope [doup] I. n inf 1. (drugs) drogas fpl; (marijuana) maría f 2. SPORTS dopaje m 3. (person) capullo, -a m, f II. vt drogar; SPORTS dopar

dope dealer, dope pusher n inf camello, -a m, f

dop(e)y ['dou·pi] adj <-ier, -iest> sl 1. (drowsy) grogui, abombado, -a AmS 2. (stupid) lelo, -a

dormer n buhardilla f

dormitory ['dɔr·mə·tɔr·i] <-ies> n UNIV residencia f de estudiantes

dorsal ['dɔr·səl] adj dorsal

dosage ['dou·sɪdʒ] n dosis f inv

dose [dous] n a. fig dosis f

dossier ['das·i·eɪ] n expediente m

dot [dat] n 1. punto m; **on the ~** en punto 2. ~**s** TYPO puntos m pl suspensivos

doting adj muy cariñoso, -a

double ['dʌb·əl] I. adj (double; **it is ~ that** es el doble de eso; ~ **meaning/life** doble sentido/vida; **in ~ digits** de varias cifras; **a ~ 's'** dos eses; ~ **room** habitación doble II. adv doble; **to see** ~ ver doble; **to fold sth** ~ doblar algo por la mitad; **he's ~ your age** te dobla la edad III. vt doblar; (efforts) redoblar IV. vi 1. duplicarse 2. CINE, THEAT doblar (**for** a) V. n 1. (quantity) doble m 2. (person) doble mf 3. **to play ~s** jugar una partida de dobles ▶ **on** [or **at**] **the ~** inmediatamente

double up vi 1. (bend over) retorcerse; **to ~ with laughter** troncharse de risa 2. (share room) compartir habitación

double bass <-es> n contrabajo m

double bed n cama f de matrimonio

double-check vi, vt comprobar por segunda vez

double-click vi hacer doble clic; **to ~ on**

the left mouse button hacer doble clic con el botón izquierdo

double-cross I. *vt* traicionar **II.** **<-es>** *n* traición *f*

double-decker *n* (*bus*) autobús *m* de dos pisos

double-edged *adj a. fig* de doble filo

double feature *n* programa *m* doble

double-park *vi, vt* aparcar en doble fila

double talk *n* palabras *f pl* ambiguas

double time *n* COM, ECON paga *f* doble

doubt [daʊt] **I.** *n* duda *f*; **no** ~ sin duda; **without a shadow of a** ~ sin lugar a dudas; **there is no** ~ **about it** no cabe la menor duda; **to cast** ~ **on sth** poner algo en tela de juicio **II.** *vt* **1.** (*not believe*) dudar de **2.** (*question*) poner en duda **3.** (*feel uncertain*) dudar; **to** ~ **that** dudar que +*subj*; **to** ~ **if** [*or* **whether**]... dudar si...; **I** ~ **it very much** lo dudo mucho

doubtful ['daʊt·fəl] *adj* **1.** (*person*) indeciso, -a; **to be** ~ **whether to...** dudar si... **2.** (*unlikely*) incierto, -a **3.** (*questionable*) dudoso, -a

doubtless ['daʊt·lɪs] *adv* sin duda

dough [doʊ] *n* **1.** CULIN masa *f* **2.** *sl* pasta *f AmS*

doughnut ['doʊ·nʌt] *n* donut *m*

dove[1] [dʌv] *n* paloma *f* blanca

dove[2] [doʊv] *pt of* **dive**

down[1] [daʊn] *n* (*feathers*) plumón *m*; (*hairs*) pelusa *f*; (*on body*) vello *m*

down[2] [daʊn] **I.** *adv* **1.** (*movement*) abajo; **to fall** ~ caerse; **to lie** ~ acostarse **2.** (*from another point*) **to go** ~ **to the lake** bajar al lago; ~ **South** hacia el sur **3.** (*volume, intensity*) **to be worn** ~ estar gastado; **the sun is** ~ se ha puesto el sol; **the price is** ~ el precio ha bajado **4.** (*temporal*) **from 1900** ~ **to the present** desde 1900 hasta el presente; ~ **through the ages** a través de la historia **5.** (*in writing*) **to write/get sth** ~ apuntar algo **6.** (*not functioning*) **to be** ~ no funcionar; (*server*) estar caído; (*telephone lines*) estar cortado ▶ **to be** ~ **on sb** tener manía a alguien **II.** *prep* **to go** ~ **the stairs** bajar las escaleras; **to run** ~ **the slope** correr cuesta abajo

downcast ['daʊn·kæst] *adj* alicaído, -a

downfall ['daʊn·fɔl] *n* ruina *f*; (*government*) caída *f*

downgrade [ˌdaʊn·'greɪd] **I.** *vt* **1.** (*demote*) bajar de categoría **2.** (*disparage*) minimizar; **to** ~ **the importance** minimizar la importancia (**of** de) **II.** *n* bajada; **to be on the** ~ *fig* ir cuesta abajo

downhearted [ˌdaʊn·'har·tɪd] *adj* descorazonado, -a

downhill [ˌdaʊn·'hɪl] **I.** *adv* cuesta abajo; **to go** ~ ir cuesta abajo; *fig* ir de mal en peor **II.** *adj* cuesta abajo; **it's all** ~ **from now on** *fig* lo que queda es pan comido *inf*

download ['daʊn·loʊd] *vt* bajar(se)

down-market *adj* (*neighborhood, newspaper*) popular; (*shop, store*) barato, -a; (*program*) de masas

down payment *n* entrada *f*, cuota *f* inicial *AmL*; **to make a** ~ **on sth** dar la entrada para algo

downplay ['daʊn·pleɪ] *vt* restar importancia a

downpour ['daʊn·pɔr] *n* chaparrón *m*

downright ['daʊn·raɪt] **I.** *adj* (*refusal*) rotundo, -a; (*disobedience*) completo, -a; (*fool*) de remate; **that's** ~ **stupid** eso es una solemne tontería **II.** *adv* completamente; **to be** ~ **difficult** ser dificilísimo; **to refuse** ~ negarse rotundamente

downside ['daʊn·saɪd] *n* inconveniente *m*

downstairs [ˌdaʊn·'sterz] **I.** *adv* abajo; **to go** ~ bajar; **to run** ~ bajar corriendo **II.** *adj* (del piso) de abajo **III.** *n* planta *f* baja

downstream [ˌdaʊn·'strim] *adv* río abajo

Down syndrome *n* síndrome *m* de Down

down-to-earth *adj* realista; (*person*) práctico, -a

downtown [ˌdaʊn·'taʊn] **I.** *n* centro *m* (de la ciudad) **II.** *adv* **to go** ~ al centro; **to live** ~ vivir en el centro **III.** *adj* (*in the city center*) céntrico, -a; (*related to the city center*) del centro (de la ciudad)

downturn ['daʊn·tɜrn] *n* empeoramiento *m*

downward ['daʊn·wərd] **I.** *adj* (*movement*) descendente; (*direction*) hacia abajo; (*path*) cuesta abajo; (*tendency, prices*) a la baja **II.** *adv* hacia abajo

downwards ['daʊn·wərdz] *adv* hacia abajo

doz. *abbr of* **dozen** docena *f*

doze [doʊz] **I.** *vi* dormitar; **to ~ off** dormirse **II.** *n* cabezada *f*; **to have a ~** echar un sueño

dozen ['dʌz·ən] *n* **1.** (*twelve*) docena *f*; **half a ~** media docena; **two ~ eggs** dos docenas de huevos **2.** (*many*) **~s of times** cientos de veces

dozy ['doʊ·zi] *adj* <-ier, -iest> soñoliento, -a

Dr. *abbr of* **Doctor** Dr. *m*, Dra. *f*

drab [dræb] *adj* <drabber, drabbest> soso, -a; (*existence*) monótono, -a

draft [dræft] **I.** *n* **1.** (*air*) corriente *f* de aire **2.** (*drawing*) boceto *m* **3.** (*first version*) borrador *m* **4.** (*beer*) **on ~** de barril **II.** *vt* **1.** (*first version*) redactar el borrador de; (*plan*) trazar **2.** MIL llamar a filas **III.** *adj* (*beer*) de barril

drafty ['dræf·ti] *adj* <-ier, -iest> **it's ~ here** hay corriente

drag [dræg] **I.** <-gg-> *vt a.* COMPUT arrastrar **II.** <-gg-> *vi* **1.** (*trail along*) arrastrarse por el suelo **2.** (*meeting, time*) hacerse interminable **3.** (*lag behind*) rezagarse **III.** *n* **1.** (*hindrance*) estorbo *m*; **to be a ~ on sb** ser una carga para alguien **2.** *sl* (*boring person*) pelmazo, -a *m, f*; (*boring experience*) lata *f*; **what a ~!** ¡qué rollo! **3. to be in ~** ir vestido de mujer **4.** *inf* (*inhalation*) calada *f*; **to take a ~** dar una calada **5.** *sl* **the main ~** la calle principal

◆**drag along** *vt* arrastrar con dificultad

◆**drag away** *vt* arrancar

◆**drag behind** *vi* seguir con atraso

◆**drag down** *vt* hundir; (*make weak*) debilitar

◆**drag in** *vt* (*person*) involucrar; (*subject*) traer por los pelos

◆**drag on** *vi* hacerse interminable

◆**drag out** *vt* alargar

◆**drag up** *vt* sacar a relucir

dragon ['dræg·ən] *n* dragón *m*

dragonfly ['dræg·ən·flaɪ] <-ies> *n* libélula *f*, alguacil *m* *RíoPl*

drain [dreɪn] **I.** *vt* **1.** AGR, MED drenar;

(*pond*) vaciar; (*food, dishes*) escurrir **2.** (*drink*) apurar **3.** (*exhaust*) agotar **II.** *n* **1.** (*sewer*) alcantarilla *f*, resumidero *m* *AmL*; (*in sink*) desagüe *m* **2.** *fig* **to throw sth down the ~** tirar algo por la borda; **to go down the ~** irse al traste **3.** (*outflow*) fuga *f*

◆**drain away** *vi* irse; (*energy*) agotarse

drainage ['dreɪ·nɪdʒ] *n* TECH desagüe *m*; **~ system** alcantarillado *m*

drainboard *n* escurridero *m*

drainpipe *n* tubo *m* de desagüe

drama ['dra·mə] *n* **1.** LIT, CINE *a. fig* drama *m* **2.** THEAT arte *m* dramático

dramatic [drə·'mæt·ɪk] *adj a. fig* dramático, -a; (*artist, production*) teatral; (*rise, discovery*) espectacular

drank [dræŋk] *pt of* **drink**

drastic ['dræs·tɪk] *adj* drástico, -a

draw [drɔ] **I.** <drew, drawn> *vt* **1.** ART dibujar **2.** (*pull*) arrastrar; (*curtains*) correr; **to ~ sb aside** llevarse a alguien aparte **3.** (*attract*) atraer; **to be ~n toward(s)** sentirse atraído por; **to ~ attention to** llamar la atención sobre **4.** (*elicit*) conseguir (**from** de) **5. to ~ a conclusion** sacar una conclusión **6.** (*take out*) sacar **7.** (*obtain*) obtener; (*salary, pension*) cobrar **8.** (*money*) sacar; **to ~ a check** extender un cheque **9.** SPORTS, GAMES empatar **II.** <drew, drawn> *vi* **1.** ART dibujar **2.** (*move*) **to ~ ahead/away** adelantarse/apartarse **3.** (*approach*) acercarse; **to ~ to a close/an end** finalizar **4.** SPORTS, GAMES empatar **III.** *n* **1.** (*attraction*) atracción *f* **2.** SPORTS, GAMES empate *m* **3.** (*raffle*) sorteo *m*

◆**draw apart** *vi* distanciarse

◆**draw aside** *vt always sep* apartar

◆**draw away** **I.** *vi* (*move off*) alejarse; (*move away*) apartarse; **to ~ from sb** dejar atrás a alguien2 **II.** *vt* apartar

◆**draw down** *vt* bajar

◆**draw in** **I.** *vi* llegar; (*days*) acortarse **II.** *vt* atraer

◆**draw off** *vt* (*boots*) quitarse

◆**draw on** *vt* **1.** (*use*) usar **2.** (*put on*) ponerse **II.** *vi* **1.** (*time, day*) seguir su curso **2.** (*approach*) acercarse

◆**draw out** **I.** *vt* **1.** (*prolong*) alargar

D

2. (*elicit*) sacar **3.** FIN, ECON, COM retirar **II.** *vi* **1.** (*car, bus, train*) salir **2.** (*day*) hacerse más largo

◆**draw together I.** *vt* juntar **II.** *vi* acercarse

◆**draw up I.** *vt* **1.** (*draft*) redactar; (*plan*) trazar **2.** (*bring near*) arrimar **II.** *vi* pararse

drawback *n* inconveniente *m*

drawer [drɔr] *n* cajón *m*

drawing *n* dibujo *m*

drawing room *n* salón *m*

drawn [drɔn] *pp of* **draw**

dread [dred] **I.** *vt* temer; **I ~ to think...** me da miedo pensar... **II.** *n* terror *m* **III.** *adj* aterrador *m*

dreadful ['dred·fəl] *adj* **1.** (*terrible*) terrible; **I feel ~ about it** me da mucha pena **2.** (*bad quality*) fatal

dreadfully ['dred·fə·li] *adv* **1.** ~ **late** tardísimo **2.** (*poorly*) fatal

dream [drim] **I.** *n* sueño *m*; **a bad ~** una pesadilla; **to be in a ~** estar en las nubes; **to go like a ~** ir como la seda; **a ~ come true** un sueño hecho realidad; **in your ~s!** ¡ni lo sueñes! **II.** <dreamed *or* dreamt, dreamed *or* dreamt> *vi* soñar; **to ~ of** (*doing*) sth soñar con (hacer) algo; **~ on!** ¡ni de coña!; **I wouldn't ~ of** (*doing*) **that** no se me pasaría por la cabeza (hacer) eso **III.** <dreamed *or* dreamt, dreamed *or* dreamt> *vt* soñar; **I never ~ed that...** nunca se me había ocurrido que... +*condicional* **IV.** *adj* ideal; **his ~ house** la casa de sus sueños

◆**dream up** *vt* idear

dreamt [dremt] *pt, pp of* **dream**

dreary ['drɪr·i] *adj* <-ier, -iest> deprimente

drench [drentʃ] *vt* empapar (**in** de)

dress [dres] **I.** *n* <-es> vestido *m* **II.** *vi* vestirse; **to ~ in blue** ir de azul **III.** *vt* **1.** (*put on*) vestir **2.** CULIN aliñar **3.** (*decorate*) adornar; (*hair*) peinar

◆**dress up** *vi* ponerse elegante; **to ~ as** disfrazarse de

dressing ['dres·ɪŋ] *n* CULIN aliño *m*

dressing-down *n* reprimenda *f*

dressing gown *n* bata *f*, albornoz *m*

dressing table *n* tocador *m*

dress rehearsal *n* ensayo *m* general

dressy ['dres·i] *adj* <-ier, -iest> elegante

drew [dru] *pt of* **draw**

dribble ['drɪb·əl] **I.** *vi* (*person*) babear; (*water*) gotear **II.** *n* (*saliva*) baba *f*; (*water*) chorrito *m*

dried [draɪd] **I.** *pt, pp of* **dry** **II.** *adj* seco, -a; ~ **milk** leche en polvo

dried-up *adj* seco, -a

drift [drɪft] **I.** *vi* (*move aimlessly*) dejarse llevar **II.** *n* **1.** NAUT deriva *f* **2.** *inf* (*sense*) onda *f*; **to catch sb's ~** captar a alguien

drill [drɪl] TECH **I.** *n* taladro *m* **II.** *vt, vi* perforar

drink [drɪŋk] **I.** <drank, drunk> *vi* beber; **to ~ heavily/in moderation** beber en exceso/con moderación; **to ~ to** brindar por **II.** <drank, drunk> *vt* beber; **to ~ a toast** brindar (**to** por) **III.** *n* bebida *f*; (*alcoholic*) copa *f*; **to have a ~** tomar algo

◆**drink in** *vt* absorber

drinkable ['drɪŋ·kə·bəl] *adj* potable

drinker *n* bebedor(a) *m(f)*

drinking *n* bebida *f*; (*drunkenness*) alcoholismo *m*

drinking fountain *n* fuente *f*

drinking water *n* agua *f* potable

drip [drɪp] **I.** <-pp-> *vi* gotear **II.** <-pp-> *vt* chorrear **III.** *n* **1.** (*act*) goteo *m* **2.** (*drop*) gota *f* **3.** *sl* (*person*) pánfilo, -a *m, f*

dripping ['drɪp·ɪŋ] **I.** *adj* **1.** (*faucet, pipe*) que gotea **2.** (*wet*) empapado, -a **II.** *adv* **to be ~ wet** estar chorreando **III.** *n* ~s pringue *m* o *f*

drive [draɪv] **I.** <drove, driven> *vt* **1.** AUTO conducir, manejar *AmL*; (*race car*) pilotar; **to ~ sb home** llevar a alguien a casa **2.** **to ~ sb to** (**do**) sth forzar a alguien a (hacer) algo **3.** (*render, make*) volver; **to ~ sb crazy** sacar a alguien de quicio, mover **II.** <drove, driven> *vi* **1.** (*operate*) conducir, manejar *AmL* **2.** (*travel*) ir **3.** (*function*) funcionar **III.** *n* **1.** (*journey*) viaje *m*; **to go for a ~** ir a dar una vuelta en coche **2.** (*street*) calle *f* **3.** (*driveway*) entrada *f* **4.** TECH tracción *f* **5.** PSYCH impulso *m*; **to have ~** ser emprendedor **6.** (*campaign*) campaña *f* **7.** COMPUT unidad *f* de disco

drive at vt inf insinuar

drive off I. vt always sep ahuyentar II. vi irse

drive out vt expulsar

drive up vi acercarse

driven ['drɪv·ən] pp of **drive**

driver ['draɪ·vər] n 1. conductor(a) m(f); truck ~ camionero, -a m, f; taxi ~ taxista mf 2. COMPUT driver m

driver's license n carné m de conducir

driving n conducción f, manejo m AmL

driving force n fuerza f motriz

driving instructor n profesor(a) m(f) de autoescuela

driving lessons npl prácticas f pl de conducir

driving school n autoescuela f

driving test n examen m de conducir

drizzle ['drɪz·əl] METEO I. n llovizna f, garúa f AmL II. vi lloviznar, garuar AmL

drone [droʊn] n 1. ZOOL a. fig zángano m 2. (sound) zumbido m

droop [druːp] I. vi (person) desanimarse II. vt inclinar

drop [drɑp] I. n 1. (liquid) gota f; ~ by ~ gota a gota; **to have had a ~ too much** llevar una copa de más 2. (trace) pizca f 3. (vertical distance) declive m 4. (decrease) disminución f 5. (fall) caída f ▶ **it's a ~ in the bucket** es una gota de agua en el mar; **at the ~ of a hat** en un abrir y cerrar de ojos II. <-pp-> vt 1. (allow to fall) dejar caer 2. (lower) bajar 3. (give up) renunciar a; **to ~ sb** romper con alguien 4. (leave out) omitir; **let's ~ the subject** cambiemos de tema III. <-pp-> vi 1. (descend) bajar 2. **to ~ into a bar** pasarse por un bar 3. inf (be exhausted) estar agotado, -a ▶ **to let it ~** dejarlo caer; **to let it ~ that...** dar a entender que...

drop behind vi quedarse atrás

drop by vi pasarse

drop down vi caer

drop in vi inf entrar un momento; **to ~ on sb** pasarse por casa de alguien

drop off I. vt inf (passenger) dejar II. vi 1. (decrease) disminuir 2. inf (fall asleep) quedarse dormido 3. (fall off) caerse

drop out vi darse de baja (of en)

drop-down menu n menú m desplegable

droplet ['drɑp·lət] n gotita f

drought [draʊt] n sequía f

drove¹ [droʊv] n 1. (animals) rebaño m 2. ~s inf manada f; **in ~s** a montones

drove² [droʊv] pt of **drive**

drown [draʊn] I. vt a. fig ahogar II. vi 1. ahogarse 2. **to be ~ing in work** estar hasta arriba de trabajo

drowsy ['draʊ·zi] <-ier, -iest> adj soñoliento, -a

drug [drʌg] I. n fármaco m; (illegal) droga f; **to take ~s** tomar drogas II. <-gg-> vt drogar

drug addict n drogadicto, -a m, f

drug addiction n drogadicción f

drug bust n incautación f de droga

drug pusher n camello, -a m, f

drugstore n farmacia-droguería f

drum [drʌm] n 1. MUS, TECH tambor m; ~s batería f 2. (for oil) bidón m 3. ANAT tímpano m

drumstick n CULIN muslito m

drunk [drʌŋk] I. vt, vi pp of **drink** II. adj (inebriated) borracho, -a, jumo, -a AmL; **to be ~** estar borracho; **to get ~** emborracharse III. n borracho, -a m, f

drunkard ['drʌŋ·kərd] n borracho, -a m, f

drunken ['drʌŋ·kən] adj borracho, -a

dry [draɪ] I. <-ier or -er, -iest or -est> adj 1. (not wet) seco, -a; **to go ~** secarse 2. (climate, soil) árido, -a ▶ **to run** agotarse II. <-ie-> vt secar III. <-ie-> vi secarse; **to put sth out to ~** sacar algo para que se seque

dry up I. vi 1. (become dry) secarse 2. inf (become silent) quedarse en silencio 3. (run out) agotarse II. vt secar

dry cleaner's n tintorería f

dry land n tierra f firme

dryness ['draɪ·nɪs] n a. fig sequedad f

dry run n prueba f; (tryout) ensayo m

dual ['duː·əl] adj inv doble

dual citizenship n doble nacionalidad f

dub [dʌb] <-bb-> vt 1. (film) doblar; **to be ~bed into English** estar doblado al inglés 2. (give sb/sth a nickname) apodar

dubbing ['dʌb·ɪŋ] n doblaje m

dubious ['du·bi·əs] adj 1. (doubtful) dubitativo, -a 2. (untrustworthy) dudoso, -a

duchess ['dʌtʃ·ɪs] n duquesa f

duck [dʌk] I. n pato m ▶ like a ~ to water como pez en el agua II. vi 1. (dip head) agachar la cabeza 2. to ~ out of sth escaquearse de algo III. vt 1. (lower) bajar 2. (avoid) esquivar; fig eludir

ducky ['dʌk·i] n sl a pedir de boca

dude [dud] n (guy) tío, -a m, f

due [du] I. adj 1. (payable) pagadero, -a; (owing) debido, -a; ~ date fecha límite; ECON fecha de vencimiento 2. (appropriate) conveniente; in ~ course a su debido tiempo; with all ~ respect con el debido respeto 3. (expected) esperado, -a; I'm ~ in Mexico City this evening esta noche me esperan en la Ciudad de México 4. ~ to debido a II. n 1. to give sb his/her ~ dar a alguien su merecido 2. ~s (debts) deudas fpl; (obligations) deberes mpl; (payment) cuota f

duel ['du·əl] n duelo m

duet [du·'et] n dúo m

duffle bag ['dʌf·əl·bæg] n talego m

duffle coat n trenca f

dug [dʌg] pt, pp of **dig**

duke [duk] n duque m

dull [dʌl] I. adj 1. (boring) aburrido, -a 2. (not bright: sky) gris; (weather) desapacible; (color) apagado, -a; (light) pálido, -a 3. (sound) sordo, -a 4. (not sharp) desafilado, -a II. vt 1. (alleviate) aliviar 2. (desensitize) insensibilizar

duly ['du·li] adv 1. (appropriately) debidamente 2. (on time) a su debido tiempo

dumb [dʌm] adj 1. often offensive (mute) mudo, -a; **deaf and ~** sordomudo, -a 2. inf (stupid) estúpido, -a; to play ~ hacerse el tonto

dumbstruck ['dʌm·strʌk] adj mudo, -a (de asombro)

dummy ['dʌm·i] I. <-ies> n 1. (mannequin) maniquí mf 2. (duplicate) imitación f 3. (fool) tonto, -a II. adj (false) falso, -a

dump [dʌmp] I. n 1. (for waste) basurero m 2. fig sl (dirty place) tugurio m II. vt 1. (drop) verter; (get rid of) deshacerse de; (boyfriend) plantar 2. COMPUT volcar III. vi sl to ~ on sb pagarla con alguien

dumping n dumping m

dune [dun] n duna f

dungarees [ˌdʌŋ·gə·'riz] npl (workman's) mono m; (jeans) vaqueros mpl

dungeon ['dʌn·dʒən] n mazmorra f

dunk [dʌŋk] vt mojar

dup. n abbr of **duplicate** dup.

duplicate¹ ['du·plɪ·kət] I. adj inv duplicado, -a m II. n duplicado

duplicate² ['du·plɪ·keɪt] vt 1. (replicate) duplicar 2. (copy) copiar

durability [ˌdʊr·ə·'bɪl·ə·ti] n 1. (permanence) permanencia f 2. (life of a product) durabilidad f

durable ['dʊr·ə·bəl] adj 1. (hard-wearing) resistente 2. (long-lasting) duradero, -a

duration [dʊ·'reɪ·ʃən] n duración f; for the ~ hasta que se acabe

during ['dʊr·ɪŋ] prep durante; ~ work/the week durante el trabajo/la semana

dusk [dʌsk] n crepúsculo m; at ~ al atardecer

dust [dʌst] I. n polvo m ▶ to bite the ~ morder el polvo; to leave sb in the ~ dejar a alguien atrás II. vi limpiar el polvo

dust bunny n inf pelusa f

duster ['dʌs·tər] n trapo m

dust mite n ácaro m del polvo

dustpan n recogedor m

dustup n sl bronca f

dusty ['dʌs·ti] <-ier, -iest> adj polvoriento, -a; (grayish) ceniciento, -a; ~ brown marrón grisáceo

Dutch [dʌtʃ] I. adj holandés, -esa II. n 1. pl the ~ los holandeses 2. LING holandés

duty ['du·ti] <-ies> n 1. (moral) deber m; (obligation) obligación f; out of ~ por compromiso; to do one's ~ cumplir con su obligación 2. (task) función f 3. (work) tarea f; to do ~ for sb sustituir a alguien; to be on/off ~ estar/no estar de servicio 4. (tax) impuesto m

duty-free *adj* libre de impuestos

duvet [du·'veɪ] *n* edredón *m* nórdico

DVD [ˌdi·vi·'di] *n inv abbr of* **Digital Video Disk** DVD *m*

dwarf [dwɔrf] <-s *or* -ves> *n* enano, -a *m, f*

dwell [dwel] <dwelt *or* -ed, dwelt *or* -ed> *vi* to ~ **on sth** insistir en algo; to ~ **on a subject** explayarse en un tema

dwelt [dwelt] *pp, pt of* **dwell**

dwindle ['dwɪn·dəl] *vi* menguar

dye [daɪ] I. *vt* teñir II. *n* tinte *m*

dyke [daɪk] *n see* **dike**

dynamic [daɪ·'næm·ɪk] *adj* dinámico, -a

dynamite ['daɪ·nə·maɪt] *n* dinamita *f*

dynamo ['daɪ·nə·moʊ] <-s> *n* dinamo *f*

dyslexia [dɪ·'sleksiə] *n* dislexia *f*

dyslexic [dɪs·'lek·sɪk] *adj* disléxico, -a

E

E, e [i] *n* **1.** (*letter*) E, e *f*; ~ **as in Echo** E de España **2.** MUS mi *m*

E *abbr of* **east** E

each [itʃ] I. *adj* cada II. *pron* cada uno, cada una; **$70** ~ 70$ cada uno

each other *pron* uno a otro, una a la otra; **to help** ~ ayudarse mutuamente; **to be made for** ~ estar hechos el uno para el otro

eager ['i·gər] *adj* ansioso, -a, ávido, -a; **to be** ~ **to start** estar ansioso por empezar

eagerness *n* entusiasmo *m*

eagle ['i·gəl] *n* águila *f*

ear[1] [ɪr] *n* ANAT oído *m*; (*outer part*) oreja *f*; ~, **nose and throat specialist** otorrinolaringólogo, -a *m, f*; **to have a good** ~ tener buen oído ▶ **to play it by** ~ *inf* tocarlo de oído, improvisar sobre la marcha

ear[2] [ɪr] *n* BOT espiga *f*

earache ['ɪr·eɪk] *n* dolor *m* de oído

eardrum *n* tímpano *m*

ear infection *n* infección *f* de oído

earl [ɜrl] *n* conde *m*

earlobe ['ɪr·loʊb] *n* lóbulo *m* de la oreja

early ['ɜr·li] I. <-ier, -iest> *adj* **1.** (*ahead of time, near the beginning*) temprano, -a; **to be** ~ llegar temprano; **in the** ~ **15th century** a principios del siglo XV; **in the** ~ **morning** de madrugada; **in the** ~ **afternoon** a primera hora de la tarde; **he is in his** ~ **twenties** tiene poco más de veinte años; **at an** ~ **age** a una edad temprana; **to make it an** ~ **night** acostarse temprano; **the** ~ **days/years of sth** los primeros tiempos de algo **2.** *form* (*prompt: reply*) rápido, -a; **at your earliest (possible) convenience** tan pronto como te sea posible **3.** (*first*) primero, -a II. *adv* **1.** (*ahead of time*) anticipadamente; **to get up** ~ madrugar; ~ **in the morning** por la mañana temprano; **an** ~ **death** una muerte prematura; **the** ~ **hours** la madrugada **2.** (*soon*) pronto; **as** ~ **as possible** tan pronto como sea posible; **book your tickets** ~ compren sus entradas con tiempo **3.** (*prematurely*) prematuramente; **to die** ~ morir joven

earmark ['ɪr·mark] *vt* (*put aside*) reservar; (*funds*) destinar

earmuffs ['ɪr·mʌfs] *npl* orejeras *fpl*

earn [ɜrn] *vt* **1.** (*be paid*) ganar; **to** ~ **a living** ganarse la vida **2.** (*interest*) devengar

earnest ['ɜr·nɪst] I. *adj* (*sincere*) sincero, -a II. *n* seriedad *f*; **in** ~ de verdad

earnestly *adv* **1.** (*speak*) seriamente **2.** (*desire*) de todo corazón

earnings ['ɜr·nɪŋz] *npl* (*of a person*) ingresos *mpl*

earphones ['ɪr·foʊnz] *npl* auriculares *mpl*

earpiece ['ɪr·pis] *n* **1.** (*of a phone*) auricular *m* **2.** (*of glasses*) patilla *f*

earplug ['ɪr·plʌg] *n* tapón *m* para el oído

earring ['ɪr·rɪŋ] *n* pendiente *m*, caravana *f CSur*, candonga *f Col*

earshot ['ɪr·ʃat] *n* alcance *m* del oído; **in/out of** ~ al alcance/fuera del alcance del oído; **within** ~ al alcance del oído

earth [ɜrθ] *n* **1.** (*planet*) Tierra *f*; **on** ~ en el mundo **2.** (*soil*) tierra *f* ▶ **to come back (down) to** ~ bajar de las nubes; **what/who/where/why on** ~ ...? *inf* ¿qué/quién/dónde/por qué diablos...?

earthling ['ɜrθ·lɪŋ] *n* terrícola *mf*

earthly ['ɜrθ·li] adj (concerning life on earth) terreno, -a; (existence, paradise) terrenal

earthquake ['ɜrθ·kweɪk] n terremoto m, temblor m AmL

earwax ['ɪr·wæks] n cerumen m

ease [iz] I. n 1. (effortlessness) facilidad f; **to do sth with ~** hacer algo con facilidad 2. (comfort) comodidad f; **to feel at ~** sentirse cómodo; **to be at ~** estar a sus anchas; (stand) **at ~!** MIL ¡descansen! II. vt 1. (relieve: pain) aliviar; **to ~ one's conscience** descargarse la conciencia 2. (burden) aligerar III. vi (pain) aliviarse; (tension, prices) disminuir

◆**ease off** vi, **ease up** vi (pain) aliviarse; (person) relajarse

easel ['i·zəl] n caballete m

easily ['i·zə·li] adv (without difficulty) fácilmente; **to be ~ the best** ser con mucho el mejor

east [ist] I. n este m; **further ~** más hacia el este; **Far East** Extremo m Oriente; **Middle East** Oriente m Medio II. adj del este; **~ coast** costa f este

Easter ['i·stər] n (holiday) Pascua f; **during ~** en Semana Santa

Easter Bunny n conejo m de Pascua

Easter Day n Domingo m de Pascua

Easter egg n huevo m de Pascua

Easter holidays npl vacaciones f pl de Semana Santa

easterly ['i·stər·li] adj, adv 1. (towards the east) hacia el este 2. (from the east) del este

Easter Monday n lunes m de Pascua

eastern ['i·stərn] adj del este, oriental

Easter Sunday n Domingo m de Pascua

East Germany [,ist·'dʒɜr·mə·ni] n HIST Alemania f oriental

eastward ['ist·wərd] adj, adv hacia el este

eastwards ['ist·wərdz] adv hacia el este

easy ['i·zi] <-ier, -iest> I. adj 1. (simple) fácil; **the hotel is within ~ reach of the beach** el hotel está muy cerca de la playa; **~ to get along with** de trato fácil 2. (relaxed: manner) natural; **an ~ disposition** una buena disposición; **to be ~ on sb** ser poco severo con alguien II. adv 1. (cautiously) con cuidado; **~ does it** inf despacio y buena letra 2. (lenient) **to go ~ on sb** inf no ser demasiado severo con alguien 3. inf **take it ~!** ¡cálmate! ▸ **come, ~ go** inf tan fácil como viene, se va

easy chair n poltrona f

easy-going adj (person) de trato fácil

eat [it] I. <ate, eaten> vt comer; **to ~ breakfast** tomar el desayuno, desayunar; **to ~ lunch/dinner** comer/cenar, almorzar/comer AmL II. vi comer

◆**eat away** vt (acid) corroer; (termites) carcomer

eaten ['i·tən] pp of **eat**

eatery ['i·tə·ri] n inf restaurante m

eating disorder n trastorno m alimenticio

eau de Cologne [,ou·də·kə·'loun] n (agua f de) colonia f

eavesdrop ['ivz·drɑp] <-pp-> vi **to ~ on sth/sb** escuchar algo/a alguien a escondidas

echelon ['ef·ə·lɑn] n 1. (strata) nivel m; (of society) capa f 2. MIL escalón m

echo ['ek·ou] I. <-es> n eco m II. <-es, -ing, -ed> vi resonar III. <-es, -ing, -ed> vt (repeat) repetir

eclectic [ek·'lek·tɪk] I. n form ecléctico, -a m, f II. adj form ecléctico

eclipse [ɪ·'klɪps] I. n eclipse m II. vt eclipsar

ecological [,i·kə·'lɑdʒ·ɪ·kəl] adj ecológico, -a

ecologically [,i·kə·'lɑdʒ·ɪk·li] adv ecológicamente; **~ -friendly** ecológico, -a

ecologist [i·'kɑl·ə·dʒɪst] n 1. (expert) ecólogo, -a m, f 2. POL ecologista mf

ecology [i·'kɑl·ə·dʒi] n ecología f

ecology movement n movimiento m ecologista

economic [,i·kə·'nɑm·ɪk] adj POL, ECON económico, -a

economical [,i·kə·'nɑm·ɪ·kəl] adj económico, -a

economics [,i·kə·'nɑm·ɪks] npl 1. + sing vb (discipline) economía f 2. + pl (matter) aspecto m económico

economist [ɪ·'kɑn·ə·mɪst] n economista mf

economize [ɪ·'kɑn·ə·maɪz] vi ahorrar; **to**

~ on sth economizar en algo

economy [ɪˈkan·ə·mi] <-ies> n 1. (*frugality*) ahorro m 2. (*monetary assets*) economía f

economy class n AVIAT clase f turista

ecstasy [ˈek·stə·si] <-ies> n (*psychological state*) éxtasis m inv

ecstatic [ekˈstæt·ɪk] adj extático, -a; (*rapturous*) eufórico, -a

Ecuador [ˈek·wə·dɔr] n Ecuador m

Ecuadorian [ˌek·wəˈdɔr·i·ən] I. n ecuatoriano, -a m, f II. adj ecuatoriano, -a

ecumenical [ˌek·juˈmen·ɪ·kəl] adj ecuménico, -a

eczema [ˈek·sə·mə] n eczema m

Eden [ˈi·dən] n Edén m

edge [edʒ] I. n sing 1. (*limit*) borde m; (*of a lake, pond*) orilla f; (*of a page*) margen m; (*of a knife*) filo m; (*of a table*) canto m 2. SPORTS ventaja f II. vi **to ~ forward** ir avanzando

edgy [ˈedʒ·i] <-ier, -iest> adj inf nervioso

edible [ˈed·ɪ·bəl] adj comestible

edify [ˈed·ɪ·faɪ] <-ie-> vt form edificar

edifying adj form edificante

edit [ˈed·ɪt] vt editar

edition [ɪˈdɪ·ʃən] n edición f; (*set of books*) tirada f

editor [ˈed·ɪ·tər] n (*of book*) editor(a) m(f); (*of article*) redactor(a) m(f); (*of newspaper*) director(a) m(f)

editorial [ˌed·əˈtɔr·i·əl] I. n editorial m II. adj editorial; **~ staff** redacción f

editor-in-chief [ˌed·ɪ·tər·ɪnˈtʃif] n redactor(a) m(f) jefe

educate [ˈedʒ·ə·keɪt] vt 1. (*bring up*) educar 2. (*teach*) instruir

educated [ˈedʒ·ə·keɪ·ṯɪd] adj culto, -a

education [ˌedʒ·ʊˈkeɪ·ʃən] n 1. SCHOOL educación f 2. (*training*) formación f 3. (*teaching*) enseñanza f; (*study of teaching*) pedagogía f

educational [ˌedʒ·ʊˈkeɪ·ʃə·nəl] adj 1. SCHOOL (*system*) educativo, -a 2. (*instructive*) pedagógico, -a

eel [il] n anguila f

eerie [ˈɪr·i] adj, **eery** <-ier, -iest> adj espeluznante

effect [ɪˈfekt] I. n 1. (*consequence*) efecto m; **to have an ~ on sth** afectar

a algo; (*result*) resultado m; **to take ~** (*medicine, alcohol*) hacer efecto 2. LAW vigencia f; **to come into** [or **to take**] **~** entrar en vigor 3. **~s** (*belongings*) efectos mpl II. vt realizar

effective [ɪˈfek·tɪv] adj 1. (*giving result*) efectivo, -a; (*medicine*) eficaz 2. (*operative*) vigente; **to become ~** entrar en vigor

effectively adv 1. (*giving result*) eficazmente 2. (*really*) realmente

effectiveness n (*efficiency*) efectividad f; (*of a plan*) eficacia f

effeminate [ɪˈfem·ə·nɪt] I. adj afeminado, -a II. n afeminado m

effervescent [ˌef·ərˈves·ənt] adj 1. efervescente 2. fig eufórico, -a

efficiency [ɪˈfɪʃ·ən·si] n 1. (*of a person*) eficiencia f; (*of a method*) eficacia f 2. (*of a machine*) rendimiento m

efficient [ɪˈfɪʃ·ənt] adj (*person*) eficiente

effigy [ˈef·ɪ·dʒi] n efigie f

effort [ˈef·ərt] n a. PHYS esfuerzo m; **to be worth the ~** valer la pena

effortless [ˈef·ərt·lɪs] adj fácil, sin esfuerzo aparente

e.g. [ˌiˈdʒi] abbr of **exempli gratia** (= **for example**) p.ej.

egalitarian [ɪˌgæl·ɪˈter·i·ən] adj igualitario, -a

e-generation [ˌi·dʒen·əˈreɪ·ʃən] n generación f de internet

egg [eg] n huevo m; **fried/boiled ~s** huevos fritos/pasados por agua; **hard-boiled ~** huevo duro; **scrambled ~s** huevos revueltos

egg cell n óvulo m

eggnog n ponche m de huevo

eggplant n berenjena f

egg roll n rollito m de primavera

eggshell n cáscara f de huevo

egg yolk n yema f de huevo

ego [ˈi·goʊ] n <-s> 1. PSYCH ego m 2. (*self-esteem*) amor m propio

egocentric [ˌi·goʊˈsen·trɪk] adj egocéntrico, -a

egoist [ˈi·goʊ·ɪst] n egoísta mf

egoistic [ˌi·goʊˈɪs·tɪk] adj, **egoistical** [ˌi·goʊˈɪs·tɪ·kəl] adj egoísta

ego surfing n COMPUT introducir en un buscador de Internet el propio nombre

egotistic [ˌi·goʊ·ˈtɪs·tɪk] *adj*, **egotistical** [ˌi·goʊ·ˈtɪs·tɪ·kəl] *adj* **1.** (*selfish*) egoísta **2.** (*self-important*) egotista

ego trip [ˈi·goʊ·trɪp] *n* **to be on an ~** darse autobombo

egregious [ɪ·ˈgri·dʒəs] *adj* escandaloso, -a

Egypt [ˈi·dʒɪpt] *n* Egipto *m*

Egyptian [ɪ·ˈdʒɪp·ʃən] **I.** *n* egipcio, -a *m, f* **II.** *adj* egipcio, -a

eh [eɪ] *interj* **1.** (*what did you say?*) ¿qué? **2.** *Can* (*isn't it; aren't you/they/ we?*) ¿verdad?

eight [eɪt] **I.** *adj* ocho *inv;* **there are ~ of us** somos ocho; **it's ~ o'clock** son las ocho; **~ and a quarter/half** ocho y cuarto/media; **~ o'clock** las ocho; **it's ~ o'clock** son las ocho; **it's half past ~** son las ocho y media; **at ~ twenty/ thirty** a las ocho y veinte/media **II.** *n* ocho *m*

eighteen [ˌeɪ·ˈtin] **I.** *adj* dieciocho **II.** *n* dieciocho *m; s. a.* **eight**

eighteenth [ˌeɪ·ˈtinθ] **I.** *adj* decimoctavo, -a *n* **1.** (*order*) decimoctavo, -a *m, f* **2.** (*date*) ocho *m* **3.** (*fraction*) dieciochoavo *m;* (*part*) decimoctava parte *f; s. a.* **eighth**

eighth [eɪtθ] **I.** *adj* octavo, -a; **~ note** corchea *f* **II.** *n* **1.** (*order*) octavo, -a *m, f* **2.** (*date*) ocho *m;* **the ~** el día ocho; **the ~ of December** el ocho de diciembre **3.** (*fraction*) octavo *m;* (*part*) octava parte *f* **III.** *adv* (*in lists*) octavo

eightieth [ˈeɪ·tɪ·əθ] **I.** *adj* octogésimo, -a **II.** *n* (*order*) octogésimo, -a *m, f;* (*fraction*) octogésimo *m;* (*part*) octogésima parte *f; s. a.* **eighth**

eighty [ˈeɪ·ti] **I.** *adj* ochenta *inv;* **he is ~ (years old)** tiene ochenta años **II.** *n* <-ies> **1.** (*number*) ochenta *m* **2.** (*decade*) **the eighties** los (años) ochenta

either [ˈi·ðər] **I.** *adj* **1.** (*one of two*) **~ way** de una manera u otra; **I don't like ~ one** no me gusta ninguno de los dos **2.** (*each*) cada; **on ~ side of the river** a cada lado del río **II.** *pron* cualquiera (de los dos); **which one? — ~** ¿cuál? — cualquiera **III.** *adv* tampoco **IV.** *conj* **~ ... or ...** o ... o ...

ejaculate [ɪ·ˈdʒæk·jʊ·leɪt] **I.** *vt* (*semen*)

eyacular **II.** *vi* ANAT eyacular

ejaculation [ɪ·ˌdʒæk·jʊ·ˈleɪ·ʃən] *n* (*of semen*) eyaculación *f*

eject [ɪ·ˈdʒekt] **I.** *vt* echar, expulsar; (*liquid, gas*) expeler **II.** *vi* eyectarse

eke out [ˈik·ˌaʊt] *vt* **to ~ a living** ganarse la vida a duras penas

EKG [ˌi·keɪ·ˈdʒi] *n abbr of* **electrocardiogram** electrocardiograma *m*, electro *m*

elaborate[1] [ɪ·ˈlæb·ər·ət] *adj* (*complicated*) complicado, -a; (*very detailed: excuse*) rebuscado, -a; (*meal*) de muchos platos

elaborate[2] [ɪ·ˈlæb·ə·reɪt] **I.** *vt* elaborar **II.** *vi* entrar en detalles

elaboration [ɪ·ˌlæb·ə·ˈreɪ·ʃən] <-(s)> *n* **1.** (*of texts*) explicación *f* **2.** (*complexity*) complicación *f*

elapse [ɪ·ˈlæps] *vi form* transcurrir

elastic [ɪ·ˈlæs·tɪk] **I.** *adj* elástico, -a **II.** *n* (*material*) elástico *m*

elasticity [ˌe·læ·ˈstɪs·ə·ti] *n a. fig* elasticidad *f*

elate [ɪ·ˈleɪt] *vt* regocijar

elated *adj* eufórico, -a

elbow [ˈel·boʊ] **I.** *n* (*of people*) codo *m;* (*of animals*) codillo *m* **II.** *vt* dar un codazo a

elbow grease *n inf* fuerza *f;* **to put some ~ into sth** poner empeño en algo

elbow room *n* (*space*) espacio *m*

elder[1] [ˈel·dər] **I.** *n* (*senior person*) anciano, -a *m, f* **II.** *adj* mayor

elder[2] [ˈel·dər] *n* BOT saúco *m*

elderly [ˈel·dər·li] **I.** *adj* anciano, -a **II.** *n* **the ~** los ancianos

eldest [ˈel·dɪst] *adj superl of* **old** mayor; **her ~** (**child**) su hijo mayor

elect [ɪ·ˈlekt] **I.** *vt* (*by vote or otherwise*) elegir **II.** *adj* **the president ~** el presidente *m* electo, la presidenta *f* electa

election [ɪ·ˈlek·ʃən] *n* **1.** (*event*) elecciones *fpl* **2.** (*action*) elección *f*

election campaign *n* campaña *f* electoral

election defeat *n* derrota *f* electoral

electioneering [ɪ·ˌlek·ʃə·ˈnɪr·ɪŋ] *n* campaña *f* electoral; *pej* promesas *f pl* electoralistas

election speech *n* discurso *m* electoral

elective [ɪ·ˈlek·tɪv] **I.** *adj* (*optional*) optativo, -a **II.** *n* SCHOOL, UNIV optativa *f*

electoral [ɪˈlek·tər·əl] *adj* electoral *m*

electorate [ɪˈlek·tər·ət] *n* electorado *m*

electric [ɪˈlek·trɪk] *adj* ELEC eléctrico, -a; (*fence*) electrificado, -a; ~ **shock** descarga *f* eléctrica

electrical [ɪˈlek·trɪ·kəl] *adj* eléctrico, -a; ~ **tape** cinta *f* aislante

electrician [ɪˌlekˈtrɪʃ·ən] *n* electricista *mf*

electricity [ɪˌlekˈtrɪs·ə·ti] *n* electricidad *f*

electrocute [ɪˈlek·trə·kjut] *vt* electrocutar

electrocution [ɪˌlek·trəˈkju·ʃən] *n* electrocución *f*

electrode [ɪˈlek·troʊd] *n* electrodo *m*

electrolysis [ɪˌlekˈtral·ə·sɪs] *n* electrólisis *f*

electromagnet [ɪˈlek·troʊ·mæg·nɪt] *n* electroimán *m*

electromagnetic [ɪˌlek·troʊ·mægˈnet·ɪk] *adj* electromagnético, -a

electron [ɪˈlek·tran] *n* electrón *m*

electronic [ɪˌlekˈtran·ɪk] *adj* electrónico, -a

electronics [ɪˌlekˈtran·ɪks] *n + sing vb* electrónica *f*

electron microscope *n* microscopio *m* electrónico

elegance [ˈel·ɪ·gəns] *n* elegancia *f*

elegant [ˈel·ɪ·gənt] *adj* elegante

elegy [ˈel·ə·dʒi] *n* elegía *f*

element [ˈel·ə·mənt] *n* **1.** *a.* CHEM, MATH elemento *m* **2.** (*factor*) factor *m* **3.** ELEC resistencia *f*

elemental [ˌel·əˈmen·təl] *adj* elemental; (*feelings, needs*) primario, -a

elementary [ˌel·əˈmen·tə·ri] *adj* elemental; (*course*) básico, -a

elementary school *n* escuela *f* (de enseñanza) primaria

elephant [ˈel·ə·fənt] *n* elefante *m*

elevate [ˈel·ə·veɪt] *vt* (*raise*) elevar; (*prices*) aumentar

elevated [ˈel·ə·veɪ·tɪd] *adj* **1.** (*raised*) elevado, -a **2.** (*position*) importante

elevation [el·ɪˈveɪ·ʃən] *n* **1.** GEO elevación *f* (del terreno) **2.** ARCHIT alzado *m*

elevator [ˈel·ə·veɪ·tər] *n* (*for people*) ascensor *m*, elevador *m* AmL; (*for goods*) montacargas *m inv*

eleven [ɪˈlev·ən] **I.** *adj* once **II.** *n* once *m*; *s. a.* **eight**

eleventh [ɪˈlev·ənθ] **I.** *adj* undécimo, -a **II.** *n* **1.** (*order*) undécimo, -a *m, f* **2.** (*date*) once *m* **3.** (*fraction*) onceavo *m*; (*part*) onceava parte *f*; *s. a.* **eighth**

eligible [ˈel·ɪ·dʒə·bəl] *adj* **1.** elegible; ~ **to vote** con derecho a voto **2.** (*desirable*) deseable; **to be ~ for the job** reunir los requisitos necesarios para el puesto

eliminate [ɪˈlɪm·ɪ·neɪt] *vt* **1.** (*eradicate*) eliminar **2.** (*exclude from consideration*) descartar

El Salvador *n* El Salvador *m*

else [els] *adv* **1.** (*in addition*) más; **anyone/anything ~** cualquier otra persona/cosa; **anywhere ~** en cualquier otro lugar; **anyone ~?** ¿alguien más?; **anything ~?** ¿algo más?; **everybody ~** (todos) los demás; **everything ~** todo lo demás; **someone/something ~** otra persona/cosa; **it's something ~!** ¡es algo fuera de serie!; **how ~?** ¿de qué otra forma?; **what/who ~?** ¿qué/quién más? **2.** (*otherwise*) **or ~** si no; **come here or ~!** ¡ven, o ya verás!

elsewhere [ˈels·wer] *adv* en otro sitio

e-mail [ˈi·meɪl] **I.** *n abbr of* **electronic mail** (*message of*) correo *m* electrónico, e-mail *m* **II.** *vt* mandar por correo electrónico

e-mail address *n* dirección *f* de correo electrónico

embark [emˈbark] *vi* embarcar(se)

embarrass [emˈbær·əs] *vt* (*make feel uncomfortable*) avergonzar

embarrassed *adj* avergonzado, -a; **to be ~** pasar vergüenza

embarrassing *adj* embarazoso, -a, penoso, -a *Méx, Col, Pan, Ven, CRi*

embarrassment [emˈbær·əs·ment] *n* (*shame*) vergüenza *f*, pena *f Méx, Col, Pan, Ven, CRi*

embassy [ˈem·bə·si] <-ies> *n* embajada *f*

embed [emˈbed] <-dd-> *vt* (*fix*) hincar; (*in rock*) incrustar; (*in memory*) grabar

embers [ˈem·bərz] *npl* ascuas *fpl*

emblem [ˈem·bləm] *n* emblema *m*

embody [emˈbad·i] <-ied> *vt* **1.** (*personify*) personificar **2.** (*include*) incorporar

embolism ['em·bə·lɪz·əm] n MED embolia f

embrace [em·'breɪs] I. vt (hug) abrazar II. vi abrazarse III. n abrazo m

embroider [em·'brɔɪ·dər] I. vi bordar II. vt bordar; fig adornar

embroidery [em·'brɔɪ·də·ri] n bordado m; ~ **frame** bastidor m

embryo ['em·bri·ou] n embrión m

emerald ['em·ər·əld] I. n esmeralda f II. adj de esmeraldas; (color) esmeralda

emerge [ɪ·'mɜrdʒ] vi (come out) salir; (ideas) surgir

emergency [ɪ·'mɜr·dʒən·si] I. <-ies> n **1.** (dangerous situation) emergencia f; **in an** [or**in case of**] ~ en caso de emergencia **2.** MED urgencia f; ~ **room** sala f de urgencias **3.** POL crisis f inv; **national** ~ crisis nacional; **to declare a state of** ~ declarar el estado de excepción II. adj (exit) de emergencia; (services) de urgencia; (brake) de mano; (landing) forzoso, -a; (rations) de reserva; ~ **exit** salida de emergencia; ~ **landing** aterrizaje forzoso

emerging adj emergente

emery board n lima f de uñas (de esmeril)

emigrant ['em·ɪ·grənt] n emigrante mf

emigrate ['em·ɪ·greɪt] vi emigrar

emigration [ˌem·ɪ·'greɪ·ʃən] n emigración f

eminent ['em·ɪ·nənt] adj eminente

emission [ɪ·'mɪʃ·ən] n emisión f

emit [ɪ·'mɪt] <-tt-> vt (radiation, light) emitir; (smoke) echar

emoticon n COMPUT emoticón m

emotion [ɪ·'mou·ʃən] n **1.** (feeling) sentimiento m **2.** (affective state) emoción f

emotional [ɪ·'mou·ʃə·nəl] adj **1.** (relating to the emotions) emocional; (involvement, link) afectivo, -a **2.** (moving) conmovedor(a) **3.** (governed by emotion) emocionado, -a; **to get** ~ emocionarse

emotionless adj impasible

emotive [ɪ·'mou·tɪv] adj emotivo, -a

empathy ['em·pə·θi] n empatía f

emperor ['em·pər·ər] n emperador m

emphasis ['em·fə·sɪs] <emphases> n **1.** (importance) énfasis m inv **2.** LING acento m

emphasize ['em·fə·saɪz] vt **1.** (insist on) poner énfasis en, enfatizar AmL; (fact) hacer hincapié en **2.** LING acentuar

emphatic [em·'fæt·ɪk] adj (forcibly expressive) enfático, -a; (strong) enérgico, -a; **to be** ~ **about sth** hacer hincapié en algo

empire ['em·paɪr] n imperio m

employ [em·'plɔɪ] vt **1.** (give a job to) emplear; **to** ~ **sb to do sth** contratar a alguien para hacer algo **2.** (put to use) utilizar

employee ['em·plɔɪ·'i] n empleado, -a m, f

employer [em·'plɔɪ·ər] n empresario, -a m, f

employment ['em·plɔɪ·mənt] n (of a person) empleo m

empower [em·'pau·ər] vt **to** ~ **sb to do sth** (give ability to) capacitar a alguien para hacer algo; (authorize) autorizar a alguien a hacer algo

empress ['em·prɪs] n emperatriz f

emptiness ['emp·ti·nɪs] n vacío m; fig vacuidad f elev

empty ['emp·ti] I. <-ier, -iest> adj **1.** (with nothing inside) vacío, -a; (truck, ship, train) sin carga; (house) desocupado, -a **2.** (threat) vano, -a II. <-ie-> vt (pour) verter; (deprive of contents) vaciar III. <-ie-> vi vaciarse; (river) desembocar

empty-handed [ˌemp·tɪ·'hæn·dɪd] adj con las manos vacías

emu ['i·mju] n emú m

emulate ['em·jʊ·leɪt] vt emular

emulsion [ɪ·'mʌl·ʃən] n **1.** a. PHOT emulsión f **2.** (paint) pintura f emulsionada

enable [ɪ·'neɪ·bəl] vt **1.** **to** ~ **sb to do sth** permitir a alguien que haga algo **2.** COMPUT activar

encase [en·'keɪs] vt encerrar

enchant [en·'tʃænt] vt **1.** (charm) encantar **2.** (bewitch) hechizar

enchanting adj encantador(a)

encircle [en·'sɜr·kəl] vt rodear

enclose [en·'klouz] vt **1.** (surround) cercar; (field) rodear; **to** ~ **sth in brackets** poner algo entre paréntesis **2.** (include) adjuntar, adosar AmL

enclosed [en·'klouzd] adj **1.** (confined)

cerrado, -a; (*garden*) vallado, -a **2.** (*included*) adjunto, -a

enclosure [enˈkloʊ·ʒər] *n* **1.** (*enclosed area*) recinto *m*; (*for animals*) corral *m* **2.** (*letter*) documento *m* adjunto

encode [enˈkoʊd] *vt a.* COMPUT codificar; LING cifrar

encompass [enˈkʌm·pəs] *vt* **1.** (*surround*) rodear **2.** (*include*) abarcar

encore [ˈɑn·kɔr] **I.** *n* repetición *f*; **as** [*or* **for**] **an ~** como bis **II.** *interj* otra

encounter [enˈkaʊn·tər] **I.** *vt* encontrar **II.** *n* encuentro; **a close ~** avistamiento *m*

encourage [enˈkɜr·ɪdʒ] *vt* **1.** (*give confidence*) alentar; (*give hope*) animar a alguien a hacer algo **2.** (*support*) fomentar

encouragement [enˈkɜr·ɪdʒ·mənt] *n* estímulo *m*; **to give ~ to sb** animar a alguien

encouraging *adj* alentador(a)

encyclopedia [enˌsaɪ·klə·ˈpi·di·ə] *n* enciclopedia *f*

end [end] **I.** *n* **1.** (*finish*) fin *m* **2.** (*extremity*) extremo *m* **3.** (*boundary*) límite *m* **4.** (*stop*) fin *m* **5.** **~s** (*goal*) fin *m*; (*purpose*) intención *f* **6.** (*phone line*) **who is on the other ~?** ¿quién está al otro lado de la línea? **7.** (*death*) muerte *f*; **he is nearing his ~** está a punto de morir **8.** (*obligation*) **to uphold one's ~ of the deal** [*or* **bargain**] cumplir su parte del trato **9.** SPORTS lado *m* **10.** COMPUT tecla *f* de fin ▶ **~ of story** punto y final, se acabó; **to be at the ~ of one's rope** no poder más; **it's not the ~ of the world** no es el fin del mundo; **to go off the deep ~** *inf* subirse por las paredes; **to make ~s meet** llegar a fin de mes; **to put an ~ to oneself** [*or* **it all**] acabar con su vida; **in the ~** a fin de cuentas **II.** *vt* **1.** (*finish*) acabar **2.** (*bring to a stop: reign, war*) poner fin a **III.** *vi* acabar; **to ~ in sth** terminar en algo

◆ **end up** *vi* terminar; **to ~ in prison** acabar en la cárcel; **to ~ doing sth** terminar haciendo algo

endanger [enˈdeɪn·dʒər] *vt* poner en peligro; **an ~ed species** una especie en

peligro de extinción

endeavor [enˈdev·ər] **I.** *vi* **to ~ to do sth** esforzarse por hacer algo **II.** *n* esfuerzo *m*

ending [ˈen·dɪŋ] *n* fin *m*; LING terminación *f*

endive [ˈen·daɪv] *n* CULIN endibia *f*

endless [ˈend·lɪs] *adj* interminable, inacabable

endorse [enˈdɔrs] *vt* **1.** (*declare approval for*) aprobar; (*product*) promocionar; (*candidate*) respaldar, apoyar **2.** FIN endosar

endorsement *n* **1.** (*support: of a plan*) aprobación *f*; (*of a candidate*) respaldo, apoyo *m*; (*recommendation*) recomendación *f* **2.** FIN endoso *m*

endowment *n* **1.** FIN dotación *f* **2.** (*talent*) talento *m*

endurance [enˈdʊr·əns] *n* resistencia *f*

endure [enˈdʊr] **I.** *vt* **1.** (*tolerate*) soportar, aguantar **2.** (*suffer*) resistir **II.** *vi* *form* durar

ENE *abbr of* **east-northeast** ENE

enema [ˈen·ə·mə] <-s *or* enemata> *n* enema *m*

enemy [ˈen·ə·mi] **I.** *n* enemigo, -a *m, f* **II.** *adj* enemigo, -a

energetic [ˌen·ər·ˈdʒet·ɪk] *adj* enérgico, -a; (*active*) activo, -a

energy [ˈen·ər·dʒi] <-ies> *n* energía *f*; **to have the ~ to do sth** tener energías para hacer algo

energy crisis *n* crisis *f inv* energética

energy resources *npl* fuentes *f pl* energéticas [*or* de energía]

energy-saving *adj* que ahorra energía

enforce [enˈfɔrs] *vt* aplicar; (*law*) hacer cumplir

enforcement [enˈfɔrs·mənt] *n* (*of a law*) aplicación *f*; (*of a regulation*) ejecución *f*

engage [enˈgeɪdʒ] **I.** *vt* **1.** *form* (*hold interest*) atraer **2.** (*put into use*) activar **3.** TECH (*cogs*) engranar; **to ~ the clutch** embragar, enclochar *Col, Méx* **4.** MIL (*the enemy*) entablar combate con **II.** *vi* MIL trabar [*or* librar] batalla

engaged *adj* **1.** (*to be married*) prometido, -a; **to get ~** (*to sb*) prometerse (con alguien) **2.** (*occupied*) ocupado, -a

engagement [ɪn·'ɡeɪdʒ·mənt] n 1. (*appointment*) compromiso m 2. (*marriage*) compromiso m 3. MIL combate m

engagement ring n anillo m de compromiso

engaging *adj* atractivo, -a

engine ['en·dʒɪn] n 1. (*motor*) motor m; **diesel/gasoline ~** motor diesel/de gasolina; **jet ~** motor a reacción 2. RAIL máquina f

engineer [ˌen·dʒɪ·'nɪr] I. n 1. (*with a degree*) ingeniero, -a m, f; **civil ~** ingeniero de caminos 2. (*technician*) técnico, -a m, f 3. RAIL maquinista mf II. vt construir; *fig* maquinar

engineering [ˌen·dʒɪ·'nɪr·ɪŋ] n ingeniería f

England ['ɪŋ·ɡlənd] n Inglaterra f

English ['ɪŋ·ɡlɪʃ] I. n *inv* 1. (*language*) inglés m 2. pl (*people*) **the ~** los ingleses II. *adj* inglés, -esa; **a movie in ~** una película en inglés; **an ~ class** una clase de inglés

English Channel n Canal m de la Mancha

English muffin n bollo de pan que se corta en dos y se toma tostado y untado en mantequilla

English speaker n persona f de habla inglesa

English-speaking *adj* de habla inglesa

enjoy [en·'dʒɔɪ] I. vt 1. (*get pleasure from*) disfrutar de; **~ yourselves!** ¡que lo paséis bien! 2. (*have: health*) poseer; **to ~ good health** gozar de buena salud II. vi pasarlo bien

enjoyable [en·'dʒɔɪ·ə·bəl] *adj* agradable; (*film, book, play*) divertido, -a

enjoyment [en·'dʒɔɪ·mənt] n disfrute m

enlarge [en·'lardʒ] vt 1. (*make bigger*) agrandar 2. PHOT ampliar

enlargement n aumento m; PHOT ampliación f

enlightenment [en·'laɪ·tən·mənt] n 1. REL iluminación f 2. PHILOS **the (Age of) Enlightenment** el Siglo de las Luces 3. (*explanation*) aclaración f

enlist [en·'lɪst] I. vi MIL alistarse II. vt MIL alistar, reclutar

enormous [ɪ·'nɔr·məs] *adj* enorme; **~ difficulties** grandes dificultades *fpl*

enough [ɪ·'nʌf] I. *adj* (*sufficient*) suficiente, bastante II. *adv* bastante; **to have seen ~** haber visto demasiado; **she was kind** [*or* **friendly**] **~ to help me** tuvo la amabilidad de ayudarme; **oddly** [*or* **strangely**] **~** por extraño que parezca III. *interj* basta IV. *pron* bastante; **more than ~** más que suficiente; **to have had ~ (of sb/sth)** estar harto (de alguien/ algo); **as if that weren't ~** por si fuera poco; **that's (quite) ~!** ¡basta ya!; **~ is ~** basta y sobra

enquire [en·'kwaɪr] vi, vt see **inquire**

enquiry [en·'kwaɪr·i] <-ies> n 1. (*question*) pregunta f 2. (*investigation*) investigación f; **an ~ into sth** una investigación sobre algo

enraged [en·'reɪdʒd] *adj* enfurecido, -a

enrich [en·'rɪtʃ] vt enriquecer

enroll <-ll-> vt, **enrol** [en·'roʊl] I. vi inscribirse; **to ~ for/in a course** matricularse para/en un curso II. vt inscribir; (*in a course*) matricular

enrol(l)ment [en·'roʊl·mənt] n inscripción f; (*in a course*) matriculación f

en route [ˌan·'rut] *adv* en el camino

ensuing *adj* siguiente

en suite bathroom [ˌan·swit·'bæθ·rum] n baño m incorporado

ensure [en·'ʃʊr] vt asegurar; (*guarantee*) garantizar

entail [en·'teɪl] vt 1. (*involve*) acarrear 2. (*necessitate*) **to ~ doing sth** implicar hacer algo

entangle [en·'tæŋ·ɡəl] vt enredar

enter ['en·tər] vt 1. (*go into*) entrar en 2. (*insert*) introducir; (*into a register*) inscribir; COMPUT **to ~ data** introducir datos 3. (*compete in*) inscribirse en; **to ~ a competition** presentarse a un concurso 4. (*begin*) entrar en; **to ~ politics** meterse en el mundo de la política 5. (*make known*) anotar; (*claim*) presentar; (*plea*) formular II. vi THEAT entrar

enter key n COMPUT tecla f intro

enterprise ['en·tər·praɪz] n 1. (*business firm*) empresa f 2. (*initiative*) iniciativa f

enterprising *adj* emprendedor(a)

entertain [ˌen·tər·'teɪn] I. vt 1. (*amuse*) entretener 2. (*guests*) recibir 3. (*con-*

sider) considerar **II.** vi (*invite guests*) recibir en casa

entertaining adj entretenido, -a; (*person*) divertido, -a

entertainment [,en·tər·'teɪn·mənt] n **1.** (*amusement*) diversión f **2.** (*show*) espectáculo m

enthusiasm [en·'θu·zi·æz·əm] n entusiasmo m; ~ **for sth** entusiasmo por algo

enthusiastic [en·,θu·zi·'æs·tɪk] adj entusiasta; **to be ~ about sth** estar entusiasmado con algo

enticement n tentación f

enticing adj tentador(a); (*smile*) atractivo, -a

entire [en·'taɪr] adj **1.** (*whole: life*) todo, -a; **the ~ day** todo el día; **the ~ world** el mundo entero **2.** (*total: commitment, devotion*) total **3.** (*complete*) entero, -a

entirely adv enteramente; **she's/he's ~ to blame** la culpa es enteramente suya; **to agree ~** estar completamente de acuerdo; **to disagree ~** estar del todo en desacuerdo

entirety [en·'taɪr·ə·ti] n **in its ~** en su totalidad

entitle [en·'taɪ·təl] vt **1.** (*give right*) autorizar; **to ~ sb to a holiday** dar a alguien derecho a vacaciones **2.** (*book*) titular

entitled adj **1.** (*person*) autorizado, -a **2.** (*book*) titulado, -a

entity ['en·tə·ti] <-ies> n form entidad f; **legal ~** persona f jurídica

entrance[1] ['en·trəns] n (*act of entering; way in*) entrada f

entrance[2] [en·'træns] vt (*cast spell*) encantar

entrance fee n cuota f de entrada [*or* de inscripción]

entrance hall n vestíbulo m

entrance requirement n requisito m de entrada

entrant ['en·trənt] n participante mf

entrée ['an·treɪ] n plato m principal [*or* fuerte], principio m Col

entrepreneur [,an·trə·prə·'nɜr] n empresario, -a m, f

entrust [en·'trʌst] vt confiar; **to ~ sth to sb** [*or* **to ~ sb with sth**] confiar algo a alguien

entry ['en·tri] <-ies> n **1.** (*act of entering*) entrada f; (*joining an organization*) ingreso m **2.** (*right to enter*) acceso m; **to refuse sb ~** negar el acceso a alguien **3.** (*in dictionary*) entrada f

entry fee n cuota f de entrada

entry-level job n empleo m raso (*empleo en el nivel más bajo de la jerarquía de una empresa*)

enunciate [ɪ·'nʌn·si·eɪt] vt **1.** (*sound*) pronunciar, articular **2.** (*theory*) enunciar

envelop [en·'vel·əp] vt envolver

envelope ['en·və·loup] n sobre m, cierro m Chile

enviable ['en·vi·ə·bəl] adj envidiable

envious ['en·vi·əs] adj envidioso, -a; **to be ~ of sb/sth** tener envidia de alguien/algo

environment [en·'vaɪ·ərn·mənt] n entorno m; **the ~** ECOL el medio ambiente; **working ~** ambiente m de trabajo

environmental [en·,vaɪ·ərn·'men·təl] adj ambiental; ECOL medioambiental; ~ **damage** daños m pl ecológicos

environs [en·'vaɪ·rənz] npl form alrededores mpl

envoy ['en·vɔɪ] n enviado, -a m, f

envy ['en·vi] **I.** n envidia f ▶ **to be green with ~** reconcomerse de envidia **II.** <-ie-> vt envidiar

enzyme ['en·zaɪm] n enzima f

epic ['ep·ɪk] **I.** n epopeya f **II.** adj épico, -a; ~ **poetry** poesía épica

epicenter ['ep·ɪ·sen·tər] n epicentro m

epilog ['ep·ɪ·lag] n epílogo m

episode ['ep·ɪ·soud] n episodio m

epitome [ɪ·'pɪt·ə·mi] n **1.** (*embodiment*) personificación f **2.** (*example*) arquetipo m; **the ~ of poor taste** el colmo del mal gusto

equal ['i·kwəl] **I.** adj (*the same*) igual; (*treatment*) equitativo, -a; **on ~ terms** en igualdad de condiciones **II.** n igual mf **III.** vt **1.** MATH ser igual a **2.** (*match*) igualar

equality [ɪ·'kwal·ə·ti] n igualdad f

equalize ['i·kwə·laɪz] vt nivelar

equalizer ['i·kwə·laɪ·zər] n **1.** MUS ecualizador m **2.** (*in soccer*) gol m del empate

equally ['i·kwə·li] *adv* igualmente

equal opportunity *n* igualdad *f* de oportunidades

equal(s) sign *n* MATH signo *m* de igual

equate [ɪ·'kweɪt] *vt* equiparar

equation [ɪ·'kweɪ·ʒən] *n* ecuación *f*

equator [ɪ·'kweɪ·tər] *n* ecuador *m*

equatorial [,ek·wə·'tɔr·i·əl] *adj* ecuatorial

equidistant [,i·kwɪ·'dɪs·tənt] *adj* equidistante

equilateral [,i·kwɪ·'læt·ər·əl] *adj* MATH equilátero, -a

equip [ɪ·'kwɪp] <-pp-> *vt* **1.** (*fit out*) equipar; **to ~ sth/sb with sth** proveer algo/a alguien de algo **2.** (*prepare*) preparar

equipment [ɪ·'kwɪp·mənt] *n* equipo *m*; **camping ~** accesorios *m pl* de cámping

equitable ['ek·wɪ·tə·bəl] *adj* equitativo, -a

equivalence [ɪ·'kwɪv·ə·ləns] *n* equivalencia *f*

equivalent [ɪ·'kwɪv·ə·lənt] **I.** *adj* equivalente; **to be ~ to sth** equivaler a algo **II.** *n* equivalente *m*

era ['ɪr·ə] *n* era *f*

eradicate [ɪ·'ræd·ɪ·keɪt] *vt* erradicar

erase [ɪ·'reɪs] *vt a.* COMPUT borrar; **to ~ a deficit** eliminar un déficit

eraser [ɪ·'reɪ·sər] *n* goma *f* de borrar

erect [ɪ·'rekt] **I.** *adj* erguido, -a; ANAT erecto, -a **II.** *vt* erigir; (*construct*) construir

erode [ɪ·'roʊd] **I.** *vt* erosionar **II.** *vi* erosionarse

erosion [ɪ·'roʊ·ʒən] *n* erosión *f*

erotic [ɪ·'rɑt·ɪk] *adj* erótico, -a

err [ɜr] *vi* errar; **to ~ on the side of sth** pecar (por exceso) de algo ▶ **to ~ is human** *prov* errar es humano *prov*

errand ['er·ənd] *n* recado *m*; **to run an ~** (salir a) hacer un recado

erratic [ɪ·'ræt·ɪk] *adj* **1.** (*inconsistent: heartbeat*) irregular; (*behavior*) imprevisible **2.** (*course*) errático, -a

erroneous [ɪ·'roʊ·ni·əs] *adj* erróneo, -a; **~ assumption** suposición equivocada

error ['er·ər] *n* error *m*; **to do sth in ~** hacer algo por equivocación; **human ~** error humano

error message *n* COMPUT mensaje *m* de error

erupt [ɪ·'rʌpt] *vi* **1.** (*explode: volcano*)

entrar en erupción; *fig* estallar **2.** MED salir

eruption [ɪ·'rʌp·ʃən] *n* erupción *f*; *fig* estallido *m*

escalate ['es·kə·leɪt] **I.** *vi* (*increase*) aumentar; (*incidents*) intensificarse **II.** *vt* intensificar

escalator ['es·kə·leɪ·tər] *n* escalera *f* mecánica

escapade [,es·kə·'peɪd] *n* aventura *f*; (*mischievous*) travesura *f*

escape [ɪ·'skeɪp] **I.** *vi* escaparse; (*person*) huir de; **to ~ from** escaparse de; **to ~ from a program** COMPUT salir de un programa **II.** *vt* escapar a; (*avoid*) evitar; **to ~ sb('s attention)** pasar desapercibido a alguien **III.** *n* **1.** (*act*) fuga *f* **2.** (*outflow*) escape *m*

escort ['es·kɔrt] **I.** *vt* acompañar; (*politician*) escoltar **II.** *n* **1.** (*companion*) acompañante *mf* **2.** (*paid companion*) chico, -a *m, f* de compañía **3.** (*guard*) escolta *f*

ESE *n abbr of* **east-southeast** ESE *m*

ESOL ['i·sɑl] *n abbr of* **English for speakers of other languages** inglés para extranjeros

esophagus [ɪ·'sɑf·ə·gəs] *n* esófago *m*

ESP [,i·es·'pi] *n abbr of* **extrasensory perception** percepción *f* extrasensorial

especially [ɪ·'speʃ·ə·li] *adv* **1.** (*particularly*) especialmente **2.** (*in particular*) en particular

espionage ['es·pi·ə·nɑʒ] *n* espionaje *m*; **industrial ~** espionaje industrial

espresso [ɪ·'spres·oʊ] <-s> *n* café *m* exprés

essay[1] ['es·eɪ] *n* **1.** LIT ensayo *m* **2.** SCHOOL redacción *f*

essay[2] [e·'seɪ] *vt* **1.** (*try*) intentar hacer **2.** (*test*) probar

essence ['es·əns] *n* **1.** esencia *f* **2.** (*in food*) esencia *f*, extracto *m*

essential [ɪ·'sen·ʃəl] **I.** *adj* esencial; (*difference*) fundamental **II.** *n* **the ~s** los elementos básicos [*or* esenciales]

essentially [ɪ·'sen·ʃə·li] *adv* esencialmente

essential oil *n* aceite *m* esencial

establish [ɪ·'stæb·lɪʃ] **I.** *vt* **1.** (*found*)

fundar; (*commission, hospital*) crear; (*dictatorship*) instaurar **2.** (*set: precedent*) sentar; (*priorities, norm*) establecer; **to ~ a reputation as a pianist** hacerse un nombre como pianista **3.** (*determine*) determinar, establecer; (*facts*) verificar; (*truth*) comprobar; **to ~ whether/where...** determinar si/dónde... **4.** ADMIN **to ~ residence** fijar la residencia **II.** *vi* establecerse

established [ɪ·ˈstæb·lɪʃt] *adj* **1.** (*founded*) fundado, -a **2.** (*fact*) comprobado, -a; (*procedures*) establecido, -a

establishment [ɪ·ˈstæb·lɪʃ·mənt] *n* **1.** (*business*) empresa *f*; **family ~** empresa *f* familiar **2.** (*organization*) establecimiento *m*; **educational ~** centro *m* educativo; **financial ~** institución *f* financiera; **the Establishment** POL la clase dirigente

estate [ɪ·ˈsteɪt] *n* **1.** (*piece of land*) finca *f*; **country ~** finca *f*, hacienda *f* AmL **2.** LAW (*possessions after death*) patrimonio *m*

esteemed *adj* apreciado, -a, valorado, -a; **highly ~** muy apreciado

esthetics *n* estética *f*

estimate[1] [ˈes·tɪ·meɪt] *vt* calcular; **to ~ that...** calcular que...

estimate[2] [ˈes·tɪ·mɪt] *n* cálculo *m* (aproximado); **a rough ~** *inf* un cálculo aproximado

estimated [ˈes·tɪ·meɪ·tɪd] *adj* estimado, -a

estimation [ˌes·tɪ·ˈmeɪ·ʃən] *n* opinión *f*; **in my ~** a mi juicio

Estonia [es·ˈtoʊ·ni·ə] *n* Estonia *f*

Estonian [es·ˈtoʊ·ni·ən] **I.** *adj* estonio, -a *n* **1.** (*person*) estonio, -a *m, f* **2.** LING estonio *m*

estranged *adj* (*distance*) distanciado, -a; (*state*) separado, -a

estrogen [ˈes·trə·dʒən] *n* estrógeno *m*

estuary [ˈes·tʃu·er·i] <-ies> *n* estuario *m*

etc. *abbr of* **et cetera** etc.

etch [etʃ] *vt* grabar (al agua fuerte)

ETD *abbr of* **estimated time of departure** hora *f* prevista de salida

eternal [ɪ·ˈtɜr·nəl] *adj* **1.** (*lasting forever: life*) eterno, -a **2.** (*constant: complaints*) constante, incesante

eternally [ɪ·ˈtɜr·nə·li] *adv* **1.** (*forever*) eternamente **2.** (*constantly*) constantemente, incesantemente

eternity [ɪ·ˈtɜr·nə·ti] *n* eternidad *f*

ethical *adj* ético, -a

ethics *n* + *sing vb* ética *f*

ethnic [ˈeθ·nɪk] *adj* étnico, -a; **~ cleansing** limpieza étnica

ethos [ˈi·θɑs] *n* espíritu *m*; **the working-class ~** los valores de la clase trabajadora

etiquette [ˈet·ɪ·kɪt] *n* etiqueta *f*

EU [i·ˈju] *n abbr of* **European Union** UE *f*

Eucharist [ˈju·kər·ɪst] *n* REL **the ~** la Eucaristía

eulogy [ˈju·lə·dʒi] <-ies> *n form* **1.** (*high praise*) elogio *m* **2.** LIT panegírico *m*

euphemism [ˈju·fə·mɪz·əm] *n* eufemismo *m*

EUR *n abbr of* **Euro** EUR *m*

euro [ˈjʊr·oʊ] *n* euro *m*

Europe [ˈjʊr·əp] *n* Europa *f*

European [jʊr·ə·ˈpi·ən] **I.** *adj* europeo, -a **II.** *n* europeo, -a *m, f*

European Union *n* Unión *f* Europea

evacuate [ɪ·ˈvæk·ju·eɪt] *vt* (*people*) evacuar; (*building*) desocupar

evacuation [ɪ·ˌvæk·ju·ˈeɪ·ʃən] *n* evacuación *f*; **~ of the bowels** MED evacuación *f*

evacuee [ɪ·ˌvæk·ju·ˈi] *n* evacuado, -a *m, f*

evade [ɪ·ˈveɪd] *vt* (*responsibility, person*) eludir; (*police*) escaparse de; (*taxes*) evadir

evaluate [ɪ·ˈvæl·ju·eɪt] *vt* (*result*) evaluar; (*person*) examinar

evaluation [ɪ·ˌvæl·ju·ˈeɪ·ʃən] *n* evaluación *f*; (*of a book*) crítica *f*

evangelical [ˌi·væn·ˈdʒel·ɪ·kəl] **I.** *n* evangélico, -a *m, f* **II.** *adj* evangélico, -a

evaporate [ɪ·ˈvæp·ə·reɪt] **I.** *vt* evaporar **II.** *vi* evaporarse; *fig* desaparecer

evasion [ɪ·ˈveɪ·ʒən] *n* **1.** (*of tax, responsibility*) evasión *f* **2.** (*avoidance*) evasiva *f*

evasive [ɪ·ˈveɪ·sɪv] *adj* evasivo, -a

eve [iv] *n* víspera *f*; **on the ~ of** en vísperas de; **Christmas Eve** Nochebuena *f*; **New Year's Eve** Nochevieja *f*

even [ˈi·vən] **I.** *adj* **1.** (*level*) llano, -a;

(*surface*) liso, -a **2.** (*equalized*) igualado, -a; **to get ~ with sb** ajustar cuentas con alguien **3.** (*of same size, amount*) igual **4.** (*constant, regular*) uniforme; (*rate*) constante **5.** (*fair*) ecuánime **6.** MATH par II. *vt* **1.** (*make level*) nivelar; (*surface*) allanar **2.** (*equalize*) igualar III. *adv* **1.** (*indicates the unexpected*) incluso; **not ~** ni siquiera **2.** (*despite*) **~ if...** aunque... +*subj;* **~ so...** aun así...; **~ though...** aunque... +*subj* **3.** (*used to intensify*) hasta **4.** + *comp* (*all the more*) aún

◆**even out** I. *vi* (*prices*) nivelarse II. *vt* igualar

◆**even up** *vt* igualar

evening ['iv·nɪŋ] *n* (*early*) tarde *f*; (*late*) noche *f;* **good ~!** ¡buenas tardes/noches!; **in the ~** por la tarde/noche; **that ~** esa noche; **the previous ~** la noche anterior; **on Monday ~** el lunes por la noche; **during the ~** durante la tarde; **8 o'clock in the ~** las 8 de la tarde; **all ~** (**long**) toda la tarde

evening class *n* clase *f* nocturna

evening dress *n* (*for woman*) vestido *m* [*or* traje *m*] de noche; (*for man*) traje *m* de etiqueta; **to wear ~** ir de etiqueta

evening prayer *n* oración *f* de la tarde

evenly ['i·vən·li] *adv* **1.** (*calmly*) apaciblemente; **to state sth ~** decir algo sin alterarse **2.** (*equally*) igualmente

event [I·'vent] *n* **1.** (*happening*) acontecimiento *m*, evento *m* **2.** (*case*) caso *m;* **in any** [*or* **either**] **~** en cualquier caso; **in the ~** (**that**) **it rains** en caso de que llueva

even-tempered ['i·vən·'tem·pərd] *adj* ecuánime

eventful [I·'vent·fəl] *adj* (*journey, week*) muy movido, -a; (*decision*) memorable

eventual [I·'ven·tʃʊ·əl] *adj* final

eventuality [I·ven·tʃʊ·'æl·ə·ti] <-ies> *n inv* eventualidad *f*

eventually [I·'ven·tʃʊ·ə·li] *adv* **1.** (*finally*) finalmente **2.** (*some day*) con el tiempo

ever ['ev·ər] *adv* **1.** (*on any occasion*) alguna vez; **have you ~ been to Hawaii?** ¿has estado alguna vez en Hawai?; **for the first time ~** por primera vez; **the**

hottest day ~ el día mas caluroso; **better than ~** mejor que nunca; **would you ~ dye your hair?** ¿te teñirías el pelo? **2.** (*in negative statements*) nunca, jamás; **nobody has ~ heard of him** nadie ha oído nunca hablar de él; **never ~** nunca jamás; **hardly ~** casi nunca; **nothing ~ happens** nunca pasa nada **3.** (*always*) **~ after** desde entonces; **as ~** como siempre; **~ since...** desde que...; **~ since** (*since then*) desde entonces **4.** (*used to intensify*) **all he ~ does is** +*infin* lo único que hace es +*infin*

everglade ['ev·ər·gleɪd] *n* tierra baja pantanosa cubierta de altas hierbas

everlasting [ˌev·ər·'læs·tɪŋ] *adj* (*undying*) imperecedero, -a; (*gratitude, love*) eterno, -a *f*

every ['ev·ri] *adj* **1.** (*each*) cada; **~ time** cada vez; **her ~ wish** su más mínimo deseo **2.** (*all*) todo, -a; **~ one of them** todos y cada uno de ellos; **in ~ way** de todas las maneras **3.** (*repeated*) **~ other week** una semana sí y otra no; **~ now and then** [*or* **again**] de vez en cuando ▶ **~ little bit helps** *prov* cualquier ayuda es buena

everybody ['ev·ri·ˌbad·i] *pron indef,* todos, todo el mundo; **~ but Paul** todos menos Paul; **~ who agrees** todos los que están de acuerdo

everyday ['ev·ri·deɪ] *adj* diario, -a; (*clothes*) de diario; (*event*) ordinario, -a; (*language*) corriente; (*life*) cotidiano, -a

everyone ['ev·ri·wʌn] *pron see* **everybody**

everything ['ev·ri·θɪŋ] *pron indef, sing* todo; **is ~ all right?** ¿está todo bien?; **~ they drink** todo lo que beben; **to do ~ necessary/one can** hacer todo lo necesario/lo posible; **money isn't ~** la riqueza no lo es todo

everywhere ['ev·ri·wer] *adv* en todas partes; **~ else** en cualquier otro sitio; **to look ~ for sth** buscar algo por todas partes

evict [I·'vɪkt] *vt* desahuciar

eviction [I·'vɪk·ʃən] *n* desahucio *m*

evidence ['ev·I·dəns] *n* **1.** (*sign*) indicios *mpl* **2.** (*proof*) prueba *f* **3.** (*tes-*

timony) testimonio *m* **4.** (*view*) evidencia *f*

evident ['ev·ɪ·dənt] *adj* evidente; **to be ~ to sb** ser evidente para alguien; **to be ~ in sth** manifestarse en algo; **it is ~ that...** está claro que...

evil ['i·vəl] **I.** *adj* malo, -a; **~ spirit** espíritu maligno *m*; **social ~** lacra *f* social; **good and ~** el bien y el mal

evocative [ɪ·'vak·ə·tɪv] *adj* evocador(a); **an ~ image** una imagen sugerente

evoke [ɪ·'vouk] *vt* evocar

evolution [ˌev·ə·'lu·ʃən] *n* evolución *f*; *fig* desarrollo *m*

evolve [ɪ·'valv] **I.** *vi* (*gradually develop*) desarrollarse; (*animals*) evolucionar; **to ~ into sth** convertirse en algo **II.** *vt* desarrollar

ewe [ju] *n* oveja *f*

ex [eks] <-es> *n inf* ex *mf*

exact [ɪg·'zækt] **I.** *adj* exacto, -a; **the ~ opposite** justo lo contrario **II.** *vt* exigir; **to ~ sth from sb** exigir algo a alguien

exacting *adj* exigente

exactly [ɪg·'zækt·li] *adv* exactamente; **~ like...** justo como...; **how/what/where ~...** cómo/qué/dónde exactamente...; **I don't ~ agree with that** no estoy del todo de acuerdo en eso; **not ~** no precisamente; **~!** ¡exacto!

exaggerate [ɪg·'zædʒ·ə·reɪt] *vi, vt* exagerar

exaggerated [ɪg·'zædʒ·ə·reɪ·tɪd] *adj* exagerado, -a; **greatly ~** muy exagerado

exaggeration [ɪg·ˌzædʒ·ə·'reɪ·ʃən] *n* exageración *f*; **it's no ~ to say that...** no es exagerado decir que...

exam [ɪg·'zæm] *n* examen *m*

examination [ɪg·ˌzæm·ɪ·'neɪ·ʃən] *n* **1.** (*exam*) examen *m* **2.** (*investigation*) investigación *f*; **medical ~** reconocimiento *m* médico

examine [ɪg·'zæm·ɪn] *vt* **1.** (*study*) estudiar **2.** MED hacer un reconocimiento médico de

examinee [ɪg·ˌzæm·ɪ·'ni] *n* examinando, -a *m, f*

examiner [ɪg·'zæm·ɪn·ər] *n* examinador(a) *m(f)*

example [ɪg·'zæm·pəl] *n* (*sample, model*) ejemplo *m*; **for ~** por ejemplo; **to follow**

sb's ~ seguir el ejemplo de alguien; **to set a good ~** dar (un) buen ejemplo

exasperating [ɪg·'zæs·pə·reɪ·tɪŋ] *adj* irritante

exasperation [ɪg·ˌzæs·pə·'reɪ·ʃən] *n* exasperación *f*

excavate ['ek·skə·veɪt] **I.** *vt* **1.** (*expose*) desenterrar **2.** (*hollow*) excavar **II.** *vi* excavar

excavation [ˌek·skə·'veɪ·ʃən] *n* excavación *f*

exceed [ɪk·'sid] *vt* exceder; (*outshine*) sobrepasar

exceedingly *adv* excesivamente

excel [ɪk·'sel] <-ll-> **I.** *vi* sobresalir; **to ~ at** [*or* **in**] **sth** destacar en algo **II.** *vt* **to ~ oneself** lucirse

excellence ['ek·sə·ləns] *n* excelencia *f*

excellent ['ek·sə·lənt] *adj* excelente

except [ɪk·'sept] **I.** *prep* **~ (for)** excepto, salvo, zafo *AmL*; **to do nothing ~ wait** no hacer nada más que esperar **II.** *vt form* exceptuar

excepting *prep* excepto, salvo

exception [ɪk·'sep·ʃən] *n* excepción *f*; **to be an ~** ser una excepción; **to make an ~** hacer una excepción; **to take ~ (to sth)** ofenderse (por algo)

exceptional [ɪk·'sep·ʃə·nəl] *adj* excepcional

exceptionally [ɪk·'sep·ʃə·nə·li] *adv* excepcionalmente

excerpt ['ek·sɜrpt] *n* extracto *m*

excess [ɪk·'ses] <-es> *n* exceso *m*; **to eat to ~** comer en exceso; **in ~ of** superior a

excess baggage *n see* **excess luggage**

excessive [ɪk·'ses·ɪv] *adj* excesivo, -a; (*claim*) exagerado, -a

excess luggage *n* exceso *m* de equipaje

exchange [ɪks·'tʃeɪndʒ] **I.** *vt* **1.** (*trade for the equivalent*) cambiar **2.** (*interchange*) intercambiar; **to ~ words** discutir **II.** *n* **1.** (*interchange, trade*) intercambio *m*; **in ~ for sth** a cambio de algo; **~ of (gun)fire** tiroteo *m* **2.** FIN, ECON cambio *m*; **foreign ~** divisas *fpl*

exchangeable *adj* cambiable; (*goods*) canjeable; **to be ~ for sth** ser intercambiable por algo

exchange rate n tipo m de cambio

exchange student n estudiante mf de intercambio

excise [ek·sáiz] vt form 1. quitar; (tumor) extirpar 2. fig eliminar, suprimir

excitable [ɪk·sái·t̬ə·bəl] adj excitable

excite [ɪk·sáit] vt 1. (move) emocionar 2. (stimulate) estimular

excited [ɪk·sái·t̬ɪd] adj emocionado, -a

excitement [ɪk·sáit·mənt] n emoción f; **what ~!** ¡qué emoción!

exciting [ɪk·sái·t̬ɪŋ] adj emocionante

exclaim [ɪk·skléim] vi, vt exclamar

exclamation [ˌek·sklə·méi·ʃən] n exclamación f

exclamation mark n, **exclamation point** n signo m de exclamación

exclude [ɪk·sklúd] vt 1. (keep out) excluir; **to ~ sb from a group** excluir a alguien de un grupo 2. (possibility) descartar

excluding [ɪk·sklú·dɪŋ] prep excepto, salvo

exclusion [ɪk·sklú·ʒən] n exclusión f

exclusive [ɪk·sklú·sɪv] I. adj exclusivo, -a; **~ interview** entrevista f en exclusiva; **~ of** sin; **to be ~ of** no incluir II. n exclusiva f

exclusively adv exclusivamente

excommunication [ˌeks·kə·ˌmju·nɪ·kéi·ʃən] n excomunión f

excrement [ék·skrə·mənt] n excremento m

excruciating [ɪk·skrú·ʃi·ei·t̬ɪŋ] adj 1. agudísimo, -a; (pain) atroz, insoportable 2. (intense: accuracy) extenuante

excursion [ɪk·skʒ·ʒən] n excursión f; **to go on an ~** ir de excursión

excusable [ɪk·skjú·zə·bəl] adj perdonable

excuse[1] [ɪk·skjúz] vt 1. (justify: behavior) justificar; (lateness) disculpar; **to ~ sb for sth** excusar a alguien por algo 2. (forgive) perdonar; **~ me!** ¡perdón! 3. (allow not to attend) **to ~ sb from sth** dispensar a alguien de algo 4. (leave) **after an hour she ~d herself** después de una hora se disculpó y se fue

excuse[2] [ɪk·skjús] n 1. (explanation) excusa f, disculpa f, agarradera f AmL

2. (pretext) pretexto m; **poor ~** mal pretexto; **to make ~s for sb** justificar a alguien

execute [ék·sɪ·kjut] vt 1. (carry out) realizar; (maneuver) efectuar; (plan) llevar a cabo; (order) cumplir 2. (put to death) ejecutar

execution [ˌek·sɪ·kjú·ʃən] n 1. (carrying out) realización f 2. (putting to death) ejecución f

executioner [ˌek·sɪ·kjú·ʃə·nər] n verdugo m

executive [ɪg·zék·jʊ·t̬ɪv] I. n (senior manager) ejecutivo, -a m, f II. adj ejecutivo, -a; **~ branch** poder ejecutivo

exempt [ɪg·zémpt] I. vt eximir II. adj exento, -a; **to be ~ from (doing) sth** estar exento de (hacer) algo

exemption [ɪg·zémp·ʃən] n exención f

exercise [ék·sər·saiz] I. vt 1. (muscles) ejercitar 2. (apply: authority, control) ejercer II. vi hacer ejercicio III. n 1. (physical training) ejercicio m; **to do ~s** hacer ejercicios 2. SCHOOL, UNIV ejercicio m 3. MIL maniobras fpl 4. (action, achievement) acción f 5. (use) uso m

exercise book n cuaderno m

exert [ɪg·zʒt] vt ejercer; (apply) emplear; **to ~ oneself** esforzarse

exertion [ɪg·zʒ·ʃən] n 1. (application: of authority, influence) ejercicio m 2. (physical effort) esfuerzo m

exhale [eks·héil] I. vt espirar; (gases, scents) despedir II. vi espirar

exhaust [ɪg·zɔst] I. vt a. fig agotar II. n (pipe) tubo m de escape

exhausted adj agotado, -a

exhausting adj agotador(a)

exhaustion [ɪg·zɔs·tʃən] n agotamiento m

exhaustive [ɪg·zɔs·t̬ɪv] adj exhaustivo, -a

exhaust pipe n tubo m de escape

exhaust system n sistema m de escape

exhibit [ɪg·zíb·ɪt] I. n 1. (display) objeto m expuesto 2. LAW prueba f presentada en juicio II. vt (show) enseñar; (rudeness, confidence) demostrar

exhibition [ˌek·sɪ·bíʃ·ən] n (display) exposición f; (performance) exhibición f

▶ **to make an ~ of oneself** ponerse en ridículo

exhibitor [ɪɡˈzɪb·ɪ·tər] *n* expositor(a) *m(f)*

exhilarating [ɪɡˈzɪl·ə·reɪ·t̬ɪŋ] *adj* estimulante; **an ~ performance** un espectáculo emocionante

exhilaration [ɪɡˈzɪl·ə·reɪ·ʃən] *n* regocijo *m*

exhume [ɪɡˈzum] *vt* exhumar

ex-husband *n* ex marido *m*

exile [ˈek·saɪl] **I.** *n* **1.** (*banishment*) exilio *m*; **political ~** exilio político; **to go into ~** exiliarse **2.** (*person*) exiliado, -a *m, f* **II.** *vt* exiliar

exist [ɪɡˈzɪst] *vi* **1.** (*be*) existir **2.** (*live*) vivir; **to ~ without sth** sobrevivir sin algo

existence [ɪɡˈzɪs·təns] *n* **1.** (*being*) existencia *f*; **to be in ~** existir **2.** (*life*) vida *f*

existing [ɪɡˈzɪs·tɪŋ] *adj* existente

exit [ˈeɡ·sɪt] **I.** *n* salida *f*; (*of road*) desvío *m* **II.** *vt* salir de **III.** *vi* a. COMPUT (*leave*) salir

exit visa *n* visado *m* de salida

exodus [ˈek·sə·dəs] *n* éxodo *m*

exorbitant [ɪɡˈzɔr·bə·tənt] *adj* exorbitante; (*demand*) excesivo, -a; (*price*) desorbitado, -a

exorcism [ˈek·sɔr·sɪz·əm] *n* exorcismo *m*

exotic [ɪɡˈzɑt̬·ɪk] *adj* exótico, -a

expand [ɪkˈspænd] **I.** *vi* **1.** (*increase*) expandirse **2.** (*spread*) extenderse **3.** PHYS dilatarse **II.** *vt* **1.** (*make larger*) ampliar; (*wings*) extender **2.** PHYS dilatar **3.** (*elaborate*) desarrollar

expandable [ɪkˈspæn·də·bəl] *adj* expansible

expansion [ɪkˈspæn·ʃən] *n* **1.** (*spreading out*) expansión *f*; (*of a metal*) dilatación *f* **2.** (*elaboration*) desarrollo *m*

expatriate[1] [eks·ˈpeɪ·tri·ət] *n* expatriado, -a *m, f*

expatriate[2] [eks·ˈpeɪ·tri·eɪt] *vt* expatriar

expect [ɪkˈspekt] *vt* esperar; (*imagine*) imaginarse; **to ~ sb to do sth** esperar que alguien haga algo; **you are ~ed to return books on time** debes devolver los libros puntualmente; **to be ~ing (a baby)** esperar un bebé; **I ~ed as much**

ya me lo esperaba; **to ~ that** esperar que +*subj*

expectancy [ɪkˈspek·tən·si] *n* esperanza *f*; **life ~** esperanza *f* de vida

expectant [ɪkˈspek·tənt] *adj* expectante; (*look*) de esperanza; **~ mother** futura madre

expectation [ˌek·spek·ˈteɪ·ʃən] *n* **1.** (*hope*) esperanza *f* **2.** (*anticipation*) expectativa *f*; **in ~ of sth** en espera de algo

expedient [ɪkˈspi·di·ənt] **I.** *adj* **1.** (*advantageous*) conveniente **2.** (*necessary*) necesario, -a **II.** *n* recurso *m*

expedite [ˈek·spɪ·daɪt] *vt form* acelerar

expedition [ˌek·spɪ·ˈdɪʃ·ən] *n* expedición *f*; **to be on an ~** estar de expedición; **to go on an ~** ir de expedición

expel [ɪkˈspel] <-ll-> *vt* expeler, arrojar; (*person*) expulsar; **to ~ sb from school** expulsar a alguien del colegio

expenditure [ɪkˈspen·dɪ·tʃər] *n* (*money*) gasto *m*; **public ~s** gasto público

expense [ɪkˈspens] *n* gasto *m*(*pl*); **all ~(s) paid** con todos los gastos pagados; **at great ~** por un precio muy elevado; **at sb's ~** *a. fig* a costa de alguien

expense account *n* cuenta *f* de gastos de representación

expensive [ɪkˈspen·sɪv] *adj* caro, -a

experience [ɪkˈspɪr·i·əns] **I.** *n* experiencia *f*; **to have translating ~** tener experiencia en traducción; **to know sth from ~** saber algo por experiencia **II.** *vt* experimentar; **to ~ happiness/pain** sentir alegría/dolor; **to ~ a loss** sufrir una pérdida

experienced [ɪkˈspɪr·i·ənst] *adj* experimentado, -a

experiment [ɪkˈsper·ɪ·mənt] **I.** *n* experimento *m*; **as an ~** como experimento; **by ~** experimentando **II.** *vi* experimentar; **to ~ with mice** hacer experimentos con ratones

experimental [ɪkˌsper·ɪ·ˈmen·t̬əl] *adj* experimental; **to be still at the ~ stage** estar todavía en fase experimental

expert [ˈek·spɜrt] **I.** *n* experto, -a *m, f*; **to be a computer ~** ser un experto en ordenadores [*or AmL* computadoras] **II.** *adj* **1.** (*skilful*) experto, -a; **she's an**

E

~ **swimmer** es una experta nadadora
2. LAW pericial
expert advice *n* **to seek** ~ asesorarse
con un experto
expertise [ˌek·spɜr·'tiz] *n* pericia *f*; (*knowledge*) conocimientos *mpl*
expiration date *n* (*of a contract*) fecha
f de vencimiento; (*of food or medicine*)
fecha *f* de caducidad
expire [ɪk·'spaɪr] I. *vi* 1. (*contract, license*) expirar; (*passport, food*) caducar
2. (*die*) expirar II. *vt* espirar
expiry [ɪk·'spaɪ·ri] *n see* **expiration**
explain [ɪk·'spleɪn] I. *vt* explicar; **to**
~ **how/what/where/why...** explicar
cómo/qué/dónde/por qué...; **that ~s
everything!** ¡eso lo aclara todo! II. *vi*
explicar
explanation [ˌek·splə·'neɪ·ʃən] *n* explicación *f*; **by way of** ~ como explicación
explanatory [ɪk·'splæn·ə·tɔr·i] *adj* explicativo, -a
expletive ['ek·splɪ·t̬ɪv] *n* palabrota *f*
explicit [ɪk·'splɪs·ɪt] *adj* 1. (*exact*) explícito, -a; ~ **directions** instrucciones explícitas 2. (*vulgar*) vulgar; ~ **language**
lenguaje *m* vulgar
explode [ɪk·'sploʊd] I. *vi* 1. (*blow up*)
explotar; (*bomb*) estallar; (*tire*) reventar; **to** ~ **with anger** montar en cólera
2. (*grow rapidly*) dispararse II. *vt*
(*blow up: bomb*) hacer explotar; (*ball*)
reventar
exploit ['ek·splɔɪt] I. *vt* explotar, pilotear *Chile* II. *n* hazaña *f*
exploitation [ˌek·splɔɪ·'teɪ·ʃən] *n* explotación *f*
exploration [ˌek·splə·'reɪ·ʃən] *n* 1. *a.*
MED exploración *f* 2. (*examination*) estudio *m*
exploratory [ɪk·'splɔr·ə·tɔr·i] *adj* (*voyage*)
de exploración; (*test*) de sondeo; (*meeting*) preliminar
explore [ɪk·'splɔr] I. *vt* 1. *a.* MED, COMPUT
explorar 2. (*examine*) analizar; **to** ~
sb's past investigar sobre el pasado de
alguien II. *vi* explorar
explorer [ɪk·'splɔr·ər] *n* explorador(a) *m(f)*
explosion [ɪk·'sploʊ·ʒən] *n* explosión *f*;
population ~ explosión demográfica

explosive [ɪk·'sploʊ·sɪv] I. *adj* explosivo,
-a; ~ **device** artefacto explosivo; **an** ~
issue un asunto espinoso; **to have an** ~
temper tener un genio muy vivo II. *n*
explosivo *m*
export I. [ɪk·'spɔrt] *vt* exportar II. ['ek·
spɔrt] *n* 1. (*product*) artículo *m* de exportación 2. (*selling*) exportación *f*; ~
taxes aranceles *m pl* de exportación
exportation [ˌek·spɔr·'teɪ·ʃən] *n* exportación *f*
expose [ɪk·'spoʊz] *vt* 1. (*uncover*) enseñar 2. (*leave vulnerable to*) exponer; **to**
~ **sb to ridicule** poner a alguien en ridículo 3. (*reveal: person*) descubrir; (*plot*)
desvelar; (*secret*) sacar a la luz
exposé [ˌek·spoʊ·'zeɪ] *n* revelación *f*
exposed [ɪk·'spoʊzd] *adj* 1. (*vulnerable*)
expuesto, -a 2. (*uncovered*) descubierto,
-a 3. (*unprotected*) desprotegido, -a
exposure [ɪk·'spoʊ·ʒər] *n* 1. (*contact*)
exposición *f* (**to** a); ~ **to new ideas**
contacto *m* con nuevas ideas 2. MED
hipotermia *f*; **to die of** ~ morir de frío
3. *a.* PHOT exposición *f* 4. (*revelation*)
descubrimiento *m* 5. (*media coverage*)
publicidad *f*
exposure meter *n* PHOT exposímetro *m*
express [ɪk·'spres] I. *vt* (*convey:
thoughts, feelings*) expresar; **to** ~ **oneself** expresarse; **I would like to** ~ **my
thanks for...** querría expresar mi gratitud por... II. *adj* 1. (*rapid*) rápido,
-a; ~ **train** tren expreso; ~ **mail** correo
urgente 2. (*precise*) explícito, -a; **by** ~
order por orden expresa III. *n* (*train*)
expreso *m* IV. *adv* **to send sth** ~ enviar
algo por correo urgente
expression [ɪk·'spreʃ·ən] *n* expresión *f*;
(*of love, solidarity*) demostración *f*; **as
an** ~ **of thanks** en señal de agradecimiento
expressionist [ɪk·'spreʃ·ə·nɪst] *n* expresionista *mf*
expressionless [ɪk·'spreʃ·ən·lɪs] *adj*
inexpresivo, -a
expressive [ɪk·'spres·ɪv] *adj* expresivo, -a
expressly [ɪk·'spres·li] *adv* 1. (*clearly*) claramente 2. (*especially*) expresamente

expressway [ɪk·ˈspres·weɪ] *n* autopista *f*

ex-prisoner *n* ex prisionero, -a *m, f*

expulsion [ɪk·ˈspʌl·ʃən] *n* expulsión *f*

exquisite [ˈek·skwɪ·zɪt] *adj* **1.** (*delicate*) exquisito, -a **2.** (*intense*) intenso, -a

extend [ɪk·ˈstend] **I.** *vt* **1.** (*enlarge: house*) ampliar; (*street*) alargar **2.** (*prolong: deadline*) prorrogar; (*holiday*) prolongar **3.** (*offer*) ofrecer; **to ~ one's thanks to sb** dar las gracias a alguien **4.** FIN (*credit*) conceder **II.** *vi* extenderse (*beyond* más allá de)

extended *adj* extenso, -a; **~ family** clan *m* familiar; **an ~ holiday** unas vacaciones prolongadas

extension [ɪk·ˈsten·ʃən] *n* **1.** (*increase*) extensión *f*; (*of rights*) ampliación *f*; **by ~** por extensión **2.** (*of a deadline*) prórroga *f* **3.** TEL extensión *f*, supletorio *m AmL*, anexo *m Chile*

extension cord *n* alargador *m*, alargue *m RíoPl*

extension ladder *n* escalera *f* extensible

extensive [ɪk·ˈsten·sɪv] *adj* **1.** *a.* fig extenso, -a; (*experience*) amplio, -a **2.** (*large: repair*) importante; **~ damage** daños *m pl* de consideración **3.** AGR (*farming*) extensivo, -a

extent [ɪk·ˈstent] *n* **1.** (*size*) extensión *f*; **to its fullest ~** en toda su extensión **2.** (*degree*) alcance *m*; **to go to the ~ of hitting sb** llegar al extremo de golpear a alguien; **to a great ~** en gran parte; **to the same ~ as...** en la misma medida que...; **to some ~** hasta cierto punto; **to such ~ that...** hasta tal punto que...; **to what ~...?** ¿hasta qué punto...?

exterior [ɪk·ˈstɪr·i·ər] **I.** *adj* exterior **II.** *n* **1.** (*outside surface*) exterior *m* **2.** (*outward appearance*) aspecto *m* **3.** CINE exteriores *mpl*

exterminate [ɪk·ˈstɜr·mɪ·neɪt] *vt* exterminar

extermination [ɪk·ˌstɜr·mɪ·ˈneɪ·ʃən] *n* exterminio *m*, exterminación *f*

external [ɪk·ˈstɜr·nəl] **I.** *adj* **1.** (*exterior*) externo, -a; (*influence*) del exterior; (*wall*) exterior **2.** (*foreign*) exterior **3.** MED tópico, -a **II.** *npl* las apariencias

extinct [ɪk·ˈstɪŋkt] *adj* (*practice*) extinto,

-a; **to become ~** extinguirse

extinction [ɪk·ˈstɪŋk·ʃən] *n* extinción *f*

extinguish [ɪk·ˈstɪŋ·gwɪʃ] *vt* (*candle, cigar*) apagar; (*love, passion*) apagar; (*life, memory*) apagar; (*debt*) amortizar

extinguisher [ɪk·ˈstɪŋ·gwɪʃ·ər] *n* extintor *m*

extort [ɪk·ˈstɔrt] *vt* extorsionar; (*confession*) arrancar

extortion [ɪk·ˈstɔr·ʃən] *n* extorsión *f*

extortionate [ɪk·ˈstɔr·ʃə·nɪt] *adj* abusivo, -a; **~ prices** precios *m pl* exorbitantes

extra [ˈek·strə] **I.** *adj* adicional; **~ clothes** ropa *f* de repuesto; **it costs an ~ \$2** cuesta dos dólares más; **meals are ~** el precio no incluye las comidas **II.** *adv* (*more*) más; (*extraordinarily*) extraordinariamente; **to charge ~ for sth** cobrar algo aparte **III.** *n* **1.** ECON suplemento *m*; AUTO extra *m* **2.** CINE extra *mf*

extract [ɪk·ˈstrækt] **I.** *vt* **1.** (*remove*) extraer **2.** (*obtain: information*) sacar **3.** MATH (*square root*) sacar **II.** *n* **1.** (*concentrate*) extracto *m* **2.** (*excerpt*) fragmento *m*

extraction [ɪk·ˈstræk·ʃən] *n* **1.** (*removal*) extracción *f* **2.** (*descent*) origen *m*

extracurricular [ˌek·strə·kə·ˈrɪk·jə·lər] *adj* extraescolar, extracurricular; **~ activities** actividades extraescolares

extradite [ˈek·strə·daɪt] *vt* extraditar

extradition [ˌek·strə·ˈdɪʃ·ən] *n* extradición *f*

extramarital [ˌek·strə·ˈmer·ɪ·təl] *adj* extramatrimonial

extraordinary [ɪk·ˈstrɔr·də·ner·i] *adj* **1.** *a.* POL extraordinario, -a **2.** (*astonishing*) asombroso, -a

extravagant [ɪk·ˈstræv·ə·gənt] *adj* **1.** (*wasteful*) despilfarrador(a) **2.** (*luxurious*) lujoso, -a **3.** (*exaggerated: praise*) excesivo, -a; **~ price** precio *m* exorbitante **4.** (*elaborate*) extravagante

extreme [ɪk·ˈstrim] **I.** *adj* extremo, -a; **an ~ case** un caso extremo; **with ~ caution** con sumo cuidado; **~ pain** dolor agudo; **in the ~ north** en la zona más septentrional; **~ sport** deporte de alto riesgo; **to be ~ in sth** ser extremista en algo **II.** *n* extremo *m*; **at the ~** fig en el

E

peor de los casos; **in the ~** sumamente;
to go from one ~ to the other pasar
de un extremo a otro; **to go to ~s** llegar
a extremos

extremely *adv* extremadamente; **to be
~ sorry** estar muy arrepentido

extremist [ɪk·'stri·mɪst] **I.** *adj* extremista
II. *n* extremista *mf*

extroverted *adj* extrovertido, -a

exuberant [ɪg·'zu·bər·ənt] *adj* **1.** (*luxuriant*) exuberante **2.** (*energetic*) desbordante

exultant [ɪg·'zʌl·tənt] *adj form* regocijado,
-a, exultante

ex-wife *n* ex mujer *f*, ex esposa *f*

eye [aɪ] **I.** *n* **1.** ANAT ojo *m*; **to blink
one's ~s** parpadear; **to keep an ~ on
sth/sb** *inf* echar un ojo a algo/alguien;
to roll one's ~s poner los ojos en blanco; **to rub one's ~s** restregarse los ojos;
visible to the naked ~ visible a simple
vista; **he couldn't take his ~s off the
girl** *inf* no le quitaba ojo a la chica **2.** BOT
yema *f* ▶ **to have ~s in the back of
one's** head *inf* tener ojos en la nuca; **an
~ for an ~, a tooth for a tooth** *prov*
ojo por ojo y diente por diente; **to give
sb a** black **~** poner a alguien un ojo a
la funeral [*or* negro]; **to turn a** blind
~ (**to sth**) hacer la vista gorda (a algo);
as far **as the ~ can see** hasta donde
alcanza la vista; **to have a** good **~ for
sth** tener (buen) ojo para algo; **there's**
more **to this than meets the ~** las
apariencias engañan; **to keep one's ~s**
open **mantener los ojos bien abiertos;
to be able to do sth with one's ~s
closed** *inf* poder hacer algo con los ojos
cerrados; (**right**) **before** [*or* under] **my**
very **~s** delante de mis propios ojos; **to
not** believe **one's ~s** no dar crédito
a sus ojos; **to** catch **sb's ~** llamar la
atención de alguien; **to (not)** see **~ to
~ with sb** (no) estar de acuerdo con alguien; **in the** public **~** a la luz pública
II. <-ing> *vt* mirar; (*observe*) observar;
to ~ sb up and down mirar a alguien de
arriba abajo

eyeball ['aɪ·bɔl] **I.** *n* globo *m* ocular
II. *vt inf* mirar de arriba abajo

eyebrow *n* ceja *f*; **to raise one's ~s at**

sth asombrarse ante algo

eyebrow pencil *n* lápiz *m* de cejas

eye contact *n* contacto *m* visual

eyedrops *npl* colirio *m*

eyelash <-es> *n* pestaña *f*; **false ~es**
pestañas *f pl* postizas

eyelid *n* párpado *m*

eyeliner ['aɪ·laɪ·nər] *n* delineador *m* de
ojos

eye opener *n inf* revelación *f*

eyepiece *n* ocular *m*

eye shadow *n* sombra *f* de ojos

eyesight *n* vista *f*; **his ~ is failing** le está
fallando la vista

eyesore *n* **to be an ~** ofender a la
vista

eyestrain *n* vista *f* cansada

eyewitness <-es> *n* testigo *mf* ocular

e-zine ['i·zin] *n* revista *f* electrónica

F

F, f [ef] *n* **1.** (*letter*) F, f *f*; **~ as in Foxtrot**
F de Francia **2.** MUS fa *m*

f *abbr of* **feminine** f

F *abbr of* **Fahrenheit** F

fable ['feɪ·bəl] *n* **1.** (*story*) fábula *f* **2.** (*lie*)
cuento *m*

fabric ['fæb·rɪk] *n* **1.** (*cloth, textile*) tejido *m*; **cotton ~** tela *f* de algodón **2.** *fig*
the ~ of society el tejido social

fabulous ['fæb·jə·ləs] *adj* fabuloso, -a; **to
look absolutely ~** estar estupendo

face [feɪs] **I.** *n* **1.** *a.* ANAT cara *f*; **a happy/sad ~** una cara de felicidad/de tristeza; **a smiling ~** un rostro sonriente;
to keep a smile on one's ~ no perder
la sonrisa; **to keep a straight ~** mantenerse impávido; **to laugh in sb's ~**
reírse en la cara de alguien; **to make a
~** (**at sb**) hacer una mueca (a alguien);
to tell sth to sb's ~ decir algo a la cara
de alguien **2.** (*front: of building*) fachada *f*; (*of coin*) cara *f*; (*of clock*) esfera *f*,
carátula *f Méx*; (*of mountain*) pared *f*
3. (*respect, honor*) prestigio *m*; **to lose
~** desprestigiarse; **to save ~** guardar las
apariencias ▶ **to** fly **in the ~ of logic/
reason** oponerse abiertamente a la lógi-

ca/razón; **on the ~ of it** a primera vista II. *vt* 1. (*turn towards*) mirar hacia; **to ~ the audience** volverse hacia el público 2. (*confront*) **the two teams will ~ each other next week** los dos equipos se enfrentarán la próxima semana; **to ~ the facts** enfrentarse a los hechos; **to ~ one's fears/problems** afrontar los miedos/problemas de uno; **to be ~d with sth** verse frente a algo; **we are ~d with financial problems** estamos pasando por problemas financieros 3. ARCHIT recubrir 4. FASHION forrar ▸ **to ~ the music** *inf* afrontar las consecuencias III. *vi* **to ~ towards the street** dar a la calle; **about ~!** ¡media vuelta!

facecloth *n* toallita *f*

face cream *n* crema *f* facial

facetious [fə'si:ʃəs] *adj* chistoso, -a, faceto, -a *Méx*; **stop being so ~** deja de hacerte el gracioso

face value *n* 1. ECON valor *m* nominal 2. *fig* **to take sth at ~** creer algo a pie juntillas

facility [fə'sɪl·ə·ti] *n* <-ies> 1. (*services*) servicio *m* 2. (*ability, feature*) facilidad *f* 3. (*building for a special purpose*) complejo *m*

facing ['feɪ·sɪŋ] *n* 1. ARCHIT revestimiento *m* 2. (*cloth strip*) vuelta *f*

fact [fækt] *n* hecho *m;* **the bare ~s** los hechos concretos; **to stick to the ~s** atenerse a los hechos ▸ **~s and figures** *inf* información *f* detallada; **a ~ of life** ley de vida; **the ~s of life** los detalles de la reproducción; **as a matter of ~...** de hecho...; **the ~ of the matter is that ...** la verdad es que...; **in ~** de hecho

fact-finding ['fækt·faɪn·dɪŋ] *adj* investigador(a)

factor ['fæk·tər] *n* factor *m*

factory ['fæk·tə·ri] *n* <-ies> fábrica *f;* **car ~** fábrica de coches

factual ['fæk·tʃu·əl] *adj* basado, -a en hechos reales; **a ~ error** un error de hecho

faculty ['fæk·əl·ti] *n* <-ies> 1. (*teachers*) cuerpo *m* docente 2. UNIV facultad *f* 3. (*ability*) facultad *f*

fad [fæd] *n inf* 1. (*fashion*) moda *f;* **a passing ~** una moda pasajera 2. (*obsession*) manía *f*

fade [feɪd] I. *vi* 1. (*lose color*) desteñirse 2. (*lose intensity: light*) apagarse; (*sound*) debilitarse; (*smile*) borrarse; (*interest*) decaer; (*hope, optimism, memory*) desvanecerse; (*plant, beauty*) marchitarse; (*life*) apagarse 3. (*disappear*) desaparecer; **to ~ from sight/view** perderse de vista 4. CINE, TV fundirse II. *vt* desteñir

◆ **fade away** *vi* (*hope, memory*) desvanecerse; (*sound, love, grief*) apagarse

◆ **fade in** I. *vi* (*picture*) aparecer progresivamente; (*sound*) subir gradualmente II. *vt* (*picture*) hacer aparecer progresivamente; (*sound*) subir gradualmente

◆ **fade out** *vi* (*picture*) desaparecer gradualmente; (*sound*) desvanecerse

fail [feɪl] I. *vi* 1. (*not succeed: person*) fracasar; (*attempt, plan, operation*) fallar; **if all else ~s** como último recurso; **to ~ to do sth** no conseguir hacer algo; **I ~ to see why that matters** no veo qué importancia tiene 2. SCHOOL, UNIV suspender, ser reprobado *AmL* 3. TECH, AUTO (*brakes, steering*) fallar; (*engine*) averiarse; (*eyesight, hearing, heart*) fallar 4. (*crops*) perderse II. *vt* 1. (*not pass: exam, subject, pupil*) suspender 2. (*not help*) **her courage ~ed her** le abandonó el coraje III. *n* SCHOOL, UNIV suspenso *m*, reprobado *m AmL* ▸ **without ~** (*definitely*) sin falta; (*always*) sin excepción

failing ['feɪ·lɪŋ] I. *adj* (*health*) débil II. *n* (*of mechanism*) defecto *m;* (*of person*) debilidad *f* III. *prep* a falta de

failure ['feɪl·jər] *n* 1. (*lack of success*) fracaso *m;* **to be doomed to ~** estar destinado al fracaso; **the ~ to answer** el no responder 2. TECH, ELEC (*breakdown*) fallo *m*

faint [feɪnt] I. *adj* 1. (*scent, odor, taste*) leve; (*sound, murmur*) apenas perceptible; (*light, glow*) tenue; (*line, outline, scratch*) apenas visible; (*memory*) confuso, -a; (*smile*) ligero, -a 2. (*slight: resemblance, sign, suspicion*) vago, -a;

(*chance, hope, possibility*) ligero, -a; **not to have the ~est idea** *inf* no tener ni idea 3. (*weak*) **to be ~ with hunger** estar desfallecido por el hambre; **to feel ~** sentirse mareado II. *vi* desmayarse III. *n* desmayo *m*

fair¹ [fer] I. *adj* 1. (*just: society, trial, wage*) justo, -a; (*price*) razonable; **a ~ share** una parte equitativa; **~ enough** está bien 2. *inf* (*quite large: amount*) bastante; **it's a ~ size** es bastante grande 3. (*reasonably good: chance, prospect*) bueno, -a 4. (*not bad*) aceptable 5. (*light in color: skin*) blanco, -a, güero, -a *AmL*; (*hair*) rubio, -a 6. METEO **~ weather** tiempo *m* agradable ▸ **~'s ~** *inf* lo justo es justo II. *adv* **to play ~** jugar limpio ▸ **~ and square** (*following the rules*) con todas las de la ley; (*directly*) de lleno

fair² [fer] *n* feria *f*; **trade ~** feria comercial

fair game *n* caza *f* legal; *fig* objeto *m* legítimo

fairground ['fer·graʊnd] *n* parque *m* de atracciones

fair-haired [ˌfer·'herd] *adj* rubio, -a

fairly ['fer·li] *adv* 1. (*quite*) bastante 2. (*justly*) con imparcialidad 3. *liter* (*almost*) prácticamente

fairness *n* 1. (*justice*) justicia *f*; **in (all) ~ ...** para ser justos... 2. (*of skin*) blancura *f*; (*of hair*) lo rubio

fairy ['fer·i] <-ies> *n* (*creature*) hada *f*

fairy tale *n* cuento *m* de hadas; *fig* cuento *m* chino

faith [feɪθ] *n* fe *f*; **to have/lose ~ in sb/sth** tener fe/perder la fe en alguien/algo; **to put one's ~ in sb/sth** confiar en alguien/algo; **to keep the ~** mantener la fe

faithful ['feɪθ·fəl] I. *adj* fiel II. *n* **the ~** los fieles

faithfully *adv* 1. (*loyally: serve*) lealmente 2. (*exactly: copy, translate*) fielmente

fake [feɪk] I. *n* 1. (*painting, jewel*) falsificación *f* 2. (*person*) impostor(a) *m(f)* II. *adj* **~ fur** piel sintética; **~ jewel** joya falsa III. *vt* 1. (*counterfeit*) falsificar 2. (*pretend to feel*)

fingir IV. *vi* fingir

fall [fɔl] <fell, fallen> I. *vi* 1. (*drop down*) caerse; (*rain, snow*) caer; (*tree*) venirse abajo; **to ~ flat** (*joke*) no tener gracia; (*plan, suggestion*) no tener éxito; **to ~ down the stairs** caerse por las escaleras; **to ~ flat on one's face** caerse de morros *inf* 2. (*decrease: prices*) bajar; (*demand*) descender 3. (*accent, stress*) recaer 4. (*in rank, on charts*) bajar 5. (*be defeated*) caer 6. *liter* (*die in battle*) caer 7. (*occur*) caer **~ on a Monday** caer en lunes 8. (*happen: darkness, silence*) caer; **night was ~ing** anochecía 9. (*belong*) **to ~ into a category** pertenecer a una categoría 10. (*hang down: hair, cloth*) colgar 11. (*go down: cliff, ground, road*) descender 12. + *adj* (*become*) **to ~ asleep** dormirse; **to ~ due** tocar (pagar); **to ~ ill** caer enfermo 13. (*enter a particular state*) **to ~ madly in love** (**with sb/sth**) enamorarse perdidamente (de alguien/algo); **to ~ out of favor** perder popularidad II. *n* 1. (*drop from a height*) caída *f* 2. (*decrease*) disminución *f*; **~ in temperature** descenso *m* de la temperatura 3. (*defeat*) caída *f* 4. (*autumn*) otoño *m* 5. **~s** (*waterfall*) cascada *f*; **Niagara Falls** las cataratas del Niágara 6. REL **the Fall** la Caída III. *adj* (*occurring in autumn: festival, sale*) en otoño; (*of autumn: colors, temperatures, weather*) otoñal

◆**fall back** *vi* 1. (*move backwards: crowd*) quedarse atrás 2. (*retreat: army*) replegarse 3. SPORTS (*runner*) perder posiciones

◆**fall behind** *vi* 1. (*become slower*) quedarse atrás 2. (*achieve less: team, country*) quedarse rezagado 3. (*fail to do sth on time*) retrasarse 4. SPORTS quedarse atrás

◆**fall down** *vi* 1. (*person*) caerse; (*building*) derrumbarse 2. (*be unsatisfactory: person, plan*) fallar

◆**fall for** *vt* **to ~ sb** enamorarse de alguien; **to ~ a trick** caer en una trampa

◆**fall in** *vi* 1. (*into water, hole*) caerse 2. (*collapse: roof, ceiling*) venirse abajo 3. MIL formar filas

◆**fall off** vi 1. (*become detached*) desprenderse 2. (*decrease*) reducirse

◆**fall out** vi 1. (*drop out: of container*) caer; (*teeth, hair*) caerse 2. inf (*argue*) pelearse 3. MIL romper filas

◆**fall over** I. vi insep caerse II. vt tropezarse con; **to ~ oneself to do sth** inf desvivirse por hacer algo

◆**fall through** vi fracasar

fallen ['fɔ·lən] adj caído, -a

false [fɔls] adj 1. (*untrue: idea, information*) falso, -a; **~ economy** falso ahorro m; **~ move** movimiento m en falso; **to take a ~ step** dar un paso en falso; **to give a ~ impression** dar una impresión equivocada; **to raise ~ hopes** crear falsas esperanzas 2. (*artificial: beard, eyelashes*) postizo, -a; **a ~ bottom** un doble fondo 3. (*name, address, identity*) falso, -a LAW, FIN; **~ accounting** falsificación f de la contabilidad; **under ~ pretenses** con engaños 4. (*insincere: smile, laugh, manner*) falso, -a; **~ modesty** falsa modestia f

falsehood ['fɔls·hʊd] n 1. (*untruth*) falsedad f 2. (*lie*) mentira f

false teeth npl dientes m pl postizos

falsetto [fɔl·'set·oʊ] I. n falsete m II. adv **to sing ~** cantar en falsete

falsify ['fɔl·sɪ·faɪ] vt falsificar

fame [feɪm] n fama f; **to rise to ~** hacerse famoso

familiar [fə·'mɪl·jər] adj 1. (*well-known*) familiar; (*face*) conocido, -a 2. (*acquainted*) familiarizado, -a; **to be ~ with sth** estar familiarizado con algo 3. (*friendly*) de familiaridad; **~ form of address** LING forma f de trato informal; **to be on ~ terms** (**with sb**) tener un trato de confianza (con alguien)

familiarize [fə·'mɪl·jə·raɪz] vt acostumbrar; **to ~ oneself with sth** familiarizarse con algo

family ['fæm·ə·li] <-ies> I. n familia f; **to be ~** ser familia; **to run in the ~** venir de familia; **to start a ~** formar una familia II. adj familiar

family allowance n Can subsidio m familiar

family doctor n médico m de cabecera

family man n (*enjoying family life*) hombre m casero; (*with wife and family*) padre m de familia

family name n apellido m

family planning n planificación f familiar

family tree n árbol m genealógico

famine ['fæm·ɪn] n hambruna f

famous ['feɪ·məs] adj famoso, -a; **to become ~ for sth** hacerse célebre por algo

famously adv **to get on ~** llevarse divinamente

fan¹ [fæn] I. n 1. (*hand-held*) abanico m 2. (*electrical*) ventilador m II. <-nn-> vt (*cool with fan*) abanicar; **to ~ oneself** abanicarse

fan² [fæn] n (*admirer: of person*) admirador(a) m(f); (*of team*) hincha mf; (*of music*) fan mf

fanatic [fə·'næt̬·ɪk] n 1. entusiasta mf 2. pej fanático, -a m, f

fanatical adj fanático, -a

fan belt n AUTO correa f del ventilador

fan club n club m de fans

fancy ['fæn·tsi] I. adj <-ier, -iest> 1. (*elaborate: decoration, frills*) de adorno 2. inf (*expensive*) carísimo, -a; **~ hotel** hotel m de lujo 3. (*whimsical: ideas, notions*) extravagante II. n <-ies> 1. (*liking*) **to take a ~ to sth/ sb** quedarse prendado de algo/alguien; **it tickled his ~** le hizo gracia 2. (*imagination*) fantasía f 3. (*whimsical idea*) capricho m III. <-ie-> vt (*imagine*) **~ (that)!** ¡lo que son las cosas!; **~ meeting you here!** ¡qué casualidad encontrarnos aquí!

fancy-free [ˌfæn·tsi·'fri] adj libre

fang [fæŋ] n (*of dog, lion*) colmillo m; (*of snake*) diente m

fan mail n cartas f pl de admiradores

fantastic [fæn·'tæs·tɪk] adj 1. (*excellent*) fantástico, -a 2. (*unbelievable: coincidence*) increíble; (*notion, plan*) absurdo, -a

fantasy ['fæn·tə·si] <-ies> n fantasía f

fanzine ['fæn·zin] n fanzine m

far [far] <farther, farthest or further, furthest> I. adv 1. (*a long distance*) lejos; **how ~ is it from Boston to Maine?** ¿qué distancia hay entre Boston y Maine?; ~ **from it** todo lo contrario **2.** (*distant in time*) **as ~ back as I remember...** hasta donde me alcanza la memoria...; **to be not ~ off sth** faltar poco para algo; **so ~** hasta ahora **3.** (*in progress*) **to go too ~** ir demasiado lejos **4.** (*much*) **~ better** mucho mejor; **to be the best by ~** ser el/la mejor con diferencia; **to be ~ too expensive** ser demasiado caro **5.** (*connecting adverbial phrase*) **as ~ as I know...** que yo sepa...; **as ~ as possible** en lo posible ▶ **so ~ so good** hasta ahora todo va bien **II.** *adj* lejano, -a; **in the ~ distance** a lo lejos; **the ~ left/right** la extrema izquierda/derecha

faraway ['far·ə·wer] *adj* **a ~ land** una tierra lejana

fare [fer] **I.** *n* **1.** (*for journey*) tarifa *f;* **one way ~** billete *m* [*or* pasaje *m*] **; round trip ~** billete *m* [*or* pasaje *m*] de ida y vuelta **2.** (*taxi passenger*) pasajero, -a *m, f* **3.** CULIN comida *f;* **simple home-style ~** comida *f* casera **II.** *vi* to ~ **badly/well** salir mal/bien parado

Far East *n* the ~ el Lejano Oriente

farewell [ˌfer·'wel] **I.** *interj form* adiós; **to bid ~ to sb/sth** despedirse de alguien/algo **II.** *n* despedida *f* **III.** *adj* de despedida

far-fetched [ˌfar·'fetʃt] *adj* inverosímil

farm [farm] **I.** *n* (*small*) granja *f*, hacienda *f* AmL, chacra *f* CSur, Perú; (*large*) hacienda *f* **II.** *vt* cultivar **III.** *vi* cultivar la tierra

farmer ['far·mər] *n* granjero, -a *m, f*, hacendado, -a *m, f*, chacarero, -a *m f* CSur, Perú

farm hand *n* mozo *m* de labranza

farmhouse *n* <-s> casa *f* de labranza

farmyard *n* corral *m*

far-off [ˌfar·'af] *adj* (*place, country*) lejano, -a; (*time*) remoto, -a

far-reaching [ˌfar·'ri·tʃɪŋ] *adj* de grandes repercusiones

farsighted [ˌfar·'saɪ·tɪd] *adj* (*decision, policy*) con visión de futuro

far-sighted *adj* MED hipermétrope

fart [fart] *sl* **I.** *n* pedo *m* **II.** *vi* tirarse un pedo

farther ['far·ðər] **I.** *adv comp of* **far** (*dis-*

tance) más allá; **~ away from...** más lejos de...; **~ down/up** más abajo/arriba **II.** *adj comp of* **far** más lejano, -a

farthest ['far·ðɪst] **I.** *adv superl of* **far** más lejos **II.** *adj superl of* **far** (*distance*) más lejano, -a; (*time*) más remoto, -a

fascinate ['fæs·ə·neɪt] *vt* fascinar

fascinating ['fæs·ə·neɪ·t̬ɪŋ] *adj* fascinante

fascination [ˌfæs·ə·'neɪ·ʃən] *n* fascinación *f*

fascist ['fæʃ·ɪst] **I.** *n* fascista *mf* **II.** *adj* fascista

fashion ['fæʃ·ən] **I.** *n* **1.** (*popular style*) moda *f;* **to be in ~** estar de moda; **to be out of ~** estar pasado de moda; **to be all the ~** estar muy de moda; **the latest ~** la última moda **2.** (*manner*) manera *f;* **in the usual ~** como de costumbre **II.** *vt* dar forma a; (*create*) crear

fashionable ['fæʃ·ə·nə·bəl] *adj* (*clothes, style*) moderno, -a; (*nightclub, restaurant*) de moda; (*person, set*) a la moda

fashion designer *n* diseñador(a) *m(f)* de moda

fashion show *n* desfile *m* de moda

fast[1] [fæst] **I.** <-er, -est> *adj* **1.** (*quick*) rápido, -a; **the ~ lane** el carril de adelantamiento; **to be a ~ worker** trabajar rápido **2.** (*clock*) **to be ~** ir adelantando **3.** (*firmly fixed*) fijo, -a; **to make ~, to make sth ~** (*to sth*) fijar algo (a algo) **II.** *adv* **1.** (*quickly*) rápidamente; **not so ~!** ¡no tan rápido! **2.** (*firmly*) firmemente; **to hold ~ to sth** agarrarse bien a algo **3.** (*deeply*) profundamente; **to be ~ asleep** estar profundamente dormido

fast[2] [fæst] **I.** *vi* (*go without food*) ayunar **II.** *n* (*period without food*) ayuno *m*

fasten ['fæs·ən] *vt* **1.** (*do up*) atar **2.** (*fix securely*) fijar, sujetar; **to ~ one's seatbelt** abrocharse el cinturón **3. to ~ sth together** (*with paper clip*) unir algo

fastener ['fæs·ə·nər] *n* cierre *m*

fat [fæt] **I.** *adj* **1.** gordo, -a; **to get ~** engordar **2.** (*thick*) grueso, -a **3.** (*large*) grande; **a ~ check** un cheque sustancioso ▶ **~ chance!** *inf* ¡para nada!, ¡ni soñarlo! **II.** *n* grasa *f;* **animal/vegetable ~** grasa animal/vegetal ▶ **to live off the ~ of the** <u>land</u> vivir a cuerpo de rey

fatal ['feɪṯ·əl] *adj* 1. (*causing death*) mortal 2. (*disastrous*) desastroso, -a 3. *liter* (*consequences*) funesto, -a

fatality [feɪ·'tæl·ə·ṯi] <-ies> *n* fatalidad *f*

fatally *adv* 1. (*causing death*) mortalmente; ~ **ill** enfermo de muerte 2. (*disastrously*) desastrosamente

fate [feɪt] *n* (*destiny*) destino *m*; (*one's end*) suerte *f*; **to meet one's** ~ hallar su destino; **a** ~ **worse than death** un destino peor que la muerte

fated ['feɪ·ṯɪd] *adj* predestinado, -a

fat-free *adj* sin grasas

fathead ['fæt·ˌhed] *n sl* imbécil *mf inf*

father ['fɑ·ðər] I. *n* 1. (*parent*) padre *m*; **to be like a** ~ **to sb** ser como un padre para alguien; **on your ~'s side** por parte paterna 2. (*founder*) fundador *m* 3. ~**s** *liter* (*ancestors*) antepasados *mpl* ▸ **like son, like ~, like son** de tal palo, tal astilla II. *vt* (*child*) engendrar; (*idea*) crear

fatherhood ['fɑ·ðər·hʊd] *n* paternidad *f*

father-in-law ['fɑ·ðər·ɪn·lɔ] <fathers--in-law *or* father-in-laws> *n* suegro *m*

fatherless ['fɑ·ðər·lɪs] *adj* huérfano, -a de padre

fatherly ['fɑ·ðər·li] *adj* paternal

Father's Day *n* Día *m* del Padre

fatigue [fə·'tig] I. *n* 1. (*tiredness*) cansancio *m*, fatiga *f* 2. TECH fatiga *f* 3. MIL faena *f* II. *vt* 1. *form* (*tire*) cansar 2. TECH (*weaken*) debilitar

fatten ['fæt·ən] *vt* engordar

fattening *adj* que hace engordar

fatty ['fæt·i] I. *adj* 1. (*food*) graso, -a 2. (*tissue*) adiposo, -a II. <-ies> *n inf* (*person*) gordinflón, -ona *m, f*

faucet ['fɔ·sɪt] *n* grifo *m*, bitoque *m Chile, Col, Méx*, canilla *f Río Pl*; **to turn the ~ on/off** abrir/cerrar el grifo

fault [fɔlt] I. *n* 1. (*responsibility*) culpa *f*; **it's not my ~** yo no tengo la culpa; **to be sb's ~** (*that...*) ser culpa de alguien (que...) 2. (*character weakness*) debilidad *f*; **to have its ~s** tener sus defectos 3. (*defect*) fallo *m* 4. GEO falla *f* 5. SPORTS falta *f*; **double ~** doble falta; **foot ~** falta de pie; **to call a ~** pitar una falta II. *vt* encontrar defectos en

faultless ['fɔlt·lɪs] *adj* impecable

faulty ['fɔl·ṯi] *adj* defectuoso, -a

favor ['feɪ·vər] I. *n* 1. (*approval*) favor *m*, aprobación *f*; **to be in ~ of sb/sth** estar a favor de alguien/algo; **to decide/vote in ~ of (doing) sth** decidir/votar a favor de (hacer) algo; **to be out of ~** no tener aceptación; **to reject sth in ~ of sth else** rechazar una cosa por otra cosa; **to find in ~ of sb** LAW fallar a favor de alguien; **to find ~ with sb** caer en gracia a alguien; **to win sb's ~** ganarse la simpatía de alguien 2. (*advantage*) **to have sth in one's ~** tener algo a favor 3. (*helpful act*) favor *m*, valedura *f Méx*; **to do sb a ~** hacer un favor a alguien; **do me a ~!** *inf* ¡hazme el favor! 4. (*small gift*) detalle *m* II. *vt* 1. (*prefer*) preferir 2. (*give advantage to*) favorecer

favorable ['feɪ·vər·ə·bəl] *adj* 1. (*approving*) favorable 2. (*advantageous*) ventajoso, -a (**to a**)

favorite ['feɪ·vər·ɪt] *adj, n* favorito, -a *m, f*

fawning ['fɔ·nɪŋ] *adj* adulador(a)

fax [fæks] I. *n* fax *m* II. *vt* mandar por fax

fax machine *n* fax *m*

fear [fɪr] I. *n* miedo *m*; **to have a ~ of sth** tener miedo de algo; ~ **of heights** miedo a las alturas; **for ~ that** por temor a que II. *vt* 1. (*be afraid of*) tener miedo de; **to have nothing to ~** no tener nada que temer 2. *form* (*feel concern*) temer ~ (**that...**) temer (que...) III. *vi liter* tener miedo; **never ~!** ¡pierde cuidado!

fearful ['fɪr·fəl] *adj* 1. (*anxious*) temeroso, -a; ~ **of doing sth** temeroso de hacer algo 2. (*terrible: pain, accident*) terrible 3. *inf* (*very bad: noise, mess*) horrendo, -a

feasibility [ˌfi·zə·'bɪl·ə·ṯi] *n* viabilidad *f*

feasible ['fi·zə·bəl] *adj* 1. (*plan*) factible 2. (*story*) plausible

feast [fist] I. *n* 1. (*meal*) banquete *m*; **a ~ for the eye** una fiesta para los ojos 2. REL festividad *f* II. *vi, vt* **to ~ on sth** darse un banquete con algo; **to ~ one's eyes on sth** regalarse la vista con algo

feat [fit] *n* hazaña *f*; ~ **of agility** proeza *f* de agilidad; ~ **of engineering** logro *m* de la ingeniería

feather ['feð·ər] I. *n* pluma *f* II. *vt* **to ~ one's own nest** barrer para dentro

featherweight ['feð·ər·weɪt] n SPORTS peso m pluma

feature ['fi·tʃər] I. n 1. (*distinguishing attribute*) característica f; (*specialty*) peculiaridad f; **sb's/sth's best** ~ lo mejor de alguien/algo; **a distinguishing** ~ un rasgo distintivo 2. ~s (*of face*) facciones fpl 3. (*in newspaper, magazine*) reportaje m 4. CINE largometraje m II. vt 1. (*have as performer, star*) presentar 2. (*give special prominence to*) ofrecer (como atracción principal); **to** ~ **sth** (*article, report*) destacar algo III. vi 1. (*appear*) constar; **to** ~ **in...** constar en... 2. (*be an actor in*) **to** ~ **in a movie** aparecer en una película

feature film n largometraje m

feature story n reportaje m

February ['feb·ru·er·i] n febrero m; s. a. **April**

federal ['fed·ər·əl] adj federal; ~ **republic** república f federal

federation [ˌfed·ə·'reɪ·ʃən] n federación f

fed up adj inf harto, -a; **to be** ~ **with sth/sb** estar harto de algo/alguien

fee [fi] n (*for doctor, lawyer*) honorarios mpl; (*for membership*) cuota f de miembro; (*for school, university*) tasas f pl de matrícula; **to charge/receive a** ~ **for sth** cobrar/recibir unos honorarios por algo

feeble ['fi·bəl] adj (*person, attempt*) débil; (*performance*) flojo, -a

feeble-minded [ˌfi·bl·'maɪn·dɪd] adj lelo, -a

feed [fid] <fed> I. vt 1. (*give food to: person, animal*) alimentar; (*plant*) nutrir; (*baby*) amamantar; **to** ~ **the fire** avivar el fuego 2. (*provide food for: family, country*) dar de comer a 3. (*supply*) proporcionar II. vi alimentarse; (*baby*) mamar III. n 1. (*for farm animals*) pienso m; **cattle** ~ pienso para ganado 2. inf (*meal*) comida f 3. TECH tubo m de alimentación

◆**feed on** vt insep, a. fig alimentarse de

◆**feed up** vt (*person*) alimentar; (*animal*) cebar

feedback ['fid·bæk] n 1. (*evaluation*) reacción f; **positive/negative** ~ reacción f positiva/negativa 2. ELEC reali-

mentación f

feeder n 1. TECH alimentador m 2. (*river*) afluente m; ~ **road** carretera f de acceso

feel [fil] <felt> I. vi 1. + adj/n (*sensation or emotion*) sentir; **to** ~ **well** sentirse bien; **to** ~ **hot/cold** tener calor/frío; **to** ~ **hungry/thirsty** tener hambre/sed; **to** ~ **certain/convinced** estar seguro/convencido; **to** ~ **as if...** sentirse como si... +subj; **to** ~ **like a walk** tener ganas de dar un paseo; **to** ~ **free to do sth** sentirse libre para hacer algo; **to** ~ **one's age** notar el peso de los años; **it** ~**s wonderful/awful** me parece maravilloso/fatal; **how do you** ~ **about him?** ¿qué opinas de él?; **how would you** ~ **if...?** ¿qué te parece si...? 2. + adj (*seem*) parecer 3. (*search*) **to** ~ (**around**) **somewhere** buscar palpando por algún sitio II. vt 1. (*experience*) experimentar; **not to** ~ **a thing** no sentir nada; **to** ~ **the cold/heat** sentir frío/calor 2. (*think, believe*) **to** ~ (**that**)... creer (que)...; **to** ~ **it appropriate/necessary to do sth** considerar adecuado/necesario hacer algo 3. (*touch*) tocar; (*pulse*) tomar III. n 1. (*texture*) textura f; **the** ~ **of sth** el tacto de algo 2. (*act of touching*) tacto m 3. (*character, atmosphere*) ambiente m 4. (*natural talent*) talento m natural; **to have a** ~ **for sth** tener talento natural para algo; **to get the** ~ **of sth** acostumbrarse a algo

◆**feel for** vt **to** ~ ~ **sb** sentirlo por alguien, compadecer a alguien

feeling ['fi·lɪŋ] n 1. (*emotion*) sentimiento m; **mixed** ~**s** sentimientos entremezclados [or encontrados]; **to hurt sb's** ~**s** herir los sentimientos de alguien 2. (*sensation*) sensación f; **a dizzy** ~ una sensación de vértigo 3. (*impression*) impresión f; **to have the** ~ (**that**)... tener la impresión (de que)...; **to have a bad** ~ **about sth/sb** tener un mal presentimiento acerca de algo/alguien 4. (*opinion*) opinión f; **to have strong** ~**s about sth** tener firmes convicciones sobre algo 5. (*strong emotion*) sentimiento m; **to say sth with** ~ decir algo con emoción 6. (*physical sensation*) sensibilidad f

feet [fiːt] *n pl of* **foot**

fell¹ [fel] *pt of* **fall**

fell² [fel] *vt* **1.** (*cut down*) talar **2.** (*knock down: boxer*) derribar

fell³ [fel] *adj* HIST feroz, terrible ▶ **at** [*or* **in**] **one ~** <u>swoop</u> de un solo golpe

fellow ['fel·oʊ] **I.** *n* **1.** *inf* (*man*) tío *m*; **an odd ~** un tipo raro **2.** UNIV profesor(a) *m(f)* **3.** *form* (*colleague*) compañero, -a *m, f* **II.** *adj* **~ student** compañero, -a *m, f* de clase

fellow member *n* consocio *mf*

fellowship ['fel·oʊ·ʃɪp] *n* **1.** (*comradely feeling*) compañerismo *m* **2.** *form* (*group*) asociación *f*, sociedad *f* **3.** UNIV **research ~** beca *f* de investigación

felon ['fel·ən] *n* criminal *mf*

felony ['fel·ə·ni] <-ies> *n* crimen *m*

felt¹ [felt] *pt, pp of* **feel**

felt² [felt] **I.** *n* (*material*) fieltro *m* **II.** *adj* de fieltro

female ['fiː·meɪl] **I.** *adj* femenino, -a; ZOOL, TECH hembra **II.** *n* (*woman*) mujer *f*; ZOOL hembra *f*

feminine ['fem·ə·nɪn] **I.** *adj* femenino, -a **II.** *n* LING **the ~** el femenino

femininity [ˌfem·ə·'nɪn·ə·ti] *n* feminidad *f*

feminist ['fem·ɪ·nɪst] **I.** *n* feminista *mf* **II.** *adj* feminista

fence [fens] **I.** *n* (*barrier*) cerca *f*; **to sit on the ~** nadar entre dos aguas **II.** *vi* SPORTS practicar esgrima **III.** *vt* (*enclose*) cercar

fencer *n* esgrimista *mf*

fencing *n* esgrima *f*

ferocious [fə·'roʊ·ʃəs] *adj* (*battle, criticism*) feroz; (*temper*) violento, -a

Ferris wheel ['fer·ɪs·ˌhwiːl] *n* noria *f*

ferry ['fer·i] <-ies> **I.** *n* (*ship*) ferry *m*; (*smaller*) balsa *f* **II.** *vt* (*in boat*) llevar en barca

ferryman <-men> *n* barquero *m*

fertile ['fɜr·təl] *adj a. fig* fértil

fertility [fər·'tɪl·ə·ti] *n* fertilidad *f*

fertilize ['fɜr·təl·aɪz] *vt* **1.** BIO fertilizar **2.** AGR abonar

fertilizer ['fɜr·təl·aɪ·zər] *n* fertilizante *m*

festival ['fes·tɪ·vəl] *n* **1.** (*special event*) festival *m* **2.** REL festividad *f*, fiesta *f*

festive ['fes·tɪv] *adj* festivo, -a

festivity [fes·'tɪv·ə·ti] <-ies> *n* **1.** **festivities** (*festive activities*) festejos *mpl* **2.** (*festival*) fiesta *f*

fetch [fetʃ] *vt* **1.** (*bring back*) traer; **to ~ sb sth** (*from somewhere*) traer algo a alguien (de algún sitio) **2.** (*be sold for*) venderse por

fetching ['fetʃ·ɪŋ] *adj* atractivo, -a

fetus ['fiː·təs] *n* feto *m*

feud [fjuːd] **I.** *n* enemistad *f* (heredada); **a family ~** una enemistad entre familias **II.** *vi* pelearse

fever ['fiː·vər] *n* **1.** MED fiebre *f*; **to have** [*or* **run**] **a ~** tener fiebre **2.** (*excited state*) emoción *f*

feverish ['fiː·vər·ɪʃ] *adj* **1.** MED con fiebre **2.** (*frantic*) febril

few [fjuː] <-er, -est> **I.** *adj det* **1.** (*small number*) pocos, pocas; **one of her ~ friends** uno de sus pocos amigos; **quite a ~ people** bastante gente; **not ~er than 100 people** no menos de 100 personas; **to be ~ and far between** ser poquísimos, ser contadísimos **2.** (*some*) algunos, algunas **II.** *pron* pocos, pocas; **a ~** unos pocos; **I'd like a ~ more** quisiera unos pocos más; **the ~ who have the book** los pocos que tienen el libro; **the happy/lucky ~** los pocos felices/afortunados

fiancé [ˌfiː·ɑn·'seɪ] *n* prometido *m*

fiancée [ˌfiː·ɑn·'seɪ] *n* prometida *f*

fib [fɪb] <-bb-> *inf* **I.** *vi* decir mentirijillas **II.** *n* mentirijilla *f*, pepa *f And*

fibber ['fɪb·ər] *n* mentirosillo, -a *m, f*

fiber ['faɪ·bər] *n* **1.** fibra *f* **2.** *fig* carácter *m*

fiberglass ['faɪ·bər·ˌglæs] *n* fibra *f* de vidrio

fickle ['fɪk·l] *adj* inconstante

fiction ['fɪk·ʃən] *n* **1.** *a.* LIT ficción *f* **2.** (*false statement*) invención *f*

fictional ['fɪk·ʃə·nəl] *adj* ficticio, -a

fictitious [fɪk·'tɪʃ·əs] *adj* **1.** (*false, untrue*) falso, -a **2.** (*imaginary*) ficticio, -a; **~ character** personaje *m* de ficción

fiddle ['fɪd·l] **I.** *vi* **1.** (*play the violin*) tocar el violín **2. to ~ (around) with sth** (*fidget with*) juguetear con algo **II.** *n* **1.** (*violin*) violín *m*; **to play the ~** tocar el violín **2.** (*fraud*) trampa *f*

fidget ['fɪdʒ-ɪt] I. *vi* no parar quieto *inf* II. *n* persona *f* inquieta

fidgety ['fɪdʒ-ɪ-t̮i] *adj* inquieto, -a

fiefdom ['fif-dəm] *n* feudo *m*

field [fild] I. *n* 1. *a.* ELEC, AGR, SPORTS campo *m;* (*meadow*) prado *m* 2. + *sing/ pl vb* (*contestants*) competidores *mpl;* **to play the ~** *fig* tantear el terreno 3. (*sphere of activity*) esfera *f;* **it's not my ~** no es mi campo 4. COMPUT campo *m* II. *vt* 1. (*return*) **to ~ the ball** recoger la pelota**; to ~ a question** sortear una pregunta 2. (*candidate*) presentar

field day *n* 1. SPORTS día *m* de competición 2. MIL día de maniobras *fpl* ► to **have a ~** divertirse muchísimo

fielder ['fil-dər] *n* SPORTS fildeador(a) *m(f) (una de las posiciones en béisbol)*

field glasses *n* prismáticos *mpl*

field mouse *n* ratón *m* de campo

fieldwork ['fild-ˌwɜrk] *n* trabajo *m* de campo

fieldworker *n* investigador(a) *m(f)* de campo

fierce [fɪrs] *adj* <-er, -est> 1. (*animal*) salvaje 2. (*competition, opposition*) intenso, -a; (*debate, discussion*) acalorado, -a; (*wind*) fuerte 3. *inf* (*hard*) difícil

fiery ['faɪr-i] <-ier, -iest> *adj* 1. (*heat*) abrasador(a) 2. (*passionate*) apasionado, -a 3. (*very spicy*) muy picante

fifteen [ˌfɪf·'tin] I. *adj* quince II. *n* quince *m; s. a.* **eight**

fifteenth I. *adj* decimoquinto, -a II. *n* 1. (*order*) decimoquinto, -a *m, f* 2. (*date*) quince *m* 3. (*fraction*) quinceavo *m;* (*part*) decimoquinta parte *f; s. a.* **eighth**

fifth [frfθ] I. *adj* quinto, -a II. *n* 1. (*order*) quinto, -a *m, f* 2. (*date*) cinco *m* 3. (*fraction*) quinto *m;* (*part*) quinta parte *f; s. a.* **eighth**

fiftieth ['fɪf·ti·əθ] I. *adj* quincuagésimo, -a II. *n* (*order*) quincuagésimo, -a *m, f;* (*fraction*) quincuagésimo *m;* (*part*) quincuagésima parte *f; s. a.* **eighth**

fifty ['fɪf·ti] I. *adj* cincuenta II. <-ies> *n* cincuenta *m; s. a.* **eighty**

fig [fɪg] *n* 1. (*fruit*) higo *m* 2. (*tree*) higuera *f* ► **to be not worth a ~** no valer nada

fight [faɪt] I. *n* 1. (*physical*) pelea *f;* (*argument*) disputa *f;* **to put up a ~** defenderse bien 2. MIL combate *m* 3. (*struggle*) lucha *f* 4. (*spirit*) combatividad *f* II. <fought, fought> *vi* 1. (*exchange blows*) pelear; MIL combatir; **to ~ with each other** pelearse; **to ~ with sb** (*against*) luchar contra alguien; (*on same side*) luchar junto a alguien 2. (*dispute*) discutir; **to ~ about sth** discutir sobre algo 3. (*struggle to overcome*) luchar; **for/against** por/contra) III. *vt* 1. (*exchange blows with, argue with*) pelearse con 2. (*wage war, do battle*) luchar con; **to ~ a battle** librar una batalla; **to ~ a duel** batirse en duelo 3. (*struggle to overcome*) combatir; **to ~ a case** LAW llevar un caso a los tribunales 4. (*struggle to obtain*) **to ~ one's way through the crowd** hacerse paso entre la multitud; **to ~ one's way to the top** hacerse camino luchando hasta la cima

◆**fight back** I. *vi* (*defend oneself*) defenderse; (*counterattack*) contraatacar II. *vt* **to ~ one's tears** contener las lágrimas

◆**fight off** *vt* (*repel*) rechazar; (*master, resist*) resistir

fighter ['faɪ-t̮ər] *n* 1. (*person*) luchador(a) *m(f)* 2. AVIAT caza *m*

fighting ['faɪ-t̮ɪŋ] I. *n* lucha *f;* (*battle*) combate *m* II. *adj* combativo, -a ► **there's a ~ chance that...** existen grandes posibilidades de que... +*subj*

figurative ['fɪg-jər-ə-t̮ɪv] *adj* 1. LING figurado, -a 2. ART figurativo, -a

figuratively *adv* en sentido figurado

figure ['fɪg-jər] I. *n* 1. (*shape*) figura *f;* **mother ~** figura materna; **to cut a fine ~** causar buena impresión; **to keep one's ~** guardar la línea 2. ART estatua *f;* (*human being*) figura *f* 3. (*numeral*) cifra *f;* **to have a head for ~s** ser bueno para los números; **in round ~s** en cifras redondas 4. (*price*) precio *m* 5. (*diagram*) figura *f;* (*illustration*) ilustración *f* II. *vt* 1. (*think*) figurarse; **to ~ that...** figurarse... 2. (*in diagram*) representar 3. (*calculate*) calcular III. *vi* (*feature*) figurar; **to ~ as sth/sb** figurar como algo/alguien; **that ~s!** es natural

figure out vt (comprehend) entender; (work out) resolver

figure skating n patinaje m artístico

Fiji ['fiːdʒi] n the ~ Islands las Islas Fiji

file¹ [faɪl] I. n 1. (folder) carpeta f 2. (record) expediente m; to open a ~ abrir un expediente; to keep sth on ~ guardar algo archivado 3. COMPUT fichero m, archivo m 4. (row) fila f; in single ~ en fila india II. vt 1. (record) archivar, failear AmC, RíoPl 2. (present: claim, complaint) presentar III. vi 1. LAW to ~ for divorce presentar una demanda de divorcio 2. (move in line) desfilar

◆**file in** vi entrar en fila

◆**file out** vi salir en fila

file² [faɪl] I. n (tool) lima f II. vt limar III. vi to ~ sth down limar algo

file name n nombre m de archivo [or fichero]

filigree ['fɪlɪɡriː] n filigrana f

filing ['faɪlɪŋ] n 1. (archiving) clasificación f 2. LAW presentación f 3. ~s (bits of metal) limaduras fpl

filing cabinet n archivador m

fill [fɪl] I. vt 1. (make full) llenar; (space) ocupar; to ~ a vacancy cubrir una vacante; to ~ a need satisfacer una necesidad 2. (seal) empastar, emplomar AmL 3. CULIN rellenar 4. (fulfil: order, requirement) cumplir II. vi llenarse III. n 1. to drink/eat one's ~ hartarse de beber/comer 2. (dirt) relleno m

◆**fill in** I. vt 1. (seal opening) llenar 2. (document) rellenar 3. (color in) colorear 4. (inform) informar; to fill sb in on the details poner a alguien al corriente de los detalles 5. (time) ocupar II. vi to ~ (for sb) hacer las veces (de alguien)

◆**fill out** I. vt (document) rellenar II. vi (put on weight) engordar

◆**fill up** I. vt llenar; (completely) colmar II. vi llenarse

fillet ['fɪlɪt] I. n filete m II. vt cortar en filetes

filling n 1. (substance) relleno m 2. (in tooth) empaste m, emplomadura f AmL II. adj sólido, -a; to be ~ que llena (el estómago)

filling station n gasolinera f, bencine-

ra f Chile, grifo m Perú

film [fɪlm] I. n 1. PHOT, CINE película f; to see [or watch] a ~ ver una película 2. (fine coating) capa f; a ~ of oil una película de aceite II. vt filmar III. vi rodar

film buff n cinéfilo, -a m, f

film camera n cámara f cinematográfica

film star n estrella f de cine

film studio n estudio m de cine

filter ['fɪltər] I. n filtro m II. vt filtrar III. vi filtrarse

◆**filter out** vi llegar a saberse II. vt quitar filtrando

◆**filter through** vi filtrarse

filter paper n papel m de filtro

filter tip n filtro m

filth [fɪlθ] n 1. (dirt) mugre f 2. (obscenity) obscenidad f

filthy ['fɪlθi] I. adj 1. (very dirty) inmundo, -a 2. (obscene) obsceno, -a II. adv inf to be ~ rich estar forrado

fin [fɪn] n aleta f

final ['faɪnəl] I. adj 1. (last) final 2. (irrevocable) definitivo, -a; to have the ~ say (on sth) tener la última palabra (sobre algo); and that's ~ inf sanseacabó II. n 1. SPORTS final f; to get (through) to the ~s llegar a la final 2. pl UNIV exámenes m de fin de carrera pl

finale [fɪ'næli] n final m; grand ~ gran escena final

finalist ['faɪnəlɪst] n finalista mf

finalize ['faɪnəlaɪz] vt ultimar

finally ['faɪnəli] adv 1. (at long last) finalmente; (expressing impatience) por fin 2. (in conclusion) en conclusión

finance ['faɪnænts] vt financiar

financial [faɪ'næntʃəl] adj financiero, -a; sb's ~ affairs los asuntos financieros de alguien

finch [fɪntʃ] n ZOOL pinzón m

find [faɪnd] I. <found, found> vt 1. (lost object, person) encontrar 2. (locate) localizar, hallar; to be nowhere to be found no encontrarse por ningún sitio; to ~ no reason why... no hallar razón alguna por la que algo...; to ~ (the) time sacar tiempo inf; to ~ the strength (to do sth) hallar las fuerzas (para hacer algo) 3. (experience) sentir; to ~ oneself

alone sentirse solo **4.** (*conclude*) **to ~ sb guilty/innocent** declarar a alguien culpable/inocente **5.** (*discover*) descubrir **II.** n hallazgo m

◆**find out I.** vt descubrir; (*dishonesty*) desenmascarar; **to ~ when/where/who...** averiguar cuándo/dónde/quién... **II.** vi to ~ **about sth/sb** informarse sobre algo/alguien

finder ['faɪn·dər] n (*of sth unknown*) descubridor(a) m(f); (*of sth lost*) persona f que encuentra (algo)

finding ['faɪn·dɪŋ] n **1.** LAW fallo m **2.** (*recommendation*) recomendación f **3.** (*discovery*) descubrimiento m

fine[1] [faɪn] **I.** adj **1.** (*slender, light*) fino, -a; (*feature*) delicado, -a; (*nuance*) sutil **2.** (*good*) bueno, -a; (*satisfactory*) satisfactorio, -a; ~ **weather** buen tiempo m; **how are you? — I'm ~, thanks** ¿qué tal estás? — bien, gracias; **to be ~ by sb** estar bien para alguien **3.** (*excellent*) excelente **II.** adv **1.** (*all right*) muy bien; **to feel ~** sentirse bien; **to work ~** funcionar bien **2.** (*fine-grained*) fino, -a

fine[2] [faɪn] **I.** n (*penalty*) multa f, boleta f AmS **II.** vt (*order to pay penalty*) multar

fine arts n bellas artes fpl

finger ['fɪŋ·gər] **I.** n dedo m; **little/middle** ~ dedo meñique/corazón ▶ **to have sb wrapped around one's little** ~ hacer que alguien baile al son que le tocan; **to keep one's ~s crossed** tener los dedos cruzados; **to lay a ~ on sb** poner la mano encima a alguien **II.** vt **1.** (*touch*) manosear **2.** sl (*reveal*) delatar

fingernail n uña f

fingerprint n huella f dactilar

fingertip n punta f del dedo

finish ['fɪn·ɪʃ] **I.** n **1.** (*end*) final m, fin m; SPORTS meta f **2.** (*sealing, varnishing: of fabric*) acabado m; (*of furniture*) pulido m **II.** vi terminar(se), acabar(se); **to ~ doing sth** terminar de hacer algo **III.** vt **1.** (*bring to end*) terminar, acabar; **to ~ a sentence** completar una oración **2.** (*make final touches to*) acabar

◆**finish off I.** vt **1.** (*end*) terminar, acabar, rematar; (*use up*) terminar **2.** (*defeat*) acabar con **3.** inf (*murder*) liquidar **II.** vi concluir

◆**finish up I.** vi to ~ **at** ir a parar a **II.** vt (*food, drink*) terminar

◆**finish with** vt terminar con; **to ~ sb** romper con alguien

finished adj (*product*) terminado, -a, acabado, -a

finishing line n, **finishing post** n línea f de meta

finite ['faɪ·naɪt] adj a. LING finito, -a

fir [fɜr] n abeto m

fire ['faɪr] **I.** n **1.** (*flames*) fuego m; (*in fireplace*) lumbre f; (*accidental*) incendio m; **to set sth on** ~ prender fuego a algo; **to catch** ~ encenderse **2.** TECH calefacción f; (*stove*) hornillo m **3.** MIL **to open** ~ **on sb** abrir fuego contra alguien; **to be under** ~ MIL estar en la línea de fuego; fig ser criticado ▶ **to set the world on** ~ hacerse famoso; **to play with** ~ jugar con fuego **II.** vt **1.** (*burn*) encender; (*ceramics*) cocer **2.** (*weapon*) disparar **3.** inf (*dismiss*) despedir, botar AmL, fletar Arg **III.** vi **1.** (*with gun*) disparar; **to ~ at sb** disparar contra alguien **2.** AUTO encenderse

fire alarm n alarma f contra incendios

firearm n arma f de fuego

firecracker n petardo m

fire department n cuerpo m de bomberos

fire engine n coche m de bomberos

fire escape n escalera f de incendios

fire extinguisher n extintor m

firefighter n bombero mf

firefly n luciérnaga f, cocuyo m AmL

fire house n parque m de bomberos

fireman <-men> n bombero m

fireplace n chimenea f, hogar m

fireproof adj a prueba de incendios

fireside n hogar m

fire station n parque m de bomberos

firewoman <-women> n mujer f bombero

firewood n leña f

fireworks npl **1.** fuegos m artificiales pl **2.** pl, fig explosión f (de cólera)

firm[1] [fɜrm] **I.** adj **1.** (*secure*) firme;

(*strong*) fuerte; **a ~ offer** una oferta en firme **2.** (*dense, solid*) duro, -a **3.** (*resolute*) decidido, -a **II.** *adv* firmemente; **to stand ~** mantenerse firme

firm² [fɜrm] *n* (*company*) empresa *f;* **law ~** bufete *m* de abogados

first [fɜrst] **I.** *adj* (*earliest*) primero, -a; **for the ~ time** por primera vez; **at ~ sight** a primera vista; **the ~ of December/December ~** el primero de diciembre, el uno de diciembre *inf* ▶ **~ and foremost** ante todo **II.** *adv* primero; (*firstly*) en primer lugar; **~ of all** ante todo; **at ~** al principio; **to go head ~** meterse de cabeza ▶ **~ come ~ served** *inf* por orden de llegada **III.** *n* **the ~** el primero, la primera

first aid *n* primeros auxilios *mpl*

first class I. *n* primera clase *f* **II.** *adv* **to travel ~** viajar en primera

first-class *adj* de primera clase

first floor *n* planta *f* baja

firstly [ˈfɜrst·li] *adv* en primer lugar

first name *n* nombre *m* (de pila)

first night *n* noche *f* de estreno

first-rate [ˌfɜrst·ˈreɪt] *adj* de primer orden

fish [fɪʃ] **I.** *<-(es)> n* **1.** zool pez *m* **2.** culin pescado *m* ▶ **(like) a ~ out of water** como pez fuera del agua **II.** *vi* pescar; **to ~ for compliments** andar a la caza de cumplidos **III.** *vt* pescar

fishbone [ˈfɪʃ·boʊn] *n* espina *f* (de pescado)

fishcake [ˈfɪʃ·keɪk] *n* croqueta *f* de pescado

fisherman [ˈfɪʃ·ər·mən] *<-men> n* pescador *m*

fishing I. *n* pesca *f* **II.** *adj* pesquero, -a

fishing line *n* sedal *m*

fishpond [ˈfɪʃ·pɑnd] *n* estanque *m* para peces

fishy [ˈfɪʃ·i] *<-ier, -iest> adj* **1.** (*taste*) que sabe a pescado; (*smell*) que huele a pescado **2.** *inf* (*dubious*) dudoso, -a ▶ **to smell ~** oler a chamusquina

fission [ˈfɪʃ·ən] *n* phys fisión *f;* bio escisión *f*

fissure [ˈfɪʃ·ər] *n* fisura *f*

fist [fɪst] *n* puño *m;* **to clench one's ~s** cerrar los puños

fistfight *n* pelea *f;* **to have a ~** liarse a golpes *inf*

fit¹ [fɪt] **I.** *<-tt-> adj* **1.** (*apt, suitable*) apto, -a, apropiado, -a; (*competent*) capaz; **~ to eat** bueno para comer **2.** sports en forma **3.** med sano, -a ▶ **to be ~ to be tied** estar fuera de sí **II.** *<-tt-> vt* **1.** (*adapt*) ajustar **2.** (*clothes*) quedar bien **3.** (*facts*) corresponder con **4.** tech caber en, encajar en **III.** *vi <-tt-> * **1.** (*be correct size*) ir bien **2.** (*correspond*) corresponder **IV.** *n* ajuste *m*

◆ **fit in I.** *vi* **1.** (*conform*) encajar **2.** (*get along well*) llevarse bien **II.** *vt* tener tiempo para

◆ **fit out** *vt* equipar

◆ **fit together** *vi* encajar

◆ **fit up** *vt* equipar

fit² [fɪt] *n* **1.** med ataque *m;* **coughing ~** acceso *m* de tos **2.** (*outburst of rage*) arranque *m;* **they were in ~s of laughter** se morían de (la) risa

fitness [ˈfɪt·nɪs] *n* **1.** (*good condition*) (buena) condición *f* física; (*health*) (buena) salud *f* **2.** (*competence, suitability*) conveniencia *f*

fitted [ˈfɪt·ɪd] *adj* (*adapted, suitable*) idóneo, -a; (*tailor-made*) a medida

fitting [ˈfɪt·ɪŋ] **I.** *n* **1.** **~s** (*fixtures*) accesorios *mpl* **2.** (*of clothes*) prueba *f* **II.** *adj* apropiado, -a

five [faɪv] **I.** *adj* cinco **II.** *n* cinco *m;* **gimme ~!** *sl* ¡choca esos cinco!; *s. a.* **eight**

fiver [ˈfaɪ·vər] *n inf* billete *m* de cinco dólares

fix [fɪks] **I.** *vt* **1.** (*repair*) arreglar **2.** (*fasten*) sujetar; **to ~ one's eyes on sb** fijar los ojos en alguien **3.** (*determine*) fijar **4.** (*arrange*) arreglar **5.** *inf* (*lunch, dinner*) preparar **6.** *inf* (*manipulate: election, result*) amañar **7.** *inf* (*take revenge on*) ajustar las cuentas con; **I'll ~ him** me las pagará **8.** phys, phot (*color*) fijar **II.** *n inf* (*dilemma*) aprieto *m*

◆ **fix on** *vt* **1.** (*choose*) escoger **2.** (*make definite*) fijar

◆ **fix up** *vt* **1.** (*supply with*) **to fix sb up (with sth)** proveer a alguien (de algo) **2.** *inf* (*arrange a date*) **to fix sb up (with sb)** arreglárselo a alguien (con alguien) **3.** (*repair*) arreglar

fixed *adj* fijo, -a; **to be of no ~ abode** LAW no tener domicilio permanente

fixings *npl inf* guarnición *f*

fixture ['fɪkst·ʃər] *n* (*in bathroom and kitchen*) instalación *f* fija; **light ~s** iluminación *f*

fizz [fɪz] **I.** *vi* burbujear **II.** *n* **1.** (*bubble, frothiness*) efervescencia *f* **2.** (*soda*) gaseosa *f*

fizzle ['fɪz·l] *vi* chisporrotear

fizzy ['fɪz·i] <-ier, -iest> *adj* (*bubbly*) efervescente; (*carbonated*) gaseoso, -a

FL *n*, **Fla.** *n abbr of* **Florida** Florida *f*

flabby ['flæb·i] <-ier, -iest> *adj pej* **1.** (*body*) fofo, -a **2.** (*weak*) débil

flag[1] [flæg] **I.** *n* **1.** (*national*) bandera *f*; (*pennant*) estandarte *m*; **to raise a ~** izar una bandera **2.** (*marker*) señalizador *m* **II.** <-gg-> *vt* (*mark*) señalar; (*label computer data*) etiquetar **III.** <-gg-> *vi* flaquear

flag[2] [flæg] *n* (*stone*) losa *f*

flagpole ['flæg·poʊl] *n* asta *f* (de una bandera)

flagrant ['fleɪ·grənt] *adj* flagrante

flair [fler] *n* **1.** (*genius*) don *m*, talento *m* **2.** (*style*) estilo *m*

flake [fleɪk] **I.** *vi* (*skin*) pelarse; (*paint*) desconcharse; (*wood*) astillarse; (*plaster*) descascararse **II.** *n* (*shaving, sliver*) viruta *f*; (*of skin*) escama *f*; (*of snow*) copo *m*

◆**flake out** *vi sl* caer rendido

flaky ['fleɪ·ki] <-ier, -iest> *adj* **1.** (*skin*) escamoso, -a; (*paint*) de láminas **2.** *sl* (*strange*) chiflado, -a

flamboyant [flæm·'bɔɪ·ənt] *adj* (*manner, person*) exuberante; (*air, clothes*) vistoso, -a

flame [fleɪm] **I.** *n* **1.** llama *f*; **to be in ~s** arder en llamas; **to burst into ~** estallar en llamas **2.** (*lover*) (*old*) **~** antiguo amor *m* **II.** *vi* (*blaze, burn*) llamear; (*glare*) brillar

flaming ['fleɪ·mɪŋ] *adj* **1.** (*burning*) en llamas *fig* (*quarrel*) acalorado, -a

flamingo [flə·'mɪŋ·goʊ] <-(e)s> *n* flamenco *m*

flammable ['flæm·ə·bəl] *adj* inflamable

flan [flæn] *n* tarta *f*

Flanders ['flæn·dərz] *n* Flandes *m*

flannel ['flæn·l] *n* **1.** (*material*) franela *f* **2.** **~s** (*trousers*) pantalones *m pl* de franela

flap [flæp] **I.** <-pp-> *vt* (*wings*) batir; (*shake*) sacudir **II.** <-pp-> *vi* **1.** (*wings*) aletear; (*flag*) ondear **2.** *inf* (*become nervous*) agitarse **III.** *n* **1.** (*of cloth*) faldón *m*; (*of skin*) colgajo *m*; (*of pocket, envelope*) solapa *f*; (*of table*) hoja *f* **2.** AVIAT flap *m* **3.** (*of wing*) aleteo *m* **4.** *inf* (*commotion*) jaleo *m*; **to cause a ~** armar un lío

flare [fler] **I.** *n* **1.** (*blaze*) llamarada *f* **2.** (*signal*) cohete *m* de señales **3.** MIL bengala *f* **4.** (*of clothes*) vuelo *m* **II.** *vi* (*blaze*) llamear; (*light*) resplandecer **III.** *vt* **to ~ one's nostrils** resoplar

flash [flæʃ] **I.** *vt* **1.** (*shine: light*) enfocar; **to ~ a light in sb's eyes** dirigir un rayo de luz a los ojos de alguien **2.** (*show quickly*) mostrar (rápidamente) **3.** (*communicate*) transmitir; (*smile, look*) lanzar **II.** *vi* **1.** (*lightning*) relampaguear; *fig* (*eyes*) brillar **2.** *sl* (*expose oneself in public*) exhibirse **III.** *n* **1.** (*of light*) destello *m*; **~ of lightning** relámpago *m* **2.** PHOT flash *m* ▶ **in a ~** en un instante **IV.** <-est> *adj sl* llamativo, -a

flashback ['flæʃ·bæk] *n* CINE, LIT, THEAT escena *f* retrospectiva, flashback *m*

flashbulb ['flæʃ·bʌlb] *n* bombilla *f* de flash

flasher ['flæʃ·ər] *n sl* exhibicionista *m*

flashgun ['flæʃ·gʌn] *n* disparador *m* de flash

flashlight ['flæʃ·laɪt] *n* linterna *f* eléctrica

flashy ['flæʃ·i] <-ier, -iest> *adj* ostentoso, -a, llamativo, -a

flask [flæsk] *n* CHEM matraz *m*; (*thermos*) termo *m*; **hip ~** petaca *f*

flat[1] [flæt] **I.** *adj* <-tt-> **1.** (*surface*) llano, -a, plano, -a **2.** (*unexciting*) soso, -a *inf* **3.** (*drink*) sin gas **4.** (*tire*) desinflado, -a **5.** (*absolute: refusal, rejection*) categórico, -a; **and that's ~** y no hay más que hablar **6.** COM (*not changing*) fijo, -a **7.** MUS desafinado, -a **II.** <-tt-> *adv* **1.** (*level*) horizontalmente **2.** *inf* (*absolutely*) completamente ▶ **to be**

~ broke no tener ni un duro; **in five minutes ~** *inf* en sólo cinco minutos **III.** *n* **1.** (*level surface: of sword, knife*) plano *m* **2.** (*low level ground*) llanura *f*; **salt ~s** salinas *fpl* **3.** (*flat tire*) pinchazo *m* **4.** MUS bemol *m*

flat² [flæt] *n* (*apartment*) piso *m*, apartamento *m Ven, Col*, departamento *m Méx, CSur*

flat-footed [ˌflæt·'fʊt·ɪd] *adj* de pies planos

flatten ['flæt·n] *vt* **1.** (*make level*) allanar **2.** MUS bajar el tono

flatter ['flæt·ər] *vt* **1.** (*gratify vanity*) adular **2.** (*make attractive*) favorecer

flattering *adj* **1.** (*clothes, portrait*) que favorece **2.** (*remark, description*) halagador(a)

flattery ['flæt·ə·ri] *n* adulación *f*; **~ will get you nowhere** adulando no conseguirás tu propósito

flatulence ['flætʃ·ə·ləns] *n form* flatulencia *f*

flavor ['fleɪ·vər] **I.** *n* **1.** (*taste*) gusto *m*; (*ice cream, fizzy drink*) sabor *m* **2.** *fig* sabor *m* **II.** *vt* sazonar

flavoring ['fleɪ·vər·ɪŋ] *n* condimento *m*; (*in industry*) aromatizante *m*

flaw [flɔ] **I.** *n* (*in machine*) defecto *m*; (*in argument, character*) fallo *m*; (*in cloth*) imperfección *f* **II.** *vt* dañar

flea [fli] *n* pulga *f*

flea market *n* rastro *m*

fled [fled] *pp of* **flee**

fledgeling, fledgling ['fledʒ·lɪŋ] **I.** *n* (*young bird*) polluelo *m* **II.** *adj* (*inexperienced*) inexperto, -a

flee [fli] <**fled**> **I.** *vt* (*run away from*) huir de **II.** *vi* (*run away*) escaparse; *liter* desaparecer

fleet [flit] *n* **1.** NAUT flota *f* **2.** (*of airplanes*) escuadrón *m*; **car ~** parque *m* móvil

fleeting ['fli·t̬ɪŋ] *adj* (*encounter, romance*) pasajero, -a; (*idea*) fugaz

flesh [fleʃ] *n* (*body tissue*) carne *f*; (*pulp*) pulpa *f* ▸ **in the ~** en persona

flew [flu] *pp, pt of* **fly**

flex [fleks] **I.** *vt* flexionar ▸ **to ~ one's muscles** medir sus fuerzas **II.** *n* ELEC cable *m*

flexible ['flek·sə·bəl] *adj* (*material; policy*) flexible

flick [flɪk] **I.** *vt* chasquear; **to ~ the light switch on/off** encender/apagar la luz; **to ~ channels** cambiar los canales **II.** *n* **1.** (*sudden movement, strike*) golpecito *m* (rápido) **2.** *sl* (*movie*) peli *f*

flicker ['flɪk·ər] **I.** *vi* parpadear **II.** *n* parpadeo *m*

flier ['flaɪ·ər] *n* **1.** (*leaflet*) folleto *m* **2.** (*in airplane*) aviador(a) *m(f)*

flight [flaɪt] *n* **1.** (*movement through air*) vuelo *m* **2.** (*group: of birds*) bandada *f* **3.** (*retreat*) huida *f*; **~ of investment** fuga *f* de inversión; **to take ~** darse a la fuga **4.** (*series: of stairs*) tramo *m*

flight attendant *n* auxiliar *mf* de vuelo

flight deck *n* **1.** (*cockpit*) cabina *f* de pilotaje **2.** (*on aircraft carrier*) cubierta *f* de aterrizaje

flight number *n* número *m* de vuelo

flimsy ['flɪm·zi] <-ier, -iest> *adj* **1.** (*light: dress, blouse*) ligero, -a **2.** (*construction*) débil **3.** (*argument, excuse*) poco sólido, -a

fling [flɪŋ] <**flung**> **I.** *vt* (*throw*) lanzar; **to ~ oneself in front of a train** tirarse al tren **II.** *n* **1.** (*short pleasant time*) rato *m* de juerga **2.** (*relationship*) aventura *f* (amorosa) **3.** *inf* (*try*) **to have a ~ at sth** intentar algo

◆ **fling out** *vt inf* (*throw out*) tirar

flip [flɪp] <-pp-> **I.** *vt* (*turn over quickly*) dar la vuelta a; **to ~ a coin** echar a cara o cruz ▸ **to ~ one's lid** poner el grito en el cielo **II.** *vi* **1.** (*turn quickly*) **to ~ over** dar una vuelta de campana **2.** *sl* (*go crazy*) perder la chaveta

flip chart *n* rotafolio *m*

flip-flop ['flɪp·flɑp] *n* chancla *f*

flipper ['flɪp·ər] *n* (*for diving*) *a.* ZOOL aleta *f*

flirt [flɜrt] **I.** *n* (*woman*) coqueta *f*; (*man*) galanteador *m* **II.** *vi* **1.** (*be sexually attracted*) flirtear **2.** (*toy with*) **to ~ with sth** jugar con algo

flirtatious [flɜr·'teɪ·ʃəs] *adj* (*woman*) coqueta; (*man*) galanteador

float [floʊt] **I.** *vi* **1.** (*in liquid, air*) flotar, boyar *AmL* **2.** (*move aimlessly*) moverse sin rumbo **3.** ECON fluctuar **II.** *vt* (*keep* *afloat* poner a flote III. *n* 1. NAUT flotador *m;* (*for people*) salvavidas *m inv* 2. (*vehicle*) carroza *f*

◆**float off** *vi* irse a la deriva

floatation [flou·'ter·ʃən] *n see* **flotation**

flock [flak] I. *n* 1. (*group: of goats, sheep*) rebaño *m;* (*of birds*) bandada *f,* parvada *f AmL;* (*of people*) multitud *f* 2. REL grey *f* II. *vi* congregarse

flood [flʌd] I. *vt* inundar; **to ~ an engine** AUTO ahogar un motor II. *vi* METEO (*town*) inundarse; (*river*) desbordarse; *fig* **refugees have been ~ing in** ha estado llegando un aluvión de refugiados III. *n* 1. METEO inundación *f* 2. REL **the Flood** el Diluvio 3. *fig* (*outpouring*) torrente *m; ~ **of tears** mar de lágrimas

floodlight ['flʌd·laɪt] I. *n* foco *m* II. *vt irr* iluminar (con focos)

floor [flɔr] I. *n* 1. (*of room*) suelo *m;* **dance ~** pista *f* de baile; **to take the ~** (*in debate*) tomar la palabra 2. (*level in building*) piso *m;* **sea ~** fondo *m* [*or* lecho] del mar *m* 3. FIN (*lowest limit*) mínimo *m* II. *vt* (*knock down*) tumbar; **the question ~ed her** la pregunta la dejó sin respuesta

floorboard ['flɔr·bɔrd] *n* tabla *f* del suelo

flooring *n* solado *m;* **wooden ~** entablado *m*

flop [flap] <-pp-> I. *vi* 1. (*fall*) dejarse caer 2. *inf* (*fail*) fracasar II. *n inf* (*failure*) fracaso *m*

floppy ['flap·i] I. <-ier, -iest> *adj* (*ears*) caído, -a; (*hat*) flexible II. <-ies> *n* diskette *m*

Florida ['flɔr·ɪ·də] *n* Florida *f*

florist ['flɔr·ɪst] *n* florista *mf;* **the ~'s** la floristería

flour ['flaʊ·ər] I. *n* harina *f* II. *vt* enharinar

flourish ['flɜr·ɪʃ] I. *vi* florecer II. *vt* hacer gala de

flourishing *adj* (*place*) esplendoroso, -a; (*business, market, trade*) próspero, -a

flow [floʊ] I. *vi* fluir, correr II. *n* (*of water, ideas*) flujo *m;* (*of goods*) circulación *f* ▶ **to go with the ~** seguir la corriente

flowchart *n,* **flow diagram** *n* organigrama *m*

flower ['flaʊ·ər] I. *n* (*plant, bloom*) flor *f;* **to be in ~** estar en flor II. *vi* florecer, florear *AmL; fig* desarrollarse

flower arrangement *n* arreglo *m* floral

flowerbed *n* arriate *m* de flores

flowerpot *n* maceta *f*

flown [floʊn] *pp of* **fly**[1]

flu [flu] *n* gripe *f,* gripa *f Col*

fluctuation [ˌflʌk·tʃʊ·'er·ʃən] *n* fluctuación *f*

fluent ['flu·ənt] *adj* (*style, movement*) con fluidez

fluffy ['flʌf·i] <-ier, -iest> *adj* (*furry: animal*) peludo, -a; (*toy*) de peluche; CULIN (*light*) esponjoso, -a

fluid ['flu·ɪd] I. *n* fluido *m* II. *adj* (*liquid*) líquido, -a

flung [flʌŋ] *pp, pt of* **fling**

flunk [flʌŋk] *vt inf* (*student*) catear, tronar *Méx argot,* rajarse *Col;* (*subject: math, history*) caer a alguien

fluoride ['flɔr·aɪd] *n* fluoruro *m*

flurry ['flɜr·i] <-ies> *n* agitación *f;* (*of snow*) ráfaga *f;* **a ~ of excitement** un frenesí

flush[1] [flʌʃ] I. *vi* (*blush*) ruborizarse II. *vt* **to ~ the toilet** tirar de la cadena III. *n* (*blush*) rubor *m*

flush[2] [flʌʃ] *adj* (*level*) llano, -a

flushed [flʌʃt] *adj* emocionado, -a; **~ with success** emocionado con el éxito

fluster ['flʌs·tər] I. *vt* **to ~ sb** poner nervioso a alguien II. *n* **to be in a ~** estar nervioso

flute [flut] *n* MUS flauta *f*

flutter ['flʌt·ər] I. *n* 1. (*sound*) revoloteo *m* 2. *fig* (*nervousness*) agitación *f* II. *vi* 1. (*quiver*) temblar 2. (*flap*) agitarse III. *vt* (*flap*) agitar; **to ~ one's wings** aletear

fly[1] [flaɪ] <flew, flown> I. *vi* 1. (*through air*) volar; (*travel by aircraft*) viajar en avión 2. (*move rapidly*) lanzarse; **to ~ at sb** precipitarse sobre alguien 3. *inf* (*leave*) salir corriendo ▶ **to ~ high** volar muy alto II. *vt* 1. (*aircraft*) pilotar 2. (*make move through air*) hacer volar; **to ~ a kite** hacer volar una cometa

◆**fly away** *vi* irse volando

◆**fly in** *vi* **to ~ from somewhere** llegar (en avión) desde algún sitio

fly² [flaɪ] n (*insect*) mosca *f;* **he wouldn't harm** a ~ sería incapaz de matar una mosca

flyer ['flaɪ·ər] n 1. (*leaflet*) folleto *m* 2. (*in airplane*) aviador(a) *m(f)*

flying ['flaɪ·ɪŋ] I. n el volar II. *adj* to **pass an exam with** ~ **colors** aprobar un examen sin problemas

flying fish n pez *m* volador

flying saucer n platillo *m* volante

flyover ['flaɪ·ˌoʊ·vər] n desfile *m* aéreo

foam [foʊm] I. n (*bubbles, foam rubber*) espuma *f* II. *vi* to ~ **with rage** echar espuma de (pura) rabia

foam rubber n goma espuma *f*

focal ['foʊ·kəl] *adj* focal; ~ **point** foco *m*

focus ['foʊ·kəs] <-es *or* foci> I. n 1. foco *m;* to **be in/out of** ~ estar enfocado/desenfocado 2. (*center*) centro *m;* ~ **of interest** centro de interés II. <-s- *or* -ss-> *vi* enfocar; to ~ **on sth** (*concentrate*) concentrarse en algo III. *vt* enfocar

fog [fɑg] n niebla *f;* to **be in a** ~ *fig* estar confundido

foggy ['fɑ·gi] <-ier, -iest> *adj* 1. (*weather*) nebuloso, -a 2. (*unclear: memory*) vago, -a ▸ to **not have the foggiest** (**idea**) no tener la más remota idea

foil¹ [fɔɪl] n (*aluminum*) papel *m* de aluminio

foil² [fɔɪl] *vt* (*cause to fail*) frustrar

fold¹ [foʊld] I. *vt* 1. (*bend*) plegar; to ~ **sth back/down** plegar algo 2. (*wrap*) to ~ **sth** (**in sth**) envolver algo (en algo) II. *vi* 1. (*bend over*) doblarse 2. (*fail, go bankrupt*) fracasar III. n pliegue *m*
◆**fold up** *vt* doblar

fold² [foʊld] n (*sheep pen*) redil *m*

folder ['foʊl·dər] n a. COMPUT carpeta *f*, fólder *m* Col, Méx

folding ['foʊl·dɪŋ] *adj* plegable; ~ **door** puerta *f* plegadiza

folk [foʊk] n 1. *pl* pueblo *m;* ordinary ~ gente *f* corriente; ~ **wisdom** sabiduría *f* popular 2. ~**s** (*parents*) viejos *mpl*

folk music n música *f* folk

folk song n canción *f* popular

follow ['fɑl·oʊ] I. *vt* 1. (*take same route as*) seguir 2. (*happen next*) to ~ **sth** suceder a algo 3. (*understand*) to ~ **sb/**

sth seguir a alguien/algo II. *vi* 1. (*take same route as*) seguir 2. (*happen next*) suceder
◆**follow on** *vi* seguir
◆**follow through** I. *vt* 1. (*study*) investigar 2. (*see through to end*) terminar II. *vi* SPORTS acompañar (un golpe)
◆**follow up** *vt* 1. (*consider, investigate*) investigar 2. (*do next*) to ~ **sth by** [*or* with]... hacer algo después de...

follower n seguidor(a) *m(f)*

following ['fɑl·oʊ·ɪŋ] I. n *inv* 1. **I'd say the** ~ diría lo siguiente 2. (*supporters: of idea*) partidarios, -as *m, fpl;* (*of doctrine*) seguidores, -as *m, fpl* II. *adj* (*next*) siguiente; **the** ~ **ideas** las siguientes ideas III. *prep* después de

follow-up n seguimiento *m*

fond [fɑnd] <-er, -est> *adj* 1. (*with liking for*) **he is** ~ **of...** le gusta... 2. (*loving*) cariñoso, -a; ~ **memories** tiernos recuerdos *mpl* 3. (*hope*) vano, -a

fondle ['fɑn·dl] <-ling> *vt* acariciar

food [fud] n comida *f* ▸ to **give sb** ~ **for thought** dar a alguien algo en que pensar

food chain n cadena *f* alimentaria

food poisoning n intoxicación *f* por alimentos

food processor n procesador *m* de alimentos

food stamps n vales emitidos por el gobierno estadounidense para la compra de comida

fool [ful] I. n idiota *mf;* to **act like a** ~ hacer el tonto; **any** ~ cualquiera II. *vt* engañar; **you could have** ~**ed me!** *inf* ¡no me lo puedo creer! III. *vi* (*joke around*) bromear IV. *adj inf* (*silly*) tonto, -a

foolish ['fu·lɪʃ] *adj* tonto, -a

foolproof ['ful·pruf] *adj* a prueba de tontos

foot [fʊt] I. <feet> n 1. (*of person*) pie *m;* (*of animal*) pata *f* 2. (*unit of measurement*) pie *m* (30,48 cm) 3. (*bottom or lowest part*) at **the** ~ **of one's bed** al pie de la cama; at **the** ~ **of the page** a pie de página ▸ to **get a** ~ **in the door** abrirse una brecha, introducirse; to **be back on one's feet** haberse recuperado;

to have/get cold feet estar/ponerse nervioso; **to get off on the wrong ~** empezar con mal pie; **to put one's ~ down** no ceder; **to put one's ~ in it** [*or* **in one's mouth**] meter la pata; **to be under sb's feet** estar siempre pegado a alguien **II.** *vt inf* **to ~ the bill** pagar

foot-and-mouth disease *n* fiebre *f* aftosa

football ['fʊt·bɔl] *n* **1.** (*sport*) fútbol *m* americano **2.** (*ball*) balón *m* de fútbol americano

footbridge ['fʊt·brɪdʒ] *n* puente *m* peatonal

footer ['fʊt·ər] *n* pie *m* de página

footing ['fʊt·ɪŋ] *n* **1.** to lose one's ~ resbalar **2.** (*basis*) posición *f*

footpath ['fʊt·pæθ] *n* sendero *m*

footprint ['fʊt·prɪnt] *n* huella *f*

footrest ['fʊt·rest] *n* reposapiés *m inv*

footstep ['fʊt·step] *n* paso *m*

footwear ['fʊt·wer] *n* calzado *m*

for [fɔr] **I.** *prep* **1.** (*destined for*) para; **this is ~ you** esto es para ti **2.** (*in order to help*) por; **to do sth ~ sb** hacer algo por alguien **3.** (*intention, purpose*) ~ **sale/rent** en venta/alquiler; **sth ~ a headache** algo para el dolor de cabeza; **it's time ~ lunch** es hora del almuerzo; **to wait ~ sb** esperar a alguien; **to go ~ a walk** ir a dar un paseo; **fit ~ nothing** bueno para nada; **what ~?** ¿para qué?; **what's that ~?** ¿para qué es eso?; **~ this to be possible** para que esto sea posible **4.** (*to acquire*) **eager ~ power** ávido de poder; **to search ~ sth** buscar algo; **to ask/hope ~ news** pedir/esperar noticias; **to apply ~ a job** solicitar un trabajo **5.** (*towards*) **the train ~ Boston** el tren hacia Boston; **to make ~ home** dirigirse hacia casa **6.** (*distance*) **to walk ~ 8 miles** caminar durante 8 millas **7.** (*time*) ~ **now** por ahora; ~ **a while/a time** por un rato/un momento; **to last ~ hours** durar horas y horas; **I'm going to be here ~ three weeks** voy a estar aquí durante tres semanas; **I haven't been there ~ three years** hace tres años que no estoy allí; **I have known her ~ three years** la conozco desde hace tres años **8.** (*on date of*) **to have**

sth finished ~ Sunday acabar algo para el domingo; **to set the wedding ~ May 4th** fijar la boda para el 4 de mayo **9.** (*in support of*) **is he ~ or against it?** ¿está a favor o en contra?; **to fight ~ sth** luchar por algo **10.** (*employed by*) **to work ~ a company** trabajar para una empresa **11.** (*in substitution*) **say hello ~ me** dile hola de mi parte **12.** (*price*) **a check ~ $100** un cheque por valor de cien dólares; **I paid $10 ~ it** pagué diez dólares por ello **13.** (*concerning*) **as ~ me/that** en cuanto a mí/eso; **two are enough ~ me** dos son suficientes para mí; **sorry ~ doing that** perdón por hacer eso; **the best would be ~ me to go** lo mejor sería que me fuese **14.** (*cause*) **excuse me ~ being late** siento llegar tarde; **as the reason ~ one's behavior** como razón por su comportamiento **15.** (*because of*) **to do sth ~ love** hacer algo por amor; ~ **fear of doing sth** por miedo a hacer algo; **to cry ~ joy** gritar de alegría **16.** (*despite*) ~ **all I know** que yo sepa **17.** (*as*) ~ **example** por ejemplo; **he ~ one** empezando por él ▶ **that's kids ~ you!** ¡así son los niños! **II.** *conj form* para

forbid [fər·'bɪd] <forbade, forbidden> *vt* prohibir; **to ~ sb from doing sth** prohibir a alguien hacer algo

forbidden [fər·'bɪd·ən] *pp of* **forbid**

forbidding [fər·'bɪd·ɪŋ] *adj* **1.** (*threatening*) que intimida **2.** (*disapproving: frown, look*) severo, -a; (*bearing rain: sky, clouds*) amenazador, -a

force [fɔrs] **I.** *n* **1.** (*power*) fuerza *f*; ~ **of gravity** PHYS fuerza de la gravedad; **to combine ~s** unir esfuerzos **2.** (*large numbers*) **in ~** en grandes cantidades **3.** (*influence*) influencia *f*; **by ~ of circumstance** debido a las circunstancias; **by ~ of habit** por costumbre; **the ~s of nature** las fuerzas de la naturaleza **4.** (*validity*) validez *f*; **to come into ~** entrar en vigor **5.** MIL **police ~** cuerpo *m* de policía; **Air Force** Fuerzas *f* Aéreas; **the armed ~s** fuerzas *f pl* armadas **II.** *vt* **1.** (*use power*) forzar; **to ~ a door** forzar una puerta **2.** (*oblige to do*) obligar; **to ~ sb to do sth** obligar a alguien a hacer algo; **to ~ sb into** (**doing**) **sth** forzar a alguien a (hacer) algo; **to ~ sth on sb** imponer algo a alguien

forced [fɔrst] (*smile, friendliness*) forzado, -a; **~ landing** aterrizaje *m* forzoso

force-feed ['fɔrs·fid] *vt* dar de comer a la fuerza

forceful ['fɔrs·fəl] *adj* enérgico, -a

forcibly *adv* a la fuerza

forearm[1] ['fɔr·arm] *n* (*body part*) antebrazo *m*

forearm[2] [fɔr·'arm] *vt liter* (*prepare for battle*) **to ~ oneself** (**against sth**) prevenirse (contra algo)

forecast ['fɔr·kæst] <forecast *or* forecasted> I. *n* predicción *f*; **weather ~** previsión *f* meteorológica II. *vt* pronosticar

forecourt ['fɔr·kɔrt] *n* patio *m* delantero

forefinger ['fɔr·fɪŋ·gər] *n* índice *m*

forefront ['fɔr·frʌnt] *n* primer plano *m*

forego [fɔr·'gou] <forewent, foregone> *vt see* **forgo**

foregone [fɔr·'gɑn] *pp of* **forego**

foreground ['fɔr·graund] I. *n a.* ART **the ~** el primer plano II. *vt* destacar

forehand ['fɔr·hænd] *n* (*tennis shot*) golpe *m* de derechas

forehead ['fɔr·hed] *n* frente *f*

foreign ['fɔr·ɪn] *adj* 1. (*from another country*) extranjero, -a *m* 2. (*involving other countries*) exterior; **~ relations** relaciones *f pl* exteriores; **~ trade** comercio *m* exterior 3. (*unknown*) extraño, -a; (*uncharacteristic*) impropio, -a 4. (*not belonging*) ajeno, -a; **a ~ body** un cuerpo extraño

foreign affairs *npl* asuntos *m pl* exteriores

foreign correspondent *n* corresponsal *mf* en el extranjero

foreign currency *n* divisa *f*

foreigner ['fɔr·ɪ·nər] *n* extranjero, -a *m, f*

foreign exchange *n* 1. (*system*) cambio *m* de divisas 2. (*currency*) divisa *f*

foreign policy *n* política *f* exterior

foreman ['fɔr·mən] <-men> *n* (*in factory*) capataz *m*

foremost ['fɔr·moust] *adj* 1. (*most important*) principal 2. (*furthest forward*) delantero, -a

forename ['fɔr·neɪm] *n form* nombre

m (de pila)

foreplay ['fɔr·pleɪ] *n* juegos *m pl* eróticos preliminares

forerunner ['fɔr·rʌn·ər] *n* precursor(a) *m(f)*

foresee [fɔr·'si] *irr vt* prever

foreseeable *adj* previsible

foreshadow [fɔr·'ʃæd·ou] *vt* anunciar

foresight ['fɔr·saɪt] *n* previsión *f*

foreskin ['fɔr·skɪn] *n* prepucio *m*

forest ['fɔr·ɪst] I. *n* (*woods*) bosque *m*; (*tropical*) selva *f* II. *adj* forestal

forestall [fɔr·'stɔl] *vt* anticiparse a

forester ['fɔr·ɪ·stər] *n* guardabosques *mf inv*

forestry ['fɔr·ɪ·stri] *n* silvicultura *f*

foretaste ['fɔr·teɪst] *n* anticipo *m*

forever [fɔr·'ev·ər] *adv* 1. (*for all time*) para siempre 2. *inf* (*continually*) continuamente

forewarn [fɔr·'wɔrn] *vt* prevenir

forewent [fɔr·'went] *pp of* **forego**

foreword ['fɔr·wɜrd] *n* prefacio *m*

forfeiture ['fɔr·fə·tʃər] *n* pérdida *f*

forgave [fər·'geɪv] *n pt of* **forgive**

forge [fɔrdʒ] I. *vt* 1. (*make illegal copy*) falsificar 2. (*metal*) forjar II. *vi* **to ~ into the lead** adelantarse mucho III. *n* 1. (*furnace*) fragua *f* 2. (*smithy*) herrería *f*

forgery ['fɔr·dʒə·ri] <-ies> *n* falsificación *f*

forget [fər·'get] <forgot, forgotten> I. *vt* 1. (*not remember*) olvidar; **to ~ to do sth** olvidarse de hacer algo; **to ~ (that)...** olvidar (que)... 2. (*leave behind*) **to ~ one's keys** dejarse las llaves 3. (*stop thinking about*) **to ~ sth/sb** dejar de pensar en algo/alguien 4. (*give up*) **to ~ sth** dejar algo; **~ it** olvídalo II. *vi* 1. (*not remember*) olvidarse; **to ~ about sth/sb** olvidarse de algo/alguien 2. (*stop thinking about*) **to ~ about a plan** desistir de un plan 3. **~ it!** (*no*) ¡ni lo sueñes!

forgetful [fər·'get·fəl] *adj* olvidadizo, -a

forgive [fər·'gɪv] <forgave, forgiven> I. *vt* 1. (*pardon*) perdonar; **to ~ sb for sth** perdonar algo a alguien 2. (*pardon*) **~ me** discúlpeme II. *vi* perdonar

forgiven *pp of* **forgive**

forgiveness *n* perdón *m*

F

forgiving *adj* misericordioso, -a

forgo [fɔrˈgoʊ] *irr vt* privarse de

forgot [fərˈgɑt] *pt of* **forget**

forgotten [fərˈgɑtn] I. *pp of* **forget** II. *adj* olvidado, -a

fork [fɔrk] I. *n* 1. (*cutlery*) tenedor *m* 2. (*tool*) horca *f* 3. (*in road*) bifurcación *f* 4. *pl* (*on bicycle*) horquilla *f* II. *vt* coger con tenedor, agarrar con tenedor *AmL* III. *vi* (*road*) bifurcarse

forked *adj* bifurcado, -a

forklift [ˌfɔrkˈlɪft] *n* carretilla *f* elevadora

form [fɔrm] I. *n* 1. (*type, variety*) tipo *m*; **in any way, shape or ~** de cualquier modo 2. (*outward shape*) forma *f*; (*of an object*) bulto *m*; **to take ~** tomar forma; **in liquid/solid ~** en estado líquido/sólido 3. LING (*of word*) forma *f*; **the singular ~** LING el singular 4. (*document*) formulario *m*; **an application/entry ~** un formulario de solicitud/admisión; **to fill in a ~** rellenar un formulario 5. SPORTS forma *f*; **to be in ~** estar en forma; **to be out of ~** estar en baja forma 6. (*correct procedure*) **in due ~** de la debida forma 7. (*mol, a. for baking*) molde *m* II. *vt* (*make*) formar; **to ~ a line** formar una cola; **to ~ an opinion** formarse una opinión 2. (*shape*) moldear 3. (*set up*) establecer

formal [ˈfɔrməl] *adj* (*official, ceremonious*) formal; **~ dress** traje *m* de etiqueta; **~ procedures** procedimientos *m pl* oficiales

formality [fɔrˈmæl·ə·t̬i] <-ies> *n* formalidad *f*

formalize [ˈfɔr·mə·laɪz] *vt* formalizar

format [ˈfɔr·mæt] I. *n* formato *m* II. <-tt-> *vt* COMPUT formatear

formation [fɔrˈmeɪ·ʃən] *n* formación *f*; **in ~** en formación

formatting *n* COMPUT formateo *m*

former [ˈfɔr·mər] *adj* 1. (*previous*) anterior 2. (*first of two*) primero, -a

formerly *adv* antes; **~ known as** anteriormente conocido como

formidable [ˈfɔr·mə·də·bəl] *adj* (*person*) extraordinario, -a; (*opponent, task*) difícil

formula [ˈfɔr·mjʊ·lə] <-s *or* -lae> *n*

1. MATH *a. fig* fórmula *f* 2. COM (*recipe for product*) receta *f* 3. (*baby milk*) leche *f* para lactantes

forsake [fɔrˈseɪk] <forsook, forsaken> *vt* (*abandon*) abandonar; (*give up*) renunciar a

forsaken [fɔrˈseɪ·kən] I. *pp of* **forsake** II. *adj* abandonado, -a

forsook [fɔrˈsʊk] *pt of* **forsake**

fort [fɔrt] *n* fuerte *m*

forte [ˈfɔr·teɪ, fɔrt] *n* (*strong point*) fuerte *m*

forth [fɔrθ] *adv* **to go ~** irse; **back and ~** de acá para allá

forthcoming [ˌfɔrθˈkʌm·ɪŋ] *adj* 1. (*happening soon*) venidero, -a; (*film*) de próximo estreno 2. (*informative*) **to be ~ (about sth)** estar dispuesto a hablar (de algo)

forthright [ˈfɔrθ·raɪt] *adj* directo, -a

forthwith [ˌfɔrθˈwɪθ] *adv* *form* en el acto

fortieth [ˈfɔr·t̬i·əθ] I. *adj* cuadragésimo, -a II. *n* (*order*) cuadragésimo, -a *m, f*; (*fraction*) cuadragésimo *m*; (*part*) cuadragésima parte *f*; *s. a.* **eighth**

fortify [ˈfɔr·t̬ə·faɪ] <-ie-> *vt* 1. MIL fortificar 2. **fortified with vitamins and minerals** enriquecido con vitaminas y minerales

fortnight [ˈfɔrt·naɪt] *n* quince días *mpl*; (*business*) quincena *f*

fortunate [ˈfɔr·tʃə·nɪt] *adj* afortunado, -a; **to be ~ to do sth** tener la suerte de hacer algo

fortunately *adv* afortunadamente

fortune [ˈfɔr·tʃən] *n* 1. (*money*) fortuna *f*; **to be worth a ~** valer una fortuna; **to cost a ~** costar un dineral; **to make a ~** hacer una fortuna 2. *form* (*luck, destiny*) suerte *f*; **good/ill ~** buena/mala suerte; **to tell sb's ~** decir la buenaventura a alguien 3. *liter* (*luck personified*) la fortuna

fortune teller *n* adivino, -a *m, f*

forty [ˈfɔr·t̬i] I. *adj* cuarenta II. <-ies> *n* cuarenta *m*; *s. a.* **eighty**

forward [ˈfɔr·wərd] I. *adv* 1. (*towards the front*) hacia adelante; **to lean ~** inclinarse hacia adelante; **a step ~** *fig* un paso hacia adelante 2. (*in time*) en adelante; **to set one's watch/the clock**

~ adelantar el reloj; **to look ~ to** sth esperar algo (con ansia) **II.** adj **1.** (towards the front) hacia adelante; **~ gear** AUTO marcha f adelante **2.** (in a position close to front) en la parte delantera **3.** (near front of plane) delantero, -a; (ship) de proa **4.** (relating to the future) **~ buying** compra f a plazos; **~ planning** planes m pl de futuro **5.** (bold, not modest) descarado, -a **III.** n SPORTS delantero, -a m, f; **center ~** delantero centro **IV.** vt **1.** (letter, e-mail) remitir; (e-mail) reenviar; **please ~** por favor, hacer seguir **2.** (help to progress) promover

forward-looking adj con miras al futuro

forwards ['fɔr·wərdz] adv **1.** (towards the front) hacia adelante **2.** (in time) en adelante

forwent [fɔr'went] pt of **forgo**

fossil ['fas·əl] n **1.** GEO fósil m **2.** fig inf (person) carca mf

foster ['fa·stər] vt **1.** (look after) acoger **2.** (encourage) fomentar

foster child n hijo, -a m, f acogido

foster father n padre m de acogida

foster home n casa f de acogida

foster mother n madre f de acogida

fought [fɔt] pt, pp of **fight**

foul [faʊl] **I.** adj **1.** (disagreeable: mood, temper) insoportable; (air) sucio, -a **2.** (rotten: taste) asqueroso, -a; (smell) fétido, -a **3.** (vulgar: language) ordinario, -a **II.** n SPORTS falta f, penal m AmL **III.** vt **1.** (pollute) ensuciar **2.** SPORTS **to ~ sb** hacer una falta a alguien

foul play n **1.** SPORTS juego m sucio **2.** (crime) delito m

found[1] [faʊnd] pt, pp of **find**

found[2] [faʊnd] vt **1.** (establish) fundar **2.** (base) basar **3.** (build) **to be ~ed on** sth estar construido sobre algo

found[3] [faʊnd] vt MIN fundir

foundation [faʊn·'deɪ·ʃən] n **1.** pl (of building) cimientos mpl; **to lay the ~(s)** (of sth) poner los cimientos (de algo) **2.** fig (basis) base f **3.** (evidence) fundamento m **4.** (act of establishing) establecimiento m **5.** (organization) fundación f **6.** (make-up) maquillaje m de base

founder[1] ['faʊn·dər] n (of organization) fundador(a) m(f)

founder[2] ['faʊn·dər] vi **1.** (sink) hundirse **2.** fig (fail) fracasar

fountain ['faʊn·tən] n fuente f

fountain pen n pluma f estilográfica

four [fɔr] **I.** adj cuatro **II.** n **1.** cuatro m **2.** (group of four) cuarteto m ▶ **to go on all ~s** andar a gatas; s. a. **eight**

fourteen [ˌfɔr·'tin] **I.** adj catorce **II.** n catorce m; s. a. **eight**

fourteenth I. adj decimocuarto, -a **II.** n **1.** (order) decimocuarto, -a m, f **2.** (date) catorce m **3.** (fraction) catorceavo m; (part) catorceava parte f; s. a. **eighth**

fourth [fɔrθ] **I.** adj cuarto, -a **II.** n **1.** (order) cuarto, -a m, f **2.** (date) cuatro m **3.** (fraction) cuarto m; (part) cuarta parte f **4.** MUS cuarta f; s. a. **eighth**

Fourth of July n Día m de la Independencia de Estados Unidos

four-wheel drive n tracción f a las cuatro ruedas

fox [faks] **I.** n **1.** (animal) zorro m **2.** (fur) piel f de zorro **3.** inf (cunning person) **an old ~** un viejo zorro **4.** sl (sexy woman) tía f buena **II.** vt **1.** (mystify) mistificar **2.** (trick) engañar

foyer ['fɔɪ·ər] n **1.** (in house) vestíbulo m, hall m **2.** (in hotel, theater) vestíbulo m

fraction ['fræk·ʃən] n fracción f; **at a ~ of the cost** por parte del costo

fracture ['fræk·tʃər] **I.** vt **1.** MED fracturar; **to ~ one's leg** fracturarse la pierna **2.** (break) romper **II.** vi (leg) fracturarse **III.** n MED fractura f

fragile ['frædʒ·əl] adj delicado, -a; (object, peace) frágil

fragment ['fræg·mənt] **I.** n fragmento m **II.** vi **1.** (break into pieces) fragmentarse **2.** fig (break up) romperse **III.** vt **1.** (break into pieces) fragmentar **2.** fig (break up) romper

fragrance ['freɪ·grəns] n fragancia f

fragrant ['freɪ·grənt] adj fragante

frame [freɪm] **I.** n **1.** (for door, picture) a. COMPUT marco m **2.** pl (spectacles) montura f **3.** (of building) armazón m o f **4.** (body) cuerpo m; **a slight/sturdy**

~ un cuerpo esbelto/robusto **5.** CINE, TV fotograma *m* **II.** *vt* **1.** (*picture*) enmarcar **2.** (*conceive: proposal*) elaborar; (*put into words*) **3.** *inf* (*falsely incriminate*) incriminar dolosamente

frame-up ['freɪm·ʌp] *n inf* montaje *m* (*para inculpar a alguien*)

framework ['freɪm·wɜrk] *n* **1.** (*supporting structure*) armazón *m* o *f* **2.** *fig* (*set of rules, principles*) sistema *m*

France [fræns] *n* Francia *f*

franchise ['fræn·tʃaɪz] **I.** *n* franquicia *f* **II.** *vt* conceder en franquicia

frank [fræŋk] **I.** *adj* franco, -a; **to be ~,...** sinceramente,... **II.** *vt* franquear

frankfurter ['fræŋk·fɜr·tər] *n* salchicha *f* de Frankfurt

frankly *adv* sinceramente

frantic ['fræn·tɪk] *adj* (*hurry, activity*) frenético, -a; **to be ~ with worry** andar loco de inquietud

fraud [frɔd] *n* **1.** *a.* LAW fraude *m* **2.** (*person*) impostor(a) *m(f)*

fraudulent ['frɔ·dʒə·lənt] *adj* fraudulento, -a

fray¹ [freɪ] *vi* (*rope, cloth*) deshilacharse; **tempers were beginning to ~** la gente estaba perdiendo la paciencia

fray² [freɪ] *n* (*fight*) lucha *f*

freak [frik] **I.** *n* **1.** (*abnormal person, thing*) monstruo *m*; **a ~ of nature** un fenómeno de la naturaleza **2.** (*enthusiast*) fanático, -a *m, f* **II.** *adj* anormal **III.** *vi see* **freak out I**

◆freak out I. *vi* flipar **II.** *vt* **to freak sb out** alucinar a alguien

freckle ['frek·l] *n* peca *f*

free [fri] **I.** <-r, -est> *adj* **1.** (*not constrained: person, country, elections*) libre; **to break ~** soltarse (de algo); **to break ~ of sth** despegarse de alguien; **to go ~** salir en libertad; **to set sb ~** poner en libertad a alguien **2.** (*not affected by*) **to be ~ of sth** no estar afectado por algo **3.** (*not busy*) **to be ~ to do sth** estar libre para hacer algo **4.** (*not occupied*) libre **5.** (*costing nothing*) gratis; **~ ticket** entrada *f* gratis; **~ of charge** gratis; **~ sample** muestra *f* gratuita **6.** (*generous*) **to be ~ with sth** dar algo en abundancia ▶ **~ and**

easy despreocupado **II.** *adv* gratis; **~ of charge** gratis **III.** *vt* **1.** (*release: person*) poner en libertad **2.** (*make available*) permitir

freebie ['fri·bi] *n* obsequio *m*

freedom ['fri·dəm] *n* **1.** (*of person, country*) libertad *f*; **~ of the press** libertad *f* de prensa; **~ of speech/thought** libertad *f* de expresión/pensamiento **2.** (*right*) derecho *m* **3.** (*room for movement*) libertad *f* **4.** (*unrestricted use*) usufructo *m*

free enterprise *n* libre empresa *f*

freehold ['fri·hoʊld] **I.** *n* plena propiedad *f* **II.** *adj* de plena propiedad **III.** *adv* en propiedad absoluta

free kick *n* SPORTS tiro *m* libre

freelance ['fri·læns] **I.** *n* freelance *mf* **II.** *adj* autónomo, -a **III.** *adv* por cuenta propia **IV.** *vi* trabajar por cuenta propia

freely *adv* **1.** (*without obstruction*) libremente **2.** (*frankly: speak, criticize*) francamente

free-range [ˌfri·'reɪndʒ] *adj* de granja

free-range chicken *n* pollo *m* de corral

free-range egg *n* huevo *m* de granja

free speech *n* libertad *f* de expresión

freestyle ['fri·staɪl] *n* estilo *m* libre

freeware *n* COMPUT programa *m* de libre distribución

freeway *n* autopista *f*

freewheel ['fri·hwil] *vi* ir en punto muerto

free will *n* libre albedrío *m*

freeze [friz] <froze, frozen> **I.** *vi* **1.** (*liquid*) helarse; (*food*) congelarse **2.** (*become totally still*) quedarse completamente quieto, -a **II.** *vt* (*liquid*) helar; (*food, prices*) congelar **III.** *n* **1.** METEO ola *f* de frío **2.** ECON congelación *f*

freezer *n* congelador *m*, congeladora *f AmS*

freezing I. *adj* glacial; **it's ~** hiela; **I'm ~** estoy helado **II.** *n* congelación *f*

freight [freɪt] *n* **1.** (*type of transportation*) flete *m* **2.** (*goods*) mercancías *fpl* **3.** (*charge*) porte *m* **II.** *adv* por flete **III.** *vt* fletar

freight car *n* RAIL vagón *m* de mercancías

freighter ['freɪ�·tər] n **1.** (ship) buque m de carga **2.** (plane) avión m de mercancías

freight train n tren m de mercancías

French [frentʃ] I. adj francés, -esa; **~ speaker** francófono, -a m, f II. n **1.** (person) francés, -esa m, f **2.** (language) francés m

French dressing n vinagreta f

French fried potatoes npl, **French fries** npl patatas f pl fritas

French horn n trompa f de llaves

Frenchman <-men> n francés m

French toast n torrija f

Frenchwoman <-women> n francesa f

frenzy ['fren·zi] n frenesí m

frequency ['fri·kwən·tsi] <-cies> n frecuencia f

frequent[1] ['fri·kwənt] adj (occurring often) frecuente, tupido, -a Méx

frequent[2] [frɪ·'kwent] vt (visit regularly) frecuentar

fresh [freʃ] adj **1.** (not stale: air, water, food) fresco, -a; (bread) recién hecho, -a **2.** (new) nuevo, -a; **to make a ~ start** volver a empezar **3.** (not tired) como nuevo, -a **4.** inf (disrespectful) descarado, -a

freshen ['freʃ·ən] vt refrescar; (one's breath) refrescarse el aliento

fret[1] [fret] <-tt-> vi (worry) inquietarse

fret[2] [fret] n MUS traste m

friction ['frɪk·ʃən] n **1.** (rubbing) fricción f **2.** fig (disagreement) desavenencia f

Friday ['fraɪ·di] n viernes m inv; **on ~s** los viernes; **every ~** todos los viernes; **this (coming) ~** este (próximo) viernes; **on ~ mornings** los viernes por la mañana; **on ~ night** el viernes por la noche; **last/next ~** el viernes pasado/que viene; **every other ~** un viernes sí y otro no; **on ~ we are going on vacation** el viernes nos vamos de vacaciones

fridge [frɪdʒ] n nevera f, refrigeradora f AmS

fried [fraɪd] adj frito, -a

fried chicken n pollo m frito

fried egg n huevo m frito

friend [frend] n amigo, -a m, f; **to be ~s** ser amigos; **to make ~s (with sb)** ha-

cerse amigo (de alguien); **a ~ of mine/ yours/his/hers** un amigo mío/tuyo/ suyo

friendly ['frend·li] <-ier, -iest> adj (person) simpático, -a, entrador(a) Arg; (house, environment) acogedor(a); (nation) cordial; **to be ~ with sb** llevarse bien con alguien

friendship ['frend·ʃɪp] n amistad f

fries [fraɪz] npl inf patatas f pl fritas

fright [fraɪt] n **1.** (feeling of fear) terror m **2.** (frightening experience) susto m, jabón m Arg, Méx, PRico; **to give sb a ~** dar un susto a alguien

frighten ['fraɪt·ən] I. vt asustar II. vi asustarse

frightened adj asustado, -a

frightful ['fraɪt·fəl] adj espantoso, -a

fringe [frɪndʒ] I. n **1.** (decorative edging) flecos mpl, barbitas f Méx **2.** (edge) margen m; fig **on the ~ of society** al margen de la sociedad **3.** (fringe benefit) extra m II. adj secundario, -a

fringe group n grupo m marginal

frisk [frɪsk] I. vi juguetear II. vt cachear

fritter[1] ['frɪt·ər] n CULIN buñuelo m, picarón m AmL

fritter[2] ['frɪt·ər] vt (reduce) **to ~ (away)** desperdiciar

frivolous ['frɪv·ə·ləs] adj frívolo, -a

frizzy ['frɪz·i] adj (hair) encrespado, -a

fro [froʊ] adv **to and ~** de un lado a otro

frock [frak] n vestido m

frog[1] [frag] n ZOOL rana ▶ **to have a ~ in one's throat** tener carraspera

frog[2] [frag] n offensive sl (French person) gabacho, -a m, f

from [fram] prep **1.** (as starting point) de; **where is he ~?** ¿de dónde es?; **the flight ~ Boston** el vuelo procedente de Boston; **to fly ~ New York to Tokyo** volar de Nueva York a Tokio; **shirts ~ $10** camisas desde 10$; **~ inside** desde dentro **2.** (temporal) **~ day to day** día tras día; **~ time to time** de vez en cuando; **~ that date on(wards)** desde esa fecha **3.** (at distance to) **100 miles ~ the river** a 100 millas del río; **far ~ doing sth** lejos de hacer algo **4.** (one to another) **to go ~ door to door** ir de puerta en puerta; **to tell good ~ evil**

distinguir el bien del mal **5.** (*originating in*) **a card ~ Paul/Corsica** una tarjeta de Paul/Córcega **6.** (*in reference to*) **~ what I heard** según lo que he escuchado; **to judge ~ appearances** juzgar según las apariencias; **different ~ the others** diferente de los demás **7.** (*caused by*) **~ experience** por experiencia; **to die ~ thirst** morirse de sed **8.** (*removed*) **to steal/take sth ~ sb** robar/quitar algo a alguien; **to prevent sb ~ doing sth** evitar que alguien haga algo; **to keep sth ~ sb** mantener algo alejado de alguien

front [frʌnt] **I.** *n* **1.** (*forward-facing part*) frente *f*; (*of building*) fachada *f* **2.** PUBL (*outside cover*) cubierta *f* exterior; (*first pages*) principio *m* **3.** (*front area*) parte *f* delantera; **in ~ of** delante de **4.** THEAT auditorio *m* **5.** (*deceptive appearance*) apariencias *fpl* **6.** MIL frente *m*; *fig* **on the domestic/work ~** en el terreno doméstico/laboral **7.** POL frente *m* **8.** (*promenade*) paseo *m* marítimo **9.** METEO frente *m* **II.** *adj* **1.** (*at the front*) delantero, -a **2.** (*first*) primero, -a **III.** *vt* **1.** (*be head of*) liderar **2.** TV presentar **IV.** *vi* estar enfrente de; **to ~ for** servir de fachada [*or* tapadera]

front door *n* puerta *f* principal

front-end *n* COMPUT frontal *m*

frontier [frʌn·'tɪr] *n* **1.** (*border*) *a. fig* frontera *f* **2.** (*outlying areas*) **the ~** los límites

frontier station *n* puesto *m* fronterizo

front line *n* primera línea *f*

front page *n* primera página *f*

front-runner *n* líder *mf*

front-wheel drive *n* tracción *f* delantera

frost [frast] **I.** *n* (*crystals*) escarcha *f*; (*on ground*) helada *f* **II.** *vt* **1.** (*cover with frost*) cubrir de escarcha **2.** (*cover with icing: cake*) escarchar

frostbite ['frast·baɪt] *n* congelación *f*

frosted *adj* **1.** (*covered with icing*) escarchado, -a **2.** (*opaque: glass*) esmerilado, -a

frosty ['fra·sti] <-ier, -iest> *adj* **1.** (*with frost*) escarchado, -a **2.** (*unfriendly*)

frío, -a

frothy ['fra·θi] <-ier, -iest> *adj* espumoso, -a

frown [fraʊn] **I.** *vi* **1.** fruncir el ceño **2.** *fig* (*disapprove of*) **to ~ on sth** no ver algo con buenos ojos **II.** *n* ceño *m* fruncido

froze [froʊz] *pt of* **freeze**

frozen ['froʊ·zn] **I.** *pp of* **freeze** **II.** *adj* congelado, -a

fruit [frut] *n* **1.** (*for eating*) fruta *f*; (*on tree, product*) fruto *m* **2.** (*results*) fruto *m* ▶ **to bear ~** dar fruto; *fig* dar resultado

fruitcake ['frut·keɪk] *n* **1.** (*cake*) tarta *f* de frutas **2.** *sl* (*crazy person*) chiflado, -a *m*, *f*

fruitful ['frut·fəl] *adj* (*productive*) provechoso, -a; (*discussion*) productivo, -a

fruition [fru·'ɪʃ·ən] *n* **to bring sth to ~** llevar algo a buen término; **to come to ~** realizarse

fruit knife *n* cuchillo *m* de la fruta

fruitless ['frut·lɪs] *adj* infructuoso, -a

fruit salad *n* macedonia *f*

fruity ['fru·ti] <-ier, -iest> *adj* **1.** afrutado, -a **2.** *sl* (*crazy*) loco, -a, chiflado, -a

frustrate ['frʌs·treɪt] <-ting> *vt* frustrar

frustrated *adj* frustrado, -a

frustration [frʌ·'streɪ·ʃən] *n* frustración *f*

fry[1] [fraɪ] <-ie-> **I.** *vt* freír **II.** *vi* **1.** (*be cooked*) freírse **2.** *inf* (*get burned*) quemarse

fry[2] [fraɪ] *n* **small ~** (*unimportant person*) don nadie *mf*; (*young person*) renacuajo, -a *m*, *f inf*

frying pan *n* sartén *f*, paila *f AmL*

ft. *abbr of* **foot, feet** pie

fudge [fʌdʒ] **I.** *n* (*candy*) dulce *m* de azúcar **II.** <-ging> *vt* (*issue*) esquivar; (*numbers, figures*) falsear

fuel ['fju·əl] **I.** *n* combustible *m* **II.** *vt* **1.** (*provide with fuel*) aprovisionar de combustible **2.** (*increase: tension, controversy*) avivar

fuel consumption *n* AUTO consumo *m* de gasolina

fuel gauge *n* indicador *m* del nivel de gasolina

fulfil <-ll-> *vt*, **fulfill** [fʊlˈfɪl] *vt* (*ambition, task*) realizar; (*condition, requirement*) cumplir; (*need*) satisfacer; (*function, role*) desempeñar; **to ~ oneself** realizarse

fulfilment *n*, **fulfillment** *n* (*of condition, requirement*) cumplimiento *m*; (*of function, role*) desempeño *m*; (*satisfaction*) realización *f*

full [fʊl] **I.** <-er, -est> *adj* **1.** (*container, space*) lleno, -a; (*vehicle*) completo, -a **2.** (*total: support*) total; (*recovery*) completo, -a; (*member*) de pleno derecho; **to be in ~ dress** estar de gala; **to be in ~ swing** estar en pleno apogeo **3.** (*maximum: employment*) pleno, -a; **~ of mistakes** lleno de errores; **at ~ speed** a toda velocidad **4.** (*rounded*) redondo, -a **5.** (*wide*) amplio, -a **6.** (*wine*) con cuerpo **7.** (*not hungry*) **to be ~** estar lleno **8.** (*conceited*) **to be ~ of oneself** ser un creído **II.** *adv* **1.** (*completely*) completamente **2.** (*directly*) directamente **3.** (*very*) muy; **to know ~ well (that...)** saber muy bien (que...) **III.** *n* **in ~** sin abreviar; **to the ~** al máximo

fullback [ˈfʊlˌbæk] *n* SPORTS defensa *mf*

full-blown [fʊlˈbloʊn] *adj* (*disaster, scandal*) auténtico, -a

full-bodied [ˌfʊlˈbad·ɪd] *adj* (*taste*) fuerte; (*wine*) con mucho cuerpo

full-grown *adj* crecido, -a

full moon *n* luna *f* llena

full-page *adj* de página entera

full stop *n* punto *m*; **to come to a ~** paralizarse

full-time *adj* de horario completo

fully [ˈfʊl·i] *adv* **1.** (*completely*) completamente **2.** (*in detail*) detalladamente **3.** (*at least*) al menos

fumble [ˈfʌm·bəl] **I.** *vi* **to ~ around for sth** buscar algo a tientas; **to ~ for words** titubear buscando las palabras **II.** *vt* SPORTS **to ~ the ball** dejar caer la pelota

fume [fjum] *vi* **1.** (*be angry*) estar furioso, -a; **to ~ at sb** echar pestes de alguien **2.** (*emit gases*) humear

fun [fʌn] **I.** *n* diversión *f*; **to do sth for ~** hacer algo por placer; **to do sth in ~** hacer algo en broma; **to have (a lot of) ~** divertirse (mucho); **have ~ on your**

weekend! ¡pásalo bien el fin de semana!; **have ~!** ¡diviértete!; **to make ~ of sb** reírse de alguien; **what ~!** ¡qué divertido! ► **~ and games** *pej* odisea *f* **II.** *adj* **1.** (*enjoyable*) agradable **2.** (*funny*) divertido, -a

function [ˈfʌŋk·ʃən] **I.** *n* **1.** *a.* MATH función *f*; **in my ~ as mayor,...** como alcalde,... **2.** (*formal ceremony*) ceremonia *f* **II.** *vi* funcionar

functional [ˈfʌŋk·ʃə·nəl] *adj* **1.** *a.* LING funcional **2.** (*operational, working*) práctico, -a

fund [fʌnd] **I.** *n* fondo *m*; **to be short of ~s** ir mal de fondos **II.** *vt* financiar

fundamental [ˌfʌn·dəˈmen·təl] **I.** *adj* fundamental; (*difference*) esencial; (*principles*) básico, -a; **to be of ~ importance** ser de vital importancia **II.** *n* **the ~s** los principios básicos

fundamentalist **I.** *n* integrista *mf* **II.** *adj* integrista

fundamentally *adv* **1.** (*basically*) fundamentalmente **2.** (*in the most important sense*) esencialmente

funeral [ˈfju·nər·əl] *n* entierro *m*; **to attend a ~** asistir a un funeral

funeral home *n* funeraria *f*

funeral parlor *n* funeraria *f*

fungus [ˈfʌŋ·gəs] *n* (*wild mushroom*) hongo *m*; (*mold*) moho *m*

funky [ˈfʌn·ki] <-ier, -iest> *adj* **1.** (*musty*) **a ~ taste/smell** un sabor/olor raro **2.** *sl* (*cool*) genial **3.** (*music*) funky

fun-loving *adj* marchoso, -a

funnel [ˈfʌn·əl] **I.** *n* (*tool*) embudo *m* **II.** <-l-> *vt* canalizar

funny [ˈfʌn·i] <-ier, -iest> *adj* **1.** (*amusing*) divertido, -a **2.** *inf* (*witty*) gracioso, -a; **to try to be ~** *inf* hacerse el gracioso **3.** (*odd, peculiar*) raro, -a **4.** (*slightly ill*) **to feel ~** no encontrarse bien

funny bone *n* *inf* hueso *m* de la alegría

fur [fɜr] *n* **1.** (*animal hair*) piel *f* **2.** (*garment*) prenda *f* de pieles

furious [ˈfjʊr·i·əs] *adj* (*very angry*) furioso, -a, enchilado, -a *Méx*, caribe *Ant*; **to be ~ about sth** estar furioso por algo

furl [fɜrl] *vt* (*flag, sail*) recoger

furnish [ˈfɜr·nɪʃ] *vt* **1.** (*supply*) proporcionar; **to ~ sb with sth** suministrar algo a alguien **2.** (*provide furniture for*) amueblar

furnished ['fɜr·nɪʃt] *adj* amueblado, -a

furniture ['fɜr·nɪ·tʃər] *n* mobiliario *m*; **piece of** ~ mueble *m*

furniture van *n* camión *m* de mudanzas

furry ['fɜr·i] <-ier, -iest> *adj* **1.** peludo, -a **2.** (*looking like fur*) peloso, -a; ~ **toy** peluche *m*

further ['fɜr·ðər] **I.** *adj comp of* **far 1.** (*greater distance*) más lejano **2.** (*additional*) otro, -a; **until** ~ **notice** hasta nuevo aviso **II.** *adv comp of* **far 1.** (*greater distance*) más lejos; ~ **on** más adelante; ~ **and** ~ cada vez más lejos **2.** (*more*) más ▶ **to not go any** ~ no ir más allá **III.** *vt* fomentar; **to** ~ **sb's interests** favorecer los intereses de alguien

furthermore ['fɜr·ðər·mɔr] *adv* además

furthest ['fɜr·ðɪst] **I.** *adj* **1.** *superl of* **far 2.** (*greatest*) mayor **3.** (*at the greatest distance*) más lejano, -a **II.** *adv* **1.** *superl of* **far 2.** (*greatest distance*) más lejos

fury ['fjor·i] *n* furor *m*; **fit of** ~ ataque *m* de furia

fuse [fjuz] **I.** *n* **1.** ELEC fusible *m*; **the** ~ **has blown** han saltado los plomos **2.** (*ignition device, detonator*) espoleta *f*; (*string*) mecha *f* ▶ **to have a short** ~ tener mucho genio **II.** *vi* **1.** ELEC fundirse **2.** (*join together*) fusionarse **III.** *vt* **1.** ELEC fundir **2.** (*join*) fusionar

fuse box <-es> *n* caja *f* de fusibles

fusion ['fju·ʒən] *n* **1.** (*joining together*) fusión *f* **2.** PHYS fusión *f*; **nuclear** ~ fusión nuclear

fuss [fʌs] **I.** *n* alboroto *m*; **to make a** ~ armar un escándalo **II.** *vi* preocuparse; **to** ~ **over sth/sb** preocuparse en exceso por algo/alguien

fussy ['fʌs·i] <-ier, -iest> *adj* **1.** (*overly particular*) puntilloso, -a **2.** (*quick to criticize*) quisquilloso, -a **3.** (*baby*) llorón, -ona

futile ['fju·təl] *adj* inútil; ~ **attempt** intento *m* en vano

future ['fju·tʃər] **I.** *n* **1.** *a.* LING futuro *m*; **to have plans for the** ~ tener planes

de futuro; **in the** ~ **tense** en futuro; **the distant/near** ~ el futuro lejano/próximo **2.** (*prospects*) porvenir *m* II. *adj* futuro, -a

fuze [fjuz] **I.** *n* (*ignition device, detonator*) espoleta *f*; (*string*) mecha *f* **II.** *vt* poner mecha (a algo)

fuzz [fʌz] *n* **1.** (*fluff*) pelusa *f* **2.** (*fluffy hair*) pelo *m* crespo **3.** (*short growing hair*) vello *m*; **peach** ~ *fig* piel *f* de melocotón

fuzzy ['fʌz·i] *adj* **1.** (*unclear*) borroso, -a **2.** (*short, soft: hair*) velloso, -a; (*curly*) rizado, -a

G

G, g [dʒi] *n* G, g *f*; ~ **as in Golf** G de Granada

g *abbr of* **gram** g

Gabon [gæ·'boʊn] *n* Gabón *m*

Gabonese [ˌgæb·oʊ·'niz] *I.* *adj* gabonés, -esa *II.* *n* gabonés, -esa *m, f*

gadget ['gædʒ·ɪt] *n* artilugio *m*

Gaelic ['geɪ·lɪk] **I.** *n* gaélico *m* **II.** *adj* gaélico, -a

gag [gæg] **I.** *n* **1.** (*cloth*) mordaza *f* **2.** (*joke*) broma *f* **II.** <-gg-> *vt* amordazar; (*silence*) hacer callar **III.** <-gg-> *vi inf* (*to joke*) contar chistes

gage [geɪdʒ] *n vt see* **gauge**

gaily ['geɪ·li] *adv* alegremente

gain [geɪn] **I.** *n* **1.** (*increase*) aumento *m*; ~ **in weight** aumento de peso **2.** ECON, FIN (*profit*) beneficio *m*; **net** ~ beneficio neto **3.** *fig* (*advantage*) ventaja *f* **II.** *vt* **1.** (*obtain*) ganar **2.** (*acquire*) adquirir; **to** ~ **weight** ganar peso ▶ **to** ~ **ground** ganar terreno **III.** *vi* **1.** (*benefit*) beneficiarse de, sacar provecho de **2.** (*increase*) aumentar; (*experience, confidence*) adquirir **3.** (*put on weight*) engordar **4.** (*clock, watch*) adelantarse

gala ['geɪ·lə] **I.** *n* gala *f* **II.** *adj* (*festive*) de gala

galaxy ['gæl·ək·si] <-ies> *n* (*space*) galaxia *f*

gale [geɪl] *n* temporal *m*; **a** ~-**force wind**

un vendaval

gale warning *n* aviso *m* de temporal

gall [gɔl] *n* 1. (*bile*) hiel *f inv* 2. (*impertinence*) impertinencia *f*; **to have the ~ to do sth** tener agallas para hacer algo; *pej* tener la cara de hacer algo

gallery ['gæl·ə·ri] <-ries> *n* 1. (*for displaying art*) museo *m*; (*for paintings*) galería *f* 2. ARCHIT, THEAT tribuna *f*

gallon ['gæl·ən] *n* galón *m (3,79 l)*

gallop ['gæl·əp] I. *vi* galopar II. *n* galope *m*; **at a ~** *fig* al galope

Gallup poll ['gæl·əp·poʊl] *n* sondeo *m* de la opinión pública

gamble ['gæm·bəl] I. *n* apuesta *f* II. *vi* jugar; **to ~ on sth** confiar en algo III. *vt* (*money*) jugarse; (*one's life*) arriesgar

gambler ['gæm·blər] *n* jugador(a) *m(f)*

gambling *n* juego *m*

game[1] [geɪm] *n* 1. (*in sports*) partido *m*; **the Olympic Games** los Juegos Olímpicos 2. (*in games*) partida *f*; **~ of chance** juego de azar; **a ~ of chess** una partida de ajedrez ▶ **to beat sb at his/her own ~** ganar a alguien con sus propias armas II. *adj* (*willing*) animoso, -a; **to be ~ (to do sth)** animarse (a hacer algo)

game[2] [geɪm] *n* (*in hunting*) caza *f*; **big ~** caza mayor

game show *n* concurso *m* de televisión

gammon ['gæm·ən] *n* jamón *m*

gang [gæŋ] *n* 1. (*criminal group*) banda *f* 2. (*organized group*) cuadrilla *f* 3. *inf* (*group of friends*) pandilla *f*, barra *f AmL*, trinca *f AmL, CSur*

gangly ['gæŋ·gli] <-ier, -iest> *adj* larguirucho, -a

gangster ['gæŋ·stər] *n* gángster *mf*

gangway ['gæŋ·weɪ] I. *n* (*gangplank*) pasarela *f*; (*ladder*) escalerilla *f* II. *interj inf* ¡paso!

gap [gæp] *n* 1. (*opening*) abertura *f*; (*empty space*) hueco *m*; (*in text, memory*) laguna *f* 2. (*break in time*) intervalo *m* 3. (*difference*) diferencia *f*; **age ~** diferencia de edad

gape [geɪp] I. *vi* abrirse; (*person*) quedarse boquiabierto II. *n* (*look*) mirada *f* pasmada; (*yawn*) bostezo *m*

gaping *adj* (*hole*) enorme; (*wound*)

abierto, -a

garage [gə·ˈrɑʒ] *n* 1. (*of house*) garaje *m*, cochera *f* 2. (*for repair*) taller *m*

garage sale *n* venta de objetos usados en casa de un particular venta *f* de garaje *Col*

garbage ['gar·bɪdʒ] *n* basura *f*; **to take out the ~** sacar la basura

garbage can *n* cubo *m* [*or AmL* tacho *m*] de la basura

garbage disposal *n* triturador *m* de basura

garbage dump *n* vertedero *m*

garbage truck *n* camión *m* de la basura

garble ['gar·bəl] *vt* (*distort: message*) distorsionar

garbled *adj* (*distorted: message*) distorsionado, -a

garden ['gar·dən] I. *n* jardín *m*; **vegetable ~** huerto *m*; **botanical ~** jardín *m* botánico II. *vi* (*with flowers*) trabajar en el jardín; (*with vegetables*) cultivar el huerto

gardener ['gard·nər] *n* 1. (*of flowers*) jardinero, -a *m, f* 2. (*of vegetables*) hortelano, -a *m, f*

gardening ['gard·nɪŋ] *n* (*of flowers*) jardinería *f*; (*of vegetables*) horticultura *f*

garden party <-ies> *n* fiesta *f* al aire libre

gargle ['gar·gəl] I. *vi* hacer gárgaras II. *n* gárgaras *fpl*

garlic ['gar·lɪk] *n* ajo *m*; **clove of ~** diente *m* de ajo

garlic press <-es> *n* triturador *m* de ajos

garment ['gar·mənt] *n* prenda *f* de vestir

gas [gæs] I. <-s(s)es> *n* 1. a. MED, CHEM gas *m*; **natural ~** gas natural 2. (*fuel*) gasolina *f*; **leaded/unleaded ~** gasolina con plomo/sin plomo; **to step on the ~** acelerar 3. (*flatulence*) gases *fpl*, ventosidad *f* II. <-ss-> *vt* asfixiar con gas

gaseous ['gæs·i·əs] *adj* gaseoso, -a

gas-guzzler *n inf* (*vehicle*) esponja *f*, vehículo *m* de alta consumición

gash [gæʃ] <-es> *n* (*deep cut*) tajo *m*; (*wound*) cuchillada *f*

gas heating *n* calefacción *f* de gas

G

gas mask n máscara f antigás

gas meter n contador m del gas

gasoline ['gæs·ə·lin] n gasolina f, nafta f CSur

gasp [gæsp] I. vi 1. (breathe with difficulty) jadear; **to ~ for air** [or **breath**] hacer esfuerzos para respirar 2. (in shock) dar un grito ahogado II. n jadeo m; **he gave a ~ of astonishment** dio un grito ahogado de asombro ▶ **to be at one's last ~** estar en las últimas

gas pedal n acelerador m

gas pipe n tubería f de gas

gas pump n surtidor m de gasolina

gas station n gasolinera f, bomba f And, Ven, estación f de nafta RíoPl, bencinera f Chile, grifo m Perú

gas stove n cocina f de gas

gassy ['gæs·i] <-ier, -iest> adj 1. (full of gas) lleno, -a de gas 2. (gas-like) gaseoso, -a

gastritis [gæ·'strai·təs] n gastritis f inv

gastroenteritis [,gæs·trou·en·tə·'rai·təs] n gastroenteritis f inv

gastronomy [gæ·'stran·ə·mi] n gastronomía f

gate [geit] n 1. (entrance barrier) puerta f; RAIL barrera f 2. SPORTS entrada f 3. AVIAT puerta f de embarque

gatecrash ['geit·kræʃ] I. vt colarse en II. vi colarse

gatecrasher n sl (at party, concert) intruso, -a m, f (que se cuela sin pagar o sin haber sido invitado), colado, -a m, f Col

gatekeeper n portero, -a m, f; RAIL guardabarrera mf

gatepost n poste m

gateway n 1. (entrance) entrada f 2. (means of access) puerta f

gather ['gæð·ər] I. vt 1. (convene: people) reunir, juntar 2. (harvest) cosechar; (flowers) recoger 3. (information) reunir 4. (muster) **to ~ one's strength** cobrar fuerzas 5. (infer) deducir; **to ~ that...** sacar la conclusión de que... II. vi 1. (convene) reunirse 2. (accumulate: things) amontonarse

gathering n reunión f

gauge [geidʒ] I. n 1. (measure) medida f 2. (instrument) indicador m 3. RAIL

ancho m de vía II. vt 1. (measure) medir 2. (assess) determinar

gauntlet ['gɔnt·lɪt] n guante m; HIST guantelete m

gauze [gɔz] n a. MED gasa f

gave [geiv] pt of **give**

gawk [gɔk] vi papar moscas; **to ~ at** mirar embobado

gawky ['gɔ·ki] adj torpe; (tall, awkward) desgarbado, -a

gay [gei] I. adj 1. (homosexual) gay 2. (cheerful) alegre II. n (man) gay m; (woman) lesbiana f

gaze [geiz] I. vi mirar fijamente II. n mirada f fija

GB [,dʒi·'bi] n 1. COMPUT abbr of **gigabyte** GB 2. abbr of **Great Britain** GB

GDP [,dʒi·di·'pi] n abbr of **gross domestic product** PIB m

gear [gir] n 1. TECH engranaje m 2. AUTO marcha f 3. (equipment) equipo m

gearbox ['gir·baks] <-es> n caja f de cambios

gearshift ['gir·ʃift] n palanca f de cambio

geezer ['gi·zər] n sl tío m; **old ~** vejestorio m

gem [dʒem] n 1. (jewel) piedra f preciosa 2. (person) joya f fig

Gemini ['dʒem·ɪ·nai] n Géminis mf

gender ['dʒen·dər] n 1. (sexual identity) sexo m 2. LING género m

gene [dʒin] n gen m

genealogist [,dʒi·ni·'æl·ə·dʒɪst] n genealogista mf

gene bank n banco m genético

general ['dʒen·ər·əl] I. adj general; **as a ~ rule** por regla general II. n MIL general mf; **lieutenant ~** teniente mf general; **four-star ~** capitán, -ana m, f general

general director n director(a) m(f) general

general election n elecciones f pl generales

generalize ['dʒen·ər·ə·laiz] vi, vt generalizar

generally ['dʒen·ər·ə·li] adv 1. (usually) generalmente 2. (mostly) en general 3. (widely, extensively) por lo general

general manager n director(a) m(f) general

general practitioner n médico, -a m, f de cabecera

general store n tienda f

general view n opinión f general

generate ['dʒen·ə·reɪt] vt generar

generation [,dʒen·ə·'reɪ·ʃən] n generación f; **for ~s** durante generaciones

generator ['dʒen·ə·reɪ·tər] n a. ELEC generador m

generous ['dʒen·ər·əs] adj 1. (magnanimous: person) generoso, -a, rangoso, -a AmS 2. (ample: serving) abundante

gene therapy [,dʒin·'θer·ə·pi] n terapia f génica

genetic [dʒɪ·'net·ɪk] adj genético, -a; **~ disease** enfermedad f genética

genetically [dʒɪ·'net·ɪk·ə·li] adv genéticamente; **~ engineered** genéticamente modificado, -a

geneticist [dʒɪ·'net·ə·sɪst] n genetista mf

genitalia [dʒen·ɪ·'ter·li·ə] npl form, **genitals** ['dʒen·ə·təlz] npl genitales mpl

genitive ['dʒen·ɪ·tɪv] I. adj genitivo, -a II. n genitivo m

genius ['dʒin·jəs] n <-ses> genio mf

genocide ['dʒen·ə·saɪd] n genocidio m

gent [dʒent] n inf abbr of **gentleman** caballero m

gentle ['dʒen·təl] adj 1. (kind) amable; (calm) suave 2. (moderate) moderado, -a; (tap on the door) suave, pasito Col, quedito Méx

gentleman ['dʒen·təl·mən] <-men> n 1. (man) señor m; **ladies and gentlemen** señoras y señores 2. (well-behaved man) caballero m

gentleness ['dʒen·təl·nɪs] n delicadeza f

genuine ['dʒen·ju·ɪn] adj 1. (not fake) genuino, -a 2. (real, sincere) verdadero, -a

genus ['dʒi·nəs] <-nera> n BIO género m

geographer [dʒi·'ɑɡ·rə·fər] n geógrafo, -a m, f

geography [dʒi·'ɑɡ·rə·fi] n geografía f

geological [,dʒi·ə·'lɑdʒ·ɪ·kəl] adj geológico, -a

geologist [dʒi·'ɑl·ə·dʒɪst] n geólogo, -a m, f

geology [dʒi·'ɑl·ə·dʒi] n geología f

geometry [dʒi·'ɑm·ə·tri] n geometría f

germ [dʒɜrm] n germen m

German ['dʒɜr·mən] I. n 1. (person) alemán, -ana m, f 2. (language) alemán m II. adj alemán, -ana

Germanic [dʒər·'mæn·ɪk] adj germánico, -a

German measles n + sing vb rubeola f

German shepherd n pastor m alemán

Germany ['dʒɜr·mə·ni] n Alemania f

germinate ['dʒɜr·mə·neɪt] vi, vt germinar

germination [,dʒɜr·mə·'neɪ·ʃən] n germinación f

germ warfare n guerra f bacteriológica

gerontologist [,dʒer·ən·'tɑl·ə·dʒɪst] n gerontólogo, -a m, f

gerund ['dʒer·ənd] n gerundio m

gestation [dʒe·'steɪ·ʃən] n gestación f

gesticulate [dʒe·'stɪk·jə·leɪt] vi form gesticular

gesture ['dʒes·tʃər] I. n 1. (body movement) gesto m 2. (act) muestra f; **a ~ towards sb** un detalle con alguien II. vi hacer un ademán III. vt indicar con un ademán

get [get] I. <got, gotten> vt 1. (obtain) obtener; (a massage) recibir; (a manicure) hacerse; **to ~ the impression that...** dar a alguien la impresión de que... 2. (receive: letter, present) recibir; **to ~ sth from sb** recibir algo de alguien 3. (catch: plane, train) coger; (the flu) coger; **do you ~ channel 4?** ¿pillas el canal 4?, ¿te entra el canal 4? Col 4. (hear, understand) comprender; (message) captar; (picture) entender; **to ~ it** no lo pillo, no agarro la onda 5. (answer) **to ~ the door** inf abrir la puerta; **to ~ the phone** inf coger el teléfono 6. (buy: groceries) comprar 7. (cause to be done) **to ~ sth done** hacer algo; **to ~ sb to do sth** hacer que alguien haga algo 8. (start) **to ~ sb to do sth** conseguir que alguien haga algo 9. inf (irk) repatear; **that really ~s me** eso me afecta realmente 10. inf (start) **to ~ going** poner en marcha; **to ~ cracking** poner manos a la obra II. vi 1. + n/adj (become) volverse; **to ~ married** casarse; **to ~ upset** enfadarse; **to ~ used to sth** acostumbrarse a algo; **to ~ to be sth** llegar a ser algo; **to ~ to**

G

like sth coger afición a algo **2.** (*have opportunity*) **to ~ to do sth** llegar a hacer algo; **to ~ to see sb** lograr ver a alguien **3.** (*travel*) llegar; **to ~ home** llegar a casa

◆**get across** *vt* hacer llegar; **to get a point across to sb** hacer llegar una idea a alguien

◆**get along** *vi* **1.** (*have a good relationship*) llevarse bien **2.** (*manage*) arreglárselas

◆**get around** **I.** *vt insep* (*avoid*) evitar **II.** *vi* **1.** (*spread*) llegar a **2.** (*travel*) viajar mucho

◆**get at** *vt insep* **1.** (*reach*) llegar a **2.** (*suggest*) apuntar a

◆**get away** *vi* irse

◆**get back** *vt* recuperar

◆**get back at** *vt* vengarse de

◆**get back to** *vt* (*letter*) contestar; (*call*) devolver

◆**get behind** *vi* atrasarse

◆**get by** *vi* (*manage*) arreglárselas

◆**get down** **I.** *vt always sep* (*disturb*) deprimir **II.** *vi* **1.** (*descend*) bajar **2.** *inf* (*enjoy oneself*) pachanguear *Méx*, rumbear *Col*

◆**get down to** *vt* ponerse con; **to ~ doing sth** ponerse a hacer algo

◆**get in** **I.** *vi* **1.** (*arrive*) llegar a casa **2.** (*enter*) entrar **3.** (*become member*) ser aceptado **II.** *vt* **1.** (*say*) lograr decir **2.** (*bring inside*) llevar dentro **3.** (*accomplish*) lograr

◆**get into** *vt insep* **1.** (*become interested in*) interesarse por **2.** (*involve*) meter; **to get sb into trouble** meter a alguien en problemas

◆**get off** **I.** *vi* **1.** (*avoid punishment*) librarse **2.** (*leave work*) salir **3.** (*have audacity*) atreverse **4.** *sl* (*have orgasm*) correrse, venirse *Col, Méx* **II.** *vt always sep* **1.** (*shot*) disparar **2.** (*help avoid punishment*) librar de **3.** (*work*) acabar

◆**get on** **I.** *vi* (*manage*) arreglárselas **II.** *vt sl* **let's get it on** (*enthusiastically begin*) ¡pongamos manos a la obra!; (*have sex*) hagámoslo

◆**get out** **I.** *vi* **1.** (*leave home*) salir **2.** (*spread*) correr la voz **3.** (*escape*)

escaparse, volarse *Col, Méx* **II.** *vt* (*make leave*) echar

◆**get over** *vt insep* **1.** (*recover from*) recuperarse de; (*illness*) reponerse de; (*difficulty*) superar **2.** (*forget about*) **to ~ sb/sth** olvidarse de alguien/algo

◆**get through** **I.** *vt* **1.** (*survive*) pasar; (*exam*) aprobar **2.** (*finish*) terminar **II.** *vi* **to ~ to sth/sb** comunicarse con algo/alguien

◆**get together** **I.** *vi* reunirse **II.** *vt* **1.** (*meet*) juntarse **2.** (*gather*) reunir **3.** (*organize*) preparar

◆**get up** **I.** *vt* **1.** *always sep* (*wake*) levantarse **2.** (*muster: courage*) conseguir **3.** *insep* (*climb*) subir **4.** *inf* (*dress*) ataviar **II.** *vi* **1.** (*get out of bed*) levantarse **2.** (*rise*) subir

getaway ['geṭ·ə·weɪ] *n* fuga *f*

get-together ['geṭ·tə·ˈgeð·ər] *n* reunión *f*

get-up ['geṭ·ʌp] *n* *inf* atuendo *m*

ghastly ['gæst·li] <-ier, -iest> *adj* (*frightful*) horroroso, -a

gherkin ['gɜr·kɪn] *n* pepinillo *m*

ghetto ['geṭ·oʊ] <-s *or* -es> *n* gueto *m*

ghetto blaster *n sl* loro *m* [*or Col, Méx* grabadora *f*] portátil

ghost [goʊst] *n a.* *fig* (*spirit*) fantasma *m*, espanto *m AmL*, azoro *m AmC*; **to believe in ~s** creer en fantasmas ▶ **not to have a ~ of a chance** no tener ni la más mínima oportunidad

ghostly ['goʊst·li] <-ier, -iest> *adj* **1.** (*ghost-like*) fantasmal **2.** (*spooky*) escalofriante

ghost story *n* historia *f* de fantasmas

GI[1] [ˌdʒiː·ˈaɪ] *n* soldado *m* norteamericano (*especialmente en la II Guerra Mundial*)

GI[2] *abbr of* **government issue** reglamentario, -a

giant ['dʒaɪ·ənt] **I.** *n* gigante *m* **II.** *adj* gigantesco, -a

giddy ['gɪd·i] <-ier, -iest> *adj* mareado, -a

gift [gɪft] *n* **1.** (*present*) regalo *m* **2.** (*talent*) don *m*; **to have the ~ of gab** *inf* tener mucha labia

gift certificate *n* vale *m* de [*or por un*] regalo

gifted *adj* **1.** (*talented: musician*) de (gran) talento **2.** (*intelligent*) brillante; **~ child** niño *m* superdotado

gift shop *n* tienda *f* de regalos

gig¹ [gɪg] *n sl* (*musical performance*) concierto *m*

gig² [gɪg] *n* COMPUT *abbr of* **gigabyte** giga *m*

gigantic [dʒaɪ·ˈgæn·tɪk] *adj* gigantesco, -a

giggle [ˈgɪg·əl] **I.** *vi* reír(se) tontamente **II.** *n* **1.** (*laugh*) risita *f* **2.** *pl* **to get the ~s** tener un ataque de risa

gimmick [ˈgɪm·ɪk] *n* (*trick*) truco *m* (*para vender más*); **sales ~** truco publicitario

gimmicky [ˈgɪm·ɪk·i] *adj* efectista

gin¹ [dʒɪn] *n* ginebra *f*; **~ and tonic** gin tonic *m*

gin² [dʒɪn] *n* AGR **cotton ~** desmotadora *f* de algodón

gin³ [dʒɪn] *n* (*card game*) juego de cartas parecido al rummy

ginger [ˈdʒɪn·dʒər] **I.** *n* **1.** (*root spice*) jengibre *m* **2.** (*color*) rojo *m* anaranjado **II.** *adj* rojizo, -a

gingerbread [ˈdʒɪn·dʒər·bred] *n* pan *m* de jengibre

gingerly [ˈdʒɪn·dʒər·li] *adv* con cautela

ginger snap *n* galleta *f* de jengibre

gipsy [ˈdʒɪp·si] *n see* **gypsy**

giraffe [dʒə·ˈræf] *n* <-(s)> jirafa *f*

girdle [ˈgɜr·dəl] *n* **1.** *a. fig* (*belt*) cinturón *m* **2.** (*corset*) faja *f*

girl [gɜrl] *n* **1.** (*child*) niña *f*; (*young woman*) chica *f*, piba *f Arg* **2. the ~s** *pl* (*at work*) las compañeras; (*friends*) las amigas

girlfriend [ˈgɜrl·frend] *n* **1.** (*of man*) novia *f*, polola *f And* **2.** (*of woman*) amiga *f*

girlhood [ˈgɜrl·hʊd] *n* juventud *f*

girlie [ˈgɜr·li] *adj* de destape

girlish [ˈgɜr·lɪʃ] *adj* de [*or* como una] niña

Girl Scout *n* exploradora *f*

gist [dʒɪst] *n* **to get the ~ of sth** entender lo básico de algo

give [gɪv] **I.** *vt* <gave, given> **1.** (*offer*) dar, ofrecer; (*kiss, signal*) dar; (*a seat*) ceder; **to ~ sb an excuse for sth** dar una excusa a alguien para algo; **given**

the choice... si pudiera elegir...; **to ~ sb something to eat/drink** dar a alguien algo de comer/beber; **don't ~ me that!** *inf* ¡venga ya, tú me la quieres dar con queso!; **~ me a break!** ¡dame un respiro!; **I don't ~ a damn** *inf* me importa un bledo; **to ~ sb the creeps** producir a alguien escalofríos; **to ~ (it) one's all** [*or* **best**] dar todo de sí mismo; **to ~ anything for sth/to do sth** dar cualquier cosa por algo/por hacer algo; **to ~ one's life to sth** dedicar la vida a algo **2.** (*lecture, performance*) dar; (*speech*) pronunciar; (*strange look*) echar; (*headache, trouble*) producir, dar; **to ~ sb a call** llamar a alguien (por teléfono); **to ~ sth a go** intentar algo **3.** (*organize*) dar, organizar **4.** (*pass on*) contagiar **II.** *vi* <gave, given> **1.** (*offer*) dar, ofrecer **2.** (*stretch*) estirarse, dar de sí; **something will have to ~** *fig* algo tendrá que cambiar **3. what ~s?** *inf* ¿qué hay? ▶ **it is better to ~ than to <u>receive</u>** *prov* es mejor dar que recibir *prov* **III.** *n* elasticidad *f*

◆ **give away** *vt* **1.** (*for free*) regalar **2.** (*reveal*) revelar **3.** *form* (*bride*) entregar en matrimonio **4.** SPORTS regalar al (equipo) contrario

◆ **give back** *vt* devolver, regresar *Méx*

◆ **give in I.** *vi* rendirse **II.** *vt* entregar

◆ **give off** *vt* emitir; (*odor*) despedir

◆ **give out I.** *vt* **1.** (*distribute*) repartir **2.** (*announce*) anunciar **3.** (*emit*) producir; (*noise*) emitir **II.** *vi* **1.** (*run out*) acabar(se) **2.** (*machine*) estropearse; (*legs*) ceder

◆ **give up I.** *vt* **1.** (*renounce*) renunciar; **to ~ smoking** dejar de fumar **2.** (*hand over*) ceder **3.** (*lose hope*) **to give sb up for dead** dar a alguien por muerto **4.** (*surrender*) entregar; **to give oneself up (to the police)** entregarse (a la policía) **II.** *vi* **1.** (*quit*) abandonar **2.** (*cease trying to guess*) rendirse

give-and-take [ˌgɪv·ən·ˈteɪk] *n* (*compromise*) toma y daca *m*

giveaway [ˈgɪv·ə·weɪ] *n* **1.** *inf* (*free gift*) regalo *m* **2.** *inf* (*exposure*) prueba *f* (que delata algo); **the way he dresses is a dead ~** su forma de vestir lo delata

given ['gɪv·ən] **I.** *pp of* give **II.** *adj* **1.** (*specified*) determinado, -a, dado, -a; **at a ~ time and place** a una hora y en un lugar determinados **2. to be ~ to** (*doing*) **sth** ser dado a (hacer) algo **III.** *prep* **~ that** dado que +*subj*, en el caso de que +*subj*; **~ the chance, I would go to Japan** si tuviese la oportunidad, iría a Japón **IV.** *n* dato *m* conocido; **that's a ~** eso se sobreentiende

giver ['gɪv·ər] *n* donante *mf*

glacial ['gleɪ·ʃəl] *adj* GEO glacial

glacier ['gleɪ·ʃər] *n* glaciar *m*

glad [glæd] <gladder, gladdest> *adj* contento, -a; **to be ~ about sth** alegrarse de algo; **I'd be ~ to go with you** me encantaría ir contigo

gladly ['glæd·li] *adv* con mucho gusto

glamorous ['glæm·ə·rəs] *adj* glamoroso, -a, atractivo, -a; (*outfit*) sofisticado, -a

glance [glæns] **I.** *n* mirada *f*, vistazo *m*; **at first ~** a primera vista **II.** *vi* **1.** (*look cursorily*) **to ~ over sth** echar un vistazo a algo **2.** (*shine*) brillar

glance off *vi* (chocar y) rebotar

glare [gler] **I.** *n* **1.** (*mean look*) mirada *f* (feroz); **to give sb a ~** fulminar a alguien con la mirada **2.** (*reflection*) resplandor *m*; **to give off ~** deslumbrar **II.** *vi* **1.** (*look*) fulminar con la mirada **2.** (*shine*) resplandecer

glaring *adj* **1.** (*obvious: error*) que salta a la vista; **~ weakness** debilidad *f* manifiesta **2.** (*sun*) deslumbrante **3.** (*hostile: eyes*) desafiante

glass [glæs] <-es> *n* **1.** (*material*) vidrio *m*, cristal *m*; **pane of ~** hoja *f* de vidrio **2.** (*for drinks*) vaso *m*; **a ~ of milk** un vaso de leche **3.** (*drink*) copa *f* **4.** **~s** gafas *fpl*, lentes *fpl AmL*

glassful ['glæs·fʊl] *n* vaso *m* (lleno) (**of** de)

glasshouse ['glæs·haʊs] *n* invernadero *m*

glassworks *npl* fábrica *f* de vidrio

glaze [gleɪz] **I.** *n a.* CULIN glaseado *m*; (*painting*) barniz *m*; (*pottery*) vidriado *m* **II.** *vt* **1.** (*pottery*) vidriar **2.** (*donut*) glasear

glazier ['gleɪ·zi·ər] *n* vidriero, -a *m, f*

gleam [glim] **I.** *n* reflejo *m*, destello *m*;

~ of hope rayo *m* de esperanza **II.** *vi* brillar, relucir

glee [gli] *n* júbilo *m*

gleeful ['gli·fəl] *adj* eufórico, -a

glide [glaɪd] **I.** *vi* **1.** (*move smoothly*) deslizarse **2.** AVIAT planear **II.** *n* **1.** (*sliding movement*) deslizamiento *m* **2.** AVIAT planeo *m*

glider ['glaɪ·dər] *n* planeador *m*

glider pilot *n* piloto *mf* de planeador

gliding ['glaɪ·dɪŋ] *n* vuelo *m* sin motor

glimmer ['glɪm·ər] **I.** *vi* brillar tenuemente **II.** *n* (*light*) luz *f* tenue; **~ of hope** atisbo *m* de esperanza

glimpse [glɪmps] **I.** *vt* (*signs*) vislumbrar **II.** *n* **to catch a ~** vislumbrar

glint [glɪnt] **I.** *vi* destellar **II.** *n* destello *m*

glisten ['glɪs·ən] *vi* brillar, relucir

glitch [glɪtʃ] <-es> *n* fallo *m*

glitter ['glɪt·ər] **I.** *vi* brillar, relucir **II.** *n* **1.** (*sparkling*) brillo *m*, destello *m* **2.** (*shiny material*) purpurina *f*

glittering *adj* (*sparkling, impressive*) brillante

glitzy ['glɪt·si] <-ier, -iest> *adj inf* ostentoso, -a; (*party*) esplendoroso, -a, suntuoso, -a

gloat [gloʊt] **I.** *vi* disfrutar con regocijo; **to ~ over sth** manifestar (gran) satisfacción por algo; **to ~ at sth** regodearse con algo **II.** *n* regocijo *m*

global ['gloʊ·bəl] *adj* **1.** (*worldwide*) (a nivel) mundial, global **2.** (*complete*) global, total, general; COMPUT **~ search and replace** buscar y reemplazar en todo el documento

global warming *n* calentamiento *m* global

globe [gloʊb] *n* (*object*) globo *m*

globetrotter ['gloʊb·trɑt·ər] *n* trotamundos *mf inv*

gloom [glum] *n* **1.** (*hopelessness*) pesimismo *m*, melancolía *f* **2.** (*darkness*) oscuridad *f*

gloomy ['glu·mi] <-ier, -iest> *adj* **1.** (*dismal*) lúgubre; (*thoughts*) melancólico, -a; **to turn ~** abatirse **2.** (*dark: corner, day*) oscuro, -a

glorify ['glɔr·ə·faɪ] <-ie-> *vt* **1.** (*make seem better*) glorificar **2.** (*honor*) alabar

glorious [ˈglɔr·i·əs] adj 1. (honorable, illustrious) glorioso, -a 2. (splendid: day, weather) espléndido, -a 3. iron (extreme) enorme

glory [ˈglɔr·i] I. n 1. (honor) gloria f; **to get all the ~ for sth** conseguir toda la gloria por algo 2. (splendor) esplendor m; **in all her ~** en todo su esplendor 3. (state of delight) **to be in one's ~** estar en la gloria 4. (adoration, praise) adoración f ▶ **be!** (thank God!) ¡gracias a Dios! II. <-ie-> vi vanagloriarse; **to ~ in sth** vanagloriarse de algo

glossary [ˈglas·ə·ri] <-ies> n PUBL, LIT glosario m

glossy [ˈglas·i] I. <-ier, -iest> adj (shiny) brillante, lustroso, -a; (paper) satinado, -a II. <-ies> n PHOT fotografía f brillante

glove [glʌv] n guante m; **leather ~s** guantes m pl de piel; **a pair of ~s** unos guantes

glove compartment n AUTO guantera f

glow [gloʊ] I. n 1. (light) luz f 2. (warmth and redness) ardor m 3. (good feeling) sensación f grata II. vi 1. (illuminate) brillar 2. (be red and hot) arder 3. (look radiant) estar radiante

glower [ˈglaʊ·ər] vi mirar con el ceño fruncido

glucose [ˈɡlu·koʊs] n glucosa f; **~ syrup** jarabe m de glucosa

glue [glu] I. n cola f, pegamento m; **to fix sth with ~** fijar algo con cola; **to sniff ~** esnifar pegamento II. vt encolar; **to ~ sth together** pegar algo; **to ~ sth on** encolar algo; **to be ~d to sth** fig estar pegado a algo

glue stick n pegamento m en barra

glum [glʌm] <glummer, glummest> adj (morose, downcast) taciturno, -a; **to be/feel ~ (about sth)** estar/sentirse melancólico (por algo)

gluten [ˈɡlu·tən] n gluten m

gnat [næt] n BIO mosquito m, jején m AmS

gnaw [nɔ] I. vi 1. (chew) **to ~ at** [or **on**] **sth** roer algo 2. (bother) atormentar; **to ~ at sb** atormentar a alguien II. vt (chew) roer

gnawing adj persistente; (pain) punzante; (doubt) que atormenta

GNP [ˌdʒi·enˈpi] abbr of **Gross National Product** PNB

go [ɡoʊ] I. <went, gone> vi 1. (proceed) ir; **to ~** (and) **do sth** ir a hacer algo; **to ~ home** irse a casa 2. (travel) viajar; **to ~ on a trip** irse de viaje; **to ~ abroad** viajar al extranjero 3. (adopt position) **when I ~ like this, my back hurts** cuando hago esto, me duele la espalda 4. (leave) marcharse; **to have to ~** tener que irse; **when does the bus ~?** ¿a qué hora sale el autobús? 5. (do) hacer; **to ~ camping/fishing/shopping** ir de camping/pesca/compras; **to ~ jogging** hacer footing; **to ~ swimming** ir a nadar 6. (attend) asistir; **to ~ to a concert** ir a un concierto; **to ~ to a movie** ir a ver una película 7. + adj or n (become) volverse; **to ~ bankrupt** caer en bancarrota; **to ~ public** hacerse público; **to ~ adrift** fallar; **to ~ bald** quedarse calvo; **to ~ haywire** volverse loco; **to ~ to sleep** dormirse; **to ~ wrong** salir mal 8. + adj (exist) **to ~ hungry/thirsty** pasar hambre/sed; **to ~ unnoticed** pasar desapercibido 9. (happen) **to ~ badly/well** ir mal/bien; **to ~ from bad to worse** ir de mal en peor; **the way things are ~ing** tal como van las cosas 10. (pass) pasar; **time seems to ~ faster as you get older** parece que pasa el tiempo más rápido a medida que envejeces 11. (begin) empezar; **ready, set, ~** preparados, listos, ya 12. (belong) pertenecer; **where does this ~?** ¿dónde va esto? 13. (fit) quedar bien; **that old picture would ~ well on that wall** ese viejo cuadro quedaría bien en aquella pared; **two ~es into eight four times** MATH ocho entre dos da cuatro 14. (lead) conducir 15. (function) funcionar; **to get sth to ~** hacer que algo funcione; **to keep a conversation ~ing** mantener una conversación 16. (be sold) venderse; **to ~ for $50** venderse por 50 dólares 17. (contribute) contribuir; **love and friendship ~ to make a lasting relationship** el amor y la amistad contribuyen a hacer duradera una relación 18. (sound) sonar; **the ambulance had**

sirens ~ing la ambulancia hacía sonar las sirenas 19. (be told) as the saying ~es como dice el refrán 20. GAMES tocar; I ~ now ahora me toca a mí 21. inf (use the toilet) do any of the kids have to ~? ¿alguno de los niños tiene que ir al lavabo? ▶ what he **says** ~es lo que él dice va a misa; **anything** ~es cualquier cosa vale; **here** ~es! ¡vamos allá! II. <went, gone> vt 1. inf (say) decir; **and then he goes, "Knock it off!"** y entonces es cuando dice: "¡Ya basta!"; **ducks ~ 'quack'** los patos hacen 'cuac' 2. (make) hacer; **to ~ it alone** hacerlo solo III. <-es> n 1. (attempt) intento m; **all in one** ~ todo de un tirón 2. (a success) éxito m; **to be no** ~ ser imposible 3. (activity) actividad f; **to be on the** ~ trajinar ▶ **from the word** ~ desde el principio

◆**go about** I. vt insep 1. (proceed with) ocuparse de 2. (perform a task) llevar a cabo II. vi andar (por ahí)

◆**go after** vt insep 1. (follow) seguir; **to ~ sb** ir detrás de alguien 2. (chase) perseguir 3. (try to get) andar tras

◆**go against** vt insep 1. (contradict) contradecir 2. (oppose) estar en contra de, oponerse a 3. (disobey) desobedecer

◆**go ahead** vi 1. (begin) empezar 2. (go before) ir delante 3. (proceed) seguir adelante; ~! ¡sigue!

◆**go along** vi 1. (move onward) ir hacia delante 2. (proceed) proceder a

◆**go around** vi 1. (move around) andar (de acá para allá) 2. (move in a curve) girar 3. (rotate) rotar 4. (be in circulation) estar circulando; **it's going around that...** se dice que...

◆**go away** vi 1. (travel) viajar 2. (leave) marcharse 3. (disappear) desaparecer

◆**go back** vi 1. (move backwards) retroceder 2. (return) volver, regresarse AmL 3. (date back) remontarse

◆**go by** vi 1. (move past) pasar (junto a) 2. (pass) transcurrir; **in days gone by** form en tiempos pasados; **to let sth ~** no aprovechar algo

◆**go down** I. vt insep bajar, descender;

to ~ a mine MIN bajar a una mina II. vi 1. (set) caer; (sun) ponerse; (ship) hundirse; (plane) estrellarse; **to ~ on all fours** ponerse [or en cuatro patas] a gatas 2. (medicine) tragar 3. (decrease) disminuir; FIN ir a la baja; (decrease in quality) empeorar 4. sl (happen) pasar; **what's going down, my man?** ¿qué pasa, tío? 5. (lose) perder; SPORTS perder frente a alguien/algo; **to ~ without a fight** rendirse sin luchar 6. (travel southward) ir hacia el sur; **we're going down to Los Angeles for the weekend** vamos a bajar a Los Ángeles por el fin de semana 7. (be received) ser recibido; **to ~ well/badly (with sb)** ser bien/mal recibido (por alguien)

◆**go for** vt insep 1. (fetch) ir a por, ir a buscar 2. (try to achieve) intentar conseguir; (try to grasp) intentar alcanzar; **~ it!** ¡a por ello! 3. (choose) elegir 4. (attack) atacar; **to ~ sb with sth** atacar a alguien con algo 5. (sell for) venderse por 6. inf (like) molar; (believe) creer en

◆**go in** vi 1. (enter) entrar 2. (belong in) ir en; **those forks ~ the drawer** esos tenedores van en el cajón

◆**go into** vt insep 1. (enter) entrar en 2. (fit into) encajar en; **does two ~ six?** ¿seis es divisible por dos? 3. (begin) empezar; **to ~ a coma/trance** MED entrar en coma/en trance; **to ~ action** pasar a la acción; **to ~ effect** entrar en vigor 4. (begin) **to ~ production** empezar a producirse 5. (examine and discuss) examinar; **to ~ detail** entrar en detalles 6. (be used in) ser utilizado en 7. (join) unirse; **to ~ the military** enrolarse en el ejército 8. (crash into) dar de lleno contra

◆**go off** vi 1. (explode: bomb) estallar 2. (make sound: alarm clock, siren) (empezar a) sonar 3. (proceed) pasar 4. (leave) irse 5. (digress) salirse; **to ~ the subject** salirse del tema ▶ **to ~ the deep end** perder los estribos

◆**go on** I. vi 1. (move on) seguir su camino, seguir adelante 2. (continue) seguir; (continue speaking) continuar 3. (go further) ir más allá; **to ~ ahead** seguir adelante **4.** (*extend*) extenderse **5.** (*pass*) pasar **6.** (*happen*) suceder **7.** (*start*) empezar; (*begin functioning*) empezar a funcionar; THEAT, MUS salir (a escena); **the show must ~** el espectáculo debe continuar **II.** *vt insep* basarse en **III.** *interj* (*as encouragement*) vamos; (*express disbelief*) anda ya

◆**go out** *vi* **1.** (*leave*) salir; **to ~ to dinner** salir a cenar **2.** (*on a date*) salir; **to ~ with sb** salir con alguien **3.** (*stop working*) estropearse, dañarse; (*light*) apagarse; (*fire*) extinguirse **4.** (*recede*) retirarse **5.** (*become unfashionable*) pasarse de moda

◆**go over I.** *vt insep* **1.** (*examine*) examinar **2.** (*cross*) atravesar; **to ~ a border/river/street** cruzar una frontera/un río/una calle **3.** (*exceed*) exceder **II.** *vi* **to ~ to** (*visit*) visitar

◆**go through** *vt insep* **1.** (*pass*) pasar por **2.** (*experience*) vivir; (*operation*) sufrir **3.** (*review, discuss*) repasar **4.** (*use up*) gastar

◆**go under** *vi* **1.** NAUT (*sink*) hundirse **2.** (*move below*) ir por debajo de **3.** (*fail*) fracasar; (*be defeated*) ser derrotado

◆**go up** *vi* **1.** (*move higher*) subir **2.** (*increase*) aumentar; FIN, ECON ascender **3.** (*approach*) **to ~ to sb/sth** acercarse a alguien/algo **4.** (*travel*) subir, viajar hacia el norte; **to ~ to Baltimore** subir a Baltimore **5.** (*be built*) ser construido **6.** (*burn up*) arder; **to ~ in flames** ser presa de las llamas

◆**go with** *vt insep* **1.** (*accompany*) ir con **2.** (*match: clothing, food and drink*) pegar con **3.** (*agree with*) estar de acuerdo con **4.** (*date*) salir con

◆**go without** *vt insep* pasar sin, prescindir de

go-ahead ['gou·ə·hed] *n* (*permission*) luz *f* verde

goal [goul] *n* **1.** (*aim*) objetivo *m*, meta *f*; **to achieve/set a ~** conseguir/fijar un objetivo **2.** SPORTS (*scoring area*) portería *f*; **to play in ~** ser portero **3.** SPORTS (*point*) gol *m;* **to score a ~** marcar un gol; **a penalty ~** un gol de penalty

goalie ['gou·li] *n inf,* **goalkeeper** ['goul·

·ki·pər] *n* SPORTS portero, -a *m, f*

goal line *n* SPORTS línea *f* de gol

goalpost *n* SPORTS poste *m* de la portería

goat [gout] *n* **1.** ZOOL cabra *f;* **~'s milk/cheese** leche *f* /queso *m* de cabra **2.** (*scapegoat*) chivo *m* expiatorio

goatee [gou·'ti] *n* perilla *f*

gobble ['gab·əl] **I.** *vi* **1.** (*devour*) jalar **2.** (*turkey*) gluglutear **II.** *vt inf* (*devour*) jalar **III.** *n* (*of turkey*) gluglú *m*

go-between ['gou·bə·,twin] *n* mediador(a) *m(f);* **to act as a ~** hacer de intermediario

goblin ['gab·lɪn] *n* duende *m*

go-cart ['gou·kart] *n* AUTO, SPORTS kart *m*

god [gad] *n* **1.** REL **God** Dios; **God bless** que Dios te/le... bendiga; **God bless America** Dios bendiga a los EEUU; **God forbid** no lo permita Dios; **God (only) knows** sólo Dios lo sabe; **for God's sake!** ¡por el amor de Dios! **2.** REL **Greek/Roman ~s** dioses *m pl* griegos/romanos

godchild *n* ahijado, -a *m, f*

goddaughter *n* ahijada *f*

goddess ['gad·ɪs] <-es> *n* **1.** REL diosa *f* **2.** (*idolized woman*) musa *f*

godfather *n* padrino *m*

godforsaken *adj* dejado, -a de la mano de Dios

godmother *n* madrina *f*

godparents *npl* padrinos *mpl*

godsend *n* **to be a ~ (to sb)** ser un regalo celestial (para alguien)

godson *n* ahijado *m*

goes [gouz] *3rd pers sing of* **go**

go-getter [,gou·'geʧ·ər] *n inf* persona *f* emprendedora

goggle-eyed ['gag·əl·aɪd] *adj* con ojos desorbitados; (*person*) con [*or* de] ojos saltones

goggles ['gag·əlz] *n* (*glasses*) gafas *fpl;* **safety ~** gafas de protección; **ski/swim ~** gafas de esquí/natación

going ['gou·ɪŋ] **I.** *n* **1.** (*act of leaving*) ida *f;* (*departure*) salida *f* **2.** (*conditions*) **easy/rough ~** condiciones *f pl* favorables/adversas; **while the ~ is good** mientras las condiciones lo permitan **3.** (*progress*) progreso *m* ▶ **when the**

~ **gets tough** (**the tough get** ~) cuando las cosas se ponen feas (los fuertes entran en acción) **II.** *adj* **1.** (*available*) disponible **2.** (*in action*) en funcionamiento; **to get sth** ~ poner algo en funcionamiento **3.** (*current*) actual; ~ **price** precio *m* actual, precio *m* de mercado **III.** *vi aux* **to be** ~ **to do sth** ir a hacer algo

goings-on [ˌgoʊˈɪŋzˈɒn] *npl* **1.** (*events*) sucesos *mpl* **2.** (*activities*) tejemanejes *mpl*

go-kart [ˈgoʊˌkɑːt] *n see* **go-cart**

gold [goʊld] **I.** *n* **1.** (*metal*) oro *m*; **to pan for** ~ lavar oro **2.** SPORTS (*medalla f de*) oro; **to win the** ~ llevarse el oro ▶ **to be good as** ~ portarse como un ángel; **all that glitters is not** ~ *prov* no es oro todo lo que reluce *prov* **II.** *adj* de oro; **a** ~ **ring** un anillo de oro

golden [ˈgoʊldən] *adj* **1.** de oro; ~ **anniversary** bodas *f pl* de oro **2.** (*color*) dorado, -a **3.** (*very good*) excelente; ~ **oldies** MUS melodías *f pl* de ayer

goldfish *n inv* pez *m* de colores

gold medal *n* SPORTS medalla *f* de oro

goldmine *n* **1.** (*mine*) mina *f* de oro **2.** FIN filón *m*

golf [gɒlf] **I.** *n* golf *m*; **to play** ~ jugar al golf; **miniature** ~ minigolf *m* **II.** *vi* jugar al golf

golf ball *n* pelota *f* de golf

golf club *n* **1.** (*stick*) palo *m* de golf **2.** (*sports association*) club *m* de golf

golf course *n* campo *m* de golf

golfer [ˈgɑːlfər] *n* golfista *mf*

gone [gɒn] **I.** *pp of* **go II.** *adj* **1.** (*absent*) ausente **2.** (*used up*) acabado, -a **3.** *inf* (*dead*) muerto, -a **4.** (*lost: hope*) perdido, -a

goner [ˈgɔːnər] *n sl* **to be a** ~ (*bound to die*) ser hombre muerto; (*broken*) estar para tirar

goo [guː] *n inf* (*substance*) sustancia *f* viscosa

good [gʊd] **I.** <better, best> *adj* **1.** (*of high quality*) bueno, -a; ~ **ears** buen oído; ~ **eyes** buena vista; ~ **thinking!** ¡buena idea!; **to do a** ~ **job** hacer un buen trabajo; **to be in** ~ **shape** estar en buena forma; **to be/to be not** ~ **enough** ser/no ser lo suficientemente

bueno **2.** (*skilled*) capacitado, -a; **to be** ~ **at** [*or in*] **sth/doing sth** estar capacitado para algo/hacer algo; **to be** ~ **at sth** dársele bien algo; **to be** ~ **with one's hands** ser bueno con las manos **3.** (*pleasant*) placentero, -a; **to have a** ~ **day/evening** tener un buen día/pasar una velada placentera; **to have a** ~ **time** pasarlo/pasársela bien **4.** (*appealing to senses*) **to feel** ~ sentirse bien; **to have** ~ **looks** ser guapo; **to look** ~ tener buen aspecto; **to smell** ~ oler bien **5.** (*favorable*) **the** ~ **life** la buena vida; ~ **luck (in sth)** buena suerte (en algo); ~ **times** buenos tiempos; **to be a** ~ **thing that...** ser bueno que... +*subj* **6.** (*beneficial*) beneficioso, -a; **a** ~ **habit** una buena costumbre; **to be** ~ **for sb/sth** ser bueno para alguien/algo **7.** (*useful*) útil **8.** (*appropriate*) adecuado, -a; (*choice, decision*) correcto, -a; **a** ~ **time to do sth** un buen momento para hacer algo **9.** (*kind*) amable; ~ **deeds/work** buenas obras/buen trabajo **10.** (*moral*) **the Good Book** la Biblia; **a** ~ **name/reputation** un buen nombre/una buena reputación **11.** (*well-behaved*) de buenos modales; **a** ~ **loser** un buen perdedor; **to be on** ~ **behavior** comportarse bien **12.** (*thorough*) completo, -a; **a** ~ **beating** una buena paliza **13.** (*valid*) válido, -a; (*not forged*) auténtico, -a; (*useable*) útil, provechoso, -a; **to be** ~ **for nothing** ser completamente inútil **14.** (*substantial*) sustancial; **a** ~ **many/few** muchos/unos pocos **15.** CULIN en su punto **16.** (*almost, virtually*) **it's as** ~ **as done** está prácticamente terminado; **to be as** ~ **as new** estar como nuevo **17.** (*said to emphasize*) **to be** ~ **and ready** estar listo **18.** (*said to express affection*) **the** ~ **old days** los buenos tiempos **II.** *n* **1.** (*moral force, not evil*) bien *m*; **to be no** ~ ser inútil; **to be up to no** ~ estar tramando algo **2.** (*profit, benefit*) beneficio *m*; **this soup will do you** ~ esta sopa te sentará bien; **for one's own** ~ en beneficio propio; **to do** ~ hacer bien; **to be not much** ~ no valer mucho ▶ **for** ~ definitivamente **III.** *adv inf* (*well*) bien **IV.** *interj* **1.** (*to* *express approval*) bien **2.** (*to express surprise, shock*) ~ **God!** ¡Dios mío!; ~ **grief!** ¡madre mía! **3.** (*said as greeting*) ~ **afternoon/evening** buenas tardes; ~ **morning** buenos días; ~ **night** buenas noches

goodbye I. *interj* adiós **II.** *n* (*departing word*) adiós *m*; **to say** ~ (**to sb**) decir adiós (a alguien); **to say** ~ despedirse

good-for-nothing [ˈgʊd·fər·ˌnʌθ·ɪŋ] **I.** *n* inútil *mf* **II.** *adj* inútil

Good Friday *n* Viernes *m* Santo

good-humored [ˌgʊd·ˈhju·mərd] *adj* afable

good-looking [ˌgʊd·ˈlʊk·ɪŋ] <better-looking, best-looking> *adj* guapo, -a

good looks *n* atractivo *m*

goodly [ˈgʊd·li] <-ier, -iest> *adj* agradable

good-natured <better-natured, best-natured> *adj* **1.** (*pleasant*) afable **2.** (*inherently good*) bonachón, -ona

goodness [ˈgʊd·nɪs] **I.** *n* **1.** (*moral virtue*) bondad *f* **2.** (*kindness*) amabilidad *f* **3.** (*quality*) buena calidad *f* **4.** (*said for emphasis*) **my** ~! ¡madre mía!; **for** ~' **sake** ¡por Dios!; **thank** ~! ¡gracias a Dios! **II.** *interj* ~ **gracious!** (*surprise*) ¡Dios mío!; (*annoyance*) ¡vaya por Dios!

goods [gʊdz] *npl* (*wares*) productos *mpl*; **to deliver the** ~ entregar la mercancía; *fig* dar la talla

good-sized [ˌgʊd·ˈsaɪzd] <better-sized, best-sized> *adj* bastante grande

good-tempered [ˌgʊd·ˈtem·pərd] <better-tempered, best-tempered> *adj irr* afable

goodwill [ˌgʊd·ˈwɪl] *n* buena voluntad *f*

goody [ˈgʊd·i] **I.** <-ies> *n* CULIN golosina *f* **II.** *interj childspeak* qué bien

gooey [ˈgu·i] <gooier, gooiest> *adj* (*sticky*) pegajoso, -a; CULIN (*dessert*) empalagoso, -a

goof [guf] **I.** *vi sl* pifiarla **II.** *n sl* **1.** (*mistake*) pifia *f* **2.** (*silly person*) bobo, -a *m, f*

goofy [ˈgu·fi] <-ier, -iest> *adj sl* bobo, -a

goose [gus] <geese> *n* ganso, -a *m, f*

gooseberry [ˈgus·ber·i] <-ies> *n* grosella *f* espinosa

goose bumps *npl* carne *f* de gallina

gorge [gɔrdʒ] **I.** *n* **1.** GEO cañón *m* **2.** ANAT garganta *f* **II.** *vt* **to** ~ **oneself on sth** atiborrarse de algo

gorgeous [ˈgɔr·dʒəs] **I.** *adj* **1.** (*attractive: woman, man*) atractivo, -a; (*dress*) precioso, -a **2.** *inf* (*pleasant: weather*) formidable **II.** *n* **hello,** ~! ¡hola, ricura!

gorilla [gəˈrɪl·ə] *n* gorila *m*

gory [ˈgɔr·i] <-ier, -iest> *adj* **1.** (*bloody*) sangriento, -a **2.** *fig* **the** ~ **details about sth** los detalles morbosos de algo

gospel [ˈgas·pəl] *n* REL evangelio *m*; **to spread/preach the** ~ extender/predicar el evangelio; ~ **singer** cantante *mf* de gospel

gossip [ˈgas·əp] **I.** *n* **1.** (*rumor*) chismorreo *m*; **the latest** ~ los últimos chismes; ~ **columnist** periodista *mf* de prensa rosa **2.** (*person*) chismoso, -a *m, f* **II.** *vi* (*spread rumors*) chismorrear; **to** ~ **about sb** cotillear acerca de alguien

gossip column *n* columna *f* de cotilleo

got [gat] *pt of* **get**

Gothic [ˈgaθ·ɪk] **I.** *adj* **1.** ARCHIT, LIT gótico, -a; ~ **architecture** arquitectura *f* gótica **2.** (*of Goths*) godo, -a **3.** TYPO ~ **script** escritura *f* gótica **II.** *n* **1.** LING gótico *m* **2.** TYPO letra *f* gótica

gotten [ˈgat·ən] *pp of* **get**

gourmet [ˈgʊr·meɪ] CULIN **I.** *n* gastrónomo, -a *m, f* **II.** *adj* gastronómico, -a

govern [ˈgʌv·ərn] **I.** *vt* **1.** POL, ADMIN (*country*) gobernar; (*organization*) dirigir **2.** (*regulate*) regular; **to** ~ **how/when/what...** regular cómo/cuándo/qué... **3.** LAW (*contract*) regir **4.** (*control*) controlar **5.** LING regir **II.** *vi* POL, ADMIN gobernar

governing *adj* directivo, -a

government [ˈgʌv·ərn·mənt] *n* (*ruling body*) gobierno *m*, administración *f Arg*; ~ **organization** organización *f* gubernamental; ~ **policy** política *f* estatal

governor [ˈgʌv·ər·nər] *n* **1.** POL gobernador(a) *m(f)* **2.** (*of organization*) director(a) *m(f)*; **the board of** ~s el consejo de dirección **3.** TECH regulador *m*

grab [græb] **I.** <-bb-> *vt* **1.** (*snatch*) quitar; **to** ~ **sth out of sb's hands** quitar algo a alguien de las manos **2.** (*take hold of*) agarrar, hacerse con; **to ~ hold of sth** hacerse con algo **3.** (*arrest*) detener **4.** *inf* (*get, acquire*) conseguir; **to ~ some sleep** dormir un rato; **to ~ sb's attention** captar la atención de alguien; **how does this ~ you?** *inf* ¿qué te parece esto? II. <-bb-> *vi* **1.** (*snatch*) arrebatar **2.** (*hold on*) asir III. *n* **to be up for ~s** *sl* estar libre

grace [greɪs] I. *n* **1.** (*movement*) elegancia *f*, gracia *f* **2.** (*elegant proportions*) elegancia *f* **3.** REL gracia *f* **4.** (*favor*) favor *m;* **to be in/get into sb's good ~s** congraciarse con alguien; **to fall from ~** caer en desgracia **5.** (*politeness*) cortesía *f* **6.** (*prayer*) bendición *f* (de la mesa); **to say ~** bendecir la mesa **7.** (*leeway*) demora *f* **8.** (*Highness*) **Your/His/Her Grace** su Excelencia **9.** (*sister goddesses*) **the Graces** las Gracias II. *vt* (*honor*) honrar

grace period *n* FIN periodo *m* [*or* período] de gracia

gracious [ˈgreɪʃəs] I. *adj* **1.** (*kind: host*) hospitalario, -a **2.** (*tactful: humor*) sutil **3.** (*merciful*) clemente II. *interj* **goodness ~** ¡Dios mío!

grade [greɪd] I. *n* **1.** SCHOOL curso *m;* **to skip a ~** perder un curso **2.** (*mark*) nota *f;* **good/bad ~s** buenas/malas notas **3.** (*level of quality*) clase *f*, calidad *f;* **high/low ~** alta/baja calidad **4.** GEO pendiente *f* **5.** (*rank*) rango *m* ▶ **to make the ~** dar la talla II. *vt* **1.** SCHOOL, UNIV (*evaluate*) evaluar **2.** (*categorize*) clasificar

grade school *n* SCHOOL escuela *f* primaria

grading [ˈgreɪdɪŋ] *n* **1.** (*gradation*) gradación *f* **2.** (*classification*) clasificación *f*

gradual [ˈgrædʒ·u·əl] *adj* **1.** (*not sudden: erosion, improvement*) gradual **2.** (*not steep: slope*) suave

gradually [ˈgrædʒ·u·ə·li] *adv* **1.** (*not suddenly: improve*) progresivamente, paulatinamente **2.** (*not steeply*) suavemente

graduate¹ [ˈgrædʒ·u·ət] *n* **1.** UNIV licenciado, -a *m, f;* **university ~** licenciado *m* universitario **2.** SCHOOL graduado,

-a *m, f* **3.** (*postgraduate*) pos(t)graduado, -a *m, f*

graduate² [ˈgrædʒ·u·eɪt] I. *vi* **1.** UNIV licenciarse; SCHOOL graduarse; **to ~ cum laude** graduarse cum laude **2.** (*move to a higher level*) subir de categoría; **to ~ to...** ascender a... II. *vt* graduar

graduated *adj* graduado, -a

graduate school *n* escuela *f* de pos(t)grado

graduation [ˌgrædʒ·u·ˈeɪ·ʃən] *n* **1.** SCHOOL, UNIV graduación *f*, egreso *m* Arg, Chile **2.** (*promotion*) ascenso *m*

graft [græft] I. *n* **1.** BOT, AGR, MED injerto *m;* **a skin ~** un injerto de piel **2.** POL corrupción *f* II. *vt* BOT, AGR, MED injertar III. *vi* POL sobornar

grain [greɪn] I. *n* **1.** (*cereal*) cereal *m* **2.** (*smallest piece*) grano *m;* **~ of sand/salt** grano de arena/sal **3.** (*smallest quantity*) pizca *f* **4.** (*direction of fibers*) fibra *f;* **wood ~** hebra *f* de madera ▶ **to take sth with a ~ of salt** no creerse algo del todo II. *vt* (*granulate*) granular

gram [græm] *n* gramo *m*

grammar [ˈgræm·ər] *n* gramática *f*

grammar book *n* libro *m* de gramática

grammar school *n* SCHOOL escuela *f* (de enseñanza) primaria

grammatical [grəˈmæt̬·ɪ·kəl] *adj* gramatical

grand [grænd] I. *adj* **1.** (*splendid*) magnífico, -a; **to make a ~ entrance** hacer una entrada triunfal; **the Grand Canyon** el Cañón del Colorado **2.** (*excellent*) sublime **3.** (*far-reaching*) importante; **~ ambitions/ideas** grandes ambiciones/ideas **4.** (*large*) grande; **on a ~ scale** a gran escala **5.** (*overall*) the **~ total** el importe total II. *n* **1.** *inf, sl* (*money*) mil dólares *mpl* **2.** MUS piano *m* de cola; **baby ~** piano *m* de cola

grandchild <-children> *n* nieto, -a *m, f*

granddad *n* **1.** *inf* (*grandfather*) abuelito *m* **2.** (*old man*) abuelo *m*

granddaughter *n* nieta *f*

grandfather *n* abuelo *m*

grand jury <- -ies> *n* LAW gran jurado *m*

grandma *n inf* abuelita *f*

grandmaster *n* GAMES (*chess pro*) gran

maestro *m*

grandmother *n* abuela *f*

grandpa *n inf* abuelito *m*

grandparents *npl* abuelos *mpl*

grand piano *n* piano *m* de cola

grandson *n* nieto *m*

grandstand *n* tribuna *f;* ~ **ticket** entrada *f* de tribuna

granite ['græn·ɪt] *n* granito *m*

grannie, granny ['græn·i] *n* 1. *inf* abuelita *f* 2. *inf* (*fussy person*) cascarrabias *mf inv* 3. *reg: esp. Southern* (*midwife*) matrona *f*

grant [grænt] I. *n* 1. UNIV beca *f;* **research** ~ subvención *f* a una investigación; **to give sb a** ~ conceder una beca a alguien 2. (*a government grant*) subvención *f* 3. (*from authority*) concesión *f;* **federal** ~ ayuda *f* estatal; **to apply for a** ~ solicitar una subvención 4. LAW cesión *f* II. *vt* 1. (*allow*) otorgar 2. (*transfer legally*) ceder; (*asylum*) dar; **to** ~ **sb a pardon** conceder un indulto a alguien 3. *form* (*consent to fulfill*) **to** ~ **sb a favor** hacer un favor a alguien; **to** ~ **sb a request** acceder a la petición de alguien; **to** ~ **sb a wish** conceder un deseo a alguien 4. (*admit to*) reconocer, admitir; ~**ed** de acuerdo; **to** ~ **that...** estar de acuerdo en que... +*subj* ▶ **to take sth for** ~**ed** dar algo por sentado; **to take sb for** ~**ed** no valorar a alguien como se merece

granulated ['græn·jə·leɪ·t̬ɪd] *adj* (*in grains*) granulado, -a; ~ **sugar** azúcar *m* cristalizado

grape [greɪp] *n* (*fruit*) uva *f;* **a bunch of** ~**s** un racimo de uvas

grapefruit ['greɪf·fruːt] *n inv* pomelo *m*

grapevine *n* vid *f;* (*climbing plant*) parra *f* ▶ **to hear sth on the** ~ saber algo por los rumores que corren

graph [græf] *n* gráfica *f;* (*diagram*) gráfico *m;* **temperature** ~ gráfico de temperaturas

graph² [græf] *n* LING grafía *f*

graphic ['græf·ɪk] *adj* gráfico, -a; **to describe sth in** ~ **detail** describir algo de forma gráfica

graphics *n* + *sing vb* 1. (*drawings*) artes *f pl* gráficas 2. COMPUT gráficos *mpl*

graphics card *n* tarjeta *f* gráfica

grapple ['græp·əl] *vi* **to** ~ **for/with sth** luchar a brazo partido por/con algo

grasp [græsp] I. *n* 1. (*grip*) agarre *m* 2. (*attainability*) alcance *m;* **to be beyond sb's** ~ estar fuera del alcance de alguien 3. (*understanding*) comprensión *f* II. *vt* 1. (*take firm hold*) agarrar; **to** ~ **sb by the arm/hand** agarrar a alguien del brazo/de la mano 2. (*understand*) entender III. *vi* (*try to hold*) intentar coger

grasping *adj* avaro, -a

grass [græs] <-es> *n* 1. hierba *f* 2. (*area of grass*) prado *m;* (*lawn*) césped *m;* **to cut the** ~ cortar el césped 3. *sl* (*marijuana*) hierba *f inf*, traba *f AmL inf* ▶ **the** ~ **is (always) greener on the other side (of the fence)** *prov* las manzanas siempre parecen mejores en el huerto del vecino *prov*

grasshopper ['græs·hɑp·ər] *n* saltamontes *m inv*, chapulín *m AmC, Méx*, saltagatos *m inv AmC, Méx*

grass snake *n* culebra *f* de collar

grate¹ [greɪt] *n* 1. (*covering an opening*) rejilla *f* 2. (*in fireplace, furnace*) hogar *m*, parrilla *f AmS*

grate² [greɪt] I. *vi* 1. (*annoy: noise*) rechinar; **to** ~ **on sb** irritar a alguien 2. (*rub together*) rozar; **to** ~ **against each other** rozar uno con otro II. *vt* 1. CULIN rallar 2. (*one's teeth*) rechinar

grateful ['greɪt·fəl] *adj* agradecido, -a; **to be** ~ **(to sb) for sth** agradecer algo (a alguien)

grater ['greɪ·t̬ər] *n* rallador *m*

gratifying *adj* gratificante

grating ['greɪ·t̬ɪŋ] I. *n* rejilla *f* II. *adj* 1. (*scraping*) que rasca; (*squeaking*) chirriante 2. (*annoyingly harsh*) áspero, -a; ~ **voice** voz *f* rasgada

gratitude ['græt·ə·tud] *n form* gratitud *f*, reconocimiento *m;* **as a token of my** ~ como muestra de mi gratitud

gratuitous [grə·'tu·ə·t̬əs] *adj* 1. (*unnecessary: criticism, violence*) innecesario, -a, gratuito, -a 2. (*free*) gratuito, -a

gratuity [grə·'tu·ə·t̬i] <-ies> *n form* propina *f*

grave¹ [greɪv] *n* tumba *f*, sepultura *f;*

mass ~ fosa *f* común; **to go to one's** ~ irse a la tumba

grave² [greɪv] *adj* **1.** (*serious: crisis, wound*) grave **2.** (*quite important: decision*) importante

gravel ['græv·əl] *n* **1.** (*small stones*) gravilla *f*; GEO grava *f*; **a** ~ **path** un camino de grava **2.** MED arenilla *f*

gravel pit *n* gravera *f*

gravestone *n* lápida *f*

graveyard *n* cementerio *m*

graving dock ['greɪ·vɪŋ·ˌdak] *n* dique *m* seco [*or* de carena]

gravitational [ˌgræv·ɪ·ˈteɪ·ʃə·nəl] *adj* gravitacional; ~ **force** fuerza *f* gravitatoria

gravity ['græv·ə·t̬i] *n* gravedad *f*; **the law of** ~ la ley de la gravedad

gravy ['greɪ·vi] *n* **1.** CULIN *salsa hecha con el jugo de la carne* **2.** *sl* (*easy money*) ganga *f*; **to make some** ~ conseguir un chollo

gravy boat *n* salsera *f*

gray [greɪ] **I.** *adj* **1.** (*colored gray*) gris; **to be dressed in** ~ ir de gris **2.** ~ **weather** tiempo *m* gris **3.** *fig* (*gloomy: mood*) triste **4.** (*grey-haired*) canoso, -a; **he has started to go** ~ empieza a tener canas **II.** *n* **1.** (*color*) gris *m* **2.** (*horse*) rucio, -a **II.** *n* **1.** (*color of horse*) rucio, -a **II.** *n* **1.** (*color*) gris *m* **2.** (*horse*) rucio, -a **III.** *vi* (*become old*) envejecer

graying *adj* con canas

graze¹ [greɪz] **I.** *n* roce *m* **II.** *vt* rozar

graze² [greɪz] AGR **I.** *vi* pastar **II.** *vt* apacentar

grease [gris] **I.** *n* **1.** (*fat*) grasa *f* **2.** (*lubricant*) lubricante *m* **II.** *vt* engrasar; (*in mechanics*) lubricar

greasepaint *n* maquillaje *m* teatral

greasy ['gri·si] <-ier, -iest> *adj* (*food*) grasiento, -a; (*hair, skin*) graso, -a

great [greɪt] **I.** *n* grande *mf*; **Alexander the** ~ Alejandro *m* Magno **II.** *adj* **1.** (*very big*) enorme; **a** ~ **amount** una gran cantidad; **a** ~ **deal of time/money** muchísimo tiempo/dinero; **a** ~ **many people** muchísima gente; **the** ~ **majority of people** la gran mayoría (de la gente) **2.** (*famous and important*) famoso, -a; ~ **minds think alike** las mentes más prestigiosas piensan parecido **3.** (*wonderful*) magnífico, -a; **she's** ~ **at playing**

tennis *inf* se le da muy bien el tenis; **to be a** ~ **one for doing sth** encantar a uno hacer algo; **the** ~ **thing about sth/ sb is** (**that**) lo mejor de algo/alguien es (que); **I had a** ~ **time with you** lo he pasado fenomenal contigo; ~! ¡estupendo! **4.** (*very healthy*) sano, -a; **to feel** ~ estar estupendamente **5.** (*for emphasis*) **they're** ~ **friends** son muy amigos; **he's a** ~ **big...** es un gran(dísimo)... **6.** (*good*) excelente

great-aunt *n* tía *f* abuela

greatcoat *n* sobretodo *m*

great-grandchild *n* bisnieto, -a *m, f*

great-grandparents *npl* bisabuelos *mpl*

greatly ['greɪt·li] *adv form* sumamente; **to be** ~ **impressed** estar muy impresionado

greatness ['greɪt·nɪs] *n* grandeza *f*

great-uncle *n* tío *m* abuelo

Greece [gris] *n* Grecia *f*

greed [grid] *n* codicia *f*; (*for food*) gula *f*; (*for money*) avaricia *f*; (*for power*) ambición *f*

greedy ['gri·di] <-ier, -iest> *adj* (*wanting too much*) codicioso, -a; (*wanting food*) glotón, -ona; (*wanting money, things*) avaricioso, -a

Greek [grik] **I.** *n* **1.** (*person*) griego, -a *m, f* **2.** (*language*) griego *m* **II.** *adj* griego, -a ▶ **it's all** ~ **to me** eso me suena a chino

green [grin] **I.** *n* **1.** (*color*) verde *m* **2.** ~**s** (*green vegetables*) verduras *fpl* **3.** (*lawn*) césped *m* **4.** SPORTS pista *f* **II.** *adj* **1.** (*green-colored*) verde; **to turn** ~ (*traffic lights*) ponerse en verde **2.** (*not ripe*) verde, tierno, -a *Chile, Ecua, Guat* **3.** (*inexperienced*) novato, -a, verde **4.** (*covered with plants*) cubierto, -a de vegetación **5.** *fig* (*jealous*) ~ **with envy** verde de envidia **6.** ECOL, POL verde

greenback *n inf* billete *m* de un dólar

green belt *n* cinturón *m* verde

green card *n* permiso *m* de residencia y de trabajo

greenery ['gri·nə·ri] *n* vegetación *f*

greenhouse *n* invernadero *m*

greenhouse effect *n* **the** ~ el efecto invernadero

greenish ['gri·nɪʃ] *adj* verdoso, -a

greenness ['ɡriːn·nɪs] n verdor m

green pepper [ˌɡriːn·'pep·ər] n pimiento m verde

green thumb n to have a ~ tener habilidad para la jardinería

greet [ɡriːt] vt 1. (welcome) saludar; (receive) recibir; **to ~ each other** saludarse 2. (react) **to ~ sth** acoger algo 3. fig (make itself noticeable) presentarse

greeting n saludo m; (receiving) recibimiento m

grenade [ɡrɪ·'neɪd] n granada f; **hand ~** granada de mano

grew [ɡruː] pt of **grow**

grey [ɡreɪ] adj, n vi, vt see **gray**

greyhound n galgo m

grid [ɡrɪd] n parrilla f; SPORTS parrilla de salida

gridlock n paralización f del tráfico; fig inactividad f

grid square n cuadrícula f

grief [ɡriːf] n (extreme sadness) aflicción f; (individual mournful feelings) pesar m; (pain) dolor m; **to cause sb ~** causar aflicción a alguien; **to give sb (a lot of) ~** hacer sentir (muy) mal a alguien ▶ **good ~!** inf ¡caramba!

grievance ['ɡriː·vəns] n 1. (complaint) queja f, reivindicación f; **to harbor a ~ against sb** presentar una queja contra alguien 2. (sense of injustice) injusticia f

grieve [ɡriːv] I. vi sufrir; **to ~ for sth/sb** llorar por algo/alguien II. vt 1. (distress) causar dolor; (make sad) afligir; **it ~s me to see your situation** me apena ver tu situación 2. (mourn) llorar; **to ~ the death of...** llorar la pérdida de...

grill [ɡrɪl] I. n 1. (part of oven) parrilla f; (for barbecue) parrilla f, grill m 2. (informal restaurant) asador m II. vt (cook) asar a la parrilla

grille [ɡrɪl] n rejilla f; (of windows) reja f; (of doors) verja f; (of car) calandra f, parrilla f AmS (rejilla del radiador)

grilling ['ɡrɪl·ɪŋ] n inf interrogatorio m

grim [ɡrɪm] adj 1. (very serious: expression) severo, -a 2. (unpleasant) desagradable; (horrible) horrible; **to feel ~** sentirse muy mal 3. (without hope) ~ **outlook** mirada f inexorable; **the**

future looks ~ el futuro parece muy desalentador

grimy ['ɡraɪ·mi] <-ier, -iest> adj (face, hands) mugriento, -a; (sooty) sucio, -a

grin [ɡrɪn] I. n amplia sonrisa f II. vi (with amusement) sonreír de oreja a oreja; (with glee) sonreír alegremente; (with embarrassment) sonreír nerviosamente; **to ~ impishly at sb** dirigir una sonrisa traviesa a alguien ▶ **to ~ and bear it** poner al mal tiempo buena cara

grind [ɡraɪnd] I. n inf 1. (tiring work) trabajo m pesado 2. (boring work) rutina f; **the daily ~** la rutina diaria II. <ground, ground> vt 1. (crush) aplastar; (mill) moler; **to ~ sth (into flour/a powder** reducir algo a harina/polvo 2. (sharpen) afilar III. vi 1. (pulverize) pulverizar 2. inf (dance seductively) bailar meneando la cadera 3. (in skateboarding) girar

grindstone ['ɡraɪnd·stoʊn] n muela f, afiladora f ▶ **to keep one's nose to the ~** inf trabajar como un enano

grip [ɡrɪp] I. n 1. (hold) agarre m; fig control m; **to keep a firm ~ on sth** agarrar algo fuertemente; **to be in the ~(s) of sth** estar en poder de algo 2. (way of holding) asidero m 3. (bag) maletín m ▶ **to get to ~s with sth** enfrentarse a algo; **to get a ~ on oneself** controlarse II. <-pp-> vt 1. (hold firmly) agarrar 2. (overwhelm) **to be ~ped by emotion** estar embargado por la emoción 3. (interest deeply) absorber la atención de III. vi agarrarse

gripping ['ɡrɪp·ɪŋ] adj (exciting: story) apasionante

gristle ['ɡrɪs·əl] n cartílago m

grit [ɡrɪt] I. n (small stones) arenilla f II. <-tt-> vt (press together) **to ~ one's teeth** a. fig apretar los dientes

gritty ['ɡrɪt·i] <-ier, -iest> adj (sandy) con arenilla; (brave: decision) valiente

grizzly ['ɡrɪz·li] I. <-ier, iest> adj gris II. <-ies> n oso m pardo americano

groan [ɡroʊn] I. n gemido m II. vi 1. (make a noise) gemir; **to ~ in pain** gemir de dolor 2. (express dissatisfaction) gruñir 3. (complain) quejarse (**about** de)

G

grocer ['groʊ·sər] *n* **1.** (*store owner*) tendero, -a *m*, *f* **2.** (*food store*) tienda *f* de comestibles

groceries ['groʊ·sə·riz] *n pl* provisiones *fpl*, víveres *mpl*

groggy ['grag·i] <-ier -iest> *adj* grogui

groin [grɔɪn] *n* ingle *f*

groom [grum] **I.** *n* **1.** (*for horses*) mozo *m* de cuadra **2.** (*bridegroom*) novio *m* **II.** *vt* **1.** (*clean: an animal*) cepillar; (*a horse*) almohazar **2.** (*prepare: a person*) acicalar

groove [gruv] *n* ranura *f*; MUS surco *m*; *fig* onda *f*

groovy ['gru·vi] <-ier, -iest> *adj sl* guay

grope [groʊp] **I.** *vi* a tientas; **to ~ for sth** buscar algo a tientas **II.** *vt*: **to ~ one's way** ir a tientas

gross [groʊs] **I.** *adj* **1.** (*vulgar*) grosero, -a **2.** LAW grave **3.** (*revolting*) asqueroso, -a **4.** (*total*) total; (*without deductions*) bruto, -a **II.** *vt* FIN (*earn before taxes*) ganar en bruto

gross income *n* ingreso *m* bruto

grossly *adv* (*in a gross manner*) groseramente; (*extremely*) enormemente; **to be ~ unfair** ser completamente injusto

gross profit *n* ganancia *f* bruta

grotto ['grat·oʊ] <-oes *or* -os> *n* gruta *f*

grouch [graʊtʃ] **I.** *n* (*grumpy person*) refunfuñón, -ona *m*, *f* **II.** *vi* refunfuñar; **to ~ about sth/sb** quejarse de algo/alguien

grouchy ['graʊ·tʃi] <-ier, -iest> *adj* malhumorado, -a

ground[1] [graʊnd] **I.** *n* **1.** (*the Earth's surface*) tierra *f*; **above/below ~** sobre el nivel del suelo/bajo tierra **2.** (*soil*) suelo *m* **3.** (*area of land*) terreno *m*; **breeding ~** zona *f* de cría **4.** (*reason*) motivo *m*; **to have ~s to do sth** tener motivos para hacer algo; **on the ~s that...** porque... **5.** (*area of knowledge*) tema *m*; **to be on one's own ~** estar en su propio terreno; **to give ~** ceder terreno; **to stand one's ~** mantenerse firme **II.** *vt* **1.** AVIAT no dejar despegar **2.** (*unable to move*) **to be ~ed** estar encallado, -a **3.** *fig inf* no dejar salir

ground[2] [graʊnd] **I.** *vt pt of* **grind** **II.** *adj* (*coffee*) molido, -a; (*meat*) picado, -a **III.** *n* **~s** sedimentos *mpl*; **coffee ~s** poso *m* de café

ground crew *n* personal *m* de tierra

ground floor *n* planta *f* baja, primer piso *AmS*; **on the ~** en la planta baja, en el primer piso *AmS*; **~ apartment** entresuelo *m*

groundless ['graʊnd·lɪs] *adj* infundado, -a

groundskeeper *n* cuidador(a) *m(f)* del terreno de juego

groundwork ['graʊnd·wɜrk] *n* trabajo *m* preliminar; (*for further study*) trabajo *m* preparatorio; **to lay the ~ for sth** *fig* establecer las bases de algo

group [grup] **I.** *n* **1. a.** CHEM grupo *m*; **~ photo** foto *f* de grupo; **~ of trees** arboleda *f*; **to get into ~s** formar grupos **2.** (*specially assembled*) colectivo *m* **3.** (*musicians*) conjunto *m* musical **II.** *vt* agrupar **III.** *vi* agruparse; **to ~ together around sb** agruparse en torno a alguien

group therapy <-ies> *n* terapia *f* de grupo

grow [groʊ] <grew, grown> **I.** *vi* **1.** (*increase in size*) crecer; (*flourish*) florecer; **to ~ taller** crecer en estatura **2.** (*increase*) aumentar; **to ~ by 2%** aumentar un 2% **3.** (*develop*) desarrollarse **4.** (*become*) volverse; **to ~ old** hacerse viejo; **to ~ to like sth** llegar a gustarle algo **II.** *vt* **1.** (*cultivate*) cultivar **2.** (*let grow*) dejar crecer; **to ~ a beard** dejarse (crecer la) barba

◆ **grow into** *vt insep* llegar a ser; *fig* acostumbrarse a

◆ **grow up** *vi* (*become adult*) crecer; (*behave like an adult*) madurar; **oh, ~! stop your whining!** ¡a ver si creces de una vez! ¡deja de lloriquear!; **when I grow up I'd like to...** cuando sea mayor me gustaría...

growing ['groʊ·ɪŋ] **I.** *n* crecimiento *m* **II.** *adj* **1.** (*developing*) **a ~ boy/girl** un chico/una chica en edad de crecimiento **2.** ECON que se expande **3.** (*increasing*) que aumenta

growing pains *npl* **1.** (*pains in the*

joints) dolores *m pl* del crecimiento **2.** (*adolescent emotional problems*) problemas *m pl* de la adolescencia

growl [graʊl] **I.** *n* **1.** (*low throaty sound: of a dog*) gruñido *m*; (*of a person*) refunfuño *m* **2.** (*rumble*) ruido *m* sordo **II.** *vi* (*dog*) gruñir; (*person*) refunfuñar

grown [groʊn] **I.** *adj* adulto, -a **II.** *pp* of **grow**

grown-up ['groʊn-ʌp] *n* adulto, -a *m, f*

growth [groʊθ] *n* **1.** (*increase in size*) crecimiento *m* **2.** (*stage of growing*) madurez *f* **3.** (*increase*) aumento *m*; **rate of ~** tasa *f* de crecimiento **4.** (*development*) desarrollo *m* **5.** MED bulto *m*

grub [grʌb] **I.** *n sl* (*food*) manduca *f*, mandado *m* Méx **II.** <-bb-> *vi* cavar

grubby ['grʌb·i] <-ier, -iest> *adj inf* roñoso, -a

grudge [grʌdʒ] *n* rencor *m*, roña *f* Cuba, Méx, PRico; **to have** [or **hold**] **a ~ against sb** guardar rencor a alguien

grudgingly ['grʌdʒ·ɪŋ·li] *adv* de mala gana

grueling ['gru·lɪŋ] *adj* duro, -a, penoso, -a

gruesome ['gru·səm] *adj* horripilante

gruff [grʌf] *adj* (*reply*) brusco, -a; **a ~ voice** una voz bronca

grumble ['grʌm·bəl] **I.** *n* (*complaint*) queja *f* **II.** *vi* (*person*) quejarse; (*stomach*) sonar; **to ~ about sth/sb** quejarse de algo/alguien

grumpy ['grʌm·pi] <-ier, -iest> *adj inf* (*bad tempered*) gruñón, -ona; (*annoyed*) cabreado, -a

grunt [grʌnt] **I.** *n* **1.** (*snort*) gruñido *m*; (*groan*) resoplido *m* **2.** *sl* (*soldier*) soldado *mf* **3.** *sl* (*laborer*) currante *mf* [or cargaladrillos] *mf* Col **II.** *vi* **1.** (*snort*) gruñir **2.** (*groan*) resoplar

G-string ['dʒi·strɪŋ] *n* tanga *m*

guarantee [ˌger·ən·'ti] **I.** *n* **1.** (*certainty*) garantía *f*; **there's no ~ that...** no hay ninguna garantía de que... +*subj* **2.** (*for repair or replacement*) garantía *f* **3.** (*a promise*) promesa *f*; **to give sb one's ~** garantizar algo a alguien **4.** (*responsibility for debt*) aval *m* **5.** (*security*) prenda *f* **II.** *vt* **1.** (*promise*) prometer **2.** (*promise to correct faults*) ofrecer

una garantía; **to be ~d for three years** tener una garantía de tres años **3.** (*make certain*) **to ~ that** asegurar que **4.** (*another's debt*) avalar

guarantor [ˌger·ən·'tɔr] *n* garante *mf*

guard [gard] **I.** *n* **1.** (*person*) guardia *mf*; **prison ~** carcelero, -a *m, f*; **security ~** guardia de seguridad; **to be on one's ~ (against sth/sb)** estar en alerta (contra algo/alguien); **to be under ~** estar bajo guardia y custodia; **to drop one's ~** bajar la guardia; **to keep ~ over sth/ sb** vigilar algo/a alguien **2.** (*in basketball*) base *mf* **3.** (*in football*) escolta *mf* **4.** (*protective device*) resguardo *m* **5.** MIL **the National Guard** la Guardia Nacional **II.** *vt* **1.** (*protect*) proteger; (*prevent from escaping*) vigilar **2.** (*keep secret*) guardar **3.** SPORTS defender

guard dog *n* perro *m* guardián

guard duty <-ies> *n* guardia *f*

guarded ['gar·dɪd] *adj* cauteloso, -a

guardian ['gar·di·ən] *n* **1.** (*responsible person*) guardián, -ana *m, f* **2.** *form* (*protector*) protector(a) *m(f)*

guardian angel *n* REL *a. fig* ángel *m* de la guarda

guardianship *n* **1.** (*being a guardian*) custodia *f* **2.** *form* (*care*) cuidado *m*; **to be in the ~ of sb** estar bajo la tutela de alguien

Guatemala [ˌgwa·ṭə·'ma·lə] *n* Guatemala *f*

guess [ges] **I.** *n* conjetura *f*; **a lucky ~** un acierto por casualidad; **to take a ~** adivinar; **to take a wild ~** hacer una conjetura al azar; **your ~ is as good as mine!** ¡vaya Vd. a saber! ▶ **it's anybody's ~** ¿quién sabe? **II.** *vi* **1.** (*conjecture*) conjeturar; **to ~ right/wrong** adivinar/equivocarse; **~ what I'm doing now?** ¿adivinas qué estoy haciendo ahora?; **to ~ that...** imaginar que...; **how did you ~?** ¿cómo lo has adivinado? **2.** (*believe, suppose*) suponer; (*suspect*) sospechar; **I ~ you're right** supongo que estás en lo cierto **III.** *vt* adivinar ▶ **to keep sb ~ing** tener a alguien en suspense; **~ what?** ¿sabes qué?

guesswork ['ges·wɜrk] *n* conjeturas *fpl*

guest [gest] *n* **1.** (*invited person*) invitado, -a *m, f*; **paying ~** (*person renting*) inquilino, -a *m, f*; (*lodger*) huésped *mf* **2.** (*hotel customer*) cliente *mf* ▶ **be my ~** *inf* ¡adelante!

guesthouse *n* casa *f* de huéspedes

guestroom *n* habitación *f* de invitados

guidance ['gaɪ·dəns] *n* (*help and advice*) consejo *m*; (*direction*) orientación *f*

guide [gaɪd] **I.** *n* **1.** (*person*) guía *mf*; **tour/mountain ~** guía turístico/de montaña **2.** (*book*) guía *f* **3.** (*help*) orientación *f* **II.** *vt* **1.** (*show*) guiar **2.** (*instruct*) orientar **3.** (*steer, influence*) dirigir

guidebook *n* guía *f*

guided ['gaɪ·dɪd] *adj* **1.** (*led by a guide*) dirigido, -a; **~ed tour** excursión *f* con guía **2.** (*automatically steered*) teledirigido, -a

guide dog *n* perro-guía *m*

guideline *n* directriz *f*; (*figure*) pauta *f*

guiding hand ['gaɪ·dɪŋ·'hænd] *n fig* mano *f* amiga

guiding principle *n* principio *m* rector

guild [gɪld] *n* (*of craftsmen*) gremio *m*; **Writers' Guild** asociación *f* de escritores

guilder ['gɪl·dər] *n* florín *m* holandés

guillotine ['gɪl·ə·tin] *n* guillotina *f*

guilt [gɪlt] *n* **1.** (*shame for wrongdoing*) culpabilidad *f* **2.** (*responsibility for crime*) culpa *f*; **to admit one's ~** confesarse culpable

guiltless ['gɪlt·lɪs] *adj* inocente

guilty ['gɪl·ti] <-ier, -iest> *adj* culpable; **to have a ~ conscience** tener un sentimiento de culpabilidad; **to feel ~ about sth** sentirse culpable por algo; **to plead ~ to a crime** declararse culpable de un crimen

Guinean I. *adj* guineano, -a **II.** *n* guineano, -a *m, f*

guinea pig *n* conejillo *m* de Indias, cuy *m AmS*

guitar [gɪ·'tar] *n* guitarra *f*; **to play the ~** tocar la guitarra

guitarist [gɪ·'tar·ɪst] *n* guitarrista *mf*

gulf [gʌlf] *n* **1.** (*area of sea*) golfo *m*; **the Gulf of Mexico** el Golfo de Méjico; **the Persian Gulf** el Golfo Pérsico **2.** (*chasm*) abismo *m* **3.** (*difference of opinion*) diferencias *fpl*

gull¹ [gʌl] *n* ZOOL gaviota *f*

gull² [gʌl] *vt* **to ~ sb** estafar a alguien

gullible ['gʌl·ə·bəl] *adj* crédulo, -a

gully ['gʌl·i] *n* (*narrow gorge*) barranco *m*; (*channel*) hondonada *f*

gulp [gʌlp] **I.** *n* trago *m*; **in one ~** de un trago **II.** *vt* tragar; (*liquid*) beber **III.** *vi* (*swallow with emotion*) tragar saliva

gum¹ [gʌm] **I.** *n* **1.** (*soft sticky substance*) goma *f*; BOT resina *f* **2.** **chewing ~** chicle *m* **II.** *vt* pegar

◆ **gum up** *vt* estropear

gum² [gʌm] *n* ANAT encía *f*

gumdrop ['gʌm·drap] *n* pastilla *f* de goma

gun [gʌn] **I.** *n* **1.** (*weapon*) arma *f* de fuego; (*pistol*) pistola *f*; (*revolver*) revólver *m*; (*rifle*) fusil *m*; **to carry a ~** llevar pistola **2.** SPORTS pistoletazo *m*; **to jump the ~** salir antes de tiempo **3.** (*device*) pistola *f* inyectora **4.** (*person*) pistolero, -a *m, f* ▶ **to stick to one's ~s** mantenerse en sus trece **II.** <-nn-> *vi* (*vehicle*) salir disparado

gunfight *n* tiroteo *m*

gunfire *n* **1.** (*gunfight*) tiroteo *m*; (*shots*) disparos *mpl* **2.** (*cannon fire*) cañoneo *m*

gung-ho ['gʊŋ·hoʊ], **gung ho** *adj sl* entusiasmado, -a

gunk [gʌŋk] *n inf* porquería *f*

gunman <-men> *n* pistolero *m*

gunpowder *n* pólvora *f*

gunshot ['gʌn·ʃat] *n* disparo *m*

gurgle ['gɜr·gəl] **I.** *n* (*noise of water*) borboteo *m*; (*of baby*) gorjeo *m* **II.** *vi* **1.** (*water*) borbotear **2.** (*baby*) gorjear

gush [gʌʃ] **I.** <-es> *n* chorro *m*; *fig* efusión *f*; **a ~ of water** un chorro de agua **II.** *vi* (*any liquid*) chorrear **III.** *vt* derramar a borbollones

gushing *adj* (*excesivamente*) efusivo, -a

gust [gʌst] **I.** *n* (*of wind*) ráfaga *f*; (*of rain*) chaparrón *m* **II.** *vi* soplar

gusty ['gʌs·ti] <-ier -iest> *adj* borrascoso, -a

gut [gʌt] **I.** *n* **1.** (*intestine*) intestino *m*; **a ~ reaction/feeling** una reacción visceral/un instinto **2.** (*string from animal intestine*) tripa *f* **3.** **~s** *sl* (*bowels*) entrañas *fpl* **4. ~s** (*courage*) valor *m;* (*strength of character*) determinación *f* **II. <-tt->** *vt* **1.** (*remove the innards*) destripar **2.** (*emotional suffering*) destrozar

gutless ['gʌt·lɪs] *adj sl* (*lacking courage*) cobarde; (*lacking enthusiasm*) apático, -a

gutsy ['gʌt·si] **<-ier, -iest>** *adj* **1.** (*brave*) valiente; (*adventurous*) atrevido, -a **2.** (*powerful*) vigoroso, -a

gutter ['gʌt·ər] *n* (*on the roadside*) alcantarilla *f;* (*on the roof*) canalón *m*

guy [gaɪ] *n inf* (*man*) tío *m;* **hi ~s** ¿qué hay, colegas?

guzzle ['gʌz·əl] **I.** *vt* (*of person: alcohol*) beber como si fuera agua; (*of car: gas*) chupar **II.** *vi* zampar

gym [dʒɪm] *n* **1.** (*gymnasium*) gimnasio *m* **2.** (*school subject*) gimnasia *f,* educación *f* física

gymnasium [dʒɪm·'neɪ·zi·əm] *n* gimnasio *m*

gymnast ['dʒɪm·næst] *n* gimnasta *mf*

gymnastic [dʒɪm·'næs·tɪk] *adj* gimnástico, -a

gymnastics [dʒɪm·'næs·tɪks] *npl* gimnasia *f*

gym shoes *n* zapatillas *fpl* de deporte

gynecologist *n* ginecólogo, -a *m, f*

gypsy ['dʒɪp·si] **<-ies>** **I.** *n* gitano, -a *m, f* **II.** *adj* gitano, -a

H

H, h [eɪtʃ] *n* H, h *f;* **~ as in Hotel** H de Huelva

ha [ha] *interj a. iron* ¡ajá!

habit ['hæb·ɪt] *n* **1.** (*customary practice*) hábito *m,* costumbre *f;* **to do sth out of ~** hacer algo por costumbre; **to get into the ~ (of doing sth)** acostumbrarse (a hacer algo); **to get out of the ~ of doing sth** perder la costumbre de hacer algo; **don't make a ~ of it** no lo vuelvas una costumbre **2.** (*dress*) hábito *m* **3.** (*addiction*) adicción *f;* **to have a heroin ~** ser adicto a la heroína

habitable ['hæb·ɪ·t̬ə·bəl] *adj* habitable

habitat ['hæb·ɪ·tæt] *n* hábitat *m*

habitual [hə·'bɪtʃ·u·əl] *adj* **1.** (*usual*) habitual **2.** (*describing person*) empedernido, -a; (*liar, drug user*) empedernido, -a

hack¹ [hæk] **I.** *vt* **1.** (*chop violently*) cortar a tajos **2.** *sl* (*cope with*) aguantar; **I can't ~ this job** este trabajo me la puede **II.** *vi* **1.** (*chop*) hacer tajos; **to ~ at sth** cortar algo a tajos **2.** (*cough*) toser (con tos seca)

hack² [hæk] *vt* COMPUT **to ~ (into) a system** introducirse ilegalmente en un sistema

hacker ['hæk·ər] *n* COMPUT hacker *mf,* pirata *mf* informático, -a

hacksaw ['hæk·sɔ] *n* sierra *f* para metales

had [hæd, *unstressed:* həd] *pt, pp of* **have**

haddock ['hæd·ək] *n* abadejo *m*

hadn't ['hæd·ənt] = **had not** *see* **have**

hag [hæg] *n* (*woman*) bruja *f*

haggle ['hæg·əl] *vi* regatear; **to ~ over sth** regatear el precio de algo

hail¹ [heɪl] **I.** *n* METEO granizo *m;* (*of stones, insults*) lluvia *f* **II.** *vi* granizar

hail² [heɪl] **I.** *vt* **1.** (*call*) llamar; **to ~ a taxi** parar un taxi **2.** (*acclaim*) aclamar **3.** (*welcome*) acoger **II.** *vi* **to ~ from** (*person*) ser de; (*thing*) proceder de

hair [her] *n* **1.** (*on head*) cabello *m,* pelo *m* Col; (*on chest, a. head*) pelo *m;* (*on armpits, legs, pubic*) vello *m;* **to do one's ~** arreglarse el pelo; **to have one's ~ cut** cortarse el pelo; **to wash one's ~** lavarse el pelo **2.** (*on animal*) pelo *m* **3.** (*on plant*) pelusa *f* ▶ **to make sb's ~ curl** *inf* poner los pelos de punta a alguien; **to get in sb's ~** poner a alguien nervioso; **to split ~s** buscarle tres pies al gato

hairbrush <-es> *n* cepillo *m* (del pelo)

hairclip *n* pasador *m,* clip *m* para el pelo

hair conditioner *n* acondicionador *m* del cabello, bálsamo *m*

haircut *n* corte *m* de pelo; **to get a ~** cortarse el pelo

hairdo *n inf* peinado *m*

hairdresser *n* peluquero, -a *m, f;* **the ~'s** la peluquería

hair dryer n secador m (de pelo)

hairless ['her·lɪs] adj (head) calvo, -a, pelado, -a AmS

hairline n (edge of the hair) nacimiento m del pelo; **he has a receding ~** tiene entradas

hairline crack n, **hairline fracture** n grieta f fina

hairnet n redecilla f

hairpiece n postizo m

hairpin n horquilla f, gancho m AmL, pinza f Col

hairpin curve n, **hairpin turn** n curva f muy cerrada

hair-raising adj espeluznante

hair remover n crema f depilatoria

hair restorer n tónico m capilar

hairstyle n peinado m

hairy ['her·i] <-ier, -iest> adj 1. (having much hair) peludo, -a 2. sl (difficult, dangerous: escape, problem) peliagudo, -a

half [hæf] I. <halves> n (equal part) mitad f; **~ an apple** media manzana; **in ~** por la mitad; **to cut sth into halves** partir algo por la mitad; **a pound and a ~** una libra y media; **to go halves with sb** ir a medias con alguien; **my better ~** fig mi media naranja; **first/second ~** SPORTS primer/segundo tiempo; **the first/second ~ of a century** la primera/segunda mitad de un siglo II. adj medio, -a; **~ an hour** media hora; **she's the player she used to be** esta jugadora no es ni sombra de lo que era III. adv 1. (almost) casi; **to be ~ sure** estar casi seguro 2. (partially) a medias; **~ asleep** medio dormido; **~ cooked** medio crudo; **~ naked** medio desnudo; **~ empty/full** medio vacío/lleno 3. (by fifty percent) **~ as many/much** la mitad; **~ as much again** la mitad más 4. inf (most) la mayor parte; **~ (of) the time** la mayor parte del tiempo 5. (thirty minutes after) (at) **~ past three** (a) las tres y media; **at ~ past** a y media IV. pron la mitad; **only ~ of them came** sólo vino la mitad de ellos

half and half I. adj **to split sth ~** dividir algo mitad y mitad II. n (for coffee) leche f con crema

halfback n (in rugby) medio m de melé y medio de apertura; (in football) corredor m

half-baked adj 1. (food) medio cocido, -a 2. inf (plan) sin sentido, estúpido, -a

half-dozen adj media docena f

half-empty adj (glass) medio vacío, -a

halfhearted adj poco entusiasta; **a ~ attempt** un intento desganado

half-price n **at ~** a mitad de precio

halfway ['hæf·weɪ] I. adj 1. (midway) medio, -a; **~ point** punto medio; **~ stage** etapa f intermedia 2. (partial) parcial II. adv 1. (half the distance) a mitad de camino; **to be ~ through sth** ir por la mitad de algo; **~ through the year** a mediados de año; **~ up** a media cuesta; **to meet sb ~** fig llegar a un acuerdo con alguien 2. (nearly, partly) **the proposals only went ~ toward meeting their demands** las propuestas sólo satisfacían en parte sus exigencias

hall [hɔl] n 1. (corridor) pasillo m, corredor m 2. (entrance room) vestíbulo m 3. (large public room) sala f; **concert ~** sala f de conciertos; **town** [or **city**] **~** ayuntamiento m 4. UNIV colegio m mayor; **residence ~** residencia f universitaria

hallelujah [ˌhæl·ɪ·ˈlu·jə] I. interj ¡aleluya! II. n aleluya m

Halloween [ˌhæl·ə·ˈwin] n víspera f de Todos los Santos, Día f de las Brujas

hallucinate [hə·ˈlu·sɪ·neɪt] vi a. fig alucinar

hallucination [hə·ˌlu·sɪ·ˈneɪ·ʃən] n alucinación f

hallucinogenic adj alucinógeno, -a

halo ['heɪ·loʊ] <-s or -es> n 1. a. fig REL aureola f 2. a. fig ASTR halo m

halogen bulb n bombilla f halógena

halt [hɔlt] I. n 1. (standstill, stop) parada f; **to bring sth/sb to a ~** detener algo/a alguien; **to come** [or **grind**] **to a ~** pararse 2. (interruption) interrupción f II. vt (stop permanently) parar; (stop temporarily) interrumpir III. vi (permanently) parar; (temporarily) interrumpirse IV. interj ~! ¡alto!

halve [hæv] I. vt 1. (lessen) reducir a la

mitad; (*number*) dividir por dos **2.** (*cut in half*) partir por la mitad **II.** *vi* reducirse a la mitad

ham [hæm] *n* **1.** (*cured*) jamón *m* (serrano); (*cooked*) jamón *m* (cocido); **a slice of ~** una loncha *f* [*or* Col tajada *f*] de jamón **2.** (*actor*) histrión *m*

hamburger ['hæm·bɜr·gər] *n* **1.** (*patty*) hamburguesa *f* **2.** (*meat*) carne *f* picada

hammer ['hæm·ər] **I.** *n* **1.** (*tool*) martillo *m*; **~ blow** *a. fig* martillazo *m*; **to go under the ~** *a. fig* (*painting*) salir a subasta **2.** (*of gun*) percutor *m* **II.** *vt* **1.** (*hit with tool: metal*) martillear; (*nail*) clavar; **to ~ sth into sb** *fig* meter algo en la cabeza a alguien **2.** *inf* SPORTS (*beat easily*) dar una paliza **3.** *inf* (*become very drunk*) **to get ~ed (on sth)** emborracharse (de algo) **III.** *vi* **1.** (*use a hammer*) martillear **2.** (*beat heavily*) golpear

hammock ['hæm·ək] *n* hamaca *f*

hamper¹ ['hæm·pər] *vt* (*hinder*) dificultar; **to ~ sb/sth** poner trabas a alguien/algo

hamper² ['hæm·pər] *n* **1.** (*picnic basket*) cesta *f* (*con tapa*) **2.** (*for dirty laundry*) cesto *m* de la ropa

hamster ['hæm·stər] *n* hámster *m*

hamstring ['hæm·strɪŋ] *n* ANAT tendón *m* de la corva; ZOOL tendón *m* del corvejón

hand [hænd] **I.** *n* **1.** ANAT mano *f*; **to be good with one's ~s** tener habilidad manual; **to deliver a letter by ~** entregar una carta en mano; **to do sth by ~** hacer algo a mano; **to shake ~s with sb** estrechar la mano a alguien; **to take sb by the ~** llevar a alguien de la mano; **sword in ~** espada en ristre; **~ in ~** de la mano; **get your ~s off!** ¡no toques!; **~s up!** ¡manos arriba!; **to ask for sb's ~** (*in marriage*) pedir la mano de alguien **2.** (*handy, within reach*) **at ~** muy cerca; **to keep sth close at ~** tener algo a mano; **on ~** (*available to use*) disponible; **to be on ~** (*object*) estar a mano **3.** (*what needs doing now*) **the problem at ~** el problema que nos ocupa; **in ~** (*being arranged*) entre manos;

preparations are in ~ los preparativos están en marcha **4.** **~s** (*responsibility, authority, care*) **to be in good ~s** estar en buenas manos; **to fall into the ~s of sb** caer en manos de alguien; **to put sth into sb's ~s** poner algo en manos de alguien; **at the ~s of sb** (*because of*) a manos de alguien **5.** (*assistance*) **to give (sb) a ~ (with sth)** echar (a alguien) una mano (con algo) **6.** (*control*) **to get out of ~** (*things, situation*) irse de las manos; (*person*) descontrolarse; **to have sth well in ~** tener algo bajo control; **to have a ~ in sth** intervenir en algo **7.** GAMES **to have a good/ poor ~** tener una buena/mala mano; **to show one's ~** *a. fig* enseñar las cartas; **a ~ of poker** una mano de póquer **8.** (*on clock*) manecilla *f*; **the hour ~** la aguja de las horas; **the minute ~** el minutero; **the second ~** el segundero **9.** (*manual worker*) obrero, -a *m, f*; (*sailor*) marinero, -a *m, f*; **farm ~** peón, -a *m, f* **10.** (*skillful person*) **old ~** veterano, -a *m, f*; **to be an old ~ at sth** tener mucha experiencia en algo; **to try one's ~ at sth** intentar algo alguna vez **11.** (*applause*) aplauso *m*; **let's have a big ~ for ...** un gran aplauso para... **12.** (*measurement for horses*) palmo *m* de alzada **13.** (*handwriting*) letra *f*; **in his own ~** de su puño y letra ▶ **to make money ~ over fist** hacer dinero a espuertas [*or* a lo loco]; **to be ~ in glove with sb** ser uña y carne con alguien; **with a firm ~** con mano dura; **at first ~** de primera mano; **to have one's ~s full** estar muy ocupado; **with a heavy** [*or* an **iron**] **~** con mano dura; **on the one ~ ... on the other (~)...** por un lado..., por otro (lado)...; **to have one's ~s tied** tener las manos atadas; **to have sb eat out of one's ~** meterse a alguien en el bolsillo, poner a alguien a comer de la mano de otro; **to force sb's ~** forzar la mano a alguien; **to get one's ~s on sb** atrapar a alguien, ponerle la mano encima a alguien; **to lay one's ~s on sth** hacerse con algo **II.** *vt* **1.** (*give*) dar; **will you ~ me my bag?** ¿puedes pasarme mi bolso? **2.** (*give credit to*) **you've got to ~ it to him** hay que reconocer que lo hace muy bien

◆**hand back** vt devolver

◆**hand down** vt **1.** (*knowledge, tradition*) transmitir; (*objects*) pasar **2.** LAW (*judgment*) pronunciar, dictar

◆**hand in** vt (*task, document*) entregar

◆**hand on** vt (*knowledge*) transmitir; (*object*) pasar

◆**hand out** vt **1.** (*distribute*) repartir **2.** (*give: advice*) dar; (*punishment*) aplicar

◆**hand over** vt **1.** (*give, submit: money, prisoner*) entregar; (*check*) extender **2.** (*pass: power, authority*) transferir; (*property*) ceder **3.** TEL pasar; **to hand sb over to sb** pasar a alguien con alguien

handbag n bolso m, cartera f AmL

handbook n manual m

handcuff vt esposar

handcuffs npl esposas fpl; **a pair of ~** unas esposas

handful ['hænd·fʊl] n **1.** a. fig (*small amount*) puñado m; **a ~ of people** un puñado de gente **2.** (*person*) **to be a real ~** (*child*) ser un bicho [or terremoto]; (*adult*) ser una buena pieza

hand grenade n granada f de mano

handgun n pistola f

handicapped I. adj physically **~** minusválido, -a; **mentally ~** discapacitado psíquico **II.** n **the ~** los minusválidos

handicap ['hæn·dɪ·kæp] **I.** n **1.** (*disability*) discapacidad f; **mental ~** discapacidad f mental; **physical ~** invalidez f **2.** (*disadvantage*) desventaja f **3.** SPORTS hándicap m **II.** <-pp-> vt perjudicar; **to be ~ped** estar en una situación de desventaja

handicraft ['hæn·dɪ·kræft] n **1.** (*work*) trabajo m artesanal **2.** (*product*) artesanía f

handkerchief ['hæn·kər·tʃɪf] n pañuelo m

handle ['hæn·dəl] **I.** n **1.** (*of pot, basket, bag*) asa f; (*of drawer*) tirador m; (*of knife*) mango m **2.** (*knob*) pomo m **3.** sl RADIO (*name*) código m ▶ **to fly off the ~** inf perder los estribos; **to get a ~ on**

sth dar con el clavo [or truco] de algo **II.** vt **1.** (*touch*) tocar **2.** (*move, transport*) llevar; **~ with care** frágil **3.** (*machine, tool, weapon*) manejar; (*chemicals*) manipular; **I don't know how to ~ her** no sé cómo tratarla **4.** (*direct*) ocuparse de; (*case*) llevar; **I'll ~ this** yo me encargo de esto; **he doesn't know how to ~ other people** (*business*) no sabe dirigir; (*socially*) no tiene don de gentes **5.** (*control*) dominar; (*work, difficult situation*) poder con **III.** vi + adv/prep responder; **to ~ poorly** no responder bien

handlebars npl manillar m

handling n **1.** (*management*) manejo m; (*of goods*) manipulación f; (*of subject*) tratamiento m **2.** COM (*fee*) porte m

hand luggage n equipaje m de mano

handmade adj hecho, -a a mano

hand-operated adj manual

handout ['hænd·aʊt] n **1.** (*money*) limosna f **2.** (*leaflet*) folleto m **3.** (*press release*) comunicado m de prensa **4.** (*written information*) apuntes mpl, hojas fpl

hand-picked adj cuidadosamente seleccionado, -a

handrail n (*on stairs*) pasamanos m inv; (*on bridge*) barandilla f

handshake n apretón m de manos

handsome ['hæn·səm] adj **1.** (*man*) guapo; (*animal, thing*) bello, -a; **the most ~ man** el hombre más apuesto **2.** (*impressive*) magnífico, -a **3.** (*large*) considerable; (*price, salary*) elevado, -a; (*donation*) generoso, -a **4.** (*gracious: gesture*) noble

hands-on adj **1.** (*practical*) práctico, -a; **~ approach** enfoque práctico **2.** COMPUT manual

handspring n salto m mortal; **backward ~** salto mortal hacia atrás

handstand n pino m; **to do a ~** hacer el pino, pararse en las manos Col

handwriting n letra f

handwritten adj manuscrito, -a

handy ['hæn·di] <-ier, -iest> adj **1.** (*convenient, available*) a mano; (*nearby*) cercano, -a; **to keep sth ~** tener algo a mano **2.** (*user-friendly*) manejable;

(*form, guide*) sencillo, -a **3.** (*skillful*) hábil; **to be ~ with sth** ser mañoso [*or* habilidoso] para algo; **to be ~ around the house** ser un manitas **4.** (*convenient*) práctico, -a; (*useful*) útil, venir bien; **to come in ~** (*for sb*) venir muy bien (a alguien)

handyman ['hæn·dɪ·mæn] <-men> *n* manitas *m inv*

hang [hæŋ] I. <hung, hung> *vi* **1.** (*be suspended*) colgar; (*picture*) estar colgado; **to ~ by/on/from sth** colgar de algo **2.** (*lean over or forward*) inclinarse **3.** (*float: smoke, fog*) flotar; **to ~ above sb/sth** cernirse sobre alguien/ algo; **to leave a question ~ing** dejar una pregunta en el aire **4.** (*die*) morir en la horca **5.** (*fit, drape: clothes, fabrics*) caer; **to ~ well** tener buena caída **6.** *sl* (*be friendly with*) **to ~ with sb** mantenerse con alguien; (*spend time at*) pasársela con alguien ► **~ in there!** ¡aguanta! II. <hung, hung> *vt* **1.** (*attach*) colgar; (*laundry*) tender; (*door*) colocar; **to ~ wallpaper (on a wall)** empapelar (una pared); **to ~ the curtains** colgar las cortinas **2.** (*lights, ornaments, decorations*) adornar **3.** (*one's head*) bajar **4.** (*execute*) ahorcar ► **to ~ it up** acabar con algo III. *n* FASHION caída *f* ► **to get the ~ of sth** *inf* coger el truquillo a algo

◆**hang around** I. *vi* **1.** *sl* (*waste time*) perder el tiempo **2.** (*wait*) esperar **3.** (*idle*) no hacer nada **4.** (*be friendly with*) **to ~ with sb** andar por ahí con alguien II. *vt insep* rondar; **to ~ a place** andar rondando por un sitio

◆**hang back** *vi* **1.** (*be reluctant to move forward*) quedarse atrás **2.** (*hesitate*) vacilar

◆**hang behind** *vi* rezagarse

◆**hang on** I. *vi* **1.** (*wait briefly*) esperar; **to keep sb hanging on** hacer esperar a alguien; **~!** *inf* ¡espera un momento!; **she's on the other phone — would you like to ~?** está hablando por la otra línea, ¿quiere esperar? **2.** (*hold on to*) **to ~ to sth** agarrarse a algo; **~ tight** agárrate fuerte **3.** (*persevere*) mantenerse firme; (*resist*) aguantar II. *vt insep*

1. (*depend upon*) depender de **2.** (*give attention*) estar pendiente de; **to ~ sb's every word** estar pendiente de lo que dice alguien

◆**hang out** I. *vt* (*laundry*) tender II. *vi* **1.** **let it all ~!** *sl* (*be relaxed*) ¡suéltate la melena! *fig* **2.** *sl* (*spend time at*) andar; **where does he ~ these days?** ¿por dónde anda estos días?

◆**hang together** *vi* **1.** (*make sense*) ser coherente **2.** (*remain associated*) permanecer unidos

◆**hang up** I. *vi* **1.** colgar; **to ~ on sb** colgar a alguien **2.** *inf* **to get hung up on sth** (*have trouble with*) quedar varado II. *vt* **1.** (*curtains, receiver*) colgar **2.** (*give up*) **to ~ one's cleats/boxing gloves** *fig* colgar las botas/los guantes **3.** (*delay*) causar un retraso a

hanger ['hæŋ·ər] *n* (*clothes*) percha *f*, gancho *m* de colgar ropa

hang-gliding *n* SPORTS vuelo *m* con ala delta

hangout *n sl* guarida *f*; **a favorite ~ of artists** un lugar frecuentado por artistas

hangover *n* **1.** (*after drinking*) resaca *f*, goma *f AmL*, guayabo *m Col* **2.** (*leftover*) vestigio *m*

hang-up *n inf* complejo *m*; **to have a ~ about sth** estar acomplejado por algo

hankie *n*, **hanky** ['hæŋ·ki] *n inf abbr of* **handkerchief** pañuelo *m*

Hanukkah ['hɑ·nə·kə] *n* Hanukah *m*

haphazard [hæp·'hæz·ərd] *adj* **1.** (*random, arbitrary*) caprichoso, -a **2.** (*badly planned*) hecho, -a de cualquier manera

happen ['hæp·ən] *vi* **1.** (*occur*) pasar; **if anything ~s to me...** si me ocurre algo...; **these things ~** son cosas que pasan; **whatever ~s** pase lo que pase; **what ~ed to your hand?** ¿qué te ha pasado en la mano? **2.** (*chance*) **I ~ed to be at home** dio la casualidad de que estaba en casa; **it ~ed (that)...** resultó que...; **he ~s to be my best friend** pues resulta que es mi mejor amigo

happily ['hæp·ɪ·li] *adv* **1.** (*contentedly*) felizmente; **they lived ~ ever after** fueron felices y comieron perdices **2.** (*will-*

ingly) con mucho gusto **3.** (*fortunately*) afortunadamente

happiness ['hæp·ɪ·nɪs] *n* felicidad *f*

happy ['hæp·i] <-ier, -iest> *adj* **1.** (*feeling very good*) feliz; **to be ~ that...** estar contento de que...; **to be ~ to know that...** alegrarse de saber que...; **I'm so ~ for you** me alegro mucho por ti; **to be ~ to do sth** estar encantado de hacer algo; **~ birthday!** ¡feliz cumpleaños!; **many ~ returns (of the day)!** ¡que cumplas muchos más! **2.** (*satisfied*) contento, -a; **to be ~ about sb/sth** estar contento con alguien/algo; **are you ~ with the idea?** ¿te parece bien la idea? **3.** (*fortunate*) afortunado, -a; **a ~ coincidence** una feliz coincidencia **4.** (*suitable: phrase, behavior*) acertado, -a

harassment [hə·ˈræs·mənt] *n* **1.** (*pestering*) acoso *m*; **sexual ~** acoso sexual **2.** (*attack*) hostigamiento *m*

harbor ['har·bər] I. *n* **1.** (*port*) puerto *m*; **fishing ~** puerto pesquero **2.** *fig* (*shelter*) refugio *m* II. *vt* **1.** (*give shelter to*) dar cobijo a **2.** (*keep: feelings*) albergar; (*hopes*) abrigar; **to ~ suspicions** tener sospechas; **to ~ a grudge (against sb)** guardar rencor (a alguien) **3.** (*keep in hiding*) esconder; (*criminal*) encubrir

hard [hard] I. *adj* **1.** (*firm, rigid*) duro, -a; (*rule*) estricto, -a; **~ times** malos tiempos; **to have a ~ time** pasarlo mal; **to give sb a ~ time** hacérselo pasar mal a alguien; **to have ~ luck** tener mala suerte **2.** (*intense, concentrated*) **to take a (good) ~ look at sth** analizar algo detenidamente; **to be a ~ worker** ser muy trabajador **3.** (*forceful*) fuerte **4.** (*difficult, complex*) difícil; **~ landing** AVIAT aterrizaje forzado, -a; **to be ~ to please** ser difícil de contentar; **to learn the ~ way** *fig* aprender a base de errores [*or* palos] **5.** (*severe*) severo, -a **6.** (*hostile, unkind*) **to be ~ on sb/sth** ser duro con alguien/algo **7.** (*extremely cold*) riguroso, -a **8.** (*solid: evidence*) concluyente; (*fact*) innegable; **~ and fast information** información veraz **9.** (*with alcohol*) **~ cider/punch** sidra/ponche fuerte [*or* cargado, -a] **10.** CHEM (*water*) duro, -a II. *adv* **1.** (*forcefully*) fuerte; **to hit sb ~** pegar fuerte a alguien; **to press/pull ~** apretar/estirar con fuerza **2.** (*rigid*) **frozen ~** helado, -a **3.** (*energetically, vigorously*) mucho; **to fight ~** *fig* luchar con todas sus fuerzas; **to study/work ~** estudiar/trabajar mucho; **to try ~** to do sth esforzarse en hacer algo; **think ~** concéntrate; **to die ~** *fig* tardar en desaparecer **4.** (*intently*) detenidamente; **to look ~ at sth** estudiar algo con detenimiento **5.** (*closely*) muy cerca; **to be ~ up** no tener ni un céntimo **6.** (*heavy*) mucho; **it rained ~** llovió fuerte; **to take sth ~** tomarse algo muy mal; **I would be ~ pressed to choose one** me costaría mucho decidirme por uno

hardback ['hard·bæk] I. *n* (*book*) libro *m* de tapa dura; **in ~** con tapa dura II. *adj* con tapa [*or* pasta] dura

hard-boiled *adj* (*egg*) duro, -a; (*person*) endurecido, -a

hard copy <-ies> *n* COMPUT impresión *f*

hardcover *n* (*book*) tapa [*or* pasta] *f* dura

hard currency <-ies> *n* FIN moneda *f* fuerte

hard disk *n* COMPUT disco *m* duro

hard drive *n* COMPUT disco *m* duro

hard drug *n* droga *f* dura

hard-earned *adj* (*money*) ganado, -a con el sudor de la frente; (*rest, vacation*) merecido, -a

harden ['har·dən] I. *vt* **1.** (*make more solid, firmer*) endurecer; (*steel*) templar **2.** (*make tougher*) curtir; **to ~ oneself to sth** insensibilizarse a algo; **to become ~ed** curtirse **3.** (*opinions, feelings*) afianzar II. *vi* **1.** (*become firmer: character*) endurecerse **2.** (*attitude*) volverse inflexible **3.** (*become confirmed: idea*) confirmarse; (*feeling, intention*) afianzarse

hard feelings *npl* resentimiento *m*; **no ~!** ¡olvidémoslo!

hardly ['hard·li] *adv* **1.** (*barely*) apenas; **~ anything** casi nada; **~ ever** casi nunca; **she can ~...** apenas puede...; **she can ~ wait until tomorrow** tiene unas ganas locas de que llegue mañana **2.** (*certainly not*) **you can ~ expect him to**

do that no puedes esperar que haga eso; **~!** ¡qué va! *inf*

hardship ['hɑːdˌʃɪp] *n* (*suffering*) penas *fpl*; (*adversity*) adversidad *f*; (*deprivation*) penuria *f*; **to suffer great ~** pasar muchos apuros

hardware *n* **1.** (*household articles*) ferretería *f*; **~ store** ferretero, -a *m, f*; (*home improvement center*) centro *m* de mejoramiento para el hogar **2.** (*articles of metal*) quincallería *f* **3.** COMPUT hardware *m*; **computer ~** soporte *m* físico del ordenador **4.** MIL armamento *m*

hard-wearing *adj* resistente

hard-working *adj* trabajador(a)

hare [her] *n* BIO liebre *f*

harem ['herˌəm] *n* harén *m*

harm [hɑːm] **I.** *n* daño *m*; **to do ~ to sb/sth** hacer daño a alguien/algo; **to do more ~ than good** hacer más mal que bien; **(to put) out of ~'s way** (poner) a salvo; **to see no ~ in sth** no ver nada malo en algo; **I meant no ~** no pretendía hacer daño; **there's no ~ in trying** no se pierde nada con intentarlo **II.** *vt* **1.** (*hurt, ruin*) hacer daño; (*reputation*) perjudicar **2.** (*spoil*) estropear

harmful ['hɑːmfəl] *adj* dañino, -a; (*thing*) nocivo, -a; **to be ~ to sth** ser perjudicial para algo

harmless ['hɑːmlɪs] *adj* (*animal, person*) inofensivo, -a; (*thing*) inocuo, -a; (*fun, joke*) inocente

harmonium [hɑːˈmoʊniəm] *n* MUS armonio *m*

harmony ['hɑːməni] <-ies> *n* armonía *f*; **in ~ (with sb/sth)** en armonía (con alguien/algo)

harsh [hɑːʃ] *adj* **1.** (*severe: parents*) severo, -a; (*punishment*) duro, -a **2.** (*unfair: criticism*) cruel; (*words, reality*) duro, -a **3.** (*unfriendly*) desabrido, -a **4.** (*uncomfortable: light*) fuerte; (*climate, winter*) riguroso, -a; (*terrain*) desolado, -a **5.** (*unaesthetic: color*) chillón, -ona **6.** (*unpleasant to the ear: sound*) discordante; (*voice*) estridente

harvest ['hɑːvɪst] **I.** *n* (*of crops*) cosecha *f*; (*of grapes*) vendimia *f*; (*of vegetables*) recolección *f*; **the apple ~** la cosecha de la manzana **II.** *vt a. fig* cosechar; (*grapes*) vendimiar; (*vegetables*) recolectar; **to ~ a field** hacer la cosecha en un campo **III.** *vi* cosechar

has [hæz, *unstressed:* həz] *3rd pers sing of* **have**

has-been *n inf* vieja gloria *f*; **to be a ~** ser alguien que ya ha pasado a la historia

hash [hæʃ] **I.** *vt* CULIN picar **II.** *n* CULIN picadillo *m*

hash browns *npl* patatas hervidas y después fritas

hasn't ['hæzˌənt] = **has not** *see* **have**

hassle ['hæsəl] **I.** *n inf* (*trouble*) lío *m*; **to give sb a ~** fastidiar a alguien; **it's such a ~** es un jaleo **II.** *vt inf* fastidiar; **to ~ sb to do sth** estar encima a alguien para que haga algo

haste [heɪst] *n* prisa *f*; **to make ~** apresurarse; **in ~** de prisa

hasten ['heɪsən] **I.** *vt* acelerar; **to ~ sb along** dar prisa a alguien **II.** *vi* apresurarse; **to ~ to do sth** apresurarse a hacer algo

hasty ['heɪsti] <-ier, -iest> *adj* **1.** (*fast*) rápido, -a **2.** (*not thought out*) precipitado, -a; **to make ~ decisions** tomar decisiones irreflexivas; **to be ~ in doing sth** precipitarse en algo

hat [hæt] *n* sombrero *m*; **to pass around the ~** pasar la gorra ▸ **at the drop of a ~** con nada; **to hang one's ~ somewhere** quedarse a vivir en algún sitio; **to keep sth under one's ~** no decir ni una palabra sobre algo

hatch[1] [hætʃ] **I.** *vi* salir del cascarón **II.** *vt* **1.** (*chick*) incubar, empollar **2.** (*devise in secret*) tramar

hatch[2] [hætʃ] <-es> *n* trampilla *f*; NAUT escotilla *f* ▸ **down the ~!** ¡salud!

hatch[3] [hætʃ] *vt* ART sombrear

hatchback ['hætʃˌbæk] *n* AUTO coche *m* con puerta trasera

hate [heɪt] **I.** *n* odio *m* **II.** *vt* odiar; **to ~ sb's guts** *sl* odiar a alguien a muerte

hate crime *n* delito de carácter xenófobo, racista, antihomosexual, etc.

hateful ['heɪtfəl] *adj* odioso, -a

hatred ['heɪtrɪd] *n* odio *m*

hat trick *n* SPORTS tres goles marcados por un mismo jugador; **to score a ~** marcar tres tantos

haul [hɔl] I. vt 1. (pull with effort) arrastrar; **to ~ up the sail** izar la vela; **to ~ a boat out of the water** sacar una barca del agua 2. inf (force to go) forzar, jalar 3. (transport goods) transportar II. n 1. (distance) trayecto m; **in** [or **over**] **the long ~** fig a la larga 2. (quantity caught: of fish, shrimp) redada f; (of stolen goods) botín m

♦**haul up** vt inf **to haul sb up before sb** hacer que alguien dé explicaciones a alguien

haunt [hɔnt] I. vt 1. (ghost) aparecerse 2. (bother, torment) perseguir; **to be ~ed by sth** estar obsesionado por algo 3. (frequent) frecuentar; **to ~ a place** rondar un lugar II. n lugar m preferido

haunted adj 1. (by ghosts) embrujado, -a 2. (troubled: look) angustiado, -a, preocupado, -a

have [hæv, unstressed: həv] I. <has, had, had> vt 1. (own) tener, poseer; **I have two brothers** tengo dos hermanos; **to ~ sth to do** tener algo que hacer 2. (engage in) **to ~ a talk with sb** hablar con alguien 3. (eat) **to ~ breakfast/a snack** desayunar/merendar; **to ~ lunch** comer, almorzar Col; **to ~ dinner** cenar, comer Col; **I ~n't had shrimp in ages!** ¡hace años que no como gambas!; **to ~ some coffee** tomar un poco de café 4. (give birth to) **to ~ a child** tener un hijo 5. (receive) tener, recibir; **to ~ visitors** tener visita 6. (show trait) **to ~ patience/mercy** tener paciencia/compasión; **to ~ doubts/second thoughts** tener dudas/reservas 7. (cause to occur) **to ~ dinner ready** tener la cena preparada; **I'll ~ Bob give you a ride home** le pediré [or diré] a Bob que te lleve a casa; **I won't ~ him doing that** no dejo que haga esto ▶ **to ~ it in for sb** inf tenerla tomada con alguien; **to ~ it in** one **to do sth** ser capaz de hacer algo; **I didn't think she had it in her!** ¡no pensaba que fuera capaz de eso!; **to ~ had it with sb/sth** inf haber tenido más que suficiente de alguien/algo II. <has, had, had> aux 1. (indicates perfect tense) **he has never been to**

California nunca ha estado en California; **we had been swimming** habíamos estado nadando; **had I known you were coming,...** form si hubiera sabido que ibas a venir,... 2. (must) **to ~ (got) to do sth** tener que hacer algo; **do we ~ to finish this today?** ¿tenemos que acabar esto hoy? III. n pl **the ~s and the have-nots** los ricos y los pobres

♦**have back** vt always sep **can I have it back?** ¿me lo devuelves?

♦**have in** vt always sep invitar; **they had some experts in** llamaron a algunos expertos

♦**have on** vt always sep 1. (wear: clothes) llevar (puesto); **he didn't have any clothes on** estaba desnudo 2. (carry) **to have sth on oneself** llevar algo encima; **have you got any money on you?** ¿llevas dinero contigo?

♦**have out** vt always sep 1. (remove) sacar 2. inf (argue) **to have it out with sb** poner las cosas en claro

♦**have over** vt always sep invitar

haven ['heɪ·vən] n refugio m

haven't ['hæv·ənt] = **have not** see **have**

hawk [hɔk] I. n halcón m II. vt (wares) pregonar III. vi carraspear

hay [heɪ] n heno m ▶ **to hit the ~** inf acostarse

hay fever n fiebre f del heno

haystack n almiar m

haywire adj inf **to go/be ~** (person) volverse/estar loco; (machine) estropearse

hazard ['hæz·ərd] I. n 1. (danger) peligro m 2. (risk) riesgo m; **fire ~** peligro de incendio; **health ~** riesgo para la salud II. vt 1. (dare) aventurar 2. (endanger) arriesgar

hazard lights npl AUTO luces f pl de emergencia

hazardous ['hæz·ər·dəs] adj (dangerous) peligroso, -a; (risky) arriesgado, -a

haze [heɪz] I. n 1. (mist) neblina f; (smog) calima f 2. (mental) aturdimiento m II. vt ESP. UNIV novatada a

hazelnut ['heɪ·zəl·nʌt] n BOT avellana f

hazy ['heɪ·zi] <-ier, -iest> adj 1. (with bad visibility) neblinoso, -a 2. (confused, unclear) vago, -a

he [hi] I. pron pers 1. (male person or

H

animal) él; ~'s [*or* ~ **is**] **my father** (él) es mi padre; ~'s **gone away but** ~'ll **be back soon** se ha ido, pero volverá pronto; **here** ~ **comes** ahí viene **2.** (*unspecified sex*) **if somebody comes,** ~ **will buy it** si alguien viene, lo comprará; ~ **who...** *form* aquél que... **II.** *n* (*of baby*) varón *m*; (*of animal*) macho *m*

head [hed] **I.** *n* **1.** ANAT cabeza *f*; **to nod one's** ~ asentir con la cabeza; **to go straight to sb's** ~ (*alcohol, wine*) subírse a la cabeza a alguien **2.** (*unit*) cabeza *f*; **a** [*or* **per**] ~ por cabeza; **a hundred** ~ **of cattle** cien cabezas de ganado **3.** (*mind*) **to clear one's** ~ aclararse las ideas; **to get sth/sb out of one's** ~ sacarse algo/a alguien de la cabeza **4.** (*top: of line*) cabeza *f*; (*of bed, table*) cabecera *f*; (*of a page, column*) parte *f* superior **5.** BOT cabeza *f*; **a** ~ **of lettuce** una lechuga **6.** ~**s** FIN (*face of coin*) cara *f*; ~**s or tails?** ¿cara o cruz? **7.** (*beer foam*) espuma *f* **8.** GEO (*of river*) nacimiento *m* **9.** (*boss*) jefe, -a *m, f* **10.** TECH (*device*) cabezal *m* **11.** COMPUT **read/write** ~ cabeza *f* de lectura/escritura **12.** NAUT (*toilet*) baño *m* ▶ **to have one's** ~ **in the <u>clouds</u>** tener la cabeza [*or* en las nubes] llena de pájaros; **to be** ~ **over <u>heels</u> in love** estar locamente enamorado; **to fall** ~ **over <u>heels</u> in love with sb** enamorarse locamente de alguien; **to bury one's** ~ **in the <u>sand</u>** hacer como el avestruz; **to not be able to make** ~ (**n**)*or* **tail of sth** no entender ni jota de algo, no encontrarle pies ni cabeza a algo; ~**s I win, <u>tails</u> you lose** o gano yo o gano yo; **to bang one's** ~ **against a <u>wall</u>** darse de cabeza contra la pared; **to keep one's** ~ **above <u>water</u>** mantenerse a flote; **to keep one's** ~ **<u>down</u>** (*avoid attention*) mantenerse al margen; (*work hard*) no levantar la cabeza; **to hold one's** ~ **<u>high</u>** mantener la cabeza alta; **to <u>bite</u> sb's** ~ **off** echar una bronca a alguien; **to <u>bring</u> sth to a** ~ llevar algo a un punto crítico; **to <u>laugh</u> one's** ~ **off** desternillarse de risa; ~**s <u>up</u>!** ¡cuidado!, ¡pilas! *Col,* ¡aguas! *Méx* **II.** *vt* **1.** (*lead*) encabezar; (*a company, organization*) dirigir; (*team*)

capitanear **2.** PUBL encabezar **3.** SPORTS (*ball*) cabecear **III.** *vi* **to** ~ (**for**) **home** dirigirse hacia casa

◆ **head back** *vi* volver, regresar

◆ **head off I.** *vt* cortar el paso a **II.** *vi* **to** ~ **toward** salir hacia

◆ **head up** *vt* dirigir

headache ['hed-eɪk] *n* dolor *m* de cabeza

headband *n* cinta *f* de pelo

head cold *n* resfriado *m*

header ['hed-ər] *n* **1.** SPORTS cabezazo *m* **2.** COMPUT cabecera *f*

headhunter *n* **1.** ECON cazatalentos *mf inv* **2.** (*warrior*) cazador *m* de cabezas

headlamp *n*, **headlight** *n* faro *m*

headline I. *n* titular *m* ▶ **to <u>hit</u> the** ~**s** salir en primera plana **II.** *vt* titular

headmaster *n* director *m* de colegio

headmistress <-es> *n* directora *f* de colegio

head-on I. *adj* (*collision*) frontal **II.** *adv* frontalmente, de frente

headphones *npl* auriculares *mpl*, audífonos *mpl AmL*

headquarters *n* + *sing/pl vb* MIL cuartel *m* general; (*of company*) oficina *f* central; (*of political party*) sede *f*; (*of the police*) jefatura *f* de policía

headrest *n* reposacabezas *m inv*

headroom *n* altura *f*

headscarf <-scarves> *n* pañuelo *m* para la cabeza

headset *n* auriculares *mpl*, audífonos *mpl AmL*

head start *n* ventaja *f*; **to give sb a** ~ dar ventaja a alguien

headway *n* progreso *m*; **to make** ~ hacer progresos

heal [hil] **I.** *vt* (*wound*) curar; (*differences*) salvar **II.** *vi* (*wound, injury*) cicatrizar

health [helθ] *n* salud *f*; **to be in good/bad** ~ estar bien/mal de salud; **to drink to sb's** ~ beber a la salud de alguien

health care *n* asistencia *f* sanitaria [*or* médica]

health center *n* centro *m* médico

health certificate *n* certificado *m* médico

health club *n* gimnasio *m*

health food *n* alimentos *m pl* naturales

health food shop n, **health food store** n tienda f de productos naturales

health insurance n seguro m médico

healthy ['hel·θi] <-ier, -iest> adj 1. MED sano, -a 2. FIN (strong) próspero, -a; (profit) sustancial 3. (positive: attitude) positivo, -a

heap [hip] I. n (pile) pila f, montón m; a (whole) ~ of work inf un montón de trabajo II. vt amontonar, apilar

hear [hɪr] <heard, heard> I. vt 1. (perceive) oír 2. (be told) enterarse de; to ~ that... enterarse de que..., oír que... 3. (listen) escuchar; Lord, ~ our prayers REL escúchanos, Señor 4. LAW to ~ a case ver un caso; to ~ a witness oír a un testigo II. vi 1. (perceive) oír 2. (get news) enterarse; to ~ of [or about] sth enterarse de algo

heard [hɜrd] pt, pp of **hear**

hearing ['hɪr·ɪŋ] n 1. (sense) oído m; to be hard of ~ ser duro de oído, no oír bien 2. (act) audición f 3. LAW vista f

hearing aid n audífono m

heart [hart] n 1. ANAT corazón m 2. (center of emotions) to break sb's ~ partir el corazón a alguien; to have a cold ~ ser duro de corazón; to have a change of ~ cambiar de opinión; to have a good [or kind] ~ tener buen corazón; to lose ~ desanimarse; to take ~ animarse; her ~ sank se le cayó el alma a los pies 3. (core) centro m; to get to the ~ of the matter llegar al fondo de la cuestión 4. CULIN (of lettuce) cogollo m; artichoke ~s corazones m pl de alcachofa 5. pl (card suit) corazones mpl; (in Spanish pack) copas fpl ▶ to one's ~'s content hasta quedarse satisfecho; to have a ~ of gold/stone tener un corazón de oro/piedra, ser todo corazón; to have one's ~ in the right place tener buen corazón; to wear one's ~ on one's sleeve ir con el corazón en la mano; with all one's ~ con toda su alma; to not have the ~ to do sth no tener el valor para hacer algo; by ~ de memoria

heart attack n ataque m al corazón

heartbreaking adj desgarrador(a)

heartbroken adj con el corazón partido

heartburn n MED acidez f de estómago

heart disease n enfermedad f coronaria

heartening ['har·tə·nɪŋ] adj alentador(a)

heartfelt adj sincero, -a

heart murmur n MED soplo m cardíaco

heart-to-heart I. n conversación f franca y abierta II. adj franco, -a y abierto, -a

heat [hit] I. n 1. (warmth, high temperature) calor m; to cook sth on a high/low ~ cocinar algo a fuego alto/bajo 2. (heating system) calefacción f; to turn down/up the ~ bajar/subir la calefacción 3. (emotional state) acaloramiento m; in the ~ of the argument en el momento más acalorado de la discusión 4. (sports race) eliminatoria f 5. ZOOL celo m; to be in ~ estar en celo ▶ to put the ~ on sb presionar a alguien; to take the ~ off sb dar un respiro a alguien II. vt 1. (make hot) calentar 2. (excite) acalorar III. vi (become hot) calentarse; fig (inflame) acalorarse

◆**heat up** I. vi calentarse II. vt calentar

heated adj 1. (window) térmico, -a; (pool) climatizado, -a; (room) caldeado, -a 2. (argument) acalorado, -a

heater ['hi·t̬ər] n calefactor m; water ~ calentador m de agua, radiador m

heat gauge n termostato m

heather ['heð·ər] n BOT brezo m

heating n calefacción f

heat rash <-es> n sarpullido m

heat-resistant adj, **heat-resisting** adj resistente al calor

heat stroke n MED insolación f

heaven ['hev·ən] n cielo m; to go to ~ ir al cielo; it's ~ fig inf es divino, es fantástico; to be in (seventh) ~ a. fig estar en el (séptimo) cielo; the ~s (sky) el cielo ▶ what/where/when/who/why in ~'s name...? ¿qué/dónde/cuándo/quién/por qué demonios...?; for ~'s sake! ¡por Dios!; good ~s! ¡santo cielo!; ~ only knows sólo Dios lo sabe; ~ help us que Dios nos ayude; thank ~s gracias a Dios

heavy ['hev·i] I. adj <-ier, -iest>

1. (*weighing a lot*) pesado, -a; ~ **food** comida pesada 2. (*difficult*) difícil; (*schedule*) apretado, -a 3. (*strong*) fuerte; ~ **fall** a. ECON fuerte descenso 4. (*not delicate, coarse*) poco delicado, -a 5. (*severe*) severo, -a; (*responsibility*) fuerte; (*sea*) grueso, -a; ~ **casualties** muchas bajas 6. (*abundant*) abundante; (*investment*) cuantioso, -a; ~ **frost/rain** helada/chubasco fuerte; **to go** ~ **on sth** consumir mucho de algo; **the tree was** ~ **with fruit** el árbol estaba cargado de frutas 7. (*excessive*) ~ **drinker/ smoker** bebedor/fumador empedernido 8. (*thick*) grueso, -a; (*beard*) denso, -a II. *n* <-ies> *sl* matón *m*

heavy-duty *adj* (*machine*) resistente

heavy going *adj* dificultoso, -a

heavy-handed *adj* 1. (*clumsy*) torpe 2. (*harsh*) duro, -a

heavyweight I. *adj* 1. SPORTS (de la categoría de los) pesos pesados 2. (*important*) serio, -a *e* importante II. *n a. fig* peso pesado *m*

Hebrew ['hi·bru] I. *n* 1. (*person*) hebreo, -a *m, f* 2. LING hebreo *m* II. *adj* hebreo, -a

hectare ['hek·ter] *n* hectárea *f*

hectic ['hek·tɪk] *adj* ajetreado, -a; ~ **fever** fiebre hé(c)tica; ~ **pace** ritmo intenso

he'd [hid] = **he had, he would** *see* **have, will**

hedge [hedʒ] I. *n* 1. (*row of bushes*) seto *m* vivo 2. FIN (*protection*) cobertura *f* II. *vi* (*avoid action*) dar rodeos; FIN cubrirse III. *vt* cercar (con un seto vivo)

hedgehog ['hedʒ·hɔg] *n* erizo *m*

hedgerow *n* seto *m* vivo

heed [hid] I. *vt form* hacer caso de; **to** ~ **advice** seguir los consejos II. *n* **to pay** (**no**) ~ **to sth, to take** (**no**) ~ **of sth** (no) prestar atención a algo, hacer caso omiso de algo

heel [hil] I. *n* 1. (*of foot*) talón *m* 2. (*of shoe*) tacón *m*, taco *m AmL* 3. (*of the hand*) base *f* de la mano 4. (*of loaf of bread*) cuscurro *m*, punta *f* 5. *inf* (*cad*) canalla *m* ▶ **to follow** <u>close</u> **on the** ~**s of sth** seguir inmediatamente a algo;

to be <u>hard</u> **on sb's** ~**s** pisar los talones a alguien; <u>under</u> **the** ~ **of sb/sth** sometido a alguien/algo; **to** <u>come</u> **to** ~ acceder a obedecer, acudir; **to** <u>dig</u> **one's** ~**s in** mantenerse en sus trece II. *interj* (*to dogs*) ven aquí

hefty ['hef·ti] *adj* <-ier, -iest> (*person*) corpulento, -a; (*profit, amount*) cuantioso, -a; (*book*) gordo, -a; (*price increase*) alto, -a

height [haɪt] *n* 1. (*of person*) estatura *f*; (*of thing*) altura *f* 2. ~**s** (*high places*) alturas *fpl*; **to be afraid of** ~**s** tener vértigo; **to scale** (**new**) ~**s** *fig* alcanzar (nuevas) cotas 3. ~**s** (*hill*) cerros *mpl* 4. (*strongest point*) cima *f*; **to be at the** ~ **of one's career** estar en la cima de su carrera 5. (*the greatest degree*) cumbre; **the** ~ **of stupidity** el colmo de la estupidez

heighten ['haɪ·tən] I. *vi* aumentar II. *vt* 1. (*elevate*) elevar 2. (*increase*) aumentar; **to** ~ **the effect of sth** acentuar el efecto de algo

heir [er] *n* heredero *m*; **to be** (**the**) ~ **to sth** ser el heredero de algo; ~ **apparent** heredero forzoso; ~ **to the throne** heredero del trono

heiress ['er·ɪs] *n* heredera *f*

heirloom ['er·lum] *n* reliquia *f*; **family** ~ reliquia familiar

held [held] *pt, pp of* **hold**

helicopter ['hel·ɪ·kap·tər] *n* helicóptero *m*

helipad ['hel·ɪ·pæd] *n* plataforma *f* de aterrizaje de los helicópteros

heliport ['hel·ɪ·pɔrt] *n* helipuerto *m*

hell [hel] I. *n* 1. (*place of punishment*) infierno *m*; ~ **on earth** infierno en vida; **to be** (**pure**) ~ ser un (auténtico) infierno; **to go to** ~ ir al infierno; **to go through** ~ pasar un calvario; **to make sb's life** ~ *inf* hacer la vida imposible a alguien 2. *inf* (*as intensifier*) **as cold as** ~ un frío de mil demonios; **as hot as** ~ un calor infernal; **as hard as** ~ duro a más no poder; **to annoy the** ~ **out of sb** molestar horrores a alguien; **to beat the** ~ **out of sb** dar a alguien una paliza de padre y muy señor mío; **to frighten the** ~ **out of sb** dar a alguien un susto

H

de miedo; **to hurt like ~** hacer un daño de mil demonios; **to run like ~** correr (uno) que se las pela; **a ~ of a decision** una decisión muy importante; **that's a ~ of a way to treat your mother!** ¡qué manera de tratar a tu madre! ▶ **the road to ~ is paved with good intentions** *prov* el camino que lleva al infierno está lleno de buenas intenciones; **come ~ or high water** contra viento y marea; **to have been to ~ and back** haber pasado un calvario; **all ~ broke loose** se armó la gorda; **to catch ~** recibir una bronca; **to do sth for the ~ of it** hacer algo porque sí; **to give sb ~ (for sth)** echar un rapapolvo a alguien (por algo), hacérselas pasar negras a alguien *AmL*; **go to ~!** *inf* (*leave me alone*) ¡déjame en paz!; **to have ~ to pay** *inf* armarse la gorda II. *interj* (*emphasis*) ¡demonios! ▶ **what the ~...!** ¡qué diablos...!

he'll [hil] = **he will** *see* **will**

hellish ['hel·ɪʃ] *adj* infernal; (*experience*) horroroso, -a

hellishly *adv* endemoniadamente

hello [hə·'loʊ] I. <hellos> *n* hola *m;* **a big ~** un gran saludo II. *interj* **1.** (*greeting*) hola; **to say ~ to sb** saludar a alguien **2.** (*beginning of phone call*) diga, dígame, aló *AmC, AmS* **3.** (*to attract attention*) oiga **4.** (*surprise*) anda, ¡ey!; ~,~ pero bueno

helm [helm] *n* timón *m;* **to be at the ~** llevar el timón; *fig* (*lead*) llevar el mando

helmet ['hel·mɪt] *n* casco *m;* **crash ~** casco protector

help [help] I. *vi* **1.** (*assist*) ayudar **2.** (*make easier*) facilitar **3.** (*improve situation*) mejorar II. *vt* (*assist*) ayudar; **nothing can ~ him now** ya no se puede hacer nada por él; **can I ~ you?** (*in shop*) ¿en qué puedo servirle?; **to ~ sb with sth** ayudar a alguien con algo **2.** (*improve*) (ayudar a) mejorar; **this medicine will ~ your headache** esta medicina te aliviará el dolor de cabeza **3.** (*contribute to a condition*) contribuir [*or* ayudar] a **4.** (*prevent*) evitar; **it can't be ~ed** es así y no hay más remedio; **to not be able to ~ doing sth** no poder

dejar de hacer algo; **I can't ~ it** no puedo remediarlo; **he can't ~ the way he is** él es así, ¿qué se le va hacer?; **to not be able to ~ but...** no poder menos de... **5.** (*take sth*) **to ~ oneself to sth** (*at table*) servirse algo; (*steal*) llevarse III. *n* **1.** (*assistance*) ayuda *f;* **to be a ~** ser una ayuda **2.** (*servant*) mujer *f* de la limpieza; (*in a shop*) ayudante *mf* IV. *interj* **~!** ¡socorro!; **so ~ me God** y que Dios me asista

◆ **help out** *vt* ayudar

helper ['hel·pər] *n* ayudante *mf*

helpful ['help·fəl] *adj* **1.** (*willing to help*) servicial **2.** (*useful*) útil

helping ['hel·pɪŋ] I. *n* (*food*) ración *f,* porción *f AmL* II. *adj* **to give sb a ~ hand** echar una mano a alguien

helpless ['help·lɪs] *adj* indefenso, -a

helpline ['help·laɪn] *n* teléfono *m* de asistencia

hem [hem] I. *n* dobladillo *m,* basta *f AmL;* **to take the ~ up/down** meter/sacar [*or* subir/bajar] el dobladillo II. *vt* hacer el dobladillo [*or* la bastilla] a III. *vi* <-mm-> **to ~ and haw** titubear

hemophilia [ˌhi·moʊ·'fɪl·i·ə] *n* hemofilia *f*

hemophiliac [ˌhi·moʊ·'fɪl·i·æk] *n* hemofílico, -a *m, f*

hemorrhage ['hem·ər·ɪdʒ] I. *n* hemorragia *f;* **brain ~** derrame *m* cerebral II. *vi* MED tener una hemorragia

hemorrhoids ['hem·ər·ɔɪdz] *npl* hemorroides *fpl*

hemp [hemp] *n* cáñamo *m*

hen [hen] *n* (*female chicken*) gallina *f;* (*female bird*) hembra *f*

hence [hens] *adv* **1.** (*therefore*) de ahí **2.** *after n* (*from now*) dentro de

hencoop ['hen·kup] *n,* **henhouse** ['hen·haʊs] *n* gallinero *m*

hepatitis [ˌhep·ə·'taɪ·tɪs] *n* hepatitis *f inv*

heptathlon [hep·'tæθ·lɑn] *n* heptatlón *m*

her [hɜr] I. *adj pos* su; ~ **dress/house** su vestido/casa; ~ **children** sus hijos II. *pron pers* **1.** (*she*) ella; **it's ~** es ella; **older than ~** mayor que ella; **if I were ~** si yo fuese ella **2.** *direct object* la *indirect object* le; **look at ~** mírala;

I saw ~ la vi; **he told ~ that...** le dijo que...; **he gave ~ the pencil** le dio el lápiz (a ella) **3.** *after prep* ella; **it's for/from ~** es para/de ella

herb [ɜrb] *n* hierba *f*

herbivorous [hɜr·ˈbɪv·ər·əs] *adj* herbívoro, -a

herd [hɜrd] I. *n + sing/pl vb* **1.** (*of animals*) manada *f*; (*of sheep*) rebaño *f* **2.** (*of people*) multitud *f*; **to follow the ~** seguir a la masa II. *vt* (*animals*) llevar en manada; (*sheep*) guardar; **they ~ed us into the press room** nos reunieron en la sala de prensa III. *vi* ir en manada [*or* rebaño]

here [hɪr] I. *adv* **1.** (*in, at, to this place*) aquí; **over ~** acá; **give it ~** *inf* dámelo; **~ and there** aquí y allá **2.** (*in introductions*) **here is...** aquí está... **3.** (*show arrival*) **they are ~** ya han llegado **4.** (*now*) **where do we go from ~?** ¿dónde vamos ahora?; **~ you are, ~ you go** (*giving sth*) aquí tienes; **the ~ and now** el presente; **~ goes** *inf* allá voy; **~ we go** ya estamos otra vez II. *interj* (*in roll call*) ¡presente!, ¡aquí!

hereafter [hɪr·ˈæf·tər] I. *adv* en lo sucesivo II. *n* **the ~** el más allá

herewith [hɪr·ˈwɪθ] *adv form* adjunto, -a

heritage [ˈher·ɪ·tɪdʒ] *n* **1.** (*objects*) patrimonio *m* histórico **2.** (*tradition*) patrimonio *m* cultural

hermetic [hər·ˈmet·ɪk] *adj* hermético, -a; **~ seal** cierre hermético

hermit crab *n* cangrejo *m* ermitaño

hero [ˈhɪr·oʊ] <heroes> *n* **1.** (*brave man*) héroe *m* **2.** (*main character*) protagonista *m* **3.** (*idol*) ídolo *m* **4.** (*sandwich*) sándwich *m* de carne fría, queso y lechuga

heroic [hɪ·ˈroʊ·ɪk] *adj* **1.** (*brave, bold*) heroico, -a; **~ deed** hazaña *f* **2.** (*epic*) heroico, -a

heroin [ˈher·oʊ·ɪn] *n* heroína *f*

heroin addict *n* MED heroinómano, -a *m, f*

heroine [ˈher·oʊ·ɪn] *n* (*brave woman*) heroína *f*; (*of film*) protagonista *f*

heroism [ˈher·oʊ·ɪz·əm] *n* heroísmo *m*

heron [ˈher·ən] <-(s)> *n* garza *f* (real)

herpes [ˈhɜr·piz] *n* herpes *m inv*

herring [ˈher·ɪŋ] <-(s)> *n* arenque *m*

hers [hɜrz] *pron pos* (el) suyo, (la) suya, (los) suyos, (las) suyas; **it's not my bag, it's ~** no es mi bolsa, es la de ella; **this house is ~** esta casa es suya; **this glass is ~** este vaso es suyo; **a book of ~** un libro suyo

herself [hɜr·ˈself] *pron* **1.** *reflexive* se *after prep* sí (misma); **she lives by ~** vive sola **2.** *emphatic* ella misma; **she hurt ~** se hizo daño

he's [hiz] **1.** = **he is** *see* **be 2.** = **he has** *see* **have**

hesitant [ˈhez·ɪ·tənt] *adj* **1.** (*indecisive*) indeciso, -a; **to be ~ about doing sth** no estar decidido a hacer algo **2.** (*shy, uncertain*) vacilante

hesitantly *adv* con indecisión

hesitate [ˈhez·ɪ·teɪt] *vi* (*be indecisive*) vacilar, trepidar *AmL*; **to (not) ~ to do sth** (no) dudar en hacer algo

hesitation [ˌhez·ɪ·ˈteɪ·ʃən] *n* vacilación *f*; **without ~** sin titubear

heterogeneous [ˌhet·ər·ə·ˈdʒi·ni·əs] *adj* heterogéneo, -a

heterosexual [ˌhet·ə·roʊ·ˈsek·ʃu·əl] I. *n* heterosexual *mf* II. *adj* heterosexual

hexagon [ˈhek·sə·gɑn] *n* hexágono *m*

hexagonal [hek·ˈsæg·ə·nəl] *adv* hexagonal

hey [heɪ] *interj inf* eh, oye, órale *Méx*

heyday [ˈheɪ·deɪ] *n* apogeo *m*; **in his/her/its ~** en su apogeo

hi [haɪ] *interj* hola

hibernate [ˈhaɪ·bər·neɪt] *vi* hibernar

hibernation [ˌhaɪ·bər·ˈneɪ·ʃən] *n* hibernación *f*

hibiscus [hɪ·ˈbɪs·kəs] <-es> *n* BOT hibisco *m*

hiccup, hiccough [ˈhɪk·ʌp] I. *n* hipo *m*; **to have the ~s** tener hipo II. *vi* <-p(p)-> tener hipo

hid [hɪd] *pt of* **hide²**

hidden [ˈhɪd·ən] I. *pp of* **hide²** II. *adj* (*person, thing*) escondido, -a; (*emotion, information*) oculto, -a

hide¹ [haɪd] *n* (*of an animal*) piel *f*

hide² [haɪd] <hid, hidden> I. *vi* (*be out of sight*) esconderse, escorarse *Cuba, Hond* II. *vt* (*conceal: person, thing*) esconder; (*emotion, information*) ocultar;

to ~ one's face taparse la cara

♦ hide away vt esconder

♦ hide out vi, hide up vi esconderse

hide-and-seek n escondite m; to play ~ jugar al escondite

hideaway ['haɪd·ə·weɪ] n escondite m

hideous ['hɪd·i·əs] adj 1. (very unpleasant, ugly) espantoso, -a 2. (terrible) terrible

hideout ['haɪd·aʊt] n escondrijo m; secret ~ guarida f secreta

hiding[1] ['haɪ·dɪŋ] n a. fig paliza f

hiding[2] ['haɪ·dɪŋ] n to be in ~ estar escondido; to go into ~ ocultarse

hieroglyphics npl jeroglíficos mpl

hi-fi ['haɪ·faɪ] I. n abbr of high-fidelity alta fidelidad f II. adj abbr of high-fidelity de alta fidelidad

high [haɪ] I. adj 1. (elevated) alto, -a; one yard ~ and three yards wide una yarda de alto y tres yardas de ancho; knee/waist-~ hasta la rodilla/cintura; to fly at ~ altitude volar a gran altitud 2. (above average) superior; to have ~ hopes (for sb/sth) tener grandes esperanzas (puestas en alguien/algo); to have a ~ opinion of sb estimar mucho a alguien; ~ blood-pressure/fever presión/fiebre alta 3. (important, eminent) elevado, -a; of ~ rank de alto rango; to have friends in ~ places tener amigos en las altas esferas; (regarding job) tener enchufe; to be ~ and mighty ser un engreído 4. (under influence of drugs) colocado, -a 5. (of high frequency, shrill: voice) agudo, -a; a ~ note una nota alta 6. FASHION with a ~ neckline/waistline con escote a (la) caja 7. (at peak, maximum) máximo, -a; ~ noon mediodía m; ~ priority alta prioridad ▸ to leave sb ~ and dry dejar a alguien colgado II. adv 1. (at or to a great point or height) a gran altura 2. (rough or strong) con fuerza ▸ to search for sth ~ and low buscar algo por todas partes III. n 1. (high(est) point) punto m máximo; an all-time ~ un récord de todos los tiempos; to reach a ~ alcanzar un nivel récord 2. sl (from drugs) to be on a ~ estar colocado, estar drogado 3. (heaven) on ~ en el cielo

highchair n silla f alta

high court n tribunal m superior de justicia

high-density adj a. COMPUT de alta densidad

higher education n enseñanza f superior

higher-up n inf superior m

high frequency adj de alta frecuencia

high-grade adj (fruit, beef) de primera calidad; (minerals) de alto grado (de pureza)

high heels npl tacones m pl altos

highjack vt see hijack

high jump n salto m de altura

high-level adj de alto nivel

highlight I. n 1. (most interesting part) aspecto m más interesante 2. ~s (in hair) mechas fpl II. vt (draw attention to) destacar; (a problem) señalar

highlighter n rotulador m

highly ['haɪ·li] adv 1. (very) muy 2. (very well) to speak ~ of sb hablar muy bien de alguien

high-octane n ~ gasoline gasolina de alto octanaje

high-performance adj a. AUTO de gran rendimiento

high-pitched adj 1. (sloping steeply) escarpado, -a 2. (sound) agudo, -a; a ~ voice una voz aguda

high point n the ~ (most successful state) el clímax; (of career) la cima, la cúspide; (most enjoyable state) súmmum m

high-powered adj 1. (powerful) de gran potencia 2. (influential, important) poderoso, -a

high pressure n METEO presión f alta

high-pressure I. adj 1. METEO a ~ area una zona de altas presiones 2. (aggressive) enérgico, -a 3. (stressful: job) de mucha responsabilidad, estresante II. vt presionar

high-protein adj rico, -a en proteínas

high-ranking adj de categoría

high-resolution adj COMPUT (image, screen, shot) de alta resolución

high-risk adj de alto riesgo; (investment) arriesgado, -a

high school n instituto m de enseñanza

secundaria (grados 9 a 12)

high-speed *adj* de alta velocidad

high-spirited *adj* (*cheerful, lively*) animoso, -a

high spirits *npl* buen humor *m*

high-tech *adj* de alta tecnología

high technology *n* alta tecnología *f*

high-tension *adj* ELEC de alta tensión

high tide *n* 1. (*of ocean*) marea *f* alta 2. *fig* (*most successful point*) apogeo *m*

high water *n* marea *f* alta

high-water mark *n* (*showing water level*) línea *f* de pleamar

highway ['haɪ·weɪ] *n* carretera *f*

hijack ['haɪ·dʒæk] I. *vt* 1. (*take over by force: plane*) secuestrar un avión 2. *fig* (*adopt as one's own*) to ~ **sb's ideas/ plans** hacer propias las ideas/los planes de alguien II. *n* secuestro *m*

hijacker ['haɪ·dʒæk·ər] *n* secuestrador (a) *m(f)* (aéreo)

hijacking ['haɪ·dʒæk·ɪŋ] *n* secuestro *m* (aéreo)

hike [haɪk] I. *n* 1. (*long walk*) caminata *f*; **to go on a ~** dar una caminata; **take a ~!** *sl* ¡vete al diablo! 2. (*increase*) aumento *m* II. *vi* ir de excursión (a pie)

hiker ['haɪ·kər] *n* excursionista *mf*

hiking ['haɪ·kɪŋ] *n* excursionismo *m*

hilarious [hɪ·'ler·i·əs] *adj* (*very funny*) divertidísimo, -a

hill [hɪl] *n* 1. (*in landscape*) colina *f*; **the ~s** la sierra 2. (*in road*) cuesta *f* 3. (*small heap*) montoncito *m* 4. POL **The Hill** Capitolio *m*, Congreso *m*
► **as old as the ~s** tan viejo como el mundo; **to be over the ~** *inf* ser demasiado viejo

hillbilly ['hɪl·bɪl·i] <-ies> *n* palurdo, -a *m, f*, montañés *m*

hillside ['hɪl·saɪd] *n* ladera *f*

hilltop ['hɪl·tap] I. *n* cumbre *f* II. *adj* de la cima

hilly ['hɪl·i] <-ier, -iest> *adj* montañoso, -a

him [hɪm] *pron pers* 1. (*he*) él; **it's ~** es él; **older than ~** mayor que él; **if I were ~** yo en su lugar 2. *direct object* lo, le *indirect object* le; **she gave ~ the pencil** le dio el lápiz (a él) 3. *after prep* él; **it's for/from ~** es para/de él 4. (*un-specified sex*) **if somebody comes, tell ~ that...** si viene alguien, dile que...

Himalayas [ˌhɪm·ə·'leɪ·əz] *npl* el Himalaya

himself [hɪm·'self] *pron* 1. *reflexive* se *after prep* sí (mismo); **for ~** para él (mismo); **he lives by ~** vive solo 2. *emphatic* él mismo; **he hurt ~** se hizo daño

hindrance ['hɪn·drəns] *n* 1. (*obstruction*) estorbo *m* 2. (*obstacle*) obstáculo *m*

hindsight ['haɪnd·saɪt] *n* percepción *f* retrospectiva; **in ~** a posteriori

hinge [hɪndʒ] I. *n* bisagra *f* II. *vi* **to ~ on/upon sb/sth** depender de alguien/algo

hint [hɪnt] I. *n* 1. (*trace: of anger, suspicion*) asomo *m*, atisbo *m* 2. (*allusion*) indirecta *f*; **to drop a ~** lanzar una indirecta; **to take a ~** pillarse una indirecta 3. (*practical tip*) consejo *m* 4. (*slight amount: of salt, curry*) pizca *f* II. *vi* soltar indirectas; **to ~ at sth** hacer alusión a algo

hip [hɪp] I. *n* 1. ANAT cadera *f* 2. BOT escaramujo *m* II. *adj sl* (*fashionable*) moderno, -a

hipbone ['hɪp·boʊn] *n* hueso *m* de la cadera

hip flask *n* petaca *f*

hippo ['hɪp·oʊ] *n inf abbr of* **hippopotamus** hipopótamo *m*

hippopotamus [ˌhɪp·ə·'pat·ə·məs] <-es or -mi> *n* hipopótamo *m*

hippy ['hɪp·i] <-ies> *n* hippy *mf*

hire [haɪr] I. *n* 1. (*hired person*) contratación *f*; **a new ~** un nuevo empleado II. *vt* (*employ*) contratar, conchabar *AmL*; **to ~ more staff** ampliar la plantilla

◆ **hire out** *vt* alquilar; **to ~ oneself out as sth** trabajar de algo

his [hɪz] I. *adj pos* su (de él); **~ car/ house** su coche/casa; **~ children** sus hijos II. *pron pos* (el) suyo, (la) suya, (los) suyos, (las) suyas, de él; **it's not my bag, it's ~** no es mi bolsa, es la suya; **this house is ~** esta casa es suya; **this glass is ~** este vaso es suyo; **a book of ~** un libro suyo

Hispanic [hɪs·'pæn·ɪk] I. *adj* hispánico,

-a **II.** n hispano, -a m, f

hiss [hɪs] **I.** vi **1.** (tea kettle, crowd) silbar **2.** (cat) bufar **II.** vt silbar **III.** n silbido m

historic [hɪˈstɔr·ɪk] adj histórico, -a; **this is a ~ moment...** es un momento clave...

historical adj histórico, -a

history [ˈhɪs·tə·ri] n historia f; **to make ~** hacer época; **sb's medical ~** historia médica de alguien

hit [hɪt] **I.** n **1.** (blow, stroke) golpe m **2.** inf (shot) tiro m certero **3.** SPORTS punto m; **to score a ~** marcar un tanto [or punto] **4.** (success) éxito m **5.** sl (murder) golpe, ataque m **II.** <-tt-, hit, hit> vt **1.** (strike) golpear, pepenar Méx **2.** (crash into) chocar contra; **to ~ one's head on a shelf** dar con la cabeza contra un estante **3.** (arrive at, reach target) alcanzar **4.** (affect) afectar; **to ~ sb where it hurts** dar a alguien donde más le duele **5.** (reach) tocar; **to ~ rock bottom** fig tocar fondo **6.** (encounter) tropezar con **7.** inf (arrive in or at) llegar a; **to ~ 100 mph** alcanzar las 100 m/h **III.** vi (strike) **to ~ against sth** chocar con algo

◆**hit back** vi devolver el golpe; **to ~ at sb** defenderse de alguien

◆**hit off** vt **to hit it off (with sb)** hacer buenas migas (con alguien)

◆**hit on** vt **1.** (show sexual interest) ligar con **2.** (think of) dar con

◆**hit out** vi lanzar un ataque

hit-and-run adj **~ attack** MIL ataque relámpago; **~ driver** conductor que se da a la fuga tras atropellar a alguien

hitch [hɪtʃ] **I.** <-es> n **1.** (obstacle) obstáculo m; **technical ~** problema m técnico; **to go off without a ~** salir a pedir de boca **2.** (sudden pull) tirón m **3.** (for a trailer) enganche m **II.** vt **1.** (fasten) atar; **to ~ sth to sth** atar algo a algo **2.** inf (hitchhike) **to ~ a lift** [or ride] hacer dedo [or autostop] **III.** vi inf hacer dedo

◆**hitch up** vt (fasten) **to hitch sth up to sth** atar algo a algo

hitcher [ˈhɪtʃ·ər] n autostopista mf

hitch-hiking n autostop m

HIV [ˌeɪtʃ·aɪˈvi] abbr of **human immunodeficiency virus** VIH m

hive [haɪv] n **1.** (beehive) colmena f **2.** + sing/pl vb (swarm of bees) enjambre m

hives [haɪvz] n MED urticaria f

ho [hoʊ] interj inf (expressing scorn, surprise) oh; (attracting attention) oiga; **land ~!** NAUT ¡tierra a la vista!

hoagie [ˈhoʊ·gi] n sándwich de carne fría, queso y lechuga

hoard [hɔrd] **I.** n acumulación f **II.** vt acumular; (food) amontonar

hoarse [hɔrs] adj ronco, -a

hoax [hoʊks] **I.** <-es> n (joke) broma f de mal gusto; (fraud) engaño m **II.** vt engañar

hobble [ˈhab·əl] vi cojear; **to ~ around** ir cojeando

hobby [ˈhab·i] <-ies> n hobby m

hockey [ˈhak·i] n hockey m

hodgepodge [ˈhadʒ·padʒ] n batiburrillo m

hog [hɔg] **I.** n **1.** (pig) puerco m, chancho m AmS **2.** inf (person) egoísta mf ▶ **to live high on the ~** sl vivir como un rajá **II.** <-gg-> vt inf (keep for oneself) acaparar; (food) devorar; **to ~ sb/sth (all to oneself)** acaparar a alguien/algo (para uno mismo)

hoist [hɔɪst] vt (raise up) alzar; (flag) enarbolar

hold [hoʊld] **I.** n **1.** (grasp, grip) agarre m; **to take ~ of sb/sth** asirse de [or a] alguien/algo **2.** (wrestling) presa f; **no ~s barred** fig sin restricciones **3.** (control) dominio m **4.** NAUT, AVIAT bodega f **5.** (delayed) **to be on ~** estar en espera; TEL **to put sb on ~** poner a alguien en espera **6.** (understand) **to get ~ of sth** comprender algo; **to have a ~ of sth** tener idea de algo **7.** (prison cell) prisión f **II.** <held, held> vt **1.** (keep) tener; (grasp) agarrar; **to ~ a gun** sostener un arma; **to ~ hands** agarrarse de la mano; **to ~ sth in one's hand** sostener algo en la mano; **to ~ sth (tight)** sujetar a alguien/algo (con fuerza); **to ~ the door open for sb** aguantar la puerta abierta a alguien **2.** (support) soportar; **to ~ one's head high** mantener la cabeza alta **3.** (*cover up*) **to ~ one's ears/nose** taparse los oídos/la nariz **4.** (*keep, retain*) mantener; **to ~ sb's attention/interest** mantener la atención/el interés de alguien; **to ~ sb hostage** retener a alguien como rehén; **to ~ a note** MUS sostener una nota **5.** (*make keep to*) **to ~ sb to his/her word** [*or promise*] hacer cumplir a alguien su palabra **6.** (*delay, stop*) detener; **~ it!** ¡para! ; **to ~ one's breath** contener la respiración; **to ~ one's fire** MIL detener el fuego; **to ~ sb's phone calls** TEL retener las llamadas de alguien **7.** (*contain*) contener; **it ~s many surprises** conlleva muchas sorpresas; **what the future ~s** lo que depara el futuro **8.** (*possess, own*) poseer; (*land, town*) ocupar; **to ~ an account** (*with a bank*) tener una cuenta (en un banco); **to ~ a position** (*as sth*) mantener un puesto (como algo); **to ~** (**down**) **the fort** MIL quedarse al cargo; *fig* hacerse cargo de **9.** (*make happen*) **to ~ a conversation** (*with sb*) mantener una conversación (con alguien); **to ~ an election/a meeting/a news conference** convocar elecciones/una reunión/una rueda de prensa; **to ~ talks** dar charlas **10.** (*believe*) creer; **to be held in great respect** ser muy respetado; **to ~ sb responsible for sth** considerar a alguien responsable de algo; **to ~ sb/sth in contempt** despreciar alguien/algo **III.** *vi* **1.** (*continue*) seguir; **to ~ still** pararse; **to ~ true** seguir siendo válido; **~ tight!** ¡quieto! **2.** (*believe*) sostener

◆**hold against** *vt always sep* **to hold sth against sb** hacerse una mala idea de alguien por algo

◆**hold back I.** *vt* (*keep*) retener; **to ~ information** ocultar información; (*stop*) detener; (*impede development*) parar; **to ~ tears** contener las lágrimas ▶ **there's no holding me back** nada me retiene **II.** *vi* **1.** (*be unforthcoming*) refrenarse **2.** (*refrain*) **to ~ from doing sth** abstenerse de hacer algo

◆**hold down** *vt* sujetar; (*control, suppress*) oprimir; **to ~ a job** mantener un trabajo

◆**hold in** *vt* (*emotion*) contener

◆**hold off I.** *vt* (*enemy*) detener; (*reporters*) dar largas a **II.** *vi* mantenerse a distancia; (*wait*) esperar, posponer

◆**hold on** *vi* **1.** (*attach*) agarrarse bien; **to be held on by/with sth** estar sujeto a/con algo **2.** (*manage to keep going*) **to ~** (*tight*) aguantar **3.** (*wait*) esperar

◆**hold onto** *vt insep* **1.** (*grasp*) agarrarse bien **2.** (*keep*) guardar

◆**hold out I.** *vt* extender **II.** *vi* **1.** (*offer, chance*) ofrecer **2.** (*manage to resist*) resistir; **to ~ for sth** resistir hasta conseguir algo **3.** (*refuse to give sth*) **to ~ on sb** no acceder a los deseos de alguien

◆**hold over** *vt* **1.** (*defer*) aplazar **2.** (*extend*) alargar

◆**hold to** *vt insep* atenerse a

◆**hold together I.** *vi* mantenerse unidos **II.** *vt* mantener unidos

◆**hold up I.** *vt* **1.** (*raise*) levantar; **to ~ one's hand** levantar la mano; **to be held up by** (*means of*)/**with sth** ser sostenido por (mediante)/con algo; **to hold one's head up high** *fig* mantener la cabeza alta **2.** (*delay*) atrasar **3.** (*rob with violence*) atracar **4.** (*offer as example*) **to hold sb up as an example of sth** mostrar a alguien como ejemplo de algo **II.** *vi* (*weather*) seguir bueno; (*material*) durar

◆**hold with** *vt insep* estar de acuerdo con

holdall ['hoʊld.ɔl] *n* bolsa *f* de viaje

holder ['hoʊl.dar] *n* **1.** (*device*) soporte *m;* **cigarette ~** boquilla *f* **2.** (*person: of shares, of account*) titular *mf;* (*of title*) poseedor(a) *m(f);* **world record ~** plusmarquista *mf* mundial

hole [hoʊl] *n* **1.** (*hollow space*) agujero *m; fig* (*in an argument, sb's reasoning*) laguna *f*, vacío *m;* **to be in the ~** estar endeudado **2.** (*in golf*) hoyo *m* **3.** (*of mouse*) ratonera *f*

◆**hole up** *vi inf* esconderse

holiday ['hal·ɪ·deɪ] *n* (*public day off*) día *m* festivo

holiday resort *n* centro *m* turístico

holiness ['hoʊ·lɪ·nɪs] *n* santidad *f;* **His/Your Holiness** Su Santidad

holistic [hoʊ·'lɪs·tɪk] *adj* holístico, -a

H

Holland ['hal·ənd] n Holanda f

hollow ['hal·oʊ] I. adj 1. (empty) hueco, -a 2. (worthless, empty: promise) vano, -a; (victory) vacío, -a; (laughter) falso, -a 3. (sound) sordo, -a. II. n hueco m; (valley) hondonada f III. vt to ~ (out) (pumpkin) vaciar; (tree trunk) ahuecar IV. vi (become hollow: tree) ahuecarse

holly ['hal·i] n BOT acebo m

holocaust ['hal·ə·kɔst] n holocausto m

hologram ['hal·ə·græm] n holograma m

holy ['hoʊ·li] <-ier, -iest> adj (sacred) santo, -a; (water) bendito, -a

Holy Communion n Sagrada Comunión f

Holy Father n Santo Padre m

Holy Scripture n the ~ las Sagradas Escrituras

Holy Spirit n Espíritu m Santo

homage ['ham·ɪdʒ] n homenaje m; to pay ~ to sb rendir homenaje a alguien

home [hoʊm] I. n 1. (residence) casa f; at ~ en casa; to leave ~ salir [or irse] de casa; away from ~ fuera de casa; make yourself at ~ ponte cómodo, estás en tu casa 2. (family) hogar m 3. (institution) asilo m; (for old people) residencia f; children's ~ orfanato m II. adv 1. (one's place of residence) to be ~ estar en casa; to go/come ~ ir/venir a casa; to take work ~ llevarse trabajo a casa 2. (understanding) to hit ~ ➤ causar impacto, dar en el blanco ➤ to be ~ <u>free</u> tener la victoria asegurada; this is nothing to <u>write</u> ~ about esto no es nada del otro mundo III. adj 1. (from own country) nacional 2. (from own area) local; (team) de casa; (game) en casa; the ~ **ground** el campo de casa

home address n dirección f particular, domicilio m

homebody n persona f hogareña

homecoming n regreso m (a casa)

home cooking n cocina f casera

home fries npl CULIN papas f pl fritas

homeland n (country of birth) tierra f natal; (of cultural heritage) patria f

homeless I. adj sin hogar II. n + pl vb the ~ los sin techo

homely ['hoʊm·li] <-ier, -iest> adj 1. (ugly) feúcho, -a 2. (simple) sen-

cillo, -a 3. (domestic) casero, -a, doméstico, -a

homemade adj casero, -a

homeopath ['hoʊ·mi·oʊ·pæθ] n homeópata mf

homeopathic [ˌhoʊ·mi·oʊ·ˈpæθ·ɪk] adj homeopático, -a

homeopathy [ˌhoʊ·mi·ˈap·ə·θi] n homeopatía f

homesick ['hoʊm·sɪk] adj nostálgico, -a; to feel ~ (for) tener morriña (de)

home team n equipo m local [or de casa]

hometown n ciudad f natal, pueblo m natal

home truth n to tell sb a few ~s decir a alguien unas cuantas verdades

homeward ['hoʊm·wərd] I. adv de camino a casa II. adj (journey) de regreso

homework ['hoʊm·wɜrk] n SCHOOL deberes mpl, tareas fpl Col

homey ['hoʊ·mi] <-ier, -iest> adj 1. (cozy) casero, -a 2. sl (home boy or girl) paisano, -a

homicide ['ham·ə·saɪd] n 1. (crime) homicidio m 2. (criminal) homicida mf

homogeneous adj, **homogenous** [ˌhoʊ·moʊ·ˈdʒi·ni·əs] adj homogéneo, -a

homosexual [ˌhoʊ·mə·ˈsek·ʃu·əl] I. adj homosexual II. n homosexual mf

Honduras [han·ˈdʊr·əs] n Honduras f

honest ['an·ɪst] adj 1. (trustworthy) honesto, -a 2. (truthful) sincero, -a; to be ~ with oneself ser sincero consigo mismo; ~ (to God) inf como Dios manda 3. (fair: wages, day's work) justo, -a, equitativo, -a

honestly adv (truthfully) sinceramente; (with honesty) honradamente

honesty ['an·ɪ·sti] n 1. (trustworthiness) honestidad f 2. (sincerity) sinceridad f; in all ~ para ser sincero

honey ['hʌn·i] n 1. CULIN miel f 2. (term of endearment) cariño m

honeybee n abeja f

honeycomb n panal m

honeydew (melon) n melón m dulce

honeymoon n luna f de miel

honeysuckle n BOT madreselva f

honk [haŋk] I. vi 1. ZOOL graznar 2. AUTO tocar la bocina [or Col el pito] II. n 1. ZOOL graznido m 2. AUTO bocinazo m [or pitazo] m Col

honor ['ɑn·ər] **I.** n **1.** (respect) honor m; **in ~ of sb/sth** en honor de alguien/algo; **to be (in) ~ bound to…** estar moralmente obligado a… **2.** LAW **Her/His/Your Honor** Su Señoría **3.** ~s (distinction) honores mpl; **final ~s** honras f pl fúnebres; **to graduate with ~s** licenciarse [or graduarse] con matrícula de honor **II.** vt **1.** (fulfil: promise, contract) cumplir (con) **2.** (confer honor) honrar; **to be ~ed** sentirse honrado

honorable adj **1.** (worthy of respect: person) honorable; (agreement) honroso, -a **2.** (honest) honrado, -a

honorary ['ɑn·ə·rer·i] adj **1.** (conferred as an honor: title) honorario, -a **2.** (without pay) no remunerado

honor roll n UNIV, SCHOOL lista f de honor académica

hood[1] [hʊd] n **1.** (covering for head) capucha f **2.** AUTO capó m **3.** (on machine) cubierta f

hood[2] [hʊd] n **1.** sl (gangster) matón, -ona m, f **2.** sl (urban neighborhood) barrio m

hoof [hʊf] <hooves or hoofs> n casco m, pezuña f

hook [hʊk] **I.** n **1.** (for holding sth) gancho m; (for clothes) percha f; (fish) anzuelo m; **to leave the phone off the ~** dejar el teléfono descolgado **2.** (in boxing) gancho m ▶ **by ~ or by crook** por las buenas o por las malas; **to fall for sth ~, line and sinker** tragárselo [or creérselo] todo; **to be off the ~** librarse **II.** vt **1.** (fasten) enganchar **2.** (fish) pescar **3.** (capture attention) atraer, atrapar **III.** vi (clothes) abrocharse (con corchetes o ganchitos); (parts) engancharse

hook up I. vt **1.** (hang: curtains) poner **2.** (link up) enganchar; (connect) conectar; **to hook sb up with sb** sl (arrange date) reunirse con alguien **II.** vi (connect) conectarse

hooked [hʊkt] adj **1.** (nose) ganchudo, -a **2.** (fascinated) atrapado, -a **3.** (addicted) enganchado, -a

hooker ['hʊk·ər] n sl (prostitute) prostituta f

hooky ['hʊk·i] n inf **to play ~** hacer novi-

llos, capar clase Col

hooligan ['hu·lɪ·gən] n hooligan mf, vándalo m

hoot [hut] **I.** vi (owl) ulular **II.** n (of owl) ululato m; (factory whistle) sirena f; (of horn) bocinazo m; (of train) pitido m; **to give a ~ of laughter** soltar una carcajada; **to give a ~ of disgust** dar un grito de repugnancia; **to not give a ~ (about sth)** importar algo un pito a alguien ▶ **to be a (real) ~** inf ser muy cómico

hop[1] [hɑp] n BOT lúpulo m

hop[2] [hɑp] <-pp-> **I.** vi **1.** (on 1 foot) saltar; fig **to ~ to it** ponerse manos a la obra **2.** inf (be busy) **to ~ping** (city streets, restaurant) tener mucho ajetreo [or movimiento] **II.** vt inf (bus, train) subir a **III.** n **1.** (leap) salto m; (using only one leg) salto m a la pata coja, brinco m de cojito Méx **2.** inf (informal dance) baile m ▶ **a ~, skip and a jump** inf un salto, estar a un paso

hope [hoʊp] **I.** n esperanza f; **to give up ~** perder la(s) esperanza(s) **II.** vi (wish) esperar; **to ~ for the best** esperar que la suerte lo acompañe a uno

hopeful ['hoʊp·fəl] **I.** adj **1.** (person) esperanzado, -a; **to be ~** ser optimista **2.** (promising) esperanzador(a) **II.** n candidato, -a m, f; **young ~s** jóvenes aspirantes mfpl

hopefully adv **1.** (in a hopeful manner) con ilusión **2.** (one hopes) ~! ¡ojalá!; ~ **we'll be in Sweden at 6.00 P.M.** si todo sale bien estaremos en Suecia a las 6 de la tarde

hopeless ['hoʊp·lɪs] adj (situation) desesperado, -a; (effort) imposible; **to be ~** inf (person) ser inútil; (service) ser un desastre; **to be ~ at sth** ser negado para algo

hopelessly adv **1.** (without hope) sin esperanzas **2.** (totally, completely) ~ **lost** totalmente perdido

hopping mad adj furioso, -a

horizon [hə·'raɪ·zən] n a. fig horizonte m

horizontal [ˌhɔr·ɪ·'zɑn·təl] **I.** adj horizontal **II.** n horizontal f

hormone ['hɔr·moʊn] n hormona f

horn [hɔrn] n 1. ZOOL cuerno m 2. MUS trompa f 3. AUTO bocina f ▶ to lock ~s (over sth) tener un enfrentamiento (por algo); to toot [or blow] one's own ~ echarse flores

hornet ['hɔr·nɪt] n avispón m

horoscope ['hɔr·ə·skoʊp] n horóscopo m

horrendous [hɔ·'ren·dəs] adj 1. (crime) horrendo, -a 2. (losses) terrible

horrible ['hɔr·ə·bəl] adj horrible

horrid ['hɔr·ɪd] adj (unpleasant) horrible

horrific [hɔ·'rɪf·ɪk] adj horroroso, -a

horrify ['hɔr·ə·faɪ] <-ie-> vt horrorizar

horror ['hɔr·ər] n horror m, espantosidad f AmC, Col, PRico; ~ film película f de terror

horror-stricken adj, **horror-struck** adj horrorizado, -a

horse [hɔrs] n 1. ZOOL caballo m; to ride a ~ montar a caballo; to eat like a ~ comer como una lima [or como un caballo] 2. SPORTS potro m ▶ to get sth straight from the ~'s mouth saber algo de buena tinta; don't look a gift ~ in the mouth prov a caballo regalado, no le mires el dentado prov; to flog a dead ~ perder el tiempo (intentando algo), arar en el mar; to be on one's high ~ inf tener muchos humos; hold your ~s! inf ¡espera un minuto!, ¡no te aceleres!

horseback ['hɔrs·bæk] I. n on ~ a caballo II. adj ~ riding equitación f

horse chestnut n (tree) castaño m de Indias; (nut) castaña f de Indias

horseplay ['hɔrs·pleɪ] n jugueteo(s) m(pl)

horsepower inv n caballo m (de vapor)

horseshoe n herradura f

horse van n remolque m para transportar caballos

hose [hoʊz] n 1. (in garden) manguera f 2. (in motor) manguera f 3. (pantyhose) medias f pl pantalón [or Méx de nylon] [or Col veladas]

hospice ['has·pɪs] n 1. (hospital) residencia f para enfermos terminales 2. (house of shelter) hospicio m

hospitable ['has·pɪ·tə·bəl] adj hospitalario, -a

hospital ['has·pɪ·təl] n hospital m

hospitality [ˌhas·pɪ·'tæl·ə·ti] n hospitalidad f

hospitalize ['has·pɪ·tə·laɪz] vt hospitalizar

host¹ [hoʊst] I. n 1. (person who receives guests) anfitrión, -ona m, f 2. (presenter) presentador(a) m(f) 3. BIO huésped m 4. COMPUT servidor m II. vt 1. (party) dar; (event) ser la sede de 2. TV, RADIO (program) presentar

host² [hoʊst] n multitud f

hostage ['has·tɪdʒ] n rehén mf; to take/hold sb ~ tomar/tener a alguien como rehén

host country <-ies> n país m anfitrión

hostel ['has·təl] n (inexpensive hotel) hostal m; youth ~ albergue m juvenil

hostess ['hoʊ·stɪs] <-es> n 1. (woman who receives guests) anfitriona f 2. (presenter) presentadora f 3. (in restaurant) mesonera f

hostile ['has·təl] adj hostil; ~ aircraft avión enemigo

hostility [ha·'stɪl·ə·ti] <-ies> n hostilidad f

hot [hat] I. adj 1. (very warm: food, water) caliente; (day, weather) caluroso, -a; (climate) cálido, -a; it's ~ hace calor 2. (spicy) picante, bravo, -a AmL 3. inf (skillful) hábil 4. (dangerous) peligroso, -a 5. sl (sexually attractive) to be ~ estar bueno 6. (exciting: music, party) animado, -a 7. sl (stolen) robado, -a ▶ to be all ~ and bothered estar sulfurado II. n to have the ~s for sb estar interesado (sentimentalmente) en alguien

hot air n fig palabras f pl huecas; to be full of ~ ser sólo palabrería

hot dog n CULIN perrito m caliente, pancho m Arg

hotel [hoʊ·'tel] n hotel m

hotel bill n factura f del hotel

hotel staff n personal m del hotel

hotfoot ['hat·fʊt] I. adv a toda prisa II. vt to ~ it somewhere inf ir volando a algún sitio

hothead ['hat·hed] n persona f alocada

hothouse ['hat·haʊs] I. n invernadero m II. adj de invernadero

hotly adv apasionadamente

hot potato <-oes> n fig patata f caliente

hot seat n (*difficult position*) **to be in the ~** estar en la línea de fuego

hotshot n sl hacha f

hot spot n inf **1.** (*popular place*) lugar m concurrido **2.** (*nightclub*) club m nocturno

hot stuff n **1.** (*good*) **to be ~ at sth** ser un as en algo **2.** (*sexy*) **to be ~** estar bueno

hot-tempered adj irascible

hot-water bottle n bolsa f de agua caliente

hound [haʊnd] **I.** n perro m de caza **II.** vt perseguir

hour [aʊr] n **1.** (*60 minutes*) hora f; **to be paid by the ~** cobrar por horas **2. ten minutes to the ~** diez minutos para en punto; **till all ~s** hasta [or las tantas] muy tarde; **after ~s** fuera del horario establecido **3.** (*time for an activity*) **lunch ~** hora de comer [or almorzar]; **opening ~s** horario m (comercial) **4.** (*period of time*) momento m; **at any ~** en cualquier momento; **to keep irregular/regular ~s** llevar un horario variable/regular; **to work long ~s** trabajar hasta muy tarde; **~ after ~** hora tras hora

hour hand n manecilla f

hourly adv (*every hour*) cada hora; (*pay*) por horas

house[1] [haʊs] n **1.** (*inhabitation*) casa f **2.** (*family*) familia f **3.** (*business*) empresa f; **it's on the ~** invita la casa **4.** (*legislative body*) cámara f **5.** (*audience*) público m; **full ~** (teatro m) lleno; **to bring the ~ down** inf ser todo un éxito

house[2] [haʊz] vt **1.** (*give place to live*) alojar **2.** (*contain*) albergar

houseboat n casa f flotante

housebroken adj adiestrado, -a

household ['haʊs·hoʊld] **I.** n hogar m **II.** adj doméstico, -a

householder n (*owner*) propietario, -a m, f de una casa; (*head*) cabeza m de familia

house-hunt vi inf buscar casa

housekeeper ['haʊs·ˌki·pər] n ama f de llaves

housekeeping n organización f doméstica

houseplant n planta f de interior

housewife <-wives> n ama f de casa

housework n tareas f pl del hogar, el oficio m

housing ['haʊ·zɪŋ] n (*for living*) vivienda f

housing conditions npl condiciones f pl de habitabilidad

housing development n urbanización f, condominio m

housing project n vivienda f de interés social

hover ['hʌv·ər] vi **1.** (*stay in air*) cernerse **2.** (*wait near*) rondar **3.** (*be in an uncertain state*) estar vacilante

hovercraft ['hʌv·ər·kræft] <-(s)> n aerodeslizador m

how [haʊ] **I.** adv **1.** (*in this way*) como; (*in which way?*) cómo **2.** (*in what condition?*) **~ are you?** ¿qué tal?; **~ do you do?** encantado de conocerle **3.** (*for what reason?*) **~ come...?** inf ¿cómo es que...? **4.** (*suggestion*) **~ about...?** ¿qué tal si... ?; **~ about that!** ¡mira por dónde! **5.** (*intensifier*) **~ pretty she looked!** ¡qué guapa estaba!; **and ~!** ¡ni que lo digas!; **well, ~ about that!** (*expressing surprise, approval*) ¡caramba! **II.** n modo m; **to know the ~(s) and why(s) of sth** saber el cómo y el porqué de algo

however [haʊ·'ev·ər] **I.** adv **1.** (*no matter how*) por más que +subj; **~ hard she tries...** por mucho que lo intente... **2.** (*in whichever way*) como; **do it ~ you like** hazlo como quieras **II.** conj (*nevertheless*) sin embargo

howl [haʊl] **I.** vi **1.** (*person, animal*) aullar; (*wind*) silbar; **to ~ in** [or with] **pain** dar alaridos de dolor **2.** (*cry*) chillar; (*child*) berrear **3.** sl (*laugh*) morirse de risa **II.** n **1.** (*person, animal*) aullido m **2.** (*cry*) chillido m; (*of child*) berrido m

◆**howl down** vt hacer callar a gritos

howler ['haʊ·lər] n sl error m garrafal

howling adj aullador(a)

hp [ˌeɪtʃ·'pi] abbr of **horsepower** CV

HP [ˌeɪtʃ·'pi] abbr of **high pressure** alta presión

HTML [ˌeɪtʃ·ti·em·'el] COMPUT abbr of **Hypertext Markup Language** HTML

hub [hʌb] n **1.** (*of wheel*) cubo m **2.** fig

H

(*center*) centro *m*

hubcap ['hʌb·kæp] *n* tapacubos *m inv,* copa *m* del carro *Col*

huckleberry ['hʌk·əl·ber·i] <-ies> *n* BOT arándano *m*

huddle ['hʌd·əl] **I.** *vi* apiñarse **II.** *n* (*close group*) piña *f*

◆ **huddle down** *vi* acurrucarse

◆ **huddle together** *vi* amontonarse

◆ **huddle up** *vi* acurrucarse

huff [hʌf] **I.** *vi* to ~ and puff (*breathe loudly*) jadear; *inf* (*complain*) quejarse **II.** *n inf* enfado *m;* to get into a ~ enfadarse; to go off in a ~ irse ofendido

huffy ['hʌf·i] <-ier, -iest> *adj* **1.** (*offended*) ofendido, -a **2.** (*touchy*) susceptible

hug [hʌg] **I.** <-gg-> *vt* **1.** (*embrace*) abrazar **2.** *fig* (*idea, belief*) aferrarse a **II.** *n* abrazo *m*

huge [hjudʒ] *adj* (*extremely big*) enorme; (*impressive*) imponente

hugely *adv* enormemente

hum [hʌm] <-mm-> **I.** *vi* **1.** (*bee*) zumbar **2.** (*sing*) tararear **3.** (*be full of activity*) bullir de animación **II.** *vt* tararear **III.** *n* zumbido *m;* (*of traffic*) murmullo *m*

human ['hju·mən] **I.** *n* humano *m* **II.** *adj* humano, -a

human being *n* ser *m* humano

humane [hju·'meɪn] *adj* humanitario, -a

humanitarian [hju·mæn·ə·'ter·i·ən] **I.** *n* humanitario, -a *m, f* **II.** *adj* humanitario, -a; ~ aid ayuda humanitaria

humanity [hju·'mæn·ə·t̬i] *n* humanidad *f*

humanly *adv* humanamente

human resources *npl* recursos *m pl* humanos

human rights *npl* derechos *m pl* humanos

humble ['hʌm·bəl] **I.** *adj* **1.** (*meek*) humilde; in my ~ opinion,... en mi modesta opinión,... **2.** (*lowly: cottage, furnishings, abode*) modesto, -a **II.** *vt* humillar

humid ['hju·mɪd] *adj* húmedo, -a

humidifier [hju·'mɪd·ɪ·faɪ·ər] *n* humidificador *m*

humidity [hju·'mɪd·ə·t̬i] *n* humedad *f*

humiliate [hju·'mɪl·i·eɪt] *vt* (*shame*) avergonzar, achunchar *AmC;* (*humble*) humillar

humiliating *adj* humillante

humiliation [hju·mɪl·i·'eɪ·ʃən] *n* humillación *f*

humility [hju·'mɪl·ə·t̬i] *n* humildad *f*

hummingbird ['hʌm·ɪŋ·bɜrd] *n* colibrí *m,* chupaflor *m AmC*

humor ['hju·mər] *n* **1.** (*capacity for amusement*) humor *m;* sense of ~ sentido *m* del humor **2.** *form* (*mood*) talante *m*

humorous ['hju·mər·əs] *adj* (*speech*) humorístico, -a; (*situation*) divertido, -a

hump [hʌmp] *n* joroba *f,* petaca *f AmC* ▶ to be over the ~ haber pasado lo más difícil

humpback ['hʌmp·bæk] *n* joroba *f*

humpbacked ['hʌmp·bækt] *adj* jorobado, -a

hunch [hʌntʃ] *n* <-es> presentimiento *m;* to have a ~ that... tener la corazonada de que... **II.** *vi* encorvarse **III.** *vt* curvar

hunchback ['hʌntʃ·bæk] *n* (*person*) jorobado, -a *m, f*

hundred ['hʌn·drəd] <-(s)> **I.** *n* cien *m;* ~s of times cientos de veces **II.** *adj* ciento; (*before a noun*) cien

hundredth ['hʌn·drədθ] **I.** *n* centésimo *m* **II.** *adj* centésimo, -a

hung [hʌŋ] **I.** *pt, pp of* hang **II.** *adj* colgado, -a; ~ jury LAW jurado que se disuelve porque no se llega a ningún acuerdo

Hungarian [hʌŋ·'ger·i·ən] **I.** *adj* húngaro, -a **II.** *n* **1.** (*person*) húngaro, -a *m, f* **2.** LING húngaro *m*

Hungary ['hʌŋ·gə·ri] *n* Hungría *f*

hunger ['hʌŋ·gər] **I.** *n* **1.** hambre *f,* filo *m AmC* **2.** *fig* (*desire*) ansia *f* **II.** *vi fig* to ~ after [*or* for] ansiar

hungry ['hʌŋ·gri] <-ier, -iest> *adj* **1.** (*desiring food*) hambriento, -a; to be/go ~ tener/pasar hambre **2.** *fig* (*wanting badly*) ansioso, -a; to be ~ for sth estar ávido de algo

hunk [hʌŋk] *n* **1.** (*piece*) trozo *m* **2.** *sl* (*man*) cachas *m inv*

hunky dory [ˌhʌŋ·ki·'dɔr·i] *adj sl* guay,

muy bien

hunt [hʌnt] I. vt 1. (chase to kill) cazar 2. (search for) buscar II. vi 1. (chase to kill) cazar; to go ~ing ir de caza 2. (search) to ~ for buscar III. n 1. (chase) cacería f 2. (search) búsqueda f

hunter n (person) cazador(a) m(f)

hunting n caza f

hunting season n temporada f de caza

hurdle ['hɜr·dəl] I. n 1. a. SPORTS (fence) valla f, obstáculo m 2. (difficulty) obstáculo m II. vi SPORTS saltar vallas [or obstáculos] III. vt SPORTS saltar

hurdler n SPORTS vallista mf

hurdle race n SPORTS carrera [or obstáculos] de vallas

hurl [hɜrl] vt (throw) lanzar

hurrah [hə·ˈra] interj, **hurray** [hə·ˈreɪ] interj hurra

hurricane ['hɜr·ɪ·keɪn] n huracán m

hurried ['hɜr·id] adj apresurado, -a, apurado, -a AmL

hurry ['hɜr·i] <-ie-> I. vi darse prisa, apurarse AmL II. vt (rush) meter prisas, apurar AmL III. n prisa f, apuro m AmL; to leave in a ~ irse disparado; to do sth in a ~ hacer algo de prisa; what's (all) the ~? ¿a qué viene tanta prisa?

◆ **hurry along** I. vi apresurarse II. vt always sep meter prisas

◆ **hurry away, hurry off** I. vi marcharse de prisa II. vt (person) hacer marchar de prisa; (object) hacer llevar de prisa

◆ **hurry on** vi continuar rápidamente

◆ **hurry up** I. vi darse prisa II. vt meter prisa

hurt [hɜrt] I. <hurt, hurt> vi (physically, emotionally) doler II. vt 1. (wound) herir 2. (cause pain) lastimar; it ~s me me duele 3. (offend) ofender 4. (damage) dañar III. adj (in pain, injured) dañado, -a; (grieved, distressed) dolido, -a IV. n 1. (pain) dolor m 2. (offence) ofensa f 3. (damage) daño m

hurtful ['hɜrt·fəl] adj perjudicial

hurtle ['hɜr·təl] I. vi lanzarse II. vt lanzar

husband ['hʌz·bənd] I. n marido m, esposo m II. vt economizar

hush [hʌʃ] I. n silencio m II. interj ~!

¡chitón! III. vi callarse IV. vt (make silent) hacer callar; (soothe) acallar

◆ **hush up** vt encubrir

hush-hush adj infsecreto, -a

hush money n infunto m (que se utiliza para comprar el silencio de alguien)

husky¹ ['hʌs·ki] <-ier, -iest> adj 1. (low, rough: voice) ronco, -a 2. (big, strong) fornido, -a; euph (well-built) robusto, -a

husky² ['hʌs·ki] <-ies> n perro m esquimal

hustle ['hʌs·əl] I. vt 1. (hurry) dar prisa a 2. (achieve) hacerse con II. n ajetreo m

hustler ['hʌs·lər] n (persuader) camelador(a) m(f)

hustling ['hʌs·lɪŋ] n ajetreo m

hut [hʌt] n cabaña f

hutch [hʌtʃ] n 1. (box for animals) jaula f 2. (cupboard) aparador m

hybrid ['haɪ·brɪd] n híbrido, -a m, f

hydrant ['haɪ·drənt] n boca f de riego, hidrante m

hydrocarbon [ˌhaɪ·droʊ·ˈkar·bən] I. n hidrocarburo m II. adj de hidrocarburo

hydroelectric [ˌhaɪ·droʊ·ɪ·ˈlek·trɪk] adj hidroeléctrico, -a

hydrofoil ['haɪ·drə·fɔɪl] n hidroala m

hydrogen ['haɪ·drə·dʒən] n hidrógeno m

hydrogen bomb n bomba f de hidrógeno

hydroponics [ˌhaɪ·drə·ˈpan·ɪks] n + sing vb hidroponía f

hyena [haɪ·ˈi·nə] n hiena f

hygiene ['haɪ·dʒin] n higiene f, salubridad f AmL

hygienic [ˌhaɪ·dʒi·ˈen·ɪk] adj higiénico, -a

hymn [hɪm] n himno m

hymnal ['hɪm·nəl] n, **hymnbook** n himnario m

hype [haɪp] I. n COM bombo publicitario II. vt dar bombo publicitario a

hypermarket ['haɪ·pər·mar·kɪt] n hipermercado m

hypertext [ˌhaɪ·pər·ˈtekst] n COMPUT hipertexto m

hyphen ['haɪ·fən] n TYPO guión m

hyphenate ['haɪ·fə·neɪt] vt separar con guiones

H

hypnosis [hɪp·'nou·sɪs] *n* hipnosis *f inv*; **to be under ~** estar hipnotizado

hypnotherapy [hɪp·nou·'θer·ə·pi] *n* hipnoterapia *f*

hypnotist ['hɪp·nə·tɪst] *n* hipnotizador(a) *m(f)*

hypnotize ['hɪp·nə·taɪz] *vt* hipnotizar

hypochondriac [haɪ·pə·'kan·dri·æk] **I.** *n* hipocondríaco, -a *m, f* **II.** *adj* hipocondríaco, -a

hypocrite ['hɪp·ə·krɪt] *n* hipócrita *mf*

hypotenuse [haɪ·'pat·ə·nus] *n* MATH hipotenusa *f*

hypothermia [haɪ·pou·'θɜr·mi·ə] *n* hipotermia *f*

hypothetical [haɪ·pə·'θeṭ·ɪ·kəl] *adj* hipotético, -a

hysterectomy [hɪs·tə·'rek·tə·mi] *n* MED histerectomía *f*

hysteric [hɪ·'ster·ɪk] **I.** *adj* histérico, -a **II.** *n* histérico, -a *m, f*

hysterical *adj* histérico, -a

I

I, i [aɪ] *n* I, i *f*; **~ as in India** I de Italia

I [aɪ] *pron pers* (*1st person sing*) yo; **~'m coming** ya voy; **~'ll do it** (yo) lo haré; **am ~ late?** ¿llego tarde?; **she and ~** ella y yo; **it was ~ who did that** fui yo quien lo hizo

IAEA *n abbr of* **International Atomic Energy Agency** OIEA *f*

ice [aɪs] **I.** *n* (*frozen water*) hielo *m* ▶ **to break the ~** *inf* romper el hielo **II.** *vt* **1.** (*chill a drink*) enfriar con hielo **2.** (*put icing on*) escarchar

Ice Age *n* era *f* glacial

iceberg *n* iceberg *m*; **the tip of the ~** *fig* la punta del iceberg

icebox <-es> *n* **1.** (*freezer*) congelador *m* **2.** (*fridge*) nevera *f*, refrigeradora *f AmL*

ice cap *n* casquete *m* de hielo

ice-cold *adj* helado, -a

ice cream *n* helado *m*, nieve *f AmC*

ice cube ['aɪs·kjub] *n* cubito *m* de hielo

iced [aɪst] *adj* **1.** (*drink*) con hielo **2.** (*covered with icing*) escarchado, -a

ice hockey *n* hockey *m* sobre hielo

ice pack *n* bolsa *f* de hielo

ice rink *n* pista *f* de patinaje

ice-skate *vi* patinar sobre hielo

icicle ['aɪ·sɪ·kəl] *n* carámbano *m*

icing ['aɪ·sɪŋ] *n* glaseado *m*

icon ['aɪ·kan] *n* icono *m*

ICU [aɪ·si·'ju] *n abbr of* **intensive care unit** UCI *f*

icy ['aɪ·si] <-ier, -iest> *adj* **1.** (*with ice*) helado, -a **2.** (*unfriendly*) frío, -a

ID¹ [aɪ·'di] **I.** *n abbr of* **identification** identificación *f* **II.** *vt inf abbr of* **identify** identificar

ID² [aɪ·'di] *n abbr of* **Idaho** Idaho *m*

I'd [aɪd] **1.** = I would *see* would **2.** = I had *see* have

ID card [aɪ·'di·ˌkard] *n see* **identity card** carné *m* de identidad

idea [aɪ·'di·ə] *n* **1.** (*opinion*) idea *f* **2.** (*notion*) noción *f*

ideal [aɪ·'di·əl] **I.** *adj* ideal **II.** *n* ideal *m*

identical [aɪ·'den·tɪ·kəl] *adj* idéntico, -a, individual *CSur*

identifiable [aɪ·ˌden·tə·'faɪ·ə·bəl] *adj* identificable

identification [aɪ·ˌden·tə·fɪ·'keɪ·ʃən] *n* identificación *f*

identification papers *npl* documentación *f*

identifier [aɪ·'den·tə·faɪ·ər] *n* COMPUT identificador *m*

identify [aɪ·'den·tə·faɪ] <-ie-> *vt* identificar

identity [aɪ·'den·tə·ti] <-ies> *n* identidad *f*

identity card *n* carné *m* de identidad

ideological [ˌaɪ·di·ə·'ladʒ·ɪ·kəl] *adj* ideológico, -a

ideology [ˌaɪ·di·'al·ə·dʒi] <-ies> *n* ideología *f*

idiom ['ɪd·i·əm] *n* LING **1.** (*phrase*) modismo *m* **2.** (*style of expression*) lenguaje *m*

idiomatic [ˌɪd·i·ə·'mæṭ·ɪk] *adj* idiomático, -a

idiot ['ɪd·i·ət] *n* idiota *mf*

idiotic [ˌɪd·i·'aṭ·ɪk] *adj* tonto, -a

idle ['aɪ·dəl] **I.** *adj* **1.** (*lazy*) holgazán, -ana **2.** (*not busy*) desocupado, -a; (*machine*) parado, -a, desocupado,

-a **3.** (*frivolous: pleasures*) frívolo, -a
4. (*unfounded*) vano, -a; (*gossip*) insustancial **5.** (*ineffective: threat*) inútil
6. FIN de paro **II.** *n* AUTO ralentí *m* **III.** *vi*
(*engine*) marchar al ralentí, funcionar en
vacío; (*person*) haraganear

idol ['aɪ·dəl] *n* ídolo *m*

idolatry [aɪ·'dɑl·ə·tri] *n* idolatría *f*

idolize ['aɪ·də·laɪz] *vt* idolatrar

if [ɪf] **I.** *conj* **1.** (*supposing that*) si; ~
it snows si nieva; ~ **not** si no; **as** ~ **it
were true** como si fuera verdad; ~ **they
exist at all** si es que en realidad existen;
~ **A is right, then B is wrong** si A es
verdadero, entonces B es falso; **I'll stay,
~ only for a day** me quedaré, aunque
sea sólo un día **2.** (*every time that*) ~ **he
needs me, I'll help him** si me necesita,
le ayudaré **3.** (*whether*) **I wonder ~
he'll come** me pregunto si vendrá **II.** *n*
pero *m*; **no ~s, ands, or buts!** ¡no hay
peros que valgan!

iffy ['ɪf·i] <-ier, -iest> *adj inf* dudoso, -a;
(*person*) sospechoso, -a

igloo ['ɪg·lu] *n* iglú *m*

ignite [ɪg·'naɪt] **I.** *vi* incendiarse **II.** *vt
form* incendiar

ignition [ɪg·'nɪʃ·ən] *n* **1.** AUTO encendido *m* **2.** *form* (*causing to burn*) ignición *f*

ignition key *n* llave *f* de contacto, suiche *m* Méx

ignition switch <-es> *n* interruptor *m*
de encendido

ignorance ['ɪg·nər·əns] *n* ignorancia *f*
▶ ~ **is bliss** ojos que no ven, corazón
que no siente

ignorant ['ɪg·nər·ənt] *adj* ignorante; **to be
~ about sth** desconocer algo

ignore [ɪg·'nɔr] *vt* no hacer caso de, ignorar

IL *n*, **Ill.** *n abbr of* **Illinois** Illinois *m*

ill [ɪl] **I.** *adj* **1.** (*sick*) enfermo, -a **2.** (*bad*)
malo, -a; (*harmful*) nocivo, -a; (*unfavorable*) perjudicial; **an ~ omen** un mal
presagio **II.** *adv form* (*badly*) mal; **to
speak ~ of sb** hablar mal de alguien

I'll [aɪl] = **I will** *see* **will**

ill-advised [ˌɪl·əd·'vaɪzd] *adj* imprudente

illegal [ɪ·'li·gəl] *adj* ilegal

illegal immigrant *n* inmigrante *mf* ilegal

illegible [ɪ·'ledʒ·ə·bəl] *adj* ilegible

illegitimate [ˌɪl·ɪ·'dʒɪt·ə·mət] *adj* ilegítimo, -a

ill-informed ['ɪl·ɪn·fɔrmd] *adj* (*wrongly
informed*) mal informado, -a

illiterate [ɪ·'lɪt·ər·ət] **I.** *adj* analfabeto,
-a; *pej, fig* inculto, -a **II.** *n* analfabeto, -a *m, f*

ill-mannered [ˌɪl·'mæn·ərd] *adj* mal educado, -a

illness ['ɪl·nɪs] <-es> *n* enfermedad *f*

illogical [ɪ·'lɑdʒ·ɪ·kəl] *adj* ilógico, -a

ill-tempered *adj* de mal genio

ill-timed *adj* inoportuno, -a

illuminate [ɪ·'lu·mə·neɪt] *vt* iluminar; *fig*
aclarar

illuminating [ɪ·'lu·mɪ·neɪ·t̬ɪŋ] *adj form*
aclaratorio, -a

illumination [ɪ·ˌlu·mɪ·'neɪ·ʃən] *n a.* ART
iluminación *f*

illusion [ɪ·'lu·ʒən] *n* (*misleading appearance*) apariencia *f*; (*false impression*)
ilusión *f*

illustrate ['ɪl·ə·streɪt] *vt* ilustrar; *fig* ejemplificar

illustration [ˌɪl·ə·'streɪ·ʃən] *n* **1.** (*drawing*) ilustración *f* **2.** (*example*) ejemplo *M*

illustrator ['ɪl·ə·streɪ·t̬ər] *n* ilustrador(a) *m(f)*

illustrious [ɪ·'lʌs·tri·əs] *adj form* ilustre

I'm [aɪm] = **I am** *see* **am**

image ['ɪm·ɪdʒ] *n* **1.** (*likeness*) imagen *f*
2. (*picture*) retrato *m* **3.** (*reputation*)
reputación *f*

imagery ['ɪm·ɪdʒ·ri] *n* LIT imágenes *fpl*

imaginable [ɪ·'mædʒ·ə·nə·bəl] *adj* imaginable

imaginary [ɪ·'mædʒ·ə·ner·i] *adj* imaginario, -a

imagination [ɪ·ˌmædʒ·ə·'neɪ·ʃən] *n* imaginación *f*; (*inventiveness*) inventiva *f*

imaginative [ɪ·'mædʒ·ə·nə·t̬ɪv] *adj* imaginativo, -a

imagine [ɪ·'mædʒ·ɪn] *vt* **1.** (*form mental
image*) imaginar **2.** (*suppose*) figurarse;
~ **that!** ¡figúrate!

imaging *n* COMPUT tratamiento *m* de
imágenes

imbalance [ˌɪm·'bæl·əns] *n* desequilibrio *m*

imbecile ['ɪm·bə·sɪl] *n* imbécil *mf*

IMF [ˌaɪ·em·'ef] *n abbr of* **International Monetary Fund** FMI *m*

imitate ['ɪm·ɪ·teɪt] *vt* imitar; (*copy*) copiar

imitation [ˌɪm·ɪ·'ter·ʃən] I. *n* 1. (*mimicry*) imitación *f*; **in ~ of sb/sth** a imitación de alguien/algo 2. (*copy*) reproducción *f* II. *adj* de imitación

immaculate [ɪ·'mæk·jʊ·lət] *adj* 1. (*spotless, neat*) inmaculado, -a 2. (*flawless*) impecable

immature [ˌɪm·ə·'tʃʊr] *adj* 1. (*young*) inmaduro, -a; (*people, animals*) joven 2. (*childish: behavior*) infantil

immaturity [ˌɪm·ə·'tʃʊr·ə·ti] *n* inmadurez *f*

immeasurable [ɪ·'meʒ·ər·ə·bəl] *adj* 1. (*boundless*) inconmensurable 2. (*effect*) incalculable

immediacy [ɪ·'mi·di·ə·si] *n* inmediatez *f*; (*nearness*) proximidad *f*

immediate [ɪ·'mi·di·ɪt] *adj* inmediato, -a; **the ~ family** los familiares directos; **in the ~ area** en las inmediaciones; **in the ~ future** en un futuro inmediato

immediately *adv* (*time*) inmediatamente; **~ after...** justo después de...

immense [ɪ·'mens] *adj* inmenso, -a; (*importance*) extremo, -a

immerse [ɪ·'mɜrs] *vt* sumergir; **to be ~d in sth** *fig* estar absorto en algo

immersion heater *n* calentador *m* de inmersión

immigrant ['ɪm·ɪ·grənt] *n* inmigrante *mf*

immigrate ['ɪm·ɪ·greɪt] *vi* inmigrar

immigration [ˌɪm·ɪ·'greɪ·ʃən] *n* inmigración *f*

imminent ['ɪm·ɪ·nənt] *adj* inminente

immobilize [ɪ·'moʊ·bə·laɪz] *vt* inmovilizar

immodest [ɪ·'mad·ɪst] *adj* 1. (*conceited*) creído, -a 2. (*slightly indecent*) descarado, -a

immoral [ɪ·'mɔr·əl] *adj* inmoral

immortal [ɪ·'mɔr·təl] I. *adj* 1. (*undying*) inmortal 2. (*remembered forever*) imperecedero, -a II. *n* inmortal *mf*

immortality [ˌɪ·mɔr·'tæl·ə·ti] *n* inmortalidad *f*

immovable [ɪ·'mu·və·bəl] *adj* 1. (*not*

moveable) inamovible 2. (*not changeable*) inalterable

immune [ɪ·'mjun] *adj* 1. MED inmune 2. POL, LAW exento, -a

immune system *n* sistema *m* inmunológico

immunity [ɪ·'mju·nə·ti] *n* 1. MED inmunidad *f* 2. **diplomatic ~** inmunidad *f* diplomática

immunize ['ɪm·jə·naɪz] *vt* inmunizar

impact ['ɪm·pækt] I. *n* 1. (*striking, contact*) choque *m*; **on ~** por impacto 2. (*effect*) impacto *m* II. *vt* incidir en III. *vi* to ~ **on sb/sth** impactar en alguien/algo

impaired *adj* (*speech, vision, hearing*) dañado, -a; (*health*) perjudicado, -a; **to be visually ~** estar impedido visualmente

impartial [ɪm·'par·ʃəl] *adj* imparcial

impartiality [ɪm·ˌpar·ʃɪ·'æl·ə·ti] *n* imparcialidad *f*

impassable [ɪm·'pæs·ə·bəl] *adj* intransitable; *fig* infranqueable

impasse ['ɪm·pæs] *n a. fig* callejón *m* sin salida; **to have reached an ~** haber llegado a un punto muerto [*or a un atolladero*]

impassioned [ɪm·'pæʃ·ənd] *adj* formapasionado, -a

impassive [ɪm·'pæs·ɪv] *adj* impasible

impatience [ɪm·'per·ʃəns] *n* impaciencia *f*

impatient [ɪm·'per·ʃənt] *adj* impaciente; **to be ~ to do sth** estar impaciente por hacer algo

impeach [ɪm·'pitʃ] *vt* acusar, (someter a un proceso de incapacitación presidencial)

impeachment [ɪm·'pitʃ·mənt] *n* acusación *f* (*proceso de incapacitación presidencial*)

impede [ɪm·'pid] *vt* impedir

imperative [ɪm·'per·ə·tɪv] I. *adj* 1. (*urgently essential*) imprescindible 2. LING imperativo, -a II. *n a.* LING imperativo *m*

imperceptible [ˌɪm·pər·'sep·tə·bəl] *adj* imperceptible

imperfect [ɪm·'pɜr·fɪkt] I. *adj* imperfecto, -a II. *n* LING (pretérito *m*) imperfecto

imperfection [ˌɪm·pər·ˈfek·ʃən] *n* imperfección *f*

imperial [ɪm·ˈpɪr·i·əl] *adj* imperial

imperialism [ɪm·ˈpɪr·i·ə·lɪz·əm] *n* imperialismo *m*

impersonal [ɪm·ˈpɜr·sə·nəl] *adj a.* LING impersonal

impersonate [ɪm·ˈpɜr·sə·neɪt] *vt* hacerse pasar por; (*imitate*) imitar

impertinent [ɪm·ˈpɜr·tə·nənt] *adj* impertinente

impetuous [ɪm·ˈpetʃ·u·əs] *adj* impetuoso, -a

impetus [ˈɪm·pɪ·təs] *n* 1. (*push*) impulso *m* 2. (*driving force*) ímpetu *m*

implacable [ɪm·ˈplæk·ə·bəl] *adj form* implacable

implant [ɪm·ˈplænt] I. *n* implante *m* II. *vt* (*add surgically*) implantar

implausible [ɪm·ˈplɔ·zə·bəl] *adj* inverosímil

implement [ˈɪm·plɪ·mənt] I. *n* (*tool*) instrumento *m;* (*small tool*) utensilio *m* II. *vt* implementar

implicate [ˈɪm·plɪ·keɪt] *vt* 1. (*show sb's involvement*) implicar 2. (*involve*) involucrar

implication [ˌɪm·plɪ·ˈkeɪ·ʃən] *n* 1. (*hinting at*) insinuación *f* 2. (*showing of involvement*) implicación *f*

implicit [ɪm·ˈplɪs·ɪt] *adj* (*suggested*) implícito, -a

implore [ɪm·ˈplɔr] *vt* implorar; **to ~ sb to do sth** suplicar a alguien que haga algo

imploring [ɪm·ˈplɔr·ɪŋ] *adj* implorante; (*voice*) suplicante

imply [ɪm·ˈplaɪ] <-ie-> *vt* (*suggest*) sugerir

impolite [ˌɪm·pə·ˈlaɪt] *adj* descortés; (*rude*) grosero, -a

impoliteness *n* descortesía *f*

import I. [ɪm·ˈpɔrt] *vt* ECON, COMPUT importar II. [ˈɪm·pɔrt] *n* (*product*) producto *m* de importación

importance [ɪm·ˈpɔr·təns] *n* importancia *f*

important [ɪm·ˈpɔr·tənt] *adj* importante

importantly *adv* significativamente

importation [ˌɪm·pɔr·ˈteɪ·ʃən] *n* ECON importación *f*

import duty <-ies> *n* derecho *m* de aduana

impose [ɪm·ˈpoʊz] I. *vt* 1. (*implement*) imponer 2. (*force on*) obligar II. *vi* aprovecharse; **I don't want to ~** no quiero molestar

imposing [ɪm·ˈpoʊ·zɪŋ] *adj* imponente

imposition [ˌɪm·pə·ˈzɪʃ·ən] *n* 1. (*forcing, application*) imposición *f* 2. (*inconvenience*) molestia *f*

impossibility [ɪm·ˌpas·ə·ˈbɪl·ə·t̬i] *n* imposibilidad *f*

impossible [ɪm·ˈpas·ə·bəl] I. *adj* (*not possible*) imposible II. *n* **the ~** lo imposible

imposter *n*, **impostor** [ɪm·ˈpas·tər] *n* impostor(a) *m(f)*

impotence [ˈɪm·pə·təns] *n* impotencia *f*

impotent [ˈɪm·pə·tənt] *adj* impotente

impound [ɪm·ˈpaʊnd] *vt* incautar

impoverish [ɪm·ˈpav·ər·ɪʃ] *vt* (*make poor*) empobrecer

impracticable [ɪm·ˈpræk·tɪ·kə·bəl] *adj* impracticable

impractical [ɪm·ˈpræk·tɪ·kəl] *adj* poco práctico, -a

imprecise [ˌɪm·prɪ·ˈsaɪs] *adj* impreciso, -a

impregnable [ɪm·ˈpreg·nə·bəl] *adj* (*unable to be taken*) inexpugnable

impregnate [ɪm·ˈpreg·neɪt] *vt* 1. (*inseminate*) fecundar 2. (*saturate*) impregnar

impress [ɪm·ˈpres] I. *vt* 1. (*affect*) impresionar 2. (*stamp*) estampar; **to ~ sth on** [*or* **upon**] **sb** (*make realize*) inculcar algo a alguien II. *vi* impresionar

impression [ɪm·ˈpreʃ·ən] *n* 1. (*general opinion*) impresión *f;* **to be of** [*or* **under**] **the ~ that...** tener la impresión de que... 2. (*feeling*) sensación *f;* **to make an ~ on sb** causar impresión a alguien 3. (*imprint*) impresión *f; fig* huella *f*

impressionable [ɪm·ˈpreʃ·ə·nə·bəl] *adj* impresionable

impressionism [ɪm·ˈpreʃ·ə·nɪz·əm] *n* impresionismo *m*

impressive [ɪm·ˈpres·ɪv] *adj* impresionante

imprint I. [ɪm·ˈprɪnt] *vt* (*stamp*) estampar; (*paper*) imprimir II. [ˈɪm·prɪnt] *n* 1. (*mark*) marca *f; fig* huella *f* 2. TYPO pie *m* de imprenta

imprison [ɪm·ˈprɪz·ən] vt encarcelar

imprisonment [ɪm·ˈprɪz·ən·mənt] n encarcelamiento m; **life** ~ cadena f perpetua

improbability [ˌɪm·prab·ə·ˈbɪl·ə·t̬i] n improbabilidad f

improbable [ɪm·ˈprab·ə·bəl] adj improbable

improper [ɪm·ˈprap·ər] adj 1. (incorrect) incorrecto, -a; (showing bad judgment) injusto, -a 2. (not socially decent) indecoroso, -a

improve [ɪm·ˈpruv] vt, vi mejorar

improvement [ɪm·ˈpruv·mənt] n 1. (betterment) mejora f; (progress) progreso m 2. (of illness) mejoría f

improvisation [ɪm·ˌprav·ɪ·ˈzeɪ·ʃən] n improvisación f

improvise [ˈɪm·prə·vaɪz] vi, vt improvisar

imprudent [ɪm·ˈpru·dənt] adj form imprudente

impudence [ˈɪm·pju·dəns] n descaro m

impudent [ˈɪm·pju·dənt] adj impertinente

impulse [ˈɪm·pʌls] n a. ELEC, PHYS, BIO impulso m; **to do sth on** (an) ~ hacer algo por impulso

impulsive [ɪm·ˈpʌl·sɪv] adj impulsivo, -a

impunity [ɪm·ˈpju·nə·t̬i] n impunidad f

impure [ɪm·ˈpjʊr] adj impuro, -a

impurity [ɪm·ˈpjʊr·ə·t̬i] <-ies> n impureza f

in [ɪn] I. prep 1. (inside, into) en, dentro de; **to be ~ bed** estar en la cama; **there is sth ~ the drawer** hay algo dentro del cajón; ~ **town/jail** en la ciudad/cárcel; ~ **Canada/Mexico** en Canadá/México 2. (within) ~ **sb's face/the picture** en el rostro de alguien/la fotografía; ~ **the snow/sun** en la nieve/el sol; **the best ~ New England/town** lo mejor de Nueva Inglaterra/de la ciudad 3. (position of) ~ **the beginning/end** al principio/final; **right ~ the middle** justo en medio 4. (during) ~ **the twenties** en los (años) veinte; **to be ~ one's thirties** estar en los treinta; ~ **May/the spring** en mayo/primavera; ~ **the afternoon** por la tarde 5. (at later time) ~ **a week/three hours** dentro de una

semana/tres horas; ~ (**the**) **future** en el futuro 6. (in less than) **to do sth ~ 4 hours** hacer algo en 4 horas 7. (for) **he hasn't done that ~ years/a week** no ha hecho eso desde hace años/una semana 8. (in situation, state of) ~ **fashion** de moda; ~ **search of sth/sb** en busca de algo/alguien; ~ **this way** de esta manera; **when ~ doubt** en caso de duda; ~ **earnest** sinceramente; **to be ~ a hurry** tener prisa; **to be ~ love** (**with sb**) estar enamorado (de alguien); **dressed ~ red** vestido de rojo 9. (concerning) **deaf ~ one ear** sordo de un oído; **to be interested ~ sth** estar interesado en algo; **to have faith ~ God** tener fe en Dios; **to have a say ~ the matter** tener algo que decir al respecto; **a change ~ attitude** un cambio de actitud; **a rise ~ prices** un aumento de los precios 10. (by) ~ **saying sth** al decir algo 11. (taking the form of) **to speak ~ French** hablar en francés; ~ **the form of a request** en forma de petición 12. (made of) ~ **wood/stone** de madera/piedra 13. (sound of) ~ **a whisper** en un murmullo; **to speak ~ a loud/low voice** hablar en voz alta/baja 14. (aspect of) **6 feet ~ length/height** 2 metros de largo/alto 15. (ratio) **two ~ six** dos de cada seis; **to buy sth ~ twos** comprar algo de dos en dos; ~ **part** en parte; ~ **tens** en grupos de diez 16. (substitution of) ~ **your place** en tu lugar; ~ **lieu of sth** form en lugar de algo 17. (as consequence of) ~ **return** a cambio; ~ **reply** como respuesta ▶ ~ **all** con todo; **all** ~ **all** en resumen II. adv 1. (inside, into) dentro, adentro; **to go** ~ entrar; **to put sth** ~ meter algo 2. (to a place) **to be** ~ inf estar en casa; **to hand sth** ~ entregar algo 3. (popular) **to be** ~ estar de moda ▶ **to be** ~ **for sth** inf estar a punto de recibir algo III. adj de moda IV. n the ~s and outs los pormenores

inability [ˌɪn·ə·ˈbɪl·ə·t̬i] n incapacidad f, ineptitud f pey

inaccessible [ˌɪn·æk·ˈses·ə·bəl] adj inaccesible

inaccuracy [ɪn·ˈæk·jər·ə·si] <-ies> n

1. (*fact*) error *m* 2. (*quality*) imprecisión *f*, inexactitud *f*

inaccurate [ɪnˈæk·jər·ət] *adj* 1. (*inexact*) inexacto, -a 2. (*wrong*) equivocado, -a

inaction [ɪnˈæk·ʃən] *n* inacción *f*

inactive [ɪnˈæk·tɪv] *adj* inactivo, -a

inactivity [ˌɪn·æk·ˈtɪv·ə·t̬i] *n* inactividad *f*

inadequate [ɪnˈæd·ɪ·kwət] *adj* inadecuado, -a; (*inept*) inepto, -a

inadvertent [ˌɪn·əd·ˈvɜr·tənt] *adj* involuntario, -a

inadvisable [ˌɪn·əd·ˈvaɪ·zə·bəl] *adj* desaconsejable

inanimate [ɪnˈæn·ɪ·mət] *adj* inanimado, -a

inapplicable [ɪnˈæp·lɪ·kə·bəl] *adj* inaplicable

inappropriate [ˌɪn·ə·ˈproʊ·pri·ət] *adj* inapropiado, -a; (*not suitable*) inadecuado, -a

inarticulate [ˌɪn·ɑr·ˈtɪk·jʊ·lət] *adj* 1. (*unable to express*) incapaz de expresarse 2. (*unclear*) inarticulado, -a

inasmuch as [ˌɪn·əzˈmʌtʃ·əz] *conj form* 1. (*because*) dado que 2. (*to the extent that*) en tanto que +*subj*

inattentive [ˌɪn·ə·ˈten·tɪv] *adj* distraído, -a; **to be ~ to sb/sth** no prestar atención a alguien/algo

inaudible [ɪnˈɔ·də·bəl] *adj* inaudible

inauguration [ɪn·ˌɔ·gjʊ·ˈreɪ·ʃən] *n* inauguración *f*

inauspicious [ˌɪn·ɔ·ˈspɪʃ·əs] *adj* poco propicio, -a

inborn [ˈɪn·bɔrn] *adj* innato, -a

inbuilt [ˈɪn·bɪlt] *adj* integrado, -a; *fig* inherente, innato, -a

Inc. [ɪŋk] *abbr of* **incorporated** Inc.

incalculable [ɪnˈkæl·kjʊ·lə·bəl] *adj* incalculable

incandescent [ˌɪn·kən·ˈdes·ənt] *adj* incandescente

incapable [ɪnˈkeɪ·pə·bəl] *adj* incapaz; **to be ~ of doing sth** ser incapaz de hacer algo

incapacity [ˌɪn·kə·ˈpæs·ə·t̬i] *n* incapacidad *f*

incendiary [ɪnˈsen·di·er·i] *adj a. fig* incendiario, -a

incense¹ [ˈɪn·sents] *n* incienso *m*

incense² [ɪnˈsents] *vt* indignar

incentive [ɪnˈsen·tɪv] *n* incentivo *m*

inception [ɪnˈsep·ʃən] *n* inicio *m*

incessant [ɪnˈses·ənt] *adj* incesante

incest [ˈɪn·sest] *n* incesto *m*

inch [ɪntʃ] <-es> *n* pulgada *f* ► **give someone an ~ and they'll take a mile** *prov* les das la mano y te cogen el brazo *prov;* **to do sth ~ by ~** hacer algo paso a paso

◆inch forward *vi* avanzar lentamente

incidence [ˈɪn·sɪ·dənts] *n* incidencia *f*

incident [ˈɪn·sɪ·dənt] *n* incidente *m;* **an isolated ~** un incidente aislado

incidental [ˌɪn·sɪ·ˈden·təl] *adj* (*related, of lesser importance*) secundario, -a

incidentally *adv* por cierto, a propósito

incinerate [ɪnˈsɪn·ə·reɪt] *vt* incinerar

incinerator [ɪnˈsɪn·ə·reɪ·tər] *n* incinerador *m*

incision [ɪnˈsɪʒ·ən] *n* MED incisión *f*

incisive [ɪnˈsaɪ·sɪv] *adj* 1. (*clear*) incisivo, -a 2. (*keen, acute*) agudo, -a

incite [ɪnˈsaɪt] *vt* instigar

inclination [ˌɪn·klɪˈneɪ·ʃən] *n* 1. (*tendency*) propensión *f* 2. (*slope*) inclinación *f*

incline¹ [ˈɪn·klaɪn] *n* inclinación *f;* (*of hill, mountain*) pendiente *f*

incline² [ɪnˈklaɪn] I. *vi* 1. (*tend*) tender 2. (*lean*) inclinarse II. *vt* 1. (*make sth tend*) predisponer 2. (*make lean*) inclinar

inclined [ɪnˈklaɪnd] *adj* predispuesto, -a; **to be ~ to do sth** estar dispuesto a hacer algo

inclose [ɪnˈkloʊz] *vt see* **enclose**

include [ɪnˈklud] *vt* incluir; (*in a letter*) adjuntar

including [ɪnˈklu·dɪŋ] *prep* incluso; (*not*) **~ tax** impuesto (no) incluido; **up to and ~ June 6th** hasta el 6 de junio inclusive

inclusion [ɪnˈklu·ʒən] *n* inclusión *f*

inclusive [ɪnˈklu·sɪv] *adj* incluido, -a

incoherent [ˌɪn·koʊ·ˈhɪr·ənt] *adj* incoherente

income [ˈɪn·kʌm] *n* ingresos *mpl*

income tax *n* impuesto *m* sobre la renta

incoming [ˈɪn·ˌkʌm·ɪŋ] I. *adj* entrante II. *interj* MIL se presenta

incomparable [ɪn·ˈkam·pər·ə·bəl] *adj* incomparable

incompatible [ˌɪn·kəm·ˈpæt̬·ə·bəl] *adj* incompatible

incompetence [ɪn·ˈkam·pə·təns] *n*, **incompetency** *n* incompetencia *f*

incompetent [ɪn·ˈkam·pə·tənt] **I.** *adj* incompetente; **mentally ~** deficiente mental **II.** *n* incompetente *mf*

incomplete [ˌɪn·kəm·ˈplit] *adj* incompleto, -a

incomprehensible [ˌɪn·kam·prɪ·ˈhen·sə·bəl] *adj* incomprensible

inconceivable [ˌɪn·kən·ˈsi·və·bəl] *adj* inconcebible

inconclusive [ˌɪn·kən·ˈklu·sɪv] *adj* (*not convincing*) inconcluyente

inconsequential [ɪn·ˌkan·sɪ·ˈkwen·ʃəl] *adj* (*illogical*) inconsecuente

inconsiderate [ˌɪn·kən·ˈsɪd·ər·ət] *adj* desconsiderado, -a; (*insensitive*) insensible

inconsistent [ˌɪn·kən·ˈsɪs·tənt] *adj* **1.** (*changeable*) incoherente **2.** (*lacking agreement*) contradictorio, -a

inconsolable [ˌɪn·kən·ˈsou·lə·bəl] *adj* inconsolable

inconspicuous [ˌɪn·kən·ˈspɪk·ju·əs] *adj* desapercibido, -a

inconstant [ɪn·ˈkan·stənt] *adj* (*changing*) inconstante

incontrovertible [ɪn·ˌkan·trə·ˈvɜr·t̬ə·bəl] *adj* incontrovertible; **~ proof** prueba *f* irrefutable

inconvenience [ˌɪn·kən·ˈvin·jəns] **I.** *n* inconveniencia *f* **II.** *vt* causar molestias

inconvenient [ˌɪn·kən·ˈvin·jənt] *adj* inconveniente; (*time*) inoportuno, -a

incorporate [ɪn·ˈkɔr·pə·reɪt] *vt* **1.** (*integrate*) incorporar; (*work into*) integrar **2.** (*include*) incluir **3.** LAW, ECON constituir

incorrect [ˌɪn·kə·ˈrekt] *adj* (*wrong, untrue*) incorrecto, -a; (*diagnosis*) erróneo, -a; **it is ~ that...** no es cierto que...

incorruptible [ˌɪn·kə·ˈrʌp·tə·bəl] *adj* (*not able to be corrupted*) incorruptible; (*morally incorruptible*) íntegro, -a

increase[1] [ˈɪn·kris] *n* (*raised amount*) incremento *m;* (*willful*) subida *f* **2. to be on the ~** ir en aumento

increase[2] [ɪn·ˈkris] **I.** *vi* (*become more*) incrementarse; (*grow*) crecer; **to ~ ten-fold/threefold** multiplicarse por diez/tres **II.** *vt* (*make more*) incrementar; (*make larger*) aumentar

increasing *adj* creciente

increasingly *adv* cada vez más

incredible [ɪn·ˈkred·ə·bəl] *adj* increíble

incriminate [ɪn·ˈkrɪm·ɪ·neɪt] *vt* incriminar; **to ~ oneself** autoinculparse

incubation period *n* período *m* de incubación

incur [ɪn·ˈkɜr] <-rr-> *vt* FIN, ECON (*debt*) contraer; (*costs*) incurrir en; (*losses*) sufrir

incurable [ɪn·ˈkjʊr·ə·bəl] *adj* incurable; *fig* incorregible; **he is an ~ romantic** es un romántico empedernido

indebted [ɪn·ˈdet̬·ɪd] *adj* **1.** (*obliged*) en deuda; **to be ~ to sb** (**for sth**) estar en deuda con alguien (por algo) **2.** (*having debt*) endeudado, -a

indecent [ɪn·ˈdi·sənt] *adj* indecente, indecoroso, -a

indecipherable [ˌɪn·dɪ·ˈsaɪ·frə·bəl] *adj* indescifrable

indecision [ˌɪn·dɪ·ˈsɪʒ·ən] *n* indecisión *f,* irresolución *f elev*

indecisive [ˌɪn·dɪ·ˈsaɪ·sɪv] *adj* (*unable to make decisions*) indeciso, -a

indeclinable [ɪn·dɪ·ˈklaɪ·nə·bəl] *adj* LING indeclinable

indeed [ɪn·ˈdid] **I.** *adv* **1.** (*really*) realmente; **this is good news ~!** ¡eso sí que es una buena noticia! **2.** (*expresses affirmation*) en efecto **II.** *interj* ya lo creo; **he's a lovely boy! — ~!** es un chico encantador — ¡ya lo creo!

indefensible [ˌɪn·dɪ·ˈfen·sə·bəl] *adj* insostenible; MIL indefendible

indefinable [ˌɪn·dɪ·ˈfaɪ·nə·bəl] *adj* indefinible

indefinite [ɪn·ˈdef·ə·nɪt] *adj* indefinido, -a; **for an ~ period** por un tiempo indeterminado

indelible [ɪn·ˈdel·ə·bəl] *adj* imborrable; (*colors, stains, ink*) indeleble

indemnify [ɪn·ˈdem·nɪ·faɪ] <-ie-> *vt* **1.** (*insure against damage*) asegurar **2.** (*compensate for damage*) indemnizar

indemnity [ɪn·ˈdem·nə·t̬i] <-ies> *n* form

1. (*insurance for damage*) indemnidad *f*
2. (*compensation*) indemnización *f*

ndependence [ˌɪn·dɪ·ˈpen·dəns] *n* independencia *f*

ndependence Day *n* día *m* de la Independencia

independent [ˌɪn·dɪ·ˈpen·dənt] **I.** *adj* independiente **II.** *n* POL diputado, -a *m, f* independiente

in-depth [ˈɪn·depθ] *adj* exhaustivo, -a, a fondo

indescribable [ˌɪn·dɪ·ˈskraɪ·bə·bəl] *adj* indescriptible

indestructible [ˌɪn·dɪ·ˈstrʌk·tə·bəl] *adj* indestructible

index [ˈɪn·deks] **I.** *n* **1.** <-es> (*alphabetical list*) índice *m* **2.** <-ices *or* -es> ECON índice *m*; **consumer price ~** índice de precios al consumo **3.** <-ices *or* -es> (*indication*) indicador *m* **4.** <-ices> MATH exponente *m* **II.** *vt* **1.** (*provide with a list*) poner índice a **2.** (*enter in a list*) indexar **3.** ECON **to ~ wages to inflation** equilibrar los sueldos a la inflación

index card *n* ficha *f*

indexer [ˈɪn·dek·sər] *n* clasificador *m*

index finger *n* dedo *m* índice

Indian [ˈɪn·di·ən] **I.** *adj* **1.** (*of India*) indio, -a, hindú **2.** (*of America*) indio, -a, indígena **II.** *n* **1.** (*of India*) indio, -a *m, f,* hindú *mf* **2.** (*of America*) indio, -a *m, f,* indígena *mf*

indicate [ˈɪn·dɪ·keɪt] *vt* indicar; **to ~ (to sb) that...** señalar (a alguien) que...

indication [ˌɪn·dɪ·ˈkeɪ·ʃən] *n* **1.** (*evidence*) indicio *m*; **an ~ of willingness** una muestra de voluntad **2.** *a.* MED indicación *f*

indicative [ɪn·ˈdɪk·ə·tɪv] **I.** *adj* indicativo, -a **II.** *n* indicativo *m*

indicator [ˈɪn·dɪ·keɪ·tər] *n* indicador *m*

indices [ˈɪn·dɪ·siz] *n pl of* **index**

indict [ɪn·ˈdaɪt] *vt* **to ~ sb for sth** LAW acusar a alguien de algo

Indies [ˈɪn·diz] *npl* Indias *fpl*; **the West ~** las Antillas

indifference [ɪn·ˈdɪf·rəns] *n* indiferencia *f*

indifferent [ɪn·ˈdɪf·rənt] *adj* (*not interested*) indiferente, valemadrista *inv Méx*

indigenous [ɪn·ˈdɪdʒ·ə·nəs] *adj* indígena

indigestible [ˌɪn·dɪ·ˈdʒes·tə·bəl] *adj* **1.** (*food*) indigesto, -a **2.** *fig* indigerible

indigestion [ˌɪn·dɪ·ˈdʒes·tʃən] *n* indigestión *f*; **to give oneself ~** empacharse

indignant [ɪn·ˈdɪg·nənt] *adj* indignado, -a; **to become ~** indignarse

indignation [ˌɪn·dɪg·ˈneɪ·ʃən] *n* indignación *f*

indignity [ɪn·ˈdɪg·nə·t̬i] <-ies> *n* (*humiliation*) indignidad *f*

indirect [ˌɪn·dɪ·ˈrekt] *adj* indirecto, -a

indiscreet [ˌɪn·dɪ·ˈskrit] *adj* indiscreto, -a; (*tactless*) falto, -a de tacto

indiscretion [ˌɪn·dɪ·ˈskreʃ·ən] *n* (*lack of discretion*) indiscreción *f*

indiscriminate [ˌɪn·dɪ·ˈskrɪm·ə·nɪt] *adj* (*random*) indiscriminado, -a

indispensable [ˌɪn·dɪ·ˈspen·sə·bəl] *adj* indispensable

indistinct [ˌɪn·dɪ·ˈstɪŋkt] *adj* indistinto, -a

indistinguishable [ˌɪn·dɪ·ˈstɪŋ·gwɪ·ʃə·bəl] *adj* indistinguible; (*not perceptible*) imperceptible

individual [ˌɪn·dɪ·ˈvɪdʒ·u·əl] **I.** *n* individuo, -a *m, f* **II.** *adj* individual; (*particular*) particular; **an ~ style** un estilo propio

individualism [ˌɪn·dɪ·ˈvɪdʒ·u·ə·lɪz·əm] *n* individualismo *m*

individualist *n* individualista *mf*

indivisible [ˌɪn·dɪ·ˈvɪz·ə·bəl] *adj* indivisible

indoor [ˌɪn·ˈdɔr] *adj* interior; (*pool*) cubierto, -a

indoors [ˌɪn·ˈdɔrz] *adv* dentro

induce [ɪn·ˈdus] *vt* **1.** (*persuade*) *a.* ELEC, PHYS inducir **2.** (*cause*) provocar

indulge [ɪn·ˈdʌldʒ] *vt* **1.** (*allow*) consentir **2.** **to ~ oneself in...** darse el lujo de..., permitirse...

indulgent [ɪn·ˈdʌl·dʒənt] *adj* **1.** (*lenient*) indulgente **2.** (*tolerant*) tolerante

industrial [ɪn·ˈdʌs·tri·əl] **I.** *adj* industrial; (*dispute*) laboral; **for ~ use** para uso industrial **II.** *npl* FIN acciones *f pl* industriales

industrialist *n* industrial *mf*

industrialization [ɪn·ˌdʌs·tri·ə·lɪ·ˈzeɪ·ʃən]

n industrialización *f*

industrialize [ɪnˈdʌs·tri·ə·laɪz] **I.** *vi* industrializarse **II.** *vt* industrializar

Industrial Revolution *n* Revolución *f* Industrial

industrious [ɪnˈdʌs·tri·əs] *adj* trabajador(a)

industry [ˈɪn·dəs·tri] *n* **1.** (*manufacturing production*) industria *f* **2.** <-ies> (*branch*) sector *m*

inedible [ɪnˈed·ə·bəl] *adj* (*unsuitable as food*) no comestible

ineffective [ˌɪn·ɪˈfek·tɪv] *adj* ineficaz

ineffectual [ˌɪn·ɪˈfek·tʃu·əl] *adj* ineficaz, inútil

inefficient [ˌɪn·ɪˈfɪʃ·ənt] *adj* ineficiente

ineligible [ɪnˈel·ɪdʒ·ə·bəl] *adj* inelegible; **to be ~ for sth** no reunir los requisitos para algo

inept [ɪnˈept] *adj* (*unskilled*) inepto, -a; **to be ~ at sth** ser inepto para algo

inequality [ˌɪn·ɪˈkwal·ə·ti] <-ies> *n* desigualdad *f*

inequitable [ɪnˈek·wə·tə·bəl] *adj* injusto, -a

inert [ɪnˈɜrt] *adj* **1.** (*not moving*) inerte; *fig* inmóvil **2.** PHYS inactivo, -a

inescapable [ˌɪn·ɪˈskeɪ·pə·bəl] *adj* ineludible

inevitable [ɪnˈev·ɪ·tə·bəl] **I.** *adj* inevitable; (*conclusion, consequence*) inexorable **II.** *n* **the ~** lo inevitable

inexact [ˌɪn·ɪgˈzækt] *adj* inexacto, -a

inexcusable [ˌɪn·ɪkˈskju·zə·bəl] *adj* imperdonable

inexhaustible [ˌɪn·ɪgˈzɔs·tə·bəl] *adj* inagotable

inexpensive [ˌɪn·ɪkˈspen·sɪv] *adj* económico, -a

inexperienced [ˌɪn·ɪkˈspɪr·i·ənst] *adj* inexperto, -a

inexplicable [ˌɪn·əkˈsplɪk·ə·bəl] **I.** *adj* inexplicable **II.** *n* **the ~** lo inexplicable

infallible [ɪnˈfæl·ə·bəl] *adj* indefectible; (*incapable of being wrong*) infalible

infamous [ˈɪn·fə·məs] *adj* **1.** (*shocking*) infame **2.** (*notorious*) de mala fama

infancy [ˈɪn·fən·si] *n* infancia *f*; **from ~** desde niño

infant [ˈɪn·fənt] *n* (*very young child*) bebé *m*; **a newborn ~** un recién nacido

infantile [ˈɪn·fən·taɪl] *adj* infantil

infant mortality *n* mortalidad *f* infantil

infantry [ˈɪn·fən·tri] *n* + *sing/pl vb* MIL infantería *f*

infatuated [ɪnˈfætʃ·u·eɪ·ʧɪd] *adj* encaprichado, -a; **to become ~ with sb/sth** encapricharse con alguien/algo

infect [ɪnˈfekt] *vt* infectar; *a. fig* (*person*) contagiar

infection [ɪnˈfek·ʃən] *n* infección *f*; **risk of ~** riesgo *m* de contagio

infectious [ɪnˈfek·ʃəs] *adj* infeccioso, -a; *a. fig* contagioso, -a

infer [ɪnˈfɜr] <-rr-> *vt* inferir

inference [ˈɪn·fər·əns] *n form* **1.** (*conclusion*) conclusión *f* **2.** (*process of inferring*) inferencia *f*

inferior [ɪnˈfɪr·i·ər] **I.** *adj* inferior **II.** *n* inferior *mf*

inferiority [ɪnˌfɪr·i·ˈɔr·ə·ʧi] *n* inferioridad *f*

inferiority complex <-es> *n* complejo *m* de inferioridad

infernal [ɪnˈfɜr·nəl] *adj* infernal

inferno [ɪnˈfɜr·noʊ] *n* infierno *m*

infertile [ɪnˈfɜr·təl] *adj* estéril

infertility [ˌɪn·fərˈtɪl·ə·ʧi] *n* esterilidad *f*

infest [ɪnˈfest] *vt* infestar

infestation [ˌɪn·fesˈteɪ·ʃən] *n* plaga *f*, infestación *f*

infidelity [ˌɪn·fə·ˈdel·ə·ʧi] *n* infidelidad *f*

infighting [ˈɪn·faɪ·tɪŋ] *n* lucha *f* interna

infiltrate [ɪnˈfɪl·treɪt] *vt* infiltrarse en

infinite [ˈɪn·fə·nɪt] *adj* infinito, -a

infinitesimal [ˌɪn·fɪn·ɪ·ˈtes·ɪ·məl] *adj form* infinitesimal

infinitive [ɪnˈfɪn·ə·tɪv] LING **I.** *n* infinitivo *m* **II.** *adj* infinitivo, -a

infinity [ɪnˈfɪn·ə·ʧi] <-ies> *n* **1.** MATH infinito *m* **2.** (*huge amount*) infinidad *f*

infirm [ɪnˈfɜrm] *adj* enfermizo, -a; (*weak*) débil

infirmary [ɪnˈfɜr·mə·ri] <-ies> *n* **1.** (*hospital*) hospital *m* **2.** (*room*) enfermería *f*

inflame [ɪnˈfleɪm] *vt* **1.** *a.* MED inflamar **2.** (*stir up*) encender

inflammable [ɪnˈflæm·ə·bəl] *adj* inflamable

inflammation [ˌɪn·flə·ˈmeɪ·ʃən] *n* MED inflamación *f*

inflammatory [ɪn·ˈflæm·ə·tɔr·i] *adj*
1. MED inflamatorio, -a 2. (*speech*) incendiario, -a

inflatable [ɪn·ˈfleɪ·tə·bəl] *adj* hinchable

inflate [ɪn·ˈfleɪt] I. *vt* 1. (*fill with air*) hinchar, inflar 2. ECON (*prices*) disparar II. *vi* hincharse

inflated [ɪn·ˈfleɪ·tɪd] *adj* 1. (*filled with air*) hinchado, -a 2. (*exaggerated*) exagerado, -a 3. ECON (*price*) excesivo, -a

inflation [ɪn·ˈfleɪ·ʃən] *n* inflación *f*

inflationary *adj* FIN inflacionario, -a

inflexible [ɪn·ˈflek·sə·bəl] *adj* inflexible

inflict [ɪn·ˈflɪkt] *vt* infligir

influence [ˈɪn·flu·əns] I. *n* influencia *f*; **to drive under the ~** *fig* conducir bajo los efectos del alcohol II. *vt* influir

influential [ˌɪn·flu·ˈen·ʃəl] *adj* influyente

influenza [ˌɪn·flu·ˈen·zə] *n* gripe *f*

influx [ˈɪn·flʌks] *n* influjo *m*

inform [ɪn·ˈfɔrm] I. *vt* informar; **to be ~ed about sth** estar enterado de algo II. *vi* **to ~ against sb** delatar a alguien

informal [ɪn·ˈfɔr·məl] *adj* informal; (*tone, manner*) familiar; (*person*) afable

informant [ɪn·ˈfɔr·mənt] *n* informante *mf*

information [ˌɪn·fər·ˈmeɪ·ʃən] *n* 1. (*data*) información *f*; **a lot of/a little ~** mucha/poca información; **to ask for ~** pedir información; **for further ~** para más información 2. COMPUT datos *mpl* 3. (*knowledge*) conocimientos *mpl* 4. LAW denuncia *f*

information science *n* ciencias *f pl* de la información

information superhighway *n* autopista *f* de la información

information technology *n* tecnologías *f pl* de la información

informative [ɪn·ˈfɔr·mə·tɪv] *adj* informativo, -a

informer [ɪn·ˈfɔr·mər] *n* informante *mf*, informador(a) *m(f)*

infrared [ˈɪn·frə·ˈred] *adj* infrarrojo, -a

infrequent [ɪn·ˈfri·kwənt] *adj* poco frecuente

infringe [ɪn·ˈfrɪndʒ] I. *vt* LAW infringir II. *vi* **to ~ on** [*or* **upon**] **sth** usurpar

infuriate [ɪn·ˈfjʊr·i·eɪt] *vt* enfurecer

infusion [ɪn·ˈfju·ʒən] *n a.* MED infusión *f*;

ECON inyección *f*

ingenious [ɪn·ˈdʒin·jəs] *adj* (*creatively inventive*) inventivo, -a; (*idea, method, plan*) ingenioso, -a

ingenuity [ˌɪn·dʒɪ·ˈnu·ə·ti] *n* ingenuidad *f*; **to use one's ~** utilizar el ingenio

ingoing [ˈɪn·goʊ·ɪŋ] *adj* entrante

ingrained [ɪn·ˈgreɪnd] *adj* 1. (*embedded: dirt*) incrustado, -a 2. (*deep-seated*) arraigado, -a

ingratitude [ɪn·ˈgræt·ə·tud] *n* ingratitud *f*

ingredient [ɪn·ˈgri·di·ənt] *n* 1. CULIN ingrediente *m* 2. (*component*) *a.* MED componente *m*

ingrowing [ˈɪn·groʊ·ɪŋ] *adj* que crece hacia dentro (de la piel); **~ toenail** uñero *m*

ingrown [ˈɪn·groʊn] *adj* que crece hacia dentro (de la piel); **~ toenail** uñero *m*

inhabit [ɪn·ˈhæb·ɪt] *vt* habitar

inhabitable *adj* habitable

inhabitant [ɪn·ˈhæb·ɪ·tənt] *n* habitante *mf*

inhale [ɪn·ˈheɪl] I. *vt* aspirar; MED inhalar II. *vi* inhalar

inhaler [ɪn·ˈheɪ·lər] *n* inhalador *m*

inherit [ɪn·ˈher·ɪt] I. *vt* heredar II. *vi* recibir una herencia

inheritance [ɪn·ˈher·ɪ·təns] *n* herencia *f*; *fig* legado *m*

inhibit [ɪn·ˈhɪb·ɪt] *vt* (*hinder*) impedir; (*impair*) inhibir

inhibition [ˌɪn·ɪ·ˈbɪʃ·ən] *n* inhibición *f*

inhospitable [ˌɪn·has·pɪ·tə·bəl] *adj* inhospitalario, -a; (*place*) inhóspito, -a

in-house [ˈɪn·haʊs] COM I. *adj* interno, -a II. *adv* dentro de la empresa

inhuman [ɪn·ˈhju·mən] *adj* (*not human*) inhumano, -a

inhumane [ˌɪn·hju·ˈmeɪn] *adj* (*cruel*) inhumano, -a, cruel

initial [ɪ·ˈnɪʃ·əl] I. *n* inicial *f*; **one's ~s** las iniciales de uno II. *adj* inicial; (*first*) primero, -a; **in the ~ phases** en las primeras etapas III. <-ll-, -l-> *vt* marcar con las iniciales

initially [ɪ·ˈnɪʃ·ə·li] *adv* en un principio

initiate [ɪ·ˈnɪʃ·i·eɪt] *vt* 1. (*start*) iniciar, dar comienzo a 2. (*admit to group*) admitir (como miembro)

initiation [ɪˌnɪʃ·ɪ·'eɪ·ʃən] n 1. (*starting*) inicio m 2. (*introducing*) iniciación f; (*as a member*) admisión f

initiative [ɪ·'nɪʃ·ə·tɪv] n iniciativa f; to **show** ~ demostrar iniciativa

inject [ɪn·'dʒekt] vt 1. a. MED inyectar 2. (*introduce*) introducir; (*funds, money*) inyectar

injection [ɪn·'dʒek·ʃən] n inyección f

injunction [ɪn·'dʒʌŋk·ʃən] n mandato m; LAW mandato m judicial

injure ['ɪn·dʒər] vt 1. (*wound*) herir, victimar AmL 2. (*do wrong to*) perjudicar

injured adj 1. (*wounded*) herido, -a, lastimado, -a AmL 2. (*damaged*) dañado, -a 3. (*wronged*) perjudicado, -a

injury ['ɪn·dʒə·ri] <-ies> n (*physical*) lesión f, herida f

injustice [ɪn·'dʒʌs·tɪs] n injusticia f

ink [ɪŋk] n tinta f

inkling ['ɪŋk·lɪŋ] n (*suspicion*) sospecha f

inland ['ɪn·lənd] I. adj (*not coastal: sea, shipping*) interior; (*town, village*) del interior m II. adv (*direction*) tierra adentro

in-laws ['ɪn·lɔz] npl suegros mpl

inlet ['ɪn·let] n 1. GEO ensenada f; (*of sea*) cala f 2. TECH entrada f

inmate ['ɪn·meɪt] n (*prison*) preso, -a m, f

inn [ɪn] n posada f

inner ['ɪn·ər] adj 1. (*located in the interior*) interno, -a, interior 2. (*deep*) íntimo, -a

innermost ['ɪn·ər·moʊst] adj más íntimo, -a

inner tube n cámara f de aire

inning ['ɪn·ɪŋ] n SPORTS (*part of baseball game*) inning m

innocence ['ɪn·ə·səns] n inocencia f; in all ~ inocentemente

innocent ['ɪn·ə·sənt] adj, n inocente mf; to **be** ~ **of sth** ser inocente de algo; an ~ **bystander** un testigo casual

innovate ['ɪn·ə·veɪt] vi innovar

innovation [ˌɪn·ə·'veɪ·ʃən] n novedad f, innovación f

innovative ['ɪn·ə·veɪ·tɪv] adj (*model, product*) novedoso, -a; (*person*) innovador(a)

innuendo [ˌɪn·ju·'en·doʊ] <-(e)s> n 1. (*insinuation*) insinuación f; to **make an** ~ (**about sth**) hacer una insinuación (sobre algo) 2. (*suggestive remark*) indirecta f

innumerate [ɪ·'nu·mər·ət] adj to **be** ~ ser incapaz de realizar cálculos

inoculate [ɪ·'nak·jə·leɪt] vt to ~ **sb** (**against sth**) inocular a alguien (contra algo)

inoculation [ɪ·ˌnak·jə·'leɪ·ʃən] n inoculación f

inoffensive [ˌɪn·ə·'fen·sɪv] adj inofensivo, -a

inoperable [ˌɪn·'ap·ər·ə·bəl] adj inoperable

inoperative [ˌɪn·'ap·ər·ə·tɪv] adj inoperante

inordinate [ɪn·'ɔr·dɪn·ɪt] adj desmesurado, -a; an ~ **amount of sth** una cantidad excesiva de algo

input ['ɪn·pʊt] I. n (*contribution*) contribución f, aportación f; COMPUT entrada f II. <-tt-> vt COMPUT introducir

inquest ['ɪn·kwest] n LAW pesquisa f judicial; to **hold an** ~ (**into sth**) llevar a cabo una investigación (sobre algo)

inquire [ɪn·'kwaɪr] I. vi 1. (*ask*) preguntar; to ~ **about sb** preguntar por alguien; to ~ **about sth** pedir información sobre algo 2. (*investigate*) investigar II. vt preguntar

inquiry [ɪn·'kwaɪ·ri] n 1. (*question*) pregunta f 2. (*investigation*) investigación f

inquisitive [ɪn·'kwɪz·ɪ·tɪv] adj (*curious*) curioso, -a; (*look, expression*) interrogante; (*child*) preguntón, -ona

ins and outs npl pormenores mpl

insane [ɪn·'seɪn] adj demente; a. fig (*crazy*) loco, -a

insanitary [ɪn·'sæn·ɪ·ter·i] adj antihigiénico, -a

insanity [ɪn·'sæn·ə·ti] n 1. (*mental illness*) demencia f 2. a. fig (*craziness*) locura f

inscription [ɪn·'skrɪp·ʃən] n inscripción f; (*dedication*) dedicatoria f

insect ['ɪn·sekt] n insecto m; ~ **bite** picadura f de insecto

insecticide [ɪn·'sek·tɪ·saɪd] n insecticida m

insecure [ˌɪn·sɪ·ˈkjʊr] *adj* inseguro, -a

insensitive [ɪn·ˈsen·sɪ·tɪv] *adj* insensible

inseparable [ɪn·ˈsep·rə·bəl] *adj* inseparable, indisoluble

insert[1] [ˈɪn·sɜrt] *n* (*page*) encarte *m*

insert[2] [ɪn·ˈsɜrt] *vt* 1. (*put into*) insertar; (*coins*) introducir 2. (*add within a text*) intercalar

in-service [ˈɪn·sɜr·vɪs] *adj* en funcionamiento

inside [ɪn·ˈsaɪd] **I.** *adj* 1. (*internal*) interno, -a; **the ~ door** la puerta interior 2. (*from within: information*) confidencial **II.** *n* 1. (*internal part or side*) interior *m;* **on the ~** por dentro; **to turn sth ~ out** volver algo del revés; **to turn the whole room ~ out** *fig* revolver toda la habitación; **to know a place ~ out** conocer muy bien un lugar 2. **~s** *inf* (*entrails*) tripas *fpl* **III.** *prep* (*within*) **(of)** dentro de; **to go ~ the house** entrar en casa **IV.** *adv* 1. (*within something*) dentro; **to go ~** entrar 2. (*internally*) interiormente

insider [ˈɪn·saɪ·dər] *n* persona *f* de la casa; (*with special knowledge*) persona *f* enterada

insight [ˈɪn·saɪt] *n* 1. (*capacity*) perspicacia *f* 2. (*instance*) nueva percepción *f;* **to gain ~ into sth/sb** entender mejor algo/a alguien

insignificant [ˌɪn·sɪɡ·ˈnɪf·ɪ·kənt] *adj* insignificante; (*trivial*) trivial

insincere [ˌɪn·sɪn·ˈsɪr] *adj* poco sincero, -a

insist [ɪn·ˈsɪst] **I.** *vi* insistir; **to ~ on doing sth** obstinarse en hacer algo; **if you ~** si insistes **II.** *vt* 1. (*state*) insistir 2. (*demand*) exigir

insistence [ɪn·ˈsɪs·təns] *n* insistencia *f;* **to do sth at sb's ~** hacer algo por insistencia de alguien

insistent [ɪn·ˈsɪs·tənt] *adj* insistente; **to be ~ (that)...** insistir en (que)...

insofar as [ˌɪn·soʊ·ˈfar·əz] *adv form* en tanto que +*subj*

insole [ˈɪn·soʊl] *n* plantilla *f*

insolent [ˈɪn·sə·lənt] *adj* insolente

insoluble [ɪn·ˈsal·jə·bəl] *adj* insoluble

insomnia [ɪn·ˈsam·ni·ə] *n* insomnio *m*

insomniac [ɪn·ˈsam·ni·æk] *n* insomne *mf*

inspect [ɪn·ˈspekt] *vt* 1. (*examine carefully*) inspeccionar, examinar 2. MIL **to ~ the troops** pasar revista

inspection [ɪn·ˈspek·ʃən] *n* inspección *f;* MIL revista *f*

inspector [ɪn·ˈspek·tər] *n* inspector(a) *m(f)*

inspiration [ˌɪn·spə·ˈreɪ·ʃən] *n* a. MED inspiración *f*

inspire [ɪn·ˈspaɪr] *vt* (*stimulate*) inspirar

instability [ˌɪn·stə·ˈbɪl·ə·ti] *n* inestabilidad *f*

instal <-ll->, **install** [ɪn·ˈstɔl] **I.** *vt* 1. a. TECH, COMPUT instalar 2. (*place*) colocar; **to ~ sb** colocar a alguien (en un cargo) **II.** *vr* **to ~ oneself** instalarse

installation [ˌɪn·stə·ˈleɪ·ʃən] *n* instalación *f*

installment *n*, **instalment** [ɪn·ˈstɔl·mənt] *n* 1. RADIO, TV entrega *f* 2. COM plazo *m;* **to pay (for sth) in ~s** pagar (algo) a plazos; **to be payable in monthly ~s** ser pagadero a plazos mensuales

installment plan *n* compra *f* a plazos

instance [ˈɪn·stəns] *n* 1. (*case*) caso *m;* **in this ~** en este caso; **for ~** por ejemplo 2. (*order*) pedido *m;* **to do sth at sb's ~** hacer algo a petición de alguien

instant [ˈɪn·stənt] **I.** *n* instante *m,* momento *m;* **for an ~** por un momento; **in an ~** al instante; **to do sth this ~** hacer algo inmediatamente **II.** *adj* 1. (*immediate*) inmediato, -a 2. CULIN instantáneo, -a; **~ coffee** café *m* instantáneo

instantaneous [ˌɪn·stən·ˈteɪ·ni·əs] *adj* instantáneo, -a; (*effect, reaction*) inmediato, -a

instantly [ˈɪn·stənt·li] *adv* al instante

instant replay *n* (*action replay*) repetición *f*

instead [ɪn·ˈsted] **I.** *adv* en cambio, en lugar de eso **II.** *prep* **~ of** en vez de, en lugar de; **~ of him** en su lugar; **~ of doing sth** en lugar de hacer algo

instigate [ˈɪn·stɪ·ɡeɪt] *vt* 1. (*initiate*) instigar 2. (*incite*) incitar

instil [ɪn·ˈstɪl] <-ll-> *vt*, **instill** *vt* **to ~ sth (into sb)** infundir algo (a alguien)

instinct [ˈɪn·stɪŋkt] *n* instinto *m;* **to do sth by ~** hacer algo por instinto

instinctive [ɪn·ˈstɪŋk·tɪv] *adj* instintivo, -a; (*innate*) innato, -a

institute ['ɪn·stɪ·tut] I. n academia f;
(of education) instituto m II. vt form
1. (establish: system, reform) instituir
2. (initiate: steps, measures) iniciar

institution [,ɪn·stɪ·'tu·ʃən] n 1. (act) institución f, establecimiento m 2. (society) asociación f 3. (home) asilo m

instruct [ɪn·'strʌkt] vt 1. (teach) instruir 2. (order) ordenar; (give instructions) dar instrucciones 3. LAW dar instrucciones

instruction [ɪn·'strʌk·ʃən] n 1. (teaching) instrucción f 2. (order) orden f; to give sb ~s dar órdenes a alguien; to carry out ~s cumplir órdenes 3. ~s (information on method) instrucciones fpl

instructive [ɪn·'strʌk·tɪv] adj instructivo, -a

instructor [ɪn·'strʌk·tər] n 1. (teacher) instructor(a) m(f); ski ~ profesor(a) m(f) de esquí 2. UNIV profesor(a) m(f)

instrument ['ɪn·strə·mənt] n 1. MUS, LAW instrumento m 2. (tool) herramienta f

instrumental [,ɪn·strə·'men·təl] adj 1. MUS instrumental 2. (greatly influential) to be ~ in doing sth jugar un papel decisivo en algo

instrument board n, **instrument panel** n AUTO salpicadero m; AVIAT, NAUT cuadro m de mandos

insufficient [,ɪn·sə·'fɪʃ·ənt] adj insuficiente

insular ['ɪn·sə·lər] adj GEO insular

insularity [,ɪn·sə·'ler·ə·ti] n GEO insularidad f

insulate ['ɪn·sə·leɪt] vt aislar; to ~ sth (against sth) aislar algo (de algo)

insulating ['ɪn·sə·leɪ·tɪŋ] adj aislante

insulation [,ɪn·sə·'leɪ·ʃən] n aislamiento m

insult I. [ɪn·'sʌlt] vt insultar II. ['ɪn·sʌlt] n insulto m, insultada f AmL ▶ to add ~ to injury... y por si fuera poco...

insurance [ɪn·'ʃʊr·əns] n 1. (financial protection) seguro m; life ~ seguro de vida; to have ~ (against sth) tener un seguro (contra algo); to take out ~ (against sth) hacerse un seguro (contra algo) 2. (measure) medida f preventiva

insurance policy <-ies> n póliza f de seguros

insure [ɪn·'ʃʊr] vt asegurar

insured [ɪn·'ʃʊrd] I. adj asegurado, -a II. n the ~ el asegurado

insurer [ɪn·'ʃʊr·ər] n (company) aseguradora f

intact [ɪn·'tækt] adj intacto, -a

intake ['ɪn·teɪk] n 1. TECH (mechanical aperture) toma f; fuel ~ toma de combustible 2. (of air, water) entrada f 3. (amount taken in) consumo m; the recommended daily ~ of fiber la cantidad diaria recomendada de fibra

integer ['ɪn·tɪ·dʒər] n MATH número m entero

integral ['ɪn·tə·grəl] adj 1. (central, essential) esencial 2. (part of the whole) integrante 3. (complete) integral

integrated ['ɪn·tɪ·greɪ·tɪd] adj (coordinating different elements) integrado, -a

integrity [ɪn·'teg·rə·ti] n (incorruptibility, uprightness) integridad f; a man of ~ un hombre íntegro

intellect ['ɪn·təl·ekt] n 1. (faculty) intelecto m 2. (thinker, intellectual) intelectual mf

intellectual [,ɪn·tə·'lek·tʃʊ·əl] I. n intelectual mf II. adj intelectual

intelligence [ɪn·'tel·ə·dʒəns] n inteligencia f; artificial ~ inteligencia artificial

intelligence test n test m de inteligencia

intelligent [ɪn·'tel·ə·dʒənt] adj inteligente

intend [ɪn·'tend] vt 1. (aim for, plan) pretender; I ~ed no harm no quería hacer daño 2. (earmark, destine) to be ~ed for sth estar destinado a algo

intended [ɪn·'ten·dɪd] I. adj (planned, intentional) intencional; (sought) deseado, -a II. n inf prometido -a m, f

intense [ɪn·'tens] adj 1. (acute, concentrated, forceful) intenso, -a; (feeling, hatred, friendship) profundo, -a; (love) apasionado, -a; (pain, pressure, wind) fuerte 2. (demanding) agotador(a)

intensify [ɪn·'ten·sɪ·faɪ] <-ie-> I. vt intensificar; (joy, sadness) aumentar; (pain) agudizar II. vi intensificarse; (joy, sadness) aumentar; (pain) agudizarse

intensity [ɪn·'ten·sə·ti] n intensidad f

intensive [ɪn·'ten·sɪv] *adj* intensivo, -a
intensive care *n* cuidados *m pl* intensivos
intent [ɪn·'tent] I. *n* propósito *m;* **to all ~s and purposes** a efectos prácticos; **with ~ to** con el objeto de; **with good/evil ~** con buenas/malas intenciones II. *adj* 1. (*absorbed, concentrated, occupied*) abstraído, -a; (*look*) atento, -a; **to be ~ on sth** estar concentrado en algo 2. (*decided, set*) decidido, -a; **to be/seem ~ on doing sth** estar/parecer resuelto a hacer algo
intention [ɪn·'ten·tʃən] *n* intención *f;* **to have no ~ of doing sth** no tener ninguna intención de hacer algo; **with the best of ~s** con la mejor intención
intentional [ɪn·'ten·tʃə·nəl] *adj* intencional; (*insult*) deliberado, -a
interactive [ˌɪn·tər·'æk·tɪv] *adj* interactivo, -a
interactive TV *n* televisión *f* interactiva
intercept [ˌɪn·tər·'sept] *vt* interceptar; MATH cortar; **to ~ sb** cerrar el paso a alguien
interception [ˌɪn·tər·'sep·ʃən] *n* 1. (*act of intercepting*) interceptación *f;* MATH intersección *f* 2. SPORTS (*football play*) intercepción *f*
interchange [ˌɪn·tər·'tʃeɪndʒ] I. *n* 1. intercambio *m* 2. (*of roads*) enlace *m,* periférico *m* Méx II. *vt* (*exchange: ideas, knowledge*) intercambiar; COMPUT (*data*) intercambiar
interchangeable [ˌɪn·tər·'tʃeɪn·dʒə·bəl] *adj* intercambiable
intercom ['ɪn·tər·kam] *n* (*on a plane or ship*) intercomunicador *m;* (*in a building*) portero *m* automático; **to speak over the ~** hablar por el portero automático
intercourse ['ɪn·tər·kɔrs] *n* 1. sexual ~ contacto *m* sexual; **to have sexual ~ with sb** tener relaciones sexuales con alguien 2. *form* **social ~** trato *m* social
interest ['ɪn·trɪst] I. *n* 1. (*hobby*) interés *m;* **to take an ~ in sth** interesarse por algo 2. (*curiosity*) **to lose ~ in sb/sth** perder el interés por alguien/algo 3. ~s (*profit, advantage*) interés *m;* **a conflict of ~s** un conflicto de intereses;

to look after the ~s of sb velar por los intereses de alguien; **to pursue one's own ~s** perseguir los propios intereses; **in the ~ of liberty** en pro de la libertad 4. (*power to excite attentiveness*) interés *m;* **this is of no ~ to me** eso no me interesa 5. FIN interés *m;* ~ **rate** tipo *m* de interés; **at 5%** con un interés del 5%; **to bear ~** devengar interés; **to earn/pay ~ on sth** percibir/pagar intereses por algo; **to pay back with ~** pagar con intereses; *fig* pagar con creces 6. (*legal right*) participación *f;* **to have an ~ in sth** tener una participación en algo II. *vt* interesar; **may I ~ you in this encyclopedia?** ¿puedo mostrarle esta enciclopedia?
interested ['ɪn·trɪ·stɪd] *adj* interesado, -a; **to be ~ in sth/sb** estar interesado en algo/alguien
interest-free *adj* FIN sin intereses
interesting ['ɪn·trɪ·stɪŋ] *adj* interesante
interfere [ˌɪn·tər·'fɪr] *vi* 1. (*become involved*) interferir; **to ~ between two people** entrometerse entre dos personas 2. (*disturb*) molestar 3. RADIO, TECH (*hamper signals*) producir interferencias 4. SPORTS (*get in way*) obstaculizar
interference [ˌɪn·tər·'fɪr·əns] *n* 1. (*hindrance*) intromisión *f* 2. RADIO, TECH, SPORTS interferencia *f*
interim ['ɪn·tər·ɪm] I. *n* ínterin *m* II. *adj* provisional; (*payment*) a cuenta; ~ **dividend** FIN dividendo *m* a cuenta; ~ **coach/manager** entrenador/manager interino
interior [ɪn·'tɪr·i·ər] I. *adj* 1. (*inner, inside, internal*) interno, -a; (*lighting*) interior 2. (*central, inland, remote*) del interior II. *n* 1. (*inside*) interior *m* 2. POL (*home affairs*) **the U.S. Department of the Interior** el departamento del Interior de EE.UU.
interior decoration *n* interiorismo *m*
interior designer *n* interiorista *mf*
intermediate [ˌɪn·tər·'mi·di·ət] I. *adj* intermedio, -a; ~ **course** curso *m* de nivel intermedio II. *n* intermediario, -a *m, f*
intermission [ˌɪn·tər·'mɪʃ·ən] *n* 1. intermedio *m;* **without ~** sin pausa 2. CINE, THEAT descanso *m*

intermittent [ˌɪn·tər·ˈmɪt·ənt] *adj* intermitente

intern[1] [ˈɪn·tɜrn] *n* estudiante *mf* en prácticas; **hospital ~** médico *m* asistente

intern[2] [ɪn·ˈtɜrn] I. *vt* recluir II. *vi* MED trabajar como interno, -a; SCHOOL hacer (las) prácticas

internal [ɪn·ˈtɜr·nəl] *adj* a. MED interno, -a; **for ~ use only** sólo para uso interno

international [ˌɪn·tər·ˈnæʃ·ə·nəl] I. *adj* a. LAW internacional; (*trade*) exterior II. *n* POL Internacional *f*

internationalize [ˌɪn·tər·ˈnæʃ·ə·nə·laɪz] *vt* internacionalizar

Internet [ˈɪn·tər·net] *n* COMPUT internet *m o f*; **to access the ~** entrar en internet; **over the ~** a través de internet

internship *n* prácticas *f pl* como interno, -a *m, f*, pasantía *f* Col

interplay [ˈɪn·tər·pleɪ] *n* interacción *f*

Interpol [ˈɪn·tər·pɑl] *n abbr of* **International Criminal Police Organization** Interpol *f*

interpret [ɪn·ˈtɜr·prɪt] I. *vt* interpretar II. *vi* interpretar; **to ~ from English into Spanish** interpretar del inglés al español

interpreter [ɪn·ˈtɜr·prɪ·tər] *n* intérprete *mf*

interrogate [ɪn·ˈter·ə·geɪt] *vt* interrogar

interrogation [ɪn·ˌter·ə·ˈgeɪ·ʃən] *n* 1. a. COMPUT interrogación *f* 2. LAW interrogatorio *m*; **police ~** interrogatorio policial

interrogative [ˌɪn·tə·ˈrɑg·ə·tɪv] I. *n* LING (*word*) palabra *f* interrogativa II. *adj* LING interrogativo, -a

interrupt [ˌɪn·tə·ˈrʌpt] *vi, vt* interrumpir

interruption [ˌɪn·tə·ˈrʌp·ʃən] *n* interrupción *f*

intersection [ˌɪn·tər·ˈsek·ʃən] *n* 1. (*crossing of lines*) intersección *f* 2. AUTO cruce *m*

interval [ˈɪn·tər·vəl] *n* a. MUS intervalo *m*; **at ~s of five minutes** a intervalos de cinco minutos; **at regular ~s** a intervalos regulares

intervene [ˌɪn·tər·ˈvin] *vi* 1. (*involve oneself to help*) intervenir; **to ~ militarily/personally** intervenir militarmente/personalmente; **to ~ on sb's behalf** interceder por alguien 2. (*meddle unhelpfully*) **to ~ in sth** mezclarse en algo

3. (*elapse*) sobrevenir

intervening *adj* **in the ~ period** en el ínterin

intervention [ˌɪn·tər·ˈven·ʃən] *n* intervención *f*; **military ~** MIL intervención militar

interview [ˈɪn·tər·vju] I. *n* (*formal conversation*) entrevista *f*; **telephone ~** encuesta *f* telefónica; **to have a job ~** tener una entrevista de trabajo; **to give an ~** conceder una entrevista II. *vt* entrevistar; **to ~ sb about sth** encuestar a alguien sobre algo

interviewee [ˌɪn·tər·vju·ˈi] *n* entrevistado, -a *m, f*

interviewer [ˈɪn·tər·vju·ər] *n* entrevistador(a) *m(f)*

intestine [ɪn·ˈtes·tɪn] *n* intestino *m*

intimacy [ˈɪn·tə·mə·si] <-ies> *n* 1. (*familiarity*) intimidad *f* 2. (*sexual relations*) relaciones *f pl* íntimas

intimate[1] [ˈɪn·tə·mət] *adj* 1. (*close, sexual*) íntimo, -a; **~ relationship** relaciones *f pl* íntimas; **to be on ~ terms with sb** tener confianza con alguien 2. (*personal: letter*) personal 3. (*link*) estrecho, -a

intimate[2] [ˈɪn·tə·meɪt] *vt form* insinuar

intimidate [ɪn·ˈtɪm·ɪ·deɪt] *vt* intimidar; **to ~ sb into doing sth** coaccionar a alguien para que haga algo

intimidating *adj* intimidante

intimidation [ɪn·ˌtɪm·ɪ·ˈdeɪ·ʃən] *n* intimidación *f*

into [ˈɪn·tə] *prep* 1. (*to the inside of*) en; (*towards*) hacia; **to walk ~ a place** entrar en un sitio; **to get ~ bed** meterse en la cama; **~ the future** hacia el futuro 2. (*indicating an extent in time or space*) **deep ~ the forest** en lo más profundo del bosque 3. (*against*) contra; **to drive ~ a tree** chocar contra un árbol; **to bump ~ a friend** tropezar con un amigo 4. (*to the state or condition of*) **to burst ~ tears** echarse a llorar; **to grow ~ a woman** hacerse una mujer; **to translate from Spanish ~ English** traducir del español al inglés; **to turn sth ~ sth** convertir algo en algo 5. *inf* (*interested in*) **she's really ~ her new job** está entusiasmada con su nuevo trabajo; **I think they are ~ drugs** creo que andan metidos en drogas **6.** MATH **two goes ~ five two and a half times** cinco dividido entre dos es igual a dos y medio

intolerable [ɪn·'tal·ər·ə·bəl] *adj* intolerable

intolerant [ɪn·'tal·ər·ənt] *adj* intolerante; **to be ~ of different opinions** ser intolerante con las opiniones diferentes; **to be ~ of alcohol** MED no tolerar el alcohol

intoxicate [ɪn·'tak·sɪ·keɪt] **I.** *vt* **1.** *a. fig* (*induce inebriation*) embriagar **2.** MED intoxicar **II.** *vi* **1.** *a. fig* (*cause intoxication*) embriagar **2.** MED intoxicar

intoxicating [ɪn·'tak·sɪ·keɪ·t̬ɪŋ] *adj* **1.** (*exhilarating, stimulating*) embriagador(a) **2.** (*substance*) estupefaciente; (*causing drunkenness*) alcohólico, -a

intoxication [ɪn·ˌtak·sɪ·'keɪ·ʃən] *n* **1.** *a. fig* (*drunkenness*) embriaguez **2.** MED intoxicación *f*

intransitive [ɪn·'træn·sɪ·t̬ɪv] *adj* LING, MATH intransitivo, -a

intravenous [ˌɪn·trə·'vi·nəs] *adj* MED intravenoso, -a; **~ feeding** alimentación *f* por vía intravenosa

intricate ['ɪn·trɪ·kət] *adj* **1.** (*detailed*) intrincado, -a **2.** (*complicated: mechanism*) complejo, -a

intrigue **I.** [ɪn·'trig] *vt* intrigar; **to be ~d by sth** estar intrigado con algo **II.** *vi* (*plot*) intrigar **III.** ['ɪn·trig] *n* intriga *f*

intriguing [ɪn·'tri·gɪn] *adj* **1.** (*mysterious*) intrigante **2.** (*fascinating*) fascinante; (*smile*) enigmático, -a

introduce [ˌɪn·trə·'dus] *vt* **1.** (*acquaint*) presentar; **allow me to ~ myself** permítame que me presente **2.** (*raise interest in subject*) **to ~ sb to sth** iniciar a alguien en algo **3.** (*insert*) introducir; **to ~ sth into sth** introducir algo en algo

introduction [ˌɪn·trə·'dʌk·ʃən] *n* **1.** (*making first acquaintance*) presentación *f*; **letter of ~** carta *f* de presentación; **to do the ~s** hacer las presentaciones **2.** (*first contact with sth*) iniciación *f* **3.** (*establishment*) introducción *f*; (*of a bill*) presentación *f* **4.** (*insertion*) introducción *f* **5.** (*preface*) prólogo *m*; MUS

introducción *f*

introductory [ˌɪn·trə·'dʌk·tə·ri] *adj* **1.** (*elementary, preparatory*) de introducción; (*course*) de iniciación **2.** COM (*price*) de lanzamiento **3.** (*beginning*) introductorio, -a; **~ remarks** aclaraciones *f pl* preliminares

intrude [ɪn·'trud] **I.** *vi* **1.** (*meddle*) entrometerse; **to ~ into sth** inmiscuirse en algo **2.** (*disturb*) estorbar; **am I intruding?** ¿molesto? **II.** *vt* **to ~ sth on sb** importunar a alguien con algo

intruder [ɪn·'tru·dər] *n* intruso, -a *m, f*

intrusion [ɪn·'tru·ʒən] *n* **1.** (*encroachment, infringement*) intrusión *f* **2.** (*meddling*) intromisión *f*

intrusive [ɪn·'tru·sɪv] *adj* (*noise*) molesto, -a; (*question*) indiscreto, -a; (*person*) entrometido, -a

intuition [ɪn·tu·'ɪʃ·ən] *n* intuición *f*

intuitive [ɪn·'tu·ɪ·t̬ɪv] *adj* intuitivo, -a; **an ~ feeling** una intuición

invade [ɪn·'veɪd] **I.** *vt* invadir; **to ~ sb's privacy** invadir la intimidad de alguien **II.** *vi* invadir

invader [ɪn·'veɪ·dər] *n* invasor(a) *m(f)*

invalid¹ ['ɪn·və·lɪd] **I.** *n* (*incapacitated person*) inválido, -a *m, f* **II.** *adj* (*disabled*) inválido, -a *f*

invalid² [ɪn·'væl·ɪd] *adj* **1.** LAW (*not legally binding*) nulo, -a; **to become ~** caducar **2.** (*unsound*) no válido, -a

invalidate [ɪn·'væl·ɪdeɪt] *vt* **1.** (*argument, decision*) invalidar; (*results*) anular **2.** LAW anular; **to ~ a judgment** revocar una sentencia

invalidity [ˌɪn·və·'lɪd·ə·ti] *n* **1.** (*inadmissibility: of a contract*) nulidad *f*; (*of evidence*) invalidez *f* **2.** (*faultiness: of a theory*) invalidez

invaluable [ɪn·'væl·ju·ə·bəl] *adj* inestimable; **to be ~ to sb** tener un valor inestimable para alguien

invariable [ɪn·'ver·i·ə·bəl] *adj form* (*custom*) invariable

invasion [ɪn·'veɪ·ʒən] *n* **1.** MIL invasión *f* **2.** (*interference*) violación *f*; **~ of privacy/of a right** violación de la intimidad/ de un derecho

invent [ɪn·'vent] *vt* inventar

invention [ɪn·'ven·ʃən] *n* **1.** (*gadget*)

invento m **2.** (*creativity*) inventiva f **3.** (*falsehood*) invención f

inventive [ɪn·ˈven·tɪv] adj inventivo, -a

inventor [ɪn·ˈven·tər] n inventor(a) m(f)

inventory [ˈɪn·vən·tɔr·i] <-ies> I. n **1.** (*catalog*) inventario m; **to draw up an ~** levantar un inventario **2.** (*stock*) stock m II. vt inventariar III. adj (*audit, level, number*) de inventario

inverse [ɪn·ˈvɜrs] I. adj inverso, -a II. n **the ~ of sth** lo contrario de algo

invert [ɪn·ˈvɜrt] vt invertir

invest [ɪn·ˈvest] I. vt **1.** (*put in*) invertir **2.** (*bestow attributes*) investir II. vi invertir; **to ~ in sth** invertir en algo

investigate [ɪn·ˈves·tɪ·geɪt] vt investigar

investigation [ɪn·ˌves·tɪ·ˈgeɪ·ʃən] n investigación f

investigator [ɪn·ˈves·tɪ·geɪ·tər] n investigador(a) m(f)

investment [ɪn·ˈvest·mənt] I. n a. fig inversión f; **long-term ~s** inversiones f pl a largo plazo II. adj de inversión

investor [ɪn·ˈves·tər] n inversor(a) m(f)

invigorating [ɪn·ˈvɪg·ə·reɪ·tɪŋ] adj vigorizante

invincible [ɪn·ˈvɪn·sə·bəl] adj invencible

invisible [ɪn·ˈvɪz·ə·bəl] adj invisible

invitation [ˌɪn·vɪ·ˈteɪ·ʃən] n invitación f; **an ~ to sth** una invitación a algo

invite¹ [ˈɪn·vaɪt] n inf invitación f

invite² [ɪn·ˈvaɪt] vt **1.** (*request to attend*) invitar; **to ~ sb for/to sth** invitar a alguien a algo **2.** (*request*) pedir; **to ~ offers** solicitar ofertas **3.** (*provoke*) buscarse; **to ~ trouble** buscar(se) problemas

inviting [ɪn·ˈvaɪ·tɪŋ] adj (*attractive*) atractivo, -a, atrayente

invoice [ˈɪn·vɔɪs] I. vt facturar II. n factura f; **~ for sth** factura de algo

involuntary [ɪn·ˈval·ən·ter·i] adj involuntario, -a

involve [ɪn·ˈvalv] vt (*implicate*) implicar, involucrar; **to be ~d in sth** estar metido [or envuelto] en algo

involved [ɪn·ˈvalvd] adj (*implicated*) involucrado, -a

inward [ˈɪn·wərd] adj **1.** (*inner*) interior, íntimo, -a **2.** (*moving in: flow*) hacia adentro

inwardly [ˈɪn·wərd·li] adv interiormente

inwards [ˈɪn·wərds] adv hacia adentro, para dentro

I/O COMPUT abbr of **input/output** E/S

iodine [ˈaɪ·ə·daɪn] n yodo m

ion [ˈaɪ·ən] n ión m

IOU [ˌaɪ·oʊ·ˈju] n inf abbr of **I owe you** pagaré m

IQ [ˌaɪ·ˈkju] n abbr of **intelligence quotient** CI m

IRA [ˌaɪ·ar·ˈeɪ] n abbr of **Irish Republican Army** IRA m

Iran [ɪ·ˈræn] n Irán m

Iranian [ɪ·ˈreɪ·ni·ən] I. n iraní mf II. adj iraní

Iraq [ɪ·ˈrak] n Irak m

Iraqi [ɪ·ˈrak·i] I. n iraquí mf II. adj iraquí

Ireland [ˈaɪr·lənd] n Irlanda f; **Republic of ~** República f de Irlanda; **Northern ~** Irlanda del Norte

iris [ˈaɪ·rɪs] <-es> n **1.** BOT lirio m **2.** ANAT iris m

Irish [ˈaɪ·rɪʃ] I. adj irlandés, -esa II. n **1.** pl (*people*) **the ~** los irlandeses **2.** LING irlandés m; **~ Gaelic** gaélico m irlandés

Irishman [ˈaɪ·rɪʃ·mən] <-men> n irlandés m

Irishwoman [ˈaɪ·rɪʃ·wʊm·ən] <-women> n irlandesa f

irk [ɜrk] vt fastidiar

iron [ˈaɪ·ərn] I. n **1.** (*metal*) hierro m, fierro m AmL **2.** (*for pressing clothes*) plancha f **3.** SPORTS (*golf club*) hierro m II. vt planchar; fig allanar III. vi planchar IV. adj de hierro; (*discipline*) férreo, -a

Iron Age I. n edad f del hierro II. adj de la edad del hierro

Iron Curtain n HIST, POL Telón m de Acero, Cortina f de Hierro

ironic [aɪ·ˈran·ɪk] adj, **ironical** [aɪ·ˈran·ɪ·kəl] adj irónico, -a

ironing [ˈaɪ·ə·rɪŋ] n planchado m; **to do the ~** planchar

ironing board n tabla f de planchar, burro m de planchar Méx

irony [ˈaɪ·rə·ni] <-ies> n ironía f

irrational [ɪ·ˈræʃ·ə·nəl] adj irracional

irregular [ɪ·ˈreg·jə·lər] adj irregular; (*behavior*) anómalo, -a; (*life*) desordenado, -a

irrelevance [ɪrˈrel·ə·vənts] *n*, **irrelevancy** <-ies> *n* irrelevancia *f*

irrelevant [ɪrˈrel·ə·vənt] *adj* irrelevante; **to be ~ to sth** no ser relevante para algo

irreparable [ɪˈrep·ər·ə·bəl] *adj* irreparable

irreplaceable [ˌɪr·ɪˈpleɪ·sə·bəl] *adj* irreemplazable

irresistible [ˌɪr·ɪˈzɪs·tə·bəl] *adj* irresistible

irrespective [ˌɪr·ɪˈspek·tɪv] *prep* **~ of** aparte de; **~ of sth/sb** sin tener en cuenta algo/a alguien

irresponsible [ˌɪr·ɪˈspan·sə·bəl] *adj* irresponsable

irretrievable [ˌɪr·ɪˈtri·və·bəl] *adj* irrecuperable

irreverent [ɪˈrev·ər·ənt] *adj* irreverente

irreversible [ˌɪr·ɪˈvɜr·sə·bəl] *adj* irreversible

irrevocable [ɪˈrev·ə·kə·bəl] *adj* irrevocable

irrigate [ˈɪr·ɪ·geɪt] *vt* **1.** AGR regar **2.** MED irrigar

irrigation [ˌɪr·ɪˈgeɪ·ʃən] **I.** *n* **1.** AGR riego *m* **2.** MED irrigación *f* **II.** *adj* de riego; **~ canal** acequia *f*

irrigation plant *n* planta *f* de riego

irritable [ˈɪr·ɪ·tə·bəl] *adj* irritable

irritant [ˈɪr·ɪ·tənt] *n* irritante *m*

irritate [ˈɪr·ɪ·teɪt] *vt* **1.** (*aggravate*) irritar, molestar **2.** MED irritar

irritation [ˌɪr·ɪˈteɪ·ʃən] *n* irritación *f*

IRS [ˌaɪ·ɑrˈes] *n abbr of* **Internal Revenue Service** Oficina de la Renta de EE.UU

is [ɪz] *vt, vi 3rd pers sing of* **to be**

ISDN [ˌaɪ·es·di·ˈen] *n abbr of* **integrated services digital network** RDSI *f*

Islam [ɪzˈlam] *n* islam *m*

Islamic [ɪzˈlam·ɪk] *adj* islámico, -a; **~ law** ley islámica

island [ˈaɪ·lənd] *n* isla *f*; **~ of calm** *fig* refugio *m* de paz

islander [ˈaɪ·lən·dər] *n* isleño, -a *m, f*

isn't [ˈɪz·ənt] **= is not**

isolate [ˈaɪ·sə·leɪt] *vt* aislar

isolated [ˈaɪ·sə·leɪ·tɪd] *adj* (*outlying, disconnected*) aislado, -a

isolation [ˌaɪ·sə·ˈleɪ·ʃən] *n* **1.** (*separation*) aislamiento *m* **2.** (*loneliness*) soledad *f*

isosceles triangle [aɪˈsas·ə·liz ˌtraɪ·æŋ·gəl] *n* MATH triángulo *m* isósceles

issue [ˈɪʃ·u] **I.** *n* **1.** (*problem, topic*) cuestión *f*; **side ~** asunto *m* menor; **the real ~s** las cuestiones de fondo; **the point at ~** el punto en cuestión; **at ~** a debate **2.** PUBL (*copy*) número *m*; **latest ~** último número **3.** FIN, ECON (*of shares, stamps*) emisión *f*; (*of checks*) expedición *f* **4.** *form* (*offspring, children*) descendencia *f* **II.** *vt* **1.** (*supply*) emitir; (*passport*) expedir **2.** (*ultimatum*) presentar **3.** (*publish*) publicar **III.** *vi* **to ~ from** (*be born out of*) surgir de; (*come out of*) provenir de

it [ɪt] **I.** *pron dem* la, le, lo *en muchos casos 'it' se omite cuando se refiere a una información ya conocida;* **who was ~?** ¿quién era?; **~'s in my bag** está en mi bolso; **~'s Paul who did that** fue Paul quien lo hizo **II.** *pron pers* **1.** él, ella, ello *direct object:* lo, la *indirect object:* le, se; **~ went off badly** aquello fue mal; **your purse? I took ~** ¿tu monedero? lo cogí yo; **~'s your cat, give ~ something to eat** es tu gato, dale algo de comer; **I'm afraid of ~** le tengo miedo; **I fell into ~** me caí dentro **2.** (*time*) **what time is ~?** ¿qué hora es? **3.** (*weather*) **~'s cold** hace frío; **~'s snowing** está nevando **4.** (*distance*) **~'s 5 miles to town from here** hay 8 km hasta el pueblo **5.** (*empty subject*) **~ seems that...** parece que... **6.** (*passive subject*) **~ is said/hoped that...** se dice/espera que...

IT [ˌaɪ·ˈti] *n* COMPUT *abbr of* **Information Technology** informática *f*

Italian [ɪˈtæl·jən] **I.** *adj* italiano, -a **II.** *n* **1.** (*person*) italiano, -a *m, f* **2.** LING italiano *m*

italics [ɪˈtæl·ɪks] *npl* cursiva *f*; **in ~** en cursiva

Italy [ˈɪt·ə·li] *n* Italia *f*

itch [ɪtʃ] **I.** *vi* **1.** MED picar **2.** *fig inf* **to be ~ing to do sth** morirse por hacer algo *fig* **II.** *n* MED comezón *f*, rasquiña *f* *Arg*

itchy [ˈɪtʃ·i] <-ier, -iest> *adj* que pica; **my arm feels ~** siento picazón en el brazo

item [ˈaɪ·təm] *n* **1.** (*thing*) artículo *m*, objeto *m*; ~ **of clothing** prenda *f* de vestir **2.** (*topic*) asunto *m*; ~ **on the agenda** asunto a tratar; ~ **by** ~ punto por punto **3.** COM partida *f* **4.** PUBL noticia *f* **5.** *inf* (*couple*) parejita *f*

itemize ['aɪ·tə·maɪz] *vt* detallar

itinerary [aɪ·'tɪn·ə·rer·i] <-ies> *n* itinerario *m*

it'll ['ɪt·əl] = **it will**

its [ɪts] *adj pos* su; ~ **color/weight** su color/peso; ~ **mountains** sus montañas; **the cat hurt ~ head** el gato se lastimó la cabeza

it's [ɪts] **1.** = **it is 2.** = **it has**

itself [ɪt·'self] *pron reflexive* él mismo, ella misma, ello mismo *direct, indirect object*: se *after prep*: sí mismo, -a; **the place ~** el sitio en sí; **by ~** solo

IUD [aɪ·ju·'di] *n abbr of* **intrauterine device** DIU *m*

I've [aɪv] = **I have** *see* **have**

ivory ['aɪ·və·ri] <-ies> *n* marfil *m*

Ivory Coast *n* Costa *f* de Marfil

ivory tower *n fig* torre *f* de marfil

ivy ['aɪ·vi] <-ies> *n* hiedra *f*

J

J, j [dʒeɪ] *n* J, j *f*; ~ **as in Juliet** J de Juan

J *n* PHYS *abbr of* **joule** J

jab [dʒæb] **I.** *n* **1.** (*with a pin*) pinchazo *m*; (*with an elbow*) codazo *m* **2.** (*in boxing*) golpe *m*) corto *m* **II.** <-bb-> *vt* **to ~ a needle into sth** pinchar algo con una aguja **III.** <-bb-> *vi* **to ~ at sb/sth** (**with sth**) dar a alguien/algo (con algo)

jabbering *n* farfulla *f*

jack [dʒæk] *n* **1.** AUTO gato *m* **2.** (*in cards*) jota *f*; (*in a Spanish pack*) sota *f* **3.** *sl* (*anything*) **you don't know ~!** ¡tú no sabes un carajo!

♦**jack up** *vt* **1.** (*object*) levantar **2.** *sl* (*prices*) subir

jacket ['dʒæk·ɪt] *n* **1.** (*short coat*) chaqueta *f*, percha *f AmC*, chapona *f RíoPl*, cuácara *f Chile* **2.** (*of a book*) sobrecubierta *f*

jacket potato *n* patata *f* asada (*con piel*)

jack-in-the-box ['dʒæk·ɪn·ðə·baks] <-xes> *n* caja *f* de sorpresas

jackpot ['dʒæk·pat] *n* (premio *m*) gordo *m* ▶ **to hit the ~** *inf* llevarse el gordo

Jacuzzi® [dʒə·'ku·zi] *n* jacuzzi® *m*

jaded ['dʒeɪ·dɪd] *adj* **to be ~ with sth** estar harto de algo

jagged ['dʒæg·ɪd] *adj* irregular; (*coastline, rocks*) recortado, -a; (*cut, tear*) desigual

jail [dʒeɪl] **I.** *n* cárcel *f*, prisión *f*; **to put sb in ~** encarcelar a alguien **II.** *vt* encarcelar; **she was ~ed for life** la condenaron a cadena perpetua

jailbreak *n* fuga *f*

jailer *n*, **jailor** ['dʒeɪ·lər] *n* carcelero, -a *m, f*

jam¹ [dʒæm] *n* CULIN mermelada *f*

jam² [dʒæm] **I.** *n* **1.** *inf* (*awkward situation*) aprieto *m*; **to get into a ~** meterse en un lío **2.** (*blockage*) **traffic ~** atasco *m*; **paper ~** COMPUT atasco de papel **II.** <-mm-> *vt* **1.** (*cause to become stuck*) atascar; (*door*) obstruir; **to ~ sth into sth** embutir algo en algo **2.** (*a wheel*) trabar **III.** <-mm-> *vi* **1.** (*become stuck*) atrancarse; (*brakes*) bloquearse **2.** (*play music*) tocar, improvisar

jam-packed [,dʒæm·'pækt] *adj inf* **the streets were ~ with people** las calles estaban atestadas de gente

janitor ['dʒæn·ɪ·tər] *n* conserje *mf*

January ['dʒæn·ju·er·i] <-ies> *n* enero *m*; *s. a.* **April**

Japan [dʒə·'pæn] *n* Japón *m*

Japanese [,dʒæp·ə·'niz] **I.** *adj* japonés, -esa **II.** *n* **1.** (*person*) japonés, -esa *m, f* **2.** LING japonés *m*

jar¹ [dʒar] *n* (*container*) tarro *m*

jar² [dʒar] **I.** <-rr-> *vt* (*shake*) sacudir **II.** <-rr-> *vi* (*cause unpleasant feelings*) **to ~ on sb's nerves** crispar los nervios a alguien **III.** *n* (*shake*) sacudida *f*

jargon ['dʒar·gən] *n* jerga *f*

jaundice ['dʒɔn·dɪs] *n* MED ictericia *f*

javelin ['dʒæv·lɪn] *n* (*spear*) jabalina *f*

jaw [dʒɔ] *n* **1.** ANAT mandíbula *f* **2.** ~**s** (*mouth*) boca *f*; *fig* fauces *fpl* **3.** ~**s** TECH mordazas *fpl*

jaywalking n cruce m imprudente de calzada

jazz [dʒæz] n jazz m; ~ **band/club** grupo m/club m de jazz ▶ **and all that** ~ sl y todo ese rollo

◆**jazz up** vt sl crear ambiente

jazzy ['dʒæz·i] <-ier, -iest> adj **1.** MUS de jazz **2.** sl (flashy) llamativo, -a

jealous ['dʒel·əs] adj **1.** (envious) envidioso, -a; **to be ~ of sb** tener celos de alguien **2.** (fiercely protective) celoso, -a; **to be ~ of sth** ser celoso de algo

jealousy ['dʒel·ə·si] <-ies> n **1.** (possessiveness) celos mpl **2.** (envy) envidia f

jeans [dʒinz] npl vaqueros mpl; **a pair of** ~ unos vaqueros

jeep [dʒip] n jeep m

jeer [dʒɪr] **I.** vt abuchear **II.** vi mofarse **III.** n burla f

jeez [dʒiz] interj inf (expressing surprise) ¡hala!; (expressing annoyance) ¡vaya, hombre!

jelly ['dʒel·i] <-ies> n **1.** (soft transparent substance) gelatina f **2.** (jam) mermelada f

jellyfish <-es> n medusa f

jeopardy ['dʒep·ər·di] n peligro m

jerk [dʒɜrk] **I.** n **1.** (jolt) sacudida f **2.** (movement) tirón m **II.** vi sacudirse **III.** vt **1.** (shake) sacudir **2.** (pull) tirar bruscamente de

jerky¹ ['dʒɜr·ki] <-ier, -iest> adj (not smooth: ride) dando botes [or tumbos], a tirones Méx

jerky² ['dʒɜr·ki] n CULIN beef ~ cecina f

jersey ['dʒɜr·zi] n **1.** (garment) jersey m **2.** (sports shirt) camiseta f **3.** (cloth) tejido m de punto **4.** (type of cow) Jersey f (raza de ganado vacuno)

Jesuit ['dʒez·u·ɪt] **I.** n jesuita m **II.** adj jesuita

Jesus ['dʒi·zəs] **I.** Jesús **II.** interj inf ¡por Dios!

Jesus Christ I. n Jesucristo m **II.** interj inf ¡Dios mío!

jet¹ [dʒet] **I.** n **1.** (aircraft) avión m a reacción, jet m **2.** (stream) chorro m **3.** (nozzle) surtidor m **II.** <-tt-> vi volar

jet² [dʒet] n (stone) azabache m

jet engine n motor m a reacción

jet fighter n caza m a reacción

jetfoil n hidroala f a reacción

jet lag n desfase m horario, jet lag m

jet plane n avión m a reacción

jet-propelled adj a reacción

jet set n inf **the** ~ la jet-set

jetty ['dʒet·i] n embarcadero m

Jew [dʒu] n judío, -a m, f

jewel ['dʒu·əl] n **1.** (piece of jewelry) a. fig joya f **2.** (watch part) rubí m

jeweler ['dʒu·ə·lər] n, **jeweller** ['dʒu·ə·lər] n joyero, -a m, f

jewelry ['dʒu·əl·ri] n joyas fpl; **a piece of** ~ una joya

Jewish ['dʒu·ɪʃ] adj judío, -a

jiffy ['dʒɪf·i] n inf **in a** ~ en un santiamén

jigsaw ['dʒɪg·sɔ] n sierra f de vaivén

jigsaw puzzle n puzzle m, rompecabezas m inv

jingle ['dʒɪn·gəl] **I.** vt hacer tintinear **II.** vi tintinear **III.** n **1.** (noise) tintineo m **2.** (in advertisements) jingle m

jinx [dʒɪŋks] **I.** vt gafar II. n gafe f; **to put a ~ on sb/sth** echar una maldición a alguien/algo

jitters ['dʒɪt·ərz] npl inf (nervousness) nervios mpl; **he got the** ~ le entró el canguelo

jittery ['dʒɪt·ər·i] <-ier, -iest> adj inf nervioso, -a; **he felt** ~ le dió el temblequé

job [dʒab] n **1.** (piece of work, employment) trabajo m; **to apply for a** ~ presentarse para un trabajo **2.** (duty) deber m; **to do one's** ~ cumplir con su deber; **it's not her** ~ no es asunto suyo

job description n descripción f del puesto

job interview n entrevista f de trabajo

jobless ['dʒab·lɪs] **I.** adj desocupado, -a **II.** npl **the** ~ los parados mpl

job market n mercado m laboral

job rating n evaluación f del lugar de trabajo

jobseeker n demandante mf de empleo

jock [dʒak] n **1.** sl (athlete) atleta m **2.** (jockstrap) suspensorio m

jockey ['dʒak·i] **I.** n jockey mf **II.** vi **to** **for sth** competir por algo

J

jockstrap n suspensorio m

jog [dʒɑg] I. n 1. (run) trote m; **to go for a ~** hacer footing 2. (nudge) golpe m II. <-gg-> vi correr III. <-gg-> vt **to ~ sb's memory** refrescar la memoria a alguien

◆**jog along** vi inf ir tirando

jogger ['dʒɑg·ər] n persona f que hace footing

jogging ['dʒɑg·ɪŋ] n footing m; **to go (out) ~** hacer footing

john [dʒɑn] n sl (toilet) váter m

join [dʒɔɪn] I. vt 1. (connect) juntar, unir; **to ~ hands** cogerse de la mano 2. (come together with sb) reunirse [or juntarse] con 3. (become member of: club) unirse a; (society) ingresar en; (army) alistarse en II. vi 1. (unite) unirse 2. (become member) hacerse socio 3. (participate) **to ~ in sth** tomar parte en algo

joiner ['dʒɔɪ·nər] n carpintero, -a m, f

joint [dʒɔɪnt] I. adj conjunto, -a II. n 1. ANAT articulación f; **to come out of ~** dislocarse 2. (connection) unión f, juntura f 3. TECH conexión f 4. sl (nightclub) garito m

jointed adj articulado, -a

jointly adv conjuntamente

joint venture n empresa f conjunta

joke [dʒoʊk] I. n 1. (amusing story) chiste m; (trick, remark) broma f; **to play a ~ on sb** gastar una broma a alguien; **to not be able to take a ~** no aceptar una broma 2. inf (easy thing) **to be no ~** no ser cosa de broma 3. inf (ridiculous thing or person) ridiculez f; **what a ~!** ¡qué farsa! II. vi bromear; **to ~ about sth** hacer bromas sobre algo

joker ['dʒoʊ·kər] n 1. (one who jokes) bromista mf 2. inf (annoying person) idiota m 3. (playing card) comodín m

joking I. adj jocoso, -a II. n bromas fpl

jokingly adv en broma

jolly ['dʒɑl·i] <-ier, -iest> adj (happy: tune) alegre

jolt [dʒoʊlt] I. n (sudden jerk) sacudida f II. vt 1. (jerk) sacudir 2. (shock) sobresaltar III. vi dar una sacudida; (vehicle) traquetear

jostle ['dʒɑs·əl] I. vt empujar II. vi 1. (push) empujarse 2. (compete) disputarse; **to ~ for position** luchar por hacerse un hueco

jot [dʒɑt] <-tt-> vt **to ~ sth down** apuntar algo

jottings npl apuntes mpl

journal ['dʒɜr·nəl] n 1. (periodical) revista f especializada 2. (diary) diario m

journalism ['dʒɜr·nə·lɪz·əm] n periodismo m, diarismo m AmL

journalist ['dʒɜr·nə·lɪst] n periodista mf

journey ['dʒɜr·ni] I. n viaje m II. vi liter viajar

joy [dʒɔɪ] n 1. (gladness) alegría f; **to jump for ~** saltar de alegría 2. (cause of joy) placer m

joyful ['dʒɔɪ·fəl] adj feliz

joyless ['dʒɔɪ·lɪs] adj falto, -a de alegría

joyous ['dʒɔɪ·əs] adj liter de júbilo

joy ride ['dʒɔɪ·raɪd] n paseo en un coche robado

joystick ['dʒɔɪ·stɪk] n 1. AVIAT palanca f de mando 2. COMPUT joystick m

jubilant ['dʒu·bɪ·lənt] adj jubiloso, -a; (crowd) exultante

jubilation [ˌdʒu·bɪ·ˈleɪ·ʃən] n júbilo m

jubilee ['dʒu·bə·li] n 1. (anniversary) aniversario m 2. REL jubileo m

judge [dʒʌdʒ] I. n 1. LAW juez mf 2. (referee) árbitro m; **panel of ~s** jurado m II. vi a. LAW juzgar; (give one's opinion) opinar III. vt 1. a. LAW juzgar; (question) decidir; (assess) valorar; (consider) considerar; **to ~ that...** opinar que... 2. (as a referee) arbitrar

judg(e)ment ['dʒʌdʒ·mənt] n 1. LAW fallo m 2. (opinion) opinión f 3. (discernment) criterio m

judicial [dʒu·ˈdɪʃ·əl] adj judicial

judiciary [dʒu·ˈdɪʃ·i·er·i] n form poder m judicial

judicious [dʒu·ˈdɪʃ·əs] adj form acertado, -a

judo ['dʒu·doʊ] n judo m

jug [dʒʌg] n (container) jarra f

juggernaut ['dʒʌg·ər·nɔt] n fuerza f irresistible

juggle ['dʒʌg·əl] I. vi a. fig hacer juegos malabares II. vt a. fig hacer juegos malabares con

juggler n malabarista mf

jugular vein n vena f yugular

juice [dʒus] n 1. (drink) zumo m 2. (of meat) jugo m 3. sl (electricity) luz f; (fuel) sopa f

juicy ['dʒu·si] <-ier, -iest> adj 1. (fruit, steak) jugoso, -a 2. inf (profit) sustancioso, -a 3. (details) picante

jukebox ['dʒuk·baks] n máquina f de discos

July [dʒu·'laɪ] n julio m; s. a. **April**

jumble ['dʒʌm·bəl] I. n revoltijo m II. vt mezclar

jumbo ['dʒʌm·boʊ] I. adj gigante m II. n inf gigante, -a m, f

jump [dʒʌmp] I. vi 1. (leap) saltar; to ~ up and down pegar saltos 2. (skip) brincar; to ~ for joy brincar de alegría 3. (increase suddenly) subir de golpe II. vt 1. (leap across or over) fig saltar 2. (attack) atacar ▸ to ~ the gun precipitarse III. n (leap) salto m

◆**jump at** vt (an opportunity) no dejar escapar

◆**jump in** vi entrar deprisa

◆**jump up** vi levantarse de un salto

jumper ['dʒʌm·pər] n 1. (person, animal) saltador(a) m(f) 2. (dress) pichi m

jumper cables npl AUTO cables m pl de arranque

jumpsuit n FASHION mono m

jumpy ['dʒʌm·pi] <-ier, -iest> adj inf nervioso, -a

junction ['dʒʌŋk·ʃən] n cruce m

June [dʒun] n junio m; s. a. **April**

jungle ['dʒʌŋ·gəl] n 1. (forest) selva f 2. fig (tangled mass) maraña f

junior ['dʒun·jər] I. adj 1. (younger) más joven 2. SPORTS juvenil 3. (lower in rank) subalterno, -a; (partner) comanditario, -a II. n 1. (younger person) he is five years my ~ es cinco años menor que yo 2. UNIV, SCHOOL estudiante mf de tercer año

junk¹ [dʒʌŋk] I. n (objects of no value) trastos mpl, tiliches mpl AmC, Méx II. vt inf tirar a la basura

junk² [dʒʌŋk] n (boat) junco m

junk food n comida f basura

junkie ['dʒʌŋ·ki] n 1. sl (addict) yonqui mf 2. sl (fanatic) fanático, -a m, f

junk mail n propaganda f postal

junkyard n chatarrería f

juror ['dʒʊr·ər] n miembro mf del jurado

jury ['dʒʊr·i] n jurado m

just [dʒʌst] I. adv 1. (very soon) enseguida; we're ~ about to leave estamos a punto de salir 2. (now) precisamente; to be ~ doing sth estar justamente haciendo algo 3. (very recently) ~ after 10 o'clock justo después de las 10; she's ~ turned 15 acaba de cumplir 15 años 4. (exactly, equally) exactamente, justo; ~ like that justo así; ~ as I expected tal y como yo esperaba; ~ now ahora mismo; not ~ yet todavía no 5. (only) solamente; ~ a minute espera un momento 6. (simply) simplemente; ~ in case it rains por si llueve 7. (barely) ~ (about), (only) ~ apenas; ~ in time justo a tiempo 8. ~ about (nearly) casi 9. it's ~ as well that... menos mal que... ▸ ~ my luck! ¡me tenía que pasar a mí! II. adj (fair) justo, -a

justice ['dʒʌs·tɪs] n 1. justicia f 2. (judge) juez mf

justifiable [ˌdʒʌs·tə·'faɪ·ə·bəl] adj justificable

justification [ˌdʒʌs·tə·fɪ·'keɪ·ʃən] n justificación f

justify ['dʒʌs·tɪ·faɪ] vt justificar; to ~ oneself to sb dar explicaciones a alguien

justly ['dʒʌst·li] adv justamente

jut [dʒʌt] <-tt-> vi to ~ out sobresalir

juvenile ['dʒu·və·naɪl] adj 1. form (young) juvenil 2. pej (childish) infantil

juxtapose ['dʒʌk·stə·poʊz] vt yuxtaponer

K

K, k [keɪ] n K, k f; ~ as in Kilo K de kilo

K 1. COMPUT abbr of **kilobyte** K m 2. (thousand) $30~ 30.000 dólares

kaiser roll ['kaɪ·zər·roʊl] n panecillo con semillas de amapola

kamikaze attack n ataque m kamikaze

kangaroo [ˌkæŋ·gə·'ru] <-(s)> n canguro m

kangaroo court n tribunal m desautorizado

kaput [ka·'put] adj inf (appliance, car, etc.) escacharrado, -a, dañado, -a; (relationship) finito, -a, acabado, -a

karat ['ker·ət] <-(s)> n quilate m

karate [kə·'ra·ţi] n kárate m

karate chop n golpe m de kárate

kayak ['kaɪ·æk] n kayak m

kayaking n I love ~ me encanta ir en kayak

kebab [kə·'bab] n kebab m

keel [kil] n NAUT quilla f

keen [kin] I. adj 1. (intent, eager) entusiasta; **to be ~ on sth** ser aficionado, -a a algo 2. (perceptive: intelligence) agudo, -a; **to have a ~ sense of smell** tener un agudo sentido del olfato 3. (extreme) fuerte; **a ~ interest** un vivo interés II. n lamento m fúnebre III. vi lamentar

keep [kip] I. n (livelihood) subsistencia f; **to earn one's ~** ganarse el sustento ▶ **for ~s** para siempre II. <kept, kept> vt 1. (have: shop) tener; (animals) criar 2. (store: silence, secret) guardar; **~ my seat** guárdame el sitio; **~ the change** quédese con el cambio 3. (maintain) mantener; **to ~ sb under observation** tener a alguien en observación; **to ~ one's eyes fixed on sth/sb** no apartar los ojos de algo/alguien; **to ~ sth going** mantener algo a flote fig 4. (detain) **~ sb waiting** hacer esperar a alguien; **to ~ sb in prison** tener a alguien en la cárcel; **what kept you?** ¿qué es lo que te ha entretenido? 5. (fulfill) cumplir; **to ~ an appointment** acudir a una cita; **to ~ one's word** cumplir su palabra 6. (record: diary) escribir; (accounts) llevar 7. (person's expenses) mantener; **to earn enough to ~ oneself** ganar lo bastante para mantenerse 8. (obey, respect) obedecer; ▶ (law) observar ▶ **to ~ one's balance** mantener el equilibrio; **to ~ time** marcar la hora III. <kept, kept> vi 1. a. fig (stay fresh) conservarse 2. (stay) mantenerse; **to ~ fit** mantenerse en forma; **to ~ silent (about sth)** guardar silencio (sobre algo); **to ~ to the left** circular por la izquierda; **~ quiet!** ¡cállate!; **~ still!** ¡estate quieto!

3. (continue) **to ~ going** (person) ir tirando; (machine) seguir funcionando; **to ~ doing sth** seguir haciendo algo; **he ~s losing his keys** siempre pierde las llaves

◆**keep ahead** vi seguir en cabeza

◆**keep away** I. vi mantenerse alejado, -a; **he can't ~ from it** no puede dejarlo; **~!** ¡no te acerques! II. vt always sep mantener alejado, -a

◆**keep back** I. vi (stay away) **to ~ from sth/sb** mantenerse alejado de algo/alguien II. vt 1. **to ~ one's tears** contener las lágrimas 2. (hide) ocultar 3. (retain sth) **to keep sth back** quedarse con algo; (slow down) retrasar algo

◆**keep down** vt 1. **to keep one's voice down** no levantar la voz; **to keep prices down** controlar los precios 2. (not vomit) retener

◆**keep in** vt (person) no dejar salir; (emotions) contener II. vi **to ~ line** comportarse bien

◆**keep off** I. vi (stay off) mantenerse alejado, -a; '**~**' 'prohibido el paso'; '**~ the grass**' 'prohibido pisar el césped' II. vt 1. mantener alejado, -a; **to keep the rain off sth/sb** resguardar algo/a alguien de la lluvia; **keep your hands off!** ¡no lo toques! 2. (avoid) evitar

◆**keep on** I. vi (continue) seguir; **to ~ doing sth** seguir haciendo algo II. vt always sep seguir teniendo; (not to dismiss) no despedir

◆**keep out** I. vi no entrar; **~!** ¡prohibido el paso! **to ~ of trouble** no meterse en líos II. vt **to keep sth/sb out (of sth)** no dejar que entre algo/alguien (en algo); **to keep the rain/cold out** resguardar de la lluvia/del frío

◆**keep together** I. vt mantener juntos, -as II. vi mantenerse unidos, -as; **please, ~** por favor, no se separen

◆**keep up** I. vt 1. (trousers) sujetar; (ceiling) sostener 2. (continue) seguir; **~ the good work!** ¡sigue así!; **keep it up!** ¡sigue! 3. (stop sb sleeping) tener en vela II. vi 1. (moral) no decaer 2. (continue) seguir; **the rain kept up all night** siguió lloviendo durante toda la noche 3. (to stay level with) to

~ **(with sb/sth)** seguir el ritmo (de alguien/algo); **to ~ with the Joneses** *fig* no ser menos que los demás **4.** (*remain informed*) **to ~ with sth** mantenerse al tanto de algo; **to ~ with the times** estar al día

keeper ['ki·pər] *n* **1.** (*in charge*) guarda *mf*; (*museum*) conservador(a) *m(f)*; (*jail*) carcelero, -a *m*, *f* **2.** SPORTS portero, -a *m*, *f*, arquero, -a *m*, *f Arg*, golero, -a *m*, *f Urug*

keeping ['ki·pɪŋ] *n* **1.** (*guarding*) cargo *m* **2. in ~ with sth** de acuerdo con algo

kelp [kelp] *n* tipo de alga marrón usada en comidas

kennel ['ken·əl] *n* **1.** (*doghouse*) perrera *f* **2. ~s** (*boarding*) residencia *f* canina; (*breeding*) criadero *m* de perros

kept [kept] **I.** *pt, pp of* **keep II.** *adj* mantenido, -a

kerosene ['ker·ə·sin] *n* queroseno *m*

ketchup ['ketʃ·əp] *n* ketchup *m*

kettle ['ket·əl] *n* tetera *f*, pava *f AmL*; **to put the ~ on** poner agua a hervir

key¹ [ki] **I.** *n* **1.** (*doors*) llave *f*; **master ~** llave maestra **2. a.** COMPUT tecla *f*; **caps lock ~** tecla de bloqueo de mayúsculas; **to hit a ~** pulsar una tecla **3.** (*list*) clave *f*; (*exercises*) soluciones *fpl* **4.** MUS tono *m*; **in the ~ of C major** en (tono de) do mayor; **to go off ~** desafinar **II.** *adj* (*factor, figure, role*) clave; **~ decision** decisión *f* clave [*or* fundamental] **III.** *vt* (*type*) **to ~ (in)** teclear

◆ **key in** *vt* COMPUT picar, teclear

◆ **key up** *vt* emocionar; **to be keyed up** estar emocionado, -a

key² [ki] *n* (*island*) cayo *m*

keyboard ['ki·bɔrd] *n* teclado *m*

keyboarding *n* introducción *f* desde teclado

keyboard instrument *n* instrumento *m* de teclado

keyhole ['ki·houl] *n* ojo *m* de la cerradura

key money *n* adelanto *m*; **as ~** en concepto de adelanto

keynote address *n* discurso *m* central

keynote speech *n* discurso *m* central

keypad ['ki·pæd] *n* COMPUT teclado *m* numérico

key ring *n* llavero *m*

Key West *n* Cayo Hueso *m*

KIA *adj abbr of* **killed in action** fallecido, -a en acto de servicio

kick [kɪk] **I.** *n* **1.** (*person*) patada *f*; (*horse*) coz *f*; (*in football*) tiro *m* **2.** (*exciting feeling*) placer *m*; **to do sth for ~s** hacer algo para divertirse; **to get a ~ out of sth** encontrar placer en algo **3.** (*craze*) **he is on an exercise ~ at the moment** ahora le ha dado por hacer ejercicio **II.** *vt* **1.** dar una patada; **to ~ sth open** abrir algo de una patada; **to ~ a ball** chutar una pelota **2.** (*stop*) dejar; **to ~ a habit** dejar un vicio **III.** *vi* **1.** (*person*) dar patadas a; (*horse*) dar coces a; SPORTS chutar **2. to be alive and ~ing** *inf* estar vivito y coleando

◆ **kick around, kick around I.** *vi inf* (*hang about*) andar por ahí; (*thing*) andar rodando **II.** *vt* (*a ball*) dar patadas a

◆ **kick around** *vt inf* **1.** (*treat badly*) tratar a patadas **2.** (*ponder: idea*) plantearse, dar vueltas a

◆ **kick away** *vt* apartar de un golpe

◆ **kick back I.** *vt* (*football*) devolver **II.** *vi inf* **1.** (*recoil*) retroceder **2.** *sl* (*give a kickback*) sobornar

◆ **kick in** *vt* derribar a patadas; **to kick sb's teeth in** romper la cara a alguien

◆ **kick off I.** *vi* (*begin*) empezar, arrancar *inf*; (*in football*) hacer el saque de centro **II.** *vt* quitar de un puntapié

◆ **kick out** *vt* **he was kicked out of the party** lo echaron de la fiesta

◆ **kick up** *vt* **to ~ dust a.** *fig* levantar polvo

kickoff ['kɪk·ɔf] *n* **1.** SPORTS saque *m* inicial **2.** *inf* (*beginning*) arranque *m*

kid [kɪd] **I.** *n* **1.** (*child*) niño, -a *m*, *f*, chavito, -a *m*, *f Méx*, pelado, -a *m*, *f Col, Ecua*; **~ brother** hermano *m* pequeño; **as a ~...** de niño... **2.** (*young person*) chico, -a *m*, *f*, muchacho, -a *m*, *f* **3.** *sl* (*term of address*) nene, -a *m*, *f* **4.** ZOOL cría *f*; (*young goat*) cabrito *m* ▶ **that's ~'s stuff** eso está tirado [*or* regalado] *inf* **II.** <-dd-> *vi* bromear; **are you ~ding?** ¿bromeas?; **just ~ding** es broma **III.** *vt* **to ~ sb (about sth)** tomar el pelo a alguien (con algo) **IV.** *vr* stop ~**ding yourself!** ¡desengáñate!

kidnap ['kɪd·næp] **I.** <-pp-> *vt* secuestrar, plagiar *AmL* **II.** *n* secuestro *m*, plagio *m AmL*

kidnapper ['kɪd·næp·ər] *n* secuestrador(a) *m(f)*

kidnapping *n* secuestro *m*

kidney ['kɪd·ni] *n* riñón *m*; ~ **disease** enfermedad *f* renal

kidney bean *n* judía *f*, poroto *m CSur*

kidney stone *n* MED cálculo *m* renal

kill [kɪl] **I.** *n* **1.** (*slaughter*) matanza *f* **2.** (*hunting*) pieza *f* ▶ **to go in for the** ~ entrar a matar **II.** *vi* matar; **thou shalt not** ~ (*Bible*) no matarás **III.** *vt* **1.** (*cause to die*) matar; **to** ~ **oneself** suicidarse **2.** (*destroy*) acabar con; **my feet are** ~**ing me!** ¡los pies me están matando! **to** ~ **sb with kindness** abrumar a alguien con atenciones

◆ **kill off** *vt* exterminar

killer ['kɪl·ər] *n* (*sb who kills*) asesino, -a *m, f*; **to be a** ~ (*person*) ser un asesino; (*disease*) cobrar muchas víctimas; **the test was a real** ~ *fig sl* el examen ha sido mortal

killer whale *n* orca *f*

killing ['kɪl·ɪŋ] **I.** *n* (*of a person*) asesinato *m*; (*of an animal*) matanza *f* ▶ **to make a** ~ *inf* hacer su agosto **II.** *adj* **1.** (*murderous*) asesino, -a **2.** (*exhausting*) mortal

kilo ['ki·loʊ] *n* kilo *m*

kilobyte ['kɪl·ə·baɪt] *n* COMPUT kilobyte *m*

kilogram ['kɪl·ə·græm] *n* kilogramo *m*

kilometer [kɪ·'lɑm·ɪ·tər] *n* kilómetro *m*

kilt [kɪlt] *n* falda *f* escocesa, pollera *f* escocesa *CSur*

kin [kɪn] *n* **next of** ~ parientes *m pl* más cercanos

kind¹ [kaɪnd] *adj* amable; **to be** ~ **to sb** ser amable con alguien; **he was** ~ **enough to...** tuvo la amabilidad de...; **would you be** ~ **enough/so** ~ **as to...?** ¿me haría usted el favor de...?; **with** ~ **regards** (*in a letter*) muchos recuerdos

kind² [kaɪnd] **I.** *n* **1.** (*type*) clase *f*; **he is not that** ~ (*of person*) no es de esa clase (de personas); **what** ~ **of...?** ¿qué clase de...?; **all** ~**s of...** todo tipo de...; **to hear/say nothing of the** ~ no haber oído/dicho nada parecido **2.** (*sth similar to*) especie *f*; **a** ~ **of soup** una especie de sopa **3.** (*sth equal to*) **he repaid her betrayal in** ~ pagó su traición con la misma moneda **4.** (*limited*) **in a** ~ **way** en cierta manera **5.** (*payment*) **to pay sb in** ~ pagar a alguien en especies **II.** *adv inf* **I** ~ **of like it** bueno, no está mal; **he was** ~ **of sad** estaba como triste; **"do you like it?" — "** ~ **of"** "¿te gusta?" — "no está mal"

kindergarten ['kɪn·dər·gɑr·gdən] *n* guardería *f*, jardín *m* infantil *Chile*, jardín *m* de infantes *RíoPl*

kindle ['kɪn·dəl] **I.** *vt a. fig* encender; **to** ~ **sb's interest** despertar el interés de alguien **II.** *vi a. fig* encenderse

kindly ['kaɪnd·li] **I.** <-ier, -iest> *adj* amable **II.** *adv* **1.** (*in a kind manner*) amablemente **2.** (*please*) **you are** ~ **requested to leave the building** se ruega abandonen el edificio; ~ **put that book away!** ¡haz el favor de guardar ese libro! **3.** (*favorably*) **to take** ~ **to sth** aceptar algo de buen grado

kindness ['kaɪnd·nɪs] <-es> *n* **1.** (*act of being kind*) amabilidad *f* **2.** (*kind act*) favor *m*

kinetic [kɪ·'net̮·ɪk] *adj* PHYS cinético, -a

king [kɪŋ] *n* **1.** *a.* GAMES rey *m*; **the** ~ **of beasts** el rey de la selva **2.** (*in checkers*) dama *f*

kingdom ['kɪŋ·dəm] *n* reino *m*; **animal/ plant** ~ reino animal/vegetal; **the** ~ **of God** REL el Reino de Dios ▶ **to blow sth to** ~ **come** hacer saltar algo en pedazos

kingfisher ['kɪŋ·fɪʃ·ər] *n* ZOOL martín *m* pescador

kink [kɪŋk] *n* **1.** (*twist: in a pipe, rope*) retorcimiento *m*; (*in hair*) rizo *m* **2.** (*sore muscle*) tortícolis *f inv*; **to have a** ~ **in one's neck** tener tortícolis **3.** (*problem*) fallo *m*; **to iron out** (**a few**) ~**s** pulir algunos defectos

kinky ['kɪŋ·ki] <-ier, -iest> *adj* **1.** (*twisted*) retorcido, -a **2.** (*with tight curls*) ensortijado, -a **3.** (*unusual*) raro, -a

kiosk ['ki·ask] *n* (*stand, pavilion*) quiosco *m*

kipper ['kɪp·ər] *n* arenque *m* ahumado

kiss [kɪs] **I.** <-es> *n* beso *m*; ~ **of life** respiración *f* boca a boca; ~ **of death** *fig* beso de la muerte; **to blow sb a** ~ lanzar un beso a alguien **II.** *vi* besarse **III.** *vt* besar; **to** ~ **sb goodnight/good-bye** dar un beso de buenas noches/despedida a alguien

kisser ['kɪs·ər] *n* (*person*) **he's a wonderful** ~! ¡beso muy bien!

kiss-off ['kɪs·ɔf] *n sl* **to give the** ~ dar calabazas

kit [kɪt] *n* **1.** (*set*) utensilios *mpl*; **first aid** ~ botiquín *m* de primeros auxilios; **tool** ~ caja *f* de herramientas **2.** (*parts to put together*) kit *m*

kitchen ['kɪtʃ·ɪn] *n* cocina *f*

kitchen cabinet *n* POL camarilla *f*

kitchenette [ˌkɪtʃ·ɪ·'net] *n* cocinita *f*, rincón *m* cocina

kitchen foil *n* papel *m* de aluminio

kitchen paper *n* papel *m* de cocina

kitchen sink *n* fregadero *m*, lavaplatos *m* *inv And*, pileta *f RíoPl*

kitchen towel *n* (*dishtowel*) paño *m* de cocina

kitchen unit *n* módulo *m* de cocina

kite [kaɪt] *n* **1.** ZOOL milano *m* **2.** (*toy*) cometa *f*, volantón *m AmL*; **to fly a** ~ hacer volar una cometa; *fig* tantear el terreno ▶ **go fly a** ~! *inf* ¡vete a freír espárragos!

kitten ['kɪt·ən] *n* gatito, -a *m, f*

kitty ['kɪt·i] <-ies> *n* **1.** (*kitten or cat*) minino *m* **2.** (*money*) fondo *m*

kiwi ['ki·wi] *n* **1.** ZOOL, BOT kiwi *m* **2.** *inf* (*New Zealander*) neozelandés, -esa *m, f*

kJ *abbr of* **kilojoule** kJ

Kleenex® ['kli·neks] *n* kleenex® *m*

kleptomania [ˌklep·tou·'meɪ·ni·ə] *n* cleptomanía *f*

kleptomaniac [ˌklep·tou·'meɪ·ni·æk] *n* cleptómano, -a *m, f*

km/h, kmph *abbr of* **kilometers per hour** km/h

knack [næk] *n* habilidad *f*; **to have a** ~ **for sth** tener facilidad para algo; **to get**

the ~ **of sth** coger el tranquillo a algo, tomar la mano a algo *AmL*

knee [ni] **I.** *n* rodilla *f*; **to get down on one's** ~**s** ponerse de rodillas; **on your** ~**s!** ¡de rodillas! **II.** *vt* **to** ~ **sb** dar un rodillazo a alguien

kneecap ['ni·ˌkæp] *n* rótula *f*

kneel [nil] <knelt *or* kneeled, knelt *or* kneeled> *vi* arrodillarse

knee sock *n* media *f*, calcetín *m*

knelt [nelt] *pt of* **kneel**

knew [nu] *pt of* **know**

knickers ['nɪk·ərz] *npl* bombachos *mpl*

knickknack ['nɪk·næk] *n inf* cachivache *m*

knife [naɪf] <knives> **I.** *n* **1.** cuchillo *m* **2.** (*dagger*) puñal *m*; **to wield a** ~ blandir un puñal *elev* **3.** (*in a machine*) cuchilla *f* **II.** *vt* apuñalar

knife-edge *n* filo *m*

knife sharpener *n* afilador *m*

knifing ['naɪ·fɪŋ] *n* pelea *f* con navajas

knight [naɪt] **I.** *n* **1.** (*man given honorable rank*) sir *m* **2.** HIST (*man of high social position*) caballero *m* **3.** (*chess figure*) caballo *m* ▶ ~ **in shining armor** príncipe *m* azul **II.** *vt* HIST armar caballero; (*give honorable title*) conceder el título de 'sir'

knighthood *n* título *m* de 'sir'

knit [nɪt] **I.** *vi* (*wool*) hacer punto; (*with a machine*) tejer **II.** *vt* (*wool*) tejer

◆**knit together I.** *vi* (*combine or join*) unirse **II.** *vt fig* (*join*) unir

knitting *n* **1.** (*the product of knitting*) tejido *m* de punto **2.** (*material being knitted*) labor *f* de punto **3.** (*action of knitting*) **she likes** ~ le gusta hacer punto

knitwear ['nɪt·wer] *n* géneros *m pl* de punto

knob [nab] *n* **1.** (*round handle: of a door*) pomo *m*; (*of a drawer*) tirador *m* **2.** (*lump*) bulto *m*

knock [nak] **I.** *n* **1.** (*blow*) golpe *m* **2.** (*sound*) golpe *f* **3.** *fig* crítica *f* **II.** *vi* **1.** (*hit*) golpear; **to** ~ **on the window/at the door** llamar a la ventana/puerta **2.** TECH (*engine, pipes*) martillear **III.** *vt* **1.** (*hit*) golpear; **to** ~ **sb** dar un

golpe a alguien **2.** *inf* (*criticize*) criticar
◆**knock about** *vi, vt see* **knock around**
◆**knock around I.** *vi inf* andar vagando, vagabundear **II.** *vt* (*person*) pegar; (*ball*) golpear
◆**knock back** *vt inf* **1.** (*drink quickly*) pimplar rápidamente **2.** (*surprise*) pasmar
◆**knock down** *vt* **1.** (*cause to fall*) derribar **2.** (*demolish*) demoler **3.** (*reduce*) **to knock the price down** bajar el precio
◆**knock off I.** *vt* **1.** (*cause to fall off*) hacer caer **2.** (*reduce*) rebajar; **to knock $5 off the price** rebajar 5 dólares el precio **3.** *sl* (*murder*) cargarse **4.** (*stop*) **to knock it off** dejarlo; **knock it off!** ¡déjalo! **II.** *vi inf* terminar; **to ~ work at 3 p.m.** soltar a las 3 de la tarde
◆**knock out** *vt* **1.** (*render unconscious*) dejar sin sentido; SPORTS dejar K.O.; (*cause to sleep*) hacer dormir; (*exhaust*) agotar **2.** (*eliminate*) eliminar **3.** (*produce quickly*) hacer (en un momento), producir
◆**knock over** *vt* atropellar; (*an object*) volcar
◆**knock together** *vt* construir deprisa, improvisar
knockdown *adj* **1.** (*very cheap*) baratísimo, -a; **~ price** precio *m* de saldo; (*at auction*) precio *m* inicial **2.** (*violent: blow*) duro, -a; (*argument*) arrollador(a); (*fight*) violento, -a
knocker ['nɑk·ər] *n* (*on door*) aldaba *f*
knockout I. *n* **1.** (*competition*) eliminatoria *f* **2.** SPORTS (*boxing*) K.O. *m;* **to win sth by a ~** ganar algo por K.O. **3.** *sl* (*attractive*) bombón *m* **II.** *adj* **1.** (*competition*) eliminatorio, -a **2.** (*boxing*) **~ blow** golpe *m* duro; *fig* duro revés *m* **3.** *sl* (*attractive*) macizo, -a
knot [nɑt] **I.** *n* **1.** (*tied join*) *a.* NAUT nudo *m;* **to tie/untie a ~** hacer/deshacer un nudo **2.** (*bow*) lazo *m* **3.** (*chignon*) moño *m*, chongo *m Méx* **4.** (*small group*) corrillo *m* **5.** (*in a wooden board*) nudo *m* ▶ **to tie the**

~ *inf* prometerse **II.** <-tt> *vt* anudar
know [nou] **I.** <knew, known> *vt* **1.** (*have information*) saber; **to ~ a bit of English** saber un poco de inglés; **she ~s all of their names** se sabe los nombres de todos; **to ~ how to do sth** saber hacer algo; **to ~ all there is to ~ about sth** saber todo lo que se ha de saber sobre algo; **to ~ what one is talking about** saber de lo que uno habla; **to ~ sth by heart** saberse algo de memoria; **not to ~ the first thing about sth/sb** no saber nada de algo/alguien; **do you ~ what I mean?** ¿entiendes?; **you ~ what?** *inf* ¿sabes qué? **2.** (*be acquainted with*) conocer; **to ~ sb by sight/by name/personally** conocer a alguien de vista/por el nombre/personalmente; **~ing Mary,...** conociendo a Mary,...; **to get to ~ each other** llegar a conocerse (bien) **3.** (*recognize*) conocer, reconocer; **to ~ sb for sth** reconocer a alguien por algo **II.** <knew, known> *vi* **1.** (*be informed*) saber; **as far as I ~** por lo que sé; **to ~ better (than sb)** saber más (que alguien); **to ~ of** [*or* about] **sth** saber de algo, estar enterado de algo; **you ~** (*you remember*) ya sabes; (*you understand*) tú ya me entiendes; (*well*) **what do you ~!** *iron* ¡no me digas!; **I ~!** (*I've got an idea!*) ¡ya lo tengo!; (*said to agree with sb*) lo sé **2.** (*be certain*) estar seguro; **one never ~s** nunca se sabe **III.** *n* **to be in the ~ about sth** estar al tanto de algo
know-how *n* know-how *m*
knowing ['nou·ɪŋ] *adj* astuto, -a; (*grins, look, smile*) de complicidad
knowingly *adv* **1.** (*meaningfully*) con conocimiento **2.** (*with full awareness*) a sabiendas
know-it-all ['nou·ɪt̬·ɔl] *n inf* sabelotodo *mf*
knowledge ['nɑl·ɪdʒ] *n* **1.** (*body of learning*) conocimiento *m;* **to have a thorough ~ of sth** conocer algo a fondo **2.** (*acquired information*) saber *m;* **to have (no) ~ about sth/sb** (no) saber de algo/alguien; **to my ~** que yo sepa **3.** (*awareness*) conocimiento *m;* **to do**

sth without sb's ~ hacer algo sin que alguien lo sepa

knowledgeable ['nal·ɪdʒ·ə·bəl] *adj* entendido, -a

known [noun] I. *vt, vi pp of* **know** II. *adj* (*expert*) reconocido, -a; (*criminal*) conocido, -a; **no ~ reason** sin razón aparente; **to make sth ~** dar a conocer algo

knuckle ['nʌk·əl] *n* nudillo *m*

kooky ['ku·ki] <-ier, -iest> *adj sl* majareta

Koran [kə·'ræn] *n* **the ~** el Corán

kosher ['kou·fər] *adj* autorizado, -a por la ley judía

kumquat ['kʌm·kwat] *n* quinoto *m*, naranja *f* china

Kwanzaa ['kwan·zə] *n* kwanzaa *m festival cultural afroamericano*

L

L, l [el] *n* L, l *f;* **~ as in Lima** L de Lisboa

l *abbr of* **liter** l.

LA [,el·'eɪ] *n* **1.** *abbr of* **Los Angeles** Los Ángeles *m* **2.** *abbr of* **Louisiana** Luisiana *f*

lab [læb] *n abbr of* **laboratory** laboratorio *m*

label ['leɪ·bəl] I. *n* **1.** (*on bottle, clothing*) etiqueta *f* **2.** (*brand name*) marca *f* II. <-l- *or* -ll-, -l- *or* -ll-> *vt* (*affix label*) etiquetar

labor ['leɪ·bər] I. *n* **1.** (*work*) trabajo *m;* **manual ~** trabajo manual **2.** ECON (*workers*) mano *f* de obra; **skilled ~** mano de obra cualificada **3.** MED (*childbirth*) parto *m;* **to be in ~** estar de parto II. *vi* **1.** (*work*) trabajar **2.** (*do sth with effort*) esforzarse; **to ~ over sth** esforzarse en algo

laboratory ['læb·rə·,tɔr·i] <-ies> *n* laboratorio *m*

Labor Day *n* Día *m* del Trabajo *(primer lunes de septiembre)*

laborer *n* peón *m*

laborious [lə·'bɔr·i·əs] *adj* (*task*) laborioso, -a

labor union *n* sindicato *m*

labyrinth ['læb·ə·rɪnθ] *n* laberinto *m*

lace [leɪs] I. *n* **1.** (*cloth*) encaje *m*, cinta *f;* (*edging*) puntilla *f* **2.** (*cord*) cordón *m;* **shoe ~s** cordones *m pl* (de zapatos) II. *vt* **1.** (*fasten*) atar **2.** (*add alcohol to*) echar licor a

◆**lace up** *vt* atar

lack [læk] I. *n* falta *f;* **~ of funds** escasez *f* de fondos; **for ~ of ...** por falta de... II. *vt* carecer de; **she ~s talent/experience** le falta talento/experiencia

lacking ['læk·ɪŋ] *adj* **he is ~ in talent/experience** le falta talento/experiencia

lackluster ['læk·,lʌs·tər] *adj* **1.** (*not shiny*) deslustrado, -a **2.** (*dull*) gris

lad [læd] *n inf* chico *m*

ladder ['læd·ər] *n* **1.** (*for climbing*) escalera *f* (de mano) **2.** (*hierarchy*) escala *f;* **to climb the social ~** subir en la escala social

laden ['leɪ·dən] *adj* cargado, -a; **to be ~ with...** estar cargado de...

ladies' room *n* servicio *f* [*or* baño *m*] de señoras

ladle ['leɪ·dəl] I. *n* cucharón *m*, ramillón *m Col, Ven* II. *vt* (*soup*) servir *(con cucharón)*

lady ['leɪ·di] <-ies> *n* señora *f;* (*aristocratic*) dama *f;* **young ~** señorita *f;* **the ~ of the house** la señora de la casa; **cleaning ~** mujer de la limpieza; **ladies and gentlemen!** ¡señoras y señores!

lag [læg] I. *n* (*lapse*) lapso *m* II. <-gg-> *vi* rezagarse; **to ~ behind** (sb/sth) quedarse atrás (con respecto a alguien/ algo)

lager ['la·gər] *n* cerveza *f* rubia

lagging ['læg·ɪŋ] *n* revestimiento *m*

laid [leɪd] *pt, pp of* **lay**[1]

lain [leɪn] *pp of* **lie**[2]

laity ['leɪ·ə·ti] *n* **the ~** el laicado

lake [leɪk] *n* lago *m*

lamb [læm] *n* **1.** (*animal*) cordero *m* **2.** (*meat*) (carne *f* de) cordero *m*

lamb chop *n* chuleta *f* de cordero

lame [leɪm] *adj* **1.** (*person, horse*) cojo, -a **2.** *inf* (*argument*) flojo, -a; (*excuse*) débil, poco convincente

lament [lə·'ment] I. *n* MUS, LIT elegía *f* II. *vt* lamentar III. *vi* **to ~ over sth** lamentarse de algo

lamentable [lə·'mən·tə·bəl] *adj* lamentable

laminated ['læm·ɪ·neɪ·tɪd] *adj* (*document*) plastificado, -a; (*glass, wood*) laminado, -a

lamp [læmp] *n* lámpara *f;* **street ~** farola *f*

lamppost ['læmp·poʊst] *n* farola *f*

lampshade ['læmp·ʃeɪd] *n* pantalla *f* (de lámpara)

land [lænd] I. *n* 1. GEO, AGR tierra *f;* **on ~** en tierra; **to travel by ~** viajar por tierra; **to work (on) the ~** trabajar (en) el campo 2. (*for building*) terreno *m* 3. (*country*) país *m* II. *vi* 1. (*plane, bird*) aterrizar 2. (*arrive by boat*) arribar 3. (*set down, fall on: bird, fly*) posarse 4. (*person, ball*) caer III. *vt* 1. (*bring onto land: aircraft*) (hacer) aterrizar; (*boat*) amarrar 2. (*obtain*) conseguir; **to ~ a job** conseguir un trabajo 3. (*cause*) **to ~ sb in trouble** meter a alguien en un lío

landing ['læn·dɪŋ] *n* 1. AVIAT aterrizaje *m;* **to make a ~** realizar un aterrizaje 2. NAUT desembarco *m* 3. (*on staircase*) rellano *m*

landing gear *n* AVIAT tren *m* de aterrizaje

landing strip *n* pista *f* de aterrizaje

landlady ['lænd·ˌleɪ·di] <-ies> *n* (*of house*) propietaria *f;* (*of boarding house*) patrona *f*

landless *adj* sin tierra

landlocked *adj* cercado, -a de tierra; **a ~ country** un país sin acceso al mar

landlord *n* (*of house*) propietario *m;* (*of boarding house*) patrón *m*

landmark *n* 1. (*object serving as a guide*) mojón *m;* (*point of recognition*) punto *m* destacado, marca *f* 2. (*monument*) monumento *m* histórico II. *adj* (*significant: decision, ruling*) que marca un hito

land mine *n* mina *f* terrestre

landowner *n* terrateniente *mf*

land reform *n* reforma *f* agraria

landscape ['lænd·skeɪp] I. *n* 1. (*scenery, painting*) paisaje *m* 2. *fig* panorama *m* 3. COMPUT impresión *f* apaisada

II. *vt* ajardinar

landslide ['lænd·slaɪd] *n* 1. GEO corrimiento *m* de tierras 2. POL victoria *f* arrolladora; **to win by a ~** ganar por mayoría abrumadora

lane [leɪn] *n* 1. (*marked strip: on highway*) carril *m;* SPORTS calle *f;* **bus/bike ~** carril bus/de bicicleta; **to change ~s** cambiar de carril 2. (*small road*) vereda *f*

language ['læŋ·gwɪdʒ] *n* 1. (*system of communication*) lenguaje *m;* **computer programming ~** lenguaje de programación (de ordenadores); **bad ~** palabrotas *fpl;* **formal/spoken/written ~** lengua formal/oral/escrita 2. (*of particular community*) idioma *m;* **native ~** lengua *f* materna; **the English ~** la lengua inglesa; **to speak the same ~** hablar el mismo idioma

lank [læŋk] *adj* 1. (*hair*) lacio, -a 2. (*person*) larguirucho, -a

lanky ['læŋ·ki] *adj* desgarbado, -a

lantern ['læn·tərn] *n* linterna *f;* (*light*) farol *m*

lap¹ [læp] *n* falda *f*

lap² [læp] SPORTS I. *n* vuelta *f* II. <-pp-> *vt* SPORTS doblar

lap³ [læp] <-pp-> I. *vt* (*drink*) beber dando lengüetazos II. *vi* (*hit gently*) **to ~ against sth** chocar suavemente contra algo

◆**lap up** *vt* 1. (*drink*) beber dando lengüetazos 2. *fig* aceptar entusiasmado; **he lapped up the praise** saboreaba las alabanzas

lapel [lə·'pel] *n* solapa *f*

lapse [læps] I. *n* 1. (*failure*) lapsus *m inv;* **~ of memory** lapsus de memoria 2. (*period*) lapso *m* II. *vi* 1. (*deteriorate*) deteriorarse 2. (*end*) terminar; (*contract*) vencer; (*subscription*) caducar 3. (*revert to*) **to ~ into sth** reincidir en algo; **to ~ into one's native dialect** recurrir al dialecto nativo

lapsed [læpst] *adj* (*membership, subscription*) caducado, -a

laptop (*computer*) ['læp·tap] *n* (ordenador *m*) portátil *m*

larch [lartʃ] *n* BOT alerce *m*

lard [lard] *n* manteca *f* de cerdo

larder ['lar·dər] n despensa f

large [lardʒ] adj grande; **a ~ number of people** un gran número de gente; **a ~ family** una familia numerosa ▶ **to be at ~** andar suelto; **by and ~** por lo general

largely ['lardʒ·li] adv en gran parte

large-scale adj a gran escala

lark[1] [lark] n (bird) alondra f ▶ **to be up with the ~** levantarse con las gallinas

lark[2] [lark] n 1. (joke) broma f 2. (adventure) **to go on a ~** irse a la aventura

laryngitis [ˌler·ɪn·'dʒaɪ·tɪs] n laringitis f inv

laser ['leɪ·zər] n láser m

lash[1] [læʃ] <-es> n (eyelash) pestaña f

lash[2] [læʃ] n. <-es> n 1. (whip) látigo m; (flexible part of a whip) tralla f 2. (stroke of whip) latigazo m II. vt 1. (whip) azotar 2. (criticize) vituperar

◆**lash about** vi, **lash around** vi golpear a diestro y siniestro

◆**lash down** vt atar firmemente

◆**lash out** vi **to ~ at sb** atacar a alguien; (verbally) arremeter contra alguien

last[1] [læst] n (for shoes) horma f

last[2] [læst] I. adj 1. (final: time, opportunity) último, -a; **to have the ~ word** tener la última palabra; **to wait till the ~ minute (to do sth)** esperar hasta el último minuto (para hacer algo) 2. (most recent) último, -a; **~ week** la semana pasada; **~ night** anoche II. adv 1. (at the end) por último; **~ but not least** por último, pero no por eso menos importante 2. (most recently) por última vez III. n **the ~ to do sth** el último en hacer algo; **the second to ~** el penúltimo; **that was the ~ of the cake** era todo lo que quedaba del pastel ▶ **at (long) ~** al fin

last[3] [læst] I. vi durar II. vt **this coat has ~ed me five years** hace cinco años que tengo este abrigo

lasting ['læs·tɪŋ] adj duradero, -a

lastly ['læst·li] adv por último

last name n apellido m

latch [lætʃ] <-es> n pestillo m

late [leɪt] I. adj 1. (after appointed time) retrasado, -a; **you're ~!** ¡llegas tarde!; **the train was an hour ~** el tren llegó con una hora de retraso 2. (after the usual time) tardío, -a 3. (towards end of) ~ **night TV show** programa m de televisión de noche; **in the ~ nineteenth century** a finales del siglo XIX 4. (recent: development) reciente; **~est news** noticias f pl de última hora 5. (deceased) fallecido, -a, difunto, -a II. adv 1. (after usual time) tarde; **too little, too ~** poco y tarde inf; **to work ~** trabajar hasta (muy) tarde 2. (towards end of) ~ **in the day** a última hora del día; **~ at night** (muy) entrada la noche 3. (recently) **as ~ as the 1980s** aún en los años ochenta; **of ~** últimamente ▶ **better ~ than never** prov más vale tarde que nunca prov

latecomer ['leɪt·kʌm·ər] n persona o cosa que llega tarde

lately ['leɪt·li] adv (recently) últimamente, ultimadamente Méx; **until ~** hasta hace poco

later ['leɪ·tər] I. adj comp of **late** posterior II. adv comp of **late** más tarde; **~ on** después; **see you ~!** ¡hasta luego!

latest ['leɪ·tɪst] I. adj superl of **late** último, -a; **the ~...** el más reciente...; **his ~ movie** su última película; **at the ~** a más tardar II. n **the ~** las últimas noticias; **the ~ in art/physics** lo último en arte/física; **at the (very) ~** a más tardar

lathe [leɪð] n torno m

Latin ['læt·ən] I. adj latino, -a II. n 1. LING latín m 2. (person) latino, -a m, f

Latin America n Latinoamérica f, América f Latina

Latin American I. adj latinoamericano, -a II. n (person) latinoamericano, -a m, f

latish ['leɪ·tɪʃ] I. adj (algo) tardío, -a II. adv algo tarde

latitude ['læt·ɪ·tud] n 1. GEO latitud f 2. (freedom) libertad f

latter ['læt·ər] adj (second of two) **the ~** el último; **in the ~ half of the year** en la segunda mitad del año

latterly adv últimamente

laugh [læf] I. n 1. (sound) risa f; **to get a ~** hacer reír; **to do sth for a ~** [or **~s**] hacer algo para divertirse 2. (sth *absurd*) ridículo, -a; **his answer was a ~** su respuesta fue ridícula **II.** *vi* reír(se); **to ~ aloud** reírse a carcajadas; **to make sb ~** hacer reír a alguien; **to ~ at sb/sth** *a. fig* reírse de alguien/algo; **to ~ until one cries** llorar de la risa; **don't make me ~** ¡no me hagas reír! ► **he who ~s last ~s best** *prov* quien ríe el último, ríe mejor *prov*

laughable ['læf·ə·bəl] *adj* de risa

laughing gas *n* gas *m* de la risa [*or* hilarante]

laughter ['læf·tər] *n* risa(s) *f(pl);* **to roar with ~** echarse a reír ► **~ is the best medicine** *prov* quien canta, sus males espanta *prov*

launch [lɒntʃ] **I.** <-ches> *n* **1.** (*boat*) lancha *f* **2.** (*of a boat*) botadura *f* **3.** (*of a missile*) lanzamiento *m* **4.** (*introduction: of exhibition*) inauguración *f* **II.** *vt* **1.** (*set in the water*) botar **2.** (*set in motion: missile*) lanzar **3.** (*start: investigation*) emprender; (*exhibition*) inaugurar

◆**launch into** *vt* emprender

◆**launch out** *vi* lanzarse

launching pad *n,* **launch pad** *n* rampa *f* de lanzamiento

laundry ['lɒn·dri] *n* **1.** (*dirty clothes*) ropa *f* sucia; **to do the ~** hacer la colada **2.** (*washed clothes*) ropa *f* lavada **3.** <-ies> (*place*) lavandería *f*

laundry basket *n* cesto *m* de la ropa sucia

laundry service *n* servicio *m* de lavandería

lavatory ['læv·ə·tɔr·i] <-ies> *n* lavabo *m,* lavatorio *m AmL*

lavish ['læv·ɪʃ] **I.** *adj* (*banquet*) opíparo, -a; (*reception*) fastuoso, -a; (*praise*) abundante **II.** *vt* **to ~ sth on sb** [*or* **to ~ sb with sth**] prodigar algo a alguien

law [lɔ] *n* **1.** *a.* PHYS ley *f* **2.** (*legal system*) derecho *m;* (*body of laws*) ley *f;* **~-and-order** ley y el orden; **his word is ~** lo que él dice va a misa; **to be against the ~** ser ilegal; **to take the ~ into one's own hands** tomarse la justicia por su mano; **the ~ of the jungle** la ley de la selva

law-abiding *adj* observante de la ley

law enforcement *n* aplicación *f* de la ley

lawful ['lɔ·fəl] *adj* (*legal*) legal; (*demands*) legítimo, -a; **~ owner** propietario, -a *m, f* legítimo

lawless ['lɔ·lɪs] *adj* sin ley; (*country*) anárquico, -a

lawn [lɔn] *n* césped *m,* pasto *m AmL*

lawn mower *n* cortacésped *m*

law school *n* facultad *f* de derecho

law student *n* estudiante *mf* de derecho

lawsuit *n* proceso *m* (judicial); **to bring a ~ against sb** presentar una demanda contra alguien

lawyer ['lɔ·jər] *n* abogado, -a *m, f*

lax [læks] *adj* **1.** (*lacking care*) descuidado, -a; **~ security** seguridad *f* poco rigurosa **2.** (*rules*) poco severo, -a, laxo, -a

laxative ['læk·sə·tɪv] **I.** *n* laxante *m* **II.** *adj* laxante

lay¹ [leɪ] **I.** *n* (*situation*) situación *f;* **the ~ of the land** la configuración del terreno; *fig* la situación actual **II.** <laid, laid> *vt* **1.** (*place*) poner; **to ~ sth on/ over sth** poner algo en/encima de algo; **to ~ the blame on sb** echar la culpa a alguien **2.** (*install*) colocar; (*cable*) tender; (*pipes*) instalar; **to ~ the foundation for sth** *a. fig* poner los cimientos de algo **3.** (*egg*) poner **4.** (*state*) presentar; **to ~ sth before sb** poner algo frente a alguien; **to ~ claim to sth** reclamar algo **III.** <laid, laid> *vi* poner huevos

◆**lay about** *vt* **to ~ sb** emprenderla a golpes con alguien

◆**lay aside** *vt* (*put away*) guardar

◆**lay back** *vt* reposar

◆**lay by** *vt* reservar

◆**lay down** *vt* **1.** (*put down*) poner a un lado; (*arms*) deponer; (*life*) sacrificar **2.** (*establish*) estipular; (*law*) dictar

◆**lay into** *vt sl* **1.** (*assault*) atacar **2.** (*criticize*) arremeter contra

◆**lay off I.** *vt* despedir (temporalmente) **II.** *vi sl* dejar; **to ~ sb** dejar en paz a alguien; **to ~ smoking** dejar de fumar

◆**lay on** *vt* **1.** (*provide: food, drink*) proveer de **2.** *sl* (*reveal*) **to ~ sth on sb** contarle algo a alguien

◆**lay out** vt **1.** (*organize*) organizar **2.** (*explain*) presentar **3.** (*spread out*) extender **4.** inf (*money*) gastar

◆**lay up** vt **1.** (*store*) guardar **2.** (*ship*) desarmar; (*car*) dejar en el garaje **3.** (*in bed*) **to be laid up** guardar cama

lay² [leɪ] adj **1.** (*not professional*) lego, -a; **in ~ terms** en términos profanos **2.** REL laico, -a

lay³ [leɪ] pt of **lie²**

layabout ['leɪ-ə-ˌbaʊt] n inf vago, -a m, f

layaway ['leɪ-ə-ˌweɪ] n **to buy/put on ~** comprar/reservar (mediante el pago de un depósito)

layer¹ ['leɪ-ər] I. n **1.** (*of dust, paint*) capa f; **ozone ~** capa de ozono **2.** (*level*) estrato m, capa f II. vt acodar

layer² ['leɪ-ər] n ZOOL (*hen*) gallina f ponedora

layered adj en capas

layout ['leɪ-aʊt] n **1.** (*of letter, magazine*) diseño m; (*of town*) trazado m **2.** TYPO maquetación f

layover ['leɪ-oʊ-vər] n (*on journey*) parada f; AVIAT escala f

laziness ['leɪ-zɪ-nɪs] n holgazanería f

lazy ['leɪ-zi] <-ier, -iest> adj (*person*) vago, -a; (*day*) en el/la que no se hace nada, sin hacer nada

lead¹ [lid] I. n **1.** (*front position*) delantera f; **to be in the ~** estar en cabeza; **to hold the ~** llevar la delantera; **to move into the ~** ponerse en cabeza; **to take the ~** tomar la delantera **2.** (*example*) ejemplo m; (*guiding*) iniciativa f; **to follow sb's ~** seguir el ejemplo de alguien **3.** THEAT papel m principal; **to play the ~** representar el papel principal **4.** (*clue, tip*) pista f; **to get a ~ on sth** recibir una pista acerca de algo **5.** (*connecting wire*) cable m, conductor m **6.** (*dog leash*) correa f II. <led, led> vt **1.** (*be in charge of*) dirigir; (*discussion, inquiry*) conducir **2.** (*conduct*) conducir, llevar; **to ~ the way** ir primero; fig mostrar el camino **3.** (*induce*) inducir; **to ~ sb to do sth** llevar a alguien a hacer algo; **to ~ sb to believe that...** hacer creer a alguien que... **4.** COM, SPORTS (*be ahead of*) liderar **5.** (*live a particular*

way: life) llevar; **to ~ a life of luxury** llevar una vida de lujo III. <led, led> vi **1.** (*be in charge*) dirigir **2.** (*guide followers*) guiar **3.** (*conduct*) llevar; **to ~ to/into sth** conducir a/hacia algo **4.** (*be ahead*) ser líder; **to ~ by 2 laps** tener una ventaja de 2 vueltas

◆**lead along** vt llevar (de la mano)

◆**lead aside** vt llevar a un lado

◆**lead astray** vt llevar por mal camino

◆**lead away** vt llevar

◆**lead back** vt hacer volver

◆**lead off** I. vt (*person*) llevar afuera; (*room*) comunicar con II. vi empezar

◆**lead on** vt (*trick, fool*) engañar; (*encourage*) incitar a; **she doesn't want to lead him on** no quiere darle falsas expectativas

lead² [led] n **1.** (*metal*) plomo m **2.** (*in pencil*) mina f **3.** NAUT sonda f

leaded ['led-əd] adj emplomado, -a; **~ fuel** gasolina f con plomo

lead-free [led-fri] adj sin plomo

leading ['li-dɪŋ] I. adj (*main, principle*) principal II. n mando m

lead pencil n lápiz m de mina

lead poisoning n saturnismo m

lead singer n cantante mf principal

lead story n PUBL artículo m principal

leader ['li-dər] n **1.** (*of group*) líder mf **2.** (*guide*) guía mf

leadership ['li-dər-ʃɪp] n **1.** (*ability to lead*) liderazgo m; **~ qualities** dotes fpl de mando **2.** (*leaders*) dirección f

leaf [lif] <leaves> n **1.** (*of plant*) hoja f **2.** (*foliage*) follaje m **3.** (*piece of paper*) hoja f; **~ of paper** hoja de papel **4.** (*thin layer*) **gold/silver ~** baño m en oro/plata **5.** (*of table*) tablero m ▶ **to shake like a ~** temblar como una pluma; **to turn over a new ~** hacer borrón y cuenta nueva

leaflet ['lif-lɪt] n folleto m

leafy ['li-fi] <-ier, -iest> adj frondoso, -a

league [lig] n **1.** a. SPORTS liga f; **soccer ~** liga de fútbol; **to be/not to be in the same ~ as sb/sth** fig estar/no estar a la altura de alguien/algo; **to be out of sb's ~** no tener comparación con alguien **2.** (*measurement*) legua f

leak [lik] I. n (*of gas, water*) fuga f; (*of in-*

formation) filtración f; (in roof) gotera f
II. vi **1.** (let sth escape) tener una fuga;
(tire) perder aire; (hose, bucket) perder
(agua); (faucet) gotear **2.** (information)
filtrarse **III.** vt **1.** (let escape) derramar;
to ~ water perder (agua) **2.** (information) filtrar

leaky ['liˑki] <-ier, -iest> adj que tiene fugas

lean¹ [liˑn] **I.** <-ed, -ed> vi inclinarse; **to
~ against sth** apoyarse en algo **II.** <-ed,
-ed> vt apoyar; **to ~ sth against algo**
apoyar algo contra algo

◆**lean on** vt **1.** (rely on) apoyarse en
2. sl (pressure) ejercer presión sobre

◆**lean over I.** vt inclinarse sobre **II.** vi
inclinarse

lean² [liˑn] adj **1.** (thin) flaco, -a; (face) enjuto, -a; (with little fat: meat) magro, -a
2. (efficient: company) eficiente

leaning ['liˑnɪŋ] n inclinación f

leap [liˑp] **I.** <leaped or leapt, leaped
or leapt> vi saltar; **to ~ forward** saltar hacia adelante; **to ~ to sb's defense** saltar en defensa de alguien; **his
heart ~ed** le dio un vuelco el corazón
II. <leaped or leapt, leaped or leapt>
vt saltar **III.** n salto m; **to take a ~**
dar un salto ▸ **by ~s and bounds** a
pasos de gigante; **a ~ in the dark** un
salto al vacío

◆**leap out** vi saltar

◆**leap up** vi (jump up) ponerse en pie
de un salto

leapfrog ['liˑp,frɔg] **I.** n potro m, pídola f;
to play a game of ~ jugar a saltar al potro, jugar a la pídola, saltar el burro Méx
II. <-gg-> vt pasar por encima de

leapt [lept] vt, vi pt, pp of **leap**

leap year n año m bisiesto

learn [lɜrn] **I.** <learned, learned> vt
aprender; **to ~ that** enterarse de que
II. <learned, learned> vi aprender; **to
~ to do sth** aprender a hacer algo; **to ~
from one's mistakes** aprender de los
propios errores

learned ['lɜrnɪd] adj erudito, -a

learner ['lɜrnər] n aprendiz mf; **to be a
quick ~** aprender rápido

learning ['lɜrnɪŋ] n **1.** (acquisition of
knowledge) aprendizaje m **2.** (extensive

knowledge) saber m

learning disability n <-ies> dificultad f
de aprendizaje

lease [liˑs] **I.** vt alquilar **II.** n (act) arrendamiento m ▸ **a new ~ on life** el co-
mienzo de una nueva vida

leaseholder ['liˑs,hoʊl,dər] n arrendatario, -a m, f

leash [liˑʃ] n correa f ▸ **to keep sb on a
tight ~** atar corto a alguien

least [liˑst] **I.** adj mínimo, -a; (age) menor **II.** adv menos; **the ~ possible** lo
menos posible **III.** n lo menos; **at (the
very) ~** por lo menos, al menos; **not in
the ~!** ¡en absoluto!; **to say the ~** para
no decir más

leather ['leð·ər] n cuero m

leathery ['leð·ə·ri] adj (skin) curtido, -a;
(meat) correoso, -a

leave¹ [liˑv] **I.** <left, left> vt **1.** (depart
from) salir de; (school, college) aban-
donar; (work) dejar; **to ~ home** irse
de casa **2.** (not take away with) dejar;
(forget) olvidar(se); **to ~ sth to sb** dejar
algo a alguien **3.** (put in a situation) **to
~ sb alone** dejar a alguien en paz; **to be
left homeless** quedarse sin hogar ▸ **to
~ a lot to be desired** dejar mucho que
desear; **to ~ it at that** dejarlo **II.** <left,
left> vi marcharse, despabilarse AmL
III. n partida f; **to take (one's) ~ (of sb)**
despedirse (de alguien)

◆**leave behind** vt **1.** (forget) olvidar
2. (progress beyond) dejar atrás

◆**leave off** **I.** vt **1.** (give up) dejar de
2. (omit) omitir **II.** vi acabar

◆**leave on** vt dejar(se) puesto; (light) dejar encendido

◆**leave out** vt **1.** (omit) omitir **2.** (exclude) excluir

◆**leave over** vt dejar; **there's nothing
left over** no queda nada

leave² [liˑv] n permiso m; **to go/be on ~**
MIL salir/estar de permiso

lecture ['lek·tʃər] **I.** n a. UNIV conferencia f, clase f; **a ~ on sth** una conferencia
acerca de algo; **to give sb a ~** fig
sermonear a alguien **II.** vi (give a lecture)
dar una conferencia; (teach) dar clases
III. vt (give a lecture) dar una conferencia a; (teach) dar clases a

lecture notes *npl* apuntes *m pl* (de clase)

lecturer ['lek·tʃər·ər] *n* conferenciante *mf*; UNIV profesor(a) *m(f)* universitario, -a

lecture tour *n* gira *f* de conferencias

led [led] *pt, pp of* **lead**[1]

LED [ˌel·iˈdi] *n abbr of* **light-emitting diode** LED *m*

ledge [ledʒ] *n* (*shelf*) repisa *f*; (*on building*) cornisa *f*; (*on cliff*) saliente *m*; **window ~** alféizar *m*

ledger ['ledʒ·ər] *n* COM libro *m* mayor

leek [lik] *n* CULIN puerro *m*

leery ['lɪr·i] *adj* desconfiado, -a, receloso, -a; **to be ~ of sb/sth** desconfiar de alguien/algo

leeway ['li·wei] *n* flexibilidad *f*

left[1] [left] *pt, pp of* **leave**[1]

left[2] [left] **I.** *n* **1.** (*direction, sight*) izquierda *f*; **the ~** la izquierda; **to turn to the ~** girar a la izquierda; **on/to the/her ~** en/a la/su izquierda **2.** POL izquierda *f*; **on the ~** de izquierda(s) **II.** *adj* izquierdo, -a **III.** *adv* a [*or* hacia] la izquierda; **to turn ~** girar hacia la izquierda

left-hand *adj* a la izquierda; **~ side** lado *m* izquierdo; **~ turn** curva *f* a la izquierda

left-handed *adj* zurdo, -a; **~ scissors** tijeras *f pl* para zurdos

left-hander *n* zurdo, -a *m, f*

leftist ['lef·tɪst] POL **I.** *adj* izquierdista **II.** *n* izquierdista *mf*

leftovers ['left·ˌoʊ·vərz] *npl* **1.** (*food*) sobras *fpl* **2.** (*remaining things*) restos *mpl*

left wing *n* POL izquierda *f*

left-wing *adj* POL de izquierda

left-winger *n* POL izquierdista *mf*

leg [leg] *n* **1.** (*of person*) pierna *f*; (*of animal, furniture*) pata *f* **2.** (*of pants*) pernera *f* **3.** CULIN (*of lamb, pork*) pierna *f*; (*of chicken*) muslo *m* **4.** (*segment of journey*) etapa *f* ▶ **to be on one's last ~s** estar para el arrastre; **break a ~!** ¡mucha suerte!; **to pull sb's ~** *inf* tomar el pelo a alguien

legal ['li·gəl] *adj* **1.** (*in accordance with law*) legal **2.** (*concerning the law*) jurídico, -a

legality [liˈgæl·ə·ți] *n* legalidad *f*

legalize ['li·gə·laɪz] *vt* legalizar

legally ['li·gə·li] *adv* legalmente

legend ['ledʒ·ənd] *n* leyenda *f*; **~ has it that...** dice la leyenda que...

legendary ['ledʒ·ən·der·i] *adj* legendario, -a

leggings ['leg·ɪŋz] *npl* mallas *fpl*

leggy ['leg·i] <-ier, -iest> *adj* patilargo, -a

legible ['ledʒ·ə·bəl] *adj* legible

legitimacy [ləˈdʒɪt·ə·mə·si] *n* legitimidad *f*

legitimate[1] [ləˈdʒɪt·ə·mɪt] *adj* **1.** (*legal*) legal; **a ~ government** un gobierno legítimo **2.** (*reasonable*) válido, -a

legitimate[2] [ləˈdʒɪt·ə·meɪt] *vt* legitimar

legroom ['leg·rum] *n* espacio *m* para las piernas

leisure ['li·ʒər] *n* **1.** ocio *m* **2. call me at your ~** llámame cuando tengas tiempo

leisurely I. *adj* pausado, -a **II.** *adv* pausadamente

leisure time *n* tiempo *m* libre

lemon ['lem·ən] *n* **1.** (*fruit*) limón *m*; **a slice of ~** una rodaja de limón **2.** (*color*) amarillo *m* limón **3.** *inf* (*defective object*) patata *f*

lemonade [ˌlem·əˈneɪd] *n* limonada *f*

lemon juice *n* zumo *m* de limón

lemon peel *n* corteza *f* de limón

lend [lend] <lent, lent> **I.** *vt* **1.** (*give temporarily*) prestar; **to ~ money to sb** prestar dinero a alguien **2.** (*impart, provide*) dar; **to ~ support to a view** apoyar una opinión ▶ **to ~ a hand to sb** echar una mano a alguien; **to ~ one's name to sth** ofrecer su nombre para algo **II.** *vi* prestar dinero

lender ['len·dər] *n* FIN prestamista *mf*

lending ['len·dɪŋ] *n* préstamo *m*

length [leŋkθ] *n* **1.** (*measurement*) longitud *f*; **it's 3 yards in ~** tiene 3 yardas de largo; (*along*) **the ~ of sth** a lo largo de algo **2.** (*piece: of pipe, rope*) trozo *m* **3.** (*of swimming pool*) largo *m* **4.** (*duration*) duración *f*; (*for*) **any ~ of time** (por) cualquier lapso de tiempo; **at ~** al fin, finalmente; **at great ~** detalladamente ▶ **to go to great ~s to do sth** dar el máximo para hacer algo

lengthen ['leŋk·θən] I. vt 1. (in time) prolongar 2. (physically) alargar II. vi (physically) alargarse

lengthways ['leŋkθ·weɪz] adv, adj, **lengthwise** ['leŋkθ·waɪz] adv, adj a lo largo

lengthy ['leŋk·θi] <-ier, -iest> adj prolongado, -a; (speech) prolijo, -a

lenience ['li·ni·ənts] n, **leniency** n indulgencia f

lenient ['li·ni·ənt] adj (judge) indulgente; (punishment) poco severo, -a

lens [lenz] <-es> n 1. (of glasses) lente m o f; **contact ~es** lentes f pl de contacto, lentillas fpl 2. (of camera) objetivo m; **zoom ~** lente de acercamiento 3. ANAT cristalino m

lent [lent] pt, pp of **lend**

Lent [lent] n Cuaresma f

lentil ['len·təl] n lenteja f

Leo ['li·oʊ] n Leo m

leopard ['lep·ərd] n leopardo m ▶ **a ~ can't change its spots** prov el árbol que nace torcido jamás sus ramas endereza prov, el que nace barrigón ni que lo fajen chiquito Ven prov

leotard ['li·ə·tard] n malla f

lesbian ['lez·bi·ən] I. n lesbiana f II. adj lésbico, -a

less [les] comp of **little** I. adj (in degree, size) menor; (in quantity) menos; **sth of ~ value** algo de menor valor; **~ wine/fat** menos vino/grasa II. adv menos; to drink ~ beber menos; to see sb ~ ver menos a alguien; **~ than 10** menos de [or que] 10; **not him, much ~ her** él no, y mucho menos ella III. pron menos; **~ than...** menos que...; **~ and ~** cada vez menos; **the ~ you eat, the ~ you get fat** cuanto menos comas, menos gordo estarás IV. prep menos

lessen ['les·ən] I. vi (danger) reducirse; (pain) aliviarse II. vt (diminish) disminuir; (risk) reducir; (pain) aliviar

lesser ['les·ər] adj comp of **less** menor; **to a ~ extent** en menor grado

lesson ['les·ən] n 1. SCHOOL clase f; **~s** lecciones fpl 2. fig lección f; **to learn one's ~** aprenderse la lección; **to teach sb a ~** dar a alguien una lección

lest [lest] conj liter 1. (for fear that) no sea que +subj; **I didn't do it ~ he should come** no lo hice por si venía 2. (if) en caso de que +subj

let¹ [let] n SPORTS let m

let² [let] vt <let, let> 1. (allow) dejar; **~ sb do sth** dejar a alguien hacer algo; **to ~ sb know sth** hacer saber algo a alguien; **to ~ sth pass** pasar algo por alto; **~ him be!** ¡déjalo en paz! 2. (in suggestions) **~'s go!** ¡vámonos!; **~'s say...** digamos...; **~ us pray** oremos 3. inf (filler while thinking) **~'s see** veamos; **~ me think** déjame pensar ▶ **~ alone...** (y) menos aún...; **to ~ sb have it** decir cuatro verdades a alguien; **to ~ sth lie** dejar algo como está; **to ~ it rip** correr

◆ **let by** vt dejar pasar

◆ **let down** vt 1. (disappoint) decepcionar 2. (lower) bajar; (hair) soltar; **to let one's hair down** a. fig soltarse el pelo

◆ **let in** vt (person) dejar entrar; (light) dejar pasar ▶ **to let sb in on sth** revelar un secreto a alguien

◆ **let off** vt (forgive) perdonar; **to let sb off with a fine** poner sólo una multa a alguien

◆ **let on** vi inf (divulge) **to not ~ about sth** callarse algo

◆ **let out** vt 1. (release) dejar salir; (prisoner) poner en libertad; (laugh) soltar; **to ~ a scream** pegar un grito inf 2. (reveal: secret) revelar

◆ **let up** vi 1. (become weaker, stop) debilitarse; (rain) amainar; (cold) suavizarse 2. (relent) aflojar; **to ~ on sb** ser menos duro con alguien; **to ~ on the gas** soltar el acelerador

lethal ['li·θəl] adj letal; (poison) mortífero, -a; (weapon) mortal

lethargic [lɪ·'θɑr·dʒɪk] adj (lacking energy) letárgico, -a

letter ['let̬·ər] n 1. (message) carta f; **~ of recommendation** carta de recomendación; **~ of credit** letra de crédito 2. (symbol) letra f ▶ **to the ~** al pie de la letra

letter bomb n carta f bomba

letterhead n (logo) membrete m; (paper) papel m membretedado

lettering ['let̬·ər·ɪŋ] n caracteres mpl

lettuce ['let̬·ɪs] n lechuga f

leukemia [luˈkiˑmiˑə] n leucemia f

level [ˈlev·əl] I. adj 1. (horizontal) horizontal; (flat) plano, -a; (spoonful) raso, -a 2. (having same height) **to be ~ with sth** estar a la misma altura que algo 3. (in same position) **to be ~ with sb/sth** estar a la par de alguien/algo 4. (of same amount) igual 5. (voice) mesurado, -a; **to keep a ~ head** no perder la cabeza II. adv a nivel III. n 1. (position, amount) nivel m 2. (height) altura f; **above sea ~** sobre el nivel del mar; **at ground ~** a ras de tierra 3. (position in hierarchy) categoría f; **at the (very) highest ~** en el nivel más alto 4. (quality of performance) nivel m; **intermediate ~ students** estudiantes mf pl de nivel intermedio 5. (meaning) **on another ~** en otro sentido ▶ **to be on the ~** (business, person) ser serio IV. <-l- or -ll-> vt 1. (smoothen, flatten) nivelar 2. (demolish completely) arrasar 3. (point) **to ~ sth at sb** apuntar con algo a alguien

◆**level off** vi, **level out** vi (aircraft) nivelarse; (inflation) equilibrarse

◆**level up** vt igualar

◆**level with** vt inf sincerarse con

lever [ˈlev·ər] I. n palanca f II. vt apalancar, palanquear AmL

levy [ˈlev·i] I. <-ies> n tasa f II. <-ie-> vt imponer; **to ~ a tax on sth** gravar algo con un impuesto

lewd [lud] adj (person) lascivo, -a; (gesture, remark) obsceno, -a

liability [ˌlaɪ·ə·ˈbɪl·ə·t̬i] n 1. FIN, LAW responsabilidad f; **to accept ~ for sth** hacerse responsable de algo f 2. FIN **liabilities** deudas fpl

liable [ˈlaɪ·ə·bəl] adj 1. (prone) propenso, -a; **to be ~ to do sth** ser propenso a hacer algo 2. LAW responsable; **to be ~ for sth** ser responsable de algo

liaison [liˑeɪ·zan] n 1. a. LING (contact) enlace m; (person) oficial mf de enlace 2. (sexual affair) aventura f

liar [ˈlaɪ·ər] n mentiroso, -a m, f

lib [lɪb] n inf abbr of **liberation** liberación f

libel [ˈlaɪ·bəl] n LAW libelo m; PUBL difamación f; **to sue sb for ~** demandar a alguien por difamación

libelous [ˈlaɪ·bə·ləs] adj LAW, PUBL difamatorio, -a

liberal [ˈlɪb·ər·əl] I. adj 1. (tolerant) a. POL liberal 2. (generous) generoso, -a 3. (not strict: interpretation) amplio, -a II. n liberal mf

liberate [ˈlɪb·ə·reɪt] vt (free) liberar; **to ~ oneself from sth/sb** librarse de algo/alguien

liberation [ˌlɪb·ə·ˈreɪ·ʃən] n liberación f

liberty [ˈlɪb·ər·t̬i] n form 1. (freedom) libertad f; **to take the ~ of doing sth** tomarse la libertad de hacer algo; **to take liberties with sb** tomarse libertades con alguien 2. **liberties** pl (rights) derechos mpl

Libra [ˈli·brə] n Libra m

librarian [laɪ·ˈbrer·i·ən] n bibliotecario, -a m, f

library [ˈlaɪ·brer·i] n <-ies> (place) biblioteca f; **film ~** filmoteca f; **newspaper ~** hemeroteca f

lice [laɪs] npl see **louse**.

license [ˈlaɪ·səns] I. n 1. (document) licencia f, permiso m; **driver's ~** carnet m [or permiso m] de conducir; **gun ~** permiso m de armas 2. (freedom) libertad f; **artistic ~** libertad artística II. vt autorizar

licensed adj autorizado, -a; **to be ~ to do sth** tener la autorización para hacer algo

lick [lɪk] I. n 1. (with tongue) lamedura f 2. inf (try) **to give sth a ~** intentar algo 3. (salt stick) bloque m de sal (para el ganado) II. vt 1. (with tongue) lamer 2. sl (defeat) derrotar 3. sl (beat up) dar una paliza a

lid [lɪd] n 1. (for container) tapa f, tape m Cuba, PRico 2. fig (limit) tope m 3. (eyelid) párpado m ▶ **to keep the ~ on sth** ocultar algo

lie[1] [laɪ] I. <-y-> vi mentir; **to ~ about sth** mentir sobre algo II. <-y-> vt **to ~ oneself out of sth** salvarse de algo por una mentira III. n mentira f, guayaba f AmL, boleto m Arg; **to be an outright ~** ser una falsedad total; **to live a ~** vivir en la mentira

lie[2] [laɪ] I. <lay, lain> vi 1. (be lying

down: *person*) estar tumbado; **to ~ in bed** estar acostado en la cama; **to ~ on the ground** estar tumbado en el suelo; **to ~ still** quedarse inmóvil **2.** (*be positioned*) hallarse; **to ~ off the coast** (*boat*) hallarse lejos de la costa; **to ~ to the east of...** quedar al este de...; **to ~ in wait** estar a la espera **3.** *form* (*be buried*) estar enterrado, -a **4. to ~ with sb/sth** (*be responsibility of*) corresponder a alguien/algo; (*be the reason for sth*) ser culpa de alguien/algo **5.** SPORTS ubicarse **II.** *n* posición *f*

◆**lie around** *vi* **1.** (*be somewhere*) estar por ahí tirado **2.** (*be lazy*) holgazanear

◆**lie back** *vi* recostarse

◆**lie down** *vi* (*act*) acostarse **2.** *inf* (*do nothing*) **to ~ on the job** no hacer su trabajo; **to take sth lying down** aceptar algo sin protestar

lien [lɪn] *n* derecho *m* de retención

lieu [lu] *n* **in ~ of** en lugar de

lieutenant [luˈten·ənt] *n* **1.** MIL teniente *mf* **2.** (*assistant*) lugarteniente *mf*

life [laɪf] <lives> *n* **1.** vida *f*; **plant ~** vida vegetal; **private ~** vida privada; **to be full of ~** estar lleno de vida; **to lose one's ~** perder la vida; **to take sb's ~** matar a alguien; **to take one's (own) ~** quitarse la vida, suicidarse **2.** (*existence*) existencia *f*; **to want sth out of ~** querer algo de la vida **3.** (*duration*) vida *f* (*útil*), duración *f* **4.** *sl* (*prison sentence*) cadena *f* perpetua; **to get ~** ser condenado a cadena perpetua ► **to be a matter of ~ and death** ser un asunto de vida o muerte; **to take one's ~ in one's hands** jugarse la vida; **to risk ~ and limb** (**to do sth**) jugarse la vida (para hacer algo); **to lay one's ~ on the line** poner la vida en peligro; **to be the ~ of the party** ser el alma de la fiesta; **to live the good ~** darse la buena vida; **~ is hard!** *iron inf* ¡qué le vamos a hacer!; **to breathe (new) ~ into sth** infundir (nueva) vida a algo; **to bring sth to ~** animar algo; **to come to ~** volver a la vida; **to frighten the ~ out of sb** dar un susto de muerte a alguien; **to give one's ~ for sb/sth** dar la vida por alguien/algo; **to make a new ~** em-

pezar una nueva vida; **~** de por vida; **I'm not able for the ~ of me to...** por mucho que lo intente no puedo...; **not on your ~!** *inf* ¡ni hablar!; **that's ~!** ¡así es la vida!; **this is the ~ (for me)!** ¡esto sí es vida!

lifeboat *n* bote *m* salvavidas

life cycle *n* ciclo *m* vital

life expectancy <-ies> *n* esperanza *f* de vida

life form *n* forma *f* de vida

lifeguard *n* socorrista *mf*, salvavidas *mf inv AmL*

life insurance *n* seguro *m* de vida

life jacket *n* chaleco *m* salvavidas

lifeless [ˈlaɪf·lɪs] *adj* **1.** (*dead*) sin vida **2.** *fig* flojo, -a

lifelike [ˈlaɪf·laɪk] *adj* natural

lifelong [ˌlaɪfˈlɒŋ] *adj* de toda la vida

life raft *n* bote *m* salvavidas

lifesaver *n* socorrista *mf*

life sentence *n* condena *f* a cadena perpetua

lifestyle *n* estilo *m* de vida

life-threatening *adj* mortífero, -a

lifetime *n* **1.** (*of person*) vida *f*; **in my ~** durante mi vida; **to happen once in a ~** suceder una vez en la vida; **~ guarantee** garantía *f* de por vida **2.** *inf* (*eternity*) eternidad *f*

lift [lɪft] **I.** *n* **1.** (*upward motion*) elevación *f* **2.** AVIAT fuerza *f* de ascensión **3.** *fig* (*positive feeling*) ánimos *mpl* **4.** (*hoisting device*) montacargas *m inv* **5.** *inf* (*help*) ayuda *f* **6.** *inf* (*car ride*) viaje *m* en coche (*gratuito*) aventón *m Méx*; **to give sb a ~** llevar (en coche) a alguien **II.** *vi* levantarse **III.** *vt* **1.** (*move upwards*) levantar; (*slightly*) alzar; **to ~ one's eyes** alzar los ojos; **to ~ one's head** levantar la cabeza; **to ~ one's voice to sb** (*yell at*) levantar la voz a alguien **2.** (*stop*) suprimir; **to ~ restrictions** levantar las restricciones **3.** (*encourage*) animar; **to ~ sb's spirits** levantar los ánimos de alguien **4.** (*move by air*) transportar (en avión) **5.** *inf* (*steal*) mangar

◆**lift down** *vt* bajar con cuidado

◆**lift off** *vi* AVIAT despegar

◆**lift up** *vt* alzar; **to ~ one's head** levantar la cabeza

ligament ['lɪg·ə·mənt] *n* ligamento *m*

light [laɪt] I. *n* 1. (*energy, brightness*) luz *f;* **by the ~ of the moon** a la luz de la luna 2. (*daytime*) luz *f* (de día) 3. (*source of brightness*) luz *f;* (*lamp*) lámpara *f;* **to turn a ~ off/on** apagar/ encender una luz; **~s out** *inf* (*bedtime*) hora *f* de apagar la luz 4. (*traffic light*) semáforo *m* 5. (*flame*) fuego *m;* **do you have a ~?** ¿tienes fuego? 6. (*clarification, insight*) comprensión *f;* **to bring sth to ~** sacar algo a la luz; **to cast** [*or* **shed**] **~ on sth** arrojar luz sobre algo; **to come to ~** salir a la luz 7. (*perspective*) perspectiva *f;* **to see things in a new ~** ver las cosas desde otra perspectiva 8. *fig* (*joy, inspiration*) sol *m;* **you are the ~ of my life** eres mi sol ▶ **to see the ~ at the end of the tunnel** ver la luz al final del túnel; **to go out like a ~** *inf* (*fall asleep quickly*) quedarse dormido enseguida II. *adj* 1. (*not heavy*) ligero, -a; **a ~ touch** un pequeño toque 2. (*not dark: color*) claro, -a; (*skin*) blanco, -a; (*room*) luminoso, -a 3. (*not serious*) ligero, -a; **~ opera** opereta *f* 4. (*not intense: breeze, rain*) leve; **to be a ~ sleeper** tener el sueño ligero 5. CULIN frugal; **a ~ meal** una comida ligera 6. (*with few calories*) bajo, -a en calorías, dietético, -a, light III. *adv* ligeramente ▶ **to get off ~** salir bien parado; **to make ~ of sth** no dar importancia a algo IV. *vt* <lit *or* lighted> 1. (*illuminate*) iluminar; **to ~ the way** mostrar el camino 2. (*start burning*) encender, prender *AmL;* **to ~ a cigarette** encender un cigarrillo V. *vi* <lit *or* lighted> (*catch fire*) encenderse

◆**light up** I. *vt* 1. alumbrar, iluminar 2. (*cigarette*) encender II. *vi* 1. (*become bright*) iluminarse 2. (*become animated*) animarse; **his face lit up se** le iluminó la cara 3. (*start smoking*) encender un cigarrillo

light bulb *n* bombilla *f,* foco *m AmL*

lighten ['laɪ·tən] I. *vi* 1. (*become brighter*) clarear 2. (*become less heavy*) aligerarse; (*mood*) alegrarse II. *vt* 1. (*make less heavy*) aligerar 2. (*bleach, make*

paler) aclarar

lighter ['laɪ·tər] *n* mechero *m,* encendedor *m AmL*

lightheaded *adj* 1. (*faint*) mareado, -a 2. (*excited*) delirante

lighthouse *n* faro *m*

lighting ['laɪ·tɪŋ] *n* iluminación *f*

lightly ['laɪt·li] *adv* ligeramente; (*to rest, touch*) levemente; **to take sth ~** tomar algo a la ligera; **to get off ~** salir bien parado

lightning ['laɪt·nɪŋ] *n* relámpago *m;* **a bolt of ~** un relámpago; **thunder and ~** rayos y centellas

lightning rod *n* pararrayos *m inv*

lightweight I. *adj* (*clothing, material*) ligero, -a II. *n* 1. SPORTS peso *m* ligero 2. *sl* (*unimpressive person*) persona *f* de poco peso

light-year *n* año *m* luz; **to be ~s away** *inf* estar a años luz de distancia

likable ['laɪ·kə·bəl] *adj* simpático, -a

like¹ [laɪk] I. *vt* 1. (*find good*) **I ~ it** (esto) me gusta; **she ~s apples** le gustan las manzanas; **I ~ swimming** me gusta nadar; **I ~ her** (ella) me cae bien; **he ~s classical music** le gusta la música clásica; **I ~ it when/how...** me gusta cuando/cómo... 2. (*desire, wish*) querer; **I would ~ to go to...** me gustaría ir a...; **would you ~ a cup of tea?** ¿quieres un té?; **I'd ~ to know...** quisiera saber...; **I'd ~ a steak** querría un filete II. *n* **~s** gustos *mpl;* **sb's ~s and dislikes** las preferencias de alguien

like² [laɪk] I. *adj* semejante; **to be of ~ mind** pensar de la misma manera II. *prep* 1. **to be ~ sb/sth** ser como alguien/algo; **what was it ~?** ¿cómo fue?; **what does it look ~?** ¿cómo es?, ¿qué aspecto tiene?; **to work ~ crazy** *inf* trabajar como un burro; **there's nothing ~...** no hay nada que se parezca a... 2. *sl* **to be ~ ...** (*say*) decir ▶ **anything** a más no poder III. *conj inf* como si +*subj;* **he speaks ~ he was drunk** habla como si estuviera borracho; **he doesn't do it ~ I do** él no lo hace como yo IV. *n* 1. (*similar things*) **toys, games and the ~** juguetes, juegos y cosas por el estilo 2. *inf* **the ~s of sth/sb**

algo/gente como algo/alguien

likeable adj see **likable**

likelihood ['laɪk·li·hʊd] n probabilidad f; **in all** ~ con toda probabilidad

likely ['laɪk·li] I. <-ier, -iest> adj probable; **it is** ~ **(that...)** es probable (que... +subj); **to be quite/very** ~ ser bastante/muy probable; **to be a** ~ **story** iron ser un cuento chino, ser puro cuento AmL; **not** ~! inf ¡ni hablar! II. adv probablemente; **most/very** ~ muy probablemente

like-minded adj del mismo parecer

liken ['laɪ·kən] vt comparar; **to** ~ **sb to sb** comparar alguien con alguien

likeness ['laɪk·nɪs] <-es> n (similarity) semejanza f

likewise ['laɪk·waɪz] adv de la misma forma, asimismo; **to do** ~ hacer lo mismo; **thank you for your help —** ~ gracias por la ayuda — lo mismo digo

liking ['laɪ·kɪŋ] n afición f; (for particular person) simpatía f; **to develop a** ~ **for sb/sth** tomar cariño a alguien/algo; **it's too sweet for my** ~ es demasiado dulce para mi gusto

lilac ['laɪ·læk] I. n 1. (bush) lila f 2. (color) lila m II. adj lila

lily ['lɪl·i] <-ies> n lirio m; **water** ~ nenúfar m

limb [lɪm] n 1. BOT rama f 2. ANAT extremidad f ▶ **to be/go out on a** ~ (to do sth) estar/ponerse en una situación arriesgada (para hacer algo)

limber ['lɪm·bər] adj (person) ágil; (material) flexible

lime¹ [laɪm] I. n 1. (fruit) lima f 2. (tree) limero m 3. (juice) zumo m de lima 4. (color) verde m lima II. adj de color verde lima

lime² [laɪm] I. n CHEM cal f II. vt abonar con cal

lime³ [laɪm] n (linden tree) tilo m

limelight ['laɪm·laɪt] n foco m proyector; **to be in the** ~ estar en el candelero

limit ['lɪm·ɪt] I. n límite m; **speed** ~ AUTO límite m de velocidad; **to put a** ~ **on sth** poner un límite a algo; **to overstep the** ~ pasarse del límite; **to know no** ~s no tener límites; **within** ~s dentro de ciertos límites; **to be off** ~s (to sb)

quedar prohibido el acceso (a alguien) II. vt limitar; **to** ~ **oneself to sth** limitarse a algo

limitation [ˌlɪm·ɪ·ˈteɪ·ʃən] n 1. (lessening) restricción f; (of pollution, weapons) limitación f 2. ~s limitaciones fpl; **she knows her** ~s ella sabe sus limitaciones 3. LAW prescripción f

limited ['lɪm·ɪ·tɪd] adj limitado, -a; **to be** ~ **to sth** estar limitado a algo

limp¹ [lɪmp] I. vi cojear II. n cojera f; **to walk with a** ~ cojear

limp² [lɪmp] adj flojo, -a; (lettuce) mustio, -a

line¹ [laɪn] <-ning> vt revestir; (clothes) forrar

line² [laɪn] I. n 1. (mark) a. MATH línea f; **dividing** ~ línea divisoria; **to be in a** ~ estar en línea 2. (for waiting) fila f, cola f AmL; **to get in** ~ ponerse en fila; **to stand in** ~ hacer cola; **to wait in** ~ esperar en la cola 3. (chronological succession) linaje m; **a (long)** ~ **of disasters/kings** una (larga) sucesión de desastres/reyes 4. (cord) cuerda f; **clothes** ~ cuerda para colgar la ropa 5. TEL línea f; **to be/stay on the** ~ estar/seguir al habla; **hold the** ~! no cuelgue(s) 6. COMPUT **on** ~ en línea; **off** ~ desconectado 7. (defense) frente m; **front** ~ línea del frente 8. (set of tracks) vía f; (train route) línea f; **the end of the** ~ el final de la línea 9. (transport company) línea f; **cruise** ~ línea de cruceros 10. (of text, poem) línea f, renglón m; **to drop sb a** ~ inf escribir a alguien 11. MUS melodía f 12. (comment) comentario m 13. (position, attitude) línea f; ~ **of reasoning** razonamiento m; **to be divided along ethnic** ~s estar dividido según criterios étnicos 14. (field, pursuit, interest) especialidad f; **what** ~ **are you in?** ¿a qué se dedica? 15. (product type) línea f; FASHION línea f de moda ▶ **somewhere along the** ~ en algún momento; **to cross the** ~ pasarse de la raya; **to be out of** ~ estar fuera de lugar; **to be out of** ~ **with sb/sth** no estar de acuerdo con alguien/algo II. <-ning> vt **to** ~ **the streets** ocupar las calles

line up I. *vt* alinear II. *vi* 1. (*stand in row*) alinearse 2. (*wait for sth*) ponerse en fila, hacer cola

linear ['lɪn·i·ər] *adj* lineal

linen ['lɪn·ɪn] *n* lino *m;* **bed ~s** sábanas *fpl;* **table ~s** mantelería *f*

liner ['laɪ·nər] *n* 1. (*lining*) forro *m;* (*garbage bag*) bolsa *f* de basura 2. (*ship*) transatlántico *m*

linger ['lɪŋ·gər] *vi* 1. entretenerse; (*film*) hacerse largo; **to ~ over sth** tomarse tiempo para (hacer) algo 2. (*die slowly*) **to ~ on** permanecer, perdurar

linguist ['lɪŋ·gwɪst] *n* lingüista *mf*

lining ['laɪ·nɪŋ] *n* 1. (*of coat, jacket*) forro *m;* (*of boiler, pipes*) revestimiento *m* 2. ANAT pared *f*

link [lɪŋk] I. *n* 1. (*in chain*) eslabón *m* 2. (*connection*) conexión *f;* **rail ~** enlace *m* ferroviario 3. COMPUT vínculo *m,* enlace *m* II. *vt* 1. (*connect*) conectar 2. (*be related to*) relacionar

linseed ['lɪn·sid] *n* linaza *f*

lion ['laɪ·ən] *n* león *m* ► **the ~'s share** la parte del león

lioness [laɪ·ə·'nes] <-sses> *n* leona *f*

lip [lɪp] *n* 1. ANAT labio *m;* **my ~s are sealed** mis labios están sellados 2. (*rim: of cup, bowl*) borde *m* 3. *sl* (*impudence*) insolencia *f*

lip service *n inf* jarabe *m* de pico; **to pay ~ to sth** apoyar algo sólo de boquilla

lipstick *n* barra *f* de labios

liqueur [lɪ·'kɜr] *n* licor *m*

liquid ['lɪk·wɪd] I. *n* líquido *m* II. *adj* líquido, -a

liquidate ['lɪk·wɪ·deɪt] *vt a. fig* liquidar

liquidation [ˌlɪk·wɪ·'deɪ·ʃən] *n* liquidación *f;* **to go into ~** ECON entrar en liquidación

liquidize ['lɪk·wɪ·daɪz] *vt* licuar

liquidizer ['lɪk·wɪ·daɪ·zər] *n* licuadora *f*

Lisbon ['lɪz·bən] *n* Lisboa *f*

lisp [lɪsp] I. *n* ceceo *m* II. *vi* cecear III. *vt* pronunciar ceceando

list¹ [lɪst] I. *n* lista *f;* **~ price** precio *m* según catálogo; **shopping ~** lista de la compra; **to make a ~ (of sth)** hacer un listado (de algo) II. *vt* 1. (*make a list*) listar 2. (*enumerate*) enumerar

list² [lɪst] NAUT I. *vi* escorar II. *n* escora *f*

listen ['lɪs·ən] *vi* 1. (*hear*) escuchar; **to ~ to sth/sb** escuchar algo/a alguien 2. (*pay attention*) estar atento; **to ~ for sth** estar atento para oír algo

listen in *vi* escuchar (a escondidas); **to ~ on sth** escuchar algo (a escondidas)

listener ['lɪs·nər] *n* oyente *mf*

lit [lɪt] *pt, pp of* **light**

litany ['lɪt·ə·ni] <-ies> *n* letanía *f*

liter ['li·tər] *n* litro *m*

literacy ['lɪt·ər·ə·si] *n* alfabetización *f;* **~ rate** índice *m* de alfabetización

literal ['lɪt·ər·əl] *adj* literal

literally ['lɪt·ər·ə·li] *adv* literalmente; **to take sth/sb ~** tomar algo/a alguien al pie de la letra

literary ['lɪt·ə·rer·i] *adj* literario, -a

literate ['lɪt·ə·rɪt] *adj* 1. (*able to read and write*) que sabe leer y escribir; **to be ~** saber leer y escribir 2. (*well-educated*) culto, -a

literature ['lɪt·ə·rə·tʃər] *n* 1. (*novels, poems*) literatura *f;* **nineteenth-century ~** literatura del siglo XIX 2. (*promotional material*) material *m* informativo

Lithuania [ˌlɪθ·ʊ·'eɪ·ni·ə] *n* Lituania *f*

Lithuanian I. *n* 1. (*person*) lituano, -a *m, f* 2. LING lituano *m* II. *adj* lituano, -a

litmus test *n* prueba *m* de tornasol; *fig* prueba *f* de fuego

litter ['lɪt·ər] I. *n* 1. (*refuse*) basura *f* 2. ZOOL camada *f* II. *vt* 1. (*make untidy*) ensuciar (tirando basura) 2. *inf* (*scatter*) esparcir; **the floor was ~ed with clothes** el suelo estaba cubierto de ropa

litter box *n* bandeja *f* para la arena del gato

little ['lɪt·əl] I. *adj* 1. (*in size, age*) pequeño, -a; **a ~ old man/woman** un viejecito/una viejecita; **the ~ ones** *inf* los niños; **my ~ brother/sister** mi hermanito, -a, mi hermano pequeño/ mi hermana pequeña 2. (*in amount*) poco, -a; **a ~ bit (of sth)** un poco (de algo); **a ~ something** alguna cosita; (*to eat or drink*) algo (de comer o de beber); **~ hope** pocas esperanzas; **~ by ~** poco a poco **3.** (*in duration*) breve; **for a ~ while** durante un ratito **II.** *n* poco *m*; **a ~ un poco**; **to know ~** saber poco; **we see ~ of him** lo vemos poco; **to have ~ to say** tener poco que decir **III.** *adv* poco; **~ less than...** poco menos que...; **~ more than an hour** poco más de una hora; **to make ~ of sth** sacar poco en claro de algo

liturgy ['lɪt·ər·dʒi] <-ies> *n* REL liturgia *f*

live¹ [laɪv] **I.** *adj* **1.** (*living*) vivo, -a **2.** RADIO, TV en directo; THEAT, MUS en vivo **3.** ELEC que lleva corriente; (*wire*) conectado, -a **4.** (*cartridge*) cargado, -a; (*bomb*) con carga explosiva **II.** *adv* RADIO, TV en directo; THEAT, MUS en vivo

live² [lɪv] **I.** *vi* vivir; **long ~ the king!** ¡viva el rey!; **to ~ on sth** (*eat*) alimentarse de algo ▶ **to ~ and let** ~ vivir y dejar vivir **II.** *vt* vivir; **to ~ a happy life** llevar una vida feliz

◆**live down** *vt* lograr superar

◆**live in** *vi* vivir en el lugar donde uno trabaja

◆**live on** *vi* vivir; (*tradition*) seguir vivo

◆**live out** *vt* vivir; (*dreams*) realizar

◆**live through** *vt* (*experience*) vivir

◆**live together** *vi* vivir juntos

◆**live up to** *vt* vivir conforme a; **to ~ expectations** estar a la altura de lo esperado

lively ['laɪv·li] *adj* (*person, conversation*) animado, -a; (*imagination, interest*) vivo, -a

liven up ['laɪ·vən·ʌp] **I.** *vi* animarse **II.** *vt* animar

liver ['lɪv·ər] *n* hígado *m*

livestock ['laɪv·stak] *n* ganado *m*

livid ['lɪv·ɪd] *adj* **1.** (*discolored*) lívido, -a **2.** (*furious*) furioso, -a

living ['lɪv·ɪŋ] **I.** *n* **1.** (*livelihood*) vida *f*; **to make a ~** ganarse la vida **2.** (*way of life*) (modo *m* de) vida *f* **3.** *pl* (*people*) **the ~** los vivos **II.** *adj* vivo, -a; (*creature*) viviente

living conditions *npl* condiciones *f pl* de vida

living quarters *npl* alojamiento *m*

living room *n* cuarto *m* de estar, living *m AmL*

lizard ['lɪz·ərd] *n* lagarto *m*; (*small*) lagartija *f*

llama ['la·mə] *n* llama *f*

load [loʊd] **I.** *n* **1.** ELEC *a.* fig carga *f*; **that took a ~ off my mind!** eso me quitó un (gran) peso de encima **2.** (*amount of work*) cantidad *f* (de trabajo); **a heavy/light ~** mucho/poco trabajo **3.** *inf* (*lots*) montón *m*; **~s** [*or* a ~] **of...** un montón de... ▶ **to get a ~ of sth** fijarse en algo **II.** *vt a.* AUTO, PHOT, COMPUT cargar **III.** *vi* cargarse

◆**load down** *vt* recargar; fig agobiar

◆**load up** *vt* cargar **II.** *vi* cargarse

loaded ['loʊ·dɪd] *adj* **1.** (*filled*) cargado, -a **2.** (*unfair: question*) tendencioso, -a **3.** *sl* (*rich*) forrado, -a

loaf¹ [loʊf] <**loaves**> *n* pan *m*; **a ~ of bread** una barra *f* de pan, un pan

loaf² [loʊf] *vi* gandulear; **to ~ around** hacer el vago

loan [loʊn] **I.** *vt* prestar **II.** *n* préstamo *m*, avío *m AmS*

lobby ['lab·i] **I.** <-ies> *n* **1.** ARCHIT vestíbulo *m* **2.** POL grupo *m* de presión **II.** <-ie-> *vi* **to ~ against/for sth** presionar en contra de/en pro de algo **III.** <-ie-> *vt* presionar

lobbyist ['lab·i·ɪst] *n* miembro *m* de un grupo de presión

lobster ['lab·stər] *n* (*with claws*) bogavante *m*; (*spiny*) langosta *f*

local ['loʊ·kəl] **I.** *adj* local; (*people*) del lugar; (*official, police*) municipal; TEL urbano, -a; **~ color** color *m* local **II.** *n* **1.** (*inhabitant*) lugareño, -a *m, f* **2.** (*bus*) autobús *m* de línea; (*train*) tren *m* de cercanías

local call *n* llamada *f* local

local government *n* administración *f* municipal

localization [ˌloʊ·kə·lɪ·'zeɪ·ʃən] *n a.* COMPUT localización *f*

local time *n* hora *f* local

locate ['loʊ·keɪt] *vt* **1.** (*find*) localizar **2.** (*situate*) situar; **to be ~d near sth** estar situado cerca de algo

location [loʊ·'keɪ·ʃən] *n* **1.** (*place*) posición *f* **2.** (*act of locating*) localización *f* **3.** CINE exteriores *mpl*; **to film sth on ~** rodar algo en exteriores

loch [lak] *n Scot* **1.** (*lake*) lago *m* **2.** (*in-*

let) brazo *m* de mar

lock¹ [lak] *n* (*of hair*) mechón *m*

lock² [lak] **I.** *n* **1.** (*fastening device*) cerradura *f*, chapa *f Arg, Méx* **2.** (*on canal*) esclusa *f* ▶ **to be under ~ and <u>key</u>** estar cerrado bajo llave **II.** *vt* **1.** (*fasten with lock*) cerrar con llave; (*confine safely: thing*) guardar bajo llave **2.** (*make immovable*) bloquear; **be ~ed** estar bloqueado **III.** *vi* cerrarse con llave

◆**lock away** *vt* (*jewels, document*) guardar bajo llave; (*person*) encerrar

◆**lock on** *vi*, **lock onto** *vi* MIL localizar y seguir

◆**lock out** *vt* impedir la entrada a; **to lock oneself out** dejarse las llaves dentro

◆**lock up** *vt* (*jewels, document*) guardar bajo llave; (*person*) encerrar

locker [ˈlak·ər] *n* (*at train station*) consigna *f* automática; (*at school*) taquilla *f*

locker room *n* vestuario *m*, desvestidero *m Col*, vestidor *m Méx*

lockjaw [ˈlak·dʒɔ] *n* MED trismo *m*

lockout [ˈlak·aʊt] *n* cierre *m* patronal

locksmith [ˈlak·smɪθ] *n* cerrajero, -a *m, f*

locust [ˈloʊ·kəst] *n* langosta *f*, chapulín *m Méx*

lodge [ladʒ] **I.** *vi* **1.** (*stay in rented room*) alojarse **2.** (*become fixed*) quedarse clavado, -a **II.** *vt* **1.** (*accommodate*) alojar **2.** (*insert*) meter **3.** (*register officially: appeal*) interponer; (*complaint, protest*) presentar **III.** *n* **1.** (*inn*) albergue *m* **2.** (*for organizations*) logia *f*

lodger [ˈladʒ·ər] *n* inquilino, -a *m, f*

lodging [ˈladʒ·ɪŋ] *n* **1.** (*accommodations*) alojamiento *m* **2.** ~s (*room to rent*) habitación *f* de alquiler

loft [laft] **I.** *n* **1.** (*space under roof*) buhardilla *f*; **hay ~** pajar *m* **2.** (*upstairs living space*) loft *m* **II.** *vt* (*ball*) lanzar por lo alto

log¹ [lɔg] **I.** *n* **1.** (*tree trunk*) tronco *m* **2.** (*firewood*) leño *m* ▶ **to sleep like a ~** dormir como un tronco **II.** <-gg-> *vt* talar *Am* **III.** <-gg-> *vi* talar árboles

log² [lɔg] *inf abbr of* **logarithm** log.

log³ [lɔg] **I.** *n* registro *m* **II.** *vt* (*record*) registrar

logarithm [ˈlɔ·gə·rɪð·əm] *n* logaritmo *m*

logic [ˈladʒ·ɪk] *n* lógica *f*

logical [ˈladʒ·ɪ·kəl] *adj* lógico, -a

login [ˈlɔg·ɪn] *n* COMPUT inicio *m* de sesión

logo [ˈloʊ·goʊ] *n* logo(tipo) *m*

logoff [ˈlɔg·ɔf] *n* COMPUT fin *m* de sesión

loin [lɔɪn] **I.** *n* **1.** ~s (*body area*) bajo vientre *m* **2.** ~s *liter* **the fruit of his ~s** el hijo/la hija de sus entrañas **3.** CULIN lomo *m* **II.** *adj* de lomo

loiter [ˈlɔɪ·tər] *vi* **1.** (*linger*) pasar el rato **2.** *a.* LAW merodear

loll [lal] *vi* colgar; **to ~ about** holgazanear

lollipop [ˈlal·i·pap] *n* chupachups® *m inv*

London [ˈlʌn·dən] *n* Londres *m*

lone [loʊn] *adj* solitario, -a

loneliness [ˈloʊn·li·nɪs] *n* soledad *f*

lonely [ˈloʊn·li] <-ier, -iest> *adj* **to feel ~** sentirse solo, -a; (*life*) solitario, -a; (*place*) aislado, -a

loner [ˈloʊ·nər] *n* solitario, -a *m, f*

long¹ [lɔŋ] **I.** *adj* (*distance, time, shape*) largo, -a; **to have a ~ way to go** tener mucho camino por recorrer; **it's been a ~ time since...** hace mucho tiempo desde que...; **~ time no see!** *inf* ¡cuánto tiempo (sin verte)! **II.** *adv* **1.** (*a long time*) mucho (tiempo); **~ after/before** mucho después/antes; **~ ago** hace mucho (tiempo); **to take ~ to do sth** tardar mucho (en hacer algo); **~ live the king!** ¡viva el rey! **2.** (*for the whole duration*) **all day ~** todo el día; **as ~ as I live** mientras viva; **so ~ as** mientras **3.** *in comparisons* **as ~ as** mientras +*subj*; **to no ~er do sth** ya no hacer algo ▶ **so ~** *inf* ¡hasta luego!

long² [lɔŋ] *vi* **to ~ for sb** echar de menos a alguien; **to ~ for sth** estar deseando algo; **to ~ to do sth** anhelar hacer algo

long-distance I. *adj* (*flight*) de largo recorrido; (*race, runner*) de fondo; (*negotiations, relationship*) a distancia; **~ call** llamada *f* de larga distancia **II.** *adv* **to phone ~** hacer una llamada interurbana

longing [ˈlɔŋ·ɪŋ] **I.** *n* **1.** (*nostalgia*) nostalgia *f* **2.** (*strong desire*) anhelo *m* **II.** *adj* anhelante

longish [ˈlɔŋ·ɪʃ] *adj inf* tirando a largo, -a

longitude ['lan·dʒə·tud] *n* longitud *f*
long jump *n* salto *m* de longitud, salto *m* largo *AmL*
long-lived *adj* (*person*) longevo, -a
long-lost *adj* perdido, -a hace mucho tiempo
long-range *adj* (*missile*) de largo alcance; (*aircraft*) transcontinental; (*policy*) a largo plazo
long shot *n* 1. (*not likely*) **to be a ~** ser una posibilidad muy remota 2. (*at all*) **not by a ~** ni de lejos
long-sighted *adj* 1. (*far-sighted*) hipermétrope 2. (*having foresight*) previsor(a)
long-standing *adj* antiguo, -a
long-suffering *adj* sufrido, -a
long-term *adj* (*care*) prolongado, -a; (*loan, memory, strategy*) a largo plazo
long wave *n* onda *f* larga
long-winded *adj* prolijo, -a
loofa(h) ['lu·fə] *n* esponja *f* vegetal
look [lʊk] I. *n* 1. (*act of looking: at person, thing*) mirada *f*; (*examination: of book, face*) ojeada *f*; **to take** [*or* **have**] **a ~ at sth** echar un vistazo a algo 2. (*appearance*) aspecto *m*; **good ~s** guapura *f* 3. (*style*) look *m* II. *vi* 1. (*use sight*) mirar; **to ~ at sth/sb** mirar algo/a alguien; **to ~ out (of) the window** mirar por la ventana; **oh, ~!** ¡mira!; **~ here** ¡oye, tú! 2. (*search*) buscar; **to ~ for sth/sb** buscar algo/a alguien 3. (*appear, seem*) parecer; **to ~ like sb/sth** parecerse a alguien/algo; **to ~ bad/good** tener mala/buena cara; **to ~ tired** parecer cansado; **to ~ as if...** parecer como si... +*subj*; **~ alive!** ¡espabila! 4. (*face*) **to ~ north** mirar [*or* dar] al norte ► **before you leap** *prov* mira lo que haces *prov* III. *vt* 1. (*examine*) mirar; **to ~ sb in the eye** mirar a alguien a los ojos [*or* a la cara] 2. (*seem*) parecer; **to ~ one's age** aparentar su edad ► **to ~ the other way** hacer la vista gorda
◆**look about** *vi* mirar alrededor
◆**look after** *vi* 1. (*take care of*) cuidar 2. (*take responsibility for*) encargarse de
◆**look ahead** *vi* mirar hacia adelante; **looking ahead to...** de cara a...

◆**look around** I. *vi* 1. (*look behind oneself*) girarse 2. (*look in all directions*) mirar alrededor 3. (*search*) **to ~ for** buscar II. *vt* (*inspect*) inspeccionar
◆**look away** *vi* apartar la mirada
◆**look back** *vi* 1. (*look behind oneself*) mirar (hacia) atrás 2. (*remember*) recordar
◆**look down** *vi* 1. (*from above*) mirar hacia abajo; (*lower eyes*) bajar la vista 2. (*feel superior*) **to ~ on sth/sb** menospreciar algo/a alguien
◆**look for** *vi* 1. (*search for*) buscar 2. (*expect*) esperar
◆**look forward** *vi* **to ~ to sth** tener muchas ganas de algo; **I ~ to hearing from you** espero tener pronto noticias suyas
◆**look in** *vi* **to ~ on sb** ir a ver a alguien
◆**look into** *vi* investigar
◆**look on** *vi* 1. (*watch*) mirar 2. (*view*) ver
◆**look out** *vi* 1. (*face a particular direction*) **to ~ on** (*window*) dar a 2. (*watch out*) tener cuidado; **~!** ¡cuidado!; **to ~ for** tener cuidado con; (*look for*) buscar
◆**look over** *vt* (*report*) revisar; (*house*) inspeccionar
◆**look through** *vt* 1. (*look*) mirar por 2. (*examine*) revisar 3. (*peruse*) **to ~ sth** echar un vistazo a algo
◆**look to** *vi* 1. (*attend to*) mirar por 2. (*depend on*) depender de 3. (*count on*) contar con
◆**look up** I. *vt* 1. (*consult*) buscar 2. (*visit*) ir a ver II. *vi* 1. (*raise one's eyes upward*) mirar hacia arriba; **to ~ to sb** *fig* tener a alguien de [*or* como] ejemplo 2. (*improve*) mejorar; **things are looking up!** ¡las cosas van mejorando!
looking glass <-es> *n* espejo *m*
lookout ['lʊk·ˌaʊt] *n* 1. (*observation post*) puesto *m* de observación 2. (*person*) centinela *mf*; **to be on the ~** estar alerta
loom [lum] *n* (*for weaving*) telar *m*
loony ['lu·ni] *sl* I. <-ier, -iest> *adj* (*person*) chiflado, -a; (*idea*) disparatado, -a II. <-ies> *n* loco, -a *m, f*, chiflado, -a *m, f*
loop [lup] I. *n* 1. (*bend*) curva *f*; (*of*

string) lazada f **2.** ELEC circuito m cerrado **3.** COMPUT bucle m **4.** (contraceptive coil) espiral f ▶ **to throw sb for a ~** sl dejar a alguien de piedra **II.** vi serpentear **III.** vt atar con un lazo; **to ~ sth around...** pasar algo alrededor de... ▶ **to ~ the loop** AVIAT rizar el rizo

loophole ['lup·hoʊl] n fig escapatoria f; **legal ~** laguna legal

loose [lus] **I.** adj **1.** (not tight: clothing) holgado, -a; (knot, rope, screw) flojo, -a; (skin) fláccido, -a **2.** (not confined) suelto, -a; **~ change** (dinero m) suelto m, sencillo m AmS **3.** (not exact: instructions) poco preciso, -a; (translation) libre **4.** (not strict or controlled: discipline) relajado, -a; **~ tongue** lengua f desatada **5.** (sexually immoral) disoluto, -a **II.** n **to be on the ~** estar en libertad **III.** vt soltar

loosely ['lus·li] adv **1.** (not tightly) sin apretar **2.** (not exactly: translate) libremente; (speak) en términos generales **3.** (not strictly: organized) de forma flexible

loosen ['lu·sən] **I.** vt (belt, knot) aflojar; (tongue) desatar **II.** vi aflojarse

loot [lut] **I.** n **1.** (plunder) botín m **2.** sl (money) pasta f, lana f AmL **II.** vt, vi saquear

looting n saqueo m

lope [loʊp] vi (person, animal) andar con paso largo

lopsided [ˌlɑp·ˈsaɪ·dɪd] adj **1.** (leaning to one side) torcido, -a, chueco, -a AmL **2.** (biased) parcial

lord [lɔrd] n señor m

lose [luz] <lost, lost> **I.** vt perder; **to get lost** (person) perderse; (object) extraviarse **II.** vi perder

loser ['lu·zər] n perdedor(a) m(f)

loss [lɔs] <-es> n pérdida f; **to be at a ~** no saber cómo reaccionar; **to be at a ~ for words** no encontrar palabras con que expresarse

loss-making adj deficitario, -a

lost [lɔst] **I.** pt, pp of **lose II.** adj **1.** perdido, -a; **to get ~** perderse; **to give sth/ sb up for ~** dar algo/a alguien por perdido; **to be ~ in a book** estar enfrascado

en la lectura de un libro **2.** (preoccupied) perplejo, -a; **to be ~ in thought** estar ensimismado

lot [lɑt] n **1.** (for deciding) **to cast ~s** echar a suertes **2.** (destiny) destino m **3.** (plot of land) terreno m **4.** (in auction) lote m **5.** inf (large quantity) **a ~ of, lots of** mucho(s); **a ~ of wine** mucho vino; **~s of houses** muchas casas; **I like it a ~** me gusta mucho; **the whole ~** todo

lotion ['loʊ·ʃən] n loción f

lottery ['lɑt·ə·ri] <-ies> n lotería f, quiniela f CSur

lotus ['loʊ·təs] <-es> n loto m

loud [laʊd] **I.** adj **1.** (voice) alto, -a; (shout) fuerte **2.** (noisy) ruidoso, -a **3.** (vigorous: complaint) enérgico, -a **4.** fig (color) chillón, -ona **II.** adv alto; **to laugh out ~** reír a carcajadas

loudmouth ['laʊd·maʊθ] n inf escandaloso, -a m, f

loudspeaker [ˌlaʊd·ˈspi·kər] n altavoz m

lounge [laʊndʒ] **I.** n **1.** (room) salón m **2.** (bar) bar m **II.** vi **1.** (recline) repanchi(n)garse **2.** (be idle) hacer el vago

louse [laʊs] n **1.** <lice> (insect) piojo m **2.** <-es> sl (person) canalla mf

lousy ['laʊ·zi] <-ier, -iest> adj **1.** (infested with lice) piojoso, -a **2.** (of poor quality) pésimo, -a; **to feel ~** sentirse fatal **3.** (nasty) asqueroso, -a

lout [laʊt] n patán m, jallán m AmC

loutish ['laʊ·tɪʃ] adj patán

love [lʌv] **I.** vt querer, amar; **I ~ swimming, I ~ to swim** me encanta nadar **II.** n **1.** (affection) amor m; **to be in ~ (with sb)** estar enamorado (de alguien); **to fall in ~ (with sb)** enamorarse (de alguien); **to make ~ to sb** hacer el amor con alguien **2.** inf (darling) cariño m **3.** (in tennis) cero m ▶ **not for ~ or money** por nada del mundo **III.** vi querer, amar

love-hate relationship n relación f de amor y odio

love letter n carta f de amor

love life n vida f amorosa [or sentimental]

lovely ['lʌv·li] <-ier, -iest> adj (house,

present) bonito, -a; (*weather*) precioso, -a; (*person*) encantador(a)

lover ['lʌv·ər] *n* amante *mf*

lovesick ['lʌv·sɪk] *adj* locamente enamorado, -a, volado, -a *AmL*

love song *n* canción *f* de amor

love story *n* historia *f* de amor

loving ['lʌv·ɪŋ] *adj* cariñoso, -a

low[1] [loʊ] **I.** *adj* **1.** (*not high, not loud*) bajo, -a; **to be ~ on sth** (*coffee, gas*) tener poco de algo; **to cook sth on ~ heat** hacer algo a fuego lento **2.** (*poor: opinion, quality*) malo, -a; (*self-esteem*) bajo, -a; (*visibility*) poco, -a; **a ~ trick** una mala jugada **II.** *adv* bajo, -a; **to feel ~** estar deprimido; **stocks are running ~** las existencias están casi agotadas; **the batteries are running ~** se están gastando las pilas **III.** *n* (*minimum*) mínimo *m*; **an all-time ~** un mínimo histórico

low[2] [loʊ] **I.** *vi* (*cow*) mugir **II.** *n* mugido *m*

low-cal *adj*, **low-calorie** *adj* bajo, -a en calorías

low-cut *adj* escotado, -a

low-down *adj* inf bajo, -a; **a ~ trick** una mala jugada

lower[1] ['loʊ·ər] **I.** *vt* bajar; (*flag, sails*) arriar; (*lifeboat*) echar al agua; **to ~ one's eyes** bajar la vista; **to ~ oneself to do sth** rebajarse a hacer algo **II.** *vi* bajar **III.** *adj* inferior

lower[2] [laʊr] *vi* (*person*) fruncir el ceño

lower-case *adj* minúsculo, -a; **in ~ letters** en minúsculas

low-key *adj* (*affair*) discreto, -a; (*debate, discussion*) mesurado, -a

lowly ['loʊ·li] <-ier, -iest> *adj* humilde

low-pitched *adj* (*voice*) grave

low profile *n* **to keep a ~** tratar de pasar desapercibido

low season *n* temporada *f* baja

low tide *n*, **low water** *n* marea *f* baja, bajamar *f*

lox [lɑks] *n* CULIN salmón *m* ahumado

loyal ['lɔɪ·əl] *adj* leal; **to remain ~ (to sb/ sth)** permanecer fiel a (alguien/algo)

loyalty ['lɔɪ·əl·ti] <-ies> *n* lealtad *f*

lubricant ['lu·brɪ·kənt] *n* lubricante *m*

lubricate ['lu·brɪ·keɪt] *vt* lubricar

luck [lʌk] *n* suerte *f*; **good/bad ~** buena/ mala suerte; **to bring sb ~** traer suerte a alguien; **to wish sb (good) ~** desear a alguien (buena) suerte; **with any ~** con un poco de suerte; **with no ~** sin éxito ► **no such ~!** *inf* ¡qué va!; **to press one's ~** tentar a la suerte

lucky ['lʌk·i] <-ier, -iest> *adj* afortunado, -a; **to be ~ in love** tener suerte en el amor; **to be ~ (in that...)** tener la suerte (de que...) +*subj*; **to make a ~ guess** acertar por (pura) casualidad; **~ day** día *m* de suerte; **~ number** número *m* de la suerte

lucrative ['lu·krə·t̬ɪv] *adj* lucrativo, -a

ludicrous ['lu·dɪ·krəs] *adj* absurdo, -a

luggage ['lʌg·ɪdʒ] *n* equipaje *m*

luggage rack *n* baca *f*

lukewarm [ˌluk·'wɔrm] *adj* **1.** (*liquid*) tibio, -a **2.** *fig* (*unenthusiastic*) poco entusiasta

lullaby ['lʌl·ə·baɪ] <-ies> *n* nana *f*

lumbar puncture *n* MED punción *f* lumbar

lumber[1] ['lʌm·bər] *vi* moverse pesadamente

lumber[2] ['lʌm·bər] **I.** *n* madera *f* **II.** *vt* aserrar

lumberjack *n* leñador *m*

luminous ['lu·mə·nəs] *adj* luminoso, -a

lump [lʌmp] **I.** *n* **1.** (*solid mass*) masa *f*; (*of coal*) trozo *m*; (*of sugar*) terrón *m*; **~ sum** cantidad *f* única **2.** (*swelling: in breast, on head*) bulto *m* ► **to have a ~ in one's throat** tener un nudo en la garganta **II.** *vt* <to ~ (together)> agrupar

lump-sum payment *n* pago *m* único

lumpy ['lʌm·pi] <-ier, -iest> *adj* (*custard, sauce*) grumoso, -a; (*surface*) desigual

lunacy ['lu·nə·si] *n* locura *f*

lunar ['lu·nər] *adj* lunar

lunatic ['lu·nə·tɪk] **I.** *n* loco, -a *m, f* **II.** *adj* lunático, -a

lunch [lʌntʃ] **I.** *n* comida *f*; **to have ~** comer **II.** *vi* comer

lunch break *n* descanso *m* para comer

luncheon ['lʌn·tʃən] *n form* almuerzo *m*

luncheon meat *n* fiambre de cerdo en conserva

lunch hour *n* hora *f* de comer

lunchtime I. *n* hora *f* de comer II. *adj* (*concert*) de mediodía

lung [lʌŋ] *n* pulmón *m;* **to shout at the top of one's ~s** decir a voz en grito

lung cancer *n* cáncer *m* de pulmón

lurch [lɜrtʃ] I. *vi* (*people*) tambalearse; (*car, train*) dar sacudidas II. <-es> *n* sacudida *f* ▶ **to leave sb in the ~** *inf* dejar a alguien colgado

lure [lʊr] I. *n* 1. (*attraction*) atractivo *m* 2. (*bait*) cebo *m;* (*decoy*) señuelo *m* II. *vt* atraer; **to ~ sb into a trap** hacer que alguien caiga en una trampa

lurk [lɜrk] *vi* merodear, esconderse

luscious ['lʌʃ·əs] *adj* 1. (*fruit*) jugoso, -a 2. *inf* (*girl, curves*) voluptuoso, -a; (*lips*) carnoso, -a

lush [lʌʃ] I. *adj* (*vegetation*) exuberante II. *n* <-es> *sl* borracho, -a *m, f*

lust [lʌst] *n* 1. (*sexual desire*) lujuria *f* 2. (*strong desire*) anhelo *m;* **~ for sth** ansia de algo

Lutheran ['lu·θər·ən] I. *adj* luterano, -a II. *n* luterano, -a *m, f*

Luxembourg ['lʌk·səm·bɜrg] *n* Luxemburgo *m*

Luxembourger *n* luxemburgués, -esa *m, f*

luxurious [lʌg·'ʒʊr·i·əs] *adj* lujoso, -a

luxury ['lʌk·ʃər·i] <-ies> *n* lujo *m;* **~ apartment** piso *m* de lujo

lying ['laɪ·ɪŋ] I. *n* mentiras *fpl* II. *adj* mentiroso, -a

lyric ['lɪr·ɪk] I. *adj* lírico, -a II. *n* 1. (*poem*) poema *m* lírico 2. **~s** (*words for song*) letra *f*

lyricist ['lɪr·ɪ·sɪst] *n* letrista *mf*

M

M, m [em] *n* M, m *f;* **~ as in Mike** M de María

M *n* 1. *abbr of* **male** H 2. *abbr of* **medium** M

m 1. *abbr of* **million** millón *m* 2. *abbr of* **minutes** min. 3. *abbr of* **meter** m

m. *n abbr of* **mile** milla *f*

MA [ˌem·'eɪ] *n* 1. *abbr of* **Master of Arts** máster *m (de Humanidades o de Filoso-*

fía y Letras) 2. *abbr of* **Massachusetts** Massachusetts *m*

ma [ma] *n inf* mamá *f*

ma'am [mæm] = **madam** (*form of address*) señora *f*

macabre [mə·'kab·rə] *adj* macabro, -a

macaroni [ˌmæk·ə·'rou·ni] *n* macarrones *mpl*

machine [mə·'ʃin] *n* (*mechanical device*) máquina *f*

machine gun *n* ametralladora *f*

machinery [mə·'ʃi·nə·ri] *n a. fig* (*machines*) maquinaria *f*

macho ['matʃ·ou] *adj* machista

mackerel ['mæk·rəl] <-(s)> *n* caballa *f*

macroeconomics [ˌmæk·rou·ek·ə·'nam·ɪks] *n* macroeconomía *f*

mad [mæd] *adj* 1. (*upset*) furioso, -a 2. (*insane: person*) loco, -a; **to go ~** volverse loco; **to drive sb ~** volver loco a alguien 3. (*enthusiastic*) **to be ~ about sb** estar loco por alguien

madam ['mæd·əm] *n* señora *f*

madden [mæd·ən] *vt* enfurecer

made [meɪd] *pp, pt of* **make**

made-up ['meɪd·ʌp] *adj* (*invented*) inventado, -a

madhouse ['mæd·haus] *n inf* loquero *m*

madly ['mæd·li] *adv* 1. (*frantically*) frenéticamente 2. (*intensely*) **she's ~ in love with him** está locamente enamorada de él

madman ['mæd·mən] <-men> *n* loco *m*

madness ['mæd·nɪs] *n* locura *f,* loquera *f AmL*

madwoman ['mæd·wʊm·ən] <-women> *n* loca *f*

magazine ['mæg·ə·zin] *n* 1. (*periodical publication*) revista *f* 2. MIL (*of gun*) recámara *f*

magic ['mædʒ·ɪk] I. *n* magia *f;* **as if by ~** como por arte de magia II. *adj* mágico, -a

magical *adj* 1. (*power*) mágico, -a 2. (*extraordinary, wonderful*) fabuloso, -a

magician [mə·'dʒɪʃ·ən] *n* mago, -a *m, f*

magistrate ['mædʒ·ɪ·streɪt] *n* juez que se ocupa de los delitos menores

magnate ['mæg·neɪt] *n* magnate *mf*

magnet ['mæg·nɪt] *n* imán *m*

M

magnetic [mæg·ˈnet·ɪk] *adj* 1. (*force*) magnético, -a 2. (*personality*) atrayente

magnetism [ˈmæg·nə·tɪz·əm] *n* magnetismo *m*

magnificent [mæg·ˈnɪf·ɪ·sənt] *adj* magnífico, -a

magnify [ˈmæg·nɪ·faɪ] <-ie-> *vt* 1. (*make larger*) ampliar; (*voice*) amplificar 2. (*make worse: problem*) exagerar

magnifying glass *n* lupa *f*

magnitude [ˈmæg·nɪ·tud] *n* magnitud *f*

magpie [ˈmæg·paɪ] *n* (*bird*) urraca *f*

mahogany [mə·ˈhag·ə·ni] *n* caoba *f*

maid [meɪd] *n* 1. (*female servant*) criada *f*, mucama *f* AmL 2. liter (*girl, young woman*) doncella *f*

maiden [ˈmeɪ·dən] **I.** *n* liter doncella *f* **II.** *adj* 1. (*unmarried*) soltera 2. (*first: voyage*) primero, -a

maiden name *n* apellido *m* de soltera

maid of honor *n* dama *f* de honor

mail¹ [meɪl] **I.** *n* a. COMPUT correo *m*; **electronic ~** COMPUT correo electrónico; **incoming/outgoing ~** COMPUT correo entrante/saliente; **by ~** por correo; **to open the ~** abrir el correo **II.** *vt* mandar por correo

mail² [meɪl] *n* (*armor*) malla *f*

mailbox *n* 1. (*for postal deliveries*) buzón *m* 2. COMPUT (**electronic**) **~** buzón *m* electrónico

mailing list *n* lista *f* de direcciones (*a las que se envía publicidad o información*)

mailman *n* cartero *m*

maim [meɪm] *vt* lisiar

main [meɪn] **I.** *adj* (*problem, reason, street*) principal **II.** *n* 1. (*pipe*) cañería *f* principal; **the water ~** la cañería maestra; **the gas ~** la cañería principal de gas 2. (*cable*) cable *m* principal ▶ **in the ~** en general

mainframe [ˈmeɪn·freɪm] *n* COMPUT ordenador *m* central, computadora *f* central *AmL*

mainland [ˈmeɪn·lənd] **I.** *n* continente *m* **II.** *adj* **~ China** China continental; **~ Spain** España peninsular

mainly [ˈmeɪn·li] *adv* principalmente

main office *n* oficina *f* central

main road *n* carretera *f* general

mainsail *n* vela *f* mayor

mainspring *n* motivo *m* principal

mainstream *adj* 1. (*ideology*) dominante 2. (*film, novel*) comercial

maintain [meɪn·ˈteɪn] *vt* 1. (*preserve, provide for*) mantener 2. (*claim*) sostener

maintenance [ˈmeɪn·tə·nəns] *n* (*repair work, preservation*) mantenimiento *m*

majesty [ˈmædʒ·ɪ·sti] <-ies> *n* majestuosidad *f*; **Her/His/Your Majesty** su Majestad

major [ˈmeɪ·dʒər] **I.** *adj* 1. (*important, significant*) fundamental 2. (*serious: illness*) grave 3. MUS mayor; **in C ~** en do mayor **II.** *n* 1. MIL comandante *mf* 2. UNIV especialidad *f*

Majorca [mə·ˈjɔr·kə] *n* Mallorca *f*

Majorcan I. *adj* mallorquín, -ina **II.** *n* mallorquín, -ina *m, f*

majorette [ˌmeɪ·dʒər·ˈet] *n* batonista *f*

majority [mə·ˈdʒɔr·ə·ti] <-ies> *n* 1. (*greater part/number*) mayoría *f* 2. (*most powerful group*) grupo *m* mayoritario 3. (*full legal age*) mayoría *f* de edad; **to reach the age of ~** alcanzar la mayoría de edad

make [meɪk] **I.** *vt* <made, made> 1. (*produce: coffee, soup, dinner*) hacer; (*product*) fabricar; (*clothes*) confeccionar; (*record*) grabar; (*film*) rodar; **to make sth out of sth** hacer algo con algo; **to ~ time** hacer tiempo 2. (*cause: trouble*) causar; **to ~ noise** hacer ruido; **to ~ a scene** montar una escena 3. (*cause to be*) **to ~ sb sad** poner triste a alguien; **to ~ sb happy** hacer feliz a alguien; **to ~ oneself heard/understood** hacerse oír/entender; **to ~ sth easy** hacer que algo sea fácil 4. (*perform, carry out*) **to ~ a call/reservation** hacer una llamada/reserva; **to ~ a decision** tomar una decisión 5. (*force*) obligar; **to ~ sb do sth** hacer que alguien haga algo 6. (*amount to, total*) ser; **two plus two ~s four** dos y dos son cuatro 7. (*earn, get*) **to ~ friends** hacer amigos; **to ~ money** hacer [*o* ganar] dinero; **to ~ a living** ganarse la vida 8. *inf* (*get to, reach*) **to ~ it to somewhere** llegar a un sitio; **to ~ it** alcanzar el éxito 9. (*make perfect*) **that made my day!** ¡eso me alegró el día! ▸ **to ~ do** (**with sth**) arreglárselas (con algo) II. *vi* (*amount to, total*) **today's earthquake ~s five since the beginning of the year** el terremoto de hoy es el quinto de este año ▸ **to ~ as if to do sth** fingir hacer algo III. *n* 1. (*brand*) marca *f* 2. (*identification*) **to get a ~ on sb** identificar [*or* tener] a alguien ▸ **to be on the ~** *sl* (*for money, power*) intentar sacar tajada

◆**make for** *vt insep* (*head for*) dirigirse a

◆**make out** I. *vi* 1. (*succeed, cope: person*) arreglárselas 2. *sl* (*kiss passionately*) **to ~ with sb** darse el lote con alguien II. *vt* 1. (*discern: writing, numbers*) distinguir; (*sth in the distance*) divisar 2. (*pretend*) **he made himself out to be rich** se hizo pasar por rico 3. (*write out*) **to ~ a check for \$100** extender un cheque por valor de 100 dólares

◆**make up** I. *vt* 1. (*invent*) inventar 2. (*prepare*) preparar 3. (*compensate*) **to ~ for sth** compensar algo 4. (*constitute*) constituir 5. (*decide*) **to ~ one's mind** decidirse II. *vi* reconciliarse

◆**make up to** *vt* **to make it up to sb** compensar a alguien

make-believe ['meɪk·bɪ·ˌliv] *adj* imaginario, -a; (*weapon*) de mentira; **a ~ world** un mundo de fantasía

maker ['meɪ·kər] *n* (*manufacturer*) fabricante *mf*

makeshift ['meɪk·ʃɪft] *adj* provisional

make-up ['meɪk·ʌp] *n* 1. (*cosmetics*) maquillaje *m*; **to put on ~** maquillarse; **to wear ~** ir maquillado 2. (*structure*) estructura *f* 3. (*character*) carácter *m*

making ['meɪ·kɪŋ] *n* 1. (*production*) producción *m*; (*of clothes*) confección *f*; (*of meals*) preparación *f* 2. **~s** (*essential qualities*) **to have the ~s of sth** tener madera de algo

malaise [mæ·'leɪz] *n* malestar *m*

malaria [mə·'ler·i·ə] *n* malaria *f*

male [meɪl] I. *adj* (*hormone, sex*) masculino, -a; (*animal*) macho; **~ chauvinism** machismo *m* II. *n* (*person*) varón *m*; (*animal*) macho *m*

malfunction [ˌmæl·'fʌŋk·ʃən] I. *vi* 1. (*not work properly*) funcionar mal 2. (*stop functioning*) fallar II. *n* 1. (*defective functioning*) mal funcionamiento *m* 2. (*sudden stop*) fallo *m*

malice ['mæl·ɪs] *n* malicia *f*

malicious [mə·'lɪʃ·əs] *adj* malicioso, -a

malign [mə·'laɪn] *adj form* maligno, -a

malignant [mə·'lɪɡ·nənt] *adj* maligno, -a

mall [mɔl] *n* centro *m* comercial

malleable ['mæl·i·ə·bəl] *adj* maleable

mallet ['mæl·ɪt] *n* mazo *m*

malnutrition [ˌmæl·nu·'trɪʃ·ən] *n* desnutrición *f*

malpractice [ˌmæl·'præk·tɪs] *n* conducta *f* incorrecta; **medical ~** negligencia *f* médica

malt [mɔlt] I. *n* malta *f* II. *vt* maltear

Malta ['mɔl·tə] *n* Malta *f*

maltreatment *n* malos tratos *mpl*

mammal ['mæm·əl] *n* mamífero *m*

mammary gland ['mæm·ə·ri·ˌɡlænd] *n* glándula *f* mamaria

mammoth ['mæm·əθ] *n* mamut *m*

man [mæn] I. *n* <men> 1. (*male human*) hombre *m* 2. (*the human race*) ser *m* humano ▸ **to talk** (**as**) **~ to ~** hablar de hombre a hombre; **as one ~** unánimemente II. *vt* <-nn-> (*operate*) encargarse de; (*ship*) tripular; **to ~ a factory** contratar personal para una fábrica; **some volunteers ~ the phones** algunos voluntarios cogen el teléfono III. *interj* ¡hombre!; **~, was that cake good!** ¡pues sí que estaba bueno el pastel!

manage ['mæn·ɪdʒ] I. *vt* 1. *a.* ECON (*control, be in charge of*) dirigir; (*money, time*) administrar 2. (*accomplish*) lograr; **to ~ to do sth** conseguir hacer algo II. *vi* **to ~ on a few dollars a day** arreglárselas con un par de dólares al día

manageable ['mæn·ɪ·dʒə·bəl] *adj* (*vehicle*) manejable; (*person, animal*) dócil; (*amount*) razonable

management ['mæn·ɪdʒ·mənt] *n* 1. (*direction*) manejo *m* 2. *a.* ECON dirección *f*, gestión *f*

manager ['mæn·ɪ·dʒər] *n* 1. COM (*administrator*) administrador(a) *m(f)*; (*of business unit*) gerente *mf* 2. (*of performer,* *artist*) representante *mf* artístico, -a; (*of a sports team*) manager *mf*

managing director *n* director(a) *m(f)* general

mandarin ['mæn·də·rɪn] *n* mandarín *m*

Mandarin *n* LING mandarín *m*

mandate ['mæn·deɪt] *n a.* POL mandato *m*

mandatory ['mæn·də·tɔr·i] *adj form* obligatorio, -a

mane [meɪn] *n* (*of horse*) crin *f*; (*of person, lion*) melena *f*

maneuver [mə·'nu·vər] I. *n a.* MIL maniobra *f* II. *vt* hacer maniobrar III. *vi* maniobrar

maneuverable [mə·'nu·vər·ə·bəl] *adj* maniobrable

manger ['meɪn·dʒər] *n* pesebre *m*

mangle ['mæn·gəl] *vt* (*body, text*) mutilar

manhandle ['mæn·hæn·dəl] *vt* **1.** (*treat roughly: person*) maltratar **2.** (*move by hand: heavy object*) empujar

manhole ['mæn·hoʊl] *n* registro *m*, boca *f* de visita *Ven*

manhood ['mæn·hʊd] *n* **1.** (*adulthood*) edad *f* adulta **2.** (*masculinity*) virilidad *f*

manhunt ['mæn·hʌnt] *n* persecución *f*

mania ['meɪ·ni·ə] *n* (*obsession*) manía *f*

maniac ['meɪ·ni·æk] *n* maníaco, -a *m, f*

manicure ['mæn·ɪ·kjʊr] *n* manicura *f*

manifest ['mæn·ɪ·fest] I. *adj form* manifiesto, -a; **to make sth ~** poner algo de manifiesto II. *vt form* declarar; **to ~ symptoms of sth** manifestar síntomas de algo

manifesto [ˌmæn·ɪ·'fes·toʊ] <-stos *or* -stoes> *n* manifiesto *m*

manipulate [mə·'nɪp·jə·leɪt] *vt* manipular

manipulation [mə·ˌnɪp·jə·'leɪ·ʃən] *n* manipulación *f*

manipulative [mə·ˌnɪp·jə·'lə·tɪv] *adj* manipulador(a)

mankind [ˌmæn·'kaɪnd] *n* humanidad *f*

manly ['mæn·li] <-ier, -iest> *adj* varonil

man-made ['mæn·meɪd] *adj* (*lake*) artificial; (*fiber*) sintético, -a

manned [mænd] *adj* AVIAT tripulado, -a

mannequin ['mæn·ɪ·kɪn] *n* (*dummy*) maniquí *mf*

manner ['mæn·ər] *n* **1.** (*way, fashion*) manera *f*; **in the ~ of sb** al estilo de alguien; **in a ~ of speaking** por así decirlo; **a ~ of speech** una forma de hablar **2.** (*behavior*) **~s** modales *mpl*; **it's bad ~s to...** es de mala educación... **3.** *form* (*kind, type*) clase *f*; **what ~ of man is he?** ¿qué tipo de hombre es?

mannerism ['mæn·ə·rɪz·əm] *n* amaneramiento *m*

manor ['mæn·ər] *n* **1.** (*house*) casa *f* solariega **2.** HIST (*territory*) feudo *m*

manpower ['mæn·paʊ·ər] *n* mano *f* de obra

mansion ['mæn·ʃən] *n* mansión *f*

manslaughter ['mæn·slɔ·tər] *n* homicidio *m* involuntario

mantelpiece ['mæn·təl·pis] *n* repisa *f* de la chimenea

manual ['mæn·ju·əl] I. *adj* manual; **~ dexterity** habilidad manual II. *n* manual *m*; **instruction ~** manual de instrucciones

manually ['mæn·ju·ə·li] *adv* manualmente, con las manos

manufacture [ˌmæn·ju·'fæk·tʃər] I. *vt* (*produce*) fabricar; **~d goods** artículos manufacturados II. *n* **1.** (*production*) manufactura *f* **2.** (*product*) producto *m* manufacturado

manufacturer [ˌmæn·ju·'fæk·ʃər·ər] *n* fabricante *mf*; **~'s label** etiqueta *f* de fábrica

manufacturing [ˌmæn·jə·'fæk·tʃər·ɪŋ] *adj* (*region, company*) industrial; **~ industry** industria *f* manufacturera

manure [mə·'nʊr] *n* abono *m*

manuscript ['mæn·ju·skrɪpt] *n* manuscrito *m*

many ['men·i] <more, most> I. *adj* muchos, muchas; **how ~ bottles?** ¿cuántas botellas?; **too/so ~ people** demasiada/tanta gente; **one too ~** uno de más; **~ times** muchas veces; **as ~ as...** tantos como... II. *pron* muchos, muchas; **~ think that...** muchos piensan que...; **so ~** tantos/tantas; **too ~** demasiados/demasiadas

many-sided [ˌmen·i·'saɪ·dɪd] *adj* polifacético, -a

map 703 marmalade

map [mæp] *n* 1. (*of region, stars*) mapa *m;* (*of town*) plano *m;* ~ **of the world** mapamundi *m;* **road** ~ mapa de carreteras 2. (*simple diagram*) plano *m* ▶ **to** blow [*or* wipe] **sth off the** ~ borrar algo del mapa; **to** put **a town on the** ~ dar a conocer a un pueblo

♦**map out** *vt* planear, proyectar; **to** ~ **a course/a plan** proyectar un curso/un plan

maple ['meɪ·pəl] *n* (*tree*) arce *m*

maple syrup *n* jarabe *m* de arce

mar [mar] <-rr-> *vt* (*ruin*) echar a perder

marathon ['mær·ə·θən] *n a. fig* maratón *m o f*

marble ['mar·bəl] *n* 1. (*stone*) mármol *m;* ~ **table** mesa *f* de mármol 2. (*glass ball*) canica *f,* bolita *f CSur;* **to play** ~**s** jugar a las canicas

marble cake *n* pastel de molde con chocolate

march [martʃ] I. <-es> *n a.* MIL marcha *f;* **funeral** ~ marcha fúnebre; **a 20 mile** ~ una marcha de 32 km; **to be on the** ~ estar en marcha II. *vi a.* MIL marchar; (*parade*) desfilar; **to** ~ **into a country** invadir un país

March [martʃ] *n* marzo *m; s. a.* **April**

mare [mer] *n* yegua *f*

margarine ['mar·dʒər·ɪn] *n* margarina *f*

margin ['mar·dʒɪn] *n a.* TYPO margen *m;* **narrow** ~ margen reducido; ~ **of error** margen de error

marina [mə·'ri·nə] *n* puerto *m* deportivo

marinate ['mær·ɪ·neɪt] *vt* marinar

marine [mə·'rin] I. *adj* (*of the sea*) marino, -a; NAUT marítimo, -a; MIL naval II. *n* infante *m* de marina

marital ['mær·ɪ·təl] *adj* marital *f;* ~ **problems** problemas *m pl* conyugales

mark¹ [mark] I. *n* 1. (*spot, stain*) mancha *f;* (*scratch*) marca *f;* (*trace*) huella *f;* **to leave one's** ~ **on sth/sb** *fig* dejar sus huellas en algo/alguien 2. (*written sign*) raya *f* 3. (*required standard*) norma *f;* **to be up to the** ~ ser satisfactorio 4. (*target*) blanco *m;* **to hit the** ~ dar en el blanco 5. (*starting line*) línea *f* de salida; **on your** ~, **get set, go!** ¡preparados, listos, ya! 6. LING signo *m;* **punctuation** ~ signo de puntuación ▶ **to**

be wide **of the** ~ fallar por mucho, estar lejos de la verdad II. *vt* 1. (*make a spot, stain*) manchar 2. (*make written sign, indicate*) marcar; **the bottle was** ~**ed 'poison'** la botella llevaba la etiqueta 'veneno' 3. (*characterize*) distinguir; **to** ~ **sb as sth** distinguir a alguien como algo 4. (*commemorate*) conmemorar; **to** ~ **the beginning/end of sth** conmemorar el principio/final de algo; **to** ~ **the 10th anniversary** celebrar el 10° aniversario

♦**mark down** *vt* 1. (*reduce prices*) rebajar 2. (*jot down*) apuntar 3. SCHOOL **to mark sb down** bajar las calificaciones de alguien 4. *fig* (*assess*) **to mark sb down as sth** catalogar a alguien como algo

♦**mark off** *vt* 1. (*divide land*) demarcar 2. (*cross out*) tachar

♦**mark out** *vt* trazar

♦**mark up** *vt* aumentar

mark² [mark] *n* FIN marco *m*

marked [markt] *adj* 1. (*improvement, difference*) marcado, -a 2. (*with distinguishing marks*) marcado, -a 3. (*liable to be attacked*) **to be a** ~ **man/woman** estar en el punto de mira

marker ['mar·kər] *n* 1. (*sign, symbol*) señal *f* 2. (*pen*) rotulador *m* 3. SPORTS (*indicator*) marcador *m*

market ['mar·kɪt] I. *n* mercado *m;* **the housing** ~ el mercado inmobiliario; **the stock** ~ la bolsa de valores; **on the** ~ a la venta II. *vt* comercializar

marketing *n* 1. (*discipline*) marketing *m* 2. (*commercialization*) comercialización *f*

marketplace *n* 1. ECON mercado *m* 2. (*square*) plaza *f* (del mercado)

market research *n* estudio *m* de mercado

market trader *n* comerciante *mf*

marking *n* (*identification*) señal *f;* (*on animal*) pinta *f*

marksmanship ['marks·mən·ʃɪp] *n* puntería *f*

markup ['mark·ʌp] *n* margen *m* de ganancia

marmalade ['mar·mə·leɪd] *n* mermelada *f* (*de cítricos*)

M

marquee [mar·'ki] *n* **1.** (*rooflike structure*) marquesina *f* **2.** (*scrolling text*) letrero con el nombre de los artistas en la fachada de un teatro u otro local

marriage ['mær·ɪdʒ] *n* **1.** (*wedding*) boda *f* **2.** (*relationship, state*) matrimonio *m*; **he is a relative by ~** es pariente político **3.** *fig* (*of organizations*) unión *f*

married *adj* (*person*) casado, -a; **~ couple** matrimonio *m*

married name *n* apellido *m* de casada

marrow ['mær·oʊ] *n* MED médula *f*

marry ['mær·i] <-ie-> **I.** *vt* **1.** (*become husband or wife*) **to ~ sb** casarse con alguien; **to get married (to sb)** casarse (con alguien) **2.** (*priest*) casar **II.** *vi* casarse

Mars [marz] *n* Marte *m*

marsh [marʃ] <-es> *n* ciénaga *f*

marshal ['mar·ʃəl] *n* **1.** LAW alguacil *mf* **2.** (*police or fire officer*) comisario, -a *m, f*

marshland ['marʃ·lænd] *n* pantanal *m*

marshmallow ['marʃ·mel·oʊ] *n* **1.** (*sweet*) dulce *m* de malvavisco, carlotina *f Ven* **2.** (*plant*) malvavisco *m*

marshy ['mar·ʃi] <-ier, -iest> *adj* pantanoso, -a

martial ['mar·ʃəl] *adj* marcial

martial arts *n* SPORTS artes *m pl* marciales

martial law *n* ley *f* marcial; **to impose ~ on a country** imponer la ley marcial en un país

Martian ['mar·ʃən] **I.** *adj* marciano, -a **II.** *n* marciano, -a *m, f*

martyr ['mar·t̬ər] **I.** *n* mártir *mf* **II.** *vt* martirizar

marvel ['mar·vəl] **I.** *n* **1.** (*thing*) maravilla *f* **2.** (*person*) joya *f* **II.** <-ll-, -l-> *vi* **to ~ that...** maravillarse de que... +*subj*; **to ~ at sb/sth** maravillarse de alguien/algo

marvel(l)ous ['mar·və·ləs] *adj* maravilloso, -a; **to feel ~** sentirse espléndido

marzipan ['mar·zɪ·pæn] *n* mazapán *m*

mascara [mæ·'skær·ə] *n* rímel *m*

mascot ['mæs·kat] *n* mascota *f*

masculine ['mæs·kjə·lɪn] *adj a.* LING masculino, -a

mash [mæʃ] **I.** *n* **1.** AGR (*animal feed*) afrecho *m*, salvado *m* **2.** (*fermentable mixture*) malta *f* **II.** *vt* machacar; **to ~ potatoes** hacer puré de patatas

mask [mæsk] **I.** *n a.* *fig* máscara *f*; **oxygen ~** máscara de oxígeno **II.** *vt* enmascarar; **to ~ sth with sth** encubrir algo con algo

masked *adj* enmascarado, -a

masochist ['mæs·ə·kɪst] *n* masoquista *mf*

mason ['meɪ·sən] *n* **1.** (*stonecutter*) cantero *m* **2.** (*bricklayer*) albañil *m* **3.** (*Freemason*) masón, -ona *m, f*

masonry ['meɪ·sən·ri] *n* **1.** (*occupation*) albañilería *f* **2.** (*stonework*) mampostería *f* **3.** (*Freemasonry*) masonería *f*

mass [mæs] *n* **1.** *a.* PHYS masa *f* **2.** (*formless substance*) bulto *m* **3.** (*large quantity*) montón *m*; **the ~ of the people** la muchedumbre **II.** *vi* (*gather*) juntarse; (*troops*) concentrarse **III.** *adj* de masas

Mass [mæs] *n* misa *f*; **to attend ~** ir a misa

massacre ['mæs·ə·kər] **I.** *n* (*killing*) *a.* *fig* masacre *f* **II.** *vt* (*kill*) *a.* *fig* masacrar

massage [mə·'sadʒ] **I.** *n* masaje *m*; **to give sb a ~** dar a alguien un masaje; **water ~** hidromasaje *m* **II.** *vt* **1.** dar masajes a **2.** *fig* manipular

masseur [mæ·'sɜr] *n* masajista *m*

masseuse [mæ·'sɜz] *n* masajista *f*

massive ['mæs·ɪv] *adj* masivo, -a, enorme; **~ amounts of money** grandes cantidades de dinero

mass media *n* **the ~** los medios de comunicación de masas

mass production *n* fabricación *f* en serie

mast [mæst] *n* **1.** NAUT mástil *m* **2.** (*flag pole*) asta *m*; **at half ~** a media asta **3.** RADIO, TV antena *f*

master ['mæs·tər] **I.** *n* **1.** (*of house*) señor *m*; (*of slave*) amo *m*; (*of dog*) dueño *m* **2.** (*one who excels*) maestro *m* **3.** (*instructor*) instructor *m* **4.** (*master copy*) original *m* ▶ **to be one's own ~** no depender de nadie **II.** *vt* **1.** (*cope with*) vencer; **to ~ one's fear of flying** superar el miedo a volar **2.** (*become* *proficient at*) dominar

master copy <-ies> *n* original *m*

masterful ['mæs·tər·fəl] *adj* **1.** (*authoritative*) autoritario, -a **2.** (*skillful*) magistral

master key *n* llave *f* maestra

masterly ['mæs·tər·li] *adj* magistral

mastermind ['mæs·tər·maɪnd] **I.** *n* cerebro *m* **II.** *vt* (*activity*) planear; (*crime*) ser el cerebro de

Master of Arts *n* licenciado, -a *m, f,* con máster *(en Humanidades o en Filosofía y Letras)*

masterpiece *n* obra *f* maestra

master switch <-es> *n* interruptor *m* principal

masturbate ['mæs·tər·beɪt] **I.** *vi* masturbarse **II.** *vt* masturbar

mat¹ [mæt] *n* **1.** (*on floor*) estera *f;* (*decorative*) tapiz *m;* **bath ~** alfombra *f* de baño **2.** (*on table*) salvamanteles *m inv* **3.** SPORTS (*in gymnastics*) colchoneta *f*

mat² *adj,* **matte** [mæt] *adj* mate

match¹ [mætʃ] <-es> *n* (*for making fire*) cerilla *f,* fósforo *m;* **box of ~es** caja de fósforos

match² [mætʃ] **I.** *n* **1.** (*competitor*) contrincante *mf;* **to be no ~ for sb** no poder competir con alguien; **to meet one's ~** encontrar la horma de su zapato **2.** (*similarity*) **to be a good ~** combinar bien **3.** (*in marriage*) **to make a good ~** casarse bien **4.** SPORTS partido *m;* **wrestling ~** combate *m* de lucha libre **II.** *vi* (*harmonize: design, color*) armonizar, pegar; (*description*) coincidir **III.** *vt* **1.** (*have same color*) hacer juego con **2.** (*equal*) igualar

matchbox ['mætʃ·bɑks] <-es> *n* caja *f* de cerillas, cerillero *m*

matching ['mætʃ·ɪŋ] *adj* que hace juego

match point *n* SPORTS bola *f* de partido

matchstick ['mætʃ·stɪk] *n* cerilla *f,* fósforo *m*

mate¹ [meɪt] **I.** *n* **1.** (*partner*) pareja *f* **2.** ZOOL (*male*) macho *m;* (*female*) hembra *f* **3.** NAUT oficial *m* de a bordo **II.** *vi* aparearse **III.** *vt* AmL

mate² [meɪt] *n* GAMES mate *m*

material [mə·'tɪr·i·əl] **I.** *n* **1.** PHILOS, PHYS materia *f* **2.** (*physical substance*) mate-

rial *m;* **raw ~** materia *f* prima **3.** (*information*) **publicity ~** material *m* publicitario **4.** (*textile*) tejido *m* **5.** **~s** (*equipment*) materiales *mpl* **II.** *adj* **1.** (*physical*) material; **~ damage** daño *m* material **2.** (*important*) importante

materialize [mə·'tɪr·i·ə·laɪz] *vi* **1.** (*take physical form*) materializarse **2.** (*hope, idea*) realizarse

maternal [mə·'tɜr·nəl] *adj* **1.** (*feeling*) maternal **2.** (*relative*) materno, -a

maternity [mə·'tɜr·nə·ţi] *n* maternidad *f*

maternity leave *n* baja *f* por maternidad

math [mæθ] *n inf abbr of* **mathematics** mates *fpl*

mathematical [ˌmæθ·ə·'mæţ·ɪ·kəl] *adj* matemático, -a

mathematician [ˌmæθ·ə·mə·'tɪʃ·ən] *n* matemático, -a *m, f*

mathematics [ˌmæθ·ə·'mæţ·ɪks] *n* matemáticas *fpl*

matinee ['mæt·ə·neɪ] *n* CINE primera sesión *f;* THEAT función *f* de tarde

mating ['meɪ·ţɪŋ] *n* apareamiento *m*

matriculation [mə·ˌtrɪk·jə·'leɪ·ʃən] *n* matrícula *f*

matrimony ['mæt·rə·moʊ·ni] *n* matrimonio *m*

matrix ['meɪ·trɪks] <-ices> *n a.* MATH matriz *f*

matted *adj* enmarañado, -a

matter ['mæt·ər] **I.** *n* **1.** (*subject*) materia *f;* (*question, affair*) asunto *m;* **the ~ at hand** el asunto a tratar; **it's a ~ of life or death** es una cuestión de vida o muerte; **money ~s** asuntos financieros; **a ~ of opinion** una cuestión de opinión **2.** **~s** (*situation*) situación *f;* **to make ~s worse** por si eso fuera poco; **to help ~s** mejorar las cosas **3.** (*wrong*) problema *m;* **what's the ~ with you?** ¿qué te pasa? **4.** (*material*) material *m;* **advertising ~** material publicitario **5.** (*amount*) **a ~ of...** cosa de...; **in a ~ of seconds** en cuestión de segundos **6.** (*substance*) materia *f* **II.** *vi* importar; **it really ~s to me** me importa mucho; **no ~ what they say** digan lo que digan; **it doesn't ~ if...** no importa si...

matter-of-fact [ˌmæt·ər·əv·'fækt] *adj*

(*practical*) práctico, -a

mattress ['mæt·rɪs] *n* colchón *m*

mature [mə·'tʃur] **I.** *adj* **1.** (*person, attitude*) maduro, -a; (*animal*) adulto, -a **2.** (*wine*) añejo, -a; (*cheese*) curado, -a; (*fruit*) maduro, -a FIN vencido, -a **II.** *vi* **1.** *a. fig* madurar **2.** FIN vencer **III.** *vt* (*cheese, ham*) curar; (*wine*) añejar

maturity [mə·'tʃur·ə·ti] *n* <-ies> **1.** (*of person, attitude*) madurez *f*; **to come to ~** llegar a la madurez **2.** FIN vencimiento *m*

mauve [mouv] *adj* malva

maximize ['mæk·sɪ·maɪz] *vt* maximizar

maximum ['mæk·sɪ·məm] **I.** *n* máximo *m*; **to do sth to the ~** hacer algo al máximo **II.** *adj* máximo, -a; **this car has a ~ speed of 100 mph** este coche alcanza una velocidad máxima de 160 km/h

may[1] [meɪ] <might, might> *aux* **1.** *form* (*be allowed*) poder; **~ I come in?** ¿puedo pasar?; **~ I ask you a question?** ¿puedo hacerle una pregunta? **2.** (*possibility*) ser posible; **it ~ rain** puede que llueva; **be that as it ~** en cualquier caso **3.** (*hope, wish*) **~ she rest in peace** que en paz descanse

may[2] [meɪ] *n* (*bush*) espino *m*; (*flower*) flor *f* de espino

May [meɪ] *n* mayo *m*; *s. a.* **April**

maybe ['meɪ·bi] *adv* (*perhaps*) quizás

mayday ['meɪ·deɪ] *n* S.O.S. *m*

mayhem ['meɪ·hem] *n* caos *m inv*

mayonnaise [ˌmeɪ·ə·'neɪz] *n* mayonesa *f*

mayor ['meɪ·ər] *n* alcalde(sa) *m(f)*

maypole ['meɪ·poul] *n* mayo *m (palo)*

maze [meɪz] *n* laberinto *m*

MD [ˌem·'di] *n* **1.** *abbr of* **Doctor of Medicine** Dr. *m*, Dra. *f* **2.** *abbr of* **Maryland** Maryland *m*

me [mi] *pron* **1.** me; **look at ~** mírame; **she saw ~** me vio; **he told ~ that...** me dijo que... **2.** (*after verb 'to be'*) yo; **it's ~** soy yo; **she is older than ~** ella es mayor que yo **3.** (*after prep*) mí; **is this for ~?** ¿es para mí esto?

ME [meɪn] *n abbr of* **Maine** Maine *m*

meadow ['med·ou] *n* pradera *f*

meager ['mi·gər] *adj* escaso, -a

meal[1] [mil] *n* comida *f*; **a heavy/light ~** una comida pesada/ligera

meal[2] [mil] *n* (*flour*) harina *f*

mealtime ['mil·taɪm] *n* hora *f* de comer

mean[1] [min] *adj* **1.** (*unkind*) vil; **to be ~ to sb** tratar mal a alguien; **to have a ~ streak** tener muy mala uva *inf* **2.** *sl* (*excellent*) de la hostia

mean[2] [min] <meant, meant> *vt* **1.** (*signify: word, event*) significar; **does that name ~ anything to you?** ¿te suena ese nombre? **2.** (*express, indicate: person*) querer decir; **what do you ~?** ¿a qué te refieres?; **I ~ what I say** digo lo que pienso **3.** (*intend for particular purpose*) destinar; **to be meant for sth** estar destinado a algo; **to be meant for each other** estar hechos el uno para el otro **4.** (*intend*) pretender; **to ~ to do sth** tener la intención de hacer algo; **to ~ well** tener buenas intenciones; **I ~ to say...** quiero decir... ▶ **to ~ business** *inf* hablar muy en serio

meaning ['mi·nɪŋ] *n* significado *m*; **to give sth a whole new ~** dar a algo un significado completamente nuevo; **what is the ~ of this?** ¿qué significa esto?; **to have ~ for sb** tener significado para alguien

meaningful ['mi·nɪŋ·fəl] *adj* **1.** (*difference, change*) significativo, -a **2.** (*look, smile*) expresivo, -a **3.** (*relationship*) importante

meaningless ['mi·nɪŋ·lɪs] *adj* sin sentido

means [minz] *npl* **1.** (*instrument, method*) medio *m*; **~ of transport** medio de transporte **2.** *pl* (*resources*) medios *mpl*; **by ~ of sth** por medio de algo **3.** *pl* (*income*) recursos *mpl*; **a person of ~** una persona acaudalada; **private ~** fondos *m pl* privados; **to live beyond one's ~** vivir por encima de sus posibilidades ▶ **by all ~!** ¡por supuesto!; **by no ~** de ninguna manera

meant [ment] *pt, pp of* **mean**

meantime ['min·taɪm] **I.** *adv* mientras tanto **II.** *n* **in the ~** mientras tanto

meanwhile ['min·hwaɪl] *adv* mientras tanto

measles ['mi·zəlz] *n* sarampión *m*

measure ['meʒ·ər] I. *vt* medir II. *vi* medir; **the box ~s 4 in. by 4 in. by 6 in.** la caja mide 10 cm por 10 cm por 15 cm III. *n* 1. (*size*) medida *f* 2. (*measuring instrument*) metro *m*; (*ruler*) regla *f* 3. (*proof*) medición *f* 4. **~s** (*action*) medidas *fpl*; **to take ~s to do sth** tomar medidas para hacer algo 5. (*degree, amount*) grado *m* 6. MUS compás *m*

measured *adj* (*response*) moderado, -a; (*voice, tone*) comedido, -a

measurement ['meʒ·ər·mənt] *n* 1. (*size*) medida *f* 2. (*dimension of body*) medida; **to take sb's ~s** tomar a alguien las medidas 3. (*act of measuring*) medición *f*

measuring cup *n* vaso *m* medidor

measuring spoon *n* cuchara *f* medidora

meat [mit] *n* 1. carne *f* 2. *fig* (*essence*) sustancia *f* 3. *fig* (*target*) **this guy is fresh ~** ese tío es carne fresca

meatball *n* albóndiga *f*

meat grinder *n* picadora *f* de carne

meat loaf *n* pastel *m* de carne

Mecca ['mek·ə] *n* REL La Meca

mechanic [mɪ·'kæn·ɪk] *n* mecánico, -a *m, f*

mechanical *adj* 1. (*relating to machines*) mecánico, -a 2. (*without thinking*) mecánico, -a

mechanics [mɪ·'kæn·ɪks] *npl* 1. AUTO, TECH mecánica *f* 2. *inf* (*how things are organized*) mecanismo *m*

mechanism ['mek·ə·nɪz·əm] *n* mecanismo *m*

medal ['med·əl] *n* medalla *f*

medalist ['med·əl·ɪst] *n* medallista *mf*

medallion [mə·'dæl·jən] *n* medallón *m*

meddle ['med·əl] *vi* **to ~ in sth** entrometerse en algo

media ['mi·di·ə] *n* 1. *pl of* **medium** 2. **the ~** los medios; **the mass ~** los medios de comunicación de masas

mediate ['mi·di·eɪt] *vi* mediar (**between** entre)

mediator ['mi·di·eɪ·tər] *n* mediador(a) *m(f)*

medic ['med·ɪk] *n* médico, -a *m, f*

medical ['med·ɪ·kəl] I. *adj* médico, -a II. *n inf* reconocimiento *m* médico

medical history *n* historial *m* clínico

Medicare ['med·ɪ·ker] *n* programa de asistencia sanitaria para personas mayores de 65 años

medicate ['med·ɪ·keɪt] *vt* (*treat medically*) medicar

medication [ˌmed·ɪ·'keɪ·ʃən] <-(s)> *n* medicamento *m*

medicine ['med·ɪ·sɪn] *n* 1. (*substance*) medicamento *m* 2. (*medical knowledge*) medicina *f* 3. (*remedy*) remedio *m* ▶ **to give sb a taste of his/ her own** ~ pagar a alguien con su misma moneda

medicine cabinet *n* botiquín *m*

medieval [ˌmi·di·'i·vəl] *adj* medieval

mediocre [ˌmi·di·'ou·kər] *adj* mediocre

meditate ['med·ɪ·teɪt] *vi* (*engage in contemplation*) meditar

Mediterranean [ˌmed·ɪ·tə·'reɪ·ni·ən] I. *n* Mediterráneo *m* II. *adj* mediterráneo, -a

Mediterranean Sea *n* mar *m* Mediterráneo

medium ['mi·di·əm] I. *adj* 1. (*not big or small*) mediano, -a 2. CULIN a punto II. *n* 1. <media *or* -s> (*method*) medio *m* 2. COMPUT medio *m*; **data ~** soporte de datos 3. <-s> (*spiritualist*) médium *mf*

medium-dry *adj* semi seco, -a

medium-rare *adj* CULIN poco hecho, -a

meek [mik] *adj* manso, -a

meet [mit] <met, met> I. *vt* 1. (*encounter*) encontrarse con; (*intentionally*) reunirse con; (*for first time*) conocer a; **to arrange to ~ sb** quedar con alguien 2. (*wait for: at train station, airport*) ir a buscar a alguien 3. (*confront: opponent*) enfrentarse con; (*problem*) tropezar con 4. (*fulfill*) reunir; (*cost*) correr con; (*demand*) atender; (*obligation*) cumplir 5. (*join: lines*) unirse II. *vi* 1. (*encounter*) encontrarse; (*intentionally*) reunirse; (*for first time*) conocerse; **to arrange to ~** quedar 2. (*join: lines*) unirse 3. SPORTS enfrentarse

◆ **meet with** *vt insep* reunirse con; **to ~ success** tener éxito

meeting ['mi·tɪŋ] *n* 1. (*gathering*) reunión *f*; **to call a ~** convocar una re-

M

unión **2.** POL mitin *m* **3.** (*casual*) encuentro *m*

meeting point *n* punto *m* de encuentro

melody ['mel·ə·di] <-ies> *n* melodía *f*

melon ['mel·ən] *n* melón *m;* (*watermelon*) sandía *f*

melt [melt] **I.** *vt* (*metal*) fundir; (*ice, chocolate*) derretir **II.** *vi* **1.** (*metal*) fundirse; (*ice, chocolate*) derretirse **2.** *fig* enternecerse

meltdown ['melt·daʊn] *n* fusión *f*

melting point *n* punto *m* de fusión

melting pot *n a. fig* crisol *m*

member ['mem·bər] *n* miembro *mf;* (*of society, club*) socio, -a *m, f*

membership *n* (*state of belonging*) calidad *f* de miembro; (*to society, club*) calidad *f* de socio; **to apply for ~ to a club** solicitar ingreso en un club

membership card *n* carnet *m* de socio

membrane ['mem·breɪn] *n* membrana *f*

memo ['mem·oʊ] *n abbr of* **memorandum** **1.** (*message*) memorándum *m* **2.** (*note*) nota *f*

memoir ['mem·war] *n* **1.** (*record of events*) memoria *f* **2.** *pl* (*autobiography*) memorias *fpl*

memorable ['mem·ər·ə·bəl] *adj* memorable

memorial [mə·'mɔr·i·əl] **I.** *n* monumento *m* conmemorativo **II.** *adj* conmemorativo, -a

Memorial Day *n* Día *m* de los Caídos

memorize ['mem·ə·raɪz] *vt* memorizar

memory ['mem·ə·ri] <-ies> *n* **1.** (*ability to remember*) memoria *f;* **to recite sth from ~** recitar algo de memoria **2.** (*remembered event*) recuerdo *m;* **to bring back memories** evocar recuerdos **3.** COMPUT memoria *f*

men [men] *n pl of* **man**

menace ['men·əs] *n* **1.** (*threat*) amenaza *f* **2.** (*child*) demonio *m*, peligro *m*

menacing *adj* amenazador(a)

mend [mend] **I.** *n* **1.** (*repair*) reparación *f* **2.** (*patch*) remiendo *m* **II.** *vt* **1.** (*repair*) reparar **2.** (*darn: socks*) zurcir **III.** *vi* (*improve*) mejorar; (*broken bone*) soldarse

menopause ['men·ə·pɔz] *n* menopausia *f*

men's room ['menz·ˌrum] *n* lavabo *m* de hombres

mental ['men·təl] *adj* **1.** (*of the mind*) mental **2.** *offensive sl* (*crazy*) chiflado, -a

mentally *adv* mentalmente; **~ disturbed** trastornado, -a

mention ['men·ʃən] **I.** *n* mención *f;* **to make ~ of sth** mencionar algo **II.** *vt* mencionar; **don't ~ it!** ¡no hay de qué!; **not to ~...** sin contar...

menu ['men·ju] *n* **1.** (*list of dishes*) carta *f;* (*fixed meal*) menú *m* **2.** COMPUT menú

menu bar *n* barra *f* de menús

meow [mi·'aʊ] **I.** *n* miau *m* **II.** *vi* maullar

mercenary ['mɜr·sə·ner·i] **I.** *n* <-ies> mercenario, -a *m, f* **II.** *adj* mercenario, -a

merchant ['mɜr·tʃənt] *n* comerciante *mf*

merchant marine *n* marina *f* mercante

merchant ship *n* mercante *m*

merciful ['mɜr·sɪ·fəl] *adj* misericordioso, -a

merciless ['mɜr·sɪ·lɪs] *adj* despiadado, -a

mercury ['mɜr·kjə·ri] *n* mercurio *m*

Mercury ['mɜr·kjə·ri] *n* Mercurio *m*

mercy ['mɜr·si] *n* **1.** (*compassion*) compasión *f;* **to have ~ on sb** tener compasión de alguien **2.** (*forgiveness*) misericordia *f;* **to be at the ~ of sb** estar a merced de alguien; **to plead for ~** pedir clemencia

mere [mɪr] *adj* mero, -a; **a ~ formality** una simple formalidad

merely ['mɪr·li] *adv* solamente

merge [mɜrdʒ] **I.** *vi* unirse; ECON, POL fusionarse **II.** *vt* unir; ECON, POL, COMPUT fusionar

merger ['mɜr·dʒər] *n* ECON fusión *f*

meridian [mə·'rɪd·i·ən] *n* meridiano *m*

merit ['mer·ɪt] **I.** *n* **1.** (*virtue*) cualidad *f* **2.** (*advantage*) ventaja *f* **3.** (*commendable quality or act*) mérito *m;* **to achieve sth on one's own ~s** conseguir algo por mérito propio **II.** *vt* merecer

merry ['mer·i] <-ier, -iest> *adj* alegre

merry-go-round ['mer·i·goʊ·ˌraʊnd] *n* tiovivo *m*

mesmerize ['mez·mə·raɪz] vt hipnotizar

mesmerizing [mez·'mer·ɪk] adj hipnótico, -a

mess [mes] <-es> n 1. (confusion) confusión f; (disordered state) desorden m; **to be in a ~** estar revuelto; **to make a ~ of sth** echar a perder algo 2. (things) caos m inv 3. (trouble) lío m, merengue m Arg

♦**mess around** vi 1. (joke) hacer el tonto 2. (waste time) pasar el rato

♦**mess up** I. vt inf 1. (make untidy) desordenar 2. (dirty) ensuciar 3. (screw up) echar a perder II. vi cagarla inf

message ['mes·ɪdʒ] n mensaje m; **error ~** COMPUT mensaje m de error

messenger ['mes·ɪn·dʒər] n mensajero, -a m, f

mess-up ['mes·ʌp] n inf follón m

messy ['mes·i] <-ier, -iest> adj 1. (untidy) desordenado, -a 2. (dirty) sucio, -a

met [met] vi, vt pt of **meet**

metal ['met·əl] I. n (element) metal m II. adj metálico, -a

metal detector n detector m de metales

metallic [mə·'tæl·ɪk] adj metálico, -a

metaphor ['met·ə·fɔr] n metáfora f

meteorite ['mi·ti·ə·raɪt] n meteorito m

meteorological [,mi·ti·ər·ə·'lɑdʒ·ɪ·kəl] adj meteorológico, -a

meteorology [,mi·ti·ə·'rɑl·ə·dʒi] n meteorología f

meter[1] ['mi·tər] n contador m, medidor m AmL; (parking) ~ parquímetro m; (taxi) ~ taxímetro m

meter[2] ['mi·tər] n metro m

method ['meθ·əd] n método m

methodical [mə·'θɑd·ɪ·kəl] adj metódico, -a

metric(al) ['met·rɪk] adj métrico, -a

metro[1] ['met·rou] n RAIL (subway) metro m

metro[2] ['met·rou] adj abbr of **metropolitan** metropolitano, -a

metropolis [mə·'trɑp·ə·lɪs] <-es> n metrópoli f

metropolitan [,met·rə·'pɑl·ə·tən] adj metropolitano, -a

Mexican ['mek·sɪ·kən] adj, n mexicano, -a m, f

Mexico ['mek·sɪ·kou] n México m; **New ~** Nuevo México

Mexico City n Ciudad f de México

MI ['mɪʃ·ɪ·gən] n abbr of **Michigan** Michigan m

MIA [,em·aɪ·'eɪ] abbr of **missing in action** desaparecido, -a en combate

mic [maɪk] n inf 1. abbr of **microphone** 2. abbr of **Michigan**

mice [maɪs] n pl of **mouse**

microbe ['maɪ·kroub] n microbio m

microbiology [,maɪ·krou·baɪ·'ɑl·ə·dʒi] n microbiología f

microchip ['maɪ·krou·,tʃɪp] n microchip m

microorganism [,maɪ·krou·'ɔr·gə·nɪz·əm] n microorganismo m

microphone ['maɪ·krə·foun] n micrófono m

microprocessor ['maɪ·krou·,prɑs·es·ər] n microprocesador m

microscope ['maɪ·krə·skoup] n microscopio m

microscopic [,maɪ·krə·'skɑp·ɪk] adj microscópico, -a

microwave ['maɪ·krou·weɪv] n 1. (wave) microonda f 2. (oven) microondas m inv

midday [,mɪd·'deɪ] n mediodía m; **at ~** al mediodía; **~ meal** almuerzo m

middle ['mɪd·əl] I. n (center) medio m; **in the ~ of sth** en medio de algo; **in the ~ of the night** en plena noche II. adj 1. (equidistant) central 2. (medium) medio, -a

middle-aged adj de mediana edad

Middle Ages npl Edad f Media

middle-class adj de la clase media

Middle East n Oriente m Medio

middleman ['mɪd·əl·mæn] <-men> n intermediario m

middle name n segundo nombre m

middle-of-the-road adj moderado, -a

middling ['mɪd·lɪŋ] adj inf 1. (average) mediano, -a 2. (not very good) regular, flojo, -a

Mideast n Oriente m Medio

midget ['mɪdʒ·ɪt] I. n enano, -a m, f II. adj en miniatura

midlife crisis [,mɪd·'laɪf·'kraɪ·sɪs] n crisis f inv de los cuarenta

M

midnight ['mɪd·naɪt] n medianoche f

midst [mɪdst] n **in the ~ of** en medio de

midsummer [,mɪd·'sʌm·ər] n pleno verano m

midterm [,mɪd·'tɜrm] I. n UNIV (exam) parcial m II. adj de mitad del trimestre; **~ vacation** vacaciones f pl de mitad de trimestre

midway [,mɪd·'weɪ] I. adv a medio camino II. n feria f (con juegos de azar, espectáculos...)

midweek [,mɪd·'wik] adv entre semana

midwife ['mɪd·waɪf] <-wives> n comadrona f

miffed [mɪft] adj ofendido, -a; **to be ~ at sb** estar picado con alguien

might[1] [maɪt] pt of **may**; **it ~ be that...** podría ser que... +subj; **how old ~ she be?** ¿qué edad tendrá?

might[2] [maɪt] n **1.** (power) poder m **2.** (strength) fuerza f

mighty ['maɪ·ti] <-ier, -iest> adj **1.** (powerful) fuerte **2.** (great) enorme

migraine ['maɪ·greɪn] <-(s)> n migraña f

migrate ['maɪ·greɪt] vi emigrar

migration [maɪ·'greɪ·ʃən] <-(s)> n (person) emigración f; (animal) migración f

mike [maɪk] n inf micro m

mild [maɪld] <-er, -est> adj **1.** (not severe) apacible; (criticism) moderado, -a; (penalty) leve **2.** (in taste) suave **3.** METEO templado, -a

mildly ['maɪld·li] adv **1.** (gently) suavemente **2.** (slightly) ligeramente

mile [maɪl] n milla f (1,61 km); **to walk for ~s (and ~s)** andar kilómetros y kilómetros ▶ **to smell sth a ~ away** ver algo a la legua

mileage ['maɪ·lɪdʒ] n AUTO kilometraje m

milestone ['maɪl·stoʊn] n **1.** (marker) mojón m **2.** fig hito m

militant ['mɪl·ɪ·tənt] I. adj militante II. n militante mf

military ['mɪl·ɪ·ter·i] I. n **the ~** los militares II. adj militante

military academy n academia f militar

military police n policía f militar

military service n servicio m militar

milk [mɪlk] I. n leche f II. vt **1. to ~ a cow** ordeñar una vaca **2.** fig inf (exploit) **to ~ sb dry** chupar la sangre a alguien

milk chocolate n chocolate m con leche

milkman <-men> n lechero m

milkshake n batido m, malteada f Méx

milk tooth n diente m de leche

milky ['mɪl·ki] <-ier, -iest> adj **1.** (color) lechoso, -a **2.** (coffee) con mucha leche

mill [mɪl] I. n **1.** (for grain) molino m; (for coffee) molinillo m **2.** (factory) fábrica f (de tejidos) II. vt (grain) moler

millennium [mɪ·'len·i·əm] <-s or -ennia> n milenio m

miller ['mɪl·ər] n molinero, -a m, f

milligram ['mɪl·ɪ·græm] n miligramo m

milliliter ['mɪl·ɪ·li·tər] n mililitro m

millimeter ['mɪl·ɪ·mi·tər] n milímetro m

million ['mɪl·jən] <-(s)> n millón m; **two ~ people** dos millones de personas; **a ~ times** inf un millón de veces; **to be one in a ~** ser único

millionaire [,mɪl·jə·'ner] n millonario, -a m, f

millipede ['mɪl·ɪ·pid] n milpiés m inv

mimic ['mɪm·ɪk] I. vt <-ck-> imitar II. n imitador(a) m(f)

min. 1. abbr of **minute** min. **2.** abbr of **minimum** mín.

mince [mɪns] I. vt **1.** (shred) picar **2.** (use tact) **to not ~ words** no andarse con rodeos II. n carne f picada

mincemeat n **1.** (meat) carne f picada **2.** (fruit) picadillo m de fruta ▶ **to make ~ of sb/sth** sl hacer picadillo a alguien/algo

mind [maɪnd] I. n **1.** (brain) mente f; **to be out of one's ~** estar fuera de juicio **2.** (thought) pensamiento m; **to bear sth in ~** tener algo presente; **to bring sth to ~** recordar algo **3.** (intention) intención f; **to change one's ~** cambiar de parecer; **to have sth in ~** tener pensado algo; **to make up one's ~** decidirse **4.** (consciousness) conciencia f; **this will take your ~ off (of) it** esto te distraerá **5.** (opinion) opinión f; **to be of the same ~** ser de la misma opinión;

to give sb a piece of one's ~ cantar las cuarenta a alguien **II.** vt **1.** (be careful of) tener cuidado con; ~ **what you're doing!** ¡cuidado con lo que haces! **2.** (look after) estar al cuidado de; **don't ~ me** no te preocupes por mí **3.** (bother) sentirse molesto por; **do you ~ my smoking?** ¿te molesta si fumo?; **would you ~ opening the window?** ¿haces el favor de abrir la ventana?; **I wouldn't ~ a beer** no me vendría mal una cerveza **III.** vi **never ~!** ¡no importa!; **I don't ~** me es igual; **if you don't ~, I prefer...** si no te importa, prefiero...; **would you ~ if...** ¿te importa si...?

mindful ['maɪnd·fəl] adj form cuidadoso, -a; **to be ~ of sth** tener presente algo

mindless ['maɪnd·lɪs] adj **1.** (job) mecánico, -a **2.** (violence) gratuito, -a **3.** (heedless) descuidado, -a

mine¹ [maɪn] pron pos (el) mío, (la) mía, (los) míos, (las) mías; **it's not his bag, it's ~** no es su bolsa, es la mía

mine² [maɪn] **I.** n MIN, MIL mina f; **a ~ of information** fig una fuente abundante de información **II.** vt **1.** MIN extraer **2.** MIL minar **III.** vi MIN explotar minas; **to ~ for silver/gold** buscar plata/oro

minefield ['maɪn·fild] n **1.** campo m de minas **2.** fig terreno m minado

miner ['maɪ·nər] n minero, -a m, f

mineral ['mɪn·ər·əl] adj, n mineral m

mineral water n agua f mineral

minestrone [ˌmɪn·ɪ·'stroʊ·ni] n sopa f de verduras

mingle ['mɪŋ·gəl] **I.** vi mezclarse (with con) **II.** vt mezclar

miniature ['mɪn·i·ə·tʃər] n miniatura f

minibus ['mɪn·i·bʌs] n microbús m

minimal ['mɪn·ɪ·məl] adj mínimo, -a

minimize ['mɪn·ɪ·maɪz] vt minimizar; fig menospreciar

minimum ['mɪn·ɪ·məm] **I.** <-s or minima> n mínimo m; **to reduce sth to a ~** reducir algo al mínimo **II.** adj mínimo, -a; ~ **requirements** requisitos m pl básicos

mining ['maɪ·nɪŋ] n minería f

miniskirt ['mɪn·i·skɜrt] n minifalda f

minister ['mɪn·ɪ·stər] n **1.** POL ministro, -a m, f **2.** REL pastor m

ministry ['mɪn·ɪ·stri] <-ies> n **1.** REL sacerdocio m **2.** POL ministerio m

minivan ['mɪn·i·væn] n vehículo m mixto, minivan m Col, Méx

minor ['maɪ·nər] **I.** adj (not great) pequeño, -a; (role) secundario, -a; (detail) sin importancia; ~ **offense** delito m de menor cuantía; **B** = MUS si menor **II.** n **1.** (person) menor mf de edad **2.** UNIV asignatura f secundaria

Minorca [mɪ·'nɔr·kə] n Menorca f

Minorcan adj, n menorquín, -ina m, f

minority [maɪ·'nɔr·ə·ti] <-ies> n minoría f; **to be in the ~** estar en minoría

mint¹ [mɪnt] n **1.** (herb) hierbabuena f **2.** (candy) caramelo m de menta

mint² [mɪnt] **I.** n FIN casa f de la moneda **II.** vt acuñar **III.** adj (coin) de reciente acuñación; (stamp) nuevo, -a

minus ['maɪ·nəs] **I.** prep **1.** a. MATH menos; **5 ~ 2 equals 3** 5 menos 2 igual a 3; ~ **ten degrees Celsius** diez grados bajo cero **2.** inf (without) sin **II.** adj MATH menos **III.** n MATH (signo m) menos m

minute¹ ['mɪn·ɪt] n **1.** (sixty seconds) minuto m **2.** (moment) momento m; **any ~** de un momento a otro; **at the last ~** a última hora; **in a ~** en seguida; **this very ~** ahora mismo; **to the ~** puntual; **wait a ~** espera un segundo **3.** ~s (of meeting) acta(s) f(pl)

minute² [maɪ·'nut] adj diminuto, -a

minute hand n minutero m

miracle ['mɪr·ə·kəl] n milagro m

miraculous [mɪ·'ræk·jə·ləs] adj milagroso, -a

mirror ['mɪr·ər] **I.** n espejo m **II.** vt reflejar

misbehave [ˌmɪs·bɪ·'heɪv] vi portarse mal

misbehavior [ˌmɪs·bɪ·'heɪv·jər] n mala conducta f

misc. adj abbr of **miscellaneous** diverso, -a

miscalculate [ˌmɪs·'kæl·kjə·leɪt] vt, vi calcular mal

miscalculation [ˌmɪs·ˌkæl·kjə·'leɪ·ʃən] n error m de cálculo

miscarriage ['mɪs·ˌkær·ɪdʒ] n MED aborto m (espontáneo)

miscarry ['mɪs·ˌkær·i] <-ied, -ying> vi

1. MED abortar **2.** *fig* fracasar

mischief ['mɪs·tʃɪf] *n* **1.** (*naughtiness*) travesura *f* **2. to get (oneself) into ~** meterse en problemas **3.** (*wickedness*) malicia *f*

mischievous ['mɪs·tʃə·vəs] *adj* **1.** (*naughty*) travieso, -a **2.** (*malicious*) malicioso, -a; **~ rumors** rumores *m pl* malintencionados

misconception [,mɪs·kən·'sep·ʃən] *n* idea *f* equivocada

misconduct [,mɪs·'kan·dʌkt] *n* (*misbehavior*) mala conducta *f*

miser ['maɪ·zər] *n* avaro, -a *m, f*

miserable ['mɪz·rə·bəl] *adj* **1.** (*unhappy*) triste **2.** (*unpleasant*) lamentable **3.** (*inadequate*) mísero, -a; **a ~ amount** una miseria

miserably *adv* **1.** (*unhappily*) tristemente; **to feel ~** sentirse abatido **2.** (*completely*) **to fail ~** fallar miserablemente

misery ['mɪz·ə·ri] *n* **1.** (*unhappiness*) infelicidad *f* **2.** (*suffering*) sufrimiento *m* **3.** (*extreme poverty*) miseria *f*, lipidia *f AmC*

misfire [,mɪs·'faɪr] *vi* **1.** (*weapon*) encasquillarse **2.** (*engine*) fallar

misfit ['mɪs·fɪt] *n* inadaptado, -a *m, f*

misfortune [,mɪs·'fɔr·tʃən] *n* infortunio *m*

misguided [mɪs·'gaɪ·dɪd] *adj* desencaminado, -a

mishap ['mɪs·hæp] *n form* percance *m*

mishear [,mɪs·'hɪr] *vt irr* oír mal

misinform [,mɪs·ɪn·'fɔrm] *vt* informar mal, desinformar *Méx*

misjudge [,mɪs·'dʒʌdʒ] *vt* juzgar mal

mislead [,mɪs·'lid] *vt irr* **1.** (*deceive*) engañar **2. to let oneself be misled** dejarse engañar

misleading *adj* engañoso, -a

misplace [,mɪs·'pleɪs] *vt* (*lose*) extraviar

misprint ['mɪs·ˌprɪnt] *n* errata *f*

mispronounce [,mɪs·prə·'naʊns] *vt* pronunciar mal

misread [,mɪs·'rid] *vt irr* **1.** (*read badly*) leer mal **2.** (*interpret badly*) malinterpretar

misrepresent [,mɪs·,rep·rɪ·'zent] *vt* tergiversar

miss¹ [mɪs] *n* (*form of address*) señorita *f*

miss² [mɪs] **I.** <-es> *n* fallo *m* **II.** *vi* fallar **III.** *vt* **1.** (*not hit*) fallar **2.** (*not catch*) perder; **to ~ the bus** perder el bus; **to ~ a deadline** no cumplir con una fecha límite **3.** (*avoid*) evitar **4.** (*not notice*) no fijarse en; **you didn't ~ much** no te has perdido nada **5.** (*not hear*) no oír **6.** (*overlook*) saltarse; **to ~ a meeting** faltar a una reunión **7.** (*not take advantage*) dejar pasar; **to ~ an opportunity** perder una oportunidad **8.** (*regret absence*) echar de menos **9.** (*notice loss*) echar en falta

♦ **miss out** *vi* perdérselo

missile ['mɪs·əl] *n* (*rocket*) misil *m*; (*projectile*) proyectil *m*

missing ['mɪs·ɪŋ] *adj* **1.** (*lost: person*) desaparecido, -a; (*thing or object*) perdido, -a **2.** (*absent*) ausente

mission ['mɪʃ·ən] *n a.* REL (*task*) misión *f*; **peace ~** misión de paz; **rescue ~** operación *f* de rescate; **his ~ in life** su misión en la vida; **~ accomplished** misión cumplida

missionary ['mɪʃ·ə·ner·i] <-ies> *n* misionero, -a *m, f*

Mississippi [mɪs·ɪ·'sɪ·pi] *n* Misisipí *m*

Missouri [mɪ·'zʊr·i] *n* Misuri *m*

misspell [,mɪs·'spel] *vt irr* escribir mal

mist [mɪst] *n* **1.** (*light fog*) neblina *f*; **to be shrouded in ~** estar cubierto por la neblina **2.** (*condensation*) vaho *m*

mistake [mɪ·'steɪk] **I.** *n* error *m*; **typing ~** errata *f*; **to learn from one's ~s** aprender de los propios errores; **to make a ~** cometer un error; **by ~** por error **II.** *vt irr* confundir

mistaken [mɪ·'steɪ·kən] **I.** *pp of* mistake **II.** *adj* (*belief*) equivocado, -a; (*identity*) confundido, -a; **to be (very much) ~** estar (muy) equivocado

Mister ['mɪs·tər] *n* señor *m*

mistook [mɪ·'stʊk] *pt of* mistake

mistreat [,mɪs·'trit] *vt* maltratar

mistress ['mɪs·trɪs] *n* **1.** (*sexual partner*) amante *f* **2.** (*woman in charge*) ama *f*; **the ~ of the house** la dueña de la casa

mistrust [,mɪs·'trʌst] **I.** *n* desconfianza *f* **II.** *vt* **to ~ sb/sth** recelar de alguien/algo

mistrustful [,mɪs·'trʌst·fəl] *adj* receloso, -a; **to be ~ of sb/sth** recelar de alguien/algo

misty ['mɪs·ti] <-ier, -iest> *adj* (*foggy*) neblinoso, -a; (*window, glasses*) empañado, -a

misunderstand [,mɪs·ʌn·dər·'stænd] *vt irr* entender mal

misunderstanding *n* 1. (*failure to understand*) malentendido *m* 2. (*disagreement*) desacuerdo *m*

misuse [,mɪs·'jus] *n* 1. (*wrong use*) mal uso *m* 2. (*abuse*) abuso *m*

mitten ['mɪt·ən] *n* manopla *f*

mix [mɪks] I. *n* mezcla *f* II. *vt* 1. CULIN (*ingredients*) mezclar; (*cocktails*) preparar 2. (*combine*) combinar; **to ~ business with pleasure** combinar los negocios con el placer III. *vi* 1. (*combine*) mezclarse 2. (*socially*) **to ~ well** llevarse bien

◆**mix up** *vt* 1. (*confuse*) confundir 2. (*put in wrong order*) revolver

mixed *adj* 1. mezclado, -a; **person of ~ race** mestizo, -a *m, f* 2. (*contradictory*) contradictorio, -a

mixer ['mɪk·sər] *n* (*machine*) batidora *f*

mixture ['mɪks·tʃər] *n* mezcla *f*

mix-up ['mɪks·ʌp] *n* confusión *f*

MMR [,emem'ar] *n* MED *abbr of* **measles, mumps and rubella** SPR *f*

MN [,mɪn·ɪ·'soʊ·tə] *n abbr of* **Minnesota** Minnesota *f*

MO *n* 1. *abbr of* **modus operandi** procedimiento *m* 2. *abbr of* **Missouri** Misuri *m* 3. *abbr of* **money order** giro *m*

moan [moʊn] I. *n* 1. (*sound*) gemido *m* 2. (*complaint*) quejido *m* II. *vi* 1. gemir; **to ~ with pain** gemir de dolor 2. (*complain*) lamentarse (**about** de)

mob [mab] I. *n* + *sing/pl vb* 1. (*crowd*) muchedumbre *f*; **angry ~** turba *f* 2. *inf* **the Mob** la mafia II. <-bb-> *vt* acosar; **he was ~bed by his fans** sus fans se aglomeraron en torno a él

mobile ['moʊ·bəl] I. *n a.* TEL móvil *m* II. *adj* (*able to move*) móvil; **to be ~** *inf* tener coche

mobile home *n* caravana *f*

mobster ['mab·stər] *n* gángster *mf*

mock [mak] I. *adj* 1. (*imitation*) artificial 2. (*fake*) ficticio, -a; **~ approval** aprobación simulada II. *vi* burlarse (**at** de) III. *vt* 1. (*ridicule*) mofarse de 2. (*imitate*) remedar

mode [moʊd] *n* 1. *a.* LING, PHILOS (*manner*) modo *m* 2. *form* (*fashion*) moda *f*; **in ~** de moda

model ['mad·əl] I. *n* (*version, example*) *a.* ART modelo *m*; (*of car, house*) maqueta *f* II. *adj* modélico, -a; **a ~ student** un alumno modelo III. <-ll-> *vt* 1. modelar 2. (*show clothes*) desfilar IV. *vi* hacer de modelo

modem ['moʊ·dəm] *n* COMPUT módem *m*

moderate[1] ['mad·ər·ət] *adj* 1. (*average*) mediano, -a 2. *a.* POL (*not extreme: speed*) moderado, -a; (*increase*) mesurado, -a; (*price*) módico, -a

moderate[2] ['mad·ə·reɪt] I. *vt* moderar II. *vi* 1. (*act as moderator*) hacer de moderador 2. (*become less extreme*) moderarse

moderation [,mad·ə·'reɪ·ʃən] *n* moderación *f*; **in ~** con moderación

moderator ['mad·ə·reɪ·tər] *n* moderador(a) *m(f)*

modern ['mad·ərn] *adj* moderno, -a

modernize ['mad·ər·naɪz] *vt* modernizar

modest ['mad·ɪst] *adj* modesto, -a

modesty ['mad·ɪ·sti] *n* modestia *f*

modification [,mad·ɪ·fɪ·'keɪ·ʃən] *n* modificación *f*

modify ['mad·ɪ·faɪ] <-ie-> *vt a.* LING modificar

modular ['madʒ·ə·lər] *adj* modular; (*construction*) por módulos

module ['madʒ·ul] *n* módulo *m*

moist [mɔɪst] *adj* húmedo, -a

moisten ['mɔɪ·sən] I. *vt* humedecer II. *vi* humedecerse

moisture ['mɔɪs·tʃər] *n* humedad *f*

moisturizer *n* hidratante *m*

molar[1] ['moʊ·lər] *n* muela *f*

molar[2] ['moʊ·lər] *adj* CHEM molar

mold[1] [moʊld] I. *n* molde *m* II. *vt* moldear

mold[2] [moʊld] *n* BOT moho *m*

moldy ['moʊl·di] <-ier, -iest> *adj* mohoso, -a

mole[1] [moʊl] *n* ANAT lunar *m*

mole² [moʊl] n **1.** ZOOL topo m **2.** (spy) topo mf

molecular [mə·ˈlek·jə·lər] adj molecular

molecule [ˈmɑl·ɪ·kjul] n molécula f

molehill [ˈmoʊl·hɪl] n topera f

mollusk [ˈmɑl·əsk] n molusco m

molten [ˈmoʊl·tən] adj fundido, -a

mom [mɑm] n inf mamá f

moment [ˈmoʊ·mənt] n momento m; **at the ~** por el momento; **at any ~** en cualquier momento; **at the last ~** en el último momento; **in a ~** enseguida; **not for a ~** ni por un momento; **the ~ that...** en cuanto... +subj

momentarily [ˌmoʊ·mən·ˈter·ɪ·li] adv **1.** (briefly) por un momento **2.** (soon) en un momento

momentary [ˈmoʊ·mən·ter·i] adj momentáneo, -a

momentous [moʊ·ˈmen·təs] adj (fact) trascendental; (day) memorable

momentum [moʊ·ˈmen·təm] n PHYS momento m; fig impulso m; **to gather ~** coger velocidad

monarch [ˈmɑn·ərk] n monarca mf

monarchy [ˈmɑn·ər·ki] <-ies> n monarquía f

monastery [ˈmɑn·ə·ster·i] <-ies> n monasterio m

Monday [ˈmʌn·di] n lunes m inv

monetary [ˈmɑn·ə·ter·i] adj monetario, -a

money [ˈmʌn·i] n dinero m; **to be short of ~** ir escaso de dinero; **to change ~** cambiar dinero; **to make ~** hacer dinero; **to raise ~** recolectar fondos ► **~ doesn't grow on trees** prov el dinero no cae del cielo prov

money order n giro m postal

monitor [ˈmɑn·ɪ·tər] I. n **1.** COMPUT monitor m; **15-inch ~** monitor de 15 pulgadas **2.** (person) supervisor(a) m(f) II. vt controlar; **to ~ sb/sth closely** seguir a alguien/algo de muy cerca

monk [mʌŋk] n monje m

monkey [ˈmʌŋ·ki] n mono, -a m, f

monkey wrench n <-es> llave f inglesa

monkfish n rape m

monogamy [mə·ˈnɑg·ə·mi] n monogamia f

monologue [ˈmɑn·ə·lag] n monólogo m

monopolize [mə·ˈnɑp·ə·laɪz] vt monopolizar

monopoly [mə·ˈnɑp·ə·li] <-ies> n monopolio m

monorail [ˈmɑn·oʊ·reɪl] n monorraíl m

monotonous [mə·ˈnɑt·ən·əs] adj monótono, -a

monotony [mə·ˈnɑt·ən·i] n monotonía f

monsoon [mɑn·ˈsun] n monzón m

monster [ˈmɑn·stər] n monstruo m

monstrous [ˈmɑn·strəs] adj **1.** (big) enorme **2.** (awful) monstruoso, -a

month [mʌnθ] n mes m

monthly [ˈmʌnθ·li] I. adj mensual II. adv mensualmente

monument [ˈmɑn·jə·mənt] n monumento m

monumental [ˌmɑn·jə·ˈmen·təl] adj (very big) monumental

moo [mu] I. <-s> n mugido m II. vi mugir

mood¹ [mud] n humor m; **in a good ~** de buen humor; **to not be in the ~ to do sth** no tener ganas de hacer algo

mood² [mud] n LING modo m

moody [ˈmu·di] <-ier, -iest> adj **1.** (changeable) voluble **2.** (bad-tempered) malhumorado, -a

moon [mun] n luna f; **full/new ~** luna llena/nueva ► **once in a blue ~** de higos a brevas; **to be over the ~** estar como un niño con zapatos nuevos

moonlight I. n luz f de la luna II. vi inf estar pluriempleado

moonlit adj iluminado, -a por la luna

moor¹ [mʊr] n (area) páramo m

moor² [mʊr] vt NAUT amarrar

mooring [ˈmʊr·ɪŋ] n amarra f

moose [mus] n ZOOL alce m americano

mop [mɑp] I. n **1.** (for cleaning) fregona f, trapeador m Chile, Méx **2.** **a ~ of hair** una mata de pelo II. <-pp-> vt fregar

moped [ˈmoʊ·ped] n ciclomotor m

moral [ˈmɔr·əl] I. adj moral; **~ support** apoyo moral II. n **1.** (message) moraleja f **2.** (standards) moralidad f

morale [mə·ˈræl] n moral f

morality [mɔ·ˈræl·ə·ti] <-ies> n moralidad f

moralize ['mɔr·ə·laɪz] vi moralizar

more [mɔr] comp of **much**, **many** I. adj más; ~ **money/coins** más dinero/monedas; **a few** ~ **coins** unas pocas monedas más; **no** ~ **money at all** nada más de dinero; **some** ~ **money** un poco más de dinero II. adv más; ~ **beautiful than me** más guapo que yo; **to drink (a bit/much)** ~ beber (un poco/mucho) más; **once** ~ una vez más; **never** ~ nunca más; ~ **than 10** más de 10 III. pron más; ~ **and** ~ más y más; **to have** ~ **than sb** tener más que alguien; **to cost** ~ **than sth** costar más que algo; **what** ~ **does he want?** ¿qué más quiere? ▶ **all the** ~ tanto más

moreover [mɔr·'ou·vər] adv form además

morgue [mɔrg] n depósito m (de cadáveres)

Mormon ['mɔr·mən] n mormón, -ona m, f

morning ['mɔr·nɪŋ] I. n mañana f; **good** ~! ¡buenos días!; **that** ~ esa mañana; **the** ~ **after** la mañana siguiente; **every** ~ cada mañana; **every Monday** ~ cada lunes por la mañana; **(early) in the** ~ por la mañana (temprano); **6 o'clock in the** ~ las 6 de la mañana; **from** ~ **until night** de la mañana a la noche II. interj inf ¡buenas!

morning-after pill [ˌmɔr·nɪŋ·'æf·tər·ˌpɪl] n píldora f del día después

morning sickness n náuseas f pl matutinas

moron ['mɔr·ɑn] n capullo, -a m, f

morsel ['mɔr·səl] n (of food) bocado m

mortal ['mɔr·təl] I. adj mortal; ~ **danger** peligro m de muerte II. n liter mortal mf

mortality [mɔr·'tæl·ə·t̮i] n form mortalidad f

mortar ['mɔr·tər] n a. MIL, TECH mortero m

mortgage ['mɔr·gɪdʒ] I. n hipoteca f II. vt hipotecar

mortify ['mɔr·tə·faɪ] vt <-ie-> (embarrass) avergonzar

mortuary ['mɔr·tʃu·er·i] n tanatorio m

mosaic [mou·'zeɪ·ɪk] n mosaico m

Moscow ['mɑs·kaʊ] n Moscú m

Moslem ['mɑz·ləm] adj, n musulmán,

-ana m, f

mosque [mɑsk] n mezquita f

mosquito [mə·'ski·tou] <-(e)s> n mosquito m, zancudo m AmL

moss [mɑs] <-es> n musgo m

mossy ['mɑs·i] <-ier, -iest> adj musgoso, -a

most [moʊst] superl of **many**, **much** I. adj la mayoría de; ~ **people** la mayoría de la gente; **for the** ~ **part** en su mayor parte II. adv más; **the** ~ **beautiful** el más bello, la más bella; **what I want** ~ lo que más quiero; ~ **of all** más que nada; ~ **likely** muy probablemente III. pron la mayoría; **at the (very)** ~ a lo sumo; ~ **of them** la mayoría de ellos; ~ **of the time** la mayor parte del tiempo; **to make the** ~ **of sth/of oneself** sacar el máximo partido a [or de] algo/ sí mismo

mostly ['moʊst·li] adv 1. (mainly) sobre todo 2. (usually) en general

motel [mou·'tel] n motel m, hotel-garaje m AmL

moth [mɔθ] n polilla f

mothball ['mɔθ·bɔl] n bola f de naftalina

moth-eaten ['mɔθ·ˌi·tən] adj apolillado, -a

mother ['mʌð·ər] I. n madre f II. vt mimar

motherhood n maternidad f

mother-in-law n suegra f

motherly ['mʌð·ər·li] adj maternal

mother tongue n lengua f materna

motion ['moʊ·ʃən] I. n 1. (movement) movimiento m; **in slow** ~ a cámara lenta; **to put sth in** ~ poner algo en marcha 2. (proposal) moción f II. vt indicar con un gesto; **to** ~ **sb to do sth** indicar a alguien que haga algo III. vi hacer señas

motionless adj inmóvil

motion picture n película f

motivate ['mou·tə·veɪt] vt 1. (cause) motivar 2. (arouse interest of) animar

motivation [ˌmoʊ·tə·'veɪ·ʃən] n 1. (reason) motivo m 2. (ambition) motivación f

motive ['mou·tɪv] n motivo m

motor ['mou·tər] I. n a. fig motor m

M

II. adj a. PHYS motor, motriz
motorbike n moto f
motorboat n lancha f motora
motorcycle n motocicleta f
motorcycling n motociclismo m
motorcyclist n motociclista mf
motor home n autocaravana f
motorist ['mou·tər·ɪst] n conductor(a) m(f)
motor racing n automovilismo m
motor vehicle n form automóvil m
motto ['mɑt·ou] <-(e)s> n lema m
mound [maund] n 1. (elevation) montículo m 2. (heap) montón m
mount [maunt] I. n 1. (horse) montura f 2. (frame) marco m II. vt 1. (get on: horse) montar; to ~ a ladder subirse a una escalera 2. (organize) organizar; to ~ a rescue organizar un rescate III. vi montarse
mountain ['maun·tən] n 1. GEO montaña f 2. inf (amount) montón m ▶ to **move** ~s mover cielo y tierra
mountain bike n bicicleta f de montaña
mountaineer [,maun·tə·'nɪr] n montañero, -a m, f
mountaineering n montañismo m
mountainous ['maun·tə·nəs] adj GEO montañoso, -a
mountain range n GEO sierra f
mourn [mɔrn] I. vi lamentarse II. vt llorar la muerte de
mourner ['mɔr·nər] n doliente mf
mourning ['mɔr·nɪŋ] n luto m
mouse [maus] <mice> n ZOOL, COMPUT ratón m
mouse pad n COMPUT alfombrilla f del ratón
mousetrap n ratonera f
moustache ['mʌs·tæʃ] n bigote m
mouth[1] [mauθ] n 1. (of person, animal) boca f; to shut one's ~ inf cerrar el pico 2. (opening) abertura f; (of bottle, jar, well) boca f; (of cave) entrada f; (of river) desembocadura f ▶ it made her ~ <u>water</u> se le hizo la boca agua con eso
mouth[2] [mauð] vt 1. (form words silently) articular 2. (say insincerely) soltar; to ~ an excuse soltar la excusa de rigor

mouthful ['mauθ·ful] n (of food) bocado m; (of drink) sorbo m
mouthpiece n TEL micrófono m
mouthwash n enjuague m bucal
mouthwatering adj apetitoso, -a
move [muv] I. n 1. (movement) movimiento m; to be on the ~ (traveling) estar de viaje; (very busy) no parar; to get a ~ on darse prisa 2. (change of abode) mudanza f; (change of job) traslado m 3. GAMES jugada f; it's your ~ te toca (a ti) 4. (action) paso m; to make the first ~ dar el primer paso II. vi 1. (change position) moverse; (make progress) hacer progresos 2. (in games) mover 3. (change abode) mudarse; (change job) cambiar de trabajo ▶ ~ it! inf ¡apúrate! III. vt 1. (change position) mover; (reschedule) cambiar la fecha de 2. (cause emotions) conmover; to be ~d by sth estar conmovido por algo
◆**move away** I. vi mudarse II. vt apartar
◆**move back** I. vi retirarse II. vt colocar más atrás
◆**move down** vi, vt bajar
◆**move in** vi 1. (move into abode) instalarse 2. (intervene) intervenir 3. (advance to attack) avanzar; to ~ on enemy territory invadir territorio enemigo
◆**move on** vi 1. (leave) partir 2. (continue to move) seguir adelante; to ~ to another subject pasar a otro tema
◆**move out** vi 1. (stop inhabiting) dejar la casa 2. (depart) irse
◆**move over** vi 1. (make room) dejar sitio; (on seat) correrse hacia un lado II. vt mover a un lado
◆**move up** I. vi 1. (make room) hacer sitio; (on seat) correrse hacia un lado 2. (increase) subir 3. (advance) ascender II. vt subir
movement ['muv·mənt] n 1. a. MUS (act) movimiento m 2. FIN, COM actividad f 3. (tendency) tendencia f
movie ['mu·vi] n película f; the ~s el cine
movie camera n cámara f cinematográfica
moviegoer n cinéfilo, -a m, f
movie star n estrella f de cine

movie theater *n* cine *m*

moving ['muːvɪŋ] *adj* **1.** (*that moves*) móvil; **~ stairs** escaleras mecánicas **2.** (*motivating*) motriz; **the ~ force** la fuerza motriz **3.** (*causing emotion*) conmovedor(a)

mow [moʊ] <mowed, mown *or* mowed> *vt* (*grass*) cortar; (*hay*) segar

mower ['moʊ-ər] *n* (*for lawn*) cortacésped *m*

mown [moʊn] *pp of* **mow**

MP [ˌem-'piː] *n abbr of* **Military Police** policía *f* militar

mpg *n abbr of* **miles per gallon** millas *f pl* por galón

mph [ˌem-piː-'eɪtʃ] *abbr of* **miles per hour** m/h

Mr. ['mɪs-tər] *n abbr of* **Mister** Sr.

Mrs. ['mɪs-ɪz] *n abbr of* **Mistress** Sra.

MS [ˌem-'es] **1.** *abbr of* **Mississippi** Misisipí *m* **2.** *abbr of* **Master of Science** máster *m*

Ms. [mɪz] *n* forma de tratamiento que se aplica tanto a mujeres solteras como casadas

MT *n abbr of* **Montana** Montana *f*

Mt. *abbr of* **Mount** mte.

much [mʌtʃ] <more, most> **I.** *adj* mucho, mucha; **how ~ milk?** ¿cuánta leche?; **too/so ~ water** demasiada/tanta agua; **as ~ as** tanto como; **three times as ~** tres veces más **II.** *adv* mucho; **better** mucho mejor; **thank you very ~** muchas gracias; **to be very ~ surprised** estar muy sorprendido; **~ to my astonishment** para gran sorpresa mía **III.** *pron* mucho; **~ of the day** la mayor parte del día; **I don't think ~ of it** no le doy mucha importancia

muck [mʌk] *n* (*dirt*) suciedad *f*

mucky ['mʌk-i] <-ier, -iest> *adj inf* guarro, -a

mud [mʌd] *n* barro *m* ▶ **to drag sb's name through the ~** ensuciar el nombre de alguien

muddle ['mʌd-əl] **I.** *vt* **1.** (*mix up*) desordenar **2.** (*confuse*) confundir **II.** *n* desorden *m*

muddy ['mʌd-i] <-ier, -iest> *adj* (*dirty*) lleno, -a de barro; (*water*) turbio, -a **II.** *vt* (*make dirty*) manchar de barro

▶ **to ~ the waters** complicar las cosas

mudslide *n* (*flow*) avalancha *f* de lodo

muffin ['mʌf-ɪn] *n especie de magdalena*

muffle ['mʌf-əl] *vt* amortiguar

mug¹ [mʌg] *n* tazón *m*; (*for beer*) jarra *m*

mug² [mʌg] **I.** *n inf* jeta *f*, escracho *m RíoPl* **II.** <-gg-> *vt* atracar

mugger ['mʌg-ər] *n* atracador(a) *m(f)*

muggy ['mʌg-i] <-ier, -iest> *adj* bochornoso, -a

mule [mjuːl] *n* (*animal*) mulo, -a *m, f* ▶ **as stubborn as a ~** terco como una mula

mull [mʌl] *vt* **to ~ sth over** meditar algo

multicolored [ˌmʌl-ti-'kʌl-ərd] *adj* multicolor

multilingual [ˌmʌl-ti-'lɪŋ-gwəl] *adj* plurilingüe

multimedia [ˌmʌl-ti-'miː-di-ə] *adj* multimedia *inv*

multimillionaire [ˌmʌl-ti-mil-jə-'ner] *n* multimillonario, -a *m, f*

multinational [ˌmʌl-ti-'næʃ-ə-nəl] *adj, n* multinacional *f*

multiplayer ['mʌl-ti-pleɪ-ər] *adj* (*computer game*) multijugador

multiple ['mʌl-tə-pəl] *adj* múltiple

multiplication [ˌmʌl-tə-plɪ-'keɪ-ʃən] *n* multiplicación *f*

multiply ['mʌl-tə-plaɪ] <-ie-> **I.** *vt* multiplicar **II.** *vi* multiplicarse

multipurpose [ˌmʌl-ti-'pɜr-pəs] *adj* multiuso

multitude ['mʌl-tə-tud] *n* multitud *f*; **the ~s** *liter* las masas

mum [mʌm] *adj* **to keep ~** *inf* guardar silencio

mumble ['mʌm-bəl] *vi* hablar entre dientes

mummy ['mʌm-i] <-ies> *n* momia *f*

mumps [mʌmps] *n MED* paperas *fpl*

munch [mʌntʃ] *vi, vt* masticar

mural ['mjʊr-əl] *n* mural *m*

murder ['mɜr-dər] **I.** *n* (*killing*) asesinato *m*; LAW homicidio *m*; **to commit ~** cometer un asesinato; **this job is ~** *fig* este trabajo es matador; **he gets away with ~** *fig* se le consiente cualquier cosa **II.** *vt* (*kill*) asesinar, ultimar *AmL*

M

murderer ['mɜr·dər·ər] n (killer) asesino, -a m, f; LAW homicida mf, victimario, -a m, f AmL

murderous ['mɜr·dər·əs] adj 1. mortífero, -a 2. (instinct, look) asesino, -a; (plan) criminal 3. inf (heat) insufrible

murky ['mɜr·ki] <-ier, -iest> adj (water, past) turbio, -a; (night) nublado, -a

murmur ['mɜr·mər] I. vi, vt murmurar II. n murmullo m

muscle ['mʌs·əl] n ANAT músculo m

muscular ['mʌs·kjə·lər] adj 1. (pain, contraction) muscular 2. (arms, legs) musculoso, -a

muse [mjuz] I. vi to ~ (on sth) cavilar (sobre algo) II. n musa f

museum [mju·'zi·əm] n museo m

mushroom ['mʌʃ·rum] n champiñón m; (wild) seta f

music ['mju·zɪk] n 1. (art) música f 2. (notes) partitura f

musical ['mju·zɪ·kəl] adj, n musical m

music box n caja f de música

musician [mju·'zɪʃ·ən] n músico, -a m, f

music stand n atril m

Muslim ['mʌz·ləm] n musulmán, -ana m, f

mussel ['mʌs·əl] n mejillón m

must [mʌst] I. aux 1. (obligation) deber; ~ you leave so soon? ¿tienes que irte tan pronto?; you ~n't do that no debes hacer eso 2. (probability) deber de; I ~ have lost it debo de haberlo perdido; you ~ be hungry supongo que tendrás hambre II. n cosa f imprescindible; this book is an absolute ~ este es un libro de lectura obligada

mustache ['mʌs·tæʃ] n bigote m

mustard ['mʌs·tərd] n mostaza f

mustn't ['mʌs·ənt] = must not s. must

mutant ['mju·tənt] adj mutante

mutation [mju·'teɪ·ʃən] n mutación f

mute [mjut] I. n MUS sordina f II. adj mudo, -a

mutiny ['mju·tɪ·ni] n <-ies> motín m

mutter ['mʌt·ər] I. vi 1. (talk) murmurar 2. (complain) refunfuñar II. vt murmurar

mutton ['mʌt·ən] n carne f de oveja

mutual ['mju·tʃu·əl] adj (understanding) mutuo, -a; (friend, interest) común

muzzle ['mʌz·əl] I. n 1. (of horse,

dog) hocico m 2. (for dog) bozal m 3. (of gun) boca f II. vt (dog) poner un bozal a

my [maɪ] I. adj pos mi; ~ dog/house mi perro/casa; ~ children mis hijos; this car is ~ own este coche es mío; I hurt ~ foot/head me he hecho daño en el pie/la cabeza II. interj ¡madre mía!

myopia [maɪ·'oʊ·pi·ə] n miopía f

myopic [maɪ·'ap·ɪk] adj form 1. (short-sighted) miope 2. fig corto, -a de miras

myself [maɪ·'self] pron reflexive 1. (direct, indirect object) me; I hurt ~ me hice daño; I deceived ~ me engañé a mí mismo; I bought ~ a handbag me compré un bolso 2. emphatic yo (mismo, misma); my brother and ~ mi hermano y yo; I'll do it ~ lo haré yo mismo; I did it (all) by ~ lo hice yo solo 3. after prep mí (mismo, misma); I said to ~ me dije (a mí mismo); I am ashamed of ~ estoy avergonzado de mí mismo; I live by ~ vivo solo

mysterious [mɪ·'stɪr·i·əs] adj misterioso, -a

mystery ['mɪs·tə·ri] <-ies> n misterio m

mystic ['mɪs·tɪk] adj místico, -a

mystical ['mɪs·tɪ·kəl] adj místico, -a

myth [mɪθ] n mito m

mythical ['mɪθ·ɪ·kəl] adj 1. (legendary) mítico, -a 2. (supposed) supuesto, -a

mythology [mɪ·'θal·ə·dʒi] n <-ies> mitología f

N

N, n [en] n N, n f; ~ as in November N de Navarra

n abbr of **noun** n m

N abbr of **north** N m

nab [næb] <-bb-> vt inf (person) pillar, pescar; (thing) agarrar

nag¹ [næg] n (horse) jamelgo m

nag² [næg] I. <-gg-> vi 1. (pester) fastidiar; to ~ at sb dar la lata a alguien inf 2. (scold) regañar 3. (complain) quejarse II. <-gg-> vt 1. (pester) fastidiar 2. (scold) regañar, dar la lata a inf III. n *inf* quejica *mf*

nagging ['næg·ɪŋ] I. *n* quejas *fpl* II. *adj* 1. (*pain, ache*) persistente 2. (*pestering: husband, wife*) refunfuñón, -ona

nail [neɪl] I. *n* 1. (*tool*) clavo *m* 2. ANAT uña *f* II. *vt* (*fasten*) clavar

nail-biting *adj fig* angustioso, -a

nail clippers *npl* cortaúñas *m inv*

nail file *n* lima *f* de uñas

nail polish *n* esmalte *m* de uñas

nail scissors *npl* tijeras *f pl* para uñas

naive [na·'iv] *adj* ingenuo, -a

naked ['neɪ·kɪd] *adj* 1. (*unclothed*) desnudo, -a 2. (*aggression*) manifiesto, -a; (*ambition*) puro, -a

name [neɪm] I. *n* 1. nombre *m*; (*surname*) apellido *m*; **by ~ de** nombre; **to know sb by ~** conocer a alguien de oídas; **under the ~ of...** bajo el seudónimo de...; **to call sb ~s** llamar a alguien de todo 2. (*reputation*) fama *f*; **to make a ~ for oneself** hacerse un nombre 3. (*list*) nombrar II. *vt* 1. (*call*) poner nombre a 2. (*list*) nombrar

name day *n* santo *m*; **today is my ~** hoy es mi santo

namely ['neɪm·li] *adv* a saber

nameplate ['neɪm·pleɪt] *n* placa *f* con el nombre

nanny ['næn·i] <-ies> *n* niñera *f*, nurse *f AmL*

nap¹ [næp] *n* (*sleep*) siesta *f*; **to take a ~** echarse una siesta

nap² [næp] *n* (*on fabric*) pelo *m*

napkin ['næp·kɪn] *n* servilleta *f*

narcotic [nar·'kaṭ·ɪk] I. *n* narcótico *m* II. *adj* narcótico, -a

narrate ['nær·eɪt] *vt* 1. (*tale, story*) narrar, relatar 2. TV (*documentary*) hacer de comentarista de

narrator ['nær·eɪ·ṭər] *n* narrador(a) *m(f)*; TV comentarista *mf*

narrow ['nær·ou] I. <-er, -est> *adj* 1. (*thin*) estrecho, -a 2. (*small: margin*) escaso, -a, reducido, -a II. *vi* estrecharse; (*gap*) reducirse III. *vt* (*reduce width of*) estrechar; (*gap*) reducir

narrowly *adv* (*barely*) por poco

narrow-minded [,nær·ou·'maɪn·dɪd] *adj* de mentalidad cerrada

nasal ['neɪ·zəl] *adj* nasal; (*voice*) gangoso, -a

nasty ['næs·ti] <-ier, -iest> *adj* 1. (*bad: person*) malvado, -a; (*habit*) feo, -a; (*smell, taste*) asqueroso, -a; (*surprise*) desagradable 2. (*dangerous*) peligroso, -a 3. (*serious*) serio, -a; (*accident*) grave

nation ['neɪ·ʃən] *n* (*country*) nación *f*, país *m*

national ['næʃ·ə·nəl] I. *adj* nacional II. *n* ciudadano, -a *m*, *f*; **foreign ~** extranjero, -a *m*, *f*

national anthem *n* himno *m* nacional

national holiday *n* fiesta *f* nacional

nationalism ['næʃ·ə·nə·lɪz·əm] *n* nacionalismo *m*

nationality [,næʃ·ə·'næl·ə·ṭi] <-ies> *n* nacionalidad *f*; **to adopt American/Spanish ~** adoptar la nacionalidad estadounidense/española

nationwide [,neɪ·ʃən·'waɪd] *adv* (*operate*) a nivel nacional

native ['neɪ·ṭɪv] I. *adj* 1. (*indigenous*) nativo, -a; (*plant, animal*) autóctono, -a, originario, -a 2. (*of place of origin*) nativo, -a, natural; **~ country** país *m* natal 3. (*indigenous*) indígena 4. (*original*) nativo, -a; (*innate*) innato, -a; (*language*) materno, -a II. *n* nativo, -a *m*, *f*, natural *mf*; **to speak English like a ~** hablar el inglés como un nativo

native American *n* indígena *mf* americano, -a

native speaker *n* hablante *mf* nativo, -a

NATO ['neɪ·tou] *n abbr of* **North Atlantic Treaty Organization** OTAN *f*

natter ['næṭ·ər] *vi inf* charlar

natural ['nætʃ·ər·əl] I. *adj* 1. natural; **~ father** padre *m* natural 2. (*usual, to be expected*) normal II. *n* 1. *inf* **to be a ~ for sth** tener un talento innato para algo 2. MUS nota *f* natural

natural childbirth *n* parto *m* natural

natural gas *n* gas *m* natural

natural history *n* historia *f* natural

naturalist ['nætʃ·ər·ə·lɪst] I. *n* naturalista *mf* II. *adj* naturalista

naturally *adv* naturalmente

natural resources *npl* recursos *m pl* naturales

N

natural science(s) *n(pl)* ciencias *f pl* naturales

natural selection *n* selección *f* natural

nature ['neɪ·tʃər] *n* **1.** (*environment*) naturaleza *f* **2.** (*quality*) naturaleza *f*; **things of this ~** cosas de esta índole; **it's in the ~ of things** es natural; **to be in sb's ~** estar en la naturaleza de alguien ▶ **second** ~ hábito muy arraigado en una persona

nature conservation *n* conservación *f* natural

nature lover *n* amante *mf* de la naturaleza

nature reserve *n* reserva *f* natural

naught [nɔt] *pron liter* nada *f*; **to be all for** ~ quedarse en nada

naughty ['nɔ·t̬i] <-ier, -iest> *adj* (*child*) desobediente, travieso, -a

nausea ['nɔ·zi·ə] *n* **1.** náusea *f* **2.** *fig* repugnancia *f*

nauseating ['nɔ·zi·eɪ·t̬ɪŋ] *adj* nauseabundo, -a

nautical ['nɔ·t̬ɪ·kəl] *adj* náutico, -a

nautical mile *n* milla *f* marina

naval ['neɪ·vəl] *adj* naval; ~ **battle/force** batalla *f*/fuerza *f* naval

navel ['neɪ·vəl] *n* ombligo *m* ▶ **to contemplate one's** ~ rascarse el ombligo

navigate ['næv·ɪ·geɪt] **I.** *vt* **1.** (*steer*) llevar; AUTO guiar **2.** (*sail*) navegar por **3.** (*cross*) atravesar **4.** COMPUT **to ~ the Internet** navegar por la red, surfear **II.** *vi* NAUT, AVIAT navegar; AUTO guiar, hacer de copiloto

navigation [ˌnæv·ɪ·ˈɡeɪ·ʃən] *n* navegación *f*

navigator ['næv·ɪ·ɡeɪ·t̬ər] *n* navegante *mf*; AUTO copiloto *mf*

navy ['neɪ·vi] **I.** <-ies> *n* (*military*) **the Navy** la Marina **II.** *adj* (*color*) azul marino

nay [neɪ] **I.** *adv form* no **II.** *n* (*negative vote*) voto *m* en contra

NC [ˌnɔrθ·ˌkær·ə·ˈlaɪ·nə] *n abbr of* **North Carolina** Carolina *f* del Norte

ND [ˌnɔrθ·də·ˈkoʊ·də] *n abbr of* **North Dakota** Dakota *f* del Norte

NE 1. *abbr of* **Nebraska** Nebraska *f* **2.** *abbr of* **New England** Nueva Inglaterra *f* **3.** *abbr of* **northeast** NE *m*

near [nɪr] **I.** *adj* **1.** (*spatial*) cercano, -a **2.** (*temporal*) próximo, -a; **in the ~ future** en un futuro próximo **3.** (*dear*) **a ~ and dear friend** un amigo íntimo **4.** (*similar: portrait*) parecido, -a **5.** **that was a ~ miss** faltó poco **II.** *adv* (*spatial or temporal*) cerca; **to be ~** estar cerca; **to come ~** aproximarse, acercarse; ~ **at hand** a mano; **to come ~er to sb/sth** acercarse más a alguien/algo **III.** *prep* **1.** (*in proximity to*) ~ (**to**) cerca de; ~ (**to**) **the house** cerca de la casa; ~ **the end of the film** hacia el final de la película **2.** (*almost*) **it's ~ midnight** es casi medianoche **3.** (*about ready to*) **to be ~ to doing sth** estar a punto de hacer algo **IV.** *vt* acercarse a; **it is ~ing completion** está casi terminado

nearby [ˌnɪr·ˈbaɪ] **I.** *adj* cercano, -a **II.** *adv* cerca; **is it ~?** ¿está cerca?

Near East *n* Oriente *m* Próximo

nearly ['nɪr·li] *adv* casi; ~ **certain** casi seguro; **to be ~ there** estar casi ahí; **to very ~ do sth** estar a punto de hacer algo; **she's ~ as tall as her father** es casi tan alta como su padre

near-sighted [ˌnɪr·ˈsaɪ·t̬ɪd] *adj a. fig* miope

neat [nit] *adj* **1.** (*orderly, well-ordered*) cuidado, -a, ordenado, -a; ~ **appearance** apariencia *f* cuidada; ~ **and tidy** ordenado **2.** (*deft*) cuidadoso, -a; ~ **solution** solución *f* exacta **3.** *sl* (*excellent*) guay *inf*

neatly *adv* **1.** (*with care*) cuidadosamente **2.** (*in orderly fashion*) de forma ordenada **3.** (*deftly*) con estilo

necessarily [ˌnes·ɪ·ˈser·ə·li] *adv* necesariamente; **not** ~ no necesariamente

necessary ['nes·ɪ·ser·i] *adj* necesario, -a; **a ~ evil** un mal necesario; **strictly** ~ estrictamente necesario; **that won't be** ~ no será necesario; **to do what is** ~ hacer lo que es necesario; **if** ~ si es necesario

necessity [nə·ˈses·ə·t̬i] <-ies> *n* (*need*) necesidad *f*; **in case of** ~ en caso de necesidad; **when the ~ arises** cuando surja la necesidad; **by** ~ por necesidad; **bare** ~ primera necesidad

neck [nek] **I.** *n* **1.** ANAT cuello *m*; (*nape*) nuca *f* **2.** FASHION (*also of bottle, violin*)

cuello m ▶ **to be up to one's ~ in sth** *inf*estar (metido) hasta el cuello en algo II. *vi inf*besuquearse

necklace ['nek·lɪs] n collar m

neckline ['nek·laɪn] n escote m

necktie n corbata f

née [neɪ] *adj* de soltera

need [nid] I. n necesidad f; **in** ~ necesitado, -a; **basic** ~**s** necesidades básicas; ~ **for sb/sth** necesidad de alguien/algo; **to be in** ~ **of sth** necesitar (de) algo; **if** ~**(s)** be si es necesario; **there's no** ~ **to shout so loud** no hace falta gritar tanto II. *vt* 1. (*require*) necesitar; **to** ~ **sb to do sth** necesitar que alguien haga algo 2. (*ought to have*) **to** ~ necesitar; **to not** ~ **sth** no necesitar (de) algo 3. (*must, have*) **to** ~ **to do sth** tener que hacer algo; ~ **we/I/you?** ¿nos/me/te hace falta?

needed *adj* necesario, -a

needle ['ni·dəl] I. n aguja f; **hypodermic** ~ jeringa f; **knitting** ~ aguja f de hacer punto; ~ **and thread** aguja e hilo; **to thread a** ~ enhebrar una aguja ▶ **it's like looking for a** ~ **in a haystack** es como buscar una aguja en un pajar II. *vt* (*prick*) pinchar; (*annoy*) provocar

needless ['nid·lɪs] *adj* innecesario, -a; ~ **to say...** no hace falta decir...

needy ['ni·di] <-ier, -iest> *adj* necesitado, -a

negate [nɪ·ˈgeɪt] *vt* negar

negation [nɪ·ˈgeɪ·ʃən] n negación f

negative ['neg·ə·tɪv] I. *adj* 1. (*not positive*) negativo, -a; ~ **answer** respuesta f negativa 2. a. MED negativo, -a; ~ **pole** polo m negativo; ~ **number** número m negativo II. n 1. (*rejection*) negativa f 2. (*saying no*) negación f 3. PHOT negativo m III. *vt* negar

neglect [nɪ·ˈglekt] I. *vt* desatender; **to** ~ **to do sth** descuidar hacer algo II. n negligencia f; (*poor state*) deterioro m

neglected *adj* descuidado, -a; (*undervalued*) infravalorado, -a; ~ **child** niño, -a m, f abandonado, -a

neglectful [nɪ·ˈglekt·fəl] *adj* negligente

negligence ['neg·lɪ·dʒəns] n a. LAW negligencia f

negligible ['neg·lɪ·dʒə·bəl] *adj* insignificante

negotiable [nɪ·ˈgoʊ·ʃi·ə·bəl] *adj*negociable; **non**~ no negociable

negotiate [nɪ·ˈgoʊ·ʃi·eɪt] I. *vt* 1. (*discuss*) negociar 2. (*convert into money*) **to** ~ **securities** negociar títulos II. *vi* negociar; **to** ~ **on sth** negociar algo

negotiation [nɪ·ˌgoʊ·ʃi·ˈeɪ·ʃən] n negociación f

negotiator [nɪ·ˈgoʊ·ʃi·eɪ·tər] n negociador(a) $m(f)$

neigh [neɪ] I. n relincho m II. *vi* relinchar

neighbor ['neɪ·bər] I. n vecino, -a m, f; (*fellow human*) prójimo, -a m, f II. *vi*to ~ **on sth** lindar con algo

neighborhood ['neɪ·bər·hʊd] n 1. (*surroundings*) vecindario m; (*people*) vecinos *mpl*; **in the** ~ en el vecindario 2. (*vicinity*) alrededores *mpl*; **in the** ~ **of the airport** en los alrededores del aeropuerto 3. (*approximately*) **in the** ~ **of** alrededor de

neighboring ['neɪ·bər·ɪŋ] *adj* (*nearby*) cercano, -a; (*bordering*) adyacente; ~ **house** casa f adyacente; ~ **country** país m vecino

neighborly ['neɪ·bər·li] *adj* amable

neither ['ni·ðər] I. *pron* ninguno, -a; ~ **which one?** — (of them) ¿cuál? — ninguno (de los dos) II. *adv* ni; ~**... nor...** ni... ni... III. *conj* tampoco; **if he won't eat,** ~ **will I** si él no come, yo tampoco IV. *adj* ningún, -una; ~ **book is good** ninguno de los dos libros es bueno

neon ['ni·ɑn] n neón m

neo-Nazi [ˌni·oʊ·ˈnɑt·si] n neonazi mf

neon sign n letrero m de neón

nephew ['nef·ju] n sobrino m

Neptune ['nep·tun] n Neptuno m

nerd [nɜrd] n *pej sl* 1. (*awkward person*) empollón, -ona m, f m 2. (*foolish person*) pardillo, -a m, f

nerve [nɜrv] n 1. ANAT nervio m 2. ~**s** nerviosismo m; **to be a bundle of ~s** *fig* ser un puñado de nervios; **to get on sb's ~s** *inf*poner los nervios de punta a alguien 3. (*courage*) **to lose one's** ~

N

perder el valor; **to have the ~ to do sth** *inf* tener el morro de hacer algo **4.** (*apprehension*) **~s** ansiedad *f*

nervous ['nɜr·vəs] *adj* (*jumpy*), -a; (*edgy*) ansioso, -a; **to make sb ~** poner nervioso a alguien; **to be ~ about sth** estar nervioso por algo

nervous breakdown *n* ataque *m* de nervios

nervousness *n* (*condition*) nerviosismo *m;* (*fearfulness*) ansiedad *f*

nervous system *n* sistema *m* nervioso

nervy ['nɜr·vi] <-ier, -iest> *adj* **1.** (*rude*) descarado, -a **2.** (*courageous*) atrevido, -a

nest [nest] **I.** *n* nido *m;* **to leave the ~** dejar el nido *f* **II.** *vi* anidar

nest egg *n* ahorros *mpl*

net¹ [net] **I.** *n* **1.** (*material*) malla *f;* **mosquito ~** mosquitera *f* **2.** (*for fishing*) *a.* SPORTS red *f* **II.** <-tt-> *vt* (*catch: fish*) pescar

net² [net] **I.** *adj* **1.** ECON neto, -a; **~ income** ingreso *m* neto, -a; (*weight*) neto, -a **II.** *vt* **to ~ sth** ganar algo en neto

Net [net] *n* COMPUT **the ~** la red

Netherlands ['neð·ər·ləndz] *n* **the ~** los Países Bajos, Holanda *f*

nett [net] *adj, vt see* **net¹** II., **net²**

netting ['net·ɪŋ] *n* **1.** (*net*) malla *f* **2.** SPORTS red *f*

nettle ['net·əl] **I.** *n* ortiga *f* **II.** *vt* irritar

network ['net·wɜrk] **I.** *n* **1.** COMPUT, TEL red *f;* **computer ~** red informática **2.** TV cadena *f* **II.** *vt* **1.** (*link together*) conectar **2.** (*broadcast*) retransmitir **III.** *vi* interconectar

networking *n* COMPUT interconexión *f*

neurological [ˌnʊr·ə·ˈlɑdʒ·ɪ·kəl] *adj* neurológico, -a

neuron ['nʊr·ɑn] *n* neurona *f*

neurosurgeon [ˌnʊr·oʊ·ˈsɜr·dʒən] *n* neurocirujano, -a *m, f*

neurosurgery [ˌnʊr·oʊ·ˈsɜr·dʒə·ri] *n* neurocirugía *f*

neurotic [nʊ·ˈrɑt·ɪk] *adj* neurótico, -a

neuter ['nu·tər] **I.** *adj* neutro, -a **II.** *vt* **1.** (*castrate: male*) castrar **2.** (*sterilize: female*) esterilizar **3.** (*neutralize*) neutralizar

neutral ['nu·trəl] **I.** *adj* **1.** (*uninvolved*)

neutral; **to remain ~** mantenerse al margen **2.** *a.* CHEM, ELEC neutro, -a **3.** (*unemotional*) objetivo, -a **II.** *n* AUTO punto *m* muerto

neutrality [nu·ˈtræl·ə·t̬i] *n* neutralidad *f*

neutralize ['nu·trə·laɪz] *vt* neutralizar

neutron ['nu·trɑn] *n* neutrón *m*

never ['nev·ər] *adv* nunca, jamás; **~ again!** ¡nunca más!; **~ fear!** ¡no te preocupes!; **well I ~ (did)** ¡no me digas!; **as ~ before** como nunca; **~ ever** nunca jamás; **~ mind** qué más da

never-ending ['nev·ər·'en·dɪŋ] *adj* interminable

nevermore *adv* nunca más

nevertheless [ˌnev·ər·ðə·'les] *adv* sin embargo, no obstante

new [nu] *adj* **1.** (*latest, recent*) nuevo, -a, reciente; **~ technology** tecnología *f* punta **2.** (*changed*) nuevo, -a; **~ boy/girl** SCHOOL novato, -a *m, f* **3.** (*inexperienced*) nuevo, -a, novato, -a; **she's ~ to the job** es nueva en el trabajo **4.** (*in new condition*) nuevo, -a; **brand ~** nuevo flamante **5.** (*fresh*) fresco, -a; **~ blood** *fig* sangre *f* fresca **6.** (*new*) fresco, -a, reciente

newbie ['nu·bi] *n* novato, -a *m, f*

newborn *adj* reciente; **~ baby** recién nacido, -a *m, f*

New Caledonia *n* Nueva Caledonia *f*

newcomer *n* **1.** (*just arrived*) recién llegado, -a *m, f* **2.** (*stranger*) nuevo, -a *m, f* **3.** (*beginner*) principiante *mf*, novato, -a *m, f*

New England *n* Nueva Inglaterra *f*

Newfoundland ['nu·fən·lənd] *n* Terranova *f*

newish ['nu·ɪʃ] *adj inf* bastante nuevo, -a

newly ['nu·li] *adv* **1.** (*discovered, diagnosed, released*) recientemente **2.** (*named, phrased*) de otra manera

newly-wed ['nu·li·wed] *npl* recién casados *mpl*

New Mexico [ˌnu·'mek·sɪ·koʊ] *n* Nuevo México *m*

new moon *n* luna *f* nueva

New Orleans [ˌnu·'ɔr·li·ənz] *n* Nueva Orleans *f*

news [nuz] *n + sing vb* **1.** noticias *fpl;* **bad/good ~** malas/buenas noticias; **to**

break the ~ to sb dar la noticia a alguien; **when the ~ broke** cuando se supo la noticia; **really! that's ~ to me** ¿de veras? no lo sabía **2.** (*broadcast*) noticias *fpl*, informativo *m*; **to be ~** ser noticia ▶ **no ~ is good ~** *prov* si no hay noticias, buena señal

news agency <-ies> *n* agencia *f* de noticias

newscast *n* informativo *m*

newsflash <-es> *n* noticia *f* de última hora

newsgroup *n* COMPUT foro *m* de discusión

news item *n* noticia *f*

newsletter *n* nota *f* de prensa

newspaper *n* periódico *m*

news report *n* reportaje *m* informativo

newsroom *n* sala *f* de redacción

newsstand *n* quiosco *m*

newsworthy *adj* de interés periodístico

newsy ['nu·zi] <-ier, -iest> *adj* lleno, -a de noticias

New Year *n* **1.** año *m* nuevo; **Happy ~** feliz año nuevo **2.** (*opening weeks of year*) principios *m pl* de año

New Year's Day *n* día *m* de año nuevo

New Year's Eve *n* nochevieja *f*

New York [,nu·'jɔrk] *n* Nueva York *f*

New Yorker *n* neoyorquino, -a *m, f*

New Zealand [,nu·'zi·lənd] *n* Nueva Zelanda *f*

New Zealander *n* neozelandés, -esa *m, f*

next [nekst] **I.** *adj* **1.** (*in location*) siguiente **2.** (*in time*) próximo, -a, que viene; **the ~ day** el día siguiente; **~ month** el mes que viene; **the ~ thing** el siguiente paso; (**the**) **~ time** la próxima vez **3.** (*following in order*) siguiente; **to be ~** ser el siguiente; **~ to sth/sb** cerca de algo/alguien **II.** *adv* **1.** (*afterwards, subsequently*) después, luego **2.** (*almost as much*) **~ to** después de **3.** (*again, once more*) de nuevo **4.** (*almost*) casi; **~ to impossible** casi imposible **5.** (*second*) **the ~ best thing** lo segundo mejor **III.** *prep* **1.** (*beside*) **~ to** junto a; **my room is ~ to yours** mi habitación está al lado de la tuya **2.** (*almost*) casi; **to cost ~ to nothing** no valer casi nada

next door [,nekst·'dɔr] *adv* al lado

next of kin *n* pariente *mf* cercano, -a

nexus ['nek·səs] *n inv* nexo *m*

NF *n abbr of* **Newfoundland** Terranova *f*

NH [,nu·'hæmp·ʃər] *n abbr of* **New Hampshire** New Hampshire

Niagara Falls [naɪ·æg·,rə·'fɔlz] *n* (**the**) **~** las cataratas del Niágara

nib [nɪb] *n* punta *f*; (*of pen*) plumilla *f*

nibble ['nɪb·əl] **I.** *n* mordisco *m*, bocado *m*; **to take a ~** (**at sth**) dar un mordisco (a algo) **II.** *vt* **1.** (*bite*) mordisquear; (*rat*) roer **2.** (*pick at*) picar **III.** *vi a. fig* picar

Nicaragua [,nɪk·ə·'rag·wə] *n* Nicaragua *f*

Nicaraguan *n adj* nicaragüense *mf*

nice [naɪs] **I.** *adj* **1.** (*pleasant, agreeable*) bueno, -a; **~ one!, ~ work!** *inf* ¡bien hecho!; **~ weather** buen tiempo *m*; **it is ~ to do sth** es agradable hacer algo **2.** (*amiable*) simpático, -a; (*kind*) amable; **to be ~ to sb** ser amable con alguien; **it is/was ~ of sb to do sth** es/fue un detalle por parte de alguien hacer algo **3.** *iron inf* (*unpleasant*) **that's a ~ thing to say to your brother** ¡vaya cosa bonita para decirle a un hermano! **4.** (*subtle*) sutil, delicado, -a; (*fine*) fino, -a **II.** *adv* bien

nicely ['naɪs·li] *adv* **1.** (*well, satisfactorily*) bien **2.** (*having success*) espléndidamente **3.** (*pleasantly, politely*) amablemente

nicety ['naɪ·sə·ti] <-ies> *n* **1.** (*subtle distinction*) sutileza *f* **2.** (*precision*) precisión *f* **3.** (*precise differentiations*) **niceties** matices *mpl*; (*in negative sense*) nimiedades *fpl*

niche [nɪtʃ] *n* **1.** (*alcove*) nicho *m* **2.** (*desired job*) buen puesto *m*; (*suitable position*) buena posición *f*

nick [nɪk] **I.** *n* (*chip in surface*) mella *f* ▶ **in the ~ of** <u>**time**</u> por los pelos **II.** *vt* **1.** (*chip*) mellar; (*cut*) cortar **2.** *sl* (*cheat*) engañar

nickel ['nɪk·əl] *n* **1.** CHEM níquel *m* **2.** (*coin*) moneda *f* de cinco centavos

nickname ['nɪk·neɪm] *n* apodo *m*

nicotine ['nɪk·ə·ˌtin] *n* nicotina *f*

niece [nis] *n* sobrina *f*

nifty ['nɪf·ti] <-ier, -iest> *adj sl* (*stylish*)

N

chulo, -a; (*skilful*) hábil

niggardly ['nɪg·ərd·li] *adj* (*stingy*) tacaño, -a; (*meager*) miserable

niggle ['nɪg·əl] I. *vi* fastidiar II. *vt* 1. (*nag*) reparar en minucias 2. (*irritate*) enfurecer, irritar

niggling ['nɪg·lɪŋ] *adj* (*irritating*) molesto, -a

night [naɪt] *n* noche *f*; **good ~!** ¡buenas noches!; **last ~** anoche; **10 (o'clock) at ~** las 10 de la noche; **the ~ before** la noche anterior; **~ and day** de noche y día; **during the ~** durante la noche; **during Tuesday ~** durante la noche del martes; **to work ~s** trabajar de noche

night bird ['naɪt·bɜrd] *n* 1. zool pájaro *m* nocturno 2. (*person*) noctámbulo, -a *m, f*, trasnochador(a) *m(f)*

night blindness *n* ceguera *f* nocturna

nightcap *n* (*cap*) gorro *m* de dormir

nightclothes *npl* ropa *f* de dormir

nightclub *n* club *m* (nocturno)

nightdress <-es> *n* camisón *m*

nightfall *n* atardecer *m*

nightgown *n* camisón *m*

nightie ['naɪ·ti] *n inf* camisón *m*

nightingale ['naɪ·tɪŋ·geɪl] *n* ruiseñor *m*

nightlight *n* lamparilla *f*

nightlong *adv* durante toda la noche

nightly ['naɪt·li] I. *adv* cada noche II. *adj* (*visits, TV program*) de todas las noches

nightmare ['naɪt·mer] *n* pesadilla *f*

nightmarish ['naɪt·mer·ɪʃ] *adj* espeluznante

night-nurse *n* enfermera *f* de noche

night school *n* escuela *f* nocturna

night shift *n* turno *m* de noche

nightshirt *n* camisa *f* de dormir

nightstand *n* mesita *f* de noche

night watchman *n* vigilante *m* nocturno, nochero *m CSur*

nihilism ['naɪ·ə·lɪz·əm] *n* nihilismo *m*

nihilistic [ˌnaɪ·ə·ˈlɪs·tɪk] *adj* nihilista

nil [nɪl] *n* (*nothing, zero*) nada *f*, cero *m*

Nile [naɪl] *n* **the ~** el Nilo

nimble ['nɪm·bəl] *adj* (*agile*) ágil; (*quick and light in movement*) diestro, -a; (*quick-thinking*) listo, -a

nine [naɪn] I. *adj* nueve *inv* ▶ **~ times out of ten** casi siempre II. *n* nueve *m*; *s. a.* **eight**

9-11, 9/11 [naɪn·ɪ·ˈlev·ən] *n* el 11-S *m*

nineteen [ˌnaɪn·ˈtin] I. *adj* diecinueve II. *n* diecinueve *m*; *s. a.* **eight**

nineteenth I. *adj* decimonoveno, -a II. *n* 1. (*order*) decimonoveno, -a *m, f* 2. (*date*) diecinueve *m* 3. (*fraction*) diecinueveavo *m*; (*part*) diecinueveava parte *f*; *s. a.* **eighth**

ninetieth ['naɪn·ti·əθ] I. *adj* nonagésimo, -a II. *n* (*order*) nonagésimo, -a *m, f*; (*fraction*) noventavo *m*; (*part*) noventava parte *f*; *s. a.* **eighth**

ninety ['naɪn·ti] I. *adj* noventa II. <-ies> *n* noventa *m*; *s. a.* **eighty**

ninth [naɪnθ] I. *adj* noveno, -a II. *n* 1. (*order*) noveno, -a *m, f* 2. (*date*) nueve *m* 3. (*fraction*) noveno *m*; (*part*) novena parte *f*; *s. a.* **eighth**

nip [nɪp] I. <-pp-> *vt* 1. (*bite*) mordisquear 2. (*pinch, squeeze: pliers*) pellizcar 3. (*remove: dead leaves*) arrancar ▶ **to ~ sth in the** **bud** *fig* cortar algo de raíz II. *n* 1. (*sip*) traguito *m* 2. (*pinch, tight squeeze*) pellizco *m* 3. (*bite*) mordisquito *m* 4. (*coldness*) helada *f*

nipple ['nɪp·əl] *n* ANAT pezón *m*

nippy ['nɪp·i] <-ier, -iest> *adj inf* helado, -a

nit [nɪt] *n* zool liendre *f*

nitpicking ['nɪt·pɪk·ɪŋ] I. *adj inf* criticón, -ona II. *n inf* pega *f*

nitrate ['naɪ·treɪt] *n* nitrato *m*

nitric ['naɪ·trɪk] *adj* nítrico, -a

nitrite ['naɪ·traɪt] *n* nitrito *m*

nitrogen ['naɪ·trə·dʒən] *n* nitrógeno *m*

nitroglycerin(e) [ˌnaɪ·troʊ·ˈglɪs·ər·ɪn] *n* nitroglicerina *f*

nitrous ['naɪ·trəs] *adj* nitroso, -a

nitty-gritty [ˌnɪt·i·ˈgrɪt·i] *n inf* **the ~** el meollo; **to get down to the ~** ir al grano

nitwit ['nɪt·wɪt] *n inf* idiota *mf*

NJ [ˌnu·ˈdʒɜr·zi] *n abbr of* **New Jersey** Nueva Jersey *f*

NM [ˌnu·ˈmek·sɪ·koʊ] *n abbr of* **New Mexico** Nuevo México *m*

NNE *abbr of* **north-northeast** NNE *m*

NNW abbr of **north-northwest** NNO m

no [nou] I. adj 1. (not to any degree) no; ~ **parking** prohibido estacionar; ~ **way** de ninguna manera; ~ **can do** inf no se puede; ~ **less than sth/sb** nada menos que algo/alguien 2. (equivalent to a negative sentence) no; (emphasizes previous statement's falsity) and can do II. n <-(e)s> n (denial, refusal) no m; **to not take ~ for an answer** no admitir un no por respuesta III. interj (word used to deny) no; (emphasizes distress) qué me dices

no., No. abbr of **number** núm., nº

Nobel prize [,nou·bel·'praɪz] n premio m nobel

nobility [nou·'bɪl·ə·ti] n 1. + sing/pl vb (aristocracy) nobleza f 2. (nobleness of character) generosidad f; (selflessness) altruismo m

noble ['nou·bəl] I. adj 1. noble; (action) generoso, -a; ~ **act** acto m noble 2. (splendid) majestuoso, -a 3. (excellent) magnífico, -a; (horse) noble II. n noble mf

nobleman ['nou·bəl·mən] <-men> n aristócrata m

noble-minded adj honesto, -a

nobly ['nou·bli] adv noblemente

nobody ['nou·bad·i] I. pron indef, sing nadie; **we saw ~** (else) no vimos a nadie (más); **he told ~** no se lo dijo a nadie II. n inf don nadie m; **those people are nobodies** esas personas son un cero a la izquierda

nocturnal [nak·'tɜr·nəl] adj form nocturno, -a

nod [nad] I. n cabezada f, inclinación f de cabeza II. <-dd-> vt to ~ one's **head** asentir con la cabeza; **to ~ one's head at sth** indicar algo con la cabeza III. <-dd-> vi 1. asentir con la cabeza; **to ~ to sb** saludar a alguien con una inclinación de cabeza 2. inf (when sleepy) dar cabezadas

◆ **nod off** vi quedarse dormido

nodding ['nad·ɪŋ] adj **to have only a ~ acquaintance** with sth conocer algo sólo por encima

node [noud] n 1. ANAT (tissue) ganglio m 2. BOT (on a stem) nódulo m 3. COMPUT

nodo m

nodule ['nadʒ·ul] n a. ANAT, BOT nódulo m

no-go area [nou·gou·'er·i·ə] n MIL zona f prohibida

nohow ['nou·hau] adv sl de ninguna manera

noise [nɔɪz] n 1. (sound) ruido m; **to make a ~** hacer ruido 2. (loud, unpleasant sounds) estruendo m 3. ELEC interferencia f ▶ **to make ~ about sth** inf quejarse mucho de algo

noise barrier n barrera f del sonido

noiseless ['nɔɪz·lɪs] adj silencioso, -a

noise pollution n contaminación f acústica

noise prevention n prevención f del ruido

noisy ['nɔɪ·zi] <-ier, -iest> adj 1. (making noise: crowd) ruidoso, -a 2. (full of noise: restaurant, street) bullicioso, -a 3. ELEC (signal) acústico, -a

nomad ['nou·mæd] n nómada mf

nomadic [nou·'mæd·ɪk] adj nómada

no man's land ['nou·mænz·lænd] n tierra f de nadie

nominal ['nam·ə·nəl] adj 1. (in name) nominal 2. (small: sum) pequeño, -a

nominally ['nam·ə·nə·li] adv nominalmente

nominate ['nam·ə·neɪt] vt 1. (propose) proponer; (for an award) nominar 2. (appoint) nombrar

nomination [,nam·ə·'neɪ·ʃən] n 1. (proposal) propuesta f 2. (appointment) nombramiento m; (for an award) nominación f

nominative ['nam·ə·nə·tɪv] I. n nominativo m II. adj nominativo, -a

nominee [,nam·ə·'ni] n candidato, -a m, f; (for an award) nominado, -a m, f

nonagenarian [,nan·ə·dʒə·'ner·i·ən] adj nonagenario, -a

nonalcoholic [,nan·æl·kə·'hal·ɪk] adj sin alcohol

nonaligned [,nan·ə·'laɪnd] adj no alineado, -a

nonchalant [,nan·ʃə·'lant] adj despreocupado, -a

nonconformist [,nan·kən·'fɔr·mɪst] adj inconformista

nonconformity [,nan·kən·'fɔr·mə·ti] n

N

inconformidad *f*

non-deposit bottle [ˌnan-dɪ-ˌpaz-ɪt-ˈbat-əl] *n* envase *m* no retornable

nondescript [ˌnan-dɪ-ˈskrɪpt] *adj* sin nada de particular; (*person*) anodino, -a; (*color*) indefinido, -a

none [nʌn] **I.** *pron* **1.** (*nobody*) nadie, ninguno, -a; ~ **of them** ninguno de ellos; ~ **of you helped me** ninguno de vosotros me ayudó **2.** (*not any*) ninguno, -a **3.** (*not any*) nada; ~ **of that!** ¡déjate de eso! **II.** *adv* **1.** (*not*) ~ **the less** sin embargo; **to be** ~ **the wiser** seguir sin entender nada **2.** (*not very*) **it's** ~ **too soon** ya era hora; **it's** ~ **too warm** no hace mucho calor

nonentity [nan-ˈen-tə-ti] <-ies> *n* **1.** (*person*) cero *m* a la izquierda **2.** (*insignificance*) insignificancia *f*

non-iron [ˌnan-ˈaɪ-ərn] *adj* que no necesita plancha

nonplus [ˌnan-ˈplʌs] <-ss-> *vt* dejar perplejo; **to be ~sed** quedarse perplejo

nonprofit [ˌnan-ˈpraf-ɪt] *adj* no lucrativo, -a

nonrefundable [ˌnan-rɪ-ˈfʌn-də-bəl] *adj* no reembolsable; ~ **down payment** pago *m* a fondo perdido

nonresident [ˌnan-ˈrez-ɪ-dənt] *adj* no residente

nonsense [ˈnan-sens] **I.** *n* tonterías *fpl;* **to talk** ~ *inf* decir tonterías **II.** *interj* tonterías

nonsensical [ˌnan-ˈsen-sɪ-kəl] *adj* absurdo, -a

nonskid [ˌnan-ˈskɪd] *adj* antideslizante

nonsmoking *adj* para no fumadores

nonstop [ˌnan-ˈstap] **I.** *adj* **1.** (*without stopping, direct*) sin parar; (*flight*) directo, -a **2.** (*uninterrupted*) incesante **II.** *adv* sin pausa

noodle[1] [ˈnu-dəl] *n* fideo *m*

noodle[2] [ˈnu-dəl] *n sl* **1.** (*head*) coco *m* **2.** (*person*) tontolaba *mf*

nook [nʊk] *n liter* rincón *m*

noon [nun] *n* mediodía *m;* **at** ~ a mediodía; **about** ~ alrededor de mediodía

no one [ˈnoʊ-wʌn] *pron see* **nobody**

noose [nus] *n* **1.** (*loop of rope*) soga *f* **2.** (*for catching*) lazo *m*

nope [noʊp] *adv inf* no

nor [nɔr] *conj* **1.** (*and also not*) tampoco; ~ (**do**) **I** ni yo tampoco **2.** (*not either*) ni

Nordic [ˈnɔr-dɪk] *adj* nórdico, -a

norm [nɔrm] *n* norma *f*

normal [ˈnɔr-məl] *adj* normal; **as** (**is**) ~ como es normal

normalize [ˈnɔr-mə-laɪz] *a.* COMPUT **I.** *vt* normalizar **II.** *vi* normalizarse

normally [ˈnɔr-mə-li] *adv* normalmente

north [nɔrθ] **I.** *n* **1.** (*cardinal point*) norte *m;* **to lie 3 miles to the** ~ **of sth** estar a 5 km al norte de algo; **to go/drive to the** ~ ir/viajar hacia el norte; **further** ~ más al norte **2.** GEO norte *m;* **in the** ~ **of France** en el norte de Francia **II.** *adj* del norte, septentrional; ~ **wind** viento *m* del norte; ~ **coast** costa *f* norte; **the North Sea** El Mar del Norte; **North Star** Estrella *f* Polar; **the North Pole** el Polo Norte

North America *n* América *f* del Norte

North American I. *n* norteamericano, -a *m, f* **II.** *adj* norteamericano, -a

North Carolina [ˌnɔrθ-ˌkær-ə-ˈlaɪ-nə] *n* Carolina *f* del Norte

North Dakota [ˌnɔrθ-də-ˈkoʊ-də] *n* Dakota *f* del Norte

northeast [ˌnɔrθ-ˈist] *n* nordeste *m*

northeastern [ˌnɔrθ-ˈi-stərn] *adj* nororiental

northerly [ˈnɔr-ðər-li] *adj* del norte

northern [ˈnɔr-ðərn] *adj* del norte, norteño, -a, nortino, -a *Chile, Perú;* ~ **hemisphere** hemisferio *m* norte; ~ **lights** aurora *f* boreal

northerner [ˈnɔr-ðər-nər] *n* norteño, -a *m, f*

northernmost *adj* más septentrional

Northern Territory *n* territorio *m* norte

North Pole [ˈnɔrθ-poʊl] *n* **the** ~ el Polo Norte

North Sea *n* Mar *m* del Norte

North-South divide *n* ECON división *f* Norte-Sur

northward [ˈnɔrθ-wərd] *adv* hacia el norte

northwest [ˌnɔrθ-ˈwest] **I.** *n* noroeste *m;* **to the** ~ (**of**) al noroeste (de) **II.** *adj* del noroeste; ~ **Texas** el noroeste de Texas **III.** *adv* en dirección noroeste

northwesterly [ˌnɔrΘ·ˈwes·tər·li] *adj* en dirección noroeste; (*from the northwest*) del noroeste

Northwest Territories *n pl* territorios *m pl* del noroeste

Norway [ˈnɔr·weɪ] *n* Noruega *f*

Norwegian [nɔrˈwi·dʒən] I. *adj* noruego, -a II. *n* 1. (*person*) noruego, -a *m, f* 2. LING noruego *m*

nose [nouz] I. *n* 1. ANAT nariz *f*; (*of animal*) hocico *m*; **to blow one's ~** sonarse la nariz 2. AVIAT (*front*) morro *m* ▸ **to follow one's ~** inf (*trust instincts*) guiarse por su olfato; (*go straight ahead*) seguir adelante; **to have a (good) ~ for sth** tener buen olfato para algo; **to poke one's ~ into sth** inf meter las narices en algo; **to rub sb's ~ in it** restregar algo a alguien por las narices; **right out from under sb's ~** inf delante de las narices de alguien II. *vi* fisgonear III. *vt* **to ~ one's way in/out/up** entrar/salir/pasar lentamente

nosebag [ˈnouz·bæg] *n* morral *m*

nosebleed *n* hemorragia *f* nasal

nose cone *n* AVIAT cabeza *f*

nosedive *vi* 1. AVIAT descender en picado 2. FIN caer en picado

nose job *n* inf arreglo *m* de nariz

nosey [ˈnou·zi] <-ier, -iest> *adj see* **nosy**

nosh [naʃ] I. *n* inf papeo *m* II. *vi* papear

nostalgia [nɑ·ˈstæl·dʒə] *n* nostalgia *f*

nostalgic [nɑ·ˈstæl·dʒɪk] *adj* nostálgico, -a

nostril [ˈnɑs·trəl] *n* ventana *f* de la nariz

nosy [ˈnou·zi] <-ier, -iest> *adj* fisgón, -ona

not [nɑt] *adv* no; **it's a woman, ~ a man** es una mujer, no un hombre; **he's asked me ~ to do it** me ha pedido que no lo haga; **~ all the children like singing** no les gusta cantar a todos los niños; **~ me!** ¡yo no!; **why ~?** ¿por qué no?; **he is ~ ugly** no es feo; **or ~** o no; **~ at all** (*nothing*) en absoluto; (*no need to thank*) de nada; **~ only... but also...** no sólo... sino también; **~ just** [or *simply*] no sólo; **~ much** no mucho

notable [ˈnou·tə·bəl] *adj* 1. (*remarkable*)

notable 2. (*eminent*) eminente

notably [ˈnou·tə·bli] *adv* notablemente

notary [ˈnou·tə·ri] <-ies> *n* ~ (**public**) notario, -a *m, f*

notation [nou·ˈteɪ·ʃən] *n* MATH, MUS notación *f*

notch [nɑtʃ] <-es> *n* I. *vt* 1. (*cut*) hacer una muesca 2. (*achieve*) conseguir II. *n* 1. (*cut*) muesca *f*; (*hole*) agujero *m* 2. (*degree*) punto *m* 3. (*narrow valley*) valle *m*

note [nout] I. *n* 1. (*annotation*) nota *f*; **to take ~** tomar nota 2. LIT apunte *m* 3. MUS nota *f*; (*sound*) tono *m*; **to strike the right ~** fig dar con el tono apropiado 4. (*money*) billete *m* 5. (*importance*) **of ~** form notable; **nothing of ~** nada importante II. *vt* form anotar; (*mention*) observar; **to ~ (that)...** hacer notar (que)...

notebook [ˈnout·bʊk] *n* cuaderno *m*

noted [ˈnou·tɪd] *adj* célebre; **to be ~ for sth** ser conocido por algo

notepad [ˈnout·pæd] *n* bloc *m*

notepaper [ˈnout·ˌpeɪ·pər] *n* papel *m* de carta

noteworthy [ˈnout·ˌwɜr·ði] *adj* form de interés; **nothing/something ~** nada/algo digno de atención

nothing [ˈnʌθ·ɪŋ] I. *pron indef, sing* 1. (*no objects*) nada; **~ happens** no pasa nada; **we saw ~** (*else/more*) no vimos nada (más); **~ new** nada nuevo 2. (*not anything*) **~ came of it** no salió nada (de ahí); **~ doing!** inf ¡para nada!; **fit for ~** bueno para nada; **to make ~ of it** no darle importancia; **there is ~ to laugh at** no tiene ninguna gracia 3. (*not important*) **that's ~!** ¡no es nada! 4. (*only*) **~ but** tan sólo; **she is ~ if not patient** es paciente por encima de todo; **~ much** poca cosa II. *adv* **~ less than** ni más ni menos que III. *n* 1. nada *f* 2. MATH, SPORTS cero *m*; **three to ~** tres a cero

nothingness [ˈnʌθ·ɪŋ·nɪs] *n* (*emptiness*) vacío *m*; (*worthlessness*) nada *f*

notice [ˈnou·tɪs] I. *vt* 1. (*see*) ver; (*perceive*) fijarse en; **to ~ (that)...** darse cuenta de (que)... 2. (*recognize*) reconocer II. *vi* darse cuenta III. *n*

1. (*attention*) interés *m;* **to take ~ of sb/sth** prestar atención a alguien/algo; **that escaped my ~** se me pasó por alto **2.** (*display*) letrero *m;* (*in newspaper, magazine*) anuncio *m* **3.** (*warning*) aviso *m;* **to give sb ~ (of sth)** avisar a alguien (de algo); **at short ~** a corto plazo; **at a moment's ~** a un momento; **until further ~** hasta nuevo aviso **4.** LAW preaviso *m;* **to give (in) one's ~** presentar la dimisión; **to give sb their ~** despedir a alguien

noticeable ['nou·tɪs·ə·bəl] *adj* (*change, improvement*) evidente; (*difference, increase, lack of friendliness*) notable

notifiable ['nou·tə·faɪ·ə·bəl] *adj* (*disease*) que hay que notificar

notification [,nou·tə·fɪ·'keɪ·ʃən] *n* notificación *f*

notify ['nou·tə·faɪ] <-ie-> *vt* informar; **to ~ sb of sth** notificar algo a alguien

notion ['nou·ʃən] *n* **1.** (*idea*) noción *f;* **to have some ~ of sth** tener algunas nociones de algo; **to have no ~ of sth** no tener ni idea de algo **2.** (*silly idea*) burrada *f*

notional ['nou·ʃə·nəl] *adj form* teórico, -a

notoriety [,nou·tə·'raɪ·ə·ti] *n* mala fama *f*

notorious [nou·'tɔr·i·əs] *adj* de mala reputación; (*thief*) bien conocido, -a; **she's a ~ liar** tiene fama de mentirosa; **to be ~ for sth** tener mala fama por algo

notwithstanding [,nat·wɪθ·'stæn·dɪŋ] *form* **I.** *prep* a pesar de **II.** *adv* no obstante

nougat ['nu·gət] *n* ≈ turrón *m*

nought [nɔt] *pron see* **naught**

noun [naʊn] *n* nombre *m;* LING sustantivo *m*

nourish ['nɜr·ɪʃ] *vt* alimentar

nourishing ['nɜr·ɪʃ·ɪŋ] *adj* nutritivo, -a; (*rich*) rico, -a

nourishment *n* **1.** (*food*) alimento *m* **2.** (*providing with food*) alimentación *f*

Nova Scotia [,nou·və·'skou·ʃə] *n* Nueva Escocia *f*

novel[1] ['nav·əl] *n* LIT novela *f*

novel[2] ['nav·əl] *adj* (*new*) novedoso, -a

novelist ['nav·ə·lɪst] *n* novelista *mf*

novelty ['nav·əl·ti] <-ies> *n* **1.** (*newness*) novedad *f* **2.** (*innovation*) innovación *f*

November [nou·'vem·bər] *n* noviembre *m; s. a.* **April**

novice ['nav·ɪs] *n* novato, -a *m, f;* REL novicio, -a *m, f*

now [naʊ] **I.** *adv* **1.** ahora; **just ~** ahora mismo **2.** (*currently*) actualmente **3.** (*then*) entonces; **any time ~** en cualquier momento; (**every**) **~ and then** de vez en cuando **4.** (*give emphasis*) **~, where did I put her book?** ¿se puede saber dónde he puesto su libro?; **~ we're talking!** ¡parece que empezamos a entendernos!; **~ then** ¡vamos a ver! ▶ (**it's**) **~ or never** (es) ahora o nunca **II.** *n* (*present*) presente *m; before ~* antes; **by ~** ahora ya; **for ~** por ahora; **as of ~** a partir de ahora **III.** *conj* **~** (**that**)... ahora que...

nowadays ['nau·ə·deɪz] *adv* hoy en día

nowhere ['nou·hwer] *adv* en ninguna parte; **to appear out of ~** aparecer de la nada; **to be going ~** *a. fig* no llevar a ninguna parte

noxious ['nak·ʃəs] *adj form* nocivo, -a; (*very unpleasant*) desagradable

nozzle ['naz·əl] *n* tobera *f;* (*of a gas pump*) inyector *m;* (*of a gun*) boquilla *f*

NT *abbr of* **Northwest Territories** Northwest Territories (Canadá)

nuance ['nu·ans] *n* matiz *m*

nub [nʌb] *n* **1.** (*point*) quid *m* **2.** (*piece*) trozo *m*

nubile ['nu·bɪl] *adj* núbil

nuclear ['nu·kli·ər] *adj* nuclear

nucleic acid [nu·'kli·ɪk·'æs·ɪd] *n* ácido *m* nucleico

nucleus ['nu·kli·əs] <-ei *or* -es> *n* núcleo *m*

nude [nud] *adj* desnudo, -a

nudge [nʌdʒ] **I.** *vt* dar un codazo a; *fig* empujar **II.** *n* (*push*) codazo *m*

nudism ['nu·dɪz·əm] *n* nudismo *m*

nudist ['nu·dɪst] *adj* nudista

nudity ['nu·də·ti] *n* desnudez *f*

nugget ['nʌg·ɪt] *n* MIN pepita *f*

nuisance ['nu·səns] *n* molestia *f*

nuke [nuk, njuk] *vt sl* **1.** MIL bombardear

con armas atómicas **2.** (*cook*) cocinar en el microondas

null [nʌl] *adj* nulo, -a; **~ and void** sin efecto

nullification [ˌnʌl·ɪ·fɪ·ˈkeɪ·ʃən] *n* anulación *f*

nullify [ˈnʌl·ɪ·faɪ] <-ie-> *vt* anular

numb [nʌm] **I.** *adj* entumecido, -a; **to go ~** entumecerse **II.** *vt* entumecer; (*desensitize*) insensibilizar

number [ˈnʌm·bər] **I.** *n* **1.** MATH número *m*; (*symbol*) cifra *f*; **telephone ~** número de teléfono **2.** (*amount*) cantidad *f*; **(a) small/large ~(s) (of children)** (una) pequeña/gran cantidad (de niños); **for a ~ of reasons** por una serie de razones; **to be 3 in ~** ser 3; **to be few in ~** ser pocos **3.** PUBL, MUS, THEAT número *m* ▸ **to be (the) ~ one** ser el mejor **II.** *vt* **1.** (*assign a number to*) poner número a; **to ~ sth from... to...** numerar algo del... al... **2.** (*count*) contar **3.** (*amount to*) sumar; **each group ~s 10 members** cada grupo tiene 10 miembros

numbering *n* numeración *f*

numberless *adj* innumerable

numbness [ˈnʌm·nɪs] *n* **1.** (*on part of body*) entumecimiento *m* **2.** (*lack of feeling*) insensibilidad *f*

numeracy [ˈnu·mər·ə·si] *n* capacidad *f* para la aritmética

numeral [ˈnu·mər·əl] *n* número *m*

numeration [ˌnu·mə·ˈreɪ·ʃən] *n form* numeración *f*

numerical [nu·ˈmer·ɪ·kəl] *adj* numérico, -a; **in ~ order** por orden numérico

numeric keypad [nu·ˌmer·ɪk·ˈki·pæd] *n* COMPUT teclado *m* numérico

numerous [ˈnu·mər·əs] *adj* numeroso, -a

nun [nʌn] *n* monja *f*

nunnery [ˈnʌn·ə·ri] <-ies> *n* convento *m* de monjas

nuptial [ˈnʌp·ʃəl] *adj* nupcial

nurse [nɜrs] **I.** *n* **1.** MED enfermero, -a *m, f* **2.** (*nanny*) niñera *f*; (*wet nurse*) nodriza *f* **II.** *vt* **1.** (*care for*) cuidar **2.** (*nurture*) nutrir **3.** (*harbor*) abrigar **4.** (*breastfeed*) amamantar **III.** *vi* dar de mamar

nursery [ˈnɜr·sə·ri] <-ies> *n* (*school*) guardería *f*

nursery rhyme *n* canción *f* infantil

nursery school *n* parvulario *m*, jardín *m* de infancia

nursing **I.** *n* enfermería *f* **II.** *adj* de enfermería

nurture [ˈnɜr·tʃər] **I.** *vt* alimentar; (*a plant*) cuidar **II.** *n* nutrición *f*

nut [nʌt] *n* **1.** BOT nuez *f* **2.** TECH tuerca *f* **3.** *sl* (*madman*) chiflado, -a *m, f*; (*enthusiast*) entusiasta *mf*

nutcracker [ˈnʌt·ˌkræk·ər] *n* cascanueces *m inv*

nuthatch <-es> *n* trepatroncos *m inv*

nuthouse <-s> *n sl* manicomio *m*

nutmeg [ˈnʌt·meg] *n* nuez *f* moscada

nutrient [ˈnu·tri·ənt] **I.** *n* nutriente *m* **II.** *adj* nutritivo, -a

nutrition [nu·ˈtrɪʃ·ən] *n* nutrición *f*

nutritionist [nu·ˈtrɪʃ·ə·nɪst] *n* nutricionista *mf*

nutritious [nu·ˈtrɪʃ·əs] *adj*, **nutritive** [ˈnu·trɪ·ˌtɪv] *adj* nutritivo, -a

nuts [nʌts] *adj* loco, -a; **to be ~** estar chiflado; **to go ~** volverse loco

nutshell [ˈnʌt·ʃel] *n* cáscara *f* de nuez ▸ **in a ~** en resumidas cuentas

nutty [ˈnʌt·i] <-ier, -iest> *adj* **1.** (*cake*) con nueces; (*flavor*) de nuez **2.** *sl* (*crazy*) chiflado, -a; **to be (as) ~ as a fruitcake** estar más loco que una cabra

nuzzle [ˈnʌz·əl] **I.** *vt* acariciar con el hocico **II.** *vi* acurrucarse; **to ~ closer** arrimarse

NV [nə·ˈva·də] *abbr of* **Nevada** Nevada *f*

NW *abbr of* **northwest** NO *m*

NY [ˌnu·ˈjɔrk] *abbr of* **New York** Nueva York *f*

nylon [ˈnaɪ·lan] *n* nailon *m*

nymph [nɪmf] *n* ninfa *f*

nymphomaniac [ˌnɪm·fou·ˈmeɪ·ni·æk] *n* ninfómana *f*

O

O, o [ou] *n* **1.** (*letter*) O, o *f*; **~ as in Oscar** O de Oviedo **2.** (*zero*) cero *m*

oak [oʊk] n (tree, wood) roble m

oar [ɔr] n remo m

oarsman ['ɔrz·mən] <-men> n reme- ro m

oarswoman ['ɔrz·wʊm·ən] <-women> n remera f

oasis [oʊ·'eɪ·sɪs] <-es> n oasis m inv

oath [oʊθ] n juramento m; **under ~** bajo juramento

oats [oʊts] npl avena f

obedience [oʊ·'bi·di·əns] n obediencia f

obedient [oʊ·'bi·di·ənt] adj obediente

obese [oʊ·'bis] adj obeso, -a

obesity [oʊ·'bi·sə·ti] n obesidad f

obey [oʊ·'beɪ] vt (person) obedecer; (or- der, the law) cumplir

object¹ ['ab·dʒɪkt] n 1. (unspecified thing) objeto m 2. (purpose, goal) propósito m, objetivo m; **the ~ of the exercise is...** el objeto del ejercicio es... 3. (obstacle) **money is no ~** el dinero no importa 4. LING complemento m

object² [əb·'dʒekt] I. vi oponerse II. vt objetar; **to ~ that...** objetar que...

objection [əb·'dʒek·ʃən] n objeción f; **to raise ~s to sth** protestar contra algo

objective [əb·'dʒek·tɪv] I. n objetivo m II. adj objetivo, -a

objector n objetor(a) m(f)

obligation [ab·lə·'geɪ·ʃən] n obligación f; **to be under an ~ to do sth** tener la obligación de hacer algo

oblige [ə·'blaɪdʒ] vt 1. (force) obli- gar 2. (perform service for) hacer un favor a

obliging [ə·'blaɪ·dʒɪŋ] adj servicial, co- medido, -a AmL

oblivion [ə·'blɪv·i·ən] n olvido m; **to fall into ~** caer en el olvido

oblivious [ə·'blɪv·i·əs] adj inconsciente; **~ of sth** inconsciente de algo

oblong ['ab·lɑŋ] adj rectangular, oblon- go, -a

obnoxious [əb·'nak·ʃəs] adj detestable

obscene [əb·'sin] adj (indecent) obs- ceno, -a

obscenity [əb·'sen·ə·ti] <-ies> n obsce- nidad f, indecencia f

obscure [əb·'skjʊr] I. adj oscuro, -a II. vt 1. (from vision) oscurecer 2. (from un- derstanding) complicar

observant [əb·'zɜr·vənt] adj observador(a); (of one's duty) cumplidor(a)

observation [ab·zər·'veɪ·ʃən] n 1. (act of seeing) observación f; LAW vigilan- cia f; **to keep sth under ~** vigilar algo/a alguien; **under ~** MED en ob- servación 2. (remark) comentario m, observación f

observation tower n atalaya f

observatory [əb·'zɜr·və·tɔr·i] n obser- vatorio m

observe [əb·'zɜrv] vt 1. (watch close- ly) observar; (notice) fijarse en; **to ~ sb doing sth** ver a alguien haciendo algo 2. (remark) comentar 3. (obey: rules) observar; (silence, religious holi- day) guardar

observer [əb·'zɜr·vər] n observa- dor(a) m(f)

obsess [əb·'ses] vt obsesionar; **to be ~ed by sb/sth** obsesionarse por al- guien/algo

obsession [əb·'seʃ·ən] n obsesión f

obsessive [əb·'ses·ɪv] adj obsesivo, -a

obsolete [ab·sə·'lit] adj obsoleto, -a

obstacle ['ab·stə·kəl] n obstáculo m; **insurmountable ~** un obstáculo in- salvable; **to overcome an ~** superar un obstáculo

obstinate ['ab·stə·nɪt] adj obstinado, -a

obstruct [əb·'strʌkt] vt 1. (block) obs- truir; (traffic) bloquear; (view) tapar 2. (hinder) dificultar; (progress) obs- taculizar

obstruction [əb·'strʌk·ʃən] n 1. (action) a. MED, POL obstrucción f 2. (impedi- ment) obstáculo m

obstructive [əb·'strʌk·tɪv] adj (tactic, at- titude) obstruccionista; (person) que pone obstáculos

obtain [əb·'teɪn] vt obtener; **to ~ sth from sb/sth** obtener algo de alguien/ algo

obtainable [əb·'teɪ·nə·bəl] adj que se puede conseguir

obtrusive [əb·'tru·sɪv] adj form (ques- tion, presence) inoportuno, -a; (noise) molesto, -a; (color, design) (demasiado) llamativo, -a

obtuse [ab·'tus] adj obtuso, -a

obvious ['ab·vi·əs] adj obvio, -a; **for ~**

reasons por razones obvias; **it is ~ to me that...** me doy perfecta cuenta de que...; **to make sth ~ to sb** hacer algo patente a alguien

obviously *adv* obviamente, claramente; **~,...** como es lógico,...

occasion [əˈkeɪ·ʒən] *n* **1.** (*particular time*) ocasión *f;* **on ~** de vez en cuando; **on one ~** en una ocasión; **on several ~s** en varias ocasiones **2.** (*event*) acontecimiento *m;* **on the ~ of...** con motivo de... **3.** (*reason*) motivo *m;* **to give ~ to sth** dar lugar a algo **4.** (*opportunity*) ocasión; **should the ~ arise** si se presenta la ocasión

occasional [əˈkeɪ·ʒə·nəl] *adj* ocasional; **I smoke an ~ cigarette** fumo un cigarrillo de vez en cuando

occasionally *adv* ocasionalmente, de vez en cuando

Occident [ˈak·sə·dənt] *n* **the ~** Occidente

occidental [ˌak·səˈden·təl] *adj* occidental

occupancy rate *n* tasa *f* de ocupación

occupant [ˈak·jə·pənt] *n form* **1.** (*of building, vehicle*) ocupante *mf;* (*tenant*) inquilino, -a *m, f* **2.** (*of post*) titular *mf*

occupation [ˌak·jəˈpeɪ·ʃən] *n* **1.** *a.* MIL ocupación *f* **2.** (*profession*) profesión *f* **3.** (*pastime*) pasatiempo *m*

occupational [ˌak·jəˈpeɪ·ʃə·nəl] *adj* profesional

occupier [ˈak·jə·paɪ·ər] *n* (*of territory, building*) ocupante *mf;* (*tenant*) inquilino, -a *m, f*

occupy [ˈak·ju·paɪ] <-ie-> *vt* **1.** (*room, position*) *a.* MIL ocupar; **the bathroom's occupied** el lavabo está ocupado **2.** (*engage*) **to be occupied with sth** estar ocupado con algo; **to keep sb occupied** mantener a alguien ocupado; **to ~ oneself** entretenerse **3.** (*hold*) **to ~ a post** ocupar un cargo **4.** (*dwell in*) **to ~ a house** vivir en una casa **5.** (*employ*) dar trabajo

occur [əˈkɜr] <-rr-> *vi* **1.** (*happen*) ocurrir; (*change, problem*) producirse; (*symptom*) presentarse; **to ~ once every two years** tener lugar una vez cada dos años **2.** (*come into mind*) **to ~ to**

sb ocurrírsele a alguien; **did it ever ~ to you that...?** ¿no se te ha ocurrido nunca que...?

occurrence [əˈkɜr·əns] *n* **1.** (*event*) acontecimiento *m;* **an unexpected ~** un suceso inesperado **2.** (*case*) caso *m* **3.** (*incidence: of disease*) incidencia *f*

ocean [ˈoʊ·ʃən] *n* océano *m*

Oceania [ˌoʊ·ʃiˈeɪ·ni·ə] *n* Oceanía *f*

oceanic [ˌoʊ·ʃiˈæn·ɪk] *adj* oceánico, -a

o'clock [əˈklak] *adv* **it's one ~** es la una; **it's two ~** son las dos

octagon [ˈak·tə·gən] *n* octógono *m*

octane [ˈak·teɪn] *n* octano *m*

octave [ˈak·tɪv] *n* LIT, MUS octava *f*

October [akˈtoʊ·bər] *n* octubre *m; s. a.* **April**

octogenarian [ˌak·tou·dʒɪˈner·i·ən] **I.** *adj* octogenario, -a **II.** *n* octogenario, -a *m, f*

octopus [ˈak·tə·pəs] <-es *or* -pi> *n* pulpo *m*

oculist [ˈak·jə·lɪst] *n* oculista *mf*

odd [ad] *adj* **1.** (*strange*) extraño, -a; **an ~ person/thing** una persona/cosa rara; **how (very) ~!** ¡qué raro!; **it is ~ that...** es raro que +*subj;* **to look ~** tener un aspecto extraño **2.** (*number*) impar **3.** (*approximately*) **30 ~ people** 30 y pico personas **4.** (*occasional*) ocasional; **at ~ times** algunas veces **5.** (*unmatched: glove, sock*) suelto, -a

oddly *adv* **1.** (*in a strange manner*) de forma extraña **2.** (*curiously*) curiosamente; **~ enough** por extraño que parezca

odds [adz] *npl* (*probability*) probabilidades *fpl;* **the ~ against/in favor of sth** las probabilidades en contra/a favor de algo; **the ~ are against us** tenemos las de perder; **the ~ are in his favor** tiene todas las de ganar; **the ~ are that...** lo más seguro es que +*subj* ► **~ and ends** *inf* (*bits*) cosas *f pl* sueltas; **against all (the) ~** contra todo pronóstico; **to be at ~ with sb** estar en desacuerdo con alguien

odor [ˈoʊ·dər] *n* (*smell*) olor *m;* (*fragrance*) aroma *m*

odorless *adj form* inodoro, -a

odyssey [ˈad·ɪ·si] *n* odisea *f*

O

of |əv, *stressed*: ʌv| *prep* **1.** de **2.** (*belonging to*) de; **the works ~ Twain** las obras de Twain; **a friend ~ mine/ theirs** un amigo mío/de ellos **3.** (*done by*) de; **it's kind ~ him** es amable de su parte **4.** (*representing*) de; **a drawing ~ Paul** un dibujo de Paul **5.** (*without*) **a tree bare ~ leaves** un árbol sin hojas; **free ~ charge** sin cargo; **free ~ tax** libre de impuestos; **to cure sb ~ a disease** curar a alguien de una enfermedad **6.** (*with*) **a man ~ courage** un hombre de valor; **a city ~ wide avenues** una ciudad con amplias avenidas **7.** (*away from*) **to be north ~ Atlanta** estar al norte de Atlanta **8.** (*temporal*) **the 4th ~ May** el 4 de mayo **9.** (*to*) **it is ten/ (a) quarter ~ two** son las dos menos diez/cuarto **10.** (*consisting of*) de; **a ring ~ gold** un anillo de oro; **to smell/ to taste ~ cheese** oler/saber a queso **11.** (*characteristic*) **with the patience ~ a saint** con la paciencia de un santo; **this idiot ~ a plumber** el idiota del fontanero **12.** (*concerning*) **his love ~ jazz** su amor por el jazz; **to know sth ~ sb's past** saber algo del pasado de alguien; **to approve ~ sb's idea** estar de acuerdo con la idea de alguien; **what has become ~ him?** ¿qué ha sido de él?; **what do you think ~ him?** ¿qué piensas de él? **13.** (*cause*) **because ~** a causa de algo/alguien; **to die ~ grief** morir de pena; **it happened ~ itself** sucedió de por sí **14.** (*a portion of*) **there's a lot ~** hay mucho de eso; **one ~ the best** uno de los mejores; **the best ~ friends** los mejores amigos; **many ~ them came** muchos de ellos vinieron; **there are five ~ them** hay cinco de ellos; **he knows the five ~ them** los conoce a los cinco; **two ~ the five** dos de los cinco; **he ~ all people knows that** él lo sabe mejor que nadie; **today ~ all days** precisamente hoy **15.** (*to amount of*) **80 years ~ age** 80 años de edad

off |ɔf| **I.** *prep* **1.** (*near*) **to be just ~ the main road** estar muy cerca de la carretera principal **2.** (*away from*) **to take sth ~ the shelf** coger algo del estante; **keep**

~ the grass prohibido pisar el césped **3.** (*down from*) **to fall/jump ~ a ladder** caer/saltar de una escalera; **to get ~ the train** bajarse del tren **4.** (*from*) **to eat ~ a plate** comer de un plato; **to cut a piece ~ the cheese** cortar un pedazo del queso; **to take 10 dollars ~ the price** rebajar 10 dólares del precio **5.** (*stop using*) **to be ~ caffeine/drugs** dejar la cafeína/las drogas **6.** (*as source of*) **to run ~ batteries** funcionar con pilas **II.** *adv* **1.** (*not on*) **to switch/turn sth ~** apagar algo; **it's ~ between them** *fig* lo han dejado **2.** (*away*) **the town is 5 miles ~ to the east** el pueblo está 8 km más al este; **not far ~** no lejos (de); **a way's ~** a bastante distancia; **to drive/ run ~** irse en coche/corriendo; **~ with him** fuera con él; **it's time I was ~** ya debería haber salido **3.** (*removed*) **the lid is ~** la tapa está fuera; **with one's coat ~** con el abrigo quitado; **~ with that hat!** ¡quítate el sombrero! **4.** (*free from work*) **to get ~ at 4:00 p.m.** salir (del trabajo) a las cuatro; **to get a day ~** tener un día libre **5.** (*completely*) **to kill ~** exterminar; **to pay sth ~** acabar de pagar **6.** COM **5% ~** 5% de descuento **7.** (*until gone*) **to walk ~ the dinner** caminar para bajar la comida; **to sleep ~ the wine** dormir el vino **8.** (*separating*) **to fence sth ~** cercar algo ▶ **straight** |*or* **right**| **~ the bat** enseguida; **~ and on** on and **~** de cuando en cuando **III.** *adj* **1.** (*not on: light*) apagado, -a; (*faucet*) cerrado, -a; (*water*) cortado, -a **2.** (*canceled: engagement, wedding, deal*) suspendido, -a **3.** (*free from work*) **to be ~ at 5:00 p.m.** salir (del trabajo) a las cinco; **I'm ~ on Mondays** los lunes estoy libre **4.** (*provided for*) **to be well ~** tener dinero; **to be not well ~** andar mal de dinero **5.** (*substandard*) **to be ~ one's game** SPORTS estar en mala forma **6.** *inf* **to go ~ on sb** echar la bronca a alguien

off-center *adj* **1.** (*diverging from the center*) descentrado, -a **2.** (*unconventional*) poco convencional

off chance |ˈɔf·tʃæns| *n* **on the ~** por si acaso

off-color [ˌɔf·ˈkʌl·ər] *adj* **1.** (*unwell*) indispuesto, -a; **to feel ~** encontrarse mal; **to look ~** tener mala cara **2.** (*in bad taste: joke*) subido, -a de tono

off-duty *adj* fuera de servicio

offend [əˈfend] I. *vi* **1.** (*cause displeasure*) ofender **2.** (*violate*) **to ~ against sth** atentar contra algo **3.** LAW infringir la ley; (*commit a crime*) cometer un delito II. *vt* ofender; **to be ~ed by sth** ofenderse por algo

offender [əˈfen·dər] *n* infractor(a) *m(f)*; (*guilty of crime*) delincuente *mf*; **first ~** delincuente sin antecedentes; **previous** [*or* **repeat**] **~** reincidente *mf*

offense [əˈfens] *n* **1.** (*crime*) delito *m*; **minor ~** infracción *f*; **traffic ~** infracción de tráfico **2.** (*affront*) atentado *m*; **an ~ against sth** un atentado contra algo **3.** (*upset feeling*) ofensa *f*; **to cause ~ (to sb)** ofender (a alguien); **to take ~ (at sth)** ofenderse (por algo); **no ~ (intended)** *inf* sin ánimo de ofender **4.** SPORTS ofensiva *f*

offensive [əˈfen·sɪv] I. *adj* **1.** (*remark, joke*) ofensivo, -a; (*language, word*) grosero, -a; (*tone*) desagradable; **to be ~ to sb** insultar a alguien **2.** (*disagreeable: smell*) repugnante II. *n* MIL ofensiva *f*; **to go on the ~** pasar a la ofensiva

offer [ˈɔ·fər] I. *vt* **1.** (*proffer: help, advice, money*) ofrecer; **to ~ sb sth** ofrecer algo a alguien; **to ~ an apology** pedir disculpas; **can I ~ you a drink?** ¿quiere tomar algo?; **to ~ a good price for sth** ofrecer un buen precio por algo; **to ~ a reward** ofrecer una recompensa; **to ~ an explanation** dar una explicación; **to ~ shelter** dar cobijo; **to have much to ~** tener mucho que ofrecer **2.** (*give: gift*) dar **3.** (*volunteer*) **to ~ to do sth** ofrecerse para [*or* a] hacer algo **4.** (*excuse*) presentar; (*opinion*) expresar II. *n* (*proposal*) propuesta *f*; (*of help*) ofrecimiento *m*; (*of a job*) oferta *f*; **that's my last ~** es mi última oferta; **to make** [*or* **put in**] **an ~ of $1000 for sth** ofrecer 1000 dólares por algo

offering [ˈɔ·fər·ɪŋ] *n* **1.** (*thing given*) ofrecimiento *m* **2.** (*contribution*) donativo *m* **3.** REL (*sacrifice*) ofrenda *f*

offhand [ˌɔf·ˈhænd] I. *adj* **1.** (*without previous thought*) improvisado, -a; **an ~ remark** una observación que no viene al caso **2.** (*uninterested*) brusco, -a; **to be ~ about sth** pasar (de algo) *inf* II. *adv* de improviso; **to judge sb/sth ~** juzgar algo/a alguien a la ligera; **~, I'd say...** así de pronto, yo diría...

office [ˈɔ·fɪs] *n* **1.** (*of a company*) oficina *f*; (*room in house*) despacho *m*; **they've got ~s in Los Angeles and Miami** tienen oficinas en Los Ángeles y Miami; **to stay at the ~** quedarse en la oficina; **doctor's ~** consultorio *m*; **lawyer's ~** bufete *m* **2.** POL (*authoritative position*) cargo *m*; **to hold ~** ocupar un cargo; **to be in ~** (*person*) estar en funciones; (*party*) estar en el poder; **to be out of ~** haber dejado el cargo; **to take ~** entrar en funciones **3.** REL oficio *m*

office building *n* bloque *m* de oficinas

office hours *npl* horas *f pl* de oficina

officer [ˈɔ·fɪ·sər] *n* **1.** MIL oficial *mf* **2.** (*policeman*) policía *mf*; **police ~** agente *mf* de policía **3.** (*in organization*) directivo, -a *m, f*; (*in political party*) dirigente *mf* **4.** (*official*) funcionario, -a *m, f*

office staff *n* personal *m* de oficina

office supplies *npl* artículos *m pl* de oficina

office worker *n* oficinista *mf*

official [əˈfɪʃ·əl] I. *n* **1.** POL oficial *mf* **2.** (*civil servant*) funcionario, -a *m, f* II. *adj* oficial

officially [əˈfɪʃ·ə·li] *adv* oficialmente

off-key MUS I. *adv* **to play/sing ~** desafinar II. *adj* desafinado, -a

off-limits *adj* fuera de los límites (permitidos)

offline [ˌɔf·ˈlaɪn] *adj* COMPUT sin conexión

off-peak [ˌɔf·ˈpik] *adj* (*fare, rate*) fuera de las horas punta

off-putting [ˈɔf·ˌpʊt·ɪŋ] *adj* **1.** (*smell, manner, appearance, person*) desagradable **2.** (*experience*) desalentador(a)

off-road vehicle *n* vehículo todoterreno *m*

off-season [ˈɔf·ˌsi·zən] *n* temporada *f* baja

offset [ˈɔf·set] I. *n* **1.** (*compensation*) compensación *f* **2.** BOT vástago *m*

II. <offset, offset> vt (*compensate*) compensar

offshore [ˌɔfˈʃɔr] I. adj 1. (*from the shore: breeze, wind*) terral 2. (*at sea*) a poca distancia de la costa; ~ **fishing** pesca de bajura; ~ **oilfield** yacimiento m petrolífero marítimo 3. (*in foreign country*) en el exterior II. adv mar adentro; **to anchor** ~ anclar a cierta distancia de la costa

offside [ˌɔfˈsaɪd] SPORTS I. n fuera de juego m II. adj en fuera de juego

offspring [ˈɔfsprɪŋ] n inv 1. (*animal young*) cría f 2. pl (*children*) prole f

off-white [ˌɔfˈhwaɪt] adj de color hueso

often [ˈɔfən] adv a menudo; **we** ~ **go there** solemos ir allí; **as** ~ **as** siempre que; **as** ~ **as not** la mitad de las veces; **every so** ~ alguna que otra vez; **how** ~? ¿cuántas veces?; **it's not** ~ **that...** no es frecuente que +subj; **more** ~ **than not** la mayoría de las veces

oh [oʊ] interj 1. oh; ~ **dear!** ¡Dios mío!; ~ **no!** ¡ay, no!; ~ **well** bueno; ~ **yes?** ¿ah, sí? 2. (*by the way*) ah

OH [oʊˈhaɪ-oʊ] n abbr of **Ohio** Ohio m

oil [ɔɪl] I. n 1. (*lubricant*) aceite m; **sunflower** ~ aceite de girasol 2. (*petroleum*) petróleo m; **to strike** ~ encontrar petróleo 3. (*grease*) grasa f II. vt engrasar

oil field n yacimiento m petrolífero

oil level n TECH nivel m de aceite

oil painting n óleo m

oil pipeline n oleoducto m

oil-producing adj productor(a) de petróleo

oil production n producción f de petróleo

oil rig n plataforma f petrolífera

oilskin n 1. (*cloth*) hule m 2. ~**s** (*clothing*) impermeable m

oil slick n marea f negra

oil tanker n NAUT petrolero m

oil well n pozo m de petróleo

oily [ˈɔɪli] <-ier, -iest> adj 1. (*oil-like*) oleoso, -a 2. (*greasy: hands*) grasiento, -a; (*food*) aceitoso, -a; (*skin, hair*) graso, -a

ointment [ˈɔɪntmənt] n MED pomada f

OK¹, okay [ˌoʊˈkeɪ] inf I. adj 1. (*ac-ceptable*) **is it** ~ **with you if...?** ¿te importa si...?; **it's** ~ **with me** por mí no hay problema 2. (*not bad*) **to be** ~ no estar mal II. interj vale inf, okey AmL inf, órale Méx III. <OKed, okayed> vt **to** ~ **sth** dar el visto bueno a algo IV. n visto bueno m; **to give (sb/sth) the** ~ dar (a alguien/algo) el visto bueno V. adv bastante bien

OK² [ˌoʊ-klə-ˈhoʊ-mə] n abbr of **Oklahoma** Oklahoma f

old [oʊld] I. adj 1. (*not young*) viejo, -a; ~ **people** la gente mayor; **to grow** ~**er** envejecer 2. (*not new*) viejo, -a; (*food*) pasado, -a; (*wine*) añejo, -a; (*furniture, house*) antiguo, -a 3. (*denoting an age*) **how** ~ **are you?** ¿cuántos años tienes?; **he's five years** ~ tiene cinco años; **she's three years** ~**er than I** me lleva tres años 4. (*former: job, partner*) antiguo, -a 5. (*of long standing*) de siempre; ~ **friend** viejo amigo; **the same** ~ **faces** las mismas caras de siempre II. n (*elderly people*) **the** ~ los viejos, los ancianos AmL; **young and** ~ grandes y chicos

old age n vejez f; **to reach** ~ llegar a viejo

old-fashioned [ˌoʊld-ˈfæʃ-ənd] adj pej 1. (*not modern: clothes*) pasado, -a de moda; (*views*) anticuado, -a 2. (*traditional*) tradicional

old school adj de la vieja escuela

olive [ˈal-ɪv] n 1. (*fruit*) oliva f, aceituna f 2. (*tree*) olivo m

Olympic [oʊˈlɪm-pɪk] adj olímpico, -a; **the Olympic Games** SPORTS los Juegos Olímpicos

omelet(te) [ˈam-lət] n tortilla f

omen [ˈoʊ-men] n indicio m, augurio m

omission [oʊ-ˈmɪʃ-ən] n omisión f

omit [oʊ-ˈmɪt] <-tt-> vt (*person, information*) omitir; **to** ~ **any reference to sb/sth** evitar toda referencia a alguien/algo

omnivorous [am-ˈnɪv-ər-əs] adj omnívoro, -a

on [an] I. prep 1. (*place*) sobre, en; ~ **the table** sobre la mesa; ~ **the wall** en la pared; **to be** ~ **the plane** estar en el avión; **to hang** ~ **a branch** colgar de una rama; **to have sth ~ one's mind** *fig* tener algo en mente **2.** (*by means of*) **to go ~ the train** ir en tren; **to go ~ foot** ir a pie; **to keep a dog ~ a leash** llevar (a) un perro con correa **3.** (*source of*) con; **to run ~ gas** funcionar con gasolina; **to live ~ $2,000 a month** vivir con 2.000 dólares al mes **4.** MED **to be ~ drugs** tomar medicamentos **5.** (*spatial*) ~ **the right/left** a la derecha/izquierda; ~ **the corner/back of sth** en la esquina/la parte posterior de algo; **a house ~ the river** una casa junto al río **6.** (*temporal*) ~ **Sunday** el domingo; ~ **Sundays** los domingos; **at 2:00 p.m.** ~ **the dot** a las dos en punto de la tarde **7.** (*at time of*) **to leave ~ time** salir a tiempo; ~ **her arrival** a su llegada; ~ **arriving there** al llegar allí; **to finish ~ schedule** acabar puntualmente **8.** (*about*) sobre; **a lecture ~ Shakespeare** una conferencia sobre Shakespeare; **to compliment sb ~ sth** felicitar a alguien por algo; **to be there ~ business** estar ahí por negocios **9.** (*through medium of*) ~ **TV/video/CD** en televisión/vídeo/CD; **to speak ~ the radio/the phone** hablar en la radio/por teléfono; **to work ~ a computer** trabajar con un ordenador; **to play sth ~ the flute** tocar algo con la flauta **10.** (*with basis in*) ~ **the principle that** en el supuesto de que; **to do sth ~ purpose** hacer algo a propósito **11.** (*in state of*) ~ **sale** en venta; **to set sth ~ fire** prender fuego a algo; **to go ~ vacation/a trip** ir de vacaciones/de viaje; ~ **the whole** en general **12.** (*involved in*) **to work ~ a project** trabajar en un proyecto; **to be ~ page 10** estar en la página 10; **two ~ each side** dos en [*or* a] cada lado **13.** (*because of*) ~ **account of sth/sb** a causa de algo/alguien; **to depend ~ sb/sth** depender de alguien/algo **14.** (*against*) **to turn ~ sb** volverse contra alguien; **to cheat ~ sb** hacer trampa [*or* engañar] a alguien **15.** (*paid by*) **to buy sth ~ credit** comprar algo a crédito; **this is ~ me** *inf* esto corre por mi cuenta **II.** *adv* **1.** (*covering one's body*) **to put a hat ~** ponerse un sombrero; **to have sth ~**

llevar algo (puesto); **to try ~ sth** probarse algo **2.** (*connected to sth*) **to screw sth ~** enroscar algo **3.** (*aboard*) **to get ~ a train** subir a un tren; **to get ~ a horse** montarse en un caballo **4.** (*not stopping*) **to keep ~ doing sth** seguir haciendo algo; **to get ~ with sth** ponerse a hacer algo **5.** (*in forward direction*) hacia delante; **to move ~** avanzar; **to urge sb ~** *fig* animar a alguien; **from that day ~** desde aquel día; **later ~** más tarde; **and so ~** y así sucesivamente **6.** (*in operation*) **to turn ~** encender; (*tap*) abrir **7.** (*performing*) en escena; **to go ~** salir a escena ▸ ~ **and off** de vez en cuando; ~ **and** sin parar **III.** *adj* **1.** (*functioning: light*) encendido, -a; (*faucet*) abierto, -a; (*brake*) puesto, -a; **to leave the light ~** dejar la luz encendida **2.** (*scheduled*) **what's ~ at the movies this week?** ¿qué dan en el cine esta semana? **3.** THEAT (*performing*) **to be ~** estar en escena; (*performing well*) hacerlo muy bien **4.** (*job*) **to be ~ duty** estar de servicio; (*doctor*) estar de guardia **5.** (*good: day*) bueno, -a **6.** (*acceptable*) **you're ~!** ¡de acuerdo!

once [wʌns] **I.** *adv* **1.** (*one time*) una vez; ~ **a week** una vez por [*or* a la] semana; ~ **in a lifetime** una vez en la vida; (*every*) ~ **in a while** de vez en cuando; ~ **again** de nuevo; ~ **and for all** de una vez por todas; **just for ~** sólo una vez; ~ **more** (*one more time*) otra vez; (*again, as before*) una vez más; ~ **or twice** una o dos veces; **at ~** (*simultaneously*) al mismo tiempo; (*immediately*) en seguida **2.** *liter* (*at one time past*) hace tiempo; ~ **upon a time there was...** *liter* érase una vez... **II.** *conj* una vez que +*subj*; **but ~ I'd arrived,...** pero una vez que llegué... ▸ **at ~** en seguida

oncoming [ˈɒn·kʌm·ɪŋ] *adj* que se aproxima; (*traffic, vehicle*) que viene en dirección contraria

one [wʌn] **I.** *n* (*number*) uno *m* ▸ (**all**) **in ~** todo en uno; **as ~** *form* a la vez; **in ~** de una sola pieza **II.** *adj* **1.** *numeral* un, uno, -a; ~ **hundred** cien; **it's ~ o'clock** es la una; **as ~ man** todos a una; **~ man out of** [*or* **in**] **two** uno de cada dos hombres **2.** *indef* un, uno, -a; **we'll meet ~ day** nos veremos un día de estos; **~ winter night** una noche de invierno **3.** (*sole*) único, -a; **her ~ and only hope** su única esperanza **4.** (*single*) mismo, -a, único, -a; **all files on the ~ disk** todos los archivos en un único disco **III.** *pron pers* **1.** *impers, no pl* **what can ~ do?** ¿qué puede hacer uno?; **to wash ~'s face** lavarse la cara **2.** (*person*) no ~ nadie; **every ~** cada uno; **the little ~s** los pequeños; **the ~ who...** el que...; **I for ~** al menos yo **3.** (*particular thing or person*) **any ~** cualquiera; **this ~** éste; **which ~?** ¿cuál (de ellos)?; **the ~ on the table** el que está en la mesa; **the thinner ~** el más fino

one-armed [ˌwʌn·ˈɑrmd] *adj* manco, -a

one-eyed [ˌwʌn·ˈaɪd] *adj* tuerto, -a

one-handed I. *adv* con una sola mano **II.** *adj* manco, -a

one-night stand [ˌwʌn·naɪt·ˈstænd] *n sl* (*relationship*) ligue *m* de una noche

one-piece (swimsuit) [ˈwʌn·pis] *n* bañador *m*

oneself [wʌn·ˈself] *pron reflexive* **1.** se *emphatic* sí (mismo, misma); **to deceive ~** engañarse a sí mismo; **to express ~** expresarse **2.** (*same person*) uno mismo

one-sided [ˌwʌn·ˈsaɪ·dɪd] *adj* (*contest*) desigual; (*decision*) unilateral; (*view, account*) parcial

one-way street [ˌwʌn·weɪ·ˈstrit] *n* calle *f* de sentido único

one-way ticket *n* billete *m* sencillo

ongoing [ˈɑn·ɡoʊ·ɪŋ] *adj* en curso

onion [ˈʌn·jən] *n* cebolla *f*

online *adj, adv* COMPUT en línea

onlooker [ˈɑn·lʊk·ər] *n* espectador(a) *m(f)*; **there were many ~s at the accident site** había muchos curiosos en el lugar del accidente

only [ˈoʊn·li] **I.** *adj* único, -a; **the ~ glass he had** el único vaso que tenía; **the ~ way of doing sth** la única manera de hacer algo; **I'm not the ~ one** no soy el único; **the ~ thing is...** la única cosa es... **II.** *adv* sólo, nomás *AmL*; **not ~... but also** no sólo... sino también; **I can ~**

say... sólo puedo decir...; **he has ~ two** sólo tiene dos; **~ Paul can do it** sólo Paul puede hacerlo; **I've ~ just eaten** acabo de comer ahora mismo **III.** *conj inf* sólo que

onset [ˈɑn·set] *n* comienzo *m*; (*of winter*) llegada *f*; (*of illness*) aparición *f*

onside [ˈɑn·saɪd] *adj* SPORTS **to be ~** (*player*) estar en posición correcta

onto [ˈɑn·tu] *prep*, **on to** *prep* **1.** (*in direction of*) sobre; **to put sth ~ the chair** poner algo sobre la silla; **to step ~ the road** pisar la calzada; **to come ~ a subject** tocar un tema **2.** (*connected to*) **to hold ~ sb's arm** aferrarse al brazo de alguien; **to be ~ sb** ver a alguien su juego

onward [ˈɑn·wərd] **I.** *adj* hacia delante **II.** *adv* hacia delante; **from today ~** de hoy en adelante

oops [ups] *interj inf* ¡huy!

ooze [uz] *vi* **1.** (*seep out*) exudar; **to ~ with sth** rezumar algo **2.** *fig* (*be full of*) rebosar

open [ˈoʊ·pən] **I.** *adj* **1.** (*not closed*) abierto, -a; **wide ~** completamente abierto; **to push sth ~** abrir algo de un empujón **2.** (*undecided*) sin concretar; **to keep one's options ~** dejar abiertas todas las alternativas **3.** (*not secret, public: scandal*) público, -a; (*hostility*) abierto, -a, manifiesto, -a; **to be an ~ book** *fig* ser un libro abierto; **an ~ secret** una cosa sabida **4.** (*unfolded: map*) desplegado, -a **5.** (*frank: person*) abierto, -a; **to welcome sb with ~ arms** recibir a alguien con los brazos abiertos **6.** (*accessible to all*) abierto, -a; (*discussion*) abierto, -a al público; (*session*) a puertas abiertas; (*trial*) público, -a **7.** (*willing to listen to new ideas*) abierto, -a de mente; **to have an ~ mind** tener una actitud abierta **8.** (*still available: job*) vacante **II.** *n* **1.** (*outdoors, outside*) (**out**) **in the ~** al aire libre **2.** (*not secret*) **to get sth (out) in the ~** sacar algo a la luz **III.** *vi* **1.** (*door, window, box*) abrirse **2.** (*trial*) público, -a **IV.** *vt* **1.** (*door, box, shop*) abrir; **to ~ the door to sth** *fig* abrir la puerta a algo; **to ~ sb's eyes (to sb/sth)** *fig* abrir a alguien los ojos (sobre alguien/algo); **to ~ fire (on sb)** abrir fuego (contra alguien) **2.** (*reveal feelings*) **to ~ one's heart to sb** abrir su corazón a alguien

◆**open up** *vi* **1.** (*unfold*) abrirse **2.** (*shop*) abrir **3.** (*become wider*) ensancharse **II.** *vt* abrir; (*map*) desplegar

open-air [ˌoʊ·pʌn·'er] *adj* al aire libre

open-ended [ˌoʊ·pʌn·'en·dɪd] *adj* (*contract*) de duración indefinida; (*question*) abierto, -a

opener ['oʊ·pə·nər] *n* abridor *m*, destapador *m AmL*; **bottle ~** abrebotellas *m inv*; **can ~** abrelatas *m inv*

opening ['oʊ·pə·nɪŋ] *n* **1.** (*gap, hole*) abertura *f*; (*in forest*) claro *m* **2.** (*job opportunity*) vacante *f* **3.** (*beginning*) apertura *f*; (*of book, film*) principio *m* **4.** (*ceremony*) inauguración *f*; (*new play, film*) estreno *m*

opening balance *n* FIN saldo *m* de apertura

opening bid *n* oferta *f* inicial

opening night *n* THEAT noche *f* del estreno

openly ['oʊ·pʌn·li] *adv* **1.** (*frankly*) honestamente **2.** (*publicly*) abiertamente

open-minded [ˌoʊ·pʌn·'maɪn·dɪd] *adj* (*accessible to new ideas*) de actitud abierta

openness ['oʊ·pʌn·nəs] *n* franqueza *f*

open-source *adj* de software libre

opera ['ɑp·rə] *n* ópera *f*

operate ['ɑp·ə·reɪt] **I.** *vi* **1.** (*work, run*) funcionar **2.** (*have or produce an effect*) actuar, surtir efecto **3.** (*perform surgery*) operar (**on** a) **4.** (*be in business*) operar **II.** *vt* **1.** (*work*) manejar **2.** (*run, manage*) llevar, tener

operating ['ɑp·ə·reɪ·t̬ɪŋ] *adj* **1.** ECON (*profit, costs*) de explotación **2.** TECH (*speed*) de funcionamiento **3.** MED de operaciones; **~ room** quirófano *m*

operation [ˌɑp·ə·'reɪ·ʃən] *n* **1.** (*way of working*) funcionamiento *m*; **to be in ~** estar en funcionamiento; **to come into ~** (*machines*) entrar en funcionamiento **2.** a. MED, MIL, MATH operación *f*

operational [ˌɑp·ə·'reɪ·ʃə·nəl] *adj* **1.** (*relating to operations*) operativo, -a **2.** (*working*) **to be ~** estar en funcio-

namiento

operative ['ɑp·ə·rə·t̬ɪv] **I.** *n* (*worker*) operario, -a *m, f* **II.** *adj* **1.** (*rules*) en vigor **2.** MED quirúrgico, -a

operator ['ɑp·ə·reɪ·t̬ər] *n* **1.** (*person*) operador(a) *m(f)*; TEL telefonista *mf*; **machine ~** maquinista *mf* **2.** (*company*) empresa *f*; **a tour ~** un(a) agente de viajes

opinion [ə·'pɪn·jən] *n* opinión *f*

opinionated [ə·'pɪn·jə·neɪ·t̬ɪd] *adj pej* dogmático, -a

opinion poll *n* encuesta *f* de opinión

opium ['oʊ·pi·əm] *n* opio *m*

opponent [ə·'poʊ·nənt] *n* **1.** POL opositor(a) *m(f)* **2.** SPORTS contrincante *mf*, rival *mf*

opportunity [ˌɑp·ər·'tu·nə·t̬i] <-ies> *n* oportunidad *f*

oppose [ə·'poʊz] *vt* **1.** (*be against*) oponerse a **2.** (*resist*) combatir

opposed *adj* opuesto, -a; **to be ~ to sth** oponerse a algo, estar en contra de algo

opposing *adj* contrario, -a

opposite ['ɑp·ə·zɪt] **I.** *n* contrario *m*; **quite the ~!** ¡todo lo contrario! ▶ **~s attract** los extremos se atraen **II.** *adj* **1.** (*absolutely different*) contrario, -a; **the ~ sex** el sexo opuesto **2.** (*facing*) de enfrente; **~ to sth** enfrente de algo **III.** *adv* (*facing*) enfrente; **they live ~** viven enfrente **IV.** *prep* enfrente de, frente a; **~ to sth** enfrente de algo; **~ me** frente a mí; **to sit ~ one another** estar sentados uno frente al otro

opposition [ˌɑp·ə·'zɪʃ·ən] *n* **1.** POL oposición *f* **2.** (*contrast*) contraposición *f* (**to** a) **3.** (*opponent*) adversario, -a *m, f*; ECON competencia *f*

oppression [ə·'preʃ·ən] *n* **1.** (*submission*) opresión *f* **2.** (*feeling*) agobio *m*

oppressive [ə·'pres·ɪv] *adj* **1.** (*harsh: regime, measures*) opresivo, -a **2.** (*burdensome*) agobiante

opt [ɑpt] *vi* optar (**for** por)

optic ['ɑp·tɪk] *adj* óptico, -a

optical ['ɑp·tɪ·kəl] *adj* óptico, -a

optician [ɑp·'tɪʃ·ən] *n* MED óptico, -a *m, f*

optics ['ɑp·tɪks] *n* óptica *f*

optimism ['ɑp·tə·mɪz·əm] *n* optimismo *m*

optimist [ˈap·tə·mɪst] n optimista mf

optimistic [ˌap·tə·ˈmɪs·tɪk] adj optimista

optimum [ˈap·tə·məm] adj óptimo, -a

option [ˈap·ʃən] n 1. (choice) a. ECON opción f 2. (possibility) posibilidad f

optional [ˈap·ʃə·nəl] adj opcional; (subject) optativo, -a

or [ɔr] conj o; (before o, ho) u; (between numbers) ó; **seven ~ eight** siete u ocho; **6 ~ 7** 6 ó 7; **either... ~...** o... o...; **to ask whether ~ not sb is coming** preguntar si alguien viene o no; **I can't read ~ write** no sé leer ni escribir

OR n 1. abbr of **operating room** quirófano m, sala f de operaciones 2. abbr of **Oregon** Oregón m

oracle [ˈɔr·ə·kəl] n oráculo m

oral [ˈɔr·əl] adj oral

orange [ˈɔr·ɪndʒ] I. n naranja f II. adj naranja

orangeade [ˌɔr·ɪndʒ·ˈeɪd] n naranjada f

orange juice n zumo m de naranja

orange peel n cáscara f de naranja

orange tree n naranjo m

orbit [ˈɔr·bɪt] I. n 1. ASTR órbita f; **to go into ~** entrar en órbita 2. (range of action, field) campo m de influencia II. vt orbitar alrededor de

orbital [ˈɔr·bɪ·təl] adj orbital; **~ trajectory** trayectoria f orbital

orchard [ˈɔr·tʃərd] n huerto m

orchestra [ˈɔr·kɪ·strə] n orquesta f

orchestral [ɔr·ˈkes·trəl] adj orquestal

orchestra pit n foso m orquestal

orchid [ˈɔr·kɪd] n orquídea f

ordeal [ɔr·ˈdil] n calvario m

order [ˈɔr·dər] I. n 1. (sequence) orden m; **to put sth in ~** poner en orden algo; **in alphabetical ~** por orden alfabético 2. (instruction) a. LAW, REL orden f; **to give/receive an ~** dar/recibir una orden; **by ~ of sb** por orden de alguien 3. (working condition, satisfactory arrangement) orden m; **to keep ~** mantener el orden; **the car is in perfect working ~** el coche funciona perfectamente bien; **to be out of ~** no funcionar; (toilet) estar fuera de servicio; **are your immigration papers in ~?** ¿tienes los papeles de inmigración en regla? 4. (appropriate behavior) out

of ~ improcedente 5. (purpose) **in (not) to** para (no) +infin; **in ~ for, in ~ that** para que +subj 6. COM pedido m; **to put in an ~ for sth** hacer un pedido de [or encargar] algo; **made to ~** hecho por encargo II. vi pedir; **are you ready to ~?** ¿ya han decidido qué van a pedir? III. vt 1. (command) **to ~ sb to do sth** ordenar a alguien que haga algo; **to ~ sb out** echar a alguien 2. (request goods or service) encargar 3. (arrange) ordenar, poner en orden

order form n hoja f de pedidos

orderly [ˈɔr·dər·li] <-ies> I. n 1. (hospital attendant) celador(a) m(f) 2. MIL ordenanza mf II. adj 1. (tidy) ordenado, -a 2. (well-behaved) disciplinado, -a

ordinal (number) [ˈɔr·də·nəl] n ordinal m

ordinary [ˈɔr·də·ner·i] I. n out of the ~ fuera de lo común II. adj normal, corriente; **in the ~ way...** normalmente...

ordnance [ˈɔrd·nəns] n artillería f

ore [ɔr] n mena f; **iron ~** mineral m de hierro

Oregon [ˈɔr·ɪ·gən] n Oregón m

organ [ˈɔr·gən] n órgano m

organ donor n donante mf de órganos

organic [ɔr·ˈgæn·ɪk] adj 1. (disease, substance, compound) orgánico, -a 2. (produce, farming method) biológico, -a 3. (fundamental: part) inherente 4. (systematic: change) sistemático, -a

organism [ˈɔr·gə·nɪz·əm] n organismo m

organist [ˈɔr·gə·nɪst] n organista mf

organization [ˌɔr·gə·nɪ·ˈzeɪ·ʃən] n organización f

organizational [ˌɔr·gə·nɪ·ˈzeɪ·ʃə·nəl] adj organizativo, -a

organize [ˈɔr·gə·naɪz] I. vt organizar II. vi organizarse

organizer n 1. (person) organizador(a) m(f) 2. COMPUT agenda f electrónica

orgasm [ˈɔr·gæz·əm] n orgasmo m

orgy [ˈɔr·dʒi] <-ies> n orgía f

Orient [ˈɔr·i·ənt] n the ~ (el) Oriente

oriental [ˌɔr·i·ˈen·təl] adj oriental

orientation [ˌɔr·i·ən·ˈteɪ·ʃən] n orientación f

origin ['ɔr·ə·dʒɪn] n origen m

original [ə·'rɪdʒ·ɪ·nəl] I. n original m II. adj 1. (new, unusual) original 2. (first) originario, -a

originality [ə·ˌrɪdʒ·ɪ·'næl·ə·t̬i] n originalidad f

originally [ə·'rɪdʒ·ɪ·nə·li] adv 1. (initially) originariamente 2. (unusually) con originalidad

originate [ə·'rɪdʒ·ɪ·neɪt] I. vi originarse II. vt crear

ornament ['ɔr·nə·mənt] n adorno m

ornamental [ˌɔr·nə·'men·t̬əl] adj ornamental, decorativo, -a

ornithology [ˌɔr·nə·'θɑl·ə·dʒi] n ornitología f

orphan ['ɔr·fən] n huérfano, -a m, f, guacho, -a m, f Arg, Chile

orphanage ['ɔr·fə·nɪdʒ] n orfanato m, orfelinato m

orthodontist [ˌɔr·θə·'dɑn·tɪst] n ortodoncista mf

orthodox ['ɔr·θə·dɑks] adj ortodoxo, -a

orthographic(al) [ˌɔr·θə·'græf·ɪk(·əl)] adj ortográfico, -a

orthography [ɔr·'θɑg·rə·fi] n ortografía f

ostrich ['ɑs·trɪtʃ] n avestruz f

other ['ʌð·ər] I. adj 1. (different) otro, -a 2. (remaining) the ~ one el otro; the ~ three los otros tres; any ~ questions? ¿alguna otra pregunta? 3. (being vague) some ~ time en algún otro momento; the ~ day el otro día; every ~ day un día sí y otro no II. pron 1. (people) the ~s los otros, los demás; no ~ than he form nadie excepto él 2. (different ones) each ~ uno a(l) otro, mutuamente; some eat, ~s drink algunos comen, otros beben 3. sing (either/or) to choose one or the ~ escoger uno u otro 4. (being vague) someone or ~ alguien III. adv de otra manera; somehow or ~ de una manera u otra

otherwise ['ʌð·ər·waɪz] I. adj form distinto, -a II. adv 1. (differently: behave, act) de otro modo 2. (in other ways) ~,... por lo demás,... III. conj si no

ouch [aʊtʃ] interj ay

ought [ɔt] aux 1. (have as duty) deber; you ~ to do it deberías hacerlo 2. (be

likely) tener que; he ~ to be here tendría que [or debería] estar aquí; they ~ to win merecerían ganar 3. (probability) she ~ to have arrived by now debe de haber llegado ya

ounce [aʊns] n 1. (weight) onza f (28,4 g) 2. (of decency, common sense) pizca f

our [aʊr] adj pos nuestro, -a; ~ house nuestra casa; ~ children nuestros hijos

ours [aʊrz] pron pos el nuestro, la nuestra; it's not their bag, it's ~ no es su bolsa, es la nuestra; a book of ~ un libro nuestro; ~ is bigger el nuestro es mayor

ourselves [aʊr·'selvz] pron reflexive 1. nos emphatic nosotros mismos, nosotras mismas; we hurt ~ nos lastimamos 2. after prep nosotros, -as (mismos, mismas)

out [aʊt] I. adj 1. (absent: person) fuera 2. (released: book, news) publicado, -a 3. BOT (in blossom) en flor 4. (visible) the moon is ~ ha salido la luna 5. (finished) before the week is ~ antes de que acabe la semana 6. (not functioning: fire, light) apagado, -a 7. SPORTS (out of bounds) fuera 8. (unfashionable) pasado, -a de moda 9. (not possible) to be ~ estar descartado, ser imposible II. adv 1. (not inside) fuera, afuera; to go ~ salir fuera; get ~! ¡fuera! 2. (outside) afuera; keep ~! ¡prohibido el paso!; to eat ~ comer fuera 3. (remove) to cross ~ words tachar palabras; to get a stain ~ sacar una mancha; to put ~ a fire apagar un fuego 4. (away) to be ~ (person) no estar; to be ~ at sea estar mar adentro; the tide is going ~ la marea está bajando 5. (unconscious) to pass ~ perder el conocimiento; to be ~ cold estar fuera de combate ▸ to be ~ and about (on the road) estar en camino; (healthy) estar repuesto; ~ with it! ¡desembucha! III. prep 1. (towards outside) ~ of fuera de; to go ~ of the room salir de la habitación; to take sth ~ of a box sacar algo de una caja; to look ~ of the window mirar por la ventana 2. (outside from) ~ of sight/ of reach fuera de vista/de alcance; to drink ~ of a glass beber de un vaso; to be ~ of it estar en otra onda *inf* 3. (*away from*) to be ~ of town/the country estar fuera de la ciudad/del país; to get ~ of the rain resguardarse de la lluvia; ~ of the way! ¡quita de en medio! 4. (*without*) to be ~ of money/work estar sin dinero/trabajo; ~ of breath sin aliento; ~ of order averiado, -a; his dog is ~ of control su perro está fuera de control 5. (*from*) made ~ of wood/steel hecho de madera/acero; to copy sth ~ of a file copiar algo de un archivo; to get sth ~ of sb sacar algo a alguien; in 3 cases ~ of 10 en 3 de cada 10 casos 6. (*because of*) to do sth ~ of politeness hacer algo por cortesía

outboard (motor) ['aʊt·bɔrd] *n* fueraborda *m*

outbreak ['aʊt·breɪk] *n* (*of the flu, violence*) brote *m*; (*of war*) estallido *m*

outburst ['aʊt·bɜrst] *n* arrebato *m*

outcast ['aʊt·kæst] *n* paria *mf*; social ~ marginado, -a *m, f* de la sociedad

outclass [ˌaʊt·ˈklæs] *vt* superar, aventajar

outcome ['aʊt·kʌm] *n* 1. (*result*) resultado *m* 2. (*consequence*) consecuencia *f*

outcry ['aʊt·kraɪ] <-ies> *n* gran protesta *f*

outdated [aʊt·ˈdeɪ·tɪd] *adj* anticuado, -a, pasado, -a de moda

outdo [aʊt·ˈduː] *vt irr* superar, mejorar; to ~ sb in sth superar a alguien en algo; to ~ oneself mejorarse

outdoor [ˌaʊt·ˈdɔr] *adj* al aire libre; (*clothing*) de calle; (*plants*) de exterior

outer ['aʊ·tər] *adj* exterior; ~ ear oído *m* externo

outermost ['aʊ·tər·moʊst] *n* más exterior

outfit ['aʊt·fɪt] *n* 1. (*clothing*) conjunto *m* 2. (*team*) equipo *m*

outgoing ['aʊt·goʊ·ɪŋ] *adj* 1. (*sociable*) sociable, extrovertido, -a 2. (*departing: president*) saliente

outgrow [ˌaʊt·ˈgroʊ] *vt irr* 1. (*become bigger than*) crecer más que; she's ~n her pants se le han quedado pequeños los pantalones 2. (*habit*) pasar de la edad de

outing ['aʊ·tɪŋ] *n* excursión *f*

outlast [ˌaʊt·ˈlæst] *vt* to ~ sth durar más que algo; to ~ sb sobrevivir a alguien

outlaw ['aʊt·lɔ] I. *n* forajido, -a *m, f* II. *vt* (*product, practice*) prohibir; (*person*) proscribir

outlet ['aʊt·let] *n* 1. ECON punto *m* de venta; retail ~ tienda *f* al por menor 2. (*means of expression*) válvula *f* de escape 3. (*vent: for air*) respiradero *m*; (*for water*) desagüe *m* 4. ELEC toma *f* de corriente

outline ['aʊt·laɪn] I. *n* 1. (*draft*) esbozo *m* 2. (*shape*) perfil *m* 3. (*general description*) resumen *m* II. *vt* 1. (*draw outer line of*) perfilar 2. (*describe*) describir a grandes trazos; (*summarize*) resumir

outlive [ˌaʊt·ˈlɪv] *vt* sobrevivir a

outlook ['aʊt·lʊk] *n* 1. (*prospects*) perspectivas *fpl* 2. (*attitude*) punto *m* de vista 3. (*view*) vista *f*

outnumber [ˌaʊt·ˈnʌm·bər] *vt* superar en número a

out-of-date [ˌaʊt·əv·ˈdeɪt] *adj* anticuado, -a

out-of-the-way [ˌaʊt·əv·ðə·ˈweɪ] *adj* apartado, -a

outplay [ˌaʊt·ˈpleɪ] *vt* jugar mejor que

output ['aʊt·pʊt] *n* ECON producción *f*; (*of machine*) rendimiento *m*

output device *n* COMPUT dispositivo *m* de salida

outrage ['aʊt·reɪdʒ] I. *n* 1. (*atrocity*) atrocidad *f* 2. (*scandal*) escándalo *m* II. *vt* (*offend*) ultrajar

outrageous [aʊt·ˈreɪ·dʒəs] *adj* 1. (*shocking: behavior*) escandaloso, -a; (*person*) atrevido, -a 2. (*cruel, violent*) atroz

outright ['aʊt·raɪt] I. *adj* (*disaster, defeat*) total; (*winner*) indiscutible II. *adv* 1. (*defeat, ignore*) totalmente; (*win*) indiscutiblemente 2. (*declare, ask*) descaradamente

outset ['aʊt·set] *n* principio *m*

outshine [ˌaʊt·ˈʃaɪn] *vt irr* eclipsar

outside [ˌaʊt·ˈsaɪd] I. *adj* 1. (*external*) externo, -a, exterior; (*world*) exterior; the ~ door la puerta exterior 2. (*not likely*) an ~ chance that... una posibilidad remota de que... +*subj* 3. (*extreme*) extremo, -a II. *n* 1. (*external* part or side) exterior *m;* **judging from the** ~ a juzgar por el aspecto exterior **2.** (*at most*) **at the** ~ a lo más **III.** *prep* **1.** (*not within*) fuera de; **to wait** ~ **the door** esperar en la puerta; ~ **business hours** fuera de horas de oficina **2.** (*besides*) además de **IV.** *adv* (*outdoors*) fuera, afuera; **to go** ~ salir fuera; **to go** ~ **the house** salir de casa; **to live an hour** ~ **Detroit** vivir a una hora de Detroit

outsider [ˌaʊtˈsaɪ·dər] *n* (*person not from a group*) persona *f* de fuera

outskirts [ˈaʊt·skɜrts] *npl* afueras *fpl;* **on the** ~ en las afueras

outsourcing [ˈaʊt·ˌsɔr·sɪŋ] *n* externalización *f*

outstanding [ˌaʊtˈstæn·dɪŋ] *adj* **1.** (*excellent*) destacado, -a **2.** FIN (*debt*) pendiente (de pago) **3.** (*unsolved*) por resolver

outstretched [ˌaʊtˈstretʃt] *adj* extendido, -a

outthink [aʊtˈθɪŋk] *irr vt* ser más listo que

outward [ˈaʊt·wərd] **I.** *adj* **1.** (*visible: indication*) externo, -a **2.** (*exterior: appearance, beauty*) exterior **3.** (*apparent: similarities, differences*) aparente **II.** *adv* hacia fuera

outwardly [ˈaʊt·wərd·li] *adv* aparentemente

outwards [ˈaʊt·wərdz] *adv* hacia fuera

oval [ˈoʊ·vəl] **I.** *n* óvalo *m* **II.** *adj* ovalado, -a, oval

Oval Office *n* **the** ~ el despacho oval

ovary [ˈoʊ·və·ri] *n* ovario *m*

ovation [oʊˈveɪ·ʃən] *n* ovación *f*

oven [ˈʌv·ən] *n* horno *m*

ovenproof [ˈʌv·ən·pruf] *adj* refractario, -a

oven-ready [ˌʌv·ənˈred·i] *adj* listo, -a para hornear

over [ˈoʊ·vər] **I.** *prep* **1.** (*above*) encima de, por encima de; **the bridge** ~ **the freeway** el puente sobre la autopista; **to fly** ~ **the sea** volar sobre el mar **2.** (*on*) **to drive** ~ **sth** arrollar algo; **to spread a cloth** ~ **the table** extender un mantel sobre la mesa **3.** (*across*) **to go** ~ **the bridge** cruzar el puente; **the house** ~ **the road** la casa de enfrente; **it rained**

all ~ **New England** llovió por toda Nueva Inglaterra **4.** (*behind*) **to look** ~ **sb's shoulder** mirar por encima del hombro de alguien **5.** (*during*) durante; ~ **the winter** durante el invierno; ~ **time** con el tiempo; ~ **a two-year period** durante un período de dos años **6.** (*more than*) **to speak for** ~ **an hour** hablar más de una hora; ~ **150** más de 150; **children** ~ **14** niños mayores de 14 (años); ~ **and above that** además de eso **7.** (*through*) **I heard it** ~ **the radio** lo oí por la radio; **to hear sth** ~ **the noise** escuchar algo a pesar del ruido; **what came** ~ **him?** ¿qué le picó? *inf* **8.** (*in superiority to*) **to have command** ~ **sth** tener mando sobre algo; **to have an advantage** ~ **sb** tener ventaja sobre alguien **9.** (*about*) ~ **sth** acerca de algo **10.** (*for checking*) **to go** ~ **a text** revisar un texto; **to watch** ~ **a child** cuidar a un niño **11.** (*past*) **to be** ~ **the worst** haber pasado lo peor **12.** MATH **4** ~ **12 equals a third** 4 entre 12 es igual a un tercio **II.** *adv* **1.** (*moving above: go, jump*) por encima; **to fly** ~ **the city** sobrevolar la ciudad **2.** (*at a distance*) **to move sth** ~ apartar algo; ~ **here** acá; ~ **there** allá; ~ **the road** cruzando la calle **3.** (*moving across*) **to come** ~ **here** venir para acá; **to go** ~ **there** ir para allá; **he has flown** ~ **to Europe** se ha ido a Europa; **he swam** ~ **to me** nadó hacia mí; **he went** ~ **the enemy** *fig* se cambió al bando enemigo **4.** (*on a visit*) **come** ~ **tonight** pásate por aquí esta noche **5.** (*changing hands*) **to pass/hand sth** ~ pasar/dar algo **6.** (*downwards*) **to fall** ~ caerse; **to knock sth** ~ tirar algo **7.** (*another way up*) **to turn the page** ~ pasar la página **8.** (*in exchange*) **to change** ~ intercambiar **9.** (*completely*) **to look for sb all** ~ buscar a alguien por todos lados; **to think sth** ~ pensar algo (detalladamente) **10.** (*again*) **to count them** ~ **again** contarlos otra vez; **I repeated it** ~ **and** ~ lo repetí una y otra vez; **to do sth all** ~ hacer algo desde el principio **11.** (*more*) **children 14 and** ~ niños de 14 años en adelante **12.** RADIO, AVIAT ~ **cambio;** ~ **and out** cambio y corto

III. *adj* **1.** (*finished*) acabado, -a; **it's all ~** se acabó; **the snow is ~** se acabó la nieve **2.** (*remaining*) restante; **there are three left ~** quedan tres

overall ['ou·vər·ɔl] **I.** *adj* **1.** (*general*) global **2.** (*above all others*) total; **~ winner** campeón absoluto **II.** *adv* en conjunto **III.** *n* **~s** mono *m*; **a pair of ~s** un peto

overboard ['ou·vər·bɔrd] *adv* al agua; **to fall ~** caer al agua; **man ~!** ¡hombre al agua!; **to go ~** *inf* exagerar

overbook [,ou·vər·'buk] *vt* sobrecontratar, sobrevender *Col*

overcast ['ou·vər·kæst] *adj* nublado, -a

overcharge [,ou·vər·'tʃardʒ] *vi* cobrar de más

overcoat ['ou·vər·kout] *n* abrigo *m*

overcome [,ou·vər·'kʌm] *irr* **I.** *vt* **1.** (*defeat*) vencer **2.** (*cope with*) superar **II.** *vi* *irr* vencer; **we shall ~** venceremos

overconfident [,ou·vər·'kan·fə·dənt] *adj* demasiado seguro, -a de sí mismo, -a

overcrowded [,ou·vər·'krau·dɪd] *adj* abarrotado, -a

overdo [,ou·vər·'du] *vt* **1. to ~ things** pasarse; (*work too hard*) trabajar demasiado **2.** *inf* (*exaggerate*) exagerar

overdone [,ou·vər·'dʌn] *adj* (*overexaggerated*) exagerado, -a

overdose ['ou·vər·dous] *n* sobredosis *f inv*

overdraft ['ou·vər·dræft] *n* FIN descubierto *m*

overdraw [,ou·vər·'drɔ] *irr vi, vt* girar en descubierto

overdue [,ou·vər·'du] *adj* **1.** (*late*) atrasado, -a; **to be ~** llevar retraso **2.** FIN (*debt*) pendiente (de pago)

overestimate¹ [,ou·vər·'es·tɪ·mɪt] *n* sobreestimación *f*

overestimate² [,ou·vər·'es·tə·meɪt] *vt* sobreestimar

overexcited [,ou·vər·ɪk·'saɪ·tɪd] *adj* sobreexcitado, -a

overflow [,ou·vər·'flou] **I.** *n* (*excess: of liquid, people*) exceso *m* **II.** *vi* rebosar; (*river*) desbordarse

overgrown [,ou·vər·'groun] *adj* (*garden*) abandonado, -a

overhang [,ou·vər·'hæŋ] *irr* **I.** *n* (*cliff*) saliente *m;* ARCHIT alero *m* **II.** *vt* **to ~ sth** sobresalir por encima de algo

overhead [,ou·vər·'hed] **I.** *n* gastos *m pl* generales **II.** *adj* de arriba, encima de la cabeza; **~ cable** cable *m* aéreo; **~ light** luz *f* de techo

overhear [,ou·vər·'hɪr] *irr vt* oír por casualidad

overheat [,ou·vər·'hit] **I.** *vt* sobrecalentar **II.** *vi* recalentarse

overjoyed [,ou·vər·'dʒɔɪd] *adj* encantado, -a

overland ['ou·vər·lænd] *adj* terrestre; **~ vehicle** vehículo *m* todoterreno; **by ~ mail** por vía terrestre

overlap ['ou·vər·læp] *n* superposición *f*

overleaf ['ou·vər·lif] *adv* al dorso

overload¹ ['ou·vər·loud] *n* **1.** ELEC sobrecarga *f* **2.** (*of work*) exceso *m*

overload² [,ou·vər·'loud] *vt* ELEC sobrecargar; **to be ~ed with sth** *fig* estar agobiado de algo

overlook [,ou·vər·'luk] **I.** *n* vista *f* **II.** *vt* **1.** (*look out onto*) tener vistas a **2.** (*not notice*) pasar por alto **3.** (*forget*) olvidar

overnight [,ou·vər·'naɪt] **I.** *adj* de noche *f;* **~ stay** estancia *f* de una noche; **~ delivery** envío *m* para la mañana siguiente **II.** *adv* durante la noche; **to stay ~** pasar la noche

overpass ['ou·vər·pæs] *n* paso *m* elevado

overpay [,ou·vər·'peɪ] *irr vt* pagar de más

overpopulated [,ou·vər·'pap·jə·leɪ·tɪd] *adj* superpoblado, -a

overpower [,ou·vər·'pau·ər] *vt* dominar

overpowering [,ou·vər·'pau·ər·ɪŋ] *adj* (*person, attack*) abrumador(a); (*taste, smell*) muy fuerte

overrate [,ou·vər·'reɪt] *vt* sobrevalorar

overreact [,ou·vər·ri·'ækt] *vi* reaccionar de forma exagerada

overreaction [,ou·vər·ri·'æk·ʃən] *n* reacción *f* exagerada

override [,ou·vər·'raɪd] **I.** *n* anulación *f* de automatismo **II.** *vt* **1.** (*not accept*) anular **2.** (*interrupt*) cancelar

overriding [,ou·vər·'raɪ·dɪŋ] *adj* primordial

overrule [ˌouˈvərˈrul] *vt* anular; **to ~ an objection** LAW rechazar una objeción

overrun [ˌouˈvərˈrʌn] **I.** *vt irr* **1.** (*invade*) invadir; **to be ~ with sth** estar plagado de algo **2.** (*budget*) exceder **II.** *vi irr* prolongarse más de lo previsto

overseas [ˌouˈvərˈsiz] **I.** *adj* extranjero, -a; (*trade*) exterior **II.** *adv* **to go/travel ~** ir/viajar al extranjero

oversee [ˌouˈvərˈsi] *irr vt* supervisar

overshadow [ˌouˈvərˈʃædou] *vt* **1.** (*cast shadow over*) ensombrecer **2.** (*make insignificant*) eclipsar

oversight [ˈouˈvərˈsaɪt] *n* **1.** (*omission*) descuido *m* **2.** (*supervision*) supervisión *f*

oversleep [ˌouˈvərˈslip] *irr vi* quedarse dormido

overspend [ˌouˈvərˈspend] *vi* gastar demasiado

overstaffed [ˌouˈvərˈstæft] *adj* con exceso de personal

overstay [ˌouˈvərˈsteɪ] *vt* **to ~ one's welcome** quedarse más de lo conveniente

overstep [ˌouˈvərˈstep] *irr vt* sobrepasar ▶ **to ~ the mark** pasarse de la raya

overtake [ˌouˈvərˈteɪk] *irr* **I.** *vt* **1.** AUTO adelantar **2.** (*in contest*) superar **II.** *vi* adelantar

overthrow [ˌouˈvərˈθrou] **I.** *n* POL derrocamiento *m* **II.** *vt irr* POL derrocar

overtime [ˈouˈvərˈtaɪm] *n* **1.** (*work*) horas *f pl* extra **2.** SPORTS prórroga *f*

overturn [ˌouˈvərˈtʌrn] **I.** *vi* volcar, voltearse *AmL* **II.** *vt* volcar; POL derrumbar

overview [ˈouˈvərˈvju] *n* perspectiva *f* general

overweight [ˌouˈvərˈweɪt] *adj* **to be ~** pesar más de la cuenta

overwhelm [ˌouˈvərˈwelm] *vt* **1.** (*overcome by force*) abrumar, sobrecoger **2.** (*swamp*) inundar

overwhelming [ˌouˈvərˈwelˈmɪŋ] *adj* abrumador(a); **~ grief** dolor inconsolable

overwork [ˌouˈvərˈwɜrk] **I.** *n* agotamiento *m* **II.** *vi* trabajar demasiado

ovum [ˈouˈvəm] <ova> *n* óvulo *m*

owe [ou] **I.** *vt* deber **II.** *vi* tener deudas

owing [ˈouˈɪŋ] *adj* por pagar

owing to *prep* debido a

owl [aul] *n* búho *m*, tecolote *m AmC, Méx;* **barn ~** lechuza *f*

own [oun] **I.** *adj* propio, -a; **with one's eyes** con sus propios ojos ▶ **in one's right** por derecho propio; **to do one's thing** ir a su aire; **in one's ~ time** en su tiempo libre; **to hold one's ~** mantenerse firme **II.** *vt* poseer ▶ **as if one ~ed the place** como Pedro por su casa

◆ **own up** *vi* confesar

owner [ˈouˈnər] *n* propietario, -a *m, f*

ownership [ˈouˈnərˈʃɪp] *n* posesión *f;* **to be under private ~** ser de propiedad privada

ox [aks] <-en> *n* buey *m*

oxidize [ˈakˈsɪˈdaɪz] **I.** *vi* oxidarse **II.** *vt* oxidar

oxygen [ˈakˈsɪˈdʒən] *n* oxígeno *m*

oyster [ˈɔɪˈstər] *n* ostra *f*

oz *n abbr of* **ounce** onza *f (28,4 g)*

ozone [ˈouˈzoun] *n* ozono *m*

ozone layer *n* capa *f* de ozono

P

P, p [pi] <-'s> *n* P, p *f;* **~ as in Papa** P de París

p *abbr of* **page** pág. *f*

pa [pa] *n inf* papá *m*

PA *n abbr of* **Pennsylvania** Pensilvania *f*

p.a. [ˌpiˈeɪ] *abbr of* **per annum** por año

pace [peɪs] **I.** *n* **1.** (*speed*) velocidad *f;* **to set the ~** marcar el ritmo; **to keep ~ with sth** avanzar al mismo ritmo que algo; **to keep up/stand the ~** llevar/mantener el ritmo **2.** (*step*) paso *m;* **to quicken one's ~** acelerar el paso **II.** <pacing> *vt* **1.** (*walk up and down*) pasearse por **2.** (*measure in strides*) medir a pasos

pacemaker [ˈpeɪsˈmeɪˈkər] *n* MED marcapasos *m inv*

Pacific [pəˈsɪfˈɪk] **I.** *n* **the ~** el Pacífico; **the ~ Ocean** el Océano Pacífico **II.** *adj* del Pacífico

pacifier [ˈpæsˈəˈfaɪˈər] *n* (*for baby*) chupete *m*

P

pacifist ['pæs-ə-fɪst] *adj, n* pacifista *mf*

pacify ['pæs-ə-faɪ] <-ie-> *vt* 1. (*establish peace*) pacificar 2. (*calm*) calmar

pack [pæk] I. *n* 1. (*bundle*) fardo *m;* (*backpack*) mochila *f;* (*packet*) paquete *m;* (*of cigarettes*) cajetilla *f* 2. (*group*) grupo *m;* (*of wolves, hounds*) manada *f;* *inf* (*of lies*) montón *m,* sarta *f* II. *vi* (*luggage*) hacer las maletas III. *vt* 1. (*fill: box, train*) llenar 2. (*wrap*) envasar; (*put in packages*) empaquetar; **to ~ one's suitcase** hacer la maleta

◆**pack in** I. *vt* 1. (*put in*) meter 2. *inf* (*stop*) dejar; **pack it in!** ¡déjalo! 3. (*attract audience*) captar II. *vi* apiñar

◆**pack off** *vt inf* **to pack sb off** deshacerse de alguien

◆**pack up** I. *vt* 1. (*put away*) guardar 2. *inf* (*finish*) terminar II. *vi inf* (*stop work*) dejar de trabajar

package ['pæk-ɪdʒ] I. *n* paquete *m;* **software ~** paquete de software II. *vt* (*pack*) empaquetar

package deal *n* acuerdo *m* global con concesiones mutuas

packaging *n* 1. (*wrapping*) embalaje *m* 2. (*action*) envasado *m*

packet ['pæk-ɪt] *n* 1. (*parcel*) paquete *m;* (*of cigarettes*) cajetilla *f* 2. *inf* (*money*) dineral *m*

packing *n* (*action, material*) embalaje *m*

pad[1] [pæd] I. *n* 1. (*cushion*) almohadilla *f;* **knee ~** rodillera *f;* **mouse ~** COMPUT alfombrilla *f* (del ratón); **shin ~** espinillera *f;* **shoulder ~** hombrera *f* 2. (*of paper*) bloc *m* II. <-dd-> *vt* 1. acolchar 2. *inf* (*inflate: the budget*) inflar

pad[2] [pæd] <-dd-> *vi* (*walk*) andar silenciosamente

padded *adj* acolchado, -a

padding *n a. fig* relleno *m*

paddle ['pæd-əl] I. *n* 1. (*type of oar*) canalete *m* 2. (*act of paddling*) chapoteo *m* II. *vt* 1. (*row*) remar 2. *inf* (*spank*) zurrar III. *vi* (*row*) remar

padlock ['pæd-lak] *n* candado *m*

page[1] [peɪdʒ] *n* (*in book*) *a.* COMPUT página *f;* **front ~** primera plana *f*

page[2] [peɪdʒ] I. *n* 1. (*of knight*) paje *m* 2. (*in hotel*) botones *m inv* II. *vt* (*by*

pager) llamar (a alguien) por el busca

page layout *n* diseño *m* de página

pager ['peɪ-dʒər] *n* busca *m*

paid [peɪd] I. *pt, pp* of **pay** II. *adj* pagado, -a

pain [peɪn] *n* 1. dolor *m;* **to be in ~** estar sufriendo; **I have a ~ in my foot** me duele el pie 2. **~s** (*great care*) gran cuidado *m;* **to be at ~s to do sth** esmerarse en hacer algo ▶ *inf* **to be a ~ in the backside** [*or vulg* **ass**] ser un plomo

painful ['peɪn-fəl] *adj* 1. (*physically*) doloroso, -a 2. (*emotionally*) angustioso, -a

painkiller ['peɪn-ˌkɪl-ər] *n* analgésico *m*

painless ['peɪn-lɪs] *adj* 1. (*not painful*) indoloro, -a 2. *fig* (*easy*) fácil

painstaking ['peɪnz-ˌteɪ-kɪŋ] *adj* (*research*) laborioso, -a; (*search*) exhaustivo, -a

paint [peɪnt] I. *n* pintura *f* II. *vi* pintar III. *vt* pintar

paintbrush <-es> *n* (*for pictures*) pincel *m;* (*for walls*) brocha *f*

painter ['peɪn-tər] *n* pintor(a) *m(f)*

painting *n* 1. (*painted picture*) cuadro *m* 2. (*art*) pintura *f*

paint stripper *n* quitapintura *m*

pair [per] I. *n* 1. (*things*) par *m* (**of** de); **a ~ of glasses** unas gafas; **a ~ of scissors** unas tijeras; **a ~ of pants** un pantalón 2. (*people, animals*) pareja *f;* **in ~s** de dos en dos II. *vi* aparearse

pajamas [pə-'dʒa-məz] *npl* pijama *m;* **in (one's) ~** en pijama

Pakistan ['pæk-ɪ-stæn] *n* Paquistán *m*

Pakistani I. *n* paquistaní *mf* II. *adj* paquistaní

pal [pæl] *n inf* 1. (*friend*) amigo, -a *m, f* 2. (*form of address*) tío, -a *m, f,* colega *mf*

palace ['pæl-əs] *n* palacio *m*

palate ['pæl-ət] *n* paladar *m*

pale [peɪl] I. *adj* 1. (*lacking color*) pálido, -a; **to look ~** tener mal color 2. (*not dark*) claro, -a II. *vi* palidecer

paleness ['peɪl-nɪs] *n* palidez *f*

paleontology [ˌpeɪ-li-an-'tal-ə-dʒi] *n* paleontología *f*

Palestine ['pæl-ə-staɪn] *n* Palestina *f*

Palestinian I. *n* palestino, -a *m, f* II. *adj*

palestino, -a

palette ['pælɪt] n ART paleta f

palm¹ [pam] **I.** n (of hand) palma f; **to read sb's ~** leer la mano a alguien **II.** vt **1.** (hide) escamotear **2.** (steal) robar

palm² [pam] n (tree) palmera f

◆**palm off** vt **to palm sth off on sb** encajar algo a alguien; **to palm sb off with sth** apartar a alguien con algo

palmtop n COMPUT palmtop m

pamper ['pæm·pər] vt mimar

pamphlet ['pæm·flɪt] n folleto m; POL panfleto m

pan¹ [pæn] n (for cooking) cazuela f; **frying ~** sartén f

pan² [pæn] n CINE panoramizar

◆**pan out** vi inf (develop) resultar; **to ~ well** salir bien

Panama ['pæn·ə·ma] n Panamá m

Panama City n Ciudad f de Panamá

Panamanian [ˌpæn·ə·'meɪ·ni·ən] **I.** adj panameño, -a **II.** n panameño, -a m, f

Pan-American ['pæn·ə·'mer·ɪ·kən] adj panamericano, -a

pancake ['pæn·keɪk] n crep m, panqueque m AmL

panda ['pæn·də] n panda m

pane [peɪn] n cristal m; **window ~** hoja f de cristal de una ventana

panel ['pæn·əl] n **1.** (wooden) tabla f; (metal) placa f **2.** FASHION paño m **3.** (of cartoon strip) tabla f **4.** (team) panel m; (in exam) tribunal m **5.** (instrument board) panel m; **instrument ~** AUTO, AVIAT cuadro m de mandos

panel discussion n mesa f redonda

paneling n paneles mpl

panelist ['pæn·ə·lɪst] n (in discussion) miembro mf de una mesa redonda

panic ['pæn·ɪk] **I.** n pánico m; **to be in a ~** estar nervioso **II.** <-ck-> vi ponerse nervioso

panicky ['pæn·ɪ·ki] <-ier, iest> adj (person) inquieto, -a; (feeling) de pánico

panic-stricken adj preso, -a del pánico

panoramic [ˌpæn·ə·'ræm·ɪk] adj panorámico, -a; **~ view** vista f panorámica

pansy ['pæn·zi] <-ies> n **1.** BOT pensamiento m **2.** offensive sl (wimp) nenaza f; (homosexual) maricón m

pant [pænt] **I.** vi jadear **II.** vt decir jadeando

panther ['pæn·θər] n **1.** pantera f **2.** (puma) puma m

panties ['pæn·tiz] npl bragas fpl

pantomime ['pæn·tə·maɪm] n **1.** (gestures) gestos mpl **2.** (mime) pantomima f **3.** (performer) mimo mf

pantry ['pæn·tri] <-ies> n despensa f

pants [pænts] npl **1.** (trousers) pantalones mpl **2.** (underpants) calzoncillos mpl ▶ **to be caught with one's ~ down** inf ser cogido en fuera de juego

pantsuit n traje m pantalón (de mujer)

pantyhose npl medias fpl

papal ['peɪ·pəl] adj papal

paper ['peɪ·pər] **I.** n **1.** papel m; **a sheet of ~** una hoja de papel; **to put sth down on ~** poner algo por escrito; **on ~** (in writing) sobre papel; (in theory) sobre el papel **2.** (newspaper) periódico m **3.** (official document) **~s** papeles mpl **4.** (academic discourse) conferencia f; **to give a ~** dar un discurso **II.** vt (walls) empapelar

paperback ['peɪ·pər·bæk] n libro m de bolsillo

paper bag n bolsa f de papel

paper clip n sujetapapeles m inv, clip m

paper cup n vaso m de papel

paperknife <-knives> n abrecartas m inv

paper mill n fábrica f de papel

paper money n papel m moneda

paper napkin n servilleta f de papel

paper-thin adj fino, -a como el papel

paperweight n pisapapeles m inv

paperwork n trabajo m administrativo, papeleo m inf

paprika [pæ·'pri·kə] n pimentón m dulce

par [par] n **1.** (standard) **to be on a ~ with sb** estar al mismo nivel que alguien; **below ~** por debajo de la media; **to feel below ~** no sentirse del todo bien **2.** (in golf) par m **3.** FIN (face value) valor m nominal; **at/above/below ~** a/sobre/bajo la par

par. abbr of **paragraph** párrafo m

parachute ['pær·ə·ʃut] n paracaídas m inv

parade [pə·'reɪd] **I.** n desfile m **II.** vi

P

desfilar **III.** *vt* **1.** (*exhibit*) lucir **2.** *fig* (*show off*) ostentar; **to ~ one's knowledge** hacer alarde de erudición

paradise ['pær·ə·daɪs] *n* paraíso *m*

paradox ['pær·ə·daks] <-es> *n* paradoja *f*

paragliding ['pær·ə·ˌglaɪ·dɪŋ] *n* parapente *m*

paragraph ['pær·ə·græf] *n* LING párrafo *m*

Paraguay ['pær·ə·gwaɪ] *n* Paraguay *m*

Paraguayan [ˌpær·ə·'gwaɪ·ən] **I.** *adj* paraguayo, -a **II.** *n* paraguayo, -a *m, f*

parallel ['pær·ə·lel] **I.** *adj* a. MATH paralelo, -a (**to** a) **II.** *n* **1.** MATH paralela *f* **2.** GEO paralelo *m* **3.** ELEC **in ~** en paralelo **4.** (*similarity*) similitud *f* **5. without ~** sin igual

parallel bars *npl* SPORTS barras *f pl* paralelas

paralysis [pə·'ræl·ə·sɪs] <-ses> *n* parálisis *f inv*

paralytic [ˌpær·ə·'lɪt·ɪk] *adj* MED paralítico, -a

paralyze ['pær·ə·laɪz] *vt* paralizar

paramedic [ˌpær·ə·'med·ɪk] *n* paramédico, -a *m, f*

paramilitary [ˌpær·ə·'mɪl·ɪ·ter·i] *adj* paramilitar

paranoid ['pær·ə·nɔɪd] *adj* paranoico, -a

paraphrase ['pær·ə·freɪz] **I.** *vt* parafrasear **II.** *n* (*reformulation*) paráfrasis *f inv*

parasite ['pær·ə·saɪt] *n* a. *fig* parásito *m*

paratrooper ['pær·ə·ˌtru·pər] *n* MIL paracaidista *mf*

paratroops ['pær·ə·trups] *npl* MIL paracaidistas *mpl*

parboil ['par·bɔɪl] *vt* CULIN sancochar

parcel ['par·səl] *n* **1.** (*package*) paquete *m* **2.** (*of land*) terreno *m*, parcela *f*

parcel post *n* servicio *m* de paquetería

parched *adj* **1.** (*dried-out*) seco, -a **2.** *fig inf* (*thirsty*) **to be ~** estar muerto de sed

pardon ['par·dən] **I.** *vt* (*forgive*) disculpar; (*prisoner*) indultar; **~ me for interrupting** siento interrumpir; (**I beg your**) **~?** (*requesting repetition*) ¿cómo dice?; **~ me!** (*after interrupting*) ¡perdone!; (*after burping*) ¡perdón!; (*requesting to pass*) ¡disculpe! **II.** *n* indulto *m*

parent ['per·ənt] *n* (*father*) padre *m*; (*mother*) madre *f*; **~s** padres *mpl*

parental [pə·'ren·təl] *adj* de los padres

parent company <-ies> *n* sociedad *f* matriz

parenthesis [pə·'ren·θə·sɪs] <-ses> *n* **1.** TYPO paréntesis *m inv*; **in parentheses** en [o entre] paréntesis **2.** (*remark*) paréntesis *m*

parenthood ['per·ənt·hʊd] *n* (*of man*) paternidad *f*; (*of woman*) maternidad *f*

Paris ['pær·ɪs] *n* París *m*

parish ['pær·ɪʃ] <-es> *n* **1.** REL parroquia *f* **2.** (*in Louisiana*) condado *m*

Parisian [pə·'ri·ʒən] *n* parisino, -a *m, f*

parity ['pær·ə·ți] <-ies> *n* paridad *f*

park [park] **I.** *n* **1.** parque *m* **2.** (*stadium*) **baseball ~** estadio *m* de béisbol **3.** AUTO (posición *f* de) estacionamiento *m* **II.** *vt* (*vehicle*) aparcar, estacionar **III.** *vi* aparcar, estacionar

parking *n* aparcamiento *m*, estacionamiento *m*

parking brake *n* freno *m* de mano

parking fine *n* multa *f* de aparcamiento

parking lot *n* aparcamiento *m*

parking meter *n* parquímetro *m*

parking space *n* sitio *m* (de aparcamiento), estacionamiento *m* AmL

parking ticket *n* multa *f* de aparcamiento

parkway ['park·weɪ] *n* avenida *f* ajardinada

Parl. *abbr of* **Parliament** Parlamento *m*

parliament ['par·lə·mənt] *n* parlamento *m*

parliamentary [ˌpar·lə·'men·tə·ri] *adj* parlamentario, -a

parlor ['par·lər] *n* **1.** (*store*) **beauty ~** salón *m* de belleza; **pizza ~** pizzería *f* **2.** (*in house*) salón *m*

parody ['pær·ə·di] *n* **1.** (*humorous*) parodia *f* **2.** (*poor imitation*) burda imitación *f* **II.** <-ie-> *vt* parodiar

parole [pə·'roʊl] **I.** *n* LAW libertad *f* condicional; **to be out on ~** estar en libertad condicional **II.** *vt* **to be ~d** ser puesto en libertad condicional

parquet [par·'keɪ] *n* parqué *m*

parrot ['pær·ət] **I.** *n* loro *m*, papagayo *m* **II.** *vt pej* repetir como un loro

parsley ['pars·li] n perejil m

parsnip ['pars·nɪp] n CULIN chirivía f

part [part] I. n 1. (not the whole) parte f (of de); the **easy/hard** ~ la parte fácil/difícil; **in** ~ en parte; **for the most** ~ en la mayor parte 2. (component) componente m; **spare** ~s piezas f pl sueltas 3. (area, region) zona f; **in these** ~s inf por aquí 4. (in ratios, measure) parte f 5. (role) papel m; **to want no** ~ **in sth** no querer tener nada que ver en algo 6. (episode, chapter) capítulo m 7. CINE, THEAT papel m; **to play the** ~ **of the King** desempeñar el papel del rey 8. (in hair) raya f ▶ **for my** ~ por mi parte; **to take sb's** ~ tomar partido por alguien; **on sb's** ~ de parte de alguien II. adv parcialmente; **to be** ~ **African** ser en parte africano III. vt 1. (detach, split) separar; **to** ~ **sb from sb/sth** separar a alguien de alguien/algo 2. (divide) partir, dividir; **to** ~ **sth in two** partir algo en dos; **to** ~ **sb's hair** hacer la raya (del pelo) a alguien IV. vi 1. (separate) separarse 2. (say goodbye) despedirse

partake [par·'teɪk] vi irr 1. (participate) **to** ~ **in sth** tomar parte en algo 2. **to** ~ **of sth** (eat) comer algo; (drink) beber algo

parted adj 1. (opened: lips) entreabierto, -a 2. (separated) **to be** ~ **from sb** estar separado de alguien

partial ['par·ʃəl] adj 1. (incomplete) parcial 2. (biased) parcial

partially adv parcialmente, en parte

participant [par·'tɪs·ə·pənt] n participante mf

participate [par·'tɪs·ə·peɪt] vi participar

participation [par·ˌtɪs·ə·'peɪ·ʃən] n participación f

participle ['par·tɪ·sɪ·pəl] n participio m

particle ['par·tɪ·kəl] n PHYS, LING partícula f

particular [pər·'tɪk·jə·lər] I. adj 1. (particular; **no** ~ **reason** ninguna razón en concreto; **in** ~ en especial 2. (fussy, meticulous) quisquilloso, -a; (demanding) exigente; **he is very** ~ **about his appearance** es muy maniático con su imagen II. n detalle m

particularly [pər·'tɪk·jə·lər·li] adv espe-

cialmente, particularmente

parting ['par·tɪŋ] I. n 1. (separation) separación f 2. (saying goodbye) despedida f II. adj de despedida; ~ **words** palabras f pl de despedida

partisan ['par·tɪ·zən] n (supporter) partidario, -a m, f

partition [par·'tɪʃ·ən] n 1. (wall) tabique m 2. (of country) división f 3. COMPUT partición f

partly ['part·li] adv en parte, en cierto modo

partner ['part·nər] n 1. (companion) compañero m 2. COM socio, -a m, f 3. (in relationship, sports) pareja f

partnership ['part·nər·ʃɪp] n 1. (association) asociación f 2. COM sociedad f (colectiva)

part ownership n copropiedad f

part-time [ˌpart·'taɪm] adj a tiempo parcial

part-time job n empleo m a tiempo parcial

part-timer n (worker) empleado, -a m, f a tiempo parcial; (student) estudiante mf a tiempo parcial

party ['par·ti] I. n <-ies> 1. fiesta f; **to have** [or **throw**] **a** ~ hacer una fiesta 2. + sing/pl vb POL partido m; **opposition/ruling** ~ partido en la oposición/en el poder 3. + sing/pl vb (group) grupo m; **to make a reservation for a** ~ **of two/eight** reservar una mesa para dos/ocho 4. a. LAW parte f; **the guilty** ~ la parte inculpada; **to be a** ~ **to sth** ser partícipe en algo 5. inf (person) individuo m II. <-ie-> vi ir de fiesta

party headquarters n POL sede f del partido

party line n 1. TEL línea f de varios abonados 2. POL línea f política del partido

party politics npl política f de partidos

party pooper n aguafiestas mf inv

pass [pæs] I. <-es> n 1. **mountain** ~ puerto m [or **paso** m] de montaña 2. (in football, soccer) pase m 3. (in exam, class) aprobado m 4. (authorization) pase m; (for festival, concert) entrada f 5. (for bus, train) abono m (de transportes) 6. SCHOOL (permit to leave class) permiso m II. vt 1. (go past) pasar;

(*cross*) cruzar **2.** (*exceed: a limit*) sobrepasar **3.** (*hand to*) **to ~ sth to sb** pasar algo a alguien **4.** (*in football, soccer*) pasar **5.** (*exam, class*) aprobar **6.** POL (*bill, law*) aprobar **II.** *vi* **1.** (*move by*) pasar; **we often ~ed on the stairs** a menudo nos cruzábamos en la escalera **2.** (*come to an end*) desaparecer; **it'll soon ~** se olvidará pronto **3.** (*in exam*) aprobar **4.** (*elapse: time*) pasar, transcurrir

◆ **pass away** *vi euph* (*die*) fallecer *elev*

◆ **pass by** *vi* **1.** (*elapse*) pasar **2.** (*go past*) pasar de largo

◆ **pass off I.** *vt* **1.** (*treat as unimportant*) disimular **2.** (*give appearance of*) **he tried to pass himself off as an expert** intentó hacerse pasar por experto **II.** *vi* **1.** (*take place successfully*) tener lugar **2.** (*fade away, wear off*) desaparecer

◆ **pass on I.** *vi* **1.** (*continue moving*) seguir su camino; **to ~ to a different topic** pasar a un tema diferente **2.** (*die*) fallecer *elev* **II.** *vt* **1.** BIO (*transmit*) contagiar **2.** (*information, advice*) **3.** (*refer*) **to pass sb on to** poner a alguien con alguien

◆ **pass out** *vi* (*faint*) perder el conocimiento

◆ **pass over** *vt* pasar por alto

◆ **pass through** *vt* pasar por

◆ **pass up** *vt* desperdiciar

passage ['pæs·ɪdʒ] *n* **1.** (*corridor*) pasillo *m*; (*path*) pasadizo *m* **2.** LIT, MUS pasaje *m* **3.** (*onward journey*) viaje *m* **4.** (*sea voyage*) travesía *f*

passageway ['pæs·ɪdʒ·weɪ] *n* pasillo *m*

passbook ['pæs·bʊk] *n* libreta *f* de ahorros

passenger ['pæs·ən·dʒər] *n* pasajero, -a *m, f*

passenger list *n* lista *f* de pasajeros

passerby [ˌpæs·ər·'baɪ] <passersby> *n* transeúnte *mf*

passing I. *adj* **1.** (*going past*) que pasa **2.** (*brief: fad, infatuation*) pasajero, -a; (*glance*) rápido, -a; (*remark*) de pasada **II.** *n euph* (*death*) fallecimiento *m elev*

passion ['pæʃ·ən] *n* (*emotion*) pasión *f*

passionate ['pæʃ·ə·nɪt] *adj* (*emotional*) apasionado, -a

passive ['pæs·ɪv] *adj* pasivo, -a

passport ['pæs·pɔrt] *n* pasaporte *m*; *fig* **sb's ~ to success** su llave hacia el éxito

password ['pæs·wɜrd] *n* COMPUT contraseña *f*

past [pæst] **I.** *n* pasado *m*; **to be a thing of the ~** ser una cosa del pasado; **sb with a ~** alguien con historia; **simple ~** LING pasado *m* simple **II.** *adj* pasado, -a; **the ~ week** la semana pasada; **in times ~** en otros tiempos; **that's ~ history** eso pertenece a la historia **III.** *prep* **1.** (*temporal*) después de; **ten/quarter/half ~ two** dos y diez/cuarto/media **2.** (*spatial*) después de **3.** (*beyond*) **to be ~ thirty** pasar de los treinta; **~ belief** increíble; **~ description** indescriptible; **I'm ~ that now** *iron* ya he superado eso **IV.** *adv* por delante; **to go/run/march ~ (sb/sth)** ir/correr/pasar por delante (de alguien/algo)

pasta ['pas·tə] *n* CULIN pasta *f*

past continuous *n* LING pasado *m* continuo

paste [peɪst] **I.** *n* pasta *f* **II.** *vt a.* COMPUT pegar

pasteurize ['pæs·tʃə·raɪz] *vt* pasteurizar

past participle *n* LING participio *m* pasado

past perfect *n* LING pretérito *m* perfecto

pastry ['peɪ·stri] <-ies> *n* **1.** (*dough*) masa *f* **2.** (*sweet bun*) pastel *m*

past tense *n* LING tiempo *m* pasado

pasture ['pæs·tʃər] **I.** *n* AGR pasto *m* **II.** *vt* apacentar **III.** *vi* pacer

pasty ['peɪ·sti] <-ier, -iest> *adj* (*texture*) pastoso, -a

pat¹ [pæt] **I.** <-tt-> *vt* (*touch softly*) dar palmaditas a; **to ~ sb on the back** *fig* felicitar a alguien **II.** *n* **1.** (*tap*) palmadita *f* **2.** (*of butter*) porción *f*

pat² [pæt] *adj pej* (*answer*) fácil

patch [pætʃ] **I.** *n* **1.** (*piece of cloth*) *a.* COMPUT parche *m* **2.** (*of land*) parcela *f* de tierra; (*of fog*) zona *f* **3.** *inf* (*phase*) fase *f* **II.** *vt* (*hole*) remendar

◆ **patch up** *vt* **1.** (*mend*) hacer un arreglo provisional a **2.** *fig* (*friendship*) arreglar; **to patch things up** hacer las paces

patchy ['pætʃ·i] <-ier, -iest> *adj* (*performance, novel*) desigual; (*weather*) variable; (*results*) irregular

pâté [pa·'teɪ] *n* paté *m*

patent ['pæt·ənt] I. *n* LAW patente *f* II. *adj* (*unconcealed*) evidente, patente III. *vt* LAW patentar

paternal [pə·'tɜr·nəl] *adj* paternal; **~ grandfather** abuelo paterno; **~ grandmother** abuela paterna

paternity leave *n* permiso *m* de paternidad

path [pæθ] *n* 1. (*footway, trail*) camino *m*; **bike ~** carril *m* bicicleta; **to clear a ~** abrir un sendero; **to follow a ~** seguir una senda 2. (*way*) trayecto *m*; **to cross sb's ~** tropezar con alguien 3. COMPUT ruta *f*

pathetic [pə·'θet·ɪk] *adj* 1. (*arousing sympathy*) conmovedor(a); **a ~ sight** una escena lastimosa 2. (*arousing scorn*) patético, -a; **a ~ performance** una pésima actuación

pathfinder ['pæθ·faɪn·dər] *n* explorador(a) *m(f)*

pathway ['pæθ·weɪ] *n* sendero *m*

patience ['peɪ·ʃəns] *n* paciencia *f*

patient ['peɪ·ʃənt] I. *adj* paciente; **to be ~ with sb** tener paciencia con alguien; **just be ~!** ¡ten paciencia! II. *n* MED paciente *mf*

patio ['pæt·i·oʊ] <-s> *n* 1. (*paved area*) área pavimentada contigua a una casa 2. (*courtyard*) patio *m*

patriot ['peɪ·tri·ət] *n* patriota *mf*

patriotic [ˌpeɪ·tri·'at·ɪk] *adj* patriótico, -a

patrol [pə·'troʊl] I. <-ll-> *vi* patrullar II. <-ll-> *vt* patrullar por III. *n* patrulla *f*; **to be on ~** patrullar

patrol car *n* coche *m* patrulla

patrol duty *n* servicio *m* de patrulla

patrolman *n* policía *m*

patronize ['peɪ·trə·naɪz] *vt* 1. (*be customer*) ser cliente de 2. (*treat condescendingly*) tratar con condescendencia

patronizing ['peɪ·trə·naɪ·zɪŋ] *adj* condescendiente

patter ['pæt·ər] I. *n* 1. (*of rain*) golpeteo *m* 2. (*talk*) labia *f* II. *vi* (*make sound*) golpetear

pattern ['pæt·ərn] *n* 1. (*model*) modelo *m* 2. ART (*design, motif*) diseño *m* 3. FASHION patrón *m*

paunch [pɔntʃ] *n* barriga *f*

pauper ['pɔ·pər] *n* indigente *mf*

pause [pɔz] I. *n* pausa *f* II. *vi* hacer una pausa

pave [peɪv] *vt* pavimentar; **to ~ the way for sth** *fig* preparar el terreno para algo

pavement ['peɪv·mənt] *n* calzada *f*

pavilion [pə·'vɪl·jən] *n* pabellón *m*

paw [pɔ] *n* pata *f*; (*of cat, lion*) garra *f*, zarpa *f*; *fig inf* (*of person*) manaza *f*

pawn[1] [pɔn] *n* GAMES peón *m*; *fig* títere *m*

pawn[2] [pɔn] *vt* empeñar

pawnbroker ['pɔn·ˌbroʊ·kər] *n* prestamista *mf* (sobre prenda), agenciero, -a *m, f Chile*; **the ~'s** la casa de empeños

pawn shop *n* casa *f* de empeños

pay [peɪ] I. *n* paga *f* II. <paid, paid> *vt* 1. (*with money*) pagar; **to ~ cash** pagar al contado; **to ~ one's debts** liquidar las deudas de uno 2. (*be worthwhile for*) ser provechoso, -a 3. (*give, render*) **to ~ attention (to sb/sth)** prestar atención (a alguien/algo); **to ~ a call (on sb), to ~ (sb) a call** hacer una visita (a alguien); **to ~ sb a compliment** hacer un cumplido a alguien III. <paid, paid> *vi* 1. (*settle, recompense*) pagar 2. (*benefit*) ser provechoso, -a

◆**pay back** *vt* devolver

◆**pay in** *vt* ingresar

◆**pay off** I. *vt* 1. (*debt*) liquidar 2. *inf* (*bribe*) sobornar II. *vi* *fig* merecer la pena

◆**pay out** I. *vt* (*money*) desembolsar II. *vi* pagar

◆**pay up** *vi* pagar (lo que se debe)

payable ['peɪ·ə·bəl] *adj* pagadero, -a; **to make a check ~ to sb** extender un cheque a favor de alguien

payback ['peɪ·bæk] *n* FIN (*return on investment*) restitución *f*, retorno *m* de la inversión; (*equaling the sum invested*) amortización *f*

paycheck *n* cheque *m* del salario

pay deal *n* acuerdo *m* salarial

pay desk *n* caja *f*

payee [peɪ·'i] *n* beneficiario, -a *m, f*

payer ['peɪ·ər] *n* pagador(a) *m(f)*; **bad ~** moroso, -a *m, f*

P

pay freeze n congelación f salarial

paying adj rentable

payment ['peɪ·mənt] n 1. (sum of cash) pago m 2. (installment) plazo m

payoff ['peɪ·ɔf] n 1. (payment) pago m; (debt payment) liquidación f 2. inf (bribe) soborno m, coima f CSur, mordida f Méx 3. inf (positive result) beneficios mpl; (on bet) ganancias fpl

pay-per-view n pago m por visión

pay phone n teléfono m público

pay raise n aumento m de sueldo

payroll n nómina f

payslip n nómina f

pay-TV n televisión f de pago

PC [ˌpiˈsi] n abbr of **personal computer** PC m, pecé m

PDT n abbr of **Pacific Daylight Time** Hora f del Pacífico

PE [ˌpiˈi] n abbr of **physical education** educación f física

pea [pi] n guisante m

peace [pis] n 1. (absence of war) a. REL paz f 2. (social order) orden m público; **to keep the ~** mantener el orden; **to make ~** hacer las paces 3. (tranquility) tranquilidad f; **~ of mind** tranquilidad de ánimo; **~ and quiet** paz y tranquilidad; **to give sb no ~** no dejar a alguien en paz; **to leave sb in ~** dejar a alguien en paz ▶ **to be at ~ with the** <u>world</u> estar satisfecho de la vida; **speak now or forever** <u>hold</u> **your ~** que hable ahora o que calle para siempre

peaceful ['pis·fəl] adj 1. (calm, quiet: animal) manso, -a; (place, person) tranquilo, -a 2. (non-violent) pacífico, -a

peacekeeper n (soldier) soldado mf en misión de paz

peace-loving adj amante de la paz

peacemaker ['pis·ˌmeɪ·kər] n conciliador(a) m(f)

peacemaking ['pis·ˌmeɪ·kɪŋ] n (between countries) pacificación f; (between friends) conciliación f

peace movement n movimiento m pacifista

peace negotiations npl negociaciones f pl de paz

peace pipe n pipa f de la paz

peacetime n tiempo m de paz

peace treaty <-ies> n tratado m de paz

peach [pitʃ] <-es> n 1. (fruit) melocotón m, durazno m Arg, Chile 2. (tree) melocotonero m, duraznero m Arg, Chile

peach tree n melocotonero m, duraznero m Arg, Chile

peacock ['pi·kak] n 1. ZOOL pavo m real 2. (vain person) engreído, -a m, f ▶ **to strut like a ~** pavonearse

peak [pik] I. n 1. (mountain top) cima f 2. (highest point, summit) punto m máximo; (of a roof) pico m; **to be at the ~ of one's career/power** estar en la cúspide de su carrera/poder II. adj máximo, -a

peal [pil] I. n 1. (sound: of bell) repique m; (of thunder) trueno m; **a ~ of laughter** una carcajada 2. (set) ~ **of bells** carillón m II. vi (thunder) tronar; (bell) repiquetear

peanut ['pi·nʌt] n 1. (nut) cacahuete m, maní m AmL, cacahuate m Méx 2. inf **to pay ~s** pagar una miseria

peanut butter n manteca f de cacahuete

pear [per] n pera f

pearl [pɜrl] n 1. perla f 2. fig (a drop) gota f 3. fig (a fine example) joya f ▶ **to cast one's ~s before the** <u>swine</u> prov echar margaritas a los cerdos prov

pear tree n peral m

peasant ['pez·ənt] n 1. (poor farmer) campesino, -a m, f 2. pej inf (crude person) paleto, -a m, f

pebble ['peb·əl] n guijarro m

peck [pek] I. n 1. (of bird) picotazo m 2. inf (quick kiss) besito m II. vt 1. (bird) picar, picotear 2. (kiss) dar un besito III. vi picar

peckish ['pek·ɪʃ] adj irritable

peculiar [pɪˈkjul·jər] adj 1. (strange) extraño, -a, raro, -a 2. (belonging to) propio, -a, peculiar

pedal ['ped·əl] I. n pedal m II. <-l- or -ll-, -l- or -ll-> vi pedalear

pedal bin n cubo m de la basura (con pedal)

pedal boat n pedaleta f

peddler ['ped·lər] n vendedor(a) m(f) ambulante

pedestrian [pə·'des·tri·ən] I. n peatón, -ona m, f II. adj (for walkers) peatonal

pedestrianize [pə·'des·tri·ə·naɪz] vt convertir en zona peatonal

pediatrician [ˌpi·di·ə·'trɪʃ·ən] n MED pediatra mf

pediatrics [ˌpi·di·'æt·rɪks] n MED pediatría f

pedigree ['ped·ɪ·gri] I. n (genealogy: of animal) pedigrí m II. adj (animal) de raza

peek [pik] I. n mirada f rápida II. vi 1. (look) mirar furtivamente; **to ~ at sth** echar una mirada furtiva a algo 2. (become visible) asomar

peel [pil] I. n piel f; (of fruit) cáscara f; (peelings) mondas fpl II. vt (fruit) pelar; (skin) levantar III. vi (person) pelarse; (paint) desconcharse; (bark) descortezarse

♦**peel off** I. vt (paint) quitar; (bark) descortezar; (clothes) quitarse II. vi (come off: paper) despegarse; (paint) desconcharse; (skin) pelarse

peeler ['pi·lər] n pelapatatas m inv

peelings ['pi·lɪŋz] npl (of fruit) peladuras fpl

peep [pip] I. n (sound: of bird) pío m; **to not say a ~** no decir ni pío II. vi piar

peep² [pip] I. n (look) vistazo m; **to have a ~ at sth** echar una ojeada a algo II. vi 1. (look quickly) mirar rápidamente 2. (become visible) asomar

peephole ['pip·hoʊl] n mirilla f

peer¹ [pɪr] vi **to ~ at sth** escudriñar algo; **to ~ into the distance** fijar la mirada en la distancia

peer² [pɪr] n (equal) igual mf, par mf; **to have no ~s** no tener par

peg [peg] I. n 1. (for coat) colgador m 2. (in furniture, for tent) estaquilla f II. <-gg-> vt 1. (with pegs) enclavijar 2. ECON fijar; **to ~ prices** congelar precios 3. inf (throw) lanzar

♦**peg away** vi inf darle duro; **to ~ at sth** persistir en algo

♦**peg out** vt señalar con estacas

pejorative [pɪ·'dʒɔr·ə·tɪv] adj peyorativo, -a

pelican ['pel·ɪ·kən] n pelícano m

pellet ['pel·ɪt] n 1. (small ball) bolita f 2. inf (animal excrement) cagadita f 3. (gunshot) perdigón m

pelt¹ [pelt] n (of animal) pellejo m; (fur) piel f

pelt² [pelt] I. vt (throw) lanzar II. vi 1. (rain) llover a cántaros 2. (run, hurry) apresurarse; **to ~ after sb** salir disparado tras alguien III. n 1. (smack) golpe m 2. (quick pace) paso m ligero; **at full ~** a todo correr

pen¹ [pen] I. n (fountain pen) pluma f; (ballpoint pen) bolígrafo m, birome f Arg; **felt-tip ~** rotulador m II. <-nn-> vt escribir

pen² [pen] n 1. (enclosure) corral m; **pig ~** pocilga f 2. inf (jail) **the ~** el talego m

penalty ['pen·əl·ti] <-ies> n 1. LAW pena f; **death ~** pena de muerte f 2. (punishment) castigo m 3. SPORTS castigo m; (in soccer) penalti m

penalty area n SPORTS área f (de penalti)

penalty box <-es> n (in ice hockey) banquillo m

penalty kick n SPORTS (tiro m de) penalti m

pencil ['pen·səl] n lápiz m

pencil case n estuche m (para lápices)

pencil sharpener n sacapuntas m inv, tajalápiz m Col

pendant ['pen·dənt] I. n colgante m II. adj colgante

pending ['pen·dɪŋ] adj pendiente; **~ deal** negocio m pendiente; **patent ~** patente en trámite

penetrate ['pen·ɪ·treɪt] vt 1. (move into or through) penetrar; **to ~ a market** introducirse en un mercado 2. (spread through) impregnar, calar en

penetrating adj penetrante

penguin ['peŋ·gwɪn] n pingüino m

penholder ['pen·ˌhoʊl·dər] n portalápices m inv

penicillin [ˌpen·ɪ·'sɪl·ɪn] n penicilina f

peninsula [pə·'nɪn·sə·lə] n península f

P

penitence ['pen·ɪ·təns] n REL penitencia f

penitentiary [ˌpen·ɪ·ten·tʃə·ri] n prisión f penitenciaria

penknife ['pen·naɪf] <-knives> n navaja f

penniless ['pen·ɪ·lɪs] adj **to be ~** no tener un duro

Pennsylvania [ˌpen·sɪl·ˈveɪ·ni·ə] n Pensilvania f

penny ['pen·i] n centavo m ▶ **to pinch pennies** apretarse el cinturón

pen pal n amigo, -a m, f por correspondencia

pension ['pen·ʃən] I. n FIN pensión f; **to draw a ~** cobrar una pensión II. vt **to ~ sb off** jubilar a alguien

pensioner ['pen·ʃə·nər] n pensionista mf

pension fund n fondo m de pensiones

pentagon ['pen·tə·ɡən] n pentágono m

pentathlon [pen·ˈtæθ·lən] n pentatlón m

penthouse ['pent·haʊs] n ático m de lujo

pent-up [ˌpent·ˈʌp] adj (emotion) contenido, -a, reprimido, -a

penultimate [pɪ·ˈnʌl·tə·mət] adj penúltimo, -a

people ['pi·pəl] n 1. pl (plural of person) gente f; **city/country ~** gente de ciudad/de campo 2. (nation, ethnic group) pueblo m; **~'s republic** república f popular 3. pl (ordinary citizens) ciudadanos, -as m, fpl; **of/by/for the ~** del/por/para el pueblo

pepper ['pep·ər] I. n 1. (spice) pimienta f 2. (vegetable) pimiento m II. vt 1. (add pepper) poner [or echar] pimienta a 2. (pelt) **to ~ sb with questions** acribillar a alguien a preguntas

peppercorn ['pep·ər·kɔrn] n grano m de pimienta

pepper mill n molinillo m de pimienta

peppermint ['pep·ər·mɪnt] n 1. (mint plant) menta f 2. (sweet) caramelo m de menta

pep talk n inf **to give sb a ~** dar ánimos a alguien

per [pər] prep 1. (for a) por; **$5 ~ pound/hour** $5 por libra/hora 2. (in a) por, a; **100 miles ~ hour** 100 millas por hora 3. form **as ~...** (as stated in) de acuerdo con...; **as ~ usual** como siempre

per annum adv al año, por año

per capita adj, adv per cápita

perceive [pər·ˈsiv] vt 1. (see) ver; (sense) percibir, notar; **to ~ that...** percibir que... 2. (view, regard) considerar; **how do the young ~ the old?** ¿qué piensan los jóvenes de los viejos?

percent [pər·ˈsent] n porcentaje m; **25 ~** 25 por ciento

percentage [pər·ˈsen·tɪdʒ] n 1. (proportion) porcentaje m; **what ~...?** ¿qué porcentaje...?; **to get a ~ of sth** recibir un tanto por ciento de algo 2. (advantage) tajada f inf

percentage point n punto m porcentual

perception [pər·ˈsep·ʃən] n 1. percepción f 2. (insight) perspicacia f, agudeza f

perceptive [pər·ˈsep·tɪv] adj perspicaz, agudo, -a

perch¹ [pɜrtʃ] I. <-es> n (for birds) percha f II. vi (person) sentarse; (bird) posarse

perch² [pɜrtʃ] n (fish) perca f

percussion [pər·ˈkʌ·ʃən] n MUS percusión f

percussionist n MUS percusionista mf

perennial [pə·ˈren·i·əl] adj 1. BOT perenne 2. (constant) constante

perfect¹ ['pɜr·fɪkt] I. adj perfecto, -a; (calm) total; **in ~ condition** en perfecto estado; **the ~ crime** el crimen perfecto; **to be a ~ stranger** ser un completo desconocido; **to be far from ~** estar (muy) lejos de ser perfecto II. n LING perfecto m

perfect² [pɜr·ˈfekt] vt perfeccionar

perfection [pər·ˈfek·ʃən] n perfección f; **to ~ a la perfección

perfectly adv perfectamente; **~ clear** completamente claro

perforate ['pɜr·fə·reɪt] vt perforar; (ticket) picar

perform [pər·ˈfɔrm] I. vt 1. MUS, THEAT, TV interpretar 2. (do, accomplish) realizar; **to ~ one's duty** cumplir con su

deber; to ~ miracles hacer milagros; **to ~ a task** llevar a cabo una tarea **II.** *vi* **1.** THEAT actuar; MUS tocar **2.** (*operate*) funcionar

performance [pər·ˈfɔr·məns] *n* **1.** (*of play*) representación *f*; (*by actor*) actuación *f*; **to give a ~** hacer una representación **2.** SPORTS actuación *f*

performer [pər·ˈfɔr·mər] *n* **1.** THEAT artista *mf*; **star ~** estrella *f* **2.** (*achiever*) **top ~** (*at work*) empleado, -a *m, f* modelo; **bad ~** (*at school*) mal(a) estudiante *mf*; (*at work*) mal(a) trabajador(a) *m(f)*

perfume [ˈpɜr·fjum] **I.** *n* perfume *m* **II.** *vt* perfumar

perhaps [pər·ˈhæps] *adv* quizá(s), tal vez

peril [ˈper·əl] *n form* peligro *m*; **to be in ~** correr peligro

perilous [ˈper·ə·ləs] *adj form* peligroso, -a

perimeter [pə·ˈrɪm·ə·tər] *n* perímetro *m*

period [ˈpɪr·i·əd] **I.** *n* **1.** **a.** GEO período *m*; **in/over a ~ of sth** en/durante un período de algo **2.** ECON plazo *m* **3.** SCHOOL (*lesson*) hora *f* **4.** (*distinct stage*) época *f* **5.** (*menstruation*) período *m*, regla *f*; **to have one's ~** tener la regla **6.** LING punto *m* final **II.** *interj* ¡y punto! *inf*

periodical [ˌpɪr·i·ˈad·ɪ·kəl] **I.** *n* (*general*) publicación *f* periódica **II.** *adj* periódico, -a

peripheral [pə·ˈrɪf·ər·əl] **I.** *adj* **1.** (*importance, role*) secundario, -a **2. a.** ANAT, COMPUT periférico, -a **II.** *n* COMPUT periférico *m*

periscope [ˈper·ɪ·skoup] *n* periscopio *m*

perish [ˈper·ɪʃ] *vi liter* **1.** (*die*) perecer **2.** (*disappear: motivation, hope*) desaparecer

perishable [ˈper·ɪʃ·ə·bəl] *adj* perecedero, -a *elev*

perjury [ˈpɜr·dʒə·ri] *n* perjurio *m*

perk [pɜrk] *n inf abbr of* **perquisite 1.** (*advantage*) ventaja *f* **2.** (*benefit m*) extra *m*

◆perk up I. *vi* **1.** (*cheer up*) alegrarse **2.** (*improve*) mejorar **II.** *vt* (*cheer up*) alegrar

perm [pɜrm] **I.** *n inf* (*hair*) permanente *f* **II.** *vt* **to ~ one's hair** hacerse la

permanente

permanent [ˈpɜr·mə·nənt] *adj* (*job*) fijo, -a; (*damage*) irreparable; (*exhibition, situation, position*) permanente; (*ink*) indeleble

permission [pər·ˈmɪʃ·ən] *n* permiso *m*

permit¹ [ˈpɜr·mɪt] *n* **1.** permiso *m* (por escrito); **to hold a ~** tener un permiso **2. fishing/gun/building ~** licencia *f* de pesca/armas/construcción

permit² [pər·ˈmɪt] <-tt-> **I.** *vt* permitir; **I will not ~ you to go there** no te permito que vayas allí **II.** *vi* **weather ~ing** si el tiempo no lo impide; **if time ~s** si hay tiempo

perpendicular [ˌpɜr·pən·ˈdɪk·ju·lər] *adj* perpendicular

perpetual [pər·ˈpetʃ·u·əl] *adj* (*lasting forever*) perpetuo, -a

perplex [pər·ˈpleks] *vt* desconcertar

persecute [ˈpɜr·sɪ·kjut] *vt a.* POL perseguir

persecution [ˌpɜr·sɪ·ˈkju·ʃən] *n* persecución *f*

persevere [ˌpɜr·sə·ˈvɪr] *vi* perseverar

persist [pər·ˈsɪst] *vi* (*continue: cold, heat, rain*) continuar; (*habit, belief, doubts*) persistir

persistence [pər·ˈsɪs·təns] *n* **1.** (*of cold, belief*) persistencia *f* **2.** (*of person*) insistencia *f*

persistent [pər·ˈsɪs·tənt] *adj* **1.** (*cold, belief*) persistente **2.** (*person*) insistente

person [ˈpɜr·sən] <people *or form* -s> *n* (*human*) **a.** LING persona *f*; **per ~** por persona

personal [ˈpɜr·sə·nəl] *adj* **1.** (*property*) privado, -a; (*data, belongings, account*) personal **2.** (*done in person*) en persona **3.** (*matter*) privado, -a, personal; (*life*) privado, -a **4. to get ~** llevar las cosas al plano personal; **it's nothing ~** no es nada personal **5.** (*bodily, physical: appearance*) personal; (*hygiene*) íntimo, -a

personal computer *n* ordenador *m* personal, computadora *f* personal *AmL*

personality [ˌpɜr·sə·ˈnæl·ə·t̬i] <-ies> *n* **1.** (*character*) personalidad *f* **2.** (*famous person*) personalidad *f*, figura *f*

personally *adv* **1.** (*in person*) personalmente **2.** (*as offensive*) **to take sth ~** ofenderse con [*or* por] algo **3.** (*referring to oneself*) ~... personalmente... **4.** (*referring to sb's character*) como persona; **I don't like him ~** no me gusta como persona

personnel [ˌpɜr·sə·'nel] *n pl* (*staff, employees*) personal *m*

personnel department *n* departamento *m* de personal

personnel director *n* director(a) *m(f)* de personal

perspective [pər·'spek·tɪv] *n* perspectiva *f*

perspiration [ˌpɜr·spə·'reɪ·ʃən] *n* transpiración *f*

perspire [pər·'spaɪr] *vi* transpirar

persuade [pər·'sweɪd] *vt* convencer; **to ~ sb into/out of sth** convencer/disuadir a alguien de algo; **to ~ sb to do sth** convencer a alguien de que haga algo

persuasion [pər·'sweɪ·ʒən] *n* **1.** (*act*) persuasión *f* **2.** (*conviction*) creencia *f*

persuasive [pər·'sweɪ·sɪv] *adj* (*person, manner*) persuasivo, -a; (*argument*) convincente

Peru [pə·'ru] *n* Perú *m*

Peruvian [pə·'ru·vi·ən] **I.** *adj* peruano, -a **II.** *n* peruano, -a *m, f*

perverse [pər·'vɜrs] *adj* perverso, -a

perversion [pər·'vɜr·ʒən] *n* (*sexual*) perversión *f*; (*of the truth*) distorsión *f*

pervert[1] ['pɜr·vɜrt] *n* (*sexual*) pervertido, -a *m, f*

pervert[2] [pər·'vɜrt] *vt* pervertir

pessimism ['pes·ə·mɪz·əm] *n* pesimismo *m*

pessimist *n* pesimista *mf*

pessimistic [ˌpes·ə·'mɪs·tɪk] *adj* pesimista

pest [pest] *n* **1.** (*animal*) plaga *f* **2.** *inf* (*person*) pesado, -a *m, f*

pest control *n* (*insects*) fumigación *f*

pester ['pes·tər] *vt* molestar

pesticide ['pes·tə·saɪd] *n* pesticida *m*

pet [pet] **I.** *n* **1.** (*house animal*) animal *m* doméstico, mascota *f* **2.** *pej* (*favorite person*) mimado, -a *m, f*; **he's the teacher's ~** es el mimado del profesor **II.** *adj* **1. my ~ cat** el gato que tengo de mascota, mi gato **2.** (*favorite: project,*

theory) favorito, -a **III.** <-tt-> *vi* besarse y acariciarse

petal ['pet·əl] *n* BOT pétalo *m*

peter ['pi·tər] *vi* **to ~ out** (*trail, track, path*) desaparecer; (*conversation, interest*) decaer

petition [pə·'tɪʃ·ən] **I.** *n* **1.** POL petición *f* **2.** LAW demanda *f* **II.** *vi* POL **to ~ for sth** elevar una petición solicitando algo

petrified *adj* **1.** GEO petrificado, -a **2.** (*terrified*) aterrorizado, -a

petrify ['pet·rɪ·faɪ] <-ies> **I.** *vi* GEO petrificarse **II.** *vt* (*terrify*) aterrorizar

petroleum [pə·'trou·li·əm] *n* petróleo *m*, canfín *m AmC*

pet shop *n* ≈ pajarería *f*

petticoat ['pet·i·kout] *n* enagua *f*, combinación *f*, fondo *m Méx*

petty ['pet·i] <-ier, -iest> *adj* **1.** *pej* (*detail, amount*) trivial, insignificante **2.** LAW menor

pew [pju] *n* banco *m* (de iglesia)

pg. *abbr of* **page** pág. *f*

phantom ['fæn·təm] **I.** *n* fantasma *m* **II.** *adj* **1.** (*ghostly*) fantasma **2.** (*imaginary*) ilusorio, -a

pharmaceutical I. *adj* farmacéutico, -a **II.** *n* ~s fármacos *mpl*

pharmacist ['far·mə·sɪst] *n* farmacéutico, -a *m, f*

pharmacy ['far·mə·si] <-ies> *n* farmacia *f*

pharynx ['fær·ɪŋks] <pharynges> *n* faringe *f*

phase [feɪz] *n* (*stage*) fase *f*; (*period*) etapa *f*; **to go through a ~** pasar por una etapa

♦ **phase in** *vt* introducir paulatinamente

♦ **phase out** *vt* (*service*) retirar progresivamente; (*product*) dejar de producir paulatinamente

PhD [ˌpi·eɪtʃ·'di] *n abbr of* **Doctor of Philosophy 1.** (*award*) doctorado *m* **2.** (*person*) Dr. *m*, Dra. *f*

pheasant ['fez·ənt] <-(s)> *n* faisán *m*

phenomenal *adj* (*success, achievement*) espectacular; (*strength*) increíble

phenomenon [fɪ·'nam·ə·nan] <phenomena *or* -s> *n* fenómeno *m*

phew [fju] *interj inf* ¡uf!

philosopher [fɪ·'las·ə·fər] *n* filósofo,

-a *m, f*

philosophize [fɪ'las·ə·faɪz] *vi* filosofar

philosophy [fɪ'las·ə·fi] *n* filosofía *f*

phobia ['fou·bi·ə] *n* PSYCH fobia *f*

phone [foun] **I.** *n* teléfono *m;* **to hang up the ~** colgar el teléfono; **to pick up the ~** coger el teléfono; **to be on the ~** estar hablando por teléfono **II.** *vt* llamar (por teléfono), telefonear

◆**phone back** *vt* volver a llamar (por teléfono)

◆**phone in I.** *vi* llamar (por teléfono); **to ~ sick** llamar (por teléfono) para dar parte de enfermo **II.** *vt* llamar por teléfono

◆**phone up** *vt* llamar (por teléfono)

phone book *n* guía *f* (telefónica), directorio *m* Col, Méx

phone booth <-es> *n* cabina *f* (telefónica)

phone call *n* llamada *f* (telefónica)

phone number *n* número *m* (de teléfono), teléfono *m*

phonetic [fə'net·ɪk] *adj* fonético, -a; **~ transcription** transcripción *f* fonética

phonetics [fə'net·ɪks] *n* fonética *f*

phony ['fou·ni] <-ier, -iest> *adj inf (person, address)* falso, -a; *(documents)* falsificado, -a

phosphorescent [ˌfas·fə·'res·ənt] *adj* fosforescente

phosphorus ['fas·fər·əs] *n* fósforo *m*

photo ['fou·tou] <-s> *n inf abbr of* **photograph** foto *f*

photo album *n* álbum *m* de fotos

photocopier [ˌfou·tou·'kap·i·ər] *n* fotocopiadora *f*

photocopy ['fou·tou·ˌkap·i] **I.** <-ies> *n* fotocopia *f* **II.** *vt* fotocopiar

photo finish *n* SPORTS foto *f* finish

photoflash *n* flash *m*

photograph ['fou·tou·græf] **I.** *n* fotografía *f;* **color ~** fotografía en color; **take a ~** sacar una fotografía (**of** de) **II.** *vt* fotografiar

photograph album *n* álbum *m* de fotos

photographer [fə·'tag·rə·fər] *n* fotógrafo, -a *m, f*

photographic [ˌfou·tə·'græf·ɪk] *adj* fotográfico, -a

photography [fə·'tag·rə·fi] *n* fotografía *f*

photojournalism [ˌfou·tou·'dʒɜr·nə·lɪz·

əm] *n* periodismo *m* gráfico

photometer [fou·'tam·ɪ·t̬ər] *n* fotómetro *m*

photomontage [ˌfou·tou·man·'taʒ] *n* fotomontaje *m*

photo reporter *n* reportero, -a *m, f* fotográfico, -a

photosynthesis [ˌfou·tou·'sɪn·θɪ·sɪs] *n* fotosíntesis *f*

phrasal verb [ˌfreɪ·zəl·'vɜrb] *n* LING verbo *m* con partícula

phrase [freɪz] **I.** *n* frase *f;* *(idiomatic expression)* expresión *f* **II.** *vt* **to ~ sth well/badly** expresar algo bien/mal

phrase book *n* libro *m* de frases

physical ['fɪz·ɪ·kəl] **I.** *adj* físico, -a; **to be in poor ~ condition** estar en bajo estado de forma; **to have a ~ disability** sufrir una discapacidad física; **~ exercise** ejercicio *m* físico **II.** *n* MED reconocimiento *m* médico

physical education *n* educación *f* física

physician [fɪ·'zɪʃ·ən] *n* médico, -a *m, f*

physicist ['fɪz·ɪ·sɪst] *n* físico, -a *m, f*

physics ['fɪz·ɪks] *n* física *f*

physique [fɪ·'zik] *n* físico *m*

pianist ['pi·æn·ɪst] *n* pianista *mf*

piano [pi·'æn·ou] <-s> *n* piano *m*

pick [pɪk] **I.** *vt* **1.** *(select)* elegir **2.** *(harvest: fruit, vegetables)* recoger **3.** *(touch)* tocar; **to ~ one's nose** hurgarse la nariz **4.** *(steal)* robar; **to ~ a lock** forzar una cerradura; **to ~ sb's pocket** robar algo del bolsillo de alguien **5.** *(provoke)* **to ~ a fight (with sb)** buscar camorra (con alguien) **II.** *n* **1.** *(selection)* elección *f;* *(of people)* selección *f;* **to take one's ~** elegir; **to have one's ~** poder elegir **2.** *(pickax)* pico *m*

◆**pick off** *vt (shoot)* abatir (a tiros)

◆**pick on** *vt insep* **1.** *(victimize)* meterse con **2.** *(select)* **to ~ sb for sth** escoger a alguien para algo

◆**pick out** *vt* **1.** *(choose)* elegir **2.** *(recognize)* distinguir

◆**pick over** *vt* ir revolviendo y examinando

◆**pick up I.** *vt* **1.** *(lift)* levantar; **to ~ the phone** coger el teléfono; **to ~ the pieces** *fig* empezar de nuevo **2.** *(get)* conseguir; *(conversation)* captar; **to ~**

a bargain conseguir una ganga; **to ~ an illness** pillar una enfermedad *inf;* **to ~ speed** coger velocidad; **to ~ the bill** [*or* **tab**] *inf* pagar la cuenta **3.** (*collect*) recoger; **to pick sb up** recoger a alguien **4.** (*clean: one's room, the living room*) ordenar **5.** (*buy*) adquirir **6.** (*detect: noise, signal*) detectar **7.** (*learn*) aprender **8.** *sl* (*sexually*) **to pick sb up** ligarse a alguien **9.** *inf* (*halt*) detener; (*arrest*) arrestar **10.** *inf* (*earn*) ganar **II.** *vi* **1.** (*improve*) mejorar; (*numbers*) ir a mejor; MED reponerse **2.** (*continue*) continuar; **to ~ where one left off** reanudar donde uno lo dejó

pickax [ˈpɪkˌæks] *n* (*tool*) pico *m,* azadón *m* de pico

picket [ˈpɪkˌɪt] *n* **1.** (*stake*) estaca *f* **2.** (*striker*) a. MIL piquete *m*

picket line *n* piquete *m;* **to be on the ~** participar en un piquete

pickle [ˈpɪkˌəl] **I.** *n* **1.** (*pickled item*) encurtido *m* **2.** (*pickled cucumber*) pepinillo *m* en vinagre al eneldo **II.** *vt* (*vegetables*) conservar en vinagre; (*fish*) conservar en escabeche

pickled *adj* **1.** (*vegetables*) encurtido, -a; (*fish*) en escabeche **2.** *fig sl* (*drunk*) borracho, -a; **to get ~** emborracharse

pickpocket [ˈpɪkˌpak·ɪt] *n* carterista *mf,* bolsista *mf AmC, Méx*

pickup *n* **1.** *inf* (*collection*) recogida *f,* recolección *f* **2.** (*increase*) aumento *m*

pickup truck *n* camioneta *f* con plataforma

picnic [ˈpɪkˌnɪk] *n* picnic *m;* **to go on a ~** ir de picnic; **to be no ~** *fig* no ser nada agradable

picnicker *n* excursionista *mf*

picture [ˈpɪkˌtʃər] **I.** *n* **1.** (*image*) imagen *f;* (*painting*) pintura *f;* **to draw a ~** hacer un dibujo; **to paint a ~** pintar un cuadro **2.** (*photo*) fotografía, foto *f;* **to take a ~** sacar una foto **3.** (*film*) película *f* **4.** (*mental image*) imagen *f* **5.** *fig* (*description*) representación *f;* **to paint a ~ of sth** representar algo; **to paint a very black ~** pintar un panorama muy negro ▶ **a ~ is worth a thousand words** *prov* una imagen vale más que mil palabras; **to get the ~** entender

II. *vt* imaginarse

picture book *n* libro *m* ilustrado

picture frame *n* marco *m* (para cuadro)

picture gallery *n* galería *f* de arte

picture postcard *n* (tarjeta *f*) postal *f*

picturesque [ˌpɪk·tʃə·ˈresk] *adj* (*scenic*) pintoresco, -a

pidgin [ˈpɪdʒ·ɪn] *n* LING pidgin *m*

pie [paɪ] *n* tarta *f,* pay *m AmS* ▶ (**as**) **easy as ~** pan comido

piece [pis] *n* **1.** (*small unit: of wood, metal, food*) trozo *m;* (*of land*) terreno *m;* **a ~ of paper** (*scrap*) un trozo de papel; (*sheet*) una hoja; **in one ~** en una sola pieza; **to break sth to/in ~s** hacer algo pedazos; **to tear sth into ~s** desgarrar algo **2.** (*item, one of set*) unidad *f;* **~ of luggage** bulto *m;* **~ of clothing** prenda *f* de vestir **3.** (*in games*) pieza *f* **4.** (*with mass nouns*) **a ~ of advice** un consejo **5.** ART, MUS pieza *f* **6.** (*coin*) moneda *f;* **a 50 cent ~** una moneda de 50 centavos ▶ **to be a ~ of cake** *inf* ser pan comido

piece rate *n* precio *m* por unidad

piecework [ˈpis·wɜrk] *n* trabajo *m* a destajo

pieceworker *n* trabajador(a) *m(f)* a destajo

pier [pɪr] *n* **1.** (*at the water*) muelle *m* **2.** ARCHIT (*pillar*) columna *f,* pilar *f;* (*buttress*) contrafuerte *m*

pierce [pɪrs] **I.** *vt* (*perforate*) perforar; **to ~ a hole in sth** agujerear algo; **to have one's ears ~d** hacerse agujeros en las orejas **II.** *vi* (*drill*) **to ~ through sth** atravesar algo

piercing I. *adj* **1.** (*wind*) cortante; **it's ~ cold** hace un frío que pela **2.** (*eyes, gaze, look*) penetrante; (*question, reply, wit*) punzante **3.** (*cry*) desgarrador(a) **II.** *n* piercing *m*

pig [pɪg] *n* **1.** ZOOL cerdo *m* **2.** *inf* (*person*) cochino, -a *m, f;* **to be a ~** ser un cerdo ▶ **to make a ~ of oneself** ponerse como un cerdo

◆**pig out** <-gg-> *vi sl* ponerse morado; **to ~ out on sth** comer demasiado de algo

pigeon [ˈpɪdʒ·ən] *n* (*bird*) paloma *f*

pigeonhole [ˈpɪdʒ·ən·hoʊl] **I.** *n* casilla f. **II.** vt **to ~** sb/sth encasillar a alguien/algo

piggyback ['pɪg·i·bæk] n **to carry** sb/**ride ~** llevar/montar a caballito

piggy bank n alcancía f en forma de cerdito

pigheaded [,pɪg·'hed·ɪd] adj testarudo, -a

piglet ['pɪg·lɪt] n cochinillo m

pigment ['pɪg·mənt] n pigmento m

pigsty ['pɪg·staɪ] n a. fig, pej pocilga f

pigtail ['pɪg·teɪl] n (hair) trenza f

pile [paɪl] **I.** n **1.** (stack) pila f **2.** (heap) montón m; **to have ~s of** sth inf tener montones de algo **3.** ELEC pila f **II.** vt amontonar

◆**pile in** vi ~! ¡todos dentro, que nos vamos!

◆**pile on** vt **1.** (enter) entrar desordenadamente **2.** (heap) amontonar **3.** inf (exaggerate) **to** (**really**) **pile it on** exagerar (mucho)

◆**pile up I.** vi **1.** (accumulate) acumularse **2.** (form a pile) apilarse **II.** vt amontonar

piles npl inf almorranas fpl

pileup ['paɪl·ʌp] n accidente m múltiple

pilfer ['pɪl·fər] vt ratear

pilgrim ['pɪl·grɪm] n peregrino, -a m, f

pilgrimage ['pɪl·grə·mɪdʒ] n peregrinación f

pill [pɪl] n **1.** pastilla f, píldora f; **the ~** (contraception) la píldora **2.** inf (pesky person) pesado, -a m, f ▶ **to sweeten** [or **sugar**] **the ~** dorar la píldora

pillage ['pɪl·ɪdʒ] **I.** vt saquear **II.** n saqueo m

pillar ['pɪl·ər] n **1.** ARCHIT pilar m, columna f **2.** fig (of support) sostén m, puntal m; **to be a ~ of** strength ser firme como una roca

pillow ['pɪl·oʊ] n **1.** (for bed) almohada f **2.** (cushion) cojín m

pillowcase n funda f de almohada

pilot ['paɪ·lət] **I.** n **1.** AVIAT piloto mf **2.** NAUT práctico mf **3.** TV programa m piloto **4.** TECH (flame) piloto m **II.** vt **1.** (plane) pilotar **2.** (boat) guiar

pilot boat n bote m del práctico

pilot burner n (on boiler) piloto m (de una caldera)

pilot light n piloto m

pilot plant n planta f piloto

pilot program n programa m piloto

pilot's license n licencia f de vuelo

pilot survey n estudio m experimental

pimple ['pɪm·pəl] n grano m

pimply ['pɪm·pli] <-ier, -iest> adj lleno, -a de granos

pin [pɪn] **I.** n **1.** (needle) alfiler m; **tie ~** alfiler m de corbata **2.** (brooch) prendedor m **3.** pl, fig (legs) patas fpl ▶ **to have ~s and needles** sentir un hormigueo **II.** <-nn-> vt (attach with a pin) **to ~** sth **on** prender algo con un alfiler

◆**pin down** vt **1.** (define) precisar **2.** (locate) concretar **3.** (pressure to decide) presionar (a alguien) para que se defina **4.** (restrict movement) inmovilizar

◆**pin up** vt (attach using pins) recoger con alfileres; (on the wall) fijar con chinchetas; **to ~** one's **hair** recogerse el pelo con horquillas

PIN [pɪn] n abbr of **personal identification number** PIN m (número de identificación personal)

pinball machine n (máquina f de) petacos mpl

pincers ['pɪn·sərz] npl **1.** ZOOL pinzas fpl **2.** (tool) tenazas fpl

pinch [pɪntʃ] **I.** vt **1.** (with fingers) pellizcar **2.** (be too tight) apretar **3.** inf (steal) birlar **II.** vi (with fingers) estrujar **III.** n **1.** (nip) pellizco m; **to give** sb **a ~** dar un pellizco a alguien **2.** (small quantity) pizca f

pine¹ [paɪn] n pino m

pine² [paɪn] vi **1.** (waste away) **to ~** (**away**) languidecer **2.** (long for) **to ~ for** sb suspirar por alguien

pineapple ['paɪn·æp·əl] n (fruit) piña f

pinecone n piña f

pine needle n aguja f de pino

pine tree n pino m

ping [pɪŋ] **I.** n (sound: of bell) tintín m; (of glass, metal) sonido m metálico **II.** vi tinear

pink [pɪŋk] **I.** n (color) rosa m ▶ **to be in the ~** rebosar de salud **II.** adj rosado, -a

pinkie ['pɪŋ·ki] n inf dedo m meñique

P

pinpoint ['pɪn·pɔɪnt] I. *vt* (*location, reason*) indicar con toda precisión II. *adj* exacto, -a; **~ accuracy** gran precisión *f*

pinprick ['pɪn·prɪk] *n* pinchazo *m*

pinstripe ['pɪn·straɪp] *n* (*stripe*) raya *f* fina; (*suit*) traje *m* de raya diplomática

pint [paɪnt] *n* pinta *f (0,47 l)*; **a ~ of beer/milk** una pinta de cerveza/leche

pinup ['pɪn·ʌp] *n* (*poster*) póster *m* (*de una persona atractiva*)

pioneer [‚paɪ·ə·'nɪr] *n* pionero, -a *m, f; fig* pionero, -a *m, f*

pious ['paɪ·əs] *adj* REL a. *iron* piadoso, -a

pip [pɪp] *n* BOT pepita *f*

pipe [paɪp] I. *n* 1. TECH (*tube*) tubo *m*; (*for gas, water*) cañería *f*, tubería *f* 2. (*for smoking*) pipa *f*, cachimba *f AmL* 3. MUS (*wind instrument*) **~s** gaita *f* II. *vt* (*transport*) transportar por tuberías

♦ **pipe down** *vi inf* (*be quiet*) callarse; (*become quieter*) calmarse

pipe dream *n* sueño *m* imposible

pipeline ['paɪp·laɪn] *n* tubería *f;* **oil ~** oleoducto *m;* **gas ~** gasoducto *m;* **to be in the ~** *fig* estar tramitándose

piper ['paɪ·pər] *n* gaitero, -a *m, f*

piping ['paɪ·pɪŋ] *n* (*pipes*) tubería *f*

piracy ['paɪ·rə·si] *n* NAUT, COM piratería *f*

pirate ['paɪ·rət] I. *n* pirata *m* II. *adj* pirata; **~ copy** copia *f* pirata

Pisces ['paɪ·siz] *n* Piscis *m*

pistachio [pɪ·'stæʃ·i·oʊ] <-s> *n* pistacho *m*, pistache *m Méx*

pistol ['pɪs·təl] *n* pistola *f*

piston ['pɪs·tən] *n* TECH pistón *m*

pit[1] [pɪt] *n* 1. (*in ground*) hoyo *m;* (*on metal*) muesca *f;* (*on face*) marca *f;* **in the ~ of one's stomach** en la boca del estómago 2. (*mine*) mina *f* 3. **the ~s** *pl, fig inf* lo peor 4. THEAT (*seating area*) patio *m* de asientos; (*orchestral area*) platea *f* 5. **the ~s** *pl* SPORTS los boxes

pit[2] [pɪt] <-tt-> I. *n* (*of fruit*) hueso *m* II. *vt* CULIN deshuesar

pitch[1] [pɪtʃ] I. *n* 1. (*in baseball*) lanza-

miento *m* 2. (*slope*) grado *m* de inclinación; **low/steep ~** pendiente *f* suave/pronunciada 3. (*volume*) volumen *m* 4. MUS, LING tono *m* 5. (*spiel*) rollo *m;* **sales ~** labia *f* para vender; **to make a ~** soltar un rollo II. *vt* 1. (*throw*) lanzar 2. SPORTS (*throw*) tirar 3. (*fix level of sound*) **this tune is ~ed** (*too*) **high/low** esta afinación es (demasiado) alta/baja 4. (*direct at: speech, advertisement*) **to ~ sth at sb** diseñar algo para alguien 5. (*set up*) **to ~ camp/a tent** montar el campamento/una tienda (de campaña) 6. (*sell forcefully: product*) vender (de forma agresiva) III. *vi* 1. (*fall headlong*) caerse de morros *inf* 2. (*boat*) cabecear 3. SPORTS (*throw baseball*) lanzar 4. (*slope*) inclinarse

♦ **pitch in** *vi inf* contribuir

pitch[2] [pɪtʃ] *n* (*bitumen*) brea *f*

pitch-black [‚pɪtʃ·'blæk] *adj* (*extremely dark*) muy oscuro, -a; (*very black*) muy negro, -a

pitcher[1] ['pɪtʃ·ər] *n* (*jug: large*) cántaro *m;* (*smaller*) jarra *f*

pitcher[2] ['pɪtʃ·ər] *n* (*in baseball*) lanzador(a) *m(f)*

pitchfork ['pɪtʃ·fɔrk] *n* horca *f*

pitfall ['pɪt·fɔl] *n* escollo *m*

pith [pɪθ] *n* 1. BOT médula *f* 2. *fig* (*main point*) meollo *m*

pithy ['pɪθ·i] <-ier, -iest> *adj* (*remark*) sucinto, -a

pitiful ['pɪt·ɪ·fəl] *adj* 1. (*terrible*) lamentable; **a ~ sight** una escena patética 2. (*unsatisfactory*) insatisfactorio, -a; **~ excuse** excusa *f* pobre

pitiless ['pɪt·ɪ·lɪs] *adj* despiadado, -a

pit stop *n* 1. (*in racing*) parada *f* en boxes 2. *fig* (*quick stop*) parada *f* rápida

pity ['pɪt·i] I. *n* 1. (*compassion*) compasión *f;* **to feel ~ for sb** compadecerse de alguien; **to take ~ on sb** apiadarse de alguien 2. (*shame*) (**it's a**) **~ that...** (es una) lástima que...; **what a ~!** ¡qué pena! II. <-ies, -ied> *vt* compadecerse de

pivot ['pɪv·ət] I. *n* 1. TECH eje *m* 2. (*focal point*) punto *m* central, pivote *m* II. *vi* pivotar

pizza [ˈpiːt·sə] n pizza f

placard [ˈplæk·ard] n pancarta f

placate [ˈpleɪ·keɪt] vt 1. (soothe) aplacar 2. (appease) apaciguar

place [pleɪs] I. n 1. (location, area) lugar m; ~ **of birth** lugar de nacimiento; **people in high** ~s gente f bien situada; **to be in** ~ estar en su sitio; fig estar listo; **if I were in your** ~,... yo en tu lugar...; **in** ~ **of sb/sth** en vez de alguien/algo; **it is not your** ~ **to say that** no eres quién para decir eso 2. inf (house) casa f; **at my** ~ en mi casa 3. (building) edificio m 4. (commercial location) local m 5. (position) posición f; **to take first/second** ~ quedar en primer/segundo lugar; **in the first** ~ primero; **in the second** ~ segundo 6. (seat) sitio m; (in theater) localidad f; **is this** ~ **taken?** ¿está ocupado este sitio?; **to change** ~s **with sb** cambiar el sitio con alguien; **to save sb a** ~ guardar un sitio a alguien 7. MATH **decimal** ~ decimal m 8. inf (in location) **any** ~ en/a cualquier sitio; **every** ~ en todas partes; **some** ~ (a) algún sitio; **no** ~ en ningún sitio ► **to fall into** ~ encajar; **to go** ~s inf (become successful) llegar lejos; **to know one's** ~ saber cuál es el lugar de uno; **to put sb in his/her** ~ poner a alguien en su sitio; **all over the** ~ por todas partes; **to feel out of** ~ sentirse fuera de lugar II. vt 1. (position, put) colocar; **to** ~ **sth somewhere** colocar algo en un sitio; **to** ~ **an advertisement in the newspaper** poner un anuncio en el periódico; **to** ~ **sth on the agenda** apuntar algo en la agenda 2. (impose) imponer; **to** ~ **an embargo on sth** prohibir algo; **to** ~ **a limit on sth** poner un límite a algo; **to** ~ **sb under arrest** arrestar a alguien 3. (ascribe) poner; **to** ~ **the blame on sb** echar la culpa a alguien; **to** ~ **one's hopes on sb/sth** poner sus esperanzas en alguien/algo; **to** ~ **one's faith in sb** depositar su confianza en alguien 4. (arrange for) hacer; **to** ~ **an order for sth** hacer un pedido de algo; **to** ~ **a bet** hacer una apuesta; **to** ~ **sth at sb's disposal** poner algo a disposición de alguien 5. (appoint to a position) to

~ **sb in charge** (of sth) poner a alguien a cargo (de algo); **to** ~ **sth under the control of sb** poner algo bajo el control de alguien; **to** ~ **sb under pressure** someter a alguien a presión; **to** ~ **sth above sth** poner algo por encima de algo; **to be** ~d **first/second** SPORTS quedar en primer/segundo lugar III. vi SPORTS clasificarse

place card n tarjeta f (indicadora del puesto que se ocupa)

place mat n salvamanteles m inv

placement [ˈpleɪs·mənt] n colocación f

place name n topónimo m

plague [pleɪg] I. n peste f; (infestation of insects) plaga f; (source of annoyance) pesadez f; **the** ~ la peste; **to avoid sb like the** ~ huir de alguien como de la peste II. vt fastidiar; **to** ~ **sb for sth** acosar a alguien por algo

plaice [pleɪs] inv n (fish) platija f

plain [pleɪn] I. adj 1. sencillo, -a; (monochrome) de un solo color; (without additions) sin aditivos; ~ **yogurt** yogur m natural 2. (uncomplicated) fácil; ~ **and simple** liso y llano 3. (clear, obvious) evidente; **it is** ~ **that...** es evidente que...; **to be** ~ **enough** estar lo suficientemente claro; **to make sth** ~ dejar algo claro; **to be** ~ **with sb** ser franco con alguien 4. (mere, pure) puro, -a; **the** ~ **truth** la pura verdad 5. (not pretty) sin atractivo; **a** ~ **girl** una chica más bien fea II. adv inf (downright) y punto; ~ **awful** horrible III. n GEO llanura f; **the great Plains** la grandes llanuras (norteamericanas)

plainclothes n LAW (of policeman) ropa f de paisano

plainly [ˈpleɪn·li] adv 1. (simply) simplemente 2. (clearly) claramente; (obviously) evidentemente; **to be** ~ **visible** ser muy visible 3. (undeniably) sin duda

plaintiff [ˈpleɪn·tɪf] n LAW demandante mf

plait [plæt] I. n trenza f II. vt trenzar

plan [plæn] I. n 1. (scheme, program) plan m; **to draw up a** ~ elaborar un plan; **to go according to** ~ ir de acuerdo con lo previsto; **to change** ~s cambiar de planes; **do you have any** ~s **for this**

weekend? ¿tienes planes para este fin de semana? **2.** FIN, ECON (*policy*) seguro *m;* **healthcare ~** seguro *m* médico; **savings ~** plan *m* de ahorro **3.** (*diagram*) plano *m* II. <-nn-> *vt* **1.** (*work out in detail*) planificar; (*prepare*) preparar **2.** (*intend*) proponerse; **to ~ to do sth** proponerse hacer algo III. <-nn-> *vi* **1.** (*prepare*) hacer proyectos; **to ~ carefully** hacer proyectos detallados **2.** (*reckon with*) **to ~ on sth** tener pensado algo

plane¹ [pleɪn] I. *n* (*level surface*) nivel *m;* MATH plano *m* II. *adj* plano, -a; MATH llano, -a; **~ angle** ángulo *m* plano

plane² [pleɪn] *n* (*airplane*) avión *m;* **by ~** en avión

plane³ [pleɪn] I. *n* (*tool*) cepillo *m* (de carpintero) II. *vt* cepillar

planet ['plæn·ɪt] *n* planeta *m; ~* **Earth** la Tierra; *~* **Jupiter** el planeta Júpiter

planetarium [ˌplæn·ɪ·'ter·i·əm] <-s *or* -ria> *n* planetario *m*

plank [plæŋk] *n* tabla *f*

planner *n* planificador(a) *m(f);* **city ~** urbanista *mf*

planning *n* planificación *f*

plant [plænt] I. *n* **1.** BOT planta *f* **2.** (*factory*) fábrica *f* **3.** (*machinery*) maquinaria *f* II. *vt* **1.** AGR (*put in earth*) plantar; **to ~ sth with sth** sembrar algo de algo **2.** (*put*) colocar; **to ~ oneself somewhere** *inf* meterse en algún sitio; **to ~ a bomb** poner una bomba; **to ~ a secret agent** introducir a un agente secreto **3.** *inf* (*incriminate*) **to ~ evidence on sb** colocar pruebas para incriminar a alguien III. *adj* vegetal; *~* **life** vida *f* vegetal

plantation [plæn·'ter·ʃən] *n* plantación *f;* (*of trees*) arboleda *f*

plaque [plæk] *n* **1.** (*on building*) placa *f* **2.** MED sarro *m*

plaster ['plæs·tər] I. *n* a. MED yeso *m* II. *vt* (*wall, ceiling*) enyesar

plasterboard ['plæs·tər·bɔrd] *n* cartón *m* de yeso (y fieltro)

plaster cast *n* MED escayola *f*

plastered *adj sl* (*drunk*) borracho, -a

plasterer *n* yesero, -a *m, f*

plastic ['plæs·tɪk] I. *n* **1.** (*material*) plás-

tico *m* **2.** *inf* (*credit card*) tarjeta *f* (de crédito) II. *adj* **1.** (*made from plastic*) de plástico **2.** *pej* (*artificial*) artificial

plastic surgery *n* cirugía *f* plástica

plate [pleɪt] I. *n* **1.** (*dinner plate*) plato *m* **2.** (*panel, sheet*) lámina *f;* **steel ~** lámina de acero **3.** AUTO **license ~** (placa *f* de la) matrícula *f* **4.** (*layer of metal*) capa *f;* **gold ~** capa de oro **5.** (*picture in book*) ilustración *f* ▶ **to have a lot on one's ~** tener muchos asuntos entre manos II. *vt* **to ~ sth with gold/silver** chapar algo en oro/plata

plated *adj* (*coated in metal*) chapeado, -a; (*jewelry*) chapado, -a

plateful ['pleɪt·fʊl] *n* plato *m*

plate glass *n* vidrio *m*

plate rack *n* portaplatos *m inv*

platform ['plæt·fɔrm] *n* **1.** a. COMPUT plataforma *f* **2.** RAIL andén *m* **3.** (*stage*) escenario *m* **4.** (*means for expressing view*) medio *m* **5.** POL (*policy*) programa *m* electoral

platinum ['plæt·nəm] *n* platino *m*

platonic [plə·'tan·ɪk] *adj* platónico, -a

platter ['plæt·ər] *n* **1.** (*large dish*) fuente *f* **2.** (*food*) plato *m* fuerte ▶ **to give sth to sb on a ~** servir algo a alguien en bandeja

platypus ['plæt·ɪ·pəs] <-es> *n* ornitorrinco *m*

play [pleɪ] I. *n* **1.** (*recreation*) juego *m;* **to be at ~** estar en juego **2.** SPORTS juego *m;* **to be in/out of ~** estar en/fuera de juego **3.** SPORTS (*move*) jugada *f;* **foul ~** juego sucio; **to make a bad/good ~** hacer una mala/buena jugada **4.** THEAT obra *f* de teatro **5.** (*free movement*) juego *m* **6.** (*interaction*) juego *m;* **to bring sth into ~** poner algo en juego; **to come into ~** entrar en juego II. *vi* **1.** a. SPORTS jugar; **to ~ for a team** jugar en un equipo; **to ~ fair/rough** jugar limpio/sucio **2.** (*perform*) actuar **3.** MUS tocar III. *vt* **1.** (*participate in game, sport*) jugar; **to ~ bridge/soccer** jugar al bridge/al fútbol; **to ~ a card** jugar una carta; **to ~ a match/a round** jugar un partido/una ronda **2.** (*perform a role*) interpretar; **to ~ the clown** [*or* fool] hacer el payaso **3.** MUS (*instrument*) tocar; (recording: CD, tape, video, DVD) poner; **do you have to ~ the music so loud?** ¿es necesario que pongas la música tan alta?

◆**play down** vt quitar importancia a

◆**play on I.** vt **1.** (exploit) **to ~ sb's weakness** aprovecharse de la debilidad de alguien **2.** (phrase, word) jugar con **II.** vi (keep playing) SPORTS, GAMES seguir jugando; MUS seguir tocando

◆**play up I.** vt (exaggerate: problem, difficulty) exagerar **II.** vi inf **to ~ to sb** (flatter) dar coba a alguien

play-act ['pleɪ·ækt] vi **1.** THEAT actuar **2.** fig hacer teatro

playback ['pleɪ·bæk] n (of tape) reproducción f

playboy ['pleɪ·bɔɪ] n playboy m

player ['pleɪ·ər] n **1.** SPORTS jugador(a) m(f); **card ~** jugador(a) m(f) de cartas; **soccer ~** futbolista mf; **tennis ~** tenista mf; MUS instrumentista mf; **cello ~** violoncelista mf; **flute ~** flautista mf **3.** THEAT actor m, actriz f **4.** **CD ~** reproductor m de CD; **record ~** tocadiscos m inv **5.** sl (important person) peso m pesado

playful ['pleɪ·fəl] adj **1.** (full of fun) juguetón, -ona **2.** (comment, tone) de guasa

playground ['pleɪ·graʊnd] n **1.** (at school) patio m; (in park) campo m de recreo **2.** fig (resort) lugar m de recreo

playgroup ['pleɪ·grup] n guardería f

playing card n carta f, naipe m

playing field n terreno m de juego

playoff ['pleɪ·ɔf] n desempate m; **~ match** partido m de desempate; **the ~s** las eliminatorias fpl

playpen ['pleɪ·pen] n parque m

playroom ['pleɪ·rum] n cuarto m de jugar

playtime ['pleɪ·taɪm] n SCHOOL recreo m

playwright ['pleɪ·raɪt] n dramaturgo, -a m, f

plea [pli] n **1.** (appeal) petición f, súplica f; **to make a ~ for help** pedir ayuda **2.** LAW alegato m; **to enter a ~ of not guilty** declararse inocente

plead [plid] <-ed or pled, -ed or pled> **I.** vi **1.** (implore, beg) implorar, suplicar; **to ~ for forgiveness** suplicar perdón **2.** LAW **to ~ innocent** (to a charge) declararse inocente (de un cargo) **II.** vt **1.** LAW **to ~ sb's case** defender el caso de alguien **2.** (claim as pretext) pretextar; **to ~ ignorance of sth** pretextar su ignorancia en algo

pleading ['pli·dɪŋ] **I.** n **1.** (entreaty, appeal) súplicas fpl **2.** LAW alegato m **II.** adj (look, tone) suplicante

pleasant ['plez·ənt] adj **1.** (pleasing) agradable; **what a ~ surprise!** ¡qué agradable sorpresa!; **have a ~ journey!** ¡buen viaje! **2.** (friendly) amable

please [pliz] **I.** vt **1.** (make happy) complacer; **to be hard to ~** ser difícil de contentar **2.** inf (do as one wishes) **~ yourself** haz lo que te parezca **II.** vi **1.** (be agreeable) **eager to ~** deseoso de agradar **2.** (think fit, wish) **you can do as you ~** como usted quiera; **to do whatever one ~s** hacer todo lo que se quiera **III.** interj por favor; **if you ~** form con su permiso; **more potatoes? — (yes) ~** ¿más patatas? — sí, por favor; **oh, ~!** (in annoyance) ¡oh, por favor!

pleased adj **1.** (satisfied, contented) satisfecho, -a (**with** de); **to be ~ about sth** estar contento de algo **2.** (happy, glad) contento, -a; **I'm ~ to inform you that ...** me complace informarle de que...; **(I'm very) ~ to meet you** encantado de conocerle **3.** (willing) **to be ~ to do sth** estar encantado de hacer algo

pleasing adj agradable; **~ news** buenas noticias fpl

pleasurable ['pleʒ·ər·ə·bəl] adj grato, -a

pleasure ['pleʒ·ər] n **1.** (feeling of enjoyment) placer m; **it was such a ~ to meet you** ha sido un placer conocerle; **to take ~ in sth/in doing sth** disfrutar de algo/haciendo algo; **with ~** con mucho gusto **2.** (source of enjoyment) placer m

pleat [plit] n pliegue m

pleb [pleb] n inf abbr of **plebian** plebeyo, -a m, f

pled [pled] pt, pp of **plead**

pledge [pledʒ] **I.** n **1.** (solemn promise) promesa f solemne; **to fulfill a ~** cum-

P

plir un compromiso **2.** (*symbolic sign of promise*) **a ~ of good faith** una garantía de buena fe **3.** (*promised donation*) donativo *m* prometido **4.** (*pawned item*) prenda *f* **II.** *vt* **1.** (*promise*) prometer; **to ~ loyalty** jurar lealtad; **to ~ to do sth** prometer hacer algo; **to ~ that...** prometer que... **2.** (*give as security*) **to ~ money** dar dinero como garantía

plentiful ['plen·tɪ·fəl] *adj* abundante

plenty ['plen·ti] **I.** *n* **1.** (*abundance*) abundancia *f;* **land of ~** tierra *f* de abundancia; **food in ~** comida *f* en abundancia **2.** (*a lot*) **~ of time** tiempo de sobra **II.** *adv* suficientemente; **~ more** mucho más

pliers ['plaɪ·ərz] *npl* alicates *mpl;* **a pair of ~** unos alicates

plight [plaɪt] *n* apuro *m*

plod [plad] <-dd-> *vi* **1.** (*walk heavily*) andar con paso pesado **2.** (*do without enthusiasm*) **to ~ through one's work** trabajar sin ganas

plonk [plʌŋk] *vt* see **plunk**

plop [plap] **I.** *n* plaf *m;* **to fall with a ~** caerse haciendo plaf **II.** <-pp-> *vi* (*fall*) **to ~ onto the bed** dejarse caer sobre la cama

plot [plat] **I.** *n* **1.** (*conspiracy, secret plan*) conspiración *f;* **the ~ thickens** *iron* el asunto se complica **2.** (*story line*) argumento *m* **3.** (*small piece of land*) terreno *m;* **a ~ of land** un terreno; **building ~** solar *m* **II.** <-tt-> *vt* **1.** (*conspire*) tramar **2.** (*create*) **to ~ a story line** idear un argumento **3.** (*graph, line*) trazar; **to ~ a course** planear una ruta **III.** <-tt-> *vi* **to ~ against sb** conspirar contra alguien; **to ~ to do sth** planear hacer algo

plotter ['plat·ər] *n* **1.** (*person*) conspirador(a) *m(f)* **2.** COMPUT plotter *m*

plough [plaʊ] *n vt, vi* see **plow**

plow [plaʊ] **I.** *n* arado *m* ▶ **to put one's hand to the ~** ponerse manos a la obra **II.** *vt* **1.** AGR arar **2.** (*move through*) **to ~ one's way through sth** abrirse paso por algo **3.** (*invest*) **to ~ money into a project** invertir mucho dinero en un proyecto **III.** *vi* **1.** AGR arar **2.** **to ~ through sth** (*move through*) abrirse

paso por algo

ploy [plɔɪ] *n* **1.** (*activity*) aventura *f* **2.** (*tactics*) estratagema *f*

pluck [plʌk] **I.** *n* **1.** (*sharp pull*) tirón *m* **2.** (*courage*) valor *m;* **it takes a lot of ~** hace falta mucho valor **II.** *vt* **1.** (*remove quickly*) arrancar **2.** (*remove hair, feathers*) **to ~ a chicken** desplumar un pollo; **to ~ one's eyebrows** depilarse las cejas **3.** MUS puntear

plucky ['plʌk·i] <-ier, -iest> *adj* valiente

plug [plʌg] **I.** *n* **1.** ELEC enchufe *m* **2.** (*stopper*) tapón *m* **3.** (*spark plug*) bujía *f* **II.** <-gg-> *vt* **1.** (*connect*) conectar; ELEC enchufar **2.** (*stop up, close*) **to ~ a hole** tapar un agujero **3.** (*publicize*) anunciar

♦**plug away** *vi* **to ~ (at sth)** perseverar (en algo)

♦**plug in** *vt* conectar; ELEC enchufar

plug-in *n* COMPUT plug-in *m*, enchufe *m*

plum [plʌm] **I.** *n* **1.** (*fruit*) ciruela *f* **2.** (*opportunity, reward*) chollo *m* **II.** *adj* (*color*) de color ciruela

plumber ['plʌm·ər] *n* fontanero, -a *m, f*, plomero, -a *m, f* AmL

plumbing ['plʌm·ɪŋ] *n* fontanería *f*

plummet ['plʌm·ɪt] *vi* caer en picado

plump [plʌmp] *adj* (*person*) rollizo, -a; (*animal*) gordo, -a

♦**plump up** *vt* **1.** (*pillow*) sacudir **2.** (*chicken*) cebar

plum tree *n* ciruelo *m*

plunder ['plʌn·dər] **I.** *n* **1.** (*stolen goods*) botín *m* **2.** (*act of plundering*) saqueo *m* **II.** *vt* **1.** (*village, city*) saquear **2.** (*goods, gold, treasures*) robar

plunderer ['plʌn·dər·ər] *n* saqueador(a) *m(f)*

plunge [plʌndʒ] **I.** *n* **1.** (*sharp decline*) caída *f* **2.** (*dive*) zambullida *f* de cabeza **II.** *vi* **1.** (*fall suddenly*) precipitarse **2.** (*leap, enter*) **we ~d into the sea** nos zambullimos en el mar **3.** (*begin abruptly*) **to ~ into sth** emprender algo

plunger ['plʌn·dʒər] *n* (*of syringe*) émbolo *m;* (*for drain, toilet*) desatascador *m*

plunk [plʌŋk] **I.** *n* *inf* (*sound*) ruido *m* sordo **II.** *vt inf* (*set down heavily*) dejar caer pesadamente

pluperfect ['plu·ˌpɜr·fɪkt] *n* LING pluscuamperfecto *m*

plural ['plʊr·əl] I. *n* plural *m;* **in the** ~ en plural; **second person** ~ segunda persona del plural II. *adj* 1. *a.* LING plural 2. (*multiple*) múltiple

plus [plʌs] I. *prep* más; **5** ~ **2 equals 7** 5 más 2 igual a 7 II. *conj* además III. <-es> *n* 1. (*mathematical symbol*) signo *m* más 2. (*advantage*) punto *m* a favor IV. *adj* 1. (*above zero*) positivo, -a; ~ **8** más 8; ~ **two degrees** dos grados positivos 2. (*more than*) algo más de; **200** ~ más de 200 3. (*advantageous*) **the** ~ **side** (**of sth**) el lado positivo (de algo)

plush [plʌʃ] I. *adj* (*luxurious*) lujoso, -a, elegante II. <-es> *n* felpa *f*

Pluto ['plu·toʊ] *n* Plutón *m*

plutonium [plu·'toʊ·ni·əm] *n* plutonio *m*

ply¹ [plaɪ] *n* (*of cloth, wood*) capa *f;* **two- ~ rope** cuerda *f* de dos cabos

ply² [plaɪ] <-ie-> *vt* 1. **to** ~ **one's trade** ejercer su profesión 2. **to** ~ **sb with questions** acosar a alguien a preguntas 3. (*sell*) **to** ~ **drugs** traficar con drogas; **to** ~ **one's wares** vender su mercancía

plywood ['plaɪ·wʊd] *n* contrachapado *m*

PM [,pi·'em] 1. *abbr of* **postmortem** autopsia *f* 2. *abbr of* **prime minister** primer ministro *m*, primera ministra *f*

P.M. [,pi·'em] *abbr of* **post meridiem** p.m.; **one** ~ la una de la tarde; **ten** ~ las diez de la noche

pneumatic [nu·'mæt·ɪk] *adj* neumático, -a

pneumonia [nu·'moʊn·jə] *n* neumonía *f*

poach¹ [poʊtʃ] *vt* (*eggs*) escalfar; (*fish*) cocer

poach² [poʊtʃ] *vt, vi* (*animals*) cazar furtivamente; (*fish*) pescar furtivamente

poacher ['poʊ·tʃər] *n* (*hunter*) cazador(a) *m(f)* furtivo, -a; (*fisherman*) pescador(a) *m(f)* furtivo, -a

poaching ['poʊ·tʃɪŋ] *n* (*hunting*) caza *f* furtiva; (*fishing*) pesca *f* furtiva

POB *n abbr of* **post office box** apdo. *m* de correos

pocket ['pak·ɪt] I. *n* 1. (*in pants, jacket*) bolsillo *m*, bolsa *f AmC, Méx;* **inside** ~ bolsillo interior; **to pay for sth out of**

one's own ~ pagar algo de su bolsillo 2. (*isolated group, area*) **a** ~ **of resistance** un foco de resistencia; ~ **of turbulence** AVIAT, METEO racha *f* de turbulencias 3. (*in pool table*) tronera *f* ▶ **to have** sth/sb **in one's** ~ tener algo/a alguien en el bolsillo II. *vt* 1. (*put in pocket*) **to** ~ sth meterse algo en el bolsillo 2. (*keep for oneself*) apropiarse de III. *adj* (*dictionary*) de bolsillo

pocketbook ['pak·ɪt·bʊk] *n* 1. (*handbag*) bolso *m*, cartera *f AmL* 2. (*billfold*) monedero *m* 3. (*book*) libro *m* de bolsillo

pocket calculator *n* calculadora *f* de bolsillo

pocketknife <-knives> *n* navaja *f*

pocket money *n* dinero *m* para gastos personales

pocket-sized *adj* de bolsillo

pod [pad] *n* BOT vaina *f*

podium ['poʊ·di·əm] <-s *or* -dia> *n* podio *m*

poem ['poʊ·əm] *n* poema *m*

poet ['poʊ·ət] *n* poeta *mf*

poetry ['poʊ·ɪ·tri] *n a.* fig poesía *f*

point [pɔɪnt] I. *n* 1. (*sharp end*) punta *f* 2. GEO cabo *m* 3. (*particular place*) punto *m;* **boiling/freezing** ~ punto *m* de ebullición/congelación; **starting** ~ punto de partida 4. (*particular time*) momento *m;* **to get to the** ~ **that...** llegar al extremo de...; **at this** ~ **in time** en este momento 5. (*significant idea*) cuestión *f;* **that's just the** ~! ¡eso es lo importante!; **to be beside the** ~ no venir al caso; **to get to the** ~ ir al grano; **to make one's** ~ expresar su opinión; **to miss the** ~ no captar lo relevante; ~ **taken** de acuerdo; ~ **by** ~ punto por punto 6. (*purpose*) finalidad *f;* **what's the** ~? ¿qué sentido tiene? 7. (*characteristic*) sb's **strong/weak** ~s los puntos fuertes/débiles de alguien 8. (*in score, result*) punto *m;* **percentage** ~ puntos *m pl* porcentuales; **to win** (sth) **on** ~s (*in boxing*) ganar (algo) por puntos 9. MATH **decimal** ~ coma *f*, punto *m* decimal *AmL* ▶ **to be a** ~ **of doing sth** procurar de hacer algo II. *vi* (*with finger*) señalar; (*indicate*) **to** ~ **to sth** indicar algo III. *vt* 1. (*aim*) apuntar; **the man had ~ed a knife at him** el hombre le había amenazado con un cuchillo; **to ~ a finger at sb** *a. fig* señalar con el dedo a alguien **2.** (*direct*) señalar; **to ~ sth toward sth/sb** dirigir algo hacia algo/alguien

◆ **point out** *vt* **1.** (*show*) indicar **2.** (*inform of*) **to point sth out to sb** advertir a alguien de algo; **to ~ that...** señalar que...

point-blank [ˌpɔɪntˈblæŋk] *adv* **1.** (*fire*) a quemarropa **2.** (*ask*) a bocajarro; **to refuse** ▸ negarse rotundamente

pointed [ˈpɔɪntɪd] *adj* **1.** (*implement, stick*) puntiagudo, -a **2.** *fig* (*question*) directo, -a; (*remark*) intencionado, -a

pointer [ˈpɔɪntər] *n* **1.** (*for blackboard*) puntero *m*; (*of clock*) aguja *f*, manecilla *f* **2.** COMPUT puntero *m*; **mouse ~** puntero del ratón **3.** (*advice, tip*) consejo *m*

pointless [ˈpɔɪntlɪs] *adj* inútil

point of no return *n inf* punto *m* sin retorno

point of view <points of view> *n* punto *m* de vista

poise [pɔɪz] *n* **1.** (*composure*) aplomo *m*; **to lose/regain one's ~** perder/recobrar la serenidad **2.** (*elegance*) porte *m*

poised *adj* **1.** (*suspended*) suspendido, -a; **~ in the air** suspendido, -a en el aire **2.** (*ready*) preparado, -a **3.** (*calm*) sereno, -a

poison [ˈpɔɪzən] **I.** *n* veneno *m*; **rat ~** matarratas *m inv*; **to take ~** envenenarse ▸ **what's your ~?** *fig* ¿qué tomas? **II.** *vt* **1.** (*give poison to*) envenenar **2.** (*spoil, corrupt*) emponzoñar

poison gas *n* gas *m* tóxico

poisoning *n* envenenamiento *m*

poison ivy *n* BOT hiedra *f* venenosa

poisonous [ˈpɔɪzənəs] *adj* venenoso, -a; *fig* **~ atmosphere** ambiente *m* pernicioso; **~ remark** comentario *m* malicioso

poke¹ [pouk] *n reg: esp. Southern* (*bag*) bolsa *f*, saco *m*

poke² [pouk] **I.** *n* (*push*) empujón *m*; (*with elbow*) codazo *m* **II.** *vt* **1.** (*with finger*) dar con la punta del dedo en; (*with elbow*) dar un codazo a; **to ~ a hole in sth** hacer un agujero en algo; **to** **~ one's nose into sb's business** meter las narices en los asuntos de alguien **2.** (*emerge*) asomar **III.** *vi* **to ~ at sth/sb** dar a algo/alguien; **to ~ through** (**sth**) salirse de (algo)

poker¹ [ˈpoʊkər] *n* (*card game*) póquer *m*

poker² [ˈpoʊkər] *n* (*fireplace tool*) atizador *m*

poky [ˈpoʊki] <-ier, -iest> *adj inf* **1.** (*slow*) lerdo, -a **2.** (*small*) diminuto, -a; **a ~ little room** un cuartucho

Poland [ˈpoʊlənd] *n* Polonia *f*

polar [ˈpoʊlər] *adj* GEO, MATH polar

polar bear *n* oso *m* polar

polar icecap *n* casquete *m* polar

polarity [poʊˈlærəti] *n* polaridad *f*

pole¹ [poʊl] *n* palo *m*; **fishing ~** caña *f* de pescar; **telephone ~** poste *m* de teléfonos

pole² [poʊl] *n* **1.** GEO, ELEC polo *m* **2.** *fig* bando *m*; **to be ~s apart** ser polos opuestos

Pole¹ [poʊl] *n* (*person*) polaco, -a *m, f*

Pole² [poʊl] *n* GEO **the North/South ~** el Polo Norte/Sur

pole vault *n* salto *m* con pértiga

police [pəˈlis] *n* policía *f*

police car *n* coche *m* de policía

police dog *n* perro *m* policía

police escort *n* escolta *f* policial; **under ~** con escolta policial

police force *n* cuerpo *m* de policía

policeman [pəˈlismən] <-men> *n* policía *m*, guardia *m*

police officer *n* policía *mf*, guardia *m*

police patrol *n* patrulla *f* policial

police raid *n* redada *f*, arreada *f Arg*

police record *n* **1.** (*file*) expediente *m* **2.** (*history of convictions*) antecedentes *m pl* penales

police state *n* estado *m* policíaco

police station *n* comisaría *f* (de policía)

policewoman [pəˈliswʊmən] <-women> *n* (mujer *f*) policía *f*

policy¹ [ˈpɑləsi] <-ies> *n* **1.** POL, ECON política *f*; **company ~** política de empresa **2.** (*principle*) principio *m*; **my ~ is to tell the truth** tengo por norma decir la verdad

policy² [ˈpɑləsi] <-ies> *n* FIN póliza *f*;

insurance ~ póliza de seguros

policyholder ['pal·ə·si·houl·dər] *n* asegurado, -a *m, f*

policy maker *n* responsable *mf* de los principios políticos de un partido

policy number *n* número *m* de póliza

policy owner *n* titular *mf* de una póliza

polio ['pou·li·ou] *n* MED polio *f*

polish ['pal·ɪʃ] **I.** *n* **1.** (*substance: for furniture*) cera *f*; (*for shoes*) betún *m*; (*for silver*) abrillantador *m*; (*for nails*) esmalte *m* **2.** (*sophisticated, refined style*) refinamiento *m* **II.** *vt* **1.** (*make shine*) sacar brillo a; (*shoes, silver*) limpiar **2.** *fig* (*refine*) pulir

◆**polish off** *vt* (*food*) despacharse; (*work, opponent*) liquidar

◆**polish up** *vt* **1.** (*polish to a shine*) dar brillo a **2.** (*improve, brush up*) perfeccionar

Polish ['pou·lɪʃ] **I.** *adj* polaco, -a **II.** *n* LING polaco *m*

polished *adj* (*shiny*) pulido, -a **2.** *fig* (*sophisticated*) distinguido, -a; **~ manners** modales *m pl* refinados; **a ~ performance** una actuación impecable

polite [pə·'laɪt] *adj* **1.** (*courteous*) atento, -a **2.** (*cultured*) educado, -a; (*refined*) fino, -a **3.** (*superficially courteous*) correcto, -a

politeness *n* cortesía *f*, educación *f*

political [pə·'lɪt·ɪ·kəl] *adj* político, -a

politically correct *adj* políticamente correcto, -a

politician [,pal·ə·'tɪʃ·ən] *n* político, -a *m, f*

politics *n pl* **1.** (*government*) política *f*; **to go into ~** dedicarse a la política; **to talk ~** hablar de política **2.** (*intrigue*) **company ~** intrigas en la empresa

poll [poul] **I.** *n* **1.** (*public survey*) encuesta *f*; **opinion ~** sondeo *m* de la opinión pública; **to conduct a ~** hacer una encuesta **2.** *pl* (*elections*) **to go to the ~s** acudir a las urnas **3.** (*number of votes cast*) votos *mpl* **II.** *vt* **1.** (*record the opinion*) sondear; **half the people ~ed** la mitad de los encuestados **2.** (*receive*) **to ~ votes** obtener votos

pollen ['pal·ən] *n* polen *m*

polling place *n* colegio *m* electoral

pollutant [pə·'lu·tənt] *n* agente *m* con-

taminador

pollute [pə·'lut] *vt* **1.** ECOL contaminar **2.** *fig* (*corrupt*) corromper

polluter [pə·'lu·tər] *n* contaminador(a) *m/f*

pollution [pə·'lu·ʃən] *n* contaminación *f*

polo ['pou·lou] *n* SPORTS polo *m*

polo shirt *n* polo *m*

polystyrene [,pal·i·'staɪ·rin] *n* (espuma *f* de) poliestireno *m*

polytechnic [,pal·i·'tek·nɪk] *n* escuela *f* politécnica

polyunsaturated fats *npl*, **polyunsaturates** [,pal·i·ʌn·'sætʃ·ə·rəts] *npl* grasas *f pl* poliinsaturadas

polyurethane [,pal·i·'jur·ə·θeɪn] *n* poliuretano *m*

pomp [pamp] *n* pompa *f*

pompous ['pam·pəs] *adj* **1.** pomposo, -a **2.** (*pretentious*) ostentoso, -a

pond [pand] *n* (*natural*) charca *f*; (*man-made*) estanque *m*; **fish ~** vivero *m*

ponder ['pan·dər] **I.** *vt* sopesar; **to ~ whether/why...** preguntarse si/por qué... **II.** *vi* reflexionar; **to ~ on sth** meditar sobre algo

ponderous ['pan·dər·əs] *adj* **1.** (*movement*) pesado, -a **2.** (*style*) laborioso, -a

pony ['pou·ni] <-ies> *n* poni *m*

ponytail ['pou·ni·teɪl] *n* coleta *f*

poo [pu] *sl* **I.** *n* caca *f* **II.** *vi* hacer caca

poodle ['pu·dəl] *n* caniche *m*, perro *m* de lanas

pool¹ [pul] *n* **1.** (*of water*) charca *f*; (*of oil, blood*) charco *f* **2.** (*man-made*) estanque *m*; **swimming ~** piscina *f*, pileta *f* *RíoPl*

pool² [pul] **I.** *n* **1.** (*common fund*) fondo *m* común **2.** (*common supply*) reserva *f*; **car ~** parque *m* de automóviles **3.** SPORTS billar *m* americano; **to play (a game of) ~** jugar al billar **II.** *vt* (*money, resources*) hacer un fondo común; (*information*) compartir

poor [pur] *adj* **1.** (*lacking money*) pobre **2.** (*attendance, harvest*) escaso, -a; (*memory, performance*) malo, -a; **~ visibility** visibilidad *f* escasa; **to be ~ at sth** no estar fuerte en algo; **to be in ~ health** estar mal de salud; **to be a ~ los-**

er no saber perder; **to have ~ eyesight** tener mala vista; **to have ~ hearing** ser duro de oído; **to do a ~ job of** (doing) sth hacer algo mal **3.** (deserving of pity) pobre; **you ~ thing!** ¡pobrecito!

poorly ['pʊr·li] **I.** adv **1.** (resulting from poverty) pobremente **2.** (inadequately) mal; **~ dressed** mal vestido; **to think ~ of sb** tener mala opinión de alguien **II.** adj **to feel ~** encontrarse mal

pop¹ [pap] **I.** adj popular; **~ culture** cultura f pop **II.** n MUS (música f) pop m

pop² [pap] n inf (father) papá m

pop³ [pap] n **1. the ~ of a champagne cork** el taponazo de una botella de champán **2.** (soda pop) gaseosa f; **orange ~** naranjada f **II.** <-pp-> vi **1.** (explode) estallar; (burst) reventar; **to let the cork ~** hacer saltar el tapón **2.** (come, go quickly) **to ~ upstairs** subir un momento; **to ~ out for sth** salir un momento a por algo **III.** <-pp-> vt (make burst) hacer estallar; **to ~ popcorn** hacer palomitas

pop in vi entrar un momento en

pop out vi salir; **to ~ from somewhere** salir de pronto de un sitio; **to ~ for sth** salir un momento a hacer algo

pop up vi (appear) aparecer; **to ~ out of nowhere** surgir de la nada

popcorn ['pap·kɔrn] n palomitas f pl (de maíz), pororó m CSur, cacalote m AmC, Méx

pope [poʊp] n REL **1.** (Catholic) papa m **2.** (Orthodox) pope m

poplar ['pap·lər] n álamo m

popper ['pap·ər] n **1.** (for making popcorn) recipiente para hacer palomitas **2.** inf (drug) popper m

poppy ['pap·i] <-ies> n amapola f

popular ['pap·jə·lər] adj **1.** (liked) popular; **he is ~ with girls** tiene éxito con las chicas **2.** (by the people) popular; **~ elections** elecciones f pl democráticas; **~ support** el apoyo del pueblo; **by ~ request** a petición del público **3.** (widespread) generalizado, -a

popularity [,pap·jə·'lær·ə·t̮i] n popularidad f

population [,pap·jə·'leɪ·ʃən] n población f; **the working ~** la población activa

population density n densidad f de población

population explosion n explosión f demográfica

populous ['pap·jʊ·ləs] adj populoso, -a

porcelain ['pɔr·sə·lɪn] n porcelana f

porch [pɔrtʃ] n **1.** (over entrance) porche m; (church) pórtico m **2.** (verandah) veranda f

porcupine ['pɔr·kjʊ·paɪn] n puercoespín m

pore [pɔr] n poro m

pork [pɔrk] n (carne f de) cerdo m, (carne f de) puerco m Méx, (carne f de) chancho m Chile, Perú

porn [pɔrn] n abbr of **pornography** porno m

pornographic [,pɔr·nə·'græf·ɪk] adj pornográfico, -a

pornography [pɔr·'nag·rə·fi] n pornografía f

porous ['pɔr·əs] adj poroso, -a

porpoise ['pɔr·pəs] n marsopa f

porridge ['pɔr·ɪdʒ] n ≈ gachas f pl de avena

port¹ [pɔrt] n **1.** NAUT (harbor) puerto m; **to come into ~** tomar puerto; **to leave ~** zarpar **2.** COMPUT puerto m; **parallel/serial ~** puerto paralelo/serial

port² [pɔrt] n AVIAT, NAUT (left side) babor m; **to ~ a** babor

port³ [pɔrt] n (wine) oporto m

portable ['pɔr·t̮ə·bəl] adj portátil

porter ['pɔr·t̮ər] n mozo m de equipajes; (on expedition) porteador m

portfolio [pɔrt·'foʊ·li·oʊ] n **1.** (case) portafolio(s) m (inv) **2.** (of drawings) carpeta f de trabajos **3.** FIN, POL cartera f; **minister without ~** Can ministro, -a m, f sin cartera

portion ['pɔr·ʃən] **I.** n **1.** (part) parte f **2.** (serving) ración f; (of cake, cheese) trozo m **II.** vt **to ~ out sth** repartir algo

portly ['pɔrt·li] <-ier, -iest> adj corpulento, -a

portrait ['pɔr·trɪt] **I.** n ART, LIT retrato m **II.** adj TYPO de formato vertical

portraitist n retratista mf

portray [pɔr·'treɪ] vt **1.** ART (person) retratar; (object) pintar; (scene, environment) representar **2.** *fig* describir

portrayal [pɔr·'treɪ·əl] *n* **1.** ART retrato *m* **2.** *fig* descripción *f*

Portugal ['pɔr·tʃə·gəl] *n* Portugal *m*

Portuguese [ˌpɔr·tʃə·'giz] **I.** *adj* portugués, -esa **II.** *n* **1.** (*person*) portugués, -esa *m, f* **2.** LING portugués *m*

pose¹ [poʊz] *vt* (*difficulty, problem*) plantear; (*question*) formular; **to ~ a threat to sb** representar una amenaza para alguien

pose² [poʊz] **I.** *vi* **1.** ART, PHOT posar **2.** (*pretend to be*) **to ~ as sb/sth** hacerse pasar por alguien/algo **II.** *n* (*body position*) pose *f*

poser ['poʊ·zər] *n inf* (*question*) pregunta *f* difícil; (*problem*) dilema *m*

posh [pɑʃ] *adj inf* (*stylish: area*) elegante; (*car, hotel, restaurant*) de lujo, pijo, -a *pey*

position [pə·'zɪʃ·ən] **I.** *n* **1.** *a.* MIL, SPORTS posición *f*; **they took up their ~s** ocuparon sus puestos; **to be in ~** estar en su sitio; **to be out of ~** estar fuera de lugar **2.** (*rank*) posición *f*, puesto *m*; (*social*) rango *m*; (*job*) puesto *m* (de trabajo); **the ~ of director** el cargo de director; **a ~ of responsibility** un puesto de responsabilidad **3.** (*opinion*) postura *f*; **to take a ~ on sth** adoptar una postura sobre algo **4.** (*situation*) situación *f*; **financial ~** situación económica; **to be in a ~ to do sth** estar en condiciones de hacer algo; **to be in no ~ to do sth** no estar en condiciones de hacer algo **II.** *vt* (*place*) colocar; MIL apostar

positive ['pɑz·ɪ·t̬ɪv] *adj* **1.** *a.* ELEC, MATH positivo, -a **2.** MED HIV **~** seropositivo, -a **3.** (*certain*) definitivo, -a; (*proof*) concluyente; **to be ~ about sth** estar seguro de algo; (**absolutely**) **~!** ¡segurísimo!

positively *adv* **1.** (*think*) positivamente; **to answer ~** contestar afirmativamente; **to think ~** pensar en positivo **2.** (*completely*) totalmente; **to ~ refuse to do sth** negarse rotundamente a hacer algo

possess [pə·'zes] *vt* **1.** (*own, have*) poseer **2. to ~ sb** (*anger, fear*) apoderarse de alguien; (*evil spirit*) poseer a alguien

possessed [pə·'zest] *adj* poseso, -a, poseído, -a; **to be ~ with sth** estar obsesionado con algo

possession [pə·'zeʃ·ən] *n* **1.** (*having*) posesión *f*; **illegal ~ of arms** tenencia *f* ilícita de armas; **to take ~ of sth** tomar posesión de algo; **to come into ~ of sth** hacerse con algo; **to gain ~ of sth** apoderarse de algo; **to be in sb's ~** estar en poder de alguien **2.** (*item of property*) bien *m* **3.** POL dominio *m* **4.** SPORTS **to be in ~ of the ball** llevar la bola

possessive [pə·'zes·ɪv] *adj* posesivo, -a; **to be ~ about sb** comportarse de manera posesiva con alguien

possibility [ˌpɑs·ə·'bɪl·ə·t̬i] *n* <-ies> **1.** (*sth feasible*) posibilidad *f* **2.** (*likelihood*) perspectiva *f*; **within the realm of ~** dentro de lo posible; **is there any ~ (that)...?** ¿hay alguna posibilidad de que +*subj*...?

possible ['pɑs·ə·bəl] *adj* posible; **as clean/good as ~** lo más limpio/lo mejor posible; **as far as ~** en lo posible; **as soon as ~** lo antes posible; **if ~** si es posible

possibly ['pɑs·ə·bli] *adv* **1.** (*perhaps*) quizás, posiblemente; **could you ~ help me?** ¿sería tan amable de ayudarme? **2.** (*by any means*) **we did all that we ~ could** hicimos todo lo posible; **I couldn't ~ do it** me es totalmente imposible hacerlo

post¹ [poʊst] **I.** *n* correo *m* **II.** *vt* **1.** (*letter, package*) echar (al correo); **to ~ sth to sb** enviar algo por correo a alguien **2.** (*inform*) **to keep sb ~ed on sth** tener a alguien al corriente de algo

post² [poʊst] *n* (*job*) puesto *m* (de trabajo); **to apply for a teaching ~** solicitar un empleo de profesor; **to take up a ~** entrar en funciones; **to desert one's ~** MIL desertar del puesto

post³ [poʊst] **I.** *n* **1.** *a.* SPORTS poste *m*; **starting/finishing ~** línea *f* de salida/ de meta **2.** *inf* (*goalpost*) poste *m* (de la portería) **II.** *vt* **~ no bills** prohibido fijar carteles

postage ['poʊ·stɪdʒ] *n* franqueo *m*; **~ and handling** gastos *m pl* de envío

postal ['poʊ·stəl] *adj* postal

post card *n* (tarjeta *f*) postal *f*

P

poster ['pou·stər] *n* 1. (*picture*) póster *m* 2. (*notice*) cartel *m*

postgraduate [,poust·'grædʒ·u·ɪt] I. *n* postgraduado, -a *m, f* II. *adj* de postgrado; ~ **studies** (estudios *m pl* de) postgrado *m*

posting ['pou·stɪŋ] *n* destino *m*

postman ['poust·mən] <-men> *n* cartero *m*

postmark ['poust·mark] I. *n* matasellos *m inv* II. *vt* matasellar

post meridiem *adv see* **P.M.**

postmortem [,poust·'mɔr·təm] *n* autopsia *f*; **to carry out a** ~ realizar una autopsia

post office *n* (oficina *f* de) correos *m*

post office box *n* apartado *m* de correos, casilla *f* postal *CSur*

postpone [poust·'poun] *vt* aplazar, posponer

postponement *n* aplazamiento *m*

postscript ['poust·skrɪp] *n* 1. (*at end of letter*) pos(t)data *f* 2. *fig* epílogo *m*; **as a** ~ **to sth** como colofón de algo

posture ['pas·tʃər] I. *n* postura *f*, actitud *f* II. *vi* tomar una postura, adoptar una actitud

postwar [,poust·'wɔr] *adj* de (la) posguerra

pot¹ [pat] I. *n* 1. (*container*) bote *m* 2. (*for cooking*) olla *f*; ~**s and pans** cacharros *mpl* 3. (*of food*) tarro *m*; (*of drink*) jarro *m*; (*for coffee*) cafetera *f*; (*for tea*) tetera *f* 4. maceta *f*, tiesto *m* 5. *inf* GAMES **to win the** ~ llevarse el bote 6. (*common fund*) fondo *m* común 7. *inf* (*a lot*) montón *m*; ~**s of money** montones de dinero 8. *fig* (*beer belly*) barriga *f inf* II. <-tt-> *vt* 1. (*put in a pot: food*) conservar en un tarro; **to** ~ (**up**) (*plants*) plantar 2. (*shoot*) cazar 3. SPORTS (*ball*) meter (en la tronera)

pot² [pat] *n sl* (*marijuana*) hierba *f*, maría *f*, mota *f Méx*; **to smoke** ~ fumar maría

potato [pə·'teɪ·toʊ] <-es> *n* patata *f*, papa *f AmL*; **sweet** ~ batata *f*; **baked** ~ patata al horno; **mashed** ~**es** puré *m* de patatas; **fried/roast(ed)** ~**s** patatas fritas/asadas

potato chips *npl* patatas *f pl* fritas (en

bolsa), papas *f pl* chip *AmL*

potato masher *n* pasapurés *m inv*

potato peeler *n* pelapatatas *m inv*, pelapapas *m inv AmL*

potent ['pou·tənt] *adj* potente; (*drink, poison, symbol*) fuerte; (*motive*) poderoso, -a

potential [pə·'ten·ʃəl] I. *adj* 1. posible 2. LING, PHYS potencial II. *n* potencial *m*; **to have** (**a lot of**) ~ tener (un gran) potencial

potentially [pə·'ten·ʃə·li] *adv* potencialmente

pothole ['pat·,houl] *n* 1. (*in road*) bache *m*, pozo *m CSur* 2. (*underground hole*) sima *f*

pot roast *n* estofado *m*

potshot ['pat·ʃat] *n* tiro *m* al azar

potted ['pat·ɪd] *adj* 1. (*plant*) en tiesto, en maceta 2. (*food*) en conserva

potter ['pat·ər] *n* alfarero, -a *m, f*; ~**'s wheel** torno *m* de alfarero

pottery ['pat·ə·ri] *n* 1. (*art*) cerámica *f* 2. <-ies> (*workshop*) alfarería *f*

potty ['pat·i] <-ies> *n* (*for baby*) orinal *m*; **to go** (**to the**) ~ (*small child*) (ir a) hacer pis

pouch [pautʃ] *n* 1. *a.* ANAT, ZOOL bolsa *f* 2. (*handbag*) bolso *m*; (*for mail*) valija *f*; **tobacco** ~ petaca *f*

poultry ['poul·tri] *n* 1. (*birds*) aves *f pl* de corral 2. (*meat*) carne *f* de ave

pounce [pauns] I. *n* (*spring*) salto *m* II. *vi* 1. (*jump*) saltar; **to** ~ **on sth** abalanzarse sobre algo 2. *fig* **to** ~ **on an opportunity** no dejar escapar una oportunidad

pound¹ [paund] *n* 1. (*weight*) libra *f* (*454 g*); **by the** ~ por libras 2. (*currency*) libra *f*; ~ **sterling** libra esterlina

pound² [paund] *n* (*for cars*) depósito *m*; (*for dogs*) perrera *f*; (*for sheep*) redil *m*

pound³ [paund] I. *vt* 1. (*hit repeatedly*) aporrear; (*beat*) golpear; (*with a hammer*) martillear; **the waves** ~**ed the ship** las olas batían contra el barco 2. (*walk heavily*) patear; **I could hear him** ~**ing the floor upstairs** podía oír sus pasos en el piso de arriba 3. (*crush*) machacar; (*meat*) golpear, ablandar 4. MIL batir; **to** ~ **sth to**

rubble reducir algo a escombros II. *vi* 1. (*beat*) dar golpes; (*on a door, table*) aporrear; (*heart, pulse*) latir con fuerza; **my head is ~ing!** ¡la cabeza me va a estallar! 2. (*run*) **to ~ downstairs** bajar corriendo 3. *fig* **to ~ away at sth** insistir en algo

pounding *n* 1. (*noise*) golpeteo *m;* (*of heart*) fuerte latido *m;* (*of sea*) embate *m;* (*in head*) martilleo *m* 2. (*crushing*) trituración *f* 3. (*attack*) ataque *m; a. fig* (*beating*) paliza *f inf;* **to take a ~** *a. fig* llevarse una paliza; **the film took a heavy ~** la película tuvo muy malas críticas

pour [pɔr] I. *vt* 1. (*cause to flow*) verter; **to ~ coffee/wine** echar café/vino; **to ~ sb sth** servir algo a alguien 2. (*give in large amounts*) verter; (*money, resources*) invertir; **to ~ time into sth** dedicar tiempo a algo; **to ~ energy into sth** volcarse en algo II. *vi* 1. (*flow in large amounts: water*) fluir; (*letters, messages*) llegar en grandes cantidades; **to ~ into sth** (*sunshine*) entrar a raudales en algo; **refugees are ~ing into the country** no cesan de llegar refugiados al país 2. *impers* **it's ~ing** llueve a cántaros

◆**pour in** *vi* llegar en abundancia

◆**pour out** I. *vt* 1. (*from container*) verter 2. (*cause to flow quickly: smoke, water*) echar 3. (*tell*) **to ~ sth to sb** revelar algo a alguien II. *vi* (*liquid*) salir; (*people*) salir en tropel

pout [paʊt] I. *vi* hacer un mohín II. *vt* **to ~ one's lips** hacer un mohín III. *n* mohín *m*

poverty ['pɑv·ər·t̬i] *n* 1. (*lack of money*) pobreza *f* 2. *fig* (*lack of ideas, imagination*) escasez *f*

poverty-stricken ['pɑv·ər·t̬i·ˌstrɪk·ən] *adj* muy pobre

POW [ˌpi·oʊ·ˈdʌb·əl·ju] *n abbr of* **prisoner of war** prisionero, -a *m, f* de guerra

powder ['paʊ·dər] I. *n* 1. (*dust*) polvo *m;* **to crush** [*or* **reduce**] **sth to a ~** reducir algo a polvo 2. (*makeup*) polvos *mpl;* **talcum ~** polvos (de) talco II. *vt* 1. (*cover with powder*) empolvar; **to ~ one's face** empolvarse; **to ~ one's**

nose *fig* ir al servicio 2. (*sprinkle*) espolvorear

powdered *adj* en polvo; **~ sugar** azúcar *m* glas

powdery ['paʊ·də·ri] *adj* como de polvo

power ['paʊ·ər] I. *n* 1. (*ability to control*) poder *m;* **to be within one's ~ to do sth** estar en manos de alguien hacer algo 2. (*country, organization, person*) potencia *f* 3. (*right*) derecho *m* 4. (*ability*) capacidad *f;* **sb's ~s of concentration/persuasion/observation** la capacidad de concentración/persuasión/observación de alguien 5. (*strength*) fuerza *f* 6. (*electricity*) electricidad *f;* **to cut (off) the ~** cortar la corriente 7. (*energy*) energía *f* 8. MATH potencia *f;* **two to the ~ of five** dos elevado a la quinta potencia II. *vt* impulsar

powerboat *n* lancha *f* fuera borda

power brakes *npl* AUTO frenos *m pl* asistidos, servofrenos *mpl*

power cable *n* cable *m* de energía eléctrica

powerful ['paʊ·ər·fəl] *adj* 1. (*influential, mighty*) poderoso, -a 2. (*physically strong*) fuerte 3. (*having a great effect*) convincente 4. (*anger, jealousy*) intenso, -a 5. (*able to perform well*) potente

powerfully ['paʊ·ər·fə·li] *adv* 1. (*using great force*) con potencia 2. (*argue, speak*) de forma convincente

powerless ['paʊ·ər·lɪs] *adj* impotente; **to be ~ against sb** no poder hacer nada contra alguien

power line *n* línea *f* eléctrica

power plant *n* central *f* eléctrica; **nuclear ~** central *f* nuclear

power station *n* central *f* eléctrica

power steering *n* dirección *f* asistida

pox [pɑks] *n* 1. MED (*chickenpox*) varicela *f;* (*smallpox*) viruela *f;* (*syphilis*) sífilis *f inv*

pp. *abbr of* **pages** págs.

PR ['pi·ˈɑr] *n* 1. *abbr of* **public relations** relaciones *f pl* públicas 2. GEO *abbr of* **Puerto Rico** Puerto Rico *m*

practicable ['præk·tɪ·kə·bəl] *adj form* factible

practical ['præk·tɪ·kəl] I. *adj* práctico, -a

P

II. *n* examen *m* práctico

practical joke *n* broma *f* pesada, trastada *f*

practically ['præk·tɪk·li] *adv* 1. (*almost*) casi 2. (*of a practical nature*) **to be ~ based** basarse en la práctica; **to be ~ minded** tener sentido práctico

practice ['præk·tɪs] I. *n* 1. (*act of practicing*) práctica *f*; **to be out of ~** estar desentrenado; **~ makes perfect** se aprende con la práctica 2. (*custom, regular activity*) costumbre *f*; **standard ~** práctica *f* habitual 3. (*training session*) entrenamiento *m* 4. (*of a profession*) ejercicio *m* 5. (*business, office*) bufete *m*; (*medical*) consulta *f* II. *vt* 1. (*do, carry out*) practicar 2. (*improve skill*) hacer ejercicios de; **to ~ the piano** estudiar el piano 3. (*work in: medicine, law*) ejercer ▶ **to ~ what one preaches** predicar con el ejemplo III. *vi* 1. (*improve skill*) practicar; SPORTS entrenarse 2. (*work in profession*) ejercer; **to ~ as a doctor** ejercer de médico

practiced ['præk·tɪst] *adj* (*experienced, skilled*) experto, -a; **a ~ liar** un mentiroso consumado

practicing ['præk·tɪs·ɪŋ] *adj* (*doctor, lawyer*) en ejercicio; (*Catholic, Jew*) practicante

practitioner [præk·'tɪʃ·ə·nər] *n* (*of a skill*) profesional *mf*; (*doctor*) médico, -a *m, f*; **legal ~** abogado, -a *m, f*

praise [preɪz] I. *vt* 1. (*express approval*) elogiar 2. (*worship*) alabar II. *n* 1. (*expression of approval*) elogio *m* 2. (*worship*) alabanza *f*

praiseworthy ['preɪz·wɜr·ði] *adj* loable

prank [præŋk] *n* broma *f*; **to play a ~ on sb** gastar una broma a alguien

prattle ['præt·əl] I. *vi* parlotear; (*child*) balbucear II. *n* parloteo *m*; (*of child*) balbuceo *m*

prawn [prɔn] *n* gamba *f*

pray [preɪ] I. *vi* 1. REL rezar 2. (*hope*) **to ~ for sth** rezar para obtener [*or* que ocurra] algo II. *vt* suplicar; **and what, ~ tell, are you doing?** ¿qué estás haciendo, si se puede saber?

prayer [prer] *n* 1. REL oración *f*; **to say a ~** [*or* one's **~s**] rezar 2. (*action of*

praying) rezo *m* 3. **~s** (*church service*) **morning/evening ~s** misa matinal/ vespertina 4. *fig* (*hope*) súplica *f*

praying mantis ['preɪ·ɪŋ·'mæn·tɪs] *n* mantis *f inv* religiosa

preach [pritʃ] I. *vi* predicar; **to ~ at sb** *pej* sermonear a alguien II. *vt* 1. REL (*a sermon, the Gospel*) predicar 2. (*advocate*) abogar por ▶ **to practice what you ~** predicar con el ejemplo

preacher ['pri·tʃər] *n* predicador(a) *m(f)*

precarious [prɪ·'ker·i·əs] *adj* precario, -a

precaution [prɪ·'kɔ·ʃən] *n* precaución *f*

precautionary [‚prɪ·'kɔ·ʃə·ner·i] *adj* de precaución; **~ measure** medida *f* preventiva

precede [prɪ·'sid] *vt* preceder

precedence ['pres·ə·dəns] *n* 1. (*priority*) prioridad *f*; **to take ~ over sb** tener prioridad sobre alguien 2. (*order of priority*) preferencia *f*

precedent ['pres·ə·dent] *n* precedente *m*; **to set a ~** (*for sth/doing sth*) sentar un precedente (para algo/hacer algo)

preceding [prɪ·'si·dɪŋ] *adj* precedente; **the ~ day** el día anterior

precinct ['pri·sɪŋkt] *n* 1. (*police district*) distrito *m* policial 2. (*electoral district*) distrito *m* 3. *form* (*environs*) alrededores *mpl*

precious ['preʃ·əs] *adj* 1. (*valuable: stone, metal*) precioso, -a 2. (*beloved: child, pet*) querido, -a 3. (*affected*) afectado, -a; (*person*) amanerado, -a

precipice ['pres·ə·pɪs] *n* precipicio *m*

précis [preɪ·'si] I. *n* resumen *m* II. *vt form* resumir

precise [prɪ·'saɪs] *adj* preciso, -a

precisely *adv* 1. (*exactly*) precisamente; **~!** ¡eso es! 2. (*carefully*) meticulosamente

precision [prɪ·'sɪʒ·ən] *n* 1. (*accuracy*) precisión *f* 2. (*meticulous care*) exactitud *f*

preclude [prɪ·'klud] *vt form* excluir

precocious [prɪ·'kou·ʃəs] *adj* precoz

precociousness *n*, **precocity** [prɪ·'kas·ə·ti] *n form* precocidad *f*

preconceived [‚pri·kən·'sivd] *adj* preconcebido, -a

preconception [‚pri·kən·'sep·ʃən] *n* idea

f preconcebida

precondition [ˌpriˈkən·dɪʃ·ən] *n* condición *f* previa

predate [priˈdeɪt] *vt* preceder

predator [ˈpred·ə·tər] *n* depredador *m*

predatory [ˈpred·ə·tɔr·i] *adj* depredador(a)

predecessor [ˈpred·ə·ses·ər] *n* predecesor(a) *m(f)*; (*ancestor*) antepasado, -a *m, f*

predestination [ˌpri·des·tɪ·ˈneɪ·ʃən] *n* predestinación *f*

predicament [prɪˈdɪk·ə·mənt] *n* apuro *m*

predict [prɪˈdɪkt] *vt* predecir

predictable [prɪˈdɪk·tə·bəl] *adj* previsible

prediction [prɪˈdɪk·ʃən] *n* 1. (*forecast*) pronóstico *m* 2. (*act of predicting*) predicción *f*

predominance [prɪˈdam·ə·nəns] *n* predominio *m*

predominant [prɪˈdam·ə·nənt] *adj* predominante

predominate [prɪˈdam·ə·neɪt] *vi* predominar

preemptive [priˈemp·tɪv] *adj* 1. (*right*) prioritario, -a 2. (*attack*) preventivo, -a

prefab [ˈpri·fæb] *adj inf abbr of* **prefabricated** prefabricado, -a

prefabricate [ˌpriˈfæb·rɪ·keɪt] *vt* prefabricar

preface [ˈpref·ɪs] *n* prefacio *m*

prefect [ˈpri·fekt] *n* prefecto *m*

prefer [prɪˈfɜr] <-rr-> *vt* preferir

preferable [ˈpref·ə·bəl] *adj* preferible

preferably [ˈpref·ə·bli] *adv* preferentemente, preferiblemente

preference [ˈpref·rəns] *n* 1. (*liking better*) preferencia *f* 2. (*priority*) preferencia *f*

preferential [ˌpref·ə·ˈren·ʃəl] *adj* preferente; ECON preferencial

preferred [prɪˈfɜrd] *adj* preferido, -a

prefix [ˈpri·fɪks] <-es> *n* prefijo *m*

pregnancy [ˈpreg·nən·si] *n* 1. (*condition: woman*) embarazo *m*; ZOOL preñez *f* 2. (*period of time*) embarazo *m*

pregnancy test *n* prueba *f* de embarazo

pregnant [ˈpreg·nənt] *adj* 1. (*woman*) embarazada; (*animal*) preñado; **to become ~** (*woman*) quedarse embarazada; **to get sb ~** dejar embarazada a alguien 2. *fig* (*silence, pause*) muy significativo, -a

prehistoric [ˌpri·hɪˈstɔr·ɪk] *adj* prehistórico, -a

prehistory [ˌpriˈhɪs·tə·ri] *n* prehistoria *f*

prejudge [ˌpriˈdʒʌdʒ] *vt* prejuzgar

prejudice [ˈpred·ʒə·dɪs] *n* 1. (*preconceived opinion*) prejuicio *m* 2. (*bias*) parcialidad *f*; LAW perjuicio *m*

prejudiced [ˈpred·ʒə·dɪst] *adj* (*person*) lleno, -a de prejuicios; (*attitude, judgment, opinion*) parcial; **to be ~ in favor of/against sb** estar predispuesto a favor de/contra alguien

prejudicial [ˌpred·ʒə·ˈdɪʃ·əl] *adj form* perjudicial

preliminary [prɪˈlɪm·ə·ner·i] I. *adj* preliminar II. <-ies> *n* 1. (*introduction*) preparativos *mpl* 2. SPORTS (*heat*) rondas *f pl* previas 3. *form* (*preliminary exam*) examen *m* preliminar

prelude [ˈprel·jud] *n* preludio *m*

premarital [ˌpriˈmær·ɪ·təl] *adj* prematrimonial

premature [ˌpri·mə·ˈtʃʊr] *adj* prematuro, -a

premeditated [ˌpriˈmed·ɪ·ter·ɪd] *adj* premeditado, -a

premier [prɪˈmɪr] *n* POL primer ministro *m*, primera ministra *f*

première [prɪˈmɪr] *n* estreno *m*

premise [ˈprem·ɪs] *n* 1. (*of argument*) premisa *f*; **on** [*or* **under**] **the ~ that...** en el supuesto de que... 2. *pl* (*land and building on it*) recinto *m*

premium [ˈpri·mi·əm] I. *n* 1. (*insurance payment*) prima *f* 2. (*extra charge*) recargo *m*; (*high price*) precio *m* con prima [*or* inflado] 3. (*bonus*) prima *f* 4. (*importance*) **to put a ~ on sth** darle (gran) importancia a algo 5. (*gasoline*) súper *f* II. *adj* de primera calidad

preoccupation [ˌpri·ak·jə·ˈpeɪ·ʃən] *n* preocupación *f*

preoccupied [priˈak·ju·paɪd] *adj* preocupado, -a

preoccupy [priˈak·ju·paɪ] <-ie-> *vt* preocupar

P

prep [prep] I. *adj abbr of* **preparatory** preparatorio, -a II. *n inf abbr of* **preparation** preparación *f*

prepaid [ˌpriːˈpeɪd] *adj* pagado, -a por adelantado; **~ phone** [*or* **calling**] **card** tarjeta (telefónica) de prepago

preparation [ˌprep·əˈreɪ·ʃən] *n* 1. (*getting ready*) preparación *f* 2. (*substance*) preparado *m* 3. *pl* (*measures*) preparativos *mpl*

preparatory [prɪˈpær·ə·tɔːr·i] *adj* preliminar, preparatorio, -a

prepare [prɪˈper] I. *vt* preparar; **to ~ sb for sth** preparar a alguien para algo II. *vi* prepararse; **to ~ for action** prepararse para actuar

prepared [prɪˈperd] *adj* 1. (*ready*) listo, -a 2. (*willing*) dispuesto, -a 3. (*food, speech*) preparado, -a de antemano

prepay [ˌpriːˈpeɪ] *vt irr* pagar por adelantado

prepayment [ˌpriːˈpeɪ·mənt] *n* pago *m* por adelantado

preposition [ˌprep·əˈzɪʃ·ən] *n* preposición *f*

preschool [ˈpriː·skuːl] I. *n* jardín *m* de infancia II. *adj* preescolar

prescribe [prɪˈskraɪb] I. *vt* 1. MED recetar; (*rest, diet*) recomendar 2. *form* (*order*) prescribir; **~d by law** establecido por la ley II. *vi* MED hacer una receta

prescription [prɪˈskrɪp·ʃən] *n* 1. MED receta *f*; **only available with a ~** sólo con receta médica; **to make out a ~** extender una receta 2. *form* (*act of prescribing*) prescripción *f*

presence [ˈprez·əns] *n* 1. (*attendance*) presencia *f*; **~ of mind** presencia de ánimo; **in sb's ~** en presencia de alguien; **in my ~** delante de mí; **your ~ is requested** se ruega su asistencia; **to make one's ~ felt** hacerse notar 2. (*personality*) carisma *m*

present[1] [ˈprez·ənt] I. *n* presente *m* ▶ **at ~** en este momento; **for the ~** por ahora II. *adj* 1. (*current: address, generation*) actual; **at the ~ moment** [*or* **time**] en este momento; **the ~ year** el año en curso; **in the ~ case** en este caso; **up to the ~ time** hasta la fecha 2. (*in attendance*) presente; **to be ~**

at sth asistir a algo; **all those ~** todos los presentes

present[2] [ˈprez·ənt] *n* (*gift*) regalo *m*; **to give sb a ~** hacer un regalo a alguien; **I got it as a ~** me lo regalaron

present[3] [prɪˈzent] *vt* 1. (*give*) presentar; **to ~ one's apologies to sb** *form* presentar sus disculpas a alguien; **to ~ one's credentials** presentar sus credenciales; **to ~ sth** (**to sb**) entregar algo (a alguien) 2. (*introduce*) presentar; **to ~ sb to sb** presentar alguien a alguien; **may I ~ my wife?** permítame presentarle a mi esposa 3. (*to an audience: play, musical, concert*) presentar; **~ing X as Julius Caesar** con X en el papel de Julio César 4. (*confront*) **to ~ sb with sth** enfrentar a alguien con algo; **to be ~ed with a complicated situation** verse frente a una situación complicada 5. (*constitute*) constituir; **to ~ a problem for sb** significar [*or* suponer] un problema para alguien 6. (*offer*) ofrecer; (*view, atmosphere*) presentar 7. (*exhibit: argument, plan, theory*) exponer; (*check, passport, ticket*) presentar; **to ~ a petition to sb** elevar una petición a alguien *elev* 8. MIL **to ~ arms** presentar armas 9. (*appear*) **to ~ oneself for sth** presentarse a algo

presentable [prɪˈzen·tə·bəl] *adj* presentable; **to make oneself ~** arreglarse

presentation [ˌpre·zənˈteɪ·ʃən] *n* 1. (*act*) presentación *f*; (*of theory, dissertation*) exposición *f*; **to make** [*or* **give**] **a ~** hacer una exposición; **on ~ of this voucher** al presentar este vale 2. (*of prize, award*) entrega *f*

present-day [ˌprez·əntˈdeɪ] *adj* actual; **~ Boston** el Boston de hoy (en) día

presenter [prɪˈzen·tər] *n* presentador(a) *m(f)*

presently [ˈprez·ənt·li] *adv* 1. (*soon*) pronto; **I'll be there ~** voy enseguida 2. (*now*) ahora

present participle *n* LING participio *m* presente

present tense *n* LING tiempo *m* presente

preservation [ˌprez·ərˈveɪ·ʃən] *n* 1. (*of*

building) conservación *f;* **to be in a poor/good state of ~** estar en mal/buen estado de conservación **2.** (*of species, custom*) preservación *f*

preservative [prɪˈzɜːvətɪv] **I.** *adj* preservativo, -a **II.** *n* conservante *m;* **without artificial ~s** sin conservantes (artificiales)

preserve [prɪˈzɜːv] **I.** *vt* **1.** (*maintain: customs, peace*) mantener; (*dignity, sense of humor, building*) conservar; (*appearance, silence*) guardar **2.** (*food*) conservar **3.** (*protect*) proteger; **to ~ sb from sth** proteger a alguien de algo **II.** *n* **1.** **~s** (*jam*) confitura *f* **2.** (*reserve*) coto *m,* vedado *m;* **wildlife ~** reserva *f* de animales **3.** *fig* (*domain*) terreno *m;* **to be the ~ of the rich** ser dominio exclusivo de los ricos

preserved *adj* **1.** (*maintained*) conservado, -a; **to be badly ~** estar mal conservado **2.** (*food*) en conserva; **~ food** conservas *fpl*

presidency [ˈprezɪdənsi] *n* POL presidencia *f;* (*of president*) presidencia *f;* (*of company*) dirección *f* **2.** (*tenure as president*) mandato *m* (presidencial)

president [ˈprezɪdənt] *n* POL presidente, -a *m, f;* (*of company*) director(a) *m(f)*

presidential [ˌprezɪˈdenˌtʃəl] *adj* presidencial

press [pres] **I.** *vt* **1.** (*push: button, switch*) pulsar; (*doorbell*) tocar; (*trigger*) apretar; **to ~ sth down** apretar algo **2.** (*squeeze*) apretar; **the crowd ~ed us against the locked door** la multitud nos apretujaba contra la puerta cerrada **3.** (*flatten: flowers, grapes, olives*) prensar **4.** (*extract juice*) exprimir **5.** (*iron: shirt, dress*) planchar **6.** MUS (*album, disk*) imprimir **7.** (*try to force*) presionar; **to ~ sb to do sth** presionar a alguien para que haga algo; **to ~ sb for payment** acosar a alguien para que pague **8.** (*find difficult*) **to be (hard) ~ed to do sth** tener dificultad para hacer algo **9.** (*be short of*) **to be ~ed for money/time** andar escaso de dinero/tiempo **10.** (*pursue*) insistir; **to ~ a claim/one's case** insistir en una petición/sus argumentos; **to ~ a point** insistir en algo

11. LAW **to ~ charges** presentar cargos **II.** *vi* **1.** (*push*) apretar; **to ~ hard** apretar fuerte; **to ~ on the brakes** pisar el freno **2.** (*crowd*) apiñarse; **to ~ through the crowd** abrirse paso entre el gentío; **to ~ down (on sth)** hacer presión (sobre algo) **3.** (*be urgent*) urgir; **time is ~ing** el tiempo apremia **4.** (*put under pressure*) hacer presión; **to ~ for sth** insistir para conseguir algo **III.** *n* **1.** (*push*) presión *f;* (*with hand*) apretón *m;* **at the ~ of a button** apretando un botón **2.** (*ironing*) planchado *m;* **to give sth a ~** planchar algo **3.** (*crush*) apiñamiento *m* **4.** (*machine*) prensa *f;* **printing ~** imprenta *f;* **to be in ~** estar en prensa; **to go to ~** (*newspaper, book*) ir a imprenta **5.** PUBL **the ~** la prensa; **to have bad/good ~** (*publicity*) tener mala/buena prensa

press on *vi* seguir adelante

press agency *n* agencia *f* de prensa

press card *n* acreditación *f* de prensa

press conference *n* rueda *f* de prensa; **to hold a ~** dar una rueda de prensa

press coverage *n* cobertura *f* periodística

pressing I. *adj* (*issue, matter*) urgente; (*need*) apremiante **II.** *n* (*of clothes*) planchado *m;* (*of records, fruits*) prensado *m*

press office *n* oficina *f* de prensa

press release *n* comunicado *m* de prensa; **to issue a ~** emitir un comunicado

pressure [ˈpreʃər] **I.** *n* **1. a.** PHYS presión *f;* **high/low ~** presión alta/baja; **to put ~ on sth** hacer presión sobre algo; **at full ~** a toda presión; **to be under ~ a.** *fig* estar bajo presión **2.** (*influence*) **to put ~ on sb (to do sth)** presionar a alguien (para que haga algo); **under the ~ of circumstances** presionado por las circunstancias **3.** **~s** (*stressful circumstances*) **the ~s of life/work** tensiones en la vida/el trabajo **4.** MED tensión *f;* **blood ~** tensión arterial **5.** PHYS (*force*) presión *f* **II.** *vt* **to ~ sb to do sth** presionar a alguien para que haga algo

pressure cooker *n* olla *f* a presión

pressure gauge *n* manómetro *m*

pressure group *n* POL grupo *m* de presión

pressurize ['preʃ·ə·raɪz] *vt* **1.** (*control air pressure*) presurizar **2.** *inf* (*person, government*) presionar; **to ~ sb into doing sth** forzar a alguien a hacer algo

prestige [preˈstiːʒ] *n* prestigio *m*

prestigious [preˈstɪdʒ·əs] *adj* prestigioso, -a

presumably [prɪˈzuː·mə·bli] *adv* presumiblemente

presume [prɪˈzum] **I.** *vt* **1.** (*suppose*) suponer; **to ~ that...** imaginarse que...; **~d dead** dado por muerto; **to be ~d innocent** ser presuntamente inocente **2.** (*dare*) **to ~ to do sth** atreverse a hacer algo **II.** *vi* **1.** (*be presumptuous*) presumir; **I don't wish to ~, but...** no quisiera parecer impertinente, pero... **2.** (*assume*) **Dr Smith, I ~?** usted debe de ser el Dr. Smith

presumption [prɪˈzʌmp·ʃən] *n* **1.** (*assumption*) suposición *f*; **the ~ of innocence** LAW la presunción de inocencia **2.** *form* (*arrogance*) presunción *f* **3.** (*daring*) atrevimiento *m*

presumptuous [prɪˈzʌmp·tʃu·əs] *adj* **1.** (*arrogant*) impertinente **2.** (*forward*) osado, -a

pretax [ˌpriːˈtæks] *adj* antes de impuestos, bruto, -a

pretend [prɪˈtend] **I.** *vt* **1.** (*make believe*) fingir; **to ~ to be interested** fingir interés; **to ~ to be dead** hacerse el muerto; **to ~ to be sb** hacerse pasar por alguien **2.** (*claim*) pretender; **I don't ~ to know** no pretendo saber **II.** *vi* fingir; **he's just ~ing** sólo está fingiendo

pretender *n* pretendiente *mf*

pretense ['priː·tens] *n* **1.** (*simulation*) fingimiento *m*, apariencia *f*; **to make a ~ of sth** fingir algo; **to make no ~ of sth** no disimular algo **2.** (*pretext*) pretexto *m*; **under (the) ~ of...** con el pretexto de...; **to do sth under false ~s** hacer algo bajo un falso pretexto **3.** (*claim*) pretensión *f*; **to make no ~ to objectivity/innocence** no pretender ser totalmente objetivo/inocente

pretentious [prɪˈten·ʃəs] *adj* pretencioso, -a

pretext ['priː·tekst] *n* pretexto *m*; **a ~ for doing sth** un pretexto para hacer algo; **on the ~ that...** con el pretexto de que...; **under the ~ of doing sth** so pretexto de hacer algo *elev*

pretty ['prɪt·i] **I.** *adj* <-ier, -iest> **1.** (*beautiful: thing*) bonito, -a, lindo, -a *AmL*; (*child, woman*) guapo, -a, lindo, -a *AmL*; **not a ~ sight** nada agradable de ver **2.** *inf* (*considerable*) menudo, -a; **~ mess** menudo lío *m* **II.** *adv* **1.** (*quite*) bastante **2.** **~ much** más o menos; **to be ~ much the same** ser prácticamente lo mismo; **~ well everything** casi todo

prevail [prɪˈveɪl] *vi* **1.** (*triumph*) prevalecer; **to ~ over/against sth** prevalecer sobre/contra algo; **to ~ over/against sb** triunfar sobre/contra alguien **2.** (*predominate*) predominar; (*conditions, situation*) imperar **3.** (*convince*) **to ~ (up)on sb (to do sth)** *form* convencer a alguien (para que haga algo)

prevailing *adj* predominante; (*atmosphere, feelings*) reinante; **under the ~ circumstances** en las circunstancias actuales

prevent [prɪˈvent] *vt* **1.** (*hamper*) impedir; **to ~ sb from doing sth** impedir que alguien haga algo **2.** (*avoid*) prevenir; (*confusion, panic, crime*) evitar

prevention [prɪˈven·ʃən] *n* prevención *f*; **for the ~ of crime** para evitar la delincuencia ► **~ is better than cure** *prov* más vale prevenir que curar *prov*

preventive [prɪˈven·tɪv] *adj* preventivo, -a

preview ['priː·vjuː] *n* CINE, THEAT preestreno *m*; (*of TV program, exhibition*) adelanto *m*

previous ['priː·vi·əs] *adj* **1.** (*former*) anterior; **on the ~ day/week** el día/ la semana anterior; **no ~ experience required** no se necesita experiencia **2.** (*prior*) previo, -a

previously *adv* **1.** (*beforehand*) previamente **2.** (*formerly*) anteriormente; **to have met sb ~** haber visto a alguien antes

prey [preɪ] *n* **1.** (*animal*) presa *f*; **bird of ~** ave *f* de presa **2.** (*person*) víctima *f*; **to be easy ~ for sb** ser presa fácil para alguien; **to fall ~ to** (*animal*) ser presa de; (*person*) ser víctima de

price [praɪs] I. n 1. COM precio m; oil ~s, the ~ of oil el precio del petróleo; to ask a high/low ~ pedir un precio alto/bajo; to be the same ~ valer [or costar] lo mismo; to go up/down in ~ subir/bajar de precio; to name a ~ pedir un precio; what ~ are apples? ¿a cuánto están las manzanas? 2. FIN (of stocks) cotización f, precio m 3. fig (disadvantage) precio m; the ~ of fame el precio de la fama; beyond [or without] ~ sin precio; to set a high ~ on sth valorar mucho algo ▶ to set a ~ on one's head poner precio a la cabeza de alguien; at any ~ a toda costa; not at any ~ por nada del mundo; to pay a heavy ~ pagarlo caro; to pay the ~ pagar caro; at a ~ a un precio muy alto II. vt 1. (mark with price tag) poner el precio a 2. (fix price) poner precio a; to be reasonably ~d tener un precio razonable

price bracket n gama f de precios

price control n control m de precios

priceless ['praɪs·lɪs] adj 1. (invaluable) incalculable; to be ~ no tener precio 2. fig (funny) divertidísimo, -a; that's ~! ¡eso es para partirse de risa! inf

price list n lista f de precios

price tag n 1. (label) etiqueta f (del precio) 2. inf (cost) precio m

pricey ['praɪ·si] adj <pricier, priciest> inf (object) carillo, -a; (shop) carero, -a

pricing ['praɪ·sɪŋ] n fijación f de precios

prick [prɪk] I. vt 1. (jab) pinchar, picar; to ~ sb's conscience hacer que a alguien le remuerda la conciencia 2. (mark with holes) agujerear 3. (listen: animal) to ~ one's ears levantar las orejas; (person) aguzar el oído II. vi 1. (pin) pinchar 2. (hurt: eyes, skin) escocer III. n 1. (act, pain) pinchazo m 2. (mark) agujero m

prickle ['prɪk·əl] I. n 1. (thorn: of plant) pincho m; (of animal) púa f 2. (tingle) picor m; to feel a ~ of excitement sentir un cosquilleo de emoción II. vi 1. (cause prickling sensation) picar 2. (tingle) sentir picor 3. (prick) pinchar III. vt (prick) pinchar, picar

prickly ['prɪk·li] <-ier, -iest> adj 1. (thorny: plant) espinoso, -a; (animal con púas 2. (tingling) que pica; (beard) que pincha; ~ sensation picor m

pride [praɪd] I. n 1. (proud feeling) orgullo m; to take ~ in sth enorgullecerse de algo; (one's work) esmerarse en algo; to be sb's ~ and joy ser el orgullo de alguien 2. (self-respect) amor m propio; to hurt sb's ~ herir el orgullo de alguien; to swallow one's ~ tragarse el orgullo 3. (arrogance) soberbia f II. vt to ~ oneself on (doing) sth enorgullecerse de (hacer) algo; to ~ oneself that... preciarse de que...

priest [prist] n REL cura m

priesthood ['prist·hʊd] n REL 1. (position, office) sacerdocio m; to enter the ~ ser ordenado sacerdote 2. (priests in general) clero m

primarily [praɪ'mer·ə·li] adv principalmente

primary ['praɪ·mer·i] I. adj 1. (principal) fundamental; (aim) prioritario, -a 2. (basic) primario, -a; (industry) de base, primario, -a II. <-ies> n POL elecciones f pl primarias

primary school n escuela f (de enseñanza) primaria

prime [praɪm] I. adj 1. (main) principal; (objective) prioritario, -a; of ~ importance de importancia primordial 2. (first-rate) excelente; (beef) de primera calidad; in ~ condition en perfecto estado II. n 1. (best stage) apogeo m elev; to be in one's ~, to be in the ~ of life estar en la flor de la vida 2. (prime number) número m primo III. vt 1. (apply undercoat: surface) aplicar una capa de base sobre 2. (prepare for exploding: gun, pump, motor) cebar 3. (brief) informar; (prepare) to ~ sb for doing sth preparar a alguien para hacer algo 4. (make drunk) emborrachar

prime minister n POL primer(a) ministro, -a m, f

prime number n MATH número m primo

primer ['praɪ·mər] n 1. (paint) (pintura f for al de) imprimación f; a ~ coat una primera mano 2. (explosive) cebo m 3. (textbook) manual m; (for learning to read) cartilla f

prime time *n* RADIO, TV horas *f pl* de máxima audiencia

primitive ['prɪm·ɪ·t̬ɪv] I. *adj a.* ART, HIST, ZOOL primitivo, -a II. *n* ART, HIST, SOCIOL primitivo, -a *m, f*

primrose ['prɪm·roʊz] *n,* **primula** ['prɪm·jə·lə] *n* BOT prímula *f,* primavera *f*

prince [prɪns] *n* príncipe *m;* **crown ~** príncipe heredero; **Prince Charming** príncipe azul; **Prince of Wales** Príncipe de Gales

princess ['prɪn·sɪs] *n* princesa *f*

principal ['prɪn·sə·pəl] I. *adj* principal II. *n* (*head of a school*) director(a) *m(f)*

principle ['prɪn·sə·pəl] *n* principio *m;* **in ~** en principio; **on ~** por principio

print [prɪnt] I. *n* 1. (*handwriting*) texto *m* impreso; (*type*) **bold ~** negrita *f* 2. (*printed form*) **to appear in ~** publicarse; **to go out of ~** agotarse 3. (*of artwork*) copia *f;* (*engraving*) grabado *m;* PHOT positivo *m* 4. (*printed pattern*) estampado *m* 5. **~s** *pl* (*fingerprints*) huella *f* II. *vt* 1. (*publish*) publicar 2. (*put into printed form*) imprimir 3. COMPUT (*make printout of*) imprimir 4. PHOT positivar 5. (*mark fabric*) estampar III. *vi* 1. (*appear in printed form*) imprimirse 2. (*write in unjoined letters*) escribir con letra de imprenta

printer ['prɪn·t̬ər] *n* COMPUT impresora *f;* **inkjet/laser ~** impresora de chorro de tinta/láser

printing *n* 1. (*art*) imprenta *f* 2. (*action*) impresión *f*

printing press *n* prensa *f,* imprenta *f*

printout ['prɪnt·aʊt] *n* COMPUT impresión *f,* listado *m*

print run *n* tirada *f*

prior ['praɪ·ər] I. *adv form* (*before*) antes; **~ to doing sth** antes de hacer algo II. *adj form* 1. (*earlier*) previo, -a; **without ~ notice** sin previo aviso 2. (*preferred*) preferente III. *n* REL prior *m*

priority [praɪ·'ɔr·ə·t̬i]. I. <-ies> *n* 1. (*being most important*) prioridad *f;* (*in time*) anterioridad *f* 2. *pl* (*order of importance*) prioridades *fpl;* **to set priorities** establecer un orden de prioridades II. *adj* 1. (*of utmost importance*)

prioritario, -a 2. (*claim, right*) *a.* FIN preferente

priory ['praɪ·ə·ri] *n* priorato *m*

prism ['prɪz·əm] *n* prisma *m*

prison ['prɪz·ən] *n* prisión *f;* **to go to ~** ir a la cárcel

prison camp *n* campo *m* de prisioneros

prison cell *n* celda *f*

prisoner ['prɪz·ə·nər] *n* preso, -a *m, f;* MIL prisionero, -a *m, f;* **to hold sb ~** detener a alguien

prison inmate *n* recluso, -a *m, f*

privacy ['praɪ·və·si] *n* intimidad *f;* **I'd like some ~** me gustaría estar a solas

private ['praɪ·vət] I. *adj* 1. (*not public*) privado, -a 2. (*confidential*) confidencial; **he's a very ~ person** es una persona muy reservada 3. (*intimate*) íntimo, -a; **~ parts** partes *f pl* pudendas II. *n* 1. **~s** *inf* (*genitals*) partes *fpl* 2. MIL soldado *m* raso

privately ['praɪ·vət·li] *adv* 1. (*in private*) en privado 2. (*secretly*) en secreto 3. (*personally*) personalmente

privatization [ˌpraɪ·və·t̬ɪ·'zeɪ·ʃən] *n* privatización *f*

privatize ['praɪ·və·taɪz] *vt* privatizar

privilege ['prɪv·ə·lɪdʒ] I. *n* 1. (*special right*) privilegio *m* 2. (*honor*) honor *m* II. *vt* **to be ~d to do sth** tener el privilegio de hacer algo

privileged *adj* 1. (*special*) privilegiado, -a 2. (*confidential*) confidencial

privy ['prɪv·i] *n* (*toilet*) retrete *m*

prize[1] [praɪz] I. *n* 1. (*in competition*) premio *m;* **to take home a ~** ganar un premio 2. (*reward*) recompensa *f* II. *adj* 1. *inf* (*first-rate*) de primera 2. (*prize-winning*) premiado, -a III. *vt* apreciar; **to ~ sth highly** estimar algo mucho

prize[2] [praɪz] *vt see* **pry**[2]

prize list *n* lista *f* de premiados

prize money *n* SPORTS premio *m* en metálico

pro[1] [proʊ] *adj inf abbr of* **professional** profesional

pro[2] [proʊ] I. *adv* a favor II. *n inf* pro *m;* **the ~s and cons of sth** los pros y los contras de algo III. *prep* pro IV. *adj* favorable

probability [ˌprab·ə·'bɪl·ə·t̬i] *n* probabilidad f; **in all** ~ sin duda

probable ['prab·ə·bəl] *adj* **1.** (*likely*) probable **2.** (*credible*) verosímil **3.** LAW ~ **cause** motivo *m* razonable

probably *adv* probablemente

probation [prou·'beɪ·fən] *n* **1.** (*at work*) período *m* de prueba **2.** LAW libertad *f* condicional

probe [proub] **I.** *vi* (*examine*) investigar; **to ~ into the possibilities** tantear las posibilidades; **to ~ into sb's private life** indagar en la vida privada de alguien **II.** *vt* **1.** (*examine*) investigar **2.** MED sondar **III.** *n* **1.** (*examination, investigation*) investigación *f* **2.** MED, AVIAT sonda *f*

problem ['prab·ləm] *n* problema *m*

problematic [,prab·lə·'mæt·ɪk] *adj*, **problematical** [,prab·lə·'mæt·ɪ·kəl] *adj* **1.** (*creating difficulty*) problemático, -a **2.** (*questionable, disputable*) dudoso, -a

procedure [prə·'si·dʒər] *n* procedimiento *m*

proceed [prou·'sid] *vi* **1.** (*move along*) seguir; **to ~ with sth** avanzar con algo; **to ~ against sb** proceder contra alguien; AVIAT (*to a gate*) dirigirse a **2.** (*come from*) **to ~ from** provenir de, proceder de **3.** (*start, begin*) **to ~ with sth** empezar con algo; **to ~ to do sth** ponerse a hacer algo

proceedings [prou·'si·dɪŋz] *npl* **1.** LAW proceso *m* **2.** *form* (*events*) actos *mpl* **3.** *form* (*minutes of meeting*) actas *fpl*

proceeds ['prou·sidz] *n* ingresos *mpl*

process[1] ['pras·es] **I.** *n* proceso *m*; **in the ~** mientras tanto; **to be in the ~ of doing sth** estar en vías de hacer algo **II.** *vt* **1. a.** TECH, COMPUT procesar **2.** PHOT revelar

process[2] [prə·'ses] *vi form* desfilar

processing ['pras·es·ɪŋ] *n* **1. a.** TECH, COMPUT procesamiento *m*; **data ~** procesamiento de datos **2.** PHOT revelado *m*

procession [prə·'sef·ən] *n* **1.** desfile *m*; **to go in ~** desfilar **2.** REL procesión *f* **3.** *fig* serie *f*

processor [prə·'ses·ər] *n* COMPUT procesador *m*

pro-choice *adj* proabortista

proclaim [prou·'kleɪm] *vt form* proclamar; **to ~ war** declarar la guerra

procrastinate [prou·'kræs·tə·neɪt] *vi* dejar para más tarde

procreate ['prou·kri·eɪt] *vi form* procrearse

prod [prad] **I.** *n* (*poke*) golpe *m*; (*with sharp object*) pinchazo *m*; (*with sharp object*) *fig* dar un empujón a alguien **II.** <-dd-> *vt* **1.** (*poke*) golpear; (*with sharp object*) pinchar **2.** (*encourage, urge on*) **to ~ sb** (*into doing sth*) estimular a alguien (para que haga algo)

prodigy ['prad·ə·dʒi] *n* prodigio *m*; **child ~** niño, -a *m, f* prodigio

produce[1] [prə·'dus] **I.** *vt* **1.** (*create*) producir; (*manufacture*) fabricar **2.** (*give birth to*) dar a luz **3.** CINE, THEAT, TV realizar, producir **4.** (*show*) mostrar; **to ~ a knife** sacar un cuchillo; **to ~ one's passport** enseñar el pasaporte **5.** (*cause*) causar; **to ~ results** producir resultados **II.** *vi* BOT (*bear fruit*) dar frutos

produce[2] ['prou·dus] *n* AGR productos *m pl* agrícolas; **the ~ section** (*in grocery store*) la sección de frutas y verduras

producer [prə·'du·sər] *n* productor(a) *m(f)*

product ['prad·əkt] *n* **1. a.** MATH producto *m* **2.** (*result*) resultado *m*

production [prə·'dʌk·fən] *n* **1.** (*of goods*) fabricación *f*; (*output of factory*) producción *f* **2.** CINE, THEAT, TV producción *f*

production costs *npl* costes *m pl* de producción

production line *n* cadena *f* de montaje

production manager *n* encargado, -a *m, f* de producción

productive [prə·'dʌk·tɪv] *adj* productivo, -a; (*writer*) prolífico, -a

productivity [,prou·dək·'tɪv·ə·t̬i] *n* productividad *f*

profane [prou·'feɪn] *adj* **1.** (*blasphemous*) blasfemo, -a **2.** *form* (*secular*) profano, -a

profanity [prou·'fæn·ə·t̬i] *n* **1.** (*blasphemy*) blasfemia *f* **2.** (*obscene language*) blasfemia *f* **3.** (*obscene word*) palabrota *f*

profess [prə·'fes] *vt* **1.** (*declare*) profesar;

P

to ~ **little enthusiasm** manifestar poco entusiasmo **2.** (*pretend*) **to ~ to be sth** pretender ser algo **3.** (*religion, Catholicism*) profesar

professed [prə·ˈfest] *adj* **1.** (*self-acknowledged*) declarado, -a **2.** (*alleged*) supuesto, -a

profession [prə·ˈfeʃ·ən] *n* **1.** (*occupation*) profesión *f;* **the teaching ~** la docencia **2.** (*declaration*) declaración *f*

professional [prə·ˈfeʃ·ə·nəl] **I.** *adj* **1.** (*related to profession*) profesional **2.** (*competent*) profesional **II.** *n* profesional *mf*

professor [prə·ˈfes·ər] *n* UNIV profesor(a) *m(f)*

proficiency [prə·ˈfɪʃ·ən·si] *n* competencia *f*

proficient [prə·ˈfɪʃ·ənt] *adj* competente

profile [ˈproʊ·faɪl] **I.** *n* **1.** (*side view*) perfil *m;* **in ~** de perfil **2.** (*description*) descripción *f;* **user ~** COMPUT perfil *m* de usuario ▶ **to keep a low ~** tratar de pasar inadvertido **II.** *vt* (*describe*) describir

profit [ˈprɑf·ɪt] **I.** *n* **1.** FIN beneficio *m* **2.** (*advantage*) provecho *m* **II.** *vi* **1.** (*benefit*) beneficiarse; **to ~ by sth** sacar provecho de algo **2.** (*make a profit*) ganar

profitability [ˌprɑf·ɪ·t̬ə·ˈbɪl·ə·t̬i] *n* rentabilidad *f*

profitable [ˈprɑf·ɪ·t̬ə·bəl] *adj* **1.** FIN rentable **2.** (*advantageous*) provechoso, -a

profit and loss *n* FIN pérdidas *f pl* y ganancias *fpl*

profiteering *n* pej especulación *f*

profit-making *adj* lucrativo, -a; **~ movie** película *f* taquillera

profit margin *n* margen *m* de beneficio

profound [prə·ˈfaʊnd] *adj* profundo, -a

prognosis [prɑg·ˈnoʊ·sɪs] *n* pronóstico *m*

program [ˈproʊ·græm] **I.** *n a.* COMPUT programa *m* **II.** <-mm-> *vt a.* COMPUT programar

programmable [ˈproʊ·græm·ə·bəl] *adj* programable

programmer *n a.* COMPUT programador(a) *m(f)*

programming *n a.* COMPUT programa-

ción *f*

progress¹ [ˈprɑg·res] *n* progreso *m;* **to make ~** avanzar; **to be in ~** estar en curso

progress² [proʊ·ˈgres] *vi* **1.** (*improve*) progresar **2.** (*continue onward*) avanzar

progression [prə·ˈgreʃ·ən] *n* **1.** (*development*) desarrollo *m;* (*of disease*) evolución *f* **2.** MATH (*series*) progresión *f*

progressive [prə·ˈgres·ɪv] *adj* **1.** (*by successive stages*) progresivo, -a; (*disease*) degenerativo, -a **2.** POL progresista **3.** (*modern*) moderno, -a **4.** MUS progresivo, -a **5.** LING continuo, -a

prohibit [proʊ·ˈhɪb·ɪt] *vt* **1.** (*forbid*) prohibir **2.** (*prevent*) impedir

prohibition [ˌproʊ·ə·ˈbɪʃ·ən] *n* **1.** (*ban*) prohibición *f* **2.** HIST **Prohibition** la Ley Seca

prohibitive [proʊ·ˈhɪb·ɪ·t̬ɪv] *adj* prohibitivo, -a

project¹ [ˈprɑdʒ·ekt] *n* **1.** (*undertaking, plan*) proyecto *m* **2.** SCHOOL, UNIV (*essay*) trabajo *m* **3.** (*social housing*) ≈viviendas *f pl* de protección oficial

project² [prə·ˈdʒekt] *vt* **1.** (*forecast*) pronosticar **2.** (*propel*) impulsar **3.** PSYCH proyectar; **to ~ sth onto sb** proyectar algo en alguien **4.** (*promote*) promover; **to ~ oneself** promocionarse

projection [prə·ˈdʒek·ʃən] *n* **1.** (*forecast*) pronóstico *m* **2.** PSYCH proyección *f*

projectionist *n* proyeccionista *mf*

project manager *n* coordinador(a) *m(f)* de proyectos, gestor(a) *m(f)* de proyectos

projector [prə·ˈdʒek·tər] *n* proyector *m*

prolific [proʊ·ˈlɪf·ɪk] *adj* **1.** (*producing a lot*) prolífico, -a **2.** (*having many offspring*) prolífico, -a

prolong [proʊ·ˈlɑŋ] *vt* prolongar; (*agony*) alargar

prom [prɑm] *n* (*school dance*) baile *m*

promenade [ˌprɑm·ə·ˈneɪd] *n form* (*walk*) paseo *m*

prominent [ˈprɑm·ə·nənt] *adj* **1.** (*conspicuous*) prominente **2.** (*teeth, chin*) saliente **3.** (*distinguished, well-known*) importante; (*position*) destacado, -a

promiscuous [prə·ˈmɪs·kju·əs] *adj* promiscuo, -a

promise ['pram·ɪs] I. vt (*pledge, have potential*) prometer; **to ~ to do sth** prometer hacer algo II. vi (*pledge*) prometer; **I ~!** ¡lo prometo! III. n 1. (*pledge*) promesa f; **to make a ~** prometer; **~s, ~s!** iron ¡promesas, promesas! 2. (*potential*) posibilidad f; **a young person of ~** un joven con porvenir; **to show ~** demostrar aptitudes

promising adj prometedor(a)

promote [prə·'moʊt] vt 1. (*in army, company, organization*) ascender; (*soccer team*) subir 2. (*encourage*) promover 3. (*advertise*) promocionar

promoter n promotor/a m(f)

promotion [prə·'moʊ·ʃən] n 1. (*in army, company, organization*) ascenso m 2. (*encouragement, advertising*) promoción f

promotional adj

promotional material n material m de promoción

prompt [prampt] I. vt 1. (*spur*) provocar; **to ~ sb to do sth** estimular a alguien para que haga algo 2. THEAT apuntar II. adj (*quick*) rápido, -a III. adv puntualmente IV. n 1. COMPUT línea f de comandos 2. THEAT (*prompter*) apuntador(a) m(f)

prompter ['pramp·tər] n THEAT apuntador(a) m(f)

promptly ['prampt·li] adv 1. (*quickly*) rápidamente 2. inf (*immediately afterward*) de inmediato

prone [proʊn] I. adj **to be ~ to doing sth** ser propenso a hacer algo II. adv boca abajo; **to lie ~ on the floor/table** estar tumbado boca abajo sobre el suelo/la mesa

prong [praŋ] n (*of fork*) diente m; (*of antler*) punta f

pronoun ['proʊ·naʊn] n LING pronombre m

pronounce [prə·'naʊns] vt 1. (*speak*) pronunciar 2. (*declare*) declarar; (*judgment*) dictaminar

pronounced adj pronunciado, -a; (*accent*) marcado, -a

pronunciation [prə·nʌn·si·'eɪ·ʃən] n LING pronunciación f

proof [pruf] I. n a. LAW prueba f; **the bur-**

den of ~ el peso de la evidencia ▶ **the ~ of the pudding is in the eating** prov no se sabe si algo es bueno hasta que se prueba II. adj (*alcoholic strength*) de graduación III. vt impermeabilizar

proofread ['pruf·rid] vt irr TYPO, PUBL corregir, revisar

prop [prap] I. n 1. (*support*) apoyo m 2. THEAT objeto m de atrezzo II. <-pp-> vt sostener, apuntalar; **to ~ sth up with sth** aguantar algo [*or* contra] algo

propaganda [ˌprap·ə·'gæn·də] n propaganda f

propagate ['prap·ə·geɪt] I. vt 1. BOT propagar 2. (*make known: lie, rumor*) difundir II. vi propagarse

propagation [ˌprap·ə·'geɪ·ʃən] n 1. BOT, PHYS propagación f 2. (*of lies, rumors*) difusión f

propel [prə·'pel] <-ll-> vt propulsar

propellant [prə·'pel·ənt] n propelente m

propeller [prə·'pel·ər] n hélice f

proper ['prap·ər] adj 1. (*appropriate: time, place, method*) apropiado, -a; (*use*) correcto, -a 2. (*socially respectable*) **to be ~ to do sth** ser apropiado hacer algo 3. (*itself*) verdadero, -a; **it's not in Boston ~** no está en Boston propiamente dicho 4. (*real*) verdadero, -a; **a ~ job** un trabajo de verdad

properly ['prap·ər·li] adv 1. (*correctly*) correctamente; **~ speaking** hablando como es debido 2. (*behave*) como es debido 3. (*politely*) educadamente

proper name n, **proper noun** n nombre m propio

property ['prap·ər·ti] <-ies> n 1. (*possession*) propiedad f; LAW (*house, land*) bien m inmueble 2. (*house*) inmueble m; (*land*) terreno m 3. a. COMPUT (*attribute*) propiedad f

prophecy ['praf·ə·si] <-ies> pl n profecía f

prophesy ['praf·ə·saɪ] <-ie-> vt (*predict*) predecir; REL profetizar

prophet ['praf·ɪt] n adivino, -a m, f; REL profeta, -isa m, f

prophetic [prə·'fet·ɪk] adj profético, -a

proponent [prə·'poʊ·nənt] n defensor(a) m(f)

proportion [prə·'pɔr·ʃən] n 1. (*relation-*

P

ship) proporción *f;* **the ~ of A to B** el porcentaje entre A y B; **to be out of ~ to sth** estar desproporcionado con algo; **to be in ~ to sth** estar en proporción con algo; **to keep a sense of ~** mantener un sentido de la proporción **2.** (*part*) parte *f* proporcional **3.** ~s (*size*) dimensiones *fpl*

proportional [prə·ˈpɔr·ʃə·nəl] *adj* proporcional; **inversely ~** inversamente proporcional

proportioned *adj* **well-~** bien proporcionado

proposal [prə·ˈpoʊ·zəl] *n* **1.** (*suggestion*) propuesta *f;* **to put forward a ~** presentar una proposición **2.** (*offer of marriage*) proposición *f;* **to make a marriage ~** hacer una petición de mano

propose [prə·ˈpoʊz] **I.** *vt* **1.** (*put forward*) proponer; **to ~ a toast** proponer un brindis **2.** (*intend*) **to ~ to do sth** tener la intención de hacer algo **3.** (*nominate*) nombrar **II.** *vi* (*offer marriage*) **to ~ to sb** declararse (a alguien)

proposer [prə·ˈpoʊ·zər] *n* **1.** (*suggester*) autor(a) *m(f)* de una moción **2.** (*nominator*) proponente *mf*

proposition [ˌprap·ə·ˈzɪʃ·ən] **I.** *n* **1.** (*theory, argument*) proposición *f* **2.** (*business*) ofrecimiento *m* **3.** (*suggestion*) sugerencia *f* **II.** *vt* hacer proposiciones deshonestas a

proprietary [prə·ˈpraɪ·ə·ter·i] *adj* **1.** (*owning property*) propietario, -a **2.** ECON (*name, brand*) registrado, -a

proprietor [prə·ˈpraɪ·ə·tər] *n* propietario, -a *m, f*

proprietress [prə·ˈpraɪ·ə·trɪs] *n* propietaria *f*

propriety [prə·ˈpraɪ·ə·ti] <-ies> *n* **1.** (*correctness*) corrección *f,* propiedad *f* **2. proprieties** (*standard of conduct*) convenciones *f pl* sociales; **to observe the proprieties** atenerse al decoro

propulsion [prə·ˈpʌl·ʃən] *n* propulsión *f*

proscribe [proʊ·ˈskraɪb] *vt* proscribir

proscription [proʊ·ˈskrɪp·ʃən] *n form* proscripción *f*

prose [proʊz] *n* prosa *f*

prosecute [ˈpras·ɪ·kjut] **I.** *vt* **1.** LAW **to ~ sb** (**for sth**) procesar a alguien (por algo)

2. *form* (*pursue, follow up*) proseguir **II.** *vi* interponer

prosecuting *adj* acusador(a)

prosecution [ˌpras·ɪ·ˈkju·ʃən] *n* **1.** LAW (*proceedings*) proceso *m* **2.** LAW (*the prosecuting party*) **the ~** la acusación **3.** *form* (*of campaign, inquiry*) seguimiento *m*

prosecutor [ˈpras·ɪ·kju·tər] *n* LAW fiscal *mf*

prospect [ˈpras·pekt] **I.** *n* **1.** (*possibility*) posibilidad *f;* **the ~ of sth** la probabilidad de algo **2.** ~s (*chances*) perspectivas *fpl* **3.** ECON (*potential customer*) posible cliente *mf;* (*potential employee*) candidato, -a *m, f* **4.** *liter* (*view*) panorama *m;* **a ~ of/over sth** una vista de/sobre algo **II.** *vi* MIN buscar

prospective [prə·ˈspek·tɪv] *adj* posible; (*candidate, student*) futuro, -a

prospector [ˈpras·pek·tər] *n* MIN prospector(a) *m(f)*

prospectus [prə·ˈspek·təs] *n* prospecto *m;* UNIV folleto *m* informativo

prosper [ˈpras·pər] *vi* prosperar

prosperity [pra·ˈsper·ə·ti] *n* prosperidad *f*

prosperous [ˈpras·pər·əs] *adj* próspero, -a; (*business*) exitoso, -a

prostitute [ˈpras·tə·tut] **I.** *n* prostituta *f* **II.** *vt a. fig* **to ~ oneself** prostituirse

prostitution [ˌpras·tɪ·ˈtu·ʃən] *n* prostitución *f*

protagonist [proʊ·ˈtæg·ə·nɪst] *n* (*main character*) protagonista *mf*

protect [prə·ˈtekt] *vt* proteger

protection [prə·ˈtek·ʃən] *n* (*defense*) protección *f;* **to be under sb's ~** estar bajo la protección de alguien

protection factor *n* factor *m* de protección

protective [prə·ˈtek·tɪv] *adj* **1.** (*giving protection*) proteccionista; **~ custody** detención *f* preventiva **2.** (*wishing to protect: instinct*) protector(a)

protector [prə·ˈtek·tər] *n* **1.** (*person*) protector(a) *m(f)* **2.** (*device*) (aparato *m*) protector *m*

protein [ˈproʊ·tin] *n* proteína *f*

protest¹ [ˈproʊ·test] *n* **1.** (*complaint*) protesta *f;* **in ~** en señal de protesta

2. (*demonstration*) manifestación *f* de protesta

protest² [prou·'test] **I.** *vi* protestar; **to ~ about/against sth** protestar por/en contra de algo **II.** *vt* (*show dissent*) protestar en contra de

Protestant ['prɑt·ɪ·stənt] *n* protestante *mf*

protester *n* manifestante *mf*

protest march *n* marcha *f* de protesta

protest vote *n* voto *m* de protesta

protocol ['prou·tə·kɔl] *n* a. COMPUT protocolo *m*

prototype ['prou·tə·taɪp] *n* prototipo *m*

protracted [prou·'træk·tɪd] *adj* prolongado, -a

protractor [prou·'træk·tər] *n* (*for measuring angles*) transportador *m* (de grados)

proud [praud] *adj* **1.** (*pleased*) orgulloso, -a; **to be ~ of sth/sb** enorgullecerse de algo/alguien; **to be ~ to do sth** tener el honor de hacer algo **2.** (*having self-respect*) digno, -a **3.** (*arrogant*) arrogante

provable ['pru·və·bəl] *adj* demostrable

prove [pruv] <proved, proved *or* proven> **I.** *vt* (*verify: theory*) probar; (*innocence, loyalty*) demostrar; **to ~ sb innocent** probar la inocencia de alguien **II.** *vi* (*be established*) resultar; **to ~ be sth** resultar ser algo

proven ['pru·vən] **I.** *vi, vt pp of* **prove** **II.** *adj* (*verified*) comprobado, -a, probado, -a

proverb ['prɑv·ɜrb] *n* refrán *m*, proverbio *m;* **as the ~ goes...** como dice el refrán...

provide [prə·'vaɪd] **I.** *vt* **1.** proveer; **to ~ sb with sth** proveer a alguien de algo **2.** *form* LAW estipular **II.** *vi* **1.** (*prepare*) **to ~ for sth** hacerse cargo de algo **2.** (*support*) **to ~ for one's family/ children** mantener a su familia/hijos **3.** (*mandate*) prever

provided *conj* **~ that...** con tal (de) que... +*subj*

providence ['prɑv·ə·dəns] *n* providencia *f*

provider *n* **1.** (*person*) proveedor(a) *m(f)*

2. COMPUT (*for Internet services*) proveedor *m* (de Internet)

providing *conj* **~ (that)...** con tal (de) que... +*subj*

province ['prɑv·ɪns] *n* POL, ADMIN provincia *f*

provincial [prə·'vɪn·tʃəl] *adj* **1.** POL, ADMIN provincial **2.** (*unsophisticated*) provinciano, -a

provision [prə·'vɪʒ·ən] **I.** *n* **1.** (*act of providing*) suministro *m* **2.** (*thing provided*) provisión *f* **3.** (*preparation*) previsiones *fpl;* **to make ~s for sth** tomar medidas de previsión para algo **4.** LAW (*in will, contract*) disposición *f* **II.** *vt* abastecer

provisional [prə·'vɪʒ·ə·nəl] *adj* provisional

proviso [prə·'vaɪ·zou] <-s> *n* condición *f;* **with the ~ that...** con la condición de que +*subj*

provocation [ˌprɑv·ə·'keɪ·ʃən] *n* provocación *f*

provocative [prə·'vɑk·ə·t̬ɪv] *adj* **1.** (*sexually*) provocativo, -a **2.** (*thought-provoking: idea, question*) estimulante, provocador, -a **3.** (*causing anger*) provocador(a)

provoke [prə·'vouk] *vt* **1.** (*make angry*) provocar **2.** (*discussion*) motivar; (*crisis*) causar

provoking *adj* (*irritating*) irritante

prowl [praul] **I.** *vt* vagar por; **to ~ the streets for victims** merodear por las calles en busca de víctimas **II.** *vi* **to ~ (around)** rondar (por)

proximity [prɑk·'sɪm·ə·t̬i] *n form* proximidad *f;* **to be in (close) ~ to sth** estar (muy) cerca de algo

proxy ['prɑk·si] <-ies> *n* apoderado, -a *m, f;* **to do sth by ~** hacer algo por poderes

prudent ['pru·dənt] *adj* prudente

prune¹ [prun] *vt* podar; **to ~ (back) costs** reducir gastos

prune² [prun] *n* (*dried plum*) ciruela *f* pasa

pry¹ [praɪ] <pries, pried> *vi* (*be nosy*) husmear; **to ~ into sth** entrometerse en algo; **to ~ around** curiosear

pry² [praɪ] *vt* **to ~ sth off** arrancar algo; **to**

~ **sth open** abrir algo por la fuerza

PS [ˌpiˈes] abbr of **postscript** P.D.

psalm [sam] n REL salmo m

pseudonym ['suˈdəˌnɪm] n seudónimo m

PST n abbr of **Pacific Standard Time** Hora f del Pacífico

psychiatric [ˌsaɪˈkiˈætˌrɪk] adj psiquiátrico, -a

psychiatrist [saɪˈkaɪˈəˈtrɪst] n psiquiatra mf

psychiatry [saɪˈkaɪˈəˈtri] n psiquiatría f

psychic ['saɪˈkɪk] I. adj 1. (with occult powers) parapsicológico, -a 2. (of the mind) psíquico, -a II. n vidente mf

psycho ['saɪˈkoʊ] n sl (crazy person) psicópata mf

psychoanalysis [ˌsaɪˈkoʊˈəˈnælˈəˈsɪs] n psicoanálisis m inv

psychoanalyst [ˌsaɪˈkoʊˈænˈəˈlɪst] n psicoanalista mf

psychological [ˌsaɪˈkəˈlɑdˈʒɪˈkəl] adj psicológico, -a

psychologist [saɪˈkɑlˈəˈdʒɪst] n psicólogo, -a m, f

psychology <-ies> n (science, mentality) psicología f

psychopath ['saɪˈkəˈpæθ] n psicópata mf

psychopathic [ˌsaɪˈkəˈpæθˈɪk] adj psicopático, -a

psychotherapist [ˌsaɪˈkoʊˈˈθerˈəˈpɪst] n psicoterapeuta mf

psychotherapy [ˌsaɪˈkoʊˈˈθerˈəˈpi] n psicoterapia f

pt. n 1. abbr of **part** parte f 2. abbr of **pint** pinta f (≈ 0,47 litros) 3. abbr of **point** punto m

PTA [ˌpiˈtiˈeɪ] n abbr of **Parent Teacher Association** asociación f de padres y maestros

pub [pʌb] n pub m

puberty ['pjuˈbərˈti] n pubertad f

public ['pʌbˈlɪk] I. adj 1. (of/for the people, provided by state) público, -a 2. (done openly) abierto, -a; **to go ~ with sth** revelar algo II. n 1. (people collectively, audience) público m; **in ~** en público 2. (ordinary people) gente f de la calle

public appearance n aparición f pública

public appointment n designación f pública

publication [ˌpʌbˈlɪˈkeɪˈʃən] n publicación f

public defender n LAW defensor(a) m(f) de oficio

public health service n servicio m sanitario

public holiday n fiesta f oficial

publicity [pʌbˈlɪsˈəˈti] n 1. publicidad f 2. (attention) **to attract ~** atraer la atención

publicize ['pʌbˈlɪˈsaɪz] vt promocionar

public library <-ies> n biblioteca f pública

publicly adv (openly) en público

public opinion n opinión f pública

public property n bienes m pl públicos

public prosecutor n fiscal mf

public relations npl relaciones f pl públicas

public school n escuela f pública

public sector n sector m público

public servant n funcionario, -a m, f

public service n funcionariado m

public-spirited [ˌpʌbˈlɪkˈspɪrˈɪˈtɪd] adj solidario, -a

public transportation n transporte m público

publish ['pʌbˈlɪʃ] vt (book, author, result) publicar; (information) divulgar

publisher n 1. (company) editorial f 2. (person) editor(a) m(f)

publishing n industria f editorial

puck [pʌk] n SPORTS disco m

pudding ['pʊdˈɪŋ] n (baked) pudin m; **vanilla ~** crema f de vainilla; **rice ~** arroz m con leche

puddle ['pʌdˈəl] n charco m

pudgy ['pʌdʒˈi] <-ier, -iest> adj rechoncho, -a

Puerto Rican [ˌpwerˈtəˈriˈkən] I. n portorriqueño, -a m, f II. adj portorriqueño, -a

Puerto Rico [ˌpwerˈtəˈriˈkoʊ] n Puerto Rico m

puff [pʌf] I. vi 1. (blow) soplar 2. (be out of breath) jadear 3. **to ~ on a pipe/cigar/cigarette** dar una calada a una pipa/un cigarro/un cigarrillo II. vt 1. (smoke) soplar; (cigarette smoke) echar **2.** (*praise: product, book*) dar bombo a **3.** (*say while panting*) resoplar **III.** *n* **1.** *inf* (*breath, wind*) soplo *m*; (*of dust, smoke*) bocanada *f* **2.** (*drag, breathing-in*) calada *f* **3.** (*quilt*) edredón *m* **4.** *inf* (*speech, praise*) bombo *m*

♦**puff out** *vt* **1.** (*expand*) inflar **2.** (*exhaust*) dejar sin aliento

♦**puff up I.** *vt* inflar **II.** *vi* hincharse

puff pastry *n* hojaldre *m*

puffy ['pʌf·i] <-ier, -iest> *adj* hinchado, -a

puke [pjuk] *sl* **I.** *vt* vomitar **II.** *vi* vomitar; **he makes me (want to) ~!** ¡me da asco!

pull [pʊl] **I.** *vt* **1.** (*draw*) tirar de, jalar *AmL*; (*trigger*) apretar **2.** *inf* (*take out: gun, knife*) sacar **3.** MED (*extract*) sacar **4.** SPORTS, MED (*strain: muscle*) forzar **5.** (*attract: business, customers*) atraer ▶ **to ~ a fast one (on sb)** *inf* hacer una jugarreta (a alguien) **II.** *vi* **1.** (*exert force*) tirar **2.** **to ~ on a beer** dar un trago a una cerveza; **to ~ on a cigarette** dar una calada a un cigarrillo **3.** *inf* (*hope for success*) **to be ~ing for sb/sth** estar con alguien/algo **III.** *n* **1.** (*act of pulling*) tirón *m* **2.** *inf* (*influence*) influencia *f* **3.** (*on knob, handle*) tirador *m* **4.** (*attraction*) atracción *f*; (*power to attract*) atractivo *m*, tirón *m* **5.** (*of cigarette*) chupada *f*; (*of drink*) trago *m*

♦**pull apart** *vt insep* **1.** (*break into pieces*) separar **2.** (*separate using force*) hacer pedazos

♦**pull away I.** *vi* (*vehicle*) alejarse **II.** *vt* arrancar; **to pull sth away from sth** arrancar algo a algo

♦**pull back I.** *vi* **1.** (*move out of the way*) retirarse **2.** (*not proceed, back out*) dar marcha atrás **II.** *vt* retener

♦**pull down** *vt* **1.** (*move down*) bajar **2.** (*demolish*) tirar [*or* echar] abajo **3.** (*drag down, hold back*) **to pull sb down** arrastrar a alguien **4.** *inf* (*earn wages*) ganar

♦**pull in I.** *vi* (*vehicle*) llegar **II.** *vt* **1.** (*attract*) atraer **2.** (*arrest*) detener

♦**pull off I.** *vt inf* (*succeed*) lograr; **to**

pull it off lograrlo, vencer **II.** *vi* (*leave*) arrancar

♦**pull out I.** *vi* **1.** (*move out to pass*) salirse; (*drive onto road*) meterse **2.** (*leave*) dejar **3.** (*withdraw*) retirarse **II.** *vt* (*take out*) sacar

♦**pull over I.** *vt* **1.** (*cause to fall*) volcar **2.** (*police*) parar **II.** *vi* hacerse a un lado

♦**pull through** *vi* reponerse

♦**pull together** *vt* **1.** (*regain composure*) **to pull oneself together** recobrar la compostura **2.** (*organize, set up*) organizar

♦**pull up I.** *vt* **1.** (*raise*) levantar **2.** (*plant*) arrancar **II.** *vi* parar

pull-down menu *n* COMPUT menú *m* desplegable

pulley ['pʊl·i] <-s> *n* TECH polea *f*

pullover ['pʊl·oʊ·vər] *n* jersey *m*, suéter *m*

pull-up *n* (*exercise*) flexión *f* en una barra horizontal

pulp [pʌlp] *n* **1.** (*soft wet mass*) pasta *f*; (*for making paper*) pulpa *f* de papel; **to beat sb to a ~** *inf* hacer papilla a alguien **2.** (*of fruit*) pulpa *f* **3.** (*literature*) literatura *f* barata

pulpit ['pʊl·pɪt] *n* REL púlpito *m*

pulsate ['pʌl·seɪt] *vi* palpitar

pulse[1] [pʌls] **I.** *n* **1.** ANAT pulso *m*; (*heartbeat*) latido *m*; **to take sb's ~** tomar el pulso a alguien **2.** (*single vibration*) pulsación *f* **II.** *vi* latir

pulse[2] [pʌls] *n* CULIN legumbre *f*

pumice ['pʌm·ɪs] *n* ~ (**stone**) piedra *f* pómez

pump [pʌmp] **I.** *n* bomba *f*; (*for fuel*) surtidor *m* **II.** *vt* bombear

pumpkin ['pʌmp·kɪn] *n* calabaza *f*

pun [pʌn] *n* juego *m* de palabras

punch[1] [pʌntʃ] **I.** *vt* **1.** (*hit*) pegar; **to ~ sb out** *sl* dar una paliza a alguien **2.** (*push: button, key*) pulsar **3.** (*pierce*) perforar; (*ticket*) picar; **to ~ holes in sth** hacer agujeros a algo; **to ~ the clock** [*or* **card**] fichar, marcar **II.** *vi* **1.** (*hit*) pegar **2.** (*employee*) **to ~ in/out** fichar (*al entrar/al salir*) **III.** <-es> *n* **1.** (*hit*) puñetazo *m* **2.** (*tool for puncturing*) punzón *m*; (*hole*) ~ perforadora *f*; (*ticket*) ~

P

máquina f de picar billetes **3.** fig (strong effect) fuerza f ▶ **to beat sb to the ~** ganar a alguien por la mano; **to roll with the ~es** saber arreglárselas

punch² [pʌntʃ] n (beverage) ponche m

punch line n gracia f (de un chiste)

punctual ['pʌŋk·tʃu·əl] adj puntual

punctuality [ˌpʌŋk·tʃu·'æl·ə·t̬i] n puntualidad f

punctuation [ˌpʌŋk·tʃu·'eɪ·ʃən] n LING puntuación f

punctuation mark n signo m de puntuación

puncture ['pʌŋk·tʃər] I. vt **1.** (pierce) pinchar; (abscess) reventar; (lung) perforar **2.** fig (sb's confidence, self-esteem, ego) minar II. vi (tire, ball) pincharse III. n (in tire, ball) pinchazo m; **to have a ~** (driver) pinchar

pungent ['pʌn·dʒənt] adj (sharp) punzante; (taste) fuerte

punish ['pʌn·ɪʃ] vt castigar

punishable adj liter punible

punishing I. adj (difficult) duro, -a II. n **to take a ~** llevarse una paliza; **this car has taken a real ~** este coche está muy castigado

punishment ['pʌn·ɪʃ·mənt] n **1.** (for misbehavior or crime) castigo m; **capital ~** pena f capital; **to inflict a ~ on sb** castigar a alguien **2.** (rough use) maltrato m

punitive ['pju·nɪ·t̬ɪv] adj form punitivo, -a

punk [pʌŋk] I. n **1.** (punk rocker) punk mf **2.** (troublemaker) gamberro, -a m, f II. adj **1.** (music, style) punk **2.** (poor quality) de pacotilla

punt¹ [pʌnt] SPORTS I. vt (in football) despejar II. vi (in football) despejar

punt² [pʌnt] I. vi (in boat) ir en batea II. n (boat) batea f

punt³ [pʌnt] vi GAMES jugar contra la banca

puny ['pju·ni] <-ier, -iest> adj (person) enclenque; (attempt) lastimoso, -a

pup [pʌp] I. n **1.** (baby dog) cachorro, -a m, f **2.** (baby animal) cría f II. <-pp-> vi parir

pupa ['pju·pə] <pupas or pupae> n BIO crisálida f, pupa f

pupate ['pju·peɪt] vi BIO convertirse en crisálida

pupil¹ ['pju·pəl] n SCHOOL alumno, -a m, f

pupil² ['pju·pəl] n ANAT pupila f

puppet ['pʌp·ɪt] n a. fig títere m

puppeteer [pʌp·ə·'tɪr] n titiritero, -a m, f

puppy ['pʌp·i] <-ies> n cachorro, -a m, f

purchase ['pɜr·tʃəs] I. vt **1.** (buy) comprar, adquirir **2.** NAUT **to ~ the anchor** levar el ancla II. n **1.** (act of buying) compra f; **to make a ~** hacer una adquisición **2.** (hold) agarre m; **to get a ~ on sth** agarrarse a [or de] algo

purchaser n (buyer) comprador(a) m(f)

purchasing n compras fpl

purchasing power n poder m adquisitivo

pure [pjʊr] adj puro, -a; **~ air** aire m puro; **~ gold** oro m puro; **~ and simple** simple y llano

purée [pju·'reɪ] n puré m

purely ['pjʊr·li] adv **1.** (completely) puramente; **~ by chance** por pura casualidad **2.** (simply) meramente; **~ and simply** simple y llanamente

purge [pɜrdʒ] I. vt **1.** MED, POL purgar **2.** a. REL (crime, sin) expiar II. n MED, POL purga f

purify ['pjʊr·ə·faɪ] vt (cleanse) purificar; (language, water) depurar

puritan ['pjʊr·ɪ·tən] n a. fig puritano, -a m, f

puritanical [ˌpjʊr·ɪ·'tæn·ɪ·kəl] adj puritano, -a

purity ['pjʊr·ɪ·t̬i] n pureza f

purple ['pɜr·pəl] adj (reddish) púrpura; (bluish) morado, -a m, f; **to be ~ with rage** estar lívido de rabia

purpose ['pɜr·pəs] n **1.** (goal) intención f; **for the ~** al efecto; **I did that for a ~** hice eso por algo; **for that very ~s** precisamente por eso; **for practical ~s** a efectos prácticos; **not to the ~** que no viene al caso; **to have a ~ in life** tener una meta en la vida **2.** (motivation) (strength of) ~ resolución f **3.** (use) utilidad f; **to no ~** inútilmente; **to serve a ~** servir de algo; **what's the ~ of...?** ¿para qué sirve...? ▶ **on ~** a propósito

purposeful ['pɜr·pəs·fəl] adj **1.** (determined) decidido, -a **2.** (meaningful) con sentido **3.** (*intentional*) intencionado, -a

purposely ['pɜr·pəs·li] *adv* a propósito

purr [pɜr] **I.** *vi* (*cat*) ronronear; (*engine*) zumbar **II.** *n* (*of cat*) ronroneo *m*; (*of engine*) zumbido *m*

purse [pɜrs] **I.** *n* **1.** (*handbag*) bolso *m*, cartera *f* *AmL*, bolsa *f* *Méx* **2.** (*wallet*) monedero *m* **3.** (*funds*) **to be beyond one's ~** estar por encima de las posibilidades de uno **4.** (*prize*) premio *m* en efectivo **II.** *vt* (*lips*) apretar

pursue [pər·'su·] *vt* **1.** (*chase*) perseguir **2.** (*seek to find*) buscar; (*dreams, goals*) luchar por; (*rights, peace*) reivindicar **3.** (*follow: plan*) seguir; **to ~ a matter** seguir un caso **4.** (*work towards*) **to ~ a career** dedicar a una carrera profesional

pursuer [pər·'su·ər] *n* perseguidor(a) *m(f)*

pursuit [pər·'sut] *n* **1.** (*chase*) persecución *f*; **police ~** persecución policial; **to be in ~ of sth** ir tras algo; (*knowledge, happiness*) en busca de algo **2.** (*activity*) actividad *f*; **outdoor ~s** actividades al aire libre

purveyor [pər·'veɪ·ər] *n* ECON proveedor(a) *m(f)*

pus [pʌs] *n* MED pus *m*, postema *f Méx*

push [pʊʃ] **I.** *vt* **1.** (*shove*) empujar; **to ~ one's way through sth** abrirse paso a empujones por algo; **to ~ sth to the back of one's mind** intentar no pensar en algo; **to ~ the door open** abrir la puerta de un empujón; **to ~ sb out of the way** apartar a alguien a empujones **2.** (*force*) **to ~ one's luck** tentar a la suerte; **to ~ sb too far** sacar a alguien de quicio **3.** (*coerce*) obligar; **to ~ sb to do** [*or* **into doing**] **sth** presionar a alguien para que haga algo; **to ~ oneself** exigirse demasiado **4.** (*insist*) insistir en; **to ~ sb for sth** apremiar a alguien para algo **5.** (*press: button*) apretar; (*the brakes, gas pedal*) pisar **6. to be ~ing 30** rondar los 30 (años) **II.** *vi* **1.** (*force movement*) empujar **2.** (*press*) apretar **3.** (*insist*) presionar; **to ~ for sth** presionar para (conseguir) algo **III.** <-es> *n* **1.** (*shove*) empujón *m*; **to give sb a ~** *fig* dar un empujón a alguien **2.** (*press*)

at the ~ of a button apretando un botón **3.** (*strong action*) impulso *m*; (*will to succeed*) empuje *m* **4.** (*strong effort*) esfuerzo *m*; **to make a ~ for sth** hacer un esfuerzo para algo **5.** MIL (*military attack*) ofensiva *f*

◆ **push along** *vi inf* largarse

◆ **push around** *vt inf* mangonear *inf*

◆ **push away** *vt* apartar

◆ **push back** *vt* (*move backwards*) hacer retroceder; (*hair*) echar hacia atrás

◆ **push down** *vt* **1.** (*knock down*) derribar **2.** (*press down*) apretar **3.** ECON (*price, interest rate*) hacer bajar

◆ **push forward I.** *vt* **1.** (*force forward*) empujar hacia delante **2.** (*promote*) promocionar **II.** *vi* **1.** (*advance*) avanzar **2.** (*continue*) **to ~ (with sth)** seguir (con algo)

◆ **push in** *vt* **1.** (*nail*) empujar (hacia adentro) **2.** (*force in*) **to push one's way in** colarse *inf*

◆ **push off** *vi inf* largarse

◆ **push on** *vi* **1.** (*continue despite problems*) **to ~ (with sth)** seguir adelante (con algo) **2.** (*continue traveling*) **we pushed on to Veracruz** seguimos hasta Veracruz **II.** *vt* **1.** (*activate*) apresurar **2.** (*urge on*) **to push sb on to do sth** empujar a alguien a hacer algo

◆ **push out** *vt* **1.** (*force out*) **to push sb out** (**of sth**) echar a alguien (de algo) **2.** (*get rid of*) eliminar; **to push competitors out of the market** eliminar a los competidores del mercado

◆ **push over** *vt always sep* (*thing*) volcar; (*person*) hacer caer

◆ **push through I.** *vi* abrirse paso entre **II.** *vt* (*help to succeed*) llevar a buen término

◆ **push up** *vt* **1.** (*move higher*) levantar; *fig* (*help*) dar un empujón **2.** (*price, interest rate*) hacer subir

pushcart ['pʊʃ·kɑrt] *n* carretilla *f* de mano

pusher *n sl* camello *mf*

pushover ['pʊʃ·oʊ·vər] *n* **1.** (*easy success*) **to be a ~** ser pan comido **2.** (*easily influenced*) **to be a ~** ser muy fácil de convencer

pushpin ['pʊʃ·pɪn] *n* chincheta *f*

push-start *vi* AUTO arrancar empujando el coche

pushup ['pʊʃ·ʌp] *n* SPORTS flexión *f* de brazos; **to do** ~**s** hacer flexiones

pushy ['pʊʃ·i] *adj* avasallador(a), insistente

puss [pʊs] <-es> *n* (*cat*) minino, -a *m, f*; Puss in Boots el gato con botas

pussy ['pʊs·i] <-ies> *n* (*cat*) ~ (**cat**) minino, -a *m, f*

put [pʊt] <-tt-, put, put> I. *vt* 1. (*place*) poner; (*in box, hole*) meter; ~ **the spoons next to the knives** pon las cucharas junto a los cuchillos; **to** ~ **sth to one's lips** llevarse algo a los labios; ~ **it there!** (*shake hands*) ¡chócala!; **to** ~ **sth in the oven** meter algo en el horno 2. (*add*) echar; **to** ~ **sugar/ salt in sth** echar azúcar/sal a algo; **to** ~ **the date on sth** poner la fecha en algo; **to** ~ **sth on a list** apuntar algo en una lista 3. (*direct*) **to** ~ **pressure on sb** presionar a alguien; **to** ~ **one's heart into sth** poner todo el afán de uno en algo; **to** ~ **one's mind to sth** poner los cinco sentidos en algo; **to** ~ **one's trust/ hope in sb** depositar la confianza/las esperanzas de uno en alguien 4. (*invest*) **to** ~ **sth into sth** invertir algo en algo; **to** ~ **energy/time into sth** dedicar energía/tiempo a algo 5. (*bet*) apostar; **to** ~ **money on sth** jugarse dinero a algo 6. (*cause to be*) **to** ~ **sb in a good mood** poner a alguien de buen humor; **to** ~ **sb in danger** poner a alguien en peligro; **to** ~ **oneself in sb's place** [*or* **shoes**] ponerse en el lugar de alguien; **to** ~ **into practice** poner en práctica; **to** ~ **sb on the train** acompañar a alguien hasta el tren; **to** ~ **sth right** arreglar algo; **to** ~ **sb to bed** acostar a alguien; **to** ~ **sth to good use** hacer buen uso de algo; **to** ~ **sb to shame** avergonzar a alguien; **to** ~ **a stop to sth** poner fin a algo; **to** ~ **sb to work** poner a alguien a trabajar 7. (*impose*) **to** ~ **an idea in sb's head** meter una idea en la cabeza a alguien; **to** ~ **a tax on sth** gravar algo con un impuesto 8. (*attribute*) **to** ~ **the blame on sb** echar la culpa a alguien; **to** ~ **emphasis on sth** conceder especial importancia a algo 9. (*present*) **to** ~ **a question** plantear una pregunta; **to** ~ **sth to discussion** someter algo a debate; **to** ~ **sth to a vote** someter algo a votación; **to** ~ **a proposal before a committee** presentar una propuesta ante un comité; **I** ~ **it to you that...** mi opinión es que... 10. (*express*) decir; **as John** ~ **it** como dijo John; **to** ~ **one's feelings into words** expresar sus sentimientos con palabras; **to** ~ **sth into Spanish** traducir algo al español; **to** ~ **sth in writing** poner algo por escrito 11. (*judge, estimate*) **I** ~ **the number of visitors at 2,000** calculo que el número de visitantes ronda los 2.000; **I'd** ~ **her at about 35** calculo que tiene unos 35 años; **to** ~ **sb on a level with sb** poner a alguien al mismo nivel que alguien II. *vi* NAUT **to** ~ **to sea** zarpar

◆ **put about** <-tt-> *irr* I. *vt* NAUT hacer virar II. *vi* NAUT virar

◆ **put across** <-tt-> *irr vt* (*make understood*) comunicar; **to put sth across to sb** hacer entender algo a alguien

◆ **put aside** <-tt-> *irr vt* 1. (*place to one side*) dejar a un lado 2. (*save*) ahorrar; (*time*) reservar 3. (*give up*) **to put sth aside** dejar algo 4. (*reject*) rechazar

◆ **put away** <-tt-> *irr vt* 1. (*save*) ahorrar 2. *inf* (*eat a lot*) zamparse 3. (*remove*) guardar 4. *inf* (*imprison*) **to put sb away** encerrar a alguien 5. *sl* (*kill*) matar

◆ **put back** <-tt-> *irr vt* 1. (*return*) volver a poner en su sitio 2. (*postpone*) posponer 3. SCHOOL (*not be promoted*) **to put sb back a year** hacer repetir curso a alguien 4. (*set earlier: watch*) atrasar

◆ **put by** <-tt-> *irr vt* ahorrar

◆ **put down** <-tt-> *irr vt* 1. (*set down*) dejar; **to not be able to put a book down** no poder parar de leer un libro 2. (*lower*) bajar; **to put one's arm/feet down** bajar el brazo/los pies; **to put sb/ sth down somewhere** dejar a alguien/ algo en un sitio 3. (*attribute*) **to put sth down to sb** atribuir algo a alguien 4. (*write*) escribir; **to put sth down on paper** poner algo por escrito 5. (*assess*)

catalogar; **I put her down as 30** le echo
30 años **6.** (*register*) **to put sb down
for sth** inscribir a alguien en algo **7.** FIN
(*prices*) disminuir **8.** ECON (*leave as
deposit*) dejar en depósito **9.** (*stop: rebellion, opposition*) reprimir **10.** sl (*humiliate*) menospreciar **11.** (*have killed:
animal*) sacrificar

◆ **put forward** <-tt-> *irr vt* **1.** (*offer for
discussion: subject*) proponer; (*idea,
plan*) exponer; **to ~ a proposal** hacer
una propuesta **2.** (*advance: event*) adelantar; **to put the clock forward** adelantar el reloj

◆ **put in** <-tt-> *irr* **I.** *vt* **1.** (*place inside*) meter **2.** (*add*) poner; **to ~ a
comma/a period** añadir una coma/un
punto **3.** (*say*) decir; (*remark*) hacer; **to
put a word in** intervenir en la conversación; **to ~ a good word for sb** hablar
bien de alguien **4.** AGR (*plant: vegetables, trees*) plantar **5.** TECH (*install*)
instalar **6.** (*invest: money*) poner; (*time,
effort*) dedicar; **to ~ overtime** hacer
horas extra **7.** (*submit: claim, request*)
presentar; (*candidate*) presentarse; **to
put oneself in for sth** inscribirse para
algo **8.** (*make*) hacer; **to ~ an appearance** hacer acto de presencia **II.** *vi* **1.** (*apply*) **to ~ for sth** solicitar algo **2.** NAUT
(*dock*) hacer escala

◆ **put into** <-tt-> *irr vt* **1.** (*place inside*)
meter **2. to put sth into sth** (*add*) añadir algo a algo **3.** (*dress in*) **to put sb
into sth** vestir a alguien de algo **4.** TECH
(*install*) instalar **5.** FIN (*deposit*) **to put
money into a bank** ingresar dinero en
un banco **6.** (*invest*) **to put sth into
sth** (*money*) invertir algo en algo; (*time,
effort*) dedicar algo a algo **7.** (*cause to
be*) **to put a plan into operation** [*or inf*
action] poner un plan en marcha **8.** (*in-
stitutionalize*) **to put sb into sth** meter
a alguien en algo; **to put sb into prison**
meter a alguien en la cárcel

◆ **put off** <-tt-> *irr vt* **1.** (*turn off: lights,
TV*) apagar; (*take off: sweater, jacket*)
quitarse **2.** (*delay*) posponer; **to put sth
off for a week** aplazar algo una semana
3. *inf* (*make wait*) entretener; **to put sb
off with excuses** dar largas a alguien *inf*

4. (*repel*) alejar; (*food, smell*) dar asco
a **5.** (*disconcert*) desconcertar **6.** (*distract*) distraer; **to put sb off sth** distraer
a alguien de algo

◆ **put on** <-tt-> *irr vt* **1.** (*place upon*) **to
put sth on sth** poner algo sobre algo
2. (*attach*) **to put sth on sth** poner algo
a algo **3.** (*wear: shirt, shoes*) ponerse;
to ~ make-up maquillarse **4.** (*turn on*)
encender; **to ~ Mozart** poner (música
de) Mozart **5.** (*use*) **to ~ the brakes**
frenar; **to put the handbrake on** poner el freno de mano **6.** (*perform: film*)
dar; (*play*) poner en escena **7.** (*provide:
dish*) servir; **to ~ a party** dar una fiesta
8. (*begin boiling: water, soup, potatoes*)
calentar **9.** (*assume: expression*) adoptar; **to ~ a frown** fruncir el ceño; **to ~
airs** darse aires **10.** (*pretend*) fingir; (*accent*) afectar **11.** (*be joking with*) **to put
sb on** tomar el pelo a alguien **12.** (*gain:
weight*) engordar **13.** TEL **to put sb
on the** (**tele**)**phone** pasar el teléfono
a alguien; **to put sb on to sb** poner a
alguien con alguien; **I'll put him on** le
paso con él **14.** (*inform*) **to put sb on
to sb** hablar a alguien de alguien

◆ **put out** <-tt-> *irr* **I.** *vt* **1.** (*take outside*) **to put the dog out** sacar al perro
2. (*extend*) extender; **to ~ one's hand**
tender la mano **3.** (*extinguish: fire*)
extinguir; **to ~ a cigarette** apagar un
cigarrillo **4.** (*turn off: lights, TV*) apagar
5. (*eject*) expulsar **6.** (*publish: newsletter, magazine*) publicar; (*announcement*) hacer público **7.** (*spread: rumor*)
hacer circular; **to put it out that...** hacer
correr la voz de que... **8.** (*produce in-
dustrially*) producir **9.** (*sprout: leaves*)
echar **10.** (*contract out*) **to put sth out
to subcontract** subcontratar **11.** (*inconvenience*) molestar a **12.** (*offend*) **to
be ~** ofenderse **13.** (*dislocate*) dislocar;
to ~ one's shoulder dislocarse el hombro **14.** NAUT botar **II.** *vi* NAUT zarpar

◆ **put over** <-tt-> *irr vt* **1.** (*place higher*)
to put sth over sth poner algo por encima de algo **2.** (*make understood: idea,
plan*) comunicar **3.** (*fool*) **to put sth
over on sb** engañar a alguien

◆ **put through** <-tt-> *irr vt* **1.** (*insert*

through) **to put sth through sth** hacer pasar algo por algo **2.** (*complete, implement*) llevar a cabo; (*proposal*) hacer aceptar **3.** (*send*) mandar; **to put sb through college** mandar a alguien a la universidad **4.** TEL poner; **to ~ a telephone call to Montreal** contactar con un número de Montreal; **to put a call through** pasar una llamada **5.** *inf* (*make endure*) **to put sb through sth** someter a alguien a algo

◆ **put together** <-tt-> *irr vt* **1.** (*join*) juntar; (*collection*) reunir; (*assemble*) ensamblar; (*machine, model, radio*) montar; (*pieces*) acoplar **2.** *fig* (*connect: facts, clues*) relacionar **3.** (*list*) hacer; (*team*) formar; (*meal*) preparar **4.** MATH sumar

◆ **put up** <-tt-> *irr* **I.** *vt* **1.** (*hang up*) colgar; (*notice*) fijar **2.** (*raise*) levantar; (*one's collar*) subirse; (*flag*) izar; (*umbrella*) abrir; **to put one's hair up** recogerse el pelo **3.** (*build*) construir; (*tent*) montar **4.** (*increase: prices*) subir **5.** (*make available*) **to put sth up for sale** poner algo a la [*or* en] venta; **to put sth up for auction** sacar algo a subasta **6.** (*give shelter*) alojar; **I can put you up for a week** te puedes quedar una semana en casa **7.** (*provide: funds*) aportar; **to ~ the money for sth** poner el dinero para algo **8.** (*show opposition*) **to ~ opposition** oponerse; **to ~ a struggle** [*or* fight] oponer resistencia **II.** *vi* **1.** (*sleep at*) alojarse; **to ~ at a hotel** hospedarse en un hotel **2.** (*tolerate unwillingly*) **to ~ with sb/sth** soportar a alguien/algo

put-on *n sl* burla *f*; (*joke*) broma *f*

putrefy ['pju·trə·faɪ] <-ie-> *vi* pudrirse

putt [pʌt] SPORTS **I.** *vi* patear **II.** *n* golpe *m* corto (al hoyo), put *m AmL*

putter[1] ['pʌt·ər] *n* (*golf club*) putter *m*

putter[2] ['pʌt·ər] *vi* entretenerse; **to ~ around the house** pasearse por la casa

putty ['pʌt·i] *n* masilla *f*

put-up *adj inf* **a ~ job** un asunto fraudulento

put-upon *adj inf* explotado, -a

puzzle ['pʌz·əl] **I.** *vt* dejar perplejo, -a **II.** *vi* **to ~ over sth** dar vueltas a algo

III. *n* **1.** (*game*) rompecabezas *m inv*; **jigsaw ~ puzzle** *m*; **crossword ~** crucigrama *m* **2.** (*mystery*) misterio *m*, enigma *m*; **to solve a ~** resolver un enigma

puzzled *adj* perplejo, -a

puzzling *adj* desconcertante

pylon ['paɪ·lɑn] *n* ELEC torre *f* de alta tensión

pyramid ['pɪr·ə·mɪd] *n* pirámide *f*

Pyrenees ['pɪr·ə·niz] *npl* **the ~** los Pirineos

Pyrex® ['paɪ·reks] **I.** *n* pyrex *m* **II.** *adj* de pyrex

pyromaniac *n* pirómano, -a *m, f*

python ['paɪ·θən] <-(ons)> *n* pitón *f*

Q

Q, q [kju] *n* Q, q *f*; **~ as in Quebec** Q de queso

Q *abbr of* **Queen** reina *f*

Q-Tip® *n* bastoncillo *m* (para los oídos)

quack[1] [kwæk] **I.** *n* (*of duck*) graznido *m* **II.** *vi* graznar

quack[2] [kwæk] *pej* **I.** *n* **1.** (*doctor*) matasanos *m inv* **2.** (*charlatan*) fantasmón, -ona *m, f inf* **II.** *adj* falso, -a

quadrangular [kwa·'dræn·gjə·lər] *adj* cuadrangular

quadratic [kwa·'dræt·ɪk] *adj* cuadrático, -a

quadrilateral [ˌkwad·rɪ·'læt̬·ər·əl] *n* cuadrilátero *m*

quadruped ['kwad·rə·ped] *n* cuadrúpedo *m*

quadruple [kwa·'dru·pəl] **I.** *vt* cuadruplicar **II.** *vi* cuadruplicarse **III.** *adj* cuádruple

quadruplet [kwa·'dru·plɪt] *n* cuatrillizo, -a *m, f*

quaint [kweɪnt] *adj* **1.** (*charming*) pintoresco, -a **2.** *pej* (*strange*) raro, -a **3.** (*pleasantly unusual*) singular

quake [kweɪk] **I.** *n* **1.** (*shaking*) temblor *m* **2.** *inf* (*earthquake*) terremoto *m* **II.** *vi* **1.** (*move*) estremecerse **2.** (*shake*) temblar; **to ~ with fear** temblar de miedo

Quaker ['kwer·kər] *n* cuáquero, -a *m, f;* **the ~s** los cuáqueros

qualification [,kwɑl·ə·fɪ·'keɪ·ʃən] *n* **1.** (*document*) título *m;* (*exam*) calificación *f;* **academic ~** título académico; **her ~s are very good** está muy cualificada **2.** (*limiting criterion*) restricción *f;* (*condition*) reserva *f;* (*change*) matización *f;* **without ~** sin reservas

qualified ['kwɑl·ɪ·faɪd] *adj* **1.** (*trained*) titulado, -a; (*certified*) certificado, -a; (*by the state*) homologado, -a **2.** (*competent*) capacitado, -a **3.** (*limited*) limitado, -a

qualify ['kwɑl·ɪ·faɪ] <-ie-> **I.** *vi* **1.** (*meet standards*) **to ~ for sth** estar habilitado para algo; (*have qualifications*) estar acreditado para algo **2.** (*complete training*) titularse **3.** SPORTS clasificarse **II.** *vt* **1.** (*give credentials*) acreditar **2.** (*make eligible*) habilitar; **to ~ sb to do sth** dar derecho a alguien para hacer algo **3.** (*explain and limit*) limitar; **to ~ a remark** matizar un comentario **4.** LING (*modify*) calificar

qualifying ['kwɑl·ɪ·faɪ·ɪŋ] *adj* **1.** (*limiting*) matizador(a) **2.** SPORTS (*testing standard*) clasificatorio, -a; **~ round** eliminatoria *f* **3.** LING (*modifying*) calificativo, -a

quality ['kwɑl·ɪ·ti] **I.** <-ies> *n* **1.** (*degree of goodness*) calidad *f;* **~ of life** calidad de vida *f* **2.** (*characteristic*) cualidad *f;* **artistic ~** cualidades *f pl* artísticas **II.** *adj* de calidad

quality time *n* tiempo *m* para relacionarse *en especial los momentos, escasos pero intensos, que una persona dedica a sus hijos*

quantify ['kwɑn·tə·faɪ] <-ie-> *vt* cuantificar

quantitative ['kwɑn·tə·teɪ·tɪv] *adj* cuantitativo, -a

quantity ['kwɑn·tə·ti] <-ies> *n* **1.** (*amount*) cantidad *f;* **a large/small ~ of sth** una gran/pequeña cantidad de algo **2.** (*large amounts*) cantidades *fpl;* **to buy in ~** comprar al por mayor

quantity discount *n* descuento *m* por grandes cantidades

quarantine ['kwɔr·ən·,tin] **I.** *n* cuaren-

tena *f;* **to be/place under ~** estar/poner en cuarentena **II.** *vt* **to ~ sb/an animal** poner en cuarentena a alguien/a un animal

quarrel ['kwɔr·əl] **I.** *n* disputa *f* **II.** <-ll-> *vi* reñir, pelearse

quarrelsome ['kwɔr·əl·səm] *adj* **1.** (*belligerent*) pendenciero, -a **2.** (*grumbly*) enojadizo, -a, enojón, -ona *Méx*

quarry[1] ['kwɔr·i] **I.** <-ies> *n* (*rock pit*) cantera *f* **II.** <-ie-> *vt* extraer

quarry[2] ['kwɔr·i] <-ies> *n* (*prey*) presa *f*

quart [kwɔrt] *n* cuarto *m* de galón

quarter ['kwɔr·tər] **I.** *n* **1.** (*one fourth*) cuarto *m;* **three ~s** tres cuartos; **a ~ of a century/an hour** un cuarto de siglo/de hora; **(a) ~ to three** las tres menos cuarto; **(a) ~ past three** las tres y cuarto **2.** (*25 cents*) un cuarto de dólar **3.** *a.* FIN, SCHOOL trimestre *m* **4.** (*neighborhood*) barrio *m;* (*area*) zona *f;* **at close ~s** de cerca; **all ~s of the earth** en todos los confines de la tierra **5.** **~s** (*unspecified group or person*) círculos *mpl;* **in certain ~s** en ciertos círculos; **in high ~s** en altas esferas **6.** SPORTS cuarto *m* **7.** (*mercy*) cuartel *m;* **to give ~** dar cuartel; **to ask for ~** pedir cuartel **II.** *vt* **1.** (*cut into four*) cuartear; **to ~ sb** descuartizar a alguien **2.** (*give housing*) alojar; **to be ~ed with sb** estar alojado en casa de alguien **III.** *adj* cuarto; **~ hour** un cuarto de hora

quarterfinal *n* SPORTS cuarto *m* de final

quarterly ['kwɔr·tər·li] **I.** *adv* trimestralmente **II.** *adj* trimestral

quartet *n,* **quartette** [kwɔr·'tet] *n* MUS cuarteto *m*

quartz [kwɔrts] **I.** *n* cuarzo *m* **II.** *adj* de cuarzo; **~ crystal** cristal de cuarzo

quash [kwɑʃ] *vt* **1.** (*suppress*) suprimir; (*rumor*) acallar; **to ~ sb's dreams/plans** aplastar los sueños/planes de alguien **2.** LAW (*annul: conviction, verdict, sentence*) anular; (*law, bill, writ*) derogar

quaver ['kweɪ·vər] **I.** *vi* temblar **II.** *n* temblor *m*

quay [ki] *n* muelle *m*

queasy ['kwi·zi] <-ier, -iest> *adj* **1.** (*nauseous*) mareado, -a **2.** *fig* (*unsettled*)

Q

intranquilo, -a; **with a ~ conscience** con la conciencia intranquila

queen |kwin| I. *n* 1. (*monarch*) reina *f*; **~ of hearts/diamonds** (*cards*) reina de corazones/diamantes 2. (*offensive sl*) (*gay man*) loca *f* II. *vt* 1. (*make queen*) **to ~ sb** coronar reina a alguien 2. (*in chess*) coronar

queen bee *n* ZOOL abeja *f* reina

queer |kwɪr| <-er, -est> *adj* (*strange*) extraño, -a; **to have ~ ideas** tener ideas raras

quell |kwel| *vt* (*unrest, rebellion, protest*) sofocar; **to ~ sb's anger** calmar la rabia de alguien

quench |kwentʃ| *vt* 1. (*satisfy*) satisfacer; (*thirst*) saciar 2. (*put out*) sofocar; **to ~ a fire** apagar un incendio 3. (*suppress*) suprimir; **to ~ sb's desire** apagar el deseo de alguien

query |'kwɪr·i| I. <-ies> *n* pregunta *f* II. <-ie-> *vt* 1. *form* (*dispute*) cuestionar; (*doubt*) poner en duda 2. (*ask*) preguntar

quest |kwest| *n* búsqueda *f*; **the ~ for the truth/an answer** la búsqueda de la verdad/una respuesta

question |'kwes·tʃən| I. *n* 1. (*inquiry*) pregunta *f*; **frequently asked ~s** a. COMPUT preguntas frecuentes; **to pop the ~ to sb** proponer matrimonio a alguien 2. (*doubt*) duda *f*; **without ~** sin duda; **to be beyond ~** estar fuera de duda 3. (*issue*) cuestión *f*; **to be a ~ of time/money** ser una cuestión de tiempo/dinero; **to raise a ~** plantear un problema; **to be out of the ~** ser totalmente imposible; **there's no ~ of sb doing sth** sería imposible que alguien hiciera algo 4. SCHOOL, UNIV (*test problem*) pregunta *f*; **to do a ~** resolver una pregunta II. *vt* 1. (*ask*) preguntar 2. (*interrogate*) interrogar 3. (*doubt*) cuestionar

questionable |'kwes·tʃə·nə·bəl| *adj* discutible

questioner *n* interrogador(a) *m(f)*

questioning I. *n* interrogatorio *m*; **to be taken in for ~** ser detenido para ser interrogado II. *adj* inquisidor(a); **to have a ~ mind** ser inquisitivo

question mark *n* signo *m* de interrogación

questionnaire |ˌkwes·tʃə·'ner| *n* cuestionario *m*

queue |kju| *n* COMPUT cola *f*

quibble |'kwɪb·əl| I. *n* 1. (*petty argument*) sutileza *f*; **a ~ over sth** una objeción acerca de algo 2. (*criticism*) pega *f* II. *vi* poner peros a; **to ~ over sth** quejarse por algo

quiche |kiʃ| *n* quiche *f*

quick |kwɪk| I. <-er, -est> *adj* 1. (*fast*) rápido, -a; **~ as lightning** (*veloz*) como un rayo 2. (*short*) corto, -a; **the ~est way** el camino más corto 3. (*hurried*) apresurado, -a; **to say a ~ good-bye/hello** decir un adiós/hola apresurado 4. (*smart*) vivo, -a; **~ thinking** pensamiento ágil; **to have a ~ mind** tener una mente vivaz; **to have a ~ temper** tener mal genio II. <-er, -est> *adv* rápidamente; **~!** ¡rápido!; **as ~ as possible** tan pronto como sea posible III. *n* carne *f* viva; **to bite/cut nails to the ~** dejar las uñas en carne viva

quick-acting |ˌkwɪk·'æk·tɪŋ| *adj* de efecto rápido

quicken |'kwɪk·ən| I. *vt* (*make faster*) apresurar; **to ~ the pace** acelerar el paso II. *vi* 1. (*increase speed*) acelerarse 2. (*become more active*) avivarse

quick-freeze |'kwɪk·friz| *vt irr* congelar rápidamente

quickly |'kwɪk·li| *adv* rápidamente

quickness |'kwɪk·nɪs| *n* 1. (*speed*) rapidez *f* 2. (*liveliness*) viveza *f*; **~ of mind** mente *f* rápida

quicksand |'kwɪk·sænd| *n* arenas *f pl* movedizas

quicksilver *n see* **mercury** mercurio *m*

quick-tempered *adj* irascible

quick-witted *adj* perspicaz

quiet |'kwaɪ·ət| I. *n* 1. (*silence*) silencio *m* 2. (*lack of activity*) sosiego *m*; **peace and ~** paz y tranquilidad II. <-er, -est> *adj* 1. (*not loud*) silencioso, -a; **to speak in a ~ voice** hablar en voz baja 2. (*not talkative*) callado, -a; **to**

keep ~ mantenerse callado 3. (*secret*) secreto, -a; **to have a ~ word with sb** hablar en privado con alguien; **to keep ~ about sth** mantenerse callado respecto a algo 4. (*unostentatious*) discreto, -a 5. (*unexciting*) tranquilo, -a

quiet down I. *vi* 1. (*quiet*) callarse 2. (*calm*) calmarse II. *vt* 1. (*silence*) hacer callar 2. (*calm (down)*) calmar

quietly ['kwaɪət·li] *adv* 1. (*not loudly*) silenciosamente; **to speak ~** hablar en voz baja 2. (*peacefully*) tranquilamente

quietness ['kwaɪ·ət·nɪs] *n* tranquilidad *f*

quill [kwɪl] *n* 1. (*feather, pen*) pluma *f* 2. (*of porcupine*) púa *f*

quilt [kwɪlt] *n* edredón *m*

quince [kwɪns] *n* membrillo *m*

quinine ['kwaɪ·naɪn] *n* quinina *f*

quintet(te) [kwɪn·'tet] *n* quinteto *m*

quintuple [kwɪn·'tup·əl] *form* I. *adj* quíntuplo, -a II. *vt* quintuplicar III. *vi* quintuplicarse

quintuplet [kwɪn·'tʌp·lɪt] *n* quintillizo, -a *m, f*

quip [kwɪp] *n* ocurrencia *f*

quirk [kwɜrk] *n* 1. (*habit*) excentricidad *f* 2. (*oddity*) rareza *f* 3. (*sudden twist or turn*) **a ~ of fate** un capricho del destino

quit [kwɪt] <quit *or* quitted, quit *or* quitted> I. *vi* 1. (*resign*) dimitir II. *vt* 1. (*resign*) dejar 2. (*stop*) parar; (*smoking*) dejar de 3. COMPUT salir de

quite [kwaɪt] *adv* 1. (*fairly*) bastante; **~ a bit** mucho, bastantito *Méx*; **~ a distance** una distancia considerable; **to run a ~** participar en una carrera 2. (*completely*) completamente; **~ wrong** totalmente equivocado; **not ~** no tanto; **~ as clever/rich as ...** no tan inteligente/rico como...

quits [kwɪts] *adj inf* en paz; **to be ~ (with sb)** estar en paz con alguien; **to call it ~** hacer las paces

quitter *n* desertor, -a *m, f*, rajado, -a *Méx*

quiver[1] ['kwɪv·ər] I. *n* (*shiver*) estremecimiento *m* II. *vi* temblar

quiver[2] ['kwɪv·ər] *n* (*for arrows*) aljaba *f*

quiz [kwɪz] I. <-es> *n* encuesta *f* II. *vt* interrogar

quizmaster ['kwɪz·ˌmæs·tər] *n* moderador(a) *m(f)*

quiz show *n* concurso *m* (de TV)

quota ['kwoʊ·tə] *n* 1. (*fixed amount allowed*) cuota *f* 2. (*proportion*) parte *f*

quotation [kwoʊ·'teɪ·ʃən] *n* 1. (*repeated words*) cita *f* 2. FIN cotización *f*

quotation marks *npl* comillas *fpl*

quote [kwoʊt] I. *n* 1. *inf* (*quotation*) cita *f* 2. ~s (*quotation marks*) comillas *fpl* 3. (*estimate*) presupuesto *m* 4. FIN cotización *f* II. *vt* 1. (*cite*) citar 2. (*name*) nombrar 3. FIN cotizar; **a ~d company** una empresa que cotiza en bolsa III. *vi* (*repeat exact words*) citar; **to ~ from sb** citar a alguien

quotient ['kwoʊ·ʃənt] *n* 1. MATH cociente *m* 2. (*factor*) coeficiente *m*; **intelligence ~** coeficiente de inteligencia

R

r, R [ar] r, R *f*; **~ as in Romeo** R de Ramón

R CINE *abbr of* **restricted** clasificación de cine para mayores de 17 años

R. *abbr of* **River** r.

rabbi ['ræb·aɪ] *n* rabino *m*

rabbit ['ræb·ɪt] *n* conejo, a *m, f*

rabble ['ræb·əl] *n* muchedumbre *f*

rabid ['ræb·ɪd] *adj* 1. (*furious*) furibundo, -a 2. (*fanatical*) fanático, -a 3. (*suffering from rabies*) rabioso, -a

rabies ['reɪ·biz] *n* rabia *f*; **to carry ~** tener la rabia

raccoon [ræ·'kun] *n* mapache *m*

race[1] [reɪs] I. *n* 1. (*contest*) carrera *f*; **a ~ against time** una carrera contra reloj; **100-meter ~** carrera de cien metros lisos; **to run a ~** participar en una carrera II. *vi* 1. (*move quickly*) correr; SPORTS competir 2. (*engine*) acelerarse III. *vt* 1. (*compete against*) competir con; **to ~ sb home** echar una carrera hasta casa a alguien 2. (*enter for race: horse*) hacer correr

race[2] [reɪs] *n* 1. (*ethnic*) raza *f* 2. (*species*) especie *f* 3. (*lineage*) estirpe *f*

racecar *n* coche *m* de carreras, carro *m*

R

de carreras *Col*

racehorse ['reɪs·hɔrs] *n* caballo *m* de carreras

racer ['reɪ·sər] *n* **1.** (*person*) corredor(a) *m(f)* **2.** (*bicycle*) bicicleta *f* de carreras

race relations *npl* relaciones *f pl* interraciales

racetrack ['reɪs·træk] *n* (*for cars*) circuito *m*; (*for runners*) estadio *m*; (*for bicycles*) velódromo *m*; (*for horses*) hipódromo *m*

racial ['reɪ·ʃəl] *adj* racial

racing **I.** *n* carreras *fpl* **II.** *adj* de carreras

racing bicycle *n*, **racing bike** *n inf* bicicleta *f* de carreras

racism ['reɪ·sɪz·əm] *n* racismo *m*

racist ['reɪ·sɪst] *adj* racista

rack [ræk] *n* **1.** (*framework, shelf*) estante *m*; **luggage ~** portaequipajes *m inv*; **dish ~** escurreplatos *m inv* **2.** (*bar for hanging things on*) barra *f*; **towel ~** portatoallas *m inv* **3.** CULIN **~ of lamb/ beef** costillar *m* de cordero/ternera **4.** (*torture instrument*) potro *m*; **to be on the ~** *fig* estar en ascuas

racket ['ræk·ɪt] *n* **1.** SPORTS raqueta *f* **2.** *inf* (*loud noise*) barullo *m*; **to make a ~** armar un alboroto **3.** (*scheme*) chanchullo *m*

racketeer [ræk·ə·'tɪr] *n* timador(a) *m(f)*

racy ['reɪ·si] <-ier, -iest> *adj* (*film, novel*) atrevido, -a

radar ['reɪ·dar] *n* radar *m*

radar trap *n* detector *m* de velocidad

radial ['reɪ·di·əl] *adj* radial; TECH en estrella

radiant ['reɪ·di·ənt] *adj* radiante

radiate ['reɪ·di·eɪt] *vt* **1.** (*emit*) irradiar **2.** (*display: happiness, enthusiasm*) mostrar

radiation [reɪ·di·'eɪ·ʃən] *n* radiación *f*

radiation therapy *n* radioterapia *f*

radiator ['reɪ·di·eɪ·tər] *n* radiador *m*

radical ['ræd·ɪ·kəl] **I.** *n* *a.* CHEM, MATH radical *m* **II.** *adj* (*change, idea*) radical; (*measures*) drástico, -a

radio ['reɪ·di·oʊ] **I.** *n* radio *f* **II.** *vt* (*information*) radiar; (*person*) llamar por radio

radioactive [reɪ·di·oʊ·'æk·tɪv] *adj* radiactivo, -a

radioactivity [reɪ·di·oʊ·æk·'tɪv·ə·ţi] *n* radiactividad *f*

radiographer *n* radiógrafo, -a *m, f*

radiography [reɪ·di·'ag·rə·fi] *n* radiografía *f*

radio ham *n* radioaficionado, -a *m, f*

radiologist [reɪ·di·'al·ə·dʒɪst] *n* radiólogo, -a *m, f*

radiology [reɪ·di·'al·ə·dʒi] *n* radiología *f*

radio station *n* emisora *f* de radio, estación *f* de radio *AmL*

radio telescope *n* radiotelescopio *m*

radiotherapy [reɪ·di·oʊ·'θer·ə·pi] *n* radioterapia *f*

radish ['ræd·ɪʃ] <-es> *n* rábano *m*

radius ['reɪ·di·əs] <-dii> *n* radio *m*

raffle ['ræf·əl] **I.** *n* rifa *f* **II.** *vt* rifar

raft[1] [ræft] (*vessel*) **I.** *n* balsa *f* **II.** *vi* ir en balsa

raft[2] [ræft] *n* (*large quantity*) *inf* montón *m*; **a ~ of options** un montón de opciones

rafter ['ræf·tər] *n* ARCHIT viga *f*

rag [ræg] **I.** *n* **1.** (*old cloth*) trapo *m* **2.** *pl* (*worn-out clothes*) harapos *mpl* **3.** *pej sl* (*newspaper*) periodicucho *m* **II.** <-gg-> *vt sl* tomar el pelo a

rage [reɪdʒ] **I.** *n* **1.** (*anger*) furia *f*; **to be in a ~** estar hecho una furia **2.** (*fashion*) **to be all the ~** ser el último grito **II.** *vi* **1.** (*express fury*) enfurecerse; **to ~ at sb/sth** enfurecerse con alguien/algo **2.** (*continue: battle*) continuar con pleno vigor; (*wind, storm*) bramar; (*fire*) arder furiosamente

ragged ['ræg·ɪd] *adj* **1.** (*torn: clothes*) hecho, -a jirones **2.** (*wearing worn clothes*) andrajoso, -a **3.** (*rough*) recortado, -a **4.** (*irregular*) irregular

raging ['reɪ·dʒɪŋ] *adj* (*gale*) furioso, -a; (*fire*) incontenible

raid [reɪd] **I.** *n* **1.** MIL incursión *f* **2.** (*attack*) ataque *m* **3.** (*robbery*) asalto *m* **4.** (*by police*) redada *f* **II.** *vt* **1.** MIL invadir **2.** (*attack*) atacar **3.** (*by police*) hacer una redada en

rail [reɪl] **I.** *n* **1.** (*of fence*) valla *f*; (*of balcony, stairs*) barandilla *f* **2.** (*railway system*) ferrocarril *m*; **by ~** en tren, por ferrocarril 3. (*track*) raíl [*or* rail] *m*, riel *m AmL* II. *vt* to ~ sth in [*or* off] cercar algo

railing ['reɪ·lɪŋ] *n* 1. (*post*) valla *f*; iron ~ verja *f* 2. (*of stairs*) pasamanos *m inv*

railroad ['reɪl·roʊd] *n* 1. (*system*) ferrocarril *m* 2. (*track*) línea *f* de ferrocarril

railroad line *n* vía *f* del tren

railroad station *n* estación *f* del ferrocarril

railway ['reɪl·weɪ] *n* ferrocarril *m*

rain [reɪn] I. *n* lluvia *f*; ~ shower chubasco *m*; the ~s la temporada de lluvias II. *vi* llover

◆**rain out** *vt* to be rained out cancelarse por lluvia

rainbow *n* METEO arco *m* iris

rain cloud *n* nube *f* de lluvia

raincoat *n* gabardina *f*, piloto *m Arg*

raindrop *n* gota *f* de lluvia

rainfall *n* precipitación *f*

rain forest *n* selva *f* tropical

rainproof I. *adj* impermeable II. *vt* impermeabilizar

rainstorm *n* tormenta *f* de lluvia

rainwater *n* agua *f* de lluvia

rainy ['reɪ·ni] *adj* <-ier, -iest> lluvioso, -a; the ~ season la estación de las lluvias

raise [reɪz] I. *n* (*of wages, prices*) aumento *m* II. *vt* 1. (*lift*) levantar; (*periscope, window*) subir; (*arm, hand, leg*) levantar; (*flag*) izar; (*anchor*) levar 2. (*stir up*) provocar 3. (*increase: wages, awareness*) aumentar; (*bet*) subir; MATH elevar; (*standards*) mejorar 4. (*promote*) ascender 5. (*introduce: subject, problem*) plantear 6. FIN recaudar 7. (*build*) erigir; (*monument*) levantar 8. (*bring up, cultivate*) cultivar 9. (*end: embargo*) levantar 10. (*contact*) llamar, contactar *Méx, Col*; to ~ the alarm dar la voz de alarma

raisin ['reɪ·zən] *n* pasa *f*

rake[1] [reɪk] *n* (*tool*) rastrillo *m*

rake[2] [reɪk] *n* (*dissolute man*) vividor *m*

◆**rake in** *vt sl* (*money*) amasar; to be raking it in estar forrándose

◆**rake up** *vt* 1. (*gather*) reunir 2. *fig* (*refer to*) sacar a relucir

rally ['ræl·i] <-ies> I. *n* 1. (*race*) rally *m* 2. POL mitin *m* II. *vi* 1. MED mejorar; FIN

repuntar 2. MIL agruparse; to ~ behind sb apoyar a alguien III. *vt* 1. MIL reagruparse 2. (*support*) apoyar

ram [ræm] I. *n* 1. (*male sheep*) carnero *m*; (*astrology*) Aries *m* 2. MIL ariete *m* II. *vt* <-mm-> (*hit*) embestir contra

ramble ['ræm·bəl] I. *n* (*walk*) caminata *f*; to go for a ~ ir de excursión II. *vi* 1. (*person*) pasear; (*river*) serpentear; (*plant*) trepar 2. (*in speech*) divagar

rambler ['ræm·blər] *n* 1. (*walker*) excursionista *mf* 2. BOT rosa *f* trepadora

rambling ['ræm·blɪŋ] I. *n* ~s (*speech*) divagaciones *fpl* II. *adj* 1. (*estate, house*) laberíntico, -a 2. (*speech*) divagante 3. (*rose*) trepador(a) 4. (*roaming*) errante

ramp [ræmp] *n* 1. (*sloping way*) rampa *f* 2. AUTO (*on-ramp*) carril *m* de incorporación; (*off-ramp*) carril *m* de salida

rampage ['ræm·peɪdʒ] I. *n* destrozos *mpl*; to be on the ~ ir arrasando todo II. *vi* arrasar

rampant ['ræm·pənt] *adj* (*disease, growth*) exuberante; (*inflation*) galopante

ran [ræn] *pt of* run

ranch [ræntʃ] *n* <-es> granja *f*, rancho *m* II. *vi* (*run a ranch*) llevar una granja

rancher ['ræn·tʃər] *n* 1. (*owner*) hacendado, -a *m, f*, ranchero, -a *m, f Méx* 2. (*worker*) granjero, -a *m, f*

rancid ['ræn·sɪd] *adj* rancio, -a

rancor ['ræn·kər] *n* rencor *m*

R & D [ˌɑr·ənd·ˈdi] *abbr of* Research and Development I+D

random ['ræn·dəm] I. *n* at ~ al azar II. *adj* aleatorio, -a

rang [ræŋ] *pt of* ring[2]

range [reɪndʒ] I. *n* 1. (*variety*) variedad *f* 2. (*scale*) gama *f*; the full ~ of sth la gama completa de algo 3. (*extent*) distancia *f* 4. (*maximum capability*) alcance *m*; out of ~ fuera del alcance; within ~ al alcance 5. (*field*) ámbito *m*, campo *m*; shooting ~ campo *m* de tiro 6. (*pasture*) pradera *f* 7. MUS extensión *f* 8. GEO cadena *f*; mountain ~ cordillera *f*; (*shorter*) sierra *f* II. *vi* 1. (*vary*) variar 2. (*extend*) extenderse

R

3. (*rove*) deambular

ranger ['reɪn·dʒər] *n* guardabosque *mf*

rank[1] [ræŋk] I. *n* 1. (*status*) rango *m* 2. MIL graduación *f*; **the ~s** las tropas II. *vi* clasificarse; **to ~ above sb** estar por encima de alguien III. *vt* 1. (*classify*) clasificar 2. (*arrange*) situar

rank[2] [ræŋk] *adj* 1. (*smelling unpleasant*) fétido, -a 2. (*absolute*) total; (*beginner*) absoluto, -a

ranking ['ræŋ·kɪŋ] *n* clasificación *f*

rankle ['ræŋ·kəl] *vi* doler; **to ~ with sb** estar resentido con alguien; **it ~s that...** duele que... +*subj*

ransom ['ræn·səm] I. *n* rescate *m*; **to hold sb (for)** ~ secuestrar a alguien y pedir rescate; *fig* chantajear a alguien II. *vt* rescatar

rant [rænt] I. *n* despotrique *m* II. *vi* despotricar; **to ~ and rave** despotricar

rap [ræp] I. *n* 1. (*knock*) golpe *m* seco 2. MUS rap *m* II. *vt* golpear III. *vi* 1. (*talk*) charlar 2. MUS rapear

rape[1] [reɪp] I. *n* 1. (*of person*) violación *f* 2. (*of city*) saqueo *m* II. *vt* 1. (*person*) violar 2. (*city*) saquear

rape[2] [reɪp] *n* BOT, AGR colza *f*

rapeseed oil *n* aceite *m* de colza

rapid ['ræp·ɪd] *adj* (*quick*) rápido, -a

rapist ['reɪ·pɪst] *n* violador(a) *m(f)*

rapture ['ræp·tʃər] *n* éxtasis *m inv*

rapturous ['ræp·tʃər·əs] *adj* (*expression*) extasiado, -a; (*applause*) entusiasta

rare[1] [rer] *adj* 1. (*uncommon: animal, coin, disease*) raro, -a 2. (*exceptional: genius, sense of humor*) único, -a

rare[2] [rer] *adj* CULIN poco hecho, -a

rarely ['rer·li] *adv* raramente, raras veces

rarity ['rer·ə·ti] <-ies> *n* rareza *f*

rascal ['ræs·kəl] *n* granuja *mf*

rash[1] [ræʃ] *n* 1. MED sarpullido *m* 2. (*outbreak: of burglaries, etc*) racha *f*

rash[2] [ræʃ] *adj* (*decision*) precipitado, -a; (*move*) impulsivo, -a

rasher ['ræʃ·ər] *n* loncha *f* (de beicon)

raspberry ['ræz·ˌber·i] <-ies> *n* 1. (*fruit*) frambuesa *f* 2. *sl* SPORTS (*wound*) rasponazo *m*

rat [ræt] I. *n* 1. (*animal*) rata *f* 2. (*person*) canalla *mf* ▶ **I smell a ~** aquí hay gato encerrado *m* II. *vi* (*betray*) dela-

tar; **to ~ on sb** chivatear a alguien *Col, Cuba, PRico*

rate [reɪt] I. *n* 1. (*speed*) velocidad *f*; **at this ~** a este ritmo; **at one's own ~** a su propio ritmo 2. (*proportion*) índice *m*, tasa *f*; **birth/death ~** tasa *f* de natalidad/mortalidad; **unemployment ~** índice *m* de desempleo 3. (*price*) precio *m*; **~ of exchange** cambio *m*; **interest ~** tipo *m* de interés ▶ **at any ~** de todos modos II. *vt* calificar; **to ~ sb/sth as sth** considerar algo/a alguien como algo III. *vi* **to ~ as** ser considerado como

rather ['ræð·ər] I. *adv* 1. (*somewhat*) ~ **sleepy** medio dormido 2. (*more exactly*) más bien 3. (*on the contrary*) más bien 4. (*very*) bastante 5. (*in preference to*) **I would ~ stay here** preferiría quedarme aquí; ~ **you than me!** ¡no quisiera estar en tu lugar! II. *interj* por supuesto

ratify ['ræt·ə·faɪ] *vt* ratificar

rating ['reɪ·tɪŋ] *n* 1. (*estimation*) evaluación *f* 2. *pl* TV, RADIO índice *m* de audiencia

ratio ['reɪ·ʃi·oʊ] *n* proporción *f*

ration ['ræʃ·ən] I. *n* 1. (*fixed allowance*) ración *f* 2. ~**s** (*total amount allowed*) raciones *fpl*; **food ~s** víveres *mpl* II. *vt* racionar

rational ['ræʃ·ə·nəl] *adj* 1. (*able to reason*) racional 2. (*sensible*) razonable

rationalization [ˌræʃ·ə·nə·lɪ·ˈzeɪ·ʃən] *n* racionalización *f*

rationalize ['ræʃ·ə·nə·laɪz] *vt* racionalizar

rationing *n* racionamiento *m*

rat poison *n* raticida *m*

rat race *n* **the ~** la lucha para sobrevivir

rattle ['ræt·əl] I. *n* 1. (*noise*) ruido *m*; (*of carriage*) traqueteo *m* 2. (*for baby*) sonajero *m* II. *vi* hacer ruido; (*carriage*) traquetear III. *vt* 1. (*making noise*) hacer sonar 2. (*make nervous*) poner nervioso, -a

rattlesnake ['ræt·əl·sneɪk] *n* serpiente *f* de cascabel

ravage ['ræv·ɪdʒ] *vt* hacer estragos en

rave [reɪv] I. *adj inf* (*review*) elogioso, -a II. *vi* desvariar; **to ~ about sth/sb** poner algo/a alguien por las nubes; **to**

~ **against** sb/sth despotricar contra alguien/algo

raven ['reɪ·vən] n cuervo m

ravenous ['ræv·ə·nəs] adj (person, animal) hambriento, -a; (appetite) voraz

ravine [rə·'vin] n barranco m

raving ['reɪ·vɪŋ] I. adj (success) total; **a ~ madman** un loco de remate II. adv **to be ~ mad** estar como una cabra III. npl desvaríos mpl

raw [rɔ] adj 1. (uncooked) crudo, -a 2. (unprocessed: sewage) sin tratar; (data) en sucio; ~ **material** materia prima 3. (sore) en carne viva 4. (inexperienced) novato, -a 5. (unrestrained) salvaje 6. (weather) crudo, -a

ray¹ [reɪ] n 1. (of light) rayo m 2. (trace) resquicio m

ray² [reɪ] n (fish) raya f

razor ['reɪ·zər] I. n navaja f de afeitar; **electric ~** maquinilla f de afeitar II. vt afeitar

razor-sharp adj 1. (knife) muy afilado, -a 2. (person) agudo, -a

RC [ˌar·'si] 1. abbr of **Red Cross** Cruz f Roja 2. abbr of **Roman Catholic** católico, -a m, f

Rd. abbr of **road** C/

re [reɪ] n MUS re m

reach [ritʃ] I. n 1. (range) alcance m; **to be within** (sb's) ~ a. fig estar al alcance (de alguien); **to be out of** (sb's) ~ a. fig estar fuera del alcance (de alguien) 2. (of river) tramo m; **the upper/lower ~es of the Amazon** la parte alta/baja del Amazonas II. vt 1. (stretch out) alargar, extender 2. (arrive at: city, country) llegar a 3. (attain) alcanzar; (agreement) llegar a; **to ~ 80** cumplir (los) 80 (años) 4. (extend to) llegar a 5. (communicate with) ponerse en contacto con III. vi **to ~ for sth** alargar la mano para tomar algo

reach down vi **to ~ to** (land) extenderse hasta; (clothes) llegar hasta

reach out vi tender la(s) mano(s); **to ~ for sth** estirar la mano para agarrar algo

react [rɪ·'ækt] vi reaccionar; **to ~ to sth** reaccionar ante algo; MED reaccionar a algo; **to ~ against sth** reaccionar contra algo

reaction [rɪ·'æk·ʃən] n 1. a. CHEM reacción f; **chain ~** reacción en cadena 2. MED efecto m

reactionary [rɪ·'æk·ʃə·ner·i] adj reaccionario, -a

reactor [rɪ·'æk·tər] n reactor m

read¹ [rid] I. n lectura f II. vt <read, read> 1. leer; **to ~ sth aloud** leer algo en voz alta; **to ~ sb a story** leer un cuento a alguien 2. (decipher) descifrar; **to ~ sb's mind** [or **thoughts**] adivinar los pensamientos de alguien; **to ~ sb's palm** leer la mano a alguien; **to ~ sb like a book** conocer a alguien como la palma de la mano; ~ **my lips!** ¡léeme los labios! 3. (interpret) interpretar 4. (inspect) inspeccionar; (meter) leer 5. (understand) entender; **I don't ~ you** no te sigo III. vi <read, read> (person) leer; (book, magazine) leerse

read off vt leer (de un tirón)

read on vi seguir leyendo

read out vt 1. (read aloud) leer en voz alta 2. COMPUT (data) sacar

read over vt releer

read through vt leer de principio a fin

read² [red] adj leído, -a; **little/widely ~** poco/muy leído

readable ['ri·də·bəl] adj 1. (legible) legible 2. (easy to read) ameno, -a

reader ['ri·dər] n 1. (person) lector(a) m(f) 2. (book) libro m de lectura 3. TECH lector m

readership ['ri·dər·ʃɪp] n lectores mpl

readily ['red·ə·li] adv 1. (promptly) de buena gana 2. (easily) fácilmente

readiness ['red·i·nɪs] n 1. (willingness) (buena) disposición f 2. (preparedness) preparación f

reading ['ri·dɪŋ] n 1. lectura f 2. (interpretation) interpretación f 3. TECH medición f

reading glasses npl gafas f pl para leer

reading lamp n lámpara f portátil

readjust [ˌri·ə·'dʒʌst] I. vt a. TECH reajustar II. vi (objects) reajustarse; (people) readaptarse

readjustment [ˌri·ə·'dʒʌst·mənt] n TECH reajuste m

ready ['red·i] I. adj <-ier, -iest> 1. (pre-

R

pared) listo, -a; **to get ~ (for sth)** prepararse (para algo); **to get sth ~** preparar algo 2. (*willing*) dispuesto, -a 3. (*available*) disponible; **~ cash** dinero *m* en efectivo; **~ at hand** a mano 4. (*quick, prompt*) vivo, -a; **to find ~ acceptance** tener inmediata aceptación ▶ **~, set, go!** SPORTS ¡preparados, listos, ya! II. *n* **at the ~** a punto III. *vt* preparar

real |ril| I. *adj* 1. (*actual*) real; **for ~** de verdad 2. (*genuine*) auténtico, -a; **the ~ thing** [*or* **deal**] lo auténtico; **a ~ man** *iron* un hombre como Dios manda II. *adv inf* muy

realist ['ri·lɪst] *n* realista *mf*

realistic [ˌri·ə·'lɪs·tɪk] *adj* realista

reality [ri·'æl·ə·t̬i] *n* realidad *f*; **to come back to ~** volver a la realidad; **to face ~** enfrentarse a la realidad; **to become a ~** hacerse realidad; **in (all) ~** en realidad

reality television *n*, **reality TV** programación televisiva basada en la vida real

realization [ˌri·ə·lɪ·'zeɪ·ʃən] *n* 1. (*awareness*) comprensión *f* 2. a. FIN realización *f*

realize ['ri·ə·laɪz] I. *vt* 1. (*be aware of*) ser consciente de; (*become aware of*) darse cuenta de 2. (*achieve*) realizar 3. (*fulfill*) cumplir 4. FIN realizar; (*acquire*) liquidar II. *vi* (*notice*) darse cuenta; (*be aware of*) ser consciente

really ['ri·ə·li] I. *adv* 1. (*genuinely*) de verdad 2. (*actually*) en realidad 3. (*very*) muy II. *interj* 1. (*surprise and interest*) ¿ah sí? 2. (*annoyance*) pero bueno 3. (*disbelief*) ¿de veras?

realm |relm| *n* 1. (*kingdom*) reino *m* 2. (*area of interest*) campo *m*

realtor ['ri·əl·tər] *n* agente *mf* inmobiliario, -a

reap |rip| *vi, vt* cosechar

reappear [ˌri·ə·'pɪr] *vi* reaparecer

reapply [ˌri·ə·'plaɪ] I. *vi* **to ~ for sth** volver a presentar una solicitud para algo II. *vt* (*paint*) dar otra capa de

rear¹ |rɪr| I. *adj* (*light*) trasero, -a; (*leg, wheel*) posterior 2. (*back part*) parte *f* trasera 2. *inf* (*buttocks*) trasero *m* 3. MIL retaguardia *f*

rear² |rɪr| I. *vt* 1. (*bring up: child, animals*) criar 2. (*raise*) **to ~ one's head**

levantar la cabeza II. *vi* (*horse*) encabritarse

rearmost ['rɪr·moʊst] *adj* último, -a

rearrange [ˌri·ə·'reɪndʒ] *vt* 1. (*system*) reorganizar 2. (*furniture*) colocar de otra manera 3. (*meeting*) volver a concertar

rearview mirror *n* retrovisor *m*

rear-wheel drive *n* tracción *f* trasera

reason ['ri·zən] I. *n* 1. (*motive*) motivo *m*; **the ~ why...** el motivo por el que...; **for no particular ~** sin ningún motivo en concreto; **for some ~** por algún motivo 2. (*common sense*) sensatez *f*; **within ~** dentro de lo razonable; **to listen to ~** atender a razones; **to be beyond all ~** no tener ninguna lógica 3. (*sanity*) razón *f*; **to lose one's ~** perder la razón II. *vt* razonar III. *vi* razonar; **to ~ from sth** discurrir partiendo de algo

reasonable ['ri·zə·nə·bəl] *adj* 1. (*sensible*) sensato, -a; (*demand*) razonable 2. (*inexpensive*) moderado, -a

reasonably ['ri·zə·nə·bli] *adv* 1. (*fairly*) razonablemente 2. (*acceptably*) bastante

reasoning ['ri·zə·nɪŋ] *n* razonamiento *m*

reassemble [ˌri·ə·'sem·bəl] *vt* (*machine*) volver a montar; (*people*) volver a reunir

reassurance [ˌri·ə·'ʃʊr·əns] *n* (*comfort*) palabras *f pl* tranquilizadoras

reassure [ˌri·ə·'ʃʊr] *vt* tranquilizar

reassuring [ˌri·ə·'ʃʊr·ɪŋ] *adj* tranquilizador(a)

rebate ['ri·beɪt] *n* 1. (*refund*) reembolso *m*; **tax ~** devolución *f* de impuestos 2. (*discount*) rebaja *f*

rebel¹ ['reb·əl] I. *n* rebelde *mf* II. *adj* rebelde

rebel² [rɪ·'bel] <-ll-> *vi* rebelarse

rebellion [rɪ·'bel·jən] *n* rebelión *f*

rebellious [rɪ·'bel·jəs] *adj* rebelde

reboot [ˌri·'but] *vt* COMPUT reiniciar

rebound [rɪ·'baʊnd] I. *vi* 1. (*bounce back: ball*) rebotar 2. (*in basketball*) rebotear II. *vt* rebotar III. *n* 1. (*basketball*) rebote *m* 2. *fig* **to marry on the ~** casarse por despecho

recall [rɪ·'kɔl] I. *vt* 1. (*remember*) recordar 2. ECON retirar (del mercado) II. *vi* recordar III. *n* 1. (*memory*) memoria *f* 2. ECON retirada *f* (del mercado)

recap¹ ['ri·kæp] <pp-> *vi, vt inf abbr of* **recapitulate** recapitular

recap² [,ri·'kæp] <pp-> *vt* AUTO recauch(ut)ar, reencauchar *AmC*

recede [rɪ·'sid] *vi* 1. (*move backward: sea*) retirarse; (*tide*) bajar; (*fog*) desvanecerse 2. (*diminish*) disminuir; (*prices*) bajar

receding hairline *n* entradas *fpl*

receipt [rɪ·'sit] *n* 1. (*document*) recibo *m* 2. ~s COM ingresos *mpl* 3. (*act of receiving*) recepción *f*; **payment on ~** pago *m* al recibo de; **on ~ of...** al recibo de...; **to acknowledge ~ of** acusar recibo de

receive [rɪ·'siv] I. *vt* 1. (*be given*) a. TEL, RADIO recibir; (*pension, salary*) percibir 2. (*react to: proposal, suggestion*) acoger; **the book was well/badly ~d** el libro tuvo buena/mala acogida 3. (*injury*) sufrir II. *vi* SPORTS recibir

receiver [rɪ·'si·vər] *n* 1. TEL auricular *m*, tubo *m AmL*, fono *m Chile* 2. RADIO receptor *m* 3. SPORTS receptor(a) *m/f*

recent ['ri·sənt] *adj* reciente; **in ~ times** en los últimos tiempos

recently *adv* recientemente

reception [rɪ·'sep·ʃən] *n* 1. (*welcome*) acogida *f* 2. (*in hotel*) recepción *f*

reception desk *n* (mesa *f* de) recepción

receptionist [rɪ·'sep·ʃə·nɪst] *n* recepcionista *mf*

receptive [rɪ·'sep·tɪv] *adj* receptivo, -a

recess ['ri·ses] I. <-es> *n* 1. POL suspensión *f* de actividades, receso *m AmL* 2. SCHOOL recreo *m* 3. ARCHIT hueco *m* 4. MED fosa *f* 5. *often pl* (*place*) lugar *m* recóndito II. *vi* prorrogar; (*meeting, session*) suspender

recession [rɪ·'seʃ·ən] *n* 1. (*retreat*) retroceso *m* 2. ECON recesión *f*

recharge [,ri·'tʃardʒ] I. *vt* recargar II. *vi* recargarse

rechargeable [,ri·'tʃar·dʒə·bəl] *adj* recargable

recipe ['res·ə·pi] *n a. fig* receta *f*

recipient [rɪ·'sɪp·i·ənt] *n* (*of letter*) destinatario, -a *m, f*; (*of transplant*) recep-

tor(a) *m(f)*

reciprocal [rɪ·'sɪp·rə·kəl] *adj* 1. *a.* LING, MATH recíproco, -a 2. (*reverse*) mutuo, -a

recital [rɪ·'saɪ·təl] *n* 1. MUS recital *m* 2. (*description*) relación *f*

recite [rɪ·'saɪt] I. *vt* 1. (*repeat*) recitar 2. (*list*) enumerar II. *vi* dar un recitado

reckless ['rek·lɪs] *adj* imprudente; LAW temerario, -a

reckon ['rek·ən] I. *vt* 1. (*calculate*) calcular 2. (*consider*) considerar; **to ~ (that)...** creer (que)...; **I ~ not** me parece que no; **what do you ~?** ¿qué opinas? 3. (*judge*) estimar II. *vi inf* calcular

♦**reckon with** *vt insep* tener en cuenta; **she is a force to be reckoned with** es alguien a quien hay que tener muy en cuenta

♦**reckon without** *vt insep* no tener en cuenta

reckoning ['rek·ə·nɪŋ] *n* 1. (*calculation*) cálculo *m;* **to be out in one's ~** calcular mal 2. (*settlement*) ajuste *m* de cuentas

reclaim [rɪ·'kleɪm] *vt* 1. (*claim back: title, rights*) reclamar 2. (*reuse: land*) recuperar; (*material*) reciclar 3. (*reform*) regenerar

recline [rɪ·'klaɪn] I. *vi* apoyarse; **to ~ on** reclinarse contra [*or* en] II. *vt* reclinar

recliner [rɪ·'klaɪ·nər] *n* asiento *m* reclinable

recognition [,rek·əg·'nɪʃ·ən] *n a.* COMPUT reconocimiento *m;* **voice ~** reconocimiento de voz; **in ~ of** en reconocimiento de

recognizable ['rek·əg·naɪ·zə·bəl] *adj* reconocible

recognize ['rek·əg·naɪz] *vt* reconocer

recognized ['rek·əg·naɪzd] *adj* reconocido, -a

recoil¹ [rɪ·'kɔɪl] *vi* 1. (*draw back*) echarse atrás; **to ~ in horror** retroceder de miedo; **to ~ from doing sth** rehuir hacer algo 2. (*gun*) retroceder

recoil² ['ri·kɔɪl] *n* retroceso *m*

recollect [,rek·ə·'lekt] *vi, vt* recordar

recollection [,rek·ə·'lek·ʃən] *n* recuerdo *m;* **to have no ~ of sth** no recordar algo

R

recommend [ˌrek·ə·'mend] *vt* recomendar

recommendable *adj* recomendable

recommendation [ˌrek·ə·mən·'der·ʃən] *n* (*suggestion*) recomendación *f*; **on sb's ~** por recomendación de alguien

reconcile ['rek·ən·saɪl] *vt* 1. (*person*) reconciliar; **to become ~d with sb** reconciliarse con alguien 2. (*difference, fact*) conciliar; **to be ~d to sth** aceptar algo

reconciliation [ˌrek·ən·ˌsɪl·i·'er·ʃən] *n* 1. (*restoration of good relations*) reconciliación *f* 2. (*making compatible*) conciliación *f*

reconnaissance [rɪ·'kan·ə·səns] *n* reconocimiento *m*

reconsider [ˌri·kən·'sɪd·ər] I. *vt* reconsiderar II. *vi* recapacitar

reconstruct [ˌri·kən·'strʌkt] *vt* 1. (*building*) reconstruir 2. (*life*) rehacer; (*crime, event*) reconstituir

reconstruction [ˌri·kən·'strʌk·ʃən] *n* 1. (*of building*) reconstrucción *f* 2. (*of crime, event*) reconstitución *f*

record[1] ['rek·ərd] I. *n* 1. (*account*) relación *m*; (*document*) documento *m*; **medical ~** historial *m* médico; **to say sth off the ~** decir algo extraoficialmente 2. (*sb's past*) antecedentes *mpl*; **to have a good ~** tener un buen historial; **to have a clean ~** no tener antecedentes 3. **~s** archivos *mpl* 4. MUS disco *m*; **to make a ~** grabar un disco 5. SPORTS récord *m*; **to break a ~** batir un récord 6. LAW acta *f* II. *adj* récord; **to do sth in ~ time** hacer algo en un tiempo récord

record[2] [rɪ·'kɔrd] I. *vt* 1. (*store*) archivar 2. *a.* COMPUT registrar; MUS grabar 3. LAW hacer constar en acta II. *vi* grabar

record-breaking *adj* que bate todos los récords

recorded [rɪ·'kɔr·dɪd] *adj* registrado, -a; (*history*) documentado, -a; (*music*) grabado, -a

recorder [rɪ·'kɔr·dər] *n* 1. (*tape recorder*) grabadora *f* 2. MUS flauta *f* dulce

record holder *n* SPORTS plusmarquista *mf*

recording *n* (*of sound*) grabación *f*

record label *n* sello *m* discográfico

record player *n* tocadiscos *m inv*

recount[1] [rɪ·'kaʊnt] *vt* 1. (*narrate*) contar 2. (*count again*) volver a contar

recount[2] ['ri·kaʊnt] *n* POL recuento *m*

recover [rɪ·'kʌv·ər] I. *vt a.* COMPUT recuperar; **to ~ one's composure** recobrar su compostura II. *vi* (*regain health*) recuperarse

re-cover [ˌri·'kʌv·ər] *vt* retapizar

recovery [rɪ·'kʌv·ə·ri] <-ies> *n a.* MED, ECON recuperación *f*; **to be beyond ~** ser irrecuperable

recreate [ˌri·kri·'eɪt] *vt* recrear

recreation[1] [ˌri·kri·'eɪ·ʃən] *n* (*of conditions, situation*) recreación *f*

recreation[2] [ˌrek·ri·'eɪ·ʃən] *n* 1. *a.* SCHOOL recreo *m* 2. (*pastime*) diversión *f*

recreational [ˌrek·ri·'eɪ·ʃə·nəl] *adj* recreativo, -a

recreation room *n* salón *m* recreativo

recruit [rɪ·'krut] I. *vt* MIL reclutar; (*employee*) contratar II. *vi* MIL recluta *mf*

recruitment *n* MIL reclutamiento *m*; ECON contratación *f*

rectangle ['rek·tæŋ·gəl] *n* rectángulo *m*

rectangular [rek·'tæŋ·gjə·lər] *adj* rectangular

rectify ['rek·tə·faɪ] *vt* rectificar

rector ['rek·tər] *n* 1. SCHOOL director(a) *m(f)* 2. UNIV rector(a) *m(f)*

recur [rɪ·'kɜr] *vi* repetirse

recurrence [rɪ·'kɜr·əns] *n* repetición *f*

recurrent [rɪ·'kɜr·ənt] *adj* (*dream, motif*) recurrente; (*costs, expenses*) constante

recurring *adj* recurrente

recycle [ˌri·'saɪ·kəl] *vt* reciclar

recycling *n* reciclaje *m*

red [red] I. <-dd-> *adj* rojo, -a; (*hair*) pelirrojo, -a; (*wine*) tinto; **to be** [*or go*] **~** ruborizarse II. *n* rojo *m*; **to be in the ~** FIN estar en números rojos ▶ **to see** ~ salir de sus casillas

red blood cell *n* glóbulo *m* rojo

Red Crescent *n* **the ~** la Media Luna Roja

Red Cross *n* **the ~** la Cruz Roja

red deer *n inv* ciervo *m*

redden ['red·ən] I. *vi* enrojecerse; (*person*) ruborizarse II. *vt* enrojecer

reddish ['red·ɪʃ] *adj* rojizo, -a

redecorate [ˌri·'dek·ə·reɪt] *vt* redecorar; (*paint*) volver a pintar; (*wallpaper*) volver a empapelar

redeem [rɪ·ˈdim] *vt* **1.** *a.* REL (*person, soul*) redimir; (*situation*) salvar; **to ~ oneself** redimirse **2.** FIN (*policy, share*) liquidar; (*pawned item*) desempeñar; (*debt*) pagar **3.** (*fulfill: promise*) cumplir

Redeemer [rɪ·ˈdi·mər] *n* REL **the ~** el Redentor

redeeming [rɪ·ˈdi·mɪŋ] *adj* redentor(a)

redemption [rɪ·ˈdemp·ʃən] *n* **1.** *a.* REL redención *f* **2.** FIN (*of policy, share*) liquidación *f*

redevelop [ˌri·dɪ·ˈvel·əp] *vt* reurbanizar

red-haired [ˌred·ˈherd] *adj* pelirrojo, -a

red-handed [ˌred·ˈhæn·dɪd] *adj* **to catch sb ~** pillar a alguien con las manos en la masa

redhead [ˈred·hed] *n* pelirrojo, -a *m, f*

red-headed *adj* pelirrojo, -a

red herring *n fig* pista *f* falsa

red-hot [ˌred·ˈhat] *adj* **1.** (*extremely hot*) candente; **to be ~** estar al rojo vivo **2.** (*exciting*) apasionante **3.** (*up-to-the-minute: information*) de última hora

redirect [ˌri·dɪ·ˈrekt] *vt* reorientar; (*traffic*) desviar

red light *n* semáforo *m* en rojo

red-light district *n* barrio *m* de mala fama

red meat *n* carne *f* roja

redneck [ˈred·nek] *n* campesino blanco de la clase baja rural, de los estados del Sur

redness [ˈred·nɪs] *n* rojez *f*

redo [ˌri·ˈdu] *vt irr* rehacer

redouble [rɪ·ˈdʌb·əl] *vt* redoblar; **to ~ one's efforts** redoblar los esfuerzos

red pepper *n* pimiento *m* rojo

Red Sea *n* **the ~** el Mar Rojo

redskin *n offensive* piel *mf* roja

red tape *n* papeleo *m*

reduce [rɪ·ˈdus] *vt* **1.** (*diminish*) reducir; (*price*) rebajar **2.** **to ~ sb to tears** hacer llorar a alguien; **to ~ sth to rubble/ashes** reducir algo a escombros/cenizas; **to be ~d to doing sth** verse forzado a hacer algo **3.** MATH (*fraction*) simplificar

reduced [rɪ·ˈdust] *adj* (*lower*) reducido, -a; (*price*) rebajado, -a

reduction [rɪ·ˈdʌk·ʃən] *n* reducción *f*; (*in price*) rebaja *f*

redundancy [rɪ·ˈdʌn·dən·si] <-ies> *n* redundancia *f*

redundant [rɪ·ˈdʌn·dənt] *adj* (*superfluous*) superfluo, -a; LING redundante

red wine *n* vino *m* tinto

reed [rid] *n* **1.** (*plant*) junco *m*, totora *f* AmS **2.** (*straw*) caña *f* **3.** MUS lengüeta *f*

reef [rif] *n* **1.** (*ridge*) arrecife *m* **2.** (*mine*) filón *m*

reel[1] [ril] *n* (*storage or winding device*) carrete *m*; (*for film, rope, tape*) bobina *f*

reel[2] [ril] *vi* **1.** (*move unsteadily*) tambalearse **2.** (*recoil*) retroceder

re-elect [ˌri·ɪ·ˈlekt] *vt* reelegir

re-enter [ˌri·ˈen·tər] *vt* **1.** (*go in again*) volver a entrar en **2.** COMPUT teclear de nuevo

re-entry [ˌri·ˈen·tri] <-ies> *n* reingreso *m*

ref [ref] *n* **1.** *inf abbr of* **referee** árbitro, -a *m, f* **2.** *abbr of* **reference** referencia *f*

refectory [rɪ·ˈfek·tə·ri] <-ies> *n* refectorio *m*

refer [rɪ·ˈfɜr] <-rr-> *vt* **to refer sth to sb** (*article*) remitir algo a alguien; **to ~ a patient to a specialist** mandar a un paciente a un especialista

referee [ˌref·ə·ˈri] *n* SPORTS árbitro, -a *m, f*, referí *m* AmL

reference [ˈref·ər·əns] *n* **1.** (*consultation*) consulta *f* **2.** (*source*) referencia *f* **3.** (*allusion*) alusión *f*; **with ~ to what was said** en alusión a lo que se dijo **4.** ADMIN (*number*) número *m* de referencia **5.** (*for job application*) referencias *fpl*

reference book *n* libro *m* de consulta

reference library *n* biblioteca *f* de consulta

reference number *n* **1.** (*in document, on book*) número *m* de referencia **2.** (*on product*) número *m* de serie

referendum [ˌref·ə·ˈren·dəm] <-s *or*-da> *n* referéndum *m*

refill[1] [ˌri·ˈfɪl] *vt* (*fill again*) rellenar

refill[2] [ˈri·fɪl] *n* (*replacement*) recambio *m*

R

refine [rɪ·ˈfaɪn] *vt* **1.** (*oil, sugar*) refinar **2.** (*technique*) perfeccionar

refined [rɪ·ˈfaɪnd] *adj* **1.** (*oil, sugar*) refinado, -a **2.** (*sophisticated*) sofisticado, -a **3.** (*very polite*) fino, -a

refinery [rɪ·ˈfaɪ·nə·ri] <-ies> *n* refinería *f*

reflation [ˌri·ˈfleɪ·ʃən] *n* reflación *f*

reflect [rɪ·ˈflekt] **I.** *vt* reflejar **II.** *vi* **1.** (*cast back light*) reflejarse **2.** (*contemplate*) reflexionar

reflection [rɪ·ˈflek·ʃən] *n* **1.** (*image*) reflejo *m* **2.** (*thought*) reflexión *f*; **~s on sth** reflexión acerca de algo; **on ~** pensándolo bien **3.** *fig* **to be a fair ~ of sth** ser un fiel reflejo de algo

reflective [rɪ·ˈflek·tɪv] *adj* **1.** (*surface*) reflector(a) **2.** (*thoughtful*) reflexivo, -a

reflector [rɪ·ˈflek·tər] *n* (*mirror*) reflector *m*; (*of bicycle, car*) captafaros *m inv*

reflex [ˈri·fleks] <-es> **I.** *n* reflejo *m* **II.** *adj* reflejo, -a

reflexive [rɪ·ˈflek·sɪv] *adj* **1.** (*independent of will*) reflejo, -a **2.** LING reflexivo, -a

reform [rɪ·ˈfɔrm] **I.** *vt* reformar **II.** *vi* reformarse **III.** *n* reforma *f*

Reformation [ˌref·ər·ˈmeɪ·ʃən] *n* reforma *f*; **the Reformation** la Reforma

reformer *n* reformador(a) *m(f)*

refract [rɪ·ˈfrækt] *vt* PHYS refractar

refraction [rɪ·ˈfræk·ʃən] *n* refracción *f*

refrain[1] [rɪ·ˈfreɪn] *vi form* abstenerse; **to ~ from doing sth** abstenerse de hacer algo

refrain[2] [rɪ·ˈfreɪn] *n* MUS estribillo *m*

refresh [rɪ·ˈfreʃ] *vt* refrescar; **to ~ oneself** refrescarse

refreshing *adj* **1.** (*drink*) refrescante **2.** (*change, difference*) reconfortante

refreshment [rɪ·ˈfreʃ·mənt] *n* **1.** (*drink*) refresco *m* **2.** (*food*) refrigerio *m*

refrigerate [rɪ·ˈfrɪdʒ·ə·reɪt] *vt* refrigerar

refrigerator [rɪ·ˈfrɪdʒ·ə·reɪ·tər] *n* nevera *f*, refrigerador *m*

refuel [ˌri·ˈfju·əl] <-ll-, -l-> **I.** *vi* repostar combustible **II.** *vt* reabastecer de combustible; *fig* renovar

refuge [ˈref·judʒ] *n* refugio *m*; **to take ~ in sth** refugiarse en algo

refugee [ˌref·ju·ˈdʒi] *n* refugiado, -a *m, f*

refugee camp *n* campo *m* de refugiados

refund[1] [ˌri·ˈfʌnd] *vt* reembolsar

refund[2] [ˈri·fʌnd] *n* reembolso *m*

refusal [rɪ·ˈfju·zəl] *n* negativa *f*

refuse[1] [rɪ·ˈfjuz] **I.** *vi* negarse **II.** *vt* (*request, gift*) rechazar; (*permission, entry*) denegar; **to ~ sb sth** negar algo a alguien

regain [rɪ·ˈgeɪn] *vt* (*freedom, possession*) recuperar; (*consciousness, health*) recobrar

regal [ˈri·gəl] *adj* regio, -a

regard [rɪ·ˈgard] **I.** *vt* **1.** (*consider*) considerar; **to ~ sb highly** tener muy buena opinión de alguien **2.** *form* (*watch*) contemplar **3.** (*concerning*) **as ~s...** respecto a... **II.** *n form* **1.** (*consideration*) consideración *f*; **to pay no ~ to sth** no prestar atención a algo; **with ~ to...** en cuanto a... **2.** (*respect*) respeto *m*, estima *f* **3.** (*point*) respeto *m*; **in this ~** con respecto a esto **4.** **~s** (*in messages*) recuerdos *mpl*; **with kind ~s** muchos saludos

regarding *prep* en cuanto a

regardless [rɪ·ˈgard·lɪs] **I.** *adv* a pesar de todo; **to press on ~** seguir cueste lo que cueste **II.** *adj* indiferente; **~ of...** sin tener en cuenta...

regenerate [rɪ·ˈdʒen·ə·reɪt] **I.** *vt* regenerar **II.** *vi* regenerarse

regeneration [rɪ·ˌdʒen·ə·ˈreɪ·ʃən] *n* regeneración *f*

regime [rə·ˈʒim] *n* régimen *m*

regiment [ˈredʒ·ə·mənt] *n* **1.** MIL regimiento *m* **2.** *fig* multitud *f*

region [ˈri·dʒən] *n* GEO, ANAT región *f*; **in the ~ of 30** alrededor de 30 **2.** (*administrative area*) provincia *f*

regional [ˈri·dʒə·nəl] *adj* regional

register [ˈredʒ·ɪ·stər] **I.** *n* registro *m*; **class ~** lista *f* de la clase **II.** *vt* registrar; (*car*) matricular; (*voter*) inscribir; (*letter, package*) certificar **III.** *vi* **1.** (*record*) inscribirse; UNIV matricularse **2.** (*be understood*) **the information didn't ~ with him** no registró la información

registered [ˈredʒ·ɪ·stərd] *adj* registrado, -a; (*nurse*) diplomado, -a; (*student*) matriculado, -a; (*letter, package*) certificado, -a

registration [ˌredʒ·ɪ·ˈstreɪ·ʃən] *n* **1.** (*act*)

inscripción f 2. AUTO matrícula f 3. UNIV matriculación f

registration fee n cuota f de inscripción; UNIV matrícula f

registration number n matrícula f

registry ['redʒɪstri] n registro m

regret [rɪ'gret] I. <-tt-> vt lamentar; **to ~ doing sth** arrepentirse de haber hecho algo II. n arrepentimiento m; **to have ~s** tener remordimientos; **to have no ~s about sth** no arrepentirse de algo; **much to my ~** a mi pesar; **to send one's ~s** enviar sus condolencias

regretful [rɪ'gretfəl] adj arrepentido, -a

regretfully adv lamentablemente

regrettable [rɪ'gret·ə·bəl] adj lamentable

regroup [‚ri·'grup] I. vt reagrupar II. vi reagruparse

regular ['reg·jə·lər] adj 1. (pattern) regular; (appearance, customer) habitual; (procedure) normal; **to have ~ meetings** tener reuniones periódicas 2. (gas) normal 3. LING regular

regularity [‚reg·ju·'ler·ə·ti] n regularidad f

regularly adv con regularidad

regulate ['reg·ju·leɪt] vt 1. (supervise) reglamentar 2. (adjust) regular

regulation [‚reg·ju·'leɪ·ʃən] n 1. (rule) regla f; **safety ~s** reglamento m de seguridad; **in accordance with (the) ~s** de acuerdo con el reglamento 2. (adjustment) regulación f

regulator ['reg·ju·leɪ·tər] n regulador m

regulatory ['reg·jə·lə·tɔr·i] adj regulador(a)

rehab ['ri·hæb] n inf abbr of **rehabilitation** rehabilitación f

rehabilitate [‚ri·hə·'bɪl·ə·teɪt] vt rehabilitar

rehabilitation [‚ri·hə‚bɪl·ə·'teɪ·ʃən] n rehabilitación f

rehearsal [rɪ'hɜr·səl] n ensayo m

rehearse [rɪ'hɜrs] vt, vi ensayar

reign [reɪn] I. vi 1. (be monarch) reinar 2. fig (be dominant) imperar II. n 1. (sovereignty) reinado m 2. (rule) régimen m

reimburse [‚ri·ɪm·'bɜrs] vt reembolsar

reimbursement n reembolso m

rein [reɪn] n rienda f ▶ **to keep sb on a tight ~** atar corto a alguien, tener a alguien controlado; **to hold the ~s** sujetar las riendas

reincarnation [‚ri·ɪn·kar·'neɪ·ʃən] n reencarnación f

reindeer ['reɪn·dɪr] n inv reno m

reinforce [‚ri·ɪn·'fɔrs] vt a. MIL reforzar; (argument) fortalecer

reinforcement n refuerzo m

reject[1] [rɪ'dʒekt] vt a. MED, TECH rechazar; (application, request) desestimar; (accusation) negar

reject[2] ['ri·dʒekt] n 1. (cast-off) artículo m defectuoso 2. (person) persona f rechazada

rejection [rɪ'dʒek·ʃən] n rechazo m

rejoice [rɪ'dʒɔɪs] vi regocijarse; **to ~ in doing sth** regocijarse haciendo algo; **I ~d to see that...** me alegré al ver que...

rejoicing n regocijo m

rejoin [‚ri·'dʒɔɪn] I. vt (join again) volver a unirse con; (regiment) reincorporarse a II. vi reunirse

rejuvenate [rɪ'dʒu·və·neɪt] vt rejuvenecer

relapse [rɪ'læps] I. n MED recaída f II. vi a. MED recaer

relate [rɪ'leɪt] I. vt 1. (establish connection) relacionar 2. (tell) contar II. vi 1. (be connected with) **to ~ to sb/ sth** estar relacionado con alguien/algo 2. (understand) **to ~ to sth/sb** comprender algo/a alguien

related adj 1. (linked) relacionado, -a 2. (in same family) emparentado, -a; **to be ~ to sb** estar emparentado con alguien

relating to prep acerca de

relation [rɪ'leɪ·ʃən] n 1. (link) relación f; **in ~ to** en relación a; **to bear no ~ to sb/sth** no tener relación con alguien/algo 2. (relative) pariente mf 3. **~s** (contact) relaciones fpl

relationship [rɪ'leɪ·ʃən·ʃɪp] n 1. (link) relación f 2. (family connection) parentesco m 3. (between two people) relaciones fpl; **to be in a ~ with sb** tener una relación con alguien; **business ~s** relaciones comerciales

R

relative [ˈrel·ə·tɪv] I. *adj* relativo, -a II. *n* pariente *mf*

relatively *adv* relativamente

relativity [ˌrel·ə·ˈtɪv·ə·t̬i] *n* relatividad *f*

relax [rɪ·ˈlæks] I. *vi* relajarse; (*rules*) suavizarse; **relax!** ¡cálmate! II. *vt* relajar; (*rules*) suavizar; **to ~ one's efforts** disminuir sus esfuerzos

relaxation [ˌri·læk·ˈseɪ·ʃən] *n* relajación *f*

relaxed *adj* relajado, -a

relay [ˈri·leɪ] I. *vt* (*information*) pasar; TV retransmitir II. *n* 1. (*group*) turno *m;* **to work in ~s** trabajar por turnos 2. SPORTS carrera *f* de relevos 3. ELEC relé *m*

release [rɪ·ˈlis] I. *vt* 1. (*set free*) poner en libertad 2. (*cease to hold*) soltar 3. PHOT disparar 4. (*allow to escape: gas*) emitir 4. (*weaken: pressure*) aliviar 5. (*make public: information*) anunciar; (*book*) publicar; (*film*) estrenar; (*CD*) poner a la venta II. *n* 1. (*of prisoner*) excarcelación *f;* (*of hostage*) liberación *f* 2. PHOT disparador *m* 3. (*escape*) escape *m* 4. (*publication*) publicación *f;* (*of film*) estreno *m;* **press ~** comunicado *m* de prensa

relegate [ˈrel·ə·geɪt] *vt* relegar

relent [rɪ·ˈlent] *vi* (*person*) ceder; (*wind, rain*) amainar

relentless [rɪ·ˈlent·lɪs] *adj* (*pursuit, opposition*) implacable; (*pressure*) incesante; (*criticism*) despiadado, -a

relevance [ˈrel·ə·vəns] *n* pertinencia

relevant [ˈrel·ə·vənt] *adj* pertinente

reliability [rɪˌlaɪ·ə·ˈbɪl·ə·t̬i] *n* 1. (*dependability*) seguridad *f* 2. (*trustworthiness*) fiabilidad *f*

reliable [rɪ·ˈlaɪ·ə·bəl] *adj* 1. (*credible*) fidedigno, -a; (*authority*) serio, -a; (*evidence*) fehaciente 2. (*trustworthy*) de confianza

reliance [rɪ·ˈlaɪ·əns] *n* 1. (*dependence*) dependencia *f* 2. (*belief*) confianza *f*

reliant [rɪ·ˈlaɪ·ənt] *adj* **to be ~ on sb/sth** depender de alguien/algo

relic [ˈrel·ɪk] *n a. fig* reliquia *f*

relief [rɪ·ˈlif] I. *n* 1. (*relaxation*) alivio *m;* **what a ~!** ¡menos mal! 2. (*aid*) socorro *m* 3. (*replacement*) relevo *m* 4. *a.* GEO relieve *m* 5. **tax ~** desgravación *f* fiscal II. *adj* 1. de relevo; (*driver*) su-

plente 2. GEO en relieve

relief worker *n* trabajador (a) *m(f)* de una organización humanitaria

relieve [rɪ·ˈliv] *vt* 1. (*assist*) socorrer 2. (*alleviate: pain*) aliviar; (*suffering*) mitigar; (*one's mind*) tranquilizar 3. (*urinate, defecate*) **to ~ oneself** hacer sus necesidades

relieved *adj* aliviado, -a

religion [rɪ·ˈlɪdʒ·ən] *n* religión *f*

religious [rɪ·ˈlɪdʒ·əs] *adj* religioso, -a

relish [ˈrel·ɪʃ] I. *n* 1. (*enjoyment*) gusto *m;* **with ~** con gusto 2. (*enthusiasm*) entusiasmo *m* 3. CULIN condimento *m* II. *vt* deleitarse en

reload [ˌri·ˈloʊd] I. *vt* recargar II. *vi* recargarse

relocate [riˈloʊ·keɪt] I. *vi* trasladarse II. *vt* trasladar

reluctance [rɪ·ˈlʌk·təns] *n* desgana *f;* **with ~** de mala gana

reluctant [rɪ·ˈlʌk·tənt] *adj* reacio, -a; **to be ~ to do sth** tener pocas ganas de hacer algo

rely [rɪ·ˈlaɪ] *vi* **to ~ on** [*or* **upon**] (*trust*) confiar en; (*depend on*) depender de

remain [rɪ·ˈmeɪn] *vi* 1. (*stay*) quedar(se) 2. (*continue*) permanecer; **to ~ seated** quedarse sentado; **to ~ unsolved** seguir sin solucionarse; **much ~s to be done** queda mucho por hacer; **the fact ~s that...** sigue siendo un hecho que...; **it ~s to be seen** (**who/what/how**) está por ver (quién/qué/cómo)

remainder [rɪ·ˈmeɪn·dər] *n a.* MATH resto *m;* **the ~ of sb's life** lo que queda de la vida de alguien

remaining [rɪ·ˈmeɪ·nɪŋ] *adj* restante

remains [rɪ·ˈmeɪnz] *npl* restos *mpl*

remand [rɪ·ˈmænd] I. *vt* **to ~ sb to prison** [*or* **in custody**] poner a alguien en prisión preventiva; **to ~ sb on bail** poner a alguien en libertad bajo fianza II. *n* **to be on ~** estar en prisión preventiva

remark [rɪ·ˈmɑrk] I. *vi* **to ~ on sth** hacer observaciones sobre algo II. *n* observación *f;* **to make ~s about sb/sth** hacer comentarios sobre alguien/algo

remarkable [rɪ·ˈmɑr·kə·bəl] *adj* extraordinario, -a; (*coincidence*) singular

remarry [ˌri·ˈmær·i] <-ie-> *vi* volver a

remedy ['rem·ə·di] I. <-ies> n 1. remedio m; **to be beyond ~** no tener remedio 2. LAW (**legal**) **~** recurso m (legal) II. vt remediar

remember [rɪ·'mem·bər] vt 1. (recall) recordar 2. (commemorate) conmemorar

remind [rɪ·'maɪnd] vt recordar; **to ~ sb to do sth** recordar a alguien que haga algo; **he ~s me of you** me recuerda a ti; **that ~s me,...** por cierto,...

reminder [rɪ·'maɪn·dər] n 1. (note) recordatorio m 2. (warning) advertencia f 3. (memento) recuerdo m

reminisce [,rem·ə·'nɪs] vi rememorar

remission [rɪ·'mɪʃ·ən] n remisión f

remit [rɪ·'mɪt] <-tt-> vt form 1. (send) remitir; (money) enviar 2. LAW perdonar

remittance [rɪ·'mɪt·əns] n giro m

remorse [rɪ·'mɔrs] n remordimiento m; **without ~** sin remordimientos

remorseful [rɪ·'mɔrs·fəl] adj arrepentido, -a

remote [rɪ·'moʊt] adj <-er, -est> (place, possibility) remoto, -a

remote control n mando m a distancia, control m remoto Col

remote-controlled adj teledirigido, -a

removal [rɪ·'mu·vəl] n 1. (of stain, problem) eliminación f 2. (extraction) extracción f

remove [rɪ·'muv] vt 1. (take away) quitar; (clothes) quitarse 2. (get rid of) eliminar; (cork, dent) sacar; (entry, name) borrar; (doubts, fears) disipar; (problem) solucionar; **to ~ one's hair** depilarse 3. (dismiss from job) destituir

remover [rɪ·'mu·vər] n 1. agente mf de mudanzas 2. **stain ~** quitamanchas m inv 3. **nail polish ~** quitaesmalte

rename [,ri·'neɪm] vt poner un nuevo nombre a

render ['ren·dər] vt form 1. (make) hacer; **to ~ sb speechless** dejar a alguien mudo 2. (perform) representar; MUS interpretar 3. (give: thanks) ofrecer; (aid, service) prestar; (judgment) emitir 4. (translate) traducir 5. (homage) rendir

rendezvous ['ran·deɪ·,vu] n inv 1. (meeting) cita f 2. (place) lugar m de reunión

renew [rɪ·'nu] vt 1. (begin again: membership, passport) renovar 2. (mend) recuperar

renewable [rɪ·'nu·ə·bəl] adj renovable

renewed [rɪ·'nud] adj renovado, -a

renounce [rɪ·'naʊns] vt renunciar a

renovate ['ren·ə·veɪt] vt restaurar, renovar

renovation [,ren·ə·'veɪ·ʃən] n renovación f

renowned [rɪ·'naʊnd] adj renombrado, -a

rent[1] [rent] n (rip) rasgadura f

rent[2] [rent] I. vt (apartment, car, video) alquilar; (land) arrendar II. n alquiler m; **for ~** se alquila

rent-a-car n (car) coche m de alquiler; (agency) agencia f de alquiler de coches

rental ['ren·təl] I. n alquiler m II. adj de alquiler

rent-free adj exento, -a de alquiler

reopen [ri·'oʊ·pən] I. vt reabrir II. vi reabrirse

reorder [,ri·'ɔr·dər] vt 1. (reorganize) reordenar 2. COM hacer un nuevo pedido de

reorganize [ri·'ɔr·gə·naɪz] I. vt reorganizar II. vi reorganizarse

rep [rep] n inf 1. abbr of **representative** representante mf de ventas 2. THEAT abbr of **repertory** repertorio m

Rep. 1. abbr of **Republic** Rep. 2. abbr of **Republican** republicano, -a

repair [rɪ·'per] I. vt 1. (machine) reparar; (clothes) arreglar 2. (set right: damage) enmendar II. n 1. (mending: of machine) reparación f; (of clothes) arreglo m; **to be beyond ~** no tener arreglo; **to be under ~** estar en reparación 2. (state) **to be in good/bad ~** estar en buen/mal estado

repair kit n caja f de herramientas

repairman <-men> n (for cars) mecánico m; (for television) técnico m

repair shop n taller m de reparaciones

repatriate [ri·'peɪ·tri·eɪt] vt repatriar

repay [rɪ·'peɪ] <repaid> vt (money) de-

R

volver; (*debts*) liquidar; **to ~ money to sb** reintegrar dinero a alguien; **to ~ a debt** pagar una deuda

repayable |rɪ·ˈpeɪ·ə·bəl| *adj* reembolsable

repayment |rɪ·ˈpeɪ·mənt| *n* reembolso *m*

repeat |rɪ·ˈpit| **I.** *vt* (*say or do again*) repetir **II.** *vi* (*happen again*) repetirse; (*taste*) repetir

repeated *adj* repetido, -a

repel |rɪ·ˈpel| <-ll-> *vt* 1. (*ward off*) rechazar 2. MIL, PHYS repeler 3. (*disgust*) repugnar

repellent |rɪ·ˈpel·ənt| **I.** *n* repelente *m* **II.** *adj* repugnante

repentance |rɪ·ˈpen·təns| *n* arrepentimiento *m*

repetition |ˌrep·ə·ˈtɪʃ·ən| *n* repetición *f*

replace |rɪ·ˈpleɪs| *vt* 1. (*take the place of*) reemplazar; (*person*) sustituir 2. (*put back*) reponer

replacement |rɪ·ˈpleɪs·mənt| **I.** *n* 1. (*person*) sustituto, -a *m, f*; (*part*) recambio *m* 2. MIL reemplazo *m* 3. (*act of substituting*) sustitución *f* **II.** *adj* de repuesto

replay[1] |ˌri·ˈpleɪ| *vt* 1. SPORTS volver a jugar 2. MUS volver a tocar 3. TV repetir

replay[2] |ˈri·pleɪ| *n* 1. SPORTS, TV repetición *f*; **instant ~** repetición *f* instantánea 2. MUS reproducción *f*

reply |rɪ·ˈplaɪ| **I.** <-ied> *vt* contestar **II.** <-ied> *vi* 1. (*verbally*) contestar 2. (*react*) responder **III.** <-ies> *n* respuesta *f*

report |rɪ·ˈpɔrt| **I.** *n* (*account*) informe *m*; PUBL noticia *f*; (*longer*) reportaje *m*; **to give a ~** presentar un informe **II.** *vt* 1. (*recount*) relatar; (*discovery*) anunciar; **to ~ that...** informar que...; **nothing to ~** sin novedades 2. (*denounce*) denunciar **III.** *vi* 1. (*make results public*) presentar un informe 2. (*arrive at work*) presentarse; **to ~ sick** dar parte de enfermedad

report card *n* cartilla *f* escolar

reporter |rɪ·ˈpɔr·tər| *n* reportero, -a *m, f*

represent |ˌrep·rɪ·ˈzent| *vt* (*act for, depict*) representar

representative |ˌrep·rɪ·ˈzen·tə·tɪv| **I.** *adj* 1. POL representativo, -a 2. (*typical*) típico, -a **II.** *n* 1. *a.* COM representante *mf* 2. LAW apoderado, -a *m, f* 3. POL diputado, -a *m, f*

repress |rɪ·ˈpres| *vt* reprimir

repression |rɪ·ˈpreʃ·ən| *n* represión *f*

repressive |rɪ·ˈpres·ɪv| *adj* represivo, -a

reprimand |ˈrep·rə·mænd| **I.** *vt* reprender **II.** *n* reprimenda *f*

reprint[1] |ˌri·ˈprɪnt| *vt* reimprimir

reprint[2] |ˈri·prɪnt| *n* reimpresión *f*

reprisal |rɪ·ˈpraɪ·zəl| *n* represalia *f*; **to take ~s** tomar represalias

reproach |rɪ·ˈproʊtʃ| **I.** *vt* reprochar **II.** *n* reproche *m*; **beyond ~** intachable

reproachful |rɪ·ˈproʊtʃ·fəl| *adj* acusador(a)

reprocess |ˌri·ˈpras·es| *vt* reprocesar

reprocessing plant *n* ECOL, TECH planta *f* reprocesadora

reproduce |ˌri·prə·ˈdus| **I.** *vi* reproducirse **II.** *vt* reproducir

reproduction |ˌri·prə·ˈdʌk·ʃən| *n* reproducción *f*

reproductive |ˌri·prə·ˈdʌk·tɪv| *adj* reproductor(a)

reprove |rɪ·ˈpruv| *vt* reprender

reproving |rɪ·ˈpru·vɪŋ| *adj* reprobatorio, -a

reptile |ˈrep·taɪl| *n* reptil *m*

republic |rɪ·ˈpʌb·lɪk| *n* república *f*

republican |rɪ·ˈpʌb·lɪ·kən| **I.** *n* republicano, -a *m, f* **II.** *adj* republicano, -a

repugnance |rɪ·ˈpʌg·nəns| *n* repugnancia *f*

repugnant |rɪ·ˈpʌg·nənt| *adj* repugnante

repulse |rɪ·ˈpʌls| *vt* 1. (*disgust*) repulsar 2. (*ward off*) rechazar **II.** *n* repulsa *f*

repulsion |rɪ·ˈpʌl·ʃən| *n* repulsión *f*

repulsive |rɪ·ˈpʌl·sɪv| *adj* repulsivo, -a

reputable |ˈrep·jə·tə·bəl| *adj* acreditado, -a

reputation |ˌrep·jʊ·ˈteɪ·ʃən| *n* reputación *f*; **to have a good/bad ~** tener buena/mala fama

repute |rɪ·ˈpjut| *n* reputación *f*

request |rɪ·ˈkwest| **I.** *n* petición *f*; ADMIN solicitud *f*; **on ~** a petición; **to make a ~ for sth** pedir algo **II.** *vt* pedir; ADMIN solicitar

require [rɪ'kwaɪr] *vt* **1.** (*need*) necesitar **2.** (*demand*) exigir; **to ~ sb to do sth** exigir a alguien que haga algo

requirement [rɪ'kwaɪr·mənt] *n* requisito *m*

rerun [ˌri·'rʌn] *vt irr* CINE, TV repetir; THEAT reestrenar

resale ['ri·seɪl] *n* reventa *m*

reschedule [ˌri·'skedʒ·ul] *vt* reprogramar

rescue ['res·kju] **I.** *vt* (*save*) rescatar **II.** *n* rescate *m;* **to come to sb's ~** rescatar a alguien

research [ri·'sɜrtʃ] **I.** *n* investigación *f* **II.** *vi, vt* investigar

researcher *n* investigador(a) *m(f)*

resemblance [rɪ·'zem·bləns] *n* parecido *m*

resemble [rɪ·'zem·bəl] *vt* parecerse a

resent [rɪ·'zent] *vt* **to ~ sth** sentirse molesto por algo

resentful [rɪ·'zent·fəl] *adj* (*person*) resentido, -a; (*expression*) de resentimiento

resentment [rɪ·'zent·mənt] *n* resentimiento *m*

reservation [ˌrez·ər·'veɪ·ʃən] *n* **1.** (*booking*) reserva *f* **2.** (*doubt*) reserva *f;* **to have ~s about sth** tener ciertas dudas sobre algo

reserve [rɪ·'zɜrv] **I.** *n* **1.** reserva *f;* **to have sth in ~** tener algo en reserva **2.** SPORTS suplente *mf* **II.** *vt* reservar

reserved *adj* reservado, -a

reservoir ['rez·ər·vwar] *n* **1.** (*tank*) depósito *m* **2.** (*lake*) embalse *m*

reset [ˌri·'set] *vt irr* **1.** (*machine*) reajustar; COMPUT reiniciar **2.** (*jewel*) reengastar

reshuffle [ˌri·'ʃʌf·əl] *vt* (*a government*) reorganizar; (*cards*) volver a barajar

residence ['rez·ɪ·dəns] *n* **1.** (*home*) domicilio *m* **2.** (*act*) residencia *f*

residence permit *n* permiso *m* de residencia

resident ['rez·ɪ·dənt] **I.** *n* residente *mf* **II.** *adj* residente

residential [ˌrez·ɪ·'den·ʃəl] *adj* residencial

resign [rɪ·'zaɪn] **I.** *vi* **1.** (*leave job*) dimitir **2.** GAMES abandonar **II.** *vt* (*leave: job*) dimitir de; **to ~ oneself to sth** resignarse a algo

resignation [ˌrez·ɪg·'neɪ·ʃən] *n* **1.** (*from job*) dimisión *f* **2.** (*conformity*) resignación *f*

resigned [rɪ·'zaɪnd] *adj* resignado, -a

resilient [rɪ·'zɪl·jənt] *adj* (*material*) elástico, -a; (*person*) resistente

resist [rɪ·'zɪst] **I.** *vt* resistir; **to ~ doing sth** resistirse a hacer algo **II.** *vi* resistir

resistance [rɪ·'zɪs·təns] *n* resistencia *f*

resistant [rɪ·'zɪs·tənt] *adj* resistente

resistor [rɪ·'zɪs·tər] *n* resistencia *f*

resolution [ˌrez·ə·'lu·ʃən] *n a.* COMPUT, PHOT, TV resolución *f*

resort [rɪ·'zɔrt] *n* **1.** (*use*) recurso *m;* **as a last ~** como último recurso **2.** (*for holidays*) lugar *m* de veraneo; **ski ~** estación *f* de esquí

resounding *adj* **1.** (*noise*) resonante **2.** (*failure, success*) rotundo, -a

resource ['ri·sɔrs] **I.** *n* **1.** (*asset*) recurso *m* **2.** (**natural**) ~**s** recursos *m pl* naturales **3.** (*resourcefulness*) inventiva *f* **II.** *vt* financiar

resourceful [rɪ·'sɔrs·fəl] *adj* ingenioso, -a

respect [rɪ·'spekt] **I.** *n* **1.** (*relation*) respeto *m* **2.** (*esteem*) estima *f;* **with all due ~** con el debido respeto **3.** (*point*) respecto *m;* **in all/many/some ~s** desde todos/muchos/algunos puntos de vista; **in every ~** en todos los sentidos; **in this ~** a este respecto; **with ~ to** con respecto a **II.** *vt* respetar

respectable [rɪ·'spek·tə·bəl] *adj* **1.** (*person*) respetable **2.** (*behavior*) decente **3.** (*performance, result*) aceptable

respected [rɪ·'spek·təd] *adj* respetado, -a

respectful [rɪ·'spekt·fəl] *adj* respetuoso, -a

respectfully [rɪ·'spekt·fə·li] *adv* respetuosamente

respecting [rɪ·'spek·tɪŋ] *prep* respecto a

respective [rɪ·'spek·tɪv] *adj* respectivo, -a

respectively *adv* respectivamente

respirator ['res·pə·reɪ·tər] *n* respirador *m*

respiratory ['res·pər·ə·tɔr·i] *adj* respiratorio, -a

respond [rɪ·'spand] *vi* **1.** (*answer*) contestar **2.** (*react*) responder

response [rɪ·'spans] *n* **1.** (*answer*) respuesta *f* **2.** (*reaction*) reacción *f*

responsibility [rɪ·ˌspan·sə·'bɪl·ə·ti] *n* responsabilidad *f*

R

responsible [rɪ·'spɑn·sə·bəl] *adj* responsable; **to be ~ for sth/to sb** ser responsable de algo/ante alguien

responsive [rɪ·'spɑn·sɪv] *adj* (*person*) receptivo, -a; (*mechanism*) sensible; **to be ~ to sth** MED responder a algo

rest[1] [rest] **I.** *vt* **1.** (*cause to repose*) descansar **2.** (*support*) apoyar **II.** *vi* **1.** (*cease activity*) descansar **2.** (*remain*) quedar **3.** (*be supported*) apoyarse; **to ~ on sth** (*theory*) basarse en algo ▶ **you can ~** <u>assured</u> **that...** esté seguro de que... **III.** *n* **1.** (*period of repose*) descanso *m*; **to come to ~** detenerse; **at ~** (*not moving*) en reposo; (*dead*) en paz **2.** MUS pausa *f* **3.** (*support*) apoyo *m*

rest[2] [rest] *n* resto *m*; **the ~** (*the other people*) los demás; (*the other things*) lo demás; **for the ~** por lo demás

restaurant ['res·tər·ant] *n* restaurante *m*

restful ['rest·fəl] *adj* tranquilo, -a, relajante

rest home *n* residencia *f* de ancianos

restless ['rest·lɪs] *adj* **1.** (*agitated*) inquieto, -a **2.** (*impatient*) impaciente

restoration [,res·tə·'reɪ·ʃən] *n* **1.** (*act of restoring: of building, painting*) restauración *f*; (*of communication, peace*) restablecimiento *m* **2.** (*return to owner*) restitución *f*

restore [rɪ·'stɔr] *vt* **1.** (*reestablish: building, painting*) restaurar; (*communication, peace*) restablecer; **to ~ sb's faith in sth** hacer que alguien recupere la fe en algo; **to ~ sb to health** devolver la salud a alguien; **to ~ sb to power** volver a colocar a alguien en el poder **2.** *form* (*return to owner*) restituir

restrain [rɪ·'streɪn] *vt* (*person, animal*) contener; (*temper, ambition*) dominar; (*trade*) restringir; **to ~ sb from doing sth** impedir que alguien haga algo; **to ~ oneself** contenerse

restrained [rɪ·'streɪnd] *adj* (*person*) comedido, -a; (*criticism, policy*) moderado, -a

restraint [rɪ·'streɪnt] *n* **1.** (*self-control*) dominio *m* de sí mismo; **to exercise ~** *form* mostrarse comedido **2.** (*restriction*) restricción *f*

restrict [rɪ·'strɪkt] *vt* (*limit*) restringir; **to ~ oneself** limitarse

restricted *adj* **1.** (*limited*) restringido, -a; (*document*) confidencial; (*parking*) limitado, -a; **entry is ~ to...** sólo se permite la entrada a... **2.** (*small: space*) reducido, -a; (*existence, horizon*) limitado, -a

restriction [rɪ·'strɪk·ʃən] *n* restricción *f*; **speed ~** límite *m* de velocidad; **to impose ~s on sth** imponer restricciones a algo

restrictive [rɪ·'strɪk·tɪv] *adj* restrictivo, -a

restring [,ri·'strɪŋ] *irr vt* (*instrument, tennis racket*) volver a encordar; (*necklace*) reensartar

rest room *n* aseos *mpl*, baños *mpl* Col

restructuring *n* reestructuración *f*

result [rɪ·'zʌlt] **I.** *n a.* MATH, SPORTS, POL resultado *m*; (*of exam*) nota *f*; **to get ~s** obtener buenos resultados; **with no ~** sin resultado; **as a ~ of** a consecuencia de; **as a ~** por consiguiente **II.** *vi* **to ~ from** ser consecuencia de; **to ~ in** ocasionar

resume [rɪ·'zum] **I.** *vt* **1.** (*start again: work, journey*) reanudar; (*speech*) proseguir con **2.** *form* (*duties*) volver a asumir **II.** *vi form* proseguir

résumé ['rez·u·meɪ] *n* **1.** (*summary*) resumen *m* **2.** (*for jobs*) currículum *m* (vitae)

resumption [rɪ·'zʌmp·ʃən] *n* (*of journey, work*) reanudación *f*

resurrection [,rez·ə·'rek·ʃən] *n* resurrección *f*

retail ['ri·teɪl] COM **I.** *n* venta *f* al por menor **II.** *vt* vender al por menor **III.** *vi* venderse al detalle; **this product ~s at $5** el precio de venta al público de este producto es 5 dólares

retail business *n* comercio *m* minorista

retailer *n* minorista *mf*

retail price *n* COM precio *m* de venta al público

retail trade *n* ECON comercio *m* minorista

retain [rɪ·'teɪn] *vt* **1.** *form* (*keep: power*) retener; (*right*) reservarse; (*title*) revalidar **2.** (*not lose: dignity*) mantener;

(*color*) conservar **3.** (*hold in place: water*) contener **4.** (*remember*) retener

retake¹ [ˌriːˈteɪk] *vt irr* **1.** (*recapture: town*) volver a tomar; **to ~ the lead** recuperar el liderazgo **2.** SCHOOL, UNIV (*exam*) volver a presentarse a **3.** CINE volver a rodar; PHOT volver a hacer

retake² [ˈriːteɪk] *n* CINE toma *f* repetida

retaliate [rɪˈtælɪeɪt] *vi* tomar represalias

retaliation [rɪˌtælɪˈeɪʃən] *n* represalias *fpl*

retard [rɪˈtɑːd] *vt form* (*growth, development*) retardar; (*journey*) retrasar; **mentally ~ed person** retrasado, -a *m, f* mental

retch [retʃ] *vi* tener arcadas [*or* náuseas]

retentive [rɪˈtentɪv] *adj* retentivo, -a; **he's very ~** tiene muy buena memoria

rethink¹ [ˌriːˈθɪŋk] *vt irr* replantearse

rethink² [ˈriːθɪŋk] *n* replanteamiento *m*

reticent [ˈretɪsənt] *adj* reticente

retina [ˈretɪnə] <*s or* -nae> *n* retina *f*

retire [rɪˈtaɪr] **I.** *vi* **1.** (*stop working*) jubilarse; (*soldier, athlete*) retirarse **2.** *form* (*withdraw*) retirarse **3.** SPORTS (*from a race*) abandonar **II.** *vt* **1.** (*stop working*) jubilar **2.** MIL (*soldier*) retirar

retired *adj* jubilado, -a; (*soldier, athlete*) retirado, -a

retirement [rɪˈtaɪrmənt] *n* **1.** (*act of retiring*) retiro *m*; (*from race*) abandono *m* **2.** (*after working*) jubilación *f*; **to be in ~** estar jubilado; **to come out of ~** salir de su retiro **3.** MIL retirada *f*

retiring *adj* **1.** (*reserved*) reservado, -a **2.** (*worker, official*) saliente

retrace [rɪˈtreɪs] *vt* repasar; **to ~ one's steps** volver sobre sus pasos

retract [rɪˈtrækt] **I.** *vt* **1.** (*statement, offer*) retirar **2.** (*claws*) retraer; (*wheels*) replegar **II.** *vi* **1.** (*withdraw statement, offer*) retractarse **2.** (*be withdrawn: claws*) retraerse; (*wheels*) replegarse

retractable [rɪˈtræk·tə·bəl] *adj* retráctil

retrain [rɪˈtreɪn] **I.** *vt* reconvertir **II.** *vi* hacer un curso de perfeccionamiento

retreat [rɪˈtriːt] **I.** *vi* retroceder **II.** *n* **1.** (*withdrawal*) *a.* MIL retirada *f* **2.** (*safe place*) refugio *m* **3.** (*seclusion*) retiro *m*; **to go on a ~** hacer un retiro espiritual

retrial [ˈriːtraɪl] *n* nuevo juicio *m*

retribution [ˌretrəˈbjuːʃən] *n form* castigo *m* justo; **divine ~** justicia *f* divina

retrieval [rɪˈtriːvəl] *n* (*finding*) *a.* COMPUT recuperación *f*

retrieve [rɪˈtriːv] *vt* **1.** (*get back*) *a.* COMPUT recuperar **2.** (*make amends for: error*) enmendar **3.** (*repair: loss*) reparar **4.** SPORTS (*in tennis*) devolver

retrospect [ˈret·rə·spekt] *n* **in ~** mirando hacia atrás

retrospective [ˌret·rə·ˈspek·tɪv] *adj* **1.** (*looking back*) retrospectivo, -a **2.** LAW retroactivo, -a

return [rɪˈtɜːrn] **I.** *n* **1.** (*going back*) regreso *m*; (*home, to work, to school*) vuelta *f*; **on his ~** a su regreso **2.** (*to previous situation*) retorno *m*; **a ~ to sth** un restablecimiento de algo **3.** MED (*of illness*) recaída *f* **4.** (*giving back*) devolución *f* **5.** (*recompense*) recompensa *f* **6.** FIN (*proceeds*) ganancia *f*; (*interest*) rédito *m* **7.** **~s** POL resultados *m pl* de las elecciones **8.** COMPUT (*tecla f de*) retorno *m* **9.** FIN declaración *f* ▶ **many happy ~s!** ¡feliz cumpleaños!; **by ~ mail** a vuelta de correo; **in ~ for sth** a cambio de algo **II.** *adj* (*coming back: flight, journey*) de vuelta **III.** *vi* **1.** (*come back*) volver; (*home*) regresar a **2.** (*reappear*) volver a aparecer **IV.** *vt* **1.** (*give back*) devolver **2.** (*reciprocate*) corresponder a; (*compliment, favor, ball*) devolver; **to ~ sb's call** devolver la llamada a alguien **3.** (*send back*) volver a colocar; **~ to sender** devuélvase al remitente **4.** FIN (*yield*) dar; (*profit*) proporcionar **5.** ECON (*income*) declarar

return journey *n* viaje *m* de vuelta

return key *n* COMPUT tecla *f* de retorno

return ticket *n* billete *m* de vuelta

reunification [ˌriːjuːnəfɪˈkeɪʃən] *n* reunificación *f*

reunion [ˌriːˈjuːnjən] *n* **1.** (*meeting*) reunión *f* **2.** (*after separation*) reencuentro *m*

reunite [ˌriːjuːˈnaɪt] **I.** *vt* **1.** (*bring together*) volver a unir **2.** (*friends*) reconciliar **II.** *vi* reunirse

R

reusable [ˌriːˈjuːzəbəl] *adj* reutilizable

reuse [ˌriːˈjuːz] *vt* volver a usar

reveal [rɪˈviːl] *vt* **1.** (*divulge: secret, identity*) revelar; **he ~d his identity** desveló su identidad **2.** (*uncover*) descubrir

revealing [rɪˈviːlɪŋ] *adj* revelador(a)

revelation [ˌrevəˈleɪʃən] *n* revelación *f*

reveler *n*, **reveller** *n* juerguista *mf*

revenge [rɪˈvendʒ] I. *n* **1.** (*retaliation*) venganza *f*; **in ~** (**for sth**) como venganza (algo por); **to take ~** (**on sb**) **for sth** tomar venganza (en [*or de*] alguien) de [*or por*] algo **2.** SPORTS revancha *f* II. *vt* vengar; **to ~ oneself** vengarse de alguien

revenue [ˈrevəˌnuː] *n* **1.** (*income*) ingresos *mpl* **2.** (*of government*) rentas *f pl* públicas; **tax ~** declaración *f* de renta

revere [rɪˈvɪr] *vt* venerar

reverence [ˈrevərəns] *n* veneración *f*; **to pay ~ to sth/sb** rendir homenaje a algo/alguien

reverend [ˈrevərənd] *adj* reverendo, -a

reverent [ˈrevərənt] *adj* reverente

reverse [rɪˈvɜrs] I. *vt* (*turn other way*) volver al revés; (*order*) invertir; (*judgment*) revocar; **to ~ the charges** TEL llamar a cobro revertido II. *vi* (*order, situation*) invertirse III. *n* **1.** **the ~** lo contrario; **in ~** a la inversa **2.** AUTO (*gear*) marcha *f* atrás **3.** (*setback*) revés *m* **4.** (*the back*) reverso *m*; (*of cloth*) revés *m*; (*of document*) dorso *m* IV. *adj* **1.** (*inverse*) inverso, -a **2.** (*opposite: direction*) contrario, -a

reversible [rɪˈvɜrsəbəl] *adj* **1.** (*jacket*) reversible **2.** (*decision*) revocable

review [rɪˈvjuː] I. *vt* **1.** (*consider*) analizar **2.** (*reconsider*) reexaminar; (*salary*) reajustar **3.** (*look over: notes*) revisar **4.** (*criticize: book, play, film*) hacer una crítica de **5.** MIL (*inspect*) pasar revista a **6.** (*study again*) repasar II. *n* **1.** (*examination*) análisis *m inv*; **to come under ~** ser examinado **2.** (*reconsideration*) revisión *f*; **to come up for ~** estar pendiente de revisión **3.** (*summary*) resumen *m* **4.** (*criticism: of book, play, film*) crítica *f*

reviewer [rɪˈvjuːər] *n* crítico, -a *m, f*

revise [rɪˈvaɪz] *vt* (*alter: text, law*) revisar;

(*opinion*) cambiar de

revision [rɪˈvɪʒən] *n* **1.** (*of text, law*) revisión *f*; (*of policy*) modificación *f* **2.** (*book*) edición *f* corregida

revival [rɪˈvaɪvəl] *n* **1.** MED reanimación *f* **2.** (*rebirth: of interest*) renacimiento *m*; (*of idea, custom*) restablecimiento *m*; (*of economy*) reactivación *f* **3.** CINE, THEAT reestreno *m*

revive [rɪˈvaɪv] I. *vt* **1.** MED reanimar **2.** (*resurrect: interest*) hacer renacer; (*idea, custom*) restablecer; (*economy*) reactivar; (*conversation*) reanimar **3.** CINE, THEAT reestrenar II. *vi* **1.** (*be restored to life*) volver en sí **2.** (*be restored: country, interest*) resurgir; (*tradition*) restablecerse; (*style*) volver a estar de moda; (*trade, economy*) reactivarse

revocation [ˌrevəˈkeɪʃən] *n* **1.** (*of license*) suspensión *f* **2.** (*of law, decision*) revocación *f*

revoke [rɪˈvoʊk] *vt* **1.** (*cancel: decision, order*) revocar **2.** (*license*) suspender

revolt [rɪˈvoʊlt] POL I. *vi* rebelarse, alzarse *AmL*; **to ~ against sb/sth** sublevarse contra alguien/algo II. *vt* repugnar a; **it ~s me** me da asco III. *n* (*uprising*) revuelta *f*; **to rise in ~ against sb/sth** alzarse contra alguien/algo

revolting [rɪˈvoʊltɪŋ] *adj* (*disgusting*) repugnante; **to look ~** tener un aspecto horrible

revolution [ˌrevəˈluːʃən] *n* a. POL revolución *f*

revolutionary [ˌrevəˈluːʃəneri] *adj* revolucionario, -a

revolutionize [ˌrevəˈluːʃənaɪz] *vt* revolucionar

revolve [rɪˈvɑːlv] *vi* girar; **to ~ on an axis** girar en torno a un eje

revolving *adj* giratorio, -a

revolving door *n* puerta *f* giratoria

revulsion [rɪˈvʌlʃən] *n* repulsión *f*

reward [rɪˈwɔrd] I. *n* recompensa *f* II. *vt* recompensar

rewarding *adj* gratificante

rewind [ˌriːˈwaɪnd] *irr* I. *vt* (*tape*) rebobinar; (*clock, watch*) dar cuerda a II. *vi* rebobinarse

rewound [ˌriːˈwaʊnd] *pt of* **rewind**

rhetorical [rɪˈtɔrɪkəl] *adj* retórico, -a

rheumatism ['ru·mə·tɪz·əm] *n* reumatismo *m*

rhino ['raɪ·nou] *n inf abbr of* **rhinoceros** rinoceronte *m*

rhinoceros [raɪ·'nas·ər·əs] <-(es)> *n* rinoceronte *m*

rhombus ['ram·bəs] <-es *or* -i> *n* rombo *m*

rhubarb ['ru·barb] *n* ruibarbo *m*

rhyme [raɪm] **I.** *n* **1.** (*similar sound*) rima *f;* **in ~** en verso **2.** (*poem*) poesía *f* **II.** *vi* rimar

rhythm ['rɪð·əm] *n* ritmo *m*

RI *n abbr of* **Rhode Island** Rhode Island *m*

rib [rɪb] **I.** *n* **1.** (*bone*) costilla *f;* **to dig sb in the ~s** dar a alguien un codazo en el costado **2.** NAUT cuaderna *f* **II.** <-bb-> *vt inf* tomar el pelo a

ribbon ['rɪb·ən] *n* (*long strip*) cinta *f;* **to be cut to ~s** estar hecho jirones

rib cage *n* tórax *m*

rice [raɪs] *n* arroz *m*

rice pudding *n* arroz *m* con leche

rich [rɪtʃ] **I.** <-er, -est> *adj* **1.** (*person*) rico, -a; (*soil*) fértil; **to become ~** enriquecerse; **to be ~ in sth** abundar en algo **2.** (*stimulating: life, experience, history*) rico, -a **3.** (*food*) pesado, -a **4.** (*intense: color*) brillante; (*flavor*) intenso, -a **II.** *n* **the ~** los ricos

rid [rɪd] <rid *or* ridded, rid> *vt* **to ~ sth/ sb of sth** librar algo/a alguien de algo; **to be ~ of sth/sb** estar libre de algo/ alguien; **to get ~ of sb/sth** deshacerse de alguien/algo

ridden ['rɪd·ən] *pp of* **ride**

riddle¹ ['rɪd·əl] *n* **1.** (*conundrum*) adivinanza *f* **2.** *fig* (*mystery*) misterio *m;* **to speak in ~s** hablar en clave

riddle² ['rɪd·əl] *vt* acribillar; **to be ~d with mistakes** estar plagado, -a de errores

ride [raɪd] **I.** *n* (*on horse, motorcycle, car*) paseo *m;* **to give sb a ~** llevar a alguien ▸ **to take sb for a ~** *sl* tomar el pelo a alguien **II.** <rode, ridden> *vt* **1.** (*sit on*) **to ~ a bike** montar en bicicleta; **to ~ a horse** montar a caballo; **can you ~ a bike?** ¿sabes montar en bici? **2.** *inf* (*tease*) meterse con; **to ~ sb about sth** meterse con alguien por algo

III. <rode, ridden> *vi* **1.** (*on horse, bicycle*) montar; **to ~ on a horse** montar a caballo; **to ~ by bicycle** ir en bicicleta **2.** (*do well*) **to ~ high** alcanzar popularidad **3.** *inf* (*take no action*) **to let sth ~** dejar pasar algo

◆ **ride out** *vt a. fig* aguantar

◆ **ride up** *vi* (*person*) acercarse; (*dress*) subirse

rider ['raɪ·dər] *n* (*on horse*) jinete *m*, amazona *f;* (*on bicycle*) ciclista *mf;* (*on motorcycle*) motociclista *mf*

ridge [rɪdʒ] *n* **1.** GEO cresta *f* **2.** METEO sistema *m* de altas presiones **3.** (*of roof*) caballete *m*

ridicule ['rɪd·ɪ·kjul] **I.** *n* burlas *fpl;* **to be an object of ~** ser el hazmerreír **II.** *vt* ridiculizar

ridiculous [rɪ·'dɪk·ju·ləs] *adj* ridículo, -a

riding *n* equitación *f*

rifle¹ ['raɪ·fəl] *n* fusil *m*, rifle *m*

rifle² ['raɪ·fəl] **I.** *vt* **1.** (*plunder*) saquear **2.** (*steal*) robar **II.** *vt* revolver **III.** *vi* **to ~ through sth** rebuscar en algo

rifle range *n* campo *m* de tiro

rift [rɪft] *n* **1.** (*in earth*) fisura *f* **2.** *fig* ruptura *f;* **to heal the ~** cerrar la brecha

rig [rɪg] <-gg-> **I.** *vt* **1.** (*falsify*) amañar **2.** NAUT aparejar **II.** *n* **1.** TECH (*oil*) **~ platform** *f* petrolífera **2.** (*truck*) camión *m* **3.** NAUT aparejo *m* **4.** *inf* (*clothing*) atuendo *m*

rigging ['rɪg·ɪŋ] *n* **1.** (*of result*) pucherazo *m;* **ballot ~ fraude** *m* electoral **2.** NAUT jarcia *f*

right [raɪt] **I.** *adj* **1.** (*correct*) correcto, -a; (*ethical*) justo, -a; **to be ~ (about sth)** tener razón (en algo); **to do sth the ~ way** hacer algo correctamente; **to do the ~ thing** hacer lo que se debe hacer; **to be in the ~ place at the ~ time** estar en el lugar indicado en el momento indicado **2.** (*direction*) derecho, -a; **a ~ hook** SPORTS un gancho de derecha **3.** POL de derechas **4.** (*well*) bueno, -a; **to be not (quite) ~ in the head** *inf* no estar muy bien de la cabeza **II.** *n* **1.** (*entitlement*) derecho *m;* **to have the ~ to do sth** tener el derecho de hacer algo **2.** (*morality*) **to be in the ~** tener razón **3.** (*right side*) derecha *f* **4.** POL

R

the **Right** la derecha **III.** *adv* **1.** (*correctly*) correctamente; **to do ~** obrar bien **2.** (*straight*) directamente; **~ away** inmediatamente **3.** (*to the right*) hacia la derecha **4.** (*precisely*) precisamente; **~ here** justo aquí; **to be ~ behind sb** estar inmediatamente detrás de alguien **IV.** *vt* **1.** (*rectify*) rectificar; (*mistake*) enmendar **2.** (*straighten*) enderezar **V.** *interj* de acuerdo, órale *Méx*

right angle *n* ángulo *m* recto

right-angled ['raɪt·ˌæŋ·gəld] *adj* en ángulo recto

rightful ['raɪt·fəl] *adj* legítimo, -a

right-hand [ˌraɪt·'hænd] *adj* **on the ~ side** a la derecha

right-handed [ˌraɪt·'hæn·dɪd] *adj* diestro, -a

right-hander *n* **1.** (*person*) diestro, -a *m, f* **2.** (*punch*) derechazo *m*

rightly *adv* **1.** (*correctly*) correctamente; **if I remember ~** si recuerdo bien **2.** (*justifiably*) con razón; (**whether**) **~ or wrongly** con razón o sin ella

right-minded [ˌraɪt·'maɪn·dɪd] *adj* sensato, -a

right of way <-rights> *n* (*on road*) preferencia *f*

right-wing [ˌraɪt·'wɪŋ] *adj* POL de derechas

rigid ['rɪdʒ·ɪd] *adj* **1.** (*stiff*) rígido, -a; **to be ~ with fear/pain** estar paralizado, -a de miedo/dolor **2.** (*inflexible*) inflexible; (*censorship*) estricto, -a **3.** (*intransigent*) intransigente

rigorous ['rɪg·ər·əs] *adj* riguroso, -a

rim [rɪm] *n* **1.** (*of cup, bowl*) canto *m* **2.** (*frame for eyeglasses*) montura *f* **3.** GEO borde *m;* **the Pacific ~** los países de la costa del Pacífico *m.* <-mm-> *vt* **1.** (*surround*) bordear **2.** (*frame*) enmarcar

rind [raɪnd] *n* (*of fruit*) cáscara *f;* (*of bacon, cheese*) corteza *f*

ring[1] [rɪŋ] **I.** *n* **1.** (*small circle*) círculo *m;* (*of people*) corro *m;* (*around eyes*) ojera *f* **2.** (*jewelry*) anillo *m* **3.** (*arena*) ruedo *m;* (*in boxing*) cuadrilátero *m;* (*in circus*) pista *f* **II.** *vt* (*surround*) rodear; **to be ~ed by sth** estar cercado, -a con algo

ring[2] [rɪŋ] **I.** *n* **1.** (*metallic sound*) sonido *m* metálico; (*of bell*) toque *m* **2.** (*telephone call*) llamada *f;* **to give sb a ~** llamar a alguien (por teléfono) **II.** <rang, rung> *vt* (*bell*) tocar; (*alarm*) hacer sonar **III.** <rang, rung> *vi* (*telephone, bell*) sonar

♦ **ring out** *vi* resonar

♦ **ring up** *vt* COM (*at cash register*) **to ~ sb up** registrar la compra de alguien en la registradora

ring finger *n* dedo *m* anular

ringing **I.** *n* repique *m* **II.** *adj* sonoro, -a

ringleader ['rɪŋ·ˌli·dər] *n* cabecilla *mf*

ringlet ['rɪŋ·lɪt] *n* tirabuzón *m*

ringside ['rɪŋ·saɪd] **I.** **to be at the ~** estar junto al cuadrilátero **II.** *adj* (*seats*) de primera fila

ringtone *n* TEL tono *m* (del móvil)

rink [rɪŋk] *n* pista *f* de patinaje

rinse [rɪns] **I.** *vt* (*dishes, clothes*) enjuagar; (*hands*) lavar **II.** *n* **1.** (*wash*) enjuague *m;* **cold/hot ~** aclarado *m* frío/caliente **2.** (*hair coloring*) reflejos *mpl*

riot ['raɪ·ət] **I.** *n* disturbio *m;* **to be a ~** *sl* ser la monda **II.** *vi* causar disturbios **III.** *adv* **to run ~** *fig* desmandarse; **to let one's imagination run ~** dar rienda suelta a su imaginación

rioter *n* alborotador(a) *m(f)*

riot gear *n* uniforme *m* antidisturbios

rioting *n* disturbios *mpl*

rip [rɪp] **I.** <-pp-> *vi* rasgarse **II.** <-pp-> *vt* rasgar; **to ~ sth open** abrir algo de un rasgón **III.** *n* rasgón *m*

♦ **rip down** *vt* arrancar

♦ **rip off** *vt* **1.** (*remove*) arrancar **2.** *sl* (*swindle*) timar

♦ **rip out** *vt* arrancar

♦ **rip up** *vt* romper

RIP [ˌar·ar·'pi] *abbr of* **rest in peace** D.E.P.

ripe [raɪp] *adj* **1.** (*fruit*) maduro, -a; **at the ~ old age of 80** a la avanzada edad de 80 **2.** (*ready*) **the time is ~ for...** es el momento oportuno de...

ripen ['raɪ·pən] **I.** *vt* hacer madurar **II.** *vi* madurar

rip-off ['rɪp·ɔf] *n* *sl* timo *m*

ripple ['rɪp·əl] **I.** *n* onda *f* **II.** *vt* rizar

III. *vi* rizarse

riptide ['rɪp·taɪd] *n* corriente *f* de resaca

rise [raɪz] I. *n* 1. (*increase*) subida *f*; **to be on the ~** ir en aumento; **to give ~ to sth** dar lugar a algo; **to get** [*or* **take**] **a ~ out of sb** burlarse de alguien 2. (*incline*) cuesta *f* II. <rose, risen> *vi* 1. (*arise*) levantarse 2. (*become higher: ground*) subir (en pendiente); (*temperature*) aumentar; (*river*) crecer 3. (*go up: smoke*) subir; (*moon, sun*) salir; (*building*) elevarse 4. (*improve socially*) ascender; **to ~ to fame** alcanzar la fama 5. (*rebel*) sublevarse

risen ['rɪz·ən] *pp of* **rise**

riser ['raɪ·zər] *n* (*person*) **early ~** madrugador(a) *m(f)*; **late ~** dormilón, -ona *m, f*

rising ['raɪ·zɪŋ] I. *n* levantamiento *m* II. *adj* (*in number*) creciente; (*in status*) ascendente; (*floodwaters*) en aumento; (*sun*) naciente

risk [rɪsk] I. *n* 1. (*chance*) riesgo *m*; **to run the ~ of sth** correr el riesgo de algo 2. (*danger*) peligro *m*; **at one's own ~** bajo su propia responsabilidad; **to be at ~** correr peligro II. *vt* arriesgar; **to ~ doing sth** arriesgarse a hacer algo; **to ~ one's life** poner la propia vida en peligro

risky ['rɪs·ki] <-ier, -iest> *adj* arriesgado, -a, riesgoso, -a *AmL*

rite [raɪt] *n* rito *m*; **last ~s** extremaunción *f*; **~s of passage** rito de paso

ritual ['rɪtʃ·u·əl] I. *n* ritual *m* II. *adj* ritual

rival ['raɪ·vəl] I. *n* rival *mf* II. *adj* competidor(a) III. <-ll-, -l-> *vt* competir con

rivalry ['raɪ·vəl·ri] *n* rivalidad *f*

river ['rɪv·ər] *n* río *m*

river bed *n* lecho *m* de un río

riverside ['rɪv·ər·saɪd] *n* ribera *f*

riveting ['rɪv·ɪ·tɪŋ] *adj inf* fascinante

roach [roʊtʃ] <-es> *n inf* (*cockroach*) cucaracha *f*

road [roʊd] *n* 1. (*between towns*) carretera *f*; (*in town*) calle *f*; (*route*) camino *m*; **by ~** por carretera; **to be on the ~** (*fit for driving*) estar en circulación; (*traveling by road*) estar en camino;

(*performing on tour*) estar de gira 2. *fig* sendero *m*; **to be on the ~ to recovery** estar reponiéndose ▶ **all ~s lead to Rome** *prov* todos los caminos llevan a Roma *prov*; **to get sth on the ~** *inf* empezar (con) algo

road accident *n* accidente *m* de circulación

roadblock *n* control *m* de carretera

road hog *n inf* loco, -a *m, f* del volante

road map *n* mapa *m* de carreteras

road rage *n* furia *f* al volante

road safety *n* seguridad *f* vial

roadside ['roʊd·saɪd] *n* borde *m* de la carretera

road sign *n* señal *f* de tráfico

road-test *vt* **to ~ a car** someter un coche a una prueba de carretera

roadway ['roʊd·weɪ] *n* calzada *f*

roam [roʊm] I. *vi* vagar II. *vt* vagar por

roar [rɔr] I. *vi* (*lion, person*) rugir; (*cannon*) tronar; **to ~ with laughter** reírse a carcajadas II. *vt* vociferar III. *n* (*of lion, person*) rugido *m*; (*of engine*) estruendo *m*

roaring I. *adj* rugiente; (*thunder*) estruendoso, -a; (*fire*) furioso, -a II. *adv* completamente

roast [roʊst] I. *vt* 1. (*food*) asar; (*coffee*) tostar 2. (*poke fun at*) burlarse de II. *vi* (*food*) asarse; (*person*) achicharrarse III. *n* 1. (*meat*) asado *m* 2. (*party*) asado *m* IV. *adj* (*meat*) asado, -a; (*coffee*) tostado, -a

roasting ['roʊs·tɪŋ] I. *n* 1. (*baking*) asado *m* 2. *inf* (*telling off*) **to give sb a ~** echar una bronca a alguien II. *adj* abrasador(a) III. *adv* **~ hot** abrasador(a)

rob [rab] <-bb-> *vt* 1. (*person, house*) robar; **to ~ sb of sth** robar algo a alguien 2. (*deprive*) **to ~ sb of sth** privar a alguien de algo

robber ['rab·ər] *n* ladrón, -ona *m, f*; **bank ~** atracador (a) *m(f)* de bancos

robbery ['rab·ə·ri] <-ies> *n* robo *m*

robe [roʊb] *n* (*formal*) toga *f*; (*dressing gown*) traje *m*; (*after bath*) albornoz *m*; (*of a priest*) sotana *f*

robin ['rab·ɪn] *n zool* petirrojo *m*

robot ['roʊ·bat] *n* (*machine*) robot *m*

R

robotics [rou·'bat̩·ıks] *npl* robótica *f*

rock¹ [rak] *n* **1.** GEO roca *f* **2.** (*music*) rock *m* ▶ **to be stuck between a ~ and hard place** estar entre la espada y la pared; **as solid as a ~** duro como una piedra; **whisky on the ~s** whisky con hielo

rock² [rak] **I.** *vt* **1.** (*swing*) mecer **2.** (*shock*) sacudir **II.** *vi* balancearse

rock band *n* grupo *m* de rock

rock bottom *n* fondo *m;* **to hit ~** tocar fondo; **to be at ~** estar por los suelos

rock climber *n* escalador(a) *m(f)*

rock climbing *n* escalada *f* en roca

rocker ['rak·ər] *n* **1.** (*chair*) mecedora *f* **2.** *inf* (*musician, fan*) roquero, -a *m, f*

rockery ['rak·ə·ri] <-ies> *n* jardín *m* rocoso

rocket ['rak·ıt] **I.** *n* **1.** (*weapon*) misil *m* **2.** (*vehicle for space travel*) cohete *m* espacial **3.** (*firework*) cohete *m* **II.** *vi* (*costs, prices*) dispararse

Rockies ['rak·iz] *n* **the ~** las Rocosas

rocking chair ['rak·ıŋ] *n* mecedora *f,* columpio *m AmL*

rock music *n* música *f* rock

rock salt *n* sal *f* gema

rock star *n* estrella *f* del rock

rocky¹ ['rak·i] <-ier, -iest> *adj* rocoso, -a; (*ground*) pedregoso, -a

rocky² ['rak·i] <-ier, -iest> *adj* (*unstable*) inestable

Rocky Mountains *n* Montañas *f pl* Rocosas

rod [rad] *n* (*stick*) varilla *f;* (*fishing rod*) caña *f* de pescar

rode [roud] *pt of* **ride**

rodent ['rou·dənt] *n* roedor *m*

rodeo ['rou·di·ou] <-s> *n* rodeo *m*

roe¹ [rou] *n* (*fish eggs*) hueva *f*

roe² [rou] <-(s)> *n* (*deer*) corzo, -a *m, f*

roger ['radʒ·ər] *interj* RADIO recibido

rogue [roug] **I.** *n* **1.** (*rascal*) pícaro, -a *m, f* **2.** (*villain*) bribón, -ona *m, f* **II.** *adj* (*animal*) solitario, -a; (*trader, company*) deshonesto, -a

role *n*, **rôle** [roul] *n a.* THEAT papel *m;* **to play a ~** THEAT hacer un papel; *fig* desempeñar un papel

role model *n* modelo *m* a imitar

role play *n* juego *m* de imitación

role reversal *n* inversión *m* de papeles

roll [roul] **I.** *n* **1.** (*turning over*) voltereta *f* **2.** (*swaying movement*) balanceo *m;* **to be on a ~** *fig* tener buena suerte **3.** (*cylinder: of cloth, paper*) rollo *m;* (*film*) carrete *m* **4.** (*noise: of drum*) redoble *m* **5.** (*catalog of names*) padrón *m;* (*for elections*) censo *m;* **to call the ~** pasar lista **6.** (*bread*) panecillo *m* **II.** *vt* **1.** (*push: ball, barrel*) hacer rodar; (*dice*) tirar; **to ~ one's eyes** poner los ojos en blanco **2.** (*form into cylindrical shape*) **to ~ sth into sth** enrollar algo en algo; **all ~ed into one** todo unido en uno **3.** (*make: cigarette*) liar **III.** *vi* **1.** (*move*) rodar; (*with undulating motion*) ondular **2.** (*be in operation*) funcionar

◆**roll back** *vt* **1.** (*cause to retreat*) hacer retroceder **2.** ECON reducir **3.** (*return to previous state*) hacer recular

◆**roll in** *vi* llegar en abundancia

◆**roll on** *vi* seguir rodando; (*time*) pasar

◆**roll out I.** *vt* **1.** (*flatten*) estirar; (*pastry*) extender **2.** (*unroll*) desenrollar **3.** COM (*new product*) lanzar **II.** *vi* (*wake up*) despertarse

◆**roll over** *vi* (*movement*) dar vueltas

◆**roll up I.** *vi* *inf* aparecer **II.** *vt* enrollar; (*sleeves*) arremangarse

roll bar *n* AUTO barra *f* protectora antivuelco

roller ['rou·lər] *n* **1.** TECH rodillo *m* **2.** (*for hair*) rulo *m*

Rollerblade® *n* patín *m* en línea

roller coaster *n* montaña *f* rusa

roller skate I. *n* patín *m* de ruedas **II.** *vi* patinar

rolling pin *n* rodillo *m*

roll-on ['roul·an] *adj* (*deodorant*) de bola

Roman ['rou·mən] **I.** *adj* romano, -a; (*alphabet*) latino, -a; (*religion*) católico, -a **II.** *n* romano, -a *m, f*

Roman Catholic I. *n* católico, -a *m, f* **II.** *adj* católico, -a; **the ~ Church** la Iglesia católica romana

romance [rou·'mæns] *n* **1.** (*love affair*) romance *m* **2.** (*novel*) novela *f* rosa; (*film*) película *f* de amor **3.** (*glamour*) romanticismo *m*

Romania [rou·'meɪ·ni·ə] *n* Rumanía *f*

Romanian [rou·'mer·ni·ən] I. *adj* rumano, -a II. *n* 1. (*person*) rumano, -a *m, f* 2. LING rumano *m*

romantic [rou·'mæn·tɪk] *adj a.* LIT, ART romántico, -a

Rome [roum] *n* Roma *f* ► ~ was not built in a **day** *prov* no se ganó Zamora en una hora *prov;* **when in** ~ (do as the **Romans**) *prov* allí donde fueres haz lo que vieres *prov*

roof [ruf] <-s> I. *n* 1. (*of house*) tejado *m;* (*of car*) techo *m;* (*of tree*) copa *f* ► to **go through the** ~ (*prices*) estar por las nubes; (*person*) subirse por las paredes; to **hit the** ~ subirse por las paredes II. *vt* techar

roof garden *n* azotea *f* con flores y plantas

rooftop ['ruf·tap] *n* techo *m*

rook [rʊk] *n* 1. (*bird*) grajo *m* 2. (*in chess*) torre *f*

rookie ['rʊk·i] *n sl* novato, -a *m, f*

room [rum] I. *n* 1. (*in house*) habitación *m;* ~ and **board** pensión *f* completa 2. (*space*) espacio *m;* to **make** ~ for sb/sth hacer sitio para alguien/algo; **there's no more** ~ for anything else ya no cabe nada más; ~ for improvement posibilidad *f* de mejorar; **there is no** ~ for doubt no cabe duda II. *vi* to ~ with sb compartir alojamiento con alguien

roomie *n inf* (*in same room*) compañero, -a *m, f* de habitación; (*in same apartment*) compañero, -a *m, f* de piso

roommate ['rum·meɪt] *n* (*in same room*) compañero, -a *m, f* de habitación; (*in same apartment*) compañero, -a *m, f* de piso

room service *n* servicio *m* de habitaciones

roomy ['ru·mi] <-ier, -iest> *adj* amplio, -a

rooster ['ru·stər] *n* gallo *m*

root [rut] *n* 1. *a.* BOT, LING, MATH raíz *f;* to **take** ~ *a. fig* arraigar 2. (*source*) causa *f;* the ~ **of all evil** la esencia de todos los males; **the** ~ **of the problem is that...** el problema radica en que...

root vegetable *n* tubérculo *m*

rope [roup] I. *n* 1. (*cord*) cuerda *f;* (*of pearls*) sarta *f* 2. ~s (*in boxing*) cuerdas *fpl* 3. (*for capital punishment*) soga *f* ► to **learn** the ~s aprender el oficio; to **have sb on** the ~s tener a alguien contra las cuerdas II. *vt* atar con una cuerda

rope ladder *n* escalera *f* de cuerda

rose[1] [rouz] I. *n* 1. (*flower; color*) rosa *f* 2. (*on watering can*) roseta *f* 3. ARCHIT rosetón *m* ► to **come up** smelling of ~s aparecer contento; **coming up** ~s a pedir de boca II. *adj* rosa

rose[2] [rouz] *pt of* **rise**

rosebud ['rouz·bʌd] *n* capullo *m*

rose garden *n* rosaleda *f*

rosemary ['rouz·mer·i] *n* romero *m*

roster ['ras·tər] *n* lista *f*

rostrum ['ras·trəm] <-s *or* rostra> *n* (*for conductor*) estrado *m;* (*for public speaker*) tribuna *f*

rosy ['rou·zi] <-ier, -iest> *adj* 1. (*rose-colored*) rosado, -a 2. (*optimistic: viewpoint*) optimista; (*future*) prometedor(a)

rot [rat] I. *n* putrefacción *f* II. <-tt-> *vi* pudrirse III. *vt* pudrir

rotate ['rou·teɪt] I. *vt* 1. (*turn around*) dar vueltas a 2. (*alternate*) alternar; (*duties*) turnarse en; AGR cultivar en rotación II. *vi* girar; to ~ **around sth** girar alrededor de algo

rotation [rou·'teɪ·ʃən] *n a.* ASTR, AGR rotación *f*

rote [rout] *n* by ~ de memoria

rotor ['rou·tər] *n* rotor *m*

rotten ['rat·ən] *adj* 1. (*food*) podrido, -a; to **go** ~ pudrirse 2. *inf* (*nasty: behavior*) despreciable 3. *inf* (*performance, book*) malísimo, -a

rough [rʌf] I. *adj* 1. (*uneven: road*) desigual; (*surface*) áspero, -a 2. (*poorly made: work*) chapucero, -a 3. (*harsh: voice*) bronco, -a 4. (*imprecise*) aproximado, -a; ~ **work** borrador *m* 5. (*unrefined: person, manner*) tosco, -a 6. (*stormy: sea*) agitado, -a; (*weather*) tempestuoso, -a 7. (*difficult*) difícil; (*treatment*) duro, -a; to **be** ~ **on sb** *inf* ser injusto con alguien II. *n* 1. (*sketch*) borrador *m* 2. SPORTS **the** ~ el rough ► to **take the** ~ **with the smooth** es-

R

tar a las duras y a las maduras III. *adv*
to play ~ jugar duro; to live ~ vivir a
la intemperie

rough-and-tumble *n* riña *f*; *fig* juegos
m pl bruscos

roughen ['rʌf·ən] *vt* poner áspero

roughly *adv* 1. (*approximately*) aproximadamente; ~ **speaking** por así decirlo
2. (*aggressively*) bruscamente

roulette [ru·'let] *n* ruleta *f*

round |raʊnd| I. <-er, -est> *adj* 1. (*cir-
cular: object, number*) redondo, -a; (*arch*) de medio punto 2. (*not angular*)
arqueado, -a 3. (*sonorous*) sonoro, -a
II. *n* 1. (*circle*) círculo *m* 2. (*series*) serie *f*; (*of shots*) descarga *f* 3. ~**s** (*route*)
recorrido *m*; MIL ronda *f*; MED visita *f*
4. (*time period: of elections*) vuelta *f*; (*in
card games*) mano *f*; SPORTS eliminatoria *f*; (*in boxing*) asalto *m* 5. (*of drinks*)
ronda *f*; **this ~ is on me** esta ronda la
pago yo 6. (*of ammunition*) bala *f* III. *vt*
1. (*movement*) redondear; (*corner*) doblar 2. MATH aproximar

◆**round down** *vt* MATH redondear por
defecto

◆**round off** *vt* 1. (*finish*) rematar
2. (*smooth*) pulir 3. MATH redondear

◆**round out** *vt* acabar; **to ~ a list** completar una lista

◆**round up** *vt* 1. MATH redondear por exceso 2. (*gather*) reunir; (*cattle*) rodear

roundabout ['raʊnd·ə·baʊt] *adj* indirecto, -a; **to take a ~ route** ir dando
un rodeo

round-the-clock *adv* las veinticuatro horas; **to work ~** trabajar día y noche

round trip *n* viaje *m* de ida y vuelta; ~
ticket billete *m* de ida y vuelta

roundup ['raʊnd·ʌp] *n* 1. AGR rodeo *m*
2. (*by police*) redada *f*

rouse [raʊz] *vt* 1. (*awaken*) despertar
2. (*activate*) provocar; **to ~ sb to do sth**
animar a alguien a hacer algo

rousing ['raʊ·zɪŋ] *adj* (*welcome*) caluroso, -a; (*speech*) vehemente

route [raʊt] *n* 1. (*way*) ruta *f*; (*of parade, bus*) recorrido *m*; (*to success*) camino *m* 2. (*delivery path*) recorrido *m*;
to have a paper ~ hacer un reparto de
periódicos 3. (*road*) carretera *f* II. *vt* to

~ **sth via New York** mandar algo vía
Nueva York

routine [ru·'tin] I. *n* 1. *a.* COMPUT rutina *f*
2. (*of dancer*) número *m* II. *adj* 1. (*regular*) habitual; (*inspection*) de rutina
2. (*uninspiring*) rutinario, -a

row¹ [roʊ] *n* 1. (*line: of houses, cars*)
hilera *f*; (*of people, of seats*) fila *f*; **to
stand in a ~** estar en la fila 2. (*succession*) sucesión *f*; **three times in a ~** tres
veces consecutivas

row² [roʊ] I. *vi* remar II. *vt* (*boat*) llevar;
to ~ sb across the lake llevar a alguien
en bote al otro lado del lago

rowboat ['roʊ·boʊt] *n* bote *m* de remos

rowdy ['raʊ·di] <-ier, -iest> *adj* 1. (*noisy*)
alborotador(a) 2. (*quarrelsome*) pendenciero, -a

rower ['roʊ·ər] *n* remero, -a *m, f*

rowing *n* SPORTS remo *m*

royal ['rɔɪ·əl] *adj* 1. (*of monarch*) real;
the ~ we el plural mayestático 2. *fig*
regio, -a; (*welcome*) espléndido, -a

royalty ['rɔɪ·əl·ti] <-ies> *n* 1. (*sovereignty*) realeza *f*; **to treat sb like ~** tratar a
alguien a cuerpo de rey 2. **royalties**
(*payment*) derechos *m pl* de autor

RSVP [ˌar·es·vi·'pi] *vi abbr of* **répondez
s'il vous plaît** (= please reply) s.r.c.

rub [rʌb] I. *n* 1. (*act of rubbing*) frota-
miento *m*; **to give sth a ~** frotar algo
2. *liter* (*difficulty*) dificultad *f*; **there's
the ~** ahí está el quid de la cuestión
II. <-bb-> *vt* frotar; (*one's eyes*) restregarse; (*one's hands*) frotarse; **to ~ sth
clean** lustrar algo III. <-bb-> *vi* rozar

◆**rub down** *vt* 1. (*smooth*) pulir; (*horse*)
almohazar 2. (*dry*) secar frotando

◆**rub in** *vt* 1. (*spread on skin*) aplicar frotando 2. (*keep reminding*) reiterar;
pej insistir en

◆**rub off** I. *vi* (*become clean: stain*) irse
II. *vt* (*dirt*) quitar frotando

◆**rub out** *vt* (*remove: writing*) borrar;
(*dirt*) quitar

rubber ['rʌb·ər] *n* 1. (*material*) goma *f*,
hule *m Méx* 2. *sl* (*condom*) goma *f*;
forro *m RíoPl*

rubber band *n* goma *f* (elástica), caucho *m Col*

rubbernecker *n sl* mirón, -ona *m, f*

rubber-stamp I. vt (*decision*) dar el visto bueno a II. n (*device*) sello m de goma

rubber tree n árbol m del caucho

rubbery <-ier, -iest> adj (*texture*) parecido a la goma; (*food*) correoso, -a

rubbish ['rʌb.ɪʃ] n inf tonterías fpl

rubble ['rʌb.əl] n escombros mpl

rubella [ru·'bel·ə] n MED rubéola f

ruby ['ru·bi] <-ies> n rubí m

rudder ['rʌd·ər] n AVIAT, NAUT timón m

rudderless adj a. fig sin timón

ruddy ['rʌd·i] <-ier, -iest> adj 1. liter (*cheeks*) rubicundo, -a 2. (*light*) rojizo, -a

rude [rud] adj 1. (*impolite*) grosero, -a 2. (*vulgar*) vulgar; (*joke*) verde 3. (*sudden*) brusco, -a; (*surprise*) desagradable 4. liter (*unrefined*) tosco, -a

rudimentary [ˌru·də·'men·tə·ri] adj rudimentario, -a

rue [ru] vt liter lamentar

ruffle ['rʌf·əl] I. vt 1. (*agitate: hair*) alborotar; (*clothes*) fruncir; (*feathers*) erizar 2. (*upset*) alterar II. n volante m

rug [rʌg] n (*small carpet*) alfombra f

rugby ['rʌg·bi] n rugby m

rugged ['rʌg·ɪd] adj 1. (*uneven: cliff, mountains*) escarpado, -a; (*landscape, country*) accidentado, -a; (*ground*) desigual 2. (*tough: face*) de facciones duras; (*construction, vehicle*) resistente

ruin ['ru·ɪn] I. vt 1. (*bankrupt*) arruinar 2. (*destroy: city, building*) destruir 3. (*spoil: dress, surprise*) estropear II. n 1. (*bankruptcy, downfall*) ruina f; **drugs will be his ~** las drogas serán su ruina 2. pl (*remains*) ruinas fpl

rule [rul] I. n 1. (*law*) regla f; (*principle*) norma f; **~s and regulations** reglamento m; **~s of the road** normas f pl de tráfico; **to break a ~** infringir una norma; **to play (it) by the ~s** obedecer las reglas; **it is against the ~s** va contra las normas; **as a ~** por lo general 2. (*control*) gobierno m 3. (*measuring device*) regla f
► **a ~ of thumb** una regla general II. vt 1. (*govern: country*) gobernar; (*company*) dirigir 2. (*control*) dominar 3. (*draw*) trazar con una regla 4. LAW

(*decide*) dictaminar III. vi 1. (*control*) gobernar; (*monarch*) reinar 2. (*predominate*) imperar 3. LAW **to ~ for/ against sb/sth** fallar a favor/en contra de alguien/algo

♦ **rule out** vt descartar

rule book n reglamento m

ruler n 1. (*governor*) gobernante mf; (*sovereign*) soberano, -a m, f 2. (*measuring device*) regla f

ruling ['ru·lɪŋ] I. adj 1. (*governing*) gobernante; (*class*) dirigente; (*monarch*) reinante 2. (*primary*) dominante II. n fallo m; **the final ~** la sentencia definitiva

rum [rʌm] n ron m

rumble ['rʌm·bəl] I. n 1. (*sound*) ruido m sordo; (*of thunder*) estruendo m 2. sl (*fight*) pelea f II. vi hacer un ruido sordo; (*thunder*) retumbar; **my stomach is ~ing** me suenan las tripas

rumbling I. n (*sound*) ruido m sordo; (*of thunder*) estruendo m; **there were ~s of war** se hablaba de una posible guerra II. adj retumbante

rummy ['rʌm·i] n GAMES rummy m

rumor ['ru·mər] I. n rumor m II. vt **it is ~ed that...** se rumorea que...

rump [rʌmp] n 1. (*back end: of horse*) grupa f; (*of bird*) rabadilla f 2. (*cut of beef*) cuarto m trasero 3. iron (*buttocks*) trasero m

run [rʌn] I. n 1. (*jog*) **to break into a ~** echar a correr; **to go for a ~** salir a correr 2. (*trip*) viaje m; (*of train*) trayecto m; **to go for a ~ in the car** ir a dar una vuelta en el coche 3. (*series*) racha f; (*of books*) tirada f 4. (*demand*) demanda f; **a sudden ~ on the dollar** una súbita presión sobre el dólar; **a ~ on the banks** un pánico bancario 5. (*type*) categoría f 6. (*direction, tendency*) dirección f; **the ~ of events** el curso de los acontecimientos 7. (*enclosure for animals*) corral m 8. (*hole in tights*) carrera f 9. SPORTS (*in baseball, cricket*) carrera f 10. CINE, THEAT permanencia f en cartel ► **in the long ~** a la larga; **in the short ~** a corto plazo; **on the ~** deprisa y corriendo; **to be on the ~** huir de la justicia II. vi <ran, run> 1. (*move fast*)

R

correr; **to ~ for the bus** correr para no perder el autobús; **to ~ for help** correr en busca de ayuda; **~ for your lives!** ¡sálvese quien pueda! **2.** (*operate*) funcionar; **to ~ smoothly** ir sobre ruedas *fig* **3.** (*go, travel*) ir; **to ~ off the road** salirse de la carretera; **to ~ ashore/onto the rocks** NAUT embarrancar **4.** (*extend*) extenderse; **the road ~s along the coast** la carretera bordea la costa **5.** (*last*) **to ~ for two hours** durar dos horas; **to ~ and ~** ser el cuento de nunca acabar *inf* **6.** (*be*) existir **7.** (*flow: river*) fluir; (*make-up*) correrse; (*nose*) gotear *inf* **8.** (*enter election*) presentarse, postularse *AmL;* **to ~ for election/President** presentarse a las elecciones/como candidato a presidente **9.** + *adj* (*be*) **to ~ dry** (*river*) secarse; **to ~ short** (*water*) escasear II. (*say*) decir III. *vt* <ran, run> **1.** (*move fast*) **to ~ a race** participar en una carrera **2.** (*enter in race: candidate, horse*) presentar **3.** (*drive*) llevar; **to ~ sb home** llevar a alguien a casa; **to ~ a truck into a tree** chocar contra un árbol con un camión **4.** (*pass*) pasar **5.** (*operate*) poner en marcha; (*car*) llevar; (*computer program*) ejecutar; (*engine*) hacer funcionar; **to ~ a washing machine** poner una lavadora **6.** (*manage, govern*) dirigir, pilotear *AmL;* **to ~ a farm** tener una granja; **to ~ a government** estar al frente de un gobierno; **to ~ a household** llevar una casa **7.** (*conduct*) realizar; (*experiment, test*) llevar a cabo **8.** (*provide: course*) organizar **9.** (*let flow*) dejar correr; (*bath*) preparar **10.** (*show: article*) publicar; (*series*) emitir **11.** (*smuggle*) pasar de contrabando **12.** (*not heed: blockade*) romper; (*red light*) saltar(se) (en rojo) **13.** (*incur*) exponerse a; (*risk*) correr **14.** (*perform tasks*) **to ~ errands** hacer recados

◆**run about** *vi* andar de un lado para otro

◆**run across** I. *vi* cruzar corriendo II. *vt* toparse con

◆**run after** *vt* correr tras

◆**run along** *vi* marcharse

◆**run away** *vi* escaparse; (*water*) de-rramarse

◆**run away with** *vt* apoderarse de

◆**run back** *vi* volver corriendo

◆**run down** I. *vt* **1.** (*clock*) parar; (*battery*) gastarse II. *vi* **1.** (*run over*) atropellar **2.** (*disparage*) hablar mal de **3.** (*capture*) capturar

◆**run in** I. *vi* entrar corriendo II. *vt* **1.** AUTO rodar **2.** *sl* (*capture*) detener

◆**run into** *vt* dar con; AUTO chocar con

◆**run off** I. *vi* escaparse; (*water*) derramarse II. *vt* **1.** (*water*) dejar correr **2.** TYPO tirar **3.** (*make quickly*) hacer deprisa

◆**run on** *vi* **1.** (*continue to run*) seguir corriendo **2.** (*conversation*) continuar

◆**run out of** *vi* quedarse sin

◆**run over** I. *vt* (*person*) irse; (*fluid*) rebosar II. *vt* AUTO atropellar a

◆**run through** *vt* **1.** (*station*) pasar sin parar por **2.** (*money*) derrochar

◆**run up** I. *vi* **1.** subir corriendo **2. to ~ against difficulties** tropezar con dificultades II. *vt* **1.** (*flag*) izar **2.** (*make quickly*) hacer deprisa **3. to ~ debts** endeudarse

runaround [ˈrʌn·ə·ˈraʊnd] *n* **to give sb the ~** traer a alguien al retortero

runaway [ˈrʌn·ə·weɪ] *adj* **1.** (*train*) fuera de control; (*person*) fugitivo, -a; (*horse*) desbocado, -a **2.** (*enormous: success*) arrollador(a)

rundown [ˌrʌn·ˈdaʊn] I. *n* **1.** (*report*) resumen *m;* **to give sb the ~ on sth** poner a alguien al tanto de algo **2.** (*reduction*) disminución *f;* (*of staff*) reducción *f* II. *adj* **1.** (*building, town*) mal conservado, -a **2.** (*person*) debilitado, -a

rung¹ [rʌŋ] *n* **1.** (*ladder*) peldaño *m* **2.** (*level*) nivel *m*

rung² [rʌŋ] *pp of* **ring²**

run-in [ˈrʌn·ɪn] *n* **1.** *inf* (*argument*) altercado *m* **2.** (*prelude*) etapa *f* previa

runner [ˈrʌn·ər] *n* **1.** SPORTS (*person*) corredor(a) *m(f);* (*horse*) caballo *m* de carreras **2.** (*messenger*) mensajero, -a *m, f* **3.** (*smuggler*) contrabandista *mf;* **drug ~** camello *m* **4.** (*rail*) riel *m;* (*on sledge*) patín *m* **5.** (*stem*) tallo *m* rastrero **6.** (*long rug*) alfombrilla *f* estrecha

runner-up [ˌrʌn·ər·ˈʌp] *n* subcampeón, -ona *m, f*

running I. n 1. (*action of a runner*) carrera f 2. (*operation*) acción f; (*of a machine*) funcionamiento m; **the day-to-day ~ of the business** el día a día del negocio II. adj 1. (*consecutive*) sucesivo, -a; (*day*) consecutivo, -a 2. (*ongoing*) continuado, -a 3. (*operating*) que está funcionando 4. (*flowing*) que fluye

runny ['rʌn·i] <-ier, -iest> adj líquido, -a; (*sauce*) acuoso, -a

run-off ['rʌn·ɔf] n 1. POL desempate m 2. SPORTS segunda vuelta f

run-through ['rʌn·θru] n THEAT, MUS ensayo m (rápido); **to have a ~ of sth** ensayar algo

run-up ['rʌn·ʌp] n 1. SPORTS carrerilla f 2. (*prelude*) período m previo; **the ~ to sth** el preludio de algo

runway ['rʌn·weɪ] n pista f

rupture ['rʌp·tʃər] I. vi romperse II. vt romper; **to ~ oneself** herniarse III. n 1. (*act of bursting*) ruptura f 2. (*hernia*) hernia f, relajadura f Méx

rural ['rʊr·əl] adj rural

ruse [ruz] n treta f

rush¹ [rʌʃ] n BOT junco m

rush² [rʌʃ] I. n 1. (*hurry*) prisa f; **to be in a ~** tener prisa; **to leave in a ~** salir corriendo 2. (*charge, attack*) ataque m; (*surge*) ola f; (*of air*) corriente f; (*of customers*) oleada f; **there's been a ~ on oil** ha habido una fuerte demanda de aceite; **gold ~** fiebre f del oro 3. (*dizziness*) mareo m II. vi correr deprisa III. vt 1. (*do quickly*) hacer precipitadamente 2. (*hurry*) apresurar 3. (*attack*) asaltar
♦ **rush at** vt precipitarse hacia
♦ **rush out** I. vi (*leave*) salir precipitadamente II. vt (*publish*) publicar con urgencia

rush hour n hora f punta

Russia ['rʌʃ·ə] n Rusia f

Russian ['rʌʃ·ən] I. adj ruso, -a II. n 1. (*person*) ruso, -a m, f 2. (*language*) ruso m

rust [rʌst] I. n 1. (*decay*) oxidación f 2. (*substance*) herrumbre f 3. (*color*) color m herrumbre II. vi oxidarse III. vt oxidar

rust-colored adj de color herrumbre

rustle ['rʌs·əl] I. vi (*leaves*) susurrar; (*paper*) crujir II. vt 1. (*leaves*) hacer susurrar; (*paper*) hacer crujir 2. (*steal: cattle*) robar III. n (*of leaves*) susurro m; (*of paper*) crujido m

rustler ['rʌs·lər] n ladrón, -ona m, f de ganado

rustproof ['rʌst·pruf] adj inoxidable

rusty ['rʌs·ti] <-ier, -iest> adj 1. (*metal*) oxidado, -a 2. (*in skill*) falto, -a de práctica; **my Spanish is a bit ~** tengo bastante olvidado el castellano

rut¹ [rʌt] n bache m ▸ **to be stuck in a ~** estar metido en la rutina

rut² [rʌt] n ZOOL celo m

ruthless ['ruθ·lɪs] adj (*person*) despiadado, -a; (*ambition*) implacable; **to be ~ in doing sth** hacer algo sin piedad

rye [raɪ] n centeno m

S

S [es], **s** n S, s f; **~ as in Sierra** S de Soria

s [es] abbr of **second** s m

S [es] n abbr of **south** S m

sabotage ['sæb·ə·taʒ] I. vt sabotear II. n sabotaje m

saccharin ['sæk·ər·ɪn] n sacarina f

sachet [sæ·'ʃeɪ] n bolsita f

sack¹ [sæk] I. n 1. (*large bag*) saco m; **a ~ of potatoes** un saco de patatas; (*bag*) bolsa f 2. sl **to hit the ~** irse al catre; **to get the ~** ser despedido; **to give sb the ~** despedir a alguien II. vt despedir

sack² [sæk] I. n (*plundering*) saqueo m II. vt (*plunder*) saquear

sacred ['seɪ·krɪd] adj sagrado, -a; **is nothing ~ to you?** ¿no tienes respeto por nada?

sacrifice ['sæk·rə·faɪs] I. vt sacrificar; (*time, money*) renunciar a II. n sacrificio m; **at the ~** en detrimento (**of** de)

sacrilege ['sæk·rə·lɪdʒ] n sacrilegio m

sacrilegious [ˌsæk·rə·'lɪdʒ·əs] adj sacrílego, -a

SAD [ˌes·eɪ·'di] n abbr of **seasonal affective disorder** trastorno m afectivo estacional

sad [sæd] <-dd-> adj **1.** (unhappy) triste; **it is ~ that** es una pena que +subj; **to make sb ~** poner triste a alguien; **to become ~** entristecerse **2.** (pathetic) patético, -a **3.** (deplorable) lamentable; **~ to say** lamentablemente

sadden ['sæd·ən] vt entristecer; **to be deeply ~ed** estar muy afligido

sadistic [sə·'dɪs·tɪk] adj sádico, -a

sadness ['sæd·nɪs] n tristeza f

safari [sə·'far·i] n safari m; **to go on ~** irse de safari

safe [seɪf] **I.** adj **1.** (free of danger) seguro, -a; (driver) prudente; **at a ~ distance** a una distancia prudencial; **it is not ~ to...** es peligroso... +infin; **just to be ~** por precaución **2.** (secure) salvo, -a; **to feel ~** sentirse a salvo; **in a ~ place** en un lugar seguro **3.** (certain) seguro, -a; **a ~ bet** una apuesta muy segura **4.** (trustworthy) de fiar; **to be in ~ hands** estar en buenas manos ► **to be on the ~ side** para mayor seguridad; **it is better to be ~ than sorry** más vale prevenir que curar; **~ and sound** sano y salvo **II.** n caja f fuerte

safe-deposit box n caja f de seguridad

safeguard ['seɪf·gard] **I.** vt salvaguardar **II.** vi protegerse (**against** contra) **III.** n salvaguardia f; **as a ~ against sth** para evitar algo

safekeeping [,seɪf·'ki·pɪŋ] n custodia f; **to be in sb's ~** estar bajo la custodia de alguien

safe sex [seɪf·'seks] n sexo m seguro

safety ['seɪf·ti] n seguridad f; (on gun) seguro m; **a place of ~** un lugar seguro; **for her ~** para su seguridad

safety belt n cinturón m de seguridad

safety curtain n telón m de seguridad

safety glass n vidrio m inastillable

safety margin n margen m de seguridad

safety net n red f (de seguridad); fig protección f

safety pin n imperdible m

safety regulations npl normas f pl de seguridad

safety valve n válvula f de seguridad

sag [sæg] **I.** <-gg-> vi **1.** (droop) combarse, achiguarse Arg, Chile **2.** (sink)

hundirse; (spirit) decaer; (interest) decrecer **II.** n (fall) caída f

Sagittarius [,sædʒ·ə·'ter·i·əs] n Sagitario m

said [sed] **I.** pp, pt of **say II.** adj dicho, -a

sail [seɪl] **I.** n **1.** NAUT vela f **2.** (windmill) aspa f ► **to set ~** zarpar (**for** hacia); **under full ~** a toda vela **II.** vi **1.** (travel) navegar **2.** (move smoothly) deslizarse **3. to ~ through sth** hacer algo con facilidad ► **to ~ against the wind** nadar a contracorriente **III.** vt (navigate) cruzar; **to ~ the seas** surcar los mares

sailboard ['seɪl·bɔrd] n tabla f de windsurf

sailboat ['seɪl·boʊt] n barco m de vela

sailing n **1.** NAUT navegación f **2.** SPORTS vela f **3.** (departure) salida f

sailor ['seɪ·lər] n marinero, -a m, f; SPORTS navegante mf

saint [seɪnt, sənt] n santo, -a m, f

saintly ['seɪnt·li] adj santo, -a

sake[1] [seɪk] n **for the ~ of** por ► **for Christ's ~! for goodness ~!** ¡por Dios!; **for old times'** ~ por los viejos tiempos

sake[2] n, **saki** ['sa·ki] n sake m

salable ['seɪ·lə·bəl] adj vendible

salad ['sæl·əd] n ensalada f, verde m CSur

salami [sə·'la·mi] n salami m, salame m CSur

salaried ['sæl·ə·rid] adj asalariado, -a

salary ['sæl·ə·ri] n sueldo m

sale [seɪl] n **1.** (act of selling) venta f; **the ~s** las rebajas; **benefit ~** venta benéfica f **2.** (auction) subasta f ► **to put sth up for ~** poner algo en venta; **for ~** se vende; **on ~** en venta algo

saleable ['seɪ·lə·bəl] adj see **salable**

sales executive n ejecutivo, -a m, f de ventas

salesman n dependiente m; (for company) representante m

salesperson n vendedor(a) m(f)

saleswoman n dependienta f; (for company) representante m

saliva [sə·'laɪ·və] n saliva f

salmon ['sæm·ən] n salmón m; **smoked ~** salmón ahumado

saloon [sə·'lun] n bar m

salt [sɔlt] I. n sal f; **bath ~s** sales de baño; **bath/smelling ~s** sales de baño/aromáticas ▶ **to take sth with a grain of ~** creerse la mitad de algo; **to rub ~ in a wound** hurgar en una herida II. vt 1. echar sal; (*preserve*) salar 2. (*season*) sazonar con sal III. *adj* salado, -a; (*butter*) con sal

salt water n agua f salada

salty [ˈsɔl·ti] *adj* salado, -a

salute [səˈlut] vt saludar; (*honor*) rendir homenaje

Salvadorian [ˌsæl·vəˈdɔr·i·ən] *adj, n* salvadoreño, -a m, f

salvage [ˈsæl·vɪdʒ] I. vt salvar II. n (*retrieval*) salvamento m

salvation [sælˈveɪ·ʃən] n salvación f

salve [sæv] I. n ungüento m; *fig* bálsamo m II. vt curar; (*conscience*) tranquilizar

same [seɪm] I. *adj* 1. (*identical*) **the ~** igual (**as que**) 2. (*not another*) **the ~** el mismo, la misma **at the ~ time** al mismo tiempo ▶ **to be one and the ~** ser lo mismo; **by the ~ token** del mismo modo II. *pron* 1. (*nominal*) **the ~** el mismo, la misma lo mismo *neuter*; **she's much the ~** sigue igual; **it's always the ~** siempre es lo mismo 2. (*adverbial*) **it's all the ~ to me** me da igual; **it's not the ~ as before** ya no es lo mismo; **all the ~** de todas formas; **~ to you** igualmente III. *adv* igual; **they are spelled the ~** se deletrean igual

sameness n igualdad f; (*monotony*) monotonía f

sample [ˈsæm·pəl] I. n muestra f; **free/urine ~** muestra gratuita/de orina II. vt 1. (*try*) probar 2. (*survey*) tomar muestras

sanatorium [ˌsæn·əˈtɔr·i·əm] <-s *or* -ria> n sanatorio m

sanction [ˈsæŋk·ʃən] I. n LAW, POL sanción f II. vt 1. (*approve*) aprobar 2. (*penalize*) sancionar

sanctity [ˈsæŋk·tə·ti] n inviolabilidad f; REL santidad f

sanctuary [ˈsæŋk·tʃu·er·i] n <-ies> 1. REL santuario m; (*around altar*) sagrario m 2. (*refuge*) refugio m; (*for animals*) reserva f; **wildlife ~** reserva natural

sand [sænd] I. n arena f; **grain of ~** grano m de arena ▶ **the ~s of time are running out** el tiempo se agota II. vt 1. (*make smooth*) lijar; (*floor*) pulir 2. (*cover with sand*) enarenar

sandal [ˈsæn·dəl] n sandalia f, quimba f AmL

sandbag [ˈsænd·bæg] n saco m de arena

sandbank [ˈsænd·bæŋk] n, **sandbar** [ˈsænd·bar] n banco m de arena

sandcastle n castillo m de arena

sand dune n duna f

sandpaper [ˈsænd·peɪ·pər] n papel m de lija

sandwich [ˈsænd·wɪtʃ] <-es> n bocadillo m

sandy [ˈsæn·di] *adj* <-ier, -iest> arenoso, -a; (*hair*) rojizo, -a

sane [seɪn] *adj* 1. (*not mad*) cuerdo, -a 2. (*sensible*) sensato, -a

sang [sæŋ] *pt of* **sing**

sanitary [ˈsæn·ɪ·ter·i] *adj* sanitario, -a; (*clean*) higiénico, -a

sanitation [ˌsæn·ɪˈteɪ·ʃən] n saneamiento m

sanity [ˈsæn·ə·ti] n cordura f; (*decision*) sensatez f

sank [sæŋk] *pt of* **sink**

Santa Claus n Papá m Noel

sap[1] [sæp] n 1. BOT savia f 2. (*vitality*) vitalidad f

sap[2] [sæp] <-pp-> vt (*weaken*) socavar

sap[3] [sæp] n *sl* (*fool*) papanatas *mf inv*

sapling [ˈsæp·lɪŋ] n pimpollo m

sarcasm [ˈsar·kæz·əm] n sarcasmo m

sarcastic [sarˈkæs·tɪk] *adj* sarcástico, -a

sardine [sarˈdin] n sardina f ▶ **to be packed (in) like ~s** estar como sardinas en lata

sash[1] [sæʃ] <-es> n faja f

sash[2] [sæʃ] <-es> n ARCHIT marco m

sat [sæt] *pt, pp of* **sit**

Satan [ˈseɪ·tən] n Satanás m

satchel [ˈsætʃ·əl] n cartera f, busaca f Col, Ven

satellite [ˈsæt·ə·laɪt] I. n satélite m II. *adj* por satélite

satin [ˈsæt·ən] I. n raso m II. *adj* satinado, -a

satire [ˈsæt·aɪr] n sátira f

satirical [səˈtɪr·ɪ·kəl] *adj* satírico, -a

satirize ['sæt·ə·raɪz] vt satirizar

satisfaction [ˌsæt·ɪs·'fæk·ʃən] n satisfacción f (**to** para); (*compensation*) compensación f

satisfactory [ˌsæt·ɪs·'fæk·tə·ri] adj satisfactorio, -a; SCHOOL suficiente

satisfy ['sæt·əs·faɪ] <-ie-> vt 1. (*person, desire*) satisfacer; (*condition*) cumplir; (*debt*) saldar 2. (*convince*) convencer (**that** de que)

satisfying adj satisfactorio, -a

Saturday ['sæt·ər·deɪ] n sábado m; s. a. **Friday**

Saturn ['sæt·ərn] n Saturno m

sauce [sɔs] n salsa f; **tomato ~** salsa de tomate

sauceboat n salsera f

saucepan ['sɔs·pæn] n cacerola f

saucer ['sɔ·sər] n platillo m

saucy ['sɔ·si] adj <-ier, -iest> descarado, -a

sauna ['sɔ·nə] n sauna f

sausage ['sɔ·sɪdʒ] n salchicha f; (*cured*) salchichón m

sausage meat n carne f de salchicha

savage ['sæv·ɪdʒ] I. adj 1. (*fierce*) salvaje 2. (*bad-tempered*) de mal carácter II. n salvaje mf

save¹ [seɪv] I. vt 1. (*rescue*) salvar; **to ~ sb's life** salvar la vida a alguien; **to ~ face** salvar las apariencias; **to ~ one's own skin** salvar el pellejo 2. (*keep*) a. COMPUT guardar 3. (*collect*) coleccionar 4. (*avoid wasting*) ahorrar 5. (*reserve*) reservar II. vi ahorrar (**for** para); **to ~ on** guardar

save² [seɪv] prep ~ (**for**) salvo; **all ~ the youngest** todos salvo los más jóvenes

saver ['seɪ·vər] n ahorrador(a) m(f)

saving ['seɪ·vɪŋ] I. n 1. ahorro m 2. (*rescue*) rescate m II. prep excepto

savings account ['seɪ·vɪŋz·ə·kaʊnt] n cuenta f de ahorros

savings bank n caja f de ahorros

savior ['seɪv·jər] n salvador(a) m(f)

savor ['seɪ·vər] I. n 1. (*taste*) sabor m 2. (*pleasure*) gusto m II. vt saborear

savory ['seɪ·və·ri] adj 1. (*salty*) salado, -a 2. (*appetizing*) apetitoso, -a

saw¹ [sɔ] pt of **see**

saw² [sɔ] I. n sierra f; **power ~** sierra

eléctrica II. <sawed, sawed *or* sawn> vt serrar

saw³ [sɔ] n dicho m

sawdust ['sɔ·dʌst] n serrín m

sawn [sɔn] pp of **saw**

saxophone ['sæk·sə·foʊn] n saxofón m

say [seɪ] I. <said, said> vt decir (**to** a, **that** que); **to ~ where/when** decir dónde/cuándo; **to ~ sth to sb's face** decir algo a alguien a la cara; **~ no more!** ¡no diga(s) más!; **to have something/nothing to ~** tener algo/no tener nada que decir; **people ~ that...** se dice que...; **the said lady** dicha señora; **(let's) ~...** digamos... ▶ **when all is said and done** a fin de cuentas; **having said that** una vez dicho eso; **to ~ when** decir basta; **you don't ~ (so)!** ¡no me digas!; **you said it!** ¡dímelo a mí! II. <said, said> vi **I'll ~!** ¡ya lo creo!; **I must ~...** debo admitir...; **not to ~...** incluso...; **that is to ~...** es decir... III. n parecer m; **to have a ~** tener voz y voto (**in** en)

saying ['seɪ·ɪŋ] n dicho m; **as the ~ goes** como dice el refrán; **it goes without ~** ni qué decir tiene

say-so ['seɪ·soʊ] n inf 1. (*authority*) autoridad f; **to have the ~** tener la última palabra 2. (*approval*) visto bueno m; **to get the ~** obtener el visto bueno

scab [skæb] n (*wound*) costra f; BOT, ZOOL roña f

scald [skɔld] I. vt 1. (*burn*) escaldar 2. (*clean*) esterilizar II. n MED escaldadura f

scalding ['skɔl·dɪŋ] adj que escalda; **~ hot** hirviendo

scale¹ [skeɪl] n ZOOL escama f; TECH, MED sarro m

scale² [skeɪl] n (*for weighing*) platillo m; **~s** balanza f; (*bigger*) báscula f ▶ **to tip the ~s** inclinar la balanza

scale³ [skeɪl] n (*range, magnitude, proportion*) a. MUS escala f; **on a large/small ~** a gran/pequeña escala; **to ~** a escala II. vt 1. (*climb*) escalar 2. TECH, ARCHIT reducir a escala

◆**scale down** vt reducir

scallop ['skal·əp] n ZOOL vieira f

scalp [skælp] I. n (*head skin*) cuero m cabelludo II. vt (*resell*) revender

scaly ['skeɪ·li] *adj* <-ier, -iest> escamoso, -a; (*skin*) reseco, -a

scam [skæm] *n sl* timo *m*

scamper ['skæm·pər] *vi* corretear

scan [skæn] I. <-nn-> *vt* 1. (*scrutinize*) escudriñar 2. (*look through*) dar un vistazo; (*newspaper*) hojear 3. MED explorar 4. COMPUT escanear II. *n* COMPUT escaneo *m*; MED escáner *m*

scandal ['skæn·dəl] *n* 1. (*public outrage*) escándalo *m*; to cover up a ~ tapar un escándalo; what a ~! ¡qué vergüenza! 2. (*gossip*) chismorreo *m*; to spread ~ difundir habladurías

Scandinavia [ˌskæn·dɪ·'neɪ·vi·ə] *n* Escandinavia *f*

Scandinavian *adj, n* escandinavo, -a *m, f*

scanner ['skæn·ər] *n* COMPUT, MED escáner *m*

scanning *n* escaneo *m*

scapegoat ['skeɪp·gout] *n* cabeza *mf* de turco

scar [skar] I. *n* 1. MED (*on skin*) cicatriz *f*; to leave a ~ dejar cicatriz 2. (*mark of damage*) señal *f* II. <-rr-> *vi* cicatrizar

scarce [skers] *adj* escaso, -a; to make oneself ~ esfumarse

scarcely ['skers·li] *adv* (*barely*) apenas; (*certainly not*) ni mucho menos

scare [sker] I. *vt* asustar; julepear *Arg, Par; Urug*, acholar *Chile, Perú*; to be ~d stiff estar muerto de miedo II. *vi* asustarse III. *n* susto *m*, julepe *m AmL*; to have a ~ llevarse un sobresalto; to give sb a ~ dar un susto a alguien

scarecrow ['sker·krou] *n* espantapájaros *m inv*

scarf [skarf, *pl* skarvz] <-ves *or* -s> *n* bufanda *f*; (*around head*) pañuelo *m*

scarlet ['skar·lət] *adj, n* escarlata *f*

scarlet fever *n* escarlatina *f*

scary ['sker·i] *adj* <-ier, -iest> que da miedo; (*movie*) de miedo

scat [skæt] *interj inf* fuera

scathing ['skeɪ·ðɪŋ] *adj* mordaz

scatter ['skæt·ər] I. *vt* esparcir; to ~ sth with sth salpicar algo con algo II. *vi* dispersarse

scatterbrain ['skæt·ər·breɪn] *n* cabeza *mf* de chorlito

scatterbrained *adj* atolondrado, -a

scattered *adj* disperso, -a; (*sporadic*) esporádico, -a

scene [sin] *n* 1. THEAT, CINE escena *f*; (*setting*) escenario *m*; a. *fig* behind the ~s entre bastidores; to make a ~ montar una escena 2. (*locality*) lugar *m*; the ~ of the crime la escena del crimen 3. (*view*) vista *f* 4. (*milieu*) mundo *m*; the art ~ el mundo del arte; this is/isn't my ~ esto es/no es lo mío

scenery ['si·nə·ri] *n* paisaje *m*; THEAT, CINE decorado *m*; to blend into the ~ conseguir pasar inadvertido

scent [sent] I. *n* 1. (*aroma*) aroma *m* 2. (*in hunting*) rastro *m*; to be on the ~ estar sobre la pista (of de); to put [*or* throw] sb off the ~ despistar a alguien 3. (*perfume*) perfume *m* II. *vt* 1. (*smell*) oler 2. (*sense*) intuir 3. (*perfume*) perfumar

sceptic ['skep·tɪk] *n see* skeptic

sceptical *adj see* skeptical

schedule ['skedʒ·ul] I. *n* 1. (*timetable*) horario *m*; bus/flight ~ horario de autobuses/vuelos; to stick to a ~ seguir un horario; everything went according to ~ todo fue según lo previsto 2. (*plan*) programa *m* 3. FIN inventario *m* II. *vt* 1. (*plan*) programar 2. (*list*) hacer una lista

scheduled *adj* programado, -a; (*flight*) regular

scheme [skim] *n* 1. (*structure*) esquema *m* 2. (*plot*) treta *f*

scheming ['ski·mɪŋ] *adj* intrigante

schizophrenia [ˌskɪt·sə·'fri·ni·ə] *n* esquizofrenia *f*

schizophrenic [ˌskɪt·sə·'fren·ɪk] *adj, n* esquizofrénico, -a *m, f*

scholar ['skal·ər] *n* 1. (*erudite*) erudito, -a *m, f* 2. (*scholarship holder*) becario, -a *m, f*

scholarship ['skal·ər·ʃɪp] *n* 1. (*learning*) erudición *f* 2. (*grant*) beca *f*

school[1] [skul] I. *n* escuela *f*, colegio *m*; primary ~ escuela primaria; secondary ~ instituto *m*, liceo *m Chile, Méx*; dancing ~ escuela de baile; driving ~ autoescuela; to go to ~ ir al colegio II. *adj* escolar

S

school² [skul] *n* ZOOL banco *m*

school board *n* consejo *m* escolar

schooling *n* enseñanza *f*

schoolmate *n* compañero, -a *m, f* de clase

schoolteacher *n* profesor(a) *m(f)*

science ['saɪəns] **I.** *n* ciencia *f* **II.** *adj* de ciencias

science fiction I. *n* ciencia ficción *f* **II.** *adj* de ciencia ficción

scientific [ˌsaɪən'tɪfɪk] *adj* científico, -a

scientist ['saɪəntɪst] *n* científico, -a *m, f*

scissors ['sɪzərz] *npl* tijeras *fpl;* **a pair of ~** unas tijeras

scoff [skɑf] *vi (mock)* burlarse (**at** de)

scold [skould] *vt* regañar

scone [skoun] *n* bollo *m*

scoop [skup] *n (utensil)* cucharón *m;* (*amount*) cucharada *f*

scoot [skut] *vi* largarse; **to ~ over** escabullirse

scooter ['sku�·tər] *n (toy)* patinete *m;* (*vehicle*) scooter *m*

scope [skoup] *n* **1.** *(range)* alcance *m* **2.** *(possibilities)* posibilidades *fpl*

scorch [skɔrtʃ] **I.** *vt* chamuscar **II.** *vi* chamuscarse **III.** *n* <-es> quemadura *f*

scorching *adj* abrasador(a); **it's ~ hot** hace un calor abrasador

score [skɔr] **I.** *n* **1.** SPORTS *(points)* puntuación *f;* **to keep (the) ~** llevar la cuenta **2.** SPORTS tanto *m* **3.** SCHOOL nota *f* **4.** *(twenty)* veintena *f;* **~s of people** mucha gente **5.** MUS partitura *f* **II.** *vt* **1.** *(goal, point)* marcar; *(triumph, victory)* obtener; *(drugs)* pillar **2.** *(cut)* cortar **III.** *vi* **1.** SPORTS marcar un tanto **2.** *sl (succeed)* triunfar; *(sex)* mojar; *(drugs)* pillar

scoreboard ['skɔr·bɔrd] *n* marcador *m*

Scorpio ['skɔr·pi·oʊ] *n* Escorpio *m*

scorpion ['skɔr·pi·ən] *n* escorpión *m*

Scot [skɑt] *n* escocés, -esa *m, f*

Scotch [skɑtʃ] **I.** *n* whisky *m* escocés **II.** *adj* escocés, -esa

scot-free [ˌskɑt·'fri] *adv* **1.** *(without punishment)* impunemente; **to get away** [*or* **off**] **~** salir impune **2.** *(unharmed)* sin un rasguño

Scotland ['skɑt·lənd] *n* Escocia *f*

Scots [skɑts] *adj see* **Scottish**

Scotsman ['skɑts·mən] <-men> *n* escocés *m*

Scotswoman ['skɑts·wʊm·ən] <-women> *n* escocesa *f*

Scottish ['skɑt·ɪʃ] *adj* escocés, -esa

scout [skaut] **I.** *n* explorador(a) *m(f)*, scout *mf Méx;* **talent ~** cazatalentos *mf inv* **II.** *vi* **to ~ ahead** reconocer el terreno; **to ~ around for** buscar

scowl [skaul] *vi* fruncir el ceño

scrabble ['skræb·əl] *vi* escarbar

scram [skræm] <-mm-> *vi sl* largarse, rajarse *AmC;* **~!** ¡largo!

scramble ['skræm·bəl] **I.** *vi (struggle)* luchar; **to ~ for sth** esforzarse por algo **II.** *vt* **1.** *(mix)* revolver; **~d eggs** huevos revueltos **2.** *(encrypt)* codificar **III.** *n* **1.** *(rush)* carrera *f;* *(chase)* persecución *f* **2.** *(struggle)* pelea *f,* rebatinga *f Méx*

scrap¹ [skræp] **I.** *n* **1.** *(piece)* trozo *m;* *(amount)* pizca *f;* **not a ~ of truth** ni un ápice de verdad **2.** *pl (food)* sobras *fpl* **3.** *(metal)* chatarra *f* **II.** <-pp-> *vt (get rid of)* desechar; *(abandon)* descartar; *(abolish)* abolir; *(car)* desguazar, deshuesar *Méx*

scrap² [skræp] **I.** *n (fight)* bronca *f,* agarrón *m Méx* **II.** <-pp-> *vi* pelearse

scrapbook ['skræp·bʊk] *n* álbum *m* de recortes

scrape [skreɪp] **I.** *vt* **1.** *(remove layer)* raspar; *(dirt)* limpiar **2.** *(graze)* rozar; *(scratch)* rascar **3.** *(rub against)* rozar **II.** *vi* **1.** *(rub against)* rozar **2.** *(make noise)* chirriar **3.** *(economize)* ahorrar **III.** *n* **1.** *(act)* raspado, -a *m, f* **2.** *(skin)* rozadura *f* **3.** *(sound)* chirrido *m* **4.** *(situation)* lío *m*

scrap iron *n* chatarra *f*

scrappy¹ ['skræp·i] <-ier, -iest> *adj (knowledge)* superficial; *(performance, game)* irregular

scrappy² ['skræp·i] <-ier, -iest> *adj (ready to fight)* pendenciero, -a, peleonero, -a *Méx*

scratch [skrætʃ] **I.** *n* **1.** *(on skin)* arañazo *m,* rayón *m AmL* **2.** *(mark)* raya *f*

3. (*start*) principio *m;* **from ~** desde cero **II.** *vt* **1.** (*cut*) arañar **2.** (*mark*) rayar **3.** (*relieve itch*) rascar **4.** (*erase*) tachar **5.** (*exclude*) retirar **III.** *vi* **1.** (*cat*) arañar **2.** (*relieve itch*) rascarse **IV.** *adj* improvisado, -a

scratchy ['skrætʃ·i] <-ier, -iest> *adj* **1.** (*record, voice*) rayado, -a **2.** (*irritating*) áspero, -a

scrawl [skrɔl] **I.** *vt* garabatear **II.** *n* garabato *m*

scream [skrim] **I.** *n* grito *m;* (*animal or shrill cry*) chillido *m* ▶ **to be a ~** ser la monda **II.** *vi* gritar; (*shrilly*) chillar; **to ~ with laughter** reír a carcajadas **III.** *vt* gritar; (*abuse, obscenities*) lanzar

screech [skritʃ] **I.** *n* chillido *m* **II.** *vi* chillar (**with**)

screen [skrin] **I.** *n* **1.** TV, CINE, COMPUT pantalla *f;* **split/touch ~** pantalla dividida/táctil **2.** (*framed panel*) biombo *m;* (*for protection*) *a. fig* cortina *f* **II.** *vt* **1.** (*conceal*) ocultar **2.** (*shield*) proteger **3.** (*examine*) examinar; (*revise*) revisar **4.** TV emitir; CINE proyectar

◆**screen off** *vt* separar con un biombo

screening *n* **1.** CINE proyección *f;* TV emisión *f* **2.** (*testing*) prueba *f* **3.** MED chequeo *m*

screw [skru] **I.** *n* **1.** tornillo *m;* **to tighten/loosen a ~** apretar/aflojar un tornillo **2.** (*turn*) vuelta *f* **3.** (*propeller*) hélice *f* **4.** (*twisted piece*) rosca *f* ▶ **he's got a ~** [*or* **a few ~s**] **loose** *inf* le falta (más de) un tornillo; **to put the ~s** apretar las tuercas (**on a**) **II.** *vt* **1.** (*with a screw*) atornillar; (*by twisting*) enroscar **2.** *sl* (*cheat*) timar **III.** *vi* (*turn*) enroscarse; (*become attached*) atornillarse

screwdriver ['skru·draɪ·vər] *n* (*tool*) destornillador *m*, desarmador *m AmL*

screw top *n* tapón *m* de rosca

scribble ['skrɪb·əl] **I.** *vt, vi* garabatear **II.** *n* garabatos *mpl*

Scripture ['skrɪp·tʃər] *n* Sagrada Escritura *f*

scriptwriter ['skrɪpt·raɪ·tər] *n* guionista *mf*

scroll [skroʊl] **I.** *n* (*roll*) rollo *m* **II.** *vi* desplazarse (**to** a); **to ~ down/up** bajar/subir

scrounge [skraʊndʒ] *vt, vi* gorronear

scrounger ['skraʊn·dʒər] *n* gorrón, -ona *m, f*, pedinche *mf Méx*

scrub[1] [skrʌb] <-bb-> **I.** *vt* **1.** (*clean*) fregar **2.** (*cancel*) cancelar **II.** *vi* fregar; **to ~ at** restregar **III.** *n* (*act*) fregado *m*

scrub[2] [skrʌb] *n* matorral *m*

scrubber ['skrʌb·ər] *n* fregón, -ona *m, f*

scruff [skrʌf] *n* cogote *m;* **to grab sb by the ~ of the neck** coger a alguien por el cogote

scruffy ['skrʌf·i] <-ier, -iest> *adj* desaliñado, -a, fachoso, -a *Méx*

scrumptious ['skrʌmp·ʃəs] *adj* de rechupete

scrunch [skrʌntʃ] **I.** *vi, vt* crujir **II.** *n* crujido *m*

scrutinize ['skru·tə·naɪz] *vt* escudriñar; (*votes*) escrutar; (*text*) revisar

scuba diving ['sku·bə·daɪ·vɪŋ] *n* submarinismo *m*

scuff [skʌf] **I.** *vt* **1.** (*roughen*) raspar **2.** (*drag*) arrastrar **II.** *n* rozadura *f*

scuffle ['skʌf·əl] **I.** *n* refriega *f* **II.** *vi* pelearse

sculpture ['skʌlp·tʃər] **I.** *n* escultura *f* **II.** *vt* esculpir

scum [skʌm] *n* (*people*) escoria *f*

scurry ['skɜr·i] <-ie-> *vi* corretear

scuttle[1] ['skʌt·əl] *vi* (*run*) corretear; **~ away** escabullirse

scuttle[2] ['skʌt·əl] *vt* (*sink*) hundir; (*plan*) echar por tierra

sea [si] *n* mar *m o f*; **at the bottom of the ~** en el fondo del mar; **by ~** por mar; **by the ~** junto al mar; **out at ~** en alta mar; **open ~, high ~s** mar abierto; **a ~ of people** un mar de gente

seafood ['si·fud] *n* marisco *m*

seafront ['si·frʌnt] *n* playa *f;* (*promenade*) paseo *m* marítimo, malecón *m Méx*

seagull ['si·gʌl] *n* gaviota *f*

seal[1] [sil] *n* ZOOL foca *f*

seal[2] [sil] **I.** *n* (*wax*) sello *m;* (*goods, door*) precinto *m* ▶ **~ of approval** aprobación *f* **II.** *vt a. fig* sellar; (*with tape*) precintar

S

sea level n nivel m del mar

sea lion n león m marino

seam [siːm] I. n 1. (*stitching*) costura f; **to come** [*or* **fall**] **apart at the ~s** descoserse; *fig* rebosar de gente 2. (*junction*) juntura f 3. MIN veta f II. vt (*sew*) coser

seamy ['siːmi] <-ier, -iest> adj sórdido, -a

search [sɜːtʃ] I. n a. COMPUT búsqueda f; (*building*) registro m, esculco m Col, Méx; (*person*) cacheo m; **to go in ~ of** ir en busca (**of** de) II. vi a. COMPUT **to ~** (**for**) buscar; **to ~ high and low** buscar por todas partes; **~ and replace** buscar y reemplazar III. vt 1. a. COMPUT buscar en; (*building, baggage*) registrar, escular Col, Méx; (*person*) cachear 2. (*examine*) examinar; **to ~ one's memory** hacer memoria ▸ **~ me!** ¡a mí que me registren!

◆ **search out** vt encontrar; (*information*) averiguar

search function n función f de búsqueda

searching adj 1. (*penetrating*) inquisitivo, -a 2. (*exhaustive*) minucioso, -a

searchlight ['sɜːtʃlaɪt] n reflector m

search party <-ies> n equipo m de salvamento

search warrant n orden f de registro [*or* AmL de allanamiento]

searing adj (*heat*) abrasador(a); (*pain*) punzante

sea salt n sal f marina

seashell ['siːʃel] n concha f

seashore ['siːʃɔːr] n costa f; (*beach*) playa f

seasick ['siːsɪk] adj mareado, -a; **to get ~** marearse

seasickness ['siːsɪknɪs] n mareo m

seaside ['siːsaɪd] I. n costa f; (*beach*) playa f II. adj costero, -a; **a ~ resort** un lugar de veraneo costero, un balneario AmL

season ['siːzən] I. n 1. (*of year*) estación f 2. (*epoch*) a. SPORTS temporada f; **Season's Greetings** Felices Fiestas; **the fishing/pear ~** la temporada de pesca/las peras; **to be in ~** estar en sazón; **out of ~** fuera de temporada; **high/low ~**

temporada alta/baja 3. **to be in ~** estar en celo; **the mating ~** la época de celo II. vt CULIN sazonar; (*salt and pepper*) salpimentar

seasonal ['siːzənəl] adj 1. estacional; **~ affective disorder** trastorno afectivo estacional 2. (*temporary*) temporal; **~ worker** temporero, -a m, f 3. (*food*) del tiempo

seasoning ['siːzənɪŋ] n condimento m, yuyos mpl Ecua, Perú

season ticket n abono m de temporada

seat [siːt] I. n 1. (*furniture*) asiento m; (*bicycle*) sillín m; THEAT butaca f; **back ~** asiento trasero; **is this ~ free/taken?** ¿está libre/ocupado este asiento?; **to hold a ~** guardar el sitio (**for** a); **to take one's ~** sentarse 2. (*ticket*) entrada f 3. (*buttocks*) trasero m 4. POL escaño m, banca f Arg, Par, Urug 5. (*center*) sede f ▸ **to fly by the ~ of one's pants** dejarse guiar por el instinto II. vt sentar; ARCHIT, TECH asentar

seat belt n cinturón m de seguridad; **to fasten one's ~** abrocharse el cinturón

seating n (*seats*) asientos mpl; **~ capacity** número de plazas; **~ for two thousand** aforo de dos mil personas

seawater ['siːwɔːtər] n agua f de mar

seaweed ['siːwiːd] n algas fpl, huiro m Chile

seaworthy ['siːwɜːrði] adj en condiciones de navegar

secluded [sɪ'kluːdɪd] adj aislado, -a; (*life*) solitario, -a

second[1] ['sekənd] I. adj 1. segundo, -a; **every ~ girl** una de cada dos chicas; **every ~ week** una semana sí y otra no; **to be ~** ser el segundo; **the ~ biggest town** la segunda ciudad más grande 2. (*another*) otro, -a; **to give sb a ~ chance** dar a alguien una segunda oportunidad; **to have ~ thoughts** tener dudas (**about** acerca de); **on ~ thought** pensándolo bien; **to have a ~ helping** repetir 3. **the ~ floor** el primero, en el segundo AmL II. n 1. AUTO segunda f 2. **may I have ~s?** ¿puedo repetir? III. adv en segundo lugar

second[2] ['sekənd] n segundo m; **per**

~ por segundo; at that very ~ en ese preciso instante; **just a ~!** ¡un segundo!; **it won't take (but) a ~!** ¡sólo será un momento!

secondary ['sek·ən·der·i] *adj* secundario, -a; **to be ~** ser de menor importancia (**to** que); (*industry*) derivado, -a

secondary school *n* 1. (*school*) instituto *m*, liceo *m Chile, Méx* 2. (*education*) enseñanza *f* secundaria

second best *n* segundo, -a *m, f*

second class *n* segunda *f* clase

second-class I. *adj* de segunda clase; (*mail*) regular; (*hotel, service*) de segunda categoría; (*goods*) de calidad inferior II. *adv* RAIL en segunda

second cousin *n* primo, -a *m, f* segundo, -a

secondly *adv* en segundo lugar

second-rate [,sek·ənd·'reɪt] *adj* mediocre

secrecy ['si·krə·si] *n* secreto *m;* **in ~** en secreto

secret ['si·krɪt] I. *n* 1. secreto *m;* **an open ~** un secreto a voces; **to let sb in on a ~** revelar un secreto a alguien 2. (*mystery*) misterio *m* II. *adj* secreto, -a; **to keep sth ~** ocultar algo

secretary ['sek·rə·ter·i] <-ies> *n* secretario, -a *m, f;* POL ministro, -a *m, f,* secretario, -a *Méx*

secretive ['si·krɪ·tɪv] *adj* reservado, -a

sect [sekt] *n* secta *f*

section ['sek·ʃən] I. *n* 1. *a.* MIL, MUS, PUBL sección *f;* (*object*) parte *f;* (*city*) distrito *m;* (*document*) párrafo *m;* LAW artículo *m;* (*road*) tramo *m* 2. (*group*) sector *m* 3. (*cut*) corte *m* II. *vt* (*cut*) seccionar; (*divide*) dividir

sector ['sek·tər] *n* sector *m;* **public/private ~** sector público/privado

secure [sɪ·'kjʊr] I. *adj* <-rer, -est> 1. (*safe, confident*) seguro, -a; **to be ~** estar protegido (**from** contra); **to feel ~** sentirse seguro (**about** respecto a); **to be ~ in the knowledge that...** tener la certeza de que...; **to be financially ~** tener estabilidad económica 2. (*fixed*) firme; (*foundation*) sólido, -a II. *vt* 1. (*obtain*) obtener 2. (*make firm*) asegurar; *fig* afianzar 3. (*make safe*) proteger

security [sɪ·'kjʊr·ə·ṭi] <-ies> *n* 1. (*safety*) seguridad *f;* **~ risk** peligro *m* para la seguridad 2. (*stability*) estabilidad *f;* **~ of employment** estabilidad laboral 3. (*safeguard*) salvaguardia *f* 4. (*of payment*) garantía *f*

security guard *n* guarda jurado *mf*

sedation [sɪ·'deɪ·ʃən] *n* sedación *f;* **under ~** sedado

sedative ['sed·ə·ṭɪv] *adj, n* sedante *m*

seduce [sɪ·'dus] *vt* seducir; **to ~ sb into doing sth** inducir a alguien a hacer algo

seduction [sɪ·'dʌk·ʃən] *n* seducción *f;* **~s** atractivo *m*

seductive [sɪ·'dʌk·tɪv] *adj* atrayente; (*person*) seductor(a); (*offer*) tentador(a)

see [si] <saw, seen> I. *vt* 1. ver; **to ~ sth with one's own eyes** ver algo con sus propios ojos; **it is worth ~ing** vale la pena verlo; **you were ~n entering the building** se os vio entrar en el edificio; **to ~ a little/a lot of sb** ver a alguien poco/a menudo; **~ you around!** ¡nos vemos!; **~ you (later)!** ¡hasta luego!; **as I ~ it...** a mi modo de ver...; **I don't ~ him doing that** no lo veo capaz de hacer eso; **I could ~ it coming** lo veía venir; **to ~ how/what/if...** ver cómo/qué/si...; **Mr. Brown will ~ you now** el Sr. Brown le recibirá ahora 2. **to be ~ing sb** salir con alguien 3. (*accompany*) acompañar 4. (*perceive*) darse cuenta de; **I don't ~ what you mean** no entiendo lo que quieres decir; **to ~ sth in a new light** cambiar de opinión respecto a algo 5. **~ that you are ready when we come** procura estar listo cuando vengamos II. *vi* ver; **as far as the eye can ~** hasta donde alcanza la vista; **as far as I can ~** por lo que veo; **~ for yourself!** ¡véalo usted mismo!; **let me ~** ¿a ver?; **let's ~** vamos a ver; **you'll ~** ya verás; **I ~** ya veo; **you ~?** ¿entiendes? ▶ **he can't ~ further than the end of his nose** no puede ver más allá de sus narices

♦ **see about** *vt inf* encargarse de; (*consider*) pensarse ▶ **we'll soon ~ that!** ¡eso ya lo veremos!

♦ **see in** *vt* (*welcome*) hacer pasar

◆**see off** vt despedir

◆**see out** vt (to door) acompañar hasta la puerta

◆**see through** vt 1. (not be deceived by) calar inf 2. (sustain) mantener a flote

◆**see to** vt encargarse de; **to ~ it that...** asegurarse de que...

seed [sid] I. n 1. BOT semilla f; (fruit) pepita f, pepa f AmL; (seeds) simiente f 2. (beginning) germen m; **to sow the ~s of doubt/discord** sembrar la duda/discordia II. vt 1. AGR sembrar 2. **to ~ a project with money** aportar capital a un proyecto

seedy ['si·di] <-ier, -iest> adj 1. (dubious) sórdido, -a 2. (unwell) pachucho, -a

seeing I. conj ~ (that) en vista de (que) II. n visión f; **~ is believing** ver para creer

seek [sik] <sought> vt 1. (look for, try to obtain) buscar; (help) pedir; (job) solicitar; **to ~ one's fortune** probar suerte 2. (attempt) tratar de

seem [sim] vi parecer; **it ~s that...** parece que...; **so it ~s, so it would ~** eso parece; **they ~ed to like the idea** parecía que les gustaba la idea; **to ~ as if...** parecer como si... +subj; **it is not all that it ~s** no es lo que parece; **things aren't always what they ~** las apariencias engañan

seeming adj aparente

seemingly adv aparentemente

seen [sin] pp of **see**

seep [sip] vi filtrarse

◆**seep away** vi escurrirse

see-through ['si·θru] adj transparente

segregate ['seg·rə·geɪt] vt segregar; (girls and boys) separar

segregation [ˌseg·rə·'geɪ·ʃən] n segregación f

seize [siz] vt 1. (grasp) agarrar, cachar Arg, Nic, Urug, acapullar Méx; (opportunity) no dejar escapar; (initiative, power) tomar; (criminal) detener; (property) confiscar; (drugs, weapons) incautar; **to ~ sb by the arm/by the throat** agarrar a alguien del brazo/por el cuello 2. (overcome) **he was ~d by fear** el miedo se apoderó de él 3. (un-

derstand) captar

◆**seize up** vi (stop) paralizarse; (muscles) agarrotarse; COMPUT colgarse

seizure ['si·ʒər] n (drugs) incautación f; (property) confiscación f

seldom ['sel·dəm] adv rara vez

select [sə·'lekt] I. vt seleccionar; (gift, wine) escoger II. adj (high-class) selecto, -a; (product) de primera calidad

selection [sə·'lek·ʃən] n selección f; (range) gama f; (food, drinks) surtido m

selective [sə·'lek·tɪv] adj selectivo, -a

self [self] n <selves> uno mismo, una misma **his better ~** su mejor parte; **one's other ~** su alter ego; **the ~** el yo

self-adhesive adj autoadhesivo, -a

self-assured adj seguro, -a de sí mismo, -a

self-centered adj egocéntrico, -a

self-complacent adj pej engreído, -a

self-composed adj sereno, -a; **to remain ~** no perder la serenidad

self-confessed adj confeso, -a; **she's a ~ coward** se confiesa cobarde

self-confidence n confianza f en uno mismo; **to have ~** confiar en sí mismo

self-conscious adj 1. (shy) tímido, -a 2. (unnatural) afectado, -a

self-contained adj 1. (community) autosuficiente; (apartment) con cocina y cuarto de baño 2. (reserved) reservado, -a

self-control n autocontrol m

self-critical adj autocrítico, -a

self-deception n engaño m a sí mismo

self-defeating adj contraproducente

self-defense n defensa f personal; LAW legítima defensa

self-destruct vi autodestruirse

self-discipline n autodisciplina f

self-employed I. adj **to be ~** trabajar por cuenta propia II. n **the ~** los autónomos

self-esteem n amor m propio

self-explanatory adj clarísimo, -a

self-expression n expresión f personal

self-important adj presuntuoso, -a

self-indulgent adj indulgente consigo mismo, -a

self-inflicted adj autoinfligido, -a

self-interest n interés m personal

selfish ['sel·fɪʃ] adj egoísta

selfishness n egoísmo m

selfless ['self·lɪs] adj desinteresado, -a

self-pity n autocompasión f

self-portrait n autorretrato m

self-possessed adj sereno, -a

self-preservation n instinto m de supervivencia

self-reliant adj independiente

self-respect n amor m propio; **to lose all ~** perder la dignidad

self-respecting adj **every ~ man** todo hombre que se precie

self-righteous adj farisaico, -a; (tone) de superioridad moral

self-sacrifice n abnegación f

self-satisfied adj engreído, -a

self-service adj, n ~ (store) autoservicio m; ~ restaurant self-service m

self-sufficient adj independiente, ECON autosuficiente

self-taught adj autodidacta

self-willed adj obstinado, -a, voltario, -a Chile

sell [sel] I. vt <sold, sold> 1. vender (for por); **to ~ sth at half price** vender algo a mitad de precio 2. (make accepted) convencer ▶ **to ~ oneself short** no hacerse valer II. vi <sold, sold> (product) venderse (at, for a); (company, shop) estar en venta

◆**sell off** vt liquidar; (industry) privatizar

◆**sell out** I. vi COM, FIN agotarse; fig venderse II. vt liquidar

sellable adj vendible

sell-by date ['sel·baɪ·ˌdeɪt] n fecha f límite de venta

seller n vendedor(a) m(f)

selves [selvz] n pl of **self**

semi ['sem·i] n 1. (truck) trailer m 2. pl SPORTS semifinal f

semicircle ['sem·ɪ·ˌsɜr·kəl] n semicírculo m

semicircular [ˌsem·ɪ·ˈsɜr·kjə·lər] adj semicircular

semicolon ['sem·ɪ·ˌkoʊ·lən] n punto y coma m

semiconductor [ˌsem·ɪ·kən·ˈdʌk·tər] n semiconductor m

seminar ['sem·ə·nar] n seminario m

semolina [ˌsem·ə·ˈli·nə] n sémola f

senate ['sen·ɪt] n POL senado m; UNIV consejo m

senator ['sen·ə·tər] n senador(a) m(f)

send [send] vt <sent, sent> 1. enviar, mandar; **to ~ sth by mail** enviar algo por correo; **to ~ sb to prison** mandar a alguien a la cárcel; **~ her my regards** dale recuerdos de mi parte 2. (propel) lanzar 3. RADIO transmitir ▶ **to ~ sb packing** mandar a alguien a freír espárragos

◆**send away** vt 1. (dismiss) despedir 2. (send) enviar

◆**send back** vt mandar de vuelta

◆**send for** vt (person) llamar; (assistance) pedir; (goods) encargar

◆**send in** vt 1. (send) mandar 2. (let in) hacer pasar

◆**send off** vt mandar

◆**send on** vt 1. (in advance) mandar por adelantado 2. (forward) remitir

◆**send out** vt 1. (ask to leave) echar 2. (send on errand) mandar 3. (dispatch) enviar 4. (signal, rays) emitir; (smell, heat) despedir

◆**send up** vt 1. (drive up) hacer subir 2. (mock) parodiar

sender n remitente mf

senile ['si·naɪl] adj senil

senior ['sin·jər] I. adj **James Smith, Senior** James Smith, padre; **to be ~ to sb** estar por encima de alguien II. n 1. (age) mayor mf; **she is two years my ~** me lleva dos años 2. (rank) superior mf

senior citizen n jubilado, -a m, f

senior partner n socio, -a m, f mayoritario, -a

sensation [sen·ˈseɪ·ʃən] n sensación f; **to be a ~** ser un éxito; **to cause a ~** hacer furor

sensational [sen·ˈseɪ·ʃə·nəl] adj sensacional; pej sensacionalista

sense [sens] I. n 1. sentido m; **~ of hearing/sight/smell/taste/touch** oído m /vista f/olfato m /gusto m /tacto m; **to make ~** tener sentido; **there's no ~ in doing...** no tiene sentido hacer...; **to have no ~ of occasion** ser in-

S

oportuno; **to lose all ~ of time** perder la
noción del tiempo; **in every ~** en todos
los sentidos; **in a ~** en cierto modo; **in
no ~** de ninguna manera *f (sensa-
tion)* sensación *f* **3.** *pl* PSYCH juicio *m;*
to come to one's ~s recobrar el conocimiento; *(see reason)* entrar en razón
4. common ~ sentido común; **to have
enough** *[or* **the good]** **~ to...** tener la
sensatez de... **II.** *vt* sentir; **to ~ that...**
darse cuenta de que...

senseless ['sens·lɪs] *adj* **1.** *(pointless)*
sin sentido **2.** MED inconsciente

sense organ *n* órgano *m* sensorial

sensibility [ˌsen·sə·'bɪl·ə·ţi] *n* sensibilidad *f;* **to offend sb's sensibilities** herir
la sensibilidad a alguien

sensible ['sen·sə·bəl] *adj (person, decision)* sensato, -a

sensibly *adv* prudentemente; *(decide)*
acertadamente; *(dress)* con ropa cómoda

sensitive ['sen·sɪ·ţɪv] *adj* **1.** *(sympathetic)* sensible **2.** *(touchy)* susceptible
(about a) **3.** *(delicate)* delicado, -a

sent [sent] *pp, pt of* **send**

sentence ['sen·təns] **I.** *n* **1.** LAW sentencia *f; (punishment)* condena *f;* **life ~**
cadena perpetua; **to serve a ~** cumplir
condena **2.** LING frase *f* **II.** *vt* condenar

sentimental [ˌsen·tə·'men·təl] *adj* sentimental **(about** con); *pej* sensiblero, -a

separable ['sep·ər·ə·bəl] *adj* separable

separate¹ ['sep·ər·ɪt] *adj* separado, -a;
to remain a ~ entity ser una entidad
independiente; **a ~ piece of paper** un
papel aparte; **to go one's ~ ways** ir por
caminos distintos

separate² ['sep·ə·reɪt] **I.** *vt* separar **II.** *vi*
separarse

separated *adj* separado, -a

September [sep·'tem·bər] *n* septiembre *m; s. a.* **April**

septic ['sep·tɪk] *adj* séptico, -a

sequel ['si·kwəl] *n* secuela *f; (follow-up)*
continuación *f*

sequence ['si·kwəns] *n a.* CINE secuencia *f; (events)* sucesión *f*

sequin ['si·kwɪn] *n* lentejuela *f*

Serb [sɜrb] *adj, n* serbio, -a *m, f*

Serbia ['sɜr·bi·ə] *n* Serbia *f*

Serbian ['sɜr·bi·ən] *n see* **Serb**

Serbo-Croat [ˌsɜr·boʊ·kroʊ·'æt] *n* ser-
bocroata *m*

sergeant ['sar·dʒənt] *n* sargento *m*

serial ['sɪr·i·əl] **I.** *n* serial *m;* TV serie *f*
II. *adj (in series)* consecutivo, -a; *(in
parts)* por entregas

series ['sɪr·iz] *n inv (sequence)* serie *f;
(succession)* sucesión *f*

serious ['sɪr·i·əs] *adj* **1.** *(earnest)* serio,
-a; *(problem, injury)* grave; *(argument)*
importante; *(debt, amount)* considerable
2. *(determined)* firme; **to be ~** ir en serio **(about** con)

seriously *adv* **1.** *(in earnest)* en serio
2. *(ill, damaged)* gravemente *mf
(very)* muy

sermon ['sɜr·mən] *n a. fig* sermón *m;* **to
deliver a ~** dar un sermón

serpent ['sɜr·pənt] *n* serpiente *f*

servant ['sɜr·vənt] *n* criado, -a *m, f,* mucamo, -a *m, f AmL*

serve [sɜrv] **I.** *n* SPORTS saque *m* **II.** *vt*
1. *(attend)* atender **2.** *(provide)* servir
3. *(be enough for)* servir para; **if my
memory ~s me right** si la memoria
no me falla ▸ **it ~s him/her right!**
¡se lo merece!; SPORTS sacar **III.** *vi* servir **(as** de);
▸ **serve up** *vt* CULIN servir; *fig* ofrecer

server ['sɜr·vər] *n* **1.** *(spoon)* cuchara
f de servir **2.** *(tray)* bandeja *f; (dish)*
fuente *f* **3.** *(waiter)* camarero, -a *m, f*
4. COMPUT servidor *m*

service ['sɜr·vɪs] *n* **1.** *a.* SPORTS servicio *m;*
train ~ servicio de trenes; **to be of ~**
ser de utilidad **2.** TECH mantenimien-
to *m;* AUTO revisión *f* **3.** *(set)* vajilla *f;*
tea ~ juego *m* de té ▸ **to be at sb's
~** estar al servicio de alguien; **to be in
~** estar en uso

service area *n* área *f* de servicio

service center *n (repairs)* centro *m* de
reparaciones

service charge *n* gastos *m pl* de servicio

service road *n* vía *f* de acceso

service station *n* estación *f* de servicio

serving ['sɜr·vɪŋ] *n (portion)* ración *f*

sesame ['ses·ə·mi] *n* sésamo *m*

session ['sef·ən] *n* **1.** sesión *f;* **to be in**

~ estar reunido **2.** SCHOOL trimestre *m*; **morning/afternoon** ~ sesión de mañana/tarde

set [set] **I.** *adj* **1.** (*ready*) listo, -a; **to get** ~ **prepararse** (**to** para) **2.** (*fixed*) fijo, -a **3.** (*assigned*) asignado, -a **II.** *n* **1.** (*people*) grupo *m*; (*cups, chess*) juego *m*; (*kitchen utensils*) batería *f*; (*glasses*) cristalería *f*; (*tools*) set *m*; (*teeth*) dentadura *f* **2.** (*collection*) colección *f* **3.** CINE plató *m* **4.** (*TV*) televisor *m* **5.** (*tennis*) set *m* **III.** *vt* <set, set> **1.** (*place*) poner, colocar; **a house that is** ~ **on a hill** una casa situada sobre una colina **2.** (*give*) dar; (*task*) imponer; (*problem*) plantear **3. to** ~ **sth on fire** prender fuego a algo; **to** ~ **sth in motion** poner algo en movimiento **4.** (*adjust*) ajustar; (*prepare*) preparar; (*table*) poner **5.** (*fix*) fijar; (*record*) establecer **IV.** *vi* **1.** MED soldarse **2.** (*cement*) endurecerse; (*Jell-O, cheese*) cuajar; (*sun*) ponerse

◆**set about** *vt* emprender; **to** ~ **doing sth** comenzar a hacer algo

◆**set against** *vt* **1.** (*compare*) comparar **2. to set sb against** poner a alguien en contra de

◆**set apart** *vt* **1.** (*distinguish*) diferenciar **2.** (*reserve*) reservar

◆**set aside** *vt* **1.** (*save*) reservar; (*money*) ahorrar **2.** (*put to side*) dejar de lado; **to set one's differences aside** dejar a un lado sus diferencias

◆**set back** *vt* **1.** (*delay*) retrasar **2.** (*place away*) apartar **3.** (*cost*) salir por

◆**set down** *vt* **1.** (*place on surface*) posar **2.** (*write*) poner por escrito

◆**set off** **I.** *vi* salir (**for** hacia) **II.** *vt* **1.** (*explosive*) detonar **2.** (*start*) causar **3.** (*enhance*) resaltar

◆**set out** **I.** *vi* **1.** *see* **set off 2.** (*intend*) tener la intención (**to** de) **II.** *vt* **1.** (*display*) disponer **2.** (*explain*) exponer (**for** a)

◆**set to** *vi* (*begin working*) ponerse manos a la obra

◆**set up** *vt* **1.** (*prepare*) poner **2.** (*establish*) establecer; (*arrange*) disponer; (*cause*) causar; (*committee, corporation*) crear **3. to set oneself** dárselas (**as** de) **4.** (*provide*) proveer **5.** (*deceive*) jugársela

setback ['set-bæk] *n* revés *m*; **to experience a** ~ tener un contratiempo

settee [se-'ti] *n* sofá *m*

setting ['set-ɪŋ] *n* **1.** (*sun*) puesta *f* **2.** (*scenery*) escenario *m*; (*surroundings*) entorno *m* **3.** TECH ajuste *m*

settle ['set-əl] **I.** *vi* **1.** (*residence*) establecerse **2.** (*get comfortable*) ponerse cómodo, -a **3.** (*calm down*) calmarse; (*weather, situation*) normalizarse **4.** (*decide*) llegar a un acuerdo **5.** (*pay*) saldar las cuentas **6.** (*accumulate*) acumularse; (*snow*) cuajar **7.** (*bird*) posarse **II.** *vt* **1.** (*calm down*) calmar **2.** (*decide*) acordar **3.** (*conclude*) finalizar; (*resolve*) resolver **4.** (*pay*) pagar; (*account*) liquidar **5.** (*colonize*) colonizar ► **that** ~**s it!** ¡ya no hay más que decir!

◆**settle down** *vi* **1.** (*calm down*) calmarse **2.** (*residence*) establecerse

◆**settle for** *vt* contentarse con

◆**settle in** *vi* acostumbrarse

◆**settle on** *vt* (*decide*) decidir; (*agree*) acordar

◆**settle up** *vi* ajustar cuentas

settled ['set-əld] *adj* **1.** (*established*) establecido, -a; **to feel** ~ sentirse cómodo **2.** (*calm*) calmado, -a **3.** (*fixed*) fijo, -a

settlement ['set-əl-mənt] *n* **1.** (*resolution*) resolución *f* **2.** (*agreement*) acuerdo *m* **3.** FIN, ECON liquidación *f* **4.** (*town*) asentamiento *m*

settler ['set-lər] *n* colono, -a *m, f*

set-to ['set-tu] *n* bronca *f*; **to have a** ~ tener una bronca (**with** con)

seven ['sev-ən] *adj, n* siete *m*; *s. a.* **eight**

seventeen [ˌsev-ən-'tin] *adj, n* diecisiete *m*; *s. a.* **eight**

seventeenth [ˌsev-ən-'tinθ] **I.** *adj* decimoséptimo, -a **II.** *n* **1.** (*order*) decimoséptimo, -a *m, f* **2.** (*date*) diecisiete *m* **3.** (*fraction*) diecisieteavo *m*; *s. a.* **eighth**

seventh ['sev-ənθ] **I.** *adj* séptimo, -a **II.** *n* **1.** (*order*) séptimo, -a *m, f* **2.** (*date*) siete *m* **3.** (*fraction*) séptimo *m*; *s. a.* **eighth**

seventy ['sev-ən-ti] **I.** *adj* setenta *inv* **II.** *n* <-ies> setenta *m*; *s. a.* **eighty**

several ['sev-ər-əl] **I.** *adj* varios, -as; ~

S

times varias veces; (*distinct*) distintos, -as **II.** *pron* varios, -as; **~ of us** algunos de nosotros; **we've got ~** tenemos varios

severe [sə·ˈvɪr] *adj* (*problem, illness*) grave; (*pain*) fuerte; (*criticism, punishment, person*) severo, -a; (*weather*) riguroso, -a

sew [soʊ] <sewed, sewn *or* sewed> *vt, vi* coser; **hand ~n** cosido a mano

♦**sew up** *vt* **1.** a. MED coser **2.** (*arrange*) arreglar; (*deal*) cerrar

sewage [ˈsuː·ɪdʒ] *n* aguas *f pl* residuales

sewer [ˈsuː·ər] *n* alcantarilla *f*

sewing [ˈsoʊ·ɪŋ] **I.** *n* costura *f* **II.** *adj* de costura

sewn [soʊn] *pp of* **sew**

sex [seks] <-es> *n* sexo *m;* **to have ~** tener relaciones sexuales

sex appeal *n* atractivo *m*

sex discrimination *n* discriminación *f* sexual

sex education *n* educación *f* sexual

sexism [ˈsek·sɪz·əm] *n* sexismo *m*

sexist *adj, n* sexista *mf*

sex life *n* vida *f* sexual

sexual [ˈsek·ʃu·əl] *adj* sexual

sexuality [ˌsek·ʃuˈæl·ə·t̬i] *n* sexualidad *f*

sexually *adv* sexualmente; **to be ~ abused** ser víctima de abusos sexuales

sexy [ˈsek·si] <-ier, -iest> *adj* sexy; (*exciting*) flipante *argot*

shabby [ˈʃæb·i] <-ier, -iest> *adj* **1.** (*worn*) deteriorado, -a **2.** (*ragged*) desharrapado, -a, encuerado, -a *Méx, Cuba* **3.** (*substandard*) de mala calidad

shack [ʃæk] *n* choza *f*, ruca *f Arg, Chile*, jacal *m Méx*

shade [ʃeɪd] **I.** *n* **1.** (*shadow*) sombra *f*; ART sombreado *m;* **in the ~ of** a [*or* en] la sombra de **2.** (*covering*) pantalla *f* **3.** *pl* (*blind*) persiana *f* **4.** (*variation*) matiz *m;* (*color*) tono *m* **5.** (*small amount*) pizca *f* **6.** *pl, inf* (*sunglasses*) gafas *f pl* de sol **II.** *vt* (*cast shadow*) dar sombra a; (*protect*) resguardar; ART sombrear

shading *n* sombreado *m*

shadow [ˈʃæd·oʊ] **I.** *n* **1.** a. *fig* sombra *f;* **the ~s** las tinieblas **2.** (*trace*) pizca *f;*

without a ~ of a doubt sin lugar a dudas ▶ **to have ~s under one's eyes** tener ojeras; **to be a ~ of one's former self** no ser ni la sombra de lo que fue; **to be afraid of one's own ~** tener miedo de su propia sombra; **to cast a ~ over** ensombrecer; **to be under sb's ~** estar a la sombra de alguien **II.** *vt* **1.** ART sombrear **2.** (*darken*) ensombrecer **3.** (*follow*) seguir

shadowy <-ier, -iest> *adj* **1.** (*dark*) oscuro, -a **2.** (*vague*) impreciso, -a

shady [ˈʃeɪ·di] <-ier, -iest> *adj* sombreado, -a; (*dubious*) turbio, -a; (*character*) sospechoso, -a

shaft [ʃæft] *n* **1.** (*of tool*) mango *m* **2.** TECH eje *m* **3.** (*ray*) rayo *m*

shaggy [ˈʃæg·i] <-ier, -iest> *adj* peludo, -a; (*coat*) lanudo, -a

shake [ʃeɪk] **I.** *n* **1.** (*wobble*) sacudida *f;* (*quiver*) temblor *m* **2.** (*milk*) batido *m*, malteada *f AmL* **3.** (*handshake*) apretón *m* **4.** *pl* (*trembling*) tembleque *m;* **to get the ~s** entrarle el tembleque ▶ **in two ~s of a lamb's tail** en un santiamén **II.** <shook, shaken> *vt* **1.** (*joggle*) agitar; (*person*) sacudir; **to ~ hands** darse la mano; **to ~ one's head** negar con la cabeza **2.** (*unsettle*) debilitar **3.** (*worry*) desconcertar **III.** <shook, shaken> *vi* (*tremble*) temblar; **'~ well before opening'** 'agitar antes de abrir'; **let's ~ on it** chócala

♦**shake off** *vt* librarse de

♦**shake out** *vt* sacudir

♦**shake up** *vt* **1.** (*reorganize*) reorganizar **2.** (*upset*) desconcertar

shaken [ˈʃeɪ·kən] *vi, vt pp of* **shake**

shakily [ˈʃeɪ·kɪ·li] *adv* de forma temblorosa

shaking [ˈʃeɪ·kɪŋ] *adj* tembloroso, -a

shaky [ˈʃeɪ·ki] <-ier, -iest> *adj* **1.** (*jerky*) tembloroso, -a **2.** (*wavering*) inseguro, -a **3.** (*unstable*) inestable

shall [ʃæl] *aux* **1.** (*future*) **we ~ win the match** ganaremos el partido **2.** (*ought to*) **he ~ call his mother** debería llamar a su madre

shallow [ˈʃæl·oʊ] *adj* **1.** (*not deep*) poco profundo, -a **2.** (*superficial*) superficial

sham [ʃæm] *pej* I. *n* 1. (*fake*) fraude *m* 2. (*impostor*) impostor(a) *m(f)* 3. (*cover*) funda *f* II. *adj* falso, -a; (*deal*) fraudulento, -a; (*marriage*) simulado, -a III. <-mm-> *vt, vi* fingir

shame [ʃeɪm] *n* 1. vergüenza *f*, pena *f AmC*; **to die of ~** morirse de vergüenza; **to feel no ~** no tener vergüenza; **to put sb to ~** avergonzar a alguien; **~ on you!** ¡debería darte vergüenza!; **to bring ~** deshonrar (**on** a) 2. (*pity*) pena; **what a ~!** ¡qué pena!; **what a ~ that...** qué pena que... +*subj*; **it's a crying ~** es una verdadera lástima

shameful [ˈʃeɪm·fəl] *adj* vergonzoso, -a, penoso, -a *AmC*; **it's ~ that...** es una vergüenza que... +*subj*

shameless [ˈʃeɪm·lɪs] *adj* descarado, -a, conchudo, -a *AmL*

shampoo [ʃæmˈpu] *n* champú *m*

shape [ʃeɪp] I. *n* forma *f*; **to get out of ~** perder la forma; **to take ~** adquirir forma; **in the ~ of** en forma (**of** de); **in bad/good ~** en mala/buena forma; **to get into ~** ponerse en forma II. *vt* 1. (*form*) dar forma a 2. (*influence*) condicionar

share [ʃer] I. *n* 1. parte *f*; **to do one's ~** hacer su parte (**of** de) 2. FIN acción *f*; **stocks and ~s** acciones y participaciones II. *vi, vt* compartir; (*divide*) repartir

shark [ʃark] <-(s)> *n* tiburón *m*; (*person*) timador(a) *m(f)*

sharp [ʃarp] I. *adj* 1. (*cutting*) afilado, -a; (*pointed*) puntiagudo, -a 2. (*curve*) cerrado, -a; (*pain, cry*) agudo, -a; (*look*) penetrante; (*tongue*) viperino, -a 3. (*astute*) astuto, -a; (*perceptive*) perspicaz 4. (*sudden*) súbito, -a; (*abrupt*) abrupto, -a; (*marked*) pronunciado, -a 5. (*distinct*) nítido, -a 6. MUS sostenido, -a II. *adv* 1. (*exactly*) en punto 2. (*suddenly*) de repente; **to pull up ~** frenar en seco

sharpen [ˈʃar·pən] *vt* 1. (*blade*) afilar; (*pencil*) sacar punta a 2. (*intensify*) agudizar; (*appetite*) abrir

sharpener [ˈʃar·pən·ər] *n* afilador *m*, afiladora *f Méx*; **pencil ~** sacapuntas *m inv*

sharp-eyed [ʃarp·ˈaɪd] *adj* observador(a)

sharp-tongued *adj* mordaz

sharp-witted *adj* agudo, -a

shatter [ˈʃæt·ər] I. *vi* hacerse añicos II. *vt* (*smash*) hacer añicos; (*hopes, dreams, unity*) destruir

shattering *adj* tremendo, -a

shatterproof [ˈʃæt·ər·ˌpruf] *adj* inastillable

shave [ʃeɪv] I. *n* afeitado *m*, rasurada *f Méx* ▶ **to have a close ~** librarse por los pelos II. *vi* afeitarse III. *vt* afeitar, rasurar *Méx*

shaven [ˈʃeɪ·vən] *adj* afeitado, -a; (*head*) rapado, -a

shaver [ˈʃeɪ·vər] *n* maquinilla *f* de afeitar, rasuradora *f Méx*

shawl [ʃɔl] *n* chal *m*

she [ʃi] *pron pers* (*female*) ella; **~'s my mother** (ella) es mi madre

shed¹ [ʃed] *n* cobertizo *m*, galera *f AmL*

shed² [ʃed] <shed, shed> *vt* (*cast off*) quitarse; (*hair, weight*) perder; (*skin*) mudar; (*blood, tears*) derramar; (*light*) emitir

sheep [ʃip] *n* oveja *f*; (*ram*) carnero *m* ▶ **black ~** oveja negra

sheepdog [ˈʃip·dɒg] *n* perro *m* pastor

sheepish [ˈʃi·pɪʃ] *adj* tímido, -a

sheepskin [ˈʃip·skɪn] *n* piel *f* de borrego

sheer [ʃɪr] *adj* 1. (*pure*) puro, -a; (*agony, lunacy*) total; **~ coincidence** pura coincidencia 2. (*vertical*) escarpado, -a; (*drop*) en picado 3. (*thin*) fino, -a

sheet [ʃit] *n* 1. (*bed*) sábana *f*; (*paper*) hoja *f*; (*metal, stamps*) plancha *f*; (*glass*) lámina *f* 2. (*information*) folleto *m* 3. (*layer*) capa *f*

sheik(h) [ʃik] *n* jeque *m*

shelf [ʃelf] *n, pl* felvz] <shelves> *n* estante *m*; **~s** estantería *f*; GEO arrecife *m*

shell [ʃel] *n* (*nut, egg*) cáscara *f*; (*shellfish, snail*) concha *f*; (*crab, turtle*) caparazón *m*; (*house*) estructura *f*; (*ship*) casco *m*; TECH armazón *m* ▶ **to come** [*or* **bust**] **out of one's ~** salir del cascarón

◆ **shell out** *vt, vi inf* (*pay*) aflojar; **to ~ for** apoquinar para

shellfish [ˈʃel·fɪʃ] *n* CULIN marisco *m*

shelling *n* bombardeo *m*

shelter ['ʃel·tər] I. n refugio m; **to take ~** refugiarse II. vt resguardar III. vi refugiarse

sheltered adj protegido, -a; pej sobreprotegido, -a

shield [ʃild] I. n (armor) escudo m; (animal) caparazón m; (machine) revestimiento m II. vt proteger

shift [ʃɪft] I. vt (change) mover; (reposition) cambiar de sitio; (gears, lanes) cambiar; **to ~ the blame** echar la culpa (**onto** a); **to ~ one's ground** cambiar de opinión II. vi moverse; (wind) cambiar II. n 1. (change) cambio m 2. (work) turno m; **to work in ~s** trabajar por turnos

shifting adj movedizo, -a; (values) cambiante

shift key n tecla f de las mayúsculas

shifty ['ʃɪf·ti] <-ier, -iest> adj sospechoso, -a

shin [ʃɪn] n ANAT espinilla f

shine [ʃaɪn] I. n brillo m ▶ **to take a ~** sentir simpatía (**to** por) II. <shone or shined, shone or shined> vi 1. (moon, star) brillar; (metal) relucir; (light) alumbrar; (eyes) resplandecer 2. (be gifted) destacar III. <shone or shined, shone or shined> vt **to ~ a light at** alumbrar

shiner ['ʃaɪ·nər] n inf ojo m morado

shining ['ʃaɪ·nɪŋ] adj 1. (gleaming) reluciente, abrillantada, -a AmL; (eyes) resplandeciente 2. (outstanding) magnífico, -a

shiny ['ʃaɪ·ni] <-ier, -iest> adj brillante

ship [ʃɪp] I. n barco m; **passenger ~** buque m de pasajeros; **sailing ~** velero m II. vt <-pp-> 1. (send) **to ~** (freight) enviar (mercancías) por barco 2. (transport) transportar

ship out vi embarcarse

shipwreck I. n naufragio m; (remains) restos m pl de un naufragio II. vt **to be ~ed** naufragar; fig estar hundido

shipyard n astillero m

shirk [ʃɜrk] vt, vi **to ~** (**away from**) sth escaquearse de algo

shirker ['ʃɜr·kər] n vago m, -a m, f

shirt [ʃɜrt] n camisa f ▶ **to lose** one's **~** perder hasta la camisa; **keep your ~ on!** ¡no te sulfures!

shirtsleeve ['ʃɜrt·sliv] n **to be in ~s** estar en mangas de camisa

shiver ['ʃɪv·ər] I. vi temblar; **to ~ with cold** tiritar de frío II. n escalofrío m; **to feel a ~** tener un escalofrío; **to give sb the ~s** dar escalofríos a alguien

shock[1] [ʃak] I. n 1. (surprise) conmoción f, batata f CSur (de asombro; **to give sb a ~** dar un disgusto a alguien 2. inf ELEC descarga f 3. MED shock m 4. (explosion, earthquake) sacudida f II. vt 1. (appall) horrorizar 2. (scare) asustar III. vi impactar

shock[2] [ʃak] n (hair) mata f

shock absorber n ['ʃak·əb·sɔr·bər] n amortiguador m

shocker ['ʃak·ər] n (surprising news) bombazo m

shocking ['ʃak·ɪŋ] adj 1. (distressing) espantoso, -a 2. (surprising) chocante 3. (offensive) escandaloso, -a

shockproof ['ʃak·pruf] adj fig imperturbable

shock wave n onda f expansiva; fig conmoción f

shod [ʃad] pt, pp of **shoe**

shoddy ['ʃad·i] <-ier, -iest> adj (goods) de muy mala calidad; (treatment) mezquino, -a

shoe [ʃu] I. n zapato m; **athletic ~s** zapatillas f pl de deporte ▶ **if I were in your ~s** si estuviera en tu lugar II. <shod, shod or shodden> vt calzar

shoelace n cordón m; **to tie one's ~s** atarse los cordones

shoe polish n betún m

shoestring ['ʃu·strɪŋ] n cordón m; **on a ~** con poquísimo dinero

shone [ʃoʊn] pt, pp of **shine**

shoo [ʃu] I. interj fuera II. vt espantar

shook [ʃʊk] n pt of **shake**

shoot [ʃut] I. n <shot, shot> vi 1. (fire) a. PHOT disparar (**at** a); **to ~ to kill** tirar a matar 2. (aim) aspirar (**for** a) 3. SPORTS chutar 4. CINE rodar ▶ **to ~ for the moon** [or the stars] ir a por todas II. <shot, shot> vt 1. disparar 2. CINE rodar; PHOT tomar 3. (glance) lanzar;

(*goal, basket*) meter; (*drugs*) meterse ▶ **to ~ the** <u>breeze</u> cotillear; **to ~** <u>darts</u> lanzar miradas asesinas (**at** a); **to ~ the** <u>works</u> tirar la casa por la ventana **III.** *n* **1.** (*hunt*) cacería *f* **2.** CINE rodaje *m*; PHOT sesión *f* **3.** BOT retoño *m*

shoot down *vt* (*aircraft*) derribar

shoot off I. *vt* **to shoot one's mouth off** cotorrear **II.** *vi* (*vehicle*) salir como un bólido

shoot out *vi* salir disparado

shoot up *vi* **1.** (*expand*) crecer mucho; (*child*) pegar un estirón **2.** (*drugs*) chutarse

shooting ['ʃuːtɪŋ] *n* **1.** (*killing*) asesinato *m* **2.** (*firing*) tiroteo *m* **3.** (*hunting*) caza *f*; **to go ~** ir de caza **4.** SPORTS tiro *m* al blanco

shooting star *n* estrella *f* fugaz

shop [ʃɒp] **I.** *n* tienda *f*; (*book*) librería *f*; (*workshop*) taller *m* ▶ **to** <u>set</u> **up ~** establecerse (**as** como); **to** <u>talk</u> **~** hablar de trabajo **II.** <-pp-> *vi* hacer compras

shopaholic [ʃɒp·ə·ˈhɒ·lɪk] *n* comprador(a) compulsivo, -a *m*

shopkeeper *n* comerciante *mf*

shoplifter [ʃɒp·lɪf·tər] *n* ladrón, -ona *m, f*

shoplifting *n* robo *m* (en tiendas)

shopper *n* comprador(a) *m(f)*

shopping [ʃɒp·ɪŋ] *n* compra *f*; (*purchases*) compras *fpl*; **to go ~** ir de tiendas

shopping cart *n* carrito *m* de la compra

shopping center *n* centro *m* comercial

shopping list *n* lista *f* de la compra

shopping mall *n* centro *m* comercial

shore [ʃɔr] *n* costa *f*; (*beach*) orilla *f*; **on ~** a tierra

shoreline *n* orilla *f*

short [ʃɔrt] **I.** *adj* **1.** (*not long*) corto, -a; (*memory*) malo, -a; (*vowel*) breve **2.** (*not tall*) bajo, -a, petizo, -a *CSur, Bol* **3.** (*not enough*) escaso, -a; **to be** [*or* **run**] **~** andar escaso (**on** de); **to be ~ of breath** quedarse sin aliento; **to be in ~ supply** escasear **II.** *n* **1.** CINE cortometraje *m* **2.** ELEC cortocircuito *m* **III.** *adv* **to cut ~** interrumpir

bruscamente; **to stop ~** parar en seco; **to fall ~** quedarse corto; **to fall ~ of** no alcanzar

shortage [ˈʃɔr·tɪdʒ] *n* falta *f*; (*water*) escasez *f*

short circuit *n* cortocircuito *m*

shortcoming [ˈʃɔrt·kʌm·ɪŋ] *n* defecto *m*

shortcut key *n* tecla *f* rápida

shorten [ˈʃɔr·tən] **I.** *vt* acortar **II.** *vi* acortarse

shorthand [ˈʃɔrt·hænd] *n* taquigrafía *f*

short-lived *adj* efímero, -a; (*happiness*) pasajero, -a

shortly [ˈʃɔrt·li] *adv* dentro de poco; **~ after** poco después

shorts [ʃɔrts] *npl* **1.** (*pants*) pantalón *m* corto; **a pair of ~** unos pantalones cortos **2.** (*underpants*) calzoncillos *mpl*; **boxer ~** boxers *mpl*

short-sleeved *adj* de manga corta

short-staffed *adj* falto, -a de personal

short story *n* narración *m* corta

short-tempered *adj* irascible

short-term *adj* a corto plazo

shot¹ [ʃɑt] **I.** *n* **1.** (*gun*) tiro *m*, baleo *m* *AmC*; **to fire a ~** pegar un tiro **2.** (*person*) tirador(a) *m(f)* **3.** SPORTS tiro *m*; (*tennis*) golpe *m* **4.** PHOT foto *f*; CINE toma *f* **5.** *inf* (*try*) intento *m*; **to have** [*or* **take**] **a ~** probar suerte (**at** con) **6.** (*alcohol*) chupito *m* ▶ **a ~ in the** <u>arm</u> un estímulo; **a ~ in the** <u>dark</u> un palo de ciego; **not by a** <u>long</u> **~** ni por asomo **II.** *pp, pt of* **shoot**

shot² [ʃɑt] *adj* (*worn out*) hecho, -a polvo

shotgun [ˈʃɑt·gʌn] *n* escopeta *f*

shot put *n* lanzamiento *m* de peso

should [ʃʊd] *aux* **1.** (*advisability*) **to insist that sb ~ do sth** insistir en que alguien debería hacer algo; (**why**) **~ I...?** ¿(por qué) debería...? **2.** I **~ be so lucky!** ¡ojalá! **3.** I **~ like to see her** me gustaría verla; **we ~ like to invite you** nos gustaría invitarle

shoulder [ˈʃoʊl·dər] **I.** *n* **1.** ANAT hombro *m*; **~ to ~** hombro con hombro; **to glance over one's ~** mirar por encima del hombro; **to lift a burden off one's ~s** quitarse un peso de encima **2.** CULIN

S

paletilla f 3. (road) arcén m, banquina f Arg, Urug, berma f Col ▶ **to rub ~s** codearse (**with** con); **to stand ~ to ~** apoyar (**with** a) II. vt 1. empujar; **to ~ one's way** abrirse paso a empujones 2. (carry) llevar a hombros; (responsibility) cargar con

shoulder blade n omóplato m

shoulder pad n hombrera f

shoulder strap n tirante m

shout [ʃaʊt] I. n grito m ▶ **to give sb a ~** dar un toque a alguien II. vi gritar (**at** a); **to ~ for help** pedir auxilio a gritos ▶ **to give sth to ~ about** dar una gran alegría III. vt gritar; (slogans) corear

◆**shout down** vt hacer callar a gritos

◆**shout out** vt gritar

shouting n griterío m

shove [ʃʌv] I. n empujón m, pechada f Arg, Chile; **to give sth a ~** dar un empujón a algo II. vt (push) empujar; **to ~ one's way through** abrirse paso a empujones; **to ~ sb about** [or **around**] abusar de alguien III. vi empujar; **to ~ along** largarse

◆**shove off** vi (go away) largarse

shovel [ʃʌv·əl] n (tool) pala f; (machine) excavadora f

show [ʃoʊ] I. n 1. (expression) demostración f; **~ of solidarity** muestra f de solidaridad 2. (exhibition) exposición f; **fashion ~** desfile m de modelos; **slide ~** pase m de diapositivas; **to be on ~** estar expuesto 3. (play) espectáculo m; TV programa m; THEAT representación f; **quiz ~** concurso m ▶ **~ of hands** voto a mano alzada; **let's get the ~ on the road** vamos manos a la obra; **to put on a good ~** hacer un buen papel; **the ~ must go on** el espectáculo debe continuar; **to run the ~** llevar la voz cantante II. <showed, shown> vt 1. (display) mostrar; (slides) pasar; ART exponer 2. (express) demostrar; (enthusiasm) expresar 3. (expose) exponer 4. (point out) señalar; (statistics) indicar 5. (prove) probar; **to ~ sb that...** demostrar a alguien que... 6. (escort) guiar; **to ~ sb to the door** acompañar a alguien hasta la puerta 7. (project)

proyectar; TV poner III. vi <showed, shown> 1. (be visible) verse 2. (film) proyectarse; (artist) exponer; (work of art) estar expuesto, -a 3. inf (arrive) aparecer

◆**show around** vt guiar

◆**show in** vt hacer pasar

◆**show off** I. vt lucir II. vi alardear, compadrear Arg, Urug

◆**show out** vt acompañar hasta la puerta

◆**show up** I. vi 1. inf (arrive) aparecer 2. (be apparent) ponerse de manifiesto II. vt 1. (expose) descubrir; **to show sb up as (being) sth** demostrar que alguien es algo 2. (embarrass) poner en evidencia

showdown [ˈʃoʊ·daʊn] n enfrentamiento m

shower [ˈʃaʊ·ər] I. n 1. ducha f, lluvia f Arg, Chile, Nic 2. (rain) chaparrón m; (sparks, insults) lluvia II. vi ducharse; (spray) regar III. vt 1. (spray) derramar; **to ~ sb** regar a alguien (**with** de) 2. **to ~ sb with gifts** colmar de regalos a alguien

shower gel n gel m de ducha

showery [ˈʃaʊ·ə·ri] adj lluvioso, -a

showground n recinto m ferial

showing n 1. (exhibition) exposición f 2. (broadcasting) proyección f 3. (performance) actuación f

shown [ʃoʊn] pp of **show**

showy [ˈʃoʊ·i] <-ier, -iest> adj llamativo, -a

shrank [ʃræŋk] vt, vi pt of **shrink**

shred [ʃred] I. <-dd-> vt cortar en tiras; (document) triturar II. n tira f; (hope, truth) pizca f; **to be in ~s** estar hecho jirones; **to tear to ~s** hacer trizas

shredder [ˈʃred·ər] n trituradora f

shriek [ʃrik] I. n chillido m II. vt, vi chillar; **to ~ with laughter** reírse a carcajadas

shrink [ʃrɪŋk] I. n loquero, -a m, f II. <shrank or shrunk, shrunk or shrunken> vt encoger; (costs) reducir III. <shrank or shrunk, shrunk or shrunken> vi disminuir; (clothes) encoger; **to ~ from (doing) sth** rehuir (hacer) algo

shrivel [ˈʃrɪv·əl] <-ll-, -l-> I. vi (fruit, plant) secarse; (skin) arrugarse; (person) consumirse II. vt (fruit) secar; (skin) arrugar

◆**shrivel up** vi see **shrivel** I

shrub [ʃrʌb] n arbusto m

shrug [ʃrʌg] I. n encogimiento m de hombros II. <-gg-> vt, vi to ~ (one's **shoulders**) encogerse de hombros

◆**shrug off** vt 1. (ignore) negar importancia a 2. (overcome) superar

shrunk [ʃrʌŋk] pp, pt of **shrink**

shudder [ˈʃʌd·ər] I. vi vibrar; (person) estremecerse; **to ~ at the memory of sth** temblar al recordar algo II. n vibración f; (person) estremecimiento m; **it sent a ~ down my spine** hizo que me estremeciera

shuffle [ˈʃʌf·əl] I. n (cabinet, management) reestructuración f; **with a ~** arrastrando los pies II. vt (papers) revolver; (cards) barajar; (cabinet, management) reestructurar; (feet) arrastrar III. vi (cards) barajar; (feet) arrastrar los pies

shush [ʃʊʃ] inf I. interj silencio II. vt hacer callar III. vi callarse

shut [ʃʌt] I. <shut, shut> vt cerrar; **to ~ one's ears** hacer oídos sordos (**to** a); **to ~ one's finger in the door** pillarse el dedo con la puerta II. <shut, shut> vi (door, window) cerrarse; (shop, factory) cerrar III. adj cerrado, -a; **to slam a door ~** cerrar la puerta de un portazo

◆**shut away** vt encerrar; **to shut oneself away** recluirse

◆**shut down** I. vt 1. (shop, factory) cerrar; (airport) paralizar 2. (turn off) apagar II. vi (shop, factory) cerrar; (engine) apagarse

◆**shut in** vt encerrar

◆**shut off** vt 1. (turn off) apagar 2. (isolate) aislar

◆**shut out** vt 1. (block out) ahuyentar 2. (exclude) dejar fuera

◆**shut up** I. vt 1. (confine) encerrar 2. inf (silence) hacer callar II. vi inf callarse

shuttle [ˈʃʌt·əl] I. n 1. (bus, train) enlace m; (plane) puente m aéreo II. vt transportar III. vi AVIAT volar (regularmente)

shuttle flight n puente m aéreo

shy [ʃaɪ] <-er, -est> adj 1. (timid) tímido, -a 2. (lacking) escaso, -a

shyness n timidez f

sick [sɪk] <-er, -est> adj 1. (ill) enfermo, -a; **to feel ~** sentirse mal; **to get ~** caer enfermo; **to be off ~** estar de baja 2. (nauseated) **to get ~** vomitar; **to feel ~ to one's stomach** tener el estómago revuelto; **alcohol makes me ~** el alcohol me sienta fatal 3. (disgusted) asqueado, -a (**about** de) 4. (angry) furioso, -a; **to be ~ and tired** estar (más que) harto (**of** de) 5. inf cruel; (joke) de mal gusto

sickbay n enfermería f

sickening [ˈsɪk·ən·ɪŋ] adj 1. (repulsive) repugnante 2. (annoying) ofensivo, -a

sick leave [ˈsɪk·liːv] n baja f por enfermedad; **to be on ~** estar de baja por enfermedad

sickness [ˈsɪk·nɪs] n enfermedad f; (nausea) mareo m

sick pay n subsidio m de enfermedad

side [saɪd] n 1. (surface) lado m; (of page) cara f; **at the ~** en el lado (**of** de); **at sb's ~** al lado de alguien; **~ by ~** uno al lado de otro; **from all ~s** por todas partes; **from ~ to ~** de lado a lado; **on the ~** aparte; **to leave sth on one ~** dejar algo a un lado 2. (edge) límite m; (river) ribera f; (road) arcén m; **on all ~(s)** por todas partes; (in dispute) **to take ~s** tomar partido; **to take sb's ~** ponerse de parte de alguien; **to be on the ~** ser partidario (**of** de); **to have sth on one's ~** tener algo a su favor; **on my father's ~** por parte de padre 4. (aspect) aspecto m; (story) versión f ▶ **the other ~ of the** coin la otra cara de la moneda; **to be on the** safe ~ para mayor seguridad

sideboard [ˈsaɪd·bɔrd] n aparador m, bufet m AmL

side dish n acompañamiento m

side effect n efecto m secundario

sideline [ˈsaɪd·laɪn] n 1. SPORTS (line) línea f; (area) banda f; **on the ~s** fig al margen; **from the ~s** desde fuera 2. (secondary activity) actividad f secundaria

S

side road *n* carretera *f* secundaria

sidestep ['saɪd·step] <-pp-> I. *vt* esquivar II. *vi* dar un paso hacia un lado

side street *n* calle *f* lateral

sidetrack ['saɪd·træk] I. *vt* distraer II. *n* vía *f* muerta; *fig* cuestión *f* secundaria

sidewalk ['saɪd·wɔk] *n* acera *f*, vereda *f Am*, banqueta *f Guat, Méx*

sieve [sɪv] I. *n* colador *m; (flour)* tamiz *m* II. *vt* colar; *(flour)* tamizar

sigh [saɪ] I. *n* suspiro *m; to let out a ~ of relief* soltar un suspiro de alivio II. *vi* suspirar; *to ~ with relief* suspirar aliviado

sight [saɪt] *n* **1.** vista *f; (gun)* mira *f; to be out of (one's) ~* no estar a la vista; *to come into ~* aparecer; *to catch ~ of* vislumbrar; *to know sb by ~* conocer a alguien de vista; *to lose ~ of sth* perder algo de vista; *(forget)* no tener presente algo; *at first ~* a primera vista; *within ~* a la vista (of de); *get out of my ~! inf* ¡fuera de mi vista!; *at the ~ of* al ver **2.** *pl (attractions)* lugares *m pl* de interés ▶ *to be a ~ for sore eyes* ser una alegría para los ojos; *out of ~, out of mind* ojos que no ven, corazón que no siente; ~ *unseen* sin haber visto; *I never buy anything ~ unseen* nunca compro nada sin verlo bien antes; *out of ~!* ¡fabuloso!

sightseeing ['saɪt·si·ɪŋ] *n* turismo *m; to go ~* visitar los lugares de interés

sightseer ['saɪt·si·ər] *n* turista *mf*

sign [saɪn] I. *n* **1.** *(gesture)* señal *f; to make a ~* hacer un gesto (to a); *as a ~ that* como señal de que **2.** *(signpost)* indicador *m; (signboard)* letrero *m* **3.** *(symbol)* símbolo *m* **4.** MATH, ASTR, MUS signo *m; a ~ that* un signo de que **5.** *(trace)* rastro *m; they couldn't find any ~ of him* no encontraron ni rastro de él II. *vt* **1.** *(signature)* firmar **2.** *(employ)* contratar; SPORTS fichar **3.** *(gesticulate)* indicar; *to ~ sb to do sth* indicar a alguien que haga algo **4.** *(in sign language)* decir por señas III. *vi* **1.** *(signature)* firmar; SPORTS fichar (with por); *~ here, please* firme aquí, por favor; *to ~ for sth* firmar el recibo de algo **2.** *(gesticulate)* gesticular; *to ~ to sb that...*

indicar con señas a alguien que...

◆**sign in** I. *vi* firmar en el registro de entrada II. *vt* firmar por

◆**sign off** *vi inf* terminar; RADIO, TV cerrar la emisión

◆**sign on** I. *vi* firmar un contrato; *to ~ for sth* inscribirse en algo; *he has signed on for courses in Japanese* se ha apuntado a clases de japonés II. *vt* contratar

◆**sign out** *vi* firmar en el registro de salida

◆**sign over** *vt* firmar un traspaso; *to sign property over to sb* poner una propiedad a nombre de alguien

◆**sign up** I. *vi* apuntarse II. *vt* contratar

signal ['sɪg·nəl] I. *n* **1.** *(gesture)* a. AUTO, RAIL, COMPUT seña *f; to give sb a ~ to do sth* hacer una señal a alguien para que haga algo **2.** *(indication)* signo *m; to be a ~ that* ser signo de que **3.** ELEC, RADIO señal *f* II. <-ll-, -l-> *vt* **1.** *(indicate)* indicar *(that* que) **2.** *(gesticulate)* hacer señas; *he ~ed them to be quiet* les hizo señas de que se callaran III. <-ll-, -l-> *vi* hacer una señal

signature ['sɪg·nə·tʃər] *n* firma *f*

significance [sɪg·'nɪf·ə·kəns] *n (importance)* importancia *f; (meaning)* significado *m*

significant [sɪg·'nɪf·ə·kənt] *adj* **1.** *(important)* importante; *(difference)* notable **2.** *(meaningful)* significativo, -a

signify ['sɪg·nə·faɪ] *form* I. <-ie-> *vt* **1.** *(mean)* significar **2.** *(indicate)* indicar II. <-ie-> *vi (matter)* tener importancia

sign language ['saɪn·ˌlæŋ·gwɪdʒ] *n* lenguaje *m* por señas; *(deaf)* lenguaje *m* de signos

signpost I. *n* señal *f* II. *vt* señalizar

silence ['saɪ·ləns] I. *n* silencio *m* II. *vt* silenciar; *(person)* hacer callar

silent ['saɪ·lənt] *adj* silencioso, -a; LING, CINE mudo, -a; *to be ~* no decir nada *(on* sobre); *to fall ~* callarse

silently *adv* silenciosamente; *(without speaking)* en silencio

silicon ['sɪl·ɪ·kən] *n* silicio *m*

silk [sɪlk] *n* seda *f; ~ scarf* pañuelo *m* de seda

silky ['sɪl·ki] <-ier, -iest> *adj* sedoso, -a; (*fur, voice*) suave

sill [sɪl] *n* (*door*) umbral *m;* (*window*) alféizar *m*

silly ['sɪl·i] <-ier, -iest> *adj* (*person*) tonto, -a, dundo, -a *AmC, Col*; (*idea*) estúpido, -a; **it was ~ of her to...** fue una estupidez por su parte...; **to look ~** parecer ridículo; **to laugh oneself ~** desternillarse de risa

silver ['sɪl·vər] **I.** *n* plata *f* **II.** *adj* de plata; (*color*) plateado, -a

silverware ['sɪl·vər·wer] *n* (*cutlery*) cubertería *f* de plata; (*dishes, trays*) vajilla *f* de plata

similar ['sɪm·ə·lər] *adj* similar

similarity [ˌsɪm·ə·ˈler·ə·ti] *n* semejanza *f*

simile ['sɪm·ə·li] *n* símil *m*

simmer ['sɪm·ər] **I.** *vi* hervir a fuego lento; *fig* estar a punto de estallar **II.** *vt* cocer a fuego lento **III.** *n* ebullición *f* lenta; **to bring sth to a ~** poner algo a hervir; **at a ~** hirviendo a fuego lento

◆**simmer down** *vi inf* tranquilizarse

simple ['sɪm·pəl] *adj* **1.** (*not difficult*) fácil **2.** (*not elaborate*) sencillo, -a **3.** (*honest*) honesto, -a **4.** (*ordinary*) normal **5.** (*foolish*) simple

simple-minded [ˌsɪm·pəl·ˈmaɪn·dɪd] *adj inf* (*dumb*) tonto, -a; (*naïve*) ingenuo, -a

simplicity [sɪm·ˈplɪs·ə·ti] *n* **1.** (*plainness*) sencillez *f* **2.** (*ease*) simplicidad *f*

simplification [ˌsɪm·plə·fɪ·ˈkeɪ·ʃən] *n* simplificación *f*

simply ['sɪm·pli] *adv* **1.** (*not elaborately*) sencillamente **2.** (*just*) simplemente **3.** (*absolutely*) completamente

simulation [ˌsɪm·ju·ˈleɪ·ʃən] *n* simulación *f*; (*of feeling*) fingimiento *m*

simultaneous [ˌsaɪ·məl·ˈteɪ·ni·əs] *adj* simultáneo, -a

sin [sɪn] **I.** *n* pecado *m* ▶ **to be as ugly as ~** ser más feo que Picio **II.** *vi* <-nn-> pecar

since [sɪns] **I.** *adv* (*ever*) **~** desde entonces; **long ~** hace mucho; **not long ~** hace poco **II.** *prep* desde **III.** *conj* **1.** desde que; **it's been a week now ~ I came back** ya ha pasado una semana desde que llegué **2.** (*because*)

puesto que

sincere [sɪn·ˈsɪr] *adj* sincero, -a

sincerely *adv* sinceramente

sine [saɪn] *n* seno *m*

sing [sɪŋ] <sang, sung> **I.** *vi* cantar (**to** para) **II.** *vt* cantar

◆**sing out** *vt* **to ~ sb's name** llamar a alguien a voces

singer ['sɪŋ·ər] *n* cantante *mf*

singing *n* canto *m*

single ['sɪŋ·gəl] **I.** *adj* **1.** (*one only*) único, -a; (*blow*) solo, -a; (*figure*) de un solo dígito; **not a ~ person/thing** nadie/nada; **not a ~ soul** ni un alma; **every ~ thing** cada cosa **2.** (*unmarried*) soltero, -a **3.** (*bed, room*) individual **II.** *n* **1.** (*bill*) billete *m* de un dólar **2.** MUS single *m* **3.** (*baseball*) sencillo *m*

◆**single out** *vt* señalar

single-minded *adj* resuelto, -a

single-parent family <-ies> *n* familia *f* monoparental

singleton ['sɪŋ·gəl·tən] *n* persona *f* soltera

singly ['sɪŋ·gli] *adv* uno por uno

sink [sɪŋk] <sank *or* sunk, sunk> **I.** *n* (*kitchen*) fregadero *m;* (*bathroom*) lavabo *m* **II.** *vi* **1.** (*in water*) hundirse; **to ~ to the bottom** hundirse hasta el fondo **2.** (*drop*) caer; **to ~ to the ground** caer al suelo **3.** (*decline: a. price, level*) bajar; **to ~ in sb's estimation** perder la estima de alguien; **to ~ into depression** sumirse en la depresión; **to ~ into oblivion** caer en el olvido ▶ **to ~ or swim** a su suerte **III.** *vt* **1.** (*submerge*) hundir **2.** (*ruin*) destruir **3.** (*invest*) invertir (**into** en)

◆**sink back** *vi* repantigarse

◆**sink in** *vi* **1.** (*go into surface*) penetrar; (*liquid*) calar **2.** (*be understood*) entenderse

sinking ['sɪŋ·kɪŋ] *n* hundimiento *m*

sinner ['sɪn·ər] *n* pecador(a) *m(f)*

sip [sɪp] **I.** <-pp-> *vt, vi* sorber **II.** *n* sorbo *m;* **to have a ~** dar un sorbo

sir [sɜr] *n* señor *m*

siren ['saɪ·rən] *n* sirena *f*

sis [sɪs] *n inf abbr of* **sister** hermana *f*

sissy ['sɪs·i] <-ier, -iest> *adj* <-ies> *n* mariquita *m*

sister ['sɪs·tər] n a. REL hermana f; ~ **company** empresa f asociada

sister-in-law ['sɪs·tər·ɪn·ˌlɔ] <sisters-in-law> n cuñada f, concuña f AmL

sit [sɪt] <sat, sat> I. vi 1. sentarse; (be seated) estar sentado, -a 2. ART posar 3. inf (babysit) cuidar (for a) 4. (perch) posarse; (eggs) empollar 5. (be placed) estar; **to ~ on the shelf** estar en el estante; **to ~ in Congress** ser diputado 6. (fit) **to ~ well/badly** caer [or sentar] bien/mal ▶ **to be ~ting pretty** estar bien situado; **to ~ tight** no moverse; (opinion) no dar el brazo a torcer II. vt sentar

◆**sit around** vi estar sin hacer nada

◆**sit back** vi 1. (in chair) ponerse cómodo 2. (do nothing) cruzarse de brazos

◆**sit down** I. vi sentarse; (be sitting) estar sentado II. vt sentar

◆**sit in** vi 1. (attend) asistir como oyente 2. **to ~ for sb** sustituir a alguien 3. (hold sit-in) hacer una sentada

◆**sit on** vt inf (information) guardar para sí; (secret) no revelar; (idea, plan) acabar con

◆**sit out** vt 1. (not join) no tomar parte en; **to ~ a dance** no bailar 2. (sit through) aguantar hasta el final

◆**sit through** vt aguantar hasta el final

◆**sit up** vi 1. (sit erect) sentarse derecho; ~! ¡siéntate derecho! 2. (pay attention) atender

sitcom ['sɪt·kɑm] n inf abbr of situation comedy comedia f de situación

site [saɪt] I. n 1. (place) sitio m 2. (vacant land) solar m; building ~ obra f 3. GEO, HIST yacimiento m 4. COMPUT página f, sitio; **Web ~** página [or sitio] web II. vt situar

sit-in ['sɪt·ɪn] n sentada f; **to hold a ~** hacer una sentada

sitting duck n inf blanco m fácil

sitting room n salón m

situate ['sɪtʃ·u·eɪt] vt ubicar; (in context) situar

situated ['sɪtʃ·u·eɪ·tɪd] adj situado, -a; **to be ~ near the station** estar ubicado cerca de la estación; **to be well/badly ~** estar bien/mal situado

situation [ˌsɪtʃ·u·'eɪ·ʃən] n situación f;

according to the ~ conforme a la situación

sit-up ['sɪt·ʌp] n **to do ~s** hacer abdominales

six [sɪks] adj, n seis m; **in ~ figures** por encima de cien mil

sixteen [sɪk·'stin] adj, n dieciséis m; s. a. **eight**

sixteenth [sɪk·'stinθ] I. adj decimosexto, -a II. n 1. (order) decimosexto, -a m, f 2. (date) dieciséis m 3. (fraction) dieciseisavo m; s. a. **eight**

sixth [sɪksθ] I. adj sexto, -a II. n 1. (order) sexto, -a m, f 2. (date) seis m 3. (fraction) sexto m; s. a. **eighth**

sixtieth ['sɪk·sti·əθ] I. adj sexagésimo, -a II. n (order) sexagésimo, -a m, f; (fraction) sesentavo m; s. a. **eighth**

sixty ['sɪk·sti] adj, n <-ies> sesenta m; s. a. **eighty**

size¹ [saɪz] n (person, thing, space) tamaño m; (problem) magnitud f; (clothes) talla f; (shoes) número m; **to be the same ~** ser de las mismas dimensiones (as que); **to increase/decrease in ~** aumentar/disminuir de tamaño

◆**size up** vt evaluar

size² [saɪz] n cola f

skate¹ [skeɪt] SPORTS I. n patín m II. vi patinar; **to ~ over an issue** tocar un tema muy por encima

skate² [skeɪt] n (fish) raya f

skateboard ['skeɪt·bɔrd] n monopatín m

skateboarder n skater mf

skater n patinador(a) m(f); **figure ~** patinador(a) m(f) artístico, -a

skating rink n pista f de patinaje

skeleton ['skel·ɪ·tən] n ANAT esqueleto m, cacastle m AmC, Méx; **to be reduced to a ~** quedarse en los huesos; (boat, plane) armazón m; (building) estructura f; (book, report) esquema m ▶ **to have ~s in one's closet** tener un secreto vergonzoso

skeleton key n llave f maestra

skeptic ['skep·tɪk] n escéptico, -a m, f

skeptical adj escéptico, -a

sketch [sketʃ] I. n 1. ART boceto m 2. (draft) borrador m 3. (outline) esquema m 4. THEAT, TV sketch m II. vt hacer un borrador de; ART hacer un boceto de

III. vi ART hacer bocetos

sketchy ['sketʃɪ] <-ier, -iest> adj (vague) impreciso, -a; (incomplete) incompleto, -a

skewer ['skju·ər] **I.** n pincho m **II.** vt ensartar

ski [ski] **I.** n esquí m; on ~s con esquís **II.** vi esquiar; **to ~ down a slope** bajar una pista esquiando

ski boot n bota f de esquí

skid [skɪd] **I.** <-dd-> vi **1.** (on ice) patinar, colear AmC, Ant; **to ~ to a halt** AUTO derrapar; **to ~ off the road** derrapar y salirse de la carretera **2.** (slide) deslizarse (**along, across** sobre) **II.** n AUTO derrape m ▶ **to be on the ~s** andar de capa caída

skier ['ski·ər] n esquiador(a) m(f)

skiing n esquí m; ~ **equipment** equipo m de esquiar; ~ **lesson** clase f de esquí

ski instructor n monitor(a) m(f) de esquí

ski jump n salto m de esquí; (runway) trampolín m

ski lift n telesquí m; (with chairs) telesilla m

skill [skɪl] n **1.** (ability) habilidad f; **to involve some ~** requerir cierta destreza **2.** (technique) técnica f; **communication ~s** facilidad f de comunicación; **language ~s** habilidad f para los idiomas; **negotiating ~s** artes f pl de negociación

skilled adj **1.** (trained) preparado, -a; (skillful) hábil, habiloso, -a Chile, Perú **2.** (requiring skill) cualificado, -a; ~ **labor** mano de obra f cualificada

skillful ['skɪl·fəl] adj hábil, tinoso, -a Col, Ven

skim [skɪm] <-mm-> **I.** vt **1.** CULIN espumar; (milk) desnatar **2.** (move above) rozar **II.** vi **to ~ over** pasar rozando; **to ~ through** fig hojear

ski mask n pasamontañas m inv

skin [skɪn] **I.** n **1.** piel f; (fruit) cáscara f; **to be soaked to the ~** estar calado hasta los huesos **2.** TECH revestimiento m **3.** (milk) nata f ▶ **to be all ~ and bone(s)** estar en los huesos; **it's no ~ off his/her back** ni le va ni le viene; **by the ~ of one's teeth** por los pelos; **to**

jump out of one's ~ pegarse un susto de muerte; **to get under sb's ~** afectar a alguien **II.** <-nn-> vt despellejar

skincare n cuidado m de la piel

skin-deep adj epidérmico, -a; (beauty) superficial

skinhead ['skɪn·hed] n cabeza mf rapada

skinny ['skɪn·i] **I.** <-ier, -iest> adj flaco, -a, charcón, -ona Arg, Bol, Urug **II.** n sl verdad f

skip [skɪp] **I.** <-pp-> vi saltar (**from/to** de/a); (CD) saltarse; (rope) saltar a la comba **II.** <-pp-> vt saltarse; **to ~ class** faltar a clase; **to ~ rope** saltar a la comba; **to ~ a grade** saltar un curso **III.** n brinco m

skipper ['skɪp·ər] **I.** n NAUT patrón, -ona m, f; inf jefe, -a m, f **II.** vt (aircraft) pilotar; (team) capitanear

ski rack n portaesquís m inv

ski resort n estación f de esquí

skirt [skɜrt] **I.** n falda f, pollera f AmL **II.** vt evitar; (path, road) rodear

ski slope n pista f de esquí

skull [skʌl] n calavera f; ANAT cráneo m ▶ **to be bored out of one's ~** estar más aburrido que una ostra

sky [skaɪ] <-ies> n cielo m; **under blue skies** bajo el cielo azul ▶ **the ~'s the limit** todo es posible; **to praise to the skies** poner por las nubes

sky-blue [ˌskaɪ·blu] adj azul celeste inv

skydiving ['skaɪ·ˌdaɪ·vɪŋ] n caída m libre

sky-high [ˌskaɪ·ˈhaɪ] **I.** adv por las nubes; **to go ~** (prices) dispararse **II.** adj (prices) astronómico, -a

skyjack ['skaɪ·dʒæk] vt secuestrar

skylight ['skaɪ·laɪt] n tragaluz m

skyline ['skaɪ·laɪn] n (horizon) horizonte m

skyscraper ['skaɪ·skreɪ·pər] n rascacielos m inv

slab [slæb] n (stone) losa f; (concrete) bloque m; (wood) tabla f; (cake, cheese) trozo m; (chocolate) tableta f

slack [slæk] **I.** adj (rope, piece of work) flojo, -a; (muscle) flácido, -a; (student) vago, -a; (paying) negligente; (period, season) de poca actividad **II.** n COM

S

período *m* de inactividad ▶ **to cut sb some ~** *sl* dar más tiempo a alguien III. *vi* hacer el vago

slacken ['slæk·ən] I. *vt* aflojar; (*speed, vigilance*) reducir; (*pace*) aflojar II. *vi* aflojarse, petaquearse *Col*; (*demand, intensity*) disminuir

slacker ['slæk·ər] *n* vago, -a *m, f*

slackness ['slæk·nɪs] *n* 1. (*negligence*) negligencia *f*; (*discipline*) relajamiento *m* 2. COM inactividad *f* 3. (*laziness*) pereza *f*

slacks [slæks] *npl* pantalón *m* de sport

slam [slæm] I. <-mm-> *vt* 1. (*strike*) golpear; **to ~ the door** dar un portazo 2. (*criticize*) poner por los suelos II. <-mm-> *vi* cerrarse de golpe; **to ~ against/into** chocar contra/con III. *n* (*door*) portazo *m*

slammer ['slæm·ər] *n* chirona *f*, cana *f AmS*, bote *m Méx*, guandoca *f Col*

slander ['slæn·dər] I. *n* calumnia *f* II. *vt* calumniar

slang [slæŋ] *n* argot *m*

slangy <-ier, -iest> *adj* argótico, -a

slant [slænt] I. *vi* inclinarse II. *vt* (*make diagonal*) inclinar III. *n* 1. (*slope*) inclinación *f*; **on a ~** en pendiente 2. (*perspective*) perspectiva *f*

slanting *adj* inclinado, -a; (*eyes*) rasgado, -a

slap [slæp] I. *n* palmada *f*; **a ~ in the face** una bofetada, una biaba *Arg, Urug*, un bife *Arg, Urug*; *fig* un insulto II. <-pp-> *vt* dar una palmada, guantear *AmL*; **to ~ the book onto the table** tirar el libro en la mesa III. *adv* de lleno; **to drive ~** chocar de lleno (**into** contra)

　slap down *vt* 1. tirar 2. (*silence*) hacer callar

slapdash ['slæp·dæʃ] *adj* chapucero, -a

slash [slæʃ] I. *vt* 1. (*cut*) rajar; **to ~ one's wrists** cortarse las venas 2. (*prices, spending*) rebajar drásticamente; (*budget*) recortar drásticamente II. *n* 1. (*cut*) corte *m* 2. (*swinging blow*) latigazo *m* 3. FASHION raja *f* 4. TYPO barra *f*

slate [sleɪt] I. *n* pizarra *f*; POL lista *f* de candidatos ▶ **to wipe the ~ clean** hacer borrón y cuenta nueva II. *vt* (*schedule*) programar

slaughter ['slɔ·tər] I. *vt* (*animal*) matar, beneficiar *AmL*, carnear *CSur*, (*person*) masacrar; *fig* dar una paliza a II. *n* (*animal*) matanza *f*, beneficio *AmL*, carneada *f Arg, Chile, Par, Urug*; (*person*) masacre *f*; *fig* paliza *f*

Slav [slav] *adj, n* eslavo, -a *m, f*

slave [sleɪv] I. *n* esclavo, -a *m, f* ▶ **to be a ~ to** *fashion* ser un esclavo de la moda II. *vi* trabajar como un burro

slavery ['sleɪ·və·ri] *n* esclavitud *f*

Slavic ['sla·vɪk] *adj, n* eslavo, -a *m, f*

sleaze [sliz] *n* sordidez *f*; POL corrupción *f*

sleazy ['sli·zi] <-ier, -iest> *adj* sórdido, -a; (*person*) con mala pinta; POL corrupto, -a

sled [sled] *n* trineo *m*

sledge [sledʒ], **sledgehammer** ['sledʒ·ˌhæm·ər] *n* almádena *f*

sleek [slik] *adj* (*fur, hair*) lacio, -a y brillante; (*car*) de líneas elegantes; (*person*) muy aseado, -a

sleep [slip] I. *n* 1. sueño *m*; **to go** [*or* **get**] **to ~** dormirse; **to fall into a deep ~** dormirse profundamente; **to** (**not**) **lose ~** (no) perder el sueño (**over** por); **to put sb to ~** dormir a alguien 2. *inf* (*substance*) legañas *fpl*; **to rub the ~ from one's eyes** quitarse las legañas II. <slept, slept> *vi* dormir; **to ~ sound**(**ly**) dormir profundamente; **~ tight!** ¡que duermas bien! ▶ **to ~ on it** consultarlo con la almohada

　sleep around *vi* acostarse con cualquiera

　sleep in *vi* dormir hasta tarde

　sleep off *vt* **to sleep it off** dormir la mona [*or AmL* la cruda]

　sleep out *vi* dormir al aire libre

　sleep through *vt* **to ~ noise** no despertarse con el ruido; **to ~ the entire trip** dormir durante todo el viaje

　sleep together *vi* dormir juntos; (*sex*) acostarse juntos

sleeper ['sli·pər] *n* 1. **to be a heavy/light ~** tener el sueño profundo/ligero 2. RAIL coche *m* cama

sleeping bag *n* saco *m* de dormir

sleeping car *n* coche *m* cama

sleeping pill *n* somnífero *m*

sleepless ['slip·lɪs] *adj* insomne; (*night*) en vela

sleepwalk ['slip·wɔk] *vi* caminar dormido, -a; **he ~s** es sonámbulo

sleepwalker ['slip·wɔ·kər] *n* sonámbulo, -a *m, f*

sleepy ['sli·pi] <-ier, -iest> *adj* **1.** (*drowsy*) somnoliento, -a **2.** (*quiet*) aletargado, -a

sleepyhead ['sli·pi·hed] *n* dormilón, -ona *m, f*

sleet [slit] I. *n* aguanieve *f* II. *vi* **it is ~ing** cae aguanieve

sleeve [sliv] *n* **1.** (*shirt*) manga *f*; **to roll up one's ~s** arremangarse **2.** (*cover*) manguito *m* **3.** (*record*) funda *f* ▶ **to have sth up one's ~** tener algo en la manga

sleeveless ['sliv·lɪs] *adj* sin mangas

sleigh [sleɪ] *n* trineo *m*

slender ['slen·dər] *adj* delgado, -a; (*rod, branch*) fino, -a; (*majority, resources*) escaso, -a; (*chance*) remoto, -a

slept [slept] *pt, pp of* **sleep**

slice [slaɪs] I. *n* (*bread*) rebanada *f*; (*ham*) loncha *f*; (*meat*) tajada *f*; (*cake, pizza*) trozo *m*; (*cucumber, lemon*) rodaja *f*; (*credit, profits*) parte *f* ▶ **to get a ~ of the pie** sacar tajada II. *vt* cortar ▶ **any way you ~ it** lo mires por donde lo mires

◆**slice off** *vt* cortar; (*reduce*) reducir en

◆**slice up** *vt* cortar

sliced *adj* (*bread*) en rebanadas; (*ham*) en lonchas; (*meat*) fileteado, -a; (*cake*) troceado; (*cucumber, lemon*) en rodajas

slick [slɪk] I. <-er, -est> *adj* (*person*) hábil; *pej* astuto; (*performance*) pulido, -a II. *n* (*oil*) marea *f* negra

slide [slaɪd] I. <slid, slid> *vi* (*glide*) deslizarse; (*slip*) resbalar; **the door ~s open/shut** la puerta se abre/se cierra corriéndola; **to ~ back into one's old habits** volver a las viejas costumbres II. <slid, slid> *vt* deslizar III. *n* **1.** (*act*) deslizamiento *m* **2.** (*incline*) rampa *f*; (*playground*) tobogán *m*; **water ~** tobogán acuático **3.** PHOT diapositiva *f* **4.** GEO desprendimiento *m* **5.** FIN caída *f*

slide projector *n* proyector *m* de diapositivas

slide rule *n* regla *f* de cálculo

sliding *adj* (*sunroof*) corredizo, -a; (*door*) corredero, -a

slight [slaɪt] I. <-er, -est> *adj* (*person*) delgado, -a; (*chance*) escaso, -a; (*error*) pequeño, -a; **the ~est thing** la menor tontería; **not in the ~est** en absoluto; **not to have the ~est** (*idea*) no tener ni la menor idea II. *n* desaire *m* III. *vt* despreciar

slightly *adv* un poco; **to be ~ familiar with sth** conocer algo muy poco

slim [slɪm] I. <slimmer, slimmest> *adj* (*person*) delgado, -a; (*cigarette, book*) fino, -a; (*chance*) escaso, -a II. <-mm-> *vi* adelgazar; (*diet*) hacer régimen

slimeball, slimebag *n sl* asqueroso, -a *m, f*

slimy ['slaɪ·mi] <-ier, -iest> *adj* viscoso, -a; *fig* asqueroso, -a

sling [slɪŋ] I. *n* **1.** (*bandage*) cabestrillo *m* **2.** (*for baby*) canguro *m* **3.** (*weapon*) honda *f* II. *vt* **1.** (*fling*) lanzar, aventar *Méx* **2.** (*hang*) colgar

slink [slɪŋk] <slunk> *vi* **to ~ away** [*or* **off**] escabullirse

slip [slɪp] I. <-pp-> *n* **1.** (*slipping*) resbalón *m* **2.** (*mistake*) error *m*; **~ of the tongue** lapsus *m* **3.** COM resguardo *m* **4.** (*underwear*) combinación *f* **5.** BOT esqueje *m* ▶ **to give the ~** dar esquinazo II. *vi* **1.** (*slide*) resbalarse **2.** (*move*) deslizarse; **to ~ into a pub** colarse en un bar **3.** (*decline*) decaer; **to ~ into a depression** caer en una depresión III. *vt* **1.** (*put*) deslizar; **to ~ a note/some money** pasar una nota/dinero disimuladamente (**to** a); **to ~ in a comment** dejar caer un comentario **2.** (*escape*) escabullirse de; **to ~ sb's attention** pasar desapercibido por alguien; **it ~ped my mind** se me olvidó

◆**slip away** *vi* **1.** (*leave unnoticed*) escabullirse (**from** de) **2.** (*pass*) pasar rápidamente **3.** (*die*) morirse

◆**slip by** *vi* pasar rápidamente; (*unnoticed*) pasar inadvertida, -a

◆**slip down** *vi* dejarse caer

◆**slip in** *vi* colarse

◆**slip off** I. *vi* **1.** (*leave*) escabullirse **2.** (*fall off*) caerse **II.** vt (*clothes*) quitarse

♦**slip on** vt (*clothes*) ponerse

♦**slip out** vi **1.** (*leave*) escabullirse **2.** (*say*) escaparse; **the name slipped out** se me escapó el nombre

♦**slip up** vi equivocarse

slip-on ['slɪp·ɑn] adj (*shoes*) sin cordones

slippery ['slɪp·ə·ri] <-ier, -iest> adj (*surface*) resbaladizo, -a; (*soap*) escurridizo, -a; (*character*) que no es de fiar ▶ **to be on the ~ slope** encontrarse en un terreno resbaladizo

slipshod ['slɪp·ʃɑd] adj chapucero, -a

slip-up ['slɪp·ʌp] n desliz m

slit [slɪt] I. <slit, slit> vt cortar; **to ~ one's wrists** cortarse las venas II. n (*opening*) rendija f; (*tear*) raja f

slither ['slɪð·ər] vi deslizarse (**down/on** por/sobre)

sliver ['slɪv·ər] n (*lemon*) rodajita f; (*cake*) trocito m; (*glass, wood*) astilla f

slob [slɑb] n dejado, -a m, f

slog [slɑg] inf I. <-gg-> vi (*walk*) avanzar con gran esfuerzo II. <-gg-> vt (*hit*) golpear III. n esfuerzo m

slogan ['sloʊ·gən] n eslogan m

slop [slɑp] <-pp-> inf I. n (*food*) aguachirle f II. vi derramarse; **to ~ about** [*or* **around**] salpicarlo todo III. vt derramar

slope [sloʊp] I. n inclinación f; (*up*) cuesta f; (*down*) declive m; (*ski*) pista f II. vi inclinarse; **to ~ down** descender, bajar; **to ~ up** ascender, subir III. vt inclinar

sloping adj inclinado, -a; (*shoulders*) caído, -a

sloppiness n falta f de cuidado

sloppy ['slɑp·i] <-ier, -iest> adj (*messy*) descuidado, -a

slot [slɑt] I. n **1.** (*opening*) ranura f **2.** TV espacio m II. <-tt-> vt encajar (**in** en)

slot machine ['slɑt·mə·ʃin] n tragaperras f inv

slouch [slaʊtʃ] I. vi **1.** (*bend*) encorvarse **2.** (*walk*) ir arrastrando los pies II. n **to be no ~** no ser manco

Slovakia [sloʊ·'vɑ·ki·ə] n Eslovaquia f

Slovene ['sloʊ·vin] I. adj esloveno, -a

II. n **1.** esloveno, -a m, f **2.** LING esloveno m

Slovenia [sloʊ·'vi·ni·ə] n Eslovenia f

Slovenian n see **Slovene**

slovenly ['slʌv·ən·li] adj descuidado, -a

slow [sloʊ] I. adj lento, -a; **to be ~ to do sth** tardar en hacer algo; **to be (10 minutes) ~** ir (10 minutos) retrasado **2.** (*stupid*) torpe, guanaco, -a AmL II. vi ir más despacio; **to ~ to a halt** detenerse gradualmente III. vt frenar

♦**slow down** I. vi **1.** (*speed*) reducir **2.** (*be less active*) moderar el ritmo de vida II. vt ralentizar

slowly adv lentamente; **~ but surely** lento pero seguro

slow motion n cámara f lenta; **in ~** a cámara lenta

slowpoke ['sloʊ·poʊk] n tortuga f

slow-witted adj lerdo, -a

sluggish ['slʌg·ɪʃ] adj (*person*) perezoso, -a, conchudo, -a Méx; (*progress, pace*) lento, -a; (*market*) flojo, -a

sluice [slus] I. n (*gate*) compuerta f II. vt regar; **to ~ down** enjuagar

slum [slʌm] n suburbio m

slump [slʌmp] I. n ECON (*decline*) depresión f; **~ in prices** súbita caída de precios; (*recession*) recesión f II. vi desplomarse; (*prices*) caer

slung [slʌŋ] pt, pp of **sling**

slunk [slʌŋk] pt, pp of **slink**

slur [slɜr] n **1.** (*insult*) calumnia f **2.** (*in speech*) pronunciación f incomprensible

slurp [slɜrp] inf I. vt, vi sorber II. n sorbetón m

slush [slʌʃ] n **1.** (*snow*) nieve f medio derretida **2.** (*sentimentality*) sentimentalismo m

slushy adj <-ier, -iest> **1.** (*snow*) a medio derretir **2.** (*sentimental*) sentimentaloide

sly [slaɪ] adj **1.** (*secretive*) sigiloso, -a; (*smile*) sutil; **on the ~** a hurtadillas **2.** (*crafty*) astuto, -a, songo, -a Col, Méx

smack [smæk] I. vt **1.** (*slap*) dar un manotazo **2.** (*hit*) golpear; **to ~ one's lips** relamerse los labios II. n inf **1.** (*slap*) bofetada f; (*soft blow*) palmada *f* **2.** (*kiss*) besazo *m* **3.** (*noise*) ruidazo *m* **III.** *adv* **1.** (*loudly*) haciendo un fuerte ruido **2.** (*directly*) justamente; **~ in the middle** justo en el medio

small [smɔl] **I.** *adj* **1.** pequeño, -a; (*person*) bajo, -a, petizo, -a *CSur, Bol*; (*young*) joven; **on a ~ scale** a pequeña escala; **with a ~ 'c'** TYPO minúscula; **with a ~ 'c'** con 'c' minúscula ▶ **it's a ~ world** el mundo es un pañuelo *prov* **II.** *n* **the ~ of the back** la región lumbar

small change *n* calderilla *f*, chaucha *f Bol, Chile, Perú*, chirolas *fpl Arg*

small-minded [ˌsmɔl·ˈmaɪn·dɪd] *adj* estrecho, -a de miras

smallpox [ˈsmɔl·pɑks] *n* viruela *f*

small-scale *adj* a pequeña escala

smart [smɑrt] **I.** *adj* **1.** (*clever*) inteligente **2.** (*elegant*) elegante **3.** (*quick*) rápido, -a; **at a ~ pace** rápidamente **II.** *vi* escocer; **my eyes ~** me pican los ojos **III.** *n* escozor *m*

smarten [ˈsmɑr·tən] **I.** *vt* **to ~ up** arreglar **II.** *vi* **to ~ up** arreglarse

smash [smæʃ] **I.** *vt* (*break*) romper, quebrar *AmL*; (*crush*) destruir; (*glass*) hacer pedazos; (*record*) pulverizar **II.** *vi* **1.** (*break*) romperse, quebrarse *AmL*; (*glass*) hacerse pedazos **2.** (*strike*) chocar (**into** contra) **III.** *n* **1.** (*sound*) estruendo *m* **2.** (*accident*) colisión *f*

◆ **smash in** *vt* forzar; **to smash sb's face in** partir la cara a alguien

◆ **smash up** *vt* hacer pedazos; (*car*) destrozar

smashed *adj inf* borracho, -a; **to get ~** emborracharse

smattering [ˈsmæt·ər·ɪŋ] *n* nociones *fpl*

smear [smɪr] **I.** *vt* **1.** (*spread*) untar **2.** (*attack*) desprestigiar **II.** *n* **1.** (*blotch*) mancha *f* **2.** (*accusation*) calumnia *f*

smell [smel] <smelled *or* smelt, smelled *or* smelt> **I.** *vi, vt* oler; (*animal*) olfatear; (*stink*) apestar **II.** *n* **1.** (*sense*) olfato *m* **2.** (*odor*) olor *m*; (*stink*) peste *f* **3.** (*trace*) sabor *m*; **the ~ of victory** el sabor del triunfo

smelly [ˈsmel·i] *adj* <-ier, -iest> apestoso, -a

smelt¹ [smelt] *vt* MIN fundir

smelt² [smelt] *pt, pp of* **smell**

smile [smaɪl] **I.** *n* sonrisa *f*; **to be all ~s** ser todo, -a sonrisas; **to give sb a ~** sonreír a alguien **II.** *vi* sonreír; **to ~ at/about sth** sonreírse de; **to ~ on sb/sth** mirar con buenos ojos a alguien/algo

smiling *adj* sonriente

smirk [smɜrk] **I.** *vi* sonreír afectadamente **II.** *n* sonrisa *f* afectada

smog [smɑg] *n* niebla *f* y humo

smoke [smoʊk] **I.** *n* humo *m*; (*cigarette*) pitillo *m* ▶ **where there's ~, there's fire** cuando el río suena, agua lleva; **to go up in ~** esfumarse **II.** *vt* **1.** fumar, pitar *AmS*; **to ~ a pipe** fumar en pipa **2.** CULIN ahumar ▶ **to ~ the peace pipe** fumar la pipa de la paz; **put that in your pipe and ~ it!** ¡métetelo donde te quepa! **III.** *vi* echar humo; (*tobacco*) fumar, pitar *AmS*

◆ **smoke out** *vt* (*scandal*) destapar

smoke bomb *n* bomba *f* de humo

smoked *adj* ahumado, -a; **~ salmon** salmón ahumado

smoke detector *n* detector *m* de humo

smokeless [ˈsmoʊk·lɪs] *adj* sin humo; (*tobacco*) de mascar

smoker *n* fumador(a) *m(f)*; **to be a heavy ~** fumar como un carretero

smoking *n* fumar *m*; **to give up ~** dejar de fumar; **~ ban** prohibición de fumar

smoky [ˈsmoʊ·ki] *adj* <-ier, -iest> **1.** (*filled with smoke*) lleno, -a de humo **2.** (*producing smoke*) humeante **3.** CULIN ahumado, -a

smolder [ˈsmoʊl·dər] *vi* **1.** arder sin llama; (*cigarette*) consumirse lentamente **2.** *fig* arder

smooch [smutʃ] **I.** *vi* besuquearse **II.** *n* **to have a ~** besuquearse

smooth [smuð] **I.** *adj* liso, -a; (*skin, texture, landing, drink*) suave; (*sea, flight*) tranquilo, -a; **as ~ as silk** suave como la seda; **to be a ~ talker** tener un pico de oro **II.** *vt* allanar

◆ **smooth down** *vt* alisar

◆ **smooth over** *vt* (*difficulty*) solucionar

smoothie *n*, **smoothy** [ˈsmu·ði] *n inf* zalamero, -a *m, f*

smooth-shaven *adj* bien afeitado, -a

smother [ˈsmʌð·ər] *vt* **1.** (*suffocate*) ahogar **2.** (*suppress*) contener **3.** **to be**

S

~ed estar cubierto (**in** de)

smudge [smʌdʒ] I. vt (*smear*) emborronar; (*reputation*) destruir II. vi mancharse; (*make-up*) correrse III. n mancha f

smudgy ['smʌdʒ·i] adj <-ier, -iest> manchado, -a

smug [smʌg] adj <-gg-> presumido, -a; **to be ~** presumir (**about** de)

smuggle ['smʌg·əl] vt pasar de contrabando

smuggling ['smʌg·lɪŋ] n contrabando m

smutty ['smʌt̬·i] adj <-ier, -iest> obsceno, -a; (*joke*) verde

snack [snæk] I. n refrigerio m, puntal m AmL; **to have a ~** tomarse un tentempié II. vi picar

snack bar n cafetería f

snag [snæg] I. n 1. (*problem*) dificultad f; **to hit a ~** tropezar con una dificultad 2. (*clothes*) enganchón m II. <-gg-> vt enganchar; (*cause problems*) causar problemas III. <-gg-> vi engancharse (**on** en)

snail [sneɪl] n caracol m ▸ **at a ~'s pace** a paso de tortuga

snail mail n correo m ordinario

snake [sneɪk] I. n serpiente f II. vi serpentear, viborear *Arg, Urug*

snap [snæp] <-pp-> I. n 1. (*sound*) chasquido m 2. (*fastener*) cierre m automático 3. **a cold ~** una ola de frío 4. **a ginger ~** una galleta de jengibre 5. PHOT foto f II. adj repentino, -a III. vi 1. (*break*) romperse 2. **to ~ back** recolocarse; **to ~ at sb** (*bite*) intentar morder a alguien; (*answer*) contestar a alguien de forma brusca IV. vt 1. (*break*) romper 2. (*sound*) chasquear; **to ~ one's fingers** chasquear los dedos 3. PHOT fotografiar

◆ **snap out** vi **to ~ of sth** quitarse algo de encima; **~ of it!** ¡anímate!

◆ **snap up** vt lanzarse sobre

snappy ['ʃnæp·i] adj <-ier, -iest> 1. inf FASHION de lo más elegante; **to be a ~ dresser** vestir con elegancia 2. (*quick*) rápido, -a; **make it ~!** ¡date prisa!

snarl[1] [snɑrl] I. vi gruñir II. n gruñido m

snarl[2] [snɑrl] n 1. (*tangle*) enredo m

2. (*traffic jam*) atasco m

snarl-up ['snɑrl·ʌp] n atasco m

snatch [snætʃ] I. vt 1. (*grab*) agarrar; **to ~ sth** (**away**) arrebatar algo (**from** a) 2. (*steal*) robar; **to ~ victory** hacerse con el triunfo 3. (*kidnap*) secuestrar II. vi quitar algo de las manos; **to ~ at** tratar de arrebatar III. <-es> n 1. **to make a ~ at** intentar arrebatar 2. (*kidnapping*) secuestro m

◆ **snatch up** vt agarrar

snazzy ['snæz·i] adj <-ier, -iest> de lo más elegante

sneak [snik] I. vi moverse furtivamente; **to ~ in/out** entrar/salir a hurtadillas; **to ~ away** [or **off**] escabullirse II. vt hacer furtivamente; **to ~ a look at** mirar con disimulo

sneaker ['sni·kər] n pl zapatillas f pl de deporte

sneaking adj 1. (*slight*) ligero, -a 2. (*secret*) secreto, -a

sneaky ['sni·ki] adj <-ier, -iest> furtivo, -a

sneer [snɪr] I. vi (*mock*) mofarse (**at** a) II. n expresión f desdeñosa

sneering ['snɪr·ɪŋ] adj burlón, -ona

sneeze [sniz] I. vi estornudar ▸ **that's not something to be ~d at** no es de despreciar II. n estornudo m

snicker ['snɪk·ər] I. vi reírse con disimulo (**at** de) II. n risa f disimulada

snide [snaɪd] adj vil

sniff [snɪf] I. vi (*inhale*) sorber; **to ~ at** oler; (*disdain*) despreciar; **to go ~ing around** husmear (**for** en busca de) ▸ **not to be ~ed at** no ser de despreciar II. vt olfatear; (*person*) oler III. n **to have a ~** oler; **to catch a ~ of** captar el olor de

◆ **sniff out** vt descubrir; (*by smelling*) encontrar olfateando

sniffer dog ['snɪf·ər·ˌdɔg] n perro m rastreador

sniffle ['snɪf·əl] I. vi 1. (*sniff*) sorberse los mocos 2. (*cry*) lloriquear II. npl **to have the ~s** estar acatarrado

snip [snɪp] I. vt cortar n 1. (*cut*) tijeretazo m 2. (*cloth*) recorte m

sniper ['snaɪ·pər] n francotirador(a) m(f)

snitch [snɪtʃ] inf I. vi chivarse (**on**

de) **II.** vt (*steal*) birlar **III.** <-es> n **1.** (*thief*) caco mf **2.** (*tattletale*) soplón, -ona m, f

snivel ['snɪv·əl] **I.** <-ll-, -l-> vi (*cry*) lloriquear **II.** n lloriqueo m

snobbish ['snab·ɪʃ] <more, most> adj esnob

snoop [snup] pej, inf **I.** n fisgón, -ona m, f **II.** vi fisgonear; **to ~ around** husmear

snooty ['snu·t̬i] <-ier, -iest> adj presumido, -a, pituco, -a AmS

snooze [snuz] inf **I.** vi echar una cabezada; (*lightly*) dormitar **II.** n cabezada f

snore [snɔr] MED **I.** vi roncar **II.** n ronquido m

snort [snɔrt] **I.** vi resoplar **II.** vt (*inhale*) esnifar **III.** n bufido m

snot [snat] n moco m

snotty ['snat̬·i] <-ier, -iest> adj inf **1.** lleno, -a de mocos **2.** (*rude*) petulante

snout [snaʊt] n hocico m; (*person*) napia f

snow [snoʊ] **I.** n **1.** METEO nieve f; **a blanket of ~** un manto de nieve **2.** (*cocaine*) nieve f **II.** vi nevar
♦ **snow in** vt **to be snowed in** estar aprisionado por la nieve
♦ **snow under** vt **to be snowed under** estar desbordado (**with** de)

snowball ['snoʊ·bɔl] **I.** n bola f de nieve ► **to not have a ~'s chance in hell** (**of doing sth**) no tener ni la más remota posibilidad (de hacer algo) **II.** vi fig aumentar progresivamente

snowboard n snowboard m

snowbound ['snoʊ·baʊnd] adj aprisionado, -a por la nieve

snowfall n nevada f; (*snowstorm*) tormenta f de nieve, nevazón m Arg, Chile, Ecua

snowflake n copo m de nieve

snowman n muñeco m de nieve

snowmobile ['snoʊ·moʊ·bil] n moto f de nieve, trineo m motorizado

snowstorm n tormenta f de nieve

snow tire n neumático m de nieve

snowy ['snoʊ·i] adj (*region, season*) de mucha nieve; (*street, field*) cubierto, -a de nieve; (*hair, flowers*) blanco, -a como la nieve

snub [snʌb] **I.** <-bb-> vt hacer el vacío

II. n desaire m

snub-nosed adj (*person*) de nariz respingona

snuff [snʌf] **I.** vt **1.** (*put out*) apagar **2.** inf (*end*) acabar con **II.** n rapé m

snug [snʌg] adj (*cozy*) acogedor(a); (*warm*) calentito, -a; (*tight*) ajustado, -a

snuggle ['snʌg·əl] vi acurrucarse (**up to** contra)

so [soʊ] **I.** adv **1.** (*same way*) tan, tanto; **~ do/did I** yo también; **~ to speak** por así decirlo **2.** (*like that*) así; **~ they say** eso dicen; **is that ~?** ¿de verdad?; **I hope/think ~** eso espero/creo **3.** (*degree*) tan, tanto; **~ late** tan tarde; **~ many books** tantos libros; **not ~ ugly as that** no tan feo como eso; **would you be ~ kind as to...?** ¿sería tan amable de...? **4.** (*in order that*) para; **I bought the book ~ that he would read it** compré el libro para que él lo leyera **5.** (*result*) así; **and ~ she won** y así ganó ► **and ~ on** [or **forth**] etcétera; **or ~** más o menos **II.** conj **1.** (*therefore*) por (lo) tanto **2.** (*afterwards*) ~ (**then**) **he told me...** y entonces me dijo... ¿y qué? **3.** (*summing up*) así que; **~ what?** ¿y qué? **~ now** entonces; **~, as I was saying...** entonces, como iba diciendo... **III.** interj **~ that's why!** ¡conque era eso!

soak [soʊk] **I.** vt remojar, ensopar AmS **II.** vi (*lie in liquid*) estar en remojo **III.** n remojo m
♦ **soak in** vi penetrar
♦ **soak up** vt absorber; (*money, resources*) agotar; (*people*) embelesar; (*sun*) tomar

soaking I. n remojo m; **to get a good ~** calarse hasta los huesos **II.** adj **~** (**wet**) empapado, -a

so-and-so ['soʊ·ən·soʊ] n (*person*) fulano m; (*thing*) movida f

soap [soʊp] **I.** n jabón m ► **soft ~** coba f **II.** vt enjabonar

soap opera n telenovela f

soapy ['soʊ·pi] <-ier, -iest> adj **1.** (*full of lather*) lleno, -a de jabón **2.** (*like soap*) jabonoso, -a **3.** (*flattering*) zalamero, -a

soar [sɔr] vi llegar muy alto; (*house*) elevarse mucho; (*temperature, prices*) subir bruscamente; (*hopes*) renacer; (*bird, plane*) remontar el vuelo

sob [sab] I. <-bb-> *vi* sollozar II. <-bb-> *vt* decir sollozando III. *n* sollozo *m*

sober ['sou·bər] *adj* sobrio, -a; (*mood, atmosphere, expression*) serio, -a; (*attire*) sencillo, -a; (*colors*) discreto, -a; (*assessment*) sensato, -a

◆ **sober up** *vi* (*less drunk*) espabilar la borrachera; (*serious*) ponerse serio

sob story *n* dramón *m*

so-called [ˌsou·'kɔld] *adj* presunto, -a

soccer ['sak·ər] *n* fútbol *m*

sociable ['sou·ʃə·bəl] *adj* sociable

social ['sou·ʃəl] *adj* social

socialist *n* socialista *mf*

socialize ['sou·ʃə·laɪz] I. *vi* alternar con la gente II. *vt* PSYCH socializar; POL, ECON nacionalizar

social science *n* ciencia *f* social

social security *n* seguridad *f* social

society [sə·'saɪ·ə·ti] *n* 1. (*all people*) sociedad *f*; **high** ~ alta sociedad; **to be a menace to** ~ ser una amenaza para la sociedad 2. (*organization*) asociación *f*

sociolinguistics [ˌsou·si·ou·lɪŋ·'gwɪs·tɪks] *n* sociolingüística *f*

sociology [ˌsou·si·'al·ə·dʒi] *n* sociología *f*

sock¹ [sak] *n* calcetín *m*, media *f* AmL; **knee-high** ~ calcetín largo ▶ **to knock sb's ~s off** dejar a alguien con la boca abierta

sock² [sak] I. *vt* (*hit*) dar una piña ▶ ~ **it to 'em!** ¡a por ellos! II. *n* tortazo *m*

socket ['sak·ɪt] *n* 1. ELEC enchufe *m*, tomacorriente *m* Arg, Perú; **double/triple** ~ enchufe de dos/tres entradas 2. (*eye*) cuenca *f*; (*tooth*) alvéolo *m*

sod [sad] *n* césped *m*

sodden ['sad·ən] *adj* empapado, -a

sofa ['sou·fə] *n* sofá *m*

soft [sɔft] *adj* 1. (*not hard*) blando, -a 2. (*smooth*) suave; ~ **as silk** suave como la seda 3. (*mild*) ligero, -a; (*drug*) blando, -a 4. (*not bright*) (*lighting, light*) tenue 5. (*sound, music*) agradable; (*voice*) dulce 6. (*lenient*) indulgente; **to go** ~ ser muy indulgente (**on** con) 7. (*easy*) fácil; **a** ~ **target** un blanco fácil

8. (*currency*) débil

soft-boiled [ˌsɔft·'bɔɪld] *adj* pasado, -a por agua

soften ['sɔ·fən] I. *vi* ablandarse; (*butter, ground*) reblandecerse, amelcochar Méx II. *vt* (*butter*) reblandecer; (*skin, color, voice, opinion, words*) suavizar; (*effect*) mitigar; (*blow*) amortiguar

◆ **soften up** *vt* ablandar

soft-hearted ['sɔft·ˌhar·tɪd] *adj* bondadoso, -a

softie ['sɔf·ti] *n* blandengue *mf*

softly *adv* 1. (*not roughly*) suavemente; (*shine*) tenuemente 2. (*quietly*) silenciosamente

softness ['sɔft·nɪs] *n* blandura *f*; (*smoothness*) suavidad *f*

software ['sɔft·wer] *n* software *m*; **accounting** ~ programa *m* de contabilidad

softy ['sɔf·ti] *n* blandengue *mf*

soggy ['sag·i] <-ier, -iest> *adj* empapado, -a

soil¹ [sɔɪl] *n* AGR suelo *m*; **fertile** ~ tierra *f* fértil

soil² [sɔɪl] I. *vt* form (*stain*) manchar; (*clothing, shoes*) ensuciar II. *vi* ensuciarse

solar ['sou·lər] *adj* solar

sold [sould] *pt, pp of* **sell**

soldier ['soul·dʒər] *n* soldado *mf*; (*officer*) militar *mf*; **old** ~ veterano *m*

sole¹ [soul] *adj* (*only*) único, -a; (*exclusive*) exclusivo, -a

sole² [soul] *n* (*foot*) planta *f*; (*shoe*) suela *f*

sole³ [soul] <-(s)> *n* (*fish*) lenguado *m*; **filet of** ~ filete de lenguado

solely ['soul·li] *adv* únicamente

solemn ['sal·əm] *adj* solemne; (*person, appearance*) serio, -a

solicit [sə·'lɪs·ɪt] I. *vt* solicitar II. *vi* ofrecer por la calle servicios sexuales

solid ['sal·ɪd] I. *adj* 1. (*hard*) sólido, -a; (*table, door*) robusto, -a; (*meal*) pesado, -a; **to be** (**as**) ~ **as a rock** ser duro como una piedra 2. (*not hollow*) macizo, -a 3. (*true*) real; (*facts*) verídico, -a; (*evidence*) sustancial; (*argument*) sólido, -a; (*reasons*) de peso; (*conviction*) firme; (*agreement*) concreto, -a 4. (*uninter-*

rupted) ininterrumpido, -a; (*hour, day, week*) entero, -a **II.** *adv* **to be packed/ frozen ~** estar abarrotado/como un témpano **III.** *n* sólido *m*

solidify [sə-'lɪd·ə·faɪ] <-ie-, -ying> **I.** *vi* solidificarse; *fig* concretarse **II.** *vt* solidificar; *fig* reforzar

solidly *adv* firmemente; (*unanimously*) unánimemente

solitary ['sɑl·ə·ter·i] *adj* **1.** (*alone, single*) solitario, -a **2.** (*isolated*) solo, -a, íngrimo, -a *AmL*; (*unvisited*) apartado, -a; **to go for a ~ walk** ir a pasear solo

solo ['soʊ·loʊ] **I.** *adj* solo, -a **II.** *adv* a solas; **to go ~** lanzarse como solista **III.** *n* MUS solo *m*

soloist ['soʊ·loʊ·ɪst] *n* solista *mf*

soluble ['sɑl·jə·bəl] *adj* soluble

solution [sə-'lu·ʃən] *n* solución *f*

solve [sɑlv] *vt* resolver

solvent ['sɑl·vənt] **I.** *n* disolvente *m* **II.** *adj* FIN solvente; CHEM disolvente

somber ['sɑm·bər] *adj* (*mood*) sombrío, -a; (*color*) oscuro, -a

some [sʌm] **I.** *adj indef* **1.** *pl* (*several*) algunos, -as; **~ apples** algunas manzanas; **~ people think...** algunos piensan... **2.** (*imprecise*) algún, alguna; (*at*) **~ place** (en) algún lugar; **~ day** algún día; (*at*) **~ time** (en) algún momento; **for ~ time** durante un tiempo; **~ other time** en algún otro momento; **~ time ago** hace algún tiempo; **in ~ way or another** de una u otra manera; **to have ~ idea** tener alguna idea (**of** de) **3.** (*amount*) un poco de, algo de; **~ more tea** un poco más de té; **to have ~ money** tener algo de dinero; **to ~ extent** hasta cierto punto **II.** *pron indef* **1.** *pl* (*several*) algunos, -as; **I would like ~** quisiera algunos; **~ like it, others don't** a unos les gusta, a otros no **2.** (*part of it*) algo **III.** *adv* (*about*) unos, unas; **~ more apples** unas manzanas más; **~ more wine** un poco más de vino

somebody ['sʌm·bɑd·i] *pron indef* alguien; **~ else** otra persona, otro; **~ or other** alguien

somehow ['sʌm·haʊ] *adv* **1.** (*through unknown methods*) de alguna manera **2.** (*for an unclear reason*) por algún

motivo **3.** (*come what may*) de un modo u otro

someone ['sʌm·wʌn] *pron see* **somebody**

someplace ['sʌm·pleɪs] *adv* en algún lugar

somersault ['sʌm·ər·sɔlt] **I.** *n* salto *m* mortal **II.** *vi* dar un salto mortal; (*vehicle*) dar una vuelta de campana

something ['sʌm·θɪŋ] **I.** *pron indef, sing* **1.** algo; **~ else/nice** algo más/bonito; **~ or other** alguna cosa; **one can't have ~ for nothing** quien algo quiere, algo le cuesta **2.** **or ~** o algo así; **six-foot ~** dos metros y pico; **his name is Paul ~** es Paul no sé qué **II.** *n* **a little ~** una cosita; **a certain ~** cierta cosa ▸ **that is really ~!** ¡ésa sí que es buena! **III.** *adv* **~ around \$10** alrededor de 10\$; **~ over/ under \$10** algo más/menos de 10\$

sometime ['sʌm·taɪm] *adv* en algún momento; **~ soon** pronto

sometimes ['sʌm·taɪmz] *adv* a veces

somewhat ['sʌm·hwʌt] *adv* algo; **to feel ~ better** sentirse un poco mejor

somewhere ['sʌm·hwer] *adv* **1.** (*be*) en alguna parte; (*go*) a alguna parte; **to be/ go ~ else** estar en/ir a otra parte; **to get ~** *fig* progresar; **or ~** o así **2.** (*roughly*) alrededor de; **she is ~ around 40** ronda los 40; **he earns ~ around \$40,000** gana unos 40.000\$

son [sʌn] *n* hijo *m*

song [sɔŋ] *n* canción *f*; (*act*) canto *m* ▸ **~ and dance** (*excuse*) rollo *m*; (**to go**) **for a ~** (*venderse*) a precio de saldo

songbook *n* cancionero *m*

son-in-law ['sʌn·ɪn·lɔ] <sons-in-law> *n* yerno *m*

soon [sun] *adv* pronto, mero *AmC, Méx*; **~ after** poco después de; **how ~...?** ¿para cuándo...?; **as ~ as possible** lo antes posible; **I would just as ~...** preferiría...

soot [sʊt] *n* hollín *m*

soothing *adj* tranquilizador(a); (*pain-relieving*) analgésico, -a; (*balsamic*) reparador(a)

sophisticated [sə-'fɪs·tə·keɪ·t̬ɪd] *adj* **1.** (*refined*) sofisticado, -a **2.** (*cultured*) culto, -a sophomore ['saf·ə·mɔr] n estudiante mf de segundo año

sopping ['sap·ɪŋ] inf I. adj empapado, -a II. adv ~ wet empapado, -a

soppy ['sap·i] <-ier, -iest> adj sensiblero, -a

sore [sɔr] I. adj 1. (aching) dolorido, -a; to be in ~ need of necesitar a toda costa; a ~ point fig un punto delicado 2. inf (offended) ofendido, -a; (aggrieved) resentido, -a; ~ loser mal perdedor II. n MED llaga f; fig recuerdo m doloroso; to open an old ~ abrir una vieja herida

sorely ['sɔr·li] adv form muy; he will be ~ missed lo echarán mucho de menos

sorrow ['sar·oʊ] n pena f; to feel ~ sentirse apenado (over por); to my ~ muy a mi pesar

sorry ['sar·i] I. <-ier, -iest> adj 1. triste, apenado, -a; to be ~ that sentir que +subj; to feel ~ for oneself compadecerse de sí mismo; to feel ~ tener lástima (for de) 2. (regretful) arrepentido, -a; I'm (very) ~ lo siento (mucho) (about por); to say ~ pedir perdón 3. (wretched, pitiful) desgraciado, -a; (choice) desafortunado, -a; (figure) lastimoso, -a II. interj ~! ¡perdón!; ~? ¿cómo dice?

sort [sɔrt] I. n 1. (type) tipo m; (kind) especie f; (variety) clase f; flowers of all ~s toda clase de flores; something/ nothing of the ~ algo/nada por el estilo; he was a friend of ~s se le podía considerar amigo; to not be the ~ to do sth no ser de los que hacen algo; I know your ~! ¡sé de qué pie calzas! 2. ~ of en cierto modo; (not exactly) más o menos; I ~ of feel that... en cierto modo pienso que...; that's ~ of difficult to explain es algo difícil de explicar ▶ out of ~s pachucho II. vt clasificar; COMPUT ordenar; to ~ in ascending/descending order poner en orden ascendente/descendente III. vi to ~ through revisar

◆sort out vt 1. (resolve) solucionar; (details) aclarar 2. (arrange) clasificar; (choose) separar 3. (tidy up) arreglar

SOS [ˌes·oʊ·'es] n SOS m

so-so ['soʊ·soʊ] inf I. adj regular II. adv

ni fu ni fa, así así

sought [sɔt] pt, pp of seek

soul [soʊl] n 1. alma f; bless his/her ~ que en paz descanse; not a ~ ni un alma; to be the ~ of discretion ser la discreción en persona 2. MUS soul m

soul-searching n examen m de conciencia; after much ~ tras mucha reflexión

sound¹ [saʊnd] I. n 1. a. LING, PHYS sonido m; there wasn't a ~ to be heard no se oía nada; by the ~ of it según parece; I don't like the ~ of that no me huele nada bien 2. (radio, TV) volumen m; to turn the ~ down/up bajar/subir el volumen II. vi 1. sonar 2. (seem) parecer III. vt (alarm) hacer sonar; (bell, car horn) tocar

sound² [saʊnd] I. adj 1. (healthy) sano, -a; (robust) fuerte; (character, health) bueno, -a; (basis) sólido, -a; to be of ~ mind estar en su sano juicio; to be safe and ~ estar sano y salvo 2. (trustworthy) digno, -a de confianza; (competent) competente 3. (thorough) profundo, -a; to be a ~ sleeper tener el sueño profundo II. adv to be ~ asleep dormir profundamente

sound³ [saʊnd] vt NAUT sondear; MED auscultar

sound⁴ [saʊnd] n (channel) estrecho m; (inlet) brazo m de mar

◆sound out vt tantear

soundproof ['saʊnd·pruf] I. vt insonorizar II. adj insonorizado, -a

soup [sup] n sopa f; (clear) caldo m; home-made/instant ~ sopa casera/ instantánea

sour ['saʊ·ər] I. adj a. fig agrio, -a; (milk) cortado, -a; to go ~ agriarse; (milk) cortarse II. vt agriar; fig amargar III. vi agriarse; (milk) cortarse; (person) amargarse

source [sɔrs] n fuente f; according to government ~s según fuentes gubernamentales; from a reliable ~ de una fuente fiable; to list one's ~s hacer la bibliografía; a ~ of inspiration una fuente de inspiración

south [saʊθ] I. n sur m; to lie 5 miles to the ~ quedar a 8 km al sur (of de);

to go/drive to the ~ ir hacia el sur; **further** ~ más al sur; **in the** ~ **of Bolivia** en el sur de Bolivia II. *adj* del sur, meridional; ~ **wind** viento del sur; ~ **coast** costa *f* sur

South Africa *n* Sudáfrica *f*

South African *adj, n* sudafricano, -a *m, f*

South America *n* América *f* del Sur

South American *adj, n* sudamericano, -a *m, f*

southbound ['saʊθ·baʊnd] *adj* hacia el sur

southerly ['sʌð·ər·li] I. *adj* (*location*) en el sur; **in a** ~ **direction** en dirección sur II. *n* viento *m* meridional

southern ['sʌð·ərn] *adj* del sur; **the** ~ **part of the country** la parte sur del país

southerner ['sʌð·ər·nər] *n* sureño, -a *m, f*

South Pole *n* Polo *m* Sur

southward(s) ['saʊθ·wərd(z)] *adv* hacia el sur

souvenir [ˌsu·və·ˈnɪr] *n* recuerdo *m*

Soviet Union *n* Unión *f* Soviética

sow[1] [soʊ] <sowed, sown *or* sowed> *vt, vi* AGR sembrar ▶ **as you** ~, **so shall you reap** lo que siembres cosecharás

sow[2] [saʊ] *n* (*pig*) cerda *f* ▶ **you can't make a silk purse out of a** ~**'s ear** no se le puede pedir peras al olmo

sown [soʊn] *pp of* **sow**

sox [saks] *npl* calcetines *mpl*

soy [sɔɪ] *n* soja *f*

spa [spa] *n* 1. (*spring*) manantial *m* 2. (*town*) ciudad *f* balnearia 3. (*health center*) balneario *m*

space [speɪs] I. *n* espacio *m*; **parking** ~ plaza *f* de aparcamiento; **in a short** ~ **of time** en un breve espacio de tiempo; **leave some** ~ **for dessert** deja hueco para el postre II. *vt* espaciar

space bar *n* barra *f* espaciadora

space probe *n* sonda *f* espacial

space-saving *adj* que ocupa poco espacio

spaceship ['speɪs·ʃɪp] *n* nave *f* espacial

space shuttle *n* transbordador *m* espacial

space station *n* estación *f* espacial

spacing ['speɪ·sɪŋ] *n* espaciamiento *m*; TYPO espacio *m*; **double** ~ doble espacio

spacious ['speɪ·ʃəs] *adj* espacioso, -a

spade [speɪd] *n* pala *f*; GAMES pica *f* ▶ **to call a** ~ **a** ~ llamar al pan, pan y al vino, vino

spaghetti [spə·ˈget·i] *n* espaguetis *mpl*

Spain [speɪn] *n* España *f*

spam [spæm] COMPUT I. *n* COMPUT spam *m* II. *vt* enviar spam

Spam® [spæm] *n* fiambre de cerdo enlatado

spambot ['spæm·bɒt] *n* spambot *m*

span[1] [spæn] *pt of* **spin**

span[2] [spæn] I. *n* 1. (*time*) lapso *m*; (*project*) duración *f* 2. ARCHIT luz *f* 3. AVIAT, NAUT envergadura *f* II. <-nn-> *vt* 1. (*cross*) atravesar 2. (*include*) abarcar

spangled *adj* con lentejuelas; *fig* salpicado, -a (**with** de)

Spaniard ['spæn·jərd] *n* español(a) *m(f)*

Spanish ['spæn·ɪʃ] I. *adj* español(a); ~ **speaker** hispanohablante *mf* II. *n* 1. (*people*) español(a) *m(f)*; **the** ~ los españoles 2. LING español *m*

spank [spæŋk] *vt* zurrar

spanking ['spæŋ·kɪŋ] I. *n* zurra *f*, fleta *f* AmC II. *adj* ~ **new** nuevo flamante

spare [sper] I. *vt* 1. (*pardon*) perdonar; **to** ~ **sth** ahorrar algo a alguien; **to** ~ **no effort** no escatimar esfuerzos 2. (*do without*) prescindir de; (*time*) disponer de II. *adj* 1. (*additional*) de repuesto; (*room, minute*) libre 2. (*remaining*) sobrante III. *n* (*part*) repuesto *m*

spare time *n* tiempo *m* libre

spare tire *n* rueda *f* de repuesto; *iron* michelín *m*

spark [spark] I. *n* 1. chispa *f* 2. (*small amount*) pizca *f*; **not even a** ~ ni una pizca (**of** de) II. *vt* (*debate, protest, problems*) desencadenar; (*interest*) suscitar; **to** ~ **sb into action** hacer que alguien se mueva

sparkle ['spar·kəl] I. *n* destello *m*, brillo *m* II. *vi* (*eyes*) brillar; (*fire*) chispear; (*sea*) destellar

sparkler ['spark·lər] *n* 1. (*firework*) bengala *f* 2. *inf* (*diamond*) diamante *m*

sparkling ['spark·lɪŋ] *adj* (*light, dia-*

S

mond) brillante; (*conversation, wit*) chispeante

spark plug ['spark·plʌg] *n* bujía *f*

sparrow ['sper·oʊ] *n* gorrión *m*

sparse [spars] *adj* escaso, -a

spat[1] [spæt] *pt, pp of* spit

spat[2] [spæt] **I.** *n* (*quarrel*) rencilla *f* **II.** <-tt-> *vi* (*quarrel*) reñir

spate [speɪt] *n* racha *f*; (*of letters, inquiries*) aluvión *m*

spatial ['speɪ·ʃəl] *adj* espacial

spatter ['spæt·ər] **I.** *vt, vi* salpicar (**with** de) **II.** *n* salpicadura *f*, salpicada *f Méx*; **~ of rain** cuatro gotas

spawn [spɔn] **I.** *n* ZOOL hueva(s) *f(pl)* **II.** *vt* generar **III.** *vi* desovar

speak [spik] <spoke, spoken> **I.** *vi* hablar (**to** con, **on behalf of** por); **so to ~** por así decir; **generally ~ing** en términos generales; **scientifically ~ing** desde el punto de vista científico; **strictly ~ing** en realidad **II.** *vt* hablar; (*say*) decir; **to ~ dialect/English** hablar dialecto/inglés; **to ~ one's mind** hablar claro; **to ~ the truth** decir la verdad; **to not ~ a word** no decir ni una palabra

◆ **speak for** *vi* 1. (*represent*) hablar por; **speaking for myself** en lo que a mí respecta; **it speaks for itself** habla por sí solo 2. (*advocate, support*) hablar en favor de

◆ **speak out** *vi* expresarse; **to ~ against** denunciar

◆ **speak up** *vi* 1. (*state*) decir lo que se piensa; **to ~ for sth** hablar a favor de algo 2. (*more loudly*) hablar más alto

speaker *n* 1. hablante *mf* 2. (*orator*) orador(a) *m(f)* 3. (*loudspeaker*) altavoz *m*

speaking **I.** *n* habla *f*; (*public*) oratoria *f* **II.** *adj* hablante; (*tour*) comentado, -a; **to not be on ~ terms** no dirigirse la palabra

spear [spɪr] **I.** *n* lanza *f*; (*for throwing*) jabalina *f*; (*for fishing*) arpón *m* **II.** *vt* (*fork*) pinchar

spearhead ['spɪr·hed] *n a. fig* punta *f* de lanza

special ['speʃ·əl] **I.** *adj* especial; (*aptitude, character*) excepcional; **nothing ~** nada especial **II.** *n* TV programa *m*

especial; CULIN especialidad *f* del día; COM oferta *f* especial

specialist ['speʃ·ə·lɪst] *n* especialista *mf*

specialize ['speʃ·ə·laɪz] *vi* especializarse (**in** en)

specially *adv* especialmente; **a ~ good wine** un vino especialmente bueno

specialty ['speʃ·əl·ti] *n* <-ies> especialidad *f*

species ['spi·fiz] *n inv* especie *f*

specific [spə·'sɪf·ɪk] *adj* específico, -a; **to be ~** dar detalles; **to be ~ to sth** ser propio de algo

specifically *adv* (*expressly*) expresamente; (*ask, mention*) explícitamente; (*particularly*) específicamente

specification [ˌspes·ə·fɪ·'keɪ·ʃən] *n* especificación *f*

specify ['spes·ə·faɪ] <-ie-> *vt* especificar

specimen ['spes·ə·mən] *n* 1. (*blood, urine*) muestra *f*; (*plant, animal, product*) ejemplar *m*; **a ~ copy** un ejemplar de muestra 2. (*person*) espécimen *m*

speck [spek] *n* punto *m*; (*dust*) mota *f*; **not a ~** ni pizca (**of** de)

specs [speks] *npl inf* 1. *abbr of* **spectacles** gafas *fpl* 2. *abbr of* **specifications** especificaciones *fpl*

spectacle ['spek·tə·kəl] *n* 1. espectáculo *m*; **to make a real ~ of oneself** dar el espectáculo 2. *pl* (*glasses*) gafas *fpl*, lentes *fpl AmL*; **a pair of ~** unas gafas

spectacular [spek·'tæk·jʊ·lər] **I.** *adj* espectacular **II.** *n* programa *m* especial

spectator [spek·'teɪ·tər] *n* espectador(a) *m(f)*

spectrum ['spek·trəm] <-ra *or* -s> *n* 1. PHYS espectro *m* 2. (*range*) gama *f*; **the political ~** el espectro político

speculation [ˌspek·jʊ·'leɪ·ʃən] *n* especulación *f*; **stock-market ~** especulación bursátil

sped [sped] *pt, pp of* speed

speech [spitʃ] <-es> *n* 1. (*capacity*) habla *f*; **to lose/regain the power of ~** perder/recobrar el habla 2. (*words*) palabras *fpl* 3. (*public talk*) discurso *m*; **to make** [*or* **give**] **a ~** pronunciar un discurso

speech defect *n* defecto *m* del habla

speechless ['spitʃ·lɪs] *adj* mudo, -a; **to**

leave sb ~ dejar a alguien sin palabras

speech therapist *n* logopeda *mf*

speed [spid] **I.** *n* **1.** (*velocity*) velocidad *f;* **at a ~ of** a una velocidad de **2.** (*quickness*) rapidez *f* **3.** (*gear*) marcha *f* **4.** PHOT sensibilidad *f* **5.** (*drug*) speed *m* **II.** *vi* <sped *or* speeded, sped *or* speeded> **1.** (*go fast*) ir de prisa; **to ~ by** pasar volando **2.** (*hasten*) apresurarse **3.** AUTO ir con exceso de velocidad **III.** *vt* <sped *or* speeded, sped *or* speeded> acelerar

◆**speed up** <sped *or* speeded, sped *or* speeded> **I.** *vi* (*car*) acelerar; (*process*) acelerarse; (*person*) darse prisa, apurarse *AmL* **II.** *vt* (*process*) acelerar, expeditar *AmL;* (*person*) apresurar

speedboat ['spid·bout] *n* lancha *f* motora

speed bump *n* banda *f* rugosa

speeding *n* exceso *m* de velocidad

speed limit *n* límite *f* de velocidad

speedy ['spi·di] <-ier, -iest> *adj* veloz

spell¹ [spel] <spelled *or* spelt, spelled *or* spelt> (*language*) **I.** *vt* **1.** deletrear; **how do you ~ it?** ¿cómo se deletrea? **2.** significar; **this ~s trouble** esto significa problemas **II.** *vi* escribir; **to ~ well** escribir sin faltas

◆**spell out** *vt* deletrear; *fig* explicar de forma minuciosa (for a)

spell² [spel] *n* (*magic*) encanto *m;* **to be under a ~** estar hechizado

spell³ [spel] *n* **1.** (*period*) temporada *f* **2.** (*turn*) turno *m*

spellbound ['spel·baund] *adj* hechizado, -a; *fig* fascinado, -a

spelling *n* ortografía *f;* **~ mistake** falta *f* de ortografía

spelt [spelt] *pp, pt of* **spell**

spend [spend] <spent, spent> **I.** *vt* (*use up*) agotar; (*money*) gastar; (*time*) pasar; **to ~ time doing sth** dedicar tiempo a hacer algo **II.** *vi* gastar

spending *n* gasto *m;* **public ~** el gasto público

spending money *n* dinero *m* para gastos personales

spending spree *n* derroche *m* de dinero; **to go on a ~** gastar dinero a lo loco

spent [spent] **I.** *pp, pt of* **spend II.** *adj*
(*used*) gastado, -a

sperm [spɜrm] <-(s)> *n* esperma *m o f*

spew [spju] *vi, vt* vomitar

sphere [sfɪr] *n* esfera *f;* **~ of influence** ámbito *m* de influencia

spherical ['sfɪr·ɪ·kəl] *adj* esférico, -a

spice [spaɪs] **I.** *n* **1.** CULIN especia *f,* olor *m Chile* **2.** (*excitement*) picante *m;* **to give ~ to sth** dar sabor a algo (to a); **the ~ of life** la sal de la vida **II.** *vt* condimentar

spicy ['spaɪ·si] <-ier, -iest> *adj* **1.** (*seasoned*) condimentado, -a **2.** (*sensational*) picante

spider ['spaɪ·dər] *n* araña *f*

spike [spaɪk] **I.** *n* **1.** (*object*) pincho *m* **2.** *pl* (*shoes*) zapatillas *f pl* con clavos **3.** (*increase*) pico *m* **4.** SPORTS remate *m* **II.** *vt* **1.** **to ~ a drink** echar alcohol a una bebida **2.** (*injure*) pinchar **3.** (*secure*) clavar **4.** SPORTS rematar

spiky ['spaɪ·ki] <-ier, -iest> *adj* **1.** (*sharp*) puntiagudo, -a; (*hair*) de punta **2.** *inf* chinchoso, -a

spill [spɪl] **I.** *n* **1.** derrame *m;* **oil ~** vertido *m* de petróleo **2.** *inf* (*fall*) caída *f;* **to take a ~** tener un accidente **II.** *vt* <spilled *or* spilt, spilled *or* spilt> derramar **III.** *vi* derramarse

◆**spill over** *vi* derramarse

spilt [spɪlt] *pp, pt of* **spill**

spin [spɪn] **I.** *n* vuelta *f;* **to go** [*or* **take the car**] **for a ~** dar un paseo (en coche) **II.** *vt* <spun, spun> girar; (*clothes*) centrifugar; (*ball*) dar efecto a; (*wool, cotton*) hilar; (*story, tale*) contar **III.** *vi* <spun, spun> girar; (*wool, cotton*) hilar

◆**spin out** *vi* (*car*) salirse de la calzada

spinach ['spɪn·ɪtʃ] *n* espinacas *fpl*

spine [spaɪn] *n* **1.** (*person*) columna *f* vertebral; (*animal*) espina *f* dorsal **2.** (*spike*) púa *f* **3.** BOT espina *f*

spiral ['spaɪ·rəl] **I.** *n* espiral *f* **II.** *adj* en espiral; (*staircase*) de caracol **III.** *vi* <-ll-, -l-> (*increase*) dispararse; (*decrease*) caer; **to ~ out of control** descontrolarse

spire [spaɪr] *n* ARCHIT aguja *f*

spirit ['spɪr·ɪt] *n* **1.** (*ghost*) espíritu *m;* **the ~ of the age** el espíritu de la época;

S

that's the ~! ¡muy bien! **2.** *pl* (*mood*) ánimo *mpl*; **to be in high/low ~s** estar animado/desanimado **3.** *pl* (*alcohol*) licor *m*

spirited *adj* enérgico, -a; (*discussion*) animado, -a; (*person*) animoso, -a, entrador(a) *AmS*

spiritual ['spɪr·ɪ·tʃu·əl] *adj* espiritual

spit[1] [spɪt] BIOL **I.** *n inf* saliva *f* **II.** *vt* <spat, spat> escupir; (*crackle*) chisporrotear **III.** *vt* escupir

◆ **spit out** *vt* escupir; (*say angrily*) soltar; **spit it out!** ¡desembucha!

spit[2] [spɪt] *n* **1.** CULIN asador *m* **2.** (*sandbar*) banco *m* de arena

spite [spaɪt] **I.** *n* rencor *m*; **out of ~** por despecho; **in ~ of** a pesar de **II.** *vt* fastidiar

spiteful ['spaɪt·fəl] *adj* rencoroso, -a

spitting image *n* vivo *m* retrato

splash [splæʃ] **I.** *n* **1.** (*sound*) chapoteo *m* **2.** (*drops*) salpicadura *f*; **a ~ of color** una mancha de color ▶ **to** make **a** (**big**) **~** causar sensación **II.** *vt, vi* salpicar

◆ **splash down** *vi* amerizar

splatter ['splæt̬·ər] *vi, vt* salpicar

splendid ['splen·dɪd] *adj* espléndido, -a

splendor ['splen·dər] *n* esplendor *m*; *pl* maravillas *fpl*

splint [splɪnt] **I.** *n* tablilla *f* **II.** *vt* entablillar

splinter ['splɪn·tər] **I.** *n* astilla *f* **II.** *vi* astillarse

split [splɪt] **I.** *n* **1.** (*crack*) grieta **2.** (*clothes*) desgarrón **3.** (*division*) división *f* **II.** *vt* <split, split> **1.** (*divide*) dividir; (*atom*) desintegrar; **to ~ sth between two people** repartir algo entre dos personas **2.** (*crack*) agrietar; **to ~ one's** head **open** abrirse la cabeza ▶ **to ~ one's** sides **laughing** partirse de risa; **to ~ hairs** buscarle tres pies al gato **III.** *vi* <split, split> **1.** (*divide*) dividirse **2.** (*crack*) agrietarse **3.** (*leave*) largarse

◆ **split off** **I.** *vt* separar **II.** *vi* separarse

◆ **split up** **I.** *vt* partir **II.** *vi* separarse (**with** de)

split-up ['splɪt·ʌp] *n* ruptura *m*

splutter ['splʌt̬·ər] **I.** *vi* (*person*) farfullar

(*candle, engine*) chisporrotear **II.** *n* (*candle, engine*) chisporroteo *m*

spoil [spɔɪl] **I.** *vt* <spoiled *or* spoilt, spoiled *or* spoilt> estropear, salar *AmL*; (*party*) aguar; (*child*) consentir, engreír *AmL*, papachar *Méx* **II.** *vi* <spoiled *or* spoilt, spoiled *or* spoilt> estropearse **III.** *n* **1.** *pl* (*profits*) botín *m* **2.** (*debris*) escombros *mpl*

spoilsport ['spɔɪl·spɔrt] *n* aguafiestas *mf inv*

spoilt **I.** *pp, pt of* **spoil** **II.** *adj* mimado, -a, engreído, -a *AmL*

spoke[1] [spoʊk] *pt of* **speak**

spoke[2] [spoʊk] *n* (*wheel*) radio *m*; **to put a ~ in sb's wheel** poner trabas a alguien

spoken *pp of* **speak**

spokesperson ['spoʊks·pɜr·sən] *n* portavoz *mf*, vocero, -a *m, f AmL*

sponge [spʌndʒ] **I.** *n* **1. a.** ZOOL esponja *f* **2.** (*person*) gorrón, -ona *m, f* **II.** *vi* gorronear

◆ **sponge down** *vt* limpiar con una esponja

◆ **sponge off** *vt inf* vivir a costa de

sponge cake *n* bizcocho *m*

sponger *n* gorrón, -ona *m, f*, sablero, -a *m, f Chile*

sponsor ['span·sər] **I.** *vt* patrocinar **II.** *n* patrocinador(a) *m(f)*, propiciador(a) *m(f) AmL*

spontaneous [span·'teɪ·ni·əs] *adj* espontáneo, -a

spooky ['spu·ki] <-ier, -iest> *adj inf* que da miedo

spoon [spun] *n* cuchara *f*; (*amount*) cucharada *f*

spoonful ['spun·fʊl] <-s *or* spoonfuls> *n* cucharada *f*

sport [spɔrt] *n* **1.** deporte *m* **2. to be a good/poor ~** ser buena/mala gente; GAMES, SPORTS ser buen/mal perdedor

sporting *adj* deportivo, -a, esportivo, -a *AmL*

sports car *n* deportivo *m*

sportsman ['spɔrts·mən] *n* deportista *m*

sportsmanship *n* deportividad *f*

sports page *n* página *f* de deportes

sportswear *n* ropa *f* de deporte

sportswoman ['spɔrts·wʊm·ən] *n* deportista *f*

sporty ['spɔr·ti] <-ier, -iest> *adj* deportivo, -a

spot [spat] **I.** *n* **1.** (*mark*) mancha *f* **2.** (*pattern*) lunar *m* **3.** (*skin*) grano *m* **4.** (*place*) lugar *m*; **on the ~** in situ; (*at once*) en el acto **5.** TV, RADIO espacio *m* ▶ to **really hit the ~** venir de perlas; **to have a soft ~** tener debilidad (**for** por); **to put sb on the ~** poner a alguien en un aprieto **II.** <-tt-> *vt* **1.** (*see*) divisar **2.** (*speckle*) manchar

spot check *n* control *m* al azar

spotless ['spat·lɪs] *adj* inmaculado, -a

spotlight ['spat·laɪt] **I.** *n* foco *m* ▶ **to be in the ~** ser el centro de atención **II.** <spotlighted *or* spotlit, spotlighted *or* spotlit> *vt* iluminar

spotted *adj* con manchas; (*pattern*) de lunares

spotty ['spat·i] <-ier, -iest> *adj* **1.** (*skin*) con granos **2.** (*inconsistent*) irregular

spout [spaʊt] **I.** *n* (*kettle*) pitorro *m*; (*jar*) pico *m*; (*tube*) caño *m*; (*jet*) chorro *m* **II.** *vt* **1.** echar **2.** *pej* perorar sobre **III.** *vi* **1.** chorrear **2.** *pej* perorar

sprain [spreɪn] **I.** *vt* torcer **II.** *n* torcedura *f*

sprang [spræŋ] *vi, vt pt of* **spring**

sprawl [sprɔl] *vi pej* (*person*) respantigarse; (*town*) extenderse; **to send sb ~ing** derribar a alguien

sprawling *adj* (*town*) de crecimiento descontrolado; (*handwriting*) irregular

spray¹ [spreɪ] **I.** *n* **1.** (*mist*) rocío *m* **2.** (*device*) spray *m* **II.** *vt* rociar **III.** *vi* chorrear

spray² [spreɪ] *n* rama *f*; **a ~ of flowers** un ramo de flores

spread [spred] **I.** *n* **1.** (*difusion*) propagación *f* **2.** (*range*) gama *f* **3.** (*meal*) comilona *f* **II.** <spread, spread> *vt* (*news*) difundir; (*disease*) propagar; (*butter*) untar; (*payments, work*) distribuir; (*map, blanket*) extender **III.** <spread, spread> *vi* (*news*) difundirse; (*disease*) propagarse; (*liquid*) extenderse

spreadsheet ['spred·ʃit] *n* hoja *f* de cálculo

spree [spri] *n* parranda *f*; tambarria *f AmC*; **to go on a drinking ~** ir de juerga

sprightly ['spraɪt·li] <-ier, -iest> *adj* vivaz

spring [sprɪŋ] **I.** *n* **1.** (*season*) primavera *f* **2.** (*jump*) salto *m* **3.** (*metal*) muelle *m* **4.** (*water*) manantial *m* **II.** <sprang, sprung> *vi* saltar; **to ~ to one's feet** levantarse de un salto; **to ~ shut/open** cerrarse/abrirse de golpe

springboard ['sprɪŋ·bɔrd] *n* trampolín *m*

spring-clean [ˌsprɪŋ·'klin] *vt* limpiar a fondo

spring roll *n* CULIN rollito *m* de primavera

springy ['sprɪŋ·i] <-ier, -iest> *adj* elástico, -a

sprinkle ['sprɪŋ·kəl] **I.** *vt* salpicar **II.** *n* salpicadura *f*

sprinkling ['sprɪŋ·klɪŋ] *n* **a ~** unas gotas (**of** de)

sprint [sprɪnt] SPORTS **I.** *vi* esprintar **II.** *n* (*race*) esprint *m*

sprinter ['sprɪn·tər] *n* velocista *mf*

sprout [spraʊt] **I.** *n* **1.** brote *m* **2.** *pl* (*Brussels sprouts*) coles *m pl* de Bruselas **II.** *vi* brotar **III.** *vt* echar

spruce¹ [sprus] *n* BOT picea *f*

spruce² [sprus] *adj* (*neat*) aseado, -a

sprung [sprʌŋ] *pp, Am: pt of* **spring**

spud [spʌd] *n* papa *f*

spun [spʌn] *pp, pt of* **spin**

spur [spɜr] **I.** <-rr-> *vt fig* estimular **II.** *n* espuela *f*; *fig* estímulo *m* ▶ **on the ~ of the moment** sin pensarlo

spurt [spɜrt] **I.** *n* (*jet*) chorro *m* **II.** *vi* **1.** (*gush*) salir a chorros **2.** (*accelerate*) acelerar

spy [spaɪ] **I.** *n* espía *mf* **II.** *vi* espiar (**on** a); **to ~ on sb** espiar a alguien

squabble ['skwab·əl] **I.** *n* riña *f* **II.** *vi* reñir

squad [skwad] *n* (*group*) pelotón *m*; (*police*) brigada *f*; SPORTS equipo *m*

squalid ['skwal·ɪd] *adj* **1.** (*dirty*) asqueroso, -a **2.** (*sordid*) sórdido, -a

squander ['skwan·dər] *vt* malgastar, fundir *AmL*; (*opportunity*) desperdiciar

square [skwer] **I.** *n* **1.** *a.* MATH cuadrado *m*; (*in town*) plaza *f* **2.** (*tool*) escuadra *f* ▶ **to go back to ~ one** volver al punto de partida **II.** *adj* **1.** cuadra-

S

do, -a; forty-three ~ feet cuatro metros cuadrados; **a ~ deal** un trato justo **2.** (*even*) en paz **3. be there or be ~** si no lo haces, eres un muermo **III.** *vt* cuadrar; (*settle*) acomodar; (*accounts*) saldar; MATH elevar al cuadrado **IV.** *vi* concordar (**with** con)

square root *n* raíz *f* cuadrada

squash¹ [skwɑʃ] *n* BOT calabaza *f*

squash² [skwɑʃ] **I.** *n* **1.** SPORTS squash *m* **2.** (*dense pack*) apiñamiento *m* **II.** *vt* aplastar

squashy ['skwɑʃ·i] <-ier, -iest> *adj* blando, -a

squat [skwɑt] **I.** <-tt-> *vi* **1.** (*crouch down*) agacharse, ñangotarse *PRico, RDom* **2.** (*property*) ocupar **II.** *n* **1.** (*exercise*) sentadilla *f* **2.** *sl* **to not know ~** no tener ni idea **III.** <-tt-> *adj* (*person*) rechoncho, -a

squatter ['skwɑt·ər] *n* ocupador, -a *m, f*

squeak [skwik] **I.** *n* chirrido *m* **II.** *vi* chirriar

squeal [skwil] **I.** *n* chillido *m* **II.** *vi* **1.** chillar; (*brakes, car*) chirriar **2.** (*inform*) chivarse

squeamish ['skwi·mɪʃ] *adj* remilgado, -a; **to feel ~** sentir náuseas

squeeze [skwiz] **I.** *n* **1.** estrujón *m;* **to put the ~ on** apretar **2.** ECON restricción *f* **II.** *vt* **1.** (*press together*) estrujar; **freshly ~d juice** zumo recién exprimido **2.** (*force*) presionar; **to ~ sth out of sb** sacar algo a alguien

squelch [skweltʃ] **I.** *vi* chapotear **II.** *vt* aplastar **III.** *n* chapoteo *m*

squid [skwɪd] <-(s)> *n* calamar *m*

squiggle ['skwɪg·əl] **I.** *n* garabato *m* **II.** *vi* garabatear

squint [skwɪnt] **I.** *vi* (*cross-eyed*) bizquear; (*partly closed eyes*) mirar con los ojos entrecerrados **II.** *n* **1.** bizquera *f AmL* **2.** (*quick look*) mirada *f* furtiva

squirm [skwɜrm] *vi* retorcerse; **he ~ed with embarrassment** se le caía la cara de vergüenza

squirrel ['skwɜr·əl] *n* ardilla *f*

squirt [skwɜrt] **I.** *vt* echar un chorreón de **II.** *vi* chorrear **III.** *n* **1.** chorrito *m* **2.** (*person*) farsante *mf*

stab [stæb] **I.** <-bb-> *vt* apuñalar, achurar *CSur*, carnear *Méx;* **to ~ sb in the back** dar a alguien una puñalada trapera **II.** *n* **1.** (*blow*) puñalada *f* **2.** (*pain*) punzada *f* **3. to take a ~ at** (*doing*) sth intentar (hacer) algo

stabbing I. *n* apuñalamiento *m* **II.** *adj* punzante

stability [stə·'bɪl·ə·t̬i] *n* estabilidad *f*

stabilize ['ster·bə·laɪz] **I.** *vt* estabilizar **II.** *vi* estabilizarse

stable¹ ['ster·bəl] *adj a.* ECON, MED estable; (*structure*) firme

stable² ['ster·bəl] *n* cuadra *f*

stack [stæk] **I.** *vt* apilar; (*shelves*) llenar ▶ **the cards are ~ed against us** la suerte está en contra nuestra **II.** *n* **1.** (*pile*) pila *f* **2.** (*large amount*) montón *m*, ponchada *f CSur* **3.** *pl* (*bookcase*) estantería *f*

stadium ['ster·di·əm] <-s *or* -dia> *n* estadio *m*

staff [stæf] *n* **1.** (*employees*) personal *m*, elenco *m AmL* **2.** (*stick*) bastón *m;* **~ of office** bastón de mando **3.** (*flagpole*) asta *f* **4.** <staves> MUS pentagrama *m*

stag [stæg] *n* ZOOL ciervo *m*

stage [steɪdʒ] **I.** *n* **1.** (*period*) etapa *f*, pascana *f AmS;* **at this ~ in my life** en esta etapa de mi vida; **in ~s** por etapas **2.** THEAT escena *f;* **the ~** el teatro; **to be on the ~** ser actor/actriz **II.** *vt* **1.** THEAT representar **2.** (*organize*) organizar

stage fright *n* miedo *m* escénico

stagger ['stæg·ər] **I.** *vi* tambalearse **II.** *vt* **1.** (*amaze*) asombrar **2.** (*work, payments*) escalonar **III.** *n* tambaleo *m*

staggering *adj* sorprendente

stagnant ['stæg·nənt] *adj* estancado, -a

stagnate ['stæg·neɪt] *vi* estancarse

stain [steɪn] **I.** *vt* manchar; (*dye*) teñir **II.** *vi* mancharse **II.** *n* **1.** (*mark*) mancha *f;* **grease ~** mancha de grasa **2.** (*dye*) tinte *m*

stained *adj* (*marked*) manchado, -a

stainless ['steɪn·lɪs] **I.** *adj* sin mancha **II.** *n* acero *m* inoxidable

stair [ster] *n* peldaño *m; pl* escalera *f*

staircase ['ster·keɪs] *n*, **stairway** ['ster·weɪ] *n* escalera *f*

stake [steɪk] **I.** *n* **1.** (*stick*) estaca *f*

2. (*share*) participación *f;* **to have a ~** tener interés (**in** en) **3.** (*bet*) apuesta *f;* **to play for high ~s** arriesgar mucho; **to be at ~** estar en juego **II.** *vt* (*bet*) apostar; **to ~ one's life** poner la mano en el fuego (**on** por); **to ~ a claim to** reivindicar

stakeholder ['steɪk,hoʊl,dər] *n* tenedor(a) *m(f)* de apuestas

stale [steɪl] *adj* **1.** (*not fresh*) pasado, -a; (*bread*) duro, -a; (*air*) viciado, -a; (*joke*) viejo, -a **2.** (*tired*) cansado, -a

stalk¹ [stɔk] *n* BOT tallo *m;* **her eyes were out on ~s** se le salían los ojos de las órbitas

stalk² [stɔk] **I.** *vt* (*follow*) acechar **II.** *vi* **to ~ off** marcharse airadamente

stall [stɔl] **I.** *n* **1.** (*animals*) establo *m* **2.** (*market*) puesto *m*, tarantín *m* Ven **3.** AUTO calado *m* **4. shower ~** cabina para ducharse; **toilet ~** urinario *m* **II.** *vi* **1.** AUTO calarse **2.** (*delay*) ir con rodeos; **to ~ for time** intentar ganar tiempo **III.** *vt* **1.** AUTO calar **2.** *inf* (*keep waiting*) retener

stamina ['stæm·ə·nə] *n* resistencia *f*

stammer ['stæm·ər] **I.** *vi*, *vt* tartamudear **II.** *n* tartamudeo *m*

stamp [stæmp] **I.** *n* **1.** sello *m*, estampilla *f* AmL **2.** (*character*) impronta *f* **3.** (*with foot*) pisotón *m* **II.** *vt* **1.** (*post*) pegar un sello en **2.** (*mark*) estampar **III.** *vi* patalear

stampede [stæm·'pid] **I.** *n* estampida *f;* (*people*) desbandada *f* **II.** *vi* huir en desbandada

stance [stæns] *n* postura *f*

stand [stænd] **I.** *n* **1.** (*position*) posición *f;* **to make a ~** oponer resistencia (**against** a) **2.** *pl* (*stadium*) tribuna *f* **3.** (*support, frame*) soporte *m* **4.** (*market*) puesto *m*, trucha *f* AmC **5.** AUTO parada *f;* **taxi ~** parada de taxis **6. witness ~** estrado *m* II. <stood, stood> *vi* **1.** (*be upright*) estar de pie; **to ~ 6 feet tall** medir dos metros; **to ~ still** estarse quieto **2.** (*be located*) encontrarse **3.** (*decision, law*) mantenerse en vigor **III.** <stood, stood> *vt* **1.** (*place*) colocar **2.** (*bear*) aguantar; **I can't ~ her** no la soporto **3. to ~ trial** ser juzgado

◆**stand about** *vi*, **stand around** *vi* esperar

◆**stand aside** *vi* **1.** (*move*) apartarse **2.** (*stay*) mantenerse aparte

◆**stand back** *vi* **1.** (*move*) retroceder **2.** (*be objective*) distanciarse

◆**stand by** **I.** *vi* **1.** (*observe*) mantenerse al margen **2.** (*be ready*) estar alerta **II.** *vt* (*support*) apoyar

◆**stand down** *vi* renunciar

◆**stand for** *vt* **1.** (*represent*) representar; (*mean*) significar **2.** (*tolerate*) aguantar

◆**stand in** *vi* suplir (**for** a)

◆**stand out** *vi* destacar

◆**stand over** *vt* vigilar

◆**stand up** **I.** *vi* levantarse, arriscarse Col; (*evidence, argument*) ser convincente ▶ **to ~ and be counted** declararse abiertamente **II.** *vt* dar plantón

standard ['stæn·dərd] **I.** *n* **1.** (*level*) nivel *m;* (*quality*) clase *f* **2.** (*norm*) norma *f* **3.** (*flag*) estandarte *m* **II.** *adj* normal; (*procedure*) habitual; LING estándar

standardize ['stæn·dər·daɪz] *vt* estandarizar; TECH normalizar

standby ['stænd·baɪ] **I.** *n* **1.** (*money, food*) reserva *f* **2.** AVIAT lista *f* de espera **II.** *adj* de reserva

stand-in ['stænd·ɪn] *n* suplente *mf;* CINE doble *mf*

standing ['stæn·dɪŋ] **I.** *n* **1.** (*status*) posición *f* **2.** (*duration*) duración *f;* **of long ~** desde hace mucho **II.** *adj* **1.** (*upright*) vertical **2.** (*permanent*) permanente; (*water*) estancado, -a

standpoint ['stænd·pɔɪnt] *n* punto *m* de vista

standstill ['stænd·stɪl] *n* paralización *f;* **to be at a ~** estar parado

stank [stæŋk] *pt of* **stink**

staple¹ ['steɪ·pəl] **I.** *n* **1.** (*product*) producto *m* principal **2.** (*food*) alimento *m* de primera necesidad **3.** (*component*) elemento *m* esencial **II.** *adj* principal; (*standard*) corriente

staple² ['steɪ·pəl] **I.** *n* (*fastener*) grapa *f* **II.** *vt* grapar

stapler ['steɪp·lər] *n* grapadora *f*

star [star] **I.** *n* **1.** ASTRON estrella *f* **2.** TYPO asterisco *m* **3.** (*celebrity*) famo-

S

so, -a *m, f*; **a movie ~** una estrella de cine ▸ **to thank one's lucky ~s** dar las gracias a Dios; **to reach for the ~s** apuntar a lo más alto; **to see ~s** ver las estrellas II. *vt* <-rr-> 1. THEAT, CINE tener como protagonista 2. (*mark*) señalar con un asterisco

starboard ['star·bərd] I. *n* estribor *m* II. *adj* de estribor

starch [startʃ] *n* almidón *m*; CULIN fécula *f*

starchy ['star·tʃi] <-ier, -iest> *adj* (*food*) rico, -a en almidón; (*person*) estirado, -a

stardom ['star·dəm] *n* estrellato *m*, estelaridad *f* Chile

stare [ster] I. *vi* mirar fijamente II. *vt* mirar fijamente; **to ~ sb in the face** *fig* saltar a la vista III. *n* mirada *f* fija

staring ['ster·ɪŋ] *adj* que mira fijamente; (*eyes*) desorbitado, -a

stark [stark] I. *adj* 1. (*desolate*) severo, -a; (*landscape*) inhóspito, -a 2. (*austere*) austero, -a 3. (*complete*) absoluto, -a; **a ~ contrast** un fuerte contraste II. *adv* **~ naked** en cueros, empelotado, -a *AmL*; **~ raving mad** loco de atar

starry-eyed ['star·i·ˌaɪd] *adj* soñador(a)

star-studded *adj* (*sky*) estrellado, -a; (*film*) lleno, -a de estrellas; (*cast*) estelar

start [start] I. *vi* 1. (*begin*) comenzar; **to ~ to do sth** empezar a hacer algo 2. (*begin journey*) salir (**from** de) 3. (*vehicle, motor*) arrancar 4. (*begin at level*) empezar 5. (*jump*) sobresaltarse (**at** con) II. *vt* 1. (*begin*) comenzar; **we ~ work at 6:30** entramos a trabajar a las 6:30 2. (*set in operation*) poner en marcha; (*car*) arrancar; (*business*) abrir ▸ **to ~ something** *inf* crear problemas III. *n* 1. (*beginning*) principio *m*; **to make an early/a late/a fresh ~** empezar temprano/tarde/de nuevo 2. SPORTS (*place*) salida *f*; (*time*) inicio *m* 3. (*jump*) sobresalto *m*; **to give a ~** dar un respingo; **to give sb a ~** dar un susto a alguien

◆ **start back** *vi* 1. (*jump back*) retroceder de un salto 2. (*journey*) emprender el regreso

◆ **start off** I. *vi* empezar; (*journey*) partir; (*train, plane*) salir II. *vt* empezar; **to start sb off** ayudar a alguien (**on** a)

◆ **start out** *vi* 1. (*begin*) empezar; **to ~ to do sth** ponerse a hacer algo 2. (*journey*) partir; (*train, plane*) salir

◆ **start up** I. *vt* (*organization, business*) fundar; (*vehicle, motor*) arrancar II. *vi* 1. (*vehicle, motor*) arrancar 2. (*open*) abrir 3. (*jump up*) levantarse de un salto

starter *n* 1. AUTO estárter *m* 2. CULIN entrante *m* 3. SPORTS titular *mf* ▸ **for ~s** *inf* para empezar

starting *adj* de comienzo

startle ['star·təl] *vt* sobresaltar

startling *adj* asombroso, -a; (*alarming*) alarmante

starvation [star·'veɪ·ʃən] *n* hambre *m o f*; **to die of ~** morir de hambre

starve [starv] I. *vi* pasar hambre, hambrear *AmL*; (*die*) *a. fig* morirse de hambre II. *vt* privar

stash [stæʃ] I. *vt* ocultar II. *n* <-es> *inf* 1. (*place*) escondite *m* 2. (*cache*) alijo *m*

state [steɪt] I. *n* 1. (*condition*) estado *m*; **~ of mind/war** estado de ánimo/guerra; **solid/liquid ~** estado sólido/líquido 2. (*nation*) estado *m* 3. *pl, inf* the **States** los Estados Unidos II. *adj* estatal; (*secret*) de Estado *m* III. *vt* declarar; LAW exponer

State Department *n* Departamento *m* de Estado, ≈ Ministerio *m* de Asuntos Exteriores

stateless ['steɪt·lɪs] *adj* apátrida

statement ['steɪt·mənt] *n* 1. declaración *f*; **to make a ~** LAW prestar declaración 2. (*bank*) extracto *m* de cuenta

state of the art [ˌsteɪt·əv·ði·'art] *adj* moderno, -a; (*technology*) punta *inv*

station ['steɪ·ʃən] I. *n* 1. RAIL estación *f* 2. (*place*) sitio *m*; **police ~** comisaría *f*; **gas ~** gasolinera *f*; **research ~** centro *m* de investigación 3. RADIO emisora *f*; TV canal *m* II. *vt* colocar; MIL destinar

stationary ['steɪ·ʃə·ner·i] *adj* (*not moving*) inmóvil

stationery ['steɪ·ʃə·ner·i] *n* artículos *m pl* de papelería

station wagon *n* monovolumen *m*

statistics [stə·'tɪs·tɪks] *n* **1.** (*science*) estadística *f* **2.** *pl* estadísticas

statue ['stætʃ·u] *n* estatua *f*

Statue of Liberty *n* **the ~** la Estatua de la Libertad

status ['steɪ·təs] *n* **1.** (*official position*) estatus *m* **2.** (*prestige*) prestigio *m*

stay [steɪ] **I.** *vi* **1.** (*not leave*) quedarse; **to ~ in bed** guardar cama **2.** (*reside temporarily*) alojarse **3.** (*remain*) permanecer; **to ~ friends** seguir siendo amigos **II.** *vt* (*endure*) resistir; (*hunger, thirst*) aplacar; **to ~ the course** [*or* **distance**] aguantar hasta el final **III.** *n* estancia *f*, estada *f AmL*

◆**stay away** *vi* ausentarse; **to ~ from** mantenerse alejado de

◆**stay behind** *vi* quedarse

◆**stay in** *vi* quedarse en casa

◆**stay out** *vi* no volver a casa; **to ~ all night** pasar toda la noche fuera

◆**stay up** *vi* no acostarse; **to ~ late** acostarse tarde

staying power *n* resistencia *f*

STD [ˌes·tiˈdi] *n abbr of* **sexually transmitted disease** ETS *f*

steady ['sted·i] **I.** <-ier, -iest> *adj* **1.** (*stable*) estable; (*job*) fijo, -a; (*temperature, speed*) constante **2.** (*regular*) regular; (*boyfriend*) formal **3.** (*hand*) firme **4.** (*calm*) sereno, -a **II.** *vt* **1.** (*stabilize*) estabilizar **2.** (*calm*) calmar **III.** *adv* **to be going ~** ser novios formales **IV.** *interj* cuidado

steak [steɪk] *n* (*fry, grill*) bistec *m*, bife *m AmL*; (*stew, mince*) carne *f* de ternera; (*lamb, fish*) filete *m*

steal [stil] **I.** <stole, stolen> *vt* robar, cachar *AmC*; **to ~ a glance** echar una mirada furtiva (**at** a) ▶ **to ~ the show** llevarse todos los aplausos **II.** <stole, stolen> *vi* robar; **to ~ in** entrar a hurtadillas; **to ~ away** escabullirse **III.** *n* ganga *f*; **to be a ~** ser una ganga

steam [stim] **I.** *n* vapor *m*; **to run out of ~** *fig* perder fuerza ▶ **to let off ~** desahogarse **II.** *adj* de vapor **III.** *vi* echar vapor **IV.** *vt* cocer al vapor

◆**steam up** *vi* empañarse; **to get steamed up** *inf* acalorarse (**about** por)

steamer ['sti·mər] *n* **1.** (*boat*) barco *m* de

vapor **2.** CULIN vaporera *f*

steamy ['sti·mi] <-ier, -iest> *adj* **1.** (*full of steam*) lleno, -a de vapor; (*very humid*) húmedo, -a **2.** (*sexy*) erótico, -a

steel [stil] **I.** *n* acero *m*; **nerves of ~** nervios de acero **II.** *adj* de acero **III.** *vt* **to ~ oneself** armarse de valor (**for** para)

steep[1] [stip] *adj* **1.** (*sloping*) empinado, -a **2.** (*increase, fall*) pronunciado, -a; **that's a bit ~!** ¡no hay derecho! **3.** (*expensive*) exorbitante

steep[2] [stip] **I.** *vt* remojar; **to be ~ed in history** tener mucha historia **II.** *vi* **to leave sth to ~** dejar algo en remojo

steeple ['sti·pəl] *n* torre *f*; **church ~** campanario

steer[1] [stɪr] **I.** *vt* (*direct*) dirigir; (*guide*) guiar; (*car*) conducir, manejar *AmL* **II.** *vi* (*person*) conducir, manejar *AmL*; (*vehicle*) manejarse; NAUT poner rumbo (**for** a); **to ~ clear of** evitar

steer[2] [stɪr] *n* ZOOL novillo *m*; (*castrated*) buey *m*

steering wheel *n* (*car*) volante *m*, guía *f PRico*; (*ship*) timón *m*

stem [stem] **I.** *n* **1.** (*plant*) tallo *m* **2.** (*glass*) pie *m* **3.** LING raíz *f* **II.** <-mm-> *vt* (*stop*) detener **III.** <-mm-> *vi* **to ~ from** resultar de

step [step] **I.** *n* **1.** paso *m*; (*footprint*) huella *f*; **to take a ~** dar un paso; *fig* dirigirse (**towards** hacia); **~ by ~** paso a paso; **to be in/out of ~** llevar/no llevar el paso; *fig* estar/no estar al tanto; **to watch one's ~** andar con cuidado; **watch your ~!** ¡mira por dónde pisas! **2.** (*stair*) peldaño *m* **3.** (*measure*) medida *f*; **to take ~s** tomar medidas (**to** para) **4.** MUS **whole/half ~** tono/semitono *m* **II.** <-pp-> *vi* **1.** (*tread*) pisar **2.** (*walk*) caminar

◆**step aside** *vi* hacerse a un lado

◆**step back** *vi* **1.** (*move back*) retroceder **2.** (*gain new perspective*) distanciarse

◆**step down I.** *vi* renunciar (**from** a) **II.** *vt* reducir

◆**step in** *vi* intervenir

◆**step up I.** *vt* aumentar **II.** *vi* dar la cara

stepbrother *n* hermanastro *m*

stepchild *n* hijastro, -a *m, f*

S

stepdaughter *n* hijastra *f*

stepfather *n* padrastro *m*

stepladder ['step·ˌlæd·ər] *n* escalera *f* de mano

stepmother ['step·ˌmʌð·ər] *n* madrastra *f*

stepping stone ['step·ɪŋ·stoʊn] *n* pasadera *f*; *fig* trampolín *m*

stepson ['step·sʌn] *n* hijastro *m*

stereo ['ster·i·oʊ] **I.** *n* (*hi-fi*) equipo *m* estéreo; **in** ~ en estéreo **II.** *adj* estéreo

stereotype ['ster·i·ə·taɪp] **I.** *n* estereotipo *m* **II.** *vt* estereotipar

sterile ['ster·əl] *adj* estéril

sterilize ['ster·ə·laɪz] *vt* esterilizar

sterling ['stɜr·lɪŋ] **I.** *n* (*metal*) plata *f* de ley **II.** *adj* excelente; **pound** ~ libra esterlina

stern¹ [stɜrn] *adj* estricto, -a; (*warning*) terminante

stern² [stɜrn] *n* NAUT popa *f*

stew [stu] **I.** *n* estofado *m*, hervido *m* AmS ▶ **to be in a** ~ sudar la gota gorda **II.** *vt* (*meat*) estofar; (*fruit*) hacer compota de **III.** *vi* cocer

stick¹ [stɪk] *n* **1.** (*wood*) a. SPORTS palo *m*; (*celery, rhubarb*) tallo *f*; (*deodorant, glue*) barra *f* **2.** **walking** ~ bastón *m* **3.** MUS batuta *f* **4.** **in the** ~s en el quinto pino ▶ **to get the wrong end of the** ~ coger el rábano por las hojas

stick² [stɪk] <stuck, stuck> **I.** *vi* pegarse; (*person*) quedarse parado; (*door, window*) atascarse; (*mechanism*) bloquearse; **to** ~ **in sb's mind** quedarse grabado a alguien **II.** *vt* **1.** (*affix*) pegar **2.** *inf* (*put*) poner; **to** ~ **one's head out the window** asomar la cabeza por la ventana

◆**stick around** *vi* acoplarse

◆**stick in** *vt* meter; (*knife, needle*) clavar

◆**stick out I.** *vt* asomar; **to stick one's tongue out** sacar la lengua (**at** a) ▶ **to stick one's neck out** arriesgarse **II.** *vi* **1.** (*nail, ears*) sobresalir **2.** (*be obvious*) ser evidente; **to** ~ **like a sore thumb** saltar a la vista **3.** **to stick it out** aguantar

◆**stick together I.** *vi* **1.** (*remain loyal*) mantenerse unidos **2.** (*not separate*)

no separarse **3.** (*adhere*) juntarse **II.** *vt* juntar

◆**stick up I.** *vt inf* (*rob*) atracar; **stick 'em up!** ¡manos arriba! **II.** *vi* sobresalir; (*hair*) estar de punta

sticker ['stɪk·ər] *n* pegatina *f*

stick-on ['stɪk·an] *adj* adhesivo, -a

sticky ['stɪk·i] <-ier, -iest> *adj* (*label*) adhesivo, -a; (*surface, hands*) pegajoso, -a; (*weather*) bochornoso, -a

stiff [stɪf] **I.** *n* fiambre *m* **II.** *adj* **1.** (*rigid, hard*) duro, -a; (*shirt*) tieso, -a; **to be (as)** ~ **as a board** estar más tieso que un palo **2.** (*joints*) entumecido, -a; (*muscles*) agarrotado, -a; **to have a** ~ **neck** tener tortícolis **3.** (*strong*) fuerte **4.** (*strenuous*) agotador(a) **5.** (*price*) exorbitante **III.** *adv* **to be bored** ~ estar aburrido como una ostra; **to be scared** ~ estar muerto de miedo

stiffen ['stɪf·ən] **I.** *vi* **1.** (*get tense: person*) ponerse tenso; (*muscles*) agarrotarse **2.** (*get dense*) espesarse **II.** *vt* (*penalties*) endurecer; (*competition*) hacer más difícil; (*morals*) fortalecer

stifle ['staɪ·fəl] **I.** *vt* sofocar; (*yawn, scream, desire*) contener; (*initiative, opposition*) reprimir **II.** *vi* sofocarse; (*lack of air*) ahogarse

stifling ['staɪ·flɪŋ] *adj* (*heat*) sofocante; (*room*) agobiante

still¹ [stɪl] **I.** *adj* (*calm*) tranquilo, -a; (*wind, waters*) en calma; **to keep** ~ quedarse quieto **II.** *n* CINE, PHOT fotograma *m* **III.** *vt* (*calm*) calmar

still² [stɪl] *adv* **1.** aún, todavía; **to be** ~ **alive** seguir vivo; **to want** ~ **more** querer aún más; **better** ~ aún mejor **2.** (*nevertheless*) sin embargo

still³ [stɪl] *n* (*distillery*) destilería *f*

stillborn ['stɪl·bɔrn] *adj* **1.** (*born dead*) nacido, -a muerto, -a **2.** (*unsuccessful*) malogrado, -a

stilted ['stɪl·tɪd] *adj* (*manner, style*) forzado, -a

stimulate ['stɪm·jə·leɪt] *vt* a. MED estimular

stimulus ['stɪm·jə·ləs] <-li> *n* estímulo *m*

sting [stɪŋ] **I.** *vt* **1.** (*with poison*) picar **2.** (*goad*) incitar **II.** <stung, stung> *vi*

1. (*with poison*) picar **2.** (*ache*) escocer; (*criticism*) herir **III.** n **1.** (*injury*) picotazo m **2.** (*pain*) escozor m; ~ of **remorse** remordimientos mpl

stingy ['stɪn·dʒi] <-ier, -iest> adj tacaño, -a, pijotero, -a AmL, amarrado, -a Arg, Par, PRico, Urug, coñete Chile, Perú, (*amount*) mísero, -a

stink [stɪŋk] **I.** n mal olor m; fig escándalo m; **to create a ~** montar un escándalo **II.** <stank or stunk, stunk> vi **1.** (*smell*) bufar AmL; **to ~ of money** estar podrido de dinero **2.** (*be bad*) ser patético, -a **3.** (*business, situation*) oler mal

stinker ['stɪn·kər] n inf asco m; (*person*) canalla mf

stipulate ['stɪp·jə·leɪt] vt estipular

stipulation [ˌstɪp·jə·'leɪ·ʃən] n estipulación f; **with the ~ that** a condición de que +subj

stir [stɜr] **I.** <-ring, -red> vt **1.** (*mix*) remover; (*fire*) avivar **2.** (*move*) mover **3.** (*stimulate*) estimular; (*trouble*) provocar **II.** vi **1.** (*mix*) mezclar **2.** (*move*) agitarse **3.** (*rouse*) despertarse **III.** n **1. to give sth a ~** remover algo **2.** (*excitement*) conmoción f; **to cause a ~** causar revuelo

stir-fry ['stɜr·fraɪ] <-ied, -ies> vt freír en poco aceite y removiendo constantemente

stirring adj conmovedor(a)

stitch [stɪtʃ] **I.** <-es> n (*knitting*) a. MED punto m; (*sewing*) puntada f; **cross ~** punto de cruz ► **to leave sb in ~es** hacer que alguien se tronche de risa **II.** vi, vt coser

stock [stak] **I.** n **1.** reserva f **2.** COM, ECON existencias fpl; **to have sth in ~** tener algo en stock; **to be out of ~** estar agotado; **to take ~** hacer el inventario; fig hacer un balance **3.** FIN acción f **4.** AGR, ZOOL ganado m **5.** (*descent*) linaje m **6.** (*popularity*) prestigio m; **her ~ had fallen/risen** había perdido/ganado prestigio **7. to put (no) ~ in sth** (no) dar crédito a algo **II.** adj (*model*) estándar; (*response*) típico, -a **III.** vt (*goods*) vender; (*shop*) suministrar; (*shelves*) llenar

stockbroker ['stak·ˌbroʊ·kər] n corredor(a) m(f) de bolsa

stock exchange n bolsa f

stocking ['stak·ɪŋ] n media f

stock market n mercado m bursátil

stockpile ['stak·paɪl] **I.** n reservas fpl **II.** vt almacenar

stocky ['stak·i] <-ier, -iest> adj bajo, -a y fornido, -a

stodgy ['stadʒ·i] <-ier, -iest> adj (*food*) pesado, -a; (*person, book*) aburrido, -a

stoke [stoʊk] vt (*fire*) atizar; (*furnace*) echar leña; fig avivar

stole[1] [stoʊl] pt of **steal**

stole[2] [stoʊl] n FASHION estola f

stomach ['stʌm·ək] **I.** n **1.** estómago m; **to have an upset ~** tener mal el estómago; **to have a strong ~** tener estómago **2.** (*belly*) barriga f **II.** vt inf (*drink, food*) tolerar; (*person, insult*) soportar

stone [stoʊn] **I.** n **1.** GEO piedra f; **to be a ~'s throw (away)** estar a tiro de piedra **2.** MED cálculo m **3.** (*jewel*) gema f **4.** (*fruit*) hueso m, carozo m CSur ► **to cast the first ~** tirar la primera piedra; **to leave no ~ unturned** no dejar piedra por mover; **to be carved** [or **set**] **in ~** estar grabado en piedra **II.** adv ~ **hard** duro, -a como una piedra; ~ **crazy** loco de remate

Stone Age n Edad f de Piedra

stone-cold I. adj helado, -a **II.** adv **to knock sb out ~** dejar de piedra; **to be ~ sober** no haber bebido ni una gota

stoned adj fumado, -a

stony ['stoʊ·ni] <-ier, -iest> adj (*beach, ground*) pedregoso, -a; (*expression*) frío, -a; (*silence*) sepulcral; (*feelings*) de piedra

stood [stʊd] pt, pp of **stand**

stool [stul] n (*seat*) taburete m

stoop[1] [stup] vi ARCHIT inclinarse; **to ~ to sth** rebajarse a algo; **to ~ low** caer (muy) bajo

stoop[2] [stup] n pórtico m

stop [stap] **I.** n **1.** pausa f; **to come to a ~** detenerse; **to put a ~** poner fin (**to** a) **2.** (*place*) parada f ► **to pull out (all) the ~s** desplegar todos los recursos **II.** <-ping, -ped> vt **1.** (*cease*) parar; (*payment*) suspender **2.** (*switch off*) apagar **3.** (*block*) rellenar; (*hole, ears*) tapar **III.** <- ping, -ped> *vi* pararse; (*car*) detenerse; **to ~ doing sth** dejar de hacer algo; **to ~ and think** (**about**) pararse a pensar

◆**stop by** *vi* pasar por

◆**stop in** *vi* quedarse en casa

◆**stop off** *vi* detenerse un rato

◆**stop over** *vi* pasarse por

◆**stop up** *vt* (*block*) atascar; (*hole*) tapar; (*gap*) rellenar

stopover ['stap·ou·vər] *n* parada *f*; AVIAT escala *f*

stop sign *n* stop *m*, alto *m* *Méx*

stopwatch *n* cronómetro *m*

storage ['stɔr·ɪdʒ] *n a.* COMPUT almacenamiento *m*; **to put sth in ~** almacenar algo

store [stɔr] **I.** *n* **1.** (*shop*) tienda *f*; **department ~** grandes almacenes *mpl*, emporio *m* *AmC* **2.** (*supply*) provisión *f*; (*wine*) reserva *f* **3.** (*warehouse*) almacén *m*; **what is in ~ for us?** ¿qué nos deparará el futuro? **II.** *vt* **1.** (*into storage*) almacenar **2.** (*for future use*) guardar **3.** COMPUT (*file*) guardar; (*data*) almacenar

storehouse ['stɔr·haus] *n* almacén *m*; *fig* mina *f*

stork [stɔrk] *n* cigüeña *f*

storm [stɔrm] **I.** *n* tormenta *f*; *fig* trifulca *f*; (*protest*) ola *f*; (*political*) revuelo *m*; **to take sth by ~** asaltar algo; **to take sb by ~** cautivar a alguien ▸ **to ride out** [*or* **weather**] **the ~** capear el temporal **II.** *vi* **1.** haber tormenta; (*winds*) soplar con fuerza **2.** (*speak*) bramar

storm cloud *n* nubarrón *m*

stormy ['stɔr·mi] <-ier, -iest> *adj* tormentoso, -a; (*sea, relationship*) tempestuoso, -a; (*argument*) violento, -a

story[1] ['stɔr·i] <-ies> *n* (*account*) historia *f*; (*fictional*) cuento *m*; **to tell stories** *a. fig* contar cuentos; **so the ~ goes** eso dicen ▸ **that's another ~** eso es harina de otro costal; **the same old ~** la misma historia de siempre; **a tall ~** un cuento chino

story[2] ['stɔr·i] *n* piso *m*

stout [staut] **I.** *adj* (*person*) robusto, -a; (*shoes, boots*) fuerte **II.** *n* cerveza *f* negra

stoutly ['staut·li] *adv* (*strongly*) sólidamente; (*firmly*) con firmeza

stove [stouv] *n* cocina *f*; (*heater*) estufa *f*

stowaway ['stou·ə·wei] *n* polizón, -ona *m, f*

straggle ['stræg·əl] *vi* **1.** (*lag behind*) rezagarse **2.** (*come in small numbers*) llegar poco a poco; (*move in a disorganized group*) avanzar desordenadamente

straggler ['stræg·lər] *n* rezagado, -a *m, f*

straight [streit] **I.** *adj* **1.** (*not bent*) recto, -a **2.** (*honest*) sincero, -a (**with** con) **3.** (*plain*) sencillo, -a; (*gin*) solo, -a **4.** (*consecutive*) seguido, -a **5.** (*heterosexual*) hetero **II.** *adv* **1.** (*direct*) en línea recta; **to go ~ ahead** ir todo recto; **to come/head ~** ir derecho (**at, for** a); **to get ~ to the point** ir directo al grano **2.** *inf* honestamente; **to give it to sb ~** ser franco con alguien **3.** (*see, think*) con claridad **III.** *n* recta *f*; **the finishing ~** la recta final

straightaway [ˌstreit·ə·'wei] **I.** *adv* enseguida **II.** *n* recta *f*

straighten ['strei·tən] *vt* (*hair*) alisar; (*wires*) enderezar; (*body, leg*) estirar

◆**straighten out** *vt* **1.** (*straight*) estirar **2.** (*level*) igualar **3.** (*situation*) arreglar; (*problem*) resolver **4.** (*clarify*) aclarar

◆**straighten up** *vi* ponerse derecho, arriscarse *Col* **II.** *vt* **1.** (*tidy*) ordenar **2.** (*level*) igualar

straightforward [ˌstreit·'fɔr·wərd] *adj* **1.** (*honest*) honesto, -a **2.** (*easy*) sencillo, -a

straight-out [ˌstreit·'aut] *adj inf* (*outright*) redomado, -a; (*refusal*) tajante

strain[1] [strein] **I.** *n* **1.** (*pressure*) presión *f*; **to be under a lot of ~** tener mucho estrés; **to put a ~** crear tensiones (**on** en) **2.** PHYS deformación *f* **3.** MED tensión *f* **II.** *vt* **1.** **to ~ one's eyes/ears** forzar la vista/aguzar el oído **2.** (*relationship*) crear tensiones en; (*credulity*) poner a prueba **3.** CULIN filtrar; (*vegetables*) escurrir

strain[2] [strein] *n* (*virus*) cepa *f*; (*species*) raza *f*; **~ of eccentricity** vena *f* excéntrica; **~ of puritanism** nota *f* de puritanismo

strained [streɪnd] *adj* (*relations*) tenso, -a; (*smile*) forzado, -a

strait [streɪt] *n* **1.** GEO estrecho *m*; **the Bering Strait** el estrecho de Bering **2.** apuro *m*; **to be in dire ~s** estar en grandes apuros

strand[1] [strænd] *n* (*wool*) hebra *f*; (*rope, string*) ramal *m*; (*hair*) mechón *m*; (*pearls*) sarta *f*; (*plot*) hilo *m*

strand[2] [strænd] *vt* varar; **to be ~ed** quedarse desamparado

strange [streɪndʒ] *adj* **1.** (*peculiar*) raro, -a; **I felt ~** me sentía raro; **it's ~ that** es raro que +*subj*; **~r things have happened** cosas más raras se han visto; **~ to say** aunque parezca mentira **2.** (*unfamiliar: face*) desconocido, -a; (*bed*) ajeno, -a

strangely *adv* (*behave, dress*) de forma rara; **~ enough** aunque parazca mentira

stranger ['streɪn·dʒər] *n* desconocido, -a *m, f*

strangle ['stræŋ·gəl] *vt* estrangular; (*cry*) ahogar

strap [stræp] **I.** *n* (*bag*) correa *f*; (*dress*) tirante *m* **II.** <-pp-> *vt* sujetar con una correa

strapless ['stræp·lɪs] *adj* sin tirantes

strapping ['stræp·ɪŋ] **I.** *adj inf* robusto, -a **II.** *n* esparadrapo *m*

strategy ['stræt·ə·dʒi] <-ies> *n* estrategia *f*

straw [strɔ] *n* paja *f*; (*drink*) pajita *f*, popote *m Méx*, pitillo *m And* ▸ **to be the last ~** ser el colmo; **to draw the short ~** tocarle a uno la china; **to clutch at ~s** agarrarse a un clavo ardiendo

strawberry ['strɔ·ˌber·i] <-ies> *n* fresa *f*, frutilla *f AmL*

stray [streɪ] **I.** *adj* (*dog, cat*) callejero, -a, realengo, -a *Méx, PRico*; (*hair*) suelto, -a **II.** *vi* (*wander*) errar; (*get lost*) perderse; **to ~ from** alejarse de; **to ~ off course** apartarse del camino; **to ~ from the point** divagar

streak [strik] **I.** *n* **1.** (*stripe*) raya *f*; (*hair*) mechón *m*; (*light*) rayo *m*; (*lightning*) relámpago *m* **2.** (*tendency*) vena *f*; **an aggressive ~** una vena agresiva **3.** (*spell*)

racha *f*; **to be on a winning ~** tener una buena racha ▸ **like a ~ of lightning** como un rayo; **to talk a blue ~** hablar como una cotorra **II.** *vt* rayar; **to have one's hair ~ed** hacerse mechas; **to be ~ed** estar manchado (**with** de) **III.** *vi* **1.** (*move fast*) ir rápido **2.** (*naked*) correr desnudo en público

streaky ['stri·ki] <-ier, -iest> *adj* rayado, -a

stream [strim] **I.** *n* **1.** (*river*) arroyo *m*, estero *m Chile, Ecua, Perú* **2.** (*current*) corriente *f*; **to go against the ~** ir a contracorriente **3.** (*flow: liquid*) chorrito *m*; (*people*) torrente *m*; (*insults*) sarta *f* **II.** *vi* **1.** (*flow*) fluir; (*water*) correar; (*blood*) manar; (*tears*) caer; (*sunlight*) entrar a raudales; (*nose*) gotear **2.** (*move in numbers*) afluir en masa

streamer ['stri·mər] *n* serpentina *f*

streamline ['strim·laɪn] *vt* (*vehicle*) aerodinamizar; (*method*) racionalizar

streamlined *adj* (*vehicle*) aerodinámico, -a; (*method*) racionalizado, -a

street [strit] *n* calle *f*; **in** [*or* **on**] **the ~** en la calle ▸ **to be out on the ~** no tener hogar; **to walk the ~s** deambular por las calles; (*prostitute*) hacer la calle

streetcar *n* tranvía *m*

streetwise ['strit·waɪz] *adj* espabilado, -a; (*politician*) astuto, -a

strength [streŋθ] *n* **1.** (*power*) fuerza *f*, ñeque *m Chile, Ecua, Perú*; (*feeling, light*) intensidad *f*; (*alcohol*) graduación *f*; (*economy*) solidez *f*; (*mental*) fortaleza *f* **2.** (*members*) número *m*; **to be at full ~** tener el cupo completo; **to be below ~** (*office*) estar corto de personal **3.** (*strong point*) punto *m* fuerte; **one's ~s and weaknesses** sus virtudes y defectos

strengthen ['streŋk·θən] **I.** *vt* (*muscles*) fortalecer; (*wall*) reforzar; (*financial position*) consolidar; (*chances*) aumentar; (*relations*) intensificar; (*links*) estrechar **II.** *vi* fortalecerse

strenuous ['stren·ju·əs] *adj* (*activity*) agotador(a); (*supporter*) acérrimo, -a; (*denial*) rotundo, -a

stress [stres] **I.** *n* **1.** PSYCH estrés *m* **2.** (*emphasis*) énfasis *m inv* **3.** LING acento *m* **4.** PHYS tensión *f* **II.** *vt* recalcar; LING acentuar

stressed *adj*, **stressed out** *adj* estresado, -a

stressful ['stres·fʊl] *adj* estresante

stretch [stretʃ] **I.** <-es> *n* **1.** (*elasticity*) elasticidad *f*; **at full ~** a todo gas; **not by any ~ of the imagination** ni por asomo **2.** SPORTS estiramiento *m* **3.** GEO trecho *m* **4.** (*piece*) trozo *m*; (*road*) tramo *m*; (*time*) período *m* **5.** (*race*) recta *f*; **the home ~** la recta final **II.** *vi* estirarse; (*clothes*) dar de sí; (*sea, influence*) extenderse; **to ~ (all the way) back to a)** remontarse **III.** *vt* estirar; **to ~ one's legs/the limit** estirar las piernas/el límite; **to ~ sb's patience** poner a prueba la paciencia de alguien; **to ~ a point** hacer una excepción; **now you're really ~ing it** ahora sí que estás exagerando **IV.** *adj* elástico, -a

stretcher ['stretʃ·ər] *n* camilla *f*

strict [strɪkt] *adj* (*person*) severo, -a, fregado, -a *AmC*; (*control, orders, sense*) estricto, -a; (*deadline*) inamovible; (*neutrality*) total; (*secrecy, confidence*) absoluto, -a

strictly ['strɪkt·li] *adv* **1.** (*exactly*) estrictamente; **not ~ comparable** no del todo comparable; **~ speaking** en rigor **2.** (*harshly*) severamente; (*forbidden*) terminantemente

stride [straɪd] **I.** <strode> *vi* andar a trancos; **to ~ ahead** andar dando zancadas; **to ~ across sth** cruzar algo de una zancada **II.** *n* **1.** (*step*) zancada *f* **2.** (*progress*) progreso *m*; **to make (positive) ~s forward** hacer grandes progresos; **to make ~s** acercarse (**towards** a) ▸ **to get into** [*or* **hit**] **one's ~** coger el ritmo; **to take sth in ~** tomarse algo con calma

strike [straɪk] **I.** *n* **1.** MIL ataque *m* **2.** (*workers*) huelga *f* **3.** (*discovery*) descubrimiento *m* **4.** (*baseball*) strike *m* **II.** <struck, struck *or* stricken> *vt* **1.** (*collide*) golpear; (*match*) encender; **struck by lightning** alcanzado por un rayo; **to ~ a blow** asestar un golpe (**against** a) **2.** (*achieve*) conseguir; **to ~ a balance** encontrar un equilibrio; **to ~ a bargain**

hacer un trato **3.** (*seem*) parecer; **it ~s me that...** se me ocurre que... **4.** (*impress*) impresionar; **I was struck by the news** la noticia me impactó **5.** (*discover*) descubrir; (*find*) encontrar **6.** **to ~ an attitude** adoptar una actitud; **to ~ fear** infundir miedo (**into** a) **7.** (*clock*) marcar; **the clock struck three** el reloj dio las tres ▸ **to ~ a chord** llegar a entenderse (**with** con); **to ~ sb dumb** dejar a alguien sin habla; **to ~ it rich** forrarse **III.** <struck, struck *or* stricken> *vi* **1.** (*hit*) golpear; (*attack*) atacar (**at the heart of** directamente a); **to ~ home** dar en el blanco **2.** (*worker*) declararse en huelga; **the right to ~** el derecho a la huelga; **to ~ for** hacer una huelga por

◆**strike back** *vi* contraatacar; **to ~ at sb** tomar represalias contra alguien

◆**strike down** *vt* **1.** **she was struck down by cancer** fue abatida por el cáncer **2.** LAW revocar

◆**strike off** *vt* tachar

◆**strike out I.** *vt* **1.** (*baseball*) eliminar **2.** (*delete*) borrar **II.** *vi* **1.** (*baseball*) ser eliminado, *fig* fallar **2.** (*move off*) andar resueltamente; **to ~ on one's own** hacerse independiente

◆**strike up** *vt* (*conversation, friendship*) entablar; (*relationship*) iniciar

striker ['straɪ·kər] *n* **1.** huelguista *mf* **2.** SPORTS delantero, -a *m, f*

striking ['straɪ·kɪŋ] *adj* notable; (*result, beauty*) impresionante; (*resemblance*) sorprendente; (*contrast*) acusado, -a; **visually ~** llamativo

string [strɪŋ] **I.** *n* **1.** (*twine*) *a.* MUS cuerda *f*; (*puppet*) hilo *m*; **to pull ~s** *fig* mover hilos; **with no ~s attached** sin compromiso alguno **2.** (*chain*) cadena *f*; (*pearls*) collar *m*; (*lies*) sarta *f*; (*people*) hilera *f* **3.** COMPUT secuencia *f* **II.** <strung, strung> *vt* poner una cuerda a; (*instrument, tennis racket*) encordar; (*beads*) ensartar

◆**string along** *inf* **I.** *vi* ir/venir también **II.** *vt* embaucar

◆**string out** *vt* (*extend*) espaciar; (*activity*) prolongar

◆**string up** *vt inf* colgar

string band *n* banda *f* de cuerda

strip [strɪp] **I.** vt **1.** (lay bare) dejar sin cubierta; **to ~ sb of sth** quitar algo a alguien **2.** (unclothe) desnudar **3.** (dismantle) desmontar **II.** vi desnudarse **III.** n **1.** (ribbon) tira f; (metal) lámina f; (land) franja f **2.** (striptease) striptease m **3. landing ~** pista f de aterrizaje

stripe [straɪp] n **1.** (band) raya f **2.** (type) **of every ~** de todo tipo; **governments of every ~** gobiernos de todos los colores

striped adj rayado, -a; (shirt) a rayas

stripper ['strɪp·ər] n **1.** (person) stripper mf **2.** (solvent) líquido m quitaesmaltes; (wallpaper) líquido quitapapeles

strive [straɪv] <strove, striven or strived> vi esmerarse (**to** en, **after, for** por)

strode [stroʊd] pt of **stride**

stroke [stroʊk] **I.** vt **1.** (caress) acariciar **2.** SPORTS golpear suavemente **II.** n **1.** (caress) caricia f **2.** MED derrame m cerebral; **to suffer a ~** tener una apoplejía **3.** (pencil) trazo m; (brush) pincelada f **4.** SPORTS golpe m; (billiards) tacada f; (swimming style) estilo m **5.** (clock) campanada f **6. by a ~ of fate** por cosas del destino; **a ~ of genius** una genialidad; **a ~ of luck** un golpe de suerte

stroll [stroʊl] **I.** n paseo m; **to go for a ~** ir a dar una vuelta **II.** vi dar un paseo

strong [strɔŋ] **I.** adj **1.** fuerte; (competition) duro, -a; (reason) de peso; (nerves) de acero, fervoroso, -a; (emotion) intenso, -a; (friendship) estrecho, -a; (supporter) acérrimo, -a; (color) llamativo, -a; **to be as ~ as an ox** ser tan fuerte como un toro; **to produce ~ memories** traer muchos recuerdos **2.** (very likely) muy probable; **~ chance of success** muchas posibilidades de éxito **3.** (high value) de gran valor **II.** adv inf **to come on ~ to sb** ir por alguien; **to be still going ~** seguir bien

strongly adv fuertemente; (advise) fervorosamente; (condemn, criticize) duramente; **to smell ~** tener un fuerte olor (**of** a); **to be ~ opposed** estar muy en contra (**to** de); **to be ~ biased** tener muchos prejuicios (**against** contra)

strong-minded [ˌstrɔŋ·'maɪn·dɪd] adj resuelto, -a

strove [stroʊv] pt of **strive**

struck [strʌk] pt, pp of **strike**

structure ['strʌk·tʃər] **I.** n estructura f; (building) construcción f **II.** vt estructurar

struggle ['strʌg·əl] **I.** n **1.** (effort) esfuerzo m; **to be a real ~** suponer un gran esfuerzo; **to give up the ~** dejar de esmerarse (**to** en) **2.** (skirmish) lucha f; **to put up a ~** oponer resistencia **II.** vi **1.** (effort) esforzarse **2.** (fight) luchar

strung [strʌŋ] pt, pp of **string**

stub [stʌb] **I.** n (check) talón m; (cigarette) colilla f **II.** <-bb-> vt **to ~ one's toe** tropezar (**against** con)

stubborn ['stʌb·ərn] adj (person, animal) terco, -a; **as ~ as a mule** más terco que una mula; (insistence) tenaz; (problem) persistente; (refusal) rotundo, -a; (resistance) inquebrantable

stuck [stʌk] **I.** pt, pp of **stick II.** adj **1.** (jammed) atascado, -a **2. to be ~** estar loco (**on** por)

stuck-up [ˌstʌk·'ʌp] adj inf engreído, -a

stud[1] [stʌd] n ZOOL a. fig semental m, garañón m AmL

stud[2] [stʌd] n **1.** (nail) clavo m **2. collar ~** gemelo m **3.** (tire) taco m **4.** (earring) pendiente m

student ['stu·dənt] n estudiante mf; **the ~ body** el alumnado

studied ['stʌd·id] adj estudiado, -a; (insult) premeditado, -a

studio ['stu·di·oʊ] <-s> n a. CINE estudio m; (artist) taller m

studio apartment n estudio m

studious ['stu·di·əs] adj estudioso, -a

study ['stʌd·i] **I.** vt (subject) estudiar; (evidence) examinar **II.** vi estudiar **III.** <-ies> n **1.** estudio m; (evidence) investigación f **2.** (room) despacho m

stuff [stʌf] **I.** n **1.** inf (things) movidas fpl argot; **to know one's ~** conocer su oficio **2.** (belongings) cosas fpl **3.** (material) material m; (cloth) tela f; **the (very) ~** la esencia (**of** de) **II.** vt **1.** (fill) llenar; **to ~ sth into sth** meter algo en algo; **to ~ sb's head** llenar a alguien la cabeza (**with** de); **to ~ oneself** darse un atracón

S

2. (*animal*) disecar

stuffing ['stʌf·ɪŋ] *n* relleno *m*

stuffy ['stʌf·i] *adj* (*room*) mal ventilado, -a; (*atmosphere*) cargado, -a; (*nose*) taponado, -a; (*person*) tieso, -a

stumble ['stʌm·bəl] *vi* **1.** (*trip*) tropezar (**on** con) **2.** (*talking*) balbucear

stumbling block *n* obstáculo *m*

stump [stʌmp] **I.** *n* (*plant*) tocón *m*; (*arm*) muñón *m* **II.** *vt inf* desconcertar **III.** *vi* **to ~ about** andar pisando fuerte

stun [stʌn] <-nn-> *vt* **1.** (*stupefy*) dejar pasmado **2.** (*unconscious*) dejar sin sentido

stung [stʌŋ] *pp, pt of* **sting**

stunk [stʌŋk] *pt, pp of* **stink**

stunned *adj* aturdido, -a

stunning ['stʌn·ɪŋ] *adj* **1.** (*surprising*) asombroso, -a **2.** (*impressive*) espléndido, -a; (*dress*) estupendo, -a

stupendous [stu·'pen·dəs] *adj* estupendo, -a

stupid ['stu·pɪd] *adj* estúpido, -a, cojudo, -a *AmL*, zonzo, -a *AmL*

stupidity [stu·'pɪd·ə·t̬i] *n* estupidez *f*, dundera *f AmL*

sturdy ['stɜr·di] *adj* **1.** (*robust*) robusto, -a **2.** (*resolute*) decidido, -a; **a ~ defender** un defensor acérrimo

stutter ['stʌt̬·ər] **I.** *vi, vt* tartamudear, cancanear *AmL* **II.** *n* tartamudeo *m*

sty [staɪ] *n* (*pigsty*) pocilga *f*

style [staɪl] **I.** *n* **1.** *a.* ART, ARCHIT estilo *m*; (*management*) modo *f*; (*teaching*) forma *f* **2.** (*elegance*) elegancia *f*; **to have no ~** no ser elegante; **with ~** con estilo; **to live in** (*grand*) **~** vivir a lo grande; **to travel in ~** viajar con todo el confort **3.** (*fashion*) moda *f*; **in ~** de moda **II.** *vt* (*design*) diseñar; (*hair*) peinar

styling *n* estilización *f*

stylish ['staɪ·lɪʃ] *adj* a la moda; (*elegant*) garboso, -a

stylist ['staɪ·lɪst] *n* estilista *mf*

Styrofoam® ['staɪ·rə·foʊm] *n* poliestireno *m*

sub¹ [sʌb] *n* **1.** *abbr of* **substitute** sustituto, -a *m, f* **2.** *abbr of* **submarine** submarino *m* **3.** *abbr of* **sandwich** sándwich *m* mixto

sub² [sʌb] <-bb-> *vi abbr of* **substitute** sustituir

subconscious [ˌsʌb·'kan·ʃəs] *adj, n* subconsciente *m*

subdivide [ˌsʌb·dɪ·'vaɪd] *vt* subdividir

subdue [səb·'du] *vt* (*tame*) someter; (*repress*) reprimir

subject¹ ['sʌb·dʒɪkt] **I.** *n* **1.** (*theme*) tema *m*; **to change the ~** cambiar de tema; **to wander off the ~** salirse del tema; **on the ~ of** a propósito de **2.** SCHOOL, UNIV asignatura *f*; (*research area*) ámbito *m* **3.** (*citizen*) ciudadano, -a *m, f* **4.** LING, MED sujeto *m* **II.** *adj* **to be ~** estar sujeto (**to** a); **~ to approval** pendiente de aprobación; **to be ~ to colds** ser propenso a acatarrarse; **to be ~ to many dangers** estar expuesto a muchos peligros

subject² [səb·'dʒekt] *vt* dominar

subjective [səb·'dʒek·tɪv] *adj* subjetivo, -a

subject matter *n* tema *m*; (*letter*) contenido *m*

subjunctive [səb·'dʒʌŋk·tɪv] *n* subjuntivo *m*

sublet [sʌb·'let] <sublet, sublet> *vt* subarrendar

submarine ['sʌb·mə·rin] **I.** *n* **1.** NAUT, MIL submarino *m* **2.** *inf* sándwich *m* mixto **II.** *adj* submarino, -a

submerge [səb·'mɜrdʒ] **I.** *vt* sumergir; **to ~ oneself** *fig* dedicarse de lleno (**in** a) **II.** *vi* sumergirse

submission [səb·'mɪʃ·ən] *n* **1.** (*surrender*) sumisión *f* **2.** (*proposal*) presentación *f*; (*document*) entrega *f*

submissive [səb·'mɪs·ɪv] *adj* sumiso, -a

submit [səb·'mɪt] <-tt-> **I.** *vt* **1.** (*proposal*) presentar; (*document*) entregar **2.** *form* proponer **II.** *vi* (*yield*) someterse

subordinate¹ [sə·'bɔr·dən·ɪt] **I.** *n* subordinado, -a *m, f* **II.** *adj* (*secondary*) secundario, -a; (*rank*) subordinado, -a

subordinate² [sə·'bɔr·də·naɪt] *vt* subordinar

subscribe [səb·'skraɪb] **I.** *vi* suscribirse; **to ~ to** suscribir **II.** *vt* (*contribute*) donar

subscriber [səb·'skraɪ·bər] *n* (*magazine*) suscriptor(a) *m(f)*; (*phone*) abonado, -a *m, f*

subscription [səb·'skrɪp·ʃən] n suscripción f; **to order a ~** suscribirse (**to** a)

subsequent ['sʌb·sɪ·kwənt] adj posterior; **~ to** después de

subsequently adv después; **~ to** después de

subside [səb·'saɪd] vi disminuir; (water) bajar; (ground) hundirse

subsidiary [səb·'sɪd·i·er·i] I. adj subsidiario, -a; (reason) secundario, -a; ECON filial II. <-ies> n ECON filial f

subsidize ['sʌb·sə·daɪz] vt subvencionar

subsidy ['sʌb·sɪ·di] <-ies> n subvención f; **unemployment ~** subsidio m de desempleo

subsist [səb·'sɪst] vi subsistir; **to ~ on sth** sustentarse con [or a base de] algo

substance ['sʌb·stəns] n 1. (matter) sustancia f 2. (essence) esencia f 3. (significance) valor m 4. (main point) punto m más importante; **the ~ of the conversation** el punto esencial de la conversación; **in ~** en esencia 5. (possessions) riqueza f; **a man of ~** un hombre acaudalado

substandard [ˌsʌb·'stæn·dərd] adj inferior

substantial [səb·'stæn·ʃəl] adj 1. (important) sustancial; (difference, improvement) notable; **to be in ~ agreement** estar de acuerdo en gran parte 2. (large) grande; (meal) copioso, -a; (sum, damage) considerable 3. (sturdy) sólido, -a

substantially [səb·'stæn·ʃə·li] adv (significantly) considerablemente; (in the main) esencialmente

substantive ['sʌb·stən·tɪv] n sustantivo m

substitute ['sʌb·stə·tut] I. vt sustituir; **to ~ sb for sb** reemplazar a alguien por alguien; **to ~ oil for butter, to ~ butter with oil** sustituir la mantequilla por el aceite II. vi **to ~ for** suplir III. n 1. (equivalent) sustituto m; (milk, coffee) sucedáneo m; **there's no ~ for him** no hay nadie como él 2. SCHOOL, SPORTS suplente mf

substitution [ˌsʌb·stə·'tu·ʃən] n sustitución f

subtitle ['sʌb·taɪ·tl̩] I. vt subtitular II. n subtítulo m

subtle ['sʌt·l̩] adj sutil; (flavor) suave; (nuance) tenue; (question, suggestion) inteligente; (person) astuto, -a

subtotal ['sʌb·tou·tl̩] n subtotal m

subtract [səb·'trækt] vt sustraer; **to ~ 3 from 5** restar 3 a 5

subtraction [səb·'træk·ʃən] n resta f

subtropical [ˌsʌb·'trɑp·ɪ·kl̩] adj subtropical

suburb ['sʌb·ɜrb] n barrio m periférico; **the ~s** la periferia; **to live in the ~s** vivir en las afueras

suburban [sə·'bɜr·bən] adj (area) periférico, -a; (train) de cercanías; (lifestyle) aburguesado, -a

subvention [səb·'ven·ʃən] n subvención f

subversive [səb·'vɜr·sɪv] adj subversivo, -a

subvert [sʌb·'vɜrt] vt (authority) minar; (principle) debilitar

subway ['sʌb·weɪ] n metro m, subte m Arg

sub-zero [ˌsʌb·'zɪr·ou] adj bajo cero

succeed [sək·'sid] I. vi 1. (be successful) tener éxito; **to ~ in doing sth** lograr hacer algo; **the plan ~ed** el plan salió bien 2. (follow) suceder II. vt suceder a

succeeding [sək·'si·dɪŋ] adj siguiente; (generation) venidero, -a; **in the ~ weeks** en las próximas semanas

success [sək·'ses] n éxito m; **to meet with ~, to enjoy ~** tener éxito; **to have ~ in doing sth** conseguir hacer algo; **to make a ~** tener éxito (**of** en); **to wish sb ~ with sth** desear a alguien que le vaya bien algo

successful [sək·'ses·fəl] adj (business) próspero, -a; (candidate) electo, -a; (solution) eficaz; **to be ~** (person) tener éxito; (business) prosperar

succession [sək·'seʃ·ən] n sucesión f; **in ~** sucesivamente; **a ~ of** una serie de; **an endless ~ of** un sinfín de

successive [sək·'ses·ɪv] adj sucesivo, -a; **on ~ occasions** varias veces seguidas

successor [sək·'ses·ər] n sucesor(a) m(f)

such [sʌtʃ] I. adj tal, semejante; **~ great weather/a good book** un tiempo/un libro tan bueno; **~ an honor** tanto honor; **to earn ~ a lot of money** ganar

S

tanto dinero; **or some ~ remark** o un comentario por el estilo; **to buy some fruit ~ as apples** comprar fruta como manzanas **II.** *pron* **~ is life** así es la vida; **people ~ as him** las personas que son como él; **~ as it is** tal como es; **as ~** propiamente dicho

such and such ['sʌtʃ·ən·ˌsʌtʃ] *adj* tal o cual; **to arrive at ~ a time** llegar a tal o cual hora; **to see sb in ~ a place** ver a alguien en tal o cual lugar

suck [sʌk] **I.** *vt* succionar; (*straw*) sorber; (*air*) aspirar; (*breast*) mamar; (*sweets*) chupar; **to ~ one's thumb** chuparse el dedo **II.** *vi* chupar **III.** *n* chupada *f*; (*straw*) sorbo *m*

sucker ['sʌk·ər] **I.** *n* **1.** (*person*) imbécil *mf* **2.** ZOOL ventosa *f* **II.** *vt* *inf* timar (**into** en); **to ~ sb into/out of doing sth** engañar a alguien para que haga/no haga algo

sudden ['sʌd·ən] *adj* repentino, -a, sorpresivo, -a *AmL*; (*death*) súbito, -a; (*departure*) imprevisto, -a; (*movement, drop*) brusco, -a; **to put a ~ stop to** detener de forma repentina; **all of a ~** *inf* de repente

suddenly *adv* de repente

suds [sʌdz] *npl* **1.** jabonaduras *fpl* **2.** *sl* cerveza *f*

sue [su] <**suing**> **I.** *vt* demandar; **to ~ sb for damages** demandar a alguien por daños y perjuicios; **to ~ sb for divorce** poner a alguien una demanda de divorcio **II.** *vi* presentar demanda; **to ~ for peace** pedir la paz

suede [sweɪd] *n* ante *m*

suffer ['sʌf·ər] **I.** *vi* sufrir; **the economy is ~ing** la economía se está viendo afectada (**from** por); **to ~ for sth** ser castigado por algo; **to ~ in** [*or* **by**] **comparison** salir perdiendo en comparación **II.** *vt* sufrir; MED padecer de; **to ~ the consequences** sufrir las consecuencias; **to ~ the misfortune of** tener mala suerte de

suffering ['sʌf·ər·ɪŋ] *n* sufrimiento *m*; **years of ~** años de penurias

suffice [sə·'faɪs] *vi* bastar; **~ (it) to say that** basta decir que

have ~ tener bastante; **to be ~ for** ser suficiente para

suffix ['sʌf·ɪks] *n* sufijo *m*

suffocate ['sʌf·ə·keɪt] **I.** *vi* asfixiarse **II.** *vt* asfixiar; *fig* sofocar

suffocating *adj* asfixiante; *fig* sofocante

sugar ['ʃʊg·ər] **I.** *n* **1.** CULIN azúcar *m* **2.** *inf* (*term of affection*) cariño **II.** *vt* azucarar

sugary ['ʃʊg·ə·ri] *adj* **1.** azucarado, -a **2.** (*insincere*) meloso, -a

suggest [səg·'dʒest] *vt* **1.** (*propose*) proponer; **to ~ doing sth** proponer hacer algo; **to ~ (to sb) that** sugerir a alguien que +*subj*; **an idea ~ed itself to him** se le ocurrió una idea **2.** (*indicate*) indicar **3.** (*hint*) insinuar; **what are you trying to ~?** ¿qué insinúas?

suggestion [səg·'dʒes·tʃən] *n* **1.** (*proposal*) sugerencia *f*; **to make the ~ that** sugerir que +*subj*; **at Ann's ~** a petición de Ann **2.** (*bit*) pizca *f* **3.** (*insinuation*) insinuación *f*

suggestive [səg·'dʒes·tɪv] *adj* **1.** (*lewd*) indecente **2.** (*evocative*) sugestivo, -a

suicide ['su·ə·saɪd] *n* **1.** suicidio *m*; **~ bombing** atentado *m* suicida; **to commit ~** suicidarse **2.** (*person*) suicida *mf*

suit [sut] **I.** *vt* **1.** (*be convenient*) convenir; **to ~ sb** convenirle a alguien; **that ~s me fine** eso me viene bien; **to ~ oneself** hacer lo que uno quiere; **~ yourself!** ¡haz lo que quieras! **2.** (*be right*) ir [*or* sentar] bien; **they are well ~ed** hacen buena pareja **3.** (*look good*) quedar bien; **this dress ~s you** este vestido te sienta bien **II.** *n* **1.** (*with pants*) traje *m*, terno *m Chile*, flus *m Ant, Col, Ven*; (*with skirt*) traje *m* de chaqueta; **bathing** [*or* **swim**] **~** bañador *m* **2.** LAW pleito *m* **3.** GAMES palo *m*; **to follow ~** seguir el palo; *fig* seguir el ejemplo

suitable ['su·tə·bəl] *adj* apropiado, -a (**for** para); **not ~ for children under 14** no apto para menores de 14 años

suitcase ['sut·keɪs] *n* maleta *f*, valija *f RíoPl*, petaca *f Méx*

sulfuric [sʌl·'fjʊr·ɪk] *adj* sulfúrico, -a

sulk [sʌlk] **I.** *vi* enfurruñarse, alunarse *RíoPl,* amurrarse *Chile* **II.** *n* mal humor *m;* **to be in a ~** estar enfurruñado, -a [*or RíoPl*] alunado, -a] [*or Chile* amurrado, -a]

sulky ['sʌl·ki] <-ier, -iest> *adj* enfurruñado, -a

sullen ['sʌl·ən] *adj* malhumorado, -a; (*sky*) sombrío, -a

sultana [sʌl·'tæn·ə] *n* pasa *f* sultana

sultry ['sʌl·tri] <-ier, -iest> *adj* **1.** (*weather*) bochornoso, -a **2.** (*sensual*) sensual

sum [sʌm] *n* **1.** (*money*) cantidad *f* **2.** (*total*) total *m;* **in ~** en resumen **3.** MAT cuenta *f*

summarize ['sʌm·ə·raɪz] *vt* resumir

summary ['sʌm·ər·i] *n* resumen *m*

summer ['sʌm·ər] **I.** *n* verano *m;* **a ~'s day** un día de verano **II.** *adj* de verano, veraniego, -a **III.** *vi* veranear

summertime ['sʌm·ər·taɪm] *n* verano *m;* **in the ~** en verano

summit ['sʌm·ɪt] *n a. fig* cumbre *f;* **to hold a ~** celebrar una cumbre

summon ['sʌm·ən] *vt* llamar; (*meeting*) convocar; LAW citar

summons ['sʌm·ənz] *n* llamamiento *m;* LAW citación *f*

sun [sʌn] **I.** *n* sol *m;* **the ~'s rays** los rayos del sol; **the rising/setting ~** el sol naciente/poniente; **in the ~** al sol ▶ **everything under the ~** de todo; **to call sb every name under the ~** decir a alguien de todo **II.** <-nn-> *vt* **to ~ oneself** tomar el sol

sunbathe ['sʌn·beɪð] *vi* tomar el sol

sunburn ['sʌn·bɜrn] *n* quemadura *f* de sol

sunburned *adj,* **sunburnt** *adj* quemado, -a por el sol

sundae ['sʌn·di] *n* helado con fruta, crema, *etc*

Sunday ['sʌn·deɪ] *n* domingo *m; s. a.* **Friday**

Sunday school *n* ≈ catequesis *f inv*

sundial *n* reloj *m* de sol

sundown *n see* **sunset**

sundry ['sʌn·dri] *adj* varios, -as; **~ items** objetos varios

sunflower ['sʌn·flaʊ·ər] *n* girasol *m,* maravilla *f Chile*

sung [sʌŋ] *pp of* **sing**

sunglasses ['sʌn·ˌglæs·ɪz] *npl* gafas *f pl* de sol

sunk [sʌŋk] *pp of* **sink**

sunken ['sʌŋ·kən] *adj* sumergido, -a; (*cheeks, eyes*) hundido, -a

sunlight ['sʌn·laɪt] *n* luz *f* del sol

sunlit ['sʌn·lɪt] *adj* soleado, -a

sunny ['sʌn·i] <-ier, -iest> *adj* soleado, -a; (*personality*) alegre

sunrise ['sʌn·raɪz] *n* amanecer *m;* **at ~** al alba

sunroof ['sʌn·ruf] *n* techo *m* corredizo

sunset ['sʌn·set] *n* puesta *f* de sol; **at ~** al atardecer

sunshade ['sʌn·ʃeɪd] *n* (*umbrella*) sombrilla *f;* (*awning*) toldo *m*

sunshine ['sʌn·ʃaɪn] *n* sol *m;* **in the ~** al sol

sunstroke *n* insolación *f,* asoleada *f Col, Chile, Guat;* **to have ~** tener una insolación

suntan ['sʌn·tæn] *n* bronceado *m;* **to get a ~** broncearse

suntan lotion *n* crema *f* bronceadora

suntanned *adj* bronceado, -a

suntan oil *n* aceite *m* bronceador

sunup ['sʌn·ʌp] *n see* **sunrise**

sun visor *n* visera *f*

super ['su·pər] **I.** *adj, adv* guay **II.** *n* AUTO súper *f*

superb [sə·'pɜrb] *adj* magnífico, -a

superficial [ˌsu·pər·'fɪʃ·əl] *adj* superficial

superfluous [su·'pɜr·flu·əs] *adj* superfluo, -a; **to be ~** estar de más

superglue® ['su·pər·glu] *n* superglue® *m*

superintendent [ˌsu·pər·ɪn·'ten·dənt] *n* **1.** director(a) *m(f);* (*building*) portero, -a *m, f* **2.** (*police*) superintendente *mf*

superior [sə·'pɪr·i·ər] **I.** *adj* superior; **to be ~** estar por encima (**to** de); **a ~ number** un número mayor (**of** de) **II.** *n* superior *mf*

superiority [sə·ˌpɪr·i·'ɔr·ə·ti] *n* superioridad *f*

superlative [su·'pɜr·lə·tɪv] **I.** *adj* excepcional; LING superlativo, -a **II.** *n* superlativo *m*

supermarket ['su·pər·ˌmar·kɪt] *n* supermercado *m*

superpower ['su·pər·ˌpaʊ·ər] *n* superpotencia *f*

supersonic [ˌsu·pər·ˈsan·ɪk] *adj* supersónico, -a

superstitious [ˌsu·pər·ˈstɪʃ·əs] *adj* supersticioso, -a

superstore [ˈsu·pər·stɔr] *n* hipermercado *m*

supervise [ˈsu·pər·vaɪz] *vt* supervisar; (*thesis*) dirigir

supervision [ˌsu·pər·ˈvɪʒ·ən] *n* supervisión *f*; **under the ~** bajo la supervisión (**of** de)

supervisor [ˈsu·pər·vaɪ·zər] *n* supervisor(a) *m(f)*; POL alcalde, -esa *m, f*

supervisory [ˌsu·pər·ˈvaɪ·zə·ri] *adj* de supervisor

supper [ˈsʌp·ər] *n* cena *f*; **to have ~** cenar

supple [ˈsʌp·əl] *adj* (*leather, skin*) flexible; (*person*) ágil

supplement [ˈsʌp·lə·mənt] I. *n* complemento *m*; (*newspaper*) suplemento *m*; (*book*) apéndice *m* II. *vt* complementar

supplementary [ˌsʌp·lə·ˈmen·tə·ri] *adj* adicional

supplier [sə·ˈplaɪ·ər] *n* proveedor(a) *m(f)*

supply [sə·ˈplaɪ] I. <-ie-> *vt* suministrar; COM proveer; (*information*) proporcionar; **accused of ~ing drugs** acusado de tráfico de drogas II. *n* suministro *m*; ECON oferta *f*; **~ and demand** oferta y demanda; **to be in short ~** escasear

support [sə·ˈpɔrt] I. *vt* 1. (*hold up*) sostener; (*weight*) aguantar; **to ~ oneself** apoyarse (**on** en) 2. (*sustain*) mantener; **to ~ two children** mantener a dos hijos; **to ~ oneself** ganarse la vida 3. (*pay*) financiar 4. (*encourage*) apoyar 5. (*show to be true*) confirmar II. *n* 1. (*help*) apoyo *m*; **moral ~** apoyo moral 2. (*structure*) soporte *m* 3. FIN ayuda *f* 4. confirmación *f*; **to lend ~ to** respaldar; **in ~ of** en apoyo de

supporter *n* partidario, -a *m, f*; (*fan*) seguidor(a) *m(f)*

supportive [sə·ˈpɔr·tɪv] *adj* comprensivo, -a; **to be ~** of apoyar

suppose [sə·ˈpoʊz] *vt* 1. suponer (**that** que); **I ~ not/so** supongo que no/sí; **I don't ~ so** supongo que no; **let's ~ that** supongamos que 2. (*believe*) creer

3. **to be ~d to do sth** tener que hacer algo; **you are not ~d to know that** no deberías saber eso; **she is ~d to be intelligent** dicen que es inteligente

supposed *adj* supuesto, -a; LAW presunto, -a

supposedly [sə·ˈpoʊ·zɪd·li] *adv* supuestamente

supposing *conj* **~ that** suponiendo que

suppress [sə·ˈpres] *vt* 1. reprimir; (*evidence, information*) ocultar 2. MED inhibir

supremacy [sə·ˈprem·ə·si] *n* supremacía *f*

supreme [sə·ˈprim] I. *adj* (*authority*) supremo, -a; (*commander*) en jefe; **Supreme Court** Tribunal Supremo; **to show ~ courage** mostrar una gran valentía II. *adv* **to reign ~** no tener rival

surcharge [ˈsɜr·tʃardʒ] I. *n* recargo *m* II. *vt* aplicar un recargo a

sure [ʃʊr] I. *adj* seguro, -a; **to be ~ of/ that** estar seguro de/de que; **to make ~ that** asegurarse de que; **I'm not ~ that/ if** no estoy seguro de/de si; **she is ~ to come** vendrá seguro; **I'm not ~ why/ how** no sé muy bien por qué/cómo; **~ thing!** ¡claro!; **for ~** seguro; **~ of herself** segura de sí misma II. *adv* seguro; **~ I will!** ¡seguro!; **for ~** a ciencia cierta; **~ enough** en efecto ▶ **as ~ as I'm standing here** como me llamo...

sure-footed [ʃʊrˈfʊt·ɪd] *adj* (*confident*) seguro, -a de sí mismo, -a

surely [ˈʃʊr·li] *adv* 1. (*certainly*) sin duda 2. (*astonishment*) claro; **~ you don't expect me to believe that?** ¿no esperarás que me lo crea? 3. **~!** ¡pues claro!

surf [sɜrf] I. *n* olas *fpl* II. *vi* SPORTS hacer surf III. *vt* **to ~ the Internet** navegar por internet

surface [ˈsɜr·fɪs] I. *n* superficie *f*; **on the ~** *fig* a primera vista; **to scratch the ~ of sth** tratar algo muy por encima II. *vi* salir a la superficie

surface tension *n* tensión *f* superficial

surfboard [ˈsɜrf·bɔrd] *n* tabla *f* de surf

surfer [ˈsɜr·fər] *n* surfista *mf*; COMPUT internauta *mf*

surfing [ˈsɜr·fɪŋ] *n* surf *m*

surge [sɜrdʒ] I. *vi* 1. (*rush*) abalanzarse;

surgeon ['sɜr·dʒən] n cirujano, -a m, f

surgery ['sɜr·dʒə·ri] n cirugía f; **to perform ~** practicar una intervención quirúrgica; **to undergo ~** pasar por el quirófano

surgical ['sɜr·dʒɪ·kəl] adj quirúrgico, -a; (collar, gloves) ortopédico, -a

surly ['sɜr·li] <-ier, -iest> adj hosco, -a

surname ['sɜr·neɪm] n apellido m

surpass [sər·'pæs] vt sobrepasar; **to ~ oneself** superarse

surplus ['sɜr·pləs] I. n (product) excedente m; FIN superávit m II. adj sobrante

surprise [sər·'praɪz] I. n sorpresa f; **in a ~** con sorpresa; **to sb's ~** para sorpresa de alguien II. vt sorprender; **it ~d her that** le sorprendió que +subj; **to ~ sb doing sth** sorprender a alguien haciendo algo

surprising adj sorprendente, sorpresivo, -a AmL

surprisingly adv sorprendentemente

surrender [sə·'ren·dər] I. vi rendirse; **to ~ to sb** entregarse a alguien II. n (giving up) rendición f

surrogate ['sɜr·ə·gɪt] n sustituto, -a m, f

surround [sə·'raʊnd] I. vt rodear II. n marco m

surrounding adj de alrededor

surroundings npl alrededores mpl

surveillance [sər·'veɪ·ləns] n vigilancia f; **to be under ~** estar bajo vigilancia

survey¹ [sər·'veɪ] vt 1. (poll) encuestar 2. GEO medir 3. (research) investigar 4. (watch) contemplar

survey² ['sɜr·veɪ] n 1. (poll) encuesta f 2. GEO medición f 3. (report) informe m 4. (examination) examen m

survival [sər·'vaɪ·vəl] n supervivencia f ▶ **the ~ of the <u>fittest</u>** la ley del más fuerte

survive [sər·'vaɪv] I. vi (person) sobrevivir; (thing) conservarse; **to ~ on** vivir a base de II. vt sobrevivir a; **to ~ an accident** salir con vida de un accidente

surviving adj superviviente

survivor [sər·'vaɪ·vər] n superviviente mf

susceptible [sə·'sep·tə·bəl] adj susceptible; MED propenso, -a

suspect¹ [sə·'spekt] vt sospechar; (person) sospechar de; **to ~ sb's motives** dudar de los motivos de alguien

suspect² ['sʌs·pekt] adj, n sospechoso, -a m, f

suspend [sə·'spend] vt 1. (stop) suspender; (judgment, proceedings) posponer 2. SCHOOL, UNIV expulsar temporalmente 3. (hang) colgar

suspender [sə·'spen·dər] n pl tirantes mpl, suspensores mpl AmL, calzonarias fpl Col

suspense [sə·'spens] n incertidumbre f; CINE suspense m; **in ~** en vilo

suspension [sə·'spen·ʃən] n suspensión f; SCHOOL, UNIV expulsión f temporal

suspension bridge n puente m colgante

suspicion [sə·'spɪʃ·ən] n 1. (belief) sospecha f 2. (mistrust) recelo m

suspicious [sə·'spɪʃ·əs] adj 1. (arousing suspicion) sospechoso, -a, emponchado, -a Arg, Bol, Perú 2. (lacking trust) desconfiado, -a

sustain [sə·'steɪn] vt 1. (maintain) sostener 2. (withstand) aguantar 3. (uphold: conviction) confirmar; (objection) admitir

sustainable [sə·'steɪ·nə·bəl] adj (resources, development) sostenible

sustained [sə·'steɪnd] adj continuo, -a; (applause) prolongado, -a

sustenance ['sʌs·tə·nəns] n sustento m; **to give sb ~** sustentar a alguien

swab [swab] <-bb-> vt fregar; MED limpiar

swagger ['swæg·ər] I. n arrogancia f II. vi pavonearse

swallow¹ ['swal·oʊ] (food, drink) I. vt tragar II. vi tragar saliva III. n trago m
◆ **swallow down** vt tragar

swallow² ['swal·oʊ] n zool golondrina f

swam [swæm] vi pt of **swim**

swamp [swamp] I. n pantano m, suampo m AmC, wampa f Méx II. vt inundar; **to ~ sb** abrumar a alguien (**with** con); **to**

be ~ed estar agobiado (**with** de)

swan [swɒn] n cisne m

swank [swæŋk] I. adj 1. (grand) espléndido, -a 2. (pretentious) fanfarrón, -ona II. n gran elegancia f

swanky ['swæŋ·ki] adj pijo, -a

swap [swɒp] I. <-pp-> vt, vi cambiar (**for/with** por/a) II. n cambio m

swarm [swɔrm] I. vi fig aglomerarse; **to be ~ing** estar plagado (**with** de) II. n (bees) enjambre m; (people) multitud f

swastika ['swɑs·tɪ·kə] n cruz f gamada

sway [sweɪ] I. vi balancearse II. vt 1. (move) balancear 2. (persuade) persuadir III. n 1. (influence) influencia f; **under the ~** bajo el influjo (**of** de) 2. form control m; **to hold ~ over** dominar

swear [swer] <swore, sworn> I. vi 1. jurar; **I couldn't ~ to it** no pondría la mano en el fuego 2. (curse) decir palabrotas II. vt jurar (**to** a); **to ~ sb to secrecy** hacer que alguien jure silencio
  ◆**swear in** vt tomar juramento

swearing n palabrotas mpl

sweat [swet] I. n 1. sudor m; **to break into a ~** romper a sudar 2. (effort) esfuerzo m; **no ~** sin problema 3. pl inf chándal m ► **it makes me break out in a cold ~** me hace correr un sudor frío por la espalda; **to work oneself into a ~** preocuparse mucho (**about** por) II. vi sudar (**with** de) III. vt sudar; **to ~ bullets** sudar la gota gorda
  ◆**sweat out** vt **to sweat it out** inf soportar; (await) esperar con gran impaciencia

sweater ['swet·ər] n jersey m

sweatshirt ['swet·ʃɜrt] n sudadera f

sweaty ['swet·i] <-ier, -iest> adj sudado, -a

Swede [swid] n sueco, -a m, f

Sweden ['swi·dən] n Suecia f

Swedish ['swi·dɪʃ] I. adj sueco, -a II. n 1. (person) sueco, -a m, f 2. LING sueco m

sweep [swip] <swept, swept> I. n barrido m; **to give sth a ~** barrer algo; **with a ~ of her arm** con un amplio movimiento del brazo ► **to make a ~ of an area** rastrear una zona ► **to make a clean ~** hacer tabla rasa II. vt 1. (floor) barrer 2. (remove) quitar 3. (search) rastrear 4. (win) aplastar; **to ~ a series** arrasar en una serie ► **to ~ sb off his/her feet** enamorar a alguien III. vi 1. (floor) barrer 2. **to ~ into power** llegar al poder fácilmente; **to ~ into a room** entrar en una sala majestuosamente; **the road ~s around the lake** la carretera rodea el lago 3. (extend) extenderse
  ◆**sweep aside** vt 1. (move) apartar 2. (dismiss) desechar
  ◆**sweep away** vt (remove) erradicar
  ◆**sweep out** vt barrer
  ◆**sweep up** vt 1. (brush) barrer 2. (gather) recoger

sweeper n cepillo m; (person) barrendero, -a m, f

sweeping I. adj (gesture) amplio, -a; (victory) aplastante II. npl basura f; **the ~s of society** la escoria de la sociedad

sweet [swit] I. <-er, -est> adj 1. (taste) dulce 2. (pleasant) agradable; (smile) encantador(a); **to go one's own ~ way** hacer lo que a uno le da la gana 3. (cute) mono, -a 4. **to be ~ on** estar enamorado de II. n pl caramelos mpl, dulce m Chile

sweet-and-sour [ˌswit·ən·ˌsaʊ·ər] adj agridulce

sweeten ['swi·tən] vt endulzar; **to ~ sb up** ablandar a alguien

sweetener n 1. edulcorante m 2. inf incentivo m

sweetheart ['swit·hɑrt] n 1. (kind person) encanto m 2. (term of endearment) cariño m 3. (boyfriend, girlfriend) novio, -a m, f

sweetie ['swi·ti] n inf cariño m

sweetness n dulzor m; **to be all ~ and light** estar de lo más amable

sweet-talk vt camelar

sweet tooth n **to have a ~** ser goloso, -a

swell [swel] <swelled, swelled or swollen> I. vi 1. (bigger) hincharse 2. (louder) subir 3. (more) aumentar II. vt 1. (size) hinchar 2. (number) engrosar III. n (sea) oleaje m; **a heavy ~** un fuerte oleaje IV. <-er, -est> adj inf genial

swelling n hinchazón f

sweltering *adj* sofocante

swept [swept] *vt, vi pt of* **sweep**

swerve [swɜrv] I. *vi* virar bruscamente; **to ~ from** desviarse de II. *n* (*car*) viraje *m* brusco

swift[1] [swɪft] *adj* (*fast-moving*) rápido, -a; (*occurring quickly*) súbito, -a

swift[2] [swɪft] *n* ZOOL vencejo *m*

swiftly *adv* rápidamente

swig [swɪg] *inf* I. <-gg-> *vt* beber II. *n* trago *m*

swim [swɪm] I. <swam, swum> *vi* 1. *a. fig* nadar; **her head was ~ming** la cabeza le daba vueltas 2. (*full of water*) estar inundado, -a II. <swam, swum> *vt* (*cross*) cruzar a nado III. *n* nado *m*

swimmer [swɪm·ər] *n* nadador/a *m(f)*

swimming *n* natación *f*

swimming pool *n* piscina *f*, alberca *f* Méx, pileta *f* Arg

swimming trunks *npl* bañador *m*

swimsuit [swɪm·sut] *n* bañador *m*

swindle [swɪn·dəl] I. *vt* estafar II. *n* estafa *f*

swine [swaɪn] *n* (*mean person*) cabrón, -ona *m, f*

swing [swɪŋ] I. *n* 1. (*movement*) vaivén *m* 2. (*punch*) golpe *m* 3. (*hanging seat*) columpio *m* 4. (*sharp change*) cambio *m* drástico; **a mood ~** cambio de humor 5. MUS swing *m* ▶ **to get (back) into the ~ of things** cogerle el tranquillo II. <swung, swung> *vi* 1. (*move*) oscilar 2. (*hanging seat*) columpiarse 3. (*alter*) cambiar III. <swung, swung> *vt* (*move*) balancear, chilinguear Col

◆**swing around** *vi* dar un giro

swipe [swaɪp] I. *vt* 1. (*steal*) mangar 2. (*card*) pasar; (*car*) dar un golpe a II. *n* 1. (*blow*) golpe *m* 2. (*criticism*) crítica *f*

swirl [swɜrl] I. *vi* arremolinarse II. *vt* arremolinar III. *n* remolino *m*

Swiss [swɪs] *adj, n* suizo, -a *m, f*

switch [swɪtʃ] I. <-es> *n* 1. ELEC interruptor *m*, suiche *m* Méx 2. (*substitution*) reemplazamiento *m* 3. (*change*) cambio *m* II. *vi* cambiar (**from/to** de/a); **to ~ with sb** cambiarse con alguien III. *vt* cambiar (**for** por)

◆**switch off** I. *vt* apagar; (*water, electricity*) cortar II. *vi* 1. apagarse 2. (*attention*) desconectar

◆**switch on** I. *vt* encender II. *vi* encenderse

◆**switch over** *vi* cambiar

switchman <-men> *n* guardagujas *m inv*

switchyard *n* patio *m* de maniobras

Switzerland [swɪt·sər·lənd] *n* Suiza *f*

swivel [swɪv·əl] <-ll-, -l-> *vt* girar

swivel chair *n* silla *f* giratoria

swollen [swou·lən] I. *pp of* **swell** II. *adj* hinchado, -a

swoop [swup] I. *n* 1. (*dive*) caída *f* en picado 2. *inf* (*police*) redada *f* ▶ **in one fell ~** de un tirón II. *vi* (*dive*) *a. fig* caer en picado

sword [sɔrd] *n* espada *f*

swore [swɔr] *pt of* **swear**

sworn [swɔrn] I. *pp of* **swear** II. *adj* jurado, -a

swum [swʌm] *pp of* **swim**

swung [swʌŋ] *pt, pp of* **swing**

syllable [sɪl·ə·bəl] *n* sílaba *f*; **stressed/ unstressed ~** sílaba tónica/átona; **not a ~** ni media palabra

syllabus [sɪl·ə·bəs] <-es, *form:* syllabi> *n* plan *m* de estudios; (*for one subject*) programa *m*

symbol [sɪm·bəl] *n* símbolo *m*

symbolize [sɪm·bə·laɪz] *vt* simbolizar

symmetry [sɪm·ə·tri] *n* simetría *f*

sympathetic [ˌsɪm·pə·ˈθet·ɪk] *adj* (*understanding*) comprensivo, -a; (*sympathizing*) receptivo, -a; POL simpatizante (**towards** de)

sympathize [sɪm·pə·θaɪz] *vi* (*understand*) mostrar comprensión; (*pity*) compadecerse; (*agree*) estar de acuerdo; **to ~ with** simpatizar con

sympathy [sɪm·pə·θi] *n* 1. compasión *f*; (*understanding*) comprensión *f*; **you have my deepest ~** le acompaño en el sentimiento 2. solidaridad *f*

symphony [sɪm·fə·ni] *n* sinfonía *f*; (*orchestra*) orquesta *f* sinfónica

symptom [sɪmp·təm] *n* síntoma *m*

synagogue [sɪn·ə·gag] *n* sinagoga *f*

synchronize [sɪŋ·krə·naɪz] I. *vt* sincronizar II. *vi* sincronizarse

S

syndicate¹ ['sɪn·də·kɪt] *n* ECON consorcio *m;* PUBL agencia *f* de noticias

syndicate² ['sɪn·də·keɪt] *vt* ECON agrupar; PUBL vender

syndrome ['sɪn·droʊm] *n* síndrome *m;* **acquired immune deficiency ~** síndrome de la inmunodeficiencia adquirida

synonym ['sɪn·ə·nɪm] *n* sinónimo *m*

synonymous [sɪ·'nɑn·ɪ·məs] *adj* sinónimo, -a

synopsis [sɪ·'næp·sɪs] <-es> *n* sinopsis *f inv*

synthetic [sɪn·'θeṭ·ɪk] *adj* sintético, -a; (*fake*) artificial

syringe [sə·'rɪndʒ] *n* jeringuilla *f*

syrup ['sɪr·əp] *n* **1.** CULIN almíbar *m,* sirope *m AmC, Col* **2.** MED jarabe *m;* **cough ~** jarabe para la tos

system ['sɪs·təm] *n* **1.** (*set*) sistema *m;* **music ~** equipo *m* de música **2.** (*method, order*) método *m;* POL sistema *m* ▶ **to get something out of one's ~** quitarse algo de encima

systematic [ˌsɪs·tə·'mæṭ·ɪk] *adj* sistemático, -a

system error *n* error *m* en el sistema

system registry *n* registro *m* del sistema

T

T, t [ti] *n* **1.** T, t *f;* **~ as in Tango** T de Tarragona **2. the description fits him to a ~** la descripción le va perfecta

tab [tæb] *n* **1.** (*flap*) solapa *f* **2.** (*label*) etiqueta *f* **3.** *inf* (*bill*) cuenta *f;* **to put sth on the ~** cargar algo a la cuenta **4.** (*ringpull*) anilla *f* ▶ **to keep ~s on sth/sb** no perder de vista algo/a alguien

tab key *n* tabulador *m*

table ['teɪ·bəl] *n* **1.** mesa *f;* **to clear/set the ~** recoger/poner la mesa **2.** MATH tabla *f;* **multiplication ~** tabla de multiplicar **3.** (*list*) lista *f;* **~ of contents** índice *m* ▶ **the ~s have turned** han cambiado las tornas

tablecloth ['teɪ·bəl·klɔθ] *n* mantel *m*

tablespoon *n* cucharón *m*

tablet ['tæb·lɪt] *n* (*pill*) pastilla *f*

table tennis *n* ping-pong *m*

tabloid ['tæb·lɔɪd] *n* periódico *m* sensacionalista; **the ~ press** la prensa amarilla

taboo, tabu [tə·'bu] **I.** *n* tabú *m* **II.** *adj* tabú *inv*

tabulate ['tæb·ju·leɪt] *vt* COMPUT tabular

tacit ['tæs·ɪt] *adj* tácito, -a

tack [tæk] **I.** *n* (*approach*) política *f;* **to try a different ~** intentar un enfoque distinto **II.** *vi* virar

tackle ['tæk·əl] **I.** *vt* (*issue, problem*) abordar; (*job*) emprender **II.** *n* (*equipment*) equipo *m*

tacky ['tæk·i] <-ier, -iest> *adj* **1.** (*sticky*) pegajoso, -a **2.** *inf* (*showy*) hortera

tactful ['tækt·fəl] *adj* discreto, -a

tactic ['tæk·tɪk] *n* ~(**s**) táctica *f*

tactical ['tæk·tɪ·kəl] *adj* táctico, -a

tactician [tæk·'tɪʃ·ən] *n* táctico, -a *m, f*

tactile ['tæk·təl] *adj* táctil

tactless ['tækt·lɪs] *adj* falto, -a de tacto

tad [tæd] *n* **a ~** un poquitín

tadpole ['tæd·poʊl] *n* renacuajo *m*

tag [tæg] **I.** *n* **1. a.** COMPUT etiqueta *f* **2. to play ~** jugar al pillapilla **3. question ~** cláusula final interrogativa **II.** <-gg-> *vt* etiquetar; **to ~ sth onto sth** añadir algo a algo

♦ **tag along** *vi inf* seguir; **to ~ with sb** ir detrás de alguien

tail [teɪl] **I.** *n* **1.** ANAT, AVIAT cola *f;* (*dog, bull*) rabo *m* **2.** ~**s** (*coin*) cruz *f* **3.** *inf* (*person*) perseguidor(a) *m(f)* **4.** *sl* (*bottom*) trasero *m* ▶ **to chase one's ~** pillarse los dedos; **to turn ~ and run** salir por pies **II.** *vt* seguir

♦ **tail off** *vi* disminuir

tailgate I. *n* puerta *f* de atrás **II.** *vt* AUTO pegarse

taillight *n* luz *f* trasera

tailor ['teɪ·lər] **I.** *n* sastre *m* **II.** *vt* (*clothes*) confeccionar

tailor-made [ˌteɪ·lər·'meɪd] *adj* hecho, -a a medida; (*perfect*) perfecto, -a

taint [teɪnt] **I.** *vt* (*food*) contaminar; (*reputation*) manchar **II.** *n* mancha *f*

take [teɪk] **I.** *n* **1.** (*receipts*) ingresos *mpl* **2.** PHOT, CINE toma *f* **II.** <took, taken>

vt **1.** (*accept*) aceptar; (*advice*) seguir; (*responsibility*) asumir; **to ~ sth seriously** tomar algo en serio; **to ~ one's time** tomarse su tiempo; **to ~ sth as it comes** aceptar algo tal y como es; **to ~ office** entrar en funciones **2.** (*hold*) coger, agarrar *AmL* **3.** (*eat*) comer; (*medicine, drugs*) tomar **4.** (*use*) necesitar **5.** (*bring*) llevar **6.** (*decision, bath, holiday, rest*) tomar; (*walk*) dar; (*trip*) hacer; (*photograph*) sacar; (*bus, train*) coger, tomar *AmL* **7.** (*feel, assume*) **to ~ (an) interest** interesarse (**in** por); **to ~ offense** ofenderse ▸ **~ it or leave it** ¡tómalo o déjalo!; **what do you ~ me for?** ¿por quién me has tomado?; **I ~ it that...** supongo que...; **~ that!** ¡toma!
◆**take aback** *vt* sorprender; (*shock*) abatir
◆**take after** *vt* parecerse a
◆**take along** *vt* (*take*) llevarse; (*bring*) traerse
◆**take apart** *vt* **1.** (*disassemble*) desmontar **2.** (*destroy*) despedazar
◆**take away** *vt* **1.** (*remove, subtract*) quitar **2.** (*go away with*) llevarse
◆**take back** *vt* **1.** (*return*) devolver **2.** (*accept back*) aceptar **3.** (*repossess*) recobrar
◆**take down** *vt* **1.** (*remove*) quitar **2.** (*write*) apuntar **3. to take sb down** *fig* bajar los humos a alguien
◆**take in** *vt* **1.** (*at home*) acoger **2. to take sb in one's arms** sostener a alguien entre sus brazos; **to take sth in hand** *fig* hacerse cargo de algo **3.** (*deceive*) estafar **4.** (*understand*) comprender **5.** (*include*) englobar
◆**take off** I. *vt* **1.** (*remove*) retirar; (*clothes*) quitarse **2.** (*subtract*) descontar II. *vi* **1.** AVIAT despegar **2.** *sl* (*leave*) largarse; (*flee*) salir por pies
◆**take on** *vt* **1.** (*acquire*) adoptar **2.** (*hire*) contratar II. *vi* apurarse
◆**take out** *vt* **1.** (*remove*) quitar **2.** (*bring outside*) sacar **3.** (*borrow*) coger prestado
◆**take over** *vt* **1.** (*buy*) comprar **2.** (*control*) tomar el control de **3.** (*possess*) tomar posesión de
◆**take to** *vt* (*like*) encariñarse con; **to**

~ doing sth aficionarse a hacer algo; **to ~ drink/drugs** darse a la bebida/las drogas
◆**take up** I. *vt* **1.** (*bring up*) subir **2.** (*start*) empezar **3.** (*discuss*) tratar **4.** (*accept*) aceptar **5.** (*adopt*) adoptar II. *vi* **to ~ with sb/sth** relacionarse con alguien/familiarizarse con algo
take-home pay ['teɪk·hoʊm·ˌpeɪ] *n* salario *m* neto
taken ['teɪ·kən] *vi, vt pp of* **take**
takeoff ['teɪk·ɔf] *n* AVIAT despegue *m*
takeout ['teɪk·aʊt] *n* comida *f* para llevar
takeover ['teɪk·ˌoʊ·vər] *n* POL toma *f* del poder; ECON adquisición *f*
taking ['teɪ·kɪŋ] *n* **1.** (*capture*) toma *f*; **it's yours for the ~** es tuyo si lo quieres **2.** **~s** ingresos *mpl*
tale [teɪl] *n* historia *f*; (*lie*) *a.* LIT cuento *m* ▸ **to tell ~s** chivarse
talent ['tæl·ənt] *n* talento *m*
talented *adj* con mucho talento
Taliban ['tæ·lɪ·bæn] *n* talibán, -ana *m, f*
talk [tɔk] I. *n* **1.** (*conversation*) conversación *f*, plática *f Méx* **2.** (*lecture*) charla *f* **3.** **~s** negociaciones *fpl* ▸ **to be the ~ of the town** andar de boca en boca; **to be all ~ (and no action)** mucho ruido y pocas nueces *prov* II. *vi* hablar ▸ **to ~ dirty** decir obscenidades; **look who's ~ing** ¡mira quién habla! III. *vt* decir; (*discuss*) hablar de
◆**talk back** *vi* replicar
◆**talk out** *vt* **to talk sb out of sth** disuadir a alguien de algo
◆**talk over** *vt* hablar (**with** con)
◆**talk through** *vt* **1.** (*discuss*) discutir **2.** (*explain*) explicar
talkative ['tɔk·ə·t̬ɪv] *adj* hablador(a)
talker *n* hablador(a) *m(f)*
talking-to ['tɔ·kɪŋ·tu] *n* sermón *m*
talk show *n* programa *m* de entrevistas
tall [tɔl] *adj* alto, -a; **to grow ~(er)** crecer
tally ['tæl·i] <-ies> I. *n* cuenta *f*; **to keep a ~** llevar la cuenta (**of** de) II. *vi* coincidir (**with** con)
tamarind ['tæm·ə·rɪnd] *n* tamarindo *m*
tambourine [ˌtæm·bə·ˈrin] *n* pandereta *f*
tame [teɪm] I. *adj* **1.** (*animal*) manso, -a

T

2. (*unexciting*) soso, -a **II.** *vt* (*animal*) domesticar

tamper ['tæm·pər] *vi* entrometerse

tampon ['tæm·pan] *n* tampón *m*

tan¹ [tæn] **I.** <-nn-> *vi* broncearse **II.** <-nn-> *vt* (*leather*) curtir **III.** *n* bronceado *m;* **to get a ~** ponerse moreno **IV.** *adj* marrón claro

tan² *abbr of* **tangent** tg

tandem ['tæn·dəm] *n* tándem *m;* **to work in ~** trabajar conjuntamente

tang [tæŋ] *n* olor *m* penetrante

tangent ['tæn·dʒənt] *n* tangente *f;* **to go off on a ~** salirse por la tangente

tangerine [,tæn·dʒə·'rin] *n* mandarina *f*

tangible ['tæn·dʒə·bəl] *adj* tangible; (*benefit*) palpable

tangle ['tæŋ·gəl] **I.** *n* maraña *f; fig* enredo *m* **II.** *vi* enredarse

tank [tæŋk] *n* **1.** (*container*) depósito *m* **2.** MIL tanque *m*

tanker ['tæŋ·kər] *n* (*truck*) camión *m* cisterna; **oil ~** petrolero *m*

tanned [tænd] *adj* bronceado, -a

tannery ['tæn·ə·ri] *n* curtiduría *f*

tantalize ['tæn·tə·laɪz] *vt* **1.** (*torment*) atormentar **2.** (*tempt*) tentar

tantalizing *adj* tentador(a); (*smile*) seductor(a)

tantrum ['tæn·trəm] *n* berrinche *m*, dengue *m Méx;* **to have** [*or* **throw**] **a ~** coger [*or* agarrar *AmL*] una rabieta

tap¹ [tæp] *n* (*water*) grifo *m*, canilla *f Arg, Par, Urug,* **to turn the ~ on/off** abrir/cerrar el grifo; **on ~** de barril; *fig* al alcance de la mano

tap² [tæp] **I.** *n* (*knock*) golpecito *m* **II.** <-pp-> *vi* dar golpecitos

tap dance ['tæp·ˌdæns] *n* claqué *m*

tape [teɪp] *n* (*a. cassette*) cinta *f;* (*adhesive*) cinta *f* adhesiva; MED esparadrapo *m*

tape measure *n* metro *m*

taper ['teɪ·pər] **I.** *n* (*wick*) cerilla *f* **II.** *vt* afilar

tape recorder *n* grabadora *f*

tape recording *n* grabación *f*

tapestry ['tæp·əs·tri] *n* tapicería *f;* (*object*) tapiz *m*

tapeworm ['teɪp·wɜrm] *n* tenia *f*

tap water *n* agua *f* corriente

tar [tar] *n* alquitrán *m*

tarantula [tə·'ræn·tʃə·lə] *n* tarántula *f*

tare [ter] *n* ECON tara *f*

target ['tar·gɪt] **I.** *n a.* ECON objetivo *m;* **to hit the ~** dar en el blanco; **to be on ~** ir según lo previsto **II.** *vt* centrarse en

targeted ['tar·gɪ·tɪd] *adj* elegido, -a como objetivo

target practice *n* prácticas *f pl* de tiro

tariff ['tær·ɪf] *n* (*customs duty*) arancel *m*

tarmac® ['tar·mæk], **tarmacadam**® [,tar·mə·'kæd·əm] *n* asfalto *m*

tarnish ['tar·nɪʃ] **I.** *vi* deslustrarse **II.** *vt* deslustrar; (*reputation*) manchar **III.** *n* mancha *f*

tarpaulin [tar·'pɔ·lɪn] *n* lona *f* impermeabilizada

tart¹ [tart] *adj* **1.** (*taste*) agrio, -a; (*acid*) ácido, -a **2.** (*caustic*) cortante

tart² [tart] *n* CULIN tarta *f*

tartan ['tar·tən] *n* (*design*) tartán *m*

tartar ['tar·tər] *n* MED sarro *m*

tartar(e) sauce *n* salsa *f* tártara

task [tæsk] **I.** *n* tarea *f*, tonga *f Col;* **to take sb to ~** llamar la atención a alguien **II.** *vt* **to be ~ed** estar encargado (**with** de)

task force *n* MIL destacamento *m*

taste [teɪst] **I.** *n* **1.** sabor *m;* **sense of ~** sentido del gusto **2.** (*small portion*) bocado *m;* **to have a ~ of** probar **3.** (*liking*) gusto *m;* **to get a/lose the ~** coger/perder el gusto (**for** a/por); **to have different ~s** tener gustos distintos ▶ **to leave a bad ~** (**in one's mouth**) dejar un mal sabor de boca **II.** *vt* **1.** (*food, drink*) saborear **2.** (*experience*) experimentar **III.** *vi* saber (**of, like** a); **to ~ bitter/sweet** tener un sabor amargo/dulce

taste bud ['teɪst·bʌd] *n* papila *f* gustativa

tasteful ['teɪst·fəl] *adj* con gusto; (*decorous*) con delicadeza

tasteless ['teɪst·lɪs] *adj* soso, -a; (*clothes, remark*) de mal gusto

tasty ['teɪ·sti] *adj* sabroso, -a

tattle ['tæt·əl] *n* chismorreo *m*

tattoo [tæ·'tu] **I.** *n* (*on skin*) tatuaje *m* **II.** *vt* tatuar

tatty ['tæt·i] <-ier, -iest> *adj* estropeado, -a

taught [tɔt] *pt, pp of* **teach**

taunt [tɔnt] **I.** *vt* burlarse de **II.** *n* insulto *m*

Taurus ['tɔr·əs] *n* Tauro *m*

taut [tɔt] *adj* (*wire, string*) tensado, -a; (*skin*) terso, -a; (*nerves*) de punta

tavern ['tæv·ərn] *n* taberna *f*

tax [tæks] **I.** <-es> *n* **1.** FIN impuesto *m*; **free of ~** exento de impuestos **2.** *fig* carga *f* (**on** para) **II.** *vt* FIN gravar con un impuesto

taxable ['tæk·sə·bəl] *adj* imponible

tax allowance *n* desgravación *f* fiscal

taxation [tæk·'seɪ·ʃən] *n* impuestos *mpl*; (*system*) sistema *m* impositivo

tax avoidance *n* evasión *f* de impuestos

tax bracket *n* categoría *f* impositiva

tax-deductible *adj* deducible

tax dodger *n*, **tax evader** *n* evasor(a) *m(f)* de impuestos

tax evasion *n* evasión *f* de impuestos

tax exemption *n* exención *f* fiscal

tax-free *adj* libre de impuestos

tax haven *n* paraíso *m* fiscal

taxi ['tæk·si] *n* taxi *m*

taxidermist ['tæk·sɪ·ˌdɜr·mɪst] *n* taxidermista *mf*

taxi driver *n* taxista *mf*, ruletero, -a *m, f AmC, Méx*

taxing *adj* difícil

taxi stand *n* parada *f* de taxis

taxpayer ['tæks·ˌpeɪ·ər] *n* contribuyente *mf*

tax rebate *n* devolución *f* de impuestos

tax relief *n* exención *f* de impuestos

tax return *n* declaración *f* de la renta

tax revenues *n* ingresos *m pl* fiscales

tax system *n* sistema *m* impositivo

tax year *n* año *m* fiscal

tea [ti] *n* té *m*; **strong/weak ~** té fuerte/flojo; **chamomile ~** manzanilla *f* ▶ **not for all the ~ in China** ni por todo el oro del mundo

tea bag *n* bolsita *f* de té

tea break *n* descanso *m*

teach [titʃ] <taught, taught> **I.** *vt* enseñar; **to ~ sb a lesson** dar una lección a alguien **II.** *vi* dar clase(s)

teacher ['ti·tʃər] *n* profesor(a) *m(f)*

teacher training *n* formación *f* de profesorado

teaching I. *n* **1.** docencia *f* **2.** ~s enseñanza *f* **II.** *adj* didáctico, -a

teaching staff *n* profesorado *m*

teacup *n* taza *f* de té

team [tim] **I.** *n* equipo *m* **II.** *adj* de equipo **III.** *vt* asociar

♦**team up** *vi* agruparse; **to ~ with** asociarse con

teammate *n* compañero, -a *m, f*

team effort *n* esfuerzo *m* conjunto

team spirit *n* espíritu *m* de equipo

teamwork *n* trabajo *m* en equipo

teapot ['ti·pat] *n* tetera *f*

tear[1] [tɪr] *n* (*from crying*) lágrima *f*; **to bring ~s to sb's eyes** hacer que a alguien se le salten las lágrimas; **to burst into ~s** echarse a llorar; **to not shed (any) ~s** no derramar una (sola) lágrima

tear[2] [ter] <tore, torn> **I.** *vt* (*rip*) rasgar; (*ruin*) romper; **to ~ a hole** hacer un agujero (**in** en) **II.** *vi* **1.** (*rip*) rasgarse **2.** (*rush*) lanzarse

♦**tear apart** *vt* destrozar; *fig* dividir

♦**tear at** *vt* quitar de un tirón

♦**tear away I.** *vi* salir disparado **II.** *vt* (*pull*) arrancar; **to tear sb/oneself away** sacar a alguien/irse de mala gana

♦**tear down** *vt* derribar

♦**tear into** *vt* arremeter contra

♦**tear off I.** *vt* arrancar **II.** *vi* (*leave*) salir disparado

♦**tear out** *vt* arrancar de cuajo; **to tear one's hair out** *fig* subirse por las paredes (**over** por)

♦**tear up** *vt* despedazar

teardrop ['tɪr·drap] *n* lágrima *f*

tearful ['tɪr·fəl] *adj* lloroso, -a

tear gas *n* gas *m* lacrimógeno

tease [tiz] **I.** *vt* **1.** (*make fun*) tomar el pelo (**about** por) **2.** (*provoke*) provocar **II.** *vi* bromear *mf*; (*sexually*) provocador(a) *m(f)*

teaser ['ti·zər] *n* rompecabezas *m inv*

teaspoon *n* cucharilla *f*

teaspoonful ['ti·spun·fʊl] *n* cucharadita *f*

teat [tit] *n* teta *f*

teatime ['ti·taɪm] *n* hora *f* del té

tea towel *n* paño *m* de cocina

T

technical ['tek·nɪ·kəl] *adj* técnico, -a; ~ **term** tecnicismo *m*

technician [tek·'nɪʃ·ən] *n* técnico, -a *m, f*

technique [tek·'nik] *n* técnica *f*

technological [,tek·nə·'lɑdʒ·ɪ·kəl] *adj* tecnológico, -a

technology [tek·'nɑl·ə·dʒi] *n* tecnología *f*

tedious ['ti·di·əs] *adj* aburrido, -a

tee [ti] *n* SPORTS tee *m*

♦**tee off** *sl* **I.** *vi* (*start*) arrancar(se) **II.** *vt* (*anger*) cabrear

teem [tim] *vi* rebosar; **to ~/be ~ing with** estar repleto de

teeming *adj* muy numeroso, -a

teenage(d) ['tin·eɪdʒ(d)] *adj* adolescente

teenager ['tin·eɪ·dʒər] *n* adolescente *mf*

teens [tinz] *npl* adolescencia *f*

teensy ['tin·si] *adj*, **teensy-weensy** *adj*, **teeny** ['ti·ni] *adj* chiquitín, -ina

tee shirt ['ti·ʃɜrt] *n* camiseta *f*

teeth [tiθ] *pl of* **tooth**

teethe [tið] *vi* echar los dientes

teetotal [,ti·'tou·təl] *adj* abstemio, -a

teetotaler [,ti·'tou·təl·ər] *n* abstemio, -a *m, f*

telecommunications ['tel·ɪ·kə·,mju·nɪ·'keɪ·ʃənz] *npl* telecomunicaciones *fpl*

telecommuting ['tel·ɪ·kə·,mju·tɪŋ] *n* teletrabajo *m*

teleconference ['tel·ɪ·,kɑn·fər·əns] *n* teleconferencia *f*

telecopy ['tel·ɪ·kɑp·i] *n* fotocopia *f*

telegram ['tel·ɪ·græm] *n* telegrama *m*

telepathic [,tel·ə·'pæθ·ɪk] *adj* telepático, -a

telepathy [tə·'lep·ə·θi] *n* telepatía *f*

telephone ['tel·ə·foun] **I.** *n* teléfono *m*; **mobile ~** móvil *m* **II.** *vt, vi* llamar por teléfono **III.** *adj* telefónico, -a

telephone book *n* guía *f* telefónica

telephone booth *n* cabina *f* telefónica

telephone call *n* llamada *f* telefónica

telephone conversation *n* conversación *f* telefónica

telephone directory *n* guía *f* telefónica

telephone exchange *n* central *f* telefónica

telephone information service *n* servicio *m* de información telefónica

telephone message *n* mensaje *m* telefónico

telephone number *n* número *m* de teléfono

telephone operator *n* operador(a) *m(f)* telefónico, -a

telephone rates *n* tarifa *f* telefónica

telephoto lens ['tel·ə·fou·tou·'lens] *n* teleobjetivo *m*

teleprocessing ['tel·ɪ·prɑ·,ses·ɪŋ] *n* teleproceso *m*

telescope ['tel·ə·skoup] *n* telescopio *m*

telescopic [,tel·ə·'skɑp·ɪk] *adj* telescópico, -a; (*folding*) plegable

teleshopping ['tel·ə·ʃɑp·ɪŋ] *n* telecompra *f*

televise ['tel·ə·vaɪz] *vt* televisar

television ['tel·ə·vɪʒ·ən] *n* televisión *f*; (*TV set*) televisor *m*; **to watch ~** ver la televisión; **to turn the ~ on/off** encender/apagar el televisor

television announcer *n* locutor(a) *m(f)* de televisión

television camera *n* cámara *f* de televisión

television program *n* programa *m* de televisión

television set *n* televisor *m*

television studio *n* estudio *m* de televisión

tell [tel] **I.** *<told, told> vt* **1.** (*say*) decir; **to ~ sb of sth** comunicar algo a alguien; **I told you so** te avisé **2.** (*narrate*) contar **3.** (*command*) mandar; **to ~ sb to do sth** mandar a alguien que haga algo **4.** (*make out*) reconocer; **to ~ sth from sth** distinguir algo de algo; **there is no ~ing** no hay manera de saberlo ► **to ~ it like it is** las cosas claras; **you're ~ing me!** ¡a mí me lo vas a contar! **II.** *<told, told> vi* **1.** hablar (*of* de) **2.** (*know*) saber; **you never can ~** nunca se sabe; **how can I ~?** ¡yo qué sé!; **who can ~?** ¿quién sabe?

♦**tell apart** *vt* distinguir

♦**tell off** *vt* regañar (**for** por)

teller ['tel·ər] *n* (*employee*) cajero, -a *m, f*

telling ['tel·ɪŋ] **I.** *adj* (*revealing*) revelador(a) **II.** *n* narración *f*

telling-off [,tel·ɪŋ·'ɔf] *<tellings-off> n Can* bronca *f*; **to give sb a ~ for** (*do-*

ing) sth echar una bronca a alguien por (hacer) algo

telltale ['tel·teɪl] n chivato, -a m, f

temp [temp] **I.** vi trabajar temporalmente **II.** n trabajador(a) m(f) temporal

temper ['tem·pər] **I.** n temperamento m; (*mood*) humor m; **(bad) ~** (mal) genio; **good ~** buen humor; **to keep one's ~** no perder la calma; **to lose one's ~** perder los estribos **II.** vt (*mitigate*) atenuar

temperament ['tem·prə·mənt] n temperamento m; (*moodiness*) genio m

temperamental [ˌtem·prə·'men·təl] adj temperamental; (*unpredictable*) caprichoso, -a

temperate ['tem·pər·ət] adj moderado, -a

temperature ['tem·pər·ə·tʃər] n temperatura f; MED fiebre f; **to run a ~** tener fiebre

tempest ['tem·pɪst] n tempestad f

tempestuous [tem·'pes·tʃu·əs] adj tempestuoso, -a

temple[1] ['tem·pəl] n REL templo m

temple[2] ['tem·pəl] n ANAT sien f

tempo ['tem·poʊ] <-s or -pi> n **1.** MUS tempo m **2.** (*pace*) ritmo m

temporarily ['tem·pə·rer·ə·li] adv temporalmente

temporary ['tem·pə·rer·i] adj (*improvement, relief*) pasajero, -a; (*staff, accommodation*) temporal

tempt [tempt] vt tentar; **to ~ sb into doing sth** incitar a alguien a hacer algo

temptation [temp·'teɪ·ʃən] n tentación f; (*tempting thing*) aliciente m; **to resist ~ (to do sth)** resistir la tentación (de hacer algo); **to succumb to ~** caer en la tentación

tempting ['temp·tɪŋ] adj tentador(a)

ten [ten] **I.** adj diez inv **II.** n diez m; **~ to one he comes** seguro que viene; s. a. **eight**

tenacious [tə·'neɪ·ʃəs] adj firme; (*person*) tenaz

tenacity [tə·'næs·ə·ţi] n tenacidad f

tenant ['ten·ənt] n inquilino, -a m, f

tend[1] [tend] vi (*have tendency*) tender; **to ~ to do sth** tender a hacer algo; (*usually*) soler hacer algo

tend[2] [tend] vt (*look after*) ocuparse de

tendency ['ten·dən·si] <-ies> n tendencia f; MED propensión f

tender[1] ['ten·dər] adj **1.** (*soft*) tierno, -a **2.** (*easily damaged*) vulnerable **3.** (*affectionate*) cariñoso, -a

tender[2] ['ten·dər] **I.** n COM oferta f **II.** vi hacer una oferta (**for** para)

tenderize ['ten·də·raɪz] vt ablandar

tenderloin ['ten·dər·lɔɪn] n lomo m

tenderness ['ten·dər·nɪs] n **1.** (*softness*) blandura f **2.** (*affection*) ternura f **3.** (*sensitivity*) sensibilidad f

tendon ['ten·dən] n tendón m

tenfold ['ten·foʊld] adv diez veces

tennis ['ten·ɪs] n tenis m inv

tennis ball n pelota f de tenis

tennis court n pista f de tenis

tennis racket n raqueta f de tenis

tenor ['ten·ər] n a. MUS tenor m; (*of events*) curso m

tense[1] [tens] n LING tiempo m

tense[2] [tens] **I.** adj tenso, -a **II.** vt tensar **III.** vi ponerse tenso

tension ['ten·ʃən] n tensión f

tent [tent] n (*for camping*) tienda f de campaña, carpa f AmL; (*circus*) carpa f

tentacle ['ten·tə·kəl] n tentáculo m

tentative ['ten·tə·ţɪv] adj vacilante; (*decision*) provisional

tentatively adv (*suggest*) con vacilación; (*decide*) provisionalmente

tenth [tenθ] **I.** adj décimo, -a **II.** n **1.** (*order*) décimo, -a m, f **2.** (*date*) diez m **3.** (*fraction*) décimo m; s. a. **eighth**

tent peg n estaquilla f de tienda

tent pole n mástil m de tienda

tenure ['ten·jər] n (*possession*) posesión f

tepid ['tep·ɪd] adj tibio, -a

terabyte ['ter·ə·baɪt] n terabyte m

term [tɜrm] n **1.** (*label, word, category*) término m; **~ of abuse** insulto m; **in glowing ~s** con gran admiración; **in no uncertain ~s** en términos claros; **in simple ~s** en palabras sencillas **2.** **~s** (*conditions*) condiciones fpl; **to offer easy ~s** ofrecer facilidades de pago **3.** (*limit*) plazo m; **~ of delivery** plazo de entrega; **in the short/long ~** a corto/largo plazo **4.** UNIV, SCHOOL tri-

T

mestre *m* **5. to be on good/bad ~s** llevarse bien/mal (**with** con)

terminal ['tɜr·mɪ·nəl] **I.** *adj* terminal; (*extreme*) absoluto, -a **II.** *n* RAIL, AVIAT, COMPUT terminal *f*; ELEC polo *m*

terminate ['tɜr·mɪ·neɪt] *vt* poner fin a; (*contract*) rescindir; (*pregnancy*) interrumpir

termination [ˌtɜr·mɪ·'neɪ·ʃən] *n* fin *m*; (*contract*) rescisión *f*; (*pregnancy*) interrupción *f*

terminus ['tɜr·mɪ·nəs] <-es *or* -i> *n* última parada *f*

termite ['tɜr·maɪt] *n* termita *f*

terrace ['ter·əs] *n* a. AGR terraza *f*

terraced house *n* casa *f* adosada

terrain [tə·'reɪn] *n* terreno *m*

terrible ['ter·ə·bəl] *adj* **1.** (*shocking*) terrible **2.** (*very bad*) espantoso, -a **3.** *inf* fatal

terribly ['ter·ə·bli] *adv* terriblemente; (*very*) tremendamente

terrific [tə·'rɪf·ɪk] *adj* **1.** (*terrifying*) terrorífico, -a **2.** (*excellent*) estupendo, -a **3.** (*very great*) tremendo, -a

terrified *adj* aterrorizado, -a

terrify ['ter·ə·faɪ] <-ie-> *vt* aterrar

terrifying *adj* aterrador(a)

territory ['ter·ə·tɔr·i] <-ies> *n* territorio *m*

terror ['ter·ər] *n* terror *m* (**of** a); **to strike ~** infundir terror; **a little ~** un demonio de niño

terrorism ['ter·ə·rɪz·əm] *n* terrorismo *m*

terrorist ['ter·ə·rɪst] *adj*, *n* terrorista *mf*

terrorize ['ter·ə·raɪz] *vt* aterrorizar

terror-stricken ['ter·ər·ˌstrɪk·ən] *adj*, **terror-struck** ['ter·ər·strʌk] *adj* aterrorizado, -a

terry cloth [ˌter·i·'klɔθ] *n* felpa *f*

terse [tɜrs] *adj* lacónico, -a

Tertiary ['tɜr·ʃi·er·i] *n* **the Tertiary** el Terciario

test [test] **I.** *n* **1.** SCHOOL, UNIV examen *m*; **to pass/fail a ~** aprobar/suspender un examen; **driving ~** examen de conducir **2.** MED prueba *f*; **blood ~** análisis *m inv* de sangre **3. to put sth to the ~** poner algo a prueba **II.** *vt* **1.** (*examine*) *a.* MED examinar; **to ~ sb for sth** hacer a alguien una prueba de algo **2.** (*meas-*

ure) comprobar **3.** (*try to prove*) someter a prueba

testament ['tes·tə·mənt] *n* **1.** (*will*) testamento *m* **2.** (*evidence*) testimonio *m* **3. Old/New Testament** Antiguo/Nuevo Testamento

test bench *n* banco *m* de pruebas

test drive *n* vuelta *f* de prueba

testicle ['tes·tɪ·kəl] *n* testículo *m*

testify ['tes·tɪ·faɪ] <-ie-> *vi*, *vt* testificar; **to ~ that...** declarar que...; **to ~ to sth** atestiguar algo

testimony ['tes·tɪ·moʊ·ni] <-ies> *n* testimonio *m*; **to give ~** dar testimonio

testing **I.** *n* experiencia *f* **II.** *adj* duro, -a

test pilot *n* piloto *mf* de pruebas

test stage *n* período *m* de pruebas

test tube *n* probeta *f*

testy ['tes·ti] <-ier, -iest> *adj* irritable

tetanus ['tet·ə·nəs] *n* tétano(s) *m (inv)*; **~ injection** vacuna *f* antitetánica

tetchy ['tetʃ·i] <-ier, -iest> *adj* irritable

tether ['teð·ər] **I.** *n* cuerda *f* ▶ **to be at the end of one's ~** no aguantar más **II.** *vt* amarrar; **to be ~ed to sth** *fig* estar atado a algo

Texan ['tek·sən] *adj*, *n* tejano, -a *m*, *f*

Texas ['tek·səs] *n* Tejas *m*

text [tekst] *n* texto *m*

textbook ['tekst·bʊk] *n* libro *m* de texto

textile ['teks·taɪl] **I.** *n pl* tejidos *mpl* **II.** *adj* textil

than [ðən, ðæn] *conj* que; **you are taller ~ she (is)** eres más alto que ella; **more ~ 60** más de 60; **more ~ once** más de una vez; **nothing else ~...** nada más que...; **no other ~ you** nadie más que tú; **no sooner had she told him, ~...** en cuanto se lo dijo...

thank [θæŋk] *vt* dar las gracias (**for** por); **~ you (very much)** (muchas) gracias

thankful ['θæŋk·fəl] *adj* **1.** (*pleased*) aliviado, -a; **to be ~ that...** alegrarse de que... +*subj* **2.** (*grateful*) agradecido, -a

thankfully *adv* afortunadamente

thankless ['θæŋk·lɪs] *adj* desagradecido, -a

thanks [θæŋks] *npl* gracias *fpl* (**to** a); **~ very much** muchísimas gracias; **in ~**

thanksgiving [θæŋks·'gɪv·ɪŋ] *n* acción *f* de gracias

Thanksgiving (Day) *n* Día *m* de Acción de Gracias

that [ðət, ðæt] **I.** *adj dem* <those> ese/esos, esa(s) (*more remote*) aquel/aquellos, aquella(s) *m, f;* **~ table** esa/aquella mesa; **~ book** ese/aquel libro **II.** *pron* **1.** *rel* que; **the woman ~ told me...** la mujer que me dijo...; **all ~ I have** todo lo que tengo **2.** *dem* ése/ésos, ésa(s) *m, f,* eso(s) *neuter;* **what is ~?** ¿eso qué es?; **who is ~?** ¿ése/ésa quién es?; **like ~** así; **after ~** después de eso **III.** *adv;* **it was ~ hot** hacía tanto calor **IV.** *conj* **1.** que; **I told you ~ I couldn't come** te dije que no podía ir **2.** (*in order that*) para que +*subj*

thatch [θætʃ] *n inf* (*hair*) greña *f*

thatched roof *n* techo *m* de paja

thaw [θɔ] **I.** *n* (*weather*) deshielo *m* **II.** *vi* (*weather*) deshelar; (*food*) descongelarse **III.** *vt* derretir

the [ðə, *stressed, before vowel* ði] **I.** *def art* el(la) *m(f),* los(las) *m(f)pl;* **from ~ garden** del jardín; **at ~ hotel** en el hotel; **to ~ garden** al jardín **II.** *adv* ~ **more one tries,** ~ **less one succeeds** cuanto más se esfuerza uno, menos lo logra; ~ **sooner ~ better** cuanto antes mejor

theater ['θɪ·ə·tər] *n* **1.** THEAT teatro *m* **2.** CINE cine *m* **3.** UNIV auditorio *m*

theatrical [θɪ·'æt·rɪ·kəl] *adj* teatral; **don't be so ~ about it** no hagas tanto teatro por eso

theft [θeft] *n* robo *m;* **petty ~** hurto *m*

their [ðer] *adj pos* su(s); ~ **house** su casa; ~ **children** sus hijos

theirs [ðerz] *pron pos* (el) suyo, (la) suya *m, f,* (los) suyos, (las) suyas *m, fpl;* **this house is ~** esta casa es suya; **they aren't our bags, they are ~** no son nuestras bolsas, son las suyas; **a book of ~** un libro suyo

them [ðem, ðəm] *pron pers pl* **1.** (*they*) ellos, -as; **older than ~** mayor que ellos **2.** *direct object* los(las) *m(f);* *indirect object* les; **look at ~** míralos; **I saw ~** yo los vi; **he gave ~ the pencil** les dio el lápiz **3.** *after prep* ellos, -as; **it's from/**

for ~ es de/para ellos

theme [θim] *n a.* MUS tema *m;* **on the ~ of** sobre el tema de

theme music *n* sintonía *f*

theme park *n* parque *m* temático

themselves [ðəm·'selvz] *pron* **1.** *subject* ellos mismos, ellas mismas *m, f* **2.** *object, reflexive* se; **the children behaved ~** los niños se portaron bien **3.** *after prep* sí mismos, sí mismas *m, f;* **by ~** solos, -as

then [ðen] **I.** *adj* **the ~ chairman** el entonces presidente **II.** *adv* **1.** (*at that time*) entonces; **before/since ~** hasta/desde entonces; **from ~ on(ward)** a partir de entonces; **until ~** hasta aquel momento; **(every) now and ~** de vez en cuando **2.** (*after that*) después; **what ~?** ¿y entonces qué? **3.** (*additionally*) además; **but ~** (*again*) y además **4.** ~ **he must be there** entonces debe estar allí

theologian [ˌθi·ə·'lou·dʒən] *n* teólogo, -a *m, f*

theology [θɪ·'al·ə·dʒi] <-ies> *n* teología *f*

theorem ['θi·ər·əm] *n* teorema *m*

theoretical [ˌθi·ə·'ret·ɪ·kəl] *adj* teórico, -a

theory ['θi·ə·ri] <-ies> *n* teoría *f;* **in ~** en teoría

therapeutic [ˌθer·ə·'pju·tɪk] *adj,* **therapeutical** [ˌθer·ə·'pju·tɪ·kəl] *adj* terapéutico, -a

therapist ['θer·ə·pɪst] *n* terapeuta *mf*

therapy ['θer·ə·pi] <-ies> *n* terapia *f*

there [ðer] **I.** *adv* allí [*or* allá]; **here and ~** aquí y allá; ~ **is/are** hay; ~ **will be** habrá; ~ **you are!** ¡ahí lo tienes!; ~ **'s the train** ahí está el tren; ~ **is no one** no hay nadie; ~ **and then** en el acto **II.** *interj* ¡vaya!; ~, **take this** toma esto; ~, **that's enough!** ¡bueno, basta ya!

thereabouts ['ðer·ə·bauts] *adv* por ahí

thereafter [ðer·'æf·tər] *adv* a partir de entonces

thereby [ðer·'baɪ] *adv* por eso ► ~ **hangs a tale** es una larga historia

therefore ['ðer·fɔr] *adv* por (lo) tanto

therein [ðer·'ɪn] *adv form* ahí dentro; *fig* en eso

thereupon [ˌðer·ə·ˈpan] *adv* acto seguido

thermal [ˈθɜr·məl] *adj* térmico, -a; (*water*) termal

thermal underwear *n* ropa *f* interior térmica

thermodynamic [ˌθɜr·moʊ·daɪ·ˈnæm·ɪk] *adj* termodinámico, -a

thermoelectric [ˌθɜr·moʊ·ɪ·ˈlek·trɪk] *adj* termoeléctrico, -a

thermometer [θər·ˈmam·ə·t̬ər] *n* termómetro *m*

thermos [ˈθɜr·məs] *n* termo *m*

thermostat [ˈθɜr·mə·stæt] *n* termostato *m*

thesaurus [θɪ·ˈsɔr·əs] <-es *or* -ri> *n* diccionario *m* de sinónimos y antónimos

these [ðiz] *pl of* **this**

thesis [ˈθi·sɪs] <-ses> *n* tesis *f inv*

they [ðeɪ] *pron pers* 1. (*3rd person pl*) ellos, -as ~ **are my parents/sisters** (ellos/ellas) son mis padres/hermanas 2. (*people in general*) ~ **say that...** dicen que...

they'll [ðeɪl] = **they will** *see* **will**

they're [ðer] = **they are** *see* **be**

they've [ðeɪv] = **they have** *see* **have**

thick [θɪk] I. *adj* 1. (*wall*) grueso, -a; (*coat*) gordo, -a; (*hair*) abundante; (*forest*) denso, -a; (*liquid*) espeso, -a; (*darkness*) profundo, -a 2. (*stupid*) corto, -a; **to be as ~ as two short planks** no tener dos dedos de frente 3. **to be ~ with sb** ser muy amigo de alguien II. *n* **to be in the ~ of sth** estar de lleno en algo

thicken [ˈθɪk·ən] *vt, vi* espesar

thicket [ˈθɪk·ɪt] *n* matorral *m*

thickness [ˈθɪk·nɪs] *n* grosor *m*; (*hair*) abundancia *f*; (*sauce*) consistencia *f*

thick-skinned [ˈθɪk·skɪnd] *adj* insensible; **he is ~** todo le resbala

thief [θif, θivz] <thieves> *n* ladrón, -ona *m, f*

thieving [ˈθi·vɪŋ] *adj* de dedos largos

thigh [θaɪ] *n* muslo *m*

thimble [ˈθɪm·bəl] *n* dedal *m*

thin [θɪn] <-nn-> *adj* (*person*) flaco, -a; (*clothes*) fino, -a; (*voice*) débil; (*hair*) ralo, -a; **to be ~ on top** ser calvo

◆**thin out** *vi* disminuir

thing [θɪŋ] *n* 1. cosa *f*; **all his ~s** todas sus cosas; **the lucky/best/main ~** lo

bueno/mejor/principal; **the last ~ she wants to do is...** lo último que quiere hacer es...; **above all ~s** por encima de todo; **if it's not one ~, it's another** cuando no es una cosa es otra 2. *inf* **the real ~** lo auténtico; **the very ~** lo importante 3. (*situation*) **as ~s stand, the way ~s are** tal (y) como están las cosas; **the shape of ~s to come** lo que se avecina 4. *inf* **the poor ~!** ¡el pobre!; (*children, animals*) ¡pobrecito!; **you lucky ~!** ¡qué suerte tienes!; **lazy ~!** ¡vago! ▶ **he won but it was a close ~** ganó por un pelo; **all ~s being equal** si no surge ningún imprevisto; **first ~s first** lo primero es lo primero; **to not know the first ~** no tener ni la más remota idea (**about** de); **to be onto a good ~** tener un chollo; **to have a ~ about** tener asco a; **to make a (big) ~** armar un escándalo (**out of** por)

think [θɪŋk] <thought, thought> I. *vt* 1. (*believe*) pensar; **who would have thought it!** ¡quien lo hubiese pensado! 2. (*consider*) considerar; **to ~ sb (to be) sth** considerar a alguien (como) algo II. *vi* pensar; **to ~ of sb/doing sth** pensar en alguien/hacer algo; **to ~ aloud** pensar en voz alta; **to ~ for/to oneself** pensar por/para sí mismo

◆**think ahead** *vi* pensar de cara al futuro

◆**think back** *vi* **to ~ over/to sth** hacer memoria de/recordar algo

◆**think out** *vt* 1. (*consider*) pensar muy bien 2. (*plan*) planear cuidadosamente

◆**think over** *vt* reflexionar sobre

◆**think through** *vt* estudiar detenidamente

◆**think up** *vt* inventar

thinker *n* pensador(a) *m(f)*

thinking I. *n* 1. (*thought*) pensamiento *m* 2. (*reasoning*) razonamiento *m* 3. (*opinion*) opinión *f* II. *adj* inteligente

think tank *n* gabinete *m* estratégico

thinner *n* disolvente *m*

third [θɜrd] I. *adj* tercero, -a II. *n* 1. (*order*) tercero, -a *m, f* 2. (*date*) tres *m* 3. (*fraction*) tercio *m* 4. MUS, AUTO tercera *f*; *s. a.* **eighth**

thirdly adv en tercer lugar

third party n tercero m

Third World n Tercer Mundo

thirst [θɜrst] n a. fig sed f

thirsty ['θɜr·sti] <-ier, -iest> adj sediento, -a; **to be ~** tener sed; fig estar ansioso (**for** por)

thirteen [θɜr·'tin] adj, n trece m; s. a. **eight**

thirteenth [θɜr·'tinθ] I. adj decimotercero, -a II. n 1. (order) decimotercero, -a m, f 2. (date) trece m 3. (fraction) decimotercero m; s. a. **eighth**

thirtieth ['θɜrt·i·əθ] I. adj trigésimo, -a II. n 1. (order) trigésimo, -a m, f 2. (date) treinta m 3. (fraction) trigésimo m; s. a. **eighth**

thirty ['θɜr·ţi] <-ies> adj, n treinta m; s. a. **eight**

this [ðɪs] I. <these> adj det este, -a; ~ **car** este coche; ~ **house** esta casa; ~ **one** éste, -a; ~ **morning/evening** esta mañana/tarde; ~ **time** esta vez; **these days** hoy en día II. <these> pron dem éste m, ésta f, esto neuter; **what is ~?** ¿esto qué es?; **who is ~?** ¿éste/ésta quién es?; ~ **and that** esto y aquello; ~ **is Ana (speaking)** TEL soy Ana III. adv así; ~ **late** tan tarde; ~ **much** tanto; ~ **big** así de grande

thistle ['θɪs·əl] n cardo m

thong [θɑŋ] n 1. (of leather) correa f 2. (G-string) tanga m 3. (sandal) chancla f

thorn [θɔrn] n espina f

thorny ['θɔr·ni] <-ier, -iest> adj espinoso, -a, espinudo, -a AmC, CSur; (issue) peliagudo, -a

thorough ['θɜr·oʊ] adj 1. (complete) absoluto, -a 2. (detailed) exhaustivo, -a 3. (careful) minucioso, -a

thoroughbred ['θɜr·oʊ·brɛd] I. n pura sangre mf II. adj de pura sangre

thoroughfare ['θɜr·oʊ·fɛr] n vía f pública

thoroughly adv 1. (in detail) a fondo 2. (completely) completamente

those [ðoʊz] pl of **that**

though [ðoʊ] I. conj aunque; **as** ~ como si +subj; **even** ~ aunque; **even** ~ **it's cold** aunque hace frío II. adv sin embargo; **he did it,** ~ sin embargo, sí que lo hizo

thought [θɔt] n 1. (process) reflexión f; **without** ~ sin pensar; **after much** ~ tras mucho reflexionar; **to be deep/lost in** ~ estar ensimismado 2. (idea, opinion) pensamiento m; **that's a** ~ es posible

thoughtful ['θɔt·fəl] adj 1. (pensive) pensativo, -a 2. (careful) cuidadoso, -a 3. (considerate) atento, -a

thoughtless ['θɔt·lɪs] adj irreflexivo, -a; (tactless) desconsiderado, -a; (careless) descuidado, -a

thought-out [ˌθɔt·'aʊt] adj planeado, -a

thought-provoking adj que hace pensar

thousand ['θaʊ·zənd] adj, n mil m

thousandth ['θaʊ·zəntθ] adj, n milésimo m; **the** ~ el número mil

thrash [θræʃ] vt a. fig dar una paliza

 ◆**thrash out** vt inf (problem) discutir; (agreement) llegar a

thrashing n paliza f, batida f AmL

thread [θrɛd] n hilo m ▶ **to hang by a** ~ pender de un hilo

threadbare ['θrɛd·bɛr] adj raído, -a; (argument, excuse) trillado, -a

threat [θrɛt] n amenaza f

threaten ['θrɛt·ən] vt, vi amenazar (**to** con)

threatening adj amenazador(a)

three [θri] adj, n tres m; s. a. **eight**

three-D [ˌθri·'di] adj abbr of **three-dimensional** en tres D

three-dimensional adj tridimensional

threefold ['θri·foʊld] I. adj triple II. adv por triplicado

three-part adj de tres partes

three-piece ['θri·'pis] adj de tres piezas

threshold ['θrɛʃ·hoʊld] n umbral m

threw [θru] pt of **throw**

thrice [θraɪs] adv tres veces

thrifty ['θrɪf·ti] <-ier, -iest> adj ahorrativo, -a

thrill [θrɪl] I. n estremecimiento m II. vt estremecer III. vi estremecerse

thriller ['θrɪl·ər] n novela f de suspense; CINE película f de suspense

thrilling ['θrɪl·ɪŋ] adj emocionante

thrive [θraɪv] <thrived or throve, thrived or thriven> vi crecer mucho; (business) prosperar

thriving adj próspero, -a

throat [θrout] n (external) cuello m; (internal) garganta f; **sore ~** dolor de garganta

throb [θrab] I. n vibración f; (heart) palpitación f II. <-bb-> vi vibrar; (heart) palpitar

throne [θroun] n trono m

throttle ['θrɑt·əl] n acelerador m; **to open the ~** acelerar; **at full ~** a todo gas

◆**throttle back** vi reducir (la velocidad)

through [θru] I. prep 1. (place) a través de, por; **to go right ~ sth** traspasar algo; **to go ~ the door** entrar por la puerta; **to walk ~ a room** atravesar una habitación 2. (during) durante; **all ~ my life** durante toda mi vida; **to be ~** acabar (de) 3. (until) hasta; **open Monday ~ Friday** abierto de lunes a viernes 4. (by means of) por (medio de) II. adv 1. (place) de un lado a otro; I **read the book ~** leí el libro entero; **to go ~** ir directo (to a) 2. (time) **all day ~** de la mañana a la noche; **halfway ~** a medio camino 3. **to put sb ~ to sb** poner a alguien con alguien 4. (completely) completamente; **to think sth ~** pensarse algo detenidamente ▶ **~ and ~** de cabo a rabo III. adj 1. (finished) terminado, -a; **we are ~** hemos terminado 2. (direct) directo, -a 3. SCHOOL **to get ~** aprobar

throughout [θru·'aut] I. prep 1. (place) por todas partes de; **~ the town** por toda la ciudad 2. (time) a lo largo de; **~ his stay** durante toda su estancia II. adv 1. (place) por [or en] todas partes 2. (time) todo el tiempo

through traffic n tráfico m de tránsito

through train n tren m directo

throughway ['θru·wei] n autopista f de peaje

throw [θrou] I. n 1. (toss) lanzamiento m 2. inf (chance) oportunidad f II. <threw, thrown> vi lanzar III. <threw, thrown> vt 1. (propel, cause to fall) tirar; (ball, javelin, glance) lanzar; **to ~ oneself at sb** tirar los tejos a alguien; **to ~ oneself into sth** entregarse de lleno a algo 2. inf (confuse) desconcertar 3. **to ~**

the switch pulsar el interruptor; **to ~ a party** dar una fiesta

◆**throw away** vt 1. (discard) tirar 2. (waste) malgastar; (money) despilfarrar (on en) 3. (say) soltar

◆**throw back** vt 1. (return) devolver 2. (curtains) correr 3. **to throw sth back (in sb's face)** echar algo en cara a alguien

◆**throw down** vt 1. (throw) tirar 2. (deposit) dejar

◆**throw in** vt arrojar; (include) agregar; (comment) soltar

◆**throw off** vt 1. (remove) quitarse 2. (escape from) despistar

◆**throw on** vt (clothes) ponerse

◆**throw out** vt (heat, light) despedir; (person) echar; (thing) tirar

◆**throw together** vt (make quickly) hacer en un periquete

◆**throw up** I. vt 1. (project upwards) lanzar al aire 2. (bring to light) revelar 3. (build quickly) levantar 4. inf (give up) dejar II. vi potar, buitrear CSur, revulsar Méx

throwaway ['θrou·ə·wei] adj desechable

throw-in ['θrou·ɪn] n (soccer) saque m de banda; (baseball) lanzamiento m

throwing n lanzamiento m

thrown pp of **throw**

thru [θru] prep, adj see **through**

thrush [θrʌʃ] n MED afta f

thrust [θrʌst] I. <-, -> vi (shove) empujar II. <-, -> vt (push) empujar; (insert) clavar III. n 1. (shove) empujón m 2. (impetus) empuje m 3. TECH propulsión f

thrusting ['θrʌs·tɪŋ] adj arribista

thruway ['θru·wei] n autopista f de peaje

thud [θʌd] <-dd-> vi dar un golpe sordo

thug [θʌg] n matón, -ona m, f

thumb [θʌm] n pulgar m ▶ **to be all fingers and ~s** to be all <u>thumbs</u> ser un manazas; **to stand out like a <u>sore</u> ~** cantar como una almeja

thumbnail ['θʌm·neɪl] n uña f del pulgar

thumbnail sketch n pequeña reseña f

thumbtack n tachuela f

thump [θʌmp] I. vt golpear II. vi

1. (*heart*) latir con fuerza **2. to ~ on sth** aporrear algo **III.** *n* porrazo *m*

thumping *adj inf* descomunal

thunder ['θʌn·dər] **I.** *n* **1. a** (*clap of*) ~ un trueno **2.** (*sound*) estruendo *m*

thunderclap *n* trueno *m*

thundercloud *n* nubarrón *m*

thundering **I.** *n* estruendo *m* **II.** *adj inf* escandaloso, -a; (*very great*) enorme

thunderous ['θʌn·dər·əs] *adj* estruendoso, -a

thunderstorm ['θʌn·dər·stɔrm] *n* tormenta *f*

Thursday ['θɜrz·deɪ] *n* jueves *m inv*; *s. a.* **Friday**

thus [ðʌs] *adv form* **1.** (*therefore*) por lo tanto **2.** (*like this*) de este modo; ~ **far** hasta aquí

thwart [θwɔrt] *vt* frustrar

thyme [taɪm] *n* tomillo *m*

thyroid ['θaɪ·rɔɪd] *adj* tiroides *f inv*

tick[1] [tɪk] *n* (*insect*) garrapata *f*

tick[2] [tɪk] **I.** *n* **1.** (*sound*) tic-tac *m* **2.** (*mark*) visto *m* **II.** *vt* marcar (*con un visto*)

◆**tick off** *vt* **1.** marcar (*con un visto*) **2.** (*exasperate*) dar la lata

◆**tick over** *vi fig* ir tirando

ticket ['tɪk·ɪt] *n* **1.** (*bus, train*) billete *m*, boleto *m AmL*; (*cinema, concert*) entrada *f* **2.** (*price, tag*) etiqueta *f* **3.** AUTO multa *f* ▶ **just the ~** justo lo que hacía falta

ticket agency *n* taquilla *f*

ticket counter *n* mostrador *m* de venta *de entradas o billetes*

ticket holder *n* persona *f* que tiene entrada o billete

ticket machine *n* dispensador *m* de billetes

ticket office *n* RAIL ventanilla *f* de venta de billetes; THEAT taquilla *f*

tickle ['tɪk·əl] **I.** *vi* hacer cosquillas; (*clothes*) picar **II.** *vt* hacer cosquillas; (*amuse*) hacer gracia **III.** *n* cosquilleo *m*; (*tingling*) picor *m*

ticklish ['tɪk·lɪʃ] *adj* cosquilloso, -a; (*delicate*) delicado, -a

tidal ['taɪ·dəl] *adj* de la marea

tidal wave *n* sunami *m*

tidbit ['tɪd·bɪt] *n* **1.** (*delicacy*) golosina *f* **2.** (*information*) noticia *f*; (*gossip*) cotilleo *m*

tide [taɪd] *n* marea *f*; (*of opinion*) corriente *f*; **to go against the ~** ir contracorriente; **to swim with the ~** seguir la corriente

tidy ['taɪ·di] **I.** *adj* <-ier, -iest> **1.** (*orderly*) ordenado, -a; **to have a ~ mind** ser metódico **2.** *inf* suculento, -a **II.** *vt* ordenar

tie [taɪ] **I.** *n* **1.** (*necktie*) corbata *f* **2.** (*cord*) atadura *f* **3.** ~**s** (*bonds*) lazos *mpl* **4.** SPORTS empate *m* **II.** *vi* **1.** (*fasten*) atarse **2.** SPORTS empatar **III.** *vt* atar; (*knot*) hacer; **to be ~d by/to sth** estar limitado por/limitarse a algo

◆**tie back** *vt* atar

◆**tie down** *vt* atar; **to tie sb down to sth** *inf* comprometer a alguien a algo

◆**tie in** **I.** *vt* relacionar **II.** *vi* coincidir

◆**tie up** *vt* **1.** (*bind*) atar; (*hair*) recogerse; **to ~ some loose ends** atar cabos sueltos **2. to be tied up** estar ocupado

tiebreak ['taɪ·breɪk] *n*, **tiebreaker** *n* desempate *m*

tier [tɪr] *n* (*row*) hilera *f*; (*level*) nivel *m*

tiff [tɪf] *n inf* pelea *f*

tiger ['taɪ·gər] *n* tigre *m* ▶ **to have a ~ by the tail** tener el toro por los cuernos

tight [taɪt] **I.** *adj* **1.** (*screw, knot*) apretado, -a; (*clothing*) ceñido, -a; (*rope*) tirante; (*skin*) terso, -a **2.** (*condition, discipline*) estricto, -a; (*budget*) restringido, -a; (*situation*) difícil; (*schedule*) apretado, -a; **to be ~ for money/time** ir escaso de dinero/tiempo **3.** (*hard-fought*) reñido, -a **4.** (*drunk*) como una cuba **II.** *adv* fuerte; **sleep ~!** ¡que duermas bien!

tighten ['taɪ·tən] **I.** *vt* apretar; (*rope*) tensar **II.** *vi* apretarse; (*restrictions*) intensificarse

tightrope ['taɪt·roʊp] *n* cuerda *f* floja

tights [taɪts] *npl* medias *fpl*

tightwad ['taɪt·wad] *n sl* tacaño, -a *m, f*

tigress ['taɪ·grɪs] *n* tigresa *f*

tile [taɪl] *n* (*roof*) teja *f*; (*wall, floor*) azulejo *m*

till[1] [tɪl] **I.** *prep* hasta **II.** *conj* hasta que

till² [tɪl] *n* (*cash*) caja *f*

tiller ['tɪl·ər] *n* **at the ~** al timón

tilt [tɪlt] **I.** *n* inclinación *f* ▶ (**at**) **full ~** a toda máquina **II.** *vt* inclinar **III.** *vi* inclinarse; **to ~ over** volcarse

timber ['tɪm·bər] *n* madera *f;* (*beam*) viga *f*

time [taɪm] **I.** *n* **1.** tiempo *m;* (*period*) período *m;* **to kill/spend/waste ~** matar/pasar/perder el tiempo; **to make/save ~** hacer/ganar tiempo; **as ~ goes by, in the course of ~** con el paso del tiempo; **to be a matter of ~** ser cuestión de tiempo; **of all ~** de todos los tiempos; **in ~** a tiempo; **over/given ~** con el tiempo; **free ~** tiempo libre; **after a ~** al cabo de un tiempo; **all the ~** continuamente; **some/a long ~ ago** hace algún/mucho tiempo; **for the ~ being** por ahora; **to have a good ~** pasárselo bien; **most of the ~** la mayor parte del tiempo; **in one week's ~** dentro de una semana; **it takes a long/short ~** se tarda mucho/poco; **to give sb a hard ~** hacerlas pasar canutas a alguien **2.** (*clock*) hora *f;* **arrival/departure ~** hora de llegada/salida; **train ~s** horario *m* de tren; **breakfast ~** hora de desayunar; **at any ~** a cualquier hora; **at any given ~, at (any) one ~** en un momento dado **3.** (*moment*) momento *m;* **the best ~ of day** el mejor momento del día; **this ~ tomorrow** mañana a esta hora; **at all ~s** a todas horas; **at a different ~** en otro momento; **each ~** cada vez; **the right ~** el momento oportuno; **ahead of ~** con antelación **4.** (*occasion*) vez *f;* **the last/next ~** la última/próxima vez; **~ and (~) again** una y otra vez; **lots of ~s** muchas veces; **from ~ to ~** de vez en cuando; **to remember the ~...** recordar cuando...; **it is about ~ that...** ya es hora de que... +*subj* **5.** (*right moment*) hora; **it's high ~ that...** ya es hora de que... +*subj*; **right on ~** en el momento preciso **6. to work full/part ~** trabajar a jornada completa/a tiempo parcial; **to be on short ~** estar en jornada reducida ▶ **~ is of the essence** no hay tiempo que perder; **to have ~ on one's hands** tener tiempo de sobra; **~ is a great healer** el tiempo lo cura todo; **~ is money** el tiempo es oro; **there's a ~ and a place (for everything)** todo a su debido tiempo; **there's no ~ like the present** no dejes para mañana lo que puedas hacer hoy; **~ and tide wait for no man** el tiempo no perdona; **in less than no ~** en menos que canta un gallo; **to buy ~** ganar tiempo; **~ moves on** la vida sigue **II.** *vt* SPORTS cronometrar **III.** *adj* SPORTS contrarreloj

time bomb *n* bomba *f* de relojería

timecard *n* tarjeta *f* de registro horario

time clock *n* reloj *m* de control de asistencia

time-consuming ['taɪm·kən,su·mɪŋ] *adj* laborioso, -a

time difference *n* diferencia *f* horaria

timekeeper *n* (*device*) cronómetro *m*

time lag *n* retraso *m*

timeless ['taɪm·lɪs] *adj* eterno, -a

time limit *n* límite *m* de tiempo

timely ['taɪm·li] *adj* <-ier, -iest> oportuno, -a; **in a ~ fashion** a tiempo

time-out [,taɪm·'aut] *n* descanso *m;* SPORTS tiempo *m* muerto

timer ['taɪ·mər] *n* temporizador *m*

time sheet *n* hoja *f* de asistencia

timetable *n* (*bus, train*) horario *m;* (*project, events*) programa *m*

time zone *n* huso *m* horario

timid ['tɪm·ɪd] *adj* <-er, -est> tímido, -a

timing ['taɪ·mɪŋ] *n* cronometraje *m;* **that was perfect ~** ha sido el momento oportuno

tin [tɪn] **I.** *n* **1.** (*metal*) estaño *m;* (*tinplate*) hojalata *f* **2.** (*container*) lata *f* **3.** (*for baking*) molde *m* **II.** *vt* enlatar

tin can *n* lata *f*

tinfoil *n* papel *m* de aluminio

tinge [tɪndʒ] **I.** *n* tinte *m* **II.** *vt* teñir; *fig* matizar

tingle ['tɪŋ·gəl] **I.** *vi* estremecerse **II.** *n* estremecimiento *m*

tinkle ['tɪŋ·kəl] *vi, vt* tintinear

tinsel ['tɪn·səl] *n* oropel *m*

tint [tɪnt] **I.** *n* tono *m;* (*for hair*) tinte *m* **II.** *vt* teñir

tiny ['taɪ·ni] *adj* <-ier, -iest> chiquito, -a, chingo, -a *Col, Cuba*

tip¹ [tɪp] **I.** <-pp-> *vt* cubrir **II.** *n* punta *f*; **from ~ to toe** de pies a cabeza; **it's on the ~ of my tongue** lo tengo en la punta de la lengua

tip² [tɪp] I. <-pp-> *vt* (*incline*) inclinar; **to ~ the balance** inclinar la balanza (**against** en contra de, **in favor of** a favor) II. *vi* inclinarse

tip³ [tɪp] I. *n* 1. (*for service*) propina *f*, yapa *f Méx*; **10 per cent ~** el diez por ciento de propina 2. (*hint*) aviso *m*; **to give sb a ~** dar a alguien un consejo; **to take a ~ from** sb seguir el consejo de alguien II. <-pp-> *vi, vt* dejar propina

◆**tip off** *vt* avisar

◆**tip over** *vt, vi* volcar

◆**tip up** I. *vt* inclinar II. *vi* inclinarse

tip-off [ˈtɪp.ɔf] *n inf* soplo *m*

tipsy [ˈtɪp.si] *adj* <-ier, -iest> bebido, -a, achispado, -a *AmL*

tiptoe [ˈtɪp.toʊ] I. *n* **on ~(s)** de puntillas II. *vi* ponerse de puntillas

tiptop [ˈtɪp.tɑp] *adj* de primera

tirade [ˈtaɪ.reɪd] *n* diatriba *f*

tire¹ [taɪr] *n* (*for vehicle*) neumático *m*, llanta *f Méx*, caucho *m Col, Ven*

tire² [taɪr] (*become tired*) I. *vt* cansar II. *vi* cansarse

tired [ˈtaɪrd] *adj* <-er, -est> cansado, -a; (*excuse*) trillado, -a; **to be sick and ~** estar aburrido (**of** de)

tiredness *n* cansancio *m*

tire gauge *n* medidor *m* de presión

tireless [ˈtaɪr.lɪs] *adj* incansable

tiresome [ˈtaɪr.səm] *adj* molesto, -a; (*person*) pesado, -a, molón, -ona *Guat, Ecua, Méx*

tiring [ˈtaɪ.rɪŋ] *adj* agotador(a)

tissue [ˈtɪʃ.u] *n* 1. (*handkerchief*) pañuelo *m* 2. ANAT, BIO tejido *m*

tissue paper *n* papel *m* de seda

tit [tɪt] *n* ANAT teta *f*

titanium [taɪˈteɪ.ni.əm] *n* titanio *m*

titillate [ˈtɪt.ə.leɪt] *vt* excitar

title [ˈtaɪt.əl] *n* 1. (*name*) título *m* 2. (*championship*) campeonato *m*

titleholder *n* titular *mf*

title page *n* portada *f*

title role *n* papel *m* principal

title track *n* canción *f* que da nombre al álbum

titter [ˈtɪt.ər] *vi* reírse disimuladamente

to [tu] I. *prep* 1. (*direction*) a; **to go ~ Mexico/town** ir a México/a la ciudad; **to go ~ the cinema/the dentist('s)** ir al cine/al dentista; **to go ~ bed** irse a la cama; **~ the left/right** a la izquierda/derecha 2. (*before*) **a quarter ~ five** las cinco menos cuarto 3. (*until*) hasta; **to count up ~** 10 contar hasta 10; **~ this day** hasta el día de hoy; **done ~ perfection** hecho a la perfección; **~ some extent** hasta cierto punto 4. *indirect object* **to show sth ~ sb** mostrar algo a alguien; **to talk ~ sb** hablar con alguien; **this belongs ~ me** esto es mío 5. (*towards*) con; **to be kind/rude ~ sb** ser amable/grosero con alguien 6. (*against*) contra; **elbow ~ elbow** codo con codo 7. (*comparison*) a; **3 (goals) ~ 1** 3 (goles) a 1; **superior ~ sth/sb** superior a algo/alguien 8. (*of*) de; **the top ~ this jar** la tapa de este tarro 9. (*purpose*) para ▶ **that's all there is ~ it** eso es todo II. *infinitive particle* 1. (*infinitive*) **~ do/walk** hacer/andar 2. (*command*) **I told him ~ eat** le dije que comiera 3. (*interrogative*) **she didn't know how ~ say it** no sabía cómo decirlo 4. (*wish*) **she wants ~ go** quiere irse; **he wants me ~ tell him a story** quiere que le cuente un cuento 5. (*purpose*) **he comes ~ see me** viene a verme; **to phone ~ ask sth** llamar para preguntar algo 6. (*intention*) **the work ~ be done** el trabajo que hay que hacer 7. (*result*) **too tired ~ do sth** demasiado cansado para hacer algo 8. (*ellipsis*) **he doesn't want ~ eat, but I want ~** él no quiere comer, pero yo sí III. *adv* **to push the door ~** cerrar la puerta

toad [toʊd] *n* sapo *m*; (*person*) mamarracho, -a *m, f*

toadstool [ˈtoʊd.stul] *n* seta *f* venenosa

toast [toʊst] I. *n* 1. **a (piece of) ~** una tostada 2. (*drink*) brindis *m inv* II. *vt* 1. (*cook*) tostar 2. (*drink*) brindar III. *vi* tostarse

toaster *n* tostadora *f*

tobacco [təˈbæk.oʊ] *n* tabaco *m*

tobacconist [təˈbæk.ə.nɪst] *n* estanquero, -a *m, f*

to-be [təˈbi] *adj* futuro, -a

toboggan [tə·'bag·ən] n trineo m

toboggan run n, **toboggan slide** n pista f de trineos

today [tə·'deɪ] I. adv hoy; (*nowadays*) hoy día II. n hoy m; (*nowadays*) actualidad f

toddler ['tad·lər] n niño, -a m, f que empieza a caminar

to-do [tə·'du] n inflío m

toe [toʊ] I. n dedo m del pie; (*shoe*) puntera f; **on one's ~s** de puntillas ▶ **to step on sb's ~s** pisotear a alguien *fig* II. vt **to ~ the line** conformarse

toehold n SPORTS punto m de apoyo

toenail n uña f del pie

toffee ['tɒ·fi] n toffee m

together [tə·'geð·ər] adv 1. (*jointly*) juntos, -as **all ~** todos juntos, todas juntas m, f; **~ with** junto con; **to get ~** juntarse; **to get it ~** sl organizarse 2. (*at the same time*) a la vez

toggle ['tag·əl] I. n COMPUT tecla f de conmutación II. vt pulsar

toil [tɔɪl] I. n labor f II. vi (*work hard*) afanarse

toilet ['tɔɪ·lɪt] n 1. (*room*) cuarto m de baño; (*public*) servicio m 2. (*appliance*) váter m 3. (*process*) aseo m

toilet paper n papel m higiénico

toiletries ['tɔɪ·lɪ·triz] npl artículos m pl de tocador

toiletries bag n neceser m

toilet roll n rollo m de papel higiénico

toilet water n colonia f

token ['toʊ·kən] I. n 1. (*sign*) señal f; (*affection*) muestra f; **by the same ~** por la misma razón; **in ~ of** como muestra de 2. (*for machines*) ficha f II. adj simbólico, -a

told [toʊld] pt, pp of **tell**

tolerance ['tal·ər·əns] n tolerancia f

tolerant ['tal·ər·ənt] adj tolerante

tolerate ['tal·ə·reɪt] vt 1. (*accept*) a. MED tolerar 2. (*endure*) soportar

toll[1] [toʊl] n 1. AUTO peaje m 2. TEL tarifa f 3. (*damage*) número m

toll[2] [toʊl] vi doblar

toll bridge n puente m de peaje

toll call n conferencia f

toll-free adv gratis

toll road n autopista f de peaje

tomato [tə·'meɪ·toʊ] <-es> n tomate m

tomato ketchup n ketchup m

tomb [tum] n tumba f, guaca f AmL

tomboy ['tam·bɔɪ] n marimacho m

tombstone ['tum·stoʊn] n lápida f sepulcral

tomcat ['tam·kæt] n gato m (macho)

tomorrow [tə·'mar·oʊ] I. adv mañana; **the day after ~** pasado mañana; **all** (**day**) **~** todo el día de mañana; **~ morning/evening** mañana por la mañana/tarde; **see you ~!** ¡hasta mañana! II. n mañana m ▶ **~ is another day** mañana será otro día; **never put off until ~ what you can do today** no dejes para mañana lo que puedas hacer hoy; **who knows what ~ will bring?** ¿quién sabe qué nos deparará el futuro?

ton [tʌn] n tonelada f; **~s of** montones de

tone [toʊn] I. n tono m II. vt (*muscles, skin*) tonificar

◆tone down vt moderar

tone control n control m de tonalidad

tone-deaf ['toʊn·'def] adj falto, -a de oído musical

toner ['toʊ·nər] n 1. (*for skin*) tonificante m 2. (*for printer*) tóner m; PHOT virador m

tongs [taŋz] npl tenazas fpl

tongue [tʌŋ] n lengua f; **to bite one's ~** morderse la lengua; **to hold one's ~** contenerse *(para no decir algo)*; **to have a sharp ~** tener una lengua afilada; **to speak in ~s** hablar en lenguas desconocidas ▶ **have you lost your ~?** ¿te ha comido la lengua el gato?; **to set ~s wagging** dar (de) qué hablar

tongue-tied ['tʌŋ·taɪd] adj **to be ~** cortarse

tongue twister n trabalenguas m inv

tonic ['tan·ɪk] n tónico m; **~** (**water**) tónica f

tonight [tə·'naɪt] adv (*evening*) esta tarde; (*night*) esta noche

tonne [tʌn] n tonelada f

tonsillitis [ˌtan·sə·'laɪ·t̬ɪs] n amigdalitis f inv

too [tu] adv 1. (*overly*) demasiado; **that's ~ much!** ¡es demasiado! 2. (*very*) muy 3. (*also*) también; **me ~!** ¡y yo!

4. (*moreover*) además

took [tʊk] *vt, vi pt of* **take**

tool [tul] *n* **1.** (*implement*) herramienta *f*, implemento *m AmL* **2.** (*instrument*) instrumento *m*

tool bag *n* bolsa *f* de herramientas

toolbar *n* COMPUT barra *f* de herramientas

toolmaker *n* fabricante *mf* de herramientas

toot [tut] **I.** *n* to give a ~ tocar el claxon **II.** *vi* pitar

tooth [tuθ] <teeth> *n* ANAT diente *m*; (*molar*) muela *f*; **he's cutting a ~** está echando un diente ▶ **to set sb's teeth on edge** dar dentera a alguien; **to fight ~ and nail** luchar a brazo partido; **to have a sweet ~** ser goloso; **to get one's teeth into** hincar el diente a; **to grit one's teeth** apretar los dientes; **in the ~ of sth** (*straight into*) en medio de algo; (*despite*) a pesar de algo

toothache [ˈtuθ·eɪk] *n* dolor *m* de muelas

toothbrush [ˈtuθ·brʌʃ] *n* cepillo *m* de dientes

toothpaste [ˈtuθ·peɪst] *n* pasta *f* de dientes

toothpick *n* palillo *m*, pajuela *f Bol, Col*

toots [tuts] *n sl* nena *f*

top [tɑp] **I.** *n* **1.** (*highest part*) parte *f* superior; (*mountain*) cima *f*; (*tree*) copa *f*; (*head*) coronilla *f*; (*list*) cabeza *f*; (*bottle*) tapón *m*; (*street*) final *m*; **to get on ~ of sth** llegar a lo más alto de algo; **from ~ to bottom** de arriba a abajo; **from ~ to toe** de la cabeza a los pies; **to feel on ~ of the world** estar loco de contento **2.** (*surface*) superficie *f*; **on ~ of** encima de **3.** (*highest rank*) lo mejor; **to be at the ~** estar en la cima **4.** (*clothing*) top *m* ▶ **at the ~ of one's voice** a grito pelado; **to go over the ~** exagerar **II.** *adj* **1.** (*highest, upper*) de arriba **2.** (*best*) de primera (calidad) **3.** (*successful*) exitoso, -a **4.** (*important*) mejor **5.** (*maximum*) máximo, -a **III.** <-pp-> *vt* **1.** (*head*) encabezar **2.** (*cover*) coronar **3.** (*surpass*) superar

◆**top off** *vt* rematar; CULIN coronar

◆**top up** *vt* rellenar

topcoat [ˈtɑp·koʊt] *n* sobretodo *m*

top copy *n* original *m*

top dog *n sl* **1.** (*boss*) mandamás *mf* **2.** (*victor*) ganador(a) *m(f)*

top executive *n* ejecutivo, -a *m, f* superior

top hat *n* sombrero *m* de copa, galera *f AmL*

top-heavy *adj* inestable

topic [ˈtɑp·ɪk] *n* tema *m*

topical [ˈtɑp·ɪ·kəl] *adj* de interés actual

topless [ˈtɑp·lɪs] **I.** *adj* sin parte de arriba; (*person*) en topless **II.** *adv* **to go ~** ir en topless

top-level [ˈtɑp·ˌlev·əl] *adj* (*rank*) de alto nivel; (*importance*) de primera categoría

topmost [ˈtɑp·moʊst] *adj* más alto, -a

top-notch [ˌtɑp·ˈnɑtʃ] *adj inf* de primera

topographer [tə·ˈpɑg·rə·fər] *n* topógrafo, -a *m, f*

topping [ˈtɑp·ɪŋ] *n* cobertura *f*

topple [ˈtɑp·əl] **I.** *vt* derrocar **II.** *vi* **to ~ (down)** caerse

◆**topple over** *vi* volcarse

top price *n* precio *m* máximo

top priority *n* prioridad *f* máxima

top quality *n* máxima calidad *f*

top salary *n* salario *m* máximo

top-selling *adj* de mayor venta

topsoil *n* capa *f* superior del suelo

top speed *n* velocidad *f* máxima

topsy-turvy [ˌtɑp·sɪ·ˈtɜr·vi] *adj, adv* patas arriba

torch [tɔrtʃ] <-es> *n* antorcha *f*; **to carry a ~ for sb** beber los vientos por alguien

tore [tɔr] *vi, vt pt of* **tear**

torment [ˈtɔr·ment] **I.** *n* tormento *m*; *fig* suplicio *m* **II.** *vt* atormentar

torn [tɔrn] *vi, vt pp of* **tear**

tornado [tɔr·ˈneɪ·doʊ] *n* <-(e)s> tornado *m*

torpedo [tɔr·ˈpi·doʊ] <-es> *n* torpedo *m*

torrent [ˈtɔr·ənt] *n a. fig* torrente *m*; **to rain in ~s** llover a cántaros

torrential [tɔ·ˈren·ʃəl] *adj* torrencial, torrentoso, -a *AmL*

torso [ˈtɔr·soʊ] *n* torso *m*

tortoise [ˈtɔr·təs] *n* tortuga *f*

tortoiseshell [ˈtɔr·təs·ʃel] *n* concha *f*

torture [ˈtɔr·tʃər] **I.** *n* tortura *f*; (*men-*

T

tal) tormento *m* **II.** *vt* torturar; *fig* atormentar

torturer ['tɔr·tʃər·ər] *n* torturador(a) *m(f)*

toss [tɔs] **I.** *n* lanzamiento *m* **II.** *vt* lanzar; (*pancake*) dar la vuelta; (*head*) sacudir; **to ~ a coin** echar una moneda al aire **III.** *vi* **to ~ for sth** echar algo a cara o cruz ▸ **to ~ and turn** dar vueltas en la cama

◆**toss about** *vt*, **toss around** *vt* **1.** (*shake*) zarandear **2.** (*consider*) considerar

◆**toss away** *vt* tirar

◆**toss off** *vt* hacer en un periquete; (*drink*) beberse de un trago

◆**toss out** *vt* tirar

◆**toss up** *vi* **to ~ for sth** echar algo a cara o cruz

toss-up ['tɔs·ʌp] *n* **it's a ~ between...** la cosa está entre...

total ['toʊ·təl] **I.** *adj*, *n* total *m* **II.** *vt* **1.** (*count*) sumar **2.** (*amount to*) ascender a

totalitarian [toʊ·tæl·ə·'ter·i·ən] *adj* totalitario, -a

totalitarianism *n* totalitarismo *m*

totally ['toʊ·tə·li] *adv* totalmente

tote[1] [toʊt] *n* SPORTS totalizador *m*

tote[2] [toʊt] *vt inf* (*carry*) llevar consigo [*or a cuestas*]

tote bag *n* bolsa *f* grande

totter ['tɑt·ər] *vi* tambalearse

toucan ['tu·kæn] *n* ZOOL tucán *m*

touch [tʌtʃ] <-es> **I.** *n* **1.** (*sense*) tacto *m* **2.** (*act of touching, small amount*) toque *m* **3.** (*communication*) **to be/get/keep in ~** estar/ponerse/mantenerse en contacto (**with** con); **to be out of/lose ~** no tener/perder el contacto (**with** con) **4.** (*skill*) habilidad *f* ▸ **to be a soft ~** (*person*) ser un blandengue **II.** *vt* **1.** (*feel*) tocar **2.** (*brush*) rozar **3.** (*reach*) alcanzar; **there's no painter to ~ him** no existe pintor que le iguale **4.** (*emotionally*) conmover **III.** *vi* tocar

◆**touch down** *vi* AVIAT aterrizar

◆**touch off** *vt* hacer estallar

◆**touch on** *vt* tocar

◆**touch up** *vt* retocar

◆**touch upon** *vt* tocar

touchdown ['tʌtʃ·daʊn] *n* AVIAT aterri-

zaje *m*

touched [tʌtʃt] *adj* **1.** (*moved*) conmovido, -a **2.** (*crazy*) tocado, -a

touching ['tʌtʃ·ɪŋ] *adj* conmovedor(a)

touch-sensitive *adj* sensible al tacto

touchy ['tʌtʃ·i] <-ier, -iest> *adj* susceptible (**about** en cuanto a); (*issue*) delicado, -a

tough [tʌf] **I.** *adj* **1.** (*strong*) fuerte; (*meat, person*) duro, -a **2.** (*strict*) severo, -a (**on** con) **3.** (*difficult*) difícil; **~ luck** mala suerte **II.** *n* matón, -ona *m, f*

toughen ['tʌf·ən] **I.** *vt* endurecer **II.** *vi* endurecerse

toupee [tu·'peɪ] *n* peluquín *m*

tour [tʊr] **I.** *n* **1.** (*journey*) viaje *m*; **guided ~** visita *f* guiada **2.** MUS gira *f*; **on ~** de gira **II.** *vt* **1.** (*travel*) recorrer **2.** (*visit*) visitar **III.** *vi* ir de viaje

tourism ['tʊr·ɪz·əm] *n* turismo *m*

tourist ['tʊr·ɪst] *n* turista *mf*

tourist bureau *n* oficina *f* de turismo

tourist class *n* clase *f* turista

tourist guide *n* **1.** (*book*) guía *f* **2.** (*person*) guía *mf*

tourist industry *n* industria *f* turística

tourist information office *n* oficina *f* de información y turismo

tourist ticket *n* pasaje *m* de turista

tourist visa *n* visado *m* turístico

tournament ['tɜr·nə·mənt] *n* torneo *m*

tour operator *n* operador *m* turístico

tout [taʊt] *n* revendedor(a) *m(f)*

tow [toʊ] **I.** *n* remolque *m*; **in ~** *fig* a cuestas **II.** *vt* remolcar

toward(s) [tɔrd(z)] *prep* **1.** (*time, place*) hacia **2.** (*for*) para **3.** (*regarding*) respecto a; **to feel sth ~ sb** sentir algo por alguien

tow bar *n* barra *f* de tracción

towel ['taʊ·əl] *n* toalla *f* ▸ **to throw in the ~** tirar la toalla

towel rack *n* toallero *m*

tower ['taʊ·ər] *n* torre *f* ▸ **a ~ of strength** un gran apoyo

◆**tower above** *vi*, **tower over** *vi* ser mucho más alto que

towering *adj* (*high*) altísimo, -a; (*large*) inmenso, -a

town [taʊn] *n* (*large*) ciudad *f*; (*small*)

town council pueblo *m;* **the ~** el centro ▶ **to go out on the ~** **to paint the ~ red** irse de juerga

town council *n* ayuntamiento *m* concejales

town hall *n* ayuntamiento *m* edificio

townhouse *n* casa *f* unifamiliar

town planning *n* urbanismo *m*

township ['taun·ʃɪp] *n* municipio *m*

townspeople ['taunz·ˌpi·pəl] *npl* ciudadanos *mpl*

tow truck *n* grúa *f*

toxic ['tak·sɪk] *adj* tóxico, -a

toxin ['tak·sɪn] *n* toxina *f*

toy [tɔɪ] *n* juguete *m;* **cuddly ~** muñeco *m* de peluche

toyshop *n* juguetería *f*

trace [treɪs] I. *n* (*sign, amount*) rastro *m;* **to disappear without a ~** desaparecer sin dejar rastro; **~s of a drug/poison** rastros de droga/veneno II. *vt* 1. (*locate*) localizar; **it can be ~d back to...** se remonta a... 2. (*draw*) trazar; (*with tracing paper*) calcar

trachea ['treɪ·ki·ə] <-s *or* -chae> *n* tráquea *f*

tracing *n* calco *m*

tracing paper *n* papel *m* de calco

track [træk] I. *n* 1. (*path*) *a. fig* camino *m;* RAIL vía *f;* (*in station*) andén *m;* **to be on the right/wrong ~** ir por buen/mal camino 2. (*mark*) pista *f;* (*animal*) huella *f;* **to be on the ~** seguir la pista (of a) 3. (*logical course*) curso *m;* **to get off the ~** salirse del tema 4. SPORTS, MUS pista *f* ▶ **to live on the wrong side of the ~s** *inf* vivir en los barrios pobres; **to lose/keep ~ of** perder/no perder de vista; **to make ~s** largarse; **to throw sb off the ~** despistar a alguien II. *vt* 1. (*pursue*) seguir la pista de 2. (*trace*) trazar

◆**track down** *vt* localizar

track and field *n* atletismo *m*

track event *n* carrera *f* de atletismo

tracking station ['træk·ɪŋ·ˌster·ʃən] *n* centro *m* de seguimiento

track record *n* historial *m*

track shoe *n* zapatilla *f* de atletismo

tracksuit *n* chándal *m*

tract [trækt] *n* tramo *m;* ANAT tracto *m*

traction ['træk·ʃən] *n* (*grip*) adherencia *f*

tractor ['træk·tər] *n* tractor *m*

tractor trailer *n* camión *m* articulado

trade [treɪd] I. *n* 1. (*buying and selling*) comercio *m* (**in** de) 2. (*business activity*) actividad *f* económica 3. (*type of business*) industria *f* 4. (*profession*) oficio *m;* **by ~** de profesión 5. (*swap*) intercambio *m* II. *vi* COM comerciar (**in** en); **to ~ with sb** tener relaciones comerciales con alguien III. *vt* 1. (*exchange*) intercambiar; **to ~ sth for sth** cambiar algo por algo 2. (*sell*) vender

◆**trade in** *vt* aportar como parte del pago

trade agreement *n* acuerdo *m* comercial

trade association *n* asociación *f* mercantil

trade fair *n* feria *f* de muestras

trade-in *n* **as a ~** como parte del pago

trade journal *n* periódico *m* gremial

trademark *n* 1. COM marca *f;* **registered ~** marca registrada 2. *fig* distintivo *m*

trade name *n* marca *f;* (*of a firm*) razón *f* social

trader ['treɪ·dər] *n* comerciante *mf*

trade route *n* ruta *f* comercial

trade secret *n* secreto *m* profesional

tradesman ['treɪdz·mən] <-men> *n* tendero *m*

trade union *n* sindicato *m*

trade unionist *n* sindicalista *mf*

trade war *n* guerra *f* comercial

trade wind *n* viento *m* alisio

trading ['treɪ·dɪŋ] *n* comercio *m*

tradition [trə·'dɪʃ·ən] *n* tradición *f;* **by ~** por tradición; **in the ~ of** del estilo de

traditional [trə·'dɪʃ·ə·nəl] *adj* 1. (*customary*) tradicional 2. (*conventional*) clásico, -a

traffic ['træf·ɪk] I. *n* 1. (*vehicles*) tráfico *m;* **air/commercial/passenger ~** tráfico aéreo/comercial/de pasajeros 2. (*movement*) tránsito *m;* **drug ~** tráfico de drogas II. <trafficked, trafficked> *vi* traficar (**in** con)

traffic accident *n* accidente *m* de tráfico

traffic circle *n* rotonda *f*

traffic island *n* isleta *f*

T

traffic jam *n* atasco *m*

trafficker ['træf·ɪk·ər] *n* traficante *mf;*
drug/arms ~ traficante de drogas/armas

traffic light *n* semáforo *m*

traffic sign *n* señal *f* de tráfico

tragedy ['trædʒ·ə·di] <-ies> *n* tragedia *f*

tragic ['trædʒ·ɪk] *adj* trágico, -a

trail [treɪl] I. *n* 1. (*path*) camino *m*
2. (*track*) pista *f;* **to be on the ~** seguir
la pista (**of** de) II. *vt* 1. (*follow*) seguir
la pista de; (*animal*) seguir el rastro de
2. (*drag*) arrastrar 3. (*be losing*) ir perdiendo ante [*or* contra] III. *vi* 1. (*drag*)
arrastrarse 2. SPORTS ir perdiendo

♦**trail away** *vi* esfumarse

♦**trail behind** *vi* ir detrás

trailer *n* 1. AUTO remolque *m;* (*mobile home*) caravana *f* 2. (*advertisement*)
tráiler *m*

trailer park *n* cámping *m* de caravanas

train [treɪn] I. *n* 1. (*railway*) tren *m;*
by ~ en tren 2. (*series*) serie *f;* **~ of thought** hilo *m* de pensamiento; **to put in ~** poner en marcha II. *vi* entrenarse
III. *vt* formar; (*animal*) amaestrar

train accident *n* accidente *m* ferroviario

trained [treɪnd] *adj* 1. (*educated*) formado, -a (**in** en); (*animal*) amaestrado,
-a 2. (*expert*) cualificado, -a

trainee [treɪ·'ni] *n* aprendiz *mf*

trainer *n* entrenador(a) *m(f)*

training *n* 1. (*education*) formación *f;* **~ on-the-job** formación laboral 2. SPORTS
entrenamiento *m* (**for** para)

training camp *n* campamento *m* de
instrucción

training course *n* curso *m* de formación

training program *n* programa *m* de
entrenamiento

train schedule *n* horario *m* de trenes

train service *n* servicio *m* de trenes

trait [treɪt] *n* rasgo *m*

traitor ['treɪ·tər] *n* traidor(a) *m(f)*

trajectory [trə·'dʒek·tə·ri] *n* trayectoria *f;*
fig camino *m*

tram [træm] *n* tranvía *m;* **by ~** en tranvía

tramp [træmp] I. *vi* (*walk*) ir a pie

II. *vt* (*town, miles*) patearse *inf* III. *n*
1. (*sound*) ruido *m* de pasos 2. (*walk*)
caminata *f*

trample ['træm·pəl] *vt* pisotear

trampoline ['træm·pə·lin] *n* trampolín *m*

trance [træns] *n* trance *m;* **to be in a ~**
estar en trance

tranquil ['træŋ·kwɪl] *adj* tranquilo, -a

tranquility [træŋ·'kwɪl·ə·t̬i] *n* tranquilidad *f*

tranquilizer *n* tranquilizante *m;* **to be on ~s** estar tomando tranquilizantes

transact [træn·'zækt] *vt* tramitar

transaction [træn·'zæk·ʃən] *n* transacción *f,* transa *f RíoPl*

transcend [træn·'send] *vt* (*go beyond*)
trascender; (*surpass*) superar

transcribe [træn·'skraɪb] *vt* transcribir

transcript ['træn·skrɪpt], **transcription**
[træn·'skrɪp·ʃən] *n* transcripción *f*

transfer[1] ['træns·fɜr] I. <-rr-> *vt* trasladar; (*power*) transferir; (*shop*) traspasar
II. <-rr-> *vi* trasladarse; (*change train,
plane*) hacer transbordo

transfer[2] ['træns·fɜr] *n* traslado *m;* (*information*) transmisión *f;* (*shop*) traspaso *m;* (*reassignment*) transferencia *f*

transform [træns·'fɔrm] *vt* transformar

transformation [ˌtræns·fɔr·'meɪ·ʃən] *n*
transformación *f*

transformer *n* transformador *m*

transfusion [træns·'fju·ʒən] *n* transfusión *f;* **blood ~** transfusión de sangre

transient ['træn·zi·ənt] *adj* pasajero, -a

transistor [træn·'zɪs·tər] *n* transistor *m*

transit ['træn·zɪt] *n* tránsito *m;* **in ~** de
paso

transit business *n* negocio *m* de tránsito

transition [træn·'zɪʃ·ən] *n* transición *f*

transitional [træn·'zɪʃ·ə·nəl] *adj* transitorio, -a; (*government*) de transición

transitive ['træn·sɪ·t̬ɪv] *adj* transitivo, -a

transit passenger *n* pasajero, -a *m, f*
de tránsito

transit visa *n* visado *m* de tránsito

translate [træns·'leɪt] *vt* LING traducir; **to ~ sth from English into Spanish** traducir algo del inglés al español

translation [træns·'leɪ·ʃən] *n* traducción *f*

translator *n* traductor(a) *m(f)*

translucent [træns·'lu·sənt] *adj* translúcido, -a

transmission [træns·'mɪʃ·ən] *n* transmisión *f;* **data ~** transmisión de datos

transmission speed *n* velocidad *f* de transmisión

transmit [træns·'mɪt] <-tt-> *vt* transmitir

transmitter *n* transmisor *m*

transmitting station *n* emisora *f*

transparency [træns·'per·ən·si] *n* <-ies> transparencia *f*

transparent [træns·'per·ənt] *adj* transparente

transplant[1] [træns·'plænt] *vt* trasplantar

transplant[2] ['træns·plænt] *n* trasplante *m*

transport[1] [træns·'pɔrt] *vt* transportar

transport[2] ['træns·pɔrt] *n* transporte *m;* **public ~** transporte público

transportation [ˌtræns·pər·'teɪ·ʃən] *n* transporte *m*

transpose [træns·'pouz] *vt* transponer

transsexual [træns·'sek·ʃu·əl] *adj, n* transexual *mf*

transvestite ['træns·ves·taɪt] *n* travesti *mf*

trap [træp] I. *n* 1. (*device*) trampa *f;* **to set a ~** poner una trampa 2. *sl* (*mouth*) pico *m* II. *vt* <-pp-> atrapar

trapdoor ['træp·dɔr] *n* escotillón *m*

trapeze [træ·'piz] *n* trapecio *m*

trapezoid ['træp·ɪ·zɔɪd] *n* MATH trapecio *m*

trapper ['træp·ər] *n* trampero, -a *m, f*

trash [træʃ] I. *n* 1. (*rubbish*) basura *f;* **to take the ~ out** sacar la basura 2. *sl* (*people*) gentuza *f;* (*book, film*) bazofia *f* 3. *inf* (*nonsense*) chorradas *fpl* II. *vt sl* 1. (*wreck*) hacer polvo 2. (*criticize*) poner por los suelos

trash can ['træʃ·kæn] *n* cubo *m* de la basura

trashy ['træʃ·i] *adj* cutrísimo, -a

trauma ['trɔ·mə] *n* trauma *m*

traumatic [trɔ·'mæt·ɪk] *adj* traumático, -a

traumatize ['trɔ·mə·taɪz] *vt* traumatizar

travel ['træv·əl] I. *vi* 1. (*make trip*) viajar; (*be away*) estar de viaje; **to ~ by air/car** viajar en avión/coche; **to ~ first-class** viajar en primera 2. (*light, sound*) pro-

pagarse 3. *inf* (*go fast*) ir como una bala II. *vt* viajar por III. *npl* viajes *mpl*

travel agency *n* agencia *f* de viajes

travel agent *n* agente *mf* de viajes

travel card *n* bono *m* de transporte

traveler ['træv·ə·lər] *n* viajero, -a *m, f*

traveler's check *n* cheque *m* de viaje

travel expenses *n* gastos *m pl* de viaje

travel guide *n* guía *mf* turístico, -a; (*book*) guía *f* turística

traveling *n* viajar *m*

travel insurance *n* seguro *m* de viaje

travel sickness *n* mareo *m*

trawler ['trɔ·lər] *n* pesquero *m* de arrastre

tray [treɪ] *n* bandeja *f,* charola *f AmS*

treacherous ['tretʃ·ər·əs] *adj a. fig* traicionero, -a

treachery ['tretʃ·ə·ri] *n* traición *f*

treacly ['tri·kli] *adj* meloso, -a; (*sentimental*) empalagoso, -a

tread [tred] I. <trod, trodden *or* trod> *vi, vt* pisar II. *n* (*step*) paso *m;* (*of stair*) escalón *m*

treadmill ['tred·mɪl] *n* SPORTS rueda *f* de andar; *fig* rutina *f*

treason ['tri·zən] *n* traición *f*

treasonable ['tri·zə·nə·bəl], **treasonous** ['tri·zə·nəs] *adj* traidor(a)

treasure ['treʒ·ər] I. *n* tesoro *m; fig* joya *f;* **my assistant is a ~** mi ayudante es una joya III. *vt* atesorar

treasure hunt *n* caza *f* del tesoro

treasurer ['treʒ·ər·ər] *n* tesorero, -a *m, f*

treasury ['treʒ·ə·ri] <-ies> *n* tesorería *f;* **the Treasury** Hacienda *f*

Treasury Secretary *n* ≈ Ministro, -a *m, f* de Hacienda

treat [trit] I. *vt* 1. *a.* MED tratar; **to ~ badly** tratar mal 2. (*pay for*) invitar (**to** a) II. *vi* negociar (**with** con) III. *n* (*event*) convite *m;* (*present*) regalo *m;* **it's my ~** invito yo

treatment ['trit·mənt] *n* 1. trato *m;* **to give sb the ~** hacerlas pasar canutas a alguien 2. MED tratamiento *m*

treaty ['tri·ti] <-ies> *n* tratado *m;* **peace ~** tratado de paz

treble ['treb·əl] I. *vt* triplicar II. *vi* triplicarse

treble clef *n* clave *f* de sol

tree [tri] *n* árbol *m* ▶ **you can't see the forest for the ~s** los árboles no te dejan ver el bosque; **to grow on ~s** caer del cielo

tree-lined ['tri·laɪnd] *adj* arbolado, -a

tree surgeon *n* arboricultor(a) *m(f)*

tree trunk *n* tronco *m* del árbol

trek [trek] **I.** <-kk-> *vi* caminar **II.** *n* (*walk*) caminata *f*

trekking ['trek·ɪŋ] *n* senderismo *m;* **to go ~** hacer senderismo

trellis ['trel·ɪs] <-es> *n* espaldera *f;* (*for plants*) enrejado *m*

tremble ['trem·bəl] *vi* temblar; **to ~ with cold** tiritar de frío; **to ~ like a leaf** temblar como un flan

tremendous [trɪ·'men·dəs] *adj* **1.** (*enormous*) tremendo, -a; (*crowd*) inmenso, -a; (*help*) inestimable **2.** *inf* (*excellent*) estupendo, -a

tremor ['trem·ər] *n* temblor *m;* (*of fear, excitement*) estremecimiento *m*

trench [trentʃ] <-es> *n* zanja *f;* MIL trinchera *f*

trend [trend] **I.** *n* **1.** (*tendency*) tendencia *f* (**toward(s)** hacia); **downward/upward ~** tendencia a la baja/al alza **2.** (*fashion*) moda *f;* **the latest ~** las últimas tendencias **II.** *vi* tender (**to** a)

trendsetter ['trend·ˌset·ər] *n* persona *f* que inicia una moda

trendy ['tren·di] **I.** <-ier, -iest> *adj* de moda; (*person*) moderno, -a **II.** <-ies> *n* modernillo, -a *m, f inf*

trespass ['tres·pəs] *vi* LAW entrar ilegalmente

trespasser ['tres·pæs·ər] *n* intruso, -a *m, f*

triad ['traɪ·æd] *n* tríada *f*

trial ['traɪ·əl] *n* **1.** LAW proceso *m;* **~ by jury** juicio *m* con jurado; **to stand ~** ser procesado **2.** (*test*) prueba *f;* **clinical ~s** ensayos *m pl* clínicos; **on ~** a prueba; **to give sb a ~** poner a alguien a prueba

trial period *n* período *m* de prueba

triangle ['traɪ·æŋ·gəl] *n* triángulo *m*

triangular [traɪ·'æŋ·gju·lər] *adj* triangular

tribal ['traɪ·bəl] *adj* tribal

tribe [traɪb] *n* tribu *f*

tribesman ['traɪbz·mən] <-men> *n* miembro *m* de una tribu

tribeswoman ['traɪbz·ˌwʊm·ən] <-women> *n* miembro *m* de una tribu

tribulation [ˌtrɪb·jə·'leɪ·ʃən] *n* tribulación *f*

tribunal [traɪ·'bju·nəl] *n* tribunal *m*

tribune ['trɪb·jun] *n* ARCHIT tribuna *f*

tributary ['trɪb·jə·ter·i] <-ies> *adj, n* (*river*) afluente *m*

tribute ['trɪb·jut] *n* (*homage*) homenaje *m;* **to pay ~** rendir tributo (**to** a)

trick [trɪk] **I.** *n* **1.** (*ruse*) trampa *m;* **a dirty ~** una mala pasada; **to play a ~** tender una trampa (**on** a); **to be up to one's (old) ~s again** volver a hacer de las suyas **2.** (*magician*) truco *m* **3.** (*technique*) truquillo *m* **4.** (*illusion*) ilusión *f;* **a ~ of the light** una ilusión óptica ▶ **to try every ~ in the book** intentar todos los trucos habidos y por haber; **the ~s of the trade** los trucos del oficio; **that'll do the ~** con eso solucionamos el tema **II.** *adj* **a ~ question** una pregunta con trampa **III.** *vt* (*deceive*) engañar; (*fool*) burlar; (*swindle*) timar

trickery ['trɪk·ə·ri] *n* artimañas *fpl*

trickle ['trɪk·əl] **I.** *vi* chorrear; (*drops*) gotear; **to ~ in/out** (*people*) ir entrando/saliendo **II.** *n* hilo *m;* (*drops*) *a. fig* goteo *m*

◆ **trickle away** *vi* consumirse poco a poco

tricky ['trɪk·i] <-ier, -iest> *adj* **1.** (*crafty*) astuto, -a **2.** (*difficult*) complicado, -a

tricycle ['traɪ·sɪ·kəl] *n* triciclo *m*

trifle ['traɪ·fəl] *n* (*thing*) bagatela *f;* (*amount*) insignificancia *f;* **a ~** un poquito

trifling *adj* insignificante

trigger ['trɪg·ər] **I.** *n* gatillo *m;* *fig* detonante *m* **II.** *vt* desencadenar

trigonometry [ˌtrɪg·ə·'nam·ə·tri] *n* trigonometría *f*

trike [traɪk] *n inf abbr of* **tricycle** triciclo *m*

trilingual [ˌtraɪ·'lɪŋ·gwəl] *adj* trilingüe

trillion ['trɪl·jən] *n* billón *m*

trilogy ['trɪl·ə·dʒi] <-ies> *n* trilogía *f*

trim [trɪm] **I.** *n* **1.** (*state*) (buen) estado *m;* **to be in ~** estar listo (**for** para) **2.** (*hair*) **to give a ~** dar un recorte; (*hair*) cortar las puntas **II.** *adj*

muy cuidado, -a; (*person*) esbelto, -a
III. <-mm-> *vt* (*cut, reduce*) recortar; **to ~ one's beard** recortarse la barba

◆**trim down** *vt* recortar

◆**trim off** *vt* cortar

trimming *n* **1.** (*decoration*) adorno *m* **2.** ~s CULIN guarnición *f*

Trinidad ['trɪn·ɪ·dæd] *n* Trinidad *f;* **~ and Tobago** Trinidad y Tobago

Trinidadian ['trɪn·ɪ·dæd·i·ən] **I.** *adj* de Trinidad **II.** *n* habitante *mf* de Trinidad

trinket ['trɪŋ·kɪt] *n* baratija *f*

trio ['tri·ou] *n a.* MUS trío *m;* **string ~** trío de cuerda

trip [trɪp] **I.** *n* **1.** (*journey, drugs*) viaje *m;* (*shorter*) excursión *f;* **business ~** viaje de negocios; **to go on a ~** irse de viaje **2.** (*fall*) tropezón *m* **II.** <-pp-> *vi* (*stumble*) tropezar (**on** con) **III.** <-pp-> *vt* **to ~ sb** (**up**) poner la zancadilla a alguien

◆**trip over** *vi* dar un tropezón

◆**trip up I.** *vi* tropezar; (*verbally*) equivocarse **II.** *vt* **1.** (*cause to stumble*) hacer tropezar **2.** (*cause to fail*) confundir

triple ['trɪp·əl] **I.** *adj* triple **II.** *vt* triplicar **III.** *vi* triplicarse

triplet ['trɪp·lɪt] *n* (*baby*) trillizo, -a *m, f*

tripod ['traɪ·pad] *n* trípode *m*

tripping ['trɪp·ɪŋ] *adj* ligero, -a

trite [traɪt] *adj* tópico, -a

triumph ['traɪ·ʌmf] **I.** *n* triunfo *m* (**over** sobre); **in ~** triunfalmente; **a ~ of medicine** un éxito de la medicina **II.** *vi* triunfar (**over** sobre)

triumphant [traɪ·ʌm·fənt] *adj* (*victorious*) triunfante; (*successful*) exitoso, -a; (*return*) triunfal

trivia ['trɪv·i·ə] *npl* trivialidades *fpl*

trivial ['trɪv·i·əl] *adj* **1.** (*unimportant*) irrelevante; (*dispute, matter*) trivial **2.** (*insignificant*) insignificante

trod [trad] *pt, pp of* **tread**

trolley ['tral·i] *n* (*trolley car*) tranvía *m*

trombone [tram·'boun] *n* trombón *m*

troop [trup] **I.** *n* **~s** tropas *fpl* **II.** *vi* **to ~ in/out** entrar/salir en tropel

trooper ['tru·pər] *n* (*police*) policía *mf*

trophy ['trou·fi] *n* <-ies> trofeo *m*

tropic ['trap·ɪk] *n* trópico *m;* **~ of Can-**

cer/Capricorn Trópico de Cáncer/Capricornio

tropical ['trap·ɪ·kəl] *adj* tropical

trot [trat] **I.** *n* (*horse*) trote *m* **II.** *vi* trotar; (*go busily*) ir apresurado

◆**trot off** *vi* marcharse

◆**trot out** *vt* (*excuse, explanation*) soltar

trotter ['trat·ər] *n* manita *f* de cerdo

trouble ['trʌb·əl] **I.** *n* **1.** (*difficulty*) problema *m;* **to have ~** tener dificultades; **to be in/get into ~** estar/meterse en un lío; **to be the least of sb's ~s** ser el menor de los males de alguien **2.** (*inconvenience*) molestia *f;* **to go to a lot of ~** tomarse muchas molestias (**for** por); **to go to the ~ of doing sth** tomarse la molestia de hacer algo; **to put sb to the ~ of doing sth** comprometer a alguien para que haga algo; **to be (not) worth the ~ (of doing sth)** (no) merecer la pena (hacer algo) **3.** MED enfermedad *f;* **stomach ~** dolor *m* de estómago **4.** (*malfunction*) avería *f* **II.** *vt* **1.** *form* (*bother*) molestar (**for** con) **2.** **to ~ oneself** esforzarse (**about** en) **3.** (*worry*) preocupar **III.** *vi* esforzarse; **to ~ to do sth** molestarse en hacer algo

troubled *adj* **1.** (*period, water*) turbulento, -a **2.** (*worried*) preocupado, -a; (*look*) de preocupación

trouble-free [ˌtrʌb·əl·'fri] *adj* sin problemas

troublemaker ['trʌb·əl·ˌmeɪ·kər] *n* alborotador(a) *m(f)*

troubleshooting ['trʌb·əl·ˌʃu·t̬ɪŋ] *n* localización *f* de problemas

troublesome ['trʌb·əl·səm] *adj* molesto, -a

trouble spot *n* centro *m* de fricción

trough [trɔf] *n* **1.** (*receptacle*) abrevadero *m;* **feeding ~** comedero *m* **2.** METEO, GEO depresión *f*

trousers ['trau·zərz] *npl* pantalones *mpl;* **a pair of ~** unos pantalones

trout [traut] *n* <-(s)> trucha *f*

trowel ['trau·əl] *n* (*building*) llana *f;* (*gardening*) desplantador *m*

truancy ['tru·ən·si] *n* falta *f* injustificada

truant ['tru·ənt] **I.** *n* persona *f* que hace novillos **II.** *vi* hacer novillos

truce [trus] *n* tregua *f*

T

truck [trʌk] I. n AUTO camión m II. vt transportar

truck driver, trucker n camionero, -a m, f

true [tru] adj 1. (not false) cierto, -a; **to be ~** ser verdad [or cierto] (**that** que); **to ring ~** sonar convincente 2. (real) auténtico, -a; **~ love** amor verdadero; **sb's ~ self** la verdadera personalidad de alguien; **to come ~** hacerse realidad 3. (loyal) fiel (**to** a)

truffle ['trʌf·əl] n trufa f

truly ['tru·li] adv 1. (sincerely) sinceramente 2. (as intensifier) realmente ▶ **yours ~** (letter) atentamente

trump [trʌmp] GAMES I. n triunfo m II. vt matar

◆**trump up** vt falsificar

trumpet ['trʌm·pət] n trompeta f ▶ **to blow one's own ~** echarse flores

trumpeter ['trʌm·pə·t̮ər] n trompetista mf

truncate [trʌŋ·'keɪt] vt truncar

truncheon ['trʌn·tʃən] n porra f, macana f AmL

trunk [trʌŋk] n 1. ANAT, BOT tronco m; (elephant) trompa f 2. (for storage) baúl m; (car) maletero f, baúl m AmL 3. **~s** bañador m

trust [trʌst] n 1. (belief) confianza f; **to gain sb's ~** ganarse la confianza de alguien; **to place one's ~** depositar su confianza (**in** en) 2. (responsibility) responsabilidad f 3. FIN, COM consorcio m; **investment ~** grupo m de inversión II. vt confiar; **to ~ sb to do sth** confiar a alguien (el) hacer algo; **to ~ sb with sth** confiar la responsabilidad de algo a alguien; **to ~ that...** esperar que... +subj III. vi confiar (**in** en)

trusted ['trʌs·tɪd] adj fiable; (person) leal

trustee [trʌs·'ti] n fideicomisario, -a m, f; **board of ~s** consejo m de administración

trust fund n fondo m de fideicomiso

trusting adj confiado, -a

trustworthy ['trʌst·ˌwɜr·ði] adj fiable; (person) honrado, -a

trusty ['trʌs·ti] <-ier, -iest> adj leal

truth [truθ] n verdad f; **in ~** en realidad;

to tell the ~ decir la verdad (**about** sobre); **to tell the ~,...** a decir verdad,...

truthful ['truθ·fəl] adj (true) veraz; (sincere) sincero, -a; (accurate) preciso, -a

truthfulness n (veracity) veracidad f; (sincerity) sinceridad f; (accuracy) exactitud f

try [traɪ] I. n intento m; **to give sth a ~** intentar algo II. <-ie-> vi esforzarse; **to ~ and do sth** infintentar hacer algo III. <-ie-> vt 1. (attempt) intentar; **to ~ one's best** esforzarse al máximo; **to ~ one's luck** probar suerte 2. (test, sample) probar 3. LAW juzgar

◆**try for** vt insep tratar de obtener

◆**try on** vt (put on) probarse; **to try sth on for size** probarse algo para ver la talla

◆**try out** vt probar; **to try sth out on sb** dar a probar algo a alguien

trying adj (exasperating) irritante; (difficult) difícil

tsar n see **tzar**

tsarina n zarina f

tsetse fly ['tse·tsi·ˌflaɪ] n mosca f tse-tse

T-shirt ['ti·ʃɜrt] n camiseta f, playera f Guat, Méx, polera f Chile

tub [tʌb] n 1. (container) cubo m 2. (bathtub) bañera f 3. (carton) tarrina f; **a ~ of ice cream** una tarrina de helado

tubby ['tʌb·i] <-ier, -iest> adj rechoncho, -a, requenete Ven

tube [tub] n 1. (hollow cylinder) tubo m 2. ANAT trompa f; **Fallopian ~** trompa de Falopio 3. TV tele f ▶ **to go down the ~s** irse al traste

tuberculosis [tu·ˌbɜr·kjə·'loʊ·sɪs] n tuberculosis f inv

tuberculous [tu·'bɜr·kjʊ·ləs] adj tuberculoso, -a

tuck [tʌk] I. n (fold) pliegue m II. vt (fold) plegar

◆**tuck away** vt (hide) poner a buen recaudo; **to be tucked away** estar en un sitio seguro II. vi comer con apetito

◆**tuck in** vt 1. **to tuck one's shirt in** meterse la camisa 2. (in bed) arropar

Tuesday ['tuz·deɪ] n martes m inv; s. a. **Friday**

tuft [tʌft] n (hair, grass) mata f

tug [tʌg] I. n tirón m II. <-gg-> vt tirar de

tuition [tu·ˈɪʃ·ən] n 1. (fee) tasas fpl 2. (teaching) enseñanza f

tulip [ˈtu·lɪp] n tulipán m

tumble [ˈtʌm·bəl] I. n caída f; **to take a ~** caerse II. vi caerse; fig caer

◆**tumble down** vi desplomarse

◆**tumble over** vi caerse

tumbledown [ˈtʌm·bəl·ˌdaʊn] adj en ruinas

tumbler [ˈtʌm·blər] n vaso m

tumbleweed [ˈtʌm·bəl·wid] n planta f rodadora

tummy [ˈtʌm·i] <-ies> n childspeak barriguita f

tummy ache n childspeak dolor m de tripita

tumor [ˈtu·mər] n tumor m; **brain/malignant ~** tumor cerebral/maligno

tumultuous [tu·ˈmʌl·tʃu·əs] adj 1. (noisy) tumultuoso, -a; (applause) apoteósico, -a 2. (disorderly) agitado, -a

tuna [ˈtu·nə] n <-(s)> atún m

tune [tun] I. n 1. mus melodía f; **a catchy ~** una tonada pegadiza 2. (pitch) **to be in/out of ~** estar afinado/desafinado; fig armonizar/desentonar (with con) ▶ **to change one's ~ to sing another ~** cambiar de parecer; **to the ~ of** $100 por valor de 100$ II. vt 1. mus afinar 2. auto poner a punto

◆**tune in** I. vi 1. **to ~ to a station** radio sintonizar una emisora; tv sintonizar un canal 2. fig sl sintonizar (**to** con) II. vt radio, tv sintonizar

◆**tune up** vt auto poner a punto

tuner n (radio) sintonizador m

tune-up [ˈtun·ʌp] n auto puesta f a punto

tunic [ˈtu·nɪk] n fashion casaca f

tuning n auto puesta f a punto

tuning fork n diapasón m

tunnel [ˈtʌn·əl] n túnel m

turbine [ˈtɜr·bɪn] n turbina f

turbocharged [ˈtɜr·boʊ·ˌtʃɑrdʒd] adj turboalimentado, -a

turbo engine n motor m turbo

turbulence [ˈtɜr·bju·ləns] n turbulencia f

turbulent [ˈtɜr·bju·lənt] adj turbulento, -a

turd [tɜrd] n vulg 1. (excrement) zurullo m 2. (person) guarro, -a m, f

turf [tɜrf] <-s or-ves> n 1. bot césped m 2. **the ~** las carreras de caballos 3. (territory) territorio m

Turk [tɜrk] n turco, -a m, f

turkey [ˈtɜr·ki] n 1. zool pavo m 2. sl (stupid) papanatas mf inv ▶ **to talk ~** hablar claro

Turkey [ˈtɜr·ki] n Turquía f

Turkish [ˈtɜr·kɪʃ] I. adj turco, -a II. n 1. (person) turco, -a m, f 2. ling turco m

turmoil [ˈtɜr·mɔɪl] n 1. (chaos) caos m inv; **to be thrown into ~** estar sumido en el caos 2. psych trastorno m; **to be in a ~** estar desconcertado

turn [tɜrn] I. vi 1. (rotate) dar vueltas, girar (**on** sobre) 2. (switch direction) volver; (car) girar; **to ~ around** dar media vuelta, voltearse AmL; **to ~ right/left** torcer a la derecha/izquierda 3. (change) cambiar, transformarse; (for worse) volverse II. vt 1. (rotate) girar 2. (switch direction) volver, voltear AmL; **to ~ one's head** volver la cabeza; **to ~ a page** pasar una página; **to ~ the coat inside out** volver el abrigo del revés 3. (age) cumplir 4. (hour) dar; **it has ~ed three o'clock** dieron las tres 5. **it ~ed my stomach** me revolvió el estómago ▶ **to ~ sth upside down** dejar algo patas arriba III. n 1. (change) giro m; **to make a ~ to the right** girar a la derecha; **to take a ~ for the worse/better** empeorar/mejorar 2. (period of duty) turno m; **in ~** por turnos; **it's your ~** te toca; **to be sb's ~ to do sth** tocar a alguien hacer algo; **to speak out of ~** hablar fuera de lugar 3. (twist) rotación f 4. (service) favor m; **to do sb a good ~** hacer un favor a alguien ▶ **one good ~ deserves another** favor con favor se paga

◆**turn against** vt volverse en contra de

◆**turn around** I. vi volverse II. vt 1. (move) girar 2. (change) transformar

◆**turn away** I. vi apartarse (**from** de) II. vt 1. (refuse entry) no dejar entrar 2. (deny help) rechazar

T

◆**turn back** I. *vi* retroceder II. *vt* 1. (*send back*) hacer regresar 2. (*fold*) doblar

◆**turn down** *vt* 1. (*reject*) rechazar 2. (*volume*) bajar 3. (*fold*) doblar

◆**turn in** I. *vt* (*hand over*) entregar II. *vi inf* (*go to bed*) meterse en la cama

◆**turn off** *vt* 1. ELEC, TECH desconectar; (*light*) apagar; (*motor*) parar; (*gas, faucet*) cerrar 2. *sl* dar asco

◆**turn on** *vt* 1. ELEC, TECH conectar; (*light*) encender, prender *AmL*; (*gas, faucet*) abrir 2. (*excite*) excitar; (*attract*) gustar; **to ~ the charm** desplegar el encanto

◆**turn out** *vi* 1. (*end*) salir 2. (*be revealed*) resultar; **it turned out to be true** resultó ser cierto II. *vt* 1. (*light*) apagar 2. (*kick out*) echar; **to turn sb out on the street** echar a alguien a la calle

◆**turn over** *vt* 1. (*reverse*) dar la vuelta a 2. (*give*) ceder; (*criminal*) entregar 3. (*facts, idea*) dar vueltas a 4. COM, FIN facturar 5. (*search*) revolver buscando

◆**turn up** I. *vi* 1. (*arrive*) llegar 2. (*become available*) aparecer 3. (*point upwards*) doblarse hacia arriba II. *vt* 1. (*volume*) subir 2. (*shorten*) acortar 3. (*locate*) localizar

turnabout ['tɜrn·ə·ˌbaʊt] *n*, **turnaround** ['tɜrn·ə·ˌraʊnd] *n* 1. (*change*) giro *m* en redondo 2. (*improvement*) mejora *f*

turnaround time *n* AVIAT, NAUT tiempo *m* en puerto; (*of project*) tiempo de respuesta

turning ['tɜr·nɪŋ] *n* giro *m*; (*road*) bocacalle *f*

turning point *n* momento *m* decisivo; **a ~ in one's career** un cambio decisivo en su carrera

turnip ['tɜr·nɪp] *n* nabo *m*

turnout ['tɜrn·aʊt] *n* 1. (*attendance*) número *m* de asistentes 2. POL número de votantes 3. ECON producción *f* 4. FASHION atuendo *m*

turnover ['tɜrn·ˌoʊ·vər] *n* 1. COM, FIN volumen *m* de negocios; (*sales*) facturación *f* 2. (*in staff*) rotación *f* 3. CULIN empanada *f*

turnpike ['tɜrn·paɪk] *n* AUTO autopista *f* de peaje

turnstile ['tɜrn·staɪl] *n* torniquete *m*

turntable ['tɜrn·ˌteɪ·bəl] *n* RAIL plataforma *f* giratoria

turpentine ['tɜr·pən·taɪn] *n* trementina *f*

turquoise ['tɜr·kwɔɪz] *n* 1. (*stone*) turquesa *f* 2. (*color*) turquesa *m*

turret ['tɜr·ɪt] *n* torreón *m*

turtle ['tɜr·təl] <-(s)> *n* tortuga *f*

turtleneck ['tɜr·təl·nek] *n* cuello *m* de cisne

tusk [tʌsk] *n* colmillo *m*

tussle ['tʌs·əl] I. *vi* pelearse II. *n* pelea *f*

tutor ['tu·tər] SCHOOL, UNIV I. *n* tutor(a) *m(f)*; (*at home*) preceptor(a) *m(f)* II. *vt* dar clases particulares (**in** de)

tutorial [tu·'tɔr·i·əl] *n* COMPUT tutorial *m*

tux [tʌks] *inf abbr of* **tuxedo** esmoquin *m*

tuxedo [tʌk·'si·doʊ] *n* esmoquin *m*

TV [ˌti·'vi] *n abbr of* **television** TV *f*

tweak [twik] I. *vt* pellizcar II. *n* pellizco *m*

tweezers ['twi·zərz] *npl* (**a pair of**) ~ (unas) pinzas

twelfth [twelfθ] I. *adj* duodécimo, -a II. *n* 1. (*order*) duodécimo, -a *m, f* 2. (*date*) doce *m* 3. (*fraction*) duodécimo *m; s. a.* **eighth**

twelve [twelv] *adj, n* doce *m; s. a.* **eight**

twentieth ['twen·ti·əθ] I. *adj* vigésimo, -a II. *n* 1. (*order*) vigésimo, -a *m, f* 2. (*date*) veinte *m* 3. (*fraction*) vigésimo *m; s. a.* **eighth**

twenty ['twen·ti] <-ies> *adj, n* veinte *m; s. a.* **eighty**

twerp [twɜrp] *n sl* capullo, -a *m, f*

twice [twaɪs] *adv* dos veces

twiddle ['twɪd·əl] I. *vt a.* TECH, ELEC (hacer) girar II. *vi* juguetear (**with** con) III. *n* giro *m*

twig [twɪg] *n* ramita *f*

twilight ['twaɪ·laɪt] *n* crepúsculo *m*

twin [twɪn] *adj, n* mellizo, -a *m, f*; **identical ~s** gemelos

twin bed *n* cama *f* gemela

twin brother *n* hermano *m* gemelo

twine [twaɪn] I. *vt* 1. (*wind up*) enrollar 2. (*encircle*) rodear II. *n* cordel *m*

twinge [twɪndʒ] *n* 1. MED punzada *f* 2. *fig* arrebato *m*; **a ~ of conscience** un remordimiento de conciencia

twinkle ['twɪŋ·kəl] I. *vi* brillar II. *n* brillo *m* ▶ **to do sth in a ~** hacer algo en un abrir y cerrar de ojos

twinkling ['twɪŋ·klɪŋ] I. *adj* brillante II. *n* parpadeo *m* ▶ **in the ~ of an eye** en un abrir y cerrar de ojos

twinning ['twɪn·ɪŋ] *n* hermanamiento *m* de dos ciudades

twin sister *n* hermana *f* gemela

twirl [twɜrl] I. *vi* dar vueltas (**around** alrededor de) II. *n* pirueta *f*

twist [twɪst] I. *vt* 1. (*turn*) dar vueltas a 2. (*wind around*) enrollar (**around** alrededor de) 3. (*ankle*) torcerse; (*truth*) tergiversar ▶ **to ~ sb's arm** presionar a alguien; **to ~ sb round one's little finger** manejar a alguien a su antojo II. *vi* 1. (*squirm*) (re)torcerse 2. (*river, road*) **to ~ and turn** serpentear III. *n* 1. (*turn*) vuelta *f*; **to give sth a ~** dar un giro a algo 2. (*change*) giro *m* 3. (*hair*) mecha *f*; (*lemon*) rodajita *f*; (*paper*) cucurucho *m* 4. (*dance*) twist *m*

twisted ['twɪs·tɪd] *adj* 1. (*cable, metal*) retorcido, -a; (*ankle*) torcido, -a 2. (*perverted*) pervertido, -a; (*logic, humor*) retorcido, -a

twister ['twɪs·tər] *n inf* tornado *m*

twit [twɪt] *n sl* capullo, -a *m, f*

twitch [twɪtʃ] I. *vi, vt* ANAT, MED temblar II. *n* <-es> 1. ANAT, MED tic *m* 2. (*pull*) tirón *m*

twitter ['twɪt·ər] I. *vi* gorjear; *fig* parlotear II. *n* gorjeo *m*

two [tu] *adj, n* dos *m* ▶ **that makes ~ of us** ya somos dos; **to put ~ and ~ together** sacar conclusiones; *s. a.* **eight**

two-dimensional [ˌtu·dɪ·ˈmen·ʃə·nəl] *adj* bidimensional; *fig* superficial

two-door *adj* de dos puertas

two-edged *adj* de doble filo

two-faced *adj* falso, -a, falluto, -a *RíoPl*

twofold ['tu·foʊld] I. *adv* dos veces II. *adj* doble

two-part *adj* de dos partes

two-party system *n* sistema *f* bipartidista

two-piece *n* 1. (*suit*) conjunto *m* de dos piezas 2. (*bikini*) bikini *m*

two-seater AUTO I. *n* biplaza *m* II. *adj* de dos plazas

twosome ['tu·səm] *n* (*duo*) dúo *m;* (*couple*) pareja *f*

two-way ['tu·ˈweɪ] *adj* de doble sentido; (*process*) recíproco, -a; (*conversation*) bilateral

tycoon [taɪ·ˈkun] *n* magnate *mf*

tyke [taɪk] *n* 1. (*child*) diablillo, -a *m, f* 2. (*dog*) perro *m* callejero

type [taɪp] I. *n a.* TYPO tipo *m;* (*machine*) modelo *m;* (*animal, person*) clase *f;* **he's not her ~** no es su tipo II. *vt, vi* escribir con el ordenador

◆type out *vt* escribir con el ordenador

◆type up *vt* pasar a máquina

typesetting ['taɪp·ˌset·ɪŋ] *n* composición *f* tipográfica

typewriter ['taɪp·ˌraɪ·tər] *n* máquina *f* de escribir

typewritten *adj* mecanografiado, -a

typhoid ['taɪ·fɔɪd], **typhoid fever** *n* fiebre *f* tifoidea

typhoon [taɪ·ˈfun] *n* tifón *m*

typical ['tɪp·ɪ·kəl] *adj* típico, -a (**of** de); (*symptom*) característico, -a

typically *adv* típicamente

typify ['tɪp·ɪ·faɪ] <-ie-> *vt* simbolizar

typing ['taɪ·pɪŋ] *n* mecanografía *f*

typist ['taɪ·pɪst] *n* mecanógrafo, -a *m, f*

tyranny ['tɪr·ə·ni] *n* tiranía *f*

tyrant ['taɪ·rənt] *n* tirano, -a *m, f*

tzar [zar] *n* zar *m*

tzetze fly ['te·tsi·ˌflaɪ] *n* mosca *f* tse-tse

U

U, u [ju] *n* U, u *f;* **~ as in Uniform** U de Uruguay

U[1] *abbr of* **uranium** uranio *m*

U[2] *inf abbr of* **university** universidad *f*

ubiquitous [ju·ˈbɪk·wə·təs] *adj* omnipresente

udder ['ʌd·ər] *n* ubre *f*

UFO [ˌju·ef·ˈoʊ] *n abbr of* **unidentified flying object** OVNI *m*

ugh [ʌh] *interj* uf

ugliness ['ʌg·lɪ·nɪs] *n* fealdad *f;* (*nastiness*) repugnancia *f*

ugly ['ʌg·li] <-ier, iest> *adj* 1. feo, -a, macaco, -a *Arg, Méx, Cuba, Chile*; **to be ~**

as sin ser más feo que Picio **2.** (*mood*) peligroso, -a; (*look*) repugnante **3.** (*violent*) violento, -a; **to turn ~** ponerse violento **4.** (*harsh*) desagradable; (*weather*) horroroso, -a; **~ rumors** calumnias

UHF [ju·ertʃ·'ef] *n abbr of* **ultrahigh frequency** UHF *f*

UK [ju·'keɪ] *n abbr of* **United Kingdom** RU *m*

Ukraine [ju·'kreɪn] *n* Ucrania *f*

Ukrainian I. *adj* ucraniano, -a **II.** *n* **1.** (*person*) ucraniano, -a *m, f* **2.** LING ucraniano *m*

ukulele [ju·kə·'leɪ·li] *n* MUS ukelele *m*

ulcer ['ʌl·sər] *n* **1.** MED úlcera *f*, chácara *f Col* **2.** *fig* llaga *f*

ulterior [ʌl·'tɪr·i·ər] *adj* (*secret*) secreto, -a

ultimate ['ʌl·tə·mɪt] **I.** *adj* **1.** (*best*) máximo, -a; (*experience, feeling*) extremo, -a **2.** (*final*) final; (*cost, consequences, effect*) definitivo, -a **3.** (*fundamental*) primordial **II.** *n* the **~** lo último; (*bad taste, vulgarity*) el colmo; **the ~ in fashion** el último grito en moda; **the ~ in stupidity** el colmo de la estupidez

ultimately ['ʌl·tə·mɪt·li] *adv* **1.** (*in the end*) finalmente **2.** (*fundamentally*) fundamentalmente

ultimatum [ʌl·tə·'meɪ·təm] <ultimata *or* -tums> *n* ultimátum *m*

ultrasound ['ʌl·trə·saʊnd] *n* ultrasonido *m*

ultraviolet [ʌl·trə·'vaɪ·ə·lɪt] *adj* ultravioleta

umbilical [ʌm·'bɪl·ɪ·kəl] *adj* umbilical

umbilical cord *n* cordón *m* umbilical

umbrella [ʌm·'brel·ə] *n* (*rain*) paraguas *m inv*; (*sun*) sombrilla *f*

umbrella organization *n* organización *f* paraguas

umpire ['ʌm·paɪr] SPORTS **I.** *n* árbitro *mf* **II.** *vt, vi* arbitrar

umpteen ['ʌmp·tin] *adj inf* innumerable; **~ reasons** múltiples razones

umpteenth ['ʌmp·tinθ] *adj* enésimo, -a

UN [ju·'en] *n abbr of* **United Nations** ONU *f*

unabashed [ʌn·ə·'bæʃt] *adj* desenvuelto, -a; (*behavior*) atrevido, -a

unable [ʌn·'eɪ·bəl] *adj* incapaz

unabridged [ʌn·ə·'brɪdʒd] *adj* (*whole*) íntegro, -a

unacceptable [ʌn·ək·'sep·tə·bəl] *adj* inadmisible

unaccompanied [ʌn·ə·'kʌm·pə·nid] *adj* sin compañía; MUS sin acompañamiento

unaccountable [ʌn·ə·'kaʊn·tə·bəl] *adj* **1.** (*not responsible*) no responsable **2.** (*inexplicable*) inexplicable

unaccustomed [ʌn·ə·'kʌs·təmd] *adj* raro, -a; (*new*) inusual; **to be ~ to doing sth** no tener costumbre de hacer algo

unaddressed [ʌn·ə·'drest] *adj* sin señas

unadulterated [ʌn·ə·'dʌl·tə·reɪ·tɪd] *adj* puro, -a; (*alcohol, wine*) no adulterado, -a

unadventurous [ʌn·əd·'ven·tʃər·əs] *adj* poco atrevido, -a; (*style*) poco llamativo, -a

unaffected [ʌn·ə·'fek·tɪd] *adj* **1.** (*not changed*) inalterado, -a **2.** (*not influenced*) espontáneo, -a **3.** (*down to earth*) sencillo, -a; (*manner, speech*) natural

unafraid [ʌn·ə·'freɪd] *adj* sin temor; **to be ~** no tener miedo (**of** de)

unaided [ʌn·'eɪ·dɪd] *adj* sin ayuda; **to do sth ~** hacer algo por sí solo

unaltered [ʌn·'ɔl·tərd] *adj* inalterado, -a; **to leave sth ~** dejar algo tal como estaba

unambiguous [ʌn·æm·'bɪg·ju·əs] *adj* inequívoco, -a; (*statement*) incuestionable

un-American [ʌn·ə·'mer·ɪ·kən] *adj* antiamericano, -a

unanimity [ju·nə·'nɪm·ə·ţi] *n* unanimidad *f*

unanimous [ju·'næn·ə·məs] *adj* unánime

unannounced [ʌn·ə·'naʊnst] **I.** *adj* (*without warning*) inesperado, -a; (*not made known*) fortuito, -a **II.** *adv* de repente; (*arrive, visit*) sin previo aviso

unanswerable [ʌn·'æn·sər·ə·bəl] *adj* (*with no answer*) sin respuesta; (*irrefutable*) irrefutable

unanswered [ʌn·'æn·sərd] *adj* sin contestar

unappetizing [ʌn·'æp·ə·taɪ·zɪŋ] *adj* poco apetitoso, -a

unapproachable [ʌn·ə·'prou·tʃə·bəl] *adj*

inaccesible; (*person*) intratable

unarmed [ʌn-'armd] *adj* desarmado, -a

unashamed [ʌn-ə-'ʃeɪmd] *adj* desvergonzado, -a; (*greed, selfishness*) descarado, -a; **to be ~ of sth** (*guilt*) no tener remordimientos por algo; (*shame*) no avergonzarse por algo

unasked [ʌn-'æskt] *adj* no solicitado, -a; (*spontaneous*) espontáneo, -a

unassignable [ʌn-ə-'saɪ-nə-bəl] *adj* LAW intrasferible

unassuming [ʌn-ə-'su-mɪŋ] *adj* modesto, -a

unattached [ʌn-ə-'tætʃt] *adj* **1.** (*not connected*) suelto, -a; (*part*) separable **2.** (*independent*) libre

unattainable [ʌn-ə-'teɪ-nə-bəl] *adj* inalcanzable

unattended [ʌn-ə-'ten-dɪd] *adj* **1.** (*alone*) sin compañía; **to leave the children ~** dejar a los niños sin vigilancia **2.** (*unmanned*) desatendido, -a **3.** (*not taken care of*) descuidado, -a

unattractive [ʌn-ə-'træk-tɪv] *adj* (*ugly*) poco atractivo, -a; (*unpleasant*) desagradable

unauthorized [ʌn-'ɔ-θə-raɪzd] *adj* no autorizado, -a

unavailable [ʌn-ə-'veɪ-lə-bəl] *adj* inasequible; (*person*) ocupado, -a

unavoidable [ʌn-ə-'vɔɪ-də-bəl] *adj* inevitable

unaware [ʌn-ə-'wer] *adj* ajeno (**of** a)

unawares [ʌn-ə-'werz] *adv* desprevenido

unbalanced [ʌn-'bæl-ənst] *adj* **1.** (*uneven*) desnivelado, -a; (*account*) desequilibrado, -a **2.** PSYCH trastornado, -a

unbearable [ʌn-'ber-ə-bəl] *adj* insufrible

unbeatable [ʌn-'bi-tə-bəl] *adj* (*record, team*) imbatible; (*value, quality*) inmejorable; (*meal*) insuperable

unbeaten [ʌn-'bi-tən] *adj* invicto, -a; (*record*) insuperado, -a

unbelievable [ʌn-bɪ-'li-və-bəl] *adj* increíble

unbelieving [ʌn-bɪ-'li-vɪŋ] *adj* incrédulo, -a

unbending *adj* firme; (*will*) inquebrantable

unbiased [ʌn-'baɪ-əst] *adj* imparcial; (*opinion, report, advice*) objetivo, -a

unbleached [ʌn-'blitʃt] *adj* sin blanquear; (*flour*) integral

unbolt [ʌn-'boʊlt] *vt* desatrancar

unborn [ʌn-'bɔrn] *adj* (*baby*) en gestación

unbreakable [ʌn-'breɪ-kə-bəl] *adj* inquebrantable; (*material*) irrompible

unbroken [ʌn-'broʊ-kən] *adj* **1.** (*not broken*) intacto, -a; **an ~ promise** una promesa cumplida **2.** (*continuous*) ininterrumpido, -a

unbuckle [ʌn-'bʌk-əl] *vt* desabrochar

unbusinesslike [ʌn-'bɪz-nɪs-laɪk] *adj* poco profesional

unbutton [ʌn-'bʌt-ən] *vt* desabrochar

uncalled-for [ʌn-'kɔld-fɔr] *adj* gratuito, -a; (*remark*) fuera de lugar

uncanny [ʌn-'kæn-i] *adj* <-ier, -iest> **1.** (*mysterious*) misterioso, -a **2.** (*remarkable*) extraordinario, -a; **to be ~ how...** ser sorprendente cómo...; **an ~ knack** una destreza extraordinaria

uncared-for [ʌn-'kerd-fɔr] *adj* descuidado, -a

unceasing [ʌn-'si-sɪŋ] *adj* incesante; (*support*) incondicional

uncertain [ʌn-'sɜr-tən] *adj* **1.** (*unsure*) dudoso, -a; **to be ~ of/whether/when...** no estar seguro de/de si/de cuándo...; **in no ~ terms** claramente **2.** (*chancy*) incierto, -a **3.** (*volatile*) volátil

uncertainty [ʌn-'sɜr-tən-ti] <-ies> *n* incertidumbre *f* (**about** sobre); (*hesitancy*) indecisión *f*

unchallenged [ʌn-'tʃæl-ɪndʒd] *adj* **1.** (*not questioned*) incuestionado, -a **2.** (*unopposed*) no protestado, -a; **to go ~** pasar sin protesta

unchanged [ʌn-'tʃeɪndʒd] *adj* **1.** (*unaltered*) inalterado, -a **2.** (*not replaced*) no sustituido, -a

uncharacteristic [ʌn-ˌkær-ɪk-tə-'rɪs-tɪk] *adj* poco característico, -a; **to be ~** no ser típico (**of** de)

uncharitable [ʌn-'tʃær-ɪ-tə-bəl] *adj* (*severe*) severo, -a (**in** en)

unchecked [ʌn-'tʃekt] *adj* **1.** (*unrestrained*) desenfrenado, -a **2.** (*not checked*) sin comprobar

unchristian [ʌn-'krɪs-tʃən] *adj* indigno, -a de un cristiano

uncivil [ʌnˈsɪv·əl] *adj* grosero, -a (**to** con)

unclaimed [ʌnˈkleɪmd] *adj* sin reclamar

uncle [ˈʌŋ·kəl] *n* tío *m*

unclean [ʌnˈklin] *adj* **1.** sucio, -a; (*impure*) impuro, -a **2.** (*taboo*) tabú

unclear [ʌnˈklɪr] *adj* **1.** (*not certain*) nada claro, -a; **to be ~** no estar seguro (**about** de) **2.** (*vague*) vago, -a

uncomfortable [ʌnˈkʌm·fər·t̬ə·bəl] *adj* incómodo, -a; **an ~ silence** un silencio incómodo; **it makes me ~ to...** me hace sentir incómodo (el)...

uncommon [ʌnˈkam·ən] *adj* (*rare*) poco común; **to be not ~** no ser raro (**for** para)

uncommonly *adv* raramente; (*extremely*) excepcionalmente

uncompromising [ʌnˈkam·prə·maɪ·zɪŋ] *adj* intransigente; **to take an ~ stand** adoptar una postura intransigente

unconcerned [ʌn·kənˈsɜrnd] *adj* **1.** (*not worried*) no preocupado, -a; **to be ~** no preocuparse (**about** por) **2.** (*indifferent*) indiferente (**with** con respecto a)

unconditional [ʌn·kənˈdɪʃ·ə·nəl] *adj* incondicional

unconfirmed [ʌn·kənˈfɜrmd] *adj* no confirmado, -a

unconnected [ʌn·kəˈnek·tɪd] *adj* desconectado, -a (**to** de)

unconscionable [ʌnˈkan·tʃə·nə·bəl] *adj* desmedido, -a

unconscious [ʌnˈkan·tʃəs] **I.** *adj* **1.** MED, PSYCH inconsciente; **to knock sb ~** dejar a alguien inconsciente **2.** (*unaware*) no intencional; **to be ~** no ser consciente (**of** de) **II.** *n* PSYCH inconsciente *m*

unconsciously *adv* inconscientemente

unconsciousness *n* **1.** MED pérdida *f* de conocimiento **2.** (*unawareness*) inconsciencia *f*

unconstitutional [ʌn·kan·stə·ˈtu·ʃə·nəl] *adj* inconstitucional

uncontested [ʌn·kənˈtes·tɪd] *adj* (*not disputed*) sin oposición

uncontrollable [ʌn·kənˈtrou·lə·bəl] *adj* **1.** (*irresistible*) irrefrenable **2.** (*frenzied*) incontrolable

uncontrolled [ʌn·kənˈtrould] *adj* descontrolado, -a

unconvinced [ʌn·kənˈvɪnst] *adj* **to be ~** no estar convencido (**of** de)

unconvincing [ʌn·kənˈvɪn·sɪŋ] *adj* nada convincente; **rather ~** poco convincente

uncooked [ʌnˈkʊkt] *adj* crudo, -a

uncooperative [ʌn·kouˈap·ər·ə·t̬ɪv] *adj* poco cooperativo, -a

uncork [ʌnˈkɔrk] *vt* descorchar; **to ~ one's feelings** dejar aflorar los sentimientos; **to ~ a surprise** destapar una sorpresa

uncountable noun [ʌnˈkaun·t̬ə·bəl naun] *n* substantivo *m* incontable

uncouth [ʌnˈkuθ] *adj* basto, -a

uncover [ʌnˈkʌv·ər] *vt* destapar; (*secret, truth*) desvelar

uncut [ʌnˈkʌt] *adj* **1.** (*not cut*) sin cortar; **an ~ diamond** un diamante en bruto **2.** (*not shortened*) sin cortes

undaunted [ʌnˈdɔn·t̬ɪd] *adj* impertérrito, -a; **to be ~** quedarse impávido (**by** ante)

undecided [ʌn·dɪˈsaɪ·dɪd] *adj* **1.** (*unresolved*) indeciso, -a (**about** ante); **to be ~ as to what to do** no saber qué hacer **2.** (*not settled*) no decidido, -a

undeclared [ʌn·dɪˈklerd] *adj* **1.** FIN no declarado, -a **2.** (*not official*) no oficial; **an ~ war** una guerra no declarada

undeliverable [ʌn·dɪˈlɪv·rə·bəl] *adj* que no puede ser entregado, -a

undelivered [ʌn·dɪˈlɪv·ərd] *adj* sin entregar

undemanding [ʌn·dɪˈman·dɪŋ] *adj* sencillo, -a; (*person*) poco exigente

undeniable [ʌn·dɪˈnaɪ·ə·bəl] *adj* innegable; (*evidence*) irrefutable

undeniably *adv* indudablemente

under [ˈʌn·dər] **I.** *prep* **1.** (*below*) debajo de; **~ the bed** debajo de la cama; **~ there** ahí debajo **2.** (*supporting, governed by*) bajo; **to break ~ the weight** romperse bajo el peso; **to be ~ sb's influence** estar bajo la influencia de alguien **3.** (*less*) **to cost ~ $10** costar menos de 10$; **those ~ the age of 30** los menores de 30 años **4.** **~ the circumstances** dadas las circunstancias; **~ repair** en reparación; **to classify the books ~ fiction** clasificar los libros por ficción II. *adv* 1. (*fewer*) menos 2. **to crawl/go ~** meterse debajo 3. *inf* **to go ~** quedar inconsciente

underage [ˌʌn·dərˈeɪdʒ] *adj* menor de edad

undercapitalized [ˌʌn·dərˈkæp·ɪ·tə·laɪzd] *adj* subcapitalizado, -a; **to be ~** estar descapitalizado

undercharge [ˌʌn·dərˈtʃɑrdʒ] *vt, vi* cobrar de menos

underclothes [ˈʌn·dərˌkloʊz] *npl*, **underclothing** [ˈʌn·dərˌkloʊ·ðɪŋ] *n* ropa *f* interior

undercoat [ˈʌn·dərˌkoʊt] *n* primera capa *f* de pintura

undercover [ˌʌn·dərˈkʌv·ər] I. *adj* secreto, -a II. *adv* clandestinamente

undercurrent [ˈʌn·dərˌkɜr·ənt] *n* corriente *f* submarina; *fig* trasfondo *m*

undercut [ˌʌn·dərˈkʌt] *irr vt* (*charge less*) vender más barato

underdeveloped [ˌʌn·dər·dɪˈvel·əpt] *adj* 1. ECON subdesarrollado, -a; (*resource*) infradesarrollado, -a 2. BOT inmaduro, -a

underdog [ˈʌn·dərˌdɔg] *n* desvalido, -a *m, f*

underdone [ˌʌn·dərˈdʌn] *adj* FOOD poco hecho, -a

underemployed [ˌʌn·dər·ɪmˈplɔɪd] *adj* 1. subestimado, -a en el trabajo 2. ECON **to be ~** ser poco utilizado, -a

underestimate [ˌʌn·dərˈes·tə·meɪt] I. *vt* subestimar II. *n* infravaloración *f*

underfed [ˌʌn·dərˈfed] *n* desnutrido, -a *m, f*

underfoot [ˌʌn·dərˈfʊt] *adv* bajo los pies; **to trample ~** *a. fig* pisar

undergarment [ˈʌn·dərˌgɑr·mənt] *n* prenda *f* interior

undergo [ˌʌn·dərˈgoʊ] *irr vt* experimentar; (*change*) sufrir; **to ~ surgery** ser operado

undergraduate [ˌʌn·dərˈgrædʒ·u·ət] *n* estudiante *mf* no licenciado, -a

underground [ˈʌn·dərˌgraʊnd] I. *adj* 1. subterráneo, -a 2. (*clandestine*) clandestino, -a II. *adv* 1. bajo tierra 2. (*clandestinely*) en la clandestinidad III. *n* (*lifestyle*) underground *m*

undergrowth [ˈʌn·dərˌgroʊθ] *n* male-

za *f*

underhand [ˌʌn·dərˈhænd], **underhanded** [ˌʌn·dərˈhæn·dɪd] I. *adj* (*secret*) subrepticio, -a II. *adv* (*secretly*) subrepticiamente

underline [ˌʌn·dərˈlaɪn] *vt* 1. (*word*) subrayar; **to ~ sth in red** subrayar algo en rojo 2. (*emphasize*) enfatizar; **to ~ that...** subrayar que...

underlying [ˌʌn·dərˈlaɪ·ɪŋ] *adj* subyacente

undermanned [ˌʌn·dərˈmænd] *adj* sin plantilla suficiente

undermine [ˌʌn·dərˈmaɪn] *vt* 1. (*damage, sap, weaken*) minar; **to ~ hopes** desalentar; **to ~ sb's confidence** hacer perder la confianza de alguien; **to ~ sb's health** perjudicar la salud de alguien 2. (*tunnel under*) socavar

underneath [ˌʌn·dərˈniθ] I. *prep* debajo de II. *adv* por debajo III. *adj* inferior

undernourished [ˌʌn·dərˈnɜr·ɪʃt] *adj* desnutrido, -a

underpaid [ˌʌn·dərˈpeɪd] *adj* mal pagado, -a

underpants [ˈʌn·dərˌpænts] *npl* calzoncillos *mpl*

underpass [ˈʌn·dərˌpæs] <-es> *n* paso *m* subterráneo

underpay [ˌʌn·dərˈpeɪ] *irr vt* pagar un sueldo insuficiente

underperform [ˌʌn·dər·pərˈfɔrm] *vi* rendir por debajo de lo suficiente

underprivileged [ˌʌn·dərˈprɪv·ə·lɪdʒd] *adj* sin privilegios; **the ~ class** la clase no privilegiada

underrate [ˌʌn·dərˈreɪt] *vt* subestimar; **to ~ the difficulty/importance** infravalorar la dificultad/importancia (**of** de)

underrepresented [ˌʌn·dər·rep·rɪˈzen·tɪd] *adj* con mala representación

undershirt [ˈʌn·dərˌʃɜrt] *n* camiseta *f* interior

underside [ˈʌn·dərˌsaɪd] *n* superficie *f* inferior

undersigned [ˈʌn·dərˌsaɪnd] *n* **the ~** el/la abajo firmante

understaffed [ˌʌn·dərˈstæft] *adj* falto, -a de personal

understand [ˌʌn·dərˈstænd] *irr* I. *vt* 1. (*perceive*) comprender, entender

U

(that que); **to make oneself under-stood** hacerse entender; **to not ~ a word** no entender ni una palabra; **to ~ sb's doing sth** entender que alguien haga algo **2.** *form* (*be informed*) quedar informado (**that** de que); **to ~ from sb** saber por alguien (**that** que) **3.** (*believe*) creer; (*infer*) sobreentender; **as I ~ it** según tengo entendido; **it is understood that...** se sobreentiende que... **II.** *vi* entender (**about** de)

understandable [ˌʌn·dərˈstæn·də·bəl] *adj* comprensible; **to be ~ that...** ser comprensible que...

understanding I. *n* **1.** (*grasp*) entendimiento *m;* **to not have any ~ of sth** no tener ni idea de algo *inf;* **to come to an ~** llegar a entender; **sb's ~** la interpretación de alguien (**of** de) **2.** (*agreement*) acuerdo *m;* **to come to an ~** llegar a un acuerdo **3.** (*rapport*) comprensión *f;* **a spirit of ~** un espíritu de comprensión **4.** (*condition*) condición *f;* **to do sth on the ~ that...** hacer algo a condición de que... **II.** *adj* comprensivo, -a

understatement [ʌn·dərˈsteɪt·mənt] *n* atenuación *f*

understood [ʌn·dərˈstʊd] *vt, vi pt, pp of* **understand**

understudy [ˈʌn·dər·ˌstʌd·i] <-ies> *n* THEAT suplente *mf* (**for** de)

undertake [ˌʌn·dərˈteɪk] *irr vt* **1.** (*take on*) emprender; **to ~ a journey** emprender un viaje **2.** *form* **to ~ to do sth** comprometerse a hacer algo; **to ~ (that)...** comprometerse a (que)...

undertaker [ˈʌn·dər·ˌteɪ·kər] *n* director(a) *m(f)* de una funeraria

undertaking [ˌʌn·dərˈteɪ·kɪŋ] *n* **1.** (*project*) empresa *f* **2.** (*pledge*) promesa *f* (**to** de)

undervalue [ˌʌn·dərˈvæl·ju] *vt* infravalorar

underwater [ˈʌn·dər·ˈwɔ·tər] **I.** *adj* submarino, -a **II.** *adv* bajo el agua

underwear [ˈʌn·dər·wer] *n* ropa *f* interior

underweight [ʌn·dərˈweɪt] *adj* de peso insuficiente

underworld [ˈʌn·dər·wɜrld] *n* **1.** (*criminals*) hampa *m* **2. the Underworld** el inframundo

underwrite [ˈʌn·dər·raɪt] *irr vt* **1.** (*sign*) firmar; **to ~ a contract** firmar un contrato **2.** (*insurance*) asegurar

undesirable [ʌn·dɪˈzaɪ·rə·bəl] *adj* indeseable; **to be ~ that...** no ser recomendable que...; **an ~ character** un carácter difícil

undetected [ʌn·dɪˈtek·tɪd] *adj* no descubierto, -a; **to go ~** pasar inadvertido, -a

undeveloped [ʌn·dɪˈvel·əpt] *adj* **1.** POL, ECON subdesarrollado, -a **2.** (*not used*) poco utilizado, -a **3.** BIO, PSYCH no desarrollado, -a

undid [ʌnˈdɪd] *vt, vi pt of* **undo**

undies [ˈʌn·diz] *npl inf* paños *m pl* menores

undisclosed [ʌn·dɪsˈkloʊzd] *adj* no revelado, -a; (*amount*) no desvelado, -a; (*location*) sin desvelar

undisturbed [ʌn·dɪˈstɜrbd] *adj* **they were ~ by the noise** el ruido no les molestaba

undivided [ʌn·dɪˈvaɪ·dɪd] *adj* íntegro, -a; **sb's ~ attention** toda la atención de alguien

undo [ʌnˈdu] *irr vt* **1.** (*unfasten*) soltar; (*button*) desabrochar; (*zipper*) bajar **2.** (*cancel*) anular; (*damage*) reparar ▶ **what's <u>done</u> cannot be undone** lo hecho, hecho está

undoing *n* ruina *f*

undone [ʌnˈdʌn] **I.** *vt pp of* **undo II.** *adj* **1.** (*unfastened*) desatado, -a; **to come ~** deshacerse, desatarse **2.** (*uncompleted*) por hacer; **to leave sth ~** dejar algo sin hacer

undoubted [ʌnˈdaʊ·tɪd] *adj* indudable

undoubtedly *adv* sin duda

undress [ʌnˈdres] **I.** *vt* desnudar, desvestir *AmL* **II.** *vi* desnudarse, desvestirse *AmL* **III.** *n* **1.** (*informal clothing*) ropa *f* informal **2. to be in a state of ~** estar desnudo

undressed *adj* desvestido, -a; **to get ~** desnudarse

undue [ʌnˈdu] *adj* indebido, -a

unduly [ʌnˈdu·li] *adv* indebidamente

undying [ʌnˈdaɪ·ɪŋ] *adj* imperecedero, -a

unearned [ʌnˈɜrnd] *adj* **1.** (*undeserved*)

unearth [ʌn·'ɜrθ] vt desenterrar; fig sacar a la luz; (truth) descubrir

unearthly [ʌn·'ɜrθ·li] adj sobrenatural; ~ **noise/scream** ruido/grito aterrador

unease [ʌn·'iz] n malestar m; **with growing ~** con creciente inquietud

uneasiness n inquietud f

uneasy [ʌn·'i·zi] adj <-ier, -iest> 1. (uncertain) intranquilo, -a; **to be/feel ~** estar/sentirse inquieto (about por) 2. (causing anxiety) ansioso, -a; (suspicion) inquietante; (relationship) inestable 3. (insecure) dudoso, -a

uneducated [ʌn·'edʒ·ə·keɪ·tɪd] adj inculto, -a

unemployable [ʌn·ɪm·'plɔɪ·ə·bəl] adj incapacitado, -a para trabajar

unemployed [ʌn·ɪm·'plɔɪd] I. n pl **the ~** los desempleados II. adj parado, -a

unemployment [ʌn·ɪm·'plɔɪ·mənt] n paro m

unemployment benefit n subsidio m de desempleo

unequal [ʌn·'i·kwəl] adj 1. (inequitable) desigual 2. **to be ~ to sth** no estar a la altura de algo; **to be ~ to a task** ser incapaz de realizar una tarea

unequaled adj, **unequalled** adj sin igual

unequivocal [ʌn·ɪ·'kwɪv·ə·kəl] adj inequívoco, -a; (success) indudable; **to be ~ in sth** ser claro en algo

unethical [ʌn·'eθ·ɪ·kəl] adj poco ético, -a

uneven [ʌn·'i·vən] adj 1. (not level) desnivelado, -a 2. (unequal) desigual 3. (different) distinto, -a 4. (erratic, fluctuating) cambiante

uneventful [ʌn·ɪ·'vent·fəl] adj sin acontecimientos; (unexciting) tranquilo, -a

unexceptional [ʌn·ɪk·'sep·ʃə·nəl] adj corriente

unexpected [ʌn·ɪk·'spek·tɪd] adj inesperado, -a

unfair [ʌn·'fer] adj injusto, -a

unfaithful [ʌn·'feɪθ·fʊl] adj 1. (adulterous) infiel 2. (disloyal) desleal 3. (not accurate) inexacto, -a

unfamiliar [ʌn·fə·'mɪl·jər] adj 1. (new) desconocido, -a; **to be ~ to sb** no ser familiar a alguien 2. (unacquainted) ajeno, -a

unfasten [ʌn·'fæs·ən] I. vt desatar; (belt) desabrochar; (zipper) bajar II. vi soltarse

unfavorable [ʌn·'feɪ·vər·ə·bəl] adj 1. (adverse) adverso, -a 2. (disadvantageous) desfavorable

unfilled adj sin llenar [or ocupar]

unfinished [ʌn·'fɪn·ɪʃt] adj inacabado, -a

unfit [ʌn·'fɪt] adj 1. (unhealthy) **I'm ~** no estoy en forma; **to be ~ for** no estar en condiciones para 2. (incompetent) incapaz 3. (unsuitable) no apto, -a (for para)

unfold [ʌn·'foʊld] I. vt 1. (open) desdoblar; (arms) descruzar 2. **to ~ one's ideas/plans** exponer sus ideas/planes II. vi 1. (develop) desarrollarse 2. (be revealed) revelarse

unforeseeable [ʌn·fɔr·'si·ə·bəl] adj imprevisible

unforeseen [ʌn·fɔr·'sin] adj imprevisto, -a

unforgettable [ʌn·fər·'get·ə·bəl] adj inolvidable

unforgivable [ʌn·fər·'gɪv·ə·bəl] adj imperdonable

unfortunate [ʌn·'fɔr·tʃə·nɪt] I. adj 1. (luckless) desafortunado, -a; **to be ~ that...** ser lamentable que... +subj 2. (regrettable) deplorable 3. (inopportune) inoportuno, -a II. n desafortunado, -a m, f

unfortunately adv por desgracia

unfounded [ʌn·'faʊn·dɪd] adj infundado, -a

unfriendly [ʌn·'frend·li] adj <-ier, -iest> 1. (unsociable) insociable 2. (hard to use) complicado, -a 3. (inhospitable) hostil

unfulfilled [ʌn·fʊl·'fɪld] adj 1. (unrealized) incumplido, -a 2. (unsatisfied) insatisfecho, -a 3. (frustrated) frustrado, -a

unfurnished [ʌn·'fɜr·nɪʃt] adj desamueblado, -a

ungainly [ʌn·'geɪn·li] adj <-ier, -iest> torpe

ungodly [ʌn·'gad·li] adj <-ier, -iest> inf atroz; **at this ~ hour** a esta hora intempestiva

U

ungrateful [ʌn·ˈgreɪt·fəl] *adj* ingrato, -a

unguarded [ʌn·ˈgar·dɪd] *adj* 1. (*not watched*) sin vigilancia 2. (*careless*) desprevenido, -a; **in an ~ moment** en un momento de descuido

unhappy [ʌn·ˈhæp·i] *adj* <-ier, -iest> 1. (*sad*) infeliz; **to make sb ~** hacer desdichado a alguien 2. (*unfortunate*) desafortunado, -a

unharmed [ʌn·ˈharmd] *adj* ileso, -a

unhealthy [ʌn·ˈhel·θi] *adj* <-ier, -iest> 1. (*sick*) enfermizo, -a 2. (*unwholesome*) nocivo, -a 3. (*dangerous*) arriesgado, -a

unheard [ʌn·ˈhɜrd] *adj* desoído, -a; (*ignored*) desatendido, -a

unheard-of [ʌn·ˈhɜrd·ˌʌv] *adj* sin precedentes; (*impossible*) inaudito, -a

unhelpful [ʌn·ˈhelp·fʊl] *adj* de poca ayuda

unhook [ʌn·ˈhʊk] *vt* desenganchar

unhoped-for [ʌn·ˈhoʊpt·ˌfɔr] *adj* inesperado, -a

unhurt [ʌn·ˈhɜrt] *adj* ileso, -a

unicorn [ˈju·nɪ·kɔrn] *n* unicornio *m*

unidentified [ˌʌn·aɪ·ˈden·tə·faɪd] *n* no identificado, -a; **~ flying object** objeto volante no identificado

unification [ˌju·nɪ·fɪ·ˈkeɪ·ʃən] *n* unificación *f*

uniform [ˈju·nə·fɔrm] I. *n* uniforme *m* II. *adj* (*similar*) uniforme; (*constant*) constante

uniformity [ˌju·nə·ˈfɔr·mə·ti] *n* uniformidad *f*

unify [ˈju·nə·faɪ] *vt* unificar

unilateral [ˌju·nə·ˈlæt·ər·əl] *adj* unilateral

unimaginable [ˌʌn·ɪ·ˈmædʒ·nə·bəl] *adj* inimaginable

unimportant [ˌʌn·ɪm·ˈpɔr·tənt] *adj* sin importancia

uninformed [ˌʌn·ɪn·ˈfɔrmd] *adj* desinformado, -a

uninhabitable [ˌʌn·ɪn·ˈhæb·ɪ·tə·bəl] *adj* inhabitable

uninhabited [ˌʌn·ɪn·ˈhæb·ɪtɪd] *adj* deshabitado, -a; (*deserted*) desierto, -a

uninhibited [ˌʌn·ɪn·ˈhɪb·ɪ·tɪd] *adj* desinhibido, -a

uninjured [ˌʌn·ˈɪn·dʒərd] *adj* ileso, -a

uninsured [ˌʌn·ɪn·ˈʃʊrd] *adj* sin seguro

unintelligent [ˌʌn·ɪn·ˈtel·ɪ·dʒənt] *adj* poco inteligente

unintelligible [ˌʌn·ɪn·ˈtel·ɪ·dʒə·bəl] *adj* ininteligible

unintentional [ˌʌn·ɪn·ˈten·ʃə·nəl] *adj* involuntario, -a

unintentionally *adv* sin intención

uninterested [ʌn·ˈɪn·trə·stɪd] *adj* indiferente

uninteresting *adj* aburrido, -a

uninterrupted [ʌn·ˌɪn·tər·ˈʌp·tɪd] *adj* ininterrumpido, -a

union [ˈjun·jən] *n* 1. (*act of becoming united*) unión *f* 2. (*society*) asociación *f* 3. **+** *sing/pl vb* (*of employees*) sindicato *m* 4. (*marriage*) enlace *m*

Union Jack *n* bandera del Reino Unido

unique [ju·ˈnik] *adj* único, -a; (*exceptional*) excepcional; (*characteristic*) exclusivo, -a

unisex [ˈju·nə·seks] *adj* unisex

unison [ˈju·nə·sən] *n* **in ~** al unísono; *fig* de acuerdo (**with** con)

unit [ˈju·nɪt] *n* 1. a. COMPUT, COM unidad *f*; **central processing ~** unidad central de proceso; **~ of currency** unidad monetaria 2. (*furniture*) elemento *m*

unite [ju·ˈnaɪt] I. *vt* (*join together*) juntar; (*bring together*) unir II. *vi* juntarse; **to ~ against sb** unirse para hacer frente a alguien

united *adj* unido, -a

United Arab Emirates *npl* **the ~** los Emiratos Árabes Unidos

United Kingdom *n* **the ~** el Reino Unido

United Nations *n* **the ~** las Naciones Unidas

United States *n* **+** *sing vb* **the ~** (**of America**) los Estados Unidos (de América)

unity [ˈju·nə·ti] *n* unidad *f*; (*consensus*) consenso *m*

universal [ˌju·nə·ˈvɜr·səl] I. *adj* universal; (*agreement*) global II. *n* universal *m*

universe [ˈju·nə·vɜrs] *n* universo *m*

university [ˌju·nə·ˈvɜr·sə·ti] <-ies> *n* universidad *f*

unjust [ʌn·ˈdʒʌst] *adj* injusto, -a

unjustifiable [ʌn·ˌdʒʌs·tɪ·ˈfaɪ·ə·bəl] *adj* injustificable

unjustified [ʌn·ˈdʒʌs·tɪ·faɪd] *adj* injustificado, -a; (*complaint*) no justificado, -a

unjustly *adv* injustamente

unkempt [ʌnˈkempt] *adj* descuidado, -a

unkind [ʌnˈkaɪnd] *adj* desagradable; **to be ~ to sb** tratar mal a alguien; **to be ~ to animals** ser cruel con los animales; **to be ~ to hair/skin** estropear el pelo/la piel

unkindly *adv* cruelmente; **to take sth ~** tomarse algo mal

unknown [ʌnˈnoʊn] **I.** *adj* desconocido, -a; **~ to me** sin saberlo yo **II.** *n* desconocido, -a *m, f*; **the ~** lo desconocido; MATH la incógnita

unlawful [ʌnˈlɔ·fəl] *adj* ilegal; (*possession, association*) ilícito, -a

unleaded [ʌnˈled·ɪd] *adj* sin plomo

unleash [ʌnˈliʃ] *vt* (*dog*) soltar; (*passions*) desatar

unleavened [ʌnˈlev·ənd] *adj* sin levadura

unless [ənˈles] *conj* a no ser que *+subj*, a menos que *+subj*; **he won't come ~ he has time** no vendrá a menos que tenga tiempo; **~ I'm mistaken** si no me equivoco

unlike [ʌnˈlaɪk] **I.** *adj* diferente **II.** *prep* **1.** (*different from*) diferente a; **it's ~ him** no es característico de él **2.** (*in contrast to*) a diferencia de

unlikely [ʌnˈlaɪk·li] <-ier, -iest> *adj* **1.** (*improbable*) improbable; **it seems ~** parece poco probable; **it's ~ that...** es difícil que... **2.** (*unconvincing*) inverosímil

unlimited [ʌnˈlɪm·ɪ·tɪd] *adj* ilimitado, -a; (*great*) impresionante

unlisted [ʌnˈlɪs·tɪd] *adj* FIN no cotizado, -a

unload [ʌnˈloʊd] **I.** *vt* **1.** (*goods*) descargar **2.** (*get rid of*) deshacerse de **3.** (*express*) desahogarse **II.** *vi* **1.** AUTO descargar **2.** (*be emptied*) vaciarse

unlock [ʌnˈlak] *vt* abrir; *fig* resolver

unlocked *adj* abierto, -a; *fig* resuelto, -a

unlucky [ʌnˈlʌk·i] *adj* **1.** (*person*) desgraciado, -a; (*cards, love*) desafortunado, -a; **to be ~ enough to...** tener la mala suerte de... **2.** (*bringing bad luck*) nefasto, -a

unmanned [ʌnˈmænd] *adj* no tripulado, -a

unmarried [ʌnˈmær·ɪd] *adj* soltero, -a

unmentionable [ʌnˈmen·ʃə·nə·bəl] *adj* inmencionable; (*disease*) tabú

unmentioned [ʌnˈmen·ʃənd] *adj* indecible

unmitigated [ʌnˈmɪt̬·ɪ·geɪ·t̬ɪd] *adj* absoluto, -a; (*evil*) implacable

unmoved [ʌnˈmuvd] *adj* impasible

unnatural [ʌnˈnætʃ·ər·əl] *adj* **1.** (*not natural*) poco natural; (*affected*) afectado, -a **2.** (*not normal*) anormal

unnecessarily [ʌn·nes·ə·ˈser·ə·li] *adv* innecesariamente

unnecessary [ʌnˈnes·ə·ser·i] *adj* innecesario, -a; (*uncalled for*) superfluo, -a

unnerving *adj* enervante

unnoticed [ʌnˈnoʊ·tɪst] *adj* desapercibido, -a; **to go ~ that...** pasar inadvertido que...

unobtainable [ʌn·əb·ˈteɪ·nə·bəl] *adj* inalcanzable

unobtrusive [ʌn·əb·ˈtru·sɪv] *adj* (*people*) modesto, -a; (*things*) discreto, -a

unoccupied [ʌnˈak·jə·paɪd] *adj* deshabitado, -a; (*chair, table*) libre

unofficial [ʌn·ə·ˈfɪʃ·əl] *adj* no oficial; (*figures*) oficioso, -a; (*capacity*) extraoficial

unorganized [ʌnˈɔr·gə·naɪzd] *adj* desorganizado, -a

unorthodox [ʌnˈɔr·θə·daks] *adj* poco ortodoxo, -a; (*approach*) poco convencional

unpack [ʌnˈpæk] **I.** *vt* (*car*) descargar **II.** *vi* deshacer el equipaje

unpaid [ʌnˈpeɪd] *adj* **1.** (*not remunerated*) no remunerado, -a **2.** (*not paid*) pendiente

unparalleled [ʌnˈpær·ə·leld] *adj* sin precedentes

unpleasant [ʌnˈplez·ənt] *adj* desagradable; (*unfriendly*) antipático, -a

unpleasantness *n* antipatía *f*; **the ~** lo desagradable

unplug [ʌnˈplʌɡ] <-gg-> *vt* ELEC desenchufar; (*drain, pipe*) destapar

unpolluted [ʌn·pə·ˈlu·tɪd] *adj* no contaminado, -a

unpopular [ʌnˈpap·jə·lər] *adj* que gusta poco; **to be ~ with sb** caer mal a alguien

unpopularity [ʌn·ˌpap·jə·ˈler·ə·t̬i] *n* im-

U

popularidad *f*

unprecedented [ʌn·ˈpres·ə·den·tɪd] *adj*
sin precedentes; (*action*) inaudito, -a

unpredictable [ˌʌn·prɪ·ˈdɪk·tə·bəl] *adj*
imprevisible

unproductive [ˌʌn·prə·ˈdʌk·tɪv] *adj* improductivo, -a; (*negotiations*) infructuoso, -a

unprofessional [ˌʌn·prə·ˈfeʃ·ə·nəl] *adj*
poco profesional

unprofitable [ʌn·ˈpraf·ɪ·tə·bəl] *adj* (*business*) no rentable; (*investment, meeting*)
infructuoso, -a; (*day*) improductivo, -a

unprompted [ʌn·ˈpramp·tɪd] *adj* espontáneo, -a

unpublished [ʌn·ˈpʌb·lɪʃt] *adj* inédito, -a

unqualified [ʌn·ˈkwal·ə·faɪd] *adj*
1. (*without qualifications*) sin título; **to
be ~ for sth** no estar cualificado para
algo **2.** (*unlimited*) incondicional; (*disaster*) absoluto, -a; (*success*) rotundo,
-a; (*support*) total

unquestionable [ʌn·ˈkwes·tʃə·nə·bəl] *adj*
incuestionable; (*fact*) innegable

unquestionably *adv* indudablemente

unquestioning [ʌn·ˈkwes·tʃə·nɪŋ] *adj* incondicional; (*obedience*) ciego, -a

unravel [ʌn·ˈræv·əl] <-ll-, -l-> **I.** *vt*
1. (*undo*) deshacer **2.** (*solve*) aclarar
II. *vi* deshacerse

unreadable [ʌn·ˈri·də·bəl] *adj* ininteligible; (*text*) ilegible; (*expression, face*)
inescrutable

unreal [ʌn·ˈril] *adj* **1.** irreal **2.** *sl* impresionante

unrealistic [ˌʌn·ˌri·ə·ˈlɪs·tɪk] *adj* poco realista

unreasonable [ʌn·ˈri·zə·nə·bəl] *adj* poco
razonable; (*unfair*) injusto, -a; (*demands*) excesivo, -a

unrelated [ˌʌn·rɪ·ˈleɪ·tɪd] *adj* no relacionado, -a

unrelenting [ˌʌn·rɪ·ˈlen·tɪŋ] *adj* **1.** (*not
yielding*) implacable (**in** en) **2.** (*not easing*) incesante

unreliable [ˌʌn·rɪ·ˈlaɪ·ə·bəl] *adj* informal

unrepeatable [ˌʌn·rɪ·ˈpi·tə·bəl] *adj* irrepetible; (*price*) inmejorable

unreserved [ˌʌn·rɪ·ˈzɜrvd] *adj* **1.** (*tickets,
seats*) no reservado, -a **2.** (*absolute*) incondicional **3.** (*frank*) abierto, -a

unresolved [ˌʌn·rɪ·ˈzalvd] *adj* sin resolver

unrest [ʌn·ˈrest] *n* descontento *m*; (*social*)
malestar *m*

unrestrained [ˌʌn·rɪ·ˈstreɪnd] *adj* incontrolado, -a; (*criticism, consumerism*)
desenfrenado, -a; (*laughter*) desmedido, -a

unrestricted [ˌʌn·rɪ·ˈstrɪk·tɪd] *adj* ilimitado, -a; (*access*) libre

unripe [ʌn·ˈraɪp] *adj* verde; *fig* inmaduro, -a

unroll [ʌn·ˈroʊl] *vt* desenrollar

unruffled [ʌn·ˈrʌf·əld] *adj* **1.** (*undisturbed*) sereno, -a; **to be ~** no inmutar-
se (**by** ante) **2.** (*smooth*) liso, -a

unruly [ʌn·ˈru·li] <-ier, -iest> *adj* indisciplinado, -a; (*children*) revoltoso, -a;
(*hair*) rebelde

unsafe [ʌn·ˈseɪf] *adj* inseguro, -a; (*animal*)
peligroso, -a

unsaid [ʌn·ˈsed] **I.** *vt pt, pp of* **unsay**
II. *adj* sin decir; **to leave sth ~** callarse algo; **to be better left ~** mejor
no hablar

unsatisfactory [ʌn·ˌsæt·ɪs·ˈfæk·tə·ri] *adj*
insatisfactorio, -a; (*answer*) poco convincente; (*service*) poco satisfactorio, -a;
(*grade*) insuficiente

unsatisfied [ʌn·ˈsæt·ɪs·faɪd] *adj* **1.** (*not
content*) insatisfecho, -a **2.** (*not convinced*) no convencido, -a

unsay [ʌn·ˈseɪ] *irr vt* desdecirse de
▶ **what's __said__ cannot be unsaid** lo
dicho, dicho está

unscathed [ʌn·ˈskeɪðd] *adj* ileso, -a; **to
escape ~** escapar ileso

unscheduled [ʌn·ˈskedʒ·ʊld] *adj* no programado, -a; (*train, landing*) no previsto, -a

unscientific [ʌn·ˌsaɪ·ən·ˈtɪf·ɪk] *adj* sin rigor científico

unscrupulous [ʌn·ˈskru·pjə·ləs] *adj* sin
escrúpulos

unseat [ʌn·ˈsit] *vt* POL derrocar

unsecured [ʌn·sɪ·ˈkjʊrd] *adj* no sujeto,
-a; (*stock, funds*) no garantizado, -a;
(*loan*) sin aval

unseemly [ʌn·ˈsim·li] *adj* impropio, -a

unseen [ʌn·ˈsin] *adj* (*unnoticed*) sin ser
visto, -a; **to do sth ~** hacer algo inad-

vertidamente; **sight** ~ a ciegas

unselfish [ʌnˈsel·fɪʃ] *adj* generoso, -a

unsettle [ʌnˈset·əl] *vt* alterar; (*market*) desestabilizar

unsettled [ʌnˈset·əld] *adj* 1. (*changeable*) inestable 2. (*troubled*) inquieto, -a 3. (*unresolved*) no resuelto, -a

unsettling [ʌnˈset·əl·ɪŋ] *adj* (*disquieting*) inquietante; (*perturbing*) perturbador(a)

unshakable [ʌnˈʃer·kə·bəl] *adj* inquebrantable

unshaved *adj*, **unshaven** [ʌnˈʃer·vən] *adj* sin afeitar

unsightly [ʌnˈsart·li] <-ier, -iest> *adj* feo, -a

unsigned [ʌnˈsaɪnd] *adj* sin firmar

unskilled [ʌnˈskɪld] *adj* 1. (*person*) no cualificado, -a; **to be ~ at** (**doing**) **sth** no estar cualificado para (hacer) algo 2. (*job*) no especializado, -a

unsociable [ʌnˈsou·ʃə·bəl] *adj* insociable

unsocial [ʌnˈsou·ʃəl] *adj* insociable

unsold [ʌnˈsould] *adj* sin vender

unsolved [ʌnˈsalvd] *adj* sin resolver

unsophisticated [ʌn·sə·ˈfɪs·tə·ker·tɪd] *adj* sencillo, -a; (*machine*) simple; (*person*) ingenuo, -a

unspeakable [ʌnˈspi·kə·bəl] *adj* indecible

unstable [ʌnˈster·bəl] *adj a.* PSYCH inestable

unstuck [ʌnˈstʌk] *adj* **to** (**be**)**come ~** despegarse; (*fail*) irse al garete

unsuccessful [ʌn·sak·ˈses·fəl] *adj* sin éxito; (*candidate*) fracasado, -a; **to be ~ in** (**doing**) **sth** fracasar en/no lograr hacer algo

unsuitable [ʌnˈsu·tə·bəl] *adj* inapropiado, -a (**for** para); (*moment*) inoportuno, -a *m*; **to be ~ to the occasion** no ajustarse a la ocasión

unsung [ʌnˈsʌŋ] *adj* olvidado, -a

unsure [ʌnˈʃor] *adj* inseguro, -a; **to be ~ how/what...** no ser seguro cómo/qué...; **to be ~ about sth** no estar seguro de algo

unsuspecting [ʌn·sə·ˈspek·tɪŋ] *adj* confiado, -a; **all ~** nada suspicaz

unsustainable [ʌn·sə·ˈster·nə·bəl] *adj* insostenible

untangle [ʌnˈtæŋ·gəl] *vt* desenredar; (*mystery*) desentrañar

untapped [ʌnˈtæpt] *adj* (*resources*) sin explotar

unthinkable [ʌnˈθɪŋ·kə·bəl] *adj* inconcebible; (*shocking*) impensable

unthinking [ʌnˈθɪŋ·kɪŋ] *adj* 1. (*thoughtless*) irreflexivo, -a 2. (*unintentional*) no intencionado, -a

untidy [ʌnˈtar·di] <-ier, -iest> *adj* desordenado, -a; (*appearance*) desaliñado, -a

untie [ʌnˈtaɪ] <-y-> *vt* desatar; **to ~ one's shoelaces** desatarse los cordones

until [ənˈtɪl] **I.** *adv* hasta; **~ then** hasta entonces **II.** *conj* hasta que +*subj*; **~ he comes** hasta que venga; **not ~ does sth** no hasta que alguien haga algo

untimely [ʌnˈtaɪm·li] *adj* 1. (*premature*) prematuro, -a 2. (*inopportune*) inoportuno, -a

untold [ʌnˈtould] *adj* 1. (*immense*) incalculable 2. (*not told*) nunca contado, -a

untouched [ʌnˈtʌtʃt] *adj* 1. (*not affected*) intacto, -a; **to leave sth ~** dejar algo intacto 2. (*not eaten*) sin probar; **to leave a meal ~** no probar una comida 3. (*not moved*) insensible

untreated [ʌnˈtri·tɪd] *adj* no tratado, -a

untrue [ʌnˈtru] *adj* 1. (*false*) falso, -a 2. (*unfaithful*) infiel (**to** a)

untrustworthy [ʌnˈtrʌst·ˌwɜr·ði] *adj* **to be ~** no ser de fiar

untruthful [ʌnˈtruθ·fəl] *adj* falso, -a; (*liar*) mentiroso, -a

unused [ʌnˈjuzd] *adj* no usado, -a; (*talent, energy*) malgastado, -a; (*goods, clothes*) sin estrenar

unusual [ʌnˈju·ʒu·əl] *adj* 1. (*not usual*) inusual; **to be ~ for sb** ser poco usual en alguien 2. (*atypically positive*) inusitado, -a 3. (*atypically negative*) insólito, -a

unveil [ʌnˈveɪl] *vt fig* presentar

unwanted [ʌnˈwan·tɪd] *adj* no deseado, -a

unwarranted [ʌnˈwɔr·ən·tɪd] *adj* 1. (*not justified*) injustificado, -a; (*criticism*) infundado, -a 2. (*not authorized*) no autorizado, -a

unwell [ʌnˈwel] *adj* indispuesto, -a; **to**

feel ~ sentirse mal

unwieldy [ʌn·ˈwil·di] *adj* abultado, -a; *fig* poco manejable

unwilling [ʌn·ˈwɪl·ɪŋ] *adj* no dispuesto, -a; **to be ~ to do sth** no estar dispuesto a hacer algo; **to be ~ for sb to do sth** no querer que alguien haga algo

unwillingly *adv* de mala gana

unwind [ʌn·ˈwaɪnd] *irr* I. *vt* desenrollar II. *vi* 1. (*unroll*) desenrollarse 2. (*relax*) relajarse

unwise [ʌn·ˈwaɪz] *adj* imprudente

unwitting [ʌn·ˈwɪt·ɪŋ] *adj* 1. (*unaware*) inconsciente 2. (*unintentional*) involuntario, -a

unwittingly *adv* sin darse cuenta

unworthy [ʌn·ˈwɜr·ði] <-ier, -iest> *adj* que no vale la pena; (*person*) indigno, -a

unwrap [ʌn·ˈræp] <-pp-> *vt* desenvolver; *fig* sacar a la luz

unwritten [ʌn·ˈrɪt·ən] *adj* no escrito, -a; (*agreement*) verbal

unzip [ʌn·ˈzɪp] <-pp-> *vt* abrir la cremallera de

up [ʌp] I. *adv* 1. (*movement*) (hacia) arriba; **~ here/there** aquí/allí arriba; **to look ~** mirar (hacia) arriba; **to stand/get ~** levantarse; **to go ~** subir; (*stand*) **~!** ¡arriba!; **~ in Seattle** allá en Seattle 2. **to be ~ all night** no dormir en toda la noche; **with one's head ~** con la cabeza en alto 3. (*limit*) **time's ~** se acabó el tiempo; **when 5 hours were ~** cuando pasaron 5 horas; **from the age of 18 ~** a partir de los 18 años; **to have it ~ to one's ears** estar hasta la coronilla (**with** de) 4. SPORTS (*ahead*) por delante ▶ **~ and** <u>down</u> arriba y abajo; <u>what's</u> **~?** ¿qué hay de nuevo?; <u>what's</u> **~ with him?** ¿qué le pasa? II. *prep* encima de; **to climb ~ a tree** subirse a un árbol; **to go ~ the stairs** subir las escaleras; **to run ~ the slope** correr cuesta arriba; **to go ~ the street** ir por la calle III. *n* **~s and downs** altibajos *mpl;* **to be on the ~ and ~** estar cada vez mejor IV. *adj* 1. (*position: tent*) montado, -a; (*curtains, picture*) colgado, -a; (*hand*) alzado, -a; (*person*) levantado, -a 2. (*ready*) **to be ~ and about** [*or* around] estar en buena forma; **to be ~ for** (**doing**) **sth** estar listo para (hacer) algo; **~ for sale/ trial** a la venta/en juicio

up-and-coming [ˈʌp·ən·ˈkʌm·ɪŋ] *adj* joven y prometedor(a)

upbeat [ˈʌp·bit] *adj* optimista (**about** respecto a)

upbringing [ˈʌp·brɪŋ·ɪŋ] *n* educación *f;* **to have a good ~** tener una buena educación

upcoming [ˈʌp·ˌkʌm·ɪŋ] *adj* venidero, -a

update [ˈʌp·deɪt] I. *vt* poner al día; COMPUT actualizar II. *n* puesta *f* al día; COMPUT actualización *f;* **to give sb an ~** poner a alguien al día (**on** de)

upgrade [ˈʌp·greɪd] I. *vt* mejorar; COMPUT modernizar; **to ~ sb** ascender a alguien (**to** a) II. *vi* mejorar III. *n* 1. COMPUT, TECH, COM mejora *f;* **software ~** modernización del software; **to be on the ~** ir mejorando; MED ir recuperándose 2. (*slope*) cuesta *f*

upheaval [ʌp·ˈhi·vəl] *n* 1. sacudida *f;* **political ~** convulsión *f* política 2. GEO solevamiento *m*

uphill [ʌp·ˈhɪl] I. *adv* cuesta arriba; **to run/walk ~** correr/ir cuesta arriba II. *adj* 1. ascendente 2. (*difficult*) difícil

uphold [ʌp·ˈhoʊld] *irr vt* sostener; **to ~ the principle that...** defender el principio de que...

upholster [ʌp·ˈhoʊl·stər] *vt* tapizar

upholstery *n* 1. (*covering*) tapizado *m;* **leather ~** tapizado de piel 2. (*craft*) tapicería *f*

upkeep [ˈʌp·kip] *n* mantenimiento *m;* (*cost*) gastos *m pl* de mantenimiento

uplift [ʌp·ˈlɪft] *vt* elevar; *fig* inspirar

uplifting [ʌp·ˈlɪf·tɪŋ] *adj* positivo, -a

upload [ˈʌp·loʊd] *vt* subir

upon [ə·ˈpɑn] *prep form* 1. (*on top of*) encima de; **to hang ~ the wall** colgar en la pared 2. (*around*) en 3. **~ her arrival** a su llegada; **~ this** acto seguido; **once ~ a time** érase una vez

upper [ˈʌp·ər] I. *adj* superior; **~ management** altos cargos; **the ~ Northeast** el alto nordeste II. *n* (*drug*) anfeta *f*

upper class <-es> n clase f alta

upper-class adj de clase alta

uppermost I. adj más alto, -a II. adv boca arriba; **to put sth ~** poner algo boca arriba

upright ['ʌp·raɪt] I. adj recto, -a; (post, rod) vertical; (citizen) honrado, -a II. adv verticalmente; **to stand ~** permanecer erguido; **to sit bolt ~** estar muy derecho en la silla III. n SPORTS poste m

uprising ['ʌp·raɪ·zɪŋ] n alzamiento m

uproar ['ʌp·rɔr] n alboroto m, batifondo m CSur, tinga f Méx; **to cause an ~** provocar un escándalo

uproot [ʌp·'rut] vt arrancar de raíz; fig desarraigar; **to ~ oneself** perder las raíces

upset¹ [ʌp·'set] I. vt irr 1. (unsettle) trastornar; (distress) afligir 2. (untidy) alborotar 3. (overturn) derrumbar II. adj 1. (disquieted) perturbado, -a; (sad) apenado, -a; **to get ~** enfadarse (**about** por); **to be ~ (that)**... estar enfadado (**porque**)...; **don't be ~** no te enfades 2. **to have an ~ stomach** tener el estómago revuelto 3. (overturned) trastornado, -a

upset² ['ʌp·set] n 1. (surprise) sorpresa f 2. **stomach ~** trastorno m estomacal 3. (trouble) disgusto m

upside down [ʌp·saɪd·'daʊn] adv al revés; **to turn sth ~** poner algo del revés

upstage [ʌp·'steɪdʒ] vt eclipsar

upstairs [ʌp·'sterz] I. adj de arriba II. adv arriba; **to go ~** ir arriba; **the people who live ~** los vecinos de arriba III. n piso m de arriba

upstate ['ʌp·steɪt] I. adj del norte; **in ~ New York** en el norte de Nueva York II. adv en el norte

upstream [ʌp·'strim] adv río arriba; **to swim ~** nadar contra la corriente

upsurge ['ʌp·sɜrdʒ] n aumento m (**in** de)

uptake ['ʌp·teɪk] n **to be quick on the ~** cogerlas al vuelo; **to be slow on the ~** ser algo corto

uptight [ʌp·'taɪt] adj **to be/get ~** estar/ponerse de mala leche (**about** por)

up-to-date [ʌp·tə·'deɪt] adj 1. (contemporary) moderno, -a; (book) actualizado, -a 2. (informed) al día; **to bring sb ~**

poner a alguien al corriente

up-to-the-minute [ʌp·tə·ðə·'mɪn·ɪt] adj de última hora

uptown ['ʌp·taʊn] adj residencial; **in ~ Manhattan** en el norte de Manhattan

upturn ['ʌp·tɜrn] n mejora f

upturned [ʌp·'tɜrnd] adj vuelto, -a hacia arriba; (nose) respingón, -ona

upward ['ʌp·wərd] I. adj ascendente II. adv (hacia) arriba; (in number) al alza; **to go ~** ir en aumento

upwards adv (hacia) arriba; **and ~** y más

uranium [ju·'reɪ·ni·əm] n uranio m

urban ['ɜr·bən] adj urbano, -a; **~ area** zona urbana; **~ decay** deterioro urbano

urbane [ɜr·'beɪn] adj fino, -a

urbanization [ˌɜr·bə·nɪ·'zeɪ·ʃən] n urbanización f

urchin ['ɜr·tʃɪn] n iron pilluelo, -a m, f

urethra [ju·'ri·θrə] <-s or -e> n uretra f

urge [ɜrdʒ] I. n (desire) ansia f; (compulsion) impulso m; PSYCH instinto m; **an ~ to do sth** un impulso de hacer algo; **an ~ for power** un afán de poder; **an irresistible ~** un impulso irresistible; **an uncontrollable ~** un deseo incontrolable; **to control/repress an ~** controlar/reprimir un impulso II. vt 1. (encourage) fomentar; **to ~ sb to do sth** instar a alguien a hacer algo; **to ~ sb into sth** incitar a alguien a algo 2. (recommend) recomendar ((up)on a)

urge on vt **to urge sb on** animar a alguien (**to** a)

urgency ['ɜr·dʒən·si] n urgencia f; **to be a matter of (great) ~** ser un asunto de (gran) urgencia; **to realize/stress the ~** darse cuenta de/remarcar la urgencia (**of** de)

urgent ['ɜr·dʒənt] adj urgente; (insistent) insistente; **to be in ~ need of sth** necesitar algo urgentemente

urgently adv (earnestly) insistentemente

urinal ['jʊr·ə·nəl] n urinario m

urinate ['jʊr·ə·neɪt] vi orinar

urine ['jʊr·ɪn] n orina f

urn [ɜrn] n urna f; (tea) tetera f

Uruguay ['jʊr·ə·gwaɪ] n Uruguay m

Uruguayan [jʊr·ə·'gwaɪ·ən] adj, n uruguayo, -a *m, f*

us [əs, *stressed:* ʌs] *pron pers* nos *after prep* nosotros, -as; **it's ~** somos nosotros; **look at ~** míranos; **he saw ~** nos vio; **he gave it to ~** nos lo dio

USA [ju·es·'eɪ] *n abbr of* **United States** EE.UU. *mpl*

usage ['ju·sɪdʒ] *n* **1. a.** LING uso *m;* **in common/general ~** de uso común/general **2.** (*treatment*) tratamiento *m*

use¹ [jus] *n* **1.** (*application*) uso *m;* (*possibility of applying*) empleo *m;* **in ~** en uso; **to be of/no ~** (no) ser de utilidad (**to** para); **it's no ~** es inútil; **there's no ~ doing sth** no sirve de nada hacer algo; **to make ~ of** utilizar; **to be out of ~** estar fuera de servicio; **to come into ~** empezar a utilizarse; **to go out of ~** quedar en desuso **2.** (*consumption*) consumo *m*

use² [juz] **I.** *vt* **1.** (*make use of*) usar (**to** para, **against** en contra de); (*skills, training*) hacer uso de; **I could ~ some help** no me vendría mal una mano **2.** (*employ*) emplear; **to ~ discretion** ser discreto **3.** (*consume, manipulate*) utilizar; (*exploit*) explotar; (*energy, drugs*) consumir **II.** *vi* **he ~d to...** solía...; **did you ~ to work in banking?** ¿trabajabas en banca?

♦ **use up** *vt* agotar

used [juzd] *adj* usado, -a; (*clothes, car*) de segunda mano

used to *adj* **to be ~** estar acostumbrado a; **to become ~** acostumbrarse a; **to be ~ doing sth** tener la costumbre de hacer algo

useful ['jus·fəl] *adj* **1.** (*convenient*) útil (**for** para) **2.** (*beneficial*) beneficioso, -a; (*experience*) positivo, -a **3.** (*effective*) eficaz; (*competent*) competente (**with** en)

usefulness *n* utilidad *f;* (*applicability*) aplicabilidad *f;* (*relevance*) relevancia *f*

useless ['jus·lɪs] *adj* **1.** (*in vain*) inútil; **to be ~ doing sth** ser inútil hacer algo; **to be ~ to do sth** no servir de nada el hacer algo **2.** (*unusable*) inservible; **to be/become ~** no ser/dejar de ser de utilidad (**for** para) **3.** *inf* (*incompetent*) incompetente; **to be worse than ~** no

servir para nada

user *n* **a.** COMPUT usuario, -a *m, f;* (*gas, drug*) consumidor(a) *m(f)*

user-friendly *adj* COMPUT fácil de usar

usher ['ʌʃ·ər] *n* CINE acomodador(a) *m(f)*

usual ['ju·ʒu·əl] **I.** *adj* habitual; **as ~** como de costumbre; **to be ~ for sb** (**to do sth**) ser habitual para alguien (hacer algo) **II.** *n* **the ~** lo de siempre

usually *adv* normalmente

usurp [ju·'sɜrp] *vt* usurpar

utensil [ju·'ten·səl] *n* utensilio *m;* **kitchen ~s** utensilios de cocina

uterus ['ju·tər·əs] <-ri *or* -es> *n* útero *m*

utilitarian [ju·tɪl·ə·'ter·i·ən] *adj* utilitario, -a

utility [ju·'tɪl·ə·t̬i] <-ies> *n* **1.** (*usefulness*) utilidad *f* **2.** (*public service*) empresa *f* de servicio público **3.** COMPUT herramienta *f*

utilization [ˌju·t̬ə·lɪ·'zeɪ·ʃən] *n* utilización *f*

utilize ['ju·t̬ə·laɪz] *vt* utilizar

utmost ['ʌt·moʊst] **I.** *adj* mayor; **with the ~ care** con sumo cuidado; **the ~ difficulty** la máxima dificultad; **of ~ importance** de primerísima importancia **II.** *n* **the ~** lo máximo; **to the ~** al máximo; **to try one's ~** hacer todo lo posible (**to** para, por)

utopia [ju·'toʊ·pi·ə] *n* utopía *f*

utopian *adj* utópico, -a

utter¹ ['ʌt̬·ər] *adj* (*complete*) completo, -a; **in ~ despair** en la más absoluta desesperación

utter² ['ʌt̬·ər] *vt* (*say*) pronunciar; (*warning*) dar; **to ~ a threat** amenazar; **without ~ing a word** sin mediar palabra

utterance ['ʌt̬·ər·əns] *n* **1.** LING enunciado *m* **2.** (*style*) expresión *f;* **to give ~ to a feeling** manifestar un sentimiento

utterly *adv* completamente; (*despise, hate*) profundamente

U-turn ['ju·tɜrn] *n* AUTO cambio *m* de sentido; *fig* giro *m* de 180°

UV [ju·'vi] *abbr of* **ultraviolet** UV

V

V, v [vi:] n V, v f; ~ **as in Victor** V de Valencia

V 1. abbr of **velocity** V **2.** abbr of **volt** V **3.** abbr of **volume** vol. **4.** (five) V

vac [væk] inf I. n **1.** abbr of **vacuum cleaner** aspirador m **2.** abbr of **vacuum** vacío m II. <-cc-> vt, vi pasar el aspirador (a)

vacancy ['veɪ·kən·si] <-ies> n **1.** (room) habitación f libre; '~' 'habitaciones libres'; '**no ~**' 'completo' **2.** (job) vacante f; **to fill a ~** ocupar una vacante

vacant ['veɪ·kənt] adj vacío, -a; (seat, room) libre; (job) vacante; '**~**' 'libre'; **to leave sth/become ~** dejar algo/quedarse vacante

vacate [veɪ·keɪt] vt form (place, seat) dejar libre; (room, house) desocupar; (job, post) dejar vacante

vacation [veɪ·keɪ·ʃən] n vacaciones fpl; **on ~** de vacaciones; **to take a ~** tomarse unas vacaciones

vaccinate ['væk·sə·neɪt] vt vacunar (**against** contra)

vaccination [,væk·sə·neɪ·ʃən] n vacunación f (**against** contra)

vaccine [væk·siːn] n vacuna f

vacillate ['væs·ə·leɪt] vi vacilar (**between** entre); **to ~ between hope and despair** oscilar entre la esperanza y la desesperación

vacuum ['væk·jum] I. n vacío m; **to fill/leave a ~** llenar/dejar un vacío; **to live in a ~** vivir en una burbuja II. vt pasar la aspiradora a

vacuum cleaner n aspirador m

vacuum-packaged adj, **vacuum-packed** [,væk·jum·'pækt] adj envasado, -a al vacío

vagina [və·'dʒaɪ·nə] n vagina f

vagrant ['veɪ·grənt] adj, n vagabundo, -a m, f

vague [veɪg] adj (promise) vago, -a; (word) impreciso, -a; (outline) borroso, -a; (expression) distraído, -a; (person) despistado, -a

vain [veɪn] adj (person) vanidoso, -a; (attempt, hope) vano, -a; **it is ~ to...** es

inútil...; **in ~** en vano; **it was all in ~** todo fue en vano

valentine ['væl·ən·taɪn] n **1.** (card) tarjeta de San Valentín **2.** (sweetheart) enamorado, -a m, f; **be my ~!** ¿quieres ser mi novio?

Valentine's Day n día m de los enamorados [or San Valentín]

valet [væ·'leɪ] n (car parker) aparcacoches mf inv

valid ['væl·ɪd] adj **1.** válido, -a; **no longer ~** caducado, -a **2.** LAW vigente; (binding) vinculante

validate ['væl·ə·deɪt] vt dar validez a; (document) validar; (ticket) picar

validity [və·'lɪd·ə·ti] n validez f; (law) vigencia f

valley ['væl·i] n valle m

valuable ['væl·ju·ə·bəl] I. adj (help, ring) valioso, -a; (time) precioso, -a II. n **-s** objetos m pl de valor

valuation [,væl·ju·'eɪ·ʃən] n valoración f; (estimation) tasación f

value ['væl·ju] I. n a. MATH, MUS valor m; **~-judgment** juicio de valor; **set of ~s** escala de valores; **of little ~** de poco valor; **to be of (great) ~** ser (muy) valioso (**to** para); **to be a good ~** estar bien de precio; **to put a ~** poner precio (**on** a); **to place a high ~** dar mucha importancia (**on** a) II. vt **1.** (regard highly) apreciar **2.** FIN tasar (**at** en)

valued adj apreciado, -a; (customer) valioso, -a

valueless ['væl·ju·lɪs] adj sin valor

valve [vælv] n **1.** AUTO, ANAT válvula f **2.** ELEC lámpara f

vampire ['væm·paɪr] n vampiro m

van¹ [væn] n AUTO furgoneta f; **delivery ~** furgoneta de reparto; **moving ~** camión m de mudanzas

van² [væn] n inf abbr of **vanguard** vanguardia f

vandal ['væn·dəl] n gamberro -a m, f

vandalism ['væn·də·lɪz·əm] n vandalismo m

vandalize ['væn·də·laɪz] vt destrozar

vanguard ['væn·gard] n vanguardia f

vanilla [və·'nɪl·ə] n vainilla f

vanish ['væn·ɪʃ] vi desaparecer (**from** de); **to ~ into thin air** esfumarse

vanity ['væn·ə·ţi] <-ies> n 1. (*pride*) vanidad f 2. (*dressing table*) tocador m

vanity bag n, **vanity case** n neceser m

vantage point n mirador m; *fig* posición f ventajosa

vapor ['veɪ·pər] n vapor m; **water** ~ vapor de agua; (*on glass*) vaho m, vaporizo m *Méx, PRico*

variable ['vær·i·ə·bəl] adj, n variable

variance ['vær·i·əns] n 1. (*disagreement*) discrepancia f; **at** ~ en contradicción; **to be at** ~ discrepar (**with** en); **to set two people at** ~ sembrar la discordia entre dos personas 2. (*variation*) variación f

variant ['vær·i·ənt] n variante f

variation [ˌvær·i·'eɪ·ʃən] n 1. a. BIO, MUS variación f (**on** de) 2. (*difference*) diferencia f; **wide** ~s grandes diferencias (**in** de)

varicose ['vær·ə·koʊs] adj ~ **veins** varices fpl

varied ['vær·id] adj variado, -a; (*colors*) multicolor

variety [və·'raɪ·ə·ţi] <-ies> n 1. (*diversity*) a. BIO variedad f; **to lend** ~ to variar 2. (*assortment*) surtido m; **in a** ~ **of ways** de diversas formas 3. (*sort*) tipo m ▶ ~ **is the spice of life** en la variedad está el gusto

variety show n programa m de variedades; THEAT espectáculo m de variedades

various ['vær·i·əs] adj 1. (*numerous*) varios, -as; **for** ~ **reasons** por diversas razones 2. (*diverse*) diferentes

varmint ['var·mɪnt] n a. fig alimaña f

varnish ['var·nɪʃ] I. n barniz m II. vt barnizar

vary ['vær·i] <-ie-> I. vi 1. (*change*) variar; **opinions** ~ hay diversidad de opiniones; **to** ~ **between... and...** oscilar entre... y...; **to** ~ **from...** diferenciarse de... 2. (*diverge*) desviarse; **to** ~ **from...** apartarse de... II. vt 1. (*change*) variar 2. (*diversify*) diversificar

varying adj variable

vase [veɪs] n jarrón m

vast [væst] adj enorme; (*area, region*) vasto, -a; (*importance, amount of money*) considerable; (*majority, knowledge*) amplio, -a

vastly adv sumamente; ~ **superior** infi-

nitamente superior

vat [væt] n tanque m

Vatican ['væt·ɪ·kən] n Vaticano m

vault¹ [vɔlt] n 1. ARCHIT bóveda f; (*under churches*) cripta f; (*at cemeteries*) panteón m 2. (*basement*) sótano m; (*bank*) cámara acorazada

vault² [vɔlt] (*jump*) I. n salto m II. vi, vt saltar

vaulting horse n potro m

veal [vil] n ternera f

veal cutlet n chuleta f de ternera

vector ['vek·tər] n 1. MATH vector m 2. BIO, MED portador(a) m(f)

veer [vɪr] vi (*vehicle*) virar; (*wind*) cambiar; (*road, way*) torcer; (*attitude, goal*) cambiar bruscamente; **to** ~ **towards sth** dar un giro hacia algo

vegan ['vi·gən] n vegan mf

vegetable ['vedʒ·tə·bəl] n vegetal m; (*edible*) hortaliza f; (**green**) ~ verdura f; **seasonal** ~ verdura del tiempo; **root** ~ tubérculo m; ~ **soup** sopa de verduras

vegetable garden n huerto m

vegetable kingdom n reino m vegetal

vegetable oil n aceite m vegetal

vegetarian [ˌvedʒ·ə·'ter·i·ən] adj, n vegetariano, -a m, f; **to go** ~ hacerse vegetariano

vegetate ['vedʒ·ə·teɪt] vi a. fig vegetar

vegetation [ˌvedʒ·ə·'teɪ·ʃən] n vegetación f

veg(g)ie ['vedʒ·i] n inf 1. vegetariano, -a m, f 2. ~s verdura f

veggieburger n hamburguesa f vegetariana

vehemence ['vi·ə·məns] n vehemencia f

vehement ['vi·ə·mənt] adj vehemente

vehicle ['vi·ə·kəl] n 1. AUTO vehículo m; **motor** ~ vehículo motorizado 2. (*of expression*) medio m; **to be a** ~ servir de vehículo (**for** para)

veil [veɪl] I. n velo m; **a** ~ **of secrecy** un halo de misterio; **under the** ~ bajo el pretexto (**of** de); **to draw a** ~ correr un tupido velo (**over** sobre) II. vt velar; (*disguise*) disimular

veiled adj (*wearing a veil*) cubierto, -a con velo; **thinly** ~ apenas disimulado

vein [veɪn] n ANAT, BOT vena f; GEO veta f

Velcro® ['vel·kroʊ] n velcro® m

velocity [vəˈlas·ə·t̬i] <-ies> n velocidad f; **at the ~ of** a la velocidad de; **sound/light ~** velocidad del sonido/de la luz

velvet [ˈvel·vɪt] I. n terciopelo m II. adj de terciopelo; fig aterciopelado, -a

velvety [ˈvel·və·t̬i] adj fig aterciopelado, -a

vendetta [venˈdeṯ·ə] n vendetta f

vending machine n máquina f expendedora

vendor [ˈven·dər] n vendedor(a) m(f)

veneer [vəˈnɪr] n chapado m; fig apariencia f

venereal [vəˈnɪr·i·əl] adj venéreo, -a

venetian blind [vəˌni·ʃən·ˈblaɪnd] n persiana f veneciana

Venezuela [ˌven·ə·ˈzwei·lə] n Venezuela f

Venezuelan adj, n venezolano, -a m, f

vengeance [ˈven·dʒəns] n venganza f; **to take ~** vengarse ((up)on de); **with a ~** con ganas

venison [ˈven·ɪ·sən] n venado m

venom [ˈven·əm] n veneno m; fig malevolencia f

venomous [ˈven·ə·məs] adj venenoso, -a; (malicious) maligno, -a

vent [vent] I. n conducto m de ventilación; **air ~** respiradero m II. vt (feelings) dar rienda suelta a; (opinion) expresar; (anger) descargar (**on** contra)

ventilate [ˈven·t̬ə·leɪt] vt ventilar; **artificially ~d** con respiración asistida

ventilation [ˌven·t̬ə·ˈleɪ·ʃən] n ventilación f

ventilator [ˈven·t̬ə·leɪ·t̬ər] n ventilador m; MED respirador m

ventricle [ˈven·trɪ·kəl] n ventrículo m

ventriloquist [venˈtrɪl·ə·kwɪst] n ventrílocuo, -a m, f

venture [ˈven·t̬ər] I. n aventura f; COM empresa f II. vt 1. (dare) atreverse (**to** a); (opinion) aventurar 2. (endanger) arriesgar (**on** contra) III. vi aventurarse

venture capital n capital m de riesgo

venue [ˈven·ju] n lugar m; SPORTS campo m

Venus [ˈvi·nəs] n Venus m

veranda n, **verandah** [vəˈræn·də] n porche m

verb [vɜrb] n verbo m

verbal [ˈvɜr·bəl] adj 1. (oral) verbal; ~

agreement acuerdo verbal; ~ **facility** facilidad de palabra 2. (word for word) literal

verbally adv verbalmente

verbatim [vərˈbei·t̬ɪm] I. adj literal II. adv literalmente

verbose [vərˈbous] adj verboso, -a

verdict [ˈvɜr·dɪkt] n 1. LAW fallo m; (by jury) veredicto m; **to bring in** [or **return**] **a ~** dictar sentencia; (jury) emitir un veredicto 2. (conclusion) juicio m (**on** sobre); **what is your ~?** ¿qué opinas?

verge [vɜrdʒ] n margen m; fig borde m; **to be on the ~** estar al borde (**of** de); **to be on the ~ of doing sth** estar a punto de hacer algo

verge on vt rayar en; **she is verging on fifty** ronda los cincuenta

verification [ˌver·ə·frˈkei·ʃən] n 1. (checking) verificación f 2. (confirmation) confirmación f

verify [ˈver·ə·faɪ] <-ie-> vt 1. (corroborate) confirmar 2. (authenticate) verificar

vermicelli [ˌvɜr·mə·ˈtʃel·i] n fideos m pl finos

vermin [ˈvɜr·mɪn] n 1. pl alimañas fpl; (insects) bichos mpl 2. (people) gentuza f

vermouth [vərˈmuθ] n vermut m

versatile [ˈvɜr·sə·t̬əl] adj 1. (flexible) versátil; (mind) ágil 2. (multifaceted) polifacético, -a

versatility [ˌvɜr·sə·ˈt̬ɪl·ə·t̬i] n versatilidad f; (mental) agilidad f

verse [vɜrs] n LIT verso m; MUS estrofa f; REL versículo m

versed adj **to be (well) ~** estar (muy) versado (**in** en)

version [ˈvɜr·ʒən] n versión f

versus [ˈvɜr·səs] prep frente a; SPORTS, LAW contra

vertebra [ˈvɜr·t̬ə·brə] <-ae> n vértebra f

vertebrate [ˈvɜr·t̬ə·brɪt] I. n vertebrado m II. adj vertebrado, -a

vertical [ˈvɜr·t̬ə·kəl] adj vertical; ~ **drop** caída en picado

vertigo [ˈvɜr·t̬ə·gou] n vértigo m

verve [vɜrv] n ímpetu m; **with ~** con brío

V

very ['ver·i] I. *adv* muy; (**not**) **~ much** (no) mucho; **I am ~, ~ sorry** de veras lo siento; **the ~ best** lo mejor de lo mejor; **the ~ first** el primerísimo; **at the ~ most** como mucho; **at the ~ least** por lo menos ▶ **~ well** muy bien; **to be all ~ fine, but...** estar muy bien y tal, pero... II. *adj* **at the ~ bottom** al final del todo; **the ~ fact** el mero hecho; **the ~ man** el mismísimo

vessel ['ves·əl] *n* **1.** (*boat*) embarcación *f* **2.** (*container*) recipiente *m* **3.** ANAT, BOT vaso *m*

vest[1] [vest] *n* FASHION chaleco *m*

vest[2] [vest] *vt* investir (**with** de, con); (*hopes*) depositar; **to ~ sth in sb** conferir algo a alguien

vestibule ['ves·tə·bjul] *n* vestíbulo *m*

vet[1] [vet] *inf* I. *n* (*animal doctor*) veterinario, -a *m, f* II. *vt* <-tt-> (*examine*) examinar

vet[2] [vet] *n inf* MIL veterano, -a *m, f*

veteran ['vet·ər·ən] *adj, n* veterano, -a *m, f*

veterinarian [,vet·ər·ə·'ner·i·ən] *n* veterinario, -a *m, f*

veterinary ['vet·ər·ə·ner·i] *adj* veterinario, -a

veto ['vi·toʊ] I. *n* <-es> veto *m* II. *vt* <vetoed> vetar

via ['vaɪ·ə] *prep* por; **~ Denver/the bridge** por Denver/el puente

viable ['vaɪ·ə·bəl] *adj* viable

viaduct ['vaɪ·ə·dʌkt] *n* viaducto *m*

vial ['vaɪ·əl] *n* ampolla *f*

vibrant ['vaɪ·brənt] *adj* (*personality*) enérgico, -a; (*color, light*) radiante; (*economy*) en ebullición

vibrate ['vaɪ·breɪt] *vi* vibrar; **to ~ with enthusiasm** estremecerse de entusiasmo

vibration [vaɪ·'breɪ·ʃən] *n* vibración *f*

vicar ['vɪk·ər] *n* vicario *m*

vicarage ['vɪk·ər·ɪdʒ] *n* vicaría *f*

vicarious [vɪ·'ker·i·əs] *adj* indirecto, -a

vice [vaɪs] *n* vicio *m*; **~ squad** brigada antivicio

vice versa [,vaɪ·sə·'vɜr·sə] *adv* viceversa

vicinity [və·'sɪn·ə·t̬i] *n* inmediaciones *fpl*; **in the ~ of...** en los alrededores de...

vicious ['vɪʃ·əs] *adj* (*malicious*) malicioso, -a; (*cruel*) despiadado, -a; (*fighting*) salvaje; (*pain*) atroz; (*wind*) devastador(a)

vicious circle *n* círculo *m* vicioso

victim ['vɪk·tɪm] *n* víctima *f*; **to be the ~** ser víctima (**of** de) ▶ **to fall ~** sucumbir (**to** a)

victimize ['vɪk·tə·maɪz] *vt* discriminar; **to be ~d by law** ser víctima de la ley

victor ['vɪk·tər] *n* vencedor(a) *m(f)*; **to emerge (as) the ~** salir victorioso

Victorian [vɪk·'tɔr·i·ən] *adj* victoriano, -a *m, f*

victorious [vɪk·'tɔr·i·əs] *adj* victorioso, -a

victory ['vɪk·tə·ri] <-ies> *n* victoria *f* (**over** sobre); **to win a ~** obtener una victoria (**in** en)

video ['vɪd·i·oʊ] *n* vídeo *m*; **to come out on ~** salir en vídeo

video camera *n* videocámara *f*

video game *n* videojuego *m*

videophone *n* videoteléfono *m*

video recorder *n* magnetoscopio *m*

video surveillance *n* vigilancia *f* con cámaras

videotape I. *n* cinta *f* de vídeo II. *vt* grabar en vídeo

Vietnam [,vi·et·'nam] *n* Vietnam *m*

Vietnamese [vi·et·nə·'miz] I. *adj* vietnamita II. *n* **1.** (*person*) vietnamita *mf* **2.** LING vietnamita *m*

view [vju] I. *n* **1.** (*opinion*) punto *m* de vista; **exchange of ~s** intercambio *m* de opiniones; **conflicting ~s** opiniones *f pl* contrapuestas; **to have an optimistic ~ of life** ver la vida con optimismo; **to hold strong ~s** mantener una postura fuerte (**about** sobre) **2.** (*perspective*) perspectiva *f*; **long-term ~** perspectiva a largo plazo; **to take the long ~ of sth** considerar algo a largo plazo **3.** (*sight*) vista *f*; **to block sb's ~** estar tapando a alguien; **to disappear from ~** perderse de vista ▶ **to take a dim ~ of sth** ver algo con malos ojos; **to have sth in ~** tener algo en mente; **in ~ of** en vista de; **with a ~ to** con vistas a; **to be on ~** estar expuesto; **on ~ to the public** abierto al público; **with this in ~** con este fin II. *vt* **1.** (*consider*) considerar; **to ~ sth from a different angle**

enfocar algo desde un ángulo distinto **2.** (*watch*) ver

viewer *n* (*person*) telespectador(a) *m(f)*

viewfinder ['vju·faɪn·dər] *n* visor *m*

viewing *n* visita *f;* **~ figures** índice *m* de audiencia

viewpoint ['vju·pɔɪnt] *n* punto *m* de vista

vigil ['vɪdʒ·əl] *n* **to keep ~** mantenerse alerta

vigilance ['vɪdʒ·ɪ·ləns] *n* vigilancia *f;* **to relax ~** bajar la guardia

vigilant ['vɪdʒ·ɪ·lənt] *adj* vigilante; **to be ~ in doing sth** estar atento al hacer algo

vigor ['vɪg·ər] *n* vigor *m;* (*energy*) energía *f*

vigorous ['vɪg·ər·əs] *adj* enérgico, -a; (*growth*) pujante

vile [vaɪl] *adj* **1.** vil **2.** *inf* vomitivo, -a; (*weather*) asqueroso, -a; **~ mood** humor de perros; **to smell ~** apestar

vilify ['vɪl·ə·faɪ] <-ie-> *vt* envilecer

village ['vɪl·ɪdʒ] **I.** *n* **1.** aldea *f* **2.** + *pl/sing vb* (*populace*) pueblo *m* **II.** *adj* de pueblo

villager ['vɪl·ə·dʒər] *n* aldeano, -a *m, f*

villain ['vɪl·ən] *n* villano, -a *m, f* ▶ **the ~ of the piece** el malo/la mala de la obra

vinaigrette [vɪn·ə·'gret] *n* vinagreta *f*

vindicate ['vɪn·də·keɪt] *vt* (*justify*) justificar; (*right*) reivindicar

vindictive [vɪn·'dɪk·tɪv] *adj* vengativo, -a

vine [vaɪn] *n* vid *f;* (*climbing*) parra *f*

vinegar ['vɪn·ə·gər] *n* vinagre *m*

vineyard ['vɪn·jərd] *n* viñedo *m*

vintage ['vɪn·tɪdʒ] **I.** *n* cosecha *f;* (*season*) vendimia *f* **II.** *adj* **1.** CULIN añejo, -a **2.** **~ car** coche *m* de época

vinyl ['vaɪ·nəl] *n* vinilo *m*

viola [vi·'ou·lə] *n* MUS viola *f*

violate ['vaɪ·ə·leɪt] *vt* **1.** (*break*) violar **2.** (*disturb*) perturbar

violation [vaɪ·ə·'leɪ·ʃən] *n* violación *f;* **traffic ~** infracción *f* de tráfico

violence ['vaɪ·ə·ləns] *n* violencia *f*

violent ['vaɪ·ə·lənt] *adj* **1.** (*cruel*) violento, -a **2.** (*powerful*) fuerte

violet ['vaɪ·ə·lɪt] **I.** *n* **1.** BOT violeta *f* **2.** (*color*) violeta *m* **II.** *adj* violeta

violin [vaɪ·ə·'lɪn] *n* violín *m*

violinist [vaɪ·ə·'lɪn·ɪst] *n* violinista *mf*

violoncello [vi·ə·lən·'tʃel·ou] *n* violoncelo *m*

VIP [vi·aɪ·'pi] *see* **very important person** VIP *mf*

viper ['vaɪ·pər] *n a. fig* víbora *f*

virgin ['vɜr·dʒɪn] *n* virgen *f*

virgin forest *n* selva *f* virgen

virginity [vər·'dʒɪn·ə·ti] *n* virginidad *f;* **to lose one's ~** perder la virginidad

Virgo ['vɜr·gou] *n* virgo *mf*

virile ['vɪr·əl] *adj* viril

virility [və·'rɪl·ə·ti] *n* virilidad *f*

virtual ['vɜr·tʃu·əl] *adj* virtual

virtually *adv* prácticamente

virtue ['vɜr·tʃu] *n* **1.** (*moral*) virtud *f* **2.** (*advantage*) ventaja *f* ▶ **by ~ of** en virtud de

virtuous ['vɜr·tʃu·əs] *adj* virtuoso, -a; (*chaste*) casto, -a

virulent ['vɪr·jə·lənt] *adj* MED virulento, -a

virus ['vaɪ·rəs] <-es> *n* COMPUT, MED virus *m inv*

visa ['vi·zə] *n* visado *m*

vis-à-vis [vi·zə·'vi] *prep* con relación a; (*compared to*) en comparación con

viscosity [vɪ·'skas·ə·ti] *n* viscosidad *f*

viscous ['vɪs·kəs] *adj* viscoso, -a

vise [vaɪs] *n* torno *m* de banco

visibility [vɪz·ə·'bɪl·ə·ti] *n* **1.** visibilidad *f;* **poor ~** poca visibilidad **2.** (*prominence*) notoriedad *f*

visible ['vɪz·ə·bəl] *adj* **1.** visible; **to be barely ~** ser a penas perceptible **2.** (*in the public eye*) notorio, -a

vision ['vɪʒ·ən] *n* **1.** (*sight*) vista *f* **2.** (*mental image*) visión *f*

visit ['vɪz·ɪt] **I.** *n* visita *f* (*from* de); **to pay a ~ to sb** ir a ver a alguien **II.** *vt* visitar **III.** *vi* ir de visita

visitation [vɪz·ə·'teɪ·ʃən] *n* (*visit*) visita *f*

visiting hours *npl* horario *m* de visita

visitor ['vɪz·ɪ·tər] *n* visitante *mf;* **~'s book** libro *m* de visitas

visor ['vaɪ·zər] *n* visera *f*

visual ['vɪʒ·u·əl] *adj* visual; **~ sense** sentido estético; **~ aid** soporte visual

visualize ['vɪʒ·u·ə·laɪz] *vt* visualizar

vital ['vaɪ·təl] *adj* vital; (*ingredient*) esen-

V

cial; (*part*) crucial; (*statistics*) demográfico, -a

vitality [vaɪ·ˈtæl·ə·t̬i] *n* vitalidad *f*

vitamin [ˈvaɪ·t̬ə·mɪn] *n* vitamina *f*

vitamin deficiency *n* avitaminosis *f inv*

vivacious [vɪ·ˈveɪ·ʃəs] *adj* vivaz; (*life*) animado, -a

vivid [ˈvɪv·ɪd] *adj* (*color*) vivo, -a; (*language*) vívido, -a; (*imagination*) fértil

vixen [ˈvɪk·sən] *n* **1.** ZOOL zorra *f* **2.** *pej* arpía *f*

vocabulary [voʊ·ˈkæb·jə·ler·i] *n* vocabulario *m;* **to widen one's** ~ ampliar vocabulario; **the word 'politeness' isn't in his** ~ la palabra 'modales' no entra en su vocabulario

vocal [ˈvoʊ·kəl] *adj* **1.** vocal; (*communication*) oral **2.** (*outspoken*) vehemente; **to be** ~ armar revuelo (**about** acerca de)

vocalist [ˈvoʊ·kə·lɪst] *n* vocalista *mf*

vocalize [ˈvoʊ·kə·laɪz] *vi, vt* vocalizar

vocation [voʊ·ˈkeɪ·ʃən] *n* vocación *f;* **to miss one's** ~ equivocarse de vocación

vocational [voʊ·ˈkeɪ·ʃə·nəl] *adj* vocacional; ~ **counseling/training** orientación/formación profesional

vociferation [voʊ··sɪf·ə·ˈreɪ·ʃən] *n* vocerío *m*

vociferous [voʊ·ˈsɪf·ər·əs] *adj* vociferante

vodka [ˈvad·kə] *n* vodka *f*

vogue [voʊg] *n* moda *f* ▶ **in** ~ de moda; **out of** ~ pasado de moda

voice [vɔɪs] *n* voz *f;* **in a loud** ~ en voz alta; **to raise/lower one's** ~ levantar/bajar la voz; **to lose one's** ~ quedarse afónico; **to listen to the** ~ **of reason** atender a razones; **to make one's** ~ **heard** hacerse escuchar

voice box <-es> *n inf* laringe *f*

voiced *adj* sonoro, -a

voiceless [ˈvɔɪs·lɪs] *adj* LING sordo, -a

voice mail *n* mansaje *m* de voz

voice-over *n* voz *f* en off

void [vɔɪd] **I.** *n* vacío *m* **II.** *adj* inválido, -a; **to be** ~ estar falto (**of** de) **III.** *vt* anular

volatile [ˈval·ə·t̬əl] *adj* volátil; (*situation*) inestable

volcanic [val·ˈkæn·ɪk] *adj* volcánico, -a

volcano [val·ˈkeɪ·noʊ] <-(e)s> *n* volcán *m*

vole [voʊl] *n* ratón *m* de campo

volition [voʊ·ˈlɪʃ·ən] *n* voluntad *f*

volley [ˈval·i] *n* **1.** (*salvo*) descarga *f* **2.** (*onslaught*) lluvia *f* **3.** SPORTS volea *f*

volleyball [ˈval·i·bɔl] *n* voleibol *m*

volt [voʊlt] *n* voltio *m*

voltage [ˈvoʊl·tɪdʒ] *n* voltaje *m*

voltage detector *n* voltímetro *m*

voltage drop *n* caída *f* de tensión

volume [ˈval·jum] *n* volumen *m;* ~ **of sales** volumen de ventas

volume control, volume regulator *n* control *m* de volumen

volume discount *n* rappel *m*

voluntary [ˈval·ən·ter·i] *adj* voluntario, -a

volunteer [ˌval·ən·ˈtɪr] **I.** *n* voluntario, -a *m, f* **II.** *vt* **to** ~ **oneself** ofrecerse (**for** para) **III.** *vi* ofrecerse voluntario

voluptuous [və·ˈlʌp·tʃu·əs] *adj* voluptuoso, -a

vomit [ˈvam·ɪt] **I.** *vi* vomitar; **it makes me want to** ~ me produce náuseas **II.** *vt* vomitar **III.** *n* vómito *m*

voodoo [ˈvu·du] *n* **1.** vudú *m* **2.** *inf* (*jinx*) maldición *f*

voracious [vɔ·ˈreɪ·ʃəs] *adj* voraz

vortex [ˈvɔr·teks] <-es *or* vortices> *n* vórtice *m*

vote [voʊt] **I.** *vi* votar (**for/against** a favor de/en contra de); **to** ~ **on sth** someter algo a votación **II.** *vt* votar; **to** ~ **that...** votar que... +*subj* **III.** *n* (*choice*) voto *m;* (*election*) votación *f;* **to put sth to the** ~ someter algo a votación

◆**vote down** *vt* rechazar (por votación)

◆**vote in** *vt* elegir (por votación)

◆**vote out** *vt* no reelegir (**of** en)

voter *n* votante *mf*

voting *n* votación *f*

voting booth <-es> *n* cabina *f*

vouch [vaʊtʃ] **I.** *vi* **to** ~ **for sth/sb** responder de algo/por alguien **II.** *vt* **to** ~ **that...** confirmar que...

voucher [ˈvaʊ·tʃər] *n* **1.** (*coupon*) vale *m* **2.** (*receipt*) comprobante *m*

vow [vaʊ] **I.** *vt* hacer voto de **II.** *n* voto *m*

vowel [ˈvaʊ·əl] *n* vocal *f*

voyage [ˈvɔɪ·ɪdʒ] **I.** *n* viaje *m* **II.** *vi* viajar

(**across** por)

voyeur |vɔɪˈʒɜr| n mirón, -ona m, f

vulgar |ˈvʌl·ɡər| adj **1.** (crude) ordinario, -a **2.** (commonplace) vulgar

vulgarity |vʌlˈɡær·ə·t̬i| n **1.** (crudeness) grosería f **2.** (ordinariness) vulgaridad f

vulnerable |ˈvʌl·nər·ə·bəl| adj vulnerable

vulture |ˈvʌl·tʃər| n a. fig buitre m

vulva |ˈvʌl·və| <-s or -e> n vulva f

W

W, w |ˈdʌb·əl·ju| n W, w f; ~ **as in Whiskey** W de Washington

W n **1.** abbr of **watt** W **2.** abbr of **west** O

wacko |ˈwæk·oʊ| n sl bicho m raro

wacky |ˈwæk·i| <-ier, -iest> adj sl (person) grillado, -a; (thing) estrambótico, -a

wad |wad| n (banknotes) fajo m; (cotton) bola f

waddle |ˈwad·əl| n andares m pl de pato

wade |weɪd| vi andar por el agua; **to ~ into sth** adentrarse en algo; **to ~ into sb** tomarla con alguien

wader |ˈweɪ·dər| n **1.** (bird) ave m zancuda **2.** (boot) bota f de pescador

wafer |ˈweɪ·fər| n **1.** (biscuit) barquillo m **2.** REL hostia f

waffle¹ |ˈwaf·əl| n CULIN gofre m, waffle m AmL

waffle² |ˈwaf·əl| inf **I.** vi parlotear **II.** n palabrería f

waffle iron n plancha f para gofres [or AmL waffles]

wag¹ |wæɡ| (move) **I.** <-gg-> vt menear **II.** n meneo m

wag² |wæɡ| n inf (funny person) bromista m f

wage |weɪdʒ| n sueldo m; **minimum/living ~** salario mínimo/de subsistencia

wage earner n asalariado, -a m, f

wage freeze n congelación f salarial

wage increase n aumento m salarial

wager |ˈweɪ·dʒər| **I.** n apuesta f; **to place a ~** hacer una apuesta **II.** vt apostar; fig jugarse

waggle |ˈwæɡ·əl| **I.** vt mover **II.** vi moverse

wail |weɪl| **I.** vi gemir; (wind) silbar **II.** vt lamentar **III.** n lamento m

wailing n gemidos mpl

waist |weɪst| n cintura f

waistband |ˈweɪst·bænd| n cinturilla f

waist-deep |ˌweɪstˈdip| adj hasta la cintura

waistline |ˈweɪst·laɪn| n cintura f; **to watch one's ~** guardar la línea

wait |weɪt| **I.** vi esperar; **to ~ for sth/sb** esperar algo/a alguien; **to keep sb ~ing** hacer esperar a alguien; **he cannot ~ to see her** está ansioso por verla; **~ and see** espera y verás **II.** vi esperar; **to ~ one's turn** esperar su turno **III.** n espera f

◆**wait about** vi, **wait around** vi estar a la espera (**for** de)

◆**wait behind** vi esperarse

◆**wait on** vt **1.** (serve) servir **2.** (expect) estar a la espera de

◆**wait up** vi esperar de pie (**for** a)

waiter |ˈweɪ·t̬ər| n camarero m, garzón m AmL, mesero m Méx

waiting n espera f

waiting game n **to play the ~** dejar pasar el tiempo

waiting list n lista f de espera

waiting room n sala f de espera

waitress |ˈweɪ·trɪs| n camarera f, garzona f AmL, mesera f Méx

waive |weɪv| vt (right) renunciar a; (rule) no aplicar

waiver |ˈweɪ·vər| n renuncia f

wake¹ |weɪk| n NAUT estela f; **in the ~ of** tras

wake² |weɪk| n velatorio m

wake³ |weɪk| <woke or waked, woken or waked> **I.** vi despertarse **II.** vt despertar

◆**wake up** vi, vt despertar

walk |wɔk| **I.** n **1.** (stroll) paseo m; **to take a ~** ir a dar un paseo; **it's a five minute ~** está a cinco minutos a pie **2.** (gait) andar m **3.** (pace) paso m **4.** (easy) pan m comido; **to do sth in a ~** hacer algo con los ojos cerrados ▶ **~ of life** condición f **II.** vt andarse; **to ~ sb home** acompañar a alguien a su casa;

W

to ~ **the dog** sacar a pasear al perro
III. *vi* andar; (*stroll*) pasear ▶ **to ~ on air** rebosar felicidad

◆**walk about** *vi*, **walk around** *vi* dar una vuelta

◆**walk away** *vi* irse; **to ~ from** alejarse de; *fig* desentenderse de

◆**walk back** *vi* volver a pie

◆**walk in** *vi* entrar

◆**walk off** *vi* marcharse

◆**walk on** *vi* seguir andando

◆**walk out** *vi* (*leave*) salir

◆**walk over** *vt* pisotear

◆**walk through** *vt insep* (*part*) ensayar

◆**walk up** I. *vi* 1. (*go up*) subir 2. (*approach*) acercarse (**to a**) II. *vt* subir

walker ['wɔ·kər] *n* paseante *mf*; (*as a hobby*) senderista *mf*

walkie-talkie [wɔ·ki·'tɔ·ki] *n* walkie-talkie *m*

walk-in ['wɔk·ɪn] *adj* empotrado, -a; ~ **closet** vestidor *m*

walking I. *n* paseo *m*; SPORTS marcha *f* atlética; **to do a lot of ~** andar mucho II. *adj* it is within ~ **distance** se puede ir a pie; **to be a ~ encyclopedia** ser una enciclopedia con patas

walking stick (*cane*) bastón *m*

walk-on ['wɔk·ɑn] *n* THEAT figurante *mf*; CINE extra *mf*; SPORTS cedido, -a *m, f*

walkout ['wɔk·aʊt] *n* salida *f*; (*strike*) huelga *f*

walkover ['wɔk·ˌoʊ·vər] *n inf* paseo *m*; **it was a ~** fue pan comido

walkway ['wɔk·weɪ] *n* pasarela *f*

wall [wɔl] *n* muro *m*; (*in the interior*) a. ANAT pared *f*; (*enclosing town*) muralla *f*; (*enclosing house*) tapia *f*; (*barrier*) barrera *f* ▶ **to have one's back to** [or **up against**] **the ~** estar entre la espada y la pared; **to drive sb up the ~** sacar a alguien de quicio; **to be off the wall** ser un freaky

◆**wall in** *vt* (*garden*) cercar; *fig* encerrar

◆**wall off** *vt* separar con un muro; **to wall oneself off** encerrarse en uno mismo

◆**wall up** *vt* (*opening*) tapiar

wall chart *n* gráfico *m* de pared

wallet ['wɑl·ɪt] *n* cartera *f*, billetera *f AmL*

wallflower ['wɔl·ˌflaʊ·ər] *n* BOT al(h)elí *m*

wallop ['wɑl·əp] *inf* I. *vt* zurrar II. *n* (*hit*)

guantazo *f*; **to pack a ~** causar impacto

wallow ['wɑl·oʊ] I. *n* revolcón *m* II. *vi* 1. (*animal*) revolcarse 2. (*revel*) regodearse; **to ~ in wealth** nadar en la abundancia

wallpaper ['wɔl·ˌpeɪ·pər] I. *n* papel *m* pintado II. *vt* empapelar

wall-to-wall ['wɔl·tə·'wɔl] *adj* ~ **carpeting** moqueta *f*

walnut ['wɔl·nʌt] *n* nuez *f*; (*tree*) nogal *m*

walrus ['wɔl·rəs] <**walruses** *or* **walrus**> *n* morsa *f*

waltz [wɔlts] <**-es**> I. *n* vals *m* II. *vi sl* ir tan campante

◆**waltz about** *vi*, **waltz around** *vi* dar vueltas despreocupado

◆**waltz in** *vi sl* entrar como si nada

◆**waltz off** *vi sl* **to ~ with sth** birlar algo

◆**waltz out** *vi sl* salir como si nada

wand [wɑnd] *n* varita *f* mágica

wander ['wɑn·dər] I. *vt* vagar por; **to ~ the streets** deambular por las calles, callejear II. *vi* (*roam*) vagar; (*stroll*) pasearse III. *n inf* paseo *m*

wane [weɪn] *vi* menguar

wangle ['wæŋ·gəl] *vt inf* agenciarse; **to ~ one's way into sth** arreglárselas para entrar en algo

want [wɑnt] I. *vt* querer; **to ~ to do sth** querer hacer algo; **to ~ sb to do sth** querer que alguien haga algo; **to ~ sth done** querer que se haga algo; **you're ~ed on the phone** te llaman por teléfono; **I was ~ing to leave** estaba deseando macharme II. *n* 1. (*need*) necesidad *f*; **to be in ~ of** necesitar 2. (*lack*) falta *f*; **for ~** por falta (**of** de)

◆**want in** *vi* querer entrar; **do you ~?** ¿te apuntas?

◆**want out** *vi* querer salirse (**of** de)

wanting *adj* falto, -a (**in** de); **there is sth ~** falta algo

war [wɔr] *n* guerra *f*; **the Great War** la Primera Guerra Mundial; **the Second World War** la Segunda Guerra Mundial; **to be at ~** estar en guerra; **to declare ~** *fig* hacer la vida imposible (**on** a)

war bond *n* bono *m* de guerra

war correspondent *n* corresponsal *mf* de guerra

war crime n crimen m de guerra

war criminal n criminal mf de guerra

war cry n grito m de guerra

ward [wɔrd] n **1.** (wardship) tutela f; **in ~** bajo tutela **2.** (room) sala f; **maternity ~** sala de maternidad; **geriatric/psychiatric ~** pabellón m geriátrico/psiquiátrico

♦ **ward off** vt evitar

warden ['wɔr·dən] n guardián, -ana m, f; (prison) alcaide(sa) m(f); **game ~** guardabosque mf

wardrobe ['wɔrd·roʊb] n **1.** (closet) ropero m **2.** (clothes) vestuario m

wardrobe trunk n baúl m ropero

warehouse ['wer·əhaʊs] n almacén m

warfare ['wɔr·fer] n guerra f

warhead ['wɔr·hed] n ojiva f

warily ['wer·ɪ·li] adv cautamente; (suspiciously) recelosamente

warlike ['wɔr·laɪk] adj (of war) bélico, -a

warlord ['wɔr·lɔrd] n jefe m militar

warm [wɔrm] I. adj **1.** (hot) caliente; (clothes) de abrigo; (day) caluroso, -a; (climate, wind) cálido, -a; (tracks) fresco, -a; **to be ~** (person) tener calor; (thing) estar caliente; (weather) hacer calor **2.** (affectionate) efusivo, -a; (welcome) caluroso, -a ▶ **you're getting ~** ¡caliente, caliente! II. vt calentar; **to ~ sb's heart** reconfortar a alguien

♦ **warm up** I. vi calentarse II. vt calentar; (food) recalentar; (person) hacer entrar en calor

warm-blooded [ˌwɔrm·'blʌd·ɪd] adj de sangre caliente

warm front n frente m cálido

warm-hearted [ˌwɔrm·'har·tɪd] adj bondadoso, -a; (affectionate) cariñoso, -a

warmth [wɔrmθ] n **1.** (heat) calor m **2.** (affection) calidez f

warm-up, **warmup** ['wɔrm·ʌp] n (pre)calentamiento m

warn [wɔrn] vt advertir; **to ~ sb not to do sth** advertir a alguien que no haga algo; **to ~ sb of a danger** prevenir a alguien de un peligro

warning ['wɔr·nɪŋ] n aviso m; **a word of ~** una advertencia; **to give sb a ~** advertir a alguien; **without ~** sin previo aviso; **~!** ¡atención!

warning shot n disparo m de advertencia

warp [wɔrp] vt (wood) deformar; (mind) pervertir

warpath ['wɔr·pæθ] n **to be on the ~** fig buscar pelea

warped adj deformado, -a; (mind) pervertido, -a; **to have a ~ way of looking at things** tener una manera retorcida de ver las cosas

warrant ['wɔr·ənt] I. n **1.** LAW orden f; **search ~** orden de registro **2.** COM garantía f II. vt **1.** (promise) garantizar **2.** (justify) justificar

warrantee [ˌwɔr·ən·'ti] n beneficiario, -a m, f de una garantía

warranty ['wɔr·ən·ti] <-ies> n garantía f

warren ['wɔr·ən] n fig laberinto m

warring adj en guerra

warrior ['wɔr·i·ər] n guerrero, -a m, f

warship ['wɔr·ʃɪp] n barco m de guerra

wart [wɔrt] n verruga f

wartime ['wɔr·taɪm] n tiempo m de guerra

wary ['wer·i] <-ier, -iest> adj cauteloso, -a; **to be ~** recelar (of de); **to be ~ about (doing) sth** dudar sobre (si hacer) algo

war zone ['wɔr·zoʊn] n zona f de guerra

was [waz] pt of **be**

wash [waʃ] I. vt (clean) lavar; (dishes, floor) fregar; **to ~ one's hair/hands** lavarse el pelo/las manos II. vi **1.** (person) lavarse; **that excuse won't ~ with me** esa excusa conmigo no cuela **2.** (do the laundry) lavar la ropa III. n **1.** (cleaning) lavado m; **to have a ~** darse un baño **2.** (clothes) **the ~** la ropa para lavar; **to be in the ~** estar en la lavandería **3.** (layer) baño m; (painting) mano f

♦ **wash away** vt **1.** (clean) quitar **2.** (carry away) arrastrar

♦ **wash down** vt **1.** (clean) lavar **2.** (carry away) arrastrar

♦ **wash out** I. vi quitarse II. vt (clean) lavar; (remove) quitar

♦ **wash over** vt (not affect) no afectar

♦ **wash up** I. vt lavar; **the sea washed it up** el mar lo arrojó sobre la playa II. vi (hands, face) lavarse

W

washable *adj* lavable

washbasin *n* lavabo *m;* (*bowl*) palangana *m*

washcloth *n* manopla *f*

washed-out [ˌwɑʃtˈaʊt] *adj* **1.** (*faded*) desteñido, -a **2.** (*tired*) cansado, -a

washer ['wɑʃ·ər] *n* (*machine*) lavadora *f*

washing ['wɑʃ·ɪŋ] *n* **1.** (*clothes*) ropa *f* sucia **2.** (*act*) lavado *f;* (*of clothes*) colada *f;* **to do the ~** hacer la colada

washing machine *n* lavadora *f,* lavarropas *f inv Arg*

Washington ['wɑʃ·ɪŋ·tən] *n* Washington *m*

Washington D.C. *n* Washington D.C. *m*

washout ['wɑʃ·aʊt] *n inf* desastre *m;* **a complete ~** un desastre total

wasn't ['wʌz·ənt] = **was not** *see* **be**

wasp [wɑsp] *n* avispa *f*

WASP [wɑsp] *n pej inf abbr of* **White Anglo-Saxon Protestant** *estadounidense anglosajón, blanco y protestante*

waste [weɪst] **I.** *n* **1.** (*misuse*) derroche *m* (**of** de); **it's a ~ of time** es una pérdida de tiempo; **to go to ~** echarse a perder; **what a ~!** ¡qué pena! **2.** (*refuse*) residuos *mpl;* **to recycle ~** reciclar la basura **II.** *vt* malgastar; (*time, opportunity*) perder; **to ~ one's breath** *fig* gastar saliva; **to ~ no time in doing sth** apresurarse a hacer algo

◆**waste away** *vi* consumirse

wastebasket ['weɪstˌbæs·kət] *n* papelera *m*

wasteful ['weɪst·fəl] *adj* derrochador(a)

wasteland *n* yermo *m*

waste management *n* gestión *f* de residuos

wastepaper *n* papel *m* usado

wastepaper basket *n* papelera *f*

waste pipe *n* tubo *m* de desagüe

waste product *n* residuos *mpl*

wastewater *n* aguas *f pl* residuales

watch [wɑtʃ] **I.** *n* **1.** (*on wrist*) reloj *m* (de pulsera) **2.** (*observation*) vigilancia *f;* **to be on the ~** estar pendiente (**for** de) **3.** (*period of duty*) guardia *f;* **to keep** [*or* **be on**] **~** estar de guardia **II.** *vt* **1.** (*observe*) mirar; (*to ~ TV/a film*) ver la tele/una película; **to ~ sb/ sth do sth** mirar a alguien/algo hacer

algo **2.** (*keep vigil*) vigilar; **to ~ the kids** echar un ojo a los niños **3.** (*mind*) fijarse en; **to ~ one's weight** cuidar la línea; **~ it!** ¡cuidado!, ¡aguas! *Méx;* **to ~ it** tener cuidado (**with** con); **~ yourself** cuídate **III.** *vi* fijarse

◆**watch out** *vi* tener cuidado; **~!** ¡cuidado!

watchdog ['wɑtʃ·dɔg] *n* (*dog*) perro *m* guardián; *fig* guardián, -ana *m, f*

watcher ['wɑtʃ·ər] *n* observador(a) *m(f)*

watchful ['wɑtʃ·fəl] *adj* vigilante; **to keep a ~ eye** estar pendiente (**on** de); **under the ~ eye** bajo la atenta mirada (**of** de)

watchman ['wɑtʃ·mən] <-men> *n* vigilante *m;* **night ~** vigilante nocturno

watchtower ['wɑtʃ·taʊ·ər] *n* atalaya *f*

water ['wɔ·tər] **I.** *n* agua *f;* **bottled/running ~** agua embotellada/corriente; **a drink/glass/bottle of ~** un trago/un vaso/una botella de agua; **territorial ~s** aguas jurisdiccionales; **by ~** por mar

▶ **to be ~ under the** <u>bridge</u> ser agua pasada; **like ~ off a** <u>duck's</u> **back** como si oyera llover; **to be in** <u>deep</u> **~** estar metido en un lío **II.** *vt* (*plants*) regar; (*livestock*) dar de beber a

water bottle *n* botellín *m* de agua; (*for travelers*) cantimplora *f*

water cannon *n inv* cañón *m* de agua

watercolor *n* acuarela *f*

water-cooled ['wɔ·tər·kuld] *adj* refrigerado, -a por agua

watercress *n* berro *m*

waterfall *n* cascada *f*

waterfront *n* puerto *m*

water heater *n* calentador *m* de agua

water hose *n* manguera *f*

watering can ['wɔ·tər·ɪŋˌkæn] *n* regadera *f*

water level *n* nivel *m* del agua

water lily <-ies> *n* nenúfar *m*

water line *n* línea *f* de flotación

water main *n* cañería *f* principal

watermark *n* línea *f* del agua; (*on paper*) filigrana *f*

watermelon *n* sandía *f*

water meter *n* contador *m* de agua

water pipe *n* **1.** cañería *f* **2.** (*hookah*) pipa *f* de agua

water pistol *n* pistola *f* de agua

water polo n waterpolo m

water pressure n presión f del agua

waterproof ['wɔ·tər·pruf] adj impermeable

water-repellent adj hidrófugo, -a

watershed ['wɔ·tər·ʃed] n fig punto m de inflexión

waterside n orilla f

water-ski ['wɔ·tər·ski] vi to go ~ing hacer esquí acuático

water-skiing n esquí m acuático

water softener n ablandador m de agua

water-soluble adj soluble en agua

water supply n suministro m de agua

water tank n cisterna f; (small) aljibe m

watertight ['wɔ·tər·taɪt] adj hermético, -a; fig irrecusable

water tower n depósito f de agua

waterway n canal m

waterworks n pl reserva f de abastecimiento de agua ▶ **to turn on** the ~ echarse a llorar

watery ['wɔ·tə·ri] <-ier, -iest> adj 1. (bland) aguado, -a 2. (weak) diluido, -a

watt [wat] n vatio m

wattage ['wat·ɪdʒ] n vatiaje m

wave [weɪv] I. n 1. (water) ola f; (surface) ondulación f; **to be on the crest of the** ~ fig estar en la cumbre 2. PHYS onda f ▶ **to make** ~s causar problemas II. vi (flag) ondear; **to** ~ **at** [or to] sb saludar a alguien con la mano III. vt agitar; **to** ~ **goodbye** decir adiós con la mano

◆**wave down** vt hacer señas para que pare

◆**wave on** vt hacer señas para que siga

◆**wave through** vt hacer señas para que pase

waver ['weɪ·vər] vi 1. (falter) desfallecer 2. (hesitate) titubear (**over** acerca de); **to** ~ **between... and...** dudar entre... y...

wavering adj vacilante; (between two options) titubeante

wavy ['weɪ·vi] <-ier, -iest> adj (hair) ondulado, -a; (pattern) ondulante

wax¹ [wæks] I. n cera f II. vt 1. (polish) encerar; (shoes) lustrar 2. (remove hair from) depilar con cera

wax² [wæks] vi (moon) crecer; **to** ~ **and wane** crecer y menguar; fig tener altibajos

waxy ['wæk·si] <-ier, -iest> adj (shiny) lustroso, -a

way [weɪ] I. n 1. (route) camino m; **to be (well) on the** ~ **to doing sth** fig ir encaminado a hacer algo; **under** ~ en curso; **on the** ~ de camino (**to** a); **to find one's** ~ **into/out** encontrar la manera de entrar/salir (**of** de); **to go out of one's** ~ fig tomarse la molestia (**to** de); **to go one's own** ~ a. fig irse por su lado; **to lose one's** ~ perderse; **to make one's** ~ (progress) progresar; (move) abrirse camino 2. (road) camino m; (name of road) vía f 3. (direction) dirección f; **the right/wrong** ~ around del derecho/del revés 4. (distance) trayecto m; **all the** ~ todo el trayecto; (completely) completamente; **to be a long** ~ **off** estar muy lejos; **to have a long** ~ **to go** tener un largo camino por recorrer; **to go a long** ~ a. fig llegar lejos 5. (fashion) manera f (**to** de); **in many** ~s de muchas maneras; **in some** ~s en cierto modo; **there are no two** ~s about it no tiene vuelta de hoja; **by** ~ **of** a modo de 6. (manner) modo m; **her** ~ **of life** su estilo de vida; **in a big** ~ a gran escala; **either** ~ de cualquier forma; **no** ~! ¡de ninguna manera!; **in no** ~ para nada; **to get one's own** ~ salirse con la suya; **in a** ~ en cierto modo 7. (free space) paso m; **to be in sb's** ~ estorbar a alguien; **in the** ~ en medio; **to give** ~ dar paso; fig dejar hacer (**to** a); **to make** ~ abrir paso (**for** a) 8. (condition) estado m; **to be in a bad** ~ estar en mala forma ▶ **which** ~ **the wind blows** por donde van los tiros; **to rub sb the wrong** ~ caer mal a alguien; **by the** ~ por cierto II. adv sl (very) mogollón de; **that's** ~ **cool!** ¡mola mazo!

way-out [ˌweɪ·'aʊt] adj sl (modern) ultramoderno, -a; (amazing) fuera de serie

wayside ['weɪ·saɪd] n borde m del camino

we [wi] pron pers nosotros, -as; **as** ~ **say** como decimos nosotros

weak [wik] adj 1. (not strong) débil; (cof-

W

fee, tea) claro, -a; **to be ~ with desire/thirst** languidecer de deseo/sed; **the ~ link/spot** *fig* el punto débil **2.** (*below standard*) flojo, -a (**at** en)

weaken [ˈwiˈkən] **I.** *vi* debilitarse; (*diminish*) disminuir **II.** *vt* debilitar; (*diminish*) disminuir

weakling [ˈwiˈklɪŋ] *n* enclenque *mf*

weakly [ˈwiˈkli] *adv* débilmente; (*unconvincingly*) sin convicción

weakness [ˈwiˈknɪs] <-es> *n* **1.** (*lack of strength*) debilidad *f;* **to have a ~** tener debilidad (**for** por) **2.** (*vulnerability*) punto *m* débil; (*flaw in character*) flaqueza *f*

wealth [welθ] *n* **1.** (*money*) riqueza *f;* (*fortune*) fortuna *f* **2.** (*large amount*) abundancia *f*

wealthy [ˈwelˈθi] <-ier, -iest> *adj* rico, -a

weapon [ˈwepˈən] *n* arma *f*

wear [wer] <wore, worn> **I.** *vt* **1.** (*clothes, jewelry, hair*) llevar **2.** (*deteriorate*) desgastar **II.** *vi* desgastarse **III.** *n* **1.** (*clothing*) ropa *f;* **casual/sports ~** ropa informal/deportiva **2.** (*amount of use*) desgaste *m*

♦**wear away I.** *vt* desgastar **II.** *vi* desgastarse; (*person*) consumirse

♦**wear down** *vt* (*reduce*) gastar; (*tire, resistance*) desgastar

♦**wear off** *vi* desaparecer

♦**wear on** *vi* (*time*) pasar lentamente

♦**wear out I.** *vi* gastarse **II.** *vt* gastar; (*patience*) agotar

wearing [ˈwerˈɪŋ] *adj* agotador(a)

weary [ˈwɪrˈi] <-ier, -iest> *adj* **1.** (*tired*) extenuado, -a **2.** (*tiring*) agotador(a) **3.** (*bored*) aburrido, -a; (*unenthusiastic*) desanimado, -a; **to be ~ of** estar harto de **II.** *vt* (*tire*) fatigar; (*bore*) aburrir (**with** con) **III.** *vi* (*get tired*) cansarse; (*get bored*) aburrirse

weasel [ˈwiˈzəl] *n* comadreja *f*

weather [ˈweθˈər] **I.** *n* tiempo *m;* (*climate*) clima *m; ~* **permitting** si lo permite el tiempo ► **to make heavy ~ of sth** complicar algo **II.** *vt* **1.** (*wear*) desgastar **2.** (*endure*) hacer frente a

weather-beaten [ˈweθˈərˈbiˈtən] *adj* (*face*) curtido, -a *f*

weather forecast *n* previsión *f* meteorológica

weatherman [ˈweθˈərˈmæn] <-men> *n* hombre *m* del tiempo

weathergirl [ˈweθˈərˈgɜrl] *n* mujer *f* del tiempo

weatherproof [ˈweθˈərˈpruf] *adj* impermeabilizado, -a

weave [wiv] **I.** <wove *or* weaved, woven *or* weaved> *vt* **1.** (*produce cloth*) tejer **2.** (*intertwine*) entretejer; *fig* tramar; **to ~ sth together** entrelazar algo **II.** <wove *or* weaved, woven *or* weaved> *vi* **1.** (*produce cloth*) tejer **2.** (*twist*) serpentear **III.** *n* tejido *m*

web¹ [web] *n* **1.** (*woven net*) tela *f;* **spider('s) ~** telaraña *f* **2.** *fig* (*complex network*) trama *f;* (*of lies*) sarta *f*

web² [web] COMPUT **I.** *n* red *f;* **on the ~** en la red **II.** *adj* de internet

web-footed [ˈwebˈfʊtˈɪd] *adj* palmípedo, -a

weblog [ˈwebˈlɒg] *n* blog *m*

webmaster *n* administrador(a) *m(f)*

website *n* sitio *m* web; **to visit a ~** visitar un sitio web

webzine *n* revista *f* electrónica

wed [wed] <wedded *or* wed, wedded *or* wed> **I.** *vt* contraer matrimonio con; *fig* casar **II.** *vi* contraer matrimonio

we'd [wid] **1.** = **we had** *see* **have 2.** = **we would** *see* **would**

wedded [ˈwedˈɪd] *adj* casado, -a; **lawfully ~ wife** legítima esposa; **to be ~ to** estar unido a; (*opinion*) aferrarse a; (*habit*) tener

wedding [ˈwedˈɪŋ] *n* boda *f*

wedding anniversary <-ies> *n* aniversario *m* de bodas

wedding cake *n* tarta *f* nupcial

wedding day *n* día *m* de la boda

wedding dress *n* traje *m* de novia

wedding ring *n* alianza *f*

wedge [wedʒ] **I.** *n* cuña *f;* *fig* porción *f*

wedlock [ˈwedˈlak] *n* matrimonio *m*

Wednesday [ˈwenzˈdeɪ] *n* miércoles *m inv; s. a.* **Friday**

wee [wi] *adj* (*tiny*) chiquito, -a

weed [wid] *n* **1.** mala hierba *f* **2.** (*marijuana*) maría *f* ► **to grow like a ~** crecer como la mala hierba

weedkiller [ˈwidˈkɪlˈər] *n* herbicida *m*

weedy ['wiː·di] *adj* <-ier, iest> lleno, -a de malas hierbas; (*person*) canijo, -a

week [wiːk] *n* semana *f*; last ~ la semana pasada; once a ~ una vez por semana; during the ~ durante la semana; ~ after/by ~ semana tras/a semana; a forty hour ~ cuarenta horas semanales

weekday ['wiːk·deɪ] *n* día *m* laborable; on ~s los días laborables

weekend ['wiːk·end] *n* fin *m* de semana; on/over the ~ el fin de semana

weekly ['wiːk·li] I. *adj* semanal II. *adv* semanalmente

weep [wiːp] I. *vi*, *vt* <wept, wept> llorar (with de, for/over por) II. *n* llanto *m*

weeping *adj* lloroso, -a

weeping willow *n* sauce *m* llorón

weigh [weɪ] I. *vi* pesar II. *vt* 1. pesar; to ~ oneself pesarse 2. (*consider*) sopesar; (*words*) medir; to ~ sth against sth contraponer algo a algo

◆**weigh down** *vt* doblar del peso; *fig* abrumar

◆**weigh in** *vi inf* (*take part*) intervenir; to ~ to a discussion with one's opinion intervenir en una discusión dando su opinión

weigh-in ['weɪ·ɪn] *n* pesaje *m*

weight [weɪt] *n* 1. (*amount weighed*) peso *m*; to lift a heavy ~ levantar algo pesado; to put on ~ engordar 2. (*metal*) pesa *f* 3. (*importance*) peso *m*; to carry ~ tener mucho peso ▶ to take the ~ off one's **feet** sentarse y descansar; to be a ~ off sb's **mind** ser un alivio para alguien; it's a great ~ off my mind es un peso que me quito de encima; to **pull** one's (**own**) ~ poner de su parte

weightless ['weɪt·lɪs] *adj* ingrávido, -a

weightlessness *n* ingravidez *f*

weightlifter *n* levantador(a) *m(f)* de pesas

weightlifting ['weɪt·lɪf·tɪŋ] *n* levantamiento *m* de pesas; to do ~ hacer pesas

weighty ['weɪ·ti] *adj* <-ier, -iest> 1. (*heavy*) pesado, -a 2. (*important*) importante; (*matter*) de peso

weir [wɪr] *n* presa *f*

weird [wɪrd] *adj* misterioso, -a; how ~! ¡qué raro!; ~ and wonderful extraor-

dinario

welcome ['wel·kəm] I. *vt* 1. dar la bienvenida a; to ~ sb warmly recibir a alguien con los brazos abiertos 2. (*support*) aprobar II. *n* 1. bienvenida *f* 2. (*approval*) aprobación *f* III. *adj* grato, -a; ~! ¡bienvenido, -a!; to be ~ ser bienvenido ▶ you **are** ~ de nada; you're **very** ~ no hay de qué; to **be** ~ to do sth poder hacer algo; you are ~ to use it está a su disposición

welcoming *adj* acogedor(a)

weld [weld] I. *vt* (*join metal*) soldar II. *n* soldadura *f*

welfare ['wel·fer] *n* 1. bienestar *m* 2. social ~ asistencia *f* social; to be on ~ vivir de las ayudas sociales

welfare state *n* estado *m* del bienestar

welfare work *n* trabajos *m pl* de asistencia social

welfare worker *n* trabajador(a) *m(f)* social

we'll [wiːl] = we will *see* will

well[1] [wel] I. *adj* <better, best> bien; to feel ~ sentirse bien; to get ~ recuperarse; to look ~ tener buen aspecto II. <better, best> *adv* 1. (*satisfactory*) bien; ~ enough suficientemente bien; ~ done bien hecho 2. (*thoroughly*) completamente; that's ~ east of here está muy al este; ~ enough suficiente; pretty ~ bastante a fondo; it costs ~ over... cuesta tranquilamente más de... 3. (*fairly*) justamente; you may ~ think... bien podrías pensar...; you might (just) as ~ tell her the truth más valdría que le dijeras la verdad ▶ all ~ and **good** muy bien; that's all **very** ~, but... todo eso está muy bien, pero...; **as** ~ (*also*) también; **as** ~ **as** así como; **just as** ~ menos mal III. *interj* vaya; very ~! ¡muy bien!

well[2] [wel] I. *n* (*hole*) pozo *m* II. *vi* (*flow*) manar

◆**well up** *vi* brotar

well-advised [ˌwel·əd·'vaɪzd] *adj* bien asesorado, -a; he would be ~ to stay at home haría bien en quedarse en casa

well-balanced [ˌwel·'bæl·ənst] *adj* a. PSYCH equilibrado, -a

well-behaved [ˌwel·bɪ·'heɪvd] *adj* bien

W

educado, -a; (*child, dog*) obediente

well-being [ˈwel·ˌbi·ɪŋ] n bienestar m; **a feeling of ~** una sensación de bienestar

well-bred [ˌwel·ˈbred] adj bien educado, -a; (*refined*) refinado, -a

well-chosen [ˌwel·ˈtʃoʊ·zən] adj cuidadosamente seleccionado, -a

well-connected [ˌwel·kəˈnek·tɪd] adj influyente; **to be ~** tener contactos

well-deserved [ˌwel·dɪˈzɜvd] adj merecido, -a

well-developed [ˌwel·dɪˈvel·əpt] adj muy desarrollado, -a; (*sense of humor*) agudo, -a

well-done [ˌwel·ˈdʌn] adj bien hecho, -a; (*meat*) muy hecho, -a

well-dressed [ˌwel·ˈdrest] adj bien vestido, -a

well-educated [ˌwel·ˈedʒ·ʊ·keɪ·tɪd] adj culto, -a

well-fed [ˌwel·ˈfed] adj bien alimentado, -a

well-founded [ˌwel·ˈfaʊn·dɪd] adj fundado, -a

well-heeled [ˌwel·ˈhild] adj ricachón, -ona

well-informed [ˌwel·ɪn·ˈfɔrmd] adj bien informado, -a (**about** sobre)

well-intentioned [ˌwel·ɪn·ˈten·ʃənd] **to be ~** tener buenas intenciones

well-known [ˌwel·ˈnoʊn] adj conocido, -a (**for** por); **it is ~ that...** es bien sabido que...

well-mannered [ˌwel·ˈmæn·ərd] adj con buenos modales

well-meaning [ˌwel·ˈmi·nɪŋ] adj con buenas intenciones

well-meant [ˌwel·ˈment] adj con buenas intenciones

well-off [ˌwel·ˈɔf] adj acomodado, -a; **the city is ~ for parks** la ciudad tiene muchos parques

well-oiled [ˌwel·ˈɔɪld] adj 1. (*functioning smoothly*) eficaz 2. (*drunk*) como una cuba

well-organized [ˌwel·ˈɔr·gə·naɪzd] adj bien organizado, -a

well-paid [ˌwel·ˈpeɪd] adj bien pagado, -a

well-placed [ˌwel·ˈpleɪst] adj bien situado, -a

well-read [ˌwel·ˈred] adj 1. (*knowledge-able*) culto, -a 2. (*read frequently*) muy leído, -a

well-spoken [ˌwel·ˈspoʊ·kən] adj bien-hablado, -a

well-thought-of [ˌwel·ˈθɔt·əv] adj de buena reputación; (*school*) de prestigio

well-timed [ˌwel·ˈtaɪmd] adj oportuno, -a

well-to-do [ˌwel·tə·ˈdu] I. adj de pelas II. n the ~ la gente de pelas

well-wisher [ˈwel·ˌwɪʃ·ər] n simpatizante mf

well-worn [ˌwel·ˈwɔrn] adj raído, -a; fig trillado, -a

went [went] pt of **go**

wept [wept] pt, pp of **weep**

were [wɜr] pt of **be**

we're [wɪr] = **we are** see **be**

weren't [wɜrnt] = **were not** see **be**

west [west] I. n oeste m; **in the ~ of Mexico** en el oeste de México; **to lie 5 miles to the ~ of...** quedar a 8 km al oeste de...; **to the ~** hacia el oeste; **the West** el mundo occidental; **the Wild West** el viejo oeste II. adj occidental; **~ wind** viento del oeste; **~ coast** costa oeste; **West Indies** Antillas fpl III. adv al oeste; **further ~** más al oeste ▶ **to go ~** (*thing*) estropearse; (*person*) irse al otro mundo

westbound [ˈwest·baʊnd] adj que va hacia el oeste

westerly [ˈwes·tər·li] adj (del) oeste

western [ˈwes·tərn] I. adj occidental II. n western m

westerner n occidental mf; (*western US*) del oeste de EEUU

westernize [ˈwes·tər·naɪz] vt occidentalizar

West Virginia n Virginia f Occidental

wet [wet] I. adj <-tt-> 1. (*soaked*) mojado, -a; (*damp*) húmedo, -a; (*paint*) fresco, -a; **to get ~** mojarse; **to get sth ~** mojar algo; **~ through** calado hasta los huesos 2. (*rainy*) lluvioso, -a ▶ **to be ~ behind the ears** estar con la miel en los labios; **to be all ~** estar en la parra II. <wet, wet> vt humedecer; **to ~ the bed** mojar la cama

we've [wiv] = **we have** see **have**

whack [hwæk] inf I. vt golpear II. n (*blow*) golpe m ▶ **to be out of ~**

estar fastidiado; **to have a ~ at** intentar

whacking *n* zurra *f*

whale [hweɪl] *n* ballena *f* ▸ **a ~ of a...** un(a) enorme...; **to have a ~ of a time** pasarlo bomba

whaling *n* pesca *f* de ballenas

wham [hwæm] *interj* zas

wharf [hwɔːrf] <-ves-> *n* muelle *m*

what [hwʌt] **I.** *adj interrog* qué; **~ kind of book?** ¿qué tipo de libro?; **~ time is it?** ¿qué hora es?; **~ men is he talking about?** ¿de qué hombres está hablando?; **~ an idiot!** ¡qué idiota! **II.** *pron* **1.** *interrog* qué; **~ can I do?** ¿qué puedo hacer?; **~ does it matter?** ¿qué importa?; **~'s up?** ¿qué hay?; **~ for?** ¿para qué?; **~ is he like?** ¿cómo es?; **~'s his name, ~'s it called?** ¿cómo se llama?; **~ about Paul?** ¿y Paul?; **~ about a walk?** ¿te va un paseo?; **~ if it snows?** *inf* ¿y si nieva? **2.** *rel* lo que; **~ I like is ~ he says** lo que me gusta es lo que dice; **~ is more** lo que es más **III.** *interj* **~?** ¡qué!; **so ~?** ¿y qué?; **is he coming, or ~?** ¿viene, o qué?

whatever [hwʌt·'ev·ər] **I.** *pron* **1.** *(anything)* (todo) lo que; **~ happens, happens** pasará lo que tenga que pasar **2.** *(any of them)* cualquier(a); **~ you pick is fine** cualquiera que elijas está bien **II.** *adj* **1.** *(being what it may be)* cualquiera que; **~ the reason sea** cual sea la razón **2.** *(of any kind)* de ningún tipo; **there is no doubt ~** no cabe duda

whatnot ['hwʌt·nat] *n* chisme *m;* **and ~** y demás

whatsoever [ˌhwʌt·sou·'ev·ər] *adv* sea cual sea; **nothing ~** nada de nada; **to have no interest ~** no tener interés alguno (**in** en)

wheat [hwiːt] *n* trigo *m*

wheat belt *n* zona *f* de cultivo de trigo

wheel [hwiːl] **I.** *n* **1.** AUTO rueda *f;* **alloy ~s** llantas *f pl* de aleación; **front/rear ~** rueda delantera/trasera; **to be on ~s** ir sobre ruedas **2.** *(steering wheel)* volante *m;* NAUT timón *m;* **to be at the ~** ir al volante; **to get behind the ~** ponerse al volante **3.** TECH torno *m* **4.** **~s** *sl* carro *m* ▸ **to be hell on ~s** *sl* ser un peligro al volante **II.** *vt* empujar **III.** *vi* girar ▸ **to ~ and deal** trapichear

◆ **wheel around** *vi* dar media vuelta

wheelbarrow ['hwil·ˌbær·ou] *n* carretilla *f*

wheelchair *n* silla *f* de ruedas

wheeler-dealer [ˌhwi·lər·'di·lər] *n* trapichero, -a *m, f*

wheeze [hwiz] <-zing-> *vi* resollar

when [hwen] **I.** *adv* cuándo; **since ~?** ¿desde cuándo?; **I'll tell him ~ to go** yo le diré cuándo ir **II.** *conj* **1.** *(at which time)* en que; **at the moment ~ he arrived** en el momento en que vino **2.** *(during)* **~ singing that song** cuando cantaba esa canción **3.** *(every time)* **~ it snows** cuando nieva **4.** *(although)* **he buys it ~ he could borrow it** lo compra cuando podría pedirlo prestado **5.** *(considering)* si; **how can I listen ~ I can't hear?** ¿cómo puedo escuchar si no puedo oír?

whenever [hwen·'ev·ər] **I.** *conj* **1.** *(every time)* siempre que; **~ I can** siempre que puedo **2.** *(at any time)* **he can come ~ he likes** puede venir cuando quiera **II.** *adv* **~ did I say that?** ¿cuándo he dicho yo eso?; **tomorrow or ~** mañana o un día de estos

where [hwer] *adv* **1.** *interrog* dónde; **~ does he live?** ¿dónde vive?; **~ does he come from?** ¿de dónde es?; **~ is he going (to)?** ¿adónde va? **2.** *rel* donde; **the box ~ he puts his things** la caja donde pone sus cosas

whereabouts ['hwer·ə·bauts] **I.** *n +* *sing/pl vb* paradero *m* **II.** *adv inf* dónde; **~ in Caracas do you live?** ¿en qué zona de Caracas vives?

whereas [hwer·'æz] *conj* *(while)* mientras que

whereby [hwer·'baɪ] *conj* por lo cual

wherein [hwer·'ɪn] *conj form* en donde

whereupon ['hwer·ə·ˌpan] *conj* con lo cual

wherever [ˌhwer·'ev·ər] **I.** *conj* dondequiera que; **~ I am/I go** dondequiera que esté/vaya; **~ he likes** donde le plazca **II.** *adv* **~ did she find that?** ¿dónde demonios encontró eso?; **or ~** o donde sea

W

wherewithal [ˈhwer·wɪð·ɔl] n liter recursos mpl

whet [hwet] <-tt-> vt 1. (sharpen) afilar 2. (stimulate) estimular

whether [ˈhweð·ər] conj 1. (if) si; to tell/ask ~ it's true (or not) decir/preguntar si es verdad (o no); I doubt ~ he'll come dudo que venga 2. (all the same) sea; ~ rich or poor sean ricos o pobres; ~ I go by bus or bike vaya en autobús o en bici

whew [hwu, fju] interj uf

which [hwɪtʃ] I. adj interrog qué; ~ one(s)? ¿cuál(es)? II. pron 1. interrog cuál, qué; ~ is his? ¿cuál es el suyo? 2. rel que, el que, la que lo que neuter; the book ~ I read/of ~ I'm speaking el libro que leí/del que estoy hablando; he said he was there, ~ I believed dijo que estaba ahí, lo cual creí

whichever [hwɪtʃˈev·ər] I. pron cualquiera que; you can choose ~ you like puedes escoger el que quieras II. adj cualquier, el que, la que ~ the ~ book you like puedes coger el libro que quieras

whiff [hwɪf] n 1. (smell) olorcillo m (to a) 2. (trace) indicio m

while [hwaɪl] I. n rato m; a short ~ un ratito; quite a ~ bastante tiempo; after/for a ~ después de/durante un rato; once in a ~ de vez en cuando II. conj 1. (during) mientras; I did it ~ he was sleeping lo hice mientras él dormía; ~ I'm alive mientras (que yo) viva 2. (although) aunque; ~ I like it, I won't buy it aunque me guste, no lo compraré; ~ I know it's true... a pesar de que sé que es verdad...

whim [hwɪm] n capricho m; on a ~ por capricho; as the ~ takes him según se le antoja

whimper [ˈhwɪm·pər] I. vi quejarse; (child) lloriquear II. n quejido m; to give a ~ dar un gemido

whimsical [ˈhwɪm·zɪ·kəl] adj 1. (odd) descabellado, -a 2. (capricious) caprichoso, -a

whine [hwaɪn] I. <-ning> vi gemir; (cry) lloriquear; (engine) zumbar II. n quejido m; (engine) zumbido m

whip [hwɪp] I. n (lash) látigo m, fuete m AmL II. <-pp-> vt 1. azotar; to ~ sb fig dar una paliza a alguien (at, in en) 2. CULIN batir

◆**whip back** vi 1. (bounce back) rebotar bruscamente 2. (return) volverse de golpe

◆**whip off** vt (tablecloth) sacar de un tirón

◆**whip on** vt 1. (urge on) animar 2. (put on quickly) ponerse rápidamente

◆**whip up** vt 1. (encourage) avivar; to ~ support conseguir apoyo 2. inf (prepare) improvisar 3. CULIN batir

whiplash n <-es> 1. (whip part) tralla f 2. (blow) latigazo m 3. MED traumatismo m cervical

whipped cream n nata f para montar

whipping n 1. (punishment) azotaina f; to give/get a ~ dar/llevarse una paliza 2. (gusting) azote m; the ~ of the wind el azote del viento

whipping cream n nata f para montar

whir [hwɜr] <-rr-> I. vi hacer ruido II. n ruido m; (of wings) aleteo m

whirl [hwɜrl] I. vi girar rápidamente; my head ~s la cabeza me da vueltas II. vt hacer girar; to ~ sb around dar vueltas a alguien III. n torbellino m; a ~ of dust una polvareda ► to give sth a ~ probar algo

whirlpool [ˈhwɜrl·pul] n remolino m

whirlwind n torbellino m; a ~ romance un idilio relámpago

whisk [hwɪsk] I. vt 1. CULIN batir 2. (take quickly) llevar rápidamente II. n 1. (kitchen tool) batidora f; electric/hand-held ~ batidora eléctrica/de mano 2. (movement) sacudida f; (of tail) coletazo m

whisker [ˈhwɪs·kər] n ~s pelo m de la barba; (of animal) bigotes mpl ► by a ~ por un pelo; within a ~ (of doing sth) a punto (de hacer algo)

whiskey n, **whisky** [ˈhwɪs·ki] n <-ies> whisky m

whisper [ˈhwɪs·pər] I. vi cuchichear II. vt 1. (speak softly) susurrar; to ~ sth in sb's ear decir algo al oído 2. fig (gossip) rumorear; it is ~ed... se rumorea... III. n 1. (soft sound or speech) cuchicheo m; **in a ~** en voz baja **2.** *fig* rumor m

whistle ['hwɪs·əl] **I.** <-ling> vi, vt silbar (at a); (*bird*) trinar **II.** n **1.** silbido m; **the ~ of the wind** el silbido del viento **2.** (*device*) silbato m; **to blow a ~** pitar ▶ **to blow the ~** llamar al orden (**on** a)

white [hwaɪt] **I.** adj blanco, -a; **~ sauce** bechamel f; **to turn** [or **go**] **~ with fear** palidecer de miedo **II.** n **1.** blanco m; (*egg*) clara f **2.** (*person*) blanco, -a m, f

White House n **the ~** la Casa Blanca

white lie n mentira f piadosa

whiten ['hwaɪ·tən] vi, vt blanquear; (*go pale*) palidecer

whitewash ['hwaɪt·waʃ] **I.** <-es> n **1.** (*for walls*) cal f **2.** (*coverup*) blanqueo m **3.** (*victory*) paliza f **II.** vt **1.** (*wall*) encalar **2.** (*conceal*) blanquear **3.** SPORTS dar una paliza

white wine n vino m blanco

Whitsun ['hwɪt·sən] n Pentecostés m

whittle ['hwɪt·əl] <-ling> vt tallar

whiz [hwɪz] **I.** n **1.** *inf* (*person*) hacha m **2.** (*noise*) silbido m **3.** *sl* **to take a ~** echar un meo **II.** vi ir disparado; **to ~ along** ir a toda pastilla; **to ~ by** pasar como una bala

whizz [hwɪz] n vi *see* **whiz**

who [hu] pron **1.** *interrog* quién, quiénes; **~ broke the window?** ¿quién rompió la ventana?; **~ were they?** ¿quiénes eran? **2.** *rel* que; **the people ~ work here** la gente que trabaja aquí; **all those ~ know her** todos los que la conocen; **it was your sister ~ did it** fue tu hermana quien lo hizo

whoa [hwoʊ] *interj* (*to horse*) so; (*to person*) para el carro

whoever [hu·'ev·ər] pron **1.** *rel* (*who*) quien, quienes, quienquiera que, quienesquiera que; **~ said that doesn't know me** el que dijo eso no me conoce **2.** *interrog* quién diablos; **~ said that?** ¿quién diablos dijo eso?

whole [hoʊl] **I.** adj **1.** (*entire*) todo, -a; **the ~ world** el mundo entero **2.** (*in one piece*) entero, -a; **to swallow sth ~** tragarse algo entero **3.** (*intact*) intacto,

-a; (*person*) ileso, -a **II.** n **1.** (*a complete thing*) todo m; **as a ~** en su totalidad; **taken as a ~** en conjunto; **on the ~** en general **2.** (*entirety*) totalidad f; **the ~** la totalidad; **the ~ of next week** toda la semana que viene **III.** adv *inf* completamente; **a ~ lot of people** un mogollón de gente; **to be a ~ lot faster** ser mucho más rápido

wholesale ['hoʊl·seɪl] **I.** n venta f al por mayor **II.** adj **1.** COM al por mayor; (*business, supplier*) mayorista **2.** (*on a large scale*) a gran escala **III.** adv **1.** COM al por mayor **2.** (*in bulk*) en masa

wholesaler ['hoʊl·seɪ·lər] n mayorista mf; **furniture ~** mayorista de muebles

wholesome ['hoʊl·səm] adj sano, -a

who'll [hul] = **who will** *see* **will**

wholly ['hoʊ·li] adv enteramente; **to be ~ aware/different** ser totalmente consciente/diferente

whom [hum] pron **1.** *interrog* a quién, a quiénes *after prep* quién, quiénes; **~ did he see?** ¿a quién vio?; **to ~ did he talk?** ¿con quién habló? **2.** *rel* a quien, que *after prep* quien, que; **those ~ I love** aquellos a quienes amo; **with ~** con quien

whoop [hup] **I.** vi gritar **II.** vt **to ~ it up** echar una cana al aire **III.** n grito m

whoopee ['hwu·pi] **I.** *interj* estupendo **II.** n juerga f

whooping cough ['hu·pɪŋ·kɔf] n tos f ferina

whoops [hwʊps] *interj* epa

whopper ['hwap·ər] n *iron* **1.** (*huge thing*) cosa f muy grande; **a ~ of a fish** un cacho pez **2.** (*lie*) embuste m; **to tell a ~** contar una mentira como una casa

whopping ['hwap·ɪŋ] adj *sl* enorme; **a ~ lie** una mentira como una casa

whore [hɔr] n puta f

who's [huz] **1.** = **who is** *see* **is** **2.** = **who has** *see* **has**

whose [huz] **I.** adj **1.** *interrog* de quién, de quiénes; **~ book is this?** ¿de quién es este libro?; **~ son is he?** ¿de quién es hijo? **2.** *rel* cuyo, cuyos, cuya, cuyas; **the girl ~ brother I saw** la chica cuyo hermano vi **II.** pron pos de quién, de

W

quiénes; ~ **is this pen?** ¿de quién es esta pluma?

why [hwaɪ] I. *adv* por qué; ~ **not?** ¿por qué no?; ~**'s that?** ¿y eso por qué?; **that's ~ I didn't tell you** por eso no te dije nada; **I want to know ~ you came late** quiero saber por qué llegaste tarde II. *n* porqué *m* III. *interj* ¡cómo!

wick [wɪk] *n* mecha *f*

wicked ['wɪk·ɪd] I. *adj* 1. (*evil*) malvado, -a 2. (*malicious*) retorcido, -a; (*sense of humor*) mordaz 3. *sl* de puta madre II. *n* the ~ los malos

wicker ['wɪk·ər] *n* mimbre *m*

wicket ['wɪk·ɪt] *n* (*door*) portillo *m*; **to be in a sticky ~** estar en un apuro

wide [waɪd] I. *adj* 1. (*broad*) extenso, -a; (*as a measurement*) ancho, -a; **it is 3 feet ~** tiene 1 m de ancho 2. (*varied*) amplio, -a; **a ~ range/experience** una amplia gama/experiencia 3. (*extensive*) grande; ~ **support** gran apoyo *m* II. *adv* extensamente; (*eyes*) como platos; (*door, window*) de par en par; **to be ~ apart** estar muy lejos (el uno del otro)

wide-angle [,waɪd·'æn·gəl] *adj* gran angular

wide-awake [,waɪd·ə·'weɪk] *adj* bien despierto, -a

wide-eyed ['waɪd·aɪd] *adj fig* inocente

widely *adv* 1. (*broadly*) extensamente; (*smile*) ampliamente; (*gesture*) mucho 2. (*extensively*) ampliamente; ~ **accepted/admired** muy aceptado/admirado 3. (*to a large degree*) considerablemente; ~ **differing aims** objetivos muy diferentes

widen ['waɪ·dən] I. *vt* extender; (*discussion*) ampliar II. *vi* ensancharse

wide-open ['waɪd·,oʊ·pən] *adj* 1. (*undecided*) abierto, -a 2. (*exposed*) expuesto, -a; **to be ~** estar expuesto (**to** a)

widespread ['waɪd·spred] *adj* extendido, -a; *fig* general

widow ['wɪd·oʊ] I. *n* viuda *f* II. *vt* dejar viuda; **to be ~ed** enviudar

widowed *adj* viudo, -a

widower ['wɪd·oʊ·ər] *n* viudo *m*; **to be left a ~** enviudar

width [wɪdθ] *n* 1. (*distance*) extensión *f*; (*clothes*) ancho *m*; **to be 4 inches in ~** medir 10 cm de ancho 2. (*amount, size*) amplitud *f*

wield [wild] *vt* manejar; (*weapon*) empuñar; (*power*) ejercer

wife [waɪf] <**wives**> *n* mujer *f*; **my ~** mi mujer

wig [wɪg] *n* peluca *f*

wiggle ['wɪg·əl] I. *vt* menear II. *n* (*movement*) meneo *m*; (*walking*) contoneo *m*

wild [waɪld] I. *adj* 1. (*animal*) salvaje; (*plant*) silvestre; (*landscape*) agreste 2. (*unruly*) indisciplinado, -a; (*party*) loco, -a 3. (*not sensible*) insensato, -a; (*plan*) descabellado, -a; (*guess*) disparatado, -a 4. (*extreme*) absurdo, -a 5. METEO tormentoso, -a; (*wind, weather*) furioso, -a 6. (*angry*) hecho, -a una fiera; **to drive sb ~** sacar de quicio a alguien; **to go ~** ponerse como loco 7. (*enthusiastic*) loquito, -a; (*applause*) entusiasta II. *adv* silvestre; **to grow ~** crecer libre; **to let one's imagination run ~** dejar volar la imaginación

wild card *n* GAMES, COMPUT comodín *m*

wildcat *n* 1. ZOOL gato *m* montés 2. *fig* fiera *f*

wilderness ['wɪl·dər·nɪs] *n* 1. (*desert tract*) páramo *m* 2. (*unspoiled land*) paraje *m* natural

wildfire ['waɪld·,faɪr] *n* fuego *m* incontrolado ▶ **to spread like ~** extenderse como un reguero de pólvora

wild goose <- **geese**> *n* ganso *m* salvaje

wild-goose chase *n* (*search*) búsqueda *f* inútil

wildlife *n* fauna *f* y flora *f*

wildly *adv* 1. (*frantically*) como loco; **to behave ~** portarse como un salvaje; **to talk ~** hablar sin ton ni son 2. (*haphazardly*) a lo loco; (*shoot, guess*) a tontas y a locas 3. *inf* (*very*) muy; ~ **exaggerated** superexagerado; ~ **expensive** carísimo

wilful ['wɪl·fəl] *adj see* **willful**

will[1] [wɪl] <**would, would**> *aux* 1. (*future*) **they'll be delighted** estarán encantados; **I'll be with you in a minute** estaré contigo en un minuto; **she ~ have received the letter by now** ya debe haber recibido la carta 2. (*imme-*

diate future) **we'll be off now** ya nos vamos **3.** (*tag question*) **you won't forget, ~ you?** no se te olvidará, ¿verdad? **4.** (*request*) **~ you let me speak!?** ¡déjame hablar!; **give me a hand, ~ you?** échame una mano, ¿quieres?; **~ you be having a slice of cake?** ¿quiere un trozo de tarta? **5.** (*willingness*) **who'll mail this letter for me? — I** — ¿quién me echa esta carta al buzón? — lo haré yo **6.** (*fact*) **the car won't run without gas** el no funciona sin gasolina **7.** (*persistence*) **he ~ keep doing that** se empeña en hacer eso; **the door won't open** no hay manera de abrir la puerta **8.** (*likelihood*) **they'll be tired** estarán cansados

will² [wɪl] **I.** *n* **1.** (*faculty*) voluntad *f* (**to** de); (*desire*) deseo *m*; **at ~** a voluntad; **to lose the ~** perder las ganas de vivir **2.** (*testament*) testamento *m* ▶ **where there's a ~, there's a way** querer es poder; **with the best ~ in the world** con la mejor voluntad del mundo; **to have a ~ of one's own** ser cabezón **II.** *vt* **1.** (*try to cause*) sugestionar; **to ~ sb to do sth** sugestionar a alguien para que haga algo **2.** (*bequeath*) legar

willful [ˈwɪl·fəl] *adj* **1.** (*deliberate*) intencionado, -a; (*murder*) premeditado, -a **2.** (*self-willed*) testarudo, -a

willing [ˈwɪl·ɪŋ] *adj* **1.** dispuesto, -a; **to be ~ to do sth** estar dispuesto a hacer algo **2.** (*compliant*) servicial

willingness *n* **1.** (*readiness*) disposición *f* **2.** (*enthusiasm*) entusiasmo *m*; **lack of ~** falta *f* de ánimo

willow [ˈwɪl·ou] *n* sauce *m*

willowy [ˈwɪl·ou·i] *adj* esbelto, -a

willpower [ˈwɪl·ˌpau·ər] *n* fuerza *f* de voluntad

wilt [wɪlt] *vi* (*plants*) marchitarse; (*person*) desanimarse

wily [ˈwaɪ·li] <-ier, -iest> *adj* astuto, -a

wimp [wɪmp] *n sl* endeble *mf*

win [wɪn] **I.** *n* victoria *f* **II.** <won, won> *vt* ganar; (*obtain*) obtener; (*recognition, popularity*) ganarse ▶ **to ~ the day** prevalecer; **you can't ~ them all** you ~ some, **you lose some** no se puede ganar todo **III.** <won, won> *vi* ganar ▶ **to ~ hands down** ganar con mucha facilidad; **you (just) can't ~ with him/her** con él/ella, siempre llevas las de perder; **you ~!** ¡como tú digas!

◆ **win back** *vt* recuperar

◆ **win over** *vt* ganarse; (*convince*) convencer (**to** para)

wince [wɪns] *n* mueca *f* de dolor

wind¹ [wɪnd] *n* **1.** (*current of air*) viento *m*; **gust of ~** ráfaga *f*; **a breath of ~** un poco de aire **2.** (*breath*) aliento *m*; **to get** [*or* **catch**] **one's ~** recobrar el aliento; **to have the ~ knocked out of sb** parar a alguien los pies ▶ **to take the ~ out of sb's sails** desanimar a alguien; **to sail close to the ~** estar a punto de pasarse de la raya; **to get ~ of sth** enterarse de algo; **to go** [*or* **run**] **like the ~** correr como el viento; **there's sth in the ~** se está tramando algo

wind² [waɪnd] <wound, wound> **I.** *vt* **1.** (*coil*) enrollar (**around** alrededor de); (*clock, watch*) dar cuerda a **2.** (*wrap*) envolver **II.** *vi* serpentear

◆ **wind down** **I.** *vt* (*reduce*) reducir; (*business*) limitar **II.** *vi* **1.** (*business*) tocar a su fin **2.** (*relax*) desconectar

◆ **wind up** **I.** *vt* (*finish*) acabar; (*debate, meeting, speech*) concluir **II.** *vi* **to ~ in prison** ir a parar a la cárcel

windbag [ˈwɪnd·bæg] *n* charlatán, -ana *m, f*

winder [ˈwaɪn·dər] *n* cuerda *f*

windfall [ˈwɪnd·fɔl] *n* fruta *f* caída; (*money*) ganancia *f* imprevista

wind farm *n* granja *f* con energía eólica

winding [ˈwaɪn·dɪŋ] *adj* sinuoso, -a

wind instrument *n* instrumento *m* de viento

windmill *n* molino *m* de viento; (*toy*) molinillo *m*

window [ˈwɪn·dou] *n a.* COMPUT ventana *f*; **pop-up ~** ventana emergente; (*shop*) escaparate *m*; (*vehicle*) ventanilla *f*; **rear ~** ventanilla trasera ▶ **to go out (of) the ~** (*plan*) venirse abajo

window box <-es> *n* jardinera *f*

window envelope *n* sobre *m* de ventanilla

window-shopping *n* **to go ~** ir de escaparates

windpipe ['wɪnd·paɪp] n tráquea f

windshield ['wɪnd·ʃild] n parabrisas m inv

windsock n manga f de viento

windsurfer ['wɪnd·ˌsɜr·fər] n windsurfista mf

windsurfing ['wɪnd·ˌsɜr·fɪŋ] n windsurf m

wind tunnel n túnel m aerodinámico

windward ['wɪnd·wərd] n barlovento m

windy[1] ['wɪn·di] <-ier, -iest> adj (weather) ventoso, -a

windy[2] ['waɪn·di] <-ier, -iest> adj (road) sinuoso, -a

wine [waɪn] n vino m

wine cooler n (drink) ≈ sangría f

wine list n carta f de vinos

winery ['waɪ·nə·ri] <-ies> n bodega f

wing [wɪŋ] I. n 1. ZOOL, AVIAT, ARCHIT, SPORTS, POL ala f; **the west ~ of the house** la ala oeste de la casa; **left/right ~** ala izquierda/derecha 2. ~**s** THEA bastidores mpl; **to be waiting in the ~s** estar esperando su oportunidad ▶ **to spread** [or °stretch] **one's ~s** desplegar las alas; **to take sb under one's ~** hacerse cargo de alguien II. vt (fly) volar ▶ **to ~ it** arreglárselas sobre la marcha

winger ['wɪŋ·ər] n SPORTS extremo, -a m, f; **left/right ~** extremo izquierdo/derecho

wing nut n TECH palomilla f

wingspan ['wɪŋ·spæn] n, **wingspread** ['wɪŋ·spred] n envergadura f

wink [wɪŋk] I. n guiño m; **to give sb a ~** guiñar el ojo a alguien ▶ **to have forty ~s** echarse una siestecita; **to not sleep a ~** no pegar ojo; **in a ~** en un tris II. vi guiñar el ojo (at a); (light) parpadear

winner ['wɪn·ər] n 1. (person) ganador(a) m(f) 2. inf (success) éxito m; (book) obra f premiada; **to be on to a ~** tener mucho éxito (with con)

winning ['wɪn·ɪŋ] I. adj 1. ganador(a); (ticket) premiado, -a; (point) decisivo, -a 2. (charming) encantador(a) II. n 1. triunfo m 2. ~**s** (money) ganancias fpl

winter ['wɪn·tər] I. n invierno m II. vi hibernar

winter sports npl deportes m pl de invierno

wint(e)ry ['wɪn·tri] adj invernal; fig frío, -a

wipe [waɪp] I. n 1. limpieza f; **to give the floor a ~** limpiar el suelo 2. (tissue) toallita f II. vt limpiar; (floor) fregar; (one's nose) sonarse; (disk) borrar; **to ~ dry** secar

◆**wipe down** vt limpiar

◆**wipe off** vt 1. quitar con un trapo; (data, program) borrar 2. ECON reducir ▶ **to wipe the smile off sb's face** borrar a alguien la sonrisa de la cara

◆**wipe out** vt 1. (destroy) exterminar; (economically) arruinar; (debt) liquidar 2. (tire out) dejar hecho polvo

◆**wipe up** I. vt limpiar II. vi secar

wire ['waɪr] I. n 1. (metal thread) alambre m 2. ELEC cable m 3. (hidden microphone) micro m (oculto) 4. (prison camp fence) alambrada f 5. inf **to get one's ~s crossed** tener un malentendido; **to get** (sth) **in under the ~** conseguir algo justo a tiempo II. vt ELEC conectar

wireless ['waɪr·lɪs] adj inalámbrico, -a

wiretapping ['waɪr·ˌtæp·ɪŋ] n escuchas f pl telefónicas

wire transfer n transferencia f por cable

wiring ['waɪ·rɪŋ] n ELEC 1. (system of wires) cableado m 2. (electrical installation) instalación f eléctrica

wisdom ['wɪz·dəm] n 1. sabiduría f; **with the ~ of hindsight** con la sabiduría que da la experiencia; **~ comes with age** más sabe el diablo por viejo que por diablo prov 2. (sensibleness) prudencia f

wisdom tooth <- teeth> n muela f del juicio

wise [waɪz] adj 1. (having knowledge) sabio, -a 2. (showing sagacity) acertado, -a 3. (sensible) sensato, -a 4. inf (aware) consciente; **to be ~ to sb** tener calado a alguien; **to be ~ to sth** estar al tanto de algo; **to get ~** caer en la cuenta (to de); **to be none the ~r** seguir sin enterarse (for de)

◆**wise up** sl I. vi ponerse al tanto (to de) II. vt poner al tanto (about de)

wisecrack ['waɪz·kræk] I. n coña f II. vi estar de coña

wise guy n sl gracioso, -a m, f

wish [wɪʃ] I. <-es> n 1. (desire) deseo *m;* **against my ~es** en contra de mi voluntad; **to make a ~** pedir un deseo; **to have no ~** no tener ganas (to de) **2. ~s** (*greetings*) recuerdos *mpl;* **give him my best ~es** dale muchos recuerdos de mi parte; (**with**) **best ~es** un abrazo **II.** *vt* **1.** (*desire*) desear; **I ~ he hadn't come** ojalá no hubiera venido; **I ~ you'd told me** me lo podrías haber dicho **2.** *form* (*want*) **to ~ to do sth** querer hacer algo **3.** (*hope*) **to ~ sb luck** desear suerte a alguien; **to ~ sb happy birthday** felicitar a alguien por su cumpleaños; **to ~ sb good night** dar las buenas noches a alguien **III.** *vi* **to ~ (for)** desear; **as you ~** como usted mande; **if you ~** como quieras; **everything one could ~ for** todo lo que uno podría desear

wishbone [ˈwɪʃ·boʊn] *n* espoleta *f*

wishful thinking *n* ilusión *f*

wishy-washy [ˈwɪʃ·i·ˌwɑʃ·i] *adj* insípido, -a; (*drink, soup*) aguado, -a; (*argument*) flojo, -a

wisp [wɪsp] *n* (*hair*) mechón *m*

wispy [ˈwɪs·pi] <-ier, -iest> *adj* (*hair*) ralo, -a; (*person*) menudo, -a; (*clouds*) tenue

wistful [ˈwɪst·fəl] *adj* nostálgico, -a; (*longing*) añorante

wit [wɪt] *n* **1.** (*humor*) ingenio *m;* **to have a dry ~** ser mordaz **2.** (*intelligence*) inteligencia *f;* **to be at one's ~s' end** estar para volverse loco; **to gather one's ~s** poner las ideas en orden; **to have/keep one's ~s about one** andar con mucho ojo; **to live off one's ~s** vivir del cuento **3.** (*person*) chistoso, -a *m, f*

witch [wɪtʃ] <-es> *n* bruja *f*

witchcraft [ˈwɪtʃ·kræft] *n* brujería *f,* payé *m CSur*

witch doctor *n* curandero, -a *m, f,* payé *m CSur*

witch-hunt [ˈwɪtʃ·hʌnt] *n* caza *f* de brujas

with [wɪð, wɪθ] *prep* **1.** (*accompanied by, by means of*) con; (*together*) **~ sb** (junto) con alguien; **to take sth ~ both hands** tomar algo con las dos manos **2.** (*having*) **the man ~ the umbrella** el hombre del paraguas; **~ no hesitation at all** sin ningún titubeo **3.** (*manner*)

~ all speed a toda velocidad; **~ one's whole heart** de todo corazón; **to cry ~ rage** llorar de rabia **4.** (*despite*) **~ all his faults** a pesar de todos sus defectos **5.** (*supporting*) **to be ~ sb/sth** estar de acuerdo con alguien/algo; **popular ~ young people** popular entre los jóvenes **6.** (*understanding*) **I'm not ~ you** no te sigo; **to be ~ it** estar al tanto; **to get ~ it** ponerse al día

withdraw [wɪðˈdrɔ] *irr* **I.** *vt* **1.** (*take out*) quitar; (*money*) sacar **2.** (*take back*) retirar **3.** (*cancel*) cancelar **II.** *vi* **1.** (*leave*) retirarse (**from** de) **2.** (*socially*) recluirse; (*into silence*) retraerse

withdrawal [wɪðˈdrɔ·əl] *n* **1. a.** MIL retirada *f;* **to make a ~** FIN sacar dinero **2.** (*sports*) abandono *m* **3.** PSYCH retraimiento *m* **4.** MED abstinencia *f;* **to go through ~** presentar síndrome de abstinencia

wither [ˈwɪð·ər] *vi* marchitarse; *fig* debilitarse ▶ **to ~ on the vine** desaparecer poco a poco **II.** *vt* (*plant*) marchitar; (*strength*) mermar

withering [ˈwɪð·ər·ɪŋ] *adj* destructivo, -a; (*heat, fire*) abrasador(a); (*criticism*) hiriente

withhold [wɪðˈhoʊld] *irr vt* ocultar (**from** a); (*support*) negar; (*benefits, rent*) retener

within [wɪðˈɪn] **I.** *prep* **1.** (*place*) dentro de, en; **~ the country** dentro del país; **~ sight/easy reach** al alcance de la vista/mano; **~ 5 miles of the town** a menos de 8 km de la ciudad **2.** (*time*) en (el transcurso de); **~ 3 days** en (el plazo de) tres días **3.** (*according to*) de acuerdo a; **~ the law** dentro de la legalidad **II.** *adv* dentro; **from ~** desde dentro

without [wɪðˈaʊt] *prep* sin; **~ warning** sin previo aviso; **to do ~ sth** apañárselas sin algo

withstand [wɪðˈstænd] *irr vt* resistir; (*heat, pressure*) soportar

witness [ˈwɪt·nɪs] **I.** *n* **a.** LAW testigo *mf* (**to** de); **according to ~es** según testigos **II.** *vt* **1.** (*see*) ser testigo de; (*changes*) presenciar; **to ~ sb doing sth** observar a alguien haciendo algo **2.** (*authenticate*) dar fe de

W

witness stand n tribuna f

witty ['wɪt·i] <-ier, -iest> adj ingenioso, -a; (funny) gracioso, -a

wizard ['wɪz·ərd] n mago, -a m, f; (expert) genio mf; **to be a ~ at sth** ser un genio haciendo algo

wobble ['wab·əl] I. vi tambalearse; (voice) temblar; (prices, shares) fluctuar II. n 1. (movement) tambaleo m 2. (sound) temblor m 3. ECON fluctuación f

wobbly ['wab·li] <-ier, -iest> adj tambaleante; (line) zigzagueante; (chair) cojo, -a; (voice) tembloroso, -a

woe [woʊ] n desgracia f; **~s** males mpl

wok [wak] n wok m

woke [woʊk] vt, vi pt of **wake**

woken ['woʊ·kən] vt, vi pp of **wake**

wolf [wʊlf] n. <wolves> n 1. lobo m 2. (seducer) donjuán m ▶ **a ~ in sheep's clothing** un lobo disfrazado de cordero; **to cry ~** dar una falsa alarma II. vt engullir

woman ['wʊm·ən] <women> n 1. mujer f; **~ candidate/president** candidata/presidenta f 2. inf parienta f

womb [wum] n útero m; **in the ~** en el seno materno

women's lib n inf abbr of **women's liberation** liberación f de la mujer

won [wʌn] vt, vi pt, pp of **win**

wonder ['wʌn·dər] I. vt preguntarse; **to make sb ~** hacer pensar a alguien; **I ~ why he said that** me extraña que dijera eso II. vi 1. (ask oneself) preguntarse; **to ~ about doing sth** pensar si hacer algo 2. (feel surprise) sorprenderse (at sth); **I don't ~ (at it)** no me extraña III. n 1. (marvel) maravilla f; **to do [or work] ~s** hacer maravillas; **the ~s of modern technology** los prodigios de la tecnología moderna; **it's a ~ (that)...** es un milagro que... +subj; **~ (will) never cease!** ¡eso sí es increíble! 2. (feeling) asombro m; **in ~** con asombro; **to listen in ~** escuchar estupefacto

wonder drug n remedio m milagroso

wonderful ['wʌn·dər·fəl] adj maravilloso, -a

wonderland ['wʌn·dər·lænd] n país m de las maravillas

won't [woʊnt] = **will not** see **will**

woo [wu] vt 1. (attract) atraer 2. (court) cortejar

wood [wʊd] n 1. (material) madera f; (for a fire) leña f 2. **~s** bosque m ▶ (to) **touch [or knock on] ~** tocar madera; **to be out of the ~s** estar a salvo

woodcut n grabado f en madera

wooded ['wʊd·ɪd] adj boscoso, -a

wooden ['wʊd·ən] adj 1. (of wood) de madera 2. (awkward) rígido, -a; (smile) inexpresivo, -a

woodland ['wʊd·lənd] n bosque m

woodpecker n pájaro m carpintero

woodpile n montón m de leña

woodshed ['wʊd·ʃed] n leñera f

woodwind ['wʊd·wɪnd] adj de viento

woodwork ['wʊd·wɜrk] n **to come out of the ~** salir de quién sabe dónde

woodworm n inv ZOOL carcoma f

woody ['wʊd·i] I. <-ier, -iest> adj 1. (tough like wood) leñoso, -a 2. (wooded) boscoso, -a II. n empalmada f

wool [wʊl] n lana f ▶ **to pull the ~ over sb's eyes** dar a alguien gato por liebre

woolen [wʊl] adj, **woollen** ['wʊl·ən] adj de lana

woolly n, **wooly** ['wʊl·i] <-ier, -iest> adj 1. (of wool) de lana 2. (wool-like) lanoso, -a 3. (vague) vago, -a

word [wɜrd] n 1. palabra f; **of few ~s** de pocas palabras; **to not breathe a ~** no decir ni pío (of); **in other ~s** en otros términos; **~ for ~** palabra por palabra 2. (news) noticia f; (message) mensaje m; **to get ~** enterarse (of de); **to have ~ from sb** tener un recado de alguien (from de); **to have ~ that...** tener conocimiento de que... 3. (order) orden f; **a ~ of advice** un consejo; **a ~ of warning/caution** una advertencia; **just say the ~** sólo tienes que pedirlo 4. (promise) palabra f (de honor); **to keep one's ~** cumplir su promesa 5. **~s** (lyrics) letra f ▶ **to have a quick ~** hablar en privado (with con); **by ~ of mouth** de viva voz; **to take the ~s (right) out of sb's mouth** quitar a alguien la palabra de la boca; **to put in a good ~** interceder (for por); **~s fail me!** ¡no tengo palabras!; **from the ~ go**

desde el primer momento; **mark** my ~s! ¡toma nota!; **to mince** one's ~s medir sus palabras; **to not mince** one's ~s no tener pelos en la lengua

wording n 1. (*words*) términos mpl 2. (*style*) estilo m

word order n orden m de las palabras

word processor n procesador m de textos

wordy ['wɜr·di] <-ier, iest> adj farragoso, -a

wore [wɔr] vt, vi pt of **wear**

work [wɜrk] I. n 1. a. PHYS trabajo m; **to be hard** ~ (**doing sth**) (*strenuous*) costar mucho trabajo (hacer algo); **good** ~! ¡bien hecho!; **to be out of** ~ estar en paro 2. (*product*) a. ART, MUS obra f; **reference** ~ obra de consulta 3. ~s + sing/pl vb (*factory*) fábrica f; (*clock*) mecanismo m ▶ **to get to** ~ **on sth** ponerse manos a la obra con algo; **the** ~**s** sl toda la pesca II. vi 1. (*do job*) trabajar (**as a** de) 2. (*be busy*) estar ocupado; **to get** ~**ing** poner manos a la obra; **to** ~ **hard** ser aplicado; **to do sth** dedicarse a hacer algo 3. (*be successful*) a. TECH funcionar; MED hacer efecto 4. (*affect*) obrar (**against** en contra de); **to** ~ **both ways** ser un arma de doble filo 5. + adj **to** ~ **free/loose** soltarse/desprenderse ▶ **to** ~ **like a charm** funcionar de maravilla; **to** ~ **like a dog** [or **slave**] trabajar como un esclavo; **to** ~ **around** prepararse con tranquilidad (**to** para) III. vt 1. **to** ~ **sb hard** hacer trabajar duro a alguien; **to** ~ **oneself to death** matarse trabajando; **to** ~ **a forty-hour week** trabajar 40 horas semanales 2. TECH hacer que funcione; **to be** ~**ed** ser accionado (**by** por) 3. (*move*) mover; **to** ~ **sth free/loose** liberar/desprender algo; **to** ~ **one's way** abrirse camino (**along** por) 4. (*bring about*) producir; (*cure*) efectuar; **to** ~ **it** [or **things**] **so that...** arreglárselas para que... +subj 5. (*shape*) tallar; (*bronze, iron*) trabajar

◆**work away** vi trabajar sin parar

◆**work in** vt introducir; (*fit in*) colocar; CULIN añadir

◆**work off** vt contrarrestar; (*anger, frus-*

tration) desahogar; (*stress*) aliviar; (*debt, loan*) amortizar

◆**work out** I. vt 1. (*solve*) resolver; **to** **work things out** arreglárselas 2. (*calculate*) calcular 3. (*develop*) desarrollar; (*solution*) encontrar 4. (*understand*) darse cuenta II. vi 1. (*sum*) resultar; (*cheaper*) salir 2. (*be resolved*) resolverse 3. (*be successful*) acabar bien; **to** ~ **for the best** salir perfectamente

◆**work up** vt 1. (*generate*) sacar; (*courage, energy, enthusiasm*) estimular; **to** **work oneself up** emocionarse; **to work** **sb up into a rage** sacar a alguien de quicio 2. (*develop*) desarrollar; (*plan*) llevar a cabo; (*business*) fomentar; **to work** **one's way up through the company** ir ascendiendo en la empresa

workaholic ['wɜrk·ə·ho·lɪk] n trabajador (a) m(f) compulsivo

workbench <-es> n mesa f de trabajo

workbook n cuaderno m de ejercicios

workday n (*weekday*) día m laborable; (*time*) jornada f laboral

worker ['wɜr·kər] n trabajador(a) m(f); (*in factory*) obrero, -a m, f

working adj 1. (*employed*) empleado, -a; (*population*) activo, -a 2. (*pertaining to work*) laboral 3. (*functioning*) que funciona 4. **a** ~ **knowledge** conocimientos básicos (**of** de)

working class ['wɜr·kɪŋ·klæs] <-es> n clase f obrera

working-class adj obrero, -a; (*background*) humilde

workload ['wɜrk·loʊd] n (volumen m de) trabajo m; **to have a heavy/light/unbearable** ~ tener mucho/poco/demasiado trabajo

workman ['wɜrk·mən] <-men> n obrero m

workmanlike ['wɜrk·mən·laɪk] adj profesional

workmanship ['wɜrk·mən·ʃɪp] n (*skill*) destreza f; **shoddy** ~ mala calidad; **of fine** ~ de excelente factura

work of art n obra f de arte

workout ['wɜrk·aʊt] n entrenamiento m

work permit n permiso m de trabajo

workplace n (lugar m de) trabajo m

work-sharing ['wɜrk·ʃer·ɪŋ] n sistema

en el cual dos personas comparten un puesto laboral

workshop ['wɜrk·ʃap] *n* taller *m;* UNIV seminario *m*

workstation *n* estación *f* de trabajo

workweek ['wɜrk·wik] *n* semana *f* laborable

world [wɜrld] *n* mundo *m;* the ~'s **population** la población mundial; the ~ **champion** el campeón del mundo; the **best/worst in the** ~ el mejor/peor del mundo; the (**whole**) ~ **over** en el mundo entero; **to see the** ~ ver mundo; the ~ **of dogs** el mundo del perro; the **animal** ~ el mundo animal; the **New/Old/Third** ~ el Nuevo/Viejo/Tercer Mundo ▶ **to be a** ~ **of difference between...** haber un abismo entre...; **he/she has the** ~ **at his/her feet** el ~ **is his/her oyster** tiene el mundo a sus pies; **to feel on top of the** ~ estar en el séptimo cielo; **that's the way** the ~ **is** así es la vida; **to be for all** the ~ **like...** ser exactamente como...; **to be** ~**s apart** ser como la noche y el día; **to be dead to the** ~ dormir como un tronco; **to be out of this** ~ ser algo nunca visto; **it's a small** ~! ¡el mundo es un pañuelo!; **to move up/down in the** ~ *inf* prosperar/venir a menos; **to live in a** ~ **of one's own** vivir en su mundo; **to mean (all) the** ~ serlo todo (**to** para); **to think the** ~ tener un alto concepto (**of** de); **what/who/how in the** ~**...?** ¿qué/quién/cómo demonios...?

World Bank *n* the ~ el Banco Mundial

world-class *adj* mundialmente reconocido, -a

World Cup *n* SPORTS the ~ la Copa del Mundo; the ~ **Finals** la final de la Copa del Mundo

world-famous ['wɜrld·,feɪ·məs] *adj* de fama mundial

worldly ['wɜrld·li] *adj* **1.** (*goods*) material **2.** (*having experience*) mundano, -a; (*manner*) sofisticado, -a; ~ **wise** cosmopolita

world record *n* récord *m* mundial

world war *n* guerra *f* mundial

worldwide ['wɜrld·,waɪd] I. *adj* mundial II. *adv* por todo el mundo

worm [wɜrm] I. *n a.* COMPUT gusano *m;* (*larva*) oruga *f;* **earth** ~ lombriz *f,* gusano II. *vt* (*treat for worms*) desparasitar; **to** ~ **one's way through people** colarse entre la gente; **to** ~ **a secret** sonsacar un secreto (**out of** a)

worn [wɔrn] I. *vt, vi pp of* wear II. *adj* (*deteriorated*) desgastado, -a; (*clothing*) raído, -a; (*person*) ojeroso, -a; (*expression, news, story*) tópico, -a

worn-out [,wɔrn·'aʊt] *adj* (*exhausted*) rendido, -a; (*clothing*) raído, -a

worried *adj* preocupado, -a (**about, by** por); ~ **sick** preocupadísimo; **I am** ~ **that he may be angry** tengo miedo de que esté enfadado

worry ['wɜr·i] I. <-ies> *n* (*anxiety, concern*) preocupación *f;* (*trouble*) problema *m;* **financial worries** problemas económicos; **to be a cause of** ~ dar problemas (**to** a); **to have a** ~ estar preocupado (**about** por); **it is a great** ~ **to me** me preocupa mucho II. *vt* <-ie-, -ing> **1.** (*concern*) preocupar; **she is worried that she might not be able to find a job** tiene miedo de no encontrar trabajo; **that doesn't** ~ **me** eso me tiene sin cuidado **2.** (*bother*) molestar III. <-ie-, -ing> *vi* preocuparse (**about** por); **don't** ~ no te preocupes; **not to** ~! ¡no pasa nada!

worrying *adj* preocupante

worse [wɜrs] I. *adj comp of* bad peor; **to be even/much** ~ ser aún/mucho peor (**than** que); **from bad to** ~ de mal en peor; **to get** ~ **and** ~ ser cada vez peor; **it could have been** ~ podría haber sido peor; **to make matters** ~ por si fuera poco; **so much the** ~ **for her!** ¡peor para ella!; **to get** ~ empeorar II. *n* **the** ~ el/la peor; **to change for the** ~ cambiar para mal; **to have seen** ~ haber visto cosas peores; ~ **was to follow** lo peor estaba por llegar III. *adv comp of* badly peor (**than** que); **to be** ~ (**off**) estar peor

worsen ['wɜr·sən] *vi, vt* empeorar

worship ['wɜr·ʃɪp] *vt* <-pp-, -p-> **1.** *a.* REL adorar; **to** ~ **money/sex** tener obsesión por el dinero/sexo **2.** (*admire*) idolatrar ▶ **to** ~ **the ground sb walks on**

besar el suelo que alguien pisa **II.** *n a.* REL culto *m; (adoration)* adoración *f*

worst [wɜrst] **I.** *adj superl of* **bad**; **the ~ el/la peor**; **the ~ soup I've ever eaten** la peor sopa que he comido nunca; **the ~ mistake** el error más grave **II.** *adv superl of* **badly** peor; **to be ~ affected** ser los más afectados **(by** por**) III.** *n* **the ~** lo peor; **the ~ of it, ~ of all** lo peor de todo; **the ~ is over now** ya ha pasado lo peor; **at ~** en el peor de los casos; **at her ~** en su peor momento; **to fear the ~** temerse lo peor ▶ **if (the) ~ comes to (the) ~** en el peor de los casos; **to get the ~ of it** llevarse la peor parte

worth [wɜrθ] **I.** *n* valor *m; (person)* valía *f; (wealth)* fortuna *f;* **to be of great/ little ~** tener gran/poco valor **(to** para**);** **$4,000 ~ of items** objetos por valor de 4.000$; **to get one's money's ~** sacar partido **(from** a**) II.** *adj* **1.** COM, FIN, ECON **to be ~** valer; **it is ~ about $2,000** está valorado en unos 2.000$; **it's ~ a lot** tiene mucho valor **(to** para**) 2.** *(significant, useful)* **to be ~** merecer; **to be ~ a mention/seeing** ser digno de mención/ver; **it's not ~ arguing about** no vale la pena discutir por eso; **it's ~ a try** vale la pena intentarlo ▶ **to be ~ sb's while** compensar; **for all one's ~** con todas sus fuerzas; **for what it's ~** por si sirve de algo; **to be (well) ~ it** valer la pena

worthless ['wɜrθ·lɪs] *adj (no value)* sin ningún valor; *(no use)* inútil

worthwhile [,wɜrθ·'hwaɪl] *adj* **1.** *(beneficial)* que vale la pena; **it's not ~ making such an effort** no merece la pena esforzarse tanto; **it isn't financially ~ for me** no me compensa económicamente **2.** *(useful)* útil

worthy ['wɜr·ði] <-ier, -iest> *adj* **1.** *(admirable)* encomiable; *(principles)* loable; *(cause)* noble **2.** *(appropriate)* digno, -a *(of* de*);* **to be ~ of attention** merecer atención

would [wʊd] *aux pt of* **will 1.** *(future in the past)* **he said he ~ do it later on** dijo que lo haría más tarde **2.** *(past in the past)* **we thought they ~ have done it before** pensamos que lo ha-

brían hecho antes **3.** *(intention)* **he said he ~ always love her** dijo que siempre la querría **4.** *(possibility)* **I'd go myself, but I'm too busy** iría yo, pero estoy muy liado **5.** *(conditional)* **what ~ you do if you lost your job?** ¿qué harías si te quedaras sin trabajo? **6.** *(request)* **~ you phone him, please?** ¿me harías el favor de llamarlo?; **~ you like...?** ¿te gustaría...?; **~ you like me to come with you?** ¿quieres que vaya contigo? **7.** *(regularity)* **they ~ help each other with their homework** solían ayudarse con los deberes; **he ~ say that, wouldn't he** era de esperar que lo dijera, ¿no? **8.** *(opinion)* **I ~ imagine that...** me imagino que... **9.** *(probability)* **he had an Australian accent — that ~ be Tom** tenía acento australiano — debía de ser Tom **10.** *(preference)* **I ~ rather have water** prefiero beber agua **11.** *(advice)* **I ~n't worry, if I were you** yo que tú no me preocuparía **12.** *(motive)* **why ~ anyone do something like that?** ¿por qué haría nadie algo así?

would-be ['wʊd·bi] *adj* aspirante a

wouldn't ['wʊd·ənt] = **would not** *see* **would**

wound[1] [waʊnd] *vi, vt pt, pp of* **wind**[2]

wound[2] [wund] **I.** *n* herida *f;* **a leg/ war ~** una herida en la pierna/de guerra **II.** *vt* herir

wounded ['wun·dɪd] **I.** *adj* herido, -a **II.** *npl* **the ~** los heridos

woven ['woʊ·vən] **I.** *vt, vi pp of* **weave II.** *adj* tejido, -a

wow [waʊ] *inf* **I.** *interj* hala, caray *AmL* **II.** *n* exitazo *m;* **I had a ~ of a time** me lo pasé en grande **III.** *vt* volver loco

wrap [ræp] **I.** *n* **1.** *(robe)* bata *f* **2.** *(shawl)* chal *m* **3.** *(packaging)* envoltorio *m;* **foil ~** papel *m* de aluminio **II.** *vt* <-pp-> envolver **(in** con**);** **he ~ped a scarf around his neck** se puso una bufanda; **to ~ one's fingers around sth** agarrar algo con las manos

◆ **wrap up I.** *vt* <-pp-> **1.** *(cover)* envolver **2.** *inf (finish)* poner fin a; *(deal)* cerrar; **that wraps it up for today** eso es todo por hoy **II.** *vi* **1. to ~**

W

(**well/warm**) abrigarse (bien) **2. to be wrapped up in sth** estar absorto en algo; **to be wrapped up in one's work** vivir para el trabajo **3.** (*finish*) terminar

wrapper ['ræp·ər] n **1.** (*packaging*) envoltorio m; (*book*) sobrecubierta f **2.** (*robe*) bata f

wrapping paper n papel m de regalo; (*plain*) papel de embalar

wreath [riθ] <wreaths> n corona f

wreck [rek] I. vt (*damage*) destrozar; (*demolish*) derribar; (*hopes, plan*) arruinar II. n **1.** NAUT naufragio m; AUTO accidente m; **a ~ of a car** un coche siniestrado; **an old ~** un cacharro **2.** inf (*ruin*) ruina f; (*mess*) caos m; **to feel like a complete ~** estar hecho polvo; **to be a nervous ~** tener los nervios destrozados

wreckage ['rek·ɪdʒ] n restos mpl; (*building*) escombros mpl

wren [ren] n chochín m

wrench [rentʃ] I. vt **1.** (*pull*) arrancar (**from** a); (*ankle*) torcerse; (*shoulder*) dislocarse; **to ~ oneself away** soltarse de un tirón **2.** (*take from*) separar (**from** de) II. n **1.** (*tool*) llave f inglesa **2.** (*twist*) tirón m, jalón m CSur

wrestle ['res·əl] SPORTS I. <-ling> vt **1.** a. SPORTS luchar; **to ~ sb** forcejear con alguien **2.** fig lidiar con II. <-ling> vi luchar III. n lucha f

wrestler n luchador(a) m(f)

wrestling n lucha f; **freestyle ~** lucha libre

wrestling match n combate m de lucha

wretched ['retʃ·ɪd] adj **1.** (*miserable*) desdichado, -a; (*state*) lamentable; (*house, conditions*) miserable **2.** (*despicable*) despreciable **3.** (*awful*) horrible; (*sick*) mal

wriggle ['rɪg·əl] I. <-ling> vi **1.** (*squirm*) retorcerse **2.** (*move*) deslizarse (**through** por); fig escapar (**out of** de) II. <-ling> vt menear; **to ~** (**one's way**) **out of sth** escaquearse de algo inf

wring [rɪŋ] <wrung, wrung> vt (*twist*) retorcer; (*water*) escurrir

wrinkle ['rɪŋ·kəl] I. n (*crease*) arruga f

II. <-ling> vi (*form folds, creases*) arrugarse; (*apple, fruit*) pasarse III. <-ling> vt arrugar ▶ **to ~ one's brow** fruncir el ceño

wrinkled adj, **wrinkly** ['rɪŋ·kli] adj arrugado, -a; (*fruit*) pasado, -a

wrist [rɪst] n muñeca f; (*of garment*) puño m

wristband ['rɪst·bænd] n **1.** (*sleeve*) puño m **2.** (*strap*) correa f **3.** (*sweatband*) muñequera f

wristwatch <-es> n reloj m de pulsera

write [raɪt] <wrote, written, writing> I. vt **1.** escribir; **to ~ a check** extender un cheque **2.** MUS componer; (*song*) escribir **3.** COMPUT (*save*) grabar (**to** en) ▶ **to be nothing to ~ home about** no ser nada del otro mundo II. vi escribir; **to ~ clearly** escribir con letra clara; **to ~ to sb/about sth** escribir a alguien/sobre algo

◆**write away** vi **to ~ for sth** solicitar algo por escrito

◆**write back** vt, vi contestar

◆**write down** vt apuntar

◆**write in** vt (*insert*) escribir

◆**write off** I. vi **to ~ for** solicitar por escrito II. vt (*attempt*) abandonar; (*project*) dar por perdido; (*debt*) cancelar; **~ as useless** descartar por inútil

◆**write out** vt **1.** (*copy*) copiar **2.** (*fill in*) rellenar **3.** (*remove*) suprimir

◆**write up** vt redactar; **to ~ a concert** escribir la crítica de un concierto

write-off ['raɪt·ɔf] n (*beyond repair*) siniestro m total; **the camera was a complete ~** la cámara estaba hecha trizas

write-protected ['raɪt·prə·tek·təd] adj protegido, -a contra escritura

writer ['raɪ·tər] n escritor(a) m(f); **~ of children's books** autor(a) m(f) de libros infantiles; **DVD ~** grabadora f de DVD

write-up ['raɪt·ʌp] n crítica f

writing ['raɪ·tɪŋ] n **1.** (*handwriting*) letra f; **to put sth in ~** poner algo por escrito; **there was some ~ in...** había algo escrito en... **2.** a. LIT escribir m; **creative ~** escritura f creativa **3.** (*written work*) obra f

writing desk *n* escritorio *m*

writing paper *n* papel *m* de carta

written ['rɪt·ən] I. *vt, vi pp of* **write** II. *adj* escrito, -a ▶ **to have guilt ~ all over one's face** llevar la culpa escrita en la cara

wrong [rɔŋ] I. *adj* **1.** (*not right*) incorrecto, -a; **to be ~ about sth/sb** equivocarse en algo/con alguien; **he is ~ in thinking...** se equivoca si piensa...; **to be in the ~ place** estar mal colocado; **to be plainly ~** estar completamente equivocado; **to get the ~ number** equivocarse de número **2.** (*not appropriate*) inoportuno, -a; **this is the ~ time** no es el momento oportuno (**to para**) **3.** (*bad*) mal; **it is ~ to...** está mal...; **it was ~ of him** ha hecho muy mal; **what's ~ with that?** ¿qué hay de malo en ello?; **is there anything ~?** ¿te pasa algo?; **what's ~ with you today?** ¿qué te pasa hoy?; **something's ~ with the radio** la radio no funciona bien ▶ **to fall into the ~ hands** caer en manos equivocadas II. *adv* mal; **to get sth ~** equivocarse en algo; **to get it ~** entender mal; **don't get me ~** no me malinterpretes; **to go ~** equivocarse; (*fail*) salir mal; (*machine*) estropearse, descomponerse *Méx* III. *n* mal *m*; **to put sb in the ~** echar la culpa a alguien; **to do sb no ~** no hacer nada malo a alguien; **to suffer a ~** sufrir una injusticia ▶ **to do ~** obrar mal; **he can do no ~** es incapaz de hacer nada malo

wrongdoing *n* maldad *f*; LAW delito *m*

wrongful *adj* injusto, -a; (*arrest*) ilegal; (*dismissal*) improcedente

wrongly *adv* mal; (*believe, state*) erróneamente; (*accuse, convict*) injustamente

wrote [roʊt] *vi, vt pt of* **write**

wrought iron *n* hierro *m* forjado

wrung [rʌŋ] *vt pt, pp of* **wring**

wry [raɪ] <wrier, wriest *or* wryer, wryest> *adj* (*dry and ironic*) cáustico, -a; **to make a ~ face** torcer el gesto

WSW *abbr of* **west-southwest** OSO

X

X, x [eks] *n* **1.** X, x *f;* **~ as in X-ray** X de xilófono **2.** MATH x **3. Mr./Mrs./Ms. ~** el Sr./la Sra. X **4.** (*cross*) aspa *f*

xenophobia [ˌzen·ə·'foʊ·bi·ə] *n* xenofobia *f*

xenophobic [ˌzen·ə·'foʊ·bɪk] *adj* xenófobo, -a

Xmas ['krɪs·məs] *n abbr of* **Christmas** Navidad *f*

X-ray ['eks·reɪ] I. *n* **1.** (*photo*) radiografía *f;* **~s** rayos *m pl* X **2.** (*department*) radiología *f* II. *vt* hacer una radiografía de

xylophone ['zaɪ·lə·foʊn] *n* xilófono *m*

Y

Y, y [waɪ] *n* **1.** Y, y *f;* **~ as in Yankee** Y de yema **2.** MATH y

yacht [jɑt] I. *n* yate *m;* (*for racing*) velero *m;* **~ club** club *m* náutico; **~ race** regata *f* II. *vi* navegar

yachting *n* **to go ~** navegar

yachtsman ['jɑts·mən] <-men> *n* (*owner*) dueño *m* de un yate; (*sailor*) regatista *m*

yam [jæm] *n* ñame *m;* (*sweet potato*) batata *f,* camote *m AmL*

yank [jæŋk] *inf* I. *vt, vi* **to ~ (on) sth** tirar de algo, jalar de algo *AmL;* **she ~ed at his hair** le tiró del pelo II. *n* tirón *m,* jalón *m AmL*

◆ **yank out** *vt* sacar de un tirón

Yank [jæŋk] *n,* **Yankee** ['jæŋ·ki] *n pej inf* yanqui *mf,* gringo, -a *m, f AmL*

yap [jæp] I. <-pp-> *vi* **1.** (*bark*) ladrar **2.** *sl* cotorrear II. *n* **1.** (*bark*) ladrido *m* **2.** *sl* cotorreo *m*

yard[1] [jɑrd] *n* yarda *f (0'91 m);* **square ~** yarda cuadrada

yard[2] [jɑrd] *n* **1.** (*paved area*) patio *m* **2.** (*land*) jardín *m* **3.** (*work area*) taller *m* **4.** (*storage*) almacén *m* **5.** (*livestock*) corral *m*

yardstick ['jɑrd·stɪk] *n* (*standard*) criterio *m*

yarn [jarn] *n* **1.** (*thread*) hilo *m* **2.** (*story*) trola *f;* **to spin a ~** inventarse una trola

yawn [jɔn] I. *vi* bostezar II. *n* bostezo *m;* **it was a ~** *fig* fue un rollo

yawning *adj* **1.** (*bored*) que bosteza **2.** (*chasm, crater*) enorme; **there's a ~ gap** hay un abismo (**between** entre)

yea [jeɪ] *n* voto *m* a favor

yeah [jeə] *adv inf* sí; **oh ~!** *iron* ¡no me digas!

year [jɪr] *n* **1.** año *m;* **~ of birth** año de nacimiento; **~ in, ~ out** año tras año; **fiscal ~** ejercicio *f* fiscal; **leap ~** año bisiesto; **all (the) ~ round** (durante) todo el año; **every other ~** cada dos años; **happy new ~!** ¡feliz año nuevo!; **last/next ~** el año pasado/que viene; **$5000 a ~** 5.000$ al año; **this ~** este año; **I'm eight ~s old** tengo ocho años; **~s ago** hace años; **it's been ~s since...** hacía años que no...; **it'll be ~s before...** pasarán años hasta que...; **over the ~s** con el tiempo **2.** SCHOOL, UNIV curso *m*

yearbook [ˈjɪr·bʊk] *n* anuario *m*

yearly I. *adj* anual; **on a ~ basis** cada año II. *adv* anualmente; **twice ~** dos veces al año

yearn [jɜrn] *vi* ansiar; **to ~ after/for** anhelar/añorar

yearning *n* anhelo *m* (**for** de); **to have a ~ to do sth** tener ansias de hacer algo

yeast [jist] *n* levadura *f*

yell [jel] I. *n* chillido *m;* **a ~ of laughter** una carcajada II. *vi* chillar; **to ~ at sb (to do sth)** gritar a alguien (para que haga algo); **to ~ for sb/help** llamar a alguien/pedir ayuda a gritos III. *vt* gritar

yellow [ˈjel·oʊ] I. *adj* **1.** amarillo, -a; **golden ~** amarillo canario **2.** (*cowardly*) **gallina** II. *n* amarillo *m;* (*egg*) yema *f*

yellow fever *n* fiebre *f* amarilla

Yellow Pages® *npl* **the ~** las páginas amarillas

yelp [jelp] I. *vi* gritar (**with** de); (*dog*) aullar II. *n* grito *m;* (*dog*) aullido *m*

yen [jen] *inv n* yen *m*

yep [jep] *adv inf* sí

yes [jes] *adv* sí; **~, please** sí, por favor; **to answer ~** contestar que sí (**to** a); **~ indeed** por supuesto que sí; **~, of course** claro que sí; **~?** ¿sí?; **oh ~?** ¿de verdad?

yesterday [ˈjes·tər·deɪ] *adv* ayer; **~ morning** ayer por la mañana, ayer en la mañana *AmL*, ayer a la mañana *CSur;* **the day before ~** anteayer, antes de ayer

yet [jet] I. *adv* **1.** (*till now*) aún; **it's too early ~ to...** aún es muy pronto para...; **not ~** aún no; **as ~** hasta ahora; **have you finished ~?** ¿ya has terminado?; **the best is ~ to come** aún queda lo mejor; **~ again** otra vez más; **~ more food** aún más comida; **~ bigger/more beautiful** aún más grande/bonito **2.** (*despite that*) sin embargo; (*in spite of everything*) a pesar de todo; **you'll do it ~** algún día lo conseguirás II. *conj* con todo

yew [ju] *n* tejo *m*

Yiddish [ˈjɪd·ɪʃ] *adj, n* yiddish *m*

yield [jild] I. *n* rendimiento *m;* AGR producción *f;* COM, FIN beneficio *m;* (*interest*) interés *m* II. *vt* **1.** (*results*) dar; (*information*) proporcionar; (*profit*) proporcionar **2.** AGR producir **3.** **to ~ ground** ceder terreno; **to ~ responsibility** delegar responsabilidades III. *vi* AGR, COM, FIN ser productivo; **to ~ to** ceder ante; (*give priority*) dar prioridad a

yodel [ˈjoʊ·dəl] *n* canción *f* tirolesa

yoga [ˈjoʊ·gə] *n* yoga *m*

yoghourt *n*, **yoghurt** [ˈjoʊ·gərt] *n see* **yogurt**

yogi [ˈjoʊ·gi] *n* yogui *mf*

yogurt [ˈjoʊ·gərt] *n* yogur *m*

yoke [joʊk] I. *n* yugo *m;* **to throw off the ~** liberarse del yugo II. *vt* **to ~ two things together** ligar una cosa a otra

yokel [ˈjoʊ·kəl] *n* paleto, -a *m, f,* pajuerano, -a *m, f Arg, Bol, Urug*

yolk [joʊk] *n* yema *f*

you [ju] *pron pers* **1.** *2nd pers sing* tú, vos *CSur,* *pl:* vosotros, -as, ustedes *AmL;* **I see ~** te/os veo; **do ~ see me?** ¿me ves/veis?; **it is for ~** es para ti/vosotros; **older than ~** mayor que tú/vosotros; **if I were ~** si yo fuera tú/vosotros **2.** (*2nd person sing, polite form*) usted *pl:* ustedes; **~ have a car** usted tiene/ustedes tienen un coche

you'd [jud] = **you would** *see* **would**

you'll [jul] = **you will** *see* **will**

young [jʌŋ] I. *adj* joven; **~ children**

niños pequeños; **my ~er brother/son** mi hermano/hijo menor; (*appearance, clothes*) juvenil; (*love*) de juventud ▶ **you're only** – **once!** ¡sólo se vive una vez! II. *n pl* **the ~** los jóvenes; ZOOL las crías

youngster ['jʌŋ·stər] *n* joven *mf*

your [jʊr] *adj pos* **1.** *2nd pers sing* tu(s) *pl:* vuestro(s), vuestra(s) **2.** (*2nd pers sing and pl: polite form*) su(s)

you're [jʊr] = **you are** *see* **be**

yours [jʊrz] *pron pos* **1.** *sing:* (el) tuyo, (la) tuya, (los) tuyos, (las) tuyas *pl:* vuestro, (la) vuestra, (los) vuestros, (las) vuestras, el/la de ustedes *AmL;* **this glass is ~** este vaso es tuyo/vuestro **2.** *polite form* (el) suyo, (la) suya, (los) suyos, (las) suyas; **~ truly** le saluda atentamente

yourself [jʊr·'self] *pron reflexive* **1.** *sing:* te *emphatic:* tú (mismo, misma) *after prep:* ti (mismo, misma) **2.** *polite form:* se *emphatic:* usted (mismo, misma) *after prep:* sí (mismo, misma)

yourselves *pron reflexive* **1.** os, se *AmL; emphatic, after prep:* vosotros (mismos), vosotras (mismas), ustedes (mismos, mismas) *AmL* **2.** *polite form:* se *emphatic:* ustedes (mismos, mismas) *after prep:* sí (mismos, mismas)

youth [juθ] *n* **1.** (*period*) juventud *f* **2.** (*young man*) joven *m* **3.** (*young people*) jóvenes *mpl*

youthful ['juθ·fəl] *adj* **1.** (*young-looking*) juvenil **2.** (*typical of the young*) de la juventud **3.** (*young*) joven

youth hostel *n* albergue *m* juvenil

you've [juv] = **you have** *see* **have**

yo-yo ['joʊ·joʊ] *n* yo-yo *m*

yuan [ju·'æn] *n* yuan *m*

yucky ['jʌk·i] *adj sl* asqueroso, -a

yummy ['jʌm·i] *adj* de rechupete

yuppie ['jʌp·i] *n* yuppy *mf*

Z

Z, z [zi] *n* Z, z *f;* **~ as in Zulu** Z de Zaragoza ▶ **to catch some ~'s** echar una cabezada, apolillar un poco *RíoPl*

zany ['zeɪ·ni] *<-ier, -iest> adj* (*person*) chiflado, -a; (*idea*) disparatado, -a; (*clothing*) estrafalario, -a

zap [zæp] I. *n.* <-pp-> *vt* (*destroy*) liquidar; (*send*) mandar echando leches II. <-pp-> *vi* **to ~ through the channels** hacer zapping; **to ~ somewhere** ir a un sitio echando leches III. *interj* ¡zas!

zapping ['zæp·ɪŋ] *n* zapping *m*

zealot ['zel·ət] *n* fanático, -a *m, f*

zealous ['zel·əs] *adj* ferviente; **to be ~ in** (**doing**) **sth** poner gran celo en (hacer) algo

zebra ['zi·brə] *n* cebra *f*

zero ['zɪr·oʊ] I. <-s *or* -es> *n* cero *m;* **below ~** bajo cero; **to be a ~** ser un cero a la izquierda II. *adj* cero *inv;* (*visibility*) nulo, -a; **my chances are ~** no tengo ninguna posibilidad

zigzag ['zɪg·zæg] I. *n* zigzag *m* II. *adj* zigzagueante; (*pattern*) en zigzag III. <-gg-> *vi* zigzaguear

zinc [zɪŋk] *n* zinc *m*

zip [zɪp] I. *n* **1.** (*ZIP code*) código *m* postal **2.** (*whistle*) silbido *m* **3.** (*vigor*) garra *f* **4.** *sl* (*nothing*) nada; **I know ~ about that** NPI *m* II. <-pp-> *vt* **to ~ sth open/shut/up** abrir/cerrar/subir la cremallera de algo III. <-pp-> *vi* **to ~ in/past** entrar/pasar volando; **the days ~ped by** los días pasaron volando

zipper ['zɪp·ər] *n* cremallera *f*

zippy ['zɪp·i] *<-ier, -iest> adj inf* (*fast*) veloz; (*energetic*) enérgico, -a

zodiac ['zoʊ·di·æk] *n* zodíaco *m*

zombie ['zam·bi] *n* zombi *mf*

zone [zoʊn] I. *n* zona *f;* **time ~** zona horaria II. *vt* dividir en zonas; **to ~ an area for residential use** declarar un lugar zona residencial

zoning *n* zonificación *f*

zoo [zu] *n* zoo *m*

zoological [ˌzoʊ·ə·'ladʒ·ɪ·kəl] *adj* zoológico, -a; **~ garden** parque *m* zoológico

zoologist [zoʊ·'al·ə·dʒɪst] *n* zoólogo, -a *m, f*

zoology [zoʊ·'al·ə·dʒi] *n* zoología *f*

zoom [zum] I. *n* **1.** PHOT zoom *m* **2.** (*buzz*) zumbido *m* II. *vi* (*move*) ir zumbando; **to ~ away** salir pitando;

to ~ past pasar volando; (*costs, sales*)
dispararse
◆**zoom in** *vi* enfocar en primer plano
◆**zoom out** *vi* cambiar a un plano general

zoom lens *n* zoom *m*
zucchini [zu-'ki-ni] <-(s)> *n inv* calabacín *m*, calabacita *f AmL*

Los verbos regulares e irregulares españoles
Spanish regular and irregular verbs

Abreviaturas:

pret. ind.	pretérito indefinido
subj. pres.	subjuntivo presente

Verbos regulares que terminan en *-ar*, *-er* e *-ir*

hablar

presente	imperfecto	pret. ind.	futuro	subj. pres.
hablo	hablaba	hablé	hablaré	hable
hablas	hablabas	hablaste	hablarás	hables
habla	hablaba	habló	hablará	hable
hablamos	hablábamos	hablamos	hablaremos	hablemos
habláis	hablabais	hablasteis	hablaréis	habléis
hablan	hablaban	hablaron	hablarán	hablen
gerundio hablando		**participio** hablado		

comprender

presente	imperfecto	pret. ind.	futuro	subj. pres.
comprendo	comprendía	comprendí	comprenderé	comprenda
comprendes	comprendías	comprendiste	comprenderás	comprendas
comprende	comprendía	comprendió	comprenderá	comprenda
comprendemos	comprendíamos	comprendimos	comprenderemos	comprendamos
comprendéis	comprendíais	comprendisteis	comprenderéis	comprendáis
comprenden	comprendían	comprendieron	comprenderán	comprendan
gerundio comprendiendo		**participio** comprendido		

recibir

presente	imperfecto	pret. ind.	futuro	subj. pres.
recibo	recibía	recibí	recibiré	reciba
recibes	recibías	recibiste	recibirás	recibas
recibe	recibía	recibió	recibirá	reciba
recibimos	recibíamos	recibimos	recibiremos	recibamos
recibís	recibíais	recibisteis	recibiréis	recibáis
reciben	recibían	recibieron	recibirán	reciban
gerundio recibiendo		**participio** recibido		

Verbos con cambios vocálicos

\<e → ie\>   **pensar**

presente	imperfecto	pret. ind.	futuro	subj. pres.
pienso	pensaba	pensé	pensaré	piense
piensas	pensabas	pensaste	pensarás	pienses
piensa	pensaba	pensó	pensará	piense
pensamos	pensábamos	pensamos	pensaremos	pensemos
pensáis	pensabais	pensasteis	pensaréis	penséis
piensan	pensaban	pensaron	pensarán	piensen
gerundio pensando		**participio** pensado		

\<o → ue\>   **contar**

presente	imperfecto	pret. ind.	futuro	subj. pres.
cuento	contaba	conté	contaré	cuente
cuentas	contabas	contaste	contarás	cuentes
cuenta	contaba	contó	contará	cuente
contamos	contábamos	contamos	contaremos	contemos
contáis	contabais	contasteis	contaréis	contéis
cuentan	contaban	contaron	contaron	cuenten
gerundio contando		**participio** contado		

Verbos con cambios ortográficos

<c → qu>   **atacar**

presente	imperfecto	pret. ind.	futuro	subj. pres.
ataco	atacaba	ataqué	atacaré	ataque
atacas	atacabas	atacaste	atacarás	ataques
ataca	atacaba	atacó	atacará	ataque
atacamos	atacábamos	atacamos	atacaremos	ataquemos
atacáis	atacabais	atacasteis	atacaréis	ataquéis
atacan	atacaban	atacaron	atacarán	ataquen
gerundio atacando		**participio** atacado		

<g → gu>   **pagar**

presente	imperfecto	pret. ind.	futuro	subj. pres.
pago	pagaba	pagué	pagaré	pague
pagas	pagabas	pagaste	pagarás	pagues
paga	pagaba	pagó	pagará	pague
pagamos	pagábamos	pagamos	pagaremos	paguemos
pagáis	pagabais	pagasteis	pagaréis	paguéis
pagan	pagaban	pagaron	pagarán	paguen
gerundio pagando		**participio** pagado		

<z → c>   **cazar**

presente	imperfecto	pret. ind.	futuro	subj. pres.
cazo	cazaba	cacé	cazaré	cace
cazas	cazabas	cazaste	cazarás	caces
caza	cazaba	cazó	cazará	cace
cazamos	cazábamos	cazamos	cazaremos	cacemos
cazáis	cazabais	cazasteis	cazaréis	cacéis
cazan	cazaban	cazaron	cazarán	cacen
gerundio cazando		**participio** cazado		

<gu → gü> averiguar

presente	imperfecto	pret. ind.	futuro	subj. pres.
averiguo	averiguaba	averigüé	averiguaré	averigüe
averiguas	averiguabas	averiguaste	averiguarás	averigües
averigua	averiguaba	averiguó	averiguará	averigüe
averiguamos	averiguábamos	averiguamos	averiguaremos	averigüemos
averiguáis	averiguabais	averiguasteis	averiguaréis	averigüéis
averiguan	averiguaban	averiguaron	averiguarán	averigüen
gerundio averiguando		**participio** averiguado		

<c → z> vencer

presente	imperfecto	pret. ind.	futuro	subj. pres.
venzo	vencía	vencí	venceré	venza
vences	vencías	venciste	vencerás	venzas
vence	vencía	venció	vencerá	venza
vencemos	vencíamos	vencimos	venceremos	venzamos
vencéis	vencíais	vencisteis	venceréis	venzáis
vencen	vencían	vencieron	vencerán	venzan
gerundio venciendo		**participio** vencido		

<g → j> coger

presente	imperfecto	pret. ind.	futuro	subj. pres.
cojo	cogía	cogí	cogeré	coja
coges	cogías	cogiste	cogerás	cojas
coge	cogía	cogió	cogerá	coja
cogemos	cogíamos	cogimos	cogeremos	cojamos
cogéis	cogíais	cogisteis	cogeréis	cojáis
cogen	cogían	cogieron	cogerán	cojan
gerundio cogiendo		**participio** cogido		

<gu → g> distinguir

presente	imperfecto	pret. ind.	futuro	subj. pres.
distingo	distinguía	distinguí	distinguiré	distinga
distingues	distinguías	distinguiste	distinguirás	distingas
distingue	distinguía	distinguió	distinguirá	distinga
distinguimos	distinguíamos	distinguimos	distinguiremos	distingamos
distinguís	distinguíais	distinguisteis	distinguiréis	distingáis
distinguen	distinguían	distinguieron	distinguirán	distingan
gerundio distinguiendo		**participio** distinguido		

<qu → c> delinquir

presente	imperfecto	pret. ind.	futuro	subj. pres.
delinco	delinquía	delinquí	delinquiré	delinca
delinques	delinquías	delinquiste	delinquirás	delincas
delinque	delinquía	delinquió	delinquirá	delinca
delinquimos	delinquíamos	delinquimos	delinquiremos	delincamos
delinquís	delinquíais	delinquisteis	delinquiréis	delincáis
delinquen	delinquían	delinquieron	delinquirán	delincan
gerundio delinquiendo		**participio** delinquido		

Los verbos irregulares

abolir

presente	
—	**gerundio**
—	aboliendo
abolimos	**participio**
abolís	abolido

abrir

participio:	abierto

adquirir

presente	
adquiero	**gerundio**
adquieres	adquiriendo
adquiere	
adquirimos	**participio**
adquirís	adquirido
adquieren	

andar

presente	pret. ind.	
ando	anduve	**gerundio**
andas	anduviste	andando
anda	anduvo	
andamos	anduvimos	**participio**
andáis	anduvisteis	andado
andan	anduvieron	

asir

presente	
asgo	**gerundio**
ases	asiendo
ase	
asimos	**participio**
asís	asido
asen	

aullar

presente	
aúllo	**gerundio**
aúllas	aullando
aúlla	
aullamos	**participio**
aulláis	aullado
aúllan	

avergonzar

presente	pret. ind.	
avergüenzo	avergoncé	**gerundio**
avergüenzas	avergonzaste	avergonzando
avergüenza	avergonzó	
avergonzamos	avergonzamos	**participio**
avergonzáis	avergonzasteis	avergonzado
avergüenzan	avergonzaron	

caber

presente	pret. ind.	futuro	condicional	
quepo	cupe	cabré	cabría	**gerundio**
cabes	cupiste	cabrás	cabrías	cabiendo
cabe	cupo	cabrá	cabría	
cabemos	cupimos	cabremos	cabríamos	**participio**
cabéis	cupisteis	cabréis	cabríais	cabido
caben	cupieron	cabrán	cabrían	

caer

presente	pret. ind.	
caigo	caí	**gerundio**
caes	caíste	cayendo
cae	cayó	
caemos	caímos	**participio**
caéis	caísteis	caído
caen	cayeron	

ceñir

presente	pret. ind.	
ciño	ceñí	**gerundio**
ciñes	ceñiste	ciñendo
ciñe	ciñó	
ceñimos	ceñimos	**participio**
ceñís	ceñisteis	ceñido
ciñen	ciñeron	

cocer

presente	
cuezo	**gerundio**
cueces	cociendo
cuece	
cocemos	**participio**
cocéis	cocido
cuecen	

colgar

presente	pret. ind.	
cuelgo	colgué	**gerundio**
cuelgas	colgaste	colgando
cuelga	colgó	
colgamos	colgamos	**participio**
colgáis	colgasteis	colgado
cuelgan	colgaron	

crecer

presente		
crezco	**gerundio**	
creces	creciendo	
crece		
crecemos	**participio**	
crecéis	crecido	
crecen		

dar

presente	pret. ind.	subj. pres.	
doy	di	dé	**gerundio**
das	diste	des	dando
da	dio	dé	
damos	dimos	demos	**participio**
dais	disteis	deis	dado
dan	dieron	den	

decir

presente	imperfecto	pret. ind.	futuro	subj. pres.
digo	decía	dije	diré	diga
dices	decías	dijiste	dirás	digas
dice	decía	dijo	dirá	diga
decimos	decíamos	dijimos	diremos	digamos
decís	decíais	dijisteis	diréis	digáis
dicen	decían	dijeron	dirán	digan
gerundio diciendo		**participio** dicho		

dormir

presente	pret. ind.	
duermo	dormí	**gerundio**
duermes	dormiste	durmiendo
duerme	durmió	
dormimos	dormimos	**participio**
dormís	dormisteis	dormido
duermen	durmieron	

elegir

presente	pret. ind.	
elijo	elegí	**gerundio**
eliges	elegiste	eligiendo
elige	eligió	
elegimos	elegimos	**participio**
elegís	elegisteis	elegido
eligen	eligieron	

empezar

presente	pret. ind.		
empiezo	empecé	**gerundio**	
empiezas	empezaste	empezando	
empieza	empezó		
empezamos	empezamos	**participio**	
empezáis	empezasteis	empezado	
empiezan	empezaron		

enraizar

presente	pret. ind.		
enraízo	enraicé	**gerundio**	
enraízas	enraizaste	enraizando	
enraíza	enraizó		
enraizamos	enraizamos	**participio**	
enraizáis	enraizasteis	enraizado	
enraízan	enraizaron		

erguir

presente	pret. ind.	subj. pres	subj. imp.
yergo	erguí	irga	**gerundio**
yergues	erguiste	irgas	irguiendo
yergue	irguió	irga	
erguimos	erguimos	irgamos	**participio**
erguís	erguisteis	irgáis	erguido
yerguen	irguieron	irgan	

errar

presente	pret. ind.	
yerro	erré	**gerundio**
yerras	erraste	errando
yerra	erró	
erramos	erramos	**participio**
erráis	errasteis	errado
yerran	erraron	

escribir

participio:	escrito

estar

presente	imperfecto	pret. ind.	futuro	subj. pres.
estoy	estaba	estuve	estaré	esté
estás	estabas	estuviste	estarás	estés
está	estaba	estuvo	estará	esté
estamos	estábamos	estuvimos	estaremos	estemos
estáis	estabais	estuvisteis	estaréis	estéis
están	estaban	estuvieron	estarán	estén
gerundio estando		**participio** estado		

forzar

presente	pret. ind.	
fuerzo	forcé	**gerundio**
fuerzas	forzaste	forzando
fuerza	forzó	
forzamos	forzamos	**participio**
forzáis	forzasteis	forzado
fuerzan	forzaron	

fregar

presente	pret. ind.	
friego	fregué	**gerundio**
friegas	fregaste	fregando
friega	fregó	
fregamos	fregamos	**participio**
fregáis	fregasteis	fregado
friegan	fregamos	

freír

presente	pret. ind.	
frío	freí	**gerundio**
fríes	freíste	friendo
fríe	frió	
freímos	freímos	**participio**
freís	freísteis	frito
fríen	frieron	

haber

presente	imperfecto	pret. ind.	futuro	subj. pres.
he	había	hube	habré	haya
has	habías	hubiste	habrás	hayas
ha	había	hubo	habrá	haya
hemos	habíamos	hubimos	habremos	hayamos
habéis	habíais	hubisteis	habréis	hayáis
han	habían	hubieron	habrán	hayan
gerundio habiendo		**participio** habido		

hacer

presente	imperfecto	pret. ind.	futuro	subj. pres.
hago	hacía	hice	haré	haga
haces	hacías	hiciste	harás	hagas
hace	hacía	hizo	hará	haga
hacemos	hacíamos	hicimos	haremos	hagamos
hacéis	hacíais	hicisteis	haréis	hagáis
hacen	hacían	hicieron	harán	hagan

| **gerundio** haciendo | | **participio** hecho | | |

hartar

participio:	hartado – *saturated*
	harto (*only as attribute*): estoy harto – *I've had enough*

huir

presente	pret. ind.	
huyo	huí	**gerundio**
huyes	huiste	huyendo
huye	huyó	
huimos	huimos	**participio**
huís	huisteis	huido
huyen	huyeron	

imprimir

participio:	impreso

ir

presente	imperfecto	pret. ind.	subj. pres.	
voy	iba	fui	vaya	**gerundio**
vas	ibas	fuiste	vayas	yendo
va	iba	fue	vaya	
vamos	íbamos	fuimos	vayamos	**participio**
vais	ibais	fuisteis	vayáis	ido
van	iban	fueron	vayan	

jugar

presente	pret. ind.	subj. pres.	
juego	jugué	juegue	**gerundio**
juegas	jugaste	juegues	jugando
juega	jugó	juegue	
jugamos	jugamos	juguemos	**participio**
jugáis	jugasteis	juguéis	jugado
juegan	jugaron	jueguen	

leer

presente	pret. ind.	
leo	leí	**gerundio**
lees	leíste	leyendo
lee	leyó	
leemos	leímos	**participio**
leéis	leísteis	leído
leen	leyeron	

lucir

presente		
luzco	**gerundio**	
luces	luciendo	
luce		
lucimos	**participio**	
lucís	lucido	
lucen		

maldecir

presente	pret. ind.	
maldigo	maldije	**gerundio**
maldices	maldijiste	maldiciendo
maldice	maldijo	
maldecimos	maldijimos	**participio**
maldecís	maldijisteis	maldecido – *cursed*
maldicen	maldijeron	maldito – *noun, adjective*

morir

presente	pret. ind.	
muero	morí	**gerundio**
mueres	moriste	muriendo
muere	murió	
morimos	morimos	**participio**
morís	moristeis	muerto
mueren	murieron	

oir, oír

presente	pret. ind.		
oigo	oí	**gerundio**	
oyes	oiste	oyendo	
oye	oyó		
oímos	oímos	**participio**	
oís	oísteis	oído	
oyen	oyeron		

oler

presente		
huelo	**gerundio**	
hueles	oliendo	
huele		
olemos	**participio**	
oléis	olido	
huelen		

pedir

presente	pret. ind.		
pido	pedí	**gerundio**	
pides	pediste	pidiendo	
pide	pidió		
pedimos	pedimos	**participio**	
pedís	pedisteis	pedido	
piden	pidieron		

poder

presente	pret. ind.	futuro	
puedo	pude	podré	**gerundio**
puedes	pudiste	podrás	pudiendo
puede	pudo	podrá	
podemos	pudimos	podremos	**participio**
podéis	pudisteis	podréis	podido
pueden	pudieron	podrán	

podrir, pudrir

presente	imperfecto	pret. ind.	futuro	
pudro	pudría	pudrí	pudriré	**gerundio**
pudres	pudrías	pudriste	pudrirás	pudriendo
pudre	pudría	pudrió	pudrirá	
pudrimos	pudríamos	pudrimos	pudriremos	**participio**
pudrís	pudríais	pudristeis	pudriréis	podrido
pudren	pudrían	pudrieron	pudrirán	

poner

presente	pret. ind.	futuro	
pongo	puse	pondré	**gerundio**
pones	pusiste	pondrás	poniendo
pone	puso	pondrá	
ponemos	pusimos	pondremos	**participio**
ponéis	pusisteis	pondréis	puesto
ponen	pusieron	pondrán	

prohibir

presente	
prohíbo	**gerundio**
prohíbes	prohibiendo
prohíbe	
prohibimos	**participio**
prohibís	prohibido
prohíben	

proveer

presente	pret. ind.	
proveo	proveí	**gerundio**
provees	proveíste	proveyendo
provee	proveyó	
proveemos	proveímos	**participio**
proveéis	proveísteis	provisto
proveen	proveyeron	

pudrir *see* **podrir**

querer

presente	pret. ind.	futuro	
quiero	quise	querré	**gerundio**
quieres	quisiste	querrás	queriendo
quiere	quiso	querrá	
queremos	quisimos	querremos	**participio**
queréis	quisisteis	querréis	querido
quieren	quisieron	querrán	

reír

presente	pret. ind.		
río	reí	**gerundio**	
ríes	reíste	riendo	
ríe	rió		
reímos	reímos	**participio**	
reís	reísteis	reído	
ríen	rieron		

reunir

presente		
reúno	**gerundio**	
reúnes	reuniendo	
reúne		
reunimos	**participio**	
reunís	reunido	
reúnen		

roer

presente	pret. ind.	subj. pres.	
roo/roigo	roí	roa/roiga	**gerundio**
roes	roíste	roas/roigas	royendo
roe	royó	roa/roiga	
roemos	roímos	roamos/roigamos/royamos	**participio** roído
roéis	roísteis	roáis/roigáis/royáis	
roen	royeron	roan/roigan	

saber

presente	pret. ind.	futuro	subj. pres.	
sé	supe	sabré	sepa	**gerundio**
sabes	supiste	sabrás	sepas	sabiendo
sabe	supo	sabrá	sepa	
sabemos	supimos	sabremos	sepamos	**participio**
sabéis	supisteis	sabréis	sepáis	sabido
saben	supieron	sabrán	sepan	

salir

presente	futuro	
salgo	saldré	**gerundio**
sales	saldrás	saliendo
sale	saldrá	
salimos	saldremos	**participio**
salís	saldréis	salido
salen	saldrán	

seguir

presente	pret. ind.	subj. pres.	
sigo	seguí	siga	**gerundio**
sigues	seguiste	sigas	siguiendo
sigue	siguió	siga	
seguimos	seguimos	sigamos	**participio**
seguís	seguisteis	sigáis	seguido
siguen	siguieron	sigan	

sentir

presente	pret. ind.	subj. pres.	
siento	sentí	sienta	**gerundio**
sientes	sentiste	sientas	sintiendo
siente	sintió	sienta	
sentimos	sentimos	sintamos	**participio**
sentís	sentisteis	sintáis	sentido
sienten	sintieron	sientan	

ser

presente	imperfecto	pret. ind.	futuro	subj. pres.
soy	era	fui	seré	sea
eres	eras	fuiste	serás	seas
es	era	fue	será	sea
somos	éramos	fuimos	seremos	seamos
sois	erais	fuisteis	seréis	seáis
son	eran	fueron	serán	sean
gerundio siendo		**participio** sido		

soltar

presente	
suelto	**gerundio**
sueltas	soltando
suelta	
soltamos	**participio**
soltáis	soltado
sueltan	

tener

presente	pret. ind.	futuro	
tengo	tuve	tendré	**gerundio**
tienes	tuviste	tendrás	teniendo
tiene	tuvo	tendrá	
tenemos	tuvimos	tendremos	**participio**
tenéis	tuvisteis	tendréis	tenido
tienen	tuvieron	tendrán	

traducir

presente	pret. ind.	
traduzco	traduje	**gerundio**
traduces	tradujiste	traduciendo
traduce	tradujo	
traducimos	tradujimos	**participio**
traducís	tradujisteis	traducido
traducen	tradujeron	

traer

presente	pret. ind.	
traigo	traje	**gerundio**
traes	trajiste	trayendo
trae	trajo	
traemos	trajimos	**participio**
traéis	trajisteis	traído
traen	trajeron	

valer

presente	futuro	
valgo	valdré	**gerundio**
vales	valdrás	valiendo
vale	valdrá	
valemos	valdremos	**participio**
valéis	valdréis	valido
valen	valdrán	

venir

presente	pret. ind.	futuro	
vengo	vine	vendré	**gerundio**
vienes	viniste	vendrás	viniendo
viene	vino	vendrá	
venimos	vinimos	vendremos	**participio**
venís	vinisteis	vendréis	venido
vienen	vinieron	vendrán	

ver

presente	imperfecto	pret. ind.	
veo	veía	vi	**gerundio**
ves	veías	viste	viendo
ve	veía	vio	
vemos	veíamos	vimos	**participio**
veis	veíais	vimos	visto
ven	veían	vieron	

Los verbos irregulares ingleses
English irregular verbs

Infinitive	Past	Past Participle
abide	abode, abided	abode, abided
arise	arose	arisen
awake	awoke	awaked, awoken
be	was *sing*, were *pl*	been
bear	bore	borne, born
beat	beat	beaten
become	became	become
beget	begot	begotten
begin	began	begun
behold	beheld	beheld
bend	bent	bent
beseech	besought, beseeched	besought
beset	beset	beset
bet	bet, betted	bet, betted
bid	bade, bid	bid, bidden
bind	bound	bound
bite	bit	bitten
bleed	bled	bled
blow	blew	blown
break	broke	broken
breed	bred	bred
bring	brought	brought
build	built	built
burn	burned, burnt	burned, burnt
burst	burst	burst
buy	bought	bought

Infinitive	Past	Past Participle
can	could	-
cast	cast	cast
catch	caught	caught
choose	chose	chosen
cleave *(cut)*	cleft, cleaved, clove	cleft, cleaved, cloven
cling	clung	clung
come	came	come
cost	cost, costed	cost, costed
creep	crept	crept
cut	cut	cut
deal	dealt	dealt
dig	dug	dug
dive	dived, dove	dived
do	did	done
draw	drew	drawn
dream	dreamed, dreamt	dreamed, dreamt
drink	drank	drunk
drive	drove	driven
dwell	dwelt, dwelled	dwelt, dwelled
eat	ate	eaten
fall	fell	fallen
feed	fed	fed
feel	felt	felt
fight	fought	fought
find	found	found
flee	fled	fled
fling	flung	flung
fly	flew	flown
forbid	forbade, forbad	forbidden, forbid

Infinitive	Past	Past Participle
forget	forgot	forgotten
forsake	forsook	forsaken
freeze	froze	frozen
get	got	gotten, got
gild	gilded, gilt	gilded, gilt
gird	girded, girt	girded, girt
give	gave	given
go	went	gone
grind	ground	ground
grow	grew	grown
hang	hung, LAW hanged	hung, LAW hanged
have	had	had
hear	heard	heard
heave	heaved, hove	heaved, hove
hew	hewed	hewn, hewed
hide	hid	hidden
hit	hit	hit
hold	held	held
hurt	hurt	hurt
keep	kept	kept
kneel	knelt, kneeled	knelt, kneeled
know	knew	known
lade	laded	laden, laded
lay	laid	laid
lead	led	led
leap	leaped, leapt	leaped, leapt
learn	learned, learnt	learned, learnt
leave	left	left
lend	lent	lent

Infinitive	Past	Past Participle
let	let	let
lie	lay	lain
light	lighted, lit	lighted, lit
lose	lost	lost
make	made	made
may	might	–
mean	meant	meant
meet	met	met
mistake	mistook	mistaken
mow	mowed	mown, mowed
pay	paid	paid
put	put	put
quit	quit, quitted	quit, quitted
read [rid]	read [red]	read [red]
rend	rent, rended	rent, rended
rid	rid, ridded	rid, ridded
ride	rode	ridden
ring	rang	rung
rise	rose	risen
run	ran	run
saw	sawed	sawed, sawn
say	said	said
see	saw	seen
seek	sought	sought
sell	sold	sold
send	sent	sent
set	set	set
sew	sewed	sewn, sewed
shake	shook	shaken

Infinitive	Past	Past Participle
shave	shaved	shaved, shaven
shear	sheared	sheared, shorn
shed	shed	shed
shine	shone, shined	shone, shined
shit	shit, *iron* shat	shit, *iron* shat
shoe	shod	shod, shodden
shoot	shot	shot
show	showed	shown, showed
shrink	shrank, shrunk	shrunk, shrunken
shut	shut	shut
sing	sang, sung	sung
sink	sank, sunk	sunk
sit	sat	sat
sleep	slept	slept
slide	slid	slid
sling	slung	slung
slink	slunk	slunk
slit	slit	slit
smell	smelled, smelt	smelled, smelt
smite	smote	smitten, smote
sow	sowed	sown, sowed
speak	spoke	spoken
speed	sped, speeded	sped, speeded
spell	spelled, spelt	spelled, spelt
spend	spent	spent
spill	spilled, spilt	spilled, spilt
spin	spun	spun
spit	spat, spit	spat, spit
split	split	split

Infinitive	Past	Past Participle
spoil	spoiled, spoilt	spoiled, spoilt
spread	spread	spread
spring	sprang, sprung	sprung
stand	stood	stood
steal	stole	stolen
stick	stuck	stuck
sting	stung	stung
stink	stank, stunk	stunk
strew	strewed	strewn, strewed
stride	strode	stridden
strike	struck	struck
string	strung	strung
strive	strove	striven, strived
swear	swore	sworn
sweep	swept	swept
swell	swelled	swollen, swelled
swim	swam	swum
swing	swung	swung
take	took	taken
teach	taught	taught
tear	tore	torn
tell	told	told
think	thought	thought
thrive	thrived, throve	thrived, thriven
throw	threw	thrown
thrust	thrust	thrust
tread	trod	trodden, trod
wake	woke, waked	waked, woken
wear	wore	worn

Infinitive	Past	Past Participle
weave	wove	woven
weep	wept	wept
win	won	won
wind	wound	wound
wring	wrung	wrung
write	wrote	written

Los numerales | | Numerals

Los numerales cardinales | | Cardinal numbers

cero	0	zero
uno (*apócope* un), una	1	one
dos	2	two
tres	3	three
cuatro	4	four
cinco	5	five
seis	6	six
siete	7	seven
ocho	8	eight
nueve	9	nine
diez	10	ten
once	11	eleven
doce	12	twelve
trece	13	thirteen
catorce	14	fourteen
quince	15	fifteen
dieciséis	16	sixteen
diecisiete	17	seventeen
dieciocho	18	eighteen
diecinueve	19	nineteen
veinte	20	twenty
veintiuno (*apócope* veintiún), -a	21	twenty-one
veintidós	22	twenty-two
veintitrés	23	twenty-three
veinticuatro	24	twenty-four
veinticinco	25	twenty-five
treinta	30	thirty

treinta y uno (*apócope* treinta y un) -a	31	thirty-one
treinta y dos	32	thirty-two
treinta y tres	33	thirty-three
cuarenta	40	forty
cuarenta y uno (*apócope* cuarenta y un) –a	41	forty-one
cuarenta y dos	42	forty-two
cincuenta	50	fifty
cincuenta y uno (*apócope* cincuenta y un) -a	51	fifty-one
cincuenta y dos	52	fifty-two
sesenta	60	sixty
sesenta y uno (*apócope* sesenta y un) –a	61	sixty-one
sesenta y dos	62	sixty-two
setenta	70	seventy
setenta y uno (*apócope* setenta y un) –a	71	seventy-one
setenta y dos	72	seventy-two
setenta y cinco	75	seventy-five
setenta y nueve	79	seventy-nine
ochenta	80	eighty
ochenta y uno (*apócope* ochenta y un) –a	81	eighty-one
ochenta y dos	82	eighty-two
ochenta y cinco	85	eighty-five
noventa	90	ninety
noventa y uno (*apócope* noventa y un) –a	91	ninety-one
noventa y dos	92	ninety-two
noventa y nueve	99	ninety-nine
cien	100	one hundred
ciento uno (*apócope* ciento un) -a	101	one hundred and one

ciento dos	102	one hundred and two
ciento diez	110	one hundred and ten
ciento veinte	120	one hundred and twenty
ciento noventa y nueve	199	one hundred and ninety-nine
dos cientos, -as	200	two hundred
dos cientos uno (*apócope* doscientos un) –a	201	two hundred and one
dos cientos veintidós	222	two hundred and twenty-two
tres cientos, -as	300	three hundred
cuatro cientos, -as	400	four hundred
quinientos, -as	500	five hundred
seiscientos, -as	600	six hundred
setecientos, -as	700	seven hundred
ochocientos, -as	800	eight hundred
nuevecientos, -as	900	nine hundred
mil	1 000	one thousand
mil uno (*apócope* mil un) -a	1 001	one thousand and one
mil diez	1 010	one thousand and ten
mil cien	1 100	one thousand one hundred
dos mil	2 000	two thousand
diez mil	10 000	ten thousand
cien mil	100 000	one hundred thousand
un millón	1 000 000	one million
dos millones	2 000 000	two million
dos millones quinientos, -as mil	2 500 000	two million, five hundred thousand
mil millones, un millardo	1 000 000 000	one billion
un billón	1 000 000 000 000	one trillion
mil billones	1 000 000 000 000 000	one quadrillion
un trillón	1 000 000 000 000 000 000	one quintillion

Los numerales ordinales   **Ordinal numbers**

primero (*apócope* primer), -a	1°, 1ª	1st	first
segundo, -a	2°, 2ª	2nd	second
tercero (*apócope* tercer), -a	3°, 3ª	3rd	third
cuarto, -a	4°, 4ª	4th	fourth
quinto, -a	5°, 5ª	5th	fifth
sexto, -a	6°, 6ª	6th	sixth
séptimo, -a	7°, 7ª	7th	seventh
octavo, -a	8°, 8ª	8th	eighth
noveno, -a	9°, 9ª	9th	ninth
décimo, -a	10°, 10ª	10th	tenth
undécimo, -a	11°, 11ª	11th	eleventh
duodécimo, -a	12°, 12ª	12th	twelfth
decimotercero, -a	13°, 13ª	13th	thirteenth
decimocuarto, -a	14°, 14ª	14th	fourteenth
decimoquinto, -a	15°, 15ª	15th	fifteenth
decimosexto, -a	16°, 16ª	16th	sixteenth
decimoséptimo, -a	17°, 17ª	17th	seventeenth
decimoctavo, -a	18°, 18ª	18th	eighteenth
decimonoveno, -a	19°, 19ª	19th	nineteenth
vigésimo, -a	20°, 20ª	20th	twentieth
vigésimo, -a primero, -a (o vigesimoprimero, -a)	21°, 21ª	21st	twenty-first
vigésimo, -a segundo, -a (o vigesimosegundo, -a)	22°, 22ª	22nd	twenty-second
vigésimo, -a tercero, -a (o vigesimotercero, -a)	23°, 23ª	23rd	twenty-third
trigésimo, -a	30°, 30ª	30th	thirtieth
trigésimo, -a primero, -a	31°, 31ª	31st	thirty-first
trigésimo, -a segundo, -a	32°, 32ª	32nd	thirty-second
cuadragésimo, -a	40°, 40ª	40th	fortieth

quincuagésimo, -a	50°, 50ª	50th	fiftieth
sexagésimo, -a	60°, 60ª	60th	sixtieth
septuagésimo, -a	70°, 70ª	70th	seventieth
septuagésimo, -a primero, -a	71°, 71ª	71st	seventy-first
septuagésimo, -a segundo, -a	72°, 72ª	72nd	seventy-second
septuagésimo, -a noveno, -a	79°, 79ª	79th	seventy-ninth
octogésimo, -a	80°, 80ª	80th	eightieth
octogésimo, -a primero, -a	81°, 81ª	81st	eighty-first
octogésimo, -a segundo, -a	82°, 82ª	82nd	eighty-second
nonagésimo, -a	90°, 90ª	90th	ninetieth
nonagésimo, -a primero, -a	91°, 91ª	91st	ninety-first
nonagésimo, -a noveno, -a	99°, 99ª	99th	ninety-ninth
centésimo, -a	100°, 100ª	100th	one hundredth
centésimo, -a primero, -a	101°, 101ª	101st	one hundred and first
centésimo, -a décimo, -a	110°, 110ª	110th	one hundred and tenth
centésimo, -a nonagésimo, -a quinto, -a	195°, 195ª	195th	one hundred and ninety-fifth
ducentésimo, -a	200°, 200ª	200th	two hundredth
tricentésimo, -a	300°, 300ª	300th	three hundredth
quingentésimo, -a	500°, 500ª	500th	five hundredth
milésimo, -a	1 000°, 1 000ª	1 000th	one thousandth
dosmilésimo, -a	2 000°, 2 000ª	2 000th	two thousandth
millonésimo, -a	1 000 000°, 1 000 000ª	1 000 000th	one millionth
diezmillonésimo, -a	10 000 000°, 10 000 000ª	10 000 000th	ten millionth

Numeros fraccionarios (o quebrados)		**Fractional numbers**
mitad; medio, -a	$^1/_2$	one half
un tercio	$^1/_3$	one third
un cuarto	$^1/_4$	one quarter
un quinto	$^1/_5$	one fifth
un décimo	$^1/_{10}$	one tenth
un céntesimo	$^1/_{100}$	one hundredth
un milésimo	$^1/_{1000}$	one thousandth
un millonésimo	$^1/_{1\,000\,000}$	one millionth
dos tercios	$^2/_3$	two thirds
tres cuartos	$^3/_4$	three quarters
dos quintos	$^2/_5$	two fifths
tres décimos	$^3/_{10}$	three tenths
uno y medio	$1\,^1/_2$	one and a half
dos y medio	$2\,^1/_2$	two and a half
cinco tres octavos	$5\,^3/_8$	five and three eighths
uno coma uno	1,1	one point one

Medidas y pesos

Weights and measures

Sistema (de numeración) decimal

Decimal system

giga-	1 000 000 000	G	giga-
mega-	1 000 000	M	mega-
hectokilo-	100 000	hk	hectokilo-
miria-	10 000	ma	myria-
kilo-	1 000	k	kilo-
hecto-	100	h	hecto-
deca- (o decá-)	10	da	deca-
deci- (o decí-)	0,1	d	deci-
centi- (o centí-)	0,01	c	centi-
mili-	0,001	m	milli-
decimili-	0,000 1	dm	decimilli-
centimili-	0,000 01	cm	centimilli-
micro-	0,000 001	μ	micro-

Tablas de equivalencia

Damos el llamado **imperial system** solamente en los casos en los que en el lenguaje cotidiano éste todavía se sigue usando en los EEUU. Para convertir una medida métrica en la imperial estadounidense, se debe multiplicar por el factor en **negrita**. Asimismo, dividiendo la medida imperial estadounidense por ese mismo factor, se obtiene el equivalente métrico.

Conversion tables

Only U.S. Customary units still in common use are given here. To convert a metric measurement to U.S. Customary measures, multiply by the conversion factor in **bold**. Likewise dividing a U.S. Customary measurement by the same factor will give the metric equivalent.

Sistema métrico
Metric measurement

Sistema imperial
U.S. Customary System

Medidas de longitud

Length measure

milla marina	1 852 m	–	nautical mile			
kilómetro	1 000 m	km	kilometer	**0,62**	mile (=1 760 yards)	m, mi
hectómetro	100 m	hm	hecto-meter			
decámetro	10 m	dam	decameter			
metro	1 m	m	meter	**1,09** **3,28**	yard (= 3 feet) foot (= 12 inches)	yd ft
decímetro	0,1 m	dm	decimeter			
centímetro	0,01 m	cm	centimeter	**0,39**	inch	in
milímetro	0,001 m	mm	millimeter			
micrón, micra	0,000 001 m	µ	micron			
milimicrón	0,000 000 001 m	mµ	milli-micron			
ángstrom	0,000 000 000 1 m	Å	angstrom			

Medidas de superficie

Surface measure

kilómetro cuadrado	1 000 000 m²	km²	square kilometer	**0,386**	square mile (= 640 acres)	sq. m., sq. mi.
hectómetro cuadrado	10 000 m²	hm²	square hecto-meter	**2,47**	acre (= 4 840 square yards)	a.
hectárea		ha	hectare			
decámetro cuadrado	100 m²	dam²	square decameter			
área		a	are			

metro cuadrado	1 m²	m²	square meter	**1.196** **10,76**	square yard (9 square feet) square feet (= 144 square inches)	sq. yd sq. ft
decímetro cuadrado	0,01 m²	dm²	square decimeter			
centímetro cuadrado	0,000 1 m²	cm²	square centimeter	**0,155**	square inch	sq. in.
milímetro cuadrado	0,000001 m²	mm²	square millimeter			

Medidas de volumen y capacidad

Volume and capacity

kilómetro cúbico	1 000 000 000 m³	km³	cubic kilometer			
metro cúbico	1 m³	m³	cubic meter	**1,308**	cubic yard (= 27 cubic feet)	cu. yd
estéreo		st	stere	**35,32**	cubic foot (= 1 728 cubic inches)	cu. ft
hectolitro	0,1 m³	hl	hectoliter			
decalitro	0,01 m³	dal	decaliter			
decímetro cúbico	0,001 m³	dm³	cubic decimeter	**0,26**	US gallon	gal.
litro		l	liter	**2,1**	US pint	pt
decilitro	0,000 1 m³	dl	deciliter			
centilitro	0,00001 m³	cl	centiliter	**0,338**	US fluid ounce	fl. oz
centímetro cúbico	0,000001 m³	cm³	cubic centimeter	**0,061**	cubic inch	cu. in.
mililitro	0,000001 m³	ml	milliliter			
milímetro cúbico	0,000000001 m³	mm³	cubic millimeter			

abreviaturas

Symbols and abbreviations

▶	idiom block
=	contraction
≈	approximate equivalent
–	change of speaker
®	trademark
◆	phrasal verb
1st pers	1st person
3rd pers	3rd person
a.	also
abr de, abbr of	abbreviation of
adj	adjective
ADMIN	administration
adv	adverb
AGR	agriculture
AmC	
AmL	
AmS	
ANAT	anatomy
And	
Ant	
argot	
ARCHIT, ARQUIT	architecture
Arg	
art	article
ART	art
ASTR	astronomy, astrology
AUTO	automobile, transport
aux	auxiliary verb
AVIAT	aviation, aerospace, space technology
BIO	biology
Bol	
BOT	botany
Can	Canadian English
CHEM	chemistry
Chile	
CINE	cinema
Col	
COM	commerce
comp	comparative
COMPUT	computing
conj	conjunction
CRi	

Cono Sur (República Argentina, Chile, Paraguay, Uruguay)	*CSur*	
Cuba	*Cuba*	
culinaria	CULIN	culinary
definido	*def*	definite
demostrativo	*dem*	demonstrative
deporte	DEP	
República Dominicana	*DomR*	
ecología	ECOL	ecology
economía	ECON	economics
Ecuador	*Ecua*	
electrotécnica, electrónica	ELEC	electricity, electronics
elevado, literario	*elev*	
El Salvador	*ElSal*	
enseñanza	ENS	
	EU	European Union
feminino	*f*	feminine
	FASHION	fashion and sewing
ferrocarril	FERRO	
figurativo	*fig*	figurative
Filipinas	*Fili*	
filosofía	FILOS	
finananzas, bolsa	FIN	finance, banking, stock exchange
física	FÍS	
	form	formal language
fotografía	FOTO	
	GAMES	games
geografía, geología	GEO	geography, geology
Guatemala	*Guat*	
Guayana	*Guay*	
Guinea Ecuatorial	*GuinEc*	
historia, histórico	HIST	history, historical
Honduras	*Hond*	
imperativo	*imper*	imperative
impersonal	*impers*	impersonal
indefinido	*indef*	indefinite
lenguaje informal	*inf*	informal language
infinitivo	*infin*	infinitive
	insep	inseparable
interjección	*interj*	interjection
interrogativo	*interrog*	interrogative
invariable	*inv*	invariable
irónico, humorístico	*iron, irón*	ironic, humorous
irregular	*irr*	irregular

Pesos / Weight

tonelada	1 000 kg	t	ton	**1,1**	[short] ton *Am* (= 2000 pounds)	t.
quintal métrico	100 kg	q	quintal			
kilogramo	1 000 g	kg	kilogram	**2,2**	pound (= 16 ounces)	lb
hectogramo	100 g	hg	hectogram			
decagramo	10 g	dag	decagram			
gramo	1 g	g	gram	**0,035**	ounce	oz
quilate	0,2 g	–	carat			
decigramo (o decagramo)	0,1 g	dg	decigram			
centigramo	0,01 g	cg	centigram			
miligramo	0,001 g	mg	milligram			
microgramo	0,000 001 g	µg, γ	microgram			

Temperaturas: Fahrenheit y Celsius

Temperatures: Fahrenheit and Celsius

Para convertir una temperatura indicada en grados centígrados a Fahrenheit se debe multiplicar por 1,8 y sumar 32; p. ej. 100 °C (el punto de ebullición del agua) × 1,8 = 180; 180 + 32 = 212°F.

Para convertir una temperatura indicada en Fahrenheit a centígrados se deben restar 32 y dividir por 1,8; p. ej. 212°F (el punto de ebullición del agua) − 32 = 180; 180/1,8 = 100 °C.

To convert a temperature from degrees Celsius to Fahrenheit, multiply by 1.8 and add 32; e.g. 100 °C (boiling point of water) × 1.8 = 180; 180 + 32 = 212° F.

To convert a temperature from degrees Fahrenheit to Celsius, deduct 32 and divide by 1.8; e.g. 212° F (boiling point of water) − 32 = 180; 180/1.8 = 100 °C.

		Fahrenheit	Celsius
el punto de congelación del agua	Freezing point of water	32°	0°
el punto de ebullición del agua	Boiling point of water	212°	100°
un día tremendamente frío	An extremely cold day	−40°	−40°
un día de frío	A cold day	14°	−10°
un día fresco	A cool day	50°	10°
un día templado	A mild day	68°	20°
un día de calor	A warm day	86°	30°
un día de mucho calor	A very hot day	104°	40°
la temperatura normal del cuerpo (humano)	Normal body temperature	98.6°	37°

Símbolos y abreviaturas

jurisdicción, derecho	JUR, LAW	law
lingüística, gramática	LING	linguistics, grammar
literatura, poesía	LIT	literature, poetry
	liter	literary
masculino	*m*	masculine
masculino o femenino	*m of*	
matemáticas, geometría	MAT, MATH	mathematics, geometry
medicina, farmacología	MED	medicine, pharmacology
metereología	METEO	weather, meteorology
México, Méjico	*Méx*	
masculino y femenino	*mf*	
fuerzas armadas	MIL	military
minería	MIN	mining
música	MUS, MÚS	music
	n	noun
náutica, navegación	NAUT, NÁUT	nautical, naval
negativo	*neg*	negative
Nicaragua	*Nic*	
o	*o*	or
	no art	no article
	offensive	insulting language
Panamá	*Pan*	
Paraguay	*Par*	
peyorativo	*pej, pey*	pejorative, disapproving usage
persona, personal	*pers*	person, personal
Perú	*Perú*	
	PHILOS	philosophy
	PHOT	photography
	PHYS	physics
plural	*pl*	plural
política	POL	politics
posesivo	*pos*	possessive
participio pasado	*pp*	past participle
participio presente	*pres p*	present participle
prensa	PREN	
preposición	*prep*	preposition
presente	*pres*	present
pretérito	*pret*	
Puerto Rico	*PRico*	
pronombre	*pron*	pronoun
proverbio	*prov*	proverb

Symbols and abbreviations

psicología	PSICO, PSYCH	psychology
	pt	past tense
	PUBL.	publishing, journalism
química	QUÍM	
radio	RADIO	radio
	RAIL	railways
República Dominicana	*RDom*	
regional	*reg*	regional
relativo	*rel*	relative
religión	REL	religion
Río de la Plata	*RíoPl*	
	s.	see
	s. a.	see also
	sb	somebody
	SCHOOL	school
	sep	separable
singular	*sing*	singular
	sl	slang
sociología	SOCIOL	sociology
	SPORTS	sports
	sth	something
subjuntivo	*subj*	
superlativo	*superl*	superlative
también	*t.*	
tauromaquia	TAUR	
teatro	TEAT	
técnica	TÉC, TECH	technical
teléfono	TEL	telecommunications
	THEAT	theater
tipografía, imprenta, gráfica	TIPO	
televisión	TV	television
	TYPO	typography, printing, graphic arts
Unión Europea	UE	
universidad	UNIV	university
Uruguay	*Urug*	
véase	*v.*	
Venezuela	*Ven*	
verbo	*vb*	verb
verbo intransitivo	*vi*	intransitive verb
verbo impersonal	*vimpers*	
verbo reflexivo	*vr*	
verbo transitivo	*vt*	transitive verb
véase también	*v.t.*	
lenguaje vulgar	*vulg*	vulgar language
zoología	ZOOL	zoology